Bibliography of Comparative Literature

Bibliography of Comparative Literature

by

† FERNAND BALDENSPERGER
Ancien Professeur à la Sorbonne et à l' U.C.L.A.
Harvard Emeritus
Membre ou Correspondant de plusieurs Académies

and

WERNER P. FRIEDERICH
Professor of German and Comparative Literature
University of North Carolina

New York
RUSSELL & RUSSELL

REISSUED, 1960, BY RUSSELL & RUSSELL
A DIVISION OF ATHENEUM PUBLISHERS, INC.
BY ARRANGEMENT WITH
THE DEPARTMENT OF COMPARATIVE LITERATURE
OF THE UNIVERSITY OF NORTH CAROLINA
L. C. CATALOG CARD NO: 60-5279
PRINTED IN THE UNITED STATES OF AMERICA

Table of Contents

BOOK ONE
GENERALITIES, INTERMEDIARIES, THEMATOLOGY, LITERARY GENRES.

BOOK TWO
THE ORIENT, ANTIQUITY (GREECE, ROME), JUDAISM, EARLY CHRISTIANITY, MOHAMMEDANISM AND THEIR CONTRIBUTIONS.

BOOK THREE
ASPECTS OF WESTERN CULTURE

MODERN CHRISTIANITY, LITERARY CURRENTS, INTERNATIONAL LITERARY RELATIONS, COLLECTIVE INFLUENCES UPON CONTINENTS, NATIONS AND INDIVIDUALS.

BOOK FOUR
THE MODERN WORLD

One World
Wendell Willkie

Preface

Américain d'origine alsacienne pour qui, en sa qualité d'autodidacte, la mutualité des influences littéraires réciproques était un fait d'expérience autant et plus que de doctrine, Louis P. Betz serait heureux de voir rigoureusement développé ce qu'il appelait il y a un demi-siècle "son petit bagage" bibliographique.

Le temps a, de fait, travaillé pour des vues que l'espoir du monde civilisé, de son côté, incorpore aux conditions les plus actuelles de l'effort intellectuel. Sans qu'on puisse dire que "l'esprit souffle où il lui plaît," les échanges intellectuels sont favorisés par l'aisance des relations entre peuples et par les curiosités des lecteurs. Du coup, la permanence de contacts analogues dans le passé, même soumis à des difficultés matérielles ou liés aux eventualités de l'aventure ou de la conquête, de l'apostolat ou de l'héroïsme, prend rétrospectivement une importance accrue. Il est loin, le temps où un Nisard pouvait affirmer que les nations n'échangent leurs idées qu'en courant le risque de graves inconvénients: la seule réserve demeure, comme le disait déjà Goethe, l'examen rationnel des notions importées, la valeur esthétique des oeuvres proposées.

C'est dire qu'une "somme" de l'importance de celle-ci doit avant tout permettre à maîtres et élèves, bibliothécaires et lecteurs, spécialistes et curieux, de se rendre compte des emprunts et des dettes, attestés par le labeur de l'histoire littéraire et de la critique documentaire, qui ont favorisé l'effort humain vers l'expression de sentiments, d'espérance, d'idées et d'instincts qui ne devaient point demeurer dans l'indétermination et la passivité. Du folklore à la métaphysique, du lyrisme au drame, du simple récit à la plus ambitieuse *Comédie,* divine, diabolique ou humaine, tout un monde verbal fut tributaire de curiosités qui furent en définitive à l'honneur de l'humanité.

F. B.

Der Plan zur Vollendung dieser Bibliographie wurde im Herbste 1945 kurz vor Professor Baldenspergers Rückkehr nach Europa gefasst. Im Verlaufe der Jahre hatte der Altmeister der vergleichenden Literaturwissenschaft eine reichhaltige Sammlung von ungefähr 15 000 Karten angelegt, die er im Sommer 1940 abbrach und der Universitätsbibliothek von Harvard zur Verfügung stellte. Ich meinerseits hatte ungefähr 14 000 Karten zumeist über englisch-deutsch-französisch-amerikanische literarische Beziehungen angehäuft und durch die Zusammenlegung beider Sammlungen wurde der Kern des vorliegenden Werkes geschaffen. Dabei stellte sich sofort heraus, dass die nach Herrn Baldenspergers Gesichtspunkten vorgenommene Einteilung der einzelnen Bücher und Kapitel weitaus besser war als meine eigene immer etwas unbefriedigende Einteilung; sie ist, wie jeder Leser erkennen kann, auch bedeutend besser als die von Betz vor fast fünfzig Jahren angetroffene Anordnung. Die Jahre von 1945 bis 1947 verbrachte ich mit dem Ansammeln von fast 20 000 neuen Zetteln, denn nicht nur musste die Zeitspanne von 1940 bis 1948 gefüllt werden, sondern es mussten auch viele im bereits vorhandenen Material vorgefundene Lücken ausgemerzt werden.

Nach der Aussonderung der zahllosen und unvermeidlichen Duplikate und Triplikate schrumpften die in meinen Zettelkasten vorhandenen Karten um mehr als ein Drittel auf ungefähr 33 000 zusammen, die im Verlaufe von 1948 und 1949 durch meine Frau in ein übersichtliches maschinengeschriebenes Manuskript übertragen werden mussten. Nicht nur in erster Linie ihr, sondern auch unseren unermüdlichen und fachkundigen Referenzbibliothekaren der University of North Carolina Library schulde ich unendlich viel mehr Dank als sich mit blossen Worten ausdrücken lässt, denn wenn auch immer im Verlaufe der Monate und Jahre Zweifel über die Richtigkeit einzelner Titelangaben in mir erstanden (und viele Zettel über dasselbe Thema brachten in der Tat oft diametral entgegengesetzte Auskunft) so war es mir vergönnt, durch oft stündlich vorgenommene Telephonanrufe von Miss Georgia Faison, Miss Louise Partrick, Miss Louise Hall, Mr. Donald Stave und ihren gut geschulten Helfern innerhalb von kurzer Zeit die gewünschte Richtigstellung zu erhalten. Besonders herzlichen Dank schulde ich auch Herrn Baldensperger persönlich, der, obschon er mir in allem grosszügig freie Hand liess, doch nie zu geschäftig war, mir schriftlich sofort mit Rat und Tat beizustehen, wenn ich ihn in Bezug auf verschiedene Probleme um Beistand bat. Für das Ausfertigen tausender von Karten bin ich besonders der Sekretärin unserer Abteilung, Mrs. Eslie H. Miller, verpflichtet. Durch die

Fürsprache von Herrn Charles Dédéyan in Paris, dem zuvorkommenden Sekretär der Commission internationale d'histoire littéraire moderne, gelang es mir auch, von U.N.E.S.C.O. eine namhafte Summe zur Fertigstellung des Manuskriptes zu erhalten, und auch das an unserer Universität wirkende Komitee zur Verteilung der für akademische Zwecke bestimmten Carnegie-Gelder bedachte mich mit einer ermutigenden Summe für ebendenselben Zweck. Beiden Organisationen bin ich in der Tat zu grossem Danke verpflichtet. Unter den Kollegen, die mir gelegentlich halfen, möchte ich besonders Herrn A.B. Benson (Yale) erwähnen, der meine Kapitel über skandinavische Einflüsse einer Ueberprüfung unterzog—und wertvolle Ergänzungen für meine slavischen Kapitel wurden mir von den Herren R. Wellek (Yale), O. Maslenikov (Berkeley) und M. Markovitch (Belgrad-Paris) zugestellt. Meine Unkenntnis der slavischen Sprachen möge erklären und entschuldigen, warum ich slavische Titel zumeist in der Sprache der von mir konsultierten westeuropäischen Bibliographien wiedergegeben habe.

Ich möchte es als ein günstiges und erwähnenswertes Omen auffassen, dass alle drei Männer, die sich in erster Linie mit dem Ansammeln einer Bibliographie der vergleichenden Literaturgeschichte befassten, aus den französisch-deutschen Randgebieten stammen und dass sie dieses französisch-deutsche Erbe mit einer tiefen innerlichen Verbundenheit zur Schweiz und zu den Vereinigten Staaten verknüpften : der in der Umgebung von New York aufgewachsene Elsässer Louis Betz legte in Zürich den Grundstein einer tragisch kurzen, doch glänzenden akademischen Laufbahn; der Lothringer Fernand Baldensperger bezeugte durch sein Erstlingswerk über Gottfried Keller seine Vorliebe für die Schweiz bevor er in Lyon, Paris, Harvard und Los Angeles das Studium der vergleichenden Literaturgeschichte neuen Spitzenleistungen entgegenführte; und ich als geborener Schweizer wurde in Bern, Paris, Harvard und Yale geschult bevor ich mich im Jahre 1935 in North Carolina niederliess. So scheinen rein äussere Umstände dazu beigetragen zu haben, dass durch diese beneidenswerte Kulturvermischung die bestmöglichen Vorbedingungen zu toleranter internationaler Zusammenarbeit geschaffen wurden. Möge dieses völkerversöhnende Ideal in den Seiten der vorliegenden Bibliographie einen besonders überzeugenden und fruchtbringenden Ausdruck finden!

W. P. F.

To The Reader

A repeated study of the Table of Contents will best be able to explain the arrangement of this Bibliography. The emphasis, in Books Two and Four, has always been on the emitter, never on the receiver, stressing, first, the influence of one country upon another (e.g. of Greece upon Rome) ; second, of an individual author upon a foreign country or author (e.g. of Homer on Rome or on Virgil) ; and, third, the general influences of a country upon an individual foreign author (e.g. general Greek influences upon Virgil). The arrangement also of Book Three, "Aspects of Western Culture," sandwiched in between Antiquity and the Modern Era, was relatively easy and clear-cut, for it had to deal with Modern Christianity and its variegated influences upon literature (Book Two having stopped with the Church Fathers) ; then, with the various trends of Modern Literature, from the late Middle Ages up to the twentieth century; and finally, with the various aspects of reciprocal influences and of collective actions from abroad which are not always easily classifiable. In all these discussions of modern countries matters were to some extent simplified by uniting related countries under one heading: Austrian literature, for instance, can be found under German literature, Scotland under England, Serbia under Yugoslavia, etc.

That left Book One as the vessel of the widest possible field of matters which had to be included in such a Bibliography. Certain chapters required as complete a treatment as was humanly possible—e.g., the chapters dealing with the theory of Comparative Literature, with the importance of all types of Intermediaries, or with the manifold ramifications of Thematology. Other chapters, however, seemed to call for a general outline of problems rather than for a detailed treatment of all aspects—for instance, the chapters dealing with the relationship of Literature to Politics, to the Arts and the Sciences, or again those dealing with Literary and Semi-Literary Genres and Forms, where the effort at completeness would have led much too far.

The unfortunate habit of scores of writers of articles of using vague or mysterious titles presented many a hard problem to solve. If a fourth-rate character in the *Faerie Queene* was traced back to a fourth-rate character of the *Orlando Furioso* through the medium of a third-rate French author, it was, after a while, possible to figure out the puzzling title and to place the item accurately under the heading of Ariosto's influence upon Spenser. Much more complicated (unless, of course, I was willing and able to investigate scores and hundreds of books myself) were broad titles such as "Mickiewicz and French Literature" or "Goethe and Italy." Since everything had to be arranged from the viewpoint of the emitter and not of the receiver, such titles failed to indicate whether the book dealt with French influence upon Mickiewicz or with Mickiewicz's influence upon France. The title on Goethe and Italy (and scores of similar ones) lent itself to even more interpretations and different classifications: it could mean Italy's influence upon Goethe, Goethe's influence upon Italy, Goethe as a traveller in Italy, or even Goethe as a translator from Italian literature (with the latter two interpretations placing the item under the heading of Intermediaries in Book One, instead of under Influences in Book Four). In order to avoid ambiguity and unnecessary scattering of essentially similar items, it was finally decided that the chapters on Intermediaries in Book One should contain only travellers and translators in general, whenever no particular country or literature was indicated—but that similar cards containing a direct reference to the country of origin should be included in Book Four, under the heading of that particular country. Even so I should like to warn that there may be quite a few erroneous placings of cards and that a book dealing with England's influence upon Montesquieu may have been filed not under England (as it should be), but under Montesquieu, because I may have assumed that it dealt with Montesquieu's influence upon England. In all cases where the reader does not at once find what he is looking for, it may be well to look at the problem from the second angle possible.

Another problem which often defied accurate interpretation dealt with the possibility that two authors may merely have been compared and that no tracings of influences were intended. Articles with the title "Boccaccio and Cervantes" I placed under Boccaccio, unless they stated expressly that they were a mere comparison (in which case I filed them in the Fifth Part of Book One, dealing with Similarities and Contrasts). But how about two contemporaries—e.g., "Dickens and Balzac" or "Leopardi and Espronceda?" Unless I knew of actual influences, I was inclined to place such cards about two contemporaries also in the chapter on Comparisons, for I could not be too sure whether Leopardi had influenced Espronceda or Espronceda Leopardi. Here again it may pay to turn to the chapter on Comparisons if the reader does not find what he wants in Book Four.

I deviated from the general rule of including nothing but published books and articles only in the case of certain significant American doctoral dissertations, because such dissertations, even though typewritten, are increasingly accessible in the form of abstracts, photostats, microfilms, or through our highly developed interlibrary loans—and it seems more than justified to give them their due place in a work such as this.

A word of justification about borderline-cases and about the inclusion of many items which may not always be pertaining to Comparative Literature. No apologies are needed under most headings in the large chapter on Thematology, for, comparative or not, the reader has a right to get the most complete list possible on Sophonisbe, Caesar, Joan of Arc, or the Alps in European literature. But what about other aspects in the field of Thematology: (Molière and) Physicians, (Liliencron and) War, (Wordsworth and) Nature, (Camoens and) the Sea, (Tolstoi and) Divorce, (O'Neill and) the Negro? It was evident that an exhaustive treatment, e.g., of Nature in literature would lead much too far—and I therefore restricted myself to only a few examples of such treatments, which, I hope, will not be criticized as being either too much or too little. Other borderline cases where I tried to find a happy middleground between too much and too little have to do with Literature and Politics (e.g., the Utopias), Literature and Science (e.g., Dante and Astronomy, Joyce and Freudianism, London and Darwinism), and, above all, Literature and Philosophy (see all the information on Aristotle, Plato, Kant, Hegel, etc., where it was often exceedingly hard to draw a line), or Literature and Religion (see, above all, the Fifth Part of Book Two, where I tried my best not to become too much involved e.g. with the non-literary aspects of the Church Fathers). At times it was also hard to keep away from Philology, as the various chapters on the Greek, Latin, French, German or English languages will prove, where I had to include language teachers and language boundaries without, however, becoming involved in *ablautsreihen* or weak adjective endings. A similar selectiveness had to be observed in the chapters on Literary Movements in Book Three: though I tried to make the indications about Renaissance, Classicism, Romanticism as international as possible, I thought it wise to include also a few typical authors as striking examples of each trend (e.g., Calderón and the Baroque, Marivaux and the Rococo, Stifter and Biedermeier, Carducci and Young Europe).

All these borderline cases, the reproaches that I may have included too much, or the criticisms that I may have overlooked scores of valuable books on this or that subject which may have escaped my attention, do not frighten me half as much as the mere thought of the numberless factual mistakes which may have and will have crept into this bibliography. For how do we ever know that a piece of bibliographical information is correct unless we actually hold the book or the journal in question in our hands? For years the bibliographer walks around with cards in his pocket, jotting down every new pertinent item he lays his eyes upon, perusing Marouzeau or other specialized bibliographies, examining the recurrent bibliographies in *RLC, PMLA, RLM, SPh, AGR, RR,* etc., etc. To be sure, whenever my cards differed from those Professor Baldensperger had given me, or whenever my own duplicates and triplicates on the same subject differed, I would immediately contact our reference librarians in order to find out which version was right. Yet they, too, in supplying the answer, in by far the most cases could not directly consult the book or the article in question; instead, they consulted some other "authoritative" bibliography compiled by some mortal with the help of other mortals. All I can therefore say is this: that whenever my cards showed discrepancies we checked and tried to get the accurate version—but that in the thousands of cases where I had only one card about each item, I accepted that card at its face-value and inserted it in its proper place. To reduce the number of probable errors still further, my wife and I also rechecked the entire manuscript of 1500 pages and, when it came to proof-reading, we again did the entire job ourselves, not trusting the work of any outsider. Through this meticulousness we earnestly hope greatly to have reduced the number of factual errors—and we hope, too, that the friendly cooperation of our readers will enable us to publish a supplementary volume in 1955.

W. P. F.

List of the Most Frequently Used Periodicals and of Their Abbreviations

ABAW	Abhandlungen der Bayrischen Akademie der Wissenschaften. München. (Cf. also SBAW.)
Acr.	Acropole. Revue du monde hellénique. Paris.
AFR	Anglo-French Review. London & Paris.
AGR	American-German Review. Philadelphia, Pennsylvania.
AHAW	Abhandlungen der Heidelberger Akademie der Wissenschaften. Heidelberg. (Cf. also SHAW.)
AHR	American Historical Review. New York.
AJPh	American Journal of Philology. Baltimore, Maryland.
AK	Archiv für Kulturgeschichte. Weimar.
AL	American Literature. Durham, North Carolina.
ALG	Archiv für Literaturgeschichte. Leipzig.
AM	Atlantic Monthly. Boston, Massachusetts.
Anglia Bb	Beiblatt zur Anglia. Halle.
Antike	Zeitschrift für Kunst und Kultur der Altertumswissenschaft. Berlin.
APAW	Abhandlungen der Preussischen Akademie der Wissenschaften. Berlin (Cf. also SAWB).
AR	Archivum Romanicum. Firenze.
A & R	Atene e Roma. Bullettino della Società italiana per la diffusione degli studi classici. Firenze.
Archiv	Archiv für das Studium der neueren Sprachen & Litteraturen. Braunschweig.
ARIV	Atti del Reale Istituto Veneto di Scienze, Lettere e Arti. Venezia.
ASEER	American Slavonic and East European Review. New York.
ASPh	Archiv für slavische Philologie. Berlin.
ASR	American-Scandinavian Review. New York.
Ath	Athenaeum, Studi periodici di letteratura e storia. Pavia.
Ausonia	Cahiers Franco-Italiens. Grenoble.
BA	Books Abroad. Norman, Oklahoma.
BAGB	Bulletin de l'Association Guillaume Budé. Paris.
BBG	Blätter für das Bayrische Gymnasial - Schulwesen. München.
Belfagor	Rassegna di varia umanità. Firenze.
BH	Bulletin Hispanique. Bordeaux.
BHR	Bibliothèque d'Humanisme et Renaissance. Paris.
BI	Bulletin Italien. Bordeaux.
BRL	Bulletin of the John Rylands Library. Manchester.
BSS	Bulletin of Spanish Studies. Liverpool.
BURS	Bibliothèque Universelle et Revue Suisse. Genève.
CB	Classical Bulletin. Chicago.
CFA	Cahiers Franco-Allemands (Deutsch-französische Monatshefte.) Karlsruhe.
CJ	Classical Journal. Chicago, Illinois.
CL	Comparative Literature. Eugene, Oregon.
CLN	Comparative Literature Newsletter. Chicago, Illinois.
CLS	Comparative Literature Studies. Cardiff.
Confluences	Revue de la Renaissance française. Paris.
Conv.	Convivium, Rivista di lettere, filosofia e storia, Università Catt. del Sacro Cuore. Milano-Torino.
CPh	Classical Philology. Chicago, Illinois.

CQ	Classical Quarterly. London.
CR	Classical Review. London.
C.R.	In French titles: Comptes rendus.
Crit.	La Critica. Bari.
Cult.	La Cultura. Milano.
CW	Classical Weekly. Lancaster, Pennsylvania.
DFM	Deutsch-französische Monatshefte. Karlsruhe.
Dion.	Dioniso. Siracusa.
DLZ	Deutsche Literatur-Zeitung. Leipzig.
DR	Deutsche Rundschau. Berlin.
D & V	Dichtung & Volkstum. Leipzig.
DVLG	Deutsche Vierteljahrsschrift für Literaturwissenschaft und Geistesgeschichte. Halle.
EA	Etudes Anglaises. Paris.
EC	Etudes Classiques. Namur.
EETS	Early English Text Society. London.
EF	Etudes Françaises. Paris.
EG	Etudes Germaniques. Paris.
EHLF	Etudes d'Histoire Littéraire de la France. Paris.
EHR	English Historical Review. London.
EI	Etudes Italiennes. Bordeaux.
ELH	English Literary History. Baltimore, Maryland.
EN	L'Europe Nouvelle. Paris.
EO	Echos d'Orient. Paris.
Eos.	Commentarii Societatis philologiae Polonorum. Lwow.
EPhK	Egyetemes Philologiai Közlöny. Budapest.
ER	Edinburgh Review.
E & S	Essays & Studies by Members of the English Association. Oxford.
Ensayos y Estudios	Bonn.
ESn	Englische Studien. Leipzig.
ESs	English Studies. Groningen.
ET	Expository Times. Edinburgh.
Et	Etudes, Revue catholique d'intérêt général. Paris.
Euph.	Euphorion. Stuttgart.
FAR	French-American Review. Washington.
FDPh	Forschungen zur deutschen Philologie. Leipzig.
F & F	Forschungen und Fortschritte. Berlin.
FGB	France-Grande Bretagne. Paris.
FL	Folk-Lore. London.
FNL	Forschungen zur neueren Literaturgeschichte. Weimar.
FQ	French Quarterly. London.
FR	French Review. New York.
FS	French Studies. New Haven, Connecticut.
G	Gymnasium. Heidelberg.
GD	Giornale dantesco. Firenze.
GLL	German Life and Letters. Oxford.
GQ	German Quarterly. Lancaster, Pennsylvania.
GR	Germanic Review. New York.
G & R	Greece and Rome. Oxford.
Greg.	Gregorianum. Roma.
GRM	Germanisch-romanische Monatsschrift. Heidelberg.
GS	Germanoslavica. Praha.
GSLI	Giornale Storico della letteratura italiana. Torino.
H	Hermes. Zeitschrift für klassische Philologie. Berlin.
Ha	Hermathena. A Series of Papers on Literature, Science and Philosophy. London.

HG	Humanistisches Gymnasium. Leipzig.
Hisp.	Hispania. Stanford (1918 ff.); also, Paris, 1918-22.
HJ	Hibbert Journal. London.
HLQ	Huntington Library Quarterly. San Marino, California.
HR	Hispanic Review. Philadelphia, Pennsylvania.
H & R	Humanisme et Renaissance. Paris.
HSCPh.	Harvard Studies in Classical Philology. Cambridge, Massachusetts.
HSPhL	Harvard Studies & Notes in Philology and Literature. Cambridge, Massachusetts.
Hum.	Humanités. Revue d'Enseignement Secondaire et d'Education. Paris.
ICS	L'Italia Che Scrive. Roma.
IS	Italian Studies. London.
Isis.	International Review Devoted to the History of Science and Civilization. Brussels.
Ital.	Italica. Chicago, Illinois.
JAFL	Journal of American Folklore. Lancaster, Pennsylvania.
JbDG	Jahrbuch der Dante Gesellschaft. Leipzig.
JbGG	Jahrbuch der Goethe Gesellschaft. Weimar.
JbGrG	Jahrbuch der Grillparzer Gesellschaft. Wien.
JbShG	Jahrbuch der Shakespeare Gesellschaft. Weimar.
JCL	Journal of Comparative Literature. New York.
JEGPh	Journal of English and Germanic Philology. Urbana, Illinois.
JHI	Journal of the History of Ideas. New York.
JQR	Jewish Quarterly Review. Philadelphia, Pennsylvania.
JS	Journal des Savants. Paris.
JWI	Journal of the Warburg and Courtauld Institute. London.
KK	Kwartalnik Klasyczny. Lwow.
Latomus	Revue d'Etudes Latines. Bruxelles.
Leonardo	Rassegna bibliografica. Firenze.
LE	Das literarische Echo. Berlin.
LM	Les Langues Modernes. Paris.
LNI	La Nuova Italia. Perugia.
LQHR	London Quarterly and Holborn Review.
M	Museum. Leiden.
MA	Medium Aevum. Oxford.
MB	More Books. Boston, Massachusetts.
MC	Il Mondo Classico. Torino.
MDU	Monatshefte für deutschen Unterricht. Madison, Wisconsin.
MF	Mercure de France. Paris.
Mfr	Muse Française. Paris.
Mind	A Quarterly Review of Psychology and Philosophy. London.
ML	Modern Languages. London.
MLF	Modern Language Forum. Los Angeles, California.
MLIA	Magazin für die Litteratur des In- und Auslands. Berlin.
MLJ	Modern Language Journal. Menasha, Wisconsin.
MLN	Modern Language Notes. Baltimore, Maryland.
MLQ	Modern Language Quarterly. Seattle, Washington.
MLR	Modern Language Review. London.
MPh	Modern Philology. Chicago, Illinois.
MS	Mediaeval Studies. Toronto.

NAnt	Nuova Antologia di Scienze, Lettere ed Arti. Roma.
NAR	North American Review. Boston, Massachusetts.
NC	Nineteenth Century and After. London.
NEQ	New England Quarterly. Baltimore, Maryland.
NJAB	Neue Jahrbücher für Antike & deutsche Bildung. Leipzig.
NJKA	Neue Jahrbücher für das klassische Altertum. Leipzig.
NJWJ	Neue Jahrbücher für Wissenschaft und Jugendbildung. Leipzig.
NL	Nouvelles Littéraires. Paris.
NM	Neuphilologische Monatsschrift. Leipzig.
NPh	Neophilologus. Groningen.
N & Q	Notes and Queries. London.
NR	Neue Rundschau. Berlin.
NRC	Nouvelle Revue Critique. Paris.
NRF	Nouvelle Revue Française. Paris.
NRFH	Nueva Revista de Filologia Hispánica. México.
NRI	Nouvelle Revue d'Italie. Roma.
NRS	Nuova Rivista Storica. Milano.
NSM	Nuovi Studi Medievali. Bologna.
NSp	Die neueren Sprachen. Marburg.
NSR	Neue Schweizer Rundschau. Zürich.
N & V	Nova et Vetera. Bruxelles.
OC	Open Court. Chicago, Illinois.
PBA	Proceedings of the British Academy. London.
PCA	Proceedings of the Classical Association. Cambridge.
PEGS	Publications of the English Goethe Society. London.
PJb	Preussische Jahrbücher. Berlin.
Ph.	Philologus. Zeitschrift für das klassische Altertum. Leipzig.
PhQ	Philological Quarterly. Iowa.
PhW	Philologische Wochenschrift. Leipzig.
PL	Poet Lore. Philadelphia, Pennsylvania.
PMLA	Publications of the Modern Language Association. New York.
QR	Quarterly Review. London.
RAA	Revue Anglo-Américaine. Paris.
RAF	Revue de l'Alliance française. Zürich.
RaI	Rassegna italiana. Roma.
RB	Revue Bleue. Paris.
RBPh	Revue Belge de Philologie et d'Histoire. Bruxelles.
RC	Revue Celtique. Paris.
RCC	Revue des Cours et Conférences. Paris.
RCLI	Rassegna critica della letteratura italiana. Roma.
RdF	Revue de France. Paris.
RDM	Revue des Deux Mondes. Paris.
REA	Revue des Etudes Anciennes. Paris.
REG	Revue des Etudes Grecques. Paris.
REI	Revue des Etudes Italiennes. Paris.
REL	Revue des Etudes Latines. Paris.
RELV	Revue de l'Enseignement des Langues Vivantes. Le Havre.
RES	Review of English Studies. Oxford.
RF	Romanische Forschungen. Erlangen.
RFA	Revue Franco-Allemande. Paris.
RFB	Revue Franco-Belge. Paris & Bruxelles.
RFE	Revista de Filología Española. Madrid.
RG	Revue Germanique. Paris.
RFH	Revista de Filología Hispánica. Buenos Aires.

RH	Revue Hispanique. Paris.
RHLF	Revue d'Histoire Littéraire de la France. Paris.
RhM	Rheinisches Museum für Philologie. Frankfurt.
RHPhC	Revue d'histoire de la philosophie et d'histoire générale de la civilisation. Lille.
RI	Rivista d'Italia. Roma.
RIA	Revista Iberoamericana. México.
RIE	Revue Internationale de l'Enseignement. Paris.
RLC	Revue de Littérature Comparée. Paris.
RLFE	Revue des Lettres françaises et étrangères. Bordeaux.
RLM	Rivista di letterature moderne. Firenze.
RLR	Revue des Langues Romanes. Montpellier.
RMM	Revue de Métaphysique et de Morale. Paris.
Rom.	Romania. Paris.
Romana	Rivista dell' Istituto Interuniversitario. Firenze.
RP	Revue de Paris.
RR	Romanic Review. New York.
RRh	Revue Rhénane. Mainz.
RSI	Rivista storica italiana. Torino.
RU	Revue Universitaire. Paris.
RyF	Razon y Fe. Madrid.
SAB	Shakespeare Association Bulletin. New York.
SAQ	South Atlantic Quarterly. Durham, North Carolina.
SAWB	Sitzungsberichte der Akademie der Wissenschaften. Berlin.
SAWW	Sitzungsberichte der Akademie der Wissenschaften. Wien.
SBAW	Sitzungsberichte der Bayrischen Akademie der Wissenschaften. München.
SEER	Slavonic and East European Review. London.
SFQ	Southern Folklore Quarterly. Gainesville, Florida.
SG	Studi Germanici. Firenze.
SHAW	Sitzungsberichte der Heidelberger Akademie der Wissenschaften. Heidelberg.
SIFC	Studi italiani di filologia classica. Firenze.
SKG	Srpski Kgnjizevni Glasnik. Belgrade.
SM	Studi Medievali. Torino.
Spec.	Speculum. Journal of Mediaeval Studies. Cambridge, Massachusetts.
SPh	Studies in Philology. Chapel Hill, North Carolina.
SR	Slavonic Review. London.
SRL	Saturday Review of Literature. New York.
SS	Scandinavian Studies. Lincoln, Nebraska.
SVL	Studien zur vergleichenden Literaturgeschichte. Berlin.
Symposium	Syracuse, New York.
SZ	Stimmen der Zeit. Freiburg.
TAPhA	Transactions and Proceedings of the American Philological Association. Lancaster, Pennsylvania.
TLS	Times Literary Supplement. London.
UCPPh	University of California Publications in Modern Philology. Berkeley.
UTQ	University of Toronto Quarterly. Toronto.
VBW	Vorträge der Bibliothek Warburg. Leipzig.
WBFA	Wiener Blätter für die Freunde der Antike. Wien.
WM	Westermanns Monatshefte. Braunschweig.
WS	Wiener Studien. Zeitschrift für klassische Philologie. Wien.
ZDA	Zeitschrift für deutsches Altertum und deutsche Litteratur. Leipzig.

ZDK	Zeitschrift für Deutschkunde. Leipzig.
ZDMG	Zeitschrift der deutschen morgenländischen Gesellschaft. Leipzig.
ZDPh	Zeitschrift für deutsche Philologie. Halle.
ZDU	Zeitschrift für deutschen Unterricht. Leipzig.
ZFEU (or ZEFU)	Zeitschrift für englischen und französischen Unterricht. Berlin.
ZFSL	Zeitschrift für französische Sprache und Literatur. Leipzig.
ZNS	Zeitschrift für neuere Sprachen. Marburg.
ZNU	Zeitschrift für neusprachlichen Unterricht. Berlin.
ZRPh	Zeitschrift für romanische Philologie. Halle.
ZSPh	Zeitschrift für slavische Philologie. Leipzig.
ZVL	Zeitschrift für vergleichende Literaturgeschichte. Berlin.

Other Abbreviations:

CR	Comptes rendus	Progr.	Programm
Ges.	Gesellschaft	U	University
Jb	Jahrbuch or Jahrbücher	UP	University Press
Mag.	Magazine	Zs	Zeitschrift
NS or NF	New Series	Zt	Zeitung

Festschrift, Gedenkschrift, Hommage or Mélanges: used in lieu of any memorial volume with a lengthy title.

Unless otherwise indicated, Frankfurt is Frankfurt a/M.

Of the two Freiburgs, Freiburg is in Germany, Fribourg in Switzerland.

Whenever possible, Harvard U.P. was substituted for Cambridge, Massachusetts, in order to avoid any confusion with Cambridge, England.

Whenever possible, Columbia U.P. and Oxford U.P. were used in order to facilitate the search in the two great book-centers of New York and London.

Volumes are in Arabic numbers. Roman numbers are used only for the indication of months in dates, e.g. 27.XII.1935 : December 27, 1935.

Cross-references refer to Books, Parts, and Chapters, in that order. See Longfellow, IV. XI. 9 means Book Four, Part Eleven, Chapter Nine.

BOOK ONE

Generalities, Intermediaries, Thematology, Literary Genres

FIRST PART

Comparative Literature, World Literature, European Literature

FIRST CHAPTER

Comparative Literature.

(The items of this chapter are arranged chronologically up to 1900, afterwards alphabetically.)

Gérando, J. M. de. Des communications littéraires et philosophiques entre les nations de l'Europe. Arch. litt. de l'Europe, 1, 1804.

Lamartine, A. de. Discours sur les avantages de la communication des idées entre les peuples par la littérature. Académie de Mâcon, discours prononcé en 1811. In: Reyssié, La jeunesse de Lamartine. Paris, 1892.

Scheffer, C. A. De la libre communication d'idées entre les peuples. Censeur européen, 1, 1815.

Noël et Laplace. Cours de littérature comparée. Paris, 1816ff.

Goethe, J. W. von. Gespräche mit Eckermann, 31. I. 1827.

—— Gespräche mit Mickiewicz und David, 25. VIII. 1829.

Ampère, J. J. Littérature et voyages (Préface). Paris, 1833.

Anon. Vergleichende Uebersicht der französischen, englischen und deutschen Literatur. Blätt. z. Kunde d. Litt. d. Auslands, 1836.

Chasles, P. Littérature étrangère comparée. Leçon d'ouverture à l'Athénée, 17. I. 1836.

Duquesnel, A. Histoire des lettres : cours de littérature comparée. Paris, 1846.

Benloew, L. Introduction à l'histoire comparée des littératures. Leçon d'ouverture. Dijon, 1849.

Delatouche, H. Cours de littérature comparée. Paris, 1859.

Sainte-Beuve, C. A. Définition de la littérature comparée à propos de J. J. Ampère. Nouveaux Lundis, 13 & RDM, 1868.

Graf, A. Storia letteraria e comparazione. Prolusione al corso di storia comparata delle letterature neolatine. Torino, 1876.

Shackford, C. C. Comparative Literature. Proc. of the U. Convocation. Albany (N.Y.) 1876.

Koch, M. Introduction to the Zeitschrift für vergleichende Litteraturgeschichte. N.F. 1. Berlin, 1877.

Lomenitz, M. de. Acta comparationis litterarum universarum. London, 1877.

Pucci, S. Principi di letteratura generale italiana e comparata. Genova, 1880.

Posnett, H. M. Comparative Literature. Internat. Scientific Series, 1. London, 1886.

Rod, E. De la littérature comparée. Discours d'inauguration du cours d'histoire générale des littératures modernes à l'U. de Genève. Genève, 1886. Cf. ZVL, 2, 1889.

Wetz, W. Ueber Begriff und Wesen der vergleichenden Litteraturgeschichte. In: Shakespeare vom Standpunkte der vergleichenden Litteraturgeschichte. Worms, 1890.

Texte, J. Les études de littérature comparée à l'étranger et en France. RIE, 25, 1893.

Gayley, C. M. A Society of Comparative Literature. Dial, 1. VIII. 1894.

Marsh, A. R. The Comparative Study of Literature. PMLA, 11, 1895.

Betz, L. P. Kritische Betrachtungen über Wesen, Aufgabe und Bedeutung der vergleichenden Litteraturgeschichte. ZFSL, 18, 1896.

Texte, J. L'histoire comparée des littératures. Rev. de philologie fr. et de litt. 10, 1896.

Barine, A. Du libre-échange en littérature. Journal des Débats, 4. VIII. 1897.

Brunetière, F. Conférence inédite sur la critique, prononcée en Amérique en 1897. Citée par Pierre Moreau. RHL, 1936.

Mueller, H. C. L'étude scientifique de la littérature comparée. RIE, 15. I & 15. IV. 1898.

Benazet, A. Quelques mots sur l'étude comparée des littératures. Rev. de linguist. et de philol. comparée, 1899.

Anon. The Foible of Comparative Literature. Blackwood's Mag., 1901.

Arias, A. Literatura general. Quito, 1942.

Baldensperger, F. L'enseignement de la littérature comparée aux Universités Columbia et Harvard. RIE, 1909.

—— Où nous en sommes: examen de conscience d'un comparatiste. RU, 1919.

—— Littérature comparée: le mot et la chose. RLC, 1, 1921.

Mélanges d'histoire littéraire, générale et comparée, offerts à Fernand Baldensperger. 2 vols. Paris, 1930
—— Les études de littérature comparée. Science française. Paris, 1933.
—— Starea actuala a Studiilor comparatiste. Insemnari Tesene, 15. IX. 1937.
—— Solidarité internationale et littérature comparée. CLS, 16, 1945.
—— Antécédents internationaux du 'comparatisme' actuel. (L. Betz). Symposium, 1, 1946.
—— La littérature comparée aux Etats-Unis. RLC, 21, 1947.

Barreira, I. De literatura comparada. Vasco da Gama, (July), 1926.

Baur, F. De vergelijkende methode in de literaturwetenschap. Mélanges J. Vercquille, Bruxelles, 1927.

Bertrand, J. J. Littérature comparée. Bull. de l'U. de l'Acad. de Toulouse, 1921.

Betz, L. P. La littérature comparée. Essai bibliographique. Strassburg, 1900.
—— 2e éd. augmentée—publiée par F. Baldensperger. Strassburg, 1904.
—— Litteraturvergleichung. LE, 10, 1901 & in Studien zur vergleichenden Litteraturgeschichte der neueren Zeit. Frankfurt, 1902.

Campbell, O. J. What is Comparative Literature? Festschrift Barrett Wendell. Harvard U.P. 1926.

Carré, J. M. La littérature comparée en France pendant l'occupation. CLS, 17-18, 1945.

Charbonnel, R. Le comparatisme et l'extension universitaire. RIE, 15. III & 15. IV. 1920.

Chevalley, A. Littérature comparée. MF, 1928.

Christy, A. E. A Guide to Comparative Literature. CLN, 1943-44.

Croce, B. La Letteratura comparata. Critica, 1, 1903.

Desoray, F. Littérature comparée. RBPh, 9, 1930.

Eckhardt, A. Méthodes et problèmes de la littérature comparée dans l'Europe centrale. Bull. of the Internat. Committee of Historical Sciences, 14. Paris, 1932.

Etiemble, R. Renouveau de la littérature comparée. El Katib el Masri (Le Caire), 1.I.1948.

Folkierski, W. Littérature comparée ou histoire littéraire nationale. Bull. of the Internat. Committee of Historical Sciences, 14. Paris, 1932.

Fransen, J. Iets over de vergelijkende literaturstudie: perioden en invloeden. Groningen, 1936.

Friederich, W. P. The Case of Comparative Literature. Bull. Am. Assoc. of U. Professors, 31, 1945.
—— L'organisation des comparatistes aux Etats-Unis. RLC, 22, 1948.
—— & Gohdes, C. A Department of American and Comparative Literature. MLJ, 33, 1949.

Garoglio, D. La critica letteraria (concerning Betz, La Littérature comparée). Marzocco, 22. VI. 1902.

Gayley, C. M. What is Comparative Literature? AM, 92, 1903.

Hankiss, J. La terminologie d'histoire littéraire et les littératures comparées. NPh 23, 1937-38.

Hazard, P. Les récents travaux en littérature comparée. Essai de classification. RU, 1914.
—— La littérature comparée In: Les Méthodes françaises. Civilisation française, Sept. 1919.

Hirth, F. Vom Geiste vergleichender Literaturwissenschaft. Universitas 2, (Stuttgart), 1947.

Holmes, U. T. Comparative Literature: Past and Future. American Colleges and Universities. SPh, 42, 1945.

Ijac, C. Une ancienne Revue de Littérature comparée: Acta comparationis litterarum universarum. (1877-88). RLC, 14, 1934.

Jameson, R. D. A Comparison of Literatures. London, 1935.

Jan, E. von. Französische Literaturgeschichte und vergleichende Literaturbetrachtung. GRM, 15, 1927.

Jantz, H. S. The Fathers of Comparative Literature. BA, 1936.

Jellinek, A. Bibliographie der vergleichenden Literaturgeschichte. Berlin, 1903.

Jones, H. M. & Thomas R. The Comparative Study of Literature. Longhorn Mag. (U. of Texas). 1922.

Kalff, G. Algemeene en vergelijkende letterkunde. Vragen des Tijds, 1, 1915.

Kriaras, E. La littérature comparée en France. Nea Hestia, Jan., 1948.

Kuehnemann, E. Zur Aufgabe der vergleichenden Litteraturgeschichte (concerning L. Betz, La littérature comparée). Centralbl. f. Bibliothekwesen, 1901.

Van der Laan, J. E. Comparatistische Dogmatiek. Levende Talen, 85, 1935.
Loliée, F. Histoire des littératures comparées des origines au XXe siècle. Paris, 1903.
Maury, L. Cooperation intellectuelle et littérature comparée. RB, 1927.
Neri, F. La tavola dei valori del comparatista. GSLI, 109, 1937.
Partridge, E. The Comparative Study of Literature. In: A Critical Medley. Paris, 1926.
Petersen, J. Nationale oder vergleichende Literaturgeschichte?. DVLG, 6, 1928.
Popa, N. I. Un umanism modern: literatura comparata. Insemnari Tesene, 15. IX. 1937.
—— Resistentele franzese in literatura comparata. Iasi, 1938.
Posnett, H. M. The Science of Comparative Literature. Contemp. Rev., 79, 1901.
Revon, M. Acquérir le sens des littératures étrangères. NRC, 1924.
Schoell, F. L. Littérature comparée et littérature générale aux Etats-Unis. EF, 1925.
Sittard, J. Vergleichende Literaturgeschichte. Ber. d. Hamb. Corresp., 6. IX.1903.
Smith, G. G. Some Notes on the Comparative Study of Literature. MLR, 1905.
Strich, F. Weltliteratur und vergleichende Literatur. In: Philosophie der Literaturwissenschaft (ed. by E. Ermatinger). Berlin, 1930.
Van Tieghem, P. La notion de littérature comparée. Rev. du Mois, 10. III. 1906.
—— La littérature comparée. Paris, 1931. 3. ed., 1946.
Tobin, J. E. A 1607 Concept of Comparative Literature. CLN, 1, 1943.
Trojan, F. Wege zu einer vergleichenden Wissenschaft von der dichterischen Komposition. Festschrift O. Walzel, Wildpark-Potsdam, 1924.
De Vries, D. De vergelijkende literatur-studie. NPh, 1935.
Wais, K. Zeitgeist und Volkszeit in der vergleichenden Literaturgeschichte (am Beispiel der Romantik). GRM, 1934.
—— Der zweite internationale Kongress für Literaturgeschichte. Archiv, 1935.
Will, J. S. Comparative Literature: its Meaning and Scope. UTQ, 1939.
Woodberry, G. Editorial. JCL, 1, 1903.

SECOND CHAPTER

Generalities, Scope, Definitions and Tasks of Literature.

(See also Literary Criticism, I. VII. 2.)
(The items of this chapter are arranged chronologically up to 1900, afterwards alphabetically.)

Morhofi, D. Polyhistor, in tres tomos, literarium, philosophicum et practicum. Lubecae, 1708.
Reimann, J. F. Einleitung in die Historiam literariam antediluvianam. Halle, 1708-13.
Salvini, A. M. Par qual cagione gli uomini letterati sieno più accreditati fuori delle loro patrie che nelle medesime. Discorso XIV. Firenze, 1712.
Denina, C. Tableau des révolutions de la littérature ancienne et moderne. Traduit de l'italien. Paris, 1767. London, 1771.
Batteux, C. Principes de la littérature. 5 ed., 5 vols. Paris, 1774.
Herder, J. G. Ursachen des gesunkenen Geschmackes bei den verschiedenen Völkern, da er geblühet. (1775).
—— Ueber die Wirkung der Dichtkunst auf die Sitten der Völker in alten und neuen Zeiten. (1778).
Andrés, P. J. Dell' origine, progresso e stato attuale d'ogni letteratura. 7 vols. Parma, 1782-99.
Gedicke, F. Ueber das Studium der Literarhistorie. Berliner Monatsschrift, 1783.
Schiller, F. von. Ueber naive und sentimentale Dichtung (1795).
Meusel, J. G. Leitfaden zur Geschichte der Gelehrsamkeit. 3 vols. Leipzig, 1799.
Wächler, L. Handbuch der allgemeinen Geschichte der literarischen Cultur. Marburg, 1804. (3 ed. in 4 vols. Leipzig, 1833).
Eichhorn, J. G. Geschichte der Litteratur von ihrem Anfang bis auf die neuesten Zeiten. 6 vols. Göttingen, 1805-11.
—— Literargeschichte der drei letzten Jahrhunderte. 2 vols. Göttingen, 1814.
Schlegel, F. Geschichte der alten und neuen Litteratur. Vorlesungen gehalten zu Wien 1812. Wien, 1815.
Quinet, E. De l'unité des littératures modernes. RDM, 1838.
Théry, A. F. Principes de littérature. Cours de littérature générale. Paris, 1847-60.

Schmidt, C. Vergleichende Tabellen über die Literatur- und Staatengeschichte der wichtigsten Kulturvölker der neueren Welt. Leipzig, 1865.
Linguiti, P. Sul nuovo indirizzo degli studi letterari storici e critici, riguardato nelle cause e nei suoi effetti. Salerno, 1877.
Grosse, E. Die Litteratur-Wissenschaft, ihr Ziel und ihr Weg. Halle, 1887.
Bouchet, E. Précis de littératures étrangères anciennes et modernes. Paris, 1888.
Ten Brink, B. Ueber die Aufgabe der Litteraturgeschichte. Strassburg, 1890.
Wolff, E. Das Wesen wissenschaftlicher Litteraturbetrachtung. Kiel, 1890.
Biese, A. Ueber die Aufgabe der Litteraturgeschichte. National Zt, 587 & 589, 1891.
Wetz, W. Ueber Litteraturgeschichte, eine Kritik von Ten Brink's Rede. Worms, 1891.
Falkenheim, H. Kuno Fischer und die litteraturhistorische Methode. Berlin, 1892.
Elster, E. Die Aufgaben der Litteraturgeschichte. Halle, 1894.
Wetz, W. Litteraturwissenschaft. Krit. Jahresb. über d. Fortschr. der roman. Philologie, 1894.
Mazzoni, P. Della storia letteraria. In: Ann. d. R. Instituto di studi sup. Firenze, 1894-95.
Backhaus, W. E. Das litterarische Schaffen und das Entwicklungsgesetz in der Litteratur. In: Litterarische Essays. Braunschweig, 1895.
Corson, H. The Aims of Literary Study of Literature. London, 1895.
Elster, E. Prinzipien der Litteraturwissenschaft. Halle, 1897.
Lacombe, P. Introduction à l'histoire littéraire. Paris, 1898.
Renard, G. La méthode scientifique de l'histoire littéraire. Paris, 1900.

Auerbach, E. Mimesis, dargestellte Wirklichkeit in der abendländischen Literatur. Bern, 1946.
Baldensperger, F. La littérature: création, succès, durée. Paris, 1914.
—— La littérature moyen de défense. RLC, 10, 1930. And in: Etudes d'histoire littéraire, 4e sér. Paris, 1939.
—— Divergences actuelles en histoire littéraire. Bull. of the Internat. Committee of Historical Sciences, 14. Paris, 1932.
—— Littérature générale et littératures particulières. FR, 1932.
Bartels, A. Nationale oder internationale Literaturwissenschaft. München, 1917.
Betz, L. P. Aus dem Wanderleben der Litteraturen. LE, July, 1901.
Bruch, J. Literaturgeschichte und Sprachgeschichte. Festschrift P. A. Becker. Heidelberg, 1922.
Buck, P. M. Directions in Contemporary Literature. New York, 1942.
Castro, R. S. Estado actual de los métodos de la historia literaria. Santiago (Chile), 1933.
Chadwick, H. M. & N. K. The Growth of Literature. 3 vols. Cambridge U.P., 1932-40.
Cooper, L. Methods and Aims in the Study of Literature: a Series of Extracts and Illustrations. Ithaca, 1940.
Croce, B. Osservazioni sullo stato presente della metodologia della storia letteraria. Bull. of Internat. Committee of Historical Sciences, 14. Paris, 1932.
—— Methodologie und Literaturgeschichte. DVLG, 10, 1932.
Cysarz, H. Literaturgeschichte als Geisteswissenschaft. Kritik und System. Halle, 1926.
Dilthey, W. Das Erlebnis und die Dichtung. Leipzig, 1906. 8th ed. 1922.
Dragomirescou, M. La science de la littérature. 4 vols. Paris, 1939.
DuBos, C. What is Literature? New York, 1940.
Earnest, E. A Foreword to Literature. New York, 1945.
Elster, E. Prinzipien der Litteraturwissenschaft. Halle, 1911.
Ermatinger, E. Die deutsche Literaturwissenschaft der Gegenwart. ZDK, 1925.
—— Das dichterische Kunstwerk. Berlin, 1929.
—— Die Idee in der Literaturwissenschaft. EPhK, 1931.
—— Die Idee der Literaturwissenschaft, Bull. of the Internat. Committee of Historical Sciences, 14. Paris, 1932.
Esquerra, R. Iniciación a la literatura. 3 vols. Barcelona, 1937.
Farinelli, A. Attraverso la poesia e la vita. Saggi e discorsi. Bologna, 1935.
Gayley, C. M. The Development of Literary Studies During the Nineteenth Century (and Comparative Literature). Congress of Arts and Sciences, Universal Exposition St. Louis, 1904. vol. 3. Boston & New York, 1906.
Getto, G. et al. Tecnica e teoria letteraria. Milano, 1948.
Greenlaw, E. The Province of Literary History. Baltimore, 1931.

Hall, Dorothy. The Function of Literature. Antioch Rev., 1, 1941.
Hankiss, J. Défense et illustration de la littérature. Paris, 1936.
Hazard, P. Les tendances actuelles de l'histoire littéraire. Le Mois, 1935.
Hunt, T. W. Literature: Its Principles and Problems. New York, 1906.
Kohler, P. Petites gloses sur la crise de l'histoire littéraire. Mélanges Tappolet. Bâle, 1935.
Van Kranendonk, A. G. New Methods for the Study of Literature. ESs, 17, 1935.
Lichtenberger, H. Une méthode nouvelle d'histoire littéraire. Mélanges Baldensperger. Paris, 1930.
Matthews, B. Approach to Literature. Columbia U Lectures. New York, 1911.
Mornet, D. Questions de méthode (concerning P. Hazard: La crise de la conscience européenne). RHLF, 1935.
Nadler, J. Forschungsprobleme der Literatur des 19. Jahrhunderts. Euphorion, 27, 1926.
Neri, F. Lo studio delle letterature moderne. L'Erma, 3 (Torino).
Nicholson, N. Man and Literature. Toronto, 1944.
Nicolson, Marjorie. The History of Literature and the History of Thought. English Institute Annual, 1939.
Oppel, H. Die Literaturwissenschaft in der Gegenwart. Stuttgart, 1939.
Petersen, J. Die Wissenschaft von der Dichtung. Berlin, 1939.
Pollock, T. C. The Nature of Literature: Its relations to Science, Language, and Human Experience. Princeton, 1942.
Pommier, J. De la méthode et du but de l'histoire littéraire. RIE, 1922.
Richter, W. Von der Literaturwissenschaft zur Literaturgeschichte. MDU, 33, 1941.
Rickert, E. New Methods for the Study of Literature. Chicago, 1927.
Schück, H. Allmän literatur-historia. 7 vols. Stockholm, 1919-26.
Shipley, J. T. (ed.) Encyclopedia of Literature. 2 vols. New York, 1946.
Soderhjelm, W. Henrik Schück und scine allgemeine Literaturgeschichte. Neuphilol. Mitteilungen, 25, 1924.
Spring, P. The Spirit of Literature. Winter Park, (Fla.), 1945.
Starr, N. C. The Dynamics of Literature. New York, 1945.
Thibaudet, A. Réflexions sur la littérature. Paris, 1938.
Tiander, K. Allgemeiner Kursus der Geschichte der antiken und abendländischen Literatur. Petrograd, 1915.
van Tieghem, P. La synthèse en histoire littéraire. Rev. de synthèse historique, 31, 1921.
—— Les grands écrivains étrangers. Paris, 1928.
—— La littérature générale. Bull. of the Internat. Committee of Historical Sciences, 14. Paris, 1932.
—— La question des méthodes en histoire littéraire. ibid.
—— Répertoire chronologique des littératures modernes. Paris, 1935.
van Tieghem, Ph. Tendances nouvelles en histoire littéraire. EF, 1930.
Unger, R. Literaturgeschichte als Problemgeschichte. Schriften der Königsberger gelehrten Ges., 1, 1925.
—— Literaturgeschichte und Geistesgeschichte. DVLG, 4, 1926.
Vermeylen, A. La méthode scientifique de l'histoire littéraire. Rev. de l'U de Bruxelles, 6, 1901.
Walzel, O. et al. Handbuch der Literaturwissenschaft. Berlin-Potsdam, 1923 ff.
Wellek, R. & Warren, A. The Theory of Literature. New York, 1949.
Williams, W. E. The Craft of Literature. London, 1925.

CHAPTER THREE

World Literature.

Anon. Littérature européenne et littérature universelle. Le Mois, Oct., 1935.
Arnold, R. F. Weltliteratur. Rede. Wien, 1932.
Baldensperger, F. La littérature universelle selon l'esprit occidental. Annales de l'U. de Paris, Dec., 1934.
Baumgarten, A. Geschichte der Weltliteratur. 3 vols. Freiburg, 1901-11.
Beil, E. Zur Entwicklung des Begriffs der Weltliteratur. Diss. Leipzig, 1915. Probefahrten, 28.
Benedetto, L. F. La letteratura mondiale. Ponte, 2, 1946.
Berg, L. Weltliteratur und Heimatkunst. Hannoverscher Courier. 7.II.1901.
Berthet, A. La littérature universelle. Paris, 1923.
Bodmer, M. Eine Bibliothek der Weltliteratur. Zürich, 1947.
Dizionario letterario delle opere e dei personaggi di tutti i tempi e di tutte le letterature. Valentino Bompiani editore. Milano, 1947 ff. Cf. GR, 1948.
Boyd, E. A. Studies from Ten Literatures. New York, 1925.

Brandes, G. Weltlitteratur. LE, 1.X 1899.
Buck, P. M. An Anthology of World Literature. New York, 1940.
Carter, M. Case for World Literature. School Review, 66, 1948.
Chiarini, G. L'avvenimento della letteratura universale. NAnt, 96, 1887.
Dezsi, L. Dictionnaire universel de littérature. (In Hungarian). Budapest, 1930.
Elster, E. Weltliteratur und Literaturvergleichung. Archiv, 107, 1901.
Engel, E. Was bleibt? Die Weltliteratur. Leipzig, 1928.
Eppelsheimer, H. W. Handbuch der Weltliteratur von den Anfängen bis zum Weltkrieg. Frankfurt, 1937.
Ernst, P. Völker und Zeiten im Spiegel ihrer Dichtung. Aufsätze zur Weltliteratur. München, 1940.
Farinelli, A. Il sogno di una letteratura mondiale. Roma, 1923.
—— Aufsätze, Reden und Charakteristiken zur Weltliteratur. Bonn, 1925.
—— Weltliteratur und Innenleben. In: Neue Reden und Aufsätze. Pisa, 1937.
Ford, F. M. The March of Literature: From Confucius to Modern Times. London, 1939.
Gorky, M. Préface au catalogue de la littérature mondiale. Ecrits Nouveaux, Oct, 1922.
Guérard, A. Preface to World Literature. New York, 1940.
Hankiss, J. Littérature universelle? Helicon, 1, 1938.
Hart, J. Führer durch die Weltliteratur. Berlin, 1923.
Hecht, G. Der Begriff einer allgemeinen Weltliteratur. Kritische Tribüne, 1 (München), 1912.
Holtermann, K. Kurze Geschichte der Weltliteratur. Freiburg, 1912.
Klemperer, V. Weltliteratur und europäische Literatur. Logos, 18, 1930.
Kralik, R. Die Weltliteratur der Gegenwart. Graz, 1923.
Ludkewicz, S. Die Sowjetliteratur als Vortrupp der Weltliteratur. In: Die Literatur in der Sowjetunion. Spezialnummer herausgegeben von der Ges. für kulturelle Verbindung des Sowjet mit dem Ausland, 7-8, 1934.
Macy, J. The Story of the World's Literature. New York, 1925.
Meyer, R. M. Die Weltliteratur und die Gegenwart. DR, Aug, 1900.
—— Die Weltliteratur im 20. Jahrhundert. Stuttgart, 1913.
Moulton, R. G. World Literature. London, 1911.
Nehry, J. Aus der Weltliteratur. Progr. Aschersleben, 1890.
Oberholzer, O. Kleines Lexikon der Weltliteratur. Bern, 1946.
Oehl, W. Zur Revision der deutschen Beurteilung der Weltliteratur des 16. und 17. Jahrhunderts. Das Neue Reich, 6, 1924.
Oehlke, W. Grundriss der Weltliteratur, im besonderen der deutschen Dichtung. Berlin, 1939.
Otto. Ueber die Bestrebungen um Begründung einer Universalliteratur. Braunsberg, 1852.
Poritzky, J. E. Austausch literarischer Stoffe und Formen in der Weltliteratur. Literatur, 31, 1929.
Prampolini, G. Storia universale della letteratura. 3 vols. Torino, 1933-38.
Rodenberg, J. Weltliteratur und der moderne Staat. DR, 24, 1880.
Schacht, R. Kurzgefasste Geschichte der Weltliteratur. Leipzig, 1925.
Scherr, J. Illustrierte Geschichte der Weltliteratur. 11th ed. Stuttgart, 1926-27.
Schick, H. G. Forderung einer Problemgeschichte der Weltliteratur. LE, 1922.
Shipley, J. T. (ed.) A Dictionary of World Literature: Criticism, Forms, Technique. New York, 1943.
Shoemaker, F. Aesthetic Experience through . . . World Literature. New York, 1943.
Slochower, H. No Voice Is Wholly Lost. New York, 1945.
van Tieghem, P. Histoire littéraire de l'Europe et de l'Amérique, de la Renaissance à nos jours. Paris, 1946.
Vossler, K. Nationalliteratur und Weltliteratur. Zeitwende, 4, 1928.
Walzel, O. Zusammenhänge in der Weltdichtung. NPh, 17, 1932.
Wiegler, P. Geschichte der Weltliteratur. Berlin, 1914.
Zamboni, A. Weltliteratur. Una breve rassegna bibliografica. LNI, 20.IV. 1933.

CHAPTER FOUR

European Literature.

Anon. The Poets and Poetry of Europe by H. W. Longfellow. NAR, 1845.
Arcos, R. Patrie européenne. Europe, 1923.
Babits, M. Geschichte der europäischen Literatur. Zürich, 1949.
Baldensperger, F. La littérature euro-

péenne; leçon d'ouverture du cours de littératures comparées à l'U. de Lyon. Bull. de la Société des Amis de l'U. de Lyon, 1900.
—— Geistiger Europäismus. Neue Zürcher Zt, 26.VII. 1930.
Benda, Bloch, Claudel, Lévy-Bruhl, Rolland. Esprit européen. NL, 23.XI. 1935—18.I.1936.
Benda, Bernanos, Jaspers, Spender, Guéhenno, Flora, Rougemont, Salis, Lukasc. Esprit européen. (textes in extenso des conférences et des entretiens organisés par les rencontres internationales de Genève.) 1946.
Bonsels, W. Der europäische Schriftsteller. Literatur, Sept., 1939.
Bovet, E. Les Européens. Wissen & Leben, 1921.
Brunetière, F. La littérature européenne. RDM, 1900.
Bruno, F. Concetto di europeismo. Augustea, 15.IV. 1929.
Buron, L. L. Histoire abrégée des principales littératures de l'Europe ancienne et moderne avec tableaux et sommaires. Paris, 1867.
Contini, G. Dove va la cultura europea? Fiera letteraria, 1, 1946.
Corrodi, E. Studien zur europäischen Literatur. Neue Zürcher Zt., 8.XII. 1929.
Cremieux, B. Der europäische Geist in der modernen Literatur. Rhein. Blätter, 1927.
Croce, B. European Literature in the Nineteenth Century. New York, 1924.
Curtius, E. R. Vom europäischen Geist in der modernen französischen Literatur. Wissen & Leben, 1924.
—— Europäische Literatur und lateinisches Mittelalter. Bern, 1948.
Cysarz, H. Europa Nova? Kritische Bemerkungen zur vergleichenden Schrifttumsforschung und zum ausserdeutschen Gegenwartsschrifttum. DVLG, 17.
Deshaches, G. D'une littérature européenne. L'Age nouveau, 1939.
Drake, W. A. Contemporary European Writers. New York, 1928.
Dubosq, A. Recherche du bien spirituel d'une communauté européenne. Correspondance, 25.VII. 1931.
Duehring, E. Die Grossen der modernen Litteratur. Leipzig, 1893.
Dumont-Wilden, L. L'esprit européen; essais. Paris, 1914.
—— L'évolution de l'esprit européen. Paris, 1937.
Eichoff, F. G. Coup d'oeil sur le génie littéraire de l'Europe. Discours d'ouverture prononcé à Lyon. 1850.
Ernst, F. Studien zur europäischen Literatur. Zürich, 1929.
Flora, F. Spirito europeo. Rassegna d'Italia, 1, 1946.
Guéhenno, J. Culture européenne et dénationalisation. Europe, 1929.
Haas, W. Der deutsche Europäer und der europäische Franzose. Neue Bücherschau, 4, 1924.
Hallam, H. Introduction to the Literature of Europe. London, 1838-39.
Hazard, P. Etudes européennes. La fin du XVIIe siècle, RDM, 1932.
—— La crise de la conscience européenne, 1680-1715. Paris, 1935. Hamburg, 1939. Madrid, 1941.
—— La pensée européenne au XVIIIe siècle, de Montesquieu à Lessing. Paris, 1941.
Howald, E. Humanismus und Europäertum. NSR, 1930.
Laharpe, J. F. De l'état des lettres en Europe depuis la fin du siècle qui a suivi celui d'Auguste jusqu'au règne de Louis XIV. Discours. Paris, 1797.
Lavrin, J. Studies in European Literature. London, 1929.
Levi, A. D. Précis méthodique de l'histoire ancienne et moderne des littératures européennes et orientales. Paris, 1850.
Lichtenberger, H. Le problème de la culture européenne. Cahiers alsaciens, Nov, 1912.
Maeztu, Maria de. Historia de la cultura europea. Buenos Aires, 1941.
Magnus, L. A History of European Literature. New York, 1934.
Mann, H. Europa, Reich über den Reichen. NR, 1923.
Marcello-Fabri. Si l'on veut favoriser la formation d'une littérature européenne. L'Age nouveau, 1938.
Martin du Gard, M. Un Français en Europe. Paris, 1935.
Mazzini, G. D'una letteratura europea. Antholog. d. Firenze, 1829. And in: Opere 2, Milano, 1862.
Neff, E. A Revolution in European Poetry: 1660-1900. New York, 1940.
Pannwitz, A. Der Geist Europas. NR, 1927.
Pourtalès, G. de. De l'esprit européen dans la littérature. Rev. hebdomadaire, 18.II. 1922.
Rameru, M. de. Une image des Etats-Unis européens. Cahiers romands, 1930.

Reynold, G. de. La formation de l'Europe. 4 vols. Fribourg, 1947.
Robinet. Considérations sur l'état présent de la littérature en Europe. Londres, 1762.
Rousseaux, A. La pensée européenne au 18e siècle. Le Littéraire, 23.XI.1946.
Saintsbury, G. (ed.) Periods of European Literature. 12 vols. Edinburgh, 1897-1907.
Salinari, G. B. Che cosa significa in letteratura essere europei? Cultura Neolatina, 3, 1943.
Sauvebois, G. De l'européanisme. Vie des lettres, 1923.
Ségur, N. Le génie européen. Paris, 1926.
—— Histoire de la littérature européenne. Paris, 1948 ff.
Skulima, E. Der europäische Schriftsteller. Literatur, Aug, 1939.
Smith, H. (ed.) Columbia Dictionary of Modern European Literature. New York, 1947. Cf. GR, 23, 1948.
Spanier, M. Probleme europäischer Dichtung. Literatur, 29, 1927.
Texte, J. Etudes de littérature européenne. Paris, 1898.
Van Tieghem, P. Histoire littéraire de l'Europe et de l'Amérique de la Renaissance à nos jours. Paris, 1946.
Turnell, M. The Unity of European Culture. Dublin Rev. 1947.
Valéry, P. Caractères de l'esprit européen. Rev. universelle, 1924.
Varia. Studies in European Literature. Taylorian Lectures. Oxford, 1931.
Wais, K. Die Gegenwartsdichtung der europäischen Völker. Berlin, 1939.
Wendell, B. The Traditions of European Literature, From Homer to Dante. New York, 1920.
Williams, O. Is There a European Literature? National Rev., 1932.
Wyneken, G. Der europäische Geist. Der neue Geist, (Leipzig), 1927.
Zamboni, G. La storia della cultura europa raffigurata in una tavola sinottica. LNI, 20.VI. 1935.

CHAPTER FIVE

Individual Authors.

(See also III. III. 13.)

Dumont-Wilden, L. Maurice **BARRES** et l'esprit européen. RB, 19.VI. 1907.
James, S. B. Hilaire **BELLOC**—the Good European. Catholic World, 151, 1940.
Villat, L. Un grand Européen: Albert de **BERZEVICZY**. Rev. des Etudes hongroises, 1935.
Romieu, A. Benjamin **CONSTANT** et l'esprit européen. Paris, 1933.
Delpy, G. **FEIJOO** et l'esprit européen. Paris, 1937.
Brodersen, A. Stefan **GEORGE**, Deutscher und Europäer. Berlin, 1935.
Baldensperger, F. **GOETHE** et la littérature mondiale. Bull. de l'Association des Amis de l'U. de Liège, 1933.
Betz, L. P. Weltlitteratur, Goethe und R. M. Meyer. Beilage zur Allg. Zt. 258-59. 1900.
Blankenagel, J. C. Goethe, Mme de Staël, and Weltliteratur. MLN, 40, 1925.
Frühm, T. Gedanken über Goethes Weltliteratur. Leipzig, 1932.
Grün, K. Goethe und die Weltliteratur. In: Ueber Goethe vom menschlichen Standpunkte. Darmstadt, 1846.
Leyen, F. von der. Goethe und die Weltliteratur. JbGG, 5, 1918.
Martin, E. Goethe über die Weltlitteratur. Strassburg, 1899.
Nolte, F. O. Grillparzer, Lessing and Goethe in the Perspective of European Literature. Lancaster, (Pa), 1938.
Schack, A. Frh. von. Goethe und die Weltlitteratur: Pandora. In: Vermischte Schriften. Stuttgart, 1890.
Strich, F. Goethes Idee einer Weltliteratur. In: Dichtung und Zivilisation. München, 1928.
—— Goethe und die Weltliteratur. JbGG, 18, 1932.
—— Goethe und die Weltliteratur. Bern, 1946.
Suarès, A. Goethe, le grand Européen. Paris, 1932.
Varia. Goethe européen. In: Hommage à Goethe. Paris, 1932.
Vulliod, A. Goethe, l'Allemagne et l'Europe. In: Goethe, études publiées pour le contenaire de sa mort par l'U. de Strasbourg. Paris, 1932.
Weinbarg, L. Goethe und die neueste Weltliteratur. In: Zur neuesten Literatur. Mannheim, 1835.
Jabram-Desrivaux, L. Thomas **HARDY**, Européen. Point et Virgule, 1928.
Gillies, A. **HERDER** and the Preparation of Goethe's Idea of Weltliteratur. PEGS, 1933.
Rousseau, A. Victor **HUGO** européen. Rev. universelle, 1930.
Hazard, P. **LEOPARDI** et la pensée européenne. Rev. pédagogique, 1913.
Milliex, R. Costis **PALAMAS** et l'Europe. RLC, 21, 1947.
Bagloi, D. **PUSCHKIN** und die Weltliteratur. Aufbau, 6, 1947.

Tronchon, H. Ernest **RENAN**, comparatiste. RLC, 6, 1926.

Angelloz, J. F. **RILKE** als Europäer. Das Goldene Tor, 3.

Boxberger, R. **RUECKERTS** Stellung zur Weltlitteratur. MLIA, 1888.

Merian-Genast, E. W. **VOLTAIRE'S** Essai sur la poésie épique und die Entwicklung der Idee der Weltliteratur. Leipzig, 1920.

—— Voltaire und die Entwicklung der Idee der Weltliteratur. RF, 40, 1926.

Romains, J. Stefan **ZWEIG**, Great European. New York, 1941.

SECOND PART

Literature and Politics

FIRST CHAPTER

Sociology and Politics: Bourgeoisie, Capitalism, Communism, Democracy, Marxism, Nazism, Proletarians, Socialism.

(For Saint-Simonism, see IV. VII. 22. and for Young Europe see also I. IV. 4 & III. II. 8.)

Ancona, A. d' La politica nella poesia del secolo XIII e XIV. NAnt, 1867.
Aronstein, P. Die socialen und politischen Strömungen in England im zweiten Drittel unseres Jahrhunderts in Dichtung und Roman. Archiv, 98-99, 1897.
Atkins, H. G. German Literature through Nazi Eyes. London, 1941.
Baldensperger, F. Ist die Literatur der Ausdruck der Gesellschaft? DVLG, 7, 1929.
Barzellotti. La letteratura e la rivoluzione in Italia avanti e dopo il 1848. Firenze, 1875.
Becker, C. L. The Declaration of Independence: a Study in the History of Political Ideas. New York, 1922.
Bellet, D. L'histoire du socialisme en Italie et les influences germaniques. Rev. d'économie politique, 30, 1916.
Bezold, F. von. Republik und Monarchie in der italienischen Litteratur des XV. Jahrhunderts. Historische Zs., 45, 1899.
Biese, A. Pädagogik und Poesie. In: Vermischte Aufsätze. Berlin, 1908-13.
Bowman, J. S. The Proletarian Novel in America. Diss. Pa. State College, 1940.
Bloom, S. F. The World of Nations. A Study of the National Implications in the Work of Karl Marx. New York, 1941.
Bowle, J. Western Political Thought... to Rousseau. London, 1947.
Brasch, M. Der Staatsroman oder der Sozialismus im Gewande der Poesie. 1882.
Brentano, B. von. Kapitalismus und schöne Literatur. Berlin, 1930.
Brinton, C. The Political Ideas of the English Romanticists. London, 1926.
Brotanek, R. State Poems. Beiträge zur neueren Philol. Jac. Schipper, Wien, 1902.
Brueggemann, F. Der Kampf um die bürgerliche Welt- und Lebensanschauung in der deutschen Literatu des XVIII. Jahrhunderts. DVLG, 1925.
Burgun, E. B. The Novel and the World Dilemma. New York, 1947.
Canby, H. S. Who Speaks for Ne World Democracy? Memoria del terc Congreso . . . de Lit. Iberoamerican 1944.
Cappelli, R. I poeti delle classe opera e operai poeti in Inghilterra. NAn 37, 1878.
Catlin, G. The Story of the Politic Philosophers. New York, 1939.
Challaye, F. La formation du socialism De Platon à Lénine. Paris, 1937.
Cook, T. I. History of Political Phi osophy from Plato to Burke. Ne York, 1936.
Cox, R. A. Political Disunion as a Sul ject in Recent French Drama. U. c Colorado Studies, 1941.
Deschamps, G. Littérature et politiqu In: La Vie et les Livres. Paris, 1894.
Dietz, H. Demagogie im Spiegel der eng lischen Literatur des vergangenen Jah hunderts. NM, 11.
Dohn, W. Das Jahr 1848 im deutsche Drama und Epos. Stuttgart, 1912.
Drabovitch, W. Les intellectuels françai et le bolchévisme. Paris, 1938.
Dubac, J. Revolutionslyrik. In: Streiflich ter. Leipzig, 1902.
Dunning, W. A. The Political Theorie of the German Idealists. Politica Science Quart., 28, 1913.
Elias, A. Literatura política y polític literaria. Hisp, 22, 1939.
Ely, R. T. French and German Socialisr in Modern Times. New York, 1911.
Ernst, F. Der Ursprung der Menschen rechte (Switzerland). NSR, 1939.
Farrell, J. T. Literature and Ideology College English, 3, 1942.
Faure, F. La révolution de 1848 et le écrivains britanniques. RLC, 22, 194
Fehr, I. Den politiska visan jämte med delanden om censuren och utlands literatur i Sverige. Diss. Upsala, 188
Fierens-Gevaert. L'anarchisme au théâ tre. Journal des Débats, 20.II.1898.
Francke, K. Social Forces in Germa Literature. New York, 1896.
Fundenburg, G. B. Feudal France in th French Epic. Princeton, 1918.
Gabriel, R. H. The Course of America

Democratic Thought: An Intellectual History Since 1815. New York, 1940.
Geffcken, F. H. German Socialism and Literary Sterility. Forum, 14, 1893.
Gerbi, A. La politica del settecento. Bari, 1928.
—— La politica del romanticismo. Bari, 1932.
Glaser, K. Die Bewertung der Staatsformen in der Antike. WS, 1939.
Glicksberg, C. I. Literature and the Marxist Aesthetic. UTQ, 18.
—— The Decline of Literary Marxism. Antioch Rev., 1, 1941.
—— Nihilism in Contemporary Literature. NC, 144, 1948.
Goriely, B. Les poètes dans la révolution russe. Paris, 1934.
Graham, W. The Politics of the Greater Romantic Poets. PMLA, 1921.
Grummere, F. B. Democracy and Poetry. Boston, 1911.
Guérard, A. Literature and Society. Boston, 1935.
Hanstein, A. von. Die soziale Frage in der Poesie. Leipzig, 1897.
—— Der Staatsgedanke in der dramatischen Literatur um die Mitte des 19. Jahrhunderts. Monatshefte d. Comenius Ges., 14, 1905.
Haushofer, M. Die socialen Fragen im Lichte der dramatischen Dichtung. WM, 1896.
Hedler, F. Führertum und Dichterschaft. Neue Literatur, April, 1934.
Helmut, A. Gesellschaftsideal und Gesellschaftsmoral im angehenden 17. Jahrhundert. Breslau, 1935.
Hempel, J. Politische Absicht und politisches Wirken im biblischen Schrifttum. Göttinger Nachrichten, Jahresbericht 1937-38.
Herder, J. G. Vom Einfluss der Regierung auf die Wissenschaften und der Wissenschaften auf die Regierung. (1780).
Herzen, I. Du développement des idées révolutionnaires en Russie. Paris, 1851; 2nd ed. 1856.
Hilgendag, W. Das Erlebnis der Arbeitslosigkeit in der deutschen Erzählkunst der Krisenzeit. Hamburg, 1940.
Hirsch, A. Sociologie und Literaturgeschichte. Euphorion, 29, 1928.
Hyman, S. E. The Marxist Criticism of Literature. Antioch Rev., 7, 1947.
Jaskulski, K. Ueber den Einfluss der sozialen Bewegungen auf das moderne deutsche Drama. Czernowitz, 1899.
Klovekorn, F. Die Entstehung der Erklärung der Menschen- und Bürgerrechte. Berlin, 1911.
Kniffler, C. Die sozialen Dramen der 80er und 90er Jahre des 19. Jahrhunderts und der Sozialismus. Diss. Frankfurt, 1929.
Kohn-Bramstedt, E. Aristocracy and the Middle-Classes in Germany. Social Types in German Literature, 1830-1900. London, 1937.
Launay, R. de. Les pères de la démocratie. Paris, 1903.
Langenbucher, H. Nationalsozialistische Dichtung. Berlin, 1935.
Leblond, M. A. Le roman socialiste de 1895 à 1900. Rev. socialiste, April, 1902.
Legge, J. G. Rhyme and Revolution in Germany. London, 1918.
Lehmann, K. Das Lied der Arbeit, die moderne Dichtung zwischen Hochöfen und Schloten. Leipzig, 1924.
Loise, F. De l'influence de la civilisation sur la poésie: l'Italie et la France. Bruxelles, 1862.
Lucker, Dorothy F. The American Interest in European Democracy: a Study of the Literary Reaction to the Revolutions of 1848. Diss. U. of Texas, 1942.
Manns, B. Das Proletariat und die Arbeiterfrage im deutschen Drama. Diss. Rostock, 1913.
Mattei, R. de. La politica nel teatro romano. Riv. ital. del Dramma, 1, 1937.
Mayer, J. P. et al. Political Thought. The European Tradition. New York, 1939.
McIlwain, C. H. The Growth of Political Thought in the West, from the Greeks to the End of the Middle Ages. New York, 1932.
McKenzie, R. I. Proletarian Literature in Canada. Dalhousie Rev. 19, 1939.
Mehle, K. Die soziale Frage im deutschen Roman. Diss. Haile, 1924.
Mesnard, P. L'essor de la philosophie politique au XVI siècle. Paris, 1936.
Moore, E. R. Novelists of the Mexican Revolution. Mexican Life, 16-17, 1940-41.
Mumford, L. & Spingarn, J. E. Politics and the Poet. AM, 170, 1942.
Pannekoek, A. Marxism and Darwinism. Chicago, 1912.
Petzet, C. Die Blütezeit der deutschen politischen Lyrik. München, 1908.
Pohl, G. Vormarsch ins 20. Jahrhundert. Zerfall und Neubau der europäischen Gesellschaft im Spiegel der Literatur. Leipzig, 1932.
Presber, H. Zur politischen und tendenziösen Poesie. Deutsches Museum, 1866.

Prutz, H. Zur Geschichte der politischen Komödie in Deutschland. Berlin, 1919.
Prutz, R. Literatur und Literaturgeschichte in ihren Beziehungen zur Gegenwart. Deutsches Museum, 1858.
Quinn, A. H. American Literature and American Politics. Proc. Amer. Antiq. Soc., 1944.
Routh, H. V. Money, Manners, and Morals as Revealed in Modern Literature. London, 1935.
Saint-Auban, E. de. L'idée sociale au théâtre. Paris, 1901.
Schlemmer, H. Staat und Mensch im Spiegel der neueren deutschen Dichtung. Berlin, 1920.
Schröer, C. Gegenwartsbeziehungen englischer Romane des XVIII. Jahrhunderts. NM, 1935.
Schücking, L. L. Die Soziologie der literarischen Geschmacksbildung. 2e ed. Leipzig, 1931.
—— Soziologie und Literatur. Bull. of the Internat. Committee of Historical Sciences, 14. Paris, 1932.
Schultheiss, A. Die Gesellschaft der italienischen Renaissance in Litteratur und Geschichte. Beilage Allg. Zt. 294, 301. 1902.
Skerlitch, J. L'opinion publique en France d'après la poésie politique et sociale de 1830 à 1848. Lausanne, 1901.
Smart, G. K. The Reflection of Socialistic Thought in American Literature, 1825-45. Diss. Harvard, 1942.
Socialism: see also Utopias (I. II. 4), Karl Marx (Chapter Five, below) and Saint-Simon (IV. VII. 22).
Staël, Mme G. de. De la littérature considérée dans ses rapports aves les institutions sociales. Paris, 1800.
Steadman, R. W. A Critique of Proletarian Literature. NAR, 1939.
Stovall, F. The Function of Literature in a Democracy. College English, 6, 1945.
Strodtmann, A. Die Arbeiterdichtung in Frankreich. Hamburg, 1863.
Struve, G. Twenty-five Years of Soviet Russian Literature. London, 1944; Paris, 1940.
Thomson, D. The Democratic Ideal in France and England. New York, 1941.
Thomson, G. Marxism and Poetry. London, 1946.
Tisdel, F. The Influence of Popular Customs on the Mystery Plays. JEGPh, 5, 1904.
Traeger, P. Die politische Dichtung in Deutschland. München, 1895.
Trilling, L. The Victorians and Democracy. Southern Rev., 5, 1940.
Trösch, E. Die helvetische Revolution im Lichte der deutsch-schweizerischen Dichtung. Leipzig, 1911.
Ulmann, H. Das deutsche Bürgertum in deutschen Tragödien des 18. und 19. Jahrhunderts. Giessen, 1923.
Vaughan, C. E. Studies in the History of Political Philosophy before and after Rousseau. 2 vols. Manchester, 1939.
Vossler, K. Weltgeschichte und Politik in der italienischen Dichtung vor Dante. SVL, 3, 1903.
Wesemann, H. Beiträge zur Geschichte der sozialen Lyrik in Deutschland. Diss. Freiburg, 1928.
Wilson, E. Marxism and Literature. AM, 1937.
Withington, R. Partisanship in Literature. BA, 14, 1940.
Wortelmann, F. Das Thema Revolution in der Dichtung. Prisma, 2, 1926.
Wright, L. H. Propaganda in Early American Fiction. Papers Bibl. Soc. Amer., 33, 1939.
Young Germany: see also I. IV. 4 & III. II. 8.

CHAPTER TWO

Races, Nationalism, Patriotism, Chauvinism, Imperialism, Bigotry.

(See also Reich, I. VI. 10; War, I. VI. 10; Colonial Literature I. II. 2 & II. I. 8; and State Novels, I. VII. 2.)

Anon. English Patriotic Poetry. ER, 1902.
Allers, U. S. The Concept of Empire in German Romanticism. Diss. Washington, 1948.
Ancona, A. d'. Il concetto dell' unità politica nei poeti italiani. In: Studi di critica e storia lettararia. Bologna, 1880.
Arco y Garay, R. del. La idea del imperio en la política y la literatura españolas. Madrid, 1944.
Baldi, A. Das deutsch-patriotisch nationale Lied und seine Bedeutung, 1813-70. Bamberg, 1871.
Barine, A. L'isolement intellectuel de l'Angleterre. Journal des Débats, 5.II. 1902.
Barth, J. Literatur und Drama im Dienste der nationalen Erziehung Japans. Tokio, 1935.
Beck, M. Unabhängigkeit der geistigen Kultur von der Rasse. Mass & Wert, 1938.

Bleibtreu, K. Das Nationale in der Poesie. MLIA, 21.III.1896.
Bourget, P. Le nationalisme intellectuel. Illustration. 19.XI.1921.
Bradsher, E. L. Nationalism in our Literature. NAR, 1921.
Brie, F. Imperialistische Strömungen in der englischen Literatur. Anglia, 40, 1916, & Halle, 1928.
Bulle, O. Die italienische Einheitsidee von Parini bis Manzoni. Berlin, 1893.
Cailhava. Des caractères nationaux. In: L'art de la comédie, Paris, 1786.
Canter, H. V. Praise of Italy in Classical Authors. CJ, 34, 1939.
Carruth, W. H. Expressions of German National Feeling . . . to the Time of Walther von der Vogelweide. HSPhL, 2. 1893.
Christ, F. Die römische Weltherrschaft in der antiken Dichtung. Stuttgart, 1938.
Clauss, L. F. Von Seele und Antlitz der Rassen und Völker. München, 1929.
Clement, N. H. An Aspect of the World-Conquest Motif in Literature. MPh, 24, 1927.
Corbató, H. La emergencia de la idea de nacionalidad en el México colonial. RIA, 6, 1943.
Cysarz, H. Menschheit, Volk, Dichtung. Zs. f. Aesthetik, 28, 1934.
Dana, H. W. L. Patriotic Plays in Soviet Russia. Russian Rev. 1, 1941.
Depta, M. Die Frage der Rassenmischung in der spanischen Literatur. NSp, 45, 1937.
Drinkwater, J. Patriotism in Literature. London, 1924.
Dülberg, F. Drama und Reichsgedanke. Berlin-Pankow, 1920.
Düwall, K. Die patriotische Dichtung der Deutschen seit Klopstock. Progr. Spremberg, 1878.
Farinelli, A. Gl'influssi letterari e l'insuperbire delle nazioni. Mélanges Baldensperger. Paris, 1930.
Franke, K. Vaterland in der deutschen Literatur vom Sturm und Drang bis zur Frühromantik. Zs. f. deutsche Bildung, 4.
Frey, D. Die Entwicklung nationaler Stile in der mittelalterlichen Kunst des Abendlandes. DVLG, 16.
Gide, A. Nationalismus in Literatur. NR, 1931.
Giffin, Mary E. Nationalism and English Literature. College English, 6, 1945.
Gomez de Baquero, A. Nacionalismo e Hispanismo. Madrid, 1928.
Hadas, M. From Nationalism to Cosmopolitanism in the Greco-Roman World. JHI, 4, 1943.
Hart, A. B. National Ideals Historically Traced. New York, 1907.
Heidicke, K. Völkerphilologie. Die Glocke, 25.XII. 1920.
Hertzberg, W. Patriotische Poesien der Engländer und Amerikaner. Deutsches Museum, 1853.
Hirst, W. A. The Empire in Literature. Empire Rev., 1932.
Howe, Susanne. Novels of Empire. New York, 1949.
Hubbell, J. B. Literary Nationalism in the Old South. Festschrift W. K. Boyd, Durham, (N.C.), 1940.
Jaehns, M. Der Vaterlandsgedanke und die deutsche Dichtung. Leipzig, 1896.
Jüthner, J. Hellenen und Barbaren. Geschichte des Nationalbewusstseins. Leipzig, 1923.
Kadner, S. Rasse und Humor. München, 1936.
Kindermann, H. Der grossdeutsche Gedanke in der Dichtung. Münster, 1941.
Klotz, A. Nationale und internationale Strömungen in der römischen Literatur. Erlangen, 1931.
Knauer, K. Die vaterländische Dichtung der Franzosen von der Frühzeit bis zum Anbruch des grossen nationalen Jahrhunderts. ZNU, 36.
Knight, G. W. Britain as Dramatic Artist: Poets and Imperial Destiny. TLS, 5.IV.1941.
Köhn, W. Der Rassengedanke in den englischsprechenden Ländern. ZNU, 36.
Lednicki, W. Poland and the Slavophile Idea. SR, 1928.
Le Fort, E. C. Some Trends in Contemporary Spanish-American Letters: Anti-Imperialism. U. of Miami Hispanic-American Studies. 1941.
Lenient, C. F. La poésie patriotique en France au moyen âge. Paris, 1891 and in: Le moyen âge, 4, 1892.
—— La poésie patriotique dans les temps modernes. 2 vols. Paris, 1894.
Letourneau, C. L'évolution littéraire dans les diverses races humaines. Paris, 1894.
Leyen, F. von der. Volkstum und Dichtung. Jena, 1933.
Lollis, C. de. Imperialismo letterario. RI, 1906.
Lowell, J. R. Nationality in Literature. Pioneer, 1843.
Madariaga, S. de. An Admirable Variety: Further Diversities of National Character. AM, 1928.
Mausser, O. Der Einheits- und Reichsge-

danke in der deutschen Literatur mit Berücksichtigung der Lyrik. Sammler, 90, 1921.
Mazon, P. Le mythe des races (Hesiod). REG, 54, 1914.
McKillop, A. D. The Poet as Patriot—Shakespeare to Wordsworth. Rice Institute Pamphlet, 29, 1942.
Michel, F. Histoire des races maudites de la France et de l'Espagne. 2 vols. Paris, 1847.
Michels, R. Elemente zu einer Soziologie des Nationalliedes. Archiv für Sozialwiss. & Sozialpolitik, 55, 1926.
Mokrauer-Maine, O. Die Entstehungsgeschichte patriotischer Lieder verschiedener Völker und Zeiten. Leipzig, 1895.
Mukerjee, R. Nationalism in Hindu Culture. London, 1921.
Myers, G. History of Bigotry in the United States. New York, 1943.
Nadler, J. Rassenkunde, Volkskunde. Stammeskunde. D&V, 1, 1934.
—— Nation, Staat und Dichtung. Corona, 4, 1934 & in: Deutscher Geist, deutscher Osten. München, 1937.
Oppenheim, H. B. Der Fatalismus des Rassen-Hochmuts. In: Demokratische Studien. Hamburg, 1860.
Petersen, J. Die Sehnsucht nach dem Dritten Reich in deutscher Sage und Dichtung. D&V, 1, 1934.
Peuckert, F. Völker und Kolonien in der Dichtung. Bücherkunde, 4, 1937.
Postgate R. & Vallance, A. Those Foreigners. The English People's Opinion on Foreign Affairs, as Reflected in Their Newspapers Since Waterloo. London, 1937.
Regnault, F. Y a-t-il des caractères nationaux? MF, 1933.
Roberts, W. R. Patriotic Poetry Greek and English. London, 1916.
Rohan, C. de. Nationalisme; internationalisme; transnationalisme. La Renaissance, 15.VII. 1922.
Rouché, M. L'évolution du patriotisme allemand de 1750 à 1815. EG, 3, 1948.
Sprengel, J. G. Der Staatsgedanke in der deutschen Dichtung vom Mittelalter bis zur Gegenwart. Berlin, 1933.
Stirk, S. D. The Prussian Spirit, a Survey of German Literature and Politics, 1914-40. London, 1941.
Toldo, P. Il sentimento nazionale nel teatro francese. Imola, 1900.
Tronchon, H. Littérature et nationalité. Davoser Revue, 1929.
Unruh, F. Das patriotische Drama in dem heutigen Frankreich. Progr. Königsberg, 1891.
Varia. Psychologies nationales. Séances et travaux de l'Académie des Sciences morales et politiques, March, 1933.
Velo, G. B. Del carattere nazionale del gusto italiano e di certo gusto dominante in letterature straniere. Vicenza, 1786.
Verschoor, A. D. Die ältere deutsche Romantik und die Nationalidee. Amsterdam, 1928.
Vossler, O. Der Nationalgedanke von Rousseau bis Ranke. München, 1937.
Wallbott, R. Die französische Kolonialerzählung der Gegenwart. Frankfurt, 1938.
Weddigen, C. Die patriotische Dichtung von 1870-71 unter Berücksichtigung der gleichzeitigen politischen Lyrik im Ausland. Leipzig, 1880.
Withington, R. Patriotisme et littérature. RLC, 9, 1929.

CHAPTER THREE

Cosmopolitanism and Pacifism.

Adams, R. P. Pre-Renaissance Courtly Propaganda for Peace in English Literature. Papers Michigan Acad., 32, 1947.
Betz, L. P. Internationale Strömungen und kosmopolitische Erscheinungen. In: Studien zur vergl. Litteraturgeschichte. Frankfurt, 1902.
Braga, D. Du cosmopolitisme littéraire: Expressionisme et humorisme. Rev. de Genève, 7, 1923.
Brand, G. K. Dichtung der Friedensidee. München-Gladbach, 1926.
Brunetière, F. Le cosmopolitisme et la littérature nationale. RDM, 1.X. 1895.
Busch, J. G. Ueber die Frage: Gewinnt ein Volk, in Absicht auf seine Aufklärung, wenn seine Sprache zur Universal-Sprache wird? Berlin, 1787.
Cammaerts, E. Literature and International Relations. HJ, 1922.
Carantonis, A. Le cosmopolitisme dans la poésie grecque moderne. L'Hellénisme contemporain, Nov., 1947.
Cézamy, J. de. Le cosmopolitisme littéraire. Rev. mondiale, 1931.
Davies, W. Education for Internationalism. HJ, 1922.
Einert. Ueber die weltbürgerliche Richtung unserer klassischen Litteratur. Progr. Arnstadt, 1865.
Faguet, E. Le cosmopolitisme littéraire. RB, I.IV. 1895.

Francke, K. Weltbürgertum in der deutschen Literatur von Herder bis Nietzsche. Berlin, 1929.
Geissler, E. Paneuropa in der deutschen Dichtung der Gegenwart. Langensalza, 1930.
Hazard, P. Cosmopolite. Mélanges Baldensperger. Paris, 1930.
Kovalewsky, P. Le sentiment cosmopolite dans la littérature russe. Paris, 1933.
Lalou, R. Cosmopolite, européen, humain. Europe, 1923.
Lichtenberger, H. L'esprit international. Rev. de Genève, 1928.
Mewaldt, J. Das Weltbürgertum in der Antike. Antike, 2.
Ortega y Gasset, J. Kosmopolitismus. NR, 1926.
Pange, J. de. L'esprit transnational. Monde nouveau, 1929.
Remi, Abbé. Le cosmopolitisme. Paris, 1770.
Robertson, J. G. Literary Cosmopolitanism. In: Essays and Addresses on Literature. London, 1935.
Souleyman, E. V. The Vision of World Peace in XVIIth and XVIIIth Century France. New York, 1941.
Stephen, L. The Cosmopolitan Spirit in Literature. National Rev., 34, 1899.
Thibaudet, A. La littérature cosmopolite. Rev. des idées et des livres, 25.III. 1921.
Trent, W. P. The Cosmopolitan Outlook. Columbia U. Lectures, New York, 1911.

CHAPTER FOUR

Utopias. Land of Cockaigne.

(See also Atlantis, I. VI. 10; State Novels, I. VII. 2; and Imaginary Voyages, I. VII. 1.)

Ackermann, Elfriede M. Das Schlaraffenland in German Literature and Folksong. Chicago, 1944.
Arndt, K. J. R. American Utopias and Internationalism. CLN, 3, 1945.
Bailey, J. O. An Early American Utopian Fiction. AL, 14, 1942.
—— Pilgrims through Space and Time: Trends in Utopian Fiction. New York, 1947.
Beauvois, E. L'Elysée transatlantique et l'Eden occidental. Rev. de l'histoire des religions, 7-8, 1883.
Bertalauffy, L. von. Die klassische Utopie. PJb, 1927.
Brüggemann, F. Utopie und Robinsonade. Weimar, 1914.
Calverton, V. F. Where Angels Dared to Tread (American Utopias). Newport, 1941.
Champney, F. Utopia, Ltd. Antioch Rev., 8, 1948.
Connes, G. Quelques utopistes anglosaxons. Publ. de l'U. de Dijon, 1, 1928.
Döblin, A. Die deutsche Utopie von 1933 und die Literatur. Das Goldene Tor, 2-3.
Donner, H. W. Introduction to Utopia. London, 1946.
Frensch, L. Das Land Nirgendwo und seine Geschichte. Protestant. Monatshefte, 17, 1913.
Holbrook, S. H. Brook Farm, Wild West Style. Amer. Mercury, 57, 1943.
Hommel, F. Die Insel der Seligen in Mythus und Sage der Vorzeit. München, 1901.
Imaz, E. Utopias del renacimiento: Moro, Campanella, Bacon. México, 1941.
Kirchenheim, A. von. Schlaraffia politika, Geschichte der Dichtungen vom besten Staat. Leipzig, 1892.
Krutch, J. W. Literature and Utopia. Nation, 18.X. 1933.
Le Flamane, A. Les Utopies prérévolutionnaires et la philosophie du XVIIIe siècle. Paris, 1934.
McNiff, W. J. Heaven on Earth. A Planned Mormon Society. Oxford, (Ohio), 1940.
Mannheim, K. Ideologie und Utopie. Bonn, 1930.
Morgan, A. E. Nowhere Was Somewhere. How History Makes Utopias and How Utopias Make History. Chapel Hill, (N.C.), 1946.
Müller, W. D. Geschichte der Utopia-Romane der Weltliteratur. Bochum-Langendreer, 1938.
Mumford, L. The Story of Utopias. London, 1923.
Nock, A. J. Utopia in Pennsylvania: The Amish. AM, 167, 1941.
Novati, F. Il paese che non si trova. La Domenica letteraria, 15.III. 1885.
Parrington, V. L. The Utopian Novel in America. Diss. Brown U. 1943.
—— American Dreams. A Study of American Utopias. Providence, 1948.
Patrick, J. M. Scydromedia, a Forgotten Utopia of the Seventeenth Century. PhQ, 23, 1944.
—— The Free State of Noland, a Neglected Utopia From the Age of Queen Anne. PhQ, 25, 1946.
Poeschel, J. Das Märchen vom Schlaraffenland. In: Braun's Beiträge, 5, 1877. & Leipzig, 1878.

Reiner, J. Berühmte Utopisten und ihr Staatsideal (Plato, Morus, Campanella, Cabet). Jena, 1906.
Robinsonaden. See Defoe, IV. VIII. 7.
Ross, H. Utopias Old and New. London, 1938.
Rossi, V. Il paese di Cuccagna nella letteratura italiana. In: Lettere di A. Calmo. Torino, 1888.
Russell, F. T. Utopian Esthetics. TAPhA, 16, 1929.
Saint-Simonism. See IV. VII. 22.
Schmidt, E. Das Schlaraffenland. In: Charakteristiken, 2. Berlin, 1900.
Schomann, E. Französische Utopisten des 18. Jahrhunderts und ihr Frauenideal. Diss. Greifswald, 1911.
Simon, W. Die englische Utopie im Lichte der Entwicklungslehre. Breslau, 1937.
Stearns, Bertha M. Memnonia: The Launching of a Utopia. NEQ, 15, 1942.
Thal-Larsen, Margaret W. Political and Economic Ideas in American Utopian Fiction, 1868-1914. Diss. U. of Cal. 1941.
Volk, W. Die Entdeckung Tahitis und das Wunschbild der seligen Insel in der deutschen Literatur. Diss. Heidelberg, 1934.
White, F. R. (ed.). Famous Utopias of the Renaissance, with Introductions and Notes. Chicago, 1946.
Wilson, J. B. The Antecedents of Brook Farm. NEQ, 15, 1942.
Zavala, S. The American Utopia in the XVIth Century. HLQ, 10, 1947.
Zenkovsky, V. V. Der Geist der Utopie im russischen Denken. Orient et Occident, 1934.

CHAPTER FIVE

Individual Authors.

Bouvy, E. **ALFIERI**, Monti, Foscolo. La poésie patriotique en Italie de 1789 à 1815. BI, 17.
Bricca, J. F. **ALFONSO EL SABIO** and Niccolo Machiavelli or the Return of the Pagan Idea of the State. Diss. Harvard, 1944.
Held, F. E. Johann Valentin **ANDREA'S** Christianopolis: an Ideal State of the Seventeenth Century. Diss. Illinois, 1914.
Lough, J. **D'ARGENSON** and Socialist Thought in XVIIIth Century France. MLR, 37, 1942.
Gomme, A. W. **ARISTOPHANES** and Politics. CR, 1938.
Hugill, W. M. Panhellenism in Aristophanes. Chicago U.P. 1936.
Römer, W. Die Gedanken des **ARISTOTELES** über den Staat in seiner Politik im Lichte der mittelalterlichen und modernen Staatslehre. Giessen, 1929.
Pundt, A. G. **ARNDT** and the Nationalist Awakening in Germany. New York, 1935.
Stegemann, V. **AUGUSTINS** Gottesstaat. Tübingen, 1928.
Deferrari, R. J., & Keeler, M. J. St. Augustine's City of God; its Plan and Development. AJPh, 1929.
Brezzi, P. La concezione agostiniana della Città di Dio e le sue interpretazioni medioevali. RSI, 1938.
Johns, H. H. The Mexican Revolution as Seen in the Novels of Mariano **AZUELA**. Diss. Southern Methodist U., 1943.
Blodgett, E. D. **BACON'S** New Atlantis and Campanella's Civitas Solis: A Study in Relationship. PMLA, 1931.
Minkowski, H. Die Neu-Atlantis des Francis Bacon und die Leopoldino-Carolina. AK, 26, 1936.
—— Die geistesgeschichtliche und die literarische Nachfolge der Neu-Atlantis des Francis Bacon. NPh, 22, 1936-37.
Peers, E. A. Michael **BAKUNIN** and Spanish Anarchism. Studies, an Irish Quart. Rev., 1938.
Bachelier & Dumesnil. Le cosmopolitisme dans la Comédie humaine de **BALZAC**. RP, 1924.
Bertault, P. H. de Balzac et l'idée coloniale. Etudes, 20.IX. 1935.
dell'Isola, Maria. Joel **BARLOW**, précurseur de la Société des Nations. RLC, 14, 1934.
Sadler, Elizabeth. One Book's Influence: Edward **BELLAMY'S** Looking Backward. NEQ, 17, 1944.
Levi, A. W. Edward Bellamy: Utopian. Ethics, 55, 1945.
Brandes, O. **BJOERNSON**, Deutschland und Socialismus. Zeitgeist, 1895.
Feist, E. Weltbild und Staatsidee bei Jean **BODIN**. Halle, 1930.
Mosse, G. L. The Influence of Bodin's République on English Political Thought. Medievalia & Humanistica, 1948.
Reynolds, B. Proponents of Limited Monarchy in Sixteenth Century France: Francis Hotman and Jean Bodin. New York, 1931.

Gianturco, E. Jean Bodin's View of the Venetian Constitution and His Critical Rift With F. Albergati. RLC, 18, 1938.
—— Bodin et Vico. RLC, 22, 1948.
Tobler, G. **BODMERS** politische Schauspiele. In: J. J. Bodmer Denkschrift zum 200. Geburtstag (1898). Zürich, 1900.
Mann, L. H. **BOURGET** als Kosmopolit. Gegenwart, 1894.
Triggs, O. L. **BROWNING** and Whitman; a Study in Democracy. London, 1893.
Anon. The Purport of Browning's and Whitman's Democracy. PL. Nov, 1895.
Schlesinger, A. M. Orestes **BROWNSON**, an American Marxist Before Marx. Sewanee Rev., 47, 1939.
Viëtor, K. Georg **BUECHNER** als Politiker. Bern, 1939.
Petri, A. The Coming Race von E. **BULWER-LYTTON**. Eine Quellenuntersuchung Progr. Schmöllen, 1908.
Gould, M. G. V. The Political Ideas of **BURKE** and Rousseau Compared. UTQ, 2, 1896.
Osborn, Annie M. Rousseau and Burke: A Study of the Idea of Liberty in Eighteenth-Century Political Thought. New York, 1940.
Harvey, R. F. Jean Jacques **BURLAMAQUI**: a Liberal Tradition in American Constitutionalism. Chapel Hill, (N.C.), 1937.
Patrick, J. M. Robert **BURTON'S** Utopianism. PhQ, 27, 1948.
Prutz, R. Lord **BYRON** als politischer Dichter. Deutsches Museum, 1867.
CAMPANELLA: see also Bacon.
Signorel, J. Contribution à l'étude du communisme intégral au début du XVIIe siècle: la Cité du soleil de Thomas Campanella. In: Mémoires de l'Académie de Toulouse, 12e sér., 1, 1923.
Treves, P. La filosofia politica di Tommaso Campanella. Bari, 1930.
Ducloux, W. Die metaphysische Grundlage der Staatsphilosophie des Thomas Campanella. München, 1935.
van Tieghem, P. **CARDUCCI** et la poésie nationale. Rev. du Mois, 10.II. 1910.
Guérnier, E. Jacques **CARTIER** et la pensée colonisatrice. Paris, 1946.
Jaloux, E. V. **CHERBULIEZ** et le cosmopolitisme. Le Temps, 24.IV. 1937.
How, W. W. **CICERO'S** Ideal in His De republica. Journal of Roman Studies, 1930.
Anon. The **COMTIST** Utopia. Fraser's Mag., 1869.
Cordié, C. **CONSTANT** e i limiti del liberalismo europeo. Società Nuova 1, 1945.
Zeiss, K. Die Staatsidee P. **CORNEILLES** mit einer Einleitung über die Politik und Litteratur Frankreichs von der Renaissance bis auf Corneille in ihren Hauptvertretern. Diss. Leipzig, 1898.
Bouvy, E. De **DANTE** à Alfieri: l'idée de patrie dans la poésie italienne. BI, 1914.
Garofalo, R. Idee sociologiche e politiche di Dante, Nietzsche e Tolstoi. Palermo, 1907.
Pollert, H. Daniel **DEFOE'S** Stellung zum englischen Kolonialwesen. Münster, 1928.
Courtney, W. L. **DEMOSTHENES** and the Principle of Patriotism. Fortnightly Rev., 1916.
Dunkel, H. B. Was Demosthenes a Panhellenist? CPh, 1938.
Schmitt, C. Der Staat als Mechanismus bei Hobbes und **DESCARTES**. Archiv f. Rechts- und Sozialphilosophie, 30, 1937.
Girard, H. Le cosmopolitisme d'un dilettante (Emile **DESCHAMPS**). RLC, 1, 1921.
De Jongh, A. W. **ERASMUS'** denkbeelden over staat en regeering. Amsterdam, 1928.
Adams, R. P. Designs by More and Erasmus for a New Social Order. SPh, 42, 1945.
Brachfeld, O. Un poète espagnol sur les barricades en 1830 (**ESPRONCEDA**). Rev. mondiale, 1930.
Hettich, E. L. A Study in Ancient Nationalism. The Testimony of **EURIPIDES**. Williamsport, 1933.
Haymann, F. Weltbürgertum und Vaterlandsliebe in der Staatslehre Rousseaus und **FICHTES**. Berlin, 1924.
Becher, W. Platon und Fichte. Die königliche Erziehungskunst. Jena, 1937.
—— Das erzieherische Ausleseprinzip bei Platon und Fichte. Volk und Führung, 3, 1937.
Pons, E. Les langues imaginaires dans le voyage utopique: Les grammairiens: Vairasse et **FOIGNY**. RLC, 12, 1932.
Bestor, A. E. American Phalanxes: A Study of **FOURIER'S** Socialism in the United States. Diss. Yale, 1938.
—— Fourierism in Northampton. NEQ, 13, 1940.
Smart, G. K. Fourierism in Northampton. NEQ, 12, 1939.
Gudde, E. G. **FREILIGRATHS** Entwicklung als politischer Dichter. Berlin, 1922.

Guignard, R. La paix universelle selon **GOERRES**. Cinquantenaire de la Faculté des Lettres d'Alger, 1932.

Müller-Freienfels, R. **GOETHE** als deutscher Typus. Die Tat, 1923.

Reinsch, F. H. Goethe's Political Interests prior to 1787. UCPPh, 1923.

Baldensperger, F. Goethe cosmopolite entre l'Orient et l'Occident. Rev. de Genève, 1930.

Croce, B. Un' epistola del Goethe e le storie popolari italiane del paese di Cuccagna. Critica 39, 1941.

Bataillon, M. Le cosmopolitisme de Damião de **GOIS**. RLC, 18, 1938.

Widmann, M. **HALLERS** Staatsromane und Bedeutung als politischer Schriftsteller. Biel, 1893.

Liljegren, S. B. A French Draft Constitution of 1792 modelled on James **HARRINGTON'S** Oceana: Théodore Lesueur, Idées sur l'espèce de gouvernement populaire. Edited with an Introduction on Harrington's Influence in France. Lund, 1932.

Steinhauer, H. **HAUPTMANN'S** Utopian Fantasy Die Insel der grossen Mutter. MLN, 53.

Hawthorne, M. **HAWTHORNE** and Utopian Socialism. NEQ, 12, 1939.

Doubleday, N. F. Hawthorne and Literary Nationalism. AL, 12, 1941.

Foster, M. B. The Political Philosophies of Plato and **HEGEL**. Oxford, 1935.

Marcuse, H. Reason and Revolution: Hegel and the Rise of Social Theory. New York, 1941.

Vallentin, A. 1848, Henri **HEINE** et la Révolution en marche. Europe, March, 1948.

Laufer, S. Smith and **HELVETIUS**. Diss. Bern, 1902.

Farinelli, A. L'Umanità di **HERDER** e il concetto della razza nella storia evolutiva dello spirito. Catania, 1908.

Hayes, C. J. H. Contributions of Herder to the Doctrine of Nationalism. AHR, 1927.

Eichler, G. Der nationale Gedanke bei Herder. Emsdetten, 1934.

Schmitz, R. Das Problem Volkstum und Dichtung bei Herder. Berlin, 1937.

Hadas, M. Utopian Sources in **HERODOTUS**. CPh, 1935.

Zagorski, V. A. **HERTZEN** et Michelet. La Pensée, 1946.

Smyrniadis, B. Les doctrines de **HOBBES**, Locke et Kant sur le droit d'insurrection. Vie universitaire, 1921.

Ehrenberg, V. Panhellenentum bei **HOMER**. Verhandl. der Vers. deutscher Philologen, 1929.

Lord, L. E. Two Imperial Poets, **HORACE** and Kipling. CJ, 1921.

Schroeder, R. A. Horaz als politischer Dichter. Europ. Revue, 11, 1935.

Schinz, A. Victor **HUGO**, le grand poète humanitaire; champion de la cause de la paix universelle; promoteur de l'idée des Etats-Unis d'Europe. FR, 1935.

Herder, J. C. **HUME'S** und Rousseau's Abhandlungen über den Urvertrag. Nachrichten von gelehrten Sachen, 1797.

Kimball, Marie. **JEFFERSON'S** Four Freedoms. Virginia Quar. Rev., 19, 1943.

Chinard, G. An American Philosopher in the World of Nations. ibid.

Guerster-Steinhausen, E. The Prophet of German Nihilism—Ernst **JUENGER**. Rev. of Politics, 7, 1945.

KANT: see also Hobbes.

Oncken, A. Adam Smith und Im. Kant. I. Ethik und Politik. Leipzig, 1877

Hauch, E. F. Gottfried **KELLER** as a Democratic Idealist. New York, 1916.

Hofe, H. von. Gottfried Keller's Conception of the Unique Character of Swiss Democracy. MDU, 35, 1943.

Montégut, E. Le socialisme et la littérature démocratique en Angleterre, M. **KINGSLEY**. RDM, 1.V.1851.

KIPLING: see Horace.

Wolff, H. M. Heinrich von **KLEIST** als politischer Dichter. UCPPh, 1947. Cf. MLJ, 1948.

Liebusch, G. Ueber das Vaterländische in **KLOPSTOCKS** Oden. Quedlinburg, 1874.

Schumacher, J. Klopstocks patriotische Lyrik. Hamm, 1880.

Mehnert, K. Ueber **LAMARTINES** politische Gedichte. Erlangen, 1903.

Phelps, W. G. **LESSING**, the Champion of Universal Brotherhood. Shreveport, (La.), 1939.

Melli, G. Un precursore del socialismo sul finire del settecento a Parma. (F. G. **LEVACHER**). Aurea Parma, 1, 1920.

LOCKE: see Hobbes.

Macri, O. La democrazia in **LOPE DE VEGA**. Convivium, 1947.

Santonastaso, G. Le dottrine politiche de **LUTERO** a Suarez. Milano, 1946.

Waring, L. H. The Political Theories of Martin Luther. New York, 1910.

MACHIAVELLI: see also Alfonso el Sabio and Morus.

Renaudet, A. Machiavel, étude d'histoire des doctrines politiques. Paris, 1942.
Jones, W. T. Masters of Political Thought: Machiavelli to Bentham. London, 1947.
Chevallier, J. J. Les grandes oeuvres politiques, de Machiavel à nos jours. Paris, 1948.
Seidlin, O. Thomas **MANN** and Democracy. SAQ, 43, 1944.
Borzsak, I. **MARTIAL** und das römische Nationalbewusstsein. (In Hungarian). EPhK, 1939.
Bernstein, E. Karl **MARX** und Michael Bakunin. Archiv f. Sozialwissenschaft & Sozialpolitik, 30, 1910.
Schuler, E. Pareto's Marx-Kritik. Diss. Tübingen, 1935.
Skerlitch, J. Karl Marx et les Serbes. (In Serbian). SKG, 24.
Wall, B. William Morris and Karl Marx. Dublin Rev., 202, 1938.
Lipshitz, M. The Philosophy of Art of Karl Marx. New York, 1938.
Lam, E. P. The Place of Marx in Christian Thought. Diss. Chicago, 1939.
Barzun, J. Darwin, Marx, Wagner: Critique of a Heritage. Boston, 1941.
Slochower, H. Freud and Marx in Contemporary Literature. Sewanee Rev. 49, 1941.
Glicksberg, C. Marxism, Freudianism, and Modern Writings. Queen's Quarterly, 54, 1947.
Levin, L. M. The Political Doctrine of **MONTESQUIEU'S** Esprit des Lois; its Classical Background. New York, 1936.
Fletcher, F. T. H. Montesquieu and Penal Law Reform in England. UTQ, 1937.
Ellinger, G. Thomas **MORUS** und Machiavelli. Vierteljahrschrift f. Kultur & Lit. d. Renaissance, 2, 1884.
Sherwin, P. F. Some Sources of More's Utopia. U. of New Mexico Bull., N.S., 88, 1917.
Dermenghem, E. Thomas Morus et les utopistes de la Renaissance. Paris, 1927.
Kautsky, K. Thomas More and His Utopia. New York, 1927.
Brockhaus, H. Die Utopieschrift des Thomas Morus. Leipzig, 1929.
Campbell, W. E. More's Utopia and His Social Teaching. London, 1930.
Pons, E. Les langues imaginaires dans le voyage utopique. Un précurseur: Thomas Morus. RLC, 10, 1930.
Zavala, S. La Utopia de Tomás Moro en la Nueva España. México, 1937.
Parks, G. B. More's Utopia and Geography. JEGPh, 37, 1938.
Peggram, R. E. The First French and English Translations of Sir Thomas More's Utopia. MLR, 35, 1940.
Brussone, J. L. R. La Utopia de Tomás Moro en América. U. de la Habana, 7, 1942.
Grace, W. J. The Conception of Society in More's Utopia. Thought, 22, 1947.
Ames, R. Citizen Thomas More and His Utopia. Princeton U.P., 1948.
MORRIS: see also Marx.
Ekstrom, W. F. The Social Idealism of William Morris and of William Dean Howells, a Study in Four Utopian Novels. Diss. U. of Illinois, 1947.
Rowbotham, A. La **MOTHE** le Vayer's Vertu des Payens and Eighteenth Century Cosmopolitanism. MLN, 1938.
Leibrich, L. **NIETZSCHE** et la politique. EG, 1, 1946.
Roy, C. **PETRARQUE** et Stendhal votent pour la liberté. Lettres françaises, 8. IV. 1948.
PLATO: see also Fichte and Hegel.
Salin, E. Platon und die griechische Utopie. München, 1921.
Delatte, A. L'Atlantide de Platon. Musée belge, 1922.
Herter, H. Platons Atlantis. Bonn, 1928.
Heidel, W. A. A Suggestion Concerning Plato's Atlantis. Proc. Amer. Acad., 68, 1933.
Bidez, J. L'Atlantide. Bull. de la classe des lettres de l'Acad. royale de Belgique, 1934.
Zwengel, O. Platons politische Erziehungstheorie im Lichte des national-politischen Erziehungsgedankens. Frankfurt, 1938.
Zeise, H. Der Staatsmann, ein Beitrag zur Interpretation des platonischen Politikos. Leipzig, 1938.
Morrow, G. R. Plato's Law of Slavery in its Relation to Greek Law. Urbana, 1939.
Field, G. C. Plato's Political Thought and Its Value To-day. PCA, 1939.
Murley, C. Plato's Republic, Totalitarian or Democratic? CJ, 36, 1941.
Demos, R. Was Plato a Fascist? CW, 35, 1941-42.
Hammond, M. **PLINY** the Younger's Views on Government. HSCPh, 1938.
Glicksberg, C. Ezra **POUND** and the Fascist Complex. SAQ, 45, 1947.
Pons, E. Les langues imaginaires dans le voyage utopique: Les jargons de Panurge dans **RABELAIS**. RLC, 11, 1931.
ROUSSEAU: see also Burke, Fichte and Hume.

Texte, J. J. J. Rousseau et les origines du cosmopolitisme littéraire. Paris, 1895. Cf. RDM, I. VIII. 1895 & JS, 1896.
Bizzilli, P. Rousseau et la démocratie. Annuaire de l'U. de Sofia, 24, 1928.
Houvens Post, H. La Société des Nations de l'abbé de **SAINT-PIERRE**. Amsterdam, 1935.
Nussberger, M. **SCHILLER** als politischer Dichter. In: Zwei Aufsätze zur deutschen Literaturgeschichte. Zürich, 1917.
Schröder, K. **SCHNABELS** Insel Felsenburg. Marburg, 1912.
Sipple, A. Der Staatsmann und Dichter **SENECA** als politischer Erzieher. Würzburg, 1938.
Pongs, H. **SHAKESPEARE** und das politische Drama. D&V, 37, 1936.
Thaler, A. Shakespeare and Democracy. Knoxville, (Tenn.), 1941.
Stirling, B. Anti-Democracy in Shakespeare: A Re-Survey. MLQ, 2, 1941.
Phillips, J. E. The State in Shakespeare's Greek and Roman Plays. New York, 1940.
Withington, R. Shakespeare and Race Prejudice. Festschrift George F. Reynolds. U. of Colorado, 1945.
Spitz, L. Upton **SINCLAIR** and Nazism. American Hebrew, 158, 1948.
STATE NOVELS. See p. **195**.
Brussaly, M. The Political Ideas of **STENDHAL**. New York, 1933.
Rommen, H. Die Staatslehre des F. **SUAREZ**. Gladbach-Köln, 1926.
Gianturco, E. Character, Essence, Origin and Content of the jus gentium according to Suarez and Vico. RLC, 16, 1936.
Darnall, F. M. Old Wine in New Bottles (Utopianism in **SWIFT**). SAQ, 41, 1942.
Fink, Z. S. Political Theory in Gulliver's Travels. ELH, 14, 1947.
Willibrand, W. A. Ernst **TOLLER**, Product of Two Revolutions Norman, (Okla.), 1941.
Garcia-Mausilla, E. **TOLSTOI** et le communisme. Paris, 1905.
Anon. Le tolstoïsme et l'anarchisme. Paris, 1900.
Bourdeau, J. Tolstoi, Lénin et la Révolution russe. Paris, 1921.
Gillet, L. Un pacifiste allemand à Paris (F. von **UNRUH**). RDM, 15.I.1920.
VICO: see Suarez.
Verasani, D. **VIRGILIO** poeta dell'impero. Caserta, 1932.
Ellissen, A. **VOLTAIRE** als politischer Dichter. Leipzig, 1852.
White, Florence D. Voltaire and English Liberty. OC, 1918.
Heussner, F . **WALTHER VON DER VOGELWEIDE** als politischer Dichter. Deutsche Blätter, 1873.
Boese, G. Walthers von der Vogelweide patriotische Dichtungen an den Faden der Geschichte seiner Tage gereiht. Oldenburg, 1875.
Grimm, A. Ueber die politische Dichtung Walthers von der Vogelweide. Schwerin, 1876.
Pechel, L. Die kulturhistorischen Momente in der Dichtung Walthers von der Vogelweide. Progr. Malchin, 1876.
WHITMAN: see Browning.
Vogt, O. Der goldene Spiegel und **WIELANDS** politische Ansichten. Berlin, 1904.
Scharr, E. **XENOPHONS** Staats- und Gesellschaftsideal und seine Zeit. Halle, 1919.
Zawacki, E. The Utopianism of Stefan **ZEROMSKI**. SEER, 21, 1943.

THIRD PART

Literature and Arts and Sciences

(Religion and Philosophy are often so intimately linked with Literature that it was considered unwise to detach them from the latter and give them special chapters here. Instead, religious and philosophical authors were left in the proper chronological and geographical surroundings to which they belong. Cf. Chapter Two for a few philosophical items.)

FIRST CHAPTER

Fine Arts and Gardens.

Ayscough, F. The Chinese Idea of a Garden. China Journal of Science and Arts, 1, 1923.

Babbitt, I. The New Laokoon. An Essay on the Confusion of the Arts. London, 1910.

Baldensperger, F. Le jardin à la française, signe et symbole d'une civilisation. FR, 1936.

Bebermeyer, G. Die deutsche Dicht- und Bildkunst im Spätmittalter. DVLG, 7, 1929.

Binyon, L. English Poetry in its Relation to Painting and the Other Arts. PBA, 8, 1918.

Chastel, A. Art et religion dans la Renaissance italienne. BHR, 7, 1945.

Denk, F. Dichtermaler und Malerdichter. NJWJ, 5, 1929.

Dubos, Abbé. Réflexions critiques sur la poésie et la peinture. Paris, 1719.

Erdberg, E. von. Chinese Influence on European Garden Structures. Harvard U.P., 1937.

Förster, M. Englische Literatur und bildende Kunst in ihren Wechselbeziehungen. Berlin, 1925.

Gothein, M. Der englische Landschaftsgarten in der Literatur. Verh. des 11. Neuphilologentages Köln, 1905.

Greene, T. The Arts and the Art of Criticism. Princeton, 1940.

Halliday, F. E. Fine Arts. A New Approach to Poetry through Architecture, Sculpture, Painting and Music. London, 1945.

Harnisch, K. Deutsche Malererzählungen. Die Art des Sehens bei Heinse Tieck, Hoffmann, Mörike, Stifter und Keller. Diss. München, 1938.

Hatzfeld, H. Literary Criticism through Art Criticism and Art Criticism through Literary Criticism. Journal of Aesthetics, 6, 1947.

Herzfeld, G. Werke der bildenden Kunst als Quelle von Dichtungen. Archiv, 153, 1928.

Holt, Elizabeth G. Literary Sources of Art History. Princeton U.P., 1947.

Kleinmayr, H. Die deutsche Romantik und die Landschaftsmalerei. Strassburg, 1912.

Larrabee, S. A. English Bards and Grecian Marbles. The Relationship Between Sculpture and Poetry, especially in the Romantic Period. New York, 1943.

Lee, R. W. Ut pictura poesis: the Humanistic Theory of Painting. Art Bulletin, 122, 1940.

Lessing, G. E. Laokoon. (1766).

Maury, P. Art et littérature comparés. Etat présent de la question. EF, 33, 1934.

Müller, R. Dichtung und bildende Kunst im Zeitalter des deutschen Barock. Diss. Zürich, 1937.

Müller, W. A. Die archäologische Dichtung in ihrem Umfang und Gehalt. Königsberg, 1928.

Neumeyer, Eva M. The Landscape Garden as a Symbol in Rousseau, Goethe and Flaubert. JHI, 8, 1947.

Panzer, F. Dichtung und Kunst des deutschen Mittelalters in ihren Wechselbeziehungen. NJKA, 13, 1904.

Poche, E. Jes jardins à la française et le baroque praguois. L'Europe Centrale, 16.VII. 1938.

Rapaics, R. Le jardin français en Hongrie. Nouvelle Rev. de Hongrie, 1938.

Sieveking, A. F. Gardens Ancient and Modern: an Epitome of the Literature of the Garden-Art. London, 1899.

Smith, R. H. Architecture in English Fiction. New Haven, 1937.

Sobry. Cours de peinture et de littérature comparées. Paris, 1810.

Tinker, C. B. Painter and Poet. Studies in the Literary Relations of English Painting. Harvard U.P., 1938.

Thielke, K. L. F. Literatur- und Kunstkritik in ihren Wechselbeziehungen;

ein Beitrag zur englischen Aesthetik des 18. Jahrhunderts. Halle, 1935
Wellek, R. The Parallelism between Literature and the Arts. Eng. Inst. Annual. (New York), 1941.
Wier, A. E. Thesaurus of the Arts: Drama, Music, Radio, Painting, Screen, Television, Literature, Sculpture, Architecture, Ballet. New York, 1943.
Zaloscer, H. Malende Dichter und dichtende Maler. Festschrift Strzygowski. Klagenfurt, 1932.

CHAPTER TWO

History and Philosophy.

(See also Historical Novels and Dramas, and Thematology on the Influence of English, French, German, etc. History on Literature.)

Allais, G. De l'histoire au théâtre d'après la tragédie classique. RCC, 1894.
Amador de Los Rios, J. La poesía considerada como elemento de la historia. Eco literario de Europa, 2. Madrid,
Boas, G. French Philosophies of the Romantic Period. Baltimore, 1925.
Branca, G. Bibliografia storica ossia collezione delle migliori e più recenti opere di ogni nazione intorno ai principali periodi e personaggi della storia universale. Milano, 1862.
Braun, M. History and Romance in Graeco-Oriental Literature. Oxford, 1938.
Byrne, B. Philosophy and Criticism. Thought, 22, 1948.
Canning, A. S. G. History in Fact and Fiction. London, 1897.
Chassang, A. Histoire du roman et de ses rapports avec l'histoire dans l'antiquité grecque et latine. Paris, 1862.
Cohen, J. W. Aspects of the Relations Between Philosophy and Literature. Colorado Studies, 1, 1940.
Croce, B. La storia ridotta sotto il concetto generale dell'arte. Napoli, 1893.
Eaker, J. G. Design for a Philosophy of Literature. SAQ, 39, 1940.
Einstein, L. The Relation of Literature to History. JCL, 1, 1903.
Flint, R. The Philosophy of History in Europe. Edinburgh, 1874.
Goedeke, K. Bibliographie der geschichtlichen Dichtung des Mittelalters. In: Grundriss der romanischen Philologie, 1884.
Harnack, O. Ueber die Verwendung historischer Stoffe in der Dichtung. Darmstadt, 1899.
Hohlbaum, R. Von den Grenzen der geschichtlichen und künstlerischen Wahrheit. Literatur, July, 1935.
Jockers, E. Philosophie und Literaturwissenschaft. GR, 1935.
Josephson, M. Historians and Mythmakers. Virginia Quart. Rev., 1939-40.
Landsberg, F. Das Bild der alten Geschichte in mittelalterlichen Chroniken. Basel, 1934.
Lenglet du Fresnoy. L'histoire justifiée contre les romans. Amsterdam, 1735.
Maigron, L. Le roman historique et l'histoire au XIXe siècle. In: Le roman historique à l'époque romantique. Paris, 1898.
Marchesi, C. Storia e Poesia. NAnt, 81, 1946.
Messac, P. Déterminisme et histoire littéraire. Science moderne, Sept., 1926.
Müller, H. Ueber den Einfluss der Zeitgeschichte auf die dramatische Litteratur der Italiener. Diss. Rostock, 1871.
Müller, G. E. Philosophy of Literature. New York, 1948.
Nagele, A. Geschichte und Litteratur. W. Reichspost. 143, 1903.
Neff, E. The Poetry of History: the Contribution of Literature and Literary Scholarship to the Writing of History since Voltaire. New York, 1947.
Neri, F. Storia e poesia. Torino, 1936.
Pons, J. S. Le roman et l'histoire. Mélanges Martinenche, Paris, 1939.
Quatremère de Quincy. De l'emploi des sujets d'histoire moderne dans la poésie et de leur abus dans la peinture. Rec. des Disc. prononcés dans la séance annuelle de l'Institut, Paris, 1825.
Schargo, Nelly N. History in the Encyclopédie. New York, 1947.
Spaventa, B. La filosofia italiana nelle sue relazioni con la filosofia europea. Firenze, 1938.
Tatlock, J. S. P. Interpreting Literature by History. Spec, 12, 1937.
Teggart, F. J. Prolegomena to History. The Relation of History to Literature. Berkeley, 1916.
Thompson, J. W. & Holm, B. J. A History of Historical Writing. 2 vols. New York, 1942.
Wetz, W. Ueber das Verhältniss der Dichtung zur Wirklichkeit und Geschichte: Studien zur hamburgischen Dramaturgie. ZVL, 9, 1896.
Zerby, L. Philosophy and Literature. Journal of Aesthetics, 5, 1947.

CHAPTER THREE

Music.

Ahmels, H. Dis Schallformen der Dichtungen. ZDK, 1933.
Baldensperger, F. Sensibilité musicale et romantisme. Paris, 1920.
Bonaventura, A. Saggio storico sul teatro musicale italiano. Livorno. 1913.
Brown, C. S. Music and Literature. Athens, (Ga.), 1948.
Capelli, A. Poesie musicali dei secoli XIV, XV, XVI. Bologna, 1868.
Chase, G. Origins of the Lyric Theatre in Spain. Musical Quart., 25, 1939.
Coeuroy, A. Musique et littérature. Etudes de musique et de littérature comparée. Paris, 1923.
Colby, E. The Echo-Device in Literature. New York Library, July, 1920.
Combarieu, J. Les rapports de la musique et de la poésie, considerées au point de vue de l'expression. Diss. Paris, 1893.
Evans, R. L. Les romantiques français et la musique. Paris, 1934.
Fiedler, H. German Musicians in England and Their Influence to the End of the Eighteenth Century. GLL, 4, 1939.
Fox Strangways, A. H. Words and Music in Song. E&S, 1, 1921.
Frehn, P. Der Einfluss der englischen Literatur auf Deutschlands Musiker und Musik. Düsseldorf, 1937.
Frye, N. Music in Poetry. UTQ, 11, 1942.
La Laurencie, L. de. America in the French Music of the Seventeenth and Eighteenth Centuries. Musical Quart., 7, 1921.
Mengewein, C. Die Musik im Lichte der Poesie. Tonkunst, 9, 1905.
Müller-Freienfels, R. Musik und Dichtung. ZDK, 43, 1929.
Nef, K. An Outline of the History of Music. New York, 1935.
Pattison, B. Music and Poetry of the English Renaissance. London, 1948.
Roberts, W. W. Musical Parlance in English Literature. Music & Letters, 5, 1924.
Robson, J. Tracts on Listening to Music (in Indian Literature). London, 1938.
Rubsamen, W. H. Literary Sources of Secular Music in Italy. Berkeley, 1943.
Salazar, A. Music in the Primitive Spanish Theatre Before Lope de Vega. In: Papers of the American Musicological Society Meeting, 1938. 1940.
Schueller, H. M. Literature and Music as Sister Arts. PhQ, 26, 1947.
Sorgatz, H. Musiker und Musikanten als dichterisches Motif. Eine Studie . . . vom Sturm und Drang bis zum Realismus. Würzburg, 1939.
Spindler, K. Obersachsens grosse Musiker (Bach, Wagner) in der deutschen Dichtung. Sächsische Heimat, 5.
Teigel, Eva. Das Musikalische in der romantischen Prosa. Coburg, 1912
Velten, R. Das deutsche Gesellschaftslied unter dem Einfluss der italienischen Musik. GRM, 1915.

CHAPTER FOUR

Individual Artists, Poets and Scholars.

(Poets, rather than artists or composers, determine the alphabetical arrangement of the following pages.)

Betz, S. A. E. The Operatic Criticism of the Tatler and Spectator. (**ADDISON**). Musical Quart., 31, 1945.
Aragomès, C. Marie d'**AGOULT** et François Liszt. Rev. hebdomadaire, 1936.
Marzolla, U. B. G. d'**ANNUNZIO** e l'europeismo musicale. Scuola e Cultura, 14, 1938.
Samervell, D. C. The **BACH** Passions and Greek Tragedy. Music & Letters, 27, 1946.
Marix, T. Histoire d'une amitié: F. Liszt et H. de **BALZAC**. Rev. des Etudes hongroises, 1934.
Bandy, W. T. **BAUDELAIRE** and Liszt. MLN, 53, 1938.
Macchia, G. Baudelaire e la musica. Mercurio, 3, 1946.
Alekseev, M. P. **BEETHOVEN** in der russischen Literatur des 19. Jahrhunderts. GS, 2, 1932-33.
Benz, R. Beethoven und die Dichter. Literar. Welt, 3, 1922.
Hirschberg, L. Beethoven in der Dichtung. Musik, 37, 1910.
Lebede, H. Beethoven in der Dichtung. Bad. Bühnenblätter, 7, 1927.
Schrade, L. Beethoven in France. The Growth of an Idea. New Haven, 1943.
Volkmann, H. Beethovendramen. Musik, 17, 1905.
Scenna, A. The Treatment of Ancient Legend and History in **BODMER**. New York, 1937.
Royère, J. Le Musicisme: **BOILEAU**, La Fontaine, Baudelaire. Paris, 1929.
Deutsch, O. E. Haydn's Hymn and **BUR-**

NEY'S Translation. Music Rev., 4, 1943.
Hughes, Rosemary. Dr. Burney's Championship of Haydn. Musical Quart., 27, 1941.
Curtius, E. R. **CALDERON** und die Malerei. RF, 50, 1936.
Espla, O. **CERVANTES** et la musique. Europe, 25, 1947.
Querol Gavaldá, M. La música en las obras de Cervantes. Barcelona, 1948.
Dimoff, P. Winckelmann et André **CHENIER**. RLC, 21, 1947.
Kuehn, J. **DANTES** Geschichtsphilosophie. JbDG, N.F., 17, 1946.
Gillot, H. **DELACROIX** et l'Allemagne. In: Mélanges H. Lichtenberger. Paris, 1934.
McKenzie, G. **DICKENS** and Daumier. In: Studies in the Comic. Berkeley, 1941.
Dubray, M. La storia nei romanzi di Al. **DUMAS**. Cultura Moderna, 1932.
Parigot, H. Al. Dumas et l'histoire. RP, 15.VII.1902.
Panofsky, E. **DUERERS** Stellung zur Antike. Jb. f. Kunstgeschichte (Wien), 1921.
Pauli, G. Dürer, Italien und die Antike. VBW, 1921.
Picco, F. Il dipinto di Breughel e la Tentation de Saint Antoine dei **FLAUBERT**. RLM, 1, 1946.
Maynial, E. De Stendhal à **FOGAZZARO**: La poésie de la musique chez un écrivain italien. RLC, 13, 1933.
Messedaglia, L. Aspetti della realta storica in Merlin Cocai. (Teofila **FOLENGO**). Venezia, 1939.
Federmann, A. J. H. **FUESSLI**, Dichter und Maler. Diss. Greifswald, Zürich, 1927.
Knowles, J. The Life and Writings of H. Fuseli. 3 vols. London, 1831.
Crass, E. **GOETHES** Beziehungen zur Tonkunst und den Tonkünstlern seiner Zeit. Leipzig, 1943.
Gara, E. Goethe e la musica. Illustr. italiana, 1932.
Kling, H. Goethe e Berlioz. Riv. musicale italiana, 4, 1906.
Korff, H. A. Goethe und die bildende Kunst. ZDK, 41, 1927.
Meier-Graefe, J. Delacroix und Goethe. NR, 1932.
Mondésir, E. de. Goethe et la musique italienne. Schweiz. Musik. Zt., Oct., 1947.
Popov, S. Goethe in Russian Music. (In Russian). Literaturnoe Nasledstvo, 4-6. Moskva, 1932.
Prang, H. Goethe und die Kunst der italienischen Renaissance. Berlin, 1938.
Prud'homme, J. G. Goethe et les compositeurs français. RFA, 1, 1899.
Rolland, R. Goethe et Beethoven. Paris, 1930.
Sherrington, Sir Charles. Goethe on Nature and on Science. Cambridge, 1942.
Varenne, G. Goethe et David d'Angers. In: Mélanges H. Lichtenberger. Paris, 1934.
Volbehr, T. Goethe und die bildende Kunst. Leipzig, 1895.
Necker, M. **GRILLPARZERS** Verhältnis zur Geschichte. Beilage zur Allg. Zt., 168, 1901.
Redlich, O. Grillparzers Verhältniss zur Geschichte. Wien, 1901.
Wutzky, A. Grillparzer und die Musik. Regensburg, 1940.
Owen, C. H. The Treatment of History in Gerhard **HAUPTMANN'S** Dramas. Ithaca (N.Y.), 1939.
Larrabee, S. A. **HAZLITT'S** Criticism and Greek Sculpture. JHI, 2, 1941.
Toennies, F. Neuere Philosophie der Geschichte: **HEGEL**, Marx, Comte. Archiv f. Geschichte der Philosophie, 7, 1894.
Jessen, K. D. **HEINSES** Stellung zur bildenden Kunst und ihrer Aesthetik. Berlin, 1901.
Gillies, A. **HERDER'S** Approach to the Philosophy of History. MLR, 35, 1940.
Glöckner, E. Studien zur romantischen Psychologie der Musik, besonders mit Rücksicht auf die Schriften E.T.A. **HOFFMANNS**. Diss. Bonn, 1909.
Katz, M. Die Schilderung des musikalischen Eindrucks bei Schumann, Hoffmann und Tieck. Diss. Giessen, 1910.
Schaeffer, C. Die Bedeutung des Musikalischen und Akustischen in E.T.A. Hoffmanns literarischem Schaffen. Diss. Marburg, 1909.
Gallas, K. R. Bij Victor **HUGO'S** "A Albert Dürer." NPh, 30, 1946-47.
Weise, C. J. K. **HUYSMANS'** Beziehungen zur Malerei. Diss. Jena, 1934.
Willey, N. & Prada, C. **IBSEN** and Goya. Hisp., 1938.
Schaffner, P. G. **KELLER** als Maler. Stuttgart, 1923.
Gavazzeni, G. **KIERKEGAARD**, il Don Giovanni e la musica. Rassegna d'Italia, 1947.
Morgan, D. P. Heinrich von **KLEISTS** Verhältnis zur Musik. Köln, 1940.
Bayer, K. T. Franz **LISZT** in der Dichtung. Deutsche Musikkultur, 1, 1936.
Haraszti, E. F. Liszt et la Hongrie. Nouvelle Rev. de Hongrie, Dec., 1935.
Paolillo, M. L'influsso **LUCREZIANO**

nella Primavera di Botticelli. Lucera, 1936.

Baldensperger, F. La Tragédie de l'homme de **MADACH** et les prévisions positivistes. Rev. des Etudes hongroises, 1934.

Benedetto, F. Un giudizio inedito di Xavier de **MAISTRE** sul Trattato della Pittura del Cennini. Il Vasari, 2, 1929.

Schlappner, M. Thomas **MANN** und die französische Musik. NSR, June, 1947.

Goldstein, L. Moses **MENDELSSOHN** und die deutsche Aesthetik. Königsberg, 1902.

Richter, L. Pholosophie der Dichtkunst: Moses Mendelssohns Aesthetik. Berlin, 1948.

Guillon, F. Le Roman de la Rose considéré comme document historique. (Jean de **MEUNG**). Paris, 1903.

Sulger-Gebing, E. C. F. **MEYERS** Werke in ihren Beziehungen zur bildenden Kunst. Euphorion, 23, 1921.

Praz, M. **MILTON** and Poussin. Festschrift Grierson. London, 1938.

Roberts, D. R. The Music of Milton. PhQ, 26, 1947.

Spaeth, S. G. Milton's Knowledge of Music. Diss. Princeton, 1913.

Ullrich, H. J. **MOZART** and England: his British Friends and Pupils. Music Rev., 4, 1943.

Denk, F. Fr. **MUELLER**, der Malerdichter und Dichtermaler. Speyer, 1930.

Bastian, H. Breugel und **OVID**. HG, 45, 1934.

Holde, A. Mozart's Collaborator Lorenzo da **PONTE**. AGR, 7, 1941.

Abatangel, L. Marcel **PROUST** et la musique. Paris, 1943.

Chernowitz, M. E. Proust and Painting. New York, 1945.

Salomon, R. A Trace of Dürer in **RABELAIS**. MLN, 58, 1943.

Brom, G. **REMBRANDT** in de literatuur. NPh, 21, 1936.

Fleissner, O. A. **RILKE** und van Gogh. GR, 20, 1945.

Hewett-Thayer, H. W. Rilke and the Boscoreale Frescoes. GR, 20, 1945.

Houston, C. C. Rilke and Rodin. Festschrift Fiedler, Oxford, 1938.

Paulsen, W. Rilke-Rodin: Once More. MLN, 58, 1943.

Peters, H. F. Rilke-Rodin: a Correction. MLN, 57, 1942.

—— Rilke in his Letters to Rodin. MLQ, 4, 1943.

Pitrou, R. Rilke et Van Gogh. RLC, 21, 1947.

Reichart, W. A. Rilke's Fifth Duino Elegy and Picasso's Les Saltimbanques. MLN, 61, 1946.

Block, L. D. G. **ROSSETTI**, der Malerdichter. Diss. Giessen, 1925.

Tietz, E. Das Malerische in Rossettis Dichtung. Anglia, 51, 1937.

Róbert, Ella. **ROUSSEAU** et la musique. Budapest, 1939.

Baroja, P. Chopin y Jorge **SAND** y otros ensayos. Barcelona, 1941.

Rice, P. B. George **SANTAYANA**: The Philosopher as Poet. Kenyon Rev., 2, 1940.

Arndt, K. J. R. Mozart and **SCHILLER** on the Wabash. MDU, 38, 1946.

Buchwald, R. Schiller und Beethoven. Heidelberg, 1946.

Fischer, K. Schiller als Philosoph. Heidelberg, 1891.

Janssen, J. Schiller als Historiker. Freiburg, 1879.

Ueberweg, F. Schiller als Historiker und Philosoph. Leipzig, 1884.

Sulger-Gebing, E. Die Brüder A. W. und Fr. **SCHLEGEL** in ihrem Verhältnisse zur bildenden Kunst. München, 1897.

Bauer, A. **SCHUBERT** im Roman und auf der Bühne. Moderne Welt, 7, 1926.

Brendel, U. Schubert in Dichtung und Malerei. Bayreuther Blätter, 34, 1911.

Krauss, R. Schubert im Roman und Drama. Schwäb. Merkur, 322, 1907.

Ash, Margaret. Anglo-French Relations in King John. (**SHAKESPEARE**). EA, 3, 1940.

Bates, E. S. Shakespeare as History. Gentleman's Mag., Feb., 1902.

Bitter, C. H. Ueber Gervinus, Händel und Shakespeare. Berlin, 1869.

Brandl, A. Geschichte auf der Bühne: Theater und Wahrheit bei Shakespeare. Berliner Tageblatt, 289, 1935.

Bundi, G. Verdi und Shakespeare. Der kleine Bund, 39-41 (Bern), 1936.

Daffner, H. Haydn und Shakespeare. JbShG, 50, 1914.

Einstein, A. Mozart und Shakespeare's Tempest. MDU, 36, 1944.

Fairchild, A. H. R. Shakespeare and the Arts of Design (Architecture, Sculpture, and Painting). Columbia (Mo.), 1937.

Farinelli, A. Verdi e Shakespeare. NAnt, 410, 1940.

Gervinus, G. G. Händel und Shakespeare. Zur Aesthetik der Tonkunst. Leipzig, 1868.

Istel, E. Verdi und Shakespeare. JbShG, 53, 1917.

Sampson, G. Bach and Shakespeare. QR, 1923. And in: Earl of Birkenhead's One

Hundred Best English Essays. London, 1929.
Saunders, W. Debussy and Shakespeare. ML, 1932.
Scherillo, M. Verdi, Shakespeare, Manzoni. NAnt, 244, 1912.
Schnapp, F. F. Liszt's Stellung zu Shakespeare. JbShG, 61, 1925.
Thorp, M. F. Shakespeare and the Fine Arts. PMLA, 46, 1931.
Waltershausen, H. W. von. Shakespeares Einfluss auf die Musik. JbShG, 64, 1928.
Whitridge, A. Shakspere and Delacroix. SAB, 17, 1942.
Williams, T. Shakespeare's Fidelity to History. PL, March, 1901.
Woermann, K. Shakespeare und die bildenden Künste. Leipzig, 1930.
O'Sullivan, I. **SHELLEY** und die bildende Kunst. Diss. Freiburg, 1927.
Sallenbach, F. Carl **SPITTELERS** Verhältnis zur Musik. Zürich, 1945.
Arbelet, P. L' "Histoire de la peinture en Italie" et les plagiats de **STENDHAL**. Paris, 1914.
Gentili, A. Curiosi giudizi di Stendhal sulla musica di Rossini. Dante, 1932.
Harthan, J. P. Stendhal and Mozart. Music & Letters, 27, 1946.
Jourda, P. Stendhal et Canova. REI, 1937.
Martino, P. Le "Del Romanticismo nelle arte" de Stendhal. RLC, 2, 1922.
Prunières, H. Stendhal et Rossini. Rev. critique des idées et livres, 10&25.VII. 1920.
Tiersot, J. Stendhal, Haydn et Carpani. Le Temps, 28.VIII.1932.
Novotny, F. Adalbert **STIFTER** als Maler. Wien, 1941.
Cournos, J. Gauguin and **THOREAU**: A Comparison. Bookman, 1928.
Grundy, J. B. C. **TIECK** and Runge. A Study in the Relationship of Literature and Art in the Romantic Period. Strassburg, 1930.
Beausire, P. Paul **VALERY** et Leonard de Vinci. Suisse contemporaine, 1947.
Burriss, E. E. **VERGIL** and Hector Berlioz. CW, 17.
Klemm, O. G. B. **VICO** als Geschichtsphilosoph und Völkerpsycholog. Leipzig, 1906.
Baldensperger, F. Note sur le Mozart d'Alfred de **VIGNY**. RHLF, 1927.
Delius, H. **VITRUV** und der deutsche Klassizismus. Architectura, 1, 1933.
Guérard, A. The New History, H. G. Wells and **VOLTAIRE**. Scribner's Mag., Nov., 1924.
Dessauer, E. **WACKENRODERS** Herzensergiessungen in ihrem Verhältnis zu Vasari. SVL, 6, 1906.
Carpenter, E. **WAGNER**, Millet and Whitman: in Relation to Art and Democracy. Progressive Rev., Oct., 1896.
Liess, A. L. van Beethoven und Richard Wagner im Pariser Musikleben. Hamburg, 1940.
C. M. von **WEBER'S** Freischütz: See Goethe's Faust, IV. X. 6.
Eichbaum, G. Die impressionistischen Frühgedichte O. **WILDES** unter besonderer Berücksichtigung des Einflusses von J. M. N. Whistler. NSp, 40, 1932.
Fierz, J. Heinrich **WOELFFLIN** und die Literaturwissenschaft. GRM, 31, 1943.
Shackford, M. H. **WORDSWORTH'S** Interest in Painters and Pictures. Wellesley (Mass.), 1946.
Olney, C. Wordsworth and Haydn. N&Q, 193, 1948.

CHAPTER FIVE

Science and Technology.

1. Science, especially Astronomy, Darwinism and Freudianism.

(For individual topics, e.g. Moon, Stars, Sun, Machines, etc. see Thematology.)

Anon. Darwinismus und Dichtung. Hannoverscher Courier, 113, 1909.
Aikin, J. An Essay on the Application of Natural History to Poetry. Warrington, 1777.
Allen, D. C. The Star-Crossed Renaissance: The Quarrel about Astrology and Its Influence in England. Durham, (N.C.), 1941.
Bab, J. Die Poesie der Technik. Schaubühne, 10, 1914.
Barzun, J. Darwin, Marx, Wagner: Critique of a Heritage. Boston, 1941.
Basler, R. P. Sex, Symbolism, and Psychology in Literature. New Brunswick, 1948.
Brace, C. L. Darwinism in Germany. NAR, 1870.
Brett, G. S. Psychology, Ancient and Modern. In: Our Debt to Greece and Rome. New York, 1928.
Cazamian, L. La psychanalyse et la critique littéraire. RLC, 4, 1924.
Conner, F. W. Cosmic Optimism: The Influence of Darwinian Evolution on American Poets. Diss. U. of Pa., 1944.
Davidson, M. The Stars and the Mind: A Study of the Impact of Astronomical

Development on Human Thought. London, 1947.
Entralgo, P. L. La acción catartica de la tragedia o sobre las relaciones entre la poesía y la medicina. Madrid, 1943.
Fay, B. L'Amérique et l'esprit scientifique en France à la fin du XVIIIe siècle. RLC, 3, 1923.
Foster, R. E. The Influence of Freud on the Autobiographical Novel. Diss. Vanderbilt U., 1941.
Friedrich, P. Das Problem der Vererbung in der deutschen Literatur. Kultur, 2, 1906 & Deutsche Renaissance, 2, (Leipzig), 1913.
Gantz, K. F. The Beginnings of Darwinian Ethics, 1859-71. U. of Texas Studies in English, 1939.
Glicksberg, C. I. Literary Criticism and Science. UTQ, 12, 1943.
—— Literature and Science: A Study in Conflict. Scientific Mo., 59, 1944.
—— Poetry and Freudian Aesthetic. UTQ, 17, 1948.
Gode-von-Aesch, A. Natural Science in German Romanticism. New York, 1941.
Henkin, L. J. Darwinism in the English Novel, 1860-1910. The Impact of Evolution on Victorian Fiction. New York, 1940.
Hoffman, F. J. Freudianism in the Literary Mind. Baton Rouge, (La.) 1945.
Hofstadter, R. Social Darwinism in American Thought, 1860-1915. Philadelphia, 1944.
Hyman, S. E. The Psychoanalytic Criticism of Literature. Western Rev., 12, 1948.
Johnson, F. R. Astronomical Thought in Renaissance England. Baltimore, 1937.
Jones, R. F. Science and Criticism in the Neo-Classical Age of English Literature. JHI, 1, 1940.
Karpe, L. Technik und Literatur. Die Arbeit, 6, 1906.
Kirchbach, V. Das Problem der Vererbung in Religion, Literatur und Naturwissenschaft. Freidenker, 11, 1914.
Lacroix, P. Science and Literature in the Middle Ages and at the Period of the Renaissance. London, 1878.
Laurent, E. La poésie décadente devant la science psychiatrique. Paris, 1897.
Loewenberg, B. J. Darwinism Comes to America. Miss. Valley Hist. Rev., 1941.
Martin, A. R., Trilling, L. & Vivas, E. The Legacy of Sigmund Freud: An Appraisal. Kenyon Rev., 2, 1940.
Mayer, E. Die Leistungen der modernen Technik in der Dichtung Englands und der Vereinigten Staaten. Diss. Freiburg. Endigen, 1938.
McCoffery, Ellen. Astrology: Its History and Influence in the Western World. New York, 1942.
McColley, G. (ed.). Literature and Science: An Anthology from English and American Literature, 1600-1900. Chicago, 1940.
Messac, P. Déterminisme et histoire littéraire. Science moderne, Sept., 1926.
Messac, R. Le detective novel et l'influence de la pensée scientifique. Paris, 1929.
Montagu, M. F. A. Suggestions for the Better Correlation of Literature and Science. Festschrift George Sarton. New York, 1947.
Muller, H. J. Scientist and Man of Letters. Yale Rev., 31, 1941.
Müller-Freienfels, R. Die Aufgaben einer Literaturpsychologie. LE, 16, 1913-14.
Myers, F. W. H. Modern Poets and Cosmic Law. In: Science and a Future Life. London, 1893.
Nicolson, Marjorie. The Microscope and English Imagination. Northampton, (Mass.), 1935.
—— The New Astronomy and English Literary Imagination. SPh, 32, 1935.
—— A World in the Moon: a Study of the Changing Attitude Toward the Moon in the Seventeenth and Eighteenth Centuries. Northampton, (Mass.), 1936.
Pernot, H. Mythes astrales et traditions littéraires. Paris, 1944.
Picard, R. La poésie romantique, la science et la révolution industrielle. RR, 35; 1944.
Rowbotham, A. H. The "philosophes" and the Propaganda for Inoculation of Smallpox in Eighteenth Century France. UCPPh, 18, 1935.
Sanctis, F. de. Il Darvinismo nell'arte. Napoli, 1883.
Schmidt, A. M. La poésie scientifique en France au XVIe siècle. Paris, 1939.
—— Haute science et poésie française au XVIe siècle. Cahiers d'Hermès, 1, 1947.
Sherwood, M. Vital Study of Literature and the Influence of Science. ER, 1919.
Slochower, H. Freud and Marx in Contemporary Literature. Sewanee Rev., 49, 1941.
Stucken, E. Astralmythen. Leipzig, 1896-1907.
Taylor, F. S. The March of Mind. A Short History of Science. New York, 1939.
Thorndike, L. A History of Magic and Experimental Science During the First

Thirteen Centuries of our Era. 2 vols. New York, 1923.
Wagman, F. H. Magic and Natural Science in German Baroque Literature. Columbia U.P., 1942.
Wilson, A. Science and Poetry. In: Humboldt Library, 100, 1888.
Wolff, W. Technik und Dichtung. Leipzig, 1923.
Zimmermann, F. Die Wiederspiegelungen der Technik in der deutschen Dichtung seit Goethe. Diss. Leipzig, 1913.
Zinner, E. Geschichte und Bibliographie der astronomischen Literatur in Deutschland zur Zeit der Renaissance. Leipzig, 1941.

2. Book-Printing and its History

Barge, H. Geschichte der Buchdruckerkunst von ihren Anfängen bis zur Gegenwart. Leipzig, 1940.
Bernard, A. De l'origine et des débuts de l'imprimerie en Europe. Paris, 1853.
Birge, J. K. The Printing of Books in Turkey in the Eighteenth Century. Moslem World, 33, 1943.
Butler, P. The Origin of Printing in Europe. Chicago U.P., 1940.
Crapelet, G. A. Des progrès de l'imprimerie en France et en Italie au XVIe siècle et de son influence sur la littérature. Paris, 1836.
Fauteux, A. The Introduction of Printing into Canada. Montreal, 1929.
Griselle, E. L'entrée des livres en Angleterre. Bull. du Bibliophile, 15.V. 1899.
Haebler, K. Deutsche Buchdrucker in Spanien und Portugal. Gutenberg Festschrift. Leipzig, 1902.
—— Die deutschen Buchdrucker des XV. Jahrhunderts im Auslande. München, 1924.
Jezerniczky, M. Les impressions en français de Hongrie (1707-1848). Diss., Szeged, 1933.
Kugelmann, J. Histoire de l'imprimerie en Portugal. Paris, 1867.
Leonard, I. A. & Green, O. H. On the Mexican Book Trade in 1600: A Chapter in Cultural History. HR, 1941
Oliveira, J. O primeiro impressor portugués e a su obra. Porto, 1942.
Pastorello, E. Bibliografia storico-analitica dell'arte della stampa in Venezia. Venezia, 1933.
Proctor, R. Printing of Greek in the Fifteenth Century. In: Illustrated Monographs, Bibliographical Society, 8, 1900.
Ruppel, A. Deutsche Pioniere der Druckkunst in Spanien. In: Klimschs Druckerei Anzeiger, Frankfurt, 64, 1939.
Scholderer, V. Geneva as a Centre of Early Printing. Library, 2, 1948.
Sonne, I. The Beginning of Hebrew Printing in Spain. Kirjath Sepher (Jerusalem), 14, 1939.
Steiger, E. Dreiundfünfzig Jahre Buchhändler in Deutschland und Amerika. New York, 1902.
Torre Revello, J. El libro, la imprenta y el periodismo en América durante la dominación española. Buenos Aires, 1940.
—— Origenes de la imprenta en España y su desarrollo en América Española. Buenos Aires, 1940.
Varia. Studi e ricerche sulla storia della stampa del quattrocento. Omaggio dell'Italia a Giovanni Gutenberg nel V. centenario della sua scoperto. Milano, 1942.
Van den Wijngaert, F. De expansie van de vlaamsche prentkunst in de XVIe en XVIIe eeuw. De Gulden Passer, 21, 1943.
Winship, G. P. Gutenberg to Plantin: An Outline of the Early History of Printing. Harvard U.P., 1926.
Zulaica Garate, R. Los franciscanos y la imprenta en México en el siglo XVI. México, 1939.

3. Individual Authors.

(Here again we try to show trends in scholarship rather than to compile a "complete" bibliography of authors influenced by the sciences. For Dreams, Insanity, etc., see also Thematology.)

Johnson, A. F. Books Printed at Heidelberg for Thomas **CARTWRIGHT.** Library, 2, 1948.
Rosenberg, E. Giacopo **CASTELVETRO:** Italian Publisher in Elizabethan London. HLQ, 6, 1943.
Carter, B. G. Alphonse **DAUDET** and Darwinism. MLQ, 6, 1945.
Winter, W. **DICKENS** and the Psychology of Dreams. PMLA, 63, 1948.
Nicolson, Marjorie. Kepler, the Somnium, and John **DONNE.** JHI, 1, 1940.
Bernard, A. Les **ESTIENNE** et les types grecs de François Ier. Paris, 1856.
Elliott, Leota W. & Kercheville, F. M. **GALDOS** and Abnormal Psychology. Hisp. 23, 1940.
Elia, P. d' Echi della scoperta galileiana in Cina, vivente ancora **GALILEO.** Rendiconti dell' Accad. Naz. dei Lincei, 8, 1946.

Reis, J. H. O. **GOETHE** en Camper als voorloopers van Darwin. In: Vragen van den dag, 24, 1909.

Berthelot, R. Lamarck et Goethe: l'évolutionisme de la continuité au début du XIXe siècle. RMM, 1929.

Gross, J. Darwinistisches in Goethes Faust. Baltische Monatsschrift, 72, 1911.

Hildebrandt, K. Goethe und Darwin. Archiv f. Gesch. d. Philos., 41, 1932.

Krappe, A. H. Le thème de la science stérile chez **GOWER** et chez Goethe. RLC, 12, 1932.

Barenbach, F. von. **HERDER** als Vorgänger Darwins in der modernen Naturphilosophie. Berlin, 1877. And in WM, 1878.

Karppe, S. Herder, précurseur de Darwin. In: Essais de critique et d'histoire de la philosophie. Paris, 1902.

Goetz, H. War Herder ein Vorgänger Darwins? Vierteljahrsschrift für wiss. Philosophie, 26, 1903.

Fechter, P. **IBSEN**, Sophokles und Darwin. Propylaen, 35, 1906.

Halstead, F. The Attitude of **LOPE DE VEGA** toward Astrology and Astronomy. HR, 7, 1939.

Baldensperger, F. La Tragédie de l'homme **(MADACH)** et les prévisions positivistes. Rev. des Etudes hongroises, 1934.

Cantoni, C. Terenzo **MAMIANI** e H. Lotze: o il mondo secondo la scienza e secondo il sentimento. NAnt, 11, 1869.

Schueck, J. Aldus **MANUTIUS** und seine Zeitgenossen in Italien und Deutschland. Berlin, 1862.

Johnson, F. R. **MARLOWE'S** Astronomy and Renaissance Skepticism. ELH, 13, 1946.

Schmid, G. **MATTHISSON** und Linné. Berlin, 1935.

Delen, A. J. J. Christophe **PLANTIN**, imprimeur de l'humanisme. Bruxelles, 1944.

Lind, S. E. **POE** and Mesmerism. PMLA, 62, 1947.

Spears, M. K. Matthew **PRIOR'S** Attitude toward Natural Science. PMLA, 63, 1948.

Nugent, E. M. Sources of John **RASTELL'S** The Nature of the Four Elements. PMLA, 57, 1942.

Parks, G. B. Rastell and Waldseemüller's Map. PMLA, 58, 1943.

Parr, J. More Sources of Rastell's Interlude of the Four Elements. PMLA, 60, 1945.

François, A. **J. J. ROUSSEAU** et la science genevoise du XVIIIe siècle. RCC, 31, 1924 and RHLF, 1924.

Tomaschek, K. **SCHILLER** in seinem Verhältnis zur Wissenschaft. Wien, 1862.

Roth, E. Die Mainzer Buchhändlerfamilie **SCHOEFFER** in Livorno und Venedig im XVI. Jahrhundert. Centralblatt für Bibliothekwesen, 9, 1892.

Fraser-Harris, D. **SHAKESPEARE** and the Influence of the Stars. Discovery, 8, 1927.

Schark, F. Shakespeare und die Astrologie. Hamburger Fremdenblatt, 24.VII, 1926.

Ewing, S. B. Scientists and Shakespeare. SAB, 23, 1948.

Ellis, O. C. Shakespeare as a Scientist. Papers of the Manchester Literary Club, 59, 1933.

Barbensi, G. Biologia e medicina in B. **SHAW**. Il Mondo, 37, 1946.

Glicksberg, C. I. Shaw versus Science. Dalhousie Rev., 28, 1948.

Bonno, G. Hans **SLOANE** et les relations intellectuelles franco-anglaises au 18e siècle. RR, 34, 1943.

Burroughs, J. **WHITMAN'S** and **TENNYSON'S** Relations to Science. Dial, 16.III. 1893.

Drennon, H. J. **THOMSON'S Contact** with Newtonianism and His Interest in Natural Philosophy. PMLA, 1934.

Bernard, A. Geoffroy **TORY**, peintre et graveur, premier imprimeur royal. Paris, 1857.

Ives, S. A. Geoffrey Tory and Catharine de Medici. New York, 1944.

Potter, G. R. **WORDSWORTH** and the Traité élémentaire de Chimie of Lavoisier. PhQ, 17, 1938.

Pottle, F. A. Wordsworth and Freud. Bull. General Theological Seminary, 34, 1948.

Wiener, P. Chauncey **WRIGHT'S** Defense of Darwin and the Neutrality of Science. JHI, 6, 1945.

FOURTH PART

Intermediaries

CHAPTER ONE

Countries: The Alsace

(In order to avoid scattering names of countries and individuals over too many chapters, most great intermediaries [e.g. Switzerland and Holland] have been discussed in the chapters assigned to them. Cities can be found in the space allotted to them in the chapter on Thematology. That leaves the Alsace as the sole intermediary not given a chapter elsewhere.
For Normans, see IV. XII. 1.)

Anon. Das Deutschtum im Elsass. Europa, 32, 1856.

Baldensperger, F. L'Alsace et la sensibilité romantique française. L'Alsace française, 4.VI. 1927.

Barthel, E. De l'Alsace et des mentalités française et allemande. Rev. mondiale, 1928.

Trautwein von Belle. Das deutsche Element in der elsässischen Journalistik. MLIA, 23, 1868.

Boudinot, A. Les écrivains alsaciens dans la littérature allemande. Paris, 1937.

Breitenbucher, J. R. Trends in Alsatian Literature. BA, 14, 1941.

Bury, J. P. Quelques voyageurs anglais en Alsace, 1680-1860. Annuaire de la Société . . . du Club vosgien, 3, 1935.

Gillet, L. L'Alsace, école de l'Allemagne. NL, 26, III. 1938.

Hirsing, A. Das Elsass in der Romanliteratur. Kölnische Volks Zt., 13.IX. 1922.

Koszul, A. Les relations entre l'Alsace et l'Angleterre au XVIe siècle. RLC, 9, 1929.

Krause, K. Das Elsass und die Deutschen. Grenzboten, 4, 1845.

Kurz, H. Die deutsche Litteratur im Elsass. Berlin, 1874.

Lamey, A. La poésie allemande en Alsace. RDM, 1.VIII.1857.

Lebert, H. Les écrivains alsaciens dans la littérature allemande. L'Alsace française, 10.VIII.1938.

Pöschel, K. Die elsässische Lyrik des 19. Jahrhunderts in ihrer Abhängigkeit von den literarischen Strömungen in Deutschland. Frankfurt, 1932.

Tronchon, H. Alsace et littératures modernes comparées. Vie en Alsace, 1926.

Weis, E. Der Elsässer im französischen Roman des 19. und 20. Jahrhunderts. Diss. Tübingen, 1938.

Loeper, von. GOETHES Strassburger Freunde. Beilage zur Allg. Zt. Aug. 1884.

Pange, Mme. J. de. Goethe en Alsace. Paris, 1925.

Redslob, R. Goethe, l'Alsace et les deux Allemagnes. Le Temps, 26.VIII. 1932.

Traumann, E. Goethe der Strassburger Student. Leipzig, 1923.

Vermeil, E. Goethe à Strasbourg. In: Goethe. Etudes publiées pour le centenaire de sa mort par l'U. de Strasbourg. Paris, 1932.

Koszul, A. Les SIDNEY à Strasbourg. Bull. de la Fac. des Lettres de Strasbourg, 1938.

Baldensperger, F. STRASBOURG et les grands courants européens. Alsace française, 1923.

Froitzheim, J. Zu Strassburgs Sturm und Drangperiode, 1770-76. Strassburg, 1888.

Pfleger, L. Das Strassburger Münster und die deutsche Dichtung. Strassburg, 1909.

CHAPTER TWO

Translations.

(Only works of a general character are contained here; for specific translations [e.g. English translations from the Italian], see specific country of origin.)

Anon. On Oriental Translation. Asiatic Journ. N.S., 21, 1836.

—— The Art of Translation. QR, 182, 1895.

—— De las traducciones. Norte, 1.IX. 1935.

—— Index Translationum. Répertoire international des traductions. Institut de Cooperation intellectuelle, 1932.

—— Verzeichnis der (in's Deutsche) übersetzten Werke der Gegenwartsdichtung europäischer Völker. In: Die Gegenwartsdichtung der europäischen Völker. Berlin, 1939.

Amos, F. R. Early Theories of Translation. New York, 1920.
Baites, E. S. Modern Translations. London, 1936.
Baragiola, Elsa N. Beitrag zur Frage des lyrischen Uebersetzens. Festschrift Louis Gauchat. Aarau, 1926.
Bellanger, S. Histoire de la traduction en France. Paris, 1903.
Du Bellay, J. Défense et illustration de la langue française (1549).
Belloc, H. On Translation. Oxford, 1931.
Bianquis, G. Kann man Dichtung übersetzen? D&V, 37, 1936.
Bignan, A. Des traductions et de l'imitation. MF, 20, 1828.
Binni, W. Le traduzioni preromantiche. RLM, 2, 1947.
Boyd, E. The Way of the Translator. Literary Rev., 1922.
Bynner, W. On Translating Chinese Poetry. Asia, Dec., 1921.
Chandibine, M. De la traduction. Hum, 8, 1932.
Clements, A. F. Tudor Translations. Oxford, 1929.
Descaves, P. Le problème de la traduction peut-il être résolu par la création d'un ordre de traducteurs? Courrier de Berne, 24.VII. 1947.
Drescher, P. Die ungarische Uebersetzungsliteratur, 1920-28. Ungarische Jb, 9, 1930.
Egger, E. L'art de traduire et les traducteurs français d'Hérodote. Mém. du Congrès scientifique tenu à Amiens en 1867.
Engel, E. Die Uebersetzungsmanie in Deutschland. MLIA, 1879.
L'Estang, de. De la traduction, ou règles pour apprendre à traduire la langue latine en langue françoise. Paris, 1670.
Farrar, Clarissa P. & Evans, A. P. Bibliography of English Translations from Medieval Sources. New York, 1946.
Fränzel, W. Geschichte des Uebersetzens im 18. Jahrhundert. Leipzig, 1914.
Fuchs, G. Studien zur Uebersetzungstheorie und Praxis des Gottsched-Kreises. Leipzig, 1936.
Genzmer, F. Ist die Skaldendichtung übersetzbar? JEGPh, 47, 1948.
Glasenapp, G. von. Ueber poetische Uebersetzungen. Baltische Monatschrift, 1897.
Goedeke, K. (On German Translators of English and French Works: Dyck, Mylius, Schmid, Faber, Huber. etc.) Grundr. z. Gesch. d. deutsch. Dichtung, 5, 1884-98.
Golitsyn, Prince (Prince Galitzin). Réflexions sur les traducteurs russes. Saint-Petersbourg, 1811.
Granville-Barker, H. On Translating Plays. Transactions of the Royal Soc. of Lit., N.S., 5, 1925.
Grasset, B. Traductions et Traducteurs. RDM, 1938.
Grierson, H. J. C. Verse Translation. English Association. Oxford U.P., 1948.
Gruppe, O. F. Deutsche Uebersetzungskunst. Hannover, 1866.
Guthrie, W. N. Translation: A Method for the Study of Literature. Sewanee Rev., 17, 1909.
Hartwig, O. Die Uebersetzungslitteratur Unteritaliens. Centralblatt f. Bibliothekwesen, 1886.
—— Die Uebersetzungsliteratur Unteritaliens in der normannisch-sicilischen Monarchie. Innsbruck, 1904.
Haskins, C. H. North-Italian Translators of the Twelfth Century. In: Studies in the History of Medieval Science, Cambridge, 2nd ed., 1927.
—— Translators in Syria during the Crusades. ibid.
Hatcher, O. L. Aims and Methods of Elizabethan Translators. ESn, 1911-12.
Heck, P. Uebersetzungsprobleme im frühen Mittelalter. Tübingen, 1931.
Huet, P. D. De Interpretatione libri duo: de optime genere interpretandi; de claris interpretibus. Paris, 1661.
Hugo, V. Les traducteurs. RdF, 15.III. 1937.
Kliger, S. The Gothic Revival and the German Translatio. MPh, 45, 1947.
Krueger, H. A. Uebersetzungen ausländischer Erzähler. Beil. zum litter. Centralblatt, 15.IX.1902.
Larwill, P. H. La théorie de la traduction au début de la Renaissance. München, 1934.
Lebègue, R. Les traductions en France pendant la Renaissance. Actes du Congrès G. Budé à Strasbourg. Paris, 1939.
Lebeuf, Abbé. Recherches sur les plus anciennes traductions en langue française. In: Mémoires de l'Académie des Inscriptions et Belles-Lettres, 17, 1751.
Leibowitz, N. Die Uebersetzungstechnik der jüdisch-deutschen Uebersetzungen des 15. und 16. Jahrhunderts dargestellt an den Psalmen. In: Beitr. zur Gesch. der deutschen Sprache & Literatur, 55, 1931.
Luther, M. Sendbrief vom Dolmetschen (1530).
Matthiessen, F. O. Translation—an Elizabethan Art. Harvard U.P., 1931.

Oldaker, W. H. Translating Poetry. G&R, 7, 1938.
Ortega y Gasset, J. Miseria e bellezza della traduzione. Poesia, June, 1947.
Pellicer y Saforcada, J. A. Ensayo de una Bibliotheca de traductores Españoles donde se da noticia de las traducciones que hay en Castellano. Madrid, 1778.
Phillimore, J. S. On Translation and Translators. English Association, 42. Oxford, 1919.
Postgate, J. P. Translators and Translations: Theory and Practice. London, 1922.
Raleigh. Tudor Translations. Fortnightly Rev., 1895.
Richter, H. E. Uebersetzen und Uebersetzungen in der römischen Literatur. Koburg, 1938.
Roscommon, W. D. An Essay on Translated Verse. In: Works, London, 1709.
Rosenberg, R. P. Problems in Translation with Reference to Dantons Tod. GQ, 15, 1942.
—— The Use of the Critical Edition in Literary Translation. MLJ, 27, 1943.
Rossetti, C. I traduttori e il linguaggio marinaro. Lingua Nostra, 7, 1946
Saint-Evremond, C. de. Réflexions sur nos traducteurs. In: Oeuvres complètes, Paris, 1740.
Sarrasin, J. Zur Uebersetzungspoesie. MLIA, 1883.
Schleger, H. Das Uebersetzungsproblem bei den spanischen Bühnenklassikern. Ibero-amerikan. Rundschau, 7, 1941.
Schwarz, W. Translation into German in the Fifteenth Century. MLR, 39, 1944.
—— The Theory of Translation in 16th Century Germany. MLR, 40, 1945.
Staël, Mme. G. de. Sulla maniera e la utilità delle traduzioni. In: Biblioteca italiana, January, 1816.
Starnes, D. T. Bilingual Dictionaries of Shakespeare's Day. PMLA, 1937.
Svoboda, K. Les conceptions de la traduction dans l'antiquité. (In Czech). Listy Filologicke, 1941.
Swingler, D. T. Apropos of Translation. G&R, 1937.
Tallgren, O. J. Savoir, comprendre, traduire. Neuphilol. Mitteil., (Helsingfors), 1925.
Tardieu, J. De la traduction d'un rythme. Mesures, 15.X. 1935.
Theuriet, A. De la traduction des poètes. RDM, 1.II. 1877.
Toyoda, M. On Translating Japanese Poetry into English. Studies in English Literature (Tokyo), 14, 1934.
Ungaretti, G. Del tradurre. Fiera letteraria, 1, 1946.
Weidle, V. L'art de traduire. NL, 30.V. 1939.
West, Constance B. La théoric dc la traduction au XVIIIe siècle par rapport surtout aux traductions françaises d'ouvrages anglais. RLC, 12, 1932.
Whibley, C. Translations. In: The Cambridge History of English Literature, 4. Cambridge, 1909.
Wolfskehl, K. Vom Sinn und Rand des Uebersetzens. In: Bild und Gesetz, 1930.
Woodworth, D. C. Meaning and Verse Translation. CJ, 1938.
Workman, S. K. Fifteenth Century Translation as an Influence on English Prose. Princeton, 1940.

CHAPTER THREE

Travelling.

(Only general works are contained in this chapter; for travels to specific countries and cities, see specific country or city in question. For travels as a literary genre, see Voyages, I. VII. 1.)

Ancona, A. d'. Viaggiatori e avventurieri. Firenze, 1911.
Arentzen, K. Danish Travellers at the End of the Previous Century. (In Danish). København, 1884.
Atkinson, G. Les relations de voyages au XVIIe siècle et l'évolution des idées. Paris, 1925.
Bastide, C. Le voyage de Paris à Londres sous Louis XIV. Foi et Vie, 16.IV. 1911.
Brown, W. C. English Travel Books, 1775-1825. PhQ, 1937.
Cawley, R. R. The Voyagers and Elizabethan Drama. Boston, 1938.
—— Unpathed Waters: Studies in the Influence of the Voyagers on Elizabethan Literature. Princeton, 1940.
Cox, E. G. A Reference Guide to the Literature of Travel. Seattle, 1935.
Faure, G. Pèlerinages passionés. Paris, 1922.
Frantz, R. W. The English Traveller and the Movement of Ideas (1660-1732). U. of Nebraska, 1935.
Gigli, L. Viaggiatori dell'ottocento. I libri del Giorno, 1928.
Hantzsch, V. Deutsche Reisende des XVI. Jahrhunderts. Leipzig, 1895.

Hazard, P. L'Europe des voyageurs en 1700. L'Europe centrale, 1933.
Howard, C. English Travellers of the Renaissance. London, 1914.
Kaeppel, C. Off the Beaten Track in the Classics. Melbourne, 1936.
Lambert, R. S. (ed.). Grand Tour. A Journey in the Tracks of the Age of Aristocracy. New York, 1937. Cf Journal of Modern History, 9, 1937.
Mazzoni, G. I viaggi nella letteratura italiana. Rendiconti della R. Accademia dei Lincei, 7.VI. 1931.
Newton, A. P. Travel and Travellers in the Middle Ages. New York, 1926.
Park, R. E. Human Migration and the Marginal Man. Amer. Journal of Sociology, 1928.
Parkes, J. Travel in England in the 17th Century. London, 1925.
Pavel, J. Autour de l'heureux voyage de trois gentilshommes tchèques dans l'Europe du XVIIe siècle. L'Europe centrale, 11.IX.1937.
Penrose, B. Urbane Travelers, 1591-1635. Philadelphia, 1942.
Robertson, J. G. The Spirit of Travel in Modern Literature. In: Essays and Addresses on Literature. London, 1935.

CHAPTER FOUR

Emigrants, Foreign Colonies, Groups in Exile.

(See also Religious Sects, III. I. 2, and Collective Influences, III. III.)

1. Generalities.

Anon. Etwas über die Lage der Ausländer im Russischen Reiche. Journal von Russland, May, 1796.
Alesius, M. Ueber Réfugiés in Deutschland. Theolog. Jahresber., 14, 1895.
Balogh, E. Political Refugees in Ancient Greece. Johannesburg, 1943.
Clarke, T. W. Emigrés in the Wilderness. New York, 1941.
Imhoof, W. Der Europamüde in der deutschen Erzählungsliteratur. Frauenfeld-Leipzig, 1930.
Kieve, R. S. The Psychology of a Refugee Writer. BA, 15, 1941.
Kirkconnell, W. The European Canadians and Their Press. Annual Report of the Canadian Historical Assoc., 1940.
Lawrence, E. The Influence of the Immigrant on American Fiction. 1890-1925. Diss. Western Reserve U. 1942.
Leacock, S. Emigration in English Literature. QR, 1938.
Lindt, P. M. Schriftsteller im Exil. New York, 1944.
Liubimenko, I. Les étrangers en Russie avant Pierre le Grand. Rev. des Etudes slaves, 1923-24.
Lonn, E. Foreigners in the Confederacy. Chapel Hill (N.C.), 1939.
Morgan, B. Q. Literature in Exile. BA, 18, 1944.
Norwood, F. A. The Reformation Refugees as an Economic Force. Chicago, 1942.
Robb, N. Four in Exile. London, 1946.
Tindall, W. Y. Exiles: Rimbaud to Joyce. Amer. Scholar, 14, 1945.
Valette, J. Ecrivains et artistes étrangers en Angleterre. La Nef, 1946.
Weiskopf, F. C. What Refugee Writers Are Doing. BA, 15, 1941.
Zukermann, W. Refugees in England. QR, 1939.

2. Emigrants or Refugees from England.

Anon. Anglais réfugiés en Suisse en 1557. Conservat. Suisse, 1814.
Aydelotte, F. Elizabethan Seamen in Mexico. AHR, 48, 1942.
Boutet de Monvel, R. Les Anglais à Paris de 1800 à 1850. Paris, 1911.
Dancoisne, Abbé. Histoire des établissements religieux britanniques fondés à Douai avant la Révolution française. Douai, 1880.
Du Boscq de Beaumont & Bernos, M. La Cour des Stuarts à Saint-Germain-en-Laye, 1689-1718. Paris, 1912.
Fortolis, L. Les Anglais en France. Des cachots de la Terreur aux geôles de l'Empire. Paris, 1923.
Jung, R. Die englische Flüchtlings-Gemeinde in Frankfurt a.M. 1554-59. Frankfurt, 1910.
Lechat, R. Les réfugiés anglais dans les Pays-Bas espagnols durant le règne d'Elisabeth. Louvain, 1914.
Leith, W. F. Bibliographie des livres publiés à Paris et à Lyon par les savants écossais réfugiés en France au XVIe siècle. Paris, 1912.
Locke, J. The First Englishmen in India. London, 1930.
Lubimenko, J. Les marchands anglais en Russie au XVIe siècle. Revue historique, 109, 1912.
Martin, C. Les Protestants anglais réfugiés à Genéve au temps de Calvin, 1555-60. Leur église, leurs écrits. Genève, 1915.
Merriden, F. M. La colonie anglaise à

Boulogne depuis deux cent cinquante ans. XXVIIe Congrès de l'Association pour l'avancement des sciences, Boulogne, 1899.
Michel, F. Les Ecossais en France et les Français en Ecosse. 2 vols. Paris, 1862.
O'Mahony, D. English Footprints on the Continent (Irish Saints and Schools). London, 1927.
Puiseux, L. L'émigration normande et la colonisation anglaise en Normandie au XVe siècle. Caen, 1866. 2nd ed. Paris, 1885.
Vetter, T. Englische Flüchtlinge in Zürich während der 1. Hälfte des 16. Jahrhunderts. Neujahrsblatt der Stadtbibliothek Zürich, 1893-94.

3. Emigrants or Refugees from France. The Huguenots.

(See also French Influences upon Canada, IV. VII. 3, and French Revolution, IV. VII. 25.)

Anon. The Early French in India. Calcutta Rev., 31, 1858.
—— French Calvinists in North America. NAR, 80, 1855.
—— French India at its Zenith. Calcutta Rev., 43, 1866.
—— The Huguenot Emigration to America. AM, 1885.
Agnew, D. French Protestant Exiles. 3 vols. London, 1886.
Ancillon, C. Histoire de l'établissement des Français réfugiés dans les Etats de Brandebourg. Berlin, 1690.
Arnal, J. De l'influence des réfugiés français aux Pays-Bas Bull. de la Commission de l'histoire des églises wallonnes. Leyden, 1929.
Arx, F. von. Die französischen Emigranten in Solothurn. Sonntagsblatt des Bund, (Bern), 1892.
Bainville, J. Les descendants de réfugiés et d'émigrés français dans l'Allemagne contemporaine. Revue des Revues, 1.II. 1900.
Baird, C. W. History of the Huguenot Emigration to America. New York, 1885; Toulouse, 1886.
Baldensperger, F. Le mouvement des idées dans l'émigration française. 2 vols. Paris, 1924.
—— La littérature des émigrés français de 1789 à 1815. Bruxelles, 1924.
—— Goethe et les émigrés français à Weimar. RG, 1911.
—— Klopstock et les émigrés français à Hambourg. RHLF, 1913.
Barthold, F. W. Deutschland und die Hugenotten. Bremen, 1848.
Bartholmess, C. Histoire philosophique de l'Académie de Prusse (and French refugees in Germany). 2 vols. Paris, 1851.
Bastide, C. Huguenot Thought in England. JCL, 1, 1903.
Bercet, E. La colonie française de Friedrichsdorf. Bull. de la Soc. arch. de Vervins, 15, 1892.
Béringuier, R. Metzer Réfugiés in Berlin. Jb. der Ges. für Lothring. Geschichte & Altertumskunde, 1.
Bertaut, J. Les émigrés français à Londres. Le Monde nouveau, 1925.
Besson, E. Les Francs-Comtois en Russie au XVIIIe siècle. Mem. de la Soc. d'émulation du Doubs, Besançon, 7, 1893.
Bonnet, J. Ministres réfugiés à Londres après la Sainte-Barthélemy. Bull. de la Soc. de l'hist. du Protestantisme fr., 2, 1854.
Boussey, A. Les Francs-Comtois à Ferrare au XVe et au XVIe siècle. Académie de Besançon, 1903-04.
Brandon. A French Colony in Michigan. MLN, 13, 1898.
Burns, J. S. The History of the French, Waloon, Dutch, and other Foreign Protestant Refugees Settled in England. London, 1846.
Carré, A. L'influence des Huguenots français en Irlande aux XVIIe et XVIIIe siècles. Paris; Belfast, 1937.
Cazenave, M. Les émigrés bonapartistes de 1815 aux Etats-Unis. Rev. d'hist. diplom., 1929.
Chambrier, Mme. A. de. Les réfugiés français en Suisse de 1593 à 1699. In: Bull. du Protesantisme fr., 58, 1909.
Chavannes, J. Les réfugiés français dans le pays de Vaud. Lausanne, 1874.
Childs, F. S. French Refugee Life in the United States (1790-1800). Baltimore, 1940.
Chinard, G. Les Réfugiés huguenots français en Amérique. Paris, 1925.
Cohen, G. Ecrivains français en Hollande. La Flambeau, April, 1921.
Curzon, A. de. Les Français en Angleterre sous le Premier Empire. NRC, 1924-25.
Dohm, E. von. Ueber die Aufnahme der verjagten protestantischen Franzosen in den Kurbrandenburgischen Landen. In: Denkwürdigkeiten, vol. 5, 1819.
Dompierre de Jonquières. Les pasteurs de l'Eglise réformée française de Copenhague (1685-1856). Bull. du Protestantisme fr., 7, 1858.

Durrien, P. Les Gascons en Italie. Rev. de Gascogne, 25, 1884.

Ebrard. Die französisch-reformierte Gemeinde in Frankfurt a.M., 1554-1904. Frankfurt, 1906.

Eckardt, J. Französische Emigranten in Russland. Baltische Monatsschrift, 35, 1888.

Erman & Réclam. Mémoires pour servir à l'histoire des réfugiés français dans les Etats du Roi. 9 vols. Berlin, 1782-1800.

Ferréol, A. Les proscrits français en Belgique. Paris, 1871.

Fosdick, L. J. The French Blood in America. New York, 1906.

Fournier-Marcigny, F. Les Français à Genève au XVIe siècle. Journal des Débats, 26.IX. 1942.

France, H. de. Les Montalbanais et le refuge. Montauban, 1887.

Gaillardet, F. Souvenirs français du Texas: le champ d'asile. Constitutionnel, 22-29.VIII. 1841.

Graziani, A. Emigrati illustri a Vicenza. Archivo veneto, 5 ser., 64, 1934.

Harkensee & Hennecke. Beiträge zur Their Descendants in Plymouth. N&Q, 187, 1944.

Harkensee & Hennecke. Beiträge zur Geschichte der Emigranten in Hamburg. I. Das französische Theater. Hamburg, 1894-96. Cf. RHLF, 3.

Hauser, H. Les Huguenots français au Brésil (1560-1584) d'après des documents portugais. Bull. du Protestantisme fr, 1937.

Hecht, L. Les colonies lorraines et alsaciennes en Hongrie. Mémoires de l'Académie de Stanislas, Nancy, 1879.

Henriot, E. Goethe et les émigrés français. Le Temps, 5.I. 1932.

Lee, Hannah, F. The Huguenots in France and America. 2 vols. Boston, 1852.

Lee, G. L. The Huguenot Settlements in Ireland. London, 1936.

Marmier, C. Geschichte und Sprache der Huguenottencolonie Friedrichsdorf a.T. Marburg, 1901.

Michel, F. Les Portugais en France et les Français en Portugal. Paris, 1882.

Morel, L. Goethe et les Français de passage. Zürich, 1901.

Murray, E. French Exiles of 1793 in North Pennsylvania. Légion d'honneur, 1935.

Nemeth, E. Les colonies françaises de Hongrie. Szeged, 1936.

Pagès, G. Les réfugiés à Berlin d'après la correspondance du comte de Rebenac (1681-88). Bull. du Protestantisme fr., 51, 1902.

—— Les réfugiés français à Baireuth en 1686. Bull. du Protestantisme fr., 52, 1903.

Pariset, G. L'état et les églises en Prusse sous Frédéric Guillaume Ier (and French refugees). Paris, 1897.

Paul, A. Les réfugiés huguenots et wallons dans le Palatinat du Rhin. Rev. hist., 1928.

Perez de Guzman, J. Los emigrados de Francia. Recuerdos de la revolución. La Illustración española y americana, 1908.

Pingaud, L. Les Français en Russie et les Russes en France. Paris, 1886.

Poulet, H. Les Lorrains en Toscane. Paris, 1912.

Puaux, F. Histoire de l'établissement des protestants français en Suède. Paris, Stockholm, 1891.

Reeves, J. S. The Napoleonic Exiles in America, 1815-19. Johns Hopkins Studies, 1905.

Reverdin, F. Prosélytes et réfugiés à Genève (1714-17). Bull. du Protestantisme fr., 1930.

Revesz, E. La Hongrie et les réfugiés huguenots. Nouvelle Rev. de Hongrie, 1933.

Reyer, C. Histoire de la colonie française en Prusse. Paris, 1855.

Richemond, L. de. La Rochelle d'outremer (Huguenots in England). Ann. de l'Acad. de la Rochelle, 23, 1885.

Robert, C. Les émigrés bretons réfugiés à Bath pendant la Révolution. Rev. de Bretagne, de Vendée et d'Anjou, 20. Nantes, 1898.

Ruskowski, L. F. French Emigre Priests in the United States, 1791-1815. Diss. Catholic U. of America, 1940.

Schickler, B. de. Les églises du refuge en Angleterre. 3 vols. Paris, 1892.

Schmidt, G. Geschichte und Sprache der Hugenottenniederlassung Friedrichsdorf im Taunus. ZFSL, 13, 1891.

Smiles, S. The Huguenots in England and Ireland (Appendix: The Huguenots in America). New York, 1868.

Stapleton, A. Memorials of the Huguenots in America, with Special Reference to Their Emigration to Pennsylvania. Carlisle, (Pa), 1901.

Sugenheim, S. Der Widerruf des Edictes von Nantes und seine Folgen für Frankreich und Deutschland. In: Aufsätze und biographische Skizzen zur französischen Geschichte. Strassburg, 1872.

Tantet, V. Les réfugiés politiques français en Amérique sous la convention. Revue, 52, 1905.

Tastevin, F. Histoire de la colonie française de Moscou. Moscou, Paris, 1908.

Thomas, A. Emigrants auvergnats en Espagne sous Charles VII (1449). Homenaje a Menéndez Pidal, 3. Madrid, 1925.

Tollin, H. Urkunden zur Geschichte hugenottischer Gemeinden in Deutschland. Gesch. Blätter d. Hug. Vereins, 1900.

Urtel, H. Die Hugenottensprache in Friedrichsdorf. Beilage zur Allg. Zt., 135, 1902.

Vedder, C. S. & Demarest, W. H. S. The French Protestant Church in the City of Charleston. Charleston, 1912.

Villers, C. de. Idées sur la destination des hommes de lettres sortis de France et qui séjournent en Allemagne. Spectateur du Nord, 7, 1798.

Weightman, J. G. French Writing on English Soil. A Choice of French Writing Published in London, 1940-44. London, 1945.

Weiss, C. Mémoire sur les protestants de France au XVIIe siècle. Séances et Trav. de l'Acad. des Sc. mor. et pol., 20, 1851.

—— Mémoire sur l'influence littéraire des réfugiés protestants de France en Hollande. ibid. 25-26, 1853.

—— Histoire des réfugiés protestants de France depuis la révocation de l'Edit de Nantes jusqu'à nos jours. 2 vols. Paris, 1853.

Wildbolz, H. Die französische Kolonie von Bern, 1689-1850. Bern, 1920.

Wühr, W. Jean Paul und die französische Emigration. Jean Paul Blätter (Bayreuth), 1940.

4. Emigrants or Refugees from Germany

(See also German influences upon America, IV. X. 2.)

Anon. Etwas über die Lage, Lebensart und Vorteile der Deutschen in Russland und vorzüglich in St. Petersburg. Journal von Russland, 1795.

—— Die Deutschen in Paris. Beilage zur Allg. Zt, 9.X. & 24.XII, 1842, 14.I. & 15.II, 1843.

—— Die deutsche Niederlassung in Missouri. Beilage zur Allg. Zt. 2.II.1843.

—— German Emigration to America. NAR, 82, 1856.

—— Die Deutschen in New York. Grenzboten, 45, 1886.

Althaus, F. Beiträge zur Geschichte der deutschen Colonie in England. Unsere Zeit, N.F., 9, 1873.

Beidelmann, W. The Story of the Pennsylvania Germans. Easton (Pa.), 1898.

Bentley, E. R. German Writers in Exile, 1933-43. BA, 17, 1943.

Bloesch, H. Die Deutschen in Paris 1830-50. Beilage zur Allg. Zt, 103, 1903.

Bookstahler, O. L. Contributions to American Literature by Hoosiers of German Ancestry. Indiana Mag. of History, 38, 1942.

Bosse, G. von. Das deutsche Element in den Vereinigten Staaten. Stuttgart, 1908.

Cipolla, F. & C. Dei coloni tedeschi nei XII communi veronesi. Arch. glott. 8, 1866.

Cronau, R. Drei Jahrhunderte deutschen Lebens in Amerika. Berlin, 1909.

Cunz, D. The Maryland Germans: A History. Princeton, 1948.

Davis-Du Bois, R. & Schweppe, E. The Germans in American Life. New York, 1936.

Faust, A. B. Das Deutschtum in den Vereinigten Staaten I. in seiner Bedeutung für die amerikanische Kultur, II. in seiner geschichtlichen Entwickelung. Leipzig, 1912.

—— The German Element in the United States. New York, 1927.

Franck, W. La littérature de l'émigration allemande. Grande Revue, 1935.

Giordani. La colonia tedesca di Alagna-Valsesia. Torino, 1891.

Goebel, J. Das Deutschtum in den Vereinigten Staaten von Nordamerika. München, 1904.

Graefer, G. Deutsche in Frankreich. NM. 1936.

Graevenitz, G. von. Deutsche in Rom: Studien und Skizzen aus elf Jahrhunderten. Leipzig, 1902.

Hofe, H. von. German Literature in Exile. GQ, 17, 1944.

Jacob, E. G. Die Deutschen in Spanien und Portugal, 1147-1934. Berlin, 1935.

Kapp, F. Die Achtundvierziger in den Vereinigten Staaten. In: Demokratische Studien, 1, (Hamburg), 1860.

Katscher, L. German Life in London. NC, 1887.

Kayser, R. Deutsches Leben in Dänemark. PJb, 132, 1908.

Koerner, G. Das deutsche Element in den Vereinigten Staaten von Amerika (1818-48). Cincinnati, 1880. Cf. WM, 1881.

Krauss, H. Deutsche Einwanderungen und Kultureinfluss in Rumänien seit dem 13. Jahrhundert. Vossische Zt, 383-85, 1892.

Kruener, F. Brandenburger in Italien. Archiv f. Brandenburgia, 9, 1902.

Kuhns, O. The German and Swiss Settlements of Colonial Pennsylvania. A Study of the so-called Pennsylvania Dutch. New York, 1901. Cf. DR, 1901.

Lalor, J. J. The Germans in the West. AM, 1873.

Lehmann, H. Das Deutschtum in Ostkanada. Das Deutschtum in Westkanada. 2 vols. Berlin, 1939.

Lengyel, E. German Emigré Literature. BA, 1938.

Leroux, A. La colonie germanique de Bordeaux (1462-1870). 2 vols. Bordeaux, 1870.

Loehrer, F. Geschichte und Zustände der Deutschen in Amerika. Cincinnati, 1847.

Loewenfeld, R. Eine deutsche Tafelrunde in Kopenhagen. Nord & Süd, 83, 1897.

Mann, E. & K. Escape to Life (The German Exiles). Boston, 1939.

Mathorez, J. Histoire de la formation de la population française: les étrangers en France sous l'Ancien Régime. vol. II: les Allemands, les Hollandais, les Scandinaves. Paris, 1921.

—— Les catholiques de langue allemande à Paris au XVIIe siècle. Bull. de bibliophile et du bibliothécaire, 1921.

Mollmann, A. Das Deutschtum in Montreal. Marburg, 1937.

Morel-Fatio, A. Les Allemands en Espagne du XVe au XVIIIe siècle. RFE, 1922.

Noack, F. Deutsches Leben in Rom; 1700 bis 1900. Stuttgart, 1907.

—— Das Deutschtum in Rom seit dem Ausgang des Mittelalters. Stuttgart, 1927.

Pick, O. La contribution des émigrants allemands à la culture de l'Europe centrale. L'Europe centrale, 26.VIII. 1933.

Pogatscher, H. Deutsche in Avignon im XIV. Jahrhundert. Römische Quartalschrift, 1899.

Ratton, M. H. The Saxon Borgo in Rome. National Review, 1938.

Robacker, E. F. Pennsylvania German Literature: Changing Trends from 1683 to 1942. Philadelphia, 1943.

Rod, E. Les Allemands à Paris. Paris, 1880.

Roger-Henrichsen, G. German Refugee Literature. London Mercury, 39, 1939.

Rosenberger, J. L. The Pennsylvania Germans. Chicago, 1923.

Schaefer, K. H. Deutsche in Avignon und ihre Wohnungen zur Zeit Johannes XXII. Römische Quartalschrift, 20, 1906.

—— Deutsche Ritter und Edelknechte in Italien während des 14. Jahrhunderts. Paderborn, 1911.

Schaible, K. H. Geschichte der Deutschen in England. Von den ersten germanischen Ansiedlungen in Britannien bis zu Ende des 18. Jahrhunderts. Strassburg, 1885.

Schirmunsky, V. Das kolonistische Lied in Russland. Zs. des Vereins für Volkskunde, 1927-28.

Schmidt, H. Die deutschen Flüchtlinge in der Schweiz, 1833-36. Zürich, 1899.

Schoen, H. Les institutions allemandes en France. Rev. alsacienne illustrée, 11, 1909.

Schönemann, F. Das Deutschtum in den Vereinigten Staaten von Amerika. ZNU, 38.

Schott, A. Die deutschen Kolonien in Piemont, ihr Land, ihre Mundart und Herkunft. Stuttgart, 1842.

Schünemann, G. Das Lied der deutschen Kolonisten in Russland. München, 1923.

Schuett, M. Die germanische Besiedlung Britanniens in der englischen Geschichtsschreibung besonders des 16. und 17. Jahrhunderts. Britannia, 13, 1936.

Semmig, H. Deutsche Studien in Frankreich: Die deutschen politischen Flüchtlinge. MLIA, 1869.

Taube, E. German Craftsmen in England during the Tudor Period. Economic History, 3, 1939.

Trautwein von Belle. Die Deutschen in Ungarn und Siebenbürgen. MLIA, 1882.

Weiskopf, F. C. Bitter Bread, Exiled German Writers in the Belligerent Countries. BA, 14, 1940.

Wentz, A. R. The Beginnings of the German Element in York County, Pennsylvania. Diss. George Washington U., 1916.

Wiltberger, O. Die deutschen politischen Flüchtlinge in Strassburg, 1830-49. Strassburg, 1908.

Wood, R. (ed.). The Pennsylvania Germans. Princeton, 1942.

5. Emigrants and Refugees from Italy.

Arnaud, J. Les Italiens prosateurs français. Etudes sur les émigrations italiennes depuis Brunetto Latini jusqu'à nos jours. Milan, 1861.

Benedetto, L. F. Vigny e gli esuli della Giovine Italia. Marzocco, 19.XI.1922.

Bonifacio, G. Esuli italiani in Corsica. Rassegna ital., 1939.
Cantarella, M. Italian Writers in Exile: a Bibliography. BA, 1938.
Carloni, F. F. Gl'Italiani all'estero. In: Poeti e letterati. Città di Castello, 1890.
Charpin-Feugerolles, de. Les Florentins à Lyon. Mém. Acad. Lyon, 1890-91.
Crémieux, B. L'émigration politique italienne en France sous la Monarchie de Juillet. REI, 1936.
Dejob, C. Un bel libro da fare (On the Italians in France). Festschrift A. d'Ancona, Firenze, 1901.
—— Nota per servire alla storia degli esuli italiani in Francia sotto Luigi Filippo. Atti del Congresso di scienze storiche, 1903. Roma, 1904.
Facchini, C. Gli esuli italiani in Francia. In: La Scuola letteraria bolognese, Bologna, 1888.
Fournier, L. Les Florentins en Pologne. Lyon, 1893.
Galiffe. Le refuge italien de Genève au XVIe et au XVIIe siècle. Genève, 1881.
Giacosa, G. Gli Italiani a New York ed a Chicago. NAnt, Aug., 1892, March, 1893.
Manzoni, R. Gli esuli italiani nella Svizzera. Milano, 1922.
Marraro, H. R. Italo-Americans in XVIIIth Century New York. New York History, 1940.
—— Italo-Americans in Pennsylvania in the XVIIIth Century. Pennsylvania History, 1940.
Mathorez, J. Notes sur les Italiens en France du XIII siècle jusqu'au règne de Charles VIII. BI. 17.
—— Les Italiens à Nantes et dans le pays nantais. BI, 1913.
Michel, E. Esuli italiani in Algeria, 1815-61. Bologna, 1935.
Monaci, E. Gli italiani in Francia durante il medio evo. Roma, 1895.
Nunziante, F. Gli italiani in Inghilterra durante i secoli XV e XVI. NAnt, 1.VIII. & 1.X.1906.
Paolucci di Calboli, B. I girovaghi italiani in Inghilterra. Città di Castello, 1893.
Picot, E. Les Italiens en France au XVIe siècle. BI, 1901-03.
Piton. Les Lombards en France et à Paris. Paris, 1893.
Rava, L. La sfida degli esuli romagnoli a Vittor Hugo. NAnt, 16.III.1902.
Roberti, G. Per la storia dell'emigrazione cisalpina in Francia durante il periodo austro-russo, 1799-1800. Riv. st. Risorgimento ital., 3, 1898.
Rodocanachi, E. Les médecins et astrologues italiens en France. In: Etudes et fantaisies historiques. Paris, 1919.
Rusconi, C. Le emigrazione italiane da Dante ai nostri giorni. Torino, 1853.
Varia, Gli italiani di New York. New York, 1939.
Wicks, M. C. W. The Italian Exiles in London, 1816-48. Manchester, 1937.
Zagaria, R. Per la storia degli esuli italiani in Francia. Rassegna storica d. Risorgimento, 1920.

6. Emigrants and Refugees from Poland.

Boye, P. La cour polonaise de Lunéville. Nancy, 1926.
Coleman, Marian M. The Polish Writer Abroad: Three Years of Emigration Literature. SEER, 21, 1944.
Edmond, C. La colonie polonaise à Paris. In: Paris-Guide, par les principaux écrivains et artistes de la France, Paris, 1867.
Krosnowski, Cte T. de. Almanach historique ou souvenir de l'émigration polonaise. Paris, 1847.
Sokolnicki, M. Les origines de l'émigration polonaise en France, 1830-32. Diss. Berne. Paris, 1910.
Wloszewski, S. L'installation des Polonais en France avant la Révolution. La Pologne, 1934.

7. Emigrants and Refugees from Russia.

Aleksandrova, V. A. Russian Emigrés in Western European Literature. Russian Rev., 3, 1944.
Astafiev-Alter, M. L'apport de l'émigration à la littérature russe des temps actuels. L'Age nouveau, 23.
Beucler, A. Russes de France. RP. 15.IV. 1937.
Brueckner, A. Die Russen im Auslande im 17. Jahrhundert. Baltische Monatsschrift, 1877. And in: Culturhistorische Studien. Riga, 1878.
Daudet, E. L'émigration en Russie de 1708 à 1801. Société historique et Cercle Saint-Simon, 4, 1886.
Gronsky, P. L'établissement des Russes en Californie. Rev. d'histoire moderne, 1929-30.
Iswolsky, Helen. Twenty-five Years of Russian Emigré Literature. Russian Rev., 1, 1942.
—— Russian Emigré Literature in World War II. Russian Rev., 6, 1946-47.
Leikine, N. Nos gens à l'étranger. Petersbourg, 1899.
Pingaud, L. Les Russes à Paris de 1800

à 1830. Le Correspondant, 215, 1904.
—— Les Russes en France. Paris, 1886.
Schtschepetew, A. Russen in Paris. Süddeutsche Monatshefte, 1916.

8. Emigrants and Refugees from Spain and Portugal.

Beaurepaire, C. de. La société espagnole de Rouen au XVIIe siècle. C.R. de l'Assemblée générale des bibliophiles normands du 10.VI.1888.
Carvalho, A. de. Os portugueses em Bordeus durante o seculo XVII. O Instituto, 1936.
Hilton, R. Spaniards in Marseille in the XVIIIth Century. BH, 40, 1938.
Marañón Posadillo, G. Españoles fuera de España. Madrid, 1948.
Martinez Ruiz, J. Españoles en Paris, 2 ed. Buenos Aires, 1942.
Mathorez, J. Notes sur les Espagnols et les Portugais à Nantes. Bordeaux, 1912.
—— Note sur la pénétration des Espagnols en France du XIIe au XVIe siècle. BH, 1, 1922.
—— Notes sur l'infiltration des Espagnols en France aux XVIIe et XVIIIe siècles. BH, 1932.
Michel, T. Les Portugais en France. Paris, 1882.
Peers, E. A. The Literary Activities of the Spanish Emigrados in England (1814-34). MLR, 19, 1924.
Sarrailh, J. L'émigration et le romantisme espagnol. RLC, 10, 1930.
Sorbelli, A. Bibliografia e cultura iberica in Bologna: la Casa degli Spagnuoli. Biblioteca dell'Archiginnasio, ser. II, 48, 1936.

9. Emigrants and Refugees from Various Countries.

Bayer, H. G. The Belgians, first Settlers in New York and in the Middle States. New York, 1925.
Bréhier, L. Les colonies d'Orientaux en Occident au commencement du moyen âge. Byzantinische Zs, 12, 1903.
Burns, J. S. The History of the (French), Waloon, Dutch and other Foreign Protestant Refugees Settled in England. London, 1846.
Kratchkovsky, I. Die Literatur der arabischen Emigranten in Amerika, 1895-1915. Le Monde oriental, 21, 1927.
Kuhns, O. The (German and) Swiss Settlements of Colonial Pennsylvania. New York, 1901.
Lyng, J. The Scandinavians in Australia, New Zealand and the Western Pacific. Melbourne, 1939.
Mathorez, J. Les étrangers en France sous l'Ancien Régime. I. Les orientaux et les extra-européens. Paris, 1919.
—— Les éléments de population orientale en France. Les Grecs en France du XVe au XIXe siècle. REG, 29.
—— Histoire de la formation de la population française: (les Allemands), les Hollandais, les Scandinaves. Paris, 1921.
Petri, F. Köln und die niederländischen Flüchtlinge. Joost van den Vondel Festschrift. Jena, 1937.
Robinson, W. G. The American Colony in Paris. Cosmopolitan, Oct., 1900.
Sagher, H. E. de. L'immigration des tisserands flamands et brabançons en Angleterre sous Edouard III. Mélanges Henri Pirenne. Bruxelles, 1926.
Schaedelin. Les émigrés suisses ou prétendus suisses dans le Haut-Rhin. Revue d'Alsace, 1935.
Sipos, L. Les Hongrois de Paris devant Lamartine. Nouvelle Rev. de Hongrie, 1934.
Varia, Les Danois à Paris à travers les âges. (In Danish) (800-1820). København, 1936.

CHAPTER FIVE

Periodicals and Newspapers.

(Specific influences of a country upon a journal are listed under the country in question.)

Anon. Die deutsche Presse in Paris. Strickers Germania, 1, 1847.
—— Die Revue germanique. Grenzboten, 17, 1858.
—— Kinkels deutsche Zeitung in London. Europa, 1859.
—— French Newspaper in the U.S. before 1800. Bibliographical Society of America, 14, Chicago, 1923.
Baldensperger, F. Goethes Lieblingslektüre, 1826-30: Die Zeitschrift Le Globe. GRM, 1932.
Beckwith, F. The Bibliothèque britannique 1733-47. Trans. of the Bibliogr. Society, The Library, 1931.
Bédarida, H. Voltaire collaborateur de la Gazette littéraire de l'Europe (1764). Mélanges Baldensperger, Paris, 1929.
Betz, L. P. Pierre Bayle und die Nouvelles de la République des lettres. Erste populär-wissenschaftliche Zeitschrift 1684-87. Zürich, 1896.

Bevington, Merle M. The Saturday Review, 1855-68: Representative Educated Opinion in Victorian England. New York, 1941.
Brisson, A. Les Allemands chez eux: un journal parisien en Allemagne. Le Temps, 21.VIII.1897.
Carlson, C. The First Magazine. A History of the Gentleman's Magazine (with an Account of the Notice Given America in the Magazine). Brown U.P., 1938.
Clark, H. Literary Criticism in the North American Review 1815-35. Trans. Wisconsin Acad. Sciences, Arts, and Letters, 32, 1940.
Davies, T. R. French Romanticism and the Press: the Globe. Cambridge U.P., 1906.
Deiters, H. Un journal allemand pour la littérature étrangère (1836-40). RLC, 21, 1947.
Digby, W. The Struggle for Existence of the English Press in India. Calcutta Review, 62, 1876.
Esdaile, A. Forerunners of the Anglo-French Review. AFR, 1919.
De Filippi. I giornali italiani a Parigi dall' 1803. La Perseveranze (Milano) 4.IV.1883.
Geiger, L. Eine deutsche Zeitschrift in Frankreich (1805). ZVL, 10-11, 1897.
Gohdes, C. The Periodicals of American Transcendentalism. Durham, (N.C.), 1931.
Graham, W. English Literary Periodicals. New York, 1930.
Hazard, P. Le Spectateur du Nord. RHLF, 13, 1906.
—— Les littératures étrangères et les débuts de la Revue des Deux Mondes. In: Cent ans de vie française dans la Revue des Deux Mondes. Paris, 1929.
Hohenhausen, F. von. Die deutschen Schriftstellerinnen und die Revue des Deux Mondes. MLIA, 1869.
Isopescu, C. La stampa periodica romeno-italiana, in Romania e in Italia. Roma, 1937.
Jones, Kathleen. La Revue britannique, son histoire et son action littéraire (1825-40). Paris, 1939.
Kraeger, H. The German Spy (1738). ESn, 29, 1901.
Lachèvre, F. Bibliographie sommaire de l'Almanach des Muses de 1765 à 1833. Paris, 1928.
Le Gentil, G. Les revues littéraires de l'Espagne pendant la première moitié du XIXe siècle. Paris, 1909.
Luehrs, P. M. Der nordische Aufseher: ein Beitrag zur Geschichte der moralischen Wochenschriften. Heidelberg, 1909.
Luna, J. L. La Revue de l'Amérique Latine y la literatura hispano-americana. RIA, 4, 1941.
Maingard, L. F. La Revue européenne: étude bibliographique. RHLF, 1922.
Marchand, L. A. The Athenaeum, A Mirror of Victorian Culture. Chapel Hill, (N.C.), 1941.
Martin, R. La fondation et les débuts de la Revue germanique de 1858. RG, 1931.
Milberg, E. Die moralischen Wochenschriften des 18. Jahrhunderts. Meissen, 1880.
Miller, E. E. Der Zuschauer, 1739-43. MLN, 1931.
Moore, Margaret. Les doctrines littéraires du Constitutionnel, 1815-30. Diss. Chicago, 1941.
Morino, L. La Nouvelle Revue française dans l'histoire des lettres. Paris, 1939.
Palfrey, T. R. L'Europe littéraire, 1833-34. Paris, 1927.
Pariset, G. La Revue germanique de Dollfus et Nefftzer (1858-68) d'après la correspondance inédite des deux auteurs. Paris, 1906.
Pettinari, A. La Rivista europea, 1838-48. In: La Lombardia nel Risorgimento italiano, 15, 1928.
Russ, K. Deutsche Zeitschriften in Amerika. MLIA, 1870.
Shelley, P. A. Annuals and Gift Books as American Intermediaries of Foreign Literature. CLN, 3, 1945.
Speaight, R. La Revue française et le romantisme anglais. RHPhC, 1946.
Van Tieghem, P. L'Année littéraire (1754-90) comme intermédiaire en France des littératures étrangères. Paris, 1917.
Zoraveva, B. V. Les origines de la Revue des Deux Mondes et les littératures européennes (1831-42). Sophia, 1930.
Zucker, A. E. Two German American Periodicals. AGR, 10, 1943.

CHAPTER SIX

Academic Intermediaries.

1. Universities, Schools, Libraries, Education.

Anon. European and American Universities. NAR, 80, 1855.
—— Französische, englische und deutsche Universitäten. Mag., 75, 1869.

—— L'histoire et l'oeuvre de l'Ecole française de Rome. Paris, 1931.
Allwood, M. S. Universiteten i en ny värld. Stockholm, 1944.
Boethius, A. Das schwedische Institut in Rom. Gnomon, (Berlin), 1932.
Bonnerot, J. L'Université de Paris, du moyen âge à nos jours. Paris, 1933.
Burton, E. H. (ed.). The Douai College Diaries. London, 1911 ff.
Burton, M. Famous Libraries of the World, Their History, Collections and Administration. London, 1937.
Daffis, H. Litteratur und Universität. LE, 12, 1901.
Demersnay. Les Briançonnais Libraires en Italie. Bull. de la Société d'études des Hautes-Alpes, 5, 1886.
Destombes, C. J. B. Mémoires sur les séminaires et collèges anglais fondés à la fin du XVIe siècle dans le nord de la France. Cambrai, 1854.
Dureault, A. Une académie italienne à Mâcon. Annales de l'Acad. de Mâcon, 13, 1908.
Fabre, F. Le Collège anglais de Douai: son histoire héroïque. RLC, 10, 1930.
Geffroy, A. L'Ecole française de Rome, ses origines, ses premiers travaux. Mém. de l'Acad. des sciences morales, 1876.
Gervinus. Ueber deutsches und französisches Unterrichtswesen. Blätter f. literarische Unterhaltung, 40-47, 1834.
Goyau, G. Les origines de l'Ecole française de Rome. RP, 1931.
Hallberg, E. Les académies littéraires en Italie et en Allemagne au XVIIe siècle. Mémoires de l'Acad. de Toulouse, 1894.
Haumant, E. La Sorbonne et la Russie. RIE, 1903.
Hazard, P. Harvard et la France. Paris, 1936.
Hinsdale, B. A. Foreign Influence upon Education in the United States. Report of the Commissioner of Education for 1897-98. Washington.
Irsay, S. d'. Histoire des universités françaises et étrangères des origines à nos jours. 2 vols. Paris, 1933 ff.
Jansen, F. L'université médiévale. Nouv. Rev. théologique (Louvain), 64, 1937.
Joseph, M. Die deutschen Universitäten im Urteil französischer Gelehrter in der Zeit von 1900-1920. Berlin, 1923.
Jourdain, C. Un collège oriental à Paris au XIIIe siècle. Revue des Sociétés savantes, 2, 1861.
Keller, A. Die Schweiz und die fremden Universitäten. Wissen & Leben, Sept., 1919.
Kibre, P. The Intellectual Interests Reflected in Libraries of the 14th and 15th Centuries. JHI, 1946.
Lalanne. Influence des Pères de l'Eglise sur l'éducation publique pendant les cinq premiers siècles de l'ère chrétienne. Paris, 1851.
Lanning, J. T. Academic Culture in the Spanish Colonies. London, 1940.
Lavisse, E. Les universités allemandes et les universités françaises. RDM, 1.VI.1884.
Leblanc. L'étude et l'enseignement des lettres profanes dans les premiers siècles de l'église. Paris, 1852.
Ledos, E. G. L'Ecole française de Rome. Revue des questions historiques, 19, 1931.
Maistre, L. Les écoles monastiques et épiscopales de l'occident depuis Charlemagne jusqu'à Philippe-Auguste. Paris, 1866.
Mellon, P. Les universités protestantes et les Ecossais. Revue chrétienne, 1907 & 1911.
Neudigate, C. A. Notes on the Seventeenth Century Printing Press of the English College at Saint-Omers. The Library, 3rd ser., 10, 1919.
Neve, F. Mémoire historique et littéraire sur le Collège des trois langues à l'Université de Louvain. Bruxelles, 1856.
Pierling, R. P. La Sorbonne et la Russie. Paris, 1882.
Platzhoff-Lejeune, E. Die ausländische Literatur in den französischen Schulen. Vossische Zt., 279, 1907.
Rashdall, H. The Universities of Europe in the Middle Ages. 3 vols. Oxford, 1936.
Rubio, D. La Universidad de S. Marcos de Lima durante la colonización española. Madrid, 1933.
Schachner, N. The Mediaeval Universities. London, 1938.
Simon, P. Die Idee der mittelalterlichen Universität und ihre Geschichte. Tübingen, 1932.
Willm. L'Université de France, jugée en Allemagne. Nouvelle Rev. germanique, 47, 1832.
Wischnitzer, M. Die Universität Göttingen und die Entwicklung der liberalen Ideen in Russland im ersten Viertel des XIX. Jahrhunderts. Berlin, 1907.
Wong, V. L. Libraries and Book-Collecting in China from the Epoch of the Five Dynasties to the End of Ch'ing. T'ien Hsia Monthly, 8, 1939.

2. Students and Professors.

(See under Humanism for the study of Greek and Latin and also for the internationalism of scholars [e.g. Italian-Hungarian relations] during the Renaissance. For the study of foreign languages, see under French, English, German, etc. Languages Abroad.)

Anon. Studenti germanici nelle Università italiane. Arch. veneto, 31.
—— Was ein französischer Schulmeister von Leipzig erzählt. Europa, 1865.
—— Gli studenti tedeschi e la S. Inquisizione a Padova nella 2a metà del secolo XVI. ARIV, 52.
Aström, S. E. Finländska studerande vid Uppsala universitet, 1595-1632. Historisk Tidskrift för Finland, 30, 1946.
—— Studerande från Sverige vid Abo akademi. ibid, 31, 1946.
Barycz, H. Les Polonais à Rome et leurs études à l'époque de la Renaissance. Bull. de l'Acad. polonaise de Cracovie, Nov., 1935.
Bryce, G. C. The English-German Nation in the University of Paris during the Middle Ages. Vassar College Series. Bruges, 1927.
Budinsky, Z. Die Universität Paris und die Fremden an derselben im Mittelalter. Berlin, 1876.
Cohn, A. Opportunities for University Study in France. Columbia U. Quarterly, 1903.
Dejob, C. Trois italiens, professeurs en France sous le Gouvernement de Juillet. BI, 1912.
Denis, S. La Nation germanique à l'Université d'Orléans. RLC, 10, 1930.
De Vries, H. Les étudiants des Pays-Bas à Genève au temps de Théodore de Bèze. Genève, 1918.
Doinel, J. Liste des étudiants scandinaves à l'Université d'Orléans (1384-1687). Bull. de la Société archéol. et hist. de l'Orléanais, 8, 1886.
Fournier, M. La Nation allemande à Orléans au XIVe siècle. Paris, 1888.
Gabriel, A. Etudiants hongrois dans le Paris du moyen âge. Nouvelle Rev. de Hongrie, March, 1940.
Geffroy, A. Les étudiants suédois à Paris au XIVe siècle. Rev. des Sociétés savantes, 2, 1858.
Geiger, L. Wie ein Franzose deutsche Litteratur lehrt. Berliner Tageblatt, 20, 1891.
Jakobowsky, C. V. Svenska studenter i Oxford, ca 1620-1740. Penarhistoriska tidskr., 1927.
Jourdain, C. Un compte de la nation d'Allemagne de l'Université de Paris au XVe siècle. Mém. de la Soc. de l'hist. de Paris et de l'Acad. de France, 1, 1875.
Kirkpatrick, J. La Nation Ecossaise à l'Université d'Orléans. RIE, 1904.
Knod, G. Deutsche Studenten in Bologna, 1289-1562. Berlin, 1899.
Lévy, R. G. Les étudiants américains en France. RIE, 15.II.1897.
Luschin, A. Studenti tedeschi nello studio di Siena. Blätter des Vereins f. Handelskunde von Niederösterreich, 1880-82.
Matthey, L. A. Ecoliers français à l'Académie de Genève. BHR, 1949.
Maury, L. Les étudiants scandinaves à Paris (XIe-XVe siècles). Annales de l'U. de Paris, 1934.
Neumann, A. Ein Studienaufenthalt in den französischen Universitätsstädten Nancy, Caen, Tours, Montpellier, Grenoble, Besançon. Marburg, 1901.
Plon, E. Les maîtres italiens au service de la maison d'Autriche. Paris, 1889.
Porter, N. An American Student in German Universities. New Englander, 1857.
Ristelhuber, P. Heidelberg et Strasbourg: recherches biographiques et littéraires sur les étudiants alsaciens immatriculés à l'Université de Heidelberg de 1386 à 1662. Paris, 1889.
—— Strasbourg et Bologne: recherches biographiques et littéraires sur les étudiants alsaciens immatriculés à l'Université de Bologne de 1289 à 1562. Paris, 1891.
Rodrigue, E. M. French Educators in the Northern States during the 18th Century. FR, 14, 1940.
Shumway, D. B. The American Students of the University of Göttingen. German American Annals, N.S., 8, 1910.
Stremooukhoff, D. Les étudiants russes à Strasbourg au XVIIIe siècle. Rev. d'Alsace, 1934.
Toulouse, M. La nation anglaise-allemande de l'Université de Paris des origines à la fin du XVe siècle. Paris, 1939.
Verrua, P. Precettori italiani in Ispagna durante il regno di Ferdinando il Cattolico. Adria, 1919.

CHAPTER SEVEN

Miscellaneous Intermediaries, Diplomats. Salons, Dual Nationality.

Berchet, G. Le antiche ambasciate giapponesi in Italia. Archivio veneto, 13, 1877.
Garrisson, R. La maison d'un ambassadeur à Parme au XVIIIe siècle. REI, 1938.
Ghennady, G. Les écrivains franco-russes: bibliographie des ouvrages français publiés par des Russes. Dresde, 1874.
Jean-Aubry, G. Poètes français d'Angleterre. MF, 1.V.1918.
Keating, L. C. Studies in the Literary Salon in France, 1550-1615 Cambridge, 1941.
Klemm, A. Four German-American Novelists of New World Adventure. AGR, 7, 1941.
Léger, L. Les premières ambassades russes à l'étranger. In: Russes et Slaves. Paris, 1890.
Lubimenko, I. Les étrangers en Russie avant Pierre le Grand: diplomates, militaires, intellectuels. Rev. des Etudes slaves, 4, 1924.
Ortlieb, C. Les Alsaciens à l'ambassade suédoise de Paris. La Vie en Alsace, 1926.
Picard, R. Les salons littéraires et la société française, 1680-1769. New York, 1943.
Pastor, A. Un embajador de España en la escena inglesa. Homenaje a Menéndez Pidal. Madrid, 1925.
Tetrault, L. Three Franco-American Poets. FR, 16, 1943.
Varia. Enquête sur l'institution d'attachés littéraires français à l'étranger. Minerve française, 15.IX.1920.
van de Weyer, S. Lettres sur les Anglais qui ont écrit en français. Mél. de la Soc. des philobibl. et Choix d'opuscules, London, 1863.
Wrangel E. Diplomates français en Suède. Stockholm, 1891.

CHAPTER EIGHT

Individual Intermediaries: Translators, Essayists, Travellers, Refugees, Emigrants, Scholars, Students, Diplomats, Bi-lingual Authors.

(The following pages contain lists mainly of minor rather than of major figures. Titles which indicated the country to which the intermediaries were indebted were filed under these respective countries; but cards with two or more contributing countries are mentioned here. See also Collective Influences, III. III. 13-14.)

Baudouin, A. Jacques **ABBADIE**, Prediger der französischen Gemeinde zu Berlin, in der Geschichte der französischen Literatur. Berlin, 1939.
Fleury, V. Un salon cosmopolite vers 1843: chez Mme d'**AGOULT**. RLC, 10, 1930.
Monod, M. O. Daniel Stern, comtesse d'Agoult. Paris, 1937.
Gugenheim, Suzanne. Mme. d'Agoult et la pensée européenne de son époque. Paris, 1938.
Hauvette, H. Luigi **ALAMANNI**. Paris, 1903.
Vogt, W. de. Les écrivains russes en France: Marc **ALDANOV**. Figaro, 18. V.1929.
Treat, I. Un cosmopolite italien du XVIIIe siècle: Francesco **ALGAROTTI**. Trevoux, 1913.
Calcaterra, C. Mme. du Boccage e F. Algarotti. RI, June 1913.
Szigethy, V. de. H. F. **AMIEL**, traducteur. Son européanisme. Ses relations avec la Hongrie. Szeged, 1929.
Champagny, F. de. Essai sur **AMYOT** et les traducteurs français au XVIe siècle. Le Correspondant. 29, 1851.
Kars, H. **ARIGO**. Diss. Halle, 1932.
Praz. M. Stanley, Sherburne and **AYRES** as Translators and Imitators of Italian, Spanish and French Poets. MLR, 1925.
Beaussire, E. Deux étudiants de l'Université de Poitiers, **BACON** (1578) et Descartes (1616). Mémoires de la Soc. des Inst. de l'Ouest, 1868.
Lenna, N. di. Giosafat **BARBARO** e i suoi viaggi nella regione russa (1436-51) e nella Persia (1474-78) Nuovo archivio veneto, N.S., 28, 1914.
Morandi, L. Episodi della vita dell' **BARETTI** a Londra. NAnt, 67, 1883.
Collison-Morley, L. Giuseppe Baretti, with an Account of his Literary Friendships. London, 1909.
Zucchetti, M. G. Baretti e il rinnovamento letterario della seconda meta del settecento. Firenze, 1921.
Devalle, A. La critica letteraria nel 700. G. Baretti nei suoi rapporti con Voltaire, Johnson e Parini. Milano, 1932.
Piccioni, L. Un maestro italiano in una famiglia inglese. GSLI, 102, 1933.
– Baretti davanti ai giudici inglesi. Pan, 1934.

—— Giuseppe Baretti, difensore dell'Italia in Inghilterra. Pan, 3, 1935.
—— Bibliografia analitica di Giuseppe Baretti. Torino, 1942.
Segré, C. Baretti ed Ester Thrale. In: Relazioni letterarie fra Italia e Inghilterra. Firenze, 1911.
Engel, E. Ein geistiger Vermittler zwischen Deutschland und Frankreich (J. **BAUMGARTEN**). MLIA, 1880.
Le Dantec, Y. G. **BAUDELAIRE** traducteur. Le Correspondant, Dec., 1931 & Jan., 1932.
Ashbee, H. S. Les Anglais qui ont écrit en français: William **BECKFORD**. Le Livre, 1882.
Las Vergnas, R. Une personnalité anglo-française, Hilaire **BELLOC**. RDM, 15.VII.1935.
Palfrey, T. R. Louise Swanton **BELLOC** (1796-1881) as an Intermediary Between France and America. MLF, 27, 1942.
Ligotti, E. H. Giovanni **BERÇHET**, 1783-1851. Firenze, 1933.
Monglond, A. Le rôle littéraire d'un réfugié: **BITAUBE** et la prose poétique. RLC, 3, 1923.
Gill-Mark, G. Une femme de lettres au XVIIIe siècle: Anne-Marie du **BOCCAGE**. Paris, 1927.
Anon. **BOERNE** als Vermittler zwischen Deutschland und Frankreich. Blätter für liter. Unterhaltung, March, 1836.
Kolloff, E. Börne in Paris. Jahrbücher d. Litt., (Hamburg), 1, 1839.
Anon. Börne in einer französischen Apotheose. Blätter für lit. Unterh., 14. VIII.1849.
Morsier, E. de. Un écrivain franco-allemand: Louis Boerne (1786-1837). Grande Revue, 1902.
Ras, G. Boerne als Vermittler zwischen deutscher und französischer Kultur. NPh, 3, 1918.
Adler, M. Börne, Deutschland und Frankreich. RRh, 1922.
Rosenberg, R. Ludwig Boerne and the French. Jewish Forum, 29, 1946.
Baldensperger, F. Une grande anglaise de France: Lady **BOLINGBROKE**. RP, 15.IX.1930 and in: Etudes d'histoire littéraire, 4e sér., Paris, 1939.
Heigl. Giamb. **BOLZA** als Vermittler zwischen der deutschen und italienischen Litteratur. Progr. Innsbruck, 1897; cf. GSLI, 38.
Bodemann, Julie **BONDELI** und ihr Freundeskreis. Hannover, 1874.
Herking, M. L. Charles-Victor de **BONSTETTEN**, sa vie, ses oeuvres (1745-1832). Lausanne, 1920.
Bézard, Yvonne. Deux voyageurs suisses d'Italie et de Provence. (Saussure, Bonstetten). RLC, 17, 1937.
La Harpe, Jacqueline de. Intermédiares et serviteurs littéraires: Mme **BONTEMPS**. Hommage à l'Ecole Vinet, Lausanne, 1937.
Baldensperger, F. L'émigration du chevalier de **BOUFFLERS**. RP, 1912.
Boeri, A. Una contesa franco-italiana del secolo XVIII (**BOUHOURS**-Orsi). Palermo, 1900.
Calmette, J. Un protestant de Montpellier réfugié à Londres en 1680 (**BOYER**). Soc. de l'hist. du Protestantisme fr., 1904.
Tillier, L. Un huguenot français à Londres: Abel Boyer. La France libre, 3, 1941.
Loisy, A. George Tyrrell et Henri **BREMOND**. Paris, 1836.
Reynold, G. de. Le doyen **BRIDEL** et les origines de la littérature suisse romande. Lausanne, 1909.
Boyce, B. Tom **BROWN** of Facetious Memory: Grub Street in the Age of Dryden. Harvard U.P., 1939.
Riewald, J. G. Sir Thomas **BROWNE'S** Supposed Visit to the Continent. ESs, 28, 1947.
Pellegrini, A. M. Giordano **BRUNO** on Translations. ELH, 10, 1943.
Dufour, A. Un voyageur hollandais à Corbeil. Arnold van **BUCHEL**, d'Utrecht. (1586). Bull. de la Société hist. et archéol. de Corbeil, 8. Paris, 1902.
Warenghien, Baron de. Un Hollandais à l'Université de Douai. Journal d'Arnold van Buchel, 1584-85. Mém. de la Société d'agricult. du dép. du Nord, 3e sér., 1900-02, Douai, 1904.
Martin, R. Une femme de lettres française à Berlin (1857-65): Mme. Cosima de **BULOW** (Cosima Wagner). RLC, 11, 1931.
Delachaux, Eugénie. Fanny **BURNEY**, intermédiare manquée entre l'Angleterre et la France. RLC, 15, 1935.
Bentley, N. E. Hudibras's **BUTLER** Abroad (1670). MLN, 60, 1945.
Maychrzak, F. Lord **BYRON** als Uebersetzer. ESn, 21, 1895.
Everson, Ida G. George Henry **CALVERT**, American Literary Pioneer. New York, 1944.
Lozinski, G. Le prince Antioche **CANTEMIR**, poète français. Rev. des Etudes slaves, 5, 1925.
Ehrhardt, Marcelle. Un ambassadeur de Russie à la Cour de Louis XV. Paris, 1938.

Benaglia, G. Relazione del viaggio fatto da Vienna a Constantinopoli e ritorno in Germania del conte Alberto **CAPRARA.** Roma, 1684; Frankfurt, 1887.
Dell'Isola, M. G. **CARDUCCI**, traducteur de poèmes. Mélanges Hauvette. Paris, 1934.
Binazzi, B. Annibal **CARO** tradutiore. In: Antichi, moderni e altro. Firenze, 1941.
Croce, B. Un insegnante di lingua italiana in Germania: Nicolò di **CASTELLI.** In: Nuovi Saggi del Seicento. Bari, 1931.
Alemanni, V. Un filosofo delle lettere, M. **CESAROTTI.** Torino, 1894.
Roddier, H. Robert **CHALLES**, inspirateur de Richardson et de l'abbé Prévost. RLC, 21, 1947.
Hueser. Wie **CHAMISSO** ein Deutscher wurde. Halle, 1847.
Riegel, R. Adalbert de Chamisso, sa vie et son oeuvre. 2 vols. Paris, 1934.
Noth, E. E. Adalbert de Chamisso, gentilhomme français, poète allemand. NL, 24.IX.1938.
Godet, P. Mme de **CHARRIERE** et ses amis. Genève, 1906.
Valkhoff, P. Une Hollandaise romancière française: Mme de Charrière. Gaz. de Hollande, 1926.
Morgulis, G. Caliste de Mme de Charrière et l'Idiot de Dostoievski. RLC, 15, 1935.
Kimstedt, Charlotte. Frau von Charrière (1740-1805). Ihre Gedankenwelt und ihre Beziehungen zur französischen und deutschen Literatur. Berlin, 1938.
Martin, R. Philarète **CHASLES** et la Revue germanique de 1858: un projet de revue anglo-américaine vers 1860. RAA, 1933.
Maricourt, A. de. Les amitiés franco-américaines au XVIIIe siècle: le marquis de **CHASTELLUX.** France-Etats-Unis, 1922.
Varnum, F. Un philosophe cosmopolite du XVIIIe siècle: le chevalier de Chastellux. Paris, 1936.
Le Braz, A. Au pays d'exil de **CHATEAUBRIAND**, RP, 15.VII & 15.IX. 1908.
Boillot, F. Chateaubriand théoricien de la traduction. RHLF, 1912.
Baldensperger, F. A propos de Chateaubriand traducteur. RHLF, 1913.
—— Le grand amour d'exil de Chateaubriand. RP, 1931.
Pratt, R. **CHAUCER** and the Visconti Libraries. ELH, 6, 1939.
La Force. Un Anglais de chez nous, éducateur et humaniste: Lord **CHESTERFIELD.** RdF, 1.II.1930.
Baldensperger, F. Une américaine de Paris: Mrs. Lee **CHILDE.** Etudes d'histoire littéraire, 3e sér., Paris, 1939.
Claretta, G. La regina **CRISTINA** di Svezia in Italia. GSLI, 21, 1893.
Benaducci, G. La regina Cristina di Svezia in Tolentino. Tolentino, 1895.
Wrangel, F. U. La première visite de Christine à la cour de France en 1656. Paris, 1930.
Cuendet, G. **CICERON** et S. Jérôme traducteurs. REL, 1933.
Thomas, J. W. James Freeman **CLARKE** as a Translator. AGR, 10, 1943.
Smith, M. E. Une anglaise intellectuelle en France sous la Restauration: Mary **CLARKE.** Paris, 1927.
Griggs, E. L. S. T. **COLERIDGE** at Malta. MPh, 1929.
Jusserand, J. J. A French ambassador at the court of Charles the Second, the Cte. de **COMMINGES.** London, 1892.
Dick, H. G. Giacomo **CONCIO**: A Renaissance Exile. MLF, 26, 1940-41.
Brown, E. K. James and **CONRAD.** Yale Rev., 35, 1945.
Freisler, E. W. J. Conrad in Deutschland. NR, Jan., 1929.
Bradbrook, Muriel C. Joseph Conrad, Poland's English Genius. Cambridge U.P., 1941.
Jean-Aubry, G. La Pologne dans la vie et l'oeuvre de Joseph Conrad. Pologne littéraire, 15.V.1932.
Morf, G. The Polish Heritage of Joseph Conrad. London, 1930.
Ettlinger, J. Benjamin **CONSTANT.** Berlin, 1909.
Léon, P. Benjamin Constant. Paris, 1930.
Constant, B. Cf. special number of Gazette de Lausanne, 14.VI.1930, commemorating the 100th anniversary of his death.
Ferrari, L. L'Abate A. **CONTI** e Madama de Caylus. ARIV, 1934-35.
Shepard, O. H. A Seventeenth Century Traveller (Th. **CORYAT**). In: Papers of the Manchester Literary Club, 59, 1933.
Rice, H. C. Le cultivateur américain: étude de St. John de **CREVECOEUR.** Paris, 1932.
Shelley, P. A. Crèvecoeur's Contribution to Herder's Neger-Idyllen. JEGPh, 37, 1938.
Fess, G. M. Catharine Sedgwick and Crèvecoeur. AL, 15, 1944.
Hogberg, P. Le genevois Isaacus Cujacius (Isaac de CUYAUX) premier

lecteur de français à Uppsala. Zs. für schwedische Geschichte, 6, 1926.
Ashbee, H. S. Frenchmen who have Written in English: Voltaire, O. **DALEPIERRE**, Motteux. The Bookworm, 1890-91.
Eccles, M. Samuel **DANIEL** in France and Italy. SPh., 1937.
Power, W. John **DAVIDSON**: the Doom of an Exile. The Modern Scot, 1930.
Maurois, A. Madame Du **DEFFAND** et Horace Walpole. In: Etudes anglaises, Paris, 1927.
Naughton, A. E. A. Some Literary Opinions of Mme Du Deffand. Stanford Studies in Language & Literature, 1941.
Oetter, K. Richard **DEHMEL** als Uebersetzer romantischer Dichtungen. Würzburg, 1936.
Baldensperger, F. L'émigration de Jacques **DELILLE**. RHLF, 1911.
Negri, L. Carlo **DENINA**, un accademico piemontese del settecento. Torino, 1933.
Monglond, A. Sénancour et un voyageur au Brésil. Lettres inédites à Ferdinand **DENIS**. RLC, 11, 1931.
Girard, H. Le cosmopolitisme d'un dilettante: Emile **DESCHAMPS** et les littératures étrangères. RLC, 1, 1921.
—— Un bourgeois dilettante à l'époque romantique: Emile Deschamps, 1791-1871. Paris, 1921.
Deslisle, L. Sir Kenelm **DIGBY** et les anciens rapports des Bibliothèques françaises avec la Grande-Bretagne. Library Assoc. of the U.K. London, 1892.
Bennett, R. E. **DONNE'S** Letters from the Continent in 1611-12. PhQ, 19, 1940.
Kerr, W. H. The Treatment of **DRAKE'S** Circumnavigation in Hakluyt's Voyages, 1589. Papers of the Bibliographical Soc. of America, 34, 1940.
Wackernagel, W. **DROLLINGER**. Basel, 1841.
Löhlein, T. Drollinger. Karlsruhe, 1873.
Wallerstein, R. C. The Style of **DRUMMOND** of Hawthornden in Its Relation to His Translations. PMLA, 1933.
Morel, A. Etude sur l'Abbé **DUBOS**, ses voyages en Allemagne, en Hollande, en Italie. Paris, 1859.
Bellessort, A. Les voyages d'Alexandre **DUMAS**. RDM, 1932.
Joret, C. Auguste **DUNAU**, traducteur, critique, biographe et naturaliste, 1771-1831. Paris, 1921.
Burtin, P. M. N. Un semeur d'idées au temps de la Restauration: le baron d'**ECKSTEIN**. Paris, 1931.
Brun, A. Le Baron d'Eckstein, policier et journaliste marseillais. RLC, 21, 1947.
Oomkens, R. Les écrits français de Justus van **EFFEN**. Rev. de Hollande, 1916-17.
Pienaar, W. J. B. English Influences in Dutch Literature and Justus van Effen as Intermediary. Cambridge U.P., 1929.
Zuydam, W. Justus van Effen. Gouda, 1922.
Mathorez, J. Un étudiant pangermaniste à Orléans en 1517 (**EICHHOLZ**). Bull. du bibliophile, 1913.
Liebemann, F. Königin **ELIZABETH** als Uebersetzerin. Archiv, 144, 1923.
Wortham, J. Sir Thomas **ELYOT** and the Translation of Prose. HLQ, 1948.
Sommer, F. Wilhelm Ludwig von **ESCHWEGE** (1775-1855). Stuttgart, 1928.
Venturi, A. Les beaux-arts et la maison d'**ESTE**, le cardinal de Ferrare en France. Annales de la Soc. historique et archéologique du Gatinais, 21, 1903.
Fey, J. Albrecht von **EYB** als Uebersetzer. Halle, 1888-89.
Fucilla, J. G. The Spanish and Portuguese Imitations from the Italian of Manuel **FARIA Y SOUSA**. PhQ, 1929.
Anon. Zwei deutsch-spanische Dichter (Hartzenbusch und **FASTENRATH**). Europa, 1872.
William, C. Ein Vermittler zwischen Deutschland und Spanien. MLIA, 1880.
Lejeune, F. Die deutsch-spanischen Bestrebungen und Freundschaft von Johannes Fastenrath. Greifswald, 1926.
Fellheimer, Jeannette. Notes on Geoffrey **FENTON'S** Minor Translations. PhQ, 22, 1943.
Havet, J. Maître **FERNAND** de Cordue et l'Université de Paris au XVe siècle. Mém. de la Soc. de l'hist. de Paris et de l'Ile-de-France, 9, 1882.
Severus, E. von. Lupus von **FERRIERES**. Gestalt und Werk eines Vermittlers antiken Geistesgutes an das Mittelalter im 9. Jahrhundert. Münster, 1940.
Longworth-Chambrun, A. de. Giovanni **FLORIO**, un apôtre de la Renaissance en Angleterre à l'époque de Shakespeare. Paris, 1921.
Spampanato, V. Giovanni Florio. Un amico del Bruno in Inghilterra. Critica, 21-22, 1923-24.
Orsini, G. N. L'Inghilterra di Shakespeare

definita da G. Florio. Civiltà moderna, 4, 1932.
Yates, F. A. John Florio: the Life of an Italian in Shakespeare's England. Cambridge, 1934.
Page, F. Shakespeare and Florio. N&Q, 184-85, 1943.
Holinger, Cora. Charles FOLLEN. A Sketch of his Life in New England. AGR, 14, 1948.
Bianchi, D. Ugo FOSCOLO e le traduzioni. GSLI, 1929.
Anon. Charles de la Mothe FOUQUE et Suzanne de Robitard. Rev. de la Saintonge et de l'Aunis, 10, 1890.
Walz, J. A. Kuno FRANCKE, the American and the German. AGR, 6, 1940.
Weddigen, O. F. FREILIGRATH als Vermittler englischer und französischer Dichtung. Archiv, 61, 1879 & 66, 1881.
Richter, K. Freiligrath als Uebersetzer. Berlin, 1899.
Treumann-Kroner, B. Käthe FREILIGRATH-KROCKER. Die Frau, 4, 1897.
Wade, M. Margaret FULLER: Whetstone of Genius. New York, 1940.
Stern, Madeleine B. The Life of Margaret Fuller. New York, 1941.
Detti, Emma. Margaret Fuller Ossoli e i suoi corrispondenti. Firenze, 1942.
Caro, E. M. L'abbé GALIANI en exil et sa correspondance. Acad. des Sciences morales et politiques, 1882.
Niccolini, F. Il pensiero dell' abate Galiani. Bari, 1909.
—— Amici e corrispondenti dell' abate F. Galiani. Archivio storico italiano, 1929.
Croce, B. Una lettera inedita della signora d'Epinay e il Dialogue sur les femmes dell' abate Galiani. Mélanges Baldensperger. Paris, 1929.
Troilo, E. Considerazioni sul pensiero filosofico dell' abate Galiani. ARIV, 90, 1932.
Magnotti, L. L'Abbé F. Galiani, sa philanthropie et ses rapports avec la France. Naples, 1933.
Palmieri, G. Viaggio in Germania, Baviera, Svizzera, Olanda e Francia (1761-63). Diario del cardinal GARAMPI. Roma, 1889.
Stone, G. The Journal of David GARRICK, describing his visit to France and Italy in 1763. New York, 1939-40.
Frois, E. Théophile GAUTIER voyageur. RAF, 1931.
San Lazzaro, Clementina di. Stefan GEORGE als Uebersetzer. GRM, 28, 1940.
Loeper, G. von. Zu GOETHES Uebersetzungen aus fremden Sprachen. ALG, 2, 1872.
Bataillon, M. Le cosmopolitisme de Damião de GOIS. RLC, 18, 1938.
—— Damião de Gois et Reginald Pole. O Instituto, 79, 1930.
Golding, L. T. An Elisabethan Puritan: Arthur GOLDING the Translator. New York, 1937.
Tegen, G. Jascha GOLOWANJUK, Russian-Swedish Novelist. BA, 17, 1943.
Moore, E. R. Estebanillo GONZALEZ'S Travels in Southern Europe. HR, 8, 1940.
Baldensperger, F. Une anglaise intellectuelle dans l'emmêlement des races: Lady Duff GORDON. In: Etudes d'histoire littéraire, 3e sér. Paris, 1939.
Fuchs, G. Studien zur Uebersetzungstheorie und Praxis des GOTTSCHED-Kreises. Leipzig, 1936.
Carlton, W. N. C. H. Walpole's Edition of De GRAMONT'S Memoirs. American Collector, 1927.
Darbelnet, J. Un écrivain américain d'expression française: Julian GREEN. Bull. des Etudes fr., 25, 1945.
Geiger, L. GRIMMS Correspondance littéraire und die deutsche Litteratur. Beilage zur Allg. Zt., 26.IV.1882.
Koch, A. Baron Melchior von Grimm und seine Pariser Briefe. ZFSL, 7, 1885.
Wohlfeil, P. Friedrich Melchior Grimms Beziehungen zu Frankreich. Festschrift zum 15. Neuphilologentage, Frankfurt, 1912.
Jones, A. C. In Defence of M. Grimm. PMLA, 1928.
Smiley, J. R. Grimm's Alleged Authorship of Certain Articles on the Theater in Paris. MLN, 63, 1948.
Thomson, S. H. A Note on GROSSETESTE'S Work of Translation. Journal of Theolog. Studies, 1933.
Delpech, J. Albert GUERARD. NL, 29. VII.1948.
Palmerocchi, R. L'ambasceria di GUICCIARDINI in Spagna. Archivio storico italiano, 97.
Anon. Les femmes touristes: la Csse Ida HAHN-HAHN. Le Correspondant, 10, 1845.
Van de Weyer, S. Lettres sur les Anglais qui ont écrit en français: Thomas HALE. London, 1855.
Clark, R. Anthony HAMILTON, his Life and Works and his Family. London, 1921.
Parry, A. Henry HARLAND: expatriate. The Bookman, 76, 1933.

Long, O. W. Frederick Henry **HEDGE**: A Cosmopolitan Scholar. Portland (Me.), 1940.

Gronicka, A. von. Henry von **HEISELER**: a Russo-German Writer. New York, 1944.

Guillois, A. Le salon de Mme **HELVETIUS**. Paris, 1894.

González del Valle, F. **HEREDIA** en La Habana. La Habana, 1939

Henriquez Ureña, M. El aporto hispánico de Heredia en la poesía francesa. Annales Acad. de Cuba, 23, 1942.

Schoenbach, A. E. W. **HERTZ** als Uebersetzer. LE, 2, 1900.

Hackenberg, F. Elisa von **HOHENHAUSEN**. Eine Vorkämpferin und Uebersetzerin englischer und nordamerikanischer Dichtung. Diss. Münster, 1913.

Anon. Baron von **HOLBACH**: Denkmal für einen Deutschen von einem Franzosen. Neues Deutsches Museum, 1790.

Augustin-Thierry A. Un salon anglais à Paris: Lady **HOLLAND**. Correspondant, March, 1925.

Segré, C. Lady Holland e i suoi ospite italiani. In: Relazioni letterarie fra Italia e Inghilterra. Firenze, 1911.

Baldensperger, F. Etudiants américains en France: O. W. **HOLMES**. Bull. Maison fr. de Columbia U. New York, 1918.

Duméril, H. Un guide anglais sur le continent au XVIIe siècle. (J. **HOWELL**, 1642). RELV, 1930.

Eggli, E. Un émigré germanisant: L'abbé **HUBERT** (1760-1842). Mélanges Baldensperger, Paris, 1929.

Remenyi, J. Hugo V. **IGNOTUS**, Refugee Hungarian Poet and Critic. BA, 16, 1942.

JAMES: see also Conrad.

Foley, R. N. Criticism in American Periodicals of the Works of Henry James from 1866-1916. Washington, 1944.

JEROME: see Cicero.

Brown, H. Un cosmopolite du grand siècle: Henri **JUSTEL**. Bull. de la Soc. du Protestantisme fr., July, 1933.

Corovic, V. Vuk **KARADZIC**. SEER, 1938.

Martin, M. Un aventurier intellectuel sous la Restauration et la Monarchie de Juillet: le Dr. **KOREFF**. Paris, 1925.

Johannes, W. Christophorus **KORMART** als Uebersetzer französischer und holländischer Dramen. Diss. Berlin, 1892.

Kohler, P. "Valérie" ou maîtres et imitateurs de Mme de **KRUDENER**. Bull. de l'Institut national genevois. 45, 1922.

Knapton, E. The Lady of the Holy Alliance: The Life of Julie de Krüdener. New York, 1939.

LABOULAYE, E. Paris en Amérique. Paris, 1863. Cf. Grenzboten, 25, 1866.

Ducarre, J. Une supercherie littéraire de l'abbé Prévost: Les voyages de Robert **LADE**. RLC, 16, 1936.

Mattlé, R. **LAMARTINE** voyageur. Paris, 1936.

Jaloux, E. Valéry **LARBAUD**, voyageur. Intentions, 1, 1922.

LE BLANC, Abbé. Lettres d'un François. 3 vols. La Haye, 1745.

Monod-Cassidy, Hélène. Un voyageur-philosophe au XVIIIe siècle, l'abbé Jean-Bernard Le Blanc. Harvard U.P., 1941.

Barnes, A. Jean **LE CLERC** (1657-1736) et la république des lettres. Paris, 1938.

Gragger, R. **LENAU** und Fontane. Budapesti Szemle, July, 1912.

—— Lenaus ungarische Sprachkenntnisse. Ungarische Rundschau, 2. (Leipzig), 1913.

Kohut, A. Nicolaus Lenau und Ungarn. MLIA, 1885.

Meyer, R. M. **LESSING** als Uebersetzer. MLIA, 1893.

Ernst, A. W. H. **LEUTHOLD** als Uebersetzer. Schweiz. Rundschau, 4, 1894.

Betz, L. P. Heinrich Leuthold, der Dichter und der Dichter Dolmetsch. Die Wage, 1899.

Milch, W. J. Georg Christoph **LICHTENBERG**. MLR, 37, 1942.

Dorfman, J. & Tugwell, R. G. Francis **LIEBER**: German Scholar in America. Columbia U. Quarterly, Sept., 1938.

Wittner, L. Le prince de **LIGNE**, Jean de Muller, Frédéric de Gentz et l'Autriche. Paris, 1925.

Oulié, Marthe. Le cosmopolitisme du Prince de Ligne (1735-1814). Paris, 1926.

Hochdorf, M. Der Fürst von Ligne. Zürich, 1934.

Dumont-Wilden, L. Le bicentenaire du Prince de Ligne. Acad. royale de langue et de litt. françaises de Belgique, 1935.

Perrochon, H. Un ami suisse du Prince de Ligne: le général Frossard. Annales du Prince de Ligne, 16, 1935.

Gössler, P. Jakob **LINCKH**. Ein württembergischer Italienfahrer, Philhellene, Kunstsammler und Maler. Stuttgart, 1930.

Helber, O. Paul **LINDAU** als Uebersetzer. MLIA, 1880.
Delines, M. Un Russe parmi les sectaires chinois (**LOBZA**). Nouvelle Revue, 1.IX.1900.
Lorch, M. Francisco **LONBAYSSIN DE LAMARCA**, romancier franco-espagnol du XVIIe siècle. Auch, 1929.
Johnson, C. L. Professor **LONGFELLOW** of Harvard. U. of Oregon P., 1944.
Doyle, H. G. Longfellow as Professor at Harvard. Hisp., 27, 1944.
Marshall, D. C. Professor Longfellow of Harvard. BSS, 1944.
Gates, W. B. The Dramatic Works and Translations of Sir William **LOWER**. Philadelphia, 1932.
Kluge, J. W. H. **MACKENZIE**, sein Leben und seine Werke. Leipzig, 1910. Cf. Anglia, 22, 1911.
MADRISIO, N. Viaggi in Italia, Francia, Germania. Venezia, 1718.
Benvenuti, E. Andrea **MAFFEI** poeta originale e traduttore. Pro Cultura, 1911.
Stadler, H. Paul-Henri **MALLET**. Lausanne, 1924.
Vogels, J. Das Verhältniss der italienischen Version der Reisebeschreibung **MANDEVILLE'S** zur französischen. Progr. Crefeld, 1885.
Jourda, P. **MARGUERITE D'ANGOULEME**. Paris, 1930.
Sayous, E. Xavier **MARMIER**, voyageur dans l'Europe méridionale. Acad. des Sciences de Besançon, 1891.
Charlier, G. **MARNIX**, écrivain de langue française. In: Marnix van Sint Aldegonde, Bruxelles, 1940.
Lograsso, Angeline H. Poe's Piero **MARONCELLI**. PMLA, 58, 1943.
Rossi, J. The Italian Poems of Thomas James **MATHIAS**. MLQ, 4, 1943.
Soeight, K. An English Writer of Italian Verse. SPh, 43, 1946.
Natali, G. Un'Arcado inglese. NAnt, 1929.
Lanoire, M. Un anglo-français, Georges du **MAURIER**. RP, 15.III.1940.
Magne, E. Un salon français à Londres au XVIIe siècle (Mme de **MAZARIN**). AFR, 1920.
Breitinger, H. Heinrich **MEISTER**, der Mitarbeiter Melchior Grimms. In: Studien und Wandertage. Frauenfeld, 1890.
Betz, L. P. Altes und Neues aus dem Leben Jacob Heinrich Meisters. Schweiz. Rundschau, 4, 1895.
Lavater-Sloman, M. Henri Meister. Neuchâtel, 1938.
Babou, H. Un Français de Russie: Elim **MESTCHERSKI**. Revue nouvelle, 13, 1847.
Mazon, A. Le prince Elim Mestcherski (in Russian). In: La Civilisation russe et la France, vol. 2. Moscou, 1937.
Vinant, G. Un esprit cosmopolite au XIXe siècle: Malwida de **MEYSENBURG** (1816-1903). Paris, 1932.
Taylor, M. E. William Julius **MICKLE** (1734-88). Washington, 1937.
Byse, F. **MILTON** on the Continent: a Key to l'Allegro and The Penseroso. MLQ, 3, 1901 and London, 1905.
Mutschmann, H. Die Beweggründe zu Miltons Festlandreise. Anglia Bb, 50, 1939.
MONTAIGNE, M. de. Journal de voyage en Italie par la Suisse et l'Allemagne en 1580 et 1581. Introduction, notes et variantes par C. Dédéyan. Paris, 1946.
Dédéyan, C. Essai sur le Journal de Voyage de Montaigne. Paris, 1947.
Buffum, I. L'influence du voyage de Montaigne sur les Essais. Princeton, 1946.
Lallemand, P. de. **MONTALEMBERT** et ses relations littéraires avec l'étranger jusqu' en 1840. Paris, 1927.
Betz, L. P. Emile **MONTEGUT**, ein französischer Vermittler der Weltlitteratur. In: Studien, Frankfurt, 1902.
Fournier de Flaix. Les voyages de **MONTESQUIEU**. Réforme sociale, 1e sér., 1897.
MOORE, J. Lettres d'un voyageur anglais sur la France, la Suisse et l'Allemagne. 4 vols. Genève, 1781.
Mavrondis, A. **MOREAS** en Grèce. Figaro, 25.V.1912.
Eggli, E. Quelques suggestions de Lady **MORGAN** à Mérimée et à Vigny. CLS, 11-12, 1943.
Charlanne, L. Un Français, écrivain anglais au XVIIe siècle: Pierre Antoine **MOTTEUX**. RB 26.VIII & 2.IX. 1911.
Cunningham, R. N. Peter Anthony Motteux (1663-1716). Oxford, 1933.
Prod'Homme, J. G. Une grande dame cosmopolite: la comtesse de **MOUCHAROFF**. (Mme. Kabergis). Rev. de Hollande, 1916.
Shelley, P. A. Niclas **MUELLER**, German-American Poet and Patriot. Festschrift J. A. Walz, Lancaster, (Pa.), 1941.
Greyerz, O. von. Beat Ludwig von **MURALT**. Frauenfeld, 1888.
Dejob, C. Marc-Antoine **MURET**, un professeur français en Italie dans la

seconde moitié du XVIe siècle. Paris, 1881.
Hitzig. Ueber die zahlreichen Uebersetzungen französischer und englischer Romane von MYLIUS. Gelehrtes Berlin, 1825.
Baldensperger, F. Le premier instructeur de français à Harvard: NANCREDE. Harvard Advocate, Dec., 5, 1913.
Haussonville, O. d' Le salon de Mme NECKER. Paris, 1882.
Jones, R. A. Mme. Necker et Mrs. Elizabeth Montagu d'après des lettres inédites. RLC, 13, 1933.
Perrochon, H. Un foyer helvétique de préciosité au XVIIIe siècle. RLC, 16, 1936.
Betz, L. P. Gérard de NERVAL. Ein Dichterbild aus Frankreichs deutschfreundlichen Tagen. Beilage z. Allg. Zt., 3.V.1897 and in: Studien, Frankfurt, 1902.
Cartier, J. Un intermédiaire entre la France et l'Allemagne: Gérard de Nerval. Genève, 1904.
Marie, A. Gérard de Nerval, le poète, l'homme. Paris, 1914.
Clouard, H. La déstinée tragique de Gérard de Nerval. Paris, 1928.
Neri, F. Gérard de Nerval. In: Il Maggio delle Fate. Torino, 1944.
Pelliot, P. Le juif NGAI, informateur du P. Mathieu Ricci. T'oung Pao, 20, 1921.
Spenlé, J. E. NIETZSCHE médiateur spirituel entre la France et l'Allemagne. MF, 1.VI.1937.
Ennis, L. Anthony NIXON: Jacobean Plagiarist and Hack. HLQ, 3, 1940.
Salamon, M. Charles NODIER et le groupe romantique. Paris, 1908.
Morance, A. Le salon de Ch. Nodier. Paris, 1927.
Mönch, W. Charles Nodier und die deutsche und englische Literatur. Berlin, 1931.
Cavrois, L. O'CONNELL et le collège anglais à St. Omer. Bull. historique trimestriel. St. Omer, 1866.
Patrick, G. Z. A. N OSTROVSKI: Slavophile or Westerner. In: Slav Studies. Ithaca, 1943.
Soeteman, C. Untersuchungen zur Uebersetzungstechnik OTFRIEDS von Weissenburgs. Museum, 50, 1943.
Bradford, G. OVID among the Goths. Yale Review, 4, 1915.
Anon. Thomas PAINE in England, Amerika und Frankreich. WM, 14, 1863
Lapp, J. C. An Explorer-Poet: Jean PARMENTIER. MLQ, 6, 1945.
Mayer, T. H. Ein deutscher Franzose: PELADAN. Roseggers Heimgarten, 44.
Levati, A. Viaggi di PETRARCA in Francia, in Germania ed in Italia descritti. 5 vols. Milano, 1820.
Bartoli, A. Il Petrarca viaggiatore. NAnt, 76, 1884.
Penco, E. Il Petrarca viaggiatore. Genova, 1932.
Bisson, L. A. Amédée PICHOT: a Romantic Prometheus. Oxford, 1942.
Bourguignon, J. Un empereur de Russie dans les Ardennes: le passage de PIERRE LE GRAND à son depart de France en 1717. Sedan, 1902.
Biadego, G. Il PINDEMONTE poeta e traduttore. In: Da libri e manoscritti, Verona, 1883.
Cobb, L. Antoine de la PLACE, sa vie et son oeuvre, 1707-93. Paris, 1928.
Marraro, H. R. Da PONTE and Foresti: the Introduction of Italian at Columbia. Columbia U. Quarterly, 18, 1941.
Sarrailh, J. Un intermédiaire, POUGENS. RLC, 3, 1923 and in: Enquêtes romantiques, France-Espagne. Paris, 1932.
Engel, C. E. Figures et aventures du XVIIIe siècle: Voyages et découvertes de l'abbé PREVOST. Paris, 1939.
Hazard, P. L'amitié franco-anglaise ne date pas du XXe siècle. NL, 18.III. 1939.
Staab, J. Das Journal étranger unter dem Abbé Prévost und seine Bedeutung für die literarischen Beziehungen zwischen England und Frankreich. Strassburg, 1912.
Feher, R. François RAKOCZI II dans les mémoires françaises de son temps. Pecs, 1931.
Zolnai, B. Un écrivain français du XVIIIe siècle: François Rakoczi. Nouvelle Rev. de Hongrie, 1936.
Hallo, R. Rudolf Erich RASPE, ein Wegbereiter von deutscher Art und Kunst. Stuttgart, 1934.
Spanheimer, Mary E. Heinrich Armin RATTERMANN, German-American Author, Poet, and Historian, 1832-1923. Diss. Catholic U. of America, 1938.
Herriot, E. Mme RECAMIER et ses amis. Paris, 1904.
Sedgwick, H. D. Mme. Récamier. Indianapolis, 1940.
Larne, E. Prinz August von Preussen

und Madame Récamier. Berliner Tageblatt, 20, 1892.
Lang, W. Graf **REINHARD.** Ein deutsch-französisches Lebensbild. Bamberg, 1896.
Crosby, E. A. Une romancière oubliée: Mme **RICCOBONI**, sa vie, ses oeuvres, sa place dans la littérature anglaise et française du XVIIIe siècle. Paris, 1924.
Price, L. M. Charlotte Buff, Mme. Riccoboni and Sophie Laroche. GR, 1931.
Furst, N. **RILKE'S** Translations of English, French, and Italian Sonnets. SPh, 39, 1942.
Le Breton, A. **RIVAROL**, sa vie, ses idées, son talent. Paris, 1895.
Baker, J. M. Henry Crabb **ROBINSON.** London, 1937.
Szikszay, E. Louis-Auguste **ROGEARD** (in Hungarian). Pecs, 1936.
Iorga, N. Un éducateur français: Antonin **ROQUES** (professeur en Roumanie dans la seconde moitié du XIXe siècle). Bull. de l'Acad. roumaine, 1.I. 1920.
Dupré, H. Un italien d'Angleterre: le poète peintre D. G. **ROSSETTI.** Paris, 1922.
Waller, R. D. The Rossetti Family. Manchester, 1932.
Las Vergnas, R. Le britannisme de Rossetti. RAA, Dec., 1933.
Winwar, F. The Rossettis and Their Circle. London, 1934.
Vincent, R. Gabriele Rossetti in England. Oxford, 1937.
Macke, K. Friedrich **RUECKERT** als Uebersetzer. Progr. Siegburg, 1896.
Wagner, M. M. **RUFINUS** the Translator. Washington, Catholic U.P., 1945.
Anon. Fremde Dichtungen im deutschen Gewande (**RUPERTI**-Lann). Europa, 1862.
Schrader, F. F. Otto **RUPPIUS**: a Career in America. AGR, 9, 1943.
Ivanoff, N. La marquise de **SABLE** et son salon. Paris, 1927.
Baldensperger, F. L'émigration de la comtesse de **SABRAN.** In: Etudes d'histoire littéraire, 3e sér. Paris, 1939.
Harvitt, H. J. Hugues **SALEL**, Poet and Translator. MPh, 16, 1919.
Chaponnière. Les premières années d'exil de **SAINT-EVREMOND.** RHLF, 1922.
Puaux, F. Saint-Evremont et les réfugiés de la Révocation à Londres. Rev. de l'histoire du Protestantisme fr., 1918.
Jaspar, M. H. Saint-Evremond à Londres. France Libre, 10, 1945.
Horsley, Phyllis M. Themiseul de **SAINT-HYACINTHE**, 1684-1746. CLS, 4, 1941.
Pierrotet. **SAINTE-BEUVE** in seinen metrischen Uebersetzungen. SVL, 6, 1906.
Seliger, P. **SCHACK** als Uebersetzer und Dichter. Gegenwart, 1891.
Walter, E. Ad. Fried. Graf von Schack als Uebersetzer. Leipzig, 1908.
Schirmer, W. F. The Odyssey of A. W. **SCHLEGEL.** GLL, 3, 1939.
Cunz, D. C. H. **SCHNAUFFERS** literarische Versuche. PMLA, 59, 1944
Barth, T. Karl **SCHURZ**, der Vermittler zweier Nationen. Nation, 25, 1899.
Blumenhagen, K. Sir Walter **SCOTT** als Uebersetzer. Diss., Rostock, 1900.
Hohlfeld, A. R. Scott als Uebersetzer. SVL, 3, 1903.
Faust, A. B. Charles **SEALSFIELD** (Carl Postl). A Study of his Style, his Influence upon American Literature. Baltimore, 1892.
—— Ch. Sealsfield, der Dichter beider Hemisphären. Weimar, 1897.
Mueller, K. Charles Sealsfield und Ad. Stifter. Blätter f. literar. Unterhaltung, 6, 1893.
Weiss, A. Postl-Sealsfield und Grillparzer. Gegenwart, 1896.
Heller, O. Charles Sealsfield und der Courier des Etats-Unis. Euphorion, 14, 1907.
Ludwig, A. Der Entdecker Amerikas. LE, 1923.
Popa, N. Les sources de Gérard de Nerval dans Jemmy. RLC, 10, 1930.
Djordjewitsch, M. Sealsfields Auffassung des Amerikanertums und seine literarische Stellung. Weimar, 1932.
Dallmann, W. P. The Spirit of America as Interpreted in the Works of Charles Sealsfield. Diss. Washington U. (St. Louis), 1938.
Ashby, Nanette M. The Sealsfield Controversy. Diss. Stanford U, 1939.
Dallmann, W. P. Sealsfield and Balzac Again. JEGPh, 39, 1940.
Waldinger, E. Charles Sealsfield. Southwest Rev, 25, 1940.
Arndt, K. J. & Groen, H. Sealsfield: "The Greatest American Author." AGR, 7, 1941.
Willey, N. L. Charles Sealsfield in Amerika. ZDPh, 66, 1941.
Castle, E. Sealsfield in Amerika. ZDPh, 67, 1942.
Arndt, K. J. R. Sealsfield's Early Reception in England and America. GR, 18, 1943.

—— The Cooper-Sealsfield Exchange of Criticism. AL, 15, 1943.

Wright, J. Un intermédiare entre l'esprit germanique et l'esprit français sous le Second Empire: Camille **SELDEN**, sa vie, son oeuvre. Paris, 1931.

Casati, E. Un carnet de **SHAFTESBURY** pendant son voyage en France et en Italie (1711-13). RLC, 16, 1936.

Elton, C. J. An Account of **SHELLEY'S** Visits to France, Switzerland and Savoy in the Years 1814, 1816. London, 1895.

Salis, J. R. de. **SISMONDI** et son temps. Rev. de Genève, 1929.

—— Sismondi (1775-1842). La vie et l'oeuvre d'un cosmopolite philosophe. Paris, 1932.

—— Sismondi. Lettres et documents inédits, suivies d'une liste des sources et d'une bibliographie. Paris, 1932.

Chancellor, E. B. **SMOLLETT** as a Traveller. Fortnightly Rev., 1921.

Morize, A. Samuel **SORBIERE** (1610-70). ZFSL, 1908.

Trautwein von Belle. Ludwig **SPACH**, ein Vermittler zwischen deutschem und französischem Geiste, MLIA, 1880.

Friedland, L. S. **SPENSER'S** Earliest Translations. JEGPh, 12, 1913.

Waschnitius, V. Heinrich **STEFFENS**. Ein Beitrag zur nordischen und deutschen Geistesgeschichte. Neumünster, 1939.

Borvitz, W. Die Uebersetzungstechnik Heinrich **STEINHOEWELS**. Diss. Halle, 1914.

Dollot. Les journées adriatiques de **STENDHAL**. Paris, 1929.

Pozzi, J. Stendhal diplomate. Le Temps, 11.IV.1939.

Herzfeld, G. William **TAYLOR** von Norwich. Halle, 1897.

Farkas, G. Un compagnon d'exil de Victor Hugo: le comte Alexandre de **TELEKI**. RLC, 16, 1936.

Masson, P. M. Madame de **TENCIN**. Paris, 1909.

Beck, R. Steingrimur **THORSTEINSSON**—Lyric Poet and Master Translator. SS, 20, 1948.

Baldensperger, F. Le touriste de l'émigration française, le chevalier de La **TOENAYE**. BURS, 1914.

Cushing, Mary G. Pierre Le **TOURNEUR**. New York, 1908.

Derocquigny, J. **TURBERVILLE** traducteur. RG, 1912.

Sutherland, B. Pierre Henri **TREYSSAC** de Vergy, 1738-74. MLQ, 4, 1942.

Ciampi, J. Pietro della **VALLE**, il pellegrino. NAnt, 47-48, 1879.

Durand, J. Pierre Des **VIGNES**, chancelier de l'empereur Frédéric II. Paris, 1851.

Bourdeau, J. Ch. de **VILLERS** et Mme. de Staël. Journal des Débats, 14-15.IV. 1880.

Seillrère, E. Charles de Villers. RP, 1.X. 1903.

Gautier, P. Un idéologue sous le Consulat et le Premier Empire. RDM, 1.III.1906.

Graeter, F. A. Charles de Villers und Mad. de Staël. Progr. Rastenburg, 1881-82.

Kohn, M. Ein geistiger Vermittler zwischen Deutschland und Frankreich. Deutschland, 22, 1890.

Ulrich, O. Charles de Villers. Leipzig, 1899.

Wittmer, L. Etude de littérature comparée: Charles de Villers. Genève, 1908.

Baldensperger, F. Charles de Villers. Semaine littéraire (Genève), 1908.

—— Un précurseur lorrain de Mme. de Staël: Charles de Villers. Le Pays lorrain, 20.XI.1909.

Eggli, E. L'Erotique comparée de Charles de Villers. Paris, 1927.

Weiss, R. Cornelio **VITELLI** in France and England. JWI, 2.

Ashbee, H. Frenchmen who have written in English: **VOLTAIRE**. The Bookworm, 1890-91.

Vries de Heckelingen, H. de. Correspondance de Bonaventura **VULCANIUS** pendant son séjour à Cologne, Genève et Bâle (1573-77). Den Haag, 1928.

Bodmer, J. J. Denkmal, dem Uebersetzer Butlers, Swifts und Luzians errichtet (Heinrich **WASER**). Deutsches Museum, 1784.

Witkowski, G. Diederich von dem **WERDER**. Leipzig, 1887.

Ischer, R. Ein Beitrag zur Kenntniss von **WIELANDS** Uebersetzungen. Euphorion, 14, 1907.

Strauss, E. Der Uebersetzer N. von **WYLE**. Berlin, 1911.

Harrison, T. P. Bartholomew **YONG**, Translator. MLR, 21, 1926.

Langfelder, E. M. Les séjours en Suisse, en France et en Belgique du comte **ZINZENDORF** (1764-70). Szeged, 1933.

FIFTH PART

Comparisons, Sources, Imitations

CHAPTER ONE

Similarities and Contrasts.

1. Among Nations.

a. Generalities.

Anon. Literary Coincidences (between writers probably not connected). Cornhill Mag., Oct., 1878.
Loane, G. G. Parallel Passages. N & Q, 3.IX.1938.
Munson, G. Twelve Decisive Battles of the Mind. New York, 1942.
Smith, C. A. Literary Contrasts Selected and Edited. Boston, 1925.
Wechssler, E. Esprit und Geist. Bielefeld, 1927. Cf. Literatur, 1928.

b. America and Others.

(The titles are arranged under the first national adjective mentioned; comparisons with America can be found also in the English, French, German etc. subchapters. See also Collective Influences, III. III. 1.)

Anon. American and English Literature Compared. American Quart. Observer, 2, 1833.
Stone, T. T. American and English Literature Compared. Lit. and Theol. Rev., 2, 1835.
Van Doren, C. & M. American and British Literature Since 1890. New York, 1939.

c. Asia and Others.

Chatterjee, S. Theories of Knowledge in Indian and Western Philosophy. Calcutta Rev., 3rd Ser., 54, 1935.
Clerke, E. M. Arabic Analogies in Western Speech. Asiatic Quart. Rev., 2, 1885.
Clouston, W. A. Parallel Passages from European and Asiatic Writers. ibid. 10, 1890.
Freeburg, V. O. A Sanscrit Parallel to an Elizabethan Plot. MLN, 1912.
Heimann, B. Indian and Western Philosophy: a Study in Contrasts. London, 1937.
Hughes, E. R. The Individual in East and West. Oxford, 1937.
Linden, G. Arische und semitische Dichtung. Bonn, 1925.
Poel, W. Hindu Drama and the English Stage. Asiatic Quart. Rev., N.S., 1, 1913.
Reichwein, A. China and Europe: Intellectual and Artistic Contrasts in the 18th Century. New York, 1925.
Spalding, H. N. Civilization in East and West: an Introduction to the Study of Human Progress. London, 1939.

d. England and Others.

Anon. English and French Literature. ER, 1821.
—— Fragments d'un Essai sur le théâtre anglais, comparé au théâtre français. Ann. de la litt. et des arts, 10, 1823.
—— English and French Fiction in the 19th Century. Academy, 1.II.1902.
Bulwer, E. L. England and the English (comparison with the French). London, 1833 and RP, 1833.
Carrel, F. English and French Manners. Fortnightly Rev., 1894.
Charpentier, J. Humour anglais et humour américain. A propos du centenaire de Mark Twain. MF, 15.XII.1935.
Demiashkevich, M. J. The National Mind: English, French, German. New York, 1938.
Gerothwohl, M. English and French Attitude towards Poetry. Fortnightly Rev., 1912.
Gerould, G. H. The Patterns of English and American Fiction: a History. Boston, 1942.
Grierson, G. A. A Supplement to Early English Theater and the Bengali Drama. Calcutta Rev., 3rd Ser., 9, 1923.
Herder, J. G. Von der Aehnlichkeit der mittleren englischen und deutschen Dichtkunst. (1777).
Howells, W. D. A Possible Difference in English and American Fiction. NAR, 1901.
Madariaga, S. de. Inglaterra, Francia, España, su evolución literaria. Rivista de Estudios Hispánicos, 1928.
—— Ingleses, Franceses, Españoles. Ensayo de psicologia colectiva comparada. Madrid, 1942.
—— Englishmen, Frenchmen, Spaniards. London, 1930.

Martin, E. Caractères spéciaux de la poésie en Angleterre et en France. FQ, 1932.

Metcalfe, F. The Englishman and the Scandinavian; or, A Comparison of Anglo-Saxon and Old Norse Literature. London, 1880.

Mukhopadhvay, M. M. Early English Theatre and the Bengali Drama. Calcutta Rev., 3rd Ser., 8, 1923.

Muralt, B. L. de. Lettres sur les Anglois et les François et sur les voyages (1725) ed. by Charles Gould. Paris, 1933. Cf. Anon. Apologie du caractère des Anglais et Français, ou Observations sur le livre intitulé: Lettre sur les Anglais et les Français. Paris, 1726.

Russell, J. Essai sur les moeurs et la littérature des Anglais et des Français. Paris, 1822.

Saintsbury, G. The Contrasts of English and French Literature. Macmillan's Mag. March, 1891 and in: Collected Essays, 4. London, 1924.

Scott, C. Dramatic Art in England and America. Munsey's Mag. Nov., 1900.

Sedgwick, H. D. English as Against French Literature. AM, 81, 1898.

Symons, A. On English and French Fiction. In: Dramatis Personae. Indianapolis, 1923.

Weidlé, W. Esprit anglais et esprit français. NL, 1938.

Whitman, S. England and Germany. Harpers Mag, 1898.

Zucker, A. E. Théâtre elizabethain et théâtre chinois. RLC, 3, 1923.

e. France and Others.

Anon. Sur les Français et les Allemands, ou l'après-dinée de Mad. la Marquise de R. Deutsches Museum, July, 1777.

—— Lettre d'un jeune homme à son ami sur les Français et les Anglais. Essai d'un parallèle. Amsterdam, 1779.

—— Bemerkungen über das Pariser und das Wiener Theater. Deutsches Museum, Oct., 1781.

Braga, G. C. La filosofia francese e italiana del settecento. Arezzo, 1920.

Busch, J. G. Ueber französische und deutsche Philosophie. Deutsches Museum, March, 1783.

Carré, J. M. Lettres françaises et portugaises, aujourd'hui. Bull. des Etudes Portugaises, 5, 1938.

Constant, B. Du théâtre français et du théâtre étranger. MF, 13.XII.1817.

Cruice, Mgr. Etudes littéraires sur l'apologue, la poésie lyrique, la poésie épique chez les Français, les Anglais, les Allemands, les Italiens et les Espagnols, et sur la poésie hébraïque et la poésie orientale. Paris, 1840.

Desmarets de Saint-Sorlin, J. La comparaison de la langue et de la poésie française avec la grecque et la latine, et des poètes grecs, latins et français. Paris, 1670.

Dollfuss, C. De l'esprit français et de l'esprit allemand. Paris, 1864.

Dumont, A. Les études d'érudition en France et en Allemagne. In: Notes et Discours. Paris, 1885.

Halbach, K. H. Franzosentum und Deutschtum in höfischer Dichtung des Stauferzeitalters. Hartmann von Aue und Crestien de Troyes. Berlin, 1939.

Jay, A. Du théâtre français et du théâtre étranger. MF, 20.XII.1817.

Lamothe Le Vayer. Discours de la contrariété d'humeurs qui se trouvent entre certaines nations et singulièrement entre la françoise et l'espagnole. Paris, 1636.

Macaulay, T. C. French and English Drama in the XVIIth Century: some Contrasts and Parallels. E & S, 1935.

Maugain, G. Le silence au théâtre en France et en Italie au XVIIIe siècle. Ausonia, 1937.

Merian-Genast, E. Das Problem der Form in der französischen und deutschen Klassik. GRM, 27.

Needham, H. A. La développement de l'esthétique sociologique en France et en Angleterre au XIXe siècle. Paris, 1926.

Noetzel, C. Der französische und der deutsche Geist. Jena, 1916.

Purves, J. Some Contrasts Between the French and English Literature of the Renaissance. Bull. de la Soc. des Amis de l'U. de Lyon, 1903.

Spronck, M. Français et Anglais. RB, 1897.

Starrenburg, C. Quelques observations sur les rythmes français et néerlandais. NPh, 1947.

Steinbömer, G. Le théâtre français et le théâtre allemand. CFA, 1939.

Stewart, J. Poetry in France and England. London, 1931.

Strayer, J. R. The Laicization of French and English Society in the Thirteenth Century. Spec., 15, 1940.

Symons, A. Studies in Two Literatures: France and England. London, 1897.

Toth, K. Französische und deutsche Kultur. DR. 1921.
Travis, J. Parallels in Poetic Device Between the Old French Epic and the Old Welsh Elegy. PMLA, 59, 1944.

f. Germany and Others.

Anon. Deutsches und französisches Theater. Europa, 1869.
Ancillon, F. Préface des mélanges de littérature et de philosophie. (Parallelisms between German and French philosophy). Paris, 1809.
Boemar, O. Deutsch, französisch, englisch, eine vergleichende Charakterstudie. NSp, 50.
Diels, P. Deutsche und russische Literatur in älterer Zeit. Intern. Monatsschrift f. Wissenschaft, Kunst &Technik, 13, 1918-19.
Friederich, W. P. German and French Dramatic Topics of the XVIIth Century. SPh, 34, 1937.
Garve, C. Ueber die Frage: warum stehen die Deutschen, nach dem Geständnis ihrer besten Schriftsteller, in Ansehung einer guten prosaischen Schreibart, gegen Griechen und Römer, vielleicht auch gegen Franzosen und Engländer, zurück? Neue Bibl. der schönen Wissenschaften, 62.
Kellermann, W. Altdeutsche und altfranzôsische Literatur. Epische Vergleichsprobleme. GRM, 26, 1938.
Lindau, P. Ueber Bühnendichtung in Deutschland und Frankreich. Gegenwart, 13, 1878.
Masson-Oursel, P. L'illimité selon le germanisme et selon l'Inde. Recherches philosophiques, 3, 1934.
Meyerfeld, M. Von Sprach' und Art der Deutschen und Engländer. Berlin, 1903.
Muensterberg, H. The Germans and the Americans. AM, July, 1899.
Petersen, C. Deutscher und nordischer Geist. Breslau, 1932.
Richter, W. Deutscher Geist und französische Literatur im Lichte der Säkularisierung. MDU, 35, 1943.
Saint-René Taillandier. Publications sur le XVIe siècle en Allemagne et en France. RDM, 15.II.1848.
Salm, Constance de. Des Allemands comparés aux Français, dans leurs moeurs, leurs usages, leur vie intérieure et sociale. Rev. encyclopédique, 30, 1826.
Schoenemann, F. Deutsche und amerikanische Romane. German Soc. Quarterly, 3, 1916.
Spanke, H. Deutsche und französische Dichtung des Mittelalters. In: Frankreich, sein Weltbild und Europa. Stuttgart, 1943.

g. Italy and Others.

Calepio, P. de'. Paragone della poesia tragica d'Italia con quella di Francia. Zürich, 1732. Venezia, 1770.
Flasche, H. Grundlagen moderner Kulturpolitik in Italien und Portugal. GRM, 26, 1938.
Moritz, P. Italien und Deutschland in Rücksicht auf Sitten, Gebräuche, Litteratur und Kunst. Berlin, 1892.
Neri, G. Saggi di letteratura italiana, francese, inglese. Napoli, 1936.
Nicolai, F. Vergleichung der italienischen und deutschen Dichter. Briefe, die neueste Literatur betreffend, XXIII, 332-33, Berlin, 1765.
Paroletti, M. Discours sur le caractère des deux langues, l'italienne et la française. Turin, 1810.
Santoli, V. La lingua letteraria in Italia e in Germania. Lingua Nostra, 3, 1941.
Vossler, K. Lingua e nazione in Italia e in Germania. Firenze, 1936.

h. Other Nations.

Anon. Russian and English Fiction. Academy, 3.I.1903.
Boltz, A. Ueber das altrussische Heldenlied in Vergleich mit der Arthursage. In: Beiträge zur Völkerkunde. Oppenheim, 1868.
Dyroff, A. Zur griechischen und germanischen Kosmogonie (Anaximandros, Pherekydes und Völuspa). Archiv f. Religionswissenschaft, 1934.
Filon, A. Le théâtre espagnol et le théâtre anglais. Journal des Débats, 20.XII. 1899.
Gandolphe, M. Essai sur quelques distinctions entre un esprit suédois et un esprit français. In: La vie et l'art des Scandinaves, Paris, 1899.
Hatzfeld, H. El estilo nacional en los símiles de los místicos españoles y franceses. NRFH, 1, 1947.
Johnson, S. Old Norse and Ancient Greek Ideals. Ethics, 49, 1938.
Knapp, C. Literature in Early Rome and Literature in Early America. CW, 21, 1928.
Oppermann, H. Griechen, Römer, Deutsche im Spiegel ihrer Nationalepen: Ilias, Aeneis, Nibelungenlied. Die alten Sprachen, 3, 1938.
Rostagni, A. Genio greco e genio romano nella poesia. Rivista di filologia e d'istruzione classica, 7, 1929.

Umphrey, G. W. Spanish American Literature Compared with That of the United States. Hisp., 26, 1943.
Vedenski. La réalité occidentale et l'idéal russe. Moscou, 1894.
Williams, A. Russian and British Poets a Hundred Years Ago. TLS, 24.V.1923.
Zielinski, T. L'istoriosofia graeca paragonata a quella degli Ebrei. In: La Pologne au Congr. internat. des Sciences hist. Oslo, 1928. Varsovie, 1930.

2. Among Individuals.

(It was often quite difficult to distinguish books and articles dealing with comparisons from those dealing with the influence of one writer upon the other. Consequently it is possible that items dealing with actual influences have erroneously been filed here and that other items dealing with mere parallelisms have been filed under influences. The titles are again arranged alphabetically, under the first name mentioned.)

Zanella, G. Paralleli letterari. Studi: **ADDISON** - Gozzi; Shelley - Leopardi; poemi d'Ossian e Melchior Cesarotti; Ippolito Pindemonte e gli inglesi, ecc. Verona, 1885.
Zdarski. Vergleichung einiger Tragödien des **ALFIERI**, Schiller und Voltaire. Die Ameise von Posen, Poln. Zs., 2, 1821.
Croce, B. **ARIOSTO**, Shakespeare e Corneille. Bari, 1920.
Nencioni, E. Orlando, Lear, Don Chisciotte. In: Saggi critici di letteratura italiana. Firenze, 1898.
Sanvisenti, B. Ariosto, Cervantes, Manzoni. Boll. della R. U. di Perugia, 7.XI.1931 and in: Convivium, 1932.
Hippel, E. von. **BACON** und Goethe als Staatsdenker. Freiburg, 1941.
Anon. **BALZAC** and Thackeray; a Little Comparison. Dublin U. Rev., 64, 1864.
Abbott, L. F. Honoré de Balzac and S. Lewis. The Outlook, 6.VII.1927.
Flat, P. Les personnages excessifs chez Dickens et Balzac. In: Essais sur Balzac. Paris, 1893.
Stanley, H. M. Balzac and Shakespeare: Which is the Greater? Dial, 16.V.1900.
Strindberg, A. Balzac, Goethe, Schiller. Neues Magazin, 7, 1904.
Hartsook, J. H. **BECQUER** and Heine: a Comparison. Diss. U. of Illinois, 1939.
Castagnaro, R. A. Bécquer and Gutiérrez Nájera. Some Literary Similarities. Hisp., 27, 1944.
Brandl, A. **BEOWULF**-Epos und Aeneis in systematischer Vergleichung. Archiv, 171, 1937.
Cook, A. S. Beowulfian and Odyssean Voyages. New Haven Academy, 1926.
—— Greek Parallels to Certain Features of the Beowulf. PhQ, 5, 1926.
Haber, T. B. A Comparative Study of the Beowulf and the Aeneid. Princeton, 1931.
Hulbert, J. R. Beowulf and the Classical Epic. MPh, 44, 1946.
Schröbler, Ingeborg. Beowulf and Homer. Beiträge zur Gesch. der deutschen Sprache & Literatur, 63, 1939.
Woolf, H. B. Beowulf and Grendel: An Analogue from Burma. MLN, 62, 1947.
Caprin, G. **BISMARCK** e Shakespeare. Divagazioni comparative. Marzocco, 13, 1908.
McNerney, R. F. A Famous Paralelo entre **BOLIVAR** y Washington (1832) and its Authorship. Hisp. 24, 1941
Loomba, R. M. **BRADLEY** and Bergson: a Comparative Study. Lucknow, 1938.
Goldschmidt, K. W. **BUDDHA** und Dionysos. Berlin, 1925.
Smyth, M. W. Puritan **BUNYAN** and Catholic Dante. NC, 1928.
Le Fèvre, L. **PAUL BUNYAN** and Rip van Winkle. Yale Rev., 36, 1946.
Mory, Mary M. Russian Bylini and American Paul Bunyan Tales. Slavonic Monthly, 1, 1942.
Candreas, G. Der Begriff des Erhabenen bei **BURKE** und Kant. Diss. Strassburg, 1894.
Maignien, C. A. N. Sur Lord **BYRON**, comparé à quelques poètes sous le rapport de la pensée (Homère, Sophocle, Shakespeare, Corneille, Racine, Bossuet, etc.) In: Etudes littéraires. Paris, 1837.
Gurteen, S. H. The Epic of the Fall of Man: a Comparative Study of **CAEDMON**, Dante, and Milton. London, 1896. Cf. Athenaeum 3625, 1897.
Anon. **CALDERON** und Shakespeare. Beilage zur Allg. Zt., 4-5, I. 1870.
Carrière, M. Calderons Arzt seiner Ehre und Shakespeares Othello. Nord & Süd, 1881.
Fey, E. Calderon und Shakespeare. NM, 1, 1930.
Pereira. Calderón y Shakespeare. Revista de España, 1884.
Reade, H. How did Calderon Know Shakespeare's Plays? Westminster Rev., 1903.
Schütt, M. Hat Calderon Shakespeare gekannt? JbShG, 61, 1925.

Cecchi, P. L. Il **CAMOENS** e il Tasso. Crepuscolo, 1856.

Hofrichter, Ruth. Three Poets and Reality: Study of a German, an Austrian, and a Swiss Contemporary Lyricist (**CAROSSA**, Weinheber, Steffen). New Haven, 1942.

Anon. **CERVANTES** and Shakespeare. N & Q, 1874.

Brandes, G. Don Quixote and Hamlet. Fortnightly Rev., Oct., 1913.

Fitzmaurice Kelly, J. Cervantes and Shakespeare. PBA, 1916.

González Ruiz, N. Dos genios contemporáneos : Cervantes, Shakespeare. Barcelona, 1945.

Hagberg, C. A. Cervantes et Walter Scott, parallèle littéraire. Diss. Lund, 1838.

Lister, J. T. A Comparison of Two Works of Cervantes With a Play by Massinger. Hisp., 5.

M'Carty, D. F. Cervantes and Shakespeare. Athenaeum, 26.III.1864.

Starkie, W. Cervantes et Shakespeare. Revista Nacional de Educación, 7, 1947.

Prescott. **CHATEAUBRIAND'S** English Literature (Parallelism with Scott). In: Critical and Historical Essays, 1850.

Schlauch, M. **CHAUCER'S** Merchant Tale and a Russian Legend of King Solomon. MLN, 1934.

Belden, H. M. Observation and Imagination in **COLERIDGE** and Poe; a Contrast. Festschrift C. F. Johnson. Hartford, 1928.

Legouvé, E. **CORNEILLE** et Shakespeare. RU, 15.VII.1894.

Reymond, W. Corneille, Shakespeare et Goethe. Berlin, 1864.

Potez, H. **CYRANO** et Shakespeare. Journal des Débats, 22.VIII.1899.

Ludwig, A. **DAHN**, Fouqué, Stevenson. Euphorion, 19, 1910.

Augustin, H. **DANTE**, Goethe, Stifter: Das fromme Weltbild des Dichters. Basel, 1944.

Costa, A. della. La metà della vita in Dante, Goethe, Schopenhauer, Wagner e Leopardi. Milano, 1938.

Osgood, C. G. Poetry as a Means of Grace: Dante, Spenser, Milton, and Johnson. Princeton, 1941.

Pacheu, J. Dante, Spenser, Bunyan, Shelley. Revue des fac. cath. de l'Est, 1895.

—— De Dante à Verlaine. Etudes d'idéalistes et mystiques: Dante-Spenser, Bunyan-Shelley, Huysmans-Verlaine. Paris, 1897.

Pardo Bazán, Emilia. Los poetas épicos cristianos (Dante, Tasso, Milton). Madrid, 1895.

Paur, T. Vergleichende Bemerkungen über Dante, Milton und Klopstock. Neisse, 1847 and in: Zur Litteratur- und Kulturgeschichte. Leipzig, 1876.

Reckert, S. Alcuni parallelismi fra i simboli concreti della Divina Commedia e del Pilgrim's Progress. Ital. 25, 1948.

Topin, H. Parallèle entre Dante et Klopstock. In: Etudes sur la langue italienne, 1855, and in his translation of Paradiso. Paris, 1862.

Trezza, G. Dante, Shakespeare, Goethe nella rinascenza europea. Verona, 1888.

Wagner, G. H. A. Zwei Epochen der modernen Poesie in Dante, Petrarca, Bocaccio, Goethe, Schiller und Wieland. Leipzig, 1806.

Hubert, R. **DESCARTES** et Bacon: ressemblances et différences. Revue de Synthèse, 14, 1937.

Fuerst, R. Literarische Verwandtschaften (**DICKENS** und Marie von Ebner-Eschenbach; Sue und Rostand). Zeit, 420, 1902.

Klett, Ada M. Doom and Fortitude: A Study of Poetic Metaphor in Annette von **DROSTE-HUELSHOFF** (1797-1848) and Emily Dickinson (1830-1886). MDU, 37, 1946.

Schottlaender, R. Two Dionysians: **EMERSON** and Nietzsche. SAQ, 39, 1940-41.

Weygandt, C. A. E., the Irish Emerson. Sewanee Rev., 15, 1907.

Tenhoeff, N. B. **ERASMUS** en Voltaire als exponenten van hun tijd. Groningen, 1939.

Steiger, H. **EURIPIDES**, ein antiker Ibsen? Ph., 1924.

Furst, N. The Structure of l'Education sentimentale and Der grüne Heinrich. (**FLAUBERT**-Keller). PMLA, 56, 1941.

Besouchet, Lidia. Amando **FONTES** y Steinbeck. Nosotros, 7, 1942.

Van Doren, C. Anatole **FRANCE** and T. Hardy. Century, 1925.

Saix, G. de. Anatole France et Oscar Wilde. NL, 1945.

Frick, H. **GHAZALIS** Selbstbiographie. Ein Vergleich mit Augustins Confessionen. Leipzig, 1919.

Ungnad, A. **GILGAMESCH**-Epos und Odyssee. Breslau, 1923.

Anon. **GOETHE** and J. S. Mill Contrasted. Westminster Review, 102.

Dovski, L. von. Genie und Eros: Goethe, Beethoven, Shelley, Poe. Bern, 1947.
Pollak, G. International Perspective in Criticism: Goethe, Grillparzer, Sainte-Beuve, Lowell. New York, 1914.
Sand, George. Essai sur le drame fantastique: Goethe, Byron, Mickiewicz. RDM, 1839.
Vogel von Vogelstein, C. Die Hauptmomente aus Goethes Faust, Dantes Divina Commedia und Virgils Aeneis. München, 1862.
Heimerle, M. **GOTTFRIED** und Thomas: ein Vergleich. Frankfurt. 1942.
Friedrichs, E. **GOTTSCHED**, Shakespeare, Tolstoi. NSp, 24, 1917.
Roch, H. Richter ihrer Zeit: **GRIMMELSHAUSEN**, Swift, Gogol. Berlin, 1940.
Friederich, W. P. From Ethos to Pathos: The Development from **GRYPHIUS** to Lohenstein. (Parallelism with Aeschylus and Euripides). GR, 10, 1935.
Keppler, E. Gryphius und Shakespeare. Diss. Tübingen, 1921.
O'Brien, J. Henry **HARLAND**, an American Forerunner of Proust. MLN, 54.
Trumbauer. **HAUPTMANN** and Galsworthy, a Parallel. Diss. U. of Pa., 1917.
Astrov, V. **HAWTHORNE** and Dostoievski as Explorers of the Human Conscience. NEQ, 15, 1942.
Betz, L. P. **HEINE** und Alfred de Musset. Eine biographisch-litterarische Parallele. Zürich, 1897.
Anon. **HOFFMANNS** Doge und die Dogaresse und Byrons Marino Faliero. Wiener Jb., 16, 1821.
Boisjollin, S. de. Hoffmann, Thomas de Quincey, Edgar Poe, Gérard de Nerval. Rev. des Etudes historiques, 1899.
Wenzel, G. F. **HOELDERLIN** und John Keats als geistesverwandte Dichter. Progr. Magdeburg, 1896.
Anon. **HOMER** und Ossian, Tocco und Wilhelm Tell, Till Eulenspiegel und Don-Quixote. Isis, March, 1806.
—— Homer und Klopstock. Allg. Modezeitung, 41. (Leipzig), 1824.
—— Similes of Homer, Virgil and Milton. In: Monthly Mag. and British Repertory, 1796-97.
Ashby, A. M. Poetic Imagery in Homer and Virgil. G&R, 2, 1932-33.
Becker, J. Homerische Ansichten und Ausdrucksweisen mit altfranzösischen zusammengestellt. SAWB. 1867.
Beni, P. Comparazione di Homero, Virgilio e Torquato Tasso e a chi di loro si debbe la palma nell'heroica poema. Padova, 1607.
Bock, W. Homerische Poesie mit vergleichender Berücksichtigung des Epos von anderen Völkern. Progr. Marienburg, 1882.
Boehm, F. Ilias und Nibelungenlied. Znaim, 1885.
Bogan, Z. Homerus Hebraizon, sive Comparatio Homeri cum Scriptoribus sacris. Oxoniae, 1658.
Dahl. Comparatio Homeri et Ossiani. Upsala, 1792.
Dobschütz, E. von. Homer und die Bibel, eine überlieferungsgeschichtliche Vergleichung. NJWJ, 1925.
Duckworth, G. E. Foreshadowing and Suspense in the Epics of Homer, Apollonius and Vergil. Princeton, 1933
Gambirasio, L. Omero, Dante e Shakespeare e la poesia biblica. Milano, 1887.
Herder, J. G. Homer und Ossian. Horen, 1795.
Inez, M. Homeric and Beowulfian Funeral Rites. CB, 12, 1935-36.
Keith, A. L. The Taunt in Homer and Vergil. CJ, 19.
Mauro, D. Omero, Dante, Shakespeare. Rivista contemporanea, 46, 1866.
Mierow, H. E. Some Aspects of the Literary Technique of the Aeneid and the Odyssey. CW, 20, 1927.
Milatovic, L. Dreiheit und Dreigliederungsprinzip bei Homer im Vergleich mit dem serbischen Heldenlied. Leipzig, 1941.
Montanari, G. J. Omero, Virgilio e Dante Alighieri. Pesaro, 1865.
Nardis, V. de. Omero e Dante nei loro tempi. Roma, 1884.
Penei, E. Omero e Dante, Schiller e il dramma. Milano, 1882.
Petrettini, G. Orazione intorno ad Omero e a Dante. Padova. 1821.
Reinach, S. Homère et Turold. Revue archéologique, 1914.
Schnorr von Carolsfeld. Litteraturvergleichende Bemerkungen zu den Homerischen Gedichten. ALG, 10, 1881.
Scott, J. A. Similes in Homer and in Virgil. CJ, 13.
—— Some Biblical and Homeric Parallels. CJ, 16.
Shephard, W. P. Chansons de geste and the Homeric Problem. AJPh, 42, 1921.
Spera, G. Parallelo tra Omero, Virgilio, Shakespeare, Klopstock e Dante. In: Saggio estetico-storico-critico. Potenza, 1870.
Tuerk, M. Zur Vergleichung der Iliade und des Nibelungenliedes. Progr. Kronstadt, 1873.
Zell, C. Ueber die Iliade und das Nibelungenlied. Karlsruhe, 1843.

Anon. Réflexions sur le génie d'**HORACE**, de Despréaux et de Rousseau. MF, 1851.

Mierow, C. C. Horace and Omar Khayyam. CW, 11.

Schubert, L. The Realism in Romanticism: **HUGO** and Wordsworth. Festschrift A. M. Drummond. Ithaca, 1944.

Kohn-Bramstedt, L. The Intellectual as an Ironist: Aldous **HUXLEY** and Thomas Mann. Contemporary Rev., April, 1939.

Wood, F. T. Individualism in the Religious Thought in the Plays of **IBSEN** and Bernard Shaw. Calcutta Rev., 3rd Ser., 55, 1935.

Schinz, A. Samuel **JOHNSON**, le Boileau anglais. RDM, 1935.

Leser, E. On the Relation of Ben **JONSON'S** Epicoene to Molière's Médecin malgré lui and Femmes Savantes. MLN, 7, 1892.

Samter, F. Ben Jonson und Molière. Eine Parallele. In: Studien zu Ben Jonson. Diss., Bern, 1903.

Stanger, H. Gemeinsame Motive in Ben Jonsons und Molières Lustspielen. SVL, 3, 1903.

Arnold, M. Essays in Criticism (**JOUBERT** and Coleridge). London, 1880.

Sorrento, L. Il pastore-filosofo in **JOUFFROY** e in Leopardi. In: Mélanges Baldensperger. Paris, 1929-30.

Summer, M. Les héroines de **KALIDASA** et les héroines de Shakespeare. Paris, 1879.

Joseph, H. W. B. A Comparison of **KANT'S** Idealism with that of Berkeley. London, 1929.

Benkowitz, C. F. Der Messias von **KLOPSTOCK**, ästhetisch beurtheilt und verglichen mit der Iliade, der Aeneide und dem Verlornen Paradiese. Breslau, 1797. Cf. A. W. Schlegel: Schriften, 11.

Léger, L. La jeunesse de deux idéalistes: S. **KRASINSKI** et Henry Reeve. RDM, 1.V.1903.

Morice, C. **LAMARTINE**, Baudelaire, Shelley. Rev. contemporaine, 4, 1886.

Donna, Sister Rose B. Despair and Hope. A Study in **LANGLAND** and Augustine. Washington, 1947.

Owen, D. L. Piers Plowman, a Comparison with some Earlier and Contemporary French Allegories. London, 1912.

Mejia Nieto, Q. El descontento de **LAWRENCE** y Unamuno. La Nación, 2.VI. 1940.

Faggi, A. **LENAU** e Leopardi. Palermo, 1898.

Duesterdieck, M. Lenau und Leopardi. Gegenwart, 1899.

Barzun, J. Truth in Biography: **LEONARDO** and Freud. University Rev., 6, 1940.

Bickersteth, G. L. **LEOPARDI** and Wordsworth. PBA, 1927.

Chiappelli, A. Leopardi e Shelley. Marzocco, 17.VII.1927.

Del Mastro, V. Le pessimisme de deux contemporains, Jacques Leopardi et Alfred de Musset. Naples, 1896.

Farinelli, A. Ueber Leopardis und Lenaus Pessimismus. Hannover, 1898.

—— Del pessimismo di Leopardi e di Lenau. Riv. mens. di lett. tedesca, 2, 1908.

Necco, J. Leopardi e Hölderlin. Romania, 1938.

Rentsch, J. **LUCIAN** und Voltaire, eine vergleichende Charakteristik. Progr. Plauen, 1895.

Grisy, A. de. **LUCILIUS** et Béranger ou deux poètes populaires. Nîmes, 1876.

Dornseiff, F. Das Geheimnis der Form von **MANRIQUES** coplas und Villons Ballade. ZFSL, 64.

Galletti, A. **MANZONI**, Shakespeare e Bossuet. In: Saggi e Studi. Bologna, 1915.

Cassères, B. de. **MENCKEN** and Shaw, the Anatomy of America's Voltaire and England's Other John Bull. Newton, 1930.

Anon. Lettre où l'on compare le Paradis perdu de **MILTON** avec le poème intitulé Sarcothis du P. Jacques Masenius. Mémoires de Trévoux, 1755.

Gilbert, A. H. A Parallel between Milton and Boiardo. Ital, 20, 1943.

Scharf, L. John Milton und Jean Jacques Rousseau: eine vergleichende Studie. Progr. Freudenthal, 1873, and in: Studien & Skizzen. Braunschweig, 1882.

Bouchier, J. **MOLIERE**, Bacon, Shakespeare. N&Q, 13.XI.1886.

Coquelin, C. Molière and Shakespeare. Century Mag., 1889 and in: Grande Revue, 1901.

Francisci, C. Molière et Shakespeare. In: Fantaisies littéraires. Perugia, 1909.

Humbert, C. Molière-Harpax und Shakespeare-Othello. Franco-Gallia, 9, 1892.

—— Zu Molières Leben und Wirken und zu Shakespeares Hamlet. Progr. Bielefeld, 1899.

Stapfer, P. Molière et Shakespeare. Paris, 1887. 4th ed. 1899.

Stoll, E. E. Molière and Shakespeare. RR, 35, 1944.

Addis, J. Parallel Passages (in **MON-**

TAIGNE, Molière, Homer, etc.). N&Q, 25.IV.1874.
Gregor, D. B. Plagiarism or Parallelism? (MONTI-Byron). N&Q, 90, 1946.
Anon. Comparaison du Philoclée de MORGAN avec la Cour bergère d'Ant. Maréschal. Ann. Litt., 5, 1755.
San Jurjo, P. Sobre el romanticismo, paralelo entre MUSSET y Espronceda. Hisp., 8, 1926.
Lütcke, H. MUSSOLINI und Klopstock. Quedlinburg, 1937.
Hamburger, L. L'epopea dei NIBELUNGHI, le sue analogie coi poemi Omerici, e le sue fonti storiche e mitologiche. Napoli, 1884.
Nusch, A. Zur Vergleichung des Niebelungenliedes mit der Ilias. Progr. Speyer, 1863.
Stolte, F. Der Nibelunge Not verglichen mit der Ilias. Progr. Rielberg, 1869, & Progr. Paderborn, 1877.
Olivero, F. NOVALIS e Keats. Convivium, 14, 1942.
Gurlitt. Ueber OSSIAN mit Hinsicht auf Homer. Hamburg, 1802.
Simões, J. G. Fernando PESSOA e Paul Valéry, afinidades ignoradas. RLC, 19, 1939.
Trabalza, C. PETRARCA, Fauriel e Racine nell' inedita digressione sull' amore nei romanzi. In: Dipanature critiche. Bologna, 1920.
Bhattacharjee, U. PLATO and the Bhagavad-Gita. Calcutta Rev., 3rd Ser., 24, 1927.
Connely, W. When PLAUTUS is Greater than Shakespeare. CJ, 19.
Dubedout, E. J. Edgar POE et Musset. MLN, 1907.
Holsapple, C. K. The Masque of the Red Death and I promessi sposi. Texas Studies in English, 1938.
Jones, P. M. Poe and Baudelaire: the Affinity. MLR, 40, 1945.
Meter, A. van. PROUST and Santayana. In: The Aesthetic Way of Life. Chicago, 1937.
Chasles, P. (RABELAIS') Panurge, Falstaff et Sancho. RP, 2, 1829.
Ampère, J. J. Le théâtre comparé de RACINE et de Shakespeare. Globe, 9.VII.1825.
Duport, F. Racine, Shakespeare et Rivarol. Ephémérides universelles, April, 1829.
Owenson, S. (Dupin, C.) Lettre à Milady Morgan sur Racine et sur Shakespeare. Paris, 1818.
Merian-Genast, C. Racine und Goethe; ein Vergleich zwischen französischer und deutscher Klassik. Archiv, 1935.
Stendhal. Racine et Shakespeare. (1823). (ed. by Pierre Martino with Notes, Preface). Paris, 1925. Cf. RCC, 21.
Barzilai Gentilli, E. Jean François REGNARD e il suo teatro, e di alcune analogie con quello di C. Goldoni. NAnt., 1925.
Schmidt, E. RICHARDSON, Rousseau und Goethe. Jena, 1875.
Traverso, L. RILKE, Baudelaire, Kleist. Firenze, 1945.
Wood, F. Rilke and D. H. Lawrence. GR, 15, 1940.
Woelker, E. M. Menschengestaltung in vorhöfischen Epen des 12. Jahrhunderts: Chanson de ROLAND, Rolandslied, König Rother. Berlin, 1940.
Mason, E. Two Christian Poets (Christina G. ROSSETTI & Paul Verlaine) In: A Book of Preferences in Literature. London, 1914.
Wolff, H. M. ROTROUS Venceslas und Kleists Prinz von Homburg. MPh, 37, 1939.
Schmidt, W. Der Kampf um den Sinn des Lebens: ROUSSEAU, Carlyle, Ibsen. Berlin, 1907.
Cassirer, E. Rousseau, Kant, Goethe. Two Essays. Princeton, 1945.
Kahn, L. W. Freedom: an Existentialist and an Idealist View. (SARTRE & Schiller). PMLA, March, 1949.
Humbert, C. SCHILLER, Lessing, Goethe, Molière und Herr Dr. Paul Lindau. Progr. Bielefeld, 1885.
Raschen, J. F. L. An Arabian Parallel to Schiller's Ballad Die Bürgschaft: the Hostage. MPh, 17, 1919-20.
Seiler, F. Die Behandlung des sittlichen Problems in Schillers Kampf mit dem Drachen, der Erzählung bei Livius (VIII,7), Kleists Prinz von Homburg und Sophokles' Antigone. Progr., 1890.
Wiener, M. Orientalische Parallelen zu Schillers Bürgschaft. Deutsche Wochenschrift, 5, 1854.
David, J. Le pessimiste et l'optimiste, SCHOPENHAUER et Joubert. Rev. de la Soc. des études historiques, 4e sér., 3, 1885. And in: Annales de la Société philotechnique, 44. Paris, 1886.
Anon. Parallèle de SHAKESPEARE et des poètes dramatiques grecs et français, avec quelques remarques sur les jugements faux portés par M. de Voltaire. Année litt., 1769.
Bailly, H. Le théâtre grec et le théâtre de Shakespeare: Hamlet; le Roi Léar. Bull. de la Société académique de Brest, 2e sér., 11. 1886.
Beck, A. Shakespeare und Homer. Leipzig, 1865.

Berthelot, R. La sagesse de Shakespeare et de Goethe. Paris, 1930.
Brown, H. A Philosopher's Tragedy: Shakespeare and Spinoza. HJ, 1929.
Civello, I. Amleto, Faust, Manfredo, Gonsalvo. In: Studi critici. Palermo, 1900.
Claretie, J. Shakespeare and Molière. Fortnightly Rev., 66, 1899.
Corney, B. Shakespeare and Cervantes. Athenaeum, 2.IV.1864.
Crawford, J. P. W. A 16th Century Spanish Analogue of Measure for Measure (Juan de la Cueva, 1579). MLN, 1925.
Decreus, J. Forces constructives dans Hamlet et dans La Princesse Maleine de Maeterlinck. CLS, 11.
Farinelli, A. Shakespeare, Kant, Goethe. Drei Reden. Berlin, 1942.
Helbig, F. W. Shakespeare und Hartmann von der Aue. Allg. litterar. Correspondenz, 3, 1879.
Hense, C. C. Beseelende Personification in griechischen Dichtungen mit Berücksichtigung lateinischer Dichter und Shakespeares. Parchim, 1874-77.
Herford, C. H. Shakespeare and Descartes. HJ, 1925.
Jacob, E. Shakespeares Naturverbundenheit im Vergleich mit Schillers und Goethes Verhältnis zur Natur. Hamburg, 1937.
Koch, M. Shakespeare und Lope de Vega. ESn, 20, 1896.
Koenig, W. Shakespeare als Dichter, Weltweiser und Christ. Durch eine Vergleichung mit Dante dargestellt. Leipzig, 1873.
Lewinski, M. Shakespeare und Goethe in ethischer Betrachtung. Archiv f. Gesch. der Philosophie, 29. 1916.
Losini, F. Amleto e Don Chisciotte. Fanfulla della Domenica, 1908.
Ludwig, A. Shakespeare, Calderon und Lope. PJb, 1919.
Montagu, Mrs. E. An Essay on the Writings and Genius of Shakespeare, Compared with the Greek and French Dramatic Poets. London, 1769. Paris, 1777. Firenze, 1828.
Murray, A. T. Hamlet and Orestes; a Study in Traditional Types. London, 1914.
Navone, G. Amleto e Don Chisciotte. Rassegna Nazionale (Firenze), 1897.
Oppell, Baron von. Beauty in Shakespeare and in Kant. HJ, 40.
Overmaus, J. Hamlet, Don Quijote, Deutschland. Stimmen der Zeit, 91, 1916.
Petsch, R. Die dramatischen Figuren bei Shakespeare, Goethe, Kleist und anderen Dramatikern. Archiv, 173, 1938.
Proelss, R. Shakespeare und Molière. Allg. litt. Correspondenz, 2.
Roetscher, H. T. Ueber Shakespeares dramatische Kunst und sein Verhältniss zu Calderon. In: Dramaturgische Skizzen. Berlin, 1847.
Saint-Victor, P. de. Shakespeare et le théâtre classique français. RB, 27.V. 1882.
Sapienza, V. Shakespeare contro Omero. Milano, 1930.
Schlegel, J. E. Vergleichung Shakespeares und Andreas Gryphius bei Gelegenheit einer Uebersetzung von Shakespeares Julius Caesar. Kritische Beiträge. Berlin, 1741. And in: Sämtliche Werke 5. Kopenhagen, 1771.
Silvain, R. La formule dramatique de Shakespeare et de Racine. Confluences, 2, 1942.
Stone, W. G. Shakespeare, Cicero and Dante. N&Q, 12.IV.1879.
Turguenieff, I. Hamlet et Don Quichotte. Revue Suisse, 1879. And in: Fortnightly Rev., 56, 1894.
Turner, L. M. Du conflit tragique chez les Grecs et dans Shakespeare. Paris, 1913.
Ulrici, H. Shakespeares dramatische Kunst und sein Verhältniss zu Calderon und Goethe. Halle, 1839.
Vaske, T. Shakespeare und Euripides. Eine Parallele. JbShG, 4, 1869.
Verlaine, P. Shakespeare and Racine. Fortnightly Rev., 56, 1894.
Witte, H. Shakespeare und Molière. Wiesbaden, 1881.
Wolff, M. Shakespeare und Racine. Zukunft, 42, 1903.
Yardley, E. Shakespeare and Calderon. N&Q, 13.VII.1889.
Masvidal, A. B. La dramatica de **SHAW** y Pirandello. Universidad de la Habana, 1934.
Salvador de Madariaga, S. de. **SHELLEY,** Calderon and Other Essays on English and Spanish Poetry. London, 1920.
Verkoren, L. Over Shelley en Hölderlin. NPh, 24, 1938-39.
Zanella, G. Shelley e G. Leopardi. NAnt., 1, 1881. And in: Paralleli letterari. Verona, 1885.
Riccoboni, D. Dei sistemi tragici di **SOFOCLE** e Shakespeare. Venezia, 1862.
Smith, L. H. Ars tragica Sophoclea cum Shakespeariana comparata. London, 1896.
Saurat, D. Spiritual Attitudes in **SPEN-**

SER, Milton, Blake and Hugo. CLS, 13-14, 1944-45.
Martineau, H. **STENDHAL**, Molière, Shakespeare. Paris, 1930.
Trompeo, P. P. De quelques rapports entre la critique littéraire de Stendhal et celle de Manzoni. Annales de l'U. de Grenoble, 26, 1915.
Eyre, J. Prince A. A. Shakhovskoi, the new **STERNE**. SEER, 4, 1945.
Monti, G. Il dolore nelle opere del **TASSO** e dello Shakespeare. In: La poesia del dolore. Modena, 1892.
Portugal de Faria, A. de. Torquato Tasso a Luis de Camões. Leorne, 1898.
Buchanan, R. **TENNYSON**, Heine and de Musset. In: Master-Spirits. London, 1873.
Nuys, F. van. The Spirit of Tennyson's and Longfellow's Poetry Compared. U. of Virginia Mag., May, 1897 and Jan., 1902.
Rose, F. Tennyson and V. Hugo: Two Poets, Two Nations, One Epoch. Poetry Rev., 1939.
Spencer, R. Literary Coincidences. Calcutta Rev., 83, 1886.
Anon. **TOLSTOI** Compared with Ibsen. The Chautauquan, 31, 1900.
Rose, E. The Fighting Temeraire: William **TURNER**, Henry Newbolt, Detlev von Liliencron. GR, 15, 1940.
Olivera, M. A. **UNAMUNO** y Chesterton a través de dos novelas. Argentina libre, 15.VIII.1940.
Lehmann, R. P. Henry **VAUGHAN** and Welsh Poetry: a Contrast. PhQ, 25, 1946.
Goretta, M. **VERGA**, Goethe, Ibsen. Verona, 1940.
Furst, N. **VIGNY**, Leopardi, Hölderlin. MLF, 24, 1939.
Buxton, C. R. Prophets of Heaven and Hell: **VIRGIL**, Dante, Milton, Goethe. New York, 1945.
Haenni, R. Der Vergilische und der Faustische Mensch. NSR, 1932.
Tissot, P. Etudes sur Virgile, comparé avec tous les poètes épiques et dramatiques des anciens et des modernes. Paris, 1825-28.
Smith, W. F. **VIVES** and Montaigne as Educators. Hisp., 29, 1946.
Dejob, C. La tragédie historique chez **VOLTAIRE** et Shakespeare. RCC, 1899.
Bentley, E. R. The Theatres of **WAGNER** and Ibsen. Kenyon Rev., 6, 1945.
Dandieu, A. **WELLS** et Diderot. MF, 15. III.1927.
Collin, C. **WERGELAND**, Byron og Lamartine. Atlantis, 1, 1919.
Moore, S. H. **WESLEY** and Fénelon. LQHR, 1944.
Beal, P. B. **WHITMAN** and Verhaeren: A Comparison. Diss. U. of Washington, 1943.
Randall, H. F. Whitman and Verhaeren: Priests of Human Brotherhood. FR, 15-16, 1942.
Schumann, D. W. Enumerative Style and Its Significance in Whitman, Rilke, Werfel. MLQ, 3, 1942.
Glunz, H. H. Die Literaturästhetik des europäischen Mittelalters, **WOLFRAM**, Rosenroman, Chaucer, Dante. Bochum-Langendreer, 1937.
Rosenkranz, C. Ueber den Titurel und Dante's Komödie. Halle, 1829.
Anon. **YEATS**, Synge, Ibsen and Strindberg. Scrutiny, 1936.
Doty, G. L. **ZABALETA** et Parini: leurs satires et leur critique des milieux contemporains. RLC, 10, 1930.
Dahlström, C. E. W. L. Theomachy: **ZOLA**, Strindberg, Andreyev. SS, 17, 1942.
Rauhut, F. Zola, Hauptmann, Pirandello. Von der Verwandtschaft dreier Dichtungen. GRM, 26.

CHAPTER TWO

Sources.

1. Generalities.

Brandl, A. Quellen des weltlichen Dramas in England vor Shakespeare. Strassburg, 1898.
Cazamian, L. The Aims and Method of Higher Literary Studies. The Lure of Sources. Rice Institute Pamphlet, 1929.
Clark, W. S. The Sources of the Restoration Heroic Play. RES, 1928.
Genelin, T. Unsere höfischen Epen und ihre Quellen. Progr. Triest, 1890.
Langbaine, G. An Account of the English Dramatic Poets. Oxford, 1691.
Lancaster, H. C. A History of French Dramatic Literature in the 17th Century. 9 vols. Baltimore, 1929-42.
Stiefel, A. L. Zur Schwankdichtung im 16. und 17. Jahrhundert. ZVL, 12.
Wolff, E. Die Sturm und Drang-Komödien und ihre fremden Vorbilder. ZVL, 1.

2. Individual Authors and Works.

(If source is a single foreign author, see, of course, under that author. For many source-items not mentioned here [e.g. on Cain, Roland, etc.] see under the chapter on Thematology. See also under Collective Influences, III. III. 13.)

Orcibal, J. Les sources étrangères du Cherubinischer Wandersmann (1657) d' après la bibliothèque d'**ANGELUS SILESIUS.** RLC, 18, 1938.
Thovez, E. I fonti segreti del Signor d'**ANNUNZIO.** Gaz. letteraria, 18.I. 1896.
Croce, B. Fonti dannunziane Critica, 8, 1910.
Duplessy, L. Quelques sources de Gabriele d'Annunzio. MF, 15.XI.1934.
Rajna, P. Le fonti dell' Orlando Furioso (**ARIOSTO**). Firenze, 1876.
Steins, F. Die Quellen von **BALZACS** Roman La Peau de chagrin. ZFSL, 36, 1910.
Vianey, J. Les antiquitez de Rome (Du **BELLAY**), leurs sources latines et italiennes. BI, 1, 1921.
Bartoli, A. I precursori del **BOCCACCIO.** Firenze, 1876.
Duméril, E. Des sources du Décameron et de ses imitations. In: Histoire de la poésie scandinave. Paris, 1839.
Francia, L. di. Alcune novelle del Decameron illustrate nelle fonti. GSLI, 49, 1907.
Groeber, G. Ueber die Quellen von Boccaccio's Dekameron. Strassburg, 1913.
Landau, M. Die Quellen des Dekameron. Stuttgart, 1884.
Lee, A. C. The Decameron, Its Sources and Analogues. London, 1909.
Löhmann, O. Die Rahmenerzählung des Decameron, ihre Quellen und Nachwirkungen. Halle, 1935.
Schofield, W. H. The Source and History of the Seventh Novel of the Seventh Day. Boston, 1899.
Ibershoff, C. H. **BODMER** as a Literary Borrower. PhQ, 1922.
Berdoe, E. The **BROWNING** Cyclopaedia. London, 1931.
Holmes, S. T. The Sources of Browning's Sordello. SPh, 1937.
Moulton, R. G. Balanstion's Adventure as a Beautiful Misrepresentation of the Original. Browning Society Papers, 3, 1891.
Koch, L. De Musset, Feuillet, Turgenief en **BUSKEN HUETS'** Lidenejde. De nieuwe Taalgids, 20, 1928.
Cotton, E. **CADALSO** and his Foreign Sources. BSS, 1940.
Olmedo, F. G. Las fuentes de la Vida es sueño (**CALDERON**). Madrid, 1928.
Acchiardi, P. Antecedentes de La Vida es sueño. Instituto nacional de estudios de teatro, 12, Buenos Aires, 1940.
Icaza, F. A. Las novelas ejemplares de **CERVANTES** . . . sus modelos literarios. Madrid, 1901.
Koeppel, E. Quellen-Studien zu den Dramen G. **CHAPMANS**, Ph. Massingers und J. Fords. Strassburg, 1897.
Dempsey, M. A Contribution to the Sources of the Génie du Christianisme (**CHATEAUBRIAND**). Paris, 1928.
Chinard, G. Quelques origines littéraires de René. MLN, 1928.
Bryan, W. F. & Dempster, Germaine. Sources and Analogues of **CHAUCER'S** Canterbury Tales, Chicago, 1941.
Tatlock, J. S. P. Development and Chronology of Chaucer's Works. Chaucer Society, 1907.
Ungemach, H. Die Quellen der fünf ersten **CHESTER** Plays. Archiv, 86, 1891.
Lefèvre, F. Les sources de Paul **CLAUDEL.** Paris, 1927.
Riddle, L. M. The Genesis and Sources of Pierre **CORNEILLE'S** Tragedies from Médée to Pertharite. Baltimore, 1926.
Boorsch, J. L'invention chez Corneille. Comment Corneille ajoute à ses sources. Mélanges Albert Feuillerat. New Haven, 1943.
Guggenheim, J. Quellenstudien zu S. **DANIELS** Sonettencyklus Delia. Berlin, 1898.
Anon. The Sources of the Divina Commedia (**DANTE**). NAR, 1847.
Ancona, A. d'. I precursori di Dante. Firenze, 1874.
Delff, H. K. Dante und seine Meister. JbDG, 4, 1877.
Gorra, E. Per la genesi della Divina Commedia. In: Fra drammi e poemi. Milano, 1899.
Labitte, C. La Divine Comédie avant Dante, les prédécesseurs et les inspirateurs de Dante. RDM, 1.IX.1842.
Ozanam, A. F. Etudes sur les sources poétiques de la Divine Comédie. Paris, 1845. Cf. Correspondant, 9, 1845.
Savj-Lopez, P. Precursori spagnuoli di Dante. GD, 4, 1896.
Albrecht, L. **DRYDEN'S** Sir Martin Mar-All in Bezug auf seine Quellen. Diss. Rostock, 1906.
Allen, N. B. The Sources of Dryden's Comedies. Ann Arbor, 1935.
Jünemann, W. Drydens Fabeln und ihre Quellen. Hamburg, 1932.

Zeidler, V. Die Quellen von Rudolphs von **EMS** Wilhelm. ZVL, 1895.
Appelt, T. C. Studies in the Contents and Sources of **ERASMUS'** Adagia. Chicago, 1942.
Kriaras, E. Recherches sur les sources de l'**EROTOKRITOS**, poème crétois du XVIIIe siècle. Athènes, 1938.
Brereton, G. Quelques précisions sur les sources d'**ESPRONCEDA**. Paris, 1933.
Stiefel, A. L. Ueber die Quellen von J. **FLETCHERS** Island Princess. Archiv, 103, 1899.
Günther. Die Quellen der Fabeln **FLORIANS**. Progr. Plauen, 1900.
Fleury, V. Les sources de **FREILIGRATH**. RG, 1922.
Lunn, H. C. How Theophile **GAUTIER** Made Use of his Sources in Le Roman de la Mamie. FQ, 1919.
Coleman, A. Some Sources of the Roman de la Mamie. MPh, 1922.
Hammer, J. Les sources de **GEOFFREY DE MONMOUTH**, Historia regum Britanniae. Latomus, 5, 1946.
Machin, I. W. **GIBBON'S** Debt to Contemporary Scholarship. RES, 1939.
Ellmer, W. Ueber die Quellen der Reimchronik Roberts von **GLOUCESTER**. Halle, 1886.
Davidson, L. J. Forerunners of **GOLDSMITH'S** The Citizen of the World. MLN, 1921.
Baudin, M. Une source de She Stoops to Conquer. PMLA, 1930.
Pruvost, R. Robert **GREENE** et ses romans. Paris, 1938.
Lambert, E. Eine Untersuchung über die Quellen der Jüdin von Toledo (**GRILLPARZER**). JbGrG, 19, 1910.
Haase, F. K. Die altenglischen Bearbeitungen von **GROSSETESTES** Chateau d'amour verglichen mit der Quelle. Anglia, 12, 1889.
Pariser, L. Quellenstudien zu Andreas **GRYPHIUS'** Trauerspiel Katharina von Georgien. ZVL, 5.
Neubauer, K. Zur Quellenfrage von Andreas Gryphius' Cardenio und Celinde. SVL, 2, 1902.
Spencer, F. E. & Schevill, E. The Dramatic Works of Luis **VELEZ DE GUEVARA**: Their Plots, Sources and Bibliography. Berkeley, 1937.
Arnandoff, J. W. **HAUFFS** Märchen und Novellen. Quellenforschungen und stilistische Untersuchungen. Diss. München, 1915.
Thauiès, R. Etude sur les sources de J. M. de **HEREDIA** dans les 57 premiers sonnets des Trophées. RLR, 53, 1910.
Baldensperger, F. Les grands thèmes romantiques dans les Burgraves de V. **HUGO**. Archiv, 1908.
Giraud, J. Etudes sur quelques sources des Burgraves. RHLF, 1909.
O'Connor, Sister Mary I. A Study of the Sources of Han d'Islande and Their Significance in the Literary Development of V. Hugo. Diss. Catholic U. of America, 1942.
Cornell, J. G. A propos des notes sur les sources de la préface de Cromwell. RHLF, 1936.
Frick, R. Hernanis Stammbaum. ZVL, 17.
Huguet, E. Quelques sources de Notre Dame de Paris. RHLF, 8, 1901.
Koeppel, E. Quellenstudien zu den Dramen Ben **JONSONS**, J. Marstons, Beaumonts und Fletchers. Münchener Beiträge. Erlangen, 1895.
Espiner-Scott, J. G. Louise **LABE'S** Sources. CLS, 6-8, 1942.
Guillemin, H. Le Jocelyn de **LAMARTINE**. Paris, 1936.
Ehrhard, M. A. L. Sources historiques des Maximes de **LA ROCHEFOUCAULD**. Diss. Heidelberg, 1891.
Schmidt, E. Quellen der komischen Einfälle und Züge **LESSINGS**. SAWB, 1897.
—— Quellen und Parallelen zu Lessing. Euphorion, 8, 1901.
Morin, P. Les sources de l'oeuvre d'Henry Wadsworth **LONGFELLOW**. Paris, 1913.
Varnhagen, H. Longfellow's Tales of a Wayside Inn und ihre Quellen, nebst Nachweisen und Untersuchungen über die vom Dichter bearbeiteten Stoffe. Berlin, 1884.
Worden, J. P. Longfellow's Tales and Their Origin. Anglia, 23, 1900. Cf. Anglia Bb, 13, 1902.
Jameson, A. K. The Sources of **LOPE DE VEGA'S** Erudition. HR, 1937.
Burd, L. A. Le fonti letterarie di **MACHIAVELLI** nell' Arte della guerra. Atti d. R. Accad. dei Licei, Roma, 1897.
Gilbert, A. H. Machiavelli's Prince and its Forerunners. Duke U.P., 1938.
Ptasnik, G. Un precursore di Machiavelli in Polonia (Filippo Buonacorsi detto Callimaco). Europa orientale, 18, 1938.
Counson, A. **MALHERBE** et ses sources. Liège, 1905.
Busetto, N. La genesi e la formazione dei Promessi Sposi (**MANZONI**). Bologna, 1921.
Orne, J. The Sources of I Promessi Sposi. MPh, 38, 1940-41.

Telle, E. V. La source de la nouvelle 55 de l'Heptaméron (**MARGUERITE DE NAVARRE**). RR, 39, 1948.
Mango, F. Le fonti dell' Adone del **MARINO**. Palermo, 1891.
Harrison, T. P. Further Background for the Jew of Malta and The Massacre of Paris (**MARLOWE**). PhQ, 1948.
Guy, H. De fontibus Clementis **MAROTI** poetae; antiqui et medii aevi scriptores. Diss. Paris, 1898.
Ortiz, R. Dall' indifferenza alla libertà: radicie propaggini francesi, rumene e spagnuole della Libertà di Pietro **METASTASIO**. In: Varia romanica. Firenze, 1932.
Langlois, E. Origines et sources du Roman de la Rose. (Jean de **MEUNG**). Paris, 1890.
Hardaway, R. T. C. F. **MEYER'S** Der Heilige in Relation to Its Sources. PMLA, 58, 1943.
Essarts, E. des. Les prédécesseurs de **MILTON**. Clermont-Ferrand, 1874.
Lander, W. An Essay on Milton's Use and Imitation of the Moderns in his Paradise Lost. London, 1750.
McColley, G. Paradise Lost. An Account of its Growth and the Major Origins, with a Discussion of Milton's Use of Sources and Literary Patterns. Chicago, 1940.
Scheludko, D. Quellen und Vorbilder von **MISTRALS** Calendan. Diss. Halle, 1931.
Knoerich, W. Die Quellen des Avare von **MOLIERE**. ZFSL, 8, 1886.
Villey, P. Les sources et l'évolution des Essais de **MONTAIGNE**. 2 vols. Paris, 1908, 1933.
Fey, E. Der literarische Charakter **MUSSETS** und das Problem seiner Beeinflussung. Erlangen, 1933.
Giraud, J. Notes sur quelques sources de la Coupe et les Lèvres d'A. de Musset. RU, 15.II & 15.III.1912.
Constans, F. Artemis ou les fleurs du désespoir. Etude sur les sources et la portée d'un sonnet de Gérard de **NERVAL**. RLC, 14, 1934.
Ancona, A. d'. Le fonti del **NOVELLINO**. In: Studi di critica e storia lett. Bologna, 1880.
Sarrazin, G. Ueber die Quellen des **ORMULUM**. ESn, 6, 1883.
Hassell, J. W. A Study of the Sources of the First Forty-five of the Nouvelles Récréations et Joyeux Devis. (Des **PERIERS**). Diss. U. of N.C., 1941.
Saintyves. Les contes de **PERRAULT** et les récits parallèles, leurs origines. Paris, 1923.
Nozick, M. A Source of Don **RAMON DE LA CRUZ**. MLN, 1948.
Castro Guisasola, F. Observaciones sobre las fuentes literarias de la Celestina. (F. de **ROJAS**). Madrid, 1924.
Lancaster, H. C. The Ultimate Source of **ROTROU'S** Venceslas and of Rojas Zorrilla's No hay ser padre siendo rey. MPh, 15.
Stiefel, A. L. Jean Rotrou's Cosroes und seine Quellen. ZFSL, 23.
Havens, G. R. The Sources of **ROUSSEAU'S** Edouard Bomston. MPh, 17, 1919. Cf. MLN, 35, 1920.
Krueger, G. Fremde Gedanken in J. J. Rousseaus erstem Discours. Diss. Halle, 1886.
Lida, María R. Notas para la interpretación, influencia, fuentes y texto del Libro de Buen Amor (Juan **RUIZ**, Arcipreste de Hita). RFH, 2, 1940.
Geiger, E. Hans **SACHS** als Dichter in seinen Fastnachtspielen im Verhältnis zu seinen Quellen betrachtet. Halle, 1904.
Stiefel, A. L. Zu den Quellen der Fabeln und Schwänke des Hans Sachs. SVL, 2.
—— Ueber die Quellen der Hans Sachsischen Dramen. Germania, 36, 1903.
Krappe, A. H. Les sources du Libro de exemplos (C. **SANCHEZ**). BH, 39, 1937.
Poll, M. Die Fabeln von G. C. **SCHEFFEL** und ihre Quellen. Strassburg, 1888.
Abramczyk, R. Ueber die Quellen zu W. **SCOTT'S** Roman Ivanhoe. Diss. Halle, 1903.
Schweitzer, J. W. Georges de **SCUDERY'S** Almahide. Authorship, Sources and Structure. Baltimore, 1939.
Schroeder, A. E. New Sources of Charles **SEALSFIELD**. JEGPh, 46, 1947.
Plueckhahn, E. Die Bearbeitung ausländischer Stoffe im englischen Drama am Ende des 17. Jahrhunderts dargelegt an Sir Charles **SEDLEY'S** The Mulberry Garden und Bellamira or the Mistress. Diss. Rostock, 1904.
Allen, P. **SHAKESPEARE**, Jonson and Wilkins as Borrowers. London, 1928.
Boas, F. S. Shakespeare and his Predecessors. New York, 1936.
Bullough, G. The Murder of Gonzago (a possible source of Hamlet). MLR, 30, 1935.
Collins, J. C. The Predecessors of Shakespeare. QR, 141, 1885.
Dempewolf, W. Shakespeares angebliche Modelle. Jena, 1914.
Eschenburg, J. J. Ueber Shakespeares

Gelehrsamkeit. In: Ueber W. Shakespeare. Zürich, 1787.
Farmer, R. An Essay on the Learning of Shakespeare. Cambridge, 1767. Cf. E. Malone: A Letter to the Rev. Richard Farmer Relative to the Editor of Shakespeare publ. in 1790. London, 1792.
Fleay, F. G. On Shakespeare's Knowledge of Foreign Languages. Literary World, 16. (Boston), 1883.
Guttman, Selma. The Foreign Sources of Shakespeare's Works. New York, 1947.
Lanier, S. Shakespeare and his Forerunners. 2 vols. New York, 1902.
Lennox, Mrs. Shakespeare Illustrated; or, the Novels and Histories on which the Plays of Shakespeare are founded, collected and translated from the original Authors, with critical Remarks. 3 vols. London, 1753-54.
Messiaen, P. L'érudition de Shakespeare. RB, May, 1939.
Simrock, K. et al. Quellen des Shakespeare in Novellen, Märchen und Sagen. 4 vols. Berlin, 1831.
Whitaker, V. K. Shakespeare's Use of his Sources. Festschrift Hardin Craig, PhQ, 20, 1941.
Meissner, H. Die Quellen zu Shakespeare's Was ihr wollt. Progr. Lyck, 1895.
Groene, J. Zwei neu entdeckte Quellen zu Shakespeares Komödie der Irrungen. JbShG, 1894.
Leonhardi, B. Ueber die Quellen Cymbelines. Anglia, 6, 1883.
Ohle, R. Ueber die romanischen Vorläufer von Shakespeares Cymbeline. Diss. Leipzig, 1890. Cf. G. Paris. Miscellanea A. Graf. Bergamo, 1903.
Caro, J. Sources of Shakespeare's Love's Labor's Lost. Steinhausens Zs. f. Kulturgeschichte, N.F., 1.
Sarrazin, G. Die Entstehung von Shakespeares Verlorner Liebesmühe. JbShG, 31, 1895.
Phelps, J. The Source of Love's Labour's Lost. SAB, 12, 1942.
Stoll, E. E. Source and Motive in Macbeth and Othello. RES, 19.
Proescholdt, L. On the Sources of Shakespeare's Midsummer Night's Dream. Diss. Halle, 1878.
Weichberger, K. Die Urquelle von Shakespeares Much Ado about Nothing. JbShG, 1898.
Holleck-Weithmann, F. Zur Quellenfrage von Shakespeares Lustspiel Much Ado About Nothing. Kieler Studien. Heidelberg, 1902.
Urbach, R. Das Verhältnis des Shakespeareschen Lustspiels The Taming of the Shrew zu seinen Quellen. Diss. Rostock, 1887.
Dorrer, E. Die Quelle zu Shakespeares Sturm. MLIA, 1885.
Perott, J. The Probable Source of the Plot of Shakespeares Tempest. Publ. of the Clark U. Library, 1905.
Gray, H. D. The Sources of the Tempest. MLN, 1920.
Ackermann, R. Quellen, Vorbilder, Stoffe zu **SHELLEY'S** poetischen Werken. Münchener Beiträge. Erlangen, 1890.
Sweet, H. A Source of Shelley's Alastor. Festschrift Dr. Furnivall. London, 1901.
Hertmann, H. Ueber die Vorlagen zu **SHERIDANS** Rivals. Diss. Königsberg, 1888.
Knecht, H. Ueber Sprache und Quelle des mittelenglischen Heldengedichts von dem **SOWDAN OF BABYLON**. ZRPh, 3, 1879.
Bennett, Josephine W. The Evolution of The Faerie Queene (**SPENSER**). Chicago, 1942.
Hankins, J. E. The Sources of Spenser's Britomartis. MLN, 58.
Jones, H. S. V. Spenser's Defense of Lord Grey. Urbana, 1919.
McPeek, J. A. S. The Major Sources of Spenser's Epithalamion. JEGPh, 1936.
Eddy, W. A. A Source for Gulliver's Travels (**SWIFT**). MLN, 1921.
Faggi, A. Le fonti dei viaggi di Gulliver. Marzocco, 1924.
Poll, M. The Sources of Gulliver's Travels. Bull. U. of Cincinnati, 3.II.1909.
Vivaldi, V. Sulle fonti della Gerusalemme liberata. (**TASSO**). Catanzaro, 1893.
Multineddu, S. Le fonti della Gerusalemme liberata. Sassari, 1895.
Stiefel, A. L. **TRISTAN** l'Hermites Le Parasite und seine Quelle. Archiv, 86, 1891.
Suchier, H. Ueber die Quelle Ulrichs von dem **TURLIN** und die älteste Gestalt der Prise d'Orange. Marburg, 1873.
Eichholtz, P. Quellenstudien zu **UHLANDS** Balladen. Berlin, 1878.
Rochet, H. L'Astrée, ses origines, son importance dans la formation de la littérature classique. (d'**URFE**). Diss. Genève, 1923.
Rice, W. H. The European Ancestry of **VILLON'S** Satirical Testaments. Syracuse U. Monographs, 1, 1941.
Seele, W. **VOLTAIRE'S** Roman Zadig ou la Destinée. Eine Quellen-Forschung. Leipzig, 1891. Cf. RFE, 7

Krappe, A. H. The Sources of Voltaire's Zaïre. MLR, 20, 1925.
Koehler, R. Die Quelle von WIELANDS Hann und Gulpenheh. ALG. 3, 1874.
Goodale, O. Some of Walt WHITMAN'S Borrowings. AL, 10, 1938.
Bernacki, L. Les sources de quelques comédies de ZABLOCKI. In: Mémoires littéraires. Cracovie, 1907.

CHAPTER THREE

Originality, Influence, Imitation, Plagiarism.

Anon. Progress of Plagiarism. Monthly Mirror, 1796-97.
Adkins, N. F. Chapter on American Cribbage : Poe and Plagiarism. Papers Bibliograph. Soc. of America, 42, 1948.
Arnould, E. De l'invention originale. Paris, 1849.
Auriant. Un écrivain original: M. André Maurois. MF, 202, 1928.
Bandy, W. T. A propos des plagiats présumés de Gérard de Nerval. RLC, 23, 1949.
Barine, A. Des influences étrangères en littérature. Journal des Débats, 8.I.1895.
Batteux, Abbé. Les beaux-arts réduits à un seul principe (imitation). Paris, 1746.
Bignan, A. Des traductions et de l'imitation. MF, 1928.
Bozzelli, F. Della imitazione tragica. Firenze, 1861.
Brechler, O. Kontagiösität des Geistes. Wien, 1926.
Cajot, D. J. Les plagiats de J. J. Rousseau sur l'éducation. La Haye, 1766.
Carré, J. M. Les problèmes d'influence en littérature comparée. Davoser Revue, 15.V.1929.
Cazamian, L. Quelques réflexions sur les problèmes d'influence. RG, 12, 1921.
Croiset, Bloch et al. L'imitation des littératures étrangères. Bull. de la Société des humanistes français, 1.IV.1896.
DeClerq, W. Verhandeling over den invloed der vreemde letterkunden. Amsterdam, 1824.
Duclos. Sur l'imitation en littérature. In: Mémoires de l'Académie des Inscriptions et Belles-Lettres, 1751.
Eisenstaedter, J. Elementargedanke und Uebertragungstheorie in der Völkerkunde. Stuttgart, 1912.
Englisch, P. Meister des Plagiats, oder die Kunst der Abschriftstellerei. Berlin, 1933.
Flamini, F. I plagi di F. Desportes. In: Studi di storia letteraria e straniera. Livorno, 1895.
France, A. Apologie pour le plagiat. In: La vie littéraire, 4.
Gide, A. Les influences en littérature. In: Prétextes. Paris, 1903.
Gmelin, H. Das Prinzip der Imitatio in den romanischen Literaturen der Renaissance. Erlangen, 1932.
Gourmont, R. de. L'influence étrangère. In: Le problème du style. Paris, 1902.
Grandgent, C. H. Imitation and Other Essays. Harvard U.P., 1934.
Hallays, A. De l'influence des littératures étrangères. RP, 15.II.1895.
Hazard, P. Les plagiats de Stendhal. RDM, 1921.
Izambart, G. Le plagiat en 1895. RB, 15.II.1896.
Jasinski, R. La Duchesse d'Abrantès, plagiaire. Annales de l'U. de Paris, 1947.
Kraemer, C. J. On Imitation and Originality. CW, 20.
La Drière, C. Horace and the Theory of Imitation. AJPh, 1939.
Mann, Elizabeth. The Problem of Originality in English Literary Criticism, 1750-1800. PhQ, 18, 1939.
Margraf, H. Goethe von einem Franzosen des Plagiats beschuldigt. Blätter f. literar. Unterhaltung, 3.IX.1863.
Maurevert, G. Le livre des plagiats. Paris, 1923.
Nisard. Discours de réponse à Saint-René Taillandier à l'Académie, 22.I.1874.
Nodier, C. Questions de littérature légale. Paris, 1812.
Peyre, H. André Gide et les problèmes d'influence en littérature. MLN, 57, 1942.
Schwabe, J. C. Wie kann die Nachahmung sowohl alter als neuer fremder Werke der schönen Wissenschaften den vaterländischen Geschmack entwickeln und vervollkommen? Berlin, 1789.
Stemplinger, E. Das Plagiat in der griechischen Literatur. Berliner Philolog. Wochenschrift, 1914.
Stranik, E. Ueber das Wesen des Plagiats. DR, 211, 1927.
—— Plagiat in der Literatur. Prisma, 6, 1930.
Thilorier. Discours sur l'émulation des nations de l'Europe. Académie de La Rochelle, 15. VI. 1747 & MF, 1749.
Van Tieghem, P. Influences et simultanéités en histoire littéraire. RR, 1929.
White, H. O. Plagiarism and Imitation During the English Renaissance: A Study in Critical Distinction. Harvard U.P., 1935.

SIXTH PART

Literary Themes (Stoffgeschichte)

CHAPTER ONE

Generalities.

Bauerhorst, K. Bibliographie der Stoff- und Motivgeschichte der deutschen Literatur. Leipzig, 1933.
Baym, M. I. Recurrent Poetic Themes. SAB, 12, 1937.
Gilbert, P. Thèmes littéraires méditerranéens. Chronique d'Egypte, 19, 1944.
Hoffmann, Käte. Themen der französischen Lyrik im 12. und 13. Jahrhundert. Freiburg, 1936.
Karpa, L. Themen der französischen Lyrik im 17. Jahrhundert. Diss. Bonn, 1933.
Körner, J. Erlebnis-Motiv-Stoff. In: Festschrift O. Walzel, Potsdam 1924.
Leroux, P. V. Dictionnaire comique, satirique, critique, burlesque, libre et proverbial. Paris, 1750.
Ludwig, A. Motivstudien zur neueren Literaturgeschichte. Berlin-Lichterfelde, 1913.
Petersen, J. Das Motiv in der Dichtung. D&V, 38, 1937.
Poritzky, I. E. Austausch literarischer Stoffe und Formen in der Weltliteratur. Literatur, 12, 1930.
Rotunda, D. P. A Tabulation of Early Italian Tales. Berkeley, 1930.
—— Motif-Index of the Italian Novella in Prose. Indiana U. Publications, 1942.
Sauer, E. Bemerkungen zum Versuch einer Stoffgeschichte. Euphorion, 26, 1925.
Taylor, A. The Themes Common to English and German Poetry. MLQ, 1940.
Vulpius, C. A. Curiositäten der physischen, literarischen, artistischen, historischen Vor- und Mitwelt. 10 vols. Weimar, 1811-25.

CHAPTER TWO

Fables and Fabliaux.

(See also Chapter Nine on Individual Authors and Eleven on Animals)

Bédier, J. Les fabliaux; étude de littérature populaire et d'histoire littéraire au moyen âge. Paris, 1893. 5th ed., 1925.
Cederschiold & Wulff. Versions nordiques du fabliau français Le Mantel mautaillié. Lund, 1877.
Cesari, A. Il fabliau francese e la novella italiana. Vita italiana, N.S., 2, 1896.
Ebeling, E. Die babylonische Fabel und ihre Bedeutung für die Literaturgeschichte. Leipzig, 1927.
Hart, W. M. The fabliau and Popular Literature. PMLA, 23, 1908.
Hervieux, L. Les fabulistes latins depuis le siècle d'Auguste jusqu'à la fin du moyen âge. 2 vols. Paris. 1884 and 1893-99.
Heybroek, J. E. De fabel. Ontwikkeling van een litteratuursoort in Noord-Nederland en in Vlaanderen. Amsterdam, 1941.
Hjertén, I. Fabel och anekdot inom Sveriges 1700-talslitteratur. Stockholm, 1910.
Julien, S. Contes et apologues indiens, inconnus jusqu'à ce jour, suivis de fables et de poésies chinoises. Paris, 1860.
Keller, O. Untersuchung über die Geschichte der griechischen Fabel. Jb. für class. Philologie. Leipzig, 1861-67.
Lange, M. Vom Fabliau zu Boccaccio und Chaucer. Hamburg, 1935.
Loiseleur-Deslongchamps, A. Essai sur les fables indiennes et sur leur introduction en Europe. Paris, 1838.
Neri, F. Fiabe. L'Erma, 5 (Torino), 1934.
Newbigging, T. Fables and Fabulists. Papers of the Manchester Literary Club, 13, 1894.
Plessow, M. Geschichte der Fabeldichtung in England bis zu John Gay (1726). Berlin, 1906.
Smith, M. E. The Fable and Kindred Forms. JEGPh, 14, 1915.
Staege, M. Die Geschichte der deutschen Fabeltheorie. Sprache & Dichtung, Bern.
Ursing, U. Studien zur griechischen Fabel. Lund, 1930.
Wache, K. Die Tierfabel in der Weltliteratur. Zs. f.d. österreichischen Gymnasien, 69, 1919.
Weber. Ueber indische und griechische Fabeln. Indische Studien, 3. Berlin, 1870.
Weddigen, O. Das Wesen und die Theorie der Fabel und ihre Hauptvertreter in Deutschland. Leipzig, 1893.
Weinreich, O. Fabel, Aretalogie, Novelle. Beiträge zu Phädrus, Petron, Martial und Apuleius. SHAW, 1930.

Wienert, W. Die Typen der griechisch-römischen Fabel, mit einer Einleitung über das Wesen der Fabel. Helsingfors, 1925.

CHAPTER THREE

Fairy Tales.

Anon. La féerie considérée dans la littérature. Le Globe, 11 & 13.I.1827.
Aarne, A. Leitfaden der vergleichenden Märchenforschung. Helsinki, 1910.
—— Verzeichnis der Märchentypen. Helsinki, 1910.
Benz, R. Die Märchendichtung der Romantiker. Gotha, 1908.
Burnell. Samavidhana Brahmana (Introduction). London, 1873.
Cumings, E. K. The Literary Development of the Romantic Fairy-Tale in France. Bryn Mawr, 1934.
Denewa, W. S. Das österreichische Märchendrama in der Biedermeierzeit. Berlin, 1940.
Eberhard, A. Wandernde Märchen. Neue Zürcher Zt., 21.III.1947.
Eberhard, W. Typen chinesischer Volksmärchen. Helsinki, 1937.
Eckhardt, E. Ein irisches Volksmärchen und seine literarische Sippe. GRM, 31, 1943.
Ehrentreich, A. Gibt es angloamerikanische Volksmärchen? ZNS, 1943.
Engel, E. Deutsche Kindermärchen in englischer Bearbeitung. MLIA, 1879.
Fife, R. H. The German Romantic Märchen. MPh, 9, 1911-12.
Gaster, M. The Modern Origin of Fairy-Tales. FL, 1887.
Goebel, F. M. Jüdische Motive im märchenhaften Erzählungsgut. Diss. Greifswald, 1932.
Grimm, W. Kleinere Schriften. Berlin, 1883.
Gunkel, H. Das Märchen im Alten Testament. DLZ, 1919.
Guterman, N. Russian Fairy Tales. New York, 1945.
Hahn, J. G. von. Griechische und Albanesische Märchen. Leipzig, 1864.
Hartland, E. S. The Science of Fairy Tales. London, 1891.
Hausrath, A. Germanische Märchenmotive in griechischen Tierfabeln. NJWJ, 1937.
Huttemann, W. Eigenes und Fremdes im deutschen Volksmärchen. ZVL, 15, 1904.
Jacob, G. Märchen und Traum mit besonderer Berücksichtigng des Orients. Hannover, 1923.
Jehle, Mimi I. Das deutsche Kunstmärchen von der Romantik zum Naturalismus. Illinois Stud. in Lang. and Lit., 1935.
Katann, O. Das Kunstmärchen. Der Gral, 19, 1935.
Koechlin, E. Wesenszüge des deutschen und französischen Volksmärchens. Basel, 1945.
Koehler, R. Aufsätze über Märchen und Volkslieder. Ed. by Johannes Bolte & E. Schmidt. Berlin, 1894.
Lambertz, M. Vom goldenen Horn. Griechische Märchen aus dem Mittelalter. Leipzig, 1922.
Lenz, L. Die neuesten englischen Märchensammlungen und ihre Quellen. Kassel, 1902.
Leskoschek, A. von. Märchen und Legenden aus den Gesta Romanorum. Leipzig, 1926.
Leyen, F. von der. Das Märchen. Berlin, 1911.
Lüders, E. Buddhistische Märchen (mit einer Einleitung). Jena, 1921.
Lüthi, M. Das europäische Volksmärchen: Form und Wesen. Bern, 1947.
Müller, M. Ueber die Wanderung der Märchen. In: Essays. Leipzig, 1870.
Naumann, H. Märchennovelle und Märchenmotiv. In: Faust, eine Monatsschrift. Berlin, 1923-24.
Niebergall, V. Die Bedeutung des Märchens für die Welt des antiken Geistes. In: Die Welt als Geschichte. Stuttgart, 1942.
Panzer, F. Märchen, Sage und Dichtung. München, 1905.
Pieper, M. Das ägyptische Märchen. Ursprung und Nachwirkung ältester Märchendichtung bis zur Gegenwart. Morgenland, 27.
Pratt, F. From the Fairy Tale of Science to the Science of Fairy Tale. Pacific Spectator, 2, 1948.
Ranke, F. Märchenforschung. Ein Literaturbericht. DVLG, 1936.
Rosenfeld, P. The Conscious Faerie-Tale: History of the Origin of a Romantic Genre. Commonweal, 43, 1946.
Rutgers, H. W. Märchen und Sage. Groningen, 1923.
Schmidt, B. Griechische Märchen, Sagen, und Volkslieder. Leipzig, 1877.
Spanner, W. Das Märchen als Gattung. Giessen, 1939.
Spence, L. The Fairy Tradition in Britain. London, 1948.
Stemplinger, E. Antike Motive in deutschen Märchen. NJKA, 1922.
Storer, M. La mode des contes de fées, 1685 à 1700. Paris, 1928.

Sydow, C. W. von. Das Märchen als indogermanische Tradition. Niederdeutsche Zs. für Volkskunde, 4, 1926.
Thimme, A. Antike Märchen in deutschem Gewande. Grenzboten, 45, 1886.
Uffer, L. Rätoromanische Märchen und ihre Erzähler. Basel, 1945.
Wesselski, A. Versuch einer Theorie des Märchens. Reichenberg, 1930.

CHAPTER FOUR

Folklore.

(See also Popular Literature, I. VII. 2.)

Abbot, G. F. Macedonian Folklore. Cambridge, 1903.
Astley, H. J. D. Biblical Anthropology Compared with and illustrated by the Folklore of Europe and the Customs of Primitive Peoples. London, 1929.
Benfey, T. Kleinere Schriften. Ed. by Bezzenberger. Berlin, 1892.
Boggs, R. S. Bibliography of Latin American Folklore. New York, 1940.
—— Folklore in Pan Americanism. U. of Miami Hispanic-American Studies, 1, 1940.
—— Spanish Folklore in America. Ibid.
—— The Development of Folklore in a University. SPh, 42, 1945.
Bonneau, G. L'expression poétique dans le folk-lore japonais. 3 vols. Paris, 1933.
Brand, J. Observations on Popular Antiquities. 2 vols. London, 1813.
Brewer, J. M. Negro Folklore in North America: A Field of Research. New Mexico Quarterly Rev., 16, 1946.
Browney, W. J. Essay in Slavonic Folklore. Contemporary Rev., 156, 1939.
Butterworth, W. Celtic Song and Folklore. Papers of the Manchester Literary Club, 13, 1894.
Clough, W. O. Has American Folklore a Special Quality? SFQ, 8, 1944.
Cosquin, E. Etude de folk-lore comparé. Le conte de la chaudière bouillante et la feinte maladresse dans l'Inde et hors de l'Inde. Rennes, 1910.
Dennys, N. B. The Folklore of China and its Affinities With That of the Aryan and Semitic Races. London, 1876.
Frazer, J. G. Folk-lore in the Old Testament. Studies in Comparative Religion, Legend, and Law. London, 1919 & Paris, 1924.
Gaidoz, H. De l'influence de l'Académie celtique sur les études de folklore. Paris, 1807. Cf. Livre du Centenaire de la Société nationale des antiquaires de France, 1904.
Gaster, M. Studies and Texts in Folklore, Magic, Medieval Romance. 3 vols. London, 1925-28.
Genner, A. van. Manuel de folk-lore français contemporain. Paris, 1938.
Gielen, J. J. Folklore en thematologie. NPh, 20, 1935.
Halliday, W. R. Folklore Studies Ancient and Modern. London, 1924.
—— Greek and Roman Folklore. In: Our Debt to Greece and Rome. New York, 1927.
Herskovits, M. J. Folklore After a Hundred Years: A Problem in Redefinition. JAFL, 59, 1946.
Jameson, R. D. Three Lectures on Chinese Folklore. Peiping, 1932.
Kaun, A. Folk Motives in Soviet Poetry. American Rev. of the Soviet Union, 4, 1941.
Köhler, R. Kleinere Schriften. 3 vols. Weimar, 1898-1900.
Krappe, A. H. The Science of Folklore. London, 1930.
Krauss, S. Jewish Giants in the Gentile Folklore. Jewish Quart. Review, 38, 1948.
Krohn, K. Die folkloristische Arbeitsmethode. Oslo, 1926.
Lawson, J. C. Modern Greek Folklore and Ancient Greek Religion. Cambridge, 1910.
Leisy, E. E. Folklore in American Literature. College English, 8, 1946.
Lichtenstaedter, I. Folklore and Fairy-Tale Motifs in Early Arabic Literature. Folklore, 51, 1940.
Lomax, A., & Cowell, S. R. American Folk Song and Folk Lore: A Regional Bibliography. New York, 1942.
McCartney, E. S. The Lure of Greek and Roman Folklore. Michigan Alumnus, 41, 1935.
Monnier, D., & Vingtrinier, A. Traditions populaires comparées. Paris, 1854.
Patai, R. Problems and Tasks of Jewish Folklore and Ethnology. JAFL, 59, 1946.
Pitre, G. Bibliografia delle tradizioni popolari in Italia. Torino, 1894.
Rappoport, A. S. The Folklore of the Jews. London, 1937.
Saintyves, P. Essais de folklore biblique. Magie, mythes et miracles dans l'Ancien et le Nouveau Testament. Paris, 1923.
—— Les origines de la méthode comparative et la naissance du folklore. Des superstitions aux survivances. Rev. de l'Hist. des Religions, 105, 1932.
Schlauch, Margaret. Folklore in the Soviet Union. Science & Society, 8, 1944.
Sikes, W. British Goblins: Welsh Folk-

lore, Fairy Mythology, Legends and Traditions. London, 1880.
Sinaiski, V. Théorie du folk-lore comme science ancienne. Annali del R. Istituto Orientale di Napoli, 5, 1932.
Sokolov, I. Le folklore russe. Paris, 1945.
Thompson, S. Motiv-Index of Folk-Literature: a Classification of Narrative Elements in Folk-Tales, Ballads, Myths, Fables, Mediaeval Romances, Exempla, Fabliaux, Jest-Books, and Local Legends. 5 vols. Bloomington, 1932-35.
—— Folklore and Literature. PMLA, 55, 1940.
Tronchon, H. Quelques notes sur le premier mouvement folkloriste en France. Mélanges Baldensperger. Paris, 1930.
Urwin. K. Folklore Influences in Aucassin et Nicolette. CLS, 10, 1943.
Wijnpersse, W. M. A. van de. Le folklore en rapport avec la philologie grecque. Festschrift Schrijnen. Nijmegen, 1929.
Wimberley, L. C. Folklore in the English and Scottish Ballad. U. of Chicago P. 1928.

CHAPTER FIVE

Legends.

Bédier, J. Les légendes épiques. Recherches sur la formation des chansons de geste. 3rd ed. Paris, 1926-29.
Carini, B.di. Leggenda storica popolare del secolo XVI nella poesia siciliana. Palermo, 1873.
Castelli, D. Leggende talmudiche. Pisa, 1869.
Dorson, R. M. New England Popular Tales and Legends. Cambridge (Mass.), 1943.
Eis, G. Beiträge zur mittelhochdeutschen Legende und Mystik. Berlin, 1935.
Franco, A. La leyenda, bosquejo de un estudio folklorico. Buenos Aires, 1940.
Gennep, A. van. La formation des légendes. Paris, 1910.
Ginzberg, L. The Legends of the Jews. 6 vols. Philadelphia, 1909-28.
Gould, B. S. Legends of Old Testament Characters. London, 1871.
Graf, A. Il tramonto delle leggende. In: La Vita italiana nel trecento. Milano, 1891.
Guarducci, M. Leggende dell'antica Grecia relative all'origine dell'umanità, e analoghe tradizioni di altri paesi. Rendiconti della R. Accademia dei Lincei, 6.
Guenther, J. Legende, Mythe, Märchen im neueren Schrifttum. Literatur, 1925.
Herpin, E. Au pays des légendes (Bretagne). Bibliothèque bretonne. (Rennes), 1901.
Ittner, R. T. The Christian Legend in German Literature since Romanticism. Urbana, St. Louis, 1937.
Kern, O. Griechische Kultlegenden. Archiv f. Religionswissenschaft, 26, 1928.
King, L. W. Legends of Babylon and Egypt in Relation to Hebrew Tradition. London, 1916.
Lanzoni, F. Genesi, svolgimento e tramonto leggende storiche. Roma, 1925.
Leon, G. von. Rabbinische Legenden. Wien, 1821.
Leroux de Lincy. Le livre des légendes. Paris, 1836.
Levi, G. Parabole, leggende e pensieri raccolti dai libri talmudici dei primi cinque secoli dell' E.C. Firenze, 1861.
Loomis, C. G. Legend and Folklore. California Folklore Quarterly, 2, 1943.
Luzel. Légendes chrétiennes de la Basse-Bretagne. Paris, 1881.
Maury, A. Essai sur les légendes pieuses du moyen âge. Paris, 1843.
McGrady, S. J. Legends and Myths of Greece and Rome. London, 1936.
Menéndez Pidal. Relaciones entre las leyendas moriscas y las cristianas. Mélanges Marshall Elliott. Baltimore, 1911.
Muro, B. de. Legends of France and Spain. Stamford (Conn.), 1937.
Nissen, T. Zu den ältesten Fassungen der Legende vom Judenknaben. ZFSL, 62, 1939.
Paris, G. Poèmes et légendes du moyen âge (Chanson de Roland; Huon de Bordeaux; Aucassin et Nicolette; Tristan; Saint Josaphat; Infants de Lara; Romance mauresque). Paris, 1900.
—— Légendes du moyen âge (Roncevaux; Paradis de la reine Sibylle; Tannhäuser; Juif errant; le Lai de l'oiselet). Paris, 1903.
Pineau, L. La légende divine et héroïque. In: Les vieux chants populaires scandinaves. Paris, 1901.
Reinsberg-Dueringsfeld. Traditions et légendes de la Belgique. Bruxelles, 1870.
Sparnaay, H. Verschmelzung legendarischer und weltlicher Motive in der Poesie des Mittelalters. Groningen, 1922.
Villemarqué, H. de la. La légende celtique et la poésie des cloîtres en Irlande, en Cambrie et en Bretagne. Paris, 1864.
Waldman, M. Origin and Development of Judeo-German and the Old German Legends. PhQ, 19, 1940.

Zink, G. Derniers échos des légendes allemandes au XVe et au XVIe siècle. EG, 3, 1948.

CHAPTER SIX

Literary Types: Generalities.

(See also Chapter Eleven below.)

Bouzenot, A. De quelques types nationaux en littérature. France littéraire, 8, 1834.

Calvet, J. Les types universels dans la littérature française. 3 vols. Paris, 1932.

Celler, L. Les types populaires au théâtre. Paris, 1870.

Doutrepont, G. Les types populaires de la littérature française. 2 vols. Bruxelles, 1926-28.

Ehrenpreis, J. The Types Approach to Literature. New York, 1945.

Fehr, B. Psychologische Typen in der Literaturgeschichte. NSp, 1923.

Guechot. Types populaires crées par les grands écrivains. Paris, 1907.

Huysmans, C. Quatre types: Le Renard et Ulenspiegel, le Démon et le Diable. Anvers, 1937.

Mantz, H. E. Types in Literature. MLR, 1917.

Montégut, E. Types littéraires et fantaisies esthétiques. Paris, 1882.

Nodier, C. Des types en littérature. RP., 1830. And in: Rêveries littéraires, morales et fantastiques. Bruxelles, 1832.

Piercy, J. K. Studies in Literary Types in 17th Century America. New Haven, 1939.

CHAPTER SEVEN

Myths and Mythology.

(See also Greek, Roman, Hebrew, Germanic Influences.)

Altheim, F. Griechische Götter im alten Rom. Giessen, 1930.

Arbois de Jubainville, H. d'. Le cycle mythologique irlandais et la mythologie grecque. Paris, 1884.

Basler, O. Vom griechischen Mythos zum modernen Humanismus. NSR, June, 1947.

Bechstein, L. Mythe, Sage, Märe und Fabel im Leben und Bewusstsein des deutschen Volkes. Leipzig, 1856.

Beckwith, Martha W. Hawaiian Mythology. New Haven, 1940.

Bethe, E. Mythus, Sage, Märchen. Leipzig, 1922.

Bezold, F. von. Das Fortleben der antiken Götter im mittelalterlichen Humanismus. Bonn, 1922.

Bluemner, H. Die klassische Mythologie in der Metapher. Grenzboten, 18, 1892.

Bourne, E. The Medieval Wanderings of a Greek Myth. JEGPh, 1925.

Bradley, A. C. Old Mythology in Modern Poetry. Macmillan Mag., 1881.

Bush, D. Mythology and the Renaissance Tradition in English Poetry. Minneapolis, 1932.

—— Mythology and the Romantic Tradition in English Poetry. Harvard U.P., 1937.

Chase, R. Myth as Literature. English Institute Essays, 1947.

Clarke, H. A. Ancient Myths in Modern Poets. New York, 1910.

Clemen, C. Die Anwendung der Psychoanalyse auf Mythologie und Religionsgeschichte. Leipzig, 1928.

Croce, B. Dei antichi nella tradizione mitologica del medio evo e del rinascimento. La Parola del Passato, 1, 1947.

Curtin, J. Seneca Indian Myths. Boston, 1923.

Daremberg, C., & Saglio, E. Dictionnaire des antiquitês grecques et romaines. 5 vols. Paris, 1877-1919.

Dietz, H. Nordischer Mythus in der englischen Literatur. NM, 10, 1939.

Erkes, E. Chinesisch-amerikanische Mythenparallelen. T'oung Pao, 1926.

Fairbanks, A. The Mythology of Greece and Rome. New York, 1907.

Falter, O. Der Dichter und sein Gott bei den Griechen und Römern. Würzburg, 1934.

Fox, W. S. Greek and Roman Mythology. In: The Mythology of All Races. Boston, 1916.

Franz, E. Die Beziehungen der japanischen Mythologie zur griechischen. Bonn, 1932.

Frazer, J. G. The Golden Bough. A Study in Magic and Religion. London, 1922.

—— Aftermath. A Supplement to the Golden Bough. London, 1936.

Frey Sallmann, A. Aus dem Nachleben antiker Göttergestalten. Die antiken Gottheiten in der Bilderbeschreibung des Mittelalters und der italienischen Renaissance. Leipzig, 1931.

Friedemann, H. Die Götter Griechenlands von Schiller bis zu Heine. Diss. Berlin, 1905.

Gayley, C. M. The Classic Myths in English Literature and in Art. Boston, 1911.

Gayton, A. H. English Ballads and Indian Myths. JAFL, 55, 1942.
Golther, W. Handbuch der germanischen Mythologie. Leipzig, 1895.
Goti, L. Origen semita de la mitologia ibérica. Judaica (Buenos Aires), 12, 1939.
Gould, S. Curious Myths of the Middle Ages. London, 1877.
Graf, A. Miti, leggende e superstizioni del medio evo. Torino, 1892.
Grimm, J. Deutsche Mythologie. 3 vols. Berlin, 1930.
Guerber, H. A. Myths of Greece and Rome. New York, 1893.
—— Myths and Legends of the Middle Ages, their Origin and Influence on Literature and Art. London, 1909.
Guild, E. C. A List of Poems Illustrating Greek Mythology in the English Poetry of the Nineteenth Century. Bowdoin College Library Bull., 1891.
Harrington, K. P. & Tolman, H. C. Greek and Roman Mythology. Boston, 1897.
Harrison, J. E. Mythology. In: Our Debt to Greece and Rome. London, 1925.
Haymaker, M. Some Contrasts between Greek and Norse Mythology. English Journal, 27, 1938.
Howald, E. Mythos und Tragödie. Tübingen, 1927.
Jung, E. Germanische Götter und Helden in christlicher Zeit. München, 1939.
Keeble, T. W. Some Mythological Figures in Golden Age Satire and Burlesque. BSS, 25, 1948.
Krappe, A. H. Etudes de mythologie et de folklore germaniques. Paris, 1928.
—— Mythologie universelle. Paris, 1930.
—— La genèse des mythes. Paris, 1938.
Lambrechts, P. Contributions à l'étude des divinités celtiques. Brugge, 1942.
Law, Helen H. Bibliography of Greek Myth in English Poetry. New York, 1941.
Lévêque, E. Les mythes et les légendes de l'Inde et de la Perse dans Aristophane, Platon, Aristote, Virgile, Ovide, Tite-Live, Dante, Boccace, Arioste, Rabelais, Perrault, Lafontaine. Paris, 1880.
Liebert, A. Mythos und Kultur. Berlin, 1925.
Liebeschütz, H. Fulgentius Metaforalis. Ein Beitrag zur Geschichte der antiken Mythologie im Mittelalter. VBW, 1926.
Marshall, L. Greek Myths in Modern English Poetry. Studi di fil. mod., 4, 1911.
Meyer, E. H. Germanische Mythologie. Berlin, 1891.
Michetschlaeger, H. Mythologische Enzyklopädie. Die Götter-, Heroen-, und Nymphensagen aller Zeiten und Länder. Wien, 1927.
Mogk, E. Germanische Religionsgeschichte und Mythologie. Berlin, 1927.
Niebergall, V. Griechische Religion und Mythologie in der ältesten Literatur der Römer. Giessen, 1937.
Opler, M. E. Myths and Legends of the Lipan Apache Indians. Memoirs of the American Folk-Lore Society, 36. (New York), 1940.
Otto, W. F. Die Götter Griechenlands. Das Bild des Göttlichen im Spiegel des griechischen Geistes. Bonn, 1929.
—— Der Dichter und die alten Götter. Frankfurt, 1942.
Paton, L. A. Studies in the Fairy Mythology of Arthurian Romance. Boston, 1903.
Pauly, A. F., Wissowa, G. & Kroll, W. Real-Encyclopädie der klassischen Altertumswissenschaft. 13 vols. (incomplete). Stuttgart, 1894-1922.
Peschel, O. Der Ursprung und die Verbreitung einiger geographischen Mythen im Mittelalter. DVLG, 2.
Preller, L. Griechische Mythologie. Berlin, 1894-1926.
Radermacher, L. Mythos und Sage bei den Griechen. Leipzig, 1938.
Rahner, H. Griechische Mythen in christlicher Deutung. In: Gesammelte Aufsätze. Zürich, 1945.
Robertson, J. G. The Gods of Greece in German Poetry. Oxford, 1924. And in: Essays and Addresses on Literature. London, 1935.
Roscher, W. H. Ausführliches Lexikon der griechischen und römischen Mythologie. Leipzig, 1885. Supplement: Geschichte der klassischen Mythologie und Religionsgeschichte während des Mittelalters im Abendland und während der Neuzeit, von Otto Gruppe. 1921.
Rose, H. J. A Handbook of Greek Mythology, Including its Extension to Rome. New York, 1928.
Rose, W. Men, Myths, and Movements in German Literature. London, 1931.
Sabin, F. E. Classic Myths that Live To-Day. New York, 1927 & 1940.
Saxl, F. Antike Götter in der Spätrenaissance. Leipzig, 1927.
Schoen, F. Die antiken mythologischen Elemente in der mittelhochdeutschen Lyrik. Bonn, 1912.
Schrader, A. Germanische Mythologie. Berlin, 1843.
Seznec, J. Les manuels mythologiques italiens et leur diffusion en Angleterre à la fin de la Renaissance. Mélanges

d'archéologie et d'histoire de l'école fr. de Rome. 1933.
—— La survivance des dieux antiques. Essai sur le rôle de la tradition mythologique dans l'humanisme et dans l'art de la Renaissance. London, 1939.
Stinchcomb, J. Classical Mythology in Contemporary American Poetry. CW, 26, 1933.
Strich, F. Die Mythologie in der deutschen Literatur von Klopstock bis Wagner. München, 1910.
Sühnel, R. Die Götter Griechenlands und die deutsche Klassik. Würzburg, 1935.
Thomas, J. Les mythes antiques dans le théâtre français contemporain. Lettres d'humanité, 3. (Paris), 1944.
Uehli, E. Nordisch-germanische Mythologie als Mysteriengeschichte. Basel, 1926.
Van Tieghem, P. La mythologie et l'ancienne poésie scandinaves dans la littérature européenne au XVIIIe siècle. Edda, 11-12, 1919-20.
—— La découverte de la mythologie et de l'ancienne poésie scandinave. In: Le Préromantisme. Paris, 1924.
Wallen, E. Nordisk mythologie i svensk romantik. Stockholm, 1918.
—— Studier over romanisk mythologie i svensk literatur. Malmö, 1923.

CHAPTER EIGHT

Sagas.

Albert. Die altdeutsche Heldensage in der neueren Dichtung. Diss. Wien, 1922.
Baumgartner, W. Israelitisch-griechische Sagenbeziehungen. Schweiz. Archiv f. Volkskunde, 41, 1944.
Bohning, Elizabeth E. The Concept Sage in Nibelungen Criticism. Bethlehem (Pa.), 1944.
Braun, M. Zum Themenbestand des serbokroatischen Heldenliedes. Beiträge z. Gesch. d. deutschen Sprache & Lit. 64, 1940.
Bützler, J. Geschichte der rheinischen Sage und die Romantik in ihrem Einfluss auf deren Wiederbelebung. Elberfeld, 1928.
Dähnhardt, O. Natursagen. Leipzig, 1907-12.
Graesse, J. G. T. Die grossen Sagenkreise des Mittelalters. Dresden, 1842.
—— Beiträge zur Litteratur und Sage des Mittelalters. Dresden, 1850.
Heinzel, R. Ueber die ostgothische Heldensage. SAWW, 119, 1889.
Heusler, A. Lied und Epos in germanischer Sagendichtung. Dortmund, 1905.
Jiriczek, O. L. Deutsche Heldensagen. Strassburg, 1898.
Leyen, F. von der. Deutsches Sagenbuch. 2 vols. München, 1923-24.
Manitius, M. Mittelalterliche Umdeutung antiker Sagenstoffe. ZVL, 15, 1903.
Nover, J. Deutsche Sagen in ihrer Entstehung, Fortbildung und poetischen Gestaltung. Giessen, 1895.
Oja. Finlands äldsta såginrättningar. Historiallinen Aikakauskirja, 1945.
Philippson, E. A. Ueber das Verhältnis von Sage und Literatur. PMLA, 62, 1947.
Radermacher, L. Nordische und hellenische Sage. F&F, 1938.
Radin, P. Winnebago Hero Cycles : A Study in Aboriginal Literature. Baltimore, 1948.
Raszmann, A. Die deutsche Heldensage und ihre Heimat. Hannover, 1857-58.
Saran, G. Deutsche Heldengedichte des Mittelalters. Halle, 1922.
Sarrazin, G. Germanische Sagenmotive im Tristan-Roman. ZVL, 1888.
Schneider, H. Germanische Heldensage. Berlin, 1930 ff.
Schröder, F. R. Germanische Heldendichtung. Tübingen, 1935.
Stadtmueller, G. Althellenisches Sagengut in albanischen Märchen? Stimmen aus dem Südosten, 1940-41.
Strömholm, D. Nordens Gudar och Greklands heroer. Deras sagors danande och inbördes släktskap. Uppsala, 1938.
Teske, H. Die abendländischen Sagenkreise in der deutschen Dichtung des Mittelalters. Brüssel, 1943.
Thurneysen, R. Die irische Helden- und Königsage bis zum siebzehnten Jahrhundert. Halle, 1921.
Tobler, L. Ueber sagenhafte Völker des Altertums und Mittelalters. Zs. für Völkerpsychologie & Sprachwissenschaft, 18, 1888.
Uhland, L. Sagengeschichte der germani schen und romanischen Völker. Gesammelte Werke, 7.
Wild, F. Odin und Euemeros. Spiegelung germanischer Göttersage im englischen Schrifttum. SAWW, 1941.
Wolters, F. & Petersen, C. Die Heldensagen der germanischen Frühzeit. Breslau, 1925.
Wright, C. E. The Cultivation of Saga in Anglo-Saxon England. Edinburgh, 1939.

CHAPTER NINE

Individual Authors.

Kliger, S. Hebraic Lore in Maxwell **ANDERSON'S** Winterset. AL, 18, 1946.

Lemmi, C. W. The Classic Deities in **BACON**. Baltimore, 1933.

Fick, R. **BENFEY** als Begründer der vergleichenden Märchenkunde. Göttingen, 1931.

Köhler, R. Ueber J. F. **CAMPBELLS** Sammlung gaelischer Märchen. Orient & Occident, 2, 1864.

Lewis, C. B. Classical Mythology and Arthurian Romance. A Study of the Sources of **CHRESTIEN DE TROYES**. London, 1932.

Piper, F. Ueber die Benützung mythologischer Vorstellungen in **DANTES** Komödie. In: Mythologie und Symbolik der christlichen Kunst. Weimar, 1847.

Villari, P. Alcune leggende e tradizioni che illustrano la Divina Commedia. Annali della U. toscana, 8. Pisa, 1866.

Bassi, D. La mitologia nelle prime imitazioni della Divina Commedia. Aevum, 1937.

Ristelhuber, P. Une fable de **FLORIAN**. Paris, 1881.

Otto, W. F. Der griechische Göttermythos bei **GOETHE** und Hölderlin. Berlin, 1939.

Magnini, G. B. C. **GOZZI** e le fiabe. In: Saggi storici. Cremona, 1876.

Boltc, J. & Polívka, G. Anmerkungen zu den Kinder- und Hausmärchen der Brüder **GRIMM**. 5 vols. Leipzig, 1913-32.

Tonnelat, E. Les contes des frères Grimm. Paris, 1912.

Anon. On Translations from Beracha **HANAKDAN'S** Fables. In: Briefe, die neueste Literatur betreffend, 1. (Berlin), 1759.

Tabak, I. Judaic Lore in **HEINE**. Diss. Baltimore, 1942.

Aly, W. Volksmärchen, Sage und Novelle bei **HERODOT** und seinen Zeitgenossen. Göttingen, 1921.

Panitz, H. Mythos und Orakel bei Herodot. Greifswald, 1935.

Tacke, O. Die Fabeln des Erzpriesters von **HITA** im Rahmen der mittelalterlichen Fabelliteratur. RF, 31, 1912.

Herzog-Hauser, G. Märchenmotive in **HOMERS** Ilias. Geistige Arbeit, 1937.

Calhoun, G. M. Homer's Gods. Myth and Märchen. AJPh, 1939.

Carpenter, R. Folk Tale, Fiction and Saga in the Homeric Epics. Berkeley, 1946.

Wheeler, C. F. Classical Mythology in the Plays, Masques and Poems of Ben **JONSON**. Princeton, 1938.

Talbert, E. W. The Classical Mythology and Structure of Cynthia's Revels. PhQ, 22, 1943.

Mayer, A. Die Quellen zum Fabularius des **KONRAD VON MURE**. Nürnberg, 1916.

Joly, A. Histoire de deux fables de **LAFONTAINE**, leurs origines et leurs pérégrinations. Mém. de l'Académie de Caen, 1877-78.

Osgood, C. G. The Classical Mythology of **MILTON'S** English Poems. New York, 1900.

Herbst, E. L. Classical Mythology in Paradise Lost. CPh, 1934.

Hoare, A. D. M. The Works of **MORRIS** and Yeats in Relation to Early Saga Literature. Cambridge, 1937.

Bleich, E. Die Märchen des **MUSAEUS**, vornehmlich nach Stoffen und Motiven. Archiv, 108-09, 1902.

Pletscher, T. Die Märchen **PERRAULTS**. Berlin, 1906.

Tesdorpf, P. Beiträge zur Würdigung Charles Perraults und seiner Märchen. Stuttgart, 1910.

Fehr, K. Die Mythen bei **PINDAR**. Zürich, 1936.

Frutiger, P. Les mythes de **PLATON**. Paris, 1930.

Sleeman, J. H. The Myths of Plato. Religion, 13, 1935.

Stewart, J. A. The Myths of Plato. New York, 1900.

Wolters, X. F. M. G. Notes on Antique Folklore on the Basis of **PLINY'S** Natural History Book XXVIII. Amsterdam, 1935.

Azadovski, M. **POUCHKINE** et le folklore. Festschrift Pouchkine. Moscou, 1939.

Kramer, C. Les tragédies mythologiques de **RACINE**. NPh, 25, 1940.

Anon. Folk-lore of **SHAKESPEARE**. Leisure Hour, March, 1884.

Boas, F. S. Aspects of Classical Legend and History in Shakespeare. PBA, 29, 1943-44.

Nutt, A. T. The Fairy Mythology of Shakespeare. London, 1900.

Root, R. K. Classical Mythology in Shakespeare. New York, 1903.

Sarrazin, G. Germanische Heldensagen in Shakespeares Titus Andronicus. Archiv, 1896.

Tschischwitz, B. Nachklänge germanischer Mythen in Shakespeares Werk. Halle, 1865.

Sawtelle, A. E. The Sources of **SPEN-**

SER'S Classical Mythology. New York, 1896.
Lotspeich, H. G. Classical Mythology in the Poetry of Edmund Spenser. Princeton, 1932.
Adrian, W. Die Mythologie in Carl **SPITTELERS** Olympischem Frühling. Sprache & Dichtung, Bern.
Wagner, H. **TASSO** und die nordische Heldensage. Euphorion, 6, 1899.
Walzel, O. Der Begriff Mythus bei D. F. **STRAUSS**. NPh, 26, 1940-41.
Schneider, H. **UHLAND** und die deutsche Heldensage. Abhandlungen der Kaiserl. Akad. d. Wissenschaften, Berlin, 1918.
Paris, G. La mythologie allemande dans Girart de **VIANE**. Romania, 1, 1872.
Saxl, F. Antike Götter in der Spätrenaissance. Ein Freskenzyklus und ein Discorso des Jacobo **ZUCCHI**. Leipzig, 1927.

CHAPTER TEN

Individual Motifs.

—A—

Sabatini, F. **ABELARDO** ed Eloisa nella tradizione popolare romana. Romania, 9, 1880.
Matulka, B. On the European Diffusion of the Last of the **ABENCERAGES** Story in the 16th Century. Hisp. 16, 1933.
Anon. Pièces de théâtre relatives au Sacrifice d'**ABRAHAM**. Polybiblion, 1882-83.
Bernard, A. Histoire de la survivance **ACADIENNE**, 1755-1935. Montréal, 1935.
Landau, M. Vittoria **ACCOROMBONA** in der deutschen Dichtung im Verhältnis zur wahren Geschichte. Euphorion, 9, 1902.
Atwood, E. B. The Story of **ACHILLES** in the Seege of Troye. SPh, 39, 1942.
Fries, A. Goethe und Hebbel als Sänger Achills. Reichsbote, Sonntagsblatt 41, 1902.
Hibernicus. Achilles and the Critics. N&Q, 13.VIII.1938.
Kern, F. Goethes Achilleis und der letzte Gesang der Ilias. Vossische Zt, 2-3, 1890.
Patzig, E. Die Achillestragödie der Ilias im Lichte der antiken und der modernen Tragik. NJKA, 1923.
—— Achills tragisches Schicksal bei Diktys und den Byzantinern. Byzantin. Zs, 25, 1925.
Schlosser, R. Ueber R. Wagners Beschäftigung mit einem Drama Achilleus. Bayr. Blätter, 19, 1896.
Wendling, E. Achilleus, das homerische Ur-Epos. Karlsruhe, 1927.
Laumonier, A. L'**ACROPOLE** d'Athènes dans la littérature française. In: Mélanges P. Laumonier. Paris, 1934.
Hibernicus. **ACTAEON**: Myth and Moralizing. N&Q, 30.VII.1938.
Pompecki, B. St. **ADALBERT** in der deutschen Dichtung. Westpreuss. Volksblatt, 235, 1912.
Breuer, H. Untersuchungen zum lateinisch-altfranzösischen **ADAMSSPIEL**. ZRPh, 51-52, 1931-32.
Croce, B. La trilogia de **ADELAIDE** e Comingio e il signor Gualzetti. Critica, 1928.
Plaumann, E. Die Mythe von **ADMETOS** und Alcestis. Neue Jb. f. Philologie & Pädagogik, 156, 1897.
ADULTERY: See Chapter Eleven below.
AENEAS: See also Virgil, II. IV. 6.
Crosland, Jessie. Eneas and the Aeneid. MLR, 29, 1934.
Dressler, A. Der Einfluss des altfranzösischen Eneasromanes auf die altfranzösische Litteratur. Borna-Leipzig, 1907.
Hoepffner, E. L'Enéas et Wace. AR, 15-16, 1931-32.
—— Marie de France et l'Enéas, SM, 5, 1932.
Means, T. A Comparison of the Treatment by Vergil and by Ovid of the Aeneas-Dido Myth. CW, 23, 1929.
Parodi, E. I rifacimenti dell'Eneide. Studi di filologia romanza, 2, 1887.
Pauphilet, A. Enéas et Enée. Romania, 1929.
Sage, E. T. The Non-Virgilian Aeneas. CJ, 15.
Salverda de Grave, J. J. Caxtons Eneydos 1490 englisht from the French Liure d'Eneydes (1483). London, 1890.
—— Un imitateur du Roman d'Enéas au XIIIe siècle en France. SM, 5, 1932.
Schur, W. Die Aeneassage in der späteren römischen Literatur. Strassburg, 1914.
Slijper, E. Les origines de la fable d'Enée. Mélanges Salverda de Grave, Groningen, 1933.
Sorrento, L. La storia di Enea in lingua siciliana del Trecento. SM, 5, 1932.
Teusink, D. Das Verhältnis zwischen Veldekes Eneide und dem Alexanderlied. Museum, 52, 1947.

Warren, F. M. On the Latin Sources of Thebes and Eneas. MLN, 16, 1901.
AESOP: See under Greek Literature, II. III. 13.
Möller, J. **AGAMEMNONS** Einzug bei Aeschylos und in der neueren Literatur. NJKA, 23, 1908.
Rugani, R. L'Agamennone di Vittorio Alfieri. LNI, 12, 1941.
Crundell, H. W. Shakespeare and **AGINCOURT**. N&Q, 26.X.1935.
Lazar, B. **AGIS** dans la littérature universelle. Progr. Budapest, 1894.
Anon. **AGNES BERNAUER** in Dichtung und Drama. Bayerland, 12, 1900.
Behrens, C. Agnes Bernauer i historiens og digtringens lys. København, 1906.
Garin, P. Die beiden Agnesen. Allg. Zt., 102, 1901.
Gessler, A. Zur Dramaturgie des Bernauerstoffes. Progr. Basel, 1906.
Golz, B. Die Wandlungen literarischer Motive. Leipzig, 1920.
Petri, J. Der Agnes Bernauer-Stoff im deutschen Drama. Diss. Rostock, 1893.
—— Agnes Bernauer in Dichtung und Drama. Bayerland, 12, 1900.
Prehn, A. Agnes Bernauer in der deutschen Dichtung. Progr. Nordhausen, 1907.
Voeller. Agnes Bernauer. Augsburger Post, 26, 1900.
Gamba, V. Di alcuni influssi della leggenda **AGNESIANA** nella produzione latina medievale. ARIV, 1940
AHASVERUS. See Wandering Jew below.
Perrotta, G. L'**AIACE** di Sofocle. A&R, 1934.
Lang, F. **ALBOIN** und Rosamunde in Sage und Dichtung, mit besonderer Berücksichtigung von Fr. W. Schusters gleichnamigem Drama. Cluj, 1938.
Arnavon, J. La légende d'**ALCESTE**. RdF, 1, 1929.
Butler, E. M. Alkestis in Modern Dress (Rilke). JWI, 1, 1937.
Doerrie, H. Zur Dramatik der euripideischen Alkestis. NJAB, 1939.
Drew, D. L. Euripides' Alcestis. AJPh, 1931.
Ellinger, G. Alkeste in der modernen Literatur. Halle, 1885.
Gaster, M. Zur Alkestis-Sage. Byz.-neugriech. Jahrbücher, 15, 1939.
Kittredge, G. L. Chaucer's Alceste. MPh, 6, 1909.
Lesky, A. Alkestis, der Mythus und das Drama. Wien, 1925.
Megas, G. Die Sage von Alkestis. Archiv f. Religionswiss., 30, 1933.
Michaut, G. Un débat récent sur la légende d'Alceste. Ann. Univ. 4, Paris, 1929.
Momigliano, A. Il mito di Alcesti ed Euripide. Cult, 10, 1931.
Séchan, L. Le dévouement d'Alceste. RCC, 18, 1927.
Tisdel, F. M. Balanstion's Adventure (by Browning) as an Interpretation of the Alcestis of Euripides. PMLA, 1917.
Valgimigli, M. L'Alcesti di Euripide. ARIV, 92, 1932-33.
Weber, L. Die Alkestissage. RhM, 1936.
Wiener, F. Der Alkestis-Stoff in der deutschen Literatur. Breslau, 1921.
Bahder, K. von. Lamprechts **ALEXANDERLIED** und seine Heimat. Germania, 30, 1885.
Berzunza, J.J A Tentative Classification of Books, Pamphlets and Pictures Concerning Alexander the Great and the Alexander Romances. Durham (N.H.), 1939.
—— Preliminary Notes on the Three Italian Versions of Quintus Curtius Rufus' Historiae Alexandri Magni. Ital., 18, 1941.
Bruhl, A. Le souvenir d'Alexandre le Grand et les Romains. Mélanges d'archéologie et d'histoire de l'Ecole fr. à Rome, 1930.
Carraroli, D. La leggenda di Alessandro Magno. Torino, 1891. Cf. NAnt, 1892.
Friedlaender, I. Die Chadhirlegende und der Alexanderroman. M., 1914.
Gaster, M. An Old Hebrew Romance of Alexander. Journal of the Royal Asiatic Society, 1897.
Gomez, E. G. Un texto arabe occidental de la leyenda de Alejandro. Madrid, 1929.
Grammel, E. Studien über den Wandel des Alexanderbildes in der deutschen Dichtung des 12. und 13. Jahrhunderts. Limburg, 1931.
Hampe, T. Ueber die Quellen der Strassburger Fortsetzung von Lamprechts Alexanderlied und deren Benutzung. Diss. Bonn, 1890.
Harczyk, J. Zu Lamprechts Alexander. ZDPh, 4, 1872.
Héron, A. La légende d'Aristote et d'Alexandre. Rouen, 1892.
Lascelles, M. M. Alexander and the Earthly Paradise in Mediaeval English Writings. MA, 1936.
Levi. La légende d'Alexandre dans le Talmud. Rev. des études juives, 1, 1888.
Magoun, F. P. The Gests of King Alexander of Macedon. Harvard U.P., 1929.
Mederer, E. Die Alexanderlegende bei den

ältesten Alexanderhistorikern. Stuttgart, 1936.
Meyer, P. Alexandre le Grand dans la littérature française du moyen âge. 2 vols. Paris, 1886.
Pfister, F. Eine orientalische Alexandergeschichte in mittelenglischer Prosabearbeitung. ESn, 74, 1940.
—— Das Nachleben der Ueberlieferung von Alexander und den Brahmanen. H., 76, 1941.
—— Studien zu mittelalterlichen deutschen Alexandergeschichten. ZDA, 79, 1942.
Pistoles, L. Del posto che spetta al Libro de Alexandro nella storia della letteratura spagnola. RLR, 46, 1903.
Rochat, A. Ueber die Quelle des deutschen Alexanderliedes. Germania, 1, 1856.
Schmidt, A. Ueber das Alexanderlied des Alberic von Besançon und sein Verhältniss zur antiken Ueberlieferung. Diss. Bonn, 1886.
Steele, R. B. Some Features of the Later Histories of Alexander. CPh, 1915
Storost, J. Studien zur Alexandersage in der älteren italienischen Literatur. Halle, 1935. Cf. ZRPh, 1938.
Talbot, E. Essai sur la légende d'Alexandre-le-Grand dans les romans français du XIIe siècle. Paris, 1850.
Willis, R. S. The Relationship of the Spanish Libro de Alexandre to the Alexandreis of Gautier de Châtillon. Princeton, 1934.
—— The Debt of the Spanish Libro de Alexandre to the French Roman d'Alexandre. Princeton, 1935.
Wünsche, A. Der Alexanderroman in der Literatur. Jb. f. jüdische Gesch. & Lit. 1, 1898.
Amiaud, A. La légende syriaque de Saint **ALEXIS**. Bibl. de l'École des Hautes Etudes, 79. Paris, 1889.
Andersen, H. Zu den späteren Bearbeitungen der Alexiuslegende. ZFSL, 42.
Blau, M. F. Zur Alexiuslegende. Diss. Leipzig, 1888.
Brauns. Ueber Quelle und Entwicklung der altfranzösischen. Cançun de Saint Alexis, verglichen mit der provenzalischen Vida. Diss. Kiel, 1884.
Joret, C. La légende de Saint Alexis en Allemagne. Paris, 1881.
Koerting, G. Studien über altfranzösische Bearbeitungen der Alexius-Legende mit Berücksichtigung deutscher und englischer Alexiuslieder. Progr. Trier, 1890.
Leffson, A. Geschichte des Alexis-Stoffes in der dramatischen Literatur. In: Immermanns Alexis. Gotha, 1904.
Mueller, P. Studien über drei dramatische Bearbeitungen der Alexiuslegende. Diss. Berlin, 1888.
Paris, G. La vie de Saint Alexis. Paris, 1885.
Renier, R. Qualche nota sulla diffusione della leggenda di Sant' Alessio in Italia. Mélanges A. D'Ancona. Firenze, 1901.
Rösler, Margarethe. Beziehungen der Celestina zur Alexiuslegende. ZRPh., 58, 1938.
Schneegans, E. Die romanhafte Dichtung der Alexiuslegende. MLN, 1888.
Arnold, J. L. King **ALFRED** in English Poetry. Diss. Leipzig, 1898.
Bettex, G. & Guillon, E. Les **ALPES** suisses dans la littérature et dans l'art. Lausanne, 1915.
Coolidge, W. A. B. The Alps in Nature and History. London, 1908.
DeWitt, N. J. Polybius, Livy and the Alps. CW, 37, 1943-44.
Dreyer, A. Geschichte der alpinen Literatur. München, 1938.
Dübi, H. Der Alpensinn in der Litteratur und Kunst der Berner von 1537-1839. Neujahrsblatt der litt. Gesellschaft. Bern, 1901.
Engel, C. E. La littérature alpestre en France et en Angleterre aux XVIIIe et XIXe siècles. Diss. Paris. Chambéry, 1930.
Greyerz, O. von. Die Alpen in der Dichtung. Schweiz. Monatshefte, 1932.
Gysi. Die Alpen und ihre Darstellung im Lied. Schweiz. musikpädagog. Blätter, 12, 1923.
Huna, L. Die Alpen in der Dichtung. Heimgarten, 37, 1911.
Jenny, E. Schweizerische Alpenliteratur vor hundert Jahren. Die Alpen, 1, 1927.
Jenny, H. E. Die Alpendichtung der deutschen Schweiz. Bern, 1905.
Lindner, Tilly. Die Geburt der Alpendichtung. Karlsruher Beobachter, 22.VI. 1927.
Müller, K. Jens Baggesen und sein Alpengedicht Die Parthenäis. Schweiz. Monatshefte, 24, 1945.
Roux, R. Les Alpes et les lettres grecques. CLS, 16, 1945.
Spindler, R. Die Alpen in der englischen Literatur und Kunst. Leipzig, 1932.
Thorps, C. O. Two Augustans Cross the Alps: Dennis and Addison on Mountain Scenery. SPh, 1935.
Weiss, R. Das Alpenerlebnis in der deutschen Literatur des 18. Jahrhunderts. Diss. Zürich. Frauenfeld, 1934.
Wichmann, F. Die Alpen in der deutschen Lyrik. Münchner Zt., 132, 1904.

Zollinger, M. Die Alpen in der deutschen Dichtung. Schweiz. pädagog. Zs., 1908.
ALSACE: See Intermediaries, I. IV. 1.
AMADIS DE GAULA: See Spanish Contributions, IV. IV. 4.
Adler, A. A Note on the **AMAZONS** in Anseÿs de Mes. MLN, 61, 1946.
Klein, H. Die antiken Amazonensagen in der deutschen Literatur. Diss. München, 1919.
Kühn, L. Amazonen. Die Frau, 45, 1937-38.
Leonard, I. A. Conquerors and Amazons in Mexico. Hisp. Amer. Hist. Rev., 24, 1945.
Ninck, M. Das Amazonenproblem. Schweiz. Monatshefte, 20, 1940-41.
Rosenthal, A. The Isle of the Amazons, a Marvel of Travellers. JWI, 1, 1937.
Wolf, M. J. Die Amazonensage. Atlantis, 6, 1934.
Wolff, H. Kleists Amazonenstaat im Lichte Rousseaus. PMLA, 53, 1938.
Wright, Celeste T. The Amazons in Elizabethan Literature. SPh, 37, 1940.
Wilmart, A. Saint **AMBROISE** et la légende dorée. Ephemerides Liturgicae, 50, 1936.
Bar, F. Les Epîtres latines de Raoul Le Tourtier. La légende d'**AMIS ET AMILE**. Paris, 1937.
Bauerfeld, W. Die Sage von Amis und Amiles, ein Beitrag zur mittelalterlichen Freundschaftssage. Ohlau, 1941.
Bédier, J. Amis et Amile. In: Les légendes épiques. Paris, 1926-29.
Gerould, G. H. Amis and Amiles. In: The Grateful Dead. London, 1908.
Hibbard, Laura A. Amis and Amilous. In: Mediaeval Romance in England. New York, 1924.
Leach, M. Amis and Amiloun. London, 1937.
Morris, W. The Friendship of Amis and Amile. In: Old French Romances. London, 1896.
Schwieger, P. Die Sage von Amis und Amilis in Frankreich und in Deutschland. Progr. Berlin, 1885.
AMOR (and Psyche): See also Cupid, Eros, Psyche and Apuleius.
Bluemner, H. Das Märchen von Amor und Psyche in der deutschen Dichtkunst. NJKA, 11, 1903.
Boethke, K. Amor und Psyche. National Zt. (Berlin), 129-147, 1895.
Bolte, J. Amor und Tod. Euphorion, 5, 1897.
Calonne, E. de. Préface de l'Amour et Psyche. Paris, 1842.
Calzavara, G. Il mito di Amore e Psiche nella favola di Apuleio. ARIV, 80.
Conton, L. Amore nella letteratura e nelle arti figurative degli antichi. Adria, 1902.
Cristini, G. Alcuni cenni sulle personnificazioni d'Amore nelle letterature di Francia e d'Italia nel medio evo. Bergamo, 1910.
Graf, A. La leggenda dell' amore. Torino, 1881.
Helm, R. Das Märchen von Amor und Psyche. NJKA, 33, 1914.
Keller, V. Amor und Tod. Euphorion, 6, 1898.
Köhler & Bolte. Stoffgeschichtliches zu Hans Sachs: Amor und Tod. Euphorion, 3, 1896.
Kroll, W. Das Märchen von Amor und Psyche. Pädagog. Zentralbl., 12, 1932.
Ladendorf, O. Zum Märchen von Amor und Psyche in der deutschen Dichtkunst. NJKA, 13, 1904.
Maria, U. de. La favola di Amore e Psiche nella letteratura e nell' arte italiana. Bologna, 1899.
Meyer, G. Amor und Psyche. Berlin, 1885.
Minor, J. Amor und Tod. Euphorion, 4, 1907.
Ritter, O. Amor und Tod. ESn, 32, 1903.
Stumfall, B. Das Märchen von Amor und Psyche in seinem Fortleben in der französischen, italienischen und spanischen Literatur bis zum 18. Jahrhundert. Leipzig, 1907.
Tegethoff, E. Studien zum Märchentypus von Amor und Psyche. Bonn, 1922.
Bener, F. Die **AMPHIARAOSSAGE** in der griechischen Dichtung. Diss. Zürich, 1945.
Rossi, S. Il mito di Amphiaraos nella letteratura e nell' arte figurata. Firenze, 1898.
AMPHITRYON: See also Plautus, II. IV. 4.
Anfossi, N. Anfitrione classico, prezioso e romantico. Annali dell' Instituto sup. di Piemonte, 1929.
Bock, N. Molières Amphitryon im Verhältniss zu seinen Vorgängern. Diss. Marburg, 1887. Cf. ZFSL, 10, 1888.
Bondurant, A. L. The Amphitruo of Plautus, Molières Amphitryon and the Amphitryon of Dryden. Sewanee Rev., 1925-26.
Leeuwe, H. H. J. de. Molières und Kleists Amphitryon. NPh, 31, 1947.
Leo, U. Molières Amphitryon und seine Vorgänger. ZFSL, 47, 1925.
Nordmeyer, H. W. Kleists Amphitryon: Zur Deutung der Komödie. MDU, 38, 1946 ff.

Peggram, R. E. A Neglected Dutch Amphitryon of 1679. MLR, 36, 1941.
Reinhardstoettner, C. von. Die Plautinischen Lustspiele in spätern Bearbeitungen: I. Amphitruo. Leipzig, 1880.
Wolff, T. Die Verwandlungen des Amphitrion (Fulda, Kleist). Berliner Tagblatt, 12.XII.1901.
Giese, F. Der romantische Charakter. I. Die Entwicklung des ANDROGYNEN-problems in der Frühromantik. Langensalza, 1919.
Merrill, R. V. The Pléiade and the Androgyne. CL, 1, 1949.
Koegel, K. W. Aesthetische Bemerkungen über die ANDROMAQUE des Racine mit besonderer Berücksichtigung der Antigone des Sophokles. Progr. Quedlinburg, 1864.
Mager, A. Andromaque dans la littérature française. Progr. Marburg, 1890.
Sells, A. L. From Euripides to Racine: Two Incarnations of Andromache. CLS, 5-7, 1942.
Soto y Sagarra, L. de. El carácter de Andromaca a través de la literatura. Rev. de la fac. de letras y ciencias de la Havana, 29, 1919.
Spotorno, J. Andromaca nella letteratura e nell' arte greca e latina. Palermo, 1930.
Wheatley, K. E. Andromaque as the Distrest Mother. RR, 39, 1948.
Zielinski, T. Andromaque dans la littérature postérieure à Homère et la tragédie d'Euripide. Hermes, messager de l'antiquité classique en Russie, 1915.
—— De Andromacha posthomerica. Eos, 1928.
DeVane, W. C. The Virgin and the Dragon. (ANDROMEDA). Yale Rev., 37, 1947.
Amato, A. d'. La lotta dell'ANGELO e del diavolo nella tradizione irpina. Annuario del R. Liceo-ginnasio d'Avellino, 1933-34.
Jung, L. Fallen Angels in Jewish, Christian and Mohammedan Literature. Philadelphia, 1926.
Thompson, E. N. S. The Rebel Angel in Later Poetry. PhQ, 27, 1948.
Kleinschmidt, B. Die heilige ANNA. Ihre Verehrung in Geschichte, Kunst und Volkstum. Düsseldorf, 1930.
Krogmann, W. Vom Fräulein aus Brittania, ANNA VON DER BRETAGNE im deutschen Lied. Halle, 1940.
Sussman, J. ANNE BOLEYN im deutschen Drama. Wien, 1916.
Bousset, W. Der ANTICHRIST. Göttingen, 1895.
Jeremias, A. Der Antichrist in Geschichte und Gegenwart. Leipzig, 1930.
Levi, E. La leggenda simbolica del pessimismo: l'avvento del Anticristo. Mélanges G. A. Cesareo. Palermo, 1924.
Meyer, W. Der Ludus de Antichristo. SBAW, 1882.
Pflueger, J. H. L. On the English Translation of the Ludus de Antichristo. JEGPh, 44, 1945.
Rigaux, B. L'Antéchrist et l'opposition au royaume messianique dans l'Ancien et le Nouveau Testament. Paris, 1932.
Alewyn, R. Vorbarocker Klassizismus und griechische Tragödie: Analyse der ANTIGONE-Uebersetzung des Martin Opitz. Heidelberg, 1926.
Beyfuss, E. Die Antigone-Sage in der Weltliteratur. Diss. Leipzig, 1921.
Binaut, L. A. Antigone: d'une tentative romantique sur Sophocle (Vacquerie et Meurice). Le Correspondant, 8, 1844.
Buchetmann, E. Jean de Rotrous Antigone und ihre Quellen. Leipzig, 1901.
Fiedler, H. Walter Hasenclevers Antigone. Von Sophokles zu den Jüngsten. Nord & Süd, 1919.
Gantner, M. Wie hat Garnier in seiner Antigone die antiken Dichtungen benutzt? Progr. Passau, 1887.
Maulnier, T. L'Antigone de Garnier. RP, 53, 1946.
Pluess, T. Goethe und Antigone. NJKA, 1898.
Schacht, T. Ueber die Tragödie Antigone nebst einem vergleichenden Blick auf Sophokles und Shakespeare. Darmstadt, 1842.
Schröder, C. Das Enthymema der Antigone und Goethe. PhW, 1933.
Schwarze, W. Der Einfluss Rotrous Antigone auf Racines Thébaïde. Münster, 1913.
Sheldon, W. L. The Antigone of Sophocles and Shakespeare's Isabel. PL, Dec., 1892.
Ulargiu, V. L'Antigone di Sofocle e di Vittorio Alfieri. Iglesias, 1936.
Weisstein, G. Antigone in Berlin. Beilage, National Zt, 36, 1903.
Leblond, M. A. Rayonnement des ANTILLES dans la littérature et l'art. Illustration, 23.XI.1935.
Drohojowska, Comtesse. Légende de Saint ANTOINE de Padoue. Paris, 1878.
Facchinetti, P. V. Le Saint du peuple. Antoine de Padoue. Paris, 1931.
List, J. Das Antoniusleben des hl. Athanasius d. Gr. Eine literar-historische Studie zu den Anfängen der byzantinischen Hagiographie. Athen, 1930.

Morawski, J. La légende de Saint Antoine, ermite. Poznan, 1939.
Santos, J. E. dos. Santo' Antonio na literatura e na arte portuguesas. Lisboa, 1935.
Vrancken, S. Das **ANTONIUS**-Cleopatramotiv in der deutschen Literatur. Bonn, 1930.
Demolli, L. Sant' **APOLLONIA** nella storia e nella leggenda. Milano, 1938.
Hagen, von den. Der Roman von König **APOLLONIUS** in seinen verschiedenen Bearbeitungen. Berlin, 1878.
Lewis, C. B. Die altfranzösischen Prosaversionen des Apollonius-Romans. Erlangen, 1913.
Klebs, E. Die Erzählung von Apollonius aus Tyrus. Berlin, 1899.
Singer, S. Apollonius von Tyrus. Das Fortleben des antiken Romans in späteren Zeiten. Halle, 1895.
Schlisske, O. Die **APOSTEL** in der deutschen Dichtung des Mittelalters. Diss. Münster, 1931.
Rumbaur, O. Die Geschichte von **APPIUS** und Virginia in der englischen Literatur. Breslau, 1890.
Price, R. & Chapman, J. A Bibliography of Johnny **APPLESEED** in American History, Literature, and Folklore. Paterson (N.J.), 1944.
Bertana, E. **ARCADIA** lugubre e preromantica. Spezia, 1899. And in: Arcadia, Saggi e Profili. Napoli, 1909.
Torraca, F. La materia dell' Arcadia del Sannazaro. Città di Castello, 1888.
Wendel, H. Arkadien im Umkreis bukolischer Dichtung in der Antike und in der französischen Literatur. Giessen, 1933-34.
Boulger, D. C. The Romance of the **ARDENNES**. British Review, May, 1913.
Tomsin, A. La légende des amours d'**ARETHUSE** et d'Alphée. L'Antiquité Classique. 1940.
ARGENIS: see Novels, I. VII. 2, and Barclay, IV. VIII. 14.
Bacon, J. R. The Voyage of the **ARGONAUTS**. London, 1925.
Daniel, S. Zur Entstehung und Entwicklung der Argonauten und Medeasage. Jb. d. Fakultät. München, 1920.
Ferri, F. Basinio e l'Argonautica di Apollonio Rodio. Rendiconti del R. Istituto Lombardo di scienze e lettere, 53.
Dubitzky, F. **ARIADNE**-Opern. Bühne & Welt, 15, 1913.
Nicolai, P. Der Ariadne-Stoff in der Entwicklungsgeschichte der deutschen Oper. Diss. Rostock, 1920.
Bergner, H. Der christliche Ritter in Dichtung und bildender Kunst. (**ARISTOCRACY**). Zs. f. Bücherfreunde, 6, 1914.
Linnartz, K. Stimmen über den Adel in der neueren Literatur. Kölnische Volks-Zt, Beilage 52, 1906.
Bradner, L. Poems on the Defeat of the **ARMADA**. JEGPh, 43, 1944.
Brooke, T. Some Pre-Armada Propagandist Poetry in England. Proc. Amer. Philos. Soc., 135, 1941.
Dabney, L. E. A Sixteenth Century French Account of the Spanish Armada. MLN, 61, 1946.
Entwistle, W. J. Cervantes' Two Odes on the Invincible Armada. BSS, 24, 1947.
Lapp, J. C. The Defeat of the Armada in French Poetry of the XVIth Century. JEGPh, 43, 1944.
Creizenach, W. **ARMINIUS** in Poesie und Litteraturgeschichte. PJb, 36, 1893.
Hauff, G. Hermann und die Hermannschlacht, hauptsächlich in der lyrischen Poesie des deutschen Volkes. Archiv, 67, 1882.
Hirschberg, L. Verschollene Hermanndichtungen. Zeitgeist, 33, 1909.
Holl, K. Hermann und die Hermannschlacht in der deutschen Dichtung. In: Hermann der Cherusker. Detmold, 1925.
Hwolp (Hofmann von Wellenhof). Zur Geschichte des Arminius-Cultus in der deutschen Literatur. Progr. Graz, 1886-91.
Jacobi, Lucie. Die dramatische Behandlung des Arminiusstoffes von den Befreiungskriegen bis 1888. Diss. Giessen, 1923.
Landau, P. Die Hermannsschlacht in der deutschen Dichtung. Rhein-westfäl. Zt., 769, 1909.
—— Die Hermannsschlacht in der deutschen Dichtung. Neues Tageblatt (Stuttgart), 282, 1913.
Riffert, J. E. Die Hermannschlacht in der deutschen Literatur. Archiv, 63, 1880.
Scherillo, M. L'Arminio del Pindemonte e la poesie bardita. NAnt, 16.IV.1892.
Wehrhan, K. Hermann der Cherusker in der erzählenden Literatur. Lippische Landes-Zt., 28.X. & 10.XI.1927.
Ponte, A. **ARNALDO DA BRESCIA** nelle tragedie di Giambattista Niccolini e di Carlo Marenco. Sondrio, 1879.
ARTHURIAN ROMANCES: See Celtic Influences, IV. I. 2.
Laufer, B. **ASBESTOS** and Salamander. An Essay in Chinese and Hellenistic Folk-Lore. T'oung Pao, Arch. pour l'Asie orientale, 1915.

ASSISI: See Francis of Assisi below.
Kern, H. Der antike **ASTYANAX**-Mythus und seine späteren Auswüchse. Ph. 75.
Mertz, R. Die deutschen Bruchstücke von **ATHIS UND PROPHILIAS** in ihrem Verhältnis zum altfranzösischen Roman. Leipzig, 1914.
ATLANTIS: See also Utopias, I. II. 4.
Amendola, G. B. La tradizione d'Atlantide. Nuova Parola, 1902.
Bessmertny, A. Das Atlantisrätsel. Leipzig, 1932.
Cheffaud, P. H. Une consultation sur le cas de l'Atlantide (R. Haggard et P. Benoît). RLC, 1, 1921.
Hackforth, R. The Story of Atlantis, its Purpose and its Moral. CR, 1944.
Heidel, A. W. A Suggestion Concerning Plato's Atlantis. Proc. American Acad. of Arts & Sciences, 1933.
Hirmenech, H. P. L'Atlantide et les Atlantes. In: Les Celtes. Paris, 1906.
Magden, H. L'Atlantide de Pierre Benoît. FQ, 1919.
Meunier, M. L'Atlantide: le mythe et sa leçon. NL, 15.IX.1934.
Sander, F. Ueber die platonische Insel Atlantis. Progr. Bunzlau, 1893.
Spenle, L. The History of Atlantis. London, 1931.
Stella, L. A. L'Atlantide di Platone e la preistoria egea. Rendiconti del R. Istituto lombardo di scienze e lettre, 65, 1932.
Dinsmore, C. A. **ATONEMENT** in Literature and Life. (Homer, Dante, Shakespeare, Milton, G. Eliot, Hawthorne.) Boston, 1906.
Jacob, F. Die Fabel von **ATREUS** und Thyestes in den wichtigsten Tragödien der englischen, französischen und italienischen Literatur. Münchener Beiträge. Leipzig, 1906-07.
Ancona, A. d'. La storia d'**ATTILA** "flagellum Dei." RI, 1862.
—— La leggenda d'Attila flagellum Dei in Italia. In: Studi critici e storia letteraria. Bologna, 1880.
Boor, H. de. Das Attilabild in Geschichte, Legende und heroischer Dichtung. Bern, 1932.
Foss, R. Attila in der Geschichte und Sage. Gütersloh, 1910.
Krappe, A. H. La légende de la naissance miraculeuse d'Attila, roi des Huns. Moyen Age, 41, 1931.
Suchier, W. Zu **AUCASSIN** und Nicolette in Deutschland. Archiv, 35, 1916.
Wagner, G. Aucassin et Nicolette comme imitation de Floire et Blanchefleur et comme modèle de Treue um Treue. Progr. Arnstadt, 1883.
Zettl, J. Aucassin und Nicolette in Deutschland. Progr. Eger, 1911.
Getzeny, H. Kaiser **AUGUSTUS** in der christlichen Geschichtstheologie und in der Legende des Mittelalters. Magazin f. Pädagogik, 100, 1927.
Marchetti Longhi, G. La memoria di Augusto e dei suoi monumenti nel medio evo. Roma, 1939.
Monteverdi, A. Augusto nella tradizione medievale. In: Augustus: Studi in occasione del bimillenario augusteo, ed. by A. Ruiz et al. Roma, 1938.
Santini, E. Augusto negli scrittori del rinascimento. Ann. Fac. di Lett. & Filos., 9. Cagliari, 1938.
Bianquis, G. La poésie autrichienne de Hofmannsthal à Rilke. (**AUSTRIAN**). Paris, 1926.
Ebner, T. Vom Oestreicherthum in der Litteratur. Deutsches Wochenblatt, 46.
Klemeng, H. Die Deutschen Oesterreichs im Spiegel des Zeitromans. Deutsche Blätter in Polen, 2.
Kollmann, E. C. Characteristics of Austrian Literature. MDU, 34, 1942.
Tibal, A. L'Autrichien. Essais sur la formation d'une individualité nationale. Paris, 1936.
Bruce, J. D. Human **AUTOMATS** in Classical Tradition and Medieval Romance. MPh, 10, 1913.
Heilborn, E. Hoffmann und das Automat. Literatur, Nov., 1925
Preston, K. Aspects of **AUTUMN** in Roman Poetry. CPh, 1918.
Beck, A. Herbst und Herbstgefühl in der deutschen Lyrik. Schwabenspiegel, 19, 1925.
Van Tieghem, P. L'automne dans la poésie ouest-européenne, de Brockes à Lamartine (1720-1820). Mélanges Baldensperger. Paris, 1930.
Trevedy, J. La légende de La Tour d'**AUVERGNE**. La poésie et La Tour d'Auvergne. Bull. archéol. de l'Ass. bretonne, Saint-Brieuc, 3e série, 19, 1901.

—B—

Unger, E. **BABYLON**, die heilige Stadt. Berlin, 1931.
Montarel, A. **BACCHUS** dans la mythologie et dans l'opéra de Massenet. Ménestrel, 75, 1908.
Muret, M. Michel **BAKOUNINE** dans le roman. Journal des Débats, 9.XI.1928.
Kauffmann, F. **BALDER**: Mythus und Sage nach ihren dichterischen und re-

ligiösen Elementen untersucht. Strassburg, 1902.

Krappe, A. H. The Myth of Balder. A Study in Comparative Mythology. London, 1923.

Losch, F. Mythologische Studien im Gebiet des Baldermythus. Archiv f. Religionswissenschaft, 5, 1900.

Reichert, H. W. The Characterization of **BANCBANUS** in Grillparzer. SPh, 46, 1949.

Peine, S. Sankta **BARBARA**, die Schutzheilige der Bergleute und der Artillerie und ihre Darstellung in der Kunst. Leipzig, 1898.

BARBARIANS: See Primitivism below.

Braunholtz, E. Die erste nichtchristliche Parabel des **BARLAAM** und Josaphat, ihre Herkunft und Verbreitung. Halle, 1884.

Cosquin, E. La légende des saints Barlaam et Josaphat, son origine. Revue des questions historiques, Oct., 1880.

González, S. Una fuente de la Historia de Barlaan y Josafat. RyF, 119, 1940.

Jacobs, J. Barlaam and Josaphat, English Lives of Buddha. London, 1896.

Kuhn, E. Barlaam und Josaphat. SBAW, 1893.

Liebrecht, F. Die Quellen des Barlaam und Josaphat. Jb. f. rom. & engl. Literatur, 2. And in: Zur Volkskunde. Heilbronn, 1879.

Moldenhauer, G. Die Legende von Barlaam und Josaphat auf der iberischen Halbinsel. Halle, 1929.

Zotenberg, H. Notice sur le livre de Barlaam et Joasaph. In: Notices et extraits des manuscr. de la Bibl. Nationale, 28, 1886.

Bartley, J. Harrington and Saint **BASIL**. MLR, 42, 1947.

Krappe, A. H. La vision de Saint Basile et la légende de la mort de l'empereur Julien. RBPh. 1928.

Friedrich, E. Baskenland und **BASKEN** bei Pierre Loti. Diss. Würzburg, 1934.

Iriarte, D. M. de. L'influence basque dans Cervantes. Revue internat. des Etudes basques, 1933.

Reicher, G. Les Basques dans la littérature espagnole. RLC, 18, 1938.

Hermann, L. Das Bier im Volksmund (**BEER**). Berlin, 1930.

BELLS: See Clocks below.

Axon, W. E. A. The Story of **BELFAGOR** in Literature and Folklore. Transact. of Royal Society of Literature, 23, 1902.

Hosken, J. D. Christopher Marlowe and Belphegor. London, 1896.

Schreiber, W. I. Belphegor. JEGPh, 44, 1945.

Lebermann, N. **BELISAR** in der Literatur der romanischen und germanischen Nationen. Diss. Heidelberg. Nürnberg, 1899-1900.

Glenk, W. Belsazar in seinen verschiedenen Bearbeitungen. Progr. München, 1910.

Christophe, P. **BELLEROPHON** et sa légende. RBPh, 1943.

BEOWULF: See Comparisons, I. V. 1, and English Influences, IV. VIII. 14.

Anon. Ueber **BERLIN** (French influences). Berliner Monatsschr., 1784.

—— Berlin in französischer Beleuchtung. Gegenwart, 1874.

Friedemann, H. Berlin im Roman. LE, 10.

Hicks, F. C. **BERMUDA** in Poetry, 1610-1908. Hamilton (Bermuda), 1915.

BERNAUER: See Agnes Bernauer above.

Heinermann, T. Untersuchungen zur Entstehung der Sage von **BERNARDO DEL CARPIO**. Halle, 1927.

Merbach, P. A. **BERNHARD** von Weimar als dramatis persona. Bühnenvolksbund, 2, 1927.

Feist, A. Zur Kritik der **BERTASAGE**. Marburg, 1885.

Johnston, O. M. The Legend of Berte aux grands piés and the Märchen of Little Snowwhite. RLR, 51, 1908.

Karl, L. Die Sage von der Königin Berta. Budapest, 1909.

Memmer, A. Die altfranzösische Bertasage und das Volksmärchen. Halle, 1935.

Reinhold, J. Ueber die verschiedenen Fassungen der Bertasage. ZRPh, 35, 1911.

Stronski, S. La légende amoureuse de **BERTRAN DE BORN**. Paris, 1914.

BESTIAIRES' See Animals, I. VI. 11.

Matzke, J. E. The Oldest Form of the **BEVES** Legend. MPh, 10, 1912.

BIBLE: See II. V. 2.

Anon. **BISMARCK** in der Volksdichtung. Rhein.-Westph. Zt., 47, 1903.

Biese, A. Bismarck im Leben und in deutscher Dichtung. Berlin, 1916.

Landau, P. Bismarck in der deutschen Dichtung. Berliner Börsen Courier, 141, 1915.

Pasig, J. Bismarck im deutschen Lied. Friedenau-Berlin, 1910.

—— Bismarck in der deutschen Dichtung. Germania (Brüssel), 5, 1903.

Schäfer, H. R. Bismarck in der schwäbischen Dichtung. Heilbronn, 1895.

Singer, A. Bismarck in der Literatur. Würzburg, 1909.

Kellner, L. Caxton's **BLANCHARDYN** and Eglantine. London, 1890.

Strack, H. L. Der Blutaberglaube in der Menschheit, Blutmorde und Blutritus. (**BLOOD**). München, 1892.

Gombel, H. Die Fabel vom Magen und den Gliedern in der Weltliteratur (**BODY**). Halle, 1934.

Matzke, J. E. The Legend of the Eaten Heart. MLN, 26, 1911.

Kurath, M. Bohême, **BOHEMIEN** und Gesellschaft. ZFSL, 50, 1927.

Mathorez, J. Notes sur les Bohémiens en France. Bull. du Comité des Travaux historiques et géographiques. Paris, 1915.

BOLEYN: See Ann Boleyn above.

Sorbelli, A. **BOLOGNA** negli scrittori stranieri. Bologna, 1927-33.

Sieber, S. Cesare **BORGIA** in der Dichtung. Zs. f. Wissenschaft, Beilage der Hamburger Nachrichten, 34, 1912.

Campori, G. Una vittima della storia: Lucrezia Borgia. NAnt., 2, 1866.

Carruth, F. W. **BOSTON** in Fiction. Bookman (New York), Dec., 1901 & Jan., 1902.

Counson, A. Introduction à l'histoire poétique de Godefroid de **BOUILLON**, essai sur l'épopée moderne. Bruxelles, 1912.

Pigeonneau, H. Le cycle de la croisade et de la famille de Bouillon. Paris, 1877.

Lievsay, J. L. **BRAGADOCHIO**: Spenser's Legacy to the Character-Writers. MLQ, 2, 1941.

Boughner, D. C. The **BRAGGART** in Italian Renaissance Comedy. PMLA, 58, 1943.

Crawford, J. P. W. The Braggart Soldier and the Ruffian in the Spanish Drama of the Sixteenth Century. RR, 2, 1911.

Rüdiger, H. Zur Typologie des Aufschneiders. Literatur, June, 1938.

Urstaedt, Karoline. Der Kraftmeier im deutschen Drama von Gryphius bis zum Sturm und Drang. Diss. Giessen, 1926.

Brill. Van Sinte **BRANDANE.** In: Moltzer, Bibliothek van middelnederlandsche letterkunde. Groningen, 1871.

De Goeje. La légende de Saint Brandan. In: Actes du 8e Congrès intern. des Orientalistes tenu en 1889 à Stockholm. Leyden, 1891.

Jubinal, A. La légende latine de St. Brandaines. Paris, 1836.

Michel, F. Les voyages merveilleux de Saint Brandan. Paris, 1878.

Palgen, R. Brandansage und Purgatorio. Heidelberg, 1934.

Schirmer. Zur Brendanus-Legende. Leipzig, 1888.

Selmer, C. The Beginnings of the St. Brendan Legend on the Continent. Catholic Historical Rev., 29, 1943.

—— The Irish St. Brendan Legend in Lower Germany and on the Baltic Coast. Traditio, 4, 1947.

Suchier, H. Brandans Seefahrt. Roman. Studien, 1871-75.

Wright, T. St. Brandan, a Medieval Legend of the Sea in English Verse and Prose. London, 1844.

Tardel, H. **BREMEN** in Volksreim und Volkslied. Niederdeutsche Zs. für Volkskunde, 9, 1931.

Weber, C. A. **BRISTOLS** Bedeutung für die englische Romantik und die deutsch-englischen Beziehungen. Halle, 1935.

Koeppel, E. Spensers Florimell und die **BRITOMARTIS**-Sage des Antonius Liberalis. ALG, 107, 1901.

Talbert, J. K. John **BROWN** in American Literature. Diss. U. of Kansas, 1941.

Glazer, K. Georges Rodenbach, der Dichter des toten **BRUEGGE.** Marburg, 1917.

Bohning, Elizabeth E. **BRUNHILD** in Medieval Tradition. Delaware Notes, 17, 1945.

Gildersleeve, Virginia C. Brynhild in Legend and Literature. MPh, 1909.

Rothe, C. Brunhild und Kriemhild in deutscher Sage und Dichtung. Mitteil. d. deutschen Sprachvereins, 7, 1896.

Lowis von Menar, A. Die Brunnhildesage in Russland. Leipzig, 1923.

BRUT: See Celtic Contributions, IV. I. 7.

Brie, F. Popes **BRUTUS.** Anglia, 63, 1939.

Jones, R. E. Brutus in Cicero and Shakespeare. CJ, 38, 1943.

Koch, F. Geschichte der dramatischen Behandlung des Brutus-Lucretia-Stoffes. In: Albert Lindner als Dramatiker. Weimar, 1914.

McKee, K. N. Voltaire's Brutus During the French Revolution. MLN, 56, 1941.

Anderson, A. R. **BUCEPHALAS** and his Legend. TAPhA, 24, 1929.

BUDDHA: See Oriental Influences, II. I. 9.

Smith, H. N. **BUFFALO BILL**, Hero of the Popular Imagination. Southwest Rev., 33, 1948.

Anon. The Paul **BUNYAN** Tales. Minnesota History, 21, 1940.

Ames, C. C. Paul Bunyan—Myth or Hoax. Ibid.

Felton, H. W. The Legends of Paul Bunyan. New York, 1947.

Haney, Gladys J. Paul Bunyan Twenty-five Years After. JAFL, 55, 1942.
Le Fèvre, L. Paul Bunyan and Rip van Winkle. Yale Rev., 36, 1946.
Newton, S. Paul Bunyan of the Great Lakes. Chicago, 1946.
Turney, Ida V. Paul Bunyan Marches On. Portland (Ore.), 1942.
Krappe, A. H. The Legend of **BURIDAN** and the Tour de Nesle. MLR, 23, 1928.

—C—

Allen, J. C. The Julius **CAESAR** of Shakespeare and of History. PL, N.S., 5, 1901.
Altkamp, J. Die Gestaltung Cäsars bei Plutarch und Shakespeare. Bonn, 1933.
Asch, M. Shakespeare's and Voltaire's Julius Caesar Compared. Gardelegen, 1881.
Collischonn, G. A. O. Jacques Grévins Tragödie Caesar in ihrem Verhältniss zu Muret, Voltaire und Shakespeare. Marburg, 1886.
Dedecek, V. L. Etude littéraire et linguistique de Li Hystore de Julius Cesar de Jehan de Tuin. Philadelphia, 1926.
Delius, N. Shakespeares Julius Caesar und seine Quellen im Plutarch. JbShG, 17, 1882.
Doutrepont, H. G. La légende de César en Belgique. In: CR. des travaux du Congrès scientifique international catholique à Bruxelles, 1895.
Dunn, F. S. Julius Caesar in the English Chronicles. CJ, 14.
Guichard. La tragédie Julius Caesar de Marc-Antoine Muret. REL, 1943-44.
Gundolf (Gundelfinger), F. Caesar in der deutschen Literatur. Berlin, 1904.
—— Caesar, Geschichte seines Ruhmes. Berlin, 1924. Milano, 1932.
—— Caesar im neunzehnten Jahrhundert. Berlin, 1926.
—— Zur Geschichte von Cäsars Ruhm. NJWJ, 1930.
Gottschall, R. von. Die Cäsaren-Dramen. Berlin, 1892.
Hunter, M. Politics and Character in Shakespeare's Julius Caesar. Trans. of the Royal Society of Literature, 10, 1931.
Kohlrausch, R. Shakespeares Julius Cäsar und Cäsars Rom. Bühne & Welt, 1902.
Max, G. Zur Geschichte der Cäsar-Tragödien. Progr. Friedeberg, 1890. Cf. ZVL, 4.
Morf, H. Die Cäsartragödien Voltaires und Shakespeares. Oppeln, 1888 and ZFSL, 10, 1888.
Parodi, E. G. Le Storie di Cesare nella letteratura italiana dei primi secoli. Studi di filologia romanza, 4. Roma, 1889.
Peters, J. Ueber die Voltairesche Uebersetzung des Julius Caesar von Shakespeare. Archiv, 47, 1871.
Rosa, L. de. Shakespeare, Voltaire e Alfieri e la tragedia di Cesare. Camerino, 1900.
Sanctis, N. de. Cesare e Marco Bruto nei poeti tragici. Palermo, 1895.
Spiegelberger, W. Shakespeares Caesarbild. NM, 10.
Trabaud, P. Etude comparative sur le Jules César de Shakespeare et le même sujet par Voltaire. Mém. de l'Académie des sciences de Marseille, 1888-92.
Wesemann, H. Die Cäsarfabeln des Mittelalters. Progr. Löwenberg, 1879.
Bernès, H. Le Qain de Leconte de Lisle et ses origines littéraires. (**CAIN**). RHLF, 1911.
Brieger, A. Kain und Abel in der deutschen Dichtung. Berlin, 1934.
Duerrschmidt, H. Die Sage von Kain in der mittelalterlichen Literatur Englands. Bayreuth, 1919.
Graf, A. La poesia di Caino. NAnt, 134.
Guli, A. La figura di Caino nella letteratura moderna. Palermo, 1922.
Messac, R. Cain et le problème du mal dans Voltaire, Byron et Leconte de Lisle. RLC, 4, 1924.
Mornet, D. Une source négligée du Qain de Leconte de Lisle. Mélanges Baldensperger, Paris, 1930.
Schaffner, A. (Byron's) Cain und seine Quellen. Strassburg, 1880.
Devot, L. Notes pour servir à l'histoire poétique de la reprise de **CALAIS**. Almanach de la ville et du canton de Calais, 1858.
Moffat, M. M. Le Siège de Calais et l'opinion publique en 1765. RHLF, 1932.
Hankins, J. E. **CALIBAN** the Bestial Man. PMLA, 62, 1947.
Toynbee, P. Hugh **CAPET** in the Divina Commedia and the Satyre Ménippée. Academy, 24.VI.1893.
Castle, E. Zur Stoffgeschichte von **CARDENIO** und Celinde. AR, 23, 1939.
Ricci, J. L'histoire de Cardenio et Celinde dans le théâtre allemand. Paris, 1948.
Vogeler. Cardenio und Celinde des Andreas Gryphius und Shakespeares Romeo und Julia. Archiv, 79, 1887.
CARLOS: See Don Carlos below.
Ludwig, A. Lope de Vegas Dramen aus dem **KAROLINGISCHEN** Sagenkreise. Berlin, 1898.

Pausa, G. L'epopea carolingia in Abruzzo. Casalbordino, 1899.
Templin, E. H. Carolingian Heroes and Ballad Lines in Non-Carolingian Dramatic Literature. HR, 7, 1939.
Yocca, G. S. Saggio su l'Entrée de Spagne ed altre chansons de geste medioevali franco-italiane. Roma, 1895.
Smith, H. N. Kit **CARSON** in Books. Southwest Rev., 28, 1943.
Davreux, J. La légende de la prophétesse **CASSANDRE.** Liège, 1942.
Railo, E. The Haunted-**CASTLE:** A Study of the Elements of English Romanticism. London, 1927.
CASTRO: See Inés de Castro below.
Ottone, T. da. La leggenda di **CATERINA** vergine e martire di Alessandria. Genova, 1940.
Kunst, H. Geschichte der Legenden der heiligen Katharina von Alexandrien und der heiligen Maria Aegyptica. Halle, 1890.
Mussafia, A. Zur Katharinenlegende. SAWW, 1885.
Bilbassoff, B. A. von. Katharina II von Russland im Urteile der Weltliteratur. 2 vols. Berlin, 1897.
Vogt, A. Ben Jonson's Tragödie **CATILINE** and his Conspiracy und ihre Quellen. Diss. Halle, 1903.
Speck, H. B. G. Katilina im Drama der Weltliteratur. Leipzig, 1906.
Mitzka, W. Die deutschen **CATO**dichtungen des Mittelalters. ZDPh, 54, 1929.
Garcia Villada, Z. La batalla de **CAVADONGA** en la tradición y en la leyenda. RyF, 1918.
CELESTINA: See Spanish Contributions, IV. IV. 4.
CENCI: see also Shelley, IV. VIII. 12.
Gay, F. M. Two Notes on Les Cenci of Stendhal. RR, 1930.
Haselmayer, L. A. Hawthorne and the Cenci. NPh, 27, 1941-42.
Lombard, A. Stendhal et B. Cenci. Revue de Genève, 1.I.1927.
Montenevosi, O. Beatrice Cenci davanti alla giustizia dei suoi tempi e della storia. Roma, 1928.
Pincherle, B. Stendhal, Beatrice Cenci e la Repubblica Romana. Aretusa, 2, 1945.
Stratton, S. The Cenci Story in Literature and Fact. U. of Pa. Studies in English Drama, 1917.
Dumézil, G. Le problème des **CENTAURES.** Paris, 1929.
Novati, F. L'Anti**CERBERUS.** Rivista storica. (Mantova), 1884.
Fertig, R. Die Dramatisierungen des Schicksals Karls I. von England, besonders A. G. Butlers Tragödie **CHARLES THE FIRST.** Diss. Erlangen, 1912.
Peyre, R. A propos de la Vision de **CHARLES XI** de Mérimée. RHLF, 1, 1914.
Benson, A. B. **CHARLES XII** on the American Stage. SS, 17, 1943.
Wright, H. Some English Writers and Charles XII. Festschrift Ekwall. Uppsala, 1942.
Arens, E. Kaiser Karls Sage in Romanzen und Liedern. (**CHARLEMAGNE**). Köln, 1924.
Bartsch, K. Ueber Karl Meinet. Ein Beitrag zur Karlssage. Nürnberg, 1865.
Buckler, F. W. Harunu'l-Rashid and Charles the Great. Publications of the Mediaeval Academy. Cambridge (Mass.), 1931.
Duméril, A. La légende politique de Charlemagne au 18e siècle. Mémoires de l'Acad. de Toulouse, 10, 1878.
Herrtage. The English Charlemagne Romances. Romania (London), 11, 1879-81.
Hoffmann, H. Karl der Grosse im Bilde der Geschichtsschreibung des frühen Mittelalters (800-1250). Berlin, 1919.
Köster, R. Karl der Grosse als politische Gestalt in der Dichtung des deutschen Mittelalters. Hamburg, 1939.
Labanca, B. Carlomagno e i due papi Adriano e Leone III nell'arte christiana. Torino, 1903.
Masing, W. Karlssage und Rolandslied. Balt. Monatsschrift, 53, 1902.
Osterhage, G. Anklänge an die germanische Mythologie in der französischen Karlssage. ZRPh, 11, 1887.
Paris, G. Histoire poétique de Charlemagne. Paris, 1865.
Rauschen, G. Die Legende Karls des Grossen im 11. und 12. Jahrhundert (Vita Karoli Magni). Leipzig, 1890.
Reuschel, K. Die Sage vom Liebeszauber Karls des Grossen in dichterischer Behandlung der Neuzeit. Festschrift K. Vollmöller. Erlangen, 1908.
Walpole, R. N. Charlemagne and Roland, a Study of the Source of Two Middle English Metrical Romances. UCPPh, 1944.
Hanoteau, C. **CHARYBDE** et Scylla dans l'oeuvre virgilienne. L'Antiquité classique, 1939.
Paris, G. Le roman du **CHATELAIN DE COUCI.** Romania, 8, 1879.
Frappier, J. La **CHASTELAINE DE VERGI,** Marguerite de Navarre et

Bandello. Mélanges Strasbourg, Paris, 1945.

Lorenz, E. Die Castellanin von Vergi in der Literatur Frankreichs, Italiens, der Niederlande, Englands und Deutschlands. Halle, 1909.

Stiefel, A. L. Die Chastelaine de Vergy bei Marguerite von Navarra und bei Matteo Bandello. ZFSL, 38, 1911.

Anon. A Classic on **CHESS** (Tahsia's translation of 1584, of Ruy López' work of 1561). MB, 16.

Macdonnell. Origin and Early History of Chess. Journal Royal Asiatic Society, 1898.

Dell, F. **CHICAGO** in Fiction. Bookman, Nov., 1913.

Zart, G. **CHIDHER** in Sage und Dichtung. In: Sammlung Virchow. Hamburg, 1897.

CHIVALRY: See also Courtesy below.

Kilgour, R. L. The Decline of Chivalry as Shown in the French Literature of the Late Middle Ages. Harvard U.P., 1937.

Eicheler, S. Studien über die Mâze. Ein Beitrag zur Begriffs- & Geistesgeschichte der höfischen Kultur. Würzburg, 1942.

Lefèbvre St. Ogan. Essai sur l'influence française. (La Chevalerie). Paris, 1884.

Naumann, H. & Müller, G. Höfische Kultur. Halle, 1929.

Painter, S. French Chivalry: Chivalric Ideas and Practices in Mediaeval France. Baltimore, 1940.

Pitre, G. Le tradizioni cavalleresche popolari in Sicilia. Romania, 13, 1884.

Anon. Traité des trois imposteurs (**CHRIST**, Moise, Mohamet). Yverdon, 1768.

—— Das Leben Jesu von Strauss in England und Frankreich. Blätter z. Kunde der Litt. des Auslands, 1839.

—— Strauss's Leben Jesu in England. Beilage z. Allg. Zt., 18.X.1842.

—— Christus im Drama. New Yorker Staatszeitung, Sonntagsblatt, 15.III. 1903.

Beck, M. Ueber den deutschen Messiasgedanken. Neue Zürcher Zt., 20.IV. 1940.

Behn, F. Mithras, Wodan, Christus. WM, 155, 1933-34.

Bostick, W. F. Jesus and Socrates. Biblical World, 1916.

Brake, G. Das Leben Jesu als Drama. Protestant. Kirchen-Zt, 1882.

Brandes, G. Die Jesus-Sage. Berlin, 1925.

Clarke, G. H. Christ and the English Poets. Queen's Quarterly, 55, 1948.

Eastman, F. Christ in the Drama . . . of England and America. New York, 1947.

Ellis, C. The Christ in Shakespeare's Dramas and Sonnets. London, 1902.

Featherstum, H. W. The Christ of Our Poets. Nashville, 1901.

Friedrich, P. Das Christusdrama der Gegenwart. Bühne & Welt, 14, 1912.

Glover, T. R. The Influence of Christ in the Ancient World. Cambridge, 1929.

Godoretzky, N. The Humiliated Christ in Modern Russian Thought. London, 1938.

Grimm, W. Die Sage vom Ursprung der Christusbilder. Abhandlungen der K. Akad. der Wissenschaften. Berlin, 1842.

Guidi, A. La figura di Cristo nel poema di Milton. Humanitas, 1, 1946.

Günther, R. Das deutsche Christuslied des 19. Jahrhunderts. Eckart 3, 1908.

Hedler. Heilsbringer- und Erlöseridee in Roman und Drama seit 1890. Diss. Köln, 1922.

Heine, G. Dichtungen über Christus und Christen. Christl. Welt, 16, 1902.

Heuser, A. Die Erlösergestalt in der belletristischen Literatur seit 1890 als Deuterin der Zeit. Diss. Bonn, 1935.

Hillekamps, C. Christus im Roman. Literar.-musikal. Monatshefte, 4, 1922.

Hughes, M. Y. The Christ of Paradise Regained and the Renaissance Heroic Tradition. SPh, 35, 1938. Cf. ibid, 36, 1939.

Kappstein, T. Le Christ dans la littérature d'aujourd'hui. RRh. 1929.

Lange, Dorothea. Das Christusdrama des 19. und 20. Jahrhunderts. Diss. München, 1921.

Leixner, O. von. Christusgestalt und Jesugedanken in der deutschen Dichterei (1883-1903). Tägl. Rundschau, 50-57, 1903.

Luther, A. Jesus und Judas in der Dichtung. Hanau, 1909.

Luther, P. Christusdarstellungen. Deutsche Monatsschrift, 1903.

Merejkovsky, D. Jésus l'inconnu: son visage dans l'histoire. MF, 15.VI.1934.

Mims, E. The Christ of the Poets. Nashville, 1948.

Minnigerode, I. von. Die Christusanschauung des Novalis. Berlin, 1941.

Nippold, F. Das deutsche Christuslied des 19. Jahrhunderts. Leipzig, 1902.

Petzold, Gertrud von. Heilandsbilder im deutschen Roman der Gegenwart. Giessen, 1924.

Petzold, H. Das französische Jesus Christus Drama nach dem Verfall der mittelalterlichen Mysterienspiele (1539-1936). Diss. Leipzig. Dresden, 1937.

Pfannmüller, G. Jesus im Urteil der Jahrhunderte. Leipzig, 1908.

Pfleger, K. Christus in west- und ostchristlicher Beleuchtung. Hochland, Aug., 1933.
Philippi, F. Das Jesusdrama. Christl. Welt, 21, 1906.
Preuss, H. Das Bild Christi im Wandel der Zeiten. Leipzig, 1915.
Reinisch, R. Die Pseudoevangelien von Jesu und Marias Kindheit in der romanischen und germanischen Litteratur. Diss. Leipzig, 1879.
Renier, R. Il Gelindo, dramma sacro piemontese della Natività di Cristo. Illustr. letter., 3. (Torino), 1896.
Richter, J. Hölderlins Christusmythus und die deutsche Gegenwart. München, 1941.
Schmidt, K. Die Darstellung von Christi Höllenfahrt. Diss. Marburg, 1915.
Schönfeld, F. Das Jesusbild nach der Darstellung moderner Dichter. Progr. Strehlen, 1907.
Sinchowitz, S. Jesus als dramatisches Problem. Kultur, 1903.
Spiero, H. Die Heilandsgeschichte in der neueren deutschen Dichtung. Berlin, 1926.
Suchier, H. Ueber provençalische Bearbeitung der Kindheit Jesu. ZRPh, 7, 1884.
Visser, W. J. A. Die Entwicklung des Christusbildes in Literatur und Kunst in der frühchristlichen und frühbyzantinischen Zeit. Bonn, 1934.
Weidemann, K. A. Die neuesten Darstellungen des Lebens Jesu von Renan, Schenkel und Strauss. Gotha, 1864.
Werner, R. M. Moderne Messiasdichtungen. In: Vollendete und Ringende. Minden, 1900.
Wittmann. Christus im Drama. Neue Freie Presse, 22.II.1903.
Wolfe, D. M. The Role of Milton's Christ. Sewanee Rev., 51, 1943.
Bockemühl, E. Weihnacht in der modernen Dichtung. (**CHRISTMAS**). Ostdeutsche Monatshefte, 7, 1927.
Boner, E. G. Natale e capo d'anno nella letteratura nordica. In: Saggi d. letteratura straniera. Messina, 1896.
Bülow, P. Der Weihnachtsabend in der deutschen Dichtung. Türmer, 29, 1927.
Freybe, A. Weihnachten in deutscher Dichtung. Leipzig, 1906.
—— Deutsche Weihnachtsdichtung. Konservat. Monatsschrift, 66, 1908.
Kornfeld, E. M. Der deutsche Weihnachtsbaum in der Dichtung. Hamburg. Nachrichtenblatt, 52, 1905.
—— Der Weihnachtsbaum. Oldenburg, 1906.
Martin, E. Weihnachtsspiele. Mitteilungen f. Gottesdienst & Kunst, 18.
Novati, F. I misteri del Natale nel medio evo. Emporium, 2, 1895-96.
Saintyves, P. Saint **CHRISTOPHE** successeur d'Anubis, d'Hermès et d'Héracles. Paris, 1936.
Rosenfeld, H. F. Der hl. **CHRISTOPHORUS**, seine Verehrung und seine Legende. Leipzig, 1937.
The **CID**: See Spanish Contributions, IV. IV. 5.
Hansen, M. W. The Society of the **CINCINNATI**. SAQ, 44, 1945.
Bleich, E. Das Märchen vom Aschenbrödel vornehmlich in der deutschen Volks- und Kunstdichtung. (**CINDERELLA**). ZVL, N.F., 18.
Cox, M. R. Cinderella. London, 1893.
Klemm, K. Sunabai Dschai. Ein Aschenbrödelmärchen. Zs. des Vereins für Volkskunde, 5, 1895.
Lang, A. Three Hundred and Forty Five Variants of Cinderella, Catskin, and Cap of Lushes. London, 1893.
Hughes, M. Y. Spenser's Acrasia and the **CIRCE** of the Renaissance. JHI, 4, 1943.
Goldschmidt, R. K. Die Kleinstadt im Drama. (**CITY**). Blätter d. württemberg. Volksbundes, 4, 1922.
Hermann, G. Der Grosstadtroman. Stettin, 1931.
Kardel, H. Die Stadt in der Literatur. Diss. Kiel, 1921.
Schröter, W. Die deutsche Kleinstadt in der Dichtung. Progr. Oschersleben, 1906.
Werder, P. von. Literatur im Bann der Verstädterung. Leipzig, 1943.
Heltzel, V. B. "The Rules of **CIVILITY**" (1671) and its French Source. MLN, 1928.
Rebora, P. Civiltà italiana e Civiltà inglese (Shakespeare). Firenze, 1937.
Aiken, P. Chaucer's Legend of **CLEOPATRA** and the Speculum historiale. Spec., 1938.
Ellis, O. C. Cleopatra in the Tide of Time. London, 1947.
Horner, E. Das Aufkommen des englischen Geschmackes in Wien und Ayrenhoffs Trauerspiel Kleopatra und Antonius. Euphorion, 4, 1895.
Mather, F. J. On Chaucer's Cleopatra and her Pit of Serpents. Nation, 1898.
Moeller, G. H. Die Auffassung der Kleopatra in der Tragödienlitteratur der romanischen und germanischen Völker. Diss. Freiburg. Ulm, 1888.
—— Beitrag zur dramatischen Kleopatra-Literatur. Progr. Schweinfurt, 1907.
Neri, F. La prima tragedia di Etienne

Jodelle (and his probable source, Cleopatra by de Cesari). GSLI, 74.
Traub, W. Auffassung und Gestaltung der Cleopatra in der englischen Literatur. Würzburg, 1938.
Billon, D. Campanologie. Etude sur les cloches et les sonneries françaises et étrangères. (**CLOCKS AND BELLS**). Caen, 1866.
Morel, G. Die Glocke im Lichte der deutschen Dichtung. Glarus, 1894.
Pesch, J. Die Glocken in Geschichte, Sage, Volksglauben, Volksbrauch und Dichtung. Dülmen i.W., 1918.
Sauveterre, Abbé. Essai sur le symbolisme de la cloche dans ses rapports et ses harmonies avec la religion. Paris, 1883.
Schick, E. Die Glocken in der Dichtung. Reformierte Schweiz, July, 1947.
Wins, A. L'horloge à travers les âges. Mém. et Pub. de la Soc. des Sciences, des Arts et des Lettres du Hainaut, 67, 1924.
Goedheer, A. J. Irish and Norse Traditions about the Battle of **CLONTARF**. Haarlem, 1938.
Hadas, M. **CLYTEMNESTRA** in Elizabethan Dress (Lady Macbeth). CW, 32, 1939.
Buechner, A. Klytämnestra und Maria Stuart. Deutsches Museum, 36-37, 1864.
Bastier, P. Christophe **COLOMB** et la littérature mondiale. Hispaniola, 1938.
Bédarida, H. Christoph Colomb dans la littérature française. Genova, 7.VII. 1930.
Celle, M. G. Gli elementi umanistici nella tradizione colombiana primitiva. MC, 1932.
Gleis, P. G. Columbus in Forgotten German Literature. AGR, 9, 1942.
Loevinson, E. Cristoforo Colombo nella letteratura tedesca. Torino, 1893.
Nunn, G. E. Marinus of Tyre's Place in the Columbus Concepts. Imago Mundi, 2, 1937.
Terenzi, A. Cristoforo Colombo e l'epica italiana del '400 al '900. Genova, 1939.
Wetzel, E. Der Kolumbus-Stoff in dem deutschen Geistesleben. Breslau, 1935.
COLONIAL Literature: See African Contributions, II. I. 8 & also I. II. 2.
Allen, D. C. Symbolic **COLOR** in the Literature of the English Renaissance. PhQ, 15, 1936.
Ellis, H. The Colour-Sense in Literature. Contemp. Rev., 69, 1896. & London, 1931.
Jacobsohn, M. Die Farbe in der mittelhochdeutschen Dichtung der Blütezeit. Diss. Zürich, Leipzig, 1915.
Mann, M. La couleur perse en ancien français et chez Dante. Romania, 49, 1923.
Mead, W. E. Color in Old English Poetry. PMLA, 14, 1899.
—— Colour in the English and Scottish Ballads. Festschrift Furnivall. Oxford, 1901.
Peltzer, A. Die ästhetische Bedeutung von Goethes Farbenlehre. Heidelberg, 1903.
Pratt, A. E. The Use of Color in the Verse of the English Romantic Poets. Chicago, 1898.
Richter, M. Das Schrifttum über Goethes Farbenlehre. Diss. Dresden, 1938.
Skard, S. The Use of Color in Literature. Proc. Amer. Philos. Soc., 90, 1946.
Turmann, M. Die Farbenbezeichnungen in der Dichtung der englischen Renaissance. Diss. Berlin, 1934.
Veckenstedt, E. Die Farbenbezeichnungen im Chanson de Roland und in der Nibelunge Not. Zs. f. Völkerpsychol. & Sprachwiss., 17, 1887.
Wackernagel, W. Die Farben- und Blumensprache des Mittelalters. In: Kleinere Schriften, 1. Leipzig, 1872.
Willms, J. E. Untersuchung über den Gebrauch der Farbenbezeichnung in der Poesie Altenglands. Münster, 1902.
Widmann, W. Der Komet in der deutschen Dichtung. (**COMET**). Magdeburger Zt., 49, 1910.
Baudin, M. The **CONQUEROR** in XVIIth Century French Drama. MLN, 1937.
Dvornik, F. Les légendes de **CONSTANTIN** et de Méthode vues de Byzance. Byzantinoslavica, (Praha), 1933.
Laehr, G. Die konstantinische Schenkung in der abendländischen Literatur des Mittelalters bis zur Mitte des 14. Jahrhunderts. Berlin, 1926.
Levison, W. Konstantinische Schenkung und Silvesterlegende. Festschrift Ehrle, 2. Roma, 1924.
Luecke, E. Das Leben der **CONSTANZE** bei Trivet, Gower und Chaucer. Anglia, 14, 1892.
Cocchia, E. La leggenda di **CORIOLANO** e l'origine della poesia in Roma. NAnt. Nov. 1895 & Apr. 1896.
Pascal, F. Les **COSAQUES** et la littérature. RP, 1.X.1915.
Lot, F. Les thèmes poétiques: le sentiment **COSMIQUE**. Mfr. 15.I.1933.
Platt, J. H. The Cosmic Sense as Manifested in Shelley and Whitman. Conservator, 1894.
Stiefel, A. L. Jean Rotrous **COSROES**,

seine Quellen und Nachahmungen. ZFSL, 23, 1900.
COURTS: See Law below.
Anitchkof, E. Joachim de Flore et les milieux **COURTOIS.** Roma, 1931.
Barnett, G. L. Gabricl Harvey's Castillo, sive Aulicus and De Aulica; A Study of their Place in the Literature of Courtesy. SPh, 42, 1945.
Bezzola, R. R. Les origines et la formation de la littérature courtoise en Occident. Paris, 1944. Cf. CL, 1, 1949.
Bhattacherje, M. M. Courtesy in Shakespeare. Calcutta, 1940.
Crane, T. F. Italian Social Customs of the XVIth Century and their Influence on the Literature of Europe. New Haven, 1920.
Magendie, M. La politesse mondaine et les théories de l'honnêteté en France, au XVIIe siècle, de 1600 à 1660. Paris, 1925.
West, C. B. Courtoisie in Anglo-Norman Literature. Oxford, 1938. Cf. Spec. Oct. 1938.
Lunsford, Juanita. The Louisiana **CREOLE** in Literature. Diss. La. State U, 1940.
Hilka, A. Zum **CRESCENTIASTOFF.** Archiv, 133, 1915.
Mussafia, A. Ueber eine italienische metrische Uebersetzung der Crescentiasage. SAWW, 51, 1865-66.
Stefanovic, S. Die Crescentia-Florence Sage. RF, 29, 1911.
Law, Helen H. **CROESUS:** From Herodotus to Boccaccio. CJ, 43, 1948.
Filon, A. Les drames de Victor Hugo et l'histoire d'Angleterre I. **CROMWELL.** Journal des Débats, 26.XI.1902.
Parker, V. T. Cromwell in der schönen Literatur Englands. Diss. Zürich, 1919.
Sée, H. Le Cromwell de V. Hugo et le Cromwell de l'histoire. MF, 1927.
Tillotson, K. Michael Drayton as a Historian in the Legend of Cromwell. MLR, 34, 1939.
Tournier, G. Les points de départ du Cromwell de Victor Hugo. RLC, 7, 1927.
Trost, K. Cromwell als Held der Tragödie. Norddeutsche Allg. Zt., 359, 1894.
Tardel, II. Zur Stoffgeschichte von Chamissos Künstlerlegende Das **KRUZIFIX.** Archiv, 124, 1910.
Bédier, J. Les Chansons de Croisade. (**CRUSADES**). Paris, 1909.
Brognoligo, G. Ivanhoe e i Lombardi alla prima Crociata. In: Studi di storia letteraria. Roma, 1904.
Cahen, C. Indigènes et Croisés: quelques mots à propos d'un médecin d'Amaury et de Saladin. Syria, 15, 1934.
Curtius, E. R. Der Kreuzzugsgedanke und das altfranzösische Epos. Archiv, 169, 1936.
Dreesbach, E. Der Orient in der altfranzösischen Kreuzzugslitteratur. Diss. Breslau, 1901.
Hatem, A. Les poèmes épiques des croisades. Essai sur l'activité littéraire dans les colonies franques de Syrie au moyen-âge. Paris, 1932.
Hoepffner, E. Deux notes sur le troubadour Giraut de Borneil. Romania, 63, 1937.
Lewent, K. Das altprovenzalische Kreuzlied. RF, 21, 1908.
Roy, E. Les poèmes français relatifs à la première croisade. Le poème de 1356 et ses sources. Romania, 55, 1929.
Schindler, H. Die Kreuzzüge in der altprovenzalischen und mittelhochdeutschen Lyrik. Progr. Dresden-Altstadt, 1889.
Throop, P. A. Criticism of Papal Crusade Policy in Old French and Provençal. Spec., Oct., 1938.
—— Criticism of the Crusade: A Study of Public Opinion and Crusade Propaganda. Amsterdam, 1940.
Trebe, J. H. Les trouvères et leur exhortations aux croisades. Progr. Leipzig, 1886.
Wright, J. K. The Geographical Lore of the Time of the Crusades. New York, 1925.
Niedermann, J. Kultur, Werden und Wandlungen des Begriffs von Cicero bis Herder. (**CULTURE**). Firenze, 1941.
Schulz-Tharau, O. Die Kultur der Gegenwart als Stoff der Dichtung. Xenien, 4, 1911.
CUPID: See also Amor above.
Boberg, I. M. The Tale of Cupid and Psyche. Classica & Mediaevalia, 1. København), 1938.
Spencer, F. A. The Literary Lineage of Cupid. CW, 25, 1932.
Radermacher, L. **CYPRIAN** der Magier. Archiv f. Religionswissenschaft, 21.
Reitzenstein, R. Cyprian der Magier. Nachrichten d. Ges. d. Wissenschaft zu Göttingen, 1917.
Grivec, F. Die Slavenapostel **CYRILLUS** und Methodius. Mainz, 1928.
Ledit, J. Les légendes slaves des S.S. Cyrille et Méthode. Gregorianum (Roma), 1933.
Maly, P. La vie des S.S. Cyrille et Méthode et leurs rapports avec Rome et Byzance. Hlinsko, 1936.

—D—

Albers, J. H. König **DAGOBERT** in Geschichte, Legende und Sage. Progr. 1882.

Raschen, J. F. L. Earlier and later Versions of the Friendship Theme: **DAMON** and Pythias. MPh, 11, 1921.

Megas, G. A. Die Sage von **DANAOS** und den Danaiden. H, 1933.

Kurtz, L. P. The **DANCE OF DEATH** and the Macabre Spirit in European Literature. New York, 1934.

Beltrami, A. Le danze macabri. Comment. dell' Ateneo di Brescia, 1894.

Buchheit, G. Der Totentanz. Seine Entstehung und Entwicklung. Leipzig, 1927.

Dimier, L. Les danses macabres et l'idée de la mort dans l'art chrétien. Paris, 1902.

Dollriess, J. Totentanztexte seit dem 16. Jahrhundert. Diss. Königsberg, 1928.

Fehse, W. Das Totentanzproblem. ZDPh, 1910.

Hirschberg, L. Totentänze in neuerer Zeit. Zs. f. Bücherfreunde, 7, 1903.

Kastner, G. La danse des morts. Dissertations et recherches historiques, philosophiques, littéraires et musicales sur les divers monuments de ce genre qui existent ou qui ont existé tant en France qu' à l'étranger. Paris, 1852.

Kozaky, J. Geschichte der Totentänze. Budapest, 1936.

Lambrecht, N. Der Totentanz in der modernen Literatur. Literar. Warte, 6, 1905.

Manasse, E. M. The Dance Motive of the Latin Dance of Death. Medievalia & Humanistica, 4, 1946.

Stegemeier, H. G. The Dance of Death in Folksong. Diss. Chicago, 1939.

Walton, T. La danse aux aveugles. Festschrift L.E. Kastner. Cambridge, 1932.

Goldstein, M. **DARIUS,** Xerxes und Artaxerxes im Drama der neueren Literaturen. Münchener Beiträge, 54. Leipzig, 1912.

Dannenberg, M. Die Verwendung des biblischen Stoffes von **DAVID** und Bathseba im englischen Drama. Diss. Königsberg, 1905.

Krempien, H. H. Der Stil der Davideis von Abraham Cowley im Kreis ihrer Vorläufer. Hamburg, 1936.

Bunston, A. The German Idea of **DEATH.** British Review, July, 1915.

Adler, A. Falstaff's Holy Dying, Pagan as Well as Christian. MLN, 61, 1946.

Bluemner, H. Die Schilderung des Sterbens in der griechischen Dichtkunst. NJKA, 1917.

Bornstein, P. Der Dichter des Todes in der modernen Literatur. Berlin, 1899.

—— Der Tod in der modernen Literatur und andere Essays. Leipzig, 1900.

Borriello, A. La visione della morte in G. Leopardi. Napoli, 1936.

Cappuccio, C. Il pensiero della morte nella lirica del Carducci. Conv., 1933.

Collin, J. Heinrich von Kleist, der Dichter des Todes. Euphorion, 27, 1926.

Döring-Hirsch, E. Tod und Jenseits im Spätmittelalter. Berlin, 1927.

Fisquill, R. Death and La Mort. NAR, 1914.

Fontinoy, C. Le thème de la mort par amour dans la littérature latine. RBPh, 1942.

Fougère, J. Thomas Mann ou la séduction de la mort. Paris, 1947.

Freybe, A. Das memento mori in deutscher Sitte . . . und Dichtung. Gotha, 1909.

Garnier, A. P. Les thèmes poétiques: La mort dans la poésie. Mfr, 10.XI.1926.

Gehl, W. Das Todesproblem im Spätwerk Rilkes. D&V, 42, 1942.

Gilbert, A. H. Robert Herrick on Death. MLQ, 5, 1944.

Göring, Bertha. Der Tod in Literatur und Kunst. Christl. Frau, 13, 1915.

Grolmann, A. von. Das Problem von Leben und Tod in der zeitgenössischen Literatur. ZDK, 44, 1930.

Grützmacher, B. G. Die moderne Auffassung des Todes (Th. Mann & Goethe). Geisteskultur, 36, 1927.

Hartmann, C. Der Tod in seiner Beziehung zum menschlichen Dasein bei Augustinus. Diss. Giessen, 1932.

Hauvette, H. La morte vivante (Julia, etc.). Paris, 1933.

Isola, M. dell'. L'invocation à la mort chez quelques poètes italiens. EI, 1935.

Kohn-Bramstedt, E. & Henderson, P. The Problem of Death: a) in German Literature and b) in English Literature. The Aryan Path, 1939.

Krapp, L. Das Todesproblem in der modernen Literatur. Kultur, 4 (Wien), 1903.

Kroll, J. Tod und Teufel in der Antike. Verhandlungen der Versammlung deutscher Philologen, 56, 1927.

Landenberger, A. Kindertotenlieder. Monatsblätter f. deutsche Literatur, 8, 1904.

Lockwood, P. Post-mortem Wit in Folk Tale, Literature, and Roman Law. TAPhA, 17, 1921.

Longi, Olga. La terre et les morts dans l'oeuvre de Chateaubriand. Baltimore, 1934.
Mahler, E. Die russische Totenklage. Leipzig, 1935.
Nolte, F. Der Todesbegriff bei R. M. Rilke, H. von Hofmannsthal und Thomas Mann. Heidelberg, 1934.
O'Connor, Sister Mary C. The Art of Dying Well: the Development of the Ars moriendi. New York, 1942.
Popa, N. J. Le sentiment de la mort chez G. de Nerval. Mélanges de l'Ecole Roumaine en France. Paris, 1927.
Portier, L. Le thème de la mort chez Leopardi. RLC, 17, 1937.
Praz, M. La Carne, la Morte, e il Diavolo nella letteratura romantica. Milano, 1930.
Rauch, B. Tod und Sterben in der modernen Lyrik. Progr. Melten, 1912.
Regenbogen, O. Schmerz und Tod in den Tragödien Senecas. VBW, 7.
Rehm, W. Der Todesgedanke in der deutschen Dichtung vom Mittelalter bis zur Romantik. Halle, 1928.
Riboni, D. Le thème de la mort chez Hermann Hesse. Suisse contemp, 4.II. 1947.
Sauer, K. Untersuchungen zur Darstellung des Todes in der griechisch-römischen Geschichtsschreibung. Frankfurt, 1930.
Schmid, W. & Wucherpfennig, H. Die Volksballaden vom Totenamt. Beispiele deutscher und schottischer Balladenkunst. NM, 9.
Schwebel, O. Der Tod in deutscher Sage und Dichtung. Berlin, 1876.
Sexau, R. Der Tod im deutschen Drama des 17. und 18. Jahrhunderts. Bern, 1907.
Suchier, W. Der Schwank von der viermal getöteten Leiche in der Literatur des Abend- und Morgenlandes. Halle, 1922.
Thompson, W. M. Der Tod in der englischen Lyrik des siebzehnten Jahrhunderts. Breslau, 1935.
Unger, R. Herder, Novalis und Kleist. Studien über die Entwicklung des Todesproblemes. Frankfurt, 1922.
Vordtriede, W. Der Tod als ewiger Augenblick (Droste-Hülshoff & Hofmannsthal). MLN, 63, 1948.
Wentzlaff-Eggebert, F. W. Das Problem des Todes in der deutschen Lyrik des 17. Jahrhunderts. Leipzig, 1932.
Gottschall, R. Die **DEMETRIUS**-Dramen. Berlin, 1892.
Alexeev, P. Boris Godunov et le faux Dmitrij dans le drame de l'Europe occidentale. Leningrad, 1936.
Flex, W. Die Entwicklung des tragischen Problems in den deutschen Demetriusdramen von Schiller bis zur Gegenwart. Diss. Erlangen, 1912.
Hagemann, A. Der falsche Demetrius in Geschichte und Dichtung. Tagesbote, 29, (Brünn), 1906.
Henzen, W. Die Demetrius-Dramen. Leipziger Tageblatt, 248, 1900.
Lachmann, E. Die Natur des Demetrius. Frankfurt, 1941.
Plantenius, T. H. Der falsche Demetrius. Bielefeld, 1904.
Popek, A. Der falsche Demetrius in der Dichtung. Progr. Linz, 1892-93.
Woczwak, J. Zwei Demetrius-Fragmente. Progr. Lemberg, 1913.
Landi, C. **DEMOGORGONE**, con saggio di nuova edizione delle Genealogie Deorum Gentilium del Boccaccio. Palermo, 1930.
Slaughter, E. Milton's Demogorgon. PhQ, 1931.
Callois, R. Les spectres de midi dans la **DEMONOLOGIE** slave. Rev. des Etudes slaves, 16, 1937.
Graf, A. Demonologia di Dante. GSLI, 9, 1887.
Mortier, A. Le démon dans ses incarnations dramatiques. Paris, 1924.
Siepen, B. Dämonisches Menschentum in der neuen Dichtung. LE, 1921.
Tegethoff, E. Ueber die Dämonen im deutschen und französischen Märchen. Schweiz. Archiv f. Volkskunde, 24, 1924.
Treffenfeld, H. J. Der alte **DERFFLINGER** in Sage und Geschichte. Daheim, 42, 1906.
Appleton, R. B. The **DEUS EX MACHINA** in Euripides. CR, 34.
Duncan, T. S. The deus ex machina in Greek Tragedy. PhQ, 1935.
Malge, J. **DEUX-PONTS**, ville d'influence française au XVIIIe siècle. RRh, 1923.
DEVIL: See also Satan below.
Abu'L-Faraj Ibn Al-Jawzi. The Devil's Delusion. Islamic Culture, 12, 1938.
Barowicz, W. Der Teufel in der Poesie. Oesterr.-Ungar. Revue, 1896.
Baumgarten, S. I Bulgari, gli Ungheresi e il diavolo in un poema epico del seicento. L'Europe orientale, 1934.
Billanovich. Diavolo e vangelo nella Commedia dell'arte. Riv. ital. del Dramma, 1938.
Bolte, J. Der Teufel in der Kirche. ZVL, 11, 1897.

Burton, Dorothy J. The Compact with the Devil in the Middle-English Vision of Piers the Plowman. Calif. Folklore Quarterly, 5, 1946.
Cobbe, F. P. The Devil: His Origin, Greatness and Decline. New York, 1871.
Cocchiara, G. Il diavolo nella tradizione popolare italiana. Palermo, 1945.
Cochrane, C. N. Diabolism in Graeco-Roman Thought. Journal of Hellenic Studies, 1939.
Crawford, J. P. W. The Devil as a Dramatic Figure in the Spanish Religious Drama Before Lope de Vega. RR, 1, 1910.
Cushman, L. W. The Devil and the Vice in the English Dramatic Literature Before Shakespeare. Halle, 1900.
Delines, M. Le Diable et le satanisme dans les littératures européennes. BURS, 1, 1904.
Dreyer, M. Der Teufel in der deutschen Dichtung des Mittelalters. I. Von den Anfängen bis auf das XIV. Jahrhundert. Diss. Rostock, 1884.
Graf, A. Il diavolo. Torino, 1889. Cf. also NAnt, 1889.
Grillet, C. Le diable dans la littérature du XIXe siècle. Lyon, 1935.
Hacks, C. & Taril, L. Le diable au XIXe siècle. Paris, 1892-95.
Haslinghuis, E. De Duivel in het drama der middeleuwen. Diss. Leiden, 1913.
Jallonghi, E. Fra Diavolo nella storia e nell' arte. Città di Castello, 1911.
Kahle, A. Der Teufel in der Poesie. Gegenwart, 12-13, 1896.
Krappe, A. H. The Vassal of the Devil. AR, 7, 1923.
Louandre, C. Le diable, ses moeurs, etc. RDM, 15.VIII.1842.
Matuszewski. Der Teufel in der Poesie. (In Polish). Ateneum 1, 1893 & Warschau, 1894.
Newald, R. Die Teufelsliteratur und die Antike. Blätter f. d. Gymnasialwesen, 53, 1927.
Osborn, M. Die Teufelliteratur des XVI. Jahrunderts. Berlin, 1893. Cf. Euphorion, 3. & Zs. f. Kulturgeschichte, 4.
Roskoff, G. Geschichte des Teufels. 2 vols. Leipzig, 1869.
Rudwin, M. J. Der Teufel in den deutschen geistlichen Spielen. Göttingen, 1915.
—— The Devil in Legend and Literature. Chicago, 1931.
—— Les écrivains diaboliques de France. Paris, 1937.
Sequi, G. I diavoli di Dante e di Milton. Giornale di politica e di letteratura, 15, 1939.
Turmel, J. Histoire du diable. Paris, 1931.
Wolthius, G. W. Vitzliputzli: Een mexicaanse oorlogsgod als duivel in de poppenkast. (Vitzliputzli en Faust, in Nederland, in Duitsland). Tijdschrift voor Taal en Letteren, 28.
Wünsche, A. Der Sagenkreis vom geprellten Teufel. Leipzig, 1905.
Bargetzki, K. F. **DIDO** in der Geschichte und in der Dichtung. Progr. Wien, 1898.
Cram, R. V. Dido, Queen of Hearts. CJ, 27, 1931.
Eyer, C. Boisrobert's La Vraye Didon ou la Didon chaste. RR, 32, 1941.
Friedrich, J. Die Didodramen des Dolce, Jodelle und Marlowe in ihrem Verhältniss zu einander und zu Vergils Aeneis. Diss. Erlangen, 1888.
Kowalski, J. De Didone graeca et latina. Bull. de l'Acad. polonaise de Cracovie, 1929.
Lida, María R. Dido y su defensa en la literatura española. RFH, 4-5, 1942-43.
Meier, K. Ueber die Didotragödien des Jodelle, Hardy und Scudéry. Diss. Leipzig. Zwickau, 1891.
Oppenheim, D. E. Vergils Dido. Zs. f. Individualpsychologie, 3.
Perrotin, L. Pour Dido. Mélanges Laumonier. Paris, 1935.
Raeli, V. Il dramma di Didone. Virgilio, Metastasio e gli operisti pugliesi. Iapygia (Bari), 1930.
Semrau, E. Dido in der deutschen Dichtung. Leipzig, 1930.
Vysoky, Z. K. Les sources de l'épisode de l'amour de Didon dans l'Eneide. (In Czech). In: Pio Vati. Praha, 1930.
Altaner, B. **DIETRICH VON BERN** in der neueren Literatur. Breslau, 1912.
Friese, H. Thidreksaga und Dietrichsepos. Berlin, 1914.
Studer, Ella. Russisches in der Thidreksaga. Sprache & Dichtung, Bern.
Axon, W. E. A. The Legend of the **DISGUISED KNIGHT.** Trans. Royal Society of Literature, 9, 1870.
Ulrich, H. Beiträge zur Geschichte der Tauchersage. (**DIVER**). Progr. Dresden, 1884.
—— Die Tauchersage in ihrer litterarischen und volksthümlichen Entwicklung. ALG, 10, 14.
Barth, E. Die Puppe und ihre Dichter. (**DOLLS**). Literatur, 28, 1925.
Mussafia, A. Ueber die Quellen des altfranzösischen **DOLOPATHOS.** Wien, 1865.
Anon. **DON CARLOS** von Schiller ins

Englische übersetzt. Blätter zur Kunde der Litt. des Auslands, 1837.
—— Schillers Don Carlos in französischer Bearbeitung. Europa, 30, 1856.
—— Die Quellen des Schillerschen Don Carlos. Europa, 27.
Bastier, P. Lezay-Marnesia et Don Carlos. Alsace française, 18 & 25.VII.1925.
Bibl, V. Don Carlos in Geschichte und Dichtung. Zs. f.d. österr. Gymnasien, 68, 1917.
Cattaneo, C. Il Don Carlos dello Schiller e il Filippo dell' Alfieri. In: Opere edite e inedite, a cura di A. Bertino, 1. Firenze, 1881.
Doyle, H. G. The Don Carlos Theme. MLN, 40, 1926.
Elster, G. Zur Entstehungsgeschichte des Don Carlos. Halle, 1889.
Geffroy, G. Don Carlos de Schiller, adaptation de M. Charles Raymond. Rev. Encyclopédique, 31.X.1896.
Gensel, W. Don Carlos in Paris. MLIA, 45, 1896.
Goedeke, K. Don Carlos Dichtungen und Nachahmungen. In: Grundriss zur Geschichte der deutschen Dichtung, 6, 1884-98.
Heller, H. J. Die Quellen des Schillerschen Don Carlos. Archiv, 1859.
Levi, E. Storia poetica di Don Carlos. Parma, 1914.
—— Il principe Don Carlos nella leggenda e nella poesia. Publ. dell' Instituto Cristoforo Colombo, 9.
Lieder, F. W. C. The Don Carlos Theme in Literature. JEGPh, 9, 1910 and HSPhL, 12, 1930.
—— Bayard Taylor's Adaptation of Schiller's Don Carlos. JEGPh, 16, 1917.
Loewenberg, J. Ueber Otways und Schillers Don Carlos. Diss. Heidelberg, 1886.
Mueller, E. Otways, Schillers und Saint-Réals Don Carlos. Tübingen, 1888.
Nordau, M. Zeitgenössische Franzosen. (Schiller's Don Carlos). Berlin, 1901.
—— Don Carlos in Paris. Wiener Freie Presse, Dec. 1896.
Pappritz, R. Don Carlos in der Geschichte und in der Poesie. Progr. Naumburg, 1913.
Ruge, A. Schiller's Don Carlos und unsere Schillerkritiker in England. Blätter für lit. Unterhaltung, 12.XI.1837.
Thomas, Anneliese. Don Carlos und Hamlet. Bonn, 1933.
Treverret, A. de. Don Carlos, fils de Philippe II, dans les oeuvres de Saint Réal, d'Otway, d'Alfieri, de Schiller et de Nuñez de Arec. Actes de l'Acad. de Bordeaux, 44-45, 1883.
Utpott, H. Das geistige Bild des Don Carlos. Diss. Berlin, 1928.
Valbert, G. Don Carlos dans la poésie et dans l'histoire. RDM, 1.XII.1891.

DON JUAN: See Tirso de Molina, IV. IV. 9.

DON QUIJOTE: See Cervantes, IV. IV. 7.

Buurmans, E. La fin du monde dans la littérature latine. (**DOOMSDAY**). RBPh, 1942.
Jessen, P. Die Darstellung des Weltgerichts bis auf Michelangelo. Berlin, 1883.
Nigra, C. & Orsi, D. Il giudizio universale nel Canavese. Torino, 1896.
Reitzenstein, R. Die nordischen, persischen und christlichen Vorstellungen vom Weltuntergang. VBW, 2, 1923.
Valroger, H. de. La tradition indienne du déluge. Le Correspondant, 32, 1853.
Kraus, A. Beiträge zum **DOPPELGAENGERMOTIV** bei E. T. A. Hoffmann. Progr. Rostock, 1918.
Krauss, W. Das Doppelgängermotiv in der Romantik. Berlin, 1931.
Rank, O. Der Doppelgänger, eine psychoanalytische Studie. Wien, 1925.
Bossi, L. Dei basilischi, **DRAGONI** ed altri animali creduti favolosi. Milano, 1792.
Clerke, E. M. Dragon Myths of the East. Asiatic Quarterly Rev., 4, 1887.
Roheim, G. Drachen und Drachenkämpfer. Berlin, 1912.
Siecke, E. Drachenkämpfe. Leipzig, 1907.
Smith, G. E. The Evolution of the Dragon. London, 1919.
Ray, J. A. **DRAKE** dans la poésie espagnole, 1570-1732. Diss. Paris, 1906.

DREAMS: See also Freudianism, I. III. 5.

Arnold, M. Die Verwendung des Traummotivs in der englischen Dichtung von Chaucer bis auf Shakespeare. Diss. Kiel, 1912.
Baldensperger, F. Le Songe de Jean-Paul. In: Alfred de Vigny. Paris, 1912.
Bassi, D. I sogni nei tragici greci. Aevum, 1943.
Béguin, A. L'âme romantique et le rêve: essai sur le romantisme allemand et la poésie française. 2 vols. Marseille, 1937. Cf. Yggdrasill, 25.IX.1937 and RR. Feb. 1938.
Binswanger, L. Wandlungen in der Auffassung und Deutung des Traumes von den Griechen bis zur Gegenwart. Berlin, 1928.
Blum, P. Die Geschichte von träumenden Bauern in der Weltliteratur. Progr. Teschen, 1908.
Farinelli, A. El sueño maestro de la vida en dos dramas de Grillparzer y del

duque de Rivas. La Nación (Buenos Aires), 15.V.1927.
Fioroni, M. Sonno e sogni nell' arte di Dante. Avezzano, 1911.
Franke, O. Der Traum in der deutschen Dichtung. In: A. J. J. Ratcliff, Traum und Schicksal. Dresden, 1925.
Hock, S. Der Traum, ein Leben. (Grillparzer). Stuttgart, 1904.
Hughes, R. Vers la Contrée du rêve: Balzac, Gautier et Baudelaire disciples de Quincy. MF, 1.VIII.1939.
Ittner, R. T. Comments on Hebbel's Use of Dreams. GQ, 15, 1942.
Jahn, F. Traumwelt und Poesie. Festschrift Realgymnasium. Berlin, 1925.
Klamroth, H. Beiträge zur Entwicklungsgeschichte der Traumsatire im 17. und 18. Jahrhundert. Diss. Bonn, 1912.
Koella, C. E. La puissance du rêve chez Julien Green. PMLA, 54, 1939.
Lanzoni, F. Il sogno presago della madre incinta nella letteratura medievale e antica. Analecta Bollandiana, 45, 1927.
Le Gallienne, R. Dreams, Children of Literature. In: Attitudes and Avowals. New York, 1910.
Lersch, P. Der Traum in der deutschen Romantik. München, 1924.
Luria, S. Studien zur Geschichte der antiken Traumdeutung. Bull. Acad. des Sciences de L'U.R.S.S., 1927.
Messer, W. S. The Dream in Homer and Greek Tragedy. New York, 1918.
Ritzler, Paula. Der Traum in der Dichtung der deutschen Romantik. Bern, 1943.
Sartorius, E. Der Traum und das Drama. München, 1936.
Schneider, Elisabeth. The Dream of Kubla Khan. PMLA, 40, 1945.
Stearns, J. B. Studies of the Dream as a Technical Device in Latin Epic and Drama. Lancaster (Pa.), 1927.
Stekel, W. Die Träume der Dichter. Wiesbaden, 1912.
Thomas, L. P. La genèse de la philosophie et le symbolisme de la Vida es sueño. Mélanges Wilmotte. Paris, 1910.
Weber, L. Träume in Dichtungen. Kunstwart, 20, 1906.
Albrecht, K. Der Zweikampf mit blanken Waffen in der deutschen Literatur. (**DUEL**). Burschenschaftl. Blätter, 23.
Bennetton, N. A. Social Significance of the Duel in XVIIth Century French Drama. Baltimore, 1938.
Bryson, F. R. The XVIth Century Italian Duel. Chicago, 1938.
Heyking, A. Russian and English Ideas about Duelling. Asiatic Quarterly Rev., N.S., 12, 1917.
Wassmannsdorff, K. Das älteste in französischer Sprache gedruckte Fechtbuch vom Jahre 1538 ist eine Uebersetzung des ältesten deutschen Fechtbuches vom Jahre 1516. Monatsschrift f.d. Turnwesen, 11, 1892.
Roberts, W. Claude **DUVAL** in Literature. National Review, 85, 1925.
McRittchie, D. Zwerge in Geschichte und Ueberlieferung. (**DWARFS**). Globus, 82, 1902.
Seifert, C. Zwerge und Riesen. NJKA, 10, 1902.

——E——

Merry, E. C. **EASTER**—the Legends and and the Fact. London, 1938.
Wendlandt, R. Ostern im Liede. Tägl. Rundschau, 176, 1906.
Birkenfeld, G. Die Gestalt des treuen **ECKART** in der deutschen Sage und Literatur. Diss. Berlin, 1923-24.
Crooks, Esther J. Contemporary **ECUADOR** in the Novel and Short Story. Hisp., 23, 1940.
Hutton, L. Literary Landmarks of **EDINBURGH**. New York, 1891.
Liebau, G. König **EDUARD III** von England und die Gräfin von Salisbury. Berlin, Heidelberg, 1900-01. Cf. Archiv, 109, 1902.
May, H. Die Behandlung der Sage von **EGINHARD** und Emma. Berlin, 1900.
Muret, E. **EILHARD** d'Oberge et sa source française. Romania, 16, 1887.
Kopp, A. **EISENBART** im Leben und Lied. Berlin, 1900.
Mitzschke, P. Das Eisenbartlied in Frankreich. Zs. f. Bücherfreunde, 9, 1906.
Weiss, K. Hohentwiel und **EKKEHARD** in Geschichte, Sage und Dichtung. St. Gallen, 1901.
Berkowitz, H. C. Galdos' **ELECTRA** in Paris. Hisp., 1939.
Du Molard. Dissertation sur les principales tragédies anciennes et modernes qui ont paru sur le sujet d'Electre et en particulier sur celle de Sophocle. London, 1750.
Federn, K. Hofmannsthals Elektra und die griechische Tragödie. München, 1904.
Heyfelder, E. Elektra in klassischer und moderner Dramatik. DLZ, 30, 1908.
Pistelli, E. Introduzione all' Elettra. Pegaso, 1, 1929.
Zambra, V. I caratteri nell' Electra di

Sofocle confronto con Eschilo, Euripide, Crébillon, Voltaire ed Alfieri. Progr. Trient, 1876.

Klein, K. K. Der **ELGASTOFF** bei Grillparzer und Gerhart Hauptmann. Wächter, 11, 1929.

Wolf-Cirian, Fanny. Elga. Oesterr. Rundschau, 17.

Ittameier, M. Die **ELIASSAGE.** Zs. f. kirchl. Wissenschaft und kirchl. Leben, 1883.

Fehrle, H. Die **ELIGIUSSAGE.** Frankfurt, 1940.

Kölbing, E. Die nordische **ELISSAGA** ok Rosamundu und ihre Quelle. In: Beiträge zur vergleichenden Geschichte der romantischen Poesie und Prosa des Mittelalters. Breslau, 1876.

Balazs, I. Sainte **ELISABETH** de Hongrie dans la littérature française du XIIIe siècle. Budapest, 1930.

Barcza, E. Die Literatur über die heilige Elisabeth. Bibliographie. Budapest, 1907.

Grünenberg, Hildegard. Die heilige Elisabeth in der dramatischen Dichtung. Diss. Münster, 1928.

Karl, L. Die heilige Elisabeth aus dem Aspadenhause und die Sage von der unschuldigen verfolgten Gattin. Budapest, 1908.

Krapp, L. Das Bild der heiligen Elisabeth in der neueren Dichtung. Christliche Frau, 3, 1908.

Lebon, H. Vies de sainte Elisabeth de Hongrie et de sainte Elisabeth de Portugal. Paris, 1870.

McNabb, V. St. Elizabeth of Portugal. New York, 1939.

Seppelt, F. X. Die heilige Elisabeth in Kunst und Dichtung. Hochland, 1906.

Zurbonsen, F. Die heilige Elisabeth von Thüringen in der neueren deutschen Poesie. Stuttgart, 1900.

Wilson, E. C. England's Eliza. Cambridge (Mass.), 1939.

Beeley, J. H. Queen Elizabeth in Fiction. Papers of the Manchester Literary Club, 51, 1925.

Grew, J. H. Elisabeth d'Angleterre dans la littérature française. Diss. Paris, 1932.

Lesser, E. Queen Elizabeth and Essex in English and Foreign Drama. TLS, 24. I.1929.

Meise, H. Die Gestalt der Königin Elisabeth von England in der deutschen Literatur. Diss. Greifswald, 1941.

EMBLEM Literature: See Genres and Forms, I. VII. 3.

Kranz, W. **EMPEDOKLES:** antike Gestalt und romantische Neuschöpfung. Zürich, 1949.

Le Comte, E. S. **ENDYMION** in England: The Literary History of a Greek Myth. New York, 1944.

Köllmann, E. Die Ermordung Erzbischofs **ENGELBERT** von Köln (1225) im Spiegel der Dichtung. ZDK, 1927.

Firth, C. H. **ENGLISH HISTORY** in English Poetry, from the French Revolution to the Death of Queen Victoria. London, 1911.

Hill, R. T. The **ENUEG.** PMLA, 27, 1912.

—— The enueg and plazer in Medieval French and Italian. PMLA, 30, 1915.

Wilkins, E. H. The enueg in Petrarch and in Shakespeare. MPh, 13, 1915.

Widow of **EPHESUS:** See Chapter Eleven, below.

EREC: See Celtic Influences, IV. I. 6.

Langer, R. **ERICH** XIV von Schweden in der deutschen Literatur. Progr. Berndorf, 1915-16.

Brady, Caroline. The Legends of **ERMANARIC.** Berkeley, 1943.

Bartsch, K. Herzog **ERNST.** Wien, 1869.

Heselhaus, C. Die Herzog-Ernst-Dichtung. DVLG, 20, 1942.

Hildebrand, E. Ueber die Stellung des Liedes vom Herzog Ernst in der mittelalterlichen Literaturgeschichte und Volkskunde. Halle, 1937.

Sonneborn, K. Die Gestaltung der Sage von Herzog Ernst in der deutschen Literatur. Diss. Göttingen, 1914.

Arcy, M. C. d'. The Mind and Heart of Love, Lion and Unicorn: A Study in **EROS** and Agape. New York, 1947.

Lasserre, F. La figure d'Eros dans la poésie grecque. Diss. Lausanne, 1946.

Lasson, A. Eros und Psyche. DR, Dec., 1900.

Reitzenstein, R. Noch einmal Eros und Psyche. Archiv f. Religionswissenschaft, 28, 1930.

Weinreich, O. Eros und Psyche bei den Kabylen. Ibid.

Gigas, E. **ESAU** og Jakob som dramatiske Figuur. København, 1894.

Stapledon, O. **ESCAPISM** in Literature. Scrutiny, 1939.

Banks, J. The Unhappy Favourite; or, the Earl of **ESSEX** (1696). Ed. by Th. M. H. Blair. (Cf. Introduction). New York, 1939.

Bärwolff, W. Der Graf von Essex im deutschen Drama. Diss. Tübingen, 1920.

MacMillan, D. Some Notes on XVIIIth Century Essex Plays. MLN, 55, 1940.

Schiedermair, R. Der Graf von Essex in der Literatur. Diss. München, 1908.

Schneider, A. Aeltere Essexdramen. Progr. Wien, 1901.
Stirling, B. Daniel's Philotas and the Essex Case. MLQ, 3, 1942.
Anon. Pièces de théâtre concernant **ESTHER**. Polybiblion, 1882.
—— Racine's and Masefield's Esther. TLS, 9.II.1922.
Claudel, P. Le livre d'Esther. NRF, Nov., 1935.
Geiger, L. Der Estherstoff in der neuen Litteratur. Ost & West. Monatsschrift für modernes Judentum, 1, 1901. And in: Die deutsche Literatur und die Juden. Berlin, 1910.
Krauss, R. Esther im deutschen Drama und auf der deutschen Bühne. Beilage Vossische Zt., 38-39, 1902.
—— Die Quellen der Grillparzerschen Esther. Internat. Literaturberichte, 9, 1902.
—— Grillparzers Esther und ihre Fortsetzung. Bühne & Welt, 4, 1902.
Kuechler, W. Esther bei Calderon, Racine und Grillparzer. Jb. f. Philologie, 1, 1925.
Rosenberg, F. Der Estherstoff in der germanischen und romanischen Literatur. Festschrift Tobler. Braunschweig, 1905.
Schwartz, R. Esther im deutschen und neulateinischen Drama des Reformationszeitalters. Oldenburg, 1894.
—— Das Estherdrama des Chrysostomus Schultze von 1636. ZVL, 9.
Oehler, H. Prinz **EUGEN** in Volkslied und Flugschrift. Giessen, 1941.
Schwering, J. Prinz Eugen von Savoyen als Erwecker des deutschen Nationalgefühls und der vaterländischen Dichtung. In: Festgabe F. Philippi. Münster, 1923.
Wallerstein, M. Die Legende von der heiligen **EUGENIA**. Nord & Süd, 1896.
Messenger, R. E. The Legend of St. **EULALIA** in Mozarabic Hymns. CW, 38, 1944-45.
Brie, F. Die englischen Ausgaben des **EULENSPIEGEL** und ihre Stellung in der Geschichte des Volksbuches. Diss. Breslau, 1903.
—— Eulenspiegel in England. Berlin, 1903.
Bostelmann, J. M. Der niederdeutsche Ulenspiegel und seine Entwicklung in den Niederlanden. Hamburg, 1940.
Gosche, R. Zum französischen Eulenspiegel. ALG, 1870.
Hernried, E. Eulenspiegel-Dramen. National Zt., 158, 1914.
Hirsch, F. E. Eulenspiegel auf der Bühne. Wiener Abendpost, 263, 1900.
Lappenberg, J. M. Dr. Thomas Murners Ulenspiegel (and its influence in France). Leipzig, 1854.
Meridies, W. Eulenspiegels Weg zum Mythos. Gral, 17, 1923 & Zs. f. deutsche Bildung, 3, 1927.
—— Die Eulenspiegelgestalt in der deutschen Dichtung bis auf die Gegenwart. Diss. Breslau, 1924.
Plisnier, C. La légende d'Ulenspiegel. La Nef, March, 1946.
Roloff, E. A. Ewiger Eulenspiegel. Wie der Schalk war, und was die Welt aus ihm macht. Braunschweig, 1940.
Lombard, A. Un mythe dans la poésie et dans l'art, l'enlevèment d'**EUROPE**. Neuchâtel, 1946.
Déléhaye, H. La légende de saint **EUSTACHE**. Bull. de l'Académie royale de Belgique, 4, 1919.
Krappe, A. H. La leggenda di S. Eustachio. NSM, 3, 1926-27.
Winzer, J. Die ungleichen Kinder **EVAS** in der Literatur des 16. Jahrhunderts. Diss. Greifswald, 1908.
Anon. La leggenda di Ognuno. (**EVERYMAN**). Il Boccadoro, 30.IX.1933.
Brecht, W. Die Vorläufer von Hofmannsthals Jedermann. Oesterr. Rundchau, 20, 1924.
Goedeke, K. Every-man, Homulus und Hekastus. Hannover, 1859.
Lindner, H. Hofmannsthals Jedermann und seine Vorgänger. Diss. Leipzig, 1928.
Tigg, E.. R. Is Elckerlijc prior to Everyman? NPh, 26.
Zandvoort, R. W. Elckerlije—Everyman. ESs, 23.
Hazard, P. Le problème du mal dans la conscience européenne du XVIIIe siècle. (**EVIL**). RR, 32, 1941.
Bødtker, A. T. A Study in the Colour of **EYES**. Festschrift H. Falk. Oslo. 1927.
Elworthy, F. T. The Evil Eye: an Account of an Ancient and Wide-Spread Superstition. London, 1895.
Krappe, A. H. Balor with the Evil Eye. New York, 1927.
Seligmann, S. Der böse Blick und Verwandtes. Berlin, 1910.
Bianchi, L. Eichendorffs **EZELIN** von Romano und Mussatos Ecerinide. ZDPh, 64, 1939.
Schiff, O. Zu den Quellen der Ezzelintragödie Eichendorffs. ZVL, 12.
Stieve, F. Der Charakter des Ezellino von Romano in Anekdoten und Dichtungen. Histor. Vierteljahrsschrift, 13.

—F—

Faure-Goyau, L. F. La vie et la mort des fées. (**FAIRIES**). Paris, 1910.
Maury, L. F. A. Les fées au moyen âge. Paris, 1843.
Montégut, E. Des fées et de leur littérature en France. RDM, 1.I. & 15. IV.1862.
Mushacke, W. Beiträge zur Geschichte des Elfenreiches in Sage und Dichtung. Progr. Crefeld, 1891.
Krause, F. Byrons Marino **FALIERO**. Breslau, 1897.
Barone, G. Di un antenato italiano di **FALSTAFF**. Roma, 1895-96.
Bettoli, P. Il padre di Falstaff. Vita italiana, 1, 1895.
Borgese, G. A. The Dishonor of Honor. From Giovanni Mauro to Sir John Falstaff. RR, 32, 1940-41.
Braggio. Falstaff e il grottesco nel rinascimento europeo. La Bibl. d. scuole italiane, 5, 1892.
Burns, M. Falstaff. Dalhousie Rev., 19, 1940.
Giovagnoli, R. I progenitori di Falstaff. NAnt, 78, 15.IV.1893.
Vollhardt, W. Ein italienischer Falstaff. SVL, 7, 1907.
Friedmann, G. Die Bearbeitungen der Geschichte des Bergmanns von **FALUN**. Diss. Berlin, 1887.
Lorenz, E. F. Der Bergmann von Falun. Imago, 3, 1914.
Reuschel, K. Ueber Bearbeitungen der Geschichte des Bergmanns von Falun. SVL, 3, 1902.
Wassermann, F. **FAMA**. Geschichte eines Motivs in der antiken Dichtung. Giessen, 1921.
Bleiler, E. F. The Checklist of Fantastic Literature: A Bibliography of **FANTASY**, Weird, and Science Fiction Books. Chicago, 1948.
Flechtner, H. Die phantastische Literatur. Zs. f. Aesthetik & Allg. Kunstwissenschaft, 24, 1930.
Gallaher, C. Le conte fantastique dans le romantisme espagnol. Diss. Paris, 1947.
Schmidt, E. Der Kampf gegen die Mode in der Literatur des 17. Jahrhunderts. (**FASHION**). In: Charakteristiken, 1. Berlin, 1912.
FATE & FATALISM: See also Fate-Tragedies, I. VII. 2.
Baldensperger, F. Les grands thèmes romantiques dans les Burgraves de V. Hugo. Archiv 121, 1909.
Buttmann, A. Die Schicksals-Idee in Schillers Braut von Messina und ihr innerer Zusammenhang mit der Geschichte der Menschheit. Berlin, 1882.
Engel, W. Die Schicksalsidee im Altertum. Erlangen, 1926.
Greene, W. C. Fate, Good and Evil in Early Greek Poetry. HSCPh, 1935.
Klemann, E. Die Entwicklung des Schicksalbegriffs in der deutschen Klassik und Romantik. Würzburg, 1936.
Papacostea, C. Le problème du destin dans la tragédie grecque. Orpheus, 1 (Bucuresti), 1925.
Patch, H. R. Fate in Boethius and the Neoplatonists. Spec., 1929.
Rice, W. G. Fate in Paradise Lost. Papers Michigan Acad., 31, 1945-47.
Rostenscher, J. H. Germanischer Schicksalsglaube und angelsächsische Elegiendichtung. ESn, 73, 1939.
Weber, C. A. Der germanische Schicksalsgedanke bei Shakespeare. Tübingen, 1942.
Williams, E. E. Tragedy of Destiny, Oedipus Tyrannus, Macbeth, Athalie. Cambridge (Mass.), 1940.
FAUST: See Goethe, IV. X. 6.
Walcutt, C. C. **FEAR** Motifs in the Literature between Wars. SAQ, 46, 1947.
Blanke, F. Die Entstehung der Legende von **FELIX** und Regula. NSR, 5, 1937.
Buhlmann, C. Gestaltung der Chanson de geste **FIERABRAS** im Italienischen. Diss. Marburg, 1880.
Reichel, C. Die mittelenglische Romanze Sir Fyrumbras und ihr Verhältniss zum altfranzösischen und provenzalischen Fierabras. Diss. Breslau, 1892.
Weltrich, R. Schillers **FIESKO** und die geschichtliche Wahrheit. Marbacher Schillerbuch. Berlin, 1909.
Funck-Brentano, F. **FIGARO** et ses devanciers. Paris, 1909.
Monnier, M. Les aïeux de Figaro. Paris, 1868.
Toldo, P. Figaro et ses origines. Milano, 1893.
FIRE: See Chapter Eleven, below.
Blanck, A. **FLOIRES ET BLANCEFLOR** et l'épisode de Haidee dans le Don Juan de Byron. Mélanges Baldensperger. Paris, 1929.
Ernst, L. Floire und Blantscheflur. Strassburg, 1912.
Herzog, H. Die beiden Sagenkreise von Flore und Blancheflur. Wien, 1884.
Meier, J. Die Ballade Des Grafen Töchterlein und der Roman von Flore und Blanscheflur. Jb. f. Volksliedforschung, 7, 1941.
Reinhold, J. Floire et Blancheflor. Paris, 1906.
Schwalbach, F. C. Die Verbreitung der

Sage von Flore und Blancheflor in der europäischen Literatur. Progr. Krotoschin, 1869.

Sprenger, R. Zu Konrad Flecks Flore und Blancheflur. Progr. 1887.

Stefan, F. Entstehung und äussere Form der romantischen Sage von Flore und Blancheflur. Progr. Brünn, 1913.

Sundmacher, H. Die altfranzösische und mittelhochdeutsche Bearbeitung der Sage von Flore und Blancheflur. Göttingen, 1872.

Draper, J. W. Shakespeare and **FLORENCE** and the Florentines. Ital., 23, 1947.

Faure, G. A Florence, avec Corinne. Rassegna di Studi Francesi, 1930.

Hoffmann, E. Florenz in der Dichtung von Dante bis Goethe. Berlin, 1911.

Maugain, G. Thiers et son histoire de la République de Florence. Annales de l'U. de Grenoble, Dec., 1918.

Walzel, O. Florenz in deutscher Dichtung. Köln, 1937.

Wenzel, R. Die Fassungen der Sage von **FLORENCE DE ROME** und ihr gegenseitiges Verhältnis. Diss. Marburg, 1890.

Risop, A. Ungelöste Fragen zum **FLORIMONT**. Abhandlungen Tobler. Halle, 1895.

Duhem, J. Rabelais aéronaute. (**FLYING**). Bull. du Bibliophile, 1948.

Klinckowstroem, C. Luftfahrten in der Literatur. Zs. f. Bücherfreunde, N. F. 3.

Leppmann, F. Der Menschenflug in der Dichtung von Goethe bis Keller. Neue Zürcher Zt., 1180, 1922.

Minor, J. Ueber die Luftfahrten in der deutschen Literatur. Zs. f. Bücherfreunde, N. F. 1, 1908.

Panzer, F. Das Flugproblem in Mythus, Sage und Dichtung. Denkschrift der internat. Luftschiffahrt-Ausstellung. Berlin, 1909.

Patuzzi, G. L. L'aereostatica nella fiaba e nella poesia. Verona, 1902.

Pernerstorfer, E. Flugproblem und Dichtung. LE, 11, 1908.

Bonner, W. H. The **FLYING DUTCHMAN** of the Western World. JAFL, 59, 1946.

Golther, W. Der Fliegende Holländer in Sage und Dichtung. Bayr. Blätter, 1893. And in: Bühne und Welt, 3, 1900-01.

Allen, D. C. Renaissance Remedies for Fortune: Marlowe and the Fortunati. (**FORTUNA**). SPh, 38, 1940-41.

Cioffari, V. The Conception of Fortune and Fate in the Works of Dante. Dante Society of America. Cambridge (Mass.), 1940.

—— The Conception of Fortune in the Decameron. Ital, 17, 1940.

—— The Function of Fortune in Dante, Boccaccio and Machiavelli. Ital., 24, 1947.

Coleman-Norton, P. R. The Conception of Fortune in Roman Drama. Festschrift Capps. Princeton, 1936.

Doren, L. Fortuna im Mittelalter und in der Renaissance. VBW, 2.

Farwick, L. Die Auseinandersetzung mit der Fortuna im höfischen Barockroman. Münster, 1941.

Galpin, S. L. Fortune's Wheel in the Roman de la rose. PMLA, 24, 1909.

Hammerle, K. Das Fortunamotiv von Chaucer bis Bacon. Anglia, 65.

Ortiz, R. Fortuna labilis. Bucarest, 1928.

Patch, H. R. The Tradition of the Goddess Fortuna. Smith College Studies, 3, 1922.

—— Fortuna in Old French Literature. Smith College Studies, 4, 1923.

—— The Goddess Fortuna in Mediaval Literature. Harvard U. P., 1927.

Robinson, D. M. The Wheel of Fortune. CPh, 41, 1946.

Tappan, E. Julius Caesar and Fortuna. TAPhA, 27-28, 1927.

Asmus, W. Eine Bereicherung der **FORTUNATUSLITERATUR**. Allg. Zt. Beilage, 198, 1896.

Bolte, J. Zwei Fortunatus-Dramen aus dem Jahre 1643. Euphorion, 31, 1930.

Harms, P. Das deutsche Fortunatusdrama. Hamburg, 1892.

Lazar, B. Ueber das Fortunatas-Märchen. Leipzig, 1897.

Ransmeier, J. C. Uhland's Fortunat and the Histoire de Fortunatus et de ses enfants. PMLA, 1910.

Scherer, H. Old Fortunatus by Th. Dekker. Münchener Beiträge, 21. Erlangen, 1901.

Begani, O. **FRA DOLCINO** nella tradizione e nella storia. Milano, 1901.

FRANCESCA DA RIMINI: See Dante, IV. III. 9.

Busnelli, M. D. S. **FRANCESCO D'ASSISSI** e la poesia di Francia. Boll. della R. U. di Perugia, 12.IX.1931.

Groeteken, A. Die goldene Legende. Franciskus von Assisi in der Poesie der Völker. München-Gladbach, 1912.

Steinen, W. von den. Heilige und Helden des Mittelalters. Franziskus und Domenikus. Breslau, 1926.

Styra, A. Franziskus von Assisi in der

neueren deutschen Literatur. Breslau, 1928.
Blanchard, R. Was Sir R. Steele a **FREEMASON**? PMLA, 1948
Fay, B. Origine et esprit de la Franc-Maçonnerie. Rev. universelle, 1936.
Grainha, M. B. Histoire de la Franc-Maçonnerie en Portugal, 1733-1912. Lisbonne, 1913.
Jan, E. Der französische Freimaurerroman im 18. Jahrhundert. GRM, 1925.
Jaray, G. L. La Maçonnerie française, l'Angleterre et les Etats-Unis au XVIII siècle. MF, 1937.
Laboulaye, R. de. Calvin et la Maçonnerie. Revue des Questions historiques, 47, 1939.
Lantoine, A. Les franc-maçons au théâtre. Paris, 1919.
—— Un précurseur de la franc-maçonnerie, John Toland. Paris, 1927.
Pietsch, J. Goethe als Freimaurer. Festschrift. Leipzig, 1880.
Schneider, F. L. Die Freimaurerei und ihr Einfluss auf die geistige Kultur in Deutschland am Ende des 18. Jahrhunderts. Prag, 1901.
Schneider, H. Quest for Mysteries. The Masonic Background for Literature in XVIIIth Century Germany. Ithaca, 1947.
FREISCHUETZ: See also Faust, IV. X. 6.
Apel, J. A. Die Freischützsage und ihre Wandlungen. Detmold, 1941.
Komorzynski, E. von. Zwei Vorläufer von Webers Freischütz. ZDU, 15, 1900.
Dierks, O. Die dramatische Bearbeitung nationaler Stoffe in Frankreich. (**FRENCH HISTORY**). Hannover, 1911.
Dyggve, H. P. Personnages historiques figurant dans la poésie française des XIIe et XIIIe siècles. Neuphilolog. Mitteilungen, 36-37, 1935-36.
Marchangy, F. de. La Gaule poétique, ou l'histoire de France considérée dans ses rapports avec la poésie, l'éloquence et les beaux-arts. 8 vols. Paris, 1813-17.
Muret, T. L'histoire de France par le théâtre. 3 vols. Paris, 1865-66.
Picot, E. Chants historiques français du XVIe siècle. RHLF, 1, 1894.
Schwanz, H. Der Kamisardenaufstand in der deutschen Literatur des 19. Jahrhunderts. Diss. Münster, 1911.
Gould, C. N. The **FRIDHJOFSSAGA**, an Oriental Tale. SS, 7, 1919.
Krappe, A. An Oriental Theme in the Fridjofs Saga. MLN, 56, 1941.
Koch, E. Die Sage vom Kaiser **FRIEDRICH** im Kyffhäuser. Leipzig, 1886.
Schultheiss, F. G. Die deutsche Volkssage vom Fortleben und der Wiederkehr Kaiser Friedrichs. Berlin, 1911.
Bartholomaeis, V. de. Osservazioni sulle poesie provenzali relative a **FEDERICO** II. Mem. d. R. Accad. di Bologna, I, 6.
Deetjen, W. Immermann's Kaiser Friedrich II. In: Litterarische Forschungen. Berlin, 1901.
Hampe, K. Kaiser Friedrich II. in der Auffassung der Nachwelt. Stuttgart, 1925.
Stefano, A. de. Federico II. e le correnti spirituali del suo tempo. Roma, 1922.
Torraca, F. Federico Secondo e la poesia provenzale. In: Studi sulla lirica italiana del Duecento. Bologna, 1907.
FRIEDRICH II (der Grosse): see also German Contributions, IV. X. 12., and Voltaire, IV. VII. 20.
Amelung, H. Der alte Fritz im Liede. Neue Preuss. Kreuz Zt., 42, 1917.
Hisserich, W. Der alte Fritz als Bühnenheld. Bühne & Leben, 3, 1895.
Isolani, E. Friedrich der Grosse auf der Bühne. Deutsche Bühne, 4.
Lüscher, F. Friedrich der Grosse im historischen Volkslied. Diss. Bern, 1915.
Stümcke, H. Das älteste Friedrich-Drama (1746). Bühne & Welt, 14.
Volz, B. Friedrich der Grosse im Drama. In: Aus der Zeit Friedrichs des Grossen. Gotha, 1907.
Belling, E. Der Grosse Kurfürst in der Dichtung. (**FRIEDRICH WILHELM**). Berlin, 1888.
Stümcke, H. Der Grosse Kurfürst im deutschen Drama. Norddeutsche Allg. Zt., 121 & 172, 1902.
Fuchs, G. Die Aussagen über die Freundschaft im Neuen Testament verglichen mit denen des Aristoteles. (**FRIENDSHIP**). Leipzig, 1914.

——G——

Holl, K. **GALLIEN** in der lateinischen Literatur. Geistige Arbeit, 20.V.1939.
Carnoy, H. Les Légendes de **GANELON**. Romania, 1882.
Coeuret, L. Ganelon d'après Théroulde dans son poème de Roncevaux et d'après Pulci dans son poème de Morgant. L'Investigateur. (Paris), 1874.
Sauerland, E. Ganelon und sein Geschlecht im altfranzösischen Epos. Marburg, 1886.
Mutius, G. von. Die Entführung des **GANYMED**. Zs. f. Aesthetik & allg. Kunstwissenschaft, 1939.
GARGANTUA: See Rabelais, IV. VII. 17.

Bourgin, H. **GARIBALDI** et la France en Uruguay. NRI, 1920.
Rod, E. Garibaldi dans la littérature italienne. BURS, 1901.
Stiavelli, G. Garibaldi nella letteratura italiana. Roma, 1901.
Zimei, A. Garibaldi nella poesia italiana. Roma, 1940.
Gonzalez Palencia, A. Precedentes islamicos de la leyenda de **GARIN**. Al-Andalus, 1. (Madrid), 1933.
Lot, F. L'élément historique de Garin le Lorrain. Mélanges G. Monod. Paris, 1896.
Lage, B. von der. Studien zur **GENESIUS**legende. Progr. Berlin, 1898-99.
Bohnenblust, G. Genf und der deutsche Geist. (**GENEVA**). Zürich, 1923.
Bordeaux, H. La romanesque Genève. Figaro, 24.II.1932.
Engel, C. E. Genève et l'Angleterre: Les De Luc (1727-1817). Revue d'histoire suisse, 4, 1946.
Ferrero, G. Genève et le Contrat Social. Annales J. J. Rousseau, 1934.
Gribble, F. Lake Geneva and its Literary Landmarks. London, 1901.
Tallent-Bateman, C. T. Lake Léman and English Literature. Papers of the Manchester Literary Club, 6, 1887.
Traz, R. de. L'esprit de Genève. Paris, 1929.
Condeescu, N. La légende de **GENEVIEVE** de Brabant et ses versions roumaines. Bucarest, 1938.
Dieckmann, H. Diderot's Conception of **GENIUS**. JHI, 2, 1941.
Hutchings, C. M. The Examen de Ingenios and the Doctrine of Original Genius. Hisp., 1936.
Kaufman, P. Heralds of Original Genius. Festschrift Barrett Wendell. Harvard U. P., 1926.
Thüme, H. Beiträge zur Geschichte des Geniebegriffs in England. Studien z. engl. Philol., 71 (Halle), 1927.
Tuerck, H. Der geniale Mensch. 6th ed. Berlin, 1903.
Wolf, H. Versuch einer Geschichte des Geniebegriffes in der deutschen Aesthetik des 18. Jahrhunderts. Heidelberg, 1923.
Zilzel, E. Die Entstehung des Geniebegriffes. Tübingen, 1926.
Broche, G. E. Pages françaises sur Gênes la Superbe. (**GENOA**). Paris, 1928.
Rosi, M. Contribuzione alla storia dei rapporti fra Genova e l'Inghilterra. Roma, 1899.
Viglione, F. Genova nella storia della letteratura inglese. Genova, 1937.
Finkous, E. Die **GENOVEFA**-Schauspiele des Böhmerwaldes. In: Mitteil. des Vereins f. Geschichte der Deutschen in Böhmen, 58. (Prag), 1919.
Goerres, F. Neue Forschungen zur Genovefa-Sage. Ann. des histor. Vereins des Niederrheins, 1898.
Golz, B. Pfalzgräfin Genovefa in der deutschen Dichtung. Diss. Leipzig, 1897.
—— Die neueste Genoveva-Literatur. ZVL, 14, 1900.
Gorm, L. Die Technik der Genovevadramen. Euphorion, 17, 1910.
Koehler, R. Die deutschen Volksbücher von der Pfalzgräfin Genovefa und von der Herzogin Hirlanda. ZDPh, 5, 1874. And in: Kleine Schriften, 2. Weimar.
Meszlény, R. F. Hebbels Genoveva. Berlin, 1910.
Müller, A. Die dramatischen Bearbeitungen der Genovevalegende. Progr. Muri, 1902.
Nagel, W. Die neueren dramatisch-musikalischen Bearbeitungen der Genovefa-Legende. Diss. Zürich, 1888.
Puckett, H. W. The Genoveva Theme with Particular Reference to Hebbel's Treatment. MPh, 13, 1916.
Seuffert, B. Die Legende von der Pfalzgräfin Genovefa. Progr. Würzburg, 1877.
Seyboth, H. Dramatische Technik und Weltanschauung in Tiecks Genoveva. Diss. Erlangen, 1928.
Brison, F. R. The Point of Honor in 16th Century Italy: an Aspect of the Life of the **GENTLEMAN**. New York, 1935.
Cady, E. H. The Concept of the Gentleman in Representative American Authors. Diss. U. of Wisconsin, 1943.
Eichler, A. Werden und Wesen der englischen Vorstellung vom Gentleman. NSp, 51.
McEachran, F. The Gentleman Ideal. NC, 1928.
Nyrop, K. Qu'est-ce qu'un Gentleman? In: Mélanges posthumes. Paris, 1934.
Frech, F. Die **GEOLOGIE** in der deutschen Dichtung. Hamburgischer Correspondent, Beilage, 25, 1910.
Aufhauser, J. B. Das Drachenwunder des heiligen **GEORG**, in der griechischen und lateinischen Ueberlieferung. BBG, 1915.
Budge, E. A. W. The Martyrdom and Miracles of St. George. London, 1888.
Cumont, F. La plus ancienne légende de saint Georges. Rev. de l'histoire des religions, 114, 1936.
Krefting, A. St. Michael und St. Georg

in ihren geistesgeschichtlichen Beziehungen. Jena, 1937.
Krumbacher, K. Der heilige Georg in der griechischen Ueberlieferung. BBG, 1914.
Matzke, J. E. Contributions to the Legend of Saint-George. PMLA, 17, 1903.
Sandkuehler, K. Der Drachenkampf des hl. Georg in englischer Legende und Dichtung vom 14. bis 16. Jahrhundert. Progr. Pasing, 1913.
Williams, M. E. Whence Came St. George? Bull. de la Société archéologique d'Alexandrie (Egypte), 30, 1936.
Appel, C. Deutsche Geschichte in der provenzalischen Dichtung. (**GERMAN HISTORY**). Breslau, 1907.
Baumann, M. Strömungen und Ereignisse der früheren deutschen Geschichte im Spiegel gleichzeitiger Dichtung. Progr. Berlin, 1898.
Carruth, W. H. Expressions of German National Feeling in Historical and Poetical Literature from the Middle of the Tenth Century to the Time of Walther von der Vogelweide. HSPhL, 2, 1893.
Kaiser, R. Lateinische Dichtungen zur deutschen Geschichte des Mittelalters. München, 1927.
Kreyssig, F. Die nationale Bewegung im Spiegel der zeitgenössischen Literatur. In: Literarische Studien und Charakteristiken. Berlin, 1882.
Luther, A. Deutsche Geschichte in deutscher Erzählung. Ein literarisches Lexikon. Leipzig, 1940.
Möllenbrock, K. Die historischen Lieder vom Ende des 30 jährigen Krieges bis zum Beginn des 7 jährigen. ZDPh, 64.
Woodbridge, H. E. Mark Twain and the **GESTA ROMANORUM**. Nation, 118, 1919.
Falkenfeld, H. Florian **GEYER** im Spiegel der Dichtung. Bad. Bühnenblätter, 5.
Guggenheim, E. Der Florian Geyerstoff in der deutschen Dichtung. Diss. Leipzig, 1908.
Knudsen, H. Zum Florian Geyerstoff. Euphorion, 18, 1910.
Kutzschbach, E. Florian Geyer in Roman und Drama. Neues Tageblatt 350, (Stuttgart), 1913.
Bennett, E. Apparitions and Haunted Houses. (**GHOSTS**). London, 1939.
Bonnerjea, B. Some Finno-Ugrian Ghosts and Spirits. N&Q, 23.IV.1938.
Collin de Plancy, J. Dictionnaire infernal; répertoire universel des êtres, des personnages, des livres, des faits et des choses qui tiennent aux esprits. Paris, 1818. 6th ed., 1863.
Collison-Morley, L. Greek and Roman Ghost Stories. Oxford, 1912.
Diederich, B. Von Gespenstergeschichten, ihrer Technik und ihrer Literatur. Leipzig, 1903.
Dingwall, E. J. Ghosts and Spirits in the Ancient World. London, 1930.
Edgcombe, F. J. S. Ghosts, Present and Past. Fraser's Mag., Nov., 1869.
Egan, M. F. The Ghost in Hamlet, and Other Essays in Comparative Literature. Chicago, 1906.
Hackmann, H. Chinesischer Gespensterglaube. China, 6, 1931-32.
Heilborn, E. Das deutsche Gespenst (in der Dichtung). LE, 17, 1914.
Krauss, R. Gespensterrosse und Gespensterritte in der deutschen Dichtung. Staatsanzeiger f. Württemberg, 1926.
Lang, A. The Comparative Study of Ghost Stories. NC, 1885.
Noch, C. Wiener Geisterkomödien und Gespensterpossen. In: Grillparzers Ahnfrau. Leipzig, 1911.
Stanford, W. B. Ghosts and Apparitions in Homer, Aeschylus and Shakespeare. Ha, 56, 1940.
Wagner, M. Hollands Geisterdramen und ihre Beziehungen zu der übrigen europäischen Literatur. Diss. München, 1913.
Weicker, G. Antike Gespenster. WBFA, 1924.
Weiser, L. Germanische Hausgeister und Kobolde. Niederdeutsche Zs. f. Volkskunde, 4, 1926.
Léger, L. Un poème tchèque sur la bataille de **GICY**. JS, 1902.
Longnon, A. **GIRARD DE ROUSSILLON** dans l'histoire. Revue historique, 8, 1878.
Meyer, P. La légende latine de Girart de Roussillon. Romania, 7.
Stimming, A. Ueber den provenzalischen Girart von Rossillon. Halle, 1888.
Brachvogel, C. Der Graf von **GLEICHEN** und seine Vettern. Velhagen & Klasings Monatshefte, 30, 1915.
Pernice, Magdalene. Drei Gleichendramen aus der Zeit des deutschen Idealismus. Diss. Greifswald, 1927.
Sauer, E. Die Sage vom Grafen von Gleichen in der deutschen Literatur. Diss. Strassburg, 1911.
Weilen, A. von. Der Graf von Gleichen in der deutschen Dichtung und Sage. Zs. f. allg. Geschichte & Literatur, 1885.

Weisert, J. J. Graf von Gleichen Redivivus. MDU, 40, 1948.
Routh, H. V. **GOD**, Man and Epic Poetry. 2 vols. Cambridge, 1927.
Schröder, C. Gott und Seele in der jüngsten katholischen Dichtung. Paderborn, 1927.
Spiero, E. Zwei Bücher vom vergotteten Menschen (Hauptmann, Villales). Archiv, 154, 1928.
Häfele, K. Die **GODIVASAGE** und ihre Behandlung in der Literatur. Heidelberg, 1929.
Burd, H. **GOLDEN AGE** Idea in Eighteenth Century Poetry. Sewanee Rev., 23, 1915.
Epps, P. H. The Golden Age. CJ, 29, 1934.
Lipsker, E. Der Mythos vom goldenen Zeitalter in den Schäferdichtungen Italiens, Spaniens und Frankreichs zur Zeit der Renaissance. Diss. Berlin, 1933.
Manni, E. La leggenda dell'età dell'oro nella politica dei Caesari. A&R, 16, 1938.
Meissner, P. Das goldene Zeitalter in der englischen Renaissance. Anglia, 1935.
Petersen, J. Das goldene Zeitalter bei den deutschen Romantikern. Festschrift Muncker. Halle, 1926.
GOLDEN LEGEND. See also Saints, below.
Anon. Comparison of Faust and the Golden Legend. Fraser's Mag., 1853.
Butler, P. Legenda aurea. Legende dorée. Golden Legend: A Study of Caxton's Golden Legend. Diss. Baltimore, 1899. Cf. ESn, 29, 1901.
Mary Jeremy, Sister. The English Prose Translation of Legenda Aurea. MLN, 59, 1944.
—— Caxton's Golden Legend and Voragine's Legenda Aurea. Spec., 21, 1946.
—— Caxton's Golden Legend and De Vignai's Légende Dorée. Mediaeval Studies, 8, 1946.
Meunier, M. La légende dorée des dieux et des héros. Paris, 1934.
Meyer, H. Untersuchungen über die elsässische Uebersetzung der Legenda aurea. Freiburg, 1939.
Monceaus, P. La vraie Légende Dorée. Paris, 1928.
Roze, M. Jacques de Voragine, la légende dorée, nouvelle traduction française avec notices, notes et recherches sur les sources. 3 vols. Paris, 1901.
Saintyves, P. En marge de la Légende Dorée. Songes, miracles et survivances. Paris, 1930-31.
Seybolt, R. F. Fifteenth Century Editions of the Legenda Aurea. Spec., 21, 1946-47.
—— The Legenda Aurea, Bible and Historia Scholastica. Ibid.
Wilmart, A. Saint Ambroise et la Légende dorée. Ephemerides Liturgicae, 1936.
Zuidweg, J. J. A. De werkwijze van Jacobus de Voragine in de Legenda Aurea. Oud-Beijerland, 1941.
Ludwig, A. Der **GOLEM**. Literatur, 26.
Rosenfeld, B. Die Golemsage und ihre Verwertung in der deutschen Literatur. Breslau, 1934.
Zweig, A. Der Golem. Schaubühne, 11, 1915.
Reimerdes, E. E. Karfreitag in der deutschen Dichtung. (**GOOD FRIDAY**). Reformation, 9, 1910.
GOTHIC LITERATURE: See also Gothic Novels, I. VII. 2., and Sepulchral Poetry, below.
Addison, Agnes. Romanticism and the Gothic Revival. New York, 1938.
Appell, J. W. Die Ritter-, Räuber- und Schauerromane. Leipzig, 1859.
Aubin, R. A. Grottoes, Geology and the Gothic Revival. SPh, 1934.
Blanck, A. Geijers gotiska diktning. Stockholm, 1918.
Clark, K. The Gothic Revival. London, 1928.
Coad, O. S. The Gothic Element in American Literature before 1835. JEGPh, 24, 1925.
Eimer, M. Einflüsse deutscher Räuber- und Schauerromantik auf Shelley, Mrs. Shelley und Byron. ESn, 48, 1914-15.
Evans, B. Gothic Drama from Walpole to Shelley. Berkeley, 1947.
Freyl, W. The Influence of Gothic Literature on Sir Walter Scott. Rostock, 1902.
Haferkorn, R. Gotik und Ruine in der englischen Dichtung des 18. Jahrhunderts. Leipzig, 1924.
Heilman, R. B. Fielding and the First Gothic Revival. MLN, 57, 1942.
Holbrook, W. C. The Adjective 'Gothique' in the XVIIIth Century. MLN, 56, 1941.
Kliger, S. The 'Goths' in England: An Introduction to the Gothic Vogue in XVIIIth Century Aesthetic Discussion. MPh, 43, 1945.
—— George Perkins Marsh and the Gothic Tradition in America. NEQ, 19, 1946.
—— The Gothic Revival and the German Translatio. MPh, 45, 1947.

Lovejoy, A. O. The First Gothic Revival and the Return to Nature. MLN, 1932.
Lundblatt, J. Nathaniel Hawthorne and the Tradition of the Gothic Romance. Harvard U.P., 1946.
Summers, M. The Gothic Quest. London, 1938.
—— A Gothic Bibliography. New York, 1941.
Thomas H. What Cervantes Meant by Gothic Letters. MLR, 33, 1938.
Ebrich, E. **GRACCHUS**-Dramen. Zs. f. Bücherfreunde, 5, 1901.
GRAIL: See Celtic Influences, IV. I. 4.
Pomezny, F. **GRAZIE** und Grazien in der deutschen Litteratur des 18. Jahrhunderts. Beiträge zur Aesthetik, 7. (Hamburg), 1900.
Allen, C. G. The Relation of the German **GREGORIUS** auf dem Stein to the Old French Poem La Vie de Saint Grégoire. Matzke Memorial, Leland Stanford Junior University, 1911.
Bieling, H. Ein Beitrag zur Ueberlieferung der Gregorlegende. Berlin, 1874.
Kölbing, E. Die englische Version der Gregoriussage in ihrem Verhältnis zur französischen und zu Hartmanns Bearbeitung. In: Beiträge zur vergleichenden Geschichte der romantischen Poesie und Prosa des Mittelalters. Breslau, 1876.
Krappe, A. H. La légende de saint Grégoire. Le Moyen Age, 46, 1936.
Lippold, F. Ueber die Quelle des Gregorius Hartmanns von Aue. Altenburg, 1869.
Luzarche, V. Vie du Pape Grégoire le Grand, légende française. Tours, 1857.
Littré. Légende sur le Pape Grégoire. In: Histoire de la langue française. Paris, 6e ed., vol. 2. 1873.
Neussel, O. Ueber die altfranzösische, mittelhochdeutsche und mittelenglische Bearbeitung der Sage vom Gregorius. Diss. Halle, 1887.
Seelisch, F. Die Gregoriuslegende. ZDPh, 19, 1887.
Ovidio, F. d'. Fonti dantesche: Dante e Gregorio VII. NAnt, 69, 1897.
GRISELDIS: See Boccaccio, IV. II. 8.
Bergmeier, F. Dedekinds **GROBIANUS** in England. Greifswald, 1903.
Clark, E. F. The Grobianus of Sachs and its Predecessors. JEGPh, 16, 1917.
Ruehl, R. Grobianus in England. Palaestra, 38. Berlin, 1904.
Benedict, S. Die **GUDRUNSAGE** in der neueren deutschen Litteratur. Rostock, 1902.
Boesch, B. Kudrunepos und Ursprung der deutschen Ballade. GRM, 28, 1940.
Fécamp, A. Le poème de Gudrun. Paris, 1892.
Kübel, Martha. Das Fortleben des Kudrunepos. Leipzig, 1929.
Menéndez Pidal, R. Supervivencia del poema de Kudrun. RFE, 20, 1933.
Rapp, H. Das Problem des Tragischen in der Gudrunliteratur. Diss. Köln, 1928.
Sandbach, F. E. The Nibelungenlied and Gudrun in England and America. London, 1903.
Wilmanns, W. Die Entwicklung der Kudrundichtung. Halle, 1873.
Saltzmann, H. Der historisch-mythologische Hintergrund und das System der Sage im Cyklus des **GUILLAUME D'ORANGE.** Progr. Königsberg, 1890.
Goetz, E. Der Schuldbegriff in der deutschen Volkssage der Gegenwart. **(GUILT).** In: Niederdeutsche Zs. f. Volkskunde, 6, 1928.
Moore, J. B. The Role of **GULLIVER.** MPh, 1928.
Schröder, F. R. **GUNTHERS** Brautwerbung und die GongurHrolfs Saga. Festschrift Eugen Mogk. Halle, 1924.
Benson, A. B. Colonial Americans Applauded **GUSTAVUS VASA.** American-Swedish Monthly, 1942.
—— Gustavus Vasa on the Foreign Stage: An Addendum and List of Operas by European Composers. SS, 18, 1944.
Hoenig, B. Memoiren englischer Offiziere im Heere **GUSTAV ADOLPHS** und ihr Fortleben in der Literatur. Festschrift J. Schipper. Wien, 1902.
Milch, W. Das Gustav Adolf-Bild der deutschen Literatur im Zusammenhang mit der Schwedischen. Diss. Breslau, 1927.
Nordstrom, J. Lejonet frán Norden (Gustavus Adolphus). Samlaren, N.S., 15, 1934.
Röhrig, K. Gustav Adolf in der Dichtung. Leipzig, 1909.
Stirk, S. D. Heinrich Laubes Jugenddrama Gustav Adolf. ZDPh, 63.
Willig, E. Gustav Adolf II, König von Schweden im deutschen Drama. Diss. Rostock, 1908.
Benson, A. B. **GUSTAVUS** III in the Librettos of Foreign Operas. SS (Festschrift Flom), 1942.
Lublinski, S. **GUTENBERG,** ein dramatisches Problem. Bühne & Welt, 2, 1900.
Vely, W. Johannes Gutenberg im Drama. Bühne & Welt, 2, 1900.
Hibbard, Laura A. **GUY OF WARWICK**

and the Second Mystère of Jean Louvet. MPh, 1915.

Weyrauch, M. Die mittelenglischen Fassungen der Sage von Guy of Warwick und ihre altfranzösische Vorlage. Diss. Breslau, 1899.

Bickel, E. **GYGES** und sein Ring. Zum Begriff Novelle und zu Hebbels tragischer Kunst. NJKA, 1921.

Ites, M. Die Gyges-Geschichte des Herodot als Lehre vom Menschen. BBG, 1932.

Reinhardt, K. Gyges und sein Ring. Europ. Revue, 15, 1939.

Smith, K. F. The Literary Tradition of Gyges and Candaules. AJPh, 1920.

Zilliacus, E. Die Sage von Gyges und Kandaules bei einigen modernen Dichtern. Oeversikt af finska Vetenskapssocietens förhandlingar, 51, 1908.

Baldensperger, F. L'entrée pathétique des Tziganes dans les lettres occidentales. (**GYPSIES**). RLC, 18, 1938.

Borrow, G. H. The Zincali, or an Account of the Gypsies in Spain. London, 1841.

Ebhardt, W. Die Zigeuner in der hochdeutschen Literatur bis zu Goethes Götz von Berlichingen. Diss. Göttingen, 1928.

Gosche, H. R. A. Die Zigeuner als Typus in Dichtung und Kunst. Berlin, 1879.

Grierson, G. Arabic and Persian References to Gipsies. Indian Antiquary, 16, 1887.

—— Gipsies in England and in India. Ibid.

Walters, J. C. Elizabeth Canning and the Gipsies. Papers Manchester Literary Club, 51, 1925.

Ward, H. G. Herder on the Gypsies. Journal of the Gypsy Lore Society, 3rd. Ser., 14, 1935.

Winstedt, E. O. Hans Sachs and Grimmelshausen on the Gypsies. Journal of the Gypsy Lore Society, 3rd Ser., 14, 1935.

——H——

Cook, Mercer. The **HAITIAN** Novel. FR, 19, 1946.

Wittko, P. **HAMBURG** in der neuzeitlichen Literatur. Niedersachsen, 1925.

HAMLET: See Shakespeare, IV. VIII. 11.

Borst, J. **HANNIBAL** in der deutschen Dichtung. WBFA, 4.

Funk, F. Die englischen Hannibaldramatisierungen mit Berücksichtigung der Bearbeitungen des Stoffes in den übrigen Literaturen. Diss. München, 1912.

Peter, F. Der Hannibalstoff in der deutschen Literatur. Progr. Sternberg, 1915.

HARLEKIN: See Italian Contributions, IV. III. 6.

Schladebach, K. Tennysons und Wildenbruchs **HAROLD**dramen. SVL, 2, 1902.

Ende, Clara von. Introduction à une bibliographie raisonnée de Gaspar **HAUSER** suivie d'un aperçu chronologique de la question. RG, 2, 1909.

Jungmann, O. Kaspar Hauser. Stoff und Problem in ihrer literarischen Gestaltung. Würzburg, 1935.

Peitler, H. & Ley, H. Kaspar Hauser. Ueber tausend bibliographische Nachweise. Ansbach, 1927.

Stern, Olga. Kaspar Hauser in der Dichtung. Diss. Frankfurt, Leipzig, 1925.

Hinkeldeyn, A. Die Heide im Spiegel der Dichtung. (**HEATH**). Monatsblätter f. deutsche Lit., 10, 1905.

Hüber, K. Die Heide in der Dichtung. LE, 20, 1918.

Reinhold, F. Die norddeutsche Heide als Gegenstand der Dichtung bei A. von Droste-Hülshoff, Th. Storm und H. Löns. Diss. Leipzig, 1932.

Becker, E. J. A Contribution to the Comparative Study of the Mediaeval Visions of **HEAVEN AND HELL**. Diss. Baltimore, 1899.

Amelineau, E. L'enfer égyptien et l'enfer virgilien. Annales Ecole Hautes Etudes, 1914.

Bautz, J. Die Hölle. Mainz, 1882.

Beauvois, E. L'autre vie dans la mythologie scandinave. Museon, 1883.

Beilby, A. E. Two Other World Explorers: Dante and Swedenborg. London, 1915.

Boyce, B. News from Hell. Satiric Communications with the Nether World in English Writing of the XVIIth and XVIIIth Centuries. PMLA, 58, 1943.

Buxton, C. R. Prophets of Heaven and Hell: Virgil, Dante, Milton, Goethe. Cambridge, 1945.

Collin de Plancy, J. Dictionnaire infernal; répetoire universel des êtres, des personnages, des livres, des faits et des choses, qui tiennent aux esprits. Paris, 1818.

Coulter, C. The Happy Otherworld in the Odyssey. TAPhA, 56, 1925.

Delepierre, O. L'Enfer, essai philosophique et historique sur les légendes de la vie future. London, 1876.

Dobs, M. Forerunners of Dante. An Account of Some of the More Important Visions of the Unseen World from the Earliest Times. Edinburgh, 1903.
Funaioli, G. L'oltretomba nell' Eneide di Virgilio. Palermo, 1925.
Kirkconnell, W. Avitus' Epic on the Fall. Quebec, 1947.
Landau, M. Hölle und Fegfeuer in Volksglaube, Dichtung und Kirchenlehre. Heidelberg, 1909.
Lawton, W. C. The Underworld in Homer, Virgil and Dante. AM, 1884.
Messenger, R. E. The Descent Theme in Medieval Latin Hymns. TAPhA, 1936.
Pavano, G. La discesa di Orfeo nell'Ade in Vergilio e in Ovidio. MC, 1937.
Rüegg, A. Die Jenseitsvorstellungen vor Dante. Einsiedeln, 1945.
Siuts, H. Jenseitsmotive im deutschen Volksmärchen. Leipzig, 1911.
Weatherhead, L. D. Shelley's Hell Complex. QR, 1928.
Jakobsohn, S. **HEDDA** und Hermione. Die Schaubühne, 38, 1906.
Ussani, V. Su le fortune medievali dell'**EGESIPPO.** Rendiconti della Pontificia Accademia romana di Archeologia, 9, 1933.
Goldschmit, R. K. Das **HEIDELBERGER** Schloss in der deutschen Dichtung. PJb, 191, 1923.
—— Heidelberg als Stoff und Motiv der deutschen Dichtung. Berlin, 1929.
Sauer, F. Das Heidelberger Schloss im Spiegel der Literatur. Heidelberg, 1910.
—— Alt-Heidelberg im Burschenlied. Heidelberg, 1910.
Witkop, P. Heidelberg und die deutsche Dichtung. Leipzig, 1916.
Armer **HEINRICH:** See Poor Henry, below. For others: See under Henry.
Becker, M. **HELENA,** ihr Wesen und ihre Wandlungen im klassischen Altertum. Leipzig, 1939.
Content, A. Der Helena-Mythos und die Anthroposophie. Die Drei, 7.
—— Die Helena-Saga und ihr Zusammenhang mit unserer Zeit. Dornach, 1929.
Funck-Brentano, F. La belle Hélène, reine de Sparte. Paris, 1935.
Goethe, J. W. Helena in Edinburg, Paris und Moskau. Kunst und Alterthum, 6, 1828.
Kakridis, J. T. Helena. RhM, 1931.
Moravcsik, J. Zur Quellenfrage der Helenaepisode in Goethes Faust. Byzant. neugriech. Jb, 8, 1931.
Nemethy, G. Helena und Faust. HG, 1924.
Oswald, E. The Legend of Fair Helen. London, 1905.
Voglar, F. Die Helenasage in der griechischen Dichtung. Progr. Marburg, 1914.
Zielinski, T. La bella Elena. Rivista di studi filosofici e religiosi, 4, 1923.
Charrier, C. **HELOISE** dans l'histoire et dans la légende. Paris, 1933. Cf. RLC, 15, 1935.
Souriau, M. L'oraison funèbre d'**HENRIETTE** d'Angleterre et la vérité historique. Caen, 1890.
Moore, O. The Young King, **HENRY** Plantagenet in Provençal and Italian Literature. RR, 4, 1913.
Rauschning, Hildegard. Heinrich I. in der deutschen Literatur. Diss. Breslau, 1920.
Baptistella, J. Kaiser Heinrich II., der Heilige, in der bildenden Kunst. In: Der Mainbote von Oberfranken, 1925.
Brenner, D. C. Henri IV on the French Stage in the XVIIIth Century. PMLA, 1931.
Koeppel, E. König Heinrich IV. von Frankreich im Spiegel der zeitgenössischen englischen Bühne. In: Zur Quellenkunde des Stuart-Dramas. Archiv, 97, 1896.
Parker, A. A. Henry VIII in Shakespeare and Calderon. MLR, 43, 1948.
Roncaglia, A. La questione matrimoniale di Enrico VIII e due umanisti contemporanei. GSLI, 110, 1937.
Wurzbach, W. Shakespeares Heinrich VIII und Calderons La Cisma de Inglaterra. JbShG, 32, 1896.
Riesenfeld, P. **HEINRICH VON OFTERDINGEN** in der deutschen Literatur. Berlin, 1914.
HELL: See Heaven, above.
Anderson, A. R. **HERACLES** and his Successors. A Study of a Heroic Ideal and the Recurrence of a Heroic Type. HSCPh, 39, 1928.
Hendrickson, G. L. The Heracles Myth and its Treatment by Euripides. Festschrift C. F. Smith. Madison, 1919.
Hennig, R. Eine arabische Umdeutung der hellenischen Sage von den Säulen des Herakles und ihre Fortwirkung bis auf die Gegenwart. AK, 26, 1935-36.
Herbig, R. Herakles im Orient. Heroenglaube und Geschichtserlebnis. Festschrift Curtius. Stuttgart, 1937.
Pfister, F. Herakles und Christus. Archiv f. Religionswissenschaft, 1937.
Stoessl, F. Der Tod des Herakles. For-

men der antiken Sagendichtung. Zürich, 1945.
Brandl, A. **HERCULES** und Beowulf. SAWB, 14, 1928.
Castiglioni, L. La tragedia di Ercole in Euripide e in Seneca. Rivista di filologia e d'istruzione classica, 1926.
Pavolini, P. E. Il mito d'Ercole in alcune poesie moderne. A&R, 10, 1908.
Piggott, S. The Hercules Myth, Beginnings and Ends. Antiquity, 12, 1938.
Riedl, F. Der Sophist Prodikus und die Wanderung seines Herkules am Scheidewege durch die römische und deutsche Literatur. Progr. Laibach, 1908.
Vasters, P. Hercules auf germanischem Boden. Jb. der phil. Fak. Münster, 1920.
HERMANN der Cherusker: See Arminius, above.
Cowper, F. A. G. The **HERMIT** Story, As Used by Voltaire and Mark Twain. Festschrift Ch. F. Johnson. Hartford, 1928.
Hirn, Y. Eremiter och pilgrimer. In: Landskaperomantiken och La Grande Chartreuse. Stockholm, 1924.
Rohde, O. Die Erzählung vom Einsiedler und dem Engel in ihrer geschichtlichen Entwicklung. Diss. Leipzig, 1894.
Williams, C. A. Oriental Affinities of the Legend of the Hairy Anchorite. U. of Illinois Studies in Lang. and Literature, 10-11, 18, 1925-26, 1935.
—— The German Legends of the Hairy Anchorite; with Two Old French Tcxts of La Vie de Saint Jehan Paulus, ed. by L. Allen. Urbana, 1935.
Frick, R. **HERNANI** als litterarischer Typus. In: Hernani und seine Vorläufer in der Weltlitteratur. Diss. Tübingen, 1903.
Bentley, E. R. A Century of **HERO**-Worship: A Study of the Idea of Heroism in Carlyle and Nietzsche. Philadelphia, 1944.
—— Modern Hero-Worship: Notes on Carlyle, Nietzsche, and Stefan George. Sewanee Rev., 52, 1944.
Conrad, M. G. Der deutsche Held in deutscher Dichtung. Neue Zeit, 5, 1923.
Farnell, L. R. Greek Hero Cults and Ideas of Immortality. Oxford, 1921.
Kraeger, H. Der Byronische Heldentypus. München, 1898.
Lowis von Menar, A. Der Held im deutschen und russischen Märchen. Jena, 1912.
Martens, H. Unheldenhafte und heldenhafte Menschen bei den Wiener Dichtern um 1900. Bonn, 1929.
Miller, O. Heroes, Outlaws and Funny Fellows of American Popular Tales. New York, 1939.
Morales, J. R. Carácter y empresa del heroe romantico. Atenea (Chile), 58, 1939.
Raglan, Lord. The Hero. A Study in Tradition, Myth and Drama. London, 1936.
Rank, O. Der Mythus von der Geburt des Helden. 2nd. ed. Leipzig, 1922.
Strauss und Tornay, Lulu von. Vom Helden in der Dichtung. Tat, 18, 1927.
Telberg, Ina. Heroes and Villains of Soviet Drama. American Sociological Rev, 9, 1944.
Wecter, D. The Hero in America: A Chronicle of Hero-Worship. New York, 1941.
Bush, D. **HERO AND LEANDER** and Romeo and Juliet. PhQ, 1930.
Chabauer, L. Héro et Léandre, poème de Chr. Marlowe et G. Chapman et sa fortune en Angleterre. Paris, 1911.
Jellinek, M. H. Die Sage von Hero und Leander in der Dichtung. Berlin, 1890. Cf. ZVL, 5, 1891; ESn, 17; ZDA, 1894.
Sahr, S. Die Schwimmersage. Leipziger Zt. Beilage, 30-34, 1907.
Beckmann, E. Die Motivierung in den bedeutenderen **HERODES**- und Mariamnedramen. NSp, 23, 1915.
Beermann, M. Die Herodierzeit im Spiegel moderner Dramen. Brülls Monatshefte, 25, 1905.
Borcherdt, H. H. Der Bethlemitische Kindermord und die Racheklage in der Literatur. Gottesmann, 6, 1911.
Gnerich, E. A. Gryphius und seine Herodesepen. Leipzig, 1906.
Grack, W. Studien über die dramatische Behandlung der Geschichte von Herodes und Marianne in der englischen und deutschen Litteratur. Diss. Königsberg, 1901.
Landau, M. Die Dramen von Herodes und Marianne. ZVL, 8-9, 1895-96.
Lebègue, R. L'Herodes infanticida en France (Heinsius). NPh, 23, 1937.
Reinhardstoettner, K. von. Herodes-Dramen. In: Aufsätze und Abhandlungen. Berlin, 1887.
Tomlinson, W. E. Der Herodes-Charakter im englischen Drama. Leipzig, 1936.
Valency, M. J. The Tragedies of Herod and Marianne. New York, 1940.
Benary, W. **HERVIS** von Metz und die

Sage vom dankbaren Toten. ZRPh, 37, 1913.

Eckhardt, A. Franco-Hungarica. l. Hervis de Metz et les Hongrois. Mélanges Baldensperger. Paris, 1930.

Legler, H. E. Longfellow's **HIAWATHA**; Bibliographical Notes Concerning its Origin, its Translations and its Contemporary Parodies. Literary Collector, 9, 1904.

Thompson, S. The Indian Legend of Hiawatha. PMLA, 37, 1922.

Anthes, C. Das deutsche **HILDEBRANTLIED** und die iranische Sohrabsage. Weimar. Jb. f. d. Sprachen, Lit. & Kunst, 4, 1856.

Baesecke, G. Die indogermanische Verwandtschaft des Hildebrandslieds. Göttingen, 1940.

Anon. Euripides' **HIPPOLYT** und Racines Phädra. Europa, 37, 1851.

Batteux, C. Observations sur l'Hippolyte d'Euripide et la Phèdre de Racine. Mém. de l'Acad. des Inscriptions et Belles Lettres, 41, 1786.

Chicoteau, M. Légende d'Hippolyte et régionalisme littéraire. CLS, 3, 1941.

Dohm, H. Welches ist das Verhältniss von Garniers Hippolyte zu seinen Quellen? Diss. München, 1889.

Flygt, S. G. Treatment of Character in Euripides and Seneca: the Hippolytus. CJ, 29, 1934.

Georges, C. W. Hippolyti Euripidei cum Racinii Phaedra comparati Specimen. Lüneburg, 1796.

Grene, D. The Interpretation of the Hippolytus of Euripides. CPh, 1939.

Meridier, L. Hippolyte d'Euripide, étude et analyse. Paris, 1930.

Weck, G. Quelques remarques sur l'Hippolyte d'Euripide et la Phèdre de Racine. Progr. Ratibor, 1874.

Weigert, A. Der Hippolyt des Euripides und die Phädra des Racine nebst einer vorausgesandten Würdigung des Euripides. Diss. Freiburg, 1869.

Dörrer, A. Andreas **HOFER** auf der Bühne. Brixen, 1911.

Dreyer, A. Andreas Hofer im Spiegelbild deutscher Dichtung. Warte, 7, 1906.

Freytag-Apolda, H. Andreas Hofer in der deutschen Dichtung. Tägl. Rundschau, Beilage, 181, 1909.

Frankl, L. A. Andreas Hofer im Liede. Innsbruck, 1884.

Glaser, F. Andreas Hofer im Lied und auf der Bühne. Sammler, 90, 1921.

Isolani, E. Andreas Hofer auf der Bühne. Deutsche Bühne, 2, 1910.

Kosch, W. Andreas Hofer im Leben und in der Dichtung. München-Gladbach, 1916.

Menghin, O. Andreas Hofer im volkstümlichen Liede. Brixen, 1912.

Gabriel, A. Friedrich von Heyden mit besonderer Berücksichtigung der **HOHENSTAUFEN**dichtungen. Breslau, 1900.

Warnecke, R. Grabbes Hohenstaufendramen und ihre Bedeutung für die Gegenwart. Bühne & Welt, 17, 1915.

Wolff, E. Raupachs Hohenstaufendramen. Diss. Leipzig, 1912.

Friedrich. Ueber **HOHENZOLLERN**-Dramen. Progr. Potsdam, 1891.

Höffner, E. Hohenzollerns Fürsten im deutschen Drama. Dresdner Nachrichten, 292, 1915.

Krauss, R. Hohenzollernfürsten im Drama. Beilage Allg. Zt., 241, 1903.

Landau, P. Hohenzollern auf der Bühne. Rheinisch-westfäl. Zt., 1255, 1914.

Stuemcke, H. Hohenzollern-Fürsten im Drama. Leipzig, 1903.

Weddigen, O. Die Hohenzollern und die deutsche Literatur. Berlin, 1883.

McKnight, G. H. Germanic Elements in the Story of King **HORN**. PMLA, 15, 1900.

Bartolomäus, R. Das Grauenvolle in der Kunst. (**HORROR**). Gegenwart, 76, 1905.

Boutet, F. Dichter des Grauens. Zeitgeist, 37, 1905.

Brendel, K. Das Uebersinnliche in der Theorie und im Drama der romantischen Schule. Diss. Leipzig, 1923.

Hamecher, P. Die Dichter des Grauens. Rhein.-westfäl. Zt., 997, 1912.

Lovecraft, H. P. Supernatural Horror in Literature. New York, 1945.

Seifert, G. The Supernatural in 19th Century Fiction. ER, April, 1903.

HUGUENOTS: See Emigrants, I. IV. 4.

Gebauer, C. Das **HUMANITAETSIDEAL** in der Zeit der Aufklärung und der Empfindsamkeit. Geisteskultur und Volksbildung, May, 1920.

Hope, W. G. The Suffering Humanitarian Theme in Shelley's Prometheus Unbound and in Certain Poems of Alfred de Vigny. FR, 12, 1939.

Klingberg, F. J. The Evolution of the Humanitarian Spirit in Eighteenth-Century England. Penna. Mag. of Hist. and Biog., 66, 1942.

Nestle, W. Die Humanitätsidee und die Gegenwart. Stuttgart, 1931.

Seidlin, O. Das Humane und der Dichter. MDU, 32, 1940.

Spranger, E. Wilhelm von Humboldt und die Humanitätsidee. Berlin, 1909.
Whitney, E. A. Humanitarianism and Romanticism. HLQ, 2, 1938-39.
Wind, E. Humanitätsidee und heroisiertes Porträt in der englischen Kultur des 18. Jahrhunderts. VBW, 9, 1932.
Anon. American **HUMOUR.** New Brit. Rev., 1860.
Baldensperger, F. Les définitions de l'humour. In: Etudes d'histoire littéraire, 1. sér. Paris, 1907.
—— La tradition de l'humour. RCC, 1913-14.
Blair, W. Horse Sense in American Humor from Benjamin Franklin to Ogden Nash. Chicago, 1942.
Constans, L. A. Plaute et l'humour romain. RCC, 28, 1926.
Donnelly, F. P. Humor: a Denatured Fallacy. Truth, Sept., 1934.
Gmelin, H. Zum Problem des Humors in der französischen Literatur. NSp, 41, 1933.
Haweis, H. R. American Humourists. London, 1883.
Hewitt, J. W. Humor in Homer and Vergil. CW, 22, 1929.
Johnston, C. The Essence of American Humour. AM, 1901.
Jongejan, E. De humor-cultus der Romantick in Nederland. Zutphen, 1933.
Kadner, S. Rasse und Humor. München, 1939.
Loesser, A. Humor in American Song. New York, 1942.
Neumann-Hofer. Französischer und deutscher Bühnenhumor. MLIA, 11, 1893.
Previtera, C. La poesia giocosa e l'umorismo. Milano, 1939.
Rearden, A. A Study of Humor in Greek Tragedy. U. of Calif. Chron., 16, 1914.
Remenyi, J. Hungarian Humor. SEER, 21, 1943.
Soyter, G. Humor und Satire in der byzantinischen Literatur. BBG, 1928.
Benzmann, H. Die Jagd im deutschen Liede. **(HUNT).** Sammler, 90, 1921.
Burg, A. Die Jagd im deutschen Lied. Berliner Morgenpost, 239, 1912.
Saupe, G. The Hunt is up. GRM, 28, 1940.
Fletcher, J. B. **HUON** of Bordeaux and the Faerie Queene. JEGPh, 2, 1899.
Hummel. Das Verhältniss des Ortnit zum Huon de Bordeaux. Archiv, 1878.
Kinnu, M. Possible Traces of Huon de Bordeaux in English Ballad Form. RR, 1, 1910.
Lindner, F. Ueber die Beziehungen des Ortnit zu Huon von Bordeaux. Diss. Rostock, 1872. Cf. Romania, 12 and SVL, 2, 1902.
Longnon, A. L'élément historique de Huon de Bordeaux. Romania, 1879.
McArthur, J. R. The Influence of Huon of Bordeaux upon the Faerie Queene. JEGPh, 4, 1903.
Riedl, C. Huon de Bordeaux in Geschichte und Dichtung. ZVL, 3, 1889.
Vancura, J. **HUS** in der böhmischen Geschichte und Literatur. Zs. f. Brüdergeschichte, 9.
Kraus, A. Der Hussitismus in der Literatur, besonders der deutschen vom 15.-19. Jahrhundert. (In Czech). 3 vols. Prag, 1917-24.
Korrodi, E. Ulrich von **HUTTEN** in der deutschen Dichtung. Wissen & Leben, 5, 1911.
Merbach, P. A. Ulrich von Hutten in der deutschen Dichtung. Kölnische Zt., 599, 1923.
Voigt, G. Ulrich von Hutten in der deutschen Literatur. Leipzig, 1905.
Schoo, J. Der Kampf mit der **HYDRA.** Mnemosyne, 7. (Leiden), 1939.
Moreau, P. Les trois **HYLAS.** Mélanges J. Vianey. Paris, 1934.
Asmus, R. **HYPATHIA** in Tradition und Dichtung. SVL, 7, 1907.
Schubert, H. von. Hypatia von Alexandrien in Wahrheit und Dichtung. PJb, 124, 1906.

—I—

Brückner, A. Die Echtheit des **IGOR**-liedes. ZSPh, 14, 1937.
Grégoire, H. Jakobson, R. et al. La geste du Prince Igor, épopée russe du XIIe siècle. New York, 1948. Cf. CL, 1, 1949.
Mazon, A. Les bylines russes (and the Igor Problem). RCC, 33, 1932.
Landsberg, H. **IKARUS** im Gedicht. Allg. Zt., 35, 1910.
Anon. The Red Man in Life and Literature. **(INDIAN).** TLS, 6.XII.1928.
Bissell, B. The American Indian in English Literature of the 18th Century. New Haven, 1925.
Canfield, D. L. Spanish Literature in Indian Languages of New Spain. Spanish Rev., 1935.
Carleton, P. D. The Indian Captivity. AL, 15, 1943.
Coleman, L. F. Aspects of Indian Civilization as Revealed in Representative Mexican Novels. Diss. Southern Methodist U., 1939.

David, J. Voltaire et les Indiens d'Amérique. MLQ, 9, 1948.

Debidour, A. L'indianisme de Voltaire. RLC, 4, 1924.

Driver, D. M. The Indian in Brazilian Literature. New York, 1942.

Foreman, Carolyn T. Indians Abroad, 1493-1938. Norman (Okla.), 1943.

Huff, Martha R. The Indian Element in XXth Century Spanish-American Novels. Diss. U. of Texas, 1940.

Manzoni, Aida C. El indio en la poesía de la América española. Buenos Aires, 1939.

Meléndez, Concha. Ia novela indianista en Hispanoamérica, 1832-89. Madrid, 1934, & Puerto Rico, 1935.

—— La literatura indianista en el Peru de hoy. Memoria del primer Congreso . . . de Lit. Iberoamer., 1940.

Mello Franco, A. A. de. O Indio brasileiro e a Revolução francesa. As origines brasileiras da theoria da bondade natural. Rio de Janeiro, 1937.

Morris, Mabel. Charles Brockden Brown and the American Indian. AL, 18, 1946.

Sherwin, R. T. The Viking and the Red Man. The Old Norse Origin of the Algonquin Language. New York, 1940 ff.

Sypher, W. Thomas Anburey on the Indian: his Plagiarism from Raynal. FAR, 1938.

Wogan, D. S. The Indian in Mexican Poetry. Diss. U. of North Carolina, 1940.

Yorba, E. J. The Indian in Contemporary Mexican Literature as Portrayed in the Works of Gregorio López y Fuentes. Diss. U. of Southern Calif., 1942.

Anon. **IGNEZ DE CASTRO**, episodio extrahido do canto terceiro do poema epico Os Lusiadas de Luiz de Camoes. Edição em quatorze linguas. Lisboa, 1873.

Almeida Carvalhães, P. P. d'. Inês de Castro na Opera e na Choreographia Italianas. Lisboa, 1908.

Araujo, J. de. Ignes de Castro, notas de bibliographia. Florença, 1891.

Bork, W. La Balada Inglesa y la Leyenda de Doña Inés de Castro. Anuario de la Sociedad Folklorica de Mexico, 4, 1943.

Heinemann, H. T. Inez de Castro, die dramatischen Bearbeitungen der Sage in den romanischen Literaturen. Diss. Münster, 1914.

Kreisler, K. Der Inez de Castro-Stoff im romanischen und germanischen, besonders im deutschen Drama. Progr. Krems, 1908-09. Cf. Literaturblatt. f. german. & roman. Philologie, 1914.

Price, L. M. **INKLE AND YARICO** Album. Berkeley, 1937.

Schmid, C. H. Ueber die Dichter, welche die Geschichte von Inkle und Yarico bearbeitet haben. Deutsche Monatsschrift, 1799.

Usteri, P. Inkel und Jariko (mainly Gessner's). Archiv, 122, 1909.

Roeger, J. Das Märchen von der Unsichtbarkeit in den homerischen Gedichten. (**INVISIBILITY**). Graz, 1924.

Baschmakoff, A. Origine tauridienne du mythe d'**IPHIGENIE**. BAGB, 1939.

Beck, A. Goethes Iphigenie und Maler Müllers Niobe. D&V, 40.

Bodmer, J. J. Critische Betrachtungen über einige Auftritte der von Gottscheden übersetzten Iphigenie des Racine mit historischen Vorbemerkungen. In: Critische Betrachtungen. Bern, 1743.

Boyd, J. Goethe's Iphigenie auf Tauris. Oxford, 1942.

Brandmann, P. A. Euripides Iphigenia in Aulide cum Racini Francogalli ejusdem nominis tragoedia comparata. Diss. Iena, 1836.

Desonay, F. Le personnage d'Iphigénie chez Goethe. Bruxelles, 1933.

Dubois, L. L'Iphigénie d'Euripide et celle de Racine. Progr. Riga, 1869.

Ernst, F. Iphigeneia. Mélanges Baldensperger. Paris, 1930.

—— Iphigeneia und andere Essays. München, 1933.

Fazio, S. Ifigenia nella poesia e nell'arte figurata. Palermo, 1932.

Hall, F. A. Iphigenie in Literature. St. Louis, 1910-11.

Hérenger, A. La religion de la vérité dans Iphigénie (Goethe). RLC, 12, 1932.

Houben. Euripidis Iphigenia in Aulide tragoedia cum Racini comparata. Progr. Trier, 1850.

Jacobson, M. De Fabulis ad Iphigeniam pertinentibus. Diss. Königsberg, 1888.

Jansen, H. Die Sage der Iphigenie auf Delphi in der deutschen Dichtung. Diss. Münster, 1911.

Krzysanowski, J. Source of Suckling's Brennovalt (Iphigenie, by P. Camus). TLS, 9.IV.1938.

Luzzatto, G. L. L'Ifigenia di Racine e l'imitazione di Euripide. Dioniso, 4, 1933.

Mueller, H. F. Goethes Iphigenie. Ihr Verhältnis zur griechischen Tragödie und zum Christentum. In: Beiträge zum

Verständnis der tragischen Kunst. Wolfenbüttel, 1909.
Parmentier, L. L'Iphigénie à Aulis d'Euripide. Bull. Acad. royale de Belgique. 1926.
Post, L. A. Iphigenia Among the Taurians and Trader Horn. CW, 23, 1930.
Reichart, W. A. The Genesis of Hauptmann's Iphigenia Cycle. MLQ, 9, 1948.
Schmidtmayer, R. Schillers Iphigenie in Aulis und ihr Verhältniss zum gleichnamigen Drama des Euripides. Progr. 1892.
Schoenwaelder, C. F. Die Iphigenie von Euripides, Racine und Goethe. Progr. Brieg, 1865.
Schultz, F. Die Nachbildung der Antike in Goethes Iphigenie. Extrait, 1881.
Schunck, E. Goethes Iphigenie auf Tauris und das gleichnamige Euripideische Stück. Progr. 1891.
Schwarz, C. W. Die Iphigenien-Sage und ihre dramatischen Bearbeitungen. Diss. Rostock, 1869.
Souchon, P. Les trois Iphigénies. MF, March, 1904.
Susini, E. L'Iphigénie à Delphes de Gerhart Hauptmann. EG, 3, 1948.
Tauber, G. Ueber die grundverschiedene Verwertung des Iphigenienstoffes durch Euripides und Goethe. Progr. Prag, 1897.
Thuemen, F. Die Iphigeniensage in antikem und modernem Gewande. Berlin, 1896.
Trunk, J. Ueber Euripides und Goethes Iphigenie in Tauris. Freiburg, 1865 & Offenburg, 1868.
Vogeler, A. Iphigenie im Drama der Griechen und bei Goethe. Progr. Hildesheim, 1900.
Wittich, W. Ueber Euripides' Iphigenie unter den Tauriern und Goethes Iphigenie auf Tauris. Progr. Cassel, 1888.
Zuntz, G. Die taurische Iphigenie des Euripides. Antike, 1933.
Koelbing, E. **IPOMEDON** in drei englischen Bearbeitungen. Breslau, 1889.
Oeftering, M. Die Geschichte der schönen **IRENE** in den modernen Litteraturen. Würzburg, 1897 & ZVL, 13, 1899.
Trostler, J. Zu den deutschen Bearbeitungen der Geschichte von der schönen Irene. Ungar. Rundschau, 3 & EPhK, 1914.
Heidenreich, H. Das Eiserne Kreuz im Spiegel deutscher Dichtung 1813, 1870, 1914. (**IRON CROSS**). Leipzig, 1915.
Luskey, A. E. Tieck's Romantic **IRONY**. Chapel Hill (N.C.), 1932.
Löschhorn, H. **ISABELLA** von Este. Progr. Berlin, 1914.
Bartholomaeis, V. de. Poesie provenzali storiche relative all' **ITALIA**. 2 vols. Roma, 1931.
Canter, H. V. Praise of Italy in Classical Authors. CJ, 33, 1938.
Reumont, A. Bibliografia dei lavori pubblicati in Germania sulla storia d'Italia. Berlin, 1863.
IWEIN: See Celtic Contributions, IV. I. 6.

—J—

Heidler, J. B. The **JAMAICA** Insurrection and Englishmen of Letters. PhQ, 1929.
Boertzler, F. **JANUS** und seine Deuter. Abhandlungen & Vorträge der Bremer Wiss. Ges. 1930.
Huth, O. Janus. Ein Beitrag zur altrömischen Religionsgeschichte. Bonn, 1932.
Refait, R. Le dieu Janus, sa légende, son histoire. Aesculape, 28, 1938.
Hadas, M. The Tradition of a Feeble **JASON**. CPh, 1936.
Barbier, A. **JEANNE D'ARC** jugée par Shakespeare. In: Etudes littéraires et artistiques. Paris, 1888.
Baurdeaux, H. Jeanne d'Arc et l'Allemagne. Rev. universelle, 77, 1939.
Bersancourt, A. de. Jeanne d'Arc et Shakespeare. Rev. mondiale, 15.VI. 1929.
Blaze de Bury, H. Jeanne d'Arc dans la littérature. RDM, I.VI.1885.
Blennerhasset, Charlotte von. Die Jungfrau von Orleans. Bielefeld, 1926.
Bloy, L. Jeanne d'Arc et l'Allemagne. Paris, 1915.
Bostock, J. K. The Maid of Orleans in German Literature. MLR, 1927.
Bradi, L. de. Jeanne d'Arc dans la littérature anglaise. Paris, 1921.
Brandes, G. Jeanne d'Arc in Dichtung und Geschichte. NJKA, 1911.
Buechner, A. Jeanne d'Arc in der Dichtung bei Chapelain, Shakespeare, Voltarire, und Schiller. Morgenblatt f. gebildete Leser, 66, 1862.
Bulthaupt, H. Die Jungfrau von Orleans in Geschichte und Dichtung. Masken, 6, 1912.
Cazamian, L. Andrew Lang et Jeanne d'Arc. RAA, 1932.
Cohen, G. Sainte Jeanne d'Arc dans la poésie du XVe siècle. Paris, 1947.
Crouslé, L. Jeanne d'Arc dans la poésie dramatique. In: Soirées littéraires et

scientifiques de la Sorbonne. Paris, 1867.

Delaitre, C. Un drame du XVe siècle sur Jeanne d'Arc, le Mystère du siège d'Orléans. Le Temps, 20.V.1898.

Duprey, P. Mémoires sur les oeuvres littéraires et artistiques inspirées par Jeanne d'Arc. Congrès scientifique de France, Orléans, 1852.

Evans, M. Die Jungfrau von Orleans, a Drama of Philosophical Idealism. MDU, 35, 1943.

French, A. Gower on Joan of Arc. In: Dial, 15, 1893 & in: Spectator, 71, 1893.

Goyau, G. Jeanne d'Arc devant l'opinion allemande. Paris, 1907.

Grenzmann, W. Die Jungfrau von Orleans in der Dichtung. Berlin, 1929.

Guillot de Saix. Jeanne d'Arc dans la littérature espagnole (Zamora). Hispania. (Paris), 1919.

Hanebuth, K. Ueber die hauptsächlichsten Jeanne d'Arc-Dichtungen des XV. XVI. und beginnenden XVII. Jahrhunderts. Diss. Marburg, 1893.

Hanotaux, G. Jeanne d'Arc. Paris, 1911.

Hasenow, F. Voltaire, Schiller und die Jungfrau von Orleans. MLIA, 1866.

Haudecoeur, A. Jeanne d'Arc dans la littérature et devant l'opinion en Angleterre. Travaux de l'Acad. nationale de Reims, 95, 1895.

Hebler, C. Jeanne d'Arc bei Shakespeare, Voltaire und Schiller. In: Philosophische Aufsätze. Leipzig, 1869.

Jan, E. von. Das literarische Bild der Jeanne d'Arc, 1429-1926. Halle, 1928.

Jeanne, E. L'image de la Pucelle d'Orléans dans la littérature historique française depuis Voltaire. Diss. Paris. Liège, 1925.

Klemperer, V. Jeanne d'Arc als dichterische Gestalt. Die Ernte, F. Muncker überreicht. Halle, 1926.

Krumpelmann, J. T. Schiller and Saint Joan of Arc. MDU, 34, 1942.

Kummer, C. F. Die Jungfrau von Orleans in der Dichtung (Shakespeare, Voltaire, Schiller). Wien, 1874.

Lanery d'Arc, P. Le livre d'or de Jeanne d'Arc. Paris, 1894.

Lehmann, H. Ueber Schillers Jungfrau von Orleans. Progr. 1864.

Louandre. Jeanne d'Arc dans l'histoire et dans la poésie. RDM, 1846.

Mahrenholz, R. Jeanne d'Arc in Geschichte, Legende, Dichtung auf Grund neuer Forschung. Leipzig, 1890.

—— Unberufene Verbesserer von Schillers Jungfrau von Orleans. MLIA, 1890.

Mausser, O. Die Jungfrau von Orleans in der Literatur. Walhalla, 8, 1911.

Pender, Beatrice C. Jeanne d'Arc in French Romantic Drama. Diss. Indiana U. 1937.

Porchat, J. J. Etudes sur les drames consacrés à Jeanne d'Arc par Schiller, L. d'Avrigny, A. Soumet, et spécialement sur La Mission de Jeanne d'Arc, drame en 5 journées et en vers. Lyon, 1844.

Puymaigre, de. Jeanne d'Arc au théâtre (1439-1890). Paris, 1890.

Quiquerez, J. Quellenstudien zu Schillers Jungfrau von Orleans. Diss. Leipzig, 1893.

Rabbe, F. Jeanne d'Arc en Angleterre. Paris, 1891.

Rapp, M. Jeanne d'Arc in der englischen und amerikanischen Literatur. Diss. Tübingen, 1935.

Rudler, G. L'Angleterre et Jeanne d'Arc: de Michelet à Anatole France. FQ, 2, 1920.

Sikora, A. Die Jungfrau von Orleans im tyrolischen Volksschauspiel. SVL, 6, 1906.

Soons, J. Jeanne d'Arc au théâtre. Diss. Amsterdam, 1929.

Storz, G. Jeanne d'Arc und Schiller, München, 1947.

Thurston, H. S. J. Shakespeare and Blessed Jeanne d'Arc. America, 1, 1909.

Toldo, P. Un rapporto a Benedetto XIV contro la Pucelle di Voltaire. Rendiconti Ac. Sc. Ist. di Bologna, 5, 1920.

Gartmann, B. Georg **JENATSCH** in der Literatur. Disentis, 1946.

Pohl, J. **JEPHTAS** Tochter. Festschrift Johann von Kelle. 1908.

Porwig, Johanna. Der Jephtastoff im deutschen Drama. Breslau, 1931.

Sypherd, W. O. Jephthah and his Daughter. Delaware Notes, 1939.

—— Jephthah and his Daughter. A Study in Comparative Literature. Newark (Delaware), 1948. Cf. GR, 1950.

Staude, P. **JEREMIA** in Malerei und Dichtkunst. Langensalza, 1907.

Suchier, W. Ueber das altfranzösische Gedicht von der Zerstörung **JERUSALEMS**. ZRPh, 1900.

JESUS: See Christ, above.

JEWS: See especially also II. V. 3.

Lambert, E. La Juive de Tolède de Grillparzer. RLC, 2, 1922.

—— Alphonse de Castille et la Juive de Tolède. BH, 1923.

Wurzbach, W. von. Die Jüdin von Toledo in Geschichte und Dichtung. JbGrG, 9, 1899.
Wolter, E. Die Legende vom Judenknaben. Halle, 1879.
Lindblom, J. **JOB** and Prometheus. Festschrift Nilsson. Lund, 1939.
Goebel, S. **JOHANNES** der Täufer. Dichtung und Wahrheit. Beweis des Glaubens, 35, 1898.
Gombert, L. J. Aals Spiel von Johannes dem Täufer und die älteren Johannesdramen. Breslau, 1908.
Rehse, L. Johannes der Täufer in zwei neuen Dichtungen. Deutsches Protestantenblatt, 30, 1898.
Sachse. Ueber Johannes den Täufer im Mittelalter. Progr., 1866.
Thulin, O. Johannes der Täufer im geistlichen Schauspiel des Mittelalters und der Reformationszeit. Leipzig, 1930.
Faverty, F. E. The Story of **JOSEPH** and Potiphar's Wife in Medieval Literature. HSPhL, 13, 1931.
Hamburger, K. Thomas Manns Roman Joseph und seine Brüder. Stockholm, 1945.
Poppenberg, F. Der weibliche Joseph, eine litterarische Parallele (Eugenia by G. Keller and El Joseph de las mugeres by Calderon). Bund, 45. (Bern), 1891.
Priebatsch, H. Die Josephsgeschichte in der Weltliterateur. Breslau, 1937.
Slochower, H. Thomas Mann's Joseph Story. New York, 1938.
Spann, M. Der Josephroman in Thomas Manns Gesamtwerk. PMLA, 57, 1942.
Stucki, Clara. Grimmelshausens und Zesens Josephsromane. Zürich, 1933.
Weilen, A. von. Der ägyptische Joseph im Drama des XVI. Jahrhunderts. Wien, 1887.
Paris, G. Saint **JOSAPHAT**. RP, 1895. And in: Poèmes et Légendes du moyen âge. Paris, 1900.
Anon. Das **JUDAS**problem in Wissenschaft und Literatur. Tag, 151, 1922.
Ancona, A. d'. La leggenda di vergogna e la leggenda di Giuda. Bologna, 1869.
Baum, P. F. The Mediaeval Legend of Judas Iscariot. PMLA, 31, 1916.
Buechner, A. Judas Ischarrioth in der deutschen Dichtung. Freiburg, 1921.
Creizenach, W. Judas Ischarioth in Legende und Sage des Mittelalters. In: Beiträge zur Geschichte der deutschen Sprache und Litteratur, Halle, 1875.
Engel, J. Judas Ischariot in der erzählenden und dramatischen Dichtung der Neuzeit. Deutsch-evangel. Rundschau, 1, 1906.
Freytag, H. Judas Ischarioth in der deutschen Wissenschaft, Predigt, Dichtung und bildenden Kunst unseres Jahrhunderts. Protest. Kirchenzeitung, 43, 1896.
Hand, W. D. The Birthday of Judas Iscariot: A Study in Folklore. MLF, 25, 1940.
—— A Dictionary of Words and Idioms Associated with Judas Iscariot, a Compilation Based Mainly on Material Found in the Germanic Languages. Berkeley, 1942.
Heller, B. Ueber Judas Ischariotes in der jüdischen Legende. Monatsschrift Gesch. Jud., 40, 1932.
Kinzenbach, K. Das Judasdrama in der neueren deutschen Literatur. Pfarrhaus, 19, 1903.
Rand, E. K. Mediaeval Lives of Judas Iscariot. Kittredge Anniversary Papers. Boston, 1913.
Vries, J. de. De Judas-figur in het drama. De Witte Mier, 1925.
Wünsche, A. Die Judas-Dramen in der neueren deutschen Literatur. Internat. Litt. berichte, 8, 1901.
Baltzer, O. Dramatische Bearbeitungen des **JUDITH**stoffes. Diss. Greifswald, 1922.
—— Judith in der deutschen Literatur. Berlin, 1930.
Fitzgerald, J. D. La historia de Judit y Holofernes en la literatura española. Hisp., 14, 1931.
Mortier, A. De quelques Judith antérieures à celle de M. Henry Bernstein. Nouvelle Revue, 1.II.1923.
Penten, H. The Tragedy of Judith. Internat. Journal of Apocryphes, 1907.
Purdie, E. The Story of Judith in German and English Literature. Paris, 1928.
Sommerfeld, M. Judith-Dramen des 16. und 17. Jahrhunderts. Berlin, 1933.
Teuber, V. Die mittelalterlichen Geschichten von der Judith. Progr. Komotau, 1907.
Cons, L. Montaigne et **JULIEN L'APOSTAT**. H&R, 4, 1937.
Foerster, R. Kaiser Julian in der Dichtung alter und neuer Zeit. SVL, 5, 1905.
Hoffmann, J. G. E. Julianos der Abtrünnige. Leyden, 1880.
Krappe, A. La vision de Saint Basile et la légende de la mort de l'empereur Julien. RBPh, 1928.

Oberziner, M. La leggenda di S. Giuliano il parricida. ARIV, 93, 1933.
Philip, K. Julianus Apostata in der deutschen Literatur. Berlin, 1929.
Tobler, A. Zur Legende vom heiligen Julianus. Archiv, 100-02, 1898-99.
Ruehl. Die Verbreitung des **JUSTINUS** im Mittelalter. Leipzig, 1871.

——K——

Anderson, W. **KAISER** und Abt, die Geschichte eines Schwankes. Helsingfors, 1923.
Colshorn, T. Die deutschen Kaiser in Geschichte und Sage. Leipzig, 1863.
Kampers, F. Die deutsche Kaiseridee in Prophetie und Sage. München, 1896. Cf. MLIA, 26.IX.1896.
—— Vom Werdegang der abendländischen Kaisermystik. Leipzig, 1924.
Landau, M. Das Märchen vom Blendwerk und von des Kaisers neuen Kleidern auf seiner Wanderung durch die Weltliteratur. Bühne und Welt, 1, 1899.
Lemcke, P. Der deutsche Kaisertraum und der Kyffhäuser. Magdeburg, 1887.
Ostlender, H. Dantes Kaiser und sein Veltro. JbDG, 26, 1946.
Pfister, F. Die deutsche Kaisersage und ihre antiken Wurzeln. Würzburg, 1928.
Scherer, F. J. Die Kaiser-Idee des deutschen Volkes in Liedern seiner Dichter seit 1806. Progr. 1879.
Schoenberger, J. K. Zur deutschen Kaisersage. Würzburger Jb. f.d. Altertum, 1, 1946.
Speyer, C. E. Die deutschen Kaiser in der Dichtung C. F. Meyers. Archiv, 133, 1915.
Tobler, A. Dante und vier deutsche Kaiser. Berlin, 1891.
Vollmer, H. Der Kaisergedanke in Prophetie, Sage und Dichtung. Christl. Welt, 27, 1913.
Zink, P. Die Kaiseridee im deutschen Lied. ZDU, 20, 1906.
Deutsch, Babette. Heroes of the **KALEVALA**, Finland's Saga. New York, 1940.
Fluegel, H. Das Kalewala und der Ursprung der Poesis. Literatur, 42, 1939.
Krohn, K. Kalevala-Studien. Helsinki, 1924.
Lodrone, R. La voce di una razza: il Kalevala. L'Europa Orientale, 22, 1942.
Meyer, R. Das Geisteserbe Finnlands: finnischer Mythos und das Volksepos Kalewala. Basel, 1940.
Salvini, L. Kalevala e non Kalevala. NAnt, 1943.
Guntert, H. **KALYPSO**. Halle, 1919.
Baudin, M. The Profession of **KING** in Seventeenth Century French Drama. Baltimore, 1941.
Berg, L. Die Königstragödien. LE, 3, 1901.
Burns, J. J. The Story of English Kings According to Shakespeare. New York, 1900.
Krappe, A. H. The Ploughman King. A Comparative Study in Literature and Folklore. RH, 46, 1919.
Meuli, H. Der König in der griechischen Tragödie. Diss. Zürich, 1945.
Morf, H. Ein italienisches Volksbuch (Reali di Francia). Nation, 1888.
Nauhardt, W. Das Bild des Herrschers in der griechischen Dichtung. Berlin, 1940.
Pater, W. Shakespeare's English Kings. In: Appreciations. London, 1890.
Rajna, P. Ricerche intorno ai Reali di Francia. Bologna, 1872. Cf. Romania, 7.
Schmidt, H. Der Mythos vom wiederkehrenden König im Alten Testament. 2. ed. Giessen, 1933.
Scholz, W. von. Shakespeares fünf Königsdramen. RFA, 1901.
Sciava, R. Der König in der Dichtung. RI, 1909.
Stobart, J. C. Shakespeare's Monarchs. London, 1926.
Wesselofsky. Legend of a King Struggling Against an Exiled Prince. ZRPh, 2, 1878.
Cappiello, L. Il bacio di Rossana e la poesia erotica antica e moderna. (**KISS**). Rassegna di studi francese, 1934.
Nyrop, K. Kysset og dets histoire. København, 1897.
Anon. **KLONDYKE** in American Literature. Athenaeum, 6.I.1900.
Gorra, E. Il cavaliere errante di Tommasso III di Saluzzo. (**KNIGHTS**). Stud. d. crit. letter. Bologna, 1892.
Koehler, R. Die Legende von dem Ritter in der Kapelle. Jb. f. romanische Litteratur, 1865. And in: Kleine Schriften, 2, 1868.
Wilkins, A. S. **KNOW THYSELF** in Greek and Latin Literature. Chicago, 1917.
Burckhardt, C. A. Der historische Hans Kohlhase und Heinrich von Kleists Michael **KOHLHAAS**. Leipzig, 1864.

Merbach, P. A. Michael Kohlhaasdramen. Brandenburgia, 24, 1915.
Ruppersberg, M. Michael Kohlhaas in der Dichtung und Geschichte. Wannseebuch, 1927.
Wolff, E. Der Michael Kohlhaas-Stoff auf der Bühne. Bühne & Welt, 2, 1899.
Hisserich, W. Die Prinzessin von Ahlden und Graf **KOENIGSMARK** in der erzählenden Dichtung. Diss. Rostock, 1906.
Nush, A. Kaiser **KONRAD** II in der deutschen Sage und Poesie. Progr., 1875.
Jellinek, A. L. **KONRADIN**-Dramen. SVL, 2, 1902.
Sauer, W. Konradin im deutschen Drama. Diss. Marburg. Halle, 1926.
Arnold, R. F. Tadeusz **KOSCIUSZKO** in der deutschen Litteratur. Berlin, 1898. Cf. ZVL, 13, 1899.
Niedermann, J. **KULTUR:** Werden und Wandlungen des Begriffs und seiner Ersatzbegriffe von Cicero bis Herder. Museum, 51, 1943.

—L—

LAKE: See Sea, below.
LANCELOT: See Celtic Contributions, IV. I. 6.
Böheim, J. Das Landschaftsgefühl des ausgehenden Mittelalters. (**LANDSCAPE**). Leipzig, 1934.
Dargel, F. A. Die Landschaftsschilderung in der erzählenden Dichtung Goethes, Hölderlins und der älteren Romantik. Diss. Heidelberg, 1921.
Disselhoff, H. D. Die Landschaft in der mexikanischen Lyrik. Diss. Würzburg, 1931.
Harms, S. Cl. Brentano und die Landschaft der Romantik. Diss. Würzburg, 1932.
Hauser, S. Die Entwicklung der Landschaftsschau in der englischen Reiseliteratur. Diss. Zürich, 1937.
Jan, E. von. Die Landschaft des französischen Menschen. Weimar, 1935.
Kammerer, F. Zur Geschichte des Landschaftsgefühls im frühen 18. Jahrhundert. Berlin, 1909.
Knapp, I. Die Landschaft im modernen englischen Frauenroman. Diss. Tübingen, 1935.
Messerschmidt-Schulz, J. Zur Darstellung der Landschaft in der deutschen Dichtung des ausgehenden Mittelalters. Breslau, 1938.
Meyer, C. Die Landschaft Ossians. Diss. Jena, 1906.
Palsgrave, J. Landscape in Poetry. London, 1897.
Funaioli, G. Sul mito di **LAOCOONTE** in Virgilio. Atti del 1o Congresso nazionale di Studi romani. Roma, 1928.
Nolte, F. O. Lessing's Laocoon. Lancaster (Pa.), 1940.
Pannier, L. Les **LAPIDAIRES** français du moyen âge, des XIIe, XIIIe et XIVe siècles. Paris, 1883.
Menéndez Pidal, R. La legenda de los Infantes de **LARA**. Historia y Epopeya. Madrid, 1934.
Anuda, M. Die Gerichtsverfahren im modernen Drama. (**LAW**). Wien, 1892.
Fehr, H. Das Recht in der Dichtung. Bern, 1931.
Herwitt. Der Rechtsgedanke im modernen Drama. Deutsche Juristen Zt., 32.
Müller, G. Recht und Staat in unserer Dichtung. Hannover, 1924.
Strethmann, F. W. Gerichtsverhandlungen als literarisches Motiv im Mittelalter. Köln, 1930.
Gressmann, H. Vom reichen Mann und armen **LAZARUS**: eine literaturgeschichtliche Studie mit ägyptologischen Beiträgen von G. Möller. APAW, 1918.
Harder, P. Dis Schuld des reichen Mannes in Urteilen der späteren Literatur. Beitr. zur Geschichte d. deutschen Sprache, 50, 1927.
Nahde, E. Der reiche Mann und der arme Lazarus im Drama des 16. Jahrhunderts. Diss. Leipzig, 1928.
Schultze-Jahde, K. Führergestalten und ihr Widerspiel in der Dichtung. (**LEADER**). Zs. f. deutsche Bildung, 2, 1927.
LEONORE: See also Bürger, IV. X. 12.
Arbesmann, R. The Dead-Bridegroom Motif in South American Folklore. Thought, 19, 1944.
Krumbacher, K. Die Leonorensage. ZVL, 1887. And in: Populäre Aufsätze. Leipzig, 1909.
Sozonovic, J. Bürgers Lenore und ihr verwandte Vorwürfe in der europäischen und russischen Volkspoesie. (In Russian). Warschau, 1893.
Wlislocki, H. von. Zur Lenorensage. ZVL, 11.
De Bin, U. **LEOPOLDO** I imperatore e la sua corte nella letteratura italiana. Trieste, 1910.
Grigorovitza, E. **LIBUSSA** in der deutschen Literatur. Berlin, 1901.
Müller, G. Die Libussa-Dichtungen Bren-

tanos und Grillparzers. Euphorion, 24, 1922.
Hieble, J. **LILI MARLENE**, A Study of a Modern Song. MLJ, 31, 1947.
Killen, A. M. La légende de **LILITH** et quelques interprétations modernes de cette figure légendaire. RLC, 12, 1932.
Lumbroso, A. La battaglia di **LISSA** nella storia e nella leggenda. Roma, 1910.
Luetgert, W. Die Erschütterung des Optimismus durch das Erdbeben von **LISSABON**. Gütersloh, 1901.
Rohrer, B. Das Erdbeben von Lissabon in der französischen Literatur des 18. Jahrhunderts. Diss. Heidelberg, 1933.
LOHENGRIN: See Celtic Contributions, IV. I. 3.
Anon. **LONDON** in Fiction. London News, 26.IX.1891.
Binz, G. Deutsche Besucher im Shakespeare'schen London. Beilage zur Allg. Zt, 23-25.VIII.1902.
Boynton, P. H. London in English Literature. Chicago, 1917.
Cazamian, L. Le Londres de M. Paul Morand. RAA, Dec., 1933.
Goetze, G. Der Londoner Lehrling im literarischen Kulturbild der Elizabethanischen Zeit. Diss. Jena, 1918.
Lang, E. M. Literary London. New York, 1907.
Ordish, T. P. Shakespeare's London. London, 1904.
Wyrouboff, G. Londres et Paris. La Philosophie positive, July, 1868.
LORELEY: See also Heine, IV. X. 8.
Leimbach, K. Die Lorelei, die Loreleidichtungen mit besonderer Rücksicht auf die Ballade von H. Heine. Wolfenbüttel, 1879.
Seeliger, H. Die Loreley-Sage in Dichtung und Musik. Leipzig, 1898.
—— Vorheinische Lorelei-Dichtungen. Heine-Kalender, 1911.
Büchner, G. W. F. Das altfranzösische **LOTHRINGER**-Epos. Betrachtungen über Inhalt, Form und Entstehung des Gedichts. Leipzig, 1887.
Willems, L. L'élément historique dans le Coronement **LOOIS**. Gand, 1896. Cf. Romania, 25.
Ramsey, R. W. Dante and Saint Louis. Transactions of the Royal Society of Literature, 4, 1924.
Sayous, E. La France de Saint Louis d'après la poésie nationale. Paris, 1866.
Dehne, W. Ludwig XI von Frankreich in der Literatur. RF, 42, 1930.
Mosher, O. W. Louis XI dans l'histoire et la littérature. Diss. Toulouse, 1925.
Neri. La leggenda di Louis XII. Genova, 1882.
LOUIS XIV: See also French Contributions, IV. VII. 22.
Despois, E. Les influences royales en littérature. I. Louis XIV; II. Frédéric II. RDM, 1853.
Held, M. A. Ludwig XIV und sein Hof in der englischen Prosadichtung. Diss. Zürich, 1922.
Ssymank, P. Ludwig XIV in seinen Schriften und im Spiegel der zeitverwandten Dichtung. Diss. Leipzig, 1899.
Sinhart, M. **LUDWIG DER BAYER** und Friedrich der Schöne im Drama. Bayerland, 25, 1914.
Belling, E. Die Königin **LOUISE** in der Dichtung. Berlin, 1886.
Dreyhaus, H. Die Königin Luise in der Dichtung ihrer Zeit. Berlin, 1926.
Kircheisen, F. M. Die Königin Luise in der Geschichte und Literatur. Jena, 1906.
LOVE, Eroticism, Courtly Love, Minne: See also Chapter Eleven and Platonism, II. III. 12.
Adam, A. La théorie mystique de l'amour dans l'Astrée et ses sources italiennes. Revue d'histoire de la philos., 15.VII. 1936.
Allen, P. S. The Origins of German Minnesang. MPh, 3, 1905-06.
Arnold, R. F. Die Natur verrät heimliche Liebe. Zs. d. Vereins f. Volkskunde, 12, 1902.
Aschner, S. Das Motiv der künftigen Geliebten. GRM, 6, 1914.
Bab, J. Das Drama der Liebe. Stuttgart, 1924.
Babb, L. The Physiological Conception of Love in the Elizabethan and Early Stuart Drama. PMLA, 56, 1941.
—— Love Melancholy in the Elizabethan and Early Stuart Drama. Bull. of the History of Medicine, 13, 1943.
Barth, B. Liebe und Ehe in altfranzösischer Fabel und in der mittelhochdeutschen Novelle. Berlin, 1910.
Bortone, G. Fra il voto e l'amore. Note critiche sul Monaco del Lenoir, sul Templaro dello Scott, sull'Arcidiacono dell' Hugo, etc. Napoli, 1908.
Brinkmann, H. Anfänge lateinischer Liebesdichtung im Mittelalter. NPh, 9.
—— Entstehungsgeschichte des Minnesangs. Halle, 1926.
Brusendorffe, O. Erotikens historie fra Graekenlands oldtid til vore dage. København, 1936.
Bullock, W. L. On Re-Reading Three Thwarted Romances: La Nouvelle

Héloïse, Die Leiden des jungen Werther, Jacopo Ortis. OC, 1932.
Burck, E. Die Entwicklungsgeschichte eines Motivs der antiken Liebesdichtung. HG, 1932.
Closs, H. M. Courtly Love in Literature and Art. Symposium, 1, 1948.
Denomy, A. J. An Inquiry into the Origins of Courtly Love. Mediaeval Studies, 6, 1944.
Diaz-Plaja, G. El sentimiento del amor a través de la poesía espanñola. Barcelona, 1942.
Dietrich, H. Die Freundesliebe in der deutschen Literatur. Diss. Leipzig, 1930.
Dornseiff, F. Aegyptische Liebeslieder, Hoheslied, Sappho, Theokrit. ZDMG, 1936.
Dumas, G. Tolstoy et la philosophie de l'amour. Paris, 1893.
Entwistle, W. J. From Cantigas de amigo to Cantigas de amor. RLC, 1938.
Feuerlicht, J. Vom Ursprung der Minne. AR, 23, 1939.
Englisch, P. Geschichte der erotischen Literatur. Stuttgart, 1927.
Fowler, E. B. Spenser and the System of Courtly Love. Louisville (Ky.), 1934.
Françon, M. Un motif de la poésie amoureuse au XVIe siècle. PMLA, 56, 1940.
Fucilla, J. G. Materials for the History of a Popular Classical Theme. CPh, April, 1931.
Gist, Margaret A. Love and War in the Middle English Romances. Philadelphia, 1947.
Gleichen-Russwurm, A. von. Frau Minne, LE, 12, 1908.
—— Das Liebesmotiv in der Renaissance. LE, 13, 1910.
Görner, O. Liebes- und Gesellschaftskasuistik im Mittelalter und Rokoko. AK, 22, 1931-32.
Graf, A. Liebe nach dem Tod. NAnt, Nov., 1905.
Green, O. H. Courtly Love in the Spanish Cancioneros. PMLA, 1949.
Grolmann, A. von. Das Problem der Liebe in der Dichtung der Gegenwart. ZDK, 1931.
Guillemin, A. M. L'amour dans la littérature antique. Culture, 1939-40.
Haller, W. & Malleville. The Puritan Art of Love. HLQ, 5, 1942.
Heyl, K. Die Theorie der Minne in den ältesten Minneromanen Frankreichs. Marburg, 1911.
Horne, H. H. Shakespear's Philosophy of Love. Bradenton Beach (Fla.), 1946.
Horner, E. Die ewige Liebe (Lustspielmotiv auf der Wanderung). ZVL, 11, 1897.
Irmen, F. Liebe und Freundschaft in der französischen Literatur des XVII. Jahrhunderts. Diss. Heidelberg, 1937.
Isbasescu, M. Minne und Liebe. Ein Beitrag zur Begriffsdeutung und Terminologie des Minnesangs. Stuttgart, 1940.
Kirchbach, W. Die Liebesleidenschaft in der Literatur. Wartburgstimmen, 1, 1903.
Kirby, T. A. Chaucer's Troilus: A Study in Courtly Love. University (La.), 1940.
Kluckhohn, P. Die Auffassung der Liebe in der Literatur des 18. Jahrhunderts und in der deutschen Romantik. Halle, 1922.
Koerte, A. Das Liebesmotiv in Epos und Drama der Griechen. Versammlung d. Freunde des Humanist. Gymnasiums. Erfurt, 1927.
Koltonovskaia, E. The Problem of Sex and its Treatment by the Neorealists. (In Russian). Obrazovanie, 1908.
Lewandowski, H. Das Sexualproblem in der modernen Literatur und Kunst. Dresden, 1927.
Lewis, C. S. The Allegory of Love: A Study in Medieval Tradition. Oxford, 1936.
Linge, T. La conception de l'amour dans le drame de Dumas fils et d'Ibsen. Paris, 1935.
Lippmann, J. Die Liebe in der dramatischen Literatur. Berlin, 1903.
Lot-Borodine, Myrrha. Sur les origines et les fins du service d'amour. Mélanges Jeanroy. Paris, 1928.
Luederitz, A. Die Liebestheorie der Provencalen bei den Minnesingern der Stauferzeit. Berlin, 1904.
Mann, A. The Love Theme in French Drama. FR, 1935.
Martellière. L'amour chez les classiques et les romantiques. Paris, 1911.
Martin, E. Die Carmina burana und die Anfänge des deutschen Minnesangs. ZDA, 20, 1876.
Maynard, T. Coventry Patmore's Doctrine of Love. Thought, 20, 1945.
Meyer, P. Le salut d'amour dans les littératures provençale et française. Bibl. de l'Ecole des Chartes, 6e sér. 3, 1867.
Mordell, A. The Erotic Motive in Literature. London, 1920.
Morsier, E. de. La Déclaration d'amour dans le théâtre moderne. RB, 1903.
Mott, L. F. The System of Courtly Love. New York, 1896.
Neilson, W. A. The Origin and Sources

of the Court of Love. Boston, 1889. Cf. also HSPhL, 6, 1900.
Nowak, W. Liebe und Ehe im deutschen Roman zu Rousseaus Zeit. Bern, 1906.
Paret, R. Früharabische Liebesgeschichten. Sprache & Dichtung. Bern.
Parry, J. J. The Art of Courtly Love by Andreas Capellanus. (Cf. Introduction). New York, 1941.
Pearson, L. E. Elizabethan Love Conventions. Berkeley (Cal.), 1933.
Pflugk-Harttung, J. von. Moderne Liebesliteratur. In: Splitter und Späne. Berlin, 1908.
Richardson, C. C. Love: Greek and Christian. Journal of Religion, 23, 1943.
Rowbotham, J. F. The Troubadours and Courts of Love. London, 1895.
Roy, P. N. The Poetry of Chivalrous Love. Calcutta Review, 3rd. Ser., 66-67, 1938.
Scheludko, D. Ueber die Theorien der Liebe bei den Trobadors. ZRPh, 60, 1940.
Schmid, P. Die Entwicklung der Begriffe Minne und Liebe im deutschen Minnesang bis Walther. ZDPh, 66, 1941.
Scholz, H. Eros und Caritas. Die platonische Liebe und die Liebe im Sinne des Christentums. Halle, 1929.
Schönbach, A. E. Die Anfänge des deutschen Minnesangs. Graz, 1898.
Schumann, A. Geschichte der erotischen Literatur. Leipzig, 1905.
Slaughter, E. Love and the Virtues and Vices in Chaucer. Bull. Vanderbilt U., 47, 1947.
Spitzer, L. L'amour lointain de Jaufré Rudel. Chapel Hill (N.C.), 1944.
Spanke, H. Untersuchungen über die Ursprünge des romanischen Minnesangs. Göttingen, 1940.
Stern, B. Illustrierte Geschichte der erotischen Literatur aller Zeiten und Völker. 2 vols. Wien, 1908.
Stern, G. W. Die Liebe im deutschen Roman des 17. Jahrhunderts. Berlin, 1932.
Symonds, A. The Idea of Love in Plato's Dialogues and in the Vita Nuova, the Lyrics and the Divina Commedia. Contemporary Rev., 1890.
Tieghem, Ph. van. Les droits de l'amour et l'union libre dans le roman français et allemand (1750-90). NPh, 12, 1926-27.
Tonelli, L. L'amore nella poesia e nel pensiero del Rinascimento. Firenze, 1933.
Villers, C. de. Erotique comparée, ou Essai sur la manière essentiellement différente dont les poètes français et allemands traitent l'amour. Paris, 1807.
Voort, D. van de. Love and Marriage in the English Medieval Romance. Nashville, 1938.
Wechssler, E. Die Kulturprobleme des Minnesangs. Halle, 1926.
Wiley, W. L. Pierre Le Loyer's Version of the Ars Amatoria (Cf. Introduction). Chapel Hill (N.C.), 1941.
Zelinski, W. Die Sprachen der Liebe. Leipzig, 1900.
LOVERS: See also Chapter Eleven, below.
Baldensperger, F. Les deux amants de Lyon dans la littérature. Revue d' histoire de Lyon, 1902.
Cotarelo, E. Sobre el origen y desarrollo de la legenda de Los Amantes de Teruel. Rev. de Archivos, Bibliotecas y Museos, 1903-09.
Dejob, C. Les amoureux éconduits ou transis dans Corneille et dans Racine, dans Apostolo Zeno et dans Métastase. Paris, 1897.
Farnham, W. E. The Contending Lovers. PMLA, 35, 1920.
Hammond, Eleanor P. The Lover's Mass in England and in Spain. MPh, 14, 1916.
Pinches, T. G. Legend of the Divine Lovers: Enlil and Ninlil. Journ. of the Royal Asiatic Society, 185, 1919.
Reval, G. Les grandes amoureuses romantiques. Paris, 1929.
Salomon, L. B. The Devil Take Her: A Study of the Rebellious Lover in English Poetry. Philadelphia, 1932.
Spargo, J. W. Chaucer's Shipman's Tale: The Lover's Gift Regained. Helsingfors, 1930.
Dustoor, P. E. Legends of **LUCIFER** in Early English and in Milton. Anglia, 54, 1930.
Gubernatis, de. Le type indien de Lucifer chez le Dante. Congrès international des orientalistes. Genève, 1894.
Hentschel, E. Die Mythen von Luzifers Fall und Satans Rache in der altsächsischen Genesis. Stuttgart, 1935.
Müller, U. Die Gestalt Lucifers in der Dichtung vom Barock bis zur Romantik. Berlin, 1940.
Croce, B. Intorno a **LUCREZIA** nella poesie e nella casistica morale. Critica, 35, 1937.
Dabney, L. E. An Anonymous XVIth Century French Play on the Death of Lucretia. MLN, 59.
Galinsky, H. Der Lucretia-Stoff in der Weltliteratur. Breslau, 1932.

Soltau, W. Lucretia und Virginia. PJb, 140, 1910.
Vallette, J. La légende de Lucrèce. RCC, 33.
Voigt, G. Die Lucretia-Fabel und ihre literarischen Verwandten. Leipzig, 1893.
LUDWIG, LUISE: See Louis, Louise.
Kippenberg, A. Die Sage vom Herzog von **LUXEMBURG**. Leipzig, 1901.
Cox, E. M. **LYONS** as a Literary Center in the 15th and 16th Century. Trans. of the Bibliographical Society, 14, 1919.
Romier, L. Lyon et le cosmopolitisme. BHR, 11, 1949.

—M—

Münzer, H. Die Stellung der Makkabäer in der deutschen Dichtung (**MACCABEANS**). Generalanzeiger f. d. Judentum, 17, 1902.
Hertel, G. Ein vergessenes Drama über die Eroberung von **MAGDEBURG**. Magdeburg Zt, 39, 1900.
Bolyte, J. Die schöne **MAGELONE**. Weimar, 1894.
Westermann, R. Die niederdeutschen und dänischen Uebertragungen von Victor Warbecks Schöne Magelone. Diss. Greifswald, 1932.
Freybe, A. Der Dreikönigstag und seine Feier der Kirche in deutscher Dichtung und Sitte. (**MAGI**). Allg. Evangel. Lutheran. Kirchen Zt., 42, 1908.
Hartmann, K. A. M. Ueber das altspanische Dreikönigspiel. Bautzen, 1879. Cf. Romania, 9.
Kehrer, H. Die heiligen Drei Könige in Literatur und Kunst. 2 vols. Leipzig, 1908.
MAGIC, Miracles, Merveilleux.
Anon. The Supernatural in XIXth Century Fiction. ER, April, 1903.
—— Frozen Sound (in Rabelais). N&Q, 22.I.1938.
Ansermaz-Dubois, F. Le merveilleux dans la littérature américaine. Labyrinte, 1. (Genève), 1944-45.
Baerg, G. The Supernatural in the Modern German Drama. Diss. Cornell U., 1920.
Bila, C. La croyance à la magie au XVIIIe siècle en France dans les contes, romans et traités. Paris, 1925.
Brewer, E. C. A Dictionary of Miracles: imitative, realistic, and dogmatic. London, 1884.
Butler, Eliza. The Myth of the Magus. Cambridge U.P., 1948.
Caillet, E. The Themes of Magic in XIXth Century French Fiction. Paris, 1933.
Deenen, M. Le merveilleux dans l'oeuvre de Villiers de l'Isle-Adam. Paris, 1939.
Delaporte, P. V. Du merveilleux dans la littérature française sous le règne de Louis XIV. Diss. Paris, 1891.
Doran, Madeleine. On Elizabethan Credulity, with Some Questions Concerning the Use of the Marvelous in Literature. JHI, 1, 1940.
Duncan, E. H. Jonson's Alchemist and the Literature of Alchemy. PMLA, 61, 1946.
Easter, D. B. A Study of the Magic Elements in the Romans d'Aventure and the Romans Bretons. Baltimore, 1906.
Eitrem, S. La magie comme motif littéraire chez les Grecs et les Romains. Symbolae Osloenses, 21, 1941.
Eliphas, L. The History of Magic. New York, 1948.
Friedrich, E. Die Magie im französischen Theater des XVI. und XVII. Jahrhunderts. Leipzig, 1908.
Graf, M. Die Wundersucht und die deutsche Literatur des 18. Jahrhunderts. München, 1890.
Hederer, E. Magie und Mystik in der Sprache der Dichtung. NR, June, 1937.
Lawrence, R. M. The Magic of the Horseshoe. London, 1898.
Libby, M. S. The Attitude of Voltaire to Magic and the Sciences. New York, 1935.
Loomis, C. G. White Magic: An Introduction to the Folklore of Christian Legend. Cambridge (Mass.), 1948.
Lowe, J. E. Magic in Greek and Latin Literature. Oxford, 1929.
Mabille, P. Le miroir du merveilleux. Paris, 1940.
Massonneau, E. La magie dans l'antiquité romaine. Paris, 1934.
Matthey, H. Essai sur le merveilleux dans la littérature francaise depuis 1800. Lausanne, 1915.
Pancritius, M. Die magische Flucht, ein Nachhall uralter Jenseits-Vorstellungen. Anthropos, 1913.
Polivka, J. Du surnaturel dans les contes slovaques. Rev. des Etudes slaves, 2, 1922.
Poortman, J. J. Over eenige min or meer occulte motieven in de wereldliteratur. Assen, 1937.
Ritter, H. Picatrix, ein arabisches Hand-

buch hellenischer Magie. VBW, 1921-22.
Roheim, G. Spiegelzauber. Leipzig, 1919.
Saurat, D. Literature and Occult Traditions. New York, 1930.
Scheible, J. Bibliothek der Zauber-, Geheimniss- und Offenbarungsbücher . . . aller Nationen. Stuttgart, 1849-51.
Thorndike, L. History of Magic and Experimental Science. 6 vols. New York, 1923-41.
Vogel, R. Das Wunder in der Dichtkunst. Türmer, 11, 1908.
Wahl, J. Magie et Romantisme: Notes sur Novalis et Blake. Hermes, 71, 1936.
Williams, R. C. The Merveilleux in the Epic. Paris, 1925.
Zender, R. Die Magie im englischen Drama des elisabethanischen Zeitalters. Halle, 1907.
Suchier, H. Die Quellen der **MAGUS**-sage. Germania, 20.
Wulff, F. A. Notices sur les Sagas de Magus et de Geirad et leurs rapports aux épopées françaises. Lund, 1874.
Ropa, L. **MALTE** et sa littérature. Grande Revue, Nov., 1935.
Schlosser, A. Die Sage vom Galgenmännlein im Volksglauben und in der Literatur. (**MANDRAKE**). Diss. Münster, 1912.
Lohmann. Byrons **MANFRED** und sein Verhältniss zu Dichtungen verwandten Inhalts. Anglia, 5, 1882.
Minoia, M. **MANFREDI** nella Divina Commedia. Lodi, 1900.
Frick, U. **MANON LESCAUT** als Typus. GRM, 1919.
Hollannd W. L. Die Legende der heiligen **MARGARETE**. Hannover, 1863.
Jeonroy, A. Vie provençale de sainte Marguerite. Annales du Midi, 1899.
Koltay-Kastner, E. La leggenda della beata Margherita d'Ungheria. Studi italo-ungheresi della R. Acc. d'Ungheria di Roma, 3, 1938-39.
Rode, A. Ueber die Margaretenlegende des Hartwig von der Hage. Kiel, 1890.
Vogt, F. Ueber die Margaretenlegenden. In: Pauls Beiträge, 1, 1873.
Wiese, B. Zur Margarethenlegende. Festschrift A. Tobler. Halle, 1895.
Tancredi, G. Il **MARGUTTE** del Pulci, il Cingar del Folengo e il Panurgo del Rabelais. In: Atti del Congresso intern. di scienze storiche, 4. Roma, 1903.
Alameda, S. La Virgen en la Biblia y en la primitiva iglesia. (**MARIA**). Barcelona, 1939.
Ashmann, M. Le culte de la Sainte Vierge et la littérature française profane du moyen âge. Utrecht-Nimègue, 1930.
Baldensperger, F. Le motif de Maria dans le romantisme français. Euphorion, 7, 1900.
Bockemühl, E. Neudeutsche Mariendichtung. Christl. Welt, 37, 1922.
—— Die moderne Mariendichtung. Gotha, 1927.
Ermini, F. Lo Stabat Mater e i pianti della Vergine nella lirica del medio evo. Città di Castello, 1916.
Goenner, Sister Mary E. Mariendichtung in the Teutonic Order. Washington, 1943.
Gripkey, Sister, M. V. The Blessed Virgin Mary as Mediatrix in the Latin and Old French Legend Prior to the Fourteenth Century. Washington, 1938.
Hellinghaus, O. Hundert lateinische Marienhymnen mit den Nachildungen deutscher Dichter. München-Gladbach, 1921.
Heyden, A. B. The Blesed Virgin Mary in Early Christian Latin Poetry. Washington, 1918.
Hofstetten, F. A. Maria in der deutschen Dichtung des Mittelalters. Frankfurt, 1895.
Isola, M. dell'. L'Ave Maria nel canto dei più grandi poeti. Bilychnis, 1930.
Kaltenbaeck, J. Die Mariensagen in Oesterreich. Wien, 1845.
Kirpitahnikof. L'Assomption de la Vierge dans la légende et dans l'art. Mémoires de la Société d'archéol. d'Odessa, 1888.
Kober, A. Geschichte der deutschen Mariendichtung. ZDU, 28, 1914.
Kuechenthal, P. Die Mutter Gottes in der altdeutschen schönen Litteratur bis zum Ende des XIII. Jahrhunderts. Göttingen, 1899.
Lumini, A. La Madonna nell'arte italiana da Dante a Torquato Tasso. Città di Castello, 1888.
Meyer, R. M. O. Ludwigs Maria. Euphorion, 6, 1899-1900.
Mussafia, A. Studien zu den mittelalterlichen Marienlegenden. SAWW, 113, 115, 119, 123, 139, 1886-98.
Neuhaus. Die Quellen zu Adgars Marienlegenden. Erlangen, 1882.
Paul-Emile, Soeur. Le renouveau marial dans la littérature française depuis Chateaubriand jusqu'à nos jours. Paris, 1939.
Salzer, A. Die Symbolik in den deutschen Mariendichtungen des Mittelalters. Kultur, 4. (Wien), 1903.

Sinding, O. Mariä Tod und Himmelfahrt. Kristiania, 1903.
Watenpuhl, H. Die Geschichte der Marienlegende von Beatrix der Küsterin. Diss. Göttingen, 1904.
Wechsler, E. Die romanischen Marienklagen. Ein Beitrag zur Geschichte des Dramas im Mittelalter. Halle, 1893.
Wibbelt, A. Die unbefleckte Empfängniss in Calderons Autos sacramentales. Der Katholik, 1897.
Becker, Marie L. **MARIA MAGDALENA** in der Kunst. Bühne & Welt, 5, 1903.
Brierre, J. Vie de sainte Marie-Madeleine, suivie de trois traités. Paris, 1933.
Chabaneau, C. Sainte Marie-Madeleine dans la littérature provençale. RLR, 27-28, 1885.
Doncieux, G. Le cycle de Marie-Madeleine dans la chanson populaire. Paris, 1892.
Eggert, C. E. The Middle Low German Version of the Legend of Mary Magdalen. JEGPh, 4, 1903.
Gazay, J. Etudes sur les légendes de sainte Marie-Madeleine et Joseph d'Arimathie. Annales du Midi, 51, 1939.
Hansel, H. Maria-Magdalena im Wandel der Zeiten. F&F, 1935.
—— Die Maria-Magdalena-Legende. Eine Quellen - Untersuchung. Greifswald, 1937.
Rüdiger, Gertrud von. Magdalenenliteratur vom Mittelalter bis zur Gegenwart. Frau, 18, 1911.
Chasles, P. Shakespeare, **MARIE STUART** et l'Arétin. Paris, 1852.
Fiaschi, Tima. La Maria Stuarda di V. Alfieri e quella di F. Schiller. Grosseto, 1903.
Fockens, P. Maria Stuart, eine literarhistorische Studie (Swinburne, Björnson, Schiller, Vondel). Diss. Leipzig, 1887.
Halluin, J. d'. Marie Stuart et les Poèmes de la Cassette. La Table Ronde, 2, 1946.
Henri-Bordeaux, Paule. Marie Stuart. 2 vols. Paris, 1938. Cf. Le Temps, 29.XI. 1938.
Kipka, K. Maria Stuart im Drama der Weltliteratur. Leipzig, 1907.
Koeppel, E. Zur Quellenkunde des Stuart-Dramas. ALG, 97, 1896.
Loghem, M. G. L. van. Maria Stuart und ihre Dichtung. Nederland, Sept., 1903.
Marquigny. Marie Stuart dans l'histoire, dans le drame et le roman. In Etudes religieuses . . . par les Pères de la Congrégation de Jésus, 21-22, 1864.
Morel, L. Trois Tragédies sur Maria Stuart. Progr., 1908.
Mueller, P. La tragédie de Marie Stuart dans l'idée de Schiller et dans l'histoire. Genève, 1880.
Neri, A. Una fonte dell'Ecossaise di Voltaire. Rassegna bibliografia della lett. ital., 1899.
Rassow, M. Maria Stuart 1820 in Paris. Euphorion, 17, 1910.
Reboux, P. Le calvaire de Marie Stuart. Paris, 1948.
Schulz, F. Maria Stuart vor Schiller. Königsberger Blätter, 70, 1912.
Sirven, P. Sur la Marie Stuart de V. Alfieri. Mélanges Lanson. Paris, 1922.
Tannenbaum, S. A. & Dorothy R. Marie Stuart, Queen of Scots (a Concise Bibliography). 3 vols. New York, 1944-46.
Woerner, R. Die älteste Maria Stuart-Tragödie. Festschrift H. Paul. Strassburg, 1902.
Yates, F. A. Some New Light on l'Ecossaise of A. de Montchrétien. MLR, 1927.
Fambri, P. **MARIA TUDOR** sotto la penna di Hugo e di Tennyson. NAnt, 62, 1882.
Filon, A. Les drames de Victor Hugo et l'histoire d'Angleterre. II. Marie Tudor. Journal des Débats, 24.XII.1902.
Piaget, A. Poésies françaises sur la bataille de **MARIGNAN.** Mém. et doc. de la Soc. d' histoire de la Suisse Romande, 4, 1892.
Küchler, W. **MARLBOROUGH** auf der Bühne. NSp, 33.
Chabot, J. B. Les origines de la légende de saint Jean **MARON.** Paris, 1935.
Loane, G. G. **MARTHA** and Mary. N&Q, 1.X.1938.
David, C. Die drei Mysterien des heiligen **MARTIN** von Tours. Frankfurt, 1899.
Reitzenstein, R. Bemerkungen zur **MARTYRIEN**literatur, I. Die Bezeichnung "Märtyrer." Göttingen, 1916.
Ovaa, W. A. Dekker and The Virgin Martyr. ESs, 1922.
Croce, B. Un dramma tedesco su **MASANIELLO.** In: Nuovi Saggi. Bari, 1931.
Kohlrausch, R. Masaniello. Bühne & Welt, 152, 1913.
Kistenmacher, H. W. **MASCHINE** und Dichtung. Diss. München, 1913.
Lublinski, G. Die Maschinenkultur in der modernen Dichtung. Tag, 174, 1910.
Richepin, J. Les grands types classiques du répertoire: Le **MATAMORE.** Journal de l' U. des Annales, 15.II.1912.
Versényi, G. König **MATTHIAS** in der

ungarischen Dichtung. (In Hungarian). In: Gedenkbuch für König Matthias. Budapest, 1902.
Herzberg, A. J. Der heilige **MAURITIUS**. Düsseldorf, 1936.
Hornung. König **MAXIMILIAN** von Bayern im Lichte der zeitgenössischen Literatur. Diss. München, 1921.
Waas, G. E. The Legendary Character of Kaiser Maximilian. New York, 1941.
Lewickyj, W. **MAZEPPA** in der deutschen Literatur. Ruthenische Revue, 2, 1904.
Arendt, R. La **MEDEE** de Corneille comparée à celle de Sénèque. Progr. Kempen (Posen), 1875.
Buehler, F. G. Aehnlichkeiten und Verschiedenheiten der Medea des Euripides, Seneca, und Corneille. Progr. Donaueschingen, 1876.
Byrne, L. A Comparison of the Medea of Euripides and the Medea of Seneca. Diss. Chicago, 1899.
Caimo, I. Umanità e verità della figura di Medea in Euripide. Dioniso, 6, 1937.
Deile, G. Klingers und Grillparzers Medea miteinander und mit den antiken Vorbildern des Euripides und Seneca verglichen. Progr. Erfurt, 1901.
Dunham, T. C. Medea in Athens and Vienna. MDU, 38, 1946.
Ferrel, C. C. The Medea of Euripides and the Medea of Grillparzer. Sewanee Rev., 1901.
Heine, T. C. H. Corneille's Médée in ihrem Verhältnisse zu den Medea-Tragödien des Euripides und des Seneca betrachtet, mit Berücksichtigung der Medea-Dichtungen Glovers, Klingers, Grillparzers und Legouvés. Diss. Münster, 1881.
Herold, F. Médée dans la tragédie grecque, la tragédie latine et la tragédie française. Revue d'Art dramatique, 20.I.1899.
Ischer, R. Medea. Vergleichung der Dramen von Euripides bis Grillparzer. Progr. Leipzig, 1906.
Mallinger, L. Médée. Etude de littérature comparée. Paris, 1898.
McCracken, G. Medea in Modern Dress. (M. Anderson's Wingless Victory). CJ, 33, 1937.
Mueller, H. F. Euripides' Medea und Das goldene Vliess von Grillparzer. Progr. Blankenburg, 1896.
Purtscher, H. Die Medea des Euripides verglichen mit der von Grillparzer und Klinger. Progr. 1880.
Renner, R. Medea, eine Studie. BBG, 62, 1927.
Schiller, L. Medea im Drama alter und neuer Zeit. Progr. Ansbach, 1865.
Séchan, L. La légende de Médée. REG, 40, 1927.
Behnke, F. Diego Ximenez de Encisos Los **MEDICIS** de Florencia, Giovanni Rosinis Luisa Strozzi und Alfred de Mussets Lorenzaccio in ihrem Verhältnis zur Geschichte. Diss. Berlin, 1910.
Buser. Die Beziehungen der Mediceer zu Frankreich. Leipzig, 1879.
Eckert, K. Die dramatische Behandlung der Ermordung des Herzogs A. de Medici durch seinen Vetter Lorenzino in der englischen Literatur. Diss. Königsberg, 1907.
Paccard, J. E. Les Médicis ou la renaissance des sciences, des lettres et des arts en Italie et en France. Paris, 1812.
Varia. England and the **MEDITERRANEAN** Tradition. Studies in Art, History and Literature. Warburg Institute. London, 1946.
Garnier, C. M. Les poètes anglais et la Méditerranée. FGB, 1938.
Rocca, M. Il Mediterraneo nell' opera di un poeta corso (Padovani). Giornale di politica e di letteratura, 14, 1938.
Komorzynski, E. von. Die **MEISTERSINGER** und ihre literarische Tradition. Bayreuther Blätter, 30, 1906.
Anderson, W. Die **MELEAGROSSAGE** bei den Tschuwaschen. Ph, 1914.
—— Die Meleagrossage bei den Letten. Ph, 1923.
Hanslik, R. Zur Meleagroserzählung bei Homer. Mitteil. der Arbeitsgemeinschaft der Altphilologen Oesterreichs, 10, 1936-37.
Lawrence, W. W. The Tale of **MELIBEUS**. Festschrift Carleton Brown, Oxford U.P., 1940.
Froehlicher, H. Th. von Ringoltingens **MELUSINE**, Wilhelm Ziely's Olivier und Artus und Valentin und Orsus und das Berner Cleomadesfragment mit ihren französischen Quellen verglichen. Diss. Zürich, 1889.
Hofrichter, L. Die ältesten französischen Bearbeitungen der Melusinensage. Halle, 1927.
Kohl, R. Das Melusinenmotiv. Schriften der Bremer Wiss. Ges. 11, 1933.
Mulertt, W. Rabelais und die Melusinen-Geschichte. ZFSL, 62, 1938.
Nowack, M. Die Melusinen-Sage, ihr mystischer Hintergrund, ihre Verwandtschaft mit anderen Sagenkreisen und ihre Stellung in der deutschen Litteratur. Diss. Zürich, 1886.

Saivre, L. de. Le mythe de la mère Mélusine, étude critique et bibliographique. Mém. de la Société de Statistique de Sèvres, 1882. Saint-Maixent, 1883.
Wachler, E. Die Bearbeitungen des Melusinenstoffes. Bühne & Welt, 16, 1914.
Stevens, C. H. A Study of the **MENAECHMI** Theme in Spanish Literature. In Lope's El palacio confuso. New York, 1939.
MEPHISTOPHELES: See Goethe's Faust, IV. X. 6.
Crammer-Byng L. Who was **MERLIN**? QR, 1929.
Gaster, M. The Legend of Merlin (and King Solomon). FL, 1905.
Hangwitz, C. Il mago Merlino. Memorie, tradizioni, leggende raccolte. Milano, 1865.
Hight, G. S. Tennyson's Merlin. SPh, 44, 1947.
Holzamer, W. Merlin-Dichtungen. LE, 4, 1900.
Mabbott, T. O. Tennyson's Merlin, N&Q, 193, 1948.
Paur, T. Einiges von Merlin in Sage und Dichtung. 1878.
Sanesi, I. La storia di Merlino di Paolino Pieri (and Merlin's fame in Italy). Bibl. stor. d. letter., Bergamo, 1898.
San Marte. Die Sagen von Merlin. Halle, 1853.
—— Merlin der Prophet und Zauberer, in Rückblick auf Dichtungen und Sagen des deutschen Mittelalters. Quedlinburg, 1872.
Schiprowski, E. Der Zauberer Merlin in der deutschen Dichtung. Diss. Breslau, 1933-34.
Smith, R. M. King Lear and the Merlin Tradition. MLQ, 7, 1946.
Sommer, O. Le Roman de Merlin, or The Early History of King Arthur. London, 1894.
Villemarque, H. de la. Myrdhinn, ou l'Enchanteur Merlin, son histoire, ses oeuvres, son influence. Paris, 1862.
Zumthor, P. Merlin le prophète, un thème de la littérature polémique de l'historiographie et des romans. Lausanne, 1943.
Bouvy, E. La **MEROPE** de Maffei en France et la Mérope de Voltaire en Italie. BI, 2, 1902.
Canonica, G. Merope nella storia del teatro tragico greco, latino e italiano. Milano, 1893.
Croce, B. La Mérope de Pomponio Torelli et l'Andromaque de Racine. REI, 1938-39.
Hartmann, G. Merope im italienischen und französischen Drama. Münchener Beiträge. Erlangen, 1892.
—— Merope im englischen und französischen Drama. Archiv, 95, 1896.
Oliver, T. E. The Merope of George Jeffreys as a Source of Voltaire's Mérope. Ill. Studies in Lang. and Lit. 12, 1928.
Payer von Thurn, R. Paul Weidmanns Merope (1772). SVL, 3, 1903.
Schloesser, P. Zur Geschichte und Kritik von F. W. Gotters Merope. Leipzig, 1890.
Teichmann. Merope im italienischen und französischen Drama. Progr. Borna, 1896.
Wendt, G. Die italienischen und französischen Bearbeitungen der Merope-Fabel. Diss. Jena, 1876.
Kurth, G. L'histoire poétique des **MEROVINGIENS**. Paris, 1893.
Saint **METHODE:** See Constantin and Cyrille, above.
Krefting, A. St. **MICHAEL** und St. Georg in ihren geistesgeschichtlichen Beziehungen. Jena, 1937.
Courten, C. de. **MILANO** romantica e la Francia della Restaurazione (1815-30). Milano, 1926. Cf. Libri del Giorno, June, 1926.
De Castro. La storia nella poesia popolare milanese. Milano, 1879.
MILES GLORIOSUS: See also Braggarts, above, and Plautus, II. IV. 4.
Drexler, H. Zur Interpretation des plautinischen Miles. H., 1929.
Duckworth, G. E. The Structure of the Miles Gloriosus. CPh, 1935.
Fest, O. Der Miles gloriosus in der französischen Komödie vom Beginn der Renaissance bis zu Molière. Erlangen, 1897.
Graf, H. Der Miles Gloriosus im englischen Drama bis zur Zeit des Bürgerkrieges. Diss. Rostock, 1892.
Thuemmel, J. Der Miles gloriosus bei Shakespeare. JbShG, 13, 1878.
Bruneck, H. von. Das Bergwerk in der Literatur. (**MINING**). Rhein.-westfäl. Zt., 99, 1912.
Duerler, J. Die Bedeutung des Bergbaus bei Goethe und in der deutschen Romantik. Frauenfeld, 1936.
Sébillot, P. Les travaux publics et les mines dans les traditions et les superstitions de tous les pays. Paris, 1894.
MINNE, MINNESANG: See Love, above.
Hertz, W. Spielmannsbuch. (**MINSTRELS**). Stuttgart, 1931.
Menéndez Pidal. Poesia juglaresca y juglares. Madrid, 1924.

Pillet, A. Das fabliau von den Trois bossus ménestrels und verwandte Erzählungen. Halle, 1901.
MIRACLES & MERVEILLEUX: See Magic, above.
Langen, A. Zur Geschichte des Spiegelsymbols in der deutschen Dichtung (MIRROR). GRM, 1940.
Vordtriede, W. The Mirror as Symbol and Theme in the Works of Mallarmé and George. MLF, 1947.
A'Bdurrashid Khan, N. The Play Mahomet in England. (MOHAMMED). Asiatic Quarterly Rev., 2 Ser., 1, 1891.
Ancona, A. d'. La leggenda di Maometto in Occidente. GSLI, 13, 1889. And in: Studi di critica e storia letteraria, 2. Bologna, 1912.
Bernays, M. Der französische und deutsche Mohamet. In: Zur neueren Litteraturgeschichte. Stuttgart, 1895-96.
Cailliet, E. Blaise Pascal on Mohammed. Moslem World, 36, 1946.
Krüger, H. Mohammed in der deutschen Dichtung. Post (Berlin), 17.V.1903 & Hamburger Nachrichten, Beilage 21, 1904.
Lopez, R. S. Mohammed and Charlemagne: A Revision. Spec., 18, 1943.
Martino, P. Mahomet en France au XVIIe et au XVIIIe siècle. Actes du XIVe Congrès des Orientalistes (Alger), 3.
Nolte, F. O. Voltaire's Mahomet as a Source of Lessing's Nathan der Weise and Emilia Galotti. MLN, 1933.
Otto, F. Mohammed in der Anschauung des Mittelalters. MLN, 1889.
Pirenne, H. Mahomet et Charlemagne. RBPh, 1, 1922.
—— Mohammed and Charlemagne. London, 1939.
Prutz, H. Ueber des Gautier von Compiègne Otia de Machomete. SBAW, 1903.
Tatlock, J. S. P. Mohammed and his Followers in Dante. MLR, 1932.
Forkey, L. O. The Role of MONEY in French Comedy during the Reign of Louis XIV. Baltimore, 1947.
MONKS, MONASTERIES, NUNS: See Chapter Eleven.
Martin, E. Histoire des MONSTRES depuis l'Antiquité jusqu'à nos jours. Paris, 1880.
Reich, H. Der Mann mit dem Eselskopf. Ein Mimodrama vom klassischen Altertum verfolgt bis auf Shakespeares Sommernachtstraum. Weimar, 1904.
Ancona, A. d'. I dodici mesi dell' anno nella tradizione popolare. (MONTHS). Archivio per lo studio delle tradiz. pop., 2, 1883.
Bertini, H. M. L'abazia di MONTSERRAT nella vita letteraria. Conv., 1931.
Dammert, F. Historia über den Monserrat. Benedikt. Monatsschrift Beuren, 21, 1939.
Schreiber, G. Der Montserrat im deutschen Erinnerungsbild. Span. Forschungen der Görres-Ges. 1, 1938.
Bettex, S. Der Mond in Dichtung und Volksglauben. (MOON). Du, May (Zürich), 1947.
Liljegren, S. B. Romantiken och månen. Arbok d. Vetenskaps-Societeten i Lund, 1923.
Nicolson, Marjorie H. Voyages to the Moon. New York, 1948.
Petsch, R. Goethes Mondlyrik. Zs. f. deutsche Bildung, 4, 1928.
Pompecki, B. Der Mond in der neueren deutschen Lyrik. Heimat & Welt, 24-28, 1911.
Schulz, H. Anschauung und Darstellung des Mondes in Goethes Werken. Diss. Greifswald, 1912.
Chambers, R. W. The Saga and the Myth of Sir Thomas MORE. PBA, 1926.
—— The Place of St. Thomas More in English Literature and History. London, 1937.
Distel, T. Kurfürst MORITZ zu Sachsen auf der Bühne. ZVL, 14, 1900.
Merbach, P. A. Kurfürst Moritz von Sachsen im deutschen Drama. Zwinger, 5, 1921.
Abraham, M. Légendes juives apocryphes sur la vie de Moïse. (MOSES). Paris, 1925.
Halévy, A. Moïse dans l'histoire et dans la légende. Paris, 1927.
MOUNTAINS: See also Alps, above.
Amiguet, P. Technique et poésie de la montagne. Paris, 1936.
Das, P. K. James Thomson's Appreciation of Mountain Scenery. ESn, 64, 1929.
Engel, C. E. La haute montagne romancée. Les Alpes, 1, 1937.
Fischmann, Hedwig. Die dichterische Entdeckung des Hochgebirges. Dresdner Anzeiger, 21.VIII.1923.
Hillebrand, Lucie. Das Riesengebirge in der deutschen Dichtung. Diss. Breslau, 1921.
Lioy, P. I poeti della montagna. NAnt, 110, 1890.
Negri, L. G. Carduci e la montagna. La Cultura moderna, 6, 1935.
Vallot, C. & Engel, C. E. Tableau lit-

téraire du massif du Mont-Blanc. Chambéry, 1930.
Fuchs, R. Lügen-**MUENCHHAUSEN**. Niedersachsen, 26, 1921.
Gudde, E. G. An American Version of Munchhausen. AL, 13, 1942.
Müller-Fraureuth, C. Die deutschen Lügendichtungen bis auf Münchhausen. Halle, 1881.
Rapp, A. The Genealogy of Baron Münchhausen. CJ, 32, 1937.
Schweitzer, W. Die Wandlungen Münchhausens. Leipzig, 1921.
Zobeltitz, F. von. Münchhausen und Münchhausiaden. Zs. f. Bücherfreunde, 1898.
Lehmann, A. Das Schicksal **MUSTAPHAS**, des Sohnes Solimans II. in Geschichte und Literatur. Diss. München, 1908.
Streibich, A. Mustapha und Zeangir, die beiden Söhne Solimans des Grossen in Geschichte und Dichtung. Stuttgart, 1903.
Becker, G. H. Ubi sunt qui ante nos. (**MUTABILITY**). Festschrift Ernst Kuhn. Breslau, 1916.
Dziech, J. De mortalium fragilitate antiquitus cognita. Mélanges Cwiklinski. Posnan, 1936.
Gilson, E. De la Bible à François Villon: tables pour l histoire du thème Ubi sunt? In: Les Idées et les Lettres. Paris, 1932.
Imelmann, J. Donec gratus eram tibi. Berlin, 1899.
Wais, K. K. T. Das Motiv des Vergangenen in der neueren Literatur. DVLG, 10, 1932.

—N—

Rank, O. Die Nacktheit in Sage und Dichtung. (**NAKEDNESS**). Imago, 2, 1913.
Krüger, G. Eigennamen als Gattungsnamen. (**NAMES**). Progr. Berlin, 1890-91.
Scott, E. L. Les noms de baptême et les prénoms. Nomenclature, signification, tradition, légende, histoire, arts de nommer. Paris, 1857.
Mathorez, J. Notes sur les rapports de **NANTES** avec l'Espagne. BH, 1912.
Cione, E. L'amore per **NAPOLI** nei romantici: 1830-46. Napoli, 1936.
Croce, B. La corte delle Tristi Regine a Napoli. Napoli, 1894.
—— Il tipo del Napoletano nella commedia. In: Saggi sulla letteratura italiana del seicento. Bari, 1911.
Letts, M. Some French Travellers in Naples in the 16th Century. EHR, Oct., 1919.
Mele, E. Napoli nei romanzi stranieri: Mme. de Staël. Nap. nobiliss., 7, 1898.
—— Napoli nelle descrizioni dei poeti. Corriere di Napoli, Oct., 1898.
Mitlacher, H. Die Entwicklung des **NARZISS**begriffs. GRM, 21, 1933.
Wesselski, A. Narkissos oder des Spiegelbild. Archiv Orientalni, 7, 1935.
NATHAN: See Shylock, below.
NATURE: See also Landscape, above, and Primitivism, below.
Adam, J. Der Natursinn in der deutschen Dichtung. Wien, 1906.
Allen, K. The Treatment of Nature in the Poetry of the Roman Republic. Bull. U. of Wisconsin, 28, 1899.
Batt, M. The Treatment of Nature in German Literature from Günther to the Appearance of Goethe's Werther. Diss. Chicago, 1902.
Beach, J. W. The Concept of Nature in Nineteenth-Century English Poetry. New York, 1936.
Bell, A. F. G. The Spanish Attitude towards Nature. BSS, 24, 1947.
Biese, A. Die Entwicklung des Naturgefühls bei den Griechen und Römern. Kiel, 1882-84.
—— Die Entwicklung des Naturgefühls im Mittelalter und in der Neuzeit. Leipzig, 1888.
—— Das Naturgefühl im Wandel der Zeiten. Leipzig, 1926.
Blunden, E. Nature in Literature. London, 1929.
Boheim, J. Das Landschaftsgefühl des ausgehenden Mittelalters. Diss. Leipzig, 1930.
Bollmann, H. Beiträge zur Geschichte des Naturgefühls in der alt- und mittelfranzösischen Dichtung. Diss. Rostock, 1923.
Caspari, T. Norsk Naturfølelse i det nittende Aarhundrede. Kristiania, 1917.
Charlier, G. Le sentiment de la nature chez les romantiques français. Bruxelles, 1912.
Clement, N. H. Nature and the Country in XVIth and XVIIth Century Poetry. PMLA, 1929.
Crump, P. E. Nature in the Age of Louis XIV. London, 1928.
Dauzat, A. Le sentiment de la nature et son expression artistique. Paris, 1914.
Desfeuilles, P. Le sentiment de la nature

dans la poésie populaire roumaine. Yggdrasill, 25.VI.1938.

Fairclough, H. R. Love of Nature Among the Greeks and Romans. In: Our Debt to Greece and Rome. New York, 1930.

Fleming, W. Der Wandel des deutschen Naturgefühls vom 15. bis zum 18. Jahrhundert. Halle, 1931.

Foerster, N. Nature in American Literature. New York, 1923.

Friedlaender, L. Die Entwicklung des Gefühls für das Romantische in der Natur im Gegensatz zum antiken Naturgefühl. In: Darstellungen aus der Sittengeschichte Roms. Leipzig, 1921.

Ganzenmüller, W. Das Naturgefühl im Mittelalter. Leipbig, 1914.

Guillemin, A. M. Le sentiment de la nature chez les Latins. Hum., 15, 1938.

Haas, C. E. de. Nature and the Country in English Poetry of the First Half of the XVIIIth Century. Amsterdam, 1928.

Haas, J. Ueber die Anfänge der Naturschilderung im französischen Roman. ZFSL, 26, 1904.

Hanscom, E. D. The Feeling for Nature in Old English Poetry. JEGPh, 5, 1905.

Hansen, J. Le sentiment de la nature et l'inspiration poétique. Luxembourg, 1939.

Heide, A. von der. Das Naturgefühl in der englischen Dichtung im Zeitalter Miltons. Heidelberg, 1915.

Hervier, M. Le sentiment de la nature au XVIIe siècle. RU, 1937-38.

Hjelmqvist, T. Naturskildringarna i den norröna diktningen. Diss. Stockholm, 1891.

Hoerner, M. Die Naturanschauung des Spätbarock in Literatur und bildender Kunst. Zs. f. Aesthetik, 25, 1931.

Hoffmann-Krayer, E. Die Entwicklung des Naturgefühls in der Dichtung und Kunst. SVL, 1.

Hornaday, C. L. Nature in the German Novel of the Late Eighteenth Century, 1770-1800. New York, 1940.

Hulme, F. E. Natural History Lore and Legends. London, 1895.

Huscher, H. Ueber Eigenart und Ursprung des englischen Naturgefühls. Festschrift M. Förster, Leipzig, 1929.

—— Die englische Naturdichtung im Lichte der vergleichenden Literaturbetrachtung und der jüngsten Kritik. Anglia, 62, 1938.

Isaza y Calderón, B. El retorno a la naturaleza. Los origenes del tema y sus direcciones fundamentales en la literatura española. Madrid, 1934.

Jackson, K. Studies in Early Celtic Nature Poetry. Cambridge, 1935.

Jacob, E. Shakespeares Naturverbundenheit im Vergleich mit Schillers und Goethes Verhältnis zur Natur. Hamburg, 1937.

Krech, P. Die Rolle der Natur im Sturm- und Drangdrama. Diss. Erlangen, 1929. With the title: Die Landschaft im Sturm- und Drangdrama. Berlin, 1933.

Kuhns, L. O. The Treatment of Nature in Dante's Divina Commedia. MLN, 11, 1896 & London, 1897.

Langlois, C. V. La connaissance de la nature et du monde au moyen âge. Paris, 1911.

Lederer, M. Die Gestalt des Naturkindes im 18. Jahrhundert. Progr. Bielitz, 1908.

Lewis-Jones, W. The Celt and the Poetry of Nature. Trans. Soc. Cymmrodorion, 1892-93.

Lüning, O. Die Natur, ihre Auffassung und poetische Verwendung in der altgermanischen und mittelhochdeutschen Epik. Diss. Zürich, 1888.

MacCann, G. L. Le sentiment de la nature en France dans la première moitié du 17e siècle. Diss. Paris, 1926.

Moesch, V. Naturschau und Naturgefühl in den Romanen der Mrs. Radcliffe und in der zeitgenössischen englischen Reiseliteratur. Diss. Zürich, 1924.

Moorman, F. W. The Interpretation of Nature in English Poetry from Beowulf to Shakespeare. Strassburg, 1905.

Moret, A. Les différentes conceptions de la nature et du paysage dans le lyrisme allemand du baroque. RG, 1936.

Morgan, B. Q. Nature in Middle High German Lyrics. Göttingen, 1912.

Mornet, D. Le sentiment de la nature en France de J. J. Rousseau à Bernardin de Saint-Pierre. Paris, 1907.

Nadler, J. Stamm und Landschaft in der deutschen Dichtung. Groningen, 1935.

Oertel, K. O. Die Naturschilderung bei den deutschen geographischen Reisebeschreibern des 18. Jahrhunderts. Diss. Leipzig, 1899.

Palgrave, F. T. Landscape in Poetry from Homer to Tennyson. London, 1897.

Pons, E. Le thème et le sentiment de la nature dans la poésie anglo-saxonne. Strasbourg, 1925.

Reynold, G. de. Un précurseur du Ro-

mantisme: Gessner et le sentiment de la nature. MF, 1908.
Reynolds, M. The Treatment of Nature in English Poetry Between Pope and Wordsworth. 2nd ed. Chicago, 1909.
Richter, B. Die Entwicklung der Naturschilderung in den deutschen geographischen Reisebeschreibungen. Diss. Leipzig. Euphorion, 1901.
Rochon, A. Le sentiment de la nature dans l'oeuvre de Laurent le Magnifique. Ausonia, 9, 1944.
Schneider, L. Die Naturdichtung des deutschen Minnesangs. Diss. Heidelberg, 1938.
Schütze, G. Das Naturgefühl um die Mitte des 18. Jahrhunderts in der Lyrik von Pyra bis Claudius. Diss. Leipzig, 1933.
Soutar, G. Nature in Greek Poetry. Studies Partly Comparative. London, 1939.
Stockmayer, G. Ueber Naturgefühl in Deutschland im 10. und 11. Jahrhundert. Leipzig, 1910.
Stoecklin, A. Die Schilderung der Natur im deutschen Minnesang und im älteren deutschen Volkslied. Diss. Basel, 1913.
Tinker, C. B. Nature's Simple Plan. Princeton, 1922.
Van Tieghem, P. Le sentiment de la nature. Revue du Mois, 1906.
—— Les divers aspects du sentiment de la nature dans la littérature ouest-européenne du XVIIIe siècle. Omagiu lui Ramiro Ortiz. Bucarest, 1930.
—— Goethe et le sentiment de la nature dans le préromantisme européen. RLC, 12, 1932.
Veitch, J. The Feeling for Nature in Scottish Poetry. Edinburgh, 1887.
Vianey, J. Les grands poètes de la nature en France. RCC, 27, 1925-26.
—— La nature dans la poésie française au XVIe siècle. Mélanges P. Laumonier. Paris, 1934.
Voigt, J. Das Naturgefühl in der Litteratur der französischen Renaissance. Berlin, 1898.
Wainright, S. H. Appreciation of Nature in Japanese Poetry. Transactions of the Asiatic Society of Japan, 2. Ser., 2, 1925.
Wilson, H. S. Some Meanings of Nature in Renaissance Literary Theory. JHI, 2, 1941.
Heilborn, J. NAUSIKAA in der deutschen Dichtung. Breslau, 1921.
Horner, E. Nausikaa-Dramen. Bühne & Welt, 13.
Peretti, A. Nausicaa nella poesia. A&R, 9, 1928.
Pizzagalli, A. M. Nausicaa e Miranda. Riflessi omerici in Shakespeare. MC, 1932.
Nassen, J. Die deutsche Flotte und die deutsche Dichtung. (NAVY). Breslau, 1898.

NEGROES: See also Slavery, below, and African Contributions, II. I. 8.

Aguirre Beltrán, G. La población negra de México, 1519-1810. México, 1946.
Ames, R. Art in Negro Folksong. JAFL, 56, 1943.
Bond, F. W. The Direct and Indirect Contribution which the American Negro has Made to Drama and the Legitimate Stage. Diss. New York U., 1939.
Brawley, B. G. The Negro in Literature and Art. Atlanta, 1910.
Brewer, J. Negro Folklore in North America. New Mexico Quarterly Review, 16, 1947.
Calverton, V. F. The Negro and American Culture. SRL, 22, 1940.
—— Sviluppo della letteratura negra. Poesia, 5, 1946.
Carter, W. T. Negrophile Literature and Slavery Polemic in France, 1802-1848. Diss. U. of Michigan, 1941.
Chasca, E. de. The Phonology of the Speech of the Negroes in Early Spanish Drama. HR, 14, 1946.
Cook, W. M. Five French Negro Authors. Washington, 1943.
Dykes, Eva B. The Negro in English Romantic Thought. Washington, D. C., 1942.
Glicksberg, C. I. Negro Fiction in America. SAQ, 45, 1946.
—— Negro Poets and the American Tradition. Antioch Rev., 6, 1946.
Gloster, H. M. Chief Trends of Thought in American Negro Literature Since 1900. Diss. New York U., 1943.
—— Negro Voices in American Fiction. Chapel Hill (N.C.), 1948.
Greene, L. J. The Negro in Colonial New England, 1620-1776. New York, 1943.
Holmes, H. A. Ildefonso Pereda Valdés y su libro Negros esclavos y negros libres. RIA, 8, 1944.
Huggins, Kathryn. Aframerican Fiction. Southern Lit. Messenger, 3, 1941.
Isaacs, E. J. The Negro in the American Theatre. Theatre Arts, 26, 1942 & New York, 1947.
Labarthe, P. J. El tema negroide en la poesía de Luis Palés Matos. Hisp., 31, 1948.

Landa, M. J. Der Neger auf der Bühne. Kultur, 1 (Köln), 1903.
Lanuza, J. L. Negros de Góngora y Quevedo. La Prensa (Buenos Aires), 28.V.1939.
Lash, J. S. The American Negro and American Literature. A Check List of Significant Commentaries. Bull. of Bibliogr. 19, 1946-47.
Lawson, Hilda J. The Negro in American Drama. Bull. of Bibliogr. 17, 1940.
Locke, A. The Negro Minority in American Literature. Eng. Journal, 35, 1946.
Longini, Muriel D. Folk Songs of Chicago Negroes. JAFL, 52, 1939.
Lowell, J. Eugene O'Neill's Darker Brother. Theatre Arts, 32, 1948.
Marquina, R. El negro en el teatro español antes de Lope de Vega. Ultra, 4.
Moore, W. L. The Literature of the American Negro prior to 1865. Diss. New York, 1942.
Nelson, J. H. The Negro Character in American Literature. Humanistic Studies of the U. of Kansas, 4, 1932.
Ortiz, F. El negro en el teatro español. Ultra, 4.
Pange, Mme J. de. Mme de Staël et les nègres. RdF, 1934.
Piccioni, L. Poesia negra e musica jazz. Poesia, 5, 1946.
Poag, T. E. The Negro in Drama and the Theater. Diss. Cornell U., 1943.
Porter, Dorothy B. Early American Negro Writings: A Bibliographical Study. Papers Bibl. Soc. Amer., 39, 1945.
Redding, J. S. To Make a Poet Black. Chapel Hill (N.C.), 1939.
Rodríguez-Embil, L. La poesía negra en Cuba. Havana, 1939.
Schons, Dorothy. Negro Poetry in the Americas. Hisp., 25, 1942.
Spratlin, V. B. Juan Latino, Slave and Humanist (and Negro). New York, 1938.
Troesch, Helen D. The Negro in Dramatic Literature. Diss. Western Reserve U., 1941.
Vignols, L. Les sources du Tamango de Mérimée et la littérature négrière à l'époque romantique. MF, 1927.
Weinreich, O. Der Trug des **NEKTABENOS**. Wandlungen eines Novellenstoffes. Leipzig, 1911.
Thouvenin, G. La légende orientale de **NEMROD** et Le Glaive de V. Hugo. RHLF, 1933.

Baudrillart, A. Le roman de Quo vadis et l'histoire. (**NERO**). Le Correspondant, 25.I.1901.
Engel, J. Kaiser Nero in der Dichtung. PJb, 1901.
Fluch, J. F. J. Nerodarstellungen, insbesondere in der deutschen Literatur. Diss. Giessen. Mainz, 1924.
Ittameier, M. Die Sage von Nero als dem Antichrist. Zs. für kirchl. Wissenschaft und kirchl. Leben, 1882.
Muellbach, E. Die englischen Nerodramen des 17. Jahrhunderts, insbesondere Lee's Nero. Diss. Leipzig, 1910.
Maurice, A. B. **NEW YORK** in Fiction. New York, 1901.
Wilson, R. R. New York in Literature. Elmira (N.Y.), 1947.
Dow, C. M. Anthology and Bibliography of **NIAGARA FALLS**. 2 vols. Albany, 1921.
NIBELUNGEN: See also Comparisons, I. V. 1.
Anon. Die Nibelungen in England. Grenzboten, 10, 1851.
—— Die Nibelungen in italienischer Uebersetzung. DR, July, 1890.
Abeling, T. Das Nibelungenlied und seine Literatur. 2 vols. Leipzig, 1907-09.
Antoniewicz, J. von. Das Nibelungenlied in polnischer Sprache. Beilage zur Allg. Zt., Jan., 1884.
Boer, R. C. Untersuchungen über den Ursprung und die Entwicklung der Nibelungensage. 3 vols. Halle, 1906-09.
Carlyle, T. The Nibelungenlied. Westminister Rev., 15, 1831.
Fischer, H. Die Forschungen über das Nibelungenlied seit K. Lachmann. Leipzig, 1874.
Genzmer, F. La poesia dei Nibelunghi nell' Edda. SG, 5, 1941.
Gottschall, R. von. Nibelungen-, Cäsar-, Demetriusdramen. In: Studien. Berlin, 1892.
Grégoire, H. Le berceau belge des Nibelungen. L'Europe centrale, 9 & 16.VI. 1934. Cf. also Byzantion, 9, 1934.
Gruener, G. The Nibelungenlied and Sage in Modern Poetry. PMLA, 11, 1896.
Henning. Nibelungenstudien. Strassburg, 1874.
Heusler, A. Nibelungensage und Nibelungenlied. Dortmund, 1929.
Holz, G. Der Sagenkreis der Nibelungen. Leipzig, 1914.
Hunfalvy. Das Nibelungenlied und die ungarischen Chroniken. MLIA, 1882.
Lichtenberger, H. Le poème et la légende des Nibelungen. Paris, 1891.
Meinck, E. Hebbels und Wagners Nibelungen-Trilogien. Leipzig, 1905.

Naumann, H. Das Nibelungenlied, eine staufische Elegie oder ein deutsches Nationalepos? Bonn, 1942. Cf. Euphorion 42.
Periam, A. Hebbel's Nibelungen, its Sources, Method and Style. New York, 1906.
Rehorn, K. Die deutsche Sage von den Nibelungen in der deutschen Poesie. Frankfurt, 1877.
Richter, E. Th. Carlyle über das Nibelungenlied. Bayreuther Blätter, 1896.
Sandbach, F. A. The Nibelungenlied in English. MLQ, 3, 1901.
—— The Nibelungenlied and Gudrun in England and America. London, 1903.
Schroefl, A. Der Urdichter des Liedes von der Nibelunge Not. München, 1927.
Thorp, Mary. The Study of the Nibelungenlied. Being the History of the Story of the Epic and Legend from 1755 to 1937. Oxford U.P., 1940.
Tonnelat, E. La Chanson des Nibelungen, étude sur la composition et la formation du poème épique. Paris, 1926.
Vries, J. de. Het Nibelungenlied en het Rolandslied. Nederland, 95-96, 1943-44.
Wilmans, W. Der Untergang der Nibelungen in alter Sage und Dichtung. Berlin, 1903.
Kressner, A. Saint **NICOLAS** in der Tradition und in der mittelalterlichen Dichtung. Archiv, 1878.
Fissen, K. Das Leben des heiligen Nikolaus in der altfranzösischen Literatur und seine Quellen. Göttingen, 1921.
Fowlie, W. The Theme of **NIGHT** in Four Sonnets of Mallarmé. MPh, 44, 1947.
Gross, Ruth. Die Nacht in der Dichtung von der Renaissance bis zur Romantik. Diss. Frankfurt, 1923.
Muomi. Poesia notturna preromantica. Milano, 1908.
Renéville, R. de. Le sens de la nuit. NRF, Nov., 1936.
Reuschel, K. Die Nacht in deutscher Lyrik. Kunstwart, 16, 1902.
San Lazzaro, G. di. Die Nacht in der Persönlichkeit und Dichtung Rilkes. ZDPh, 65, 1940.
Schaab, A. Das Nachtgefühl in unserer Poesie. Monatsblätter f. deutsche Lit., 7, 1903.
Van Tieghem, P. La poésie de la Nuit et des Tombeaux en Europe au XVIIIe siècle. Paris, 1921.
Nuffelen, M. van. De **NIOBE**-mythe in de letterkunde en in de plastiek. RBPh, 1938.
Schopper. Der Niobemythus in der deutschen Literatur mit besonderer Berücksichtigung der Antike. Progr. Landeskron, 1914.
Nyrop, K. Nej, et Motivs Historie. (**NO**). København, 1891.
Mill, Anna J. **NOAH'S** Wife Again. PMLA, 56, 1941.
Welle-Strand, E. **NORDLAND** i Norges literatur. Finsk Tidskrift, Feb., 1915.
Bosquet, A. La **NORMANDIE** romanesque et merveilleuse. Rouen, 1844.
NORMANS: See French Language, IV. VII. 24., and Scandinavia, IV. XII. 1.

——O——

Glaesener, H. Les points de départ méridionaux de l'**OBERON** de Wieland. RLC, 14, 1934.
Koch, M. Das Quellenverhältniss zu Wielands Oberon. Marburg, 1879.
Lindner, F. Zur Geschichte der Oberonsage. Rostock, 1902.
Aram, K. Neue okkulte Literatur. (**OCCULT**). Literatur, 32, 1930.
Mayer, T. H. Okkulte Romane. Roseggers Heimgarten, 49, 1926.
Rockenbach, M. Okkulte Dichtung. München-Gladbach, 1925.
Streve, P. Die **OCTAVIAN**-Sage. Diss. Erlangen, 1884.
Beck, T. J. The **ODIN** Legend and the Oriental Fascination. Vol. 2 of Northern Antiquities in French Learning and Literature. New York, 1935.
ODYSSEUS: See Ulysses, below.
Brack, W. Der **OEDIPE** von Corneille und der von Voltaire, verglichen mit dem Oedipus rex des Sophokles. Leipzig, 1914.
Constans, L. La légende d'Oedipe étudiée dans l'antiquité, au moyen-âge et dans les temps modernes. Paris, 1880.
Croiset, M. Oedipe roi de Sophocle. Etude et analyse. Paris, 1932.
Gevers, G. Ueber Schillers Braut von Messina und den König Oedipus des Sophocles. Progr. Verden, 1873-74.
Gordon, W. von. Die dramatische Handlung in Sophokles König Oidipus und Kleists Der zerbrochene Krug. Halle, 1926.
Hamel, A. G. V. De Oedipus der Frankschе Klassiecken. De Gids, Feb., 1897.
Howald, E. Oedipus, Geschichte eines literarischen Stoffes. Neue Zürcher Zt., 547-550, 1915.

Joerdens, W. Die französischen Oedipusdramen. Bochum-Langendreer, 1933-34.
Kohm, J. Schillers Braut von Messina und ihr Verhältnis zu Sophokles' Oidipus Tyrannos. Gotha, 1901.
Lejeune-Dehousée, R. Quatre interprétations de la légende d'Oedipe. RFB, 1933.
Luria, S. Die Oedipussage und Verwandtes. In: Festschrift F. Ramorino, Milano, 1928.
Marignac, A. de. Les imitations françaises de l'Oedipe Roi de Sophocle. Pub. de la Fac. des Lettres du Caire, 1946.
Novakovic. Die Oedipussage in der südslavischen Volksdichtung. ASPh, 11, 1888.
Richter, J. J. Oedipus und Lear. Progr. Lörrach, 1884-85.
Robert, C. Oidipus. Geschichte eines poetischen Stoffs im griechischen Altertum. 2 vols. Berlin, 1915.
Rod, E. Le développement de la légende d'Oedipe dans l'histoire de la littérature. Lausanne, 1879.
Schrader, H. Hölderlins Deutung des Oedipus und der Antigone. Mnemosyne, 10, 1933.
Stoll, E. E. Oedipus and Othello: Corneille, Rymer and Voltaire. RAA, June, 1935.
Teichmann, R. Die beiden hervorragendsten Gestaltungen der Oedipus-Sage im klassischen Drama der Franzosen. Progr. Grünberg, 1894.
Wittich, W. Ueber Sophocles' König Oedipus und Schillers Braut von Messina. Progr. Cassel, 1887.
Wolff, H. M. Der zerbrochene Krug und König Oidipus. MLN, 54, 1939.
Stevanovic, S. Ein Beitrag zur angelsächsischen **OFFA**-Sage. Anglia, 35.
Cerf, B. The Franco-Italian Chevalier **OGIER**. MPh, 8, 1911.
Matthes, J. C. De Nederlandsch Ogier. Romania, 19, 1890.
Rajna, P. Uggeri il Danese nella letteratura romanzesca degli italiani. Romania, 1873-75.
Smyser, H. M. The Middle English and Old Norse Story of **OLIVE**. PMLA, 56, 1941.
Wolff, H. M. Die **OMNIPOTENZ** als literarisches Motiv. NPh, 25, 1937.
Roescher, W. H. Der **OMPHALOS**gedanke bei verschiedenen Völkern, besonders den semitischen. Sächsische Ges. der Wiss., 70, 1918.
Gaide. Du sortilège de l'**OPIUM** dans la littérature. Mémoires de l'Acad. de Vaucluse, 3rd. Ser., 3, 1938.
Silvy, R. L'opium dans la littérature. Nouvelle Revue, 1.IX.1937.
Sowerby, A. Opium and Narcotics in China. China Journal of Science and Arts, 1, 1923.
Ker, W. P. Notes on **ORENDEL** and Other Stories. FL, 1897.
Peeters, P. La légende de S. **ORENTIUS** et de ses six frères martyrs. Analecta Bollandiana (Bruxelles), 1938.
Heintze, A. Versuch einer Parallele zwischen dem sophokleischen **ORESTES** und dem shakespearischen Hamlet. Progr. Treptow, 1857.
Heuner, C. Die Sage von Orest in der tragischen Dichtung. Progr. Linz, 1896.
Lesky, A. Die Orestie des Aischylos. H., 1931.
Longi, E. L'Oreste di Giovanni Rucellai. Dioniso, 3, 1932.
Magnani, I. Il dramma di Oreste ed Elettra nel suo valore religioso ed umano. Milano, 1934.
Magnino, B. Oreste nella poesia tragica. A&R, 9, 1928-29.
Murray, G. Hamlet and Orestes: a Study in Traditional Types. Oxford, 1914.
Trahndorff. Ueber den Orestes der alten Tragödie und den Hamlet des Shakespeare. Berlin, 1833.
Turel, A. L'Oréstie d'Eschyle et le Faust de Goethe. RG, 18, 1936.
Glabbatz. Orgel und Orgelspiel in der neueren deutschen schönen Literatur. (**ORGAN**). Mitteilungen f. Gottesdienst & Kunst, 13, 1908.
ORLANDO: See Roland, below.
Guthrie, W. K. C. **ORPHEUS** and Greek Religion: A Study of the Orphic Movement. London, 1935.
Heurgon, J. Orphée et Eurydice avant Virgile. Mélanges d'archéologie de l'Ecole française de Rome, 1932.
Kistler, M. Orphism and the Legend of Orpheus in German Literature of the 18th Century. Diss. U. of Illinois, 1948.
Wirl, J. Orpheus in der englischen Literatur. Wien, 1913.
Berger, A. E. Die **OSWALDLEGENDE** in der deutschen Literatur, ihre Entwicklung und ihre Verbreitung. Diss. Leipzig. Halle, 1886.
Treutler, H. Die **OTINELSAGE** im Mittelalter. ESn, 5, 1882.
Noll, G. Dramatische Bearbeitungen der Sage von **OTTO** dem Schützen. Zs. f. Bücherfreunde 5, 1901.
—— Otto der Schütz in der Literatur. Diss. Tübingen. Strassburg, 1907.

Morgenroth. Kaiser Otto III. in der deutschen Dichtung. Diss. Berlin, 1922.
Kilian, E. König **OTTOKAR** im Drama. Bad. Bühnenblätter, 3.

——P——

Krey, A. C. **PADUA** in the English Renaissance. HLQ, 10, 1947.
Olsen, M. Roma e la poesia del **PAGANESIMO** nordico. SG, 1, 1936 and 4, 1939.
Sokommodau, H. Heidnischer und christlicher Geist in der französischen Lyrik des 16. Jahrhunderts. RF, 54, 1940.
Timmer, B. J. Heathen and Christian Elements in Old English Poetry. NPh, 1944.
Usener, H. Legenden der **PALAGIA.** Festschrift für die 34. Versammlung deutscher Philologen, Trier. Bonn, 1879.
Stephan, H. Das heilige Land in der neueren Dichtung. **(PALESTINE).** Köln, 1931.
Krailsheimer, A. J. Rabelais and the **PAN** Legend. French Studies, 2, 1948.
Guarducci, M. Il mito di **PANDORA.** Studi e Materiali di Storia delle Religioni, 3, 1927.
Schell, H. Das Verhältnis von Form und Inhalt in Goethes Pandora. Würzburg, 1939.
Séchan, L. Pandora, l'Eve grecque. BAGB, 23, 1929.
Tuerck, H. Pandora und Eva. Menschwerdung und Schöpfertum im griechischen und jüdischen Mythus. Weimar, 1931.
Wilamowitz-Möllendorff, U. von. Goethes Pandora. JbGG, 1898.
Tobler, A. Il **PANFILO** in antico veneziano. Archivio glottologico italiano, 10, 1886-88.
Fox, Bernice. Revision in Browning's **PARACELSUS.** MLN, 55, 1940.
Reclam, E. H. Die Gestalt des Paracelsus in der Dichtung. Leipzig, 1938.
PARADISE: See also Heaven and Hell, above.
Coli, E. Il paradiso terrestre dantesco. (and the legend). Firenze, 1897.
Cooper, L. The Abyssinian Paradise in Coleridge and Milton. MPh, 3, 1906.
Kampers. Mittelalterliche Sagen vom Paradiese und vom Holze des Kreuzes Christi. Köln, 1897.
Koehler, R. Zur Legende vom italienischen jungen Herzog im Paradiese. ZDPh, 14, 1882. And in: Kleine Schriften, 2.
Paris, G. Le Paradis de la reine Sybille. RP, 15.XII.1897. And in: Légendes du moyen âge. Paris, 1903.
Peters, Elisabeth. Quellen und Charakter der Paradiesvorstellungen in der deutschen Dichtung des 9. bis 12. Jahrhunderts. Breslau, 1915.
Siuts, H. Jenseitsmotive im deutschen Volksmärchen. Teutonia. Leipzig, 1911.
Creuzes, F. Der Mythos von **PARIS UND HELENA** nach seinen Quellen, Wanderungen und Deutungen. Deutsche Schriften, 2. (Leipzig), 1847.
Toynbee, P. Paris and Tristan in the Inferno. Academy, June, 1888. And in: Studies and Researches. London, 1902.
Bertrand, J. J. A. Nach **PARIS.** (German travellers). RELV, 1932.
Boucher, F. American Footprints in Paris. New York, 1921.
Boutet de Monvel, R. Les Anglais à Paris, 1800-1850. Paris, 1911.
Bressie, Ramona. Was Chaucer at the Siege of Paris? JEGPh, 39, 1940.
Delafarge, D. Paris dans la poésie romantique et chez les précurseurs du Parnasse. RCC, 1934-35.
Durtain, L. Le Portugal et la "Capitale de l'Esprit." NL, 29.IV.1939.
Ellis, H. Early Impressions of Paris. Bookman, 74, 1932.
Franck, W. Rilke et Paris. MF, 1.IV.1938.
Goll, J. Paris, Stern der Dichter. NR, June, 1922.
Greder, L. Opinions de Frédéric de Schlegel sur Paris (1804-05). Bull. de la Société de l'Histoire de Paris, 26, 1899.
Hillebrand, K. Pariser Zustände im Lichte des englischen Romans. In: Aus und über England. Strassburg, 1892.
Kohn, A. Börne, chroniqueur de la vie parisienne. RG, April, 1938.
Kovalovsky, N. Paris dans les lettres hongroises. Nouvelle Rev. de Hongrie, 1937.
Luna, J. L. La influencia de París en la obra de Gómez Carrillo y otros modernistas. Diss. U. of Cal., 1940.
Maurice, A. B. The Paris of the Novelists. London, 1920.
Szirmai, M. Paris dans la presse hongroise contemporaine. Budapest, 1937.
Valkhoff, P. Parjse Indrukken van 1666. NPh, 23, 1938.
Varia. Danske i Paris gennem tidene. 2 vols. København, 1936-38.
Vaszary, G. Monpti, roman hongrois sur Paris. Budapest, 1934.
—— O (Elle), roman hongrois sur Paris. Budapest, 1933.

Wittmann, H. Paris in deutschen Schilderungen (1789-1814). WM, 1881.
Zanette, E. La monaca di **PARMA**. Conviv., 1935.
Zelinskii, F. The Motif of **PARTING** (Ovid, Shakespeare, Pushkin) (in Russian). Vestnik Evropy, 1903.
Koelbing, E. Die verschiedenen Gestaltungen der **PARTONOPEUSSAGE**. Germanische Studien, 2, 1872-75.
—— Ueber die nordischen Gestaltungen der Partonopeussage. Breslau, 1873.
—— Englische und französische Versionen der Partonopeussage. In: Beiträge zur vergleichenden Geschichte der romantischen Poesie und Prosa des Mittelalters. Breslau, 1876.
Look, H. van. Der Partonopier Konrads von Würzburg und der Partonopeus de Blois. Diss. Strassburg, 1881.
Massmann, H. Partonopeus und Melior, altfranzösische Gedichte des XIII. Jahrhunderts, in mittelniederländischen und mittelhochdeutschen Bruchstücken herausgegeben. Berlin, 1847.
Moret, A. Partonopeus de Blois, conte de fée et roman de chevalerie dans la littérature européenne du moyen âge. Lille, 1933.
Pfeiffer, F. Ueber Konrad von Würzburg (Partonopier, Alexius). Wien, 1867.
Sneyders de Vogel. La suite de Parthonopeus de Blois et la version hollandaise. RLR, 48, 1905.
Weingaertner, F. Die mittelenglischen Fassungen der Partonopeussage und ihr Verhältniss zum altfranzösischen Originale. Diss. Breslau, 1888.
PARZIVAL: See Celtic Contributions, IV. I. 4.
Gilson, E. La **PASSION** dans la pensée française du moyen âge. Rev. des questions historiques, July, 1934.
Maistre **PATHELIN:** See French Contributions, IV. VII. 22.
Concannon, T. Saint **PATRICK**, his Life and Mission. Dublin, 1931.
Frati, L. Il purgatorio di S. Patrizio secondo Stefano di Bourbon e Uberto da Romans. GSLI, 8, 1886.
Krapp, G. P. The Legend of Saint Patrick's Purgatory: Its Later Literary History. Baltimore, 1900.
Leslie, S. Saint Patrick's Purgatory. A Record from History and Literature. London, 1932.
McBride, P. St. Patrick's Purgatory in Spanish Literature. Studies, (an Irish Quarterly), 25, 1936.
Solalinde, A. G. La primera version española de El Purgatorio de San Patricio y la difusión de esta legenda en España. Homenaje Menéndez Pidal. Madrid, 1925.
Brandes, H. Ueber die Quellen der mittelenglischen **PAULUS**-Vision. ESn, 7, 1883.
—— Visio S. Pauli. Ein Beitrag zur Visionslitteratur. Halle, 1885.
Emrich, W. Paulus im Drama. Berlin, 1934.
PEACE: See War, below.
Kennett, W. T. E. The Theme of **PENGUIN** Island. RR, 33, 1942.
Fries, C. Zu Kleists **PENTHESILEA**. PhW, 48, 1928.
Monery, A. L'âme des parfums. (**PERFUME**). Paris, 1924.
Herter, H. Ovids **PERSEPHONE**-Erzählungen und ihre hellenistischen Quellen. RhM, 90, 1941.
Hartland, E. S. The Legend of **PERSEUS**; a Study of Tradition in Story, Custom and Belief. 3 vols. London, 1894-96.
Krappe, A. H. La légende de Persée. Neuphilol. Mitt., 34, 1933.
Woodward, J. M. Perseus. A Study in Greek Art and Legend. Cambridge U.P., 1937.
Hering, G. F. **PERSIUS**, Geschichte seines Nachlebens und seiner Uebersetzungen in der deutschen Literatur. Berlin, 1935.
Allais, G. Le **PESSIMISME** romantique. RCC, June, 1897.
Bertrand. Le pessimisme de Leopardi. EI, 1919.
Braun, W. Types of Weltschmerz in the German Poetry. New York, 1905.
Brunetière, F. La philosophie de Schopenhauer et les conséquences du pessimisme. In: Essais. Paris, 1892.
Collison-Morley, L. Pessimism in Poetry. ER, 1923.
Diels, H. Der antike Pessimismus. Berlin, 1921.
Dyer, A. S. The Folk-Lore of the Miserere. Calcutta Review, 91, 1890.
Glaser, K. Der antike Pessimismus. Mitteilungen des Vereins klass. Philologen Wien, 2, 1925.
Gourmont, R. de. Le pessimisme de Leopardi. MF, 1913.
Greeves, F. Omar Khayyam, Modern Pessimism and Christian Thought. Cornhill Mag., 158, 1938.
Guérard, A. J. French and American Pessimism. Harper's Mag., 1945.
Hentschel, C. The Byronic Teuton. As-

pects of German Pessimism, 1800-1833. London, 1939-40.
Joubert, M. Pessimism in French Literature. Contemporary Rev., March, 1939.
Kazin, A. Kafka e il dolore del secolo. Il Ponte, 3, 1947.
Marcantonio, J. D. Some Thoughts on Pessimism in Classical Literature. CW, 28, 1935.
Monti, G. La poesia del dolore. Modena, 1892.
Nestle, W. Der Pessimismus und seine Ueberwindung bei den Griechen. NJKA, 1921.
Palmer, H. A Brief History of the Poetry of Despair. English, 3, 1941.
Rose, W. Weltschmerz and Origins of Pessimism. Psyche, 1923.
—— From Goethe to Byron: the Development of Weltschmerz in German Literature from Werther to the Beginning of the Romantic Movement. London, 1924.
Salinger, B. Der Weltschmerz in der Literatur. Voss. Zt. Beilage, 39-40, 1903.
Schmidt, M. Formen der Angst bei Villiers de l'Isle-Adam. Diss. Zürich, 1934.
Sergio, A. La vera fonte del pessimismo Leopardiano. Ital., 20, 1943.
Sickels, E. M. The Gloomy Egoist: Moods and Themes of Melancholy from Gray to Keats. New York, 1932.
Whitridge, A. Vigny and Housman: A Study in Pessimism. American Scholar, 10, 1941.
Woodbridge, B. M. Poets and Pessimism: Vigny, Housman et alii. RR, 35, 1944.
Schons, E. Leconte de Lisle's Poems on **PETER** the Cruel. MPh, 1934.
Minslow, R. Pierre le Grand dans la littérature étrangère. St. Petersbourg, 1872.
Shmurlo, E. Voltaire et son oeuvre, Histoire de l'Empire de Russie sous Pierre le Grand. Prague, 1929.
Burg, F. Ueber die Entwicklung des **PETER-SQUENZ**-Stoffes bis Gryphius. ZDA, 25, 1881.
Cullmann, F. Der Apostel **PETRUS** in der älteren deutschen Literatur. Diss. Giessen, 1928.
Drews, A. Die Petruslegende. Jena, 1924.
PHAEDRA: See also Hippolytus, above.
Amodeo, E. Da Euripide a d'Annunzio. Fedra e Ippolito nella tragedia classica e nella moderna. Roma, 1930.
Bergmann, A. La Phèdre de Racine comparée à celle d'Euripide. Diss. Rostock, 1872.
Chiarchiaro, C. La Fedra di Seneca. Studio critico estetico. Palermo, 1929.
Chicoteau, M. Phèdre et les poisons. CL, 1949.
Collins, H. I. von. Vergleichung der Phädra des Racine mit der des Euripides. In: Sämtliche Werke, 6. Wien, 1814.
Czerny, J. Richard Wagners Tristan und die Phaedra-Dramen von Euripides, Seneca und Racine. Bayreuther Blätter, 58, 1935.
Dubois, P. F. Les fausses critiques de Schlegel sur Phèdre. Le Globe, 23.X. 1827.
Jones, R. Racine's Phèdre and d'Annunzio's Fedra. CLS, 6-7, 1942.
Kolar, A. Vier Phädra-Tragödien. Festschrift J. Kral. Prag, 1913.
Krug. Etude sur la Phèdre de Racine et l'Hippolyte de Sénèque. Colmar, 1883.
Kunke, G. Comparaison entre la Phèdre de Racine et l'Hippolyte d'Euripide. Progr. Schneidemühl, 1874.
Liebmann, J. A. Racine's Phèdre and its Relation to the Hippolytus of Euripides. Royal Soc. of Lit. of the United Kingdom, 2nd. ser., 20, 1899.
Maas, M. Racine's Phèdre in den beiden Uebersetzungen von Schiller und Viehoff. Archiv, 1863.
May, G. Contributions à l'étude des sources grecques de Phèdre. MLQ, 8, 1947.
Moricca, U. Le fonti della Fedra di Seneca. SIFC, 1915.
Newton, Winifred. Le thème de Phèdre et d'Hippolyte dans la littérature française. Diss. Paris, 1939.
Pommier, J. Phèdre avant Racine. Revue des Sc. hum., 45, Jan., 1947.
Schlegel, A. W. Comparaison de la Phèdre de Racine avec celle d'Euripide. Paris, 1807.
Steiert, H. Vergleichung der Phèdre des Racine mit dem Hippolytos des Euripides. Progr. Offenburg, 1878.
Wheatley, K. E. The Relation of Edmund Smith's Phaedra and Hippolitus to Racine's Phèdre and Racine's Bajazet. RR, 37, 1946.
Back, R. Ein indianischer **PHAETON.** WBFA, 4, 1928.
Hubaux, J. & Leroy, M. Le mythe du **PHENIX** dans les littératures grecque et latine. Paris, 1939.
Landau, M. Die Erdenwanderungen der Himmlischen und die Wünsche der Menschen. (**PHILEMON** & Baucis). ZVL, 14, 1900.

Malten, L. Motivgeschichtliche Untersuchungen zur Sagengeschichte. Philemon und Baukis. H, 1939-40.
Boghen-Conegliani, E. Il Filippo di V. Alfieri e il Don Carlos di F. Schiller. (**PHILIP II**). Pensiero italiano, 15, 1895.
Bratli, C. Philippe II. roi d'Espagne. Paris, 1912.
Mensi, E. Il Filippo dell'Alfieri e il Don Carlos dello Schiller. Firenze, 1924.
Oldengott, Paula. Philipp II. im Drama der romanischen Literaturen (16. & 17. Jahrhundert). Diss. Münster. Lengerich i.W., 1938.
Visconti, F. Il Filippo di V. Alfieri e il Don Carlos di Schiller. Avellino, 1906.
Goldstaub, M. & Wendriner, K. Ein Toscovenezianischer **PHYSIOLOGUS**. Halle, 1892.
Lauchert, F. Geschichte des Physiologus. Strassburg, 1889.
—— Der Einfluss des Physiologus auf den Euphuismus (and on Shakespeare). ESn, 14, 1890.
Mann, F. Der Physiologus des Philipp von Thaun und seine Quelle. Leipzig, 1884 & Anglia, 7-9.
Mayer, A. (ed.) Der waldensische Physiologus. RF, 5, 1890.
Menhardt, H. Wanderungen des ältesten deutschen Physiologus. ZDA, 74.
Peebles, R. J. The Anglo-Saxon Physiologus. MPh, 8, 1910-11.
Polioka. Zur Geschichte des Physiologus in den slavischen Literaturen. ASPh, 14, 1892.
PICARO: See Spanish Contributions, IV. IV. 4.
Axon, W. E. A. The Story of the **PIED PIPER** of Hamelin. Papers of the Manchester Literary Club, 16, 1890.
Krogmann, W. Der Rattenfänger von Hammeln. Eine Untersuchung über das Werden der Sage. Berlin, 1934.
Meinardus, O. Der historische Kern der Rattenfängersage. Hannover, 1882.
Randolph, Mary Claire. Rat Satires and the Pied Piper of Hamelin Legend. SFQ, 5, 1941.
Meyer, A. **PILATUS** als dramatische Figur. Mitteil. f. Gottesdienst & Kunst, 11, 1906.
Salverda de Grave, J. J. Over de middel-nederl. vertaling van de Pèlerinage de la vie humaine van Guillaume de Deguileville. (**PILGRIMAGE**). Tijdschrift voor nederl. tal en letterkunde, 23, 1903.
Lohmann Villena, G. Francisco **PIZARRO** en el teatro clásico español. Arbor, 15, 1946.
Harnack, E. Das Gift in der dramatischen Dichtung und in der antiken Literatur. (**POISON**). Leipzig, 1908.
Harrison, T. P. The Literary Background of Renaissance Poisons. Texas Studies in English, 27, 1948.
Hertz, W. Die Sage vom Giftmädchen. München, 1893.
Loomis, C. G. The Ring of **POLYCRATES** in the Legends of the Saints. JAFL, 54, 1941.
Hackman, O. Die **POLYPHEMSAGE** in der Volksüberlieferung. Helsingfors, 1904.
Settegast, F. Das Polyphemmärchen in altfranzösischen Gedichten. Leipzig, 1917.
Wuest, P. Die deutschen Prosaromane von **PONTUS** und Sidonia. Marburg, 1903.
Andro, L. Die Dichtungen vom Armen Heinrich. (**POOR HENRY**). Merker, 7, 1915.
Jacoby, H. Der Arme Heinrich. (Hartmann, Longfellow, Hauptmann). Deutsch-evangelische Blätter, 33, 1908.
Jellinek, A. L. Der arme Heinrich im Drama. LE, 1903.
Krumpelmann, J. J. Longfellow's Golden Legend and the Armer Heinrich Theme in Modern German Literature. JEGPh, 25, 1926.
Meyer, R. M. Zur Geschichte des armen Heinrich. Die Zeit, 35 (Wien), 1903.
Muenzner, F. Die Quellen zu Longfellow's Golden Legend. Festschrift der 44. Versammlung d. Philologen, Dresden, 1897.
Polheim, K. Der arme Heinrich. Grenzboten, 67.
Schmitz, B. Ein alter Sagen- und Legendenstoff und seine Wandlungen. Gottesminne, 4, 1906.
Tardel, H. Der Arme Heinrich in der neueren Dichtung. In: Munckers Forschungen 30, Berlin, 1905.
Wieruszowski, Jenny. Der arme Heinrich bei Longfellow. LE, 1.IV.1903.
POPES: See Chapter Eleven, below.
Müller, E. Die **POST** in der Poesie im 18. 19. und 20. Jahrhundert. Heimatblätter d. roten Erde, 164-71, 1926.
Kiesskalt, E. Die Post in der Dichtung. Straubing, 1914.
Brunet, G. La légende du **PRETRE JEAN**. Bordeaux, 1877.
Hennig, R. Das Christentum im mittelalterlichen Asien und sein Einfluss auf

die Sage vom Priester Johannes. Histor. Vierteljahrsschrift, 29, 1934.
Langlois, C. V. Les marveilles du Prêtre Jean. La vie en France au moyen âge, 35.
Oppert, G. Der Presbyter Johannes in Sage und Geschichte. Berlin, 1864; 2. ed., 1876.
Uzielli, G. Il Prete Gianni. Boll. d. Sez. fior. d. Società Afr. ital., 8, 1892.
Zarncke, F. Der Priester Johannes. Abhandl. der sächs. Ges. der Wissenschaften. Leipzig, 1879.
Boas, G. Essays on **PRIMITIVISM** and Related Ideas in the Middle Ages. Baltimore, 1948.
Chinard, G. (Bougainville's) Contribution à l'histoire du primitivisme (with Diderot's) Supplément au voyage de Bougainville. Baltimore, 1935.
David, J. Les Scythes et les Tartares dans Voltaire et quelques-uns de ses contemporains. MLN, 1938.
Fairchild, H. N. The Noble Savage: a Study in Romantic Naturalism. New York, 1928.
Fairlie, A. Leconte de Lisle's Poems on the Barbarian Races. Cambridge U.P., 1947.
Fitzgerald, M. M. Primitivism in English Poetry, 1725-50. New York, 1947.
Harrison, T. P. Aspects of Primitivism in Shakespeare and Spenser. U. of Texas Studies in English, 1940.
La Honton, Baron de. Dialogues curieux entre l'auteur et un sauvage de bon sens qui a voyagé (1703). (Ed. by G. Chinard), Baltimore, 1931.
Lovejoy, A. O. & Boas, G. Primitivism and Related Ideas in Antiquity. Baltimore, 1935.
Mayer, E. Das antike Idealbild von den Naturvölkern und Nachrichten des Caesar und Tacitus. ZDA, 62.
Millhauser, M. The Noble Savage in Mary Shelley's Frankenstein. N&Q, 190, 1946.
Neri, F. La maschera del Selvaggio. GSLI, 59, 1912.
Pearce, R. H. The Eighteenth-Century Scottish Primitivists: Some Reconsiderations. ELH, 12, 1945.
—— Primitivistic Ideas in the Faerie Queene. JEGPh, 44, 1945.
Pike, R. E. The Book of the Savages. RLC, 22, 1948.
Roy, A. Les sauvagesses de Chateaubriand et leurs réalités historiques. RCC, 1931.
Runge, Edith A. Primitivism and Related Ideas in Sturm and Drang Literature. Baltimore, 1946.
Van Tieghem, P. L'homme primitif et ses vertus dans le pré-romantisme européen. Bull. de la Société d'histoire moderne, 1922.
Whitney, L. Primitivism and the Idea of Progress in English Popular Literature of the 18th Century. Baltimore, 1934-35.
Wright, L. E. The Noble Savage of Madagascar in 1640. JHI, 4, 1943.
PRINCE: See also King, Ruler, Kaiser, and State Novels.
Born, L. K. The Perfect Prince According to the Latin Panegyrists. AJPh, 1934.
Geldner, F. Die Staatsauffassung und Fürstenlehre des Erasmus von Rotterdam. München, 1930.
Gilbert, A. The Humanist Concept of the Prince and the Prince of Machiavelli. Journal of Mod. History, 11, 1939.
Meyer, R. M. M. Die Audienz beim Fürsten. MPh, 2, 1904.
PRODIGAL SON: See Chapter Eleven, below.
Lippmann, J. Die Erfindung der Buchdruckerei im Spiegel der Poesie. (**PRINTING**). Frankfurter Zt., 156, 1900.
Aly, W. Die literarische Ueberlieferung des **PROMETHEUS**mythos. RhM, 68, 1913.
Antcliffe, H. Prometheus in Literature. NC, 1924.
Bruggen, C. van. Prometheus. Eene bijdrage tot het begrip der ontwikkeling van het individualisme in de litteratuur. Rotterdam, 1920.
Buri, F. Prometheus und Christus. Grösse und Grenzen von Carl Spittelers religiöser Weltanschauung. Bern, 1945.
Coman, J. Titanul Prometheu. Cultul si elementele pre-hesiodice si hesiodice ale istoriei sale. Bucuresti, 1935.
Declerq, M. Origine et évolution du mythe de Prométhée dans l'antiquité grecque. Diss. Louvain, 1943.
Döblin, A. Prometheus und das Primitive. Mass & Wert, 1938.
Driesmans, H. Die Prometheus-Dichtung. LE, 11, 1908.
Fraenkel, J. Wandlungen des Prometheus. Bern, 1910.
Grabo, C. Prometheus Unbound: an Interpretation. Chapel Hill (N.C.), 1935.
Graf, A. Prometeo nella poesia. Torino, 1880.

Guérard, A., Jr. Prometheus and the Aeolian Lyre. Yale Rev., 33, 1944.
Headlam, W. Prometheus and the Garden of Eden. CQ, 1934.
Hecht. Prometheus in der englischen Dichtung. HG, 1930.
Kellner, L. Shellys Prometheus in deutscher Uebersetzung. ESn, 22, 1896.
Kitto, H. D. F. The Prometheus. Journal of Hellenic Studies, 1934.
Krappe, A. H. Prométhée. Rev. de l'Histoire des Religions, 119, 1939.
Lindskog, C. Prometeus hos Aiskylos och hos V. Rydberg. Var tyd, 8, 1923.
Ludwig, G. S. Drei Gestaltungen des Prometheus. Neue Zeit, 31, 1913.
Mann, O. Der Prometheusmythus in der modernen Dichtung. Progr. Frankfurt a/O., 1878.
May. Prometheus in der deutschen Dichtung. HG, 1930.
Mullens, H. G. Prometheus in Cult, Legend and Tragedy. TAPhA, 1938.
Pohlenz. Die Prometheusgestalt bei den Griechen. HG, 1930.
Rascoe, B. Prometheans: Ancient and Modern. London, 1934.
Roussel, L. Le folklore dans Prométhée. REA, 1934.
Salac, A. Le mythe de Prométhée et Pandore chez Hésiode. Listy Filologicke, 43.
Schwartz, E. Prometheus bei Hesiod. SAWB, 1915.
Terzaghi, N. Il mito di Prometeo prima di Esodio. Atti della R. Accad. di archeologia di Napoli, 1916.
Wagschal, F. Goethes und Byrons Prometheusdichtungen. GRM, 1912.
Walzel, O. F. Das Prometheussymbol von Shaftesbury zu Goethe. Leipzig, 1910.
Weaver, B. Prometheus Bound and Prometheus Unbound. PMLA, March, 1949.
Wlastoff, G. Prométhée, Pandore et La Légende des siècles. Essai d'analyse de quelques légendes d'Hésiode. Saint-Petersbourg, 1883.
Moore, C. H. **PROPHECY** in the Ancient Epic. HSCPh, 1921.
Lipari, A. Il De raptu **PROSERPINAE** di Claudio Claudiano e il mito del rapimento nelle sue origini e nel suo sviluppo. Trapani, 1936.
Piaget, A. L'enlèvement de Proserpine, poème français du XVe siècle. Mélanges Niedermann. Neuchâtel, 1944.
Meyer-Benfey, H. Preussendramen. **(PRUSSIA)**. Neue Zeit, July, 1923.
Dermenghem, E. Le mythe de **PSYCHE** dans le folklore nord-africain. Revue africaine, (Alger), 1945.
Erdmann, H. Molières Tragödie-Ballet Psyche im Vergleich zu den ihr vorangehenden Bearbeitungen der Psyche-Sage. Diss. Königsberg, 1893.
Latour, A. de. Psyché en Espagne. Paris, 1879.
Le Maître, H. Essai sur le mythe de Psyché dans la littérature française des origines à 1890. Paris, 1939.
Weidling, F. Drei deutsche Psyche-Dichtungen. Jauer, 1903.
PULCINELLA: See Commedia dell'arte, IV. III. 6.
Glasenapp, G. von. Schillers Gang nach dem Eisenhammer. Wanderungen des Novellenstoffes durch acht Jahrhunderte. **(PUNISHMENT)**. Baltische Monatsschrift, 72, 1911.
Reinhard, J. R. Burning at the Stake in Mediaeval Law and Literature. Spec., 16, 1941.
—— Setting Adrift in Mediaeval Law and Literature. PMLA, 56, 1941.
PURGATORY: See also Heaven and Hell, and Saint Patrick.
Bautz, J. Das Fegefeuer. Mainz, 1883.
Buske, W. **PYGMALION**-Dichtungen des 18. Jahrhunderts. GRM, 7, 1915.
Spell, J. R. Pygmalion in Spain. RR, 1934.
Bonnard, J. Une traduction de **PYRAME** et Thisbé en vers français du XIIIe siècle. Lausanne, 1892.
Hart, G. Ursprung und Verbreitung der Pyramus und Thisbe-Sage. Diss. München, 1889.
—— Die Pyramus- und Thisbe-Sage in Holland, England, Italien und Spanien. Progr. Leipzig, 1891.
Penon, G. Pyramus en Thesbe. In: Bijdragen tot de geschiedenis der Nederlandsche letterkunde. Groningen, 1884.
Picot, E. Moralité nouvelle de Pyramus et Tisbée (cf. Introduction). Paris, 1901.
Schaer, A. Die dramatische Bearbeitung der Pyramus und Thisbe-Sage in Deutschland. Schkeuditz, 1909.
Fourcassié, J. Le romantisme et les **PYRENEES**. Diss., Paris, 1940. And NRF, 1940.
Guillaumie, G. Les Pyrénnées dans la littérature gasconne. RCC, 30.VI.1934.
Walker, J. Studies of the Pyrenees. Papers of the Manchester Literary Club, 18, 1899.
Lévy, I. Recherches sur les sources de

la légende de **PYTHAGORE.** Paris, 1926.
—— La légende de Pythagore de Grèce en Palestine. Paris, 1927.
—— Autour de la légende de Pythagore. RBPh, 1930.

—R—

Krappe, A. H. Sur un épisode de la Saga de **RAGNAR LODBROK.** Acta Philologica Scandinavica, 15, 1941.
Brencker, F. Die Eisenbahn in der Dichtung. **(RAILROAD).** ZDU, 25, 1911.
Poethen, W. Das Vordringen der Eisenbahn und die deutsche Dichtung. ZDK, 35, 1921.
Foulché-Delbosc, R. & Krappe, A. H. La légende du roi **RAMIRE.** RH, 78, 1930.
Beach, J. W. **REASON** and Nature in Wordsworth. JHI, 1, 1940.
Clough, W. O. Reason and Genius—An Eighteenth Century Dilemma. PhQ, 23, 1944.
Bousset, W. Die Geschichte eines Wiedererkennungsmärchens. **(RECOGNITION).** Nachr. d. Ges. der Wissenschaften zu Göttingen, 1916.
Gmur, A. Das Wiedererkennungsmotiv in den Dramen des Euripides. Freiburg, 1920.
REGIONALISM: See also Regional Novels, I. VII. 2.
Bartels, A. Heimatkunst. Strassburg, 1916.
Bentley, P. The English Regional Novel. London, 1942.
Bielschowsky, A. Geschichte der deutschen Dorfpoesie im 13. Jahrhundert. Berlin, 1891.
Coleman, R. A. Literature and Region. Pacific Northwest Quart., 39, 1948.
Homberger, T. & Herron, I. H. Literary Regionalism. Southwest Review, 1941.
Jan, E. von. Zum Problem des Regionalismus in der französischen Literatur. Archiv, 173.
Knauer, K. Charakterköpfe der französischen Heimatdichtung. ZNU, 37.
MacCarthy, B. G. Irish Regional Novelists of the Early XIXth Century. Dublin Mag., 21, 1946.
McDowell, T. Regionalism in the United States. Minnesota History, 20, 1940.
Moldenhauer, G. Wurzeln und Wesen des französischen Kulturregionalismus. NSp, 47.
Roche, A. V. Le régionalisme provençal, l'Allemagne et l'idée latine. Canada français, 29, 1942.
Savage, G. M. Regionalism in American Drama. Diss. U. of Washington, 1935.
Stewart, R. Regional Characteristics in the Literature of New England. College English, 3, 1941.
—— The Regional Approach to Literature. College English, 9, 1948.
Tate, A. The New Provincialism. Va. Quarterly Review, 21, 1945.
Walcutt, C. Regionalism—Practical or Aesthetic? Sewanee Rev., 49, 1941.
—— The Regional Novel and Its Future. Arizona Quarterly, 1, 1945.
Waldinger, E. Von der Heimatkunst zur Blut- und Bodendichtung. GQ, 13, 1940.
Ohly, E. F. Zum **REICHSGEDANKEN** des deutschen Rolandsliedes. ZDA, 77, 1940.
Petersen, J. Die Sehnsucht nach dem Dritten Reich in deutscher Sage und Dichtung. D&V, 1934.
Reitterer, N. Der Glaube an die Fortdauer des römischen Reiches im Abendlande. Diss. Münster, 1899-1900.
Vermeil, E. Germany's Three Reichs. London, 1944.
RELIGION: See II. V. & III. I.
Bleek, W. H. I. **REYNARD THE FOX** in South Africa, or Hottentot Fables and Tales. London, 1864.
—— Reineke Fuchs in Afrika. Weimar, 1870.
Buettner, H. Der Reinhart Fuchs und seine französischen Quellen. Strassburg, 1891.
—— Roman de Renard und Reinhart Fuchs. Berichte d. freien deutschen Hochstifts. Frankfurt, 7, 1891.
Busken-Huet, G. Sur le Roman du Renard. Revue de Hollande, Jan., 1916.
Chotzen, T. M. Een iersche Reinaertparallel. NPh, 21, 1936.
Foulet, L. Le Roman de Renard. Paris, 1914.
Graf, A. Die Grundlagen des Reineke Fuchs. Helsingfors, 1920.
Jonckbloet, W. J. A. Etude sur le Renart. Groningen, 1863.
Knorr, W. Die zwanzigste Branche des Roman de Renart und ihre Nachbildungen. Progr. Eutin, 1866.
Lange, J. Les rapports du Roman de Renart au poème allemand de Henri de Gleissner. Progr. Neumarkt i.W., 1887-89.
Lecompte, J. C. Chaucer's Prestes Tale and the Roman de Renard. MPh, 1917.
Morawski, J. Quelques sources méconnues du Roman de Renart, le contrefait. ZRPh, 49, 1929.

Paris, G. Nouvelle étude sur le Roman de Renart. Paris, 1860.
Raynouard, F. J. M. Le Roman de Renart. JS, 1826-27.
Reissenberger, K. Reinhart Fuchs. Halle, 1886.
Rothe, A. Les Romans de Renart examinés, analysés et comparés. Paris, 1845.
Schirokauer, A. Ein unbekannter hochdeutscher Reineke Fuchs von 1577. MLN, 63, 1948.
Sudre, L. Les sources du Roman de Renart. Paris, 1893. Cf. JS, 1895.
Voretzsch, C. Der Reinhardt Fuchs Heinrich des Glichezare und der Roman de Renart. Diss. Halle, 1890.
Willoughby, L. A. Samuel Naylor and Reynard the Fox. A Study in Anglo-German Literary Relations. London, 1914. Cf. Archiv, 1916.
Gray Wright, J. A Study of the Themes of the **RESURRECTION** in the Mediaeval French Drama. Bryn Mawr, 1935.
Paris, G. Le conte du trésor du roi **RHAMPSINITE.** Rev. de l'histoire des religions, 55, 1907.
Prato, S. La leggenda del tesoro di Rampsinite. Como, 1881.
Barnetzki, H. D. Die **RHEINDICHTUNG** seit der Romantik. Festschrift z. Lehrerversammlung. Düsseldorf, 1927.
Carré, J. M. Le Rhin et la littérature française. In: Le Rhin, Nil de l'Occident. Paris, 1946.
Van Duinkerken, A. & Tielrooy, J. Le Rhin et la littérature néerlandaise. ibid.
Las Vergnas, R. Le Rhin et les littératures anglo-américaines. ibid.
Schwab, L. Le Rhin et la littérature allemande. ibid.
Cohn, F. L. The Controversy over Becker's Deutscher Rhein (1840). MLF, 26, 1941.
Escholier, R. Victor Hugo et le Rhin. RRh, 1923.
Harnack, O. Lord Byron und der Rhein. Die Rheinlande, 2, 1902.
Plönes, H. Der Niederrhein im Schrifttum alter und neuer Zeit. Mörs, 1927.
Pongh, H. Rheinische Stammesseele in der Dichtung der Gegenwart. D&V, 1938.
Raphael, G. Le Rhin allemand. Cahiers de la Quinzaine, 1.V.1903.
Stang, S. Rheinlandsdramen. Stimmen der Zeit, 112.
Stephen, H. Die Entstehung der Rheinromantik. Diss. Köln, 1922.
Thérive, A. Les romantiques et le Rhin. RRh, 1927.
Tonnelat, E. Le Rhin dans la littérature allemande. NL, 1945.
Walzel, O. Rheinromantik. In: Vom Geistesleben Alter und Neuer Zeit. Leipzig, 1923.
Wolff, E. Guillaume Apollinaire und das Rheinland. Diss. Bonn, 1937.
Wolff, M. La genèse des Burgraves et le Rhin de V. Hugo. Figaro, 11.VIII. 1928.
Jentsch, F. Die mittelenglische Romanze **RICHARD COEUR DE LION** und ihre Quellen. ESn, 15, 1891.
Needler, G. H. Richard Coeur-de-Lion in Literature. Diss. Leipzig, 1890.
Qualia, C. B. French Dramatic Sources of Bulwer Lytton's **RICHELIEU.** PMLA, 42, 1927.
Giese, W. Trancosos Tres preguntas do rei. **(RIDDLES).** RLC, 18, 1938.
Vries, J. de. Die Märchen von klugen Rätsellösern. Helsinki, 1928.
Mason, A. E. W. Great **RIDES** in Literature. Transactions, Royal Society of Literature, N.S., 8, 1928.
Temple, R. C. Folklore of the Headless Horseman in Northern India. Calcutta Review, 77, 1883.
Gabrielli, A. Cola **RIENZI** e il theatro. NAnt, 136.
Toffano, F. **RINALDO DA MONTALBANO** nella letteratura romanzesca italiana. Venezia, 1891.
Vulpius, W. **RINALDO RINALDINI** als ein Lieblingsthema seiner Zeit. Diss. München, 1922.
Pauls. Der **RING** des Fastranes. Eine mythologische Studie. Aachen, 1896.
Paris, G. La parabole des trois anneaux. Paris, 1885. And in: Leçons et lectures sur la poésie du moyen âge, 1895.
RISORGIMENTO: See Italian Contributions, IV. III., & Literature and Politics, I. II. 2.
Fuckel, A. Der Fluss als Sinnbild des Lebenslaufes in der deutschen Dichtung. **(RIVER).** ZDU, 27, 1913.
Sander, E. Die deutschen Flüsse in der deutschen Dichtung. Kölnische Zt., 294, 1903.
Wilson, H. A. Rivers and Waters in Literature. Contemp. Review, Oct., 1946.
Beneze, E. Orendel, W. von Orense und **ROBERT DER TEUFEL.** In: Sagen- und litterarhistorische Untersuchungen. Halle, 1897.
Borinski, K. Eine ältere deutsche Bearbeitung von Robert le Diable. Germania, 37, 1892.

Breul, K. Sir Gowther (Legend of Robert le Diable). Oppeln, 1886.
Kippenberg, A. Die Sage von Robert dem Teufel in Deutschland und ihre Stellung gegenüber der Faustsage. SVL, 4, 1904.
Lincoln, J. N. The Conde de Matisio and Robert the Devil. Papers of the Michigan Academy, 28, 1943.
Tardel, H. Die Sage von Robert le Diable in neueren deutschen Dichtungen und in Meyerbeers Oper. Berlin, 1900.
—— Neuere Bearbeitungen der Sage von Robert dem Teufel. SVL, 4, 1904.
Barry, E. Les vicissitudes et les transformations du cycle poétique de **ROBIN HOOD.** Paris, 1832.
Gable, J. H. Bibliography of Robin Hood. U. of Nebraska Studies, 1939.
Houdek, I. Janosik, The Slovak Robin Hood. Slovak Review, 1, 1947.
Ritson, J. Robin Hood: A Collection of all the Ancient Poems, Songs and Ballads now extant, relative to that Celebrated Outlaw, to which are prefixed Historical Anecdotes of his Life. 2 vols. London, 1795.
Verrier, P. Robin Hood. Romania, Jan., 1936.
ROBINSON CRUSOE and Robinsonaden: See Defoe, IV. VIII. 7.
Buhlmann, J. L. Der **RODENSTEINER** in Sage, Lied und Geschichte. Monatsrosen, 1902.
Langguth, A. Der Rodensteiner in Sage und Dichtung. Burschenschaftl. Blätter, 18, 1904.
Lorentzen, T. Die Sage vom Rodensteiner. Heidelberg, 1903.
Ammann, J. J. Das Verhältnis von Strickers Karl zum Rolandslied des Pfaffen Konrad mit Berücksichtigung der Chanson de **ROLAND.** Progr. Krumau, 1897.
Armelin, G. Roland en Espagne. Paris, 1931.
Bandi di Vesme, B. Rolando marchese della marca brettone e le origini della leggenda di Aleramo. Atti del Congresso . . . di Scienze storiche, 1903. Roma, 1904.
Baret, E. Du poème du Cid dans ses analogies avec la chanson de Roland. Paris, 1863.
Bertoni, G. Il Cid e la Chanson de Roland. Cultura Neolatina, 1, 1941.
Chassé, C. Le souvenir de Roland hors de France. Humanités, May, 1948.
Chines, A. Poesia epica e romanzesca: imitazione dal francese nella poesia epica. La Chanson de Roland e l'Orlando furioso. Catania, 1921.
Chiri, G. L'epica latina medioevale e la Chanson de Roland. Genova, 1936.
Crescini, V Orlando nella Chanson de Roland e nei poemi del Bojardo e dell'Ariosto. Bologna, 1880.
Dufauret, V. Les variantes allemandes de la légende de Roland. RB, 1899.
Eicke, T. Zur neuen Litteraturgeschichte der Rolandsage in Deutschland und Frankreich. Diss. Marburg. Leipzig, 1891.
Fassbender, L. Die französischen Rolandshandschriften in ihrem Verhältniss zu einander und zur Karlmagnussage. Diss. Bonn, 1887.
Golther, W. Das Rolandslied des Pfaffen Konrad. München, 1886-87. Cf. Romania, 15.
Hagberg, T. Rolandssagan till sin historiska koerna och poetiska omklaedning. Upsala, 1884.
Liebemann, F. Shakespeare und Chanson de Roland. Archiv, 142, 1921.
De Monge. Roland et le Cid. Le Muséon, 1883.
Morf, H. Vom Rolandslied zum Orlando Furioso. DR, Sept., 1898.
Ohly, E. F. Zum Reichsgedanken des deutschen Rolandsliedes. ZDA, 77, 1940.
Paris, G. La Chanson de Roland et les Nibelungen. Rev. germanique et francaise, 1.IV.1863.
Pei, M. A. French Precursors of the Chanson de Roland. Columbia U.P., 1949.
Picco, F. Rolando nella storia e nella poesia. Torino, 1901.
Rajna, P. La genealogia dell'Orlando. NAnt, 29, 1875.
—— Le fonti dell'Orlando Furioso. Firenze, 1876. 2e ed., 1900.
Röhr, H. Die politische Umwelt des deutschen Rolandsliedes. Beiträge zur Gesch. d. deutschen Sprache & Literatur, 64, 1940.
Schleich, H. Prolegomena ad carmen de Rolando anglicum. Diss. Berlin, 1879.
Sello, G. Die deutschen Rolande. Forsch. z. brand. & preuss. Geschichte, 3, 1890.
Tavernier, W. Beiträge zur Rolandsforschung. (Aeneid, Pharsalia, Roland). ZFSL, 36, 1910.
Voigt, F. T. A. Roland-Orlando dans l'épopée française et italienne. Leiden, 1938.
Wichmann, C. Das Abhängigkeitsverhältniss des altenglischen Rolandliedes

zur altfranzösischen Dichtung. Diss. Münster, 1889.
Wilmotte, M. Une source latine de la Chanson de Roland. (Waltharius). Mélanges Gustave Lanson. Paris, 1922.
Zastrau, A. Das deutsche Rolandslied als nationales Problem. Potsdam, 1937.
Anon. Das sinkende ROM in der neueren deutschen Poesie. Grenzboten, 1882.
—— Winckelmann in Rome. TLS, 15.IX. 1927.
Ampère, J. J. A. Portraits de Rome. RDM, 15.VII.1835.
Angeli, D. Roma romantica. Marzocco, 1930.
Bellonci, G. L'idea di Roma nell'opera di Corneille. Roma, 1938.
Bernardi, A. Roma e l'Italia nell'opera di F. M. Crawford. NAnt, 1.IX.1903.
Besso, M. Roma e il Papa nei proverbi e nei modi di dire. Roma, 1899. 2e. ed., 1904.
Bonfante, P. Rome et Amérique. Scientia Organo internaz. di sintesi scientifica, 35, 1924.
Bournet, A. Voyageurs (surtout français) à Rome. In: Rome, études de littérature et d' art. Paris, 1883.
Brackmann, A. Der römische Erneuerungsgedanke und seine Bedeutung für die Reichspolitik der deutschen Kaiserzeit. SAWB, 1932.
Buriot-Darsiles, H. Un Germain amoureux de Rome: l'arrivée de Waiblinger dans la Ville éternelle. Dante, 1934. And in: Le Trésor des Lettres, 1935.
Chini, M. Roma e l'Italia nella renascita neo-provenzale. Rassegna di studi francesi, 1935.
Costa, G. Dante e il mito etico di Roma. Religio, 1937.
Cotard, R. Rome et la langue française. Hum, 7, 1934.
Damiani, E. G. Echi di Roma nei poeti bulgari. Bulgaria, 2, 1940.
—— L'idea di Roma nei poeti romantici della Polonia. Il Risveglio, 1, 1945.
Falchi, A. Il nome di Roma nel mondo. NAnt, 1.V.1910.
Faries, R. Ancient Rome in the English Novel. Diss. Philadelphia, 1923.
Flynn, V. J. Englishmen in Rome (1450-1510). TLS, 12.XII.1935.
—— Englishmen in Rome During the Renaissance. MPh, 36, 1938.
Formichi, C. Roma nell'opera di Shakespeare. Roma, 1938.
Goethe in Rome: See Italian Contributions, p. 438.
Graf, A. Roma nella memoria e nelle immaginazioni del medio evo. 2 vols. Torino, 1882-83. Cf. ZRPh, 6.
Grana, S. Il mito di Roma. Firenze, 1927.
Graevenitz, G. von. Deutsche in Rom. Leipzig, 1902.
Guglia, E. Deutsche Romantiker in Rom (1804-23). Beilage zur Allg. Zt., 20.V. 1898.
Hammer, W. The Concept of the New or Second Rome in the Middle Ages. Spec., 1944.
Heckscher, W. S. Die Romruinen. Die geistigen Voraussetzungen ihrer Wertung im Mittelalter und in der Renaissance. Würzburg, 1936.
Iorga, N. Roma nel pensiero e nella letteratura dei Romeni. Gli Studi Romani nel Mondo, 3, (Roma), 1936.
Isopescu, C. Roma e la poesia romena dell' 800. Osservatore romano, 21.IV. 1948.
Kliger, S. The Urbs Aeterna in Paradise Regained. PMLA, 61, 1946.
Kluge, O. Der Romgedanke von der Antike zur Renaissance. Gymnasium, 1941.
Lebermann, N. Das sinkende Rom in der neueren deutschen Poesie. Grenzboten, 41, 1882.
Magoun, F. P. The Rome of Two Northern Pilgrims: Archbishop Sigeric of Canterbury and Abbot Nikolas of Munkathverá. Harvard Theological Rev., 33, 1940.
Marraro, H. R. American Travellers in Rome, 1848-50. Cath. Hist. Rev., 29, 1944.
Maugain, G. Rome et le gouvernement pontifical au XVIIIe siècle, d'après des voyageurs français. EI, 1928-29.
Mazzoni, G. Roma imperiale e Roma italiana nella nostra poesia. NAnt, 1926.
Naumann, G. Rom im Liede. Leipzig, 1896.
Olsen, M. Roma e la poesia del paganesimo nordico. SG, 1936 & 1939.
Paris, G. La légende de Rome au moyen âge. JS, Oct., 1884.
Pfeil, E. Die fränkische und deutsche Romidee des frühen Mittelalters. München, 1929.
Piccoli, U. Roma nell'opera e nel pensiero di U. Foscolo. Roma, 1940.
Ponti, E. Roma nei canti di Byron. Messagero, April, 1924.
Rehm, W. Der Untergang Roms im abendländischen Denken. Leipzig, 1930.
—— Romdichtung im Zeitalter Goethes. Gymnasium, 49, 1938.

—— Europäische Romdichtung. München, 1939.

Schneider, F. Rom und Romgedanke im Mittelalter. München, 1926.

Schramm, P. E. Kaiser, Rom und renovatio. VBW, 17, 1929.

Skeel, C. Some Mediaeval Travellers to Rome. PCA, 1924.

Sorrento, L. L'idea di Roma nei poeti siciliani durante la dominazione spagnola. Bologna, 1935.

Stein, W. L. Spiritualità di Goethe: la Germania a Roma nel secolo XIX. Antieuropa, 1932.

Torri, M. Roma nella poesia francese e tedesca del secolo XIX. Parma, 1907.

Villari, L. Canti inglesi su Roma antica. NAnt, 16.II.1938.

Wocke, H. Rilke und Rom. ZDPh, 64, 1939.

Beurlier. Essai sur le culte rendu aux empereurs romains. (**ROMAN HISTORY**). Paris, 1890.

Büsser, M. Die Römerdramen in der Theatergeschichte der deutschen Schweiz. (1500-1800). Diss. Fribourg. Luzern, 1938.

MacCallum, M. W. Shakespeare's Roman Plays and Their Background. London, 1910.

Ross, W. Das Bild der römischen Kaiserzeit in der französischen Literatur des 19. Jahrhunderts. Diss. Bonn, 1938.

ROMEO AND JULIET: See Shakespeare, IV. VIII. 11.

Monteverdi, A. Un episodio della battaglia di **RONCISVALLE** nella poesia castigliana e portoghese. Studi di filologia mod., 5, 1912.

Rajna, P. La rotta di Roncisvalle nella letteratura cavalleresca italiana. Bologna, 1871.

Vaganay, H. Le **ROSAIRE** dans la poésie. Essai de bibliographie. Mâcon, 1907.

Heltzel, V. B. Fair **ROSAMOND**, a Study of the Development of a Literary Theme. Northwestern U. Studies, 1947.

Baldensperger, F. Le siège de **ROUEN** et son importance pour l'information de Shakespeare. CLS, 3, 1941.

ROUND TABLE: See Celtic Contributions, IV. I. 2.

Blum, P. Der Troubadour Jaufre **RUDEL** und sein Fortleben in der Literatur. Jahresbericht der K. K. Realschule in Brünn, 1912.

Paludan, H. H. Sagn om borgtapeter; til orientering i Jaufre Rudel problemerne. Festskrift til Valdemar Vedel. København, 1935.

Viglione, F. La leggenda di Jaufre Rudel nei canti dei poeti italiani e stranieri. Roma, 1916. Cf. RI, 19.

Zade, L. Der Troubadour J. Rudel und das Motiv der Fernliebe in der Weltliteratur. Diss. Greifswald, 1919.

Soffé, E. **RUDOLF** von Habsburg im Spiegel der deutschen Dichtung. Progr. Brünn, 1893.

Vancsa, M. Rudolf von Habsburg in der Dichtung. Oesterr. Rundschau, 55.

Michéa, R. La poésie des **RUINES** au XVIIIe siècle et la contribution de l'Italie à la sensibilité préromantique. EI, 1935.

Moorhead, M. D. Les Ruines de Volney. FQ, June, 1927.

Sauer, A. Die Ruinen des Campo Vaccino. JbGrG, 7, 1897.

Schmidt, E. Die Ruine als dichterisches Motiv. DLZ, 33, 1911.

Stoldt, H. H. Geschichte der Ruinenpoesie in der Romantik. Diss. Kiel, 1925.

Anon. Milton's History of **RUSSIA**. Calcutta Review, 104, 1897.

Mongault, H. Mérimée et l'histoire russe. Le Monde slave, 1932.

—S—

Chastel, A. La légende de la reine de **SABA**. Rev. de l'histoire des Religions, 119, 1939.

Koehler, R. Zur Legende von der Königin von Saba oder der Sibylla und dem Kreuzholze. Germania, 29, 1884. Cf. also Kleine Schriften, 2.

Kahn, A. Der **SABBAT** in der Poesie. Jüd. Presse, Beilage, 1904.

Baker, A. T. **SAINTS'** Lives Written in Anglo-French: Their Historical, Social and Literary Importance. Trans. of the Royal Society of Literature, 4, 1924.

Daxlberger, R. Der Heilige in der deutschen Dichtung zur Zeit des Expressionismus, 1910-27. Diss. München, 1937.

Déléhaye, H. Les légendes hagiographiques. Bruxelles, 1905; London, 1907.

Desjardins, P. La vie des saints au théâtre. La Quinzaine, 1.XII.1896.

Faesi, R. Der Heilige in der modernen Dichtung. ZDK, 1, 1926.

—— Die Heilige in der modernen Literatur. Didaskalia, 103, 1926.

Ford, J. D. M. The Saint's Life in the Vernacular Literature of the Middle Ages. Cath. Hist. Review, 17, 1931.

Fülöp-Miller, R. The Saints That Moved the World. New York, 1945.

Gennep, A. van. Vie des saints et roman-feuilleton. Revue des Idées, July, 1910.

Gerould, G. H. Saints' Legends. Boston, 1916.

Gougaud, L. Les saints irlandais hors d'Irlande. Louvain, 1936.

Jones, C. W. Saints' Lives and Chronicles in Early England. Ithaca, 1947.

Kapp, R. Heilige und Heiligenlegenden in England. Studien zum 16. und 17. Jahrhundert. Halle, 1934.

Koehler, R. Leggenda di un sant'uomo bruciato e rigenerato. Arch. d. tradiz. pop., 1883. And in: Kleine Schriften, 2.

Mayer, A. Der Heilige und die Dirne. Eine motivgeschichtliche Studie zu Hrotsvits Abraham und Pafnutius. BBG, 1931.

Mecklin, J. M. The Passing of the Saint: A Study of a Cultural Type. Chicago, 1941.

Priessnig, A. Die biographischen Formen der griechischen Heiligenlegenden in ihrer geschichtlichen Entwicklung. München, 1924.

Prins, A. A. Some Remarks on Aelfric's Lives of Saints and His Translation from the Old Testament. NPh, 25, 1940.

Saintyves, P. Les saints successeurs des dieux. Paris, 1907.

Steinen, W. von den. Heilige als Hagiographen. Historiche Zs, 143.

Toldo, P. Leben und Wunder der Heiligen im Mittelalter. SVL, 1901.

Tommasini, A. M. Irish Saints in Italy. London, 1937.

Vaganay, H. Les saints dans la littérature. Theolog. Jahresberichte, 1901.

Wilk, K. Führende Gestalten. Eine Kirchengeschichte in Heiligenleben. Paderborn, 1935.

Goetz, B. **SANKT PETERSBURG** im Spiegel der russischen Dichtung. Atlantis (Zürich), 6, 1947.

Fioravanti, A. Il **SALADINO** nelle leggende francesi e italiane del medio evo. Reggio-Calabria, 1891.

Paris, G. La légende de Saladin. JS, 1893. Italian translation in: La Bibl. crit. d. lett. ital., Firenze, 1896.

Becker, Maria L. **SALOME** in der Kunst des letzten Jahrtausends. Bühne & Welt, 4, 1901. And in: Internat. Literaturbericht, 10, 1903.

Cansinos Asseus, R. Salome en la literatura. Madrid, 1920.

Daffner, H. Salome. Ihre Gestalt in Geschichte und Kunst. München, 1912-13.

Drewska, Hélène. Quelques interprétations de la légende de Salome dans les littératures contemporaines. Diss. Montpellier, 1912.

Poppenberg, F. Salome-Variationen. Frankfurter Zt., 119, 1913.

Reimarus Secundus. Geschichte der Salome von Cato bis Oscar Wilde gemeinverständlich dargestellt. Leipzig, 1907-08 & 1913.

Vaucaire, M. Salome à travers l'art et la littérature. Nouvelle Revue, 1907.

Vitaletti, G. Salome nella leggenda e nell'arte. Roma, 1908.

Krappe, A. H. **SAMSON**. Revue archéologique, 6, 1933.

Gerlach, K. Der Simsonstoff im deutschen Drama. Berlin, 1929.

Rossberg, F. Die Samson-Tragödie. Bühnen-Roland, 14, 1913.

Widmann, W. Simson und Dalila in der dramatischen Dichtung. Schwäb. Merkur, 564, 1911.

SATAN: See also Devil, above.

Bailly, M. H. Origines et caractère du Satan de Milton. Bull. de la Société acad. de Brest, 1881.

Brincourt, A. Satan et la poésie. Paris, 1946.

Dufay, P. J. K. Huysmans, Madame Courrière et l'abbé Van Haecke. MF, 15.IV.1935.

Gilbert, A. H. The Theological Basis of Satan's Rebellion. MPh, 1940.

Grillet, C. Le satanisme littéraire. Satan, héros romantique. Correspondant, 1922.

Hamilton, G. R. Hero or Fool? A Study of Milton's Satan. London, 1944.

Hermann, M. Un sataniste polonais: Stanislas Przybyszewski. Paris, 1939.

Langton, E. Satan, a Portrait: A Study of the Character of Satan through all the Ages. New York, 1947.

Michelet, J. Satanism and Witchcraft. A Study in Medieval Superstition. New York, 1947.

Reinach, S. Satan et ses pompes. Revue de l'U. de Bruxelles, 8, 1902.

Rudwin, M. Supernaturalism and Satanism in Chateaubriand. OC, 36, 1922.

—— Satanism in French Romanticism. OC, 1923.

—— Satan et le satanisme dans l'oeuvre de V. Hugo. Paris, 1926.

—— Romantisme et satanisme. Grande Revue, 1927.

—— The Salvation of Satan in Modern Poetry. OC, 1931.

Schantz, B. T. Motley's The Chevalier de Sataniski. AL, 13, 1941.

Slochower, H. Satanism in Celine. BA, 18, 1944.
Torczyner, H. How Satan Came Into the World. ET, 48, 1936-37.
Anon. Le **SAULE** de Shakespeare, de Musset, de la Malibran et de l'inconnu. MF, 1.X.1936.
Baldini, M. La genesi del Saul di V. Alfieri. Firenze, 1934.
Calcaterra, C. Addenda zu Baldinis La genesi del Saul di V. Alfieri. GSLI, 1935.
Ciafardini, E. Saul nel primo libro dei Re e nella tragedia dell'Alfieri. Caserta, 1928.
Estève, E. De Shakespeare à Musset; variations sur la romance du Saule. RHLF, 1922. And in: Etudes de littérature préromantique. Paris, 1923.
Hirschberg, L. Saul-Tragödien. Allg. Zt. des Judentums, 74, 1910.
Thiel, A. La figure de Saul et sa représentation dans la littérature dramatique française. Amsterdam, 1926.
Wykoff, G. S. A Possible Source of Browning's Saul. PhQ, 1928.
Yocom, H. W. Some Additional Sources of Browning's Saul. N&Q, 181, 1941.
For **SAVAGE** (noble, or otherwise): See Primitivism, above.
SAVIOR: See Messiah, above.
Brie, M. **SAVONAROLA** in der deutschen Litteratur. Diss. Heidelberg. Breslau, 1903.
Prosch. Lenaus Savonarola. Zs. für die österreichischen Gymnasien, 43, 1892.
Schnitzer, J. Savonarola im Lichte der neuesten Litteratur. Hist. polit. Blätter für d. kath. Deutschland, 1898.
Teichmann, A. Savonarola in der deutschen Dichtung. Berlin, 1937.
Atkins, S. Peter **SCHLEMIHL** in Relation to the Popular Novel of the Romantic Period. GR, 21, 1946.
Ludwig, A. Schlemihle (Chamisso in England). Archiv, April, 1920.
Benjamin, C. Das deutsche Gymnasium im Spiegel der Dichtung seit 1830. (**SCHOOL**). Progr. Berlin, 1904.
Pagel, F. Das Schulproblem im Lichte moderner Literatur. Schule, 15, 1911.
Bain, M. J. Les voyageurs français en Ecosse (1770-1830) et leurs curiosités intellectuelles. (**SCOTLAND**). Paris, 1931.
Etzrodt, H. Schottlandreisen im 18. Jahrhundert. Wie der Engländer die Hochlande sah. Berlin, 1939.
Thomson, G. M. The Pre-Discovery of Scotland. London, 1929.
Magoun, F. P. Scottish History in the Lay of Gurun. Stud. Neoph., 14, 1941-42.
Baccelli, A. La poesia del mare. (**SEA**). NAnt, 256, 1914.
Bassett, F. S. Legends and Superstitions of the Sea and Sailors in All Lands and at All Times. Chicago, 1886.
Bertuccioli, A. Les origines du roman maritime. Livorno, 1937.
Biese, A. Die Poesie des Meeres und das Meer in Poesie. PJb, 88, 1897.
Blecua, J. M. El mar en la poesía española. Madrid, 1945.
Bolles, E. C. The Literature of Sea Travel Since the Introduction of Steam, 1830-1930. Philadelphia, 1943.
Buckhurst, H. & McMillan, T. Terms and Phrases for the Sea in Old English Poetry. Festschrift F. Klaeber. Minneapolis, 1929.
Ditchy, J. K. Le thème de la mer chez les Parnassiens. Paris, 1927.
Dupouy, A. La poésie de la mer dans la littérature française. Paris, 1948.
Farinelli, A. Poesía del agua y del mar en Camoens. Nación, 11.II.1940.
Froude, J. A. Sea Studies. In: Short Studies on Great Subjects. London, 1886.
Fuchs, R. Seefahrt und Dichtung. Flotte, 7, 1903.
Glässer, E. Zur Geistesgeschichte des Meer-Sinnbildes im französischen Schrifttum. ZFSL, 62.
Göbel, A. Das Meer in den homerischen Dichtungen. Zs. f. Gymnasialwesen, 9, 1855.
Guy, G. La mer, ce mauvais sujet. MF, 15.VIII.1933.
Herescu, N. I. Un thème traditionnel de la poésie latine: le naufrage. Rivista clasica (Bucarest), 1932-33.
Hodnett, M. P. The Sea in Roman Poetry. CJ, 15, 1919-20.
Hoppe, G. Das Meer in der deutschen Dichtung von F. L. Graf zu Stolberg bis Heinrich Heine. Marburg, 1929.
Kahlmeyer, J. Seesturm und Schiffbruch als Bild im antiken Schrifttum. Greifswald, 1934.
Kruemmel, O. Nautische Märchen und Sagen. DR, 1896.
Lange, K. Eugen Sue's Seeromane, ihre Herkunft und Eigenart. Diss. Greifswald, 1915.
Le Breton, M. Hermann Melville et la mer. RHPhC, 41, 1946.
Le Franc, A. Les navigations de Rabelais. Paris, 1905.
Le Goffic, C. La mer et la littérature. NL, 19.VII.1924.

Lewis, C. L. American Short Stories of the Sea. U. S. Naval Institute Proceedings, 57, 1941.
—— Books of the Sea: An Introduction to Nautical Literature. Annapolis, 1943.
MacGillycuddy, G. V. Das Meer und das Fischervolk in J. M. de Peredas Werken. Diss. Würzburg, 1934.
Martin, E. Joseph Conrad et le romancier de la mer. LM, May, 1948.
Melchior, F. Das Meer in deutscher Dichtung. In: Heines Verhältnis zu Byron. Berlin, 1903.
Müller, C. Zur deutschen Seepoesie. In: Germanist. Erinnerungen der Alma Mater Wratislaviensis. Berlin, 1911.
Opp, M. Die See in der Dichtung der englischen Romantiker. Diss. Leipzig, 1913.
Poeck, W. Der See in der Erzählung. Eckart, 6, 1911.
—— Der See in der plattdeutschen Dichtung. Grenzboten, 67.
Saint-Denis, E. de. Le rôle de la mer dans la poésie latine. Paris, 1935-36.
Salvatorelli, A. M. Racine, poeta del mare. La Nuova Europa, 3, 1946.
Schneider, A. Die Entwicklung des Seeromans in England im 17. und 18. Jahrhundert. Leipzig, 1901.
Sébillot, P. Légendes, croyances et superstitions de la mer. 2 vols. Paris, 1886.
Shay, F. American Sea Songs and Chanteys. New York, 1948.
Sorrento, L. La poesia popolare del mare e i suoi rapporti con l'anima e la storia marinara d'Italia. Atti IV Congr. di Arti & Trad. pop. Venezia, 1940. Udine, 1942.
Treneer, A. The Sea in English Literature from Beowulf to Donne. Liverpool, 1926.
Vallese, R. Le thème de la mer dans l'oeuvre de Chateaubriand. Napoli, 1934.
Van Tieghem, P. Les débuts de la poésie de la mer au XVIIIe siècle. NPh, 23, 1938.
Vezinet, F. La Bouteille à la mer et les croisières australiennes. RHLF, 26.
Kommerell, M, Calderons Beschreibung der SEMIRAMIS. RF, 53, 1939.

SENTIMENTS, Sensibility, Senses: See also Pessimism, Solitude.

Crane, R. S. Suggestions Toward a Genealogy of the Man of Feeling. ELH, 3, 1934.
Doyle, Mildred D. Sentimentalism in American Periodicals, 1741-1800. New York, 1944.
Erhardt-Siebold, E. von. Harmony of the Senses in English, German and French Romanticism. PMLA, 47, 1932.
Fehr, B. Empfindsamkeitsliteratur. Anglica, A. Brandl überreicht. Leipzig, 1926.
Garey, Doris B. XVIIIth Century Sentimentalism: an Essay Toward Definition. Diss. U. of Wisconsin, 1941.
Hazard, P. Les origines philosophiques de l'homme de sentiment. RR, 1937.
Mauclair, C. Le sentimentalisme littéraire et son influence sur le siècle. Grande Revue, 1.V.1900. And in: L'art en silence. Paris, 1901.
Spinner, K. Die Ausdrücke für Sinnesempfindungen in der angelsächsischen Poesie. Diss. Halle, 1924.
Van Tieghem, P. La sensibilité et la passion dans le roman européen au XVIIIe siècle. RLC, 6, 1926.
—— Quelques aspects de la sensibilité préromantique dans le roman européen au XVIIIe siècle. Edda, 26, 1927.

SEPULCHRAL POETRY: See also Gothic Literature, above.

Besouw, R. Untersuchungen über den Einfluss der heidnischen auf die Form und die Vorstellungswelt der christlichen lateinischen Grabespoesie. Bonn, 1943.
Burgada, G. Sulla poesia sepolcrale francese e italiana. Fanfulla della Domenica. 21, 1900.
Calabritto, G. Sulla fortuna dei Sepolcri in Inghilterra. Malta's Empire Press, 1932.
Cian, V. Per la storia del sentimento e della poesia sepolcrale in Italia ed in Francia prima dei Sepolcri del Foscolo. GSLI, 20, 1892.
Draper, J. W. The Funeral Elegy and the Rise of English Romanticism. New York, 1929.
Michéa, R. Le tombeau dans la pensée du XVIIIe siècle. Annales de l'U. de Grenoble, 14, 1937.
—— Le plaisir des tombeaux au XVIIIe siècle. RLC, 18, 1938.
Momigliano, A. La poesia dei Sepolcri. RI, 1928.
Parrot, A. Malédictions et violations de tombes. Paris, 1939.
Reed, A. L. The Background of Gray's Elegy: A Study in the Taste for Melancholy Poetry, 1700-51. Columbia U.P., 1924.
Rizzo, T. L. La poesia sepolcrale in Italia. Genova, 1927.
Van Tieghem, P. La poésie de la nuit

et des tombeaux en Europe au XVIIIe siècle. Paris, 1921.
Zumbini, B. La poesia sepolcrale straniera e italiana e il carme del Foscolo. NAnt, 1899, and in: Studi di letteratura italiana, Firenze, 1906.
Vlekke, B. H. M. St. **SERVATIUS**. De eerste nederlandse bisschop in historie en legende. Maastricht, 1935.
Campbell, K. A Study of the Romance of the **SEVEN SAGES** with Special Reference to the Middle English Version. Diss. Baltimore, 1898. Boston, 1907.
Delatte, A. Le déclin de la légende des Sept Sages et les prophéties théosophiques. Musée Belge, 1923.
Krappe, A. H. Studies on the Seven Sages of Rome, AR, 8, 1924; 9, 1925; 11, 1927; 16, 1932; 19, 1935.
Mussafia, A. Ueber eine italienische Bearbeitung der Sieben Weisen Meister. Jb. f. romanische & englische Sprache & Litteratur, 4, 1862.
Petras, P. Ueber die mittelenglischen Fassungen der Sage von den sieben weisen Meistern. Diss. Breslau, 1885.
Schmitz, J. Die ältesten Fassungen des deutschen Romans von den sieben weisen Meistern. Diss. Greifswald, 1904.
Selmer, C. A Latin Collection of Pseudo-Aristotelian Paroimia and its Relation to the Sayings of the Seven Sages. PhQ, 19, 1940.
Wiersma, W. The Seven Sages and the Prize of Wisdom. Mnemosyne (Leiden), 1.
Allgeier, A. Der Ursprung der griechischen Siebenschläferlegende. (**SEVEN SLEEPERS**). Byzant.-neugriech. Jb, 3.
Heller, B. Eléments, parallèles et origine de la Légende des Sept Dormants. REG, 49, 1904.
Huber, P. M. Die Wanderlegende von den Siebenschläfern. Leipzig, 1910.
Koch, J. Die Siebenschläferlegende. Leipzig, 1883.
Peers, E. A. Periodical Contributions of **SEVILLA** to Romanticism. BH, 1922.
Depken, F. **SHERLOCK HOLMES**, Raffles und ihre Vorbilder. Heidelberg, 1914.
Bolte, J. Der Jude von Venetien. (**SHYLOCK**). JbShG, 22, 1887.
—— Zur Shylockfabel. JbShG, 1892.
Draper, J. W. The Psychology of Shylock. Bull. Hist. Medicine, 8, 1940.
Flatter, R. Shylock, ein Spiegel der Zeiten. Neue Zürcher Zt, 2.VI.1947.
Graetz, H. Shylock in der Sage, im Drama, und in der Geschichte. 2nd. ed. Krotoschin, 1899.
Grisebach, R. Ueber Ursprung und Bedeutung der Sage von Shylock. WM, 145, 1868.
Heinemann, H. Shylock und Nathan. Frankfurt, 1886.
Lee, S. L. The Original of Shylock (R. Lopez). Gentleman's Mag., Feb., 1880.
Montanari, E. Due tipi d'Ebrei (Shylock e Nathan). Rivista abruzzese, 22, 1907.
Piccini, G. La questione semitica nel Mercante di Venezia: la interpretazione del carattere di Shylock. Firenze, 1895.
Samnely, N. Shylock und Nathan. Lemberg, 1881.
Sinsheimer, H. Shylock: The History of a Character of the Myth of the Jew. London, 1947.
Smith, F. M. Shylock on the Rights of Jews and Emilia on the Rights of Women. West Virginia U. Bull., 1947.
Winkler, H. A. Aegyptische Volkskunde. (Shylock). Stuttgart, 1936.
Alekseiev, M. P. **SIBERIA** in the Knowledge of the Western-European Tourists and Writers. (In Russian). Irkutsk, 1932. Cf. GS, 3, 1935.
Manning, C. A. Siberia in Russian Literature. Asia, Dec., 1934.
Guiraud, A. Les **SIBYLLES**. Le Correspondant, 9, 1845.
Benedetti, A. La **SICILIA** nel teatro di Shakespeare. Archivio storico siciliano, 45.
Capnana, L. La Sicilia nei canti populari e nella novellistica contemporanea. 1894.
Paris, G. La Sicile dans la littérature française du moyen âge. Romania, 5.
Tuzet, H. Voyageurs français en Sicile au temps du romantisme (1802-48). Paris, 1946.
Buelbring, K. **SIDRAC** in England. Festschrift Foerster. Halle, 1902.
Brockstedt, G. Das altfranzösische **SIEGFRIEDLIED.** (Cf. Schlusswort). Kiel, 1908.
Bunge, E. F. Siegfried in German Literature. PhQ, 19, 1940.
Fechter, W. Siegfrieds Schuld und das Weltbild des Nibelungenliedes. Hamburg, 1948.
Kralik, D. von. Die Siegfriedtrilogie im Nibelungenlied und in der Thidreksaga. Halle, 1941.
Rutgers, H. W. Märchen und Sage mit besonderer Rücksicht auf die Sigfridsagen. Groningen, 1923.

Schneider, H. Die deutschen Lieder von Siegfrieds Tod. Weimar, 1947.
Comparetti, D. Researches Respecting the Book of **SINDIBAD**. Folk-Lore Society, 1882.
Nicaise, Abbé C. Les **SIRENES**, ou Discours sur leur forme et figure. Paris, 1691.
Elsner, W. Untersuchungen zu dem mittelenglischen Fabliau Dame **SIRIZ**. Diss. Strassburg, 1887.
SLAVERY, Abolitionism: See also Negroes, above, and Mrs. Beecher-Stowe, IV. XI. 9.
Derbyshire, E. Anti-Slavery Opinion in France During the Second Half of the XVIIIth Century. Baltimore, 1937.
Etienne, S. L'opinion antiesclavagiste en France sous l'Ancien Régime. RFB, 1938.
Ford, N. A. Henry David Thoreau, Abolitionist. NEQ, 19, 1946.
Johnson, Louise H. The Source of the Chapter on Slavery in Dickens' American Notes. AL, 14, 1943.
Lucas, E. E. La littérature antiesclavagiste au XIXe siècle: étude sur Mme Beecher Stowe et son influence en France. Paris, 1930.
Moody, Marjory M. The Evolution of Emerson as an Abolitionist. AL, 17, 1945.
Morrow, G. R. Plato's Law of Slavery in Its Relation to Greek Law. Ill. Stud. in Lang. and Lit. Urbana, 1939.
—— Plato and Greek Slavery. Mind, 1939.
Pitt, A. S. Franklin and the Quaker Movement Against Slavery. Bull. Friends' Hist. Assoc., 32, 1943.
Scudder, H. H. Mrs. Trollope and Slavery in America. N&Q, 187, 1944.
Seeber, E. D. Anti-Slavery Opinion in the Poems of Some Early French Followers of James Thomson. MLN, 50, 1935-36.
—— Anti-Slavery Opinion in France During the Second Half of the XVIIIth Century. Baltimore, 1937.
Sypher, W. Guinea's Captive Kings: British Anti-Slavery Literature of the XVIIIth Century. Chapel Hill (N.C.), 1942.
Vlastos, G. Slavery in Plato's Thought. Journal of Philosophy, 1939.
Wilson, Janet. The Early Anti-Slavery Propaganda. MB, 19, 1944.
Deville, E. Le premier texte de la Belle au Bois Dormant. (**SLEEPING BEAUTY**). Bull. du Bibliophile, 1908.
Spiller, R. Zur Geschichte des Märchens vom Dornröschen. Progr. Frauenfeld, 1893.
Vogt, F. Dornröschen-Thalia. Festschrift K. Weinhold. Breslau, 1896.
Goodell, Margaret M. Three Satirists of Snobbery: Thackeray, Meredith, Proust; with an Introductory Chapter on the History of the Word **SNOB** in England, France and Germany. Hamburg, 1939.
Bocklen, E. Schneewittchensagen. (**SNOW WHITE**). Leipzig, 1915.
SOLDIERS: See Chapter Eleven, below.
Sieper, E. Die Geschichte von **SOLIMAN** und Perseda in der neueren Litteratur. ZVL, 9-10, 1895-96.
SOLITUDE: See also Pessimism, Sentiment.
Chazel, P. Quelques romanciers de la solitude: Estaunié, Proust, Mauriac. Foi et Vie, 28, 1925.
Crump, P. E. The Theme of Solitude: an Aspect of the Sentiment de la Nature in the XVIIIth Century. FQ, 1925.
Heilborn, E. Das Motiv der Vereinsamung in neuesten Romanen. Literatur, 27, 1926.
Hyde, R. The Singers of Loneliness. T'ien Hsia Monthly, 7, 1938.
Maduschka, L. Das Problem der Einsamkeit im 18. Jahrhundert, insbesondere bei J. G. Zimmermann. Diss. München, 1932.
Melzer, F. J. G. Zimmermann's Einsamkeit und ihre Stellung im Geistesleben des ausgehenden 18. Jahrhunderts. Breslau, 1930.
Rehm, W. Der Dichter und die neue Einsamkeit. ZDK, 1931.
Steindecker, W. Studien zum Motiv des einsamen Menschen bei Novalis und Tieck. Breslau, 1937.
Vossler, K. Poesie der Einsamkeit in Spanien. SBAW, 1935-38. (La soledad en la poesía española. Madrid, 1941.)
Wonderley, A. W. The Concept of Seclusion in German Literature. JEGPh, 47, 1948.
Krappe, A. H. **SOLOMON** and Ashmodai, AJPh, 54, 1933.
Saintyves, P. Les cinquante jugements de Salomon ou les arrêts des bons juges d'après la tradition populaire. Paris, 1933.
Arnold, R. F. Dramatische Bearbeitungen der Geschichte der Prinzessin **SOPHIE** Dorothea. Zs. f. Bücherfreunde, 5, 1901.
Andrae, A. **SOPHONISBE** in der französischen Tragödie mit Berücksichtigung der Sophonisbebearbeitungen

in anderen Litteraturen. Diss. Göttingen, 1889. And in: ZFSL, 1891.
Feit, P. Sophonisbe, Tragödie von G. G. Trissino eingeleitet und übersetzt. Sophonisbe in Geschichte und Dichtung. Lübeck, 1888. Cf. ZVL, 1.
Fries, L. Montchrestiens Sophonisbe, seine Vorgänger und Quellen. Diss. Marburg, 1886.
Kayser, W. Lohensteins Sophonisbe als geschichtliche Tragödie. GRM, 29, 1941.
Kohler, P. Sur la Sophonisbe de Mairet et les débuts de la tragédie classique. RHLF, 46.
Morel, L. La Sophonisbe de Mairet et Sophonisbe de Geibel. Zürich, 1896. Cf. Bull. de l'Institut national genevois, 34, 1897.
Muir, K. Macbeth and Sophonisba. TLS, 9.X.1948.
Porcher, J. La date de la Sophonisbe de Mellin de Saint-Gelais. Bull. du Bibliophile, April, 1946.
Ricci, C. Sophonisbe dans la tragédie classique italienne et française. Grenoble, 1904.
Holmes, S. W. Browning's **SORDELLO** in the Light of Jung's Theory of Types. PMLA, 56, 1941.
Batiouchkov, T. La dispute entre l'âme et le corps. (**SOUL**). Journal russe de l'instruction publique. St. Petersbourg, 1891. Cf. Romania, 20, 1891.
Moore, C. H. Ancient Beliefs in the Immortality of the Soul, with some Account of their Influence on Later Views. In: Our Debt to Greece and Rome. New York, 1931.
Varnhagen, H. Ein indisches Märchen auf seiner Wanderung durch die asiatischen und europäischen Litteraturen. (Transfer of a Soul). Berlin, 1882.
Gormann, H. Grillparzers **SPARTAKUS** auf seine Quellen geprüft und gewürdigt. Diss. Münster, 1908.
Müller, E. Spartacus und der Sklavenkrieg in Geschichte und Dichtung. Progr. Salzburg, 1905.
Muszkat-Muszkowski, J. Spartacus. Stoffgeschichte. Diss. Leipzig, 1909.
Ollier, F. Le mirage spartiate. Paris, 1933.
Laistner, L. Das Rätsel der **SPHINX**. 2 vols. Berlin, 1889.
Schwarz, J. Der Mythos vom Weltgeist in der deutschen Dichtung. (**SPIRIT**). DVLG, 19, 1941.
Doughty, O. The English Malady of the 18th Century. (**SPLEEN**). RES, 1926.
Abmeier, H. Der Frühling in der deutschen Lyrik des 17. Jahrhunderts. (**SPRING**). Diss. Greifswald, 1912.
Bosch, J. Der Frühling in der deutschen Dichtung. Dichterstimmen der Gegenwart, 23, 1908.
Wentzel, J. A. Der Frühling im Lied der Völker. Neue Zürcher Zt., 428, 1914.
Taylor, A. The Motif of the Vacant **STAKE** in Folklore and Romance. RR, 9, 1918.
STARS. See also Literature & Science, I. III. 5.
Lange, H. Der Heliakische Aufgang der Fixsterne bei Dante und Chaucer. JbDG, 21, 1939.
Scheffer, T. von. Die Legenden der Sterne im Umkreis der antiken Welt. Stuttgart, 1939.
Smith, C. W. Browning's Star-Imagery. Princeton, 1941.
Leland, C. G. Legends of Florence. (**STATUES**). London, 1895.
Silverstein, H. T. The Weeping Statue and Dante's Gran Veglio. HSPhL, 13, 1931.
Schreiber, G. **STEPHAN** I in der deutschen Sakralkultur. Archivum Europae Centro Orientalis, 4.
Gombos, A. F. Saint Etienne dans l'historiographie du moyen âge. Ibid.
STONES: See Chapter Eleven, below.
Albrecht, K. **STOERTEBECKER** in der Dichtung. In: Unser Pommerland, 13, 1928.
STRASSBURG: See Intermediaries, I. IV. 1.
Kennedy, Ruth L. The Theme of **STRATONICE** in the Drama of the Spanish Peninsula. PMLA, 55, 1940.
Loewinson, E. Jakob **STROEMER**, der Geigenmacher von Absam in Geschichte und Dichtung. Innsbruck, 1892.
Erler, O. Die tragischen Probleme des **STRUENSEE**-Stoffes. (Hebbel). Leipzig, 1916.
Ziegler, S. Struensee im deutschen Drama. Dithmar, 1921.
STUARTS: See also Mary Stuart, above.
Renmont. Gli ultimi Stuardi e V. Alfieri. Archiv. stor. ital., 4e ser., 8, 1881.
Hoffmann, P. Der **STUDENT** in der deutschen Literatur des 17. Jahrhunderts. Neuphilol. Blätter, 15.
Kisch, P. & Werner, A. Der Prager Student im Gedicht. Deutsche Hochschulwarte (Prag), 1930.
Konrad, K. Der Student in deutschen Schwankbüchern des 16. und 17. Jahr-

hunderts. Akad. Monatshefte, 307, 1910.
—— Die deutsche Studentenschaft in ihrem Verhältnis zu Bühne und Drama. Berlin, 1912.
—— Beitrag zur Literaturgeschichte des deutschen Studententums. Deutsche akad. Rundschau, 7, 1927.
Lange, K. Der Student in der deutschen Literatur des 18. Jahrhunderts. Diss. Breslau, 1930.
Mechow, M. Deutsches Studententum in Drama und Roman seit der Romantik. Landsmannschafter Zt., 38, 1924.
Nemtzow, Sarah. El estudiante en la comedia del siglo de oro. MLF, 31, 1947.
Patzschke, H. Der studentische Roman der Gegenwart. ZDK, 1927.
Schmidt, E. Komödien vom Studentenleben aus dem 16. und 17. Jahrhundert. Leipzig, 1880.
Stranik, E. Der Student als Motiv seit Wickram. Literatur, 27, 1924.
Brenning, E. Der Selbstmord in der Literatur. (**SUICIDE**). Bremen, 1885.
Lécrivain, C. Le suicide dans l'antiquité grecque. Mémoires de l'Acad. des Sciences de Toulouse, 12e sér., 11, 1933.
Morand, P. Le suicide en littérature. RP, 1.VI.1932.
Drasenovich, E. Sommerwende im altdeutschen und christlichen Glauben und Brauch des deutschen Volkes, in Dichtung, Lied und Tanz, in Rede und Spruch. (**SUMMER**). Graz, 1923.
Golde, K. Der Sonnenmythos im Nibelungenliede und in der Ilias. (**SUN**). Nordische Welt, 4, 1937.
Thorond, F. Anschauung und Darstellung der Sonne in Goethes Werken. Diss. Kiel, 1922.
Pasig, P. Der Sonntag im Spiegel deutscher Dichtung. (**SUNDAY**), Leipziger Zt. Beilage 66, 1903.
SUPERMEN. See also Heroes, Princes, Titans, Tyrants.
Berg, L. Der Uebermensch in der modernen Literatur. Leipzig, 1897.
—— Der Uebermensch im Drama. D. Tag, 604, 1903.
Borak, J. Der Uebermensch bei Byron, Slowacki, Ibsen und Nietzsche. Xenien (Leipzig), Oct., 1912.
Caffi, E. L'evoluzione del superuomo nella letteratura moderna. RI, Sept., 1905.
Dünnebier, H. Der Uebermensch bei Gottfried Keller und Friedrich Hebbel. Wissen & Leben, 7, 1914.
Fischmann, H. Der Uebermensch. LE, 20, 1918.
Sarolea, C. The Religion of the Blood. (Nordic Superman). Contemp. Rev., Oct., 1935.
Sirey de Villers. La faillite du surhomme et la psychologie de Nietzsche. Paris, 1920.
Walcutt, C. C. Naturalism and the Superman in the Novels of Jack London. Papers of the Michigan Academy, 24, 1939.
Baumgartner, W. **SUSANNA.** Die Geschichte einer Legende. Archiv. f. Religionswissenschaft, 1926.
Coffey, Sister Loyola M. Adrien Jourdan's Susanna (1653), a Critical Edition of the Latin Text with a Study of the Play and Its Influence. Baltimore, 1942.
Heller, B. Die Susannaerzählung: ein Märchen. Zs. f.d. alttestamentliche Wissenschaft, 1936.
Lévy, I. L'histoire de Suzanne et des deux vieillards dans la littérature juive. Rev. des Etudes juives, 96, 1934.
Pilger, R. Dramatisierungen der Susanna. ZDPh, 11, 1879.
Weilen, A. von. Ein neues Susannadrama. LE, 1900.
Hartmann, J. Geschichte Schwabens im Munde der Dichter. (**SWABIA**). Stuttgart, 1881.
Irw, B. Die literarische Gestaltung der Volkssage von den sieben Schwaben. Germania, 28.
Krauss, R. Schwäbische Literaturgeschichte. Freiburg, 1897.
Radlkofer, M. Die sieben Schwaben und ihr hervorragendster Historiograph, L. Auerbacher. Hamburg, 1895.
Landolf, G. Von den Anfängen der Eidgenossenschaft in Geschichte und Dichtung. (**SWITZERLAND**). Schweiz. Volkshochschule, 4, 1926.
SYNAESTHESIA: See Literary Criticism, I. VII. 2.

——T——

Rosières, R. Une historiette de **TALLEMAND** des réaux, annotée par un folkloriste. Paris, 1894.
Degenhart. **TAMERLAN** in den Literaturen des westlichen Europas. Archiv, 123, 1909.
Intze, O. Tamerlan und Bajazet in den Literaturen des Abendlandes. Diss. Erlangen, 1912.

Barto, P. S. **TANNHAEUSER** and the Mountain of Venus. New York, 1916.
Brissaud. La légende de Tannhäuser. Mémoires de l'Acad. de Toulouse, 9e sér., 5, 1893.
Elster, E. Tannhäuser in Geschichte, Sage und Dichtung. Bromberg, 1908.
Golther, W. Tannhäuser. Bayreuther Blätter, 1889.
—— Die französische und die deutsche Tannhäuser-Dichtung. Die Musik, 2, 1903.
—— Tannhäuser in Sage und Dichtung des Mittelalters und der neueren Zeit. Walhalla, 3, 1906.
Graesse, J. G. T. Der Tannhäuser und der Ewige Jude. Zwei deutsche Sagen. 2e ed. Dresden, 1861.
Junk, V. Tannhäuser in Sage und Dichtung. München, 1911.
Koegel, Dora. Auswertung der Tannhäusersage in der deutschen Literatur des 19. und 20. Jahrhunderts. Diss. München, 1922.
Krappe, A. H. La légende du Tannhäuser. MF, 1.VI.1938.
Paris, G. La légende du Tannhäuser. RP, 15.III.1898. And in: Légendes du moyen âge Paris, 1903.
Remy, A. F. J. The Origin of the Tannhäuser-Legend. JEGPh, 12, 1912.
Schmidt, E. Tannhäuser in Sage und Dichtung. Nord & Süd, 1892. Cf. his Charakteristiken. Berlin, 1901.
Simpson, C. M. Wagner and the Tannhäuser Tradition. PMLA, 63, 1948.
Söderhjelm, W. Antoine de la Sale et la légende de Tannhäuser. Mém. de la Société néo-phil. à Helsingfors, 1897.
Emard, P. **TARTUFFE**, sa vie, son milieu et la comédie de Molière. Paris, 1932.
Walsh, J. M. **TEA**: its History and Mystery. Philadelphia, 1892.
Justesen, P. T. **TELEMACH** und Hamlet. WBFA, 6, 1929.
Anon. Wilhelm **TELL** von Sabatier. Grenzbote, 10, 1851.
Glaser, E. Die Tellsage und Schillers Tell. Der prakt. Schulmann, 48, 1899.
Hallberg. Guillaume Tell au théâtre. Mém. de l'Académie de Toulouse, 9e sér., 6, 1894.
Heinemann, F. Tell-Ikonographie, mit Berücksichtigung der Tell-Poesie. Leipzig, 1902.
Kittner, G. Wilhelm Tell. Berlin, 1909.
Merz, E. Tell im Drama vor und nach Schiller. Diss. Basel. Bern, 1925.
Meszleny, R. Tell-Probleme. Berlin, 1910.
Moore, W. G. Horace et Wilhelm Tell. RLC, 19, 1939.
Moraviu, V. Horia, tragedie de Ghita Popp si W. Tell de Schiller. Codrul Cosminuliu, 9, 1935.
Nover, J. Wilhelm Tell in Poesie und Wirklichkeit. Virchow - Holtzendorff Vorträge, N.F., 2. Hamburg, 1887.
Petsch, R. Wilhelm Tell und Julius Caesar. Festschrift Ludwig Geiger. Berlin, 1918.
Rochholtz, E. L. Tell und Gessler in Sage und Geschichte. Heilbronn, 1877.
Roethe, G. Die dramatischen Quellen des Schillerschen Tell. FDPh, 1894.
Schirmer, G. Ueber James Sheridan Knowles William Tell. Anglia, 12, 1889.
Tardel, H. Die **TESTAMENTS**idee als dichterisches Formmotiv. Niederdeutsche Zs. f. Volkskunde, 4-5, 1926-27.
Kruuse, J. La légende de **THAIS**. In: Digter og Traditioner. København, 1939.
Wietzorek, Margareta. Die Legenden der Thais und der Maria Aegyptiaca in den romanischen Literaturen vornehmlich des Mittelalters. Münster, 1939.
THEATRE: See Professions, I. VI. 11., and Genres, I. VII. 2.
Koeppel, E. Lydgate's Story of **THEBES**: eine Quellenuntersuchung. Diss. München, 1884. Cf. Litteraturblatt f. german. und roman. Philologie, 6.
Otto, G. Der Einfluss des Roman de Thèbes auf die altfranzösische Litteratur. Coburg, 1909.
Rodeffer. Chaucer and the Roman de Thèbes. MLN, 17, 1902.
Billicsich, F. Das Problem der **THEODIZEE** im philosophischen Denken des Abendlandes, I: Von Platon bis Thomas von Aquino. Innsbruck, 1936.
Heuser, W. Eine neue mittelenglische Version der **THEOPHILUS**-Sage. ESn, 32, 1903.
Kölbing, E. Englische Fassungen der Theophilussage. In: Beiträge zur vergleichenden Geschichte der romantischen Poesie und Prosa des Mittelalters. Breslau, 1876.
Ludorff, F. William Forrest's Theophiluslegende. Anglia, 7, 1884.
Plenzat, K. Die Theophiluslegende in den Dichtungen des Mittelalters. Berlin, 1926.
Sommer, A. De Theophili cum Diabolo foedere. Berlin, 1848.
Agard, W. R. **THESEUS** as a National Hero. Arch. Inst. Amer. Cincinnati, 1927.
Dugas, C. L'évolution de la légende de Thésée. REG, 1943.

Wolgensinger, F. H. Theseus. Affoltern, 1935.

Brookes, E. H. Legends of St. **THOMAS** in South India. Calcutta Review, 115, 1902.

Monaci, E. La leggenda di Santo Tomaso. Rend. dell'Acc. d. Lincei, ser., 5, 12, 1894.

Brown, P. A. The Development of the Legend of **THOMAS BECKET**. Philadelphia, 1930.

Jaeger, F. Thomas a Becket, in Sage und Dichtung, mit besonderer Berücksichtigung des neueren englischen Dramas. Diss. Breslau, 1909.

Walberg, E. Die älteste Lebensbeschreibung des Thomas Becket. Lund, Leipzig, 1915.

Rosenbaum, R. Die **TIROLERIN** in der deutschen Literatur des 18. Jahrhunderts. Zs. f. d. Kulturgeschichte, 5, 1898.

TITANISM: See also under Heroes, Princes, Prometheus, Superman, Tyrants.

Cerny, V. Quelques remarques sur la critique masarykienne du titanisme romantique. RLC, 14, 1934.

—— Essai sur le titanisme dans la poésie romantique occidentale entre 1815 et 1850. Prague, 1935.

Vincenti, L. Il motivo titanico nell'opera di F. Hölderlin. Atti della R. Accad. di Torino, 1944-45.

TITUS AND GISIPPUS: See Boccaccio, IV. III. 8.

Spies, J. Otway's **TITUS** and Berenice and Racine's Bérénice, a Parallel. Progr. Wetzlar, 1891.

Kopp, A. Internationale Tabakspoesie. **(TOBACCO)**. ZVL, 13, 1899.

Erismann, O. Die Tabakspfeife in der deutschen Dichtung. Bern, 1917.

Diez, Katharina. **TOBIAS**. In: Dichtungen nach dem alten Testament. Berlin, 1852.

Liljeblad, S. Die Tobiasgeschichte und andere Märchen mit toten Helfern. Lund, 1927-28.

Wick, A. Tobias in der dramatischen Litteratur Deutschlands. Diss. Heidelberg, 1899.

Abrahams, J. The **TOBIT** Drama in the 17th Century. Festschrift Hermann Cohen. Berlin, 1912.

Paris, G. Le petit poucet et la grande ourse. **(TOM THUMB)**. Paris, 1875.

Solymossi, A. L'histoire de Petite Babette (Red Riding Hood) et les aventures du Petit Poucet. Nouvelle Rev. de Hongrie, 1939.

Wagstaff, W. A Comment upon the History of Tom Thumb. In: Miscellaneous Works. London, 1726.

Ferrando, G. Amor di **TOSCANA** e scrittori inglesi dell'ottocento. Marzocco, Feb., 1931.

Herron, I. H. The Small **TOWN** in American Literature. Durham (N.C.), 1939.

Hirn, Y. Les jeux d'enfants. **(TOYS)**. Paris, 1928.

Höttges, V. Die Sage vom Riesenspielzeug. Jena, 1931.

Barbi, M. La leggenda di **TRAIANO**, nei volgarizzamenti del Breviloquium de virtutibus di Fra Giovanni Gallese. Firenze, 1895.

Krappe, A. H. Un parallèle oriental de la légende de l'empereur Trajan et du pape Grégoire le grand. Moyen Age, 36, 1926.

Paris, G. La légende de Trajan. Mélanges de l'Ecole des Hautes Etudes, 35, 1878. Cf. JS, 1884.

Feeg, A. M. Das Motiv der Verwandlung. **(TRANSFORMATION)**. Diss. Prag, 1925.

TRAVELS: See Genres and Forms, I. VII. 1.

Marmorstein, A. Das Motiv vom veruntreuten Depositum in der jüdischen Volkskunde. **(TREASURE)**. Monatsschr. f. Gesch. & Wissensch. des Judentums, 1934.

Henning, J. **TRENCK** and Britain. MLR, 41, 1946.

Pogány, I. Frédéric Trenck et la littérature française. Budapest, 1933.

TRISTAN and Isolde: See Celtic Contributions, IV. I. 5.

Crisafulli, A. S. Montesquieu's Story of the **TROGLODYTES:** Its Background, Meaning, and Significance. PMLA, 58, 1943.

TROILUS: See also Boccaccio, IV. III. 8.

Chiantera, R. Troilo e Criseida in Guido delle Colonne. Mélanges F. Torraca. Napoli, 1922.

Eitner, K. Die Troilus-Fabel in ihrer litteraturgeschichtlichen Entwickelung. JbShG, 3, 1868.

Gordon, R. R. The Story of Troilus as Told by Benoît de St. Maure, G. Boccaccio, G. Chaucer, R. Henryson. London, 1934.

Hamilton, G. L. The Indebtedness of Chaucer's Troilus and Criseyde to Guido delle Colonne. London, 1903.

Young, K. The Origin and Development of the Story of Troilus and Criseyde. London, 1908.

Zenke, H. Drydens Troilus and Cressida im Verhältnis zu den übrigen Bearbeitungen des Stoffes. Rostock, 1905.

TROY: See also Homer, Greek and Roman dramatists and Virgil.

Atwood, E. B. The Exicidium Troiae and Medieval Troy Literature. MPh, 1937.

—— Some Minor Sources of Lydgate's Troy Book. SPh, 35, 1938.

Bartsch, K. Anmerkungen zu Konrad's Trojanerkrieg. Publicat. des Lit. Vereins Stuttgart. Tübingen, 1877.

Becker, P. A. Jean Lemaire, der erste humanistische Dichter Frankreichs. (Les illustrations de Gaule et singularités de Troie.) Strassburg, 1893.

Bethe, E. Die Sage vom troischen Kriege. In: Homer, Dichtung und Sage, III. Leipzig, 1927.

Bock, W. Zur Destruction of Troy, eine Sprach- und Quellenuntersuchung. Diss. Halle, 1883.

Dippe, O. Die fränkischen Trojanersagen und ihr Einfluss auf die Geschichtsschreibung im Mittelalter. Progr. Leipzig, 1896.

Dollfus, L. La légende troyenne à travers le moyen âge espagnol. In: Etudes sur le moyen âge espagnol. Paris, 1894.

Dunger, H. Die Sage vom trojanischen Kriege in den Bearbeitungen des Mittelalters und ihren antiken Quellen. Progr. Dresden. Leipzig, 1869.

Eichinger, K. Die Trojasage als Stoffquelle für John Gowers Confessio Amantis. Diss. München, 1900.

Fischer, C. Der altfranzösische Roman de Troie des Benoît de Saint-More als Vorbild für die mittelhochdeutschen Trojadichtungen des Herbart von Fritzlar und des Konrad von Würzburg. Diss. Marburg, 1883..

Gorra, E. Testi inediti di storia trojana. (Cf. Introduction.) Torino, 1887. Cf. Romania, 20.

Granz, E. T. Ueber die Quellengemeinschaft des mittelenglischen Gedichtes Seege od Batayle of Troye und des Gedichtes vom Trojanischen Kriege des Konrad von Würzburg. Leipzig, 1888.

Greif, M. Die mittelalterlichen Bearbeitungen der Trojanersage. Marburg, 1886.

Griffin, N. E. Dares and Dictys, An Introduction to the Study of Medieval Versions of the Story of Troy. Baltimore, 1907.

Hamilton, G. L. Gower's Use of the Enlarged Roman de Troie. PMLA, 20, 1905.

Heeger, G. Die Trojanersage der Britten. Diss. München, 1887. Cf. Romania, 15.

—— Ueber die Trojanersagen der Franken und Normannen. Progr. Landau, 1890.

Hiebel, F. Troja im Bewusstsein gegenwärtiger Dichtung. Das Goetheanum, 8. 1929.

Jaeckel. K. Dares Phrygius und Benoît de Sainte-More. Diss. Breslau, 1875.

Joly, A. Benoît de Sainte More et le Roman de Troie, ou les métamorphoses d' Homère et de l'épopée gréco-latine au moyen âge. 2 vols. Paris, 1870-71.

Joseph E. Darès de Phrygie considéré comme source de l'épisode de Briseis dans le Roman de Troie de Benoît de Sainte-More. ZRPh, 8. 1884.

Kempe, D. A Middle English Tale of Troy. ESn, 29, 1901.

Koerting, G. Dictys und Dares. Beiträge zur Geschichte der Troja-Sage in ihrem Uebergange aus der antiken in die romantische Form. Halle, 1874.

Luethgen, E. Die Quellen und der historische Werth der fränkischen Trojasage. Diss. Bonn, 1875.

Mazon, A. La dernière transformation de la légende de Troie chez les Slaves du Sud au XVe siècle. C. R. de l'Acad. des Inscriptions et Belles-Lettres. 1942.

McKenzie, K. & Silber, G. R. Troia and Ilion in Virgil and Dante. SM, 5, 1932.

Morf, H. Notes pour servir à l'histoire de la légende de Troie en Italie. Romania, 23-24, 1892.

Mussafia, A. Ueber die spanischen Versionen der Historia Trojana. SAWW, 1871.

Oliver, T. E. Jacques Milet's Drama, La destruction de Troie la grant; Its Principal Source, Its Dramatic Structure. Heidelberg, 1899.

Parsons, A. E. The Trojan Legend in England. MLR, 1929.

Perret, J. Les origines de la légende troyenne de Rome. Paris, 1942.

Rey, A. & Solalinde, A. G. Ensayo de una bibliografía de las leyendas troyanas en la literatura española. Bloomington, 1942.

Roth, K. L. Die Trojasage der Franken. Germania, 1, 1856.

Schuhl, P. M. Le cheval de Troie. Revue archéologique, 7, 1936.

Witte, R. Der Einfluss von Benoîts Roman de Troie auf die altfranzösische Literatur. Göttingen, 1904.

Zarncke, F. Ueber die Trojanersage der

Franken. Sächs. Akad. d. Wissenschaften, 1866.
Zietsch, A. Ueber Quelle und Sprache des mittelenglischen Gedichtes Seege od Batayle of Troye. Diss. Göttingen, 1883.
Fassnacht, M. Die drei Wahrheiten in der Volksdichtung. (**TRUTH**). Bühl, 1937.
Krappe, A. H. La leggenda della bocca della verità. NSM, 2, 1925-26.
Hill, L. A. The **TUDORS** in French Drama. Baltimore, 1932.
Bernardis, L. M. de. La leggenda di **TURANDOT**. Genova, 1932. Cf. RLC, 1933.
Francia, L. de. La leggenda di Turandot nella novellistica e nel teatro. Trieste, 1932.
Armstrong, W. A. The Elizabethan Conception of the **TYRANT**. RES, 22, 1946.
Deratani, N. La figure du tyran dans le Prométhée Enchaîné d'Eschyle. C. R. de l'Acad. des Sciences de Russie, 1929.
Heintzeler, G. Das Bild des Tyrannen bei Platon. Stuttgart, 1928.
Schoenstedt, F. Der Tyrannenmord im Spätmittelalter. Berlin, 1938.
Walsen, E. Die Gestalt des tragischen und des komischen Tyrannen in Mittelalter und Renaissance. Festschrift W. Götz, Leipzig, 1927.

—U—

UGOLINO: See Dante, IV. III. 9.
Borschak, E. L'**UKRAINE** dans la littérature de l'Europe occidentale. Le Monde slave, Aug., 1934 and Paris, 1936.
Yakobson, S. & Whitfield, F. J. Selected List of Books on the Ukraine Published in English, French, German and Italian. Library of Congress, Washington, D. C., 1942.
Hirsch, A. Die deutschen Prosabearbeitungen der Legende vom heiligen **ULRICH**. München, 1915.
ULYSSES: See also Homer, II. III. 11.
Bertoni, G. Ulisse nella Divina Commedia e nei poeti moderni. Atti dell'Accad. degli Arcadi, 5-6, 1930.
Cappon, J. The Legend of Ulysses in Dante and Tennyson. Queen's Quarterly, 1894.
Cesareo, P. L'evoluzione storica del carattere d'Ulisse. Messina, 1899.
Cook, A. S. The Literary Genealogy of Tennyson's Ulysses. PL, 1891.
Cressman, E. D. Beyond the Sunset. (Ulysses in Dante & Tennyson). CJ, 27, 1932.
Fraser, A. D. A Scottish Version of the Odysseus-Polyphemus Myth. CW, 25, 1932.
Garassino, A. Ulisse nel teatro greco. A&R, 11, 1930.
Gaude, P. Das Odysseusthema in der neueren deutschen Literatur. Diss. Greifswald. Halle, 1916.
Gettmann, R. A. Tennyson's Ulysses. Explicator, 1, 1943.
Gilde, J. A. A. Die dramatische Behandlung der Rückkehr des Odysseus bei N. Rowe, R. Bridges und St. Philips. Diss. Königsberg, 1903.
Glaser, O. Der deutsche Ulixes. Ein Beitrag zur deutschen Heldensage. Wörter & Sachen, 14, 1932.
Hibbard, Esther L. The Ulysses Motif in Japanese Literature. JAFL, 59, 1946.
Jax, K. Odysseemotive in der Sage des Nordens. BBG, 65, 1929.
—— Ein Odysseemotiv im Volksmärchen der österreichischen Alpenländer. WBFA, 7, 1930.
Loiseau, A. La légende d'Ulysse dans la littérature portugaise. Revue de la Société des études historiques, 4e sér., 3, 1885.
Pisanti, G. Ulisse nella poesia di Tennyson e in quella di Pascoli. Giuseppe Vesuviano, 1937.
Tolstoi, J. Einige Märchenparallelen zur Heimkehr des Odysseus. Ph, 1934.
Tosi, G. Gabriele d'Annunzio et la rencontre d'Ulysse. Revue des Sciences humaines, N. S., 45, 1947.
Toynbee, P. Uno studio sull'Ulisse di Joyce. Letteratura, 1947.
Dauner, L. Myth and Humor in the **UNCLE REMUS** Fables. AL, 20, 1948.
Bidou, H. **UNDINE** (La Motte-Fouqué), Hoffmann et Giraudoux. Le Temps, 20.V.1939.
Pfeiffer, W. Ueber Fouqués Undine. Heidelberg, 1903.
Bunt, C. G. E. The Lion and the **UNICORN**. Antiquity, 4, 1930.
Cohn, C. Zur litterarischen Geschichte des Einhorns. Progr. Berlin, 1897.
Godbey, A. H. The Unicorn in the Old Testament. American Journal of Semitic Lang. and Lit., 56, 1939.
Shepard, O. The Lore of the Unicorn. Boston, 1930.
Brühl, H. J. Die heilige **URSULA** in Geschichte, Legende und Dichtung. Hamm, 1906.
Lincoln, J. N. Saint Ursula, the Infanta

Isabel, and Lope de Vega. Ann Arbor, 1947.
UTOPIAS: See I. II. 4.

—V—

Bolte, J. Fahrende Leute in der Literatur des 15. und 16. Jahrhunderts. (**VAGABOND**). SAWB, 1928.
Compton-Rickett, A. The Vagabond in Literature. London, 1906.
Gäfgen, H. Der Landstreicher in der Dichtung. Hallesche Zt., 15, 1923.
Kurz-Elsheim, F. Das fahrende Volk in der Lyrik. Artist, 1076, 1905.
Lehmann, P. Beiträge zur Vagantenpoesie. NPh, 9.
Löpelmann, M. Himmel und Hölle der Fahrenden. Dichtungen der grossen Vaganten aller Zeiten und Länder. Berlin, 1940.
Moll, W. H. Ueber den Einfluss der lateinischen Vagantendichtung auf die Lyrik Walters von der Vogelweide und die seiner Epigonen im 13. Jahrhundert. Amsterdam, 1925.
Poritzky, J. E. Vagabundenromane. Berliner Börsen Courier, 195, 1908.
Süssmilch, H. Die lateinische Vagranten-Poesie der 12. und 13. Jahrhunderte als Kulturerscheinung. Leipzig, 1917.
Dickson, A. **VALENTINE** and Orson. A Study in Late Medieval Romance. New York, 1929.
Donahue, C. The **VALKYRIES** and the Irish War-Goddesses. PMLA, 56, 1941.
Clapp, E. R. La Belle Dame as **VAMPIRE**. PhQ, 27, 1948.
Fellows, A. The Vampire Legend. Occult Review, 1.IX.1908.
Hock, S. Die Vampyrsagen und ihre Verwertung in der deutschen Litteratur. Berlin, 1900.
Jellinek, A. Zur Vampyrsage. Zs. d. Vereins f. Volkskunde, 14, 1904.
Murgoci, A. The Vampire in Roumania. FL, 31.XII.1926.
Nethercot, A. H. The Road to Tryermaine; a Study of Coleridge's Christabel. Cambridge U.P., 1939.
Wiedemann, A. Vampyrvorstellungen. Sphinx, 18, 1914.
Mroz, Sister Mary. Divine **VENGEANCE:** A Study in the Philosophical Backgrounds of the Revenge Motif as it Appears in Shakespeare's Chronicle History Plays. Washington, D. C., 1941.
Avrett, E. A Brief Examination into the Historical Background of Martinez de la Rosa's La conjuración de **VENEZIA**. RR, 1930.
Cattan, L. La Venise de Byron et la Venise des romantiques français. RLC, 5, 1925.
Chiarini, G. Le due leggende del Mercante di Venezia. NAnt, 1.IV.1892.
Dollot, R. Stendhal à Venise. RLC, 7, 1927.
Fedelini, E. Il Veneto nell-opera di Gabriel Faure. NAnt, 1.XII.1927.
Fink, Z. S. Venice and English Political Thought in the Seventeenth Century. MPh, 38, 1940.
Gianturco, E. Bodin's Conception of the Venetian Constitution and His Critical Rift with Fabio Albergati. RLC, 18, 1938.
Hutton, L. Literary Landmarks of Venice. New York, 1896.
Isopescu, C. Venezia, Napoli e Roma nella poesia romena. Osservatore romano, 3.IX.1948.
Johnson, A. Etude sur la littérature comparée de la France et de l'Angleterre à la fin du XVIIe siècle: Lafosse, Otway, Saint-Réal. (Venice Preserved). Diss. Paris, 1902.
Medin, A. La storia della Republica di Venezia nella poesia. Milano, 1904.
Melia, J. Stendhal et Venise de 1801 à 1839. MF, 15.IX.1935.
Molmenti, P. G. Venezia nell'arte e nella letteratura francese. Archivio Veneto, 37, 1889.
Nolhac, P. de. Venise au temps d'Alfred de Musset. Correspondant, 25.V.1929.
Perkinson, R. H. Volpone and the Reputation of Venetian Justice. MLR, 35, 1940.
Perret, P. Histoire des relations de la France avec Venise du XIIe siècle à l'avènement de Charles VIII. Paris, 1896.
Pompeati, A. Venezia nelle pagine di H. de Régnier. Marzocco, 14.VI.1928.
Rava, B. Venise dans la littérature française depuis les origines jusqu'à la mort de Henri IV. Paris, 1916.
Riva, S. Otway, Saint-Réal e la Venezia Salvata. Dante, 1935.
Seuffert, T. von. Venedig im Erlebnis deutscher Dichter. Köln, 1937.
Thomas, W. Venise et son prestige dans la littérature d'Outre-Manche. Revue de l'U. de Lyon, 1928.
Winther, F. Venice Preserved: Otway, La Fosse and Hofmannsthal. TAPhA, 40, 1909.
Huet, G. La légende de la statue de

VENUS. Rev. de l'hist. des religions, 68, 1913.

La Borderie, A. de. La légende originale de la Venus d'Ille. Arch. historiques, 1, 1889.

Kühne, W. Venus, Amor und Bacchus in Shakespeares Dramen. Braunschweig, 1902.

Palme, J. Die deutschen **VERONIKA**-legenden des XII. Jahrhunderts; ihr Verhältnis untereinander und zu den Quellen. Progr. Prag, 1892.

Oravetz, V. Les impressions françaises de **VIENNE**. Szeged, 1930.

Strobl, K. H. Wien im Roman, LE, 10, 1908.

Werner, A. & Arne, P. Gay Vienna—an Autopsy. BA, 15, 1941.

Brown, Elsie K. Pancho **VILLA** en la novela mexicana. Diss. U. of Mexico, 1943.

Fogelquist, D. F. The Figure of Pancho Villa in the Literature of the Mexican Revolution. Diss. U. of Wisconsin, 1941.

—— The Figure of Pancho Villa in the Corridos of the Mexican Revolution. U. of Miami Hispanic-American Studies. Coral Gables (Fla.), 1942.

VILLAGE: See also Heimat-novels, I. VII. 2.

Patton, J. The English Village, a Literary Study, 1750-1850. London, 1918.

Koch, K. **VINETA** in Poesie und Prosa. Stettin, 1905.

Pudor, H. Vineta in der Dichtung. Unser Pommerland, 11, 1927.

Roettenbacher, L. Die französischen **VIRGINIA**-Dramen mit Einschluss derjenigen des Montiano, Alfieri und von Ayrenhoff. Diss. München, 1909.

Rumbauer, O. Die Geschichte von Appius und Virginia in der englischen Litteratur. Diss. Breslau, 1890.

Whitfield, J. H. The Doctrine of **VIRTU**. Italian Studies, 3, 1946.

Vitale, V. Barnabò **VISCONTI** nella novella e nella cronaca contemporanea. Archivio storico Lombardo, 28, 1901.

Ciechanowska, Z. Le drame **VISIONNAIRE**. Helicon, 2, 1940.

Fritzsche, C. Die lateinischen Visionen des Mittelalters bis zur Mitte des 12. Jahrhunderts. Halle, 1885. And RF, 2-3, 1886-87.

Knight, G. W. The Starlit Dome: Studies in the Poetry of Vision. London, 1941.

Raveggi, P. I poeti della visione celeste, Dante, Milton, Klopstock. In: L'idealità spirituale in Dante. Firenze, 1903.

Voigt, M. Beiträge zur Geschichte der Visionenliteratur im Mittelalter. 2 vols. Leipzig, 1924.

Meyer, R. M. **VITALIS** und seine Genossen. In: Gestalten und Probleme. Berlin, 1904.

Landau, M. **VITTORIA ACCORAMBONA** in der Dichtung im Verhältnis zu ihrer wahren Geschichte Euph. 9, 1902.

Pellegrini, L. L'abdicazione di **VITTORIO AMEDEO** II in un dramma di Roberto Browning. Ateneo Veneto, 125, 1939.

Arnavon, J. **VOLPONE**: de Ben Jonson (1605) à Jules Romains (1928). FGB, 1929.

—W—

Brown, W. N. The Silent **WAGER** Stories, Their Origin and Their Diffusion. AJPh, 1922.

Haak, E. L. Achim von Arnims **WALDEMAR**dramen. Diss. Greifswald, 1927.

Ragatz, J. Die dramatischen Bearbeitungen der Geschichte H. **WALDMANNS**. Chur, 1898.

Becher, G. Schillers **WALLENSTEIN** in wahrer Gestalt als Lösung des Wallenstein-Rätsels. München, 1940.

Gallas, K. R. La place du Wallenstein de B. Constant (1809) dans l'évolution de la tragédie française. NPh, 1928.

Harzen-Mueller, A. N. Wallenstein Dramen und Aufführungen vor Schiller. Jahresberichte für neuere deutsche Litteraturgeschichte, 11, 1903.

Hoenig, B. Die Gestalt Wallensteins in der Volksmythe und auf der Bühne. D. Arbeit, 1903.

John, A. Wallenstein im Roman. Unser Egerland, 18, 1915.

Kohlrausch, R. Wallensteins Tod in Geschichte und Dichtung. Bühne & Welt, 7, 1905.

—— Die älteste Wallensteintragödie. Frankfurter Zt, 183, 1912.

Krejci, J. Waldstein im deutschen Drama und Roman. Cesky Casopis Historicky, 1899.

Meyer, E. Benjamin Constants Wallenstein. Progr. Weimar, 1898.

Rippl, E. Wallenstein in der tschechischen Literatur. GS, 2, 1932-33.

Schmid, G. Die Wallenstein-Literatur. 1626-1878-1895-1900, mit Ergänzungen. Prag, 1884-1902.

Schweizer, P. Die Wallensteinfrage in der Geschichte und im Drama. Zürich, 1900.

Sommer, Charlotte. Die dichterische

Gestaltung des Wallensteinstoffes. Diss. Breslau, 1903.

Valtolina, F. Carmagnola e Wallenstein (Per l'inaugurazione del Monumento ad Aless. Manzoni). Milano, 1883.

Veit, V. Wallenstein After Three Centuries. SR, 1935.

Vetter, T. Wallenstein in der dramatischen Dichtung des Jahrzehntes seines Todes. Frauenfeld, 1894.

Widmann, W. Wallenstein in der dramatischen Dichtung. Bühne, 6, 1914.

Warnatsch, O. Die Sage vom **WANDERER** und den Saligen in ihrer literarischen Gestaltung. Festschrift des germanist. Vereins Breslau. Leipzig, 1902.

Anon. Der ewige Jude und der Teufel in der jüngsten deutschen Poesie. (**WANDERING JEW**). Grenzboten, 3, 1895.

Ancona, A. d'. La leggenda dell'ebreo errante. NAnt, 1.X.1880.

Anderson, G. K. The Wandering Jew Returns to England. JEGPh, 45, 1946.

—— The History of Israel Jobson. PhQ, 25, 1946.

—— Popular Survivals of the Wandering Jew in England. JEGPh, 46, 1947.

—— The Neo-Classical Chronicle of the Wandering Jew. PMLA, 63, 1948.

Baer, G. Edgar Quinets Ahasvérus und seine Beziehungen zu Herders Geschichtsphilosophie. Diss. Rostock, 1917.

Bergsträsser, L. Die Entstehung von Eugène Sues Juif errant. Archiv, 179.

Boudout, J. Faust et Ahasvérus. RLC, 16, 1936.

Cassel, P. Ahasverus. Die Sage vom ewigen Juden. Berlin, 1885.

Champfleury. La légende gothique du Juif Errant. Revue germanique et française, 1.VIII.1864.

Collin de Plancy, J. de. La légende du Juif Errant. Paris, 1847.

Conway, M. D. The Wandering Jew. London, 1881.

Eschelbach, H. Ueber die poetischen Bearbeitungen der Sage vom Ewigen Juden. Baden-Baden, 1896.

Fuerst, R. Ahasver-Dichtungen. LE, 1-15.VIII.1904.

Gessler, J. Ahasveriana. Leuvensche Bijdragen, 28.

Gielen, J. J. De wandelende Jood in volkskunde en letterkunde. Amsterdam, 1931. Cf. NPh, 17, 1931.

Gillet, J. E. Traces of the Wandering Jew in Spain. RR, 22, 1931.

Glaesener, H. Le type d'Ahasvérus aux XVIIIe et XIXe siècles. RLC, 11, 1931.

Glasheen, Adaline E. & Francis J. The Publication of the Wandering Jew. MLR, 33, 1943.

Graesse, J. G. T. Die Sage vom Ewigen Juden. Dresden, 1844.

Hartwich, M. Faust, Don Juan und Ahasver. Der getreue Eckart, Dec., 1930.

Hauff, G. Die Sage vom Ewigen Juden und ihre dichterische Behandlung. Deutsches Museum, 1867.

Helbig, F. Die Sage vom Ewigen Juden, ihre poetische Wandlung und Fortbildung. Berlin, 1874.

—— Der ewige Jude und der Teufel in der jüngsten Poesie. Grenzboten, 1895.

Heller, O. Ahasver in der Kunstdichtung. MPh, 3, 1905.

Van't Hooft, B. H. Der Ewige Jude bei Goethe und A. Vermeylen. NPh, 18, 1933.

Jacobs, W. Die Sage vom Ewigen Juden. Kieler Zt., 82, 87, 1903.

Kappstein, T. Ahasver in der Weltlitteratur. Berliner Tageblatt, 183, 1903.

—— Ahasver in der Weltpoesie. Mit einem Anhang: Die Gestalt Jesu in der modernen Dichtung. Berlin, 1906.

Killen, A. M. L'évolution de la Légende du Juif errant. RLC, 5, 1925.

Koenig, E. Ahasver der Ewige Jude, nach seiner ursprünglichen Idee und seiner literarischen Verwertung betrachtet. Gütersloh, 1907.

Koost, J. Die Sage vom ewigen Juden in der neueren Literatur. Leipzig, 1905.

Krappe, A. H. Sur l'origine de la légende du Juif errant. NPh, 20, 1935.

Magnin, C. Ahasvérus, et de la nature du génie poétique. RDM, 1.XII.1833.

Minor, J. Goethes Fragmente vom ewigen Juden. Stuttgart, 1904.

Morpurgo, S. L'ebreo errante in Italia. Firenze, 1890. Cf. JS, Nov., 1891.

Neubaur, L. Die Sage vom Ewigen Juden. Leipzig, 1884. 2nd ed., 1893.

—— Zur Bibliographie der Sage vom Ewigen Juden. Centralblatt f. Bibliothekswesen, 28, 1911.

Nover, J. Deutsche Sagen in ihrer Entstehung. I : Der ewige Jude. Giessen, 1895.

Paris, G. Le Juif errant. Encyclopédie des sciences religieuses. Paris, 1880.

Pfungst, A. Neuere Dichtungen vom ewigen Juden. Neue literar. Blätter, 3.

Prost, J. Die Sage vom Ewigen Juden in der neueren deutschen Literatur. Leipzig, 1904.

Renier, R. Contributo alla storia dell'Ebreo errante in Italia. GSLI, 3, 1884.
Ruhemann, A. Die Sage vom ewigen Juden in Italien. Nord & Süd, 1896.
Schoebel, C. La légende du Juif errant. Paris, 1877.
Scholz, W. von. Der Meister von Palmyra und Ahasver. In: Gedanken zum Drama. München, 1905.
Soergel, A. Ahasver-Dichtungen seit Goethe. Leipzig, 1905.
Suchomel. Die Sage vom ewigen Juden. Progr. Prag, 1881-83.
Thümmel, C. Mittelalterliche Volkssagen als Ausdruck religiös-politischer Kämpfe. Hamburg, 1898.
Wesselofsky. Der ewige Jude. ASPh, 5.
Zirus, W. Der ewige Jude in der Dichtung, vornehmlich in der englischen und deutschen. Palaestra, 162. Leipzig, 1928.
—— Ahasverus, der ewige Jude. Berlin, 1930.
Anon. Die Perserkriege in der griechischen Kunst und Dichtung. (**WAR AND PEACE**). Eos, 1, 1864.
Alexandrova, V. A. The Soviet Writer in War. (In Russian). Novosele, June, 1942.
Arnold, F. Die Dichter der Befreiungskriege. Prenzlau, 1908.
Bab, J. Die deutsche Kriegslyrik, Stettin, 1920.
Baldi, A. Das deutsch-patriotische nationale Lied und seine Bedeutung (1813-70). Bamberg, 1871.
Beers, H. A. Literature and the Civil War. AM, Dec., 1901.
Beller, E. A. Propaganda in Germany during the Thirty Years War. Princeton, 1940.
Biese, A. Die Poesie des Krieges und der Krieg in der Poesie. Konservat. Monatsschrift, 72, 1914.
Bostock, J. K. Some Well-Known German War Novels, 1914-30. Oxford, 1931.
Bulloch, J. M. British Prisoners of War in France, 1803-13. N&Q, 5, 11.II.1938.
Carantonis, A. La guerre dans la littérature grecque. L'Hellénisme contemporain, Jan., 1947.
Cysarz, H. Zur Geistesgeschichte des Weltkrieges. Halle, 1931.
Deschamps, G. La guerre de 1870 et la littérature. In: La Vie et les Livres. Paris, 1894.
De Vries, P. Poetry and the War. College English, 5, 1943.
Dykes, Eva B. The Poetry of the Civil War. Negro Hist. Bull., 7, 1944.
Fritsche, E. G. O. Die französische Kriegslyrik des Jahres 1870 in ihrem Verhältniss zur gleichzeitigen deutschen. Progr. Zwickau, 1899.
Glicksberg, C. I. Poetry and the Second World War. SAQ, 44, 1945.
Greiner, A. La poésie allemande de la grande guerre. Yggdrasil, 4, 1939.
Grimmrath, H. Der Weltkrieg im französischen Roman. Berlin, 1935.
Gunther, M. Der englische Kriegsroman und das englische Kriegsdrama, 1919-30. Berlin, 1936.
Hardt, E. Französische Kriegslyrik. NR, Feb., 1939.
Herrig, H. Die französische Kriegs- und Revanchedichtung. MLIA, 1877.
Hertford, C. H. The Post-War Mind of Germany. Oxford, 1927.
Hochdorf, M. Die Dichtung vom Kriege. Sozialist. Monatshefte, 21, 1915.
Huyssen, G. Die Poesie des Krieges und die Kriegspoesie. Berlin, 1883.
—— War and Poetry. ER, 196, 1902.
Iswolsky, Helen. War and Soviet Literature. Commonweal, 37, 1942.
Janicke, K. Das deutsche Kriegslied. Berlin, 1871.
Kalkschmidt, T. Weltkrieg und Literaturwissenschaft. Zs. f. Aesthetik & allg. Kunstwissenschaft, 33, 1939.
Kindermann, H. Die Weltkriegsdichtung der Deutschen im Ausland. Berlin, 1940.
Klancar, A. J. The Balkan Wars and Serbian Literature. BA, 14, 1940.
Koberstein, K. Die deutsche Dichtung und die Befreiungskriege. WM, July, 1887.
Koch, Vivienne. Poetry in World War II. Briarcliff Quar., 3, 1946.
Koschwitz, E. Die französische Novellistik und Romanlitteratur über den Krieg 1870-71. Berlin, 1893.
Krebs, R. Der Bauernkrieg in der neueren Literatur. Welt, 13, 1911.
Laughbaum, A. B. Some English Novels that Deal with the Crimean War. Diss. U. of Illinois, 1948.
Lutz, G. Europas Kriegserlebnis: ein Ueberblick über das ausserdeutsche Kriegsschrifttum. D&V, 39, 1938.
Matuszewski, R. Polish Literature and the War. Poland of Today, 2, 1947.
Müller, O. Kriegslyrik und Volksseele bei uns und anderen Völkern. NSp, 46.
—— Vergleichende Durchnahme eines englischen und deutschen Kriegsgedichtes. NSp, 47.
Muret, M. La littérature allemande pendant la guerre. Paris, 1920.

Neumann, R. Die Kriegsdichtung von 1870-71. Diss. München, 1911.
Northrup, C. S. War and Literature. Sewanee Rev., July, 1917.
Oppeln-Bronikowski, F. von. Krieg und Kriegslieder (1500-1900). Voss. Zt. Beilage, 15-16, 1911.
Panchaud. La poésie patriotique à Lyon pendant la guerre. Valence, 1873.
Peacock, R. The Great War in German Lyrical Poetry, 1914-18. Leeds Philosophical Society Proc., 3, 1934.
Pfeiler, W. K. War and the German Mind; the Testimony of Men of Fiction Who Fought at the Front. New York, 1941.
Plessow, G. L. Das amerikanische Kriegsschauspiel zwischen 1910 und 1930. Halle, 1933.
Pongs, H. Krieg als Volksschicksal im deutschen Schrifttum. Stuttgart, 1934.
Reed, H. Poesia inglese in tempo di guerra. Poesia, 1947.
Scherrer, M. Kampf und Krieg im deutschen Drama von Gottsched bis Kleist. Zürich, 1919.
Schlachter, F. Spottlieder in französischer Sprache, besonders auf die Franzosen im Beginne des 7 jährigen Krieges. Diss. Erlangen, 1901.
Schlueter. Die französische Kriegs- und Revanchedichtung. Heilbronn, 1878.
Schultze-Jahde, K. Dreissigjähriger Krieg und deutsche Dichtung. Histor. Zs, 143, 1931.
Smith, Rebecca W. The Civil War and Its Aftermath in American Fiction. Diss. U. of Chicago, 1932.
Spaulding, O. L. Pen and Sword in Greece and Rome. Princeton, 1937.
Spiegelberg, W. E. Frankreichs Niederlage von 1940 im Spiegel der französischen Literatur. NSp, 50.
Spitzer, L. Classical and Christian Ideas of World Harmony. Traditio, 2, 1944.
Stauffer, D. A. War and Poetry. Yale Review, 32, 1943.
Stümcke, H. Theater und Krieg. Oldenburg, 1915. Cf. Kölnische Zt. Beilage, 7, 1915.
Walcutt, C. C. Fear Motifs in the Literature between Wars. SAQ, 46, 1947.
Walter, B. Friedenssehnsucht und Kriegsabschluss in der deutschen Dichtung. Breslau, 1940.
Warstat, W. Deutsche Kriegsdichtung heut und vor hundert Jahren. Grenzboten, 19, 1915.
Weddigen, O. Die patriotische Dichtung von 1870-71 unter Berücksichtigung der gleichzeitigen politischen Lyrik des Auslandes. Leipzig, 1880.
Weevers, T. The Poetry of Dutch Resistance. MLR, 40, 1945.
Wendling, K. Der Weltkrieg in der Dichtung. Stuttgart, 1918.
Weyand, H. Der englische Kriegsroman. Bonn, 1935.
Whittridge, A. English Poetry and the Spanish War. Dalhousie Rev., 19, 1940.
Williams, A. M. An English Critic Appraises Russian War Poets. Daily Worker, 4.I.1945.
Williams, G. British Poetry of Two World Wars. Rice Institute Pamphlet, 29, 1942.
Witkowski, G. Nochmals der siebenjährige Krieg im Drama der Zeit. Vossische Zt, Beilage 24, 1902.
Courtney, W. L. Aristophanes the Pacifist. Fortnightly Rev., 1916.
Fuchs, H. Augustin und der antike Friedensgedanke. Berlin, 1926.
Stillwell, G. & Webb, H. J. Chaucer's Knight and the Hundred Years' War. MLN, 59, 1944.
Peltier, P. La terreur prussienne et Dumas père. MF, 1.III.1917.
Baldensperger, F. Goethe et la guerre actuelle. Edda, 1917.
Hildebrandt, K. Die Idee des Krieges bei Goethe, Hölderlin, Nietzsche. Stuttgart, 1941.
McCourt, E. A. Thomas Hardy and War. Dalhousie Rev., 20, 1940.
Anon. V. Hugo und sein Verhältniss zum deutsch-französischen Kriege. Leipziger Zt, Beilage, 60, 1895.
Kilbourne, H. R. Dr. Johnson and War. ELH, 12, 1945.
Messières, R. de. La guerre et les relations internationales dans les fables de La Fontaine. FR, 13, 1940.
Reilly, J. J. War and More's Utopia. Catholic World, 154, 1941.
Church. Friedrich Rückert als Lyriker der Befreiungskriege. New York, 1916.
Reilly, J. J. Ruskin and War. Catholic World, 152, 1940.
Schilling, K. Bild und Deutung des Krieges bei Schiller. Stuttgart, 1941.
Delattre, F. Shakespeare et la guerre. LM, 1947.
Rowe, K. Values for the War in Hamlet, Othello, King Lear and The Tempest. College English, 5, 1944.
Varia. Articles et poésies de Zola, Sully-Prudhomme, J. J. Weiss etc., sur la guerre de 1870. Figaro, 31.VIII.1895.
Gleichen-Russwurm, A. von. Die **WART-**

BURG und ihre Sänger. Stuttgart, 1911.
Trinius, A. Die Wartburg in Sage und Dichtung. In: Die Wartburg, 7, 1908.
Frey, J. R. George **WASHINGTON** in American Fiction. Virginia Mag. Hist. & Biog., 55, 1947.
Bolte, J. Die Wochentage in der Poesie. (**WEEK**). Archiv, 98-100, 1897-98.
WELTSCHMERZ: See Pessimism, above.
Crum, R. H. The **WEREWOLF** Again. CW, 26, 1933.
Eckels, R. P. Greek Wolf-Lore. Philadelphia, 1937.
Hertz, W. Der Werwolf. Stuttgart, 1862.
Kroll, J. Etwas vom Werwolf. WS, 1937.
Spaeth, J. W. Petronius and H. M. Tomlinson, the Werewolf Again. CW, 26, 1933.
—— In the Werewolf Tradition. CW, 28, 1935.
Summers, M. The Werewolf. London, 1933.
WERTHER: See Goethe, IV. X. 6.
Cook, M. The Literary Contribution of the French **WEST INDIAN**. Journal of Negro Hist., 25, 1940.
Sypher, W. The West-Indian as a Character in the Eighteenth Century. SPh, 36, 1939.
Eberhard. Ueber den Ursprung der Fabel von der weissen Frau. (**WHITE LADY**). Berlinische Monatsschrift, Jan., 1783.
Gedicke, F. Nachtrag zu der Legende von der weissen Frau. Ibid.
Minutoli, J. von. Die weisse Frau. Geschichtliche Prüfung der Sage und Beobachtung dieser Erscheinung seit dem Jahre 1486 bis auf die neuste Zeit. Berlin, 1850.
Nagel. Dissertatio historico-metaphysica de celebri spectro quod vulgo Die weisse Frau nominant. Vitembergae, 1743.
Maurus, P. Die **WIELAND**sage in der Litteratur. Diss. Erlangen. Leipzig, 1902.
—— Die Wielandsage in der Literatur. Weitere neuzeitliche Bearbeitungen. Progr. München, 1911, 1921, 1926.
Plischke, H. Die Sage vom wilden Heere im deutschen Volke. (**WILD HOST**). Diss. Leipzig, 1914.
Schweda, V. Die Sagen vom Wilden Jäger und vom Schlafenden Heer in der Provinz Posen. (**WILD HUNTSMAN**). Diss. Greifswald, 1915.
Bacon, S. A. The Source of Wolframs **WILLEHALM**. Tübingen, 1910.
Becker, P. A. Die altfranzösische Wilhelmsage und ihre Beziehung zu Wilhelm dem Heiligen. Halle, 1876.
Clarus, L. (Wilhelm Volk). Herzog **WILHELM VON AQUITANIEN**, ein Grosser der Welt, ein Heiliger der Kirche und ein Held der Sage und Dichtung. Münster, 1865.
San-Marte. Ueber **WILHELM VON ORANGE** und sein Verhältnis zu den altfranzösischen Dichtungen. Quedlinburg, 1871.
Kaluza, M. Ueber das Verhältniss des mittelenglischen alliterierenden Gedichtes **WILLIAM OF PALERNE** zu seiner französischen Vorlage. Diss. Breslau, 1881 & ESn, 4, 1881.
Gatterer, C. W. J. Literatur des Weinbaues aller Nationen von den ältesten bis auf die neuesten Zeiten, nebst Kritiken und den wichtigsten literarischen Nachweisungen. (**WINE**). Heidelberg, 1832.
Landau, P. Deutscher Wein im deutschen Lied. Faust, 4, 1925.
Treuheit, H. Der Wein in Prosa und Poesie. In: Weines Wahrheit. Nürnberg, 1894.
Züge, P. Der Wein in der Dichtung. Rhein.-westfäl. Zt., 334, 1903.
Anon. Der **WINTER** in der deutschen Lyrik. Hamburgischer Correspondent, Beilage, 7, 1898.
Buchholz, P. Der Eislauf in der Literatur des 18. und 19. Jahrhunderts. Daheim, 39, 1903.
Clausen, E. Schnee und Eis in der deutschen Dichtung. Wartburgstimmen, 2, 1904.
Dreyer, A. Der Wintersport in der Dichtung. Bayerland, 36, 1925.
Jessen, H. Der Winter in der schlesischen Barockdichtung. Wanderer im Riesengebirge, 3, 1927.
Davies, R. T. Four Centuries of **WITCH** Beliefs. London, 1947.
Hole, Christina. Witchcraft in England. New York, 1947.
Keenan, Sister M. E. The Terminology of Witchcraft in the Works of Augustine. CPh, 35, 1940.
Kittredge, G. L. Witchcraft in Old and New England. Harvard U.P., 1929.
Knortz, K. Hexen, Teufel und Blocksbergspuk in Geschichte, Sage und Literatur. Annaberg, 1913.
Kocher, P. H. The Witchcraft Basis in Marlowe's Faustus. MPh, 38, 1940.
Lea, H. C. Materials Toward a History of Witchcraft. 3 vols. Philadelphia, 1939.

Murray, A. The Witch Cult in Western Europe. Oxford, 1926.
Notestein, W. A History of Witchcraft in England, 1558-1718. Washington, 1911.
Seabrook, W. B. Witchcraft. New York, 1940.
WONDERS: See Magic, above.

—Y—

Wünsche, A. Das Rätsel vom Jahr (**YEAR**) und seinen Zeitabschnitten in der Weltliteratur. ZVL, 9, 1896.

—Z—

Asmus, R. **ZENOBIA** von Palmyra in Tradition und Dichtung. Euphorion, 18, 1911-12.
Herold, T. Friedr. Aug. Clemens Werthes und die deutschen **ZRINY**dramen. Münster, 1898.

CHAPTER ELEVEN.

Collective Motifs.

1. American Types and Trends

Bradsher, E. L. Americanism in Literature. Sewanee Rev., 35, 1927.
Caillava, D. A. Historia de la literatura gauchesca en el Uruguay, 1810-1940. Montevideo, 1945.
Chinard, G. Thomas Jefferson, the Apostle of Americanism. Boston, 1929.
Clavería, C. El americanismo de Gabriela Mistral. BSS, 23, 1946.
Coan, O. W. & Lillard, G. America in Fiction, an Annotated List of Novels that Interpret Aspects of Life in the United States. Stanford, 1941.
Coni, E. A. El gaucho. Buenos Aires, 1945.
Daskam, J. D. The Distinction of American Poetry. AM, May, 1901.
Dorson, R. The Yankee on the Stage—A Folk Hero of American Drama. NEQ, 13, 1940.
Eich, L. M. The Stage Yankee. Quar. Jour. Speech, 27, 1941.
Fellow, R. American History on the Stage. AM, 50, 1882.
Fox, D. Yankees and Yorkers. New York, 1940.
Franklin, A. B. La realidad americana en la novela hispano-americana. Hisp, 22, 1939.
González, M. P. Importancia del espíritu de frontera en la literatura argentina. Memoria del Primer Congreso de Literatura Iberoamericana, 1940.
—— Trayectoria del gaucho y su cultura. I. El hombre y su medio; II. Su expresión artística. Havana, 1943.
—— Sobre la antiguedad del gaucho en la Argentina y el Uruguay. Rev. Hisp. Mod., 8, 1943.
Haefner, J. H. The West as Seen Through Frontier Biography. Diss. U. of Iowa, 1943.
Hazard, Lucy L. The Frontier in American Literature. New York, 1927. New ed., 1941.
Languasco, N. La poesía gauchesca Argentina. Quaderni Ibero-Americani, 1947.
Lomax, J. & A. Cowboy Songs ant Other Frontier Ballads. (Cf. Introduction). New York, 1945.
MacLeish, A. The American Writers and the New World. Yale Rev., 31, 1941.
McCloskey, J. C. The Campaign of Periodicals After the War of 1812 for National American Literature. PMLA, 1935.
Morley, S. G. La novelística del Cowboy y la del gaucho. RIA, 7, 1944.
Moya, I. El americanismo en el teatro de Sarmiento. Buenos Aires, 1940.
Nichols, Madaline W. The Gaucho Motiv in Rio de la Plata Life. Spanish Rev., Nov., 1935.
—— Der Gaucho als literarische Figur. Ibero-Amerikanisches Archiv, 1939.
—— The Gaucho. Cattle Hunter, Cavalryman, Ideal of Romance. Duke U.P., 1942.
Nunn, M. The Americanismo of Ruben Darío. Hisp., Feb., 1937.
Oviedo Villegas, J. J. La literatura gauchesca dentro de la literatura argentina. Diss. U. of Mexico, 1935.
Power, R. The Hoosier as an American Folk-Type. Indiana Mag. of Hist., 38, 1942.
Reid, J. Recent Theories of Americanismo. Hisp., 23, 1940.
—— Spanish American Jungle Fiction. Inter-American Quarterly, 2, 1940.
—— El americanismo en la literatura americana. Quito, 1943.
Smith, Rebecca W. Catalogue of the Chief Novels and Short Stories by American Authors Dealing with the Civil War and Its Effects, 1861-99. Bull. of Bibl., 16-17, 1939-41.
Tinker, E. L. Cult of the Gaucho and the

Creation of a Literature. Proc. Amer. Antiq. Soc., 57, 1948.
Tyler, M. C. The Literary History of the American Revolution, 1763-83. 2 vols. New York, 1941.
Wershow, I. Aspects of Gaucho Literature. Diss. Yale U., 1942.
West, E. The Gaucho in Argentine Life and Literature. Diss. U. of Maryland, 1939.

2. Animals, Beasts, Bestiaires, Birds Insects.

(See also: Fables, Reynard and Pied Piper).

Aarne, A. Die Tiere auf der Wanderschaft. Eine Märchenstudie. Hamina, 1913.
Ahrens, H. Die Fabel vom Löwen und der Maus in der Weltliteratur. Diss. Rostock, 1920.
Andrée, L. Das Schwein in poetischer, mythologischer und sittengeschichtlicher Beziehung. Zürich, Paris, 1903.
Arlington, L. C. Birds in the Poetry of the Chinese. China Journal of Science & Arts, 2, 1924.
Austin, H. D. The Origin and Greek Versions of the Strange-Feathers Fable. Festschrift M. Elliott, Baltimore, 1911.
Bangert, F. Die Tiere im altfranzösischen Epos. Marburg, 1885.
Baterean, O. Die Tiere in der mittelhochdeutschen Literatur. Diss. Leipzig, 1909.
Bernhart, J. Mensch und Tier in der Legende. Hochland, Nov., 1937.
Blümlein, C. Vom Flohmotiv in der Literatur. Frankfurter Zt., 104, 1923.
Boas, G. The Happy Beast in French Thought of the 17th Century. Baltimore, 1933.
Bonwit, Marianne. The Dog in Flaubert's Education sentimentale. PMLA, 62, 1947.
Bouvy. Sur une version italienne de la fable Le Meunier, son fils et l'âne. Actes de l'Acad. de Bordeaux, 63e année, 3e sér., 1901.
Brown, C. Shakespeare and the Horse. Library 111, 1912, & London, 1912.
Brun, F. L'alouette; histoire littéraire d'un petit oiseau. Nouvelle Revue, 87, 1894.
Bulard, M. Le scorpion symbole du peuple juif dans l'art religieux des XIVe, XVe, XVIe siècles. Paris, 1935.
Burger, C. P. De haring in de geschiedenis en in de literatuur. Het Bock, 10, 1921.
Caylus, A. C. Cte. de. Les chats (in legend and proverbs). In: Oeuvres badines complettes, 11. Amsterdam, 1787.
Cazin, P. Bestiaire des deux testaments. Paris, 1928.
Chandler, A. R. The Nightingale in Greek and Latin Poetry. CJ, 30, 1934.
Churchill, A. P. Birds in Literature. London, 1911.
Cosquin, E. Le conte du chat et de la chandelle dans l'Europe du moyen âge et en Orient. Romania, 1912.
Cronin, G. The Bestiary and the Mediaeval Mind — Some Complexities. MLQ, 2, 1941.
Deny, M. J. La légende de l'eau des sauterelles et de l'oiseau qui détruit ces sauterelles. Journal asiatique, 1933.
Drule, G. C. The Elephant in Mediaeval Legend and Art. Archaeological Journal, 2nd ser., 26, 1919.
Eick, H. Ueber das Seelenleben der Tiere in der Dichtung. Oesterr. Rundschau, 25, 1911.
Ewert, M. Ueber die Fabel Der Rabe und der Fuchs. Diss. Rostock, 1894.
Feist, S. Die Sage vom Binger Mäuseturm. ZDU, 9, 1895.
Field, J. E. The Myth of the Pent Cuckoo. London, 1913.
Fischer, E. Zur deutschen Thiersage in poetischer Beziehung. Progr. 1869.
Franke, E. Gestalten der Tierdichtung. Bonn, 1934.
Fuchs, M. Die Fabel von der Krähe, die sich mit fremden Federn schmückt, in der abendländischen Litteratur. Diss. Berlin, 1886.
Gabelentz, H. von. Die Lebensalter und das menschliche Leben in Tiergestalt. Weimar, 1938.
Galos, R. L'amour et les abeilles. Influence des élégies latines de P.S. Santel sur le poète hongrois Verseghy. Irodalomtorteneti Kozlemenyek, 45, 1937.
Garnier, A. P. Les thèmes poétiques: le rossignol dans la poésie française. Mfr. 10.V.1925.
Garver, M. S. Sources of the Beast Similes in the Italian Lyrics of the Thirteenth Century. RF, 21, 1907.
Goldemann, E. Das Schicksal des Tieres in der Literatur. Literatur, Jan., 1935.
Gorski, K. Die Fabel vom Lowenanteil in ihrer geschichtlichen Entwicklung. Diss. Berlin, 1888.
Gossen, H. Die Tiere bei den griechischen Lyrikern. Archiv f. Geschichte der Medizin, 30, 1938.
Gotzes, H. Die Tiersage in der neueren Dichtung. Frankfurt, 1907.
Grion, G. Il Mare Amoroso di B. Latini

e Il Bestiario d'Amore di Riccardo di Fourneval volgarizzato nel secolo XIII. Il Propugnatore, 1, 1868.
Hastings, Hester. Man and Beast in French Thought of the Eighteenth Century. Baltimore, 1936.
—— Man and Beast: Lamartine's Contribution to French Animal Literature. PMLA, 61, 1946.
Heller, E. K. The Story of the Sorcerer's Serpent: A Puzzling Mediaeval Folk Tale. Spec., 15, 1940.
Hensel, W. Die Vögel in der provenzalischen und nordfranzösichen Lyrik des Mittelalters. RF, 26, 1909.
Herrlinger, G. Totenklage um Tiere in der antiken Dichtung. Stuttgart, 1930.
Hilka, A. Die Wanderung einer Tiernovelle. Mitteilungen der Ges. f. Schlesische Volkskunde, 17, 1915.
Hirsch, S. Das Volkslied von der Nachtigall, eine weltanschauliche Dichtung. ZDPh, 62.
Holmstrom, H. Studier over svan jungfrumotivet i Volundarkvida och annorstädes. Malmö, 1919.
Howey, M. O. The Horse in Magic and Myth. London, 1923.
Hubaux, J. & Leroy, M. Le mythe du phénix dans les littératures grecque et latine. Paris, 1939.
Imbriani, V. La Pulce: saggio di zoologia letteraria. Catanzaro, 1875.
Johnston, M. Catullus and the Literature of Pets. CW, 23, 1929.
Jones, H. S. V. The Cleomades, the Meliacin and the Arabic Tale of the Enchanted Horse. JEGPh, 1906.
Jordan, G. Mäusegeschichten. Grenzboten, 1900.
Junge, L. Die Tierlegenden des heiligen Franz von Assisi. Leipzig, 1932.
Kellen, Toni. Dichter, Künstler und Tiere. Bühne & Welt, 12, 1910.
Kitze, A. Das Ross in den altfranzösischen Artus- und Abenteuerromanen. Diss. Marburg, 1887.
Klocke, E. Das Tier in Literatur und Kunst. Ueber den Wassern, 4, 1911.
Knortz, K. Die Insekten in Sage, Sitte und Literatur. Annaberg, 1910.
—— Reptilien und Amphibien in Sage, Sitte und Literatur. Annaberg, 1911.
—— Die Vögel in Geschichte, Sage, Brauch und Literatur. München, 1913.
Konrad, K. Tierstücke. Bühne, 4, 1911.
Körner, O. Die homerische Tierwelt. München, 1930.
Koszolla, L. Das Floh-Motiv in der Literatur. Diss. München, 1924.
Krappe, A. H. The Animal Tale. In: The Science of Folk-Lore. New York, 1930.
Krohn, K. Bär (Wolf) und Fuchs. Journal de la Société finno-ougrienne, 6, 1889.
—— Mann und Fuchs. Drei vergleichende Märchenstudien. Commentationes variae, 3-4. Helsingfors, 1891.
Kuntze, F. Der Schmetterling in der Literatur. Vossische Zt., Sonntagsblatt, 24, 1907.
Lancaster, H. C. The Horse in French Plays of the Seventeenth Century. Mélanges Albert Feuillerat. New Haven, 1943.
Landsberg, H. Der Hund des Aubri (de Montdidier). Zs. f. Bücherfreunde, 11.
Leppmann, F. Kater Murr und seine Sippe. München, 1908.
Levie, D. de. The Modern Idea of the Prevention of Cruelty to Animals and its Reflection in English Poetry. New York, 1947.
Lida, M. R. El ruiseñor de las Geórgicas y su influencia en la lírica española de la edad de oro. Volkstum & Kultur d. Romanen, 11, 1938.
Luria, S. L'asino nella pelle del leone. Riv. di filologia classica, 1934.
Martin, E. W. The Birds of the Latin Poets. Stanford U., 1914.
Martin, E. Le chat dans la littérature. Intermédiaire des Chercheurs et des Curieux, July, 1939.
McDermott, W. C. The Ape in Roman Literature. TAPhA, 1936.
Micheli, P. I cani nella letteratura. In: Saggi e conferenze. Livorno, 1893.
Moravcsik, J. La légende de la biche merveilleuse chez les auteurs byzantins. EPhK, 38.
Nauroy, G. Le chat dans la littérature. Intermédiaire des Chercheurs et des Curieux, 47, 1903.
Olbrich, K. Die Katze in Literatur und Volkskunde. Mitteilungen d. Ges. f. Schles. Volkskunde, 11, 1910.
Owre, J. R. Los animales en las obras de Benito Lynch. RIA, 3, 1941.
Pecci, G. Le api in Virgilio e nel Rucellai. Faenza, 1937.
Peter, C. W. Die Tierwelt im Lichte der Dichtung. Leipzig, 1902.
—— Tiere in lyrischen Gedichten. Pädagog. Warte, 10, 1904.
Pfeiffer, F. Das Ross im Altdeutschen. Diss. Breslau, 1855.
Quarone, L. B. Le leggende della salamandra nella letteratura. A&R, 1921.
Riegler, R. Spinnenmythus und Spinnenaberglaube. Schweiz. Archiv f. Volkskunde, 26.
Robin, P. A. Animal Lore in English Literature. London, 1932.
Rosenfield, Leonora C. Descartes and

Henry More on the Beast Machine. Annals of Science, 1936.
—— Un chapitre de l'histoire de l'animal-machine (1645-1749). RLC, 17, 1937.
—— Essai bibliographique sur les principaux ouvrages concernant la controverse de l'animal-machine en Angleterre. Ibid.
Royds, T. F. The Beasts, Birds and Bees of Virgil. Oxford, 1918.
Sabbe, M. Dierkennis en diersage bij Vondel. Anvers, 1917.
Schoell, F. Vom Vogel Phönix. Heidelberg, 1890.
Schuster, M. Der Phönix und der Phönixmythus in der Dichtung des Lactantius. Commentationes Vindobonenses, 1936.
Senaveratna, J. M. Kindness to Birds and Beasts in Ancient India and Ceylon. Antiquary and Literary Register, 6, 1920.
Silcher, G. Tierfabel, Tiermärchen und Tierepos. Reutlingen, 1905.
Starkloff, E. Die literarische Entdeckung des Reiches der Tiere. Literatur, 41.
Steiner, J. Die Tierwelt nach ihrer Stellung in Geschichte und Literatur. Gotha, 1891.
Stockelbach, Lavonia. The Birds of Shakespeare. Verona (N. J.), 1940.
Stokvis, B. Het paard in de literatuur. Lochem, 1948.
Suchier, W. Tierepik und Volksüberlieferung. Archiv, 143, 1922.
Taylor, G. C. Shakespeare's Use of the Idea of the Beast in Man. SPh, 42, 1945.
Topsell, E. The Elizabethan Zoo: A Book of Beasts Both Fabulous and Authentic. London, 1926.
Tyroller, F. Die Fabel von dem Mann und dem Vogel in ihrer Verbreitung in der Weltliteratur. Berlin, 1912.
Vernon, A. The History and Romance of the Horse. Boston, 1939.
Visser, M. W. de. The Snake in Japanese Superstition. Asiatische Studien, 14-15, 1911.
Wackernagel, W. Von der Thiersage und den Dichtungen aus der Thiersage. In: Kleinere Schriften. Leipzig, 1872-73.
Weicker, G. Der Seelenvogel in der alten Literatur und Kunst. Leipzig, 1902.
Wells, C. & Everett, L. O. The Cat in Verse. Boston, 1936.
Willoughby, L. A. The Image of the Horse and Charioteer in Goethe's Poetry. PEGS, N.S., 15, 1946.
Yoder, Audrey. Animal Analogy in Shakespeare's Character Portrayal. New York, 1947.
Zeuch, J. Die moderne Tierdichtung. Diss. Giessen, 1924.

3. Characters and Types.

(See also Subdivisions 11 and 12 below)

Bolin, W. Der Menschenfeind. Euphorion, 19, 1911.
Castle, E. Die Isolierten. Varietäten eines litteraturischen Typus. Berlin, 1899.
Christensen, A. Les sots dans la tradition populaire des Persans. Acta Orientalia, 1, 1923.
Davillier, C. Les curieux dans les pièces de théâtre. In: L'Antiquaire, de J. de la Porte. Paris, 1870.
Drouhet, C. Les originaux du barbon de J. L. Guez de Balzac. (Parasite and Pedant). RHLF, 1908.
Fermaud, J. A. The Confidant in Literature and Life. MLR, 41, 1946.
Gottschalk, W. Die humoristische Gestalt in der französischen Literatur. Heidelberg, 1928.
Grassi, C. L'avaro nella commedia. Roma, 1900.
Grund, K. A. Die schöne Seele im Wandel der Zeiten. LE, 17, 1914.
Guntrum, Hedi. Die Emanzipierte in der Dichtung des Naturalismus. Diss. Giessen, 1928.
Hendrix, W. S. Some Native Comic Types in the Early Spanish Drama. Columbus (Ohio), 1924.
Holz, H. J. Der neue Philister in der Literatur. LE, 21, 1922.
Klapp, A. L'avare ancien et moderne, tel qu'il a été peint dans la littérature. Progr. Parchim, 1877.
Kurz, H. European Characters in French Drama of the 18th Century. New York, 1916.
Landau, P. Vom deutschen Hanswurst. Allg. Zt., 192, 1908.
Lingelbach, Helene. Der Enterbte und Verfemte als tragischer Typus. Jena, 1928.
Ludwig, A. Der Lügner. LE, 23, 1921.
McIlvenna, E. The Philistine in Sturm und Drang. MLR, 1938.
—— Heine and the Philistine. GLL, 4, 1939.
—— Novalis and the Philistine. CLS, 2, 1941.
Merlini, D. Saggio di ricerche sulla satira contro il villano. Torino, 1894.
Meyer, H. Der Typus des Sonderlings in der deutschen Literatur. Amsterdam, 1943.
Obenauer, K. J. Die Problematik des ästhetischen Menschen in der deutschen Literatur. München, 1933.
Reuling, C. Die komische Figur in den wichtigsten deutschen Dramen bis zum

Ende des 17. Jahrhunderts. Stuttgart, 1890.
Röhl, H. Charaktere in der deutschen Dichtung des 19. Jahrhunderts. ZDK, 35, 1922.
Schlüchtern, H. Der Typus der Naiven im deutschen Drama des 18. Jahrhunderts. Berlin, 1910.
Wenger, J. Character-Types of Scott, Balzac, Dickens, Zola. PWLA, 62, 1947.
Westerkamp, U. Beitrag zur Geschichte des literarischen Philistertypus mit besonderer Berücksichtigung von Brentanos Philisterabhandlung. München, 1941.
Whittuck, C. The Good Man of the XVIIIth Century. London, 1901.
Wieser, M. Der sentimentale Mensch. Stuttgart, 1924.

4. Disease, Infirmity, Madness, Plague.

(See also Freudianism, I. III. 5., and Doppelgänger, I. VI. 10.)

Anderson, F. M. B. The Insanity of the Hero, an Intrinsic Detail of the Orestes Vendetta. TAPhA, 1927.
Anthéaume, A. & Dromard, G. Poésie et folie: essai de psychologie et de critique. Paris, 1908.
Baum, O. Der Blinde auf der Bühne. Merker, 2, 1911.
Cohen, G. Le thème de l'aveugle et du paralytique dans la littérature française. Mélanges Picot, Paris, 1913.
Crawford, R. Plague and Pestilence in Literature and Art. Oxford, 1914.
Debenedetti, S. Un riscontro orientale della parabola di P. Cardinal (Apologue of the man not touched by folly). Rendiconti d. R. Accad. dei Lincei, 39, 1920.
Delcourt, M. Stérilités mystérieuses et naissances maléfiques dans l'Antiquité classique. Liège, 1939.
Ebstein, E. Die Lungenschwindsucht in der Weltliteratur. Zs. f. Bücherfreunde, 5, 1913.
Franzos, K. E. Die Suggestion in der Dichtung. Berlin, 1892.
Friedrichs, E. Der Hunger in der Dichtung. Der Deutsche, 7.XI.1922.
Fuchs, H. Die Homosexualität im Drama der Gegenwart und Zukunft. Kritik, 1902.
Fürst, L. Das Pathologische auf der Bühne. Bühne & Welt, 5, 1903.
Gaulke, J. Die Homosexualität in der Weltliteratur. Der Eigene, Feb., 1903.
Gaupp, R. Das Pathologische in der Kunst und Literatur. DR, 36, 1911.
Gron, K. Lepra in Literatur und Kunst. In: Handbuch der Haut- und Geschlechtskrankheiten, 2, (Berlin), 1930.
Hoche, A. E. Die Geisteskranken in der Dichtung. München, 1939.
Holzhausen, P. Irrsinn und psychologische Grenzzustände im Spiegel der dramatischen Dichtung. Kölnische Zt., 717-47, 1923.
Kellner, L. "Der Andere". Neue Freie Presse, 10913, 1895.
Keys, T. E. The Plague in Literature. Bull. Medical Library Assoc., 32, 1944.
Köhm, J. Zur Auffassung und Darstellung des Wahnsinns im klassischen Altertum. Mainz, 1928.
Krzyzanowski, J. La fable du boîteux et de l'aveugle dans la littérature polonaise. Bull. intern. de l'Acad. polonaise. Cracovie.
Kunkel, G. Die Darstellung körperlicher Krankheit im deutschen Drama seit Lessing. Diss. Münster, 1926.
Kupfer, E. von. Lieblingsminne und Freundschaftsliebe in der Weltliteratur. Berlin-Neurahnsdorf, 1900.
Luzio-Renier. Contributo alla storia del mal francese ne' costumi e nella letteratura italiana del secolo XVI. GSLI, 5, 1885.
Möller, A. Die künstlerische Verwertung der Geistesstörungen im Drama. Der Neue Weg, 41, 1911. And in: Psychologie und Medizin, 4, (Berlin), 1929.
Näcke, P. Zur homosexuellen Lyrik. Archiv f. Kriminal-Anthropologie, 10, 1902.
O'Brien-Moore, A. Madness in Ancient Literature. Weimar, 1924.
Oesterreich, T. K. Les possédés: la possession démoniaque chez primitifs dans l'antiquité, au moyen âge et dans la civilisation moderne. Paris, 1927.
Paschall, Dorothy M. The Vocabulary of Mental Aberration in Roman Comedy and Petronius. Baltimore, 1937.
Pflugk-Harttung, J. Eine trübselige Literatur. (Sadism). Der Tag, 39, 1904.
Pötsch, Anna. Der Blinde im modernen Drama. Beilage Allg. Zt., 61, 1903.
Prätorius, N. Bibliographie der Homosexualität II: Belletristik. Jb. f. sexuelle Zwischenstufen, 9, 1908.
Regis, E. La folie dans l'art dramatique. Revue des Revues, 42, 1902.
Reuss, A. von. Blindenheilungen in der schönen Literatur. Der Stein der Weisen, 11, 1906.
Schertel, E. Der Flagellantismus als literarisches Motiv. Leipzig, 1930.
Schmidt, W. Der Blinde in der Literatur (besonders des 19. Jahrhunderts). Literatur, 27, 1925 & Berlin, 1930.

Schumann, P. Der Taubstumme in der schönen Literatur. Freie Wohlfahrtspflege, 5, 1930. And in: Bull. für Taubstummenbildung, 44, 1931.

Stern, E. Krankheit als Gegenstand dichterischer Darstellung. Literatur, 28, 1927.

Ure, P. The Deformed Mistress Theme and the Platonic Convention. N&Q, 193, 1948.

Weisfert, J. N. Das Problem des Schwindsuchtskranken in Drama und Roman. Deutscher Journalistenspiegel, 3, 1927.

Wolff, G. Psychiatrie und Dichtung. Wiesbaden, 1903.

Würtz, H. Der Krüppel in der Literatur. Mediz. Mitteilungen, 4, 1932.

5. Ecclesiastical Characters and Localities.

(See also Hermit and Saints, I. VI. 10., and Religious Denominations, III. I. 2.)

Ambroise, G. Les moines du moyen âge, leur influence intellectuelle et politique en France. Paris, 1946.

Bötticher, G. Pfarrertypen in der modernen deutschen Literatur. Neue Chrisoterpe, 26, 1905.

Bulle, O. Die Kirche im Roman. Beilage Allg. Zt. 219, 1904.

Bünger, W. Kirche und Geistlichkeit im Spiegel der Literatur. Nürnberg, 1928.

Busnelli, M. D. Per la genesi della Signora di Monza. (Diderot). ARIV, 92, 1933.

—— Les couvents tragiques de Stendhal. EI, 1934.

Danneil, H. Pfarrergestalten in neueren Dichtwerken. Grenzboten, 66, 1906.

Delre, A. Die Darstellung des Weltgeistlichen bei den französischen Romantikern. Berlin, 1912.

Ditchfield, P. H. The Parson in Literature. Trans. of the Royal Society of Literature, 1, 1921.

Doyon. Les prêtres mariés ou non mariés dans le roman et dans l'histoire. Paris, 1940.

Dugnani, D. F. Dissertazione sopra l'origine del chierico celibato. In: N. Raccolta d'Opuscoli, 8. Venezia, 1761.

Eckart, R. Die Jesuiten in der deutschen Dichtung und im Volksmund. Bamberg, 1906.

Falk, H. Der Pfarrer in der modernen Literatur. Protest. Monatshefte, 16, 1911.

Golz, B. Wandlungen literarischer Motive. Leipzig, 1920.

Graf, Emma. Die Pfarrergestalt in der deutschen Erzählungsliteratur des 19. Jahrhunderts. Konstanz, 1922.

Guiette, R. La légende de la Sacristine. Paris, 1927.

Haack, H. Die Pfarrergestalten bis G. Hauptmann. Berlin, 1930.

Hochdorf, M. Die Legende von der sehnsüchtigen Nonne. MLIA, 73, 1904.

Kennard, J. S. La religieuse dans le roman italien. Paris, 1930.

Kohlschmidt, O. Der evangelische Pfarrer in moderner Dichtung. Berlin, 1901.

——Pfarrergestalten in neueren Dichterwerken. Magdeburger Zt., 643, 1903.

Kraft, W. Die Päpstin Johanna, eine motivgeschichtliche Untersuchung. Frankfurt, 1925.

Lippmann, P. Das Hinscheiden der Päpste im Drama. Deutsche Bühnengenossenschaft, 32, 1903.

Martin, H. A propos de la genèse de la Signora di Monza. (Diderot). Dante, 1934.

McKee, K. N. The Role of the Priest on the Parisian Stage During the French Revolution. Baltimore, 1939.

Mensch, Ella. Der Geistliche auf der Bühne. Bühne & Welt, 15, 1913.

Russo, L. De Diderot à Manzoni. La religieuse de Longchamp et la religieuse de Monza. Mélanges Hauvette. Paris. 1934.

Scheible, J. Das Kloster, weltlich und geistlich. Meist aus der älteren Volks-, Wunder-, Curiositäten-, und vorzugsweise komischen Literatur. 12 vols. Stuttgart, 1845-49.

Schneider, R. Der Mönch in der englischen Dichtung. Leipzig, 1928.

Schuck, E. C. Clergymen in Representative American Novels, 1830-1930. Diss. U. of Wisconsin, 1943.

Spek, C. van der. The Church and the Churchman in English Dramatic Literature Before 1642. Amsterdam, 1930.

Toldo, Die Geschichte von dem im Speckschranke versteckten Priester. Zs. des Vereins f. Volkskunde, 13, 1903.

—— Le moine bridé: à propos d'un conte de Piron. RLC, 2, 1922.

Wolff, E. W. Der Geistliche in der modernen Literatur. LE, 4, 1900.

—— Die Jesuiten im Lichte moderner Dichtung. Ambrosius, 29, 1904.

—— Der Leumund der Jesuiten bei den Dichtern. Aus Höhen & Tiefen, 7, 1904.

Zeidler, J. Beiträge zur Geschichte des Klosterdramas. ZVL, 9.

6. The Elements and Their Spirits.

(See also Fairies, Magic, etc.)

Ebermann, O. Feuersegen in der Dichtung. Hessische Blätter f. Volkskunde, 25, 1927.
Ellis, O. C. A History of Fire and Flame. London, 1932.
Ewert, M. Feuerbestattungspoesie. Tag, 327, 1902.
Floeck, O. Die Elementargeister bei Fouqué und anderen Dichtern der romantischen und nachromantischen Zeit. Heidelberg, 1909.
Frazer, J. Myths of the Origin of Fire. London, 1930.
Landrum, Grace W. Imagery of Water in the Faerie Queene. ELH, 8, 1941.
Lienhard, F. Elementargeister. In: Wege nach Weimar, 6, 1908.
Lorde, A. de. Les tremblements de terre et le théâtre. Minerva, 1, 1902.
Mushacke, W. Beiträge zur Geschichte des Elfenreichs in Sage und Dichtung. Progr. Crefeld, 1891.
Puckett, H. W. Elementargeister as Literary Characters in the Middle High German Epic. JEGPh, 15, 1916.
Saintyves. Corpus du folklore des eaux en France et dans les colonies françaises (Cf. Introduction). Paris, 1934.
Seeber, E. D. Sylphs and Other Elemental Beings in French Literature Since Le Comte de Gabalis (1670). PMLA, 59, 1944.
Tudisco, A. El agua en la poesía de Juan Ramón Jiménez. Rev. Hisp. Mod., 5, 1939.

7. Flowers, Plants, Forests, Stones.

Baumgart, W. Der Wald in der deutschen Dichtung. Diss. Leipzig. Berlin, 1936.
Buchoz, J. P. Monographie de la rose et de la violette. Paris, 1804.
Eichrodt, F. Der Schwarzwald im Spiegel deutscher Lyrik. Stuttgart, 1921.
Fischer, H. Die deutsche Lindenpoesie. Neuphilolog. Blätter, 16, 1908.
Folkard, R. Plant Lore, Legends, and Lyrics. London, 1884.
Foster-Melliar, A. The Book of the Rose. London, 1894.
Garrett, R. M. Precious Stones in Old English Literature. Diss. München, 1909.
Graffinder, P. Die Rose in Sage und Dichtung. Gemeinnützige Vorträge. Prag, 1897.
Grawi, E. Die Fabel vom Baum und dem Schilfrohr in der Weltliteratur. Diss. Rostock, 1911.
Grierson, G. The Hemp Plant in Sanskrit and Hindi Literature. Indian Antiquary, 23, 1894.
Gubernatis, A. de. La mythologie des plantes, ou les légendes du règne végétal. Paris, 1878-82.
—— Le pietre e le piante nella leggenda. NAnt, 52, 1880.
Guy, H. "Mignonne, allons voir si la rose . . ." Réflexions sur un lieu commun (Petrarch, Ariosto, etc.). Bordeaux, 1902.
Hecker, J. Das Symbol der Blauen Blume im Zusammenhang mit der Blumensymbolik der Romantik. Diss. Jena, 1931.
Joret, C. La rose dans l'antiquité et au moyen âge. Paris, 1892.
Klinkhardt, F. Der Edelstein und insbesondere der Diamant im Spiegel der Poesie. ZDU, 19, 1905.
Landrum, Grace W. Images in the Faerie Queene Drawn from Flora and Fauna. SAB, 16, 1941.
Laufer, B. The Diamond: A Study in Chinese and Hellenistic Folklore. Chicago, 1915.
Macmillan, H. The Poetry of Plants. London, 1902.
Paris, G. Le conte de la rose dans le roman de Perceforest. Romania, 23, 1894.
Perez de Guzman. Manajo de la poesia castellana formada con las mejores composiciones líricas consagradas a la rosa. Madrid, 1891.
Perger, A. von. Deutsche Pflanzensagen. Stuttgart, 1864.
Porterfield, A. W. Hebbel's Use of Jewels. PMLA, 45, 1930.
Reid, J. T. La selva en la novela hispanoamericana. Saber, 1, (México), 1940.
Reling, H. & Bohnhorst, H. Unsere Pflanzen nach ihren deutschen Volksnamen, ihrer Stellung in Mythologie und Volksglauben, in Sitte und Sage, in Geschichte und Literatur. Gotha, 1904.
Roch. Veilchenroman und Wanderung der Euriantesage. Litteraturblatt, 4, 1882.
Schnehen, V. Unsere Dichter und die Blumen. Monatsblätter f. deutsche Lit., 7, 1903.
Spiesz, K. Der Wettstreit der Bäume in Literatur und Ueberlieferung. Wiener Zs. f. Volkskunde, 34, 1930.
Starck, T. Der Alraun, ein Beitrag zur Pflanzensagenkunde. Baltimore, 1917.
Strantz, M. von. Die Blumen in Sage und Geschichte. Berlin, 1875.
Tenne, Anna. Pflanzen in Sage und Ge-

schichte. in Abhandlungen und Gedichten. Neustadt am Rübenberge, 1910.
Wille, A. M. Die Eiche in Sage und Poesie. Post, 391, 1911.
Wünsche, A. Die Pflanzenfabel in der mittelalterlichen deutschen Literatur. ZVL, 11, 1897.
—— Die Pflanzenfabel in der neueren deutschen Literatur. ZDU, 16, 1902.
—— Die Pflanzenfabel in der Weltliteratur. Wien, 1905.
—— Die Sagen vom Lebensbaum und Lebenswasser. Leipzig, 1905.

8. Foreigners, Barbarians, Gringos.

(See also Primitivism, I. VI. 10.)

Bourberis, K. I. Platon und die Barbaren. Athen, 1938.
Coon, H. R. The Foreigner in Hellenistic Comedy. Chicago, 1920.
Coulter, C. C. The Speech of Foreigners in Greek and Latin Comedy. PhQ, 1934.
Fairlie, A. Leconte de Lisle's Poems on the Barbarian Races. Cambridge U.P., 1947.
Jones, W. K. La Gringa Theme in River Plate Drama. Hisp., 25, 1942.
Lowell, J. R. On a Certain Condescension in Foreigners. In: Literary Essays. Boston, 1862.
Schweizer, F. Die Ausländer in den Romanen von Dickens. Diss. Giessen, 1924.
Seabrook, W. These Foreigners (in the U. S.). New York, 1937.
Serboni, B. Elleni e Barbari nelle orazioni di Demostene. A&R, 1940.

9. Men, Women, Children.

Virgins, Betrothals, Marriages, Brides, Widows. Family Troubles, Adolescence, Adultery, Bigamy, Divorce, Emancipation, Generationenkonflikt, Illegitimacy, Incest, Misogyny, etc. Cf. also Love, I. VI. 10., and Children's Literature, I. VII. 1.)

Alhlert, P. Mädchen und Frauen in Pindars Dichtung. Leipzig, 1942.
Amalfi, G. Eine Novellette des Vottiero in literarischen und volkstümlichen Fassungen. (Stubborn wife). Zs. des. Vereins für Volkskunde, 5, 1895.
Anderson, J. D. The Legend Sati. (The Bengali widow). Asiatic Quarterly Rev., N.S., 1, 1913.
Arfert, P. Das Motiv von der untergeschobenen Braut in der internationalen Erzählungslitteratur. Diss. Rostock, 1897.
Aron, A. W. Traces of Matriarchy in Germanic Hero-Lore. Madison, 1920.
Axon, W. E. A. The Story of the Substituted Bride. N&Q, 12, 1897.
Bach, J. Der deutsche Schülerroman und seine Entwicklung. Diss. Münster. Bad Homburg, 1922.
Bächtold-Stäubeli, H. Die Verlobung im Volks- und Rechtsbrauch. Diss. Basel, 1913.
Barnett, J. H. The American Divorce Novel. Diss. U. of Pa., 1939.
Barth, B. Liebe und Ehe in altfranzösischen Fabeln und in der mittelhochdeutschen Novelle. Berlin, 1910.
Bascoul, J. M. F. La chaste Sappho de Lesbos et le mouvement féministe à Athènes au IVe siècle avant J. C. Paris, 1911.
Baudin, M. The Stateswoman in XVIIth Century French Tragedy. MLN, 53, 1938.
Baum, P. F. The Young Man Betrothed to a Statue. PMLA, 34, 1919.
Bechstein, R. Zum Spiel von den zehn Jungfrauen. Diss. Jena. Rostock, 1872.
Beck, Vera. Las heroinas en la novelistica argentina. Rev. Hisp. Mod., 10, 1944.
Beckmann, E. & Stoss, J. Die Frau in der griechischen Sage und Dichtung. Berlin, 1930.
Beljame, A. Introduction à l'Enoch Arden de Tennyson (le retour du marin). 2e ed. Paris, 1893.
Bell, C. H. The Sister's Son in the Medieval German Epic. Berkeley, 1922.
Berger, W. Das Ehebruchsmotiv im älteren deutschen Drama. Diss. Würzburg, 1912.
Bergsträsser, L. Eugene Sue und die Frauenemanizipation. GRM, 29, 1941.
Bett, H. Nursery Rhymes and Tales: Their Origin and History. London, 1924.
Beyer, P. Das nordische Frauenbild in der deutschen Volksballade. D&V, 1936.
Bieber, H. Die junge Witwe. LE, 17, 1915.
Blanchard, R. The French Source of Two Early English Feminine Tracts, (1699 and 1705). MLN, 1929.
Bock, H. Die Bedeutung der Frauen für die geistige Kultur Englands im 18. Jahrhundert. GRM, 27, 1939.
Bonus, A. Glossen zum Thema: Das Weib in der Literatur. Patria, 5.
Bornstein, P. Die Ehe im modernen Roman. In: Der Tod in der Literatur und andere Essays. Berlin, 1900.
Borodine, Myrrha. La femme et l'amour au XIIe siècle d'après les poèmes de Chrétien de Troyes. Paris, 1909.
Bouten, J. Mary Wollstonecraft and the Beginnings of Female Emancipation in

France and England. Diss. Amsterdam, 1922.
Brachfeld, O. Die Furcht vor der Frau in Sage, Märchen und Literatur. Internat. Zs. f. Individualpsychologie, 6, 1929.
Brietzmann, E. F. Die böse Frau in der deutschen Literatur des Mittelalters. Berlin, 1912.
Buck, A. Die Frauengestalten in Tassos Gerusalemme Liberata. GRM, 27, 1939.
Caraccio, A. Le thème littéraire de la femme angélisée et sa fortune. Austonia, 5, 1940.
Chiarini, G. Le donne nei drammi dello Shakespeare e nella Commedia di Dante. In: Studi Shakespeariani. Livorno, 1897.
Coffman, G. R. Old Age from Horace to Chaucer. Spec., 1934.
Coupel, H. Les jeunes filles dans la comédie latine. REL, 1943-44.
Cueto, L. A. de. Estudios de historia y de literatura: Los hijos vengadores en la literatura dramatica: Orestes, El Cid, Hamlet, La legenda de Virginia en el teatro. Escritores castellanos, 116, Madrid, 1900.
Dacier, A. Examen de l'histoire de la Matrone d'Ephèse. Mém. de l'Acad. des Inscript., 41, 1770.
David, S. Carol Kennicott de Main Street et sa lignée européenne. RLC, 19, 1939.
Dejob, C. Les femmes dans la comédie française et italienne au XVIIIe siècle. Paris, 1899.
Dietschy, C. Die dame d'intrigue in der französischen Komödie des XVI. und XVII. Jahrhunderts. Beiheft 64, ZRPh, 1916.
Duhamel, R. La femme dans les lettres françaises. Canada français, 29, 1942.
Duparc, E. A. Vrouwenfiguren in de werken van Menander. Amsterdam, 1937.
Eberle, Mathilde. Die Bacqueville-Legende. (Returning Husband). Bern, 1917.
Eckenstein, L. Woman under Monasticism. Chapters on Saint-Lore and Convent Life between 500 and 1500. Cambridge, 1898.
Eichbaum, Gerda. Die Krise der modernen Jugend im Spiegel der Dichtung. Erfurt, 1930.
Eisele, K. Das Kinderland im Lichte neuzeitlicher Poesie. Bremen, 1925.
Elb, R. Die Witwe von Ephesus. Masken, 3, 1908.
Evrat, E. Le féminisme dans l'Eneide de Virgile et dans la Jérusalem délivrée du Tasso. Paris, 1930.
Favez, C. Un féministe romain: Musonius Rufus. Bull. de la Soc. des Etudes d. Lettres, Lausanne, 1933.
Fehrenbach, C. G. Marriage in Wittenwiler's Ring. Washington, D. C., 1941.
Fischer, C. Die mittelalterlichen Zehnjungfrauenspiele. Archiv, 125, 1910.
Fleschenberg, O. S. von Das weibliche Schönheitsideal nach seiner Darstellung im griechischen Romane. Zs. f. Aesthetik, 1907.
Franciosi, G. L'imagine della donna nel poema dantesco e nei drammi dello Shakespeare. Sapienza, 5, 1882.
Freymann, Julie. Kritik der Schiller-, Shakespeare- und Goetheschen Frauencharactere. Giessen, 1869.
Frobenius, E. Väter und Töchter. Berlin, 1933.
Fuerst, R. Die verheiratete Frau im Roman. Beilage. Allg. Zt., 75-76, 1897.
—— Die böse Schwiegermutter. Berliner Neue Nachrichten, 517, 1899.
Gadala, M. T. Le féminisme de la Bible, I: La Genèse et l'Exode. Paris, 1930.
Gallwitz, S. D. Der neue Dichter und die Frau. Berlin, 1927.
Gatterman, H. Die deutsche Frau in den Fastnachtspielen. Diss. Greifswald, 1911.
Gaudy, Alice von. Das Kind im Drama. Bühne & Welt, 1, 1898.
Geiger, A. Die Seele des deutschen Weibes in seiner modernen Lyrik. Norddeutsche Allg. Zt. 155-66, 1902.
Giusti, A. Euripide e le donne. MC, 1935.
Glaesener, H. La malédiction paternelle dans le théâtre romantique et le drame fataliste allemand. RLC, 10, 1930.
Graf, A. L'amore dopo la morte. (The Bride of Corinth in Literature). NAnt, Dec., 1904.
Grammont, M. L'homme entre deux âges et ses deux maîtresses. Mélanges Bally. Genève, 1939.
Grisebach, E. Die Wanderung der Novelle von der treulosen Witwe durch die Weltlitteratur. Berlin, 1889.
Grolmann, A. von. Kind und junger Mensch in der Dichtung. Berlin, 1931.
Guest, C. B. The Position of Women as Considered by Representative American Authors Since 1800. Diss. U. of Wisconsin, 1943.
Hazard, P. Les livres, les enfants et les hommes. Paris, 1932.
Heilborn, E. Die Dame. Ihr Lebens- und Werdegang in der deutschen Literatur. Velhagen & Klasings Almanach, 2, 1908.
Heine, H. Shakespeares Mädchen und Frauen. Werke, 5 (ed. Elster). Leipzig, 1839.

Heisig, K. Zur Herkunft eines mittelalterlichen Schwanks (The husband turned out of his house). Archiv, 167, 1935.

Herrmann, L. La Matrone d'Ephèse dans Pétrone et dans Phèdre. BAGB, 14, 1927.

Hewitt, J. W. Gratitude to Parents in Greek and Roman Literature. AJPh, 1931.

Hinkley, Laura L. Ladies in Literature. New York, 1946.

Holbrook, Sibyl C. Husbands in Shakspere. SAB, 20, 1945-46.

Holbrook, W. C. The Young Widow in XVIIIth Century French Comedy. PMLA, 1932.

—— Secret Marriage in XVIIIth Century French Comedy. MLN, 53, 1939.

Hollander, L. M. The Faithless Wife Motive in Old Norse Literature. MLN, 1912.

Holstein, H. Das Drama vom verlorenen Sohn. Halle, 1880.

Hoppe-Meyer, E. Der Typus des Mannes in der Dichtung der Frau. ZDK, 1930.

Horner, Joyce M. The English Women Novelists and their Connection with the Feminist Movement, 1688-1797. Northampton (Mass.), 1934.

Huppé, B. F. Rape and Woman's Sovereignty in the Wife of Bath's Tale. MLN, 63, 1948.

Ihrig, Pauline. Heroines in French Drama of the Romantic Period, 1829-48. Columbia U.P., 1949.

Imbert, Comte d'. Bibliographie des ouvrages relatifs à l'amour, aux femmes et au mariage. 4 vols. Paris, Lille, 1900.

Jappe, H. Jugend deutschen Geistes. Das Bild des Jünglings in der Blüte der deutschen Dichtung. Berlin, 1939.

Jarrasch, W. Das Problem der heranwachsenden Jugend im Spiegel des zeitgenössischen englischen Romans (1900-1933). Borna, 1939.

Jax, K. Die weibliche Schönheit in der griechischen Dichtung. Innsbruck, 1933.

Jeanroy, A. Les femmes poètes dans la littérature provençale aux XIIe et XIIIe siècles. Mélanges Salverda de Grave. Groningen, 1933.

Jellinek, A. L. Die Heirat aus Rache. ZVL, 14, 1900.

Jenzer, A. Wandlungen in der Auffassung der Frau im ionischen Epos und in der attischen Tragödie bis auf Sophokles. Zürich, 1933.

Johnston, M. Once More Children in Latin Literature. CW, 23, 1929.

Jordan, L. Die Sage von den vier Haimonskindern. Erlangen, 1905.

Kahle, B. Zum Kampf des Vaters und des Sohnes. Braunes Beiträge, 26, 1900.

Kainz, F. Die Familie als dichterisches Problem. Literatur, 28, 1926-27.

Karpeles, G. Die Wanderungen eines Märchens. (Faithless Widow). In: Literarisches Wanderbuch. Berlin, 1898.

Kerbaker, M. L'eterno femminino del Goethe. Napoli, 1892.

Kiefer, Monica. American Children through their Books. U. of Pa. Press, 1948.

Kiefer, O. Der Knabe in der Literatur. LE, 18, 1916.

Klaiber, T. Dichtende Frauen der Gegenwart. Stuttgart, 1930.

Klinger, B. Les légendes populaires sur l'origine de la femme et le poème de Simonide d'Amorgos. Journal du ministère de l'instruction publique en Russie, 1914.

Knoerrich, W. Litterarische-gesellige Bestrebungen, besonders der Damen, und ihr Vorbild, sowie die Frauen-Emanzipation in Frankreich während der ersten Hälfte des 17. Jahrhunderts. Zs. für Culturgeschichte, 4, 1896.

Koeppel, E. M. G. Lewis's Gedicht The Tailor's Wife und Bulwer's Wife of Miletus. Festschrift Hermann Paul. Strassburg, 1902.

Köhn, Anna. Das weibliche Schönheitsideal in der ritterlichen Dichtung. Diss. Greifswald. Leipzig, 1930.

Kohn-Bramstedt, E. Marriage and Mesalliance in Thackeray and Fontane. GLL, 3, 1939.

Kossow, K. Der Gegensatz von Vater und Sohn im deutschen Drama. Diss. Rostock, 1925.

Koster, D. N. The Theme of Divorce in American Drama, 1871-1939. Diss. U. of Pa., 1943.

Kraeger, H. Die Darstellung des Kindes in alter und neuer Literatur. In: Vorträge & Kritiken. Oldenburg, 1911.

Kraft, G. Klingers Zwillinge, Leisewitzens Julius von Tarent und Schillers Braut von Messina. Progr. Altenburg, 1894.

Krappe, A. H. Ueber die Sagen von der Geschwisterehe im Mittelalter. Archiv, 167, 1935.

Krause, R. Die Weiber von Weinsberg im Drama. Staatsanzeiger f. Württemberg, Lit. Beilage, 7, 1921.

Krauss, R. Vater und Sohn im Drama. Staatsanzeiger f. Württemberg, 1923.

Kulka, L. Mütter und Söhne. Kunstwart, 22, 1908.

Kunst, K. Die Frauengestalten im attischen Drama. Leipzig, 1922.

Kupke, L. Die Kindsmörderin im Spiegel

der Literatur. Neue Deutsche Frauen Zt., 7, 1932.
Landau, M. Die Verlobten. ZVL, 5, 1892.
—— Ehescheidungen in der erzählenden Literatur. Gegenwart, 55, 1899.
—— Die Brautzeit in der deutschen Lyrik. Kunstwart, 16, 1902.
——Ein altindischer Schwank auf europäischen Bühnen. (Returning Husband). Bühne & Welt, 6, 1904.
—— Die feindlichen Brüder auf der Bühne. Bühne & Welt, 9, 1906-07.
Landsberg, H. Feindliche Brüder. LE, 6.
Laubengeiger, W. Die Mutter im deutschen Lied. Berlin, 1910.
Leonardi, E. La misoginia d'Euripide. Acireale tip. XX. secolo, 1922.
Lewent, K. Father and Son in Provençal Poetry. MLN, 57.
Lingelbach, H. Der Enterbte und der Verfemte als tragischer Typus. Jena, 1928.
Lisi. U. Poetesse greche (Saffo, Corinna, Telesilla, Prassilla, Erinna, Anite, Miro, Nosside, Edila, Melinno). Catania, 1933.
Lissauer, E. Das Kinderland im Bilde der deutschen Lyrik (Cf. Nachwort). Stuttgart, 1925.
Lo Gatto, E. La donna nella letteratura sovietica. Cultura Sovietica, 1, 1945.
Lorin, T. Quelques observations littéraires sur le conte de la matrone d'Ephèse. Mém. de la Soc. d'agricult. de Valenciennes, 3, 1841.
Ludwig, A. Die Tragödie des Alters. Voss. Zt. Beilage, 31, 1913.
—— Das Motiv vom kritischen Alter. Euphorion, 21, 1914.
MacCarthy, B. G. Women Writers: Their Contribution to the English Novel, 1621-1744. Cork U.P., 1944. New York, 1948.
MacCulloch, J. A. The Childhood in Fiction: A Study of Folktales and Primitive Thought. New York, 1905.
Martin, M. A. La jeune fille française dans la littérature et dans la société (1850-1914). Rennes, 1938.
Maynadier, G. H. The Wife of Bath's Tale, its Sources and Analogues. London, 1901.
Menck, Ursula. Die Auffassung der Frau in den frühen moralischen Wochenschriften. Köln, 1940.
Meyer, R. M. Die bösen Buben in der Literatur. Nation, 24 (Berlin), 1906.
—— Der Fluch des Alters. LE, 11, 1908.
Miomandre, F. de. La femme dans le roman contemporain. Nouvelle Revue, 12, 1901.
Morel-Fatio, A. El puñal en la liga (Spanish Women). RLC, 1, 1921.
Oberheiden, A. Haltung und Wertung der deutschen Frau im erzählenden Schrifttum der Gegenwart. Greifswald, 1939.
Obremer, Sharon d'. Les rôles des femmes dans la comédie française de Molière à Marivaux. Paris, 1942.
O'Brien, J. The Novel of Adolescence in France. New York, 1937.
O'Connor, W. V. The New Woman of the Renaissance. New York, 1942.
Oñate, María del Pilar. El feminismo en la literatura española. Madrid, 1940.
Ornstein, J. La misoginia y el profeminismo en la literatura castellana. RFH, 3, 1941-42. Misogyny and Pro-Feminism in Early Castilian Literature. MLQ, 3, 1942.
Ortiz, R. Sul motivo folclorico del ritorno del marito (tentativo di classificazione). Mélanges Iorga. Cluj, 1931.
Paris, G. La légende du mari aux deux femmes. C.R. de l'Acad. des Inscriptions et Belles Lettres, 1887. And in: Leçons et Lectures sur la poésie du moyen âge. Paris, 1895.
Parrott, T. M. Two Late Dramatic Versions of the Slandered Bride Theme. J. Q. Adams Memorial Studies. Washington, 1948.
Partington, T. B. Women and the Chinese Poets. Asiatic Quarterly Rev., N.S., 19, 1923.
Patt, Gerda. Der Kampf zwischen Vater und Sohn im englischen Roman des 20. Jahrhunderts. Emsdetten, 1938.
Pearson, Lu Emily. Elizabethan Widows. Stanford U. Studies, 1941.
Petsch, R. Vater und Sohn. Bad. Bühnen Blätter, 2, 1922.
Piltz, Frieda. Die Frauenart im romantischen Roman. Diss. Freiburg, 1928.
Poritzky, J. E. Das Kind in der Weltliteratur. LE, 3-4, 1900-01.
Post, L. A. The Feminism of Menander. CW, 19, 1926.
—— Dramatic Infants in Greek. CPh, 1939.
Potter, M. A. Sohrab and Rustum: the Epic Theme of a Combat Between Father and Son. Grimm Library, 14. London, 1902.
Radel, Frieda. Die uneheliche Mutter in der Dichtung und im Leben. Leipzig, 1912.
Rameckers, I. M. Der Kindesmord in der Literatur der Sturm- und Drangperiode. Rotterdam, 1927.
Rank, O. Das Inzestmotiv in Dichtung und Sage. Wien, 1912 & Leipzig, 1926.

Rassow, Maria. Die alte Jungfer in der Dichtung. Türmer, 26, 1924.

Renier, R. Appunti sul contrasto fra la madre e la figliuola bramosa di marito. Miscell. nuziale Rossi-Teiss. Bergamo, 1897.

Reuter, Gabriele. Die Frau in der deutschen Dichtung. Tag, 43, 1901.

Rice, S. Women in Heroic Literature (of Antiquity). Asiatic Quarterly Rev., N.S., 26, 1930.

Roettger, H. Ein Motiv: der heimkehrende Gatte und sein Weib in der deutschen Literatur seit 1890. Diss. Bonn, 1934.

Rorabacher, L. A. Victorian Women in Life and in Fiction. Urbana, (Ill.), 1942.

Rosenbaum, Sidonia C. Modern Women Poets of Spanish America. New York, 1945.

Rosenkranz, K. Die poetische Behandlung des Ehebruchs. In: Studien. Berlin, 1839.

Ruggieri, J. M. S. Letteratura feminile nell' America latina. RLM, 3, 1948.

Saint-Point, V. de. La femme dans le théâtre. Nouvelle Rev., 3, 1908.

Saintyves, P. Les vierges mères et les naissances miraculeuses. Paris, 1908.

Scherb, H. Das Motiv vom starken Knaben in den Märchen der Weltliteratur. Tübingen, 1924.

Schink, W. Platon und die Frauenbewegung. Zs. f.d. Gymnasialwesen, 1915.

Schlauch, Margaret. The Women of the Icelandic Sagas. ASR, 31, 1943.

Schmidt, Dora. Die Frau in den Gesprächen des Erasmus. Basler Zs. f. Geschichte & Altertumskunde, 44, 1945.

Schmidt, R. Die Frau in der deutschen Literatur des 16. Jahrhunderts. Diss. Strassburg, 1917.

Schneck, Erna H. Women in the Works of Thomas Mann. MDU, 32, 1940.

Schneider, Lina. Ein englisches Kinderbuch in Deutschland. MLIA, 1880.

Schossleitner, K. Das Blaubart-Thema. Brenner, 15, 1901-02.

Schreiber, Etta S. The German Woman in the Age of Enlightenment. Columbia U.P., 1949.

Schultze, K. Das Eheproblem in neueren Romanen. Kunstwart, 21, 1908.

Siefken, O. Das geduldige Weib in der englischen Literatur bis auf Shakespeare. Diss. Leipzig, 1902.

Smith, F. P. Un conte fantastique chez Irving, Borel et Dumas père (La femme au collier de velours). RLC, 18, 1938.

Smith, Thelma M. Feminism in Philadelphia, 1790-1850. Pa. Mag. Hist. and Biog., 68, 1944.

Sneyers, G. Le roman féminin dans la littérature contemporaine. Revue générale, 15.X.1934.

Soederhjelm, W. La dama senza merceda, version italienne du poème d'A. Chartier La belle dame sans merci. RLR, 5, 1891.

Spengler, F. Der verlorene Sohn im Drama des 16. Jahrhunderts. Innsbruck, 1888.

Spiero, H. Geschichte der deutschen Frauendichtung. Leipzig, 1913.

Splettstösser, W. Der heimkehrende Gatte und sein Weib in der Weltliteratur. Diss. Berlin, 1899.

Stang, S. Frauenlos in jüngsten Romanen. Stimmen der Zeit, 55, 1926.

Stiefel, A. L. Zum Schwank von der Rache eines betrogenen Ehemannes. ZFSL, 32, 1908.

Strauch, E. Vergleichung von Sibotes Vrouwenzucht mit den anderen mittelhochdeutschen Darstellungen derselben Geschichte. Progr. Breslau, 1892.

Strinz, Martha. Der Mann in der modernen Frauenliteratur. Die Frau, 10, 1903.

Stuart, D. M. The Child in Medieval English Verse. English, 5, 1944.

Suchier, W. Der Schwank von der viermal getöteten Leiche in der Literatur des Abend- und des Morgenlandes. Halle, 1922.

Svoboda, K. L'enfant dans la littérature grecque. (In Czech). Listy Filologicke (Praha), 1931.

—— L'enfant dans la littérature romaine. (In Czech). Ibid., 1936.

Tille, V. Das Märchen vom Schicksals-Kind. Zs. des Vereins f. Volkskunde. Berlin, 1919.

Traver, Hope. The Four Daughters of God; a Study of the Versions of this Allegory with a Special Reference to Those in Latin, French and English. Diss. Bryn Mawr, 1907.

Trinker, Martha K. de. Las mujeres en el Don Quijote de Cervantes comparadas con las mujeres en los dramas de Shakespeare. Mexico, 1938.

Upham, A. H. English Femmes savantes at the End of the Seventeenth Century. JEGPh, 12, 1913.

Utley, F. L. The Crooked Rib, an Analytical Index to the Argument about Women in English and Scots Literature to the End of the Year 1568. Columbus (Ohio), 1944.

Vries, J. de. Die Brautwerbungssagen. GRM, 1921-22.

Wahl, V. Die Gestaltung des Kindes in deutschen Dichtungen. Diss. Freiburg, 1923.

Wais, K. Das Vater-Sohn Motiv in der Dichtung bis 1880. Berlin, 1931.

Wallenshoeld, A. Le conte de la femme chaste convoitée par son beau-frère. Acta Societatis Scientiarum Fennicae. Helsingfors, 1907.

Watson, F. Vives and the Renascence Education of Women. New York, 1912.

Weinberg, Margarete. Das Frauenproblem im Staatsroman der Renaissance. Archiv f. Frauenkunde & Eugenik, 7, 1921.

—— Das Frauenproblem in utopistischen Dichtungen und Abhandlungen des 18. Jahrhunderts. Ibid, 8, 1922.

Weinhold, K. Die deutschen Frauen in dem Mittelalter. 2 vols. Wien, 1897.

Werner, O. H. The Unmarried Mother in German Literature with Special Reference to the Period 1770-1800. New York, 1917.

Wesly, M. Das junge Mädchen im deutschen Roman des 18. Jahrhunderts bis zum Beginn des Sturm und Dranges. Diss. Leipzig, 1934.

Wiegand, F. Die Frau in der neueren deutschen Literatur. Bremen, 1903.

—— Frauenfragen im Drama. Tag, 583, 1903.

Winterholer, H. Eltern und Kinder in der deutschen Literatur des 18. Jahrhunderts. Giessen, 1924.

Witkowski, G. J. Les accouchements dans les beaux-arts, dans la littérature et au théâtre. Paris, 1894.

—— Curiosités médicales, littéraires et artistiques sur les seins et l'allaitement. Paris, 1898.

Wolff, Hilde. Die Darstellung des Kindes in der deutschen Dichtung des ausgehenden 18. Jahrhunderts. Diss. Köln, 1923.

Wright, F. A. Feminism in Greek Literature from Homer to Aristotle. New York, 1923.

Wyrembek, A. & Morawski, J. Les légendes du Fiancé de la Vierge dans la littérature médiévale. Posen, 1934.

Zimmermann, P. Frauenschönheit und Romanliteratur. Schönheit, 41, 1913.

Zollinger, M. Die Rolle der Mutter im bürgerlichen Trauerspiel. Literatur, 27, 1926.

10. Numbers

(For Seven Sages, Seven Sleepers, etc. See I. VI. 10.)

Chapman, C. O. Numerical Symbolism in Dante and the "Pearl." MLN, 54, 1939.

Groenman, A. W. Die Zahl 24 bei den Juden im Altertum. Acta Orientalia, 7, 1929.

Hopper, V. F. Medieval Number Symbolism: Its Sources, Meaning, and Influence on Thought and Expression. New York, 1938.

Kozminsky, I. Numbers: Their Meaning and Magic. New York, 1927.

Liebermann, F. 365 als Lieblingszahl der Sage. Archiv, 81, 1928.

Müller, R. Die Zahl 3 in Sage, Dichtung und Kunst. Progr. Teschen, 1903.

Noelle, G. Legende von den fünfzehn Zeichen. Diss. Halle, 1879.

Vitocolonna, A. La leggenda del mille nella storia c nella letteratura. Roma, 1920.

11. Professions, Occupations, Talents, Artists

(See also Subdivision 12, below.)

Anon. Journalisten auf der Bühne. Bohemia, 304, 1902.

Abendroth, W. Künstlerromane. Deutsches Volkstum, July, 1936.

Abrahams, P. The Mercator-Scenes in Mediaeval French Passion-Plays. MA, 1934.

Adam, G. Der Arzt in der Literatur. LE, 5, 1903.

Aly, D. Der Soldat im Spiegel der Komödie. PJb, 79, 1895.

Antropp, T. Der Offizier im Spiegel der deutschen Dichtung. Deutsch-Oesterreich, 4, 1915.

Baudin, M. The King's Minister in XVIIth Century French Drama. MLN, 54.

Beck, F. Der schwäbische Bauer auf der Bühne. Diöcesan-Archiv Schwaben, 15, 1898.

Becker, Marie L. Moderne Theaterromane. Bühne & Welt, 10.

Beiswanger, G. Politicians in American Plays. Theatre Arts, 24, 1943.

Benedikt, E. Advokatur und Literatur. Wage, 12, 1908.

Bettelheim, A. Der Advokat in der deutschen Literatur. Nation, 20, 1903.

Boguslawski, A. von. Der Offizier auf der Bühne und im Roman. Tägl. Rundschau, Beilage 270-72, 1903.
Bonnet-Roy, F. Balzac, les médecins, la médecine et la science. Paris, 1944.
Bornstein, P. Die Darstellung der Künstlerbohème in der modernen Literatur. Nord & Süd, Dec., 1903.
—— Der Kaufmannstand in der modernen Poesie. WM, 94, 1903 & Propyläen, 4, 1906.
Boutarel. La médecine dans notre théâtre comique depuis ses origines jusqu'au XVIe siècle. Paris, 1918.
Braibant, C. Le paysan français à travers la littérature. Paris, 1941.
Brand, G. K. Der Arzt in der Literatur. Literatur, 26, 1924.
Braun, S. D. The Courtesan in the French Theater (1831-80): an Attempt at Classification. FR, 20, 1946.
—— The Courtisane in the French Theatre from Hugo to Bècque. Baltimore, 1947.
Brisson, A. Le soldat au théâtre depuis un siècle. Le Théâtre, 8e sér., 1913.
Brivet, A. M. L. La médecine et les médecins dans l'oeuvre de quelques écrivains russes contemporains. Bordeaux, 1927.
Brombacher, K. Der deutsche Bürger im Literaturspiegel von Lessing bis Sternheim. München, 1920.
Bruyère, J. Histoire littéraire des gens de métier en France. Paris, 1932.
Büring, W. Der Kaufmann in der Literatur. Leipzig, 1916.
Buxbaum, E. Reitergeist und Reitertat in deutscher Dichtung. Halle, 1909.
Camp, C. W. The Artisan in Elizabethan Literature. New York, 1923.
Case, J. La courtisane. Nouvelle Revue, 102, 1896.
Chamberlain, J. The Business Man in Fiction. Fortune, 38, 1948.
Coleman, A. P. The Polish Peasant in Recent Literature. Journal of Central European Affairs, 1, 1941.
Collins, R. S. The Artist in Modern German Drama (1885-1939). Baltimore, 1940.
Couchoud, P. L. Le mythe de la danseuse obscène. MF, 213, 1929.
Cruchet, R. La médecine et les médecins dans la littérature française. Paris, 1939.
Darenberg, O. Der Lehrer als Romanfigur. Päd. Zt., 42, 1913.
Daucé, F. L'avocat vu par les littérateurs français. Rennes, 1947.
Dejob, C. Le soldat dans la littérature française au XVIIIe siècle. RB, 7.X. 1899.
Dohse, H. Der Schauspieler im deutschen Drama des 19. Jahrhunderts. Diss. Rostock, 1923.
Dolderer, A. Ueber Martials Epigramme auf Aerzte. Tübingen, 1933.
Doutrepont, G. La littérature et les médecins en France. Bull. de l'Acad. royale de langue et de litt. françaises. Bruxelles, 1933.
Dubitzky, F. Dichter und Tondichter als Opernhelden. Bühne & Welt, 14, 1911.
—— Bühnenkünstler als Opernhelden. Bühne & Welt, 15, 1913.
Duncan, C. S. The Scientist as a Comic Type. MPh, Sept., 1916.
Ebner, E. Der Mathematiker in der neueren Literatur. Umschau, 9, 1905 & Zeitgeist, 6-7, 1910.
—— Der Professor in der modernen Literatur. ZDU, 21, 1906.
—— Magister, Oberlehrer, Professoren. Wahrheit und Dichtung in Literaturausschnitten aus 5 Jahrhunderten. Nürnberg, 1908.
Ester, K. d'. Die Zeitung und ihre Leute im Spiegel der Satire. Kölnische Zt., 608, 1923 & Würzburg, 1941.
Fauler, L. Der Arzt im Spiegel der deutschen Literatur vom ausgehenden Mittelalter bis zum 20. Jahrhundert. Freiburg-Emdingen, 1941.
Francé-Harrar, A. Die Courtisane, ihr Prophet und die Literatur. Telos, 1925-26.
Fries, W. Der Schulmeister in Dichtungen. Kath. Zs. f. Erziehung & Unterricht, 59, 1910.
Fritz, G. Der Spieler im deutschen Drama des 18. Jahrhunderts. Diss. Berlin, 1896.
Fürst, L. Der Kaufherr in der deutschen Literatur. LE, 24, 1922.
Gerber, Dora. Studien zum Problem des Künstlers in der modernen deutschschweizerischen Literatur. Bern, 1948. Cf. GR, 1950.
Gerster, M. Der Lehrer im Spiegel der schwäbischen Dichtung. Stuttgart, 1911.
Gest, J. M. Lawyer in Literature. London, 1915.
Gill, A. The Doctor in the Farce and Molière. French Studies, April, 1948.
Gleichen-Russwurm, A. von. Dienstboten in Leben und Dichtung. Zeit, No. 1920, 1908.
Goldschmidt, Helene. Das deutsche Künstlerdrama von Goethe bis R. Wag-

ner. Forschungen zur neueren deutschen Lit. Gesch., 57, Weimar.
Götze, A. Zum Schwank vom bestochenen Richter. NJKA, 20, 1917.
Gouldson, Kathleen. The Spanish Peasant in the Drama of Lope de Vega. BSS, 19, 1942.
Graetzer, F. Theaterromane. Bühne & Welt, 16, 1914.
Haag, H. Der Gestaltwandel der Kupplerin in der französischen Literatur des 16. und 17. Jahrhunderts. Marburg, 1936.
Hafner, G. Die Gestalt des Lehrers im deutschen Drama. Württemb. Lehrer Zt., 84, 1924.
Handl, W. Journalisten im Drama. Schaubühne, 3, 1906.
Hauschild, H. Die Gestalt der Hetäre in der griechischen Komödie. Leipzig, 1933.
Hauser, H. Les métiers dans la littérature française du XVIe siècle. Mélanges J. Vianey, Paris, 1934.
Heckel, H. Die Gestalt des Künstlers in der Dichtung der Romantik. Jb. d. Görres Ges., 1927.
Heinrich, E. Der Arzt im Spiegel der Dichtkunst. Münchener Med. Wochenschrift, 1908.
Hirsch, F. E. Der Bauer in der Stadt. ZVL, N.F., 2, 1910.
Hirsing, A. Diplomaten als Romanfiguren. Kölnische Volks Zt., 840, 1922.
Hübscher, A. Der Spieler in der Literatur. LE, 25, 1923.
Hügli, Hilde. Der deutsche Bauer im Mittelalter. Bern, 1929.
Hutten, L. Der Dichter in Roman und Drama. Deutscher Journalistenspiegel, 3, 1927.
Ilutowicz, S. Le peuple dans le théâtre de Molière. Diss. Toulouse, 1932.
Jung, G. Die Dirne in der neueren Lyrik. Archiv f. Menschenkunde, 1, 1925.
Kaisler, J. Offizier und Prediger im modernen Drama. Norddeutsche Allg. Zt., 259, 1900.
Kaufmann, M. R. Der Kaufmannstand in der deutschen Literatur. Diss. Bern, 1908. Cf. Grenzboten, 69.
Kiefer. Der Offizier in der deutschen Literatur. LE, 17, 1914.
Kienzl, H. Die Aerzte im Lustspiel. Rampe, 1912.
Knortz, K. Der Schulmeister in Literatur und Folklore. Pädagog. Archiv, 44, 1902.
Kocher, P. H. The Physician as Atheist in Elizabethan England. HLQ, 10, 1947.
Kohlschmidt, W. Selbstgefühl und Todesschicksal im Liede des deutschen Soldaten. Frankfurt, 1940.
—— Die Welt des Bauern im Spiegel von Immermanns Münchhausen und Gotthelfs Uli. D&V, 39.
Koller, G. Der Beruf des Skalden. Berlin, 1939.
Kraemer, E. von. Le type du faux mendiant dans les littératures romanes depuis le moyen âge jusqu'au XVII siècle. Helsingfors, 1944.
Krappe, A. H. Sur une légende de G. A. Becquer (le chasseur maudit). NPh, 17, 1932.
Krauss, R. Theaterromane. LE, 14.
Krinnitz, W. Das deutsche Künstlerdrama in der ersten Hälfte des 19. Jahrhunderts. Diss. Leipzig, 1922.
Landau, M. Schauspieler als Bühnenfiguren. Bühne & Welt, 3, 1901.
—— Der Spieler in der Dichtung. Breslauer Zt., 165, 1912.
Landsittel, F. Die Figur der Kurtisane im deutschen Drama des 18. Jahrhunderts. Diss. Heidelberg, 1929.
Laserstein, K. Die Gestalt des bildenden Künstlers in der Dichtung. Berlin, 1931.
Lasson, A. Der Lehrer auf der modernen Bühne. Woche, 9, 1906.
Levy, Erna. Die Gestalt des Künstlers im deutschen Drama von Goethe bis Hebbel. Diss. Frankfurt, Berlin, 1928.
Lindner, G. Die Henker und ihre Gesellen in der altfranzösischen Mirakel- und Mysteriendichtung. Diss. Greifswald, 1908.
Liptzin, S. The Weavers in German Literature. Göttingen, 1926.
Lohr, A. Der deutsche Soldat bei Maupassant. Allg. Zt., Beilage 88, 1906.
Loose, G. The Peasant in Wilhelm Heinrich Riehl's Sociological and Novelistic Writings: A Contribution to the Problem of Primitivism. GR, 15, 1940.
Ludwig, A. Der Detektiv. LE, 21, 1918.
Luis, W. Das Bauerntum im grenz- und volksdeutschen Roman der Gegenwart. Berlin, 1940.
Manning, C. A. The French Tutor in Russian Literature. RR, Jan., 1936.
Marcuse, H. Der deutsche Künstlerroman. Diss. Freiburg, 1922.
Martini, F. Das Bauerntum im deutschen Schrifttum von den Anfängen bis zum 16. Jahrhundert. DVLG, Buchreihe 27. Halle, 1944.
Maubach, H. Das Charakterbild des Apothekers in der Literatur. Berlin, 1898.

Meissner, P. Der Bauer in der englischen Literatur. Bonn, 1922-23.

Meschel, K. Die Historie von vier Kaufmännern und deren dramatische Bearbeitungen in der deutschen Literatur des 16. und 17. Jahrhunderts. Diss. Halle, 1914.

Möller, N. Die Bauern in der deutschen Literatur des 16. Jahrhunderts. Berlin, 1902.

Müller-Freienfels, R. Der Dichter in der Literatur. LE, 18, 1916.

Müller-Rastatt, C. Der Kaufmann im Roman. LE, 16, 1914.

Mulot, A. Das Bauerntum in der deutschen Dichtung unserer Zeit. Stuttgart, 1937.

—— Der Soldat in der deutschen Dichtung unserer Zeit. Stuttgart, 1938.

—— Der Arbeiter in der deutschen Dichtung unserer Zeit. Stuttgart, 1938.

Nanta, G. A. Marion Delorme. Le chariot d'enfant (courtisane réhabilitée). NPh, 20, 1935.

Neuhäuser, E. Dichter als Soldaten. Stuttgart, 1939.

Neumann-Hecker, A. Das Bajaderenmotiv im modernen Drama. Südwestdeutsche Rundschau, 2, 1902.

Nolte, P. Der Kaufmann in der deutschen Sprache und Literatur des Mittelalters. Diss. Göttingen, 1909.

Osborne, Nancy F. The Doctor in the French Literature of the Sixteenth Century. New York, 1946.

Ostrop, M. Deutsche Dichter im Roman. LE, 20-21, 1918.

Pessoa, A. C. O médico de ontem e o médico de hoje vistos pelos homens de letras. Coimbra Médica, 6, 1939.

Peters, R. Der Bauer im französischen Roman von Marivaux bis zur Gegenwart. Diss. Strassburg, 1914.

Petersen, C. E. The Doctor in French Drama, 1700-75. New York, 1938.

Petsch, R. Der Kleinbürger in der deutschen Literatur. Blätt. d. württemberg. Volksbundes, 4, 1922.

Porterfield, A. W. Poets as Heroes of Epic and Dramatic Works in German Literature. MPh, 12, 1914.

Prümes, A. Musikerromane. Neue Zs. f. Musik, 80, 1913.

Ricek, L. G. Die Gestalt des Volksschullehrers im Roman und auf der Bühne. Wien, 1914.

Richmond, Admiral Sir H. The Naval Officer in Fiction. E&S, 30, 1944.

Roberts, C. E. Handwerk und Handwerker in der deutschen Erzählung vom Ausgang des 18. Jahrhunderts bis zur Gegenwart. Breslau, 1939.

Robinson, C. N. The British Tar in Fact and Fiction. London, 1909.

Roggen, E. Der Bauer in der deutschen Dichtung. Der kleine Bund, 29-30. Bern, 1916.

Rolleston, J. D. Voltaire and English Doctors. 5e Congrès internat. d'histoire de la médecine. Genève, 1926.

Rosenthal, F. Der Schauspieler in der Literatur. LE, 18, 1916.

—— Der Musiker im Drama. LE, 20, 1917.

Rosikat, A. Der Oberlehrer im Spiegel der Dichtung. ZDU, 18, 1904.

Saint-Hieble, C. de. L'instrument des apothicaires: le clystère dans l'humour et dans la littérature. Paris, 1920.

Saisset, L. & F. Un type de l'ancienne comédie: le valet. MF, 15.X.1924.

Sauvageot, A. Le paysan dans la littérature hongroise contemporaine. Essais et études universitaires, 1, 1945.

Schindler, J. Zur Einführung in die deutsche Literatur über den Kaufmann. Progr. Aussig, 1911.

Schlesier, E. Der Volksschullehrer in der deutschen Literatur. ZDU, 23.

Schneider, E. Der Kaufmann in der erzählenden Poesie. Balt. Monatsschrift, 44, 1902.

Schnemacher. Der Zöllner in Geschichte und Literatur. Tübingen, 1910.

Schultz, A. Der deutsche Schulmann im Spiegel der vaterländischen Literatur des 16. und 17. Jahrhunderts. Bielefeld, 1907.

Schulze, S. Die Darstellung der Landbevölkerung im englischen Roman. Düsseldorf, 1938.

—— Der ländliche Mensch im englischen Roman. NSp., 46.

Schütze, K. Die Wertung bäuerlicher Arbeit in der antiken Dichtung. NJAB, 1938.

Schwann, M. Die Bauern in der deutschen Literatur. Voss. Zt. Beilage 43, 1907.

Schwartz, W. L. Diplomats in Modern French Literature. Stanford U. Studies, 1941.

Silvette, H. The Doctor on the Stage. Annals of Medical History, N.S., 9, 1937.

Slagle, K. C. The English Country Squire as Depicted in English Prose Fiction from 1740 to 1800. Diss. Philadelphia, 1938.

Sommerfeld, M. Der Schulmeister in der Dichtung. LE, 18, 1916.

Sorgatz, H. Musiker und Musikanten als dichterisches Motiv. Würzburg, 1939.

Sosnosky, T. von. Der Arzt im Roman. Gegenwart, 62, 1902.

Spallici, A. I medici e la medicina in Marziale. Milano, 1934.

Stockmayer, K. H. von. Das deutsche Soldatenstück des 18. Jahrhunderts seit Lessings Minna von Barnhelm. Weimar, 1898.

Stowell, E. The Legal Profession in the Tradiciones peruanas of Ricardo Palma. Diss. U. of Washington, 1941.

Trarieux, G. Les médecins au théâtre. Rev. de l'art dramatique, 17, 1902.

Ulmann, H. Das deutsche Bürgertum in deutschen Tragödien des 18. und 19. Jahrhunderts. Diss. Giessen. Elberfeld, 1923.

Urdang, G. Der Apotheker im Spiegel der Literatur. Berlin, 1921.

—— Der Apotheker als Subjekt und Objekt in der Literatur. Berlin, 1926 & Pharmazeutische Zt., 76, 1931.

Vallery-Radot, P. La médecine et les médecins dans l'oeuvre de Montaigne. Paris, 1942.

Varia. La peinture des conditions sociales dans le théâtre français: I. le Soldat. Minerve française, 1.XII.1919.

Venglaire, A. Les types excessifs du soldat en France. BURS, 24, 1884.

Vordtriede, W. The Conception of the Poet in the Works of Stéphane Mallarmé and Stefan George. Diss. Northwestern U., 1947.

Wachsmuth, B. Der Arzt in der Dichtung unserer Zeit. Stuttgart, 1939.

Wade, I. O. The philosophe in the French Drama of the 18th Century. Diss. Princeton, 1926.

Waetzoldt, W. Malerromane und Gemäldegedichte. WM, 116, 1914.

Watson, H. F. The Sailor in English Fiction and Drama, 1550-1800. Columbia U.P., 1932.

Wells, J. M. The Artist in the English Novel, 1850-1919. West Virginia U. Bull., 1943.

Wentzel, H. Der Officier in der deutschen Dichtung. Progr., 1874.

Wohlrabe, M. Der Lehrer in der Litteratur. Freiburg, 1898. Osterwiek, 1905.

Wysk, H. Die Gestalt des Soldaten in der griechisch-römischen Komödie. Giessen, 1921.

Yearsley, M. Doctors in Elizabethan Drama. London, 1934.

Young, F. B. The Doctor in Literature. Trans. of the Royal Society of Literature, 15, 1936.

Zobeltitz, F. von. Der Offizier in der modernen Darstellung. Neue Freie Presse, 1904.

—— Der deutsche Soldatenroman. Velhagen & Klasings Monatshefte, Jan., 1925.

Zucker, A. E. The Courtiers in Hamlet and The Wild Duck. MLN, 54.

12. Virtues, Vices, Crimes

(See also Subdivisions 3, 4, 9, and 11 above. For Courtesans, etc., see Professions.)

Anon. Crime in Current Literature. Westminster Rev., 147, 1898.

Anwand, O. Dichtungen des Hasses. Post, Beilage 6, 1904.

Baurmann, W. Vertu: Die Bedeutung des Wortes in der französischen Renaissance. Berlin, 1939.

Bellen, E. C. van. Trois Joueurs. (Regnard). NPh, 1924.

Borgese, G. A. The Dishonor of Honor: from Giovanni Mauro to Sir John Falstaff. RR, 32, 1941.

Brandes, G. Dichterische Behandlung von Verbrechen und Strafe. In: Gestalten und Gedanken. Essays. München, 1903.

Dunn, E. Catherine. The Concept of Ingratitude in Renaissance English Moral Poetry. Washington, D. C., 1946.

Falk, N. Die Rolle des Bösewichtes auf der Bühne. Berliner Illustr. Zt., 12, 1903.

Ferri, E. Das Verbrechertum im modernen Roman. Neue Zeit, 18, 1900.

—— Les criminels dans l'art et la littérature. Paris, 1902.

Frick, G. Karl Moors Vorbilder und Nachläufer. Korrespondenzblatt f. d. Realschulen Württembergs, 14, 1906.

Fürst, R. Kriminalromantik. LE, 10.

Goerschen, F. Die Geizkomödie im französischen Schrifttum. GRM, 25, 1937.

Harder, F. Die Schuld des reichen Mannes in den Urteilen der späteren Literatur. Braunes Beiträge, 50, 1927.

Heynen, W. Der Sonnenwirt in Schrift und Dichtung bis zu H. Kurz. In: Der Sonnenwirt von H. Kurz. Berlin, 1913.

Hirsch, F. Wahrheitsfanatismus und Autosuggestion in der Dichtung. Progr. Teschen, 1909.

Hoegel, H. Verbrechertum in der Literatur und im Kino. Oesterr. Rundschau, 51.

Iannucci, R. J. The Treatment of the Capital Sins and the Decalogue in the

German Sermons of Berthold von Regensburg. Washington, D. C., 1942.
Jostmann. Die Treue in der deutschen Poesie. Erziehung & Unterricht, 15.
Klapp, A. L'avare ancien et moderne, tel qu'il a été peint dans la littérature. Progr. Parchim, 1877.
Korobka, N. Usurers in Gogol. (In Russian). Literaturnyi Vestnik, 1, 1904.
Lewin, H. Der Verbrecher im deutschen Drama von Lessing bis Hauptmann. Diss. Giessen, 1916.
List, W. Preussische Ehre im klassischen Drama. D&V, 42, 1942.
Luft, F. Ueber die Verletzbarkeit der Ehre in den altfranzösischen Chansons de geste. Berlin, 1907.
Menéndez Pidal, R. Der Ehrbegriff im spanischen Schrifttum der Blütezeit. D&V, 42, 1942.
Messenger, R. E. Ethical Teachings in the Latin Hymns of Medieval England, with Special Reference to the Seven Deadly Sins and the Seven Principal Virtues. Columbia U.P., 1930.
Minor, J. Wahrheit und Lüge auf dem Theater und in der Literatur. Euphorion, 3.
Norman, H. L. Swindlers and Rogues in French Drama. Chicago, 1928.
Piazza, E. Il tipo dell' avaro in Plauto e nei principali suoi imitatori. Foligno, 1887.
Pongs, H. Soldatische Ehre in der Dichtung der Gegenwart. D&V, 42, 1942.
Ranneckers, J. Der Kindesmord in der Literatur der Sturm- und Drangperiode. Diss. Amsterdam. Rotterdam, 1927.
Röthe, G. Deutsche Treue in Dichtung und Sage. Langensalza, 1925.
Stern, J. Ueber den Wert der dichterischen Behandlung des Verbrechens für die Strafrechtswissenschaft. Zs. f.d. gesamte Strafrechtswissenschaft, 26, 1905.
Stöss, W. Die Bearbeitungen des Verbrechers aus verlorner Ehre. Stuttgart, 1913.
Stövesandt, O. Verbrechen und Wahnsinn in der Literatur. Gegenwart, 56, 1899.
Strobl, K. H. Der Verbrecher in der Literatur. LE, 14, 1911.
Stümcke, H. Das Sexualverbrechen in der dramatischen Dichtung. Zs. f. Sexualwissenschaft, 2, 1915.
Trinkaus, C. E. Adversity's Noblemen: The Italian Humanists on Happiness. New York, 1940.
Wright, C. The Usurer's Sin in Elizabethan Literature. SPh, 35, 1938.
Wulffen, E. Das Kriminelle in der Weltliteratur. Karl May Jahrbuch. Dresden, 1927.
Zobelitz, F. von. Diebeskomödien. Velhagen & Klasings Monatshefte, 22, 1906.

SEVENTH PART

Literary and Semi-Literary Genres and Forms.

(The titles contained on the following pages are not restricted to the theory of a specific literary genre alone; also items dealing with the international influence of a genre [or of a motif within a genre] have been included.)

CHAPTER ONE

Individual Literary Genres.

Born, L. K. Ovid and **ALLEGORY.** Spec., 1934.
Hamblin, F. R. The Development of Allegory in the Classical Pastoral. Chicago, 1928.
Kirrmann, E. N. German Theories of Allegory. Diss. Northwestern U., 1947.
Lewis, C. S. The Allegory of Love: a Study in Medieval Tradition. Oxford, 1936.
Marni, A. Allegory in the French Heroic Poem of the XVIIth Century. PMLA, 1933 & Princeton U.P., 1936.
McClennen, J. On the Meaning and Function of Allegory in the English Renaissance. U. of Michigan Press, 1947.
Tate, J. On the History of Allegorism. CQ, 1934.
Haight, E. H. The Roman Use of **ANECDOTES.** New York, 1940.
Mautner, F. H. Der **APHORISMUS** als literarische Gattung. Zs. f. Aesthetik & allg. Kunstwissenschaft, 27, 1933.
Bates, E. S. Inside Out: An Introduction to **AUTOBIOGRAPHY.** New York, 1937.
Gooch, G. P. Political Autobiography. Trans. of the Royal Society of Literature, 15, 1936.
Greatwood, E. A. Die dichterische Selbstdarstellung im Roman des Jungen Deutschland. Berlin, 1936.
Hartmann, Ursula. Typen dichterischer Selbstbiographien in den letzten Jahrzehnten. Diss. Bonn. Breslau, 1940.
Mish, G. Geschichte der Autobiographie. Leipzig, Berlin, 1931.
Anon. Ristelhubers französische Uebersetzung deutscher **BALLADEN.** MLIA, 1877.
Becker, P. A. Vom Kurzlied zum Epos. ZFSL, 63, 1940.
Belden, H. M. The Relation of Balladry to Folk-Lore. JAFL, 24, 1911.
Bondi, J. H. Aus dem Balladenjahr 1797. Freiburg, 1898.
Bonet Maury, G. Bürger et les origines anglaises de la ballade littéraire en Allemagne. Paris, 1889.
Carducci, G. Cantilen e ballate, strambotti e madrigali. Pisa, 1871.
Cecchini, L. La ballata romantica in Italia. Firenze, 1901.
Cohen, H. L. The Ballad. New York, 1915.
Cox, E. G. The Medieval Popular Ballad. Boston, 1914.
Entwistle, W. J. European Balladry. Oxford U.P., 1939.
Espinosa, A. M. An Extraordinary Example of Spanish Ballad Tradition in New Mexico. Stanford Studies, 1941.
Gottschalk, H. Strachwitz und die Entwicklung der heldischen Ballade. Würzburg, 1939.
Gummere, F. B. The Popular Ballad. Boston, 1907.
Hart, W. M. Ballad and Epic: A Study in the Development of the Narrative Art. HSPhL, 11, 1907.
Henderson, T. F. The Ballad in Literature. Cambridge, 1912.
Holzhausen, P. Die Ballade und Romanze von ihrem ersten Auftreten in der deutschen Kunstdichtung bis zu ihrer Ausbildung durch Bürger. ZDPh, 15, 1883.
Hudson, A. P. Byron and the Ballad. SPh, 42, 1945.
Hustvedt, S. B. Ballad Criticism in Scandinavia and Great Britain During the Eighteenth Century. New York, 1916.
Jolivet, A. La ballade nordique. Yggdrasill, 25.VI.1937.
Ker, W. P. On the History of the Ballads, 1100-1500. PBA, 4, 1912.
Lang, P. Die Balladik. Geschichte der Balladik. Aesthetik der Ballade. Basel, 1942.
Midbøe, H. Romantikkens Balladediktning: Mystike Motiver. Oslo, 1946.
Mossé, F. Les ballades traditionnelles dans les littératures germaniques. EG, April, 1946.
Neumann, F. W. Geschichte der russischen Ballade. Königsberg, 1937.
Ortutay, J. Ballades populaires de Tran-

sylvanie. Nouvelle Rev. de Hongrie, Nov., 1935.

Petriconi, H. Villons Ballade und Manriques Coplas. ZFSL, 59, 1935.

Pohl, Marta. Gemeinsame Themen englischer, schottischer und französischer Volksballaden. Bonn, 1940.

Purdie, E. German Influence on the Literary Ballad in England During the Romantic Revival. PEGS, 1924.

Schmidt, W. Die Entwicklung der englisch-schottischen Volksballaden. Anglia, 1933.

—— The Popular Ballads of Germany, England and Scotland. GLL, 3, 1938.

—— Gemeinsame Themen deutscher, englischer und schottischer Volksballaden. NSp, 47, 1939.

Scholz, W. von. Die Ballade. Menschen und Mächte, Schicksale und Taten. Berlin, 1942.

Taylor, A. The Themes Common to English and German Balladry. MLQ, 1, 1940.

Tuschke, Louise. Fair Janet und Kong Valdemar og Hans Søster. Ein Beitrag zur Frage der Beziehungen zwischen englisch-schottischen und skandinavischen Volksballaden. Berlin, 1940.

Umphrey, G. W. Spanish Ballads in English. MLQ, 6-7, 1945-46.

Wuescher, G. Der Einfluss der englischen Balladenpoesie auf die französische Litteratur. Diss. Zürich, 1891.

Zolnai, B. La ballade épique. Helicon, 2, 1940.

Alexander, P. J. Secular **BIOGRAPHY** at Byzantium. Spec., 15, 1940.

Evans, B. Dr. Johnson's Theory of Biography. ESs, 1934.

Leisegang, H. Die philosophische Biographie. Euph., 31, 1930.

Maurois, A. Aspects de la Biographie. Paris, 1928.

Nitsche, K. Biographie und Kulturproblematik im gegenwärtigen Frankreich. Berlin, 1932.

Overmans, I. Die Mode biographischer Dichtung. SZ, 1930.

Russel, J. C. An Introduction to the Study of Medieval Biography. MLQ, 4, 1943.

Stauffer, D. A. The Art of Biography in Eighteenth Century England. 2 vols. Princeton, 1941.

Stuart, D. R. Epochs of Greek and Roman Biography. Berkeley, 1928.

Uxkull-Gyllenband, W. von. Plutarch und die griechische Biographie. Stuttgart, 1927.

BUCOLIC Literature: See Pastorals, below.

Bond, R. P. English **BURLESQUE** Poetry, 1700-1750. Harvard U.P., 1932.

Delepierre, O. Macaroneana, ou mélanges de littérature macaronique des différents peuples de l'Europe. Brighton, 1852.

Flogel. Geschichte des Burlesken. Liegnitz, 1794.

Genthe, F. W. Geschichte der makaronischen Poesie. Leipzig, 1836.

Heiss, H. Studien über die burleske Modedichtung Frankreichs im XVII. Jahrhundert. Erlangen, 1905. And RF, 21.

Kitchin, G. A Survey of Burlesque and Parody in England. Edinburgh, 1931.

Nodier, C. Du langage factice appelé macaronique. Paris, 1834.

Richards, E. A. Hudibras and the Burlesque Tradition. New York, 1937.

Schlötke-Schröer. Die französische burleske Kunst des XVII. Jahrhunderts in geistesgeschichtlicher Bedeutung. ZFSL, 64.

West, A. H. L'influence française dans la poésie burlesque en Angleterre entre 1660 et 1700. Paris, 1930.

Davis, E. R. Dickens and the Evolution of **CARICATURE.** PMLA, 55, 1940.

Greene, R. L. The Earliest **CAROLS** and the Franciscans. MLN, 1938.

Delp'erre, O. Le **CENTON.** London, 1888.

CHANSONS DE GESTE, CHIVALROUS and **COURTLY Poetry:** See Epic Poetry, below.

Franz, A. Das literarische Porträt in Frankreich. (**CHARACTERS**). Berlin, 1906.

Gelderblom, G. Die Charaktertypen Theophrasts, Labruyères, Gellerts und Rabeners. GRM, 14, 1926.

Greenough, C. N. Studies in the Development of Character-Writing in England. Diss. Harvard U., 1904.

Hall, W. C. The Character in English Literature. Papers of the Manchester Literary Club, 58, 1932.

Polti, G. L'art d'inventer les personnages. Paris, 1918.

Schoeder, R. V. The Classical Canons of Literary Character Portrayal: A Critical Synthesis. St. Louis, 1944.

Tieje, A. The Theory of Characterization in Prose Fiction Prior to 1740. U. of Minnesota Studies, 5, 1916.

Vogt, H. Die literarische Personenschilderung des frühen Mittelalters. Leipzig, 1934.

Bogeng, G. Der Struwelpeter und sein

Vater. Geschichte eines Bilderbuchs. (**CHILDREN'S LITERATURE**). Potsdam, 1939.

Göpel, A. Der Wandel des Kinderliedes im XVIII. Jahrhundert. Diss. Kiel, 1935.

Hazard, P. La littérature enfantine en Italie. RDM, 1914.

Proszwimmer, K. La littérature enfantine en France au XVIIIe siècle et au commencement du XIXe siècle. (In Hungarian). Budapest, 1939.

Schaukal, R. von. Kindheitsdichtung in der Weltliteratur. Der Wächter, 9, 1927.

Schelling, F. E. The English **CHRONICLE** Play (with a list of plays on English historical subjects). New York, 1902.

Starke, F. J. Populäre englische Chroniken des 15. Jahrhunderts, eine Untersuchung über ihre literarische Form. Berlin, 1935.

Duméril, H. Essai sur les **CITATIONS**. Mémoires de l'Acad. de Toulouse, 12e sér., 9, 1931.

Farnham, W. Mediaeval **COMIC** Spirit in the English Renaissance. J. Q. Adams Memorial Studies. Washington, D. C., 1948.

Hélin, M. L'esprit comique dans la littérature latine du moyen âge. RFB, 12, 1932.

Jones, J. Emerson and Bergson on the Comic. CL, 1, 1949.

Starkie, W. J. M. An Aristotelian Analysis of the Comic, Illustrated from Aristophanes, Rabelais, Shakespeare, and Molière. Ha, 42, 1920.

Faral, E. Les **DEBATS** du clerc et du chevalier dans la littérature des XIIe et XIIIe siècles. Romania, 41, 1912.

Jantzen, H. Geschichte des deutschen Streitgedichtes im Mittelalter mit Berücksichtigung ähnlicher Erscheinungen in anderen Litteraturen. Diss. Breslau, 1896.

Knobloch. Die Streitgedichte im Provenzalischen und Altfranzösischen. Diss. Breslau, 1886.

Oulmont, C. Les débats du clerc et du chevalier dans la littérature poétique du moyen äge. Paris, 1911.

Pellegrini, A. M. Renaissance and Medieval Antecedents of Debate. Quar. Jour. of Speech, 28, 1942.

Pflaum, H. Les poèmes de controverse au moyen âge. Jerusalem, 1931.

—— Der allegorische Streit zwischen Synagoge und Kirche in der europäischen Dichtung des Mittelalters. AR, 18, 1934.

Selbach, L. Das Streitgedicht in der altprovenzalischen Lyrik und sein Verhältniss zu ähnlichen Dichtungen anderer Litteraturen. Diss. Marburg, 1886.

Waites, M. C. Some Aspects of the Ancient Allegorical Debate. Festschrift Agnes Irwin. Boston, 1910.

Walther, H. Das Streitgedicht in der lateinischen Literatur des Mittelalters. München, 1920.

Dickinson, G. L. **DIALOGUE** as a Literary Form. Transactions British Academy, 11, 1932.

Egilsrud, J. S. Le Dialogue des Morts dans les littératures française, allemande et anglaise, 1644-1789. Paris, 1934.

Froehlich, H. Der Dialog im französischen Volkslied. Greifswald, 1913.

Petsch, R. Der epische Dialog. Euph., 32, 1931.

Matthews, W. American **DIARIES**: An Annotated Bibliography of American Diaries Written Prior to the Year 1861. Berkeley, 1945.

Oltramare, A. Les origines de la **DIATRIBE** romaine. Lausanne, 1926.

Hentsch, Alice A. De la littérature **DIDACTIQUE** du moyen âge s'adressant spécialement aux femmes. Cahors, 1904.

Solbach, G. Beitrag zur Beziehung zwischen deutscher und italienischer Lehrdichtung im Mittelalter. Köln, 1937.

Bergenthal, M. T. Elemente der **DROLERIE** und ihre Beziehungen zur Literatur. Diss. Bonn, 1934.

Anon. Collin's Oriental or Persian **ECLOGUES**. Calcutta Rev., 6, 1846.

Bragg, M. K. The Formal Eclogue in Eighteenth-Century England. U. of Maine Studies, 28, 1926.

Fontenelle, B. de. Discours sur la nature de l'églogue. In: Oeuvres diverses vol. 2. Amsterdam, 1742.

Hulubei, Alice. L'Eclogue en France au XVIe siècle, 1515-89. Paris, 1938.

—— Répertoire des églogues en France au XVIe siècle. Paris, 1939.

Mangani, M. Origine e svolgimento dell' egloga pescatoria italiana. Nicastro, 1902. Cf. RCLI, 8.

Beissner, F. Geschichte der deutschen **ELEGIE**. Berlin, 1941.

Fischer, J. Shenstone, Gray, and the Moral Elegy. MPh, 1937.

Guillemin, A. Sur les origines de l'élégie latine. REL, 1939.
Herrmann, L. Les caractères, le développement et la valeur de l'élégie latine. Revue de l'U. de Bruxelles, 32.
Kostlivy, A. Die Anfänge der deutschen antikisierenden Elegie mit besonderer Berücksichtigung der Entwicklungsgeschichte des elegischen Versmasses. Progr. Eger, 1898.
Mahieu, R. G. L'élégie au XVIe siècle. RHLF, 46.
Nykl, A. R. La elegía árabe de Valencia. HR, 8, 1940-41.
Potez, H. L'élégie en France avant le romantisme. Paris, 1898.
Savchenko, I. S. The Lenskii Elegy and the French Elegy. (In Russian). In: Pushkin v mirovoi literature. Leningrad, 1926.
Springer, H. Das altprovenzalische Klagelied. Berlin, 1895.

EMBLEMS: See Chapter Three, below.

EPIC and Heroic **POETRY**; Chansons de geste.

Abercrombie, L. The Epic. London, 1922.
Banachevitch, N. Le cycle de Kosovo et les chansons de geste. Revue des Etudes slaves, 4, 1926.
Bédier, J. De la formation des chansons de geste. Romania, 41, 1912.
—— Les légendes épiques, recherches sur la formation des chansons de geste. 4 vols. 3e éd. Paris, 1929.
Belloni, A. Il poema epico e mitologico. Milano, 1928.
Bowra, C. M. From Virgil to Milton: A Study of the Epic. London, 1944.
Busch, E. Das Verhältnis der deutschen Klassik zum Epos. GRM, 29, 1941.
Chassang-Marcou. Les chefs-d'oeuvre épiques de tous les peuples. Paris, 1879.
Chetteoui, W. La disparition des poèmes épiques russes. Yggdrasill, March, 1937.
Clark, J. A History of Epic Poetry. Edinburgh, 1900.
Constans, L. L'épopée antique. In: Histoire de la littérature française, (ed. by L. Petit de Julleville). Paris, 1896.
Dam, J. von. Zur Vorgeschichte des höfischen Epos. Bern, 1923.
Determann, J. W. Epische Verwandtschaften im altfranzösischen Volksepos. Diss. Göttingen, 1887.
Dubsky, O. Essais sur l'évolution du genre chevaleresque dans les littératures romanes. Praha, 1932.
Fischer, R. Zu den Kunstformen des mittelalterlichen Epos. (Iwein, Nibelungen, Boccaccio, Chaucer). Wien, Leipzig, 1889.
Frings, T. Europäische Heldendichtung. NPh, 24, 1938-39 & SG, 3, 1938.
Gautier, L. Les épopées françaises. 4 vols. 2nd ed. Paris, 1878-92. Cf. Revue critique, 2, 1866.
Gerz, A. Rolle und Funktion der epischen Vorausdeutung im mittelhochdeutschen Epos. Berlin, 1930.
Grégoire, H. L'épopée byzantine et ses rapports avec l'épopée turque et l'épopée romane. Bull. de l'Acad. royale de Belgique, 1931.
Gubernatis, A. de. Storia della poesia epica. Milano, 1883.
Hamel, A. Französische und spanische Heldendichtung. NJWJ, 4, 1928.
Hatcher, Anna G. Epic Patterns in Old French. Word, 2, 1946.
Hunt, H. J. The Epic in XIXth Century France. Oxford, 1941.
Koegel, R. Heldensang und geschichtliche Lieder der althochdeutschen und altniederdeutschen Litteratur. In: Grundriss der german Philologie, II.1.1893.
Kralik, D. von. Die geschichtlichen Züge der deutschen Heldendichtung. Wien, 1940.
Meier, J. Werden und Leben des Volksepos. Halle, 1909.
Menéndez Pidal, R. La forma épica en España y en Francia. RFE, 1933.
—— La épica española y la Literarästhetik des Mittelalters de E. R. Curtius. ZRPh, 59, 1939.
—— La epopeya castellana a través de la literatura española. Buenos Aires, 1945.
Meszleny, R. C. Spitteler und das neudeutsche Epos. Halle, 1918.
Mila y Fontanals. De la poesía heroico-popular castellana. In: Obras, 7. Barcelona, 1874.
Moerner, J. von. Die deutschen und französischen Heldengedichte des Mittelalters als Quellen für die Kulturgeschichte. Leipzig, 1886.
Muirhead, J. F. Carl Spitteler and the New Epic. Royal Society of Literature, Essays, 10, 1931.
Murray, G. The Rise of the Greek Epic. Oxford U.P., 1924.
Myers, I. T. A Study in Epic Development. New York, 1901.
Nyrop, K. Old-franske Heltedigtning. København, 1883.
Olrik, A. Danmarks Heltedigtning; en oldtidstudie. 2 vols. København, 1903-10 & New York, 1919.

Perkinson, R. H. The Epic in Five Acts. SPh, 43, 1946.
Pierce, F. The Spanish Religious Epic of the Counter-Reformation: A Survey. BSS, 18, 1941.
—— Some Aspects of the Spanish Religious Epic of the Golden Age. HR, 12, 1944.
—— The Heroic Poem of the Spanish Golden Age. Oxford, 1947.
Plate, R. Voltaire als Epentheoretiker und Dichter der Henriade. Diss. Königsberg, 1917.
Rajna, P. Le origini dell' epopea francese. Firenze, 1884. Cf. Romania, 1884.
Rang, B. Vom Wesen des epischen Kunstwerkes. Hefte für Büchereiwesen, 16, 1932.
Remmers, K. Die epische Poesie bei den alten und den modernen Völkern. Progr. Nienburg, 1876.
Rolli, P. Remarks Upon M. Voltaire's Essay on the Epic Poetry of the European Nations. London, 1728.
Routh, H. V. God, Man and Epic Poetry. A Study in Comparative Literature. 2 vols. Cambridge, 1927.
Ruggieri R. Il contributo italiano allo studio delle origini delle canzoni di gesta. Cultura Neolatina, 1, 1941.
Ryan, S. J. Comparative Fluidity of French and Greek Epics. AJPh, 1927.
Salverda de Grave, J. Sur l'origine des chansons de geste. Verslagen der K. Akad. van Wetenschappen, 1.
Schirmer, W. F. Das Problem des religiösen Epos im 17. Jahrhundert in England. DVLG, 1936.
Schlumberger, G. L'épopée byzantine à la fin du Xe siècle. Paris, 1925.
Schmidt, F. Die Erneuerung des Epos. (Spitteler). Leipzig, 1928.
Schneider, H. Heldendichtung, Geistlichendichtung, Ritterdichtung. Heidelberg, 1925.
Siciliano, I. Le origini delle canzoni di gesta: teorie e discussioni . Padova, 1940.
Swedenberg, H. T. The Theory of the Epic in England, 1650-1800. Berkeley, 1944.
Throop, G. R. Epic and Dramatic. Washington U. Studies, 5. St. Louis, 1917.
Viscardi, A. Le canzoni di gesta, i temi tradizionali, le fonti letterarie e diplomatiche. Annali della R. Scuola Normale Superiore di Pisa, 6-7, 1937-38.
Voltaire. An Essay upon the Epick Poetry of the European Nations from Homer down to Milton. London, 1727. (Essai sur la poésie épique. Paris, 1732).
Way, R. A. The Neo-Classical Epic in France, 1789-1830. Diss. U. of Cal., 1942.
White, Florence D. Voltaire's Essay on Epic Poetry, a Study and an Edition. Diss. Bryn Mawr, 1915.
Whitney, L. English Primitivistic Theories of Epic Origins. MPh, 1924.
Willem, A. L'épopée, ses lois, son histoire. Bruxelles, 1927.
Williams, R. C. The Purpose of Poetry and Particularly the Epic, as Discussed by Critical Writers of the Sixteenth Century in Italy. RR, 12, 1921.
—— Two Studies in Epic Theory. (Tasso and Scudéry). MPh, 1924.
Wilmotte, M. L'épopée française. Origine et élaboration. Paris, 1939.
Witte, K. Ueber einige romantische Heldengeschichten der Italiener und ihre neueste Ausgabe. Blätter f. literar. Unterhaltung, 17-18.IV.1836.
Zumbini, B. Klopstock e i grandi epici moderni. NAnt, 82, 1885.
Brecht, F. J. Motiv- und Typengeschichte des griechischen Spott**EPIGRAMMS.** Ph. Supplbd. 22. Leipzig, 1930.
Geffcken, J. Studien zum griechischen Epigramm. NJKA, 1917.
Hommel, H. Der Ursprung des Epigramms. RhM, 88, 1939.
Hudson, H. H. The Epigram in the English Renaissance. Princeton U.P., 1947.
Kruuse, J. Histoire de l'épigramme en France jusqu'à la fin du XVIIIe siècle. In: Digter og Traditioner. København, 1939.
Rubensohn, M. Griechische Epigramme und andere kleine Dichtungen in deutschen Uebersetzungen des XVI. und XVII. Jahrhunderts. (Cf. Introduction). Weimar, 1898.
Lattimore, R. Themes in Greek and Latin **EPITAPHS.** Illinois Stud. in Lang. and Lit. 1942.
Yart, Abbé. Discours sur les épitaphes, les élégies, les panégyriques funèbres des Grecs, des Romains, des Français et des Anglais. MF, Dec., 1750.
Gärtner, A. Die englische **EPITHALAMIEN**literatur im 17. Jahrhundert und ihre Vorbilder. Diss. Erlangen, 1936.
Wilson, E. F. Pastoral and Epithalamium in Latin Literature. Spec., 23, 1948.
Roberts, G. B. The **EPITHET** in Spanish Poetry of the Romantic Period. U. of Iowa Studies, NS, 321.

Atkinson, G. La forme de l'ESSAI avant Montaigne. BHR, 1946.
Gummere, R. M. The English Essay and Some of its Ancient Prototypes. CW, 14.
Kayser, R. Wege des Essays. NR, 36, 1925.
Routh, H. V. The Origins of the Essay Compared in French and English Literatures. MLR, 15, 1920.
Wann, L. The Spirit of Charles Lamb: Some Observations on the Informal Essay. Personalist, 22, 1941.
Watson, M. R. The Spectator Tradition and the Development of the Familiar Essay. ELH, 13, 1946.
Dornseiff, F. Literarische Verwendung des Beispiels. (**EXAMPLE**). VBW, 2, 1922-23.
Gaster, M. The Exempla of the Rabbis. London, 1924.
Mosher, J. A. The Exemplum in the Early Religious and Didactic Literature of England. New York, 1911.
Welter, J. T. L'exemplum dans la littérature religieuse et didactique du moyen âge. Paris, 1927.
FABLE and **FABLIAU**: See Literary Themes, I. VI. 2.
Brentano, M. T. Relationship of the Latin **FACETUS** Literature to the Middle English Courtesy Poems. Humanistic Studies of the U. of Kansas, 5, 1936.
FAIRY TALES: See Literary Themes, I. VI. 3.
FOLKSONG and **FRAME STORY**: See Chapter Two, below.
Schwartz, R. Die **FROTTOLE** im 15. Jahrhundert. Vierteljahrsschrift f. Musikwissenschaft, 2, 1888.
Durling, D. **GEORGIC** Tradition in English Poetry. New York, 1935.
Hooker, Helene M. Dryden's Georgics and English Predecessors. MLQ, 9, 1946.
Lilly, M. The Georgic: A Contribution to the Study of the Vergilian Type of Didactic Poetry. Baltimore, 1919.
Cline, C. L. Benjamin Disraeli on the **GROTESQUE** in Literature. RES, 16, 1940.
Ebeling, F. Flogel's Geschichte des Grotesk-Komischen. Leipzig, 1887.
Steiger, H. Die Groteske und die Burleske bei Aristophanes. Ph, 1934.
HEROIC PLAYS: See Chapter Two, below.
HEROIC POETRY: See Epics, above.
Ernst, G. P. Die **HEROIDE** in der deutschen Literatur. Diss. Heidelberg, 1901.
IDYLL: See Pastoral Poetry, below.
IMAGERY: See also Emblems in Chapter Three, below.
Day, L. C. The Poetic Image. Clark Lectures, 1946. London, 1947.
Praz, M. Studies in Seventeenth-Century Imagery. London, 1947.
Tuve, Rosamond. Elizabethan and Metaphysical Imagery. Chicago U.P., 1947.
Brooks, C. **IRONY** and Ironic Poetry. College English, 9, 1948.
Thompson, A. R. The Dry Mock, A Study of Irony. Berkeley, 1948.
Thomson, J. A. K. Irony: An Historical Introduction. Harvard U.P., 1927.
Exler, F. The Form of the Ancient Greek **LETTER**. A Study in Greek Epistolography. Washington, 1923.
Hornbeak, K. G. The Complete Letter-Writer in English, 1568-1800. Northampton, (Mass.), 1934.
Meyer, E. Der deutsche poetische Liebesbrief. ZDU, 27, 1903.
Witte, M. Antonio Perez und der französische Brief am Anfang des 17. Jahrhunderts. Würzburg, 1938.
Wohlfahrt, P. Der Brief als Literaturgattung. Der Gral, 19, 1925.
LIED: See Poetry in Chapter Two, below.
MACARONIC VERSE: See Burlesque, above.
Cesari, G. Die Entstehung des **MADRIGALS** im 16. Jahrhundert. Cremona, 1909.
—— Le origini del madrigale musicale cinquecentesco. Rivista musicale ital., 19, 1912.
Einstein, A. Augenmusik im Madrigal. Monthly Journal of the Internat. Music Society, Oct., 1912.
—— Dante, or the Way to the Madrigal. Musical Quarterly 25, 1939.
—— The Italian Madrigal. Princeton U.P., 1948.
Helm, E. B. Heralds of the Italian Madrigal. Musical Quarterly, 27, 1941.
Kiwi, Edith. Studien zur Geschichte des italienischen Liedmadrigals im 16. Jahrhundert. Würzburg, 1937.
Schwartz, R. Hans Leo Hassler unter dem Einfluss der italienischen Madrigalisten. Vierteljahrsschrift f. Musikwissenschaft, 9, 1893.
Vossler, K. Das deutsche Madrigal: Geschichte seiner Entwickelung bis in die Mitte des XVIII. Jahrhunderts. Weimar, 1898.
MAERCHEN: See Fairy Tales, I. VI. 3.
Fink, A. H. **MAXIME** und Fragment. München, 1934.
Lancaster, H. C. The Origin of the Lyric **MONOLOGUE** in French Classical Tragedy. PMLA, 1927.

MacCallum, M. W. The Dramatic Monologue in the Victorian Period. British Academy, 1925.
Nollmann, E. Ursprung und Entwicklung des Monologs bis zu seiner Entfaltung in Shakespeare. Bonn, 1934.
Schadewaldt, W. Monolog und Selbstgespräch. Untersuchungen zur Formgeschichte der griechischen Tragödie. Berlin, 1926.
Scherer, J. Molière et le monologue tragique. PMLA, 54, 1939.
Urbach, O. Zur Ehrenrettung des Monologs. Literatur, June, 1937.
Rust, Isabel B. Theory of the **ODE** Applied to the English Ode before 1700. Diss. U. of Michigan, 1946.
Schuster, G. N. The English Ode from Milton to Keats. Columbia U.P., 1940.
Viëtor, K. Geschichte der deutschen Ode. München, 1923.
ORATORY: See Rhetoric, below.
Delepierre, O. La **PARODIE** chez les Romains et chez les modernes. Londres, 1870.
Grannis, V. B. Dramatic Parody in XVIIIth Century France. New York, 1931.
Guglielmino, F. La parodia nella commedia greca antica. Catania, 1928.
Ilvonen, E. Parodies de thèmes pieux dans la poésie française du moyen âge. Helsingfors, 1914.
Lehmann, P. Die Parodie im Mittelalter. München, 1922.
Lindsay, F. W. Dramatic Parody by Marionettes in Eighteenth Century Paris. New York, 1946.
Travers, S. Catalogue of XIXth Century Theatre Parodies (1789-1914). New York, 1941.
—— The Melodrama Satirized in Theatrical Parody. MLN, 61, 1946.
—— Parody in the French Theater: A Note on Its Vogue. RR, 37, 1946.
PASTORAL LITERATURE, Pastourelle, Idyls, Bucolic Poetry. See also Robinsonaden, IV. VIII. 7.
Audiau, J. La pastourelle dans la poésie occitane du moyen âge. Paris, 1923.
Audreen. Studies in the Idyl in German Literature. Rock Island, 1902.
Budde, Illa. Die Idylle im holländischen Barock. Köln, 1929.
Carducci, G. Precedenti all' Aminta del Tasso. NAnt, 136-37, 1894.
Carnap, E. Das Schäferwesen in der deutschen Literatur des 17. Jahrhunderts und die Hirtendichtung Europas. Würzburg, 1939.
Carrara, E. La poesia pastorale. In: Vallardi's Storia dei generi letterari italiani. Milano, 1907.
Castennet des Fosses, H. La poésie pastorale portugaise. Angers, 1886.
Congleton, J. E. Theories of Pastoral Poetry in England, 1684-1717. SPh, 41, 1944.
Delbouille, M. Les origines de la pastourelle. Bruxelles, 1926.
Desfontaines, Abbé. Discours sur les pastorales de Virgile. In: Oeuvres de Virgile traduites en français. Paris, 1770.
Enzensperger, F. X. Ueber alte und neue Idylle. Progr. Staubing, 1860.
Faral, E. La pastourelle. Romania, 49, 1923.
Feuerlicht, I. Vom Wesen der deutschen Idylle. GR, 22, 1947.
Gosse, E. W. An Essay on English Pastoral Poetry. In: The Complete Works in Verse and Prose of Edmund Spenser, vol. 3. London, 1882.
Greg, W. Pastoral Poetry and Pastoral Drama. London, 1906.
Hall, H. M. Idylls of Fishermen; a History of the Literary Species. New York, 1912.
Harrison, T. The Latin Pastorals of Milton and Castiglione. PMLA, 1935.
—— & Leon, H. J. The Pastoral Elegy: An Anthology (from Theocritus to Matthew Arnold). (Cf. Introduction). Austin (Texas), 1939.
Hedberg, B. N. The Bucolics and the Medieval Poetical Debate. TAPhA, 1944.
Hubaux, J. Les thèmes bucoliques dans la poésie latine. Bruxelles, 1930.
Hübner, A. Das erste deutsche Schäferidyll und seine Quellen. Diss. Königsberg, 1910.
Jeffery, V. M. Italian and English Pastoral Drama of the Renaissance. MLR, 1924.
—— La fortuna del dramma pastorale italiano in Inghilterra. NAnt, 1924-25.
Jones, W. P. The Pastourelle: a Study of the Origins and Traditions of a Lyric Type. Harvard U.P., 1931.
—— The Pastourelle and French Folk Drama. HSPhL, 13, 1931.
Ker, W. P. Cervantes, Shakespeare and the Pastoral Idea. In: Form and Style in Poetry. London, 1928.
Kohler, E. L'inspiration pastorale de Sannazaro à B. Guarini. Bull. de la Fac. des Lettres de Strasbourg, 1933.
Krauss, W. Ueber die Stellung der Bukolik in der aesthetischen Theorie des Humanismus. Archiv, 174, 1938.

Lavagnini, B. L'idillio secondo di Teocrito. Palermo, 1935.
Lord, L. E. A Translation of the Orpheus of A. Politian and the Aminta of Tasso. With an Introductory Essay on the Pastoral. Oxford U.P., 1931.
Macri-Leone, F. La bucolica latina nella letteratura italiana del secolo XIV. Torino, 1889.
Marsan, J. La pastorale dramatique. Paris, 1905.
Merker, P. Deutsche Idyllendichtung, 1700-1840. Berlin, 1934.
Moorman, F. W. William Browne, his Britannia's Pastoral and the Pastoral Poetry of the Elizabethan Age. Strassburg, 1897.
Morsier, E. de. L'idylle dans la littérature allemande. Etudes allemandes. (Paris), 1908.
Müller, N. Die deutschen Theorien der Idylle von Gottsched bis Gessner und ihre Quellen. Diss. Strassburg, 1911.
Mustard, W. P. The Pastoral, Ancient and Modern. CW, 8.
Nagel, W. Die deutsche Idylle im 18. Jahrhundert. Diss. Zürich, 1887.
Naum, T. A. Les bucoliques et les idylles théocritéennes. In: Vergilius (in Rumanian). Bucuresti, 1930.
Netoliczka, O. Schäferdichtung und Poetik im 18. Jahrhundert. DVLG, 1889.
Piguet, E. L'évolution de la pastourelle du XIIe siècle à nos jours. Diss. Berne. Bâle, 1927.
Rennert, H. A. The Spanish Pastoral Romances. Philadelphia, 1912.
Rötteken, H. Weltflucht und Idylle in Deutschland von 1720 bis zur Insel Felsenburg. ZVL, 9, 1896.
Schneider, G. Ueber das Wesen und den Entwicklungsgang der Idylle. Progr. Hamburg, 1893.
Schultz, O. Das Verhältniss der provenzalischen Pastourelle zur altfranzösischen. ZRPh, 8, 1884.
Smith, H. Pastoral Influence in the English Drama. PMLA, 12, 1897.
Vaccarello, E. L'eredità della poesia bucolica nel romanzo di Longo. MC, 1935.
Vollhardt, W. Die Beziehungen des Sommernachtstraumes zum italienischen Schäferdrama. Progr. Leipzig, 1899.
Vossler, K. Tassos Aminta und die Hirtendichtung. SVL, 6, 1906.
Vuertheim, G. Beitrag zur Entwicklungsgeschichte des antiken Hirtengesanges. Verslagen en Mededeelingen der k. Akademie van Wetenschappen, 2.
Weinberg, G. Das französische Schäferspiel in der ersten Hälfte des 17. Jahrhunderts. Frankfurt, 1884.
Wilson, E. F. Pastoral and Epithalamium in Latin Literature. Spec., 23, 1948.
Windscheid, K. Die englische Hirtendichtung von 1579 bis 1625. Diss. Halle, 1894.

PHYSIOLOGUS: See Literary Themes, I. VI. 10.

Schreiber, H. Studien zum **PROLOG** in mittelalterlicher Dichtung. Würzburg, 1935.

RHETORIC, Oratory, Preaching, Declamation.

Baldwin, C. S. Medieval Rhetoric and Poetic (to 1400) Interpreted from Representative Works. New York, 1928.
Camus, G. Precetti di rettorica scritti per Enrico III re di Francia. Modena, 1888.
Caplan, H. The Influence of Classical Rhetoric on Mediaeval Artes Praedicandi. PCA, 1929.
—— Classical Rhetoric and the Mediaeval Theory of Preaching. CPh, 28, 1933.
—— Mediaeval Artes Praedicandi; a Handlist. Ithaca, 1934.
Charland, T. M. Les Artes predicandi, contribution à l'histoire de la rhétorique au moyen âge. Paris, Ottawa, 1936.
Crane, W. G. Wit and Rhetoric in the Renaissance. New York, 1937.
Curtius, E. R. Dichtung und Rhetorik im Mittelalter. DVLG, 16, 1938.
—— Antike Rhetorik und vergleichende Literaturwissenschaft. CL, 1, 1949.
Dodsley, R. The Art of Preaching, in Imitation of Horace's Art of Poetry. London, 1738.
Engelhardt, G. J. Mediaeval Vestiges in the Rhetoric of Erasmus. PMLA, 63, 1948.
Gilman, W. E. Milton's Rhetoric: Studies in His Defense of Liberty. U. of Missouri Studies, 14. Columbia, 1939.
Herrick, M. T. The Place of Rhetoric in Poetic Theory. Quart. Journal of Speech, 34, 1948.
Hofrichter, W. Studien zur Entwicklungsgeschichte der Deklamation von der griechischen Sophistik bis zur römischen Kaiserzeit. Ohlau i/Schl., 1936.
König, E. Stilistik, Rhetorik, Poetic in Bezug auf die biblische Literatur komparativisch dargestellt. Leipzig, 1900.
Langlois, E. De artibus rhetoricae rhytmicae. Diss. Paris, 1890.

Manly, J. M. Chaucer and the Rhetoricians. British Academy, 1926.
McKeon, R. Rhetoric in the Middle Ages. Spec., 17, 1942.
Oudendijk, J. K. Een culturhistorische Vergelijking tusschen de Fransche en de Engelsche Parlamentaire Redervering. Utrecht, 1937.
Roberts, W. R. Greek Rhetoric and Literary Criticism. In: Our Debt to Greece and Rome. New York, 1928.
—— Roman Rhetoric and Literary Criticism. Ibid.
Smyth, C. The Art of Preaching. A Practical Survey of Preaching in the Church of England, 747-1939 A.D. London, 1940.
Solmsen, F. The Aristotelian Tradition in Ancient Rhetoric. AJPh, 62, 1941.
Stoll, E. Downfall of Oratory: Our Democratic Arts. JHI, 7, 1946.
Volkmann-Hammer. Rhetorik und Metrik der Griechen und Römer. München, 1901.
Wicart, A. L'orateur (rhétorique comparée). Paris, 1935.
Wood, W. A. After-Dinner Speeches and How to Make Them. Chicago, 1914.
ROMANCE: See also Epics, Novels, Celtic Contributions, Amadis, etc.
Barbeau, M. Romancero du Canada. Toronto, 1937.
Barrow, Sarah F. The Medieval Society Romances. New York, 1924.
Begley, W. Bibliography of Romance from the Renaissance to the End of the Seventeenth Century. London, 1902.
Cox, G. W. & Jones, E. H. Popular Romances of the Middle Ages. New York, 1880.
Crane, R. S. The Vogue of Medieval Chivalric Romance During the English Renaissance. Diss. U. of Pennsylvania, 1919.
Ferrario, G. Storia ed analisi d. ant. romanzi di cavalleria e dei poemi romaneschi d'Italia. 4 vols. Milano, 1826-29.
Lavagnini, B. Le origini del romanzo Greco. Pisa, 1921.
Leonard, I. A. Romances of Chivalry in the Spanish Indies. Berkeley, 1934.
Magnus, L. A General Sketch of European Literature in the Centuries of Romance. London, 1918.
Miller, C. W. The Influence of the French Heroi-Historical Romance on XVIIth Century English Prose Fiction. Diss. U. of Virginia, 1940.
Owen, S. G. Ovid and Romance. In: English Literature and the Classics. Oxford, 1912.
Spence, L. A Dictionary of Medieval Romance and Romance Writers. London, 1913.
Taylor, A. B. An Introduction to Medieval Romance. London, 1930.
Thomas, H. The Palmerin Romances. Trans. Bibliogr. Soc., 13. (London), 1915.
Alden, R. M. The Rise of Formal **SATIRE** in England under Classical Influence. Philadelphia, 1899. Cf. Anglia, 13, 1902.
Cian, V. La satira dal medioevo al Pontano. Milano, 1939.
—— La satira dall' Ariosto al Chiabrera. Milano, 1945.
Frye, N. The Nature of Satire. UTQ, 14, 1944.
Gubernatis, A. de. Storia della satira. Milano, 1884.
Hannay, J. Satire and Satirists. Redfield, 1855.
Max, H. Die Satire in der französischen Publizistik unter besonderer Berücksichtigung des französischen Witzblattes. München, 1934.
Müller, F. Zur Geschichte der römischen Satire. Ph, 1922.
Randolph, Mary C. The Medical Concept in English Renaissance Satiric Theory: Its Possible Relationships and Implications. SPh, 38, 1941.
—— The French Coq-à-l'âne as a Satiric Form. N&Q, 181, 1941.
—— Pierre Bayle's Case Against Satire and Satirists. N&Q, 181, 1941.
—— The Structural Design of the Formal Verse Satire. PhQ, 21, 1942.
—— Female Satirists of Ancient Ireland. SFQ, 6, 1942.
—— Hide-and-Seek Satires of the Restoration and XVIIIth Century. N&Q, 183, 1942.
—— Diamond Satires in the XVIIIth Century. N&Q, 184, 1943.
—— Candour in XVIIIth Century Satire. RES, 20, 1944.
Rubio y Ors, J. Apuntes para una historia de la satira. Barcelona, 1868.
Samosch, S. Italienische und französische Satiriker. Berlin, 1879.
Schneegans, H. Geschichte der grotesken Satire. Strassburg, 1894.
Stein, A. Donne and the Satiric Spirit. ELH, 11, 1944.
—— Studies in Elizabethan Satire. Diss. Harvard, 1944.
Tupper, F. Twelfth-Century Scholarship and Satire. Festschrift Carleton Brown. New York, 1940.
Worcester, D. The Art of Satire. Harvard U.P., 1940.

Niemeyer, P. Die **SENTENZ** als poetische Ausdrucksform, vorzüglich im dramatischen Stil. Berlin, 1934.
SIRVENTES: See Debate, above.
Peignot, G. Choix de **TESTAMENTS** anciens et modernes. Paris, 1829.
Perrow, E. C. The Last Will and Testament as a Form of Literature. Trans. of the Wisconsin Academy, 17, 1913.
Rice, W. H. The European Ancestry of Villon's Satirical Testaments. New York, 1941.
Tardel, H. Die Testamentsidee als dichterisches Formmotiv. Niederdeutsche Zs. f. Volkskunde, 4, 1926.
Austen, H. Remarques sur l'idée du **TRAGIQUE** et sur les théories d'Aristote et de Corneille. Progr. Guhrau, 1868.
Geffcken, J. Der Begriff des Tragischen in der Antike, ein Beitrag zur Geschichte der antiken Aesthetik. VBW, 7, 1930.
Klees, H. Ueber das Wesen des Tragischen. Zs. f. Aesthetik & allg. Kunstwissenschaft, 26, 1932.
Muschg, W. Tragische Literaturgeschichte. Bern, 1948.
Prior, M. The Language of Tragedy. Columbia U.P., 1947.
Reiss, W. Die Theorie des Tragischen im 17. Jahrhundert in Deutschland und Frankreich. Diss. Bern, 1910.
TRANSLATIONS: See I. IV. 2.
Jolles, A. Die literarischen **TRAVESTIEN.** Bull. f. deutsche Philosophie, 6, 1933.
Atkinson, G. The Extraordinary **VOYAGE** in French Literature Before 1700. New York, 1920.
—— The Extraordinary Voyage in French Literature From 1700 to 1720. Paris, 1922.
—— Les relations de voyages en France au XVIIIe siècle et l'évolution des idées. Paris, 1925.
—— La littérature géographique française de la Renaissance. Répertoire bibliographique. Paris, 1927.
—— Les nouveaux horizons de la Renaissance française. Paris, 1935.
Bonner, W. H. Captain William Dampier, Buccaneer-Author. Some Contribution of a Modest Buccaneer and of English Travel Literature in the Early XVIIIth Century. Stanford U.P., 1934.
Boulenger, J. Voyages et aventures de François Leguat en deux îles désertes, 1690-98. Paris, 1934.
Brown, W. C. English Travel Books, 1775-1825. PhQ, 1937.
Charpentier, J. Le genre littéraire du voyage. La Vie, 1.IV.1937.
Cox, E. G. A Reference Guide to the Literature of Travel Including Voyages, Geographical Descriptions, Adventures, Shipwrecks and Expeditions. Vol. 1. Europe, Asia, Africa. Vol. 2. America. U. of Washington, Seattle, 1935-38.
Deprez, E. Les grands voyages et les grandes découvertes jusqu'à la fin du XVIIIe siècle: origines, développement, consequences. Bull. of the Intern. Committee of Hist. Sciences. Paris, 1930.
Dodds, M. Les récits de voyages, sources de L'esprit des lois de Montesquieu. Paris, 1929.
Friederich, W. P. Jakob von Graviseth's Heutelia. PMLA, 1937.
Gide, A. Voyage en littérature anglaise. Verve, 1938.
Gove, P. B. The Imaginary Voyage in Prose Fiction. A History of Its Criticism and a Guide for Its Study, with an Annotated Check List of 215 Imaginary Voyages from 1700 to 1800. Columbia U.P., 1941.
Krappe, A. H. The Subterraneous Voyage. PhQ, 20, 1941.
Messac, R. Voyages modernes au centre de la terre. RLC, 9, 1929.
Nicolson, Marjorie. Cosmic Voyages. ELH, 7, 1940.
—— The Voyage to Cacklogallinia, with a Description of the Religion, Policy, Customs, and Manners of that Country by Captain Samuel Brunt. New York, 1940.
Paludan, J. Om Holbergs Niels Klim, med saerligt hensyn til tidligere satirer i form af opdigtede og vidunderlige rejser. København, 1878.
Pons, E. Le voyage, genre littéraire au XVIIIe siècle: indications bibliographiques et critiques. Bull. de la Fac. des Lettres de Strasbourg, 1926.
Roosbroeck, G. van. Persian Letters before Montesquieu. MLR, 1925 & New York, 1932.
Seeber, E. D. Ideal Languages in the French and English Imaginary Voyage. PMLA, 60, 1945.
Toldo, P. Les voyages merveilleux de Cyrano de Bergerac et de Swift et leurs rapports avec l'oeuvre de Rabelais. Revue des Etudes rabelaisiennes, 4-5, 1906-07.
Wijngaarden, N. Les Odyssées philosophiques en France entre 1616 et 1789. Harlem, 1932.

CHAPTER TWO

Collective Literary Genres.

1. Generalities.

Ampère, J. J. Histoire littéraire de la France avant le XIIe siècle. (Birth of Genres). 3rd. ed. Paris, 1870.
Berger, L. Gattung, Form und Wort. Helicon, 2, 1940.
Bovet, E. Lyrisme, épopée, drame. Paris, 1911.
Bray, R. Des genres littéraires, de leur hiérarchie et du principe de cette hiérarchie dans la littérature classique. Lausanne, 1937.
Cohen, G. L'origine médiévale des genres littéraires modernes. Helicon, 2, 1940.
Díaz-Plaja, G. Teoría e historia de los géneros literarios. Barcelona, 1940.
Donohue, J. J. Theory of Literary Kinds. Ancient Classifications of Literature. Dubuque, (Iowa), 1943.
Hankiss, J. Les genres littéraires et leur base psychologique. Helicon, 2, 1940.
Kohler, P. Contribution à une philosophie des genres. Ibid.
Taylor, A. Problems in the Literary History of a Genre. In: Problems in German Literary History of the Fifteenth and Sixteenth Centuries. New York, 1939.
Van Tieghem, P. La question des genres littéraires. Helicon, 1939-40.

2. Drama, Comedy, Tragedy.

Bourgeois Drama, Chorus, Comédie larmoyante, Costumes, Dramatic Rules, Entremes, Farce, Fate Tragedy, Heroic Tragedy, History of Theater, Marionette, Mask, Melodrama, Mimus, Miracle Play, Pantomime, Play within Play, Political Drama, Puppetry, Religious Plays, Shrovetide Plays, Staging, Tragicomedy, University Drama.

a. General Works.

Agnes, S. Provenzalisches geistliches Schauspiel. Berlin, 1869.
Aikin-Sneath, B. Comedy in Germany in the First Half of the 18th Century. Oxford, 1936.
Alexander, H. B. Drama as a Cosmic Category. Philos. Review, 1930.
Allen, J. T. Stage Antiquities of the Greeks and Romans and Their Influence. New York, 1927.
Allevym, M. A. La mise en scène en France dans la première moitié du dix-neuvième siècle. Paris, 1938.
Anderson, M. The Essence of Tragedy. Washington, 1939.
Bachmeister, E. Der deutsche Typus der Tragödie. Berlin, 1943.
Bahlsen. Die epischen Komödien und Tragödien des Mittelalters. Centralblatt f. Bibliothekswesen, 10, 1893.
Baker, H. Introduction to Tragedy. Louisiana State U.P., 1939.
Barbas, M. The Stage Controversy in France From Corneille to Rousseau. New York, 1933.
Bayer, J. Evangelische Dramen. Neues Wiener Tageblatt, 137, 1903.
Bédier, J. Les commencements du théâtre comique en France. RDM, 1890.
Bellen, E. V. van. Les origines du mélodrame. Diss. Amsterdam. Utrecht, 1927.
Bernbaum, E. The Drama of Sensibility; A Sketch of the History of English Sentimental Comedy, and Domestic Tragedy, 1696-1780. Boston, 1915.
Biaggi, G. A. Le origine del melodramma. NAnt, 9, 1868.
Boas, F. S. University Drama in the Tudor Age. Oxford, 1917.
Borcherdt, H. H. Das europäische Theater im Mittelalter und in der Renaissance. Leipzig, 1935.
Bourdon, G. Staging in French and English Theaters. Fortnightly Rev., 1902.
Bowers, F. T. Elizabethan Revenge Tragedy, 1587-1642. Princeton, 1940.
Bragaglia, A. G. Le maschere romane. Roma, 1947.
Brahm, O. Das deutsche Ritterdrama des 18. Jahrhunderts. Strassburg, 1880.
Brinkmann, H. Zum Ursprung des liturgischen Spieles. Bonn, 1929.
Brooke, Iris. Western European Costume and its Relation to the Theatre. 2 vols. London, 1939.
Brotanek, R. Die englischen Maskenspiele. Wien, 1902. Cf. ESn, 1904.
Busch, E. Die Idee des Tragischen in der deutschen Klassik. Halle, 1942.
Carrière, M. Grundzüge und Winke zur vergleichenden Litteraturgeschichte des Dramas. In: Poesie, ihr Wesen und ihre Formen mit Grundzügen der vergleichenden Literaturgeschichte. 2. ed. Leipzig, 1884.
Ceriello, G. R. Comedias de Santos a Napoli nel 1800. BH, 22.
Chambers, Sir Edmund. The Mediaeval Stage. 2 vols. Oxford, 1903.
Chaytor, H. J. Dramatic Theory in Spain. Cambridge, 1925.

Cibber, C. Short View of the English Stage. London, 1698.
Clark, B. H. European Theories of the Drama. Cincinnati, 1918.
Cleaver, J. The Theatre Through the Ages. London, 1946.
Cloetta, W. Beiträge zur Literaturgeschichte des Mittelalters und der Renaissance: I. Komödie und Tragödie im Mittelalter. II. Die Anfänge der Renaissancetragödie. Halle, 1890-92.
Coe, Ada M. Notes on Puppetry in Mexico. Hisp., 28, 1945.
Coffman, G. R. A New Theory Concerning the Origin of the Miracle Play. Menasha (Wisconsin), 1914.
—— A New Approach to Mediaeval Drama. MPh, 22, 1924-25.
—— Tragedy and a Sense of the Tragic in Some of its Ethical Implications. Sewanee Rev., 50, 1942.
Cohen, G. Histoire de la mise en scène dans le théâtre religieux français du moyen âge. Paris, 1926.
—— Le théâtre en France au moyen âge. 2 vols. Paris, 1929-31.
Commedia dell'arte: See Italian Contributions, IV. III. 6.
Constant, B. Réflexions sur la tragédie. RP, Oct., 1829.
Contaut & de Filippi. Parallèle des principaux théâtres de l'Europe et des machines théâtrales italiennes, françaises, allemandes, anglaises, etc. 2 vols. Paris, 1870.
Cougny, E. Des représentations dramatiques et particulièrement de la Comédie politique dans les collèges au XVIe siècle. Paris, 1868.
Craig, H. The Origin of the Passion Play: Matters of Theory as well as Fact. Festschrift A. H. R. Fairchild. Columbia (Mo.), 1946.
Creizenach, W. Geschichte des neueren Dramas. Halle, 1911.
Croce, B. Di un caso di antimetodica costruzione dottrinale: la teoria del comico. Crit. 20.V.1934.
Cunliffe, J. W. Italian Prototypes of the Masque and Dumb Show. PMLA, 22, 1907.
Delcourt, M. La tradition des comiques anciens en France avant Molière. Paris, 1934.
Déléhaye, H. Les passions des martyrs et les genres littéraires. Bruxelles, 1921.
Denewa, W. Das österreichische Märchendrama in der Biedermeierzeit. Berlin, 1940.
Desnoiresterres, G. La comédie satirique au XVIIIe siècle. Paris, 1885.
Devrient, E. Geschichte der deutschen Schauspielkunst. 3 vols. Leipzig, 1848.
Diès, A. Encore guignol. (Marionettes). BAGB, 14-15, 1927.
Disher, M. W. The Plots of Pantomines. TLS, 5.XI.1938.
Dixon, W. M. Tragedy. London, 1925.
Draper, J. The Theory of the Comic in XVIIIth Century England. JEGPh, 37, 1938.
Dubech, L. et al. Histoire générale illustrée du théâtre (européen). 5 vols. Paris, 1935.
Ebner, J. Beiträge zu einer Geschichte der dramatischen Einheiten in Italien. Münchener Beiträge, 15. Erlangen, 1898.
Eichert, Ellynor. Das geistliche Spiel der Gegenwart in Deutschland und Frankreich. Berlin, 1941.
Eloesser, A. Das bürgerliche Drama im 18. und 19. Jahrhundert. Berlin, 1898.
Enzinger, M. Die Entwicklung des Wiener Theaters. Berlin, 1918.
—— Das deutsche Schicksalsdrama. Innsbruck, 1922.
Ermatinger, E. Die Kunstform des Dramas. Leipzig, 1925.
Evreinoff, N. Le théâtre en Russie soviétique. Paris, 1946.
Fauconnier, R. L. Tragedy and the Modern Theatre. Queen's Quart., 55, 1948.
Feibleman, J.J In Praise of Comedy. A Study of its Theory and Practice. New York, 1939.
Flat, P. Le faux art dramatique à l'étranger. RB, 30.IX.1911.
Frank, Grace. Beginnings of Comedy in France. MLR, 31, 1936.
—— Introduction to a Study of the Mediaeval French Drama. Festschrift Carleton Brown, Oxford U.P., 1940.
Freedley, G. & Reeves, J. A. A History of the Theatre. New York, 1940.
Frenz, H. American Drama and World Drama. College English, 6, 1945.
Fricker, R. Das historische Drama in England von der Romantik bis zur Gegenwart. Bern, 1940.
Friedland, L. S. The Dramatic Unities in England. JEGPh, 10, 1911.
Gagliulo, F. Sul problema di Thespis e l'origine del dramma satiresco. Rivista Indo-Graeca-Italica, 13, 1929.
Gaiffe, F. Le drame en France au XVIIIe siècle. Paris, 1910.

—— Le rire et la scène française. Paris, 1931.
Galletti. Le teorie drammatiche e la tragedia in Italia nel secolo XVIII. Cremona, 1901.
Gardiner, H. C. Mysteries' End: An Investigation of the Last Days of the Medieval Religious Stage. New Haven, 1946.
Geffcken, J. Der Begriff des Tragischen in der Antike. VBW, 7.
Geisler, K. Das Nachwirken des Mimus in der satirischen und burlesken Literatur Frankreichs im 17. Jahrhundert. Diss. Berlin, 1935.
Giacosa, G. L'art dramatique et les comédiens italiens. RB, 25.II.1899.
Giovanni, G. The Connection Between Tragedy and History in Ancient Criticism. PhQ, 22, 1944.
Glanz, L. Das Puppenspiel und sein Publikum. Berlin, 1941.
Görland, A. Die Idee des Schicksals in der Geschichte der Tragödie. Tübingen, 1913. Cf. also Zs. f. Aesthetik, 10.
Görner, O. Vom Memorabile zur Schicksalstragödie. Berlin, 1931.
Goggio, E. Dramatic Theories in the Prologues to the Commedie Erudite of the Sixteenth Century. PMLA, 58, 1943.
Goldschmidt. Das politische Schauspiel in Frankreich unter König Ludwig XII. Archiv, 41, 1867.
Gori, G. Il teatro contemporaneo e le sue correnti caratteristiche di pensiero e di vita nelle varie nazioni. Torino, 1924.
Green, C. C. The Neo-Classic Theory of Tragedy in England During the XVIIIth Century. Harvard U.P., 1934.
Gregor, J. Weltgeschichte des Theaters. I: Von den Ursprüngen bis zum Ausgang des Barocktheaters. München, 1944.
Grysar, C. J. Der römische Mimus. SAWW, 12, 1854.
Hallberg, L. E. Le drame lyrique au point de vue littéraire. Mémoires de l'Acad. de Toulouse. 9e sér., 8, 1896.
Harbage, A. Annals of English Drama, 975-1700. An Analytical Record of All Plays, Extant or Lost, Chronologically Arranged and Indexed by Authors, Titles, Dramatic Companies, etc. Philadelphia, 1940.
Harrison, M. Modern Religious Drama in Germany and France. Stratford, 1936.
Holl, F. Das politische und religiöse Tendenzdrama des XVI. Jahrhunderts in Frankreich. Münchener Beiträge, 1903.
Hughes, L. Attitudes of Some Restoration Dramatists Toward Farce. PhQ, 19, 1940.
Hung Sheng. What is the Chinese Drama? China Journal of Science & Arts, 1, 1923.
Hytier, J. La tragédie religieuse persane. Cahiers du Sud, 1935.
Jack, W. S. The Early entremes in Spain: the Rise of a Dramatic Form. Philadelphia, 1923.
Jacobsen, J. P. Essai sur les origines de la comédie en France au moyen-âge. Paris, 1910.
Janell, W. Lob des Schauspielers, oder Mime und Mimus. Berlin, 1922.
Javons, F. B. Masks and the Origin of the Greek Drama. FL, 27, 1916.
Jourdain, E. F. Dramatic Theory and Practice in France, 1690-1808. London, 1921.
—— The Drama in Europe: Its Theory and Practice. London, 1924.
Kawatake, S. Development of the Japanese Theatre Art. Tokyo, 1935.
Kernodle, G. R. England's Religious-Drama Movement. College English, 1, 1940.
Kluckhohn, P. Die Arten des Dramas. DVLG, 19, 1941.
Körner, J. Tragik und Tragödie: ein vorläufiger Versuch über Wesen und Gestaltwandel des Tragischen. PJb, 225, 1931.
Kruuse, J. Det følsomme Drama. København, 1934. Cf. RLC, 1937.
Lancaster, H. C. The French Tragi-Comedy. Its Origin and Development from 1552-1628. Baltimore, 1907.
Lanson, G. Etudes sur les origines de la tragédie classique en France. RHLF, 10, 1903.
—— Esquisse d'une histoire de la tragédie française. Paris, 1927.
La Piana, G. Le rappresentazioni sacre nella letteratura bizantina dalle origini al secolo IX, con rapporti al teatro sacro d'Occidente. Grottaferrata, 1912.
Lebègue, R. La vie d'un ancien genre dramatique: le mystère. Helicon, 2, 1940.
—— La tragédie religieuse en France. Les débuts (1514-73). Paris, 1929.
—— La tragédie française de la Renaissance. Bruxelles, 1944.
—— Tableau de la tragédie française de 1573 à 1610. BHR, 1944.
—— Tableau de la comédie française de la Renaissance. BHR, 8, 1946.

—— Notes sur la tragédie française. BHR, 9, 1947.

Lemercier de Neuville. Histoire anecdotique des marionnettes modernes. Paris, 1892.

Levi-Malvano, E. La fortuna d'una teoria drammatica in Italia. (Bourgeois drama). GSLI, 105, 1935.

Lindner, A. Die Taufpaten des deutschen Dramas. MLIA, 1885.

Loukovitch, K. L'évolution de la tragédie religieuse classique en France. Paris, 1933.

Lynch, K. M. The Social Mode of the Restoration Comedy. New York, 1926.

Magnin, C. Les origines du théâtre antique et du théâtre moderne, ou histoire du génie dramatique, depuis le ler jusqu'au XVIe siècle. Paris, 1868.

—— Histoire des Marionnettes en Europe depuis l'Antiquité jusqu'à nos jours. Paris, 1882.

Mahr, A. C. Dramatische Situationsbilder und Bild-Typen. Stanford U., 1928.

Malnick, Bertha. Origin and History of the Early Russian Theatre. Slavonic Yearbook, 19, 1941.

Manly, J. M. The Miracle Play in Mediaeval England. Trans. of the Royal Society of Literature, 7, 1927.

Marshall, Mary H. The Dramatic Tradition Established by the Liturgical Plays. PMLA, 56, 1941.

Meozzi, A. La drammatica della Rinascita italiana in Europa. Pisa, 1940.

Michels, V. Studien über die ältesten deutschen Fastnachtspiele. Strassburg, 1895.

Milchsack, G. Die Oster- und Passionsspiele. Eine literarische Untersuchung über den Ursprung und die Entwicklung derselben bis zum XVII. Jahrhundert, vornehmlich in Deutschland. Wolfenbüttel, 1879.

Minor, J. Die Schicksalstragödie in ihren Hauptvertretern. Frankfurt, 1883.

Mornet, D. La question des règles au XVIIIe siècle. RHLF, 1914.

Mouflard, Marie-Madeleine. La comédie au XVIe siècle. Paris, 1948.

Nestriepke, S. Das Theater im Wandel der Zeiten. Berlin, 1928.

Nethercot, A. H. The Drama of Ideas. Sewanee Rev., 49, 1941.

Nicoll, A. The Origin and Types of the Heroic Tragedy. Anglia, 44, 1920.

—— A History of Restoration Drama. 2nd ed. Cambridge, 1928.

—— Stuart Masques and the Renaissance Stage. London, 1937.

—— The Development of the Theatre: A Study of Theatrical Art from the Beginnings to the Present Day. London, 1948.

Niedner, H. Die deutschen und französischen Osterspiele bis zum 15. Jahrhundert. Berlin, 1932.

Nietzsche, F. Ueber die Geburt der Tragödie aus dem Geiste der Musik. (1872).

Nillson, M. P. Der Ursprung der Tragödie. NJKA, 28, 1911.

Nolte, F. O. The Early Middle Class Drama (1696-1774). Lancaster (Pa.), 1935.

Nuffel, R. O. J. van. Il Romanticismo e le sue teorie drammatiche. RBPh, 26, 1948.

O'Connor, W. V. The Rebirth of Tragedy. SAB, 16, 1941.

Paalhorn, L. Die aesthetische Bedeutung der Aktgliederung in der Tragödie. Halle, 1929.

Paine, C. C. The Comedy of Manners (1660-1700): A Reference Guide to the Comedy of the Restoration. Boston, 1941.

Parrott, T. M. & Ball, R. H. A Short View of Elizabethan Drama, together with Some Account of its Principal Playwrights and the Conditions under which it was Produced. New York, 1943.

Parsons, A. E. The English Heroic Play. MLR, Jan., 1938.

Pascal, R. On the Origins of the Liturgical Drama of the Middle Ages. MLR, 1943.

Pastoral Drama: See Pastoral Poetry, p. 185.

Pat, Beatrice. The Development of the Christmas Play in Spain. Diss. Bryn Mawr; Microfilm Abstracts, 8, 1948.

Peiper, R. Die profane Komödie des Mittelalters. Archiv, 5, 1875.

Péricaud, L. Le théâtre des Funambules, ses mimes, ses acteurs et ses pantomimes depuis sa fondation jusqu'à sa démolition. Paris, 1897.

Pfordten, O. von der. Werden und Wesen des historischen Dramas. Heidelberg, 1901.

Pinatel, J. Le drame bourgeois en Allemagne au XVIIIe siècle. Lyon, 1938.

—— Répertoire des drames bourgeois en Allemagne au XVIIIe siècle. Lyon, 1938.

Planelli, A. Dell' opera in musica, trattato (melodrama). Napoli, 1772.

Polti, G. Les trente-six situations dramatiques. Paris, 1895; 2nd ed., 1914.

Praz, M. Il dramma inglese della Restaurazione e i suoi aspetti preromantici. Cult., 1933.
Prescott, H. W. The Antecedents of Hellenistic Comedy. CPh, 1917.
Prinsen, J. Het drama in de 18e eeuw in West-Europa. Zutphen, 1931.
Prutz, H. Zur Geschichte der politischen Komödie in Deutschland. Berlin, München, 1919.
Rapp, E. Die Marionette in der deutschen Dichtung, vom Sturm und Drang bis zur Romantik. Leipzig, 1924.
Reich, H. Der Mimus. Berlin, 1903-04.
Reynolds, A. F. Some Principles of Elizabethan Staging. MPh, 2-3, 1904-05.
Reynolds, G. F. The Staging of Elizabethan Plays at the Red Bull Theatre, 1605-25. New York, 1940.
Riccoboni, L. Réflexions historiques et critiques sur les différents théâtres de l'Europe. Paris, 1738.
Ridgeway, W. The Origin of Tragedy, with Special Reference to the Greek Tragedy. Cambridge, 1910.
—— The Dramas and Dramatic Dances of Non-European Races in Special Reference to the Origin of Greek Tragedy. Cambridge, 1915.
Rigal, E. La lutte entre le théâtre de la Renaissance et le théâtre du moyen âge. In: Histoire de la langue et de la littérature française, (ed. by Petit de Julleville). Paris, 1897.
Robert, C. Die Masken der neueren attischen Komödie. Rev. des Etudes Anciennes, 1914.
Roditi, E. The Genesis of Neoclassical Tragedy. SAQ, 46, 1947.
Roy, E. Le mystère de la passion en France du XIVe au XVIe siècle; étude sur les sources et le classement des mystères de la passion. Paris, 1905.
Ruberti, G. Il teatro contemporaneo in Europa. Bologna, 1921.
Rudwin, M. J. The Origin of the German Carnival Comedy. New York, 1920.
Rymer, T. The Tragedies of the Last Age Consider'd and Examin'd by the Practice of the Ancients, and by the Common Sense of all Ages. London, 1692.
Sargeant, G. M. The Greek Fear of Life (and the Birth of Tragedy). QR, 1924.
Schirmer, W. F. Ueber das Historiendrama in der englischen Renaissance. Archiv, 179.
Schmid, C. H. Litteratur des bürgerlichen Trauerspiels. Deutsche Monatsschrift, Nov., 1798.
Schmitt, E. H. Moderne und antike Schicksalstragödie. Berlin, 1874.
Segond, J. La signification de la tragédie. RCC, 1936.
Sepet, M. Le drame religieux au moyen âge. In: Etudes pour le temps présent. Paris, 1903.
Solerti, A. Le origini del melodramma. Torino, 1903.
Sper, F. From Native Roots: A Panorama of Our Regional Drama. Caldwell (Idaho), 1948.
Stammler, W. Das religiöse Drama des deutschen Mittelalters. Leipzig, 1925.
Steinweg, C. Studien zur Entwicklungsgeschichte der Tragödie. 7 vols. Halle, 1905-24.
Stumpff, R. Süddeutsche Bühnenformen vor Einführung der italienischen Verwandlungsbühne. ZDPh, 1928.
Stumpfl, R. Der Ursprung des Fastnachtspiels und die kultischen Männerbünde der Germanen. ZDK, 1934.
—— Kultspiele der Germanen als Ursprung des mittelalterlichen Dramas. Berlin, 1936.
Symmes, H. S. Les débuts de la critique dramatique en Angleterre. Paris, 1903.
Tièche, E. Der Ursprung der Tragödie. Jb. d. Vereins schweiz. Gymnasiallehrer, 44.
Toldo, P. La comédie française de la Renaissance. RHLF, 1897-98.
—— Etudes sur le théâtre français du moyen âge et sur le rôle de la nouvelle dans les farces et dans les comédies. Studj di filologia romanza, 9, 1903.
Tronchon, H. L'esthétique du théâtre allemand et les règles françaises jugées par un Voltairien hongrois. RLC, 5, 1925.
Untersteiner, M. Le origini della tragedia. Milano, 1942.
Valle, N. Le origini del melodramma. Roma, 1937.
Vaughan, C. E. Types of Tragic Drama. London, 1908.
Vito, M. S. de. L'origine del dramma liturgico. Napoli, 1938.
Wackernell, J. E. Altdeutsche Passionsspiele aus Tirol mit einer Abhandlung über ihre Entwicklung, Quellen etc. Graz, 1897.
Wade, I. O. Middle-Class Philosophers, Middle-Class Philosophy in the Drama of the XVIIIth Century. MPh, 1928.
Wais, K. Die nationalen Typen des neueren Dramas im genetischen Zusammenhang. Helicon, 2, 1940.
Wassermann, E. R. The Pleasures of Tragedy. ELH, 14, 1947.

Welsford, E. Italian Influence on the English Court Masque. MLR, 1923.
—— The Court Masque. A Study of the Relationship Between Poetry and Revel. Cambridge U.P., 1927.
Williams, E. E. Tragedy of Destiny: Oedipus Tyrannus, Macbeth, Athalie. Cambridge (Mass.), 1940.
Wilson, N. European Drama. London, 1937.
Winckler, E. Zur Geschichte des Begriffs Comédie in Frankreich. Heidelberg, 1937.
Winterfeld, P. von. Der Mimus im Mittelalter. München, 1927.
Winterstein, A. Der Ursprung der Tragôdie. Wien, 1925.
Wirth, L. Die Oster- und Passionsspiele bis zum XVI. Jahrhundert. Halle, 1889.
Worp, J. A. Geschiednis van het drama en het tooneel in Nederland. Groningen, 1908.
Wright, Edith A. The Dissemination of the Liturgical Drama in France. Bryn Mawr, (Pa.), 1936.
Young, K. Concerning the Origin of the Miracle Play. Festschrift J. Manly. Chicago, 1923.
—— The Drama of the Medieval Church. 2 vols. Oxford, 1933.
Zarncke, E. Schicksalstragödie in Altertum und Neuzeit. Leipzig, 1914.
Zucker, A. E. The Chinese Theater. Boston, 1925.

b. Individual Authors.

Breitinger, H. Les unités d'**ARISTOTE** avant le Cid de Corneille. Genève, 1879. Cf. Revue critique, 52, 1879.
Cooper, L. An Aristotelian Theory of Comedy. Ithaca (N.Y.), 1948.
Knoke, F. Begriff der Tragôdie nach Aristoteles. Berlin, 1906.
Lucas, F. L. Tragedy in Relation to Aristotle's Poetics. London, 1927.
Weidenbach, P. Aristoteles und die Schicksalstragödie. Progr. Dresden, 1887.
Berens, P. **CALDERONS** Schicksalstragödien. RF, 39.
Corsi, M. Un centenario dimenticato: **CALLOT** e le maschere italiane. Illustrazione italiana, 32, 1935.
Grucker, E. **CORNEILLE**, Aristote et la tragédie française. Annales de l'Est, Oct., 1893.
Gueth. Ueber **DIDEROT** und das bürgerliche Drama. Progr. Stettin, 1873.
Hathaway, B. John **DRYDEN** and the Function of Tragedy. PMLA, 58, 1943.
Trowbridge, H. The Place of Rules in Dryden's Criticism. MPh, 44, 1946.
Boll, F. **GOETHE** und Platon über die Tragödie. Berliner Philol. Wochenschrift, 1916.
Sand, G. Essai sur le drame fantastique: Goethe, Byron, Mickiewicz. RDM, 1839.
Ortiz, M. Le commedie esopiche del **GOLDONI**. Riv. teatr. ital., 1905.
Schlenther, P. Frau **GOTTSCHED** und die bürgerliche Komödie. Berlin, 1886.
Weinberg, B. The Sources of **GREVIN'S** Ideas on Comedy and Tragedy. MPh, 45, 1947-48.
Alfero, G. A. L'Ahnfrau di Franz **GRILLPARZER** e la tragedia fatalistica. RI, 15.II.1922.
Minor, J. Die Ahnfrau und die Schicksalstragödie. Festschrift R. Heinzel. Wien, 1898.
Doering, J. F. **HUME** and the Theory of Tragedy. PMLA, 1937.
Rigal, E. De **JODELLE** à Molière. Tragédie, Comédie, Tragi-comédie. Paris, 1911.
Hofmiller, J. Die ersten sechs Masken Ben **JONSONS** in ihrem Verhältnis zur antiken Literatur. Progr. Freising, 1902.
Parrott, T. M. Comedy in the Court Masque: A Study of Ben Jonson's Contribution. PhQ, 20, 1941.
Aspelin, E. **LAMOTTES** Abhandlungen über die Tragödie, verglichen mit Lessings Hamburgischer Dramaturgie. ZVL, 14, 1899.
Arias, P. E. **LESSING** e la definizione aristotelica della tragedia. A&R, 11, 1930.
Brewer, E. V. Lessing and the Corrective Virtue in Comedy. JEGPh, 1927.
Brüggemann, F. Die Entwicklung der Psychologie im bürgerlichen Drama Lessings und seiner Zeit. Euph., 26, 1925.
Nolte, F. O. Lessing and the Bourgeois Drama. JEGPh, 31, 1932.
Robertson, J. G. Lessing's Dramatic Theory. Being an Introduction to and Commentary on his Hamburgische Dramaturgie. Cambridge U.P., 1939.
Abrahmson, O. Ein Beitrag zur Entwicklungsgeschichte der Schicksalstragödie. (**LILLO** in Germany). ALG, 9, 1880.
Crawford, J. P. W. Spanish Drama before **LOPE DE VEGA**. Philadelphia, 1937.
Bywater, I. **MILTON** and the Aristo-

telian Definition of Tragedy. Journal of Philology, 27, 1901.
Lanson, G. NIVELLE DE LA CHAUSSEE et la comédie larmoyante. 2e éd. Paris, 1900.
Leo, U. Luigi PIRANDELLO: Simbolista de la Máscara. Revista Nacional de Cultura (Caracas, Venezuela), 25-27, 1941.
Lemonnier, L. Edgar POE et le théâtre de mystère et de terreur. Grande Revue, 1929.
Houben, H. Der Chor in den Tragödien des RACINE. Progr. Düsseldorf, 1893.
Gaw, A. The Impromptu Mask in SHAKESPEARE. SAB, 11, 1936.
Lebede, H. Das Rüpelspiel bei Shakespeare und Gryphius. Zwinger, 5, 1921.
Schwab, H. Das Schauspiel im Schauspiel zur Zeit Shakesperes. Wien, 1896.
Lion, H. Les tragédies et les théories dramatiques de VOLTAIRE. Paris, 1895.
Dejob, C. La tragédie historique chez Voltaire et Shakespeare. RCC, 7, 1899.
Russell, T. W. Voltaire, Dryden and Heroic Tragedy. New York, 1946.
Koehler, R. Ueber den Stoff von Zacharias WERNERS Vierundzwanzigstem Februar. Weimarer Sonntagsblatt, 3, 1857. And in: Kleinere Schriften, 3.

3. Novel and Short Story

Apprenticeship Novel, Epistolary, Exotic, Gothic, Historical, Pastoral, Political, Regional, Rustic, Sentimental, Social, State Novel; Tales of Terror; Detective Story; Frame Story; Novella; Novela. See also: Sociology, Politics, Romances, Epics.

a. General Works.

Anon. Historical Romance in Italy. NAR, April, 1838.
—— Emile Gaboriau. The Detective Novelist's Dilemma. TLS, 2.XI.1935.
Agnoli, G. Le origine del romanzo storico in Italia. RI, Dec., 1905.
Aleksandrova, V. A. The Historical Novel in Russia. (In Russian). Novyi Zhurnal, 8, 1944.
Amezúa, A. G. de. Formación y elementos de la novela cortesana. Madrid, 1929.
Atkinson, W. C. Studies in Literary Decadence. The Pastoral Novel. BSS, 4, 1927.
Auerbach, E. Zur Technik der Fruehrenaissancenovelle in Italien und Frankreich. Heidelberg, 1921.
Bader, A. L. The Structure of the Modern Short Story. College English, 7, 1945.
Baker, E. A. The History of the English Novel. From the Brontes to Meredith. Romanticism in the English Novel. London, 1937.
Barbagelata, H. D. La novela y el cuento en Hispanoamérica. Montevideo, 1947.
Bentley, Phyllis. The English Regional Novel. London, 1941.
Berger, Berta. Der moderne deutsche Bildungsroman. Bern, 1942.
Berges, W. Die Fürstenspiegel des hohen und späten Mittelalters. Leipzig, 1938.
Bernbaum, E. The Views of the Great Critics on the Historical Novel. PMLA, 1926.
Besthorn, R. Ursprung und Eigenart der älteren italienischen Novelle. Halle, 1935.
Birkhead, Edith. The Tale of Terror. A Study of the Gothic Romance. London, 1921.
Black, F. G. The Technique of English Epistolary Novels. HSPhL, 15, 1933.
—— The Epistolary Novel in the Late Eighteenth Century: A Descriptive and Bibliographical Study. Eugene, (Oregon), 1940.
Blanco, G. Historia de la Novela en España desde el romanticismo a nuestros dias. Madrid, 1909.
Block, A. The English Novel, 1740-1850: A Catalogue Including . . . Translations of Foreign Fiction. London, 1939.
Bock, H. & Weitzel, K. Der historische Roman als Begleiter der Weltgeschichte. Leipzig, 1931.
Bollatti, A. Letteratura di spionaggio. NAnt, 1.VIII.1934.
Borcherdt, H. H. Geschichte des Romans und der Novelle in Deutschland. Leipzig, 1926.
Bourland, Caroline B. The Short Story in Spain in the 17th Century. Northampton (Mass.), 1927.
Brauchli, J. Der englische Schauerroman um 1800 unter Berücksichtigung der unbekannten Bücher. Diss. Zürich, 1928.
Brodin, P. Le roman régionaliste américain, esquisse d'une géographie morale et pittoresque des Etats-Unis. Maisonneuve, 1937.
Brown, H. R. The Sentimental Novel in America, 1789-1860. Duke U.P., 1940.
Bruel, Andrée. Romans français du moyen âge, essais. Paris, 1934.
Brunetière, F. Le roman expérimental. RDM, 1880.

Buchan, J. The Novel and the Fairy Tale. E&S, 1931.
Caillois, R. Le roman policier. Buenos Aires, 1941.
Chekhov, A. Letters on the Short Story. New York, 1924.
Cholevius, L. Die bedeutendsten deutschen Romane des 17. Jahrhunderts. Leipzig, 1866.
Coan, O. W. & Lillard, R. G. America in Fiction: An Annotated List of Novels That Interpret Aspects of Life in the United States. Stanford U., 1945.
Cowei, A. The Rise of the American Novel. Cincinnati, 1948.
Daiches, D. The Novel and the Modern World. Chicago U.P., 1939.
Davray, H. Le roman de moeurs en France et en Angleterre. Revue 1.V. 1905.
Dejob, C. Le roman politique dans l'Italie contemporaine. RIE, 1896.
Depken, F. Charakter und Technik der Detektiv-Novelle. Heidelberg, 1914.
Deschamps, G. Le roman historique. In: La Vie et les Livres. Paris, 1894.
Dresch, J. Le roman social en Allemagne. Paris, 1913.
Dunlop. History of Prose Fiction. London, 1888.
Elster, H. M. Die Kurzgeschichte oder Skizze. Die Horen, 6, 1930.
Engstrom, A. G. The Formal Short Story in France and Its Development Before 1850. SPh, 42, 1945.
Eoff, Sherman H. The Spanish Novel of Ideas: Critical Opinion (1836-80). PMLA, 55, 1940.
Epstein, H. Der Detektivroman der Unterschicht. Frankfurt, 1929.
Ernle, Lord. The Light Reading of our Ancestors: Chapters in the Growth of the English Novel. Oxford, 1921.
Evans, D. O. Le roman social sous la Monarchie de Juillet. Paris, 1930.
Flanagan, J. T. The Middle Western Historical Novel. Jour. Ill. State Hist. Soc., 37, 1944.
Fosca, F. Histoire et technique du roman policier. NRC, 1937.
Foster, H. The Basic Formulas of Fiction. Norman (Okla.), 1945.
Ford, P. L. The American Historical Novel. AM, 80, 1897.
Francia, L. di. Storia dei generi letterari italiani. Novellistica. I. Dalle origini al Bandello. Milano, 1924.
Franke, H. Das Ende des psychologischen Romans der bürgerlichen Dekadenz. Geist der Zeit, 16, 1938.
Fuerst, R. Die Vorläufer der modernen Novelle im XVIII. Jahrhundert. Halle, 1897.
Gallaway, W. F. The Conservative Attitude toward Fiction, 1770-1830. PMLA, 55, 1940.
Gatti, A. Les Italiens et le roman. Rev. catholique des idées et des faits, 25.III. 1934.
Gebhard, A. Der deutsche Bauernroman seit 1900. Danzig, 1939.
Günther, H. Der Kriminalroman und die angelsächsischen Länder. ZNU, 40.
Hankiss, J. Littérature populaire et roman policier. RLC, 8, 1928.
Hayecroft, H. Murder for Pleasure: The Life and Times of the Detective Story. London, 1942.
Henkin, L. J. Problems and Digressions in the Victorian Novel (1860-1900). Bull. of Bibliography, 18, 1943-44.
Hinckey, H. B. The Framing Tale. MLN, 49, 1934.
Historical Novels: See also History, I. III. 2.
Hogarth, B. The Technique of Novel Writing. Boston, 1938.
Jacob, P. Die novellistische Einlage im deutschen Prosaroman und ihre ausländischen Vorbilder. Diss. Berlin, 1921.
Jenisch, E. Vom Abenteuer- zum Bildungsroman. GRM, 14, 1926.
Jobin, A. J. Notes on the Evolution of the French Canadian Novel. FR, 21, 1947.
Jongh, W. F. J. de. Bibliography of the Novel and Short Story in French from the Beginning of Printing till 1600. Albuquerque, (N.M.), 1945.
Kahn, G. Le roman comique au XVIIIe siècle. La Revue, 1.V.1905.
Kany, C. E. The Beginnings of the Epistolary Novel in France, Italy and Spain. Berkeley, 1937.
Karpovich, M. Soviet Historical Novel. Russian Review, 5, 1946.
Kehr, C. Der deutsche Entwicklungsroman seit der Jahrhundertwende. Dresden, 1939.
Keiter, H. & Kellen, T. Der Roman. Geschichte, Theorie und Technik des Romans und der erzählenden Dichtkunst. Essen, 1908.
Kerényi, K. Die griechisch-orientalische Romanliteratur in religionsgeschichtlicher Beleuchtung. Tübingen, 1927.
Kleinwaechter, F. Die Staatsromane. Wien, 1891.
Korrodi, E. Schweizer Erzähler der Gegenwart. Leipzig, 1924.
Körting, P. K. Geschichte des franzö-

sischen Romans im 17. Jahrhundert. Leipzig, 1885. 2nd ed., 1891.
Koskimies, R. Theorie des Romans. Helsinki, 1935.
Krauss, W. Novela, Novella, Roman. ZRPh, 60.
—— Die Kritik des Siglo de Oro am Ritter- und Schäferroman. Homenatge a Antoni Rubio i Lluch, Barcelona, 1936.
Laby, H. F. Le roman historique. Confluences, 3, 1943.
Lebel, B. Ueber das Romanwesen in Deutschland und Frankreich. MLIA, 1886.
Le Breton, A. Le roman au XVIIe siècle. Paris, 1890.
Leisy, E. E. The American Historical Novel. Festschrift George F. Reynolds. U. Colorado Studies in the Humanities, 1945.
Lot-Borodine, Myrrha. Le roman idyllique au moyen âge. Paris, 1913.
Ludvikovski, J. Le roman grec d'aventures. Etude sur sa nature et son origine. Prague, 1925.
Ludwig, A. Die Kriminaldichtung und ihre Träger. GRM, 18, 1930.
Maatz, A. Der Einfluss des heroisch-galanten Romans auf das französische Drama im Zeitalter Ludwigs XIV. Diss. Rostock, 1896.
Magendie, M. Le roman français au XVIIe siècle. Paris, 1932.
Mayo, R. D. The Gothic Short Story in the Magazines. MLR, 37, 1942.
—— How Long Was Gothic Fiction in Vogue? MLN, 58, 1943.
McCourt, E. A. The Canadian Historical Novel. Dalhousie Rev., 26, 1946.
McLuhan, H. M. Footprints in the Sands of Crime. Sewanee Rev., 44, 1946.
Menéndez y Palayo, M. Origenes de la novela. 4 vols. Madrid, 1943.
Merland, J. Le roman personnel. Paris, 1905.
Mertner, E. Zur Theorie der Short Story in England und Amerika. Anglia, 65, 1940-41.
Messac, R. Le detective novel et l'influence de la pensée scientifique. Paris, 1929.
Mielke, H. & Rehm, W. Geschichte des deutschen Romans. Berlin, 1927.
Minning, R. Der Heimatroman des 20. Jahrhunderts in Süd-England und Wales. Bleicherode, 1937.
Mirrieless, Edith R. The American Short Story. AM, 167, 1941.
Moebius, H. Die englischen Rosenkreuzer-romane und ihre Vorläufer. Progr. Hamburg, 1911.
Moore, E. R. La primera novela historica mexicana. Rev. de lit. Mex., 1, 1941.
Morgan, B. Q. The Novelette as a Literary Form. Symposium, 1, 1947.
Morgan, C. E. The Rise of the Novel of Manners. New York, 1911.
Morillat, P. Le roman en France 1610. Paris, 1894.
Morrow, C. Le roman irréaliste dans les littératures contemporaines de langues française et anglaise. Paris, 1941.
Mueller-Fraureuth, K. Die Ritter- und Räuberromane. Halle, 1894.
Nettement, A. Etudes critiques sur le feuuilleton-roman. Paris, 1845.
Pattee, F. L. The Development of the American Short Story. New York, 1923.
Peres, H. Le roman, le conte et la nouvelle dans la littérature arabe moderne. Annales de l'Institut d'Etudes orientales, 3, 1937.
Petriconi, H. Spanisch-amerikanische Romane. RF, 1937.
Petsch, R. Wesen und Formen der Erzählkunst. Halle, 1934.
Picaresque Novel: See Spanish Contributions, IV. IV. 4.
Pike, J. B. Classical Predecessors of the Short Story. In: Classical Studies and Sketches. Minnesota U.P., 1931.
Pineau, L. L'évolution du roman en Allemagne au XIXe siècle. Paris, 1908.
Prinsen, J. De Roman in de 18e eeuw in West-Europa. Groningen, 1925.
Prys, J. Der Staatsroman des 16. und 17. Jahrhunderts und sein Erziehungsideal. Würzburg, 1913.
Putnam, S. The Brazilian Social Novel (1835-1940). Inter-Amer. Quar., 2, 1940.
Queen, Ellery. The Detective Short Story: A Bibliography. Boston, 1943.
Rausse, H. Geschichte des deutschen Romans bis 1800. Kempten, 1914.
Read, L. The Mexican Historical Novel, 1826-1910. New York, 1939.
Redden, Sister Mary M. The Gothic Fiction in the American Magazines (1765-1800). Washington, D. C., 1940.
Reich, H. Der biologische Roman der Antike und das Ringen um die Neugestaltung moderner epischer Kunst. Festschrift Wechssler, Jena, 1929.
Retinger, J. H. Le conte fantastique dans le romantisme français. Paris, 1909.
Richards, P. L. The Italian Historical Novel as Influenced by English Gothic Fiction, 1820-40. Diss. Harvard, 1939.
Riemann, R. Die Entwicklung des poli-

tischen und exotischen Romans in Deutschland. Progr. Leipzig, 1911.
Robinsonaden: See Defoe, IV. VIII. 7.
Rogers, W. Form in the Art-Novel. Helicon, 2, 1940.
Rohde, E. Der griechische Roman und seine Vorläufer. Leipzig, 1914.
Rolfe, F. P. On the Bibliography of Seventeenth Century Prose Fiction. PMLA, 1934.
Rüd, E. Die deutsche Dorfgeschichte bis auf Auerbach. Diss. Tübingen, 1909.
Rychner, M. Reflexionen über den Bekenntnis-Roman. Wissen & Leben, 1923.
Saintsbury, G. The Historical Novel. In: Collected Essays and Papers, 3. London, 1923.
Schissel von Fleschenberg, C. Die griechische Novelle. Halle, 1913.
Schlotke, C. Entwicklungsstufen des humanistisch-satyrischen Romanes in England und Frankreich. Geist der Zeit, 16, 1938.
Singer, G. F. The Epistolary Novel: its Origin, Development, Decline and Residuary Influence. Pennsylvania U.P., 1933.
Söderhjelm, W. La nouvelle française au XVe siècle. Paris, 1910.
Soerensen, A. Der polnische historische Roman der Gegenwart. Berlin, 1895.
Speare, M. E. The Political Novel, its Development in England and America. New York, 1924.
Stansbury, M. H. Foreign Languages in the Romans d'aventure. PhQ., 1928.
Strauss, H. Der Klosterroman. Diss. München, 1921.
Summers, M. The Gothic Quest: A History of the Gothic Novel. Columbia U.P., 1938.
—— A Gothic Bibliography. Columbia U.P., 1941.
Taylor, A. M. The Historical Novel as a Source in History. Sewanee Rev., 1938.
Taylor, J. T. Early Opposition to the English Novel: The Popular Reaction from 1760 to 1830. New York, 1943.
Taylor, W. F. The Economic Novel in America. Chapel Hill (N.C.), 1942.
Tcheng, H. K. Le roman policier. Confluences, 3, 1943.
Thalmann, M. Der Trivialroman des 18. Jahrhunderts und der romantische Roman. Ein Beitrag zur Entwicklungsgeschichte der Geheimbundmystik. Berlin, 1923.
Thomson, H. D. Masters of Mystery: A Study of the Detective Story. London, 1931.
Tieje, A. J. The Expressed Aim of the English Prose Fiction from 1579 to 1740. JEGPh, 11, 1912.
Toldo, P. Contributo allo studio della novella francese del XV e XVI secolo, considerata specialmente nelle sue attinenze con la letteratura italiana. Roma, 1895. Cf. JS, 1895.
Torres-Rioseco, A. La novela en la América Hispana. Berkeley, 1939.
Van Doren, C. The American Novel, 1789-1939. New York, 1940.
Van Tieghem, P. Le roman rustique. (Suisse, Allemagne, France, Angleterre). RCC, 1932.
Wache, K. Der österreichische Roman. Leipzig, 1930.
Wagenknecht, E. C. Cavalcade of the English Novel from Elizabeth to George VI. New York, 1943.
Waldberg, M. von. Der empfindsame Roman in Frankreich. Strassburg, 1906.
Waldman, M. The Propaganda Novel. London, 1934.
Wells, C. The Technique of the Mystery Story. Springfield, 1913.
Wenger, K. Historische Romane deutscher Romantiker. Bern, 1905.
Wilmotte, M. Origines du roman en France. Paris, 1941.
Wolfe, B. D. The Novel in Latin America. Antioch Rev., 3, 1943.
Würtenberger, T. Die deutsche Kriminalerzählung. Erlangen, 1941.
Wurzbach, W. von. Geschichte des französischen Romans bis zum Ende des XVII. Jahrhunderts. Heidelberg, 1913.
Zellers, G. La novela histórica en España, 1828-50. New York, 1938.
Zellweger, R. Les débuts du roman rustique; Suisse, Allemagne, France, 1836-56. Paris, 1941-42.
Zephirin, M. Le roman haitien. FR, 21, 1948.

b. Individual Authors.

Kruuse, J. Le roman fantastique en France au temps d'**ANDERSEN**. In: Digter og Traditioner. København, 1939.
Bardino, L. I'Argenis di John **BARCLAY** e il romanzo greco. Palermo, 1940.
Becker, P. A. Johann Barclay. ZVL, 15.
Langford, G. John Barclay's Argenis: A Seminal Novel. Texas Studies in English, 1947.

Meyer, J. J. **DANDINS** Deçamara Karitam, ein alt-indischer Schelmenroman. Leipzig, 1902.

Bastier, P. La nouvelle individualiste en Allemagne de **GOETHE** à Keller. Paris, 1910.

Bennett, E. K. A History of the German Novelle from Goethe to Thomas Mann. Cambridge, 1934.

Gerhard, M. Der deutsche Entwicklungsroman bis zu Goethes Wilhelm Meister. Halle, 1926.

Elwert, T. Geschichtsauffassung und Erzählungstechnik in den historischen Romanen von F. D. **GUERRAZZI**. Beiheft, 84. ZRPh, 1935.

Widmann, M. Albrecht von **HALLERS** Staatsromane und Hallers Bedeutung als politischer Schriftsteller. Biel, 1894.

Horn, W. Ueber das Komische im Schauerroman: **HOFFMANNS** Elixiers des Teufels und ihre Beziehungen zur englischen Literatur. Archiv, 1924.

Fuerst, N. Three German Novels in Education: I. **HOELDERLIN'S** Hyperion; II. Stifter's Nachsommer; III. R. M. Rilke's Malte Laurids Brigge. MDU, 38, 1946.

Kleineke, W. Englische Fürstenspiegel vom Policraticus **JOHANNS VON SALISBURY** bis zum Basilikon Doron König Jakobs I. Halle, 1937.

Angelloz, J. F. Un grand Bildungsroman, Henri Le Vert. (**KELLER**). MF, 1947.

Mason, E. On the Short Story and Two Modern Examplars (**KIPLING** and Maupassant). In: Eight Essays on Preferences in Literature. London, 1914.

Rentsch, M. M. G. **LEWIS**, mit besonderer Berücksichtigung seines Romans Ambrosio or The Monk. Leipzig, 1902.

Robinson, Jane M. The Education of the Prince: A Comparative Study of **MACHIAVELLI**, Fénelon and Wieland. Diss. Stanford U. 1939.

Alonso, A. La crisis de **MANZONI** sobre la novela historica. Sur (Buenos Aires), May, 1941.

Loehmann, O. Die Rahmenerzählung von **MORRIS** Earthly Paradise. Archiv, 172, 1937.

Warren, L. C. Humanistic Doctrines of the Prince from **PETRARCH** to Sir Thomas Elyot: A Study of the Principal Analogues and Sources of the Boke Named The Governour. Chicago, 1939.

Becher, W. **PLATON** und Fichte, Die königliche Erziehungskunst. Eine vergleichende Darstellung auf philosophischer und soziologischer Grundlage. Jena, 1937.

Chasse, C. Le roman policier d'Edgar **POE** à Nick Carter. Grande Revue, 10.V.1912.

Cobb, P. E. A. Poe and F. Spielhagen. Their Theory of the Short Story. MLN, 1910.

Lemonnier, L. E. Poe et les origines du roman policier en France. MF, 15.X. 1925.

Mitchell. Poe and Spielhagen: Novelle and Short Story. MLN, 1914.

Smith, H. Poe's Extension of his Theory of the Tale. MPh, 16, 1918-19.

Van Tieghem, P. Le roman sentimental en Europe de **RICHARDSON** à Rousseau, 1740-61. RLC, 20, 1940.

Hughes, H. S. English Epistolary Fiction before Pamela. Festschrift J. Manley. Chicago, 1923.

Servais, E. Le genre romanesque en France depuis l'apparition de la Nouvelle Héloïse jusqu'aux approches de la Révolution. (**ROUSSEAU**). Paris, 1922.

Heine, M. Le marquis de **SADE** et le roman noir. NRF, 1.VIII.1933.

Küchler, W. Die cent nouvelles nouvelles. Ein Beitrag zur Geschichte der französischen Novelle. (Antoine de la **SALLE**). ZFSL, 30-31, 1906-07.

Hartland, R. W. Walter **SCOTT** et le roman frénétique. Paris, 1930.

Héraucourt, W. Waverley und der mittelalterliche Ritterroman. NSp, 49.

Koller, H. **STENDHAL'S** Rouge et Noir und Les Misérables von Victor Hugo, zwei Typen des socialen Romans. Münster, 1922.

Boynton, P. H. The Novel of Puritan Decay: From Mrs. **STOWE** to John Marquand. NEQ, 13, 1940.

Halm, A. Anton **TSCHECHOWS** Kurzgeschichte und deren Vorläufer. Weimar, 1933.

Reynier, G. Le roman sentimental avant l'Astrée (d'**URFE**). Paris, 1908.

Magendie, M. Le roman français au XVIIe siècle de l'Astrée au Grand Cyrus. Paris, 1932.

Livingston, C. H. Les Cent nouvelles nouvelles de Philippe de **VIGNEULLES** chaussettier messin. Revue du XVIe siècle, 10, 1923.

Garte, H. Kunstform Schauerroman; eine morphologische Begriffsbestimmung des Sensationsromans im 18. Jahrhundert von **WALPOLES** Castle

of Otranto bis Jean Pauls Titan. Leipzig, 1935.
Killen, Alice M. Le Roman terrifiant, ou Roman noir, de Walpole à Anne Radcliffe, et son influence sur la littérature française jusqu'en 1840. Paris, 1915.
Mehrotra, K. K. Horace Walpole and the English Novel: A Study of the Influence of the Castle of Otranto. Oxford, 1934.
Schroeder, F. W. WIELANDS Agathon und die Anfänge des modernen Bildungsromans. Diss. Königsberg, 1904.
Pease, S. J. XENOPHON'S Cyropaedia, the compleat general. CJ, 29, 1934.
Schoell, F. L. Etude sur le roman paysan naturaliste: D'Emile ZOLA à L. Reymont. RLC, 1927.

4. Poetry.

Theory and Forms of (Lyrical) Poetry.

Abrams, M. H. Romantic Theories of Poetry and Criticism. Diss. Harvard U. 1940.
Allen, P. S. The Romanesque Lyric: from Petronius to the Cambridge Poets. Chapel Hill (N.C.), 1928.
Bartsch, K. Ueber die romanischen und deutschen Tagelieder. Album des litt. Vereins in Nürnberg, 1865.
Beach, J. W. The Function of Poetry. UTQ, 9, 1940.
—— A Romantic View of Poetry. Minneapolis, 1944.
Bremond, H. La poésie pure. Paris, 1927.
Brittain, F. The Medieval Latin and Romance Lyric to A.D. 1300. Cambridge U.P., 1937.
Brunetière, F. L'évolution de la poésie lyrique au XIXe siècle. 2 vols. Paris, 1893.
Bücken, E. Das deutsche Lied. Problem und Gestalten. Hamburg, 1939.
Coffin, R. P. T. The Substance that is Poetry. New York, 1942.
Cowl, R. P. The Theory of Poetry in England; its Development in Doctrines and Ideas from the Sixteenth Century to the Nineteenth Century. London, 1914.
Engle, P. The Source of Poetry. College English, 1, 1940.
Everett, C. C. Poetry, Comedy and Duty. Boston, 1888.
Flora, F. La poesia ermetica. Bari, 1936.
Foster, C. H. Emerson's Theory of Poetry. Iowa City, 1941.
Fraenkel, L. Shakespeare und das Tagelied. Hannover, 1893.
Friedlaender, M. Das deutsche Lied im 18. Jahrhundert. Stuttgart, 1902.
Goodwin, G. The Rapture of Song: Some Aspects of Oriental Poetry. The Calcutta Review, 3rd. Ser., 15, 1925.
Grases, P. Origenes de la poesía lírica medioeval en Europa. Caracas, 1938.
Gummere, F. B. The Beginnings of Poetry. New York, 1908.
Harrison, J. S. Types of English Poetry: A Study of Literary Organisms. Indianapolis, 1941.
Kalff, G. Het Lied in de middel eeuwen. Leiden, 1884.
Kar, G. Thoughts on the Mediaeval Lyric. Oxford, 1933.
McKenzie, K. The Development of Italian Lyric Poetry before the Rise of the dolce stil nuovo. PMLA, 13, 1898.
Minnesang: See Love, I. VI. 10.
Mizener, A. Some Notes on the Nature of English Poetry. Sewanee Rev., 51, 1943.
Müller, G. Geschichte des deutschen Liedes vom Zeitalter des Barock bis zur Gegenwart. München, 1925.
Ohling, Hertha. Das deutsche Taglied vom Mittelalter bis zum Ausgang der Renaissance. Köln, 1938.
Spanke, H. Beziehungen zwischen romanischer und mittellateinischer Lyrik mit besonderer Berücksichtigung der Metrik und Musik. Berlin, 1936.
Tate, A. The Language of Poetry. Princeton, 1942.
Taylor, A. The Literary History of the Meistergesang. New York, 1937.
Trevelyan, R. C. Poetry of Ecstasy. New Statesman, 19, 1922.
Van Tieghem, P. La notion de vraie poésie dans le pré-romantisme européen. RLC, 1921.
Wells, H. W. The American Way of Poetry. New York, 1943.
Werner, H. Die Ursprünge der Lyrik. München, 1924.
Wolff, E. Das lyrische Gedicht als bildende Kraft. Festschrift G. Bäumer. Berlin, 1933.

5. Popular Literature.

Popular Tales and Plays; Folksongs.
(See also Folklore, I. VI. 4.)

Amicis, V. de. La commedia popolare latina e la commedia dell'arte. Napoli, 1882.
Bode, K. Die Bearbeitungen und Vorlagen in Des Knaben Wunderhorn. Leipzig, 1909.

Böckel, O. Handbuch des deutschen Volksliedes. Marburg, 1930.
Brouwer, O. Das Volkslied in Deutschland, Frankreich, Belgien und Holland. Diss. Groningen. Den Haag, 1930.
Bruinier, J. W. Das deutsche Volkslied. Leipzig, 1927.
Clouston, W. A. Popular Tales and Fictions, their Migrations and Transformations. 2 vols. London, 1887.
Cosquin, E. Contes populaires de Lorraine comparés avec les contes des autres provinces de France et des pays étrangers. 2 vols. Paris, 1886.
Courlander, H. Haiti's Political Folksongs. Opportunity: Journal of Negro Life, 19, 1941.
Croce, B. Poesia popolare e poesia d'arte. Bari, 1933.
Cysarz, H. Menschheitsdichtung und Volksdichtung. Zs. f. Aesthetik & allg. Kunstwissenschaft, 28, 1934.
Danckert, W. Das europäische Volkslied. Berlin, 1939.
Deutsch, L. Treasury of the World's Finest Folk Song. (Cf. Introduction). New York, 1942.
Dolph, E. A. Sound Off: Soldier Songs from the Revolution to World War II. New York, 1942.
Durry, Marie-Jeanne. L'Académie Celtique et la chanson populaire. (Paris 1807). RLC, 9, 1929.
Espinosa, A. M. Spanish Folktales from California. Hisp., 23, 1940.
Götze, A. Begriff und Wesen des Volksliedes. GRM, 1912.
Greyerz, O. von. Das Volkslied der deutschen Schweiz. Frauenfeld, 1927.
Halliday, W. B. Indo-European Folk-Tales and Greek Legends. Cambridge, 1933.
—— Notes upon the Indo-European Folktales and the Problem of their Diffusion. FL, 1923.
Hartmann, A. Volksschauspiele in Bayern und Oesterreich-Ungarn gesammelt. Leipzig, 1880.
Illyes, J. La symbolique de la chanson populaire hongroise. Nouvelle Rev. de Hongrie, Sept., 1939.
Jungbauer, G. Zur Volksliedfrage. GRM, 1913.
Kohler, P. Le problème de la poésie populaire. Mélanges Baldensperger. Paris, 1930.
Levy, P. E. Geschichte des Begriffs Volkslied. Berlin, 1911.
Margoulies, G. Quelques chants populaires de la vieille Chine (leurs rapports avec les chants russes). Yggdrasill, 25.V.1937.
Marx, F. Römische Volkslieder. RhM, 1929.
Meier, J. Das Volkslied. Strassburg, 1909.
—— Minnesang und Volkslied. Jb. f. Volksliedforschung, 7, 1941.
Mone, F. J. Uebersicht der niederländischen Volksliteratur. Tübingen, 1838.
Nisard, C. Histoire des livres populaires et de la littérature de colportage. Paris, 1864.
Novati, F. La canzone popolare in Francia e in Italia nel più alto medio evo. Mélanges Wilmotte. Paris, 1909.
Peery, W. American Folk Drama Comes of Age. American Scholar, 11, 1942.
Penkert, A. Das Gassenlied. Leipzig, 1911.
Pineau, L. Les vieux chants populaires scandinaves; étude de littérature comparée. I. Les chants de magie. II. La légende divine et héroïque. Paris, 1898-1901.
Pitre, G. Delle novelle popolari. In: Fiabe, Novelle e Racconti popolari Siciliani. Palermo, 1875.
Platel, Marguerite. Vom Volkslied zum Gesellschaftslied. Bern, 1939.
Prutz, H. Die historischen Volkslieder der Deutschen. Deutsches Museum, 1867.
Rieser, F. Des Knaben Wunderhorn und seine Quellen. Dortmund, 1907.
Rubin, Ruth. Yiddish Folksongs in New York City. N. Y. Folklore Quarterly, 2, 1946.
Santoli, V. Problemi di poesia popolare. In: Annali della R. Scuola normale sup. di Pisa, 1935.
Scheffler, W. Die deutsche und die französische Volksdichtung. Grenzboten, 42, 1883.
—— Vergleichende Charakteristik französischer und deutscher Volksdichtungen. In: Die französische Volksdichtung und Sage. 2 vols. Leipzig, 1885.
Schell, O. Das Volkslied. In: Handbuch zur Volkskunde, 3. Leipzig, 1909.
Shortliffe, G. Populism in the Novel before Naturalism. PMLA, 54, 1939.
Simmons, E. J. A History of the Folktale and its Theories. Diss. Harvard, 1928.
Solymossi, A. Folktale and Science. (In Hungarian). Budapest, 1938.
Sorrento, L. Il genere letterario e la poesia popolare. Helicon, 2, 1940.
Spiller, R. Drei Entlehnungen. (Folksongs and Students' Songs). ZVL, 1, 1888.
Taylor, A. Some Trends and Problems

in Studies of the Folk Tale. Sph, 37, 1940.

Thimme, A. Zur Charakteristik der französischen und deutschen Volkslieder. RFA, 3, 1901.

Tiersot, J. Histoire de la chanson populaire en France. Paris, 1889.

—— La chanson populaire et les écrivains romantiques. Paris, 1930.

Thompson, S. Motiv-Index of Folk Literature. 5 vols. Bloomington (Ind.), 1932-35.

—— European Tales Among North American Indians. Colorado Springs, 1919.

Warnatsch, V. Des Knaben Wunderhorn und der lai du corn. ZVL, 1898.

Winter, G. Grande littérature et littérature populaire. L'Europe centrale, 24.VI.1938.

6. Prose.

Cherel, A. La prose poétique française. Paris, 1940. Cf. NL, 20.IV.1940.

Clayton, V. The Prose Poem in the French Literature of the XVIIIth Century. New York, 1937.

Cysarz, H. Die gattungsmässigen Form-Möglichkeiten der heutigen Prosa. Helicon, 2, 1940.

Heltzel, V. B. Types of English Prose: Non-Fiction. New York, 1941.

De La Mare, W. Poetry in Prose. PBA, 21, 1935.

Margoulies, G. Evolution de la prose artistique chinoise. Munich, 1929.

Norden, E. Die antike Kunstprosa vom 6. Jahrhundert vor Christus bis in die Zeit der Renaissance. 2 vols. Leipzig, 1915-18.

Petermann, B. Der Streit um Vers und Prosa in der französischen Literatur des XVIII. Jahrhunderts. Halle, 1913.

7. Religious Genres.

Church Songs, Psalms, Hymns, Spirituals. (See also Religious Influences, III. I. 4., and Dramas, above.)

Beck, K. A. Geschichte des katholischen Kirchenlieds. Köln, 1878.

Becker, A. Vom christlichen Hymnus zum Minnesang. Verhandlungen der Versammlung deutscher Philologen, 1929; Historisches Jb, 52, 1932.

Becker, P. A. Vom geistlichen Tagelied. Diss. Leipzig, 1887.

Breed, D. R. The History and Use of Hymns and Hymn Tunes. New York, 1903.

Brémond, H. Prière et poésie. Paris, 1927.

Cambridge, M. A. The Folk-Lore of the Psalm. Calcutta Review, 117-21, 1903-05.

Eichert, E. Das geistliche Spiel der Gegenwart in Deutschland und Frankreich. Berlin, 1941.

Fredrich, E. Der Ruf, eine Gattung des geistlichen Volksliedes. Berlin, 1936.

Havelock Ellis, H. Villon and Church Hymns. The Academy, 27.V.1882.

Jackson, G. P. White and Negro Spirituals: Their Life Span and Kinship, Tracing 200 Years of Untrammeled Song Making and Singing among Our Country Folk. New York, 1944.

Kinloch, T. F. An Historical Account of the Church Hymnary. Cambridge, 1926.

Knipfer, J. Das kirchliche Volkslied in seiner geschichtlichen Entwicklung. Bielefeld, 1875.

Kober, A. Geschichte der religiösen Dichtung in Deutschland. Essen, 1920.

Koch. Geschichte des Kirchenlieds und Kirchengesangs. Stuttgart, 1847.

Kochs, T. Das deutsche geistliche Tagelied. Münster, 1927.

Kretzmann, P. E. Luther's Use of Mediaeval Latin Hymns. TAPhA, 18, 1930.

Kroll, J. Die Hymnendichtung des frühen Christentums. Antike, 2, 1926.

Lowinski, V. Zum geistlichen Kunstliede in der altprovenzalischen Literatur. ZFSL, 20, 1898.

Morison, S. English Prayer Books: An Introduction to the Literature of Christian Public Worship. Cambridge U.P., 1943.

Phillips, C. S. Hymnody Past and Present. London, 1937.

Preaching: See Rhetoric in Chapter One.

Reeves, J. B. The Hymn as Literature. Diss. Cornell, 1922. New York, 1924.

Rohr-Sauer, P. von. English Metrical Psalms from 1600 to 1660. Diss. Freiburg, 1938.

Schaaf, A. The Psalms: A Brief Introduction and Exegesis. St. Meinrad, 1919.

Scheludko, D. Ueber die religiöse Lyrik der Troubadours. Neophilolog. Mitteilungen, 20, 1937.

Sheppard, W. J. L. Great Hymns and Their Stories. London, 1923.

Singer, S. Die religiöse Lyrik des Mittelalters. Neujahrsblatt Bern, 1933.

Thompson, S. H. The Dulcis Jesu Memoria in Anglo-Norman and Middle French. MA, 11, 1943.

White, Helen C. Sixteenth-Century English Devotional Literature. J. Q. Adams Memorial Studies. Washington, D. C., 1948.

8. Literary Criticism.

a. General Works.

Alton, J. F. d'. Roman Literary Theory and Criticism. London, 1931.
Atkins, J. W. H. Literary Criticism in Antiquity. A Sketch of its Development. Cambridge U.P., 1934.
—— English Literary Criticism: The Medieval Phase. Cambridge U.P., 1943.
—— English Literary Criticism: The Renaissance. London, 1947.
Bacci, O. La critica letteraria dall'antichità classica al Cinquecento. Milano, 1911.
Baillet, A. Jugemens des Sçavans sur les principaux ouvrages des auteurs. 4 vols. Paris, 1585-86.
Baldwin, C. S. Renaissance Literary Theory and Practice; Classicism in the Rhetoric and Poetic of Italy, France and England, 1400-1600. Ed. with Introduction by D. L. Clark. New York, 1939.
Behrens, Irene. Die Lehre von der Einteilung der Dichtkunst, vornehmlich vom 16. bis 19. Jahrhundert. Halle, 1940.
Beriger, L. Die literarische Wertung: ein Spectrum der Kritik. Halle, 1938.
Blunt, A. Artistic Theory in Italy (1450-1600). Oxford, 1940.
Borgese, G. A. Storia della critica romantica in Italia. Napoli, 1905. New ed., Milano, 1920.
Borinski, K. Die Poetik der Renaissance und die Anfänge der litterarischen Kritik in Deutschland. Berlin, 1886.
—— Die Antike in Poetik und Kunsttheorie. Vom Ausgang des klassischen Altertums bis auf Goethe und Wilhelm von Humboldt. 2 vols. Leipzig, 1914-24.
—— Deutsche Poetik. Berlin, 1916.
Bosanquet. History of Aesthetic. London, 1892.
Bosch, R. Die Problemstellung der Poetik. Leipzig, 1928.
Brightfield, M. F. The Issue in Literary Criticism. Berkeley, 1932.
Brownell, W. C. An Essay on Comparative Criticism. New York, 1890.
Bühler, C. F. An Undescribed Ars Poetica Printed at Paris about 1500. Library, 5. ser., 1, 1946.
Bundy, M. W. The Theory of Imagination in Classical and Mediaeval Thought. U. of Illinois Stud. in Lang. and Lit., 12, 1927.
Burgund, E. Die Entwicklung der Theorie der französischen Schauspielkunst im 18. Jahrhundert. Breslau, 1932.
Chambers, F. P. Cycles of Taste. A Sketch of Ancient Art and Criticism. Harvard U.P., 1928.
Clements, R. J. Critical Theory and Practice of the Pléiade. Harvard U.P., 1924.
Croce, B. Iniziazione all' estetica del settecento. Crit., 20.VII.1934.
Cross, S. H. Notes on Soviet Literary Criticism. I. The Criteria of Socialist Realism. II. Schematization in Soviet Literary Criticism. Slavonic Yearbook, 20, 1941.
Curtius, E. R. Zur Literarästhetik des Mittelalters. ZRPh, 1938.
—— Mittelalterliche Literaturtheorien. ZRPh, 1942.
Denniston, J. D. Greek Literary Criticism. In: The Library of Greek Thought. New York, 1924.
Donohue, J. J. The Theory of Literary Kinds. Ancient Classifications of Literature. Dubuque, 1943.
Eaton, J. W. The Beginnings of German Literary Criticism. MLN, 53, 1938.
Ebisch, W. & Schücking, L. L. Bibliographie zur Geschichte des literarischen Geschmackes in England. Anglia, 63, 1939.
Egger, E. Essai sur l'histoire de la critique chez les Grecs. Paris, 1885.
Elton, O. The Nature of Literary Criticism. In: Essays and Addresses. London, 1939.
Engstrom, A. G. In Defence of Synaesthesia in Literature. PhQ, 25, 1946.
Erhardt-Siebold, E. von. Synästhesien in der englischen Dichtung des 19. Jahrhunderts. ESn, 53.
Faral, E. Les arts poétiques du XIIe et du XIIIe siècle. Paris, 1924.
Figueiredo, F. de. Historia da critica litteraria em Portugal. Lisboa, 1915.
Foerster, N. American Criticism. Boston, 1928.
—— Literary Scholarship: Its Aims and Methods. Chapel Hill (N.C.), 1941.
Foffano. Una polemica letteraria nel settecento. In: Ricerche letterarie. Ginesti, 1897.
Fubini, M. Studi sulla critica letteraria nel settecento. Firenze, 1934.
Gayley, C. M. & Scott, F. N. An Introduction to the Methods and Mate-

rials of Literary Criticism. Boston, 1899. Cf. DLZ, 12, 1901.
Gayley, C. M. & Kurtz, B. P. Methods and Materials of Literary Criticism: Lyric, Epic, and Allied Forms of Poetry. Boston, 1920.
Gianturco, E. The Struggle Between Italian and Spanish Criticism in the Late 18th Century. MLF, 1932.
Gilbert, Katherine E. & Kuhn, H. A History of Esthetics. New York, 1939.
Gillet, J. E. The Vogue of Literary Theories in Germany from 1500 to 1730. MPh, 14.
Giraud, V. La critique littéraire, le problème, les théories, les méthodes. Paris, 1946.
Glunz, H. H. Die Literarästhetik des europäischen Mittelalters. Bochum, 1937.
Görtner, R. Die drei Wertstufen des Wahren, Schönen und Guten in der deutschen Klassik. Bonn, 1939.
Grolman, A. von. Deutsche Dichtkunst und französischer Art poétique. Berlin, 1943.
Grucker, E. Histoire des doctrines littéraires et esthétiques en Allemagne. 2 vols. Paris, 1896.
Gruenbaum, G. Arabic Literary Criticism in the Tenth Century A.D. Journal American Oriental Society, 61, 1941.
Guérard, A. Four Ways of Criticism. Virginia Quarterly Rev., 1939-40.
Guillemin, A. M. Les querelles littéraires dans l'antiquité. Hum., 9, 1932.
Hall, V. Renaissance Literary Criticism: A Study of Its Social Content. New York, 1945.
Hooker, E. N. The Discussion of Taste from 1750 to 1770 and the New Trends in Literary Criticism. PMLA, 1934.
Horsley, Phyllis M. Comparative Criticism. CLS, 10, 1943.
Jefferson, D. W. Theories of Taste in the XVIIIth Century. Leeds Proceedings, 5.
Jørgensen, B. Aesthetic Criticism in England from 1675 to 1725. Orbis Litterarum (Copenhagen), 1947.
Leavis, F. R. Literary Criticism and Philosophy. Scrutiny (Cambridge), June, 1937.
Lempicki, Z. Les idées directrices dans l'art et les catégories esthétiques au declin du XVIIIe et au commencement du XIXe siècle. Bull. internat. de l'Académie polonaise des sciences et des lettres, 7-10, 1931.
Lobel, E. The Medieval Latin Poetics. PBA, 17, 1931.
Lotze, H. Geschichte der Aesthetik in Deutschland. München, 1913.
McKeon, R. Literary Criticism and the Concept of Imitation in Antiquity. MPh, 34, 1936.
Menéndez y Pelayo, M. Historia de las ideas estéticas en España. Madrid, 1910.
Mirabent. L'estética inglesa del siglo XVIII. Barcelona, 1937.
Monk, S. H. The Sublime: A Study of Critical Theories in XVIIIth Century England. New York, 1935.
Mueller-Freienfels, R. Poetik. Leipzig, 1921.
Needham, H. A. Développement de l'esthétique sociologique en France et en Angleterre au XIXe siècle. Paris, 1926.
Orlo, W. The Function of Literary Criticism. ER, 1921.
Padelford, F. M. The Great Critics. New York, 1932.
Patterson, W. F. Three Centuries of French Poetic Theory. (1328-1630). 2 vols. Ann Arbor, 1935.
Pellissier, G. De sexti decimi saeculi in Francia artibus poeticis. Paris, 1882.
Peschier. Des phases de la critique en France. Archiv, 11.
Peyre, H. Writers and Their Critics: A Study of Misunderstanding. Ithaca, 1944.
Pritchard, J. P. Return to the Fountains: Some Classical Sources of American Criticism. Duke U.P., 1942.
Quigley, H. Italy and the Rise of a New Criticism in the 18th Century. Glasgow, 1921.
Rehder, H. Literary Criticism in Germany during the Romantic Period. MDU, 38, 1946.
Richards, J. A. Principles of Literary Criticism. London, 1925.
Routh, J. The Classical Rule of Law in English Criticism of the 16th and 17th Centuries. JEGPh, 12, 1913.
Saintsbury, G. A History of Criticism and Literary Taste from the Earliest Texts to the Present Date. 3 vols. Edinburgh, 1900-04.
Schücking, L. L. Die Soziologie der literarischen Geschmacksbildung. München, 1923.
Smith, B. Forces in American Criticism: A Study in the History of American Literary Thought. New York, 1939.
Spector, I. Introduction to Russian Literary Criticism. Seattle, 1945.

Spencer, T. The Central Problem in Literary Criticism. College English, 4, 1942.
Spingarn, J. E. A History of Literary Criticism in the Renaissance. With Special Reference to the Influence of Italy in the Formation and Development of Modern Classicism. New York, 1899. New ed., 1908.
—— Critical Essays of the XVIIth Century. (Cf. Introduction). 3 vols. Oxford, 1908.
Stafford, J. The Social Status of Renaissance Literary Critics. U. of Texas Studies in English, 1945-46.
Staiger, E. Grundbegriffe der Poetik. Zürich, 1946.
Stauffer, D. The Intent of the Critic. Princeton, 1941.
Sweeting, Elizabeth J. Early Tudor Criticism, Linguistic and Literary. Oxford, 1940.
Théry. De l'esprit et de la critique littéraires chez les peuples anciens et modernes. 2 vols. Paris, 1832.
Thomas, P. G. Aspects of Literary Theory and Practice, 1550-1870. London, 1932.
Thorpe, C. D. & Nelson, N. E. Criticism in the Twentieth Century. A Bird's Eye View. College English, 8, 1947.
Ullmann, S. Synaesthesia in the English Decadents. EPhK, 63, 1939.
Vossler, K. Poetische Theorien in der italienischen Frührenaissance. Berlin, 1900.
Wallace, H. B. Die Kritik der rationalen Aesthetik in England im XVIII. Jahrhundert. Diss. Jena, 1912.
Wilson, E. Literary Criticism and History. AM, 168, 1941.
Winchester, C. T. Some Principles of Literary Criticism. New York, 1899.
Worsfold, W. B. The Principles of Criticism: An Introduction to the Study of Literature. London, 1897.
Young, G. M. The Technique of Criticism: Classical. E&S, 23, 1938.

b. Individual Critics.
(See also Aristotle, Horace, Boileau, Lessing, etc.)

Batteux, C. Les quatre Poétiques d'**ARISTOTE**, d'Horace, de Vida, de Despréaux, avec traduction et remarques. 2 vols. Paris, 1771.
Cooper, L. A Bibliography of the Poetics of Aristotle. Ithaca (N.Y.), 1928.
—— Aristotle on the Art of Poetry. Ithaca (N.Y.), 1947.
Gilbert, A. H. Aristotle's Four Species of Tragedy and Their Importance for Dramatic Criticism. AJPh, 68, 1947.
Herrick, M. T. Aristotle's Pity and Fear. PhQ, 9, 1930.
Nisard, A. Examen des poétiques d'Aristote, d'Horace et de Boileau. Diss. Paris, 1845.
Trowbridge, H. Aristotle and the New Criticism. Sewanee Rev., 52, 1944.
Wadsworth, P. A. A Formula of Literary Criticism from Aristotle to La Bruyère. MLQ, 7, 1946.
Croce, B. Rileggendo l'Estetica di **BAUMGARTEN.** Crit., 20.I.1933.
Peters, H. G. Die Aesthetik Alexander Gottlieb Baumgartens und ihre Beziehungen zum Ethischen. Berlin, 1934.
Riemann, A. Die Aesthetik Alexander Gottlieb Baumgartens. Halle, 1928.
Eaton, J. W. **BODMER** and Breitinger and European Literary Theory. MDU, 33, 1941.
Braitmaier, F. Geschichte der poetischen Theorie und Kritik von den Diskursen der Maler bis auf Lessing. Frauenfeld, 1888.
Charlton. **CASTELVETRO'S** Theory of Poetry. Manchester, 1913.
Searles, C. **CORNEILLE** and the Italian Doctrinaires. MPh, 13, 1915.
Allen & Clark. Literary Criticism from **DRYDEN** to Croce. New York, 1940.
Glicksberg, C. I. T. S. **ELIOT** as Critic. Arizona Quart., 4, 1948.
Zschalig, H. Die Verslehren von **FABRI,** Du Pont und Sibilet; ein Beitrag zur älteren Geschichte der französischen Poetik. Leipzig, 1884.
Arberry, A. J. **FARABI'S** Canons of Poetry. Rivista degli Studi Orientali, 17, 1937.
Litz, F. E. The Sources of Charles **GILDON'S** Complete Art of Poetry. ELH, 9, 1942.
Berthé de Besaucèle, L. G. B. **GIRALDI,** étude sur l'évolution des théories littéraires en Italie au XVI siècle. Aix-Marseille, 1920.
Guerrieri Crocetti, C. G. B. Giraldi ed il pensiero critico del secolo XVI. Milano, 1932.
Boll, F. **GOETHE** und die tragische Katharsis. Berliner Philol. Wochenschrift, 1916.
Servaes, F. Die Poetik **GOTTSCHEDS** und der Schweizer. Strassburg, 1887.
Dewey, M. H. **HERDER'S** Relation to the Aesthetic Theory of his Time. Diss. Chicago, 1920.
Thorpe, C. D. The Aesthetic Theory of

Thomas **HOBBES**, with Special Reference to His Contribution to the Psychological Approach in English Literary Criticism. Ann Arbor, 1940.

Wood, F. Hugo von **HOFMANNSTHAL'S** Aesthetics: A Survey Based on the Prose Works. PMLA, 55, 1940.

Boyancé, P. A propos de l'Art poétique d'**HORACE**. RBPh, 1936.

Cook, A. S. The Art of Poetry: the Poetical Treatises of Horace, Vida, and Boileau, with the Translations by Howes, Pitt, and Soame. Boston, 1892.

Frank, T. Horace's Definition of Poetry, CJ, 31, 1935.

Gilbert, A. H. & Snuggs, H. L. On the Relation of Horace to Aristotle in Literary Criticism. JEGPh, 46, 1947.

Herrick, M. T. The Fusion of Horatian and Aristotelian Literary Criticism, 1531-1555. U. of Illinois Studies in Lang. and Lit., 32, 1946.

Steidle, W. Studien zur Ars poetica des Horaz. Interpretation des auf Dichtkunst und Gedicht bezüglichen Hauptteiles. Würzburg, 1939.

Kühnemann, E. **KANTS** und Schillers Begründung der Aesthetik. München, 1895.

Gillet, J. E. The Catharsis-Clause in German Criticism before **LESSING**. AJPh, 1919.

Janet, P. Histoire des doctrines esthétiques en Allemagne: Lessing. JS, 1896-97.

Robertson, J. G. Lessing's Dramatic Theory, Being an Introduction to and Commentary on his Hamburgische Dramaturgie. Cambridge U.P., 1939.

Weddigen, O. Lessings Theorie der Tragödie. Berlin, 1876.

Shearer, J. F. The Poetica and Apendices of **MARTINEZ DE LA ROSA**: Their Genesis, Sources, and Significance for Spanish Literary History and Criticism. Princeton, 1941.

Reese, H. R. La **MESNARDIERE'S** Poétique (1639), Sources and Dramatic Theories. Baltimore, 1937.

Borinski, K. Die Kunstlehre der Renaissance in **OPITZ'** Buch von der deutschen Poeterei. München, 1883.

Wenderoth, G. Die poetischen Theorien der französischen Plejade in Martin Opitz' Deutscher Poeterei. Euph., 13, 1906.

Gilbert, A. Literary Criticism from **PLATO** to Dryden. Cincinnati, 1940.

Lameere, J. Les concepts du Beau et de l'Art dans la doctrine platonicienne. Rev. d' hist. de la philosophie, 1938.

Bruckschulte, E. Julius Caesar **SCALIGERS** kunsttheoretische Anschauungen und deren Hauptquellen. Bonn, 1914.

Lintilhac, E. Un coup d'état dans la république des lettres; Jules César Scaliger fondateur du Classicisme cent ans avant Boileau. Nouvelle Revue, June, 1890.

Weinberg, B. Scaliger versus Aristotle on Poetics. MPh, 39, 1941-42.

Harnack, O. Die klassische Aesthetik der Deutschen. Würdigung der kunsttheoretischen Arbeiten **SCHILLERS**, Goethes und ihrer Freunde. Leipzig, 1892.

Henel, H. Friedrich **SCHLEGEL** und die Grundlagen der modernen literarischen Kritik. GR, 20, 1945.

Aldridge, A. O. Lord **SHAFTESBURY'S** Literary Theories. PhQ, 24, 1945.

Steinberg, C. S. The Aesthetic Theory of St. **THOMAS AQUINAS**. Philosophical Review, 50, 1941.

CHAPTER THREE

Semi-Literary Genres.

Beaumont, C. W. The Complete Book of **BALLETS**. London, 1937.

—— Five Centuries of Ballet Design. New York, 1939.

Gregor, J. Kulturgeschichte des Balletts, seine Gestaltung und Wirksamkeit in der Geschichte und unter den Künsten. Zürich, 1946.

Lebègue, R. Les ballets des Jésuites. RCC, 37, 1936.

Levinson, A. Meister des Balletts. (Translated from the Russian). Potsdam, 1924.

Michaut, P. Le ballet, forme vivante du lyrisme de notre temps. Rev. hebdomadaire, 24.IX.1938.

Propert, W. A. The Russian Ballet in Europe, 1901-20. London, 1921.

Prunières, H. Le Ballet de Cour en France avant Benserade et Lulli. Paris, 1914.

Silin, C. I. Benserade and His Ballets de cour. Baltimore, 1940.

Pike, R. E. The **BLASON** in French Literature of the Sixteenth Century. RR, 27, 1936.

Clements, R. J. The Cult of the Poet in Renaissance **EMBLEM** Literature. PMLA, 59, 1944.

—— Pen and Sword in Renaissance Emblem Literature. MLQ, 5, 1944.

—— Condemnation of the Poetic Profession in Renaissance Emblem Literature. SPh, 43, 1946.

Freeman, Rosemary. English Emblem Books. London, 1948.

James, Eleanor. The Imagery of Francis Quarles' Emblems. Texas Studies in English, 1943.

Lederer, J. John Donne and the Emblematic Practice. RES, 22, 1946.

Praz, M. The English Emblem Literature. ESs, 1934.

—— A Bibliography of Emblem Books. London, 1947.

Rosenfeld, H. Das deutsche Bildgedicht. Seine antiken Vorbilder und seine Entwicklung bis zur Gegenwart. Leipzig, 1935.

Stegemeier, H. Problems in Emblem Literature. JEGPh, 45, 1946.

Yates, Frances. The Emblematic Conceit in Giordano Bruno's De Gli Eroici Furori and in the Elizabethan Sonnet Sequences. JWI, 6.

Balacs, B. Der sichtbare Mensch oder die Kultur des **FILMS**. Wien-Leipzig, 1924.

Bardèche, M. & Brasillach, R. Histoire du cinéma. Paris, 1935.

Beyfuss, E. & Kossowsky, A. Kulturfilmbuch. Berlin, 1924.

Harloff, A. J. W. L'influence pernicieuse du cinéma sur les peuples de l'Orient. Le Monde nouveau, 1935.

Jacobs, L. The Rise of the American Film: A Critical History. New York, 1939.

Jacquier, C. Cinéma et crise du roman. Confluences, 1943.

Lansaye, M. de. Le cinéma exerce-t-il une influence sur la littérature? Revue hebdomadaire, 14.I.1939.

Rehlinger, B. Der Begriff Filmisch. Emsdetten, 1938.

Stindt, G. O. Das Lichtspiel als Kunstform. Die Philosophie des Films. Bremerhaven, 1924.

(Camusat). Histoire critique des journaux. Mémoires pour servir à l'histoire des journaux et autres livres périodiques qui ont paru en France et ailleurs. (**NEWSPAPERS**). 2 vols. Amsterdam, 1734.

Bond, R. P. & Weed, K. E. Studies of British Newspapers and Periodicals. Chapel Hill (N.C.), 1946.

Ester, K. d'. Die Presse und ihre Leute im Spiegel ihrer Dichtung. Eine Ernte aus 3 Jahrhunderten. Würzburg, 1941.

Hunt, F. K. The Fourth Estate: Contributions towards a History of Newspapers. London, 1850.

Piccioni, L. Il giornalismo letterario in Italia. Torino, 1894.

Segré, C. Due fortune giornalistiche (Addison & Gozzi). NAnt. 16.V.1903.

Vitray, L. Mills, J. & Ellard, R. Pictorial Journalism. New York, 1939.

Anon. Réflexions d'un patriote sur l'**OPERA** français et sur l'opéra italien. Lausanne, 1754.

—— Folk Opera in the U.S.S.R. Theatre Arts, 25, 1941.

Beare, M. The German Popular Play Atis and the Venetian Opera. Cambridge U.P., 1939.

Bertoni, G. Giuseppe Riva e l'opera italiana a Londra. GSLI, 267, 1927.

Briqueville, E. de. Le livret d'opéra de Lully à Gluck (1672-1779). Mémoires de l'Acad. de Vaucluse, 5, 1886.

Brockway, W. & Weinstock, H. The Opera; a History of its Creation and Performance: 1600-1941. New York, 1941.

Bronson, B. H. The Beggar's Opera. Berkeley, 1941.

Bulthaupt, H. Dramaturgie der Oper. 2 vols. Leipzig, 1887.

Della Corte. L'opera comica italiana nel' 700. Bari, 1923.

Dennis, J. Essay on the Operas After the Italian Manner, which are about to be Established on the English Stage. London, 1706.

Dubitzky, F. Shakespeare in Opern. Bühne & Welt, 15.

Font, A. Favart, l'Opéra-Comique et la Comédie-Vaudeville aux XVIIe et XVIIIe siècles. Paris, 1894.

Fuchs, A. Wieland et l'esthétique de l'opéra. RLC, 10, 1930.

Gagey, E. M. Ballad Opera. New York, 1937.

Grout, D. J. The Origins of the Opéra-Comique. Diss. Harvard, 1939.

Guiet, R. L'évolution d'un genre. Le livret d'opéra en France de Gluck à la Révolution, 1774-93. Northampton (Mass.), 1936-37.

Henderson, W. J. Some Forerunners of Italian Opera. New York, 1911.

Iaguzzi, A. The European Vogue of Favart: the Diffusion of the Opéra Comique. New York, 1932.

Kahlert. Die italienische Oper in Breslau am Anfange des XVIII. Jahrhunderts. Schlesische Provinzialblätter, 1837.

Kretzschmar, A. F. H. Geschichte der Oper. Leipzig, 1919.

Lancaster, H. C. Comedy Versus Opera in France, 1673-1700. Festschrift Carleton Brown. Oxford U.P., 1940.

Leblond, Abbé. Mémoire pour servir à l'histoire de la révolution opérée en France par M. le Chevalier Gluck. Paris, 1781.

Malherbe, C. Histoire de l'opéra jusqu'à Rameau. In: Hippolyte et Aricée (1733). Paris, 1939.

Maria y Campos, A. de. Una temporada de opera italiana en Oaxaca. México, 1939.

Nicoll, A. Italian Opera in England. The First 5 Years. Anglia, 46, 1922.

Prunières, H. L'opéra italien en France avant Lulli. Paris, 1913.

Rieder, M. Literary Sources of Italian Opera. U. of Colorado Studies, 1928.

Rolland, R. Les origines du théâtre lyrique moderne. Histoire de l'opéra en Europe avant Lully. Paris, 1895.

—— L'opéra avant l'opéra. In: Musiciens d'autrefois. Paris, 1908.

Schultz, W. E. Gay's Beggar Opera: its Content, History and Influence. New Haven, 1923.

Van der Vat, D. G. The Fabulous Opera. A Study of Continuity in French and English Poetry of the Nineteenth Century. Diss. Groningen, 1936.

Welmsley, D. M. The Influence of Foreign Opera on English Operatic Plays of the Restoration Period. Anglia, 1928.

Forman, H. J. The Story of **PROPHECY**. New York, 1936.

Guillaume, A. Prophecy and Divination among the Hebrews and other Semites. London, 1938.

Heschel, A. Die Prophetie. Krakow, 1936.

Lindblom, I. Die literarische Gattung der prophetischen Literatur. Upsala, 1924.

Robinson, T. H. Prophecy and the Prophets in Ancient Israel. London, 1923.

Anon. Antike Weisheit für moderne Menschen. 600 lateinische und griechische Sprüche mit Uebersetzung. (**PROVERBS**). München, 1932.

Arthaber, A. Dizionario comparato di proverbi e modi proverbiali italiani, francesi, espagnoli, tedeschi, inglesi e greci antichi. Suppl. ai dizion. delle principali lingue mod. e antiche. Milano, 1929.

Bellezza, P. Studio comparativo sui proverbi inglesi. Milano, 1894.

Bonser, W. & Stephens, T. A. Proverb Literature. London, 1930.

Brenner, C. D. Le développement du proverbe dramatique en France et sa vogue au XVIIIe siècle. Berkeley, 1937.

Bryant, Margaret. Proverbs and How to Collect Them. Pub. American Dialect Society, 4, 1945.

Champion, S. G. Racial Proverbs: A Selection of the World's Proverbs Arranged Linguistically. New York, 1938.

—— The Eleven Religions and Their Proverbial Lore. New York, 1945.

Cott. Deutsche und französische Sprichwörter vergleichend zusammengestellt. Progr., 1864.

Davidoff, H. A World Treasury of Proverbs from Twenty-Five Languages. New York, 1946.

Edgar, M. Finnish Proverbs in Minnesota. Minnesota History, 24, 1943.

Frischbier, H. Preussische Sprichwörter und volkstümliche Redensarten. Berlin, 1865.

Furrell, J. W. Arabic Proverbs. Calcutta Review, 59, 1874.

Galloway, C. H. The Book of Spanish Proverbs. New York, 1944.

Gates, Eunice J. Proverbs in the Plays of Calderon. RR, 38, 1947.

Gottschalk, W. Die bildhaften Sprichwörter der Romanen. Heidelberg, 1935.

Haefeli, L. Sprichwôrter und Redensarten aus der Zeit Christi. Luzern, 1934.

Haller, J. Altspanische Sprichwörter und sprichwörtliche Redensarten aus den Zeiten des Cervantes etc., verglichen mit den entsprechenden der Griechen und Römer, der sämmtlichen germanischen und romanischen Völker. 2 vols. Regensburg, 1883.

Hayes, F. C. The Use of Proverbs and Motives in the Siglo de Oro Drama: HR, 6, 1938 & 15, 1947.

Heraeus, W. Die Quellen von Jakob Werners lateinischen Sprichwörtern und Sinnsprüchen des Mittelalters. Festschrift Strecker. Dresden, 1931.

Jente, R. A Review of Proverb Literature since 1920. Corona: Festschrift Samuel Singer. Durham (N.C.), 1941.

—— The Untilled Field of Proverbs. SPh, 1945.

Juliani. La nomenclature, dialogues, proverbes et heures de recréation nécessaires à ceux qui désirent parfaitement parler et écrire les langues française, italienne et espagnole. Paris, 1673.

Klancar, A. J. A Tentative Bibliography

on the Slovene Proverb. JAFL, 61, 1948.
Klein, H. W. Die volkstümlichen sprichwörtlichen Vergleiche im Lateinischen und in den romanischen Sprachen. Würzburg, 1937.
Klimenko, I. Das russische Sprichwort. Bern, 1946.
Kradolfer, J. Das italienische Spruchwort und seine Beziehungen zum deutschen. Zs. für Völkerpsychologie & Sprachwissenschaft, 1860.
Lena, F. Proverbi italiani e latini. Bologna, 1694.
Leroux de Lincy. Le livre des proverbes français, avec des recherches historiques sur les proverbes français et leur emploi dans la littérature du moyen âge et de la Renaissance. 2 vols. Paris, 1842-59.
Loubens, D. Les proverbes et locutions de la langue française, leurs origines et leur concordance avec les proverbes des autres nations. Paris, 1889.
Martin, J. Dic Proverbes au Conte de Bretaigne nebst Belegen aus germanischen und romanischen Sprachen. Progr. Erlangen, 1892.
Molera, Frances M. California Spanish Proverbs. Western Folklore, 6, 1947.
Morawski, J. Les discours et proverbes des sages publiés avec introduction, notes et tables. Bib. de la Fac. des Lettres de Paris, 14-15, 1924.
Peretz, B. Altprovenzalische Spruchwörter. Mit einem kurzen Hinblick auf den mittelhochdeutschen Freidank. Diss. Göttingen, 1887.
Pfeffer, J. A. The Proverb in Goethe. Columbia U.P., 1948.
Reinsberg-Düringsfeld, Ida & O. von. Sprüchwörter der germanischen und romanischen Sprachen vergleichend zusammengestellt. 2 vols. Leipzig, 1872-75.
Robinson, F. N. Irish Proverbs and Irish National Character. MPh, 43, 1945.
Said Abbud. 5000 Arabische Sprichwörter aus Palästina; Glossar dazu von K. Kampffmeyer. Berlin, 1936.
Singer, S. Sprichwörter des Mittelalters. 3 vols. Bern, 1944-47.
Smith, Cornelia M. Proverb Lore in The Ring and The Book. PMLA, 56, 1941.
Speroni, C. Merbury's Proverbi Vulgari. Italica, 20, 1943.
Steiner, A. The Vernacular Proverb in Mediaeval Latin Prose. AJPh, 1944.
Taylor, A. The Proverb. Harvard U.P., 1931.
—— An Introductory Bibliography for the Study of Proverbs. MPh, 30, 1932-33.
Venedey, J. Die Deutschen und Franzosen nach dem Geiste ihrer Sprachen und Sprüchwörter. Heidelberg, 1842.
Weingarten, J. A. & Vinogradoff, Naomi. Russian Proverbs; Compared with Proverbs of Other Nations. New York, 1945.
Whiting, B. J. Proverbs in Certain Middle English Romances in Relation to their French Sources. HSPhL, 15, 1933.
—— Proverbs in the Earlier English Drama, with Illustrations from Contemporary French Plays. Harvard U.P., 1938.
—— The English Proverbs of Stephane Mallarmé. RR, 36, 1945.
Wilson, R. P. English Proverbs. Bodleian Lib. Rec., 2, 1948.
Klanfer, J. Das Wortspiel und die komische Rede. (**PUNS**). Zs. für Aesthetik und allg. Kunstwissenschaft, 30, 1936.
Schultz, I. Psychologie des Wortspiels. Ibid. 21, 1927.
Filippis, M. de. The Literary **RIDDLE** in Italy to the End of the Sixteenth Century. UCPPh, 1948.
Hull, V. & Taylor, A. A Collection of Welsh Riddles. Berkeley, 1942.
Pearce, T. M. Some Spanish Riddles in New Mexico. Western Folklore, 1947.
Rudolph, R. C. Notes on the Riddle in China. Calif. Folklore Quart., 1, 1942.
Taylor, A. A Bibliography of Riddles. Helsinki, 1939.
—— The Literary Riddle before 1600. Berkeley, 1948.
Zoff, O. Riddles around the World. New York, 1945.
Berrey, L. V. & van den Bark, M. The American Thesaurus of **SLANG**: A Complete Reference Book of Colloquial Speech. New York, 1942.

CHAPTER FOUR

Literary Forms.

1. Generalities.

Brinkmann, H. Grundfragen der Stilgeschichte. Fünf Betrachtungen. ZDK, 46-47, 1932-33.
Burke, K. The Philosophy of Literary Form. University (La.), 1941.
Goldschmidt, A. Das Nachleben der

antiken Formen im Mittelalter. VBW, 1, 1921-22.

Hack, R. K. The Doctrines of Literary Forms. HSCPh, 27, 1916.

Hamm, V. M. Form in Literature. Thought, 17, 1942.

Hirt, E. Das Formgesetz der epischen, dramatischen und lyrischen Dichtung. Diss. Zürich, 1922.

Jolles, A. Einfache Formen. Halle, 1930.

Lange, A. Griechische Formen der deutschen Dichtung. DR, 20, 1879.

Merian-Genast, E. Das Problem der Form in der französischen und deutschen Klassik. GRM, 27, 1939.

Vossler, K. Lo spirito delle forme poetiche italiane e la loro importanza per le letterature europee. Poesia, Oct., 1947.

Wright, R. E. Critique of Teaching Literary Forms. Philadelphia, 1941.

Zirminsky, V. Formprobleme in der russischen Literaturwissenschaft. ZSPh, 1925.

2. Individual Forms; Versification, Metaphors, etc.

Anon. An Introduction of the Ancient Greek and Latin Measures into British Poetry. London, 1737.

Adank, H. Essai sur les fondements psychologiques et linguistiques de la métaphore affective. Genève, 1939.

Baroway, I. The Hebrew Hexameter: A Study in Renaissance Sources and Interpretation. ELH, 2, 1935.

Bartsch, K. Goethe und der Alexandriner. JbGG, 1880.

Baudisch, J. Ueber Vergleiche im Französischen und Englischen. Progr. Wien, 1888.

Becker, P. A. Zur Technik des Vers libre in der neufranzösischen Dichtung. Diss. Strassburg, 1888.

Belfrage, S. Die Entstehung der freien Rhythmen. Lund, 1941.

Benloew, L. Rhythmes français et rhythmes latins. Paris, 1862.

Biese, A. Die Philosophie des Metaphorischen. Hamburg, 1893.

Binyon, L. Terza rima in English Poetry. English, 3.

Bouchaud, M. A. Essai sur la poésie rhythmique. Paris, 1763.

Brocks, E. Die spanische Strophe und ihr Fortleben im lateinischen Kirchenliede und in der neueren deutschen Dichtung. Progr. Marienwerder, 1890.

Brown, W. C. The Triumph of Form: The Later Masters of the Heroic Couplet. Chapel Hill (N.C.), 1948.

Bullock, W. L. The Genesis of the English Sonnet Form. PMLA, 38, 1923.

Campos, A. de. Estudos sobre o soneto: 3 conferencias. Coimbra, 1936.

Carter, M. F. Role of the Symbol in French Romantic Poetry. Washington, 1946.

Clarke, Dorothy C. The copla de arte mayor. HR, 8, 1940.

Crawford, J. P. W. Notes on the Sonnets of the Spanish cancionero general of 1554. RR, 7, 1916.

Crescimbeni, G. M. Del sonetto; delle sue forme; delle variazioni del sonetto, etc. In: L'Istoria della volgar poesia, 1. Venezia, 1731.

Devel, F. Le Quatrain: son rôle dans l'histoire et dans les lettres, à la ville et au théâtre. Paris, 1871.

Eliot, T. S. Reflections on Vers libre. New Statesman, 3.III.1927.

Elst, J. van der. L'alternance binaire dans le vers français et l'oreille germanique. NPh, 2, 1916.

Floeck, O. Die Kanzone in der deutschen Dichtung. Berlin, 1910.

Flohr, O. Geschichte des Knittelverses bis zur Jugend Goethes. Berlin, 1893.

Garlanda, F. L'alliterazione nel dramma Shakespeariano e nella poesia italiana. Roma, 1906.

Giannini, G. Sulla forma primitiva dello strambotto siciliano. Lucca, 1910.

Gotthold, F. A. Ueber die Nachahmung der italienischen und spanischen Versmasse in unserer Muttersprache. Progr, 1846.

Grimm, W. Zur Geschichte des Reimes. Berlin, 1852.

Grosse, E. Die Anfänge der Kunst. (Rhythm). Leipzig, 1894.

Guillaume, J. Le vers français et les prosodies modernes. Paris, 1898.

Henríquez Ureña, P. Sobre la historia del alejandrino. RFH, 8, 1946.

Henschke, E. Die Nachbildung griechischer Metra im Deutschen. Leipzig, 1885.

Heusler, A. Deutscher und antiker Vers; der falsche Spondeus und angrenzende Fragen. Strassburg, 1917.

Hügli, E. Die romanischen Strophen in der Dichtung deutscher Romantiker. Diss. Bern. Zürich, 1900. Cf. DLZ, 1904.

Inge, W. R. Classical Metres in English Poetry. Trans. of the Royal Society of Literature, 2, 1922.

Joerder, O. Die Formen des Sonetts bei Lope de Vega. Halle, 1936 .
Jones, P. M. Whitman and the Origins of the vers libre. French Studies, 1948.
Kastner, L. E. History of the Terza Rima in France. ZFSL, 26, 1904.
Kauffmann, F. Deutsche Metrik nach ihrer geschichtlichen Entwicklung. Marburg, 1912.
Kawczynski, M. Essai comparatif sur l'origine et l'histoire des rythmes. Paris, 1889.
Koehler, R. Das älteste bekannte deutsche Sonett und sein italienisches Original. ALG, 9, 1880. And in: Kleinere Schriften, 3. Berlin, 1898.
Konrad, H. Etude sur la métaphore. Paris, 1939.
Lang, H. R. The Original Meaning of the Metrical Terms estrabot, strambotto, estribote, estrambote. Mélanges R. Renier. Torino, 1912.
Legge, J. Parallelism in Chinese Style. Asiatic Quarterly Rev, 3rd Ser., 1, 1896.
Legouis, E. A Short Parallel Between French and English Versification. Mod. Humanities Research Ass. Bull., 9, 1925.
Lentzner, K. Ueber das Sonett und seine Gestaltung in der englischen Dichtung bis Milton. Halle, 1886.
Lote, G. Les origines du vers français. Aix-en-Provence, 1939.
Mapes, E. K. Innovation and French Influence in the Metrics of R. Dario. PMLA, 1934.
Massing, W. Ueber Ursprung und Verbreitung des Reimes. Diss. Dorpat, 1866.
Meredith, D. C. The Sonnet: Its Form and Technique. Atlanta, 1939.
Meyer, W. Gesammelte Abhandlungen zur mittellateinischen Rythmik. Berlin, 1905.
Michelagnoli, A. Il sonetto nella letteratura inglese. Padova, 1938.
Minor, J. Neuhochdeutsche Metrik. Strassburg, 1903.
Mitchell, C. B. The English Sonnet in the XVIIth Century, Especially After Milton. Diss. Harvard, 1939.
Mitlacher, H. Moderne Sonettgestaltung. Leipzig, 1932.
Morel-Fatio, A. L'arte mayor et hendécasyllabe dans la poésie castillane du XVe siècle et du commencement du XVIe. Romania, 23, 1894.
—— Histoire d'un sonnet. RHLF, 1, 1894.
Pellegrini, C. La prima opera di Margherita di Navarre e la terza rima in Francia. Catania, 1920.
Pflaenzel, M. Ueber die Sonette des Joachim Du Bellay nebst einer Einleitung: Die Einführung des Sonetts in Frankreich. Diss. Leipzig, 1898.
Reynolds, P. E. The English Sonnet Sequence, 1783-1845. Diss. Harvard, 1938.
Rieser, M. Analysis of the Poetic Simile. Journal of Philosophy, 37, 1941.
Saavedra Molina, J. El octosilabo castellano. Santiago de Chile, 1945.
—— El verso de Arte Mayor. Santiago de Chile, 1946.
St. Amour, Sister Mary P. A Study of the Villancico up to Lope de Vega. Washington, D. C., 1940.
Saintsbury, G. A History of English Prose Rhythm. London, 1912.
Sanderlin, G. A Bibliography of English Sonnets, 1800-50. ELH, 8, 1941.
Schaffer, A. The Persian Quatrain. MLN, 1936.
Schipper, J. Grundriss der englischen Metrik. Wien, 1895.
Scholl, Evelyn H. English Metre Once More. PMLA, 63, 1948.
Schuchardt, H. Ritornell und Terzine. Halle, 1875.
Servien, P. Les rythmes comme introduction physique à l'esthétique. Paris, 1930.
Sievers, E. Altgermanische Metrik. Halle, 1893.
Smith, A. Of the Affinity Between English and Italian Verses. In: Essays. London, 1869.
Spoerri, T. Französische Metrik. München, 1929.
Stiefel, H. Die italienische Tenzone des 13. Jahrhunderts und ihr Verhältnis zur provenzalischen Tenzone. Halle, 1914.
Storost, J. Ursprung und Entwicklung des altprovenzalischen Sirventes bis auf Bertram de Born. Diss. Halle, 1930.
Storost, W. Geschichte der altfranzösischen und altprovenzalischen Romanzenstrophe. Diss. Halle, 1930.
Symonds, J. A. Blank Verse. London, 1895.
Tomlinson, C. The Sonnet, Its Origin, Structure and Place in Poetry. London, 1874.
Vaganay, H. Le sonnet en Italie et en France au XVIe siècle. Essai de bibliographie comparée. Lyon, 1902.
Valentin, V. Der Grundunterschied des französischen und deutschen Verses.

Berichte d. freien deutschen Hochstifts Frankfurt, 14, 1898.

Verrier, P. Le vers français, formes primitives, développement, diffusion. 3 vols. Paris, 1931-32.

Wackernagel, W. Geschichte des deutschen Hexameters und Pentameters bis auf Klopstock. Berlin, 1831.

Welti, H. Geschichte des Sonettes in der deutschen Dichtung. Leipzig, 1884.

Wentzel, J. Ueber den Reim in der neueren französischen Dichtung. Diss. Leipzig, 1907.

Wilkins, E. H. The Invention of the Sonnet. MPh, 13, 1915.

Zerolo, E. Legajo de varios: Cairasco Figueroa y el empleo del verso esdrujulo en el siglo XVI. Paris, 1897.

Zillman, L. J. John Keats and the Sonnet Tradition: A Critical and Comparative Study. Los Angeles, 1939-40.

Zschech, F. Die Kritik des Reims in England. Berlin, 1916.

BOOK TWO

The Orient, Antiquity (Greece, Rome), Judaism, Early Christianity, Mohammedanism and Their Contributions.

FIRST PART

The Orient.

(Asia, Africa, Australia)

CHAPTER ONE

Orient, Asia, Near East and Far East in General.

(For Reciprocal Influences Between Orient and Occident, see III. III. 2. For European Orient, see Slavonic Literatures.)

Anon. Asiatische Litteratur und Kunst in England. Hamburgische Address-Comptoir Nachrichten, 7.XI.1799.
—— Western Interpreters of Eastern Verse. Calcutta Review, 119, 1904.
Auriant. L'Orient à travers les lettres françaises. Les Marges, 15.VIII.1926.
Babbitt, J. T. Romanticism and the Orient. Bookman, 1931.
Barbeau, M. Asiatic Survivals in Indian Songs. Queen's Quarterly, 47, 1940. Cf. Scientific Monthly, 56, 1942.
Barker, E. Some Foreign Influences in Greek Thought. G&R, 5, 1935.
Baumgartner, L. Israelitische und altorientalische Weisheit. Tübingen, 1933.
Bordeaux, H. Les voyageurs français en Orient. RDM, May, 1926.
—— Voyageurs d'Orient. 2 vols. Paris, 1927.
Bouvier, P. L'Orient dans la littérature française pendant les premières années du romantisme. Diss. Paris, 1907.
Braun, M. History and Romance in Graeco-Oriental Literature. Oxford, 1938.
Brown, W. C. The Popularity of English Travel Books About the Near East. (1775-1825). PhQ, 1936.
—— English Travel Books and Minor Poetry About the Near East. PhQ, 1937.
—— Prose-Fiction and English Interest in the Near East, 1775-1825. PMLA, 1938.
—— The Near East in English Drama, 1775-1825. JEGPh, 46, 1947.
Clark, T. B. Oriental England: A Study of Oriental Influences in XVIIIth Century England As Reflected in the Drama. Shanghai, 1929.
Chakravarti, J. The Discovery of Our Literary Inheritance. Calcutta Review, 3rd Ser., 53, 1934.
Chaumeix, A. L'Orient et la littérature française. Revue hebdomadaire, 7.XII. 1912.
Chiappelli, A. L'Oriente e le origini della filosofia greca. A&R, 1914.
—— La propaganda dell' orientalismo in Europa e i suoi pericoli. NAnt, 16.IX. 1927.
Christy, A. E. The Orient in American Transcendentalism. Columbia U.P., 1932.
Conant, M. P. The Oriental Tale in England in the 18th Century. New York, 1908.
Cumont, F. Les religions orientales dans le paganisme romain. Paris, 1928.
Curtius, E. R. Les influences asiatiques dans la vie intellectuelle allemande. Revue de Genève, 1920.
Darmesteter, J. L'orientalisme en France. In: Essais orientaux. Paris, 1883.
Das Gupta, J. The East in English Literature. Calcutta Review, 3rd Ser., 31, 1929.
Delattre, F. L'orientalisme dans la littérature anglaise. In: De Byron à F. Thompson. Paris, 1913.
Dieulafoy, M. Les origines orientales du drame espagnol. Le Correspondant, 10.VI.1906.
Dreesbach, E. Der Orient in der altfranzösischen Kreuzzugslitteratur. Diss. Breslau, 1901.
Dufrenoy, Marie-Louise. L'Orient romanesque en France, 1704-89. Montréal, 1946-47.
Dugat, G. Histoire des orientalistes de l'Europe du XIIe au XIXe siècle. Paris, 1868.
Durant, W. Our Oriental Heritage. New York, 1935.
Fevret, A. L'orientalisme de nos écrivains. RB, 4.VI.1927.
Fichtner, J. Die altorientalische Weisheit in ihrer israelitisch-jüdischen Ausprägung. Giessen, 1933.
Filippi, F. de. I viaggiatori italiani in Asia. Roma, 1934.
Fraenkel, S. Orientalische Einflüsse auf die deutsche Sprache. Mittheilungen

der Schlesischen Ges. f. Volkskunde, 2, 1895.

Gonzalez-Llubera, J. Un aspecte de la novelistica oriental a la literatur medieval europea. Homenatge a Antoni Rubio i Lluch. Barcelona, 1936.

Gressmann, H. Die orientalischen Religionen im hellenistisch-römischen Zeitalter. Berlin, 1930.

Gruppe, O. Die griechischen Kulte und Mythen in ihrer Beziehung zu den orientalischen Religionen. Leipzig, 1887.

Gubernatis, A. de. Matériaux pour servir à l'histoire des études orientales en Italie. Paris, 1878.

Halid, H. Oriental Studies in England and on the Continent: A Comparison. Asiatic Quarterly Rev., 3rd Ser., 18, 1904.

Hanschke, P. Der Einbruch des Orientalischen in das klassische römische Schrifttum als Vorbereitung des Christentums. NJAB, 1938.

Hausherr, I. Les grands courants de la spiritualité orientale. Orientalia Christiana Periodica, 1. (Roma), 1935.

Herder, J. G. Von den deutsch-orientalischen Dichtern. In: Fragmente über die neuere deutsche Litteratur, 2te Sammlung. Riga, 1767.

Hoops, J. Orientalische Stoffe in der englischen Literatur. DR, 1906.

Hopfner, T. Orient und griechische Philosophie. Leipzig, 1925.

Jacob, G. Oestliche Kulturelemente im Abendland. Berlin, 1902.

—— Der Einfluss des Morgenlandes auf das Abendland vornehmlich während des Mittelalters. Hannover, 1924.

Jullian, C. L'orientalisme à Bordeaux. Actes de l'Acad. de Bordeaux, 1897.

Kerenyi, K. Die griechisch-orientalische Romanliteratur in religionsgeschichtlicher Beleuchtung. Tübingen, 1927.

Lehmann-Haupt, C. F. Die griechisch-römische Geschichtsschreibung im Lichte altorientalischer Quellen. Würzburg, 1923.

Levy, G. R. The Oriental Origin of Herakles. Journal of Hellenic Studies, 1934.

Liatskii, E. Oriental Motifs in the European Epic of the Middle Ages. Russkoe Bogatstvo, 5, 1899.

Lokotsch, K. Etymologisches Wörterbuch der europäischen Wörter orientalischen Ursprungs. Heidelberg, 1927.

Lucas, R. N. Crete the Bridge by Which the Culture of Asia Passed Into Europe. Asiatic Quarterly Rev., 3rd Ser., 16, 1903.

Malet, A. & Isaac, J. L'Orient et la Grèce. Paris, 1924.

Manfronti, C. L'Italia e l'Oriente asiatico. Rassegna italiana, August, 1935.

Marot, K. Die Antike und der Orient. EPhK, 1935.

Martin, A. von. Antike, Germanentum, Christentum und Orient als Aufbaufaktoren der geistigen Welt des Mittelalters. AK, 19, 1929.

Martino, P. L'Orient dans la littérature française au 17e et au 18e siècle. Paris, 1906.

Massis, H. Défense de l'Occident. Paris, 1927.

Meester, E. de. Oriental Influences in the English Literature of the Early Nineteenth Century. Diss. Heidelberg, 1915.

Munteano, B. Influences orientales sur la littérature roumaine. RLC, 14, 1934.

Osborn, E. Oriental Diction and Theme in English Verse, 1747-1840. Humanistic Studies, U. of Kansas, 2, 1922.

Otto, W. F. Der europäische Geist und die Weisheit des Ostens. Frankfurt, 1931.

Ottolenghi, R. Influenze orientali sul Rinascimento. Ateneo Veneto, 25, 1902.

Paredi, A. Influssi orientali sulla liturgia milanese antica. Scuola Cattolica, 1940.

Paris, G. Les contes orientaux dans la littérature française du moyen âge. In: La poésie au moyen âge. 2 vols. Paris, 1885-95.

Parker, E. H. Modern Russia and Asiatic Traditions. Asiatic Quarterly Rev., 3rd Ser., 3, 1897.

Rice, S. The Challenge of Asia. London, 1924.

Romito, M. Italiani del cinquecento in Estremo Oriente. Frontespizio, 11, 1939.

Ruge, A. Der asiatische Geist in seiner Herrschaft über Europa. In: Demokratische Studien. Hamburg, 1861.

Saineanu, L. Influenta orientala asupra limbei si culturei romane. 3 vols. Bucuresti, 1900.

Saurat, D. L'Orient. Les Marges, May, 1925.

Schwartz, W. L. The Imaginative Interpretation of the Far East in Modern French Literature, 1800-1925. Paris, 1927.

—— L'appel de l'Extrême-Orient dans la poésie des Etats-Unis. RLC, 8, 1928.

Seaver, H. L. The Asian Lyric and Eng-

lish Literature. Festschrift Barrett Wendell. Harvard U.P., 1926.
Tietjens, E. The Orient's Gift to American Poetry. Asia, 1936.
Tucci, G. L'Oriente nella cultura europea. Roma, 1934.
Tyrrell, F. H. English Authors and Oriental Orthography. Asiatic Quarterly Rev., N.S., 2, 1913.
Valkhoff, M. De betekenis van Amerika en Azie voor het West-Europese Gedachtenleven van de 17e en 18e eeuw. NPh, 23, 1937-38.
Waltz, P. La question d'Orient dans l'antiquité. Paris, 1942.
Walzer, R. Klassische Altertumswissenschaft und Orientalistik. ZDMG, 11, 1932-33.
Wann, L. The Oriental in Elizabethan Drama. MPh, 12, 1913.
Weber, H. W. Tales of the East, Comprising the Most Popular Romances of Oriental Origin and the Best Imitations by European Authors. 3 vols. Edinburgh, 1812.
Wellesz, E. Eastern Elements in Western Chant. Boston, 1947.
Werner, C. La philosophie grecque et la pensée de l'Orient. Revue de Théologie et de Philosophie, 1938.

CHAPTER TWO

Babylon, Syria, Persia. (Iran).

Anikov, E. Les survivances manichéennes en pays slaves et en Occident. Revue des Etudes slaves, 8, 1929.
Braaksma, M. H. Travel and Literature: An Attempt at a Literary Appreciation of English Travel-Books about Persia, from the Middle Ages to the Present Day. Groningen, 1938.
Cumont, F. La propagation du manichéisme dans l'Empire romain. Revue d'histoire et de litt. religieuses, N. S., 1910.
Edkins, J. Persian Elements in Japanese Legends. Transactions Asiatic Society in Japan, 1889.
Masani, R. P. Court Poets of Iran and India. Bombay, 1938.
Palmer, E. H. Oriental Mysticism; A Treatise on the Sufistic and Unitarian Theosophy of the Persians. Cambridge, 1867.
Pizzi, I. Le somiglianze e le relazioni tra la poesia persiana e la nostra del medioevo. Atti d. R. Acc. delle Scienze, Torino, 1892.
Przyluski, J. Influence iranienne au Grèce et dans l'Inde. Rev. de l'U. de Bruxelles, 37.
Reitzenstein & Schaeder. Studien zum antiken Synkretismus aus Iran und Griechenland. VBW, 1926.
Remy, A. F. J. The Influence of India and Persia on the Poetry of Germany. New York, 1901-02.
Ryssel, V. Der Einfluss der syrischen Literatur auf das Abendland. Theologische Zs. aus der Schweiz, 13, 1896.
—— Syrische Quellen abendländischer Erzählungsstoffe. Archiv, 45, 1896.
Samsami, N. L'Iran dans la littérature française. Paris, 1937.
Schraeder, H. H. Urform und Fortbildungen des Manichäischen Systems. VBW, 2, 1922-23.
Sykes, P. The Influence of Persia on Europe. NC, 1931.
Tyrrell, F. H. Persian Poets and English Translations. Calcutta Rev., April, 1894.

CHAPTER THREE

China (and Indo-China).

Anon. The Vogue of Chinese Poetry. ER, 1922.
Abel-Remusat, J. P. Lettre sur l'état et les progrès de la littérature chinoise en Europe. In: Le Musée des Variétés littéraires, 2, 1823.
Allen, C. F. R. A Chinese Book of Odes for English Readers. Journal of the R. Asiatic Society, N.S., 16, 1884.
Aurich, U. China im Spiegel der deutschen Literatur des 18. Jahrhunderts. Berlin, 1935.
Belevitch-Stankevitch, H. Le goût chinois en France au temps de Louis XIV. Paris, 1910.
Chuan Chen. Die chinesische schöne Literatur im deutschen Schrifttum. Diss. Kiel, 1933.
Cordier, H. La Chine en France au XVIIIe siècle. Académie des Inscriptions et Belles-Lettres, 52, 1907-08. And Paris, 1910.
—— Les études chinoises sous la Révolution et l'Empire. T'oung Pao, 19, 1920.
Dorchain, A. La Chine et les poètes. Ann. polit. et litt., 23.IX.1900.

French, J. L. Lotus and Chrysanthemus; An Anthology of Chinese and Japanese Poetry. (Cf. Introduction). New York, 1934.

Gardner, C. S. The Future of Chinese Studies in America. U. of Pa. Library Chronicle, 12, 1944.

Gulik, R. H. van. Een nieuwe fransche vertaling van chineesche Gedichten. China, 7, 1932.

—— The Lore of the Chinese Lute, an Essay in Chinese Ideology. Monumenta Nipponica, 1, 1938.

Hundhausen, V. Chinesische Dichter in deutscher Sprache. Peking, Leipzig, 1926.

Hung Cheng Fu. Un siècle d'influence chinoise sur la littérature française, 1815-1930. Paris, 1934.

Janse, O. R. T. Notes on Chinese Influences in the Philippines in Pre-Spanish Times. Harvard Journal of Asiatic Studies, 1945.

Kahle, G. Eine islamische Quelle über China von 1500. Acta Orientalia, 12, 1934.

Lach, D. F. China and the Era of Enlightenment. Journal of Modern History, 14, 1942.

Lebois, A. Une source chinoise des "Stèles" et du "Chiffre des Choses." RLC, 22, 1948.

Léger, L. L'invasion tatare dans la littérature russe du moyen âge. In: La Russie intellectuelle. Paris, 1914.

Lovejoy, A. O. The Chinese Origin of Romanticism. JEGPh, 1933.

Malleret, L. L'exotisme indo-chinois dans la littérature française. Paris, 1934.

Martin, C. C. China in English Literature. Asiatic Quarterly Rev., N.S., 11, 1917.

Mason, M. G. Western Concepts of China and the Chinese, 1840-76. New York, 1939.

Maupassant, G. de. La Chine des poètes. Gil Blas, 31.III.1885.

Maverick, L. A. Chinese Influences upon the Physiocrats. Economic History, Feb., 1938.

May, M. G. Chinoiserie. English, 2, 1938.

McKillop, A. D. The Early European View of Old China. Rice Institute Pamphlet, 35, 1948.

North, W. R. Chinese Themes in American Verse. Philadelphia, 1937.

Parker, E. H. What We May Learn from Ancient Chinese Statesmen. Asiatic Quarterly Rev., 3rd. Ser., 27, 1909.

Patris, C. La littérature française d'inspiration indo-chinoise. Belles-Lettres, June, 1922.

Pinot, V. Les physiocrates et la Chine au XVIIIe siècle. Revue d'histoire moderne et contemp., 8, 1906-07.

—— La Chine et la formation de l'esprit philosophique en France (1640-1740). Paris, 1932.

—— Documents inédits relatifs à la connaissance de la Chine en France, de 1685 à 1740. Paris, 1932.

Prato, S. Zwei Episoden aus zwei tibetanischen Novellen in der orientalischen und occidentalen Ueberlieferung. Zs. d. Vereins f. Volkskunde, 1894.

Remusat, J. P. A. On the State and Progress of Chinese Literature in Europe. Oriental Magazine, 2, 1823.

Rose, E. Das Schicksal einer angeblich chinesischen Ballade. JEGPh, 1933.

—— China und die Spätromantik. Deutsche Kultur im Leben der Völker, 15, 1940.

Rougier, L. L'influence de la Chine sur les Physiocrates et la Révolution française. Annales franco-chinoises, 3, 1929.

Rowbotham, A. H. China and the Age of Enlightenment in Europe. Chinese Social and Political Science Review, 1935.

Selden, Elizabeth. China in German Poetry from 1773 to 1833. Berkeley, 1942.

Tchao-Ts'ing. Les descriptions de la Chine par les Français, 1650-1750. Diss. Paris, 1928.

Tscharner, E. H. von. Ein chinesisches Gedicht in achtfacher deutscher Gestalt. Der Kleine Bund, 34 (Bern), 1932.

—— China in der deutschen Dichtung bis zur Klassik. Diss. Berlin, 1934. München, 1939. Cf. also Sinica (Frankfurt), 1934-37.

Tsuda, S. Chinese Thought and Japan. Contemporary Japan, Sept., 1939.

Wen Tung, II. English Translation of Chinese Poetry. Criterion, 1938.

Wolff, E. Die erste Berührung des deutschen Geisteslebens mit dem chinesischen. Frankfurter Zt., 11.II.1902.

Zung, Cecilia S. Secrets of the Chinese Drama; a Complete Explanatory Guide to Actions and Symbols as Seen in the Performance of Chinese Dramas. With Synopses of Fifty Popular Chinese Plays. Shanghai, 1937.

CHAPTER FOUR

India.

1. Old Native India.

(For Buddha and others, see Chapter Nine).

Anon. Chinese Account of India. Asiatic Journal, N.S., 20, 1836.
—— French Notions of India. Calcutta Review, 20, 1853; 27, 1856.
—— India in the Classics. Ibid. 28, 1857.
Alviella, G. d'. Des échanges philosophiques et religieux entre l'Inde et l'antiquité classique. In: Ce que l'Inde doit à la Grèce. Paris, 1897.
Blind, K. English Neglect of Old Indian Poetry. Forum, 32, 1901.
Caputo, G. Teatro greco e teatro indiano. Dioniso, 5, 1935-36.
Del Mar, A. Christendom's Debt to India. Indian Review, Dec., 1908.
Dillon, M. The Hindu Act of Truth in Celtic Tradition. MPh, 44, 1947.
Festugière, A. J. Trois rencontres entre la Grèce et l'Inde. Rev. de l'Histoire des Religions, 125, 1942-43.
Filliozat, J. Une grammaire sanscrite du XVIIIe siècle et les débuts de l'indianisme en France. Journal asiatique, 229, 1937.
Forst, J. Indien und die deutsche Literatur. Diss. New York, 1934.
Fries, K. Indisches in der griechischen Philosophie. F&F, 1939.
Happel, J. Indische Einflüsse auf altchristliche Erzählungen. Protest. Monatshefte, 5, 1900.
Hertel, J. S. Indien auf der europäischen Bühne. Beilage Allg. Zt., 6, 1903.
Johnston, C. The Dawn of Indian Research. Calcutta Review, 100, 1895.
Joseph, P. The Extent and Influence of the Indus Civilization. Journal of Oriental Research, 11, 1937.
Jullien, S. Anecdotes indiennes traduites du sanscrit en chinois dans le VIIe siècle de notre ère, et du chinois en français. Revue orientale et américaine, 3. (Paris), 1860.
Keene, H. G. India's Place in Human Evolution. Calcutta Review, 69, 1879.
Keith, A. B. The Indian Origin of the Greek Romance. Journal of the R. Asiatic Society, 2, 1915.
Krappe, A. H. The Indian Provenance of a Mediaeval Exemplum. Traditio, 2, 1944.
Lacote, F. Sur l'origine indienne du roman grec. Mélanges S. Lévi. Paris, 1913.
Leupol, L. De l'influence qu'exerceraient les études sanscrites sur la littérature française. Mém. de l'Acad. de Stanislas, Nancy, 1862.
Lévi, S. La Grèce et l'Inde. REG, 1891.
Müller, M. Coincidences. Fortnightly Review, N.S., 64, 1898.
Pisani, V. Riflessi indiani del romanzo ellenistico-romano. Annali della Scuola Normale Superiore di Pisa, 1940.
Pope, Ethel M. India in Portuguese Literature. Hyderabad, 1938.
Rawlison, H. G. India in European Thought. In: The Legacy of India, Oxford U.P., 1937.
Remy, A. F. J. The Influence of India and Persia on the Poetry of Germany. New York, 1901-02.
Ribezzo, F. Nuovi studi sulla origine e la propagazione delle favole indoelleniche. Napoli, 1901.
Scharpe, A. De betrekkingen tussen de griekse en de indiesche roman. RBPh, 1936.
Schroeder, L. Indiens geistige Bedeutung für Europa. Beilage Allg. Zt, 151, 1899.
Sencourt, R. India in English Literature. London, 1926.
Techoneyres, E. A la recherche de l'unité. Les aspirations de l'âme hindoue et les tendances de la science occidentale contemporaine. Reims, 1934.
Vallee, P. L. de la. La Grèce et l'Inde. Musée Belge, 2.
Winternitz, M. Indian Literature and World-Literature. Calcutta Review, 3rd Ser., 10, 1924.
Zachariae, T. Kleine Schriften zur indischen Philologie, zur vergleichenden Literaturgeschichte, zur vergleichenden Volkskunde. Bonn, 1920.

2. Anglo-India.

(See also Comparisons, I. V. 1.)

Anon. The Poetry of Recent Indian Warfare. Calcutta Review, 11, 1849.
—— Recent Anglo-Indian Poetry. Ibid. 29, 1857.
—— The Poetry of the (Indian) Rebellion. Ibid. 41, 1865.
—— The Poetry of Anglo-Indian Life. Ibid. 55, 1872.
Dhar, K. N. Some Indian Novels. Ibid. 127, 1908.
Dunn, T. O. D. British Poets in India. Ibid. 1917.

Harcourt-Bath, W. Anglo-Indian. N&Q, 24.XII.1938.
Laurie, W. F. B. Anglo-Indian Periodical Literature. In: Sketches of Some Distinguished Anglo-Indians, Ser. 1, London, 1875-77.
Lawrence, T. B. English Poetry in India. Being Biographical and Critical Notices of Anglo-Indian Poets. To which is Prefixed a Preliminary Essay on Anglo-Indian Poetry in Two Parts. Calcutta, 1869.
Malabari Bahramji. The Indian Muse in English Garb. Bombay, 1876.
Mitra, S. Another Supplement (to Bengali Drama). Calcutta Review, 3rd Ser., 9, 1923.
Oaten, E. F. A Sketch of Anglo-Indian Literature. London, 1908.
Sharp, Sir H. Anglo-Indian Verse. Proc. Royal Soc. Lit., 16, 1937.
Singh Bhupal. A Survey of Anglo-Indian Fiction. Oxford U.P., 1934.

CHAPTER FIVE

The Islam (Arabia).

(For Arabian Tales, Mohammed etc., See Chapter Nine)

Alcocer Martinéz, R. La corporación de los poetas en la España musulmana. Larache, 1940.
Ali, Z. Islam in the World. Lahore, 1938.
Amari, M. Storia dei Musulmani di Sicilia. 3 vols. Firenze, 1854-72.
—— Influenze degli Arabi sulla letteratura italiana. Nazione, 28.V.1872.
Arnold, T. & Guillaume, A. The Legacy of Islam. Oxford, 1931.
Arteaga, E. Della influenza degli Arabi sull'origine della poesia moderna in Europa. Roma, 1797.
Asín Palacios, M. Spiritualité musulmane et spiritualité chrétienne. Cahiers du Sud, 1935.
—— Huellas del Islam (Santo Tomás de Aquino, Turmeda, Pascal, San Juan de la Cruz). Madrid, 1941.
Axhausen, Käte. Die Theorien über den Ursprung der provenzalischen Lyrik. Diss. Marburg. Düsseldorf, 1937.
Baldwin, M. W. Western Attitudes toward Islam. Cath. Hist. Rev., 27, 1942.
Bataillon, M. L'arabe à Salamanque au temps de la Renaissance. Hesperia, 21, 1935.
Bolaños, P. Poesía árabe y poesía arábigo-andaluza. Repertorio Americano (Costa Rica), 13.III.1943.
Bose, P. N. Hindu Civilization under Moslem Influence. Calcutta Review, 96-97, 1893.
Brown, L. P. Some Romanic Words of Arabic or Germanic Origin. Los Angeles, 1938.
Buchanan, M. A. Alhambraism. HR, 1935.
Cahen, C. Quelques mots sur le rôle de l'Islam dans l'histoire européenne. Revue de Synthèse, 1938.
Cazenave, J. Le roman hispano-mauresque en France. RLC, 5, 1925.
Cedrone, N. F. The Beginnings of Poetry in Southern Europe. Diss. Harvard, 1940.
Cesareo, G. A. Le origini della poesia lirica e la poesia siciliana sotto gli Svevi. Palermo, 1924.
Chauvin, V. Bibliographie des ouvrages arabes ou relatifs aux Arabes, publiés dans l'Europe chrétienne de 1810 à 1885, (Les Mille et une Nuits, etc.). Liège, 1892 ff.
Chew, S. The Crescent and the Rose. Islam and England during the Renaissance. Oxford U.P., 1937.
Cirot, G. La maurophilie littéraire en Espagne au XVIe siècle. BH, 39-41, 1937-39.
Colin, G. S. Un petit glossaire hispanique arabo-allemand du début du XVIe siècle. Al-Andalus, 11, 1948.
Comfort, W. W. The Literary Rôle of the Saracens in the French Epic. PMLA, 55, 1940.
—— The Saracens in Italian Epic Poetry. Ibid. 59, 1944.
Dermenghem, E. Valeurs permanentes et problèmes actuels de la civilisation musulmane. Cahiers du Sud, 1935.
Deveria, G. Origine de l'Islamisme en Chine. Paris, 1895.
Diercks, G. Die Araber im Mittelalter und ihr Einfluss auf die Cultur Europas. Annaberg, 1875.
Dozy, R. & Engelmann, W. H. Glossaire des mots espagnols et portugais dérivés de l'arabe. Leyde, Paris, 1869.
Erckmann, R. Der Einfluss der arabisch-spanischen Kultur auf die Entwicklung des Minnesangs. DVLG, 1932.
Frye, R. N. Islamic Studies in the USSR and Turkey. Moslem World, 36, 1946.
Gorra, E. Delle origini della poesia lirica del medio evo. Torino, 1895.
Grunebaum, G. E. von. Medieval Islam. Chicago U.P., 1946.
—— The Arab Contribution to Trouba-

dour Poetry. Bull. of the Iranian Institute. (New York), 1946.
Haskins, C. H. Arabic Science in Western Europe. Isis, 7, 1925.
—— The Introduction of Arabic Science into England. In: Studies in the History of Mediaeval Science. Cambridge, 1927.
—— Translators from the Arabic in Spain. Ibid.
Hassan, A. Der Islam in Indien—Indien im Weltislam. Heidelberg, 1942.
Henriot, E. L'apport de l'Islam à l'Occident. Le Monde, Oct., 1946.
Jones, C. M. The Conventional Saracen of the Songs of Geste. Spec. 17, 1942.
Keene, H. G. Islam in India. Calcutta Review, 71, 1880.
Lammens, P. H. Les études arabes en Europe au XVIe siècle. Al Machriq, 22-24, 1901.
Lapa, R. Das Origens da poesía lírica em Portugal. Lisboa, 1929.
Lecerf, J. L'arabe contemporain comme langue de civilisation. Revue africaine, 74, 1933.
Levi della Vida, G. A Portuguese Pilgrim at Mecca in the Sixteenth Century. Moslem World, 32, 1942.
Levi-Provençal, E. La civilisation arabe en Espagne. Le Caire, Paris, 1938.
Mani, H. Les études arabes en Algérie, 1830-1930. Revue africaine, 74, 1933.
Maqqari. Analectes sur l'histoire et la littérature des Arabes d'Espagne. Leiden, 1855-61.
Martins, A. A literatura árabe na Europa cultura medieval. Brotéria, 26. (Lisboa), 1938.
Menéndez Pidal, R. Poesía árabe y poesía europea. Buenos Aires, 1941. Cf. BH, 50 & Revista Cubana, 7, 1937.
Morley, S. G. A Note on Arabic Poetry in European Poetry. HR, 7, 1939.
Nadvi, S. S. The Early Relations Between Arabia and India. Islamic Culture, April, 1937.
Nykl, A. R. L'influence arabe andalouse sur les troubadours. BH, 41, 1939.
—— La elegía árabe de Valencia. HR, 8, 1940-41.
—— Hispano-Arabic Poetry and its Relation with the Old Provencal Troubadours. Baltimore, 1946.
O'Leary de Lacy. Arabic Thought and its Place in History. London, 1922.
Palencia, A. G. Historia de la Literatura arábigo-española. Barcelona, 1929.
—— El Islam y Occidente. Madrid, 1931.
—— Huellas islámicas en el carácter español. HR, 7, 1939.
—— El arabismo español y los estudios literarios. BSS, 24, 1947.
Paris, G. La Romance Mauresque des Orientales. RHLF, 15.VII.1899. And in: Poèmes et Légendes du Moyen Age. Paris, 1900.
Parker, E. H. Islam in China. Asiatic Quarterly Review, 3rd Ser., 24-25, 1907-08.
Pearce, T. M. Los Moros y los Christianos: Early American Play. New Mexico Folklore Record, 1948.
Pérès, H. La poésie andalouse en arabe classique au XIe siècle. Paris, 1937.
Philpot, C. An Introduction to the Literary History of the 14th and 15th Centuries. London, 1798.
Piccolo, F. Sull' origine della poesia moderna. Napoli, 1938.
Poliak, A. N. L'arabisation de l'Orient sémitique. Revue des Etudes Islamiques, 1938.
Probst-Biraben. Espagne et Islam. Cahiers du Sud, 1935.
Ribera, J. La enseñanza de los musulmanes españoles. Saragossa, 1893.
Ristelhuber, R. La littérature musulmane en Chine. Revue du monde musulman, 4, 1908.
Rosenthal, E. Traces of Arab Influence in Spain. Islamic Culture, 11, 1937.
Schack, A. von. Poesie und Kunst der Araber in Spanien und Sicilien. 2 vols. Berlin, 1865. Mexico, 1944.
Scheludko, S. Beiträge zur Entstehungsgeschichte der altprovençalischen Lyrik. AR, 12, 1928.
Scrofani, S. Della dominazione degli stranieri in Sicilia. Parigi, 1824.
Singer, S. Arabische und europäische Poesie im Mittelalter. Berlin, 1918. Cf. ZDPh, 52, 1927.
Smith, B. P. Islam in English Literature. Beirut, 1939.
Steinschneider, M. Spanische Bearbeitungen arabischer Werke. Leipzig, 1875.
—— Die europäischen Uebersetzungen aus dem Arabischen bis Mitte des 17. Jahrhunderts. SAWW, 149, 1905.
Suter, H. Die Araber als Vermittler der Wissenschaften und deren Uebergang vom Orient zum Occident. Aarau, 1896.
Taylor, W. Etymological List of Arabic Words in English. Egyptian University, 9. Cairo, 1934.

Wüstenfeld, F. Die Uebersetzungen arabischer Werke in das Lateinische seit dem XI. Jahrhundert. Abhandl. d. kônigl. Ges. der Wissenschaften. Göttingen, 22, 1877.

CHAPTER SIX

Japan.

Bonneau, G. Le problème de la poésie japonaise; technique et traduction. Paris, 1938.
Galdi, L. La poésie japonaise d'aujourd'hui traduite en italien et vue par un Hongrois. Dante, Nov., 1935.
Gatenby, E. V. The Influence of Japan on English Literature. Studies in English Literature, 13. (Tokyo), 1933. And in: Transactions of the Japan Society, 34, 1937.
Goto, S. Un coup d'oeil sur la littérature japonaise, comparée à la littérature française. Japan Times & Mail, Dec., 1935.
Kikou, Y. La sensibilité étrangère et le Japon. NL, 21.II.1925.
Matsuo, K. Les auteurs français au Japon depuis la Restauration de Meiji. France-Japon, Jan., 1940.
Schwartz, W. L. The Influence of Japonism upon Modern French Literature. PMLA, 36, 1921.
—— Japan in French Poetry. PMLA, 1925.
—— L'influence de la poésie japonaise sur la poésie française contemporaine. RLC, 6, 1926.
Tagore, R. La génie du Japon (et les influences orientales agissant encore). Bull. de la Soc. Autour du Monde, Dec., 1921.
Thompson, D. W. Japan and the New Atlantis. SPh, 1935.

CHAPTER SEVEN

Turkey.

Gerstenberg, W. Zur Geschichte des deutschen Türkenschauspiels. Progr. Meppen, 1902.
Lajusan. Les turcophiles du XVIe siècle. Bull. de la Soc. d'histoire moderne, Nov., 1923.
Moore, S. H. The Turkish Menace in the XVIth Century (in German Literature). MLR, 40, 1945.
Pfeffermann, H. Renaissancepäpste und Sultane. Die Zusammenarbeit der Renaissancepäpste mit den Türken. Winterthur, 1946.
Reuning, K. Turkish Contributions to Western Vocabularies. MDU, 35, 1943.
Rouillard, C. D. The Turk in French History, Thought and Literature (1520-1660). Paris, 1940.

CHAPTER EIGHT

Africa, Australia, South Seas, Exotic Literature.

(See also under Negroes, I. VI. 10. and Imperialism, I. II. 2.)

Arrom, J. J. La poesía Afro-cubana. RIA, 4, 1942.
Bokanowsky, Hélène. French Literature in Algiers. BA, 19, 1945.
Brie, F. Exotismus der Sinne: eine Studie zur Psychologie der Romantik. SHAW, 1920.
Burck, E. Das Bild der Karthager in der römischen Literatur. In: Rom und Karthago, ed. by J. Vogt. Leipzig, 1943.
Caillat, J. L'Algérie dans la vie intellectuelle française entre 1830 et 1930. RU, 1931.
Carré, J. M. Voyageurs et écrivains français en Egypte. 2 vols. Le Caire, 1932.
Christie, Christina. African Influence in the Brazilian Portuguese Language and Literature. Hisp, 26, 1943.
Curzon, H. de. L'histoire de Tunis au théâtre. (Une pièce du poète espagnol José de Canizares). Revue tunisienne, 9, 1902.
Delavignette, R. L'accent africain dans les lettres françaises. La Nef, Nov., 1945.
Demp-Périer, G. Le Congo belge dans la littérature mondiale. Le Flambeau, 1.X.1928.
Frédéricq, P. L'expansion exotique des littératures européennes au XIXe siècle. Bull. de l'Acad. royale de Belgique, 1901.
Guigne, R. de. Mémoire dans lequel on s'efforce d'établir que . . . la nation chinoise est une colonie égyptienne. Mémoires de l'Acad. des Inscriptions et Belles-Lettres, 29, 1764.
Huggins, Kathryn. Aframerican Fiction. Southern Lit. Messenger, 3, 1941.
Humbert, P. Recherches sur les sources

égyptiennes de la littérature sapientale d'Israël. Neuchâtel, 1929.
Jourda, P. L'exotisme dans la littérature française depuis Chateaubriand. Le Romantisme. Paris, 1938. Cf. also RCC 1936 & 1939.
König, K. Ueberseeische Wörter im Französischen vom 16.-18. Jahrhundert. Halle, 1939.
Lancaster, H. C. L'Afrique du Nord dans le théâtre français sous les règnes de Louis XIII et de Louis XIV. Rev. de la Méditerranée, 3, 1946.
Lebel, R. Le Maroc dans la littérature francaise. Paris, 1925.
—— L'Afrique occidentale dans la littérature française depuis 1870. Paris, 1925.
—— Histoire de la littérature coloniale en France. Paris, 1931.
—— Les voyageurs français du Maroc. L'exotisme marocain dans la littérature de voyage. Paris, 1936.
—— Le Maroc chez les auteurs anglais du XVIe au XIXe siècle. Paris, 1939.
Lesher, Clara R. The South Sea Islanders in English Literature, 1519-1798. Chicago, 1940.
Mace, A. C. The Influence of Egypt on Hebrew Literature. Annals of Archeology and Anthropology, 9, 1922.
Maury, L. Les origines et la signification de l'exotisme littéraire. RB, 21.X. 1911.
Moebius, E. Ueber die Entwicklung der Naturschilderung in den englischen Reisewerken über Afrika. Progr. Kiel, 1895.
Nienaber, P. J. De Afrikaanse Roman-Tematologie. Amsterdam, 1938.
Peet, T. E. A Comparative Study of the Literatures of Egypt, Palestine and Mesopotamia. Egypt's Contribution to the Literature of the Ancient World. London, 1931.
Peixotto, A. L'exotisme littéraire. Notes pour un livre futur. RLC, 14, 1934.
Perschmann, S. Verzeichnis der in Deutschland erschienenen Bücher und Schriften über die Burenrepubliken und den Burenkrieg. Börsenblatt f.d. deutschen Buchhandel, 163-64, 1903.
Seidel, W. Exotismus in der deutschen Literatur. Monatshefte f. Literatur, 1929.
Senna, N. de. Africanos no Brasil. Bello Horizonte, 1938.
Smith, E. M. The Egypt of the Greek Romances. CJ, 23, 1928.
Sypher, W. The African Prince in London. JHI, 2, 1941.
Todt, H. Die deutsche Begegnung mit Afrika im Spiegel des deutschen Nachkriegsschrifttums. Frankfurt, 1939.
Wiedemann, A. Die ägyptische Geschichte in der Sage des Altertums. Festgabe F. von Bezold. Bonn, 1921.
Wirth, A. Deutsche überseeische Litteratur. Internat. Litteraturberichte, 1.IV. 1897.
Zucker, F. Zur Landeskunde Aegyptens aus griechischen und römischen Quellen. Festschrift Judeich. Weimar, 1929.

CHAPTER NINE

Individual Oriental Authors and Works and their Influence.

Chateaubriend, F. R. de. Les aventures du dernier **ABENCERAGE**. (ed. by P. Hazard & M. J. Durry). Paris, 1926. (Cf. Introduction).
Cirot, G. A propos de la Nouvelle de l'Abencerage. BH, 31, 1929.
Crawford, J. P. W. El Abencerrage and Longfellow's Galgano, a Parallel. Hisp, 9, 1926.
Matulka, B. On the European Diffusion of the Last of the Abencerages Story in the XVIth Century. Hisp., 16, 1933.
Primicerio, E. La historia del Abencerage y los Romances de Granada. Napoli, 1929.
Hausrath, A. **ACHIQAR** und Aesop: Das Verhältnis der orientalischen zur griechischen Fabeldichtung. SHAW, 1918.
Salmon, D. The Mediaeval Latin Translations of **ALFARABI'S** Works. New Scholasticism, 13, 1940.
Heller, B. Die Bedeutung des arabischen **ANTAR** Romans für die vergleichende Literaturkunde. Leipzig, 1931.
Anon. **ARABIAN NIGHTS** and their Origin. Foreign Quarterly Review, 24.
—— Las Mil y una noches. Influencia de la literatura oriental sobre la arabe y de estra sobre la de la edad media. Revista de España y del extranjero, 1842.
Annan, M. C. The Arabian Nights in Victorian Literature. Diss. Northwestern U., 1945.
Chauvin, V. Les Mille et une nuits. In: Bibliographie des ouvrages arabes ou relatifs aux Arabes (parts IV-VII). Liège, 1900 ff.
Dornseiff, F. Petron und 1001 Nacht.

Symbolae Osloenses, 18, 1938.
Gabrieli, F. Le Mille e una notte nella cultura europea. Mercurio, 1, 1944.
Hammer, J. de. Sur l'origine des Mille et une nuits. Journal asiatique, 1827.
—— Note sur l'origine persane des Mille et une nuit. Journal asiatique, 1839.
Henninger, J. Mohammedanische Polemik gegen das Christentum in 1001 Nacht. Neue Zs. f. Missionswissenschaft, 4. (Luzern), 1946.
Perles, J. Rabbinische Agada's in 1001 Nacht. Ein Beitrag zur Geschichte der Wanderung orientalischer Märchen. Monatsschrift f. Gesch. & Wiss. des Judentums, 22.
Sigismund, R. Shakespeare und Tausend und Eine Nacht. JbShG, 19, 1884.
Stephens, G. A. Arabian Nights and Arthurian Romances. CLS, 20, 1946.
Toldo, P. Rileggendo le Mille e una notte. Miscellanea Arturo Graf. Bergamo, 1903.
Alphandéry, P. Y a-t-il eu un **AVERROISME** populaire au XIIIe et au XIVe siècle? Rev. de l'enseignement des religions, 44, 1901.
Doncoeur, P. Notes sur les Averroistes latins. Rev. des sciences philos. et théol., 4, 1910.
Giorgiantonio, M. Per l'Averroismo napoletano. La Rinascita, 2, 1939.
Grabmann, M. Studien über den Averroisten Taddeo da Parma. Mélanges Mandonnet. Paris, 1930.
—— Der lateinische Averroismus des 13. Jahrhunderts und seine Stellung zur christlichen Weltanschauung. München, 1931.
Krzanic, G. Grandi lottatori contro l'Averroismo. Riv. di filosofia neoscolastica, 22, 1930.
Mandonnet, P. Siger de Brabant et l'Averroisme latin au XIIIe siècle. Louvain, 1908 & 1911.
Masnovo, A.A I primi contatti di San Tommaso con l'Averroismo latino. Riv. di filosofia neoscolastica, 18, 1926.
Renan, E. Averroes et l'Averroisme. Paris, 1861.
Toffanin, G. Per l'Averroismo padovano. La Rinascita, 1, 1938-39.
Troilo, E. Per l'Averroismo padovano e veneto. ARIV, 99, 1939-40.
Mills, L. The Comparative Claims of the **AVESTA** and the Veda. Asiatic Quarterly Rev., 3rd. Ser., 15, 1903.
Carcassonne, E. Le **BHAGAVAT** devant la critique contemporaine. Recherches philosophiques, 4, 1934.
McColley, G. Milton and Moses **BARCEPHA**. SPh, 38, 1941.
Nykl, A. R. Historia de los amores de **BAYAD Y RIYAD**: una chantefable oriental en estilo persa. New York, 1941.
Tilley, A. Lafontaine and **BIDPAI**. MLR, 34, 1939.
Anon. **BUDDHISMUS**-Forschungen in Sowjetrussland. Deutsche Allg. Zt., 28.VII.1921.
Bohn, W. Der Buddhismus in den Ländern des Westens. München, 1921.
Challemel-Lacour. Un bouddhiste contemporain en Allemagne. (Schopenhauer). RDM, 15.III.1870.
Chavannes, E. Une version chinoise du conte bouddhique de Kalyanamkara et Papamkara. T'oung Pao, 15, 1914.
Eliot, Sir C. Hinduism and Buddhism. London, 1921.
Falke, R. Buddha, Mohammed, Christus, ein Vergleich. Gütersloh, 1906.
Fischer, J. M. Buddha und wir. München-Gladbach, 1924.
Fries, C. Buddha und Kineas. (Plutarch). ZDMG, 1939.
Gaultier, J. de. Le bouddhisme en Occident. In: La Fiction universelle. Paris, 1903.
Glasenapp, H. von. Buddhas Stellung zur Kultur. Jb. der Schopenhauer-Ges., 21, 1934.
Guenter, H. Buddha in der abendländischen Legende. Leipzig, 1923.
Gundert, W. An Introduction to the Main Currents of Buddhist Philosophy in Japan. Transactions of the Asiatic Society of Japan, 2. Ser., 5, 1928.
Haas, H. Bibliographie zur Frage nach den Wechselbeziehungen zwischen Buddhismus und Christentum. Leipzig, 1922.
—— Buddha in der abendländischen Legende. Leipzig, 1923.
Lilly, W. S. Kant and the Buddha. Fortnightly Rev., 1906.
Lubac, H. de. Textes alexandrins et bouddhiques. (Origenes). Recherches de Science relig., 1937.
Mensi-Klarbach, A. Buddha und Franz von Assisi. Der Sammler (München), 30.VI. & 2.VII.1921.
Nakarai, T. W. A Study of the Impact of Buddhism upon Japanese Life as Revealed in the Ode of the Koku-Shu. Diss. Indianapolis, 1929. Greenfield, 1931.
Prusek, J. The Narrators of Buddhist Scriptures and Religious Tales in the

Sung Period. Archiv Orientalni, 10, 1938.
Schroeder, L. von. Buddhismus und Christenthum. Reval, 1898.
Slepcevic, P. Buddhismus in der deutschen Literatur. Diss. Fribourg. Wien, 1920.
Stein, M. Buddha in Deutschland. LE, 10, 1908.
Streeter, B. H. The Buddha and the Christ. London, 1932.
Tonelli, L. Il Buddismo di Shakespeare. In: Alla ricerca della personalità. Milano, 1923.
Bernard, H. **CHU HSI**'s Philosophy and its Interpretation by Leibniz. T'ien Hsia Monthly, Aug., 1937.
Danton, G. H. Schiller and **CONFUCIUS**. GQ, 16, 1943.
Douglas, R. Confucianism and Taouism. London, 1879.
Chauvin, V. Le **CORAN**. In: Bibliographie des ouvrages arabes ou relatifs aux Arabes (part X). Liège, 1907.
Jones, E. A. **DIALLO** and Senghor as Interpreters of the New French Africa. FR, 21, 1948.
Mukherjee, K. The First Bengali Sonneteer (M. M. **DUTTA**). Triveni, 4, 1931.
Furlani, G. L'epopea di **GILGAMES**. Belfagor, 1, 1946.
Jensen, P. Das Gilgamesch-Epos in der Weltliteratur. Strassburg, 1906-29.
—— Das babylonische Nationalepos, judäische Nationalsagen, Ilias und Odyssee. Verhandlungen der Versammlung deutscher Philologen, 55, 1925.
Ungnad, A. Gilgamesch-Epos und Odyssee. In: Kulturfragen. Breslau, 1923.
Virolleaud, C. La légende de Gilgamesh et l'Odyssée. Bull. de la Soc. nationale des Antiquaires de France, 1939-40.
Arberry, A. J. **HAFIZ** and His English Translators. Islamic Culture (Hyderabad), 20, 1946.
Veit, F. Platens Nachbildungen aus dem Divan des Hafis und ihr persisches Original. SVL, 3, 1907.
Scott, Sir W. **HAJJI BABA** in England. QR, 1829. And in: Prose Works, 66, 1835.
Levy, R. A Note on the Latin Translation of **IBN EZRA**. Isis, 37, 1947.
Mercier, R. Un précurseur arabe de la philosphie du XVIIe siècle (**IBN THOFAIL**). RLC, 23, 1949.
Darby, G. O. S. **IBN WAHSHIYA** in Mediaeval Spanish Literature. Isis, 33, 1942.
Wilhelm, R. Goethe und **LAOTSE**. Europ. Rev., 4, 1928.
MOHAMMED: See also Thematology, I. VI. 10.
Chauvin, V. Mahomet et le Mahometisme. In: Bibliographie des ouvrages arabes ou relatifs aux Arabes (parts XI-XII). Liège, 1909-22.
Valerga, P. Il Divano di **OMAR BEN AL FORED** tradotto e paragonato col Canzoniere del Petrarca. Firenze, 1874.
Moghadam, H. **OMAR KHEYYAM** et Maurice Barrès. Messages d'Orient, 1, 1926.
Pratt, T. Edward Fitzgerald and Some Recent Omar Kheyyam Literature. Papers of the Manchester Literary Club, 18, 1899.
Benfey, T. (ed.). **PANTSCHATANTRA**. Fünf Bücher indischer Fabeln, Märchen und Erzählungen. 2 vols. Leipzig, 1859. (Cf. Introduction & Notes).
Anon. Müller's Translation of the **RIG-VEDA**. NAR, 1871.
Sander, R. Rigveda und Edda; Untersuchung der alten arischen und nordischen Mythen. Stockholm, 1893.
Sauer, W. Einfluss der **SAKUNTALA** auf Faustprolog und Schillers Alpenjäger. Deutsche Wacht, 240, 1894.
Garnier, C. M. **TAGORE** et George Russell. RAA, 7, 1929.
Maitra, S. Rabindranath Tagore and Bergson. Calcutta Review, 3rd. Ser., 19, 1926.
Schrader, F. O. Beziehungen zwischen **VEDA** und Edda. ZDA, 77, 1940.
Whitney, W. D. The Translation of the Veda. NAR, 1868.
Basu, P. S. Bergson et le **VEDANTA**. Diss. Montpellier, 1930.
Nestle. Platon und **ZARATHUSTRA**. HG, 1931.
Pardinas Illanos, F. Don Quijote contra Zaratustra. Abside (México), 4.
Reitzenstein, R. Plato und Zarathustra. VBW, 4, 1927.

CHAPTER TEN

Individual Western Authors and Works Influenced by the East.

Boulger, D. The First Englishman in Japan (William **ADAMS**, 1598). Asiatic Quarterly Review, 4, 1887.
Delcourt, M. Orient et Occident chez Eschyle (**AESCHYLUS**). Mélanges Bidez. Bruxelles, 1934.

Braden, C. S. Edwin **ARNOLD**, Poet and Orientalist. Calcutta Review, 3rd. Ser., 54, 1935.

Nicholson, R. A. The **ARTHURIAN LEGEND**: A Persian Parallel. Athenaeum, 1, 1901.

Santisson, C. Exotism och Orient i Lycksalighetens ö (**ATTERBOM**). Samlaren, 1923.

Kalff, G. Francis **BACON** en de Mandarijnen. China, 9, 1934-37.

Baldensperger, F. L'appel de la fiction orientale chez Honoré de **BALZAC**. Oxford, 1927.

Grisebach, E. H. de Balzacs Novelle La Grande Bretèche und ihre orientalische Quelle. In: Die Wanderung der . . . treulosen Witwe, 2. Suppl. Berlin, 1889.

—— Le thème chinois de la Musique de perdition dans le Mystère en pleine lumière de Maurice **BARRES**. RLC, 7, 1927.

Bordeaux, H. L'appel du divin ou Maurice Barrès en Orient. Paris, 1925.

Larat, J. Barrès, Goethe et l'Orient. Mélanges Baldensperger. Paris, 1929-30.

Feuillerat, A. **BAUDELAIRE** est-il allé dans l'Inde? FR, 17, 1944.

Schwartz, W. L. **BERGERAT'S** Ramonki le casseur de pierres (et ses éléments japonais). MLN, 1926.

Bertram, G. Die religiöse Umdeutung altorientalischer Lebensweisheit in der griechischen Uebersetzung des Alten Testaments (**BIBLE**). Zs. f. d. alttestamentl. Wiss., 1936.

Emmanuel, A. La Bible et l'Inde. Clartés convergentes. Paris, 1933.

Jean, C. F. La Bible et les récits babyloniens. Paris, 1933.

Montgomery, J. A. Arabia and the Bible. Philadelphia, 1934.

Oesterley, W. O. E. The Wisdom of Egypt and the Old Testament. London, 1927.

Nanavutty, P. Some Eastern Influences on William **BLAKE**'s Prophetic Books. Diss. U. of Cambridge, 1939.

Marcocchia, G. Una novella indiana nel **BOCCACCIO** e nel Molière (Decamerone, VII, 4). Spalato, 1905.

Hoeffner, T. Mirza-Schaffy in englischer Umdichtung. (**BODENSTEDT**). MLIA, 1882.

Carré, J. M. La première description du temple de Karnak dans la littérature française. (**BOSSUET**). Chronique d'Egypte. (Bruxelles), 1932.

David, H. Les poésies chinoises de **BOUILHET**. MPh, 1918.

Anon. E. B. **BROWNING'S** Eastern Poems. Calcutta Review, 22, 1854.

Danielou, Mme. Pearl **BUCK** et la Chine. Culture, April, 1939.

Brown, W. C. **BYRON** and English Interest in the Near East. SPh, 1937.

Thiergen, O. Byrons und Moores orientalische Gedichte. Diss. Leipzig, 1880.

Wiener, H. S. L. Byron and the East: Literary Sources of the Turkish Tales. Festschrift C. S. Northup. Ithaca, 1940.

Pannier, J. **CALVIN** et les Turcs. Revue historique, Oct., 1937.

Freitas, J. de. **CAMOES** em Macau. Lisboa, 1911.

Ross, D. Camoens and his Adventures in the East. NC, July, 1938.

Clouston, W. A. A Gorgeous Oriental MSS. Asiatic Source of a Passage in the Dictes printed by **CAXTON**. The Bookworm, 1891.

Casalduero, J. Los tratos de Argel. (**CERVANTES**). CL, 1950.

Gonzalez Palencia, A. Cervantes y los moriscos. Bol. R. Acad. Española, 27, 1948.

Darbishire, R. S. Islam in the **CHANSON D'ANTIOCH**. Moslem World, April, 1938.

Conor, Marthe. **CHATEAUBRIAND** à Tunis. Revue tunisienne, 1918.

Garabed Der-Sahaghian, Père. Chateaubriand en Orient. Diss. Fribourg. Venise, 1914.

Ivray, J. d'. Chateaubriand et l'Egypte. Revue mondiale, 1927.

Braddy, H. The Oriental Origin of **CHAUCER**'s Canacee-Falcon Episode. (Squire's Tale). MLR, 1936.

Canby, H. S. Some Comments on the Sources of Chaucer's Pardoner's Tale. MPh, 2, 1904-05.

Clouston, W. A. On the Magical Elements in Chaucer's Squire's Tale. Chaucer Soc. Publ. 2. Ser., 26, 1890.

Krappe, A. H. Une hypothèse sur la source (persane) de l'Orbecca de G. G. **CINTHIO**. RLC, 7, 1927.

Decreus, J. Paul **CLAUDEL** et le Nô japonais. CLS, 19, 1946.

Auriant. Louise **COLET** et les Pachas (du Caire). MF, 15.IV.1937.

Aubry, G. J. Joseph **CONRAD** in the Congo. London, 1926.

Clemens, Florence. Conrad's Malaysia. College English, 2, 1941.

Marquet, J. Sur les traces de Conrad (in Asia). MF, 272, 1936.

Mukherjee, K. W. **COWPER** and India. Indian Review, June, 1935.

Grivec, F. Orientalische und römische Einflüsse in den Scholien der Slavenapostel **CYRILLOS** und Methodios. Festgabe Heisenberg. Leipzig, 1930.

Asín Palacios, M. La Escatología musulmana en la Divina Comedia. (**DANTE**). Madrid, 1919.

—— L'influence musulmane dans la Divine Comédie: histoire et critique d'une polémique. RLC, 4, 1924.

—— Islam and the Divine Comedy. London, 1926.

—— La Escatologıa musulmana en la Divina Comedia, seguida de la historia y crítica de una polémica. 2 ed. Madrid, 1943.

Baynes, H. Oriental Characteristics in the Divine Comedy. Transactions of the Royal Society of Lit., 2nd ser., 36, 1918.

Blochet, E. Les sources orientales de la Divine Comédie. Paris, 1901.

Gabrieli, G. Intorno alle fonte orientali della Divina Commedia. Roma, 1920.

—— Dante e l'Oriente. Bologna, 1921.

Lepore, G. Dante e l'Etiopia. Portici, 1935.

Soderhjelm, W. Dante et l'Islam. Neuphilol. Mitteilungen, 22, (Helsingfors), 1921.

Witte, K. Dante und der Orient. JbDG, 1, 1867.

Chen Shou-yi. Daniel **DEFOE**, China's Severe Critic. Nankai Social & Economic Quarterly, 8, 1935.

Flewelling, R. T. Chinese Influence in Late Cartesianism. (**DESCARTES**). Etudes cartésiennes, 3, 1937.

Babinger, F. Ein orientalischer Berater Goethes: H. F. von **DIEZ**. JbGG, 1913.

Kühn, H. Maxime **DU CAMPS** Orientreisen. Ein Beitrag zur Geschichte des französischen Orienterlebnisses im 19. Jahrhundert. GRM, 30, 1942.

Yian Tsouan Lin. Essai sur le P. **DU HALDE** et sa Description de la Chine. Fribourg, 1937.

Fan, T. C. Percy and Du Halde. RES, 21, 1945.

Carpenter, F. I. **EMERSON** and Asia. Harvard U.P., 1930.

Christy, A. The Orient in American Transcendentalism: A Study of Emerson, Thoreau and Alcott. New York, 1933.

Harris, W. T. Emerson's Orientalism. In: Sanborn, The Genius and Character of Emerson. Boston, 1885.

Williamson, G. Emerson the Oriental. U. of California Chronicle, 30, 1928.

Yohannan, J. D. Emerson's Translations of Persian Poetry from German Sources. AL, 14, 1943.

—— The Influence of Persian Poetry upon Emerson's Work. Ibid, 15, 1943.

Rose, E. Paul **ERNST** und China. MLQ, 4, 1943.

Doumic, R. Un ennemi de l'exotisme au XVIe siècle: Henri **ESTIENNE**. Journal des Débats, 3.II.1900.

Chevreuil, R. M. **FARRERE** et la Chine. Etudes, 5.VII.1938.

Thonet, J. M. H. Etude sur Edw. **FITZ GERALD** et la littérature persane, d'après les sources originales. Liège, 1929.

Hendricks, Cecilia H. Fitzgerald's Rubaiyat. Explicator, 1, 1943.

Terhune, A. M. The Life of Edward Fitzgerald. New Haven, 1947.

Maynial, E. **FLAUBERT** orientaliste et le livre posthume de Maxime Du Camp. RLC, 3, 1923.

Seznec, J. Flaubert and India. JWI, 4.

Haas, H. Schleswig-Holstein und Persien im 17. Jahrhundert (**FLEMING**). Beilage der Hamburg. Nachrichten, 6, 1912.

Spargo, J. W. The Basket Incident in **FLOIRE AND BLANCHEFLOR**. Neuphilol. Mitteilungen, 28, 1927.

Pitt, A. S. The Sources, Significance and Date of **FRANKLIN'S** An Arabian Tale. PMLA, 57, 1942.

David, H. L'exotisme hindou chez Théophile **GAUTIER**. RLC, 9, 1929.

Carré, J. M. L'Egypte antique dans l'oeuvre de Théophile Gautier. RLC, 12, 1932.

Fehr, B. Walter Paters Beschreibung der Mona Lisa und Théophile Gautiers Orientalismus. Archiv, 135, 1916.

Coomaraswamy, A. K. Sir **GAWAIN** and the Green Knight: Indra and Namuci. Spec. 19, 1944.

Lynes, C. Northern Africa in **GIDE's** Writings. PMLA, 57, 1942.

Blum, J. Karl **GJELLERUP** et l'inspiration hindoue. Revue scandinave, July, 1912.

Bloch, J. R. Les itinéraires parallèles: **GOBINEAU** et Loti en Perse. Europe, 1.X.1923.

Masson-Oursel, P. Gobineau et la logique de l'Asie. NRF. 1.II.1934.

Baumgart. **GOETHES** Geheimnisse und seine indischen Legenden. Stuttgart, 1895.

Benfey, T. Goethes Gedicht Legende und

dessen indisches Vorbild. Orient & Occident, 1862.

Biedermann, W. von. Goetheforschungen. Frankfurt, 1879.

—— Goethe und das Schriftthum Chinas. ZVL, 7, 1894.

Burdach, K. Goethes Westöstlicher Divan. Halle, 1926.

Ghafur, A. Goethe and the East. Indian Review, May, 1938.

Jenisch, E. Goethe und das ferne Asien. DVLG, 1, 1923.

Krappe, A. H. Ueber die Quelle von Goethes Adler und Taube. Archiv, 174, 1938.

Krueger-Westend, H. Goethe und der Orient. Weimar, 1903.

Loiseau, H. Goethe et l'Orient, simples notes documentaires. RELV, 1934.

Meyer, J. J. Hindu Chips for Readers of Goethe. MPh, 5, 1907.

Schaafs, G. Zu Goethes Weissagungen des Bakis. JEGPh, 12, 1913.

Schaeder, H. H. Goethes Erlebnis des Ostens. Leipzig, 1938.

Stockum, T. C. van. Goethes indische Legenden. NPh, 28, 1943.

Strich, F. Goethe der West-Oestliche. In: Dichtung und Zivilisation. München, 1928.

Weinhold, K. Zu Goethes Parislegende. Zs. des Vereins für Volkskunde, 1, 1892.

Wernecke. Goethe und die orientalischen Handschriften der Weimarer Bibliothek. Weimar, 1911.

Witt, B. Goethe und der Osten. Ostdeutsche Monatshefte, 12, 1932.

Yusuf-Ali. Goethe's Orientalism. Contemporary Review, 1906.

Chen Shou-yi. Oliver **GOLDSMITH** and the Chinese Letters. T'ien Hsia Monthly, 8, 1939.

Waterfield, G. Lucie Duff **GORDON** in England, South Africa and Egypt. London, 1937.

Adolf, Helen. Oriental Sources for **GRAIL** Romances. PMLA, 62, 1947.

Coyajee, J. C. Iranian and Indian Analogues of the Legend of the Holy Grail. Bombay, 1939.

Iselin, L. E. Der morgenländische Ursprung der Grallegende aus orientalischen Quellen erschlossen. Halle, 1909.

Schroeder, L. von. The Holy Grail and Sanskrit Nature Myths. Bayrische Blätter, 1911.

Veselovskij, A. N. The Tales of Babylon, the Tabernacle, and the Holy Grail. St. Petersburg Academy of Sciences, 64, 1896.

Anon. (**GRIFFITH's**) Idylls from the Sanscrit. Calcutta Review, 46, 1867.

House, R. T. The South-African Stories of Hans **GRIMM**. AGR, 6, 1940.

Scholte, J. H. Een Oostinjevaarder in den Simplicissimus (**GRIMMELSHAUSEN**). De Gids, 106, 1942.

Putz, K. Joseph von **HAMMERS** Geschichte der persischen Redekünste, eine Quelle Rückertscher Gedichte. ZVL, 14, 1903.

Arpad, M. Wilhelm **HAUFF** und die morgenländische Romantik in Deutschland. Die Kultur, 1, 1902.

Davis, F. H. Lafcadio **HEARN** (and Japan). Calcutta Review, 3rd Ser., 3, 1922.

Foxwell, E. Reminiscences of Lafcadio Hearn (in Japan). Transactions and Proceedings of the Japan Society, London, 8, 1907-09.

Muret, M. L. Hearn ou les dangers de l'exotisme. Journal des Débats, 15.VI. 1926.

Stempel, D. Lafcadio Hearn: Interpreter of Japan. AL, 20, 1948.

Abdullah Al Mamom Sohraworthy. **HEINE** and Persian Poetry. Journal of the Royal Asiatic Society, 1903.

Birkenbihl, M. Die orientalischen Elemente in der Poesie H. Heines. In: Analecta Germanica für Hermann Paul. Amberg, 1906.

Plotke, I. Heinrich Heines orientalische Elemente. Das neue Leben, 1, 1913.

Lopes, D. Os Arabes nos obras de Alexandre **HERCULANO**. Lisboa, 1911.

Vogt, J. **HERODOT** in Aegypten. Ein Kapitel zum griechischen Kulturbewusstsein. Stuttgart, 1929.

Pizzagalli, A. M. Un modello orientale dell'episodio di Aristagora e Cleomene in Erodoto. Rendiconti del R. Istituto Lombardo, 70, 1937.

Jordan, L. Die Quelle des **HERVIS VON METZ**. Archiv, 114, 1905.

Dornseiff, F. **HESIODS** Werke und Tage und das alte Morgenland. Ph., 1934.

—— Altorientalisches in Hesiods Theogonie. L'Antiquité classique, 1937.

Ball, H. Hermann **HESSE** und der Orient. NR, 1927.

Primrose, J. B. A London Printer's Visit to India in the Seventeenth Century. (H. **HILL** in 1674). Transactions of the Bibliographical Society, 20, 1939.

Neumann, W. Die Quelle von **HOFMANNSTHALS** Frau ohne Schatten. MLN, 59, 1944.

Dobson. **HOMER** and the East. PCA, 1926.

Gilbert, P. Homère et l'Egypte. Chronique d'Egypte, 1939.
Wirth, H. Homer und Babylon. Freiburg, 1921.
Gilbert, P. **HORACE** et l'Egypte. Aux sources du carpe diem. Latomus, 5, 1946.
Oldenberg, H. Eine indisch-französische Dichtung (La Légende des Siècles by **HUGO**). Intern. Monatsschrift für Wissenschaft, Kunst & Technik, 13, 1917.
Paris, G. La Romance moresque des Orientales. In: Poèmes et légendes du moyen âge. Paris, 1900.
Safir, El Bardali. V. Hugo et l'Orient. Paris, 1936.
Schwab, R. Hugo troublé par l'Inde. RLC, 21, 1947.
Thouvenin, G. Verset du Koran de Victor Hugo et sa source islamique. RHLF, 1923.
Bagchi, P. C. Victor **JACQUEMONT** in India. Calcutta Review, 3rd Ser., 56, 1935.
Chevrillon, A. Victor Jacquemont (1801-1832). RdF, 1933.
Morrell, P. Victor Jacquemont's Letters from India, 1829-32. Asiatic Review, 1937.
Fan Tsen-Chung. Dr. **JOHNSON** and Chinese Culture. China Society. London, 1945.
—— Sir William **JONES**'s Chinese Studies. RES, 22, 1946.
Darbishire, H. **KEATS** and Egypt. RES, 1927.
Haward, E. **KIPLING** Myths and Traditions in India. NC, 125, 1939.
Johnston, C. Rudyard Kipling. Calcutta Review, 109, 1899.
Marquardt, H. Kipling und Indien. Breslau, 1931.
Zieseniss, A. Kiplings Indienkenntnis im Lichte seiner Balladen. GRM, 31, 1943.
LAMARTINE, A. de. Souvenirs, pensées et paysages pendant un voyage en Orient (1832-33). Paris, 1861.
Ripert, E. Le centenaire du voyage de Lamartine en Orient. RAF, 1933.
Warnier, R. Autour du voyage de Lamartine en Orient. L'Europe centrale, 23. XII.1933.
Mukherjee, K. W. S. **LANDOR**, Rose Aylmer, and Their Association with Calcutta. Calcutta Review, 3rd Ser., 37, 1930.
Williams, S. T. The Story of Ghebir (by Landor). PMLA, 36.
Prévost, J. Valéry **LARBAUD** et le renouveau de l'exotisme. Confluences, 3, 1943.
Goetz, W. Brunetto **LATINI** und die arabische Wissenschaft. JbDG, 21, 1939.
Carcassonne, E. **LECONTE DE LISLE** et la philosophie indienne. RLC, 11, 1931.
Martino, P. Sur deux poèmes musulmans de Leconte de Lisle. Ibid. 1, 1921.
Lach, D. **LEIBNIZ** and China. JHI, 6, 1945.
Dastur, M. N. Sir Oliver **LODGE**'s Substance of Faith. Journal of the K. R. Cama Oriental Institute, 7, 1926.
Christy, A. E. Introduction and Notes to **LONGFELLOW'S** Leap of Roushan Beg. New York, 1931.
Briquet, P. E. Pierre **LOTI** et l'Orient. Neuchâtel, 1946.
Kalfayan, A. The Turkish Language in Pierre Loti's Works. PhQ, 18, 1939.
Keicher, O. Raymundus **LULLUS** und seine Stellung zur arabischen Philosophie. Beiträge zur Geschichte der Philosophie des Mittelalters, 7. Münster, 1909.
Forell, G. W. **LUTHER** and the War Against the Turks. Concordia Theol. Monthly, 17, 1947.
Brown, W. C. Robert **LUTTEY** and English Interest in the Near East. ELH, 1939.
Cuénot, C. L'origine des Contes Indiens de **MALLARME**. MF, 15.XI.1938.
Nykl, A. R. Arabic Phrases in El Conde Lucanor. (Juan **MANUEL**). HR, 10, 1942.
Krappe, A. H. A Persian Myth in the Alethia of Claudius **MARIUS** Victor. Spec. 17, 1942.
Frear, W. F. **MARK TWAIN** and Hawaii. Chicago, 1948.
Anon. An Early Student of the East (J. **MARSHALL**). TLS, 9.II.1928.
Lancaster, H. C. A Chinese Source for **MAUPASSANT**. MLN, 63, 1948.
Anderson, C. R. **MELVILLE** in the South Seas. Columbia U.P., 1939.
Forsythe, R. S. Hermann Melville in the Marquesas. PhQ, 1935-36.
—— More upon Herman Melville in Tahiti. Ibid. 1938.
Howarth, R. G. Melville and Australia. N&Q, 193, 1948.
Simon, J. Recherches australiennes sur Hermann Melville. RAA, 1935.
Nykl, A. R. Algunas Observações sobre as línguas orientais citadas na Peregrinacam de Fernão **MENDES PINTO**. Petrus Nonius, (Lisboa), 3, 1942.

Le Gentil, G. Les Portugais en Extreme-Orient: Fernão Mendes Pinto. Paris, 1947.

Helys, M. Les romans chinois de Louise Jordan **MILN.** Le Correspondant, 25. VIII.1928.

Naruse, M. **MONTAIGNE** et la sagesse extrême-orientale. Conférence. Paris, 1935.

Rouillard, C. D. Montaigne et les Turcs. RLC, 18, 1938.

Carcassonne, E. La Chine dans l'Esprit des Lois. (**MONTESQUIEU**). RHLF, 1924.

Rowbotham, A. H. Montesquieu and Mgr. Foucquet. CL, 1950.

MONTHERLANT, H. de. Ce que je dois aux maîtres de l'Iran. NL, 5.XII.1936.

Brown, W. C. Th. **MOORE** and English Interest in the Near East. SPh, 1937.

Jaeckel, K. Paul **MORAND** und die Erneuerung des Exotismus in der französischen Literatur der Gegenwart. ZFSL, 60, 1936.

Davis, A. K. William **MORRIS** and the Eastern Question, with a Fugitive Political Poem by Morris. Festschrift John Calvin Metcalf. Columbia U.P., 1941.

Menhardt, H. Heinrichs von **MORUNGEN** Indienfahrt. Histor. Vierteljahrsschrift, 31, 1937.

Baldensperger, F. Gérard de **NERVAL** en Egypte d'après des publications récentes. L'Alsace française, 1933.

John, A. G. de Nervals Beziehungen zum Orient. Diss. Greifswald. Berlin, 1912.

Loriman, H. Gérard de Nerval en Syrie. Le Bon Plaisir, March, 1926.

Martino, P. Le carnet du Voyage en Orient de Gérard de Nerval. RLC, 13, 1933.

Guilhou, E. Remarques sur le récit du voyage en Chine de Jean **NEUHOF.** NPh, 23, 1937-38.

Larat, J. La tradition et l'exotisme dans l'oeuvre de Charles **NODIER** (1780-1844). Paris, 1923.

Elberling, C. V. **OEHLENSCHLAEGER** og de oesterlandske eventyr. København, 1887.

Perdrizet, P. Légendes babyloniennes dans les Métamorphoses d'**OVIDE.** Paris, 1930. And in: Revue de l'histoire des religions, 105, 1932.

Curzon, H. de. La légende de **PARSIFAL** et ses origines persanes. Journal des Débats, 18.IX.1932.

Unger, M. The Cradle of the Parsifal Legend. Musical Quarterly, July, 1932.

Fan, T. C. **PERCY** and Du Halde. RES, 21, 1945.

Hadas, M. Oriental Elements in **PETRONIUS.** AJPh, 1929.

Bidez, J. **PLATON** et l'Orient. Bull. de l'Acad. royale de Belgique, 1938.

Buonamici, G. Platone e la filosofia orientale. Pisa, 1899.

Fries, C. Indisches bei Platon. F&F, 1938.

Geffcken, J. Platon und der Orient. NJWJ, 5, 1929.

Pisani, V. Platone e l'Iran. Rivista degli Studi Orientali, 14, 1933-34.

Armstrong, A. H. **PLOTINUS** and India. CQ, 1936.

Marrucchi, P. Influssi indiani nella filosofia di Plotino? Atti, XIX Congr. internaz. degli Orientalisti, 1935. Roma, 1938.

Szabo, A. Indische Elemente im plotinischen Neuplatonismus. Scholastik, 13, 1938.

Techert, M. Iranische religiöse Elemente in dem Begriff der Psyche bei Plotin. EPhK, 1929.

Manly, S. M. Marco **POLO** and the Squire's Tale. PMLA, 11, 1896.

Ross, E. D. Marco Polo and his Book. In: Transactions of the British Academy, 20, 1934.

Yule, Sir Henry (ed.) The Book of Ser Marco Polo. 2 vols. London, 1903.

Cordier, H. Ser Marco Polo, Notes and Addenda to Sir Henry Yule's Edition. New York, 1920.

Krappe, A. H. Ueber die orientalische Quelle der Tochter des Grafen von **PONTIEU.** ZRPh, 49, 1929.

Goichon, A. M. E. **PSICHARI** et ses guides musulmans. Revue hebdomadaire, 4.VII.1925.

Svirin, N. **PUSHKIN** and the Orient. Zvezda, 4, 1935.

Howorth, H. H. **PYTHAGORAS** and India. Papers of the Manchester Literary Club, 6, 1887.

Pilon, E. **REGNARD** et la littérature barbaresque. In: Figures françaises et littéraires. Paris, 1921.

Krappe, A. H. A Persian Theme in the **ROMAN DE RENARD.** MLN, 58, 1943.

Andraud, R. L'Australie dans les romans de H. H. **RICHARDSON.** EA, 3, 1939.

Starkie, E. Arthur **RIMBAUD** in Abyssinia. Oxford, 1937.

Guy-Luc, S. Rimbaud à Java. France-Asie, 15.VII.1946.

Brachfeld, A. Jorge Tulio **ROYA,** japonisant latino-américain. France-Japon, April, 1939.

Karsen, F. **RUECKERT** und Indien. Magdeburger Zt., Montagsblatt, 4, 1913.

Azmi, M. Graf Adolf Friedrich von **SCHACK** und der Orient. Berlin, 1934.

Sauer. Sanskrit Influences on **SCHILLER**'s Alpenjäger and Goethe's Faust. Korrespondenzblatt f. d. Gelehrten und Realschulen Württembergs, 40.

Körner, J. Fr. **SCHLEGELS** persische Studien. AK, 20, 1929.

Grenier, J. C. **SCHOPENHAUER** et l'Inde. Annales de l'U. de Grenoble. N.S., 2, 1925.

Zimmer, H. Schopenhauer und Indien. Jb. der Schopenhauer-Ges., 25, 1938.

Schultz, P. Die Schilderung exotischer Natur im deutschen Roman mit besonderer Berücksichtigung von C. **SEALSFIELD.** Diss. Münster. München, 1913.

Longworth-Chambrun, A. de. **SHAKESPEARE** et le Maroc. RP, 15.VI.1925.

Sohraworthy, A. A. Shakespeare and Oriental Literature. Calcutta Review, 112, 1901.

Modak, C. Some Orientalism in **SHELLEY.** Calcutta Review, 1932.

Pettit, H. J. Shelley and Denon's Voyage dans la Haute et Basse Egypte. RLC, 18, 1938.

Sen Amiyakumar. Shelley and Indian Thought. In: Studies in Shelley. Calcutta, 1936.

Zachariae, T. Eine indische Rätselaufgabe bei **SOPHOKLES.** II, 1915.

Waechter, A. Ueber Robert **SOUTHEY**'s orientalische Epen. Diss. Halle, 1890.

Maverick, L. A. A Possible Chinese Source of **SPINOZA**'s Doctrine. RLC, 19, 1939.

Czoniczer, Elizabeth. **STENDHAL,** Joinville et un conte arabe. MLN, 60, 1945.

Bermann, R. Home from the Sea (R. L. **STEVENSON** at Samoa). Indianapolis, 1939.

Fenn, W. P. Richard Henry **STODDARD**'s Chinese Poems. AL, 11, 1940.

Shahani Ranjee, G. The Asiatic Element in **SWINBURNE.** Poetry Review, 33, 1942.

Yohannan, J. D. **TENNYSON** and Persian Poetry. MLN, 57, 1942.

Paden, W. D. Tennyson and Persian Poetry Again. MLN, 58, 1943.

—— Tennyson and Persian Poetry Once More. MLN, 60, 1945.

Kruse, A. Edward **THOMPSON,** ein Dichter des heutigen Indiens. ZEFU, 31, 1934.

Hamilton, H. E. A Note on James **THOMSON**'s Sources (Jesuits in Orient). MLN, 62, 1947.

Muto, C. Kants Anthropologie und **THUNBERGS** Aufenthalt in Japan. Yamato, Zs der deutsch-japanischen Ges., 2, 1930.

Birukoff, P. **TOLSTOY** und der Orient. Zürich, 1925.

Marquet, J. Sur les pas de P. J. **TOULET** en Asie. MF, 294, 1939.

Pizzi, I. L'origine persiana del romanzo di **TRISTANO E ISOLTA.** RI, 1911.

Zenker, R. Die Tristansage und das persische Epos von Wîs und Ramîn. RF, 29, 1911.

Eoff, S. Juan **VALERA**'s Interest in the Orient. HR, 1938.

Summers, V. A. L'Orientalisme d'Alfred de **VIGNY.** Paris, 1930.

Storer, M. E. Mme. de **VILLEDIEU**'s Nouvelles africaines, MLN, 63, 1948.

Kuhn, H. **VOLNEY** und Savary als Wegbereiter des romantischen Orient-Erlebnisses in Frankreich. Diss. Leipzig, 1938.

Anon. The Orphan of China de Murphy (and comparison with **VOLTAIRE**'s drama). Journal étranger, Jan., 1760.

—— Plagiat de Voltaire (le Chien et le Cheval, dans Zadig et un roman persan). Année littéraire, 1, 1767.

Amalfi, G. Zwei orientalische Episoden in Voltaire's Zadig. Zs. des Vereins für Volkskunde, 5, 1895.

Bertaut, J. Les Turcs et Voltaire. Figaro, 17.I.1925.

Cazenave, J. Une tragédie mauresque de Voltaire: Zulime. RLC, 5, 1925.

Engemann, W. Voltaire und China. Diss. Leipzig, 1932.

Farjenel, F. Voltaire et les Chinois. Revue hebdomadaire, 6.VIII.1911.

Goto, S. L'Orphelin de la Chine et son original chinois. RLC, 12, 1932.

Lee-You Ya-Oui. Le théâtre classique en Chine et en France d'après l'Orphelin de la Chine et l'Orphelin de la famille Tchao. Paris, 1937.

Pinot, V. Les sources de l'Orphelin de la Chine. RHLF, 14, 1907.

Rovillain, E. Sur le Zadig de Voltaire. PMLA, 43, 1928.

Rowbotham, A. H. Voltaire sinophile. PMLA, 1932.

Krappe, A. H. Oriental Themes in The **VOYAGE OF MAELDUNE.** PhQ, 23, 1944.

Negelein, J. von. R. **WAGNERS** Parzival im Lichte der indischen Religionsideen. DR, May, 1927.

Carpenter, E. The Upanishads and Leaves of Grass. In: Days with Walt **WHITMAN**. London, 1906.

Mercer, Dorothy F. Leaves of Grass and Bhagavad Gita. Diss. U. of California, 1933.

Adolf, Helen. New Light on Oriental Sources for **WOLFRAM**'s Parzival and Other Grail Romances. PMLA, 62, 1947.

Snelleman, W. Das Haus Anjou und der Orient in Wolframs Parzival. Nijkerk, 1941.

Jameson, G. E. Mysticism in A. E. and in **YEATS** in Relation to Oriental and American Thought. Diss. Ohio State U., 1932.

SECOND PART

Classical Antiquity.

CHAPTER ONE

Generalities.

(See also Mythology, I. VI. 7., Renaissance, III. II. 4., and Humanism, III. II. 3.)

Anon. Das Fortleben der Antike im Mittelalter. Grenzboten, 18, 1859.

Bailey, J. Ancient Tragedy and Modern Imitations. In: Poets and Poetry. Oxford, 1911.

Baldwin, S. La culture classique et l'homme moyen. BAGB, 11, 1926.

Barrière, P. L'antiquité vivante. Paris, 1932.

Becker, C. H. Das Erbe der Antike im Orient und Okzident. Leipzig, 1931.

Beddie, J. S. The Ancient Classcis in the Mediaeval Libraries. Spec. 1930.

Belau, K. Griechisch-römische Lyrik in ihrer Beziehung zur Gegenwart. Monatsschriften f. höhere Schulen, 1918.

Benzmann, H. Antike Dichtung und modernes Empfinden. Kölner U. Zt., 10, 1925.

Bertrand, L. La fin du classicisme et le retour à l'antiquité dans la seconde moitié du XVIIIe siècle. Paris, 1897.

Biese, A. Ist die Antike eine überwundene oder eine noch heute die Geister überwindende Macht? HG, 33.

Blanckenhagen, P. H. von. Antike Dichtung—heute. Hochland, 36, 1938.

Blunt, A. W. The Ancient World and Its Legacy to Us. Oxford, 1928.

Borinski, K. Die Antike in Poetik und Kunsttheorie. 2 vols. Leipzig, 1914.

Bottermann, W. Im Kampf um die Antike. Berlin, 1930.

Bowring, J. Borrowings of Modern from Ancient Poets. Trans. of the Royal Hist. Soc., 2, 1873.

Brecht, W. Klassisches Altertum und neueste Dichtung. Mitteil. d. Wiener Vereins d. Freunde des human. Gymnasiums, 1918-19.

Bryce, V. The Worth of Ancient Literature for the Modern World. PCA, 1917.

Burgh, W. G. de. The Legacy of the Ancient World. London, 1926.

Buttenwieser, Hilda. Popular Authors of the Middle Ages: The Testimony of the Manuscripts. Spec., 17, 1942.

Caplan, H. Classical Rhetoric and the Medieval Theory of Preaching. CPh, 1933.

Carrière, M. Hellas und Rom in Religion und Weisheit, Dichtung und Kunst. WM, 20, 1866.

Caster, M. La culture classique et la vie moderne. Actes du Congrès de Nice de l'Ass. G. Budé. Paris, 1935.

Cauer, P. Das Altertum im Leben der Gegenwart. Leipzig, 1928.

Chamberlin, H. H. Translated Classics. CW, 31, 1938.

Chassang, A. Des essais dramatiques imités de l'antiquité au XVe et au XVIe siècle. Paris, 1852.

Conway, R. S. Makers of Europe. Harvard U.P., 1931.

Curtius, E. R. Mittelalter-Studien. ZRPh, 1943.

—— Antike Rhetorik und vergleichende Literaturwissenschaft. CL, 1, 1949.

Dobson, J. F. Ancient Education and its Meaning to Us. In: Our Debt to Greece and Rome. London, 1932.

Dorn, M. Die Bedeutung des Altertums für das Leben der Gegenwart. Halle, 1923.

Egger, E. D'une renaissance nouvelle des lettres grecques et latines au XIXe siècle. (Extrait). Séance publ. annuelle des cinq académies, Paris, 1866.

Fairclough, H. R. The Classics and our Twentieth-Century Poets. Stanford U. Public., 2, 1927.

Friedemann, K. Antike und Mittelalter im Lichte der Romantik. Philosoph. Jb., 1931.

Friedlaender, L. Das Nachleben der Antike im Mittelalter. DR, 12-13, 1897, & in Erinnerungen, Strassburg, 1905.

Gaselee, S. Reminiscences of the Classics in Mediaeval Latin Poetry. PCA, 1939.

Gassner, H. Die Stellung der Antike in der modernen Kultur. Pädagog. Jb. 1931.

Grassi, E. Vom Vorrang des Logos. Das Problem der Antike in der Auseinandersetzung zwischen italienischer und deutscher Philosphie. München, 1939.

Greenlaw, E. The Return to the Classics. SPh, 1924.

Gummere, R. M. Ancient Classics in a Modern World. QR, 1939.

Hadzsits, G. D. & Robinson, D. M. (eds.)

Our Debt to Greece and Rome. Boston, New York, 1922 ff.

Hamann, R. Mittelalter und Antike. Festschrift E. Wechssler. Jena, 1929.

Haug, O. Wertungen und Umwertungen der Antike. Deutsches Bildungswesen, 3, 1935.

Hautecoeur. La renaissance de l'antiquité à la fin du XVIIIe siècle. Paris, 1912.

Heinemann, I. Die Lehre von der Zurückbestimmung der Menschen im griechisch-römischen Altertum und im jüdischen Mittelalter. Breslau, 1926.

Hoffmann-Harnisch, W. Das antike Drama auf der modernen Bühne. Die Szene, 14.

Hofmannsthal, H. von. Vermächtnis der Antike. Antike, 1928.

Immisch, O. Das Erbe der Alten. Sein Wert und seine Wirkung in der Gegenwart. Leipzig, 1919.

—— Das Nachleben der Antike. 2nd ed. Leipzig, 1933.

Ingalls, J. The Classics and New Poetry. CJ, 40, 1944.

Iorga, N. Spiritul clasic in evul mediu. (In Rumanian). Rivista Clasica, 9-10, 1937-38.

Jäger, W. Antike und Humanismus. Leipzig, 1925.

—— Die geistige Gegenwart der Antike. Antike, 1929.

—— Die Antike im wissenschaftlichen Austausch der Nationen. Ibid. 1930.

—— Die Antike und das Problem der Internationalität der Geisteswissenschaften. Inter-Nationes, 1, 1931.

Kirsch, F. M. The Classics, a Symposium. Milwaukee, 1928.

Kluyver, A. Over de classieke opvoeding. NPh, 19, 1933-34.

Köhm, J. Die Ewigkeitswerte des klassischen Altertums und die Bedeutung des humanistischen Gymnasiums für unsere Zeit. Leipzig, 1924.

Kolar, A. Influence de la culture antique sur la civilisation européenne. (In Czech). Sbornik filosoficke Fakulty v Bratislave, 2, 1924.

—— Les rapports de la culture européenne avec l'antiquité. (In Czech). Praha, 1929.

Lamer, H. Wörterbuch der Antike mit Berücksichtigung ihres Fortwirkens. Leipzig, 1933.

Lange, E. R. Von der Bedeutung antiker Stoffe für Zwecke der modernen Poesie. Progr. Oels, 1848.

Lehmann, P. Pseudo-antike Literatur des Mittelalters. VBW, 3, 1927.

—— Reste und Spuren antiker Gelehrsamkeit in mittelalterlichen Texten. Ph, 1927.

Lion, F. Europa und die Antike. Der neue Merkur, 7, 1922.

Lockwood, D. P. & Bainton, R. H. Classical and Biblical Scholarship in the Age of the Renaissance and Reformation. Church History, 10.

Lunsingh Scheurleer, D. F. De invloed van de klassieken in de 2e helft van de 18de en het 1e kwart van de 19de eeuw. Maandbl. voor beeld. kunsten, 15, 1938.

Maerker, F. A. Antike Versuche auf dem modernen Theater. Leipzig, 1857.

Martin, A. von. Antike, Germanentum, Christentum und Orient als Aufbaufaktoren der geistigen Welt des Mittelalters. AK, 19, 1929.

Miner, D. The Survival of Antiquity in the Middle Ages. In: The Greek Tradition (ed. by G. Boas). Baltimore, 1939.

Morison, S. E. The Ancient Classics in a Modern Democracy. Oxford U.P., 1939.

Moulton, R. G. Classical Literature in Translation. AM, 67, 1891.

Mountford, J. F. Quotations from Classical Authors in Mediaval Latin Glossaries. New York, 1925.

Mühl, M. Die antike Menschheitsidee in ihrer geistigen Entwicklung. Leipzig, 1928.

Newald, R. Das Nachleben der Antike (1920-29). Jahresberichte über d. Fortschritte d. klass. Altertumswissenschaft, 232, 1931.

—— Die Antike in den europäischen. Literaturen. GRM, 22, 1934.

—— L'antiquité et les littératures occidentales. Actes du Congrès G. Budé à Strasbourg. Paris, 1939.

Oberlaender, H. Das antike Drama auf der modernen Bühne. Deutsche Bühnen-Genossenschaft, 30, 1901.

Osborn, E. B. The Heritage of Greece and the Legacy of Rome. New York, 1925.

Otto, W. F. Zeit und Antike. Frankfurt, 1926.

Palhoriès, F. L'héritage de la pensée antique. Paris, 1932.

Przychocki, G. Culture classique et culture moderne. (In Polish). Varsovie, 1929.

Rand, E. K. The Founders of the Middle Ages. Harvard U.P., 1928.

—— The Classics in the Thirteenth Century. Spec. 1929.

—— The Ancient Classics and the New Humanism. In: On Going to College, a Symposium. Oxford U.P., 1938.

Regenbogen, O. Das Altertum und die politische Erziehung. NJWJ, 1934.
Rodin, M. The Relation of Medieval Latin Literature to Classical Literature. TAPhA, 27, 1927.
Rostagni, A. Classicità e spirito moderno. Torino, 1939.
Sandys, Sir J. E. A History of Classical Scholarship. 3 vols. Cambridge, 1903 ff.
Schlenther, P. Antikes Drama und moderne Kunst. Neue Freie Presse, 1300, 1901.
(Schmidt), J. S. Antike Versuche auf dem modernen Theater. Grenzboten, 16, 1857.
Schnedermann. Das Nachleben des griechisch-römischen Altertums. Neue Kirchliche Zs. 32.
Schubart, W. Die Antike und die Gegenwart. Abhandl. und Vorträge d. Bremer Ges., 1928.
Selchow, B. von. Unsere geistigen Ahnen. Berlin, 1926.
Sellheim, R. Das Fortleben der antiken Komödie in Mittelalter und Neuzeit. Gymnasium, 1942.
Singer, S. Altertum und Mittelalter. NPh, 19, 1933-34.
Stemplinger, E. Die Befruchtung der Weltliteratur durch die Antike. GRM, 2, 1910.
—— Die Ewigkeit der Antike. Leipzig, 1924.
—— Griechisch-lateinischer Literaturführer von Homer bis auf unsere Zeit. München, 1934.
Stenzel, J. Was ist lebendig und was ist tot in der Philosophie des klassischen Altertums? NJWJ, 7, 1931.
Suehnel, R. Das olympische Ideal und die klassische Antikendeutung. Geistige Arbeit, 1936.
Taylor, H. O. The Classical Heritage of the Middle Ages. New York, 1911.
Ternus, I. Die Antike, ein Hauptquellgebiet der scholastischen Philosophie. Scholastik, 1.
Tièche, E. Die Wiederentdeckung der antiken Bücher im Zeitalter der Renaissance. Bern, 1936.
Ullman, B. L. Classical Authors in Certain Mediaeval Florilegia. CPh, 1932.
Varia. A Bibliography of the Survival of the Classics. London, 1931, ff.
Villemain, A. F. L'imitation de l'antiquité, originale et créatrice. In: Discours et mélanges littéraires. Paris, 1823.
Vocht, H. de. Les débuts de l'enseignement classique dans la Compagnie de Jésus et leurs rapports avec l'humanisme. EC, 13, 1945.
Vogt, J. Unsere Stellung zur Antike. Jahresber. d. Schles. Ges. f. vaterländ. Kultur, 110. (Breslau), 1937.
Voigt, G. Die Wiederbelebung des klassischen Altertums. Berlin, 1893.
Voltaire. Discours sur la tragédie ancienne et moderne. In: Préface, Sémiramis, (1748).
Warburg, A. Die Erneuerung der heidnischen Antike. In: Gesammelte Schriften, 1-2, Leipzig, 1932.
Wechssler, E. Die Antike und das abendländische Menschentum. Schule & Wissenschaft, 1, 1927.
Weiss, T. Antike und Abendland. BBG, 1924.
Weltmann, L. Ueber die Rezeption der Antike im modernen Drama. Literatur, 26.
Wilamowitz-Moellendorff, U. von. Die Geltung des klassischen Altertums im Wandel der Zeiten. Velhagen & Klasings Monatshefte, 1921.
Wundt. Einfluss der antiken Philosophie auf das neuere Denken. Verein d. Freunde des human. Gymnasiums. Erfurt, 1926.
Wustmann, G. Antike Dichtung und moderne Kunst. Grenzboten, 32, 1873.
Ydewalle, C. d'. Plaidoyer pour le monde antique. Liège, 1939.
Zielinski, T. L'influence de la civilisation antique en Europe. Rev. internationale des Etudes Balkaniques, 1, 1935.

CHAPTER TWO

Influences upon England.

Bernigau, K. F. England und die Antike. Bielefeld, 1932.
Buck, P. M. The Classical Tradition and the Study of English. CJ, 1914.
Chislett, W. J. The Classical Influence in English Literature in the 19th Century. Boston, 1918.
Conley, C. H. The First English Translations of the Classics. New Haven, 1927.
Dietz, H. Der Einfluss der antiken Literatur auf die forensische Rhetorik Englands um 1600. Archiv, 176-77, 1939.
Glücksmann, H. L. Die Gegenüberstellung von Antike-Christentum in der englischen Literatur des 19. Jahrhunderts. Hannover, 1932.

Goldmark, R. I. Studies in the Influence of the Classics on English Literature. New York, 1918; London, 1925.

Gordon, G. S. English Literature and the Classics. Oxford, 1912.

Harrison, C. T. The Ancient Atomists and English Literature of the Seventeenth Century. HSCPh, 1934.

Hastings, C. Le théâtre français et anglais, ses origines grecques et latines. Paris, 1900.

Jacob, E. F. Some Aspects of Classical Influence in Medieval England. VBW, 9, 1930-31.

Kraemer, C. J. The Influence of the Classics on English Literature. CJ, 22, 1927.

Lathrop, H. B. Translations from the Classics into English from Caxton to Chapman. U. of Wisconsin Studies in Lang. & Lit., 35, 1934.

Meissner, P. Germanentum, Christentum und Antike in der englischen Kulturideologie. GRM, 30, 1942.

Ogilvy, J. D. A. Books Known to Anglo-Latin Writers from Aldhelm to Alcuin. Harvard U.P., 1936.

Palmer, H. R. List of English Editions and Translations of the Classics Printed Before 1641. Bibliographical Society. London, 1911.

Saxl, F. et al. England und die Antike. VBW. 1932.

Schirmer, W. F. Antike, Renaissance und Puritanismus. Eine Studie zur englischen Literaturgeschichte des 16. und 17. Jahrhunderts. München, 1924.

Thomson, J. A. K. The Classical Background of English Literature. London, 1948.

Wilson, H. R. Greek and Latin in Relation to the Appreciation of English Poetry. CJ, 20.

CHAPTER THREE

Influences upon France.

Birsch-Hirschfeld. Ueber die den provenzalischen Troubadours bekannten epischen Stoffe. Leipzig, 1878.

Bleske, T. Der Einfluss des classischen Unterrichts auf die Franzosen und die französische Revolution. Deutsches Museum, 1858.

Breitinger, H. Die französischen Uebersetzer der Alten im XVI. Jahrhundert. Frauenfeld, 1865.

Charpentier, J. P. A laquelle des deux littératures, grecque ou latine, la littérature française est-elle le plus redevable? Discours. Paris, 1868.

Cherniss, R. The Ancients as Authority in Seventeenth Century France. In: The Greek Tradition (ed. by G. Boas). Baltimore, 1939.

Clerc, C. Essai sur l'inspiration antique dans la littérature française. Paris, 1926.

Crewe, Lord. The Classics in France. PCA, 1924.

Delcourt, M. Etude sur les traductions des tragiques grecs et latins en France depuis la Renaissance. Mémoires publ. par l'Acad. royale de Belgique, 19, 1925.

Delisle, L. Traductions d'auteurs grecs et latins offertes à François I. JS, Aug., 1900.

Dernedde, R. Ueber die den altfranzösischen Dichtern bekannten epischen Stoffe aus dem Altertum. Diss. Göttingen, 1887.

Deschanel, E. La tragédie antique, la tragédie au XVIIe siècle et le drame moderne. RDM, 1.IV.1847.

Hastings, C. Le théâtre français et anglais, ses origines grecques et latines. Paris, 1900.

Hennebert, F. Histoire des traductions françaises d'auteurs grecs et latins pendant le XVIe et le XVIIe siècle. Preisschrift, Gand, 1858. And in: Annales des U. de Belgique, 1858-59, and Bruxelles, 1861.

Ladborough, R. W. Translation from the Ancients in Seventeenth-Century France. JWI, 2, 1938-39.

Malye, J. Die klassische Bildung im heutigen Frankreich. HG, 41, 1930.

Marx, F. Die Beziehungen der klassischen Völker des Alterthums zu dem kelto-germanischen Norden. Beilage zur Allg. Zt., 162-63, 1897.

Meyer, P. Les premières compilations françaises d'histoire ancienne. Romania, 14, 1885.

Murarasu, D. La poésie néo-latine et la renaissance des lettres antiques en France (1500-49). Paris, 1928.

Neubert, F. Das Nachleben antiker Philosophie in der neueren französischen Literatur: I. Die idealistischen Strömungen bis zu den Anfängen des Stoizismus: II. Die Blüte des Stoizismus und des Epikureismus. NJWJ, 1927.

Parker, H. T. The Cult of Antiquity and the French Revolutionaries. Diss. Chicago, 1937.

Peyre, H. L'influence des littératures

antiques sur la littérature française moderne. New Haven, 1941.
Reclam, W. H. Fragment d'une notice bibliographique sur les traductions françaises des auteurs grecs et latins. Progr. Berlin, 1827.
Renard, G. De l'influence de l'antiquité classique sur la littérature française pendant les dernières années du XVIIIe siècle et les premières années du XIXe siècle. Diss. Lausanne, 1875.
Rousseaux, A. La culture classique et le génie français. Actes du Congrès de Nice de l' Ass. G. Budé, Paris, 1935.
Sicard, A. Les études classiques avant la Révolution. Paris, 1887.
Skommodau, H. Heidnischer und christlicher Geist in der französischen Lyrik des 16. Jahrhunderts. RF, 54, 1940.
Texte, J. Les origines antiques et italiennes de la Renaissance française. Bull. de l'U. de Lyon, 8, 1892.
Timmermans, W. F. C. La France devant l'antiquité. Groningen, 1934.
Toldo, P. Comédies du XVIe siècle, où l'inspiration classique et italienne est la plus sensible. RHLF, 15.IV.1898.
Vossler, K. Die Antike und die Bühnendichtung der Romanen. VBW, 7.
Wanscher, V. Provençalerne og Antikken. Stud. fra Sprog og Oldtidsforskning, 27. København, 1896.
Wilmotte, M. De l'origine du roman en France. La tradition antique et les éléments chrétiens du roman. Mém. Acad. Belg., 18, 1923.
Wolff, F. Zur Theorie und Praxis der Uebersetzungen aus dem klassischen Altertum im 16. Jahrhundert in Frankreich. Heidelberg, 1923.
Xivrey, J. B. de. Recherches sur les sources antiques de la littérature française. Paris, 1829.
Zilliacus, E. Den nyare franska poesin och antiken. Diss. Helsingfors, 1905.

CHAPTER FOUR

Influences upon Germany.

Berendt, H. & Schubring, G. Die Antike und der deutsche Geist. Frankfurt, 1927.
Bogner, H. Die Behandlung der Antike im nationalsozialistischen Unterricht. Vergangenheit & Gegenwart (Ergänzungsheft). Leipzig, 1935.
Busch, E. Das Erlebnis des Schönen im Antikebild der deutschen Klassik. DVLG, 18.
Bursian, C. Geschichte der classischen Philologie in Deutschland von den Anfängen bis zur Gegenwart. München, 1883.
Cholevius, C. L. Geschichte der deutschen Poesie nach ihren antiken Elementen. 2 vols. 2nd. ed. Leipzig, 1854-56.
Cohen, H. Der deutsche Idealismus und die Antike. HG, 27.
Ermatinger, E. & Hunziker, R. Antike Lyrik in modernem Gewande. Frauenfeld, 1898.
Fischer, A. Antike und deutsche Gegenwart. HG, 1929.
Friedel, V. H. L'Allemagne contre la culture classique. Grande Revue, Oct., 1916.
Gerlach, K. Das deutsche Drama zwischen Antike und Shakespeare. Der Türmer, 43.
Hartfelder, K. Deutsche Uebersetzungen klassischer Schriftsteller aus dem Heidelberger Humanistenkreis. Progr. 1884.
Horn, H. Die Antike im Weltbild der deutschen Lebensphilosophie. Antike, 1936.
Kaerst, J. Weltgeschichte, Antike und deutsches Volkstum. Leipzig, 1925.
Kahle, W. Die Antike im deutschen Schrifttum. Paderborn, 1933.
Lehmann, P. Deutschland und die mittelalterliche Ueberlieferung der Antike. Zt. f. deutsche Geistesgeschichte, 1, 1935.
Lesky, A. Deutschtum und Antike. Alpenländische Monatshefte, 1928-29.
Malye, F. La culture classique en Allemagne. BAGB, 25, 1929.
Mauersberger, A. Hellas und Rom als Grundlage deutscher Jugendbildung im humanistischen Gymnasium der Gegenwart. Leipzig, 1932.
Müller, W. A. Die archäologische Dichtung in ihrem Umfang und Gehalt. Eine Untersuchung der Beziehungen der deutschen Literatur des 19. & 20. Jahrhunderts zur klassischen Archäologie mit ihren Ergebnissen und Funden. Kônigsberg, 1928.
Ogle, B. Classical Literary Traditions in Early German and Roman Literature. MLN, 27, 1912.
Rehm, W. Die Antike und die deutsche Gegenwart. München, 1923.
Rosenthal, G. Hellas und Rom und ihre Wiedergeburt aus deutschem Geiste. Berlin, 1925.
Schissel von Fleschenberg, O. Unser Verhältnis zur Antike. Comenius Ges. (Jena), 1916.

Schlueter, J. G. K. Vollständige Sammlung aller Uebersetzungen der Griechen und Römer vom XVI. Jahrhundert bis 1784. Frankfurt, 1785.

Schneider, H. Zur Entwicklungsgeschichte der klassischen Altertumskunde in Deutschland. NJKA, 1922.

Schuster, M. Altertum und deutsche Kultur. Wien, 1926.

Schwietering, J. Einwirkung der Antike auf die Entstehung des frühen deutschen Minnesangs. ZDA, 61.

Simons, W. Die Antike und die deutsche Volksgemeinschaft. Versammlung d. Freunde d. human. Gymn., Berlin, 1927-28.

Spranger, E. Die Antike und der deutsche Geist. BBG, 1925.

Stemplinger, E. & Lamer, H. Deutschtum und Antike in ihrer Verknüpfung. Leipzig, 1920. Cf. Theolog. Revue, 1924.

Thiersch, H. Göttingen und die Antike. Göttingen, 1926.

Thompson, L. S. German Translations of the Classics Between 1450 and 1550. JEGPh, 42, 1943.

Wahnschaffe, F. Deutschland und die Antike. Bielefeld, 1931.

Weisbach, W. Deutsche Renaissance und Antike. Antike, 4, 1928.

Wolters, F. Das Bild der Antike bei den Deutschen. Breslau, 1925.

Zettel, K. Hellas und Rom im Spiegel deutscher Dichtung. 2 vols. Erlangen, 1908.

Zucker, F. Klassisches Altertum und deutsche Bildung. Student & Leben, 1. (Jena), 1934.

CHAPTER FIVE

Influences upon Other Countries.

Secchi, C. C. L'elemento classico nella lingua e nella letteratura albanese. **ALBANIA**, 1, 1940.

Anon. Classical Studies at Cambridge (**AMERICA**). NAR, 1842.

Gildersleeve, B. L. Classical Studies in America. AM, 1806.

Gummere, R. M. Early European Migration of Classical Ideas to Colonial North America. TAPhA, 1932.

Hall, T. C. Der klassische Geist in der amerikanischen Erziehung. HG, 1930.

Jones, T. B. The Classics in Colonial Hispanic America. TAPhA, 1939.

Kelsey, F. W. Latin and Greek in American Education, with Symposia on the Value of Humanistic Studies. New York, 1927.

Mullett, C. F. Classical Influences on the American Revolution. CJ, 35, 1939.

Pritchard, J. P. Return to the Fountains. Some Classical Sources of American Criticism. Durham (N.C.), 1942.

Rey, A. La influencia clásica en algunos poetas de la Nueva España. Symposium, 2, 1948.

Schauroth, E. von. Die klassischen Studien in Amerika. HG, 41, 1930.

Shaw, A. Classic Ideals and American Life. CW, 10.

Graf, A. Influences antiques dans la littérature ethnographique **BYZANTINE** à ses débuts. (In Hungarian). EPhK, 58, 1934.

Jirani, O. De Bohemicis e linguis classicis translationibus. (**CZECHOSLOVAKIA**). Acta 2. Congressus philol. class. slav. Praha, 1931.

Malye, J. La culture classique chez les Tchèques. BAGB, 20, 1928.

Svoboda, K. Les philologues classiques tchèques comme professeurs en Russie. (In Czech). Listy Filologicke, 1939.

Kardos, T. Survie de l'antiquité en **HONGRIE**. (In Hungarian). Budapest, 1942.

Vetéssy, G. Les Hongrois et la civilisation gréco-romaine. (In Hungarian). Debrecen, 1935.

Alviella, G. d'. Des influences classiques dans la culture scientifique et littéraire de l'Inde. (**INDIA**). Bull. de l'Acad. royale de Belgique, 34, 1897.

Smith, V. A. Graeco-Roman Influence on the Civilisation of Ancient India. Journal of Asiatic Soc. of Bengal, 1889-92.

Cox, E. G. Classical Traditions in Medieval Irish Literature. (**IRELAND**). PhQ, 1924.

Amicis, V. de. L'imitazione classica nella commedia italiana del secolo XVI. (**ITALY**). Pisa, 1873 & Firenze, 1897.

Gervasoni, G. Linee di storia della filologia classica in Italia. Firenze, 1928.

Grazioli, A. La tradizione classica in Italia durante il medio evo. Mélanges C. Adami. Verona, 1941.

Ortiz, R. L'élément classique dans la littérature italienne. (In Rumanian). Rivista Clasica, 1930.

Sorbelli, T. Relazioni fra la letteratura italiana e le letterature classiche. In: Letterature comparate (ed. by A. Momigliano). Milano, 1948.

Spingarn, J. E. The Growth of the Classic Spirit in Italian Criticism. In: A History of Literary Criticism. New York, 1899.

Ludvikovsky, J. La philologie classique dans la Pologne contemporaine. (**POLAND**). Listy Filologicke, 1931.
Malye, J. La culture classique en Pologne. BAGB, 1928.
Sinko, T. Reflets classiques dans la littérature polonaise. (In Polish). Cracovie, 1923.
—— Hellada i Roma w. Polace. Lwow, 1933.
Sulica, N. Clasicismul greco-roman si literatura noastrà. (**RUMANIA**). Mure, 1930.
Flickinger, R. C. The Classics in **RUSSIA**, Germany, Turkey and America. CJ, 32, 1937.
Mikhalchi, D. Ancient Literature in Russian Translations. MLR, 39, 1944.
Zebeleva, S. A. Das Studium der Antike in der USSR. Slav. Rundschau, 10, 1938.
Colburn, G. B. Greek and Roman Themes in the Spanish Drama. (**SPAIN**). Hisp, 22, 1939.
Lida, María R. Transmisión y recreación de temas grecolatinas en la poesía lírica española. RFH, 1, 1939.
Rubio, D. Classical Scholarship in Spain. Washington, 1934.

CHAPTER SIX

Influences upon Individual Authors and Works.

Johnston, M. John Quincy **ADAMS** and the Classics. CW, 23, 1930.
Robathan, D. M. John Adams and the Classics. NEQ, 19, 1946.
Sanford, E. M. **ALCUIN** and the Classics. CJ, 20.
Bolza, J. B. **ARIOSTS** Nachahmung der Alten. Jb. f. romanische & englische Literatur, 4, 1862.
Zacchetti, C. A. L'imitazione classica nell' Orlando furioso. Prop., 24, 1892.
Houghton, R. E. C. The Influence of the Classics on the Poetry of M. **ARNOLD**. Oxford, 1923.
Montgomery, H. C. Matthew Arnold Classicist. CJ, 34, 1939.
Combes, G. Saint **AUGUSTIN** et la culture classique. Paris, 1927.
Jenkins, C. Augustine's Classical Quotations in his Letters. Journal of Theological Studies, 1938.
Keenan, M. E. Classical Writers in the Letters of Augustine. CJ, 32, 1936.
Kurfess. Die Bekenntnisse des Augustins und die Antike. HG, 1932.
Marrou, H. I. Saint Augustin et la fin de la culture antique. Paris, 1938.
Harrison, C. T. **BACON**, Hobbes, Bayle and the Ancient Atomists. HSPhL, 15, 1933.
Pedde, N. L'imitazione classica nella Nautica di Bernardino **BALDI**. Sassari, 1899.
Schalk, F. **BAYLE** und die Antike. Homenatge a Antoni Rubio i Lluch. Barcelona, 1936.
Boutemy, A. & Vercauteren, F. V. de **BEAUVAIS** et l'intérêt pour l'archéologie antique au XIe et au XIIe siècle. Latomus, 1937.
Gladysz, B. Eléments classiques et post-classiques de l'oeuvre de **BEDE**, De arte metrica. Eos, 34.
Laistner, M. L. W. Bede as a Classical and Patristical Scholar. Transact. Royal Hist. Soc., 16, 1933.
Lenz, K. Joachim du **BELLAY** und die Antike. Marburg, 1923.
Jaeger, A. **BENEDIKT VON NURSIA** und die Antike. Pharus, 1929.
Coulter, C. C. **BOCCACCIO'S** Archaeological Knowledge. Am. Journal of Archeology, 1937.
Reichenberger, A. The Classical Sources of **BOSCAN**. CL, 2, 1950.
Jech, F. et al. Le poète tchèque Otokar **BREZINA** et les langues classiques. Listy Filologicke, 1941.
Schweitzer, B. Zum Antikenstudium des Angelo **BRONZINO**. Mitteil. des deutschen archäolog. Instituts, 1918.
Cressman, E. D. The Classical Poems of Robert **BROWNING**. CJ, 23, 1927.
Hood, T. L. Browning's Ancient Classical Sources. HSCPh, 33, 1922.
Jackson, C. N. Classical Elements in Browning's Aristophanes' Apology. Ibid. 20, 1909.
Lawton, W. C. The Classical Element in Browning's Poetry. AJPh, 17, 1896.
Spindler, R. Robert Browning und die Antike. Leipzig, 1930.
Vorwahl, H. Das Bild der Antike bei Jacob **BURCKHARDT**. Antike, Alte Sprachen & deutsche Bildung, 1943.
Bleiken, M. **BYRON**, Shelley und die Antike. Hamburg, 1936.
Brandl, A. Byron und die Antike. Beilage zur Allg. Zt, 122, 1893.
Trowbridge, Mary L. The Influence of the Classics on **CAMOES'** Lusiadas. Festschrift Oldfather. U. of Illinois P., 1943.
Flint, T. **CARLYLE** as a Classicist. CW, 13.

Lida, Maria R. Huella de la tradición grecolatina en el poema de Juan de **CASTELLANOS**. RFH, 8, 1946.

Schirmer, W. F. **CHAUCER**, Shakespeare und die Antike. VBW, 9, 1930-31.

Faguet, E. André **CHENIER**, le poète antique. RCC, 11, 1903.

Fallex, E. Etude sur les sources antiques d'André Chénier. In: Histoire de la langue et de la littérature française, (ed. by Petit de Julleville). Paris, 1898.

Chapeau; J. M. De la tragédie antique au drame de Paul **CLAUDEL**. BAGB, 1938.

Van der Meer, S. Bijdrage tot het onderzoek naar klassieke elementen in **COORNHERT'S** Wellevenskunste. Amsterdam, 1934.

Strehlke, F. Ueber **CORNEILLE** und Racine als Nachahmer der alten Tragödie. Progr. Danzig, 1856.

Anon. The Classical Studies of **DANTE**. ER, 1895.

Ampère, J. J. La Grèce, Rome et Dante, études littéraires d'après nature. Paris, 1848.

Hauvette, H. L'antiquité dans l'oeuvre de Dante. RCC, 36, 1935.

Oeschger, J. Antikes und Mittelalterliches bei Dante. ZRPh, 1944.

Palm, E. W. A Classical Reference in the Divina Commedia. Ital., 22, 1945.

Patroni, G. L'antichità classica nella Commedia. A&R, 1921.

Piper, F. Ueber des Verhältniss Dantes zum klassischen Alterthum. Verhandl. der Philologenversammlung zu Jena, 1846.

Silverstein, T. On the Genesis of De monarchia II, 5. Spec., 1938.

François, E. **DESCARTES** y los antiquos. In: Descartes, Homenaje. Buenos Aires, 1937.

Stegew, G. Les lectures classiques d'un clerc du XIIe siècle. (Rupert de **DEUTZ**). Archivum Latinitatis Medii Aevi, 1934.

Malein, A. **DOSTOIEVSKY** et le monde antique. In: Dostoïevsky, journal de la Société de Bibliog. Russe, 1921.

Panzner, M. John **DRYDEN** als Uebersetzer altklassischer Dichtungen. Diss. Breslau, 1887.

Wiesener, L. Des études classiques en Angleterre au XVIe siècle et particulièrement de l'éducation littéraire d'**ELISABETH**. Ann. de la Soc. philotechnique, 34. Paris, 1874.

Papacostea, C. Filosofia antica in opera lui **EMINESCU**. Iasi, 1930.

Kluge, O. Die Antike in der Bildungstheorie des **ERASMUS**. HG, 1936.

Highet, G. Classical Echoes in La Araucana. (**ERCILLA**). MLN, 62, 1947.

Konopatzki, H. Das Bild der Antike bei Paul **ERNST**. Würzburg, 1940.

Severus, P. E. Lupus von **FERRIERES**, Gestalt und Werk eines Vermittlers antiken Geistesgutes an das Mittelalter im 9. Jahrhundert. Münster, 1938.

Seznec, J. Les lectures antiques de **FLAUBERT** entre 1840 et 1850. RHPhC, 27-28, 1939.

Stemplinger, E. Gustav Flauberts Stellung zur Antike. Zs. f. d. Gymnasialwesen, 1918.

Holler, E. Kaiser **FRIEDRICH** II und die Antike. Marburg, 1922.

Newdick, R. S. Robert **FROST** and the Classics. CJ, 35, 1940.

Mysing, O. R. **GARNIER** und die antike Tragödie. Diss. Leipzig, 1891.

Thomas, R. **GEIBEL** und die Antike. Progr. Regensburg, 1914.

Mueller, P. Stefan **GEORGE** und die Antike. G, 1937.

Alewyn, R. **GOETHE** und die Antike. HG, 1932.

Boehm, K. Goethes Verhältniss zur Antike. Progr. 1892.

Buttmann. Goethe als Vermittler des Alterthums und der modernen Zeit; Festrede. Prenzlau, 1849.

Curtius, L. Goethe und die Antike. NJWJ, 1932.

Dalmeyda, G. Goethe et le drame antique. Paris, 1908.

Dornseiff, F. Die antike Quelle von Goethe: Toblers Aufsatz Die Natur. Antike, 1939.

Enzinger, M. Goethe und die Antike. Archiv, 172, 1938.

Hering, R. Der Einfluss des klassischen Altertums auf den Bildungsgang des jungen Goethe. Jb. d. freien deutschen Hoschstifts, Frankfurt, 1902.

Keller, W. J. Goethe's Estimate of the Greek and Latin Writers as Revealed by his Works, Letters, Diaries, and Conversations. Bull. U. of Wisconsin, 1916.

Maass, E. Goethe und die Antike. Berlin, 1912. Cf. Berliner Philol. Wochenschrift, 1914.

—— Neues über Goethe und die Antike. HG, 27, 1926.

—— Goethe und die Werke der antiken Kunst. JbGG, 10.

Mangold, K. Ueber Goethes Verhältnis zur Antike. HG, 25.

Mayer, P. Goethe und das klassische

Alterthum. Progr. Hildesheim. And in: Aus dem Goethejahr, Leipzig, 1900. Cf. Türmer, 2, 1900.

Michaelis, A. Goethe und die Antike. In: Strassburger Goethevorträge, Strassburg, 1899.

Mühll, H. von der. Goethe et les anciens. Bull. de la Soc. des Etudes de Lettres (Lausanne), 1933.

Netoliczka, O. Goethe und die Antike. Progr. Kronstadt, 1899.

Olbrich, K. Nachahmung der classischen Sprachen in Goethes Wortstellung und Wortgebrauch. Diss. Leipzig, 1891.

Rabbow, P. Goethe und die Antike. NJWJ, 1926.

Riese, A. Goethe und das klassische Altertum. Frankfurter Zt. 120-22, 1900.

Roethe. Goethe und das klassische Altertum. Versamml. d. Freunde d. human. Gymn. Dresden, 1927.

Schadewaldt, W. Goethe und das Erlebnis des antiken Geistes. Freiburg, 1932.

Steinweg, C. Das Seelendrama in der Antike und seine Weiterentwicklung bis auf Goethe und Wagner. Halle, 1924.

Thalmayr, F. Goethe und das klassische Altertum. Leipzig, 1897. Cf. DLZ, 40, 1897.

Thomas, R. Goethe und die Antike. BBG, 1925.

Ulrichs, L. von. Goethe und die Antike. JbGG, 3, 1882.

Vogel, T. Goethe und das klassische Altertum. NJKA, 1-2, 1898-99.

Wegner, M. Goethes Anschauung antiker Kunst. Berlin, 1944.

Wickhoff, F. Der zeitliche Wandel in Goethes Verhältnis zur Antike, dargelegt im Faust. Jahreshefte des österr. archäolog. Instituts, 1, Wien, 1898. And in: Chron. des Wiener Goethe Vereins, 14, 1900.

Grismer, R. L. Classical Allusions in the Poetic Works of **GONGORA.** Hisp., 30, 1947.

Gervais, E. Nachahmung der antiken und französischen klassischen Tragödie durch **GOTTSCHED** und seine Schüler. Progr. Hohenstein, 1864.

Van Hook, La Rue. New Light on the Classical Scholarship of Thomas **GRAY.** AJPh, 1936.

Spoerl, J. **GREGOR** der Grosse und die Antike. Deutsche Zs, 50, 1937.

Goerlich, E. **GRILLPARZER** und die Antike. G, 1942.

Hartel, W. von. Grillparzer und die Antike. JbGrG, 17, 1907.

Stoll. Grillparzers Dramen mit antiken Stoffen. Reform, 1893.

Vretska, K. **GRYPHIUS** und das antike Drama. Mitteil. des Vereins klass. Philologen in Wien, 2, 1925.

List, S. F. von **HAGEDORN** und die antike Literatur. Diss. München, 1919.

Ischer, A. Albrecht von **HALLER** und das klassische Altertum. Bern, 1928.

Gerth, K. **HARDENBERG** und die Antike. Neue Jb. f. Pädagogik, 1922.

Hoffmann, H. Christentum und Antike bei Adolf von **HARNACK** und Ernst Troeltsch. Festschrift Tièche. Bern, 1947.

Voigt, F. A. Antike und antikes Lebensgefühl im Werke G. **HAUPTMANNS.** Breslau, 1935.

Sickel, P. **HEBBEL** und die Antike. NJWJ, 1928.

Chitil, K. Friedrich **HEGEL** und die Antike. WBFA, 1927.

Filtso, M. Heinrich **HEINE** und die Antike. Diss. München, 1928.

Walzel, O. F. Heine, Goethe und die Antike. Die Zeit, 70-71, 1897.

Danz, J. T. L. **HERDERS** Ansichten des klassischen Altertums. Leipzig, 1805-06.

Kont, J. Quid Herderus de antiquis scriptoribus senserit. Diss. Paris, 1902.

Hagelberg, L. **HOFMANNSTHAL** und die Antike. Frankfurt, 1922.

Sommer, K. Das Bild der Antike bei **HOELDERLIN.** Diss. Münster, Würzburg, 1933.

Lipscomb, H. C. **HOUSMAN** and the Classics Again. CJ, 39, 1943.

Faguet, E. Les jugements littéraires de Victor **HUGO** sur l'antiquité. RCC, 6.XII.1894.

Papeloux. L'antiquité dans la Légende des Siècles. REL, 1936.

Verdeaud, G. L'inspiration grecque et latine dans la Légende des siècles de V. Hugo. REL, 1943-44.

Wilhelm, J. Victor Hugo und die Antike. München, 1924. Cf. DVLG, 1929.

Prang, H. Wilhelm von **HUMBOLDTS** Anschauung vom Wesen der Antike. Antike, 1936.

Joos, G. Eenige grieksch-latijnsche en italiaansch-Renaissance invloeden op de Basia van **JANUS SECUNDUS,** RBPh, 1941.

Sieveking, G. **JEAN PAULS** Stellung zur Antike. Hamburg, 1925.

McEuen, K. A. Classical Influence upon the Tribe of Ben **(JONSON).** Cedar Rapids (Iowa), 1939.

Heyse, H. **KANT** und die Antike. Antike, 1932.
Wild, J. **KIERKEGAARD** and Classical Philosophy. Philos. Rev., 49, 1940.
Levy, S. **KLOPSTOCK** und die Antike. München, 1923.
Muncker, F. Klopstocks Verhältniss zum klassischen Altertum. Beilage zur Allg. Zt., 26, 29.IV. and 3, 4.V.1876. And in: Klopstock, 2. ed., Berlin, 1900.
Rosenberg, K. Klopstock über die Alten. Progr. Berlin, 1856.
Kolar, A. **KOSMAS** et l'antiquité. (In Czech). Sbornik Filosofické Fakulty v Bratislava, 3, 1925.
Nitchie, Elizabeth. The Classicism of W. S. **LANDOR.** CJ, 1918.
Landor, W. S. Imaginary Conversations of Greeks and Romans. London, 1853.
Miner. The Influence of Classical Learning on English Literature in the Earlier Period, Especially as Illustrated by **LAYAMON'S** Brut. School Review, 3, 1895.
Görlich, E. Jules **LEMAITRE** und die Antike. ZNU, 41.
Casanova, Concepción. Luis de **LEON** como traductor de los clásicos. London, 1938.
Norden, E. **LESSING** als klassischer Philolog. NJWJ, 1929.
Kummer, H. Der Romantiker Otto Heinrich Graf von **LOEBEN** und die Antike. Halle, 1929.
Fucilla, J. G. A Classical Theme in **LOPE DE VEGA** and G. B. Marino. MLN, 60, 1945.
Schmidt, O. G. **LUTHERS** Bekanntschaft mit den alten Klassikern. Leipzig, 1883.
Ellinger, G. Die antiken Quellen der Staatslehre **MACHIAVELLIS.** Tübingen, 1888; cf. Berliner Philosoph. Wochenschrift, 10, 1890.
Meyncke, G. Machiavelli als Nachahmer des classischen Alterthums. MLIA, 1878.
Nourrisson, J. F. Machiavel et les classiques anciens. Mém. de l'Acad. des sciences morales, 1877.
Blum, I. Andrea **MANTEGNA** und die Antike. Strassburg, 1936.
Calderaro, G. Alessandro **MANZONI** ed il mondo latino e greco. Firenze, 1937.
Sealts, M. M. **MELVILLE'S** Reading in Ancient Philosophy. Diss. Yale U. 1941.
Morel, W. Antikes bei Conrad Ferdinand **MEYER.** HG, 1933.
Sulger-Gebing, E. C. F. Meyers Anklänge an antike Kunst. Euphorion, 1921.
—— Meyers Gedichte aus dem Gebiet der Antike. Festschrift Litzmann. Bonn, 1920.
Sinko, T. Les traditions classiques dans l'oeuvre de A. **MICKIEWICZ.** (In Polish). Cracovie, 1923.
Meybrink, E. Die Auffassung der Antike bei Jacques **MILET,** Guido de Columna und Benoît de Ste-More mit besonderer Berücksichtigung der Kampfscenen und religiösen Gebräuche. Ausgaben & Abhandl. aus dem Gebiete der roman. Philol., 54, 1886.
Anon. An Essay upon **MILTON'S** Imitations of the Ancients, in his Paradise Lost. London, 1741.
Des Essarts, E. De veterum poetarum tum Graeciae tum Romae apud Miltonem imitatione. Diss. Paris, 1871.
Schlicht, M. On the Influence of the Ancients to Be Traced in Milton's Style and Language. Progr. Riesenburg, 1873.
Tillyard, E. M. W. Milton and the Classics. PCA, 1938.
Bruns, J. **MONTAIGNE** und die Alten. Kiel, 1898.
Hensel, P. Montaigne und die Antike. VBW, 2, 1923 & 5, 1928.
Toffanin, G. Montaigne e l'idea classica. Bologna, 1940.
Ellis, W. A. Viscount **MORLEY,** Lover of the Classics. CJ, 31, 1936.
Kuester, E. C. Mittelalter und Antike bei William **MORRIS.** Berlin, 1928.
Camp, A. Influences des études classiques sur A. de **MUSSET.** Montpellier, 1895.
Blumenthal, A. **NIETZSCHE** und die klassische Altertumswissenschaft in Deutschland. In: Die Welt als Geschichte. Stuttgart, 1939.
Howald, E. Fr. Nietzsche und die klassische Philologie. Gotha, 1920.
Nuesch, E. Nietzsche et l'antiquité. Paris, 1925.
Svoboda, K. Fr. Nietzsche als klassischer Philolog. Zs. f.d. österr. Gymnasien, 1919.
Rademann, H. Versuch eines Gesamtbildes über das Verhältnis von Martin **OPITZ** zur Antike. Jena, 1926.
Sinko, T. L'érudition classique d'**ORZECHOWSKI.** Bull. de l'Acad. Polonaise de Cracovie, 1938.
Malein, A. **OSTROVSKY** et la comédie antique. Biriouteh, 8, 1918.
Anon. Considerazioni sopra le rime del **PETRARCA** e d' A. Tassoni col confronto de' luoghi de' poeti antichi di varie lingue. Modena, 1609.
Levi, G. A. Pensiero classico e pensiero

cristiano nel Petrarca. A&R, 1933 & 1937.
Nolhac, P. de. Petrarch and the Ancient World. Boston, 1907.
Ussani, V. Reminiscenze classiche (e non classiche) nei libri XX-XXIV delle Famigliari del Petrarca. Rendiconti pont. accad. romana di archeol, 1945.
Jobst, H. Ueber den Einfluss der Antike auf die Dichtung August von **PLATENS**. München, 1928.
Theiler, W. **PLOTIN** und die antike Philosophie. Museum Helveticum, 1944.
Emmerling, S. C. Antikenverwendung und Antikenstudium bei Nicolas **POUSSIN**. Würzburg, 1939.
Jong, M. de. Eça de **QUEIROZ** devant l'antiquité. RLC, 18, 1938.
Kummer, G. Das Nachwirken der antiken kosmischen Dichtung in den Werken von **RABELAIS**. Berlin, 1937.
Gehlen, J. Eine Satire Joachim **RACHELS** und ihre antiken Vorbilder. Progr. Eupen, 1900.
Dannehl, G. Sur quelques caractères dans les tragédies de **RACINE** empruntées de l'antiquité. Progr. Sängershausen, 1887.
Duening, A. Racines auf antiken Stoffen beruhende Tragödien und deren Hauptcharaktere. Progr. Quedlinburg, 1880.
Schreiter, A. Die Behandlung der Antike bei Racine. Diss. Leipzig, 1899.
Mielert, H. **RILKE** und die Antike. Antike, 1940.
Cornelia, W. B. The Classical Sources of the Nature References in **RONSARD'S** Poetry. New York, 1934.
Abele, W. Die antiken Quellen des Hans **SACHS**. Progr. Cannstatt, 1897 & 1899.
Thon, F. W. Das Verhältniss des Hans Sachs zu der antiken und humanistischen Komödie. Diss. Halle, 1889.
Bush, D. Classical Lives in the Mirror for Magistrates. (**SACKVILLE**). SPh, 1925.
Reinhardt, G. **SAINT-EVREMONDS** Urteile und Gedanken über die alten Griechen und Römer. Diss. Leipzig, 1900.
Amatucci, A. G. Le letterature classiche negli studi e nella critica di F. De **SANCTIS**. Annali dell'Istruzione media (Firenze), 1934.
Robinson, G. W. Joseph **SCALIGER'S** Estimates of Greek and Latin Authors. HSCPh, 29.
Sanford, E. M. Scaligeriana. CJ, 26, 1931.
Brinkmann, O. Nänie. (**SCHILLER**). HG, 1932.
Hirzel, L. Ueber Schillers Beziehungen zum Alterthume. Aarau, 1872.
Ruediger, H. Schillers Metaphysik und die Antike. Antike, 1936.
Schmidt, A. Schiller und die Antike. HG, 1930.
Buenemann, H. Elias **SCHLEGEL** und Wieland als Bearbeiter antiker Tragödien. Leipzig, 1928.
Emmersleben, A. Die Antike in der romantischen Theorie. Die Gebrüder Schlegel und die Antike. Berlin, 1937.
Eymer, K. **SCHOPENHAUER** über den Wert der Antike für die Geistesbildung. Neue Jb. f. Pädagogik, 1915.
Baldwin, T. W. William **SHAKSPERE'S** Small Latine & Lesse Greeke. 2 vols. Urbana, 1944.
Boas, F. S. Aspects of Classical Legend and History in Shakespeare. London, 1943.
Delius, N. Klassische Reminiscenzen in Shakespeares Dramen. JbShG, 18, 1883.
Gutermann. Shakespeare und die Antike. Progr. Heilbronn, 1900.
Hense, C. C. Das Antike in Shakespeares Drama Der Sturm. JbShG, 15, 1879.
Kranz, W. Shakespeare und die Antike. ESn, 73, 1938.
Ormilly, P. La connaissance et le sentiment de l'antiquité chez Shakespeare. Revue bordelaise, 1.XII.1879.
Staedler, E. Die klassischen Quellen der Antoniusrede in Shakespeares Julius Caesar. NM, 10.
Stapfer, P. Shakespeare et l'antiquité. 2 vols. Paris, 1880. Cf. RB, 17.VII.1880.
Tesch, A. Das Nachleben der Antike in Shakespeares Dramen. WBFA, 7, 1930.
Theobald, W. The Classical Element in the Shakespeare Plays. London, 1909.
Wolff, E. Shakespeare und die Antike. Antike, 1944.
Intze, O. Antike Einflüsse auf P. B. **SHELLEY**. 1914.
Knapp, C. The Classical Element in **SMOLLETT'S** Roderick Random. CW, 23, 1929.
Wunderer, C. Oswald **SPENGLER** und die antike Tragödie. BBG, 1925.
Nathansky, A. **SPITTELER** und die Antike. NJKA, 1922.
Chislett, W. **STEVENSON** and the Classics, 1850-94. JEGPh, 15, 1916.
Anon. **TAYLOR'S** Classical Study. NAR, 1871.
Mooney, E. A. **TENNYSON'S** Earliest Classical Parallels. CJ, 36, 1940.

Mustard, W. P. Classical Echoes in Tennyson. New York, 1904.
Paul, H. Tennyson's Classical Poems. NC, 1893.
Rand, E. K. A Friend of the Classics in the Times of St. **THOMAS AQUINAS.** Mélanges Mandonnet. Paris, 1930.
Wittman, M. Die Ethik des Thomas von Aquin in ihren antiken Quellen erforscht. München, 1933.
Fridholm, R. **THORILD** och antiken. Göteborg, 1940.
Mishchenko, F. G. L. N. **TOLSTOY'S** Thoughts on the Art and the Literature of Classical Antiquity (in Russian). Russkaia Mysl', 1899.
Delpino, M. Elementi celtici ed elementi classici nel **TRISTAN** di Thomas. AR, 23, 1939.
Jones, F. P. Anthony **TROLLOPE** and the Classics. TAPhA, 1940.
Skard, S. A. O. **VINJE** og antikken. Oslo, 1938.
Geerts, A. M. F. B. **VONDEL** als classicus bij de humanisten in de leer. Utrecht, 1932.
Frommel, G. Der Geist der Antike bei Richard **WAGNER** in Selbstzeugnissen dargestellt. Berlin, 1933.
Guenther, R. Richard Wagner und die Antike. NJKA, 16, 1913.
Oliver, A. Izaak **WALTON** and the Classics. CW, 38, 1944-45.
Doell, M. **WIELAND** und die Antike. Progr. Nikolsburg, 1896.
—— Die Einflüsse der Antike in Wielands Hermann. Progr. München, 1897.
Groschwald, P. Das Bild des klassischen Altertums in Wielands Agathon. Giessen, 1914.
Scheidl. Persönliche Verhältnisse und Beziehungen zu den antiken Quellen in Wielands Agathon. SVL, 4, 1904.
Morgenstern, C. J. **WINCKELMANN,** nebst dessen Rede über den Einfluss des Studiums der griechischen und römischen Classiker. Leipzig, 1805.
Kern, O. Die klassische Altertumswissenschaft in Halle seit Friedrich August **WOLF.** Halle, 1928.
Hadas, M. Classical Items in **ZABARA.** CJ, 29, 1933.

THIRD PART

Greek Contributions.

CHAPTER ONE

Generalities.

(See also the chapters on Mythology, I. VI. 7., and Thematology, I. VI. 10.)

Alewyn, R. Vorbarocker Klassizismus und griechische Tragödie. Heidelberg, 1926.

Bardy, G. La culture grecque dans l'Occident chrétien au IVe siècle. Recherches de Science Religieuse, 1939.

Bernarda, N. von. Griechische Tragödie und modernes Drama. PJb, 3, 1901.

Bill, C. P. Tracking the Greeks. CJ, 25, 1929.

Bissing, F. W. von. Das Griechentum und seine Weltmission. Leipzig, 1920.

Boas, G. (ed.) The Greek Tradition. Baltimore, 1939.

Bogner, H. Epos und Lyrik der Hellenen und die Gegenwart. Süddeutsche Monatshefte, 33, 1935-36.

Brandes, G. Griechische Gestalten in der neueren Poesie. Nord & Süd, 125, 1908.

Cooper, L. The Greek Genius and Its Influence. New Haven, 1917; Ithaca, 1948.

Cramer, J. F. F. De graecis medii aevi studiis. n.p. 1848 & 1852.

Dain, A. Le moyen âge occidental et la tradition manuscrite de la littérature grecque. Actes du Congrès de Nice de l'Ass. G. Budé. Paris, 1935.

Dickinson, G. L. The Contribution of Ancient Greece to Modern Life. London, 1932.

Doellinger, J. von. Einfluss der griechischen Litteratur und Kultur auf die abendländische Welt im Mittelalter. Akadem. Vorträge, 1. München, 1890.

Ephraim, C. Wandel des Griechenbildes im achtzehnten Jahrhundert. Bern, 1936.

Geffcken, J. Gegenwartswert und geschichtliche Bedeutung der griechischen Antike. Vers. d. Freunde d. human. Gymnasiums. Rostock, 1927-28.

—— Unser Ringen um das Verständnis des Griechentums. Kantstudien, 1930.

Gravino, D. Saggio d'una storia dei volgarizzamenti d'opere greche nel secolo XV. Napoli, 1896. Cf. GSLI, 29.

Haskins, C. H. The Greek Element in the Renaissance of the Twelfth Century. AHR, 25, 1920.

Heinemann, K. Die tragischen Gestalten der Griechen in der Weltliteratur. 2 vols. Leipzig, 1920.

Hody, H. De Graecis illustribus graecae linguae litterarumque humaniorum instauratoribus. Londini, 1742.

Hook, La Rue van. The Modernity of Greek Literature. CW, 21.

Howald, E. Das Griechentum des Neuhumanismus. Geistige Arbeit, 5, 1938.

Huemer, K. Das tragische Dreigestirn und seine modernen Beurteiler. Wien, 1930.

Humboldt, A. von. Ueber das Studium des Altertums und des griechischen insbesondere. In: Sechs ungedruckte Aufsätze. Leipzig, 1896.

James, H. R. Our Hellenic Heritage. 2 vols. London, 1921-24.

Jebb, R. C. The Permanent Power of Greek Poetry. AM, 1893.

—— The Growth and Influence of Classical Greek Poetry. Boston, 1894.

Kaerst, J. Das Wesen des Hellenismus. Berlin, 1926.

Kaminski, E. Griechisches Altertum im modernen Drama. Lehrproben & Lehrgänge, 48. (Halle), 1931-32.

Kriekoulis, C. & Boemer, K. Unsterbliches Hellas. Berlin, 1938.

Langlotz, E. Griechische Klassik: ihr Wesen und ihre Bedeutung für die Gegenwart. Stuttgart, 1932.

Livingstone, R. W. et al. The Legacy of Greece. Oxford, 1921.

—— Greek Ideals and Modern Life. Harvard U.P., 1935.

Loomis, L. R. Medieval Hellenism. Lancaster (Pa.), 1906.

Mahaffy, J. P. Che cosa hanno fatto gli antichi Greci per la civiltà moderna? Palermo, 1923.

Moravcsik, G. Hellénisme antique, hellénisme vivant. (In Hungarian). Parthenon, 14, 1940.

Mueller, A. Das griechische Drama und seine Wirkungen bis zur Gegenwart. Kempten, München, 1908.

Otto, W. F. Der griechische Mensch und die Nachwelt. Europ. Revue, 13, 1937.

Puaux, R. Revenons en Grèce. Paris, 1932.

Robin, L. Greek Thought and the Origins of the Scientific Spirit. London, 1928.

Schubart, W. Hellenismus und Weltreligion. NJWJ, 1926-27.

Schuster, M. Der Hellenismus und die Gegenwart. WBFA, 4, 1926.
Thomson, J. A. K. The Greek Tradition. London, 1915.
Tougard, A. L'hellénisme dans les écrivains du moyen âge. Paris, 1886.
Woodward, A. M. Greek History at the Renaissance. Journal of Hellenic Studies, 1943.
Zimmern, A. E. Greek Historians. In: Our Debt to Greece and Rome. Boston, 1923.

CHAPTER TWO

Greek Influences upon the Orient.

Alviella, G. d'. Les Grecs dans l'Inde. Bull. de l'Acad. Royale de Belgique, 33, 1896.
—— Ce que l'Inde doit à la Grece. Paris, 1897. New ed. 1926.
Banerjee Gauranga, N. Hellenism in Ancient India. Calcutta, 1919.
Blochet, E. La pensée grecque dans le mysticisme oriental. Revue de l'Orient chrétien, 7-8, 1931-32.
Camus, A. G. Des traductions des livres grecs faits en Arabe. In: Notices et Extraits de l'an IX (1799).
Chacot. Les destinées de l'hellénisme au-delà de l'Euphrate. Mém. des Antiq. de France, 63, 1902.
Festugière, A. J. Grecs et sages orientaux. Revue de l'Histoire des religions, 1945.
Gressmann, H. Die Umwandlung der orientalischen Religionen unter dem Einfluss hellenischen Geistes. VBW, 3, 1924-26.
Horowitz, J. Spuren griechischer Mimen im Orient. DLZ, 1915.
Krause, M. Die arabische Uebersetzungsliteratur. ZDMG, 1938.
Le Coq, A. Die Brücke zwischen dem Hellenismus und dem Chinesentum. Velhagen & Klasings Monatshefte, 38, 1920.
Levi, S. Quid de Graecis veterum Indorum monumenta tradiderint. Paris, 1890.
Meyer, E. Blüte und Niedergang des Hellenismus in Asien. Berlin, 1925.
Meyerhof, M. Transmission of Greek and Indian Science to the Arabs. Islamic Culture, 11, 1937.
Oldfather, C. H. The Greek Literary Texts from Greco-Roman Egypt. U. of Wisconsin Studies, 9, 1923.
Politis, A. M. L'hellénisme et l'Egypte moderne. Paris, 1930.
Schacht, J. Ueber den Hellenismus in Bagdad und Cairo im 11. Jahrhundert. ZDMG, 90, 1936.
Schaeder, H. H. Der Orient und das griechische Erbe. NSR, 1928.
Steinschneider, M. Orientalische Uebersetzungen griechischer Autoren. Das Archiv, 1. (Berlin), 1888.
Weber. Die Griechen in Indien. SAWB, 1890.
Wilson, C. The Greeks in Asia. Asiatic Quarterly Rev., 3, 1887.
Windisch. Greek Influence on Indian Drama. Transactions of the 5th Oriental Congress, Berlin, 1882.

CHAPTER THREE

Greek Influences upon Ancient Rome and Modern Italy.

Altheim, F. Griechische Götter im alten Rom. Giessen, 1930.
Bieber, Margarete. The History of the Greek and Roman Theater. Princeton U.P., 1939.
Boerner, C. F. De doctis hominibus graecis litterarum graecarum in Italia instauratoribus. Lipsiae, 1750.
Courcelle, P. Les lettres grecques en Occident de Macrobe à Cassiodore. Bibliothèque des écoles fr. d'Athènes et de Rome, 1943.
Ducati, P. Gli Italiani e le antichità greche. In: Italia e Grecia. Firenze, 1940.
Favre, G. Mélanges d'histoire littéraire (sur les hellénistes en Italie du Xe au XVe siècle). Genève, 1856.
Federici, F. Degli scrittori greci, e delle italiane versioni delle loro opere. Padova, 1828.
Ferrua, A. L'eredità letteraria della Grecia in Roma. Civiltà cattolica, 1940.
Fraenkel, E. Rome and Greek Culture: Inaugural Lecture. Oxford, 1935.
Giraud, J. L'hellénisme en Italie (au moyen âge). Bull. de l'Acad. delphinale, 3 sér., 20. Grenoble, 1886.
Haskins, C. H. Sicilian Translators of the Twelfth Century. In: Studies in the History of Mediaeval Science. Cambridge, 1927.
Hatzfeld, J. Les trafiquants italiens et l'Orient hellénique. Paris, 1919.
Illuminati, L. L'elegia romana in relazione al elegia greca. Messina, 1946.

Jachmann, G. Die Originalität der römischen Literatur. Leipzig, 1926.
Jurenka, H. Römische Lyriker mit griechischen Parallelen. Leipzig, 1912.
Kroll, W. Die griechische Bildung im Ciceronischen Rom. F&F, 1933.
Lockwood, D. P. Two Thousand Years of Latin Translation from the Greek. TAPhA, 1918.
Lorenzi, A. de. I precedenti greci della commedia romana. Napoli, 1946.
Muckle, J. T. Greek Works Translated Directly into Latin before 1350. MS, 4-5, 1942-43.
Pascal, C. Graecia capta: saggi sopra alcune fonti greche di scrittori latini. Firenze, 1905.
Popa-Lisseanu, G. L'alexandrinisme dans la littérature latine. Orpheus, 4, 1928.
Rohlfs, G. Das Fortleben des antiken Griechentums in Unteritalien. Köln, 1933.

CHAPTER FOUR

Greek Influences upon England.

Burnet, J. The Greek Strain in English Literature. E&S, 1920.
Churton Collins, J. Greek Influence on English Poetry. London, 1910.
Clarke, M. L. Greek Studies in England, 1700-1830. Cambridge U.P., 1945.
Croll, M. W. Attic Prose in the Seventeenth Century. SPh, 1921.
Dowling, T. E. & Fletcher, E. W. Hellenism in England. London, 1915.
Foster, F. M. K. English Translations from the Greek; a Bibliographical Survey. New York, 1918.
Guttling, J. F. C. Hellenic Influence on the English Poetry of the 19th Century. Amsterdam, 1922.
Lever, K. Greek Comedy on the English Stage. CJ, 42, 1946.
Murray, G. What English Poetry May Still Learn from Greek. E&S, 3, 1912.
Penick, D. A. Greek Poetry in English Translations. CW, 8.
Pierce, F. E. The Hellenic Current in English Nineteenth Century Poetry. JEGPh, 16, 1917.
Robinson, D. M. Greek Literature in English Translations. CW, 8.
Stern, B. H. The Rise of Romantic Hellenism in English Literature, 1732-86. Menasha (Wis.), 1940.
Tilley, A. Greek Studies in England in the Early Sixteenth Century. EHR, 53, 1938.
Watt, L. M. Attic and Elizabethan Tragedy. London, 1908.
Wolff, S. L. The Greek Romances in Elizabethan Prose Fiction. New York, 1912.
Wolfrum, H. Christentum und Griechentum in der viktorianischen Prosa. München, 1943.

CHAPTER FIVE

Greek Influences upon France.

Ampère, J. J. Influences grecques sur la Gaule. In: Histoire littéraire de la France avant le 12e siècle. Paris, 1839.
Canat, R. La Renaissance de la Grèce antique (1820-50): l'Hellénisme en France pendant la période romantique. Paris, 1911.
Desonay, F. Le rêve hellénique chez les poètes parnassiens. Louvain, 1928.
Ducros, J. Le retour de la poésie française à l'antiquité grecque au milieu du XIXe siècle. Paris, 1918.
Egger, E. L'hellénisme en France. 2 vols. Paris, 1869.
Hammarsköld. Jämförelse mellan grekiska och fransyska tragedien. Fosforos, 1810-11.
Huck. La Grèce antique dans la langue française. Hum., 6, 1933.
Lacour, L. La tragédie grecque au théâtre d'Orange. RP, 1.IX.1902.
Morphopoulos, P. P. L'image de la Grèce chez les voyageurs français, du XVI au début du XVIII siècle. Diss. Johns Hopkins U., 1947.
Nogué, J. Quelques aspects de l'hellénisme dans la littérature française contemporaine. BAGB, 1938.
Peyre, H. Bibliographie critique de l'hellénisme en France de 1843 à 1870. New Haven, 1932.
Schlegel, J. E. Brief über das Verhältniss der griechischen und französischen Tragödie. In: Werke. Kopenhagen, 1771.
Schoell, F. L. L'hellénisme français en Angleterre à la fin de la Renaissance. RLC, 5, 1925.
Wilhelm, J. Das Griechentum in der französischen Literatur der Gegenwart. DVLG, 13, 1935.

CHAPTER SIX

Greek Influences upon Germany.

Baeumler, A. Hellas und Germanien. In: Unsterbliches Hellas (ed. by C. Kriekoulis & K. Boemer). Berlin, 1938.

Beck, A. Griechisch-deutsche Begegnung. Stuttgart, 1947.

Butler, E. M. The Tyranny of Greece over Germany. Cambridge U.P., 1935.

Closs, A. Apollo Dionysos. CLS, 13, 1944.

Crusius, O. Der griechische Gedanke im Zeitalter der Freiheitskriege. Mitteil. des Vereins d. human. Gymnasiums, 1916.

Degen, J. F. Litteratur der deutschen Uebersetzungen der Griechen. Altenburg, 1797-98; Erlangen, 1801.

Eggert, G. Hellas und die Deutschen. Geist der Zeit, 15, 1937.

Ephraim, Charlotte. Wandel des Griechenbildes im achtzehnten Jahrhundert. Bern, 1936.

Feise, E. The Greek Tradition in Germany. In: The Greek Tradition (ed. by G. Boas). Baltimore, 1939.

Herder, J. G. Von der griechischen Litteratur in Deutschland. In: Fragmente über die neuere deutsche Litteratur, 2. Sammlung. Riga, 1767.

Hof, W. Das klassische Griechenideal und das Deutschtum. G, 1938.

Kluge, O. Deutschtum und Griechentum. HG, 1934.

Meyer, T. A. Die griechische Tragödie und das klassische Drama der Weimaraner. ZDK, 1925.

Preime, E. Ueber die Aufnahme des griechischen Geistes im achtzehnten Jahrhundert in Deutschland. Antike, 1943.

Schröder, F. R. Germanentum und Hellenismus. Heidelberg, 1924.

Worringer, W. Griechentum und Gothik. München, 1928.

CHAPTER SEVEN

Greek Influences upon Other Countries.

Plugge, D. E. History of Greek Play Production in AMERICAN Colleges and Universities from 1881 to 1936. N. Y. Teachers' College, Columbia U., 1938.

Parvan, V. La pénétration hellénique et hellénistique dans la vallée du Danube. (BALKANS). Bull. de la Section hist. de l'Acad. roumaine, 10, 1923.

Krappe, A. H. Aegean Culture Currents in the BALTIC. SS, 16, 1941.

Dottin, G. Les légendes grecques dans l'ancienne IRLANDE. REG, 1922.

Gerretzen, J. G. Schola Hemsterhusiana. De herleving der grieksche studien aan de NEDERLANDSCHE universiteiten in de achttiende eeuw. Nijmegen, 1940.

Hahn, W. De graecis apud POLONOS studiis. Acta II. Congressus philol. class. slav. Praha, 1931.

Nadolski, B. Les auteurs grecs dans les écoles polonaises au XVIe siècle. (In Polish). KK, 1931.

Golosovker, J. La poésie lyrique de la Grèce ancienne dans les traductions des poètes RUSSES. (In Russian). Moskva Academia, 1935.

Kekelidze, K. Auteurs étrangers (grecs) dans l'ancienne littérature géorgienne. Bull. U. Tiflis, 8, 1927.

Graux, C. Essai sur les origines du fonds grec de l'Escurial. (SPAIN). Paris, 1880.

—— Notices sommaires des manuscrits grecs d'Espagne et de Portugal. In: Nouv. archives des missions scientifiques et littéraires. Paris, 1892.

Legrand, E. Bibliographie hispano-grecque. In: Bibliographie hispanique. New York, 1915-17.

Mey, C. V. Una página para la historia del helenismo en España. Revista de Archivos, Bibliotecas y Museos, 1921.

Restrepo, F. La cultura popular griega a través de la lengua castellana. Bogota, 1938.

CHAPTER EIGHT

Greek Philosophy.

(See also under Aristotle, Epicure, Plato, Socrates.)

Benndorf, W. Der Islam und die Stoa. Moslem Review, 8, 1933.

Braubach, B. Stoa und Demokratie in der Ideenwelt der französischen Revolution. Schmollers Jb. für Gesetzgebung, 48.

Buehler, C. F. Greek Philosophers in the Literature of the Later Middle Ages. Spec. 1937.

Fabricius, C. L. De studio philosophiae graecae apud Arabes. Altdorf, 1735.

Faye, E. de. The Influence of Greek

Scepticism on Greek and Christian Thought in the First and Second Centuries. HJ, 1924.
Grassi, E. Vom Vorrang des Logos. Das Problem der Antike in der Auseinandersetzung zwischen italienischer und deutscher Philosophie. München, 1939.
Huit, C. Les origines grecques du stoicisme. Paris, 1900.
Jagu, A. Epictète et Platon. Essai sur les relations du stoicisme et du platonisme. Diss. Paris, 1946.
Macchioro, V. D. From Orpheus to Paul, a History of Orphism. London, 1930.
Sabbadini, R. Il traduttore latino del Liber philosophorum. ARIV, 92, 1933.
Sams, H. W. Anti-Stoicism in Seventeenth- and Early Eighteenth-Century England. SPh, 41, 1944.
Smiley, C. N. Stoicism and its Influence on Roman Life and Thought. CJ, 29, 1934.
Smith, P. A. Neo-Stoicism in English Prose of the XVIIth Century. Diss. Harvard U., 1940.
Sonnenschein, E. A. Stoicism in English Literature. Contemp. Review, 124, 1923.
Stegemann, V. Christentum und Stoizismus im Kampf um die geistigen Lebenswerte im 2. Jahrhundert nach Christus. In: Die Welt als Geschichte. Stuttgart, 1941.
Wenley, R. M. Stoicism and its Influence. In: Our Debt to Greece and Rome. Boston, 1924.
Zanta, L. La Renaissance du stoicisme au XVIe siècle. Paris, 1915.
Zeller, E. The Stoics, Epicureans and Sceptics. London, 1880.

CHAPTER NINE

The Greek Anthology.

(and other Lyrical Poetry.)

Ermatinger, E. Altgriechische Artistenlyrik. Ein Stück vergleichender Literaturbetrachtung. Die Zeit, 439, 1903.
Hutton, J. The Greek Anthology in Italy to the Year 1800. Ithaca, 1935.
—— Analogies of Shakespeare's Sonnets 153-154. MPh, 38, 1940.
—— Ronsard and the Greek Anthology. SPh, 40, 1943.
—— The Greek Anthology in France and in the Latin Writers of the Netherlands to the Year 1800. Ithaca, 1946.
Levi, A. Echi degli epigrammi della Antologia nella poesia sepolcrale del XVIII e del XIX secolo. ARIV, 87.
Mustard, W. P. Later Echoes of the Greek Bucolic Poets. AJPh, 1918.
Preisendanz, K. Eine lateinische Uebersetzung der griechischen Anthologie von Paolo Manuzio. Wochenschrift f. klass. Philologie, 1916.
Rat, M. L'Anthologie grecque en France. Revue universelle, 15.X.1938.
Schoenberger, J. K. Die älteste deutsche Uebersetzung der Eiresione. PhW, 1939.
Waltz, P. L'Anthologie grecque. BAGB, 1928.
Zilliacus, E. José Maria de Hérédia et l'Anthologie grecque. RHLF, 17, 1910.

CHAPTER TEN

Aristotle.

1. General Influences.

(See also Literary Criticism, I. VII. 2.)

Abel, A. Aristote, la légende et l'histoire. Bruxelles, 1944.
Bienenstein, K. Aristoteles in der deutschen Wissenschaft. Ostdeutsche Rundschau, 127, 1901.
Birkenmajer, A. Classement des ouvrages attribués à Aristote par le moyen âge latin. Cracovie, 1932.
Borgeld, A. Aristoteles en Phyllis. Een bijdrage tot de vergel. Litteratuur. Groningen, 1902.
Butcher, S. H. Aristotle's Theory of Poetry and Fine Art. 4th ed. London, 1927.
Callus, D. A. Aristotelian Learning at the University of Oxford in the Thirteenth Century. Bull. of the Internat. Committee of Historical Sciences, Paris, 1938.
Cooper, L. The Poetics of Aristotle, its Meaning and Influence. In: Our Debt to Greece & Rome. Boston, 1923.
Croizant, J. Aristote et les mystères. Liège, 1932.
Dittmeyer, L. Die lateinische Uebersetzung der pseudoaristotelischen Rhetorica ad Alexandrum aus dem 13. Jahrhundert. BBG, 1933.
Dowdell, V. L. Aristotle and Anglican Religious Thought. Ithaca, 1942.
Draper, J. W. Aristotelian Mimesis in Eighteenth Century England. PMLA, 36, 1921.

Franceschini, E. Aristotele nel medioevo latino. Atti IX. Congr. Naz. di Filosofia 1934. Padova, 1935.
—— La Poetica di Aristotele nel secolo XIII. ARIV, 94, 1934-35.
Garin, E. Aristotelismo e Platonismo del Rinascimento. Rinascita, 2, 1939.
Gidel, C. La légende d'Aristote au moyen âge. In: Nouvelles études sur la littérature grecque moderne. Paris, 1878.
Giles, B. Mediaeval Latin Translations of Aristotle's Art of Rhetoric. TAPhA, 1934.
Grabmann, M. Forschungen über die lateinischen Aristotelesübersetzungen des 13. Jahrhunderts. Münster, 1916.
—— Mittelaterliche lateinische Aristotelesübersetzungen und Aristoteleskommentare in Handschriften spanischer Bibliotheken. SBAW, 1928.
—— Eine lateinische Uebersetzung der pseudo-aristotelischen Rhetorica ad Alexandrum aus dem 13. Jahrhundert. SBAW, 1931-32 & F&F, 1932.
—— Studien über den Einfluss der aristotelischen Philosophie auf die mittelalterlichen Theorien über das Verhältnis von Kirche und Staat. SBAW, 1934.
—— Methoden und Hilfsmittel des Aristotelesstudiums im Mittelalter. Ibid. 1939.
Graff, E. G. Altdeutsche Uebersetzung und Erläuterung der aristotelischen Abhandlungen. Berlin, 1837.
Gudeman, A. Die syrisch-arabische Uebersetzung der aristotelischen Poetik. Ph, 1920.
Herrick, M. T. The Early History of Aristotle's Rhetoric in England. PhQ, 5, 1926.
—— The Poetics of Aristotle in England. New Haven, 1930.
Hertz, W. Aristoteles in den Alexanderdichtungen des Mittelalters. SBAW, 1891. And in: Gesammelte Abhandlungen. Stuttgart, 1905.
Madkour, I. L'Organon d'Aristote dans le monde arabe. Ses traductions, son étude et ses applications. Paris, 1934.
Mansion, A. La version médiévale de l'Ethique à Nicomaque. Revue neoscolastique de philosophie. (Louvain), 1938.
McKeon, R. Aristotelianism in Western Christianity. Festschrift S. J. Case. Chicago, 1939.
Montanari, P. L'influenza di Aristotele sul pensiero politico posteriore. "Sophia," 1936.
Moth, F. Aristotelessagnet eller elskovs magt. København, 1916.
Mulvany, C. M. Notes on the Legend of Aristotle. CQ, 20, 1926.
Peiser, W. Aristotelianism and Thomism in Romanic Literature. New Scholasticism, 16, 1942.
Petersen, P. Geschichte der aristotelischen Philosophie im protestantischen Deutschland. Leipzig, 1921.
Plessner, M. Zur arabischen Uebersetzung der Poetik des Aristoteles. Oriental. Literatur Zt., 1931.
Pritchard, J. P. Aristotle's Poetics and Certain American Literary Critics. CW, 27, 1934.
—— Aristotle's Influence upon American Criticism. TAPhA, 1936.
Rostagni, A. Aristotele e Aristotelismo nella storia dell' estetica antica. SIFC, N.S., 4. 1921-22.
Rudberg, G. Die lateinischen Aristotelesübersetzungen des Mittelalters. (In Swedish). Lychnos, 1939.
Sandys, J. The Fortunes of Aristotle in the University of Paris, 1210-54. London, 1923.
Steenberghen, F. van. Aristote en Occident. Les origines de l'aristotelisme parisien. Louvain, 1946.
Stocks, J. L. Aristotelianism. In: Our Debt to Greece and Rome. Boston, 1925.
Tkatsch, J. Die arabische Uebersetzung der Poetik des Aristoteles und die Grundlage der Kritik des griechischen Textes. Anzeiger der Akad. d. Wissenschaften in Wien, 56, 1919 & Wien, 1932.
Walzer, R. Zur Traditionsgeschichte der aristotelischen Poetik. SIFC, 11, 1934.
Wasik, W. L'Aristotélisme populaire comme fragment de la Renaissance. Rev. d'Histoire de la Philosophie, 1937.
Wülcker, R. P. Das Evangelium Nicodemi in der abendländischen Literatur Diss. Marburg, 1872.
Zeppa de Nolva, C. La Poétique d'Aristote en Italie et en France au XVIe siècle. Actes du Congrès de Nice de l'Assoc. G. Budé. Paris, 1935.
Zonta, G. Rinascimento, Aristotelismo e Barocco. GSLI, 104, 1934.

2. Influences upon Individuals.

Heidingsfelder, G. ALBERT von Sachsen. Sein Lebensgang und sein Kommentar zur Nikomachischen Ethik des Aristoteles. Münster, 1921.

Lottin, O. Saint Albert le Grand et l'Ethique à Nicomaque. Festschrift Grabmann. Münster, 1935.
Pelster, F. Beiträge zur Aristotelesbenutzung Alberts des Grossen. Philosoph. Jb. 46, 1933.
Troilo, E. **AVERROISMO** e aristotelismo padovano. Padova, 1939.
Gabrielli, F. Estetica e poesia araba nell'interpretazione della Poetica aristotelica presso **AVICENNA** e Averroé. Roma, 1930.
Sauter, C. Avicennas Bearbeitung der aristotelischen Metaphysik, Archiv f. Gesch. der Philosophie, 21.
Anon. **BACON'S** and Shakespeare's Mistake about Aristotle. Athenaeum, 3403, 1893.
Minio-Paluello, L. The Genuine Text of **BOETHIUS'** Translation of Aristotle's Categories. Medieval & Renaiss. Studies, 1. (London), 1943.
Solmsen, F. Boethius and the History of the Organon. AJPh, 65, 1944.
Menut, A. D. **CASTIGLIONE** and the Nicomachean Ethics. PMLA, 58, 1943.
Wiley, W. L. Jean **CHAPELAIN**, the Oracle of Aristotle. SPh, 37, 1940.
Stearns, M. W. A Note on **CHAUCER'S** Use of Aristotelian Psychology. SPh, 43, 1946.
Herrick, M. T. Sir John **CHEKE** and Aristotle's Poetics. CW, 18.
Mariotti, S. **CICERONE** e una fonte stoica dipendente da Aristotele. SIFC, 17, 1940.
Grabmann, M. Gentile da **CINGOLI**, ein italienischer Aristoteleserklärer aus der Zeit Dantes. SBAW, 1941.
Bridges, J. H. **COMTE**, the Successor of Aristotle and St. Paul. London, 1883.
Lemaître, J. **CORNEILLE** et la poétique d'Aristote. Paris, 1888.
Stieff. P. Corneille's, seiner Vorgänger und Zeitgenossen Stellung zu Aristoteles. Progr. Breslau, 1893.
Grabmann, M. Das Aristotelesstudium in Italien zur Zeit **DANTES**. JbDG, 23.
Moore. The Translation of Aristotle Used by Dante. Academy, 1026, 1892.
Toynbee, P. Aristotle's De Animalibus in Dante and Other Mediaeval Writers. GSLI, 34, 1899.
Luger, F. Die Unsterblichkeitsfrage bei Johannes **DUNS SCOTUS**. Ein Beitrag zur Geschichte der Rückbildung des Aristotelismus in der Scholastik. Wien, 1933.
Cooper, L. Aristotle, **GALILEO** and the Tower of Pisa. Ithaca, 1935.
Petersen, P. **GOETHE** und Aristoteles. Braunschweig, 1914.
Schlechta, K. Goethe in seinem Verhältnis zu Aristoteles. In: Goethe, 3, 1938.
Grushka, A. Maxime **GORKI** comme interprète d'Aristote. Bull. de l'Acad. des Sciences de Russie, 1930.
Powicke, F. M. Robert **GROSSETESTE** and the Nicomachean Ethics. PBA, 16.
Hartmann, N. Aristoteles und **HEGEL**. In: Beitr. z. Phil. d. deutschen Idealismus. Erfurt, 1933.
Flickinger, R. C. When Could **HORACE** Have Become Acquainted with Aristitle's Poetics? TAPhA, 1939.
Gilbert, A. H. & Snuggs, H. On the Relation of Horace to Aristotle in Literary Criticism. JEGPh, 46, 1947.
Herrick, M. T. The Fusion of Horatian and Aristotelian Literary Criticism, 1531-55. Urbana, 1946.
Pritchard, J. P. Aristotle, Horace, and Wordsworth. TAPhA, 74, 1943.
Janet, P. Aristote et M. E. **LABICHE**. RB, 8, 1887.
Arnold, B. **LESSINGS** Emilia Galotti in ihrem Verhältniss zur Poetik des Aristoteles. Progr. Chemnitz, 1880.
Baumgart, H. Aristoteles, Lessing, und Goethe. Leipzig, 1877.
Gotschlich, E. Lessings aristotelische Studien und der Einfluss derselben auf seine Werke. Berlin, 1876.
Kommerell, M. Lessing und Aristoteles. Untersuchungen über die Theorie der Tragödie. Frankfurt, 1940.
Robertson, J. G. Lessing's Interpretation of Aristotle. MLR, 12, 1917.
Sendel, K. Lessing-Aristoteles' Verhältniss zu Shakespeare. ALG, 2, 1871.
Tonnelat, E. Lessing et Corneille interprètes d'Aristote. RCC, 34, 1932.
Walther, J. Lessings und Goethes charakteristische Anschauungen über die Aristotelische Katharsis. Progr. Stockerau, 1869.
Witkowski, G. Aristoteles und Shakespeare in Lessings Hamburgischer Dramaturgie. Euphorion, 2, 1895.
Zerbst, M. Ein Vorläufer Lessings in der Aristotelesinterpretation. Diss. Jena, 1887.
Entrambasaguas, J. de. Una guerra literaria del siglo de oro: **LOPE** y los preceptistas aristotélicos. Madrid, 1932.
Wolfson, H. A. The Aristotelian Predicables and **MAIMONIDES'** Division

of Attributes. Festschrift L. R. Miller. New York, 1938.
Tapper, B. Aristotle's sweete analytikes in **MARLOWE'S** Doctor Faustus. SPh, 27, 1930.
Robles, O. Fray Tomas **MERCADO, O. P.** Traductor de Aristóteles y commentador de Pedro Hispano en la Nueva España del siglo XVI. Filosofía y Letra. (México), 1946.
Petit, H. **MILTON**, Aristotle, and the Modern Critics. CB, 25, 1948.
Leupold, W. Die aristotelische Lehre in **MOLIERES** Werken. Berlin, 1935.
Bardy, G. **ORIGENE** et l'aristotelisme. Mélanges Glotz. Paris, 1932.
Grabmann, M. Mittelalterliche lateinische Uebersetzungen von Schriften der Aristoteles-Kommentatoren Johannes **PHILOPONOS**, Alexander von Aphrodisias und Themistios. SBAW, 1929.
Garin, E. Pietro **POMPONAZZI** e l'aristotelismo del Cinquecento. NAnt, 79, 1944.
Troilo, S. Due traduttori dell'Etica Nicomachea: **ROBERTO DI LINCOLN** e Leonardo Bruni. ARIV, 91, 1932.
Gilbert, Katherine. **RUSKIN'S** Relation to Aristotle. Philosoph. Rev., 49, 1940.
Walzel, O. Aristotelisches und Plotinisches bei J. C. **SCALIGER** und Giordano Bruno. In: Vom Geistesleben alter und neuer Zeit. Leipzig, 1922.
Weinberg, B. Scaliger Versus Aristotle on Poetics. MPh, 39, 1942.
McColley, G. Christopher **SCHEINER** and the Decline of Neo-Aristotelianism. Isis, 32, 1940-47.
Deike, W. **SCHILLERS** Ansichten über die tragische Kunst, verglichen mit denen des Aristoteles. Diss. Jena, 1891.
Flagg, J. An Analysis of Schiller's Tragedy, Die Braut von Messina, after Aristoteles' Poetic. Diss. 1871.
Green, O. H. A Note on Spanish Humanism: **SEPULVEDA** and his Translation of Aristotle's Politics. HR, 8, 1940.
Symonds, J. A. **SHAKESPEARE'S** Predecessors in the English Drama (on the influence of Aristotle). London, 1888.
Baker, C. **SHELLEY'S** Translation from Aristotle. MLN, 61, 1946.
Cameron, K. N. Shelley and Aristotle. N&Q, 190, 1946.
Grabmann, M. Die Aristoteleskommentare des **SIMON VON FAVERSHAM.** SBAW, 1933.
Both, W. H. Aristotelisches Gedankengut in **SPENSERS** Faerie Queene. Hamburg, 1941.
Shanley, J. L. Spenser's Temperance and Aristotle. MPh, 43, 1946.
Bignone, E. Alcuni motivi delle opere perdute di Aristotele nella Gerusalemme Liberata. (**TASSO**). Rinascita, 2, 1939.
Meyer, H. **THOMAS VON AQUINO** der Interpret der aristotelischen Gotteslehre. Festschrift Grabmann. Münster, 1935.
Pelster, F. Die Uebersetzungen der aristotelischen Metaphysik in den Werken des hl. Thomas von Aquin. Gregorianum, 1936.
Petersen, P. Die Philosphie Fr. A. **TRENDELENBURGS.** Ein Beitrag zur Geschichte des Aristoteles im 19. Jahrhundert. Hamburg, 1913.
O'Brien, V. de P. **VERGIL'S** Aeneid and Aristotle's Poetics. CB, 10, 1933-34.
Kater, T. G. A. J. L. **VIVES** und seine Stellung zu Aristoteles. Erlangen, 1908.

CHAPTER ELEVEN

Homer.

1. General Influences.

(See also Comparisons, I. V. I., and Thematology, I. VI. 10.)

Anon. Revue des traductions françaises d'Homère. Revue Encyclopédique, 1, 1846.
—— On Translating Homer. NAR, Jan., 1862.
Arnold, M. On Translating Homer. London, 1861.
—— On Translating Homer: Last Words. London, 1862.
Beheim-Schwarzbach. Homer in der deutschen Litteratur. PJb, 66, 1890.
Bodrero, E. Die Odyssee, das Epos der Nachkriegszeit. Europ. Revue, 8, 1932.
Cadoux, C. J. Homer and Modern Thought. NC, 1924.
Costil, P. La question homérique et l'évolution du goût littéraire en France. Annales de l'U. de Grenoble, 19, 1943.
Egger, E. Mémoires de littérature ancienne (les traducteurs français d'Homère). Paris, 1862.
Eppelsheimer, H. W. Homer, ein Originalgenie. Ueber das Schicksal der

homerischen Gedichte im 18. Jahrhundert. Imprimatur, 8, 1938.
Finsler, G. Homer in der italienischen Renaissance. NJKA, 1908.
—— Homer in der Neuzeit von Dante bis Goethe. Leipzig, 1912.
Foerster, D. M. Eighteenth Century Historical Criticism of Homer in England. Bull. of the Citadel, 6, 1942.
—— Mid-eighteenth Century Scotch Criticism of Homer. SPh, 40, 1943.
—— Homer in English Criticism: the Historical Approach in the Eighteenth Century. New Haven, 1947.
Friedlaender, L. Schicksale der Homerischen Poesie. Deutsche Revue, Jan., 1886.
Ganszyniec, R. La légende de l'Odyssée d'Homère au moyen-âge. Eos, 90, 1927.
Garnett, R. On Translating Homer. In: Essays of an Exlibrarian. London, 1901.
Hallberg, E. Note sur la genèse des quatre épopées chrétiennes. Atti del Congresso internaz. di scienze storiche, 1903. Roma, 1904.
Herder, J. G. Homer, ein Günstling der Zeit. Horen, 10, 1795.
Janisch, W. Die erste englische Uebersetzung der sog. Homerischen Hymnen. Mitteil. d. Vereins klass. Philologen. Wien, 1931.
—— Nachklänge der homerischen Hymnen in der englischer Literatur. Ibid. 9, 1932.
Knight, D. Homer's Translators. TLS, 4.V.1946.
Köppel, E. Zur Entstehung des deutschen Homer. Gegenwart, 1881.
La Roche, J. Die Homerische Textkritik im Altertum. Leipzig, 1866.
Littré, E. La poésie homérique et l'ancienne poésie française. RDM, 1.VII. 1847.
Meisels, S. Klassiker der Weltliteratur im jüdisch-hebräischen Kulturkreise, I: Homer. Wien, 1930.
Morel-Fatio, A. Les deux Omero castillans. Romania, 25, 1896.
Newald, R. Die deutschen Homerübersetzungen des 16. Jahrhunderts. HG, 1932.
Newman, F. W. Homeric Translation in Theory and Practice: a Reply to Matthew Arnold, Esq. London, 1861.
Paillet, E. Notice sur Homère et sur une traduction de l'Iliade en vers français. Annuaires de la Société des Amis des Livres, Paris, 1884.
Penon, D. G. Versiones Homeri Anglicae inter se comparatae. Bonn, 1861.
Poeschel, H. Der deutsche Homer: zu seiner Problemgeschichte. Literatur, 41, 1938.
Preibisch, H. Die Dichtungen Homers in ihren Wirkungen auf die jüngste Vergangenheit und Gegenwart, Magdeburg, 1914.
Reuleaux, F. Die Einwirkung der Homer-Uebersetzung auf die deutsche Sprache. Mittheilungen d. deutschen Sprachvereins, 6.
Romizi, A. Antologia omerica e virgiliana nelle migliori versioni italiane con note confronti e riassunti. Torino, 1898.
Schoeberl, J. Homer und die deutsche Litteratur des XVIII. Jahrhunderts. Progr. München, 1866.
Schroeter, A. Geschichte der deutschen Homerübersetzung im XVIII. Jahrhundert. Jena, 1882.
Scott, J. A. Homer and His Influence. In: Our Debt to Greece and Rome. Boston, 1925.
Stemplinger, E. Studien zum Fortleben Homers. SVL, 6.
Steuart, E. M. The Roman Homer. PCA, 1927.
Toffanin, G. Omero e il Rinascimento italiano. CL, 1, 1949.
Tolkiehn, J. De Homeri auctoritate in Romanorum vita. Jb. f. klass. Philol., 23, 1897.
—— Homer und die römische Poesie. Leipzig, 1900.
Wild, F. Die Batrachomyomachia in England. Wien, 1918.
Willman-Grabowska, H. Un thème de l'Odyssée dans un Jataka indien. Bull. de l'Acad. Polonaise de Cracovie, 1934.
Wilson. Homer and his Translations. In: Essays Critical and Imaginative, 4. Edinburgh, 1857.
Witkowski, S. Jugements sur Homère en Pologne à la fin du XVIIIe et au commencement du XIXe siècle. (In Polish). Festschrift Cwiklinski. Posnan, 1936.

2. Influences upon Individuals.

Verrusio, M. Livio **ANDRONICO** e la sua traduzione dell'Odissea omerica. Napoli, 1942.
Clark, F. L. Imitations or Reminiscences of Homer in M. **ARNOLD'S** Sohrab and Rustum. CW, 17.
Mustard, W. P. Homeric Echoes in Matthew Arnold's Balder Dead. Festschrift B. L. Gildersleeve. Baltimore, 1902.

Omond, T. S. Arnold and Homer. E&S, 3, 1912.
Cook, A. S. BEDE and Homer. Archiv, 1924.
Coulter, C. C. BOCCACCIO'S Acquaintance with Homer. PhQ, 5, 1926.
Lewis, C. F. Mr. BRYANT'S Translation of the Iliad. NAR, 1871.
Kaiser, B. BUERGERS erste Aufsätze über die Verdeutschung Homers. Euphorion, 8, 1901.
Luecke, O. Bürgers Homerverdeutschung. Norden, 1891.
—— Bürgers Homerübersetzungen. Wochenschrift f. klass. Philologie, 9, 1892.
Farrington, B. Samuel BUTLER and the Odyssey. London, 1929.
Pinto, G. de. L'Omero del CESAROTTI. RI, 3, 1898.
Lettere di G. B. Arteaga al Signor G. B. C. intorno alla traduzione d'Omero dell'abbate Cesarotti. 1787.
Bartlett, Phyllis B. The Heroes of CHAPMAN'S Homer. RES, 17, 1941.
Henkel, W. Iliad und Odyssee und ihre Uebersetzer in England von Chapman bis auf L. Derby. Leipzig, 1867.
Regel, H. M. Ueber Chapmans Homerübersetzung. ESn, 5, 1882.
Briod, B. L'homérisme de CHATEAUBRIAND. Paris, 1928.
Hart, C. R. Chateaubriand and Homer. With a Study of the French Sources of his Classical Information. Baltimore, 1928.
Stahlecker, R., & Schmid, W. Martin CRUSIUS, der erste deutsche Verfasser eines Kommentars zum gesamten Homer. PhW, 1939.
Luzzato, G. L. L'Iliade di Madame DACIER. A&R, 16, 1938.
Mazon, P. Madame Dacier et les traductions d'Homère en France. Oxford, 1936.
Bohl, J. DANTE'S Betrekking tot Homeros. De Gids, 1886.
Finsler, G. Homer in der Neuzeit von Dante bis Goethe. Leipzig, 1912.
Ruutz-Rees, C. A Neglected Translation of the Iliad. (J. H. DART). CJ, 29, 1933.
Anon. Lord DERBY'S Translation of the Iliad. NAR, July, 1865.
Bassett, S. E. Homer and Sir Arthur Conan DOYLE. CW, 24, 1930.
Kameke, H. ENNIUS und Homer. Diss. Leipzig, Weida i. Th., 1926.
Patroni, G. L'Omero di FOSCOLO. Rendiconti della R. Accad. dei Lincei, 11, 1930.
Heussner, F. FREYTAGS Ingo und Ingraban im Unterricht der Prima. Progr. Kassel, 1892.
Keseling, P. Welcher vorwärts, rückwärts schaute. (GEIBEL). G, 1938.
Tibaldi-Chiesa, M. Omero e GLADSTONE. Bologna, 1921-22.
Fries, A. GOETHES Schema zur Ilias. Wissenschaftl. Beilage, Leipziger Zt, 126, 1902.
—— Zu Goethes Ilias-Studien. Chronik d. Wiener Goethe-Vereins, 16, 1903.
Hager, H. Goethe and Homer. PEGS, 2, 1886.
Hofkes-Brukker, C. Goethe en Homerus. Bull. van de Bevordering der Kennis van de Antieke Beschaving. 'sGravenhage, 1943.
Kappelmacher, A. Goethe als Homerübersetzer und Homerinterpret. Zs. f. d. österreichischen Gymnasien, 52, 1902.
Luecke, O. Goethe und Homer. Progr. Ilfeld, 1884.
Schreyer, H. Goethe und Homer. I. Bis zur Reise nach Italien. Progr. Schulpforta, 1884.
—— Das Fortleben homerischer Gestalten in Goethes Dichtung. Gymnasialbibl. Gütersloh, 8, 1893.
Stejskal, C. Goethe und Homer. Jahresbericht d. Vereins österr. Mittelschulen, 1880-81.
Suphan, B. Homerisches aus Goethes Nachlass. JbGG, 22, 1901.
Ferrari, W. Omero nella Poetica del GRAVINA. A&R, 1941.
Tamassia, N. GREGORIO DI TOURS e Omero. ARIV, 88.
Boelsche, W. Hermann GRIMM und die Errettung Homers vor den Schulmeistern. In: Hinter der Weltstadt. Leipzig, 1901.
Wright, H. G. The Life and Works of A. HALL of Grantham, M. P., Courtier and First Translator of Homer into English. NSp, 29.
Baer, L. Anklänge an Homer in der Nordsee Heinrich HEINES. JEGPh, 1930.
Braitmaier, F. Ueber die Schätzung Homers und Virgils bis HERDER. Korrespondenzblatt f. d. Gelehrten- und Realschulen Württembergs, 32, 1885.
Aguado, J. M. Homero en HORACIO. Bol. de la Acad. española, 111, 1936.
Saint-Denis, E. de. Une comparaison homérique dans Horace. EC, 1942.
Faguet, E. HOUDAR DE LA MOTTE. Ses idées sur Homère. RCC, 7, 1899.
Gilbert, S. JOYCE et Homère, les rochers errants. BURS, 150, 1930.

Koch, Vivienne. An Approach to the Homeric Content of Joyce's Ulysses. Maryland Quarterly, 1, 1944.
Prescott, J. Homer's Odyssey and Joyce's Ulysses. MLQ, 3, 1942.
Shewan, A. Andrew **LANG'S** Work for Homer. Oxford U.P., 1929.
Ross, J. B. On the Early History of **LEONTIUS**, Translator of Homer. CPh, 22, 1927.
Setti, G. Omero nei pensieri del **LEOPARDI**. Biblioteca delle Scuole italiane, Feb., 1904.
Becker. Zu **LESSINGS** Laokoon. Progr. Neustrelitz, 1915.
Flori, E. Del dottor fisico Paolo **MASPERO** traduttore dell'Odissea. In: Scorci e Figure del Romanticismo. Milano, 1938.
Heller, B. Ein homerisches Gleichnis im **MIDRASCH**. Monatsschrift f. Gesch. & Wiss. des Judentums, 40, 1932.
Riddehough, G. B. William **MORRIS'S** Translation of the Odyssey. JEGPh, 40, 1941.
Anon. **MUNFORD** on Homer's Iliad. NAR, July, 1846.
Luca, A. de. I traduttori umanistici dei poemi omerici: Vincenzo **OBSOPEO**. Palermo, 1925.
Monti, F. L'Iliade tradotta dal **PASCOLI**. La Rassegna, 46, 1938.
Cook, A. S. Odyssey, Seventh Book, as Known to **PETRARCH**. PhQ, 4, 1925.
Frost, W. The Rape of the Lock and **POPE'S** Homer. MLQ, 8, 1947.
Tobin, J. E. Pope and Homer: Some Bicentenary Observations. CB, 21, 1944.
Newald, R. Die erste deutsche Iliasübersetzung in Prosa des J. B. **REXIUS** (1584). ZDPh, 1929.
Gandar, E. **RONSARD** considéré comme imitateur d'Homère et de Pindare. Metz, 1854.
Rency, G. Un Homère annoté de la main de Ronsard. Bull. de l'Acad. Royale de Langue et de Litt. Française, Belgique, 20, 1941.
Marichal, R. La première édition de la traduction de l'Iliade par Hugues **SALEL**. H&R, 1934.
Schultz, J. Eine Homerübersetzung. (Hermann von **SCHELLING**). MLIA, 5.XII.1896.
Muehl, M. Die Wiedererkennungsszenen bei Homer im Lichte von **SCHILLERS** Schrift Ueber naive uund sentimentalische Dichtung. G, 1941.
Peppmueller. Biblisches und Homerisches in Schillers Jungfrau von Orleans. ALG, 2, 1872.
Wilkie. Homer and Sir Walter **SCOTT**. Scots Magazine, Feb., 1893.
Law, R. A. An Echo of Homer in Henry the Fifth? (**SHAKESPEARE**). U. of Texas Studies in English, 1942.
McCauley, L. P. Hamlet and the Iliad. CB, 1929.
Reforgiato, V. La parodia omerica in un dramma di Shakespeare. Catania, 1899.
Scott, J. A. An Unnoticed Homeric Phrase in Shakespeare. CPh, 1938.
Vetter, T. **SHELLEY** als Uebersetzer des homerischen Hymnus. Festgabe H. Blümner, Zürich, 1914.
Pfeiffer, R. Die Meistersinger in Augsburg und der Homerübersetzer Johannes **SPRENG**. München, 1919.
Miller, A. F. L. Graf zu **STOLBERG** als Homerübersetzer. Münster, 1908.
McCracken, G. Homerica in Gulliver's Travels. (**SWIFT**). CJ, 29, 1934.
Riccius. Dissertationes Homericae. II: De Homeri apud Virgilium et Tassum imitatione. (**TASSO**). Leipzig, 1784.
Wederver, H. Homer, Virgil, Tasso, oder das befreite Jerusalem in seinem Verhältnis zu Ilias, Odyssee und Aeneis. Münster, 1843.
Haight, E. H. **TENNYSON'S** Use of Homeric Material. PL, 12, 1900.
Perrotta, G. Le teorie omeriche di Giambattista **VICO**. In: Italia e Grecia. Firenze, 1940.
Bérard, V. **VIRGILE** et le texte de l'Odyssée. REG, 46-47, 1919.
Conway, R. S. Vergil as a Student of Homer. BRL, 1929 & Cambridge, 1930.
Rutgers, A. Het homerische epos en de Aeneis. Leiden, 1934.
Severyns, A. Virgile et Homère. MC, 1931.
Trendelenburg, A. Virgil und Homer. Persönlichkeit und Zunft. Berlin, 1930.
Wickert, L. Homerisches und Römisches im Kriegswesen der Aeneis. Ph, 39, 1930.
Heussner, F. Die **VOSS**ische Uebersetzung des Homer. Eutin, 1882.
Koch, M. Homers Odyssee von Voss. Im Neuen Reich, 6, 1881.
Roquette, O. Der Vossische Homer. MLIA, 1881.
Wieland, C. M. Briefe über die Vossische Uebersetzung des Homers. Neuer Teutscher Merkur, 1795.
Meinek, E. Homerisches bei R. **WAGNER**. Bayr. Blätter, 25, 1902.
Carriere, M. Eine neue Homerübersetzung. (E. **WIEDASCH**). Deutsches Museum, 1852.

Kraus, K. WINCKELMANN und Homer. Berlin, 1935.

Schadewaldt, W. Winckelmann und Homer. Leipzig, 1941.

Bérard, V. Un mensonge de la science allemande: Les Prolégomènes à Homère de Fr. Aug. WOLF. Paris, 1917.

Friedlaender, L. Die homerische Kritik von Wolf bis Grote. Berlin, 1853.

Pohlenz, M. Un mensonge de la science allemande? NJKA. 1919.

Volkmann, R. Geschichte und Kritik der Wolfschen Prolegomena zu Homer. Leipzig, 1874.

Zarncke, E. Der Irrgang der Homerforschung seit Fr. August Wolf. Festschrift E. Windisch. Leipzig, 1914.

CHAPTER TWELVE

Plato.

1. General Influences.

(For Early Influences upon Jews and Christians, see also II. V. 1., and for Plato's Influence upon Politics, see I. II. 5.)

Adam, J. The Vitality of Platonism and other Essays. Cambridge, 1911.

Arnou, R. De platonismo patrum. Roma, 1935.

Bigg, G. Christian Platonists of Alexandria. Oxford, 1913.

Blueher, H. Die Wiedergeburt der platonischen Akademie. Jena, 1920.

Boemer, F. Der lateinische Neuplatonismus und Neupythagoreismus. Leipzig, 1936.

Burnet, J. Platonism. Berkeley, 1928.

Colberg, E. D. Das platonisch-hermetische Christentum. Leipzig, 1710.

Elsee, C. Neoplatonism in Relation to Christianity. Cambridge, 1908.

Fite, W. The Platonic Legend. New York, 1934.

Hessen, J. Platonismus und Prophetismus. München, 1939.

Hoffmann, E. Platonismus und Mystik im Altertum. SHAW, 1935.

Lange, S. The Wisdom of Solomon and Plato. Jouurnal of Bibl. Lit., 1936.

Lester-Garland, L. V. Plato, Aristotle and Catholicism. HJ, 31, 1933.

Lichtenstein, E. Platon und die Mystik. DVLG, 10, 1932.

Macurdy, G. H. Platonic Orphism in the Testament of Abraham. Journal of Bibl. Lit., 1942.

Magyary-Techert, M. Geschichte des hellenischen Neuplatonismus. Budapest, 1934.

More, P. E. Platonism. Princeton U.P., 1931.

Notopoulos, J. A. The Divided Line of the Platonic Tradition. Journal of Philosophy, 1935.

Ritter, C. Platonismus und Christentum. Tübingen, 1934.

Schissel von Fleschenberg, O. Das Ende des Platonismus im Altertum. Philos. Jb, 42, 1929.

Shorey, P. Platonism, Ancient and Modern. Berkeley, 1938.

Speiser, A. Die platonische Lehre vom unbekannten Gott und die christliche Trinität. Eranos Jb., 1940-41.

Taylor, A. E. Platonism and its Influence. In: Our Debt to Greece & Rome. Boston, 1924.

Temple, W. Plato and Christianity. London, 1916.

Theiler, W. Die Vorbereitung des Neuplatonismus. Berlin, 1930.

Walsdorff, F. Die antiken Urteile über Platons Stil. Bonn, 1927.

Whittaker, T. The Neo-Platonists. A Study in the History of Hellenism. Cambridge, 1901 & 1928.

2. Middle Ages and Renaissance.

Baeumker, C. Der Platonismus im Mittelalter. SBAW, 1916. And in: Stud. und Char. d. Gesch. d. Philos., Münster, 1928.

Dress, W. Der Platonismus im Mittelalter und in der Renaissance. Theolog. Literaturblatt, 9, 1930.

Hoffmann, E. Platonismus und Mittelalter. VBW, 3, 1926.

Kantorowicz, E. H. Plato in the Middle Ages. Philos. Rev., 51, 1942.

Klibansky, R. The Continuity of the Platonic Tradition During the Middle Ages. Outlines of a Corpus Platonicum medii aevi. London, 1939.

—— Plato's Parmenides in the Middle Ages and the Renaissance. Medieval & Renaiss. Studies, 1. (London), 1943.

Kluge, O. Plato, Aristoteles, Homer im Geistesleben des Humanismus. Mnemosyne, 5, 1937.

Montes, E. Algunos rasgos de la estética platónica en el Renacimiento. Rev. de Ideas Estéticas, 7, 1944.

Norwin, W. Ueber den Platonismus im 12. Jahrhundert. Teologisk Tidsskrift, 1921.

Oliver, R. P. A Late Mediaeval Plato. CW, 35, 1941-42.

Rocholl. Der Platonismus der Renaissancezeit. Zs. f. Kirchengeschichte, 13, 1892.

3. In Recent Centuries.

Baker, J. E. Plato as Contemporary Essayist. CJ, 22, 1926.
Barthel, E. L'importance du platonisme pour la formation de l'esprit futur. Actes du Congrès G. Budé. Paris, 1939.
Crossman, R. H. S. Plato To-Day. Oxford U.P., 1939.
Dickinson, G. L. After Two Thousand Years. A Dialogue Between Plato and a Modern Young Man. New York, 1931.
Eckle, C. Der platonische Bildungsgedanke im 19. Jahrhundert. Leipzig, 1935.
Evans, F. B. The Background of Romantic Platonism. CW, 32, 1939.
Goodman, P. Neo-Classicism, Platonism, Romanticism. Journal of Philosophy, 1934.
Guenther, H. F. K. Platon als Hüter des Lebens: Platons Zucht- und Erziehungsgedanken uund deren Bedeutung für die Gegenwart. München, 1920.
Horneffer, E. Der Platonismus und die Gegenwart. 3. ed. Erfurt, 1927.
Howald, E. Die Platonische Akademie und die moderne Universitas litterarum. Bern, 1921.
Jaeger, W. Der Wandel des Platobildes im neunzehnten Jahrhundert. Antike, 1928.
Kutter, H. Plato und wir. München, 1927.
Leisegang, H. Die Platondeutung der Gegenwart. Karlsruhe, 1929.
Mader, L. Platon und wir. NJWJ, 1935.
Miéville, H. L. La République de Platon et l'esprit totalitaire. Suisse contemporaine, 1941.
Singer, K. Platon und die europäische Entscheidung. Hamburg, 1931.
Wichmann, O. Platons Bedeutung für die moderne Weltanschauung. Deutsche Akad. Rundschau, 8, 1926.

4. Platonic Love.

(See also Love, I. VI. 10.)

Girardin, S-M. Du Banquet de Platon et de l'amour platonique jusqu'à la fin du XVe siècle. RDM, 15.X.1847.
Hoessli, H. Eros. Die Männerliebe der Griechen, ihre Beziehungen zur Geschichte, Literatur und Gesetzgebung aller Zeiten, oder Forschungen über platonische Liebe, ihre Würdigung und Entwürdigung für Sitten-, Natur-, und Völkerkunde. Berlin, 1924.
Kelsen, H. Die platonische Liebe. Imago, 19, 1933.
Lagerborg, R. Die platonische Liebe. Leipzig, 1926.
Meylan, E. F. L'évolution de la notion d'amour platonique. H&R, 5, 1938.
Ritter, C. Platonische Liebe. Tübingen, 1931.
Robin, L. La théorie platonicienne de l'amour. Paris, 1933.
Sensabaugh, G. E. Love Ethics in Platonic Court Drama, 1625-42. HLQ, 1, 1938.
Wechsler, E. Eros und Minne. VBW, 1923.
Zenker, E. V. Das platonische Liebesideal und das Christentum. Freie Welt, 15, 1934.

5. Influences in Italy.

Bobba, R. Di alcuni commentatori italiani di Platone. Rivista ital. di filosofia, 1892.
Cantimori, D. Anabattismo e neoplatonismo nel XVI secolo in Italia. Rendiconti della R. Accad. dei Lincei, 1936.
Cuoco, V. Platone in Italia. In: Scrittori d'Italia, 74. Bologna, 1932.
Della Torre, A. Storia dell' accademia platonica di Firenze. Firenze, 1902.
Ferri, L. L'accademia platonica di Firenze. NAnt, 118, 1891.
Heitzmann, M. Etudes sur l'Académie platonicienne à Florence. Bull. de l'Acad. Polonaise de Cracovie, 1932.
Kieszkowski, B. Il platonismo del Rinascimento italiano e la dottrina degli oracoli caldaici. Giornale crit. della filosofia italiana, 1934.
—— Studi sul platonismo del Rinascimento in Italia. Firenze, 1936.
Kristeller, P. O. Florentine Platonism and its Relations with Humanism and Scholasticism. Church History, 8, 1939.
Lorenzetti, P. La bellezza e l'amore nei trattati del Cinquecento. Annali della R. Scuola Normale Superiore di Pisa, 28, 1922.
Moench, W. Die italienische Platonrenaissance und ihre Bedeutung für Frankreichs Literatur- und Geistesgeschichte (1450-1550). Berlin, 1936.
Robb, N. A. Neoplatonism of the Italian Renaissance. London, 1935.

Sieveking, R. Die Geschichte der platonischen Akademie zu Florenz. Braunschweig, 1819 & Hamburg, 1844.

6. Influences in England.

Burnet, J. How Platonism Came to England. Cambridge, 1924.
—— Platonism in England. In: Essays & Addresses. London, 1929.
Campagnac, E. T. The Cambridge Platonists. Oxford, 1911.
Cassirer, E. Die platonische Renaissance in England und die Schule von Cambridge. Leipzig, 1932.
Dannenberg, F. Das Erbe Platons in England. Berlin, 1932.
Evans, F. B. Platonic Scholarship in Eighteenth-Century England. MPh, 41, 1943.
Harrison, J. S. Platonism in English Poetry of the XVIth and XVIIth Centuries. New York, 1903.
Inge, W. R. The Platonic Tradition in English Religious Thought. New York, 1926.
Muirhead, J. H. The Platonic Tradition in Anglo-Saxon Philosophy. London, 1931.
Pauley, W. C. de. The Candle of the Lord. Studies in the Cambridge Platonists. London, 1937.
Pawson, G. P. H. The Cambridge Platonists and their Place in Religious Thought. London, 1930.
Powicke, F. J. The Cambridge Platonists. London, 1927.
Purdy, R. The Platonic Tradition in Middle English Literature. Bull. Vanderbilt U., 67, 1947.
Sensabaugh, G. F. Platonic Love and the Puritan Rebellion. SPh, 37, 1940.
Shorey, P. Platonism and English Literature. In: Platonism Ancient & Modern. Berkeley, 1938.

7. Influences in Other Countries.

Lorimer, W. A. Plato in **AFGHANISTAN** and India. AJPh, 1932.
Pochmann, H. A. Plato and Hegel Contend for the West. (**AMERICA**). AGR, 9, 1943.
Huit, C. Le Platonisme en **FRANCE** pendant la Renaissance. Ann. de Phil. chrétienne, 1898.
Kerr, W. A. R. The Pléiade and Platonism. MPh, 4, 1906-07.
Lebègue, R. La période platonicienne et la période stoicienne dans la Renaissance française. Bull. of the International Committee of Historical Sciences, 9, Paris, 1937.
—— La République de Platon et la Renaissance française. Lettres d'humanité, 2. (Paris), 1943.
Lefranc, A. Le Platonisme dans la littérature en France à l'époque de la Renaissance (1500-50). RHLF, 3, 1896.
—— Traduction française inconnue du Criton de Platon. C. R. des Séances de l'Acad. des Inscriptions et Belles-Lettres, 1927.
Neubert, F. Antikes Geistesgut in der französischen Literatur seit der Renaissance, I: Der Platonismus. Jb. f. Philol., 1, 1925.
Shorey, P. Platonism in French Literature. In: Platonism Ancient & Modern. Berkeley, 1938.
Grunsky, H. A. Platons Begriff des Staatsmannes und die deutsche Gegenwart. (**GERMANY**). Deutsche Kultur im Leben d. Völker, 13, 1938.
Holtorf, H. Der politische Platon als Mahner der deutschen Gegenwart. G, 1939.
Wagner, A. Eine moderne deutsche Platondeutung. Zt. f. deutsche Geistesgesch., 1, 1935.
Zurlinden, L. Gedanken Platons in der deutschen Romantik. Leipzig, 1910.
Nilsson, A. Svensk romantik: de platonska strömningen. (**SWEDEN**). Lund, 1916.
Rudberg, G. Svensk Platontolkning. Nysvenska Studier, 18, 1938.
Bayer, R. Les thèmes du néo-platonisme et la mystique espagnole de la Renaissance. (**SPAIN**). In: Hommage à Ernest Martinenche. Paris, 1939.
Marasso, A. Platón en la literatura española. Nación, 17.III.1940.
Menéndez y Pelayo, M. El platonismo en la literatura castellana. Madrid, 1889.
—— La filosofía platónica en España. In: Ensayos de crítica filosófica. Madrid, 1918.

8. Influences upon Individuals.

Gaul, L. **ALBERTS** des Grossen Verhältnis zur Plato. Strassburg, Münster, 1913.
Witt, R. E. **ALBINUS** and the History of Middle Platonism. Cambridge, 1937.
Garvey, M. P. Saint **AUGUSTINE**, Christian or Neo-Platonist? Milwaukee, 1939.
Grandgeorge, L. Saint Augustin et le néo-platonisme. Paris, 1896.
Hoffmann, E. Platonism in Augustine's

Philosophy of History. Festschrift Cassirer. Oxford, 1936.
Jolivet, R. Saint Augustin et le néoplatonisme chrétien. Paris, 1932.
Leisegang, H. Der Ursprung der Lehre Augustins von der Civitas Dei. AK, 16, 1926.
Meyerhoff, H. On the Platonism of St. Augustine's Quaestio de Ideis. New Scholasticism, 16, 1942.
Schoeler, H. Augustin's Verhältnis zu Plato in genetischer Entwicklung. Diss. Jena, 1897.
Switalski, B. Neoplatonizm a etyka Sw. Augustyna. Warzawa, 1938.
Winter, A. E. De doctrinae Neoplatonicae in Augustinii civitate Dei vestigiis. Diss. Freiburg, 1928.
Wolf, E. Augustin und der lateinische Neuplatonismus. Thelog. Blätter, 12, 1933.
Kieszkowski, B. **AVERROISMO** e platonismo in Italia negli ultimi decenni del secolo XV. Giornale crit. della filosofia italiana, 1933.
Anderson, F. H. **BACON** on Platonism. UTQ, 11, 1942.
Wolff, E. Francis Bacons Verhältnis zu Platon. Diss. München, 1908.
Mohler, L. Die Wiederbelebung des Platonstudiums in der Zeit der Renaissance durch Kardinal **BESSARION**. Görres Ges., 1921.
Murley, C. Parallels between Plato and the New Testament. (**BIBLE**). Anglican Theol. Rev., 1930.
Cooke, G. W. **BROWNING'S** Interpretation of Romantic Love as Compared With That of Plato, Dante and Petrarch. PL, 1894.
Plessner, M. Der Oikonomikos des Neuplatonikers **BRYSON** und sein Einfluss auf die islamische Wissenschaft. Breslau, 1925.
Battenhouse, R. The Doctrine of Man in **CALVIN** and Renaissance Platonism. JHI, 9, 1948.
Batelli, G. Platonismo in una redondilha di **CAMOES**. Rinascita, 1, 1938.
Pescetti, L. Appunti su Antonio **CASSARINO** e la sua traduzione della Repubblica di Platone. Bull. della R. Acad. di Palermo, 1929.
Pasquali, G. **CESARE**, Platone e Posidonio. SIFC, 8, 1930.
Scholem, G. Reste neoplatonischer Spekulation in der Mystik der deutschen **CHASSIDIM**. Monatsschrift f. d. Gesch. & Wiss. des Judentums, 39, 1931.
Philips, E. Madame du **CHATELET**, Voltaire and Plato. RR, 1942.
Young, K. **CHAUCER'S** Appeal to the Platonic Deity. Spec., 19, 1944.
Lange, S. Academy and Galilee. (**CHRIST**). CJ, 30, 1935.
DeGraff, T. B. Plato in **CICERO**. TAPhA, 1938. And: CPh, 1940.
Poncelet. Cicéron traducteuur de Platon dans les traités philosophiques. REL, 1937.
Rensi, G. Platone e Cicerone. Napoli, 1934.
Meifort, J. Der Platonismus bei **CLEMENS ALEXANDRINUS**. Heidelberger Abh. zur Philos. & ihrer Gesch., 17. Tübingen, 1928.
Ramsey, W. Poesia e platonismo in Hart **CRANE**. Inventario, 1947.
Philips, Edith. Voltaire and **DACIER'S** Plato. RR, 33, 1942.
Ledig, G. **DANTE** als Platoniker. JbDG, 26, 1946.
Alain. Idées: Platon, **DESCARTES**, Hegel. Paris, 1932.
Smith, J. M. A Comparison and Criticism of the Educational Philosphies of Plato and John **DEWEY**. Diss. U. of Iowa, 1941.
Kristeller, P. O. Francesco da **DIACETO** and Florentine Platonism in the Sixteenth Century. Miscellanea Giovanni Mercati. Città dell' Vaticano, 1946.
Merrill, R. V. The Platonism of Joachim **DU BELLAY**. Chicago, 1925.
Schroeder, K. Platonismus in der englischen Renaissance vor und bei Thomas **ELIOT**, nebst Neudruck von Eliot's Disputacion Platonike, 1533. Berlin, 1920.
Brown, S. G. **EMERSON'S** Platonism. NEQ, 18, 1945.
Dörries, H. **ERIGENA** und der Neoplatonismus. Tübingen, 1925.
Holtorf, H. Plato und **FICHTE** an die deutsche Jugend der Gegenwart. HG, 1934.
Ritzer, F. Fichtes Idee einer Nationalerziehung und Platons pädagogisches Ideal. Pädagog. Magazin, 8, 1913.
Vogel, C. Platon und Fichte als Erzieher. Braune Wirtschaftspost, 7, 1938.
Ferri, L. Di Marsilio **FICINO** e delle cause della Rinascenza del Platonismo nel quattrocento. Filosofia delle Scuole italiane, 14, 1883.
Jayne, S. R. Marsilio Ficino's Commentary on Plato's Symposium. U. of Missouri Studies, 1944.
Kristeller, P. O. The Theory of Immortality in Marsilio Ficino. JHI, 1, 1940.

—— The Philosophy of Marsilio Ficino. Columbia U.P., 1943.
Puccinotti, F. Di Marsilio Ficino e dell' Accademia platonica fiorentina. Firenze, 1865.
Saitta, G. La filosofia di Marsilio Ficino. Messina, 1923.
Sensabaugh, G. F. John **FORD** and Platonic Love in Court. SPh, 36.
Edison, G. Plato and **FREUD.** UTQ, 16, 1946.
Nachmansohn, M. Freuds Libidotheorie verglichen mit der Eroslehre Platos. Internat. Zs. f. ärztl. Psychoanalyse, 1915.
Cassirer, E. **GALILEO'S** Platonism. Festschrift George Sarton. New York, 1947.
Koyré, A. Galileo and Plato. JHI, 4, 1943.
Brecht, F. J. Platon und der **GEORGE**-Kreis. Leipzig, 1929.
Wensinck, A. J. La pensée de **GHAZZALI.** Paris, 1940.
Priestly, F. E. L. Platonism in William **GODWIN'S** Political Justice. MLQ, 4, 1943.
Beyschlag, F. Eine Parallele zwischen Plato und **GOETHE.** BBG, 39, 1903.
Cassirer, E. Goethe und Platon. Jahresbericht des Philol. Vereins, 48, 1922.
Delcourt, M. Platon et les Mères dans Faust. Mélanges Desrousseaux. Paris, 1937.
Fries, C. Platozitate bei Goethe. PhW, 1939.
Günther, F. Goethe und Platon. Schônheit, 1924.
Liebert, A. Goethes Platonismus. Kantstudien, 37, 1932.
Misch, G. Goethe, Platon, Kant. Logos, 1915.
Reuther, H. Platons und Goethes Naturanschauung. NJWJ, 1929.
Rotten, E. Goethes Urphänomen und die platonische Idee. Giessen, 1913.
Foster, M. B. The Political Philosophies of Plato and **HEGEL.** Oxford, 1935.
Janet, P. Etudes sur la dialectique dans Platon et dans Hegel. Paris, 1861.
Bannes, J. **HITLER** und Platon. Geisteskultur, 42, 1933.
—— Hitlers Kampf und Platons Staat. Berlin, 1933.
Kranz, W. Diotima. (**HOELDERLIN**). Antike, 1926.
Schlagdenhauffen, A. L'expérience platonicienne de Hölderlin. Mélanges Fac. des Lettres Strasbourg (1945). Paris, 1947.
Bolaffi, E. Probabili influssi platonici su Orazio. (**HORACE**). Athenaeum (Pavia), 1933.
Flackenheim, E. L. A Treatise on Love, by **IBN SINA.** MS, 7, 1946.
Burdach, K. Platonische, freireligiöse und persönliche Züge im Ackermann aus Boehmen. (**JOHANNES VON SAAZ**). Berlin, 1933.
Deussen, P. Vedanta, Platon und **KANT.** Wien, 1917.
Grimme, A. Platon und Kant. Monatschrift f. höhere Schulen, 1924.
Lovejoy, A. O. Kant and the English Platonists. Festschrift William James, New York, 1908.
Mamiani, E. Emm. Kant e la filosofia platonica. NAnt, 3, 1866.
Mollowitz, G. Kants Platoauffassung. Kantstudien, 40, 1935.
Perls, H. Platon et Kant. Anticipations et correspondances. RMM, 1946.
Romundt, H. Der Platonismus in Kants Kritik der Urteilskraft. Berlin, 1901.
Wichmann, O. Platon und Kant. Berlin, 1920.
Ford, N. F. Endymion—a Neo-Platonic Allegory? (**KEATS**). ELH, 14, 1947.
Charbonnel, J. R. La philosophie de **LAMARTINE.** MF, 1.II.1912.
Orsier, J. Le Phédon de Platon et le Socrate de Lamartine. Paris, 1919.
Schwarz, O. De **LAURENTII CORVINI** studiis platonicis. Eos, 34.
Fontanesi, G. Il problema dell'amore nell'opera di **LEONE EBREO.** Venezia, 1934.
Mackehenie, C. A. Apuntes sobre las traducciones castellanas de León Hebreo. El Mercurio Peruano, 22, 1940.
Pflaum, H. Leone Ebreo und Pico della Mirandola. Monatsschrift f. Geschichte & Wissenschaft d. Judentuums, 72, 1928.
Roth, C. (ed.) The Philosophy of Love, by Leone Ebreo (cf. Introduction). London, 1937.
Jones, T. B. Plato and **LEONARDO DA VINCI.** CW, 29, 1936.
Baker, J. E. Sinclair **LEWIS,** Plato and the Regional Escape. English Journal, 28, 1939.
Buck, A. Der Platonismus in den Dichtungen **LORENZO DE' MEDICIS.** Berlin, 1936.
Sarrano, N. Il platonismo nelle poesie di Lorenzo il Magnifico. NAnt, 130-31, 1893.
Dannenberg, F. Das Erbe Platons in England bis zur Bildung **LYLYS.** Berlin, 1932.

Mras, K. **MACROBIUS** und Chalcidius als Uebersetzer Platos. WS, 1933.

Zanoni, L. A. **MANZONI** e V. Cousin traduttori di Platone. RI, 15.XI.1913.

Lefranc, A. **MARGUERITE DE NAVARRE** et le Platonisme de la Renaissance. Paris, 1899.

Huszti, J. Etudes platoniciennes à la cour du roi **MATTHIAS**. (In Hungarian). Minerva, 1924-1925.

—— Tendenze platonizzanti alla corte di Mattia Corvino. Giornale critico della filosofia italiana, 1930.

Couch, H. N. Moby Dick and the Phaedo. (**MELVILLE**). CJ, 28, 1933.

Kampe, F. Der **MENDELSSOHNSCHE** Phaedon in seinem Verhältniss zum Platonischen. Diss. Halle, 1880.

Thomas, G. **MICHEL-ANGE** poète: étude sur l'expression de l'amour platonique dans la poésie italienne du moyen âge et de la Renaissance. Mém. de l'Acad. de Stanislas, 5. Sér., 8. Nancy, 1890.

Agar, H. **MILTON** and Plato. Princeton Studies, 2, 1928.

Baldwin, E. C. Milton and Plato's Timaeus. PMLA, 35, 1920.

Maxwell, J. C. Plato and Milton. MLR, 43, 1948.

Samuel, Irene. Milton's References to Plato and Socrates. SPh, 41, 1944.

—— Plato and Milton. Cornell U.P., 1947.

Grabmann, M. Die Proklosübersetzungen des Wilhelm von **MOERBEKE** und ihre Verwertung in der lateinischen Literatur des Mittelalters. Festgabe Heisenberg. Leipzig, 1930.

Beger, L. Thomas **MORUS** und Plato. Zs. f. d. gesammte Staatswissenschaft, 35, 1879.

Harrold, C. F. **NEWMAN** and the Alexandrian Platonists. MPh, 37, 1940.

Hildebrandt, K. **NIETZSCHES** Wettkampf mit Sokrates und Plato. Dresden, 1922.

Arnou, R. Le thème néoplatonicien de la contemplation créatrice chez **ORIGENE** et chez S. Augustin. Gregorianum, 1932.

Koch, H. Pronoia und Paideusis. Studien über Origenes und sein Verhältnis zum Platonismus. Berlin, 1932.

Folchieri, G. Influenze platoniche nella poesia del **PASCOLI**. Nuova Cultura, Sept., 1913.

Bailey, J. A Modern Platonist (W. **PATER**). In: Poets and Poetry. Oxford, 1911.

Huppé, B. F. Walter Pater on Plato's Aesthetics. MLQ, 9, 1948.

Merrill, R. V. Platonism in **PETRARCH'S** Canzoniere. MPh, 27, 1929-30.

Siegel, P. N. The Petrarchan Sonneteers and Neo-Platonic Love. SPh, 42, 1945.

Cassirer, E. Giovanni **PICO DELLA MIRANDOLA**. A Study in the History of Renaissance Ideas. JHI, 3.

Semprini, G. La filosofia di Pico della Mirandola. Milano, 1936.

Ivaldi, G. Il platonismo di **PLOTINO**, Sant Agostino, Cartesio e Leibniz. In: Luce del Pensiero. Napoli, 1922.

Lefranc, A. Le Platon de **RABELAIS**. Bull. du Bibliophile, March, 1901.

Tolomei de Pietrasanta, H. Etudes platoniciennes de Jean **RACINE**. RBPh, 1936.

Trowbridge, H. Platonism and Sir Joshua **REYNOLDS**. ESs, 21, 1939.

Witt, C. Platon und **RODBERTUS**. Eine Untersuchung über die Zusammenhänge ihrer Sozialphilosophie. Kiel, 1921.

Anon. Plato und **ROUSSEAU**. Ein Fragment aus der Schrift: Caroli Morgenstern de Platonis Republica commentatio tertia. Neuer Teutscher Merkur, March, 1795.

Inge, W. R. Plato and **RUSKIN**. Transactions of the British Academy, 14, 1928.

Asbeck, M. d'. La mystique de **RUYSBROECK**. Un écho du néo-platonisme au XIVe siècle. Paris, 1930.

Schur, W. Nachträgliches zu **SALLUST**. Klio (Leipzig), 11, 1936.

Oliver, R. P. Plato and **SALUTATI**. TAPhA, 71, 1940.

Gray, J. G. Plato the Greek and **SANTAYANA** the Cosmopolitan. American Scholar, 12, 1943.

Fries, C. Platon bei **SCHILLER**. PhW, 1938.

Herrmann, H. Forderungen musischer Erziehung bei Schiller und Plato. Zs. f. Aesthetik, 1935.

Stengel-Mugdan, B. Einige Beziehungen zwischen der Philosophie Schillers und Platos. PJb, 145, 1912.

Kalitsounakis, J. **SCHLEIERMACHER** und Platon. Praktika (Athens), 1934.

Oellacher, H. Einflüsse von Platons Ideenlehre auf die Metaphysik **SCHOPENHAUERS**. Zs. f. d. österr. Mittelschulen, 1925.

Cassirer, E. **SHAFTESBURY** und die Renaissance des Platonismus in England. VBW, 9, 1930-31.

Anon. Plato and **SHAKESPEARE.** Athenaeum, 2299, 1871.
Mercedes, Sister Anna. Two Paths from Plato: **SHELLEY** and St. Augustine. Catholic World, 159, 1944.
Notopoulos, J. A. Notes on the Text of Shelley's Translations from Plato. MLN, 56, 1941.
—— Shelley's Translation of the Ion of Plato. MLR, 36, 1941.
—— The Platonic Sources of Shelley's Hymn to Beauty. PMLA, 58, 1943.
Prieur, S. Le platonisme d'Alastor. LM, March, 1947.
Winstanley, L. Platonism in Shelley. E&S, 4, 1913.
Samuel, Irene. The Influence of Plato on Sir Philip **SIDNEY'S** Defense of Poesy. MLQ, 1, 1940.
Ryan, J. K. John **SMITH** (1616-52): Platonist and Mystic. New Scholisticism, 20, 1946.
Scupholme, A. C. John Smith, a Cambridge Platonist. Theology, 42, 1941.
Walzel, O. Platon oder Plotin? (**SOLGER**). NPh, 23, 1937-38.
Casady, E. The Neo-Platonic Ladder in **SPENSER'S** Amoretti. PhQ, 20, 1941.
Sola Pinto, V. de. Peter **STERRY**, Platonist and Puritan (1613-72). Cambridge, 1934.
Morgenstern, C. Ueber des Grafen Friedrich Leopold zu **STOLBERG** Uebersetzung auserlesener Gespräche Platons. Leipzig, 1797.
Egermann, F. Der Dialogus des Tacitus und Platons Gorgias. H, 1935.
Evans, F. G. Thomas **TAYLOR**, Platonist of the Romantic Period. PMLA, 55, 1940.
Santeler, J. Der Platonismus in der Erkenntnislehre des heiligen **THOMAS VON AQUIN.** Innsbruck, 1939.
Wittmann, M. Neuplatonisches in der Tugendlehre des Thomas von Aquin. Festschrift Geyser, Regensburg, 1930.
Kaplinskij, V. **TOLSTOI** und Platon. ZSPh, 6, 1929.
Beachcroft, T. O. **TRAHERNE** and the Cambridge Platonists. Dublin Rev., 1930.
Merrill, R. V. Platonism in Pontus de **TYARD'S** Erreurs amoureuses. MPh, 35, 1937.
Philips, Edith. Madame du Châtelet, **VOLTAIRE** and Plato. RR, 33, 1942.
Shorthouse, J. H. The Platonism of **WORDSWORTH.** In: Literary Remains, 2. London, 1905.

CHAPTER THIRTEEN

Other Greek Authors.

Goodwin, C. J. Wielands Oberon und der griechische Roman des **ACHILLES TATIUS.** ZVL, 13.
Anon. **AESCHYLOS** in Berlin. DR, Oct., 1897.
—— The Classics in English: The Oresteia of Aeschylos. Nation, 1855, & 1901.
Burkhard, M. Die Orestie des Aeschylos im Burgtheater. Zeit, 8.XII.1900.
Kirchbach, W. Aeschylos und die Modernen. Gegenwart, 49, 1900.
Luzzatto, G. L. Traduzioni di Eschilo. Dioniso, 6, 1937.
Méautis, G. Eschyle dans la littérature française. RHLF, 24, 1917.
Sheppard, J. T. Aeschylus and Sophocles, their Work and Influence. In: Our Debt to Greece and Rome. New York, 1927.
Stuemcke, H. Die Oresteia des Aeschylos auf der modernen Bühne. Bühne & Welt, 3, 1901.
Vietta, E Aeschylus und die Sendung des Abendlandes. Literatur, 60, 1938.
Jaloux, E. D'Eschyle à Giraudoux. Fribourg, 1946.
Anon. L'Agamemnon d'Eschyle jugé par Goethe. REG, 16, 1903.
Valakis, A. P. D. The Moira of Aeschylus and the Immanent Will of Thomas Hardy. CJ, 21.
Weber, C. J. Thomas Hardy's Aeschylean Phrase. CJ, 29, 1934.
Anon. Herbert's Translations from Aeschylus. NAR, Oct., 1849.
Stanford, W. B. Gerard Manley Hopkins and Aeschylus. Studies (Ireland), 30, 1941.
Schönberger, J. K. Zwei antike Vorbilder bei Eduard Mörike. (Aeschylus & Virgil). BBG, 1920.
Faguet, E. D'Eschyle à Racine: considérations générales sur les origines de la tragédie française. Revue d'Art dramatique, 1895.
Macchia, G. Sartre ed Eschilo. La Nuova Europa, 2, 1945.
Glasson, T. F. Did Shakespeare Read Aeschylus? LQHR, 173, 1948.
Wedgwood, Julia. Aeschylus and Hamlet. Contemporary Review, 1886.
Beck, A. Die Aischylos-Uebersetzung des Grafen Friedrich Leopold zu Stolberg. Berlin, 1937.
Tailhade, L. Des tragédies d'Eschyle au pessimisme de Tolstoi. In: Le pessisme de Tolstoi. Paris, 1924.
Schaefer, T. Aeschylos' Prometheus und

Wagners Loge. Festschrift Bremen, 1899.
AESOP: See also Fables, I. VI. 2., and Phaedrus, II. IV. 7.
Brueckner, A. Die polnischen Aesopusbearbeitungen. Anz. der Akad. der Wissenschaften Krakau, 1901.
—— Ezopy Polskie. Rozprawy Akademii Umiejetnosci, Wyd. Filologiczny, 1902.
Herlet, B. Beiträge zur Geschichte der Aesopischen Fabel im Mittelalter. Progr. Bamberg, 1892.
Jacobs, J. The Fables of Aesop, I: History of the Aesopic Fable. London, 1889.
Keidel, G. C. A Manuel of Aesopic Fable Literature. Baltimore, 1896. Cf. ZFSL, 19, 1898.
—— Notes on Aesopic Fable Literature in Spain and Portugal During the Middle Ages. ZRPh, 25, 1901.
—— An Aesopic Fable in Old French Prose. AJPh, 22, 1901.
Mayer, A. Studien zum Aesoproman und zu den äsopischen Fabeln im lateinischen Mittelalter. Progr. Lohr, 1916-17.
Méril, E. du. Poésies inédites du moyen âge, précédées d'une histoire de la fable ésopique. Paris, 1854.
Morel-Fatio, A. L'Ysope castillan. Romania, 1894.
Simpson, P. A Modern Fable of Aesop. MLQ, 43, 1948.
Vine, G. Around the Earliest Spanish Version of Aesop's Fables. Library Quarterly, 25.
Zeitz, H. Des Aesoproman und seine Geschichte. Aegyptus (Milano), 1936.
Hilka, A. Beiträge zur lateinischen Erzählungsliteratur des Mittelalters: Der Novus Aesopus des Baldo. Diss. Göttingen, Berlin, 1928.
Hofer, P. Francis Barlow's Aesop. Harvard Library Bull., 2, 1948.
Harry, P. W. A Comparative Study of the Aesopic Fable in Nicole Bozon. Cincinnati, 1905.
McKenzie, K. Dante's References to Aesop. Boston, 1900.
Smith, M. E. Aesop, a Decayed Celebrity: Changing Conception as to Aesop's Personality in English Writers Before Gay. PMLA, 1931.
Gayle, Margot. Georgia's Aesop (Harris' Uncle Remus). Holland's Mag., 67, 1948.
Simon, S. De Horatio fabularum Aesopicarum imitatore. (In Hungarian). EPhK, 1939.
Foerster, R. Lessings Anmerkungen zu den Fabeln des Aesop. ZVL, 8, 1895.
Schirokauer, A. Luthers Arbeit am Aesop. MLN, 62, 1947.
Sauerstein, P. Ueber Lydgates Aesopübersetzung. Diss. Leipzig, 1885.
Mall, E. Zur Geschichte der mittelalterlichen Fabelliteratur und insbesondere des Esope der Marie de France. Halle, 1885.
Oesterley, R. Die Paraphrasen des Phaedrus und die äsopische Fabel im Mittelalter. Berlin, 1870.
Perry, B. E. The Greek Source of Rinuccio's Aesop. CPh, 1934.
Kunst, H. Steinhöwels Aesop. ZDPh, 19, 1887.
Teza, E. L'Esopo tradotto da N. Tommaseo. Rassegna bibliografica della letteratura italiana, 9, 1901.
Achelis, O. Die Aesopübersetzung des Lorenzo Valla. Münchener Museum, 2, 1914.
Frank, T. How Horace Employed ALCAEUS. CPh, 22, 1927.
Brocks. Das Fortleben der alcäischen Strophe im lateinischen Kirchenlied des Mittelalters und in der neuen deutschen Dichtung. GRM, 13.
Ansfeld, F. Die deutsche ANAKREONtische Dichtung des 18. Jahrhunderts, ihre Beziehungen zur französischen und zur antiken Lyrik. Strassburg, 1907.
Ferrari, S. Di alcune imitazioni delle Anacreontiche in Italia nel secolo XVI. GSLI, 20, 1892.
Koch, G. Beiträge zur Würdigung der ältesten deutschen Uebersetzungen Anakreontischer Gedichte. Weimarer Vierteljahrsschrift, 1893.
Michelangeli, L. A. Anacreonte e la sua fortuna nei secoli, con una rassegna critica su gl' imitatori e i traduttori italiani delle Anacreontee. Bologna, 1922.
Nissen, T. Die byzantinischen Anakreonteen. SBAW, 1940.
Rubio y Lluch, A. Estudio critico-bibliografico sobre Anacreonte y su influencia en la literatura antigua y moderna. Diss. Barcelona, 1879.
Rudberg, G. En svensk Anakreon-tolkning. Eranos (Göteborg), 1939.
Sainte-Beuve, C. Anciens poètes français: Anacréon au XVIe siècle. RDM, 15.IV.1842.
Witkowski, G. Die Vorläufer der anakreontischen Dichtung in Deutschland. ZVL, 3, 1890.

Borst, J. Ein anakreontisches Lied bei Andersen. WBFA, 6, 1930.
Koch, G. Gleims scherzhafte Lieder und die sogenannten Anakreontiker. Progr. Jena, 1894.
—— Gleim als Anakreonübersetzer und seine französischen Vorgänger. SVL, 4, 1904.
Baldensperger, F. L'anacréontisme du jeune Goethe et la poésie fugitive française. Mélanges Zdziechowski. Cracovie, 1933 & Etudes d'histoire littéraire, 4e sér. Paris, 1939.
Petzet, E. Der Einfluss der Anakreontik und Horazens auf Johann Peter Uz. ZVL, 6, 1893.
Weinreich, O. **ANTIPHANES** und Münchhausen. Das antike Lügenmärlein von den gefrornen Worten und sein Fortleben im Abendland. Wien, 1942.
Del Prete, L. Storia di **APOLLONIO** di Tiro, romanzo greco, del latino ridotto in volgare italiano nel secolo XIV. Lucca, 1861.
Maerkisch, K. Die altenglische Bearbeitung der Erzählung von Apollonius von Tyrus. Diss. Berlin, 1899.
Murko, M. Die russische Uebersetzung des Apollonius von Tyrus und der Gesta Romanorum. ASPh, 14, 1892.
Pudmenzky, B. Shakespeares Perikles und der Apollonius des Heinrich von Neustadt. Progr. Detmold, 1884.
Singer, S. Apollonius von Tyrus. Untersuchungen über das Fortleben des antiken Romans in späterer Zeit. Halle, 1895.
Smyth, A. Shakespeare's Pericles and Apollonius of Tyre. Philadelphia, 1899.
Beede, Grace L. Vergil and **ARATUS**, a Study in the Art of Translation. Chicago, 1936.
Anon. **ARISTOPHANES** in Berlin. Frankfurter Zt., 17.XII.1900.
Coulon, V. Aristophane imité par les conteurs du moyen âge. Mélanges Bidez. Bruxelles, 1934.
Friedlaender, P. Aristophanes in Deutschland. Antike, 1932.
Harding, C. R. Aristophanic Wit and Humor in English and American Literature. TAPhA, 1940.
Hille, C. Die deutsche Komödie unter der Einwirkung des Aristophanes. Leipzig, 1907.
Hilsenbeck, F. Aristophanes und die deutsche Literatur des 18. Jahrhunderts. Berlin, 1908.
Hirsch, F. Aristophanische Wortfügungen in der Sprache des 19. Jahrhunderts. Zs. f. d. deutsche Wortforschung, Dec., 1910.
Lord, L. E. Aristophanes, his Plays and his Influence. In: Our Debt to Greece & Rome. Boston, 1925.
Rambaldi, P. L. Appunti sulle imitazioni italiane di Aristofane. Firenze, 1896.
Rechner, L. Aristophanes in England. Frankfurt, 1914.
Setti, G. Della Fama di Aristofane presso gli Antichi. Rivista di Filologia, 10, 1882.
Süss, W. Aristophanes und die Nachwelt. In: Das Erbe der Alten. Leipzig, 1911.
Lockwood, D. P. Leonardo Bruni's Translation of Act I of the Plutus of Aristophanes. Festschrift Rolfe. Philadelphia, 1931.
Cataudella, Q. Giovanni Crisostomo imitatore di Aristofane. Athenaeum, 1940.
Zuretti, C. O. Aristofane e Dante. Palermo, 1901.
Anon. Frere's Version of Aristophanes. NAR, Jan., 1853.
Millhauser, M. John Hookham Frere: Translations of Aristophanes. N&Q, 178, 1940. And TLS, 2.XII.1940.
Bauer. Die Vögel nach dem Aristophanes von Goethe. Progr. 1862.
Hessen, R. Aristophanes und Hauptmann. PJb, Oct., 1900.
Brandes, G. Heine und Aristophanes. In: Die Hauptströmungen der Litteratur des 19. Jahrhunderts, 4th ed. Berlin, 1894.
Gohin, F. A propos des sources de deux fables de La Fontaine. RU, 1, 1932.
Hatzfeld, A. Aristophane et Molière. RB, 14, 1899.
Gilbert, P. Musset et Aristophane. Le Flambeau, 1930.
Buchwald, O. Platen und Aristophanes. Deutsches Museum, 1867.
Kont, J. Les parabases d'Aristophane et celles de Platen. RELV, 1886.
Muff, C. Platen als Aristophanide. Grenzboten, 32, 1873.
Littré, E. Aristophane et Rabelais. Philosophie positiviste, July, 1870.
Mierow, H. E. A Roman Cloudcuckooland. (Seneca). CJ, 26, 1931.
Guerrois, C. des. Un précurseur de Lafontaine (**BABRIUS**). Mém. de la Soc. académique de l'Aube, 3e sér., 27. Troyes, 1890.
Lévêque, E. Babrius, fables ésopiques, traduites et comparées aux fables d'Horace et de Phèdre, de Corrozet et de La Fontaine, avec une étude sur leurs origines orientales et grecques, leur iconographie et leur histoire. Paris, 1890.

Blake, W. E. **CHARITON'S** Romance, the First European Novel. CJ, 29, 1934.
Faggi, A. **DEMOCRITO** che il mondo a caso pone. (Dante). Atti della Acc. delle Scienze di Torino, 74, 1939.
Adams, C. D. **DEMOSTHENES** and his Influence. In: Our Debt to Greece & Rome. New York, 1927.
Drerup, E. Demosthenes im Urteile des Altertums von Theopomp bis Tzetzes: Geschichte, Roman, Legende. In: Studien z. Gesch. & Kultur des Altertums. Würzburg, 1923.
Shorey, P. Bacon and Demosthenes. CPh, 1930.
Poland, W. Reuchlins Verdeutschung der ersten olynthischen Rede des Demosthenes. In: Bibliothek älterer deutscher Uebersetzungen. Weimar, 1899.
Robathan, D. M. **DIODORUS SICULUS** in the Italian Renaissance. CPh, 1932.
Lowes, J. L. Keats, Diodorus Siculus and Rabelais. MPh, 34, 1937.
Workman, S. K. Versions by Skelton, Caxton, and Berners of a Prologue by Diodorus Siculus. MLN, 56, 1941.
Lievsay, J. L. Some Renaissance Views of **DIOGENES** the Cynic. J. Q. Adams Memorial Studies. Washington, D. C., 1948.
Mager, A. Wielands Nachlass des Diogenes von Sinope und das englische Vorbild. Progr. Marburg, 1890.
Leclerc, L. De la traduction arabe de **DIOSCORIDES** et des traductions arabes en général. Journal Asiatique, 6e sér., 9, 1867.
Kranz, W. Lukrez und **EMPEDOKLES.** Ph., 1943.
Sharp, D. S. **EPICTETUS** and the New Testament. London, 1914.
Oldfather, W. A. Leopardi and Epictetus. Ital., 1937.
Zanta, L. La traduction française du Manuel d'Epictète d'André de Réveaudeau au XVIe siècle, Paris, 1914.
Allen, D. C. The Rehabilitation of **EPICURUS** and His Theory of Pleasure in the Early Renaissance. SPh, 41, 1944.
Bergmann, J. Das Schicksal eines Namens. Monatsschrift f. d. Gesch. & Wissenschaft des Judentums, 81, 1937.
Ferri, L. L'Epicureismo nella storia e nella scienza. NAnt, 35, 1877.
Guiffrida, P. L'epicureismo nella letteratura latina nel primo secolo a.C., I: Esame e ricostruzione delle fonti. Torino, 1941.
Haas, A. Ueber den Einfluss der epicureischen Staats- und Rechtsphilosophie auf die Philosophie des XVI. und XVII. Jahrhunderts. Diss. Berlin, 1896.
Menzel, W. Der Kampf gegen den Epikureismus in der französischen Literatur des 18. Jahrhunderts. Berlin, 1931.
Rostagni, A. La scuola epicurea di Napoli. Rivista di filologia e d'istruzione classica, 1931.
Simpson, A. D. Epicureans, Christians, Atheists in the Second Century. TAPhA, 1941.
Philippson, R. Die Quelle der epikureischen Götterlehre in Ciceros erstem Buche De natura deorum. Symbolae Osloenses, 19, 1939.
Porter-Packer, M. N. Cicero's Presentation of Epicurean Ethics. Columbia U.P., 1938.
Tescari, O. Lucretiana: L'epicureismo in Italia nell' età di Cicerone. Conv., 1935.
Uri, H. Cicero und die epikureische Philosophie. Borna-Leipzig, 1914.
Rochot, B. Les travaux de Gassendi sur Epicure. Paris, 1944.
Beck, H. K. Das Verhältnis des Horaz zum Epikureismus in historischer Entwicklung. Erlangen, 1921.
Buccheri, G. Epicureismo d'Orazio. Tradizione, 1933.
DeWitt, N. W. Epicurean Doctrine in Horace. CPh, 1939.
Porter-Packer, M. N. The Consistent Epicureanism of the First Book of the Epistles of Horace. TAPhA, 1941.
Guyau, M. La morale d'Epicure et ses rapports avec les doctrines contemporaines: La Rochefoucauld. Paris, 1885.
Sivasriyananda, W. L'épicurisme de La Rochefoucauld. Paris, 1939.
Fubini, M. Giacomo Leopardi tra Elvezio ed Epicuro. Leonardo, 1932.
Knight, A. H. J. Nietzsche and Epicurean Philosophy. Philosophy, 1933.
Timmermans, B. J. H. M. Valla et Erasme, défenseurs d'Epicure. Hommage à K. R. Gallas. (NPh, 23). Groningen, 1938.
Franke, O. **EURIPIDES** bei den deutschen Dramatikern des achtzehnten Jahrhunderts. Leipzig, 1929.
Friedrich, W. H. Euripideisches in der lateinischen Literatur. H, 1934.
Harden, M. Euripides und Sophocles in Berlin. Gegenwart, 1890.
Lucas, F. L. Euripides and his Influence. In: Our Debt to Greece & Rome. Boston, 1923.

Schapiro, E. Der Einfluss des Euripides auf die Tragödie des Cinquecento. München, 1935.

Spranger, J. A. Le letture euripidee d'un cinquecentisto, Martin Crusius. SIFC, 11, 1934.

Herzog-Hauser, G. Ennius und Euripides. Commentationes Vindobonenses, 1, 1935.

—— Ennius imitateur d'Euripide. Latomus, 1938.

Roeser, W. Ennius, Euripides und Homer. Würzburg, 1939.

Crane, F. D. Euripides, Erasmus and Lady Lumley. CJ, 39, 1944.

Fries, K. Goethe und Euripides. Archiv, 99, 1897.

Lotholz. Goethe über Euripides. JbGG, 24, 1903.

Hanne. Euripides und Ibsen. HG, 25, 1914.

Ermatinger, E. Eine moderne französische Bearbeitung des Euripideischen Ion (L'Apollonide von Leconte de Lisle). NJKA, 6, 1900.

Krick, F. J. Racines Verhältniss zu Euripides. Progr. Aachen, 1884-1890.

Mayer, P. Euripides, Racine und Goethe. Progr. Gera, 1850-54. And in: Studien zu Homer, Sophocles. Leipzig, 1874.

Jonas, F. Zu Schillers Uebersetzungen aus dem Euripides. ALG, 7, 1878.

Kohl, R. Zu Schillers Uebersetzungen des Euripides. Euphorion, 1921.

Luzzatto, G. L. Schiller traduttore di Euripide. Dioniso, 3. 1932.

Cunningham, F. Euripides and Shakespeare. Athenaeum, 2316, 1872.

Ritter, O. Thomson and Euripides. Archiv, 107, 1902.

Nolhac, P. de. Le premier travail français sur Euripide: la traduction de François Tissard. Mélanges Henri Weil. Paris, 1898.

Luzzatto, G. L. Franz Werfel e le Troiane di Euripide. Dioniso, 4, 1934.

Sciacca, M. F. L'Elogio di Elena di **GORGIA** e l'Orazione inaugurale di Ugo Foscolo. Giornale critico della filosofia italiana, 1936.

Ellinger, G. Theagenes und Chariklea. Fortleben des **HELIODORISCHEN** Romans. Vierteljahrschrift f. Litteraturgeschichte, 5, 1892.

Oeftering, M. Heliodor und seine Bedeutung für die Litteratur. Berlin, 1901.

Tuechert, A. Racine und Holiodor. Zweibrücken, 1889.

Jensen, C. **HERAKLEIDES** vom Pontos bei Philodem und Horaz. SAWB, 1936.

Walcker, N. Heraclit und die deutsche Romantik. Tübingen, 1923.

Bapp, K. Aus Goethes griechischer Gedankenwelt. Goethe und Heraklit, nebst Studien über des Dichters Beteiligung an der Altertumswissenschaft. Leipzig, 1921.

Mariano, R. Lassalle e il suo Eraclito: saggio di filosofia egheliana. Firenze, 1865.

Françon, M. Petrarch, Disciple of Heraclitus. Spec., 11, 1936.

Post, G. Petrarch and Heraclitus once more. Spec., 1937.

Mayer, G. Heraklit von Ephesus und Arthur Schopenhauer. Heidelberg, 1886.

Egger, E. L'art de traduire et les traducteurs français d'**HERODOTE.** Mém. du Congrès scient. Amiens, 1867.

Estienne, H. L'introduction au traité de la conformité des merveilles anciennes avec les modernes: ou traité préparatif à l'Apologie pour Hérodote. Lyon, 1592.

Colonna, A. Traduzioni ottocentesche di Erodoto in Italia e la questione del dialetto erodoteo. Atti della Società ital. per il Progresso delle Scienze, 28, 1940.

Fowler, H. T. Herodotus and the Early Hebrew Historians. Journal of Biblical Lit., 1930.

Raddatz, G. Herodotus' Bedeutung für die Gegenwart. Deutsches Philologenblatt. Leipzig, 1916.

Blake, W. E. Cicero's Greek Text of Herodotus. AJPh, 1944.

Anon. Dante and Herodotus. Athenaeum. 3884, 1902.

Jorgenson, C. E. Benjamin Franklin and Rabelais. CJ, 29, 1934.

Anon. Goethe, Sophokles und Herodot. Frankfurter Zt., 22.VII.1899.

Eichtal, E. d'. Hérodote et Victor Hugo, à propos du poème Les Trois Cents. REG, 1902.

Powell, J. E. Scaliger on Herodotus. CR, 1938.

Stoltenhoff, H. Wie Schiller im Ring des Polykrates Herodots Bericht benutzt hat. ZDU, 17, 1902.

Koller, K. A Source for Portions of The Witch of Atlas. (Shelley). MLN, 52, 1937.

Méautis, G. L'actualité d'**HESIODE.** RU, 2, 1929.

Cavalli, A. Reminiscenze esiodee del libro di Daniele. (Bible). Ricerche Religiose, 7, 1931.

Bennetts, J. W. Spenser's Hesiod. AJPh, 1931.

Wickert, L. De Nicolao de Valle Hesiodi et Homeri interprete. Breslau, 1922.
Engel, J. **ISOKRATES**, Machiavelli, Fichte. Progr. Magdeburg, 1889.
Beugnot, Cte. **LIBANIUS** et les Sophistes. Le Correspondant, 7, 1844.
Foerster, R. Francesco Zambeccari und die Briefe des Libanius. Stuttgart, 1878. Cf. ZRPh, 3.
Beers, Cora L. **LONGINUS** and the Disintegration of English Neo-Classicism. Diss. Stanford U., 1940.
Einarson, B. Longinus' On the Sublime and Sir Joshua Reynolds Discourses on Art. Chicago, 1945.
Elledge, S. Cowley's Ode of Wit and Longinus. MLQ, 9, 1948.
Hamel A. G. van. Een Ijslandsche Longinus-legende. NPh, 28, 1943.
Henn, T. R. Longinus and English Criticism. Cambridge, 1934.
Nitchie, E. Longinus and Later Literary Criticism. CW, 27, 1934.
Pritchard, J. P. Lowell and Longinus. TAPhA, 1945.
Rosenberg, A. Longinus in England bis zum Ende des 18. Jahrhunderts. Diss. Berlin, 1917.
Rostagni, A. Il Sublime nella storia dell'estetica antica. Annali della Scuola Normale Superiore di Pisa, 1933.
Thompson, D. W. Montani, Saint-Evremond and Longinus. MLN, 51, 1936.
Hulubei, A. Le roman de **LONGUS**, Daphnis et Chloé et les deux Eglogues latines publiées par Henri Estienne en 1555. C. R. de l'Acad. des Inscript. & Belles Lettres, 1932.
Dalmeyda, G. Henri Estienne et Longus. Revue de Philologie, 1934.
Allison, F. G. **LUCIAN**, Satirist and Artist. In: Our Debt to Greece & Rome. New York, 1927.
Crum, R. H. More Strange Islands. CW, 28, 1935.
Foerster, R. Lucian in der Renaissance. ALG, 14, 1886.
Friedman, Miriam. Lucian in English Literature, 1683-1795. Diss. Cornell U., 1938.
Peretti, A. Luciano: un intellettuale greco contro Roma. Firenze, 1946.
Schenck, L. Lukian und die französische Literatur im Zeitalter der Aufklärung. Diss. München, 1931.
Schulze, P. Lucian in der Literatur und Kunst der Renaissance. Progr. Dessau, 1906.
Sinko, T. Wojny gramatyczne. Eos, 1937.
Thompson, C. R. The Date of the First Aldine Lucian. CJ, 35, 1940.
Frantz, M. de. Ueber das Verhältnis des Lukian und des Apuleius zur Urquelle der Eselsgeschichte. Opuscula Philologica 6, (Wien), 1934.
Bauer, A. Der Einfluss des Lukian von Samosata auf die Dialogi Septem festiue candidi authore S. Abydeno des Crotus Rubeanus. Münchener Museum 3.
Craig, H. Dryden's Lucian. CPh, 1921.
Ryba, B. Eneas Silvius et Lukianos. Listy Filologicke, 1930.
Caccia, N. Note sulla fortuna di Luciano nel rinascimento. Le versioni e i dialoghi satirici di Erasmo da Rotterdam e di Ulrico Hutten. Milano, 1915.
Heep, Martha. Die Colloquia familiaria des Erasmus und Lucian. Diss. Halle-Wittenberg, 1927.
Thompson, C. R The Translations of Lucian by Erasmus and St. Thomas More. Ithaca, 1940.
—— Erasmus' Translation of Lucian's Longaevi. CPh, 1940.
Lind, L. R. Lucian and Fielding. CW, 29, 1936.
Beauvillé, G. de. Gaspare Gozzi traducteur de Lucien et de Klopstock. REI, 1938.
Cameron, K. W. John Heywood's Play of the Wether; A Study in Early Tudor Drama. Raleigh (N.C.), 1941.
Bauer, A. Der Einfluss Lukians von Samosata auf Ulrich von Hutten. Ph, 75-76, 1918.
Gewerstock, O. Lucian und U. von Hutten. Zur Geschichte des Dialogs im 16. Jahrhundert. Berlin, 1924.
Newlin, C. M. Lucian and Liutprand. Spec,. 1927.
Mele, E. Lope de Vega, Merlin Cocai e Luciano. GSLI, 112, 1938.
Becker, P. A. Clement Marot und Lukian. Neuphilol. Mitteilungen. (Helsingfors), 1922.
Disbel, T. Die erste Verdeutschung des 12. Lukianischen Todtengesprächs nach einer urtextlichen Handschrift von Joh. Reuchlin (1495) und Verwandtes aus der Folgezeit. ZVL, 8, 1895.
—— Die zweite Verdeutschung des 12. Lukianischen Todtengesprächs durch Ringmann. Ibid., 11, 1898.
Fox, S. Lucian in the Grave-Scene of Hamlet. Trans. Royal Society of Canada, 17, 1923.
Geigenmueller, P. Lucian und Wieland. NJWJ, 1927.
Kersten. Wielands Verhältnis zu Lucian. Progr. Hamburg-Cuxhaven, 1900.

Steinberger, J. Lucians Einfluss auf Wieland. Diss. Göttingen, 1902.
Tropsch. Lucian in Wielands Geschichte des Prinzen Biribinker. ZVL, 12, 1899.
Pokrovsky, M. **MENANDRE** et ses imitateurs romains. Bull. Acad. Léningrad, 1934.
Todesco, A. Da Menandro alla commedia classica italiana. A&R, 1916.
Flickinger, R. C. Terence and Menander. CJ, 1931.
—— Terence and Menander Once More. Ibid., 1933.
Klotz, A. Der Eunuchus des Terenz und seine Vorlagen. Würzburger Jb. f. d. Altertumswissenschaft, 1, 1946.
Knoche, U. Terenz oder Menander. H, 1941.
Kuiper, W. E. J. Grieksche origineelen en latijnsche navolgingen zes komedies van Menander bij Terentius en Plautus. Amsterdam, 1936.
—— Terentius en Menander. NPh, 21, 1936.
Post, L. A. Menander and Terence. CW, 26, 1932.
Bolte, J. Jacob Rosefeldts **MOSCHUS**, eine Parallele zum Kaufmann von Venedig. JbShG, 21, 1886.
Hutton, J. The First Idyl of Moschus in Imitations to the Year 1800. AJPh, 49, 1928.
Fucilla, J. G. Additions to The First Idyl of Moschus in Imitations to the Year 1800. Ibid., 1929.
—— Materials for the History of a Popular Classical Theme. CPh, 1931.
Maxwell, S. An Addition to The First Idyl of Moschus in Imitations to the Year 1800. AJPh, 1943.
Tait, Jane J. M. **PHILODEMUS'** Influence on the Latin Poets. Bryn Mawr (Pa.), 1941.
Brower, R. A. The Theban Eagle in English Plumage (**PINDAR**). CPh, 43, 1948.
Gallavotti, C. Frammenti di un ditirambo di Pindaro in una poesia bizantina. Rivista di filologia e d'istruzione classica, 1931.
Lempicki, Z. Pindare jugé par les gens de lettres du 17e et du 18e siècle. Bull. de l'Acad. polonaise de Cracovie, 1930.
Robinson, D. M. Pindar and his Influence. TAPhA, 1935.
Wagner, R. Zum Wiederaufleben der antiken Musikschriftsteller seit dem 16. Jahrhundert. Ein Beitrag zur Frage: Kircher oder Pindar? Ph, 1936.
Allen, D. C. Cowley's Pindar. MLN, 63, 1948.
Silver, I. Did Du Bellay Know Pindar? PMLA, 56, 1941.
—— Pindaric Parallelism in Du Bellay. FR, 14, 1941.
Teza, E. Un centone pindarico nelle opere di U. Foscolo. Rassegna bibliografica della letteratura italiana, 9, 1901.
Kuk, F. Goethe und Pindar. HG, 1919.
Reiff. Pindar and Goethe. MLN, 18, 1903.
Koch, W. Das Fortleben Pindars in der deutschen Literatur von den Anfängen bis Andreas Gryphius. Heidelberg, 1927. Cf. Euphorion, 28, 1927.
Hohoff, C. Ueber den Einfluss Pindars und Sophokles' auf Hölderlins Sprache. NR, 51, 1940.
Scheller, W. Pindar und Hölderlin. LE, 15.IV.1912.
Zuntz, G. Ueber Hölderlins Pindar-Uebersetzung. Jahresber. des Friedrich Gymnasiums. Kassel, 1928.
Fraenkel, E. Das Pindargedicht des Horaz. SHAW, 1932-33.
Harms, E. Horaz in seinen Beziehungen zu Pindar. Marburg, 1935.
Highbarger, E. L. The Pindaric Style of Horace. TAPhA, 1935.
Gavel, H. De Pindare à Mistral en passant par Ronsard. Hommage à Ernest Martinenche, Paris, 1939.
Silver, I. The Pindaric Odes of Ronsard. Paris, 1937.
—— Ronsard and Du Bellay on Their Pindaric Collaboration. RR, 33, 1942.
Vaganay, H. Les odes pindariques après Ronsard. Macon, 1923.
Vianey, J. Le modèle de Ronsard dans l'ode pindarique. RLR, 43, 1900-01.
Kerényi, K. Zu Vergils Aeneid VI, Pindar, Platon und Dante. PhW, 1923.
Beaussire, E. De summi apud Britannos poetas tragoediis e **PLUTARCHO** ductis. Diss. Grenoble, 1855.
Borowski, B. Zu Plutarchs Einwirkung auf die puritanische Lebensformung. Anglia, 64, 1940.
Dezeimeris, R. Etude bibliographique et critique sur une version peu connue des Moralia de Plutarque. Bordeaux, 1904.
Gabele, A. Der Einfluss der Pseudo-Plutarchischen Erziehungsschrift auf italienische und französische Humanisten. Koblenz, 1921.
Hahn, W. Plutarque dans la littérature polonaise. (In Polish). Cracovie, 1922.
Lockwood, D. P. Plutarch in the Fourteenth Century. TAPhA, 1933.
Pizzagalli, A. M. Plutarco e il cristianesimo. A&R, 1943.

Uxkull-Gyllenband, W. Plutarch und die griechische Biographie. Stuttgart, 1929.
Weinreich, O. Zur Schätzung Plutarchs im Frankreich des 17. Jahrhunderts. WS, 1940.
Albalat, A. Amyot et Plutarque. Le Foyer, 1, 1915.
Blignières, A. de. Essai sur Amyot et les traducteurs français du XVIe siècle. Paris, 1851.
Dassenbacher, J. Amyot als Uebersetzer der Lebensbeschreibung des Perikles von Plutarch. Progr. Prag, 1887.
Jaeger, J. Zur Kritik von Amyots Uebersetzungen der Moralia Plutarchs. Diss. Heidelberg, 1899.
Weinberg, B. A False First Edition of Amyot's Plutarch. MLN, 61, 1946.
Goodenough, M. L. Bacon and Plutarch. MLN, 12, 1897.
Dezeimeris, R. Remarques et corrections d'Estienne de La Boétie sur le traité de Plutarque. Paris, Bordeaux, 1867.
Anon. Plutarch's Lives. The Translation called Dryden's. NAR, Oct., 1859.
Pemberton (ed.). Queen Elizabeth's Englishings of Boethius, Plutarch, etc. London, 1901.
Delcourt, M. Jodelle et Plutarque. BAGB, 1934.
Liebeschuetz, H. John of Salisbury and Pseudo-Plutarch. JWI, 6, 1943.
Zetowski, S. La traduction des Moralia de Plutarque au XVIe siècle par Nicolas Kochanowski. (In Polish). Minerva, 1922.
Vianey, J. Comment Montaigne corrige des récits de Plutarque traduits par Amyot. Actes du Congrès G. Budé à Strasbourg. Paris, 1939.
North, Sir Thomas. Plutarch's Lives of the Noble Grecians and Romans. Preface by G. Wyndham. In: The Tudor translations (ed. by W. E. Henley). London, 1892-96.
Lefranc, A. Deux Plutarques inconnus de la bibliothèque de Rabelais. In: Extrait de l'Amateur d'autographes, 1901.
Krappe, A. H. Pierre de Ronsard's Hymne de la mort and Plutarch's Consolatio ad Apollonium. MLR, 17, 1922.
Keller, A. C. Plutarch and Rousseau's First Discours. PMLA, 54.
Fries, K. Schiller und Plutarch. NJKA, 1, 1898.
Adler, F. Das Verhältniss von Shakespeares Antony and Cleopatra zu Plutarchs Biographie des Antonius. JbShG, 31, 1895.
Delius, N. Shakespeares Coriolanus in seinem Verhältniss zum Coriolanus des Plutarch. Ibid., 11, 1876.
Heuer, H. Shakespeare und Plutarch. Anglia, 62, 1938.
John, E. Plutarch und Shakespeare. Progr. Wertheim. a.M., 1889-1891.
Law, R. A. The Text of Shakespeare's Plutarch. HLQ, 6, 1943.
Sigismund, R. Uebereinstimmendes zwischen Shakespeare und Plutarch. JbShG, 18, 1883.
Stiftar, B. Shakespeare et Plutarque. Hermes, messager scientifique et populaire de l'antiquité classique en Russie, 1918.
Vollmer, A. Shakespeare und Plutarch. Archiv, 77-78, 1887.
Chinard, G. **POLYBIUS** and the American Constitution. JHI, 1, 1940.
Bini, A. Polibio e il Machiavelli. Montevarchi, 1900.
Fluegel, E. Ueber einige Stellen aus dem Almagestum Cl. **PTOLEMEI** bei Chaucer und im Rosenroman. Anglia, 18, 1895.
Boll, F. Chaucer und Ptolemaeus. Ibid, 21, 1898.
Brunschvicg, L. Le rôle du **PYTHAGORISME** dans l'évolution des idées. Paris, 1937.
Atanassievitch, X. L'influence des Pythagoriciens sur un philosophe italien. (Bruno). Rev. de l'U. de Bruxelles, 32.
Arnold, N. The **SAPPHIC** Ode in the Swiss Drama of the XVIth Century. GR, 16, 1941.
Cipollini, A. Saffo (in modern dramas). Milano, 1890.
Cox, E. M. Sappho and the Sapphic Metre in English. London, 1916.
Miranda, E. E. Safo en castellano. Bol. de la Acad. Argentina de Letras, 7, 1939.
Moravcsik, G. Die Spuren der Kenntnis von Sappho in Byzanz. (In Hungarian). EPhK, 1937.
Robinson, D. M. Sappho and her Influence. In: Our Debt to Greece and Rome. Boston, 1924.
Rüdiger, H. Sappho, ihr Ruf und Ruhm bei der Nachwelt. Leipzig, 1933.
—— Geschichte der deutschen Sappho-Uebersetzungen. Berlin, 1934.
Weddigen, O. Die dramatischen Bearbeitungen der Sappho in der deutschen Literatur. Deutsche Dramaturgie, 1, 1895. And in: Aufsätze & Reden. Wald, 1903.
Widmann, W. Sappho in der drama-

tischen Dichtung und Musik. Merker, 9, 1918.

Bickel, E. Catulls Werbegedicht an Clodia und Sapphos Phaonklage im Hochzeitslied an Agallis. RhM, 1940.

Connely, W. Imprints of Sappho on Catullus. CJ, 20.

Franz, W. Catulls Sapphoübertragung. H, 1930.

Gallavotti, C. Interpretando Saffo e poi Catullo. A&R, 1943.

Bartoletti, V. Saffo ed Orazio. SIFC, 1938.

Murphy, R. Two Paraphrases by A. E. Housman. CJ, 37, 1941.

Miranda, E. E. Safo en La Celestina y en la Imitación de diversos de Fray Luis de León. Bol. de la Acad. Argentina de Letras, 7, 1939.

Elledge, S. Milton, Sappho (?) and Demetrius. MLN, 58, 1943.

Hubaux, J. Ovide et Sappho. Musée belge, 1926.

Bonfante, G. Pascoli e Saffo. Ital., 21, 1944.

Cranfill, T. M. Barnaby Rich's Sappho and The Weakest Goeth to the Wall. Texas Studies in English, 1945-46.

Jourdain, C. **SEXTUS EMPIRICUS** et la philosophie scolastique. Paris, 1858.

Oates, W. J. The Influence of **SIMONIDES** of Ceos upon Horace. Princeton, 1932.

Bergmann, J. **SOKRATES** in der jüdischen Literatur. Monatsschrift f. Geschichte d. Judentums, 80, 1936.

Boehm, B. Sokrates im 18. Jahrhunder.t Leipzig, 1929.

Brenning, E. Die Gestalt des Sokrates in der Litteratur des vorigen Jahrhunderts. Festschrift Bremen, 1899.

Carrière, M. Sokrates und seine Stellung in der Geschichte des menschlichen Geistes. WM, 16, 1864.

Cielen, M. Socrates' veroordeeling gezien van uit de 20e eeuw. N&V, 15, 1933.

Friedlaender, P. Socrates Enters Rome. AJPh, 1945.

Glaser, R. Sokrates und Plato und der christliche Religionsunterricht. Monatsblatt f. evang. Religionsunterricht, 17.

Hertel. Sokrates in der deutschen Dichtung der Aufklärung. München, 1921.

Meunier, M. La légende de Socrate. Paris, 1926.

Millet, R. Socrate et la pensée moderne. 4th ed. Paris, 1920.

Deman, T. Socrate dans l'oeuvre de S. Thomas d'Aquin. Rev. des Sciences philos. et théologiques, 1940.

Gummere, R. M. Socrates at the Printing Press. Benjamin Franklin and the Classics. CW, 26, 1932.

Larock, V. Socrate, Gandhi. In: Serta Leodensia. Liège, 1930.

Kupfer, J. Die Auffassung des Sokrates in Hegels Geschichtsphilosophie. Leipzig, 1927.

Spranger, E. Hegel über Sokrates. SAWB, 1938.

Boulan, E. François Hemsterhuis, le Socrate hollandais. Paris, 1924.

Wagner, G. Hölderlin und die Vorsokratiker. Würzburg, 1937.

Deman, T. Socrate et Jésus. Paris, 1944.

Rilliet, J. Kierkegaard et Socrate. Rev. de Théologie et de Philosophie, 1943.

Hasse, H. Das Problem des Sokrates bei Friedrich Nietzsche. Leipzig, 1918.

Kaufmann, W. A. Nietzsche's Admiration for Socrates. JHI, 9, 1948.

Bakelants, L. Socrate e Petrarca. Misura, 2, 1947.

Ricard, R. Notes et matériaux pour l'étude du Socratisme chrétien chez Sainte Thérèse et les spirituels espagnols. BH, 49, 1947.

Anon. **SOPHOKLES** auf der Pariser Bühne. Beilage zur Allg. Zt., 16.VI. 1844.

Luzzatto, G. L. Traduzioni e imitazioni antiche di Sofocle. Dioniso, 6, 1937-38.

Schildknecht, W. Deutscher Sophokles. Beiträge zur Geschichte der Tragödie in Deutschland. Würzburg, 1935.

Sheppard, J. T. Aeschylus and Sophocles. In: Our Debt to Greece and Rome. New York, 1927.

Moore, J. A. Sophocles and Arete. Harvard U.P., 1938.

Anon. Matthew Arnold and Sophocles. N&Q, 22.I.1938.

Humbert, C. Boileau und Racine, die grössten Verächter Senecas und die grössten Bewunderer Sophocles' und der Griechen. Franco-Gallia, 9, 1892.

Zingg, H. I. Sophokles und Cocteau. Schweizer Rundschau, 1947.

Emmert, E. Hölderlin und die griechische Tragödie. Untersuchungen der Anmerkungen und Uebersetzungen von Sophokles' Tragödien. Freiburg, 1928.

Seebass, F. Hölderlins Sophocles-Uebertragungen im zeitgenössischen Urteil. Ph, 1921.

Wolff, W. Sophokles und Hölderlin. Nationalzeitung, 105. 5.III.1947.

Gordon, W. Die dramatische Handlung in Sophokles' Koenig Oidipus und Kleist's Der zerbrochene Krug. Halle, 1926.

Hewes. Beitrag zur Würdigung der

Opitzschen Uebersetzung der Sophokleischen Antigone. Progr. Warendorf, 1890.
Notopoulos, J. A. Sophocles and Captain Craig. (E. A. Robinson). NEQ, 17, 1944.
Weber, C. J. E. A. Robinson's Translation of Sophocles. Ibid.
Henderson, W. A. Shakespeare and Sophocles. N&Q, 28.X.1893.
Lichtenstein, S. Shakespeare und Sophokles. Diss. München, 1850.
Stoll, E. E. Reconciliation in Tragedy: Shakespeare and Sophocles. UTQ, 4, 1934.
Flügel, E. Shelleys Sophocles. Anglia, 24, 1901.
Bignone, E. Modernità e italianità di **TEOCRITO**. NAnt, 16.XII.1939.
Hulubei, A. Traductions, adaptations et imitations des idylles de Théocrite, en France, au XVIe siècle. Actes du Congrès G. Budé à Strasbourg. Paris, 1939.
Kerlin, R. T. Theocritus in English Literature. Lynchburg (Va.), 1910.
Labarbe, M. Les idylles non-bucoliques de Théocrite et leur influence sur la poésie latine. RBPh, 1936.
Schaffer, A. A Theocritean Idyll in French Poetry. (Chénier). MLN, 62, 1947.
Pughe, F. John Drydens Uebersetzungen aus Theokrit. Diss. Breslau, 1894.
Hazen, A. T. & Mabbott, T. O. Dr. Johnson and Francis Fawkes's Theocritus. RES, 21, 1945.
Beatty, Frederika. Theocritus in Hampstead (Keats). CJ, 43, 1948.
Kuiper, W. E. J. Leconte de Lisle en Theocritus. NPh, 4, 1918.
McCartney, E. S. Nicean Barks Once More. (Poe). CJ, 34, 1939.
Garin, F. La Expositio Theocriti di Angelo Poliziano nello studio fiorentino. Rivista di filologia e d'istruzione classica, 1914.
Stedman, E. C. Tennyson and Theocritus. AM, Nov., 1871.
Cesareo, E. Teocrito e Virgilio bucolico. Convivium, 1934.
Kappelmacher, A. Vergil und Theocrit. WS, 47, 1929.
Paiva Boléo, M. de. O bucolismo de Teócrito e Vergilio. Coimbra, 1936.
Broughton, L. N. The Theocritean Element in the Works of W. Wordsworth. Halle, 1920.
Boyce, B. & Greenough, C. N. The **THEOPHRASTAN** Character in England to 1642. Harvard U.P., 1947.
Greenough, C. N. & French, J. M. A Bibliography of the Theophrastan Character in English. Harvard U.P., 1947.
Lichtenberg, K. Der Einfluss des Theophrast auf die englischen Characterwriters des 17. Jahrhunderts. Berlin, 1921.
Milt, B. Schweizerische Theophrastforschung und schweizerische Theophrasteditionen im 16. Jahrhundert. Gesnerus, 3, 1946.
Pfeiffer, R. Zu Uebersetzungen der Theophrastischen Charaktere. BBG, 53.
Spinck, J. S. La diffusion des idées matérialistes et anti-religieuses au début du XVIIe siècle: Le Théophrastus redivivus. RHLF, 44.
Gelderblom, G. Die Charaktertypen Theophrasts, Labruyères, Gellerts und Rabeners. GRM, 14, 1926.
Michaut, G. La Bruyère et Théophraste. Annales de l'U. de Paris, March, 1936.
Navarre, O. La Bruyère, traducteur de Théophraste. REG, 27, 1914.
Van de Woestijne, P. Un traducteur de Théophraste, Jean de la Bruyère. Musée belge, 1929.
—— Notes sur six caractères de Théophraste traduits par La Bruyère. RBPh, 1934.
—— Les sources du Discours sur Théophraste de Jean de La Bruyère. Ibid., 1936.
Senn, G. Descartes und Theophrast von Eresos. Gesnerus, 2, 1945.
Tocco, F. Leopardi e Teofrasto. A&R, 2, 1900.
Reitzenstein, E. Theophrast bei Epikur und Lukrez. In: Orient und Antike. Heidelberg, 1924.
Cochrane, C. N. **THUCYDIDES** and the Science of History. Oxford U.P., 1929.
Dain, A. Thucydide au XVIIe siècle. Actes du Congrès G. Budé à Strasbourg. Paris, 1939.
Strebel, H. G. Wertung und Wirkung des thukydideischen Geschichtswerkes in der griechisch-römischen Literatur: Eine literargeschichtliche Studie nebst einem Exkurs über Appian als Nachahmer Thukydides. München, 1935.
Lillge, F. Eine Thukydidesreminiscenz bei Goethe. Zs. f.d. Gymnasialwesen, 1916.
Schlatter, R. Thomas Hobbes and Thucydides. JHI, 6, 1945.
Bennezon. Les procédés dans les discours de Salluste et l'influence de Thucydide. REL, 1935.

Patzer, H. Sallust und Thukydides. NJAB, 1941.
Powell, J. U. The Papyri of Thucydides and the Translation of Laurentius Valla. CQ, 1929.
Westgate, R. I. W. The Text of Valla's Translation of Thucydides. TAPhA, 1936.
Muenscher, K. **XENOPHON** in der griechisch-römischen Literatur. Leipzig, 1920.
Keseling, P. Xenophons Anabasis in Livius' Buch XXI? PhW, 1936.
Gustafson, Lorraine. Xenophon and Der Tod in Venedig. (Mann). GR, 21, 1946.
Gemoll, W. Ein Xenophonzitat bei dem Apostel Paulus. PhW, 932.
Keseling, P. Xenophons Anabasis in Sallusts Bellum Iugurthinum? Ibid., 1936.
Skard, E. Xenophon-Sallust. Ibid., 1925.
Herchner, H. Die Cyropaedie in Wielands Werken. Progr. Berlin, 1892-96.

CHAPTER FOURTEEN

The Greek Language.

(See also Humanism, III. II. 3.)

Altaner, B. Die Kenntnis des Griechischen in den Missionsorden während des 13. und 14. Jahrhunderts. Zs. f. Kirchengeschichte, 1934.
Apraiz. Apuntes para una historia de los estudios elenicos en España. Madrid, 1876.
Arland. De Gallici sermonis cum Graeco convenientia. Progr. Berlin, 1826.
Bywater, I. Four Centuries of Greek Learning in England. Oxford, 1919.
Capeller, G. Die wichtigsten aus dem Griechischen gebildeten Wörter (mots savants) der französischen und englischen Sprache. Progr. Gumbinnen, 1889-92.
Comparetti, D. Saggi dei dialetti greci dell' Italia meridionale. Pisa, 1866.
Curione, A. Sullo studio del greco in Italia nei secoli XVII-XVIII. Roma, 1941.
Delaruelle, E. La connaissance du groc en Occident du Ve au IXe siècle. Bull. de l'U. de Toulouse, 45, 1937.
Drerup, E. Die Schulaussprache des Griechischen von der Renaissance bis zur Gegenwart im Rahmen einer allgemeinen Geschichte des griechischen Unterrichts. Paderborn, 1930.
Dumont, Dr. Etude du grec en France pendant les XVIe, XVIIe, XVIIIe siècles. Mém. de la Soc. académique, 23. Angers, 1868.
Estienne, H. Traité de la conformité du language françois avec le grec. Genève, 1565.
Flachel, H. Unsere griechischen Fremdwörter. Leipzig, 1902.
Gatta, M. Dizionario etimologico delle voci di origine greca più usitate. Milano, 1867.
Gerretzen, J. G. Schola Hemsterhusiana. De herleving der Grieksche studiën aan de Nederl. Universiteiten in de 18e eeuw. Nijmegen, 1940.
Heiberg, J. L. Gjenoplivelsen af studiet af Graesk. Studien fra sprog- og oldtidsforskning. 1, Kjøbenhavn, 1891.
Huit, C. Notes sur l'état des études grecques en Italie et en France du XIVe au XVIe siècle. REG, 14, 1901.
Kelsey, F. W. Latin and Greek in American Education, with Symposia on the Value of Humanistic Studies. New York, 1927.
Kent, R. G. Language and Philology. In: Our Debt to Greece & Rome. New York, 1930.
Laistner, L. W. The Revival of Greek in Western Europe in the Carolingian Age. History, 9, 1924.
Laubert, E. Die griechischen Fremdwörter im Deutschen. Berlin, 1869.
Le Glay. L'étude du grec dans les Pays-Bas, avant la Renaissance des lettres. Mém. de la Société d'émulation de Cambrai, 1828.
Mancini, A. Spirito e caratteri dello studio del greco in Italia. In: Italia e Grecia. Firenze, 1940.
Morosi. Studj sui dialetti greci della terra d'Otranto. Lecce, 1870.
Müller, M. M. Der Uebergang von der griechischen zur lateinischen Sprache in der abendländischen Kirche. Roma, 1943.
Pendzig, P. Die Anfänge der griechischen Studien und die deutschen Universitäten. Neue Jb. f. Pädagogik, 1921.
—— Die griechischen Studien im deutschen Mittelalter. Ibid., 42.
Presenti, G. La scuola di greco a Firenze nel primo rinascimento. A&R, 1931.
Prinet, M. Le grec au moyen âge. REA, 1924.
Psichari, J. Les études de grec moderne en France au XIXe siècle. RIE, 1904.
Renieri. De l'usage pratique de la langue grecque. Paris, 1864.
Robertson, D. S. The Future of Greek Studies. Cambridge U.P., 1929.

Rohlfs, G. Griechischer Sprachgeist in Süditalien. München, 1947.
Smith, N. Greek for Students of English Literature. English, 2, 1938.
Steinacker, H. Die römische Kirche und die griechischen Sprachkenntnisse des Frühmittelalters. Festschrift Theodor Gomperz. Wien, 1902.
Stemplinger, E. Von der Aeolsharfe bis zur Xanthippe. Ein kleines Handbuch antiker Redensarten im deutschen Sprachgebrauch. München, 1933.
Stürmer, F. Das Griechische in der deutschen Sprache und Bildung. Breslau, 1932.
Thompson, C. R. Some Greek and Grecized Words in Renaissance Latin. AJPh, 1943.
Tilley, A. Greek Studies in England in the Early Sixteenth Century. EHR, 53, 1938.
Vendryès, J. La connaissance du grec en Irlande au début du moyen âge. REG, 1920.
Vogelreuter, O. Geschichte des griechischen Unterrichts in deutschen Schulen seit der Reformation. Hannover, 1891.
Voigt. Ueber formale und syntaktische Aehnlichkeiten der französischen und griechischen Sprache. Progr. Eisenberg, 1875.
Weileder. Griechisch als Weltsprache. Versammlung d. Freunde d. human. Gymnasiums. Hamm, 1927.
Wilkie, J. R. The Intrinsic Adolescent Appeal in the Study of Greek. CJ, 1926.

CHAPTER FIFTEEN

Byzantium.

Ebersolt, J. Orient et Occident. Les influences byzantines et orientales en France pendant les Croisades. Paris, 1929.
Gregoire, H. & Goossens, R. Byzantinisches Epos und arabischer Ritterroman. ZDMG, 13, 1934.
Mazon, A. Byzance et la Russie. Rev. d'hist. de la philos., 15.VII.1937.
Mercier, E. La spiritualité byzantine. L'Orient grec et chrétien. Paris, 1934.
Neumann, K. Byzantinische Kultur und Renaissance Kultur. Stuttgart, 1903.
Romein, J. Die Anfänge der Byzantinistik in Holland (1568-1655). Festgabe Heisenberg. Byzantinische Zs., 30.
Théry, G. Rôle des Byzantins dans l'activité littéraire de l'abbaye de Saint-Denis au IXe siècle. C. R. de l'Acad. des Inscriptions et Belles-Lettres, 1934.
Weingart, M. Les chroniques byzantines dans la littérature slave ecclésiastique. Bratislava, 1922-23.
Wesselski, A. Die gelehrten Sklavinnen des Islams (1001 Nächte) und ihre byzantinischen Vorbilder. Archiv Orientalni, 9, 1937.

CHAPTER SIXTEEN

Modern Greece (Philhellenism).

Anon. Hellene and Philhellene. TLS, 13. V.1949.
Andreades, A. Le philhellénisme genevois. Messager d'Athènes, 25.XII.1931.
Arnold, R. F. Der deutsche Philhellenismus. Wien, 1896. Cf. Euphorion, 2.
Asse, E. L'indépendance de la Grèce et les poètes de la Restauration. In: Les Petits Romantiques. Paris, 1900.
Babeau, A. Le mouvement philhellène sous la Restauration. Monde moderne, April, 1897. And in: Frankfurter Zt., 11-12.IV.1897.
Bikelas, D. Le philhellénisme en France. Revue d'histoire diplomatique, 5, 1891.
Buk, H. A. Kleine Beiträge zur Kenntnis des deutschen Philhellenismus. Byzant.-neugriech. Jahrbücher, 1920.
Counson, A. Navarin. Poésie et liberté: un siècle de Philhellénisme. RLC, 9, 1929.
Csia, K. Der Philhellenismus. (In Hungarian). Minerva-Könyvtar, 141. (Budapest), 1941.
Dieterich, K. Deutsche Philhellenen in Griechenland, 1821-22. Hamburg, 1929.
Earle, E. M. American Interest in the Greek Cause, 1821-27. AHR, 1927.
Eloesser, A. Die jüngste litterarische Entwicklung in Frankreich, I. Neu-Hellenismus. MLIA, 1896.
Kerofilas, C. La Grecia e l'Italia nel Risorgimento italiano. Firenze, 1919.
Kosikar, A. Zur Geschichte des deutschen Philhellenismus. National-Zt., 222, 1897.
Laistner, M. L. W. Le philhellénisme allemand (1821-27). L'Acropole, 5, 1930.
—— Le philhellénisme américain (1821-28). Ibid.
Latreille, C. La guerre de l'indépendance grecque dans la littérature française. Ibid.

Lemaître, J. Le Néo-Hellénisme. RB, 15.XII.1883. And in: Les Contemporains, 1. Paris, 1898.
Maccas, L. Le philhellénisme français d'il y a cent ans. L'Acropole, 5, 1930.
Malakis, E. French Travellers in Greece, 1770-1820, an Early Phase of French Philhellenism. Philadelphia, 1925.
Nye, I. Modern Greek Tragedy (in Europe and America). TAPhA, 1938.
Penn, V. Philhellenism in England. SR, 1936.
—— Philhellenism in Europe. SEER, 1938.
Picard, C. L'indépendance grecque et la résurrection du passé hellénique (1830-1930). L'Acropole, 5, 1930.
Rice, W. G. Early English Travellers to Greece and the Levant. Ann Arbor, 1933.
Ségu, F. Le premier poète romantique philhellène. RHLF, 43.
Ziehen, J. Studien zur Geschichte des Philhellenismus in der französischen Litteratur. Festschrift zur Einweihung des Goethe-Gymnasiums in Frankfurt, 1897.

CHAPTER SEVENTEEN

Greek Influences upon Individual Authors and Works.

Danesi, A. G. Saggio critico sulle tragedie di argomento greco di V. **ALFIERI.** Urbino, 1887.
Ronzy, P. Le grec dans le misogallisme d'Alfieri. Ausonia, 6, 1941.
Del Re, R. L'ellenismo nell' opera artistica di G. d'**ANNUNZIO.** Bologna, 1928.
Tosi, G. Gabriele d'Annunzio en Grèce et la rencontre d'Ulysse. Rev. des Sciences hum., Jan., 1947 & Paris, 1948.
Lockwood, D. P. De Rinucio **ARETINO** graecarum literarum interprete. HSCPh, 24.
Stemplinger, E. Ernst Moritz **ARNDT** und das Griechentum. Neue Jb. für Pädagogik, 1923.
Altaner, B. **AUGUSTINUS** und die griechische Sprache. Doelger-Festschrift. Münster, 1939.
Chevalier, I. S. Augustin et la pensée grecque. Fribourg, 1940.
Draeseke, J. Zur Frage nach den Quellen von Augustins Kenntnis der griechischen Philosophie. Theolog. Studien & Kritiken, (Hamburg), 1916.
Gilson, E. Les sources gréco-arabes de l'augustinisme avicennisant. Archives d'hist. doctrinale et littéraire du moyen âge, 4.
Guilloux, P. Saint Augustin savait-il le grec? Rev. d'histoire ecclésiastique, 21, 1925.
Stella, L. A. Romanità di Marco **AURELIO** nei Colloqui con se stesso in lingua greca. Rendiconti della R. Accad. dei Lincei, 1935.
Lockwood, D. P. Roger **BACON'S** Vision of the Study of Greek. CW, 12.
Bardino, L. L'Argenis di John **BARCLAY** e il romanzo greco. Palermo, 1940.
Ollier, F. Maurice **BARRES** et Sparte. RHLF, 45, 1938.
Badolle, M. L'abbé **J. J. BARTHELEMY** (1716-95) et l'hellénisme en France dans la seconde moitié du XVIIIe siècle. Paris, 1926.
Jacks, L. V. St. **BASIL** and Greek Literature. Washington, 1922.
Mohler, L. Aus **BESSARIONS** Gelehrtenkreis. Abhandlungen, Reden, Briefe von Bessarion, Theodoros Gazes, Michael Apostolios, Andronikos Kallistos. Georgios Trapezuntios, Niccolò Perotti, Niccolò Capranica. Paderborn, 1942.
Allevi, L. L'ellenismo nel libro della Sapienza. **(BIBLE).** Scuola cattolica, 1943.
Brewer, R. R. The Influence of Greek Drama on the Apocalypse of John. Anglican Theolog. Review, 18, 1936.
Dodd, C. H. The Bible and the Greeks. London, 1935.
Michaelis, W. Der Attizismus und das Neue Testament. Zs. f. d. neutestamentl. Wissenschaft, 1923.
Collin, C. **BJOERNSONS** Ueber die Kraft und die griechische Tragödie. München, 1902.
Omont, H. Un helléniste du XVIe siècle: **BLASSET,** Excellence de l'affinité de la langue grecque avec la française. REG, 30, 1917.
DeVane, W. C. **BROWNING** and the Spirit of Greece. Festschrift C. S. Northup. Ithaca, 1940.
Longnon, J. Alexandre **BUCHON,** son voyage en Grèce. Marches de l'Est, 15.IV.1911.
Rebitte. Guillaume **BUDE,** restaurateur des études grecques en France. Paris, 1846.
Jovy, E. Pouvons-nous nous assimiler la pensée grecque ancienne? A propos d'un poète anglais helléniste, Sir Edward **BULWER LYTTON.** Société des Sciences et Arts de Vitry-le-François, 17, 1891-93.

Billeter, G. Jacob **BURCKHARDTS** Auffassung des Griechentums. Zürich, 1903.

Anon. **BYRON** in Greece. Westminster Review, July, 1824.

Brunner, K. Griechenland in Byrons Dichtung. Anglia, Jan., 1936.

Dawson, C. M. Byron and a Greek Folk Song. Yale Library Gazette, 20, 1945.

Hesseling, D. C. Byron en een Nieuwgrieks Volkslied. NPh, 23, 1937-38.

Jebb, R. C. Byron in Greece. In: Modern Greece. London, 1880.

Kraeger, H. Lord Byron und Griechenland. Frankfurter Zt., 23.IV.1897.

Morphopoulos, P. Byron's Translation and Use of Modern Greek Writings. MLN, 54, 1939.

Simmons, E. J. Byron and A Greek Maid. MLR, 27, 1932.

Spender, H. Byron and Greece. London, 1924.

Wyzewa, T. de. Lord Byron en Grèce. Le Temps, 13.XII.1897.

Ziehen, J. Byronstudien zur Geschichte des Philhellenismus. Berichte d. freien deutschen Hochstifts Frankfurt, 12, 1896.

Cappola, G. Il greco di **CARDUCCI.** NAnt, 381, 1935.

Bongi, V. Influssi e motivi ellenistici in due nugae di **CATULLO.** Aevum, 1944.

Hezel, O. Catull und das griechische Epigramm. Stuttgart, 1932.

Valaori, J. Les sources d'inspiration de Catulle. Orpheus, Revista pentru cultura clasica, 3, 1927.

Malakis, E. **CHATEAUBRIAND'S** Contribution to French Philhellenism. MPh, 1928.

Outrey, A. Etude critique des documents sur le séjour de Chateaubriand à Athènes. RHLF, 45, 1938.

Fremy , A. André **CHENIER** et les poètes grecs. Revue indépendante, 14, 1844.

Hartmann, K. M. Chénier-Studien. Jahresbericht d. königl. Gymnasiums. Leipzig, 1893-94.

Zyromski, E. De A. Cheniero poeta quomodo graecos poetas sit imitatus. Diss. Paris, 1897.

Bertolotto, G. G. **CHIABRERA** ellenista? Genova, 1891.

Beltrami, A. L'ellenismo e **CICERONE** oratore. A&R, 1914.

Gaffiot, F. Note sur Cicéron traducteur du grec. REG, 1934.

Humbert, J. A propos de Cicéron traducteur du grec. Mélanges Ernout. Paris, 1940.

Keim, C. Z. Lambinus and the Greek in the Text of Cicero's Letters to Atticus. CW, 32, 1939.

Nairn, J. A. Cicero and his Greek Originals. PCA, 1932.

Phillips, E. D. Cicero and Greek Political Thought. Ibid., 1938.

Poeschl, V. Römischer Staat und griechisches Staatsdenken bei Cicero. Berlin, 1936.

Schaefer, M. Ein frühmittelstoisches System der Ethik bei Cicero. Untersuchung von Ciceros drittem Buche De finibus honorum et malorum nach Aufbau und Zugehörigkeit auf Grund griechischer Quellen zur stoischen Ethik. München, 1934.

Scribner, H. S. Cicero as a Hellenist. CJ, 16.

Trouard, M. A. Cicero's Attitude Towards the Greeks. Chicago, 1942.

Warszawska, S. L'hellénophilie de Cicéron. (In Polish). KK, 5, 1931.

Sanders, L. L'hellénisme de Saint **CLEMENT** de Rome et le Paulinisme. Louvain, 1943.

Cammelli, G. I dotti bizantini e le origini dell'umanesimo, I: Manuele **CRISOLORA.** Firenze, 1941.

Honecker, M. Nikolaus von **CUES** und die griechische Sprache. In: Cusanus-Studien, 2. SHAW, 1938.

Austin, H. D. Notes on the Greek in **DANTE'S** Latin Dictionary. SPh, 44, 1947.

Kalitsounakis, I. E. Matth. **DEVARIS** et l'école hellénique de Rome. Athena, 1914.

Silver, I. **DU BELLAY** and Hellenic Poetry: A Cursory View. PMLA, 60, 1945.

Mesnard, P. **DU VAIR** et le néostoicisme. Rev. d'histoire et philosophie, 2, 1928.

Bywater, I. **ERASMIAN** Pronunciation of Greek and its Precursors. London, 1908.

Giese, R. Erasmus' Greek Studies. CJ, 29, 1934.

Pesenti, G. Vittorino da **FELTRE** e gl'inizii della scuola dí greco in Italia. Athenaeum, 1924.

Boulvé, L. De l'hellénisme chez **FENELON.** Diss. Paris, 1898. Cf. Journal des Débats, 21.V.1898.

Schuster, M. Anselm **FEUERBACH** und das Griechentum. WBFA, 5.

Vivier, R. La patrie de **FOSCOLO.** RBPh, 1935.

—— Italie et Grèce dans la poésie d'Ugo Foscolo. RLC, 15, 1935.

Mierow, C. Ancient Greece as Depicted

in a Medieval Outline of History. (Otto von **FREISING**). CW, 24, 1931.

Nietzki, M. E. **GEIBEL** und das Griechentum. Progr. Stettin, 1914.

Grégoire, H. Une source byzantine du Second Faust. (**GOETHE**). Revue de l'U. de Bruxelles, 1930-31.

Menzel, A. Goethe und die griechische Philosophie. Wien, 1932.

Morsch, H. Goethe und die griechischen Bühnendichter. Progr. Berlin, 1888.

Petsch, R. Goethe und die Griechen. GRM, 20, 1932.

Pfalz. Goethes Wettkampf mit den griechischen Dichtern. Grenzboten, 24, 1889.

Regenbogen, O. Griechische Gegenwart. Zwei Vorträge über Goethes Griechentum. Leipzig, 1942.

Rehm, W. Griechentum und Goethezeit. Leipzig, 1936.

Rouge, J. L'hellénisme à l'époque de Goethe. RG, 28, 1937.

Struve. Zwei Balladen von Goethe (Zauberlehrling, Braut von Korinth), verglichen mit den griechischen Quellen woraus sie geschöpft sind. Kônigsberg, 1826.

Trevelyan, H. The Popular Background to Goethe's Hellenism. London, 1934.

—— Goethe and the Greeks. Cambridge U.P., 1941.

Brown, T. S. Greek Influence on Tiberius **GRACCHUS**. CJ, 42, 1947.

Lascaris, M. L'abbé **GREGOIRE** et la Grèce. La Révolution française, 1932.

Sainte-Beuve, C. A. La Grèce en 1863, par A. **GRENIER**. In: Nouveaux Lundis, 5.

Anon. Ueber den Einfluss der Griechen auf **GRILLPARZER**. Deutsches Volksblatt, 5.II.1903.

Kroymann, J. Grillparzers Begegnung mit dem Griechentum. NJAB, 1942.

Niederhofer, K. Der Einfluss der Griechen auf Grillparzer. Progr. 1892.

Schwering, J. Grillparzers hellenische Trauerspiele auf ihre litterarischen Quellen und Vorbilder geprüft. Paderborn, 1891.

Muckle, J. T. Robert **GROSSETESTE'S** Use of Greek Sources in His Hexameron. Medievalia et Humanistica, 3, 1945.

Ros, J. De studie van het Bibelgrieksch van Hugo **GROTIUS** tot Adolf Deissmann. Nijmegen, 1940.

Heisenberg, A. Die byzantinischen Quellen zu **GRYPHIUS'** Leo Armenius. ZVL, 8, 1895.

Tovar, A. Nuñez de **GUZMAN** sobre el códice B de los bucólicos griegos. RFE, 29, 1945 & Emerita, 3, 1945.

Oesterreich, K. Gerhart **HAUPTMANN** und die Griechen. Eckart, 5, 1911.

Gray, J. G. **HEGEL'S** Hellenic Ideal. New York, 1941.

Stenzel, J. Hegels Auffassung der griechischen Philosophie. F&F, 7, 1931.

Sells, A. L. **HEREDIA'S** Hellenism. MLR, 37, 1942.

Vianey, J. Les sonnets grecs de Hérédia. RCC, 1911.

Loane, G. G. **HERRICK'S** Sources. N&Q, 30.III.1940.

Blanken, G. H. Prof. Dr. D. C. **HESSLING** als Neograecus en Byzantinist. NPh, 26, 1940-41.

Baker, G. M. **HOFMANNSTHAL** and Greek Tragedy. JEGPh, 12, 1913.

Beissner, F. **HOELDERLINS** Uebersetzungen aus dem Griechischen. Stuttgart, 1933.

Montgomery, M. Hölderlin and the German Neo-Hellenic Movement. Oxford U.P., 1923.

Petsch, R. Hölderlin und die Griechen. Jb d. Vereins von Altertumsfreunden im Rheinlande, 1924.

Barge, P. L'élément grec dans les Odes d'**HORACE**. REL, 1943-44.

Birt, T. Horaz und das Lied der Griechen. Velhagen & Klasings Monatshefte. 39.

Cessi, C. Orazio e la letteratura greca. In: Conferenze oraziane. Milano, 1936.

Delcourt, M. L'esthétique d'Horace et les lettres grecques. Mélanges P. Thomas. Bruges, 1930.

Englmaier, E. Was ist in des Horaz Satiren und Episteln auf griechischen Einfluss zurückzuführen? Erlangen, 1913.

Galletier, E. Horace et les souvenirs de son voyage en Grèce. Actes du Congrès de l'Ass. G. Budé à Nice, Paris, 1935.

Giver, J. Horace a-t-il donné à la philosophie grecque une couleur romaine ou personnelle dans ses Satires et ses Epîtres? REL, 1941.

Keirns, M. E. The Use of Greek Words in Horace's Satires and Epistles. TAPhA, 1932.

Laurent, F. L'hellénisme des Odes d'Horace. REL, 1937.

Schröder, O. Horaz und die griechische Verskunst. Jahresbericht des Philol. Vereins, 1916.

Smith, W. K. Horace's Debt to Greek Literature. CR, 1935.

Szabo, A. Horaz und die hellenistische

Literaturwissenschaft. (In Hungarian). EPhK, 1935.
Baldwin. Ben **JONSON'S** Indebtedness to the Greek Character-Sketch. MLN, 16, 1901.
Richards, G. C. The Composition of **JOSEPHUS'** Antiquities. CQ, 1939.
Sproedowsky, H. Die Hellenisierung der Geschichte von Joseph in Aegypten bei Flavius Josephus. Greifswald, 1937.
Reich, K. **KANT** und die Ethik der Griechen. Tübingen, 1935. Cf. Mind (London), 1939.
Texte, J. **KEATS** et le néo-hellénisme dans la poésie anglaise. In: Etudes de littérature européenne. Paris, 1898.
Cazelles, J. **LA BRUYERE** helléniste. REG, 35, 1922.
Knös, B. Janus **LASCARIS** et la tradidition gréco-byzantine dans l'humanisme français. Paris, 1946.
Kriaras, E. Le voyage de Pierre **LEBRUN** en Grèce. RLC, 22, 1948.
Luzzatto, G. L. **LECONTE DE LISLE** traduttore dei tragici greci. Dioniso, 5, 1935-36.
Kont, J. **LESSING** et l'antiquité: étude sur l'hellénisme et la critique dogmatique en Allemagne au XVIIIe siècle. Paris, 1894.
Jumeau, R. Tite-**LIVE** et l'historiographie hellénistique. REA, 1936.
Rostagni, A. Roma e la Grecia in Tito Livio. In: Studi Liviani. Roma, 1934.
Warren, F. M. A Byzantine Source for Guilllaume de **LORRIS'S** Roman de la Rose. PMLA, 1916.
De Lacy, P. **LUCRETIUS'** Debt to Greek Pastoral Poetry. TAPhA, 1939.
Korfmacher, W. C. Stoic Assault in Lucretius. Ibid., 1935.
Greene, D. H. Lady **LUMLEY** and Greek Tragedy. CJ, 36, 1941.
Triantafillis. N. **MACHIAVELLI** e gli scrittori greci. Venezia, 1875.
Leroy, M. Grégoire **MAGISTROS** et les traductions arméniennes d'auteurs grecs. Mélanges Capart. Bruxelles, 1935.
Sells, A. L. Reflexions on Stéphane **MALLARME**: Some Greek and English Reminiscences. MLR, 41, 1946.
Didot, A. F. Alde **MANUCE** et l'Hellénisme à Venise. Paris, 1875.
Santini, E. Neoellenismo romantico nella ragione drammatica del **MANZONI**. Rivista italiana del dramma, 3, 1939.
Autore, O. **MARZIALE** e l'epigramma greco. Palermo, 1937-38.
Harman, M. A Greek Proverb in **MILTON**. CPh, 1943.
Parker, W. R. Milton's Debt to Greek Tragedy in Samson Agonistes. Baltimore, 1937.
Hazard, P. Le rayonnement d'Athènes en 1786, (Francisco de **MIRANDA**). RLC, 14, 1934.
Knös, B. Les citations grecques de **MONTAIGNE**. Eranos, 1946.
Willner, K. **MONTCHRESTIENS** Tragödien und die stoische Lebensweisheit. Berlin, 1932.
Anon. **MOORE'S** Lectures on the Greek Language and Literature. NAR, 42, 1836.
Roussel, L. L'hellénisme de J. **MOREAS**. Aix-en-Provence, 1932.
Caminade, G. Les chants des Grecs et le philhellénisme de Wilhelm **MUELLER**. Paris, 1913.
Mannheimer, A. **NIETZSCHE** und die antike Sophistik. Das freie Wort, 20. IV.1901.
Knight, A. H. J. Some Aspects of the Life and Work of Nietzsche, Particularly of his Connection with Greek Literature and Thought. Cambridge U.P., 1933.
Stallman, Alfreda. The Influence of the Greeks on Nietzsche. Festschrift W. A. Oldfather. Urbana, 1943.
Anon. Latter-day Pagans. (W. **PATER**). QR, 182, 1895.
Law, H. H. Pater's Use of Greek Quotations. TAPhA 1941-42 and MLN, 58, 1943.
Nolhac, P. de. Les études grecques de **PETRARQUE**. C. R. de l'Acad. des Inscriptions et Belles Lettres, Oct., 1888.
Hauvette, H. Le professeur de grec de Pétrarque et de Boccace. (L. **PILATE**). Chartres, 1891.
Coppola, G. **PLAUTO** e la commedia greca. A&R, 1923.
Hofmann, J. B. Griechisches in Plautus. Festschrift Kretschmer. Wien, 1926.
Hough, J. N. The Use of Greek Words by Plautus. AJPh, 1934.
Jachmann, G. Plautinisches und Attisches. In: Problemata, 3. Berlin, 1931.
Knorr, M. Das griechische Vorbild der Mostellaria des Plautus. München, 1934.
Krysiniel, B. Der plautinische Poenulus und sein attisches Vorbild. München, 1932. Cf. Eos, 34.
Middelmann, F. Griechische Welt und Sprache in Plautus Komödien. Bochum, 1938.
Sonnenburg, P. E. Plautus und seine

Originale. Wochenschrift f. klass. Philol., 1917.

Loomis, L. R. The Greek Studies of **POGGIO** Bracciolini. In memoriam G. S. Loomis. Paris, New York, 1927.

Dorez, L. L'hellénisme d'Ange **POLITIEN.** Rome, 1895.

Simon, J. L'hellénisme de **QUEVEDO.** Revue de Bibliographie nationale, 6. (Madrid), 1946.

Odgers, M. O. **QUINTILIAN'S** Use of Earlier Literature. CPh, 1933.

Carpenter, Nan C. **RABELAIS** and the Greek Dances. MLN, 64, 1949.

Bonnard, A. **RACINE** et les tragiques grecs. Bull. de la Soc. des Etudes de Lettres (Lausanne), 14, 1940.

May, G. Contribution à l'étude des sources grecques de Phèdre. MLQ, 8, 1947.

Etienne, S. **RONSARD** a-t-il su le grec? Mélanges Laumonier. Paris, 1935.

Stefansky, G. Das hellenisch-deutsche Weltbild. Einleitung in die Lebensgeschichte **SCHELLINGS.** Bonn, 1925.

Arnoldt. Ueber **SCHILLERS** Auffassung und Verwertung des antiken Chors in der Braut von Messina. Progr. Kônigsberg, 1883.

Gerhard, M. Schiller und die griechische Tragödie. Weimar, 1919.

Gerlinger, J. B. Die griechischen Elemente in Schillers Braut von Messina. Progr. Neuburg, 1892.

Hasse. Das Verhältniss von Schillers Glocke zum griechischen Chorlied. Festschrift Oscar Schade. Königsberg, 1896.

Moerlin, F. A. Briefe über die Nachbildung der griechischen Tragödie in Schillers Braut von Messina. Altenburg, 1804.

Rehorn, F. Schiller und die griechische Poesie. Berichte d. freien deutschen Hochstifts Frankfurt, 6, 1890.

Roessler, J. Ueber das Verhältniss der Schillerschen Braut von Messina zur antiken Tragödie. Progr. Budissin, 1855.

Schink, J. F. Schillers Braut von Messina kritisch entwickelt. Dresden, 1827.

Stern, J. Schillers Griechentum. HG, 1932.

Suevern, J. W. Ueber Schillers Wallenstein in Hinsicht auf die griechische Tragödie. Berlin, 1800.

Teichmann, M. Ueber Schillers und F. Schlegels Stellung zur griechischen Poesie in den Abhandlungen Ueber naive und sentimentale Dichtung und Ueber das Studium der griechischen Poesie. Diss. Marburg, 1919.

Kapnukajas, C. K. Die Nachahmungstechnik **SENECAS** in den Chorliedern des Hercules Furens und der Medea. Leipzig, 1930.

Pratt, N. T. Dramatic Suspense in Seneca and in his Greek Precursors. Princeton U.P., 1939.

Brandl, A. Der Zusammenhang der **SHAKESPEARISCHEN** Tragödie mit der griechischen. SAWB, 1916.

Buechler, H. Shakespeares Dramen in ihrem Verhältnisse zur griechischen Tragödie. Nürnberg, 1856.

Burnet, J. Shakespeare and Greek Philosophy. In: Essays & Addresses. London, 1929.

Churton-Collins, J. Had Shakespeare Read the Greek Tragedies? Fortnightly Review, April, 1903.

Hertzberg, W. Eine griechische Quelle zu Shakespeares Sonetten. JbShG, 13, 1878.

Leighton, W. Shakespeare and Greek Tragedy. Shakespeariana, 1, Aug., 1884.

Morhardt, M. A la rencontre de Shakespeare. MF, 15.V.1937.

Roussel, L. Shakespeare's Greek. TLS, 2.II.1946.

Wolffhardt, E. Shakespeare und das Griechentum. Weimar, 1920.

Leon, P. The Sophists and **SHAWIANISM.** PCA, 1929.

Guzzo, A. Hellas di P. B. **SHELLEY.** Cultura, 2, 1922-23.

Hime, H. W. L. The Greek Materials of Shelley's Adonais. London, 1888.

Scudder, Vida D. The Greek Spirit in Shelley and Browning. Boston Browning Soc. Papers, 1897.

Hughes, Y. M. **SPENSER** and the Greek Pastoral Triad. SPh, 1923.

Pound, Oliavia. On the Application of the Principles of Greek Lyric Tragedy in the Classical Dramas of **SWINBURNE.** U. of Nebraska Studies, Oct., 1913.

Rutland, W. R. Swinburne: a Nineteenth Century Hellene. Oxford, 1931.

Hardinghaus, B. **TACITUS** und das Griechentum. Emsdetten, 1932.

Jurblum. L'hellénisme dans les Annales de Tacite. REL, 1936.

Weathers, W. T. Edward **TAYLOR,** Hellenistic Puritan. AL, 18, 1946.

Nissen, P. Die griechische Formung **TEGNERS.** Edda, 39, 1939.

Clifford, H. R. Dramatic Technique and

the Originality of **TERENCE.** CJ, 26, 1931.

Flickinger, R. C. On the Originality of Terence. PhQ, 7, 1928.

Alès, A. d'. **TERTULLIEN** helléniste. REG, 1937.

Pegis, A. G. St. **THOMAS** and the Greeks. Marquette U. (Milwaukee), 1939.

Cochnower, Mary E. **THOREAU** and Stoicism. Diss. U. of Iowa, 1940.

Jovy, E. François **TISSARD** et Jérome Aléandre. Contribution à l'histoire des origines des études grecques en France. Mém. de la Soc. des Sciences et Arts de Vitry-le-François, 19, 21, 1899-1902.

Omont, H. Le premier professeur de langue grecque au Collège de France: J. **TOUSSAINT** (1529). REG, 16, 1903.

Dahlmann, H. **VARRO** und die hellenistische Sprachtheorie. Berlin, 1932.

Duckett, E. S. Hellenistic Influence on the Aeneid. (**VIRGIL**). Northampton (Mass.), 1920.

—— Influence of Alexandrian Poetry upon the Aeneid. CJ, 11.

Fairclough, H. R. Virgil's Knowledge of Greek. CPh, 1930.

Zotto, A. dal. La Ciris, Virgiliano esercizio di traduzione dal greco. Mantova, 1938.

Lemaitre, J. Comment **VOLTAIRE** imita Shakespeare et les tragiques grecs. In: Hatzfeld et Meunier, Les Critiques littéraires du XIXe siècle. Paris, 1894.

Rovillain, E. E. Rapports probables entre le Zadig de Voltaire et la pensée stoicienne. PMLA, 52.

Choisy, F. Richard **WAGNER** et la pensée grecque. L'Acropole, 1930.

Grunsky, K. Richard Wagner und das griechische Drama. HG, 1933.

Kirchbach, W. R. Wagner und das zeitgenössische und altgriechische Drama. MLIA, 1889.

Wilson, P. C. Wagner's Drama and Greek Tragedy. New York, 1919.

Montgomery, H. C. **WASHINGTON** the Stoic. CJ, 31, 1936.

Rubensohn, M. Zu **WECKHERLINS** poetischen Uebersetzungen aus dem Griechischen. ZDPh, 32, 1900.

Monck, E. C. Greek Traits in W. **WHITMAN.** PL, June, 1895.

Aron, E. Die deutsche Erweckung des Griechentums durch **WINCKELMANN** und Herder. Diss. Heidelberg, 1929.

Bork, A. Die deutsche Griechenauffassung von Winckelmann bis Nietzsche im Unterricht. Erziehung, 13, 1938.

Curtius, L. Winckelmann und unser Jahrhundert. Antike, 1930.

Justi, C. Winckelmann und seine Zeitgenossen. Leipzig, 1898.

FOURTH PART

Latin Contributions.

CHAPTER ONE

General Influences.

(See also under Rome, I. VI. 10., and under other Names in the Chapter on Thematology.)

Ames, R. A. & Montgomery, H. C. The Influence of Rome on the American Constitution. CJ, 30, 1934.

Bailey, C. (ed.). The Legacy of Rome. Oxford, 1923.

Bardy, G. La culture latine dans l'Orient chrétien au IVe siècle. Irenikon, 14, 1937.

Bréal, M. Premières influences de Rome sur le monde germanique. Mém. de la Société de linguistique de Paris, 7, 1891.

Brooke, T. Latin Drama in Renaissance England. ELH, 13, 1946.

Caflisch-Einicher, E. Die lateinischen Elemente in der mittelhochdeutschen Epik des 13. Jahrhunderts. Reichenberg i.B., 1936.

Chesterton, G. K. English Literature and the Latin Tradition. Fortnightly Review, Aug., 1935.

Cohen, G. La comédie latine en France au XIIe siècle. REL, 6, 1928. And Paris, 1931.

Cousin, J. Rhétorique latine et classicisme français. RCC, 34, 1933.

Crawford, O. G. S. Our Debt to Rome. Antiquity, 2, 1928.

Creizenach, W. Einfluss altrömischer und humanistischer Vorbilder. In: Geschichte des neueren Dramas. Halle, 1903.

Deanesby, M. Roman Traditionalist Influence among the Anglo-Saxons. EHR, 1943.

Degen, J. F. Versuch einer vollständigen Litteratur der deutschen Uebersetzungen der Römer. Altenburg, 1794-97; Erlangen, 1799.

Esposito, M. Notes on Latin Learning and Literature in Mediaeval Ireland. Ha, 1930-37.

Faral, E. Recherches sur les sources latines des contes et romans courtois du moyen âge. Paris, 1913.

Faust, R. Das erste englische Lustspiel in seiner Abhängigkeit vom Moral-Play und von der römischen Komödie. Progr. 1889.

Federici, F. Degli scrittori latini, e delle italiane versioni delle loro opere. Padova, 1840.

Ferrero, G. Le génie latin et le monde moderne. Paris, 1917.

—— Roman Historians. In: Our Debt to Greece & Rome. New York, 1930.

Foligno, C. Latin Thought During the Middle Ages. Oxford, 1929.

Fraenkel, E. Die Stelle des Römertums in der humanistischen Bildung. Berlin, 1926.

Fuchs, H. Der geistige Widerstand gegen Rom in der antiken Welt. Berlin, 1938.

Gaselee, S. The Transition from the Late Latin Lyric to the Mediaeval Love Poem. Cambridge, 1931.

Grat, F. Le moyen âge et la tradition manuscrite de la littérature classique latine. Actes du Congrès de Nice de l'Ass. G. Budé. Paris, 1935.

Graziani, F. Cultura e tradizione latina in Epiro. Rivista d'Albania, 3, 1942.

Grierson, H. J. C. Verse Translation, with Special Reference to Translation from Latin. English Assoc. Oxford U.P., 1948.

Hadley, H. S. Rome and the World of To-Day. New York, 1922.

Hagendahl, H. La comédie latine au XIIe siècle et ses modèles antiques. Festschrift Nilsson. Lund, 1939.

Immisch, O. Das Römertum im Humanismus. Vers. d. Freunde d. human. Gymnasiums. Freiburg, 1927.

Johnston, M. Romans and Americans on Government. CW, 29, 1935.

Jovy, E. Le collège de Vitry et la poésie latine. Soc. des Sciences et Arts de Vitry-le-François, 1889-90; 16, 1892.

Kardos, T. La Hongrie latine. Paris, 1944.

Klotz, A. Nationale und internationale Strömungen in der römischen Literatur. Erlangen, 1931.

Koepp, F. Die Römer in Deutschland. 2nd ed. Bielefeld, 1912.

Kroll, W. Unsere Schätzung der römischen Dichtung. NJKA, 11, 1903.

Manitius, M. Beiträge zur Geschichte römischer Dichter im Mittelalter. Ph, 2, 1891.

Mauclair, C. L'esprit romain et l'art français. Renaissance latine, 15.XII. 1903.

Méril, E. du. Origines latines du théâtre moderne. Paris, 1849.

Novati, F. L'influsso del pensiero latino sopra la civiltà italiana del medio evo. Milano, 1897.

Paasche, F. Ueber Rom und das Nachleben der Antike im norwegischen und isländischen Schrifttum des Hochmittelalters. Symbolae Osloenses, 1934.

Pascu, G. L'influence de la culture latine sur l'esprit des Roumains. Per lo Studio e l'Uso del Latino, 1, 1939.

Pichon, R. L'antiquité romaine et la poésie française à l'époque parnassienne. RDM, 1911.

Reichmann, V. Römische Literatur in griechischer Uebersetzung. Leipzig, 1943.

Sanford, E. M. The Use of Classical Latin Authors in the Libri manuales. TAPhA, 1925.

Shorey, P. Roman Poetry and its Influence upon European Culture. In: Our Debt to Greece & Rome. New York, 1930.

Streckenbach, G. Stiltheorie und Rhetorik der Römer als Gegenstand der imitatio im Bereich des deutschen Humanismus. Berlin, 1932.

Strong, E. Romanità throughout the Ages. Journal of Roman Studies, 1939.

Tage, H. La tradition latine dans la tragédie française avant la période classique. (In Danish). København, 1941.

Valentini, G. Albania latina. Per lo Studio e l'uso del Latino, 2, 1939.

Vince, C. A. Latin Poets in the British Parliament. CR, 1932.

Warren, F. M. The Troubador Canso and Latin Lyric Poetry. MPh, 9, 1911-12.

Wedeck, H. E. The Latin Situation and Some Mediaeval Analogies. CJ, 28, 1933.

Wolff, M. I. Rom und die Romania. MA, 1938.

Woodring, M. N. A Study of the Quality of English in Latin Translations. New York, 1925.

Wyss, E. Roman and American Comedy. CJ, 29, 1934.

CHAPTER TWO

Horace.

1. General Influences.

Andersen, V. Horats, fra middelalder til nytid. København, 1939-40.

Blaze de Bury, H. Horace et ses traducteurs. RDM, 1.I.1875.

Csengery, J. Valeur et signification d'Horace pour le temps présent. (In Hungarian). Szemle, 699, (Budapest), 1936.

Gnoli, D. Vecchie odi barbare e traduzioni di Orazio. NAnt, 16.XII.1878.

Haeussner, J. Das Fortleben des Horaz in der Weltliteratur. Allg. Zt., 20. VIII.1907.

Haight, E. H. Lyre and Whetstone: Horatius Redivivus. CPh, 41, 1946.

Imelmann, J. Donec gratus eram tibi. Nachdichtungen und Nachklänge aus drei Jahrhunderten. Berlin, 1899.

Johnston, M. Horace in These Days, and Others. CW, 29, 1935.

Keseling, P. Horaz im Kirchenlied? Theologie & Glaube, 1921.

Klingner, F. Horazische und moderne Lyrik. Antike, 1930.

Kraemer, C. J. Horace in Present-Day Quotation. CW, 23, 1929.

Lida, María R. Horacio en la literatura mundial. RFH, 2, 1940.

Manitius, M. Analekten zur Geschichte des Horaz im Mittelalter, bis 1300. Göttingen, 1893.

Mierow, C. C. Horace et le christianisme. Orpheus, revista pentru cultura clasica, 3, 1927.

—— The Most Modern Voice from Antiquity. CJ, 23, 1928.

Monteverdi, A. Orazio nel medio evo. SM, 9, 1936-37.

Repplier, A. Horace After Two Thousand Years. AM, 1936.

Restrepo-Millan, J. M. Horacio, su lírica ante el gusto moderno. Rev. de las Indias. (Bogota), 1938.

Richter, E. Horaz in der Weltliteratur. NM, 10, 1939.

Rolandi, U. Riflessi oraziani nei libretti per musica. Giorn. di politica e di letteratura, 14, 1938.

Rupprecht, K. Gott auf Erden: Ein Beitrag zur Horaz-Erklärung und zur Geschichte des Messianismus im Westen. Würzburger Jb. f. d. Altertumswissenschaft, 1, 1946.

Saintonge, P. F., Burgevin, L. G. &

Griffith, H. Horace, Three Phases of his Influence. Chicago U.P., 1936.
Showerman, G. Horace and his Influence. In: Our Debt to Greece & Rome. Boston, 1922.
Simecek. Horace chez les écrivains chrétiens. (In Czech). In: Non Omnis Moriar. Praha, 1935-36.
Sorrento, L. Orazio e il medio evo. In: Conferenze oraziane. Milano, 1936.
Spaeth, J. W. Verse Translations and Imitations of Horace: An Index. CJ, 40, 1944.
Stemplinger, E. Horazische Motive in der Flucht der Zeiten. SVL, 4, 1904.
—— Das Fortleben der Horazischen Lyrik seit der Renaissance. Leipzig, 1906.
—— Horaz im Urteil der Jahrhunderte. Leipzig, 1921.
Varia. Orazio nella letteratura mondiale. Roma, 1936.
Viola, A. L'Arte poetica di Orazio nella critica italiana e straniera. Napoli, 1901.

2. Influences upon Individual Countries.

Castro Leal, A. Notas para el estudio de Horacio en México (**AMERICA**). Rev. de Lit. Mexicana, 1, 1940.
Erickson, M. E. A Guatemalan Translator of Horace. MLQ, 4, 1943.
Mendez Plancarte, G. Horacio en México. México, 1937.
Oroz, R. Traductores americanos de Horacio. Annales U. de Chile, 8, 1930.
Pritchard, J. P. Some American Estimates of Horace. CW, 28, 1935.
—— Horace's Influence upon American Criticism. TAPhA, 1937.
Hrdina, K. Les échos d'Horace chez les humanistes tchèques au XVIe siècle. (**CZECHOSLOVAKIA**). In: Non Omnis Moriar. Praha, 1935-36.
Novotny, F. Horace dans la philosophie tchèque. (In Czech). Ibid.
Ryba, B. Horace et la Bohême pré-humaniste. (In Czech). Ibid.
Stiebitz, F. Les échos d'Horace dans la première école poétique de la Bohême moderne. (In Czech). Ibid.
Goad, Caroline. Horace in the English Literature of the Eighteenth Century. (**ENGLAND**). New Haven, 1918.
Jackson, W. A. The First Separately Printed English Translation of Horace. Harvard Library Bull., 1, 1947.
Thayer, Mary R. The Influence of Horace on the Chief English Poets of the Nineteenth Century. New Haven, 1916.
Boudout, J. Horace et les lettres françaises. (**FRANCE**). Hum., 11, 1935.
Campaux, A. Les raisons de la popularité d'Horace en France. Annales de l'Est, April, 1895.
Chaudruc de Crazannes, J. de. Horace considéré comme poète satirique; des imitations et de la manière de l'imiter en vers français. Mellin Mag. encycl. 1. (Paris), 1809.
Lebègue, R. L'influence d'Horace sur la pensée et la littérature francaise de la Renaissance. Actes du Congrès de Nice de l'Ass. G. Budé. Paris, 1935. Cf. H&R, 3, 1936.
Marouzeau, J. Horace dans la littérature française. REL, 1935.
Bernard, W. Horaz in der modernen deutschen Lyrik. (**GERMANY**). Wien, 1943.
Bintz. Einfluss der Ars poetica des Horaz auf die deutsche Litteratur des XVIII. Jahrhunderts. Progr. Hamburg, 1892.
Essig, O. Horatius educator linguae ac litterarum germanicarum. Horaz Festschrift. Pekinger Reichsuniversität. Peking, 1935.
Joseph, A. Oden des Horaz in deutschen Uebersetzungen aus dem 17. Jahrhundert. Diss. München, 1929; Rottach, 1930.
Lehnerdt, H. Die deutsche Dichtung des XVII. und XVIII. Jahrhunderts in ihren Beziehungen zu Horaz. Königsberg, 1882.
Liliencron, R. von. Die Horazischen Metren in deutschen Compositionen des XVI. Jahrhunderts. Berlin, 1887.
Newald, R. Deutscher Horaz in fünf Jahrhunderten. Berlin, 1933.
Nissen, T. Horaz als Erwecker vorklassischer deutscher Verskunst. HG, 1936.
Schaefer, H. Horaz und Vergil im dritten Reich. HG, 1935.
Schmolke. Deutsche Horazübersetzungen. MLIA, 1878.
Schönberger, J. K. Deutsche Parallelen zu Horaz. Augsburg, 1920.
Schwabe, E. Zur Geschichte der deutschen Horaz-Uebersetzungen. Neue Jb. f. Philologie & Pädagogik, 153, 1896.
Staedler, E. Horazanalekten zur deutschen Dichtung des 19. Jahrhunderts. NJAB, 1941.
Staedler, K. Horaz' Oden an seine Freunde in Reimstrophen verdeutscht. Nebst einer Einleitung und einem Nachtrag zu den Horaz-Verdeutschungen. Progr. Berlin, 1897.
Waldapfel, E. (ed.) 'Horatius noster.

Magyar Horatius. (**HUNGARY**). Budapest, 1935.

Curcio, G. G. Q. Orazio Flacco, studiato in **ITALIA** dal secolo XIII al XVIII. Catania, 1913.

Pietrobono, L. Orazio nella letteratura italiana. "Roma," 1935.

Ogrodzinski, W. Les traducteurs polonais d'Horace. (**POLAND**). Commentationes Horatianae, 2. Cracovie, 1935.

Gonçalves, F. R. Dois conceitos de Horacio na poesia portuguesa do século XVIII. (**PORTUGAL**). Lisboa, 1930.

Laslo, N. Horatiu In literatura romāna. (**RUMANIA**). Cluj, 1935.

Lee, O. Horace as Sung in Norway During the Last Hundred Years. (**SCANDINAVIA**). CJ, 31, 1936.

Menéndez y Pelayo, D. M. Horacio en España. (**SPAIN**). 2 vols. Madrid, 1885.

3. Influences upon Individual Authors.

Gunning, J. H. Horaz und **BILDERDIJK**. Mnemosyne, 4, 1936.

Barbier, J. C. Les deux arts poétiques d'Horace et de **BOILEAU**. Paris, 1874.

Benecke, C. Boileau imitateur d'Horace et de Juvénal. Progr. 1879.

Bielefeld. Boileau dans son rapport avec Horace. Progr. Dillenburg, 1874.

Gerlach. Ein Vergleich zwischen Horaz und Boileau. Progr. Rathenow, 1869.

Herder, J. G. Boileau und Horaz. Neue deutsche Monatsschrift, 3, 1795.

Schaefer, J. Boileaus Art poétique übersetzt und erklärt mit Parallelstellen aus Horaz. Progr. Attendorn, 1881.

Voltaire. Parallèle d'Horace, de Boileau et de Pope. Contes de Guill. Vadé, 1764.

Weiser, C. S. Ueber das Verhältniss von **BYRONS** Hints from Horace zu Horaz. ESn, 1, 1877.

Gonçalves, F. R. A fala de velho do restelo: aspectos clássicos dêste episódio camoniano. (**CAMOES**). Lisboa, 1933.

Benham, A. R. **CAMPION** and Horace. PhQ, 1933.

Coppola, G. L'Orazio di **CARDUCCI**. NAnt, 379, 1935.

Herescu, N. J. Horace et Virgile dans la poésie de Giosuè Carducci. Favonius, 1. (Bucharest), 1927.

Wedeck, H. E. **CASIMIR**, the Polish Horace. PhQ, 1937.

Krokowski, G. De Septem Sideribus quae Nicolao **COPERNICO** vulgo tribuuntur: Symbolae ad carminum Horatii a Polonorum poetis latinis imitatione expressorum historiam. Cracow, 1926.

Marchiafava, E. Orazio e **DANTE**. NAnt, 381, 1935.

Lipscomb, H. C. Horace and the Poetry of Austin **DOBSON**. TAPhA, 59, 1928.

La Drière, C. Sermoni propius; a Study of the Horatian Theory of the Epistle and of **DRYDEN'S** Allusion to it in the Preface of Religio laici. CW, 32, 1939.

Dennis, H. W. M. A Note on Horace and **DU BELLAY**. CPh, 1931.

Carberry, J. S. Queen **ELIZABETH** Quotes Horace. CW, 28, 1934.

Heussner, F. Ein vergessener Uebersetzer des Horaz und sein Werk. (F. **ESCHEN**). Zs. f.d. Gymnasialwesen, 1914.

Fucilla, J. G. The Horatianism of Antonio **FERREIRA**. Vergilius, Dec., 1940.

Charlier, G. L'Horace de **FLORIAN**. In: Etudes horatiennes. Bruxelles, 1937.

Elisei, R. Tommaso **GARGALLO** traduttore d'Orazio. MC, 1933.

Tiedke, H. Anklänge an Horaz bei **GEIBEL**. Progr. Berlin, 1903.

Maass, E. **GOETHE** und Horaz. NJKA, 1917.

Morsch, H. Goethe und Horaz. Neue Jb. f. Philologie und Pädagogik, 132, 1885.

Thomas, L. P. L'art horatien de **GONGORA**. In: Etudes horatiennes. Bruxelles, 1937.

Oka, J. Horace dans les leçons de C. E. **GRODDEK**. (In Polish). In: Commentationes Horatianae, 2. Cracow, 1935.

Ooteghem, J. van. Un commentateur extravagant d'Horace, le Père **HARDOUIN**. EC, 12, 1945.

Schuster, M. Horaz und **HEINE**. Progr. Wiener-Neustadt, 1916.

Chacón y Calvo, J. M. El horacianismo en la poesía de **HEREDIA**. U. Católica Boliviana, 6, 1941.

Colmant, P. Pour le vaisseau de Virgile: Horace et J. M. de Hérédia. EC, 1942.

Regenos, G. W. The Influence of Horace on Robert **HERRICK**. TAPhA, 72, 1941 & PhQ, 26, 1947.

Ruggles, M. J. Horace and Herrick. CJ, 31, 1936.

Pritchard, J. P. The Autocrat and Horace. (O. W. **HOLMES**). CW, 25, 1932.

Varga, L. Hannulik **JANOS**, a XVIII század Horatiusa. Debrecen, 1938.

Reinsch, H. Ben **JONSONS** Poetik und seine Beziehungen zu Horaz. Diss. München, 1898.

Coffin, H. C. **KIPLING** and Horace. CW, 15.
Saint-Amans, F. D'Horace et de **KLOPSTOCK**. Agen, 1856.
Beduarowski, A. Horace et les Opera Lyrica de St. **KONARSKI**. Eos, 1923.
Hahn, W. **KRASICKI** i Horacy. Eos, 1935.
Kuiper, W. E. J. Eenige navolgingen van Horatius bij **LECONTE DE LISLE**. NPh, 3, 1918.
Llobera, J. Q. Horatius Flaccus et Aloisius **LEGIONENSIS**. In: Horatiana, Palaestra latina, 1935.
Ogrodzinski, V. De Ioanne **LIBICKI** Horatii carminum interprete Polono. Eos, 34.
Anon. Lord **LYTTON'S** Horaz. MLIA, 9, 1870.
Counson, A. **MALHERBE** et Horace. Mélanges P. Thomas. Bruges, 1930.
Finley, J. H. **MILTON** and Horace. HSCPh, 1937.
Schuster, M. **MOERIKES** Verhältniss zu Horaz und Tibull. BBG, 65, 1929.
Espinosa Polit, A. **OLMEDO** y Horacio. Las dos Aguilas. Cuenca (Ecuador), 1937.
Festa, N. Orazio e il **PARINI**. NAnt, 1929.
Pietrobono, L. Ancora di Orazio nei carmi latini di Giovanni **PASCOLI**. Atti Acc. degli Arcadi, 20, 1938-39.
Pritchard, J. P. Horace and Edgar Allen **POE**. CW, 26, 1933.
Bloom, Lillian. **POPE** as Textual Critic: A Bibliographical Study of his Horatian Text. JEGPh, 47, 1948.
Isaacs, J. Pope's Imitations of Horace. NC, 127, 1940.
Mack, M. Pope's Horatian Poems. MPh, 41, 1943.
—— A Manuscript of Pope's Imitation of the First Ode of the Fourth Book of Horace. MLN, 60, 1945.
Tupper, J. W. A Study of Pope's Imitations of Horace. PMLA, 15, 1900.
Badalic, J. **PUSKIN** i Uraz. Zagreb, 1937.
Grégoire, H. Horace et Pouchkine. EC, 1937.
Hammer, J. A Monastic Panegyrist of Horace. (**RAGINALDUS OF CANTERBURY**). PhQ, 1932.
Stemplinger, E. **RONSARD** und der Lyriker Horaz. ZFSL, 26, 1903.
Meyer, F. A. Horaz in Jakob **SCHWIEGERS** Geharnischte Venus. Vierteljahrschrift f. Litteraturgeschichte, 2, 1889.
Brandl, A. Horaz und **SHAKESPEARE**. JbShG, 1903.
Westbrook, P. D. Horace's Influence on Antony and Cleopatra. PMLA, 62, 1947.
Mustard, W. P. **TENNYSON** and Horace. Nation, 1898.
Nitchie, Elizabeth. Horace and **THACKERAY**. CJ, 13, 1918.
Ludvikovsky, J. Les paraphrases religieuses latines des Odes d'Horace de G. **TRANOVSKY**. (In Czech). In: Non Omnis Moriar. Praha, 1935-36.
TREVELYAN, R. C. Translations from Horace, Juvenal and Montaigne, with Two Imaginary Conversations. Cambridge U.P., 1940.
Kowal, A. L'Art poétique des **VAUQUELIN DE LA FRESNAYE** und sein Verhältnis zu der Ars poetica des Horaz. Progr. Wien, 1902.
Pircher. Horaz und **VIDA**. Progr. Meran, 1895. Cf. GSLI, 30, 1897.
Granges, C. M. des. Epître de **VOLTAIRE** à Horace. Hum., 11, 1935.
Brooks, B. G. **WORDSWORTH** and the Horatian Spirit. MLR, 32, 1937.
Buehler, C. F. On the Horace Printed in Rome by Wendelinus de **WYLA** or Bartholomaeus Guldinbeck. Bibliofilia, 37, 1935.
Sajdak, J. Fr. **ZABLOCTEI** traducteur d'Horace. (In Polish). Ksiega pamiatk. Dobrzyck, 1930.

CHAPTER THREE

Ovid.

1. General Influences.

Alton, E. H. The Mediaeval Commentators on Ovid's Fasti. Ha, 44, 1926.
—— Ovid in the Mediaeval Schoolroom. PCA, 1937.
Batowski, Z. Ovide dans l'Ecole des Chevaliers. (In Polish). Przeglad Warzawski, 1923.
Bellorini, E. Note sulle traduzioni italiane dell' Ars amatoria e dei Remedia amoris d'Ovidio anteriori al Rinascimento. Bergamo, 1892. Cf. ZRPh, 16.
—— Note sulle traduzioni italiane delle Eroidi d'Ovidio anteriori al Rinascimento. Torino, 1900. Cf. GSLI, 36, 1900.
Boas, F. S. Ovid and the Elizabethans. London, 1947.
Boer, C. de et al. Ovide dans la littérature française du moyen âge. In: Ovide Moralisé. Amsterdam, 1915.
Breul, K. The Cambridge Songs, A Go-

liard's Song Book of the XIth Century. Cambridge, 1915.
Brewer, W. Ovid's Metamorphoses in European Culture. Boston, 1933.
Buttenwieser, H. Manuscripts of Ovid's Fasti. The Ovidian Tradition in the Middle Ages. TAPhA, 1940.
Ciampoli, D. La leggenda di Ovidio in Sulmona. Arch. per lo studio delle trad. popolare, 4. (Palermo), 1885.
Coon, R. H. The Vogue of Ovid Since the Renaissance. CJ, 25, 1930.
Cooper, C. B. Some Elizabethan Opinions of the Poetry and Character of Ovid. Menasha (Wis.), 1914.
Duplessis, G. Essai bibliographique sur les différentes éditions des oeuvres d'Ovide. Paris, 1889.
Engels, J. Etudes sur l'Ovide Moralisé. Groningen, 1945.
Hall, F. W. An English Commentary on Ovid. CQ, 21, 1927.
Huemer, J. Ueber das Fortleben Ovids. Zs. f. österr. Gymnasien, 32, 1881.
Langlois, E. Une rédaction en prose de l'Ovide moralisé. Bibl. de l'Ecole des Chartes, 112, 1901.
Lot-Borodine, M. Ovide et l'amour courtois. Revue de Synthèse Historique, 28.
Manitius, M. Beiträge zur Geschichte des Ovidius und anderer römischer Schriftsteller im Mittelalter. Ph. Supplementband, 7, 1899.
Nino, A. de. Ovidio nella tradizione popolare di Sulmona. Casalbordino, 1886.
Pansa, G. Ovidio nel medioevo e nella tradizione popolare. Sulmona, 1924.
Paris, G. Les anciennes versions françaises de l'Art d'aimer et des Remèdes d' amour d'Ovide. In: La Poésie du moyen âge. Paris, 1885.
Rand, E. K. Ovid and his Influence. In: Our Debt to Greece and Rome. Boston, 1925.
Reuschel, H. Ovid und die angelsächsischen Elegien. Beiträge z. Gesch. d. deutschen Sprache & Lit., 62, 1938.
Rick, L. Ovid's Metamorphosen in der englischen Renaissance. Münster, 1915.
Rotondi, G. Ovidio nel medio evo. Conv., 1934.
Savage, J. J. An Old Irish Version of Laodamia and Protesilaus. Festschrift Rand, New York, 1937.
Scheludko, D. Ovid und die Trobadors. ZRPh, 1934.
Schevill, R. Ovid and the Renaissance in Spain. Berkeley, 1913.
Schrötter, W. Ovid und die Troubadours. Diss. Halle, Marburg, 1908.
Scudieri Ruggieri, J. M. Un' Ars amandi del secolo XIV. Rendiconti della classe di scienze morali e storiche della Acc. d'Italia, 2, 1941.
Sedgwick, W. B. The Influence of Ovid. NC, 122, 1937.
Stechow, W. Apollo und Daphne. Leipzig, 1932.
Stecker, K. Ovidianische Verskunst im Mittelalter. H, 62, 1927.
Sudre, L. Ovidii Nasonis Metamorphoseon libros quomodo nostrates medii aevi poetae imitati interpretatique sint. Paris, 1893.
Tafel, S. Die Ueberlieferungsgeschichte von Ovids Carmina amatoria verfolgt bis zum 11. Jahrhundert. Diss. München, 1919.
Unger, H. De Ovidiana in Carminibus Buranis imitatione. Berlin, 1915.
Waldapfel, J. Sur une traduction hongroise des Amours d'Ovide, 1819. (In Hungarian). EPhK, 1929.
Witz, E. Die englischen Ovidübersetzungen des 16. Jahrhunderts. Diss. Strassburg, Leipzig, 1915.

2. Influences upon Individual Authors.

Bartsch, K. F. **ALBRECHT** von Halberstadt und Ovid im Mittelalter. Quedlinburg, 1861.
Runge, O. Die Metamorphosen-Verdeutschung Albrechts von Halberstadt. Berlin, 1908.
Ghisalberti, F. **ARNOLFO** d'Orléans, un cultore di Ovidio nel secolo XII. Mem. del Ist. Lombardo di Scienze e Lettere, 24. Milano, 1932.
Lascu, N. Vasile **ARON** si Ovidiu. Cluj, 1943.
Hubaux, J. Ovide et Saint **AUGUSTIN**. RBPh, 1928.
Keseling, P. Augustin und Ovid. PhW, 1940.
Wiley, W. L. Antoine de **BAIF** and the Ovidian Love-Tale. SPh, 1936.
Ghisalberti, F. L'Ovidius moralizatus di Pierre **BERSUIRE**. Roma, 1933.
Coulter, Cornelia C. The Genealogy of the Gods. (**BOCCACCIO**). Vassar Mediaeval Studies, 1923.
Callan, N. Thyn Owne Book: A Note on **CHAUCER**, Gower and Ovid. RES, 22, 1946.
Connely, W. Imprints of the Heroides of Ovid on Chaucer. CW, 18, 1924.
Meech, S. B. Chaucer and an Italian

Translation of the Heroides. PMLA, 45, 1930.
Stillwell, G. Analogues to Chaucer's Manciple's Tale in the Ovide Moralisé and Machaut's Voir-dit. PhQ, 19, 1940.
Guyer, F. E. The Influence of Ovid on **CRESTIEN DE TROYES.** RR, 12, 1921.
Johnston, O. M. Similarities of Thought in **DANTE** and Ovid. PhQ, 1934.
Szombathely, J. Dante e Ovidio. Trieste, 1888.
Kuehne, H. Prolegomena zu Maitre **ELIES** altfranzösischer Bearbeitung der Ars amatoria des Ovid. Diss. Marburg, 1883.
Reko, V. A. Ovid bis **GEIBEL.** Euphorion, 9, 1902.
Cawley, F. S. An Ovidian Prototype of a Character in Wilhelm Meister. (**GOETHE**). MLN, 40, 1925.
Blake, H. M. **GOLDING'S** Ovid in Elizabethan Times. JEGPh, 14, 1915.
Leonard, E. S. Golding's Translation of Ovid's Metamorphoses. CW, 32.
Wilmotte, M. Réminiscences Ovidiennes dans le conte de **GUILLAUME d'ANGLETERRE.** Festschrift M. K. Pope. Manchester, 1939.
Leyhauff, A. François **HABERT** und seine Uebersetzung der Metamorphosen Ovids. Münchener Beiträge, 30, 1904.
Marco, L. de. Ovidio imitato dal **LA FONTAINE.** Ascoli, 1934.
Wiley, W. L. Pierre **LE LOYER'S** Version of the Ars Amatoria. RR, 1934.
Boer, C. de. Guillaume de **MACHAUT** et l'Ovide moralisé. Romania, 43, 1914.
Rand, E. K. The Metamorphosis of Ovid in Le Roman de la Rose. (**MEUNG**). In: Studies in the History of Culture. Menasha (Wis.), 1942.
Candy, H. C. H. Some Newly Discovered Stanzas Written by John **MILTON** on Engraved Scenes Illustrating Ovid's Metamorphoses. London, 1924.
Gilbert, A. H. Ovid's Mulberry in Milton's Pro Se Defensio. MLN, 63, 1948.
Hales, J. W. Milton and Ovid. MPh, 1, 1903.
Harding, D. P. Milton and the Renaissance Ovid. U. of Illinois Studies in Lang. and Lit., 30, 1946.
Carrington, F. Benedetto **MONTAGNA** and the Metamorphoses of Ovid. Print Collector's Quarterly, 38.
Drygalski, E. von. Heinrich von **MORUNGEN** und Ovid. Göttingen, 1928.
Braune, J. **NONNOS** und Ovid. Greifswald, 1935.
Ghisalberti, F. Di un epilogo latino (Antiovidianus) attribuito al **PETRARCA.** GSLI, 1933.
Lenz, F. W. De Angeli **POLITIANI** studiis Ovidianis. In: Parerga Ovidiana. Roma, 1938.
Morici, G. **PUSKIN** e Ovidio. In: Alessandro Puskin nel primo centenario della morte. Roma, 1937.
Ganzenmueller, C. **SCHILLER** und Ovid. Neue Jb. f. Pädagogik, 1920.
Boyle, R. **SHAKESPEARE** and Ovid. ESn, 27, 1899.
Diller, H. Ovid und die Geschichte von Romeo and Julia. G, 1938.
Duernhoefer, M. Shakespeares Venus und Adonis im Verhältniss zu Ovids Metamorphosen und Constables Schäfergesang. Diss. Halle, 1890.
Coe, A. H. **SPENSER** and Ovid. CW, 22, 1929.
Cooper, L. Spenser and Ovid. Ibid.
Johnston, M. Once More Spenser and Ovid. Ibid.
Sedgwick, W. B. Spenser and Ovid Again. Ibid.
Cumming, W. P. The Influence of Ovid's Metamorphoses on Spenser's Mutabilitie Cantos. SPh, 28, 1931.
Ghisalberti, F. Giovanni del **VIRGILIO** espositore delle Metamorfosi. GD, 34, 1933.

CHAPTER FOUR

Plautus.

(See also Terence in Chapter Seven and Amphithryon, I. VI. 10.)

1. General Influences.

Anon. Plautus and his Imitators. QR, 1891.
Bacon, J. R. Plautus and Posterity. PCA, 1936.
Carducci, G. Plauto nell' Italia moderna. NAnt. 16.V.1891. And in: Studi, Saggi e Discorsi. Opere 10.
Claus, G. De Aulularia Plauti fabula iisque scriptoribus, qui eam imitati sunt. Diss. Halle, 1862.
Cole, H. W. The Influence of Plautus and Terence Upon the Stonghurt Pageants. MLN, 1924.
Dittrich, P. Plautus und Terenz in Pädagogik und Schulwesen der deutschen Humanisten. Leipzig, 1915.
Galzigna, G. A. Fino a che punti i commediografi del Rinascimento abbiano imitato Plauto e Terenzio. Progr. Capodistria, 1901.
Guenther, O. Plautuserneuerungen in der

deutschen Litteratur des XV.-XVII. Jahrhunderts und ihre Verfasser. Leipzig, 1886.
Hugle, A. Einflüsse der Palliata (Plautus & Terence) auf das lateinische und deutsche Drama im 16. Jahrhundert. Heidelberg, 1921.
Johnston, M. A Latin and an English Love-Lyric. CW, 26, 1932.
Kuntze, F. Ein plautinisches Lustspielmotiv in der Weltliteratur. NJWJ, 1, 1925-26.
Norwood, G. Plautus and Terence. In: Our Debt to Greece and Rome. New York, 1932.
Reinhardstoettner, C. von. Die Plautinischen Lustspiele in späteren Bearbeitungen, I. Amphitruo. Leipzig, 1880.
—— Die klassischen Schriftsteller des Altertums und ihr Einfluss auf spätere Literaturen. I. Plautus: Spätere (lateinische, deutsche, französische, englische, spanische, etc.) Bearbeitungen Plautinischer Lustspiele. Leipzig, 1886. Cf. ZVL, 1 & DLZ, 1887.
Roeder, A. E. A. Menechmi und Amphitruo im englischen Drama bis zur Restauration 1661. Diss. Leipzig, 1904.
Swaen, A. E. H. Plautijnsche invloed? NPh, 28, 1943.

2. Influences upon Individual Authors.

Gregorini, A. Di una rassomiglianza fra i Rivali del **CECCHI** e la Casina del Plauto. GSLI, 1894.
Przychocki, G. Le Trinummus de Plaute chez **CIEKLINSKI**. Revue des Humanités, 2, 1923.
Gatto, G. L'Amphitruo di Plauto e le imitazoni di Ludovico **DOLCE** e Molière. Catania, 1921.
Denecke, A. **GOETHE** und Plautus. LE, 1. V. 1912.
Francke, O. Ueber Goethes Versuch zu Anfang unseres Jahrhunderts, die römischen Komiker Plautus und Terenz auf der weimarischen Bühne heimisch zu machen. ZVL, 1, 1888.
Gilbert, A. H. Thomas **HEYWOOD'S** Debt to Plautus, JEGPh, 12, 1913.
Koeppel, E. Die Quellen von Thomas Heywoods Drama The Captives or the Lost Recovered. Archiv, 97, 1896.
Buisman de Savornin Lohman, F. Plautus' Aulularia bij **HOOFT** en bij Molière. Hermeneus, 10, 1937.
Meurer, K. V. **LARIVEYS** Les Esprits als Quelle zu Molières Avare unter Berücksichtigung der Aulularia des Plautus. Diss. Jena, 1873.
Grismer, R. L. The Influence of Plautus in Spain before **LOPE DE VEGA** Together with Chapters on the Dramatic Technique of Plautus and the Revival of Plautus in Italy. New York, 1944.
Bassi, D. Postille inedite di Alessandro **MANZONI** a Plauto e a Terenzio. Aevum (Milano), 1932.
Bromig. Vergleichung der Komödien Aulularia des Plautus und l'Avare des **MOLIERE**. Burgsteinfurt, 1854.
Detela, F. Des Plautus Aulularia und Molières Avare. Progr. Wiener-Neustadt, 1887.
Groon, H. Comparaison entre l'Avare de Molière et l'Aululaire de Plaute. Progr. Verden, 1875.
Klingelhoeffer, W. Plaute imité par Molière et Shakespeare. Progr. Darmstadt, 1873.
Koenig, H. L'Avare de Molière et l'Aululaire de Plaute. Progr. Corbach, 1871.
Schelz, J. L'Avare de Molière et l'Aululaire de Plaute. Progr. Eisleben, 1872.
Schuster, M. Plautus und Molières Le malade imaginaire. WS, 1932.
Vincent, C. Molière imitatore di Plauto e di Terenzio. Roma, 1917.
Grismer, R. L. Another Reminiscence of Plautus in the Comedias of Torres **NAHARRO**. HR, 8, 1940.
Pischl, M. Die Menächmen des Plautus und ihre Bearbeitung durch **REGNARD**. Progr. Feldkirch, 1897.
Boehm, A. Fonti plautine del **RUZZANTE**. GSLI, 29, 1897.
Claus, W. Ueber die Menächmen des Plautus und ihre Nachbildung, besonders durch **SHAKESPEARE**. Progr. Stettin, 1861.
Coulter, C. C. The Plautine Tradition in Shakespeare. JEGPh, 1920.
Draper, J. W. Falstaff and the Plautine Parasite. CJ, 33, 1938.
Forsythe, R. S. A Plautine Source of the Merry Wives of Windsor. MPh, 18, 1920.
Fritz, A. Die Menaechmi des Plautus und die Comedy of Errors des Shakespeare in ihrem Verhältnisse als Original und nachahmende Bearbeitung. Progr. Pisino, 1874.
Gill, E. A Comparison of the Characters in The Comedy of Errors with Those in the Menaechmi. Texas Studies in English, 1925.
Isaac, H. Shakespeare's Comedy of Errors und die Menächmen des Plautus. Archiv, 70, 1883.
Lange, J. W. How Plautus and Shakespeare Make Us Laugh. CB, 9, 1932-33.

Watt, H. A. Plautus and Shakespeare; Further Comments on Menaechmi and the Comedy of Errors. CJ, 25.
Johnston, M. Parasites in Plautus and in SPENSER. CW, 26, 1933.

CHAPTER FIVE

Seneca.

1. General Influences.

Armstrong, W. A. The Influence of Seneca and Machiavelli on the Elizabethan Tyrant. RES, 24, 1948.
Barlow, C. W. Seneca in the Middle Ages. CW, 35, 1941-42.
Beckingham, C. F. Seneca's Fatalism and Elizabethan Tragedy. MLR, 32, 1937.
Boehm, K. Beiträge zur Kenntnis des Einflusses Senecas auf die in der Zeit von 1552-1562 erschienenen französischen Tragödien. Leipzig, 1902.
Charlton, H. B. Senecan Tradition in Renaissance Tragedy (1821). Manchester U. P., 1946.
Counson, A. L'influence de Sénèque le philosophe. Paris, 1903.
Cunliffe, J. W. Influence of Seneca on Elizabethan Tragedy. London, 1893.
Eustachiewicz, T. Sénèque en Pologne. Eos, 19.
Faider, P. La lecture de Sénèque dans une abbaye du Hainaut. Mélanges P. Thomas. Bruges, 1930.
Fischer, R. Nachwirkungen Senecas. In: Zur Kunstentwicklung der englischen Tragödie. Strassburg, 1893.
Gilbert, A. H. Seneca and the Criticism of Elizabethan Tragedy. PhQ, 1934.
Gummere, R. M. Seneca the Philosopher and his Modern Message. In: Our Debt to Greece & Rome. Boston, 1922.
Heller, J. L. & Grismer, R. L. Seneca in the Celestinesque Novel. HR, 12, 1944.
Hrdina, K. Sénèque dans les plus anciennes traductions tchèques du XVe et du XVIe siècle (In Czech). Cesky Casopis Filologicky, 2, 1943.
Lucas, F. L. Seneca and Elizabethan Tragedy. Cambridge, 1922.
Mendell, C. W. Our Seneca. New Haven, 1941.
Musgrove, S. Two Anonymous Verse Translations from Seneca, 1653 and 1666. N&Q, 187, 1944.
Pitollet, C. Réflexions sur Sénèque. (Spain). Hum, 7, 1935.
Renner, R. Senekas Einfluss seit dem 15. Jahrhundert. BBG, 62.
Schelling, F. E. Foreign Influences in Elizabethan Plays. New York, 1923.
Stachel P. Seneca und das deutsche Renaissancedrama. Berlin, 1907.
Strase, A. E. The Modern Touch in Seneca. CJ, 27, 1932.
Ure, P. On Some Differences between Senecan and Elizabethan Tragedy. Durham U. Journal, 10, 1948.
Wells, H. W. Senecan Influence on Elizabethan Tragedy: A Re-Estimation. SAB, 19, 1944.
Williamson, G. Senecan Style in the Seventeenth Century. PhQ, 1936.
Worp, J. A. De invloed van Seneca's treurspelen op ons tooneel. Amsterdam, 1892.

2. Influences Upon Individual Authors.

Angugliario, B. Seneca nel teatro ALFIERIANO. Messina, 1899.
Labriolle, P. de. Saint AUGUSTIN et Sénèque. Rev. de Philologie, d'histoire et de litt. anciennes, 54, 1928.
Hubaux, J. & Harsin, P. Sénèque lu à la Conciergerie. (Jean Nicolas BASSENGE). RBPh, 1932.
Schönberger, J. K. Ein Senecazitat bei Giordano BRUNO. PhW, 1926.
Ayres, H. M. CHAUCER and Seneca. RR, 1919.
Williams, E. W. Cinna, a Note on the Historical Sources (CORNEILLE). RR, 1936.
Morby, E. S. The Influence of Senecan Tragedy in the Plays of Juan de la CUEVA. SPh, 34, 1937.
Crawford, J. P. W. The Influence of Seneca's Tragedies on FERREIRA'S Castro and Bermudez's Nise lastimosa and Nise laurada. MPh, 12, 1914-15.
Schmidt-Wartenberg. Seneca's Influence on Robert GARNIER. Diss. Cornell. Darmstadt, 1888.
Swan, M. W. S. Concerning Benefyting. (GOLDING). MB, 21, 1946.
Eustachiewicz, T. Le De beneficiis dans la traduction polonaise de L. GORNICKI (1593). Eos, 20, 1914.
Smith, P. A. Bishop HALL, Our English Seneca. PMLA, 63, 1948.
Beraneck, J. Sénèque et HARDY. Diss. Leipzig, 1890.
Kahnt, P. Gedankenkreis der Sentenzen in JODELLES und Garniers Tragödien und Seneca's Einfluss auf denselben. Diss. Marburg, 1885.
Wlislocki, H. von. KLEISTS Seneca in ungarischer Bearbeitung. ZVL, 5, 1892.

Alaejos, A. Séneca, **MAIMONIDES** y Luis Vives. Contemporanea, 4, 1936.
Travert, D. **MALHERBE** traducteur des Epîtres à Lucilius. REL, 1942.
Eidson, J. O. Senecan Elements in **MARSTON'S** Antonio and Mellida. MLN, 52, 1937.
Barlow, C. W. A Sixth-Century Epitome of Seneca's De ira. (**MARTIN DE BRAGA**). TAPhA, 1937.
Francoeur, Sister M. Petronilla. The Relationship in Thought and Language Between Lucius Annaeus Seneca and Martin of Braga. Ann Arbor, 1945.
Braswell, W. **MELVILLE'S** Use of Seneca. AL, 12, 1940.
Lüst, H. **MONLEON** in seinem Thyeste als Nachahmer Senecas. Schweinfurth, 1887.
Billy, P. Sénèque dans l'oeuvre de **MONTAIGNE**. REL, 1938.
Hay, C. H. Montaigne lecteur et imitateur de Sénèque. Poitiers, 1938.
Seliga, S. O Hippolicie Seneki w ilumaczeniu St. **MORSZTYNA**. Eos, 1937.
Spearing, E. M. Alexander **NEVILLE'S** Translation of Seneca's Oedipus. MLR, 1920.
Herrick, M. T. Senecan Influence in Gorboduc. (**NORTON**). Festschrift Alexander M. Drummond. Ithaca, 1944.
Collignon, A. Un traducteur de Sénèque à Nancy pendant la Révolution (**PELLET DE BONNEVILLE**). Mém. de l'Acad. de Stanislas, 6e sér., 1905.
Kulcke, O. Senecas Einfluss auf Jean de la **PERUSES** Médée und Jean de la Tailles La Famine ou les Gabéonites. Diss. Greifswald, 1884.
Salesse. Pierre **PINTREL**, traducteur des lettres de Sénèque. Ann. de la Soc. hist. et archéol. de Chateau-Thierry, 1896.
Schmitt, A. Dietrich von **PLIENINGENS** Senecaübersetzung. ZDPh, 28, 1896.
Serafini, M. Le tragedie di Seneca nelle opere di **POLIZIANO**. Convivium, 1945.
Dreyfus-Brisac, E. **RACINE** et Sénèque (dans Phèdre et dans Hippolyte). Paris, 1903.
Préchac, F. Jean-Jacques **ROUSSEAU** traducteur de Sénèque et de Tacite. Actes du Congrès de Nice de l'Ass. G. Budé. Paris, 1935.
Engel, J. Die Spuren Senecas in **SHAKESPEARES** Dramen. PJb. 1903.
Johnson F,. R. Shakespearian Imagery and Senecan Imitation. J. Q. Adams Memorial Studies, Washington, D. C., 1948.
Wilhelm, F. Zu Seneca und Shakespeare (Richard III). Archiv, 129, 1912.
Kulcke, O. Jean de la **TAILLES** Famine im Verhältniss zu Senecas Troades. ZFSL, 3, 1880.
Atkinson, W. C. Séneca, **VIRUES**, Lope de Vega. Homenatge a A. Rubio i Lluch. Barcelona, 1936.

CHAPTER SIX

Virgil.

(See Thematology I. VI. 10 for Aeneas, Dido, Troy, etc.; see also Christianity, II. V. 1.)

1. General Influences.

Atzert, K. Der 2000. Geburtstag des Vergil. Warum feiern wir Vergil? Breslau, 1930.
Boissier, G. Virgile au moyen âge. RDM, 1.II.1877.
Bourgery, A. Les Bucoliques de Virgile dans la poésie moderne. REL, 1946.
Buxton, C. R. Prophets of Heaven and Hell, Vergil, Dante, Milton, Goethe. Cambridge U. P. 1945.
Comparetti, D. Virgilio nel Medio Evo. Livorno, 1872; Firenze, 1896 & 1937-41. (Virgil im Mittelalter. Leipzig, 1875. Virgil in the Middle Ages. London, 1895).
Conway, R. S. Studio sull'influsso di Virgilio. Pubbl. della U. cattolica del Sacro Cuore, 4, Milano.
Creizenach, T. Die Aeneis, die vierte Ecloge und die Pharsalia im Mittelalter. Frankfurt, 1864.
Curtius, E. R. Zweitausend Jahre Vergil. NSR, 1930.
Denckinger, E. M. Some Renaissance References to Sic vos non nobis. PhQ, 1931.
Deratani, N. A propos de Virgile et le moyen âge. Humanitas, 5, 1930.
Funaioli, G. Chiose e leggende virgiliane del medio evo. SM, 5, 1932.
Ganszyniec, R. De Vergilii in medio aevo memoria. Eos, 33, 1930-31.
Gebhart, E. Des raisons de la popularité de Virgile au moyen âge. RCC, 2, 1893.
Genthe, F. W. Leben und Fortleben des Virgilius Maro als Dichter und Zauberer. Leipzig, 1857.
Graesse, J. G. T. Beiträge zur Literatur und Sage des Mittelalters. Dresden, 1850.
Gutmacher, E. Der Zauberer Virgilius. Zeitgeist, 36, 1915.
Haecker, T. Vergil, Vater des Abendlandes. Leipzig, 1931. (Virgil, Father

of the West. London, 1934. Virgile, père de l'Occident. Paris, 1935.)
Heiss, H. Virgils Fortleben in den romanischen Literaturen. Festschrift Geffcken. Leipzig, 1931.
Liebrecht, F. Zur Virgiliussage. Germania, 10, 1865.
Mackail, J. W. Virgil and his Meaning to the World of To-Day. In: Our Debt to Greece & Rome. New York, 1922.
Méril, E. du. Virgile l'enchanteur. In: Mélanges archéologiques. Paris, 1850.
Michel, F. Quae vices quaeque mutationes et Virgilium ipsum et ejus carmina per mediam aetatum exceperint. Diss. Paris, 1846.
Morgan, J. S., McKenzie, K. & Osgood, C. G. The Tradition of Virgil. Three Papers on the History and Influence of the Poet. Princeton, 1930.
Müntz, E. La légende du Sorcier Virgile dans l'art du XIV, XV, et XVI siècle. Monatsberichte über Kunstwissenschaft, 2.
Nitchie, E. Master Virgil. Boston, 1930.
Nitze, W. A. A Note on Two Virgilian Commonplaces in Twelfth Century Literature. Mélanges Alfred Jeanroy. Paris, 1928.
Ogle, M. B. The Later Tradition of Vergil. CJ, 26, 1930.
Puymaigre, C. de. Virgile au moyen âge. Revue Nouvelle d'Alsace-Lorraine, 5, 1885.
Rand, E. K. The Mediaeval Virgil. SM, 5, 1932.
Rolfe, J. C. Vergil After Two Thousand Years. Proc. Amer. Philos. Soc., 64, 1930.
Romagnoli, E. Le message de Virgile. Paris, 1930.
Roth, K. L. Ueber den Zauberer Virgilius. Germania, 8, 1863.
Sage, E. T. Some Mediaeval Conceptions of Vergil and Their Origins. CJ, 25, 1930.
Savage, J. J. H. Some Possible Sources of Medieval Conceptions of Virgil. Spec., 19, 1944.
Schuchardt, H. Virgil im Mittelalter. In: Romanisches und Keltisches. Strassburg, 1880.
Schwieger, P. Der Zauberer Virgil. Berlin, 1897.
Shennan, S. E. A Message from Virgil. CJ, 19.
Simecek, K. Virgile dans l'antiquité chrétienne. (In Czech). In: Pio Vati. Praha, 1930.
Slater, D. A. Sortes Vergilianae or Vergil and Today. Oxford, 1922.
Smith, K. F. The Later Tradition of Vergil. CW, 9, 1916.
Smuszkin, B. Les mentions de Virgile dans les commentaires du XIe siècle. In: Ksiega Wergiljuszowa. Vilna, 1930.
Spargo, J. W. Virgil the Necromancer. Studies in Virgilian Legends. Harvard U. P., 1934.
Suttina, L. Virgilio nella leggenda e nella fantasia del medio evo. In: Virgilio (ed. by V. Ussani). Milano, 1930-31.
Tescari, O. Modernità nella poesia di Virgilio. Conv., 3, 1931.
Tunison, J. S. Master Virgil. The Author of the Aeneid, as He Seemed in the Middle Ages. Cincinnati, 1890.
Ullman, B. L. Virgil in Certain Mediaeval Florilegia. SM, 5, 1932.
Upson, H. R. Medieval Lives of Virgil. CPh, 38, 1943.
Valentine, T. W. The Medieval Church and Vergil. CW, 25, 1931.
Valmaggi, L. Il Virgilianismo nella letteratura. Rivista di filologia classica, 18, 1890.
Vaudoir-Lainé, O. Virgile, ses transformations et sa légende au moyen âge. Paris, 1869.
Viëtor, W. Der Ursprung der Virgiliussage. ZRPh, 1, 1877.
Weinreich, O. Obtrectatores Vergilii im 19. und 20. Jahrhundert. Ph, 49, 1942.
Wood, E. J. Virgil and To-Day. Leeds, 1945.
Zamboni. Virgilio e l'Eneide secondo i critici del cinquecento. Messina, 1895.
Zappert, G. Virgils Fortleben im Mittelalter. Wien, 1849.

2. Influences in Various Countries.

Haarhoff, T. J. Vergil in the Experience of South AFRICA. Oxford, 1930.
—— Note on Vergil and South Africa. CPh, 1933.
Cataudella, A. Sulla fortuna di Virgilio nel mondo greco-egiziano. Chron. d'Egitto, 1932.
Brinton, A. S. C. Vergilian Allusions in the New England Poets. (AMERICA). CJ, 21, 1925-26.
Johnston, M. Vergil's Eighth Eclogue, a New England Parallel. CW, 25, 1931.
Stecher. Virgile en Belgique. Arch. de l'Acad. de BELGIQUE, 1890.
Groh. V. Virgilio nella letteratura CECOSLOVACCA. Atti 2. Congr. Stud. Roma, 1931.
Hendrich, J. Les traductions tchèques de Virgile (in Czech). In: Pio Vati. Praha, 1930.

Ludvíkovsky, J. Quelques échos de la légende virgilienne dans la vieille littérature tchèque. (In Czech). Ibid.
—— La leggenda virgiliana nella letteratura ceca. SM, 5, 1932.
Novak, A. Le paysage virgilien (dans la littérature tchèque). In: Pio Vati. Praha, 1930.
Novotny, F. Virgile et la philologie tchèque. (In Czech). Ibid.
Ryba, B. La plus ancienne traduction tchèque de l'Enéide de Virgile. Listy Filologicke, 1931.
Collins, J. C. Virgil in **ENGLISH** Hexameters. In: Ephemera critica. Westminster, 1901.
Durling, D. L. Georgic Tradition in English Poetry. New York, 1935.
Fairclough, H. R. The Influence of Virgil Upon the Forms of English Verse. CJ, 26, 1930.
Frost, G. L. Caesar and Virgil Magics in England. MLN, 1936.
Galimberti, A. Correnti virgiliane nell' alta cultura britannica. Conv., 3, 1931.
Heller, J. L. The English Title of Virgil's Epic. CJ, 38, 1943.
Mustard, W. P. Vergil's Georgics and the British Poets. AJPh, 29, 1908.
Nitchie, Elizabeth. Vergil and the English Poets. New York, 1919.
—— Master Vergil. An Anthology of Poems in English on Vergil and Vergilian Themes. New York, 1930.
Olivero, F. Accenni virgiliani nella letteratura inglese nei secoli XVII e XVIII. Ann. Ist. Piemonte, 4, 1930.
Osgood, C. G. Virgil and the English Mind. In: The Tradition of Virgil. Princeton, 1930.
Raby, F. J. E. Some Notes on Virgil, mainly in English Authors, in the Middle Ages. SM, 5, 1932.
Seills, K. C. M. Vergil in the Age of Elizabeth. CJ, 6, 1910.
Stinchcomb. Virgil's Influence upon English Drama. In: Virgil Papers. U. of Pittsburgh, 1930.
Desazars de Montgailhard. La légende de Virgile à Toulouse. (**FRANCE**). Bull. de l'Acad. de Toulouse, 2, 1898-99.
Goerschen, F. Die Vergiltravestien in Frankreich. Dresden, 1937.
Hazard, P. Virgile et les poètes français. In: Le Message de Virgile (ed. by E. Romagnoli). Paris, 1930.
Héraud, M. Virgile en France. Ibid.
Fraenkel, E. Gedanken zu einer deutschen Vergilfeier. (**GERMANY**). Berlin, 1930.
Hefti, F. Virgilio in Germania LNI, 2, 1931.
Lohmeyer, H. Vergil im deutschen Geistesleben bis auf Notker III. Berlin, 1930.
Rychner, M. Vergil und die deutsche Literatur. NSR, 23, 1930. And in: Zur europäischen Literatur zwischen zwei Weltkriegen. Zürich, 1943.
Müller, F. Virgilio e l'Olanda. (**HOLLAND**). SM, 5, 1932.
Murphy, G. Vergilian Influence upon the Vernacular Literature of Medieval Ireland. Ibid.
Ferrigni, M. Virgilio poeta italiano. (**ITALY**). Milano, 1931.
Gardner, E. G. Virgil in Italian Poetry. London, 1931.
Noël, A. Virgile et l'Italie. Paris, 1865.
Paribeni, R. The Bimillenary Virgilian Celebration in Italy. Art & Archaeology, 30, 1930.
Parodi, E. G. I rifacimenti e le traduzioni italiane dell' Eneide prima del Rinascimento. Studi di filologia romanza, 2, 1887.
Santangelo, P. E. Virgilio e lo spirito della nuova Italia. Atti e Memorie della R. Accademia Virgiliana di Mantova, 1931.
—— Virgilio e la nuova Italia. Catania, 1933.
Zabughin, F. Vergilio nel Rinascimento italiano. Bologna, 1921.
Zaniboni. Virgilio e l'Eneide secondo un critico del cinquecento. Messina, 1895. Cf. GSLI, 30, 1897.
Clement, E. W. Vergil's Appeal to the Japanese. (**JAPAN**). CJ, 26, 1931.
Birkenmajer, J. Les traductions polonaises de Virgile. (**POLAND**). Eos, 33.
Chrzanowski, I. Che cosa fu Virgilio per i Polacchi dopo la perdita dell' indipendenza? Ibid.
Hahn, V. De Virgilii apud Polonos fatis saeculo XVI. Ibid.
Lempicki, S. Virgile et la Pologne. KK, 1931.
Pigon, S. Le rôle de Virgile dans le développement de la poésie messianique polonaise. In: Ksiega Wergiljuszawa. Vilna, 1930.
Rebêlo Gonçalves, F. Reminiscências de Vergilio na literatura medieval portuguesa. (**PORTUGAL**), SM, 5, 1932.
Laslo, N. Traductions roumaines de Virgile. (in **RUMANIAN**). Anuarul U. Cluj, 1928-32.
Panas, I. O. De Vergilii Aeneide in ludum iocumque deflexa apud **SLAVOS**. Acta Congr. Phil. Slav, 2. Praha, 1931.

Menéndez Pidal, R. Un episodio de la fama de Virgilio en España. (SPAIN). SM, 5, 1932.

Olwer, L. N. d'. Notules sobre Virgili a Catalunya a l'edat mitjana. Ibid.

Rodriguez-Moñino, A. La edición más antigua de la Eneida en castellano. Bibliografia Hispáncia, 6, 1947.

3. Influences upon Individuals.

Beaussire, de. Deux Virgiliens au XVIe siècle (Robert et Antoine le Chevalier d'**AGUAUX**). Mém. de l'Académie d'Amiens, 3e sér., 4, 1878.

Previale, L. Virgilio e **ALFIERI**. Conv., 2, 1930.

Fraser, A. D. An Eighteenth-Century Critic of Vergil's Military Science. (**ALGAROTTI**). CJ, 18.

Diederich, M. D. Vergil in the Works of St. **AMBROSE**. Washington, 1931. Cf. TAPhA, 1932.

Intra, B. Virgilio e l'**ARIOSTO**. Mantova, 1890.

Rocca, P. Riflessi delle Georgiche nel Furioso. Ann. Lic-Ginn. L. Ariosto di Ferrara, 6. Bologna, 1932-33.

Bassi, D. Sant' **AGOSTINO** e Virgilio. Annali dell'Istruzione Media, 6. (Firenze). 1930.

Coffin, H. C. The Influence of Vergil on St. Jerome and on St. Augustine. CW, 17.

Keseling, P. Virgil bei Augustin. PhW, 1942.

—— Nochmals Virgil bei Augustin. Ibid, 1944.

Rodríguez, C. El alma Vergiliana de San Augustin. Religión y Cultura, 11-12, 1930.

Schelkle, K. H. Virgil in der Deutung Augustins. Stuttgart, 1939.

Wijnpersse, W. M. A. van de. Virgilius bij Augustinus. Stud. Cathol. 7, 1932.

Trompeo, P. P. Da Virgilio al **BAUDELAIRE**. Cultura, 1933.

Ruediger, H. Oswald **BELLOGS** Uebersetzung der Eklogen Virgils (1649). Imprimatur, 7, 1937.

BETTINELLI, S. Lettere virgiliane. (1758).

Calcaterra, C. La questione estetica delle Lettere virgiliane. Parma, 1935.

Osgood, C. G. **BOCCACCIO'S** Knowledge of the Life of Vergil. CPh, 1930.

Pizzagalli, A. M. **CAMOENS** e Virgilio. A&R, 1936.

Monteverdi A,. Un censore di Virgilio, Simone **CAPRADORO**. SM, 5, 1932.

Baldi, R. **CARDUCCI** e Virgilio. MC, 1934.

Quadri, G. A. **CARO** e Cesare Arici nella traduzione dell' Eneide. Brescia, 1884.

Stevens, J. Un humaniste espagnol: le Père Juan-Luis de la **CERDA**, commentateur de Virgile (1558-1643). EC, 13, 1945.

Marasso, A. **CERVANTES** y Virgilio. Buenos Aires, 1937. Cf. Vertice, 2 (Buenos Aires), 1938.

Farinelli, A. **CHATEAUBRIAND** e Virgilio. NAnt, 1930. And in: Attraverso la poesia e la vita. Bologna, 1935.

Huit, C. Virgile et Chateaubriand. L'Enseignement chrétien, 1.XII.1895 .

Naylor, L. H. Chateaubriand and Vergil. Baltimore, 1930.

Atwood, E. B. Two Alternatives of Virgil in **CHAUCER'S** Dido. Spec., Oct., 1938.

Ryba, B. Mathieu **COLLINUS** et ses conférences sur Virgile à l'Université de Prague au XVIe siècle. (In Czech). In: Pio Vati. Praha, 1930.

Aceti, A. Reminiscenze virgiliane nelle opere del cosentino Tomaso **CORNELIO**. Cosenza, 1932.

Auerbach, E. **DANTE** und Virgil. HG, 1931.

Ayo, U. Dante e Vergilio. Pisa, 1931.

Bagnani, G. The Classical Technique: Virgil, Dante, and Pope. The Phoenix (Canada), 1947.

Carter, A. E. An Unrecognized Virgilian Passage in Dante. Ital., 21, 1944.

Cavarretta, G. Virgilio e Dante, confronti critici tra l'Eneide e la Divina Commedia. Palermo, 1898.

Cesareo, E. Un confronto nuovo fra Dante e Virgilio. PhW, 1930.

Cipolla, F. Dante censore di Virgilio. ARIV, 61, 1902.

Cocchia, E. Un preteso errore di Dante nell' interpretazione dell' Eneide. Atti della R. Accademia di archeologia di Napoli, 9, 1926.

Comparetti, D. Virgilio nella tradizione letteraria fino a Dante. NAnt, 1, 1866.

—— Dante e Virgilio. A&R, 1924.

Franco, C. & Méléar, P. Virgile, Dante, Camoëns et l'expansion du génie latin. Paris, 1924.

Galassi Paluzzi, C. Perche Dante scelse Virgilio a sua guida. Annuario Dantesco, 9. (Firenze), 1938.

Hardie, W. R. Virgil, Statius and Dante. Journal of Roman Studies, 6, 1916.

Ingoglia, G. Virgilio e Dante Alghieri attraverso 14 secoli. Catania, 1914.

Jullian, C. Virgile et Dante devant l'Italie. In: Le message de Virgile. (ed. by E. Romagnoli). Paris, 1930.

Lechthaler, J. Das Verhältniss Virgils zu Dante. Progr. Halle, 1887.

Mazzoni, G. Dante e Virgilio. In: Virgilio (ed. by V. Ussani & L. Suttina). Milano, 1930-31.

MacVay, A. P. Dante's Strange Treatment of Vergil. TAPhA, 1945.

Ovidio, F. d'. Due riscontri fra l'Eneide e la Divina Commedia. A&R, 2, 1900.

Patroni, G. L'episodio virgiliano di Polidoro ed i dantisti. Rendiconti dell'Istituto Lombardo di scienze e lettere, 71, 1938.

Pollard, J. R. T. Dante's Guide. Vergilius, 3, 1939.

Richardson, B. E. A Comparative Study of the Vergilian and Dantesque Topography of the Inferno and Purgatorio. TAPhA, 1932.

Sanesi, I. Polidoro e Pier della Vigna. SM, 5, 1932.

Silverstein, H. T. Dantc and Virgil the Mystic. HSPhL, 14, 1932.

Toynbee, P. Aeneidorum in Dante's De vulgari eloquentia. GSLI, 34, 1899.

Vivier, R. Ce que Virgile fut pour Dante. RCC, 39, 1937-38.

Wolfe ,A. L. Vergil as Dante Knew Him. CJ, 26, 1931.

Bennett, J. A. W. The Early Famc of Gavin **DOUGLAS'S** Eneados. MLN, 61, 1946.

Watt, L. M. Douglas's Aeneid. Cambridgc, 1920.

Brower, R. A. **DRYDEN'S** Poetic Diction and Virgil. PhQ, 18, 1939.

—— Dryden's Epic Manner and Virgil. PMLA, 55, 1940.

Diekmann, J. Dryden's Virgil Compared with the Latin Original. Diss. Rostock, 1874.

MacPherson, C. Ueber die Virgil-Uebersetzung des John Dryden. Diss. Berlin, 1910.

Nick, C. F. J. De Virgilii carminibus a Drydeno poeta in linguam Britannicam translatis. Diss. Jena, 1868.

Decker, J. de. Vergilius en **EKKEHARD.** Handel. 14. Nederl. Philologencongr., 1931.

Wagner, H. Ekkehard und Vergil. Heidelberg, 1939.

Johnston, M. John **EVELYN'S** Vergilian Pilgrimage. CW, 23, 1930.

Fucilla, J. G. Vergil and Antonio **FERREIRA.** SPh, 40, 1943.

Geld, G. Anatole **FRANCE** et Virgile. Hermes, messager classique en Russie, 1915.

Alcalá, M. Virgilio y **GARCILASO.** Tierra Nueva (México), 1, 1940.

—— Del virgilianismo de Garcilaso de la Vega. Filosofia y letras. (México), 1946.

Chapman, C. O. Virgil and the **GAWAIN**-Poet. PMLA, 60, 1945.

Bogner, H. Eine unbekannte Entlehnung **GOETHES.** Ph, 1933.

Hänni, R. Der Vergilische und der Faustische Mensch. Schweizerische Rundschau, 32, 1932.

Nissen, T. J. P. **HEBELS** Feldhüter und Vergils 7. Ekloge. Schweiz. Archiv f. Volkskunde, 35, 1936.

Dziech, J. De Vergilii cultu apud **HIERONYMUM.** Eos, 33, 1930-31.

Anon. Vergiliana in the Oliver Wendell **HOLMES** Library. Andover Press (Mass.), 1931.

Marcellino, R. E. Vergil and A. E. **HOUSMAN.** CJ., 37, 1941.

Ghisalberti, F. Le chiose virgiliane di Benvenuto da **IMOLA.** Studi Virgiliani, 9. Mantova, 1930.

Manning, C. A. The Aeneid of **KOTLYAREVSKY.** CW, 58, 1942.

Wolff, E. Die allegorische Vergilerklärung des Cristoforo **LANDINO. NJKA,** 1919.

Schullian, D. M. **LEOPARDI** and the Parco Vergiliano. Vergilius, 3, 1939.

Faider, P. Claude **LORRAIN** interprète de Virgile. Boll. Stud. Medit., 1930.

Crahay, R. Virgile et **LUCIEN.** RBPh, 1938.

Johnston, M. **MACAULAY** and Vergil. CW, 29, 1936.

Stiebitz, F. Virgile et son portrait dans la poésie de J. S. **MACHAR.** (In Czech). In: Pio Vati. Praha, 1930.

Formenti, A. Virgilio e **MANZONI.** Brescia, 1915.

Trompeo. Col Manzoni tra Virgilio e Racine. In: Rilegature gianseniste. Milano, 1930.

Bowra, C. M. From Virgil to **MILTON.** New York, 1945.

Riley, E. H. Milton's Tribute to Vergil. SPh, 27, 1929-30.

Riddehough, G. B. William **MORRIS'S** Translation of the Aeneid. JEGPh, 36, 1937.

Brussoff, V. **NAPOLEON** et Virgile. Hermes, messager classique en Russie, 1916.

Vasquez, M. Virgilio, Bolívar y **OLMEDO.** In: Estudios Virgilianos de la Com-

pania de Jesús en el Ecuador. Quito, 1931.
Kolbuszewski, C. OSINSKI traducteur de l'Enéide. In: Ksiega Wergiljuszowa. (Vilna), 1930.
Desonay, F. Virgile selon Jean d'OUTREMEUSE. SM, 5, 1932.
Sliwinska, H. De Vergili cultu apud OWENUM. Eos, 33.
Nolhac, P. de. Virgile chez Pétrarque. RDM, 59, 1930. Cf. SM, 5, 1932.
Cocchia, E. Una felice emendazione del POLIZIANO alla fine della 4. Ecloga. Atti della R. Accad. di Archeologia di Napoli, 11, 1930.
Lange, P. RONSARDS Franciade und ihr Verhältniss zu Vergils Aeneide. Progr. Wurzen i. St., Leipzig, 1887.
Mustard, W. P. SANNAZARO'S Interpretation of Vergil's Fourth Eglogue. CW, 7.
Junker, H. P. SCARRONS Virgile travesti. Oppeln, 1883.
Boltenstern, P. von. SCHILLERS Vergilstudien. Progr. Koslin, 1894, 1901.
Brosin, O. Anklänge an Virgil bei Schiller. ALG 8, 1879.
Dettmer, H. Zur Charakteristik von Schillers Umdichtungen des Vergil. Progr. Hildesheim, 1899.
Gerhardt, E. S. Schiller and Vergil. CW, 24, 1930.
Hauff, G. Schiller und Virgil. ZVL, 1, 1887-88.
Horn, P. Schillers freie Uebersetzung des 2. und 4. Gesangs der Aeneid. Marburg, 1923.
Jarislowsky, J. Schillers Uebertragungen aus Vergil im Rahmen der deutschen Aeneis-Uebersetzung des 18. Jahrhunderts. Jena, 1927.
Jonas, F. Zu Schillers Uebersetzungen aus dem Virgil. ALG, 7, 1878.
Neuhoeffer, R. Schiller als Uebersetzer des Vergil. Progr. 1893.
Oesterlein, T. Virgil in Schillers Gedichten. In: Studien zu Virgil und Horaz. Tübingen, 1885.
Pilch, S. Virgil in Schiller and Goethe. (In Polish). KK, 7, 1933.
Rubensohn, M. Zu Schillers Uebersetzung der Aeneide. Neue Jb für Philologie und Pädagogik, 1893.
Selva, E. Schiller traduttore di Virgilio. A&R, 17, 1939.
Woyte, C. Aeneis 2. und 4. Gesang in der Nachdichtung von F. Schiller (mit Anmerkungen). Leipzig, 1939.
Gammans, H. W. SHENSTONE'S Appreciation of Vergil. CW, 22, 1929.
Pilch, S. Le Lechus de Jean SIKORSKI. (In Polish). Eos, 1916.
Skimina, S. De Bernardo SILVESTRI Vergilii interprete. In: Commentationes Vergilianae. Cracow, 1930.
Riess, S. Les traductions virgiliennes de SLOWACKI. In: Ksiega Wergiljuszowa. (Vilna), 1930.
Hughes, M. Y. Virgil and SPENSER. Berkeley, 1929.
Webb, W. S. Virgil in Spenser's Epic Theory. ELH, 4, 1937.
Giavesu, A. I poemi di Virgilio in un centone di P. A. SPERA, ossia la passione di N. S. Gesù Cristo cantata coi versi di Virgilio. Napoli, 1939.
Schmidt, H. Richard STANYHURSTS Uebersetzung von Virgils Aeneide, I-IV. Diss. Breslau, 1887.
Dittes, R. Zu SURREYS Aneisübertragung. Wien, 1902.
Fest, O. Ueber Surrey's Virgilübersetzung. Berlin, 1907.
Limouze, A. S. A Note on Vergil and The Battle of the Books (SWIFT). PhQ, 27, 1948.
Beall, C. B. A Virgilian Simile in TASSO and Chateaubriand. MLN, 1931.
Grazia, D. Reminiscenze classiche dell' Eneide e della Gerusalemme liberata. Catania, 1894.
Mustard, W. P. Tasso's Debt to Vergil. CW, 13, 1920.
Anon. Virgil and TENNYSON: A Literary Parallel. QR, 1901.
Mustard, W. P. Tennyson and Virgil. AJPh, 20, 1899-1900.
Rawnsley, H. D. Virgil and Tennyson. Macmillan's Mag., 33, 1875. And in: Memories of the Tennysons. Glasgow, 1900.
Starke, F. J. Tennyson und Virgil. NM, 9, 1938.
Steffen, W. Virgile et TREMBECKI. KK, 1931.
Brinton, A. C. Maphaeus VEGIUS and his Thirteenth Book of the Aeneid. Stanford U. P., 1930.
Fairley, B. Die Eneide Heinrichs von VELDEKE und der Roman d'Enéas. Jena, 1910.
Firmery, L. L'Enéas et la traduction de Veldecke. Rev. de philologie française, 10, 1896.
Gogala di Leesthal, O. Enrico Veldeke e l'Eneit. SM, 5, 1932.
Pey, A. L'Eneide de Henri de Veldeke et le roman d'Enéas attribué à Benoît de Sainte-More. 1860.

Teusink, D. Das Verhältnis zwischen Veldekes Eneide und dem Alexanderlied. Amsterdam, 1945.

Wittkopp, W. W. Die Eneide Heinrichs von Veldecke und der Roman d'Enéas. Diss. Leipzig, 1929.

Wormer, E. Virgil und Heinrich von Veldeke. ZDPh, 3, 1871.

Thomas, A. Notice sur la Carliade, poème épique latin d'Ugolino **VERINO**, 1494. Ann. de la Faculté des lettres de Bordeaux, 4, 1882.

Alberson, H. S. Lo mio maestro. **(VIDA)**. CJ, 32, 1937.

Verdenius, A. A. Het Vergiliaanse droomverschijnings-motief bij **VONDEL**. Hermeneus, 9, 1936-37.

Vetessy, G. **VOEROESMARTY** et Virgile. In: Les Hongrois et la civilisation gréco-romaine. (In Hungarian). Debrecen, 1935.

Ivancic, J. Wie hat **WALTHER VON CHATILLON** Virgil nachgeahmt? Progr., 1878.

Espinosa Polit, A. La pastoral virgiliana de **WHICHER**. Quito (Ecuador), 1937.

Watts, N. Virgil and **WORDSWORTH**. Dublin Review, 1946.

CHAPTER SEVEN

Other Roman Authors.

APULEIUS: See also Amor and Psyche, I. VI. 10.

Cortés, H. Algunas reminiscencias de Apuleyo en la literature española. RFE, 1935.

Costanza, S. La fortuna di L. Apuleio nell'età di mezzo. Palermo, 1937.

Haight, E. H. On Certain Uses of Apuleius' Story of Cupid and Psyche in English Literature. PL, 26, 1915.

—— Apuleius and his Influences. In: Our Debt to Greece and Rome. New York, 1927.

Hoffman, A. Das Psyche-Märchen des Apuleius in der englischen Litteratur. Strassburg, 1908.

Huet, K. Le roman d'Apulée était-il connu au moyen âge? Le Moyen Age, 2e Sér, 13, 1909.

Kawczynski, M. Ist Apuleius im Mittelalter bekannt gewesen? Bausteine zur roman. Philologie, 47, 1905.

Maria, U. de. Dell' Asino d'oro di Apuleio e di varie sue imitazioni nella nostra letteratura. Roma, 1901.

Paratone, E. La novella in Apuleio. Palermo, 1928.

Reimann, A. Des Apuleius Märchen von Amor und Psyche in der französischen Litteratur des XVII. Jahrhunderts. Progr. Wohlau, 1885.

Weyman, C. Studien zu Apuleius und seinen Nachahmern. SBAW, 2, 1893.

Wibley, C. Apuleius' The Golden Ass, Translated by William Adlingtons (1566). Preface by C. Wibley. In: The Tudor Translations. London, 1892-96.

Rossi, E. Un plagio del Boiardo traduttore? GSLI, 57, 1939.

Spampanato, V. Giordano Bruno e la letteratura dell' asino. Portici, 1904.

Tamassia, N. Reminiscenze Apuleiane nei Promessi Sposi. (Manzoni). ARIV, 81.

Generosa, Sister M. Apuleius and A Midsumer Night's Dream: Analogue or Source, Which? SPh, 42, 1945.

Starnes, D. T. Shakespeare and Apuleius. PMLA, 60, 1945.

CAESAR: See also Thematology, I. VI. 10.

Bossuat, R. Traductions françaises des Commentaires de César à la fin du XV. siècle. BHR, 3, 1943.

Cuendet, G. César et la langue gauloise. Mélanges Ch. Gilliard. Lausanne, 1944.

Nearing, H. Julius Caesar and the Tower of London. MLN, 63, 1948.

Schwabe, E. Das Fortleben von Caesars Schriften in der deutschen Litteratur und Schule seit der Humanistenzeit. NJKA, 1902.

Chistoni, P. Le fonti classiche e medievali del **CATONE** dantesco. Mélanges A. d'Ancona. Firenze, 1901. Cf. GSLI, 40.

Boas, M. Een latijnsche metrische Catoparaphrase met parodie in een onbekenden italiaanschen druk van 1539. Het Boek, 17, 1927.

—— Het spaansche substantivum Caton. Ibid, 1928.

Nehab, J. Der altenglische Cato. Diss. Göttingen, 1879.

Goldberg, M. O. Die Catonischen Distichen während des Mittelalters in der englischen und französischen Litteratur. Diss. 1883.

Pietsch, K. Two Old Spanish Versions of the Disticha Catonis. Chicago, 1902.

Pritchard, J. P. Cato in Concord (Thoreau). CW, 36, 1942.

Tobler, A. Die altvenezianischen Uebersetzungen des Dionysius Cato. APAW, 1883.

—— Die altprovenzalische Version der Disticha Catonis. Berlin, 1898.

Ulrich, J. Eine altlothringische Uebersetzung des Dionysius Cato. ZRPh, 30, 1895.
—— Die Uebersetzung der Distichen des Pseudo-Cato von Jean de Paris. Der Cato Jean Lefèvres. Der Cato des Adam de Suel. RF, 15, 1903.
Zarncke, F. Geschichte der deutschen Uebersetzungen der unter dem Namen Cato bekannten Distichen bis zum Ende des XV. Jahrhunderts. Leipzig, 1852.
Anon. **CATULLS** Gedichte in neuer Verdeutschung. Europa, 1858.
Anastasi, A. Catullo e l'umanesimo. Acireale Tip. XX. secolo, 1919.
Cipolla. Catulla nel medio evo. Archivio veneto, 1887.
Coulter, C. C. A Seventeenth-Century Parody of Catullus 4. CPh, 1917.
Duckett, E. S. Catullus in English Poetry. Northampton, (Mass.). 1925.
—— Some English Echoes of Catullus. CW, 15.
Emperor, J. B. The Catullian Influence in English Lyric Poetry, circa 1600-50. U. of Missouri Studies, 3, 1928.
Harrington, K. P. Catullus and his Influence. In: Our Debt to Greece and Rome. Boston, 1923.
McPeek, J. A. S. Catullus in Strange and Distant Britain. Harvard U. P., 1939.
Naum, T. A. Catulle en roumain. Impressions et suggestions. (In Rumanian). Anuarul Institutului de studii clasice (Cluj), 2, 1933-35.
Ramminger, A. Motivgeschichtliche Studien zu Catulls Basiagedichten, mit einen Anhang: Aus dem Nachleben der catullischen Basiagedichte. Würzburg, 1937.
Savage, J. J. H. Mediaeval Echoes of Catullus. CW, 37, 1943-44.
Schuster, M. Catull und Tibull bei Jakob Balde. PhW. 1936.
Schramm, W. L. Campion, Horace and Catullus. PhQ, 1933.
Cohon, B. J. A Catullian Echo in George Chapman's The Revenge of Bussy d'Ambois. MLN, 60, 1945.
Mandra, R. Catullus and Foscolo. Classical Outlook, 19, 1942.
Lipscomb. H. C. Catullus and Ellen Glasgow. CJ, 29, 1934.
Ussani, V. Catullo e Tibullo nella Légende des siècles di V. Hugo. Rassegna italiana di lingue e letterature classiche, 2.
Wedeck, H. E. A Mediaeval Catullus, Iohannes Secundus. PhQ, 19, 1940.
Schuster, M. Eduard Mörike und Catullus. Zs. f. d. österr. Gymnasien, 1916.
Ammendola, G. L'edizione e la traduzione di Catullo di C. Pascal. Torino, 1921.
Weston, A. H. The Nicean Barks of Edgar Allen Poe. CJ, 29, 1933-34.
Lipscomb, H. C. Poe's Nicean Barks Again. Ibid.
Beach, J. W. A Perfumed Sea. Ibid.
Harrington, K. P. The Manes Catulliani of J. C. Scaliger. CJ, 27, 1932.
Bowen, E. W. Shelley and Catullus. Sewanee Rev., 7, 1899.
Mustard, W. P. Tennyson and Catullus. Nation, 1898.
Baron, H. **CICERO** and the Roman Civic Spirit in the Middle Ages and Early Renaissance. BRL, 22, 1938.
Beltrami, A. Il Sogno di Scipione di M. Tullio Cicerone e le sue imitazioni nella letteratura. Comm. dell' Ateneo di Brescia, 1901.
Bertrand, E. Cicéron au théâtre. Grenoble, 1897.
Bossuat, R. Anciennes traductions françaises du De officiis de Cicéron. Bibliothèque de l'Ecole des Chartes, 1935.
Burnett, G. A. The Reputation of Cicero Among the English Deists. Diss. U. of Southern California, 1947.
Clark, A. C. Ciceronianism. In: G. S. Gordon, English Literature and the Classics. Oxford, 1912.
Dunn, Martha B. Cicero in Maine. Boston, 1905.
Grummel, W. C. Cicero's Influence on Medieval Philosophy. TAPhA, 1945.
Gummere, R. M. Cicero in the State House. CJ, 28, 1933.
Hartfelder, K. Eine deutsche Uebersetzung von Ciceros Cato aus der Humanistenzeit. Germania, 1888.
Hayes, G. P. Cicero's Humanism To-Day. CJ, 34, 1939.
Laurand, L. La réputation et l'influence de Cicéron. Hum., 8, 1931.
Mariès, L. Une influence toujours vivante et agissante: Cicéron. Et, 218, 1934.
Modersohn, A. B. Cicero im englischen Geistesleben des 16. Jahrhunderts. Archiv, 149.
Nelson, N. E. Cicero's De officiis in Christian Thought, 300-1300. U. of Michigan Publ. Lang. and Lit., 1933.
Peaks, M. B. Cicero and American Lawyers. CJ, 22, 1927.
Rolfe, J. C. Cicero and his Influence. In: Our Debt to Greece and Rome. Boston, 1923.

Sabbadini, R. Storia del Ciceronismo e di altre questioni letterarie nell' età della Rinascenza. Torino, 1886.
Scott, I. Controversies over the Imitation of Cicero. New York, 1910.
Shaull, D. Cicero and Modern Problems. CJ, 26, 1931.
Slaughter, M. S. Cicero and his Critics. CJ, 17.
Traub, G. Studien zum Einfluss Ciceros auf die höfische Moral. Greifswald, 1934.
Zelinskii, F. Cicero in the History of European Culture (in Russian). Vestnik Evropy, 1896.
Zielinski, T. Cicero im Wandel der Jahrhunderte. Leipzig, 1912 & 1929.
Emeneau, M. B. Ambrose and Cicero. CW, 24, 1930.
Baldwin, C. S. St. Augustine and the Rhetoric of Cicero. PCA, 1925.
Eskridge, J. B. The Influence of Cicero upon Augustine in the Development of his Oratorical Theory for the Training of the Ecclesiastical Orator. Diss. Chicago, 1912.
Millar, M. F. X. The Significance of St. Augustine's Criticism of Cicero's Definition of the State. Festgabe Geyser. Regensburg, 1930.
Alfonsi, L. Studii Boeziani. Aevum, 19, 1945.
Canter, H. V. The Impeachments of Verres and Hastings: Cicero and Burke. CJ, 9, 1914.
Rossi, E. Parafrasi turca del De senectute presentata a Solimano il Magnifico dal Bailo Marino de Cavalli (1559). Rendiconti della R. Accad. dei Lincei (Roma), 1936.
Anderson, E. P. Some Notes on Chaucer's Treatment of the Somnium Scipionis. TAPhA, 33, 1902.
Achels, T. O. Erasmus über die griechischen Briefe des Brutus. RhM, 72.
Johnston, M. Gladstone, Quintilian and Cicero. CW, 27, 1934.
Wilson, H. & Forbes, C. Gabriel Harvey's Ciceronianus. U. of Nebraska Studies in the Humanities, 4, 1945.
Fluss, V. Zur alttschechischen Cicero-Uebersetzung des Rehor Hruby von Jeleni. In: Charisteria A. Rzach. Reichenberg, 1930.
Weinreich, O. Jean Paul und Ciceros Proömien. RhM, 1941.
Hritzu, J. N. Jerome, the Christian Cicero. CW, 37, 1943-44.
Maggini, F. Orazioni Ciceroniane volgarizzate da Brunetto Latini. GSLI, 114, 1939.
Hofmeister, A. Cicero in der Vita Lieberti. N. Archiv f. ältere deutsche Geschichte, 1929.
Perpolli, C. Giacomo Leopardi e il De re publica di Cicerone. Ath., 1917.
Beeson, C. H. Lupus of Ferrières as Scribe and Text Critic. Cambridge (Mass.), 1930.
—— Lupus of Ferrières and Hadoard: the Knowledge of Cicero in the 9th Century. CPh, 1948.
Mierow, H. E. Cicero and Mark Twain. CJ, 20, 1924.
Bossuat, R. Jean Miélot, traducteur de Cicéron. Bibl. de l'Ecole des Chartes, 1938.
Croce, B. Intorno al giudizio del Mommsen su Cicerone. Quaderni della critica, 2, 1946.
Alexander, W. H. The Sieur de Montaigne and Cicero. UTQ, 9, 1940.
Hortis, A. M. T. Cicero nelle opere del Petrarca e del Boccaccio. Trieste, 1878.
Mustard, W. P. Petrarch's Africa. AJPh, 1921.
Rüegg, W. Cicero und der Humanismus. Formale Untersuchungen über Petrarca und Erasmus. Zürich, 1946.
Seiver, G. O. Cicero's De Oratore and Rabelais. PMLA, 59, 1944.
Boissier, G. Cicéron et Mme de Sévigné. RDM, 15.IV.1865.
Palmer, J. F. Shakespeare and Cicero. N&Q, 6, 1900.
Regteren Altena, A. D. van. Cicero en Shakespeare. Hermeneus, 11, 1938-39.
Rand, E. K. Cicero in the Courtroom of St. Thomas Aquinas. Milwaukee, 1946.
Gates, E. J. Góngora's Indebtedness to **CLAUDIAN**. RR, 1937.
May, G. Racine avait-il lu **ENNIUS?** MLN, 62, 1947.
Brock, J. **HYGINS** Fabeln in der deutschen Literatur. München, 1913.
Whitford, R. C. **JUVENAL** in England. PhQ, 7, 1928.
Englaender, D. La Xe Satire de Boileau comparée à la VIe de Juvénal. Progr. Berlin, 1904.
Sacret, J. H. Dante's Knowledge of Juvenal. RR, 1937.
Huntley, F. L. Dryden, Rochester, and the Eighth Satire of Juvenal. PhQ, 18, 1939.
Le Saint, W. Juvenal's Rome and Johnson's London. CB, 10, 1933-34.
McEuen, Kathryn A. Jonson and Juvenal. RES, 21, 1945.
Stein, A. Joseph Hall's Imitation of Juvenal. MLR, 43, 1948.

Westgate, R. J. W. & MacKendrick, P. L. Juvenal and Swift. CJ, 37, 1942.
Baroni, A. Tito **LIVIO** nel Rinascimento. Pavia, 1889.
Berchem, D. van. Tito Livio nella Svizzera del Rinascimento. Quaderni Liviani. Roma, 1943.
Pannier, L. Notice biographique sur le bénédictin Pierre Bersuire, premier traducteur français de Tite Live. Bibl. de l'Ecole des Chartes, 1872.
Macszke, J. L. A Neglected Source of Corneille's Horace. MPh, 1, 1904.
Scherillo, M. Dante e Tito Livio. Instit. lomb. d. scienze e lett., 2, 1897.
Edwards, W. A. Macaulay and Livy. CW, 23, 1929.
Lebègue, R. La traduction de Tite-Live par Malherbe. BHR, 1, 1941.
Pigeot, G. La traduction du XXXIIIe livre de Tite-Live par Malherbe. REL, 1945.
Bernasconi. Influence de la première décade de Tite-Live sur Plutarque. REL, 1937.
Dean, Ruth, J. The Earliest Known Commentary on Livy by Nicholas Trevet. Medievalia et Humanistica, 3, 1945.
Bataillard. **LUCAIN**, son poème et ses traducteurs. Paris, 1861.
Fischli, W. Studien zum Fortleben der Pharsalia des Annaeus Lucanus. Luzern, 1943-44.
Fränkel, E. Lucan als Mittler des antiken Pathos. VBW, 2, 1924.
Maxwell, J. C. Lucan's First Translation. N&Q, 192, 1947.
Sanford, E. M. Quotations from Lucan in Mediaeval Latin Authors. TAPhA, 1932 & AJPh, 1934.
Schlayer, C. Spuren Lukans in der spanischen Dichtung. Heidelberg, 1928.
Bickel, E. Ein Motiv aus Lucan bei E. M. Arndt: Der Gott der Eisen wachsen liess. RhM, 1933.
Chambers, F. M. Lucan and the Antiquietez de Rome. (du Bellay). PMLA, 60, 1945.
Shannon, E. F. Chaucer and Lucan's Pharsalia. MPh, 16, 1919.
Ussani, V. Lectura Dantis: Dante et Lucano. Firenze, 1917.
Harris, L. J. Lucan's Pharsalia and Jonson's Catiline. MLN, 1919.
Shorey, P. Keats and Lucan. CPh, 22, 1927.
Condee, R. W. Lodge and a Lucan Passage from Mirandula. MLN, 63, 1948.
Martin, L. C. Lucan-Marlowe? Chapman. RES, 24, 1948.
Gundolf, F. Seckendorffs Lucan. SHAW, 1930.
Ackermann, R. Lucans Pharsalia in den Dichtungen Shelleys. Mit einer Uebersicht ihres Einflusses auf die englische Litteratur. Progr. Zweibrücken, 1896.
Bushnell, C. C. A Parallelism between Lucan and Linas in Tintern Abbey. (Wordsworth). JEGPh, 4, 1902.
LUCRETIUS: See also Epicure, II. III. 13.
Baillou, J. Sur les traductions françaises de Lucrèce au XVIe siècle. BAGB, 1933.
Belowski, E. Lukrez in der französischen Literatur der Renaissance. Berlin, 1934.
Counson, A. Lucrèce en France. L'anti-Lucrèce. Musée belge, 15.X.1902.
Dorez, L. Lucrèce et la poésie philosophique au XIXe siècle. Revue générale, 1884.
Fusil, C. A. Lucrèce et la pensée française au XIXe siècle. RHLF, 44, 1938.
Hadzsits, G. D. Lucretius and his Influence. In: Our Debt to Greece and Rome. London, 1935.
Hathaway, B. The Lucretian Return upon Ourselves in Eighteenth-Century Theories of Tragedy. PMLA, 62, 1947.
Hocke, G. R. Lukrez in Frankreich von der Renaissance bis zur Revolution. Bonn, 1935-37.
Hosius, C. Zur italienischen Ueberlieferung des Lucrez. RhM, 1914.
Johnston, M. Roman and Russian Restlessness. CW, 27, 1934.
Lehnerdt, M. Lucretius in der Renaissance. Progr. Königsberg, 1904.
Mustard, W. P. Humanistic Imitations of Lucretius. CW, 12.
Philippe, S. Lucrèce dans la théologie chrétienne du IIIe au XIIIe siècle. Revue de l'hist. des religions, 33, 1896.
Spaeth, J. W. Some Modern Reminiscences of Lucretius. CJ, 29, 1933.
Stroick, A. Nachahmungen von Lucretius Carus De rerum natura. PhW, 1931.
Vaganay, H. Le seizième siècle a-t-il pu lire Lucrèce en français? BAGB, 1932.
Johnston, M. Mr. Gamaliel Bradford on Lucretius. CW, 23, 1930.
Lipscomb, H. C. Lucretius and Bridge's Testament of Beauty. TAPhA, 1933 & CJ, 31, 1935.
Wagenblass, J. H. Keats and Lucretius. MLR, 32, 1937.
Goethe, J. W. von. Von Knebels Uebersetzung des Lucrez. Sämtliche Werke, 28. Berlin, 1821.
Borra, S. Spiriti e forme affini in Lucrezio e Leopardi. Bologna, 1934.
Malein, A. Molière et Lucrèce. Biriouteh, 6, 1918.

Perrotta Nosei, A. Marcello Palingenio Stellato e Lucrezio. SIFC, 5.
Teixeira de Pascoas, J. Paulus en Lucretius. De Stem, 17, 1937.
Krappe, A. H. The Sources of B. Perez Galdos Doña perfecta, cap. VI. PhQ, 7, 1928.
Sainte-Beuve, C. A. Lucrèce en vers français par M. de Pongerville. Globe, 13.IV.1830.
Martin, L. C. Lucretius and The Rape of the Lock. (Pope). RES, 20, 1944.
Neri, F. Lucrezio e la poesia di Ronsard. A&R, 1920. And in: Il Maggio delle Fate. Torino, 1944.
Birch, W. J. Shakespeare and Lucretius. N&Q, 11.IX.1886.
Greenlaw, E. Spenser and Lucretius. SPh, 1920.
Allen, K. Lucretius the Poet and Tennyson's Poem Lucretius. PL, 11, 1899.
Korfmacher, W. C. Lucretius and Tennyson's Palace of Art. CB, 9, 1932.
Wilner, O. L. Tennyson and Lucretius. CJ, 25, 1930.
Cronk, G. G. Lucretius and Thomson's Autumnal Fogs. AJPh, 1930.
Sinko, T. **MANILIUS** et Mickievicz. (In Polish). Eos, 1914.
Jong, K. H. E. de. De Bilderdijkio Manilii vestigia secuto. Mnemosyne, 4, 1936.
Amos, A. **MARTIAL** and the Moderns. Cambridge, 1858.
Bakos, J. Les Hongrois et la civilisation gréco-romaine, I: Martial dans la littérature hongroise. (In Hungarian). Debrecen, 1935.
Guilan, A. A. Martial and the Epigram in Spain in the Sixteenth and Seventeenth Centuries. Diss. Philadelphia, 1930.
Johanneau, E. Epigrammes contre Martial, ou les Mille et une drôleries . . . de ses traducteurs. Paris, 1834.
Levy, R. Martial und die deutsche Epigrammatik des siebzehnten Jahrhunderts. Stuttgart, 1903.
Nixon, P. Martial and the Modern Epigram. In: Our Debt to Greece and Rome. New York, 1927.
Whipple, T. K. Martial and the English Epigram from Sir Thomas Wyatt to Ben Jonson. Berkeley, 1925.
Parga y Poudal, S. Marcial en la preceptiva de Baltasar Gracián. Rev. arch. bibl., 34, 1930.
Nixon, P. Herrick and Martial. CPh, 5, 1910.
Briggs, W. D. Source Material for Jonson's Epigrams and Forest. CPh, 11, 1916.
Johnston, M. Ben Jonson and Martial. CW, 28, 1934.
Visghi, I. Gli Epigrammi di Valerio Marciale tradotti da Giuseppe Lipparini. Conv., 13, 1941.
Camp, T. W. Another Version of The Things that Cause a Quiet Lyfe. (Earl of Surrey). MLN, 52, 1937.
Lendrum. Wordsworth and Martial. Academy, 16.III.1895.
Kittredge, G. L. Chaucer and **MAXIMIANUS**. AJPh, 9, 1888.
Liddell, M. The Middle English Translation of **PALLADIUS'** De re rustica. Berlin, 1895.
Struever, C. Die mittelenglische Uebersetzung des Palladius. Diss. Göttingen, 1887.
Hering, G. F. **PERSIUS**. Geschichte seines Nachlebens und seiner Uebersetzungen in der deutschen Literatur. Berlin, 1935.
Galdi, M. Il Monti traduttore di Persio. Museion, Rivista di antichità, 2, 1924.
Ghisalberti, F. Paolo de Perugia commentatore di Persio. Rendiconti del R. Istituto Lombardo di Scienze e Lettere, 62, 1929.
Allen, P. S. The Romanesque Lyric. Studies in its Background and Development from **PETRONIUS** to the Cambridge Songs, 50-1050. Chapel Hill (N. C.), 1928.
Collignon, A. Pétrone au moyen âge et dans la littérature française. Les Annales de l'Est, 1893.
Johnston, M. A Spanish Parallel. CW, 24, 1931.
Knapp, C. The Cena Trimalchionis of Petronius Illustrated by a Story in the Saturday Evening Post. CW, 28, 1935.
Peck, H. T. An American Edition of Petronius. Bookman, 1903.
Pokrovskij, M. Pétrone et le folklore russe. C. R. de l'Académie des sciences de Russie, 1930.
Rini, A. Petronius in Italy from the Thirteenth Century to the Present Time. New York, 1937.
Sage, E. T. An Unidentified (16th Century) Contributor to Petronian Criticism. TAPhA, 1934.
Sterling, M. Notes on the First English Translation of Petronius. Bibliographical Notes & Queries, July, 1936.
—— Notes on the Second English Translation of Petronius. Ibid. Oct., 1936.
—— Notes on the Spanish Translations of Petronius. Ibid. Jan. & April, 1938.
Terrebrasse, H. de. Recherches bibliogra-

phiques: La traduction de Pétrone. Lyon, 1888.
Ullman, B. L. Petronius in the Mediaeval Florilegia. CPh, 1930.
—— The Text of Petronius in the Sixteenth Century. Ibid.
Johnston, M. On Toothpicks in Jane Austen and Petronius. CW, 29, 1935.
Schoenberger, J. K. Petronius bei Cervantes. PhW, 1942.
Sage, E. T. Giraldus Cambrensis and Petronius. Spec., 1927.
Constans, L. A. Le Bourgeois gentilhomme (Molière) et le Festin de Trimalchion. Mélanges d'archéologie et d'histoire de l'Ecole fr. de Rome, 1915.
Péricaud, M. A. Curiosités littéraires: Pétrarque et Pétrone. Lyon, 1862.
Sage, E. T. Petronius, Poggio and John of Salisbury. CPh, 1916.
—— Scaliger and the Text of Petronius. TAPhA, 1933.
Pilch, S. Petronius and Tacitus in Sienkiewicz. (In Polish). Eos, 1938.
Cordasco, F. Smollett and Petronius. MLQ, 9, 1948.
Cotton, G. **PHEDRE**, les plus belles fables, annotées et rapprochées de celles de La Fontaine. Namur, 1933.
Dannemann, F. **PLINIUS** und seine Naturgeschichte in ihrer Bedeutung für die Gegenwart. Jena, 1921.
Pavlu, J. Ein Götz von Berlichingen im Altertum. WBFA, 1929.
Rife, J. M. Marley's Ghost in Athens. (Dickens). CJ, 34, 1938.
McCartney, E. S. Pliny the Elder and Benjamin Franklin on the Art of Not Contradicting. CW, 25, 1931.
Bassi, P. D. Plinio il Vecchio e Leopardi. Giornale critico della filosofia italiana, 1927.
Bernthsen, S. Ueber den Einfluss des Plinius in Shelleys Jugendwerken. ESn, 30, 1902.
Shaver, C. L. Wordsworth's Adaptation of Pliny in Laodamia. MLN, 61, 1946.
Hosius, C. Zum Nachleben des **PROPERZ.** PhW, 1932.
Baldi, R. Carducci e Properzio. MC, 1932.
Leitzmann, A. Schiller und Knebels Properz. NPh, 18, 1932-33.
Forbes, C. A. Ezra Pound and Sextus Propertius. CJ, 42, 1946.
Gilkes, M. Discovery of Ezra Pound (and his Homage to Sextus Propertius). English, 2, 1938.
Hallowell, R. E. The Fortune of the Roman Elegists, Propertius and Tibullus, in XVIth Century France, with Special Reference to Ronsard. Diss. Illinois, 1942.
Bossuat, R. Vasque de Lucène, traducteur de **QUINTE-CURCE.** BHR, 8, 1946.
Gilbert, A. H. Chapman's Fortune with Winged Hands. MLN, 52, 1937.
Lehmann, P. Die Institutio oratoria des **QUINTILIANUS** im Mittelalter. Ph, 1934.
Lind, L. R. An Ancient Dred Scott Case. CW, 29, 1935.
Wychgram, M. Studien zur Geltung Quintilians in der deutschen und französischen Literatur des Barock und der Aufklärung. Langensalza, 1921.
Mollard, A. L'imitation de Quintilien dans Guibert de Nogent. Moyen Age, 5, 1934.
Otto. Quintilian und Rousseau. Progr. Neisse, 1836.
Kurfess, A. Der Historiker **SALLUST** in Augustins Gottesstaat. Theolog. Quartalschrift, 1937.
Keseling, P. Dante und Sallust. PhW, 1925.
Morr, J. Sallust und Goethe. Ibid. 1933.
Thomas, P. Les imitations de Salluste dans la Chronique de Saint Hubert. RBPh, 1924.
Cappuccio, C. I Carmina dell'Ariosto e **STAZIO.** MC, 1937.
Wise, B. A. The Influence of Statius upon Chaucer. Baltimore, 1911.
Albini, G. Se e come la Thebais ispirasse a Dante di fare Stazio cristiano. A&R, 5, 1902.
Mustard, W. P. Note on Dante and Statius, MLN, 39.
Cunningham, J. V. Statius, Keats and Wordsworth, PhQ, 27, 1948.
Donald, Dorothy. **SUETONIUS** in the Primera Crónica General through the Speculum Historiale. HR, 11, 1943.
Rand, E. K. On the History of the Vita Caesarum of Suetonius in the Early Middle Ages. HSCPh, 37, 1926.
Schepss, G. Zu Suetons Fortleben im Mittelalter. BBG, 1887.
Andreescu, C. L'influence de Suétone sur Eginhard. Orpheus, revista pentru cultura clasica, 2, 1926.
Hellmann, S. Einhards literarische Stellung. Histor. Vierteljahrsschrift, 27, 1932.
Hammer, J. Les sources de Geoffrey de Monmouth Historia Regum Britanniae, IV, 2. Latomus, 5, 1946.
Schoenberger, J. K. Ein geflügeltes Wort bei Goethe. Würzburger Jb. f. d. Altertumswissenschaft, 1, 1946.
Steevens, G. W. Suetonius' The Twelve

Caesars (translated by Philemon Holland). In: The Tudor Translations. London, 1892-96.
Berry, E. G. Hamlet and Suetonius. Phoenix, 2, 1948.
Proestler, M. Caesar did never Wrong but with just Cause. (Shakespeare). PhQ, 7, 1928.
Boase, T. S. R. A Seventeenth Century Carmelite Legend Based on **TACITUS**. JWI, 3, 1939.
De La Marre, L. Tacite et la littérature française. Paris, 1907.
Haverfield, F. Tacitus During the Late Roman Period and the Middle Ages. Journal of Roman Studies, 1916.
Joachimson, P. Tacitus im deutschen Humanismus. NJKA, 27, 1911.
Pilch, S. De Taciti apud Polonos notitia saeculis XV-XVII. Eos, 1925.
—— De Taciti in Polonorum cultu atque humanitate vi. Acta II. Congressus philol. class. slav. Praha, 1931.
Tenney, M. F. Tacitus in the Politics of Early Stuart England. CJ, 37, 1941.
Tiedemann, H. Tacitus und das Nationalbewusstsein der deutschen Humanisten Ende des 15. und Anfang des 16. Jahrhunderts. Berlin, 1913.
Wolff, E. Das geschichtliche Verstehen in Tacitus Germania. H, 1934.
Hochart, P. Boccace et Tacite. Annales de Bordeaux, 1890.
Nolhac, P. de. Boccace et Tacite. Mélanges de l'Ecole de Rome, 1892.
Firpo, L. Tacito e Terenzio nelle ignorate versioni di Traiano Boccalini. Atti dell'Accad. delle Scienze di Torino, 77, 1942.
Pilch, S. Tacitus and Choinskiego. (In Polish). Eos, 1935.
Herold, A. F. Crébillon, Tacite et l'Arménie. Rev. des Etudes arméniennes, 9, 1929.
Radlkofer. Die älteste Verdeutschung der Germania des Tacitus durch Johann Eberlin. BBG, 1, 1887.
Cornelissen, J. D. M. Hooft en Tacitus. Nijmegen, 1938.
Toffanin, G. Machiavelli e il Tacitismo. Padova, 1921.
Albert-Petit, A. Mirabeau traducteur de Tacite. Journ. des Débats, 21.III.1914.
Welschinger, H. Tacite et Mirabeau. Paris, 1914.
Hammer, J. William of Ockham and Tacitus. CJ, 1928.
Pilch, S. Tacitus in Sienkiewicz' Quo Vadis. (In Polish). Eos, 1935-36.
Janssens, E. Stendhal et Tacite. Latomus, 5, 1946.
Ardant, A. De Tacite, singulière opinion de Voltaire sur cet historien. Bull. de la Soc. royale d'agriculture, lettres et arts de Limoges, 8, 1829.
Craig, J. D. Ancient editions of **TERENCE**. St. Andrews U. Publ., 26, 1929.
Dziatzko, K. Zu Terentius im Mittelalter. Neue Jb. f. Philosophie, 1894.
Flad, K. Der erste deutsche Terenz. Tübingen, 1922.
Herrmann, M. Terenz in Deutschland bis zum Ausgange des 16. Jahrhunderts. Mittheilungen der Ges. f. deutsche Erziehungsgeschichte, 1893.
Lawton, H. W. Térence en France au XVIe siècle. Paris, 1926.
Mangold, H. W. Studien zu den ältesten Bühnen-Verdeutschungen des Terenz. Halle, 1912.
Robbins, E. W. Theories of Characterization in Commentaries on Terence before 1600. Diss. U. of Illinois, 1948.
Stembler, B. Terence in Europe to the Rise of Vernacular Drama. CW, 32, 1939.
Straumer, F. Eine deutsche Bearbeitung des Selbstpeinigers des Terenz aus dem 16. Jahrhundert. Progr. 1888.
Swaen, A. E. H. Terentian Influence. NPh, 39, 1944.
Winniczukowna, L. Térence en Pologne. (In Polish). Mélanges G. Przychocki. Varsovie, 1934.
Sismondi, J. C. L. Comédies de l'Arioste calquées sur celles de Térence et de Plaute. In: De la littérature du Midi de l'Europe. Paris, 1813.
Zecca, G. Della influenza di Terenzio nelle commedie di Ludovico Ariosto. Milano, 1914.
Russo, J. A. Did Dante Know Terence? Ital., 24, 1947.
Franceschini, E. Il commento di Giacomino da Mantova al Prologo dell' Andria di Terenzio. Studi di filologia latina medievale. Milano, 1938.
Abbick, J. Roswitha and Terence. CB, 23, 1947.
Hulme. Hroswitha and Terence. MLN, 1903.
Roberts, A. J. Did Hroswitha Imitate Terence? MLN, 17, 1902.
Coulter, C. C. The Terentian Comedies of a Tenth-Century Nun. CJ, 24, 1929.
Eckhardt, S. Le Térence janséniste de Molière. (In Hungarian). EPhK, 1928.
Humbert, C. H. Le Phormion de Térence et les Fourberies de Scapin de Molière. Progr. Elberfeld, 1859.
Psichari, J. Térence, les Adelphes, texte

latin, publié avec une introduction. Les imitations de Molière. Paris, 1887.
Bidlingmaier, E. E. Die Terenzübersetzung des Neidhart. Greifswald, 1930.
Foresti, A. Quando il Petrarca conobbe Terenzio e Plauto? Ath., 1923.
Sabbadini, R. La Philologia del Petrarca e Terenzio. Boll. di Filologia Classica, 22.
Stiefel, A. L. Hans Sachs und Terenz. Blätter für das Gymnas.-Schulwesen, 35, 1899.
Alès, A. d'. TERTULLIEN chez Bède? Recherches de Science religieuse, 1937.
Emerson, O. F. A Parallel Between the Middle English Poem Patience and an Early Latin Poem Attributed to Tertullian. PMLA, 1895.
Jones, H. M. Wycherley, Montaigne, Tertullian and Mrs. Summers. MLN, 1932.
Holshausen, F. Chaucer und THEODOLUS. Anglia, 16, 1894.
Stevenson, W. H. Chaucer and Theodolus. Athenaeum, 1, 1902.
Nash, R. Milton, Jonson and TIBERIUS. CPh, 1946.
Hartmann, E. von. Ernst Haeckel (TIBULL in Deutschland). DR, 2, 1875.
Schuster, M. Zum Nachleben der Tibullischen Dichtung. Wien, 1930.
Ullman, B. L. Tibullus in the Mediaeval Florilegia. CPh, 23, 1928.
Wilhelm, F. Zum Fortleben Tibulls bei deutschen Dichtern seit Mitte des 18. Jahrhunderts. In: Satura Viadrina altera, Festschrift zum 50 jähr. Bestehen des philol. Vereins zu Breslau, 1921. And in: Archiv, 89.
Ullman, B. L. VALERIUS FLACCUS in the Mediaeval Florilegia. CPh, 1931.
Bright. Chaucer and VALERIUS MAXIMUS. MLN, 9, 1894.
Schullian, D. M. Valerius Maximus and Walter Map. Spec., 1937.
Camus, J. Notice d'une traduction française de VEGECE faite en 1380. Romania, 25, 1896.
Webb, H. J. The Elizabethan Translation of Vegetius' De Re Militari. MLN, 56, 1941.
Jones, C. W. Bede and Vegetius. CR, 1932.
MacDonald, G. Bede and Vegetius. Ibid. 1933.
Pellati F,. VITRUVIO nel medico evo e nel Rinascimento. Boll. del R. Instituto di Archeologia. Roma, 1932.

CHAPTER EIGHT

Latin Influences upon Individual Authors.

Stanford, W. B. Traces of Sicilian Influence in AESCHYLUS. Proc. Irish Academy, 44, 1938.
Koebel, W. Die lateinischen Metaphysikübersetzungen in den Frühwerken ALBERTS DES GROSSEN. Diss. Bonn, 1933.
Romizi, A. Le fonti latine dell' Orlando furioso. (ARIOSTO). Nuova Rassegna, 1894 & GSLI, 27, 1895.
Darpe, F. BOILEAU et la satire romaine. Progr. Rheine, 1871.
Lutz, V. F. R. L. von CANITZ, sein Verhältniss zu dem französischen Klassicismus und zu den lateinischen Satirikern. Diss. Heidelberg. München, 1887.
Valgimigli, M. Una antologia latina di Giosuè CARDUCCI. NAnt., 380, 1935.
Lounsbury, T. R. Latin Sources of CHAUCER. Nation, 4.VII.1889.
Shannon, E. F. Chaucer and the Roman Poets. Harvard U. P., 1929.
Dubois, M. M. Les éléments latins dans la poésie religieuse de CYNEWULF. Paris, 1943.
Ludvikovsky, J. Les humanités classiques chez J. DOBROVSKY. Etude des influences latines sur les débuts de la renaissance nationale en Bohème. (In Czech). Bratislava, 1933.
Bottkol, J. M. DRYDEN'S Latin Scholarship. MPh, 40, 1942-43.
Raeder, H. Die Tropen und Figuren bei R. GARNIER, ihrem Inhalt nach untersucht und in der römischen Tragödie mit der lateinischen Vorlage verglichen. Wansbeck, 1886.
Franceschini, E. Roberto GROSSATESTA, vescovo di Lincoln, e le sue traduzioni latine. ARIV, 93, 1933.
Wentzlaff-Eggebert, F. W. Dichtung und Sprache des jungen GRYPHIUS. Die Ueberwindung der lateinischen Tradition und die Entwicklung zum deutschen Stil. APAW, 1936.
Duffy, Ellen M. T. Ben JONSON'S Debt to Renaissance Scholarship in Sejanus and Catiline. MLR, 42, 1947.
Danon, A. Les sources latines de LA BRUYERE. RBPh, 1940.
Carmody, F. J. Latin Sources of Brunetto LATINI'S World History. Spec., 1936.
Seldner, K. LESSINGS Verhältnis zur altrömischen Komödie. Progr. Mannheim, 1881.

Mozley, J. H. The Latinity of Nigel de **LONGCHAMPS.** Archivum Latinitatis Medii Aevi, 1939.

Peretti, A. **LUCIANO,** un intellettuale greco contro Roma. Firenze, 1946.

Rolfe, J. C. **MACAULAY'S** Lays of Ancient Rome. CJ, 29, 1934.

Mahrenholtz, R. **MOLIERE** und die römische Komödie. Braunschweig, 1876.

Hitchcock, F. R. M. The Latinity of St. **PATRICK** Compared with the Latin Translation of Irenaeus's Treatise. Ha, 54.

Hodnett, J. J. A Study of Latinity of the Sermones and the Carmina of **PETER VENERABLE,** Ninth Abbot of Cluny. CW, 32, 1939.

Hazard, P. Etude sur la latinité de **PETRARQUE.** Mélanges d'archéologie et d'histoire de l'Ecole fr. de Rome, 1904.

Zingerle, A. Petrarcas Verhältniss zu den römischen Dichtern. Progr. Innsbruck, 1870.

Hubert. **PLUTARCH,** ein Hellene unter Römerherrschaft. HG, 1932.

Richards, G. C. **POLYBIUS** of Megalopolis, the Greek Admirer of Rome. CJ, 40, 1944-45.

Maettig. J. Ueber den Einfluss der lateinischen volkstümlichen und literarischen Literatur auf **RABELAIS.** Diss. Leipzig, 1902.

Gonot, R. **RACINE** historien de Rome. REL, 1943-44.

Sanchez-Albornoz, C. Fuentes latinas de la Historia romana de **RASIS.** Buenos Aires, 1942.

Kuehne, C. R. Possible Latin Sources for an Episode in Charles **READE,** The Cloister and the Hearth. CW, 25, 1932.

Law, R. A. The Roman Background of Titus Andronicus. **(SHAKESPEARE).** SPh, 40, 1943.

Fuller, H. W. The Sources and Authorship of Titus Andronicus. PMLA, 16, 1901.

Maxwell, J. C. Demigods and Pickpockets: The Augustan Myth in **SWIFT** and Rousseau. Scrutiny, 11, 1942.

Cheek, P. M. The Latin Element in Henry **VAUGHAN.** SPh, 44, 1947.

McCracken, G. **WODEHOUSE** and Latin Comedy. CJ, 29, 1934.

Worthing, Jane. **WORDSWORTH'S** Reading of Roman Prose. Yale U. P., 1946.

CHAPTER NINE

The Latin Language.

1. Latin and Romance Languages.

Ascoli, G. J. Lateinisches und Romanisches. Kuhns Zs., 12-13, 1863-64.

Bacci, A. Il latino lingua viva nella Chiesa cattolica. Per lo Studio e l'Uso del Latino, 2, 1939.

Beger, F. A. Lateinisch und Romanisch. Berlin, 1863.

Cumont, F. Pourquoi le latin fut-il la seule langue littéraire de l'Occident? Mélanges Paul Frédéricq. Bruxelles, 1904.

Fuchs, A. Die romanischen Sprachen in ihrem Verhältniss zum Lateinischen. Halle, 1849.

Gaenssle, C. How Dead Is Latin? CJ, 28, 1933.

Hellman, S. Das Problem der mittellateinischen Philologie. Histor. Vierteljahrschrift, 29.

Lehmann, P. Vom Leben des Lateinischen im Mittelalter. BBG, 65, 1929.

Lubecki, K. De lingua latina semper vivente. Acta II. Congressus philol. class. slav. Praha, 1931.

Marouzeau, J. La survie du latin. BURS, 10, 1925.

Oldfather, W. A. Latin as an International Language. CJ, 16.

Ostern, H. Latein als Verkehrssprache. HG, 1931.

Paetow, L. J. Latin as a Universal Language. CJ, 15.

Pascal, C. Per la resurrezione del latino come lingua internazionale. Rendiconti del R. Istituto Lombardo, 1917.

Pott, A. F. Das Latein im Uebergange zum Romanischen. Zs. f. Altertumswissenschaft, 11-12, 1853-54.

Traube, L. & Lehmann, P. Einleitung in die lateinische Philologie des Mittelalters. München, 1911.

Ussani, V. La missione unificatrice del latino nella storia della civiltà. Per lo Studio e l'Uso del Latino, 1, 1939.

Wieniewski, I. Le mouvement pour l'internationalisation du Latin en Pologne. RU, 1933.

Zielinski, T. De societate linguae latinae usui internationali adaptandae Varsoviae consistente. Per lo Studio e l'Uso del Latino, 1, 1939.

2. Individual Countries.

Marouzeau, J. Les études latines aux Etats-Unis **(AMERICA).** REL, 1926.

Faider, P. **BELGIUM** latinum. Essai sur l'usage et l'étude de la langue latine en Belgique des origines à nos jours. Per lo Studio e l'Uso del Latino, 1, 1939.
Rivas Sacconi, J. M. Il latino nella letteratura e nella scuola **COLOMBIANA.** Ibid. 1941.
Ehlerding, F. German and Latin Elements in the **ENGLISH** Language. Progr. Nauen, 1877.
Myers, W. T. The Relations of Latin and English as Living Languages in England during the Age of Milton. Dayton, (Va.), 1913.
Pogatscher, A. Die lateinischen und romanischen Lehnworte im Altenglischen. Strassburg, 1888.
Bréal, M. La tradition du latin en **FRANCE.** RDM, 1.VI.1891.
Cesson, D. La méthode latine de Port-Royal. REL, 1943-44.
Lecoutre, J. Du génie de la langue française comparé à celui de la langue latine. Neuchâtel, 1894.
Strauss, F. Vulgärlatein und Vulgärsprache im Zusammenhang der Sprachenfrage im 16. Jahrhundert. (Frankreich und Italien). Marburg, 1938.
Betz. Der Einfluss des Lateinischen auf den althochdeutschen Sprachschatz. **(GERMANY).** M, 46.
Bréal, M. Anciens mots germaniques d'origine latine. Mém. de la Société de linguistes de Paris, 3, 1892.
Meszaros, M. E. De cultu litterarum et de lingua latina **HUNGARIAE** medii aevi. Per lo Studio e l'Uso del Latino, 2, 1940.
Budinsky, A. Die Ausbreitung der lateinischen Sprache über **ITALIEN** und die Provinzen des römischen Reichs. Berlin, 1881.
Gasser, V. Abstammung der italienischen und französischen Sprache und ihr Lautverhältniss zur lateinischen Schriftsprache. Progr. Sarnen, 1879.
Buceta, E. La tendencia a identificar el español con el latin. **(SPAIN).** Homenaje ofrecido a Menéndez Pidal. Madrid, 1925.
Del Real, C. A. El latin como elemento formativo de la conciencia nacional española. Per lo Studio e l'Uso del Latino, 2, 1939.
Magnabal. Du latin à l'espagnol. Revue de linguistique et de philologie comparée, 25, 1892.
Pabón, J. M. La enseñanza del latín en España. Bol. de la U. de Granada, 1932.
Sörbom, G. Vicende e condizione della lingua latina nella Svezia. **(SWEDEN).** Per lo Studio e l'Uso del Latino, 4, 1942.

3. Individual Authors.

Pitollet, C. Le latin de Don Quichotte. **(CERVANTES).** Hum, 9, 1933.
Menegazzi, G. I latinismi nella Divina Commedia. **(DANTE).** RI, 15.VIII.1913.
Friese, H. Lateinische Sprache und Lateinunterricht im Urteil **GOETHES.** HG, 1936.
Ottinger, H. Zum Latein des **RUODLIEB.** Histor. Vierteljahrsschrift, 26, 1931.
Claffin, E. F. The Latinisms in **SHAKESPEARE'S** Diction. CJ, 16.

CHAPTER TEN

Medieval and Neo-Latin Literature.

(See also Humanism, III.II.3.)

1. Generalities.

Alet, P. La tragédie latine à Rome, l'an 1600. Le Mans, 1857.
Bahlmann, P. Die lateinischen Dramen von Wimphelings Stylpho bis zur Mitte des 16. Jahrhunderts. Münster, 1893.
Baxter, J., Johnson, C. & Willard, J. F. An Index of British and Irish Latin Writers A. D. 400-1520. Archivum Latinitatis Medii Aevi. Paris, 1932.
Biadene, L. La storia comparata delle letterature neolatine. Treviso, 1901.
Bolte, J. Ueber das lateinische Drama in Frankreich. Festschrift Joh. Vahlen. Berlin, 1900.
Bonaventura, A. La poesia neo-latina in Italia dal secolo XIV al presente. Città di Castello, 1900.
Bradner, L. Musae Anglicanae: A History of Anglo-Latin Poetry, 1500-1925. New York, 1940.
—— A Check-List of Original Neo-Latin Dramas by Continental Writers Printed Before 1650. PMLA, 58, 1943.
Brinkmann, H. Geschichte der lateinischen Liebesdichtung im Mittelalter. Halle, 1925.
Buceta, E. De algunas composiciones hispano-latinas en el siglo XVII. RFE, 19, 1932.
Chiri, G. L'epica latina medioevale e la Chanson de Roland. Genova, 1936.
—— La poesia epico-storica latina dell'Italia medioevale. Modena, 1939.
Cohen, G. La comédie latine en France

dans la seconde moitié du XIIe siècle. Bull. de l'Acad. royale de Belgique, 1931.
Corti, Maria. Studi sulla latinità merovingia. Messina, 1939.
Ellinger, G. Geschichte der neulateinischen Literatur Deutschlands im sechzehnten Jahrhundert. Berlin, 1929 ff.
Francke, K. Zur Geschichte der lateinischen Schulpoesie im 12. und 13. Jahrhundert. München, 1879.
Frantzen, J. J. A. A. Ueber den Einfluss der mittellateinischen Literatur auf die französische und deutsche Poesie des Mittelalters. NPh, 4, 1919.
Ghellinck, J. de. Littérature latine au moyen âge: depuis les origines jusqu'à Saint Anselme. 2 vols. Paris, 1939.
Gragg, F. A. Latin Writings of the Italian Humanists. New York, 1927.
Gruenwald, E. Deutsche Poesie in lateinischem Gewande. ZDU, 16, 1902.
Hélin, M. Littérature d'Occident. Histoire des lettres latines du moyen âge. Bruxelles, 1943.
Hills, E. C. The Relation of Medieval Latin Literature to Medieval Vernacular Literature. TAPhA, 28, 1922.
Kasterska, M. Les poètes latins polonais jusqu'en 1589. Paris, 1918.
Kluge, F. Latein und Humanismus. In: Von Luther bis Lessing. Strassburg, 1904.
Lavollée, R. La poésie latine en Pologne. Diss. 1869. And in: Essais de littérature et d'histoire. Paris, 1891.
Lebègue, R. L'influence du théâtre néo-latin sur le théâtre sérieux en langue française. H&R, 6.
Lehmann, P. Skandinaviens Anteil an der lateinischen Literatur und Wissenschaft des Mittalalters. SBAW, 1936-37.
Lind, L. R. Medieval Latin Studies: Their Nature and Possibilities. U. of Kansas, Humanistic Studies, 26, 1941.
Manitius, M. Geschichte der lateinischen Literatur des Mittelalters. 3 vols. München, 1911-31.
Mann, W. Lateinische Dichtung in England vom Ausgang des Frühhumanismus bis zum Regierungsantritt Elisabeths. Halle, 1939.
Meister, R. Bedeutung und Umfang des lateinischen Schrifttums im Mittelalter und in der Neuzeit. Wien, 1933.
Miola, A. Notizie di Manoscritti Neo-latini. I Ms. francesi, provenzali, spagnuoli, catalani e portoghesi della Biblioteca nazionale di Napoli. Napoli, 1895.
Murarasu, D. La poésie néo-latine et la renaissance des lettres antiques en France. (1500-49). Paris, 1928.
Paoli, U. E. Prose e poesie latine di scrittori italiani. Firenze, 1926.
Raby, F. J. A History of Secular Latin Poetry in the Middle Ages. Oxford, 1934.
Rahlmann, P. Die lateinischen Dramen der Italiener im 14. und 15. Jahrhundert. Centralblatt f. Bibliothekwesen, 11, 1894.
Regenos, G. W. The Field of Medieval Latin Literature. CB, 23, 1947.
Ronca, U. Cultura medioevale e poesia latina d'Italia nei secoli XI e XII. 2 vols. Roma, 1892.
Rumpf, P. La latinité médiévale. AR, 9, 1925.
Schmid, T. Lateinische Literatur im mittelalterlichen Schweden. Lychnos, 1940.
Spanke, H. Beziehungen zwischen romanischer und mittellateinischer Lyrik mit besonderer Berücksichtigung der Metrik und Musik. Berlin, 1936.
Van Tieghem, P. La littérature latine de la Renaissance. Paris, 1944. Cf. BHR, 4, 1944 & MF, 1947.
Wright, F. A. & Sinclair, T. A. A History of Later Latin Literature from the Middle of the Fourth to the End of the Seventeenth Century. London, 1931.
Wyzewa, T.de. La Renaissance latine et les écrivains italiens. In: Ecrivains étrangers. Paris, 1896.

2. Individual Authors.

Hohenstein, L. Melibeus und Prudentia. Der Liber consolationis et consilii des **ALBERT VON BRESCIA** in zwei deutschen Bearbeitungen des 15. Jahrhunderts. Breslau, 1903.
Hortis, A. Studi sulle opere latine del **BOCCACCIO.** Trieste, 1879.
Grant, W. L. The Shorter Latin Poems of George **BUCHANAN.** CJ, 40, 1944-45.
Schoell, F. L. George **CHAPMAN** and the Italian Neo-Latinists of the Quattrocento. MPh, 1915.
Willert, P. Deutsche Übersetzungen des Waltharilliedes. **(EKKEHARD).** Jena, 1940.
Tardi, D. **FORTUNAT.** Etude sur un dernier représentant de la poésie latine dans la Gaule merovingienne. Paris, 1927.
Lumsden, Audrey. **GARCILASO DE LA VEGA** as a Latin Poet. MLR, 42, 1947.
Keeler, L. **GEOFFREY OF MONMOUTH** and the Late Latin Chroniclers, 1300-1500. Berkeley, 1946.

Kluge, O. Die Dichtung des Hugo **GROTIUS** im Rahmen der neulateinischen Kunstpoesie. Mnemosyne, 7-8, 1939-40.

Zeydel, E. H. The Reception of **HROTSVITHA** by the German Humanists after 1493. JEGPh, 44, 1945.

—— Knowledge of Hrotsvitha's Works Prior to 1500. MLN, 59.

—— A Chronological Hrotsvitha Bibliography through 1700. JEGPh, 46, 1947.

Blanchard, A. **JEAN SECOND** (1511-36) et quelques poètes français. Mfr, 15.II. 1939.

Crane, D. Johannes Secundus. His Life, Work and Influence on English Literature. Leipzig, 1931.

Pascal, C. Le scritture filiologiche latine di Giacomo **LEOPARDI.** Catania, 1919.

Sills, K. C. M. **MILTON'S** Latin Poems. CJ, 32, 1937.

Gandiglio, A. La poesia latina di G. **PASCOLI.** A&R, 1912.

Hay. D. The Ms of **POLYDORE VERGIL'S** Anglica Historia. EHR, 54.

CHAPTER ELEVEN

Ancients versus Moderns.

Anon. Controversia sul merito degli antichi paragonati coi moderni scrittori. Bibl. di antica e moderna storia letteraria, 2. Pesaro, 1776.

Albon, C. C. d'. Discours sur cette question: Si le siècle d'Auguste doit être préferé à celui de Louis XIV, relativement aux lettres et aux sciences? Paris, 1784.

Alpár, G. Streit der Alten und Modernen in der deutschen Literatur bis um 1750. Pécs, 1939.

Beyer, C. J. Gassendi, ancien ou moderne? PMLA, 63, 1948.

Brunot, F. La lutte avec le latin. La langue française au XVIe siècle. In: Petit de Julleville, Histoire de la langue et de la littérature française. Paris, 1897.

Carré, G. La lutte du latin et du français au collège de l'oratoire de Troyes. Mém. de la Soc. acad. de l'Aube, 1882.

Collier, J. A Short View of the Immorality and Profaneness of the English Stage, Together with the Sense of Antiquity upon this Argument. London, 1698. Paris, 1715.

Czerny, S. La querelle des anciens et des modernes au XVIe siècle et l'intervention de Blaise de Vigenère. Eos, 1929.

Delattre, F. La querelle des anciens et des modernes en France et an Angleterre. Revue des Pyrénées, 1913.

Diede, O. Der Streit der Alten und Modernen in der englischen Literaturgeschichte des XVI. und XVII. Jahrhunderts. Diss. Greifswald, 1912.

Ellingham, C. J. Classical versus Modern. G&R, 6, 1937.

Fouillée, A. Les classiques et les modernes en Allemagne et en France. Journal des Débats, 31.III.1901.

Gillot, H. La querelle des anciens et des modernes en France. Nancy, 1914.

Jones, R. F. Ancients and Moderns: A Study of the Background of the Battle of the Books. St. Louis, 1936.

Kelley, A. W. Literary Theories about Progress. PMLA, 1937.

Lombard, A. La querelle des anciens et des modernes: l'abbé Dubos. Paris, 1914.

McLuhan, H. M. Ancient Quarrel in Modern America. CJ, 41, 1946.

Michiels, A. La querelle des anciens et des modernes. Revue indépendante, 1, 1841.

Momet. La querelle des anciens et des modernes au ler siècle de notre ère. REL, 1935.

Morby, E. S. Una batalla entre antiguos y modernos. RIA, 4, 1941.

Myrick, A. B. The Ancients and the Moderns, an Entente Cordiale. CW, 13.

Perrault, C. Parallèle des anciens et des modernes en ce qui concerne les arts et les sciences. Paris, 1688.

Rigault, H. Histoire de la querelle des anciens et des modernes. Diss. 1856; Paris, 1859.

Rymer, T. The Tragedies of the Last Age Considered and Examined by the Practice of the Ancients. London, 1678.

Seeger, O. Die Auseinandersetzung zwischen Antike und Moderne in England bis zum Tode Dr. Samuel Johnsons. Leipzig, 1927.

Tuve, R. Ancients, Moderns, and Saxons. ELH, 6, 1939.

Vianu, F. Polémique des anciens et des modernes. Favonius, 1, (Bucharest) 1926.

FIFTH PART

Hebraism and Early Christianity.

CHAPTER ONE

Judaism and Christianity in Contact with the Graeco-Roman World, the Earliest Germanic Tribes and the Mohammedans.

1. Generalities.

(See also under Greek, Roman and Germanic Mythology).

Aall, A. The Hellenistic Elements in Christianity. London, 1931.

Allevi, L. Ellenismo e cristianesimo. Milano, 1934.

Amatucci, A. G. Storia della letteratura latina cristiana. Bari, 1929.

Anwander, F. Die literarische Bekämpfung des Christentums in der Antike. Benedictiner Monatsschrift, 1924.

Armstrong, A. H. The Neo-Platonist Attack on Christianity. Dublin Rev., 201, 1937.

Asín Palacios, M. El Islam cristianizado. Madrid, 1931.

Baumgartner, A. Die lateinische und griechische Literatur der christlichen Völker. In: Geschichte der Weltliteratur, 4. Leipzig, 1900.

Bardenhewer, O. Geschichte der altchristlichen Literatur. Freiburg, 1932.

Bardy, G. Littérature grecque chrétienne. Paris, 1927.

—— Littérature latine chrétienne. Paris, 1929.

Beloch, K. J. et al. Hellas und Rom. Die Entstehung des Christentums. In: Propyläen Weltgeschichte, 2. Berlin, 1931.

Bentwich, N. Of Jews and Hebraism in the Greek Anthology. JQR, 23, 1932.

Bevan, E. Hellenism and Christianity. London, 1921.

Bezard, J. Israël et la pensée latine. Ce qu'il a fait pour elle. Ce qu'elle a fait pour lui. Paris, 1925.

Bousset, W. Jüdisch-christlicher Schulbetrieb in Alexandria und Rom. Göttingen, 1915.

Bouttier, L. La literatura latina cristiana en España, las Galias e Italia. Anales del Instituto de Literaturas clásicas (Buenos Aires), 1940-41.

Campbell, J. M. The Greek Fathers. In: Our Debt to Greece and Rome. New York, 1929.

Capelle, W. Die antike Literatur und die Germanen. F&F, 7, 1931.

Case, S. The Evolution of Early Christianity. Chicago, 1914.

Casel, O. Antike und christliche Mysterien. BBG, 1927.

Cavallera, F. Aux origines de l'ancienne littérature chrétienne. Bull. de litt. ecclésiastique, 1941.

Classen, W. Eintritt des Christentums in die Welt. Der Sieg des Christentums auf dem Hintergrunde der untergehenden antiken Kultur. Gotha, 1930.

Clerc, C. Le génie du paganisme. Paris, 1926.

Cochrane, C. N . Christianity and Classical Culture. A Study of Thought from Augustus to Augustine. Oxford, 1940.

Conway, R. S. Ancient Italy and Modern Religion. Cambridge U. P., 1933.

Corbière, C. Le christianisme et la fin de la philosophie antique. Essai sur la polémique du néoplatonisme avec le christianisme. Paris, 1921.

Cullman, O. Le problème littéraire et historique du roman pseudo-clémentin. Etude sur le rapport entre le gnosticisme et le judéo-christianisme. Paris, 1930.

Deferrari, R. J. Early Ecclesiastical Literature and its Relation to the Literature of Classical and Medieval Times. PhQ, 1927.

Doelger, F. J. Antike und Christentum. Kultur- und religionsgeschichtliche Studien. Münster, 1929.

Doerrie, H. Die griechischen Romane und das Christentum. Ph, 1938.

Duerr, L. Die Wertung des göttlichen Wortes im Alten Testament und im antiken Orient. Leipzig, 1938.

Dupont-Sommer, A. Hellénisme et judaïsme. Rev. de l'Hist. des Religions, 1938.

Eissfeld, O. Vom Werden der biblischen Gottesanschauung und ihrem Ringen mit dem Gottesgedanken der griechischen Philosophie. Halle, 1931.

Fink, W. Der Einfluss der jüdischen Religion auf die griechisch-römische. Bonn, 1932.

Fracassini, V. - Il misticismo greco e il cristianesimo. Città di Castello, 1923.

Gabler, K. Die nordischen Barbaren in der antiken Literatur. Deutsche höhere Schule, 5, 1938.

Gamillscheg, E. Germanische Siedlung in Belgien und Nordfrankreich. Berlin, 1938.
Geffcken, J. Das Christentum im Kampf und Ausgleich mit der Antike. Theolog. Revue, 1924.
Glücksmann, H. L. Die Gegenüberstellung von Antike-Christentum in der englischen Literatur des 19. Jahrhunderts. Hannover, 1932.
Goguel, M. Jésus et les origines du christianisme; la naissance du christianisme. 1946.
Gorce, M. & Mortier, R. (eds.). Histoire générale des religions: Indo-Iraniens, Judaïsme, Origines Chrétiennes, Christianisme, Orientaux. 1945.
Graf, G. Geschichte der christlichen arabischen Literatur. Città del Vaticano, 1944.
Gutenbrunner, S. Germanische Frühzeit in den Berichten der Antike. Halle, 1939.
Halliday, W. R. The Pagan Background of Early Christianity. Liverpool, 1925.
Harder, H. Das germanische Erbe in der deutschen Dichtung von der Frühzeit bis zur Gegenwart. Potsdam, 1939.
Hatch, E. The Influence of Greek Ideas and Usages upon the Christian Church. London, 1891.
Helm, R. Heidnisches und Christliches bei spätlateinischen Dichtern. Festschrift Geffcken. Leipzig, 1931.
Hempel, J. Die althebräische Literatur und ihr hellenistisch-jüdisches Nachleben. Potsdam, 1930-34.
Herte, J. Die Begegnung des Germanentums mit dem Christentum. Paderborn, 1935.
Herwegen, J. Antike, Germanentum und Christentum. Salzburg, 1932.
Hoffmann, H. Die Antike in der Geschichte des Christentums. Bern, 1923.
Hoffmann, E. Ueber die antike Philosophie und die Anfänge der christlichen Mystik. HG, 1933.
Horn, R. C. Greek Philosophers and Hebrew Prophets. Lutheran Church Quarterly, 5, 1932.
Hunt, T. W. Hebraism and Hellenism in Literature. Homiletic Rev., 1899.
Jaeger, W. The First Greek Records of Jewish Religion and Civilization. Journal of Religions, 1938.
Johnstone, G. S. The Contributions of Judaism and Christianity to the Drama. ET, 47, 1935.
Jolivet, R. Essai sur les rapports entre la pensée grecque et la pensée chrétienne. Bibl. d'hist. de la phil. Paris, 1931.
Kittel, G. Urchristentum, Spätjudentum, Hellenismus. Stuttgart, 1926.
Kluge, F. Germanisch-römische Beziehungen. Pauls Grundriss der germanischen Philologie, 1. Strassburg, 1901.
Knox, W. L. Some Hellenistic Elements in Primitive Christianity. London, 1944.
Kuhn, H. Das nordgermanische Heidentum in den ersten christlichen Jahrhunderten. ZDA, 79.
Labriolle, P. de. Histoire de la littérature latine chrétienne. Paris, 1924.
Laistner, M. L. W. The Christian Attitude to Pagan Literature. History, 20, 1935.
Lauha, A. Zaphon. Der Norden und die Nordvölker im Alten Testament. Annales Acad. Sc. Fennicae. Helsinki, 1943.
Lehmann. Mysticisme dans le paganisme et le christianisme. Paris, 1905.
Lewy, H. Aethiopier und Juden in der antiken Literatur. Monatsschrift f. Gesch. & Wiss. des Judentums, 81, 1937.
Livingstone, R. W. Christianity and Hellenism. HJ, 33, 1935.
Ljungberg, Helge. Die nordische Religion und das Christentum. Gütersloh, 1940.
Luria, S. L'antisémitisme dans l'antiquité. (In Russian). Petersbourg, 1922.
Meissner, P. Germanentum, Christentum und Antike in der englischen Kulturideologie. GRM, 30, 1942.
Meli, A. Dal giudaismo al cristianesimo. La Scuola Cattolica, 1936.
Michael, J. H. The Jewish Sabbath in the Latin Classical Writers. Am. Journ. Sem. Lang., 1924.
Mims, E. Great Writers as Interpreters of Religion. New York, 1945.
Moore, G. F. Judaism in the First Centuries of the Christian Era. Harvard U. P., 1927.
Moravcsik, G. Byzantine Christianity and the Magyars in the Period of their Migration. ASEER, 5, 1946.
Moricca, U. Storia della letteratura latina cristiana. Torino, 1925.
Nestle, W. Die Haupteinwände des antiken Denkens gegen das Christentum. Arch. f. Religionswiss., 37, 1941.
Newman, L. I. Jewish Influence on Christian Reform Movements. New York, 1925.
Nock, A. D. Early Christianity and its Hellenistic Background. In: A. Rawlinson: Essays on the Trinity and the Incarnation. New York, 1928.

Noye, E. Noms de Nestoriens cités dans l'histoire chinoise. Bull. catholique de Pékin, 1938.
Oelmann, F. Zur Kenntnis der karolingischen und omaijadischen Spätantike. Mittel. d. deutschen Archäologen, 38-39.
Olsen, M. Roma e la poesia del paganesimo nordico. SG, 1, 1935.
Ortega Rubio, J. Los Visigodos en España. Madrid, 1903.
Otto, W. F. Der Geist der Antike und die christliche Welt. Bonn, 1923.
Pfatschbacher, H. Hellenismus und Christentum. Der Einfluss der hellenistischen Kultur auf den Christianismus, namentlich im I. Jahrhundert unserer Zeitrechnung. Theologie & Glaube, 1929.
Pirenne, H. Geburt des Abendlandes. Untergang der Antike am Mittelmeer und Aufstieg des germanischen Mittelalters. Amsterdam, 1939.
Pohlenz, M. Stoa und Semitismus. NJWJ, 1926.
Preuss, S. Die Germanen in den Berichten der römischen Schriftsteller. Bamberg, 1915.
Puech, A. Histoire de la littérature grecque chrétienne depuis les origines jusqu'à la fin du IVe siècle. Paris, 1928-30.
Raby, F. J. E. A History of Christian-Latin Poetry from the Beginnings to the Close of the Middle Ages. Oxford, 1927.
Radin, M. Roman Knowledge of Jewish Literature. CJ, 13.
Ravisson, F. Hellénisme, judaïsme et christianisme. La Nouvelle Journée, 1922.
Ritter, C. Platonismus und Christentum. Tübingen, 1934.
Roettger, G. Altgermanien nach antiker und heutiger Kenntnis. Leipzig, 1937.
Rocquain, F. Les Germains en Gaule. RB, 1875.
Salvatorelli, L. Storia della letteratura cristiana, dalle origine alla metà del VI. secolo. Milano, 1946.
San Marte. Das letzte Geheimnis des Christentums und seine Darstellung in der Poesie. Deutsches Museum, 1865.
Saurat, D. Les éléments religieux non chrétiens dans la poésie moderne. RLC, 3, 1923.
Schiber, H. Die fränkischen und allemannischen Siedlungen in Gallien. Strassburg, 1894.
Schommodau, H. Heidnischer und christlicher Geist in der französischen Lyrik des 16. Jahrhunderts. RF, 54, 1940.
Schönbach, A. Das Christentum in der althochdeutschen Heldendichtung. Graz, 1897.
Siegmund, A. P. Die Ueberlieferung der griechischen christlichen Literatur in der lateinischen Kirche bis zum zwölften Jahrhundert. München, 1943.
Staehlin, G. Christentum und Antike. Pädagog. Hochschule, 2, 1930.
Steffens, H. Ueber die Einwirkung des Christenthums auf die nordische Mythologie. In: Nachgelassene Schriften. Berlin, 1846.
Stewart, H. L. Scholastic Philosophy in Renaissance Thought. The Personalist, 27, 1946.
Stiglmayr, J. Kirchenväter und Klassizismus. Stimmen der Vorzeit über humanistische Bildung. Freiburg, 1913.
Stob, R. Stoicism and Christianity. CJ, 30, 1935.
Treitel, L. Das Judentum als geistige Weltreligion, wie es als solche Eingang in die Kulturwelt Roms gefunden. Arch. f. Religionswissenschaft, 1927.
Vasiliev, A. A. The Goths in the Crimea. Cambridge, (Mass.), 1936.
Viscardi, A. La scuola medievale e la tradizione scolastica classica. SM, 11, 1938.
Vollhardt, W. Einfluss der lateinischen geistlichen Litteratur auf einige kleinere Schöpfungen der Uebergangsperiode. ESn, 13, 1879 & Diss. Leipzig, 1888.
Wahle, E. et al. Der Aufstieg des Germanentums und die Welt des Mittelalters. Berlin, 1940.
Wais, G. Die Alamannen in ihrer Auseinandersetzung mit der römischen Welt. M, 49, 1942.
Weigall, A. The Paganism in Our Christianity. London, 1927.
Wendland, P. Die hellenistisch-römische Kultur in ihren Beziehungen zu Judentum und Christentum. Tübingen, 1912.
West, A. F. Christian Latin Writers. In: Our Debt to Greece and Rome. Boston, 1928.
Wishnitzer, R. La Basilique et la Stoa dans la littérature rabbinique. Revue des Etudes juives, 1934.
Woltmann. Die Germanen in Frankreich. Leipzig, 1907.

2. Ancient Authors.

(See also Individual Greek and Roman Authors.)

Ogle, M. B. CICERO and Christianity. U. of Michigan Public., 27.

Minocchi, S. Lo spirito cristiano di **EURIPIDE.** Bilychnis, Rivista mensile di studi religiosi, 32, 1928.
Wright, F. A. Christian Spirit in **HORACE.** CW, 16.
Labriolle, P. de. **LUCIEN** et les chrétiens. Hum., 1929.
Pierce, E. H. **MARTIAL** and St. Paul. CJ, 27, 1932.
Much, R. Die nordischen Fabelvölker bei **MELA** und Tacitus. Festschrift Andree-Eysn. München, 1928.
Passeri, G. Intorno alla poesia e stile proprio di **PINDARO** (probable contact with Hebrew Poetry). In: Nuova Raccolta d'Opuscoli, 27. Venezia, 1775.
Cohen, H. Das soziale Ideal bei **PLATON** und den Propheten: Jüdische Schriftsteller, 1.
Richards, P. S. Plato, Aristotle and the Christian Church. Criterion, 17, 1938.
Buonaiuti, E. **PLUTARCO** e la letteratura cristiana antica. Ath, 1918.
Moffatt, J. Great Attacks on Christianity, **PORPHYRY** Against Christians. ET, 43, 1931.
Bergman, J. **PRUDENTIUS** der grösste christliche Dichter des Altertums. Dorpat, 1922.
Rodriguez-Herrera, I. Poeta christianus: Prudentius' Auffassung vom Wesen und von der Aufgabe des christlichen Dichters. München, 1936.
Benoît, P. **SENEQUE** et Saint Paul. Revue biblique, 1946.
Deissner, K. Paulus und Seneca. Gütersloh, 1917.
Faider, P. Sénèque et saint Paul. Bull. bibliogr. du Musée belge, 1926.
Koch, H. Seneca und das Urchristentum. Wochenschrift f. klass. Philol., 1919.
Schreiner, T. Seneca im Gegensatz zu Paulus. Tübingen, 1936.
Turoczi-Trostler, J. Christlicher Seneca. (In Hungarian). EPhK, 1937.
Goldschmidt, E. Die Israel-Quellen bei **TACITUS.** Morgen, 11, 1935-36.
Melander, K. R. Tacitus' Germania als Quelle der deutschen Frühgeschichte. Annales Acad. Sc. Fennicae, 47, 1940.
Norden, E. Die germanische Urgeschichte in Tacitus' Germania. Leipzig, 1923.
Schupp, F. Tacitus und die Christen. Jahresbericht des Schottengymnasiums, 125. Wien.
Teudt, W. Der Wert des Germanenbildes bei Tacitus. Germanien, 1933.
Rolffs, E. **TERTULLIAN,** der Vater des abendländischen Christentums. Berlin, 1930.
Bourne, Ella. The Messianic Prophecy in **VERGIL'S** Fourth Eclogue. CJ, 11, 1916.
Bushnell, C. C. An Interpretation of Vergil's Fourth Eclogue. TAPhA, 1932.
Carcopino, J. Virgile et le mystère de la IVe églogue. Paris, 1930.
Celle, M. G. L'ecloga IV. di Virgilio in una epistola dell' umanista Jacopo Bracelli. MC, 1934.
Heidel, W. A. Vergil's Messianic Expectations. AJPh, 1924.
Jeanmaire, H. Le messianisme de Virgile. Paris, 1930.
Kamnitzer, E. Vergil und die römische Kirche. Kathol. Gedanke, 4, 1931.
Kurfess, A. Der griechische Uebersetzer von Vergils vierter Ekloge in Kaiser Konstantins Rede an die Versammlung der Heiligen. Zs. f. d. neutestamentl. Wiss., 1936.
—— Die griechische Uebersetzung der vierten Ekloge Vergils. Mnemosyne, 5, 1937.
Romani, F. Poesia pagana e arte cristiana: I. L'inferno di Virgilio. Firenze, 1902.
Röschl, M. Vergil als Christuskünder. Die Drei, 10, 1930-31.
Smiley, C. N. Vergil, His Philosophic Background and His Relation to Christianity. CJ, 26, 1931.
Vaccari, A. Il messianismo ebraico e la IV. ecloga di Virgilio. Civilità Cattolica, 2, 1931.
Weber, W. Der Prophet und sein Gott. Eine Studie zur vierten Ekloge Vergils. Leipzig, 1925.
Witt, N. W. de. Virgil and Apocalyptic Literature. CJ, 13.

3. Modern Authors.

Moore, E. Scripture and Classical Authors in **DANTE.** In: Studies in Dante. London, 1897. Cf. GSLI, 32.
Faut, A. Griechentum und Christentum in **GOETHES** klassischem Bildungsideal. HG, 1927.
Wolf, E. Griechentum und Christentum in Goethes klassischem Bildungsideal. NJWJ, 1928.
Campbell, T. M. Gerhart **HAUPTMANN,** Christian or Pagan. MLJ, 8, 1924.
Zimmermann, W. S. Christentum und Heidentum in F. **HEBBELS** Leben und Werken. Diss. New York U., 1943.
Levi, G. A. Pensiero classico e pensiero cristiano nel **PETRARCA.** A&R, 1937.
Stedefeld, G. F. Die christlich-germanische Weltanschauung in den Werken

der Dichterfürsten WOLFRAM VON ESCHENBACH, Dante und Shakespeare. Berlin, 1871.

CHAPTER TWO

The Bible.

(For Biblical Characters, See Thematology I.VI.10.)

1. Generalities.

Albrecht, G. Die alttestamentlichen Stoffe im Schauspiel der Reformationszeit. Dramaturgie, 4, 1897.

Allgeier, A. Die altlateinischen Psalterien. (Die hieronymianischen Psalmenübersetzungen). Freiburg, 1928.

—— Die Ueberlieferung der alten lateinischen Psalmenübersetzungen und ihre kulturgeschichtliche Bedeutung. Freiburg, 1931.

—— Einfluss Spanicns in der Text - Geschichte der Psalmen. Span. Forsch. d. Goerres-Ges, 5, 1937.

Archinard. Notice sur les premières versions de la Bible en langue vulgaire. Genève, 1839.

Astaf'ev, N. An Essay in the History of the Bible in Connection with Enlightenment and Traditions. (In Russian). In: Zhurnal Mira Nravov i Prosveshcheniia, July-August, 1888.

Baroni, V. La Bible chez les controversistes catholiques du XVIIe siècle en France. Rev. d'hist. & de philos. religieuses, 19, 1939.

Baroway, I. The Lyre of David: A Further Study in Renaissance Interpretation of Biblical Form. ELH, 8, 1941.

Beerens, J. F. De Herkomst van den Bijbel. Utrecht, 1925.

Benecke, H. Der biblische Stoff und das Drama. Deutsches Museum, 1857.

Berger, S. La Bible au XVIe siècle. Paris, 1879.

—— La Bible française au moyen-âge. Etudes sur les plus anciennes versions de la Bible écrites en prose de langue d'oïl. Paris, 1884.

—— Les Bibles provençales et vaudoises. Romania, 18, 1889.

—— Nouvelles recherches sur les Bibles provençales et catalanes. Romania, 19, 1890.

Blondheim, D. S. Les parlers judéoromans et la Vetus Latina: Etude sur les rapports entre les traductions bibliques en langue romane des Juifs au moyen âge et les anciennes versions. Paris, 1925.

Blyton, W. J. Some Moderns and the Bible. QR, 1938.

Bonnard, J. Les traductions de la Bible en vers français au moyen-âge. Paris, 1884.

Bonnet, J. La poésie devant la Bible. Paris, 1858. Cf. Rev. contemporaine, 6.

Borrow, G. The Bible in Spain. London, 1843.

Burdach, K. Die nationale Aneignung der Bibel und die Anfänge der germanischen Philologie. Festschrift E. Mogk. Halle, 1924.

Burkitt, F. C. The Vulgate in England. Journal of Theolog. Studies, 35, 1934.

Butterworth, C. C. The Literary Lineage of the King James Bible, 1340-1611. Philadelphia, 1941.

—— How Early Could English Scripture be Printed in England? U. of Pa. Lib. Chron., 14, 1947.

Chumnos, G. Old Testament Legends from a Greek Poem on Genesis and Exodus. Cambridge U. P., 1925.

Cook, A. S. Biblical Quotations in Old English Prose Writers. London, 1898-1903.

Daiches, D. The King James Version of the English Bible. Chicago, 1941.

Deuschle, M. J. Die Verarbeitung biblischer Stoffe im deutschen Roman des Barock. Diss. Amsterdam, 1927.

Derjugin, T. Bibel und Griechen. Leningrad, 1925.

Deutschlander, L. Biblisch-talmudische Sentenzen und Motive in der Weltliteratur. Festschrift Jacob Rosenheim. Frankfurt, 1931.

Dodd, C. H. The Bible and the Greeks. London, 1935.

Dornseiff, F. Antikes zum Alten Testament. Zs. f. d. alttestamentl. Wissenschaft, 1934.

Fernández de Castro y Alvarez, E. F. El salterio de David en la cultura española. Madrid, 1928.

García, J. Los estudios bíblicos en el siglo de oro en la Universidad de Salamanca. Salamanca, 1921.

Glunz, H. H. History of the Vulgate in England from Alcuin to Roger Bacon. Cambridge U. P., 1933.

Hackelsperger, M. Bibel und mittelalterlicher Reichsgedanke. Diss. München, 1934.

Goebel, M. Die Bearbeitungen des Hohen Liedes im 17. Jahrhundert. Diss. Leipzig, 1914.

Hailperin, H. Jewish Influence on Christian Biblical Scholars in the Middle Ages. Historia Judaica, 4, 1942.
—— The Hebrew Heritage of Mediaeval Christian Biblical Scholarship. Ibid. 5, 1943.
Hatfield, G. B. The Bible in Medieval Civilization. Ibid.
Hatfield, J. T. The Hanseatic League and the King James Bible. AGR, 11, 1945. & Evangelical Quarterly, 20, 1948.
Hayes, D. A. Greek Culture and the Greek Testament. New York, 1925.
Hays, A. A. The Role of the Bible in the Reformation. In: The Study of the Bible Today and Tomorrow. Chicago U. P., 1947.
Hering, J. Die biblischen Grundlagen des christlichen Humanismus. Zürich, 1946 & Revue d'histoire et de philosophie religieuses. Paris, 1945-46.
Jaspis, J. S. Koran und Bibel. Ein komparativer Versuch. Leipzig, 1905.
Jones, M. The New Testament in the Twentieth Century. London, 1914.
—— The Hellenistic World Behind the New Testament. The Expositor, 1921.
Joseph, O. L. The Influence of the English Bible Upon the English Language and Upon English and American Literature. New York, 1935.
Kisch, G. Biblical Spirit in Mediaeval German Law. Spec., 14, 1939.
Kocher, P. H. Use of the Bible in English Astronomical Treatises During the Renaissance, HLQ, 9, 1946.
Koehler, W. Die älteste Ausgabe der lateinischen Bibel. F&F, 1934.
Leblois, L. Le Koran et la Bible hébraïque. Strasbourg, 1887.
Lehmann, P. L. The Reformers' Use of the Bible. Theology Today, 3, 1946.
Levin, B. Die griechisch-arabische Evangelien-Übersetzung. Upsala, 1938.
Lortsch, D. Histoire de la Bible en France. Paris, 1910.
MacDonald, D. B. The Hebrew Literary Genius. (An Introduction to the Reading of the Old Testament). Princeton U. P., 1933.
MacGregor, G. H. C. & Purdy, A. C. Jew and Greek. Tutors unto Christ. The Jewish and Hellenistic Background of the New Testament. London, 1936.
Masson, G. De l'influence de la Bible sur la littérature. Echo de la litt. et des arts, 1883.
Mergal, A. M. La Biblia en la literatura española. Luminar ((México), 2, 1938.
Moffatt, A. A Spanish Translation and Commentary of the Song of Songs. Transactions of the Glasgow U. Oriental Soc., 8, 1936.
Montet, E. Histoire de la Bible. Paris, 1924.
Moulton, R. G. The Literary Study of the Bible. New York, 1906.
Oppel, A. Das Hohelied Salomonis und die deutsche religiöse Liebeslyrik. Diss. Freiburg, 1911 & in Abhandl. zur mittl. und neueren Geschichte, 32, 1911.
Petavel, E. La Bible en France, ou les traductions françaises des Saintes Ecritures. Paris, 1864.
Pope, H. A Brief History of the English Version of the New Testament First Published at Rheims in 1582, Continued Down to the Present Day. Library, 20.
Preisker, H. Griechentum und Evangelium. Arch. f. Religionswissenschaft, 1938.
Ragon, F. Notice sur la littérature biblique en France du XVIe siècle à nos jours. In: Essais de poésie biblique. Paris, 1843.
Rappaport, S. Antikes zur Bibel und zur Agada. Kaminka-Festschrift. Wien, 1937.
Régnier, A. Quelques énigmes littéraires de l'inspiration coranique. Muséon, 1939.
Schöffler, H. Abendland und Altes Testament. Bochum-Langendreer, 1937.
Seligokowitz, B. Biblische Stoffe in der dramatischen Dichtung. Israelit. Wochenschrift, 52, 1901.
Smalley, B. The Study of the Bible in the Middle Ages. Oxford, 1941.
Smith, H. English Metrical Psalms in the Sixteenth Century and Their Literary Significance. HLQ, 9, 1946.
Smothers, E. R. The Coverdale Translation of Psalm LXXXIV. Harvard Theol. Rev., 38, 1946.
Spicq, P. C. Esquisse d'une histoire de l'exégèse latine au moyen âge. Paris, 1944.
Sprau, G. Literature in the Bible. New York, 1932.
Sypherd, W. O. The Literature of the English Bible. Oxford U. P., 1938.
Thibaut de Maisières, M. Les poèmes inspirés de la Genèse au début de la Renaissance. Louvain, 1932.
Trenel, J. L'Ancien Testament et la langue française. Revue des Etudes juives, 49, 1904.
Van Eys, W. J. Bibliographie des bibles et des nouveaux testaments en langue française des XVe et XVIe siècles. Genève, 1900-01.

Vianey, J. La Bible dans la poésie française depuis Marot. RCC, 1922.

Viering, F. C. Evangelische und katholische Schriftauslegung. Berlin, 1938.

Vollmer, H. Die Psalmenverdeutschung von den ersten Anfängen bis Luther. Potsdam, 1932-34.

Walther, W. Die deutsche Bibelübersetzung des Mittelalters. Braunschweig, 1889-92.

Wechssler, E. Hellas im Evangelium. Berlin, 1936.

Weil, G. Biblische Legenden der Muselmänner. Frankfurt, 1845.

Weir, T. H. German Critics and the Hebrew Bible. Bibliotheca Sacra, 1918.

William, A. Politics and Economics in Renaissance Commentaries on Genesis. HLQ, 7, 1944.

Wock, E. W. The Bible in English Literature. New York, 1922.

Wuelcker, R. P. Das Evangelium Nicodemi in der abendländischen Litteratur. Diss. Marburg. Paderborn, 1872.

Wuensche, A. Das biblische Epos in der neueren deutschen Literatur. Dresden, 1880.

Ziesemer, W. Studien zur mittelalterlichen Bibelübersetzung. Halle, 1928.

2. Influences upon Individual Authors.

Prins, A. A. Some Remarks on AELFRIC'S Lives of Saints and his Translations from the Old Testament. NPh, 25, 1940.

Ganshof, F. L. La revision de la Bible par ALCUIN. BHR, 9, 1947.

Trenel, J. L'élément biblique dans l'oeuvre poétique d'Agrippa d'AUBIGNE. Paris, 1904.

Lacombe, H. de. BOSSUET et les études bibliques. Le Correspondant, March, 1906.

Falkenhahn, V. Der Übersetzer der litauischen Bibel, Johannes BRETKE und seine Helfer. Königsberg, 1941.

Machen, Minnie G. The Bible in BROWNING with Particular Reference to The Ring and the Book. New York, 1903.

Poenitz, A. BYRON und die Bibel. Diss. Leipzig, 1907.

Faulhaber, M. von. CALDERON der Meistersänger der Bibel in der Weltliteratur. In: Zeitfragen und Zeitaufgaben. Freiburg, 1915.

Weidemann, C. Biblische Stilelemente bei CARLYLE. GRM, 1926-27.

Smead, J. van N. CHATEAUBRIAND et la Bible. Paris, 1924.

Méry, L. Atala et la Bible. RLC, 3, 1923.

Maurer, Klara. Die biblische Symbolik im Werke Paul CLAUDELS. Zürich, 1941.

Willoughby, H. R. The First Authorized English Bible and the CRANMER Preface. Chicago, 1942.

Bauer, G. A. L. Das Buch Hiob und DANTES Göttliche Komödie. Theolog. Studien und Kritiken. (Gotha), 28.

Poletto, G. La Santa Scrittura nelle opere e nel pensiero di Dante Alighieri. Siena, 1909.

Febvre, L. DOLET propagateur de l'Evangile. BHR, 6, 1945.

Zink, H. R. EMERSON'S Use of the Bible. U. of Nebraska Studies, 14, 1935.

Bonhöffer, A. EPIKTET und das Neue Testament. Giessen, 1911.

Sharp, D. S. Epictetus and the New Testament. London, 1914.

Tarelli, C. C. ERASMUS'S Manuscripts of the Gospels. Journal of Theological Studies, 1943.

Hammer, J. GEOFFREY OF MONMOUTH'S Use of the Bible in the Historia Regum Britanniae. BRL, 20, 1947.

Badt, B. GOETHE als Uebersetzer des Hohen-Liedes, Jb. f. Philol. & Pädagogik, 27, 1881.

Deutschländer, L. Goethe und das Alte Testament. Frankfurt, 1923.

Janzer, G. Goethe und die Bibel. Leipzig, 1929.

Schwartzkopff, A. Goethes Faust, Shakespeares Macbeth und König Lear im Lichte des Evangelii. Schönbeck, 1868.

Todt, K. Goethe und die Bibel. Wissensch. Beilage zum Jahresbericht des Gymnasiums. Steglitz, 1901.

Anon. Th. GRAY'S Elegy (and the Vulgata). In: Blätter f. literar. Unterhaltung, 16.VII.1849.

Unnik, W. C. van. Hugo GROTIUS als uitlegger van het Nieuwe Testament. Nederl. Arch. Kerkgesch., 1932.

Meusel, M. Thomas HARDY und die Bibel. Diss. Kiel, 1937.

Reu, H. Heinrich HEINE und die Bibel. Diss. München, 1909.

Windisch, E. Der HELIAND und seine Quellen. Leipzig, 1868.

Clark, R. T. HERDER, Percy and the Song of Songs. PMLA, 61, 1946.

Lewkowitz, A. Die Bedeutung der Bibel für die Weltanschauung Herders und Goethes. Monatsschr. f. Gesch. & Wissenschaft des Judentums, 1932.

Kraemer, C. J. **HOMER** and the Bible. CW, 21.

Grillet. La Bible dans V. **HUGO**. Paris 1911.

Lancaster, H. C. A Note on Hernani IV, 1, MLN, 1928.

Anon. Ueber den Einfluss des Alten Testaments auf **KLOPSTOCKS** Messias. Hamburg, 1820.

Hahn. Klopstocks Oden und die Bibel. Diss. Greifswald, 1923.

Riessler, P. **LUCIAN** von Samosata und die heilige Schrift. Theolog. Quartalschrift, 1933.

Revilla, M. Fray **LUIS DE LEON** y los estudios bíblicos en el siglo XVI. Escorial, 1928.

Wetzel, J. F. Die Sprache **LUTHERS** in seiner Bibelübersetzung. Stuttgart, 1861.

Hankins, J. E. Biblical Echoes in the Final Scene of Doctor Faustus. (**MARLOWE**). U. of Kansas Studies in English, 6, 1940.

Gouthaud. La Traduction des Psaumes de Cl. **MAROT** et de Th. de Bèze et celle de Ph. Desportes. Bull. de la Société de l'Histoire du Protestantisme fr, 15, 1866.

Lieb, F. Die biblische Botschaft und Karl **MARX**. Orient und Occident, June, 1936.

Wright, Nathalia. Biblical Allusion in **MELVILLE'S** Prose. AL, 12, 1940.

Harris, J R.. **MENANDER** and the Epistle to the Hebrews. ET, 44, 1932-33.

Baldwin, E. C. **MILTON** and the Psalms. MPh, 17, 1920.

—— Paradise Lost and the Apocalypse of Moses. JEGPh, 24, 1925.

Conklin, G. N. Biblical Criticism and Heresy in Milton. New York, 1949.

Cook, A. S. Milton's View of the Apocalypse as a Tragedy. Archiv, 129, 1912.

Fletcher, H. Milton's Use of Biblical Quotations. JEGPh, 1926-27.

—— The Use of the Bible in Milton's Prose. Illinois Stud. in Lang. and Lit., 14, 1929.

Sewell, A. Milton and the Mosaic Law. MLR, 1935.

Studley, M. H. Milton and his Paraphrases of the Psalms. PhQ, Oct., 1925.

Williams, A. Milton and the Renaissance Commentaries on Genesis. MPh, 37, 1940.

—— Renaissance Commentaries on Genesis and Some Elements of the Theology of Paradise Lost. PMLA, 56, 1941.

Hutchinson, F. E. Sir Thomas **MORE** as a Translator of the Bible. RES, 17.

Hofmann, K. **MUEHLPFORT** und der Einfluss des Hohen Liedes auf die 2te schlesische Schule. Diss. Heidelberg, 1897.

Seidmann, L. **PASCAL** und das Alte Testament. Breslau, 1937.

Garofalo, S. Il **PETRARCA** lettore della Bibbia. Ecclesia, 5, 1946.

Clar, M. Kannte **PLATON** die Religion des Alten Testaments? Gelbe Hefte, 16, 1939-40.

Forrest, W. M. Biblical Allusions in E. A. **POE**. New York, 1928.

Delfour, Abbé. La Bible dans **RACINE**. Paris, 1891.

Lichtenstein, G. Racine poète biblique. Paris, 1933.

Renan, E. De l'imitation de la Bible dans Athalie. RP, 1.VIII.1922.

Sievers, M. Die biblischen Motive in der Dichtung R. M. **RILKES**. Berlin, 1938.

Breme, M. J. Christina **ROSSETTI** und der Einfluss der Bibel auf ihre Dichtung. Münster, 1907.

Kisch, G. **SACHSENSPIEGEL** and Bible. U. of Notre Dame (Ind.), 1941.

Hatfield, G. B. The Bible in Medieval Civilization: the Saxon Code of Law in Illustration. Historia Judaica, 5, 1943.

Spitz, L. Carl **SANDBURG'S** Bible Texts. American Hebrew, 158, 1948 .

Steinherz, J. **SCHILLER** commentateur de la Bible. Annuaire de la Société littéraire israélite hongroise, 1911.

Betzinger, B. A. **SENECA** und die Bibel. Theolog. Quartalschrift, 1919.

Kurfess, A. Der Philosoph Seneca und das alte Testament. Theolog. Quartalschrift, 92, 1939.

Anon. **SHAKESPEARE** und die Bibel. Blätter f. lit. Unterhaltung, 30.IX.1850.

—— Shakespeare's Bible. TLS, 11.I.1947.

Bell, J. Biblical and Shakespearian Characters Compared. Hull, 1894.

Bullock, C. Shakespeare's Debt to the Bible. Oxford, 1879.

Eaton, J. R. Shakespeare and the Bible. London, 1858.

Hankins, J. E. Lear and the Psalmist. MLN, 61, 1946.

Noble, R. Shakespeare's Biblical Knowledge, New York, 1935.

Rees, J. Shakespeare and the Bible. Philadelphia, 1876.
Seaton, Ethel. Anthony and Cleopatra and the Book of Revelation. RES, 22, 1946.
Selkirk, J. B. (J. Brown). Bible Truths with Shakespearian Parallels. London, 1879.
Wordsworth, C. On Shakespeare's Knowledge and Use of the Bible. London, 1880.
Weaver, B. Toward the Understanding of SHELLEY. U. of Michigan P., 1932.
Hawkins, J. E. SPENSER and the Revelation of St. John. PMLA, 60, 1945.
Landrumiz, G. W. Spenser's Use of the Bible and his Alleged Puritanism. PMLA, 41, 1927.
Aalders, G. J. D. TERTULLIANUS' citaten uit de Evangelien en de oudlatijnische Bibelvertalingen. Amsterdam, 1932.
Buhle, P. A. de VIGNYS biblische Gedichte und ihre Quellen. Schwerin, 1908.
Clemenceau-Leclercq, J. G. L'inspiration biblique dans l'oeuvre poétique d'Alfred de Vigny. Diss. Aix-en-Provence. Marseille, 1937.
McKee. Alfred de Vigny and the Book of Job. MLN, 1930.
Chiapelli, A. VIRGILIO nel Nuovo Testamento. A&R, 1919.
Erdmann, G. Die Vorgeschichten des Lukas- und Matthäus-Evangeliums und Vergils vierte Ekloge. Göttingen, 1932.
Herrmann, L. Virgile a-t-il imité la Bible? L'Antiquité classique, 14, 1945.
Witt, N. W. de. Vergil and the New Testament. CJ, 27, 1932.
Schauer, H. Christian WEISES biblische Dramen. Görlitz, 1921.
Gohdes, C. A Note on WHITMAN'S Use of the Bible as a Model. MLQ, 2, 1941.
Biach, A. Biblische Sprache und biblische Motive in WIELANDS Oberon. Brüx, 1897.
Saix, G. de. Oscar WILDE et le théâtre. (Jezebel). MF, 1.XI.1937.
Beyersdorff, W. Studien zu Ph. von ZESENS biblischen Romanen Assenat und Simson. Form & Geist, 11. (Leipzig), 1928.
Brown, D. Two Naturalistic Versions of Genesis: ZOLA and Pardo Bazán. MLN, 52, 1937.
—— A Naturalistic Version of Genesis: Zola and Aluizio Azevedo. HR, 12, 1944.

CHAPTER THREE

Hebraism Ancient and Modern.

(For Biblical Characters, see Thematology, I.VI.10.)

1. Generalities.

Baron, S. W. The Jewish Factor in Medieval Civilization. Proceedings of the Am. Acad. for Jewish Research, 12, 1942.
Baumgartner, W. Israelitische und altorientalische Weisheit. Tübingen, 1933.
Blau, J. L. The Christian Interpretation of the Cabala in the Renaissance. Columbia U. P., 1944.
Breuer, I. Die rechtsphilosophischen Grundlagen des jüdischen und des modernen Rechts. Jb. der jüdisch-literar. Ges. 8. (Frankfurt), 1910.
Carrington, H. Die Figur des Juden in der dramatischen Literatur des XVIII. Jahrhunderts. Diss. Heidelberg, 1897. Cf. MLIA, 2.IV.1898.
Chabanges, R. de. Le juif au théâtre. MF, 84.
Chapman, J. J. The Effect of Hebraic Thought on Western Europe. New York, 1915.
Coudenhove-Kalergi, H. Anti-Semitism Throughout the Ages. London, 1935.
Dejob, C. Le juif dans la comédie au XVIIIe siècle. Revue des Etudes juives, 1899.
Fink, J. La première comédie en hebreu. (Leon Hebreo). RLC, 21, 1947.
Gross, H. Das Ghetto in der Dichtung. Allg. Zt. des Judentums, 72, 1908.
Guillaume, A. The Influence of Judaism on Islam. In: The Legacy of Israel. Oxford, 1926.
Herford, R. T. Talmud and Apocrypha. London, 1933.
Kayserling, M. Jüdische Frauen in Geschichte, Litteratur und Kunst. Leipzig, 1879.
Katz, S. The Jews in the Visigothic and Frankish Kingdoms of Spain and Gaul. Cambridge (Mass.), 1937.
Kroll, H. Ueber die Verwertung des jüdischen Charakters im Drama der Weltliteratur. Neuer Weg, 42, 1913.
Landa, M. J. The Jew in Drama. London, 1926.
Landau, J. Der Jude auf dem Theater. Generalanzeiger f.d. Judentum, 5, 1903.
Legband, P. Drama und Bühne der Juden. Zeitgeist, 16, 1902.
Loeb, I. Le juif de l'histoire et de la légende. Paris, 1890.

Marcus, J. R. The Jew in the Medieval World. Cincinnati, 1938.
Mauthner, Klara. Judentum in moderner erzählender Literatur. Wage, 7, 1904.
McCown, C. C. Hebrew and Egyptian Apocalyptic Literature. Harvard Theological Rev., 1925.
Menard, E. Jews in Fiction. American Hebrew, 55, 1946.
Nadler, J. Die Juden in der Literatur. Europ. Revue, 8, 1932.
Noble, S. An Introduction to Jewish Literature. CLN, 3, 1945.
Oesterley, W. A. O. The Jews and Judaism during the Greek Period. London, 1941.
Parkes, J. The Jew in the Medieval Community. London, 1938.
Pflaum, H. Les scènes des juifs dans la littérature dramatique du moyen-âge. Rev. des Etudes juives, 89, 1930.
Praag, S. van. Der Jude im Roman. In: Der Jude, 7, 1922.
—— Die Jüdin in der modernen Literatur. Menorah, 8, 1930.
Roback, A. A. The Story of Yiddish Literature. New York, 1940.
—— The Yiddish Language. Contemporary Jewish Record, 7, 1944.
Rosenberg, R. P. Bibliographies for Hebrew Translators. Jewish Forum, 25, 1942.
Rosenthal, F. Christian Hebraists of Western Europe. Diss. U. of Pittsburgh, 1946.
Roth, C. The Jewish Contribution to Civilisation. New York, 1938.
—— The Medieval Conception of the Jew. Gedenkschrift L. R. Miller. New York, 1938.
Rowley, H. H. Israel's Mission to the World. London, 1939.
Sakheim, A. Das jüdische Element in der Weltliteratur. Hamburg, 1924.
Schwab, M. Mots hébreux dans les mystères du moyen âge. Revue des Etudes juives, 46, 1903.
Slousch, N. Les juifs et le judaïsme aux Indes d'après les sources juives. Revue du monde musulman, 4, 1908.
Spire, A. Les problèmes juifs dans la littérature. In: La Renaissance religieuse. Paris, 1928.
Starr, J. The Jews in the Byzantine Empire. Athens, 1939.
Steinschneider, M. Die hebräischen Uebersetzungen des Mittelalters. Berlin, 1893.
Toussaint, C. `Introduction à l'histoire des prophètes d'Israel. RCC, 36-37, 1935-36.
Trachtenberg, J. The Devil and the Jews: The Medieval Conception of the Jew and its Relation to Modern Antisemitism. New Haven, 1943.
Vajda, G. Introduction à la pensée juive du moyen âge. Paris, 1947.
Varia. The Legacy of Israel. Oxford 1926.
Wallach, L. The Beginnings of the Science of Judaism in the Nineteenth Century. Historia Judaica, 8, 1946.
Waxman, M. A History of Jewish Literature. 4 vols. New York, 1941.
Welter, G. Le poison juif. MF, 1.IX.1927.
Werner, A. Four Tragic Jews. Jewish Outlook 6, 1942.
Williams, A. L. Adversus Iudaeos. A Bird's Eye View of Christian Apologiae until the Renaissance. Cambridge U. P., 1935.

2. In Individual Countries.

Coleman, E. D. Plays of Jewish Interest on the **AMERICAN** Stage, 1752-1821. Publ. of the American Jewish Historical Society, 33, 1934.
Friedman, L. M. Jews in Early American Literature. MB, 17, 1942.
Glanz, R. Jews in Early German American Literature. Jewish Social Studies, 4, 1942.
Labeson, A. L. Jewish Pioneers in America, 1492-1848. New York, 1932.
Mersand, J. Traditions in American Literature: A Study of Jewish Characters and Authors. New York, 1939.
Arns, K. Index der anglo-jüdischen Literatur. **(ENGLAND)** 2 vols. Bochum, 1938-39.
—— Anglo-jüdische Erzähler. NM, 10, 1939.
—— Stoffe und Probleme der neuen anglo-jüdischen Literatur. ZNU, 38.
—— Formen und Gestalten des neuen anglo-jüdischen Schrifttums. NSp, 47.
—— Deutschland und Juda im Spiegel der neuen englischen Literatur. NSp, 50.
Aufseeser, Gretel. Jüdische Gestalten im modernen englischen Roman. Zürich, 1940.
Blau, J. L. The Diffusion of the Christian Interpretation of the Cabala in English Literature. Rev. of Religion, 6, 1942.
Calisch, E. N. The Jew in English Literature, as Author and as Subject. London, 1909.
Cardozo, J. L. The Contemporary Jew in the Elizabethan Drama. Amsterdam, 1925.

Chiarini, G. Il giudeo nell' antico teatro inglese. NAnt, 124, 1892.
Coleman, E. D. The Jew in English Drama: An Annotated Bibliography. Bull. N. Y. Publ. Library, 1938 ff.
Heerwagen, H. Das Bild des Juden in der englischen Literatur. Forschungen zur Judenfrage, 5. (Hamburg), 1941.
Meyer, W. Der Wandel des jüdischen Typus in der englischen Literatur. Diss. Marburg, 1912.
Michelson, H. The Jew in Early English Literature. Amsterdam, 1926.
Modder, M. F. The Jew in the Literature of England to the End of the 19th Century. Philadelphia, 1939.
Roth, C. Anglo-Jewish Letters, 1158-1917. London, 1939.
—— A History of the Jews in England. Oxford, 1942.
Sisson, C. J. A Colony of Jews in Shakespeare's London. E&S, 23, 1938.
Van der Veen, H. R. S. Jewish Characters in 18th Century English Fiction and Drama. Diss. Groningen, 1935.
Bédaride, J. Lee juifs en **FRANCE**, en Italie, et en Espagne. Paris, 1867.
Cahen, S. De la littérature hébraïque et juive en France. Archives israélites de France, 1, 1840.
Cirot, G. Les juifs de Bordeaux. Revue historique de Bordeaux, 1938.
Cohen, A. Le juif et les romanciers français. Revue de Genève, 1923.
Fernberg, Babeth G. Treatment of Jewish Character in the XXth Century Novel in France, Germany, England and the United States. Diss. Stanford U., 1944.
Friedfertig, S. La littérature française et les lettres hébraïques. RLC, 22, 1948.
Gokkes, B. Fransch en hebreeuwsch bij enkele XVIe eeuwsche fransche grammatici. NPh, 23, 1937.
Harari, H. L'hébraïsme dans la littérature française. Rev. littéraire juive, 1930.
Lehmann, G. Der Einfluss des Judentums auf das französische Denken der Gegenwart. Berlin, 1940.
Lifschitz-Golden, M. Les juifs dans la littérature française du moyen âge. New York, 1935.
Malvezin, T. Histoire des juifs à Bordeaux. Bordeaux, 1875.
Moldenhauer, G. Frankreich und die Juden. ZNU, 36-37.
Randall, E. S. The Jewish Character in the French Novel, 1870-1914. Evanston (Ill.), 1941.
Schildener, E. H. Jüdische Bestrebungen im Spiegel französischer Literatur der Gegenwart. Diss. Bonn, 1937.
Spire, A. Les juifs dans la littérature française. La nouvelle Aurore, 1924-25.
Bass, J. Die Darstellung des Juden im deutschen Roman des 20. Jahrhunderts (**GERMANY**). Monatsschrift f. Gesch. & Wissenschaft des Judentums, 57-60, 1913-16.
Bender, H. Der Kampf um die Judenemanzipation in Deutschland im Spiegel der Flugschriften, 1815-1820. Jena, 1939.
Frankl, O. Der Judge in den deutschen Dichtungen des 15. 16. und 17. Jahrhunderts. Diss. Wien, 1905.
Frenzel, Elisabeth. Die Gestalt des Juden auf der neueren deutschen Bühne. Bühl-Baden, 1940.
Holdschmidt, H. C. Der Jude auf dem Theater des deutschen Mittelalters. Emsdetten, 1935.
Karpeles, G. Die Juden in der deutschen Literatur. Im deutschen Reich, 10, 1904.
Kraus, H. P. The Revival of Hebrew Studies in Germany. In: Catalogue 38: Sidelights on the Renaissance. New York, 1946.
Krüger, H. K. Berliner Romantik und Berliner Judentum. Bonn, 1939.
Landau, R. Der Jude im deutschen Drama. Im deutschen Reich, 10, 1904.
Liptzin, S. Germany's Stepchildren. Philadelphia, 1944.
Stoffers, W. Juden und Ghetto in der deutschen Literatur bis zum Ausgang des Weltkrieges. Graz, 1939.
Varia. L'apport des juifs d'Allemagne à la civilisation allemande. Cahiers juifs, 1933.
Witte, L. Der Jude in der deutschen Literatur. In: Kirche und Kunst. Halle, 1913.
Zweig, A. Juden auf der deutschen Bühne. Berlin, 1928.
—— Bilanz der deutschen Judenheit. Amsterdam, 1934.
Bloch, J. Hebrew Printing in Naples. (**ITALY**). Bull. of the N. Y. Publ. Libr., 46, 1942.
Mazzetti, R. Orientamenti antiebraici della vita e della cultura italiana. Modena, 1939.
Amador de los Rios, J. Estudios históricos, políticos y literarios sobre los judios de España. (**SPAIN & PORTUGAL**). Madrid, 1848 & Buenos Aires, 1942.
Anchel, R. Les juifs et les courants spirituels espagnols au XVIe siècle. Rev. des Etudes juives, 103, 1939.

Azevedo, L. de. Judeus portugueses na dispersão. Rev. de historia, 4, 1915.

Benoliel, J. A propos des juifs portugais. BH, 37, 1935.

Besso, H. V. Dramatic Literature of the Spanish and Portuguese Jews of Amsterdam in the XVIIth and XVIIIth Centuries. BH, 1937-40.

Cirot, G. Recherches sur les juifs espagnols et portugais à Bordeaux. Bordeaux, 1906.

Gelber, N. M. Contribution à l'histoire des juifs espagnols à Vienne. Rev. des Etudes juives, 1934.

Kayserling, M. Biblioteca española-portuguesa-judaica. Strassburg, 1890.

Levy, R. The Current Revival of Hebrew Studies in Spain. Jewish Forum, 24, 1941.

Millas Vallicrosa, J. M. La poesía sagrada hebraico-española. Barcelona, 1940.

Neuman, A. A. The Jews in Spain: Their Social, Political and Cultural Life During the Middle Ages. 2 vols. Philadelphia, 1942.

Pitollet, C. Sur un livre oublié de poésies judéo-espagnoles. Cultura española, 12, 1908.

Portnoy, A. Los judíos en la literatura española medieval. Buenos Aires, 1942.

Revah, I. S. Les juifs et les courants spirituels espagnols du XVIe siècle. Rev. des Etudes juives, N.S., 3, 1938.

Sonne, I. The Beginning of Hebrew Printing in Spain. Kirjath Sepher, 14. (Jerusalem).

Thomas, R. Huit romances judéo-espagnols. Hommage à E. Martinenche. Paris, 1939.

Abersten, S. Judisk litteratur på svenska. (SWEDEN). Jud. Tidskr., 6, 1933.

3. Influences upon Individual Authors.

Kliger, S. Hebraic Lore in Maxwell ANDERSON'S Winterset. AL, 18, 1946.

Adler, E. N. ARISTOTLE and the Jews. Rev. des Etudes juives, 82, 1926.

Blumenkranz, B. Die Judenpredigt AUGUSTINS. Ein Beitrag zur Geschichte der jüdisch-christlichen Beziehungen in den ersten Jahrhunderten. Basler Beitr. zur Geschichtswiss, 1946.

Spitzer, Marthe. Les juifs de BALZAC. Budapest, 1939.

Schönberg, B. BERGSONISME et judaïsme. Rev. juive de Genève, 1933.

Fehr, B. William BLAKE und die Kabbala. ESn, 1920.

Sebestyen, K. Les Mélodies hébraïques de BYRON. Annuaire de la Société littéraire israélite hongroise, 1911.

Brown, C. F. CHAUCER'S Prioresses Tale and its Analogues. PMLA, 21, 1906.

Holmes, U. T. A New Interpretation of CHRETIEN'S Conte del Graal. SPh, 44, 1947 & Chapel Hill (N.C.), 1948.

Krappe, A. H. Una leggenda talmudica nel Pugatorio di DANTE. SM, 12, 1939.

Saenger, H. Juden und Altes Testament bei DIDEROT. Diss. Würzburg, 1933.

Schaub, E. L. J. G. FICHTE and Anti-Semitism. Philosophical Review, 49, 1940.

Silberner, E. Charles FOURIER on the Jewish Question. Jewish Social Studies, 8, 1946.

Dreyfus, R. GOBINEAU est-il antisémite? Revue juive de Genève. April, 1934.

Rowbotham, A. Gobineau and the Aryan Terror. Sewanee Review, 1939.

Teweles, H. GOETHE und die Juden. Hamburg, 1925.

Lublinski, S. Jüdische Charaktere bei GRILLPARZER, Hebbel und O. Ludwig. Berlin, 1899.

Liljegren, S. B. HARRINGTON and the Jews. Bull. de la Société royale des Lettres de Lund, 4, 1931-32.

Bienenstock, M. Das jüdische Element in H. HEINES Werken. Leipzig, 1910.

Liptzin, S. Attitudes toward Heine's Jewishness in England and America. Yivo, Annual of Jewish Social Science, 2-3, 1947-48.

Plotke, G. J. H. Heine als Dichter des Judentums. Dresden, 1913.

Slochower, H. Attitudes toward Heine in German Literary Criticism. Jewish Social Studies, 3, 1941.

Tabak, I. Jewish Volkstum and Romanticism in Heine. MDU, 33, 1941.

—— Judaic Lore in Heine. Baltimore, 1948.

Apsler, A. HERDER and the Jews. MDU, 35, 1943.

Saurat, D. V. HUGO et la Cabale. Marsyas, Nov., 1927 .

Neider, C. Franz KAFKA and the Cabalists. Quart. Rev. of Lit., 2, 1945.

Dukes, L. LA FONTAINE et Berachia Hanakdan. Archives israélites de France, 9, 1848.

Bartels, A. LESSING und die Juden. Leipzig, 1935.

Moellering, R. LUTHER'S Attitude toward the Jews. Concordia Theol. Monthly, 19, 1948.

Adolf, Helen. The Esplumoir **MERLIN**: A Study of Its Cabalistic Sources. Spec., 21, 1946.
Fletcher, H. **MILTON'S** Semitic Studies. Chicago, 1927.
—— Milton's Rabbinical Readings. U. of Illinois P., 1930.
Kelley, M. Paradise Lost, VII, 8-12 and the Zohar. MLR, 1934.
Nicolson, M. H. Milton and the Conjectura Cabalistica. PhQ, 1927.
Geiger, A. Was hat **MOHAMMED** aus dem Judenthume aufgenommen? Bonn, 1833 & Leipzig, 1902.
Hirschfeld, H. Jüdische Elemente im Koran. Berlin, 1878.
Nicolaï, M. A. A propos de ce juif Michel **MONTAIGNE**. La Petite Gironde, 23.V.1938.
—— Les véritables ascendances de Montaigne. RB., 1938.
Spitz, L. Robert **NATHAN'S** Jewish Types. American Hebrew, 158, 1948.
Longbasch, R. M. F. **NIETZSCHE** und die Juden. Stockholm, 1939.
Stern, A. Nietzsche and Judaism. Contemp. Jewish Record, 8, 1945.
Beltrán, V. Un gran hebraísta olvidado: el P. **PEDRO DE VALENCIA**. Ciencia tomista, 1921.
Roth, C. Edward **POCOCKE** and the First Hebrew Printing in Oxford. Bodleian Lib. Rec., 2, 1948.
Saurat, D. Le judaïsme de **PROUST**. Les Marges, 15.X.1925.
Landsberger, F. **REMBRANDT**, the Jews and the Bible. Philadelphia, 1946.
Tronchon, H. **RENAN** et Israël. Revue d'histoire et de philosophie rel., 1927.
Krakowski, B. La psychologie des peuples allemand et juif dans les romans de Romain **ROLLAND**. Diss. Toulouse, 1931.
Busch, P. Fr. **SCHLEGEL** und das Judentum. Bottrop, 1939.
SHAKESPEARE: see also Shylock, I.VI. 10.
Flasdieck, H. M. Jüdisches im und zum Merchant of Venice. NM, 9, 1938.
Friedlander, G. Shakespeare and the Jew. London, 1921.
Stoll, E. E. Shakespeare's Jew. UTQ, 8.
Tannenbaum, S. A. Shakspere an Anti-Semite? SAB, 19, 1944.
Saurat, D. **SPENSER** and the Zohar. CLS, 1, 1941.
Sonne, I. L'ebraismo di **SPINOZA**. LNI, 1933.
Urzidil, J. Adalbert **STIFTER** and Judaism. Menorah Journal, 36, 1948.
Levy, I. **TACITE** et l'origine du peuple juif. Latomus, 5, 1946.
Emmrich, H. Das Judentum bei **VOLTAIRE**. Breslau, 1931.
Slochower, H. Franz **WERFEL** and Sholom Asch: The Yearning for Status. Accent, 5, 1945.
Spitz, L. Was **WOLFE** an Anti-Semite? American Hebrew, 158, 1948.

CHAPTER FOUR

St. Augustine.

(See also Literature and Politics, I.II.5.)

1. Generalities.

Abercrombie, N. Saint Augustine and French Classical Thought. Oxford, 1938.
Boyer, C. Christianisme et néo-platonisme dans la formation de saint Augustin. Paris, 1920.
Cherubelli, P. Le edizioni volgari delle opere di S. Agostino del Rinascimento. Firenze, 1940.
Dörries, H. Das Verhältnis des Neuplatonischen und Christlichen in Augustins De vera religione. Zs. f. neutestamentl. Wissenschaft, 1922.
Eggersdorfer, F. Augustinus und die Geisteswelt des Abendlandes. Bayr. Bildungswesen, 5, 1931.
Garvey, Sister M. Patricia. Saint Augustine: Christian or Neo-Platonist? Milwaukee, 1939.
Guzzo, A. Sant' Agostino. (Renaissance). Atti della Società ital. per il Progresso delle Scienze, 25, 1937.
Hendrix, E. Augustins Verhältnis zur Mystik. Würzburg, 1936.
Hessen, J. Augustinus und seine Bedeutung für die Gegenwart. Stuttgart, 1924.
Iscak, A. De S. Augustino in Oriente. Bohoslav., 1931.
Jolivet, R. Saint Augustin et le néoplatonisme chrétien. Paris, 1932.
Jugie, M. Saint Augustin dans la littérature théologique de l'Eglise russe. EO, 1930.
Kristeller, P. O. Augustine and the Renaissance. International Science, 1941.
Leder, H. Untersuchungen über Augustins Erkenntnistheorie in ihren Beziehungen zur antiken Skepsis, zu Plotin und zu Descartes. Diss. Marburg, 1901.
Marrou, H. I. Saint Augustin et la fin de la culture antique. Paris, 1938.

Moenius, G. Augustinus und die abendländische Welt von heute. Monatschrift f. Kultur & Politik, 2, 1937.

Mondadon, L. de. La modernité de S. Augustin. Et, 205, 1930.

Rose, H. J. St. Augustine as a Forerunner of Medieval Hymnology. Journal of Theological Studies, 1927.

Salaville, S. Saint Augustin et l'Orient. Angelicum, 8, 1931.

Semeria, P. La romanità di S. Agostino. Vita e Pensiero, 1930.

Troeltsch, E. Augustin, die christliche Antike und das Mittelalter im Anschluss an die Schrift De ciuitate dei. München, 1915.

Walzer, R. St. Augustinus und die Gegenwart. Benedictiner Monatsschrift, 12, 1930.

2. Influences upon Individual Authors.

Endter, W. König **ALFRED** des Grossen Bearbeitung der Soliloquia des Augustinus. Hamburg, 1923.

Silk, E. T. **BOETHIUS'S** Consolatio philosophiae as a Sequel to Augustine's Dialogues and Soliloquia. Harvard Theolog. Rev., 1939.

Hardy, G. Le De ciuitate Dei source principale du Discours sur l'histoire universelle. **(BOSSUET)**. Bibl. Ecole Htes. Etudes. Paris, 1913.

Guinagh, K. Sources of the Quotation from Augustine in The Parson's Tale. **(CHAUCER)**. MLN, 55.

Busnelli, G. S. Agostino, **DANTE** e il medio evo. Vita e Pensiero, 1930.

Calcaterra, R. Saint Augustin dans les oeuvres de Dante et de Pétrarque. In: S. Agostino, pubblicazione commemorativa. Milano, 1931.

Silverstein, T. On the Genesis of the De monarchia II.5. Spec., 1938.

Castellani, L. S. J. San Augustin y **DESCARTES**. In: Descartes: Homenaje en el tercer centenario, 3. Buenos Aires, 1937.

Scholz, H. Augustinus und Descartes. Blätter f. d. Philos., 5, 1931.

Vooght, P. de. La part de saint Augustin dans le De ecclesia de Jean **HUSS**. Recherches de Théologie ancienne et médiévale, 13, 1946.

Arbesmann, R. **JORDANUS** of Saxony's Vita sancti Augustini, the Source of John Capgrave's Life of St. Augustine. Traditio, 1, 1943.

Eibl, H. Von Augustinus zu **KANT**. Wien, 1933.

Jansen, B. Augustinus und Kant. Philosoph. Jb. 1930.

Godchot. **LA FONTAINE** et Saint Augustin. Paris, 1919.

Faggi, A. Echi delle Confessioni di S. Agostino nei Promessi sposi de **MANZONI**. Atti della R. Acc. di Torino, 71, 1935-36.

Alès, A. d'. Le S. Augustin de G. **PAPINI**. Et, 1931.

Dallago, C. Augustinus, **PASCAL** und Kierkegaard. Der Brenner, 6, 1921.

Gerosa, P. P. L'umanesimo agostiniano del **PETRARCA**. Didaskaleion, 1925-26.

Mariani, U. Il Petrarca e gli Agostiniani. Roma, 1946.

Martin, A. Petrarca und Augustin. AK, 1927.

Ceriani, G. L'ideologia rosminiana nei rapporti con la gnoseologia agostinianotomistica. **(ROSMINI)**. Milano, 1938.

Christ, P. Die Konfessionen Augustins und **ROUSSEAUS**. Zürich, 1894.

McCabe, J. The Confessions of St. Augustine and Rousseau. Critic, 1903.

Poux, P. **SAINTE-BEUVE** et Saint Augustin. BAGB, 19, 1928.

Gebhardt, C. **SCHOPENHAUER** gegen Augustinus. Jb. der Schopenhauer-Ges., 18, 1931.

Green, V. H. H. From St. Augustine to William **TEMPLE**: Eight Studies in Christian Leadership. London, 1948.

Molkenboer, B. Augustinus en **VONDEL**. In: Miscellanea Augustiniana. Rotterdam, 1930.

CHAPTER FIVE

Boethius.

1. Generalities.

Cappuyns, M. Le plus ancien commentaire des Opuscula sacra et son origine. Recherches de Théologie ancienne et médiévale, 1931.

Cohn, M. Die Rolle der Metra des Boethius im Streit um die Datierung der Denkmäler der angelsächsischen Poesie. Breslau, 1922.

Cossack, H. Ueber die altenglische metrische Bearbeitung von Boetius De consolatione philosophiae. Diss. Leipzig, 1889.

Courcelle, P. Boèce et l'école d'Alexandrie. Mélanges d'archéol. & d'hist. de l'Ecole française de Rome, 1935.

—— Etude critique sur les commentaires de la Consolation de Boèce. (IXe-XVe

siècles). Archives d'histoire doctrinale du moyen âge, 1939.
Delisle, L. Anciennes traductions françaises de la Consolation de Boèce conservées à la Bibliothèque Nationale. Paris, 1873.
Dolson, G. B. Boethius' Consolation of Philosophy in English Literature During the 18th Century. CW, 15.
—— Imprisoned English Authors and the Consolation of Philosophy. AJPh, 1922.
Dorogi-Ortutay, J. Boethius und das ungarische Barock im XVIII. Jahrhundert. (In Hungarian). EPhK, 1936.
Hoek, J. M. De middelnederlandse vertalingen van Boethius' De consolatione philosophiae. Hardewijk, 1943.
Hofmann, K. Ueber die Quellen des ältesten provenzalischen Gedichtes Boetius. SBAW, 1870.
Krappe, A. H. Two Medieval Derivatives of Boethius' De consolatione philosophiae. Leeuvensche Bijdragen, 18, 1926.
Leicht, A. Zur angelsächsischen Bearbeitung des Boetius. Anglia, 7, 1884.
Patch, H. R. The Tradition of Boethius. A Study of his Importance in Medieval Culture. New York, 1935.
—— The Beginnings of the Legend of Boethius. Spec., 22, 1947
Rabotine, V. Le Boèce provençal. Strasbourg, 1930.
Silk, E. T. The Study of Boethius' Consolatio philosophiae in the Middle Ages. TAPhA, 1931.
Stone, L. W. Old French Translations of the De consolatione philosophiae of Boethius. MA, 1937.
Vyver, A. van de. Les traductions du De consolatione philosophiae de Boèce en littérature comparée. H&R, 6, 1939.
Zimmermann, O. Ueber den Verfasser der altenglischen Metren des Boetius. Diss. Greifswald, 1882.

2. Influences upon Individual Authors.

Schmidt, K. H. König **ALFREDS** Boethius-Bearbeitung. Göttingen, 1934.
Milanesi, C. Il Boezio e l'**ARRIGHETTO**. Firenze, 1864.
Cline, J. M. **CHAUCER** and Jean de Meung: De consolatione philosophiae. Etudes litt. hist., l.VI.1936.
Dedeck-Héry, V. L. Le Boèce de Chaucer et les manuscrits français de la Consolatio de J. de Meun. PMLA, 59, 1944.
Koch, J. Chaucers Boethiusübersetzung. Anglia, 46.
Liddell, M. One of Chaucer's Sources. Nation, 64, 1897.
Bauer, G. A. L. Boetius und **DANTE**. Leipzig, 1874.
Falkenhausen, F. von. Dante und Boethius. JbDG, 22, 1940.
Murari, R. Boezio e Dante. GD, 5, 1897.
Riddehough, G. B. Queen **ELIZABETH'S** Translation of Boethius' De consolatione philosophiae. JEGPh, 45, 1946.
Wilkins, E. H. **LORENZO DE MEDICI** and Boethius. MPh, 15.
Nagel, F. Die altfranzösische Uebersetzung der Consolatio philosophiae des Boethius von Renault von **LOUHANS**. Diss. Halle, 1890. Cf. ZRPh, 15, 1891.
Dedeck-Héry, V. L. Jean de **MEUN** et Chaucer, traducteurs de la Consolation de Boèce. PMLA, 52, 1937.
—— The Manuscripts of the Translation of Boethius' Consolatio by Jean de Meung. Spec., 15, 1940.
Bach, W. Die althochdeutschen Boethiusglossen und **NOTKERS** Uebersetzungen der Consolatio. Halle, 1934.
Naumann, H. Notkers Boethius. Strassburg, 1913.
Sonnenburg. Bemerkungen zu Notkers Bearbeitung des Boethius. Progr. Bonn, 1887.
Dolson, G. B. **SOUTHEY** and Landor, and the Consolation of Philosophy of Boethius. AJPh, 1922.
—— I. T. Translator of Boethius. Ibid. 1921.
Hughes, M. Y. A Boethian Parallel to Faerie Queene (**SPENSER**). MLN, 63, 1948.
Houghton, W. E. Michael **WALPOLE**, Translator of Boethius' De consolatione. AJPh, 1930.
Schummer, K. John **WALTENS** metrische Uebersetzung der Consolatione philosophiae. Bonn, 1914.

CHAPTER SIX

Other Jewish and Early Christian Authors.

(See also Saints, I.VI.10.)

Cimmino, A. S. **AMBROGIO** e Dante. RCLI, 2, 1897.
Dickerman, S. O. Du Bartas and St. Ambrose, MPh, 1917.
Scherman, T. Die griechischen Quellen des hl. Ambrosius. München, 1902.
Lombard, A. De saint **ATHANASE** à Gustave Flaubert. Alma Mater (Genève), 1945.
McColley, G. Milton and Moses **BAR-CEPHA**. SPh, 38, 1941.

Courtonne, Y. Saint **BASILE** et l'hellénisme. Etude sur la recontre de la pensée chrétienne avec la sagesse antique dans l'Hexaméron de Basile le Grand. Paris, 1934.

Sanderlin, G. Quotations from St. **BERNARD** in The Parson's Tale. MLN, 54.

Schwietering, J. Der Tristan Gottfrieds von Strassburg und die Bernhardische Mystik. Berlin, 1943.

Jones, L. W. The Influence of **CASSIODORUS** on Mediaeval Culture. Spec., 1945.

—— Further Notes Concerning Cassiodorus' Influence on Mediaeval Culture. Spec., 1947.

Rougier, L. **CELSE** ou le conflit de la civilisation antique et du christianisme primitif. Paris, 1925.

Faye, E. de. **CLEMENT D'ALEXANDRIE**. Etude sur les rapports du christianisme et de la philosophie grècque au IIIe siècle. Paris, 1906.

Baur, Dom Chr. S. Jean **CHRYSOSTOME** et ses oeuvres dans l'histoire littéraire. Louvain, 1907.

Chase, F. H. Chrysostom, a Study in the History of Biblical Interpretation. Cambridge, 1897.

Naegele, A. Johannes Chrysostomos und sein Verhältnis zum Hellenismus. Byzantinische Zs., 13, 1904.

Achelis, W. Ueber das Verhältnis Meister Ekkeharts zum Areopagiten **DIONYSOS**. Marburg, 1922.

Franceschini, E. Grosseteste's Translation of the Prologos and Scholia of Maximus to the Writings of the Pseudo-Dionysius Areopagita. Journal of Theological Studies, 1933.

Grabmann, M. Pseudo-Dionysius Areopagita in lateinischen Uebersetzungen des Mittelalters. Festgabe A. Ehrhard. Bonn, 1922.

Lehmann, P. Zur Kenntnis der Schriften des Dionysius Areopagitica im Mittelalter. Revue Bénédictine, 1923.

Théry, G. L'entrée du Pseudo-Denys en Occident. Mélanges Mandonnet. Paris, 1930.

Allen, D. C. Milton and Rabbi **ELIEZER**. MLN, 63, 1948.

Théry, G. Scot **ERIGENE** traducteur de Denys. Archivum Latinitatis Medii Aevi, 6, 1931.

Gyory, J. Le système philosophique de Jean Scot Erigène et la cantilène et la cantilène de Sainte Eulalie. EPhK, 60.

Laistner, M. L. W. **FULGENTIUS** in the Carolingian Age. Festschrift Hruschewsky. Kiew, 1928.

Fletcher, H. F. Milton and Ben **GERSON**. JEGPh, 1930.

Maugeri, G. Il Petrarca e S. **GIROLAMO**. Catania, 1920.

Dewitz, A. Untersuchungen über Alfreds des Grossen westsächsische Uebersetzung der Cura pastoralis **GREGORS** und ihr Verhältniss zum Originale. Diss. Breslau, 1889.

Fleury, E. Hellénisme et christianisme. Saint Grégoire de Nazianze et son temps. Paris, 1930.

Hentrich, W. Gregor von Valencia und die Erneuerung der deutschen Scholastik im XVI. Jahrhundert. Festgabe Geyser. Regensburg, 1930.

Krebs, H. Die ags. Uebersetzung der Dialoge Gregors. Anglia, 2-3, 1878-79.

Wack, G. Ueber das Verhältniss von König Alfreds Uebersetzung der Cura Pastoralis zum Original. Diss. Greifswald, 1889.

Lundström, S. Studien zur lateinischen **IRENAEUS**übersetzung. Lund, 1943.

Allgeier, A. Die erste Psalmenübersetzung des heiligen **HIERONYMUS** und das Psalterium Romanum. Biblica (Roma), 1931.

Pease, A. S. The Attitude of Jerome Towards Pagan Literature. TAPhA, 1919.

Stummer, F. Einige Beobachtungen über die Arbeitsweise des Hieronymus bei der Uebersetzung des Alten Testaments aus der Hebraica Veritas. Biblica, 1929.

Kaiser, L. Shakespeare and St. Jerome. CJ, 41, 1946.

Bickermann, E. Sur la version vieux-russe de Flavius **JOSEPHE**. Mélanges Cumont. Bruxelles, 1936.

Brune, B. Flavius Josephus und seine Schriften in ihrem Verhältnis zum Judentum, zur griechisch-römischen Welt und zum Christentum. Gütersloh, 1913.

Creed, J. M. The Slavonic Version of Josephus' History of the Jewish War. Harvard Theolog. Rev., 25, 1932.

Dieckmann, H. Die Zeugnisse über Christus in der altslavischen Uebersetzung des Flavius Josephus. Zs. f. kath. Theol., 50, 1926.

Eisler, R. Les origines de la traduction slave de Flavius Josèphe et l'hérésie josephiniste. Actes du l. Congrès national des historiens français. Paris, 1928.

—— Die slavische Uebersetzung der Halosis tès Hierousalèm des Flavius Josephus. Byzantinoslavica, 2, (Prague), 1930.

Metcherscu, N. De la traduction russe ancienne du Bellum Iudaicum. C. R. de l'Acad. des sciences de Russie, 1930.
Parry, J. J. Geoffrey of Monmouth and Josephus. Spec., 1927.
Sproedowsky, H. Die Hellenisierung der Geschichte von Joseph in Aegypten bei Flavius Josephus. Greifswald, 1937.
Hartwell, K. E. **LACTANTIUS** and Milton. Harvard U. P., 1929.
Roth, L. Spinoza, Descartes and **MAIMONIDES**. London, 1924.
—— Maimonides and England. In: Moses Maimonides. London, 1935.
Lida, M. R. El Parsondes de Juan Valera y La Historia universal de **NICOLAO DE DAMASCO**. RFH, 4, 1942.
Murray, J. **ORIGEN**, Augustine and Plotinus. Month, 170, 1937.
Melikset-Bekov, L. M. Commentaire d'Origène sur le Cantique des cantiques de Salomon dans une version vieille-arménienne. Bull. Inst. caucasien hist. & arch. Tiflis, 1926.
Febvre, L. Origène et Des Périers, ou l'énigme du Cymbalum Mundi. BHR, 1942.
Barnett, A. E. **PAUL** Becomes a Literary Influence. Chicago U. P., 1941.
Grandgent, C. H. Dante and St. Paul. Romania, 31, 1902.
Ovidio, F. d'. Fonti dantesche: Dante e S. Paolo. RCLI, 2, 1897.
Goetz, K. G. **PETRUS** als Gründer und Oberhaupt der Kirche und Schauer von Gesichten nach den altchristlichen Berichten und Legenden. Leipzig, 1927.
Bentwich, N. From **PHILO** to Plotin. JQR, 4.
Heinemann, I. Philons griechische und jüdische Bildung. Breslau, 1932.
Drews, A. **PLOTIN** und der Untergang der antiken Weltanschauung. Jena, 1907.
Hess, W. A Quaker Plotinus. HJ, 29, 1931.
Krakowski, E. L'esthétique de Plotin et son influence. Paris, 1929.
Kraus, P. Plotin chez les Arabes. Bull. de l'Institut d'Egypte, 23, 1940-41.
Kuebler, F. Plotins Stellung zum Christentum. Erlangen, 1925.
Reiff, P. J. Plotin und die deutsche Romantik. Euphorion, 19, 1913.
Watkin, E. J. Plotin and Catholic Philosophy. Dublin Rev., 190, 1932.
Wundt, M. Plotin und die Romantik. NJKA, 1915.
Barion, J. Plotin und Augustinus. Berlin, 1935.
Henry, P. Plotin et l'Occident: Firmicus Maternus, Marius Victorinus, Saint Augustin et Macrobe. Louvain, 1934.
—— Augustine and Plotinus. Journal of Theol. Studies, 1937.
Manser, G. M. Augustins Philosophie in ihrem Verhältnis und ihrer Abhängigkeit von Plotin, dem Fürsten des Neuplatonismus. Freiburg, 1932.
Saracista, M. La filosofia di Giordano Bruno nei suoi motivi plotiniani. Firenze, 1935.
Arnou, R. Quelques idées néoplatoniciennes (plotiniennes) de David de Dinant. Festschrift Geyser. Regensburg, 1930.
Koch, F. Goethe und Plotin. Leipzig, 1925.
Wundt, M. Noch einmal Goethe und Plotin. NJKA, 1918.
Déchanet, J. M. Guillaume de St. Thierry et Plotin. Revue du moyen âge latin, 1946.
Jong, K. H. E. de. Hegel und Plotin. Leiden, 1916.
Weber-Colonius, E. Nietzsche und Plotin. Jena, 1941.
Walzel, O. Von Plotin, Proklos und Ficinus. DVLG, 19, 1941.
Koch, F. Schillers philosophische Schriften und Plotin. Leipzig, 1926.
Mueller, H. F. Shaftesbury und Plotinos. Berliner Philos. Wochenschrift, 1918.
Fletcher, H. Milton and **RASHI**. JEGPh, 1928.
Rosenthal, E. Rashi and the English Bible. BRL, 24.
Bethell, S. L. The Adoro te devote of St. **THOMAS AQUINAS** and Crashaw's English Version Compared. CLS, 6-8, 1942.
Cordovani, M. L'attualità di S. Tommaso d'Aquino. Milano, 1923.
Ryan, J. K. The Reputation of St. Thomas Aquinas among English Protestant Thinkers of the 17th Century. New Scholasticism, 22, 1948.
Thecla, Sister M. S. Thomas More and the Catena Aurea. MLN, 61, 1946.

BOOK THREE

Aspects of Western Culture. Modern Christianity, Literary Movements, International Relations.

FIRST PART

Modern Christianity.

CHAPTER ONE

Generalities.

(See also II.V.1-2.)

Anon. Das religiöse Motiv im modernen Drama. Reichsbote, 18, 1903.

Anesaki, M. Japanese Criticisms and Refutations of Christianity in the Seventeenth and Eighteenth Centuries. Transactions of the Asiatic Society of Japan, 1930.

Baechtold-Staeubli, H. et al. Handwörterbuch des deutschen Aberglaubens. 9 vols. Berlin, 1927-38.

Baker, C. D. Certain Religious Elements in the English Doctrine of the Inspired Poet during the Renaissance. ELH, 6, 1939.

Barnas, S. German Literature: Its Religious Character and Influence. Christian Review. (Boston), 1841.

Bates, E. S. American Faith: Its Religious, Political and Economic Foundations. New York, 1940.

Battenhouse, H. M. Poets of Christian Thought: Evaluations from Dante to T. S. Eliot. New York, 1947.

Bauddisson. Essai sur l'union du christianisme avec la philosophie. Paris, 1787.

Baumer, F. The Conception of Christendom in Renaissance England. JHI, 6, 1945.

Beary, R. J. Religion and the Modern Novel. Catholic World, 166, 1947.

Blennerhassett, Charlotte. Religiöse Probleme und moderne Romane. Hochland, 2, 1904.

Belloc, H. The Great Heresies. London, 1938.

Bernard, H. S. J. Christian Humanism During the Late Ming Dynasty. T'ien Hsia Monthly, 7, 1938.

Betz, L. P. Das Christentum. Eine Bibliographie. SVL, 3.

Brémond, H. Histoire littéraire du sentiment religieux en France depuis la fin des guerres de religion jusqu'à nos jours. Paris, 1916-33.

Briggs, E. R. L'incrédulité et la pensée anglaise en France au début du XVIIIe siècle. RHLF, 1934.

Buckley, G. T. Atheism in the English Renaissance. Chicago, 1932.

Busson, H. La pensée religieuse française de Charron à Pascal. Paris, 1933.

Calvet, J. La littérature religieuse de François de Sales à Fénelon. Paris, 1938.

Cantimori, D. & Feist, E. Per la storia degli eretici italiani nel secolo XVI in Europa. Roma, 1937.

Charbonnier, F. La poésie française et les guerres de religion. Diss. Grenoble, 1920.

Clemen, C. Christliche Einflüsse auf den chinesischen und japanischen Buddhismus. Orientalische Zs, 1922.

Cordier, H. Le christianisme en Chine et en Asie centrale sous les Mongols. T'oung Pao, 18, 1917.

Dale, G. I. The Religious Element in the Comedias de moros y cristianos of the Golden Age. Washington U. Studies, 7.

Diesenberg, H. Studien zur religiösen Gedankenwelt in der Spruchdichtung des 13. Jahrhunderts. Diss. Bonn, 1937.

Dunkmann, K. Das religiöse Motiv im modernen Drama. Berlin, 1903.

Duriez, G. La théologie dans le drame religieux en Allemagne au moyen âge. Paris, 1914.

Fairchild, H. N. Religious Trends in English Poetry, 1700-80. New York, 1939-42.

Fedotov, G. P. Religious Background of Russian Culture. Church History, 12, 1943.

Ferre, N. S. F. Swedish Contributors to Modern Theology. New York, 1932.

Franz, R. Die Freidenkerwelt in der Literaturgeschichte. In: Freidenkergeschichten aus der Weltliteratur. Berlin, 1930.

Giraud, V. Le problème religieux dans la littérature française. RDM, 1935.

Guenot, Abbé C. Les conquêtes du Christianisme en Asie, en Afrique, en Amérique et en Océanie. Paris, 1866.

Hardy, E. R. Militant on Earth. Twenty Centuries of the Spread of Christianity. Oxford U. P., 1940.

Henderson, A. D. Foreign Religious Influences in 17th Century Scotland. ER, 1929.

Humbert, Abbé. Les origines de la théologie moderne, I: La Renaissance de l'antiquité chrétienne (1450-1521). Paris, 1911.

Jordan, W. K. The Development of Religious Toleration in England. 4 vols. Harvard U. P., 1932-40.
—— Sectarian Thought and Its Relation to the Development of Religious Toleration, 1640-60. HLQ, 3, 1940.
Jørgensen, E. Fremmed indflydelse under den danske kirkes tidligste udvikling. Kgl. Danske videnskabenas Selskabs Skrifter, 1908.
Kaye, J. W. Christianity in India. London, 1859.
Klaiber. Religiöse Zeitprobleme in modernen deutschen Romanen. Deutsch-evangel. Blätter, 28, 1903.
Knight, G. W. The Christian Renaissance. Toronto, 1933.
Knorr, F. Die Auffassung des Christentums bei den mittelhochdeutschen Dichtern. Archiv f. Religionswissenschaft, 1938.
Latourette, K. S. A History of the Expansion of Christianity. 4 vols. New York, 1937-42.
Leach, H. G. The Relations of the Norwegian with the English Church, 1066-1399 and Their Importance to Comparative Literature. Proc. Amer. Acad. of Arts and Sciences, 44, 1909.
Liepe, W. Das Religionsproblem im neueren Drama von Lessing bis zur Romantik. Halle, 1914.
Lynd, R. The Religious Background in Literature. Trans. of the Royal Society of Literature, 8, 1928.
Marmelstein, J. W. De traditie van het Christendom in Frankrijks nieuwere letterkunde. Stemmen des tijds, 1943.
Marnas, F. La religion de Jésus ressuscitée au Japon dans la seconde moitié du XIXe siècle. 2 vols. Paris, 1897.
Menéndez y Pelayo, M. Historia de los heterodoxos españoles. 7 vols. Madrid, 1911-32.
Mensch, H. Der Pantheismus in der poetischen Literatur der Deutschen im 18. und 19. Jahrhundert. Giessen, 1893.
Mohne, E. C. Die freireligiösen Anschauungen im Drama und Roman der neueren deutschen Literatur (1885-1914). Diss. Wisconsin. St. Louis, 1926.
Plessis, J. du. A History of Christian Missions in South Africa. London, 1911.
Pradez, C. Doute et foi: influence de l'étude des sciences naturelles sur le scepticisme contemporain. Genève, 1877.
Préclin, E. Introduction à l'étude des rapports religieux entre la France et la Grande-Bretagne (1763-1848). Rev. d'Histoire moderne, 1938.
Reuter, H. Geschichte der religiösen Aufklärung im Mittelalter vom Ende des achten Jahrhunderts bis zum Anfang des vierzehnten. 2 vols. Berlin, 1875-77.
Robertson, J. M. A History of Free Thought in the 19th Century. New York, 1930.
San Marte. Das letzte Geheimniss des Christentums und seine Darstellung in der Poesie. Deutsches Museum, 1865.
Santayana, G. Interpretations of Poetry and Religion. New York, 1900.
Saunders, T. Religion and Tragedy. Dalhousie Rev., 24, 1944.
Schomerus, H. W. Indien und das Christentum. 3 vols. Halle, 1931-33.
Schroeder, R. Glaube und Aberglaube in den altfranzösischen Dichtungen. Erlangen, 1886.
Souilhé, J. La philosophie chrétienne de Descartes à nos jours. 2 vols. Paris, 1934.
Steiger, G. N. China's Attempt to Absorb Christianity. T'oung Pao, 24, 1926.
Wernle, P. Die Renaissance des Christentums im 16. Jahrhundert. Tübingen, 1906.
Withington, R. Literature and Christianity. College English, 2, 1940.
Zorb, E. H. Religiöse Strömungen in der schlesischen Literatur der Gegenwart. Leipzig, 1934.

CHAPTER TWO

Individual Denominations.

(See also Utopias, I.II.4; Emigrants, I.IV.4 and Thematology, I.VI.10.)

Guibal, G. Le poème de la croisade contres les **ALBIGEOIS**. Paris, 1864.
Hermsen, H. Die Wiedertäufer zu Münster in der deutschen Dichtung. (**ANABAPTISTS**). Diss. Breslau, Stuttgart, 1913.
Broicher, C. **ANGLIKANISCHE** Kirche und deutsche Philosophie. PJb, 1910.
Crane, R. S. Anglican Apologetics and the Idea of Progress, 1699-1745. MPh, 1934.
Fouchex, R. Le dernier chapitre de l'histoire des **BENEDICTINS** anglais de Douai. Mém. de la Soc. d'agriculture du dép. du Nord, 1900-02. Douai, 1904.
Bertrand, P. Genève et la révocation de l'Edit de Nantes. (**CALVINISM**). Genève, 1935.
Bonnet, J. Récits de la Réforme en Italie; Calvin au Val d'Aoste. Académie d.

Sciences morales et politiques, 1861.
Buitendijk, W. J. C. Het Calvinisme in de spiegel van de Zuidnederlandse literatur der Contra-Reformatie. Groningen-Batavia, 1942.
Cowell, H. J. The Sixteenth Century English-Speaking Refugee Churches at Geneva and Frankfurt. Proc. Huguenot Soc. London, 1939.
Engel, C. E. Echos de la Révocation dans le théâtre anglais. Bull. de la Soc. de l'Hist. du Prot. fr., 1932.
Groetz, J. B. Die erste Einführung des Kalvinismus in der Oberpfalz, 1559-76. Münster, 1933.
Kjöllerström, S. Striden kring Kalvinismen; Sverige under Erik XIV. Lund, 1935.
Lee, S. The Teaching of the Huguenots (America and Elizabethan England). Scribner's Mag., 1907.
Agar, W. M. CATHOLICISM and the Progress of Science. New York, 1940.
Ageorges, G. Manuel de la littérature catholique. Paris, 1939.
Allen, W. G. Renaissance in Northern Europe: the Catholic Roots of Scandinavian Culture. Tablet, 8.VIII.1942.
Anesaki, M . Psychological Observations on the Persecution of Catholics in Japan in the Seventh Century. Harvard Journal of Asiatic Studies, 1, 1936.
Baisnee, J. A. France and the Establishment of the American Catholic Hierarchy: the Myth of French Interference, 1783-84. Washington, 1934.
Baroni, V. La Contre-Réforme devant la Bible. Lausanne, 1943.
Battaglia, O. F. et al. Katholische Leistung in der Weltliteratur der Gegenwart. Freiburg, 1934.
Bougier, Marie. Essai sur la renaissance de la poésie catholique de Baudelaire à Claudel. Montpellier, 1941.
Bozza, T. Edizioni e traduzioni straniere degli scrittori politici italiani della Controriforma. Europa, 2, 1946.
Calvert, A. The Catholic Literary Revival: Three Phases in its Development from 1845 to the Present. Milwaukee, 1935.
Calvet, J. Le renouveau catholique dans la littérature contemporaine. Paris, 1927.
Caspar, E. Geschichte des Papsttums von den Anfängen bis zur Höhe der Weltherrschaft. Tübingen, 1930.
Dejob, C. De l'influence du Concile de Trente sur la littérature et les beaux-arts chez les peuples catholiques. Paris, 1884.
Fiecke, Sister M. J. The Revival of Catholic Literature in 20th Century Germany. Diss. Marquette U., 1944.
Giraud, V. Catholicisme et Romantisme. RDM, 1937.
Hatzfeld, H. A. Catholic Spirituality in Recent French Literature. Thought, 20, 1945.
Hirn, Y. Det heliga skinet: studier i den katolska kyrkens poesi och konst. Stockholm, 1909.
Hughes, P. Rome and the Counter-Reformation in England. London, 1942.
Hutton, E. Catholicism and English Literature. London, 1942.
Kolbeck, Sister M. Orestes. American Opinion of the Kulturkampf, 1871-82. Diss. Catholic U., 1942.
Leech, C. Catholic and Protestant Drama. Durham U. Journal, 33.
Levi Malvano, E. Libri proibiti nel settecento. Mélanges Hauvette. Paris, 1934.
Maklakov, G. Le catholicisme en Russie. La Vie intellectuelle, 10.XI.1938.
Marraro, H. R. Rome and the Catholic Church in Eighteenth-Century American Magazines. Cath. Hist. Rev., 32, 1946.
Maynard, T. The Story of American Catholicism. New York, 1941.
Metzger, J. Das katholische Schrifttum im heutigen England. München, 1937.
Mulvey, M. D. French Catholic Missionaries in the Present United States (1604-1791). Washington, D. C., 1936.
O'Connor, J. J. The Catholic Revival in England, 1770-1892. New York, 1942.
Odlozilik, O. Czech Missionaries in New Spain. Hispanic Amer. Histor. Review, 25, 1946.
Palmer, R. R. Catholics and Nonbelievers in Eighteenth Century France. Princeton U. P., 1939.
Ray, Sister M. A. American Opinion of Roman Catholicism in the Eighteenth Century. New York, 1936.
Riley, A. J. Catholicism in New England to 1788. Diss. Washington, D. C., 1936.
—— Catholicism and the New England Mind. Pub. Colonial Soc. Mass., 34, 1943.
Ryan, A. S. Catholic Social Thought and the Great Victorians. Thought, 23, 1948.
Shuster, G. The Catholic Spirit in Modern English Literature. New York, 1926.
—— The World's Great Catholic Literature. New York, 1943.
Soranzo, G. Il Papato, l'Europa cristiana e i Tartari. Un secolo di penetrazione occidentale in Asia. Milano, 1930.

Tarr, Sister Mary M. Catholicism in Gothic Fiction. Washington, 1946.
Thureau-Gangin, P. La renaissance catholique en Angleterre. Paris, 1912.
Thurston, H. Catholic Writers and Elizabethan Readers. The Month, 1894.
Valbuena Prat, A. El sentido católico en la literatura española. Barcelona, 1941.
Morais, H. M. **DEISM** in 18th Century America. New York, 1934. Cf. SAQ, 1935.
O'Brien, J. Le déisme en Angleterre et son influence sur les littératures anglaise et française. Progr. Köln, 1856.
Sayous, E. Les déistes anglais et le christianisme, principalement depuis Toland jusqu' à Chubb. Paris, 1882.
Torrey, N. L. The English Critical Deists and their Influence on Voltaire. Harvard U. P., 1926.
Ozanam, A. F. Les poètes **FRANCISCAINS** en Italie au XIIIe et au XIVe siècles. Paris, 1852.
FREE-MASONS: See I.VI.10.
HUGUENOTS: See Calvinism above and also Foreign Colonies I.IV.4.
Zieglschmid, A. J. E. The **HUTTERIANS** on the American Continent. AGR, 8, 1942.
Clark, R. Strangers and Sojourners at Port Royal: An Account of the Connections between the British Isles and the **JANSENISTS.** Cambridge U. P., 1932.
Codiguola, E. Le origini del Giansenismo ligure. LNI, 12, 1941.
—— Il giansenismo a Roma. Rassegna d'Italia, 1947.
Croce, B. Giansenisti e Gesuiti. Critica, 42, 1944.
Gazier, A. Histoire générale du mouvement janséniste depuis ses origines jusqu'à nos jours. Paris, 1922.
Jemolo, A. C. Dottrine teologiche dei giansenisti italiani dell' ultimo settecento. Riv. trimestrale di studi filiosofici e religiosi, 1920.
—— Il giansenismo in Italia prima della Rivoluzione. Bari, 1928.
Miguelez, R. P. Jansenismo y regalismo en España. Valladolid, 1895.
Nurra, P. Il giansenismo ligure alla fine del secolo XVIII. Giornale storico e letter. della Liguria, 1926.
Orcibal, J. Les origines du Jansénisme. Paris, 1947.
Parisi, A. I riflessi del giansenismo nella letteratura italiana. Catania, 1920.
Pompeati, A. Giansenismo e letteratura. Marzocco, 20.VII.1930.
Préclin, E. L'influence du jansénisme français à l'étranger. Rev. histor., 1938.
Ricci, C. Giansenismo e giansenisti. Il Boccadoro (Pavia), 15 & 31.I.1934.
Trompco, P. P. Rilegature gianseniste. Roma, 1929.
JESUITS: See also I.VI.11 & Colleges, I.IV.6.
Allan, C. W. Jesuits at the Court of Peking. Shanghai, 1937.
Bahlmann, P. Das Drama der Jesuiten. Euphorion, 2, 1895.
Becher, H. Die geistige Entwicklung des Jesuitendramas. DVLG, 19, 1941.
Boysse, E. Le théâtre des Jesuites. Paris, 1880.
Brodrick, J. The Origin of the Jesuits. London, 1940.
—— The Progress of the Jesuits. London, 1946.
Chadwick, H. The Scots College, Douai 1585-1613. EHR, 56.
Cian, V. L'immigrazione dei gesuiti spagnuoli letterati in Italia. Mem. dell' Acc. d. Sc., Torino, 1895
Curran, C. P. Jesuit Influence in Baroque Art. Studies: an Irish Quart. Rev., 29, 1940.
Decorme, P. G. La obra de los jesuitas mexicanos durante la época colonial, 1572-1767. 2 vols. México, 1941.
Delanglez, J. The French Jesuits in Lower Louisiana (1700-63). Washington, 1935.
Duhr, B. Geschichte der Jesuiten in den Ländern deutscher Zunge. 4 vols. Freiburg, 1907-28.
Elia, P. d'. Poeti cinesi in lode dei missionari gesuiti italiani del seicento. Civiltà Cattolica, 1947 .
Flemming, W. Geschichte des Jesuitentheaters in den Landen deutscher Zunge. Berlin, 1923.
Grainha, M. B. Histoire de la Compagnie de Jésus en Portugal (1540-1910). Lisbonne, 1915.
Harney, M. P. The Jesuits in History. New York, 1941.
Johnson, H. L. An Edition of Triunfo de los Santos, With a Consideration of Jesuit School Plays in Mexico before 1650. Philadelphia, 1941.
Kerssemakers, J. W. Jezuietenstijl. Studien, 72, 1940.
Lewalter, E. Spanisch-jesuitische und deutsch-lutherische Metaphysik des 17. Jahrhunderts. Hamburg, 1935.
Lopez Sarrelangue, D. E. Los colegios jesuitas de la Nueva España. Diss. U. of México, 1941.

McCabe, W. H. The Play-List of the English College of St. Omers, 1592-1762. RCL, 17, 1937.
—— Notes on the St. Omers College Theater. PhQ, 1938.
Misrahi, J. The Beginnings of the Jesuit Theatre in France. FR, 16, 1943.
Moule, A. C. The First Arrival of the Jesuits at the Capital of China. New China Review, 4, 1922.
Müller, J. Das Jesuitendrama in den Ländern deutscher Zunge vom Anfang (1555) bis zum Hochbarock (1665). Augsburg, 1930.
Palmer, R. R. The French Jesuits in the Age of Enlightenment: A Statistical Study of the Journal de Trévoux. AHR, 45, 1939.
Ricard, R. Les Jésuites au Brésil pendant la seconde moitié du XVI siècle (1549-97). Revue d'Hist. des Missions. 1937.
Rowbotham, A. Missionary and Mandarin: the Jesuits at the Court of China. Berkeley, 1942.
Sanchez Bawucro, J. Fundación de la Compañia de Jésus en Nueva España, 1571-80. México, 1945.
Scheid, N. Das lateinische Jesuitendrama im deutschen Sprachgebiet. Jb. der Görres Ges., 5, 1930.
Smith, G. (ed.). Jesuit Thinkers of the Renaissance. Marquette U. P., 1939.
Stender-Petersen, A. Tragoediae sacrae. Materialen und Beiträge zur Geschichte der polnisch-lateinischen Jesuitendramatik der Frühzeit. Acta et Commentationes Universitatis Dorpatensis, 25, 1931.
Smith, C. H. The Story of the **MENNONITES**. Berne (Indiana), 1941.
Douglas, P. F. The Story of German **METHODISM**. New York, 1939.
Shepherd, T. B. Methodism and the Literature of the XVIIIth Century. London, 1940.
Hock, C. H. The **MORMONS** in Fiction. Diss. U. of Colorado, 1941.
Morgan, D. Mormon Story Tellers. Rocky Mountains Rev., 7, 1942.
Bergmann, E. Die deutsche **MYSTIK**. Breslau, 1926.
Bernhard, J. Die philosophische Mystik des Mittelalters von ihren antiken Ursprüngen bis zur Renaissance. München, 1922.
Buche, J. L'Ecole mystique de Lyon, 1776-1847. Paris, 1935.
Butler, C. Western Mysticism. Neglected Chapters in the History of Religion. London, 1922.
Chérel, A. L'accent mystique de quelques grands écrivains français. Paris, 1940.
Chizhevskii, D. I. Deutsche Mystik in Russland. Geistige Arbeit, 21, 1938.
Clemen, C. Die Mystik nach Wesen, Entwicklung und Bedeutung. Bonn, 1923.
Closs, Hannah P. Chivalry versus Mysticism. In: Art and Life. New York, 1937.
Coleman, T. W. The Origin of Christian Mysticism. LQHR, 162, 1937.
Collins, J. B. Christian Mysticism in the Elizabethan Age. Baltimore, 1940.
Delacroix, H. Les grands mystiques chrétiens. Paris, 1938.
Gall, E. Mysticism through the Ages. London, 1933.
Green, O. H. The Historical Problem of Castilian Mysticism. HR, 6, 1938.
Groult, P. Lee mystiques des Pays-Bas et la littérature espagnole du XVIe siècle. Louvain, 1927.
Hatzfeld, H. Klassische Frauenmystik in Spanien und Frankreich. Span. Forschungen der Görres-Ges., 1938.
Hopfl, H. Dichtung und Mystik. Bonn, 1935.
Itrat-Husain. The Mystical Element in the Metaphysical Poets of the Seventeenth Century. Edinburgh, 1948.
Jones, R. M. The Flowering of Mysticism. The Friends of God in the XIVth Century. New York, 1939.
Peers, E. A. Spanish Mysticism. London, 1924.
—— Studies of the Spanish Mystics. 2 vols. New York, 1927-30.
—— Notes on the Historical Problem of Castilian Mysticism. HR, 10, 1942.
Thompson, E. N. S. Mysticism in Seventeenth Century England. SPh, 1921.
Tucker, W. J. The Mystic Note in English Verse. Catholic World, 167, 1948.
Varia. Concerning Mysticism. Guilford College Bull, 31, 1938.
Wieser, M. Der sentimentale Mensch gesehen aus der Welt holländischer und deutscher Mystiker im 18. Jahrhundert. Gotha, 1924.
Cazamian, L. L'intuition **PANTHEISTE** chez les poètes anglais. In: Etudes de psychologie littéraire. Paris, 1913.
Mahrhelz, W. Der deutsche **PIETISMUS**. Berlin, 1921.
Pinson, K. S. Pietism as a Factor in the Rise of German Nationalism. New York, 1934.
Pleijel, H. Der schwedische Pietismus in seinen Beziehungen zu Deutschland. Lund, 1935.
Sachse, J. F. The German Pietists of Pro-

vincial Pennsylvania. Philadelphia, 1895.

Salomoes, I. Der hallesche Pietismus in Russland zur Zeit Peters des Grossen. Helsinki, 1936.

Baruzi, J. Un moment de la luttre entre le **PROTESTANTISME** et l'Illuminisme en Espagne au XVIe siècle. Congrès d'histoire du Christianisme, 3. Paris, 1928.

Code, J. B. Protestant Tradition in Literature. Thought, March, 1938.

Dedieu, J. Le rôle politique des protestants français. Paris, 1920.

Gennrich, P. W. Evangelium und Deutschtum in Portugal. Berlin, 1936.

Hopkins, C. H. The Rise of the Social Gospel in American Protestantism, 1865-1915. Yale U. P., 1940.

Jonker, G. D. Le protestantisme et le théâtre de langue française au XVIe siècle. Groningen, 1939.

Kont, J. La littérature hongroise et le protestantisme de langue française au XVIe et XVIIe siècle. Bull. historique et littéraire, 44, 1899.

Linnhof, L. Spanische Protestanten und England. Emsdetten, 1934.

Mooij, J. Geschiedenis der protestantsche kerk in Indie. Weltevreden, 1923.

Rupp, E. G. Studies in the Making of the English Protestant Tradition. Cambridge U. P., 1947.

Schoeffler, H. Protestantismus und Literatur. Leipzig, 1922.

Soldan. Geschichte des Protestantismus in Frankreich. Leipzig, 1853.

Vaissière. Les relations de la France avec les protestants d'Allemagne sous François I. et Henri II. Paris, 1901.

Chambon, J. Der **PURITANISMUS.** Sein Weg von der Reformation bis zum Ende der Stuarts. Zürich, 1944.

Glover, T. R. Poets and Puritans. London, 1923.

Haller, W. The Rise of Puritanism. Columbia U. P., 1938.

Knappen, M. M. Tudor Puritanism: A Chapter in the History of Idealism. Chicago, 1939.

Maly-Schatter, Florence. The Puritan Element in Victorian Fiction. Zürich, 1940.

Mills, B. The Attitude of Major XIXth Century Americans towards Puritanism. Diss. U. of Wisconsin, 1942.

Plum, H. G. Restoration Puritanism: A Study of the Growth of English Liberty. Chapel Hill (N. C.), 1943.

Sheffield Clapham, H. The Influence of Puritanism on American Literature. Macmillan Mag., 1902.

Stewart, R. Puritan Literature and the Flowering of New England. William and Mary Quar., 3, 1946.

Etten, H. van. **QUAKERISM** in France. Bull. of the Friends' Historical Assoc., 26, 1937.

—— Chronique de la vie quaker française de 1750 à 1938. Paris, 1939.

Gilbert, Dorothy L. & Pope, R. Quakerism and French Quietism. Bull. of the Friends' Histor. Assoc., 29, 1940.

Gloël, Elisabeth. Die Frau bei den Quäkern des 17. Jahrhunderts in England. Halle, 1939.

Hintz, H. W. The Quaker Influence in American Literature. Friends Intelligencer 96, 1939 & New York, 1940.

Mekeel, A. J. The Society of Friends and the American Revolution. Diss. Harvard U., 1940.

Philips, Edith. Le personnage du Quaker sur la scène française. RLC, 9, 1929.

—— The Good Quaker in French Legend. Philadelphia, 1932.

Russell, E. The History of Quakerism. New York, 1942.

Burdach, K. **REFORMATION,** Renaissance, Humanismus. Berlin, 1926.

Carsano, A. Per la storia della Riforma in Italia. LNI, 12, 1941.

Chasles, P. Du movement sensualiste avant la Réforme: Rabelais, Skelton, Folengo, Luther. RDM, I.III, 1842.

Church, F. C. The Literature of the Italian Reformation. Jour. of Mod. Hist., 3, 1931.

Constant, G. The Reformation in England. New York, 1942.

Frings, T. Incontri italo-germanici nell' età della Riforma. SG, 3, 1938.

Hagedorn, M. Reformation und spanische Andachtsliteratur. Boletín bibliográfico del Centro de Intercambio Intelectual Germano-Español, 1935.

Hauser, H. La propagation de la Réforme en France. RCC, 1894.

Holstein, H. Die Reformation im Spiegelbilde der dramatischen Literatur des XVI. Jahrhunderts. Halle, 1886.

Lemmi, F. La Riforma in Italia e i riformatori italiani all' estero nel secolo XVI. Milano, 1939.

Leube, H. Reformation und Humanismus in England. Leipzig, 1930.

Monnier, M. Histoire de la littérature

moderne: La Réforme de Luther à Shakespeare. Paris, 1885.
Paux, F. Histoire de la Réformation française. 2 vols. Paris, 1859.
Sabatier-Plantier, H. de. Origines de la Réformation française. Paris, 1870.
Sembritzki, J. Die polnischen Reformisten und Unitarier in Preussen. Altpreuss. Monatsschrift, 30, 1893.
Vetter, T. Relations between England and Zürich during the Reformation. London, 1904.
Viatte, A. Les origines françaises du SPIRITISME. Rev. d'hist. de l'Eglise de France, 1935.
Watts, G. B. The WALDENSES in the New World. Duke U. P., 1941.

CHAPTER THREE

Luther and Calvin.

Anon. LUTHER in Frankreich. In: Blätter für literar. Unterhaltung, 9.VIII. 1835.
Bachman, K. Der Einfluss von Luthers Wortschatz auf die schweizerische Literatur des 16. und 17. Jahrhunderts. Freiburg, 1909.
Brophy, L. From Luther to Lenin via Liberalism. Irish Monthly, 1946.
Brunnemann, Anna. Luther in der erzählenden Dichtung. ZDU, 31, 1917.
Chérel, A. Deux responsables de l'absolutisme laïque. I. Luther. Rev. des Jeunes, 10.VII.1927.
Dallmann, W. Catholic Tributes to Luther. Concordia Theol. Monthly, 16, 1946.
—— Henry VIII's Divorce and Luther. Concordia Theol. Monthly, 18, 1949.
Hackemann, A. Martin Luther in der neueren Lyrik. Evangel. Schulblatt, 50, 1906.
Hare, J. C. Vindication of Luther Against his Recent English Assailants. London, 1855.
Haupt, O. Luther und Rabelais in ihren pädagogischen Beziehungen. Diss. Leipzig, 1890.
Herzfeld, G. Martin Luther im Drama von vier Jahrhunderten. Diss. Köln, 1922.
Hopf, C. A Sermon of Martin Luther in the English Primer. Jour. Theol. Studies, 43.
Kooiman, W. J. Luther's Kerklied in de Nederlanden. Amsterdam, 1943.
Kühlhorn, W. Luther in der dramatischen Dichtung. ZDU, 31, 1917.
Lauchert, F. Die italienischen literarischen Gegner Luthers. Freiburg, 1912.
Lehmann, H. Luther im deutschen Lied. Halle, 1910.
Leube, H. Die Anfänge der französischen Lutherauffassung. Zs. f. Kirchengeschichte, 56, 1937.
—— Deutschlandbild und Lutherauffassung in Frankreich. In: Frankreich, sein Weltbild und Europa. Stuttgart, 1941.
Lindroth, H. Luther und die Reformation in der schwedischen Theologie der Gegenwart. Theologische Zs., 3, 1947.
Marichal, R. Antoine d'Oraison, premier traducteur français de Luther. BHR, 9, 1947.
McNeill, J. T. Luther at Aldersgate. (Wesley). LQHR, 1939.
Pfandl, L. Das spanische Lutherbild des 16. Jahrhunderts. Histor. Jb, 51, 1931.
Schmidt, M. Die Bedeutung Luthers für John Wesleys Bekehrung. Luther-Jb., 20, 1938.
Schubert, R. Polens Kampf gegen Luther. Posen, 1940.
Tappert, T. G. On the Translation of Martin Luther's Works. Lutheran Church Quar., 19, 1946-47.
Villers, C. de. Essai sur l'esprit et l'influence de la réformation de Luther. Paris, 1804.
Voipio, A. Luthers Kirchenlieder in Finnland. Zs. f. systemat. Theologie, 15.
Wantula, A. The Slavonic Luther. Concordia Theol. Monthly, 17, 1946.
Warmuth, K. Martin Luther im deutschen Lied. Leipzig, 1902.
Yarmolinsky, A. Ivan the Terrible contra Luther. Bull. Public Library, 44. New York, 1940.
Zabel, A. Lutherdramen des beginnenden 17. Jahrhunderts. Diss. München, 1910.
CALVIN: See also Chapter Two above.
Crue, F. de. L'action politique de Calvin hors de Genève. Genève, 1909.
Davies, A. T. John Calvin and the Influence of Protestantism on National Life and Character. London, 1946.
Neill, T. P. Calvin and the Modern Mind. Catholic World, 164, 1946.
Rotscheidt, W. Johann Calvin im Spiegel der Dichtung. Elberfeld, 1909.
Wencelius, L. Calvin et Rembrandt. Paris, 1937.

CHAPTER FOUR

Influences upon Individual Authors.

Berthaut, P. **BALZAC** et la religion. Paris, 1942.

Kemp, F. **BAUDELAIRE** und das Christentum. München, 1939.

Woelwer, W. Hilaire **BELLOC** und sein Eintreten für den Katholizismus in England. Bonn, 1937.

Bagdasarianz, W. William **BLAKE.** Versuch einer Entwicklungsgeschichte des Mystikers. Swiss Studies in English, 2. Bern.

Saurat, D. Blake et les gnostiques. Yggdrasill, 1936.

Benz, E. Der Toleranz-Gedanke in der Religionswissenschaft: über den Heptaplomeres des Jean **BODIN.** DVLG, 12, 1934.

Sabine, G. A. The Colloquium Heptaplomeres of Jean Bodin. In: Persecution and Liberty. Festschrift G. L. Burr. New York, 1931.

Gilbert, Dorothy L. & Pope, R. The Animadversions of Bishop **BOSSUET** upon the Quakers and Quietists. PMLA, 57, 1942.

Hamm, V. M. **BOSWELL'S** Interest in Catholicism. Thought, 21, 1946.

Rajewski, Sister M. A. Sebastian **BRANT:** Studies in the Religious Aspects of His Life and Work. Washington, D. C., 1944.

Ryan, T. **BROWNSON** and the Papacy. Amer. Eccles. Rev., 114, 1946.

Martin, C. Giordano **BRUNO:** Mystic and Martyr. London, 1921.

Hopf, C. Martin **BUCER** and the English Reformation. Oxford, 1946.

Laurent, M. H. Autour de la controverse luthérienne en France: Lambert **CAMPESTER.** Rev. d'Hist. Eccles., 35, 1939.

Leopold, W. Die religiöse Wurzel von **CARLYLES** literarischer Wirksamkeit. Halle, 1922.

Hocking, G. D. A Study of the Tragoediae Sacrae of Father **CAUSSIN.** Baltimore, 1943.

Ruffini, F. I giansenisti piemontesi e la conversione della Madre di **CAVOUR.** Atti della R. Accad. di scienze di Torino, 1928-29.

Cascón M. Los jesuitas según **CERVANTES.** Bol. Bibl. Menéndez Pelayo, 23, 1948.

Teipel, H. Zur Frage des Skeptizismus bei Pierre **CHARRON.** Bonn, 1912.

Spellanzon, C. `Il P. Eusebio **CHINI,** missionario ed esploratore dell' Arizona e della California. NAnt, 1.II.1935.

Herte, A. Das katholische Lutherbild im Bann der Lutherkommentare des **COCHLAEUS.** 3 vols. Münster, 1943.

Sanders, C. R. **COLERIDGE** and the Broad Church Movement. Duke U. P., 1942.

Wright, C. J. **COMENIUS** and Methodism. LQHR, 1941.

Bluhm, H. The Douche Sources of **COVERDALE'S** Translation of the Twenty-Third Psalm. JEGPh, 46, 1947.

Berg, A. E. **CRANMER** and Lutheranism in England. Lutheran Outlook, Nov., 1946.

Allison, A. F. **CRASHAW** and St. François de Sales. RES, 24, 1948.

Baruzi, J. Saint Jean de la **CROIX** et le problème de l'expérience mystique. Paris, 1931.

Erdmann, J. E. Scholastik, Mystik und **DANTE.** JbDG, 3, 1871.

Gardner, E. E. Dante and the Mystics. London, 1913.

Ozanam, A. F. Dante et la philosophie catholique au XIIIe siècle. Paris, 1839.

Toynbee, P. The Inquisition and the Editio Princeps of the Vita Nuova. MLR, 3, 1908.

Roehnsch, M. **DEFOES** Stellung zu den religiösen Strömungen seiner Zeit. Diss. Breslau, 1933.

Stamm, R. Der aufgeklärte Puritanismus Daniel Defoes. Swiss Studies in English, 1. Bern.

Prezzolini, G. Protestant Influence on **DE SANCTIS'** Literary Criticism. In: Life and Criticism of Francesco De Sanctis. New York, 1941.

Georges-Berthier, A. **DESCARTES** et les Rose-Croix. Revue de Synthèse, 18, 1939.

Barker, J. E. **DIDEROT'S** Treatment of the Christian Religion in The Encyclopédie. New York, 1941.

Bredvold, L. I. The Religious Thought of **DONNE** in Relation to Medieval and Later Traditions. In: Studies in Shakespeare, Milton and Donne. New York, 1925.

Moloney, M. F. John Donne and the Jesuits. MLQ, 8, 1947.

Madaule, J. Le christianisme de **DOSTOIEVSKI.** Paris, 1939.

Brown, C. T. **DREISER'S** Bulwark and Philadelphia Quakerism. Bull. Friends Hist. Assn., 35, 1947.

Hartwig, G. H. **EMERSON** on Historical Christianity. HJ, 37, 1939.

Dolfen, C. Die Stellung **ERASMUS'** zur scholastischen Methode. Münster, 1936.
Humbertclaude, H. Erasme et Luther; leur polémique sur le libre arbitre. Paris, 1909.
Murray, R. H. Erasmus and Luther. London, 1920.
Pineau, J. B. Erasme, sa pensée religieuse. Paris, 1924.
Renaudet, A. Erasme, sa pensée religieuse et son action d'après sa correspondance. Paris, 1926.
Engel, C. E. John **EVELYN** et le protestantisme français. Bull. de la Société du Protestantisme fr, 1934.
Joppin, G. **FENELON** et le mystique du pur amour. Bordeaux, 1938.
Dress, W. Die Mystik des Marsilio **FICINO.** Berlin, 1929.
Hauffen, A. Johann **FISCHART,** ein Literaturbild aus der Gegenreformation. Berlin, 1921.
Kuerz, H. Quelle von Fischarts Jesuitenbüchlein. Archiv, 1863.
Zieglschmid, A. J. F. Truth and Fiction and Mennonites in the Second Part of Theodor **FONTANE'S** Novel Quitt. Mennonite Quart. Rev., 1942.
Kolbenheyer, C. Die Mystik des Sebastian **FRANCK** von Woerd. Würzburg, 1935.
Daniels, J. Les rapports entre Saint **FRANCOIS DE SALES** et les Pays-Bas. Nijmegen, 1932.
Schurhammer, G. Der. hl. **FRANZ XAVER** in Japan, 1549-51. Neue Zs. f. Missionswissenschaft, 1946.
Pendzig, P. Pierre **GASSENDIS** Metaphysik und ihr Verhältnis zur scholastischen Philosophie. Bonn, 1908.
Hewitt, T. B. Paul **GERHARDT** as a Hymn Writer and his Influence in English Hymnody. New Haven, 1918.
Mulloy, W. J. The German Catholic Estimate of **GOETHE** (1790-1939). Berkeley, 1944.
Pfund, H. W. Goethe and the Quakers. GR, 14, 1939.
Harring, W. Andreas **GRYPHIUS** und das Drama der Jesuiten. Halle, 1907.
Gilbert, Dorothy L. & Pope, R. The Cowper Translation of Mme. **GUYON'S** Poems. PMLA, 54, 1939.
Hartley, L. Cowper and Mme. Guyon: Additional Notes. Ibid. 56, 1941.
Heuser, F. W. J. The Mystical **HAUPTMANN.** GR, 7, 1932.
Weber, R. Das religiöse Problem bei Gerhardt Hauptmann. JEGPh, 15, 1916.
Mills, D. **HAWTHORNE** and Puritanism. NEQ, 21, 1948.
Voight, G. P. Hawthorne and the Roman Catholic Church. NEQ, 19, 1946.
Grauert, H. Magister **HEINRICH DER POET** und die römische Kurie. ABAW, 27, 1912.
Saurat, D. La religion de Victor **HUGO.** Paris, 1930.
Pelikan, J. Luther's Attitude toward John **HUS.** Concordia Theol. Monthly, 19, 1948.
Rehm, W. Experimentum suae medietatis. Eine Studie zur dichterischen Gestaltung des Unglaubens bei **JEAN-PAUL** und Dostoiewski. Jb. Freies deutsches Hochstift. Halle, 1940.
Rauch, E. W. Der Wiedertäuferkönig **JOHANN VON LEYDEN** in der Dichtung. Münster, 1912. Cf. Rhein. westfäl. Zt. 1354, 1912 & Kölnische VolksZt., 21, 1914.
Simpson, P. The Castle of the Rosy Cross: Ben **JONSON** and Theophilus Schweighardt. MLR, 41, 1946.
Caraceni, A. Misticismo di **KAFKA.** Mercurio, 2, 1945.
Thomas, R. H. Franz Kafka and the Religious Aspects of Expressionism. GLL, 2, 1938.
Fitzpatrick, M. **KIERKEGAARD** and the Church. Journal of Religion, 27, 1948.
Thieme, K. Sören Kierkegaard und die katholische Wahrheit. Religiöse Besinnung, 1933.
Jusserand, J. J. Piers Plowman (**LANGLAND**). A Contribution to the History of English Mysticism. London, 1894.
Schroder, T. A Contribution to the Psychology of Theism: The French Prophets and John **LARY.** Psychoanalytical Rev., 12, 1925.
Wyzewa, T. de. Un mystique protestant: Jean-Gaspard **LAVATER.** In: Excentriques et aventuriers de divers pays. Paris, 1910.
Krueger. **LENAUS** Albigenser und die Quellenschriften. Progr. Berlin, 1886.
Fittbogen, D. Die Religion **LESSINGS.** Leipzig, 1923.
Foster, H. D. International Calvinism through John **LOCKE** and the Revolution of 1688. AHR, 1927.
Nachtwey, H. J. Die Exerzitien des Ignatius von **LOYOLA** in den Dramen Jakob Bidermanns S. J. Bochum-Langendreer, 1937.
Latreille. J. de **MAISTRE** et la papauté. Paris, 1906.
Bertolini, E. Il sentimento religioso del **MANZONI** e dello Chauteaubriand. Rassegna nazionale, 1900.

Hauvette, H. La vie religieuse de Manzoni. EI, 1932-32.
Manfredi, G. S. Genesi del pensiero religioso d'Alessandro Manzoni. Conv., 4, 1932.
Portier, L. La conversion d'Alessandro Manzoni. La Vie spirituelle, 1938.
Premoli, O. La conversione di A. Manzoni. Rassegna nazionale, 1.V.1921.
Rota, E. Manzoni e il giansenismo. NRS, 1927-28.
Sarrailh, J. Note sur Clément **MAROT** et l'inquisition espagnole. RFE, 1934.
—— Note complémentaire sur Clément Marot et l'inquisition espagnole. Ibid. 21.
Francke, K. Cotton **MATHER** and August Hermann Francke. HSPhL, 5, 1896.
—— The Beginning of Cotton Mather's Correspondence with A. H. Francke. PhQ, 1926.
Landogna, F. G. **MAZZINI** e il pensiero giansenistico. Bologna, 1921.
Krakowski, E. Adam **MICKIEWICZ,** philosophe mystique. Paris, 1935.
Pritchard, J. P. The Fathers of the Church in the Works of J. **MILTON.** CJ, 33, 1937.
Wolfe, D. M. Milton in the Puritan Revolution. New York, 1941.
Dorer, M. **MONTAIGNES** Apologie des Raimund von Sabunde und ihre Bedeutung für den Skeptizismus. Philos. Jb., 40-41, 1927-28.
Dreano M,. La pensée religieuse de Montaigne. Paris, 1936.
Leonard, I. A. **MONTALBAN'S** El valor perseguido and the Mexican Inquisition, 1682. HR, 11, 1943.
Lemmonnier, L. Un résistant catholique: Thomas **MORE.** Paris, 1948.
Tappert, T. G. **MUHLENBERG** and German Religious Culture in Colonial America. AGR, 8, 1942.
Kamm, H. F. Zwei Thomas **MUENZER** Dramen. Xenien, 2.
Pfeiffer-Belli, W. Thomas **MURNER** im Schweizer Glaubenskampf. Münster, 1940.
Bouyer, L. **NEWMAN'S** Influence in France. Dublin Rev., 217, 1945.
Herbigny, M. de. Un newman russe: Vladimir Soloviev (1853-1900). Paris, 1911.
Normandin, R. Un newmaniste français (Brémond). Rev. de l'U. d'Ottawa, 15, 1945.
Simon, P. Newman and German Catholicism. Dublin Rev., 219, 1946.
Ward, W. Newman and Sabatier. Fortnightly Rev., 75, 1901.
Hazelton, R. Was **NIETZSCHE** an Anti-Christian? Journal of Religion, 22, 1942.
Jaspers, K. Nietzsche und das Christentum. Hameln, 1940.
Besset, M. **NOVALIS** et la pensée mystique. Paris, 1947.
Staehelin, E. **OECOLAMPAD** und Butzer in französischer Uebersetzung. Zs. f. Kirchengeschichte, 47, 1928.
Williams, W. M. The Genesis of John **OLDHAM'S** Satyrs upon the Jesuits. PMLA, 58, 1943.
Falk, R. P. Thomas **PAINE** and the Attitude of the Quakers to the American Revolution. Penn. Mag. of Hist. and Biography, 63, 1939.
McGloin, J. B. Francis **PARKMAN** on the Jesuits. Hist. Bull., 25, 1947.
Hoffmann, H. Die Religion im Leben und Denken **PESTALOZZIS.** Bern, 1944.
Kogan, N. Pestalozzis religiöse Haltung und die Rolle der Religion in seiner Pädagogik. Danzig, 1936.
Schmelzer, H. **PETRARKAS** Verhältnis zur vorausgehenden christlichen Philoophie des Abendlandes. Bonn, 1910.
McKee, D. R. Isaac de la **PEYRERE,** a Precursor of Eighteenth-Century Critical Deists. PMLA, 59, 1944.
Dulles, A. Princeps Concordiae: **PICO DELLA MIRANDOLA** and the Scholastic Tradition. Harvard, U. P., 1940.
Van Tieghem, Ph. La Prière universelle de **POPE** et le déisme français au XVIIIe siècle. RLC, 3, 1923.
Engel, C. E. Protestant Friends of the Abbé **PREVOST.** Proceedings of Huguenot Society of London, 16, 1938.
Hazard, P. Manon Lescaut, roman janséniste. RDM, 1924.
Spears, M. K. Mathew **PRIOR'S** Religion. PhQ, 27, 1948.
Lubac, H. de. **PROUDHON** et le Christianisme. Paris, 1946.
Febvre, L. Le problème de l'incroyance au XVIe siècle: La religion de **RABELAIS.** Paris, 1943.
Schneegans, H. Rabelais' Stellung zur Reformation. Beilage zur Allg. Zt., 10.VI.1898.
Hello, E. M. **RENAN,** l'Allemagne et l'athéisme au XIXe siècle. Paris, 1859.
Venturi, P. T. L'araldo del cristianesimo in Cina: il P. Matteo **RICCI.** NAnt, 1.X.1934.
Rodolico, N. Scipione dei Ricci. Saggio

sul giansenismo italiano. Firenze, 1920.
Wunderlich, Eva. Rainer Maria **RILKES** religiöse Ideen. GQ, 1948.

Green, O. H. The Celestina and the Inquisition. **(ROJAS)**. HR, 15, 1947.

—— Additional Note on the Celestina and the Inquisition. HR, 16, 1948.

Cook, T. I. The Influence of the Protestant Atmosphere of Geneva on the Character and Writings of **ROUSSEAU**. Economica, June, 1928.

Masson, P. M. La formation religieuse de Rousseau. Paris, 1916.

Schinz, A. La pensée religieuse de J. J. Rousseau et ses récents interprètes. Northampton (Mass.), 1928.

—— J. J. Rousseau, les déistes et les pasteurs de Genève. RR, 1937.

Beuken, W. H. **RUYSBROEC** en de middeleeuwse mystiek. Utrecht, Brussel, 1946.

Anon. Leopold **SCHEFERS** Laienbrevier in England. Blätter z. Kunde d. Litteratur des Auslandes, 1836.

Körner, J. A. W. **SCHLEGEL** und der Katholizismus. Histor. Zs. 139, 1929.

Greenewald, G. M. **SHAKESPEARE'S** Attitude towards the Catholic Church in King John. Washington, 1938.

Lanoire, M. La redécouverte de Shakespeare (as a Roman Catholic). RdF, 15.VII.1938.

Morize, A. La conversion de Samuel **SORBIERE**. Bull. de la Société d'Histoire du Protestantisme fr., 1907.

Gorino, M. G. V. **SPANZOTTI**, contributo alla storia del giansenismo piemontese. Torino, 1931.

Buyssens, E. Calvinism in the Faerie Queene of **SPENSER**. RBPh, 5, 1926.

Nelan, T. P. Catholic Doctrines in Spenser's Poetry. New York, 1946.

Padelford, F. M. Spenser and the Theology of Calvin. MPh, 12, 1914.

Siegel, P. N. Spenser and the Calvinist View of Life. SPh, 41, 1944.

Jelinek, H. Le comte F. A. de **SPORCK** et le jansénisme français en Bohème. RLC, 14, 1934.

Wichgraf, W. **SUSO'S** Horologium Sapientiae in England nach Mss. des 15. Jahrhunderts. Archiv, 169, 1936.

Looten, C. La pensée religieuse de **SWIFT** et ses antinomies. Lille, 1935.

Winter, F. Die Frömmigkeit Gerhard **TERSTEEGENS** in ihrem Verhältnis zur französisch-quietistischen Mystik. Neuwied, 1927.

Baker, F. John Wesley and the Imitatio Christi (**THOMAS A KEMPIS**). LQHR, 1941.

Fabre, J. L'Imitation de P. Corneille. Paris, 1907.

Lang, E. A. Ludwig **TIECK'S** Early Concept of Catholic Clergy and Church. Washington, 1936.

Fremont, E. E. Les idées religieuses de **TOLSTOI**. Paris, 1892.

Maffre, P. Le tolstoïsme et le christianisme. Montauban, 1896.

Higgins, M. H. The Influence of Calvinistic Thought in **TOURNEUR'S** Atheist's Tragedy. RES, 19.

Lamalle, E. La propagande du P. Nicholas **TRIGAULT** en faveur des missions de Chine (1616). Archives histor. Soc. Jesu, 9, 1940.

McKee, D. R. Simon **TYSSOT** de Patot and the XVIIth-Century Background of Critical Deism. Baltimore, 1941.

Dantas, J. Gil **VICENTE** e a Reforma. Lisboa, 1938.

Corsano, A. Umanesimo e religione in G. B. **VICO**. Bari, 1935.

Chaponnière, P. **VOLTAIRE** chez les Calvinistes. Genève, 1931 & Paris, 1936.

Jan, E. von. Voltaire und das Problem der religiösen Toleranz. GRM, 16, 1928.

Perrochon, H. Le protestantisme anglais et les Lettres philosophiques de Voltaire. Rev. de Théologie et de Philosophie, 55, 1925.

Philips, E. Le quaker vu par Voltaire. RHLF, 1932.

Torrey, N. L. Voltaire and the English Deists. New Haven, 1930.

Bashford, J. W. **WESLEY** and Goethe. Cincinnati, 1903.

Beckerlegge, O. A. John Wesley and the German Hymns. LQHR, 1940.

Bett, H. John Wesley's Translations of German Hymns in Reference to Metre and Rhyme. Ibid.

Gounelle, E. Wesley et ses rapports avec les Français. Nyons, 1890.

Hatfield, J. John Wesley's Translations of German Hymns. PMLA, 11, 1896.

Moore, S. H. Wesley and Fénelon. LQHR, 169, 1944.

Nuelsen, J. L. John Wesley und das deutsche Kirchenlied. Bremen, 1938.

Fulghum, W. B. Quaker Influences on **WHITMAN'S** Religious Thought. Diss. Northwestern U., 1943.

Griswold, M. J. American Quaker History in the Works of **WHITTIER**, Hawthorne, and Longfellow. Americana, 34, 1940.

Loserth, J. **WICLIF** and Hus. London, 1884.

Gruetzmacher, R. H. Die Stellung **WILDES** und Gorkis zu Religion und Christentum. Konservative Monatsschrift, 63, 1906.

Bender, Elizabeth H. Ernst von **WILDENBRUCH'S** Drama Der Mennonit. Mennonite Quar. Rev., 18, 1945.

Bliss, J. **YOUNG'S** Night Thoughts in Relation to Contemporary Christian Apologetics. PMLA, 1934.

Cunz, D. Ulrich **ZWINGLI**. Aarau, 1937.

SECOND PART
Literary Currents.

CHAPTER ONE

Epochs, Traditions, Generations.

Alewyn, R. Das Problem der Generation in der Geschichte. Zs. f. deutsche Bildung, 1929.

Allen, B. S. Tides in English Taste. Harvard U. P., 1937.

Baldensperger, F. The Decreasing Length of Literary Periods. Bull. des sciences historiques, 5. Paris. 1933.

—— Etablissement des périodes pour la littérature occidentale depuis la Renaissance. Bull. des sciences historiques, 5. Paris, 1933.

—— Le problème des générations spirituelles en histoire littéraire. RLC, 15, 1935.

Cazamian, L. La notion de retours périodiques dans l'histoire littéraire. Annales de l'U. de Paris, March, 1926.

Elster, E. Die Darstellungsformen litterarhistorischer Epochen. Aula, 2, 1895.

Entralgo, P. L. Las generaciones en la historia. Madrid, 1943.

Gruendel, E. G. Die Sendung der jungen Generationen. München, 1932.

Hamel, A. G. van. Literaire stroomingen. Vlaardiger, 1920.

Hankiss, J. Les périodes littéraires et la conscience collective. Bull. des sciences historiques, 9. Paris, 1937.

Hermann, R. P. G. Les courants d'idées occidentaux. Nouvelle Rev. de Hongrie, 1938.

Hoog, A. L'idée de génération. La Nef, 2, Aug., 1945.

Hoppe, K. Das Problem der Generation in der Literaturwissenschaft. ZDK, 1930.

Jantz, H. S. Herder, Goethe and Friedrich Schlegel on the Problem of the Generations. GR, 8, 1933.

—— The Factor of Generation in German Literary History. MLN, 52, 1937.

Joel, K. Wandlungen der Weltanschauung. Eine Philosophiegeschichte als Geschichtsphilosophie. Tübingen, 1928-29.

Kummer, F. Deutsche Literaturgeschichte des 19. Jahrhunderts dargestellt nach Generationen. Dresden, 1909.

Linden, W. Das Problem der Generationen in der Geistesgeschichte. Zeitwende, 8, 1932.

Lovejoy, A. O. Reflections on the History of Ideas. JHI, 1.

Mentre, F. Les générations sociales. Paris, 1920.

Meyer, R. M. Prinzipien der wissenschaftlichen Periodenbildung. Mit besonderer Rücksicht auf die Literaturgeschichte. Euphorion, 1901.

Mueller, H. von. Zehn Generationen deutscher Dichter und Denker, 1561-1892. Berlin, 1928.

Ortega y Gasset, J. La idea de las generaciones. In: El tema de nuestro tiempo. Buenos Aires, 1941.

Petersen, J. Die literarischen Generationen. Berlin, 1930.

Peyre, H. Les générations littéraires. Paris, 1948. Cf. CL, 1950.

Pinder, W. Kunstgeschichte nach Generationen. In: Zwischen Philosophie und Kunst. Festschrift Volkelt. Leipzig, 1926.

—— Das Problem der Generation in der Kunstgeschichte Europas. Berlin, 1928.

Reade, A. R. Main Currents in Modern Literature, London, 1935.

Saint-Beuve, C. A. De la tradition en littérature. Caus. du Lundi, 15, 1857-62.

Saintsbury, G. (ed.). Periods of European Literature. Edinburgh, 1897ff.

Salinas, P. El concepto de generación literaria applicado a la del 98. Revista de Occidente, 13, 1935.

Schumann, D. W. Cultural Age-Groups in German Thought. PMLA, 1936.

—— The Problem of Age-Groups: A Statistical Study. PMLA, 1937.

Van Tieghem, P. Petite histoire des grandes doctrines littéraires en France. Paris, 1946.

Wais, K. Zeitgeist in der vergleichenden Literaturgeschichte. GRM, 1934.

—— Die literarhistorischen Periodenbegriffe. In: Geistige Arbeit, 1935.

Wechssler, E. Die Generation als Jugendgemeinschaft. Festschrift Kurt Breysig, 1927.

—— Jugendreihen des deutschen Menschen, 1733-1933. Leipzig, 1934.

—— Jugendreihe und Jugendgeist in der Bildungsgeschichte der Menschheit. Bull. des sciences historiques, 9. Paris, 1937.

Wellek, R. Periods and Movements in Literary History. Engl. Institute Annual, 1940. Columbia U. P., 1941.

CHAPTER TWO

The Middle Ages.

(For Scholasticism, see also II.V.1.)

1. General Works.

Adams, G. B. Civilization During the Middle Ages, New York, 1922.

Atkinson, W. C. Mediaeval and Renaissance: A Footnote to Spanish Literary History. BSS, 25, 1948.

Baldi, S. I relitti medievali delle ballate popolari d'Inghilterra e di Scozia. RLM, 2, 1946.

Boyer, B. B. The Medieval Library. Library Quart., 10, 1940.

Coulton, G. G. Studies in Medieval Thought. London, 1940.

Curtius, E. R. Die Musen im Mittelalter. ZRPh, 59, 1939.

—— Mittelalterlicher und barocker Dichtungsstil. MPh, 38, 1941.

Doolittle D,. The Relations Between Literature and Medieval Studies in France from 1820 to 1860. Diss. Bryn Mawr, 1933.

Edelman, N. The Early Uses of Medium Aevum, Moyen Age, Middle Ages. RR, 29-30, 1938-39.

—— Attitudes of Seventh-Century France Toward the Middle Ages. New York, 1946.

Farnham, W. The Mediaeval Heritage of Elizabethan Tragedy. Berkeley, 1936.

Farrar, C. P. & Evans, A. P. Bibliography of English Translations from Medieval Sources. New York, 1946.

Frey, D. Gotik und Renaissance als Grundlagen der modernen Weltanschauung. Augsburg, 1929.

Glunz, A. Die Literarästhetik des europäischen Mittelalters. Berlin, 1937.

Haskins, C. H. The Spread of Ideas in the Middle Ages. Spec., 1, 1926.

—— Studies in Medieval Culture. Oxford, 1929.

Huizinga, J. Herbst des Mittelalters: Studien über Lebens- und Geistesformen des 14. und 15. Jahrhunderts in Frankreich und den Niederlanden. München, 1924 & London, 1927.

Jacoubet, H. Moyen âge et Romantisme. Annales de l'U. de Grenoble, 16, 1939.

Karg, F. Das literarische Erwachen des deutschen Ostens im Mittelalter. Teuthonista, 3, 1932.

Kibre, Pearl. Intellectual Interests Reflected in Libraries of the Fourteenth and Fifteenth Centuries. JHI, 7, 1946.

Lacroix, P. Le moyen âge et la Renaissance. 5 vols. Paris, 1847-52.

Laistner, M. W. Thought and Letters in Western Europe, 500-900. New York, 1931.

Loomis, R. S. Introduction to Mediaeval Literature, Chiefly in England. Columbia U. P., 1939.

McLaughlin, E. T. Studies in Mediaeval Life and Literature. New York, 1894.

Meissner, P. Mittelalterliches Lebensgefühl in der englischen Renaissance. DVLG, 15.

Nordström, J. Medeltid och Renässans. Stockhold, 1929 & Paris, 1931.

Olschki, L. Das literarische Vermächtnis des Mittelalters. DVLG, 7, 1929.

Paris, G. La poésie au moyen âge. Paris, 1890.

Pirenne, H., Cohen, G. & Focillon, H. La civilisation occidentale au moyen âge du XI au milieu du XV siècle. Paris, 1933.

Rand, E. K. Founders of the Middle Ages. Harvard U. P., 1928.

—— The Medieval Pattern of Life. U. of Pa. Bicentennial Conference, 1941.

—— A Romantic Approach to the Middle Ages. MS, 3, 1941.

Siciliano, I. Medio evo e Rinascimento. Milano, 1935.

Simone, F. Le moyen âge, la Renaissance et la critique moderne. RLC, 18, 1938.

Singer, S. Germanisch-romanisches Mittelalter. In: Aufsätze und Vorträge. Zürich, 1935.

Steenstrup, C. H. R. Vore folkeviser fra middelalderen. København, 1891.

Taylor, H. O. The Medieval Mind; a History of the Development of Thought and Emotion in the Middle Ages. 2 vols. New York, 1925.

Thompson, J. W. The Medieval Library. U. of Chicago P., 1939.
Villemain, F. Tableau de la littérature au moyen âge en France, en Italie, en Espagne et en Angleterre. 2 vols. Paris, 1864.
Vossler, K. Symbolische Denkart und Dichtung im Mittelalter und heute. Corona, 4, 1934.
Weise, G. Vom Menschenideal und von den Modewörtern der Gotik in der Renaissance. DVLG, 1936.
—— Die geistige Welt der Gotik und ihre Bedeutung für Italien. Halle, 1939.
Weisinger, H. Middle Ages and the Late Eighteenth-Century Historians. PHQ, 27, 1948.

2. Individual Authors.

Magnier, E. **DANTE** et le moyen âge. Paris, 1860.
Gilson, E. Etudes sur le rôle de la pensée médiévale dans la formation du système cartésien. (**DESCARTES**). Paris, 1930.
Berrett, P. Le moyen âge dans la Légende des siècles et les sources de Victor **HUGO**. Paris, 1911.
Kuster, E. C. Mittelalter und Antike bei William **MORRIS**. Ein Beitrag zur Geschichte des Mediaevalismus in England. Berlin, 1928.
Mommsen, T. E. **PETRARCH'S** Conception of the Dark Ages. Spec., 17, 1942.
Hübner, A. Deutsches Mittelalter und italienische Renaissance im Ackermann aus Böhmen (**SAAZ**). In: Kleine Schriften zur deutschen Philologie. Berlin, 1940.
McDowell, J. H. Conventions of Medieval Art in **SHAKESPEARIAN** Staging. JEGPh, 47, 1948.
Reichensperger, A. William Shakespeare, insbesondere sein Verhältniss zum Mittelalter und zur Gegenwart. Münster, 1872.
Taylor, G. C. The Medieval Element in Shakespeare. SAB, 12, 1937.
Kliger, S. Sir William **TEMPLE** and the Gothic Cult of the XVIIth Century. Diss. Northwestern U., 1942.
Siciliano, I. François **VILLON** et les thèmes poétiques du moyen âge. Paris, 1934.
Glunz, H. H. Die Literaturästhetik des europäischen Mittelalters: **WOLFRAM**, Rosenroman, Chaucer, Dante. Bochum, 1937.

CHAPTER THREE

Humanism.

(See also Antiquity, Greek and Latin Languages, Neo-Latin Literature, Universities, Students, and Renaissance.)

1. Generalities.

Bacherler, M. Das humanistische Bildungsideal seit vier Jahrhunderten. HG, 1925.
Bertoni, G. Vecchio e nuovo umanesimo. Rinascita, 1, 1938. And in: AR, 23, 1939.
Brachmann, W. Der humanistische Gedanke. Nat. soz. Monatshefte, 8, 1937.
Cian, V. Umanesimo e Rinascimento. Rinascita, 1 & Firenze, 1941.
Clavier, H. L'humanisme et la piété chrétienne. Etudes de théol. relig., 1931.
Curtius, E. R. L'humanisme comme initiative. RP, 1932.
Delcourt, M. Humanisme vivant. Antiquité classique, 1933.
Demain, T. Humanisme et christianisme. Vie intellectuelle, 1932.
Diesch, K. Der Humanismus im Wandel der Zeiten. HG, 1934.
Drerup, E. Perioden der klassicke philologie. Grondtlagen eener geschiedenis van het humanismus. Utrecht, 1930.
—— Der Humanismus in seiner Geschichte, seinen Kulturwerten und seiner Vorbereitung im Unterrichtswesen der Griechen. Paderborn, 1934.
Fernand, R. L'humanisme. Essai de définition. Paris, 1946.
Festa, N. Umanesimo. Milano, 1940.
Fiolle, J. La crise de l'humanisme. Paris, 1937.
Fliche, A. et al. Quelques aspects de l'humanisme médiéval. Paris, 1943.
Hermans, F. Histoire doctrinale de l'humanisme chrétien. 4 vols. Paris, 1948.
Howald, E. Humanismus und Europäertum. NSR, 23, 1930.
Iwanow, W. Christentum und Humanismus. Corona, 7, 1937.
Jaeger, W. L'umanesimo e le moderne scienze dello spirito. SG, 1, 1935.
—— Classical Philology and Humanism. TAPhA, 1936.
Korff, H. A. Humanismus und Romantik. Leipzig, 1924.
Kristeller, P. O. The Place of Classical Humanism in Renaissance Thought. JHI, 4, 1943.
Lawton, H. W. Comparative Humanism. CLS, 1, 1941.

Lebègue, R. L'humanisme latin de la Renaissance. Mélanges J. Marouzeau. Paris, 1943.
Lenz. Humanismus und Reformation. Deutsches Wochenblatt, 5, 1892.
Mackail, J. W. Studies in Humanism. London, 1938.
Maistriaux, R. Les humanités classiques et l'humanisme chrétien. Bruxelles, 1937.
Marouzeau, J. Humanisme. Nouv. Rev. de Hongrie, 1938.
Masure, E. L'humanisme chrétien. Paris, 1937.
McConnell, F. J. Humanism and Christianity. London, 1929.
Moreau, P. L'humanisme gréco-latin et la littérature. Actes du Congrès G. Budé à Strasbourg. Paris, 1939.
Nestle, W. Humanismus und Christentum. HG, 1933.
Paparelli, G. Tra umanesimo e riforma. Napoli, 1946.
Parigot, H. Le calvaire des humanités. RDM, 1927.
Pfister, F. Der politische Humanismus. BBG, 1934.
Renaudet, A. Autour d'une définition de l'humanisme. BHR, 6, 1945.
Robert, F. L'humanisme, essai de définition. BAGB, & Paris, 1946.
Ruediger, H. Wesen und Wandlung des Humanismus. Hamburg, 1937.
Ruessel, H. W. Gestalt eines christlichen Humanismus. Leipzig, 1940 & Roma, 1945.
Sandys, J. E. Harvard Lectures on the Revival of Learning. Cambridge U. P., 1905.
Théolier, L. Humanisme, humanité, catholicisme. Et, 213, 1932.
Thomas, J. L'humanisme et les temps modernes. Actes du Congrès G. Budé à Nîmes. Paris, 1932.
Toffanin, G. La fine del'umanesimo. Torino, 1920.
—— Che cosa fu l'umanesimo. Firenze, 1929.
—— Storia dell'umanesimo. Napoli, 1934.
Vellay, C. Une restauration de l'humanisme antique est-elle possible? Acr., 1934.
Voigt, G. Die Wiederbelebung des klassischen Altertums. 3 ed. Berlin, 1893.
Waldapfel, E. Principes pour l'étude de l'humanisme. EPhK, 56, 1932.
Walsh, G. G. Medieval Humanism. New York, 1942.
Weisinger, H. Renaissance Accounts of the Revival of Learning. SPh, 45, 1948.
Wolkan, R. Ueber den Ursprung des Humanismus. Zs. f. d. österr. Gymnasien, 1916.

2. Individual Countries.

Benetti-Brunelli, V. Le origini italiane della scuola umanistica, ovvero le fonti italiche della coltura moderna. (ITALY). Milano, 1918.
Boza Masvidal, A. El humanismo y el Renacimiento en Italia. In: Estudios de literatura italiana. La Habana, 1945.
Curtius, E. R. Neuere Arbeiten über den italienischen Humanismus. BHR, 10, 1948.
Kristeller, P. O. Humanism and Scholasticism in the Italian Renaissance. Byzantion, 17, 1944-45.
Meozzi, A. La poesia umanistica italiana nella lirica volgare di Europa. Rinascita, 2, 1939.
Ullman, B. L. Some Aspects of the Origin of Italian Humanism. PhQ, 20, 1941.
Weiss, R. The Dawn of Humanism in Italy. London, 1947.
Elliott-Binns, L. E. **ENGLAND** and the New Learning. London, 1937.
Funke, O. Die Frühzeit der englischen Grammatik. Bern, 1941.
Rebora, P. Aspetti dell'umanesimo in Inghilterra. Rinascita, 2, 1939.
Schirmer, W. F. Der englische Frühhumanismus. Leipzig, 1931.
—— Der englische Humanismus. NM, 1936.
Weisinger, H. The Study of the Revival of Learning in England from Bacon to Hallam. PhQ, 25, 1946.
Weiss, R. Humanism in England During the Fifteenth Century. Oxford, 1941.
Wright, E. Continuity in XVth Century English Humanism. PMLA, 51, 1936.
Delarelle, L. Recherches sur l'enseignement des humanités dans le Sud-Ouest de la **FRANCE**. Annales du Midi, 60, 1948.
Gelis, F. de. Les poètes humanistes des Jeux Floraux. Mémoires de l'Acad. des Sciences de Toulouse, 11e sér., 7, 1919.
Gottschalk, W. Die humanistische Gestalt in der französischen Literatur. Heidelberg, 1928.
Paquier, J. L'université de Paris et l'humanisme au début du XVIe siècle. Paris, 1899.
Wencelius, L. Trois pionniers de l'humanisme français au XVIe siècle. Mainz, 1948.

Bauch, G. Die Reception des Humanismus in Wien. (GERMANY). 80. Jahresbericht der Schlesischen Ges. f. vaterländ. Cultur, 1903.

Caffi, E. L'umanesimo nella letteratura e nella cultura tedesca. Roma, 1912.

Ellinger, G. Der Humanismus in Deutschland. In: Bruno Gebhardts Handbuch der deutschen Geschichte. Stuttgart, 1891.

Joachimson, P. Frühhumanismus in Schwaben. Württemberger Vierteljahrschrift, N. F., 5.

—— Der Humanismum und die Entwicklung des deutschen Geistes. DVLG, 8, 1930.

Kaegi, W. Nationale und universale Denkformen im deutschen Humanismus des 16. Jahrhunderts. Erziehung, 10, 1935.

Karstien, C. Beiträge zur Einführung des Humanismus in die deutsche Literatur. GRM, 1923.

Köhler, W. Der elsässische Humanismus. In: Deutsches Schicksal im Elsass. Heidelberg, 1941.

Kuhn, H. Die Entstehung der deutschen Aesthetik aus dem Geist des Humanismus. Antike, 1929.

Rupprich, H. Die Frühzeit des Humanismus und der Renaissance in Deutschland. Leipzig, 1939.

Taylor, A. Problems in German Literary History of the XVth and XVIth Centuries. New York, 1939.

Baitaillon, M. L'Espagne des humanistes. (SPAIN). NL, 7.I.1939.

Lanning, J. T. Academic Culture in the Spanish Colonies. Oxford U. P., 1940.

Rubió, J. Sobre els orígens de l'humanisme a Catalunya. BSS, 24, 1947.

Xirau, J. Humanismo español. Cuadernos Americanos (México), 1, 1942.

Roersch, A. L'humanisme belge à l'époque de la Renaissance. (BELGIUM). Louvain, 1933.

Hrdina, K., Young, R. F. & Kolar, A. Trois études sur l'humanisme tchèque. (CZECHOSLOVAKIA). Listy Filologicke, 55, 1928.

Léger, L. L'humanisme en DALMATIE à l'époque de la Renaissance. C. R. Acad. des Inscriptions et Belles Lettres, 1916.

Hoogewerff, G. J. Lo sviluppo del'umanesimo in Olanda fino alla fondazione dell' Università di Leida. (HOLLAND). In: Gli Studi Romani nel Mondo. Roma, 1936.

Kardos, T. Che cosa fu l'umanesimo ungherese? (HUNGARY). Studie e Documenti italo-ungheresi della R. Acc. d'Ungheria di Roma, 1936.

Peiser, W. El humanismo en la literatura MEXICANA. RIA, 4, 1942.

Malye, J. L'humanisme en Pologne. (POLAND). BAGB, 1932.

Rand, E. K. Liberal Education in Seventeenth-Century Harvard. (UNITED STATES). NEQ, 6, 1933.

3. International Influences among Humanists.

Bertoni, G. Umanisti portoghesi a Ferrara. GSLI, 1939.

Brandis, C. G. Italienische Humanisten in sächsisch-thüringischen Landen. Zentralblatt f. Bibliothekwesen, 1929.

Brie, F. Französischer Frühhumanismus in England. Anglia, 1937.

Ellinger, G. Italien und der deutsche Humanismus in der neulateinischen Lyrik. Berlin, 1929.

Galdi, L. L'influsso dell' umanesimo ungherese sul pensiero rumeno. Arch. Europ. Centro-Orientalis, 6.

Garnett, R. English Humanists in Italy in the 15th Century. Literature, 7.IV, 1900.

Grassi, E. Deutsche Dichtung und die italienische Tradition des Humanismus. In: Gedanken zum Dichterischen und Politischen. Berlin, 1939.

Hyma, A. The Continental Origins of English Humanism. HLQ, 4, 1940.

Koltay-Kaster, E. L'umanesimo italiano in Ungheria. Rinascita, 2, 1938.

Kot. Rapports de la Pologne avec l'humanisme suisse vers le milieu du XVIe siècle. Festschrift P. Vaucher. Genève, 1895.

Maugain, G. L'humanisme italien en France avant 1515. REI, 1936.

Moholi, J. English-Hungarian Connections in the Humanist Circle of Erasmus of Rotterdam. History, 32, 1947.

Monnier, P. Les humanistes d'Italie et de la Suisse du XVe siècle. Festschrift P. Vaucher. Genève, 1895.

Pellegrini, V. Umanesimo arabo e umanesimo italiano. Romana, July, 1938.

Temesi, A. Humanisme franco-hongrois. EPhK, 1938.

Várady, E. I primi contatti dell'Ungheria coll' umanesimo italiano. Romana, 2, 1938.

Vaucher, P. Les humanistes d'Italie et la Suisse du XVe siècle. Genève, 1895.

Viglione, F. L'umanesimo in Inghilterra e le sue relazioni con l'Italia. Rassegna nazionale, 1924.

4. Individual Humanists.

Paquier, J. L'humanisme et la Réforme. Jérôme **ALEANDER**. Paris, 1900; Cf. RHLF, 2, 1901.
Daxhelet, E. Adrien **BARLANDUS**, humaniste belge. Louvain, 1938.
Banfi, F. Francesco **BENINCASA**: umanista anconetano in Ungheria. Europa orientale, 18, 1933.
Mohler, L. Kardinal **BESSARION** als Theologe, Humanist und Staatsmann. 2 vols. Paderborn, 1923-27.
Taylor, J. W. Bessarion the Mediator. TAPhA, 1924.
Mayer, E. Un umanista italiano della corte di Mattia Corvino: Aurelio **BRANDOLINO**. Annuario della R. Accad. d'Ungheria di Roma, 1938.
Lebègue, R. George **BUCHANAN**. Son influence en France et au Portugal. Coimbra, 1931.
Hadas, M. George Buchanan, Scottish Humanist. SAQ, 43, 1944.
Knös, B. Guillaume **BUDE** och den franska humanismens Renässans. Stockholm, 1939.
Plattard, J. Guillaume Budé et les origines de l'humanisme français. Paris, 1923.
Sabrié, J. B. De l'humanisme au rationalisme: Pierre **CHARRON**. Paris, 1913.
Lefranc, A. Nicolas **CLENARD**, humaniste belge. H&R, 8, 1940.
MacKenzie, Kathleen. John **COLET** of Oxford. Dalhousie Rev., 21, 1941.
Rossi, V. **DANTE** e l'umanesimo. Società dantesca italiana, 1898.
Huizinga, J. **ERASMUS**. London, 1924.
Prechac, F. Erasme et l'humanisme. Lille, 1936.
Morel-Fatio, A. Maître **FERNAND DE CORDOUE** et les humanistes italiens du XVe siècle. Mélanges Julien Havet. Paris, 1895.
Wilson, H S.. **GEORGE OF TREBIZOND** and Early Humanist Rhetoric. SPh, 40, 1943.
Bell, A. F. G. Damião de **GOES**, a Portuguese Humanist. HR, 9, 1941.
Eckhardt, A. Un humaniste hongrois à la Sorbonne au début du XVIe siècle. (Jean de **GOSZTON**). Bull. Internat. Committee Hist. Sciences, 12. Paris.
Holborn, H. Ulrich von **HUTTEN** and the German Reformation. New Haven, 1937.
Strauss, D. F. Ulrich von Hutten. Leipzig, 1927.
Villemain. **LASCARIS**, ou les Grecs au XVe siècle. Paris, 1825.
Becker, P. A. Jean **LEMAIRE**, der erste humanistische Dichter Frankreichs. Strassburg, 1892.
Gerst, K. Vom ersten Humanisten Böhmens. (**LOBKOWITZ**). Mitteil. d. Vereins klass. Philologen in Wien, 2, 1925.
Banfi, C. Raffaello **MAFFI** in Ungheria. Europa orientale, 17, 1937.
Lynn, C. A College Professor of the Renaissance: Lucio **MARINEO SICULO** Among the Spanish Humanists. U. of Chicago, P., 1937.
Ronzy, P. Un humaniste italianisant, Papire **MASSON**. Paris, 1924.
Kardos, T. **MATTIA CORVINO**, re umanista. Firenze, 1941.
Richard, J. W. Ph. **MELANCHTHON**. London, 1898.
Maynard, T. Humanist as Hero: The Life of Sir Thomas **MORE**. New York, 1947
Banfi, F. Giovanni Michele **NAGONIO** panegirista di Uladislao II re di Boemia ed Ungheria. Europa orientale, 17, 1937.
Polet, A. Une gloire de l'humanisme belge, Petrus **NANNIUS**. Louvain, 1936.
Alsi, G. Il **PETRARCA** precursore degli umanisti. Messina, 1901.
Morando, F. E. Petrarca e l'umanesimo. In: Studi di letteratura e di storia. Firenze, 1940.
Nolhac, P. de. Pétrarque et l'humanisme. Paris, 1892.
Olivero Revilo P. Petrarch's Prestige as a Humanist. Festschrift W. A. Oldfather. Urbana (Ill.), 1943.
Cantimori, D. Umanesimo e luteranismo di fronte alla scolastica: Caspar **PEUCER**. SG, 2, 1937.
Weiss, A. E. S. de **PICCOLOMINI**. Sein Leben und sein Einfluss auf die literarische Cultur Deutschlands. Graz, 1897.
Paparelli, G. Il De curialium Miseriis di Enea Silvio Piccolomini e il Misaulus di Ulrico von Hutten. Ital., 24, 1947.
Banfi, F. Ugolino **PISANI** da Parma in Ungheria. Corvina, Rassegna italo-ungherese, 3, 1940.
Mazzoni, G. Il **POLIZIANO** e l'umanesimo. In: Vita italiana d. Rinascimento. Milano, 1893.
Battelli, G. La corrispondenza del Poliziano col re Don Giovanni Il di Portogallo. Rinascita, 2, 1938.
Sapegno, N. Il sentimento umanistico e la poesia del Poliziano. NAnt, 1.II.1938.
Rygiel, S. **PUTEANUS** und die Polen. Berlin, 1913.

Hoffmann, R. A. J. Italienische Humanisten und **RABELAIS** und Montaigne als Pädagogen. Progr. Stettin, 1876.
Evgeniev, B. Alexander **RADISCHEV**, a Russian Humanist of the XVIIIth Century. London, 1946.
Graves, F. P. Peter **RAMUS** and the Edcational Reformation of the XVIth Century. New York, 1912.
Kardos, T. Pietro **RANSANO** in Ungheria. Janus Pannonius, 1, 1947.
Geiger, L. **REUCHLIN**. Leipzig, 1871.
Ritter, W. Sainte-Beuve et Reuchlin. Revue critique, 1892.
Hess, G. Wege des Humanismus im Frankreich des XVII. Jahrhunderts: **SAINT-EVREMOND**. RF, 1938.
Hahn, W. Simon **SIMONOWICZ**, le plus éminent représentant de l'humanisme polonais. (In Polish). KK, 1930.
Gábriel, A. Blaise de **VARDA**, humaniste hongrois à Paris. Archivum Europae Centro-Orientalis, 7.
Banfi, F. Pier Paolo **VERGERIO** il vecchio in Ungheria. Corvina, Rassegna italo-ungherese, 2, 1939.
Corsano, A. Umanesimo e religione in G. B. **VICO**. Bari, 1935.
Ors, E. d'. **VIVES**, humaniste espagnol. Paris, 1942.
Watson, F. Juan Luis Vives. Trans. of the Royal Society of Literature, 1, 1921.
Kress, Dorothy M. Juan Luis Vives: A Study in Renaissance Theories in Methodology in Foreign Language Instruction. MLJ, 25, 1940.
Twardowski, J. Jan Ludwik Vives i Andrzej Fryez Modrzewski. Cracovie, 1921.
Scholderer, V. Jacob **WIMPHELING**, an Early Strassburg Humanist. Transactions of the Bibliog. Society, 13, 1915.

5. Neo-Humanism

Becker, A. Der Neuhumanismus. Sein Ursprung und seine Entwicklung in Deutschland. Vacha Homuth, 1924.
Cronia, A. L'umanesimo nell'interpretazione bolscevisca di un bianco-russo. Rinascita, 2, 1939.
Curtius, L. Die antike Kunst und der moderne Humanismus. Antike, 3.
Dainville, F. de. La naissance de l'humanisme moderne. Paris, 1940.
Daudet, L. Der Humanismus und die zeitgenössische Literatur Frankreichs. Antike, 6, 1930.
Drexler, H. Der dritte Humanismus. Frankfurt, 1942.
Fischer, H. Der Neuhumanismus in der deutschen Literatur. Tübingen, 1902.
Foerster, N. Humanism and America. New York, 1930.
George, R. Pour un humanisme nouveau. Le Flambeau, 21, 1938.
Helbing, L. Der dritte Humanismus. Berlin, 1932.
Immisch, O. Die Erneuerung des Humanismus. HG, 1928.
Kuhn, H. Humanismus in der Gegenwart. Kantstudien, 39, 1934.
Mercier, L. J. A. Le mouvement humaniste aux Etats-Unis. Paris, 1928.
Peeters, F. Les humanités classiques aux Etats-Unis. Le Flambeau, 14, 1931.
Rehm, A. Neuhumanismus einst und jetzt. München, 1931.
Scheffer, T. Vom heutigen Wert des Humanismus. G, 1937.
Strodtmann, A. Das humanistische Element in der deutschen Dichtung der Gegenwart. Orion, 2, 1863.

CHAPTER FOUR

Renaissance.

1. Generalities.

Akrigg, G. P. V. The Renaissance Reconsidered. Queen's Quarterly, 52, 1945.
Anagnine, E. Il concetto del Rinascimento. Romana, 1939.
Antscherl, O. Italienisch-europäische oder nationale Renaissance. GRM, 1929.
Atkinson, G. Nouveaux horizons de la Renaissance française. Paris, 1935.
Baron, H. et al. Renaissance Symposium. JHI, 4, 1943.
Bell, A. F. G. Four Poets of the Renaissance: Ronsard, Camoens, Luis de León and Spenser. Festschrift Carolina Michaelis de Vasconcellos. Coimbra, 1930.
—— El renacimiento español. Zaragoza, 1944.
Benesch, O. The Art of the Renaissance in Northern Europe: Its Relation to the Contemporary Spiritual and Intellectual Movements. Harvard U. P., 1945.
Bizilli, P. La place de la Renaissance dans l'histoire de la civilisation. RLC, 14, 1934.
Browne, H. Our Renaissance. Essays on the Reform and Revival of Classical Studies. London, 1917.
Burckhardt, J. Die Kultur der Renaissance in Italien. Leipzig, 1860; Paris, 1885; Firenze, 1886.
Bush, D. The Renaissance and English Humanism. Toronto, 1939.

Casertano, A. Saggio sul rinascimento del classicismo durante il secolo XV. Torino, 1887.
Charpentier, J. P. Histoire de la Renaissance des lettres en Europe au XVe siècle. 2 vols. Paris, 1833.
Coville, A. Origines de la Renaissance en France. Bull. des Cours et Conférences, 1, 1895.
Creighton, M. The Early Renaissance in England. Cambridge, 1895.
Eringa, S. Les premières manifestations de la Renaissance dans la poésie lyrique néerlandaise (1544-55). NPh, 4, 1919.
Ferguson, W. K. Humanist Views of the Renaissance. AHR, 45, 1939.
—— The Renaissance. New York, 1940.
—— The Renaissance in Historical Thought: Five Centuries of Interpretation. Boston, 1948.
Fife, R. H. The Renaissance in a Changing World. GR, 9, 1934.
Filippis, M. de. The Renaissance Problem Again. Ital. 20, 1943.
Folkierski, L. Renaissance et Romantisme. Bull. of the Internat. Committee of Historical Sciences, 9, 1937.
Friedrich, F. Renaissance und die Antike. Beilage zur Allg. Zt. 60-61, 1903.
Gallenga, R. Influssi del Rinascimento fuori d'Italia. Boll. della R. Univ. Ital. per stranieri, 9, 1937.
Galustre, L. La Renaissance en France. Paris, 1879.
Gebhart, E. Les origines de la Renaissance en Italie. Paris, 1879.
Geiger, L. Die Renaissance in Süd-Italien. Vierteljahrschrift f. Kultur und Literatur der Renaissance, 2, 1884.
—— Renaissance und Humanismus in Italien und Deutschland. Berlin, 1882. Milano, 1891.
Gennep, A. van. Le rôle des Germains dans la Renaissance italienne. Revue des Idées, 1906.
Goetz, W. Renaissance und Antike. Histor. Zs., 1914.
Haskins, C. H. The Renaissance of the Twelfth Century. Harvard U. P., 1927.
Hettner, H. Italienische Studien zur Geschichte der Renaissance. Braunschweig, 1879.
Hetzer, T. Die schöpferische Vereinigung von Antike und Norden in der Hochrenaissance. NJWJ, 1934-35.
Horvath, E. Il Rinascimento in Ungheria. Roma, 1939.
Huizinga, J. Le problème de la Renaissance. RCC, 40, 1938-39.
—— Das Problem der Renaissance. Parerga (Basel), 1945.
—— El problema del Renacimiento. In: El concepto de la historia y otros ensayos. México, 1946.
Hyma, A. The Christian Renaissance. A History of the Devotio Moderna. New York, 1924.
Kalff, G. West-europeesche letterkunde. (Renaissance). Groningen, 1923-24.
Kállay, N. de. Il rinascimento in Ungheria. Corvina, 5, 1942.
Kardos, T. La Renaissance en Hongrie. Nouvelle Revue de Hongrie, 1939.
Klette, T. Beiträge zur Geschichte und Litteratur der italienischen Gelehrtenrenaissance. 3 vols. Greifswald, 1888-90.
Kristeller, P. O. & Randall, J. H. The Study of the Philosophies of the Renaissance. JHI, 2, 1940-41.
Laborde, de. La Renaissance des arts à la cour de France. Paris, 1850.
Luebke, W. Geschichte der Renaissance Frankreichs. Stuttgart, 1868.
Moltzer, H. E. Invloed der Renaissance op onze letterkunde. In: Studien en Schessen van Nederlandsche letterkunde. Haarlem, 1881.
Monnier, M. Histoire de la littérature moderne: La Renaissance de Dante à Luther. Paris, 1884; Nördlingen, 1888.
Monnier, P. Le quattrocento; Essai sur l'histoire littéraire du XVe siècle italien. 2 vols. Paris, 1900.
Morris, W. M. The Renaissance and Welsh Literature. Maesteg, 1908.
Muentz, E. Les précurseurs de la Renaissance. Paris, 1882.
—— La Renaissance en Italie et en France, à l'époque de Charles VIII. Paris, 1885.
Naumann, H. Karolingische und Ottonische Renaissance. Frankfurt, 1926.
Neve, F. La Renaissance des lettres et l'essor de l'érudition ancienne en Belgique. Louvain, 1890.
Nitze, W. A. The So-Called Twelfth Century Renaissance. Spec., 23, 1948.
Owen, J. Sceptics of the Italian and French Renaissance. 2 vols. London, 1893
Paech, W. H. H. Renaissance und Humanismus in Italien. Progr. Cottbus, 1885.
Paré, G., Brunet, A., & Tremblay, P. La Renaissance du XIIe siècle. Paris, 1933.
Passuth, L. La Renaissance tardive en Hongrie. Nouvelle Revue de Hongrie, 1939.

Patzelt, E. Die karolingische Renaissance. Wien, 1924.
Petit de Julleville, L. Les origines de la Renaissance en France. RCC, 1896.
Prunel, L. La renaissance catholique en France au XVIIe siècle. Paris, 1928.
Rehm, W. Das Werden des Renaissancebildes in der deutschen Dichtung. München, 1924.
Renaudet, A. Le problème historique de la Renaissance italienne. BHR, 9, 1947.
Roxlo, C. Los poetas del Renacimiento. Montevideo, 1911.
Rubio y Lluch. El Renacimiento clásico en la literatura catalana. Barcelona, 1891.
Schaeffer, E. Das moderne Renaissance-Empfinden. NR, July, 1905.
Schulte, W. Renaissance und Barock in der deutschen Dichtung. Jb. d. Görresges., 2, 1926.
Setton, K. M. Some Recent Views of the Italian Renaissance. Annual Meeting Canadian Hist. Assoc., 1947.
Simone, F . La coscienza della Rinascita negli umanisti. Rinascita, 2, 1939. And in: RLM, 1946-47.
Symonds, J. A. Renaissance in Italy. 2 vols. London, 1877.
Taylor, A. Renaissance Guides to Books: An Inventory and Some Conclusions. Berkeley, 1945.
Terlinden, Vtc. C. et al. La Renaissance en Belgique. Bruxelles, 1945.
Texte, J. Les origines de la Renaissance française. RCC, 1894.
Thorndike, L. Renaissance or Prenaissance. JHI, 4, 1943.
Venturi, L. L'idea del Rinascimento. Poesia e verità, 1, 1945.
Waldberg, F. von. Die deutsche Renaissance-Lyrik. Berlin, 1888.
Walser, E. Studien zur Weltanschauung der Renaissance. Basler Zs. f. Geschichte & Altertumskunde, 19, 1920.
Weisbach, W. Deutsche Renaissance und Antike. Antike, 1928.
Weisinger, H. The Study of the Revival of Learning in England from Bacon to Hallam. PhQ, 25, 1946.
Wilinson, W. W. J. The Meaning of the Renaissance. Thought, 16, 1941.
Williams, A. The Two Matters: Classical and Christian in the Renaissance. SPh, 38, 1941.
Witkowski, G. Die Renaissance in der deutschen Dichtung. Grenzboten, 47, 1888.
Wölfflin, H. Renaissance und Barock. München, 1888.
—— Die Kunst der Renaissance: Italien und das deutsche Formgefühl. München, 1931.
Wolff, M. J. Die Renaissance in der englischen Literatur. Bielefeld, 1927.
Woltmann, H. Die Germanen und die Renaissance in Italien. Leipzig, 1905.
Wright, L. B. et al. Survey of Renaissance Studies. MLQ, 2, 1941.
Zonta, G. Rinascimento, aristotelismo e barocco. GSLI, 1934.

2. Individual Authors.

Spörri, T. Renaissance und Barock bei **ARIOST** und Tasso. Versuch einer Anwendung Wölfflin'scher Kunstbetrachtung. Bern, 1922.
Steenackers, F. F. Luiz de **CAMOES**, la Renaissance et les Lusiades. Lisbonne, 1880.
Prat, A. V. Camoens y Góngora, o grecoromano y Barroco. Revista de las Españas, 3, 1928.
Mabilleau, L. Etude historique sur la philosophie de la Renaissance en Italie, Cesare **CREMONINI**. Paris, 1881.
Guérard, A. L. **DANTE** and the Renaissance. Dante Sexcentenary Lectures, Rice Institute (Texas), 1921.
Vossler, K. Dante und die Renaissance. Heidelberg, 1902.
Meier, M. **DESCARTES** und die Renaissance. Münster, 1914.
Bredvold, L. I. The Naturalism of **DONNE** in Relation to Some Renaissance Traditions. JEGPh, 22, 1923.
Mezan, S. De **GABIROL** à Abravanel. Juifs espagnols promoteurs de la Renaissance. Paris, 1937.
Geiger, L. **GOETHE** und die Renaissance. Vierteljahrschrift f. Kultur und Litteratur der Renaissance, 2. And in: Vorträge und Versuche. Dresden, 1890.
Harnack, O. Goethe und die Renaissance. Atti del Congresso internaz. di Scienze storiche, 4. Roma, 1903-04.
Prang, H. Goethe und die Kunst der italienischen Renaissance. Berlin, 1938.
Eringa, S. Luc De **HEERE** et la seconde Renaissance française. NPh, 2, 1916.
Cantimori, D. Ulrico von **HUTTEN** e i rapporti tra Rinascimento e Riforma. Annali della R. Scuola Normale Superiore di Pisa, 30, 1929.
Blaser, O. C. F. **MEYERS** Renaissancenovellen. Bern, 1905 .
Bayley, C. C. **PETRARCH**, Charles IV. and the Renovatio Imperii. Spec., 17, 1942.
Whitfield, J. H. Petrarch and the Renaissance. Oxford, 1943.

Cassirer, E. Giovanni PICO DELLA MIRANDOLA: A Study in the History of Renaissance Ideas. JHI, 3, 1942.
Gebhart, E. RABELAIS, la Renaissance et la Réforme. Paris, 1895.
Eckhardt, E. Gehört SHAKESPEARE zur Renaissance oder zum Barock? Festschrift Friedrich Kluge. Tübingen, 1926.
Weibel, O. TIECKS Renaissancedichtung in ihrem Verhältnis zu Heinse und C. F. Meyer. Bern, 1925.
Banilla y San Martin, A. Luis VIVES y la filosofia del Renacimiento. Madrid, 1929.

CHAPTER FIVE

Baroque.

(Including Concettismo, Culteranismo, Euphuism, Gongorism, Marinism, Metaphysical Poetry, Préciosité, Secentismo.)

1. Generalities.

Anon. Baroque and its Aims. TLS, 19.II. 1938.
Alonso, D. Poesía barroca y desengaños de imperio. Escorial, 1944.
Arcari, P. Il seicento creatore. Il seicento nella civiltà d'Italia e d'Europa. Boll. della R. Univ. italiana per i stranieri, 12-13, 1935.
Arullani, V. A. Secentismo italiano e francese. Fanfulla della Domenica, 22, 1901.
Azorin. Il manierismo nella poesia spagnola. Poesia, 5, 1946.
Baldensperger, F. La société précieuse à Lyon au milieu du XVIIe siècle. Rev. d' histoire de Lyon, 1906. And in: Etudes d'histoire littéraire, 2e sér. Paris, 1910.
Bates, R. C. Le pèlerinage de Charlemagne: a Baroque Epic. French Studies, 1941.
Belloni, A. Il seicento. Milano, 1898.
Blasi, G. de. Concetto del barocco nella civiltà europea. Società Nuova, 2, 1946.
Brandeys, F. Une philosophie de l'âge baroque. Europe centrale, 25.I.1936.
Bray, R. La Préciosité et les précieux. Paris, 1947.
Caja, A. Secentismo spagnuolo o italiano? Avola, 1903.
Charpentier, B. Autor du précieux. MF, 1932.
Chastel, A. Sur le baroque français. Cahiers de la Restauration fr., 4, 1944.
Cicade, H. A poesia lírica cultista y conceptista. Lisboa, 1938.
Croce, B. I predicatori italiani del seicento e il gusto spagnuolo. Napoli, 1899. And in: Saggi sulla letteratura italiana del seicento. Bari, 1911.
—— Der Begriff des Barock. Die Gegenreformation. Zürich, 1925.
—— Storia della età barocca in Italia. Bari, 1929.
—— L'Arcadia e la poesia del Settecento. Quaderni della Critica, April, 1946.
Croll, M. W. The Baroque Style in Prose. Festschrift F. Klaeber. Minneapolis, 1929.
Cysarz, H. Deutsche Barockdichtung. Leipzig, 1924.
—— Zur Zeit- und Wesensbestimmung des dichterischen Barockstils. F&F, 11, 1935.
—— Der dichterische Stil- und Zeitbegriff Barock. Bull. of the Internat. Comm. of Hist. Sciences, 9, 1937.
Daniells, R. Baroque Form in English Literature. UTQ, 14, 1945.
—— English Baroque and Deliberate Obscurity. Jour. Aesthetics, 5, 1946.
Diaz-Plaja, G. El espíritu barroco. Barcelona, 1940.
Ermatinger, E. Barock und Rokoko in der deutschen Dichtung. Leipzig, 1926.
Filippon, S. Il marinismo nella letteratura tedesca. Riv. di lett. ted., 4, 1910.
Flemming, W. Die deutsche Barockzeit. Köln, 1942.
Fletcher, J. B. Précieuses at the Court of Charles I. JCL, 1, 1903.
Friederich, W. P. Spiritualismus und Sensualismus in der englischen Barocklyrik. Wien, 1932.
—— Late Renaissance, Baroque, or Counter-Reformation? JEGPh, 46, 1947.
Gillet, L. Le baroque espagnol et le Nouveau Monde. La Renaissance, Jan., 1937.
Gilman, S. An Introduction to the Ideology of the Baroque in Spain. Symposium, 1, 1946-47.
Grierson, H. J. C. European Literature in the First Half of the 17th Century. Edinburgh, 1906.
—— Cross Currents in the English Literature of the 17th Century. London, 1929.
Hassold, E. C. The Baroque as a Basic Concept of Art. College Art Jour., 6, 1946.
Hatzfeld, H. Der Barockstil der religiösen klassischen Lyrik in Frankreich. Literaturwissenschaftl. Jb. der Görresgesellschaft, 4, 1929.

—— A Clarification of the Baroque Problem in the Romance Literatures. CL, 1, 1949.
Haviland, T. P. Préciosité Crosses the Atlantic. PMLA, 59, 1944.
Heuser, Nelly. Barock und Romantik. Frauenfeld, 1942.
Hirsch, A. Bürgertum und Barock im deutschen Roman. Frankfurt, 1934.
Hornedo, R. M. Hacia una desvalorización del barroco? RyF, 125-26.
Isaacs, J. Baroque and Rococo: A History of Two Concepts. Bull. of the Internat. Committee of Historical Sciences, 9. Paris, 1937.
Kane, E. K. Gongorism and the Golden Age. Chapel Hill (N. C.), 1928.
Kettler, H. K. The Baroque Tradition in the Literature of the German Enlightenment, 1700-50. Cambridge, 1943.
Landmann, F. Der Euphuismus, sein Wesen, seine Quelle, seine Geschichte. Diss. Giessen, 1881.
Landau, M. Zur Geschichte des Barockstils in der Literatur. Beilage der Allg. Zt., 63, 1890.
Lebègue, R. Le théâtre baroque en France. BHR, 2, 1942.
López-Rey, J. Idea de la imitación barroca. HR, 11, 1943.
Lunding, E. Tysk Barok og Barokforskning. København, 1938.
Mainland, W. F. An Example of Baroque Elaboration. MLR, 41, 1946.
Mark, J. The Uses of the Term Baroque. MLR, 33, 1938.
Marzot, G. Teorici secenteschi del concettismo. LNI, 19, 1943 .
Meissner, P. Die geistesgeschichtlichen Grundlagen des englischen Literaturbarocks. München, 1935.
Meozzi, A. Il secentismo e le sue manifestazioni europee in rapporto all' Italia. Pisa, 1936.
Milch, W. Deutsche Barocklyrik und Metaphysical Poetry in England. Trivium, 1. (Zürich).
—— Deutsches Literaturbarock: Der Stand der Forschung. GQ, 13, 1940.
Moret, A. Le lyrisme baroque en Allemagne. Lille, 1936.
Mornet, D. L'idée de préciosité en France au XVIIe siècle. JHI, 1, 1940.
Nethercot, A. H. The Reputation of Native Versus Foreign Metaphysical Poets in England. MLR, 1930.
O'Connor, W. V. The Influence of the Metaphysicals on Modern Poetry. College English, 9, 1948.
Ors, E. d'. Du baroque. NRF, 1937.
—— Le baroque comme constante historique. Bull. de l'Union pour la vérité, 1937.
—— Del Barocco. Milano, 1945.
Ovidio, F. d'. Secentismo spagnolismo? NAnt, 65, 1882.
Peiser, W. El barroco en la literatura mexicana. RIA, 6, 1943.
Peixotto, A. Obscurismo o preciosidade litéraria. Revista de Philologia (Rio de Janeiro), 1933.
Plaja, D. G. El espíritu del barroco. Barcelona, 1940.
Praz, M. Secentismo e marinismo in Inghilterra. Firenze, 1925.
—— Studi sul concettismo. Cultura, 1933; Milano, 1934; Firenze, 1946.
—— Poesia metafisica inglese del 600. Poesia, 3-4, 1946.
Rehm, W. Römisch-französischer Barockheroismus und seine Umgestaltung in Deutschland. GRM, 22, 1934.
Reinhardt, K. F. The Cultural Background of the Literary Baroque in Germany. Stanford Studies in Lang. and Lit., 1941.
Rinicker, R. Rie Preziosität der französischen Renaissance Poesie. Diss. Zürich, 1898.
Robertson, J. M. Concerning Preciosity. The Yellow Book, 13, 1897.
Schücking, L. L. The Baroque Character of the Elizabethan Hero. PBA, 24, 1938.
Schürr, F. Barock, Klassizismus und Rokoko in der französischen Literatur. Leipzig, 1928.
Sharp, R. L. The Revolt Against Metaphysical Poetry. Chapel Hill (N. C.), 1940.
Simon, E. L'esprit du baroque. Valeurs, Oct., 1946.
Strich, F. Der lyrische Stil des 17. Jahrhunderts. Festschrift F. Muncker. München, 1916.
——Der europäische Barock. In: Der Dichter und die Zeit. Bern, 1947.
Thomas, L. P. Le lyrisme et la préciosité cultistes en Espagne. Halle, Paris, 1909.
—— Précieuses de France et précieuses d'Espagne. Le Flambeau, 15.I.1920.
Vancura, Z. Euphuism and Baroque Prose. Casopis pro moderni filologii, 18. (Prague), 1932.
—— Baroque Prose in America. Studies in English, Charles University. Prague, 1933.
Vedel, V. Den digteriske Barokstil omkring aar 1600. Edda, 2, 1914.
Viëtor, K. Vom Stil und Geist der deutschen Barockdichtung. GRM, 14, 1926.

—— Probleme der deutschen Barockliteratur. Leipzig, 1939.

Watkins, E. I. British Baroque. Church Quart. Rev., 142, 1946.

Weisbach, W. Der Barock als Kunst der Gegenreformation. Berlin, 1921.

Weise, G. Das gotische oder barocke Stilprinzip der deutschen und der nordischen Kunst. DVLG, 10, 1932.

Wellek, R. The Concept of Baroque in Literary Scholarship. Journal of Aesthetics & Art Criticism, 5, 1946.

Wild, F. Zum Problem des Barocks in der englischen Dichtung. Anglia, 59, 1935.

2. Individual Authors.

Pierce, F. El Bernardo of **BALBUENA**: A Baroque Fantasy. HR, 13, 1945.

Haller, Elisabeth. Die barocken Stilmerkmale in der englischen, lateinischen und deutschen Fassung von Dr. Thomas **BURNETS** Theory of the Earth. Bern, 1940.

Gilman, S. El falso Quijote, versión barroca del Quijote de **CERVANTES**. RFH, 1943.

Mahnke, D. Der Barock-Universalismus des **COMENIUS**. Zs. f. Gesch. der Erziehung & des Unterrichts, 1931-32.

Hiller, J. E. Lessing und **CORNEILLE**: Rokoko und Barock. RF, 47, 1933.

Beachcroft, T. O. **CRASHAW** and the Baroque Style. Criterion, 1934.

Warren, A. Richard Crashaw: A Study in Baroque Sensibility. University (La.), 1939.

Gillet, L. B. **CROCE** et l'Italie baroque. RDM, 1930.

Apráiz, A. de. San Juan de la **CRUZ** entre el gótico y el barroco. Rev. de Ideas estéticas, 1943.

Mann, W. **DRYDENS** heroische Tragödien als Ausdruck höfischer Barockkultur in England. Diss. Tübingen, 1933.

Praz, M. La poesia metafisica inglese del seicento: John **DONNE**. Roma, 1945.

Riemschneider-Hörner, M. Holbein, **ERASMUS** und der frühe Manierismus des 16. Jahrhunderts. Zs. f. Aesthetik & allg. Kunstwissenschaft, 33.

Warshaw, J. **GONGORA** as a Precursor of the Symbolists. Hisp. 1932.

Babelon, J. Góngora ou la Métaphore. Yggdrasill, 25.I.1938.

Croce, B. I trattatisti italiani del concettismo e Baltasar **GRACIAN**. Accad. di Napoli, 1899.

Nuglisch, O. Barocke Stilelemente in der dramatischen Kunst von A. **GRYPHIUS** und D. C. von Lohenstein. Breslau, 1938.

Castro, A. Antonio de **GUEVARA**. Un hombre y un estilo del siglo XVI. Bol. del Instituto Caro y Cuervo, 1, 1945.

Child, G. C. John **LYLY** and Euphuism. Münchener Beiträge, 7, 1894.

Farinelli, A. John Lyly, Guevara y el euphuismo en Inglaterra. In: Ensayos y Discursos de critica literaria hispanoeuropea. Milano, 1925.

Quimby, E. S. The Indebtedness of Lyly's Euphues to Certain of its Predecessors. The Colonnade, 14. (New York), 1922.

López Gon iles V,. La salvación del mundo en las coplas de Jorges **MANRIQUE** y en la cronica del condestable Miguel Lucas de Iranzo. Una generación de hombres barrocos. "Ciudad de Dios", 1943.

Jiménez Rueda, J. **QUEVEDO** y lo barroco en España. Hijo Pródigo, 10. (México), 1946.

Cogliano, H. Il barocchismo in **SENECA** e in Lucano. Messina, 1938.

Basse, M. Stijlaffectatie bij **SHAKESPEARE** vooral uit het vogpunt van het euphuisme. Gand, 1896.

Boerner, O. Shakespeare und der Barock. GRM, 25, 1937.

Deutschbein, M. Shakespeares Macbeth als Drama des Barock. Leipzig, 1936.

Landmann, F. Shakespeare and Euphuism. Euphues an Adaptation from Guevara. Shakespeare Society Transactions, 13, 1880-85.

Michels, W. Barockstil bei Shakespeare und Calderón. Diss. Frankfurt, 1928. And in: RH, 1929.

Wolff, M. J. Shakespeare als Künstler des Barocks. Internat. Monatsschrift, 11, 1917.

Gebhardt, C. Rembrandt und **SPINOZA**. Stilgeschichtliche Betrachtungen zum Barockproblem. Kant-Studien, 22, 1927.

Roditi, E. Tarquato **TASSO**: The Transition from Baroque to Neo-Classicism. Journal of Aesthetics, 6, 1948.

Brown, W. C. Edward **TAYLOR**: An American Metaphysical. AL, 16, 1944.

Warren, A. Edward Taylor's Poetry: Colonial Baroque. Kenyon Rev., 3, 1941.

Castro, A. El Don Juan de **TIRSO** y el de Molière como personajes barrocos. Hommage à Ernest Martinenche. Paris, 1939.

Peyton, M. A. Some Baroque Aspects of Tirso de Molina. RR, 36, 1945.

Mayhew, E. de N. English Baroque: Sir John **VANBRUGH** and the Baroque Country House. Baltimore, 1943.

Magne, E. VOITURE et les origines de l'hôtel de Rambouillet. MF, 1911.
Brom, G. VONDEL en de Barok. Nieuwe Taalgids, 41, 1948.
Haerten, H. Vondel und der deutsche Barock. Nijmwegen, 1935.
Schröder, R. A. Ein Klassiker des Barock, Joost van den Vondel. Hochland, 36. And in: Aufsätze und Reden. Berlin, 1939.
Friederich, W. P. J. W. ZINKGREF and his Fellow-Poets. GR, 1934.

CHAPTER SIX

Classicism, Ancient and Modern.

(Including Neo-Classicism, The Eighteenth Century in General, Enlightenment, Rationalism and Rococo.)

Alvarez Everoix, V. Poesía americana: clasicismo, romanticismo, simbolismo, futurismo. México, 1941.
Baldensperger, F. Pour une révaluation littéraire du XVIIe siècle classique. RHLF, 1937.
Banner, M. Introduction du génie classique dans la poésie française. Frankfurt, 1897.
Barton, J. E. What is the Classical Style? CLS, 3, 1941.
Bate, W. J. From Classic to Romantic: Premises of Taste in Eighteenth-Century England. Harvard U. P., 1946.
Bédarida, H. Du classicisme français au néoclassicisme du settecento. Roma, 1937.
Benedetto, L. F. La leggenda del classicismo francese. Rassegna d'Italia, 1947.
Benz. Klassik und Romantik. Berlin, 1938.
Bertrand, L. La fin du classicisme et le retour à l'antique. Diss. Paris, 1897.
Blaki, F. Dal classicismo al secentismo in Ispagna. Aquila, 1929.
Bohnstedt. Le classicisme et le romantisme en littérature. Progr. Perleberg, 1858.
Bray, R. La formation de la doctrine classique en France. Paris, 1927.
Brecht, F. J. Der Begriff des Klassischen. HG, 1930.
Brennecke, A. Die französischen Classiker des XVII. Jahrhunderts in ihrer Nachahmung der Alten und Originalität. ALG, 3, 1874.
Brie, F. Englische Rokoko-Epik. München, 1927.
Burgum, E. B. The Neoclassical Period in English Literature: A Psychological Definition. Sewanee Rev., 52, 1944.
Caudwell, H. Introduction to French Classicism. New York, 1931.
Cidade, H. Ensaio sobre a crise mental do seculo XVIII. Coimbra, 1929.
Dilthey, W. Die deutsche Aufklärung im Staat und in der Akademie Friedrich des Grossen. DR, 1901.
Doutrepont, G. Les classiques jugés par les romantiques. Bull. de l'Acad. royale de Belgique, 1927.
Drerup, E. Die klassische Schönheit der altgriechischen Dichtung. PhW, 1931.
Eliot, T. S. Che cos' è un classico? Poesia, June, 1947.
Elwell, C. E. The Influence of the Enlightenment on the Catholic Theory of Religious Education in France, 1750-1850. Harvard U. P., 1944.
Ernst, F. Der Klassizismus in Italien, Frankreich und Deutschland. Zürich, 1924.
Fidao-Justiniani J. E. Qu'est-ce qu'un classique? Paris, 1930.
Folkierski, W. Entre le classicisme et le romantisme. Cracovie, Paris, 1925.
Fraenkel, E. Die klassische Dichtung der Römer. HG, 1930.
Franz, E. Deutsche Klassik und Reformation. Halle, 1937.
Friedländer, P. Das Klassische in der griechischen Literatur. HG, 1930.
Gallaway, F. Reason, Rule and Revolt in English Classicism. New York, 1940.
Giusti, W. Studi sul pensiero illuministico e liberale russo nei secoli XVIII-XIX. L'Europe orientale, 18, 1938.
Grierson, H. J. C. Classical and Romantic. Cambridge U. P., 1923.
Haegermann, G. Die Erklärungen der Menschen- und Bürgerrechte in den ersten amerikanischen Staatsverfassungen. Berlin, 1910.
Harvey-Jellie, W. Le théâtre classique en Angleterre. Montréal, 1932.
Hatzfeld, H. Die französische Klassik in neuer Sicht. Klassik als Barock. Tijdschrift voor taal en letteren, 23, 1935.
Havens, R. Poetic Diction of the English Classicists. Kittredge Anniversary Papers. Boston, 1913.
Hazard, P. Les rationaux (1670-1700). RLC, 12, 1932.
—— Etudes européennes. La fin du XVIIe siècle. RDM, 1932.
—— La crise de la conscience européenne (1680-1715). 3 vols. Paris, 1935. Cf. RLC, 1947.

Hettner, H. Literaturgeschichte des achtzehnten Jahrhunderts (England, Frankreich, Deutschland). Braunschweig, 1872.
Hibben. The Philosophy of the Enlightenment. New York, 1910.
Jan, E. von. Französische und deutsche Aufklärungsliteratur im Rahmen des kulturkundlichen Unterrichts. NJWJ, 1928.
—— Das Aufklärungszeitalter in Spanien. GRM, 1934.
Ker, W. P. On the Value of the Terms Classical and Romantic as Applied to Literature. In: Collected Essays, 2. London, 1925.
Kimball, F. The Creation of the Rococo. JWI, 4, 1941.
Knorrek, M. Der Einfluss des Rationalismus auf die englische Sprache. Breslau, 1938.
Koerte, A. Der Begriff des Klassischen in der Antike. Verhandl. d. Sächs. Akad. d. Wiss., 86, 1934. And in: F&F, 1934.
Konrad, G. Vom Geist französischer Klassik. GRM, 30, 1942.
Köster, A. Die deutsche Literatur der Aufklärungszeit. Heidelberg, 1925.
Kraft, J. Défense de l'Aufklärung. RMM, 1936.
Landry, L. Classicisme et romantisme. Essai de définition. MF, 1927.
Lanson, G. Le dix-huitième siècle et ses principaux aspects. RCC, 1923.
Lecky, W. E. H. History of Rationalism in Europe. London, 1865.
Macri, O. T. S. Eliot e il classicismo europeo. Rassegna d'Italia, 1947.
Marega, M. La letteratura classica giapponese. Convivium, 1947.
Martí-Sabat, J. Classic? Romantic. La Revista, 1932.
Meister, R. Klassizismus im Altertum. WBFA, 1922.
Merian-Genast, E. Das Problem der Form in der französischen und deutschen Klassik. GRM, 27, 1939.
Moreau, P. Classiques et romantiques. Rev. des Jeunes, 1927.
—— Le classicisme des romantiques. Paris, 1932.
Mortensen, J. Klassicitet och Germanismen. Forum, 1920.
Murray, G. The Classical Tradition in Poetry. Harvard U. P., 1927.
Natta, A. Breve storia della parola Illuminismo. Belfagor, 1, 1946.
Neubert, F. Studien zur französischen Aufklärungsliteratur. GRM, 1921.
Partridge, E. Notes sur les débuts de la controverse classico-romantique en France. RLC, 9, 1929.
Pellissier, R. E. The Neo-Classic Movement in Spain During the XVIIIth Century. Stanford, 1918.
Peltz, Catherine W. The Neo-Classic Lyric, 1660-1725. ELH, 11, 1944.
Peyre, H. Qu'est-ce que le classicisme? Paris, 1933.
Poggioli, R. Classicismo di Pascal. Letteratura, 1947.
Postgate, J. P. Are the Classics to Go? Fortnightly Review, 1902.
Reynold, G. de. Le XVIIe siècle: Le classique et le baroque. Montréal, 1944.
Robertson, J. G. The Reconciliation of Classic and Romantic. Cambridge, 1924.
Rose, H. Klassik als künstlerische Denkform des Abendlandes. München, 1937.
Rostagni, A. Classicità e spirito moderno. Torino, 1939.
Schadewaldt, W. Begriff und Wesen der Klassik in der antiken Literatur. Antike & HG, 1930.
Schaeffer, F. Antik und romantisch. Eine Untersuchung über das Wesen der klassizistischen und antiklassizistischen Bestrebung in der deutschen Literatur des 18. Jahrhunderts. Freiburg, 1921.
Schultz, F. Klassik und Romantik der Deutschen. Stuttgart, 1940.
Stoll, E. E. Milton Classical and Romantic. PhQ, 23.
Strich, F. Deutsche Klassik und Romantik. München, 1929.
Stroux, J. Die Anschauungen vom Klassischen im Altertum. HG, 1930.
Suckling, N. A Further Contribution to the Classic-Romantic Debate. Durham U. Journal, 39, 1946.
Teesing, H. P. H. Wieland als dichter van het rococo. NPh, 30, 1946.
Thomas, R. H. The Classical Ideal in German Literature, 1755-1805. Cambridge, 1939.
Toffanin, G. Montaigne e l'idea classica. Rinascita, 3, 1940.
Tosi, T. A. Chénier e il classicismo. A&R, 6, 1903.
Villemain. Tableau du XVIIIe siècle. Paris, 1828.
Weisinger, H. English Treatment of the Classical-Romantic Problem. MLQ, 7, 1946.
Whitaker, A. et al. Latin America and the Enlightenment. New York, 1942.
Wiese, B. von. Das Humanitätsideal in der deutschen Klassik. GRM, 1932.
Willoughby, L. A. The Classical Age of German Literature. London, 1926.

Wood, P. S. The Opposition to Neo-Classicism in England. PMLA, 1928.
Woodbridge, E. Chaucer's Classicism. JEGPh, 1, 1897.
Zeydel, E. H. The Concepts Classic and Romantic: Some Fundamental Observations. GR, 19, 1944.

CHAPTER SEVEN

Romanticism.

(Including Pre-Romanticism and The Nineteenth Century in General).

1. Generalities.

Abercrombie, L. Romanticism. London, 1926.
Abril, M. Romanticismo, classicismo e goticismo. Rev. de Occidente, 1927.
Addison, Agnes. Romanticism and the Gothic Revival. Diss. Philadelphia, 1938.
Andersen, V. Guldhornene. En bidrag til den danske Romantiks historie. København, 1896.
Anderson, E. N. German Romanticism as an Ideology of Cultural Crisis. JHI, 2, 1941.
Avila, P. The Introduction of Romanticism into Mexican Literature. Diss. Stanford U., 1937.
Aynard, J. Comment définir le romantisme? RLC, 5, 1925.
Bab, J. Fortinbras oder der Kampf des 19. Jahrhunderts mit dem Geiste der Romantik. Berlin, 1913.
Babits, M. Histoire de la littérature européenne au XIXe siècles. Budapest, 1935.
Baldensperger, F. Les années 1827-28 en France et au dehors. RCC, 1928-29.
—— Romantique: Ses analogies et ses équivalents. Tableau synoptique de 1650 à 1810. HSPhL, 15, 1937.
—— Pour une interprétation équitable du romantisme européen. Helicon, 1, 1938.
—— 1793-94: Climacteric Times for Romantic Tendencies in English Ideology. JHI, 5, 1944.
Barzun, J. Romantic Historiography as a Political Force in France. JHI, 2, 1941.
—— Romanticism and the Modern Ego. Boston, 1943.
Beach, J. W. A Romantic View of Poetry. Minneapolis, 1944.
Beck, F. Der romantische Mensch als Träger des Fortschritts um die Wende des 18. und 19. Jahrhunderts. Diss. Erlangen, 1930.
Bédarida, H. Le romantisme français et l'Italie. Rev. de l'U. de Lyon, 4, 1931.
Beers, H. A. A History of English Romanticism in the Eighteenth Century. New York, 1906.
Benz, R. Die deutsche Romantik. Leipzig, 1937.
Benetti-Brunelli, V. Le origini italiane della scuola romantica. Milano 1918.
Benson, A. B. The Old Norse Element in Swedish Romanticism. New York, 1914.
Bernbaum, E. Guide through the Romantic Revolt. New York, 1930.
Berti, G. Origini politiche del Romanticismo. Società, 3, 1947.
Bertrana, E. Arcadia lugubre e preromantica. Spezia, 1899.
Bertrand, J. J. A. Le romantisme allemand et la poésie romane. RELV, 1923-24.
Bisson, L. A. Le romantisme littéraire au Canada français. Paris, 1932.
—— Le préromantisme étranger à Bordeaux. Mélanges P. Laumonier. Paris, 1934.
Blanck, A. Den nordiska Renässansen i sjuttonhundratalets litteratur. Stockholm, 1911.
Blankenagel, J. C. et al. Romanticism: A Symposium. PMLA, 55, 1940.
Blaze de Bury, H. Les grands courants de la littérature française au XIXe siècle. RDM, 1.XI.1873.
Boas, G. In Defence of Romanticism. In: Romanticism in America. Baltimore, 1940.
—— Romanticism in America. Baltimore Museum of Art, 1940.
Böök, F. Det romantiska. Samtiden. (Stockholm), 1912.
Borgese, G. A. Ottocento europeo. Milano, 1926.
Born, S. Die romantische Schule in Deutschland und Frankreich. Heidelberg, 1879.
Börries, K. Die Romantik und die Geschichte. Berlin, 1925.
Braga, T. Os iniciadores do romantismo em Portugal. In: Questiones de litteratura e arte portugueza. Lisboa, 1881.
Brandes, G. Die Hauptströmungen der Literatur des 19ten Jahrhunderts. Berlin, 1872-76. Translations: København, 1877-92; Paris, 1902; New York, 1906.
Cajumi, A. Spagna antiromantica. Cult., 1928.
Calgari, G. Il romanticismo in Germania e in Italia. Milano, 1930.
Cazamian, L. Le romantisme en France et en Angleterre: quelques différences. EA, 1, 1937.

Cerny, V. Quelques remarques sur la critique masarickienne du titanisme romantique. RLC, 14, 1934.
Chuda, J. The Czech National Revival: the Age of Romanticism. Chicago, 1934.
Churchman, P. The Beginnings of Romanticism in Spain. RH, 1910.
Croce, B. Definizioni del romanticismo. In: Problemi di estetica. Bari, 1910.
Dessauer, F. E. Fascism and Romanticism. UTQ, 15, 1946.
Deutschbein, M. Das Wesen des Romantischen. Cöthen, 1921.
—— Romantisch und romanesk. Festschrift M. Förster. Leipzig, 1929.
Diaz-Plaja, G. Introducción al estudio del romanticismo español. Madrid, 1936.
Donati, D. & Carli, F. L'Europa nel secolo XIX. Padova, 1927.
Escoffier, M. Essai de bibliographie synchronique et méthodique du movement romantique (1788-1850). Paris, 1934.
Estève, E. Etudes de littérature préromantique. Paris, 1923.
Falnes, O. J. National Romanticism in Norway. New York, 1933.
Fairchild, H. N. The Romantic Quest. New York, 1931.
—— Romanticism and the Religious Revival in England. JHI, 2, 1941.
Farkas, G. Romános, romántos, romantikus. Budapest, 1929.
—— Die ungarische Romantik. Berlin, 1931.
Farinelli, A. Il romanticismo in Germania. Bari, 1923.
—— Prolegomeni allo studio del romanticismo nel mondo latino. NAnt, 1926.
—— Il romanticismo nel mondo latino. 3 vols. Torino, 1927. Cf. RLC, 7, 1927.
—— Conferencias brasileiras. São Paolo, 1930.
—— Le romantisme et l'Espagne. RLC, 16, 1936.
Finch, M. B. & Peers, E. A. The Origins of French Romanticism. London, 1920.
Fioroni, M. I precursori del romanticismo italiano. Catania, 1915.
Fouret, L. A. Romantisme français et romantisme allemand. MF, 1927
Fournol, E. Les nations romantiques. Paris, 1931.
François, A. Le mot romantique. Annales J. J. Rousseau, 1909.
—— Encore le mot romantique. Bibliothèque universelle, 1918.
—— Romantique et romantisme. Bibliothèque universelle, 1915.
—— Où en est romantique? Mélanges Baldensperger. Paris, 1929.
Friedrich, H. Der Epochenbegriff im Lichte der französischen Préromantismeforschung, NJWJ, 10, 1934.
—— Das antiromantische Denken in modernem Frankreich. München, 1935.
Frothingham, O. B. Transcendentalism in New England. New York, 1886.
Frunck, G. Bref rörande nya skolans historia. (Romanticism). Upsala, 1886.
Giovagnoli, R. Il romanticismo nella storia del risorgimento italiano. Torino, 1904.
Girard, H. & Moncel, H. Pour et contre le romantisme: Bibliographie des travaux publiés de 1914 à 1926. Paris, 1927.
Giraud, J. Le romantisme. Paris, 1929.
Hainlein, G. Die vorromantischen Angriffe in Frankreich auf die klassische Tragödie. Diss. Jena, 1932.
Hazard, P. Romantisme italien et romantisme européen. RLC, 6, 1926.
—— De l'ancien au nouveau monde: les origines du romantisme au Brésil. RLC, 7, 1927.
—— Les origines du romantisme et les influences étrangères: le Midi. Annales de l'U. de Paris, 1928.
Henriot, E. Romanesques et romantiques. Paris, 1930.
Hermann, G. Die französische Kritik an den modernen Formen der Romantik. Prag, 1938.
Hübener, G. Theorie der Romantik. DVLG, 10, 1932.
Jacoubet, H. Le genre troubadour et les origines françaises du romantisme. Paris, 1929.
Just, W. Die romantische Bewegung der amerikanischen Literatur. Diss. Münster, 1911.
Kaufman, P. Defining Romanticism. MLN, 1923.
Kircher, E. Philosophie der Romantik. Jena, 1906.
Klemperer, V. Romantik und französische Romantik. München, 1925.
Körner, J. Romantiker und Klassiker. Berlin, 1924.
—— Die Botschaft der deutschen Romantik an Europa. Augsburg, 1920.
Kulling, J. Den svenska romantikens religiösa utveckling. Samlaren, 1936.
Languasco, B. La poesia romantica cubana. Diss. Toulouse, 1930.
Lardanchet, H. Les enfants perdus du romantisme. Paris, 1906.
Lempicki, Z. Considerations sur la genèse et l'essence du romantisme. Bull. de l' Acad. Polonaise. Cracovie, 1922.

Lerario, E. Inzii romantici in Europa ed il preromanticismo inglese. Firenze, 1940.
Lerch, E. Passion und Gefühl. AR, 22, 1938.
Lovejoy, A. O. On the Meaning of Romantic in Early German Romanticism. MLN, 1916 ff.
—— On the Discriminations of Romanticism. PMLA, 1924.
—— The Meaning of Romanticism for the Historian of Ideas. JHI, 2, 1941.
Lucas, F. L. The Decline and Fall of the Romantic Ideal. New York, 1936.
Maar, H. G. de. A History of Modern English Romanticism. Oxford U. P., 1924.
Macbeth, M. A Note on the Origins of French Romanticism. ML, 1921.
Mainenti, P. Che cosa fu il romanticismo? Napoli, 1937.
Marasca, A. Le origini del romanticismo italiano. Roma, 1909.
Marcu, A. Le romantisme italien. Bucarest, 1929.
Maver, G. Alle fonti del romanticismo polacco. Roma, 1929.
Maynial. Dans les sentiers perdus du romantisme. RB, 1927.
Mazzoni, G. Le origini del romanticismo. NAnt, 1879.
—— I precursori del romanticismo. NAnt, 1893.
McClelland, I. L. The Origins of the Romantic Movement in Spain. Liverpool, 1937.
Merz, J. T. History of European Thought in the Nineteenth Century. 4 vols. Edinburgh, 1903-14.
Michaut, G. Sur le romantisme: une poignée de définitions. In: Pages de critique et d'histoire littéraire. Paris, 1910.
Monglond, A. Histoire intérieure du préromantisme français. 2 vols. Grenoble, 1929.
Mornet, D. Le romantisme en France au XVIIIe siècle. Paris, 1912.
Mowat, R. B. The Romantic Age. London, 1937.
Natali, G. Le origini italiane del romanticismo italiano. NAnt, 16.V.1928.
Nedoncelle, M. Les leçons spirituelles du XIXe siècle. Paris, 1937.
Nillsson, A. Svensk romantik. Diss. Lund, 1916.
Ogle, M. B. Romantic Movements in Antiquity. TAPhA, 1943.
Omond, T. S. The Romantic Triumph. London, 1900.
Parodi, D. La ésencia del romanticismo. Hiperion (Montevideo), 41, 1939.
Pastor, E. G. El romanticismo argentino. Rev. de la U. de Buenos Aires, 1916.
Pauphilet, A. Romantisme et antiquité. Rev. de l'U. de Lyon, 1930.
Peers, E. A. Later Spanish Conceptions of Romanticism. MLR, 1923.
—— A History of the Romantic Movement in Spain. 2 vols. Cambridge U. P., 1939-40.
Perrochon, H. Romantisme et Protestantisme. Rev. de Théologie et de Philosophie, 16, 1928.
Petersen, J. Die Wesensbestimmung der deutschen Romantik. Leipzig, 1926.
Phelps, W. L. The Beginnings of the English Romantic Movement. Boston, 1893.
Picard, R. Romantisme et révolution. FR, 17, 1943.
Piccolo, F. Saggio d'introduzione alla critica del romanticismo. Napoli, 1920.
Picirilli, M. Per una interpretazione del romanticismo italiano nei suoi primordi. Columbia U. P., 1940.
Piggott, S. Prehistory and the Romantic Movement. Antiquity, 11, 1937.
Powell, A. E. The Romantic Theory of Poetry. New York, 1926.
Praz, M. Preromanticismo e postromanticismo. Cult, 1931.
—— The Romantic Agony. Oxford U. P., 1933.
Rasin, Sister Eunice. Evidences of Romanticism in the Poetry of Medieval England. Diss. U. of Notre Dame, 1929.
Reynaud, L. Le romantisme des origines anglo-germaniques. Paris, 1926.
Río, A. del. Present Trends in the Conception and Criticism of Spanish Romanticism. RR, 39, 1948.
Robertson, J. G. New Interpretations of Romanticism. Discovery, 1920.
—— The Genesis of Romantic Theory in the Eighteenth Century. Cambridge U. P., 1923. Cf. RLC, 1925.
Roe, C. Les véritables origines du romantisme français. RHLF, 1929.
Rouge, I. Les écrivains allemands de la première école romantique et l'histoire générale de la littérature. Mélanges Baldensperger. Paris, 1929.
Ruggiero, G. Qu'est-ce que le romantisme? Suisse contemporaine, 8.
Rusatti, N. Il romanticismo e il carattere originale della letteratura italiana. Campobasso, 1921.
Saavedra Machado, L. Conceito do romantismo. Coimbra, 1937.
Sarrazin, G. Le romantisme chez les divers peuples. Revue Idéaliste, 1902.

Schmidt, J. Zur Geschichte der Romantik in dem Zeitalter der Reformation und der Revolution. 2 vols. Leipzig, 1848.
Schulz, F. Romantik und Romantisch als literarhistorische Terminologien und Begriffsbildungen. DVLG, 1924.
Seillière, E. Sur la psychologie du romantisme français. Paris, 1933.
Smith, L. P. Four Words: Romantic, Originality, Creative, Genius. Oxford, 1924.
Souriau, M. Histoire du romantisme en France. Paris, 1927.
Strich, F. Die Romantik als europäische Bewegung. Festschrift H. Wölfflin. München, 1924.
Tarr, F. C. Romanticism in Spain. BSS, 16, 1939.
Tauro de Tintis, F. Il romanticismo nei suoi precursori in Italia, in Francia ed in Germania. Bari, 1911.
Trahard, P. Le romantisme défini par le Globe. Paris, 1924.
Tronchon, H. Romantisme et préromantisme. Paris, 1930.
Tubino, F. M. El romanticismo en España. Rev. contemporanea, 7, 1877.
Ullmann, R. Geschichte des Begriffes Romantisch in Deutschland. Berlin, 1926.
Van Tieghem, P. Le mouvement romantique. Paris, 1912.
—— La notion de vraie poésie dans le préromantisme européen. RLC, 1, 1921.
—— Le préromantisme: études d'histoire littéraire européenne. 3 vols. Paris, 1924-47.
—— Essai sur le romantisme européen. BURS, 1929.
—— La place du romantisme anglais dans le romantisme européen. Les Lettres, 5-6, 1946.
—— Le romantisme. Paris, 1948. Cf. CL. 2, 1950.
Vedel, V. Svensk romantik. København, 1894.
Vermeylen, A. Het wezen van de romantiek. Leyden, 1925.
Viatte, A. Les sources occultes du romantisme-illuminisme-théosophie, 1770-1820. Paris, 1928.
Wagner, M. L. Die Romantik im lateinischen Amerika. Internat. Monatschrift, 1921.
Wellek, R. The Concept of Romanticism in Literary History. CL, 1, 1949.
Whitney, E. A. Humanitarianism and Romanticism. HLQ, 2, 1939.
Willoughby, L. A. The Romantic Movement in Germany. Oxford U. P., 1930.
Windakiewicz, E. Spanish Literature and Romanticism. (In Polish). Pzegl. Wspolczesny, 1928.
Zanco, A. Studi recenti sul romanticismo inglese. LNI, 1938 .

2. Individual Authors.

Antscherl, O. J. B. de **ALMEIDA GARRETT** und seine Beziehungen zur Romantik. Heidelberg, 1927.
Dryssen, C. **BERGSON** und die Romantik. Marburg, 1923.
Ferretti, D. G. **CARDUCCI** e il romanticismo. Parma, 1909.
Caillet-Bois, J. **ECHEVERRIA** y los orígenes del romanticismo en América. Revista hispánica moderna, 6, 1940.
Ehrhard, M. V. A. **JOUKOVSKI** et le préromantisme russe. Paris, 1939.
Niedermeyer, G. Sören **KIERKEGAARD** und die Romantik. Leipzig, 1908.
Barzellotti, G. **LEOPARDI** fu classico o romantico. NAnt, 1907.
Rizzo, T. L. Classicismo e romanticismo nell'arte di G. Leopardi. Reggio Calabria, 1921.
Savj-Lopez, P. Romanticismo antiromantico. (Leopardi) Napoli, 1913.
Metford, J. C. J. Alberto **LISTA** and the Romantic Movement in Spain. BSS, 16, 1939.
Waille, V. Le romantisme de **MANZONI**. Alger, 1890. Cf. NAnt, 4, 1895 .
Szpotanski, S. Adam **MICKIEWICZ** et le romantisme. Paris, 1923.
Prinsen, J. **MULTATULI** en de romantiek. Rotterdam, 1909.
Wahl, J. Magie et romantisme. Notes sur **NOVALIS** et Blake. H, 1936.
Schroeder, L. Adam **OEHLENSCHLAEGER** og den romantiske skole. København, 1888.
Sipovskii, V. V. **PUSHKIN** and Romanticism. In: Pushkin i ego sovremenniki, 6-7, 1916.
Boussagol, G. Le vrai centenaire du romantisme espagnol. **(RIVAS)**. Mémoires de l'Acad. de Toulouse, 9, 1933.
Babbitt, I. **ROUSSEAU** and Romanticism. Boston, 1919.
Noack, L. **SCHELLING** und die Philosophie der Romantik. Berlin, 1859.
Tengler, R. **SCHOPENHAUER** und die Romantik. Berlin, 1923.
Sturtevant, A. M. Romantic Elements in **TEGNER'S** Religious Philosophy. SS, 1919.
Baldensperger, F. Une définition de la poésie romantique par Charles de **VILLERS**. Rev. de philol. fr. et de littérature, 16, 1902.
Rouge, I. **WACKENRODER** et le romantisme. Mélanges H. Lichtenberger. Paris, 1934.

CHAPTER EIGHT

Later Literary Currents.

(Art for Art, Young Europe, Biedermeier, Realism, Naturalism, Symbolism, Impressionism, Expressionism, Modernism, Surrealism, etc.)

1. Generalities.

(For Symbolism, etc., see also under French Influences, IV. VII. 1-8. For Young Europe, see also under Politics, I. II. 1-2.)

Anon. L'existentialisme (de Kierkegaard à Sartre). TLS, 5.X.1946.

Arrighi, P. Le vérisme dans la prose narrative italienne. Paris, 1937.

—— La poésie vériste en Italie. Paris, 1937.

Auerbach, E. Mimesis, dargestellte Wirklichkeit in der abendländischen Literatur. Bern, 1946.

Balakian, Anna. Literary Origins of Surrealism. A New Mysticism in French Poetry. Columbia U. P., 1947.

Baldensperger, F. L'art pour l'art. MLN, 1912.

—— Le grand schisme de 1830: Romantisme et Jeune Europe. RLC, 10, 1930.

Beatty, R. C. The Heritage of Symbolism in Modern Poetry. Yale Rev., 36, 1947.

Beaufret, J. A propos de l'existentialisme. Confluences, 1945.

Benoist, H. L. Le drame naturaliste en Allemagne. Paris, 1905.

Berkhout, A. P. Biedermeier und poetischer Realismus. Purmerend, 1942.

Borgerhoff, E. B. Realism and Kindred Words. PMLA, 1938.

Bowra, C. M. The Heritage of Symbolism. London, 1943.

Breysig, H. Eindruckskunst und Ausdruckskunst. Berlin, 1927 .

Brie, F. Literarisches Biedermeier in England. DVLG, 13, 1935.

Brösel, K. Veranschaulichung im Realismus, Impressionismus und Frühexpressionismus. München, 1928.

Burke, W. J. The Literature of Slang. New York Publ. Library, 1939.

Cassagne, A. La théorie de l'art pour l'art en France chez les derniers romantiques et les premiers réalistes. Paris, 1931.

Cazamian, L. Symbolisme et poésie, l'exemple anglais. Paris, 1947.

Deri, M. Naturalismus, Idealismus, Expressionismus. Leipzig, 1919.

Dohn, W. Das Jahr 1848 im deutschen Drama und Epos. Diss. Breslau. Stuttgart, 1912.

Dumont, F. Romantisme anglais et surréalisme. Les Lettres, 5-6, 1946.

Edschmid, K. Ueber den Expressionismus in der Literatur und die neue Dichtung. Berlin, 1919.

Egan, R. F. The Genesis of the Theory of Art for Art's Sake in Germany and in England. Northampton (Mass.), 1925.

Entralgo, P. L. La generación del Noventa y ocho. Madrid, 1945.

Farmer, A. J. Le mouvement esthétique et décadent en Angleterre, 1873-1900. Paris, 1931.

Faye, P. L. Dada and the Temper of 1917. U. of Colorado Studies, 1941.

Fehr, B. Expressionismus in der neuesten englischen Lyrik. Festschrift M. Förster. Leipzig, 1929.

Feibelman, J. Decline of Literary Chaos. Sewanee Rev., 54, 1946.

Filon, A. Le symbolisme anglais et l'art français. Journal des Débats, 22.II.1899.

Flora, F. Dal romanticismo al futurismo. Piacenza, 1922.

Fraenkel, C. Studien zur sozialistischen Arbeiterlyrik in Frankreich vom Beginn des 19. Jahrhunderts bis zum Ausbruch des Weltkrieges. Diss. Breslau, 1935.

Françon, M. Poésie pure et art pour art. FR, 20, 1946.

Frierson, W. C. The English Controversy over Realism in Fiction, 1885-95. PMLA, 1928.

Gabele, A. Schnörkeldichtung. Literatur, December, 1935.

Geiger, L. Das junge Deutschland. Berlin, 1907.

Gilsoul, R. La théorie de l'art pour l'art chez les écrivains belges de 1830 à nos jours. Bruxelles, 1936.

Grundmann, K. Die Entdeckung des Biedermeier in der Literatur. Neofilologa (Warschau), 1935.

Guérard, A. Art for Art's Sake. Boston, 1936.

Hamann, R. Der Impressionismus in Leben und Kunst. Marburg, 1923.

Hatzfeld, H. Der französische Symbolismus. München, 1923.

—— Discussion sur le naturalisme français. SPh, 39, 1942.

Henríquez-Ureña, P. Literary Currents in Hispanic America. Harvard U. P., 1945.

Hiler, H. Why Expressionism? Hollywood, 1946.

Hourcade, P. Panorama du modernisme littéraire en Portugal. Coimbra, 1930.
Huelsenbeck, R. En avant Dada: eine Geschichte des Dadaismus. Hannover, 1920.
Isaza y Calderón, B. El retorno a la naturaleza. Madrid, 1934.
Johansen, S. Le Symbolisme. Copenhague, 1945.
Keller, Marie V. Der Expressionismus als geschichtliche und philosophische Erscheinung. Menasha (Wis.), 1939.
Knevels, W. Expressionismus und Religion. Tübingen, 1927.
Landsberger, F. Impressionismus und Expressionismus. Leipzig, 1919.
Larrea, J. El surrealismo entre viejo y nuevo mundo. México, 1946.
Lebowitz, M. Concerning Realism in Literature. Journal of Philosophy, 39, 1942.
Lemaître, G. E. From Cubism to Surrealism in French Literature. Harvard U. P., 1941.
Levin, H. The Definition of Realism. CL, 2, 1950.
Lirondelle, A. La poésie de l'art pour l'art en Russie et sa destinée. Rev. des Etudes slaves, 1, 1921.
Lote, G. La poétique du symbolisme: poésie et musique; la synesthésie. RCC, 15, 1934.
MacAndrew, R. M. Naturalism in Spanish Poetry from the Origins to 1900. Aberdeen, 1931.
Máchal, J. O symbolismu v literature polské a ruské. Praha, 1935.
Mathews, A. J. La Wallonie, 1886-92: The Symbolist Movement in Belgium. New York, 1947.
Melegari, Dora. La giovine Italia e la giovine Europa. Milano, 1906.
Mohrenschildt, D. S. von. The Russian Symbolist Movement. PMLA, 53.
Monguió, L. Sobre la caracterización del modernismo. RIA, 7, 1943.
Morrissette, B. A. Les aspects fondamentaux de l'esthétique symboliste. Diss. Clermont-Ferrand, 1933.
Nadeau, M. Histoire du surréalisme. Paris, 1945.
Namier, L. B. 1848: The Revolution of the Intellectuals. London, 1944.
Necco, G. Realismo e idealismo nella letteratura tedesca moderna. Bari, 1937.
Panizza, O. Die deutschen Symbolisten. Gegenwart, 1895.
Paulsen, W. Expressionismus und Aktivismus. Bern, 1935.
Pierre-Quint, L. Le surréalisme fut-il un échec? Confluences, N. S., 1945.
Randall, A. W. G. The Neo-Classic Movement in 20th Century German Drama. New Europe, 13, 1919-20.
Reinhardt, K. F. The Expressionist Movement in Recent German Literature. GR, 6, 1931.
Röhl, H. Der Naturalismus. Leipzig, 1927.
Root, W. H. German Naturalism and its Literary Predecessors. GR, 23, 1948.
Rose, W. & Isaacs, J. Contemporary Movements in European Literature. London, 1928.
Rosenblatt, L. L'idée de l'art pour l'art dans la littérature anglaise pendant la période victorienne. Paris, 1931.
Rudler, M. Parnassiens, symbolistes et décadents. Paris, 1938.
Samuel, R. & Thomas, R. H. Expressionism in German Life, Literature, and the Theatre (1910-24). Cambridge, 1939.
Schmid, E. Französischer Romantizismus und deutsche Neuromantik. Das neue Leben, 1.
Schmidt, A. M. Destinée du surréalisme. Rev. des Sciences hum., 1947.
Schmidt, L. Die Stellung der Wiener Biedermeier Dichtung zu Volkstum und Volkskultur. GRM, 26.
Schuman, D. W. Expressionism and Post-Expressionism in German Lyrics. GR, 9, 1934.
Stahl, E. L. The Genesis of Symbolist Theories in Germany. MLR, 41, 1946.
Strehler, G. Vita e carattere del teatro espressionisto in Germania. Società Nuova, 1, 1945.
Symons, A. The Symbolist Movement in Literature. New York, 1919.
—— Impressionistic Writing. In: Dramatis Personae. Indianapolis, 1923.
Thon, L. Die Sprache des deutschen Impressionismus. Wortkunst. (München), 1928.
Umphrey, G. W. Fifty Years of Modernism in Spanish-American Poetry. MLQ, 1, 1940.
Utitz, T. Die Ueberwindung des Expressionismus. Stuttgart, 1927.
Volkmann, E. Zwischen Romantik und Biedermeier. Leipzig, 1938.
Vossler, K. Italienische Literatur der Gegenwart von der Romantik zum Futurismus. Heidelberg, 1914.
—— Poesía simbólica y neosimbolista. Revista cubana, 15, 1941.
Walzel, O. Biedermeier. Bull. of the Internat. Committee of Histor. Sciences. Paris, 1937.
Weigem, P. Berliner Biedermeier. Leben,

Kunst und Kultur in Alt-Berlin zwischen 1815 und 1848. Bielefeld, 1942.
Weinberg, B. French Realism: The Critical Reaction, 1830-70. New York, 1937.
Worringer, W. Nach-Expressionismus. Leipzig, 1926.
Zolnai, B. Le style biedermeier dans la littérature. Acta, 7, 1935.

2. Individual Authors.

Lauterbach, U. H. **BANG**: Studien zum dänischen Impressionismus. Breslau, 1937.
Turnell, G. M. **BAUDELAIRE**, the Symbolists, and Mr. T. S. Eliot. Cambridge Rev., 51, 1930.
Camugli, G. Les événements de la monarchie de juillet et leurs répercussions italiennes, vus à travers les sonnets en dialecte romain de G. **BELLI**. REI, 1936.
Vossler, K. Simbolismo **DANTESCO** e simbolismo moderno. Cult., 1933.
Le Fort, E. C. Some Trends in Contemporary Spanish-American Letters: Rubén **DARIO** and the Modernista Movement. U. of Miami Hispanic-American Studies. (Coral Gables, Fla.), 1941.
Walcutt, C. C. The Three Stages of Theodore **DREISER'S** Naturalism. PMLA, 55, 1940.
Weydt, G. Naturschilderung bei A. von **DROSTE-HUELSHOFF** und A. Stifter. Beiträge zum Biedermeierstil in der Literatur des 19. Jahrhunderts. Berlin, 1930.
Anon. **GERVINUS** über die der Julirevolution vorausgehende Bewegung in der europäischen Dichtung und Wissenschaft. WM, 21, 1867.
Koehler, E. E. und J. de **GONCOURT**, die Begründer des Impressionismus. Diss. Marburg. Leipzig, 1912.
Thomése, I. A. Romantik und Neuromantik mit besonderer Berücksichtigung Hugo von **HOFMANNSTHALS**. Den Haag, 1923.
Stahl, E. L. **HOELDERLIN** and Symbolism. MLR, 38, 1943.
—— Symbolism in Hoelderlin's Poetry. MLR, 39, 1944.
Kroner, A. Die Technik des realistischen Dramas bei **IBSEN** und Galsworthy. Leipzig, 1935.
Mesirca, G. Jules **LAFORGUE** e l'impressionismo. Rassegna d'Italia, 1947.
Sandomirsky, Vera. Eduard **MOERIKE**, sein Verhältnis zum Biedermeier. Erlangen, 1935.
Hudson, W. H. **ROUSSEAU** and Naturalism in Life and Thought. Edinburgh, 1903.
Richardson, Dorothy. **SAINTSBURY** and Art for Art's Sake in England. PMLA, 59, 1944.
García Bacca, J. D. Existencialismo alemán y existencialismo francés: Heidegger y **SARTRE**. Cuadernos Americanos, 6, 1947.
Hardré, J. The Existentialism of Jean Paul Sartre. Carolina Quart., 1, (Chapel Hill, N. C.) 1949.
Marchiori, I. Il verismo di Boris **STANKOVIC** narratore serbo. RLM, 1, 1946.
Jones, C. E. Proletarian Writing and John **STEINBECK**. Sewanee Rev., 48, 1940.
Holske, A. **STIFTER** and the Biedermeier Crisis. Festschrift J. A. Walz. Lancaster (Pa.), 1941.
Zeydel, E. H. L. **TIECK** und das Biedermeier. GRM, 26.
Winwar, Frances. Oscar **WILDE** and the Yellow Nineties. New York, 1940.

THIRD PART

International Literary Relations. Collective and Reciprocal Influences upon Continents, Nations and Individuals.

CHAPTER ONE

America and Europe.

(Mutual Relations and European Influences in General. For Specific Influences See Specific Countries).

Anon. Frankreich und England in Nordamerika. MLIA, 1877.

Baldensperger, F. Les contacts historiques de la civilisation alsacienne et lorraine avec les Etats-Unis d'Amérique. Messager d'Alsace-Lorraine, 1919.

—— Quelques contacts historiques avec les Etats-Unis. Alsace française, 12.XI.1921.

—— Note sur un des premiers contacts intellectuels entre l'Allemagne et l'Amérique. RLC, 8, 1928.

—— Notes pour l'histoire des relations intellectuelles entre l'Amérique du Sud et l'Europe. RLC, 11, 1931.

Barja, C. Crisis europea. Cultura americana. Memoria del tercer Congreso . . . de Lit. Iberoamer., 1944.

Baumgarten, F. et al. Ibero-Amerika und die Hansestädte. Die Entwicklung ihrer wirtschaftlichen und kulturellen Beziehungen. Hamburg, 1937.

Bernstein, H. Las primeras relaciones entre New England y el mundo hispánico. Rev. hispánica moderna, 5, 1939.

Bilgray, Ruth. Foreign Plays on the American Stage, 1870-1900. Diss. U. of Chicago, 1941.

Bjork, K. et al. Norwegian-American Studies and Records. Northfield (Minn.), 1940.

Boutroux, E. La pensée américaine et la pensée française. Revue pédagogique, 1913.

Bowers, D. F. (ed.). Foreign Influences in American Life: Essays and Critical Bibliographies. Princeton, 1944.

Boyd, Alice K. The Interchange of Plays between London and New York 1910-1939. New York, 1949.

Bruce, P. A. Some American Impressions of Europe. NC, 1901.

Cano, S. Influencias de Europa sobre la cultura de la América española. Ateneo, 141, 1938.

Chasles, P. Les Américains en Europe et les Européens aux Etate-Unis. RDM, 1843.

Coolidge, A. C. Theoretical and Foreign Elements in the Formation of the American Constitution. Diss. Freiburg, 1892.

Deschamps, G. America and France. NAR, 1902.

Duden, G. Europa und Deutschland von Nord-Amerika aus betrachtet. 2 vols. Bonn, 1833-35.

Duggan, S. Foreign Influences upon American Culture and Education. FR, 16, 1943.

Duprey, J. La culture occidentale en Europe et en Amérique latine. Cahiers français. (Montevideo), 1938.

Eidson, J. O. Innocents Abroad, Then and Now. Georgia Review, 2, 1948.

Escott, T. H. S. New World Muses and Old World Helicons. Cosmopolis, Jan., 1897.

Fay, B. Learned Societies in Europe and America in the XVIIIth Century. AHR, 1932.

Fischer, E. The Passing of the European Age. Harvard U. P., 1943.

Fischer, W. Angloamerikanische Kultur- und Literaturbeziehungen in neuerer Zeit. Archiv, 184, 1943.

Frenz, H. American Drama and World Drama. College English, 6, 1945.

Friederich, W. P. Werden und Wachsen der U. S. A. in 300 Jahren. Bern, 1939.

Friederici, G. Der Charakter der Entdeckung und Eroberung Amerikas durch die Europäer. 3 vols. Stuttgart, 1925-36.

Goggio, E. First Personal Contacts Between American and Italian Leaders of Thought. RR, 1936.

Gordon, G. S. Anglo-American Literary Relations. Oxford U. P., 1942.

Hagemann, W. Lateinischer und angelsächsischer Geist in Amerika. DR, 1927.

Hall, R. A. Appunti d'italo-americano. Lingua Nostra, 8, 1947.

Hanotaux, G. North America and France. NAR, 1912.

Hazard, P. Les relations intellectuelles entre l'Europe et l'Amérique latine. RLC, 1931.

Imhoof, W. Der Europamüde in der deutschen Erzählungsliteratur. Zürich, 1930.

Jones, H. M. The Influence of European Ideas in XIXth Century America. AL, 1935.
—— American Literature and the Melting Pot. Southwest Rev., 26, 1941.
Kapp, F. Amerikanisch-deutsche Beziehungen. DR, 1880.
Kirkconnell, W. European Elements in Canadian Life. Toronto, 1940.
Kraus, M. Literary Relations Between Europe and America in the Eighteenth Century. William & Mary Quart., 1, 1944.
Laboulaye, E. Les Etats-Unis et la France. Paris, 1862.
Lamb, G. F. Some Anglo-American Literary Contacts. QR, 1947.
Long, O. W. Literary Pioneers, Early American Explorers of European Culture. Harvard U. P., 1935.
Lowell, J. R. The Study of Modern Languages and their Addition to our Resources. In: Latest Literary Essays and Adresses. Boston, 1889.
Parkman, F. Frankreich und England in Nordamerika. Vorwort von Fr. Kapp. Stuttgart, 1876.
Patrick, W. & Taylor, C. A Louisiana French Plantation Library, 1842. FAR, 1, 1948.
Pochmann, H. A. Early German-American Journalistic Exchanges. HLQ, 11, 1948.
Richardson, Ruth. Corrientes recíprocas entre el teatro hispánico y el nuestro. Memoria del segundo Congreso . . . de Lit. Iberoamer., 1941.
Rosenthal, L. America and France. New York, 1881.
Schönemann, F. Die Beziehungen der Vereinigten Staaten von Amerika zu Europa. NM, 11.
—— Die Dankesschuld der U. S. A. gegen Europa. ZNS, 1943.
Scott, J. B. Les Etats-Unis et la France: quelques opinions sur la reconnaissance internationale. Paris, 1928.
Sellin, A. W. Deutsche Dichtungen in Brasilien und brasilianische Dichtungen in Deutschland. MLIA, 1885.
Shelley, P. A. Annuals and Gift-Books as American Intermediaries of Foreign Literature. CLN, 3, 1945.
Thoreau, H. Advantages and Disadvantages of Foreign Influence on American Literature. (1836).
Urwin, K. Uruguayan Literature and Europe. CLS, 16, 1945.
Vossler, O. Die amerikanischen Revolutionsideale in ihrem Verhältnis zu den europäischen. München, 1930.
Williams, S. T. Tradition and Rebellion: European Patterns in the Literature of America. In: Studies in Civilization. Philadelphia, 1941.
Wilson, R. R. Foreign Authors in America. Bookman, Jan., 1901 ff.
Wittke, C. Melting-Pot Literature. College English, 7, 1946.
Yancey, Myra L. Some Notes on the Knowledge of Foreign Literatures in Nineteenth Century Mexico. Hisp., 24, 1941.
Yvon, P. Les crises de la morale et de la moralité dans l'histoire de la civilisation et de la littérature des pays anglosaxons. RCC, 1936.

CHAPTER TWO

Asia and Europe.

(Mutual Relations and Western Influences upon the East. For Asiatic Influences in Europe, see II. I. 1-7. See also Comparisons, I. V. 1.)

Anon. Orient et Occident. Nouvelles Essais critiques, July, 1926.
Alsdorf, L. Deutsch-indische Geistesbeziehungen. Heidelberg, 1942.
Autremart, F. d'. Les premiers rapports de l'Europe et du Japon. Revue hebdomadaire, 23.III.1895.
Bachofen, J. J. Der Mythos von Orient und Occident. München, 1926.
Baldensperger, F. Où l'Orient et l'Occident s'affrontent. RLC, 2, 1922. And in: Etudes d'histoire littéraire, 4. Paris, 1939.
Barbagallo, C. L'Oriente e l'Occidente nel mondo romano. NRS, 6, 1922.
Benfey, T. Orient und Occident, insbesondere in ihren gegenseitigen Beziehungen. 3 vols. Göttingen, 1862-65.
Bernard, H. S. J. Les premiers rapports de la culture européenne avec la civilisation japonaise. Paris, 1938.
Chew, S. C. The Crescent and the Rose. Islam and England during the Renaissance. Oxford, 1937.
Childe, V. G. India and the West Before Darius. Antiquity, March, 1939.
—— The Orient and Europe. American Journal of Archeology, 43, 1939.
Conradi, A. Kulturbeziehungen zwischen China und dem Abendlande. Die Erde, 2, 1914.
Crewdson, W. The Dawn of Western Influence in Japan. Transactions and Proceedings of the Japan Society, 6. London, 1906.

Dasgupta, J. K. Western Influence on Bengali Literature. Calcutta Review, 3rd Ser., 41, 1931.
—— Western Influence on Some Bengali Poets. Ibid. 50-52, 1934.
Duprat, E. Les relations de la Provence et du Levant du Ve siècle aux Croisades. Séances et Travaux du Congrès français de la Syrie, 2, 1919.
Duyvendak, J. J. L. De betrekkingen tusschen China en het Westen in den loop der geschiednis. China, 2, 1927.
Faure, E. Orient et Occident. MF, 1931.
Franke, O. Beziehungen der Inder zum Westen. ZDMG, 1893.
Goetz, W. Orient und Abendland. AK, 16, 1925-26.
Gotô, S. Les premiers échanges de civilisation entre l'Extrême-Orient et l'Occident dans les temps modernes. RLC, 8, 1928.
Hempel, J. Westliche Kultureinflüsse auf das alte Palästina. Palästina Jb., 23, 1927.
Horn, P. Morgenland und Abendland. ZVL, 15, 1903.
Hudson, G. F. Europe and China: A Survey of their Relations from the Earliest Times to 1800. London, 1931.
Hughes, E. R. The Invasion of China by the Western World. London, 1937.
Janse, O. L'Empire des steppes et les relations entre l'Europe et l'Extrême-Orient dans l'antiquité. Rev. des Arts asiatiques, 9, 1935.
Kohn, H. Die Europäisierung Asiens. Berlin, 1934.
—— Western Civilization in the Near East. New York, 1936.
Kuemmel, O. Die ältesten Beziehungen zwischen Europa und Ostasien nach den Ergebnissen neuerer Ausgrabungen in China. Deutsche Forschung, 5, 1928.
Levi, S. L'Inde et le monde. Paris, 1926.
—— Essai sur l'humanisme. RP, 1925.
Littmann. Abendländisches Sprachgut im Morgenlande. Sprachkunde, 1943.
Malraux, A. La tentation de l'Occident. Paris, 1926.
Massis, H. Orient et Occident. Revue des Jeunes, 1926.
—— Défense de l'Occident. Paris, 1927. Cf. Oberländer Tagblatt (Thun), 1927.
Mazeaud, L. L'oeuvre française de collaboration intellectuelle au Japon. France-Japon, 43-44, 1939.
Miller, W. The Latins in the Levant: a History of Frankish Greece, (1204-1566). New York, 1908.
Montbrial, F. de. Les influences intellectuelles du monde occidental au Japon. Revue des Sciences politiques, 1935.
Nissen, H. Der Verkehr zwischen China und dem Römischen Reiche. Bonner Jb., 95, 1894.
Nitobé, J. et al. Western Influences in Modern Japan. U. of Chicago P., 1932.
Ouang-Ki-Tseng. Influence des ouvrages étrangers traduits en chinois pendant les dix dernières années. Bull. de l'Assoc. amicale franco-chinoise, 1909.
Rawlinson, H. G. Intercourse between India and the Western World from the Earliest Times to the Fall of Rome. Cambridge U. P., 1916.
Reichwein, A. China and Europe. Intellectual and Artistic Contacts in the XVIIIth Century. New York, 1925.
Siassi, A. A. La Perse au contact de l'Occident. Diss., Paris, 1931.
Steffen, R. Der Künstler zwischen Westen und Osten. Zürich, 1925.
Tagore, R. Western Influence in Bengali Literature. Calcutta Review, 3rd. Ser., 46, 1933.
Tanigawa, T. Orient et Occident. France-Japon, 45, 1939.
Tongas, G. Les relations de la France avec l'empire ottoman durant la première moitié du 17e siècle. Paris, 1942.
Vambery, A. La culture occidentale en Orient. (In Hungarian). Magyar Tud. Akad., 1906.
Vindel, F. La cultura y la imprenta europeas en el Japón durante los siglos XVI y XVII. La iniciativa española. Madrid, 1943.
Wesselski, A. Einstige Brücken zwischen Orient und Occident. Archiv Orientalni, 1, 1929.
Wilke, G. Kulturbeziehungen zwischen Indien, Orient und Europa. Würzburg, 1913.

CHAPTER THREE

The Slavs and the Western World.

(Mutual Relations and Western Influences in General. For Specific Influences See Specific Countries. For Individual Authors, See Chapter Thirteen).

Alekseev, M. P. Russian Literature and the West. In: Russian Literature in the West. Acad. of Sciences, Leningrad, 1945.
Alekseev, N. A. Das russische Westertum. Der Russische Gedanke, 2, 1929.
Ancel, J. Slaves et germains. Paris, 1945.

Berkovskii, N. I. The West and Questions of Russian Peculiarities in Literature. In: Russian Literature in the West. Leningrad, 1945.
Bielozerskaia, Mme. Influence des traductions de romans et de la civilisation occidentale sur la culture russe du XVIIIe siècle. Antiquité russe, 1895.
Bittner, K. Methodologisches zur vergleichenden germanisch-slavischen Literaturwissenschaft. GS, 3, 1935.
Brackmann, A. Die Anfänge der abendländischen Kulturbewegung in Osteuropa und deren Träger. Jb. f. d. Geschichte Osteuropas, 1938.
Brehièr, L. Normal Relations Between East and West Before the Schism of the XIth Century. Constructive Quart., 4, 1916.
Brueckner, A. Die Europäisierung Russlands. Gotha, 1888.
Brueggen, E. van der. Wie Russland europäisch wurde. In: Studien zur Kulturgeschichte. Leipzig, 1885.
Cross, S. H. American-Soviet Relations. SEER, 22, 1944.
Danilevsky. La Russie et l'Europe. (In Russian). Saint-Pétersbourg, 1871.
Deanovic, M. Sui rapporti culturali fra gli italiani e gli slavi meridionali attraverso i secoli. L'Europa orientale, 20, 1940.
Dumont-Wilden, L. Le slavisme et la culture française. Curieux (Neuchâtel), 6.II.1947.
Lo Gatto, E. Europa e Russia nella storia e nel pensiero russo. L'Europe Orientale, 1928.
Lappo-Danilevski. Rapports des russes avec l'Europe occidentale. Journal du Ministère de l'Instruction Publique, May, 1884.
Lieb, F. Das westeuropäische Gedankenleben im Urteil russischer Religionsphilosophie. Tübingen, 1929.
Masaryk, T. G. Russland und Europa. 2 vols. Jena, 1913.
Maver, G. I contatti letterari della Polonia con le nazioni occidentali. Bull. of the Internat. Committee of Historical Sciences, 5. Paris, 1933.
Orvicz, A. La pensée européenne du XVIe au XVIIIe siècle et la littérature slovène. RLC, 14, 1934.
Paquet, A. Deutsche und Slawen. Der Neue Merkur, 6, 1922.
Peisker, J. Die älteren Beziehungen der Slawen und Turko-Tartaren und Germanen. Vierteljahrsschrift für Social- und Wirtschaftsgeschichte, 3, 1905.
Pezold, T. Westeuropäische Einflüsse auf den Entwicklungsgang der neueren russischen Litteratur. Baltische Monatsschrift, 1, 1898.
Seifert, L. J. Das Abendland und die Slaven. Das Abendland, 1.III.1926.
Simmons, E. J. Russian and Western Culture. Queens Quarterly, 51, 1944.
Sozonovitch. Les influences occidentales dans la poésie slave et russe. (In Russian). Varsovie, 1898.
Spina, F. Beiträge zu den deutsch-slavischen Literaturbeziehungen. Prag, 1909.
Vasmer M,. Bausteine zur Geschichte der deutsch-slavischen geistigen Beziehungen. Berlin, 1939.
Veselovskii (Wesselowsky), A. Influences occidentales dans la littérature russe. (In Russian). Moskva, 1896.
—— Der westeuropäische Einfluss in der Literatur der Russisch-Armenier. In: Pod znamenem nauki. Moskva, 1902.
—— Western Influence in the New Russian Literature. (In Russian). Moskva, 1910.

CHAPTER FOUR

Romania and Germania.

(Western Traditions, Romance and Germanic Literatures and their Inter-Relations.)

Baldensperger, F. Les influences étrangères dans le romantisme français: le Nord. Annales de l'U. de Paris, 1928.
Bertoni, G. Origini delle letterature romanze nel pensiero dei romantici tedeschi. AR, 23, 1939.
Bidermann, H. J. Die Romanen und ihre Verbreitung in Oesterreich. Graz, 1877.
Carstensen, R. Skandinavisch-romanische Wechselbeziehungen. NM, 10.
Chamberlain, H. S. Classicität und Germanismus. Wiener Rundschau, 7, 1900.
Chasles, P. Du Nord et de son influence sur la civilisation actuelle. Rev. du Nord, 1, 1835.
Counson, A. La pensée romane. Paris, 1912.
Curtius, E. R. Civilisation et germanisme. BURS, 1927.
Errante G,. Sulla lirica romanza delle origini. New York, 1943.
Finzi, G. Lira italica e lira nordica; saggio sopra le due grandi correnti della letteratura europea. Torino, 1914.
Franco, C. & Méléar, P. Virgile, Dante, Camoëns et l'expansion du génie latin. Paris, 1924.

Frings, T. Französisch und fränkisch. ZRPh, 62-63, 1942-43.
Gamillscheg, E. Französisch und fränkisch. ZFSL, 62.
Gebhart, E. Etudes méridionales. Paris, 1887.
Giuliano, B. Latinität und Deutschtum. Köln, 1941.
Glaser, K. Germanisme. ZFSL, 53, 1929.
Harder, H. Das germanische Erbe in der deutschen Dichtung von der Frühzeit bis zur Gegenwart. Potsdam, 1939.
Hazard, P. Les premiers contacts des littératures du Nord avec l'esprit latin en Italie. SVL, 9, 1909.
—— L'invasion des littératures du nord dans l'Italie du XVIIIe siècle. RLC, 1, 1921.
Heidenstam, V. von. Klassicität und Germanismus. Wien, 1900.
Heiss, H. Schürr, F. & Jeschke, H. Die romanischen Literaturen des 19. und 20. Jahrhunderts. In: Handbuch der Literaturwissenschaft. Potsdam, 1935.
Kaluza, M. Romanische Einflüsse auf die englische Litteratur des Mittelalters. Krit. Jahresbericht über d. Fortschritte der roman. Philologie, 5, 1903.
Klemperer, V., Hatzfeld, H. & Neubert, F. Die romanischen Literaturen von der Renaissance bis zur frangösischen Revolution. In: Handbuch der Literaturwissenschaft. Potsdam, 1928.
Klemperer, V. L'idée de latinité en Allemagne. Dante, 1934.
Koch, C. F. Der Angelsachse im Kampfe mit dem Normannen. Progr. Eisenach, 1858.
Koelbing, E. Romanische Einflüsse auf die nordische und englische Litteratur des Mittelalters. Krit. Jahresbericht über Fortschritte der roman. Philologie, 1-4, 1890-1900.
Koerting, G. Encyclopädie und Methodologie der romanischen Philologie. Litteraturwissenschaft, 1894.
Kossina, G. Germanische Kultur im ersten Tausend nach Christus. Leipzig, 1932.
Lear, F. S. et al. Western Tradition from Rome to Britain. Rice Institute Pamphlet, 29, (Texas), 1942.
Le Cardonnel, G. Latinisme et germanisme. Rev. universelle, 1920.
Lemaître, J. De l'influence récente des littératures du Nord. RDM, 1894.
Magin-Marrens. De l'influence de l'élément germanique dans la civilisation moderne. Mém de la Société royale des Sciences. Nancy, 1844.
Mariana, G. Romania e Germania, il mondo germanico secondo le relazione di Tacito nei suoi veri caratteri, rapporti ed influenza sul mondo romano. Wochenschrift f. klass. Philologie, 19, 1892 & Jena, 1900.
Missiroli, M. Romanità e germanesimo. Roma, 1942.
Moenius, G. Le germanisme contre la romanité. Rev. universelle, 15.VI.1929.
Mortensen, J. Klassicitet och germanismen. Forum, May, 1920.
Neubert, F. Gegenwartsaufgaben der Romanistik. Neuphilol. Monatshefte, 9, 1938.
Oppel, H. Die Begegnuug romanischer Sprache mit germanisch-deutscher Dichtung. D&V, 39, 1938.
Pagano, A. Il concetto di latinità. Augustea, 31.III.1929.
Peiser, W. Forma latina y espíritu romano, como base de la literatura iberoamericana. Memoria del segundo Congreso . . . de Lit. Iberoamer., 1941.
Pogatscher, A. Angelsachsen und Romanen. ESn, 19, 1895.
Rohlfs, G. Germanisches Spracherbe in der Romania. ABAW, 1947.
Rosenqvist, A. Ueber Wanderung romanischer Fremdwörter im Deutschen. Annales Acad. Scientiarum Fennicae. Helsinki. 1942.
Roux, G. Germanisme et latinité. Nouvelle Rev. de Hongrie, 1935.
Sazo, L. L'Europe latine: les deux soeurs. Ibid, 1939.
Sismondi. Histoire des littératures du Midi de l'Europe. 4 vols. Paris, 1813.
Stengel, E. Beiträge zur Geschichte der romanischen Philologie in Deutschland. Marburg, 1886.
Suhr E,. G. Two Currents in the Thought Stream of Europe. Baltimore, 1942.
Thurau, G. Romanisches im deutschen Liederschatz. Teutonia. (Königsberg), 1902.
Valette, J. Echanges poétiques internationaux. MF, 1947.
Varia. England and the Mediterranean Tradition. Oxford U. P., 1946.
Villari, P. La civiltà latina e la civiltà germanica. In: Saggi storici e critici. Bologna, 1890.
Voretzsch, C. Die Anfänge der romanischen Philologie an den deutschen Universitäten. Tübingen, 1904.
Vossler, K. Die romanischen Kulturen und der deutsche Geist. München, 1926.
—— Südliche Romania. München, 1940.
Wallenskoeld, A. Les rapports entre la poésie lyrique romane et la poésie al-

lemande au moyen âge. Neuphilol. Mitteilungen. (Helsingfors), 1900.
Weckowski, S. Die romanischen Einflüsse in der polnischen Litteratur bis zum Ausgange des XVII. Jahrhunderts. Diss. Breslau, 1901.
Weisgerber, L. Deutsch und Welsch. Die Anfänge des Volksbewusstseins in Westeuropa. Bonn, 1943.
Winkler, E. Vom Geiste romanischer Dichtung. Zs. f. deutsche Geisteswissenschaft, 1939.

CHAPTER FIVE

England and Other Nations.

(See also Comparisons, I. V. 1.)

Lefèvre, J. L'Angleterre et la **BELGIQUE** à travers les cinq derniers siècles. Paris, 1946.
Vocadlo, O. Anglie a Cechy. (**CZECHOSLOVAKIA**). Lumir, 57, 1931.
Christopherson, C. Early Anglo-**DANISH** Literary Relations. Norseman, Oct., 1945.
Downs, B. W. Anglo-Danish Literary Relations, 1867-1900. MLR, 39, 1944.
Lukman, N. British and Danish Traditions. Some Contacts and Relations. Classica et Mediaevalia, 6, 1944.
Anon. La **FRANCE** et la Grande-Bretagne: des rapports littéraires. Revue Européenne, Aug. 1824.
Baldensperger, F. Quelques-uns de nos préférés anglo-français. Annual Bull. of the Mod. Human. Research Assoc., 1931.
Bastide, C. Anglais et Français au XVIIe siècle. Paris, 1912.
—— The Anglo-French Entente in the Seventeenth Century. London, 1914.
Battur, G. B. De l'Angleterre et de la France dans leurs rapports moraux et littéraires. Paris Monthly Rev., Dec., 1822.
Bezzola, R. R. Der französisch-englische Kulturkreis und die Erneuerung der europäischen Literatur im 12. Jahrhundert. ZRPh, 62, 1942.
Bond, D. American Scholarship in the Field of XVIIIth Century Anglo-French Studies. RR, 1938.
Bréreton, C. Intellectual Combines in France and England. Contemp. Rev., 1923.
Caussy, F. Propos sur l'influence mutuelle de la France et de l'Angleterre. Ermitage, 15.XII.1905.
Elkington, M. E. Les relations de société entre l'Angleterre et la France sous la Restauration (1814-30). Paris, 1929.
Gosse, E. France et Angleterre: l'avenir de leurs relations intellectuelles. RDM, 1.X.1916.
Green, F. C. Minuet: A Critical Survey of French and English Literary Ideas in the Eighteenth Century. London, 1935.
Hamilton, G. Les rapports franco-britanniques. RHPhC, 1946.
Hood, A. An Englishwoman and a Frenchman. Literature, 1.VI.1901.
Jusserand, J. J. Anciennes relations littéraires entre la France et l'Angleterre. In: Shakespeare en France. Paris, 1898.
Liebermann, F. England und Frankreich im 12. Jahrhundert. Archiv, 104, 1900.
Littleboy, A. L. Relations between French and English Literature in the XVIth and XVIIth Century. London, 1895.
Lockitt, C. H. The Relations of French and English Society (1763-93). London, 1920.
Mackenzie, F. Les relations de l'Angleterre et de la France d'après le vocabulaire. Paris, 1939.
Mortimer, R. La France et la littérature anglaise. RHPhC, 1946.
Rathéry, J. B. Des relations sociales et intellectuelles entre la France et l'Angleterre. Rev. Contemporaine 1855, & Paris, 1860.
Reinach, J. The Proper Sympathy Between France and England. NC, 1885.
Rivers, J. How Great Minds Jump. The Library, 1903.
Saroléa, C. Le commerce des idées entre la France et l'Angleterre. Revue de Belgique, 1896-97.
—— Le caractère anglais et le caractère français. In: Essais de littérature et de politique. Bruxelles, 1906.
Strachey, L. Books and Characters, French and English. London, 1922.
Symons, A. Studies in Two Literatures. London, 1897.
Temple, Ruth Z. Some Notes on Anglo-French Literary Relations in the Late Nineteenth Century. CLN, 2, 1944.
Tinker, C. B. The Salon and the English Letters. New York, 1915.
Troplong, E. De la fidélité des Gascons aux Anglais pendant le moyen âge. Rev. d'hist. diplomatique, 16, 1902.
Witt, C. de. La société française et la société anglaise au XVIIIe siècle. Paris, 1864.

Woods, M. L. A Literary Entente. Fortnightly Rev., 1921.
Woodward. Charactères généraux des relations franco-anglaises entre 1815 et 1870. Rev. d'histoire moderne, 1938.
Yvon, P. Traits d'union normands avec l'Angleterre, avant, pendant et après la Révolution. Diss. Caen. London, 1919.
Allen, D. C. Early 18th Century Literary Relations Between England and **GERMANY**. MLN, 1934.
Franz, W. Der Wert der englischen Kultur für die deutsche Entwicklung. Tübingen, 1913.
Herford, C. H. Studies in the Literary Relations of England and Germany in the Sixteenth Century. Cambridge, 1886.
Hohlfeld, A. R. Der Litteraturbetrieb in der Schule mit besonderer Rüchsicht auf die gegenseitigen Beziehungen der englisch-deutschen Litteratur. Pädagog. Monatshefte, 1902.
Koch, M. Ueber die Beziehungen der englischen Litteratur zur deutschen im XVIII. Jahrhundert. Leipzig, 1883.
Koszul, A. Les relations entre l'Alsace et l'Angleterre au XVIe siècle. RLC, 9, 1929.
Price, L. M. English-German Literary Influences. Bibliography and Survey. Berkeley, 1919.
Seidensticker, O. The Relation of English to German Literature in the 18th Century. PL, 2, 1890.
Waterhouse, G. The Literary Relations of England and Germany in the Seventeenth Century. Cambridge, 1914.
Ziegler, T. Beiträge zur Geschichte der deutsch-englischen Literaturbeziehungen. SVL, 1901.
Bense, J. F. The Anglo-Dutch Relations from the Earliest Times to the Death of William the Third. **(HOLLAND)**. 's Gravenhagen, 1924; London, 1926.
Downs, B. W. Anglo-Dutch Literary Relations, 1867-1900. MLR, 31, 1936.
Hoog, W. de. Studien over de nederlandsche en engelsche taal en letterkunde. Dordrecht, 1902-03.
Russel, J. A. Dutch Poetry and English. Amsterdam, 1939.
Fraenkel, L. Romanische, insbesondere italienische Wechselbeziehungen zur englischen Literatur. **(ITALY)**. Erlangen, 1900.
Praz, M. Ricerche anglo-italiane. Roma, 1944.
—— Rapporti tra la letteratura italiana e la letteratura inglese. In: Letterature comparate (ed. by A. Momigliano). Milano, 1948.
Segré, C. Relazioni letterarie fra Italia e Inghilterra. Firenze, 1911.
Trevelyan, G. M. Englishmen and Italians: Some Aspects of their Relations Past and Present. PBA, 9, 1920.
Kozlowski, W. M. Notes sur les échanges des idées philosophiques entre l'Angleterre et la **POLOGNE**. RLC, 3, 1923.
Prestage, E . Chapters in Anglo-**PORTUGUESE** Relations. Watford, 1935.
Lubimenko, J. Les relations diplomatiques de l'Angleterre avec la **RUSSIE** au XVIIe siècle. Rev. histor., 153, 1926.
Tolstoy, G. The First Forty Years of Intercourse Between England and Russia, 1553-93. St. Petersburg, 1875.
Leach, H. G. Angevin Britain and **SCANDINAVIA**. Harvard U. P., 1921.
Litzenberg, K. The Victorians and the Vikings: A Bibliographical Essay on Anglo-Norse Literary Relations. Ann Arbor, 1947.
Seaton, E. Literary Relations of England and Scandinavia in the Seventeenth Century. Oxford, 1935.
Truschke, L. Fair Janet und Kong Valdemar og hans søster. Ein Beitrag zur Frage der Beziehungen zwischen englisch-schottischen und skandinavischen Volksballaden. Berlin, 1940.
Hume, M. Españoles e ingleses en el siglo XVI. **(SPAIN)**. London, 1903.
Madariaga, S. de. Ensayos anglo-españoles. Madrid, 1922.
Mathews, E. G. Studies in Spanish-English Cultural and Literary Relations. Diss. Harvard, 1938.
Varia. Sverige i England. **(SWEDEN)**. Göteborg, 1923.
Bonjour, E. Die Schweiz und England. **(SWITZERLAND)**. Ein geschichtlicher Rückblick. Bern, 1934.
Funke, O. Die Schweiz und die englische Literatur. Bern, 1937.
Lätt, A. Les relations intellectuelles entre la Grande-Bretagne et la Suisse. BURS, 1919 & Délémont, 1920.
Sismondi. Considérations sur Genève dans ses rapports avec l'Angleterre et les états protestants. Londres, 1814.
Vetter, T. Litterarische Beziehungen zwischen England und der Schweiz im Reformationszeitalter. Zürich, 1901.
Vreeland, W. W. D. Etude sur les rapports littéraires entre Genève et l'Angleterre jusqu'à la publication de la Nouvelle Héloïse. Diss. Genève, 1901.
Dusan, S. Anglo-**YUGOSLAV** Cultural Relations. Contemporary Rev., 1940.

CHAPTER SIX

France and Other Nations.

(See also Comparisons, I. V. 1.)

Koninckh, A. W. Les relation littéraires entre la **BELGIQUE** et la France. La Nef, Oct., 1946.

Anon. Eine Umfrage bei Deutschen und Franzosen. (**GERMANY**). Neue Deutsche Rundschau 7, 1893.

Abbé, D. van. Some Notes on Cultural Relations between France and Germany in the Nineteenth Century. MLQ, 8, 1947.

Becker, A. Frankreich und wir. ZEFU, 24, 1925.

Betz, L. P. Von Hüben und Drüben. LE, 1903.

Blanc, L . D'un projet d'alliance intellectuelle entre l'Allemagne et la France. Rev. Indépendante, 10.XI.1843.

Bornecque, H. & Hengesbach, J. Histoire de la littérature et de la pensée françaises dans leurs rapports avec la littérature allemande et l'histoire de l'art. Berlin, 1928.

Buechner, A. Les rapports littéraires entre la France et l'Allemagne au XVIIIe siècle. Caen, 1889.

Clement, F. Deutschland-Frankreich seit hundert Jahren. Die literar. Welt, 1929.

Closen, F. von. Die Verhältnisse von Deutschland zu Frankreich. Deutsche Vierteljahrsschrift, 1843.

Curtius, E. R. Français et Allemande peuvent-ils se comprendre? Rev. de Genève, 1922.

Despois, E. Français et Allemands. RB, 18.V.1872.

Dresch, J. France-Allemagne. NL. 4.II. 1939.

Dupouy, A. France et Allemagne: littérature comparée. Paris, 1913.

Guilbeaux, H. Sur les rapports littéraires entre la France et l'Allemagne. Revue des Français, 25.IX.1911.

Joret, C. Les rapports intellectuels et littéraires de la France avec l'Allemagne avant 1789. Paris, 1884.

—— Additions et corrections. Revue critique, 1884.

Kellermann, W. Altdeutsche und altfranzösische Literatur. GRM, 1938.

Kraemer, P. Deutscher und französischer Geist in ihren literarischen Berührungen. ZEFU, 24, 1925.

Lichtenberger, H. Psychologische Grundlagen der deutsch-französischen Annäherung. RRh, 1930.

Lote, R. Les relations franco-allemandes. Paris, 1921.

Mann, T. Deutsch-französische Beziehungen. Der neue Merkur, 5, 1922.

Marteau, J. Le romantisme, base d'entente intellectuelle entre la France et l'Allemagne. Tribune de Genève, 5.I.1938.

Mauvillon, E. Lettres françaises et germaniques ou réflexions militaires, littéraires et critiques sur les Français et les Allemands. Londres, 1740.

Maxe, J. Les relations intellectuelles franco-allemandes. MF, 15.IX.1924.

Nicolai, F. A. Die Beziehungen zwischen der deutschen und französischen Poesie im Mittelalter. Progr. Meerane, 1877.

Peyre, H. Franco-German Literary Relations in the XIXth Century. CL, 2, 1950.

Platz, H. Die Verflochtenheit des deutsch-französischen Schicksals. Abenland, 4, 1928.

Ranke, L. Deutschland und Frankreich. Histor.-polit. Zs., 1 (Hamburg), 1932.

Reinach, J. France et Allemagne. In: Etudes de littérature et d'histoire. Paris, 1889.

Reynaud, L. France et Allemagne. Paris, 1931.

Rosenberg, A. Oesterreich-französische Kulturverbindungen. Wiener Presse, 14.II.1948.

Rosenberg, R. P. American Studies in Franco-German Literary Relations. CLN, 4, 1945.

Rossel, V. Histoire des relations littéraires entre la France et l'Allemagne. Paris, 1897. Cf. RHLF, 4; MLIA, 1897; ZVL, 1898.

Rychner, M. Die intellektuellen Beziehungen zwischen Franzosen und Deutschen. Wissen & Leben, 10.V.1922.

Schirmacher, K. Deutschland und Frankreich seit 35 Jahren. Beitrag zur Kulturgeschichte. Berlin, 1907.

Semmig, H. Deutschland und Frankreich. Sonst und jetzt. MLIA, 1888.

Singer, K. Die Wende des deutschen und des französischen Geistes. Cahiers alsaciens, May, 1912.

Stössinger, F. Was ist uns Frankreich? Weltbühne, 18, 1922.

Ten Brink, J. Het jonge Duitschland en het Franschland. Amsterdammer Weekblaad, 1886.

Texte, J. Les relations littéraires de la France avec l'Allemagne avant le milieu du XVIIIe siècle. RCC, 1896.

Tissot, E. Eine Enquête über die intel-

lektuelle Annäherung Frankreichs und Deutschlands. Deutsche Revue, 1908.
Wechssler, E. Germanisches in der altfranzösischen Dichtung. Einflüsse der altfranzösischen Literatur auf die altdeutsche. Jahresbericht, 5, 1903.
Zebrowski, M. La littérature allemande et la littérature française. RCC, 1901-02.
Baldensperger, F. HOLLANDE-France. Figaro, 25.IV.1929.
Davids, W. Français et Hollandais. Revue du mois, 10.V.1912.
Cohen, G. La France à l'étranger: France-Hollande. Civilisation française, Nov., 1919.
—— Les relations littéraires de la France et de la Hollande. Monde nouveau, July, 1925.
Gallas, K. R. Les recherches sur les rapports littéraires entre la France et la Hollande pendant trois siècles. RLC, 7, 1927.
Mathorez, J. Rapports intellectuels de la France et de la Hollande, du XIIIe au XVIIIe siècle. JS, 1921.
Panne, M. C. van de. Recherches sur les rapports entre la littérature française et le théâtre hollandais. Amsterdam, 1927.
Salverda de Grave, J. J. Hollandais et Français. Revue de Hollande, 1916.
Chelard, R. De l'impossibilité d'une alliance politique et de la nécessité d'une alliance intellectuelle avec la **HONGRIE.** MF, 1901.
Olay, F. d'. Les relations littéraires franco-hongroises au XVIIIe siècle. Gazette de Hongrie, 25.III.1933.
Sörer, I. Relations hungaro-françaises. (In Hungarian). Budapest, 1946.
Zrinyi, J. Le récent rapprochement intellectuel entre la Hongrie et la France. MF, 1900.
Anon. Studi su **ITALIA** e Francia nel settecento. Marzocco, 18.V.1930.
Ancona, A. d'. Lettere di illustri scrittori francesi ad amici italiani. Rassegna bibliografica della lett. ital., 9, 1901.
Bédarida, H. Relations et échanges intellectuels entre la France et l'Italie de 1830 à 1848. REI, 1936.
Benassi, U. Una guerra letteraria italo-francese nel secolo XVIII. GSLI, 83, 1924.
Blanc, J. Bibliographie italico-française. Milano, 1886.
Bourgin, G. Sources et travaux français sur l'histoire des rapports franco-italiens de 1830 à 1848. REI, 1936-38.
Ciccotti, P. Les relations entre les romantiques français et italiens. MF, 1930.
Evola, N. D. Letteratura comparata francese-italiana. Contributo bibliografico, 1920-1926. Rass. di studi francesi, 1926.
Flamini, F. Studi di storia letteraria italiana e straniera. Livorno, 1895.
Hauvette, H. Les relations littéraires entre la France et l'Italie. Annales U. de Grenoble, 1895.
Jourda, P. Les journées d'études franco-italiennes. RCC, 1937.
Mascarel, A. France et Italie. Paris, 1926.
Meyer-Luebke, W. Franco-italienische Studien. ZRPh, 11, 1887.
Mignon, M. Les affinités intellectuelles de l'Italie et de la France. Paris, 1921.
Moretti, A. Saggio storico delle relazioni letterarie fra l'Italia e la Francia. Cortona, 1902.
Narjoux. Français et Italiens. Paris, 1891.
Neri, F. Gli studi franco-italiani nel primo quarto del secolo XX. Roma, 1928.
—— Italia e paesi di lingua francese. Festschrift V. Rossi. Firenze, 1936.
Ortolani, G. Italie et France au XVIIIe siècle. EI, 1928-29.
Pellegrini, C. Relazioni tra la letteratura italiana e la letteratura francese. In: Letterature comparate (ed. by A. Momigliano). Milano, 1948.
Picco, F. Dame di Francia e poeti d'Italia. Genova, 1921.
Reinach, J. La France et l'Italie devant l'histoire. Paris, 1893.
Riquier R,. Enquête sur les rapports intellectuels entre la France et l'Italie. Rev. fédéraliste des pays rhodaniens, 1924.
Scoppa, A. Traité de la poésie italienne, rapportée à la poésie française. Paris, 1803.
Varia. France-Italie au XVIIIe siècle. Bull. de la Commission nationale ital. pour la cooperation intellect., 1936.
Baldensperger, F. Quelques anciennes affinités polonaises dans la France de l'Est. **(POLAND).** Petit Courier de France et de Pologne, 1929.
Brandes, G. Polen und Frankreich. In: Polen. München, 1898.
Francastel, P. Les relations artistiques entre la Pologne et la France. Rev. des Etudes slaves, 1937.
Lukasik, S. La France et la Pologne à travers les siècles. Paris, 1933.
Rudwin, M. J. The Intellectual Relations between France and Poland. New York, 1925.

Francisque-Michel, R. Les Portugais en France et les Français en **PORTUGAL.** Paris, 1882.
Nemesio, V. Relaçoes francesas do romantismo portugues. Coimbra, 1936.
Iorga, N. Histoire des relations entre la France et les **ROUMAINS.** Jassy, 1917.
Bém, A. Relations littéraires entre la France et la **RUSSIE.** Casopis pro moderni filologii, 1932.
Iakobson, L. Russland und Frankreich in den ersten Regierungsjahren der Kaiserin Katherina II. Berlin, 1929.
Larivière, C. de. La France et la Russie au XVIIIe siècle. Paris, 1909.
Makashin, S. (ed.). La culture russe et la France. In: L'Héritage littéraire. (In Russian). Moscou, 1937 ff.
Patouillet, J. Relations intellectuelles entre France et Russie. RP, 1920.
Veuclin, V. E. L'amitié franco-russe; ses origines. Verneuil, 1896.
Maury, L. Les **SCANDINAVES** et nous. Essai d'explication des relations littéraires franco-scandinaves. MF, 1947.
Anon. Quelques rapports entre l'Ecosse et la France. **(SCOTLAND).** CLS, 21-22, 1946.
Rait, R. S. Scotland and France: the Parting of the Ways. Transactions Royal Soc. of Literature, 37, 1919.
Steuart, A. F. Scotland and France. AFR, 1919.
Anon. Antipathie des Français et des Espagnols. **(SPAIN).** Journal étranger, June, 1755.
Barrès, M. Les liens spirituels de la France et de l'Espagne. RDM, 1924.
Droulers, C. & Bocquet, L. Les poètes de la Flandre française et l'Espagne. Paris, 1917.
Espiner-Scott, Janet. Quelques érudits français du XVIe siècle et l'Espagne. RLC, 20, 1940.
Farinelli, A. España y Francia. In: Ensayos y discursos de critica literaria hispano-europea. Roma, 1925.
Fournier, E. Espagne et France. RB, 1879.
Franca, J. C. Bibliographie générale de la mutua influencia entre la littérature française et la littérature castillane. In: Historia de la lengua y literatura castellana, 14. Madrid, 1932.
García, C. Antipatía de los franceses y españoles. In: La desordenada codicia, 1619.
Girard. A. L'Espagne et les lettres françaises. MF, 1937.
Hilton, R. Four Studies in Franco-Spanish Relations. Toronto, 1943.
Imbart de la Tour, P. Une entente intellectuelle avec l'Espagne. Revue des lettres françaises et étrangères, 1899.
Lanson, G. Etudes sur les rapports de la littérature française et de la littérature espagnole au XVIIe siècle. RHLF, 1896-1901.
Martinenche, E. L'Espagne et le romantisme français. Paris, 1922.
Mulertt, F. Franko-spanische Kulturberührungen. Hamburg, 1930.
Puibusque, A. de. Histoire comparée des littératures espagnole et française. 2 vols. Paris, 1843.
Sarrailh, J. Enquêtes romantiques: France-Espagne. Paris, 1932.
Sorrento, L. Francia e Spagna nel settecento. Milano, 1928.
Blank, A. La Suède et la littérature française. **(SWEDEN).** Paris, 1947.
Strindberg, A. Les relations de la France avec la Suède. Paris, 1891.
Castell, A. La Suisse et les Français. **(SWITZERLAND).** Paris, 1920.
Deny, J. Les échanges littéraires entre la France et la **TURQUIE.** NL, 8.VII.1939.
Arnaoutovitch, A. Les vers franco-yougoslaves. **(YUGOSLAVIA).** Glasnik, 1927.
Popovitch, P. Les relations intellectuelles franco-serbes. (In Serbian). SKG, 14. 1925.
Tchorovitch, V. Relations franco-serbes dans le passé. (In Serbian). SKG, 14. 1925.
Zujovic, J. La politique intellectuelle franco-serbe. Paris, 1918.

CHAPTER SEVEN

Germany and Other Nations.

(See also Comparisons, I. V. 1.)

Mahnke, D. Deutsch-tschechische Wechselwirkungen in der Geistesgeschichte Mitteleuropas. **(CZECHOSLOVAKIA).** Das innere Reich, Dec., 1938.
Anon. Litterarische Wechselbeziehungen zwischen Deutschland und Griechenland. **(GREECE).** MLIA, 1897.
Frings, T. Die Stellung der Niederlande im Aufbau des Germanischen. **(HOLLAND).** Halle, 1944.
Pluim, T. Deutschland und Holland. MLIA, 18.VI.1892.
Trunz, E. Dichtung und Volkstum in den Niederlanden im 17. Jahrhundert. Ein Vergleich mit Deutschland und ein

Ueberblick über die niederländisch-deutschen Beziehungen in diesem Jahrhundert. München, 1937.

Neugeboren, E. Ungarn, Deutschland und Deutschtum. **(HUNGARY)**. Grenzboten, 11, 1912.

Belli, A. Wechselseitige Einwirkungen der italienischen und deutschen Kultur. **(ITALY)**. Venezia, 1905.

Carriere, M. Wechselbeziehungen deutscher und italienischer Kunst. Deutsche Bücherei. (Breslau), 1882.

Engel, E. Zur deutsch-italienischen Uebersetzungslitteratur. MLIA, 1882.

Grassi, E. Beziehungen zwischen deutscher und italienischer Philosophie. DVLG, 17, 1939.

Hartmann, H. Die Beziehungen der deutschen und der italienischen Kultur. ZNU, 39.

Natali, G. Appunti sulla coltura tedesca in Italia e italiana nei paesi tedeschi nel secolo XVIII. RI, 1928.

Quinet, E. Allemagne et Italie. Paris, 1839.

Reumont, A. Delle relazioni fra la letteratura italiana e quella di Germania nel seicento. In: Saggi di storia e letteratura. Firenze, 1880.

Rossi, G. Italia e Germania nel settecento. Conv. 30.VI.1939.

Santoli, V. La letteratura italiana, la tedesca e le nordiche. In: Letterature comparate (ed. by A. Momigliano). Milano, 1948. Cf. CL, 2, 1950.

Stiefel, A. L. Wechselbeziehungen zwischen deutscher und italienischer Literatur im 16. Jahrhundert. SVL, 6, 1906.

Ciechanowska, Z. Les relations littéraires entre la Pologne et l'Allemagne au XVIIIe siècle. **(POLAND)**. Varsovie, 1934.

Kleczkowski, A. Die deutsch-polnischen Beziehungen in sprachlicher und literarischer Hinsicht. Bull. de l'Acad. polonaise des Sciences et des Lettres. Cracovie, 1936.

Anon. **PORTUGAL** und Deutschland. Internat. Litteraturberichte, 2, 1895.

Cordeiro, R. G. Die deutsch-portugiesischen Kulturbeziehungen. Portugal: Festschrift der U. Köln, 1940.

Saint-René Taillandier. Allemagne et **RUSSIE**. Paris, 1856.

Magon, L. Ein Jahrhundert geistiger und literarischer Beziehungen zwischen Deutschland und **SKANDINAVIEN** 1750-1850. Dortmund, 1926; cf. ZDPh, 1927.

—— Deutschland und Skandinavien in ihren geistigen Wechselbeziehungen. Deutschtum & Ausland, 10, 1927.

Merker, P. Tysk-skandinavisk Kultur forbindelser. Nordisk tidskrift, 6, 1927.

Petersen, C. et al. Deutschland und der Norden. Breslau, 1931.

Schriewer, F. Literarische Beziehungen zwischen dem Norden und Deutschland. Bücherei und Bildungspflege, 12, 1932.

Strauss & Torney, L. von. Nordische Literatur und deutsches Geistesleben. Schleswig-Holstein Zs., 1, 1906.

Wahlgren, E. Scandinavian and Germanic Studies. MLF, 25, 1941.

Anon. La espiritualidad española y Alemania. **(SPAIN)**. Ensayos y Estudios, 3, 1941.

Ebert, A. Litterarische Wechselwirkungen Spaniens und Deutschlands. Deutsche Vierteljahrsschrift, 2, 1857.

Farinelli, A. Die Beziehungen zwischen Spanien und Deutschland in den Literaturen der beiden Länder. ZVL, 5, 1895 ff.

Flegler, A. Spanien und Deutschland in geschichtlicher Vergleichung. Winterthur, 1845.

Klaiber, L. Der Vocabulari catalá-alemany von 1502 und seine italienische Vorlage. Homenatge Antoni Rubió i Lluch. Barcelona, 1936.

Lewalter, E. Spanisch-jesuitische und deutsch-lutherische Metaphysik des 17. Jahrhunderts. Hamburg, 1935.

Lyte, H. O. A Tentative Bibliography of Spanish-German Literary and Cultural Relations. Minneapolis, 1936.

Schreiber, G. Deutschland und Spanien: Volkskundliche und kulturkundliche Beziehungen. Düsseldorf, 1936.

Schulten, A. Spanien und Deutschland. Intern. Monatsschrift f. Wiss., Kunst & Technik, 10, 1916.

Schwering, J. Literarische Beziehungen zwischen Spanien und Deutschland. Eine Streitschrift gegen Arturo Farinelli. In: Kritische Studien. Münster, 1902. Cf. SVL, 3, 1903.

Wrangel, E. Till belysning af de litterara forbindelserna mellan **SVERIGE** och Tyksland under 1600-talet. Lund, 1899.

—— Die Literatur Deutschlands im 18. Jahrhundert vor Klopstock und ihr Verhältniss zu der schwedischen. Samlaren, 1901.

CHAPTER EIGHT

Italy and Other Nations.

(See also Comparisons, I. V. 1.)

Croce, B. Italia e Boemia. (**CZECHOSLOVAKIA**). NAnt, 1945 & Quaderni della Critica, 1945.

Rosendorfsky, J. Relazioni intellettuali fra Italia e Cecoslovaccia. Dante, June, 1934.

Okkonen, O. La **FINLANDIA** e l'Italia. Giornale di politica e letteratura, 19, 1943.

Mazzoni, G. et al. Italia e **GRECIA**. Saggi su le due civilità e i loro rapporti attraverso i secoli. Firenze, 1939-40.

For Relations between Italian and **HUNGARIAN** Humanists See: Humanism, III. II. 3.

Bronarski, A. L'Italie et la **POLOGNE** à travers les siècles. Lausanne, 1945.

Contini, G. Per una concordanza italo-portoghese. (**PORTUGAL**). Leonardo, 2, 1940.

Faria, A. de. Portugal e Italia. Leorne, 1898.

Pascu, S. Relazioni culturali tra la **ROMANIA** e l'Italia. Rassegna italo-romena, 22, 1942.

Deanovic, M. Sui rapporti culturali fra gli italiani e gli slavi meridionale attraverso i secoli. (**SLAVS**). L'Europa orientale, 20, 1940.

Anon. Literarische Beziehungen zwischen Italien und Spanien im XVIII. Jahrhundert. (**SPAIN**). Frankfurter Zt., 30.IX. & 2.X.1896.

—— Relazioni di cultura italo-ispaniche nel settecento. La civilità cattolica, 4, 1938.

Belloni, G. Per la storia del teatro italo-spagnuolo nel secolo XVII. Bibl. d. scuole ital., 10, 1904.

Cian, V. Italia e Spagna nel secolo XVIII. Torino, 1896.

Croce, Alda. Relazioni della letteratura italiana con la letteratura spagnuola. In: Letterature comparate (ed. by A. Momigliano). Milano, 1948.

Croce, B. Primi contatti fra Spagna e Italia. Memoria. Napoli, 1893.

—— La corte spagnuola di Alfonso d'Aragona a Napoli. Memoria. Napoli, 1894.

Farinelli, A. Primi contatti fra Italia e Spagna. GSLI, 24, 1894.

—— Italia e Spagna. Torino, 1929.

—— La Spagna e i romantici d'Italia. NAnt, 1936.

Levi, E. Un poeta italo-catalano del quattrocento. Homenatge a Antoni Rubio i Lluch. Barcelona, 1936.

Marinis, T. de. La biblioteca napoletana dei re d'Aragona. Milano, 1947.

Montlaur, J. de. De l'Italie et de l'Espagne. Paris, 1852.

Nicolini, F. Aspetti della vita spagnuola nel cinque e seicento. Napoli, 1934.

Teza, E. Italiani e spagnuoli. RCLI, 2.

Mauerhofer. Les rapports italo-suisses pendant la première guerre d'indépendance italienne. (**SWITZERLAND**). Rassegna storica del Risorgimento, 1938.

Mazzucchetti, L. & Lohner, A. Die Schweiz und Italien, Kulturbeziehungen aus 2 Jahrhunderten. Zürich, 1941.

CHAPTER NINE

Spain and Other Nations.

(See also chapters 5-8)

Dam, C. F. A. van. Las relaciones literarias entre España y **HOLANDA**. Amsterdam, 1923.

Davids, W. Betrekkingen tuschen de nederlandsche en de spaansche letterkunde in de 16-18. eeuw. The Hague, 1918.

Looten, C. Rapports littéraires entre la Néerlande et l'Espagne. RLC, 17, 1937.

Varenbergh, E. Les relations des Pays-Bas avec le Portugal et l'Espagne. Anvers, 1869.

Morawski, J. Espagne et **POLOGNE**. Coup d'oeil sur les relations des deux pays dans le passé et le présent. RLC, 16, 1936.

Sulima, Z. L. (Przyborowski). Poles and Spaniards. (In Polish). Warsaw, 1888.

Figueiredo, F. de. Ponto de vista para uma introduçao a historia comparada des literaturas **PORTUGUESA** e espanhola. Lisboa, 1935.

Ortiz, R. Per la storia dei contatti ispano-**RUMENI** (1710-1932). AR, 18, 1935.

Strindberg, A. Relations de la **SUEDE** avec l'Espagne et le Portugal jusqu'à la fin du XVIIe siècle. Bol. Real Acad. d. l. Hist., 17.

CHAPTER TEN

Inter-Relations Among Smaller Countries.

For Inter-Slavonic Relations, see IV. XIII. 2.)

Rez, H. Ungarn als Vermittler der westlichen geistigen Strömungen nach Süden and Südosten. (**HUNGARY**). Archivum Europae centro-orientalis, 5, 1939.

Szenczi, N. J. East and West in Hungarian Literature. SR, 1937.

Meuleman. Norge i Nederland. (**NORWAY**). M, 46.

Jong, M. de. Relaçoes literarias entre **PORTUGAL** e a Holanda. Biblos, 12. (Coimbra), 1937.

Thieurry, J. Le Portugal et la Normandie jusqu'à la fin du XVIe siècle. Paris, 1860.

Wrangel, E. Sveriges litterära forbindelser med Holland. (**SWEDEN**). Lund, 1897.

—— De betrekkingen tuschen Zweden en de Nederlanden op het gebied van letteren en wetenschap, voornamelijk gedurende de zeventiende eeuw. Leyden, 1901.

Hoiningen-Huene, Christina von. Beiträge zur Geschichte der Beziehungen zwischen der Schweiz und Holland im 17. Jahrhundert. (**SWITZERLAND**). Berlin, 1899.

Roth, P. Umrisse geistiger Beziehungen zwischen Basel und Prag. Basler Nachrichten, 11.IV.1948.

CHAPTER ELEVEN

Non-Specified Influences from "Abroad."

(See also Sources, I. V. 2.)

Dontchev, N. Les influences des littératures étrangères sur les lettres bulgares. (**BULGARIA**). Revue bulgare, 1930.

—— Influences étrangères dans la littérature bulgare. Sofia, 1934. Cf. Europo centrale 6.IV. & 1.VI.1935.

Paludan, J. Fremmed indflydelse paa den danske nationallitteratur i det 17. og 18. Aarhundrede. (**DENMARK**). København, 1887.

Anon. The Foreign Actor on the English Stage. (**ENGLAND**). Literature, 6.VII.1901.

Avery, E. L. Foreign Performers in the London Theaters in the Early 18th Century. PhQ, 1937.

Behn-Eschenburg, H. Die Wechselbeziehungen der englischen und festländischen Litteratur vor dem Zeitalter Shakespeares. Zürich, 1865.

Block, A. The English Novel, 1740-1850. A Catalogue including . . . Translations of Foreign Fiction. London, 1939.

Gosse, E. W. A View of the Influences upon English Literature from Shakespeare to Pope. London, 1885.

Harris, W. J. The First Printed Translations into English of the Great Foreign Classics. London, 1909.

Heuser, W. Festländische Einflüsse im Mittelenglischen. Bonn, 1902.

Magnus, L. English Literature in its Foreign Relations. New York, 1928.

Schelling, F. E. Foreign Influences in Elizabethan Plays. New York, 1923.

Tucker, T. G. The Foreign Debt of English Literature. London, 1907.

Anon. De la connaissance progressive des langues étrangères en **FRANCE**. Revue indépendante, 7, 1845.

—— Literarische Einflüsse auf Frankreich. Neue Rundschau, 1925.

Ampère, J. J. De la littérature française au moyen âge dans ses rapports avec les littératures étrangères. RDM, 1.I.1833 And in: Littérature et Voyages, Paris, 1833.

Baldensperger, F. Le XVIIe siècle français et les langues étrangères. RLC, 13, 1933. And in: Etudes d'hist. litt., 4e sér. Paris, 1939.

Bordeaux, H. L'invasion étrangère dans la littérature française. Le Correspondant, 25.XII.1901.

Boulan, H. R. Les mots d'origine étrangère en français. (1650-1700). Amsterdam, 1934.

Brandes, G. Die fremden Anregugen des französischen Romanticismus. Gegenwart, 1882.

Demogeot, J. Histoire des littératures étrangères considérées dans leurs rapports avec le développement de la littérature française. 2 vols. Paris, 1884.

Dumont-Wilden, L. La France d'aujourd'hui et l'étranger. L'Opinion, 17.VIII. 1912.

Jullien, J. Le théâtre moderne et l'influence étrangère. Revue d'art dramatique, 1, 1886. And in: Revue encyclopédique, 11.IV.1896.

—— Vom Einfluss der fremden Litteratur auf das junge Frankreich. Zeit, 1896.

Kurz, H. European Characters in the

French Drama of the XVIIIth Century. New York, 1916.
Lanson, G. La fonction des influences étrangères dans le développement de la littérature française. RDM, 1917.
Levallois, J. Le public français et le théâtre étranger. Paris, 1863.
Mauclair, C. Das neue Frankreich. Zukunft, 6.V.1899.
—— La critique française devant l'étranger. Revue de Genève, Aug., 1920.
Maury, L. Les littératures étrangères en France. RB, 15. & 22.XI.1919.
Michiels, A. Histoire des idées littéraires en France. 2 vols. Bruxelles, 1848.
Navarre, C. Les grands écrivains étrangers et leur influence sur la littérature française. Paris, 1930.
Prévost, M. La culture étrangère en France. Figaro, 31.V.1897.
Rigal, E. Equisse d'une histoire des théâtres de Paris de 1548-1653. Paris, 1887.
Roz, F. L'étranger et nous. Revue de la Semaine, 15.IV.1921.
Savard, J. L'étranger et la culture française. Esprit, June, 1945.
Texte, J. Les relations littéraires de la France avec l'étranger de 1799 à 1848. In: Petit de Julleville: Histoire de la langue et de la littérature française, 7. Paris, 1900.
Varia. Enquête sur l'influence réciproque de la littérature française et des littératures étrangères. EN, 10.X.1920.
Anon. Das deutsche Publikum und die fremde Belletristik. (GERMANY). Grenzboten, 4, 1850.
—— Deutsche Literatur im Auslande und ausländische Literatur in Deutschland. MLIA, 1879.
Bartels, A. Die fremden Einflüsse in der deutschen Litteratur. Grenzboten, 2, 1894.
Conrad, M. G. Verdeutschtes Auslandgut. Die Gesellschaft, 1, 1900.
Fleschlen, C. Graphische Litteratur-Tafel. Die deutsche Litteratur und der Einfluss fremder Litteraturen auf ihren Verlauf. Stuttgart, 1890.
Friederich, W. P. et al. Outline-History of German Literature (emphasizing comparative aspects). New York, 1948.
Gebhard, A. Uebersetzungen ausländischer Novellen und Erzählungen. Literarisches Centralblatt, Beilage, 7.II. 1903.
Gottschall, R. von. Die Ausländerei auf den deutschen Bühnen. In: Kritik des modernen Dramas. Berlin, 1900.
Hatzfeld, H. Wechselbeziehungen zwischen der deutschen Literatur und den übrigen europäischen Literaturen. Bielefeld, 1927.
Koischwitz, O. German Readers Turn to Foreign Countries. BA, 13, 1939.
Leist, A. Das Ausland in der deutschen Litteratur. MLIA, 1885.
Natzmer, G. von. Ausländerei im Geistesleben. Der Tag, 263, 1921.
Petersen, J. & Trunz, E. Lyrische Weltdichtungen in deutschen Uebertragungen aus sieben Jahrhunderten. (Cf. Introduction). Berlin, 1933.
Piquet, F. De quelques éléments étrangers dans la culture allemande. RG, 1936.
Vermeil, E. L'Allemagne et les démocraties occidentales. Les relations intellectuelles dans le passé. Paris, 1931.
—— L'Allemagne et l'Occident européen. LM, 1935.
Wolff, E. Von Shakespeare zu Zola. Zur Entwicklungsgeschichte des Kunststils in der deutschen Dichtung. Berlin, 1902.
Vassiliadis-Nicvas, A. Les influences étrangères dans la littérature néohellénique. (GREECE). Le Mois, Oct. 1935.
Paraschos, C. La Grèce et les influences intellectuelles occidentales. Hellénisme contemporain, Sept. 1948.
Declerq, W. Verhandeling over den invloed der vreemde Letterkunden op de onzere. (HOLLAND). Amsterdam, 1824.
Hankiss, J. Europa und die ungarische Literatur. (HUNGARY). Budapest, 1942.
Apollonio, M. Note sulla storia del teatro italiano nelle sue relazioni con il teatro europeo. (ITALY). Studi Urbinati, 1938.
Collavecchia, C. L'influence de la poésie moderne en Italie. Paris, 1860.
Eyssenhardt, F. Italienische Schilderungen alter und neuer Dichter. Hamburg, 1890.
Gargallo, T. Di alcune novità introdotte nella letteratura italiana. Milano, 1838.
Monnier, M. Les sympathies littéraires des Italiens. Journal des Débats, 25. I.1876.
Pellegrini, C. Gli studi di letteratura straniera in Italia. Romana, 1938.
Varia. L'Italia e la letteratura straniera. Festschrift V. Rossi. Firenze, 1937.
—— Ce que les écrivains polonais doivent aux littératures étrangères: Enquête. (POLAND) Pologne littéraire, 1928.

Cartojan. Les premiers éléments occidentaux dans la littérature roumaine. (ROUMANIA). RLC, 14, 1934.
Guillermou, A. La littérature roumaine et l'Europe. RLC, 23, 1949.
Munteano, B. La littérature comparée en Roumanie. Ouvrages récents sur les relations intellectuelles et politiques des Roumains avec l'Occident. RLC, 11, 1931.
Adams, N. B. Notes on Spanish Plays at the Beginning of the Romantic Period. (SPAIN). RR, 1926.
Eguia Ruiz, C. Las adaptaciones teatrales en España. RyF, 50-51, 1918.
Givanel i Mas, J. El teatre estranger en llengua catalana. La Revista, 1935.
Lorenz, Charlotte M. Translated Plays in Madrid Theatres, 1808-18. HR, 9, 1941.
Afzelius, N. Sverige i utlandsk och utlandet i svensk litteratur. En bibliografisk oversikt. (SWEDEN)... Biblioteksbl., 15, 1930.
Nyblom, C. R. Svenska literaturens förhallande till andra länders under olika tider. In: Estetiska studier. Stockholm, 1873.
Hergesic, I. La part de l'étranger dans le répertoire du Théâtre national de Zagreb. (YUGOSLAVIA). RLC, 14, 1934.

CHAPTER TWELVE

Collective Contributions Involving Three or More Countries.

(See also Intermediaries, I. IV. 2-4.)

Anon. Les théâtres italiens et français à Londres. RP, May, 1836.
Blassneck, M. Frankreich als Vermittler englisch-deutscher Einflüsse im XVIIten und XVIIIten Jahrhundert. Leipzig, 1934.
Bond, D., McDermott, J. & Tucker, J. Anglo-French and Franco-American Studies. RR, 1938 ff.
Broche, G. E. Archives marseillaises d'intérêt italien et espagnol. Mélanges Hauvette. Paris, 1934.
Carrillo, C. La lutte entre l'influence française et l'influence allemande en Espagne. Revue, 15.XI.1911.
Childs, F. S. French Opinion of Anglo-American Relations, 1795-1805. FAR, 1948.
Deanovic, M. Le théâtre français et le théâtre italien à Zagreb du moyen âge au milieu du XIXe siècle. Mélanges Hauvette. Paris, 1934.
Delavaud, H. Les Français dans le nord. Notes sur les premières relations de la France avec les royaumes scandinaves et la Russie septentrionale depuis l'antiquité jusqu'à la fin du XVIe. siècle. Rouen, 1911.
Denina, Abbé. De l'influence de la littérature française sur l'anglaise et de l'anglaise sur l'allemande. Berlin, 1790.
Dessoff, A. Ueber englische, italienische und spanische Dramen in den Spielverzeichnissen deutscher Wandertruppen. SVL, 1, 1901.
—— Ueber spanische, italienische und französische Dramen in den Spielverzeichnissen deutscher Wandertruppen. ZVL, 4.
Dieperink, G. J. Studien zum Valentin und Namulos. Ein Beitrag zur Geschichte der literarischen Beziehungen zwischen Flandern, Mittel- und Niederdeutschland und Schweden zur Zeit der Hanse. Haarlem, 1933.
Duvivier. Les influences française et germanique en Belgique au XIIIe siècle. Bruxelles, 1894.
Farinelli, A. Historia del drama holandes y español en Alemania. Revista critica de historia y literatura españolas, portuguesas e espano-americanas, 1, 1896.
—— Divagazioni erudite: Inghilterra e Italia; Germania e Italia; Italia e Spagna; Spagna e Germania. Torino, 1925.
Frierson, W. C. The English Novel in Transition, 1885-1940. U. of Okla. P., 1942.
Gáldi, L. Le origini italo-greche della versificazione rumena. Studi e documenti italo-ungheresi della R. Acc. d'Ungheria di Roma, 3, 1938-39.
García Martí, V. La voz de los mitos. Diálogos entre Fausto, Don Quijote, Don Juan, Hamlet, Dulcinea, Margarita, Doña Inés y Ofelia. Madrid, 1941.
Graf, A. Gallomania, gallofobia, anglomania nell'Italia del settecento. NAnt, 1910.
Hadrovits, L. Incontro di influenze culturali italiane e ungheresi in Croazia. Corvina, 5, 1942.
Harden, M. Deutschland, Frankreich, England. Berlin, 1923.
Hazard, P. Anglais, Espagnols et Français. RDM, 1929.
Isopescu, C. Saggi romeno-italo-ispanici. Roma, 1943.
Joret, C. La littérature allemande au XVIIIe siècle dans ses rapports avec

la littérature française et avec la littérature anglaise. Aix, 1876.
Loudun, E. L'Angleterre et l'Allemagne en France. Paris, 1854.
Madariaga, S. de. Campos eliseos. Diálogo entre Goethe, María Estuardo, Voltaire, Napoléon, Carlos Marx y el presidente Wáshington sobre el facismo, el comunismo, la paz y la guerra. Buenos Aires, 1939.
Nicolini, F. Su taluni rapporti di cultura tra l'Italia, l'Olanda e l'Inghilterra al principio del settecento. Napoli, 1930.
Piccoli, R. Poesia e vita spirituale. Saggi sulla letteratura e la civiltà inglese e americana e sui loro rapporti con l'Italia. Bari, 1934.
Pollio, J. Des influences littéraires en France et en Italie. Galatz, 1902.
Reymond, W. Corneille, Shakespeare et Goethe. Etude sur l'influence anglogermanique en France au XIXe siècle. Berlin, 1864.
Santoli, V. La letteratura italiana, la tedesca e le nordiche. In: Letterature comparate (ed. by A. Momigliano). Milano, 1948.
Schanz, J. Italien, Deutschland, Oesterreich im Spiegel moderner Dichtung. Leipzig, 1879.
Schwering, J. Zur Geschichte des niederländischen und spanischen Dramas in Deutschland. Münster, 1895.
Siegfried, A. La contribution de la France, de l'Angleterre et des Etats-Unis à la civilisation occidentale. RP, 1939-40.
Smyser, H. M. & Magoun, F. P. Survivals in Old Norwegian of Medieval English, French and German Literature, together with the Latin Versions of the Heroic Legend of Walter of Aquitaine. Connecticut College Monograph, 1. Baltimore, 1941.
Sorrento, L. Italiani e spagnuoli contro l'egemonia intellettuale francese del settecento. Milano, 1924.
Soudin, E. Influence des idées anglaises et germaniques sur l'esprit français. Paris, 1855.
Stern, A. Die französische Dichtung unter italienischen und spanischen Einwirkungen. In: Gesch. d. neueren Litt., 4, Leipzig, 1882.
Trezza, G. Dante, Shakespeare, Goethe nella rinascenza europea. Verona, 1888.
Tronchon, H. Etudes (France, Allemagne, Italie, Hongrie, Pays baltiques). Paris, 1935.

CHAPTER THIRTEEN

Influences upon Individual Authors.

(See also Intermediaries, I. IV. 8.)

Bronzini, G. Romanità di S. **AGOSTINO.** Conv., 3, 1931.
Bach, J. Des **ALBERTUS MAGNUS** Verhältniss zur Erkenntnisslehre der Griechen, Lateiner, Araber und Juden. Wien, 1881.
Kelsos, A. P. Matthew **ARNOLD** on Continental Life and Literature. Oxford, 1914.
Baldensperger, F. Orientations étrangèrs chez H. de **BALZAC.** Paris, 1927.
Eicke, W. Léon **BAZALGETTE** und seine Anschauungen über Latinität und Germanentum. Bonn, 1937.
Pierce, F. E. **BEDDOES** and Continental Romanticists. PhQ, 1927.
Wells, A. L. Les soeurs **BRONTE** et l'étranger. Paris, 1937.
Peytavi de Faugères, G. G. **CARDUCCI,** poète de la romanité. MF, 1938.
Taylor, A. C. **CARLYLE** et la pensée latine. Paris, 1937.
Hulbert, J. R. **CHAUCER'S** Romance Vocabulary. PhQ, 26, 1947.
Kirk, R. **COOPER** and the European Puzzle. College English, 7, 1946.
Poincaré, R. **DANTE** colonne miliaire de la latinité. Revue hebdomadaire, 18.VI.1921.
Dasgupta, J. K. Western Influence on the Poetry of Madhusudan **DATTA.** Bull. of the School of Oriental Studies, 7, 1933-35.
Girard, H. Le cosmopolitisme d'un dilettante: Emile **DESCHAMPS** et les littératures étrangères. RLC, 1, 1921.
Levaillant, M. Emile Deschamps et les littératures étrangères. Mfr., 1930.
Lo Gallo, E. **DOSTOJEVSKY** e l'Occidente. I Libri del Giorno, Nov., 1926.
Rychner, M. Dostojewski und der Westen. NSR, 1926.
Bourl'honne, P. George **ELIOT.** (Influences étrangères). Paris, 1933.
Hildesbrand, H. Die amerikanische Stellung zur Geschichte und zu Europa in **EMERSONS** Gedankensystem. Bonn, 1936.
Delpy, G. L'Espagne et l'esprit européen. L'oeuvre de **FEIJOO** (1725-60). Paris, 1939.
Faure, F. John **GALSWORTHY** et les littératures étrangères. RLC, 22, 1948.

Bode, W. Die Franzosen und Engländer in **GOETHES** Leben und Urteil. Berlin, 1915.
Burkhardt, C. A. H. Das Repertoire des Weimarischen Theaters unter Goethes Leitung, 1791-1817. Hamburg, 1891.
Heine, C. Die ausländischen Dramen im Spielplane des Weimarischen Theaters unter Goethes Leitung. ZVL, 4, 1890.
Maurel, A. Goethe génie latin. RP, 1.XI.1919.
Vermeil, E. La jeunesse de Goethe. Analyse des influences étrangères. RCC, 1935-36.
Vossler, K. Goethe und das Formgefühl der Romanen. F&F, 14, 1928.
—— Goethe e il mondo romanzo. Cultura, 1932.
Grozdov, J. A. Maxim **GORKI** et l'Occident. (In Russian). Moscou, 1930.
Kriessbach, E. Die Trauerspiele in **GOTTSCHED'S** Deutscher Schaubühne und im Verhältnis zur Dramaturgie und zum Theater ihrer Zeit. Diss. Halle, 1928.
Wegelin, C. Europe in **HAWTHORNE'S** Fiction. ELH, 14, 1947.
Gómez Vilá, S. **HEREDIA** influido e influyente. Revista bimestre cubana, 43, 1939.
Rigobon, M. Il teatro e la latinità di **HROTSVITHA.** Padova, 1932.
Liljegren, S. B. American and European in the Works of H. **JAMES.** Lund U. Årskrift, 15, 1920.
Farrell, J. T. **JOYCE** and the Tradition of the European Novel. N. Y. Times Book Rev., 21.I.1945.
Cornicelius, M. Romanisches in G. **KELLERS** Dichtung. Festschrift Tobler, Braunschweig, 1905.
Guyard, M. F. Les influences étrangères dans La Chute d'un Ange. (**LAMARTINE**). RLC, 21 1947.
Hazard, P. Les influences étrangères sur Lamartine. RCC, 1922.
Chaytor, H. Foreign Influences. In: Preface to La Vida de **LAZARILLO DE TORMES.** Manchester, 1922.
Biebricher, F. Jules **LEMAITRE** als Kritiker und seine Stellungnahme gegenüber dem nicht-französischen Theater. Diss. Köln, 1925 .
Johnson, C. L. **LONGFELLOW'S** Beginnings in Foreign Languages. NEQ, 20, 1947.
Mill, A. J. The Influence of the Continental Drama on **LYNDSAY'S** Satyre of the thrie estaitis. MLR, 1930.
Carré, J. M. **MAETERLINCK** et les littératures étrangères. RLC, 6, 1926.
Lecat, M. Dettes et influences de Maeterlinck. In: Le Maeterlinckisme. Bruxelles, 1939.
Boissonnade, P. Les personnages et les événements de l'histoire d'Allemagne, de France et d'Espagne dans l'oeuvre de **MARCABRU.** Romania, 48, 1922.
McKeithan, D. M. The Occasion of **MARK TWAIN'S** Speech on Foreign Critics. PhQ, 27, 1948.
—— More About Mark Twain's War with English Critics of America. MLN, 63, 1948.
Möhle, G. Das Europabild Mark Twains. Berlin, 1940.
Ortiz, R. Dall' indifferenza alla libertà: radicie propagini francesi, rumene e spagnuole della Libertà di Pietro **METASTASIO.** Mélanges Baldensperger. Paris, 1930. And in: Varia romancia. Firenze, 1932.
Cooper, L. A Concordance of the Latin, Greek and Italian Poems of John **MILTON.** Halle, 1923.
Lallemand, P. **MONTALEMBERT** et ses relations littéraires avec l'étranger. Paris, 1928.
Setchanore, L. J. Jean-Baptiste **NICCOLINI** et l'influence étrangère dans son oeuvre dramatique. Diss. Paris, 1923.
Forti, E. **NIETZSCHE** et la décadence européenne. Valeurs, Oct., 1946.
Blackburn, Clara. Continental Influences on Eugene **O'NEILL'S** Expressionistic Drama. AL, 13, 1941.
Milliex, R. Costis **PALAMAS** et l'Europe. RLC, 21, 1947.
Brian Chaminov, N. Influences européennes dans l'oeuvre de **POUCHKINE.** MF, 1936.
Girmounski, V. Pouchkine et la littérature de l'Occident. Gedenkschrift Pouchkine. Moscou, 1939.
Haumant, E. Pouchkine et l'étranger. RLC, 17, 1937.
Neustadt, V. Un génie mondial: l'Europe occidentale et Pouchkine. Gedenkschrift Pouchkine. Moscou, 1939.
Storojenko, N. I. Pouchkine et la littérature étrangère. (In Russian). Oblasti Literatury. Moskva, 1902.
Frey, E. Der Einfluss der englischen, französischen, italienischen und lateinischen Literatur auf die Dichtungen Matthew **PRIORS.** Strassburg, 1915.
Beau, A. E. Antero de **QUENTAL** in seiner Auseinandersetzung mit dem deutschen und dem französischen Geiste. RLC, 13, 1938.

Tronchon, H. Allemagne, France, Angleterre. Le jeune Edgar **QUINET** ou l'aventure d'un enthousiaste. Paris, 1937.
Dasgupta, J. Western Influence on the Poetry of **RABINDRANATH.** Calcutta Review, 3rd Ser., 47, 1933.
Tronchon, H. Ernest **RENAN** et l'étranger. Paris, 1928.
Reinhardstoettner, K. von. Graf von **SCHACK** und die romanische Litteratur. Beilage Allg. Zt., 158, 1894.
Arcari, P. La romanità dello **SHAKESPEARE.** Opere e giorni, 1932.
Plessow, G. L. Um Shakespeares Nordentum. Berlin, 1937.
Pellegrini, C. Il **SISMONDI** e la storia delle letterature dell'Europa meridionale. Genève, 1926.
Salis, H. R. von. Sismondis Geschichte der Literatur Südeuropas. NSR, 1928.
Schudt, E. Das Ausland in **SMOLLETTS** Romanen. Giessen, 1923.
Iswolski, Helene. Vladimir **SOLOVIEV** and the Western World. Russian Review, 7, 1947.
Richter, L. **SWINBURNES** Verhältnis zu Frankreich und Italien. Leipzig, 1911.
Anon. Views a Foot; or Europe Seen with Knapsack and Staff, by J. Bayard **TAYLOR.** NAR, 1847.
Foerster, N. The Intellectual Heritage of **THOREAU.** Texas Review, 2, 1916-17.
Noodt, U. H. L'occidentalisme d'Ivan **TOURGUENEV.** Paris, 1922.
Fischer, H. **UHLANDS** Beziehungen zu ausländischen Litteraturen. ZVL, 1888. And in: Beiträge z. Litteraturgeschichte Schwabens. 2 vols. Stuttgart, 1891-99.
Fraenkel, L. Ludwig Uhland als Romanist. Archiv, 1888.
Baldensperger, F. Alfred de **VIGNY** et les littératures étrangères. RCC, 1924.
Citoleux, M. Alfred de Vigny. Persistances classiques et affinités étrangères. Paris, 1924.
Koch, M. Ausländische Stoffe und Einflüsse in Richard **WAGNERS** Dichtung. SVL, 3.
Haupt, E. Ueber die deutsche Lyrik bis zu **WALTHER VON DER VOGELWEIDE:** Die romanisierenden Dichter. Progr. Schneeberg, 1896.
Beyer, H. Det norske og det europeiske hos **WERGELAND.** Samtiden, 52, 1940.
Glaesener, H. Les points de départ méridionaux de l'Obéron de **WIELAND.** RLC, 14, 1934.

CHAPTER FOURTEEN

Authors' Readings (Belesenheit.)

Ogilvy, J. D. A. Books Known to Anglo-Latin Writers from **ALDHELM** to Alcuin. Publ. of Mediaeval Academy, Cambridge, Mass., 1936.
Ragg, L. M. What Jane **AUSTEN** Read. English, 2, 1938.
Cowdrick, R. E. The Early Reading of Pierre **BAYLE.** Scottdale (Pa.), 1939.
Davis, R. **BEDE'S** Early Reading. Spec., 1933.
Champion, P. La librairie de **CHARLES D'ORLEANS.** Paris, 1910.
Duchemin, M. La bibliothèque de **CHATEAUBRIAND.** Bull. du Bibliophile, 20.X.1931.
Coffman, G. R. **CHAUCER'S** Library and Literary Heritage for the Canterbury Tales. SPh, 38, 1941.
Lounsbury, T. R. The Learning of Chaucer. In: Studies in Chaucer. Boston, 1892.
Lowes, J. L. The Road to Xanadu (**COLERIDGE**). Boston, 1927.
Snyder, A. D. Books Borrowed by Coleridge from the Library of the University of Göttingen 1799. MPh, 1928.
Isaacs, J. **CONGREVE'S** Library. Trans. of the Bibliographical Society, 20, 1939.
Guckel, W. & Günther, E. **DEFOES** und Swifts Belesenheit und ihre literarische Kritik. Berlin, 1925.
Fiedler, F. **DICKENS'** Belesenheit. Archiv, 1920.
Cameron, K. W. Ralph Waldo **EMERSON'S** Reading. Raleigh (N. C.), 1941.
Keudell, Elise von. **GOETHE** als Besucher der Weimarer Bibliothek. Ein Verzeichnis der von ihm entliehenen Werke. Weimar, 1931.
Tornius, V. Goethe als Büchersammler. Zs. f. Bücherfreunde, 1932.
Southard, G. D. Manuel **GUTIERREZ NAJERA'S** Readings in Foreign Literatures. Diss. U. of Iowa, 1940.
Warren, A. **HAWTHORNE** Reading. NEQ, 8, 1935.
Weygandt, B. M. **KIPLING'S** Reading and its Influence on his Poetry. Philadelphia, 1939.
Entwistle, W. J. The Scholarship of **LUIS DE LEON.** RR, 1935.
LOWELL, J. R. Among My Books. Boston, 1872.
Williams, S. T. **MACAULAY'S** Reading and Literary Criticism. PhQ, 1924.

Sealts, M. M. **MELVILLE'S** Reading: A Check-List of Books Owned and Borrowed. Harvard Library Bull., 2, 1948.

Dunster, C. Considerations on **MILTON'S** Early Reading and the Prima Stamina of his Paradise Lost. Edinburgh, 1800.

Bonnefon, P. La bibliothèque de **MONTAIGNE.** RHLF, 1895.

Masson, A. Notes sur la bibliothèque de Montaigne. H&R, 6.

Ullman, B. L. **PETRARCH'S** Favorite Books. TAPhA, 1923.

Marraro, H. R. Unpublished Documents on Da **PONTE'S** Italian Library. PMLA, 58, 1943.

Modzalevskii, B. L. **PUSHKIN'S** Library: a Bibliographical Description. In: Pushkin i ego sovremenniki, 3, 1910. And in: Literaturnoe Nasledstvo, 16-18, 1934.

Poetzsche, E. Samuel **RICHARDSONS** Belesenheit. Kiel, 1907.

Rhodes, S. A. Arthur **RIMBAUD'S** Readings. MLN, 53.

Reichenburg, M. Essai sur les lectures de **ROUSSEAU.** Philadelphia, 1932.

—— La bibliothèque de J. J. Rousseau. Annales J. J. Rousseau, 21, 1932.

Schiff, M. La bibliothèque du Marquis de **SANTILLANE.** Bibliothèque de l'Ecole des Hautes Etudes. Paris, 1905.

Anders, H. R. D. **SHAKESPEARE'S** Books. Berlin, 1904.

Droop, A. Die Belesenheit **SHELLEYS.** Diss. Berlin, 1906.

Riedner, W. **SPENSER'S** Belesenheit. Leipzig, 1908.

Williams, H. Dean **SWIFT'S** Library. Cambridge U. P., 1932.

Cruse, A. The Victorians and their Reading. (**TENNYSON** etc.) Boston, 1935.

Melville, L. **THACKERAY** as a Reader and Critic of Books. In: Some Aspects of Thackeray. London, 1911.

Van Doren, M. **THOREAU'S** Reading. In: H. D. Thoreau. Boston, 1916.

Grossi, E. La Biblioteca di Guido **ZANSI.** Milano, 1934.

BOOK FOUR

The Modern World

FIRST PART

Celtic and Arthurian Contributions.

CHAPTER ONE

Celtic Influences in General.

1. Generalities.

Arbois de Jubainville, H. d'. Introduction à l'étude de la littérature celtique. Paris, 1883.

Arnold, M. The Study of Celtic Literature. London, 1891.

Bauersfeld, H. Die Entwicklung der keltischen Studien in Deutschland. Halle, 1937.

Brugger, E. Ueber die Bedeutung von Bretagne, Breton in mittelalterlichen Texten. ZFSL, 20, 1898.

Buck, M. R. Gallische Fluss- und Ortsnamen in Baden. Zs. f. d. Geéschichte des Oberrheins, 3, 1888.

Denis, L. Le génie celtique et le monde invisible. Paris, 1928.

Esser, Q. Ueber gallische Ortsnamen in der Rheinprovinz. Andernach, 1874.

Feist, S. Germanen und Kelten in der antiken Ueberlieferung. Halle, 1927.

Gardner, E. G. Notes on the Matière de Bretagne in Italy. Transactions of the British Academy, 15, 1929.

Golther, W. Beziehungen zwischen französischer und keltischer Litteratur im Mittelalter. ZVL, 3, 1890.

Graf, A. Appunti per la storia del ciclo bretonne in Italia. GSLI, 5, 1885.

Grubb, H. T. H. The Ancient Celtic Muse and its Effect upon English Poetry. Poetry Rev., 29, 1938.

Hoepffner, E. Lais et romans bretons. RCC, 35, 1933.

Hoops, R. Das Keltentum in Schottland. ESn, 75, 1942.

Jirmounsky, M. M. La survivance littéraire des Matières de France et de Bretagne au delà du moyen âge. RLC, 9, 1929.

Lebesgue, P. Celtisme et germanisme. Monde nouveau, 1930.

Leslie, S. The Celt and the World: A Study of the Relation of Celt and Teuton in History. New York, 1917.

Lotspeich, C. M. Celts and Teutons. JEGPh, 12, 1913.

Neumann, W. Parenté du gaulois et du latin. Neuchâtel, 1881.

Preusler, W. Keltischer Einfluss im Englischen. Anglia, 66, 1942.

Rajna, P. Gli eroi brettoni nell' onomastica italiana del secolo XII. Romania, 17, 1887.

Snyders, E. D. The Celtic Revival in English Literature, 1760-1800. Harvard U. P., 1923.

Vasconcellos, J. L. de. Les Celtes de la Lusitanie portugaise. RC, 23, 1902.

Weisgerber, J. L. Die keltischen Völker im Umkreis von England. Marburg, 1941.

Witte, H. Deutsche und Keltoromanen in Lothringen nach der Völkerwanderung. In: Beiträge zur Landes- und Volkskunde von Elsass-Lothringen, 15, 1891. And in: Zs. f. d. Geschichte des Oberrheins, 6, 1891.

Wright, T. The Celt, the Roman and the Saxon. London, 1852.

Zachrisson, R. E. Romans, Kelts and Saxons in Ancient Britain. Leipzig, 1927.

Ziekursch, Irene. Angelsachsentum und Keltentum im heutigen Schottland. Anglis, 65, 1941.

2. Influences upon Individual Authors and Works.

Renda, U. L'elemento brettone nell' Avarchide di Luigi ALAMANNI. GSLI, 1899.

Blasche, H. Angelsachsen und Kelten im Urteil der Historia Ecclesiastica Gentis Anglorum des BEDA. Göttingen, 1940.

Boenders, F. C. M. Keltische invloeden op het Nieuwe Testament. (BIBLE). Theol. Tijdschrift, 1919.

Klinz, A. Die Keltenfrage bei CAESAR und Tacitus. Deutsche höhere Schule, 4, 1937.

Foulet, L. Le prologue du Franklin's Tale et les Lais Bretons. (CHAUCER). ZRPh, 1906.

Loomis, Laura H. Chaucer and the Breton Lays of the Auchinleck Ms. SPh, 38, 1941.

Duhouveau, F. FRANCOIS D'ASSISE, génie celtique. MF, 15.XII.1935.

Lebesgue, P. La matière de Bretagne et l'Amadis de Gaule. (LOBEIRA). Bull. des Etudes portugaises, 1, 1937.

Pound, Louise. LOWELL'S Breton Legend. AL, 12, 1940.

Tronchon, H. Ernest **RENAN** et l'âme celtique. RCC, 1928.

CHAPTER TWO

King Arthur and the Round Table.

(For Merlin, see Thematology, I. VI. 10.)

Anon. The Epic of Arthur. (Tennyson). ER, 1870.

Alton, J. Einiges zu den Charakteren der Artussage. Wien, 1883.

Bond, R. W. King Arthur on the Stage. Fortnightly Review, 57, 1895.

Breillat, P. Une traduction italienne de la Mort le Roi Artu. AR, 21, 1937.

Brinkley, R. F. Arthurian Legend in the XVIIth Century. Baltimore, 1932.

Bruce, J. D. The Evolution of Arthurian Romance from the Beginnings down to the Year 1300. 2 vols. Göttingen, 1923.

Brugger, E. Das arthurische Material in den Prophecies Merlin des Meisters Richard d'Irlande. ZFSL, 61-62, 1939.

Chambers, E. K. Arthur of Britain. London, 1927.

Cheetham, S. The Arthurian Legend in Tennyson. Contemporary Review, 1868.

Clement, N. H. The Influence of the Arthurian Romances on the Five Books of Rabelais. Berkeley, 1926.

Critchlow, F. L. Arthur in Old French Poetry not of the Breton Cycle. MPh, 6, 1908-09.

Dempf, A. Beda und die Entstehung der Artussage. Zs. f. deutsche Geistesgeschichte, 1935.

Entwistle, W. J. The Arthurian Legend in the Literatures of the Spanish Peninsula. London, 1925.

Faral, E. La légende arthurienne: études et documents. 3 vols. Paris, 1929.

Ferrando, G. La leggenda arturiana in Italia. Marzocco, 25.X.1931.

Fink, R. Der Artusstoff in der deutschen Dichtung des Mittelalters. Zs. f. deutsche Geisteswissenschaft, 2, 1939.

Fletcher, R. H. The Arthurian Material in the Chronicles of Great Britain and France. HSPhL, 10, 1906.

Frappier, J. Stude sur la Morte le roi Artu, roman du XIIIe siècle. Paris, 1936.

Freymond, E. Beiträge zur Kenntnis der altfranzösischen Artusromane in Prosa. Berlin, 1895.

—— Artus' Kampf mit dem Katzenungethüm. Die Sage und ihre Lokalisierung in Savoyen. Festschrift Gröber. Halle, 1899.

Gardner, E. G. The Arthurian Legend in Italian Literature. London, 1931.

Glennie, J. S. Arthurian Localities, Their Historical Origin. London, 1869.

Gurteen, S. H. The Arthurian Epic; A Comparative Study of the Versions of the Story, and Tennyson's Idylls of the King. London, 1895.

Jones, W. L. King Arthur in History and Legend. Cambridge, 1911.

Loomis, R. S. Celtic Myth and Arthurian Romance. New York, 1927.

—— By What Route Did the Romantic Tradition of Arthur Reach the French? MPh, 33, 1935-36.

—— Chivalric and Dramatic Imitations of Arthurian Romance. Gedenkschrift A. K. Porter. Harvard U. P., 1939.

—— The Arthurian Legend before 1139. RR, 32, 1941.

—— Arthurian Tradition and Chrétien de Troyes. Columbia U.P., 1949.

—— Breton Folklore and Arthurian Romance. CL, 2, 1950.

—— & Loomis, Laura H. Arthurian Legends in Medieval Art. New York, 1938.

Loth, J. Des nouvelles théories sur l'origine des romans arthuriens. RC, 13, 1892.

—— Contributions à l'étude des romans de la Table Ronde. Paris, 1912.

McHugh, Sheila. The Lay of the Big Fool: Its Irish and Arthurian Sources. MPh, 42, 1945.

Millican, C. B. Spenser and the Table Round. Harvard U. P., 1932.

Newell, W. W. King Arthur and the Table Round. Tales with an Account of Arthurian Romance and Notes. Boston, 1898.

Newstead, H. Bran the Blessed in Arthurian Romance. New York, 1939.

Nitze, W. A. Arthurian Romance and Modern Poetry and Music. Chicago U. P., 1940.

—— Bédier's Epic Theory and the Arthuriana of Nennius. MPh, 39, 1941.

Northrup, C. S. & Parry, J. J. The Arthurian Legends: Modern Retellings of the Old Stories. An Annotated Bibliography. JEGPh, 43, 1944.

Paris, P. Les romans de la Table Ronde. 5 vols. Paris, 1868-77.

Paris, G. De l'origine et du développement des Romans de la Table Ronde. Romanische Studien, 1872.

—— Romans en vers du cycle de la Table Ronde. RHLF, 30, 1888.

Parks, G. D. King Arthur and the Roads to Rome. JEGPh, 45, 1946.
Polidori. La Tavola Ritonda. Bologna, 1864-65.
Puetz, F. Zur Geschichte und Entwicklung der Artussage. Diss. Bonn, 1892.
Reid, Margaret J. C. The Arthurian Legend. Comparison of Treatment in Modern and Medieval Literature. Edinburgh, 1938.
Reyes, A. Influencia del ciclo artúrico en la literatura castellana. Bol. de la Acad. Argentina de Letras, 6, 1938.
Rhys, J. Studies in the Arthurian Legend. Oxford, 1891.
San Marte (A. Schulz). Die Artussage und die Märchen des Rothen Buches von Hergest. Quedlinburg, 1842.
Siebert, J. & G. Thiele. Ein ostdeutscher Artusroman des XIII. Jahrhunders. ZDA, 1940.
Singer, S. Die Artussage. Bern, 1926.
Sommer, H. O. Zur Kritik der altfranzösischen Artus-Romane in Prosa. ZRPh, 32, 1908.
—— The Vulgate Version of the Arthurian Romances. Washington, 1908-16.
Van Der Ven-Ten Bensel, E. F. The Character of King Arthur in English Literature. Diss. Amsterdam, 1925.
Villemarqué, H. de la. Contes populaires des anciens Bretons, précédé d'un Essai sur l'origine des épopées chevalresques de la Table Ronde. 2 vols. Paris, 1842.
—— Les romans de la Table Ronde et les contes des anciens Bretons. Paris, 1861.
Vincent, Ruby R. A Comparison of Malory's Morte Darthur and Tennyson's Idylls of the King. Diss. U. of Okla., 1939.
Visser, G. J. The Passing of Arthur and Ymadawiad Arthur (1902). NPh, 23, 1937.
Weston, Jessie L. The Position of Chrétien de Troyes in the Arthurian Cycle. In: The Legend of Sir Lancelot du Lake. London, 1901. Cf. also Anglia, 13, 1902.
Wuelker, R. Die Arthursage in der englischen Litteratur. Progr. Leipzig, 1895.

CHAPTER THREE

Lohengrin.

Bloete, J. F. D. Der historische Schwanritter. ZRPh, 21, 1897.
—— Das Aufkommen der Sage von Brabon Silvius, dem brabantischen Schwanritter. Amsterdam, 1904.
Blondeaux, F. La légende du chevalier au cygne. Rev. de Belgique, 38, 1903.
Doutrepont, G. La légende du chevalier au cygne pendant le XVIe siècle. Mélanges Abel Lefranc. Paris, 1936.
Frey, Anna L. The Swan Knight Legend, its Background, Early Development and Treatment in the German Poems. Nashville, 1931.
Golther, W. Ueber die deutsche Schwanrittersage und die französischen Seitenstücke. Deutsche Nationallitteratur, 5, 1882.
—— Lohengrin, Sage und Dichtung. Baireuther Taschenbuch, 1894.
—— Lohengrin-Studien. Literaturblatt f. german. & roman. Lit. & Philol, 16, 1895.
Jaffray, R. The Two Knights of the Swan, Lohengrin and Helyas. New York, 1910.
Krogman, W. Die Grundform der Schwanenrittersage. Niederdeutsche Zs. für Volkskunde, 8, 1930.
—— Die Schwanenrittersage. Archiv, 171, 1937.
Krüger, A. G. Die Quellen der Schwanritterdichtungen. Hannover, 1936.
Lampp, F. Die Schwanrittersage in der Literatur. Progr. Ratibor, 1914.
Liebermann, F. Chevalier au cygne in England. Archiv, 107, 1901.
Nover, J. Die Lohengrinsage und ihre poetische Gestaltung. Stammlung gemeinverständlicher Vorträge. Hamburg, 1899.
Panzer, F. Lohengrinstudien. Halle, 1894.
Paris, P. Le chevalier au cygne. RHLF, 22, 1895.
Poisson, G. L'origine celtique de la légende de Lohengrin. RC, 34, 1913.

CHAPTER FOUR

Parcival and the Holy Grail.

Amoretti, G. V. Il Gral romantico. Civiltà moderna, 1930.
Aubin, T. Parsifal (Wagner) jugé par Debussy. Le Ménestrel, 16.IX.1932.
Bergmann, F. Sur l'origine et la signification des romans du Saint-Graal. Strasbourg, 1842.
Bertoni, G. San Gral. Roma, 1940.
Birch-Hirschfeld, A. Die Sage vom Gral, ihre Entwicklung und dichterische Ausbildung in Frankreich und Deutschland im XII. und XIII. Jahrhunderte. Leipzig, 1877.
Breillat, P. La quête du Saint-Graal en

Italie. Mélanges d'archéologie et d'histoire, 54, 1937.
Brown, A. C. L. The Origin of the Grail Legend. Harvard U. P., 1943.
—— Irish Fabulous History and Chrétien's Perceval. MLQ, 8, 1947-48.
Burdach, K. Der Gral. Forschungen über seinen Ursprung und seinen Zusammenhang mit der Longinuslegende. Stuttgart, 1938.
Carter, Barbara B. Dante and the Holy Grail. Contemp. Rev., 153, 1938.
Dean, F. R. The Legend of the Grail. Papers of the Manchester Literary Club, 61, 1935.
Ferrari, L. La leggenda del s' Graal e i suoi echo in Italia. Ascoli, 1919.
Fourquet, J. Wolfram d'Eschenbach et le Conte del Graal. Paris, 1938.
Fritze, E. Die Gralsage und die Parzivaldichtung. Protestant. Blätter, 39, 1906.
Gaster, M. The Legend of the Grail. FL, 1891.
Gauchat, L. Parzival in Sage und Kunst. Neue Zürcher Zt., 95 ff., 1913.
Gilson, E. La mystique de la grâce dans la Queste del Saint Graal. Romania, 51, 1925.
Golther, W. Chrestiens Conte del Graal in seinem Verhältniss zum welschen Peredur und zum englischen Sir Perceval. SBAW, 1890.
—— Ursprung und Entwickelung der Sage von Parceval und dem Gral. Baireuther Blätter, 14, 1891.
—— Die Gralsage bei Wolfram von Eschenbach. Rostock, 1910.
—— Parzival und der Gral in der Dichtung des Mittelalters und der Neuzeit. Stuttgart, 1925.
—— Parzival in der deutschen Literatur. Berlin, 1929.
Hagen, P. Parzivalstudien: Wolfram von Eschenbach; Chrestien von Troies. Germania, 1892.
—— Der Gral. Strassburg, 1900.
Hamilton, W. E. M. C. L'intérpretation mystique de La queste del Saint Graal. NPh, 27, 1942.
Harper. The Legend of the Holy Grail. Baltimore, 1893.
Hatto, A. T. On Wulfram's Conception of the Graal. MLR, 43, 1948.
Heinrich, G. A. Etude sur le Parcival de Wolfram d'Eschenbach et sur la Légende de Saint-Graal. Diss. Paris, 1855.
Heinzel, R. Ueber Wolframs von Eschenbach Parzival. SAWW, 1891.
—— Ueber die französischen Gralromane. Denkschriften der kaiserl. Akademie der Wissenschaften, 40. Wien, 1892.
Hertz, W. Die Sage vom Parzival und dem Graal. Breslau, 1882.
—— Wolframs Parzival (cf. Appendix and Notes). Stuttgart, 1898.
Hurcher, E. Le Saint Graal. Paris, 1877.
Junk, V. Gralssage und Gralsdichtung im Mittelalter. Wien, 1911.
Kampers, F. Gnostisches im Parzival und in verwandten Dichtungen. Schlesische Ges. f. Volkskunde, 21, 1919.
Karg-Gasterstädt, Elisabeth. Zur Entstehungsgeschichte des Parzival. Halle, 1925.
Koelbing, E. Die nordische Parzivalsage und ihre Quelle. Diss. Leipzig, 1869.
Kuepp. Die unmittelbaren Quellen des Parzival. ZDPh, 17, 1885.
Lang, L. Ueber die Entwicklungsgeschichte der Gralsage. Progr. München, 1861.
Loomis, R. S. The Irish Origin of the Grail Legend. Spec., 8, 1933.
Lot-Borodine, Myrrha. Autour du Saint Graal. Romania, 56-57, 1930-31.
Lot, F. Les auteurs du Conte du Graal. Romania, 57, 1931.
Martin, E. E. Zur Gralsage. Strassburg, 1880.
Mensendick, D. Die Gral-Parzivalsage und Wagners Parsifal. Leipzig, 1915.
Mergell, B. Wolfram von Eschenbach und seine französischen Quellen. Wolframs Parzival. Münster, 1943.
Muncker, F. Die Gralssage bei einigen Dichtern der neueren deutschen Literatur. SBAW, 1902.
Nutt, A. Studies on the Legend of the Holy Grail with Especial Reference to the Hypothesis of its Celtic Origin. London, 1888.
Panzer, F. Die Quellen von Wolframs Parzival. F&F, 16, 1940.
Paris, G. Perceval et la légende du Saint Graal. Bull. de la Société historique et Cercle St. Simon, 1883.
Pauphilet, A. Etudes sur la Queste del Saint Graal, attribuée à Gautier Map. Paris, 1921.
Pfitzner, H. Der Parsifalstoff und seine Gestaltungen. In: Vom musikalischen Drama. München, 1915.
Ranke, F. Zur Symbolik des Grals bei Wolfram von Eschenbach. Trivium, 4, 1946.
Rochat, A. Der deutsche Parzifal, der Conte del Graal und Chrestiens Fortsetzer. Germania, 1859.

Rohr, F. Parzival und der Heilige Gral. Hildesheim, 1924.
Ruggieri, J. Versioni italiane della Questa del Saint Graal. AR, 21, 1937.
San Marte. Ueber den Bildungsgang der Graal- und Parzival-Dichtung in Frankreich und Deutschland. ZDPh, 22, 1890.
Singer, S. Ueber die Quelle von Wolframs Parzival. ZDA, 24, 1900.
—— Wolfram und der Gral. Neue Parzival Studien. Bern, 1939.
Stockum, T. C. van. Wolframs Parzival und das Problem der Quelle. NPh, 26, 1941.
Strucks, C. Der junge Parzival in Wolframs von Eschenbach Parzival, Crestiens de Troyes Conte del Gral, im englischen Syre Percyvelle und im italienischen Carduino. Leipzig, 1910.
Vercoutre, A. Un problème littéraire résolu: origine et genèse de la légende du Saint-Graal. Paris, 1901.
Veselovskij, A. N. Zur Frage über die Heimat der Legende vom Hl. Gral. ASPh, 23, 1901. And in: Journal Russian Ministry for Enlightenment, 351, 1904.
Viscardi, A. Il Graal, Giuseppe di Arimatea, l'abbazia di Glastonbury e le origini cristiane della Britannia. Cultura Neolatina, 2, 1942.
Wechssler, E. Zur Beantwortung der Frage nach den Quellen von Wolframs Parcival. Festgabe Sievers, Halle, 1896.
—— Die Sage vom Heiligen Gral in ihrer Entwicklung bis auf Richard Wagners Parsifal. Halle, 1898.
—— Untersuchungen zu den Graalromanen. ZRPh, 23, 1899.
Weston, J. L. The Perceval Legend in Literature. The Library, N. S. 5, 1904.
—— The Legend of Sir Perceval. 2 vols. London, 1906-09.
—— The Quest of the Holy Grail. London, 1913.
Wilmotte, M. Le poème du Gral et ses auteurs. Paris, 1930.
—— Le Parzival de Wolfram d'Eschenbach et ses sources françaises. Paris, 1934.

CHAPTER FIVE

Tristan and Isolde.

Adams, R. D. W. A Tristan Bibliography. Diss. U. of Southern Cal., 1935.
Bechstein, R. Tristan und Isolt in deutschen Dichtungen der Neuzeit. Leipzig, 1876.
Behagel, O. Gottfrieds von Strassburg Tristan und seine Quelle. Germania, 23. And in: Romania 15-16, 1886-87.
Benedetti, L. di. La leggenda di Tristano. Bari, 1942.
Beridze, C. Sur la possibilité de l'origine géorgienne du poème français Tristan et Iseut. L'Alliance universelle, Feb., 1934.
Block. Die Sage von Tristan und Isolde in dramatischer Form. NSp, 21.
Boor, H. de. Die Grundauffassung von Gottfrieds Tristan. DVLG, 18, 1940.
Bossert, A. Tristan et Iseult, poème de Gotfrit de Strassburg, comparé à d'autres poèmes sur le même sujet. Paris, 1865.
—— La légende chevaleresque de Tristan et Iseult. Paris, 1902.
Bruce, J. D. A Boccaccio Analogue in the Old French Tristan. RR, 1, 1910.
Clark, Mary A. Edwin Arlington Robinson's Treatment of the Tristram-Isolt Legend. Diss. U. of Illinois, 1937.
Compart, F. Die Sagenüberlieferungen in den Tristan-Epen Eilharts und Gottfrieds. Güstrow, 1876.
Czerny, J. Richard Wagners Tristan und die Phaedra-Dramen. Bayreuther Blätter, 58, 1935.
Czerwenka, Maria. Neuere Tristandichtungen. Diss. Wien, 1922.
Dam, J. van. Tristanprobleme. NPh, 15, 1929-30.
Deister, J. L. Bernart de Ventadour's Reference to the Tristan Story. MPh, 19, 1921-22.
Deutschbein, M. Eine irische Variante der Tristan-Sage. Anglia Bb., 15, 1904.
Dornbush, R. Wagner and the Iseult Legend. Musician, 54, 1939.
Dufhus, E. Tristandichtungen des 19. und 20. Jahrhunderts. Diss. Köln, 1924.
Foulet, L. Marie de France et la légende de Tristan. ZRPh, 32, 1908.
Frank, G. Marie de France and the Tristram Legend. PMLA, 63, 1948.
Golther, W. Die Sage von Tristan und Isolde, ihre Entstehung und Entwicklung im Mittelalter. München, 1887.
—— Tristan und Isolde in der französischen und deutschen Dichtung des Mittelalters. Beilage z. Allg. Zt., 11-17, 1889 & Berlin, 1929.
—— Tristan und Isolde im Epos, Drama und Bild. Bühne & Welt, 1, 1898.
—— Bemerkungen zur Sage und Dichtung von Tristan und Isolde. ZFSL, 1, 1900.
—— Tristandichtungen. LE, 4, 1902.
—— Tristan und Isolde in den Dichtungen

des Mittelalters und der neuen Zeit. Leipzig, 1907.
Heimann, E. Tristan und Isolde in der neuzeitlichen Literatur. Diss. Leipzig, 1931.
Heinzel, R. Gottfrieds von Strassburg Tristan und seine Quellen. ZDA, 14, 1888.
Hertz, W. Tristan und Isolde von Gottfried von Strassburg. (Cf. Introduction). Stuttgart, 1877.
Kelimina, J. Geschichte der Tristansage nach den Dichtungen des Mittelalters. Wien, 1923.
Koehler, R. Tristan und Isolde und das Märchen von der goldhaarigen Jungfrau und von den Wässern des Todes und des Lebens. Germania, 12, 1866. And in: Kleinere Schriften. Berlin, 1898-1900.
Koelbing, E. Die nordischen und englischen Versionen der Tristansage. Heilbronn, 1878.
Kufferath, M. Tristan et Iseult. Bruxelles, 1894.
Küpper, H. Bibliographie zur Tristansage. Jena, 1941.
Leach, H. G. Tristan in the North. In: Angevin Britain and Scandinavia. Cambridge, 1921.
Levi, E. I lais brettoni e la leggenda di Tristano. Studj romanzi, 14, 1917.
Lobedanz, E. Das französische Element in Gottfried von Strassburgs Tristan. Diss. Rostock, 1878.
Löseth, E. Le roman en prose de Tristan. Paris, 1891.
Loth, J. Un parallèle au roman de Tristan, en irlandais, au Xe siècle. C. R. des Séances de l'Acad. des Inscriptions et Belles-Lettres, 1924.
Lot-Borodine, Myrrha. Tristan et Lancelot. Gedenkschrift G. S. Loomis. New York, 1927.
Malavasi, G. La materia poetica del ciclo brettone in Italia, in particolare la leggenda di Tristano e quella di Lancillotto. Bologna, 1903.
Paris, G. Tristan et Iseut. RP, 15.IV.1894.
Parodi, E. G. Il Tristano riccardiano. (Cf. Introduction). In: Collez. d. op. ined. o rare. Bologna, 1896.
Rabe, Helene. Die Tristansage in der Bewertung des Mittelalters und der neueren Zeit. Bayr. Blätter, 36 & Leipzig, 1914.
Ranke, F. Tristan und Isolde. München, 1925.
Roettiger, W. Der heutige Stand der Tristanforschung. Hamburg, 1897. Cf. Romania, 27.
Schoepperle, Gertrude. Tristan and Isolt, a Study of the Sources of the Romance. 2 vols. Frankfurt; London, 1913.
Schuster, L. Neuere Tristan-Dichtungen. Diss. Giessen, 1912.
Schwietering, J. Der Tristan Gottfrieds von Strassburg und die Bernhardische Mystik. Berlin, 1943.
Sudre, L. Les allusions à la légende de Tristan dans la littérature du moyen âge. Romania, 15, 1886.
Szymanzig, M. Immermanns Tristan und Isolde. Marburg, 1911.
Thurneysen, R. Eine irische Parallele zur Tristansage. ZRPh, 43, 1923.
Vetter F. La légende de Tristan d'après le poème français de Thomas et les versions principales qui s'y rattachent. Diss. Marburg, 1882.
Vinaver, E. Le roman de Tristan et Iseut dans l'oeuvre de Thomas Malory. Paris, 1925.
Viotta, H. Tristan und Isolde als Sage und Drama. Caecilia, 60, 1903.
Walther, E. Hans Sachsens Tragödie Tristant und Isolde in ihrem Verhältnis zur Quelle. Diss. München, 1902.
Wangelin, Anne-Marie. Die Liebe in den Tristandichtungen der Viktorianischen Zeit. Tübingen, 1937.
Witte, A. Der Aufbau der ältesten Tristandichtungen. ZDA, 70, 1934.
Wolff, L. Tristan et Yseult dans la poésie anglaise du XIXe siècle. Annales de Bretagne, 40, 1932.

CHAPTER SIX

Erec, Iwein, Lancelot and Other Epic Characters.

Baechtold, J. Der Lanzelet des Ulrich von Zatzikhoven. Frauenfeld, 1870.
Bang, Carol K. Emotions and Attitudes in Chrétien de Troyes' Erec et Enide and Hartmann von Aue's Erec der Wunderaere. PMLA, 57, 1942.
Bartsch, K. Ueber Christians von Troies und Hartmanns von Aue Erec und Enide. Germania, 7, 1862.
Behagel, O. Zum Lanzelet Ulrichs von Zatzikhoven. Germania, 35, 1891.
Brown, A. C. L. Iwain, a Study in the Origins of Arthurian Romance. Boston, 1903.
Carman, J. N. The Relationship of the Perlesvaus and the Queste del Saint Graal. Humanistic Studies U. of Kansas, 5, 1936.
Cross, T. P. The Celtic Elements in the

Lays of Lanval and Graelent. MPh, 12, 1914-15.
——, & Nitze, W. A. Lancelot and Guenevere: A Study on the Origins of Courtly Love. Chicago, 1930.
Dreyer, K. Hartmanns Erec und seine französische Quelle. Progr. Königsberg, 1893.
Fuehrer, Sister Mary R. A Study of the Relation of the Dutch Lancelot and the Flemish Perchevael Fragments to the Mss of Chrétien's Conte del Graal. Washington, 1939.
Gaertner, G. Der Iwein Hartmanns von Aue und der Chevalier au lion des Chrestien de Troies. Diss. Breslau, 1875.
Gaster, B. Vergleich des Hartmann'schen Iwein mit dem Löwenritter Chrétiens. Diss. Greifswald, 1896.
Loomis, R. S. More Celtic Elements in Gawain and the Green Knight. JEGPh, 42, 1943.
Maertens, P. Zur Lancelotsage. Diss. Strassburg, 1880.
Minzloff, R. Deux vers du Dante et un chapître du roman de Lancelot. Bull. du bibliophile et du bibliothécaire, 36, 1898.
Nitze, W. A. The Old French Grail Romance Perlesvaus; A Study of its Principal Sources. Baltimore, 1902.
—— A New Source of the Iwain. MPh, 3, 1905-06.
Othmer, K. Das Verhältniss von Christians von Troyes Erec et Enide zu dem Mabinogion des rothen Buches von Hergest Geraint ab Erbin. Diss. Bonn, Köln, 1889.
Panzer, F. Gahmuret. Quellenstudien zu Wolframs Parzival. Heidelberg, 1940.
Paris, G. Etudes sur les romans de la Table Ronde. Le Lanzelet d'Ulrich de Zatzikhoven. Romania, 1881; Paris, 1883.
—— Etudes sur les romans de la Table Ronde: Lancelot. Romania, 1881-83.
Peter, A. Die deutschen Prosaromane von Lanzelot und ihr Verhältniss zur Quelle. Wien, 1883.
Rauch, C. Die wälische, französische und deutsche Bearbeitung der Iweinsage. Diss. Göttingen, 1869.
Ravenel, Florence L. Tydorel and Sir Gowther. PMLA, 20, 1905.
Schleich, G. Ueber das Verhältniss der mittelenglischen Romanze Iwain und Gawain zu ihrer altfranzösischen Quelle. Berlin, 1889.
Settegast, F. Hartmanns Iwein verglichen mit seiner altfranzösischen Quelle. Diss. Marburg, 1873.
Stokoe, W. C. Sources of Sir Launfal: Lanval and Graelent. PMLA, 63, 1948.
Thomas, M. C. Sir Gawayne and the Green Knight. A Comparison with the French Perceval. Diss. Zürich, 1883.
Webster, K. G. T. Ulrich von Zatzikhoven's Welsches Buch (Lancelot). HSPhL, 16, 1934.
Weston, J. L. The Legend of Sir Lancelot du Lake. London, 1901.
Whiting, B. J. Gawain: his Reputation, his Courtesy and his Appearance in Chaucer's Squire's Tale. Medieval Studies, 9, 1947.

CHAPTER SEVEN

Geoffrey of Monmouth, Wace and Other Medieval Transmittors of Celtic Lore.

Dijksterhuis, A. Thomas und Gottfried. München, 1935.
Griscom, A. The Historia regum Britanniae of Geoffrey of Monmouth, with Contributions to the Study of its Place in Early British History. London, 1929.
Hamel, A. G. van. The Old Norse Version of the Historia regum Britanniae and the Text of Geoffrey of Monmouth. Etudes celtiques, 1, 1936.
Heimerle, Magda. Gottfried und Thomas. Ein Vergleich. Frankfurt, 1942.
Hoepffner, E. Chrétien de Troyes et Thomas d'Angleterre. Romania, 55, 1929.
—— Les Lais de Marie de France. Paris, 1935.
Holmes, U. T. A Welsh Motif in Marie de France's Guigemar. SPh, 39, 1942.
Hopkins, Annette B. The Influence of Wace on the Arthurian Romances of Crestien de Troies. Menasha (Wis.), 1913.
Houck, Margaret. Sources of the Roman de Brut of Wace. Berkeley, 1941.
Jones, E. Geoffrey of Monmouth, 1640-1800. Berkeley, 1944.
Keeler, Laura. Geoffrey of Monmouth and the Late Latin Chroniclers, 1300-1500. Berkeley, 1946.
—— The Historia Regum Britanniae and Four Mediaeval Chroniclers. Spec., 21, 1946.
Krautwald, H. Layamons Brut verglichen mit Waces Roman de Brut. Diss. Breslau, 1887.
Mennung, A. Der Bel Inconnu des Renaut de Beaujeu in seinem Verhältniss zum Lybeaus Desconus Carduino und Wigalois. Diss. Halle, 1900.

Parry, J. J. Geoffrey of Monmouth and the Paternity of Arthur. Spec., 13, 1938.
Pelan, Margaret. L'influence du Brut de Wace sur les romanciers français de son temps. Paris, 1931.
Philpot, J. H. Maistre Wace, a Pioneer in Two Literatures. London, 1925.
Singer, S. Thomas von Britannien und Gottfried von Strassburg. Festschrift Tièche. Bern, 1947.
Tatlock, J. S. P. Geoffrey of Monmouth's Vita Merlini. Spec., 18, 1943.
Webster, K. G. T. Hugh de Morville. Diss. Harvard, 1902.
—— Walter Map's French Things. Spec., 15, 1940.
Willard, R. Layamon in the 17th and 18th Centuries. Texas Studies in English, 1948.
Wilson, R. H. Malory in the Connecticut Yankee. Texas Studies in English, 27, 1948.
Zetsche, A. W. Ueber den ersten Theil der Bearbeitung des Roman de Brut des Wace durch Mannyng of Brunne. Diss. Leipzig, 1887.

CHAPTER EIGHT

Ossian.

1. General Influences.

Alonzo Cortes, N. El primer traductor español del falso Ossian. Valladolid, 1920.
Hankiss, J. The Culmination of the Hungarian Ossian-Cult. Festschrift E. Ekwall. Uppsala, 1942.
Hasselqvist, T. Ossian i den svenska dikten och litteraturen. Diss. Lund. Malmö, 1895.
Hazard, P. Ossian chez les Français. NRI, 15.IV.1920.
Horstmeyer, R. Die deutschen Ossian-Uebersetzungen des 18. Jahrhunderts. Diss. Greifswald, 1926.
Kalman, C. Les poésies d'Ossian en vers hongrois. (In Hungarian). Budapest, 1911.
Leary, L. Ossian in America: A Note. AL, 14, 1942.
Leo. Ossian in Deutschland. Versuch einer Erklärung seiner tiefen Wirkung. Progr. Jena, 1909.
Peers, E. A. The Influence of Ossian in Spain. PhQ, 3, 1924.
Pilot, A. Breve storia d'una edizione ossianesca che non fu stampata (1818). Nuovo Archivio veneto, 77-78, 1920.
Ponsard, F. L'influence d'Ossian. Discours de réception à l'Académie Française, 4.XII.1856.
Schöffler, H. Ossian. Hergang und Sinn eines grossen Betrugs. Goethe-Kalender, 34, 1941.
Stern, L. C. Die ossianischen Heldenlieder. ZVL, 8.
Swaen, A. E. H. Een nieuwe Ossian. NPh, 27, 1942.
Szyjkowski, M. Ossian en Pologne. C. R. Acad. Cracovie, 17, 1912.
Tedeschi, A. Ossian, l'Homère du Nord, en France. Milano, 1911.
Tombo, R. Ossian in Germany. Columbia U. P., 1901.
Van Tieghem, P. Ossian en France, Paris, 1917. Cf. FQ, 1, 1919.
—— Ossian et l'Ossianisme dans la littérature européenne au XVIIIe siècle. La Haye, 1920.
Weitnauer K,. Ossian in der italienischen Literatur bis etwa 1832, vorwiegend bei Monti. Diss. München, 1905 & ZVL, 16, 1906.

2. Influences upon Individual Authors.

Mazzoni, G. Ossian e V. **ALFIERI.** Bibliotheca, Roma, 1883.
Grierson, H. J. C. **BLAKE** and Macpherson. TLS. 7.IV.1945.
Gantz, K. F. Charlotte **BROOKE'S** Reliques of Irish Poetry and the Ossianic Controversy. U. of Texas Studies in English, 1940.
Wilmsen, F. Ossians Einfluss auf **BYRONS** Jugendgedichte. ZVL, 15.
Zanella, G. I poemi di Ossian e M. **CESAROTTI.** NAnt, 66, 1882.
Guillard, L. Sujets tirés des poèmes d'Ossian par **CHENAVARD.** Rev. du Lyonnais, 6, 1868.
Baumgarten, A. Michael **DENIS.** Progr. Linz, 1852.
Hennig, J. **GOETHE'S** Translations of Ossian's Songs of Selma. JEGPh, 45, 1946.
—— Goethe's Translation from MacPherson's Berrathon. MLR, 42, 1947.
Mauguin, G. Ossian et Werther. MF, 1948.
Adams, N. B. A Note on Garcia **GUTIERREZ** and Ossian. PhQ, 1928.
Vos, B. J. Notes on **HEINE.** MLN, 1908.
Betteridge, T. The Ossianic Poems in **HERDER'S** Volkslieder. MLR, 30, 1935.
Gillies, A. Herder und Ossian. Berlin, 1933.
Knothe, H. C. F. **KRETSCHMANN.** Ein

Beitrag zur Geschichte des Bardenwesens. Progr. Zittau, 1858.
Poplawski, T. A. von. L'influence d'Ossian sur l'oeuvre de **LAMARTINE.** Diss. Heidelberg, 1905.
Faggi, A. I poemi d'Ossian e il **LEOPARDI.** Marzocco, 26.XII.1925.
Thovez, E. Leopardi ed Ossian. Il Campo, 1-2, 1905. And in: L'Arco di Ulisse. Napoli, 1921.
Marwell, H. **PERCEY** und die Ossian-Kontroverse. Anglia, 1934.
Leisy, E. E. **THOREAU** and Ossian. NEQ, 18, 1945.
Hubach, R. R. Walt Whitman and **TALIESSIN.** AL, 18, 1947.

CHAPTER NINE

Ireland and Wales.

Balcam, A. S. Gaelic Literature Surveyed. Dublin, 1929.
Blanke, F. Irische Mönche in Zürich und am Bodensee. NSR, 1940.
Bout, A. L'âme du terroir et les liens des peuples par la tradition. Rapprochement entre un conte traduit de l'irlandais et un conte populaire recueilli en Picardie. Congrès régional des tradit. pop. d'Abbéville en 1901. Paris, 1902.
Cross, T. P. Ancient Ireland and Spain. Festschrift J. D. M. Ford. Harvard U. P., 1948.
Duggan, G. The Stage Irishman. London, 1937.
Foucher, J. P. Les littératures celtiques contemporaines. Essais et Etudes universitaires, 2. (Paris), 1946.
Gazay, J. L'influence des moines irlandais dans l'église provençale au début du moyen âge. Annales du Midi, 47, 1938.
Gent, R. A. The Valiant Welshman. Münchener Beiträge. Erlangen, 1902.
Hennig, J. Irish Saints in Early German Literature. Spec., 22, 1947.
Hutson, A. E. Gaelic Loan-Words in America. American Speech, 22, 1947.
Jones, E. W. The Welsh in America. AM, 1876.
Kelley, Sister M. Edith. The Irishman in the English Novel of the Nineteenth Century. Washington, 1940.
Levison, W. Die Iren und die fränkische Kirche. Historische Zs., 109, 1912.
Merwin, H. C. The Irish in American Life. AM, 1896.
Mezger, F. Der Ire in der englischen Literatur bis zum Anfang des 19. Jahrhunderts. Berlin, 1930.
Morris, L. R. The Celtic Dawn. A Survey of the Renascence in Ireland, 1889-1916. New York, 1917.
Pauly, Marie H. Les voyageurs français en Irlande au temps du romantisme. Paris, 1939.
Rossman, K. R. The Irish in American Drama in the Mid-XIXth Century. N. Y. Hist., 21, 1940.
Scott, Florence R. Teg -- the Stage Irishman. MLR, 42, 1947.
Slover, C. H. Early Literary Channels between Britain and Ireland. U. of Texas Studies in English, 6-7, 1926-27.
Urwin, K. A French Refugee in 18th Century Ireland. CLS, 17-18, 1945.
Wade-Evans, A. W. The Welsh in Britain. Trans. of the H. Soc. of Cymmrodorion, 1943-44.
Walsh, A. Scandinavian Relations with Ireland During the Viking Period. Dublin, 1922.
Walsh, J. J. The World's Debt to the Irish. Boston, 1926 .
Wittig, K. Die Ulster-Frage in der angloirischen Literatur. GRM, 28, 1940.
Zimmer, H. The Irish Element in Mediaeval Culture. New York, 1891.

CHAPTER TEN

Influences upon Individual Authors.

(For Anglo-Irish Authors from Goldsmith and Hume to Shaw and Yeats, See English Contributions).

Robbins, W. Matthew **ARNOLD** and Ireland. UTQ, 17, 1947.
Boswell, C. S. An Irish Precursor of **DANTE.** London, 1908.
Michael, F. Die irischen Romane von Maria **EDGEWORTH.** Diss. Königsberg, 1918.
Wecter, D. Benjamin **FRANKLIN** and an Irish Enthusiast (Newenham). HLQ, 4, 1941.
Blind, K. **GOETHE** und Heine über die irische Frage. Nord & Süd, March, 1897.
Lilly, G. The Welsh Influence in the Poetry of Gerard Manley **HOPKINS.** MLR, 38, 1943.
Visser, G. L. James **JOYCE'S** Ulysses and Anglo-Irish. ESs, 24, 1942.
Hennig, J. Two Irish Bulls in **KANT'S** Kritik der Urtheilskraft. MLQ, 8, 1947.
Roth, G. L'Angleterre, **LAMARTINE** et l'autonomisme irlandais en 1848. **FGB,** 1937.

Hoben, J. B. **MARK TWAIN'S** A Connecticut Yankee: A Genetic Study. AL, 18, 1946.

Krueger, F. G. **MOORE** und die irische Renaissance. NM, 1935.

Clark, D. L. **SHELLEY** and Pieces of Irish History. MLN, 53, 1938.

Covington, F. F. **SPENSER'S** Use of Irish History in the Verse of the Present State of Ireland. U. of Texas Studies in English, 4, 1924.

Jenkins, R. Spenser with Lord Grey in Ireland. PMLA, 1937.

Smith, R. M. The Irish Background of Spenser's View. JEGPh, 42, 1943.

Grennan, Margaret R. Lilliput and Leprecan: Gulliver and the Irish Tradition. (**SWIFT**). ELH, 12, 1945.

Buckley, F. **THOREAU** and the Irish. NEQ, 13, 1940.

Lehmann, Ruth P. Henry **VAUGHAN** and Welsh Poetry: A Contrast. PhQ, 24, 1945.

O'Hegarty, P. S. W. B. **YEATS** and Revolutionary Ireland of his Time. Dublin Mag., 1939.

SECOND PART

Provençal Contributions.

CHAPTER ONE

The Provence and Troubadour Influences in General.

(See also Arabic Contributions, II. I. 5.)

Anglade, J. Les troubadours, leurs vies, leurs oeuvres, leur influence. 3. ed. Paris, 1922.

Appel, C. Poésies provençales inédites, tirées des ms. d'Italie. RLR, 1896.

Audiau, J. Les troubadours et l'Angleterre. Tulle, 1929.

Balaguer, V. De la poesia provenzal en Castilla y en León. Madrid, 1877. Cf. RLR, 13.

—— Historia politica y literaria de los trovadores. 2 vols. Madrid, 1878-79.

Baret, E. Espagne et Provence. L'école provençale en Catalogne. Paris, 1857.

—— Les troubadours et leur influence sur la littérature du midi de l'Europe. 2. ed. Paris, 1867.

Bartsch, K. Nachahmung provenzalischer Poesie im Deutschen. Germania, 1, 1856.

Bertoni, G. Studi e ricerche sui trovatori minori di Genova. GSLI, 36, 1900.

Birch-Hirschfeld, A. Ueber die den provenzalischen Troubadours des XII. und XIII. Jahrhunderts bekannten epischen Stoffe. Halle, 1878.

Braga, T. Trovadores gallecio-portuguezes. In: Historia da Litteratura portugueza, 8, Porto, 1871.

Briffault, R. Les troubadours et le sentiment romanesque. Paris, 1945.

Carriere, M. Eine provençalische Dichtung im deutschen Gewande. Die Gegenwart, 1893.

Chaytor, H. J. The Troubadours and England. Cambridge, 1923.

Cian, V. I contatti letterari italo-provenzali e la prima rivoluzions poetica della letteratura italiana. Messina, 1900.

Closset, N. de. Histoire de la langue et de la littérature provençales et de leur influence sur l'Espagne et sur l'Italie durant les XIe et XIIe siècles. Bruxelles, 1845.

Dabenedetti, S. Gli studi provenzali in Italia nel cinquecento. Torino, 1911.

Dange, C. Le mouvement felibréen dans le Sud-Ouest. Revue de Gascogne, 4, 1901.

Diez, F. Das Verhältniss der Poesie der Troubadours zu auswärtiger Litteratur. In: Poesie der Troubadours. Leipzig, 1883.

Fauriel, C. Histoire de la poésie provençale. 3 vols. Paris, 1846.

Galvani, G. Osservazioni sulla poesia dei trovatori, e sulle principali maniere e forme di essa confrontate colle antiche italiane. Modena, 1829.

Gaspary, A. Die sicilianische Dichterschule des XIII. Jahrhunderts. Berlin, 1878.

Gorra, E. Il reggimento e costume del Berberino ne' suoi rapporti colla letteratura provenzale e francese. In: Studi di crit. lett. Bologna, 1892.

Graf, A. Provenza e Italia. Torino, 1877.

Jeanroy, A. De nostratibus medii aevi poetis qui primum lyrica Aquitaniae carmina imitati sint. Paris, 1889.

—— Les études sur les littératures provençales à l'étranger. Revue des Pyrénées, 1893.

—— Les études provençales du XVIe siècle au milieu du XIXe siècle. Annales du Midi, 43, 1931.

—— La poésie lyrique des troubadours. 2 vols. Paris, 1934.

—— La poésie provençale dans l'Italie du sud à la fin du XIIIe siècle. Mélanges Hauvette. Paris, 1934.

Karl, L. Ungarn und die provenzalische Dichtung. ZRPh, 47, 1927.

Lang, H. R. The Relations of the Earliest Portuguese Lyric School with the Troubadours and Trouveres. MLN, 10, 1895.

Luebcke, G. Die Dichter von Montpellier in der neuprovenzalischen Literatur. Diss. Halle, 1937.

Mandalari. Una colonia provenzale nell'-Italia meridionale. Roma, 1887. And in: Saggi di storia e critica. Roma, 1888.

Manitius, J. A. Die Provence und ihre Sänger im Mittelalter mit Hinblick auf den Einfluss der provencalischen Dichter in Spanien. Dresden, 1872.

Mannucci. Voci derivati della lingua provenzale. Paris, 1840.

Meyer, P. De l'influence des troubadours sur la poésie des peuples romans. Romania, 5, 1876.

—— Des rapports de la poésie des trou-

vères avec celle des troubadours. Romania, 19, 1890.
Milá y Fontanals, M. De los trovadores en España, estudio de lengua y poesia provenzal. Barcelona, 1861.
Panzer, F. Der älteste Troubadour und der erste Minnesänger. D&V, 40, 1939.
Pellegrini, S. Studi su trove e trovatori della prima lirica ispano-portoghese. Torino, 1937.
Pombelaine, R. de. Les troubadours et le Limousin. Bull. de la Soc. du musée départemental du Bas - Limousin. (Tulle), 1900.
Raynouard, F. J. M. Grammaire comparée des langues de l'Europe latine dans leurs rapports avec la langue des troubadours. Paris, 1821.
Rees, Elinor. Provencal Elements in the English Vernacular Lyrics of Manuscript Harley 2253. Stanford Studies in Lang. and Lit., 1941.
Rivière-Dejean. Des troubadours et de l'influence qu'ils ont exercée sur la civilisation. Mém. de la Soc. des sciences et littératures d'Alais, 27, 1896.
Roque-Ferrier. Les provençaux d'Allemagne et le langage de Pinache-Serres (Wurtemberg). Occitania, 1888.
Sachs, C. In welchem Zusammenhange steht die lyrische Kunstpoesie der Provenzalen mit der mittelalterlichen Kunstpoesie der Franzosen, Italiener, Spanier, Portugiesen und Deutschen? Progr. Berlin, 1854.
Sartori. Trovatori provenzali alla corte dei marchesi in Este. Este, 1889.
Schultz, O. Die Lebensverhältnisse der italienischen Trobadors. ZRPh, 7, 1883.
Steiner, H. Ueber die deutschen Uebertragungen der Trobadors. Festschrift Louis Gauchat. Aarau, 1926.
Suchier, H. Vers provençaux de Nuremberg. ZRPh, 15, 1891.
Tardel, H. Untersuchungen zur mittelhochdeutschen Spielmannspoesie. Leipzig, 1894.
Tourtoulon, C. de. Renaissance de la littérature catalane et de la littérature provençale. Les fêtes littéraires internationales de 1868. Congrès scientifique de France, Montpellier, 1872.
—— & Bringuier. Etude sur la limite géographique de la langue d'oc et de la langue d'oil. Paris, 1876.
Ugolini, F. A. La poesia provenzale e l'Italia. Modena, 1939.
Vasconcellos, C. M. de. Trovadores gallecio-portuguezes. In: Grundriss der roman. Philologie, 2, 1888.
Viscardi, A. La poesia trobadorica e l'Italia. In: Letterature comparate (ed. by A. Momigliano) Milano, 1948.
Voretzsch, R. Reisen Deutscher nach der Provence und Süd-Frankreich in früheren Zeiten. In: Volkstum und Kultur der Romanen, 3-4, 1938.
Vossler, K. Die Dichtung der Trobadors und ihre europäische Wirkung. RF, 51, 1937-38.
—— L'importance européenne des troubadours. Investigaciones lingüisticas (México), 4-5, 1937-38

CHAPTER TWO

Individual Provençal Authors.

Appel, C. Petrarka und **ARNAULT DANIEL**. Archiv, 147, 1924.
Perrier, J. L. **BERTRAN DE BORN**, Patriot, and his Place in Dante's Inferno. RR, 11-12, 1920-21.
Scherillo, M. Dante e Bertram dal Bornio. NAnt, 71, 1897.
Bartsch, K. Ueber die Nachahmung **FOLQUETS VON MARSEILLE** durch Rudolph von Ems. ZDA, 11, 1867 & 18, 1874.
Zingarelli, N. Folchetto di Marsiglia nella Commedia di Dante. Napoli, 1887; Bologna, 1899.
Levi, E. Due trovatori antichissimi nell'onomastica italiana del secolo XII: **MARCABRU** e Cercamon. Romania, 55, 1929.
Birkas, G. **MISTRAL** en Hongrie. Budapest, 1933 & Revue des Etudes hongroises, 1935.
Coulon, M. Mistral, en traduction. MF, 103, 1928.
Roche, A. Anglo-Saxon Attitudes toward Frederic Mistral and the Felibrige. MLQ, 5, 1944.
Schultz-Gora. Le epistole del trovatore **RAMBALDO DI VAQUEIRAS** al marchese Bonifacio I. di Monferrato. Firenze, 1898.
Blum, P. Der Troubadour Jaufre **RUDEL** und sein Fortleben in der Literatur. Progr. Brünn, 1912.
Zade, L. Der Troubadour Jaufre Rudel und das Motiv der Fernliebe in der Weltliteratur. Diss. Greifswald, 1920.
De Lollis, C. Vita e poesie di **SORDELLO** di Goifo. Halle, 1896.

CHAPTER THREE

Provençal Influences upon Individual Authors.

Thomas, A. Francesco da **BARBERINO** et la littérature provençale en Italie au moyen-âge. Romania, 16, 1883. Cf. GSLI, 6.

Koehler, E. Le provençalisme de P. **BEMBO** et l'élaboration des Prose della volgar lingua. Mélanges Hauvette. Paris, 1934.

Jan, E. von. William C. **BONAPARTE-WYSE,** ein irischer Dichter der Provence. GRM, 27, 1939.

Caix, N. **CIULLO D'ALCAMO** e gli imitatori delle romanze e pastorelle provenzali e francesi. NAnt, 30, 1875.

Estrich, R. M. A Possible Provencal Source for **CHAUCER'S** Hous of Fame, 300-310. MLN, 55, 1940.

Lowell, J. R. Chaucer. NAR, 1870.

Sandras, E. G. Etude sur G. Chaucer considéré comme imitateur des trouvères. Diss. Paris, 1859.

Zimansky, C. A. Chaucer and the School of Provence: A Problem in Eighteenth Century Literary History. PhQ, 25, 1946.

Bartsch, K. Die von **DANTE** benutzten provenzalischen Quellen. JbDG, 2, 1868.

Chaytor, H. J. The Troubadours of Dante. Oxford, 1902.

Fiske, W. Dante's Obligations to Provençal Poets. Diss. Harvard, 1897.

Hauvette, H. La France et la Provence dans l'oeuvre de Dante. RLC, 9, 1929.

Mahn, K. A. F. Ueber das dichterische und sprachliche Verhältniss Dantes zu einigen Vorgängern der altitalienischen und provenzalischen Litteratur. Archiv, 38, 1865.

—— Ueber einige von Dante in seinen Werken erwähnte provenzalische Dichter. JbDG, 1, 1867.

Santangelo, S. Dante e i trovatori provenzali. Catania, 1921.

Scherillo, M. Alcune fonti provençali della Vita Nuova. Atti dell' Acc. arch. di Napoli, 1890.

Teissier, L. Le voyage de Dante en France. Dante et les troubadours. Bordeaux, 1924.

Toynbee, P. Il Provenzale in Dante's Convivio. Athenaeum, 3938, 1903.

Torraca, F. **FREDERICO** II e la poesia provençale. NAnt, 139, 1895.

Barre, H. Un Allemand en Provence sous le Consulat, C. A. **FISCHER.** Répertoire das travaux de la Société de statistique de Marseille, 47. Valence, 1908-11.

Michel, F. **HEINRICH VON MORUNGEN** und die Troubadours. Diss. Strassburg, 1879.

Lewent, K. Paul **HEYSES** Troubadour-Novellen. Archiv, 127, 1911

Espagne, A. Des influences provençales dans la langue de **MOLIERE.** Paris, 1876.

Gidel, C. A. Les troubadours et **PETRARQUE.** Angers, 1857.

Manfredi, U. La poesia provenzale e la cultura del Petrarca. Palermo, 1947.

Savj-Lopez, P. Ueber die provenzalischen Quellen der Lyrik Petrarcas. Beilage zur Allg. Zt., 283, 1901.

Scarano, N. Fonti provenzali e italiane della lirica Petrarchesca. Studi di filologia romanza, 8, 1900-01.

Schiaffini, A. Lingua e technica nella poesia d'amore dai Provenzali al Petrarca. Cultura Neolatina, 3, 1943.

Iorio, C. L'imitazione provenzale in **PIER DELLA VIGNA.** Festschrift F. Torraca. Napoli, 1922.

Armana, J. d'. **WAGNER** troubadour. Avignon, 1940.

THIRD PART

Italian Contributions.

CHAPTER ONE

Generalities.

(See also Emigrants and Refugees, I. IV. 4.)

Aldington, R. The Italian Heritage. TLS, 10.XI.1938.
Ancona, A. d'. Saggio d'una bibliografia ragionata dei viaggi e delle descrizioni d'Italia e dei costumi italiani in lingua straniera. In: Le Voyage de Montaigne. Città di Castello, 1895.
Crane, T. F. Italian Social Customs in the Sixteenth Century and Their Influence on the Literature of Europe. Yale U. P., 1920.
Glaesener, H. Au pays des conspirations: Quelques complots d'Italie sur la scène. RLC, 15, 1935.
Hauvette, H. L'Italie dans ses rapports avec les autres littératures. Bibliographie. BI, 1907-08.
Klenze, C. von. The Interpretation of Italy During the Last Two Centuries. Chicago, 1907.
Mengin, U. L'Italie des romantiques. Paris, 1902.
Meozzi, A. Azione e diffusione della letteratura italiana in Europa, secoli XV-XVII. Pisa, 1932.
Parpagliolo, L. L'Italia negli scrittori italiani e stranieri. Roma, 1938.
Pellegrini, C. Il contributo italiano agli studi nel campo delle letterature moderne. In: Un secolo di progresso scientifico italiano. Roma, 1939.
—— Tradizione italiana e cultura europea. Messina, 1947.
Quigley, H. Italy and the Rise of a New School of Criticism in the 18th Century. Perth, 1921.
Schuyler, E. Italian Influences. New York, 1903.
Sforza, C. Les étrangers et l'âme italienne. L'Europe centrale, 11.XI.1933.
Strafforello, G. L'Italia nei canti dei poeti stranieri contemporanei. Torino, 1860.
Waetzoldt, W. Das klassische Land; Wandlungen der Italiensehnsucht. Leipzig, 1927.
—— Die Kulturgeschichte der Italienreisen. PJb, 1932.
Walsh, J. J. What Civilization Owes to Italy. Boston, 1923.
Zeller, G. Les relations internationales au temps de la Renaissance: l'apport de l'Italie. RCC, 1935.

CHAPTER TWO

Italian Influences upon England.

Anon. Les Anglais en Italie. Le Globe, 8.XI.1825.
—— Les Anglais en voyage: I. Italie. Rev. Britannique, 1839.
—— Italian Renaissance. Its Influence on the Elizabethan Stage. QR, 1882.
—— Italian Influence on English Poetry. ER, 1896.
Ady, C. M. Italian Influences on English History During the Period of the Renaissance. History, 9.
Arnold, M. England and the Italian Question. (1859).
Babcock, R. W. English Interest in Italy. PhQ, 26, 1947.
Berdan, J. M. Early Tudor Poetry, 1485-1547. New York, 1921.
Boileau, H. T. Italy in the Post-Victorian Novel. Philadelphia, 1931.
Bonaschi, A. & C. Italian Currents and Curiosities in English Literature from Chaucer to Shakespeare. New York, 1937.
Bouvy, E. L'italianisme en Angleterre. In: A travers cinq siècles de littérature italienne. Paris, 1928.
Bräm, E. M. Die italienische Renaissance in dem englischen Geistesleben des 19. Jahrhunderts. Zürich, 1932.
Collison, M. L. Seventeenth Century Englishmen in Italy. ER, 1925.
Cunliffe, J. W. The Influence of Italian on Early Elizabethan Drama. MPh, 4, 1907.
Einstein, L. Italian Renaissance in England. New York, 1902. Cf. BI, 3, 1903.
Ernle, Lord. Tudor Novels and Romances. NC, 1922.
Fanchiotti, G. I ms. italiani in Inghilterra. Caserta, 1899. And in: GSLI, 34.
Fornelli, G. L'Italia nel dramma inglese dell' ottocento. Milano, 1931.
Gargano, G. S. Scapigliatura italiana a Londra ai tempi di Shakespeare. Vita

Britannica, 1918 & Firenze, 1923.
—— Influssi italiani in Inghilterra fra il XVI e il XVII secolo. Marzocco, 18.IX. 1921.
Hallam, A. H. Influence of Italian Works of the Imagination on the Same Class of Composition in England. Cambridge, 1831. And in: Remains, London, 1834.
Holme, J. W. Some Italian Ideals of Culture and Their Influence in England. Calcutta Review, 1914.
King, R. W. Italian Influence on English Scholarship and Literature during the Romantic Revival. MLR, 20-21, 1925-26.
Koeppel, E. Italienische Einflüsse auf die englische Litteratur. Krit. Jahresbericht über d. Fortschritte der roman. Philologie, 1, 1890. And in: Jahresberichte f. neuere deutsche Literaturgeschichte, 1, 1892 & 5, 1897.
—— Studien zur Geschichte der italienischen Novelle in der englischen Litteratur des XVI. Jahrhunderts. Strassburg, 1892.
Lee, V. The Italy of the Elizabethan Dramatists. Euphorion, 1, 1884 & London, 1885.
Loiseau, C. L'Angleterre et l'unité italienne. L'Europe centrale, 16.XI.1935.
Manwaring, E. W. Italian Landscape in 18th Century England. A Study Chiefly of the Influence of Claude Lorrain and Salvator Rosa on English Taste, 1700-1800. Wellesley Semi-Centennial Ser. New York, 1925.
Marshall, R. Italy in English Literature, 1755-1815. Origins of the Romantic Interest in Italy. Columbia U. P., 1934.
Massarani, T. Classici italiani nelle versioni inglese. Poeti inglesi nelle versioni italiane. In: Studi di lettere e d'arte. Firenze, 1876.
McCain, R. English Travellers in Italy during the Renaissance. Bull. of Bibliography, 19, 1947.
Mead, W. E. Italy in English Poetry. PMLA, 23, 1908.
Miles, H. Introduction to Painter's Palace of Pleasure. London, 1929.
Murray, J. R. The Influence of Italian on English Literature During the XVIth and XVIIth Centuries. Academy (Cambridge), 4.IX.1886.
Obertello, A. Influssi italiani sulla poesia e la musica elisabettiana. Giorn. di politica e di letteratura, 13, 1937.
Orsini, N. Studi sul Rinascimento italiano in Inghilterra. Firenze, 1937.
—— La scena italiana in Inghilterra. Anglica, 1, 1946.
Ott, A. Die italienische Novelle im englischen Drama von 1600 bis zur Restauration. Zürich, 1904.
Praz, M. Les Anglais en Italie pendant le Grand Tour. In: Studi e svaghi inglesi. Firenze, 1937.
—— Fortuna della lingua e della cultura italiana in Inghilterra. Romana, 3, 1939.
Radice, B. Gli Inglesi nel Risorgimento italiano. Livorno, 1903.
Rebora, P. L'Italia nel dramma inglese (1558-1642). Milano, 1925.
—— Echi di Urbino nella cultura inglese. Studi Urbinati, 1938.
Rudman, H. W. Italian Nationalism and English Letters: Figures of the Risorgimento and Victorian Men of Letters. Columbia U. P., 1940.
Savage, H. J. The Begining of Italian Influence in English Prose Fiction. PMLA, 1917.
Schanzer, M. Influssi italiani nella letteratura inglese. RI, 1901.
Scott, Mary A. Elizabethan Translations from the Italian. PMLA, 11-15, 1896-1900.
Stuart, J. M. England's Literary Debt to Italy. Fraser's Mag., 1859.
Symonds, J. A. The Debt of English to Italian Literature. Fortnightly Review, 23.
Thompson, E. N. S. The Interest of English Poets in Italian Freedom. PhQ, 1924.
Trevelyan, G. M. Wandering Englishmen in Italy. Transactions British Academy, 16, 1930.
Varia. England and the Mediterranean Tradition: Studies in Art, History and Literature. Oxford U. P., 1946.
Wilson, A. English Poets in Italy. Macmillan Mag., 1862.
Winstanley, Lillian. Othello as the Tragedy of Italy, Showing that Shakespeare's Italian Contemporaries Interpreted the Story of the Moor and the Lady of Venice as Symbolizing the Tragedy of Their Country in the Grip of Spain. London, 1924. Cf. Marzocco, 21.XII.1924.

CHAPTER THREE

Italian Influences upon France.

Anon. Die Italiener vor französischem Richterstuhl. Europa, 1859.
Anagnine, E. L'Italia vista da viaggiatori francesi del secolo XVII. NRS, 1937.

Arnould, N. Essais de théorie et d'histoire littéraire: De l'influence exercée par la littérature italienne sur la littérature française. Paris, 1858.

Auerbach, E. Zur Technik der Frührenaissancenovelle in Italien und Frankreich. Heidelberg, 1921.

Baillou, J. L'influence de la pensée philosophique de la Renaissance italienne sur la pensée française du XVIe siècle. REI, 1936.

Balzo, C. del. Gli scrittori francesi e l'Italia avanti il Rinascimento. Gazzetta lett. de Torino, 1886.

—— L'Italia nella letteratura francese dalla morte di Enrico IV alla Rivoluzione. Torino, 1907.

Beall, C. B. Un recueil italianisant du XVIIIe siècle français. MLN, 55, 1940.

Bedarida, H. Le romantisme français et l'Italie. Revue de l'U. de Lyon, 1931. Cf. Leonardo, 1932.

Bernardini, A. L'Italia e il secolo XVI in Francia. Roma, 1938.

Bertaut, J. L'Italie vue par les Français. Paris, 1911.

Blanc, J. Bibliographie des traductions françaises d'auteurs italiens littéraires. In: Bibliographie italico-française. 2 vols. Milan, Paris, 1886.

Bisi, A. L'Italie et le romantisme français. Milano, 1914.

Brimont, M. La séduction italienne sur les poètes français. Dante, July, 1934.

Cangiullo, F. Un caposcuola napoletano e un romanziere francese. Rassegna d'Italia, 1947.

Cecchi, E. Italiani tradotti in francese. Fiera letter., 10.VI.1928.

Charbonnel, J. R. La pensée italienne au XVIe siècle et le courant libertin. Paris, 1919.

Charlier, G. L'Académie française a-t-elle des origines italiennes? RdF, 15.V.1935.

Chaumeix, A. L'Italie des romantiques. Journal des Débats, 29.VI.1902.

Chevalier, A. L'Italie d'aujourd'hui vue par un Français. NRF, 1.IV.1917.

Dejob, C. Histoire de la Société d'études italiennes. Paris, 1919.

Dienne, Cte. de. Des rapports de l'Agenais avec l'Italie, principalement au XVe et XVIe siècles. Revue de l'Agenais, 30, 1903.

Dorelet, J. Sur les influences italiennes et la littérature française. Scripta, 1938.

Dumesnil, J. Voyageurs français en Italie depuis le XVIe siècle jusqu'à nos jours. Paris, 1865.

Elwert, W. T. Das Italienbild der Franzosen im XIX Jahrhundert. Archiv, 180.

Fiumi, L. Gli italianisti di Francia. LNI, 13.VIII.1929.

Fossoyeux, M. Les traductions françaises de traités d'hygiène italiens au XVIe siècle. Bull. de la Société d'histoire de la médecine, 1931.

Franci, A. Poeti italiani volti in francese. I Libri del Giorno, March, 1922.

François, A. Les origines italiennes du dictionnaire de l'Académie française. Mélanges Bouvier. Genève, 1920.

Gabotto, F. Notes sur quelques sources italiennes de l'épopée française au moyen-âge. RLR, 10, 1896-97.

Gambier, H. Italie et Renaissance poétique en France. Padova, 1936.

Gerace, G. Lingua e cultura letteraria italiana in Francia dal Rinascimento ai nostri giorni. Romana, 3-4, (Firenze), 1939-40.

Girardeau, F. Les voyageurs français en Italie. Revue contemporaine, 14, 1861.

Glasser, K. Das Italien der französischen Romantiker. ZNU, 38.

Jongh, W. F. J. de. Early French Borrowings in Novelistic Fiction from Italian Narrative Literature, 1384-1560. Diss. Harvard, 1939.

Jourda, P. L'exotisme dans la littérature française depuis le romantisme: L'Italie. RCC, 1937.

Kupka, I. Italienreisen in der französischen Literatur des 19. Jahrhunderts. Breslau, 1936.

Letts, M. Some French Travellers in Naples in the 16th Century. EHR, Oct., 1919.

Madelin, L. Le journal d'un habitant français de Rome au XVIe siècle (1509-40). Mélanges d'archéologie de l'Ecole fr. de Rome, 22, 1902.

Malvano, E. L. L'Italie et la littérature française. Ausonia, 5, 1940.

Mathorez, J. Les Italiens et l'opinion française à la fin du XVIe siècle. Bull. du Bibliophile et du Bibliothécaire, 1914.

Maugain, G. L'Italie dans quelques publications de jésuites français. Annales de l'U. de Grenoble. Paris, 1910.

Mignon, M. La culture italienne en France. In: Les affinités intellectuelles de l'Italie et de la France. Paris, 1921.

Momigliano, F. Rinascimento italiano, illuminismo francese. RI, 2, 1918.

Müntz, E. La Renaissance en Italie et en France à l'époque de Charles VIII. Paris, 1885.

Navarra, T. L'Italia nel pensiero di alcuni scrittori di Francia. Rass. di studi francesi, 1926.

Neri, F. L'italianismo in Francia nel secolo XVII. Romana, 2, 1938.
Noli, R. Les romantiques français et l'Italie. Diss. Dijon, 1928.
Peletier d'Auney. Mémoire sur cette question: Quelle a été l'influence de la langue et de la littérature italiennes sur la langue et la littérature francaises? L'Investigateur, 9, 1849.
Pelissier, L. G. Les nouvellistes italiens à Paris en 1498. Nogent, 1892.
Pellegrini, C. I romantici francesi e l'Italia. Civiltà moderna, June, 1929.
Picot, E. Les Français italianisants au XVIe siècle. Paris, 1907.
—— Pour et contre l'influence italienne en France au XVIe siècle. EI, 1920.
Pintard, R. L'influence de la pensée philosophique de la Renaissance italienne sur la pensée française du XVIIe siècle. REI, 1936.
Porcelli, G. La letteratura italiana nella critica francese durante la Monarchia di Luglio, 1830-48. Firenze, 1926.
Prezzolini, G. Come i Francesi conoscono l'Italia. ICS, 1924.
Rasmussen, W. Italiensk Kultur i Frankrig. Stud. fra Sprog- og Oldtidsforskning. Kjøbenhavn, 1898.
Rathéry, E. J. B. Influence de l'Italie sur les lettres françaises depuis le XIIIe siècle jusqu'au règne de Louis XIV. Paris, 1853.
Rivoire, P. Contributo alla storia dell'influenza della novella italiana sulla novella francese. Il Rinascimento, 2, 1896.
Searles, C. Italian Influences as Seen in the Sentiments of the French Academy on the Cid. RR, 1912.
Serre, M. La cultura italiana in Lione. NAnt, 16.XI.1919.
Sibilia, A. Les Italiens dans l'ancienne comédie française. Versailles, 1917.
Steiner, A. Florentine Influence at Avignon in 1365. Cath. Historical Review, 27, 1942.
Strauss, L. Uebersetzungen italienischer Dichtwerke in Frankreich zwischen 1789 und 1820. Diss. Heidelberg, 1931.
Texte, J. L'influence italienne dans la Renaissance française. In: Etudes de littérature européenne. Paris, 1898.
—— L'Italie et la critique française au XVIIIe siècle. RCC, 16.I.1896.
Tuzet, H. Voyageurs français en Sicile au temps du romantisme. Paris, 1945.
Vianey, J. L'influence italienne chez les précurseurs de la Pléiade. BI, 2-3, 1903.
Vidal, C. Studi sul Risorgimento in Francia. Rassegna storica del Risorgimento, 35, 1938.

CHAPTER FOUR

Italian Influences upon Germany.

Boner, E. G. L'Italia nell' antica letteratura tedesca. NAnt, 1.VI.1887.
Deetz, M. Anschauungen von italienischer Kunst in der deutschen Literatur von Winckelmann bis zur Romantik. Berlin, 1931.
Friedlaender, M. Reisen nach Italien in den letzten Jahrhunderten. DR, 1876.
Harnack, O. Deutsches Kunstleben in Rom im Zeitalter der Klassik. Weimar, 1896.
Häusler, Regina. Das Bild Italiens in der deutschen Romantik. Bern, 1939.
Jacoby, L. Deutsche Lieder aus Italien. München, 1892.
Köppel, E. Italien in deutscher Kunst und Litteratur. MLIA, 1887.
Landau, M. Die italienische Litteratur am österreichischen Hofe. Wien, 1879. Aquila, 1880. Cf. MLIA, 1880.
Molo, W. von (ed.). Italien: Erlebnisse Deutscher in Italien. Berlin, 1921.
Morpurgo, E. L'opera del genio italiano all'Estero I. Gli artisti in Austria. Roma, 1938.
Oehmann, E. Ueber den italienischen Einfluss auf die deutsche Sprache bis zum Ausgang des Mittelalters. Annales Acad. Scient. Fennicae. B. 51-53, 1942-44.
Petrone, M. L'influenza dell'Italia e della letteratura italiana sulla letteratura tedesca. Boll. della Reale U. di Perugia. 7.XI.1931.
Reinhardstoettner, K. von. Ueber die Beziehungen der italienischen Litteratur zum bayrischen Hofe und ihre Pflege an demselben. Jb. f. Münchener Geschichte, 1, 1887.
Rüdiger, H. L'Italia nella storia spirituale della Germania. Convivium, 14, 1942.
Rumpf-Fleck, J. Italienische Kultur in Frankfurt am Main im 18. Jahrhundert. Köln, 1936.
Scartazzini, G. A. La letteratura italiana in Germania nel 1869. Rivista Europea, 2, 1870.
Scelbi, J. Grandi Tedeschi nella terra del sole. Illustrazione italiana, 19.IX.1937.
Schmidt, H. Ein Jahrhundert römischen Lebens: Von Winckelmanns Romfahrt bis zum Sturze der weltlichen Papstherrschaft: Berichte deutscher Augenzeugen. Leipzig, 1904.
Wölfflin, H. Italien und das deutsche Formgefühl. Logos, 10, 1922.

CHAPTER FIVE

Italian Influences upon Other Countries.

(See also Italian Humanism, III. II. 3.)

Koliqi, E. Tradizioni e canti popolari italo-albanesi. Rivista d'ALBANIA, 1, 1940.
Bernardy, A. A. Contributi italiani alla formazione degli Stati Uniti d'AMERICA. Giornale di politica e letteratura, 18, 1942.
Garlick et al. Italy and the Italians in Washington's Time. New York, 1947.
Giannotta, R. O. Contribution of Italians to the Development of American Culture during the XVIIIth Century. Diss. St. John's U. 1942.
Goggio, E. The Dawn of Italian Culture in America. RR, 1919.
La Piana, Angelina. La cultura americana e l'Italia. Torino, 1938.
Marraro, H. R. Italian Culture in Eighteenth-Century American Magazines. Ital, 22, 1945.
—— Interpretation of Italy and the Italians in 18th Century America. Ital., 1948.
Peragallo, Olga. Italian-American Authors and their Contribution to American Literature. New York, 1949. Cf. CL, 2, 1950.
Prezzolini, G. Come gli Americani scoprirono l'Italia (1750-1850). Milano, 1933.
Shields, N. C. Italian Translations in America. New York, 1931.
Stern, Madeleine B. New England Artists in Italy, 1835-55. NEQ, 14, 1941.
Halperin Donghi, E. de. Contribución al estudio del Italianismo en la República Argentina. Buenos Aires, 1939.
Martin, J. L. A Guatemalan Man of Letters in Italy. Ital., 25, 1948.
Manfroni, C. L'Italia e l'Oriente ASIATICO. Rassegna italiana, 1935.
Fiumi, L. Italianismo e Italianisti in BELGIO. Il Libro Italiano, 3, 1939.
Donchev, N. L'Italia e le sue influenze nella letteratura BULGARA. L'Europa orientale, 18, 1938.
Kalista, Z. Motivi italiani nella poesia ceca contemporanea. (CZECHOSLOVAKIA). L'Europa orientale, 21, 1941.
Lo Gatto, E. Letteratura italiana in Boemia. L'Europa orientale, 22, 1942.
Rosendorfsky, J. La cultura italiana nella stampa ceca. L'Europa orientale, 20, 1940.
Andersen, V. Italien i dansk Digtning. (DENMARK). Festskrift Valdemar Vedel. København, 1935. And in: SG, 1, 1935-36.
Lebesgue, P. La part de l'Italie dans la Renaissance littéraire de la GRECE. Dante, 1934.
Sapori, F. Letteratura italiana in Olanda. (HOLLAND). Libri del giorni, 1921.
Galdi, L. Italia e italiani nel romanzo ungherese. (HUNGARY). Romana, 7, 1943.
Gigante, S. Italia e italiani nella storia d'Ungheria. Fiume, 1933.
Kardos, T. L'Ungheria e l'eredità di Roma. Corvina, 6, 1943.
Koltay-Kastner, T. Gli ultimi studi ungheresi sul Risorgimento italiano. Rassegna storica del Risorgimento, 1938.
Opice, V. & Galdi, L. L'Italia nella poesia ungherese. Romana, 7, 1943.
Salvini, L. L'Italia nei conti popolari magiari. Roma, 1932.
Varady, E. La letteratura italiana e la sua influenza in Ungheria. Roma, 1934. Cf. Nouvelle Rev. de Hongrie, 1935.
Wlislocki, H. von. Ueber den Einfluss der italienischen Litteratur auf die ungarische. ZVL, 6, 1893.
Krappe, A. H. The Italian Origin of an ICELANDIC Story. SS, 19, 1946.
Barycz. Viaggi di polacchi a Napoli nei secoli XVI-XVIII. (POLAND). Przeglad Wspólczesny, 17, 1938.
Bielatowicz, J. La Polonia a Bologna. Iridion, 1, 1945.
Brahamer, M. La letteratura italiana in Polonia. Roma, 1937.
Damiani, E. Influssi di poeti e prosatori italiani nella storia della letteratura polacca. Romana, 1937.
Stanghellini, A. La cultura italiana in Polonia. Ibid.
Verdiani, S. Basi storiche per una propaganda culturale italiana a carattere popolare in Polonia. Giornale di politica e di letteratura, 1935.
Battelli, G. Umanisti italiani in PORTOGALLO. Rinascita, 5, 1942.
Bertoni, G. Contatti culturali italo-portoghesi nell'età della Rinascenza. NAnt, 161, 1940.
Carvalho, J. de. L'Italia e le origini del movimento umanistico in Portogallo. Rinascita, 7, 1944.
Poppa, L. di. Romanticisma portoghese: detrattori e amici dell'Italia. Romana, 5, 1941.
Rossi, G. C. Notizie d'Italia in Portogallo in una gazzetta letteraria del settecento. Convivium, 1947.
Torraca, F. Le donne italiane nella poe-

sia provenzale. (PROVENCE). Bibl. critica d. lett. ital., Firenze, 1901.

Cioranescu, A. Italia in literatura romanuesca. (RUMANIA). Via Romanuesca, April, 1932 ff.

Isopescu, C. Le stampa periodica romena-italiana in Romania e in Italia. Roma, 1937.

—— La letteratura italiana in Romania. Meridiano di Roma, 24.XII.1939.

—— Umanesimo e Arcadia dall'Italia in Romenia. Osservatore romano, 25. VII.1948.

—— L'Italianismo e il Risorgimento italiano nella letteratura romena. Ibid. 15. VIII.1948.

—— Lingua e letteratura italiana in Romenia. Augustea, 16, 1941.

Marcu, A. Romanticii italieni si românii. Bucharest, 1924.

—— Athènes ou Rome? A propos de l'influence italienne en Roumanie vers 1820. Mélanges Baldensperger, Paris, 1930.

Ortiz, R. Per la storia della cultura italiana in Rumania. Bucharest, 1916.

—— Italia e Rumania. Firenze, 1937.

Tagliavini. La cultura italiana in Romania. Romana, 6, 1942.

Lo Gatto, E. L'Italia nelle letterature slave. (SLAVS). Studi di letterature slave, 3. Roma, 1931.

Anon. Le arti italiani in Ispagna ossia storia di quanto gli artisti italiani contribuirono ad abbellire le Castiglie. (SPAIN). Roma, 1828.

Croce, B. Di un antico romanzo spagnuolo relativo alla storia di Napoli. Napoli, 1894.

Esterlich, J. L. Antologia de poetas liricos italianos traducidos en verso castellano. (Cf. Introduction). Palma, 1889.

Fucilla, J. G. Notes on Spanish Renaissance Poetry. PhQ, 1932.

Giannini, A. Impressioni italiane di viaggiatori spagnuoli nei secoli XVI e XVII. RH, 55, 1922.

Hatzfeld, H. Italienische und spanische Renaissance. Jb. der Goerres-Ges., 1926.

Juliá, E. La influencia de Italia en el Renacimiento español. Anuario cultural Italo-Español, 1, 1942.

Meozzi, A. Lirica della Rinascita italiana nel primo Rinascimento di Spagna. Rinascita, 3, 1940.

—— Lirica della Rinascita italiana in Spagna e Portogallo. (Sec. XV-XVII). Firenze, 1943.

Milá y Fontanals, M. Notas sobre la influencia de la literatura italiana en la catalana. In: Obras completas, 3. Barcelona, 1877.

Nicolau y d'Olwer, L. Apunts sobre l'influencia italiana en la prosa catalana desde Bernat Metge a Francesch Alegre. Estudis Univ. Catal., 2, Barcelona.

Parducci, A. Motivi italiani nel romanzo picaresco spagnuolo. Conv., 30.VI.1939.

Puymaigre, C. de. La cour littéraire de Don Juan II, roi de Castile. Paris, 1873.

On Italo-Catalonian Relations see also: Homenatge a Antoni Rubió i Lluch. Estudis Univ. Catal. Barcelona, 1936.

Kleberg, T. Italien i svensk litteratur. (SWEDEN). Göteborg, 1944.

Lundstrom, V. Svenskas i Italien, 1650-1850. Sverige-Italien, 3, 1933.

Schiller, H. Italien och den Svenska litteraturen. Nya dagl. Allehanda, 20.III-16.IV. 1927.

Schück, H. Svedesi a Roma. RLM, 1, 1946.

Sibilia, S. I rapporti culturali italo-svedesi. Rivista di Cultura, 14, 1933.

Amicis, E. de. La Genève italienne. (SWITZERLAND). BURS, 1884.

Aubert, H. Pourquoi nous aimons l'Italie. BURS, 1911.

Tonelli, L. Scrittori della Svizzera italiana. ICS, 1937.

Cronia. L'influence italienne sur les Serbes. (YUGOSLAVIA). L'Europe orientale, 4.

Deanovic, M. Les influences italiennes sur la littérature croate du littoral adriatique jusqu'à la fin du XVIIIe siècle. RLC, 14, 1934.

Leger, L. L'influence italienne dans la littérature slave de la Dalmatie. JS, 1917.

Maver, G. Gli sloveni e la cultura italiana. NAnt, 165, 1941.

Skerly, S. Représentations italiennes à Ljubjana aux XVIIe et XVIIIe siècles. Mélanges Hauvette. Paris, 1934.

Torbarina, J. Italian Influence on the Poets of the Ragusan Republic. London, 1931.

Urbani, U. La lirica italiana nelle edizioni del Dott. N. Andric: 40 poeti italiani tradotti di 18 poeti croati. L'Europe orientale, 19, 1932.

CHAPTER SIX

The Italian Drama: Theatre, Commedia dell'arte, Arlecchino, Pulcinella, etc.

(For Italian Opera, see I. VII. 3.)

1. Generalities.

Anon. Italienische Bühnenkunst in Paris. Frankfurter Zt. 28.VI.1898.
—— Noticias y documentos sobre el teatro castellano, italiano y catalán en Barcelona desde el siglo XIV a principios del XIX. Rev. crit. de hist. y lit. esp., 5, 1900.
Albert, M. Une troupe d'acteurs italiens sous la Régence. RB, 12.V.1900.
Alboize, E. Histoire de la comédie italienne en France. Le Monde dramatique, 1, 1835.
Ancona, A. d'. I comici italiani in Francia. In: Varietà storiche e letterarie. Milano, 1885.
Apollonio, M. Storia della Commedia dell'arte. Roma, 1930.
Arcais, F. d'. I teatri italiani all'estero. NAnt. 79, 1885.
Arcoleo, G. Pulcinella dentro e fuori del teatro. NAnt, 1872 & Napoli, 1897.
Bader, A. L. The Modena Troupe in England. MLN, 1935.
Baschet, A. Les comédiens italiens à la cour de France sous Charles IX Henri III et Louis XIII. Paris, 1882. Cf. Lyon-Revue, 1883.
Beaumont, C. W. The History of Harlequin. London, 1927.
Bernardin, N. M. La comédie italienne en France. RCC, 8, 1899.
—— La comédie italienne en France et le Théâtre de la Foire. Paris, 1902.
Blomberg, H. von. Das Theatralische in Art und Kunst der Franzosen. Zs. f. Völkerpsychologie und Sprachwissenschaft, 1860.
Bocchia, G. Comici dei Farnesi in Francia. La compagnia del Reggente (1716). Aurea Parma, 1929.
Bolte, J. Schauspiele am Hofe des Landgrafen Moritz von Hessen. SAWB, 1931.
Bonghi R,. Le nostre commedie del secolo XV e un dramma francese del XIX. NAnt, 1887.
Brunelli, B. Una storia inedita della commedia dell'arte. Marzocco, 15.III.1931.
Campardon, E. Les Comédiens du Roi de la troupe italienne pendant les deux derniers siècles. 2 vols. Paris, 1880.
Chancerel, L. Arlequin. Jeux, Tréteaux, Personnages, 15.VIII.1931.
Croce, B. Pulcinella e il personnaggio del Napoletano in commedia. Roma, 1899.
—— Napoli e la commedia napoletana dell'arte. Crit., 1919.
—— Sul significato storico e il valore artistico della commedia dell' arte. Acc. di Scienze morali e politiche di Napoli, 1929.
Decombe, L. Les comédiens italiens à Rennes au XVIIIe siècle. Rennes, 1900.
Desboulmiers, A. J. Histoire anecdotique et raisonnée du Théâtre italien depuis son rétablissement en France jusqu'à l'année 1769. 7 vols. Paris, 1769.
Dieterich, A. Pulcinella, Pompejan. Wandbilder und römische Satyrspiele. Leipzig, 1897.
Doutrepont, G. L'évolution du type de Pierrot dans la littérature française. Bull. de l'Acad. royale de langue et litt. françaises, 1925.
Driesen, O. Der Ursprung des Harlekin. Berlin, 1903.
Duchartre, P. L. La Comédie italienne. Paris, 1924.
Eckhardt, E. Die lustige Person im älteren englischen Drama (bis 1642). Berlin, 1902.
Fassini, S. Il melodramma italiano a Londra nella prima metà del 700. Torino, 1914.
Flasdieck, H. M. Harlekin, germanischer Mythos in romanischer Wandlung. RLR, 1938.
Funck-Brentano, F. Requête de la Comédie française contre la Comédie italienne. Nouvelle Revue Rétrosp., 19, 1902.
Gherardi, E. Théâtre italien, ou recueil de toutes les comédies et scènes françaises jouées par les comédiens italiens du Roy. 6 vols. Amsterdam, 1721.
Holm, K. Italienische Schauspielerei in Berlin. MLIA, 26.V.1900.
Kellen, T. Die ersten Schauspielerinnen in Frankreich. MLIA, 2.IV.1898.
Kindermann, H. Die Commedia dell'arte und das deutsche Volkstheater. Berlin, 1938.
Klein, J. L. Das italienische Drama. In: Geschichte des Dramas. Leipzig, 1866.
Klingler, O. Die Comédie italienne in Paris. Diss. Strassburg, 1902.
Lea, K. M. Italian Popular Comedy. A Study in the Commedia dell'arte, 1569-1620, with Special Reference to the English Stage. Oxford U. P., 1934.
Leslie, J. K. Italian Plays and Players in Montevideo (1835-45). Ital. 22, 1945.

Liuzzi, F. I comici dell'arte e la musica italiana in Francia. Romana, 1937.
Lombard, A. Charlot et Scaramouche. Rev. hebdom. 27.XI.1926.
Magnin, C. Les commencements de la Comédie italienne en France. RDM, 15.XII.1847.
Marschall, W. Das Sir Thomas Moore Manuskript und die englische Commedia dell' arte. Anglia, 52, 1928.
Mattalia, D. Problemi della storia di Pulcinella. Cultura moderna, 1931.
Melese, P. A propos de l'expulsion des comédiens italiens en 1696. RHLF, 44.
Mic, C. La Commedia dell'arte ou le théâtre des comédiens italiens des XVIe, XVIIe et XVIIIe siècles. Paris, 1927.
Mignon, M. Les influences italiennes dans la Comédie française de la Renaissance. Paris, 1912.
Monnot, R. La comédie italienne en France. Dante, 1933.
Origny, d'. Annales du Théâtre italien depuis son origine jusqu'à nos jours. 3 vols. Paris, 1788.
Parducci, A. Traduzioni e riduzioni spagnuole di drammi italiani. GSLI, 117, 1941.
Parfaict. Histoire de l'ancien Théâtre italien depuis son origine en France jusqu'à sa suppression en l'année 1697. Paris, 1753.
Petraccone, E. La Commedia dell'arte: Storia, tecnica, scenari. Napoli, 1927.
Rauhut, F. Die italienische Stegreifkomödie in Bayern. Archiv, 182.
Rigal, E. Esquisse d'une histoire des théâtres de Paris, 1548-1653. Paris, 1887.
Rodocanachi, E. Une protestation des comédiens français contre les comédiens italiens, 1683. Journal des Débats, 3.X.1926.
Roy, E. Les comédiens italiens. RHLF, 1924.
Ruhlemann, M. Etymologie des Wortes Harlequin und verwandte Wörter. Diss. Halle, 1912.
Salzer, E. C. La commedia italiana dell' arte alla corte viennese. Riv. ital. del dramma, 2, 1938.
—— Il teatro allegorico italiano a Vienna. Ibid.
—— Teatro italiano in Vienna barocca. Ibid.
Sanesi, I. Note sulla Commedia dell'arte. GSLI, 111, 1938.
Scherillo, M. La commedia dell'arte. Torino, 1884.
Schlager, J. E. Comédiens italiens à Vienne au XVIe siècle. SAWW, 1851.
Schücking, L. L. Studien über die stofflichen Beziehungen der englischen Komödie zur italienischen bis Lilly. Halle, 1901.
Schwartz, I. A. The Commedia dell'Arte and its Influence on French Comedy in the 17th Century. New York, 1933.
Smith, W. Italian and Elizabethan Comedy. MPh, 5, 1908.
—— The Commedia dell'arte. A Study in Italian Popular Comedy. New York, 1912.
—— Italian Actors in Elizabethan England. MLN, 1929.
Solerti, A. La rappresentazione della Calandria a Lione nel 1548. Festschrift d'Ancona. Firenze, 1901.
Stiefel. Die Nachahmung italienischer Dramen bei einigen Vorläufern Molières. Berlin, 1904.
Toldo, P. La comédie française de la Renaissance (Influence italienne depuis Larivey jusqu'au XVIIe siècle). RHLF, 1898-1900.
Tomasi, F. Appunti sul teatro italiano e francese del seicento e del settecento. Firenze, 1926.
Trautmann, K. Italienische Schauspieler am bayrischen Hofe. Jb. f. Münchener Geschichte, 1887.
Windakiewicz. Das italienische Theater am Hofe Königs Ladislaus IV (1633-48). Anzeigen d. Akad. der Wissenschaft Krakau, 1893.
Wolff, M. J. Die Commedia dell'arte. GRM, 21, 1933.
Zabel, E. Die italienische Schauspielkunst in Deutschland. Diss. Berlin, 1892.
Zeppa de Nolva, C. Tragédie italienne et française au XVI siècle. REI, 1937.

2. Actors and Troupes

Byrn, F. A. Giovanni **CASANOVA** und die Comici italiani am polnischen-sächsischen Hofe. Neues Archiv für sächsische Gesch. und Altertumskunde, 1880.
Boutet, E. Eleonora **DUSE** a Parigi. NAnt. 1.VII.1897.
Larroumet, G. La Duse et le public parisien. In: Nouvelles Etudes. Paris, 1899.
Guillemot, J. Les oubliés. Le théâtre de **GHERARDI**. RB, 1893.
Klingler, O. Die Comédie Italienne in Paris nach der Sammlung von Gherardi. Diss. Zürich. Strassburg, 1902.
Toldo, P. Il teatro d'Evaristo Gherardi a Parigi. Rassegna nazionale, 1897.
Heilly, G. d'. Rachel et la **RISTORI**, les

80 ans d'une tragédienne, les séjours de la Ristori à Paris. RP, 1902.
Muret, M. Adelaide Ristori à Paris. Journal des Débats, 30.I.1902.
Perrens, F. T. La Comédie italienne à Paris. Mad. Ristori. RDM, 1855-57.
Gold, A. ZACCONI-Kainz, MLIA 1897.

CHAPTER SEVEN

Ariosto.

1. Generalities.

Cioranescu A. Une supercherie littéraire non dévoilée. RLC, 15, 1935.
Ferrazzi, G. G. Traduzioni dell'Orlando Furioso. In: Bibliografia Ariostesca. Bassano, 1881.
Fucilla, J. G. Four Notes on Italian Influences. RR, 1935.
Jacoubet, H. Comment le XVIIIe siècle lisait l'Orlando furioso. EI, 1933.
Koehler, R. Eine Stelle in Ariostos Orlando Furioso und Nachahmungen derselben. ALG, 5, 1876.
Pezard, A. Le thème d'Angélique dans la littérature moderne. RLC, 23, 1949.
Pitollet, C. Le quatrième centenaire de l'Arioste. Les langues méridionales, 1934.
Varia. La fortuna dell' Ariosto nel mondo. Messaggero della Libreria italiana, 1933.

2. Influences upon Individual Countries.

Bottazzi, B. Ludovico Ariosto e l'Inghilterra. (**ENGLAND**). Reggio Emilia, 1941.
Casson, T. E. Ariosto and the English Poets. Papers of the Manchester Literary Club, 62, 1937.
Faggi, A. Une traduzione inglese della Ginestra. Marzocco, 22.V.1921.
Olivero, F. La fortuna dell' Ariosto in Inghilterra. ICS, 1933.
Praz, M. Ariosto in Inghilterra. Illustrazione ital., 18.VI.1933.
Schoembs, J. Ariosts Orlando Furioso in der englischen Litteratur des Zeitalters der Elisabeth. Diss. Strassburg, 1899; cf. ESn, 26.
Cioranescu A. L'Arioste en **FRANCE** des origines à la fin du XVIIIe siècle. 2 vols. Paris, 1939.
Ferrazzi, G. L'Ariosto presso i Francesi. In: Bibliografia Ariostesca. Bassano, 1881.
Keyser, S. Contribution à l'étude de la fortune littéraire de l'Arioste en France. Leyden, Paris, 1934.
Orvieto, A. L'Ariosto in Francia. Marzocco, 20.V.1928.
Roth, T. Der Einfluss von Ariosts Orlando Furioso auf das französische Theater. Münchener Beiträge, 34, 1905.
Salvioli, G. L'Ariosto all' Hôtel de Rambouillet. Rassegna settimanale di polit. Roma, 1880.
Toldo, P. Sulla fortuna dell'Ariosto in Francia. Studi romani. Perugia, 1903.
—— Quelques notes pour servir à l'histoire de l'influence du Furioso dans la littérature française. BI, 4.
Vianey, J. L'Arioste et la Pléiade. BI, 1, 1901.
Ellinger, G. Kleine Beiträge zur Geschichte des deutschen Dramas im 17. Jahrhundert (**GERMANY**). ZVL, 5.
Gianturco, E. The Beginnings of Ariosto-Criticism in Germany. RR, 1934.
Köppel, E. Eine neue Ariostübersetzung. MLIA, 1881.
Schmidt, E. Ariost in Deutschland. In: Charakteristiken. Berlin, 1886.
Vincenti, L. La fortuna dell'Ariosto in Germania. ICS, 1933.
Wiesner, W. Ariost im Lichte der deutschen Kritik. Diss. Basel, 1941.
Colombo, J. Di una traduzione ebraica dell' Orlando Furioso. (**HEBREW**). Annuario del R. Liceo scientifico. Ferrara, 1934.
Babudri, F. L'Orlando furioso di Ludovico Ariosto in **ISTRIA**. AR, 23, 1939.
Rossi, G. C. L'Orlando Furioso in **PORTOGALLO**. Cultura Neolatina, 4-5, 1944-45.
Bertini, G. M. L'Orlando furioso nella sua prima traduzione ed imitazione spagnuola. (**SPAIN**). Aevum, 1934.
—— l'Orlando furioso e l'inquisizione spagnuola. Conv., 1935.
—— L'Orlando furioso e la Rinascenza spagnuola. LNI, 12, 1936.
Morby, E. S. Orlando furioso y El Crotalon. RFE, 1 1935.
Parducci A. La fortuna dell'Ariosto in Ispagna. ICS, 1933.
—— Note sulle traduzioni spagnuole dell' Orlando furioso. Annali della R. Scuola normale superiore di Pisa. Bologna, 1935.

3. Influences upon Individual Authors.

Horne, J. van. El Bernardo of Bernardo de **BALBUENA**. A Study of the Poem with Particular Attention to it Relations to the Epics of Boiardo and Ari-

osto and to its Significance in the Spanish Renaissance. Urbana, 1927.
Cioranescu, A. Les Rodomontades espagnoles de N. **BAUDOIN.** BH, 39, 1937.
Lachèvre, F. La dissertation de **BOILEAU** sur les deux traductions ou imitations du conte Joconde de l'Arioste faites par Bouillon et La Fontaine. RHLF, 32, 1925.
Anon. **BYRON** and Ariosto. N&Q, 172, 218, 316, 1893.
Cioranescu, A. La première rédaction de l'Ollivier de **CAZOTTE.** MLN 54, 1939.
Brecheler, R. Orlando fatato e l'elmo di Mambrino: Saggio di idee sul meraviglioso in Ariosto e in **CERVANTES.** La Rassegna d'Italia, 1, 1946.
Garrone, M. A. L'Orlando furioso considerato come fonte del Quijote. RI, 1911.
Pitollet, C. Le quatrième centenaire de l'Arioste (et l'influence de l'Arioste sur Don Quichotte). Les Langues Méridionales, 1934.
Renier, R. Cervantes e l'Ariosto. Riv. Eur., 16.XI.1878.
Sanctis, F. de. L'Ariosto e Cervantes. In: Storia della letteratura italiana, 2. Napoli, 1870.
Savj-Lopez, P. Il Cervantes poeta cavalleresco. Festschrift P. Rajna. Firenze, 1912.
Ronzy, P. Jacques **DELILLE** et l'Arioste. Ausonia, cahiers franco-italiens, 3, 1938.
Cameron, A. **DESPORTES** and Ariosto. MLN, 50, 1935.
Cioranescu, A. Les imitations de l'Arioste de Philippe Desportes. Paris, 1936.
Neri, F. Nota ai Regrets. **(DU BELLAY).** Atheneum, 7, 1919.
Gilbert, A. H. Nevizanus, Ariosto, Florio, Harrington and **DRUMMOND.** MLN, 62, 1947.
Bizzarri, E. L'influenza dell'Ariosto su La Araucana di **ERCILLA.** Rinascita, 4, 1941.
Pasini, F. La Bradamante di Roberto **GARNIER** e la sua fonte ariostesca. Ann. d. st. Trentini, 7, 1900-01.
Conliffe, J. W. Supposes and Jocasta, **(GASCOIGNE).** Boston, 1906.
Bruce, J. D. Some Unpublished Translations from Ariosto by John **GAY.** Archiv, 123, 1910.
Morris, M. Zu **GOETHES** Gedicht: Das Tagebuch. In: Goethe-Studien. Berlin, 1902.
Morrison, M. R. **GREEN'S** Use of Ariosto in Orlando furioso. MLN, 1934.
Cameron, A. The Influence of Ariosto's Epic and Lyric Poetry on the Work of Amadis **JAMYN.** Baltimore, 1933.
Cotronei, B. **LA FONTAINE** e l'Ariosto. Rassegna della lett. italiana e straniera, 1890.
Dubois, J. Lafontaine et l'Arioste. Mém. de la Société académique de l'Aube, 73, 1909.
Amico, A. d'. L'imitazione ariostesca nella Hermosura de Angelica di **LOPE DE VEGA.** Pistoia, 1921.
Parducci, A. L'Orlando furioso nel teatro di Lope de Vega. AR, 17, 1934.
Marcu, A. Un Arioste inconnu annoté par **MALHERBE.** Mélanges Drouhet. Bucarest, 1940.
Buckley, W. E. **MILTON'S** Translations from Dante and Ariosto. N&Q, 9.VI. 1888.
Ruta, E. L'Ariosto e **PEREZ DE HITA.** RH, 81, 1933.
Valli, G. Ludovico Ariosto y Ginés Pérez de Hita. RFE, 30, 1946.
Vianey, J. L'Arioste et les Discours de **RONSARD.** Rev. Univers., 12, 1903.
Bennett, M. L. **SHAKESPEARE'S** Much Ado and its Possible Italian Sources. U. of Texas Bulletin, 1937.
Prouty, C. T. George Whetstone, Peter Beverly and the Sources of Much Ado about Nothing. SPh, 38, 1940.
Segrè, C. Riflessi ariosteschi in una commedia dello Shakespeare. Fanfulla della Domenica, 27, 1905.
Townsend, Freda L. **SIDNEY** and Ariosto. PMLA, 61, 1946.
Ramat, R. **SISMONDI** e il mito di Ginevra. Firenze, 1936.
Dodge, R. E. N. **SPENSER'S** Imitations from Ariosto. PMLA, 12, 1897.
Galimberti, Alice. L'Ariosto inglese. NAnt, 1.VIII.1903.
—— Edmondo Spenser, l'Ariosto inglese. Torino, 1938.
Gilbert, A. H. Spenser's Imitations from Ariosto. PMLA, 34, 1919.
MacMurphy, S. J. Spenser's Use of Ariosto for Allegory. U. of Washington Publ. Lang. and Lit., 2, 1924.
Warton, T. On Spenser's Imitations of Ariost. London, 1754.
Purves, J. The Abregement of Roland Furious by John **STEWART OF BALDYNNEIS,** and the Early Knowledge of Ariosto in England. Italian Studies, 3, 1946.
Avalle Arce, J. B. **TIRSO** y el romance de Angelica y Medoro. NRFH, 2, 1948.
Carducci, G. L'Ariosto e il **VOLTAIRE.** Fanfulla della Domenica, 15.VI.1881. And in: Opere, 10, 1898.

Donati, L. L'Ariosto e il Tasso, giudicati dal Voltaire. Halle, 1889.
Dubled, J. L'Orlando furioso et la Pucelle de Voltaire. BI, 11-12, 1911-12.
Fasola, C. Diedrichs von dem WERDER Uebersetzung des Ariost. ZVL, 7, 1894.
Witkowski, G. Diederich von dem Werder. Leipzig, 1887.
Anon. Ueber eine Stelle im Amadis. (WIELAND). Teutscher Merkur, 1775.
Marinig, Lydia. Der Einfluss von Ariosts Orlando furioso auf Wieland. Studi di filol. moderna, 1912.
Koch, M. Das Quellenverhältnis von Wielands Oberon. Marburger Habilitationsschrift, 1879.
Tribolet, H. Wielands Verhältnis zu Ariost und Tasso. Diss. Bern, 1919.
Vaganay, H. Orlando furioso, traduit par URREA. RH, 81, 1933.

CHAPTER EIGHT

Boccaccio.

1. General Influences.

(See also Sources, I. V. 2.; for Troilus, see also I. VI. 10.)

Anon. Griseldis. LE, 11.
Anschuetz, R. Boccaccios Novelle vom Falken und ihre Verbreitung in der Litteratur. Diss. Erlangen, 1892.
Bartoli, A. Il Decamerone nelle sue attinenze colla novellistica europea. Rivista Europea, 14, 1879.
Betz, L. P. Die Griseldissage in Dichtkunst und Tonkunst. Neue Zürcher Zt., 64, 1903.
Bongini, D. La 48a novella del Decamerone ed i suoi precedenti nella letteratura e nella leggenda. Aosta, 1907.
Borgeld, A. Vrouwenlist, verbreiding en oorsprung van een novelle uit den Decamerone. NPh, 1926.
Cappelletti, L. Studj sul Decamerone. Parma, 1880.
Cate, A. The Problem of the Origin of the Griselda Story. SPh, 1932.
Cook, A. S. The First Readers of Petrarch's Tale of Griselda. MPh, 15, 1917.
Dick, H. G. The Lover in a Cask: A Tale of a Tub. Ital., 18, 1941.
Fassò, L. La prima novella del Decamerone e la sua fortuna. Annali della R. U. di Cagliari, 1930-31.
Fürst, R. Die Vorläufer der modernen Novelle im XVIII. Jahrhundert. Halle, 1897.
Groeber, G. Ueber die Quellen von Boccaccios Decameron. Strassburg, 1913.
Hauvette, H. Réminiscences de Boccace dans une légende célèbre (Morte vivante). In: Studii su G. Boccaccio. Castelfiorentino, 1913 .
Hortis, A. Studj sulle opere latine del Boccaccio con particolare riguardo alla storia delle erudizione nel medio evo e alle letterature straniere. Trieste, 1879.
Jones, F. N. Boccaccio and his Imitators in German, English, French, Spanish and Italian Literatures. Chicago, 1910.
Koehler, R. Die Griseldis-Novelle als Volksmärchen. ALG, 1870. And in: Kleinere Schriften. Berlin, 1899.
—— Griselda. Encycl. Ersch-Gruber, 1871. And in: Gesammelte Schriften. Berlin, 1900.
Laserstein, K. Der Griseldisstoff in der Weltliteratur. Weimar, 1926.
Lee, A. C. The Decameron, its Sources and Analogues. London, 1909.
Ljubibratic, W. Boccaccios Novelle Griseldis in der Weltliteratur. Nastarni Vjesnik, 17, 1910.
Loehmann, O. Die Rahmenerzählung des Decameron, ihre Quellen und Nachwirkungen. Halle, 1935.
Luetgenau, F. Troilus and Cressida. ESn, 46, 1916.
Menéndez y Pelayo. Origines de la novela. Madrid, 1907.
Murray, J. Tancred and Gismund. RES, 14, 1938.
Schmidt, W. V. Beiträge zur Geschichte der romantischen Poesie. Berlin, 1818.
Schofield, W. H. The Source and History of the Seventh Novel of the Seventh Day in the Decameron. HSPhL, 1893.
Sorieri, L. Boccaccio's Story of Tito e Gisippo in European Literature. New York, 1937.
Tatlock, J. Troilus and Cressida. PMLA, 30, 1922.
Tosi, J. Sulla leggenda di Griselda. Italia Moderna, 4, 1906.
Traversari, G. Bibliografia Boccaccesca. Città di Castello, 1907.
Westenholz, F. von. Die Griseldis-Sage in der Litteraturgeschichte. Heidelberg, 1888.
—— Griselda in der Weltliteratur. Bühne & Welt, 11.
Wilkins, E. H. Chriseida. MLN, 24, 1909.
Wurzbach, W. Zur dramatischen Behandlung der Griseldissage. Euphorion, 4, 1897.

2. Influences upon Individual Countries.

Brunnemann, M. Decamerone III[3] im englischen Drama. (ENGLAND). Diss. Rostock, 1910.
Farnham, W. England's Discovery of the Decameron. PMLA, 39, 1924.
Förster, M. Boccaccios De casibus virorum illustrium in englischer Bearbeitung. DLZ, 45, 1924.
Halstead, W. L. Collaboration on the Patient Grissill. PhQ, 18.
Malone, K. Patient Griseldus. RR, 20, 1929.
Munsterberg, Margaret. The Decameron in English. (1620). MB, 19, 1944.
Orsini, N. La novella boccaccesca di Ghismonda in una tragedia inedita (London, 1597). In: Studii sul Rinascimento italiano in Inghilterra. Firenze, 1937.
Raith, J. Boccaccio in der englischen Literatur von Chaucer bis Painters Palace of Pleasure. Leipzig, 1936. Cf. MLR, 32.
Sherwood, C. Die neuenglischen Bearbeitungen der Erzählung Boccaccios von Ghismonda und Guiscardo. Diss. Berlin, 1892.
Siefken, O. Der Constance-Griseldis-Typus in der englischen Literatur. Rathenow, 1903.
Wild, F. Ueber die Verstechnik des Verfassers der mittelenglischen Umdichtung von Boccaccios De claris mulieribus. Festschrift Luick. Marburg, 1925.
Wright, H. G. The First English Translation of the Decamerone. MLR, 1936.
—— Early English Versions of the Tales of Guiscardo and Ghismonda and Titus and Gisippus, from the Decameron. Oxford U. P., 1937.
—— The Elizabethan Translation of the Questioni d'Amore in the Filocolo. MLR, 36, 1941.
Zupitza, J. Die mittelenglischen Bearbeitungen der Erzählung Boccaccios von Ghismonda und Guiscardo. Zs. f. Kultur & Geschichte d. Renaissance, 1, 1883.

Crouzet, J. & Hauvette, H. Les plus anciennes traductions françaises de Boccace. (FRANCE). BI, 8, 1908.
Durrieu, P. Le plus ancien MS de la traduction française du Décameron. C. R. de l'Acad. des Inscriptions et Belles Lettres, 1909.
Golenistcheff-Koutouzoff, E. L'histoire de Griseldis en France au XIVe et au XVe siècle. Paris, 1933.
Groeneveld, H. Die älteste Bearbeitung der Griseldissage in Frankreich. Marburg, 1888.
Hauvette, H. Un chapître de Boccace et sa fortune dans la littérature française. BI, 3, 1903.
—— Pour la fortune de Boccace en France. Studi di filologia moderna, 1, 1908.
—— Les plus anciennes traductions françaises de Boccace. Bordeaux, 1909.
Liese, K. Der französische Roman Athis et Prophilias verglichen mit einer Erzählung von Boccaccio (X.8). Progr. der Realschule zu Görlitz, 1901.
Livingston, C. H. Decameron, VIII, 2: Earliest French Imitations. MPh, 22, 1924.
Roncaglia, A. G. Boccaccio e la critica francese dell'ultimo secolo. Il libro italiano nel mondo, 1.
Saulnier, V. L. Boccace et la nouvelle française de la Renaissance. RLC, 21, 1947.
Schuster, R. Griseldis in der französischen Literatur. Tübingen, 1909.
Torraca, F. Il Boccaccio e i novellieri francesi. Fanfulla della Domenica, 1882.

Anon. Neuere Uebersetzungen des Decameron. (GERMANY). Blätter f. literar. Unterhaltung, 21.I.1831.
Drescher, K. Untersuchungen über den Verfasser der ersten deutschen Decamerone-Uebersetzung. Strassburg, 1900.
Durrieu, P. Le Boccace de Munich. München, 1909.
Pellizzari, A. Documenti: Boccaccio in Germania. Rassegna, 24, 1916.
Stockum, T. C. van. Zwei deutsche Griseldis-Dramen. NPh, 1944.
Widmann, G. Griseldis in der deutschen Literatur des 19. Jahrhunderts. Euphorion, 13, 1906.

Verdam, J. De Griseldis-Novelle in het Nederlandsch. (HOLLAND). Tijdschrift voor nederl. taal- en letterkunde, 17, 1898.

Landau, M. Boccaccio in Ungarn (HUNGARY). ZVL, 7.
Papp, G. Il Boccaccio in Ungheria. In: Studii su G. Boccaccio. Castelfiorentino, 1913.

Bourland, C. B. Boccaccio and the Decameron in Castilian and Catalan Literature. (SPAIN). RH 12, 1905 & New York, Paris, 1905.
Casella, M. La versione catalana del Decameron. AR, 9, 1925.
Farinelli, A. Note sulla fortuna del Boccaccio in Ispagna nell' età media. Archiv, 1905.
—— Note sulla fortuna del Corbaccio nella

Spagna medievale. Festgabe A. Mussafia. Halle, 1905.
—— Boccaccio in Ispagna. In: Italia e Spagna. Torino, 1929.
Haan, F. de. El Decameron en Castellano, Ms. del Escorial. Festschrift Marshall Elliot. Baltimore, 1911.
Pagès, A. Les poésies lyriques et la traduction catalane du Décameron. Annales du Midi, 1934.
Sanvisenti, B. I primi influssi di Dante, del Petrarca e del Boccaccio nella letteratura spagnuola. Milano, 1902.
Wannemacher, F. Die Griseldissage auf der iberischen Halbinsel. Diss. Strassburg, 1894.

3. Influences upon Individual Authors.

Drescher, K. **ARIGO**, der Uebersetzer des Decameron und der Fiore di Virtu. Strassburg, 1900.
—— Zu Arigos Blumen der Tugend. ZVL, 13.
Chiurlo, U. Appunti intorno alle traduzione francese del Filostrato dovuta a Louis de **BEAUVAU**. BI, 10, 1910.
Filippi, L. La poesia di G. A. **BUERGER**. Firenze, 1920.
Hatzfeld, H. Boccacciostil in Don Quijote. **(CERVANTES)**. Festschrift O. Walzel. Potsdam, 1925.
Rotunda, D. P. A Boccaccian Theme in the Galatea of Cervantes. RR, 20, 1929.
Bardelli, M. Qualche contributo agli studi sulle relazioni del **CHAUCER** col Boccaccio. Firenze, 1911.
Borghesi, P. Boccaccio and Chaucer. Bologna, 1903.
Bright, J. W. Chaucer and Lollius. PMLA, 19.
Brown, C. Another Contemporary Allusion in Chaucers Troilus. MLN, 26, 1911.
Brown, M. L. The Hous of Fame and the Corbaccio. MLN, 32, 1917.
Bryant, F. E. Did Boccaccio Suggest the Character of Chaucer's Knight? MLN, 17, 1902.
Child, C. G. Chaucer's Hous of Fame and Boccaccio's Amorosa visione. MLN, 10, 1895.
—— Chaucer's Legend of Good Women and Boccaccio's De Genealogia Deorum. MLN, 11, 1896.
Cook, A. S. Chaucer's Troilus and Criseyde. Archiv, 119, 1908.
Cummings, H. The Indebtedness of Chaucer's Work to the Italian Works of Boccaccio. U. of Cincinnati Studies, 10, 1916.
Dempster, Germaine. Chaucer's Ms of Petrarch's Version of the Griselda Story. MPh, 41, 1943.
Epstein, H. J. The Identity of Chaucer's Lollius. MLQ, 3, 1942.
Farnham, W. E. Chaucer's Clerkes Tale. MLN, 33, 1918.
Grillo, E. Chaucer imitatore del Boccaccio. Boll. della R. U. di Perugia, 1, 1929.
Kittredge, G. L. Chaucer's Lollius. HSCPh, 28, 1917.
Koch, J. Ein Beitrag zur Kritik Chaucers. ESn, 1, 1877. And in: Essays on Chaucer, London, 1878.
Lewis, C. S. What Chaucer Really Did to Il Filostrato. E&S, 17, 1932.
Lowes, J. L. The Prologue to the Legend of Good Women as Related to the French Marguerite Poems and the Filostrato. PMLA, 19, 1904.
—— The Franklin's Tale, the Teseida and the Filocolo. MPh, 15, 1918.
Mamroth, F. Geoffrey Chaucer, seine Zeit und seine Abhängigkeit von Boccaccio. Diss. Rostock, 1873.
McNeal, T. H. Chaucer and the Decameron (V.2). MLN, 53, 1938.
Morsbach, L. Chaucers Plan der Canterbury Tales und Boccaccios Decamerone. ESn, 42, 1910.
—— Chaucers Canterbury Tales und das Decameron. Berlin, 1934.
Ogle, G. Gualtherus and Griselda: or the Clerc of Oxford's Tale. From Boccace, Petrarch, and Chaucer. London, 1739.
Pratt, R. A. Chaucer's Use of the Teseida. PMLA, 62, 1947.
Rajna, P. Le origini della novella narrata dal Frankeleyn nei Canterbury Tales del Chaucer. Romania, 32, 1903.
Root, R. K. Chaucer and the Decameron. ESn, 44, 1912.
Rossetti, W. M. Chaucer's Troylus and Cryseyde Compared with Boccaccio's Filostrato. Chaucer Society, 1873.
Schirmer, W. F. Boccaccios Werke als Quelle Geoffrey Chaucers. GRM, 12, 1924.
Schofield, W. H. Chaucer's Franklin's Tale. PMLA, 1901.
Segrè, C. Chaucer e Boccaccio. Fanfulla della Domenica, 22, 1901. And in: Studi petrarcheschi. Firenze, 1911.

Sells, A. L. Boccaccio, Chaucer and Stendhal. RLM, 2, 1947.
Severs, J. B. The Literary Relationships of Chaucer's Clerkes Tale. Yale U. P., 1942.
Shannon, E. F. The Source of Chaucer's Anelida and Arcite. PMLA, 27, 1912.
Tatlock, J. S. P. Boccaccio and the Plan of Chaucer's Canterbury Tales. Anglia, 37, 1913.
—— The Scene of the Franklin's Tale Visited. Chaucer Society, 1914.
—— The Epilogue of Chaucer's Troilus. MPh, 1921.
Toynbee, P. Chaucer and Boccaccio. Athenaeum, 18, 1905.
Trigona, F. Chaucer imitatore del Boccaccio. Catania, 1923.
Young, K. Chaucer's Use of Boccaccio's Filocolo. MPh, 4, 1906-07.
—— The Origin and Development of the Story of Troilus and Criseyde. Chaucer Society, 1908.
Jeanroy, A. Boccace et **CHRISTINE DE PISAN**: le De Claris Mulieribus principale source du Livre de la Cité de Dieu. Romania, 1922.
Lugli, V. Da Boccaccio a **COURTELINE.** Rassegna d'Italia, 1947.
Merlino, C. Boccaccio in the Works of Mario **EQUICOLA.** Ital., 12, 1935.
Moll, F. El Corbatx de G. Boccacco, traduit en catala par Narcis **FRANCH** (segle XIV). Mallorca, 1935.
Todesco, V. Un'antica traduzione catalana del Corbaccio di Narcis Franch. Conv., 10, 1938.
Dilts, D. A. John **GOWER** and the De Genealogia Deorum. MLN, 57, 1942.
Strauch, P. Erhart **GROSS,** der Verfasser der Grisardis. ZDA, 36.
Buchheim, C. A. **HALM'S** Griseldis (Cf. Introduction). Oxford, 1894.
Lemmi, C. W. The Influence of Boccaccio on **HAWES'** Pastime of Pleasure. RES, 5, 1929.
MacCracken, H. The Source of **KEATS'** Eve of Saint Agnes. MPh, 5, 1907.
Barri, V. F. Le novelle del Decameron imitate da **LA FONTAINE.** Annuario della Civica Scuola Reale. Trieste, 1914.
Cacudi, N. La Fontaine imitateur de Boccace. Rassegna di studi francesi, 1-2, 1923-24.
Dubois, J. Lafontaine et Boccace. Mém. Société acad. de l'Aube, 72, 1908.
Gaudenzi, E. La novella di Federigo Alberighi di G. Boccaccio e Le faucon del La Fontaine. Cremona, 1929.
Toldo, P. Come il La Fontaine si ispirasse al Boccaccio. Festschrift F. Torraca. Napoli, 1912.
Auer, J. W. S. **LANDOR** in seinen Beziehungen zu den Dichtern des Trecento, Dante, Boccaccio, Petrarca. Diss. Münster, 1903.
Ettlinger, E. Eine Parallele zur Parabel von den drei Ringen. **(LESSING).** Euphorion, 19, 1913.
Giannone, T. Una novella del Boccaccio e un dramma del Lessing. Riv. Abbruzzese, 15, 1901.
Henning, M. & Weber, J. Neue Beiträge zur Fabel von den drei Ringen. Das Freie Wort, 1, 1901.
Vella, G. Una novella del Decamerone e una poesia del **LONGFELLOW.** Soc. universitaria di lett. ital. dell'isola di Malta. Valletta, 1940.
Martin, H. M. **LOPE DE VEGA'S** El velloncino depro in Relation to its Sources. MLN, 39, 1924.
Menéndez y Pelayo, M. Libro de las virtuosas y claras mujeres de Alvaro de **LUNA.** (Cf. Introduction). Madrid, 1891.
Wolff, S. L. A Source of Euphues, The Anatomy of Wyt. **(LYLY).** MPh, 7, 1909.
Schiff, M. **MIRABEAU** au donjon de Vincennes. MF, 1914.
Wright, H. G. (ed.). De Claris Mulieribus, Translated by Henry Parker, Lord **MORLEY.** EETS. Oxford U. P., 1943.
Hauvette, H. **MUSSET** et Boccace. BI, 11, 1911.
Toldo, P. L'arte e la personalità di Alfredo de Musset. Mem. della R. Accad. Bologna, 10, 1915-16.
Hauvette, H. De Laurentio de **PRIMOFATO** qui primus J. Boccacii opera quaedam gallice transtulit, ineunte saeculo XV. Paris, 1903.
Koeppel, E. Laurent de Premierfaits und John Lydgates Bearbeitungen von Boccaccios De casibus virorum illustrium. München, 1886.
Smith, F. A. La traduction française de L. de Premierfait et son importance pour la fortune de Boccace en France. RLC, 14, 1934.
Renucci, P. Deux étapes d'utopisme humaniste: Le château du Décameron et l'Abbaye de Télème. **(RABELAIS).** BRL, 30, 1947.
Thorpe, L. Boccaccio and Rabelais. N&Q, 192, 1947.
Belden, H. Boccaccio, Hans **SACHS** and the Bramble Briar. PMLA, 33, 1918.
Brand, O. Hans Sachs als Humanist in

seinen Gedichten und Schwänken. München, 1907.
Drescher, K. Hans Sachs und Boccaccio. ZVL, 7, 1894.
Hartmann, J. Das Verhältnis von H. Sachs zur sog. Steinhöwelschen Decameronübersetzung. Berlin, 1912.
Hortis, A. Hans Sachs e Giovanni Boccaccio. In: Studii sulle opere latine del Boccaccio. Trieste, 1879.
MacMechan. The Relation of Hans Sachs to the Decameron. Diss. Halifax, 1894.
Monti, G. M. La novella di Simona e Pasquino in Boccaccio, Hans Sachs e De Musset. Rassegna di studi francesi, 8, 1930.
Parmentier. H. Sachs entre Boccace et Molière. Bull. de la Faculté des Lettres de Poitiers, 1884.
Bierfreund, T. Palemon og Arcite. En literaturhistorisk undersøgelse som bidrag til SHAKESPEAREkritiken. København, 1891.
Hertzberg, W. Die Quellen der Troilus-Sage in ihrem Verhältniss zu Shakespeares Troilus und Cressida. JbShG, 4, 1871.
Ohle, R. Ueber die romanischen Vorläufer von Shakespeares Cymbeline. Diss. Leipzig, 1890.
Rebora, P. Shakespeare e Boccaccio. In: Civiltà italiana e civiltà inglese. Firenze, 1936.
Segrè, C. Un'eroina del Boccaccio (III.9) e l'Elena Shakespeariana. Fanfulla della Domenica, 1901.
Gomez, E. G. Boccaccio y Castillo SOLORZANO. RFE, 15, 1928.
Briggs, W. D. SPENSER'S Faerie Queene III.2 and Boccaccio's Fiammetta. Gedenkschrift Matzke. Stanford, 1911.
Bühler, C. F. The Fifteenth-Century Editions of Petrarch's Historia Griseldis in STEINHOEWELS German Translation. Library Quar., 15, 1945.
Drescher, K. Boccaccios De claris mulieribus übersetzt von Stainhöwel. (Cf. Introduction). Stuttgart, 1895.
Wunderlich, H. Steinhoewel und das Dekameron. Braunschweig, 1889.
Axon, W. A. TENNYSON'S Lover's Tale, its Original and Analogues. Trans. of the Royal Soc. of Lit., 24, 1903.
Strauss, B. Der Uebersetzer Nicolaus von WYLE. Berlin, 1912.
Wright, H. G. The Italian Edition of Boccaccio's Fiammetta Used by Bartholomew YOUNG. MLR, 38.

CHAPTER NINE

Dante.

1. General Influences.

(See also Comparisons, I. V. I., and Sources, I. V. 2.)

Auffray, J. Dantisti e Dantofili dei secoli XVIII e XIX. GD, 1901 ff.
Bach, J. Vorlesungen über Dante und seine Stellung zur allgemeinen Geistesgeschichte. Oesterreichische Vierteljahrschrift f. kath. Theologie, 1866.
Balzo, C. del. Francesca da Rimini nell' arte e nella critica. Napoli, 1895.
—— Dante sul teatro. NAnt, 755, 1903.
Barrès, M. La grande mission de Dante. Revue hebdomadaire, 11.VI.1921.
Bassermann, A. Dante-Literatur der Neuzeit. DVLG, 2.
Besso, M. La fortuna di Dante fuori d' Italia. Firenze, 1912. Cf. NAnt. 1.VIII. 1912.
Bullowa, A. M. The Divine Comedy during the Renaissance. Dante Prize Essay, Harvard, 1930.
Chatenet, G. La Divine Comédie jugée par les critiques du XVIIIe et du XIXe siècle. In: Etudes sur les poètes italiens. Paris, 1892.
Chiminelli, P. La fortuna di Dante nella cristianità riformata. Roma, 1921.
Cian, V. Dante nel Rinascimento. Festschrift A. d'Ancona. Firenze, 1901.
Coligny, C. Revue littéraire (Fêtes de Dante à Florence). L'Artiste, 15.VI. 1865.
Counson, A. Le réveil de Dante. RLC, 1, 1921.
Demoulin, G. Dante et ses traducteurs. L'Artiste, 7-14.VI.1857.
Farinelli, A. Dante in Ispagna, Francia, Inghilterra, Germania. Torino, 1922.
—— Dante a través de los siglos. In: Ensayos y Discursos de critica literaria hispano-europea Roma, 1925.
Friederich, W. P. Dante Through the Centuries. CL, 1, 1949.
—— Dante's Fame Abroad, 1350-1850. The Influence of Dante Alighieri upon the Poets and Scholars of Spain, France, England, Germany, Switzerland and the United States. Roma & Chapel Hill (N. C.), 1950.
Géniaux, C. Retour à Dante. Cahiers du Sud, Dec., 1938.
Guérard, A. Dante and the Renaissance. Dante Sexcentenary Lectures. Houston (Texas), 1921.

Hauvette, H. Dante et la pensée moderne. RP, 1.VI.1921.
Hazard, P. Dante, poète mondial. NRI, 1921.
Heinemann, F. Dante auf der Bühne. Neue Zürcher Zt., 151, 1903.
Henderson, A. The Rimini Story in Modern Drama. Arena, 39, 1908.
Hillebrand, K. De l'apostolat de Dante et de son influence. Revue des cours littéraires, 2, 1865.
Jacobs, M. Ugolino-Dichtungen. In: Gerstenbergs Ugolino. Berlin, 1898.
Locella, G. & M. Dantes Francesca da Rimini in der Literatur, bildenden Kunst und Musik. Esslingen, 1913. Cf. also Verhandlungen d. 12. Philologentages, Erlangen, 1906.
Lo Gatto, E. La fortuna di Dante nel mondo. ICS, 1921.
Marchesi, G. B. Della fortuna di Dante nel secolo XVII. Bergamo, 1898.
Micocci, U. La fortuna di Dante nel secolo XIX. Venezia, 1890.
Oelsner, H. The Influence of Dante on Modern Thought. London, 1895.
Passerini, G. L. Dantisti e Dantofili dei secoli XVIII e XIX. Firenze, 1901.
Paur, T. Das früheste Verständnis von Dantes Commedia. Görlitz, 1887.
Perroni-Grande, L. Per la storia della varia fortuna di Dante nel seicento. Il Saggiatore, 1, 1901.
Plumptre, E. H. Estimates, Contemporary and Later. In: The Commedia and Canzoniere of Dante Alighieri. London, 1887.
Pochhammer, P. Dantes Dichtung in unserer Zeit. Beilage Norddeutsche Allg. Zt., 295, 1901.
Presutti, G. Francesca da Rimini nella storia. Torino, 1903.
Ritis, A. de. Dante intimo nella storia, nella leggenda e nell'arte. Milano, 1939.
Ronzoni, P. Per la storia della fortuna di Dante nel quattrocento. GD, 1899.
Ruffini, F. Le caractère moderne de la pensée politique de Dante. Revue hebdomadaire, 18.VI.1921.
Schlosser, F. C. Uebersetzungen: englische, französische und deutsche. In: Dante-Studien. Leipzig, 1855.
Schullern. Paolo Malatesta und Francesca da Rimini in der Geschichte. Monatsblätter der k. & k. herald. Ges. Adler, 5, 1903.
Sterkmann. Dante e la modernità. Riv. mod. d. cultura, 3, 1901.
Taillandier, S. Dante Alighieri et la littérature dantesque en Europe. RDM, 1.XII.1856.
Toynbee, P. The Earliest Illustrators of Dante. QR, 1909.
Turnbull. J. M. Dante Speaks to the Moderns. Queen's Quarterly, 1938.
Underdown, Emily. Historical Influences of the Divina Commedia. Gentleman's Mag., 1900.
Urban, G. Paolo and Francesca in History and Literature. Critic, May, 1902.
Urbano, G. Il culto di Dante Alighieri dal secolo XIV al secolo XIX. Trani, 1899.
Varia. Dante, la vita, le opere, le grandi città dantesche, Dante e l'Europa. Milano, 1921.
Yriarte, C. Françoise de Rimini dans la légende et dans l'histoire. Paris, 1883.
Zacchetti, G. La fama di Dante nel secolo XVIII. Roma, 1900.

2. Influences upon England.

Anon. Dante and his English Translators. Westminster Rev., 1861.
—— Dante and his Latest English Translators. NAR, 1886.
—— Dante in English Literature. ER, 1908.
—— Il culto di Dante e gli Anglo-Sassoni. Marzocco, 20.III.1921.
Alger, J. G. Did Dante Visit England? N&Q, 6.VIII.1892.
Axson, S. Dante and English Literature. Dante Sexcentenary Lectures. Houston (Texas), 1921.
Barbi, M. Letteratura dantesca in Inghilterra e in America. Boll. della Società Dantesca italiana, 9, 1902.
Bellezza, P. La fortuna di Dante in Inghilterra. ICS, 1921.
Bouchier, J. The Study of Dante in England. N&Q, 4.II.1888; 2.VI.1888; 9.VIII. 1890; 25.X.1890.
Butler, J. D. The Study of Dante in England. N&Q, 31.III.1888.
Cattaneo, C. G. La Divina Commedia in inglese. Le Curiosità dell' erudizione, 3, 1895.
Chambers, R. W. Long Will, Dante and the Righteous Heathen. E&S, 1923.
Cross, J. W. Dante and the New Reformation. NC, 1890.
Galimberti, Alice. Dante nel pensiero inglese. Firenze, 1921.
Gladstone, W. E. Did Dante Study at Oxford? NC, 1892. And in: Dante Society Lectures, 3. London, 1909.
Hales, J. W. Dante in England. The Bibliographer, 1882. And in: Folia litteraria. London, 1893.

Halley, A. R. The Influence of Dante on Nineteenth Century English Poets. Diss. Harvard, 1922.

Koeppel, E. Dante in der englischen Literatur des XVI. Jahrhunderts. ZVL, 3, 1890.

Kuhns, L. O. Dante's Influence on English Poetry in the XIXth Century. MLN, 14, 1899.

—— Dante and the English Poets from Chaucer to Tennyson. New York, 1904.

Newman, Florence M. The Francesca da Rimini Episode in English Literature. Dante Prize Essay, Harvard, 1942.

Pellizzi, C. Dante in Inghilterra. Idea nazionale, 13.V.1921.

Renzulli, M. Dante nella letteratura inglese. Firenze, 1925. Cf. Marzocco, 27. XI.1925.

Saffi, A. Studi recenti degl'Inglesi su Dante. Rivista di Firenze, 1857.

Scudder, Vida D. The Life of the Spirit in the Modern English Poets. (Dante, Spenser, Milton). Boston, 1895.

Sills, K. C. M. References to Dante in Seventeenth Century Literature. MPh, 3, 1905.

Tomlinson, C. The Study of Dante in England. N&Q, 7, 1890.

Toynbee, P. English Translation from Dante (14th to 17th Centuries). JCL, 1, 1903.

—— The Earliest References to Dante in the English Literature. Festschrift Arturo Graf. Bergamo, 1903.

—— The Earliest Editions of the Divina Commedia Printed in England. Athenaeum, 2.I.1904.

—— A Chronological List of English Translations from Dante, from Chaucer to the Present Day. 24th Annual Report Dante Society Cambridge (Mass.), 1905.

—— Dante in English Literature from Chaucer to Cary. 2 vols. London, 1909. Cf. Boll. Soc. dantesca ital., 17, 1910 & Italian Studies, 3, 1946.

—— Dante in English Art. 38th Annual Report Dante Society Cambridge (Mass.), 1919.

—— The Oxford Dante Society. Oxford, 1920.

—— Britain's Tribute to Dante in Literature and Art (1380-1920). London, 1921.

—— Some Mistranslations of Dante. MLR, 1929.

Valgimigli, A. Il culto di Dante in Inghilterra. GD, 6, 1898

—— La forza morale di Dante e gli Anglo-Sassoni. GD, 11, 1903.

3. Influences upon France.

Anon. Dante in Frankreich. Blätter zur Kunde der Litt. des Auslands, 3, 1838.

Arlotta, F. Sur la traduction de deux passages de Dante. Paris, 1898.

Auffray, J. La Divine Comédie. Traductions anciennes et modernes. Revue hebdomadaire, 24.XI.1900.

Auvray, L. Les manuscrits de Dante des bibliothèques de France. Paris, 1892.

Beaurepaire, C. de. De la récente admiration des Français pour Dante. Rouen, 1873.

Bouvy, E. Dante en France. Revue des lettres françaises et étrangères, 1, 1899.

Camus, J. La première version française de l'Enfer de Dante. GSLI, 37, 1901.

Canudo, R. L'heure de Dante et la nôtre. MF, 15.IX.1921.

Counson, A. Dante en France. Erlangen, Paris, 1907.

Delmont, T. Dante et la France. Revue de Lille, 1901.

Farinelli, A. Dante e la Francia dall' età media al secolo di Voltaire. 2 vols. Milano, 1908.

Gillet, L. Dante et la France. NL, 1939.

Girard, G. Essai de bibliographie française de Dante. Bull. de la Maison du livre français, July, 1921.

Hauvette, H. Dante dans la poésie française de la Renaissance. Annales de l'U. de Grenoble, 1899. And in: Etudes sur la Divine Comédie. Paris, 1922.

Hazard, P. Dante et la pensée française. Minerve française, 1920.

Labitte, C. Biographes et traducteurs de Dante. RDM, 1.X.1841.

Lamartine, A. de. Traducteurs et commentateurs de Dante. Souvenirs et Portraits. Paris, 1872.

Lamy. Dante, guide des romantiques français en Italie. Revue de l'Art, 1924.

Lollis, C. de. Dante e Goethe in Francia. Cultura, 1.V.1907.

Longnon, J. Dante et la France. Rev. critique des idées et des livres, 25.IV. 1921.

Lowositz, J. B. Dante und der Katholizismus in Frankreich. Königsberg, 1847.

Mariano, P. Dante in Francia. Portici, 1902.

Maugain, G. L'orthodoxie de Dante et la critique française de 1830 à 1860. In: Mélanges publiés à l'occasion du sixième centenaire de la mort de Dante. Paris, 1921.

—— Le voyage de Dante à Paris. RdF, 1.XII.1922.

May, D. Le sixième centenaire de Dante à Paris et en France. NRI, 25.VI.1921.
Mignon, M. Dante e la Francia. In: Dante, la vita, le opere, le grandi città dantesche, Dante e l'Europa. Milano, 1921.
—— La culture dantesque en France. In: Les affinités intellectuelles de l'Italie et de la France. Paris, 1921.
Morel, C. Les plus anciennes traductions françaises de la Divine Comédie. Paris, 1897.
Oelsner, H. Dante in Frankreich bis zum Ende des XVIII. Jahrhunderts. Diss. Berlin, 1898.
Picco, F. La fortuna di Dante in Francia. ICS, 1921.
Rajna, P. Per la questione dell'andata di Dante a Parigi. Festschrift M. Barbi. Firenze, 1920.
Ronzy, P. Dante auxiliaire du Gallicanisme dans le De Episcopis Urbis (1586). In: Mélanges publiés à l'occasion du sixième centenaire de la mort de Dante. Paris, 1921.
Sainte-Beuve, C. A. Article sur la Divine Comédie, contenant une esquisse de l'influence de Dante en France. Causeries du Lundi, 11.XII.1854.
Soulier, G. L'inspiration dantesque dans l'art français. NRI, 6, 1921.
Stengel, E. Philologischer Kommentar zu der französischen Uebertragung von Dantes Inferno. (Turiner Ms). Paris, Paris, 1925.
Topin, H. Dante en France depuis le XVe siècle jusqu'à nos jours. Il Bibliofilo, 1882.
Vasconcellos, J. de. L'inspiration dantesque dans l'art romantique français. Paris, 1925.

4. Influences upon Germany.

Anon. Die Dantefeier zu Dresden den 14. September, 1865. Dresdner Journal, 216, 1865.
—— Dante und seine neuen Uebersetzer und Erklärer. Beilage aur Allg. Zt., 145-46, 1866.
Auerbach, E. Die Entdeckung Dantes in der Romantik. DVLG, 7, 1929.
Bartsch, K. Aeltester Versuch einer deutschen Danteübersetzung. ZRPh, 6, 1882.
Bassermann, A. Zur Frage der Dante-Uebersetzungen. SVL, 1, 1901.
Belle, T. von. Dante in Deutschland. MLIA, 1881.
Bianquis, G. L'influence de Dante sur la littérature allemande. EI, 3, 1921.
Bolte, J. Ein deutsches Urtheil über Dante aus dem XVII. Jahrhundert. ZVL, 1, 1887.
Bulle, O. Ein deutscher Dante. LE, 1. VIII.1909.
Daeubler, T. Ueber die Möglichkeit einer deutschen Dante-Uebersetzung. Preuss. Akad. der Künste, 1929.
Dietrich, F. Eine neue Dante-Uebersetzung. Literatur, Oct., 1935.
Farinelli, A. La fortuna di Dante in Germania. ICS, 1921.
Friederich, W. P. Dante's Influence upon the Poets and Philosophers of Germany, 1800-1865. PhQ, 25, 1946.
Fuchs, C. C. Dante in der deutschen Romantik. JbDG, 15, 1933.
Gallo, N. La mostra del libro tedesco e della fortuna di Dante in Germania. Il Libro Italiano, 3, 1939.
Goetz, W. Deutsche Dante-Verleger. JbDG, N.F., 17, 1946.
Grauert, H. Zur Dante-Forschung. Histor. Jb. der Görres-Ges, 1895.
—— Dante in Deutschland. Hist. polit. Blätter für das kath. Deutschland, 120, 1897.
Hertkens, J. Francesca da Rimini im deutschen Drama. Diss. Münster. Dortmund, 1912.
Koch, M. Dantes Bedeutung für Deutschland. Mainz, 1921.
Kohler, J. Dante-Uebersetzung oder Nachbildung. ZVL, 11, 1898.
—— Was ist uns Dante? Zeitgeist, 11, 1902. And in: Aus Kultur und Leben. Berlin, 1904.
Köhler, R. Dantes Göttliche Komödie und ihre deutschen Uebersetzungen. Der 5. Gesang der Hölle in 22 Uebersetzungen seit 1763 bis 1865. Weimar, 1865.
Lang, W. Dante-Litteratur in Deutschland. Im Neuen Reich. (Leipzig), 1871.
Leo, U. Dante in Germany. Ital., 18, 1941.
Locella, G. Zur deutschen Dante-Litteratur, mit besonderer Berücksichtigung der Uebersetzungen von Dantes Göttlicher Komödie. Leipzig, 1889.
—— Dante in der deutschen Kunst. Dresden, 1890.
Loeher, F. Dante in Deutschland. Beilage zur Allg. Zt., 271, 1865.
Merbach, P. A. Dante in Deutschland. JbDG, 5, 1920.
Michaelis, C. Dante in Deutschland. Leipziger Tageblatt, 70, 1906.
Mugna, P. Dante Alighieri in Germania. Padova, 1869.
Ostermann, T. Dante in Deutschland: Bib-

liographie der deutschen Dante-Literatur, 1416-1927. Heidelberg, 1929.
Paur, T. Dante in Deutschland. Unsere Zeit, 1, 1865.
—— Zur Dante-Litteratur in Deutschland. Blätter für literar. Unterhaltung, 23, 1877.
Pochhammer, P. Deutsche Dantefreunde. Der Kunstwart, 1898.
—— Die Wiedergewinnung Dantes für die deutsche Bildung. Humboldt-Akademie. Berlin, 1902.
Scartazzini, G. A. Deutsche Dante-Litteratur und Kunst. Beilage zur Allg. Zt., 217-18, 1870.
—— Dante und die deutsche Philosophie. MLIA, 1871.
—— I recenti studii Danteschi in Germania. NAnt, 17, 1871.
—— Dante in Germania. 2 vols. Milano, 1881-83.
—— Bibliografia dantesca alemanna dell' ultimo decennio (1883-93). GD, 1, 1894.
Schmitthenner, H. Dante in der konfessionellen Polemik des 16. und 17. Jahrhunderts. Grenzboten, 63, 1904.
—— Dante in der deutschen Literatur. In: Aus Dichters Werkstatt, Aufsätze. Stuttgart, 1911.
Schneider, F. Deutschland und die sechshundertjährige Dantefeier. Südland, March, 1920.
—— Neuere Dante-Literatur. Histor. Zs., 134, 1926.
—— Der deutsche Weg zu Dante. Weimar, 1936.
Schubring, P. Dantes Göttliche Komödie in Zeichnungen deutscher Romantiker. Leipzig, 1921.
Schulenburg, W. von der. Dante und Deutschland. Freiburg, 1922.
Stranik, E. Dante und die deutsche Romantik. N. Wiener Tagblatt, 257, 1921 & Freie Welt, 7, 1926.
Sulger-Gebing, E. Dante in der deutschen Litteratur bis zum Erscheinen der ersten vollständigen Uebersetzung der Divina Commedia, 1767-69. ZVL, 8-10, 1895-97.
—— Ein Zeugnis deutscher Dantekenntnis im XVII. Jahrhundert. SVL, 2, 1902.
Susan, C. V. Dante-Uebersetzungen. LE, 3, 1901.
Taube, C. F. Dante und Deutschland. Das Innere Reich, 1938.
Traversi, C. A. Dante in Germania. Illustr. Ital., 3, 1883.
Valle, E. Il culto di Dante in Germania. Prov. di Vicenza, Jan., 1895.
Vossler, K. Dante in Germania. LNI, 13, 1942.
Wegele, F. X. Ueber deutsche Dante-Studien des letzten Jahrzehntes. ZVL, 2, 1889.
Witte, K. Deutsche Dante-Studien im Jahre 1855. Blätter für literar. Unterhaltung, 1856.
—— Dante-Forschungen I. & II. Halle, 1869, Heilbronn, 1879.
Zoozmann, R. Dante in Deutschland. In: Dantes Werke, 4. Leipzig, 1907.
—— Dante und das deutsche Drama. Bühne & Welt, 11, 1909.

5. Influences upon Spain.

Alòs, R. d'. De la primera traducció catalana de la Divina Comedia. Revista, 1921.
Amezúa, A. G. Fases y carácteres de la influencia del Dante en España. Madrid, 1922.
Farinelli, A. Dante in Spagna. In: Dante in Spagna, Francia, Inghilterra, Germania. Torino, 1922.
Friederich, W. P. The Unsolved Problem of Dante's Influence in Spain, 1515-1865. HR, 14, 1946.
Giannini, A. La fortuna di Dante in Ispagna. ICS, 1921.
Green, O. H. Additional Data on Dante in Spain. Romance Philology, 1, 1948.
Hutton, W. H. The Influence of Dante in Spanish Literature. MLR, 1908.
Lollis, C. de. Dante e la Spagna. In: Dante, la vita, le opere, le grandi città dantesche, Dante e l'Europa. Milano, 1921.
Post, C. R. The Beginnings of the Influence of Dante in Castilian and Catalan Literature. Cambridge (Mass.), 1908.
—— Castilian Allegory of the XVth Century with Especial Reference to the Influence of Dante. Harvard Studies in Comp. Lit. 4, 1913.
Rossi, R. Dante e la Spagna. Milano, 1929.
Sanvisenti, B. I primi influssi di Dante, del Petrarca e del Boccacio sulla letteratura spagnuola. Milano, 1902.
Savj-Lopez, P. Un imitatore spagnuolo di Dante nel 1400. GD, 3, 1896.
—— Dantes Einfluss auf spanische Dichter des 15. Jahrhunderts. Napoli, 1900.
Scartazzini, G. A. Dante Alighieri in Spanien. MLIA, 1870.
—— Eine alt-catalanische Dante-Uebersetzung. MLIA, 1878.
Schiff, M. La première traduction espagnole de la Divine Comédie. Festschrift Menéndez y Pelayo. Madrid, 1899.
Uhagon, F. R. de. Una traducción castel-

lana desconocida de la Divina Commedia. Rev. de Archivos, Bibliotecas y Museos, 5, 1901.
Vidal y Valenciano, C. Imitadores, traductores y comentadores españoles de la Divina Commedia. Revista de España, 1869.

6. Influences upon Other Countries.

Ancona, E. L. d'. Dante and his American Friends in Florence. (**AMERICA**). Wellesley Mag., 25, 1940.
Boni, G. Studi danteschi in America. RI, 1898.
Fucilla, J. G. The First Fragment of a Translation of the Divine Comedy Printed in America. Ital., 25, 1948.
Grandgent, C. H. Il contributo americano agli studî danteschi. GD, 18, 1910.
Knortz, K. Dante in Amerika. Reform. Zs. d. Allg. Vereins f. vereinfachte Rechtsschreibung, 10.
Koch, T. W. Dante in America. 15th Annual Report of Dante Society. Cambridge (Mass.) 1896.
La Piana, Angelina. Dante's American Pilgrimage: A Historical Survey of Dante Studies in the United States, 1800-1944. New Haven (Conn.), 1946. Cf. CL, 2, 1950.
Mathews, J. C. Dante and Major American Writers, 1800-67. Diss. U. of Cal., 1938.
Wood, C. J. Dante in America. Critic, Jan., 1901.
Counson, A. Dante en Belgique. (**BELGIUM**). GD, 14, 1906.
Fromm, H. G. Le Dante dans les Flandres. L'Univers, 17.I.1894.
Babler, O. F. Die tschechischen Bemühungen um Dante. (**CZECHOSLOVAKIA**). JbDG, 1942.
Cohen, J. L. Dante in de nederlandsche letterkunde. (**HOLLAND**). Haarlem, 1929.
Dupont, A. Dante aux Pays-Bas. De Wachter, 4, 1880.
Hellwald, F. von. Dante im Niederland. MLIA, 1879.
Nolet de Brauwere van Steeland. Les traducteurs de Dante Alighieri aux Pays-Bas. Bull. de l'Acad. Royale de Belgique, 47 & Bruxelles, 1879.
Persyn, J. Dante in de nederlandsche letterkunde. Korr. Vlaamsche Acad., 1921.
Anon. Dante in Ungarn. (**HUNGARY**). MLIA, 1879.
Czaszar, E. Dante in Ungarn. Ungar. Rundschau, 1, 1912.
Gluecksmann, H. Dantes Hölle in ungarischer Uebertragung. MLIA, 1886.
Kapos, J. Dante Magyarornagon. Budapest, 1911.
Kertbeny. Dante in der ungarischen Litteratur. JbDG, 1, 1867.
Pavolini, P. E. La fortuna di Dante in Ungheria e in Finlandia. ICS, 1921.
Gubernatis, A. de. Dante in **INDIEN**. Deutsche Revue, 1890.
Toynbee, P. Some Recent **JAPANESE** Publications on Dante. MLR, 1925.
Maver, G. Una enciclopedia polacca e una nuova traduzione della Divina Commedia (**POLAND**). Belfagor, 1947.
Szmydtowa, Z. Dante and Polish Romanticism. SR, 1929.
Bell, A. F. G. Dante in **PORTUGUESE** Literature. MLR, 1922.
Anon. Le sixième centenaire de Dante à Petrograd. (**RUSSIA**). EI, 1920.
Lo Gatto, E. La fortuna di Dante in Russia. In: Saggi sulla cultura russa. Napoli, 1922.
Sandomirsky, V. The New Russian Dante. Ital., 18, 1941.
Witte, K. Dante im Norden. (**SCANDINAVIA**). In: Dante Forschungen. Halle, 1869.
Daffner, H. Galeotto in einem frühen Schweizer Roman. (**SWITZERLAND**). JbDG, 9, 1925.
Friederich, W. P. Switzerland's Contribution to the International Appreciation of Dante Alighieri. SPh, 42, 1945.
Pochhammer, P. Dante und die Schweiz. Zürich, 1896.
Cronia, A. Riflessi danteschi nella poesia popolare serbo-croata. (**YUGOSLAVIA**). Romana, 4, 1940.
Naldini, L. Una celebrazione slovena di Dante. I nostri quaderni, May, 1924.
Res, A. Dante, raccolta di studi. Gorizia, 1923.

7. Influences upon Individual Authors and Scholars.

Franchi, F. de'. Dante e **BALZAC**. Rassegna di studi francesi, 1932.
Jung, A. Ein polnischer Dante (K. (**BATORNICKI**). In: Charaktere. Königsberg, 1848.
Ronzy, P. **BELLARMINE** et Dante. NRI, 1921.
Torre, H. Le Lettere virgiliane e la Difesa di Dante. (**BETTINELLI**, Voltaire & Gozzi). GD, 4, 1897.
Praz, M. Una versione inglese di Dante. (**BINYON**). Cultura, 1929.

Richter, H. William BLAKES Dantebilder. JbDG, 11, 1929.
Yeats, W. B. William Blake and his Illustrations to the Divine Comedy. London, 1896.
Croce, B. Una difesa tedesca di Dante nel 1763. (BODMER). Critica, 18, 1920.
Ibershoff, C. H. Bodmer Indebted to Dante. MLN, 1924.
Hellwald, F. von. Joan BOHLS Dante-Uebersetzung. MLIA, 1880.
Hazard, P. Un traducteur français imprévu de Dante. (BORNE). RLC, 6, 1926.
BRIDEL, L. Lettre à Carion de Nizas sur la manière de traduire Dante. Bâle, 1805.
Terrade, E. BRIZEUX poète et traducteur de Dante. In: Etudes comparées. Paris, 1904.
Defries, Esther. BROWNING and Dante. Academy, 10.I.1891.
Duff, D. An Exposition of Browning's Sordello. Edinburgh, 1906.
Mathews, J. C. BRYANT'S Knowledge of Dante. Ital., 16, 1939.
Ferguson, J. Dante and BUNYAN. American Church Review, 16, 1865.
Smyth, M. W. Puritan Bunyan and Catholic Dante. NC, 1928.
Dobelli, A. Dante e BYRON. GD, 6, 1898.
Haacke, U. Byron und Dante. Diss. Münster. Wohlau (Schlesien), 1917.
Kraeger, H. Lord Byron und Francesca da Rimini. Archiv, 98, 1897.
Monti, G. Il prigioniero di Chillon di Byron e il Conte Ugolino di Dante. In: Studi critici. Firenze, 1887.
Terrade, E. Dante et Byron. In: Etudes comparées. Paris, 1904.
Cioffari, V. CAMOES and Dante: A Source Study. Ital, 25, 1948.
Olivero, F. Dante e CARLYLE. Rassegna moderna, 1921.
King, R. W. The Translator of Dante: The Life, Work and Friendships of H. F. CARY, 1772-1844. London, 1925.
Dobelli, A. Una scena della Commedia e una del Don Chisciotte. (CERVANTES). GD, 1897.
Chiarini, C. Di una imitazione inglese della Divina Commedia, La Casa della Fama di G. CHAUCER. RI, 4, 1901 & Bari, 1902.
Clarke, H. Dante and Chaucer. N&Q, 30.VII.1892.
Dilts, Dorothy A. Observations on Dante and the Hous of Fame. MLN, 57, 1942.
Herfard, C. H. Chaucer's Hous of Fame and Prof. Ten Brink. Academy 18.V. & 15.VI.1889.
Köppel, E. Chauceriana: III. Dante. Anglia, 13.
Looten, C. Chaucer et Dante. RLC, 5, 1925.
Lounsbury, T. R. Studies in Chaucer. New York, 1892.
Lowes, J. L. Chaucer and Dante's Convivio. MPh, 13, 1915.
—— The Use of Dante in Chaucer's Parliament of Fowles. MPh, 14, 1916.
—— Chaucer and Dante. MPh, 1917.
Palgrave, F. T. Chaucer and the Italian Renaissance. NC, 1888.
—— Chaucer's Hous of Fame and Prof. Ten Brink. Academy 4.V. & 1.VI.1889.
Rambeau, A. Chaucer's Hous of Fame in seinem Verhältniss zu Dantes Divina Commedia. ESn, 3, 1879 & Altenburg, 1880.
Robinson, F. N. Chaucer and Dante. JCL, 1, 1903.
Spencer, T. The Story of Ugolino in Dante and Chaucer. Spec., 9, 1934.
Sypherd, W. O. The Hous of Fame and Dante's Divina Commedia. In: Studies in Chaucer's Hous of Fame. London, 1904.
Tatlock, J. S. P. Chaucer and Dante. MPh, 3, 1906.
—— Dante and Guinizelli in Chaucer's Troilus. MLN, 1920.
Beck, F. Un' imitazione dantesca nell' antica letteratura francese (CHRISTINE DE PISAN). L'Alighieri, 2, 1891.
Merkel, M. Le chemin de long étude. Rassegna nazionale, 1 & 16.IV.1920.
Temple, M. E. Paraphrazing in the Livre de paix, of Christine de Pisan, of the Paradiso III-V. PMLA, 37.
Toynbee, P. Two References to Dante in Early French Literature. Academy, 29.VI.1889.
Anon. COLERIDGE on Cary's Dante. Athenaeum, 7.I.1888.
Olivero, F. Dante e Coleridge. GD, 16, 1908.
Guaraldo, L. La giovinezza di A. DESCHAMPS e i suoi studi danteschi. Atti della R. Acc. delle Scienze di Torino, 74, 1939.
Villey, P. Les sources italiennes de la Deffence et Illustration de la langue françoyse (DU BELLAY). Paris, 1908.
Praz, M. T. S. ELIOT and Dante. Southern Review (Louisiana), 1936. And in: Letteratura, 1937.
Mathews, J. C. EMERSON'S Knowledge of Dante. U. of Texas Studies in English, 1942.
Daffner, H. FICHTE als Dante-Uebersetzer. JbDG, 9, 1925.

Labitte, C. Dante, traduit de M. FIORENTINO et ses anciens traducteurs. RDM, 1.XI.1840.
Toynbee, P. John FOXE and the Editio Princeps of Dante's De Monarchia. Athenaeum, 14.IV.1906.
Dorez, L. FRANCOIS I. et la Commedia. In: Mélanges de critique et d'érudition françaises publiés à l'occasion du sixième centenaire de la mort de Dante. Paris, 1921.
Gerould, G. H. The GAWAIN Poet and Dante. PMLA, 51, 1936.
Bianchi, L. Dante und Stefan GEORGE. Bologna, 1936 & Berlin, 1938.
Jacobs, M. GERSTENBERGS Ugolino. Berlin, 1898.
Klarmann, A. D. Motivation in Gerstenberg's Ugolino. GR, 16, 1941.
Toynbee, P. GIBBON and Dante. MLR, 1911.
Fischer, P. D. GILDEMEISTERS Dante-Uebersetzung. DR, 15, 1888.
Nolte, M. Eine neue Uebersetzung der Göttlichen Komödie. MLIA, 1888.
Abeken, B. Urteil eines französischen Kritikers über Inferno VI (GINGUENE). In: Beiträge, Berlin, 1826.
Anon. Dante y GOETHE. Revista cont., 15.X.1890.
Bassermann, A. Nachlese zu dem Kapitel Goethe und Dante. Euphorion, 24.
Bem, A. Goethe, Dante und Dostojevskii. Germanoslavica, 2, 1932-33.
Casella, G. Della Divina Commedia e del Fausto di Goethe. Opere ined. e post. Firenze, 1884.
Chamberlain, H. S. Dante und Goethe. NR, 1912.
Daffner, H. Goethe und Dante. JbDG, 5, 1920.
Farinelli, A. Dante e Goethe. Firenze, 1900.
—— Dante und Goethe. Zürich, 1921.
Garrod, H. B. Dante, Goethe's Faust and Other Lectures. London, 1913.
Gnoli, D. La Vita Nuova di W. Goethe. NAnt; 25, 1874.
Graefe, B. Dantes Göttliche Komödie als Quelle vom II. Theil des Goetheschen Faust. Allg. conservative Monatsschrift, 1889.
—— Briefe über Goethe und Dante. Ibid. 40, 1890.
——— An-Dante; Divina Commedia als Quelle für Shakespeare und Goethe. Leipzig, 1896.
Jacini, S. Divina Commedia. Faust. Voce, 6.III.1913.
Ladewig, P. Dantes Vita Nova bei Goethe. Darmstadt, 1934.
Maffei, L. Il simbolo in Dante e Goethe. Alba, 1906.
Meltzl von Lomnitz, H. K. Goethe und Freidank als Interpreten Dantes. Klausenburg, 1886.
Mézières, A. Dante et Goethe. Revue des cours littér., 3, 1866.
Montégut, E. Dante et Goethe. Mon. Univ., July & Sept., 1866.
Pochhammer, P. Dante im Faust. Beilage zur Allg. Zt., 11-12.V.1898.
—— Goethes Bedeutung für die Erschliessung Dantes. Festgabe Hugo Blümner. Zürich, 1914.
—— Wie steht Goethe zu Dante? Schriften zur Fortbildung, 3. Berlin, n. d.
Portmann, A. Dantes Divina Commedia und Goethes Faust. Kath. Schweizer Blätter, 14, 1896.
Rössler-Grotek, O. Ein Antifaust in Dantes Inferno. JbDG, 7, 1923.
Scherer, E. Dante et Goethe. Le Temps, 30.X.1866. And in: Etudes de littérature contemporaine, 16.
Schmidt, E. Danteskes in Faust. Archiv, 107, 1901.
Spera, G. Dante e Goethe. In: Leter. comp., Napoli, 1896.
Stern, D. (Comtesse d'Agoult). Dante et Goethe. Paris, 1866.
Sulger-Gebing, E. Faust und Göttliche Komödie. In: Stunden mit Goethe, 2, 1906.
—— Goethe und Dante. Berlin, 1907.
Terrade, E. Dante et Goethe. In: Etudes comparées. Paris, 1904.
Teza, E. Dantiana (Dante & Goethe). Atti e Memorie della R. Accad. di Padova, 1903.
Traumann, E. Dante und Goethe. Süddeutsche Monatshefte, 18, 1920-21.
Vöchting, F. Das Paradies bei Dante und im Faust. JbDG, 7, 1923.
Baldensperger, F. L'émigré GOURBILLON, traducteur de Dante. RLC, 1, 1921.
Warren, T. H. GRAY and Dante. Monthly Review, 1901.
—— Gray and Dante. Tennyson and Dante. In: Essays of Poets and Poetry. London, 1909.
Toynbee, P. Two Alleged Quotations from Dante by Robert GREENE. Athenaeum, 1, 1902.
Mari, A. Un cinquecentista spagnuolo (Diego GUILLEN DE AVILA) imitatore di Dante. Il Saggiatore, 1, 1901.
Mathews, J. C. HAWTHORNE'S Knowledge of Dante. U. of Texas Studies in English, 1940.

Pizzo, P. La Divina Commedia nei giudizi dell' **HEGEL**, di F. Th. Vischer e di Fr. De Sanctis. Festschrift Louis Gauchat. Aarau, 1926.

Scartazzini, G. A. Die Dante-Uebersetzerin Josefa von **HOFFINGER**. MLIA, 1870.

Griswold, E. N. & Wilkins, E. H. **HOLMES** and Pollock on Dante. Ital., 18, 1941.

Beall, C. B. **HOUSMAN**, Dehmel and Dante. MLN, 57, 1942.

Lange, M. Victor **HUGO** et les sources de la Vision de Dante. RHLF, 25, 1918.

Orvieto, A. Come V. Hugo parlava di Dante. Marzocco, 26.II.1902.

Terrade, E. Dante et V. Hugo. La Divine Comédie et la Légende des Siècles. In: Etudes comparées. Paris, 1904.

Olivero, F. Leigh **HUNT** ed i suoi studii sulla Divina Commedia. GD, 18, 1910.

Paur, T. **IMMANUEL** (Ben Salomo) und Dante. JbDG, 3, 1871.

Schulz, E. **IMMERMANNS** Uebersetzung aus Dante. Westfälische Studien Alois Bömer gewidmet. Leipzig, 1928.

Place, E. B. The Exaggerated Reputation of Francisco **IMPERIAL**. Spec., 21, 1946.

Savj-Lopez, P. Un imitatore spagnuolo di Dante nel '400. GD, 1896.

Mathews, J. C. Washington **IRVING'S** Knowledge of Dante. AL, 10, 1939.

Wilkins, E. H. The **JACKSON** Dante. Ital., 20, 1943.

Witte, K. **KANNEGIESSER** und Streckfuss, Uebersetzungen der Divina Commedia. Litterar. Conversationsblatt, 261, 1825.

Anon. Dante et **KEATS**. Marzacco, 4.X. 1925.

Lowes, J. L. Hyperion and the Purgatorio. TLS, 11.I.1936.

Witte, K. August **KOPISCH**, Uebersetzungen der Divina Commedia. Blätter f. literar. Unterhaltung, 17, 1838.

Zipper, A. Das Ms von **KRASZEWSKIS** Dante-Uebersetzung. ZVL, 8.

Abate, F. Dante dans les impressions de **LAMARTINE**. Messina, 1878.

Pugh, A. R. Dante: Une réminiscence possible chez Lamartine. RLC, 5, 1925.

Ruberto, L. Un articolo dantesco di Gabriele Pepe e il suo duello con A. di Lamartine. Firenze, 1898.

Foucher de Careil. Les traducteurs de Dante: **LAMENNAIS** et M. Mesnard. Revue contemporaine, 15.XI.1857.

Sanctis, F. de. Dante e Lamennais. In: Saggi critici. Napoli, 1888.

Terrade, E. Dante et Lamennais. In: Etudes comparées sur Dante et la Divine Comédie. Paris, 1904.

Villers, H. de. Le Dante et Lamennais. Le Correspondant, N. S., 37, 1856.

Auer, J. W. S. **LANDOR** in seinen Beziehungen zu den Dichtern des Trecento, Dante, Boccaccio, Petrarca. Diss. Münster, 1903.

Thompson, E. N. S. Dante and Landor. MLN, 20, 1905.

Bellezza, P. **LANGLAND** and Dante. N&Q, 4.VIII.1894.

Miramon Fitz-James, F. de. **LISZT** et la Divine Comédie. Rev. de Musicologie, 1938.

Pirro, A. Franz Liszt et la Divine Comédie. Mélanges publiés à l'occasion du sixième centenaire de la mort de Dante. Paris, 1921.

Smigelski, E. Dante und Liszt. JbDG, 21, 1939.

Auvray, L. Dante et **LITTRE**. Mélanges Hauvette. Paris, 1934.

Koch, M. Zur deutschen Dantelitteratur von Baron G. **LOCELLA**. ZVL, 3, 1890.

Anon. Mr. **LONGFELLOW'S** Translation of the Divine Comedy. Nation. 9.V. & 20.VI.1867.

Boni, J. Longfellow traduttore della Divina Commedia. NAnt, 1921.

Norton, C. E. Longfellow's Translation of the Divine Comedy. NAR, 1867.

Lomonaco, G. Dante e **LUTERO**. Napoli, 1871.

Courthope, W. J. A Consideration of **MACAULAY'S** Comparison of Dante and Milton. PBA, 1908.

Eddy, N. W. Dante and Ferran **MANUEL DE LANDO**. HR, 1936.

Clements, R. J. **MARGUERITE DE NAVARRE** and Dante. Ital., 18, 1941.

Farinelli, A. Dante e Margherita di Navarra. RI, 5, 1902.

Ronzy, P. Papire **MASSON** biographe de Dante, de Pétrarque et de Boccace. Annales de l'U. de Grenoble, 1, 1924.

Giovannini, G. **MELVILLE'S** Pierre and Dante's Inferno. PMLA, 1949.

Post, C. R. The Sources of Juan de **MENA**. RR, 1912.

Hearn, L. Dr. **MERCIER** on Dante. Time Democrat of New Orleans, 10.I.1886.

MERI DE LA CANORGUE, V. de. Françoise de Rimini. Nice, 1850.

Casella, M. Il Somni di Bernart **METGE** e i primi influssi italiani sulla letteratura catalana. AR, 3, 1919.

Guardia, J. M. Le Songe de Bernat Metge, auteur catalan du XVe siècle. Paris, 1889.

Tienhoven, G. van. Un dantista olandese (Hacke van **MIJNDEN**). Firenze, 1873.
Austin, A. **MILTON** and Dante: A Comparison and a Contrast. QR, 1909.
Barnes, C. L. Parallels in Dante and Milton. Papers of the Manchester Literary Club, 43, 1917.
Buckley, W. E. Milton's Translations from Dante and Ariosto. N&Q, 9.VI. 1888.
Byington, Jeannette G. Milton's Debt to Dante. Dante Prize Essay, Harvard, 1933.
Garlick, R. Milton and Dante. Poetry Review, Oct., 1947.
Herford, C. H. Dante and Milton. BRL, 8, 1924 & New York, 1925.
Kelley, Sister Margaret T. The Influence of Dante's Paradiso upon Milton. Diss. Cornell, 1938.
Kuhns, L. O. Dante's Influence on Milton. MLN, 12, 1897.
McKenzie, K. Echoes of Dante in Milton's Lycidas. Ital., 20, 1943.
Smith, E. V. Comparative Analysis of Dante and Milton. Crayon, 1860.
Tarelli, C. Milton and Dante. The Pilot, 2.III.1901.
Terrade, E. Le Paradis terrestre chez Dante et Milton. In: Etudes comparées sur Dante. Paris, 1904.
Dorez, L. Le Ms. de Dante offert par Jacques **MIRUT** au roi François Ier. Rev. des Bibliothèques, 1903.
Counson, A. Dante et **NAPOLEON**. Flambeau, 30.IV.1921.
Pastor, J. F. Dante y **NEBRIJA**. RFE, 21.
Cochin, H. Dante Alighieri et les catholiques français: **OZANAM**. Correspondant, 10.IX.1921.
Labaude-Jeanroy, T. G. **PERTICARI** et Raynouard: Une apologie de Dante fondée sur un paradoxe linguistique. RLC, 1, 1921.
Scartazzini, G. A. Die neue Ausgabe von **PHILALETHES'** Dante-Uebersetzung. Beilage zur Allg. Zt., 310, 1877.
Witte, K. Philalethes' Uebersetzung der Divina Commedia. Wissenschaftl. Beilage der Leipziger Zt., 1, 1866.
Warton, E. The Three Francescas (**PHILLIPS**, Crawford, D'Annunzio). NAR, 175, 1902.
Brandl, A. Dante und Adolf **PICHLER**. Festschrift Adolf Tobler. Braunschweig, 1905.
Mathews, J. C. Did **POE** Read Dante? U. of Texas Studies in English, 1938.
Lafenestre, G. Une traduction poétique de Dante (Louis **RATISBONNE**). Revue contemporaine, 14, 1860.
Altrocchi, R. The Story of Dante's Gianni Schicchi and **REGNARD'S** Légataire Universel. PMLA, 29, 1914.
Peyre, R. Dante et Regnard. Journal des Débats, 1.XII.1912.
Siebels, Eva. Dante im Erleben Rainer Maria **RILKES**. JbDG, 23.
Henriot, E. **RIVAROL** traducteur de Dante. Le Temps, 31.VIII.1926.
Croce, B. La signora **ROLAND** e la lettura di Dante. Crit., 42, 1944.
Butterworth, W. D. G. **ROSSETTI** in Relation to Dante Alighieri. Papers of the Manchester Literary Club, 31, 1912.
Gray, N. Rossetti, Dante and Ourselves. London, 1947.
Morse, B. J. D. G. Rossetti and Dante Alighieri. ESn, 68, 1933-34.
Sticco, M. Gli studi danteschi di G. Rossetti. Milano, 1940.
Marks, D. L. Dante and **ROUSSEAU**. Dante Prize Essay, Harvard, 1932.
Norton, C. E. **RUSKIN'S** Comments on Dante, with an Introduction. London, 1903.
Olivero, F. Ruskin e Dante. GD, 1925.
Witte, K. **SCARTAZZINIS** Dante. MLIA, 1880.
Raimondi, E. Del saggio di **SCHELLING** su Dante. Convivium, 1947.
Belohoubek, V. Die von A. W. **SCHLEGEL** übersetzten Bruchstücke aus der Divina Commedia in ihrem Verhältnisse zur italienischen Vorlage. Progr. Troppau, 1904-06.
Sulger-Gebing, E. A. W. Schlegel und Dante. Festschrift H. Paul. Strassburg, 1902.
Lorenzo, G. de. **SCHOPENHAUER**, Dante e Petrarca. Marzocco, 17, 1912.
Anon. The Other Poet (in **SHAKESPEARE'S** Sonnets) Identified. Blackwood's Mag., June, 1884; June, 1885; March, 1886.
Bigoni, G. Dante e Shakespeare. Milano, 1895.
Borinski, K. Dante und Shakespeare. Anglia, 18, 1896.
Bouchier, J. Dante and Shakespeare. N&Q, 25.I.1890.
Carcano, G. Dante e Shakespeare. In: Memorie di grandi. Milano, 1869.
Chiarini, C. Carlyle, Dante e Shakespeare. Biblioteca critica della lett. ital., 7. Firenze, 1896.
Franciosi, G. La virtù punitiva della coscienza nell'inferno dantesco e nei drammi dello Shakespeare. Sapienza,

5, 1882. And in: Scritti danteschi. Avellino, 1891.
Gamberale, L. Shakespeare conobbe le opere di Dante? Nuovo Convito, 1921.
Gardner, E. Dante and Shakespeare. Dublin Review, 1902.
Graefe, B. An-Dante; Divina Commedia als Quelle für Shakespeare und Goethe. Leipzig, 1896.
Hales, J. W. Dante and Romeo and Juliet. Athenaeum, 26.II.1887.
Koenig, W. Shakespeare und Dante. JbShG, 7, 1872.
Mascetta-Caracci, L. Dante in Shakespeare. GD, 4, 1896.
Piccoli, V. Dante e Shakespeare. Rassegna Italiana, 33, 1933.
Smyth, Mary W. Dante and Shakespeare. NC, 1908.
Kuhns, L. O. Dante's Influence on SHELLEY. MLN, 13, 1898.
Zacchetti, C. Shelley e Dante. Palermo, 1922.
Pellegrini, C. Dante ed altri scrittori italiani nel pensiero del SISMONDI. GD, 28, 1925.
Bayne, T. SPENSER'S Probable Knowledge of Dante. N&Q, 28.V.1892.
Palgrave, F. T. Spenser and Dante. Academy, 28.I.1888.
Toynbee, P. A Latin Translation of the Divina Commedia Quoted by STILLINGFLEET. Athenaeum, 30.XI.1901.
Sewall, F. Dante and SWEDENBORG. London, 1893.
Thackeray, F. St. J. Dante and TENNYSON. Temple Bar, 102, 1894.
Warren, T. H. Tennyson and Dante. Monthly Review, 14, 1904.
Witte, K. Lord VERNONS Dante. Beilage zur Allg. Zt., 217, 1871.
Baldensperger, F. Dante et A. de VIGNY. Mélanges Hauvette. Paris, 1934.
Mazzoni, G. Romien de VILLENEUVE e Dante. Mélanges Jeanroy. Paris, 1928.
Oelsner, H. Dante's Beatrice and VILLON'S Bietris. Literature, 24.IX.1898.
Bouvy, E. VOLTAIRE et les polémiques italiennes sur Dante. Revue des U. du Midi, 1895. Cf. GSLI, 28 & Journal des Débats, 15.II.1899.
Capelli, L. M. Dante et Voltaire. GD, 8, 1899.
Prato, S. Tre passi della Divina Commedia nell Henriade e nella Pucelle d'Orléans del Voltaire. GD, 1, 1893-94.
Torelli, G. Lettera sopra Dante contro il sig. di Voltaire. Verona, 1781.
Klarman, A. D. Franz WERFEL'S Eschatology and Cosmogony. MLQ, 7.
Mathews, J. C. Walt WHITMAN'S Reading of Dante. Texas Studies in English, 1939.
Boehmer, E. Karl WITTES Danteforschungen. Jb. für roman. & engl. Sprache & Litteratur, 10, 1869.
Scartazzini, G. A. K. Wittes Dante-Forschungen. MLIA, 1869.
—— Karl Wittes Dante-Uebersetzung. DR, 1878 & MLIA, 1879.
Sills, K. C. M. WYATT and Dante. JCL, 1, 1903.

CHAPTER TEN

Leopardi.

1. General Influences.

Carrière, J. M. A Note on Leopardi's Early Fortune in France. Ital., 21, 1944.
Charlier, G. Le premier article français sur Leopardi (1833). REI, 3, 1938.
Ciampoli, D. Leopardi in russo. RCLI, 1, 1896.
Finzi, G. Leopardi e la letteratura contemporanea. Torino, 1895.
Fiorentino, A. La fortuna del Leopardi in Francia. Dante, 1932.
Fiumi, L. Leopardi e la Francia. Giornale d'Italia, 10.VII.1937.
Koltay-Kastner, E. La fortuna di Leopardi in Ungheria. Studi italo-ungheresi della R. Acc. d'Ungheria di Roma, 2, 1937.
Marchesi, G. Leopardi e la poesia inglese. Iride, 3, 1899.
Matarrese, F. Leopardi e la Spagna. Bari, 1938.
Mititchu, A. Traduceri românesti diu Leopardi. Studii italiene, 3, 1936.
Oriol, A. Leopardi et la littérature française. BI, 2.
Rabizzani. Leopardi in Francia. Nuova Rassegna di Letterature Moderne, 1906.
Rebora, P. Traduttori e critici inglesi di Leopardi. NAnt, 1.VI.1920.
—— Leopardi nella cultura inglese. Il Libro Italiano, 1, 1940.
Schanzer, A. Il Leopardi in Inghilterra. Rassegna nazionale, April, 1900.
Serban, N. Leopardi et la France. Paris, 1913.
Torraca, F. G. Leopardi e la letteratura spagnuola. NAnt, 16.XI.1924 & Milano, 1928.
Zdiechowski, M. Ueber die Gedichte Leopardis und deren Verhältniss zu den

gleichzeitigen Hauptströmungen der europäischen Litteratur. Anz. d. Akad. d. Wissenschaften Krakau, 1892.
Zumbini, B. Leopardi presso i Tedeschi. NAnt, 22, 1873.

2. Influences upon Individual Authors.

Capdeville, J. M. ALCOVER i Leopardi. La Veu de Catalunya, 1.XII.1921.
Arullani, V. A. Leggendo il Leopardi e il BAUDELAIRE. Fanfulla della Domenica, 13, 1901.
Fiumi, L. Leopardi et Baudelaire. NL, 21.VIII.1937.
Ezban, S. Gamaliel BRADFORD et Leopardi. Ital., 22, 1945.
Caracostea, D. EMINESCU fata de Leopardi. Revista fundatilor Regale, 1938.
Pellegrini, R. Giacomo Leopardi e Mihail Eminescu. Rassegna italo-romena, 22, 1942.
Nutricati-Briganti, A. J. Enrico HEINE e G. Leopardi. Wien, 1873.
Carrière, M. Leopardis Dichtungen, übersetzt von HEYSE. Die Gegenwart, 1879.
Gelosi, G. Paul Heyses Leopardi Uebertragungen. Turin, 1936.
Carrière, J. M. Jules LAFORGUE and Leopardi. RR, 34, 1943.
Perito, E. J. M. MORRISON'S Translations from Leopardi. RCLI, 6, 1902.
Rodocanachi, E. Pages inédites d'Alfred de MUSSET sur Leopardi. Journal des Débats, 21.V.1919.
Gabetti, G. NIETZSCHE e Leopardi. Il Convegno, 30.X.1923.
Friepes, E. Il PLATEN, il Leopardi e il Ranieri. Civiltà moderna, May, 1937.
Ambruzzi, L. A. G. RESTREPO, traduttore del Leopardi. Conv., 1930.
Stern, C. Leopardi und SCHOPENHAUER. NSR, 1931.
Busnelli, M. D. Leopardi e STENDHAL. Mélanges Hauvette. Paris, 1934.
Betz, L. P. Eine Jüngerin Leopardis (Marg. SUSMAN). Neue Zürcher Zt. 16.V.1901.
Cotten, L. A. Leopardi and The City of Dreadful Night. (J. THOMSON). SPh, 42, 1945.
Olivero, F. Un seguace del Leopardi: James Thomson. In: Studi su poeti e prosatori inglesi. Torino, 1925.
Rebora, P. James Thomson e la poesia di Leopardi in Inghilterra. Boll. degli studi inglesi in Italia, 1937.
Galletti, A. Leopardi ed A. de VIGNY. In: Studi di letterature straniere. Verona, 1903.
Baldensperger, F. Un curé alsacien au berceau de Leopardi: notes sur l'abbé VOGEL. L'Alsace française, 1934.
Horne, J. van. Leopardi and WHITMAN. Ital., 23, 1946.
Mititelu, A. Influenta lui Leopardi si Carducci in poezia lui D. ZAMFIRESCU. Studii Italiene, 1938.

CHAPTER ELEVEN

Machiavelli.

1. General Influences.

Alderisio, F. La critica straniera di Machiavelli nell'ultimo quindicennio. NRS, 24, 1940.
Angelini, A. Niccolò Maciavelli nel suo Principe, ossia il Machiavellismo ed i politici del nostro secolo. Milano, 1869.
Benoist, C. Le machiavélisme de Machiavel. Revue universelle, 1&15.VIII.1934.
Borgese, C. A. Political Creeds and Machiavellian Heresy. American Scholar, 9, 1940.
Burnham, J. The Machiavellians. New York, 1943.
Christopherson, R. Old Nick and his Traducers. American Scholar, 15, 1946.
Colimore, Fifi-Dolores. Edizioni e Traduzioni della Mandragola. Ital., 18, 1941.
Collison-Morley, L. Machiavelli and the World Today. Contemporary Rev., 170, 1946.
Ferrero, G. Machiavelli and Machiavellianism. Foreign Affairs, 17.
Léglise, S. Abbé. Machiavel comparé. Paris, 1901.
Mack, S. Neo-Machiavellism and Ethical Nihilism. Ethics, 51, 1940.
Maritain, J. La fine del machiavellismo. Quaderni di Roma, 1, 1947.
Monaco, M. La fortuna della Mandragola. Biblio, 40, 1937.
Panella, A. Gli antimachiavellici. Firenze, 1943.
Peytavi de Fougères, G. La modernité de Machiavel. MF, 1932.
Sorrentino, A. Storia dell'antimachiavellismo europeo. Napoli, 1936.
Truc, G. L'actualité de Machiavel. Revue hebdomadaire, 6.V.1939.

2. Influences upon Individual Countries.

Allen, D. C. An Unmentioned Elizabethan Opponent of Machiavelli. (ENGLAND). Ital., 14, 1937.
Craig, H. Machiavelli's The Prince; an

Elizabethan Translation edited with an Introduction and Notes. Chapel Hill (N. C.), 1944.

Hauffen, A. Zu Machiavelli in England. JbShG, 1899.

Meyer, E. Machiavelli and the Elizabethan Drama. Diss. Heidelberg. Weimar, 1897. Cf. ESn, 24.

Orsini, N. Le traduzioni elisabettiane inedite di Machiavelli. In: Studii sul Rinascimento italiano in Inghilterra. Firenze, 1937.

—— Elizabethan Ms. Translations of Machiavelli's Prince. JWI, 1, 1937.

—— Nuove ricerche intorno al machiavellismo nel Rinascimento inglese. Rinascita, 1-2, 1938-39.

—— "Policy" or the Language of Elizabethan Machiavellianism. JWI, 1946.

Philipps, A. Machiavelli and the English Reformation. NC, 1896.

Praz, M. Machiavelli e gl'Inglesi dell' epoca Elisabettiana. Firenze, 1928.

—— Machiavelli and the Elizabethans. PBA, 14, 1928.

—— Machiavelli in Inghilterra ed altri saggi. Roma, 1942.

Purves, J. The First Knowledge of Machiavelli in Scotland. Rinascita, 1, 1938.

Ritter, O. Macchiavelli in England. ESn, 32, 1903.

Chérel, A. Les réactions de la pensée française contre Machiavel au XVIe siècle. **(FRANCE).** Revue des Jeunes, 10.X.1928.

—— La pensée de Machiavel en France au temps de la Fronde. RLC, 13, 1933.

—— La pensée de Machiavel en France. Paris, 1935.

Darsy, F. Machiavelli in Francia. Société d'études italiennes, 1895.

Mattei, R. Giudizi e pregiudizi francesi sul Machiavelli nel Cinquecento e nel Seicento. Atti del secondo convegno nazionale di studi sul Rinascimento. Firenze, 1940.

Reyam. Les principes de Machiavel et la politique de la France. New York, 1943.

Villefosse, L. de. Machiavel et nous. Paris, 1937.

Berr, H. Machiavel et l'Allemagne. **(GERMANY).** Paris, 1940.

Bertini, G. M. La fortuna di Machiavelli in Spagna. **(SPAIN).** Quaderni iberoamericani, 2, 1947.

Siliό Beleña, C. Maquiavelo y el maquiavelismo en España. Acad. de Ciencias morales y políticas. Madrid, 1941.

3. Influences upon Individual Authors.

Orsini, N. **BACONE** e Machiavelli. Genova, 1936.

Luciani, V. Bacon and Machiavelli. Ital., 24, 1947.

Cardascia, G. Machiavel et Jean **BODIN.** BHR, 3.

Armaingaud, D. La **BOETIE** et Machiavel. Revue philomatique de Bordeaux, 1908.

Barrière, J. Etienne de la Boëtie contre N. Machiavel. Bordeaux, 1909.

Ribner, I. **BOLINGBROKE,** A True Machiavellian. MLQ, 9, 1948.

BOZIUS, T. De Imperio Virtutis libri duo adversus Macchiavellum. Coloniae Agrippinae, 1594.

Robertson, J. Nicholas **BRETON** and The Uncasing of Machivils Instructions to his Sonne (1613). HLQ, 4, 1941.

Cardascia, G. Un lecteur de Machiavel à la cour de France: Jacopo **CORBINELLI.** H&R, 5, 1938.

Buoso, A. Il Machiavelli nel concetto del **FICHTE.** Diss. Fribourg. Portogruaro, 1920.

Hauffen, A. **FISCHART**-Studien. Der Antimacchiavell. Euphorion, 6, 1899.

Pace, A. **FRANKLIN** and Machiavelli. Symposium, 1, 1947.

Bouillé, L. J. A. de. Commentaires politiques et historiques sur le traité du Prince de Machiavel et sur l'Anti-Machiavel de **FREDERIC II.** Paris, 1827.

Schäfer, H. J. Innozenz **GENTILLET,** sein Leben und besonders sein Antimachiavel. Diss. Bonn, 1929.

Tommasini, O. Wolfgang **GOETHE** e Niccolò Machiavelli. Rendiconti d. R. Accad. dei Lincei, 10, 1901.

Boas, F. S. **GREENE,** Marlowe and Machiavelli. TLS, 3.VIII.1940.

Jameson, T. H. The Machiavellianism of Gabriel **HARVEY.** PMLA, 56, 1941.

Anon. **HEGEL** e Machiavelli, ossia la Germania e l'Italia nella presente lotta religiosa. Napoli, 1875.

Alderisio, F. La politica del Machiavelli nella rivalutazione dello Hegel e del Fichte. NRS, 15, 1931.

Malzi, A. Machiavelli nel giudizio di G. **HERDER.** Assisi, 1937.

Boughner, D. C. Clizia and Epicoene. (Ben **JONSON**). PhQ, 19, 1940.

Hollstein, E. Das Verhältniss von Ben Jonsons The Devil is an Ass und John Wilsons Belphegor, or the Marriage of the Devil, zu Machiavellis Novelle vom Belfagor. Diss. Halle, 1901.

Benito, J. de. Ruta de Maquiavelo y **LOYOLA.** Rev. de América, 12, 1947.
Butler, K. T. Louis **MACHON'S** Apologie pour Machiavelle. JWI, 3.
Merchant, W. M. **MARLOWE** and Machiavelli, CLS, 13, 1944.
Orsini, N. Gli studii machiavellici di **MILTON.** In: Studii sul Rinascimento italiano in Inghilterra. Firenze, 1937.
Bénezet, T. Machiavel et **MONTESQUIEU.** Journal des Débats, 14, 18. & 26.IX.1841.
Levi-Malvano. Montesquieu e Machiavelli. Paris, 1912.
Sclopis di Salerano, F. Montesquieu et Machiavel. Revue historique du droit français et étranger, 1856.
NAPOLEON. Machiavel commenté, manuscrit trouvé dans le carrosse de Buonaparte. Paris, 1816.
Stearns, F. P. Napoleon and Machiavelli. Cambridge, 1903.
Aniceto, N. R. Maquiavelo y **NIETZSCHE.** Madrid, 1920.
Caffi, E. Nietzsches Stellung zu Machiavellis Lehre. Wien, 1912.
Ferrara, M. Machiavelli, Nietzsche e Mussolini. Firenze, 1939.
Luciani, V. **RALEIGH'S** Discourse of War and Machiavelli's Discorsi. MPh, 46, 1948.
Aruffo, A. Machiavelli e Gianpaolo. (**RICHTER**). Rassegna nazionale, 1930.
Santonastaso, G. Machiavelli e B. de **SAINT-PIERRE.** La Città Libera, 1, 1945.
Anon. Machiavel, **SCHILLER** et Michel Cervantes. Mercure du XIXe siècle, 11, 1825.
Giovagnoli, R. Machiavelli e **SHAKESPEARE.** In: Frustula et nugae: scritti letterari. Roma, 1888.
Greenlaw, E. A. The Influence of Machiavelli on **SPENSER.** MPh, 7, 1909-10.
Anon. Machiavelli und **SPINOZA.** Neue Freie Presse, 13670, 1902.
Pollock, F. Spinoza et Machiavel. Revue des Nations, 1927.
Pintard, R. Une adaptation de Machiavel au XVIe siècle: Le Prince nécessaire de Jean de la **TAILLE.** RLC, 13, 1933.
Bertolini, F. **VILLARI** Il Macchiavelli giudicato dalla stampa straniera. NAnt, 42, 1878.
Galera, K. S. **VOLTAIRE** und der Antimachiavell Friedrich des Grossen. Halle, 1926.

CHAPTER TWELVE

Manzoni.

(For his Cinque Maggio, see under Napoleon, IV. VII. 25.)

1. General Influences.

Battistini, M. La fortuna del Manzoni nel Belgio. GSLI, 106-07, 1936.
Bellezza, P. Intorno alle versioni inglesi, tedesche e russe dei Promessi sposi. Rassegna nazionale, 128, 1902.
Christesco, D. La fortune d'Alexandre Manzoni en France. Paris, 1943.
Courten, C. de. I Promessi sposi ebbero fortuna in Francia? Vita e Pensiero, 5.V.1927.
Franzi, T. I Promessi sposi giudicati dal primo traduttore inglese. Marzocco, 25.IX.1932.
Hazard, P. Pour un Centenaire. Les Promessi sposi relus par un Français. Milano, 1927.
Neri, Nicoletta. La fortuna del Manzoni in Inghilterra. Atti della R. Accad. delle Scienze di Torino, 74, 1938-39.
Rossei, G. C. Il Manzoni e il Pellico nel Portogallo e nel Brasile. Convivium, 13, 1941.

2. Influences upon Individual Authors.

Croce, B. Un ricordo dei Promessi sposi in una lettera del **CLAUSEWITZ.** Crit., 1934.
Lollis, C. de. La Monaca di Monza e Mme. Bovary. **(FLAUBERT).** Cult., 15.V.1926.
Hennig, J. **GOETHE** and an English Critic of Manzoni. MDU, 39, 1947.
Reumont, A. Theilnahme Goethes an Manzoni. In his: Bibliografia. Berlin, 1863.
Acerra, A. Influenza di Manzoni sopra V. **HUGO** nelle dottrine drammatiche. Napoli, 1909.
Faggi, A. I Promessi sposi e I Miserabili di Victor Hugo. Marzocco, Feb., 1924.
Mengin, U. **LAMARTINE** et Manzoni. Mélanges Hauvette. Paris, 1934.
Holsapple, C. K. The Masque of the Red Death and I Promessi sposi. **(POE).** Texas Studies in English, 1938.
Anon. **STENDHAL** e I Promessi sposi. Marzocco, 20.III.1932.
Bellezza, P. Di qualche opinione dello Stendhal circa il Manzoni. Rassegna nazionale, 16.II.1896.

—— Manzoni, Giordani e Stendhal. GSLI, 1899.
Ortiz, R. Dal Manzoni allo Stendhal. Dalla Monaca di Monza a L'intérieur d'un couvent. In: Varia romanica. Firenze, 1932.
Vermale, F. Manzoni et Stendhal. Annales de l'U. de Grenoble, 21, 1945.
Villani, C. Dal Manzoni al TOLSTOI. Fanfulla della Domenica, 1889.
Mazzoni, G. E. TURQUETY e A. Manzoni. Studi di filologia moderna, 1, 1908.

Chapter Thirteen

Petrarca.

(See also Humanism and Renaissance, III. II. 3-4., Plato, II. III. 12., and Love, I. VI. 10.)

1. General Influences.

Allodoli, E. L'antipetrarchismo nel Cinquecento. R. Accad. di Arezzo, 3, 1938.
Françon, M. Une imitation du Sonnet de Pétrarque: Pace non trovo. Ital., 20, 1943.
Galletti, A. La modernità del Petrarca. In: Parma a F. Petrarca. Parma, 1934.
Graf, A. Petrarchismo e antipetrarchismo nel Cinquecento. NAnt, 85, 1886. And in: Attraverso il Cinquecento. Torino, 1888.
Marcenac, J. L'art de pétrarquiser. Les Lettres françaises, 8.IV.1948.
Meozzi, A. Il Petrarchismo europeo (secolo XVI). Pisa, 1934. Cf. PhQ, 15, 1936.
Momigliano, A. Petrarchismo europeo. In: Elzeviri. Firenze, 1945.
Wilkins, E. H. European Petrarchism. CL, 2, 1950.
Zamora, V. Sobre petrarquismo. U. de Santiago de Compostela, 1945.

2. Influences upon Individual Countries.

Billanovich, G. Studi sul Petrarca in AMERICA. GSLI, 125, 1948.
Wilkins, E. H. Manuscripts of the Canzoniere and the Triumphs of Petrarch in American Libraries. MPh, 45, 1947.
Borghesi, P. Petrarch and his Influence on English Literature. (ENGLAND). Bologna, 1906.
Chini, E. Il sorgere del Petrarchismo in Inghilterra. Civiltà Moderna, 6, 1934.
Foscolo, V. Saggi sopra il Petrarca pubblicati in inglese e tradotti in italiano. Lugano, 1824.
Fucilla, J. G. Petrarchan Translations in British Periodicals. Bull. of Bibliography, 18, 1943.
Hasselkuss, H. K. Der Petrarkismus in der Sprache der englischen Sonettdichter der Renaissance. Barmen, 1927.
Bertoli, L. Appunti sulla fortuna del Petrarca in Francia nella prima metà del secolo XIX. (FRANCE). Livorno, 1916.
—— I traduttori francesi del Petrarca nel secolo XIX. Festschrift F. Flamini. Pisa, 1918.
Clements, R. J. Anti-Petrarchism of the Pléiade. MPh, 39, 1941.
Delisle, L. Anciennes traductions françaises du traité de Pétrarque sur les remèdes de l'une et l'autre fortune. Notices et extr. des Ms., 34.
Françon, M. Sur l'influence de Pétrarque en France aux XVe et XVIe siècles. Ital., 19, 1942.
Golenitscheff-Koutouzoff, E. La première traduction des Triomphes de Pétrarque en France. Mélanges Hauvette. Paris, 1934.
Harvitt, Hélène. Les Triomphes de Pétrarque en France. RLC, 2, 1922.
Mignon, M. Le Musée de Pétrarque à Avignon. Mélanges Hauvette. Paris, 1934.
Niobe, C. Les Triomphes de Pétrarque sur un vitrail de l'église d'Ervy (Aube). Soc. acad. de l'Aube, 3.X.1897; Troyes, 1898.
Pellegrini, C. Il Petrarca nella cultura francese. RLM, 1, 1946.
—— Il Petrarca e la cultura francese. In: Tradizione italiana e cultura europea. Messina, 1947.
Praviel, A. Pétrarque en Provence et en Gascogne. RB, 75, 1937.
Sanctis, F. de. Petrarca e la critica francese. NAnt, 9, 1868.
Tourneur, C. Pétrarque dans le roman des dominicains de Toulouse. Rev. hist. de Toulouse, 25.
Vianey, J. Le Pétrarquisme en France au XVIe siècle. Montpellier, 1909.
Burdach, K. Aus Petrarcas ältestem deutschem Schülerkreise. (GERMANY). Berlin, 1929.
Livescu, J. Deutscher Petrarkismus im 18. Jahrhundert. Jassy, 1943.
Pacini, L. Petrarca in der deutschen Dichtungslehre vom Barock bis zur Romantik. Köln, 1936.
Souvageol, H. Petrarka in der deutschen

Lyrik des XVII. Jahrhunderts. Diss. Leipzig. Ansbach, 1911.
Söderhjelm, W. Petrarca in der deutschen Dichtung. München, Helsingfors, 1886. Cf. ZVL, 1.
Teza, E. Opere di Petrarca tradotte in ungherese. (**HUNGARY**). NAnt, 101, 1888.
Várady, E. Studi petrarcheschi in Ungheria. Studi petrarcheschi, 1 (Arezzo), 1948.
Rossi, G. C. La poesia del Petrarca in Portogallo. (**PORTUGAL**). Cultura Neolatina, 3, 1943.
Ortiz, R. Per la fortuna del Petrarca in **RUMANIA**. Mem. della Acad. Romêna, 5, 1930.
Farinelli, A. Il Petrarca fra gli ispani e i lusitani. Studi petrarcheschi, 1, (Arezzo), 1948.
Fucilla, J. G. Two Generations of Petrarchists in Spain. (**SPAIN**). MPh, 27, 1929.
—— Notes on Anti-Petrarchism in Spain. RR, 20, 1929.
—— The Pedigree of a Soneto a lo divino. CL, 1, 1949.
Cronia, A. Il petrarchismo nel cinquecento serbocroato. (**YUGOSLOVIA**). Studi petrarcheschi, 1 (Arezzo), 1948.

3. Influences upon Individual Authors.

Ortiz, R. Georghe **ASACHI** e il petrarchismo rumeno. In: Varia romanica. Firenze, 1932.
Benedetti, A. de. Un Petrarchista francese d'oggi: Fernand **BRISSET**. In: Parma a F. Petrarca. Parma, 1934.
Levi, E. **BYRON** and Petrarch. Athenaeum, 3847; cf. also 3851.
Schalk, F. Petrarca und **CAMOES**. Portugal Festschrift der U. Köln, 1940.
Savj-Lopez, P. Un petrarchista spagnuolo: Gutiere de **CETINA**. Vecchi, 1896.
Withers, A. M. The Sources of the Poetry of Gutierre de Cetina. Philadelphia, 1923.
Schoell, F. L. Une source nouvelle de **CHAPMAN**: Pétrarque, De contemptu mundi. RG, 1913.
Bellezza, P. **CHAUCER** s'è trovato col Petrarca? ESn, 23, 1899.
Bromby. Chaucer and Petrarch. Athenaeum, 3700, 1898.
Hornstein, Lillian H. Petrarch's Laelius, Chaucer's Lollius? PMLA, 63, 1948.
Jusserand, J. J. Did Chaucer Meet Petrarch? NC, 1896.
Mather, F. J. On the Asserted Meeting of Chaucer and Petrarch. MLN, 12, 1897.
Segrè, C. Chaucer e Petrarca. In: Studi petrarcheschi. Firenze, 1903.
Couture. Pétrarque et Jacques **COLONNE**, évêque de Lombez. Revue de Gascogne, 21. Cf. Romania, 1882.
Guggenheim, J. Quellenstudien zu S. **DANIELS** Sonettencyclen Delia. Berlin, 1908.
Clements, R. J. **DESPORTES** and Petrarch. RR, 36, 1945.
Cook, A. S. The Sad Florentine of **DU BELLAY** and Spenser. Academy,10. III.1888.
Pfänzel, M. Ueber die Sonnete des Joachim du Bellay. Saalfeld, 1898.
Vianey, J. La part de l'imitation dans les Regrets. BI, 4, 1904.
Schreiber, A. Petrarca und **ERASMUS**. Der Humanismus in Italien und im Norden. Heidelberg, 1947.
Croce, Alda. Il Petrarca spagnuolo: **GARCILASO DE LA VEGA**. Aretusa, 1, 1944.
Keniston, H. Garcilaso de la Vega: A Critical Study of his Life and Works. New York, 1922.
Flitner, W. Von Petrarca zu **GOETHE**. Goethe Kalender, 1942.
Bougouyn, S. Les Triomphes de Pétrarque traduits en vers français par H. **HARVITT**. RLC, 2, 1922.
Ceriello, G. R. Imitazioni petrarchesche di Fernando de **HERRERA**. RCLI, 17, 1911.
Auer, J. W. S. **LANDOR** in seinen Beziehungen zu den Dichtern des Trecento. Diss. Münster. Rheydt, 1903.
Fucilla, J. G. Concerning the Poetry of **LOPE DE VEGA**. Hisp., 15, 1932.
Kastner, L. E. The Sources of Olivier de **MAGNY'S** Sonnets. MPh, 7, 1909.
Pagès, A. Auzias **MARCH** et ses prédécesseurs. Paris, 1912.
Gilbert, A. H. **MILTON** Quotes from Petrarch. MLN, 60, 1945.
Bertoni, G. De Pétrarque à **MONTAIGNE**. REI, 1936.
Melton, W. F. The Influence of Petrarch upon Edward Coote **PINCKNEY**. MLN, 1913.
Anon. Pétrarque et **RONSARD**. Le Temps, 9.V.1896.
Laumonier, P. Ronsard pétrarquiste avant 1550. Mélanges Lanson. Paris, 1922.
Marmay, L. L'influence italienne au temps de Ronsard, les imitations de Pétrarque et des poètes italiens dans le premier livre des Amours. Bull. his-

torique et scientifique de l'Auvergne, 29-30, 1909-10.
Pieri, M. Le pétrarquisme au XVIe siècle. Pétrarque et Ronsard, ou de l'influence de Pétrarque sur la Pléiade française. Marseille, 1895.
Saulnier, V. L. Maurice SCEVE et Pontus de Tyard. Deux notes sur le Pétrarquisme de Pontus. RLC, 22, 1948.
Conrad, H. Petrarca als Lyriker verglichen mit seinem grössten Jünger, SHAKSPERE. PJb, 376-88, 1917.
Dannenberg, F. Shakespeare's Sonette: Herkunft, Wesen, Deutung. JbShG, 70, 1934.
Linguеglia, P. Un soneto shakespeariano del Petrarca (Passa la nave mia . . .). In: Parma a Fr. Petrarca. Parma, 1934.
Valente, P. L. Petrarca e Shakespeare. Studi petrarcheschi, 1 (Arezzo), 1948.
Wilkins, E. H. The Sonnet in Petrarch and in Shakespeare. MPh, 1915.
Wolff, M. J. Petrarkismus und Antipetrarkismus in Shakespeares Sonetten. ESn, 49, 1916.
—— Shakespeare und der Petrarkismus. NSp, 1920.
Fucilla, J. G. Un sonetto di Barahona de SOTO e uno del Petrarca. GSLI, 116, 1941.
Jusserand, J. J. SPENSER'S Visions of Petrarch. Athenaeum, 10.V.1902.
Koeppel, E. Ueber die Echtheit der Edmund Spenser zugeschriebenen Visions of Petrarch und Visions of Du Bellay. ESn, 15, 1891.
Fehse, H. Henry Howard, Earl of SURREY. Ein Beitrag zur Geschichte des Petrarkismus in England. Progr. Chemnitz, 1883.
Flamini, F. Du rôle de Pontus de TYARD dans le pétrarquisme français. Revue de la Renaissance, 43-45, 1901.
Teza, E. Tre canzoni petrarchesche tradotte in boemo (da VRCHLICKI). Padova, 1901.
Segrè, C. Due Petrarchisti inglesi del secolo XVI: I. Sir Thomas WYATT. II. Enrico conte di Surrey. NAnt, 1901. And in: Studi petrarcheschi. Firenze, 1903.

CHAPTER FOURTEEN

Tasso.

1. General Influences.

Ferrazzi, G. G. Traduzioni della Gerusalemme Liberata. In: Torquato Tasso, Studi. Bassano, 1880.
Pitou, S. French and English Echoes of a Descriptive Passage in Tasso. MLN, 1937.
Robertis, G. de. La fortuna dell' Aminta. In: Studi. Firenze, 1944.
Tortoreto, A. Gli studi tassiani in AMERICA. Boll. di letterature moderne, 1, 1947.
Grillo, E. Tasso's Aminta. (ENGLAND). London, 1924.
Koeppel, E. Die englischen Tasso-Uebersetzungen des XVI. Jahrhunderts. Anglia, 11-13, 1888-90.
Murphy, Joan. Elizabethan Lyrics from Tasso. MLN, 58, 1943.
Wiffen, J. H. Jerusalem Delivered with a Prefatory Dissertation on Existing Translations. London, 1821.
Baletti-Riccovoni, E. Lettre de Mlle. R. à M. l'abbé C. au sujet de la nouvelle traduction du poème de la Jérusalem de Tasse. (FRANCE). Paris, 1725.
Beall, C. B. Noterelle sulla fortuna del Tasso in Francia. Bergomum (Bergamo), 1937.
—— Deux romans peu connus du XVIIe siècle français. MLN, 52, 1937.
—— The First French Imitation of Tasso's Invocation to the Muses. MLN, 53, 1938.
—— Note sur la Jérusalem délivrée et le roman français. RLC, 19, 1939.
—— La fortune du Tasse en France. Eugene (Oregon), 1942.
Mazzoni, G. Un ape d'alveare italiano in Francia. Marzocco, 15.XI.1925.
Puglisi Pico, M. Il Tasso nella critica francese. Arcireale, 1896.
Williams, R. C. French Allusions to Tasso. MLN, 1932.
Cattani, J. M. Studien zum deutschen Tassobild des 17. & 18. Jahrhunderts. (GERMANY). Diss. Freiburg, 1941.
Wagner, H. Tasso daheim und in Deutschland. Einwirkungen Italiens auf die deutsche Literatur. Berlin, 1905.
Camariano, N. Torquato Tasso in literatura greaca. (GREECE). Studii italiene, 3, 1936.
Pollak, R. La fortuna del Tasso in Polonia. (POLAND). GSLI, 113, 1939.
Rossi, G. L. Tasso na literatura portuguesa. (PORTUGAL). Rev. da Faculdade de letras (Lisboa), 11.
Marcu, A. Torquato Tasso in romantica romaneasca. (RUMANIA). Studii italiene, 3, 1936.
Amador de los Rios. Estudios criticos sobre la Jerusalén liberada del Tasso. (SPAIN). Revista Española de Ambos Mundos, 4, 1885.

Farinelli, A. La più antica versione spagnuola della Gerusalemme del Tasso manoscritta alla nazionale di Madrid. Rassegna bibliografica della lett. ital., 3, 1895.
Pizzagalli, A. M. Un'eco spagnola del Tasso. Convivio letterario, 7, 1939.

2. Influences upon Individual Authors.

Beall, C. B. Guez de BALZAC and Tasso. MLN, 1934.
Gallagher, M. BAOUR and Tasso. In: Baour-Lormian, Life and Works. Philadelphia, 1938.
Beall, C. B. Le Père BOUHOURS et le Tasse. MLN, 1935.
—— CHATEAUBRIAND et le Tasse. Paris, Baltimore, 1934.
Ormesson, W. d'. Chauteaubriand à Rome et le souvenir du Tasse. RLC, 23, 1949.
Marcu, A. Un motiv din Tasso în Tiganiada lui Budai DELEANU. Studii italiene, 5, 1938.
—— Dela Torquato Tasso la EMINESCU: Coincidente tematice. Ibid., 4, 1938.
Fucilla, J. G. The Influence of Ercilla and Tasso on ESCOIQUIZ'S Mexico Conquistada. HR, 14, 1946.
Crawford, J. P. W. Suarez de FIGUEROA'S España Defendida and Tasso's Gerusalemme Liberata. RR, 4, 1913.
Köppel, E. Abraham FRAUNCES Amyntas Pastoral. Anglia, 11, 1888.
Bosco, U. Il Tasso e il GOETHE. In: Aspetti del romanticismo. Roma, 1942.
Bouchaud, P. de. Goethe et le Tasse. Paris, 1907.
Cora, M. Sul Tasso di Goethe. La Ronda, 1920.
Croce, B. Un contrasto tra la vecchia età e la nuova: Il Paleophron und Neoterpe di Volfgango Goethe. Crit., 20. III.1932.
Delp, W. E. Goethe's Tasso in the Light of Chekov. CLS, 12, 1944.
Kern, F. Goethes Tasso und Kuno Fischer, nebst einem Anhange: Goethes Tasso und Goldonis Tasso. Berlin 1892,
Michéa, R. L'italianisme de "Torquato Tasso", RG, 1934.
Ruoff, H. Zur Entstehungsgeschichte von Goethes Tasso. Marburg, 1910.
Wilkinson, E. M. Goethe's Tasso. The Tragedy of a Creative Artist. PEGS, N. S., 15, 1946.
Teza, E. Il Tasso e il GUIZOT. Rassegna bibliografica della lett. ital., 8, 1901.
Bucchioni, U. T. Tasso e LOPE FELIX DE VEGA. Rocca S. Casciano, 1910.
Lapesa, R. La Jerusalén de Tasso y la de Lope. Bol. de la Real Acad. Española, 25, 1946.
Lucie-Lary, Mme. La Jerusalén conquistada de Lope de Vega et la Gerusalemme liberata du Tasse. RLR, 1, 1898.
Beall, C. B. A Spanish Sonnet Imitated from Tasso. (Luis MARTIN DE LA PLAZA). Hisp., 25, 1942.
—— Francisco de MEDRANO'S Imitations from Tasso. HR, 11, 1943.
Hall, Bettie M. A Further Tasso Imitation in Francisco de Medrano. HR, 14, 1946.
Benedetto, U. F. Le osservazioni inedite di G. MENAGE sopra l'Aminta del Tasso. BI, 10, 1910.
Beall, C. B. Cristóbal de MESA and Tasso's Rime. MLN, 60, 1945.
Massarani, T. Tasso e MILTON. In: Studi di letteratura e d'arte. Firenze, 1873.
Pommerich, E. Miltons Verhältnis zu Torquato Tasso. Diss. Leipzig, 1902.
Marcu, A. Gerusaleme liberata in traducera lui A. PACLEANU. Studii italiene, 2, 1935.
Benedetto, U. F. Jean Jacques ROUSSEAU tassofilo. Festschrift R. Renier. Torino, 1912.
Wagner, H. Ist SCHILLER bei der Jungfrau von Orleans durch Tasso Gerusalemme liberata beeinflusst worden? Euphorion, 1898.
Lee, S. Tasso and SHAKESPEARE'S England. In: Elizabethan and Other Essays. Oxford, 1929.
Beall, C. B. A Tasso Quotation in SHELLEY. MLQ, 2, 1941.
—— A Tasso Imitation in SPENSER. MLQ, 3, 1942.
Blanchard, H. S. Imitations from Tasso in the Faerie Queene. SPh, 1925.
Castelli, A. La Gerusalemme liberata nella Inghilterra di Spenser. Milano, 1936.
Koeppel, E. Edmund Spensers Verhältniss zu Tasso. Anglia, 11, 1888.
Lascaris, M. Rhodolinos, tragédie de J. A. TROILOS et l'influence du Tasse sur le théâtre crétois. Athènes, 1938.
Banti, C. L'Amyntas du Tasse e l'Astrée d'Honoré d'URFE. Milano, 1895.
Ronzy, P. Une imitation inédite du Tasse: la Judith d'Anne d'Urfé. L'Italie classique et moderne, 1, 1908.
Mickle, W. J. Dissertation on the Machinery of Tasso's Jerusalem and VOLTAIRE'S Henriade. Oxford, 1776.
Kalff, G. VONDEL'S vertaling van La

Gerusalemme liberata. Tijdschrift voor nederl. taal- en letterkunde, 14, 1895.
Tribolet, H. WIELANDS Verhältnis zu Ariost und Tasso. Diss. Bern, 1919.
Beall, C. B. Un Tassista americano di cent' anni fa, R. H. WILDE. Bergomum, 17, 1939.

CHAPTER FIFTEEN

Other Italian Authors.

Froger, L. Ronsard et **ALAMANNI**. Annales fléchoises. La Flèche, 3, 1904.
Fucilla, J. G. De morte et amore. (**ALCIATO** in England). PhQ, 1935.
Cipolla, F. & Fasola, C. **ALEARDI** e Freiligrath. Riv. mens. di lett. ted., 1, 1907.
Pettinati, C. Alphonse de Lamartine e Aleardo Aleardi. Rassegna Nazionale, 1920.
Bassi, B. Vittorio **ALFIERI** e la Svezia. Annali Alfieriani, 2, 1943.
Costanzi, O. Cenni sulla fortuna di V. Alfieri in Germania. Rassegna Nazionale, 1939.
Ortiz, R. Vittorio Alfieri e l'influsso esercitato dalle sue tragedie sul Risorgimento nazionale della Romania. Boll. della R. U. di Perugia, 1931.
Parducci, A. Traduzioni spagnole di tragedie alfieriane. Annali Alfieriani, 1, 1942.
Peers, E. A. The Vogue of Alfieri in Spain. HR, 1933.
Rossi, G. C. L'Alfieri e il Portogallo. Annali Alfieriani, 1, 1942.
Pudbres, Anna. Lord Byron, Admirer and Imitator of Alfieri. ESn, 33, 1903.
Landau, M. Alfieri und Byron. Frankfurter Zt., 277-78, 1903.
Zanco, A. L'Alfierismo del Byron. Rivista italiana del dramma, 5, 1941.
Montera, P. de. André Chénier et Vittorio Alfieri. EI, 4.
Ellet, E. F. Alfieri and Schiller. Southern Literary Messenger, Oct., 1836.
ALGAROTTI: See Intermediaries, I. IV. 8.
Munsterberg, M. Precursor of Paradise Lost. (**ANDREINI**). MB, 19, 1944.
Fucilla, J. G. **ANGERIANO** and Antonio Ferreira. PhQ, 25, 1946.
Hutton, J. Germain Colin Bucher and Girolamo Angeriano. MLN, 57, 1942.
Begozzi, L. G. d'**ANNUNZIO** nei saggi critici di H. von Hofmannsthal. Convivium, 13, 1941.
Fucilla, J. G. & Carrière, J. M. D'Annunzio Abroad. A Bibliographical Essay. 2 vols. New York, 1935-37.
Sprigge, C. J. S. D'Annunzio's Italy and England. Fortnightly Rev., 1938.
Stuart, R. A. G. D'Annunzio giudicato in Inghilterra. Rassegna internaz., 15.IX. 1900.
Tosi, G. D'Annunzio à son traducteur Georges Hérelle. Paris, 1946. Cf. RLM, 1947.
Paoli, M. L'**ARETIN** au théâtre. BI, 4.
Spicker, S. H. Der spanische Aretin. Serapeum, 1847.
Stocchi, B. L'Orazia dell' Aretino e l'Horace del Corneille. Napoli, 1912.
Dublin, P. G. Molière et l'Arétin. MF, 15.X.1935.
Hewlett, M. Two Translations from the Italians (**BANDELLO**, Vittoria Colonna). Academy, 1189, 1895.
Kaulfuss-Diesch, K. Bandellos Novella Timbreo und Fenicia im deutschen Drama . des 17. Jahrhunderts. Festschrift A. Köster. Leipzig, 1912.
Kiesow, K. Die verschiedenen Bearbeitungen der Novelle von der Herzogin von Amalfi des Bandello in der Litteratus des XVI. und XVII. Jahrhunderts. Diss. Leipzig. Anglia, 17, 1894-95.
Pruvost, R. Matteo Bandello and Elizabethan Fiction. Paris, 1937.
Sturel, R. Bandello en France au XVIe siècle. BI, 1918.
Ebert, W. Beaumont und Fletcher's Triumph of Love und Triumph of Death und ihre Quellen. Diss. Halle, Wittenberg, 1904.
Langton, D. Fenton's Tragicall Discourses. (Cf. Introduction). London, 1892-96.
Kohler, E. Lope et Bandello. Festschrift Ernest Martinenche. Paris, 1939.
Fellheimer, Jeannette. The Source of Richard Lynche's Amorous Poeme of Dom Diego and Gineura. PMLA, 58, 1943.
Bédarida, H. Une nouvelle de Matteo Bandello et la Barbérine d'A. de Musset. RHLF, 1920.
Gordon, D. J. Much Ado About Nothing: A Possible Source for the Hero-Claudio Plot. SPh, 39, 1942.
Osella, G. Andrea da **BARBERINO** nel giudizio degli stranieri. Convivium, 14, 1942.
BARETTI: See Intermediaries, I. IV. 8.
Faggi, A. Daniello **BARTOLI** e Federigo Schiller. Marzocco, 27.IV.1930.
Hauvette, H. Un précurseur italien de Corneille: Girolamo **BARTOLOMMEI**. Annales de l'U. de Grenoble, 1897.

Zambiasi, M. Giuseppe **BELLOMO**, un precursore di Goethe. Studi trentini di Scienze storiche, 16, 1935.
Battelli, G. Un grande umanista portoghese: Damiano di Goes e la sua corrispondenza col Sadoleto e col **BEMBO**. Bibliofilia, 42, 1940.
Rajna, P. I versi spagnuoli di mano di Pietro Bembo e di Lucrezia Borgia serbati da un codice ambrosiano. Festschrift Menéndez Pidal. Madrid, 1924.
Ruutz-Rees, C. A Note on Saint-Gelais and Bembo. RR, 1, 1910.
Fletcher, J. B. **BENIVIENI'S** Ode of Love and Spenser's Foure Hymnes. MPh, 8, 1910-11.
Fucilla, J. G. Una imitazione satirica di Pedro de Padilla (E. **BENTIVOGLIO**). AR, 20, 1936.
Bertoni, G. Sulle redazioni provenzale e francese della Practica oculorum di **BENVENUTO**. RLR, 47, 1904.
Bosurgi, G. C. La caricatura della donna nel **BERNI** e in due lirici spagnuoli del secolo XVII. Festschrift Fr. Torraca. Napoli, 1922.
Fucilla, J. G. A Passage in Quevedo's Buscón. Ital., 23, 1946.
Myrmex. Orme italiane nella Germania Settecentesca: G. L. **BIANCONI**. Illustrazione italiana, 40, 1933.
Behrend, F. Trajano **BOCCALINI** und die deutsche Literatur. Berlin, 1936.
Stoetzner, P. Der Satyriker Trajano Boccalini und sein Einfluss auf die deutsche Litteratur. Archiv, 103, 1899.
Williams, R. H. Boccalini in Spain. A Study of his Influence on Prose Fiction of the Seventeenth Century. Menasha (Wis.), 1946.
Gray, P. H. Suckling's A Session of the Poets as a Ballad: Boccalini's Influence Examined. SPh, 36, 1939.
Thijssen-Schoute, C. L. Nicolaas Jarichides Wieringa, een zeventiende-eeuws vertaler van Boccalini, Rabelais, Barclai. Assen, 1939.
Parducci, A. L'Orlando innamorato nel teatro spagnuolo. (**BOIARDO**). Annali della R. Scuola Normale Superiore di Pisa, 1934.
Gilbert, A. H. A Parallel between Milton and Boiardo. Ital., 20, 1943.
Draper, J. W. Shakespeare's Orlando Innamorato. MLQ, 2, 1941.
Weiss, R. Leonardo **BRUNI** Aretino and Early English Humanism. MLR, 36, 1941.
Anon. Giordano **BRUNO** in England. QR, 1902.
Auvray, L. Giordano Bruno à Paris, d'après le témoignage d'un contemporain (1585-86). Mém. de la Société de l'Histoire de Paris, 1901.
Elton, O. Giordano Bruno in England. In: Modern Studies. London, 1907.
Hauser, O. G. Bruno im Drama der jüngsten Zeit. Hamburgischer Correspondent, Beilage, 19, 1903.
Limentani, L. G. Bruno a Oxford. Civiltà moderna, 9, 1937.
Looten, C. Giordano Bruno à Londres. RLC, 19, 1939.
Pellegrini, A. M. Giordano Bruno and Oxford. HLQ, 5, 1942.
Scholz, W. von. Giordano Bruno Dramen. LE, 1903.
Stanepanato, V. Alcuni antecedenti e imitazioni francesi del Candelajo. Riv. bibl. ital., 12, 1907.
Steffens, H. Ueber das Leben des Jordanus Brunus (im Ausland). Berlin, 1846.
Wendt. Giordano Bruno in Deutschland. Göttingische Gelehrte Anzeigen, 26. VIII.1830.
Yates, F. A. Giordano Bruno's Conflict with Oxford. JWI, 2.
Snyder, A. D. Coleridge on Giordano Bruno. MLN, 1927.
Broad, C. D. The New Philosophy: Bruno to Descartes. Cambridge Hist. Jour., 8, 1944.
Kuhlenbeck, L. G. Brunos Einfluss auf Goethe und Schiller. Leipzig, 1907.
Sänger, W. Goethe und G. Bruno. Berlin, 1931.
Orsini, N. Giordano Bruno ad Oxford nella testimonianza di Harvey (June, 1583). In: Studii sul Rinascimento italiano in Inghilterra. Firenze, 1937.
Liljegren, S. B. La pensée de Milton et Giordano Bruno. RLC, 3, 1923.
Beyersdorff, R. Giordano Bruno und Shakespeare. Progr. Oldenburg, 1889 & JbShG, 26, 1891.
Capasso, A. L'ispiratore italiano di Shakespeare. Giorn. d'Italia, 7.V.1916.
Croci, P. Il maestro italiano di Shakespeare. Corriere della Sera, 177, 1921.
König, W. Shakespeare und Giordano Bruno. JbShG, 11, 1876.
Orano, P. Amleto è Giordano Bruno? Lanciano, 1916.
Tschischwitz, B. Shakespeare und Giordano Bruno. In: Shakespeare-Forschungen. Halle, 1868.
Cook, A. S. Sidney and G. Bruno. MLN, 8, 1893.
Ferruolo, A. Sir Philip Sidney e Giordano Bruno. Convivium, N. S., 1948.

Pellegrini, A. M. Bruno, Sidney and Spenser. SPh, 40, 1943.
Lovejoy, A. O. The Dialectic of Bruno and Spinoza. U. of Cal. Pub. in Philosophy, 1, 1904.
Paris, G. La source italienne de la Courtisane amoureuse de la Fontaine (Girolamo **BRUSONI**: La cortigina innamorata). Festschrift A. d'Ancona. Firenze, 1901.
Funck, H. Lavater und **CAGLIOSTRO.** WM, 67, 1922.
Sypesten, C. van. Voltaire, Saint-Germain, Cagliostro, Mirabeau in Nederland. S'Gravenhage, 1861 & Den Haag, 1896.
Zaniboni, E. Goethe e il Cagliostro. Marzocco, Nov., 1925.
McColley, G. The Debt of Bishop John Wilkins to the Apologia Pro Galileo of T. **CAMPANELLA.** Annals of Science, 4.
Anon. **CARDUCCI** in English. TLS, 16.I. 1930.
Azzolini, M. Giosuè Carducci und die deutsche Literatur. Tübingen, 1910.
Benedetto, U. F. Carducci e la Francia. Pan, Sept., 1935.
Buriot-Darsiles, H. Quelques transcriptions françaises de poèmes de Carducci. NRI, 15.XII.1920.
—— Carducci en France. Dante, 1935.
Dell'Isola, Maria. Giosuè Carducci en France. RLC, 10, 1930.
—— Carducci nella letteratura europea. Paris, 1936.
Ferretti, L. Carducci e la letteratura inglese. Milano, 1927.
Giavesu, A. Giosuè Carducci. Studio di letteratura comparata. Roma, 1933.
Hazard, P. Les traductions de G. Carducci devant le public de langue anglaise. EI, 1935.
Maugain, G. Carducci et la France. Paris, 1914.
Mele, E. Per la fortuna del Carducci in Ispagna. Cult., 20.XI.1910.
Salvadori del Prato, T. G. Carducci nella critica letteraria francese. Tempo nostro, 1935.
Scalia, S. E. Carducci et la critique anglo-saxonne. RLC, 15, 1935.
—— Carducci, his Critics and Translators in England and America, 1881-1932. New York, 1937.
Witte, J. K. Giosuè Carducci und seine deutschen Uebersetzer. MLIA, 1880.
Damiani, F. H. Auguste Barbier e Giosuè Carducci. Bologna, 1913.
Albertazzi, A. Carducci e Leconte de Lisle. Natura ed Arte, 11, 1909.
Dionisotti, C. Carducci e Mallarmé. La Nuova Europa, 2, 1945.
Battelli, G. Le Saudades paganas di Antero de Quental e la poesia classica di G. Carducci. Byblos, 5, 1930.
Amram, B. B. Swinburne and Carducci. Yale Rev., 5, 1916.
Bleackley, H. **CASANOVA** in England 1763-64. London, 1923.
Maynial, E. Casanova et son temps. Paris, 1911.
—— Les Mémoires de Casanova et les conteurs français au XVIIIe siècle. MF, 1928.
—— Balzac et Casanova. RHLF, 45, 1938.
Curiel, C. L. Ancora Casanova e Stendhal. Marzocco, 1.VI.1924.
Neri, F. Casanova e Stendhal. In: Il Maggio delle Fate. Novara, 1929 & Torino, 1944.
Andreas, W. Graf Baldassare **CASTIGLIONE** und die Renaissance. AK, 10, 1913.
Krebs, E. El Cortesano de Castiglione en España. Bol. de la Acad. Argentina de Letras, 8-10, 1940-42.
Reinhardstoettner, K. von. Die erste deutsche Uebersetzung von Baldassare Castigliones Cortegiano. Jb. f. Münchener Geschichte, 2, 1888.
Schrinner, W. Castiglione und die englische Renaissance. Diss. Breslau. Berlin, 1939.
Toldo, P. Le courtisan dans la littérature française et ses rapports avec l'oeuvre du Castiglione. Archiv, 104, 1900.
Green, O. H. Boscan and Il Cortegiano. Bol. Inst. Caro y Cuervo, 4, 1948.
Nitze, W. A. Corneille's Conception of Character and the Cortegiano. MPh, 15, 1917.
Hogrefe, Pearl. Elyot and The Boke called Cortigiano in Ytalion. MPh, 27, 1929-30.
Ruutz-Rees, C. Some Notes of G. Harvey's in Hoby's Translation of Castigliones Courtier (1561). PMLA, 1910.
Marasso, A. Fernando de Herrera y El Cortesano de Castiglione. Bol. de la Acad. Argentina de Letras, 8, 1940.
Bang, W. Ben Jonson und Castigliones Cortegiano. ESn, 36, 1906.
Ziino, M. Castiglione e Montaigne. Relazioni tra Essais e Cortegiano. Conv., 10, 1938.
Praz, M. Shakespeare, il Castiglione e le facezie. Riv. italiana del dramma, 4, 1940.
Torraca, F. La grazia secondo il Castiglione e secondo lo Spenser. Antologia

della nostra crit. lett. moderna. Città di Castello, 1894.
Prezzolini, G. Castiglione and Alfonso de Valdès. RR, 1938.
Praz, M. De Foe and **CELLINI**. ESs. 13, 1931. And in: Studi e Svaghi inglesi. Firenze, 1937.
Lumbroso, A. Il Cellini del Goethe. Marzocco, 20.X.1929.
Vossler, K. Goethes Cellini-Uebersetzung. Beilage zur Allg. Zt., 253, 1900.
Anon. Cellini and Shakespeare. N&Q, 8, 1901.
Moseley, B. D. Cellini and Shakespeare. N&Q, 9, 1902.
Levin, H. La Citadelle de Parme: Stendhal et Benvenuto Cellini. RLC, 18, 1938.
CENCI: see Thematology, I. VI. 10.
Scorza, M. Gongora e **CHIABRERA**. Modena, 1934.
Meregazzi, G. Un melodramma del **CIMAROSA** tradotto dal Goethe. Riv. mens. di lett. ted., 2, 1908.
Praz, M. Swinburne and the Hypnerotomachia Poliphili. (F. **COLONNA**). ESs, 25, 1943.
—— Some Foreign Imitators of the Hypnerotomachia Poliphili. Ital., 24, 1947.
Soeltoft-Jensen. Le cinquième livre de Rabelais et le Songe de Poliphile. RHLF, 3, 1896.
Hamilton, G. L. Chaucer's Indebtedness to Guido delle **COLONNE**. New York, 1903.
Axon, W. E. A. L. **CORNARO** in English. Library, N. S., 2, 1901.
Kastner, L. E. Desportes et Angelo di **COSTANZO**. RHLF, 15, 1908.
Ginuzburg, L. **CROCE** e Valéry. Rassegna d'Italia, 1, 1946.
Barberi, C. La fortuna del Bertoldo (by J. C. Croce) in Romania. Rassegna italo-romena, 23, 1943.
Schoell, F. Leo **FERRERO** et la France. Lausanne, 1945.
Festugière, J. La philosophie de l'amour de Marsile **FICIN** et son influence sur la littérature française au XVIe siècle. Revista da U. de Coimbra, 1923 & Paris, 1941.
Schoell, F. L. Les emprunts de G. Chapman à Marsile Fissin, philosophus platonicus. RLC, 3, 1923.
Croce, B. Intorno a un giudizio del Macaulay su Vincenzo da **FILICAIA**. In: Nuovi Saggi sulla letteratura italiana del Seicento. Bari, 1931.
Ferrante, G. L'opera di Lionelli **FIUMI** nella critica dell'America latina. Dante, Nov., 1939.
John **FLORIO**: See Intermediaries, I. IV. 8.
Begey, M. B. **FOGAZZARO** e le correnti messianiche polacche. Przeglad Wspólczesny, 1938.
Crawford, J. P. W. Teofilo **FOLENGO'S** Moschaea and José de Villarviciosa's La Mosquea. PMLA, 1912.
Lo Forte-Randi, A. Fr. Rabelais et T. Folengo. Revue internationale, 10.III. 1885.
Luzio, A. Spigolature Folenghiane (Imitazioni Folenghiane del Rabelais). Bergamo, 1897. And in: Studi Folenghiani. Firenze, 1899.
Zumbini, B. Folengo precursore del Cervantes. Napoli letter., Jan., 1885.
—— Gli episodi dei montoni e della tempesta presso il Folengo e presso il Rabelais. In: Studi di letteratura comparata. Bologna, 1931.
Bassi, O. Interpretazioni foscoliane in Francia. (**FOSCOLO**). Convivium, 1936.
Caraccio, A. Ugo Foscolo comparatiste. RCL, 17, 1937.
Cézilly, M. Ugo Foscolo et quelques-uns de nos écrivains. NRI, 19, 1922.
Cortese, C. Ugo Foscolo e l'Inghilterra. Napoli, 1935.
Evola, N. D. Bibliografia foscoliana, 1920-27. I Libri del Giorno, 1927.
Hazard, P. Foscolo et Gray au Nouveau-Monde. RLC, 11, 1931.
Ottolini, A. Bibliografia foscoliana. Firenze, 1921.
Prezzolini, G. Monti, Pellico, Manzoni, Foscolo, veduti da viaggiatori americani. Pegaso, 1932.
Vigneron, R. Stendhal, Foscolo et l'Edinburgh Review. RLC, 10, 1930.
Minolfi, G. Foscolo e Byron. Catania, 1904.
Petrucci, G. Lo Jacopo Ortis del Foscolo e il René di Chateaubriand. Tutto, 24, 1926.
Sóriga, R. Ugo Foscolo e il suo amico anglo-italo Augusto Bozzi Granville. Milano, 1928.
Vincent, E. R. Foscoliana in Hudson Gurney's Work. Italian Studies, 1938.
Bédarida, H. De Foscolo à José Maria de Hérédia: une adaptation cubaine des Sepolcri. Festschrift E. Martinenche. Paris, 1939.
Caraccio, A. Stendhal, Foscolo et les Ultime lettere di Jacopo Ortis. Le Divan, 1932.
Garrone, M. A. Un poeta sardo in due opere di M. Cervantes (Antonio del **FRASSO**). Fanfulla della Domenica, 33, 1911.

Enriques, F. Descartes et GALILEE. RMM, 1937.
Gilbert, A. H. Milton and Galileo. SPh, 1922.
Liljegren, S. B. Milton and Galileo. In: Studies in Milton. Lund, 1918.
Faggi, A. Pascal e Galileo. Marzocco, May, 1923.
Boselli, A. Il Galileo di G. Carducci e quello di Shelley. Fanfulla della Domenica, 23.V.1909.
Greg, W. W. GIRALDI CINTIO and the English Drama. MLQ, 1902.
Panella, I. G. B. Giraldi ferrarese e la fortuna d'una novella dei suoi Hecatommithi. Romagna, 1, 1904.
Evardsen, H. Mrs. Centlivre's Drama The Cruel Gift und seine Quellen. Diss. Kiel, 1912.
Fusco, A. La Sapho del Daudet e una novela del Giraldi. Napoli, 1901.
Kohler, E. Lope de Vega et Giraldi Cintio. Mélanges de la Faculté des Lettres de l'U. de Strasbourg, 1945. Paris, 1946.
Morby, E. S. Gli Ecatommiti, El favor agradecido, and Las burlas y enredos de Benito. HR, 10, 1942.
Ball, R. H. Cintio's Epitia and Measure for Measure. (Shakespeare). Festschrift G. F. Reynolds. Boulder (Colorado), 1945.
Osztoya, A. H. von. Zur Quelle von Shakespeares Mass für Mass. ZVL, 7.
Krappe, A. H. The Source of Voltaire's Zadig. MLR, 1925.
Carli, P. La Terra dei Morti di Giuseppe GIUSTI e il Lamartine. Rassegna d' Italia, 1947.
Bertoni, G. Carlo GOLDONI e il teatro francese del suo tempo. In: Modena a Carlo Goldoni. Modena, 1907.
Bos, M. du. Curiosités Goldoniennes. L'Italie et la France, revue illustrée, 2, 1907.
Clarétie, J. Goldoni et la Comédie Française. Ibid.
Gagliardi, E. Goldoni e Gallina in Germania. Marzocco, July, 1925.
Ginisty, P. Goldoni en France. Journal des Débats, 23.II.1906.
Kühle, M. Carlo Goldonis Komödien auf dem deutschen Theater des 20. Jahrhunderts. Köln, Stuttgart, 1943.
Maddalena, E. La fortuna della Locandiera fuori d'Italia. RI, 1907.
—— Goldoni in America. Marzocco, 15.I. 1922.
—— Goldoni in inglese. Marzocco, 7.I.1923.
——Goldoni in Inghilterra e in America. RI, 15.IX.1923.
—— Goldoni in Germania. Marzocco, June, 1924.
Marffy, O. La fortuna del Goldoni in Ungheria. GSLI, 119, 1942.
Mathar, L. Carlo Goldoni auf dem deutschen Theater des XVIII. Jahrhunderts. Diss. München, 1910.
Moretti, A. C. Goldoni in Francia. Cortona, 1907.
Ortiz, M. Goldoni in Francia. Chorus, 11. (Napoli), 1908.
Ortiz, R. Goldoni e la Francia. Accad. romana: Mem. sect. liter., 3, 1927.
—— Attività del Goldoni alla Comédîe Italienne. Venezia, 1946.
Ortolani, G. Goldoni e la Francia. GSLI, 1929.
Palinkas, L. Goldoni nel teatro nazionale ungherese. Corvina, 4, 1941.
Radu, C. Goldoni in România. Revista de cultura italiana, 1931.
Rodocanachi. Goldoni en France. Journal des Débats, 25.II.1907.
Rogers, P. P. Goldoni in Spain. Oberlin (Ohio), 1941.
Sarti, C. G. Gli ultimi anni di C. Goldoni a Parigi. NAnt, 1928.
Toldo, P. Tre commedie francesi inedite di C. Goldoni. GSLI, 1897.
Vaccalluzzo, N. Arlequin franc-maçon e Le donne curiose del Goldoni. Mélanges Hauvette. Paris, 1934.
Verdeil, H. La Locandiera de Goldoni sur la scène française. Dante, 1933.
Young, B. Goldoni and the French Theater. MLJ, 1935.
Simionescu, D. Ion Vodà Caragea si traducerile lui din Goldoni. Studii italiene, 2, 1935.
Toldo, P. Se il Diderot abbia imitato il Goldoni. GSLI, 26, 1895.
Maddalena, E. Goldoni e Favart. Ateneo Veneto, 22, 1899.
—— Goethe e Goldoni. Fanfulla della Domenica, 24.IX.1892.
Petsch, R. A Jest of Goldoni's in Goethe's Faust. MLR, 1912.
Gatti, J. F. Una imitacion de Goldoni por Juan Ignacio González del Castillo. RFH, 5, 1943.
Maddalena, E. Lessing e Goldoni. GSLI, 1906.
—— Moratin e Goldoni. Pagine italiane, 2. Capodistria, 1905.
Sarrailh, J. Note sur le Café de Moratín. BH, 1934.
Rozanov, M. N. Pushkin and Goldoni. (In Russian). In: Pushkin i ego sovremenniki, 38-39, 1930.
Busnelli, M. D. Stendhal traducteur de

Goldoni. Annales de l'U. de Grenoble, 1926.
Chasles, P. D'un théâtre espagnol-vénitien au XVIIIe siècle et de Charles **GOZZI**. In: Etudes. Paris, 1847.
Koester, A. Gozzi in Deutschland. In: Schiller als Dramaturg. Berlin, 1891.
Rusack, H. H. Gozzi in Germany: A Survey of the Rise and Decline of the Gozzi Vogue in Germany and Austria. New York, 1930.
Wildberg, B. Gozzi und die moderne Bühne. Vossische Zt., 15.VI.1909.
Dahmen, H. E. T. A. Hoffman und Carlo Gozzi. Hochland, 26, 1929.
Gugenheim, S. A propos de Ch, Nodier et de C. Gozzi. Milano, 1916.
Horn, F. Ueber Carlo Gozzis dramatische Poesie, insbesondere über dessen Turandot und Schillers Bearbeitung derselben. Penig, 1804.
Graban, C. The Bugbears. Komödie aus der Zeit vor Shakespeare (und **GRAZZINIS** La Spiritata). 9rchiv, 1897-98.
Krebs. The Earliest French Version of **GUARINIS** Pastor Fido. Academy, 21. I.1882.
Olschki, L. G. B. Guarinis Pastor fido in Deutschland. Leipzig, 1909.
Rossi, G. C. Censori portoghesi del Pastor Fido. Conv., 13, 1941.
Waldberg, F. von. Einfluss Guarinis auf die Schäferpoesie. In: Renaissance-Lyrik. Berlin, 1888.
Beall, C. B. Kenelm Digby's Thuscan Virgil. MLN, 57, 1942.
Kastner, L. E. Desportes et Guarini. RHLF, 17, 1910.
Friebe, K. Ueber C. Hofman von Hofmanswaldau und die Umarbeitung seines Getreuen Schäfers. Greifswald, 1886.
Lievsay, J. L. Notes on The Art of Conversation. (**GUAZZO**). Ital., 17, 1940.
—— Robert Greene, Master of Arts, and Mayster Steeven Guazzo. SPh, 36, 1939.
—— A Suggested New Source for Sebastian Mey's Fabulario. RR, 30, 1939-40.
Draper, J. W. Shakespeare and the Conversazione. Ital., 23, 1946.
Anderson, M. L. Webster's Debt to Guazzo. SPh, 36, 1939.
Michéa, R. **GUERAZZI** vu par un critique allemand. REI, 1936.
Counson, A. L. **GUICHARDIN** et la Belgique. Festschrift R. Rénier. Torino, 1912.
Graillot, H. François Guichardin dans le midi de la France et en Espagne. Annales du Midi, 1933.
Luciani, V. Fr. Guicciardini and his European Reputation. New York, 1936.
—— Il Guicciardini e la Spagna. PMLA, 56, 1941.
Mele, E. & Alonso Cortés, N. Apuntes bibliograficos sobre las traducciones de Guicciardini en España. Valladolid, 1931.
Orsini, N. I ricordi del Guicciardini nell' Inghilterra elisabettiana. In: Studii sul Rinascimento italiano in Inghilterra. Firenze, 1937.
Luciani, V. Bacon and Guicciardini. PMLA, 62, 1947.
Fellheimer, Jeannette. Barnabe Barnes' Use of Geoffrey Fenton's Historie of Guicciardin. MLN, 57, 1942.
—— Geoffrey Fenton's History of Guicciardin and Holinshed's Chronicles of 1587. MLQ, 6, 1945.
Gottfried, R. B. Geoffrey Fenton's Historie of Guicciardin. Bloomington (Ind.), 1940.
Beall, C. B. Un écho de **GUINICELLI** dans Philippe Desportes. MLN, 57, 1942.
Mascetta-Caracci, L. Shakespeare e i classici italiani a proposito di un sonetto di Guido Guinizelli. Lanciano, 1902. Cf. GSLI, 42.
Monnot, R. **LEONARD DE VINCI** traduit par Péladan. Dante, March, 1934.
Brunelli, B. Il giudizio di Voltaire intorno ad una tragedia italiana. (**LIVIERA**). Rivista ital. del dramma, 2, 1938.
Weiss, R. Henry Wotton and Orazio **LOMBARDELLI**. RES, 19.
Rossi, L. Un precursore di Montesquieu: Scipione **MAFFEI**. Milano, 1941.
Trotter, Margret G. Harington's Sources. (**MALATESTA**). TLS, 30.XII.1944.
Briard, E. Le poète Munzio **MANFREDI** et Dorothée de Lorraine, duchesse de Brunswick. Journ. de la Soc. d'archéol. lorraine, Nancy, 38, 1889.
Mustard, W. P. The Eclogues of B. **MANTUANUS** (cf. Introduction). Baltimore, 1911.
Rossi, G. C. **MARIA PIA DI SAVOIA** nei poeti portoghesi. Romana, 5, 1941.
Chasles, P. Le **MARINO** en France et en Italie. In: Etudes. Paris, 1847.
Neri, F. Il Marino e i poeti francesi. GSLI, 111, 1938.
Nunziante, F. Il Cavalier Marino alla corte di Luigi XIII. NAnt, 1887.
Picco, F. Il Cavalier Marino. Roma, 1928.
Zamboni, G. B. H. Brockes (and Marino). ARIV, 90, 1932.
Croce, B. Ricordi personali del Chapelain sul Marino. Crit., 20.VII.1931.

Picco, F. Chapelain e Marino. Fanfulla della Domenica, 28.
Thomas, L. P. Etude sur Gongora et le gongorisme, considérés dans leurs rapports avec le marinisme. Mém. Acad. Roy. Belgique. Bruxelles, 1911.
Geibel, H. Der Einfluss Marinos auf Christian Hofmann von Hofmannswaldau. Giessen, 1938.
Panarese, L. Lope de Vega e Giambattista Marino. Maglie, 1935.
Finney, G. L. Comus, Dramma per Musica. (Milton). SPh, 37, 1940.
Adam, A. Le Prince déguisé de Scudéry et l'Adone de Marini. Rev. d'hist. de la Philosophie (Lille), 1937.
Fucilla, J. G. G. B. Marino and the Conde de Villamediana. RR, 32, 1940-41.
Lograsso, Angeline H. Poe's Piero **MARONCELLI**. PMLA, 58, 1943.
Gillet, J. E. A Note on the Lazarillo de Tormes. **(MASUCCIO)**. MLN, 1940.
Croce, G. **MAZZINI** e la Polonia. Iridion, 1, 1945.
Gay, H. N. Mazzini e A. Gallenga, apostoli dell'indipendenza italiana in Inghilterra. NAnt, 16.VII.1928.
Jaszay, M. Mazzini et les peuples danubiens. Rev. d'histoire comparée, 5, 1947.
Menghini, M. Mazzini et Madame d'Agoult. Imola, 1915.
Nencioni, E. Mazzini, Carlyle e Swinburne. Fanfulla della Domenica, 13.IV. 1884.
Rip van Winkle. Mazzini e la Signora Carlyle. Gazetta letteraria, artistica e scientifica, 29.VIII.1885.
Rostenberg, Leona. Mazzini to Margaret Fuller, 1847-49. AHR, 47, 1941.
Giusti, W. A. J. Herzen e i suoi rapporti con Mazzini e l'Italia. L'Europa orientale, 11-12, 1935 .
Anon. Mazzini, George Sand und der Papst. Europa, 1848.
Cioranescu, A. Theatrul lui **METASTASIO** in Romania. Studii Italiene. (Bucarest), 1934.
Coester, A. Influences of the Lyric Drama of Metastasio on the Spanish Romantic Movement. HR, 1938.
Fucilla, J. G. Metastasio's Lyrics in Eighteenth Century Spain and the Octavilla Italiana. MLQ, 1, 1940.
Guiet, R. La tragédie française au XVIIIe siècle et le théâtre de Métastase. PMLA, 53, 1938.
Ortiz, R. Pietro Metastasio, il settecento rumeno, e i poeti Vacaresti. Boll. della R. U. di Perugia, 19.IX.1931.
Santi, L. de. La Partenza de Métastase (en France). Mém. de l'Acad. de Toulouse, 12e sér., 6, 1928.
Stoudemire, S. A. Metastasio in Spain (1736-78). HR, 9, 1940-41.
Zambra, A. Metastasio and Hungary. (In Hungarian). EPhK, 1919.
Litto, V. del. Stendhal, Métastase et Sismondi. Ausonia, 1, 1936.
Gelosi, G. Wielands Verhältnis zu Metastasio. Archiv, 152, 1927.
Gilbert, C. **MICHAEL ANGELO'S** Poetry in English Verse. Ital., 24, 1947.
Hofmiller, J. Deutsche Uebersetzungen von Michelangelos Gedichten. Allg. Zt., 16, 1910.
Calendini, P. Lazare de Baif et Michel-Ange. Annales Fléchoises, La Flèche, 1, 1903.
Mazzoni, G. Un sonetto di Michelangelo tradotto da Emerson. Marzocco, 25.X. 1931.
Gilbert, C. On Longfellow's Translation of a Michael Angelo Sonnet. PhQ, 27, 1948.
Goggio, E. The Sources of Longfellow's Michel Angelo. RR, 1935.
Furst, N. Rilke's Translations of English, French and Italian Sonnets. SPh, 39, 1942.
Wocke, H. Rilkes Michelangelo-Uebertragungen. GRM, 9-10, 1936.
Beckford, W. Michel-Ange en rapport avec Shakespeare. Londres, 1802.
Curry, K. Uncollected Translations of Michelangelo by Wordsworth and Southey. RES, 1938.
Evans, B. I. An Unacknowledged Sonnet by Wordsworth. TLS, 12.III.1938.
Gilbert, A. H. The Prosperous Wittol in Giovanni Battista **MODIO** and Thomas Middleton. SPh, 41, 1944.
Menghini, M. **MONTI**, Sherlock e Zacchiroli. NAnt, 1895.
Rossetti, W. M. Browning's Sordello. **MURATORI** and Browning. Browning Soc. Papers, 3, 1891.
Bianchi, L. Eichendorffs Ezzelin von Romano und **MUSSATOS** Ecerinide. ZDPh, 66, 1939.
Françon, M. **NAVAGERO** et Ronsard. Italica, 25, 1948.
Zanella, G. Relazioni poetiche tra l'Italia e la Spagna nel secolo XVI: G. Boscán ed Andrea Navagero. NAnt, 1883.
Tillman, B. Leibniz' Verhältnis zu **NIZOLIUS**. Bonn, 1910.
Hanford, J. Milton and **OCHINO**. MLN, 1921.
Pellegrini, F. Mme. de Maintenon ed uno scrittore italiano del seicento. **(PAIOLI)**. Civiltà moderna, 15.IV.1930.

Porena, M. La prima traduzione inglese del Giorno del **PARINI**. NAnt, 1930.
Grimaldi, V. André Chénier et Giuseppe Parini. Rassegna Nazionale, 112, 1900.
Rizzi, F. Un passo del Parini e un episodio del Dickens. Rivista d. Letture, 1937.
Lo Gatto, E. Puskin e Parini. In: Puskin Gedenkschrift. Roma, 1937.
Fiumi, L. La fortuna del **PASCOLI** in Francia. Tempo nostro, Dec., 1934.
Arullani, V. A. G. C. **PASSERONI** in Germania. RI, 1909.
Battistini, M. La fortuna del **PELLICO** in Belgio. Rassegna storica del Risorgimento, 1933.
Bédarida, H. La fortune des Prisons de Silvio Pellico en France (1832-1932). RLC, 12-13, 1932-33.
Frati, C. Una rarissima traduzione inglese delle Mie Prigioni e dei Doveri dell' Uomo di Silvio Pellico. La Bibliofilia, 1924.
Pannella, A. Il Confanolieri in America e la fortuna delle Mie Prigioni. Pegaso, 1932.
Sprietsma, C. Douze lettres inédites de Silvio Pellico; introduction aux études italiennes en Bourgogne de 1821 à 1847. RLC, 16, 1936.
Mazzoni, G. Le Mie Prigioni del Pellico e Picciola del Saintine. Marzocco, 24.I. 1932.
Noyes, G. R. Slowacki i Silvio Pellico. Sprawozdania z czynnosci i posiedzen Polskiej Akademiji Uniejçtnosci, 32, 1927.
Vianey, J. Marcello **PHILOXENO** et Melin de Sainct-Gelays. BI, 4.
Rouault, J. Une recontre spirituelle de Joachim du Bellay avec **PIC DE LA MIRANDOLE** et Saint Thomas More. Eurydice, 1938-39.
Paparelli, G. Il De Curialium Miseriis di Enea Silvio **PICCOLOMINI** e il Misaulus di Ulrico von Hutten. Humanitas, 1947.
Alley, J. N. French Periodical Criticism of **PIRANDELLO'S** Plays. Ital., 25, 1948.
La Vecchia Musti, M. La diffusione dell' opera pirandelliana all'estero. Romana, 1939.
Masvidal, A. B. La dramatica de Shaw y Pirandello. In: Estudios de literatura. La Habana, 1940.
Piellat. Première traduction française des épitres d'Ange **POLITIEN** par un chanoine de Saint-Paul de Lyon en 1682. Revue du Lyonnais, 3e sér., 12, 1871.
Rasupe, M. Il Poliziano in Lettonia. Rinascita, 2, 1939.
Allodoli, E. Poliziano e Johnson. Rinascita, 5, 1942.
Busson, H. L'influence du De incantatianibus de P. **POMPONAZZI** sur la pensée française. RLC, 9, 1929.
Ferri, L. Pomponazzi e gli scettici della Rinascenza. NAnt, 133, 1894.
Gordon, D. L. Middleton's No Wit, No Help Like a Woman's and della **PORTA'S** La Sorella. RES, 17.
Neri, R. Il Lorenzino di G. **ROVERE** e Une nuit à Florence di A. Dumas père. Pagine Istriane, 8, 1910.
Roy, E. Les premiers cercles du XVIIe siècle. Mathurin Régnier et Guidobaldo Bonarelli della Rovere. RHLF, 4, 1897.
Neri, F. Il De **SANCTIS** e la critica francese. GSLI, 79.
Rossi, J. I critici inglesi e americani del De Sanctis. Ital., 1938.
Rossi, G. C. Il **SANNAZARO** in Portogallo. Romana, 7, 1943.
Torraca, F. Gl' imitatori stranieri di J. Sannazaro. Roma, 1882.
Fucilla, J. G. Bernardo de Balbuena's Siglo de Oro and its Sources. HR, 15, 1947.
Sainati. Jacopo Sannazaro e Joachim Du Bellay. Pisa, 1915.
Ruutz-Rees, C. C. Fontaine's Fontaine d'Amour and Sannazaro. MLN, 1912.
Fucilla, J. G. Sannazaro's Arcadia and Galvez de Montalvo's El Pastor de Filida. MLN, 57, 1942.
Serra, L. Sannazaro e Garcilaso. Convivium, N. S., 1948.
Mele, E. Lope de Vega e due epigrammi del Sannazaro. GSLI, 113, 1939.
Berdan, J. M. Migration of a Sonnet (Sannazaro, Saint-Gelais, Wyatt). MLN, 23, 1908.
Genouy, H. L'Arcadia de Sidney dans ses rapports avec l'Arcadia de Sannazaro et la Diana de Montemayor. Paris, 1928.
Dunlop, G. A. The Sources of the Idyls of Jean Vauquelin de la Fresnay. MPh, 12, 1914-15.
Vaganay, H. & Vianey, J. Un modèle de Desportes non signalé encore: Pamphilo **SASSO**. RHLF, 1903.
Bataillon, M. Sur la diffusion des oeuvres de **SAVONAROLE** en Espagne et en Portugal. Mélanges Joseph Vianey. Paris, 1934.
—— De Savonarole à Louis de Grenade. RLC, 16, 1936.
Teichmann, A. Savonarola in der deutschen Dichtung. Berlin, 1937.

Wendeler, M. Lindner als Uebersetzer Savonarolas. ALG, 7, 1878.

Swift, B. A Note on Savonarola and Rabelais. Athenaeum, 3719, 1899.

Bataillon, M. Une source de Gil Vicente et de Montemayor: La Méditation de Savonarole sur le Miserere. Bull. des Etudes Portugaises, 3, 1936.

Gillet, J. E. Was **SECCHI'S** Gl' Inganni Performed before Philip of Spain? MLN, 1920.

Pratt, R. A. Chaucer's Shipman's Tale and **SERCAMBI**. MLN, 55, 1940.

Bruce, Dorothy H. The Merry Wives and Two Brethren. (**STRAPAROLA**). SPh, 39.

Gargano, G. S. Una problematica fonte shakespeariana: Le piacevoli notti di F. Straparola. Marzocco, 1927.

Jannet, P. Imitations de Straparole. Paris, 1857.

Prato, S. Una novellina popolare italiana nello Straparola e nel Des Périers. Archivio per lo studio delle Tradizioni populari, 6, 1887.

Hutton, J. Germain Colin Bucher and the **STROZZI**. MLN, 58, 1943.

Ortiz, R. Per la fortuna in Ispagna e in Rumenia di un motivo madrigalesco italiano. In: Varia Romanica. Firenze, 1932.

Fucilla, J. G. On the Vogue of **TANSILLO'S** Lagrime di San Pietro in Spain and Portugal. Rinascita, 2, 1939.

—— A (Spanish) Ms Imitation of Tansillo's Lagrime di San Pietro. PMLA, 53, 1938.

Bini, E. Di un poemetto giovanile di François de Malherbe. Pisa, 1903.

Thurston, H. Tansillo and Southwell. The Month, Sept., 1905.

Hall, R. A. A Possible Italian Model for Don Quixote. (Bernardo **TASSO**). Ital., 24, 1947.

Tatlock, J. Bernardo Tasso and Sidney. Ital., 12, 1937.

Schiffer, E. **TASSONI** in Frankreich. Berlin, 1915. Cf. Archiv, 1916.

Zimmer, H. J. Friedrich Wilhelm Zacharia und sein Renommist. (Tassoni). Leipzig, 1892.

Todesco, V. Marco da Lisbona traduttore da **TODI**? La Rassegna, 1935.

Plattard, J. Une source des Tragiques: le Pimandre de Mercure **TRISMEGISTE**. Mélanges Laumonier. Paris, 1935.

Dargan, E. P. **TRISSINO**, a Possible Source for the Pléiade. MPh, 1916.

Allen, D. C. John Donne and Pierio **VALERIANO**. MLN, 58.

Lafoscade, L. De G. Sand à Musset. (**VARCHI**). RLC, 7, 1927.

Wilkins, E. H. **VELLUTELLO'S** Map of Vaucluse and the Carte de Tendre. MPh, 1932.

Gallo, U. Un **VERGA** peruviano: Enrique Lopez Albujar. NAnt, 1945.

Soto, R. A. Un olvidado precursor del modernismo francés. N. A. della Rocca de **VERGALO**. New York, 1928.

Gemelli, F. A. La posizione di G. B. **VICO** nella storia del pensiero. Münster, 1935.

Hall, R. A. G. B. Vico and Linguistic Theory. Ital., 18, 1941.

Hazard, P. La pensée de Vico. Son influence sur la pensée française. RCC, 1931-32.

Papu, E. Vico in cultura românească. Studii italiene, 2, 1935.

Varia. Opinioni e giudizi di alcuni illustri italiani e stranieri sull' opera di G. B. Vico. Napoli, 1863.

Chaix-Ruy, J. Un disciple hétérodoxe de J. B. Vico: Nicolas Boulanger. RLC, 21, 1947.

Fisch, M. H. The Coleridges, Dr. Prati, and Vico. MPh, 41, 1943.

Auerbach, E. Vico und Herder. DVLG, 10, 1932.

Clark, R. T. Herder, Cesarotti and Vico. SPh, 44, 1947.

Gemmingen, O. von. Vico, Hamann und Herder. Diss. München. Borna, 1919.

Gianturco, E. Critical Reflections on Karl Joel's Appraisal of Vico. Ital., 17, 1940.

—— Joseph de Maistre and Giambattista Vico. Columbia U. P., 1937.

Clarke, Margaret I. Rimbaud, Michelet, Vico. MLR, 37, 1942.

Donati, B. Notes sur Vico. Souvenirs d'une lecture dans les archives de Michelet. NRI, 25.III.1922.

Estève, E. Vico, Michelet et Vigny. Revue Univers., 1919.

Nicolini, F. Rapporti ideali tra il Vico e il Rousseau. Aretusa, 1, 1944.

Fériaud, T. Solution d'une énigme littéraire: le sonnet d'Arvers est-il traduit de l'italien? (**ZANELLA**). Grande Revue latine, Feb., 1911.

Rotondi, G. Il Corrado di G. Zanella e il Ventiquattro Febbraio di Z. Werner. Athenaeum, 1920.

Toffanin, G. Zanella e Longfellow. RI, 1920.

CHAPTER SIXTEEN

The Italian Language.

Damiani, E. La fortuna della lingua italiana in Bulgaria. Firenze, 1939.
Gabrieli, F. La lingua italiana in Levante. NAnt, 1946.
Gáldi, L. Italianismi diretti e italianismi indiretti in rumeno. Lingua nostra, 2, 1940.
Kahane, H. & R. Turkish Nautical Terms of Italian Origin. Journal American Oriental Society, 62, 1942.
Kastner, J. Le passé et l'avenir des études italiennes en Hongrie. Revue des Etudes hongroises, 3, 1925.
Marraro, H. R. The Teaching of Italian in America in the Eighteenth Century. MLJ, 25, 1940.
Massarani, T. Gli studi italiani in Francia. In: Studi di letteratura e d'arte. Firenze, 1899.
Oehmann, E. Der italienische Einfluss auf die deutsche Sprache bis zum Ausgang des Mittelalters. Annales Acad. Scientiarum Fennicae. Helsinki, 1942-44.
Terlingen, J. H. Los italianismos en español desde la formación del idioma hasta principios del siglo XVII. Amsterdam, 1943.

CHAPTER SEVENTEEN

Italian Influences upon Individual Authors.

Segré, C. Il viaggio dell'ADDISON in Italia. NAnt. 1 & 16.III.1930.
Camillucci, M. Vasile ALECSANDRI e l'Italia. NAnt, 161, 1940.
Marcu, A. V. Alecsandri e l'Italia. Roma, 1929.
Avalle, A. Mateo ALEMAN en Italia. RFH, 6, 1944.
Rotunda, D. P. Guzman de Alfarache and Italian Novellistica. RR, 24, 1933.
Stensgård, E. H. C. ANDERSON i Italien. Milano, 1935.
Flamini, F. Di alcune inosservate imitazioni italiane nei poeti francesi del cinquecento (De BAIF, Passerat). Atti del Congresso di Scienze storiche, 1903. Roma, 1904.
Ingraham, E. S. The Sources of les Amours de Baif. Diss. U. of Pennsylvania, 1903.
Trencsenyi-Waldapfel, G. Le fonti italiane della poesia di BALASSI. Studi italo-ungheresi della R. Acc. d'Ungheria di Roma, 2, 1937.
David, H. BALZAC italianisant: autour de Sarrasine. RLC, 13, 1933.
Pisani, M. L'Italia nella Comédie humaine. Napoli, 1927.
Prior, H. Portrait de Balzac. Balzac et ses amis d'Italie. Milano, 1920.
—— Balzac à Milan, 1837. RP, 1925.
—— Balzac à Venise. RdF, 1.XII.1927.
Marcu, A. Simeon BARNUTIU, Al. Papiu Ilarian et Josif Hodos. (In Rumanian). Bucarest, 1935.
Melia, J. Venise et Maurice BARRES. Figaro litt., 7.XI.1925.
Pensa, M. BJOERNSON e l'Italia. SG, 5, 1941.
Ancona, A. d'. Madama du BOCCAGE in Italia. Fanfulla della Domenica, 1882.
Donati, L. BODMER und die italianische Litteratur. Denkschrift Bodmer. Zürich, 1900.
Chiarini, M. Un adversaire de l'influence italienne en France: Nicolas BOILEAU Despréaux. Imola, 1911.
Maugain, G. Boileau et l'Italie. Paris, 1912.
Canchie, M. Le voyage de BOIS-ROBERT en Italie. In: Documents pour servir à l'histoire littéraire du XVIIe siècle. Paris, 1924.
Gargano, S. G. Bois-Robert e il suo viaggio in Italia. Marzocco, 26.X.1924.
Warnock, R. BOSWELL and Wilkes in Italy. ELH, 1936.
—— Boswell and Some Italian Literati. Interchange, 1, 1940.
Marcheix. Sur le voyage en Italie de BOUCHARD en 1634. Société d'Etudes italiennes, 1896.
Barrière, P. Gabriel BOUQUIER: notes sur un voyage en Italie (1776-80). RHLF, 1932.
Dubois, J. BOURSAULT et la comédie italienne. Mém. de la Soc. acad. de l'Aube, 67, 1903.
Ruffini, M. L'influenza italiana in Valacchia nel epoca di Constantin-Voda BRANCOVEANU. Milano, 1933.
Cipolla, C. Il viaggio letterario del card. de BRIENNE in Italia (1789-90). Nuovo Archivio Veneto, 24, 1912.
Auvray, L. En marge des Lettres sur l'Italie du Président de BROSSES. EI, 1932.
Bézard, Yvonne. Comment le Président de Brosses a écrit ses Lettres d'Italie. EI, 1922.
—— Les Lettres du Président de Brosses à Ch.-C. Loppin de Géméaux, publiées

pour la première fois avec une introduction et des notes. Paris, 1929.

Leoni, G. D. Come il Presidente De Brosses ha scritto le sue Lettres d'Italie. Archiginnasio, Sept., 1928.

Michéa, R. Le Président de Brosses en Italie. RLC, 14, 1934.

Socio, G. de. Le Président de Brosses et l'Italie. Paris, 1923.

Baccetti, N. Andrea del Sarto nella poesia di **BROWNING**. Il Boccadoro, 28. II.1933.

—— Filippo Lippi nella poesia del Browning. Il Boccadoro, 18.II.1934.

Benedetti, A. de. Impressioni d'Italia nella poesia di R. Browning. NAnt, 1930.

Clarke, H. A. Browning's Italy: A Study of Italian Life and Art in Browning. New York, 1907.

Hogreve, P. Browning and Italian Art and Artists. Kansas U. Bulletin, 1914.

Nencioni, E. R. Browning e l'Italia. NAnt, 109, 1890.

Raymond, W. O. Browning's First Mention of the Documentary Sources of The Ring and the Book. MLN, 1928.

Minckwitz, M. J. Zu dem Casa guidi Windows, dem Dichtstück der E. B. Browning. Anglia, 50, 1926.

Pratesi, L. L'Italianità nei Canti di Elisabetta Barrett Browning. Rocca San Casciano, 1928.

Moreau, P. Notes sur F. **BRUNETIERE** et l'Italie. Rassegna di studi francesi, 1928.

Majut, R. **BUECHNER** und das italienische Theater. In: Studien um Büchner. Berlin, 1932.

Christ, Salome. Jacob **BURCKHARDT** und die Poesie der Italiener. Basel, 1940.

Guarnieri, R. Burckhardt in Italia. Rinascita, 1, 1938.

Ricci, C. **BURNEY**, Casanova e Farinelli a Bologna. Milano, 1890.

Anon. **BYRON** and Shelley at Ravenna. Athenaeum, 3474, 1894.

—— Byron in Venice. Academy, 28.VII. 1900.

Boutet de Manvel, R. Lord Byron en Italie. Rev. de la Semaine, 30.XII.1921.

Cattolica, B. della. L'Italia e Byron. L'Eroica, Dec., 1938.

Foresi, M. Italianità di G. Byron. Rass. nazionale, April, 1924.

Koelbing, E. Byron und Dupatys Lettres sur l'Italie. ESn, 1892.

Krause, F. Byrons Marino Faliero. Progr. Breslau, 1897 & 1898.

Leitgeb, O. von. Zu Byrons venetianischem Aufenthalt. Beilage zur Allg. Zt., 262, 1893.

Lorenzo, G. de. L'Italia di Byron e di Schopenhauer. In: Oriente ed Occidente. Bari, 1931.

Lüder, A. Lord Byrons Urtheile über Italien und seine Bewohner, ihre Sprache, Literatur und Kunst. Progr. Dresden, 1893. Cf. Anglia, 15 & ESn, 18.

Maurois, A. Lord Byron en Italie. Alsace française, 8.IV.1939.

Meneghetti, N. Lord Byron à Venise. Venezia, 1911.

Messinese, G. Byron and Italy. Tripoli, 1937.

Panella, J. Byron in Romagna. La Romagna, 1, 1904.

Poujoulat. Le séjour de Lord Byron à Pise. 1839.

Quennell, P. Byron in Italy. London, 1941.

Rava, L. Lord Byron e P. B. Shelley a Ravenna e Teresa Guiccioli Gamba. Roma, 1929.

Ross, M. Byron at Pisa. NC, 1901.

Sencourt, R. Byron and Shelley in Venice. QR, 1947.

Strahan, J. A. Byron in Italy. ER, 1922.

Tribolati, P. Lord Byron a Pisa. NAnt, 26, 1874.

Vitelli, A. Byron e l'Italia. Le Lettere, 30.IV.1920.

Wiel, T. Lord Byron e il suo soggiorno a Venezia. Ateneo Veneto, 28.

Zacchetti, C. Lord Byron e l'Italia. Palermo, 1920.

Farinelli, A. Il **CAMOES** e i poeti d'Italia. In: Nuovi saggi e nuove memorie. Torino, 1941.

Tueselmann, O. Eine Studienreise nach Italien im Jahre 1562. Nach Briefen des Johann **CASELIUS**. Nordhausen, 1896.

Mazzi, C. Il conte di **CAYLUS** a Siena (1714). Siena, 1896.

Mele, E. Di alcuni versi di poeti italiani nel Don Quijote. (**CERVANTES**). RCLI, 5, 1901.

Speziale, A. Il Cervantes e le imitazioni della novellistica italiana. Messina, 1914.

Picco, F. Appunti intorno alla cultura italiana in Francia nel secolo XVII: Jean **CHAPELAIN**. Festschrift Guido Mazzoni. Firenze, 1907.

Stiefel, A. L. George **CHAPMAN** und das italienische Drama. JbShG, 1899.

Bédarida, H. Le monument de **CHATEAUBRIAND** à Rome. EI, 1935.

Bordeaux, H. Chateaubriand à Rome. RP, 15.III.1928.

Bowen, B. L. The Place of Chateaubriand as a Critic of Italian Literature. Festschrift Marshall Elliott. Baltimore, 1911.
Dollot, R. En marge de l'Itinéraire: Chateaubriand à Venise et à Trieste (1806). Le Correspondant, 10.XI.1929.
Durry, M. J. Chateaubriand ambassadeur à Rome. RHLF, 1925-26.
Faure, G. Voyage en Italie précédé d'une étude sur les six voyages de Chateaubriand en Italie. Grenoble, 1921.
—— Chauteaubriand à Rome. Figaro, 7.V. 1932.
Gallettier, E. Chateaubriand à Pompei. (1804). Annales de Bretagne, 41, 1934.
Lancellotti, A. Chateaubriand in Italia. Cultura moderna, 1935.
Lejeune, R. Chateaubriand en Italie. Rev. crit. des idées et des livres, 1922.
Monti, G. Un grande innamorato dell'Italia: Chateaubriand. Emporium, 1935.
Trompeo, P. P. Ritorno a Roma di Chateaubriand. NAnt, 16.XII.1934.
Axon, W. E. A. Italian Influence on **CHAUCER**. In: Chaucer Memorial Lectures. London, 1900.
Bellezza, P. Introduzione allo studio dei fonti italiani di G. Chaucer. Milano, 1895.
Fluegel, E. & Hinckley, H. B. Chaucer in Italy. Nation, 63, 1896.
Kissner, A. Chaucer in seinen Beziehungen zur italienischen Litteratur. Diss. Marburg, 1867.
Koch, J. Chaucers italienische Periode. ESn, 27, 1900.
Kuhl, E. P. Why Was Chaucer Sent to Milan in 1378? MLN, 62, 1947.
Marley, J. M. Chaucer's Mission to Lombardy. MLN, 1934.
Mather, F. J. Chaucer's First Italian Journey. Nation, 63, 1896.
—— An Inedited Document Concerning Chaucer's First Italian Journey. MLN, 11, 1896.
Palgrave, T. Chaucer and the Italian Renaissance. NC, 1888.
Pollard, A. W. Date of Chaucer's Italian Period. Academy, 3.IX.1892.
Scott, Mary A. Chaucer in Italy. Nation, 63, 1896.
Tatlock, J. S. P. The Duration of Chaucer's Visit to Italy. JEGPh, 12, 1913.
Montera, P. de. A. **CHENIER** et l'Italie. NRI, 1921.
—— Quelques jugements d'André Chénier sur la littérature italienne. NRI, 1922.
Olivero, F. **COLERIDGE** e la letteratura italiana. In: Studi su poeti e prosatori inglesi. Torino, 1925.
Pergoli, B. **CONDILLAC** in Italia. Faenza, 1903.
Goggio, E. The Italy of James Fenimore **COOPER**. MLJ, 29, 1945.
Searles, C. **CORNEILLE** and the Italian Doctrinaires. MPh, 1915.
Gentile, G. V. **COUSIN** e l'Italia. Rassegna bibliografica della lett. italiana, 6, 1898.
Carle, N. Un ami grenoblois de l'Italie: souvenirs sur J. de **CROZALS**. Ausonia, Jan., 1936.
Kastner, L. E. The Italian Sources of **DANIEL'S** Delia. MLR, 7, 1912.
Rolland de Villarceaux, H. La comédie italienne et **DEBUREAU**. Revue moderne, 1.VII.1845.
Varia. Ch. **DEJOB** et l'Italie. Rassegna di studi francesi, 1931.
Isopescu, C. Lo scrittore rumeno Aron **DENSUSIANU** e l'Italia. Napoli, 1936.
Bartol, L. Antoni **DESCHAMPS** e l'Italia. Roma, 1913.
Beaufils, E. Antoni Deschamps en Italie. Revue du Berry et du Centre, 1935 & REI, 1938.
Anon. Recontres des Muses de France et d'Italie. **(DESPORTES)**. RHLF, 1906.
Busnelli, V. **DIDEROT** et l'Italie. Paris, 1925. Cf. Revue critique, 1.XI.1926.
Lovat-Fraser, J. A. With **DISRAELI** in Italy (1826). Contemp. Review, 1930.
Addamiano, N. Quelques sources italiennes de la Deffence de J. **DU BELLAY**. RLC, 3, 1923.
Menasci, G. Un poeta francese del secolo XVI a Roma. Fanfulla della Domenica, 22, 1900.
Merrill, R. V. Du Bellay's Olive LXII and the Rime diverse. MLN, 60, 1945.
Moulié, C. Joachim du Bellay à Rome: les amours de Faustine. Rev. crit. idées et livres, 25.VIII.1920.
Pompeati, A. La giovinezza di du Bellay e l'Italia. Marzocco, 22.I.1922.
Vaganay, H. Joachim du Bellay et les rime diversi di molti eccellentissimi autori. RHLF, 1901.
Vianey, J. Les Antiquitez de Rome, leurs sources latines et italiennes. BI, 1901.
—— Les sources italiennes de l'Olive de Du Bellay. Annales internat. d'histoire. Paris, Macon, 1901. Cf. GSLI, 39, 1902.
Croce, B. Al. **DUMAS** a Napoli nei primi anni della nuova Italia. Crit., 1926.
Dubray, M. Al. Dumas e le Impressioni di Viaggio in Italia. Cultura moderna, 1928.
Bianchi, L. Italien in **EICHENDORFFS** Dichtung. Bologna, 1937.

Goggio, E. **EMERSON'S** Interest in Italy and Italian Literature. Ital., 17, 1940.
Galdi, L. La culture italienne chez Michel **EMINESCU**. Dante, Dec., 1936.
Cantimori, D. Note su **ERASMO** e l'Italia. SG, 1, 1936.
Nolhac, P. de. Erasme et l'Italie, RDM, 1888.
—— Erasme en Italie. Paris, 1888 & 1925.
Kuhnke, A. Ch. **ESTIENNES** Les Abusés und ihre Quelle Gl'Ingannati nebst Beiträgen zur Stellung der letzteren in der Weltliteratur. Diss. Breslau, 1912.
Tracconaglia, G. Contributo allo studio dell'italianismo in Francia: H. Estienne. Lodi, 1907.
Espiner-Scott, Janet, G. Claude **FAUCHET** et l'Italie. H&R, 6, 1939.
Barbiera, R. G. **FAURE** e l'Italia. Libri del giorno, Sept., 1925.
Cannaro, F. L'Italia nei libri di Gabriel Faure. RI, 31.XII.1917.
Chevalier, A. L'Italie de G. Faure. Rassegna di studi francesi, 1928.
Navarra, T. G. Faure e le sue Ore d'Italia. Ibid.
Sapori, F. L'Italia nell' opera di Gabriel Faure. NAnt, 1.IV.1917.
Telin, R. Inspirations italiennes d'un écrivain français. Idea latina, Oct., 1918.
Terrin, C. L'Italie dans l'oeuvre de Gabriel Faure. MF, 15.VII.1938.
Anon. Claude **FAURIEL** in Italia. NAnt, 50, 1880.
Negri, L. Riflessi italiani nelle novelle di A. **FERNANDEZ DE AVELLANEDA**. GSLI, 113, 1939.
Faure, G. L'Italie de **FLAUBERT**. In: Pèlerinages passionés. Paris, 1919.
Jeffery, V. M. Italian Influences in **FLETCHER'S** Faithful Shepherdess. MLR, 1926.
Rua, G. Di alcune fonti italiane di un vecchio libro francese. (Jeanne **FLORE**) Bibl. d. scuole ital. Verona, 5, 1892.
Maugain, G. **FONTENELLE** et l'Italie. RLC, 3, 1923.
Bédarida, M. H. Anatole **FRANCE** et l'Italie. RCC, 1926.
Parisi, P. Pellegrinaggi napoletani di A. France. La Lettera, 1927.
Petraccone, G. Anatole France e l'Italia. Il Lavoro d'Italia, 10.VIII.1927.
Flamini, F. Le lettere italiane alla corte di **FRANCESCO** I, re di Francia. In: Studi di storia letteraria. Livorno, 1895.
Ancona, A. d'. **FREDERICO IL GRANDE** e gli Italiani. NAnt, 1904.
Rostenberg, Leona. Margaret **FULLER'S** Roman Diary. Journal of Mod. History, 12, 1940.
Croce, B. Intorno al soggiorno di **GARCILASSO DE LA VEGA** in Italia. Rassegna stor. napol. di lettere ed arti, 1894.
Flamini, F. Imitazioni italiane in Garcilasso de la Vega. La Bibl. d. scuole ital., 1.VII.1899.
Frattoni, O. Influssi prepetrarcheschi nei sonetti di Garcilaso. Italica, 25, 1948.
Bédarida, H. Impressions d'art dans le Voyage en Italie de Th. **GAUTIER**. Rev. de l'U. de Lyon, 1933.
—— Th. Gautier et l'Italie. Paris, 1934.
Capograssi, A. L'espulsione di T. Gautier dal regno di Napoli. NAnt, 1930.
Matulka, B. Th. Gautier et l'Italie. RR, 26, 1936.
Angeli, D. Il viaggio di Madama di **GENLIS**. Marzocco, 27.X.1929.
Rosenfeld, E. Visioni d'Italia nella poesia di Stefan **GEORGE**. Conv., 11, 1939.
Longaker, J. M. The Della Cruscans and William **GIFFORD**. Diss. U. of Pennsylvania, 1924.
Bellezza, P. G. **GLADSTONE** ed i suoi studi di letteratura italiana. Firenze, 1895.
Zumbini, B. W. E. Gladstone nelle sue relazioni con l'Italia. NAnt, 16.VI.1910.
Anon. Il soggiorno veneziano di Giovanni Gaspare **GOETHE**. Marzocco, 17.VII. 1932.
Farinelli, A. Il padre di Goethe in Italia. NAnt, 16.III.1932.
Pompeati, A. Il viaggio in Italia del padre di Goethe. Marzocco, 1.V.1932.
Alfero, G. A. Goethe e la Sicilia. NAnt, 1928.
Angeli, D. Come Goethe vide l'Italia. Illustr. ital., 1932.
Barzellotti. W. Goethe in Italia. Giorn. d'Italia, 24.VI.1903.
Bertrand, J. J. A. Sur les pas de Goethe en Italie. RG, 23, 1927.
Blok, P. J. Goethe in Rome. Oonze Eeuw, Oct., 1906.
Bottachiari, R. Un maestro italiano di Goethe e il suo biografo. Il Mattino, 11.XII.1937.
Bottazzi, L. Il viaggio in Italia di Goethe. Corr. della Sera, 22.III.1932.
Brandeis, A. Auf Goethes Spuren von Verona bis Rom. Chronik des Wiener Goethe-Vereins, 16, 1902-03.
Buriot-Darsiles, H. Une renommée injustifiée: le Voyage en Italie de Goethe. EI, 1932.
Carletta. Gli amori romani di Goethe. Riv. moderna, 2, 1902.

Carlo, E. di. Goethe a Messina. Perugia, 1933.
—— Goethe a Palermo. Palermo, 1934.
Cart, T. Goethe en Italie. Neuchâtel, 1881.
Contarino, G. Goethe und die sizilianische Mundartdichtung. GRM, 30, 1942.
Croce, B. Wolfango Goethe a Napoli. GSLI, 1903.
—— Una poesiola giovanile del Goethe e il suo probabile originale in un canto popolare italiano. Aretusa, 1, 1944.
Dowden, E. Goethe in Italy. Fortnightly Review, 1888.
Duentzer, H. Goethes Tagebücher und Briefe aus Italien. Die Gegenwart, 1882.
Farinelli, A. Goethe e il Lago Maggiore. Bellinzona, 1894.
—— Goethe und Rom. JbGG, 18, 1932.
—— Goethe und Italien. In: Neue Reden und Aufsätze. Pisa, 1937.
Faure, G. Goethe et Heine en Italie. In: Pèlerinages passionnés. Paris, 1919.
—— Avec Goethe à Padoue. In: Les rendez-vous italiens. Paris, 1932.
Fucilla, G. Goethe in Italia. Leonardo, 13, 1942.
Gentile, G. Goethe in Italien. Berliner Tageblatt, 22.III.1932.
Gerstenberg, K. Goethe und die italienische Landschaft. DVLG, 1. 1923.
Gnoli, D. W. Goethe a Roma. NAnt, 28, 1875.
Graevenitz, G. Goethe unser Reisebegleiter in Italien. Berlin, 1904.
—— Italien in Goethes Leben vor der italienischen Reise. Tägl. Rundschau, 199-202, 1907.
Grimm, H. Goethe in Italien. Berlin, 1861.
Gubernatis, A. de. Goethe und Italien. Deutsche Revue, 1903.
Haarhaus, J. R. Auf Goethes Spuren in Italien. Leipzig, 1897.
Hérenger, A. Goethe en Italie. RDM, 1930 & Paris, 1931.
Herford, C. H. Goethe's Italian Journey. In: Taylorian Lectures. Oxford, 1900.
Hirzel, L. Goethes italienische Reise. Basel, 1871.
Imperatori, G. Giudizi Goethiani su scrittori d'Italia. Via dell'Impero (Pisa), Dec., 1934.
—— Goethe e gli scrittori d'Italia. Udine, 1937.
Kampmann, W. Goethes Kunsttheorie nach der italienischen Reise. JbGG, 15, 1929.
Locella, G. Goethe in Italien. Berichte d. freien deutschen Hochstifts Frankfurt, 7, 1891.
Löwenthal. Goethe, fils d'Italie. Revue mondiale, 1923.
Macan, R. W. Goethe in Rome. Fortnightly Rev., 101, 1914.
Meyer, K. Goethe und seine italienische Reise. Hamburg, 1886.
Meyer, R. M. Goethe in Venedig. Die Nation, 24.VII.1897.
—— Goethes italienische Dramen. JbGG, 26, 1905.
Michéa, R. Le Voyage en Italie de Goethe devant l'opinion européenne. EI, 1933 & Paris, 1945.
Neugass, F. Goethe et l'Italie. RB, 19. III.1932.
Occella, I. Una canzonetta italiana ed una imitazione del Goethe. Torino, 1902.
Prang, H. Goethe als Benützer von italienischen Reiseführern. Goethe Vierteljahrsschrift, 1936.
—— Goethe und die Kunst der italienischen Renaissance. Berlin, 1938.
Riese, J. Goethes italienische Reise. Progr., 1893.
Schneegans, A. Goethe in Messina. Die Gegenwart, 1881.
Schrenck, E. von. Wie hat Italien auf Goethe gewirkt? PJb, 1900.
Schulz, O. T. Goethe und Rom. Bielefeld, 1926.
Viëtor, K. Goethe in Italien. GR, 7, 1932.
Vogel, J. Aus Goethes römischen Tagen. Leipzig, 1905.
—— Goethe in Venedig. Leipzig, 1924.
Wauer, G. A. Die Redaktion von Goethes Italienischer Reise. Leipzig, 1904.
Wickhoff, F. Goethes Briefe aus Italien. Grenzboten, 1887.
Zanella, G. W. Goethe a Vicenza (1786). Vicenza, 1863.
Zaniboni, E. Il Goethe nell'Umbria. Augusta Peruvia, 1, 1906.
Zumbini, B. Per Wolfango Goethe (e la letteratura italiana). Napoli, 1903. Cf. LE, 5.
Wickersham-Crawford, J. P. Italian Sources of **GONGORA'S** Poetry. RR, 20, 1929.
Calvi, B. Alojz **GRADNIT** e la letteratura italiana. Convivium, 1947.
Roe, F. C. Le voyage de **GRAY** et Walpole en Italie. RLC, 6, 1926.
Wolff, S. L. Robert **GREENE** and the Italian Renaissance. ESn, 37, 1907.
San Lazzaro, C. L'Italia nei Wanderjahre del **GREGOROVIUS**. Conv., 6, 1935.
Michéa, R. Quelques détails inédits sur le voyage en Italie de **GREUZE** et de Gougenot. EI, 1934.
Rossi, G. C. L'epica italiana in Germania

nelle traduzioni del romantico **GRIES.** Conv., 13, 1941.

Picot, E. P. **GRINGOIRE** et les comédiens italiens. Paris, 1878. Cf. Romania, 1878.

Santa, G. dalla. Il viaggio di **GUSTAVO** III re di Svezia negli stati veneti. Venezia, 1902.

Rosenberg, Csse W. de. Du séjour des comtes du Nord à Venise. (Gustav III). Paris, 1782.

Hutton, J. Michel **GUY DE TOURS.** Some Sources and Literary Methods. MLN, 58, 1943.

Pearson, N. H. **HAWTHORNE'S** French and Italian Notebooks. Diss. Yale U., 1941.

Bédarida, H. L'Italie dans la vie et dans l'oeuvre de Paul **HAZARD.** RLC, 20, 1946.

HAZLITT, W. Notes on a Journey through France and Italy. London, 1826.

Bottacchiari, R. **HEINE** e l'Italia. Cult., 1929.

Schanz, G. Enrico Heine in Italia. Como, 1868.

Amoretti, G. V. Wilhelm **HEINSE** e il suo Ardinghello. Bologna, 1932.

Brecht, W. Heinse und der ästhetische Immoralismus. Zur Geschichte der italienischen Renaissance in Deutschland. Berlin, 1911.

Sulger-Gebing, E. Heinses Beiträge zu Wielands Teutschem Merkur in ihren Beziehungen zur italienischen Litteratur und zur bildenden Kunst. ZVL, 12, 1899.

Zippel, A. W. Heinse und Italien. Jena, 1930.

Praz, M. **HEMINGWAY** in Italy. Partisan Review, 15, 1948.

Nolhac, P. de & Solerti, A. Le roi **HENRI** III et l'influence italienne en France. GSLI, 17.

—— Il viaggio in Italia di Enrico III re di Francia e le feste a Venezia. Torino, 1890. Cf. GSLI, 1891.

Anon. **HERDER** in Italien. Europa, 17, 1860.

Necco, G. Herder e la letteratura italiana. Romana, 6, 1942.

Zehender, F. Herders italienische Reise. Progr. Zürich, 1882.

Bertaux, A. L'ode de **HERRERA,** La Soledad. BH, 1932.

Carriere, M. **HEYSE** und die italienische Poesie. Gegenwart, 1889.

Fester, R. P. Heyse und Italien. DR, 1910.

Fischer, P. D. Italienische Novellisten in deutscher Uebersetzung, herausgegeben von Paul Heyse. MLIA, 1878.

—— Paul Heyses italienische Dichter. DR, 1890.

Anon. **HOWELLS:** Modern Italian Poets. AM, 1888.

Damiani, E. Echi italiani nell'opera di Kiril **HRISTOV.** NAnt, 1945.

Carli, A. de. L'Italia nell'opera di V. **HUGO.** Torino, 1930.

Crump, P. Victor Hugo's Italian Plays. FQ, 1922.

Franchetti, A. V. Hugo e il melodramma italiano. Marzocco, 26.II.1902.

Grant, E. M. Victor Hugo, Vesuvius and Etna. Northampton (Mass.), 1930.

Roberti, G. Victor Hugo e l'Italia. Scuola e Cultura, 1936.

Valente, M. Victor Hugo e la lirica italiana. Torino, 1907.

Vorluni, G. Victor Hugo et l'Italie. L'Européen, 1902.

Fischer, Erika. Leigh **HUNT** und die italienische Literatur. Diss. Freiburg, 1936.

Bull, F. Le premier séjour à Rome d'**IBSEN** et de Björnson. RLC, 1929.

Goggio, E. Washington **IRVING** in Italy. RR, 1930.

Anon. J. **IWASZKIEWICZ** e l'Italia. RLM, 2, 1947.

—— J. **JANIN** e il suo viaggio in Italia. Marzocco, 1.IV.1926.

Berveiller, M. Influencias italianas en las comedias de Ben **JONSON.** Filosofía y Letras. (México), 1942.

Gilbert, A. H. The Italian Names in Every Man Out of his Humour. SPh, 44, 1947.

Praz, M. L'Italia di Ben Jonson. Riv. ital. del Dramma, 1937.

Allodoli, E. John **KEATS** e l'Italia. Nuova Rassegna bibl. lett. mod., 1904.

Benedetti Anna. Correnti italiane nella poesia di G. Keats. NAnt, 210, 1921.

Olivero, J. John Keats et la littérature italienne. Studi di filologia moderna, 1908-09.

Wright, L. B. Will **KEMP** and the Commedia dell' arte. MLN, 1926.

Mutterer, M. L'attrait de Rome pour un fils de Charlotte, August **KESTNER.** RLC, 12, 1932.

Gubernatis, A. de. **KRASZEWSKI** a Firenze. NAnt, 38, 1878.

Picco, F. La culture italienne de Louise **LABE.** NRI, 25.IV.1922.

Paris, G. La source italienne de la Courtisane amoureuse de **LA FONTAINE.** Festschrift A. d'Ancona. Firenze, 1901.

Toldo, P. Fonti e propaggini italiane delle favole del La Fontaine. GSLI, 59, 1912.

Allais, G. **LAMARTINE** en Toscane et

les harmonies poétiques et religieuses. Paris, 1908.
Benedetto, L. F. La ritrattazione di Lamartine sull'Italia. La Rassegna, 1921.
Cenzatti, G. Alfonso de Lamartine e l'Italia. Livorno, 1903.
Dejob, C. Lamartine, Chateaubriand et l'Italie. In: Vita italiana nel Risorgimento, 3. Firenze, 1899.
Farges, L. Lamartine à Florence (1826-28). RP, 1.VIII.1900.
Gentili di Giuseppe, F. Lamartine, de Jussieu et l'Italie. Dante, 1933.
Guillemin, H. Lamartine, Byron et Mme. Guiccioli. RLC, 19, 1939.
Hazard, P. Les Alpes ou Vallombrosa. Festschrift G. A. Cesareo. Palermo, 1924.
Jannone, G. Il duello Pope-Lamartine. Terni, 1912.
Mazzanti, M. Pelegrinaggi livornesi di A. de Lamartine. Liburni Civitas, 6, 1933.
Mengin, U. Lamartine à Naples et à Ischia. RLC, 4, 1924.
Ortensi, M. Lamartine le poète et l'Italie. Città di Castello, 1910.
Pitollet, C. Lamartine: deux témoignages anglais sur son séjour à Florence. RLC, 5, 1925.
Pirazzini, A. The Influence of Italy on the Literary Career of A. de Lamartine. Diss. Columbia U. 1918.
Benedetto, L. F. Due recapiti fiorentini del **LAMENNAIS.** Marzocco, 31.V.1931.
Robertson, J. G. Sources italiennes des paradoxes dramatiques de **LA MOTTE.** RLC, 3, 1923.
Toldo, P. Quelques sources italiennes du théâtre comique de Houdart de la Motte. BI, 1, 1901.
Elkin, F. Walter Savage **LANDOR'S** Studies of Italian Life and Literature. Diss. Philadelphia, 1934.
Fornelli, G. W. S. Landor e l'Italia. Forli, 1931.
Schuyler, E. Landor and Italy; Dickens and Genoa. In: National Influences. London, 1901.
Linati, C. **LAWRENCE** e l'Italia. Pegaso, April, 1933.
Baym, M. I. A Neglected Translator of Italian Poetry: Emma **LAZARUS.** Ital., 21.
Maddalena, E. **LESSING** e l'Italia. Atti del Congresso internaz. di Scienze storiche, 4. Roma, 1904.
Muncker, F. Eine Hauptquelle für Lessings Tagebuch seiner italienischen Reise. Festschrift H. Paul. Strassburg, 1902.
Vanni, A. Lessing e l'Italia. Venezia, 1923.
Kastner, L. E. Thomas **LODGE** as an Imitator of the Italian Poets. MLR, 1907.
Walker, A. Italian Sources of Lyrics of Th. Lodge. MLR, 1927.
Adkins, N. F. **LONGFELLOW** and the Italian Risorgimento. PMLA, 1933.
Gargàno, G. S. Longfellow e l'Italia. Marzocco, 23.IX.1928.
Giovanni, Margaret di. The Italian Friends of Longfellow. Ital., 17, 1940.
Goggio, E. Italian Influences on Longfellow's Works. RR, 1925.
Iannetta, S. H. W. Longfellow and Montecassino. Boston, 1940.
Tosi, J. Longfellow e l'Italia. Bologna, 1906.
Weidlich, E. Longfellow e l'Italia. Marzocco, 1923.
Stiefel, A. L. **LOPE DE RUEDA** und das italienische Lustspiel. ZRPh, 15, 1891.
Villela de Chasca, E. Lope de Rueda's Comedia de los Engañados. Chicago, 1941.
Arjona, J. H. La introducción del gracioso en el teatro de **LOPE DE VEGA.** HR, 7, 1939.
Levi, E. Lope de Vega e l'Italia. Firenze, 1935.
Place, E. B. Does Lope de Vega's Gracioso Stem in Part from Harlequin? Hisp., 1934.
Nolhac, P. de. Pierre **LOTI** et les Italiens. Pegasus, 5.III.1931.
Lucas, M. Two Englishwomen in Rome 1871-1900 (Anne & Mathilda **LUCAS**). London, 1938.
Hausrath. Martin **LUTHERS** Romfahrt. Berlin, 1894.
Bond, R. W. Note on Italian Influences in **LYLY'S** Plays. In: Complete Works of John Lyly. Oxford, 1902.
Boughner, D. C. The Background of Lyly's Tophas. PMLA, 54, 1939.
Jefferey, V. M. John Lyly and the Italian Renaissance. Paris, 1928.
Torretta, L. L'Italofobia di John Lyly e i rapporti dell'Euphues col Rinascimento italiano. GSLI, 1934.
Mignon, M. L'italianisme de **MARGUERITE DE NAVARRE.** In: Les affinités intellectuelles de l'Italie et de la France. Paris, 1921.
Pellegrini, C. Riflessi di cultura italiana in Margherita di Navarra. In: Tradizione italiana e cultura europea. Messina, 1947.
Luporini, M. La comédie de **MARIVAUX.** Lucques, 1921.
Bertoni, G. Clement **MAROT** à Ferrare. REI, 1946.

Lenoir, V. M. Une critique d'art et l'Italie: Camille **MAUCLAIR**. EI, 1925.
Post, C. R. The Sources of Juan de **MENA**. RR, 3, 1913.
Chuquet, A. **MERIMEE** et l'Italie de 1859. Revue hebdomadaire, 2.X.1920.
Casella, M. I Somni di Bernat **METGE** e i primi influssi italiani sulla letteratura catalana. AR, 1919.
Kalischer, E. **MEYER** in seinem Verhältnis zur italienischen Renaissance. Berlin, 1907.
Monod, G. **MICHELET** et l'Italie. RI, 1903.
Sorani, A. Michelet in Italia. Marzocco, 24.II.1924.
Alladoli, E. H. Giovanni **MILTON** e l'Italia. Prato, 1907.
Egle, A. Milton und Italien. Freiburg, 1940.
Ferrando, G. Milton in Toscana. Illustrazione italiana, 1924.
Ferrara Mirenzi, L. Milton a Roma. "Roma", 1930.
Finney, G. L. Comus, dramma per mucica. SPh, 37, 1940.
Fumio Ochi. Milton in Florence (in Japanese). In: Studies in Engl. Liter. Tokyo, 1940.
Glaesener, H. Le voyage de Milton en Italie: Prélude au Paradis Perdu. RLC, 16, 1936.
Hanford, J. H. A Milton Handbook. (Cf. Appendix). New York, 1946.
Liljegren, S. B. Miltons italienische Reise. Anglia, 1938.
Mari, A. Un precursore siciliano di G. Milton. Atti e Rendiconti dell' Accad. Dafnica di Acireale, 9, 1903.
Martin, J. Milton en Italie. BI, 1910.
Praz, M. Milton e Poussin alla scuola dell' Italia. Romana, 2, 1938.
Schmidt, I. Miltons Jugendjahre und Jugendwerke. Sammlung gemeinverständlicher Vorträge. Hamburg, 1896.
Zicari da Paola, F. Sulla scoperta dell' originale italiano da cui Milton trasse il suo Poema del Paradiso Perduto. Napoli, 1844.
Anon. **MIRABEAU** e i giardini del Renascimento italiano. NAnt, 16.XI.1919.
Arnavon, J. Les influences italiennes dans l'oeuvre de **MOLIERE**. NRI, 1922.
Corsi, M. Scaramuccia, maestro di Molière. Riv. ital. del dramma, 15.VII.1939.
Gillet, J. E. A Possible New Source for Molière's Tartuffe. MLN, 1930.
Joung, M. V. Molières Stegreifkomödien, insbesondere Le médecin volant. ZFSL, 22, 1900.
Kugel, A. Untersuchungen zu Molière's Médecin malgré lui und seine Hauptquellen. Diss. Jena, 1897.
Lanson, G. Molière et la farce. RP, 1.V. 1901.
Levi, C. Molière e il teatro italiano. Marzocco, 15.I.1922.
Marletta, F. La materia dell'Ecole des femmes in un ignota farsa. Rassegna di studi francesi, 1934.
Matic, T. Molières Tartuffe und die italienische Stegreifkomödie. SVL, 1, 1901.
Mère, C. Molière et la Comédie italienne. Nouvelle Revue, 1.IV.1911.
Moland, L. Molière et la comédie italienne. Paris, 1867.
Mortier, A. Un ancêtre italien de Georges Dandin. RLC, 6, 1926.
Toldo, P. A proposito d'una fonte italiana del Tartuffe. GSLI, 23, 1894.
Vitu, A. Molière et les Italiens. Le Molièriste, 1879-80.
Waechter, A. Les sources du Tartuffe de Molière. Progr. Erfurt, 1901.
Wolff, M. J. Italienisches zum Tartuffe. Archiv, 139, 1920.
Refuge, E. de. Deux lettres de **MONGE** relatives à sa mission littéraire et artistique en Italie (1796-97). L'Amat. d'Autogr., 15.IV.1899.
Ancona, A. d'. L'Italia alla fine del secolo XVI: Giornale del viaggio di Michele de **MONTAIGNE** in Italia nel 1580 e 1581. Città di Castello, 1895.
Forkey, L. O. Montaigne's Trip to Italy. FR, 13, 1939.
Hazard, P. A l'Italie que doit Montaigne? Dante, 1933.
Henriot, E. Montaigne en Italie. Bull. des Amis de Montaigne, 2 sér., 8, 1940.
Liber, M. Montaigne à Rome. Revue des Etudes juives, 55, 1908.
Maurel, A. Le voyage de Montaigne en Italie. NRI, 1920.
Montecorboli, H. Montaigne en Italie. Nouvelle Revue, 60, 1888.
Moreau, P. Le voyage de Montaigne en Italie. Bull. des Amis de Montaigne, 2 sér., 7, 1939.
Neri, F. I saggi del **MONTEGUT** sulla letteratura italiana. Mélanges Vianey. Paris, 1935.
Anon. **MONTESQUIEU** in Italy. LQHR, July, 1899.
Cantù, C. Montesquieu in Italia. NAnt, 138, 1894.
Fabureau, H. Montesquieu à Venise. Dante, 1934.
Nicolini, F. Viaggiatori stranieri a Napoli. Il presidente Montesquieu. In: Napoli nobilissima, 14, 1905.

Flamini. G. **MUELLER** e Roma. Pisa, 1908.
Faure, G. L'Italie de **MUSSET**. Minerve française, 15.VI.1919.
Gaio, A. Musset. Marzocco, 28.IX.1930.
Giraud, J. Musset et l'Histoire littéraire d'Italie de Ginguené. Mélanges Lanson. Paris, 1922.
Lafoscade, L. Le théâtre d'Alfred de Musset. Paris, 1902.
—— La genèse de Lorenzaccio. RDM, 15. XII.1927.
Mignon, M. Musset et l'Italie. In: Etudes de littérature italienne. Paris, 1912.
Moroncini, E. Alfred de Musset e l'Italia. Roma, 1921.
Pommier, L. Le théâtre d'Alfred de Musset. Bull. Fac. des Lettres de Strasbourg, 1934.
Rabizzani, G. L'effimera Italia del Musset. Marzocco, 15, 1910.
Werner, P. Alfred de Musset og Italien. Edda, 26, 1927.
Bianconi, G. Voyageurs mineurs en Italie. (Paul de Musset). Dante, 1936.
Mazzei, P. Contributo allo studio delle fonti italiane del teatro di Torres **NAHARRO**. Lucca, 1922.
Moreau, P. Notes sur Gérard de **NERVAL** et l'Italie. Rassegna di studi francesi, 1931.
Bédarida, H. Italianizante all'estero: P. de **NOLHAC**. Leonardo, Nov., 1925.
Picco, F. Pierre de Nolhac e i sui studi franco-italiani. La Rassegna, 1929.
Rosendorfsky, J. Arne **NOVAK** e l'Italia. L'Europa orientale, 21, 1941.
Donati, L. Giovanni Gasparo degli **ORELLI** e le lettere italiane. Progr. Zürich, 1894.
Young, F. B. The Triumph of Death Translated out of Italian by the Countess of **PEMBROOKE**. PMLA, 1912.
Balderston, Katherine C. (ed.). Thraliana: The Diary of Mrs. Hester Lynch Thrale (Later Mrs. **PIOZZI**), 1776-1809. 2 vols. Oxford U. P., 1942.
Clifford, J. L. Hester Lynch Piozzi (Mrs. Thrale). New York, 1941.
—— Mrs. Piozzi's Letters. Festschrift David Nichol Smith. Oxford, 1945.
Chindemi, S. **PLATEN** e l'Italia. Cimento, 2. (Torino). 1853.
Gentile, A. Platen a Trieste. Indipendente, July, 1900.
Ghezzo-Bellen, D. Augusto Platen in Italia. Bologna, 1907.
Lollis, C. de. Platen in Italia. NAnt, 16.X.1897. And in: Natura ed Arte. Milano, 1899-1900.
Martin, N. Platen et l'Italie. In: Poètes contemporains de l'Allemagne. Paris, 1860.
Mele, E. Platen a Napoli. In: Napoli nobilissima, 5, 1896.
Muscogiuri, F. Augusto Platen in Italia. NAnt, 98, 1888.
Reuter, F. Drei Wanderjahre Platens in Italien, 1826-29. Jahresbericht d. histor. Vereins f. Mittelfranken, 1901.
Sarento, L. Aug. von Platen. Il suo amore per l'Italia e la morte in Siracusa. Studi di filol. moderna, 3, 1910.
Scheffler, L. von. Platens letzte Wanderfahrt in Italien. Allg. Zt., 132-33, 1899.
Schmidt, H. Platen in Rom. ZDU, 6, 1892.
Schulz, H. W. Platen und die Italiener. Morgenblatt, 98-99, 1836.
Setti, G. A. von Platen in Italia. NAnt, March, 1879.
Zardo, A. Platen e Venezia. NAnt, 142, 1895.
Hazard, P. L'Italie de l'abbé **PREVOST**. Mélanges Hauvette. Paris, 1934.
Duranti, F. Un libello di **PROUDHON** contro l'Italia. Quadrinio, 7, 1939.
Lo Gatto, E. **PUSKIN** in Italia. RLC, 17, 1937.
Verkhovskii, I. N. Pushkin and the Italian Language. (In Russian). In: Pushkin i ego sovremenniki, 3, 1910.
Gay, J. Edgar **QUINET** et l'Italie. In: Les deux Romes et l'opinion française. Paris, 1931.
Pellegrini, C. Edgar Quinet e la letteratura italiana. Festschrift F. Flamini. Pisa, 1918.
—— Edgar Quinet et l'Italia. Pisa, 1919.
Sorrento, L. Garibaldi, E. Quinet e l'Italia. Rendiconti del R. Istituto lombardo, 1932.
Tronchon, H. L'Italie dans les Carnets d'Edgar Quinet. Mélanges Hauvette. Paris, 1934.
Heulhard, A. **RABELAIS**, ses voyages en Italie, son exil à Metz. Paris, 1891.
Guerrini, O. Rabelais in Italia. Roma, 1883.
Toldo, P. L'arte italiana nell'opera di Rabelais. Archiv, 1899.
Waille, V. Les voyages de Rabelais à Rome et l'influence que l'art italien de la Renaissance a pu exercer sur lui. Atti del Congresso intern. di scienze storiche, 7. Roma, 1903-04.
Santoro, D. Una canzone popolare del Parzanese e l'Ode alla croce di Giov. **REBOUL**. Studi di filologia mod., 1912.
Chaponnière, P. Les notes de **REGNARD** pour le théâtre italien. RLC, 2, 1922.

Bertrand, L. L'Italie dans l'oeuvre de H. de REGNIER. RDM, 1.VI.1921.
Valeri, D. Henri de Régnier veneziano. NAnt, 1936.
Vianey, J. Mathurin Régnier. Paris, 1896.
Heilig, I. Philipp Joseph von REHFUES. Ein Beitrag zur Entwicklung der geistigen Beziehungen Deutschlands zu Italien Ende des 18. und Anfangs des 19. Jahrhunderts. Breslau, 1941.
Calisse, C. L'Italia e Ernesto RENAN. Pegaso, 8, 1931.
Lefranc, A. Le premier voyage d'Ernest Renan en Italie. RP, 1926.
—— Ernest Renan en Italie. Paris, 1938.
Tronchon, H. Renan et la leçon de l'Italie moderne. Grande Revue, April, 1928.
Genevois, P. Impressions d'Italie dans les poèmes de RENAULD. REI, 1938.
Façon, N. RILKE e l'Italia. In: Saggi di Filologia et Filosofia, 1. Bucarest, 1946.
Wocke, H. Rilke und Italien. Giessen, 1940.
Jones, W. P. The William ROBINSONS in Italy, HLQ, 4, 1941.
Nolhac, P. de. RONSARD et les contemporains italiens. EI, 3, 1921.
Williams, R. C. Italien Influence on Ronsard's Theory of the Epic. MLN, 1920.
Dupré, H. L'Italie dans l'oeuvre artistique et littéraire de D. G. ROSSETTI. BI, 4, 1904.
Simonini, R. C. Rossetti's Poems in Italian. Ital., 25, 1948.
Stiefel, A. L. Unbekannte italienische Quellen Jean ROTROUS. ZFSL Suppl., 5 & Oppeln, 1891 & ZVL, 6, 1893.
Vianey, J. Deux sources inconnues de Rotrou. Arch. hist., art. et litt. Dôle, 1891.
Cérésole, V. J. J. ROUSSEAU à Venise, 1743-44. Notes et documents publiés par Th. de Saussure. Genève, 1885.
Culcas, C. Gl'influssi italiani nell' opera di G. G. Rousseau. Roma, 1907.
Derche, R. Autour du séjour de J. J. Rousseau à Venise. Annales de l'U. de Grenoble, 1, 1924.
Faugère, P. J. J. Rousseau à Venise. Correspond., 1888.
Fulin, R. Partenza di Rousseau da Venezia. Archivio veneto, 1877.
Girardin, S.-M. Du séjour de J. J. Rousseau à Venise. Journal des Débats, 22.I.1862.
Mignon, M. J. J. Rousseau et l'Italie. In: Les affinités intellectuelles de l'Italie et de la France. Paris, 1921.
Mongland, A. Rousseau secrétaire de M. de Montaigu, ambassadeur de France à Venise. Annales J. J. Rousseau, 24, 1938.
Plan, P. P. Jean-Jacques Rousseau à Venise. MF, 1923.
Petrone, A. SÁ DE MIRANDA e l'Italia. Romana, 5, 1941.
Cesano, A. H. SACHS ed i suoi rapporti con la letteratura italiana. Roma, 1904. Cf. Archiv, 1905.
Manacorda, G. Beziehungen Hans Sachsens zur italienischen Literatur. SVL, 6, 1906.
Angeli, D. Il viaggio di SAINTE-BEUVE. (Roma). Marzocco, 11.V.1930.
Faure, G. Sainte-Beuve en Italie. RdF, 1.IV.1921.
—— (ed.). Voyage en Italie de Sainte-Beuve. Paris, 1922.
Oliva, G. Sainte-Beuve e la letteratura italiana. Milano, 1915.
Pellegrini, C. Sainte-Beuve et la littérature italienne. NRI, 15.IV.1920.
Toldo, P. Ce que SCARRON doit aux auteurs d'Italie. Pavia, Roma, 1893.
Bolte, J. Zu den von Christoph von SCHALLENBERG übersetzten italienischen Liedern. Archiv, 92, 1894.
Toldo, P. Due leggende tragiche ed alcuni riscontri col teatro dello SCHILLER. ZRPh, 22, 1898.
Mazzuchetti, L. A. W. SCHLEGEL und die italienische Literatur. Zürich, 1917.
Beer, E. S. de. François SCHOTT'S Itinerario d'Italia (1600). Library, N. S., 23.
Angeli, D. Vignette romane, l'ultimo viaggio di Walter SCOTT. Illustrazione italiana, 1932.
Coleman, A. A Source of Ibrahim ou l'illustre Bassa. (SCUDERY). RR, 1938.
Friedmann, C. La cultura italiana di Madame de SEVIGNE. GSLI, 60, 1912.
Toldo, P. La signora di Sévigné e l'Italia. Festschrift R. Rénier. Torino, 1912.
Anon. SHAKESPEARE and Venice. QR, 1889.
—— Shakespeares inneres Verhältnis zu Italien. Neue Züricher Zt., 479, 1917.
Benedetti, A. La Sicilia nel teatro dello Shakespeare. Archivio storico siciliano, N. S., 45, 1925.
Bennett, M. L. Shakespeare's Much Ado and Its Possible Italian Sources. Texas Studies in English, 17, 1937.
Boas, F. S. Shakspere Italianate. In: Shakspere and his Predecessors. London, 1896.
Boughner, D. C. Don Armado (in Love's Labor's Lost) and the Commedia dell' arte. SPh, 37, 1940.
Campbell, O. J. The Italianate Back-

ground of the Merry Wives of Windsor. In: Essays and Studies in English and Comparative Literature. Ann Arbor, 1932.
Capocci, V. Il dramma shakespeariano e la commedia dell'arte. Quaderni della Critica, 1, 1945.
Conrad, H. War Shakespeare in Italien? National-Zt., 13.II.1900.
—— Shakespeares Twelfth Night (Gli Ingannati). ESn, 46, 1912.
Coote. Shakespeare and Italian Law. Athenaeum, Feb., 1884.
Croce, B. Shakespeare e la commedia napoletana. In: Nuove curiosità storiche. Napoli, 1921.
—— Shakespeare, Napoli e la commedia napoletana dell'arte. In: Nuovi saggi sulla letteratura italiana del seicento. Bari, 1931.
Doccioli, M. Fonti italiane dei drammi di G. Shakespeare. Lodi, 1914.
Draper, J. W. Shakespeare and Florence and the Florentines. Ital., 23, 1946.
—— Shakespeare and the Doge of Venice. JEGPh, 46, 1947.
Elze, T. Shakespeares muthmassliche Reisen. JbShG, 8, 1873.
—— Italienische Skizzen zu Shakespeare. JbShG, 13-15, 1878-80.
—— Venezianische Skizzen zu Shakespeare. München, 1900.
Engel, E. War Shakespeare in Italien? Der Türmer, 1902. And in: Saarbrücker Blätter f. Theater & Kunst, 2, 1923-24.
Farinelli, A. Shakespeares Italien. JbShG, 75, 1939.
—— La visión de Italia en la obra de Shakespeare. La Nación, (Buenos Aires), 9 & 16.VII.1939.
Flamstead Walters, C. Italian Influence on Shakespeare. Gentleman's Mag., Dec., 1895.
Gordon, D. J. Twelfth Night and Gli Ingannati; A Note. Boll. degli studi inglesi in Italia, 7.
Henneberger, Olive P. Proximate Sources for the Italianate Elements in Shakespeare. Diss. U. of Illinois, 1936.
Hutton, J. Analogues of Shakespeare's Sonnets 153-54: Contributions to the History of a Theme. MPh, 38, 1941.
Keller, W. Zu Shakespeares italienischer Reise. JbShG, 35, 1899.
Koenig, W. Ueber die Entlehnungen Shakespeares, insbesondere aus Rabelais und einigen italienischen Dramatikern. JbShG, 9, 1874.
Koeppel, E. War Shakespeare in Italien? JbShG, 35, 1899.
Lawrence, W. J. Shakespeare and the Italian Comedies. TLS, 11.XI.1920.
Lee, S. Shakespeare and the Italian Renaissance. PBA, 1915. And in: Elizabethan and Other Essays. Oxford, 1929.
Levi, A. R. Gli originali di Otello. Nuova rassegna delle lett. moderne, 4, 1906.
Mascetta-Carasci, L. Shakespeare e i classici italiani. Lanciano, 1902.
Morsier, E. de. Shakespeare a-t-il été en Italie? BURS, 1903.
Nemi. E stato Shakespeare in Italia? NAnt, 189, 1903.
Paladino, S. Shakespeare sarebbe pseudonimo di un poeta italiano? Reggio Calabria, 1929.
Rebora, P. La Tempesta di Shakespeare e la commedia popolare italiana. Boll. della R. U. per gli Stranieri di Perugia, 8.VIII.1931.
—— Di alcune fonti italiane di Shakespere. Rinascita, 6, 1943.
Sarrazin, G. Shakespeare in Mantua? JbShG, 29-30, 1894.
—— Neue italienische Skizzen zu Shakespeare. JbShG, 39, 1903.
—— Shakespeare in Mailand? JbShG, 46, 1910.
Segrè, C. Due novelle italiane e Le allegre comari di Windsor. In: Relazioni letterarie fra Italia e Inghilterra. Firenze, 1911.
—— Le fonti italiane dell'Otello. Ibid. And in: NAnt, 223.
—— Shakespeare a Milano? Ibid. And in: Fanfulla della Domenica, 32, 1910.
Sullivan, E. Shakespeare and the Water Ways of North Italy. NC, 1908.
Tarchiani, N. Shakespeare e l'arte italiana. Marzocco, 21, 1916.
Tilley, M. P. Shakespeare and Italian Geography. JEGPh, 16, 1917.
Wokatsch, W. Zur Quelle des Othello und zu Shakespeare's Kenntnis des Italienischen. Archiv, 118.
Wolff, M. J. Shakespeare und die Commedia dell'arte. JbShG, 46, 1910.
Angeli, D. SHELLEY e l'Italia. Giornale d'Italia, 17.XI.1922.
Angeli, H. R. Shelley and his Friends in Italy. London, 1911.
Caldana, G. Giudizi di P. B. Shelley sui poeti italiani. NAnt, 16.VI.1907.
Courten, M. L. de. Shelley e l'Italia. Milano, 1923.
Fontanarosa, V. Gli amori di P. B. Shelley e le due poesie sull'Italia. Napoli, 1897.
Giesen, J. P. B. Shelley als Uebersetzer

aus dem Italienischen. Diss. Freiburg, Bonn, 1910.
Mazzanti, M. Un nostro grande ospite (Shelley in Livorno). Liburni Civitas, 1, 1928.
Olivero, F. P. B. Shelley e il paesaggio italico. NAnt, 1.III.1911.
Raimondi, R. Percy Bysshe Shelley in Italia. Padova, 1920.
Croce, B. Un viaggiatore in Italia nel settecento, apostolo dello Shakespeare. (**SHERLOCK**). Crit., 20.XI.1928.
Schanzer, A. Influssi italiani nella letteratura inglese: Sir Ph. **SIDNEY**. RI 4, 1901.
Stratton, C. The Italian Lyrics of Sidney's Arcadia. Sewanee Review, 1917.
SISMONDI: See also Intermediaries, I. IV. 8.
Alpino, E. Il Sismondi storico della letteratura italiana. Milano, 1944.
Bariola, F. Un amico dell'Italia e degli Italiani, Sismonde de Sismondi. Boll. d. Società Pavese di Storia Patria, 1921.
Pellegrini, C. Il Sismondi e l'Italia. NAnt, 171, 1942.
Anon. **SLAVEIKOV** in Italia. RLM, 2, 1947.
Ferrando, G. Le impressioni italiane di Tobia **SMOLLET**. Marzocco, 15.V.1921.
Brandenburg, J. **SOLOMOS** et l'Italie. Diss. Leiden, 1935.
Praz, M. Robert **SOUTHWELL'S** Saint Peter's Complaint and its Italian Source. MLR, 1924.
Bizzarri, E. L'influenza italiana sugli Amoretti di E. **SPENSER**. Romana, 6, 1942.
Gottfried, R. B. Spenser and the Italian Myth of Locality. SPh, 1937.
Meli, F. **SPINOZA** e due antecedenti italiani dello spinozismo. Firenze, 1934.
Pange, Mme. J. de. Albertine de **STAEL** en Italie, 1815. RLM, 3, 1948.
Aulard, A. Mme. de Staël en Italie. Révolution française, 45, 1903.
Berti, D. La Staël a Roma. In: Scritti vari. Torino, 1892.
Dejob, C. Mme. de Staël et l'Italie. Paris, 1890.
Gennari, G. Le premier voyage de Mme. de Staël en Italie et la genèse de Corinne. Paris, 1948. Cf. Convivium, 1947.
Lanfredini, Dina. Mme. de Staël e i suoi amici italiani. RLM, 1-3, 1946-47.
Marcabruni, M. La connaissance de l'Italie d'après Corinne. Diss. Montpellier, 1910.
Matteucci, I. Mad. de Staël e il suo studio sull'Italia al principio del secolo XIX. Siena, 1900.
Porta, M. T. Mme. de Staël e l'Italia. Firenze, 1910. Cf. GSLI, 56.
Trojandt, Gerda. Das Italienerlebnis bei Frau von Staël und Henri Beyle. Göttingen, 1938.
Bersano-Begey, M. Viaggio in Italia di Stanislao **STASZIC**. Iridion, 1, 1945.
Allodoli, E. La littérature italienne en 1825 selon **STENDHAL**. NRI, 15.XII. 1920.
Arbelet, P. Les origines de la Chartreuse de Parme. RP, 1922.
Barbero, G. L'Italia e l'Italiano dello Stendhal. Marzocco, 16, 1911.
—— Gli originali delle Chroniques italiennes. Casale, 1912.
Barbiera, R. Stendhal in Italia. Illustraz. italiana, 1892.
Benedetto, L. F. Giornale fiorentino dello Stendhal. Pegaso, 1933.
—— I viaggi a Siena del console Beyle. Mélanges Vianey. Paris, 1935.
—— Arrigo Beyle Milanese. Bilancio dello Stendhalismo italiano. Firenze, 1942.
Boppe, R. Stendhal à Rome. Paris, 1946.
Carrère, J. Stendhal à Cività-Vecchia. Le Temps, 24. & 27.VII.1924.
Cavalli, J. Lo Stendhal a Trieste. Il Palvese. (Trieste), 1907.
Cordié, C. Arrigo Beyle Milanese. Leonardo, 1947.
Dollot, R. Stendhal à Venise. RLC, 7, 1927.
—— Les logis de Stendhal à Milan. EI, 1935.
—— Stendhal à la Scala. MF, 1935.
Faure, G. Avec Stendhal à Parme. Le Temps, 16.VI.1928.
Ferlar, K. Stendhals Italien. Kjøbenhavn, 1925.
Giglio, A. Stendhal e la letteratura italiana. Milano, 1921.
Hazard, P. Stendhal et l'Italie. RDM, 1926-27.
—— Stendhal à la Scala. NL, 22.VI.1935.
Jourda, P. Stendhal en Italie. RCC, 1924.
—— Stendhal et la littérature italienne. Mélanges Hauvette. Paris, 1934.
Kühnau, R. Quellen-Untersuchungen zu Stendhal-Beyles Jugendwerken. Marburg, 1908.
Madini, P. Stendhal il Milanese. Illustrazione italiana, 1935.
Martineau, H. Stendhal et la police de Florence, MF, 1933.
Metalli, R. Stendhal console a Trieste. Giornale di politica e di letteratura, 8, 1933.
Nasalli-Rocca, G. Stendhal e Piacenza. Strenna piacentine, 19, 1893.

Novati, F. Stendhal e l'anima italiana. Milano, 1915.
Oppeln-Bronikowski, F. von. Die Quellen zu Stendhals Renaissance-Novellen. ZEFU, 7, 1908.
Osterling, A. Stendhal och Italien. Edda, 4, 1917.
Pellegrini, C. Nota stendhaliena. Gedenkschrift Fr. Flamini. Città di Castello, 1931.
Piroli, E. Se Stendhal fu a Parma e quando. Aurea Parma, 1938.
Serao, M. L'Italia di Stendhal. In: La Vita italiana nel Risorgimento, 3, 1898.
Trompeo, P. P. Nell' Italia romantica sulle orme di Stendhal. Roma, 1924. Cf. Marzocco, 1.VI.1924.
Waldmann, E. Stendhals italienisches Tagebuch. Pan, 2, 1912.
Streckfuss, K. A. F. Karl STRECKFUSSENS früheste Verdeutschung italienischer Dichterwerke. JbDG, 26, 1946.
Eddy, W. A. Gulliver's Travels and Le théâtre italien. (SWIFT). MLN, 1929.
Faggi, A. SWINBURNE e l'Italia. Marzocco, May, 1926.
Renauld, C. A. Ch. Swinburne et l'Italie. NRI.15.X.1920.
Richter, L. Swinburne's Verhältnis zu Frankreich und Italien. Leipzig, 1911.
Luzzatto, G. L. TAINE e la scuola bolognese. L'Archiginnasio, 1935.
Roy, P. N. Italian Influence on the Poetry of TENNYSON. Benares, 1936.
THRALE, H. L.: See H. L. Piozzi, above.
Valli, G. Las fuentes italianas de la patraña IX de TIMONEDA. RFE, 30, 1946.
Mioni, A. B. Italianisti in Boemia: Nina TUCKOVA. L'Europe orientale, 19, 1939.
Koeppel, E. George TURBERVILES Verhältnis zur italienischen Litteratur. Anglia, 13, 1890.
Kawczynski. Ueber das Verhältniss des Lustspiels Les Contents von Odet de TURNEBE zu Les Esbahis von Jacques Grévin und beiden zu den Italienern. Festschrift zum 8. allg. deutschen Neuphilologen-Tag. Wien, 1898.
Longo, T. Luigi UHLAND, con speciale riguardo all' Italia. Firenze, 1908.
Adam, A. La théorie mystique de l'amour dans l'Astrée et ses sources italiennes. (d'URFE). RHPhC, 1936.
Dollot, R. Paul VALERY en Italie. MF, 1.XII.1946.
Simone, F. L'Italianità di Valéry. RLM, 1947.
Dunlop, G. A. The Sources of the Idyls of Jean VAUQUELIN DE LA FRESNAYE. MPh, 12, 1914.
Vianey, J. Les Satyres françoises de Vauquelin de La Fresnaie. Revue des U. du Midi, 1, 1895.
Fourcassié, J. Recherches sur le premier paragraphe du Cor de VIGNY. RU, 1938.
Bertini, G. Influencia de algunos renacentistas italianos en el pensamiento de Francisco de VITORIA. Salamanca, 1933.
Bouvy, E. VOLTAIRE et l'Italie. Paris, 1898.
Cioranescu, A. Tancrède de Voltaire et ses sources épiques. RLC, 19, 1939.
Hazard, P. Voltaire et la pensée philosophique de la Renaissance italienne. Mélanges A. Lefranc. Paris, 1936.
Krappe, A. H. The Source of Voltaire's Zadig. MLR, 1925.
Sirven, P. Voltaire et l'Italie. RB, 1899.
Tribolati, F. Voltaire e l'Italia. Pisa, 1860.
Allason, B. Riccardo VOSS, un romanziere della campagna romana. NAnt, 16.IV.1900.
Thiergartner, H. Der Romanschriftsteller Richard Voss und sein Italienerlebnis. Diss. Frankfurt, 1937.
Parodi, E. G. La nostra letteratura contemporanea e un suo giudice tedesco. (K. VOSSLER). Marzocco, 16.I.1916.
Croce, B. I Quattro Poeti e la edizione fattane in Germania da Adolfo WAGNER. Critica, 39, 1941.
Buriot-Darsiles, H. W. WAIBLINGER en Sicile (1829). Mélanges Hauvette. Paris, 1934.
Hagenmayer, G. W. Waiblingers Gedichte aus Italien. Berlin, 1931.
Thompson, L. S. Wilhelm Waiblinger's Interpretation of Italy. Diss. Chapel Hill (N. C.), 1938.
Carpenter. Thomas WATSON'S Italian Madrigals Englished 1590. JEGPh, 1899.
Olivero, F. La duchessa di Amalfi di John WEBSTER. RI, 15.III.1924.
Beall, C B.. Un Italofilo americano di cent' anni fa: R. H. WILDE. Bergamo, 1939.
Brooks, B. G. WORDSWORTH Reconsidered. NC, 126, 1939.
Shackford, M. H. Wordsworth's Italy. PMLA, 38, 1923.
Bellezza, P. Il primo poeta satirico inglese (Thomas WYATT) e le sue imita-

zioni italiane. Istituto lomb. d. sc. e lettere, 30.
Marchi, L. de. L'influenza della lirica italiana sulla lirica inglese nel secolo XVI, Sir T. Wyatt. NAnt, 1.VII.1895. Cf. GSLI, 27.
Arrighi, P. **ZOLA** à Rome. RLC, 8, 1928.
Jemolo, A. C. L'Italia come Zola la vide. Rassegna d'Italia, 1947.
Ternois, R. Les amitiés romaines d'Emile Zola. RLC, 21, 1947.
Giannini, A. Recuerdos y impresiones italianos in José **ZORRILLA**. In: Amigos de Zorrilla. Valladolid, 1933.

FOURTH PART

Spanish Contributions.

CHAPTER ONE

Generalities.

Ballesteros y Beretta, A. Historia de España y su influencia en la historia universal. 8 vols. Barcelona, 1918-36.
Bertrand, J. J. A. Sur les vieilles routes d'Espagne. Paris, 1931.
Cabal, J. Los Héroes Universales de la literatura española. Barcelona, 1942.
Delattre, J. De invloed van het Spaans en het Portugees op de Westeuropese talen. Brussel, n. d.
Farinelli, A. España y su literatura en el extranjero a través de los siglos. Madrid, 1902.
—— Viajes por España y Portugal desde la edad media hasta el siglo XX. Madrid, 1921.
—— España y su literatura en el extranjero. In: Ensayos y Discursos de critica literaria hispano-europea. Roma, 1925.
—— Consideraciones sobre los carácteres fundamentales de la literatura española. Ibid.
Ferrater Mora, J. España y Europa. Santiago de Chile, 1942.
Ford, J. D. M. The Influence of Spain. JCL, 1903.
Hatzfeld, H. A. El predominio del espíritu español en la literatura europea del siglo XVII. RHF, 3, 1941.
Hübner, R. Spanien im Lichte der Weltlitteratur. DR, 96, 1897.
Juderias, J. La legenda negra. Estudios acerca del concepto de España en el extranjero. Barcelona, 1917.
Lanson, G. Diffusion de la langue et de la littérature espagnoles. RHLF, 1896.
Madariaga, S. de. Le génie de l'Espagne. BURS, 1924.
—— Genius of Spain. Oxford U. P., 1928.
Pérez Goyena, A. Los maestros de teología española en naciones extranjeras. RyF, 1927.
Pfandl, L. Zur Bibliographie der Voyages en Espagne. Archiv, 133, 1915.
Peers, E. A. Literary Pilgrimages in Spain. BSS, 1, 1923.
Peset, V. Lo que debe a España la cultura mundial. Madrid, 1930.
Rubio, D. The Soul of Spain. The Americas, 1, 1945.
Varia. L'Espagne éternelle. NL, 7.I.1939.
Vossler, K. Die Bedeutung der spanischen Kultur für Europa. DVLG, 8, 1930.

CHAPTER TWO

Spanish Influences upon Individual Countries.

1. The Americas.

Arjona, Doris K. et al. Spain and America. New York, 1940.
Barón Castro, R. Españolismo y antiespañolismo en la América Hispana. Madrid, 1945.
Bernstein, H. Las primeras relaciones entre New England y el mundo hispánico, 1700-1815. Rev. Hispanica Moderna, 5, 1939.
Campa, A. L. Spanish Folk-Poetry in New Mexico. Albuquerque, 1946.
Farnham, C. E. American Travellers in Spain. Diss. New York, 1921 & RR, 13, 1922.
Green, O. H. & Leonard, I. A. On the Mexican Booktrade in 1600: A Chapter in Cultural History. HR, 9, 1941.
Hills, E. C. et al. El Español en Méjico, Los Estados Unidos y la América Central. Buenos Aires, 1938.
Jaúregui, J. F. Compendio de la historia de la literatura española y argentina. Buenos Aires, 1941.
Jeschke, H. Die spanische, portugiesische und lateinamerikanische Literatur von 1870 bis zur Gegenwart. Handbuch der Literaturwissenschaft, Romanische Literaturen, 2. Potsdam, 1935.
Levene, R. El Sentido de la Hispanidad a través de los juristas indianos. BSS, 24, 1947.
Onís, F. de. La eternidad de España en América. Memoria del tercer Congreso de Lit. Iberoamer., 1944.
Pitollet, C. Hispanophiles Yankees, RELV, 38.
Portnoy, A. Argentina's Cultural Debt to Spaniards. Nosotros, March, 1939.
Rael, J. B. Cuentos Españoles de Colorado y de Nuevo Méjico. JAFL, 52, 1939.
Reparaz-Ruiz, G. de. Les études hispani-

ques aux Etats-Unis jusqu'en 1939. BH, 47-48, 1945-46.
Ricard, R. La conquête spirituelle du Méxique. Paris, 1933.
Romero-Navarro, M. El hispanismo en Nortc-America. (Irving, Prescott, Ticknor, Longfellow, Lowell, Los Contemporaneos). Madrid, 1917.
Rubio, D. La cultura en la colonias españolas de América. U. Catholica Bolivariana, 8, 1942.
Schevill, R. Menéndez y Pelayo y el estudio de la cultura española en los Estados Unidos. Santander, 1919.
Steck, F. B. Education in Spanish America during the XVIth Century. Washington, 1943.
Torre Revello J. El libro, la imprenta y el periodismo en América durante la dominación española. Buenos Aires, 1940.
Whitman, W. The Spanish Element in Our Nationality. Letter to the Philadelphia Press, 3.VIII.1883.

2. England.

Bahlsen, L. Spanische Quellen der dramatischen Litteratur, besonders Englands zu Shakespeares Zeit. ZVL, 6, 1893.
Biaggi, Z. & Sánchez y Escribano, F. English Translations from the Spanish, 1932-38. Stonington (Conn.), 1939.
Buceta, E. El entusiasmo por España en algunos romanticos ingleses. RFE, 10, 1923.
Crow, J. A. España, pais del ensueño, vista por los romanticos ingleses. Spanish Rev., 1, 1934.
Elder, J. R. Spanish Influence in Scottish History. Glasgow, 1920.
Fischer, R. Spanische Einflüsse. In: Zur Kunstentwicklung der englischen Tragödie. Strassburg, 1893.
Fitzmaurice-Kelly, J. Un hispanofilo inglés del siglo XVII. Homenaje a Menéndez y Pelayo. Madrid, 1899.
Flores, A. Spanish Literature in English Translation: a Bibliographical Syllabus. New York, 1926.
Gayangos y Arche, P. de. Catalogue of the Mss. in the Spanish Language in the British Museum. 4 vols. London, 1875-1893. Cf. ZRPh, 1880.
Grases, P. La trascendencia de la actividad de los escritores españoles e hispano-americanos en Londres, de 1810 a 1830. Caracas, 1943.
Grossman, B. Spanien und das elisabethanische Drama. Diss. Leipzig. Hamburg, 1920.
Hume, M. Spanish Influence on English Literature. London, 1905.
Mathews, E. G. English Translations from Spanish: A Review and a Contribution. JEGPh, 44, 1945.
Moreno-Lacalle, J. Influencias españolas en la literatura inglese. Bul. of the New England Mod. Lang. Assoc., 1922.
Pane, R. U. English Translations from the Spanish, 1484-1943, a Bibliography. New Brunswick (N. J.), 1944.
Peers, E. A. Spanish Studies in England, 1920-27. MLR, 1928.
—— Our Debt to Spain. London, 1938.
Schevill, R. On the Influence of Spanish Literature upon English in the Early XVIIth Century. RF, 20, 1907.
Sturgis, C. The Spanish World in English Fiction: A Bibliography. Boston, 1927.
Thomas, H. Anti-English Propaganda in the Time of Queen Elizabeth: Being the Story of the First British Printing in the Peninsula. New York, 1946.
Umphrey, G. W. Spanish Ballads in English. MLQ, 6, 1945.
Underhill, J. G. Spanish Literature in the England of the Tudors. New York, 1899.
Ward, H. G. A Spanish Legend in English Literature. In: Gaster Anniversary Volume. London, 1936.
Watkins, J. Attention to Spanish Literature Recommended. Gentleman's Mag., June, 1801.

3. France.

Azorin. L'espagnolisme des romantiques français. MF, 16.VI.1917.
Bertaut, J. L'Espagne et les voyageurs français. Le Temps, 10.XI.1932.
Brunetière, F. L'influence de l'Espagne dans la littérature française. RDM, 1891. And in: Etudes critiques sur l'histoire de la littérature. Paris, 1891.
Chasles, P. Etudes sur l'Espagne et sur les influences de la littérature espagnole en France et en Italie. Paris, 1847.
Collier, B. Catalan France. London, 1939.
Demogeot, J. L'Espagne en France. In: Histoire des littératures étrangères considérée dans les rapports avec le développement de la littérature française. Paris, 1884.
Foulché-Delbosc, R. Un voyage en Espagne au début du règne de Charles II. Homenage a Bonilla y San Martin. Universidad Central, 1930.

Gilman, M. Some French Travellers in Spain. Hisp., 13, 1930.
Girard, A. L'Espagne et les lettres françaises. MF, 15.XI.1937.
Hazard, P. Ce que les lettres françaises doivent à l'Espagne. RLC, 16, 1936.
Huszár, G. L'influence de l'Espagne sur le théâtre français des XVIIIe et XIXe siècles. Paris, 1913.
Jourda, P. L'exotisme dans la littérature française depuis le Romantisme: L'Espagne. RCC, 38, 1936-37.
Lanson, G. Etudes sur les rapports de la littérature française et de la littérature espagnole au XVIIe siècle (1600-60). RHLF, 3-4, 1896-97.
Lopez Barrera J. La influencia española en Francia en el siglo XVII. El Instituto, 1, 1928.
Martinenche, E. Le romantisme français et l'Espagne. Hispania, 5. (Paris), 1922.
—— L'Espagne et le romantisme français. Paris, 1922.
Mérimée, E. L'école romantique et l'Espagne au XIXe siècle. Toulouse, 1889.
Michaud, G. L. The Spanish Sources of Certain XVIth Century French Writers. MLN, 1928.
Morel-Fatio, A. Comment la France a connu l'Espagne depuis le moyen âge. In: Etudes sur l'Espagne. Paris, 1888.
—— L'Espagne en France. In: Etudes sur l'Espagne. Paris, 1895.
Pons, J. S. La littérature catalane en Roussillon au XVIIe et au XVIIIe siècle. 2 vols. Toulouse, 1929.
Reparaz-Ruiz, G. de. Hispanism in France. BSS, 23, 1946.
Rogers, P. P. Spanish Influences on the Literature of France. Hisp., 9, 1926.
Sarrailh, J. Voyageurs français au XVIIIe siècle. BH, 1934.
Sas Murias, R. de. España a través de la literatura francesa. Tarragona, 1935.
Serra-Baldó, A. Une version française du sonnet A Cristo crucificado. BH, 47, 1946.
Server, A. W. L'Espagne dans La Revue des Deux Mondes, 1829-48. Paris, 1939.
Texte, J. L'Espagne et la critique française au XVIIIe siècle. RCC, 13.II.1896.
Villemain. Rapport à l'Académie française sur le concours proposé en 1840 (Quelle a été sur la littérature française, au commencement du XVIIe siècle, l'influence de la littérature espagnole?). Moniteur universel, 1.VII. 1842.

4. Germany.

Bertrand, J. J. A. Voyageurs allemands en Espagne. BH, 22, 1920.
—— L'hispanisme allemand. BH, 1935.
Eschweiler, K. Die Philosophie der spanischen Spätscholastik auf den deutschen Universitäten des 17. Jahrhunderts. Münster, 1928.
Farinelli, A. Spanien und die spanische Literatur im Lichte der deutschen Kritik und Poesie. ZVL, 5-8, 1891-94.
Giseke, R. Spanien in deutscher Dichtung. WM, 31, 1872.
Gmelin, H. Die Entdeckung der spanischen Literatur in der deutschen Romantik. Geist der Zeit, 18, 1940.
Hämel, A. The Spanish Movement in Germany. MLJ, 1928.
Lyte, H. O. Spanish Literature and Spain in Some of the Leading German Magazines of the Second Half of the XVIIIth Century. Madison (Wis.), 1932.
—— A Tentative Bibliography of Spanish-German Relations. Privately Mimeographed. Minneapolis, 1936.
Mulertt, W. Los estudios hispanistas en Alemania durante los últimos veinticinco años. Bol. de la Biblioteca Menéndez y Pelayo, 1926.
Petriconi, H. Das Spanienbild im deutschen Bewusstsein. Geist der Zeit, 19, 1941.
Pitollet, C. A propos de l'hispanisme allemand. BH, 1935.
Schneider, A. Spaniens Anteil an der deutschen Literatur des 16. and 17. Jahrhunderts. Strassburg, 1898. Cf. ZVL, 13.
Schneider, R. Spanien und der deutsche Geist. Literatur, 1934.
Schreiber, G. Spanische Motive in der deutschen Volksreligiosität. Münster, 1935.
—— Katalanische Motive in der deutschen Volksfrömmigkeit. Homenatge a Antoni Rubió i Lluch. Barcelona, 1936.
Stricker, W. Die Deutschen in Spanien und Portugal. Leipzig, 1850.
Schulhof, Hilda. Spanische Prosadichtung des Mittelalters in deutscher Uebersetzung. Reichenberg i/B., 1925.
Tiemann, H. Das spanische Schrifttum in Deutschland von der Renaissance bis zur Romantik. Hamburg, 1937.
Vogeler, C. H. Spanisches Volkstum nach älteren deutschen Reisebeschreibungen (1760-1860). Hamburg, 1941.
Woermann, K. Spanisch-deutsche Lyrik. MLIA, 1885.

5. Italy.

Bofarull y Sans, F. de. Alfonso V de Aragón en Napoles. Homenaje a Menéndez y Pelayo. Madrid, 1899.

Conti, C. B. Scelta di poesie castigliane trad. in verso toscano e illustrate. Madrid, 1782.

Croce, B. Appunti sulla letteratura spagnuola in Italia alla fine del secolo XV e nella prima metà del secolo XVI. In: Ricerche ispano-italiane. Atti dell' Accad. Pontiana, 28. Napoli, 1898.

—— Gli Spagnuoli descritti dagli Italiani. Ibid.

—— Lo Spagnuolo nelle commedie italiane. Ibid.

—— La Spagna nella vita italiana durante la Rinascenza. Bari, 1917.

—— Spanish Culture in Italy in the XVIIth Century. Hisp. 10, 1927.

—— Appunti sui costumi e la letteratura spagnuola in Italia. In: Nuovi Saggi sulla letteratura italiana del Seicento. Bari, 1931.

Farinelli, A. Sulle ricerche ispano-italiane di B. Croce. Rassegna bibliogr. della lett. italiana, 7, 1899.

—— Sobre viajos y viajeros par España y Portugal. Madrid, 1903.

—— La Spagna e i romantici d'Italia. NAnt, 1936.

Green, O. The Literary Court of the Conde de Lemos at Naples, 1610-16. HR, 1933.

Lampillas, X. Ensayo historico-apologetico de la literatura española contra las opiniones preocupadas de algunos escritores modernos italianos. Trad. del italiano por Doña J. Amar y Borbon. 2. ed. Madrid, 1789.

Lumsden, A. Spanish Viceroy of Naples in the Sixteenth Century. BSS, 23, 1946.

Marcu, A. La Spagna ed il Portogallo nella visione dei romantici italiani. Roma, 1924.

Mele, E. Due canti spagnuoli nella società ispano-napoletana del Cinquecento. RLM, 2, 1947.

Mierow, C. Some Latin Writers of Spain. CJ, 24, 1929.

Savj-Lopez, P. La lirica spagnuola in Italia nel secolo XV. GSLI, 41, 1903.

Vaganay, H. L'Espagne en Italie. RH, 9-12, 1902-05.

6. Other Countries.

Pérès, H. L'Espagne vue par les voyageurs musulmans de 1610 à 1930. (AFRICA). Alger, Paris, 1937.

Foster, R. H. The Spanish in the Cebuano Vocabulary of the Bible as a Partial Revelation of Spanish Cultural, Political, and Economic Influence in the Philippine Islands. (ASIA). Diss. U. of California, 1948.

Setton, K. M. Catalan Domination of Athens, 1311-88. (GREECE). Cambridge (Mass.), 1948.

Farinelli, A. España y Flandes. (NETHERLANDS). In: Ensayos y Discursos de critica literaria hispano-europea. Roma, 1925.

Peeters-Fontainas, F. J. Bibliographie des impressions espagnoles des Pays-Bas. Anvers, 1933.

—— Livres espagnols imprimés aux Pays-Bas. Louvain, 1939.

Winkel, J. T. De invloed der spansche letterkunde op de nederlandsche in de zeventiende eeuw. Tijdschrift voor nederlandsche taal- en letterkunde. 1, 1881.

Ciesielska-Barkowska, S. Les voyages de Pologne en Espagne et en Portugal au XVe et XVIe siècle. (POLAND). Arch. Neophil., 1934.

Wedkiewicz, S. Les études hispaniques en Pologne. (In Polish). Przegl. Wspolczesny, 1928.

Windakiewicz, S. La littérature espagnole chez les romanciers polonais. (In Polish). Prz., B., 73, 1928.

Ortiz, R. Per la storia dei contatti ispano-rumeni (1710-1932). (RUMANIA). AR, 18, 1935.

Derzhavin, K. El estudio de la literatura española e hispanoamericana en la URSS durante 25 años. (RUSSIA). La Literatura Internacional, 2. (Moscow), 1943.

Acosta, J. M. de. El movimiento hispanofilo en los paeses escandinavos. (SCANDINAVIA). Revista de las Españas, 3, 1928.

Strindberg, A. Spanish-Portuguese Influences in Swedish History. (In Swedish). Samlade Skrifter, 27. Stockholm, 1912-20.

CHAPTER THREE

The Spanish Theatre.

Abraham, J. El drama español en Nueva Orleans. Diss. Loyola U., 1935.

Alart, B. Passage des comédiens du roi d'Espagne à Perpignan (1631). Revue des Soc. Savantes, 6 sér., 3, 1877.

Bonelli, M. L. Una lirica inglese e una commedia spagnola. Convivium, 1947.
Brachfeld, O. Note sur la fortune du théâtre espagnol en Hongrie. BH, 1932.
Croce, B. Comici spagnuoli in Italia nel Seicento. Critica, 38, 1940.
Curzon, H. de. Le Théâtre espagnol et sa visite à Paris. Versailles, 1899.
Doumic, R. Le drame espagnol et notre théâtre classique. RDM, 71, 1901.
Farinelli, A. La Comedia española en Holanda y Alemania. In: Ensayos y Discursos de critica literaria hispanoeuropea. Roma, 1925.
Fournier, E. L'Espagne et ses comédiens en France au XVIIe siècle. Revue des provinces, 15.IX.1864 & RH, 25, 1911.
Hills, E. C. A Catalogue of English Translations of Spanish Plays. RR, 1919.
—— English Translations of Spanish Plays. Hisp., 1920.
Johnson, H. L. Noticias dadas por Tomás Gage, a propósito del Teatro en España, México y Guatemala (1624-37). RIA, 8, 1944.
Knoller, F. Das spanische Drama und die deutsche Bühne. D&V, 1938.
Koberstein, A. Spanische Dramen in Deutschland. In: Geschichte der deutschen Nationallitteratur, 2. Leipzig, 1884.
Lampillas, X. Examen critico apologetico de las preocupaciones de algunos escritores modernos italianos contra el teatro español antiquo y moderno. Zaragoza, 1784.
Leonard, I. A. A Shipment of Comedias to the Spanish Indies. HR, 1934.
Lisoni, A. Gli imitatori del teatro spagnuolo in Italia. Nuova Rassegna, 1894 & Parma, 1895.
Ludwig, A. Spanische Dramen auf der deutschen Bühne in den Jahren 1816-1834. Archiv, 123, 1910.
Martinenche, E. La comédie espagnole en France de Hardy à Racine. Paris, 1901. Cf. RHLF, 1901 & ZFSL, 26, 1904.
Nicholson, F. Spanish Drama on the American Stage, 1900-1938. Hisp., 22, 1939.
Praag, J. A. van. La comedia espagnole aux Pays-Bas au XVIIe et au XVIIIe siècle. Amsterdam, 1922.
Rojas Garcidueñas, J. El teatro de Nueva España en el siglo XVI. México, 1935.
Schack, A. von. Geschichte der dramatischen Literatur und Kunst in Spanien (und Frankreich). Berlin, 1845.
Schlegel, H. El problema de la traducción de los clásicos del teatro español. Ensayos y Estudios, 2, Bonn.
Spell, J. R. Hispanic Contributions to the Early Theater in Philadelphia. HR, 9, 1941.
Stiefel, A. L. Die Nachahmungen spanischer Komödien in England unter den ersten Stuarts. RF, 5 & Archiv, 99, 1897 & 119, 1907.
—— Einfluss des spanischen Dramas auf das anderer Länder. Jahresbericht, 95-96, 1900.
Verde, R. Studi sull' imitazione spagnuola nel teatro italiana del Seicento. Catania, 1912.
Zazel, E. Spanische Dramen auf der deutschen Bühne. In: Zur modernen Dramaturgie. Oldenburg, 1899.

2. Influences upon Individual Authors.

Tenner, F. François le Metel de **BOISROBERT** als Dramatiker und Nachahmer des spanischen Dramas. Diss. Leipzig, 1907.
Bolz, G. Die spanischen Vorbilder P. **CORNEILLES**. Diss. Rostock, 1878.
Brunetière, F. Corneille et le théâtre espagnol. RDM, 1.I.1903.
Hemon, F. Don Sanche d'Aragon: de quoi est faite une comédie héroïque de Corneille. RB, 1.VIII.1896.
Huszár, G. P. Corneille et le théâtre espagnol. Paris, 1903. Cf. JS, 1903.
Michaelis, G. Die sogenannten Comédies espagnoles de Th. Corneille. Berlin, 1915.
Mulertt, W. Die sogenannten Comédies espagnoles des Thomas Corneille, ihr Verhältniss zu den spanischen Vorlagen und ihre eventuellen weiteren Schicksale in den Schriften anderer Nationen. Literaturblätter für german. & roman. Philol., 41, 1920.
Reynier, G. Thomas Corneille (La Comédie espagnole). Paris, 1893.
Segall, J. B. Corneille and the Spanish Drama. New York, 1902.
Farinelli, A. **GOETHES** Aufführungen spanischer Dramen in Weimar. In: Neue Reden und Aufsätze. Stuttgart, 1937.
Carrara, E. Studio sul teatro ispano-veneto di C. **GOZZI**. Cagliari, 1900.
Mahrenholtz, R. Franz **GRILLPARZER** und das spanische Drama. Archiv, 1891.
Wurzbach, W. von. Das spanische Drama am Wiener Hoftheater zur Zeit Grillparzers. JbGrG, 1898.
Dorer, E. Ludwig **HOLBERG** und das spanische Theater. MLIA, 1886.

Levi, E. Il dramma spagnuolo preludio dei Promessi sposi. (MANZONI). Napoli, 1934.
Mahrenholtz, R. MOLIERE in seinem Verhältnisse zur spanischen Komödie. Archiv, 60, 1878.
Sorkin, M. Paul SCARRON'S Adaptations of the Comedia. New York, 1938.
Tiemann, H. Gilles van STAVEREN als Uebersetzer spanischer Comedias. NPh, 18, 1933.
Sacks, Zenia. VERDI and Spanish Romantic Drama. Hisp., 27, 1944.
Lebesgue, P. Lettres portugaises. Influence du théâtre castillan sur Gil VICENTE et Bocage. MF, 1.VII.1937.

CHAPTER FOUR

Spanish Novels and Romances.

1. Generalities.

Berchet, G. Vecchie romanze spagnuole recate in italiano. Brussella, 1837.
Bourne, J. A. Some English Translations of XVIIIth Century Spanish Novels. MLR, 1936.
Buceta, E. Traducciones inglesas de romances en el primer tercio del siglo XIX. Notas acerca de la difusión del hispanismo en la Gran Bretaña y en los Estados Unidos. RH, 62, 1924 & RFE, 1933.
—— Relaciones anglo-hispanas: Apuntes preliminares para un estudio de las traducciones inglesas de romances en el primer tercio del siglo XIX. Festschrift Bonilla y San Martin. Madrid, 1930.
Mendoza, V. T. El romance español y el corrido mexicano. México, 1939.
Krappe, A. H. A Spanish Romancero in English. Hisp., 24, 1941.
Olea, A. de. Sobre traducciones al alemán de novelas españolas modernas. Festgabe Karl Vossler. München, 1932.
Paris, G. Une romance espagnole écrite en France au XVe siècle. Romania, 1, 1872.

2. Amadis de Gaula and Other Romances

Baret, E. De l'Amadis de Gaule et de son influence sur les moeurs et la littérature au XVIe et au XVIIe siècle. Paris, 1853 & 1873.
Foulché-Delbosc, R. La plus ancienne mention d'Amadis. RH, 15, 1906.
Jameson, A. K. Was There a French Original of the Amadis de Gaule? MLR, 1933.
Koeppel, E. The Prince of the Burning Crocone and Palmerin d'Oliva. Archiv, 1898.
Koszul, A. La première traduction d'Arnalte e Lucenda et les débuts de la nouvelle sentimentale en Angleterre. Publications Fac. des Lettres, Strasbourg, Paris, 1946.
Patchell, Mary. The Palmerin Romances in Elizabethan Prose Fiction. Columbia U. P., 1947.
Pfeiffer, M. Amadis-Studien. Mainz, 1905.
Seibt, W. Einfluss des französischen Ritterthums und des Amadis de Gaule auf die deutsche Kultur. Progr. Frankfurt, 1886.
Thomas, H. The Romance of Amadis of Gaul (and its Main Translations). Transactions of the Bibliographical Society, 1911.
—— Spanish and Portuguese Romances of Chivalry. London, 1920.
Vaganay, H. Amadis en français. Florence, 1906.
—— Les romans de chevalerie italiens d'inspiration espagnole. Bibliofilia, 9-11. Firenze, 1908-09.
—— Les traductions françaises de la XIIe partie de l'Amadis espagnol. RH, 72, 1928.

3. La Celestina and Lazarillo de Tormes.

Bertini, G. M. Un Lazarillo de Tormes in italiano inedito. Quaderni Ibero-Americani, 1, 1946.
Fitzmaurice-Kelly, J. Preface to La Celestina (Tudor Translations). London, 1892.
Gillet, J. E. A Note on the Lazarillo de Tormes. MLN, 55, 1940.
Hespelt, E. The First German Translation of Lazarillo de Tormes. HR, 1936.
Laplane, G. Les anciennes traductions françaises de Lazarille de Tormes. Hommage à Ernest Martinenche. Paris, 1939.
Maeztu, R. de. Don Quijote, Don Juan y la Celestina. Buenos Aires, 1938 & 1941.
Marcu, A. Une traduction roumaine du Lazarillo de Tormes. RFE, 24, 1937.
Rosenbach, A. S. W. The Influence of the Celestina in the Early English Drama. JbShG, 1903.

Rösler, M. Beziehungen der Celestina zur Alexiuslegende. ZRPh, 58, 1938.
Sims, E. R. An Italian Translation of Lazarillo de Tormes. HR, 1935.
Sloan, A. S. Juan de Luna's Lazarillo and the French Translation of 1660. MLN, 1921.

4. Picaresque Novels.

Atkinson, W. C. Studies in Literary Decadence: The Picaresque Novel. BSS, 4, 1927.
Bataillon, M. Le roman picaresque. Paris, 1931.
Chandler, F. W. Romances of Roguery: I. The Picaresque Novel in Spain. New York, 1899.
—— The Literature of Roguery. Boston, 1907.
Greifelt, R. Die französischen Uebersetzungen des spanischen Schelmenromans im 17. Jahrhundert. RF, 50, 1936.
Habel, U. Die Nachwirkung des picaresken Romans in England. Breslau, 1930.
Hatfield, T. M. Some German Picaros of the 18th Century. JEGPh, 1932.
Herrero, M. Nuova interpretación de la novela picaresca. RFE, 24, 1937.
Hughes, L. & Scouten, A. H. Some Theatrical Adaptations of a Picaresque Tale. Texas Studies in English, 1945-46.
Payer, R. von. Der Schelmenroman. Unter besonderer Berücksichtigung seiner Verbreitung in Oesterreich-Ungarn. Oesterr.-Ungar. Revue, 1899.
Petriconi, H. Zur Chronologie und Verbreitung des spanischen Schelmenromans. In: Volkstum und Kultur der Romanen, 1. Hamburg, 1928.
Rauhut, F. Influencia de la picaresca española en la literatura alemana. RFH, 1, 1939.
—— Vom Einfluss des spanischen Schelmenromans auf das italienische Schrifttum. RF, 54, 1940.
Rausse, H. Zur Geschichte des spanischen Schelmenromans in Deutschland. Münster, 1908.
Sanvisenti, B. Picaro. BH, 1933.
Schultheiss, A. Der Schelmenroman der Spanier und seine Nachbildungen. Hamburg, 1893.
Storozhenko, N. I. Wozniknovenie realnavo Romana. In: Iz oblasti literatury. Moskva, 1902.
Todesco, V. A proposito di una nuova interpretazione del romanzo picaresco. Convivium, 14, 1942.
Valbuena Prat, L. La novela picaresca española. Madrid, 1942.
Vles, J. Le roman picaresque hollandais des XVIIe et XVIIIe siècles et ses modèles espagnols et français. La Haye, 1926.

5. Influences upon Individual Authors and Translators.

Marcu, A. Contributie la soarta romanului picaresc in literatura romana. Fratilor ALEXANDRI si Ion Lapedatu. Bucarest, 1936.
Magendie, M. A propos du personnage de Figaro (BEAUMARCHAIS). Bull. Fac. des Lettres de Strasbourg, 1936.
Mérimée, H. Le vrai et le faux Figaro. Homenaje Menéndez Pidal. Madrid, 1925.
Toldo, P. Figaro et ses origines. Milan, 1893.
Wharey, J. B. BUNYAN'S Mr. Badman and the Picaresque Novel. Texas Studies in English, 1924.
Lanson, G. Emile DESCHAMPS et le Romancero. RHLF, 15.I.1899.
Bennett, J. St. Bridget, Queen ELIZABETH and Amadis de Gaul. ELH, 10, 1943.
Bloedan, C. A. von. GRIMMELSHAUSEN'S Simplicissimus und seine Vorgänger. Berlin, 1907.
Roguette, O. Ueber den Simplicissimus und seine literarische Familie. WM, 1859.
Ten Brink, J. Nic. HEINSIUS, eene Studie over den hollandschen Schelmenroman in de 17e eeuw. Rotterdam, 1885.
Pfandl, L. Abel HUGO und seine französische Uebersetzung spanischer Romanzen. Normania, 7. (Berlin), 1911.
Baret, E. Mémoires sur l'originalité du Gil Blas de LESAGE. Paris, 1864.
Collmann, O. Gil Blas und die novela picaresca. Archiv, 46, 1870.
Franceson, F. Essai sur l'originalité de Gil Blas. Leipzig, 1857.
Haack, G. Untersuchungen zur Quellenkunde von Lesages Gil Blas de Santillane. Kiel, Erlangen, 1895.
Hugo, V. Revendication de Gil Blas par les Espagnols. In: Victor Hugo raconte, 2.
Lalanne, L. Les origines de Gil Blas. Corresp. litt., 1, 1856-57.
Lintilhac, E. Lesage (et ses sources espagnoles). Paris, 1893.
Lorenti, J. A. Observations critiques sur

le roman de Gil Blas de Santillane. Paris, 1822.
Neufchateau, F. de. Examen de la question de savoir si Lesage est l'auteur de Gil Blas. Académie française, 7.VII. 1818.
Veckenstedt, E. Die Geschichte der Gil Blas-Frage. Braunschweig, 1879.
Houck, Helen. MABBE'S Paganization of the Celestina. PMLA, 54, 1939.
Bowers, F. T. Thomas NASHE and the Picaresque Novel. Festschrift John Calvin Metcalf. New York, 1941.
Kollmann, W. Nashs Unfortunate Traveller und Heads English Rogue, die beiden Hauptvertreter des englischen Schelmenromanes. Diss. Leipzig, 1899.
Hecht, H. Th. PERCY als Bearbeiter spanischer Romanzen. Anglia, 58, 1934.
Laun, A. Eine altspanische Romanze zur Vergleichung mit SCHILLERS Handschuh. ALG, 1, 1870.
Gorra, E. Una romanza spagnuola nella poesia popolare e nel teatro: L'Alarcos di F. SCHLEGEL. In: Fra drammi e poemi. Milano, 1899.
Matulka, B. The Main Source of SCUDERY'S Le Prince Déguisé: The Primaleon. RR, 1934.
Serrurier, C. Julien SOREL, une réincarnation du Picaro. Mélanges Salverda de Grave, Groningen, 1933-34.
Atkinson, Dorothy F. Busirane's Castle and Artidon's Cave. (SPENSER). MLQ, 1, 1940.
Battaglia, R. Dalla lingua dell' Amadigi a quella della Gerusalemme. (TASSO). Cultura Neolatina, 1, 1941.
Boxberger, R. Die Quellen von UHLANDS Romanze Dom Massias. ALG, 8, 1879.
Harn, E. M. WIELANDS Neuer Amadis. Hesperia, 17. Göttingen, 1928.
Fehse, W. Chr. WIRSUNGS deutsche Celestinaübersetzung. Halle, 1902.

CHAPTER FIVE

El Cid.

1. Generalities.

Aschbach, J. De Cidi historiae fontibus. Diss. Bonn, 1843.
Baret, E. Du poème du Cid dans ses analogies avec la chanson de Roland. Paris, 1863.
Baumgarten, A. Der Cid in Geschichte und Poesie. In: Stimmen aus Maria Laach, 54, 1898.
Bormann, W. Der Cid im Drama. ZVL, 5-6, 1893.
Buceta, E. Una tragedia francesa relacionada con la leyenda de Rodrigo. RFE, 1933.
Callcott, F. The Cid as History Records Him. Hisp., 1934.
Cambouliu. Le Cid de l'histoire et le Cid de la légende. Mag. de Librairie, 11, 1860.
Castro, A. Poesia y realidad en el poema del Cid. Tierra Fierma (Madrid), 1935.
Chasles, E. Le Cid de l'histoire et celui de la poésie. Revue contemporaine, 2, 1857.
Clavería, C. Notas sobre el Cid en el Norte de Europa. RFE, 25, 1941.
Coe, Ada M. The Vitality of the Cid Theme. HR, 16, 1948.
Dozy, R. Le Cid d'après de nouveaux documents. Leyde, 1860.
Fischer, P. L. Der Cid und die Cid-Romanzen. Progr. Sarnen, 1887.
Folkierski, W. Cyd Cornela w Polsce. Krakow, 1917.
Glaesener, H. Le Cid et Wallenstein. RELV, 1907.
Hämel, A. Der Cid im spanischen Drama des 16. und 17. Jahrhunderts. ZRPh, 1910. Beiheft, 25.
Kleinschmidt, J. R. The Date of the Cid in English. MLN, 55, 1940.
Lévi-Provençal. Le Cid de l'histoire. Revue historique, July, 1937.
Lorch, M. The Cid and Raymond de Toulouse Heroes of a Novel of Chivalry. RLC, 13, 1933.
Matulka, Barbara. The Cid as a Courtly Hero from the Amadis to Corneille. New York, 1928.
—— The Courtly Cid Theme in the Primaleon. RR, 1934.
Menéndez Pidal, R. El Cid en la historia. Madrid, 1921.
Pelligrini, S. Epica francese e Cantare del Cid. Cultura Neolatina, 3, 1943.
Reynier, G. Le Cid en France avant le Cid. Mélanges Lanson. Paris, 1922.
Roosbroeck, G. L. van. The Cid Theme in France in 1600. Minneapolis, New York, 1920.
Tronchon, H. Deux adaptations préromantiques du Romancero del Cid. RHLF, 1912.

2. Influences upon Individual Authors.

Anon. Le Cid de CORNEILLE, comparé aux originaux espagnols qui en ont fourni le sujet et les situations princi-

pales. La Quinzaine littéraire, 3-4. Paris, 1817.
Bernard, G. Le Cid espagnol et le Cid français. Lille, 1910.
Collmann, O. The French Cid and his Spanish Prototype. Progr. Meseritz, 1868.
Creizenach, W. Die älteste deutsche Uebersetzung von Corneilles Cid. ZVL, 13, 1899.
Fee, A. Etudes sur l'ancien théâtre espagnol. Les trois Cid: Castro, Corneille, Diamante. Paris, 1873.
Ferrière, E. Littérature et philosophie. Corneille et G. de Castro. Paris, 1865.
Gasté. La querelle du Cid. Paris, 1897.
Gaumont, A. Comparison du Cid de Corneille avec l'original espagnol de Guillén de Castro. Berichte des freien deutschen Hochstifts Frankfurt, N. F., 5, 1889.
Gros, E. Le Cid après Corneille, suites, restitutions, imitations. RHLF, 30-31, 1923.
Hunger. Der Cidstreit in chronologischer Ordnung. Leipzig, 1891.
Reynier, G. Le Cid de Corneille. Paris, 1930.
Roosbroeck, G. L. van. The Purpose of Corneille's Cid. Minneapolis, 1921.
Ruggieri, J. Le Cid di Corneille e Las Mocedades del Cid di Guillén de Castro. AR, 1930.
Santelices, L. Las Mocedades del Cid de Guillén de Castro; Le Cid de Pierre Corneille; y El Honrador de su padre de Juan Bautista Diamante. Annales de la U. de Chile, 1933.
Searles, C. Sentiments de l'Académie française sur le Cid. Minneapolis, 1916.
Matulka, Barbara. The Courtly Cid Theme and GIRALDI CINTIO. RLC, 16, 1936.
Bertrand, J. J. A. HERDER et le Cid. BH, 23, 1921.
Koehler, R. Herders Cid und seine französische Quelle. Leipzig, 1867.
Moennich, W. B. Herders Cid und die spanischen Cidromanzen. Progr. Tübingen, 1854.
Tronchon, H. Préromantisme allemand et français: Herder et Creuzé de Lesser, adaptateurs du Romancero del Cid. RHLF, 1912.
Voegelin, A. S. Herders Cid, die französische und die spanische Quelle. Heilbronn, 1879.
Roesler, M. Sur les sources de la Légende des siècles. (V. HUGO). ZFSL, 37, 1911.
Stange, P. Le Cid dans la poésie lyrique de Victor Hugo. Progr., Erfurt, 1903.
Buceta, E. Opiniones de SOUTHEY y Coleridge sobre el Poema del Cid. RFE, 9, 1922.

CHAPTER SIX

Calderón.

1. Generalities.

Anon. Calderon in Deutschland. Grenzboten, 13, 1854.
Breymann, H. Die Calderon-Literatur. München, 1905.
Cantela, A. R. Calderón de la Barca in Italia. Roma, 1923.
Dorer, E. Calderon-Litteratur in Deutschland. Zürich, 1877; Leipzig, 1880.
—— Calderon und seine Werke nach deutschen Urtheilen. Leipzig, 1881.
Ellinger, G. Eine neue Calderon-Uebersetzung. National Zt., 670, 1892.
Farinelli, A. Calderón y la musica en Alemania. Cultura española, 1907 and in: Ensayos y Discursos de critica literaria hispano-europea. Roma, 1925.
—— Despedida de mis papeles calderonianos y de la obra sobre Calderón en las diversas literaturas. La Nación (Buenos Aires), 6.IV.1941.
Fucilla, J. G. Italian Manuscript Versions of La Vida Es Sueño and El Delincuente Honrado. Ital., 17, 1940.
Guignard, R. H. Calderon dans le Frauentaschenbuch. RLC, 10, 1930.
Heine, K. Calderon im Spielverzeichniss der deutschen Wandertruppen. ZVL, 2, 1888.
Hilborn, H. W. Calderón's agudos in Italianate Verse. HR, 10, 1942.
Iden, O. Der Einfluss Lope de Vegas und Calderons auf die deutsche Literatur. ZNU, 38, 1939.
Koch, M. Calderon in Deutschland. Im neuen Reich, 1, 1881.
Landsberg, H. Calderon in Deutschland. In: Masken, 6. (Düsseldorf), 1911.
Malkiewicz, Marie. Un remaniement français de La Vie est un songe. RLC, 19, 1939.
Moglia, P. Una representación de Calderón en Buenos Aires en el siglo XVIII. RFH, 2.
Münnig, Elisabeth. Calderon und die ältere deutsche Romantik. Berlin, 1912.
Murphy, E. English Translations of Calderon. Catholic U. Bull., 5, 1899.
Oppenheimer, M. Supplementary Data on

the French and English Adaptations of Calderon's El Astrologo Fingido. RLC, 22, 1948.
Pitollet, C. El medico de su honra à Paris. Les Langues méridionales, 1935.
Sanchez Rojas J. España fuera de España: La vida es sueño de Calderón. La España moderna, 1909.
Schmidt, J. S. Calderon in Deutschland. Grenzboten, 16, 1857.
Schuchardt, H. Neuste deutsche Calderon-Litteratur. Beilage zur Allg. Zt., 198-200, 1881.
Steiner, A. Calderon's Astrologo Fingido in France. MPh, 1926.
Turkevich, L. B. Calderón en Rusia. RFH, 1, 1939.

2. Influences upon Individual Authors.

Pitollet, C. La querelle caldéronienne de J. N. **BOEHL VON FABER** et J. J. de Mora reconstituée d'après les documents originaux. Paris, 1909.
Lista y Aragon, A. La Vida es sueño de Calderón et **BOISSY.** Ensayos literarios y criticos. Sevilla, 1844.
Lancaster, H. C. Calderon, **BOURSAULT** and Ravenscroft. MLN, 1936.
Rundle, J. More About Calderon, Boursault and Ravenscroft. MLN, 62, 1947.
Lancaster, H. C. Still more about Calderon, Boursault and Ravenscroft. Ibid.
Rundle, J. Footnote on Calderon, Ravenscroft and Boursault. MLN, 63, 1948.
Kosch, W. **EICHENDORFF** und Calderons autos sacramentales. Der Gral, 7. (Trier), 1913.
Thormann, W. E. Eichendorff als Calderon-Uebersetzer. Rheinische Thalia, 1, 1921.
Anon. **FITZ GERALD** and Calderon. Academy, 30.V.1903.
Gates, Eunice J. Antonio da **FONSECA SOARES,** an Imitator of Góngora and Calderón. HR, 9, 1941.
Carriere, M. Calderons Wundertätiger Magus und **GOETHES** Faust. Braunschweig, 1876.
Dorer, E. Goethe und Calderon; Gedenkblätter zur Calderonfeier. Leipzig, 1881. And in: Nachgelassene Schriften. Dresden, 1893.
Fastenrath, J. Die Beziehungen zwischen Calderons Wunderthätigem Magus und Goethes Faust. In: Calderon in Spanien. Leipzig, 1882.
Fernandez Merino, A. Calderón und Goethe. Revista de España, 81-82, 1881-82.
Herford, C. H. On Goethe and Calderon. PEGS, 2, 1886.
Rosenkranz, K. Ueber Calderons Tragödie vom wunderthätigen Magus, ein Beitrag zum Verständniss der Faustischen Fabel. Halle, 1829.
Sanchez Moguel, A. Calderon et Goethe, ou le Faust et le Magicien prodigieux. Paris, 1883.
Schuchardt, H. Goethe und Calderon. In: Romanisches und Keltisches. Berlin, 1886.
Schuetz-Wilson, H. Goethe and El Magico Prodigioso. Gentleman's Mag., N. S., 45, 1890.
Semeran, A. Calderon und Goethe. Beilage Leipziger Zt., 7, 1899.
Treverret. Calderon et Goethe, le Magicien prodigieux et Faust. Annales Faculté des Lettres de Bordeaux, 1883.
Wolff, K. Goethe und Calderon. JbGG, 1913.
Geiger, L. Schreyvogel über **GRIES'** Calderon-Uebersetzung. SVL, 3, 1903.
Lambel. **GRILLPARZERS** Ahnfrau und Calderons Andacht zum Kreuze. Die Presse, 16, 1884.
Schulhof, H. Grillparzer und Calderon. JbGrG, 33, 1935.
Foerster. **LORINSERS** Calderon-Uebersetzung. MLIA, 1878.
Morel-Fatio, A. **MERIMEE** et Calderon. RHLF, 1920.
RAVENSCROFT: see Boursault, above.
Kreyenborg, H. **RUECKERTS** Calderon-Uebersetzungen. Geistesleben der Gegenwart; Weg der Zeit, 5, 1926.
Anon. **SCHLEGEL'S** Criticism of Calderon. In: Spanish Drama. Foreign Quarterly Rev., 1843.
Gates, E. J. **SHELLEY** and Calderon. PhQ, 1937.
Madariaga, S. de. Shelley and Calderon and other Essays on English and Spanish Poetry. Transactions Royal Society, 37, 1920.
Farinelli, A. **WAGNER** e Calderon. NAnt, 16.I.1934.

CHAPTER SEVEN

Cervantes and Don Quijote.

1. Cervantes.

Babinger, G. Die Wanderungen und Wandlungen der Novelle von Cervantes El curioso impertinente. RF, 31, 1912.
Buck, G. Written in Imitation of the Manner of Cervantes. GRM, 29, 1941.

FitzGerald, T. A. Cervantes' Popularity Abroad. MLJ, 32, 1948.
Flores, A. & Benardete, M. J. (eds.). Cervantes Across the Centuries. New York, 1947.
Ford, J. D. M. & Lansinc, R. Cervantes. A Tentative Bibliography of his Works and of the Biographical and Critical Material Concerning Him. Harvard U. P., 1931.
Mazade, C. de. Le théâtre de Michel Cervantes. RDM, 1.III.1862.
Sender, R. 1947's Biggest Literary Anniversary. Cervantes' Quadricentennial Finds Him in Exile. SRL, 9.VIII.1947.
Singer, A. E. The Literary Progeny of Cervantes' El licenciado Vidriera. West Virginia U. Bull., 5, 1947.
Wurzbach, W. von. Die Preziosa des Cervantes. SVL, 1.
Heiser, M. F. Cervantes in the United States. (AMERICA), HR, 15, 1947.
Medina, J. T. Cervantes en las letras chilenas. Santiago de Chile, 1923.
Molina, J. Cervantes en Chile. Atenea, 88, 1947.
Remos y Rubio, J. J. Tradición cervantina en Cuba. Rev. Cubana, 22, 1947.
Sanchez, L. A. Cervantes en el Brasil. Rev. Hisp. Moderna, 8, 1942.
Torres Quintero, R. Cervantes en Colombia. Bol. Inst. Caro y Cuervo, 4, 1947.
Vegas Castillo, M. Cervantes y don Quijote en el Perú. Peruanidad, 2, 1942.
Armas, J. de. Cervantes en la literatura inglesa. (ENGLAND). Madrid, 1916.
Knowles, E. B. Cervantes and English Literature. In: Cervantes Across the Centuries. Ed. by Flores & Benardete. New York, 1947.
—— Cervantes y la literatura inglesa. Realidad, 1947.
Maxwell, B. The Source of the Principal Plot of The Fair Maid of the Inn. MLN, 59, 1944.
Peers, E. A. Cervantes in England. BSS, 24, 1947.
Rosenbach, A. The Curious Impertinent in English Dramatic Literature. MLN, 17, 1902.
Wilson, E. M. Cervantes and the English Literature of the Seventeenth Century. BH, 50, 1948.
Crooks, Esther. The Influence of Cervantes in FRANCE in the 17th Century. Baltimore, 1931.
—— French Translations of Cervantes. In: Cervantes Across the Centuries Ed. by Flores & Benardete. New York, 1947.
Hainsworth, G. La fortune de la première traduction française des Novelas ejemplares. BH, 1930.
—— Quelques opinions françaises (1614-64) sur les Nouvelles exemplaires de Cervantes. BH, 1930.
—— Cervantes en France. BH, 1932.
—— Les Novelas exemplares de Cervantes en France au XVIIe siècle. Paris, 1933.
Hämel, A. M. H. Neumann und sein literarischer Nachlass: Cervantes in Frankreich. In: Estudios sobre America y España. Halle, 1925.
Neumann, M. H. Cervantes in Frankreich, 1582-1910. RH, 1930.
Rondel, A. Commémoration de Molière, Racine, Corneille, Shakespeare et Cervantes à la Comédie française. Paris, 1919.
Bergel, L. Cervantes in GERMANY. In: Cervantes Across the Centuries. Ed. by Flores & Benardete. New York, 1947.
Bertrand, J. J. A. Cervantes et le romantisme allemand. Paris, 1914.
Burkhard, O. The Novelas exemplares of Cervantes in Germany. MLN, 1917.
Dorer, E. Cervantes und seine Werke nach deutschen Urteilen. Leipzig, 1880.
Neumann, M. H. Cervantes in Deutschland. NSp, 25, 1918.
Borgeld, A. Nederlandsch vertalingen van Cervantes' Novellen. (HOLLAND). Tijdschrift voor nederl. taal- en letterkunde, 25, 1906.
Fucilla, J. G. Italian Cervantina. (ITALY). HR, 1934.
—— Notes on the Vogue of Cervantes in Italy. HR, 8, 1940.
Hainsworth, G. Les Nouvelles exemplaires de Cervantes en Italie. BH, 31, 1929.
Mazzei, A. Cervantes en Italia. Bol. de la Acad. Argentina de Letras, 10, 1942.
Mele, E. Per la fortuna del Cervantes in Italia nel seicento. Studi di filologia moderna, 2, 1909.
—— Mas sobre la fortuna de Cervantes en Italia en el siglo XVII. RFE, 6, 1919.
—— Nuevos datos sobre la fortuna de Cervantes en Italia en el siglo XVII. RFE, 8.
Morawski, J. Cervantes a Polska. (POLAND). Kurjer Pozn, 1930.
Shepelevich, L. J. Cervantes in der russischen Literatur. (RUSSIA). In: Pod znamenem nauki. Moskva, 1902.
Turkevich, Ludmilla B. Cervantes in Russia. In: Cervantes Across the Centuries. Ed. by Flores & Benardete. New York, 1947.

Markovic, M. Cervantes dans la littérature yougoslave. (YUGOSLAVIA). RLC, 14, 1934.

2. Don Quijote.

Ashbee, H. S. The Iconography of Don Quichotte. Transactions Bibliographical Society. London, 1893.
Bardon, M. Don Quichotte en Europe. In: Introduction au Cervantes. Cent chefs-d'oeuvre étrangers. Paris.
Beinhauer, W. El españolismo del Quijote. Ensayos y Estudios, 1 (Bonn), 1939.
Biedermann, F. B. Don Quichotte et la tâche de ses traducteurs. Paris, Leipzig, 1837.
Carlesi, F. Traducendo il Don Chisciotte. NAnt, 16.IV.1935.
Chesterton, G. K. The Return of Don Quixote. Living Age, 7.IX.1912.
Fuerst, R. Don Quijote-Spuren in der Weltlitteratur. Beilage zur Allg. Zt., 61, 1898.
Gebhart, E. Récents interprètes de Don Quichotte. Rep. franc., 9.IV.1878. And in: De Panurge à Sancho Panza. Paris, 1911.
—— De la popularité universelle de Don Quichotte. Journal des Débats, 10.V. 1905. And in: De Panurge à Sancho Panza. Paris, 1911.
Hazard, P. Don Quichotte au cours des siècles. In: Don Quichotte de Cervantes. Paris, 1931.
—— La fortuna de Don Quijote en la literatura europea. Bol. del Instituto de las Españas, 1934.
Hilton, R. Four Centuries of Cervantes: The Historical Anatomy of a Best-Selling Masterpiece. Hisp., 30, 1947.
Ingles. Rambles in the Footsteps of Don Quixote. London, 1827.
Maeztu, R. de. Don Quijote, Don Juan y La Celestina. Buenos Aires, 1941.
Mazzei, P. Impressioni sul Don Chisciotte. LNI, 20.VIII.1934.
Meier, H. Zur Entwicklung der europäischen Quijote-Deutung. RF, 54, 1940.
Municio, A. Don Quijote y El Cid: El alma de Castilla. Madrid, 1945.
Romera-Navarro, M. Correspondencia entre las interpretaciones literarias del Quijote y las pictóricas. HR, 12, 1944.
Rondani, A. Don Chisciotte e certi suoi parenti. L'Italia moderna, Sept., 1905.
Salinas, P. Lo que le debemos a Don Quijote. U. Nacional de Colombia, 10, 1948.
Witkowski, S. De Don Quijotii praecursore graeco. Eos, 33.
Becker, G. Die Aufnahme des Don Quijote in die englische Literatur (1605-1770). (ENGLAND). Berlin, 1904.
—— Zur ersten englischen Don Quijotade. Archiv, 123, 1910.
Knowles, E. B. Don Quixote through English Eyes. Hisp, 23, 1940.
—— Four Articles on Don Quixote in England. New York, 1941.
—— Allusions to Don Quixote before 1660. PhQ, 20, 1941.
—— Some Textual Peculiarities of the First English Don Quixote. Papers Bibl. Soc. Amer., 37.
Koeppel, E. Don Quixote, Sancho Panza und Dulcinea in der englischen Litteratur bis zur Restauration. Archiv, 101, 1898.
Bardon, M. Don Quichotte en FRANCE au XVIIe et au XVIIIe siècle, 1605-1815. Paris, 1931.
—— Don Quichotte et le roman réaliste français. RLC, 16, 1936.
Garcia Calderón, V. Une enquête littéraire: Don Quichotte à Paris et dans les tranchées. Paris, 1916.
Legarde, P. Un Don Quichotte populiste au Guignol de Luxembourg. NL, 15.X. 1938.
Alewyn, R. Die ersten deutschen Uebersetzer des Don Quijote und des Lazarillo de Tormes. (GERMANY). ZDPh, 54, 1929.
Berger, W. Don Quichotte in Deutschland und sein Einfluss auf den deutschen Roman, 1613-1800. Heidelberg, 1902.
—— Don Quixote in Deutschland. Zs. f. Bücherfreunde, 12, 1908.
Dorer, E. Deutsche Uebersetzer des Don Quijote. MLIA, 1885.
Fischer, H. Don Quijote in Deutschland. Vierteljahrschrift f. Litteraturgeschichte, 5, 1892.
Melz, C. F. An Evaluation of the Earliest German Translation of Don Quixote: Juncker Harnisch aus Fleckenland. Berkeley, 1945.
Schwering, J. Cervantes' Don Quijote und der Kampf gegen den Roman in Deutschland. Euphorion, 29, 1929.
Steiner, A. Zum Thema des Don Quijote in Deutschland im 17. Jahrhundert. Archiv, 158, 1930.
Weiss, J. Don Quijote am Kurpfälzischen Hofe, 1613; sein öffentlicher Einzug in Deutschland. Das Bayerland, 27, 1916.
Wulfertange, R. Don Quichote reitet nach Deutschland. Berlin, 1939.

Roose, R. Don Quichotte dans la littérature néerlandaise aux XVIIe et XVIIIe siècles. **(HOLLAND).** Les Langues et Lettres romanes, 2, 1948.
Flaccomio, R. La fortuna del Don Quijote in Italia nei secoli XVII e XVIII. (ITALY). Palermo, 1928.
Garrone, M. A. Il Don Chisciotto Siciliano e il Don Chisciotto spagnuolo. Studi di filologia moderna, 4, 1911.
Fitzmaurice-Kelly, J. Don Quixote in Gujerati and Japanese. (JAPAN). RH, 1901.
Valle, R. H. ¿ Cuando llegó a MEXICO Don Quijote? Cervantes (Habana), 14, 1939.
—— El Ingenioso Hidalgo en México. Ibid.
Leonard, I. A. Don Quixote and the Book Trade in Lima, 1606. (PERU). HR, 8, 1940.
Figueiredo, F. de. O thema de Quixote na litteratura portegueza do seculo XIX. **(PORTUGAL).** RFE, 8, 1921.
Foulché-Delbosc, R. Les traductions turques de Don Quichote. (TURKEY). RH. 1899.

3. Influences upon Individual Authors.

Wilson, E. M. Don Quixote, **ANDRES** and Juan Haldudo. CL, 2, 1950.
Boulanger, M. Cervantes et **BERGSON.** Lettres Romanes, 1, 1947.
Howell, S. E. Does **BRETON'S** Marcela stem from Quijote? MLN, 53.
Babinger, G. Wanderung und Wandelung der Novelle von Cervantes El curioso impertinente mit spezieller Untersuchung von **BROSSES** Le curieux impertinent. Diss. München, 1911.
Hood, T. L. My Last Duchess and Cervantes. **(BROWNING).** Trinity Review, 1. (Hartford), 1946.
Goodfellow, D. M. The Sources of Mercedes of Castile. (J. F. **COOPER).** AL, 12, 1940.
Markovitch, M. Alphonse **DAUDET** et Cervantes. Vernac, 18, 1933.
Ashbee, K. S. Don Quixote et Pickwick. **(DICKENS).** RH, 6, 1899.
Hignard, H. Etude de littérature comparée. Don Quichotte et Pickwick-Club. Revue du Lyonnais, 7, 1889.
Romera-Navarro, M. Interpretación pictorica del Quijote por **DORE.** Madrid, 1946.
Giusti, W. Sul Donchisciottismo di alcuni personaggi del **DOSTOIEVSKI.** Cultura, 10, 1931.
Potthof, A. **EICHENDORFF** als Cervantesübersetzer. LE, 1922.
Romero, F. Don Quijote y **FICHTE.** Realidad, 1, 1947.
Buck, G. Written in Imitation of the Manner of Cervantes. **(FIELDING).** GRM, 29, 1941.
Peery, W. The Curious Impertinent in Amends for Ladies. HR, 14, 1946.
Pons, E. Fielding, Swift et Cervantes. Studia neophilologica, 15. (Upsala), 1942.
Hatzfeld, H. Don Quijote und Madame Bovary. **(FLAUBERT).** Investigación y Progreso (Madrid), 1927 & Idealist. Philologie, 3, 1927.
Lugli, V. Flaubert e il Don Chisciotte. Cultura, 15.VII.1927.
Thomas, R. Cervantes et Flaubert. Les langues néo-latines, 1939.
Bahlsen, L. Eine Komödie **FLETCHERS,** ihre spanische Quelle und die Schicksale jenes Cervanteschen Novellenstoffes in der Weltlitteratur. ESn, 23.
Grant, R. Patricia. Cervantes' El Casamiento enganoso and Fletcher's Rulc a Wife and Have a Wife. HR, 12, 1944.
Sarrailh, J. Cervantes et Anatole **FRANCE.** Poitiers, 1934.
Bickermann, J. Don Quijote und Faust; die Helden und die Werke. **(GOETHE).** Berlin, 1929; Barcelona, 1932.
García, P. F. Cervantes-Goethe. Religión y Cultura, 1932.
Vordtriede, W. The Trial of Books in Goethe and Cervantes. MLN, 62, 1947.
Rausse, H. Cervantes und Friedrich **HALM.** JbGrG, 24, 1913.
Bertrand, J. J. A. Une source inconnue du Verlorene Sohn de P. **HEYSE.** RLC, 3, 1923.
Bugge, A. Literaere Forbilleder: Cervantes, **HOLBERG.** Edda, 14, 1920.
Moore, O. H. How Victor **HUGO** Created the Characters of Notre Dame de Paris. PMLA, 57, 1942.
Peterson, Doris E. A Note on the Probable Source of **LANDOR'S** Metellus and Marius. SPh, 39, 1942.
Wolf, M. Avellanedas Don Quijote. Sein Verhältnis zu Cervantes und seine Bearbeitung durch **LESAGE.** Diss. Giessen, 1907 & ZVL, 17.
Brandes, W. Minna von Barnhelm und Don Quijote. **(LESSING).** Akad. Blätter, 16, 1884.
Michaelis, C. F. Lessings Minna von Barnhelm und Cervantes' Don Quijote. Berlin, 1883.
Pierce, F. James **MABBE** and La Española Inglesa. RLC, 23, 1949.

Spitzer, L. Thomas **MANN** y la muerte de Don Quijote. RFH, 2, 1940.
Ovidio, F. d'. **MANZONI** e Cervantes. In: Studii Manzoniani. Caserta, 1928.
Moore, O. H. **MARK TWAIN** and Don Quixote. PMLA, 37, 1922.
Roades, M. T. Cervantes and Mark Twain. Diss. U. of Kansas, 1926.
Templin, E. H. On Re-reading Mark Twain. Hisp., 24, 1941.
Levin, H. Don Quijote and Moby Dick. (**MELVILLE**). In: Cervantes Across the Centuries. Ed. by Flores and Benardete. New York, 1947.
—— Don Quijote y Moby-Dick. Realidad, 1, 1947.
Stauber, E. Carmen. (**MERIMEE**). ZFSL, 50, 1927.
Trahard, P. Cervantes et Mérimée. RLC, 2, 1922.
Bardon, M. Edition de la Critique du livre de Don Quichotte de la Manche, par Pierre **PERRAULT**, 1679. Paris, 1931.
Molina, J. S. Sobre un plagio de La **ROCHEFOUCAULD** a Cervantes. Santiago de Chile, 1935.
Anon. **SALES'S** Don Quixote: Spanish Literature in America. NAR, 1837.
Sacoto Arias, A. Hamlet y don Quijote, o la dialéctica de la locura. (**SHAKESPEARE**). América (Quito), 14, 1939.
Thornbury, W. Did Shakespeare ever read Don Quixote? N&Q, 193, 197, 204, 1871.
Turgenev, I. S. Hamlet and Don Quijote. In: Benardete & Flores: The Anatomy of Don Quixote. Ithaca, 1932.
Wyneken, H. Falstaff und Don Quichotte. Münchener Neueste Nachrichten, 113, 1939.
Fitzmaurice-Kelly, J. Preface to **SHELTON'S** Translation of Don Quixote. Tudor Translations. London, 1892.
Knowles, E. B. The First and Second Editions of Shelton's Don Quixote. HR, 9, 1941.
Cordasco, F. **SMOLLETT** and the Translation of the Don Quixote. N&Q, 193, 1948.
Cirot, G. Cervantes et les frères **THARAUD**. BH, 1921.
Heine, H. **TIECK** und Cervantes. In: Die romantische Schule. Hamburg, 1836.
Lussky, A. E. Cervantes and Tieck's Idealism. PMLA, 43, 1928.
Henry, A. Góngora et P. **VALERY**. Deux incarnations de Don Quichotte. Bruxelles, 1937.
Harland, Frances & Beall, C. B. **VOLTAIRE** and Don Quijote. MLF, 25, 1940.
Fitzmaurice-Kelly, J. The Ingenious Gentleman Don Quixote by M. de Cervantes done into English by H. E. **WATTS**. RH, 2, 1895.
Tropsch. **WIELANDS** Don Sylvio und Cervantes' Don Quijote. Euphorion, 1899.

CHAPTER EIGHT

Lope de Vega.

1. Generalities.

Levi, E. Il centenario di Lope di Vega. Leonardo, Oct., 1935.
Matulka, B. The Tercentenary of Lope de Vega: His International Diffusion. Spanish Review, 1935.
Pitollet, C. Le troisième centenaire de la mort de Lope de Vega. Les Langues méridionales, 1935.
Pomès, M. Le tricentenaire de Lope de Vega. NL, 15.VI.1935.
Esquerra, R. Note sur la fortune de Lope de Vega en **FRANCE** pendant le XVIIe siècle. BH, 1936.
Hainsworth, G. Quelques notes pour la fortune de Lope de Vega en France. BH, 1931.
—— Notes supplémentaires sur Lope en France (au XVIIIe siècle). BH, 41, 1939.
Johnson, H. L. A Recent French Adaptation of La Estrella de Sevilla. RR, 36, 1945.
Farinelli, A. Lope de Vega en Alemania. (**GERMANY**). Berlin, 1894 & Barcelona, 1936.
Iden, O. Der Einfluss Lope de Vegas und Calderons auf die deutsche Literatur. ZNU, 38, 1939.
Tiemann, H. Lope de Vega in Deutschland (1629-1935). Hamburg, 1939.
Vossler, K. Lope de Vega und wir. DVLG, 1936.
Thomas, H. A Forgotten Translation of Lope de Vega. (**ITALY**). MLR, 35, 1940.
Dam, C. F. A. van. Lope de Vega en het Nederlands. (**HOLLAND**). De nieuere Taalgids, 21, 1927.
Fevralski, A. Lope de Vega en Georgia. (**RUSSIA**). La Literatura Internacional (Moscow), 3, 1944.
Gabinski, N. Lope de Vega en la Rusia del siglo XIX. Ibid. 2, 1943.
Leonard, I. A. Notes on Lope de Vega's Works in the **SPANISH INDIES**. HR, 6, 1938.

2. Influences upon Individual Authors.

Bohning, W. H. Lope's El mayor imposible and **BOISROBERT'S** La Folle gageure. HR, 12, 1944.
Decroos, J. Guido **GEZELLE** en Lope de Vega. Leuvensche Bijdragen, 28.
Adler, F. La quinta de Florencia. **(GRILLPARZER)**. Euphorion, 20, 1913.
Farinelli, A. Grilparzer und Lope de Vega. Berlin, 1894. Madrid, 1895.
Menéndez y Pelayo, M. Lope de Vega y Grillparzer. Estudios de Critica Literaria, 2, Madrid, 1912.
Lancaster, H. C. Lope's Peregrino, **HARDY**, Rotrou and Beys. MLN, 1935.
Cotronei, B. Una commedia di Lope de Vega ed i Promessi Sposi. **(MANZONI)**. GSLI, 1899.
Kollewijn, R. A. Theodore **RODENBUGH** en Lope de Vega. De Gids, 3, 1891.
Steffens, G. Jean de **ROTROU** als Nachahmer Lope de Vegas. Berlin, 1891. Cf. Revue critique, 1893.
Margouliès, G. **SCARRON** imitateur de Lope de Vega. RLC, 8, 1928.
Barton, F. B. The Sources of the Story of Sesostris et Timarète in Le Grand Cyrus. **(SCUDERY)**. MPh, 1922.
Schmidt, E. Ludwig **UHLAND**, als Dolmetsch Lopes de Vegas. Archiv, 1899.

CHAPTER NINE

Tirso de Molina and Don Juan.

1. Generalities.

Austen, J. The Story of Don Juan: A Study of the Legend and the Hero. London, 1939.
Balmont, K. Der Typus des Don Juan in der Weltliteratur (In Russian). Mir Iskusstwa, 5-6, 1903.
Bévotte, G. de. La légende de Don Juan. Son évolution dans la littérature des origines au romantisme. Paris, 1906 & 1929.
Bolin, W. Don Juan Studier. Finsk Tidskrift, 1885.
Bolte, J. Ueber den Ursprung der Don Juan-Sage. ZVL, 13, 1899.
Bradi, L. de. Don Juan, la légende et l'histoire. Paris, 1930.
Brousson, J. J. La légende de Don Juan, du Festin de pierre au Trompeur de Séville. NL, 1937.
Bushee, Alice H. Three Centuries of Tirso de Molina. Philadelphia, 1939.
Cartia, G. La figura del Don Giovanni nella vita e nell'arte. Giornale di politica e di letteratura, 1935.
Casalduero, J. Contribución al estudio del tema de Don Juan en el teatro español. Northampton (Mass.), 1938.
Cuatrecasas, J. Donjuanismo y tenorismo. Nosotros (Buenos Aires), 8, 1938.
Daffner, H. Der Don Juan Typus. LE, 1.VIII.1920.
Engel, K. Die Don Juan-Sage auf der Bühne. Dresden, 1887.
—— Zwei Kapitel aus der Geschichte der Don Juan-Sage. ZVL, 1, 1887.
Eschelbach, H. Ueber die dramatischen Bearbeitungen der Sage von Don Juan. Montagsblätter f. deutsche Litt., 6, 1902.
Fagerström, J. Några anteckningar om Don Juansagans dramatiska bearbetning under sjuttonde seklet. Lund, 1877.
Farinelli, A. Don Giovanni. GSLI, 1896 & Milano, 1946.
—— Cuatro palabras sobre Don Juan y la literatura donjuanesca del porvenir. Homenaje a Menéndez y Pelayo. Madrid, 1899. And in: Estudios de erudición. Madrid, 1899.
—— Don Juan y la literatura donjuanesca del porvenir. In: Ensayos y Discursos de critica literaria hispano-europea. Roma, 1925.
Fastenrath, J. Die Don Juan Sage in Spanien und in der Weltlitteratur. (Preface to his translation of Zorrilla's Don Juan). Dresden, 1898.
Filippini, E. Per lo svolgimento drammatico della leggenda Dongiovannesca. RCLI, 1899.
Green, O. H. New Light on Don Juan: A Review Article. HR, 7, 1939.
Guerle, de. Don Juan et ses origines littéraires. Mém. de l'Acad. Stanislas, Nancy, 4e sér., 15, 1883.
Gutmacher, E. Der Don-Juan Stoff im 19. Jahrhundert. Bühne & Welt, 15, 1913.
Hazanas y la Rua, J. Genesis y desarrollo de la legenda de Don Juan Tenorio. Sevilla, 1893.
Heckel, H. Das Don Juan Problem in der neueren Dichtung. Stuttgart, 1915.
Heinrich, G. A. La légende de Don Juan et ses diverses interprétations. Mém. de l'Acad. de Lyon, 1857-58.
Jellinek, A. L. et al. Zur Don Juan Litteratur. LE, 1902.
Kaltaecker, H. Don Juan in der modernen Dichtung und Musik. Rhein. Musik- & Theater- Zt., 15, 1914.

Klemperer, V. Vom Aufstieg des Don Juanthemas. Zeitgeist, 3, 1910.
Kolb, Annette. Don Juan und Fra Diavolo. Wiener Rundschau, 3, 1899.
López Núñez, J. Don Juan Tenorio en el teatro, la novela y la poesía. Orígenes, antecedentes, historia y anécdotas de esta obra. Madrid, 1946.
MacKay, Dorothy E. The Double Invitation in the Legend of Don Juan. Stanford U. P., 1943.
Madariaga, S. de. Don Juan as a European Figure. Nottingham, 1946.
Maranini, L. Morte e Commedia di Don Juan. Bologna, 1937.
Marañón, G. Les origines de la Légende de Don Juan. Revue hebdomadaire, 21.I.1939.
—— Don Juan: Ensayos sobre el origen de su leyenda. Buenos Aires, 1940 & Madrid, 1942.
Margall, F. P. Observaciones sobre el carácter de Don Juan Tenorio. In: Opusculos. Madrid, 1884.
Mauclair, C. Don Juan ou Don Miguel? Revue universelle, 15.XI.1930.
Metzeler, H. Die literarische Wandlung Don Juans. Ueber den Wassern, 5, 1911.
Osma, J. M. de. Variaciones sobre el tema de Don Juan. Hisp., 15, 1932.
Picatoste, F. Estudios literarios: Don Juan Tenorio. Madrid, 1883.
Platzhoff, E. Sur la légende de Don Juan. LE, 15.XI.1901.
Rank, O. Die Don Juan Gestalt. Leipzig, 1924.
Rauter, A. Die Don Juan Sage im Lichte biologischer Forschung. Leipzig, 1899.
Revilla, M. de la. El tipo legendario de Don Juan Tenorio y sus manifestaciones en las modernas literaturas. Madrid, 1883.
Rios, Blanca de los. Don Juan en la literatura y en la musica. España moderna, Dec., 1889.
Schmitz, O. A. Don Juan, Casanova und andere erotische Charaktere. Berlin, 1905.
Schroeder, T. Die Don Juan Sage, ihre Entstehung und ihre Bearbeitungen bis auf Mozart. Deutsche Welt, Beilage zur Deutschen Zt., 4, 1912-13.
—— Die dramatischen Bearbeitungen der Don-Juan Sage in Spanien, Italien und Frankreich bis auf Molière. Beiheft zur ZRPh, 1912.
Siccardi, V. Les Don Juan célèbres. Asti, 1907.
Simone-Brouwer, F. de. Don Giovanni nella poesia e nell'arte musicale. Napoli, 1894.
Vatteone, A. C. Don Juan y la leyenda donjuanesca. Nosotros, 52, 1926.
Vigneul-Marville. Notes sur les changements du Festin de Pierre. In: Mélanges d'histoire et de littérature. 2 vols. Paris, 1699-1700.

2. Influences upon Individual Countries.

Seary, E. R. A Sequel to Don Juan. (South **AFRICA**). MLR, 35, 1940.
Johnson, D. H. Don Juan in **ENGLAND.** ELH, 11, 1944.
Lancaster, H. C. Don Juan in a **FRENCH** Play of 1630. PMLA, 38, 1923.
Oría, J. A. Don Juan en el teatro frances. Instituto Nacional de Estudios de Teatro (Buenos Aires), 9, 1940.
Lefftz, J. Strassburger Puppenspiele. Geschichtlicher Rückblick mit den alten Texten des Strassburger Don Juan und Faust. **(GERMANY).** Strassburg, 1942.
Warp, J. A. Nederlandsche Don Juan Dramen. **(HOLLAND).** Taal en Letteren, 8, 1899.
Weber, A. Don Juan en **HONGRIE.** Revue de Hongrie, 15.VIII.1912.
Costanzo, L. Don Giovanni Tenorio nel teatro spagnuolo e romano. **(ITALY).** Napoli, 1938.
Spitzer, L. Una variante italiana del tema del Condenado por desconfiado. RFH, 1, 1939.
Bittcher, E. Ein Don Juan in der japanischen Literatur. **(JAPAN).** Der Sammler, 41. (München-Augsburg), 1913.
Figueiredo, F. de. Donjuanisme et antidonjuanisme en **PORTUGAL.** Coïmbra, 1933.
Manning, C. A. **RUSSIAN** Versions of Don Juan. PMLA, 38, 1923.

3. Influences upon Individual Authors.

Feuillerat, A. **BAUDELAIRE** et la légende de Don Juan. Renaissance (New York), 2-3, 1945.
Boyd, Elizabeth. **BYRON'S** Don Juan: A Critical Study. New Brunswick (N. J.), 1945.
Santelices, V. Lidia. El Don Juan de Byron, y El Estudiante de Salamanca de Espronceda. Anales de la U. de Chile, 1931.
Trueblood, P. G. The Flowering of Byron's Genius: Studies in Byron's Don Juan. Stanford U. P., 1945.
Cabrera, J. Don Juan y **CASANOVA.** México, 1946.

Adams, N. B. A Little Known Spanish Adaptation of DUMAS Don Juan de Maraña. RR, 1929.
Pfandl, L. Wie Johannes FASTENRATH den Don Juan Tenorio übersetzte. In: Amigos de Zorilla. Valladolid, 1933.
Singer, A. E. FLAUBERT'S Une nuit de Don Juan. MLN, 55, 1940.
Denslow, S. Don Juan and Faust. (GOETHE). HR, 10, 1942.
Scheible, J. Doctor Johann Faust (Faust und seine Vorgänger; Don Juan Tenorio von Sevilla; Die Schwarzkünstler der verschiedenen Nationen, etc.) 4 vols. Stuttgart, 1846-49.
Gavazzeni, G. KIERKEGAARD, il Don Giovanni e la musica. Rassegna d'Italia, 1947.
Castro, A. El Don Juan de Tirso y el de MOLIERE como personajes barrocos. Hommage à Ernest Martinenche. Paris, 1938.
Draeger, R. Molières Don Juan historisch-genetisch neu beleuchtet. Diss. Halle, 1899.
Latour, A. de. Séville et l'Andalousie (comparaison du Don Juan de Molière avec le Burlador de Tirso do Molina). In: Etudes sur l'Espagne. Paris, 1855.
Laun, A. Tirso de Molinas und Molières Don Juan. Deutsches Museum, 1866.
—— Molière und Tellez als Bearbeiter des Don Juan. ALG, 3, 1874.
Molinier, V. Notice sur la tragi-comédie de G. Tellez, El Burlador de Sevilla et sur le Don Juan de Molière. Mém. de l'Acad. de Toulouse, 7e sér., 5, 1873.
Valera, J. Comparaison du Don Juan de Molière avec le Burlador. In: Estudios críticos sobre literatura, política y costumbres de nuestros días. Madrid, 1864.
Bidou, H. Don Juan ou la Solitude. (G. OLTRAMARE). Le Temps, 29.VI.1936.
Anon. Don Juan in deutscher Uebersetzung und auf deutschen Bühnen. (Lorenzo da PONTE). Europa, 1866.
Pappacena, E. Le ultime incarnazioni di D. Giovanni: un dramma postumo di Ed. ROSTAND. Festschrift Fr. Torraca. Napoli, 1921.
Hainsworth, G. New Details on the Nouvelles of SCARRON and Boisrobert: Plus d'effets que de paroles. BH, 49.
Reichmann, O. Th. SHADWELLS Tragödie The Libertine und ihr Verhältnis zu den vorausgehenden Bearbeitungen der Don Juan-Sage. Leipzig, 1904.
Hartz, S. W. Don Juan and Hamlet. (SHAKESPEARE). London, 1837.
Erlich, V. Beniowski and Don Juan. (SLOWACKI). Symposium, 1, 1947.
Schevill, R. SWIFT'S Hoax on Patridge the Astrologer and Similar Jests in Fiction. Transactions of the Conn. Acad. of Arts and Sciences, 15, 1909.

CHAPTER TEN

Other Spanish Authors.

Fincke, G. Le Menteur de Corneille et La Verdad sospechosa de ALARCON. Progr. Danzig, 1872.
Laun, A. Das ältere Charakterlustspiel der Spanier. Alarcóns Verdad sospechosa und Moretos El desdén con el desdén, mit besonderer Rücksicht auf Wests Bearbeitung. Archiv, 1872.
Molinier, V. Notice sur le poète espagnol Alarcón, sur sa comédie La Verdad Sospechosa et sur les diverses imitations qu'en offrent celle du Menteur de Corneille et celle de Goldoni intitulée Il Bugiardo. Mém. de l'Acad. de Toulouse, 7e sér., 4, 1872.
Monterde, F. La verdad sospechosa y Corneille. Letras de México, 2, 1939.
Schons, Dorothy. Alarcón's Reputation in Mexico. HR, 8, 1940.
Skola, J. Corneilles Le menteur und Goldonis Il bugiardo in ihrem Verhältnisse zu Alarcóns La verdad sospechosa. Progr. Pilsen, 1883.
Granges de Surgères, F. de. Les traductions françaises du Guzman d'Alfarache. (ALEMAN). Bull. du Bibliophile. Paris, 1885-86.
Leonard, I. A. Guzman de Alfarache in the Lima Book Trade, 1613. HR, 11, 1943.
Payer, R. von. Eine Quelle des Simplicissimus. ZDPh, 22, 1889.
Petriconi, H. Mérimées Histoire de Don Pèdre Ier in ihrem Verhältnis zur Chronik AYALAS und zur Geschichte. Volkstum und Kultur der Romanen, 4, 1931.
Horne, J. van. Bernardo de BALBUENA y la literatura de la Nueva España. Arbor, March, 1945.
Wilson, E. M. Rule a Wife and Have a Wife and El Sagaz Estacio. (BARBADILLO). RES, 24, 1948.
McClelland, I. L. BECQUER, Ruben Darío and Rosalía de Castro. BSS, 16, 1939.
Anon. Fernan CABALLERO in Deutschland. Europa, 1859.
Hespelt, E. H. & Williams, S. T. Washington Irving's Notes on F. Caballeros' Stories. PMLA, 1934.

Schmidt, J. F. Caballero und die spanische Litteratur in Deutschland. WM, 25, 1869.
Williams, S. T. Washington Irving and F. Caballero. JEGPh, 1930.
Jessup, M. H. Rotrou's Dom Bernard de Calrève and its Source. (Bernardoy de **CALREVA**). MLN, 1932.
Hilton, R. **CAMPOAMOR**, Spain and the World. U. of Toronto P. 1941.
Maseras, A. Solitud de Victor **CATALA** en francès. Catalunya, 10, 1939.
Bettelheim, A. Beaumarchais über Goethes **CLAVIGO**. Gegenwart, 1880.
Heinemann. Clavigo und seine Quelle. Berichte des freien deutschen Hochstifts, Frankfurt, 4, 1889.
Lindau, P. Clavijo bei Beaumarchais und Goethe. Gegenwart, 1872.
Risch, J. Ueber das Verhältniss des Goetheschen Clavigo zu seiner Quelle. Stralsund, 1861.
Rivera, G. Beaumarchais y Clavijo. Hisp., May, 1937.
Schmidt, E. Clavigo, Beaumarchais, Goethe. In: Charakteristiken. Berlin, 1901.
Filippis, M. de. Manso's Debt to Santa **CRUZ DE DUENAS**. HR, 4, 1936.
Crawford, J. P. W. A Sixteenth Century Spanish Analogue of Measure for Measure. (**CUEVA**). MLN, 1920.
Molinier, V. Notice sur la question suivante: Est-il vrai, comme l'ont affirmé Voltaire, Laharpe et Sismondi, que Corneille ait pris le sujet et les principales scènes du Cid dans une pièce espagnole du **DIAMANTE**? Mém. de l' Acad. de Toulouse, 6e sér., 3, 1865.
Mathews, E. G. Cokain's The Obstinate Lady and the Araucana. (**ERCILLA**). MLN, 57, 1942.
Wogan, D. Ercilla y la poesía mexicana. RIA, 3.
Arrieta, R. A. **ESPRONCEDA** en al Plata. La Prensa (Buenos Aires), 21.XII. 1941.
Capdevila, A. Enfoque argentino de Espronceda. Nosotros, 2, 1943.
Delpy, G. L'Espagne et l'esprit européen dans l'oeuvre de **FEIJOO**. Paris, 1937.
Matulka, B. The Novels of Juan de **FLORES** and their European Diffusion. New York, 1931.
Olmsted, E. W. The Story of Grisel and Mirabella. In: Homenaje a Menéndez Pidal. Madrid, 1925.
Praag, J. A. van. Algo sobre la fortuna de Juan de Flores. RR, 1935.
Bruton, J. G. **GALDOS** visto por un inglés y los ingleses vistos por Galdós. Rev. de las Indias (Bogotá), 17, 1943.
Heras, A. Galdós y el Nuevo Mundo. Hisp., 24, 1941.
Mathews, E. G. **GIL POLO**, Desportes, Lyly's Cupid and my Campaspe. MLN, 56, 1941.
Anon. **GONGORA** Translated. TLS, 22. VI.1932.
Cirot, G. Góngora et Musée. BH, 33, 1931.
Gates, E. J. A Nineteenth Century English Translator of Góngora. HR, 7, 1939.
—— Antonio da Fonseca, an Imitator of Góngora and Calderón. HR, 9, 1941.
Henry, A. Gongora et P. Valéry. Le Flambeau, April, 1937.
Pradal, G. La técnica poetica y el caso Góngora-Mallarmé. CL, 1950.
Schons, Dorothy. The Influence of Góngora on Mexican Literature during the XVIIth Century. HR, 7, 1939.
Thomas, H. Three Translations of Góngora and of the Spanish Poets during the 17th Century. RH, 48, 1920.
Acosta, J. M. Traductores franceses de **GRACIAN**. Rev. de las Españas, 5, 1930.
Baumgarten, S. Balthasar Gracián en Hongrie. RLC, 16, 1936.
Borinski, K. Baltasar Gracián und die Hofliteratur in Deutschland. Halle, 1893. Cf. ZVL, 9.
Brachfeld, O. Note sur la fortune de Gracián en Hongrie. BH, 1931.
Farinelli, A. Baltasar Gracián y la literatura de Corte en Alemania. Revista crítica de Historia y Literatura españolas, portuguesas e hispano-americanas, 1896. And in: Ensayos y Discursos. Roma, 1925.
Hope, F. Baltasar Gracián and his Influence in General. The Downside Rev., 57, 1939.
Lacoste M. & Bouillier, V. Note sur une traduction du Héros de B. Gracián. BH, 1934.
Praag, J. A. van. Traducciones neerlandesas de las obras de Baltasar Gracián. HR, 7, 1939.
Romera-Navarro, M. Bibliografia graciana. HR, 1936.
Sarrailh, J. Notes sur Gracian en France. BH, 1937.
Pitollet, C. Chronique espagnole. (A. France). Bull. de la Société d'Etudes des professeurs de langues méridionales, 1932.
Bouillier, V. Baltazar Gracián et Nietzsche. RLC, 6, 1926.

Mele, E. Baltasar Gracián e il Nietzsche. Cult., 1928.
Hough, G. Gracián's Oraculo Manual and the Maximes of Mme. de Sablé. HR, 4, 1936.
Morel-Fatio, A. Gracián interprété par Schopenhauer. BI, 12, 1910.
McGhee, Dorothy M. Voltaire's Candide and Gracián's El Criticon. PMLA, 52, 1937.
Clement, L. Antoine de **GUEVARA**, ses lecteurs et ses imitateurs français au XVIe siècle. RHLF, 15.X.1900.
Fellheimer, Jeannette. Hellowes' and Fenton's Translations of Guevara's Epistolas Familiares. SPh, 44, 1947.
Gálvez, J. M. Guevara in England, nebst Neudruck von Lord Berners Golden Boke of Marcus Aurelius. Berlin, 1916.
Karl, L. Note sur la fortune des oeuvres d'Antonio de Guevara à l'étranger. BH, 35, 1933.
Morawski, J. O polskim przekladzie Guevary. Poznan, 1930.
Praag, J. A. van. Ensayo de una bibliografía neerlandesa de las obras de Fray Antonio de Guevara. Homenatge a Antoni Rubío i Lluch. Barcelona, 1936.
Thomas, H. The English Translations of Guevara's Works. Madrid, 1930.
Vaganay, H. Antonio de Guevara et son oeuvre dans la lïttérature italienne: essai de bibliographie. Firenze, 1916.
GUEVARA, Luis Vélez de: See Vélez de Guevara, below.
Pitollet, C. Lettre sur la version allemande des Cavaliers de l'Apocalypse de B. **IBANEZ.** Bruxelles, 1925.
Viñas, A. Eco constante de San **JUAN DE LA CRUZ** en Francia. La Prensa, 21. V.1939.
Oria, J. Alberdi Figarillo: Contribución al estudio de la influencia de **LARRA** en el Rio de la Plata. (1830). Buenos Aires, 1936.
Alterton, A. An Additional Source for Poe's The Pit and the Pendulum (**LLORENTE'S** History of the Spanish Inquisition). MLN, 1933.
Cordasco, F. Llorente and the Originality of Gil Blas. PhQ, 26, 1947.
Crow, J. A. Federico García **LORCA** en Hispanoamérica. RIA, 1, 1939.
—— Bibliografía hispanoamericana de F. G. Lorca. RIA, 1, 1939.
Fletcher, J. G. Lorca in English. Poetry, 56, 1940.
Morby, E. S. García Lorca in Sweden. HR, 14, 1946.
Salazar y Chapela, E. García Lorca en Londres. Romance (México), 1, 1940.
Hagedorn, M. Reformation und spanische Andachtsliteratur: **LUIS DE GRANADA** in England. Leipzig, 1935.
Anthéunis, L. Un réfugié anglais traducteur de Louis de Grenade: Richard Hopkins. Rev. d'hist. ecclésiastique, 35, 1939.
Atkinson, W. **LUIS DE LEON** in Eighteenth Century Poetry. RH, 81, 1933.
Claveria, C. Sobre la traducción inglesa del Libre del Orde de Cavalleria de Ramón **LULL.** Analecta Sacra Terraconensia. (Tarragona), 1942.
Ruel. Montaigne et Raymond Lulle. Bull. des Amis de Montaigne, 2, 1939.
Batllori, M. Un lul-lista bolonyes del XVIIe segle. Homentage a Antoni Rubío i Lluch. Barcelona, 1936.
Riquer, M. de. Traducciones castellanas de Ausías **MARCH** en la edad de oro. Barcelona, 1946.
Alonso, D. Un soneto de **MEDRANO** imitado de Ariosto. HR, 16, 1948.
Crawford, J. P. W. Don Diego Hurtado de **MENDOZA** and Michele Marullo. HR, 6, 1938.
Martinenche, E. Les sources de l'Ecole des maris. RHLF, 5, 1898.
Allen, D. C. Jacques' Seven Ages and Pedro **MEXIA.** MLN, 56, 1941.
Charlier, G. Sur un passage de Comme il vous plaira de Shakespeare. (**MONTEMAYOR**). Revue du XVIe siècle, 7.
Fischer, W. Honoré d'Urfé's Sireine and the Diana of Montemayor. MLN, 1913.
Harrison, T. P. Googe's Eglogs and Montemayor's Diana. Texas Studies in English, 5, 1925.
—— A Source of Sidney's Arcadia: The Contributions of Montemayor's Diana by Perez and Gil Polo. Ibid, 1926.
—— Shakespeare and Montemayor's Diana. Ibid.
—— The Probable Source of Beaumont and Fletcher's Philaster. PMLA, 41, 1926.
—— The Faerie Queene and the Diana. PhQ, 1930.
Reyher, P. Alfred de Vigny, Shakespeare et George de Montemayor. RELV, 1920.
Schönherr, G. Jorge de Montemayor, sein Leben und sein Schäferroman, die Siete Libros de la Diana. Halle, 1886.
Tobler, R. Shakespeares Sommernachtstraum und Montemayors Diana. JbShG, 1898.
Pitollet, C. Comment la première tragédie allemande est empruntée à l'Es-

pagne, ou Lessing et **MONTIANO.** Hisp., (Paris), 1921.

Vail, C. C. D. Lessing and Montiano. JEGPh, 1935.

Ottavi, M. Carlo Gozzi, imitateur de **MORETO.** El desdén con el desdén et La principessa filosofa. Mélanges Hauvette. Paris, 1934.

Privitera, J. F. The Sources of Thomas Corneille's Comtesse d'Orgueil. MLN, 56, 1941.

Crane, W. G. Lord Berners's Translation of Diego de San **PEDRO'S** Carcel de Amor. PMLA, 49, 1934.

Marichalar, A. Un ancêtre espagnol de Descartes: Gomez **PEREIRA.** Revue hebdomadaire, 12, 1937.

Parker, J. H. A Possible Source of a jeu de scène in Molière's Ecole des Maris. (Juan **PÉREZ DE MONTALBAN**). MLN, 55, 1940.

Entralgo, P. L. **QUEVEDO** und Heidegger. DVLG, 17, 1939.

Hauffen, A. Zu den Quellen der Geschichte Philanders von Sittewald von Moscherosch. Euphorion, 7.

Léger, L. Un petit problème de littérature comparée (Quevedo-Szaczinski). Acad. des Inscriptions et Belles-Lettres, 1.III.1918.

Mérimée, E. Essai sur la vie et les oeuvres de Francisco de Quevedo. (Molière). Paris, 1886.

Morawski, J. Dwaj moralisci hiszpanscy, Quevedosi Gracian, w szacie polskiej. Poznan, 1934.

Pike, R. E. La Pinelière and Mount Parnassus in French Satirical Literature. RLC, 15, 1935.

Praag, J. A. van. Een hollandsch epigoon van Quevedo: Salomon Van Rusting. NPh, 23, 1938.

—— Ensayo de una bibliografia neerlandesa de las obras de don Francisco de Quevedo. HR, 7, 1939.

Rey, H. An English Imitation Attributed to Quevedo. RR, 20, 1929.

Thomas, H. The English Translations of Quevedo's La Vida del Buscón. RH, 81, 1933.

Adams, N. B. A Note on Mme. Cottin and the Duke of **RIVAS.** HR, 15, 1947.

Bordato, E. E. Mérimée y el duque de Rivas. Humanidades, 21, 1930.

Jensen, H. Zu Vanbrughs The False Friend. (F. de **ROJAS**-Zorrilla). Archiv, 120, 1908.

Peter, A. Francisco de Rojas' Tragödie Casarse por vengarse und ihre Bearbeitungen in den anderen Litteraturen. Progr. Dresden. Leipzig, 1898.

Przezdziecki, A. Don Pietro **RONQUILLO,** posel hiszpanski do krolowej polskiej Eleonory w r. 1674. Cracovie, 1869.

Morel-Fatio, A. Ambrosio de **SALAZAR** et l'étude de l'espagnol en France sous Louis XIII. Toulouse, 1901.

Coralnik, A. Zur Geschichte der Skepsis: Francesco **SANCHEZ.** Arch. f. Gesch. der Philosophie, 27, 1913-14.

Iriarte, J. Kartesischer oder Sanchezischer Zweifel? Diss. Bonn. Bottrop i/W, 1935.

Lancaster, H. C. Castillo **SOLORZANO'S** El celoso hasta la muerte and Montfleury's Ecole des jaloux. MLN, 54.

Gianturco, E. **SUAREZ** and Vico. Harvard Theolog. Review, 1934.

—— Character and Essence, Origin and Content of the Jus Gentium According to Vico and Suarez. RLC, 16, 1936.

Allison, A. F. Some Influences in Crashaw's Poem On a Prayer Booke Sent to Mrs. M. R. (St. **THERESA**). RES, 23, 1947.

Carayon, M. Les trois poèmes de Crashaw sur Sainte Thérèse. Hommage à E. Martinenche. Paris, 1939.

Hough, Mary E. Santa Teresa in America. Diss. Columbia U., 1939.

Richter, E. Juan **TIMONEDA** und das Imogen-Portia-Motiv. JbShG, 64, 1928.

Cione, E. Giulia Gonzaga e Juan **VALDÉS.** Meridiano di Roma, 9.VII.1939.

Meozzi, A. Per la storia del valdesianesimo in Italia. Civiltà Moderna, 12, 1940.

Place, E. B. A Note on El Diablo cojuelo and the French Sketch of Manners and Types. (**VÉLEZ DE GUEVARA**). Hisp., 1936.

Vic, J. La composition et les sources du Diable boîteux de Lesage. RHLF, 1920.

Willers, H. Le Diable boîteux; el Diablo cojuelo. RF, 1935.

Todesco, M. L'Atlandide di Jacinto **VERDAGUER** nella traduzione boema di Jaroslav Vrchlicky. L'Europa orientale, 22, 1942.

Fernandez, E. Influencia de España en la restauración de la U. de Coimbra: **VIVES** y Juan III. Hisp. (Madrid), 1940.

Günther, R. In wie weit hat L. Vives die Ideen Bacos von Verulam vorbereitet? Leipzig, 1912.

Marañón, G. Juan Luis Vives, un Español fuera de España. Madrid, 1942.

Prat, J. Luis Vives y la paz europea. Rev. de las Indias, II.10.

Smith, W. F. Vives and Montaigne as Educators. Hisp., 29, 1946.
ZORILLA'S Don Juan Tenorio. See Tirso's Don Juan in Chapter Nine, above.
Marmocchi, F. Zorilla e Mistral. Convivium, 1947.

CHAPTER ELEVEN

The Spanish Language.

Blackmar, F. W. Spanish American Words. MLN, 4, 1891.
Chabas, J. La lengua y la cultura de España en Italia. Revista de las Españas, 1927.
Croce, B. & Farinelli, A. La lingua spagnuola in Italia. Roma, 1895.
Duñaiturria, S. Observaciones sobra la enseñenza y difusión de la lengua y cultura españolas en el extranjero. Madrid, 1930.
Feyjoo y Montenegro, B. G. Paralelo de las lenguas castellana y francesa. In: Theatro critico universal. Madrid, 1726.
Helman, Edith F. Early Interest in Spanish in New England. Hisp., 29, 1946.
Jacob, E. G. Die Bedeutung der spanischen Sprache und Kultur für die nationalpolitische Erziehung. NM, 1935.
Marder, C. C. Notes for a Bibliography of American Spanish. Festschrift Marshall Elliot. Baltimore, 1911.
Oehmann, E. Zum spanischen Einfluss auf die deutsche Sprache. Neuphilol. Mitteilungen, 41, 1940.
Pastor, J. F. Las apologias de la lengua castellana en el siglo de oro. Madrid, 1929.
Scheid, P. Studien zum spanischen Sprachgut im Deutschen. Greifswald, 1936.
Wiener, L. Spanish Studies in England in the 16th and 17th Centuries. MLQ, 2, 1899.

CHAPTER TWELVE

Influence upon Individual Authors.

Lévi-Provençal, E. La Péninsule ibérique au moyen âge d'après le Kitab ar-Rawd al mi' tãr di habar alaktãr d'Ibn **ABD AL-MUN-IM AL-HIMYARI.** Texte arabe des notices relatives à l'Espagne, au Portugal et au sud-ouest de la France, publié avec une introduction, un répertoire analytique, une traduction annotée, un glossaire et une carte. Leyde, 1938.
Bergmann, H. Madame d'**AULNOY** und Spanien. Diss. Würzburg, 1934.
Foulché-Delbosc, R. (ed.). Relation du voyage d'Espagne de Mme. d'Aulnoy. Paris, 1926.
Lenz, A. Quelques survivances du Voyage d'Espagne de Mme. d'Aulnoy. RH, 81, 1933.
Levi, E. La vecchia Spagna di Mad. d'Aulnoy. Marzocco, 4.III.1928.
Mazon, J. Mme. d'Aulnoy n'aurait-elle pas été en Espagne? RLC, 7, 1927.
Praag, J. A. van. Las ediciones holandesas de Mémoires de la Cour d'Espagne y Relation du voyage d'Espagne de Mme. d'Aulnoy. BH, 1930.
Streckenbach, M. Madame d'Aulnoy, ihre Novellen und Romane. RF, 45, 1931.
Leathers, V. L. L'Espagne et les Espagnols dans l'oeuvre de H. de **BALZAC.** Paris, 1931.
Place, E. B. Spanish Sources of the Diabolism of **BARBEY D'AUREVILLY.** RR, 1928.
Hilton, R. M. **BARRÉS** and Spain. RR, 30, 1939.
Lambert, E. Maurice Barrès et l'Espagne. RLC, 20, 1940.
Roz, F. Maurice Barrès et l'Espagne. Revue française, 5.V.1912.
Gallas, K. R. **BAUDELAIRE** et l'âme espagnole. NPh, 31, 1947.
Gilman, Margaret. Le cosmopolitisme de Baudelaire et l'Espagne. RLC, 16, 1936.
Cioranescu, A. Les Rodomontades espagnoles de N. **BAUDOIN.** BH, 1937.
Courtines, P. Spain and Portugal in **BAYLE'S** Dictionnaire. Hisp., 24, 1941.
Roosbroeck, G. van. Prose Poems of Spain by Aloysius **BERTRAND.** Spanish Review, Nov., 1935.
Schevill, R. George **BORROW**: An English Humorist in Spain. U. of California Chronicle, 18, 1916.
Hanotaux, G. De l'influence espagnole en France à propos de **BRANTOME.** In: Etudes hist. sur le XVIe et le XVIIe siècle en France. Paris, 1886.
Reparaz, G. de. Jean **BRUNCHES,** hispanisant. BH, 1931.
Cicade, H. Dividas de **CAMOES** a poesia espanhola. Homenatge a Antoni Rubió i Lluch. Barcelona, 1936.
Rumeau, A. Un Français à Madrid entre 1824 et 1840: **CHALUMEAU DE VERNEUIL.** BH, 1934.
Hazard, P. Comment **CHATEAUBRIAND** écrivit une nouvelle espagnole. RP, 1924.

Bataillon, M. L'Espagne de Chauteaubriand. RLC, 23, 1949.
Martinenche, E. Les sources espagnoles d'Horace et d'Héraclius. (CORNEILLE). RLR, 43, 1900.
Valle Abad, F. del. Influencia española sobre la literatura francesa: Pedro Corneille. Bol. de la U. de Granada, 79, 1946.
Sarrailh, J. Le voyage en Espagne du Marquis de **CUSTINE.** Hommage à E. Martinenche. Paris, 1939.
Mallo, J. Ruben **DARIO** en Barcelona durante su ultimo viaje a España. Rev. Hisp. Mod., 11, 1946.
Seifert, E. Das Katalanische in den Werken von Friedrich **DIEZ.** Homenatge a Antoni Rubió i Lluch. Barcelona, 1936.
Bald, R. C. A Spanish Book of **DONNE'S.** N&Q, 193, 1948.
Muñoz Rojas, J. A. Un libro español en la biblioteca de Donne. RFE, 25, 1941.
Simpson, Evelyn M. Donne's Spanish Authors. MLR, 43, 1948.
Sarrailh, J. Le voyage en Espagne d'Al. **DUMAS** père. BH, 1928.
Schulhoff, H. **EICHENDORFF** und die spanische Lyrik. Euphorion, 22, 1920.
Bertrand, J. J. A. Johannes **FASTENRATH** et l'Espagne. BH, 1927.
Wilson, E. M. Did John **FLETCHER** Read Spanish? PhQ, 27, 1948.
Rivet, Mary M. The Influence of the Spanish Mystics on the Works of Saint **FRANCOIS DE SALES.** Washington, D. C., 1941.
Asberg, C. S. **FROEDING** och det spanska. Göteborgs Posten, 10.V.1924.
Guillaumie-Reicher, C. Théophile **GAUTIER** et la langue espagnole. BH, 1934.
Sánchez-Ocaña, V. El viaje a España de Gautier. Nación, 21.VII.1940.
Mele, E. Le fonti spagnuole della storia dell' Europa del **GIAMBULLARI.** GSLI, 59, 1912.
Fucilla, J. G. Un Italien imitateur des poètes espagnols **(GOBBI).** BH, 1934.
Farinelli, A. **GOETHE** et l'Espagne. In: G. Humboldt et l'Espagne. Paris, 1898.
Pitollet, C. Goethe und Spanien. Hamburger Fremdenblatt, 30.IV.1904.
Salvador, A. Recuerdos españoles en la obra de Goethe. Universidad (Zaragoza), Sept., 1932.
Lambert, E. La Juive de Tolède de **GRILLPARZER,** étude sur la composition et les sources de la pièce. RLC, 2, 1922.
Luciani, V. Il **GUICCIARDINI** e la Spagna. PMLA, 56, 1941.
Palmarocchi, R. L'ambasceria del Guicciardini in Spagna. Archivio Storico Italiano, 97, 1939.
Bataillon, M. Paul **HAZARD** et le monde ibérique. RLC, 20, 1946.
Gigas, E. **HEIBERG** und die spanische Litteratur. In: Literatur og Historie. København, 1898.
Parlow, H. Die Spanier und H. **HEINE.** Berliner Tageblatt, July, 1893.
Pitollet, C. La légende espagnole de la Peña de los Enamorados et le dénouement de la tragédie de Heine, Almanser. RLC, 1, 1921.
Vordtriede, W. Wilhelm **HEINSE'S** Share in the German Interest in Spanish Literature. JEGPh, 48, 1949.
Fenimore, E. English and Spanish in For Whom the Bell Tolls. **(HEMINGWAY).** ELH, 10, 1943.
Kayser, W. Die iberische Welt im Denken J. G. **HERDERS.** Hamburg, 1945.
Gigas, E. Ueber **HOLBERG** und die Spanier. In: Litteratur og Historie. København, 1898.
Wardropper, B. W. An Early English Hispanist. (Lord **HOLLAND).** BSS, 24, 1947.
Morby, E. S. William Dean **HOWELLS** and Spain. HR, 14, 1946.
Deschamps, G. Victor **HUGO** en Espagne. Le Temps, 14.X.1900.
Esquerra, R. Sur les origines d'Hernani. BH, 40, 1938.
Foulché-Delbosc, R. L'Espagne dans les Orientales de Victor Hugo. RH, 1897.
Gentil, G. le. Victor Hugo et la littérature espagnole. BH, 1899.
Guillaumie-Reicher. G. Le voyage de V. Hugo en 1843: France, Espagne, Pays Basque. Paris, 1936.
Guilloton, V. Hernani et l'honneur castillan. Northampton (Mass.), 1940.
Lanson, G. Un document espagnol sur le séjour de V. Hugo à Madrid en 1811. RHLF, 1927.
Morel-Fatio, A. L'histoire dans Ruy Blas. In: Etudes sur l'Espagne. Paris, 1895.
—— L'hispanisme dans Victor Hugo. Homenaje Menéndez Pidal. Madrid, 1925.
Rosières, R. La genèse d'Hernani. RB, 25.IV.1896.
Casariego, J. E. **HUMBOLDT** y el mundo hispánico. Ensayos y Estudios (Bonn), 3, 1941.
Farinelli, A. Guillaume de Humboldt et l'Espagne. Paris, 1898. Torino, 1924. Cf. DR, 1899.
—— Guillermo de Humboldt y el Pais Basco. Ensayos y Discursos de critica literaria hispano-europea. Roma, 1925.

—— Ancora di Humboldt e la Spagna. Colombo, 4, 1926.
Garate, J. G. de Humboldt. Estudio de sus trabajos sobre Vasconia. Bilbao, 1933.
Bowers, C. G. The Spanish Adventures of Washington **IRVING.** Boston, 1940.
Hoffman, Louise M. Irving's Use of Spanish Sources in The Conquest of Granada. Hisp., 28, 1945.
Williams, S. T. The First Version of the Writings of Washington Irving in Spanish. MPh, 38, 1930.
Flasche, H. **KRAUSE** in Spanien. DVLG, 1936.
Pitollet, C. Contributions à l'hispanisme de G. E. **LESSING.** Paris, 1909.
Wagner, G. A. Zu Lessings spanischen Studien. Progr. Berlin, 1883.
Pitollet, C. Deux types d'hispanologues allemands avant l'ère lessinguienne: Gaspard **LINDENBERG** et Christian-Heinrich Postel. Rev. de Archivos. Bibl. y Museos, 1912.
Dana, H. W. L. **LONGFELLOW** on Spain. New Masses, 1938.
Lefranc, A. **LOUIS XIII** a-t-il appris l'espagnol? Mélanges Baldensperger. Paris, 1930.
Mele, E. Ancora di alcuni spagnolismi e dello spagnuolo nei Promessi sposi. **(MANZONI).** GSLI, 62, 1913.
Morel-Fatio, A. L'espagnol de Manzoni. BI, 1901. And in: Etudes sur l'Espagne. Paris, 1904.
Izard, T. C. The Principal Source for **MARLOWE'S** Tamburlaine. MLN, 58, 1943.
Mariéjol, J. H. Un lettré italien à la cour d'Espagne (Pierre **MARTYR D'ANGHIERA**). Paris, 1887. Cf. RB, 4.VIII. 1888.
Heckmann, T. **MASSINGERS** The Renegado und seine spanischen Quellen. Diss. Halle, 1905.
Bertrand, J. J. A. M. **MASSON.** BH, 1922.
Wilson, E. M. Mr. **MAUGHAM** and Spanish Literature. Scrutiny, 4, 1935.
Bataillon, M. L'Espagne de **MERIMEE** d'après sa correspondance. RLC, 22, 1948.
Filon, A. P. Mérimée et ses amis. Paris, 1894.
Tourneux, M. P. Mérimée. In: L'Age du romantisme. Paris, 1888.
Trahard, P. Les sources de l'amour africain dans le théâtre de Clara Gazul de Mérimée. RLC, 2, 1922.
Yovanovitch, V. La Guzla de Prosper Mérimée. Paris, 1911.
Huszár, G. **MOLIÈRE** et l'Espagne. Paris, 1907.
Morley, S. G. Spanish Influence on Molière. PMLA, 19, 1904.
Hayes, R. S. Ce que **MONTAIGNE** doit à l'Espagne. Bull. des Amis de Montaigne, 2e sér., 6, 1939.
Calderon, V. G. L'espagnolisme de **MONTHERLANT.** NL, 31.VIII.1929.
—— Der Spanier in Montherlant. RRh, 1929.
Bataillon, M. L'hispanisme au Collège de France: Alfred **MOREL-FATIO.** BSS, 24, 1947.
Bertrand, J. J. H. Ch. Gottlieb von **MURR.** BH, 1928.
Fucilla, J. G. Un Italien, imitateur des poètes espagnols. **(PASTORINI).** BH, 1934.
Rice, W. G. A Principal Source of The Battle of Alcazar (**PEELE**). MLN, 58.
Gaselee, S. The Spanish Books in the Library of Samuel **PEPYS.** Suppl. Transactions Bibliograph. Society, London, 1926.
Matthews, W. Samuel Pepys and Spain. NPh, 20, 1935.
Pitollet, C. Samuel Pepys, hispanophile. RELV, 1923.
Stephensen, R. C. The English Source of **PUSHKIN'S** Spanish Themes. Texas Studies in English, 1938.
Boudout, J. Edgar **QUINET** et l'Espagne. RLC, 16, 1936.
Gebser, H. **RILKE** und Spanien. Zürich, 1940.
Sachs, G. R. M. Rilke en España. Rev. hispanica moderna, 4, 1938.
Baldensperger, F. L'arrière-plan espagnol des Maximes de La **ROCHEFOUCAULD.** RLC, 16, 1936. And in: Etudes d'histoire littéraire, 4e sér., Paris, 1939.
Crane, T. F. Jean **ROTROU'S** Saint Genest and Venceslas. Boston, 1907.
Stiefel, A. L. Jean Rotrous Cosroes und seine Quellen. ZFSL, 23, 1901.
Esquerra, R. Juicios de **SAINT-EVREMOND** sobre España. BH, 1936.
Morel-Fatio, A. George **SAND** et Majorque. Bull. du bibliophile, 1921.
Janicki, J. Les comédies de P. **SCARRON.** Contribution à l'histoire des relations littéraires franco-espagnoles au XVIIe siècle. Progr. Posen, 1907.
Morillot, P. Scarron. Diss. Paris, 1888.
Peters, R. P. Scarrons Jodelet Duelliste und seine spanischen Quellen. Münchener Beiträge. Erlangen, 1894.
Stiefel, A. L. P. Scarrons Le Marquis

ridicule und seine spanische Quelle. ZFSL, 32, 1908.
Schwartz, W. A. W. **SCHLEGELS** Verhältnis zur spanischen und portugiesischen Literatur. Halle, 1914.
Haemel, A. A. **SCHOPENHAUER** y la literatura española. Anuarios Faculdád di Filos. y Letras de Granada, 2, 1925.
Valle, R. H. Lo español en **SÉNECA**. Revista cubana, 9, 1937.
Frey, A. R. William **SHAKESPEARE** and Alleged Spanish Prototypes. New York, 1886.
Farinelli, A. G. C. L. **SISMONDI** e la Spagna. Roma, 1945.
Pfandl, L. Robert **SOUTHEY** und Spanien. RH, 28, 1913.
Vigneron, R. **STENDHAL** en Espagne (1829). MPh, 1934.
Williams, R. H. A Manuscript Document on the Translations from Spanish by Captain John **STEVENS**. RLC, 16, 1936.
Northrop, G. T. G. **TICKNOR'S** Travels in Spain. U. of Toronto Studies, 1913.
Gillies, A. Ludwig **TIECK'S** Initiation into Spanish Studies. MLR, 33, 1938.
Ludwig, A. Ein Dramenentwurf **UHLANDS** und seine spanischen Quellen. Archiv, 119, 1907.
Perrotin, L. L'Espagne vue par **VERHAEREN**. RB, Sept., 1938.
Rombauts, E. Richard **VERSTEGEN**, een pro-Spaansch pamflietsschrijver uit de XVIIe eeuw. Bijdragen voor de Geschiednis. Haarlem, 23, 1932.
Pitollet, C. L'Espagne dans l'oeuvre de M. de **VOLTAIRE**. Renaissance d'Occident, 13, 1925.
Salvio, A. de. Voltaire and Spain. Hisp., 7, 1924.
Duméril, H. Les voyageurs anglais en Espagne au XVIIIe siècle: **A. YOUNG**. Bull. de la Société académique hispano-portugaise, Toulouse, 1, 1880.

FIFTH PART

Portuguese Contributions.

CHAPTER ONE

General Influences.

Anon. Etudes sur l'histoire de l'expansion portugaise dans le monde. Rev. d'hist. moderne, 14, 1939.
Bernardes Branco, M. Portugal e os estrangeiros. 5 vols. Lisboa, 1879-95.
Boxer, C. R. Portuguese Influence in Japan in the 16th and 17th Centuries. Trans. & Proc. Japan Soc. London, 33, 1935-36.
Cardim, L. Sources portugaises de Torrent of Portyugale. Rev. de Faculdade de Letras da U. da Porto, 1920.
Carvalho, H. A. D. de. L'influence de la civilisation et de la colonisation latine et surtout portugaise en Afrique. Lisbonne, 1889.
Castro, J. de. Portugal em Roma. 2 vols. Lisboa, 1939.
Cidade, H. A cultura portuguesa no sécolo XVI e no sécolo XVII. In: Liçôes sôbre a cultura e a literatura portuguesas. Coimbra, 1933.
Cordier, H. L'arrivée des Portugais en Chine. Leide, 1911.
Coutinho, B. X. C. Bibliographie franco-portugaise. Essai de bibliographie chronologique de livres français sur le Portugal. Porto, 1939.
Fournier, E. La Rosalinda et l'origine portugaise de la Fiancée du roi de Garbe. Paris, 1851.
Fucilla, J. G. A Miscellany of Portuguese Imitations. HR, 1935.
Hazard, P. Esquisse d'une histoire tragique du Portugal devant l'opinion publique du dix-huitième siècle. RLC, 18, 1938.
Hourcade, P. Le feuilleton de la Revolução de Setembro à l'epoque de la Question de Coimbra (1863-67). RLC, 18, 1938.
Jorge, O. O nosso amorismo novelesco nos quinhentos. Sua influencia na literatura universal. Revista da Faculdade de Letras, 2. Lisboa, 1936.
Lopes, D. A expansão da Lingua Portuguesa no Oriente durante os seculos XVI, XVII e XVIII. Barcelos, 1936.
Parmelee, K. W. The Flag of Portugal in History and Legend. RR, 9, 1918.
Ricard, R. Influences portugaises au Méxique durant la période coloniale. Revista da Faculdade de Letras, 4, 1937.
Saavedra Machado, L. Os Ingleses em Portugal. Biblos (Coimbra), 12, 1936.
Thomas, H. English Translations of Portuguese Books Before 1680. The Library, 7, 1926.
Varenbergh, E. Les relations des Pays-Bas avec le Portugal. Annales de l'Acad. d'archéol. de Belgique, 25, 1869.
Walter, F. La littérature portugaise en Angleterre à l'époque romantique. Paris, 1927.

CHAPTER TWO

Camoens.

1. Generalities.

Nabuco, J. Camoës e assumptos **AMERICANOS.** São Paulo, 1943.
Adamson, J. Some Account of the Translations of the Lusiad of Camoens, with Notices Concerning the Translators. **(ENGLAND).** In: Memoirs of the Life and Writings of Camoens, London, 1810.
Braga, T. As Traduçoës inglezas dos Lusiadas. In: Questoës de Litteratura e Arte Portugueza. Lisboa, 1881.
Cardim, L. Projecção de Camoës nas letras inglesas. Lisboa, 1940.
Bois, J. et al. Camoens à Paris. **(FRANCE).** Inauguration du monument élevé à Camoens par la Société des Etudes portugaises. Paris, 1912.
Coutinho, B. Camoens en France au XVIIe siècle. RLC, 18, 1938.
Denis, F. Camoens dans l'Almanach des Muses. Paris, 1891.
Desfeuilles, P. Camoens en France. Vie des Peuples, 1924.
Gentil, G. le. Camoës e a literatura francesa. Biblos, 4, 1928.
Bertrand, J. J. A. Camoens en Allemagne. **(GERMANY).** RLC, 5, 1925.
—— Camoës na Allemanha. Portugalia, 1926.
Körner, J. Nochmals Camoens in Deutschland. RLC, 21, 1947.
Storck, W. Camoës in Deutschland. Acta

comparationis litterarum universarum. (Klausenburg), 1880.
Vasconcellos, J. de. Camoës em Allemanha. Porto, 1881.
Wilmsmeier, W. Camoens in der deutschen Dichtung des 19. Jahrhunderts. Münster, 1913.
Jong, M. de. Quelques notes sur Camoens et les Lusiades en **HOLLANDE.** NPh, 19, 1934-35.
Araujo, J. de. As traduçoës italianas dos Lusiadas. (**ITALY**). Livorno, 1897.
Salomon, A. Camoens dans la littérature **RUSSE.** Bull. Bibliographique. Circulo camoneano. Porto, 1890.
Krauss, W. Die Geltung der Lusiaden in **SPANIEN.** Portugal-Festschrift der U. Köln, 1940.

2. Influences upon Individual Authors.

Teza, E. Giudizi del **BARETTI** e del Voltaire sopra alcuni versi dei Lusiadas. Festschrift A. de Portugal de Faria: Portugal e Italia. Livorno, 1900.
Zanella, G. I Lusiadi, trad. F. **BELLOTTI.** NAnt, 57, 1881.
Orico, O. Camoens y **CERVANTES.** Madrid, 1948.
Almuzara, E. F. Relaciones de la Epica de **LOPE DE VEGA** y la de Camoës. Coimbra, 1936.
Figueiredo, F. de. Camoës e Lope. RLC, 18, 1938.
West, S. G. W. J. **MICKLE'S** Translation of Os Lusiadas. RLC, 18, 1938.
Feliciano de Castilho, A. Camoës, estudo historico-poetico, liberrimamente fundado sobre um drama francez dos senhores Victor **PERROT** e Armand Du Mesnil. Lisboa, 1863-64.
Anon. Les Lusiades travesties, parodie en vers burlesques, grotesques et sérieux. Voyage maritime et pédestre du grand portugais Vasco da Gama par J. R. M. **SCARRON II.** Porto, 1883.
Walzel, O. Der deutsche Entdecker des Camoës. (F. **SCHLEGEL**). RLC, 18, 1938.
Pango, Comtesse J. de. Madame de **STAEL** et Camoëns. RLC, 19, 1939.
Anon. Relaciones entre T. **TASSO** y Camoens. Revista critica de historia y litteratura españolas, portuguesas e hispano-americanas, 5, 1900.
Araujo, J. de. O Soneto de Torquato Tasso a Camoës e Vasco da Gama. Genova, 1897.

CHAPTER THREE

Other Portuguese Authors.

Bordeaux, H. Marianna, la religieuse portugaise. (Marianna **ALCOFORADO**). Paris, 1935.
Cardim, L. Les Lettres portugaises. Coimbra, 1931.
Larat, P. & J. Les Lettres d'une religieuse portugaise et la sensibilité française. RLC, 8, 1928.
Prestage. The Letters of a Portuguese Nun. London, 1897.
Stahl, R. Die Verdeutschungen der Lettres portugaises. Ein Beitrag zum Thema Rilke. RRh, 1929.
Gentil, G. Le. Nicolas de Grouchy traducteur de **CASTANHEDA.** Bull. des Etudes portugaises et de l'Institut fr. au Portugal, 1937.
Rebêlo Gonçalves, F. da L. Une édition brésilienne des Géorgiques de **CASTILLO.** Bull. des Etud. Port., 5, 1938.
Anon. João de **DEUS** e Paul Verlaine. Arte, Jan., 1896.
Perott, J. de. Die Hirtendichtung des **FELICIANO DE SILVA** und Shakespeares Wintermärchen. Archiv, 130, 1913.
Axon, W. E. A. **GIL VICENTE** and Lafontaine; a Portuguese Parallel of La laitière et le pot au lait. Trans. Royal Soc. of Lit., 23, 1902.
Campos, A. de. Gil Vicente, un précurseur de Lope de Vega et de Molière. Biblos., July, 1936.
Carvalho, A. de. Le centenaire de Gil Vicente à l'université de Bordeaux. Bull. des Etudes Portugaises, 1939.
Gentil, G. Le. Les thèmes de Gil Vicente dans les moralités, sotties et farces françaises. Hommage à E. Martinenche. Paris, 1939.
Franck, A. Mémoire sur **MARTINEZ PASQUALIS**, ses doctrines mystiques et son influence sur Saint-Martin. Séances et Travaux de l'Acad. des Sc. mor. et polit., 74, 1865.
Gentil, G. le. Molière et le Fidalgo Aprendiz. (F. M. de **MELO**). RLC, 1, 1921.
Peixoto, A. Le Bourgeois gentilhomme et le Gentilhomme apprenti. Hommage à Ernest Martinenche. Paris, 1939.
Jong, M. de. Ramalho **ORTIGAO** e o escritor Holandes Multatuli. Biblos (Coimbra), 1937.
Anon. Eça de **QUEIROZ** tiene en Brasil más admiradores que en Portugal. Argentina Libre, 21.III.1940.

Chapter Four

Portuguese Influences upon Individual Authors.

Prioult, A. **BALZAC** et le Portugal. RLC, 19, 1939.
Parreaux, A. Le Portugal dans l'oeuvre de William **BECKFORD.** Paris, 1935.
—— Précisions sur les séjours de William Beckford au Portugal. Bull. des Etudes portugaises, 1939.
Lizon, A. El viaje de Miguel de **CERVANTES** a Portugal. Cuadernos de literatura, 1947.
Bremond, A. Les Sonnets de la Portugaise. De Marceline **DESBORDES-VALMORE** à Elizabeth Browning. Etudes, 20.IV.1936.
Picarolo, A. Gonçalves **DIAS** et le Portugal. Bull. des Etudes portugaises, 5, 1938.
Puyvelde, L. van. De reis van Jan van **EYCK** naar Portugal. Mededeelingen der Kon. Vl. Acad. voor Taal- en Letterkunde, 1940.
Higginson, T. W. **FAYEL** and the Portuguese. In: Atlantic Essays. Boston, 1871. ....
Ricard, R. Les sources portugaises de deux vers de **HÉRÉDIA.** Revista de Historia, 12. Lisboa, 1923.
Figueiredo, F. de. **LOPE DE VEGA.** Alguns elementos portugueses na sua obra. El Eco franciscano. Santiago, 1936. And in: Revista do Arquivo Municipal, 1. Sao Paolo, 1938. And in: Ultimas aventuras. Rio de Janeiro, 1940.
West, S. G. The Work of W. J. **MICKLE,** the First Anglo-Portuguese Scholar. RES, 1934.
Sten, H. Les sources portugaises de **MOLIÈRE.** Orbis Litterarum. (København), 1947.
Boulanger, J. **MONTAIGNE** et le Portugal. Le Temps, 12.VI.1934.
Aquarone, J. B. Edgar **QUINET** et le Portugal. RLC, 18, 1938.
Campos Ferreira Lima, H. de. Quinet e Portugal. Biblos, 18, 1942.
Morby, E. S. Portugal and Galicia in the Plays of **TIRSO DE MOLINA.** HR, 9, 1941.

SIXTH PART

Dutch and Belgian Contributions.

CHAPTER ONE

General Dutch Influences.

Asselin, H. La Hollande dans le monde. Paris, 1921.

Closset, F. Great Books from Small Countries: The Literature of Holland and Flanders. BA, 20, 1946.

Dahl, F. Amsterdam, Earliest Newspaper Centre of Western Europe. Het Boek, 25, 1939.

Villiers, A. J. D. de. De hollandse taalbeweging in Suid-AFRIKA. Kaapstad, 1935.

Boxer, C. R. Jan Compagnie in Japan, 1600-1817. An Essay on the Cultural, Artistic and Scientific Influence Exercised by the Hollanders in Japan from the 17th to the 19th Centuries. (ASIA). The Hague, 1936.

Duyvendak, J. J. L. Holland door Chinese oogen. China, 1, 1925-26.

Bense, J. F. Dictionary of the Low-Dutch Element in the English Vocabulary. (ENGLAND). The Hague, 1939.

Llewellyn, E. C. The Influence of Low Dutch on the English Vocabulary. Oxford, 1936.

Lucas, E. V. The Dutch in English Literature. In: A Wanderer in Holland. London, 1905.

Price, L. M. Holland as a Mediator of English-German Literary Influences in the Seventeenth and Eighteenth Centuries. MLQ, 2, 1941.

Russell, J. A. English Men of Letters in Holland. Gazette de Hollande, 27.I & 3.II.1928.

—— English Translations of Dutch Novels. Gazette de Hollande, 28.X.1927 & 1931.

Vries, J. D. de. Holland's Influence on English Language and Literature. Chicago, 1916.

Brugmans, H. L. La Hollande du XVIIIe siècle dans l'Encyclopédie. (FRANCE). RR, 1935.

Cohen, G. Ecrivains français en Hollande dans la première moitié du XVIIe siècle. Paris, 1920.

Gellion Douglas, E. Un asile de la liberté. Journal officiel de la République française, 6-11.II.1871.

Murris, R. La Hollande et les Hollandais au XVIIe et au XVIIIe siècle vus par les Français. Paris, 1925.

Tuin, H. van der. Voyageurs français aux Pays-Bas dans la première moitié du XIXe siècle. Revue d'hist. de la philosophie, 15.X.1935.

—— De invloed der vroegere Vlaamse en Hollandse schilder op de franse literatuur in de eerste helft der 19de eeuw. NPh, 1937-38.

Bolte, J. Das Danziger Theater im 16. und 17. Jahrhundert. (GERMANY). Theatergeschichtl. Forschungen. Hamburg, 1895.

Forster, L. W. The Königsberger Zwischenspiele of 1644 and the Dutch Comedy. MLR, 36, 1941.

Graevell von Jostenoode, H. Bedeutung der Niederlande für die deutsche Bildung. Pädagog. Archiv, 1899.

Heitmüller, F. Holländische Komödianten in Hamburg (1740-41)... Theatergeschichtl. Forschungen, 8, 1894.

Junkers. Niederländische Schauspieler und niederländische Schauspiele im 17. & 18. Jahrhundert in Deutschland. Museum, 44.

Kosch, W. Ein österreichischer Dichter und türkischer Diplomat in Holland. Bijdragen tot de Nederlandsche Taal- en Letterkunde, 1937.

Ramondt, M. De middelnederlandsche sproken in hun verhouding tot de werkelijkheid en de duitse litteratuur. NPh, 27, 1942.

Pater, J. C. H. de. Nederland en HONGARIJE en 1681. In: Christendom en Historie. Kampen, 1931.

Peeters-Fontainas, J. Impressions espagnoles des Pays Bas. (SPAIN). New York, 1933.

CHAPTER TWO

Erasmus.

1. General Influences.

Alonso, B. El crepuscolo de Erasmo. Rev. de Occidente, Oct., 1932.

Mangan, J. J. Life, Character and Influence of Desiderius Erasmus of Rotterdam. 2 vols. New York, 1927.

Matthes, H. C. Umarbeitungen und Einwirkungen der Gleichnissammlung des Erasmus. Archiv, 180.

Schevill, R. Erasmus and the Fate of a Liberalistic Movement prior to the Counter Reformation. HR, 1937.

Stange, C. Erasmus und Julius II. eine Legende. Göttinger Gelehrte Anzeigen, 200, 1938.

Reyes, A. Reseña sobre el erasmismo en **AMÉRICA**. Rev. de Hist. de América, 1.

Looten, C. Erasme et ses amis de St.-Omer, Courtebourne, Tournehem et Hames. (**BELGIUM**). Bull. du Comité flamand de France, 1939.

Exner, H. Der Einfluss des Erasmus auf die englische Bildungsidee. (**ENGLAND**). Berlin, 1939.

Hudson, H. H. Current English Translations of The Praise of Folly. PhQ, 20, 1941.

Mozley, J. F. The English Enchiridion of Erasmus, 1533. RES, 20.

Philips, Margaret M. Erasmus and Propaganda. A Study of the Translations of Erasmus in English and French. MLR, 37.

Vocht, H. de. De invloed van Erasmus op de engelsche toonellitteratuur der XVI en XVII eeuwen. Gent, 1908.

—— The Earliest English Translations of Erasmus' Colloquia, 1536-66. Louvain, 1928.

Mann, M. Erasme et les débuts de la Réforme française. (**FRANCE**). Paris, 1933.

Péricaud. Erasme dans ses rapports avec Lyon. Lyon, 1838.

Ritter, G. Erasmus und der deutsche Humanistenkreis am Oberrhein. (**GERMANY**). Fribourg, 1937.

Kelényi, B. O. Glossen eines ungarischen Humanisten zu den Adagia des Erasmus. (**HUNGARY**). Budapest, 1940.

Cantimori, D. Note sur Erasmo e l'**ITALIA**. SG, 2, 1937.

Nolhac, P. de. Erasme en Italie. Paris, 1888.

Snellen, J. B. The Image of Erasmus in **JAPAN**. Trans. of the Asiatic Soc. Japan, Dec., 1934.

Bataillon, M. Erasme et la cour de **PORTUGAL**. Arquivo de historia e bibliografia, 2, Coimbra, 1927.

—— Erasme et l'Espagne. (**SPAIN**). Paris, 1937. Cf. Archiv, 175; HR, 7; Revue historique, 1938; Conv. 28.II.1939; Annales d'Hist. sociale, 1939.

Boehmer, E. Erasmus in Spanien. Jb. f. roman. und engl. Sprache & Litteratur, 4, 1862 & 1874.

Castro, A. Lo hispánico y el erasmismo. RFH, 1940-42.

Gigas, E. Erasmus fra Rotterdam og Spanien. København, 1922.

Sánchez y Escribano, F. Dos notas sobre el erasmismo. HR, 9, 1941.

2. Influences upon Individual Authors.

Castro, A. Erasmo en tiempo de **CERVANTES**. RFE, 1931.

Kommoss, R. Sebastian **FRANCK** und Erasmus von Rotterdam. Berlin, 1934.

Halkin, L. E. D'Erasme à Saint-**FRANCOIS DE SALES**. EC, 10, 1941.

Dunlop, D. M. Erasmus and **FROBEN**. N&Q, 192, 1947.

Kaegi, W. **HUTTEN** und Erasmus. Ihre Freundschaft und ihr Streit. Histor. Vierteljahrsschrift, 22, 1924.

Sánchez y Escribano, F. Los Adagia de Erasmo en La Philosophia Vulgar de Juan de **MAL LARA**. New York, 1944.

Lokkers, A. Erasmus en **MANTUANUS**. Studiën, 70, 1938.

Almoina, J. La biblioteca erasmista de Diego **MÉNDEZ**. Publ. de la U. de Santo Domingo, 35, 1945.

Mattes, H. C. Francis **MERES** und Erasmus von Rotterdam. Anglia, 63, 1939.

Giraud, V. **MONTAIGNE** et Erasme. Bull. des Amis de Montaigne, 2. sér., 6, 1939.

Errandonea, I. ¿Erasmo o **NEBRIJA**? RFE, 29, 1945.

Gebhart, E. Erasme et **RABELAIS**. Journal des Débats, 9.XI.1904.

Schoenfeld, H. Die Beziehung der Satire Rabelais' zu Erasmus' Moriae und Colloquia. PMLA, 8, 1893.

Thompson, C. R. Rabelais and Iulius Exclusus. PhQ, 22, 1943.

Franchet, H. Erasme et **RONSARD**: la lettre Contra quosdam et le Discours des misères de ce temps. RHLF, 1932.

Gee, J. A. Margaret **ROPER'S** English Version of Erasmus' Precatio Dominica. RES, 13.

Fischer, W. Ein Zwiegespräch des Erasmus von Rotterdam und **ROSTANDS** Cyrano de Bergerac. Archiv, 136, 1917.

Baskervill, C. R. **TAVERNER'S** Garden of Wisdom and the Apophtegmata of Erasmus. SPh, 1932.

White, Olive B. Richard Taverner's Interpretation of Erasmus in Proverbes or Adagies. PMLA, 59, 1944.

Prat, J. Erasmo y **UNAMUNO**. Rev. de las Indias, 4. (Bogotá), 1939.

Burger, O. Erasmus von Rotterdam und der Spanier VIVES: eine pädagogische Studie. Diss. München, 1914.
Riber, L. Erasmo y Luis Vives. Bol. de la R. Acad. Española, 24-26, 1946-47.
Reed, A. W. Erasmus and John WEBSTER. TLS, 14.VI.1947.
Usteri, M. ZWINGLI und Erasmus. Zürich, 1885.

CHAPTER THREE

Spinoza.

1. General Influences.

Baeck, L. Spinozas erste Einwirkungen auf Deutschland. Berlin, 1895.
Baumgardt, D. Spinoza und der deutsche Spinozismus. Kant-Studien, 32, 1927.
Bellange, C. Spinoza et la philosophie moderne. Paris, 1912.
Espinosa, G. Un pretendido intérprete suramericano de Spinoza. Caracas, 1943.
Francès, M. Spinoza dans les pays néerlandais de la seconde moitié du XVIIe siècle. Paris, 1938.
Gruenwald, M. Spinoza in Deutschland. Berlin, 1897.
Lanson, G. Les origines et les premières mainfestations de l'esprit philosophique de 1675 à 1748. RCC, 1908-10.
Luzzatti, L. Benedetto Spinoza e i precursori della libertà di coscienza. NAnt, 35, 1877.
Meisels, S. Spinoza als Romanheld. Vossische Zt., Sonntagsbeilage, 51, 1910.
Nourrisson, F. Spinoza et le naturalisme contemporain. Paris, 1886.
Phillips, T. M. The Influence of Spinoza on Modern Literature. Papers Manchester Literary Club, 41, 1921.
Warnant, J. de. Spinoza et la France. RFB, 1932.

2. Influences upon Individual Authors.

Maurice, F. D. Spinoza and Professor ARNOLD. The Spectator, 31.I.1863.
Brunner, K. GOETHES Verhältnis zu Spinoza. Zunkunft, 21, 1912.
Caro, E. Goethe et Spinoza. RDM, 15.X. 1865.
Danzel, W. Ueber Goethes Spinozismus. Heidelberg, 1850.
Hering, R. E. Spinoza im jungen Goethe. Leipzig, 1897.
Kaufmann, M. Spinoza, Goethe and the Moderns. QR, 1912.
Krappe, S. Le Spinozisme de Goethe. In: Essais de critique d'histoire et de philosophie. Paris, 1902.
Kühnemann, E. Goethe und Spinoza. JbGG, 15, 1929.
Schneege, G. Goethes Verhältniss zu Spinoza und seiner philosophischen Weltanschauung. Phil. Monatshefte, 1891.
Springer, R. Goethe und Spinoza. Deutsches Museum, 1866.
Suphan, B. Goethe und Spinoza, 1783-86. Festschrift Gymnasium Berlin, 1881.
Tuerck, H. Spinoza und Faust. Tägl. Rundschau Unterh. Blatt, 46-48, 1900.
—— Neue Spinoza-Elemente im Faust. Kultur, 1, 1902.
Vogel, T. Nüchterne Erwägungen über Goethes Spinozismus. ZDU, 15, 1901.
Anon. Der Spinozismus HERDERS und Goethes. MLIA, 1870.
Vollrath, W. Die Auseinandersetzung Herders mit Spinoza. Diss. Giessen, 1911.
Stockum, T. C. van. Spinoza, Jacobi, LESSING. Groningen, 1916. Cf. Museum, 25, 1917.
Timmermans, B. Le Spinozisme de MAETERLINCK. Diss. Groningen, 1924.
McEachran, F. NIETZSCHE, Spinoza and Human Pity. Contemporary Rev., Dec., 1938.
Slochower, H. Spinoza und Nietzsche. Geisteskultur, 1928.
Eckstein, W. ROUSSEAU and Spinoza. Their Political Theories and Their Conception of Ethical Freedom. JHI, 5, 1944.
Cohen, G. Le séjour de SAINT-EVREMOND en Hollande et l'entrée de Spinoza dans le champ de la pensée française. Paris, 1926.
Schmidt, P. Spinoza und SCHLEIERMACHER. Berlin, 1868.
Padovani, U. A. SCHOPENHAUER, Spinoza e il panteismo. Spinazo Gedenkschrift, Milano, 1934.
Bernthsen, S. Der Spinozismus in SHELLEYS Weltanschauung. Heidelberg, 1900. Cf. Anglia Bb, 11, 1901.
Radetti, G. Cartesianismo e spinozismo nel pensiero del TSCHIRNHAUS. Etudes cartésiennes, 3, 1937.
Hazard, P. VOLTAIRE et Spinoza. MPh, 38, 1940-41.

CHAPTER FOUR

Vondel.

Hechtle, M. Joost van den Vondel. Sein Einfluss auf das deutsche Geistesleben. Joost van den Vondel Festschrift. Jena, 1937.
Weevers, T. Vondel's Influence on German Literature. MLR, 1937.
Flemming, W. Vondels Einfluss auf die Trauerspiele des Andreas **GRYPHIUS.** NPh, 14, 1928-29.
Kollewijn, A. Gryphius' Dornrose und Vondels Leeuwendalers. Archiv, 9, 1880.
Pott, C. K. Holland-German Literary Relations in the 17th Century: Vondel and Gryphius. JEGPh, 47, 1948.
Duflou. Vondel en **MILTON.** Nederl. Spectator, 1895.
Edmundson, G. Milton and Vondel, a Curiosity of Literature. London, 1885. Cf. Athenaeum, 7. & 21.IX.1885.
Gosse, E. G. Milton and Vondel. In: Studies in the Literature of Northern Europe. London, 1879.
Grierson, H. J. C. A Note Upon the Samson Agonistes of John Milton and Samson by Joost van den Vondel. Mélanges Baldensperger. Paris, 1930.
MacIbraith, J. R. Milton and Vondel. Academy, 28, 1885.
Mody, J. R. P. Vondel and Milton. Bombay, 1942.
Moltzer, H. E. Milton en Vondel. Noord en Zuid, 9, 1886.
Moolhuizen, J. J. Vondels Lucifer en Miltons Verloren Paradijs. S'Gravenhage, 1895.
Mueller, A. Ueber Milton's Abhängigkeit von Vondel. Diss. Berlin, 1891.
Zeegers, G. Joost van den Vondel (and Milton). Antwerpen, 1888.

CHAPTER FIVE

Other Dutch Authors.

Rudder, G. de. Etude sur la vie et les oeuvres de **CATS.** (Germany). Diss. Nancy, 1898.
Schröter, S. Jacob Cats Beziehungen zur deutschen Literatur. Diss. Heidelberg, 1905.
Barnouw, A. J. Goldsmith's Indebtedness to Justus van **EFFEN.** MLR, 1913.
Brown, J. E. Goldsmith's Indebtedness to Voltaire and Justus van Effen. MPh, 1926.
Brummel, L. Van Effens spectatorische Geschriften in ihren Verband met de Duitsche. De niewe Taalgids, 22, 1928.
Tielrooy, J. Rimbaud et les frères van **EYCK.** NPh, 1935.
Malaise, J. Een engelsche vertaling van het dagboek van Geert **GROOTE.** Bijdragen tot de Nederlandsche Taal- en Letterkunde, 1937.
Cohen, G. Une biographie inédite de Hugo **GROTIUS** par Samuel Sorbière. Mélanges Salverda de Grave. Groningen, 1933-34.
Beckherrn, R. M. Opitz, P. Ronsard und D. **HEINSIUS.** Diss. Königsberg, 1888.
Lebègue, R. L'Herodes Infanticide en France. NPh, 23, 1938.
Muth, B. Ueber das Verhältnis von Martin Opitz zu Daniel Heinsius. Leipzig, 1872.
Wevers, T. The Influence of Heinsius on Two Genres of the German Baroque. JEGPh, 37, 1938.
—— Some Aspects of Heinsius' Influence on the Style of Opitz. MLR, 34, 1939.
Funder, F. Frans **HEMSTERHUIS** und die Aesthetik der Engländer und Franzosen im 18. Jahrhundert. Diss. Bonn, 1912.
Poritzky, J. E. Franz Hemsterhuys. Seine Philosophie und ihr Einfluss auf die deutschen Romantiker. Berlin, 1926.
Knippenberg, H. H. Erycius Puteanus en Constantijn **HUYGHENS,** twee vrienden in oorlogstijd. Studiën, 1940.
Jong, M. de. **MULTATULI** (Dekker) in het Portugees. NPh, 23, 1938.
—— Ramalho Ortigão e o escritor holandes Multatuli. Coimbra, 1937.
Hubbard, L. L. A Dutch Source for Robinson Crusoe. (Hendrik **SMEEKS,** 1708). Ann Arbor, 1921.
Creizenach, W. Studien zur Geschichte der dramatischen Poesie im XVII. Jahrhundert: Die Tragödien des Holländers Jan **VOS** auf der deutschen Bühne. Berichte Königl. Sächsischen Ges. der Wissenschaften, 38, 1886.

CHAPTER SIX

Dutch Influences upon Individual Authors.

Gallas, K. R. L'Invitation au Voyage de **BAUDELAIRE** et la Hollande. NPh, 3, 1918.
Charlier, G. **DIDEROT** et la Hollande. RLC, 21, 1947.
Tielrooy, J. G. **DUHAMEL** over Neder-

land. Letterk. Bijbl. N. Rott. Courier, 206, 1926.

Daniels, J. Les rapports entre St. **FRANCOIS DE SALES** et les Pays-Bas. Nijmegen, 1932.

Kollewijn, A. Ueber den Einfluss des holländischen Dramas auf Andreas **GRYPHIUS.** Amersfoort, 1880.

Wysocki, L. G. A. Gryphius et la tragédie allemande au XVIIe siècle. Paris, 1893.

Walkhoff, P. **LAMARTINE** in Nederland. In: Ontmoetingen tussen Nederland en Frankrijk. La Haye, 1943.

Weevers, T. Some Unrecorded Dutch Originals of Opitz. NPh, 23, 1938.

Guilliou, E. L'abbé **PREVOST** en Hollande. La Haye, 1934.

Feugère, A. L'abbé **RAYNAL** et les Pays-Bas. Revue de Belgique, 1912.

Opstal, A. G. van. André **RIVET.** Een invloedrijk Hugenoot aan het hof van Frederik Hendrik. Harderwijk, 1937.

Cohen, G. Le séjour de **SAINT-EVREMONT** en Hollande. RLC, 5-6, 1925-26.

—— Le voyage de Samuel **SORBIÈRE** en Hollande en 1660. Mélanges Baldensperger. Paris, 1930.

Wiarda, R. **TAINE** et la Hollande. Paris, 1938.

Alizé, F. **VOLTAIRE** à la Haye en 1713. RP, 1922.

Kennedy, W. S. Dutch Traits of Walt **WHITMAN.** In: In re Walt Whitman. Philadelphia, 1893.

Hommes, T. Holland im Urteil eines Jungdeutschen. **(WIENBARG).** Diss. Amsterdam, 1926.

CHAPTER SEVEN

Belgian Contributions.

1. Generalities.

Anders, E. Das Flamentum in Frankreich, NM, 11.

Arents, P. Flemish Writers Translated (1830-1931). A Bibliographical Essay. s'Gravenhage, 1931.

Avermaete, R. La littérature belge d'expression flamande depuis 1830. Revue belge, 1930.

Backer, de. La langue flamande en France depuis les temps les plus reculés jusqu' à nos jours. Gand, 1893.

Carco, F. Ce que nous devons aux poètes belges. NL, 9.I.1937.

Counson, A. La Belgique romano-germanique. Belgique artistique et littéraire, 85, 1912.

Dumont Wilden, L. Les Flamands dans la littérature française. Cahiers de l' Acad. septentrionale, July, 1939.

Fischer, O. L'écho de la littérature flamande en Bohème. Prague, 1927.

Franck, L. La nationalité belge et le mouvement flamand. Séances et Travaux de l'Acad. des Sciences morales et politiques, Nov., 1930.

Heiss, H. Der vlamische Anteil an der französischen Literatur. Internat. Monatsschrift für Wiss., Kunst & Technik, 11, 1917.

Lazzeri, G. Interpreti dell'anima belga. Roma, 1917.

Lejeune. Définition de la littérature wallonne. NPh, 26, 1940-41.

Masoin, F. Histoire de la littérature française en Belgique de 1815 à 1830. Bruxelles, 1902.

Nautet, F. Histoire des lettres belges d'expression française. Bruxelles, 1892-93.

2. Belgian Authors.

Trautwein von Belle, E. Henrik **CONSCIENCE** in der Weltlitteratur. MLIA. 1883.

Singleton, R. H. Milton's Comus and the Comus of **ERYCIUS PUTEANUS.** PMLA, 58, 1943.

Anon. **MAETERLINCK** in French and English. Athenaeum, 4003, 1904.

Hagemann, K. Maeterlinck und W. Boelsche. Die Propylaen, 27.XI.1903.

Lecat, M. Bibliographie de Maurice Maeterlinck. Bruxelles, 1939.

Palleske, S. O. Maurice Maeterlinck en Allemagne. Strasbourg, Paris, 1938.

Rabuse, G. J. M. Synge's Verhältnis zur französischen Literatur und besonders zu Maeterlinck. Archiv, 174, 1938.

Hatzfeld, H. The Influence of Ramon Lull and Jan van **RUYSBROECK** on the Language of the Spanish Mystics. Traditio, 4, 1947.

Oechler, W. F. The Reception of Emile **VERHAEREN** in Germany. Some Unpublished Letters of Stefan Zweig. MLN, 60, 1947.

3. Belgian Influences upon Individual Authors.

Lescure, J. Le tempérament flamand et la vie flamande dans la Recherche de l'absolu de **BALZAC**. RU, 1934.
Glaesener, H. **GOETHE** et la Belgique. RLC, 12, 1932.
Govaert, C. Victor **HUGO** proscrit en Belgique. RFB, 1933.
Vanwelkenhuyzen, G. J. K. **HUYSMANS** et la Belgique. MF, 1935.
Grégoire, H. Le berceau belge des **NIBELUNGEN**. L'Europe Centrale, 9. & 16. VI.1934 & Byzantion, 9, 1934.
Griselle, E. **RACINE** et la Flandre. Revue de Lille, April, 1899.

SEVENTH PART

French Contributions.

CHAPTER ONE

Generalities.

(See also Emigrants & Refugees, I. IV. 4. For Normans, see IV. XII. 1.)

Angel, J. Culture européenne et culture française. Europe centrale, 5.VIII.1933.

Baldensperger, F. Intellectuels français hors de France. RCC, 1934-35.

Bourdeau, J. La France et les Français jugés à l'étranger. RDM, 1.IX.1890. And in: Poètes et humoristes de l'Allemagne. Paris, 1906.

Brownell, W. C. French Traits: An Essay in Comparative Criticism. London, 1889.

Caraccioli. L'Europe française. Turin, 1776.

Cayeux, C. de. Présence française à l'étranger. Esprit, June, 1946.

Chevé, A. L'esprit européen et l'influence française au XVIIIe siècle. Revue de Pologne, 1926-27.

Cohen-Portheim, P. Der Geist Frankreichs und Europa. Potsdam, 1926.

Crabitès, P. The Spiritual Empire of France. Catholic World, 1928.

Curtius, E. R. Französischer Geist im neuen Europa. Stuttgart, 1925.

Dariac, A. Les pionniers de l'idée française. RB, 17.VI.1933.

Davray, H. D. L'expansion intellectuelle et morale de la France. AFR, 1919.

Delavaud, L. Nos amis étrangers et la pensée française. Revue scandinave, 1912.

Deschamps, E. De l'influence de l'esprit français sur l'Europe depuis deux siècles. Paris, 1846.

Dumont-Wilden, L. Le théâtre et l'influence française à l'étranger. RB, 14.III. 1908.

Dussieux, L. Les artistes français à l'étranger. Paris, 1876.

Eckhardt, A. La mission mystique de la France. Nouvelle Revue de Hongrie, 1937.

Faquet, E. French Seventeenth Century Literature and its European Influence. In: Cambridge Modern History, 5, 1908.

Gaidoz, H. & Sébillot, P. Bibliographie des traditions et de la littérature populaire des Francs d'outre-mer. Paris, 1886.

Gascogne, J. Nos oeuvres dramatiques à l'étranger. RB, 18.IV.1896.

Goizet, J. & Burtal, A. Dictionnaire universel du théâtre français à l'étranger. Paris, 1867-68.

Griswold, W. M. A Descriptive List of Novels and Tales Dealing with Life in France. Cambridge, 1894.

Hazard, P. L'esprit français, axe de la civilisation. NL, 2.IV.1938.

Hennequin, E. Ecrivains francisés. Paris, 1889.

Jemsen, Emeline M. The Influence of French Literature on Europe. Boston, 1919.

Kleinau, G. Die kulturelle Position Frankreichs (im Ausland). DR, 1938.

Leblond, M. A. Das typisch Französische in der modernen Literatur. Rhein. Blätter, 1927.

Lefèbvre Saint-Ogan. Essai sur l'influence française. Paris, 1884.

Liais, E. Suprématie intellectuelle de la France. Paris, 1872.

Mann, K. Influences françaises. Cahiers du Sud, 1938.

Martin, H. Du rôle de la France dans la philosophie du moyen âge. Rev. Indép., 3, 1842.

Michels, R. Zum Wesen des Franzosentums. NM, 1, 1930.

Mille, P. La France dans le monde. Le Thyrse, 1939.

Peyre, H. The Influence of Contemporary French Literature in the World. Sewanee Rev., 48, 1940.

Raymond, M. Réflexions sur le génie de la France. Suisse Contemporaine, 1, 1941.

Reau, L. L'Europe française au siècle des lumières. Paris, 1938.

Rossel, V. Histoire de la littérature française hors de France. (Suisse, Belgique, Canada, Hollande, Angleterre etc.) Lausanne, 1895.

Sainte-Beuve, C. A. Des jugements sur notre littérature contemporaine à l'étranger. RDM, 15.VI.1836.

Sayous, A. Histoire de la littérature française à l'étranger depuis le commencement du XVIIe siècle. 2 vols. Paris, 1853.

Stern, A. Die Nachwirkung der französischen Aufklärungslitteratur in den Litteraturen des Südens und des Nor-

dens. In: Geschichte der neueren Litteratur, 4, Leipzig, 1882.
Tarde, A. de Les préjugés étrangers sur la France. Marches de l'Est, 15.X.1910.
Texte, J. L'hégémonie littéraire de la France au XVIIIe siècle. RCC, 1896.
Varia. Influences françaises à l'étranger. NL, 6. & 13.XI.1937.
Viatte, A. La pensée française d'outremer pendant la guerre. La Vie intellectuelle, Nov., 1945.
Villemain. Examen de l'influence exercée par les écrivains français du XVIIIe siècle sur la littérature étrangère et l'esprit européen. Paris, 1829.
Villers, H. de De l'influence de la France en Europe. Paris, 1846.
Weidlé, W. Le rayonnement culturel de la France. Le Mois, 1938.

CHAPTER TWO

French Influences upon the Americas.

Anon. Lessons from a French Novel. (For Americans). The Nation, 23.VII. 1908.
Altamirano, A. I. Influence de la littérature française sur la littérature mexicaine. Mexico, 1935.
Arnavon, C. Les débuts du roman réaliste américain et l'influence française. Cahiers des langues modernes, 1, 1946.
Bailey, R. E. French Culture in Mexico in the 19th Century. Dijon, 1936.
Bonsal, S. When the French Were Here: A Narrative of the Sojourn of the French Forces in America, (1778-81). New York, 1945.
Bostsarron, Sylvie. Le théâtre français à New York. FR, 21, 1948.
Bowe, F. L. Bibliographical Notes on Early American Translations from the French. Papers of the Bibliogr. Soc. of America, 35, 1941.
Breton, M. Le. The French in Boston in the Eighteenth Century. Bordeaux, 1929.
Chinard, G. Les origines françaises du transcendentalisme américain. Paris, 1918.
—— La littérature française dans le Sud des Etats-Unis d'après le Southern Literary Messenger (1834-64). RLC, 8, 1928.
Choisy, G. Les lettres françaises aux Etats-Unis. RB, 1.IX.1900.
Croisset, F. de. L'influence au Brésil de la culture française. Le Journal, 18.XI. 1931.
Deschamps, G. Conférences d'Amérique, la littérature française outre-mer, la littérature française et les universités d'Amérique. Le Temps, 3, 10, 31.III. & 21.IV.1901.
Dorchain, A. Le théâtre français en Amérique. Annales politiques et littéraires, 18.XI.1900.
Fay, B. L'esprit révolutionnaire en France et aux Etats-Unis à la fin du XVIIIe siècle. Paris, 1925.
Fecteau, E. French Contributions to America. Methuen (Mass.), 1945.
Forbes, A. & Cadman, P. F. France and New England. Historic Monographs of the State Street Trust Co. Boston, 1929.
Frierson, W. C. & Edwards, H. The Impact of French Naturalism on American Critical Opinion, 1877-92. PMLA, 63, 1948.
Génin, A. Les Français au Méxique du XVIe siècle à nos jours. Paris, 1935.
Gentil, G. Le. L'influence parnassienne au Brésil. RLC, 11, 1931.
Harris, J. Can the Study of French Literature Survive in America? FR, 1939.
Haskins, C. G. L'histoire de France aux Etats-Unis. RP, 1920.
Hazard, P. Traductions populaires des romantiques français au Méxique. RLC, 10, 1930.
Hillebrand, K. Ein amerikanischer Novellist über seine französischen Collegen. MLIA, 1878.
Hyde, J. H. La littérature française aux Etats-Unis. In: Lectures pour tous. Corbeil, 1913.
Johnson, Margaret L. Contemporary Translations from the French. Southern Literary Messenger, 3, 1941.
Jones, H. M. America and French Culture, 1750-1848. Chapel Hill (N. C.), 1927.
—— The Importation of French Literature in New York City, 1750-1800. SPh, 28, 1931.
—— The Importation of French Books in Philadelphia, 1750-1800. MPh, 1934.
Kress, D. El peso de la influencia francesa en la renovación de la prosa hispano-americana. Hisp, May, 1937.
Lafimer, A. M. French Thought in Argentina. Inter-America, Dec., 1917.
Lima-Barbosa, M. de Les Français dans l'histoire du Brésil. Rio de Janeiro, Paris, 1923.
Loughrey, Mary E. France and Rhode Island, 1686-1800. New York, 1945.
Lowry, Hope. L'influence de la littérature française sur les poètes hispano-américains de l'école modernista. Diss. McGill (Montreal), 1931.
Mason, A. H. French Theatre in New

York: A List of Plays, 1899-1939. Columbia U. P., 1940.
Merlant, J. Soldiers and Sailors of France in the American War of Independence. New York, 1920.
Milles, W. M. A French Community in Ohio. FR, 1946.
Morrissette, B. A. Early English and American Critics of French Symbolism. Festschrift F. W. Shipley. St. Louis, 1942.
Nasatir, A. P. French Activities in California. Stanford U., 1945.
Poëte, M. L'expansion intellectuelle de la France aux Etats-Unis. RB, 23.XII. 1911.
Ponte Dominguez, A. Francia y la historia política de Cuba. U. de la Habana, 1935.
Rabinovitz, A. L. Criticism of French Novels in Boston Magazines: 1830-60. NEQ, 14, 1941.
Raeders, G. L'influence française au Brésil. France-Amérique, Jan., 1937.
Rice, H. C. Témoignages américains: Livres américains sur la France parus depuis 1940. Paru (Paris), 1945.
Riley, I. W. La philosophie française en Amérique. Rev. philosophique, Nov., 1917 & May, 1919.
Ripley, G. Jugement d'un auteur américain sur la nouvelle école philosophique française. Constitutionnel, 1.VIII.1841.
Roy, C. Le folklore français au Missouri. Le Canada français, 1936.
Roz, F. & Préclin, E. L'influence de la France sur la vie intellectuelle du Canada anglais et des Etats-Unis. France-Amérique, 1935-36.
Rudwin, M. Les lettres françaises aux Etats-Unis en 1938. France-Etats-Unis, Feb., 1939.
Sas, L. F. The Spirit of France in Argentine. FR, 15, 1942.
Schinz, A. La librairie française en Amérique au temps de Washington. RHLF, 1917.
—— Le livre français aux Etats-Unis. RP, 15.II.1936.
Schoenberger, H. W. American Adaptations of French Plays on the New York and Philadelphia Stages from 1790 to 1833. Diss. Philadelphia, 1924.
Scott, J. D. La dette spirituelle des Etats-Unis à l'égard de la France. France-Amérique, 30, 1939.
Scott, R. C. L. American Travellers in France, 1830-60. Diss. Yale U., 1940.
Sears, E. I. French Romances and American Morals. National Quarterly Rev., 2, 1860.
Seeber, E. D. The French Theatre in Charleston in the Eighteenth Century. S. C. Hist. and Genealogical Mag., 42, 1941.
Spiker, C. C. The North American Review and French Morals. West Va. U. Bull. Philol. Stud., 4, 1943.
Taupin, R. L'influence du symbolisme français sur la poésie américaine de 1910 à 1920. Paris, 1929.
—— L'interprétation américaine de la poésie française contemporaine. Paris, 1929.
Thieme, H. P. La civilisation française jugée par un Américain. RDM, 1924.
Tronchon, H. Huit mois au Brésil. (French Influences). Paris, 1938.
Ureña, M. H. Les influences françaises sur la poésie hispano-américaine. Institut des Etudes américaines, 1937.
Uzarte, M. B. Notes sur l'Amérique du Sud et la littérature française. Revue des Revues, 1899.
Wacht, E. French Theatre Through American Eyes. Le Spectateur, 1946.
Waldo, L. P. The French Drama in America in the Eighteenth Century. Baltimore, 1942.
White, Elizabeth B. American Opinion of France from Lafayette to Poincaré. New York, 1927.

CHAPTER THREE

French Influences upon Canada, Louisiana and Haiti.

Anon. La vie franco-américaine. Manchester (N. H.), 1945.
Beaubien, C. P. Le problème de la survivance française au Canada et les influences américaines. France-Amérique, 30, 1939.
Bellegarde, A. D. The Significance of French Culture in Louisiana. Southwest Journal, 1, 1945.
Bisson, L. A. Le romantisme littéraire au Canada français. Paris, 1932.
Caulfield, R. V. A. The French Literature in Louisiana. New York, 1929.
Chartier, E. La vie de l'esprit au Canada français: les survivances françaises. Mémoires de la Soc. Royale du Canada, 33, 1939 & Montréal, 1941.
Cruchet, R. France et Louisiane. Louisiana State U. P., 1939.
Dibelius, W. Die Franzosen in Canada unter den Anfängen der englischen Herrschaft. NM, 1, 1930.
Doehn, R. Frankreich in Nord-Amerika. MLIA, 1876.

Ende, E. van. Franco-amerikanische Literatur. Beilage zur Allg. Zt., 106, 1901.
Fabre, H. La société française au Canada. Réf. sociale, 1886.
Fortier, A. French Literature in Louisiana. PMLA, 2, 1886 & MLN, 6, 1891.
Fortier, E. J. Les lettres françaises en Louisiane. Mémoires du 1. Congrès de la Langue française au Canada, Quebec, 1915.
Fraser, I. F. Bibliography of French-Canadian Poetry. New York, 1935.
—— The Spirit of French Canada: A Study of the Literature. Columbia U. P., 1939.
Frégault, G. La civilisation de la Nouvelle France, 1733-44. Montréal, 1944.
Graf, I. Die Anfänge der französisch-kanadischen Dichtung. Diss. Würzburg, 1936.
Ham, B. En marge de la survivance franco-américaine. Le Canada français, 27, 1939.
Heller, O. Französische Poesie in Canada. MLIA, 1883.
Jaray, G. L. La France en Acadie France-Amérique, 1935.
—— L'héritage du passé et les Français d'Amérique. Paris, 1937.
—— L'Empire français d'Amérique, (1534-1803). Paris, 1938.
Jobin, A. J. Present and Future Trends in French Canadian Nationalist Literature. FR, 16, 1943.
Lanzac de Laborie. L'Amérique française. Correspondant, 25.VI.1930.
Léger, J. Le Canada français et son expression littéraire. Paris, 1938.
Leland, M. La vie intellectuelle au Canada français. FR, 15, 1942.
Loizeau, G. Les provinces de France au Canada. Rev. des Questions histor., 1934.
Marion, S. Le roman et le Canada français du XIXe siècle. Revue de l'U. d'Ottawa, 13, 1943.
Moraud, M. Explorateurs et pionniers français en Louisiane. FR, 13, 1940.
Morrissette, N. Quelques facteurs essentiels de la survivance française au Canada. France-Amérique, 1935.
Priestley, H. I. France Overseas Through the Old Régime. New York, 1940.
Tinker, L. Ecrits de la langue française en Louisiane au XIXe siècle. Paris, 1933.
Vattier, G. Essai sur la mentalité canadienne-française. Paris, 1927.
Viatte, A. Chez les parlants français du Nouveau Monde, Canada, Louisiane, Haïti. RdF, 1935.
—— La langue et la littérature françaises dans la République d'Haïti. France-Amérique, 1937.
—— Tendances de la littérature canadienne-française. FR, 17, 1944.
Wade, M. The French-Canadian Outlook. New York, 1946.
Walter, F. Letters in Canada; French-Canadian Letters. UTQ, 1937.

CHAPTER FOUR

French Influences upon England.

(For Normans, see IV.XII.1)

Anon. Die Edinburgh Review über die neueste französische Literatur. Blätter für literar. Unterhaltung, 24-25.I.1834.
—— Englische Kritik und französische Replik. Blätter zur Kunde der Litt. des Auslands, 1836.
—— Les Anglais en voyage: France. Rev. Brit., Nov., 1839.
—— The Pleiade and the Elizabethans. ER, 205, 1907.
—— Short-Title Catalogue of Books Printed in France and of French Books Printed in Other Countries from 1470 to 1600 Now in the British Museum. London, 1924.
—— Our Debts to France. TLS, 3.XII. 1938.
Arnold, M. The French Play in London. NC, 1879. And in: Irish Essays. London, 1882.
Bailey, J. C. English Taste and French Drama: In: The Claims of French Poetry. London, 1912.
Baldensperger, F. Un incident théâtral franco-anglais au XVIIIe siècle d'après un témoignage diplomatique. RLC, 9, 1929.
—— English Artistic Prose and its Debt to French Writers. MLF, 29, 1944.
Barine, A. Les Anglais à Blois en 1775. Journal des Débats, 19.III.1895.
Barlow, G. French Plays and English Audiences. Contemporary Rev., 1893.
Bastide, C. Les Français peints par les Anglais. Foi et Vie, 16.X.1905.
—— Anglais en France au XVIIIe siècle. Paris, 1912.
Baugh, A. C. The Chester Plays and French Influence. Schelling Anniversary Papers. New York, 1923.
Bernard, J. M. La jeune poésie française vue d'Angleterre. Revue critique des idées et des livres, 10.I.1913.

Boutelleau, C. Peg's Club. RP, 16.XII. 1936.

Cazamian, M. L. Le roman et les idées en Angleterre. Paris, 1935.

Charlanne, L. L'influence française en Angleterre au XVIIe siècle. Paris, 1906.

Churton Collins. The Literary Indebtedness of England to France. Fortnightly Review, 1908.

Conard, N. Poèmes à la France de grands poètes anglais (1939-44). Paris, 1947.

Dallington, R. The View of France, 1604, (Introduction by W. P. Barrett). Oxford U. P., 1936.

Darwall, R. M. The English in France in the Early XIXth Century. N&Q, 172, 1937.

Deschamps, G. Jugement d'un Anglais sur la France. Le Temps, 21.VII.1901.

Dukes, A. French Drama and English Stage. Theatre Art Monthly, 21, 1937.

Ellenhauge, M. English Restoration Drama: Its Relation to Past English and Past and Contemporary French Drama. Copenhagen, 1933.

Evans, D. O. French Romanticism and British Reviewers. FQ, 9, 1927.

Filon, A. Le théâtre anglais contemporain. Paris, 1896.

Freeman, E. A Proposal for an English Academy in 1660. MLR, 1924.

Frierson, W. L'influence du naturalisme français sur les romanciers anglais. Paris, 1925.

Fuchs, M. & P. Comédiens français à Londres (1738-55). RLC, 13, 1933.

Fusil, L. Le théâtre français à Londres en 1815. Suppl. du Constitutional, 23.V. 1841.

Galdemar, A. The Comédie Française in London. Fortnightly Review, 1893.

Gosse, Sir E. French Profiles. London, 1905.

Grappe, G. Les romanciers français devant la critique anglaise. L'Opinion, 5.IX.1908.

Hamilton, C. Modern France as Seen by an Englishman. London, 1933.

Hanstein, M. Die französische Literatur im Urteil der englischen Romantiker. Diss. Leipzig. Halle, 1921.

Harvey-Jellie, W. Le théâtre classique en Angleterre dans l'âge de John Dryden. Montréal, 1032.

Haviland. The Roman de longue haleine on English Soil. Diss. Philadelphia, 1931.

Hearn, L. Our Modern English Criticism, and the Contemporary Relation of English to French Literature. In: Life and Literature. New York, 1919.

Holmes, U. T. The French Novel in English Translation. Chapel Hill (N. C.), 1930.

Holthausen, F. Die Quelle des mittelenglische Gedichtes Lob der Frauen. Archiv, 108, 1902.

Jusserand, J. J. The English Novel in the Time of Shakespeare. London, 1890.

Kastner, L. E. The Scottish Sonneteers and the French Poets. MLR, 3, 1907.

—— The Elizabethan Sonneteers and the French Poets. MLR, 3, 1908.

Kinne, W. A. Revivals and Importations of French Comedies in England, 1749-1800. Columbia U.P., 1939.

Lawrence, J. Early French Players in England. In: The Elizabethan Playhouse and Other Studies. Stratford-on-Avon, 1912.

Lee, S. The French Renaissance in England. Oxford, 1910. Cf. RB, 19.XI.1910.

Lester, J. A. Some Franco-Scottish Influences on the Early English Drama. Haverford Essays (Pa.), 1909.

MacIntyre, E. J. French Influence on the Beginnings of English Classicism. PMLA, 26, 1911.

Maiberger, M. Studien über den Einfluss Frankreichs auf die elisabethanische Literatur. Diss. München, 1903.

Mathorez, J. Notes sur les intellectuels écossais en France au XVIe siècle. Bull. du Bibliophile, March, 1919.

Maxwell, C. The English Traveller in France, 1698-1715. London, 1932.

Moraud, M. The French Drama in England, 1815-40. Rice Inst. Pamphlet (Texas), 1928.

—— La France de la Restauration d'après les visiteurs anglais. Paris, 1933.

—— Le romantisme français en Angleterre. Diss. Paris, 1933.

—— Le théâtre français à Londres sous la Restauration. FR, 22, 1948.

Mortimer, R. La France et la littérature anglaise. L'Arche, 1 (Alger), 1944.

Pinto, V. de S. The English Romantics and France. Spectator, Jan., 1946.

Quesnel, L. Le théâtre anglais contemporain. RB, 1882.

Reimeringer, A. L'opinion anglaise sur les institutions françaises au XVIIIe siècle. Paris, 1938.

Roth, G. Le théâtre classique français en Angleterre. RU, 15.VII.1907.

Salvan, J. L. Le romantisme français et l'Angleterre victorienne. Diss. U. of Michigan, 1937.

Saroléa, C. Influence de la culture française sur la culture anglaise. Revue française d'Edimbourg, 1, 1897.

Scarfe, F. H. The French Background in

English Poetry, 1850-1900. Diss. Cambridge U., 1940.
Schickler, B. de. L'histoire de France dans les archives privées de la Grande-Bretagne. JS, 1878.
Smith, A. H. Les événements politiques de France dans le théâtre anglais du siècle d'Elisabeth. Diss. Paris, 1908.
Smith, J. H. French Sources for Six English Comedies, 1600-1750. JEGPh, 47, 1948.
Smith, J. M. The French Background of Middle Scots Literature. Edinburgh, 1934.
Stern, A. Die französische Schule in der englischen Dichtung. In: Geschichte der neueren Literatur, 4, Leipzig, 1882.
Taine, H. L'esprit français importé en Angleterre: Les Normands. Revue de l'instruction publique, 28.II.1856.
Tucker, J. E. English Translations from the French 1650-1700: Corrections and Additions to the Cambridge Bibliography of English Literature. PhQ, 21, 1942.
Upham, A. H. The French Influence in English Literature from the Accession of Elizabeth to the Restoration. New York, 1908.
Watson, E. B. From Sheridan to Robertson, a Study of the Nineteenth Century London Stage. Cambridge, 1926.
Weightman, J. G. French Writing on English Soil, (1940-44). London, 1945.
Wollstein, R. H. English Opinions of French Poetry. Columbia U. P., 1923.
Wood, Kathryn L. The French Theatre in the XVIIIth Century According to Some Contemporary English Travellers. RLC, 12, 1932.
Wray, E English Adaptations of French Dramas between 1780 and 1815. MLN, 1928.
Yanoski, J. Les historiens français jugés par les Anglais. National, 6.XI.1841.
Yvon, P. Les Français et la société anglaise au XVIIIe siècle. RELV, 1912.

CHAPTER FIVE

French Influences upon Germany.

Anon. Diskurs, welcher Gestalt man den Franzosen im gemeinen Leben und Wandel nachahmen solle. Leipzig, 1687.
—— Französischer Dichter und Berliner Kritiker. Blätter für litterar. Unterhaltung, 10.X.1830.
—— Répertoire du Théâtre français à Berlin, 4 vols. Berlin, 1830-48.
—— Die Einführung der französischen Mode in Deutschland. Europa, 1862.
—— Französische Romane in deutschen Uebersetzungen. Beilage zur Allg. Zt., 29.XI.1897.
—— Les comédiens français à Berlin. Le Temps, 22.I.1901.
—— Unsere Stellung zum französischen Klassicismus. Konservative Monatsschrift, Sept., 1918.
—— French Culture through German Eyes. TLS, Feb., 1923.
Babou, H. Les princes allemands à la cour de Versailles. Athenaeum français, 8.III.1856.
Bamberger, L. Die Französelei am Rheine. In: Demokratische Studien. Hamburg, 1861. And in: Studien und Meditationen. Berlin, 1897.
Barine, A. Le Français jugé par l'Allemand. RB, 13.VIII.1881.
Berry, R. M. The French Symbolist Poets in Germany: Criticism and Translations, 1870-1914. Diss. Harvard, 1944.
Bertaux, F. Le retour de l'Allemagne à la culture française. Cahiers alsaciens, May, 1912.
Betz, L. P. Das französische Theater im Kurfürstentum Pfalzbayern (1679-1770). LE, July, 1901.
Bloesch, H. Das junge Deutschland in seinen Beziehungen zu Frankreich. Bern, 1903.
Bolte, J. Französische Einflüsse auf das deutsche Schauspiel vor 1700. Archiv, 1889.
Bourdeau, J. Notre littérature en Allemagne. Journal des Débats, 21.III.1879.
Brausewetter, E. Die französischen Gesellschaftsdramen und ihr Einfluss auf die deutsche dramatische Litteratur. Bühne und Leben, 2, 1894.
Brieger, A. Französische Lyrik in deutscher Uebersetzung. Internat. Litteraturberichte, 21.III.1901.
Brochard, P. L'influence française en Allemagne. Cahiers du Sud, 1938.
Brun, L. La France jugée par un Allemand. RG, 1924.
Brunot, F. La civilisation française en Allemagne au XVIIe. siècle. RP, 1.VIII. 1915.
Chélard, R. La civilisation française dans le développement de l'Allemagne. Paris, 1900.
Cohn, F. L. France and the Poetry of the German Vormärz. Diss. U. of California, 1938.
Cramer, L. D. Ueber den schädlichen Einfluss des französischen Despotismus auf die Literatur der Deutschen. Quedlinburg, 1815.

Curtius, E. R. Was wir an Frankreich lieben. NSR, 1928.

Delbost, R. Conférances françaises en Allemagne. RB, 1902.

Dieffenbach, F. Der französische Einfluss in Deutschland unter Ludwig XIV. Dresden, 1891.

Diehl, O. L'influence de l'art français sur la poésie allemande. MF, 15.X.1938.

Duthie, E. L. L'influence du symbolisme français dans le renouveau poétique de l'Allemagne: les Blätter für die Kunst de 1892 à 1900. Paris, 1933.

Elsener, C. Die Beziehungen zwischen der deutschen und französischen Poesie im Mittelalter. Progr. Zug, 1873 & 1879.

Firmery, J. Notes critiques sur quelques traductions allemandes de poèmes français au moyen âge. Paris, 1901.

Fritsch, P. Influence du théâtre français sur le théâtre allemand de 1870 jusqu' aux approches de 1900. Diss. Paris, 1912.

Gandillac, M. de. La France devant l'Allemagne. Suisse contemporaine, Feb., 1947.

Gebauer, C. Geschichte des französischen Kultureinflusses auf Deutschland von der Reformation bis zum dreissigjährigen Kriege. Strassburg, 1911.

Goethe, J. W. von. Französisches Schauspiel in Berlin. Sämtliche Werke, 29. Berlin, 1828.

Golther, W. Einflüsse der altfranzösischen Litteratur auf die altdeutsche. Krit. Jahresbericht über die Fortschritte der roman. Philol., 1890.

Gottschall, R. Die französische Richtung der neuen deutschen Dramatik und Dramaturgie. Deutsches Museum, 1857.

Grand-Carteret, J. La France jugée par l'Allemagne. Paris, 1886. Cf. MLIA, 1887.

Guglia, E. Analekten zur deutschen Litteraturgeschichte. Aufnahme französischer Schriftsteller in Deutschland in der 2. Hälfte des 18. und zu Anfang des 19. Jahrhunderts. Progr. Wien, 1901.

Heiss, H. Deutschland und die klassische Tragödie der Franzosen. Internat. Monatschrift für Wissenschaft, 12, 1925.

Hessem, L. de. Le roman en Allemagne. Revue Encyclopédique, 7.IV.1897.

Hohenhausen, F. von. Deutsche Romane aus französischer Geschichte. MLIA, 1864.

—— Deutsche Kritik des heutigen französischen Theaters. MLIA, 1868.

Honegger, J. J. Kritische Geschichte der französischen Cultureinflüsse in den letzten Jahrhunderten. Strassburg, 1875.

Jeanroy, J. Les origines de la poésie lyrique en France. (et en Allemagne). Paris, 1889.

Kaemmel, H. J. Der Einfluss der französischen Sprache und Litteratur auf die höheren Stände Deutschlands seit der Mitte des XVI. Jahrhunderts. Progr. Zittau, 1853.

Kerr, A. Das Théâtre Libre in Berlin. MLIA, 1894.

King, A. H. The Influence of French Literature on German Prose and the Drama between 1880 and 1890. London, 1933.

Kotzebue, A. Politische Flugblätter II: Was verdanken wir den Franzosen? Königsberg, 1816.

Krauss, R. Französische Komödie am Württembergischen Hofe im Jahre 1748. Neues Tagblatt, Stuttgart, 2.V. 1906.

—— Zur Geschichte des Schauspiels am Württembergischen Hofe bis zum Tode Karl Alexanders: Französische Komödianten. Württemberg. Vierteljahrshefte für Landesgeschichte, 16, 1907.

Krieck, E. Geistige Invasion des Westens im deutschen XVIII. Jahrhundert. Volk im Werden, 1939.

Lamotte, L. A. Versuch über den Einfluss der französischen Literatur in den Sitten der deutschen Nation. Stuttgart, 1780.

Lauret, R. L'esprit français et l'Allemagne. Wissen und Leben, 1923.

Lindau, P. Das französische Theater in Berlin. Gegenwart, 1872-74.

Loen, von. Erörterung der Frage: ob die Teutschen wohl thun, dass sie den Franzosen nachahmen? In: Kleine Schriften. Frankfurt, 1741.

Maas, M. Die französische Tragödie und ihre deutschen Kritiker. MLIA, 1861.

Mayer, H. La littérature française en Allemagne. Synthèses (Bruxelles), 1946.

Meier, E. von. Französische Einflüsse auf die Staats- und Rechtsentwicklung Preussens im XIX. Jahrhundert. Leipzig, 1907-08.

Meyer, F. Welchen Wert hat für uns noch jetzt die klassische Tragödie der Franzosen? Progr. Breslau, 1892.

Moeser, L. Ein Beitrag zur Kritik der französischen Tragödie mit Beziehung auf Deutschland. Diss. Jena, 1875.

Muench, W. Zur Kunst des Uebersetzens aus dem Französischen. ZFSL, 9, 1887.

Muret, M. La France littéraire et les critiques allemands. Journal des Débats, 19.X.1919.

Naumann, H. Die ritterliche Kultur der

Stauferzeit und der französische Westen. In: Von deutscher Art in Sprache und Dichtung. Stuttgart, 1941.

Neubert, F. Studien zur französischen Aufklärungsliteratur. GRM, 1921.

Olivier, J. J. Les comédiens français dans les cours d'Allemagne au XVIIIe siècle. Paris, 1901-02.

Randall, A. W. G. French Symbolism and Modern German Poetry. AFR, 1920.

Reinach, J. De l'influence historique de la France sur l'Allemagne. RB, 7.VII. 1877.

Reynaud, L. Les origines de l'influence française en Allemagne. Paris, 1913.

—— Histoire générale de l'influence française en Allemagne. Paris, 1915.

—— La culture française en Allemagne. Minerve française, 15.XI.1920.

Rivier, A. La poésie lyrique française en Allemagne. Revue de Belgique, 29, 1878.

Roertgen, W. F. The Sources of the French Reviews in the Frankfurter Gelehrte Anzeigen of 1772. JEGPh, 47, 1948.

Roisin, F. de De l'influence française sur les moeurs et la littérature en Allemagne. Séances et Trav. de l'Acad. de Reims, 10, 1849.

Ruehs, F. Historische Entwicklung des Einflusses Frankreichs und der Franzosen auf Deutschland und die Deutschen. Berlin, 1815.

Schilling, F. Die Uebersetzungen ins Deutsche, namentlich aus dem Französischen. Progr. Liegnitz, 1898.

Schilling, H. Der Franzose im deutschen Drama. Bern, 1931.

Schmitz, O. A. H. Was uns Frankreich war. München, 1914.

Schnabel, F. Der französische Geist und unsere Zukunft. Das neue Deutschland, 10, 1922.

Schneider, F. J. Japeta (1643). Ein Beitrag zur Geschichte des französischen Klassizismus in Deutschland. Stuttgart, 1927.

Sénéchal, C. L'Allemagne à l'école de la France. Vie des Peuples, 1924.

Sieburg, F. Gott in Frankreich? Frankfurt, 1929. Dieu est-il français? (suivi d'une lettre de B. Grasset). Paris, 1930.

Steinhausen, G. Die Anfänge des französischen Litteratur- und Kultureinflusses in Deutschland in neuerer Zeit. ZVL, 7, 1894.

Stoessinger, F. Was ist uns Frankreich? Weltbühne, 18, 1922.

Strauss, B. La culture française à Francfort au XVIIIe siècle. Paris, 1914.

Strecker, K. Die Franzosenherrschaft auf der deutschen Bühne. Deutsche Monatsschrift, 1903.

Sugenheim, S. Frankreichs Einfluss auf, und die Beziehungen zu, Deutchland seit der Reformation bis zur ersten Staatsumwälzung (1517-1789). 2 vols. Stuttgart, 1845-56.

Thomasius, C. Von der Nachahmung der Franzosen (1687 & 1701). Stuttgart, 1894.

Tieck, L. Ueber die neuen französischen Stücke auf dem deutschen Theater (1827). In: Kritische Schriften, 4. Leipzig, 1852.

Trautmann, K. Französische Komödianten in Augsburg (1613). ALG, 14, 1886.

—— Französische Schauspieler am bayerischen Hofe. Jb. f. Münchener Geschichte, 2-3, 1888.

Volz, B. Das französische Theater in Berlin unter Friedrich dem Grossen. Vossische Zt. Beilage, 37-38, 1904.

Voretzsch, K. Reisen Deutscher nach der Provence und Südfrankreich in früheren Zeiten. Volkstum und Kultur der Romanen, 11, 1938.

Weber-Luskow, H. Französisches Schrifttum in deutscher Sprache. Internat. Litteraturberichte, 21.III.1900.

Wechssler, E. Einflüsse der altfranzösischen Litteratur auf die altdeutsche. Germanisches in der altfranzösischen Dichtung. Jahresberichte, 1895-96, 1900.

—— Die Auseinandersetzung des deutschen Geistes mit der französischen Aufklärung, 1732-1832. DVLG, 1923.

Wekherlin. Ueber den Herostatismus unserer Literatur. Verteidigung der französischen Literatur. Chronologen, 4, 1779.

Wilmotte, M. Les passions allemandes du Rhin dans leur rapport avec l'ancien théâtre français. Paris, 1898.

Witzenetz, J. Le théâtre français de Vienne (1752-72). Szeged, 1932.

Wyzewa, T. de. Un Allemand en France. Le Temps, 13263, 1898.

Zabel, E. Französische Gäste auf deutschen Bühnen. In: Zur modernen Dramaturgie. Oldenburg, 1899.

Zöllner, R. Französische Einflüsse auf die deutsche Literatur des XVI. und der ersten Hälfte des XVII. Jahrhunderts. Deutsches Museum, 1865.

CHAPTER SIX

French Influences upon Italy.

Anon. Sulla drammatica compagnia francese a Milano. Riv. Europea, 1840.
Arcari, P. M. Influssi francesi nell' ottocento italiano. Mélanges Baldensperger. Paris, 1930.
—— La Francia nell'opinione pubblica italiana dal 1859 al 1870. Roma, 1934.
Bédarida, H. Parme et la France de 1748 à 1789. Paris, 1928. Cf. Marzocco, 13.V. 1928.
—— Parme dans la politique française au XVIIIe siècle. Paris, 1929.
—— & Hazard, P. L'influence française en Italie au XVIIIe siècle. Paris, 1934.
Bertoni, G. L'imitazione francese nei poeti meridionali della scuola poetica siciliana. Mélanges Chabaneau & RF, 1907.
Boyer, F. Les artistes français et les amateurs italiens au XVIIIe siècle. Bull. de la Soc. de l'Histoire de l'Art français, 1938.
Calcaterra, C. Storia della poesia frugoniana. Genova, 1920.
Camus, J. Notices et extraits des ms. français de Modène antérieurs au XVIe siècle. RLR, 35, 1891.
Capone Braga, G. La filosofia francese e italiana del settecento. Arezzo, 1921.
Carli, A. de. Autour de quelques traductions et imitations du théâtre français publiées à Bologne de 1690 à 1750. Bologna, 1920.
—— L'influence du théâtre français à Bologne, de la fin du XVIIe siècle à la grande Révolution. Torino, 1925.
Cascio, A. L'influenza del teatro tragico francese in Italia. Castelvetrano, 1906.
Castets, F. Recherches sur les rapports des chansons de geste et de l'épopée chevaleresque italienne. RLR, 27.
Cesario, M. L'illuminismo francese in Italia. Rassegna di studi francesi, Nov., 1925.
Cochin, H. Ce que disaient d'eux-mêmes les Français au XVIe siècle (d'après les Italiens). In: En souvenir d'H. Cochin. Paris, 1928.
Darré, H. La littérature française en Italie. EI, 1925-26.
Dejob, C. Etudes sur la tragédie (influence du théâtre français en Italie aux XVIIIe et XIXe siècles). Paris, 1896.
Delio, E. La letteratura francese in Italia nei secoli XI, XII, XIII. Sinigaglia, 1897.
Ferrari, L. Le traduzioni italiane del teatro tragico francese nei secoli XVII e XVIII. Paris, 1925.
Gaidoz, H. Les vallées françaises du Piémont. Annales de l'Ecole libre des sciences politiques, 1887.
Galletti, A. La tragedia classica italiana del secolo XVIII. Cremona, 1901.
Gaspary, A. Sur l'épopée française en Italie. Romania, 18. And in: Storia della letteratura italiana, 1. Torino, 1887.
Graillot, H. Un prince de Toscane à la cour de Louis XIV en 1669. Mélanges Hauvette. Paris, 1934.
Guillon, A. De quelques préventions des Italiens contre la langue et la littérature des Français. Paris, Milan, 1805.
Hazard, P. La culture française en Italie. Minerve française, March, 1920.
Hermite de Soliers, dit Tristan. La Toscane française contenant les éloges historiques et généalogiques des princes, seigneurs et grands capitaines de la Toscane, lesquels ont été affectionnés à la couronne de France. Paris, 1661.
Jeanroy, A. La lirica francese in Italia nel periodo delle origini. Firenze, 1897.
Libri, G. De l'influence française en Italie. RDM, 1.III.1841.
Malvano, E. L. L'Italie et la littérature française, de la Renaissance au Romantisme. Ausonia, 5, 1940.
Maugain, G. L'évolution intellectuelle de l'Italie de 1657 à 1750 environ. Paris, 1909.
—— Les débuts de la tragédie française en Italie. Annales de l'U. de Grenoble, 1918.
Novati, F. I codici francesi dei Gonzaga secondo nuovi documenti. Romania, 19, 1890.
Ojetti, U. L'invasion du théâtre français en Italie. Renaissance latine, 15.XI. 1902.
Oliva, D. De l'influence française en Italie. Renaissance latine, 15.X.1902.
Pélissier, L. G. Notes italiennes d'histoire de la France. RLR, 7, 1894 ff.
Pingaud, A. Le théâtre français en Italie, 1806-14. NRI, 1920.
Rati Opizzoni di Torre, L. A. La culture française à Turin et dans le Piémont. Rev. de l'Alliance française, 1931.
Rota, E. L'esthétique du sensualisme français dans la littérature italienne au XVIIIe siècle. NRI, 1920.
Spont, A. La France dans l'Italie du Nord au XVe siècle. Revue des questions historiques. 1897.
Thibault, G. De la vogue de quelques livres français à Venise. H&R, 2, 1935.

Valmaggi, L. Sulla fonte francese del Trattato di virtu morali. GSLI, 10, 1887.

CHAPTER SEVEN

French Influences in Spain and Portugal.

Anon. La littérature française en Espagne. Polybiblion, 1878.
Alboize, E. Les comédiens français en Espagne, 1833. Le Monde dramatique, 1, 1835.
Bédarida, H. Le romantisme français et l'Espagne. Revue de l'U. de Lyon, 4, 1931.
Bejarano, M. M. Historia politica de los afrancesados. Madrid, 1912.
Capmany y de Montpalan, A. de. Contienda contra los Franceses. Madrid, 1801.
Castro, E. M. de L'influence du symbolisme français dans la poésie portugaise contemporaine. Paris, 1923.
Combes, F. Le gallicanisme et les idées françaises en Espagne sous Philippe V. Actes de l'Acad. de Bordeaux, 43, 1881.
Dantas, J La part de l'élément français dans la fondation de la nationalité portugaise. Bull. des Etudes portugaises, 5, 1938.
Gascogne, J. Notre exportation dramatique en Portugal. RB, 5.XI.1898.
Gentil, G. Le. Les Français en Portugal. Instituto, 1928.
Gentil, P. Le. Le cinquantenaire du symbolisme et le Portugal. Bull. des Etudes portugaises, 4, 1937.
Juretschke, H. Das Frankreichbild des modernen Spanien. Diss. Bonn, Bochum-Langendreer, 1937.
Mandon, L. De l'influence française en Espagne sous Philippe V (1700-13). Acad. de Montpellier, Mém. de la Section des Lettres, 5, 1870-73.
Maseres, A. França i Catalunya. Notes per l'estudi de la influencia de l'esperit francès en la literatura catalana moderna. La Revista, 1935.
Menéndez y Pelayo, M. El romanticismo en Francia. In: Historia de las ideas estéticas en España, 6. Madrid, 1886.
Mérimée, P. L'influence française en Espagne au XVIIIe siècle. Paris, 1936.
Nemesio, V. Relaçoēs francesas do romantismo portugues. Coimbra, 1937.
—— La poésie portugaise moderne et la France. RLC, 18, 1938.
Pagès, A. M. La poésie française en Catalogne du XIIIe siècle à la fin du XVe siècle. Paris, 1937.
Pastor, J. F. Wie sieht Spanien Frankreich? Deutsch-französische Rundschau, 4, 1931.
Qualia, C. B. The Campaign to Substitute French Neo-Classical Tragedy for the Comedia, 1737-1800. PMLA, 54, 1939.
—— The Vogue of Decadent French Tragedies in Spain, 1762-1800. PLMA, 58, 1943.
Rubiò, A. La critica del galicismo en España (1726-1832). México, 1937.
Ugarte, M. L'influence de la littérature française en Espagne. Revue, 1.IX.1903.
Zeriga-Fombona, A. Le symbolisme français et la poésie espagnole moderne. Paris, 1920.

CHAPTER EIGHT

French Influences in Other Countries.

Tchobanian, A. L'influence de la littérature française dans la littérature arménienne contemporaine. (**ARMENIA**). Annales internationales d'histoire. Paris, 1901.
Charlier, G. Les lettres françaises de Belgique. (**BELGIUM**). Bruxelles, 1938.
Culot, J. M. Bibliographie des lettres françaises de Belgique de 1880 à 1938. Bruxelles, 1939.
Deschamps. L'étude de la langue et de la littérature française en Belgique. Journal des gens de lettres belges, 1882.
Doutrepont, G. Histoire illustrée de la littérature française en Belgique. Paris, 1939.
Dumont-Wilden, L. Les Flamands et la culture française. RB, 30.IX.1911.
Faber, F. Histoire du théâtre français en Belgique depuis son origine jusqu'à nos jours. 5 vols. Bruxelles, 1878-80.
Hasselt, A. van. Essai sur l'histoire de la poésie française en Belgique. Bruxelles, 1838.
Liebrecht, H. Histoire du théâtre français à Bruxelles au XVIIe et au XVIIIe siècle. Paris, 1923.
Lobet, M. La littérature française de Belgique. RB, 1938.
Looten, C. La pénétration des lettres françaises en Flandre après le traité de Nimègue (1678). Mélanges Baldensperger. Paris, 1930.
Masoin, F. Histoire de la littérature française en Belgique de 1815 à 1850. Bruxelles, 1902.
Vanwelkenhuyzen, G. L'influence du naturalisme français en Belgique de 1875 à 1900. Bruxelles, 1930.

Wilmotte, M. La culture française en Belgique. Paris, 1912.
Pierre, A. L'influence française dans les lettres bulgares. (**BULGARIA**). L'Europe Centrale, 1.VI.1935.
Cartojan, N. Le modèle français de l'Erotokritos, poème crétois du XVIIe siècle. (**CRETE**). RLC, 16, 1936.
Chopin, J. Promenades littéraires en Tchécoslovaquie avec Mme. de Staël, Chateaubriand, George Sand. (**CZECHOSLOVAKIA**). Grenoble, 1938.
Jelinek, H. Les Tchèques et la France dans le passé. L'Europe Centrale, 21.IV. 1934.
Letty, J. La Comédie-Française à Prague. Revue française de Prague, 16.X.1936.
Pasquier, J. Influences françaises à Prague. L'Europe Centrale, 31.III.1934.
Varia. Catalogue des ouvrages français traduits en tchèque. Prague, 1889.
Winter, G. L'influence française en Tchécoslovaquie au miroir des lettres. L'Europe Centrale, 27.VI.1936.
Clausen, J. La littérature française à Copenhague au temps de Frédéric V. (**DENMARK**). Historisk Tidskrift, 1897.
Varia. Anthologie des écrivains d'Egypte d'expression française. (**EGYPT**). Le Caire, 1937.
Rudrauf, L. La culture française vue par un écrivain estonien. (**ESTONIA**). Annuaire. Akadeemiline Kooperatiiv. Tartu, 1935.
Gidel, C. Etudes sur la littérature grecque moderne. Imitations en grec de nos romans de chevalerie, depuis le XIIe siècle. (**GREECE**). Paris, 1866.
Louvet, A. L'influence française en Grèce. RB, 20.VI.1903.
Asselin, H. L'influence française en **HOLLANDE**. Revue mondiale, 15.V. 1920.
Bauwens, J. La tragédie française et le Théâtre hollandais au XVIIe siècle. Amsterdam, 1921.
Berger, L. Les oeuvres hollandaises d'expression française. Monde nouveau, 1928.
Bonet-Maury, G. De l'influence actuelle de la littérature française aux Pays-Bas. RB, 18.X.1879.
Brom, G. Franse invloed op onze Tachtigers. NPh, 23, 1938.
Dijkshorn, J. A. L'influence française dans les moeurs et les salons des Provinces-Unies. Diss. Groningen. Paris, 1925.
Dubosq, Y. Z. Le livre français et son commerce en Hollande de 1750 à 1780. Amsterdam, 1926.
Fransen, J. Les comédiens français en Hollande au XVIIe et au XVIIIe siècle. Paris, 1925.
Graaf, J. de. Le réveil littéraire en Hollande et le naturalisme français. Amsterdam, 1938.

932.

Prinsen, J. Les grands romantiques français jugés par un Hollandais de 1850. Mélanges Baldensperger. Paris, 1930.
Salverda de Grave, J. J. Français et livres français dans les Pays-Bas au XVIIIe siècle. Mélanges Baldensperger. Paris, 1930.
Schooneveldt, C. van. Over de navolging der klassiek-fransche tragedie in nederlandsche treurspelen der achttiende eeuw. Doetichem Misset, 1906.
Valkhoff, P. Le roman moderne hollandais et le réalisme français. Revue de Hollande, 1916.
—— L'influence de la littérature française dans les Pays-Bas. Leyde, 1918.
—— La littérature française en Hollande. Revue de l'Université, 1924.
Varia. Enquête sur l'influence de l'esprit français en Hollande. Revue de Hollande, 1916-17.
Worp, J. A. Invloed van het Fransche drama op het onze in het begin der 17de eeuw. Noord en Zuid, 18, 1895.
Anon. Le livre français en Hongrie. (**HUNGARY**). Cahiers de litt. comparée. Budapest, 1948.
Balogh, J. La pensée française en Hongrie. Nouvelle Rev. de Hongrie, 1934.
Baranyai, Z. La langue et la culture françaises en Hongrie au XVIIIe siècle. Budapest, 1920.
Baumgarten, S. Un épisode hongrois du gallicanisme: une controverse entre le Primat de Hongrie et le Parlement de Paris, 1682. Revue des Etudes hongroises, 1933.
Czerhalmi, H. Le romantisme français et son influence sur le théâtre hongrois. Budapest, 1894.
Eckhardt, A. Le premier philosophe hongrois et la pensée française. Nouvelle Rev. de Hongrie, 1938.
Gesmey, B. Les débuts des études françaises en Hongrie (1789-1830). Etudes francaises, 18. Szeged.
Haas, P. de. La France en Hongrie. Revue mondiale, 1931.
Karl, L. Sur le romantisme français en Hongrie. Revue de Hongrie, 8, 1911-12.
Kont, J. Etude sur l'influence de la littérature française en Hongrie, 1772 à 1896. Diss. Paris, 1902.
Szinnyei, F. Le romantisme français et

le roman hongrois avant 1848. Revue des Etudes hongroises, 1927.
Valmy-Baisse, J. L'art dramatique français et les tournées dramatiques en Hongrie. Nouvelle Rev. de Hongrie, 1935.
Villat, L. Reflets du génie français en Hongrie. Le Génie français, 1930.
Zolnai, B. La littérature de langue française en Hongrie. Nouvelle Rev. de Hongrie, 1937.
Hayes, R. Biographical Dictionary of Irishmen in France. **(IRELAND)**. Studies, 34, 1945.
Goto, S. L'influence française au Japon. **(JAPAN)**. Bull. de la Maison franco-japonaise, 8, 1937.
Naito Jokichi. La culture française au Japon. Minerve française, 15.V.1920.
Nouet, N. La poésie française au Japon. Mfr., 10.III.1928.
Björnson, B. La Norvège contre la France. **(NORWAY)**. Revue des Revues, 1896.
Jolivet, A. La culture française en Norvège. Minerve française, 1.II.1920.
Oeksnevad, R. Frankrike i norsk litteratur. Oslo, 1939.
Iorga, N. Les voyageurs orientaux en France. **(ORIENT)**. Revue hist. du Sud-Est européen, 1927.
Fabre, J. La propagande des idées philosophiques en Pologne sous Stanislas-Auguste et l'Ecole varsovienne des Cadets. **(POLAND)**. RLC, 15, 1935.
—— Stanislas Auguste et les hommes de lettres français. Archivium neophilologicum, 2, Cracovie, 1936.
Kasterska, M. La poésie française en Pologne. Mfr., 1924.
Kozlowski, W. M. Les idées françaises dans la philosophie nationale et la poésie patriotique de la Pologne. Revue française de Prague, 1924.
Szulc-Golska, B. Bibliographie des traductions polonaises de la littérature française. Poznan, 1926.
Apostolescu, N. I. L'influence des romantiques français sur la poésie roumaine. **(RUMANIA)**. Paris, 1909.
Demetrescu, A. L'influence de la langue et de la littérature françaises en Roumanie. Diss. Lausanne, 1888. Cf. RHLF, 15.I.1898.
Drouhet, C. La culture française en Roumanie. Minerve française, 15.X.1920.
Eliade, P. De l'influence française sur l'esprit public en Roumanie. 3 vols. Paris, 1898-1914.
Haseganu, I. La France dans l'oeuvre des écrivains roumains contemporains de langue française. Paris, 1940.
Munteano, B. L'influence française en Roumanie au XVIIIe siécle. L'Europe Centrale, 24.XI.1934.
Ortiz, R. L'influsso dei romantici francesi sulla poesia rumena. In: Varia romanica. Firenze, 1932.
Petrovici, J. La philosophie française en Roumanie. Séances & travaux de l'Acad. des sciences mor. et pol., 1934.
Popovici, D. La littérature roumaine à l'époque des Lumières. Paris, 1945.
Rossel, V. La poésie française en Roumanie. RHLF, 5, 1898.
Xenopol, A. D. L'influence intellectuelle française chez les Roumains (XVIII-XIXe siècles). Annales des sciences politiques, 24, 1909.
Anon. La littérature française en U. S. S. R. **(RUSSIA)**. Temps modernes, March, 1946.
Beridzé, C. La Géorgie et les lettres françaises. Paris, 1932.
Delines, M. La France jugée par la Russie. Paris, 1887.
Ghennady, G. Bibliographie des ouvrages français publiés par des Russes. Dresde, 1870.
Haumant, E. Les romans français en Russie. Journal des Débats, 20.V.1896.
—— La culture française en Russie (1700-1900). Paris, 1910.
Larivière, C. de. La langue et l'influence françaises en Russie. Revue des Etudes Franco-Russes, 2, 1902.
Léger, L. Les voyageurs russes en France. Bull. de la Société normande de Séez, 1897.
Lirondelle, A. L'influence française en Russie au XVIIIe siècle. Revue pédagogique, 15.IX.1910.
Manouvriez, A. La fin d'une influence: les Français en Russie. Revue critique des idées et des livres. 10.I.1921.
Pol, S & Quais, M. La France dans les lettres russes. Nouvelle Revue, 1.V. 1910.
Maury, L. Jugements scandinaves sur la France. **(SCANDINAVIA)**. RB, 11.II. 1911.
—— Nos classiques en Scandinavie. In: L'imagination scandinave. Paris, 1928.
Soulier, E. Les pays du Nord et la France. Corresp., 10.VIII.1917.
Mansuy, A. Le monde slave et les classiques français aux XVIe et XVIIe siècles. **(Slavs)**. Paris, 1912. Cf. RB, 1913.
Baldensperger, F. De Descartes à Gobineau: France et Suède. **(SWEDEN)**. RP, 1.VI.1917.
Blanck, A. La Suède et la littérature francaise. Stockholm, 1947.

Brachin, P. La littérature française en Suède. EG, 3, 1948.

Maury, L. La Suède et la littérature française. Paris, 1947.

Strindberg, A. Franska insatser i svenska kulturen. In: Samlade Skrifter, 27. Stockholm, 1912-20.

Thibaudet, A. La culture française en Suède. Europe nouvelle, 24 & 31.I.1920.

Wrangel, E. Aperçu de l'influence française sur la littérature suédoise. Annales internationales d'histoire, 1901.

Amiet, J. Culturgeschichtliche Bilder aus dem schweizerischen Volks- und Staatsleben zur Blütezeit des französischen Einflusses auf die Aristokratien der Schweiz. **(SWITZERLAND)**. St. Gallen, 1862.

Baldensperger, F. La Suisse et la littérature française. In: La Suisse et les Français. Paris, 1920.

Lombard, A. Influence littéraire de la France en Suisse. In: Dictionnaire historique & biographique de la Suisse. Neuchâtel, 1925.

Reynold, G. de. Préliminaires à une histoire de la littérature française en Suisse. Mélanges Lanson. Paris, 1922.

—— Influence de la littérature et de l'art français en Suisse. Le Mois, 10.VI. 1937.

Trautmann, K. Die Schauspieler des Hôtel de Bourgogne in Basel (1604). Archiv, 15, 1887.

Aumeglian, P. Le Théâtre français à Constantinople. **(TURKEY)**. Revue hebdomadaire, 2, 1902.

Malet, A. Le théâtre serbe et les oeuvres françaises. **(YUGOSLAVIA)**. RB, 7.IX. 1895.

Markovitch, M. La culture française en Yougoslavie. Paris, 1935.

Savkovitch, M. L'influence du réalisme français dans le roman serbo-croate. Paris, 1935.

CHAPTER NINE

Balzac.

1. General Influences.

Anon. American Imitators of Balzac. AM, 54, 1884.

—— Balzac in England. Athenaeum, 14. VIII.1897.

—— Balzac's Vogue in America. Harper's Weekly, 4.X.1902.

—— Perche Balzac spiacque ai Veneziani del 1837. Marzocco, 17.IV.1921.

Alekseev, M. Balzac en Russie. (In Russian). Krasny Archiv, 1923.

Bidou, H. Balzac à Manchester. Journal des Débats, 17.IX.1905.

Cajumi, A. Balzac in Italia. I libri del giorno, Sept., 1920.

Carrière, J. M. Unnoticed Translations of Balzac in American Periodicals. MLN, 60, 1945.

Casseres, B. Why Americans Prefer Balzac to Trollope. New York Sun, 12-19.XI.1910.

Dargan, E. P. Parmi la descendance de Balzac dans la vie et dans la fiction. RLC, 7, 1927.

Decker, C. R. Balzac's Literary Reputation in Victorian Society. PMLA, 1932.

Feder. Balzac in Italia. Corr. della Sera, 24, 1899.

Filon, A. Balzac et les Anglais. Journal des Débats, 27.VIII.1895.

Gigli, G. Balzac in Italia. Milano, 1920.

Griffith, M. Balzac aux Etats-Unis. Paris, 1931.

Grossmann, L. Balzac en Russie. (In Russian). In: La Civilisation russe et la France, ed. by L'Héritage littéraire. Moscou, 1937.

Korwin-Piotrowska, S. de. Balzac et le monde slave; Mme. Hanska et l'oeuvre balzacienne. Paris, 1933.

Kuenzi, A. Balzac in deutscher Sprache. NSR, 1928.

Lissoni. Difesa dell' onore dell' armi italiani oltraggiata del Signore de Balzac. Milano, 1837.

Mabbot, T O. A Newly Found American Translation of Balzac. MLN, 61, 1946.

Muret, M. Balzac en Allemagne. Journal des Débats, 15.II.1924.

Prioult, A. Balzac et le Portugal. RLC, 19, 1939.

Rzewuski, S. Le théâtre de Balzac à l'étranger. Gaulois, 30.I.1899.

Toth, K. Balzac und die deutsche Gegenwart. Essen, 1926.

Wilde, O. Balzac in English. Pall Mall Gazette, 13.IX.1886.

2. Influences upon Individuals.

Cattelani, G. Un apologista italiano di Balzac in 1831. (G. **AMEGGIO**). Vita moderna, 35, 1893.

Bettelheim, A. **ANZENGRUBERS** Jaggernaut. Euphorion, 24, 1922.

Bouteron, M. Balzac et les **APPONYI**. Nouvelle Revue de Hongrie, 1935.

Bienstock, J. W. **DOSTOJEVSKY** et Balzac. MF, 1.XII.1924.

Levinson, A. Dostojevsky et le roman occidental. RCC, 1927.

McNair, L. Balzac and **HUXLEY**: FR, 12, 1939.
Dengis, J. **KEMENY** et Balzac. Bud. Szaule, April, 1910.
Marix, T. Histoire d'une amitié: Fr. **LISZT** et H. de Balzac. Revue des Etudes hongroises, 1934.
Pilot, A. Onorato di Balzac e Camillo **NALIN**. Nuovo Archivio Veneto, N. S., 40, 1920.
Bijvanek, W. G. C. Balzac en **NEWMAN**. De Gids, 1. And in: Poezie en Leven in de 19de eeuw. Haarlem, 1889.
Pinvert, L. Deux prophètes: Balzac et **NIETZSCHE**. Revue des Etudes historiques, 84, 1918.
Eoff, S. A Phase of **PEREDA'S** Writings in Imitation of Balzac. MLN, 59, 1944.
Dallmann, W. P. **SEALSFIELD** and Balzac Again. JEGPh, 39, 1940.
Landsberg, E. Sealsfield's Morton und Balzac's Gobseck. ZFEU, 22, 1923.
Dobrzycki, S. Balzac and **SIENKIEWICZ**. (In Polish). Duch Lit., 1, 1928.
Falconer, J. A. Balzac and **THACKERAY**. ESs, 26, 1944-45.
Pacey, W. C. D. Balzac and Thackeray. MLR, 36, 1941.
Whibley, C. The Style of Thackeray and Balzac. Living Age, 84, 1865.

CHAPTER TEN

Chateaubriand.

1. General Influences.

Anon. Chateaubriand vor dem Richterstuhl der englischen Kritik. MLIA, 1837.
Baldensperger, F. La veracité de Chateaubriand: premiers doutes britanniques (1813). MLN, 58, 1943.
Baumgarten, S. La fortune de Chateaubriand en Hongrie. RLC, 23, 1949.
Chinard, G. Un frère cadet de René en Amérique. Mélanges Baldensperger. Paris, 1930.
Chopin, J. Promenades en Tchéco-Slovaquie avec Mme. de Staël, Chateaubriand, George Sand. Grenoble, 1938.
Dechamps, J. Chateaubriand en Angleterre. Paris, 1933.
Fedelini, E. Une lettre inédite de Chateaubriand et un poème italien sur Le dernier des Abencérages. EI, 1931.
Hazard, P. Chateaubriand et la littérature des Etats-Unis. RLC, 8, 1928.
—— Les Martyrs en vers espagnols. RLC, 11, 1931.
Lejeune, R. Chateaubriand en Italie. Revue critique des idées et des livres, 1922.
Markovitch, M. Chateaubriand en Russie. Mélanges Baldensperger. Paris, 1930.
—— Un prince monténégrin disciple de Chateaubriand. RLC, 23, 1949.
Moreau, P. Horizons internationaux de Chateaubriand. RLC, 23, 1949.
Napione, T. Studi sulla fortuna di Chateaubriand nella letteratura e nell'arte italiana. Torino, 1928.
Nuñez y Dominguez, J. de. Chateaubriand y México. Revue de l'Ifal, 1.
Peers, E. A. La influencia de Chateaubriand en España. RFE, 1924.
Rabbizani, G. Chateaubriand nel risorgimento italiano. RI, 2, 1918.
Reboul, P. Chateaubriand et les Anglais. RLC, 23, 1949.
Sarrailh, J. La fortune d'Atala en Espagne, 1801-33. Homenaje a Menéndez Pidal. Madrid, 1924.
Saunal, D. Chateaubriand et le Portugal. RLC, 23, 1949.
Tchobanian, A. Victor Hugo, Chateaubriand et Lamartine dans la littérature arménienne. Paris, 1936.

2. Influences upon Individual Authors.

Esquerra, R. **BALMES** i Chateaubriand. Homenatge a Antoni Rubió i Lluch. Barcelona, 1936.
Scherillo, M. La Norma di **BELLINI** e la Velleda di Chateaubriand. NAnt, 16.VI. 1892.
Kaiser, R. René und Harold. (**BYRON**). Archiv, Dec., 1936.
Ritter, O. Byron und Chateaubriand. Archiv, 109, 1902.
Tellier, E. Byron et Chateaubriand. Paris, 1947.
Gentil, G. Le. Filinto **ELYSIO**, traducteur de Chateaubriand. RLC, 18, 1938.
Elwert, W. T. Geschichtsauffassung und Erzählungstechnik in den historischen Romanen P. D. **GUERRAZZIS**. Halle, 1935.
Brown, D. F. Chateaubriand and the Story of Feliciana in Jorge **ISAACS'** Maria. MLN, 62, 1947.
Neri, F. II **LEOPARDI** ed un Mauvais maître. RI, 1915.
Druchnalski, W. **MICKIEWICZ** and Chateaubriand. (In Polish). Mélanges Balzer, Leopol, 1925.
Bem, A. On the Influence of Chateaubriand on **PUSHKIN**. (In Russian). In: Pushkin i ego sovremenniki, 4, 1911.

Sipovskii, V. Pushkin, Byron and Chateaubriand. (In Russian). In: Pushkin. St. Petersburg, 1901.
Fischer, P. D. **SCHLEIERMACHER** und Chateaubriand. MLIA, 1870.
Terrade, R. P. Quo vadis? de H. **SIENKIEWICZ** et Les Martyrs de Chateaubriand. Paris, 1902.
Böök, F. **STAGNELIUS** och Chateaubriand. Samlaren, 1909.
Pinot, V. Chateaubriand et Stagnelius. Le Temps, 11.I.1912.

CHAPTER ELEVEN

Corneille.

1. Generalities.

Baldensperger, F. Corneille vu du Danemark. Figaro, May, 1927.
Brüning, Ida. Molière et Corneille en Allemagne. Rev. d'Art dram., Feb., 1885.
Canfield, Dorothy. Corneille and Racine in England. New York, 1904.
Ellinger. Deutsche Bearbeitung von Corneilles Polyeucte. ALG, 3, 1874.
Hoffmann, K. Corneille und Racine in England. Vossische Zt., Sonntagsblatt, 22,1906. And in: Zwölf Studien zur Literatur und Ideengeschichte. Charlottenburg, 1908.
Laun, A. Die ältesten deutschen Uebersetzungen einiger Dramen von Corneille. Archiv, 3, 1874.
Leonard, I. An Early Peruvian Adaptation of Corneille's Rodogune. HR, 1937.
McCoe, A. Additional Notes on Corneille in Spain in the 18th Century. RR, 1933-34.
Meregazzi, G. Le tragedie di Pierre Corneille nelle traduzioni e imitazioni italiane del secolo XVIII. Bergamo, 1906.
Mulert, A. P. Corneille auf der englischen Bühne und in der englischen Uebersetzungslitteratur des XVII. Jahrhunderts. Diss. München, 1899; Leipzig, 1900.
Powell, P. Pierre Corneilles Dramen in deutschen Bearbeitungen auf der deutschen Bühne bis zum Anfang des XIX. Jahrhunderts. Diss. Rostock. Emsdetten, 1939.
—— Corneilles Polyeucte als deutsche Barockoper. CLS, 5, 1942.
Qualia, C. B. Corneille in Spain in the 18th Century. RR, 1933.
Raab, R. Pierre Corneille in deutschen Uebersetzungen und auf der deutschen Bühne bis Lessing. Heidelberg, 1910.
Schmid, K. H. Corneille und die deutsche Literatur. Esslingen, 1909.
Trautmann, K. Französische Komödie in der Stuttgarter Ausgabe von Dramen P. Corneilles. Eine deutsche Polyeucte-Uebersetzung vom Jahre 1698. ALG, 1870.

2. Influences upon Individual Authors.

Pellizzaro, G. B. Il freno dei tempi in Corneille e **ALFIERI:** Saggio. Vicenza, 1903.
Martin, H. M. Corneille's Andromède and **CALDERON'S** Las Fortunas de Perseo. MPh, 1926.
Schramm, E. Corneilles Heraclius und Calderóns En vida todo es verdad y todo mentira. RH, Oct., 1927.
Legouis, P. Corneille and **DRYDEN** as Dramatic Critics. Festschrift H. Grierson. Oxford U.P., 1938.
Friedwagner, M. **GOETHE** als Corneille-Uebersetzer. Progr. Währing, 1890.
Hiller, J. E. **LESSING** und Corneille; Rokoko und Barock. RF, 47, 1933.
Kurzreiter, H. Ueber die Hamburger Dramaturgie und Corneilles Discours. Graz, 1887-88.
Boost, P. F. **SCHILLER** und Corneille. Lit. Conversationsblätter, 57, 1821.
Merian-Genast, E. Corneille und Schiller. GRM, 1938.
Lang, D. M. A Russian Dramatist's Views on Corneille and Voltaire (**SUMAROKOV**). RLC, 23, 1949.
Celen, V. Werken van Michiel de **SWAEN.** Antwerpen, 1928.
Freeman, W. A Comparison Between the Horace of Corneille and the Roman Father of **WHITEHEAD.** London, 1750.

CHAPTER TWELVE

Descartes.

1. Generalities.

Barja, C. Descartes a distancia. RIA, 2, 1940.
Beyer, C. J. Du cartésianisme à la philosophie des lumières. RR, 34, 1943.
Boorsch, J. Etat présent des études sur Descartes. Paris, 1937.
Guili, G. de. Edizioni e studi cartesiani. Rivista di filosofia, 1934.
Hock, F. C. Cartesius und seine Gegner. Wien, 1935.
Hubert, R. Le cartésianisme et le mouvement des idées philosophiques au XVIIe

siècle. Rev. d'hist. de la philosophie, 1937.
Lantrua, A. Il ritorno di Cartesio. Archivio di filosofia, 1934.
Lawler, D. Influence of Descartes on Modern Science. Thought, 12, 1937.
Adam, C. Descartes et ses correspondants anglais. (**ENGLAND**). RLC, 17, 1937.
Anderson, P. R. Descartes' Influence in Seventeenth-Century England. Travaux du IXe Congrès international de philosophie, 3, 1937.
Cunningham, W. Influence of Descartes on Metaphysical Speculation in England. London, 1876.
Frondizi, R. Descartes y la filosofia inglesa del siglo XVII. In: Escritos en honor de Descartes. La Plata, 1938.
Laird, J. L'influence de Descartes sur la philosophie anglaise du XVIIe siècle. Revue philosophique, 1937.
Lamprecht, S. P. The Role of Descartes in XVIIth Century England. Columbia Studies in the History of Ideas. New York, 1935.
Lyon, G. L'idéalisme en Angleterre au XVIIIe siècle. Paris, 1888.
Nicholson, M. The Early Stages of Cartesianism in England. SPh, 26, 1929.
Pait, J. A. The Influence of Descartes on XVIIth Century English Philosophy. Diss. U. of Virginia, 1941.
Angyal, A. Zur Literaturgeschichte des deutschen Cartesianismus. (**GERMANY**). GRM, 29, 1941.
Bergmann, E. Les principaux ouvrages sur Descartes publiés en Allemagne depuis 1900. Revue de synthèse, 1937.
—— Die Einflüsse der cartesischen Philosophie in Deutschland. Etudes cartésiennes, 3, 1937.
Foucher de Careil. Descartes et la Princesse Palatine, ou l'influence du cartésianisme sur les femmes au XVIIe siècle. Paris, 1862.
Medicus, F. Descartes' Cogito und der deutsche Idealismus. Etudes cartésiennes, 3, 1937.
Schwarz. Die cartesianische Reflexion und die Methode der Denker des deutschen Idealismus. Etudes cartésiennes, 3, 1937.
Varia. Dem Gedächtnis René Descartes. Berlin, 1937.
Brugmans, H. L. Descartes et les pasteurs de Hollande. (**HOLLAND**). RLC, 17, 1937.
Cohen, G. Descartes en Hollande. NL, 24. VI.1937.
Gilson, E. Descartes en Hollande. RMM, 1921.
Guilhou, E. Descartes en Hollande et en Suède. Bull. de l'Alliance fr. en Hollande, 1937.
Halasy-Nagy, J. Le cartésianisme en Hongrie. (**HUNGARY**). Etudes cartésiennes, 3, 1937.
Turóczi-Trostler, J. Les Cartésiens hongrois. Revue des Etudes hongroises, 1934.
Berthe de Besancèle, L. Les Cartésiens d'Italie. (**ITALY**). Paris, 1920-22.
Werner, K. Die Cartesisch-Malebranche'sche Philosophie in Italien. SAWW, 102, 1882.
Vértes, A. O. Descartes chez les Lapons. (**LAPLAND**). RLC, 17, 1937.
Mauricio, D. A primeira alusão a Descartes em **PORTUGAL**. Lisboa, 1937.

2. Influences upon Individual Philosophers and Authors.

Frondizi, R. Influencia de Descartes sobre el idealismo de **BERKELEY**. In: Descartes Gedenkschrift. Buenos Aires, 1937.
Katkov, G. Descartes und **BRENTANO**. Archiv f. Rechts- und Socialphilosophie, 30, 1937.
Cassirer, E. Descartes und Königin **CHRISTINA VON SCHWEDEN**. In: Descartes. Stockholm, 1939.
Schuhl, P. M. Un souvenir cartésien dans les pensées de la reine Christine. Revue philosophique, 1937.
Müller, H. J. **CLAUBERG** und seine Stellung zum Cartesianismus. Jena, 1891.
Lindsay, J. **COLERIDGE** Marginalia in a Volume of Descartes. PMLA, 1934.
Caso, A. Don Juan Benito **DIAZ DE GAMARRA**, un filósofo mexicano discípulo de Descartes. Rev. de Lit. Mexicana, 1, 1940.
Zolnai, B. Mikes **ESZMENYEI**. Budapest, 1937.
Gazzaniga, P. Il Cartesio giudicato dal **GIOBERTI**. Rassegna di scienze moderne, Dec., 1934.
Schmitt, C. Der Staat als Mechanismus bei **HOBBES** und Descartes. Archiv f. Rechts- und Socialphilosophie, 30, 1937.
Schütz, L. H. Die Lehre von den Leidenschaften bei Hobbes und Descartes. Hagen i./W., 1921.
Giorgiantonio, M. **HUME** e Descartes. Rivista Internaz. di Fonti e Studi di Storia della filosofia (Sophia), 5, 1937.
Becker, O. **HUSSERL** und Descartes. Archiv f. Rechts- und Socialphilosophie, 30, 1937.

Romero, F. Descartes y Husserl. Descartes Gedenkschrift. La Plata, 1938.

Cohen, G. Descartes en Constantijn **HUYGENS.** Haagsch Maandschrift, Aug., 1928.

Quintero, V. El cogito cartesiano en la Crítica de la razón pura de **KANT.** Descartes Gedenkschrift. Buenos Aires, 1937.

Heimsoeth, H. Die Methode der Erkenntnis bei Descartes und bei **LEIBNIZ.** Giessen, 1912.

Nason, J. W. Leibniz's Attack on the Cartesian Doctrine of Extension. JHI, 7, 1946.

Papillon, F. De la rivalité de l'esprit leibnizien et de l'esprit cartésien au XVIIIe siècle. Séances et Trav. de l'Acad. des Sc. mor. et pol., 98, 1872.

Delbos, V. Le Cogito de Descartes et la philosophie de **LOCKE.** Année philos., 5, 1914.

Geil, G. Ueber die Abhängigkeit Lockes von Descartes. Strassburg, 1887.

Sommer, R. Lockes Verhältnis zu Descartes. Berlin, 1887.

Papillon, F. **NEWTON** considéré comme disciple de Descartes. Séances et Trav. de l'Acad. des. Sc. mor. et pol., 99, 1873.

Vrijer, M. J. A. de. Henricus **REGIUS** een Cartesiaansch hoogleeraar. Museum, 25.

Gehlen, A. Descartes im Urteil **SCHELLINGS.** Etudes cartésiennes, 3, 1937.

Brunschwicg. Descartes et **SPINOZA.** RMM, 1904.

Lachièze-Rey, P. Les origines cartésiennes du Dieu de Spinoza. Paris, 1932.

Mahler, K. Die Entstehung des Irrtums bei Descartes und bei Spinoza. Leipzig, 1910.

Roth, L. Spinoza and Cartesianism. Mind, Jan., 1923.

Chiocchetti, E. L'estetica di G. B. **VICO.** Rivista di filosofia neoscolastica, 1927.

Cuccaro, J. J. Descartes y Vico. Descartes Gedenkschrift. Buenos Aires, 1937.

Scerbo, G. Il metodo cartesiano e la riduzione vichiana della filologia a scienza. Logos, 1934.

Tocco, F. Descartes jugé par Vico. RMM, 1896.

Witzenmann, W. Giambattista Vico und René Descartes. Archiv f. Rechts- und Socialphilosophie, 30, 1937.

CHAPTER THIRTEEN

Diderot and the Encyclopédie.

1. Generalities.

Dieckmann, H. Stand und Probleme der Diderot-Forschung. Bonn, 1931.

Schalk, F. Einleitung in die Encyclopädie der französischen Aufklärung. München, 1936.

Venturi, F. Le origini dell'enciclopedia. Firenze, 1946.

Francotte. La propagande des encyclopédistes français au pays de Liège. **(BELGIUM).** Bruxelles, 1880.

Lough, J. The Encyclopédie in XVIIIth Century Scotland. **(ENGLAND).** MLR, 38, 1943.

Praz, M. An English Imitation of Diderot's La Religieuse. RES, 1930.

Abrahams, J. Diderot, Französisch und Deutsch. Eine Studie über das künstlerische Werk und seine zeitgenössische Uebersetzung. **(GERMANY).** Jena, 1936. RF, 1937.

Béranger, A. Diderot et l'Allemagne. BURS, 32, 1868.

Gandar, E. Diderot et la critique allemande. Lettres et souvenirs d'enseignement, 2. Paris, 1869.

Oberländer, H. Die geistige Entwicklung der deutschen Schauspielkunst im XVIII. Jahrhundert. Hamburg, 1898.

Schirlitz, E. E. Diderots Beziehungen zur deutschen Litteratur. Archiv, 1885.

Burgmans, H. L. La Hollande du XIXe siècle et l'Encyclopédie. **(HOLLAND).** RR, 1935.

Levi-Malvano, E. Les éditions toscanes de l'Encyclopédie. **(ITALY).** RLC, 3, 1923.

—— La fortuna d'una teoria drammatica in Italia (Père de famille). GSLI, 53, 1935.

Sorrento, L. L'incidente diplomatico franco-spagnuolo a proposito dell' Enciclopedia. **(SPAIN).** Colombo, 3, 1926.

Berg, R. G. Sverige i Diderots Encyclopedi. **(SWEDEN).** Svensk Tidskrift, 19, 1929.

2. Influences upon Individual Authors.

Patrick, H. S. Les relations de **CATHERINE II** avec Diderot et son plan d'une université pour la Russie. Diss. U. of California, 1921.

Tourneux, M. Diderot et Catherine II. Paris, 1899.

Snyder, Alice D. **COLERIDGE** and the Encyclopedists. MPh, 38, 1940.

Flaischlen, C. Otto Heinrich von **GEM-**

MINGEN. Mit einer Vorstudie über Diderot als Dramatiker. Diss. Zürich, 1890.
Anon. **GOETHE** et Diderot. Revue bordelaise, 1881.
Barbey d'Aurévilly, J. Goethe et Diderot. Paris, 1880.
Boxberger, R. Maître Jacques in Goethes Briefwechsel. Vierteljahrsschrift f. Litt.geschichte, 1888.
Dieckmann, H. Goethe und Diderot. DVLG, 10, 1932.
Doering, O. Goethe und Diderot über die Malerei. PJb, 1888.
Eggert, C. A. Goethe und Diderot: über Schauspieler und die Kunst des Schauspielers. MLN, 11, 1896 & Euphorion, 4, 1897.
Müller, J. Goethe, Diderot und das 18. Jahrhundert. ZNU, 38, 1939.
Papillon, F. Des rapports philosophiques de Goethe et de Diderot. Séances et Trav. de l'Acad. des Sc. mor. et pol., 101, 1874.
Schloesser, R. Rameaus Neffe. Studien und Untersuchungen zur Einführung in Goethes Uebersetzung des Diderotschen Dialogs. Weimar, Berlin, 1900. Cf. ZFSL, 1903.
Tronchon, H. Goethe, Herder et Diderot. In: Goethe Gedenkschrift, Strasbourg. Paris, 1932.
Willm. Goethe et Diderot. RG, 11.
Crane, R. S. & Friedman, A. **GOLDSMITH** and the Encyclopédie. TLS, 11.V.1933.
Cazes, A. **GRIMM** et les Encyclopédistes. Paris, 1935. Cf. Vie Intellectuelle, 10. IV.1935.
Kosciusko, J. Diderot et **HAGEDORN**. RLC, 16, 1936.
Gerold, K. G. **HERDER** und Diderot. Ihr Einblick in die Kunst. Frankfurt, 1941.
Hankiss, J. Diderot und Herder. Archiv, 140, 1920.
Schazmann, P. E. Une correspondante genevoise de Diderot: Marie Madeleine **JODIN**. Journal de Genève, 4.IV.1932.
Powell, L. F. **JOHNSON** and the Encyclopédie. RES, 1926.
Dikenmann, R. Beiträge zum Thema: Diderot und **LESSING**. Diss. Zürich, 1915.
Schmidt, E. Diderot und Lessing. Gegenwart, 9-10, 1882.
Schott, S. Lessing und Diderot. MLIA, 1882.
Luzio, A. **MANZONI** e Diderot. La Monaca e la Religieuse. Milano, 1884.
Scarano, N. La miscredenza di Manzoni. GSLI, 228, 1920.
Ashton, H. Diderot and **MATURIN**. Transactions of the Royal Soc. London, 1919.
Eggli, E. Diderot et **SCHILLER**. RLC, 1, 1921.
Bitterling, R. Joh. Fr. **SCHINK**, ein Schüler Diderots und Lessings. Hamburg, 1911.
Bastier, P. Le Paradoxe sur le comédien: Talma, **TIECK** et Roetscher pour et contre Diderot. RLC, 12, 1932.

CHAPTER FOURTEEN

Hugo.

1. Generalities.

Coselshi, E. Universalité de Victor Hugo. Dante, Jan., 1933.
Hooker, K. W. The Victor Hugo Legend. RR, 27, 1936.
Royer de Lescar. Victor Hugo et la critique littéraire à l'étranger. Revue hebdomadaire, 1902.
Varia. L'influence de Victor Hugo à l'étranger. Le Mois, May, 1935.
Barbagelata, H. G. V. Hugo et l'Amérique espagnole. (**AMERICA**). France-Amérique latine, 1935-36.
George, A. Early American Criticism of Hugo. FR, 1938.
Groot, R. Victor Hugo en América. Bogotá, 1889.
Hazard, P. Traductions de Lamartine et de Victor Hugo au Brésil. RLC, 11, 1931.
Smith, Virginia K. Appreciation of Hugo in Mexico. Diss. U. of Texas, 1939.
Tchobanian, A. V. Hugo, Chateaubriand et Lamartine dans la littérature arménienne. (**ARMENIA**). Paris, 1936.
—— Victor Hugo si Armenii. Ani, June, 1936.
Barthou, L. Victor Hugo et l'Angleterre. (**ENGLAND**). Conferencia, Jan., 1926.
Bowley, V. E. A. English Versions of Victor Hugo's Plays. FQ, 10, 1928.
—— Notre-Dame and Les Misérables on the English Stage. FG, 11, 1929.
Engel, C. A. Une traduction anglaise d'Hernani. RLC, 14, 1934.
Hooker, K. W. The Fortunes of Victor Hugo in England. Columbia U. P., 1938.
Roth, G. Une adaptation anglaise de Cromwell en 1859. FQ, 1927.
Anon. Un Allemand chez Victor Hugo. (**GERMANY**). Le Temps, 7.II.1900.
Sarrazin, J. Victor Hugo und die deutsche Kritik. Archiv, 74, 1885.
—— Deutsche Stimmen über die franzö-

sische Lyrik im allgemeinen und V. Hugo im besonderen. Franco-Gallia, 2, 1885.
Schmeding, G. Victor Hugo. Ein Beitrag zu seiner Würdigung in Deutschland. Braunschweig, 1887.
Hamel, A. G. van Navolgingen en vertalingen van Victor Hugo in Nederland. (**HOLLAND**). Handelingen van de Maatschappij der Nederlandsche Letterkunde, Leiden, 1901-02.
—— Victor Hugo in Nederland. De Gids, 20, 1902.
Yperlaan, Johanna. Les traductions hollandaises des poésies lyriques de V. Hugo. Bussum, 1925.
Eckhardt, A. Victor Hugo et les Hongrois. (**HUNGARY**). Revue de Hongrie, 1931.
Hankiss, J. Victor Hugo. Nouvelle Revue de Hongrie, 1935.
Hodinka, A. Victor Hugo en Hongrie. Etudes hongroises, 14-15.
Galletti, A. V. Hugo in Italia. (**ITALY**). GSLI, 1907.
Italico, I. Victor Hugo nel melodramma italiano. Riv. mod., 2, 1902.
Clarétie, J. Victor Hugo en Norvège. (**NORWAY**). Le Temps, 29.IV.1897.
Pinot, V. Victor Hugo et la Norvège. Revue scandinave, 2, 1911.
Gonçalves Viana, M. A influência de Victor Hugo na literatura portuguesa. (**PORTUGAL**). Afinidades, 13, 1945.
Alekseev, P. Victor Hugo en **RUSSIE**. (In Russian). La Civilisation russe et la France, ed. by l'Héritage littéraire. Moscou, 1937.
Morgulis, G. Autour de quelques vers des Feuilles d'automne: vicissitudes de Victor Hugo en Russie. RLC, 11, 1931.
Gabbert, T. A. Notes on the Popularity of V. Hugo's Dramas in **SPAIN** during the Years 1835-45. HR, 1936.
González Serrano, U. Victor Hugo e su influencia en la literatura española. Nuestro Tiempo, 1902.
Parker, A. & Peers, E. A. The Vogue of V. Hugo in Spain. MLR, 27, 1932-33.
Pitollet, C. Victor Hugo en Espagne. MF, 1928.
Wrangel, E. Victor Hugos lyriska Diktning. (**SWEDEN**). Nordisk Tidskrift, 1900.

2. Influences upon Individual Authors.

Granier, J. A. Some Influences of Victor Hugo's Poetry on the Writings of Olegario V. **ANDRADE**. Diss. George Washington U., 1941.
Fay, E. G. The Source of a Poem by d'**ANNUNZIO**. FR, 15, 1942.
Mundy, J. H. Some Aspects of the Poetry of Juan **AROLAS**. BSS, 17, 1940.
Bonning, W. A. Andrés **BELLO'S** Imitations of V. Hugo. HR, 13, 1945.
Charlier, G. Victor Hugo et un poète hollandais de langue française (**BELTJENS**). NPh, 23, 1938.
Wolff, M. **BISMARCK** et Victor Hugo. Nouvelle Revue, 1.VIII.1901.
Lescoffier, J. Une adaptation de Victor Hugo par **BJOERNSON**. RLC, 2, 1922.
Schinz, A. Victor Hugo, Napoléon III et Elizabeth **BROWNING**. RLC, 13, 1933.
Giubbini, A. Victor Hugo e Giosuè **CARDUCCI**. Perugia, 1912.
Isola, M. dell'. Victor Hugo e Giosuè Carducci. Studi e Memorie per la Storia dell' U. di Bologna. Imola, 1930.
Rosso, A. T. L'ispirazione hughiana nel Carducci e nel Pascoli. Torino, 1932.
Breitfeld, E. F. **FREILIGRATHS** Uebersetzungen aus V. Hugo. Progr. Plauen, 1896.
Besson, P. **HEINES** Beziehungen zu V. Hugo. SVL, 1905.
Pina, M. V. Hugo julgado par **JUNGMERO**. A Illustraçao portugueza, 20. IX.1885.
Lerner, N. O. **PUSHKIN** and Victor Hugo. Zven'ia, 5, 1935.
Aubry, G. J. Victor Hugo et **SWINBURNE**. RB, 7.III.1936.
Daryl, P. Victor Hugo jugé par un poète anglais. Le Temps, 9. & 13.VIII.1885.
Hankiss, J. V. Hugo en 1935 (étude rétrospective des relations de V. Hugo avec **TELEKI** et les émigrés hongrois). Nouvelle Revue de Hongrie, 1935.
Dejob, C. Les Pauvres Gens de V. Hugo et Enoch Arden de **TENNYSON**. RCC 5.VII.1900.
Rose, F. Tennyson and Victor Hugo. Poetry Review, March, 1939.
Breton, A. Le. La pitié sociale dans le roman: l'auteur des Misérables et l'auteur de Résurrection (**TOLSTOI**). RDM, 15.II.1902.
Kohnhorst, H. L'influence de V. Hugo sur l'oeuvre d' A. **VALAONTIS**. Museum, 41, 1935.
Riisager, V. Emile **VERHAEREN** og V. Hugo. Festskrift til Valdemar Vedel. København, 1935.
Weil, F. Victor Hugo und Richard **WAGNER**. Diss. Bern, 1926.
Peers, E. A. **ZORRILLA** y Victor Hugo. In: Amigos de Zorrilla. Valladolid, 1933.

CHAPTER FIFTEEN

Molière

(See also Amphitryon I.VI.10, Don Juan, IV.IV.9 and Comparisons, I.V.1.)

1. Influences upon Individual Countries.

Genovesi, P. Molière e la commedia moderna. Mantova, 1883.
Klemperer, V. Die Gestalt Molières auf der Bühne. Bühne & Welt, 8, 1906.
Saintonge, P. & Christ, R. W. Fifty Years of Molière Studies, a Bibliography, 1892-1941. Baltimore, 1942.
Tibal, A. Molière dans la littérature européenne. Revue de Prague, 30.III. 1922.
Copeau, J. Notes sur des représentations de Molière aux Etats-Unis. (**AMERICA**). RLC, 1, 1921.
Socin, A. Zur Metrik einiger ins Arabische übersetzter Dramen Molières. (**ARABIA**). Leipzig, 1897.
Laborde, G. Molière au Danemark. (**DENMARK**). Le Temps, 23.IV.1932.
Reumert, P. Molière sur la scène danoise. Annales de l'U. de Paris, Sept., 1932.
Anon. Estime des Anglais pour Molière. (**ENGLAND**). Le Pour et Contre, 1, 1733.
—— Molière in England. TLS, 20.IV.1946.
Donnay, M. Molière et nos amis les Anglais. Revue hebdomadaire, 4.II.1922.
Ferchlardt, H. Molières Misanthrop und seine englischen Nachahmungen. Diss. Halle, 1907.
Gillet, J. E. Molière en Angleterre. Paris, 1913.
Humbert, C. H. Molière in England. Progr. Bielefeld, 1874.
—— Englands Urtheil über Molière. Bielefeld, Leipzig, 1878. Cf. Archiv, 1879.
Kerby, W. M. Some Thoughts Concerning Molière and the Restoration Drama. ML, 23, 1942.
Lann, H. van. Les plagiaires de Molière en Angleterre. Le Moliériste, 1880-81.
Lemarquis. Molière en Angleterre, le Misanthrope. Mém. de la Soc. litt. de Bar-le-Duc, 1886.
Mandach, A. de. Molière et la comédie de moeurs en Angleterre. Neuchâtel, 1946.
Miles, D. H. The Influence of Molière on Restoration Comedy. New York, 1910.
Schmidt, K. E. Molière in der angelsächsischen Kritik. Hamburg, 1940.
Taine, H. Molière en Angleterre. In: Histoire de la littérature anglaise, 3. Paris, 1886.
Tucker, J. E. Molière in England, 1700-1750. Diss. U. of Wisconsin, 1937.
—— The Eighteenth-Century English Translations of Molière. MLQ, 3, 1942.
Upham, A. H. English Femmes Savantes at the End of the Seventeenth Century. JEGPh, 12, 1913.
Wilcox, J. The Relation of Molière to Restoration Comedy. Columbia U. P., 1938.
Anon. Ein finnländischer Molière-Uebersetzer aus dem Anfang des Jahrhunderts. (**FINLAND**). Neuphilolog. Mitteilungen. Helsingfors, 1900.
Anon. Molière in Deutschland. (**GERMANY**). RRh, Feb., 1922.
Appel, C. Der Misanthrope in der neueren deutschen Molière-Forschung. Heidelberg, 1933.
Baluffe. Molière et les Allemands. Paris, 1884.
Boehn, M. von. Deutsche Betrachtungen über Molière. RRh, 1924.
Bolte, J. Molière-Uebersetzungen des XVII. Jahrhunderts. Archiv, 82, 1889.
Brouchoud. Molière à Vienne. Le Moliériste, June, 1882.
Buriot-Darsiles, H. Molière en Allemagne. NRI, 1922.
Ehrhard, A. Les comédies de Molière en Allemagne. Paris, 1888. Cf. Archiv, 84, 1890.
Eloesser, A. Die älteste deutsche Uebersetzung Molière'scher Lustspiele. Berlin, 1893.
Farinelli, A. Un critico tedesco del Molière. NAnt, 5.IV.1930.
Fraenkel, L. Zu Molière in Deutschland. Archiv, 1893.
Friedmann, A. Deutschlands Urteil über Molière. MLIA, 1883.
Geiger, L. Molière in Deutschland. Blätter zur Allg. Zt., 156, 1892.
Hartmann, K. A. M. Molière im deutschen Gewande. Blätter f. literar. Unterhaltung, 13, 1893 & ZFSL, 15, 1893.
Horner, E. Der Stoff von Molières Femmes savantes im deutschen Drama. Zs. f. d. oesterr. Gymnasien, 47, 1896.
Humbert, C. Molière, Shakespeare und die deutsche Kritik. Leipzig, 1869.
—— Die Molière-Vorstellungen auf deutschen Bühnen. Molière-Museum, 4, 1879-80.
—— Deutschlands Urtheil über Molière. Oppeln, 1883.
Lindau, P. Molière in Deutschland. Internationale Revue, Wien, 4, 1867.
—— Molière von einem seiner Zeitgenossen übersetzt. Magazin, 1868.

—— Molières Tartuffe im Schauspielhaus. Gegenwart, 11, 1877.
—— Molière et les classiques allemands. Le Moliériste, June, 1883.
Mahrenholtz, R. Molière in Deutschland. Blätter f. literar. Unterhaltung, 6, 1890.
Mangold, W. Deutsche Quellen zur Molière-Biographie. Molière-Museum, 2, 1879-80.
Morf, H. Das Molière-Gastspiel in Frankfurt. Les Précieuses Ridicules und Tartuffe. Frankfurter Zt., 26, 1902.
Schlenther, P. Molière in Deutschland. Gegenwart, 1882.
—— Molière im Deutschen. MLIA, 15.IV. 1893.
Schuh, O. F. Sieben deutsche Molière-Uebersetzungen. Rheinische Thalia, 1, 1922.
Spirgatis, M. Die Nürnberger Molière-Uebersetzungen. Sammlung f. bibliothekswissenschaftl. Arbeiten, 10.
Stichlin, O. W. Molière und kein Ende. Anhang: Molière in Deutschland. Berlin, 1887.
Veber, P. Molière en Allemagne. Revue d'art dramatique, 1.XI.1889.
Zabel, E. Molière'sche Dramen auf deutschen Bühnen. In: Zur modernen Dramaturgie. Oldenburg, 1899.
Andel, D. van. Les médecins de Molière au théâtre classique des Pays-Bas. (**HOLLAND**). C. R. du 2e Congrès d'histoire de la médicine en 1921. Evreux, 1922.
Loon, H. E. van. Nederlandsche vertalingen naar Molière uit de 17e eeuw. Diss. Leyden. S'Gravenhage, 1911.
Mandach, A. de. The First Translation of Molière in the World. CLS, 21-22, 1946.
Deutsch, J. Molière in Ungarn. (**HUNGARY**). Molière-Museum, 1879-81.
Filippi, J. de. Tartuffe en Italie. (**ITALY**). Le Moliériste, 6, 1884.
Frajo, C. Studi letterari. Napoli, 1895.
Levi, C. Studii Molieriani. Palermo, 1922.
Mele, E. Monzu Moliero (les imitations de M. dans la comédie napolitaine du XVIIIe siècle). Flegrea, Riv. di lettere, 4, 1901.
Ronzy, P. Reflets du génie français en Italie: de Molière aux dames et poètes de la Venise mourante. Le Génie français, 1930.
Toldo, P. Molière en Italie. JCL, 1, 1903.
—— L'oeuvre de Molière et sa fortune en Italie. Torino, 1910. Cf. NAnt, 1.VII. 1911.
Estreicher, C. Molière en Pologne. (**POLAND**). Le Moliériste, 4, 1882.
Folkierski, W. Molière en Pologne. RLC, 2, 1922.
Allard, S. d'. Une adaptation portugaise du Tartuffe de Molière. (**PORTUGAL**). Annales internationales d'histoire, 1901.
Figueiredo, F. de. Quelques mots sur Molière en Portugal. Mélanges Baldensperger. Paris, 1930.
Néry, F. J. de. Molière au Portugal. Revue du monde latin. Paris, 1883.
Ashkinasi, M. Les influences françaises en Russie: Molière. (**RUSSIA**). Le Livre, 10.XI.1884.
Blavières, de. Molière in Russland. MLIA, 1880.
Patouillet, J. Mol'er v Rossii. Rev. des Etudes slaves, 1922 & Berlin, Petropolis, 1924.
Cotarelo, S. Traductores castellanos de Molière. (**SPAIN**). Homenaje a Menéndez y Pelayo. Madrid, 1899. And in: Estudios de historia literaria. Madrid, 1901.
Martinenche, E. Molière et le théâtre espagnol. Paris, 1906.
Thalasso, A. Molière en Turquie. (**TURKEY**). Paris, 1888.
Jezic, S. Une traduction slovène de Georges Dandin. (**YUGOSLAVIA**). RLC, 1, 1921.

2. Influences upon Individual Authors.

Anon. Molière übersetzt von Graf **BAUDISSIN**. Grenzboten, 24, 1865 & 26, 1867.
Freytag, G. Molière übersetzt durch Graf Baudissin. In: Vermischte Aufsätze. Leipzig, 1901.
Figueiredo, F. de. As adaptações do theatro de Molière por **CASTILHO**. In: Estudos de litteratura, 2. Lisboa, 1918.
Ornstein, J. Castilho e as suas adaptações portuguesas de Molière. Hisp., 25, 1942.
Hohrmann, F. Das Verhältniss Susanne **CENTLIVRES** zu Molière und Regnard. ZVL, 14, 1900.
Weidler, W. Das Verhältniss von Mrs. Centlivres The Busy Body zu Molières L'Etourdi und Ben Jonsons The Divell is an Asse. Diss. Halle, 1900.
Wüllenweber, A. Mrs. Centlivres Lustspiel Loves Contrivance und seine Quellen. Diss. Halle, 1900.
Schneider, W. Das Verhältniss von Colley **CIBBERS** Lustspiel The Non-Juror zu Molières Tartuffe. Diss. Halle, 1903.
Toeuse, L. Colley Cibbers Komödie The Refusal in ihrem Verhältnis zu Molières Les Femmes Savantes. Diss. Kiel, 1910.
Bennewitz, A. Molières Einfluss auf

CONGREVE. Diss. Leipzig, 1889. Cf. ESn, 16.
Roy, E. L'Avare de **DONI** et l'Avare de Molière. RHLF, 15.I.1894.
Haas, M. Das Problem des Tartuffe bei **DOSTOJEWSKI**. NSp, 1932.
Hartmann, K. Einfluss Molières auf **DRYDEN'S** komisch-dramatische Dichtungen. Diss. Leipzig, 1885.
Ott, P. Ueber das Verhältniss des Lustspieldichters Dryden zur gleichzeitigen französischen Komödie, insbesondere zu Molière. Diss. München, 1885.
Lindner, F. H. **FIELDINGS** dramatische Werke. Dresden, 1895.
Gnecca, G. Il Molière nella produzione di Stefano di **FRANCHI**. Giornale storico e letter. della Liguria, 1926.
Mangold, W. **FRIEDRICH DER GROSSE** und Molière. ZFSL, 12, 1900.
Barthélemy, A. Les jugements de **GOETHE** sur Molière. L'Alsace française, 31.VII.1932.
Humbert, C. Goethe über Molière, nebst einigen Bemerkungen von Lessing und Schiller. Progr. Bielefeld, 1886.
Beduschi, M. Molière et **GOLDONI**. Verona, 1899.
Conreil, S. de Parallelo fra Molière i Goldoni. In: Opere, 2. Livorno, 1818.
Giovagnoli, R. Goldoni a fronte di Molière. In: Meditazioni di un Cratalone. Roma, 1887.
Lueder, W. Carlo Goldoni in seinem Verhältniss zu Molière. Diss. Leipzig, 1883.
Maddalena, E. Scene e figure molieresche imitate del Goldoni. Rivista teatrale italiana, 10. Napoli, 1905.
Mignon, M. Molière et Goldoni. NRI, 1922.
Molmenti, P. Il Molière e il Goldoni. Gedenkschrift C. Goldoni. Venezia, 1893.
Rabany, C. De Goldonio, italicae scoenae correctore. Paris, 1893.
—— Carlo Goldoni. Le théâtre et la vie en Italie au XVIIIe siècle. Paris, 1896.
Sarcey, F. Le Molière de Goldoni. RCC, 6, 1897-98.
Vico, A. de Per un parallelo letterario mal falto. Milano, 1913.
Ellinger, G. Der Einfluss des Tartuffe auf die Pietisterey der Frau **GOTTSCHED** und deren Vorbild. ALG, 13, 1884.
McKenzie, K. Francesco **GRISELINI** and his Relation to Goldoni and Molière. MPh, 14, 1916.
Houben, H. Molières Tartuffe und **GUTZKOWS** Urbild des Tartuffe. MLIA, 18. V. 1899. And in: Gutzkow-Funde. Berlin, 1901.
Bull, F. **HOLBERG** and Molière. Holberg Aarbog, 1921.
—— Un grand disciple de Molière: Ludvig Holberg. RLC, 2, 1922.
Coussange, J. de Le Molière danois. Journal des Débats, 19.I.1922.
Gourdault, J. Holberg considéré comme imitateur de Molière. RDM, 15.VII. 1865.
Humbert, C. Molière und Holberg. Neue Jb. für Philologie und Pädagogik, 1881.
Laun, A. Molière und Holberg. Molière-Museum, 2, 1880.
Legrelle, A. Holberg considéré comme imitateur de Molière. Diss. Paris, 1864.
Topsøe-Jensen, H. G. Holberg og den eftermoliereske Komedie. Holberg Aarbog, 1921.
Vedel, V. Molière et Holberg. Mélanges Baldensperger. Paris, 1930.
Klemperer, V. Molière und **IBSEN**. Aus fremden Zungen, 16, 1906.
Humbert, C. Fr. **JACOBS** über Molière und die Klassiker aus dem Zeitalter Ludwigs XIV. Bielefeld, 1879.
Bach, A. Johann **KAEMPF**: Peter Squenz (1775): eine Bearbeitung von Molières Médecin malgré lui. ZFSL, 46, 1920.
Ohnsorg, R. John **LACY'S** Dumb Lady, Mrs. Centlivres Love's Contrivance und Fieldings Mock Doctor in ihrem Verhältnis zueinander und zu ihrer gemeinsamen Quelle. Diss. Rostock, 1900.
Wernicke, A. Das Verhältnis von John Lacys The Dumb Lady zu Molières Le médecin malgré lui und L'Amour médecin. Diss. Halle, 1903.
Gueth, A.Eine neue Molière-Uebersetzung von **A. LAUN**. MLIA, 1880.
Humbert, C. **LESSING** über Molière. Molière-Museum, 3, 1879-80.
Mahrenholtz, R. Lessings Jugenddichtungen in ihrer Beziehung zu Molière. Archiv, 10, 1881.
Ridenti, L. Un Molierista italiano: Cesare **LEVI**. Il Secolo XX, Dec., 1925.
Breitinger, H. **LINDAUS** Molière. Beilage zur Allg. Zt., 17.IX.1872.
Friedmann, A. Les Femmes savantes et les **MEININGER** à Vienne. Le Molièriste, 1880.
Vezinet, F. **MORATIN** et Molière; Molière, Florian et la littérature espagnole. Paris, 1909.
Mando, F. Il più prossimo precursore di Carlo Goldoni (Jacopo Angelo **NELLI**). Arezzo, 1903.
Baumann, F. Ueber die Abhängigkeit Alberto **NOTAS** von Molière und Goldoni. RF, 25, 1908.
Maruffi, G.__**PARINI** e Molière. Roma letteraria, 4, 1895-96.
Patouillet, J. **POUCHKINE** et Molière. RLC, 17, 1937.

Cirot, G. Une des imitations de Molière par **RAMON DE LA CRUZ.** RLC, 3, 1923.
Hamilton, A. Ramon de la Cruz's Debt to Molière. Hisp., 1921.
Faguet, E. **ROUSSEAU** contre Molière. Paris, 1912.
Beam, J. M. Goethe und Heine über **SCHLEGEL** und Molière. Euphorion, 23, 1920.
Bertrand, J. J. Á. G. Schlegel critique de Molière. RLC, 2, 1922.
Gerth, C. A. E. Ueber den Misanthropen des Molière, mit Bezugnahme auf das Urtheil von A. W. von Schlegel. Progr. Putbus, 1841.
Humbert, C. Deutschlands Urteile über Molière bis zum Regierungsantritt A. W. von Schlegels. Oppeln, 1883.
Crull, F. Th. **SHADWELLS** und H. Fieldings Comoedien The Miser in ihrem Verhältnis untereinander und zu ihrer gemeinsamen Quelle. Diss. Rostock, 1899.
Erichsen, A. Thomas Shadwells Komödie The Sullen Lovers in ihrem Verhältnis zu Molières Komödien Le Misanthrope und Les Fâcheux. Diss. Kiel, 1906.
Cammaerts, E. Molière and B. **SHAW.** NC., Sept, 1926.
Milne, J. M. Molière et **SHERIDAN.** Diss. Rennes, 1912.
Levinstein, K. Chr. **WEISSE** und Molière. Diss. Berlin, 1899.
Aynard, J. Molière et **WYCHERLEY.** Journal des Débats, 29.I.1922.
Klette, J. William Wycherleys Leben und dramatische Werke, mit besonderer Berücksichtigung von Wycherley als Plagiator Molières. Münster, 1883.
Sandmann, P. Molières Ecole des Femmes und Wycherleys Country Wife. Archiv, 72, 1884.
—— Molière, Wycherley und Garrick. Archiv, 77, 1887.

CHAPTER SIXTEEN

Montaigne.

1. Generalities.

Anon. Montaigne in English. TLS, 15.V. 1937.
Belleli, M. L. Modernità di Montaigne. Roma, 1934.
Bouillier, V. La renommée de Montaigne en Allemagne. Paris, 1921.
—— La fortune de Montaigne en Italie et en Espagne. Paris, 1922.
Dédéyan, C. Montaigne chez ses amis anglo-saxons. 2 vols. Paris, 1946. Cf. TLS, 13.IX.1947.
Ellerbroek, G. G. Notes sur la fortune de Montaigne en Hollande. NPh, 32, 1948.
Faure, E. Montaigne et ses trois premiers-nés: Shakespeare, Cervantes, Pascal. Paris, 1948.
Hall, Marie-Louise. Montaigne and his Translators. Diss U. of Wisconsin, 1940.
Hayes, R. S. La posteridad de Montaigne en España. Nosotros (Buenos Aires), Dec., 1936. Cf. NL, 11.II.1939.
Plattard, J. Etat présent des études sur Montaigne. Paris, 1935.
Pudor, H. Die Bedeutung Montaignes für die Pädagogik unserer Zeit. Norddeutsche Allg. Zt., 39, 1901.
Schneider, F. L. Montaigne und die Geniezeit. Euphorion, 23, 1921.
Spencer, T. Montaigne in America. AM, 177, 1946.
Teulié, H. Projet d'une prétendue traduction des Essais de Montaigne au XVIIIe siècle. Mélanges Laumonier. Paris, 1934.
Texte, J. La descendance de Montaigne. In: Etudes de littérature européenne. Paris, 1898.
Villey, P. Montaigne et les poètes dramatiques anglais du temps de Shakespeare. RHLF, 24, 1917.
—— Montaigne devant la postérité. Paris, 1935.
Yvon, P. Montaigne chez les Anglo-Saxons. Caen, 1935.

2. Influences upon Individual Authors.

Anon. Montaigne und **BACON**, eine Parallele. Archiv, 31, 1862.
Selby, F. G. Bacon and Montaigne. Criterion, Jan., 1925.
Taffe, V. Bacon et Montaigne essayistes. RAA, 1924.
Villey, P. Montaigne a-t-il eu quelque influence sur François Bacon? Revue de la Renaissance, 1911 ff.
Zeitlin, J. The Development of Bacon's Essays with Special Reference to the Question of Montaigne's Influence upon Them. JEGPh, 1928.
Ellerbroek, G. G. Un adversaire hollandais de Montaigne: Johan van **BEVERWIJCK.** NPh, 31, 1947.
Villey, P. L'influence de Montaigne sur Charles **BLOUNT** et sur les déistes anglais. Revue du XVIe siècle, 1913.
Bouillier, V. Montaigne en Allemand: Christoph **BODE,** son grand traducteur. RLC, 13, 1933.
Texte, J. La descendance de Montaigne:

Sir Thomas BROWNE. In: Etudes de littérature européenne. Paris, 1898.
Collins, A. BROWNING and Montaigne. London, 1902.
Faure, E. Montaigne et ses trois premiers-nés (CERVANTES). Paris, 1926.
Bennett, R. E. Sir W. CORNWALLIS'S Use of Montaigne. PMLA, 1933.
Nethercot, A. H. Abraham COWLEY'S Essays. JEGPh, 1930.
Turnbull. Montaigne and EMERSON. Littell's Living Age, 26, 1850.
Ustick, W. L. Emerson's Debt to Montaigne. Washington U. Studies, 9, 1922.
Young, C. L. Emerson's Montaigne. New York, 1941.
Dieckow, F. John FLORIOS englische Uebersetzung der Essais Montaignes und Lord Bacons, Ben Jonsons und Robert Burtons Verhältniss zu Montaigne. Diss. Strassburg, 1903.
Saintsbury, G. Preface to Florio's Translation of Montaigne's Essays. Tudor Translations. London, 1892-96.
Waites, A. Montaigne-Florio-Shakespeare. Shakespeariana, April, 1891.
Bouillier, V. Montaigne et GOETHE, RLC, 5, 1925.
Schneider, J. HIPPEL als Schüler Montaignes, Hamanns und Herders. Euphorion, 23, 1920.
Mehner, C. M. Der Einfluss Montaignes auf die pädagogischen Ansichten von John LOCKE. Diss. Leipzig, 1891.
McBryde. Montaigne and Jan MACLAREN. MLN, 12, 1897.
Wood, H. (ed.). Preface to the Plays of J. MARSTON. London, 1938.
Bouillier, V. Montaigne et NIETZSCHE. Bull. des Amis de Montaigne. 2. Sér., 6, 1939.
Fabureau, H. Un Montaigne suédois. (OXENSTIERNA). MF, Feb., 1948.
Barrett, W. P. Matthew PRIOR'S Alma. MLR, 1932.
Wright, H. B. William Jackson on Prior's Use of Montaigne. MLR, 1936.
Klingensfor, F. Montaigne und SHAFTESBURY in ihrer praktischen Philosophie. Diss. Erlangen, 1908.
Anon. Hamlet and Montaigne. (SHAKEPEARE). Academy, 1366, 1898.
Blind, K. Hamlet et Montaigne. Revue internationale, 4, 1884.
Collins, J. C. Shakespeare and Montaigne. Saturday Review, 85, 1897.
Deutschbein, M. Shakespeares Kritik an Montaigne in As You Like It. NM, 5, 1934.
Faure, E. Montaigne et ses trois premiers-nés (Shakespeare, Cervantes, Pascal). Paris, 1926.
Feis, J. Shakespeare and Montaigne. (Hamlet). London, 1891.
Franz, W. Shakespeare und Montaigne. NSp, 40, 1934.
Harmon, Alice. How Great Was Shakespeare's Debt to Montaigne? PMLA, 57, 1942.
Henderson, W. B. Montaigne's Apologie of Raymond Sebond and King Lear. SAB, 14-15, 1939-40.
Hooker, E. R. The Relation of Shakespeare to Montaigne. PLMA, 17, 1902.
Manovitch, M. Shakespeare et Montaigne. In: Letopis Matice Srpske, 1933.
Maxwell, J. C. Montaigne and Macbeth. MLR, 43, 1948.
Robertson, J. Montaigne and Shakespeare. London, 1898.
Smith, R. M. Shakspere, the Montaigne of England. SAB, 22.
Stapfer. Montaigne et Shakespeare. Bull. des Amis de Montaigne, 2. Sér., 6, 1939.
Stedefeld, G. E. Hamlet: ein Tendenzdrama Shakespeares gegen die skeptische und cosmopolitische Weltanschauung des Michael de Montaigne. Berlin, 1871.
Taylor, G. C. Shakespeare's Debt to Montaigne. Harvard U. P., 1925.
—— Montaigne-Shakespeare and the Deadly Parallel. PhQ, 22, 1943.
Tuerck, S. Shakespeare und Montaigne. Berlin, 1930.
Ferriar, J. Comments on STERNE. Manchester Philos. & Literary Transactions, 1793.
Neri, F. TASSONI e Montaigne? In: Fabrilia. Torino, 1930.
Crawford, C. Montaigne, WEBSTER and Marston. Collectanea, 2, Ser., 1907.

CHAPTER SEVENTEEN

Rabelais.

1. Generalities.

Boulenger, J. Rabelais à travers les âges. Paris, 1925.
Neri, F. La leggenda di Gargantua nella valle d'Aosta. Actes de l'Acad. royale de Turin, 2.II.1919.
Sainéan, L. L'influence et la réputation de Rabelais. Paris, 1930.
Sebillot, P. Gargantua dans les traditions populaires. Paris, 1887.
Anon. Rabelais in English. (ENGLAND). TLS, 13.XII.1934.
Bourgeois, A. F. Rabelais en Angleterre. Revue des Etudes rabelaisiennes, 3, 1906.

Brown, H. Rabelais in English Literature. Harvard U. P., 1933.

Campbell, O. J. The Earliest English Reference to Rabelais' Work (1533). HLQ, 2, 1938.

McKillop, A. D. Some Early Traces of Rabelais in English Literature. MLN, 1921.

Whibley, C. Rabelais en Angleterre. Revue des Etudes rabelaisiennes, 1, 1903.

Sainéan, L. Les interprètes de Rabelais en Angleterre et en Allemagne. Revue des Etudes rabelaisiennes, 7, 1910.

Hegaur, E. Auf Rabelais Spuren in Deutschland. (**GERMANY**). LE. 15.IX. 1908.

Pfeffer, G. Les études sur Rabelais parues en Allemagne. Revue des Etudes rabelaisiennes, 1, 1903.

—— Rabelais in Deutschland. Frankfurter Zt., 178, 1906 .

Thijssen-Schoute, C. L. Quelques observations sur la fortune de Rabelais en **HOLLANDE**. H&R, 6.

Bianchi, A. G. Rabelais in Italia. (**ITALY**). La Lettura, 1.III.1921.

Neri, F. La dubbia fortuna del Rabelais in Italia. RLC, 12, 1932.

Rajna, P. Il Rabelais giudicato da un italiano del secolo XVI. Revue des Etudes rabelaisiennes, 1, 1903.

Gillet, J. E. Note sur Rabelais en Espagne. (**SPAIN**). RLC, 16, 1936.

2. Influences upon Individual Authors.

Upham, A. H. Rabelaisianism in **CARLYLE**. MLN, 1918.

Gebhart, E. De Panurge à Sancho Pança. (**CERVANTES**). Paris, 1911.

Hatzfeld, H. Künstlerische Berührungspunkte zwischen Cervantes und Rabelais. Jb. f. Philologie, 1.

Buonanno, V. **FISCHART** e Rabelais. Studi di filologia moderna, 3, 1910.

Ellmer, W. Rabelais' Gargantua und Fischarts Geschichtsklitterung. Progr., 1895.

Frantzen, J. A. Fischarts Uebersetzung von Rabelais' Gargantua. Diss. Strassburg, 1892.

Ganghofer, L. Joh. Fischart und seine Verdeutschung des Rabelais. Diss. Augsburg, 1880. München, 1881.

Gelbeke, F. A. Joh. Fischart und Rabelais' Gargantua. St. Petersburg, 1874.

Rausch, H. A. Das Spielverzeichnis im 25. Kapitel von Fischarts Geschichtsklitterung. Diss. Strassburg, 1908.

Schwarz, G. Rabelais und Fischart. Diss. Zürich, 1885.

Strehlke, F. Das Verhältniss Fischarts zu Rabelais. Archiv, 1854.

Gallas, K. R. Quelques observations sur la traduction néerlandaise de Rabelais par Claudio **GALLITALO** (1682). Donum natalicum Schrijnen, Utrecht, 1929.

Engel, E. Rabelais' Gargantua und Pantagruel. Deutsch von F. A. **GELBEKE**. MLIA, 1880.

Jordan, L. **GOETHE** und Rabelais. GRM, 1911.

Thijssen-Schoute, C. L. **HUYGENS** en Rabelais. Tijdschr. v. Nederl. taal- en letterkunde, 1937.

Bonger, F. van. **MARNIX** en Rabelais. NPh, 25, 1940.

Reeves, W. P. Moby Dick and Rabelais. (**MELVILLE**). MLN, 1923.

Farmer, A. J. Une source de Eastward Ho: Rabelais. (Ben **JONSON**). EA, 1937.

Axon, W. **SHAKESPEARE** the Knavish and Rabelais. N&Q, 7,1901.

Birch, W. J. Rabelais and Shakespeare. N&Q, 3.I.1879 & 13.IX.1880.

Herpich, C. A. Shakespeare the Knavish and Rabelais. N&Q, 8, 1901.

Koenig, W. Ueber die Entlehnungen Shakespeares, insbesondere aus Rabelais und einigen italienischen Dramatikern. JbShG, 9, 1874.

Smith, W. Rabelais and Shakespeare. N&Q, 1.IX.1877. And in: Revue des Etudes rabelaisiennes, 1, 1903.

Eddy, W. A. Rabelais, a Source for Gulliver's Travels. (**SWIFT**). MLN, 1922.

Orrery, John Earl of. Remarks on the Life and Writings of Dr. J. Swift. London, 1752.

Pons, E. Rabelais et Swift. A propos des Liliputiens. Mélanges Lefranc. Paris, 1936.

Ferriar, J. Comments on **STERNE**. Manchester Philos. and Literary Transactions, 1793.

Sainéan, L. Sur la traduction de Rabelais par **URQUHART**. Revue des Etudes rabelaisiennes, 1909.

Thijssen-Schoute, C. L. Nicolas Jarichides **WIERINGA**. Assen, 1939.

CHAPTER EIGHTEEN

Racine.

1. Generalities.

Baldensperger, F. Racine et la tradition romanesque. RLC, 19, 1939.

Peyre, H. Racine et la critique contemporaine. PMLA, 45, 1930.

Williams, E. E. Racine depuis 1885: bibliographie raisonnée. Baltimore, 1940.
Bowe, F. B. Recherches sur Racine dans l'Amérique du Nord (1668-1820). (**AMERICA**). RLC, 19, 1939.
Etiemble, R. Recherches sur Racine au Méxique. RLC, 19, 1939.
Dontchev, N. Racine en Bulgarie. (**BULGARIA**). Sofia, 1939.
Lechnikova, T. Racine en Bulgarie. RLC, 19,1939.
Anon. Racine in English. (**ENGLAND**). TLS, 12.VI.1937.
—— Un-English Tastes. TLS, 22.X.1938.
Eccles, F. Y. Racine in England. Oxford, 1922.
Hoffmann, K. Corneille und Racine in England. Vossische Zt., Sonntagsblatt, 22, 1906. And in: Zwölf Studien zur Literatur und Ideengeschichte. Charlottenburg, 1908.
Stewart, W. Racine vu par les Anglais de 1800 à nos jours. RLC, 19, 1939.
Villard, L. Bérénice en Angleterre. Revue de l'U. de Lyon, May, 1928.
Wheatley, K. E. Andromaque as the Distrest Mother. RR, 39, 1948.
Bentmann, F. Racine und der deutsche Geist. (**GERMANY**). CFA, 6, 1939.
Dach, Charlotte von. Racine in der deutschen Literatur des 18. Jahrhunderts. Bern, 1941.
Grolmann, A. von. Racine-Uebersetzung und Problemlage. Die neue Literatur, July, 1939.
Monchoux, A. Une récente traduction allemande de Racine. RLC, 19, 1939.
Schröder, R. A. Racine und die deutsche Humanität. München, 1933.
Uehlin, H. Geschichte der Racine-Uebersetzungen in der vorklassischen deutschen Literatur. Heidelberg, 1903.
Geleerd, S. Les traductions hollandaises de Racine au XVIIe et au XVIIIe siècle. (**HOLLAND**). Zutphen, Amsterdam, 1936.
Looten, C. Racine et les Pays-Bas. RLC, 19, 1939.
Baumgarten, S. Racine et les résistances de l'esprit hongrois. (**HUNGARY**). RLC, 19, 1939.
Angelis, V. de Per la fortuna del teatro di Racine in Italia, notizie e appunti. (**ITALY**). Studi di filologia moderna, 6, 1913.
—— Critiche, traduzioni ed imitazioni italiane del teatro di G. Racine durante il secolo XVIII. Arpino, 1914.
Fubini, M. Racine et la critique italienne. RLC, 19, 1939.
Weintraub, V. Les débuts de l'influence de Racine en Pologne. (**POLAND**). RLC, 19, 1939.
Campos Ferreira Lima, H. de. Racine et le **PORTUGAL**. Bull. des Etudes Portugaises, 1940.
Gukovskij, G. Racine en Russie au XVIIIe siècle: la critique et les traductions. (**RUSSIA**) Revue des Etudes slaves, 7, 1927.
Brachfeld, O. Les traductions catalanes de Racine. (**SPAIN**). RLC, 12, 1932.
Qualia, C. B. Racine's Tragic Art in Spain in the XVIIIth Century. PMLA, 54, 1939.
Blanck, A. Une représentation de l'Iphigénie de Racine à Stockholm en 1684. (**SWEDEN**). RLC, 16, 1936.
Schazmann, P. E. Jean Racine et Genève. (**SWITZERLAND**). RLC, 19, 1939.

2. Influences upon Individual Authors.

Moioli, A. Jean Racine e Vittorio **ALFIERI**. Clusone, 1922.
Lugli, V. **CARDUCCI** e Racine. Convivium, 13, 1941.
Dechamps, J. Charles **FOXE** et Racine. MLR, 36, 1941.
Baldensperger, F. **FREDERIC II** appréciateur de Racine. RR, 1937. And in: Etudes d'histoire littéraire, 4e. Sér. 1939.
Anon. Zu **GOETHE** und Racine. NJKA, 2, 1899.
Glaesener, H. Notes sur Goethe et Racine. Revue hebdomadaire, 2.IV.1932.
Merian-Genast, E. Racine und Goethe, ein Vergleich zwischen französischer und deutscher Klassik. Archiv, 165, 1935.
Spitzer, L. Racine et Goethe. RHPhC, 1933.
Suphan, B. Goethes ungedruckte Uebersetzung der Chöre von Racines Athalie. JbGG, 1895.
Baldensperger, F. Encore la Cabale de Phèdre: **LEIBNIZ** du mauvais côté? MLN, 58, 1943.
Neri, F. Racine e **MANZONI**. GSLI, 69.
Pizzagalli, A. M. Il duello di Lodovico nei Promessi sposi e un passo di Racine. Rendiconti, R.Istituto lombardo di Scienze e Lettere, 1939-40.
Pellegrini, C. Ippolito **PINDEMONTE** traduttore di Racine. Mélanges Vianey. Paris, 1935.
Batiouchkof, T. **POUCHKINE** et Racine (In Russian). Gedenkschrift Pouchkine. St. Petersbourg, 1900.
Luzzato, A. **SCHILLER** traducteur de Racine. RLC, 19, 1939.
Hazlitt, W. Sir W. **SCOTT**, Racine and

Shakespeare. In: The Plain Speaker. London, 1826.
Anon. Racine et Michel de **SWAEN**. Annales du Comité flamand de France, 27, 1903.

CHAPTER NINETEEN

Stendhal.

1. Generalities.

Charlier, G. Stendhal et ses amis belges. Paris, 1931.
Dechamps, J. Stendhal et l'Espagne. BH, 1926.
Esquerra, R. Stendhal en España, 1835-1935. RLC, 16, 1936.
Green, M. L. The Stendhal of American Publications. RLC, 10, 1930.
Gunnell, Doris. Stendhal et l'Angleterre. Paris, 1909.
Hayden-Siler, J. Stendhal et l'Amérique. Diss. U. of Tennessee, 1940 & Le Divan, July, 1947.
Jourda, P. Etat présent des études stendhaliennes. In: Etudes françaises. Paris, 1930.
Kuehn, J. Deutsche Stendhal-Erinnerungen. Revue Napoléonienne, 13, 1913.
Pitollet, C. Une version latine de Stendhal. Hum., 5, 1933.
Schurig, A. Une amie allemande de Stendhal. RB, 1905.
—— Stendhals erster Leser in Deutschland. Das Inselschiff, 8, 1927.
Smith, B. Stendhal and the American Reader. N. Y. Times Book Review, 1.IV.1945.
Smith, H. E. La fortune d'une oeuvre de jeunesse de Stendhal en Amérique. Revue des Bibliothèques, 1927.
Vigneron, R. Stendhal en Espagne. MPh, 32, 1934.
Vinogradov, A. Trois rencontres russes de Stendhal. MF, 1928.
Volk, W. Stendhal im Lichte der neuesten Forschung. NM, 1935.

2. Influences upon Individual Authors.

Lafourcade, G. Stendhal et Arnold **BENNETT**. RLC, 19, 1939.
Benedetto, L. F. Stendhal jugé par **CARDUCCI**. Le Divan, Jan., 1937.
Caraccio, A. Stendhal, **FOSCOLO** et leur amie Métilde Dembowski. Ausonia, 7, 1942.
Baldensperger, F. Le dossier Stendhalien de **GOETHE**. Mélanges Vianey. Paris, 1935.
Poncheville, A. M. de. Le comte **GREPPI**, ami de Stendhal. Revue critique des idées et des livres, 25.V.1921.
Vigneron, R. Stendhal et **HAZLITT**. MPh, 1938.
Schurig, A. **HEINE** und Stendhal. 1902.
Elfelt, K. I. P. **JACOBSEN**-Stendhal. Festskrift til Valdemar Vedel. København, 1935.
Martino, P. Une rencontre italienne de Stendhal: M. de **MICCICHE**. RLC, 8, 1928.
Guibert, L. R. Stendhal et **NIETZSCHE**. RG, 1930.
Seillière, E. Un commentateur allemand de Stendhal. (**OPPELN**). RB, 1.VI.1912.
Gara, E. Giuditta **PASTA** tra Stendhal e Bellini. NAnt, 74, 1939.
Sarrailh, J. Stendhal et **VALLE-INCLAN**. In: Enquêtes romantiques. Paris, 1932.
—— Note sur Stendhal et Valle-Inclán. RLC, 14, 1934.
Vigneron, R. Stendhal et **VIGANO**. MPh, 1932.
Benedetto, T. Ermes **VISCONTI** e Stendhal. Arezzo, 1921.

CHAPTER TWENTY

Voltaire.

1. Generalities.

Rovillain, E. E. Sur le Zadig de Voltaire. Quelques influences probables. PMLA, 43, 1928.
—— L'Ingénu de Voltaire; quelques influences. PMLA, 44, 1929.
Arrom, J. J. Voltaire y la literatura dramática cubana. (**AMERICA**). RR, 34, 1943.
Barr, Mary M. Voltaire in America, 1744-1800. Baltimore, 1941.
Benson, A. B. Charles XII on the American Stage. SS, 1943.
Marion, S. Le Voltairianisme de la Gazette littéraire de Montréal. Revue de l'U. d'Ottawa, 9, 1939.
McDermott, J. F. Voltaire and the Free thinkers in Early St. Louis. RLC, 16, 1936.
Baumgaertner, G. Voltaire auf der englischen Bühne des 18. Jahrhunderts. (**ENGLAND**). Strassburg, 1913.
Bellessort, A. Voltaire en Angleterre. Revue hebdomadaire, 1925.
Bruce, H. L. Voltaire on the English Stage. Berkeley, 1918.
—— The Period of Greatest Popularity

of Voltaire's Plays on the English Stage. MLN, 1918.
Collins Churton. Voltaire, Montesquieu and Rousseau in England. London, 1908.
Crane, R. S. The Diffusion of Voltaire's Writings in England, 1750-1800. MPh, 20, 1923.
Foulet, L. Voltaire en Angleterre. RHLF, 15, 1908.
Oake, R. B. Political Elements in Criticism of Voltaire in England, 1732-47. MLN, 57, 1942.
Schilling, B. N. The English Case against Voltaire: 1789-1800. JHI, 4, 1943.
Strachey, G. L. Voltaire and England. In: Books and Characters, French and English. London, 1922.
Tallentyne, S. G. The English Friends of Voltaire. Cornhill Mag., April, 1904.
Tronchon, H. Voltaire et l'Angleterre. In: Licões Inaugurais da Missão Universitaria Francesa. Rio de Janeiro, 1937.
Wyzewa, T. de. Voltaire et Rousseau en Angleterre. RDM, 1908.
Ingler, F. Voltaire und seine Beziehungen zu Deutschland. **(GERMANY)**. MLIA, 1878.
Jung, R. Voltaires Verhaftung in Frankfurt a. M. Archiv f. Frankfurts Geschichte & Kunst, 3. Ser., 3, 1899.
Kersten, K. Voltaires Henriade in der deutschen Kritik vor Lessing. Berlin, 1914.
Korff, H. A. Voltaire im literarischen Deutschland des 18. Jahrhunderts. Heidelberg, 1918.
Koser, R. Voltaire und die Idée de la cour de Prusse. Forschungen z. brandenb. & preuss. Geschichte, 6, 1893.
Mahrenholtz, R. Voltaires Beziehungen zu Sachsen. ZFSL, 10, 1888.
Quinsonas, Chevalier de. Lettre sur l'apothéose de Voltaire en Prusse (1750). In: Barbier, Dictionnaire des ouvrages anonymes. 4 vols. Paris, 1872-79.
Ristelhuber, P. Un touriste allemand à Ferney en 1775. RB, 1878.
Sakmann, P. Voltaire und das Haus Württemberg. In: Eine ungedruckte Correspondenz Voltaires. Stuttgart, 1899.
Schultz-Bertram. Voltaire's Statue oder der Kaiser und der Atheist. Baltische Monatsschrift, 67, 1909.
Thieriot, A. Voltaire en Prusse. Paris, 1878.
Varhagen von Ense. Voltaire in Frankfurt. In: Berliner Kalender, 1846, & in: Denkwürdigkeiten und Vermischte Schriften, 8, 1869.
Vodoz, J. La lecture de Voltaire dans les classes supérieures des gymnases de l'Allemagne et de la Suisse allemande est-elle indiquée? Festschrift zum 14. Neuphilologentage Zürich, 1910.
Benoît, C. Voltaire et les libraires de **HOLLANDE**. Gazette de Hollande, March, 1926.
Minderhood, H. J. Le Henriade dans la littérature hollandaise. Paris, 1927.
Valkhoff, P. Zaïre en de Henriade in de Nederlandsche Letterkunde. De nieuwe Taalgids, 10, 1916.
—— Voltaire et la Hollande. Monde nouveau, April, 1926.
—— Voltaire en Holland. In: Nederland en Frankrijk. Den Haag, 1943.
—— & Frantsen, J. Voltaire en Hollande. Revue de Hollande, 1915-16.
Kont, J. Voltaire en Hongrie. **(HUNGARY)**. Annales internationales d'histoire. Paris, 1901.
Hennig, J. Voltaire in **IRELAND**. Dublin Mag., 19, 1944.
Anon. Due diplomatici italiani e gli ultimi giorni del Voltaire. **(ITALY)**. NAnt, 1.VI.1891.
Ademollo, A. Voltaire e i traduttori italiani della Henriade. Genova, 1891.
Bouvy, E. Zaire en Italie, BI, 1, 1901.
—— Zaire et ses quatorze traductions italiennes. Annales internationales d'histoire. Paris, 1901.
Neri, A. L'Olimpia di Voltaire in Italia. NAnt, 1904.
Tribolati, F. Sull' epistolario italiano del Voltaire academico della Crusca. Pisa, 1878.
Iasykoff, D. D. Voltaire in der russischen Literatur. **(RUSSIA)**. In: Das alte und das neue Russland. Petersburg, 1879. And in: Pod Znamenem nauki. Moskva, 1902.
Netchkina, M. Voltaire et la société russe. Moscou, 1944.
Moldenhauer, G. Voltaire und die spanische Bühne im 18. Jahrhundert. **(SPAIN)**. In: Philologisch-philosophische Studien. Jena, 1929.
Praag, J. A. van. Une traduction espagnole inconnue du Brutus de Voltaire. RLC, 16, 1936.
Qualia, C. Voltaire's Tragic Art in Spain in the XVIIIth Century. Hisp., 22, 1939.
Sarrailh, J. Notes sur une traduction espagnole de Jeannot et Colin de Voltaire. RLC, 2, 1922.
Baldensperger, F. Voltaire contre la Suisse de Jean-Jacques: la tragédie des Scythes. **(SWITZERLAND)**. RCC, 1931.
—— Voltaire et la diplomatie française dans les affaires de Genève. RLC, 11,

1931. And in: Etudes d'histoire littéraire, 4e Sér. Paris, 1939.
Caussy, F. Voltaire pacificateur de Genève. RB, 4.I.1908.
—— Voltaire seigneur de village. Paris, 1912.
Gaberel. Voltaire et les Genevois. Genève, 1856.
Perrochon, H. Voltaire et leurs excellences de Berne. Nouvelle Semaine artistique et littéraire. Neuchâtel, 13.X.1928.

2. Influences upon Individual Authors.

Chinard, G. Notes de John **ADAMS** sur Voltaire et Rousseau. MLN, 1931.
Bertana, E. **L'ALFIERI** e il Voltaire. In: V. Alfieri. Torino, 1902.
Anon. Voltaires Briefe an die Markgräfin von **BAIREUTH**. MLIA, 1865.
Horn, G. Voltaire und die Markgräfin von Baireuth. Berlin, 1865.
Angeli, D. Voltaire e **BARETTI**. Giornale d'Italia, 15.VIII.1920.
Baretti, G. A Dissertation upon the Italian Poets in Which are Interspersed Some Remarks upon M. de Voltaire's Essay on the Epic Poets. London, 1753.
Schumann, J. Baretti als Kritiker Voltaires. Archiv, 69, 1883.
Anon. L. **BASSI** ed il Voltaire. Rass. settimanale, 19.V.1878. And in: Studi e ritratti. Bologna, 1881.
Maestro, M. T. Voltaire and **BECCARIA** as Reformers of Criminal Law. Columbia U. P., 1942.
Suard, J. B. A. De Voltaire et du poète italien **BETTINELLI**. In: Mélanges de littérature. Paris, 1803.
Ibershoff, C. H. **BODMER'S** Indebtedness to Voltaire. MPh, 1925.
Lehmann, J. Voltaire, Du **BOIS-REYMOND** und die Ewigkeit der Gottesidee. MLIA, 1868.
Neri, A. Un traduttore della Henriade del Voltaire (Michele **BOLAFFI**). Rassegna bibliografica della lett. ital., 7, 1899.
Hurn, A. S. Voltaire et **BOLINGBROKE**. Diss. Paris, 1915.
Gotheim. Briefe Voltaires an den Kurpfälzischen Minister Baron von **BUKERS**. Zs. f. d. Geschichte des Oberrheins, 2, 1885.
Gardner, J. **CHESTERFIELD** and Voltaire. Cornhill Mag., 155, 1937.
Ford, C. L. **COWPER** and Voltaire. N&Q, 9.XII.1905.
Wells, J. E. Henry **FIELDING** and the History of Charles XII. JEGPh, 11, 1912.
Steel, W. **FRANKLIN** and Voltaire. Forum, 77, 1927.
Anon. Voltaire und die Schwester Friedrichs des Grossen. **(FREDERICK THE GREAT)**. Europa, 1865.
Aldington, R. Voltaire and Frederick the Great. Fortnightly Review, 1926.
Baldensperger, F. Les prémices d'une douteuse amitié: Voltaire et Frédéric II de 1740 à 1742. RLC, 10, 1930.
Beaune, H. Voltaire, Frédéric II et le Président de Brosses. Revue européenne, 14, 1861.
Benard. Frédéric II et Voltaire. Paris, 1878.
Brousson, J. J. Frédéric II disciple de Voltaire, élève de la France. NL, 17. XII. 1938.
Desnoiresterres, G. Voltaire et Frédéric. In: Voltaire et la Société française au XVIIIe siècle, 4. Paris, 1870.
Fischer, P. D. Friedrich der Grosse und Voltaire. MLIA, 1871.
Graeser, C. Eine historische Abhandlung: Voltaires Verhältniss zu Friedrich dem Grossen. Marienwerder, 1874.
Grimm, H. Voltaire and Frederick. In: Literature. London, 1886.
Henriot, E. Voltaire et Frédéric II. Revue hebdomadaire, 12.XII.1926 & Paris, 1927.
Koser, R. & Droysen, H. Briefwechsel Friedrichs des Grossen mit Voltaire. Publik. aus den kgl. Preuss. Staatsarchiven, 82, Leipzig, 1909.
Linz, F. Friedrich der Grosse und Voltaire. Hamburg, 1897.
Mönch, W. Voltaire und Friedrich der Grosse. NM, 11.
Pompéry, E. de. La correspondance de Voltaire avec le roi de Prusse. Paris, 1900.
Schulthess, R. Friedrich II und Voltaire in ihrem persönlichen und litterarischen Wechselverkehr. Nordhausen, 1850. Cf. Archiv, 9, 1851.
Stengel, E. Ungedruckte Briefe Voltaires an Friedrich den Grossen und an den Landgrafen von Hessen-Kassel. ZFSL, 7, 1885.
Strachey, L. Voltaire and Frederick the Great. In: Books and Characters. London, 1922.
Taponier, D. Voltaire et Frédéric le Grand. Mél. d'hist. et d'archéol. de la Soc. helvétique de St. Maurice en Valais, 1897.
Tuerk, M. Voltaire und die Veröffentlichung der Gedichte Friedrichs des Grossen. Forschungen z. brandenb. & preuss. Geschichte, 13, 1900.
Venedey, J. Friedrich der Grosse und Voltaire. Leipzig, 1859.

Wychgram, J. Friedrich der Grosse und Voltaire. In: Vom Fels zum Meer, 1890.
Stengel, E. Der Briefwechsel Voltaires mit dem Landgraf **FRIEDRICH II VON HESSEN.** ZFSL, 1, 1879-80.
Tronchon, H. Les oeuvres posthumes de Jean Fekete de **GALANTHA**, voltairien de Hongrie. Revue des Etudes hongroises, 1934.
Anon. Voltaire's Influence on **GOETHE.** ER, 1850.
Bertaux, P. Goethe et Voltaire. Mélanges Lichtenberger. Paris, 1934.
Bugge, A. Goethe og Voltaire. (Faust). Atlantis, 5, 1925.
Carel, G. Voltaire und Goethe als Dramatiker. Progr. Berlin, 1890 & 1898.
—— Voltaire und Goethe (bis 1770). Progr., Berlin, 1899.
Glaesener, H. Goethe imitateur et traducteur de Voltaire au théâtre. RLC, 13, 1933.
Graul, J. Goethes Mahomet und Tankred. Diss. Berlin, 1914.
Groeschl, K. Die deutschen Uebersetzungen Voltaire'scher Tragödien bis zu Goethes Mahomet und Tancred. Prag, 1912.
Mann, H. Voltaire et Goethe. Cri des Peuples, 1928.
Muench, W. Goethe als Uebersetzer Voltaire'scher Tragödien. Archiv, 51, 1877.
Schirmacher, K. Der junge Voltaire und der junge Goethe. Festschrift Morf. Halle, 1905.
Toldo, P. Attinenze fra il teatro comico di Voltaire e quello del **GOLDONI.** GSLI, 31, 1897.
Crane, R. S. & Warner, J. H. **GOLDSMITH** and Voltaire's Essai sur les moeurs. MLN, 1923.
Siegel, H. Zu **GRILLPARZERS** Der Traum ein Leben. Archiv, 64, 1880.
Duebi, H. Der Briefwechsel zwischen Voltaire und **HALLER** im Jahre 1759. Archiv, 123, 1910.
Rexrodt, F. **HEINE** und Voltaire. Diss. Marburg, 1925.
Horsley, Phyllis M. Aaron **HILL**: An English Translator of Mérope. CLS, 12, 1944.
Obser. Voltaires Beziehungen zu der Markgräfin **KAROLINE LOUISE VON BADEN-DURLACH** und dem Karlsruher Hof. Revue critique, 1902.
Sacke, G. Entstehung des Briefwechsels zwischen der Kaiserin **KATHARINA II** von Russland und Voltaire. ZFSL, 61.
Barbier, O. Voltaire et **LESSING.** Athenaeum français, 37, 1854.
Jan, E. von. Voltaire und Lessing. Mélanges Baldensperger. Paris, 1930.
Morf, H. Lessings Urteil über Voltaire. In: Aus Dichtung und Sprache der Romanen, 3. Berlin, 1922 .
Nolte, F. C. Voltaire's Mahomet as a Source of Lessing's Nathan der Weise and Emilia Galotti. MLN, 1933.
Schmidt, E. Lessings Uebersetzungen aus dem Französischen Friedrichs des Grossen und Voltaires. Berlin, 1892.
Hahn, J. Voltaires Stellung zur Frage der menschlichen Freiheit in ihrem Verhältnis zu **LOCKE** und Collins. Borna, Leipzig, 1905.
Marasca, A. La Henriade del Voltaire e l'Enrico di G. **MALMIGNATI.** Città di Castello, 1885. Cf. GSLI, 7.
Riva, S. I Promessi Sposi ed una commedia del Voltaire. **(MANZONI).** GSLI, 1933; Treviso, 1933. And in: Dante, 1934.
Zuno, M. Voltaire, Rousseau e i Promessi Sposi. GSLI, 1933.
Fiammazzio. Il Voltaire e l'abate Giovanni **MARENZI** primo traduttore italiano della Henriade. Bergamo, 1894.
Schmidt, J. Voltaire und **MARIA THERESIA**: französische Kultur des Barocks in ihren Beziehungen zu Oesterreich. Mitteilungen d. Vereins f. Geschichte d. Stadt Wien, 11, 1931.
Cervino, M. Voltaire y **MAYANS.** Bol. de la Soc. esp. de Excursiones, 7.
Ronzy, P. De la Henriade à la Marseillaise de la Paix en passant par **MONTI.** Ausonia, 5, 1940.
Sandmann. Voltaires l'Orphelin de la Chine und **MURPHYS** The Orphan of China. Neuphilolog. Centralblatt, 9, 1895.
Ryan, Mary. Alfred **NOYES** on Voltaire. Studies, 26, 1937.
Clark, H. H. Th. **PAINE'S** Relation to Voltaire and Rousseau. RAA, 1932.
Lewis, F. R. An Englishman Visits Voltaire (Thomas **PENNANT**). TLS, 20. VIII.1938.
Scafi, A. Voltaire, **PEZZANA**, Ducis. Rivista d. Biblioteche e degli Arch., 11, 1901.
Morici, G. L'Ombra di Voltaire e un sonetto attribuito al **PINDEMONTE.** GSLI, 223, 1920.
Adams, P. G. **POE**, Critic of Voltaire. MLN, 57, 1942.
Hoffmann, A. Voltaires Stellung zu **POPE.** Diss. Königsberg, 1913.
Iakubovitch, D. **PUSHKIN** and Voltaire. (In Russian). In: Literaturnoe Nasledstvo, 16-18, 1934.

Fassini, S. Paolo **ROLLI** contro il Voltaire. GSLI, 49, 1907.
Hachtmann. Voltaire und **ROUSSEAU.** Zu ihrem 150. Todestage. DR, 1928.
Landau, M. L'Enfant prodigue und die Räuber. **(SCHILLER).** ZVL, 2.
Aleksiev, M. P. Voltaire et **SCHOUVA---LOFF.** Odessa, 1928.
Haupt, H. Voltaire und Joseph Erasmus von **SENCKENBERG.** Deutsche Revue, June, 1903.
Joliat, E. **SMOLLETT,** Editor of Voltaire, MLN, 54, 1939.
Patouillet, J. Un épisode de l'histoire littéraire de la Russie: la lettre de Voltaire à **SOUMAROKHOV.** RLC, 7, 1927.
Pressense, E. de. Voltaire jugé par **STRAUSS.** Journal des Débats, Nov., 1877. And in: Etudes contemporaines. Paris, 1880 .
Quenet, C. **TCHAADAEV** et les Lettres philosophiques, contribution à l'étude du mouvement des idées en Russie. Paris, 1931.
Peairs, Edith. The Hound, the Bay Horse and the Turtle-Dove: a Study of **THOREAU** and Voltaire. PMLA, 52, 1937.
Finch, M. B. & Peers, E. A. **WALPOLE'S** Relations with Voltaire. MPh, 18, 1920-21.
Scheffer, J. D. A Note on Joseph **WARTON** and Voltaire. Bull. of the Citadel, 7, 1940.
Boost, P. F. **WIELAND** und Voltaire. Rheinisches Archiv, 5, Wiesbaden, 1814.
Droyser, H. Die Marquise du Châtelet, Voltaire und der Philosoph Christian **WOLFF.** ZFSL, 35, 1910.
Hesseling, D. C. P. de Wakker van **ZON** en Voltaire. Mélanges Salverda de Grave. Groningen, 1934.

CHAPTER TWENTY-ONE

Zola.

1. Generalities.

Saintsbury, G. The Literary Prophets of the Later Nineteenth Century. The Independent, 54, 1902.
Edwards, H. Zola and the American Critics. **(AMERICA).** AL, May, 1932.
Jones, M. B. Translations of Zola in the United States Prior to 1900. MLN, 55, 1940.
—— L'Attaque du moulin in American Translation. MLN, 57, 1942.
——Two American Zola Forgeries. FR. 16, 1942.
—— Henry Gréville et Emile Zola aux Etats-Unis (1870-1900). RLC, 22, 1948.
Lüdeke, H. Zola and the American Public. ESs, 23, 1941.
Salvan, A. J. Zola aux Etats-Unis. Brown U. Studies, 8, 1943.
Decker, C. R. Zola's Literary Reputation in **ENGLAND.** PMLA, 49, 1934.
Varia. Pernicious Literature. Debate in the House of Commons. With Opinions of the Press. National Vigilance Ass. London, 1889.
Anon. Zola im deutschen Buchhandel. **(GERMANY)** Börsenbl. f. d. deutschen Buchhandel, 16, 1898.
Bertaux, F. L'influence de Zola en Allemagne. RLC, 4, 1924.
Bleibtreu, K. Zola und die Berliner Kritik. In: Gesellschaft, 1885.
Conrad, M. G. Zola jugé par un Allemand. RFA, 1899.
Hart, J. Der Zolaismus in Deutschland. Gegenwart, 30, 1886.
Lemmermayer, F. Emile Zola in deutscher Sprache. Allg. literar. Correspondenz, 8.
Mann, H. Zola vu d'Allemagne. NL, 8. X.1927 & RRh, 1927.
Root, W. H. German Criticism of Zola, 1875-93. New York, 1931.
Vivarelli-Colonna, L. E. Zola e i Veristi. **(ITALY)** Firenze, 1880.

2. Influences upon Individual Authors.

Brown, D. Pardo **BAZAN** and Zola: Refutation of Some Critics. RR, 1936.
Fester, H. Zolas Einfluss auf die literarischen Anfänge der Gräfin Emilia Pardo Bazán. Münster, 1940.
Airoli, G. F. Zola e **BOVIO.** Firenze, 1894.
Niess, R. J. Zola's L'Oeuvre and Reconquista of **CAMBOA.** PMLA, 61, 1946.
Arpad, M. Zola und **GORKI.** Internat. Litteraturberichte, 1901.
Blankenagel, J. C. The Mob in Zola's Germinal and in **HAUPTMANN'S** Weavers. PMLA, 39, 1924.
Conrad, M. G. Von Emile Zola bis Gerhart Hauptmann. Leipzig, 1902.
Kelley, Cornelia P. Henry **JAMES** on Zola. Colby Library Quarterly, 1, 1943.
Sedgwick, Ruth. Baldomero **LILLO** y Emile Zola. RIA, 7, 1944.
Aubry, G. J. Zola et George **MOORE.** NL, 17.I.1925.
Auriant. Un disciple anglais d'Emile Zola: George Moore. MF, 297, 1940.
Gauthier-Villars. Zola et **NORDAU.** MF, 1893.
Haines, L. F. **READE,** Mill and Zola. SPh, 40, 1943.

Dahlström, C. E. W. L. Theomachy: Zola, **STRINDBERG**, Andreyev. SS, 17, 1942-43.
—— Strindberg's Naturalistiska Sorgespel and Zola's Naturalism. SS, 18, 1943-44.

CHAPTER TWENTY-TWO

Other French Authors.

Prince, F. André Antoine et le renouveau du théâtre hollandais (1880-1900). **(ACTORS)**. Amsterdam, 1941.
Hofen, F. Sarah Bernhardt in Deutschland. Bühne und Welt, Nov., 1902.
Anon. Sur la troupe de Doligny en Italie. Riv. Europea, 2, 1840.
Heilly, G. d'. La comédie française à Londres (1871-79), journal de Got et de Sarcey. Paris, 1880.
Anon. Die Rachel in Deutschland. Europa, 1850.
Beauvallet, L. Rachel et le Nouveau Monde. Paris, 1856.
Fellows, O. Rachel and America: A Reappraisal. RR, 30, 1939.
Roetscher, H. T. Mademoiselle Rachel in Berlin. Dramaturg. Skizzen. Berlin, 1847.
Lyonnet, H. Mlle. Raucourt, directrice des théâtres français en Italie (1806-07). Bull. de la Soc. de l'historie du théâtre, 1902.
Jeansson, B. G. Notre premier opéra et la troupe Rossidor en Suède. Svensk Tidskrift för Musikforskning, 1919-20.
Eggli, E. Talma à Londres en 1817. In: A Miscellany of Studies. Cambridge, 1932.
Banzer, A. Die Farce Pathelin und ihre Nachahmungen. **(ANONYMOUS)**. ZFSL, 10, 1888.
Bolte, J. Veterator (Maistre Pathelin) und Advocatus: Zwei Pariser Studentenkomödien. Berlin, 1900.
Hamilton, A. Two Spanish Imitations of Maître Pathelin. RR, 30, 1939.
Popovic, P. L'avocat Patelin dans la littérature serbo-croate de Raguse. RHLF, 22, 1915.
Schaumburg, K. Die Farce Patelin und ihre Nachahmungen. (Hans Sachs). Diss. Leipzig,1887.
Drei, G. Il d'**ALEMBERT** e l'educazione di Don Ferdinando di Parma. Aurea Parma, Jan., 1937.
Chasles, P. M. Montaigne et **AMYOT** étudiés et traduits par Shakespeare. Journal des Débats, 14.X. & 7.XI.1846.
Clark, M. E. M. **ANGELLIER** as He Appears to a Scot. Cahier Angellier, 4, 1927.
Elton, O. An English Tribute to Angellier. Cahier Angellier, 4, 1927.
Inklaar, D. François-Thomas de Baculard d'**ARNAUD**, ses imitateurs en Hollande et dans d'autres pays. Paris, 1926.
Malvano, E. L. L'étrange fortune de Baculard d'Arnaud en Italie. Ausonia, 7, 1942.
Axon, W. E. A. The Literary Wanderings of **ARNAULT'S** Feuille. Papers of the Manchester Literary Club, 32, 1913.
Littré, E. Schiller et d'**AUBIGNE**. Gazette littéraire, 25.III.1830.
Procacci, G. Un romanzo francese del seicento e una sua traduzione italiana: Vital d'**AUDIGUIER** e Maiolini Bisaccioni. BI, 1906.
Wright, H. G. Cowper's Retirement and Guez de **BALZAC'S** Entretiens. MLR, 40, 1945.
Gosse, E. A French Satirist in England. (Aug. **BARBIER**). ER, 1914.
Calderon, F. G. Maurice Barrès et l'Amérique latine. Revue de l'Amérique latine. 1.I.1924.
Farmer, A. J. The Return of Barrès. Festschrift L. E. Kastner. Cambridge, 1932.
Ashton, H. Du **BARTAS** en Angleterre. Diss. Paris, 1908.
Beckman, A. Influence de du Bartas sur la littérature néerlandaise. Poitiers, 1912.
Holmes, U. T. Lyons, J. C. & Linker, R. W. The Works of Guillaume de Salluste, sieur du Bartas. 3 vols. Chapel Hill (N. C.), 1935-41. (Cf. Introduction).
Strathmann, E. The 1595 Translation of Du Bartas' First Day. HLQ, 8, 1945.
Baldensperger, F. Un sonnet de William Drummond et son point de départ dans La Semaine de Du Bartas. MLN, 55, 1940.
Beall, C. B. John Eliot's Ortho-Epia Gallica and Du Bartas-Goulart. SPh, 43, 1946.
Tilley, M. P. Charles Lamb, Marston and Du Bartas. MLN, 53, 1938.
Taylor, G. C. Milton's Use of Du Bartas. Harvard U. P., 1934. Cf. RES, 1936.
Sykes. Peele's Borrowings from Du Bartas. N&Q, 15. & 22.XI.1924.
Taylor, G. C. The Strange Case of Du Bartas in The Taming of a Shrew. PhQ, 20, 1941.
Weller, P. Joshuah Sylvesters englische Uebersetzungen der religiösen Epen des Du Bartas. Tübingen, 1902.

Toldo, P. Il poema della creazione del du Bartas e quello di T. Tasso. Roma, 1894.
Hendricks, A. Joost van den Vondel en G. de Saluste Sr. du Bartas. Diss. Leiden, 1893.
Kraft, W. Von **BASSOMPIERRE** zu Hofmannsthal. Zur Geschichte eines Novellenmotivs. RLC, 15, 1935.
Meyer von Waldeck, F. Die Memoiren des Marschalls von Bassompierre und Goethes Unterhaltung der Ausgewanderten. Archiv, 87, 1891.
Schenker, M. Charles **BATTEUX** und seine Nachahmungstheorie in Deutschland. Leipzig, 1909.
Wolff, H. M. Zur Bedeutung Batteux's für Lenz. MLN, 56, 1941.
Anon. The influence of **BAUDELAIRE**. Blackwood's Mag., 1913.
Banzati, J. L'imitazione del Baudelaire in Italia. ARIV, 10, 1922.
Cantor, J. The Literary Reputation of Baudelaire in England and America, 1857-1934. Diss. Harvard, 1940.
Friis-Moller, K. L'influence de Baudelaire sur la poésie danoise. Revue scandinave, Aug., 1911.
Hajdu, H. Un ami hongrois de Baudelaire. Cahiers de littérature comparée. Budapest, 1948.
Hauser, O. Baudelaire in deutscher Uebersetzung. LE, 4, 1901-02.
Rechert, E. Baudelaire und die Modernen. Wien, 1895.
Sallwuerk, E. von. Verlaine und Baudelaire in Deutschland. Beilage zur Allg. Zt., 241, 1902.
Turquet-Milnes, G. The Influence of Baudelaire on France and England. London, 1913.
Woestijne, K. van der. Baudelaire. N. Rotterd. Courant, 14.VI.1915.
Trompeo, P. P. Carducci e Baudelaire. Pan, Nov., 1935.
Clapton, G. T. Carlyle and Some Early English Critics of Baudelaire. Festschrift L. E. Kastner. Cambridge, 1932.
Berger, Margaret R. The Influence of Baudelaire on the Poetry of Julián de Casal. RR, 37, 1946.
Hartstall, P. K. Phonétique: traditore. (Baudelaire translated by G. Dillon and Edna St. Vincent Millay). FR, 12, 1939.
Douglas, A. B. Lord Alfred Douglas and Baudelaire. Athenaeum, 19.XII.1919.
Sender, R. J. Speaking of Epitaphs. (Joyce). BA, 19, 1945.
Hirsch, M. L. Poésie pas morte: traduction tchèque des Fleurs du Mal par S. Kadlec. L'Europe Centrale, 19.I.1935.
Montellano, B. J. Baudelaire y Ramon Lopez Velarde. RIA, 2, 1946.
Bradley, W. A. Méryon and Baudelaire. In: Prints and Their Makers. New York, 1912.
Golzio, V. La critica di Walter Pater e il misticismo romantico. Cult., 3, 1923.
Carrier, W. Baudelaire y Silva. RIA, 7, 1943.
Hughes, R. Baudelaire, Miss Starkie and Other Critics. New English Weekly, 4, 1933.
Aubry, J. G. Baudelaire et Swinburne. MF, Oct., 1917.
Delattre, F. Charles Baudelaire et le jeune C. A. Swinburne. Mélanges Baldensperger. Paris, 1930.
Lafourcade, G. Swinburne et Baudelaire. RAA, 1924.
Nicolson, H. Swinburne and Baudelaire. Trans. of the Royal Society of Literature, 6, 1926 & Oxford, 1931.
Suepfle, T. Ein Franzose (**BAUNOIR**) als Originalverfasser eines deutschen Theaterstückes ZVL, 1, 1886.
Courtines, L. P. Some Notes on the Dissemination of **BAYLE'S** Thought in Europe. RLC, 17, 1937.
—— Bayle's Relations with England and the English. Columbia U. P.,1938.
—— Bayle, Hume and Berkeley. RLC, 21, 1947.
Serrurier, C. Pierre Bayle en Hollande. Lausanne, 1912.
Staubach, C. The Influence of Bayle on Feijoo. Hisp., 22, 1939.
Arneth, A. von. **BEAUMARCHAIS** und Sonnenfels. Wien, 1868.
Hallays, A. Ibsen et Beaumarchais. Journal des Débats, 26.IX.1895.
Lindau, P. Beaumarchais und Julian Schmidt. Gegenwart, 1872.
Mérimée, P. Une critique espagnole du Mariage de Figaro. (Huerta). RLC, 16, 1936.
Seligmann, A. Figaros Hochzeit von Beaumarchais und die deutsche Literatur. Progr. Troppau, 1910.
Wahl, E. Beaumarchais chez Franklin à Passy (1777). Bull. de la Societe hist. d'Auteuil et de Passy, 1901-03.
Addamiano, N. Delle opere poetiche francesi di J. Du **BELLAY** e delle sue imitazioni italiane. Cagliari, 1920.
Menaugh, J. J. A Possible Source of a French Quotation in the Religio Medici. N&Q, 175, 1938.
Renwick, W. L. Mulcaster and Du Bellay. MLR, 1922.
Ronault, J. Joachim du Bellay et Goethe. Eurydice, Jan., 1937.

Law, R. A. **BELLEFOREST**, Shakespeare and Kyd. J. Q. Adams Memorial Studies. Washington, 1948.
Rouleau, P. Shakespeare et Belleforest. Revue de Gascogne, N. S., 23, 1929.
Tallez, P. Shakespeare et Belleforest. Ibid.
Tremolières, D. La part de Belleforest dans trois oeuvres de Shakespeare. Bull. de la Soc. d'histoire et d'archéologie du Gers, 39.
Baumgarten, J. Eine neue Uebersetzung der Lieder von **BERANGER**. MLIA, 1883.
Foldvari, E. Le culte de Béranger en Hongrie. (In Hungarian). Pecs, 1936.
Giuriani, R. Béranger und die deutsche Lyrik. Mailand, 1902.
Jaffé, G. L'influence de Béranger en Allemagne. RLC, 21, 1947.
Matthiae, O. La gloire posthume de Béranger. Festschrift Kgl. Wilhelm Gymnasium. Berlin, 1908.
Mentz, V. Béranger im Rheinischen Volksliede. NPh, 10, 1924.
Pollak, V. Béranger in Deutschland. Progr. Wien, 1908.
Valk, B. Béranger en Russie. Littérature internationale, 1945.
Wilde, O. Béranger in England. Pall Mall Gazette, 21.IV.1886.
Musso, P. Il Béranger e il Brofferio. RI, 13, 1911.
Hoffmann. Bérangers Einfluss in Chamissos Gedichten. Progr. Suhl, 1908.
Coppola. Béranger et Giusti. Riv. Abruzzese. Teramo, 1906.
Segal. An Estimate of Béranger by Goethe. MLN, 14, 1899.
Levi, M. Mon habit (Béranger & Holtei). MLN, 1906.
Anon. Spaniens Béranger (Melendez). Blätter für literar. Unterhaltung, 5.II. 1836.
Halasz, G. Petöfi es Béranger. Progr. Bresso, 1898.
Anon. Bérangers Lieder, deutsch von Reubens. Blätter z. Kunde der Litt. des Auslandes, 1840.
Boerne, L. Béranger et Uhland. Paris, 1836. And in: Gesammelte Schriften, 4, Leipzig, 1899.
Lachèvre, F. Les successeurs de Cyrano de **BERGERAC**. Paris, 1922.
Storer, W. H. Notes on Cyrano de Bergerac: A Mythical Translation of the Histoires comiques. MLN, 1924.
Duebi, H. Zu Cyranos L'autre monde. (Godwin). Archiv, 129, 1912.
Cornetz, V. Une idée de Nietzsche chez Cyrano de Bergerac. Revues des Idées, Oct., 1912.
Baughan, D. E. Swift's Source of the Houyhnhmns Reconsidered. ELH, 5, 1938.
Bennett, R. E. A Note on the Cyrano-Swift Criticism. MLN, 1928.
Borkowsky, T. Quellen zu Swifts Gulliver: Cyrano de Bergerac. Diss. Rostock, 1893.
Eddy, W. A. Cyrano de Bergerac and Gulliver's Travels. MLN, 1923.
Delattre, F. La personnalité d'Henri **BERGSON** et l'Angleterre. RLC, 7, 1927.
Landré, L. Henri Bergson et l'Angleterre. LM, 1948.
Mathewson, L. Bergson's Theory of the Comic in the Light of English Comedy. U. of Nebraska Studies, 1920.
Scott, J. W. Bergsonism in England. The Monist, April, 1917.
Holmberg, O. Bergson och Bellman. Var tid, 1924.
Loomba, R. M. Bradley and Bergson. Lucknow, 1937.
Delattre, F. S. Butler et le Bergsonisme. RAA, 1936.
Markrich, W. L. ¿ Hay bergsonismo en la filosofía de José Enrique Rodó? Diss. U. of Washington, 1943.
Delattre, F. La durée bergsonienne dans le roman de Virginia Woolf. RAA, 1931.
Maddalena, E. La Dalmatina del Goldoni. (Mme. du **BOCAGE**). NAnt, 1927.
BODIN: See also Politics, I.II.5.
Brown, J. L. Bodin et Ben Jonson. RLC, 20, 1940.
Dean, L. F. Bodin's Methodus in England before 1625. SPh, 39, 1942.
Fubini, M. Vico e **BOUHOURS**. NRS, 24, 1940.
Backers, H. **BOILEAUS** Einfluss in Deutschland bis auf Lessing. Greifswald, 1910.
Clark, A. F. B. Boileau and the French Classical Critics in England. Paris, 1925.
Hack, A. Boileau dans la littérature hongroise. (In Hungarian). Pécs, 1933.
Kuechler, W. Eine amerikanische Uebersetzung Boileauscher Satiren. SVL, 5, 1905.
Neri, F. Disputa del Boileau e di un Italiano. RLC, 13, 1933.
Stein, H. J. M. Boileau en Hollande. Essai sur son influence aux XVIIe et XVIIIe siècles. Nimègue, 1929.
Streinu, N. Boileau si timpul nostru. Revista Fundatiilor Regale, 1937.
Walter, U. Boileaus Wirkung auf seine englischen Zeitgenossen. Diss. Strassburg, 1911.

Anon. Dissertation sur les poèmes de Messieurs Boileau, Addison et de Voltaire. MF, 1745.
Thorpe, C. D. Addison and Some of his Predecessors on Novelty. PMLA, 1937.
Reinhardstoettner, K. von. Der Hyssope des Ant. Diniz in seinem Verhältniss zu Boileaus Lutrin. Leipzig, 1877. And in: Aufsätze und Abhandlungen. Berlin, 1887.
Huntley, F. L. Dryden's Discovery of Boileau. MPh, 45, 1947.
Wichmann, O. L'art poétique de Boileau dans celui de Gottsched. Berlin, 1879.
Landré, L. Une traduction anglaise inédite du Lutrin. (Leigh Hunt, 1830). RAA, 1929.
Dejob, C. Lessing et Boileau. RCC, 29. VIII.1897.
Knaake, F. Le Lutrin de Boileau et The Rape of the Lock de Pope. Progr. Nordhausen, 1883.
Tomashevskii, B. Pushkin and Boileau. (In Russian). In: Pushkin v mirovoi literature. Leningrad, 1926.
Moore, F. The Originality of Rochester's Satire against Mankind. PMLA, 58, 1943.
Friedmann, F. La Fille de Roland von Henri de **BORNIER** in deutschen Uebertragungen. MLIA, 1880.
Douglas, L. A Severe Animadversion on **BOSSU**. (Pope). PMLA, 62, 1947.
Bon. Hobbes et **BOSSUET** considérés dans leurs doctrines politiques. Bull. de la Soc. des Sciences et Arts de l'Ile de la Réunion, 1874.
Lambin, G. Les rapports de Bossuet avec l'Angleterre. Bull. du Bibliophile et du Bibliothécaire, Sept., 1909.
Mangold, W. Nachahmungen Montesquieus und Bossuets von Friedrich dem Grossen. Archiv, 102, 1899.
Rébelliau, A. Bossuet et sa renommée en Angleterre. RAA, 1924.
Simpson, W. S. Bossuet et Leibniz. Bossuet en Angleterre. London, 1937.
Zuno, M. Echi del Bossuet in Leopardi. RCLI, 1925.
Stauber, E. Die Essais de Psychologie contemporaine von **BOURGET** und Spenglers Untergang des Abendlandes. GRM, 1925.
Hunton, C. H. Shakespeare's Compliment to **BRANTOME**. PL, SEPT., 1892.
Bézard, Yvonne. Le Président de **BROSSES** et ses amis de Genève. Paris, 1940.
Taylor, A. C. Le Président de Brosses et l'Australie. Paris, 1938. Cf. RDM, 1938.
Anderson, P. B. La **BRUYERE** and Mrs. Crackenthorpe's Female Tatler. PMLA, 52, 1937.
Digeon, A. Gulliver et La Bruyère. RAA, 1926.
Fehr, B. La Bruyère und Thackeray. Archiv, 123, 1909.
Lugli, V. Un La Bruyère italiano (A. Gatti). LNI, 1934.
Mattia, A. Gozzi e La Bruyère. Venezia, 1897.
McCormick, J. F. A Forerunner of the Scottish School. (**BUFFIER**). New Scholasticism, 15, 1941.
Brown, H. **BUFFON** and the Royal Society of London. Festschrift George Sarton. New York, 1948.
Falls, W. Buffon, Franklin et deux académies américaines. RR, 1938.
Lynskey, W. Goldsmith and the Chain of Being. JHI, 6, 1945.
Pit, A. S. The Sources, Significance and Date of Franklin's An Arabian Tale. PMLA, 57, 1942.
Sauter, E. Herder und Buffon. Diss. Basel, 1910.
Janet, P. Schopenhauer et la physiologie française. (**CABANIS**). RDM, 1.V.1880.
Kapstein, I. Shelley and Cabanis. PMLA, 1937.
Hill, H. W. La **CALPRENEDE'S** Romances and the Restoration Drama. U. of Nevada Studies, 2-3, 1910-11.
Pitou, S. La Calprenède's Faramond. A Study of the Sources, Structure and Reputation of the Novel. Baltimore, 1938.
—— A Portuguese Adaptation of La Calprenède's Faramond. MLN, 54, 1939.
Schnelle, A. Die Staatsauffassung in Anton Ulrichs Aramena im Hinblick auf La Calprenèdes Cléopâtre. Berlin, 1939.
Hausding, C. Jean Galbert de **CAMPISTRON** in seiner Bedeutung für das Theater Frankreichs und des Auslandes. Leipzig, 1903.
CALVIN: See Religion, III.I.3.
Heymach, F. Ramond de **CARBONNIERES**. Ein Beitrag zur Geschichte der Sturm- und Drangperiode. Progr. Corbach, 1887.
Tompkins, J. M. S. Ramond de Carbonnières, Grosley and Mrs. Radcliffe. RES, July, 1929.
Atkinson, D. F. The Wandering Knight, the Red Cross Knight, and Miles Dei (**CARTIGNY**). HLQ, 7, 1944.
Bouillier, V. La fortune de **CHAMFORT** en Allemagne. RLC, 3, 1923.
Hartag, P. Chamfort und Schopenhauer. ZFEU, 24, 1925.
Ruehle-Gerstel, A. Friedrich Schlegel und Chamfort. Euphorion, 24, 1922.
Flenley, R. The First English Translation

of CHAMPLAIN. Canadian Hist. Rev., 28, 1947.

Hamm, V. A XVIIth Century French Source for Hurd's Letters on Chivalry and Romance. (CHAPELAIN). PMLA, 1937.

Bullrich, G. Ueber CHARLES D'ORLEANS und die ihm zugeschriebene englische Uebersetzung seiner Gedichte. Progr. Berlin, 1893.

Sauerstein, P. Charles d'Orléans und die englische Uebersetzung seiner Dichtungen. Festschrift Reichenbach i.V., 1899.

Morgulis, G. Caliste de Mme. de CHARRIERE et l'Idiot de Dostoievski. RLC, 15, 1935.

Groehler, H. Ueber Richard Ros' mittelenglische Uebersetzung des Gedichtes von Alain CHARTIER: La belle dame sans mercy. Diss. Breslau, 1886.

Piaget, A. La belle dame sans merci et ses imitations. Romania, 30-34, 1901-05.

Wahlund, C. (ed.) La belle dame sans mercy. (Cf. Introduction). Upsala, 1893.

Baldensperger, F. Un témoignage allemand sur la mère d'André CHENIER en 1777. RLC, 21, 1947.

Courten, C. de. André Chénier et Ugo Foscolo. BI, 18.

Legros, R. P. André Chénier en Angleterre. MLR, 1924.

CHRETIEN DE TROYES: See also Celtic Contributions, IV.I.10.

Bang, C. K. Emotions and Attitudes in Chrétien de Troyes Erec et Enide and Hartmann von Aue's Erec der Wunderaere. PLMA, 57, 1942.

Becker, P. A. Chrestien de Troyes und Deutschland. In: Beiträge zur Geschichte der deutschen Sprache und Litatur, 67, 1943.

Drube, H. Hartmann und Chrestien. Münster i. W., 1931.

Foerster, W. Chrestien de Troyes und Hartmann von Aue. In: Christian von Troyes' Sämmtliche Werke. Halle, 1890.

Halbach, K. H. Franzosentum und Deutschtum in höfischer Dichtung des Stauferzeitalters. Hartmann von Aue und Crestien de Troyes. Berlin, 1939.

Hatto, A. T. Two Notes on Chrétien and Wolfram. MLR, 42, 1947.

Rochat, A. Wolfram von Eschenbach und Chrestien de Troies. Stuttgart, 1858.

Scheunemann, E. Hartmann von Aue und Chretien de Troyes. Jahresbericht der schlesischen Ges. f. vaterländ. Kultur, 1935.

Steinbach, P. Ueber den Einfluss des Chrétien de Troies auf die altenglische Litteratur. Diss. Leipzig, 1885.

Campbell, P. G. C. CHRISTINE DE PISAN en Angleterre. RLC, 5, 1925.

Fransen, J. Paul CLAUDEL inconnu et le Dr. W. G. C.Byvanck. NPh, 23, 1938.

Anon. H. Martineau's Translation of COMTE'S Philosophy. NAR, 1854.

Cecilia, J. La. Wordsworth et Aug. Comte. Figaro, 25.V.1929.

Faguet, E. August Comte et Stuart Mill. RB, 14, 1899.

Gaupp, O. Auguste Comte und Herbert Spencer. Gegenwart, 23, 1893.

Harrison, F. Aug. Comte in America. Positivist Rev., 1901.

Hawkins, R. L. Aug. Comte and the United States. Harvard U. P., 1937.

Littré, M. P. E. Auguste Comte et Stuart Mill. Paris, 1866.

Souday, P. La correspondance de Stuart Mill et d'Aug. Comte. Le Temps, 31.I. 1899.

Jobert, A. Une correspondance polonaise de CONDILLAC; le sort de la logique de Condillac en Pologne. Revue d'histoire moderne, 1936.

Pergoli, B. Il Condillac in Italia. Faenza, 1904.

Engel, E. COPPEE'S Olivier in deutscher Umdichtung von Wolf Graf Baudissin. MLIA, 1880.

Grant, R. Patricia. The Poetry of François Coppée and Gutiérrez Nájera. HR, 13, 1945.

Hobohm, M. Das Verhältniss von Susanna Centlivres Love at a Venture zu Thomas CORNEILLES Le Galant Double. Diss. Halle, 1900.

Kahn, V. Thomas Corneille et François Zablocki. In: Mémoires Littéraires. Cracovie, 1911.

Smith, J. H. Thomas Corneille to Betterton to Congreve. JEGPh, 45, 1946.

Heidelberger, E. Formen der Publizistik bei Börne und COURIER. München, 1931.

Galletti, A. A. Manzoni e la filosofia de V. COUSIN. Il Convegno, 1923.

Lièvre, P. CREBILLON a-t-il menti? RP, 15.IV.1934.

Scott, A. A. Lessing's Philotas and Crébbillon. MLR, 1922.

CREVECOEUR: See Intermediaries, I. IV.8.

Allen, J. C. Henry James and A. DAUDET. Critic, 1882.

Delattre, F. Daudet et l'Angleterre. In: Dickens et la France. Paris, 1927.

Favreau, A. R. British Criticism of Daudet, 1872-97. PMLA, 52, 1937.

Markovitch, M. Alphonse Daudet et les Serbes. RLC, 21, 1947.
Roux, T. M. Le. Alphonse Daudet à l'étranger. RB, 4.IV.1885.
Weizmann, L. Dickens und Daudet in deutscher Uebersetzung. Berlin, 1880.
Wharey, J. B. A Study of the Sources of Bunyan's Allegories, with Special Reference to **DEJULEVILLE'S** Pilgrimage of Man. Baltimore, 1904.
Baldensperger, F. Le poète Bondi et Jacques **DELILLE.** RLC, 3, 1923.
Bielak, F. Les motifs empruntés à Delille dans le Pan Tadeusz. Bull. internat. de l'Acad. polonaise, 7-10, 1931.
Waldmueller - Duboc. **DEROULEDE** in Deutschland. Gegenwart, 1886.
Janet, P. Un précurseur français de Hegel, **DESCHAMPS.** RDM, 1.VII.1865.
Brown, C. The Evolution of the Canterbury Marriage Group. (E. Deschamps). PMLA, 48, 1933.
McGalliard, J. C. Chaucer's Merchant's Tale and Deschamps' Miroir de Mariage. PhQ, 25, 1946.
Lossing, Marian. The Prologue to the Legend of Good Women and the Lai de Franchise. SPh, 39, 1942.
Lowes, J. L. The Prologue to the Legend of Good Women Considered in its Chronological Relations. PMLA, 20, 1905.
—— Chaucer and the Miroir de Mariage. MPh, 8, 1910-11.
—— Illustrations of Chaucer, Drawn Chiefly from Deschamps. RR, 2, 1911.
Berthon, H. E. & Kastner, L. E. Suckling and **DESPORTES.** MLR, 1911.
Kastner, L. E. Spenser's Amoretti and Desportes. MLR, 4, 1908.
Vaganay, H. Lodge et Desportes. Mâçon, 1922.
Ahrend. Einiges über **DESTOUCHES** in Deutschland. Neuphilol. Centralblatt, 12, 1898.
Fürst, R. Destouches in Deutschland. In: A. G. Meissner, sein Leben und seine Schriften. Stuttgart, 1894.
Schimberg, A. Ueber den Einfluss Holbergs und Destouches' auf Lessings Jugenddramen. Progr. Görlitz, 1883.
Koller, A. E. The Abbé **DU BOS,** his Advocacy of the Theory of Climate, a Precursor of J. G. Herder. Champaign (Ill.), 1937.
Leysat, R. Dubos und Lessing. Diss. Rostock, Greifswald, 1874.
Peteut, P. Influence de Dubos en Allemagne. In: J. B. Dubos. Diss. Tramelan, 1902.
Mayo, D. Ann Radcliffe and **DUCRAY-DUMINIL.** MLR, 36, 1941.
Archer, W. **DUMAS** and the English Drama. Cosmopolis, Feb., 1896.
Bulthaupt, H. Dumas, Sardou und die jetzige Franzosenherrschaft auf der deutschen Bühne. Berlin, 1887.
Durylin, S. Alexandre Dumas en Russie. (In Russian). In: La Civilisation russe et la France, ed. by l'Héritage Littéraire. Moscou, 1937.
Frenzel, K. Der jüngere Dumas in Deutschland. Cosmopolis, 1896.
Gibbens, V. E. Hawthorne's Note to Dr. Heidegger's Experiment. MLN, 60, 1945.
Hansen, J. Ibsen und Dumas. Das freie Wort, 6, 1906.
Karpeles, G. Ein Gespräch von Heine und Alexandre Dumas père. Grenzboten, 1895.
Lacour, L. Dumas et Ibsen. RP, 15.X. 1894.
Leslie, J. K. Towards the Vindication of Zorrilla: the Dumas-Zorrilla Question Again. HR, 13, 1945.
Munro, D. The Three Musketeers. TLS, 31.I. & 7. II. 1942.
Peers, E. A. The Vogue of Alexandre Dumas Père in Spain. Homenatge a Antoni Rubió i Lluch. Barcelona, 1936.
Pierre, A. Alexandre Dumas Père et le tsar Nicolas Ier. Le Temps, 17.XI.1938.
Pique, G. A. Dumas fils jugé par un Allemand. Rev. de Belgique, 13, 1873.
Reed, F. W. Edmond Dantes' Sequel. American N&Q, 5, 1945.
Roberts, W. Dumas and Sue in England. NC, Nov., 1922.
Schwartz, H. S. The Influence of Dumas on Oscar Wilde. FR, 7, 1933.
Szalczer, H. Alex. Dumas fils dans la littérature et sur la scène hongroises. Budapest, 1937.
Thompson, J. A. Alexandre Dumas Père and Spanish Romantic Drama. Baton Rouge (La.), 1938.
Woodbridge, B. M. B. Shaw's Spiritual Forbear, Dumas fils. Harvard Grad. Mag., June, 1928.
Zucker, A. E. & Henderson, P. Camille as the Translation of La Dame aux Camélias. MLN, 1934.
Templeman, W. D. Arnold's The Literary Influence of Academies, Macaulay and **ESPINASSE.** SPh, 43, 1946.
Lehner, F. The German Reaction to **ESTAUNIE.** BA, 14, 1940.
Iacuzzi, A. The European Vogue of **FAVART.** New York, 1932.
Stendhal. Walter Scott et la Princesse de Clèves. (Mme. de la **FAYETTE**). In: Racine et Shakespeare. Paris, 1823.

Stroup, T. B. The Princess of Clèves and Sentimental Comedy. RES, 1935.
Carcassonne, E. Etat présent des travaux sur Fénelon. Paris, 1939.
Chérel, A. Ramsay et la tolérance de Fénelon. Revue du XVIIIe siècle, 1918.
Cordasco, F. Smollett and the Translation of Fénelon's Telemachus. N&Q,193, 1948.
Eckhardt, A. Télémaque en Hongrie. Revue des Etudes hongroises, 1926.
Haselen H. J. L. van. Willem van Haren's Gevallen van Friso. Alphen sur Rhin, 1922.
Kosma, A. Une version hongroise en vers du Télémaque de Fénelon au XVIIIe siècle. (In Hungarian). Pécs, 1932.
Martin, H. G. Fénelon en Hollande. Diss. Amsterdam, 1927.
Maugain, G. La storia della fortuna del Fénelon in Italia. Paris, Firenze, 1910.
Trompeo, P. P. Fénelon e Pascoli. Cult., 1930.
Wieser, M. Deutsche und romanische Religiosität. Fénelon, seine Quellen und seine Wirkungen. Diss. Heidelberg, 1918.
Anon. **FLAUBERT** in English. TLS, 1.XI. 1923.
Bonwit, Marianne. Effi Briest und ihre Vorgängerinnen Emma Bovary und Nora Helmer, MDU, 40, 1948.
Chaves, C. B. A influencia de Gustave Flaubert na estetica de Eça de Queiroz. RLC, 18, 1938.
Clavería, C. Flaubert y la regenta de Clarín. HR, 10, 1942.
David, S. Carol Kennicott de Main Street et sa lignée européenne. RLC, 19, 1939.
Eloesser, A. Flaubert in Deutschland. Vossische Zt., 581, 1904.
Ferguson, W. D. The Influence of Flaubert on George Moore. Philadelphia, 1934.
Fürst, N. The Structure of L'Education sentimentale and Der grüne Heinrich. PMLA, 56, 1941.
Golovachenko, Y. Madame Bovary au théâtre Kamerny. La Littérature soviétique. Moscou, 1946.
Gordon, Caroline. Notes on Faulkner and Flaubert. Hudson Review, 1, 1948.
Helms, F. von. German Criticism of G. Flaubert. Columbia U.P., 1929.
Lafitte, G. Mme. Bovary et la Regenta. BH, 45, 1943.
L'vov, V. Flaubert and L. Andreev (in Russian). Obrazovanie, 6-7, 1907.
Michaud, R. Lafcadio Hearn et Flaubert. RG, 1912.
Pacey, D. Flaubert and his Victorian Critics. UTQ, 16, 1946.
Pierre, A. V. Flaubert et Kipling. RB, 7.IX.1929.
Seznec, J. Notes on Flaubert and the United States. The Am. Society of the Legion of Honor Magazine, 17, 1946.
Steegmuller, F. Flaubert's Sundays: Maupassant and Henry James. Cornhill Mag. 947, 1948.
Yvon, P. L'influence de Flaubert en Angleterre. Caen, 1939.
Zaleski, Z. L. Les relations polonaises de Flaubert. RLC, 11, 1931.
Mehring, S. Verblichene Lyrik. (**FLORIAN** & Bürger). Berliner Tageblatt, 661, 1907.
Schoeppl, S. Von Florians Les deux billets zu Goethes Bürgergeneral. Progr. Laibach, 1909.
Bougeault, A. Krylov, ou le La **FONTAINE** russe. Paris, 1852.
Brooks, B. G. Wordsworth and La Fontaine. TLS, 25.VII.1936.
Germain, G. La Fontaine et les fabulistes espagnols. RLC, 12, 1932.
Lugli, V. Emilio de Marchi traduttore di La Fontaine. Rendiconti dell' Istituto Lombardo, 1939-40.
Niess, R. J. La Fontaine and the Cuentos of Samaniego. RLC, 18, 1938.
Smith, M. E. Notes on the Rimed Fable in England. MLN, 1916.
Stein, F. Lafontaines Einfluss auf die deutsche Fabeldichtung des XVIII. Jahrhunderts. Progr. Aachen, 1889.
Uhlemayr, B. Der Einfluss Lafontaines auf die englische Fabeldichtung des XVIII. Jahrhunderts Diss. Heidelberg. Nürnberg, 1900.
Ibershoff, C. H. Another French Source of Bodmer (**FONTENELLE**). MLN, 1924.
Maugain, G. Fontenelle et l'Italie. RLC, 3, 1923.
Staubach, C. N. Fontenelle in the Writings of Feijóo. HR, 8, 1940.
Debu-Bridel, J. **FOURIER** psychologue et précurseur de Freud. NRF, 1937.
Liatskii, E. N. G. Chernyshevskii and Ch. Fourier. Sovremennyi Mir, 11, 1909.
Denizot, G. Anatole **FRANCE** vu par les Musulmans. L'Arche, 1 (Alger), 1944.
Fay, E. G. Borrowing from Anatole France by Willa Cather and Robert Nathan. MLN, 56, 1941.
Hilton, R. Anatole France y la America Latina. RIA, 3, 1941.
Privitera, J. F. O. Henry and Anatole France. MLF, 25, 1940.
Sarrailh, J. Le prestige d'Anatole France en Espagne. RLC, 16, 1936.

Sénéchal, C. A. France jugé par les Allemands. Vie des Peuples, March, 1925.
Thibaudet, A. A. France en Angleterre. NRF, June, 1924.
Daniels, J. Les rapports entre saint **FRANCOIS DE SALES** et les Pays-Bas, 1550-1700. Nijmegen, 1932.
Bradley. Chaucer and **FROISSART**. Academy, 1188, 1895.
Kittredge, G. L. Chaucer and Froissart. ESn, 26, 1899.
Lehmann, J. Shakespeare and Froissart. TLS, 3.III.1945.
Newbolt, H. Froissart in Britain. Leipzig, 1902.
Schleich, G. Lord Berners Froissart-Uebersetzung in ihren Beziehungen zum Original. Archiv, 1935.
—— Beiträge zur Textkritik von Lord Berners Froissart Uebersetzung. Archiv, 1936.
Smith, R. M. Froissart and the English Chronicle Plays. Diss. Columbia U., 1915.
Williams, E. **FURETIERE** and Wycherley: Le Roman bourgeois in Restoration Comedy. MLN, 53, 1938.
Edwards, H. L. R. Robert **GAGUIN** and the English Poets, 1489-90. MLR, 32, 1937.
Witherspoon, A. M. The Influence of Robert **GARNIER** on Elizabethan Drama. New Haven, 1924.
Allen, M. S. Poe's Debt to **GAUTIER**, Pascal and Voltaire. Diss. U. of Texas, 1940.
Brown, D. F. Azevedo's Naturalistic Version of Gautier's La Morte Amoureuse. HR, 13, 1945.
Coquart, A. Théophile Gautier et la Russie. Le Monde Slave, 1936.
Csaplaros, E. Théophile Gautier et les Hongrois. (In Hungarian). Pécs, 1935.
Majut, R. Büchner und Gautier. Archiv, 1934.
Moret, A. Note sur une source du Roman de la Momie. RHLF, 1899.
Baughan, D. E. Swift and **GENTILLET**. SPh, 37, 1940.
Strauch, C. F. **GERANDO**: A Source for Emerson. MLN, 58, 1943.
Curtius, E. R. A. **GIDE** vu par un critique allemand. Vie des Peuples, March, 1925.
Reyes, A. André Gide in America. Bibliography. Monterrey, 1933.
Schlappner, M. Thomas Mann und das Moralistentum André Gides. Der Kleine Bund (Bern), 30.V.1948.
Achelis, T. Zur deutschen **GOBINEAU**-Litteratur. LE, 15.II.1903.
Gjellerup, K. Graf Gobineau in Deutschland. Dresdner Anzeiger, Beilage, 28.I. 1901.
Hansson, O. Ein französischer Vorgänger Nietzsches. Nation, 45, 1903.
Mangold, A. Arthur de Gobineau und Richard Wagner. DFM, 4, 1939.
Rowbotham, A. H. Gobineau and the German Terror. Sewanee Rev., 47, 1939.
Taupin, R. The Example of R. de **GOURMONT** (in England). Criterion, July, 1931.
Ibershoff, C. H. A French Source of Bodmer's Noah (Mme de **GRAFFIGNY**). PhQ, 1924.
Braddy, H. Chaucer and the French Poet **GRAUNSON**. Baton Rouge (La.), 1947.
Fothergill, R. An Early Influence on the Poetry of Gray. (**GRESSET**). RLC, 9, 1929.
Froger, L. Gresset et Frédéric II. Annales Flèchoises, 2, 1903.
Babeau, A. Une traduction anglaise d'un ouvrage de **GROSLEY**. Mém. de la Soc. acad. de Troyes, 49, 1885.
Lesowsky, J. Der tolle Invalide auf dem Fort Ratonneau (**GROSSON** & Arnim). Archiv, 27, 1912.
Winkler, E. G. C. Deux traductions du Centaure de M. de **GUERIN**, celle de R. M. Rilke et du Néerlandais R. van Genderen Stort. NPh, 24, 1939.
Fouillée, A. Les jugements de Nietzsche sur **GUYAU**. Revue de théologie, 1901.
Hoffmann, P. Heinrich von Kleist und **HELVETIUS**, GRM, 1935.
Tronchon, H. Helvétius (De l'Esprit) jugé par un voltairien de Hongrie. Revue des Etudes hongroises, 1924.
Wolff, H. M. Fatalism in Klinger's Zwillinge. (**HOLBACH**). GR, 15, 1940.
Kocher, P. H. François **HOTMAN** and The Massacre at Paris (Marlowe). PMLA, 56, 1945.
Hanighen, F. C. **HUYSMAN'S** Influence in America. RLC, 13, 1933.
Knickerbocker, W. S. Arnold, Shelley and **JOUBERT**. MLN, 55, 1940.
Berkowitz, H. C. Mesonero's Indebtedness to **JOUY**. PMLA, 1930.
Derndarsky, D. Louise **LABE** und Rilke. RF, 60, 1947.
Fürst, N. Rilke's Translations of English, French and Italian Sonnets. SPh, 39, 1942.
Rose, E. Two German Translations of Louise Labé's Second Sonnet. MLQ, 5, 1944.
Davray, H. D. The Influence of **LAFORGUE** and Péguy on T. S. Eliot. MF, 15. VII.1937.
Greene, E. J. Jules Laforgue et T. S. Eliot. RLC, 22, 1948.

Hays, H. R. Laforgue and Wallace Stevens. RR, 25, 1934.
Alton-Shee, E. d'. Les Méditations de **LAMARTINE** en Russie. In: Mes Mémoires, 1826-48. 2 vols. Paris, 1869.
Alekseev, M. P. Turgenev and Lamartine. In: Russian Literature in the West. Leningrad, 1945.
Benedetto, L. F. Il canonico Borghi e Lamartine. Marzocco, 1931.
Fournet, C. Lamartine et Huber-Saladin, son confident genevois. Annales de l'Acad. de Mâcon, 31, 1937.
Gosse, E. Lamartine and the English Poets. In: More Books on the Table. London, 1923.
Gugenheim, Suzanne. La poésie de Lamartine en Italie. Pavie, 1919.
Guillemin, H. Lamartine en Russie. RLC, 14, 1934.
—— Un fragment de Jocelyn, traduit en vers anglais par Mme. de Lamartine. RLC, 16, 1936 .
Hazard, P. Les traductions de Lamartine au Brésil. RLC, 11, 1931.
Kool, J. H. Les Premières méditations en Hollande de 1820 à 1880. Paris, 1921.
Lichtenberger, A. Lamartine et les Yougoslaves. Les Annales 1, (Paris), 1924.
Monnet, C. Projet de Bibliographie lamartinienne française-italienne. Torino, 1910.
Nanteuil, de. Un ami italien de Lamartine (Frullani). MF, 1937.
Ozerowitch, M. Lamartine et la Yougoslavie. L'Europe centrale, 1933-34.
Palamas, C. Lamartine dans la poésie néo-hellénique. L'Acropole, 1920.
Peers, E. A. The Fortunes of Lamartine in Spain. MLN, 1922.
Raag, Laura M. Mme. de Lamartine et sa famille anglaise. RLC, 18, 1938.
Sourine, N. Tioutcheff et Lamartine. Bull. de l'Institut de l'Hist. des Arts, 3, Leningrad, 1928.
—— Lamartine russe. In: Poésie russe. Leningrad, 1929.
Trompeo, P. P. Lamartine e la marchesa di Barolo. Cult. 1926-27.
Tronchon, H. Lamartine au Brésil. RCC, 39, 1937-38.
Valkhoff, P. Lamartine in Nederland. De Gids, 1.V.1939.
Ahrens, L. **LAMENNAIS** und Deutschland. Münster, 1930.
Dudon, P. Disciples et admirateurs florentins de Lamennais. Revue des questions historiques, 1936.
Lemoine, J. Admirateurs modénois de l'Essai. Lettres inédites à Lamennais. Ibid. 1937.
Panella, A. Lamennais e l'Italia. Marzocco, 24.I.1926.
Versluys, J. C. Sur l'accueil fait en Hollande aux Paroles d'un Croyant. NPh, 19, 1934.
Zader, G. L'abate Lamennais e la fortuna delle sue opere in Italia. Brescia, 1928.
Ruffini, F. Manzoni e Lamennais. Cult., 1930.
Ziino, M. Manzoni non tradusse il Lamennais. Conv., 1932.
Zadei, G. Controversia di G. Mazzini col Lamennais. Pegaso, 1933.
Versluys, J. C. Lamennais et Gren van Prinsterer. NPh, 17, 1931.
Kozlowski, W. M. H. Wronski et Lamennais. Revue de philosophie, 1905.
Grosi, E. La Biblioteca di Guido Zansi. (Lamennais). Milano, 1934.
Eliel, A. **LAMOTTES** Abhandlung über die Tragödie verglichen mit Lessings Hamburgischer Dramaturgie, ZVL, 13.
Klimas, P. Ghillebert de **LANNOY** in Medieval Lithuania. New York, 1945.
Vianey, J. **LECONTE DE LISLE**, ouvrier de l'unité italienne. Mélanges Hauvette. Paris, 1934.
Gatti, J. F. La fuente de Inesilla (Ramón de la Cruz) **(LE GRAND)**. RFH, 5, 1943.
Markovitch, M. Jules **LEMAITRE** et Laza Kostic. (In Serbian). Prilozi za kujizevnost, 17, 1937.
Rosenblatt, Louise. Marius l'épicurien de Walter Pater et ses points de départ français. RLC, 15, 1935.
Guéroult, M. Fichte et Xavier **LEON**. Revue philosophique, 71, 1946.
Livesay, J. L. An Immediate Source for Faerie Queene, Book V, Proem. **(LE ROY)**. MLN, 59, 1944.
Smith, H. Tamburlaine and the Renaissance. U. of Colorado Studies, 1945.
Anon. Un Gil Blas en Californie. **(LE SAGE)** .MLF, 1931.
Goethe, W. von. Der deutsche Gil Blas. Sämtliche Werke, 28. Berlin, 1821.
Shorthouse, J. H. The Successor of Monsieur Le Sage (G. Borrow). In: Literary Remains, 2. London, 1905.
Guastalla, R. R. Le Sage e C. Goldoni. Marzocco, 20.IV.1924.
Knapp, L. M. Smollett and Lesage's The Devil Upon Crutches. MLN, 1932.
Lawrence, A. L'influence de Lesage sur Smollett. RLC, 12, 1932.
Wershoven, F. J. Smollett et Lesage. Berlin, 1883.
Varenne, G. Goethe et Claude **LORRAIN**. RLC, 12, 1932.
Bourgeois, M. Pierre **LOTI** and Syne. Westminster Review, 1913.

Estrich, R. M. Chaucer's Prologue to the Defence of Good Women and **MACHAUT'S** Le Jugement du Roy de Navarre. SPh, 36, 1939.

Harrison, B. S. Medieval Rhetoric in the Book of the Duchesse. PMLA, 49, 1934.

Kitchel, Anna T. Chaucer and Machaut's Dit de la fontaine amoureuse. In: Vassar Mediaeval Studies. New Haven, 1923.

Kittredge, G. L. Chauceriana. MPh, 7, 1909.

—— Guillaume de Machaut and the Book of the Duchess. PMLA, 30, 1915.

—— Chaucer's Troilus and Guillaume de Machaut. MLN, 30, 1915.

Schoeck, R. J. T. S. Eliot, Mary Queen of Scots and Guillaume de Machaut. MLN, 63, 1948.

Schofield, W. H. Chaucer's Franklin's Tale. PMLA, 16, 1901.

Blaszczyk, S. Sur une traduction en Polonais de la Sylvie de **MAIRET**. RLC, 14, 1934.

Caussy, F. Joseph de **MAISTRE** et Schopenhauer. L'Ermitage, 15.VII.1906.

—— La théorie des Sacrifices, d'après Nietzsche et Joseph de Maistre. MF, 1.II.1906.

Grauert, H. von. J. de Maistre und J. Görres vor hundert Jahren. Köln, 1922.

Holdsworth, F. Joseph de Maistre et l'Angleterre. Paris, 1936.

Lytkowski, J. Josef de Maistre à Henryk Pzeworski. Krakow, 1925.

La Fuye, M. de. Xavier de Maistre, gentilhomme européen. Tours, 1934.

Anon. Nicolas **MALEBRANCHE**. TLS, 27.VIII.1938.

Luce, A. A. Malebranche et le Trinity College de Dublin. Rev. philosoph. de la France et l'étranger, 125, 1938.

Jessop, T. E. Malebranche and Berkeley. Rev. internat. de philos., 1, 1938.

Leroux, E. Notes concernant l'influence de Malebranche sur Berkeley. RMM, 1938.

Luce, A. A. Berkeley and Malebranche. Oxford U. P., 1934.

Staubach, C. N. Feijóo and Malebranche. HR, 9, 1941.

Church, R. W. Malebranche and Hume. Rev. internat. de philosophie, 1, 1938.

Dal Verme, M. E. Di alcuni rapporti fra Malebranche e Hume. Revista di filosofia neo-scolastica, 30, 1938. And in: Malebranche Gedächtnisschrift. Milano, 1938.

Doxsee, C. W. Hume's Relation to Malebranche. Philosophical Review, 25, 1916.

Hamm, V. M. Pope and Malebranche: A Note on the Essay on Criticism. PhQ, 24, 1945.

Anon. **MALLARME** in English. TLS, 14. XI.1936.

Kellermann, W. Die jüngste deutsche Mallarmé-Exegese. GRM, 27, 1939.

Reyes, A. Mallarmé en espagnol. RLC, 12, 1932.

—Mallarmé entre nosotros. Buenos Aires, 1938.

Valéry, P. Lettre sur Mallarmé (et son influence). RP, 1.IV.1927.

Chisholm, A. R. Le symbolisme français en Australie: Mallarmé et Brennan. RLC, 18, 1938.

Chast, D. Eugénio de Castro et Stéphane Mallarmé. RLC, 21, 1947.

Dottin, P. Un mallarméen d'outre-Manche, Arthur Ellis. RELV, 1928.

Simons, H. Wallace Stevens and Mallarmé. MPh, 43, 1947.

Tosi, G. Gabriele d'Annunzio lecteur de **MALRAUX**. CL, 1950.

Sandbach, F. E. Otto von Diemeringens German Translation of **MANDEVILLES** Travels. Mod. Quarterly of Lang. and Literature, 5, 1899.

Schoener, A. Die deutschen Mandeville-Versionen. Diss. Lund, 1928.

Anderson, G. K. **MARIE DE FRANCE** and Arthur O'Shaughnessy: a Study in Victorian Adaptation. SPh, 36, 1939.

Baldwin, E. C. **MARIVAUX'** Place in Character Portrayal (and Richardson). PMLA, 27, 1912.

Busetto, N. Gertrude (in Manzoni's Promessi Sposi) e La Vie de Marianne del Marivaux. In: La Genesi e la formazione dei Promessi Sposi. Bologna, 1921.

Gatti, J. F. Un sainete de Ramón de la Cruz y una comedia de Marivaux. RFH, 3, 1941.

—— Moratin y Marivaux. RFH, 3, 1941.

Grimm, C. Encore une fois la question Marivaux-Richardson. RLC, 4, 1924.

Hughes, Helen S. Translations of the Vie de Marianne and Their Relation to Contemporary English Fiction. MPh, 15, 1917.

Laborde, P. Un problème d'influence: Marivaux et El sí de las niñas. RLR, 69, 1946.

Melloni, N. Note sur Marivaux en Italie. RLC, 1923.

Schroers, Carola. Ist Richardsons Pamela von Marivaux's Vie de Marianne beeinflusst? ESn, 49, 1916.

Swaen, A. E. H. Marianne-Pamela. NPh, 23, 1938.

Price, L. M. The Vogue of **MARMON-**

TEL on the German Stage. UCPPh, 27, 1944.
Robertson, J. G. Lessing and Marmontel. MLR, 1911.
Schmid, G. O. Marmontel; seine moralischen Erzählungen und die deutsche Literatur. Strassburg, 1935.
Wlislocki, H. von. Marmontel in Ungarn. ZVL, 7, 1894.
Buisman, J. F. **MAROT** en Spiegel. NPh, 22, 1937.
Shannon, G. P. Against Marot as a Source of Marlowe's Hero and Leander. MLQ, 9, 1948.
Moore, J. R. A New Source for Gulliver's Travels. (Jacques **MASSE**). SPh, 38, 1941.
Buseto, N. La genesi e la formazione dei Promessi Sposi (**MASSILLON**). Bologna, 1921,
Mackall, L. L. Goethe's quatrain Liegt dir gestern klar und offen a Paraphrase from **MAUCROIX**. AJPh, 1920.
Anon. **MAUPASSANT** in English. TLS, 16.X.1924.
Artinian, A. Maupassant as Seen by American and English Writers of Today. FR, 17, 1943.
Chasse, C. Maupassant et l'Angleterre. LM, 1926.
Frierson, W. C. Realism in the Eighteen-Nineties and the Maupassant School in England. FQ, 10, 1928.
Duplessys, L. Maupassant, source de G. d'Annunzio. MF, 1.XII.1927.
Kadner, S. Eine literarische Anleihe d'Annunzio's bei Maupassant. GRM, 13, 1925.
Maynial, E. Guy de Maupassant et G. d'Annunzio. MF, 52, 1904.
Braddy, H. Ambrose Bierce and Guy de Maupassant. Amer. N&Q, 1, 1941-42.
Artinian, A. Lafcadio Hearn: First Translator-Critic of Maupassant in the United States. MLF, 27, 1942-43.
Klemperer, V. Schnitzler und Maupassant. Zeitgeist, Berliner Tagblatt, 27, 1911.
Grilli, A. Renato Serra e Maupassant. NAnt, 402, 1939.
Anon. Maupassant and Sudermann. Athenaeum, 17.II.1912.
Diels, H. **MAUPERTUIS** und Friedrich der Grosse. DR, 15.III.1898.
Sokal, E. Friedrich der Grosse und Maupertuis. Beilage z. Allg. Zt., 165, 1898.
Greene, G. François **MAURIAC**, vu par un Anglais. France Libre, 10, 1945.
Hopkins, G. François Mauriac et les Anglais. MF, 1948 .
Morgan, C. & Bowen, E. François Mauriac vu par deux écrivains anglais. Echo, Oct., 1946.
Monsour, B. François Mauriac vu par un critique suédois. L'Arche, 1 (Alger), 1944.
Pusey, W. W. L. S. **MERCIER** in Germany: his Vogue and Influence in the XVIIIth Century. Columbia U .P., 1939.
San-Giorgin, J. Sébastien Merciers dramaturgische Ideen im Sturm und Drang. Basel, 1921.
Zollinger, O. Séb. Mercier's Beziehungen zur deutschen Litteratur. ZFSL, 25, 1902.
Bainville, J. Björnson et Séb. Mercier. Revue d'Art dramatique, Aug., 1898.
Fester, R. Schiller, Mercier und Huber. Beilage zur Allg. Zt., 216-18, 1904.
Mis, L. S. Mercier, Schiller und Otto Ludwig. Euphorion, 29, 1928.
Brom, G. **MERIMEE** en Heine. NPh, 28, 1943.
Diels, P. Mérimée, Chamisso, Zukovskij. In: Jb. f. Kultur & Geschichte der Slaven, N. F., 2, 1935.
Fischer, W. Th. Wilder's The Bridge of Saint Louis Rey and P. Mérimée's Le carrosse du St. Sacrement. Anglia, 1936.
Sarrailh, J. Un drame espagnol tiré de Carmen. RLC, 2, 1922.
Solalinde. Prosper Mérimée y Valle-Inclan. RFE, 1919.
Picavet, F. La **METTRIE** et la critique allemande. Paris, 1889.
Benedetto, L. F. Il Roman de la rose e la letteratura italiana. (Jean de **MEUNG**). Halle, 1910.
Cenac-Moncant. Les jardins du Roman de la Rose, comparés avec ceux des Romains et ceux du moyen âge. In: L'investigateur, 4e sér., 8, 1868.
Gorra, E. Di alcune propaggini del Romanzo della Rosa. In: Studi d. crit. letter. Bologna, 1892.
Huppe, B. F. The Translation of Technical Terms in the Middle English Romaunt of the Rose. JEGPh, 47, 1948.
Langlois, E. Origines et sources du Roman de la Rose. Paris, 1890.
Lindner, F. Die englische Uebersetzung des Roman de la Rose. ESn, 11, 1888.
Luquiens, F. B. The Roman de la Rose and Medieval Castilian Literature. RF, 20, 1905.
Monaci, E. Una redazione italiana inedita dell Roman de la Rose. Giornale di filologia romanza, 1878.
Paré, G. Le Roman de la Rose et la scolastique courtoise. Paris, 1941.
Sieper, E. Les échecs amoureux. Eine altfranzösische Nachahmung des Rosen-

romans und ihre englische Uebertragung. Weimar, 1898.

Cipriani, L. Studies in the Influence of the Romance of the Rose upon Chaucer. PMLA, 22, 1907.

Fansler, D. S. Chaucer and the Roman de la rose. New York, 1914.

Kaluza, M. Chaucer und der Rosenroman. Berlin, 1893.

Koeppel, E. Chauceriana. Jehan de Meung. Le Roman de la rose. Anglia, 14, 1891.

Magoun, F. P. Chaucer and the Roman de la Rose. RR, 17, 1926.

Koester, H. Huchown's Pistel of Swete Susan. Strassburg, 1895.

Walter, J. Astrophel and Stella and the Romaunt of the Rose. RES, 15, 1939.

Carré, J. M. **MICHELET** en Hollande. NPh, 1925.

Allen, G. W. Walt Whitman and Jules Michelet. EA, May, 1937.

Breazu, J. Michelet et les Roumains. (In Roumanian). Publications de l'U. de Cluj, 1935.

Hazard, P. Michelet, Quinet, Mickiewicz et la vie intérieure du Collège de 1838 à 1852. In: Le collège de France. Livre jubilaire. Paris, 1932.

Knapp, Adeline. Whalt Whitman and Jules Michelet. Critic, 44, 1907.

Portigliotti, G. Spiriti e motivi del Michelet nel Ça ira di G. Carducci. Scena illustrata, 45, 1909.

Zaleski, Z. L. Michelet, Mickiewicz et la Pologne. RLC, 8, 1928.

Dresch, J. Sur les traductions allemandes de l'Histoire secrète de la cour de Berlin de **MIRABEAU**. EG, 3, 1948.

Fay, B. Franklin et Mirabeau collaborateurs. RLC, 8, 1928.

Kont, I. **MONTALEMBERT** et Tolstoi. RB, 1, 1907.

Auerbach, R. von. **MONTESQUIEU** et son influence sur le mouvement intellectuel du XVIIIe siècle. Progr., Triest, 1876.

Cattelain, F. Etudes sur l'influence de Montesquieu dans les constitutions américaines. Diss. Besançon, 1927.

Spurlin, R. M. Montesquieu in America, 1760-1801. Louisiana U. P.,1940.

Baldensperger, F. Un jugement diplomatique sur Montesquieu en Angleterre. RLC, 9, 1929.

Collins Churton. Voltaire, Montesquieu and Rousseau in England. London, 1908.

Fletcher, F. T. H. English Imitators of Montesquieu. RLC, 13, 1933.

—— L'Esprit des Lois Before Early British Opinion. RLC, 14, 1934.

—— Montesquieu and Penal Law Reform in England. UTQ, 6, 1937.

—— Montesquieu and English Politics, 1750-1800. London, 1939.

Lough, G. L'Esprit des lois in a Scottish University in the Eighteenth Century. CLS, 13, 1944-45.

Knust, H. Montesquieus Esprit des lois im Lichte nationalsozialistischer Weltanschauung. NM, 9.

Smolenski, W. Montesquieu en Pologne au XVIIIe siècle. (In Polish). Warszawa, 1927.

Barrère, P. Montesquieu et l'Espagne. BH, 1947.

Brandl, A. Die Herkunft von Manfreds Astarte. (Byron). Anglia, 1936.

Pypin, A. Catherine II and Montesquieu (In Russian). Vestnik Evropy, 1903.

Fuchs, Vera. Die strafrechtlichen Anschauungen Montesquieus und Friedrich des Grossen. Diss. Zürich, 1924.

Mehring, K. Inwieweit ist praktischer Einfluss Montesquieus und Voltaires auf die strafrechtliche Tätigkeit Friedrichs des Grossen anzunehmen bezw. nachzuweisen? Breslau, 1927.

Boulan, E. Hemsterhuys et Montesquieu, et de quelques considérations sur l'esthétique. Gazette de Hollande, March, 1917.

Oake, R. B. Montesquieu and Hume. MLQ, 2, 1941.

Toldo, P. Dell' Espion di Giovanni Paolo Marana e delle sue attinenze con le Lettres persanes del Montesquieu. GSLI, 29, 1897.

Ayrault, R. Schiller et Montesquieu sur la genèse de Don Carlos. EG, 3, 1948.

Mathews, E. G. **MONTFLEURY'S** Ecole des Jaloux and Aphra Behn's The False Count. MLN, 54, 1939.

Daele, Rose-Marie. Nicolas de **MONTREULX** (Ollenix du Mont-Sacré), Arbiter of European Literary Vogues of the Late Renaissance. New York, 1947.

Wieder, R. Pierre **MOTTEUX** et les débuts du journalisme en Angleterre au XVIIe siècle. Paris, 1944.

Michaud, R. A French Friend and Inspirer of Emerson (Achille **MURAT**). U. of California Chronicle, April, 1921.

Traubel, H. L. Whitman and **MURGER**. PL., Oct., 1894.

Cioranescu, A. Rolla de **MUSSET** u literatura romina. Viata romíneasca, July, 1933.

Geist, A. Musset'sche Gedichte in deutscher Fassung. Progr. Kempten, 1897.

Morgulis, G. La véritable histoire d'Un Caprice de Musset en Russie. RLC, 10, 1930.

Södermann, S. A. de Musset i Sverige. Stockholms Dagblad, 31.XII.1893.
Ujvary, L. Arany et Musset. In: Debreceni Lzemble, 9, 1937.
Reimerdes, E. E. Mussets Beziehungen zu H. Heine. Berliner Morgenpost, 264, 1910.
Tisseau, P. H. La Confession de Musset et le Banquet de Kierkegaard. RLC, 14, 1934.
Littlefield, W. Alfred de Musset and the English Opium-Eater. (Thomas de Quincey) Bookman, July, 1902.
Swinburne, A. Tennyson and Musset. Fortnightly Rev., 1881.
Trent, W. P. Tennyson and Musset Once More. Bookman, 7, 1898. And in: The Authority of Criticism and Other Essays. New York, 1899.
Darnay, J. Tourguenieff et Musset. (Terres Vierges et la Confession). Courier Musical, 1.X.1901.
NERVAL: See Intermediaries, I.IV.8.
Broese, G. Eine der Quellen Lessings für Minna von Barnhelm: L'école des amis, Lustspiel von **NIVELLE DE LA CHAUSSEE**. Progr. Naumburg, 1902.
NODIER: See Intermediaries, I.IV.8.
Child, C. G. Nodier and (Du Maurier's) Peter Ibbetson. MLN, 10, 1895.
Gnecco, G. Il **PALAPRAT** nell' opera di Stefano di Franchi. Giornale storico e letterario della Liguria, July, 1928.
Béguin, A. **PASCAL** en Allemagne. Journal de Genève, 11.IX.1939.
Neri, F. Traduzioni italiane dei Pensieri di Pascal. Atti della R. Accad. delle Scienze di Torino, 71, 1935-36.
Stadler, T. W. Pascal deutsch. NSR, 1939.
Droulers, C. Goethe et Pascal. RLC, 15, 1935.
Gillies, A. Herder and Pascal. MLR, 37, 1942.
Tronchon, H. Un écho de Pascal outre-Rhin. (Herder). Grande Revue, 1923.
Chinard, G. Notes sur quelques pensées de Pascal (Hobbes). Festschrift A. Feuillerat. Yale U.P., 1943.
Allen, E. Pascal and Kierkegaard. LQHR, 1937.
Gandillac, M. de. Kierkegaard, le Pascal du Nord. Revue universelle, 1934.
Höffding, H. Pascal et Kierkegaard. RMM, 1923.
Ancelot. Etude comparative sur Pascal et Leibniz. Ann. scientifiques de l'Auvergne, 31, 1858.
Gerhardt. Leibnitz und Pascal. SAWB, 1891.
Arrighi, P. Leopardi et Pascal, note sur l'Infinito. RLC, 18, 1938.
Zuno, H. Note magalottiane: I. Magalotti e Pascal. II. Magalotti e una doctrina psico-fisica di Descartes. Archivio di storia della Scienza, 11, 1929.
Platz, H. Ein deutsches Pascalerlebnis (C. F. Meyer). Hochland, April, 1938.
——Nietzsche, der wiedererstandene Pascal. NM, 10, 1939.
—— Pascal in der Goeschichtsperspective Nietzsches. Theologie und Glaube, 2, 1939.
Wild, A. Pascal et Nietzsche. Suisse Contemporaine, 4, 1944.
Martin, F. R. Pascal and Miguel de Unamuno. MLR, 39, 1944.
Fess, G. M. Melendez Valdes' Vanidad de las Quejas del hombre contra su hacedar and The Pensées of Pascal. MLN, 39, 1924.
Léger, A. La jeunesse de Wesley. Paris, 1910.
Velten, H. V. The Influence of **PERRAULT'S** Contes de ma mère l'oie on German Folklore. GR, 1930.
Glaesener, H. Benoit **PICARD**, modèle de Schiller. RLC, 21, 1947.
Lynskey, Winifred. **PLUCHE** and Derham, New Sources of Goldsmith. PMLA, 57, 1942.
PREVOST: See also Intermediaries. I.IV. 8.
Foster, J. K. The Abbé Prévost and the English Novel. PMLA, 42, 1927.
Friedrich, H. Abbé Prevost in Deutschland. Heidelberg, 1929.
Heilborn, E. Abbé Prévost und seine Beziehungen zur deutschen Litteratur. Nation, 14, 1897.
Mossleny, R. Manon Lescaut und Wilhelm Meister. Euphorion, 21, 1914.
Neri, F. Prévost e l'Inghilterra. Cultura, 1928.
Robertson, M. E. I. Quelques notes sur la contrefaçon hollandaise du Pour et Contre. RLC, 15, 1935.
Labry, R. Herzen et **PROUDHON**. Paris, 1928.
Lindner, G. D. Marcel **PROUST:** Reviews and Estimates in English. Palo Alto, (Cal.), 1944.
Roberts, J. G. The American Career of **QUESNAY DE BEAUREPAIRE**. FR, 20, 1947.
Legouis, P. **QUINAULT** et Dryden. Une Source de The Spanish Fryar. RLC, 11, 1931.
Petronio, G. De Sanctis e **QUINET**. Romana, 3, 1939.
Zaleski, Z. L. Edgar Quinet et Auguste Cieszkowski. Mélanges Baldensperger. Paris, 1930.
Briggs, E. R. Gray's Elegy: A French Source? **(RACAN)** RLC, 19, 1939.

Barzilai Gentilli, E. J. Fr. **REGNARD** e il suo teatro, e di alcune analogia con quello di C. Goldoni. NAnt, 1.V.1925.
Grober, F. Das Verhältniss von Susanna Centlivres Lustspiel The Gamester zu Regnard's Lustspiel Le Joueur. Diss. Halle, 1900.
Hohrmann, F. Das Verhältnis Susanna Centlivres zu Molière und Regnard. ZVL, 14,
Ortiz, M. Goldoni e Regnard. Rivista teatrale ital., 11, 1906.
Parmentier, G. En Laponie sur les traces de Regnard. Nouvelle Revue, 1930.
Roger, N. Regnard en Laponie. Figaro, 4.IX.1930.
Roth, G. Une adaptation anglaise du Légataire universel. RHLF, 1914.
Smith, H. Ernest **RENAN** vs. an Anglo-Saxon Publisher. MLF, 27, 1942.
Angell, J. W. M. Arnold's Indebtedness to Renan's Essais de morale et de critique. RLC, 14, 1934.
Mott, L. F. Renan and Matthew Arnold. MLN, 33, 1918.
Anon. Eleonora Duse ed E. Renan. NAnt, 101, 1888.
Du Vignaux, L. Correspondence de Renan et Strauss. Journal de Genève, 22.V. 1948.
Anon. **RENAUDOT'S** Influence in the English Press. TLS, 21.I.1921.
Duehren, E. Rétif-Bibliothek. Verzeichniss der französischen und deutschen Ausgaben und Schriften von und über **RETIF DE LA BRETONNE**. Berlin, 1906.
Duentzer, H. Monsieur Nicolas in Goethes Tagebuch, Juni und Juli 1798. Euphorion, 7, 1900.
Hassler, K. Ludwig Tiecks Jugendroman William Lovell und der Paysan Perverti des Restif de la Bretonne. Diss. Greifswald, 1902.
Grits, T. Jean **RICHEPIN'S** Letters to Zaguliaev. (In Russian). Literaturnoe Nasledstvo, 31-32. Moscow, 1937.
Foster, Margaret. Arthur **RIMBAUD** and Hart Crane: an Essay in Influence and Parallels. Diss. Ohio State U., 1940.
Roditi, E. A French Poet and his English Critics. Sewanee Rev., 52, 1944.
Schwartz, D. Rimbaud in Our Time. Poetry, 55, 1939.
Fabian, E. Adeptes hongrois de **RIVAROL**. Nouvelle Revue de Hongrie, 1935.
Dreyfus-Brisac, E. La clef des Maximes de la **ROCHEFOUCAULD**, études littéraires comparées. Paris, 1904.
Hazlitt, W. Characteristics, in the Manner of Rochefoucauld's Maxims. London, 1823 & 1837.
Kaye, F. B. La Rochefoucauld and the Character of Zimri. (Dryden). MLN, 1924.
Pinot, V. Christine de Suède et La Rochefoucauld. RB, 23.IX.1911.
Götzfried, H. L. R. **ROLLAND** und die Erneuerung des deutschen Geistes. Erlangen, 1946.
Breitburg, J. M. Romain Rolland et Gorki. Novy Mir, 1945.
Schlappner, M. Thomas Mann und Romain Rolland. Der Kleine Bund (Bern), 27.IV.1947.
Bigongiari, P. Nota per una traduzione da **RONSARD.** In: Studi. Firenze, 1946.
Hincz, V. Ronsard et la Hongrie. Rev. des sciences humaines, 50, 1948.
Maugain, G. Ronsard en Italie. Paris, 1926.
Nolhac, P. de. Ronsard et la Pologne. Revue de la Semaine, 21, 1921.
Sinko, T. Ronsardum vidi. Przeglad Warzsawski, Jan., 1928.
Valkhoff, P. Ronsard en Nederland. In: Over Frankrijk's Letterkunde. Amersfoort, 1925.
Nitze, W. A. Goethe and Ronsard. PMLA, 59, 1944.
Dabney, L. E. John Hays, Plagiarist of Ronsard. MLN, 61, 1946.
Beckherrn, R. M. Opitz, P. Ronsard und Daniel Heinsius. Königsberg, 1888.
Beranek, V. Martin Opitz in seinem Verhältniss zu Scaliger und Ronsard. Progr. Wien, 1883.
Schloesser, R. Ronsard und Schwabe von der Heide. Euphorion, 6, 1899.
Baym, M. I. A Recurrent Poetic Theme (Ronsard and Shakespeare). SAB, 12, 1937.
Sturtz, S. V. Ronsard et Shakespeare. Journal des Débats, 29.VI.1927.
Dupré, A. Relations du Tasse avec Ronsard. Bull. de la Soc. archéol., Vendôme, 13, 1874.
Tonnelat, E. Deux imitateurs allemands de Ronsard: G. R. Weckherlin et Martin Opitz. RLC, 4, 1924.
Mackey, W. F. Yeats' Debt to Ronsard on a Carpe Diem Theme. CLS, 19, 1945-46.
Proffen, G. Goethe und **ROTROU**. Archiv, 13, 1885.
Wolff, H. M. Rotrous Venceslas und Kleists Prinz von Homburg. MPh, 37, 1939-40 .
Mickiewicz, A. J. B. **ROUSSEAU** accepté comme modèle par les poètes lyriques russes. In: Les Slaves, 2. Paris, 1866.
Anton, V. Degli. Confronto fra l'Adula-

tore dell Goldoni e quello di J. B. Rousseau. Giorn. arcadico, 15. Roma, 1822.
Hueffer, H. Heine und J. B. Rousseau. In: Aus dem Leben von H. Heine. Berlin, 1878.
Friedman, A. Goldsmith and Jean **ROUSSET DE MISSY**. PhQ, 19, 1940.
Aubin, R. A. **SAINT-AMAND** en Angleterre. MLN, 1935.
Woledge, G. Saint-Amand, Fairfax and Marvell. MLR, 1930.
Kastner, L. E. Saint-Amant and the English Poets. MLR, 1931.
SAINT-EVREMOND: See Intermediaries. I.IV.8.
Koeppel, E. Sir Thomas Wyatt und Mellin de **SAINT-GELAIS**. Anglia, 13, 1890.
Bianquis, G. Etude sur deux fragments d'un poème de Goethe: Zueignung, Die Geheimnisse (**SAINT-MARTIN**). Nancy, 1926.
Wallas, M. Sur la fortune de l'abbé **SAINT-PIERRE** en Angleterre au XVIIIe siècle. RLC, 20, 1940.
Blanck, A. Fritjof och Ingelborg, Paul et Virginie. En komparativ skiss. Festschrift K. Warburg. Stockholm, 1912.
Braun, E. G. Graf Tolstoi und Bernardin de St. Pierre. ZVL, 9-10, 1895-96.
Hawkins, R. L. Bernardin de St. Pierre and Peale's Philadelphia Museum. RR, 1929.
Hirn, Y. Bernardin de St. Pierre och Finland. Svenska Literatursallskapets: Finland Förhandlingar och Uppsatser, 19, 1905.
Sarrailh, J. Paul et Virginie en Espagne. In: Enquêtes romantiques. Paris, 1933.
Saussey, E. Une adaptation arabe de Paul et Virginie. Bull. d'Etudes orientales de l'Institut français de Damas, 1, 1932.
Singer, A. E. The Influence of Paul et Virginie on La Madre Naturaleza. (Pardo Bazán). West Virginia U. Bull., 4, 1944.
Ware, I. N. B. de Saint-Pierre and Charlotte Brontë. MLN, 1925.
Carnot, H. Sur le **SAINT-SIMONISME**. Académie des Sciences morales, 28, 1887-88.
Guyon, B. Une revue romantique inconnue: Le Gymnase. Etude sur les rapports du Saint-Simonisme et de la littérature étrangère. RLC, 11, 1931.
Hazard, P. Staint-Simonisme et littérature. NPh, 23, 1937-38.
Lector. Il Sansimonismo. LNI, 20.III.1932.
Polinger, E. H. Saint-Simon, the Utopian Precursor of the League of Nations. JHI, 4, 1943.
Larrabec, R. H. Henri de Saint-Simon at Yorktown: a French Prophet of Modern Industrialism in America. FAR, 1937.
Liefde, C. L. de. Le Saint-Simonisme dans la poésie française, 1825-65. Diss. Amsterdam, 1927.
Butler, E. M. The Saint-Simonian Religion in Germany: a Study of the Young German Movement. Cambridge U.P., 1926.
Gerathewohl, F. Saint - Simonistische Ideen in der deutschen Literatur. München, 1920.
Suhge, W. Saint-Simonismus und Junges Deutschland. Berlin, 1935.
Shine, H. Carlyle and the Saint-Simonians: The Concept of Historical Periodicity. Baltimore, 1941.
Murphy, E. Carlyle and the Saint-Simonians. SPh, 1936.
Chaneton, A. Intermedio polemico. Echeverría y Saint-Simon. La Nación, 17. XI. 1940.
—— Echeverría y el Sansimonismo. La Nación, 24.XI.1940.
Butler, E. M. Heine and the Saint-Simonians. MLR, 1923.
Hainds, J. R. John Stuart Mill and the Saint-Simonians. JHI, 7, 1946.
Shine, H. J. S. Mill and an Open Letter to the Saint-Simonian Society in 1832. JHI, 6, 1945.
MacClintock, L. **SAINTE-BEUVE** and America. PMLA, 60, 1945.
Mahieu, R. G. Sainte-Beuve aux Etats-Unis. Princeton, 1945.
Guyot, C. Sainte-Beuve a-t-il collaboré à la Gazette d'Augsbourg? RLC, 9, 1929.
Lang, B. Sainte-Beuve vu par les Allemands. RR, 32, 1941.
Bray, R. Sainte-Beuve à l'Académie de Lausanne. Lausanne, 1937.
Choisy, L. F. Sainte-Beuve et Genève. Mélanges Bouvier. Genève, 1920.
Monglond, A. Sainte-Beuve et la Revue Suisse. RHLF, 1919.
Anon. Matthew Arnold and Sainte-Beuve. Athenaeum, 3697, 1898.
Clark, C. C. A Possible Source of M. Arnold's Dover Beach. MLN, 1902.
Furrer, P. Der Einfluss Sainte-Beuves auf die Kritik M. Arnolds. Diss. Zürich, Wetzikon, 1926.
Whitridge, A. Matthew Arnold and Sainte-Beuve. PMLA, 53, 1938.
Harris, Julia C. An American Sainte-Beuve: Gamaliel Bradford. Emory U. Quart., 4, 1948.
Gambier, H. Emprunt de Carducci à Sainte-Beuve. RHLF, 27, 1920.
Lafleur, P. A. Sainte-Beuve, Balzac, and Thackeray. MLR, 9, 1914.

Arrighi, P. Un émule italien de Sainte-Beuve romancier (Tommaseo). RLC, 10, 1930.

Tsebikoff, Mme. George **SAND** et son influence. Annales de la Patrie, June, 1877.

Mundt, T. Geschichte der Literatur der Gegenwart (Influence of G. Sand). Berlin, 1842.

Rosenberg, R. P. George Sand in Germany, 1832-48. Diss. U. of Wisconsin, 1933.

Karenine, W. George Sand, sa vie et ses oeuvres. (Influence in Russia). Paris, 1899. Cf. Correspondant, 10.VII.1899; Le Temps, 16.VII.1899; Journal des Débats, 4.X.1899;Nouvelle Revue, 15. XII.1899.

Minckwitz, M. J. Elisabeth Barrett Browning und George Sand. Grenzboten, 1904.

Ravà-Corinaldi, B. G. Sand e Elisabetta Barrett Browning. Rassegna di Studi francesi, 1929.

Brincken, Alexandra von der. George Sand et Dostoievsky. RLC, 13, 1933.

Delines, M. George Sand et l'auteur de Crime et Châtiment. Petit Temps, 24. VII.1904.

Levinson, A. Autour des Frères Karamasoff: Dostojewski et George Sand. NL, 13.VII.1929.

Pouzyna, I. George Sand et Dostoievski; la parenté littéraire des Frères Karamazov et du Spiridion. Etudes, 5.II. 1939.

Watzke, O. George Sand et Dostoiewski. RLC, 20, 1940.

Anon. George Eliot und George Sand. MLIA, 1872.

Ponsonby, M. E. George Eliot and George Sand. NC, 50, 1901.

Larnac, J. De Sand à Gorki. Les Lettres françaises, 5, April, 1946.

Rathje, G. G. Gutzkow's Debt to George Sand. JEGPh, 35, 1936.

Fischer, K. George Sand und Gräfin Hahn-Hahn. Literatur- und Kunstblatt, 1846.

Karpeles, G. Heine und Laube bei George Sand. Gegenwart, 1885.

Rosenberg, R. P. Heine and George Sand. JEGPh, 35, 1936.

Lundeberg, O. K. The Sand-Chopin Episode in Los muertos mandan (B. Ibañez). Hisp. 1932.

Basch, V. Ibsen et G. Sand. Cosmopolis, Feb., 1898.

Karenine, W. Adam Mickiewicz e G. Sand. Messaggiero d'Europa, May, 1907.

Rosenberg, R. P. Nietzsche and George Sand. GR, 1935.

Karpeles, G. Die polnische George Sand (E. P. Orzesko). Gegenwart, 9.V.1885.

Roth, G. Kirke White et Joseph Delorme. RLC, 1, 1921.

Shepard, E. Walt Whitman's Prose (Influence of G. Sand). New York, 1938.

Séménoff, E. 1830 et le romantisme russe. George Sand, Tourgueneff et Bakounine. MF, 15.XII.1930.

Harden, M. Vom alten **SARDOU** zum jüngsten Deutschland. Gegenwart, 1890.

Wolff, E. Sardou, Ibsen und die Zukunft des deutschen Dramas. In: Deutsche Schriften. Kiel, 1891.

Leavitt, S. E. Paul **SCARRON** and English Travesty. HSPhL, 14, 1919.

Ellinger, G. Der Einfluss von Scarrons Roman comique auf Goethes Wilhelm Meister. JbGG, 9, 1888.

Schmerbach, M. Das Verhältnis von Davenant's The Man and the Master zu Scarron's Jodelet, ou le maître valet. Diss. Halle, 1899.

Stein, H. Goldsmith's Translation of the Roman comique. MLN, 1934.

Archer, W. Ibsen's Craftsmanship (**SCRIBE**). Fortnightly Review, 1906.

Doumic, R. De Scribe à Ibsen. Paris, 1899.

Schweitzer, J. W. Dryden's Use of Georges de **SCUDERY'S** Almahide. MLN, 54, 1939.

—— Another Note on Dryden's Use of Georges de Scudéry's Almahide. MLN, 62, 1947.

Reinacher, H. Studien zur Uebersetzungstechnik im deutschen Literaturbarock: Madeleine de Scudéry, Philipp von Zesen. Diss. Fribourg, 1937.

Will, H. Zesen-Scudéry. Eine Parallele. Archiv, 80, 1925 .

Tuechert, A. John Dryden als Dramatiker in seinen Beziehungen zu Mad. de Scudéry's Romandichtung. Zweibrücken, 1885.

Wrangel, E. Drottning Christina och Le grand Cyrus. Pro Novitate. Stockholm, 1898.

Gariel, P. Eulalie de **SENANCOUR** et ses amis fribourgeois, (1844-57). RLC, 13, 1933.

Anon. Mme. de **SEVIGNE** in English. TLS, 14.VI.1928.

Padelford, F. M. Sidney's Indebtedness to **SIBILET**. JEGPh, 7, 1908.

Bouillier V. **SILVAIN** et Kant ou les antécédents français de la théorie du sublime. RLC, 8, 1928.

Chmaj, L. Samuel **SORBIERE** et Wiszovaty. Bull. de l'Histoire du Protestantisme fr. 1928.
Bonno, G. Correspondance littéraire de **SUARD** avec le margrave de Bayreuth. Berkeley, 1934.
Anon. G. W. M. Reynolds and Penny Fiction (Eug. **SUE**). TLS, 24.I.1924.
Sih, E. Eug. Sue in Deutschland. Vossische Zt., 579, 1904.
Bourdon, P. La Grande Monarchie de F. de Claude de **SYSSEL** et sa traduction en italien. Mélanges de l'Ecole fr. de Rome, 28, 1908.
Wiarda, R. **TAINE** et la Hollande. Paris, 1938.
Casalduero, J. Marianela y De l'Intelligence de Taine. PMLA, 50, 1935.
Foerster- Nietzsche, E. Friedr. Nietzsche und Hipp. Taine. Deutsche Revue, 1901.
Seillière, E. Taine et Nietzsche. Séances et Travaux de l'Acad. des Sciences morales et politiques, 175, 1909.
Borsdorf, A. T. W. On the Literary Theories of Taine and Herbert Spencer. London, 1903.
Brace, R. M. **TALLEYRAND** in New England: Reality and Legend. NEQ, 16, 1943.
Gérin, M. La réputation de Claude **TILLIER** en France et à l'étranger. Bull. de la Société des sciences et des arts de Clamécy, 1905.
Meyer, R. M. Das Beste aus schlechten Büchern. (Lessing and the Abbé **TRUBLET**). Euphorion, 14, 1907.
Anon. Honoré d'**URFE** and Astrée (in England). TLS, 25.VI.1925.
Welti, A. Astrée und ihre deutschen Verehrer. ZFSL, 5, 1883.
Lynch, K. M. D'Urfé's L'Astrée and the Proviso Scenes in Dryden's Comedy. PhQ, 1925.
Hatcher, O. L. The Sources of Fletcher's Monsieur Thomas (L'Astrée). Anglia, 30, 1907.
Stiefel, A. L. Zur Quellenfrage von Fletchers Monsieur Thomas. ESn, 36, 1906.
Douglas, K. N. Translations, English, Spanish, Italian and German, of Paul **VALERY'S** Le Cimetière marin. MLQ, 8, 1947.
Darca, J. Nota per sette traduttori italiani del Cimetière marin. Poesia, 7, 1947.
Zieler, G. **VAUVENARGUES**, ein Vorgänger Nietzsches. Zs. f. lit. Kunst und Wissenschaft, Beilage des Hamburger Korrespondenten, 1907.
Gedeon, J. La fortune intellectuelle de **VERLAINE** (France, Allemagne, Autriche, Hongrie). Szeged, 1933.
Tournoux, G. A. Bibliographie verlainienne; contribution critique à l'étude des littératures étrangères et comparées. Leipzig, 1912.
Le Corbeau, A. Opinion d'un Américain sur Verlaine. Figaro, 23.VIII.1919.
Harris, F. Verlaine en Angleterre. Figaro, 5.VI.1924.
Temple, R. Z. Verlaine and his English Readers. CLN, 3, 1945.
Underwood, V. P. Paul Verlaine in England. TLS, 18.XII.1937.
Anon. Verlaine in deutschem Gewande. Germania, 37, 1903.
Clodomir. Paul Verlaine en Allemagne. La Plume, 1.I.1895.
Werner, E. Die deutschen Verlaine-Uebersetzungen. Berliner Börsen-Courier, 411, 1923 .
—— Verlaine in Deutschland. Neue Zürcher Zt., 1055, 1923.
Jean-Aubry, G. Verlaine en Hollande. MF, 14.VI.1923.
Batchelor, C. M. Verlaine and Darío. Diss. Yale U., 1940.
Aynard, J. Un critique anglais de Verlaine (Harold Nicolson). RP, 15.VIII. 1922.
Benson, A. B. The Sources of William Dunlap's Ella, a Norwegian Tale (**VERTOT**). SS, 19, 1946.
Snarely, G. E. Jehan de **VIGNAY** and his Influence on Early English Literature. RR, 1911.
Anon. Alfred de **VIGNY**. TLS, 12.XII. 1934.
Baldensperger, F. Alfred de Vigny et la Pologne. Przeglad Wspolczesny, April, 1929. And in: A. de Vigny. Paris, 1933.
Benedetto, U. F. A. de Vigny e gli esuli italiani della Giovine Italia. Marzocco, 19.XI.1922.
Kleiner, J. Vigny and Poland. (In Polish). Gazeta Lwowska, 12, 1925.
Lednicki, W. Alfred de Vigny et les Slaves. Bull. of the Polish Inst. of Arts & Sciences in America, 1, 1942.
Ascher, J. Alfred de Vigny and Thomas Campbell. FQ, 4, 1922.
Chinard, G. Vigny et l'amiral Collingwood. MLN, 1931.
Whitridge ,A. Vigny and Housman: A Study in Pessimism. American Scholar, 10, 1941.
Weiler, M. Alfred de Vigny a-t-il inspiré Le Procès de Kafka? Le Monde, 3.I. 1948.
Baldensperger, F. Thomas Moore et Alfred de Vigny. MLR, 1, 1906.

Ortiz, R. Un'imitazione rumena dal Gessner e dal Vigny (C. Negruzzi). In: Varia Romanica. Firenze, 1932.
Folkierski, W. Alfred de Vigny et Slowacki: Eloa et Eloe. RLC, 15, 1935.
Duncan, E. H. Jonson's Use of Arnald of **VILLANOVA'S** Rosarium. PhQ, 21.
VILLERS: See Intermediaries, I.IV.8.
Drougard, E. Ibsen et **VILLIERS DE L'ISLE-ADAM**. RLC, 21, 1947.
Becker, May L. List of Translations of the Works of François **VILLON** and Books About his Life. SRL, 6, 1929-30.
Vigier, H. François Villon en Angleterre. RG, 1913.
Zech, P. François Villon und seine deutschen Uebersetzer. RRh, 1929.
Aiken, Pauline. **VINCENT OF BEAUVAIS** and Chaucer's Monk's Tale. Spec., 17, 1942.
—— Vincent of Beauvais and Chaucer's Knowledge of Alchemy. SPh, 41, 1944.
Miller, C. W. Zelinda and **VOITURE**. PhQ, 22, 1943.
Munteano, B. Un écho tardif de l'Hôtel de Rambouillet en Moldavie (1783). RLC, 14, 1934.
Petri, E. R. Anklänge von **VOLNEYS** Les Ruines und Godwins Caleb Williams in Byrons Werken. Progr. Glauch, 1885.
Gobert, A. Franklin et Volney. FR, 9, 1936.
Cameron, K. N. A Major Source of The Revolt of Islam. PMLA, 56, 1941.
Kellner, L. Shelley's Queen Mab and Volney's Les Ruines. ESn, 22, 1897.
Atkinson, Dorothy F. The Source of Two Gentlemen of Verona (**YVER**). SPh, 41, 1944.

CHAPTER TWENTY-THREE

French Influences upon Individual Authors.

Le Breton, M. Henry **ADAMS** et la France. In: Harvard et la France. Paris, 1936.
Shoemaker, R. L. The France of Henry Adams. FR, 21, 1948.
Sander, C. Die Franzosen und ihre Literatur im Urteil der moralischen Zeitschriften Steeles und **ADDISONS**. Diss. Strassburg, 1903.
Pasquier, F. M. d'**AGUILAR**, gentilhomme catalan au service de la France. Académie de Toulouse, 1901.
Hauvette, H. Un exilé florentin à la cour de France au XVIe siècle: Luigi **ALAMANNI**. Paris, 1903.
Drouhet, C. De l'influence française dans la poésie de V. **ALEXANDRI**. Mélanges Lanson. Paris, 1922.
—— Vasile Alecsandri si scriitorii francezi. Bucuresti, 1924.
ALFIERI, V. The Famous Victor Alfieri's Passion for Music, Abhorrence of Dancing, and Aversion to the French Nation, Written by Himself. In: The Annual Register, (1809). London, 1811.
Jannaco, C. Usi e forme francesi dell'Alfieri. Annali d. Scuola Normale Super. di Pisa, 11, 1942.
Michel, J. R. France et Italie. Le misogallisme d'Alfieri, notice historique et littéraire. Chambéry, 1902.
Papini, G. Vittorio Alfieri. NAnt, 1935.
Remenyi, J. A Hungarian Exponent of French Realism, Zoltan **AMBRUS**. Symposium, 2, 1948.
Pineau, L. Sur **ANDERSEN** et la littérature française. Revue des Revues, 1897.
Picot, E. Gli ultimi anni di G. B. **ANDREINI** in Francia. Rassegna bibliografica della lett. italiana, 9, 1901.
Dale, H. Matthew **ARNOLD**, ami de la France. RHPhC, 1946.
Fyfe, H. & Pollock, J. Matthew Arnold and the Fall of France. HJ, 40, 1942.
Romer, C. Matthew Arnold and Some French Poets. NC, June, 1926.
Sells, I. E. Matthew Arnold and France. Cambridge U.P., 1935. Cf. MPh, 1936.
Wickelgren, F. L. Matthew Arnold's Literary Relations with France. MLR, 33, 1938.
AZORIN (pseud.) (Martínez Ruiz), J. Entre España y Francia. Barcelona, 1917.
Picco, F. I viaggi e la dimora del **BANDELLO** in Francia. Festschrift R. Rénier. Torino, 1912.
Ezban, S. Maurice **BARING** et la France. PMLA, 60, 1945.
Walton, T. J. M. **BARRIE** and the French Theatre. ML, 19, 1937.
Neumann, A. **BAUERNFELDS** Verhältnis zur französischen Lustspielliteratur. Progr. Steyn, 1911.
Morgulis, G. Un épisode de la vie de **BECKFORD** en France en 1793. RLC, 14, 1934.
Camugli, G. Les événements de la Monarchie de Juillet et leurs répercussions italiennes, vus à travers les sonnets en dialecte romain de G. **BELLI**. REI, 1936.

Evans, R. L. Arnold **BENNETT** et la France. ML, 21, 1940.
Lafourcade, G. The Sources of Bennett's Old Wives' Tales. London Mercury, Feb., 1937.
Nava, M. L. **P. A. BERNARDONI** e il melodramma. Atti e Memorie di Dep. di Storia patria per le Provincie moderne, 5, 1928.
Eckhardt, A. Le premier philosophe hongrois (G. **BESSENYEI**) et la pensée française. Nouvelle Revue de Hongrie, Dec., 1938.
Carli, A. de. Riflessi francesi nell' opera di S. **BETTINELLI.** Torino, 1928.
Larg, D. Le baron de **BIELEFELD,** informateur des historiens de Frédéric II. RLC, 7, 1927.
Smit, J. **BILDERDIJK** et la France. Amsterdam, 1929.
Lescoffier, J. **BJOERNSON** et la France. Paris, 1937.
Yvon, P. Un Ecossais en Normandie à la fin du XVIIIe siècle. (Th. **BLAIKIE**) Caen, 1933.
Mangold, W. C. von **BLUMENTHALS** Pariser Tagebücher, eine deutsche Quelle zur französischen Theatergeschichte. ZFSL, 1883.
Cidade, H. Don Raphael **BLUTEAU:** initiation du Portugal à l'esprit du siècle des lumières. RLC, 18, 1938.
Longnon, A. La famille de **BOCCACE** à Paris (1291-1332). Bull. de la Soc. de l'histoire de Paris, 5, 1878.
Pézard, A. Figures françaises dans les contes de Boccacce. RLC, 22, 1948.
Maurras, C. L'Anglais qui a connu la France (**BODLEY**). Paris, 1928.
Betz, L. P. **BODMER** und die französische Litteratur. In: Denkschrift zum 200. Geburtstage (1899). Zürich, 1900. And in: Studien. Frankfurt, 1902.
Ibershoff, C. H. A French Source of Bodmer's Noah. PhQ, 1924.
—— Another French Source of Bodmer. MLN, 1924.
Kohn, A. **BOERNE,** chroniqueur de la vie parisienne. RG, 1937.
Rosso, A. T. Echi francesi nella poesia di Arrigo **BOITO.** Rassegna di Studi francesi, 1932.
Searles, G. **BOJARDOS** Orlando innamorato und seine Beziehungen zur altfranzösischen erzählenden Dichtung. Diss. Leipzig, 1901. Cf. GSLI, 39, 1902.
Rimestad, C. **BRANDES** og Frankrike. Tilskueren, Feb., 1912.
Imelmann, R. Die 3 Nüsse von Clemens **BRENTANO.** ESn, 62, 1927.
Ratchford, Fannie (ed.) Five Essays Written in French by Emily Jane **BRONTE.** Austin, 1948.
Chassé, C. **BROWNING** et la France. FGB, Nov., 1930.
Dominique, J. Le poète Browning à Ste. Marie de Pornic. Rev. de Bretagne, de Vendée et d'Anjou, 22. (Nantes), 1899.
Du Bos, C. Note sur Browning en France. In: Approximations, 2. Sér., Paris, 1927.
Faverty, F. E. The Source of the Jules Episode in Pippa Passes. SPh, 38, 1941.
Gosse, E. Browning in France. In: More Books on the Table. London, 1923.
Minckwitz, M. J. Einige Beziehungen der englischen Dichterin E. Barrett-Browning zu Frankreich, insbesondere zur französischen Literatur. ZFSL, 1906.
Ransom, H. The Brownings in Paris, 1858. U. of Texas Studies in English, 1941.
Schmidt, K. Robert Brownings Verhältnis zu Frankreich. Berlin, 1909.
Strohl, J. George **BUECHNER** à Strasbourg. La Vie en Alsace, Sept., 1936.
Viëtor, K. Die Quelle von Büchners Drama Dantons Tod. Archiv, 54, 1933.
Rousseau, M. Filippo **BUONARROTI** et les artistes français sous la Monarchie de Juillet. REI, 1938.
Cobban, A. E. **BURKE** and the Revolt Against the 18th Century. London, 1929.
Tielroy, J. Conrad **BUSKEN HUET** et la littérature française; essai de biographie intellectuelle. Paris, 1923.
Bentley, N. E. Hudibras' **BUTLER** Abroad. MLN, 60, 1945.
Mulertt, W. Die Stellung der Marokkanischen Briefe innerhalb der Aufklärungsliteratur. (José **CADALSOS**). Halle, 1937.
Meldrum, E. Roy **CAMPBELL** et les poètes français du XIXe siècle. MF, 1947.
Erhard, M. Le prince **CANTEMIR** à Paris (1738-44). Lyon, 1938.
Benedetto, L. F. **CARDUCCI** e la Francia. Pan, 1935.
Buoni-Fabro, M. La genèse et les sources françaises du Ça ira de Carducci. Lucca, 1909.
Castellini, G. La Francia nella poesia di G. Carducci. Rassegna contemp., 15. IX.1910.
Jeanroy, A. Quelques sources françaises de G. Carducci. RP, 15.I.1911.
Maugain, G. Giosuè Carducci et la France. Paris, 1914.

Jeannerat, C. Rosalba **CARRIERA** et ses relations avec la France. EI, 1926.

Sarran d'Allard. Le centenaire de **CASTILHO**: le vicomte de Castilho et les écrivains français. Mém. et C. R. de la soc. sc. et litt. d'Alais, 30, 1899.

Ehrlich, E. Das französische Element in der Lyrik **CHAMISSOS**. Berlin, 1932.

Kuttner, M. Korsische Quellen von Chamisso und Mérimée. Archiv, 1903.

Eilers, W. Die Erzählung des Pfarrers in **CHAUCER'S** Canterbury-Geschichten und die Somme de vices et de vertus de Frère Lorens. Diss. Erlangen, 1882.

Jusserand, J. J. Chaucer and King René of Anjou. Athenaeum, 3622, 1897.

Taine, H. En quoi Chaucer est Français. Journal des Débats, 18.XII.1862.

Yvon, P. **CHESTERFIELD** et les Français. RAA, 1927.

Brest, R. Deux romanciers britanniques à Paris, Peter **CHEYNEY**, Taylor Caldwell. NL, 1.V.1947.

Neri, F. X. **CHIABRERA** e la Pléiade francese. Torino, 1920.

Calderini-De Marchi, R. J. **CORBINELLI** et les érudits français. Milano, 1914.

Soldati, P. Uomini e cose di Francia nei giudizi di Jacopo Corbinelli. GSLI, 110, 1937.

DALLINGTON, R. The View of France, 1604 (with Introduction by W. P. Barrett). Oxford U.P., 1936.

Hauvette, H. La France et la Provence dans l'oeuvre de **DANTE**. RLC, 9, 1929.

Rajna, P. Per l'andata di Dante a Parigi. In: Studi danteschi. Firenze, 1920.

Teissier, L. Le voyage de Dante en France. Bordeaux, 1924.

Terrade, E. Dante à Paris, ses idées sur la France. In: Etudes comparées. Paris, 1904.

Mapes, E. K. L'influence française dans l'oeuvre de Rubén **DARIO**. Paris, 1925.

Marasso, A. Rubén Darío y su creación poética. Biblioteca humanidades de la U. de La Plata, 13, 1934.

Laig, F. Englische und französische Elemente in Sir William **DAVENANTS** dramatischer Kunst. Diss. Münster, 1934.

Anderson, R. L. A French Source for J. **DAVIES OF HEREFORD'S** System of Psychology. PhQ, 1926.

Krautwurst, A. Die französische Literatur in **DEPPINGS** Korrespondenznachrichten des Morgenblatts für gebildete Stände. Giessen, 1924.

Neri, F. Il **DE SANCTIS** e la critica francese. GSLI, 79, 1922.

Delattre, F. **DICKENS** et la France. Paris, 1927.

Heussey, R. de. Dickens à Paris. Gazette anecdotique, 1880 & Le Livre, 7, 1886.

Usanne, O. Charles Dickens en France. Le Livre, 10, 1889.

Noyes, G. R. Introduction to the Poetical Works of **DRYDEN**. Boston, 1908.

Mahrenholtz, R. **DU BOIS-REYMOND** als Essayist über französische Litteratur. ZFSL, 10, 1887.

Titz, K. Les traces de l'influence française sur le manuscrit de Kralove **DVUR**. Revue française de Prague, 1935.

Oomkens, R. Les ouvrages français de J. van **EFFEN**. Gazette & Revue de Hollande, 1916-17.

Valkhoff, P. Justus van Effen en de franse letterkunde. De Gids, 11, 1917. And in: Ontmoetingen tussen Nederland en Frankrijk. Den Haag, 1943.

Kaboth, K. George **ELIOTS** Beziehungen zu Frankreich. Diss. Breslau, 1930.

Magny, C. E. T. S. Eliot, poète français. Une Semaine dans le Monde, 24.I.1948.

Parish, L. **EMERSON'S** View of France. Légion d'honneur, 1935.

Scorpan, G. **EMINESCU** si lirica franceza. Revista critica, 1937.

Lyonnet, H. Les comédiens français du Prince **EUGENE**. Bull. de la Soc. de l'histoire du théâtre, 1902.

Delpy, G. Bibliographie des sources françaises de B. **FEIJOO**. Diss. Paris, 1936.

Staubach, C. N. The Influence of French Thought on Feijóo. Diss. U. of Michigan, 1937.

Schoell, F. L. Leo **FERRERO** et la France. Lausanne, 1945.

Franck, W. **FICHTE** et la France. Europe, 17, 1939.

Parfitt, G. E. L'influence française dans les oeuvres de **FIELDING** et dans le théâtre anglais contemporain de ses comédies. Paris, 1928.

Hauffen, A. **FISCHART** Studien. Die Verdeutschungen politischer Flugschriften aus Frankreich. Euphorion, 8, 1902.

Aegerter, E. Theodor **FONTANE** und der französische Naturalismus. Diss. Bern, 1922.

Wiskott, Ursula. Französische Wesenszüge in Fontanes Persönlichkeit und Werk. Leipzig, 1938.

Choullier, E. Voltaire et **FRANKLIN** à

l'Académie des Sciences. Mém. de la Soc. acad. de l'Aube, 61, 1897.
Jenkins, C. F. Franklin Returns from France, 1785. Proc. American Philos. Soc., 92, 1948.
Marsh, P. M. Philip **FRENEAU** and his Circle. Pa. Mag. of Hist. & Biography, 63, 1939.
Muret, M. L'influence française à la cour de Berlin: **FREDERIC** Ier et Sophie-Charlotte. Journal des Débats, 21.IX. 1901.
Emery, L. Gallicismo di **FEDERICO IL GRANDE.** Cult., June, 1934.
Gaertner, G. Ueber Friedrich des Grossen Schrift: De la littérature allemande. Progr. Breslau, 1892.
Guiraud, C. L'éducation française d'un Roi de Prusse. Revue des Questions historiques, May, 1936.
Gundlach, W. Friedrich der Grosse und sein Vorleser de Prades. Hamburg, 1897.
Harpe, C. de la. Etude sur les oeuvres poétiques de Frédéric le Grand. Progr., 1852.
Iorga, N. Frédéric II, roi de Prusse, et l'influence française. Revue historique du Sud-Est européen, 1939.
Jagdhuhn, G. Die Dichtungen Friedrichs des Grossen. RF, 1936.
Langer, W. Friedrich der Grosse und die geistige Welt Frankreichs. Hamburg, 1932.
Lemoine, J. & Lichtenberger, A. Frédéric II poète et la censure française. RP, 15.I.1901.
Rossi, J. The Abbé **GALIANI** in France. New York, 1930.
Cru, R. L. John **GALSWORTHY** et la France. Le Temps, 25.XII.1933.
Hedgcock, F. A. David **GARRICK** and his French Friends. London, 1911.
Hopkins, A. B. Mrs. **GASKELL** in France. PMLA, 53, 1938.
Duthie, E. Some References to the French Symbolist Movement in the Correspondence of Stephan **GEORGE** and Hugo von Hofmannsthal. CLS, 9.
Hirschfeld, R. Stefan George und Frankreich. Die Horen, 5, 1928-29.
Hobuhm, Freya. Die Bedeutung französischer Dichter im Werk und Weltbild Stefan Georges. Köln, Marburg, 1931.
Jaeger, H. Stefan Georges französische Gedichte und deutsche Uebersetzungen. PMLA, 51, 1936.
Levinsonn, A. Un grand poète francisé: Stefan George. Le Temps, 24.IX.1927.
Meessen, H. J. Stefan Georges Algabal und die französische Décadence. MDU, 39, 1947.
Saint-Paul, A. S. George et le symbolisme français. Revue d'Allemagne, 1928.
Sior, M. L. Stefan George und der französische Symbolismus. Diss. Giessen, 1932.
Spenlé, J. E. Stefan George et les poètes symbolistes français. Helicon, 2, 1940.
Vordtriede, W. Direct Echoes of French Poetry in Stefan George's Works. MLN, 60, 1945.
Machin, I. W. J. **GIBBON'S** Debt to Contemporary Scholarship. RES, 15, 1939.
GILLIAM, Florence. France: A Tribute by an American Woman. New York, 1945.
Groi, S. La critica della letteratura francese di V. **GIOBERTI.** Rassegna di Studi francesi, Nov., 1928.
Bac, F. Ce que **GOETHE** doit à la France. Journal des Débats, 22.III.1932.
Baldensperger, F. Le voyage de Goethe à Paris. BURS, 1912.
Barnes, B. Goethe's Knowledge of French Literature. New York, 1937.
Bode, W. Die Franzosen und Engländer in Goethes Leben und Urteil. Berlin, 1915.
Caumont, A. Goethe et la littérature française. Progr. Frankfurt, 1885.
Englert, A. Ueber Entlehnungen Goethes aus dem Französischen. ZVL, 5, 1892.
Gaiser, K. Goethes Auseinandersetzung mit der französischen Kultur. NJWJ, 8, 1932.
Gerock, . E. Goethe en France (1792). Alsace française, 21.IV.1929.
Goedeke, K. Goethes lothringische Reise. Gegenwart, 1878.
Gromer, L. Des idées françaises dans Faust. Paris, 1931.
Heine, K. Ueber französische Dramen an der Weimarschen Bühne unter Goethe. ZVL, 1891.
Lichtenberger, H. Goethe und Frankreich. JbGG, 18, 1932.
Loiseau, H. Goethe et la France. Neuchâtel, 1930.
—— Influences françaises dans les oeuvres de Goethe. Alsace française, 30.XI.1930.
Montigny, E. Goethe et la littérature française. Rev. de l'Instruction publique, 21.XI.1867 & 16. & 23.I.1868.
Morel, L. Goethe et les Français de passage en Allemagne. Goethe et Napoléon. Progr. Zürich, 1901.
—— Influence de la littérature française chez Goethe. JbGG, 31, 1910.

Mueller, C. Goethe und die Franzosen. Strassburger Post, 735, 1899.

Sachs, C. Goethes Beschäftigung mit französischer Sprache und Litteratur. ZFSL, 23, 1901.

Seidlin, O. Goethe über Goethe auf Französisch. GR, 21, 1946-47.

Steinweg, C. Goethes Seelendramen und ihre französischen Vorlagen. Halle, 1912.

Titsworth, P. E. The Attitude of Goethe and Schiller Toward the French Classic Drama. JEGPh, 11, 1912.

Urbach, O. Goethe und Frankreich. CFA, 1938.

Wadepuhl, W. Goethes Stellung zur französischen Romantik. Madison, 1924.

Maddalena, E. Il viaggio di **GOLDONI** in Francia. NAnt, 1.XI.1921.

Merz, J. Carlo Goldoni in seiner Stellung zum französischen Lustspiel. Diss. Leipzig, 1903.

Traversi, A. Carlo Goldoni a Parigi. Natura ed Arte, 16, 1907.

Crane, R. S. & Smith, H. J. A French Influence on **GOLDSMITH'S** Citizen of the World. MPh, 19, 1921.

Duméril, H. Un voyageur anglais en France au XVIIIe siècle. Oliver Goldsmith. Mém. de l'Acad. de Toulouse, 1887-89.

Sells, A. L. Les sources françaises de Goldsmith. Paris, 1924.

Garnier. Un romancier anglais à Bar-le-Duc (Edmund **GOSSE**). Mém. de la Soc. des Lettres de Bar-le-Duc, 3e Sér., 1898.

Litzmann, B. Fr. W. **GOTTER**, sein Leben und seine Werke. Hamburg, 1895.

Blanck, K. Der französische Einfluss im 2. Teil von **GOTTSCHEDS** Kritischer Dichtkunst. Diss. München. Göttingen, 1910.

Reichel, E. Gottsched und die Franzosen. Norddeutsche Allg. Zt., 84, 1902.

Waniek, G. Gottsched und die deutsche Litteratur seiner Zeit. Leipzig, 1897.

Fowler, E. Une source française des poèmes de **GOWER**. Diss. Paris, 1905.

Koeppel, E. Gowers französische Balladen und Chaucer. ESn, 20, 1895.

Mebes, A. Ueber den Wigalois von Wirnt von **GRAVENBERG** und seine altfranzösische Quelle. Progr. Neumünster, 1879.

Briggs, E. R. **GRAY'S** Elegy: a French Source? RLC, 19, 1939.

Mahrenholtz, R. Franz **GRILLPARZER** über die französische Litteratur. ZFSL, 13, 1891.

Jones, A. C. F. M. **GRIMM** as a Critic of XVIIIth Century French Drama. Bryn Mawr, 1926.

Zygulski, Z. A. **GRYPHIUS'** Catharina von Georgien nach ihrer französischen Quelle untersucht. Lwów, 1932.

Geffroy, A. **GUSTAVE** III et la cour de France. Paris, 1867.

Levertin, O. Gustaf III som dramatisk forfattere. Stockholm, 1894.

—— Sur l'influence de la littérature française au XVIIIe siècle et sur Gustave III, auteur dramatique. RHLF, 1897.

Bondi, G. Das Verhältnis von **HALLERS** philosophischen Gedichten zur Philosophie seiner Zeit. Diss. Leipzig, 1891.

Rigal, E. Alexandre **HARDY** et le théâtre français. Paris, 1889.

Piquet, H. Etude sur **HARTMANN D'AUE**. Diss. Paris, 1898.

Corbiere, A. J. E. **HARTZENBUSCH** and the French Theatre. Diss., Philadelphia, 1927.

Feller, J. André van **HASSELT**. Bull. de l'Acad. royale de langue et de litt. francaises. Bruxelles, 1925.

Glaesener, H. Van Hasselt et ses modèles français. RHLF, 1928.

Müller, Irmgard. Gerhart **HAUPTMANN** und Frankreich. Breslau, 1939.

Anon. **HEINE** und die Franzosen. Grenzboten, 4, 1845.

Betz, L. P. Die französische Litteratur im Urtheile Heinrich Heines. Berlin, 1897.

Blankenagel, J. C. Heine on French Romantic Dramatists. PhQ, 2, 1923.

Bloesch, H. Heine in Paris. Die Nation, 41-42, 1903.

Bonnerot, J. & Hirth, F. Heine en France. RLC, 17, 1937.

Clarke, M. A. Heine et la monarchie de Juillet. Paris, 1927.

Coser, L. A. Heine en France. RLC, 17, 1937.

Elster, E. War Heine französischer Bürger? DR, 1902.

Lantoine, A. H. Haine et la France. RFA, 1899.

Legras, J. Heinrich Heine in Paris. DR, 79, 1894.

Morsier, E. Henri Heine à Paris. Jugement d'un témoin. BURS, 1902.

Ribère, A. Un ami de la France: Henri Heine. Perpignan, 1899.

Schellenberg, A. Heinrich Heines französische Prosawerke. Berlin, 1921.

Ziel, E. Heine in Paris. Frankfurter Zt., 21.II.1895.

Sulger-Gebing, E. Die französischen

Vorgänger zu **HEINSES** Kirschen. ZVL, 11, 1898.
Frank, R. **HERDERS** Frankreicherlebnis. Diss. Hamburg. Zeulenroda, 1934.
Jacobi, J. Herder und die Welt der Franzosen. ZNS, 1943.
Pange, J. de. Les voyages de Herder en France. EG, Jan., 1947.
Colquhoun, Elizabeth. Notes on French Influences in the Work of Julio **HERRERA Y REISSIG**. BSS, 21, 1944.
Schmidt, C. Le voyage d'un prince allemand (Guillaume VI, langrave de **HESSE**) en France de 1646-48. Bull. hist. et litt., 1899.
Maxwell, I. French Farce and John **HEYWOOD**. Melbourne U.P., 1946.
Young, K. The Influence of French Farce upon the Plays of John Heywood. MPh, 1904.
Anon. Karl **HILLEBRANDS** französisch-deutsche Studien. MLIA, 1868.
Daudet, A. Ein Deutscher (K. Hillebrand) über Frankreich. Gegenwart, 1.IV.1882.
Kozlowski, W. M. Les idées françaises dans la philosophie nationale et la poésie patriotique de la Pologne: J. **HOENE-WRONSKI** et Ballanche. Grenoble, 1923.
Harney, E. T. William **HOGARTH** à Calais. Bull. de la Soc. académique de Boulogne, 8, 1908-09.
Duthie, E. Some References to the French Symbolist Movement in the Correspondence of S. George and H. von **HOFMANNSTHAL**. CLS, 9.
Seillière, E. L'influence française dans la littérature allemande contemporaine (Arno **HOLZ**). RDM, 15.IV.1900.
Prinsen, J. Jean van **HONT**, l'initiateur de la Hollande aux principes de la Pléiade. Revue de la Renaissance, June, 1907.
Baldensperger, F. La première relation intellectuelle de David **HUME** en France; une conjecture. MLN, 57, 1942.
Metz, R. Les amitiés françaises de Hume et le mouvement des idées. RLC, 9, 1929.
Fay, E. G. **HUNEKER'S** Criticism of French Literature. FR, 14, 1940.
Temple, R. Z. Aldous **HUXLEY** et la littérature française. RLC, 19, 1939.
Brugmans, H. L. Le séjour de Christian **HUYGHENS** à Paris. Paris, 1935.
Edel, R. Vicente Blasco **IBANEZ** in seinem Verhältnis zu einigen neuren französischen Romanschriftstellern. Münster, 1935.
Kihlmann, E. **IBSEN** och det franska drama. Mélanges Y. Hirn. Helsingfors, 1930.
Raynaud, G. Paris en 1596 vu par un Italien (Fr. Greg. d'**IERNI**). Bull. de la Société de l'histoire de Paris et de l'histoire de France, 12, 1885.
Smith, F. P. Washington **IRVING** on French Romanticism. RLC, 17, 1937.
Williams, S. T. Washington Irving's First Stay in Paris. AL, 1930.
Jones-Evans, M. Henry **JAMES'S** Year in France. Horizon, 14, 1946.
Pacey, W. C. D. Henry James and His French Contemporaries. AL, 13, 1941.
Chinard, G. **JEFFERSON** et les idéologues. Baltimore, 1925.
—— Trois amitiés françaises de Thomas Jefferson. Paris, 1927.
Dumbauld, E. Les demeures parisiennes de Jefferson. FAR, 1948.
Kimball, L. M. Jefferson in Paris. NAR, 1939.
Koch, Adrienne. The Philosophy of Thomas Jefferson. Columbia U.P., 1943.
Minnigerode, M. Jefferson, Friend of France, (1793). New York, 1929.
Bosker, A. Literary Criticism in the Age of **JOHNSON**. Groningen, 1930.
Klenker, R. Dr. Samuel Johnsons Verhältniss zur französischen Literatur. Diss. Strassburg, 1907.
Tyson, M. & Guppy, H. The French Journals of Mrs. Thrale and Doctor Johnson. Manchester U.P., 1932.
Hourcade, P. Guerra **JUNQUEIRO** et le problème des influences françaises dans son oeuvre. Coimbra, Paris, 1932.
Galos, M. Sigismond **JUSTH** et Paris. Pécs, 1933.
Schwarz, H. Die Ueberwindung des französischen Rationalismus und des englischen Empirismus durch **KANT**. NJWJ, 1, 1925.
Bojanowski, P. von. Herzog **KARL AUGUST VON WEIMAR** in einer Sitzung der Pariser Akademie. Festschrift K. Frenzel, Berlin, 1903.
Rowbotham, A. Rudyard **KIPLING** and France. FR, 1937.
Servajean, H. Kipling et la France. L'Escholier, Dec., 1926.
Lauret, R. Un romantique ennemi de la France: Henri de **KLEIST**. Marches de l'Est, 25.VIII.1912.
Windakiewicz, S. The Literary Program of **KOCHANOWSKI**. (In Polish). Przeglad Warszawski, Nov., 1922.
Pellegrini, C. Giovanni **LAMI**, le Novelle letterarie e la cultura francese. GSLI, 116, 1940.
Hespelt, E. H. The Translated Dramas

of Mariano José de **LARRA** and Their French Originals. Hisp., 1932.
Auer, O. Ueber einige Dramen N. **LEE'S**, mit besonderer Berücksichtigung seiner Beziehung zum französischen heroisch-galanten Roman. Berlin, 1904.
Sivers, J. von. **LENZ** als französischer Briefsteller und Autor. In: J. M. P. Lenz. Riga, 1879.
Boeri, A. G. **LEOPARDI** e la lingua e la letteratura francese. Palermo, 1903.
Fiumi, L. Leopardi e la Francia. Giornale d'Italia, 10.VII.1937.
Frattini, A. La cultura francese nella formazione del pensiero del Leopardi. Poesia e Verità, 2, 1946.
Oriol, A. Leopardi et la littérature française. BI, 2, 1902.
Serban, N. Leopardi et la France. Diss. Paris, 1913.
Sorrentino, A. Cultura e poesia di G. Leopardi. Città di Castello, 1928.
Aronson, A. **LESSING** et les classiques français. Diss. Toulouse, 1935.
Crouslé, L. Lessing et le goût français en Allemagne. Paris, 1863.
Humbert, C. Lessings Stellung zur französischen Litteratur. Archiv, 1871 & 1878.
Legrand, M. Lessing et le goût français en Allemagne. Conf. de l'Assoc. phil. de Bayonne, 1880.
Lerch, E. Lessing, Goethe, Schiller und die französische Klassik. Mainzer Universitäts-Reden, 11-12, 1948.
Robertson, J. G. Lessing's Criticism of the French Drama. Some Sources. Mélanges Baldensperger. Paris, 1930.
Schuchardt, H. Riccaut de la Marlinière. Ein Beitrag zur Erklärung von Lessings Minna von Barnhelm. Progr., 1879.
Springer, R. Lessings Kritik der französischen Tragödie in Frankreich. Museum, 15-16, 1865.
Trautwein von Belle. Lessings Kampf mit dem französischen Geschmack, von einem Franzosen geschildert. MLIA, 49, 1880.
Cione, E. Cesare de **LOLLIS** e l'ottocento francese. LNI, 11, 1940.
Chinard, G. Notes sur le voyage de H. W. **LONGFELLOW** dans le Sud-Ouest de la France. Revue philomathique de Bordeaux et du Sud-Ouest, 19, 1916.
Anon. H. **LYTTON BULWER**, Parodie der neuen Schule in Frankreich. Blätter zur Kunde der Litteratur des Auslands, 1836.
Qualia, C. B. French Dramatic Sources of Bulwer Lytton's Richelieu. PMLA, 42, 1927.
Juhasz, L. Un disciple du romantisme français: **MADACH** et la Tragédie de l'homme. Diss. Szeged, 1930.
Havens, J. R. James **MADISON** et la pensée française. RLC, 3, 1923.
Citron, P. Katherine **MANSFIELD** et la France. RLC, 20, 1940.
Gabutti, E. Il **MANZONI** e gli ideologi francesi. Firenze, 1936.
Lollis, C. de. Manzoni e gli storici liberali francesi della Restaurazione. Bari, 1926.
Premoli, G. Prima dimora di Al. Manzoni a Parigi. Rassegna nazionale, 16. XII.1920.
Schevill, R. El Abate **MARCHENA** and French Thought of the XVIIIth Century. RLC, 16, 1936.
Gaspary, A. Di una fonte francese del **MARINO**. GSLI, 15, 1890.
Nunziante, F. Il cavaliere Marino alla corte di Luigi XIII. NAnt, 92, 1887.
Kocher, P. H. Contemporary Pamphlet Backgrounds for **MARLOWE'S** The Massacre at Paris. MLQ, 8, 1947.
Saviotti, A. L'imitazione francese nel teatro tragico di P. Jacopo **MARTELLI**. Bologna, 1887.
Tormic, J. A. G. **MATOS** et la littérature française. Annales de l'Institut français de Zagreb, April, 1939.
Gugenheim, Suzanne. Les romantiques français jugés par Joseph **MAZZINI**. RLC, 10, 1930.
Nolhac, P. de. Un poète rhénan ami de la Pléiade, Paul **MELISSUS**. RLC, 1, 1921.
Börne, L. **MENZEL** der Franzosenfresser. Paris, 1837.
Mackay, Mona E. **MEREDITH** et la France. Paris, 1937. Cf. TLS, 31.VII. 1937.
Baldensperger, F. C. F. **MEYER** et ses rapports avec la Suisse romande et la France. BURS, 1909.
Lerber, H. von. Der Einfluss der französischen Sprache und Literatur auf C. F. Meyer und seine Dichtung. Diss. Bern, 1924.
Merian-Genast, E. C. F. Meyer und das französische Formgefühl. Trivium, 1, (Zürich), 1942-43.
Chowaniec, C. Les amitiés françaises de **MICKIEWICZ**. Pologne littéraire, 9, 1934.
Krakowski, E. Mickiewicz et la société française de 1830. MF, 15.VI.1935.
Kridl, M. Mickiewicz et la France. Po-

logne littéraire, 15.IV.1929 & Revue de l'U. de Bruxelles, 1929.
Madacsy, M. Clement **MIKES** et les sources françaises de ses Lettres de Turquie. (In Hungarian). Szeged, 1937.
Véran, J. Le souvenir de Stuart **MILL** à Avignon. RDM, 1.IX.1937.
Borland, L. **MONTGOMERY** and the French Poets of the Early Sixteenth Century. MPh, 1913.
Hoffmann, O. Studien zu Alexander Montgomery. ESn, 20.
Halévy, D. George **MOORE** à Paris et son initiation à la littérature française. Minerve française, 1.VI.1920.
Thomas, A. B. Moore en France (1819-30). Paris, 1910.
Guyard, M. F. Charles **MORGAN** en France. RLC, 23, 1949.
Lalou, R. Ch. Morgan et la France. LM, 1945.
Buchanan, R. A Young English Positivist (J. **MORLEY**). In: Master-Spirits. London, 1873.
Hillebrand, K. J. Morleys Studien über das XVIII. Jahrhundert in Frankreich. In: Aus und über England. Strassburg, 1892.
Wilson, W. P. William **MORRIS** and France. SAQ, 1924.
Herzog, P. Johann von **MUELLER** und die französische Literatur. Frauenfeld, 1938.
Soldani, D. La cultura francese di A. **MURATORI.** Rassegna di Studi francesi, May, 1924.
Ramos Arce, Maria. Estudio de la influencia francesa en la vida y en la obra de Gutiérrez **NAJERA.** Diss. U. of Mexico, 1942.
Scherrer, M. Quelques sources des Tableaux parisiens de **NERUDA.** Revue des Etudes slaves, 1936.
Colombier, P. du. Les inspirateurs français de **NIETZSCHE.** RdF, 1.X.1921.
Foerster-Nietzsche, Elisabeth. Nietzsche und die Franzosen. Zukunft, 18.III.1899.
Lasserre, P. Nietzsche et la littérature française. Revue Encyclopédique, 6.I. 1900. And in: La morale de Nietzsche. Paris, 1902.
Lauret, R. Nietzsche et la culture française. Marches de l'Est, 15.II.1911.
Lichtenberger, H. La France et l'Allemagne jugées par Nietzsche. RP, 1.X. 1900.
Spenlé, J. E. Nietzsche à Nice. MF, 15. X.1935.
Wilhelm, Julie. F. Nietzsche und der französische Geist. Hamburg, 1940.
Biencourt, M. Une influence du naturalisme français aux Etats-Unis: Frank **NORRIS.** Paris, 1933.
Wenderoth, G. Die poetischen Theorien der französischen Plejade in Opitz' deutscher Poeterei. Euphorion, 13, 1906.
Herriot, E. **PAINE** and Priestley, French Citizens. In: The Wellsprings of Liberty. London, 1939.
Meng, J. J. Thomas Paine, French Propagandist in the United States. Am. Catholic Hist. Soc., 57. (Philadelphia), 1946.
Arrighi, P. La France vue par G. **PARINI.** Rassegna di studi francesi, 1929.
Beyer, A. Walter **PATERS** Beziehungen zur französischen Literatur und Kultur. Halle, 1931.
Behrens, C. Le répertoire français d'Emil **PAULSEN.** Revue scandinave, Oct., 1911.
Rodzevich, S. Les précurseurs de **PECHORIN** dans la littérature française. (In Russian). Kiev, 1913.
Riva Agüero, J. de la. Las influencias francesas en las obras dramáticas de don Pedro de **PERALTA.** In: Hommage à Ernest Martinenche. Paris, 1939.
Lanson, G. Antonio **PEREZ** et les origines de la préciosité. RHLF. 1896.
Imre, S. **PETOEFI** et les Français. Trodalmi tanulmanyok, 1897.
Caillet, R. & Geoffroy, C. Le souvenir de **PETRARQUE** à Carpentras. Carpentras, 1928.
Delécluze. Pétrarque au Mont-Ventoux. RP, 13, 1839.
Petit de Julleville L. Voyage de Pétrarque à Paris en 1371. RCC, 6.II.1896.
Segré, C. Il Petrarca a Montpellier. NAnt, 16.VII.1929.
Worzel, K. Gottlieb Konrad **PFEFFELS** theatralische Belustigungen. Beitrag zur Geschichte des französischen Dramas in Deutschland. Bruchsal, 1911.
Dorez, L. & Thuasne, L. **PIC DE LA MIRANDOLE** en France. Paris, 1897. Cf. GSLI, 31.
Lozinski, G. **PIERRE LE GRAND** et la Bibliothèque du Roi. Annales de la Société des amis du livre russe, 4. (Paris), 1937.
Felice, P. de. Un étudiant bâlois (Th. **PLATTER**) à Orléans en 1599. Mém. de la Soc. arch. de l'Orléanais, 17, 1880.
Lemonnier, L. Edgar **POE,** illuminé français. MF, 15.I.1928.
—— Edgar Poe et la bon sens français. Grande Revue, 1928.
Massac, R. Influences françaises dans l'oeuvre d'Edgar Poe Paris, 1929.

Matthew, J. Poe's Indebtedness to French Literature. FR, 1936.
Audra, E. L'influence française dans l'oeuvre de **POPE**. Paris, 1931.
Beljame, A. Le public et les hommes de lettres en Angleterre au XVIIIe siècle. Paris, 1881.
Bobertag, F. A. Popes Verhältnis zu der Aufklärung des 18. Jahrhunderts. ESn, 29.
Minto, W. The Literature of the Georgian Era. London, 1895.
Léger, L. **POUCHKINE** et la poésie française. BURS, 1900.
Lozinski, G. La littérature française et Pouchkine. RLC, 17, 1937.
Mongault, H. Pouchkine en France. RLC, 17, 1937.
Tomashevskii, B. Pushkin, Reader of French Poets. In: Pushkinskii sbornik, pamiati Profesora S. A. Vengerova. Moskva, 1922.
—— Pushkin and the Novels of the French Romanticists. In: Literaturnoe Nasledstvo, 1934.
Pfeifer, M. J. A. **POYSELS** Gedichte wider Ludwig XIV. und die Franzosen. Progr. Altenburg, 1889.
Seillière, E. Un Allemand d'autrefois sous le charme de la France (**PUECKLER-MUSKAU**). Figaro littéraire, 10. IX.1927.
Hourcade, P. Eça de **QUEIROS** et la France. Revista de Faculdade de Letras. Lisboa, 1935.
Oprescu, G. Eliade **RADULESCU** and France. (In Rumanian). Dacoromania, 1921-23.
Casamitjana, Francisca. **RAMON DE LA CRUZ** und der französische Kultureinfluss im Spanien des 18. Jahrhunderts. Bonn, 1935.
Crane, R. S. A Note on **RICHARDSON'S** Relation to French Fiction. MPh, 16, 1919.
Macaulay, G. C. Richardson and his French Predecessors. MLR, 8, 1913.
Bauer, M. R. M. **RILKE** und Frankreich. Diss. Bern, 1931.
Goertz, H. Frankreich und das Erlebnis der Form im Werke R. M. Rilkes. Stuttgart, 1932.
Grossmann, R. Rilke und der französische Symbolismus. Jena, 1938.
Rops, D. Rilke et la France. Revue d'Allemagne, 1928.
Wenderoth, G. Rilke in Paris. Aufbau, 1947.
Wocke, H. Rilke und Frankreich. GRM, 24, 1936.
Dutton, G. B. The French Aristotelian Formalists and Th. **RYMER**. PMLA, 29, 1914.
Redick, J. P. French Literature and the Literary Theories of Domingo Faustino **SARMIENTO**. Diss. U. of Colorado, 1939.
Besson, P. **SCHILLER** et la littérature française. Annales de l'U. de Grenoble, 17, 1905.
Cunningham, K. Schiller und die französische Klassik. Bonn, 1930.
Jan, E. von. Schiller und die französische Klassik. ZNU, 34, 1935.
Koester, A. Schiller und die französische Literatur. In: Schiller als Dramaturg. Berlin, 1891.
Neubert, F. Schiller, Goethe und die französische Klassik. CFA, 1942.
Schanzenbach, O. Französische Einflüsse bei Schiller. Stuttgart, 1885.
Titsworth, P. E. The Attitude of Goethe and Schiller toward the French Classic Drama. JEGPh, 11, 1912.
Bertrand, J. J. A. G. **SCHLEGEL** et la France. RG, 18, 1922.
Schevill, R. Aug. W. Schlegel über das Theater der Franzosen. Diss. München, 1898.
Curtius, E. R. F. Schlegel und Frankreich. ZEFU, 31, 1932.
Kluckhohn, P. Französische Einflüsse in Friedrich Schlegels Lucinde. Euphorion, 20, 1913.
Berggrün, H. Französische Einwirkungen auf J. Elias Schlegels Lustspiele. GR, 13, 1938-39.
Muehleisen, W. Französische Vorbilder von J. E. Schlegels Stumme Schönheit. SVL, 8, 1908.
Chesnier du Chesne, A. Les voyages de Walter **SCOTT** en France. Correspondant, 25.VIII.1929.
Genevrier, P. Walter Scott historien français. Tours, 1935.
Lacroix, P. Soirées de Walter Scott à Paris. Paris, 1829.
Latham, E. Le Français dans les romans de Sir Walter Scott. MF, 15.VIII.1939.
Anon. Hermann **SEMMIG**, ein deutscher Emigrant in Frankreich. MLIA, 1.IV. 1865.
Bastide, C. La France et les Français dans le théâtre de **SHAKESPEARE**. Edda, 3, 1916.
Hagen, H. von der. Ueber die altfranzösische Vorstufe des Shakespeare'schen Lustspiels Ende gut, Alles gut. Diss. Halle, 1879.
Keller, W. Die Franzosen in Shakespeares Dramen. JbShG, 76, 1940.
Lefranc, A. Les éléments français dans

Peines d'amour perdues de Shakespeare. Revue historique, 42, 1936.
Longworth-Chambrun, A. Influences françaises dans la Tempête de Shakespeare. RLC, 5, 1925.
Radoff, M. L. Influence of the French Farce in Henry V and the Merry Wives. MLN, 48, 1933.
Siler, H. D. A French Pun in Love's Labour's Lost. MLN, 60, 1945.
Wallace, C. W. Shakespeare and his (French) London Associates. U. of Nebraska Studies, 10, 1910.
Gunnell, Doris. Sutton **SHARPE** et ses amis français. Paris, 1925.
Crabo, C. The Magic Plant. The Growth of **SHELLEY'S** Thought. Chapel Hill (N.C.), 1936.
Grabowski, T. Jules **SLOWACKI** et le romantisme français. Revue de Pologne, 1924.
Joliat, E. **SMOLLETT** et la France. Paris, 1935.
Pilon, E. Un Polonais à la cour d'Henri IV: Jacques **SOBIESKI**. MF, 295, 1939.
Atkinson, Dorothy F. The Wandering Knight, The Red Cross Knight and Miles Dei. (**SPENSER**). HLQ, 7.
Hutton, J. Spenser and the Cinq Points en Amours. MLN, 57.
Renwick, W. L. The Critical Origins of Spenser's Diction. MLR, 1922.
Thorton, Frances C. The French Element in Spenser's Poetical Works. Toulouse, 1938.
Depping. Une princesse allemande à la cour de Louis XIV (**SOPHIE VON BRAUNSCHWEIG**). RB, 1, 1897.
Wind, B. H. Purisme comparé: **SPIEGHEL** imitateur de la France? NPh, 23, 1938.
Anon. **STAHR** in Paris. Europa, 1851.
Duméril, H. Un humoriste anglais à Toulouse au XVIIIe siècle. (**STERNE**). Revue des Pyrénées, 1895.
Anacker, R. d'. Les traductions d'Antoine **STETTLER**. Etude sur les premières influences de la littérature française à Berne au XVIIe siècle. Berne, 1927.
Carré, J. M. **STEVENSON** et la France. Mélanges Baldensperger. Paris, 1930.
Douglas, R. B. Stevenson et Fontainebleau. Macmillan's Mag., March, 1906.
Maclean, C. La France dans l'oeuvre de Stevenson. Paris, 1936.
Macpherson, H. D. A. L. Stevenson: a Study in French Influence. New York, 1930.
Saroléa, C. Robert L. Stevenson and France. Edinburgh, 1924.
Whiting, B. J. Diccon's French Cousin (W. Stevenson's Gammer Gurton's Needle.) SPh, 42, 1945.
Fletcher, J. G. Lytton **STRACHEY** and the French Influence on English Litture. BA, 1934.
Bannermann, E. I. Les influences françaises en Ecosse au temps de Marie **STUART**. Diss. Besançon, 1929.
Bosq de Beaumont, E. du & Bernos, M. La Cour des Stuarts à Saint-Germain-en-Laye. Paris, 1912.
Thierkoff, P. **SWIFTS** Gulliver und seine französischen Vorgänger. Progr. Magdeburg, 1899.
Delattre, F. **SWINBURNE** et la France. RCC, 1926.
Fontainas, A. Swinburne et les symbolistes. Yggdrasill, 25.IV.1937.
Mourey, G. Passé le Détroit (Swinburne et la France). Paris, 1895.
Reul, P. de. Swinburne et la France. Grande Revue, 15.XII.1904.
Richter, L. Swinburne's Verhältnis zu Frankreich und Italien. Leipzig, 1911.
Aufhauser, A. Sind die Dramen von John Millington **SYNGE** durch französische Vorbilder beeinflusst? München, 1935.
Rabuse, G. J. M. Synges Verhältnis zur französischen Literatur und besonders zu Maeterlinck. Archiv, 174, 1938.
Schoepperle, G. John Synge and his Old French Farce. NAR, 214, 1921.
Gournerie, E. de la. Voyage du **TASSE** en France, 1570-71. L'Univ. cathol., April, 1839.
Olschki, L. La lettre du Tasse sur la France et les Français. RR, 33, 1942.
Solerti, A. Le voyage du Tasse en France. RLR, 36, 1892. And in: Biographie du Tasse. Torino, 1895.
Valéry. Le Tasse en France. In: Curiosités et Anecdotes italiennes. Paris, 1842.
Gravier, M. **TEGNER** et la France. Paris, 1943.
Fuhomann, K. **TELEKI** and France. (In Hungarian). Budapest, 1929.
Anon. **THACKERAY** à Paris. In: Intermédiare des Chercheurs et des Curieux, 20.XII.1908, 10.I & 10.VI.1909.
Forest, H. A. Thackeray à Paris. Nouvelle Revue, 15.VII.1910.
Lanoire, M. Thackeray et la France. Revue hebdomadaire, 10.IX.1910.
Melville, L. Thackeray in France. AFR, 2, 1919.
Ray, G. N. Thackeray and France. Diss. Harvard, 1940.
Wyzewa, T. de. Un livre de Thackeray

sur la littérature et la vie françaises. RDM, 15.IV.1906.

Lafontaine, A. Henri **THOREAU**, un exemplaire de la culture franco-américaine. Revue hebdomadaire, 1.III.1919.

Langlois, A. Un Américain à Paris en 1817, 1838 et 1857 (G. **TICKNOR**). Correspondant, 10.X.1876.

Bezsmertny, M. **TOLSTOY** über die französischen zeitgenössischen Autoren. MLIA, 11.VII.1896.

Abruzzese, F. N. **TOMMASEO** a Parigi nel 1848. Ateneo Veneto, 125, 1939.

Gluecksmann, H. **TURGENJEW** in seinem Pariser Freundeskreise. Vossische Zt., 421, 1903.

Markovitch, M. Ivan Tourguéneff et les Français. (In Serbian). Strani Pregled, 1933.

Semenoff, E. & M. Tourguéneff et la France. Grande Revue, March, 1930.

Clark, R. Sir William **TRUMBULL** in Paris, 1685-86. Cambridge U.P., 1938.

Valette, J. Nos classiques vus par un critique anglais. (M. **TURNELL**). Le Monde, 18-19.IV.1948.

Ginzel, L. Ludwig **UHLAND** und die altfranzösische Poesie. Grenzboten, 1887.

Espla Rizo, C . **UNAMUNO**, Blasco Ibañez y Sanchez Guerra en Paris. Buenos Aires, 1940.

UEXKUELL, B. Pariser Erinnerungen eines Balten. Baltische Monatsschr. 28, 1881.

Gresig, G. Giovanni **VERGAS** Kunst und ihre Beziehungen zur Dichtung des französischen Realismus und Naturalismus. Bleicherode, 1940.

Nechaeva, V. & Durylin, S. **VIASEMSKII** and France. (In Russian). Literaturnoe Nasledstvo, 31-32, 1937.

Anon. Une lettre inédite de Richard **WAGNER**. Ses sentiments à l'égard des Français. RB, 17.II.1883.

Baudelaire, C. Richard Wagner à Paris. In: Réflexions sur quelques-uns de nos contemporains. Oeuvres compl., 2. Paris, 1888-92.

Chamberlain, H. S. Richard Wagner et le génie français. RDM, 15.VII.1896.

Prodhomme, J. G. Une source française de l'Anneau du Niebelung de Wagner. MF, 1937.

Sorilène, P. Séjour d'un Anglais en Gascogne à la fin du 18e siècle. (**WALEY**). Société archéologique du Gers, 9, 1908.

Anon. La France vue par un étranger (Horace **WALPOLE**). Bull. de l'Alliance française en Hollande, 1937.

Bioves, A. Horace Walpole à Paris. Feuilles d'histoire, 1.IX.1911.

Baldensperger, F. Un découvreur américain de la France: Barrett **WENDELL**. Living Age, 30.IV.1921.

Legouis, E. La France jugée par un Américain. RIE, 15.IX.1913.

Fuchs, A. Les apports français dans l'oeuvre de **WIELAND** de 1772 à 1789. Paris, 1934.

Lote, R. La France et l'esprit français jugés par le Mercure de Wieland. Paris, 1913.

Michel, V. C. M. Wieland: la formation et l'évolution de son esprit jusqu'en 1772. Paris, 1938.

Cook, H. L. French Sources of **WILDE'S** Picture of Dorian Gray. RR, 1929.

Hartley, K. Oscar Wilde; l'influence française dans son oeuvre. Paris, 1935.

Bonno, G. John **WILKES** et ses amis français. RFB, 1933.

Legouis, P. Une amitié franco-anglaise au XVIIIe siècle. Bull. de l'Acad. de Mâcon, 1934.

Smith, M. E. Une Anglaise intellectuelle en France sous la Restauration: Miss H. **WILLIAMS**. Paris, 1927.

Mergell, B. **WOLFRAM VON ESCHENBACH** und seine französischen Quellen. Münster 1935-43. Cf. M, 46-47.

Saltzmann, H. Wolfram von Eschenbach's Willehalm und seine französische Quelle. Progr. Pillau, 1884.

San Marte. Ueber Wolframs von Eschenbach Rittergedicht Wilhelm von Orange und sein Verhältnis zu altfranzösischen Dichtungen gleichen Inhalts. Leipzig, 1871.

Christensen, F. The Date of **WORDSWORTH'S** The Birth of Love. MLN, 1938.

Haustein, M. Die französische Literatur im Urteile der englischen Romantiker Wordsworth, Coleridge, Southey. Diss. Leipzig, 1921.

Logan, J. V. Wordsworth in France (1793). TLS, 20.XI.1937.

Wright, H. G. The Reflection of Wordsworth's Personality in his Choice of French Writers. MLR, 42, 1947.

Krause, K. **WYCHERLEY** und seine französischen Quellen. Diss. Halle, 1883.

Killen, A. M. Some French Influences in the Works of W. B. **YEATS** at the End of the Nineteenth Century. CLS, 8, 1942.

Pauly, Marie-Hélène. W. B. Yeats et les symbolistes français. RLC, 20, 1940.

Des Robert, F. Voyage d'un Anglais (A.

YOUNG) à Metz. Mém. de l'Acad. de Stanislas, 5. Sér., 10. Nancy, 1892.
Stoudemire, S. A. Gil y **ZARATE'S** Translations of French Plays. MLN, 1933.
Brull, M. Le poète romantique cubain Juan Clemente **ZENEA** et l'influence française. Paris, 1937.
Scholte, J. H. Philipp von **ZESEN** in Frankrijk. NPh, 28, 1943.

CHAPTER TWENTY-FOUR

The French Language.

1. Influences upon Individual Countries.

Arnold, F. R. Ambassadors of France. (Teachers of French). MLJ, 1921.
Baldensperger, F. Comment le XVIIIe siècle expliquait l'universalité de la langue française. Etudes d'histoire littéraire, 1. Sér. Paris, 1907.
—— Le rebondissement de la langue française aux alentours de 1830. Mélanges J. J. Salverda de Grave. Groningen, 1934.
—— A propos de la langue française dans le monde. FR, 1936.
Broche, G. E. Le Discours de Rivarol sur l'universalité de la langue française. RAF, 1930.
Brunot, F. Le Français hors de France au XVIIIe siècle. In: Histoire de la langue française. Paris, 1934.
Chambon, A. La langue française sous l'occupation. FR, 20, 1947.
Estienne, H. Précellence de la langue française (1579). Nouv. édition par Huguet. Paris, 1896.
Foncin, P. La langue française dans le monde. Paris, 1900.
Hazard, P. La langue française et la guerre. RDM, 1920.
Hovelacque, W. Les limites de la langue française. In: Revue de linguistique et de philologie comparée, 14, 1880-81.
Mohn, A. Pour la langue française. Amitié franco-suédoise de Stockholm, 1921.
Novicow, J. Le français langue internationale de l'Europe. Paris, 1911.
Pierre, A. La langue française en Europe centrale et dans les Balkans au XVIIIe siècle. L'Europe centrale, 1.XII.1934.
Plattard, J. Un chapître de l'histoire de la langue française: où et comment les étrangers séjournant en France au XVIIe siècle apprenaient le français. RCC, 28.II.1937.
Roumiguière, H. Le Français dans les relations diplomatiques. Berkeley, 1926.
Schoell, F. La langue française dans le monde. Paris, 1936.
Baldensperger, F. Rivarol à l'épreuve: vicissitudes récentes du français aux Etats-Unis. (**AMERICA**). NPh. 30, 1946.
Bayer, H. G. French Names in our Geography. RR, 1930.
Carrel, M. La question de l'enseignement du français aux Etats-Unis. Revue pédagogique, 15.VIII.1909.
Duby, C. L'enseignement du français aux Etats-Unis. Revue, 15.IV.1902.
Elliot, A. Contributions to a History of the French Language of Canada. AJPh, 6, 1885.
Fermaud, A. Le Français au Canada. Bull. de l'Institut national genevois, 34, 1897.
Fortier, Alcée. The French Language in Louisiana and the Negro-French Dialect. PMLA, 1886.
Geddes. American-French Dialect Comparison. MLN, 13, 1898.
Gresley, O. L'enseignement du français en Acadie (1604-1926). Diss. Paris, 1925.
Jones, H. M. Note on the Knowledge of French in XVIIIth Century America. SPh, 24, 1927.
McDavid, R. I. The Influence of French on Southern American English. Linguistics, 6, 1948.
Muller, H. F. La langue française aux Etats-Unis. Le Français moderne, Jan., 1935.
Pulhod, M. L'enseignement du français dans un collège américain. Revue pédagogique, 15.XII.1910.
Schoell, F. L. Le français en Amérique latine. RP, 1936.
Seybolt, R. F. Teaching of French in Colonial New York. RR, 1919.
Spurlin, P. M. The Founding Fathers' Knowledge of French. FR, 20, 1946.
Davignon, H. Les écrivains flamands et la langue française. (**BELGIUM**). NL, 4. IX. 1937.
Anon The French Language in **ENGLAND.** NAR, Oct., 1840.
—— The Use of Foreign (French) Phrases. Literature, 20.VII.1901.
Behrens, D. Beiträge zur Geschichte der französischen Sprache in England. Heilbronn, 1884.
—— Zur Lautlehre der französischen Lehnwörter im Mittelenglischen. Heilbronn, 1886.
—— Zur äusseren Geschichte der französischen Sprache in England. In: Paul's Grundriss I, Strassburg, 1901.

Berkebusch. Zur Vergleichung der französischen und englischen Syntax. Progr. Göttingen, 1873.
Betz, L. P. Französisches in der englischen Sprache. Frankfurter Zt., 182, 1901.
Bonnier, C. Le français parlé et écrit aujourd'hui en Angleterre. ZFSL, 21, 1898.
Clover, B. The Mastery of the French Language in England from the XIth to the XIVth Century. New York, 1888.
Draat, F. van. Aliens. Influx of French Words into English. ESn, 72, 1937-38.
Eckhardt, E. Der Uebergang zur germanischen Betonung bei Wörtern französischer Herkunft im Frühneuenglischen. ESh, 75, 1942.
Elze, K. Ueber die Beziehungen des Französischen und Englischen. In: Grundriss der englischen Philologie, Halle, 1888.
Feyerabend, W. In What Manner did the French Influence the Formation of the English Language? Progr. Elberfeld, 1881.
Gay. Anglo-French Words in English. MLN, 14, 1899.
Gessler, J. Fragments d'anciens traités pour l'enseignement du français en Angleterre. Paris, 1933.
Gudra, G. Das Neufranzösische im Wortbilde des Englischen. Progr. Wien, 1880.
Hamerton, G. French and English, a Comparison. AM, 58-59, 1886 & London, 1889.
Héricher, Le. Glossaire étymologique anglo-normand, ou l'anglais ramené à la langue française. Paris, 1885.
Lambley, K. The Teaching and Cultivation of the French Language in England During Tudor and Stuart Times. Manchester U.P., 1920.
Legion (pseud.). The Humble Remonstrance of the Mob of Great Britain against the Importation of French Words. In: Annual Register for 1758.
Leidig, P. Französische Lehnwörter und Lehnbedeutungen im Englischen des 18. Jahrhunderts. Diss. Kiel, 1938. Bochum, 1941.
Liebermann, F. Englisch und Französisch im 12. Jahrhundert. Archiv, 1900.
MacKenzie, F. Les relations de l'Angleterre et de la France d'après le vocabulaire. I. Les infiltrations de la langue et de l'esprit français. Paris, 1939.
Mossé, F. On the Chronology of French Loan-Words in English. ESs, 25, 1943.
Ritchie, R. L. G. Early Instances of French Loan-Words in Scots and English. Fesschrift M. K. Pope. Manchester, 1939.
Schreibner, O. Ueber die Herrschaft der französischen Sprache in England in der Zeit vom XI.-XIV. Jahrhundert. Progr. Annaberg, 1880.
Sykes, F. H. French Elements in Middle English. Oxford, 1899.
Thommerel, J. P. Recherches sur la fusion du franco-normand et de l'anglosaxon. Paris, 1841.
Thompson, A. W. French, the Chief Source of English Military Words. FR, 18, 1945.
Vising, J. Etude sur le dialecte anglonormand au XIIIe siècle. Upsala, 1881.
—— Le français en Angleterre. Mém sur les études de l'Anglo-Normand. Macon, 1901.
—— Franska språket i England. Progr. Göteborg, 1901.
Andenmatten, J. Etymologien der wichtigsten deutschen Fremdwörter französischen Ursprungs. **(GERMANY)** Progr. Amberg, 1880.
Brandstaeter, F. A. Die neuesten Gallicismen in unserer Litteratur. Archiv, 1868.
—— Die Gallizismen in der deutschen Schriftsprache, besonders in der neueren schönwissenschaftlichen Literatur. Leipzig, 1874.
Brisson, A. Une chaire française à l'Université de Berlin. Le Temps, 10.XII. 1901.
Dorfeld, C. Beiträge zur Geschichte des französischen Unterrichts in Deutschland. Beilage zum Programm des Grossherzogl. Gymnasiums Giessen, 1891-92.
Friedwagner, M. La question du français en Autriche. Neue Freie Presse, 9.VIII.1902.
Groth, K. Die Gallicismen in der deutschen Schriftsprache. Gegenwart, 5, 1873.
Kassewitz, J. Die französischen Wörter im Mittelhochdeutschen. Strassburg, 1890.
Katara, P. Das französische Lehngut in den mittelniederdeutschen Denkmälern des 13. Jahrhunderts. Annales Acad. Scientiarum Fennicae. Helsinki, 1942.
Keiper, P. Französisch in der Pfalz. Krit. Jahresbericht über die Fortschritte der roman. Philologie, 2, 1891.
Kelle, G. Die Verwälschung in der deutschen Sprache. Nord & Süd, May 1882.
Kluge, F. Französische Einflüsse. In: Deutsche Studentensprache. Strassburg, 1895.
Lange, P. A. Ueber den Einfluss des Französischen auf die deutsche Sprache im

17. und 18. Jahrhundert. Festschrift P. A. Geijer. Upsala, 1901.

Laubert, K. Die französischen Fremdwörter in unserem heutigen Verkehr. Progr. Danzig, 1866.

Leber. Quels services l'Allemagne a-t-elle rendus à l'étude de la langue française? Progr. Bonn, 1870.

Lévy, P. La langue française en Alsace et en Lorraine de 1648 à 1870. Le Français moderne, 1933.

Liesche, H. Einfluss der französischen Sprache auf die deutsche. Progr. Dresden, 1871.

Maximer, T. Beiträge zur Geschichte der französischen Wörter im Mittelhochdeutschen. Diss. Marburg, 1897.

Mentz, R. Französisches im mecklenburgischen Platt und in den Nachbardialekten. Progr. Delitzsch, 1897-99.

Moers, J. Die Form- und Begriffsveränderungen der französischen Fremdwörter im Deutschen. Progr. 1884.

Oehmann, E. Studien über die französischen Worte im Deutschen im 12. und 13. Jahrhunderte. Neuphilol. Mitteil. Helsinki, 1918.

—— Der französische Einfluss auf die deutsche Sprache im Mittelalter. Ibid. 1931.

Palander, H. Der französische Einfluss auf die deutsche Sprache im XII. Jahrhundert. Mém. de la Société néo-phil. à Helsingfors, 3, 1902.

Papillon, J. Recueil des mots français ou conservés à peu près tels, usités dans la langue allemande. Mém. de la Soc. acad. de l'Aube, 3. Sér., 27, 1890.

Poitevin, A. La langue allemande et les mots français. RB, 1890.

Rosenqvist, A. Der französische Einfluss auf die mittelhochdeutsche Sprache in der zweiten Hälfte des XIV. Jahrhunderts. Helsinki, 1943.

Schuchardt, H. Das Französische im neuen Deutschen Reich. In: Romanisches und Keltisches. Strassburg, 1886.

Suolahti, H. Der französische Einfluss auf die deutsche Sprache im 13. Jahrhundert. Helsingfors, 1933.

Varhagen, H. Ueber einen Sammelband französischer Grammatiken des XVI. Jahrhunderts auf der Erlanger Bibliothek. Neuphil. Centralblatt, 1893.

Welcker, F. Warum muss die französische Sprache weichen und wo zunächst? Giessen, 1814.

Wittstock, A. Zur Geschichte der deutschen Sprachreinigung. MLIA, 1888.

Wolff, H. Der Purismus in der deutschen Litteratur des siebzehnten Jahrhunderts. Diss. Strassburg, 1888.

Zeydel, E. H. The German Language in the Prussian Academy of Sciences. PMLA, 41, 1926.

Asselin, C. La langue française en **HOLLANDE**. L'Européen, 26.XI.1930.

Riemens, K. J. Esquisse historique de l'enseignement du français en Hollande du XVIe au XIXe siècle. Leyde, 1919.

Salverda de Grave, J. J. L'influence de la langue française en Hollande d'après les mots empruntés. Paris, 1913. Cf. also Tijdschrift voor nederl. taal en letterkunde, 21, 1903.

Vreese, de. Gallicismen in het Zuid-Nederlandsch. Museum, 8, 1900.

Delattre, R. P. Notre langue en Hongrie. (**HUNGARY**). Nouvelle Revue de Hongrie, 1934.

Allario, C. I principali francesismi da evitarsi nella lingua parlata e scritta. (**ITALY**). Torino, 1879.

Denina, C. Dell' uso della lingua francese nel Piemonte. 3 vols. Milano, 1820.

Fanfani, P. Lettera d'un tedesco sull' infrancesamento della lingua italiana. Firenze, 1871.

Gozzi, C. L'invasione della lingua francese in Italia. NAnt, 1.V.1932.

Haupt, F. Lettera d'un tedesco sull' infrancesamento dello stile italiano. Losanna, 1798.

Melon, P. Le français dans la vallée d'Aoste. Nouvelle Revue, 15.VII.1901.

Meyer, P. De l'expansion de la langue française en Italie pendant le moyen âge. Atti del Congresso internaz. di Scienze storiche, 1903. Roma, 1904.

Schioffini, A. Egemonia linguistica. Il regresso del francese. Romana, 1937.

Terracini, B. A. La lingua delle canzoni popolari piemontesi. L'elemento francese. Torino, 1914.

Doroszewski, W. La langue française en Pologne. (**POLAND**). Revue des Etudes slaves, 14, 1934.

Vasconcellos, Carolina Michaëlis de. Sources du Léxique portugais: Les éléments français. (**PORTUGAL**). Bull. des Etudes portugaises, 2, 1936.

Iordan, I. Le français en **ROUMANIE**. Le Français moderne, Oct., 1934.

Montussaint, F. La langue française en **RUSSIE** de 1803 à 1903. Revue des Etudes franco-russes, 3, 1903.

Seris, H. Los nuevos galicismos. (**SPAIN**). Hisp., May, 1925.
Nordfelt, A. Om franska lånord i svenska. (**SWEDEN**). Nyfilologiska sällskapets i Stockholm publikation, 1901.

2. Influences upon Individual Authors.

Bradley, H. **CAXTON'S** Dialogues English and French, 1481-83. EETS, 1901.
Kirby, T. A. The French of **CHAUCER'S** Prioress. Festschrift William A. Read. Baton Rouge (La.), 1940.
Elzinga, J. J. B. Les mots français et les gallicismes dans le Hollandsche Spectator de Justus van **EFFEN**. Leyden, 1923.
ERANDEL, P. A French Garden for English Ladyes and Gentlewomen to Walk in. London, 1605.
Bock, F. Französische Einflüsse in **GOETHES** Sprache. Progr. Wien, 1903.
Engel, H. Goethe in seinem Verhältnis zur französischen Sprache. Diss. Göttingen, 1937.
Weill, F. Goethe et la langue française. FR, 1932.
Kaindl, R. F. Les mots français dans **GOTTFRIED DE STRASBOURG**. ZRPh, 17, 1893.
Bourland, Caroline B. Gabriel **HARVEY** and the Modern Languages. HLQ, 4, 1940.
Curtis, J. A 16th Century English-French Phrase-Book, **HOLLYBAND'S** French Littelton. Festschrift zum 15ten Neuphilologentage Frankfurt, 1912.
Pollard, A. F. Claudius Holleyband and his French Schoolmaster and French Littelton. Transact. of Bibliog. Soc., 12, 1916.
Oriol, A. **LEOPARDI** et la langue française. BI, 1. Cf. Journal des Débats, 24.IV.1900.
Kluge, F. Das französische Element im **ORMULUM**. ESn, 22, 1896.
Philips, E. The French of E. A. **POE**. American Speech, 1927.
Pellisson, M. Un Allemand apologiste de la langue française. (**SCHWAB**). MF, 1.IX.1906.
Jobin, A. & Wilcy, N. L. **SEALSFIELD'S** Knowledge of French. Papers of the Michigan Academy, 31, 1947.
Nicholson, B. **SHAKESPEARE'S** French. N&Q, 222, 1872.
Rebillon-Lambley, K. Shakespeare's French. Festschrift L. E. Kastner. Cambridge, 1932.
:az, A. Kannte Shakespeare Französisch? Frankfurter Zt., Nov., 1887.
Hildebrand, F. L'élément français dans le Liber censualis de Guillaume Ier d'Angleterre. (**WILLIAM I**). ZRPh, 8, 1884.
Wiener, L. French Words in **WOLFRAM VON ESCHENBACH**. AJPh, 16, 1896.

CHAPTER TWENTY-FIVE

The French Revolution and Napoleon.

(See also Emigrants and Refugees, I. IV. 4.)

1. Influences upon Individual Countries.

Albert, M. Napoléon et les théâtres populaires. RP, 1902.
Baldensperger, F. La France napoléonienne et la littérature étrangère. Revue des Etudes napoléoniennes, 1914.
Bède, J. A. Quatorze Juillet et sa fortune littéraire (1789-1902). Cahiers d'histoire de la Révolution fr., 1 (New York), 1947.
Bersaucourt, A. de. Napoléon au théâtre. Revue mondiale, 1927.
Buenzod, E. Die französische Revolution als Bühnenstoff. Neue Zürcher Zt., 30. VIII.1947.
Chassé, C. Napoléon par les écrivains. Paris, 1921.
Ciampini, R. Napoleone visto dai contemporanei. Torino, 1930.
Damade, L. Histoire chantée de la Première République, 1789 à 1799. Paris, 1892.
Dechamps, J. La légende de Napoléon à travers le monde. Napoléon, 1926.
—— La légende napoléonienne. Le mot et la chose. Le Flambeau, 1927.
—— La légende de Napoléon: Remarques sur le folklore et l'imagerie. RFB, 1928.
—— La légende de Napoléon et la littérature comparée. RLC, 9, 1929.
—— La légende et l'histoire de Napoléon. FQ, 1929.
—— Sur la légende de Napoléon. Paris, 1931.
Delahaye, H. La légende de saint Napoléon. Mélanges Pirenne. Bruxelles, 1926.
Deschamps, G. Le Napoléonisme littéraire. In: La Vie et les livres, Paris, 1894.
Duret, T. Les Napoléons, réalité et imagination. Paris, 1909.
Ewert, M. Napoleon-Romane. LE, 3.

Guérard, A. Sur la légende napoléonienne: identité de la légende et de l'histoire. Le Flambeau, 1927.
Hazard, P. Tendences romantiques dans la littérature de la Révolution. RHLF, 1907.
Hellmann, O. Napoleon im Spiegel der Dichtung. Glogau, 1914.
Holzhausen, P. Napoleons Tod im Spiegel der zeitgenössischen Presse und Dichtung. Frankfurt, 1902.
Kircheisen, F. Bibliographie Napoleons. Berlin, 1902.
Larchey, L. La Marseillaise à l'étranger. Ann. polit. et litt., 17.VII.1898.
Larroumet, G. Napoléon au théâtre. Le Temps. 7.VIII.1899.
Lecomte, L. H. Napoléon et l'Empire racontés par le théâtre (1797-1899). Paris, 1900.
Lote, G. Napoléon et le romantisme français. RF, 1913.
Lumbroso, A. La Napoleonità e i suoi ricorsi storici. Marzocco, 4.XII.1932.
Mahrenholz, R. Die französische Revolution auf der Schaubühne und in der Tagesdramatik. Archiv, 94, 1895.
Monglond, A. La France révolutionnaire et impériale. Grenoble, 1931 ff.
Perennes, J. B. De l'influence des évènements politiques sur la littérature depuis 1789. Paris, 1829.
Pierray, C. Le duc de Reichstadt dans le drame. Revue des Revues, Sept., 1902.
Pilon, E. Les lettres françaises et Napoléon. RFA, 1899.
Reinhardtstoettner, C. von. Napoleon I. in der zeitgenössischen Dichtung. In: Aufsätze und Abhandlungen. Berlin, 1887.
Romero, J. L. La Revolución francesca y el pensamiento historiografico. Buenos Aires, 1940.
Salvatorelli, L. Napoleone: mito, romanzo e storia. Pegaso, 1932.
Siklosy, J. Napoleon auf der Bühne. Neues Pester Journal, 316, 1899.
Söderhjelm, A. Rapports intellectuels pendant la Révolution. Helsingfors, 1903.
Dechamps, J. Témoignages américains et anglais sur la légende de Napoléon. (**AMERICA**). RLC, 17, 1937.
Macartney, C. E. & Dorrance, G. The Bonapartes in America. Philadelphia, 1939.
Mello Franco, A. de. O Indio brasileiro e a Revolução Francesa. Rio de Janeiro, 1937.
Schalk de la Faverie, A. Napoléon et l'Amérique; histoire des relations franco-américaines. Paris, 1917.
Vallaux, C. La légende napoléonienne aux Etats-Unis. MF, 15.I.1925.
AUSTRIA: See Germany.
Verhaegen, P. La Belgique sous la domination francaise, 1797-1814. (**BELGIUM**). Bruxelles, 1922-29.
Adams, M. R. Studies in the Literary Background of English Radicalism with Special Reference to the French Revolution. (**ENGLAND**). Franklin & Marshall College Stud., 5. Lancaster (Pa.), 1947.
Alger, J. G. Englishmen in the French Revolution. London, 1889.
Bernstein, S. English Reactions to the French Revolution. Science & Society, 9, 1945.
Cestre, C. La Révolution française et les poètes anglais (1789-1809). Paris, 1906.
Dechamps, J. Napoléon en Angleterre. FQ, 10, 1928.
—— Etudes sur la formation de la légende de Napoléon: En Belgique avec les Anglais après Waterloo. RLC, 10, 1930.
—— La Révolution française et les lettres anglaises. CLS, 2, 1941.
Dowden, E. The French Revolution and English Literature. London, 1897.
Gregory, A. The French Revolution and the English Novel. New York, 1915.
Hancock, A. E. The French Revolution and the English Poets. New York, 1899.
Hudson, A. P. & Virginia M. The Coast of France How Near! French Invasion and English Literature, 1793-1805. SAQ, 40, 1941.
Klingberg, F. J. & Hustvedt, S. B. The Warning Drum: The British Home Front Faces Napoleon: Broadsides of 1803. UCPPh, 1944.
Lehmann, K. Die Auffassung und Gestaltung des Napoleonproblems im englischen Drama. Erlangen, 1931.
Mailahn, W. Napoleon in der englischen Geschichtsschreibung von den Zeitgenossen bis zur Gegenwart. Berlin, 1937.
McCourt, E. A. The Invasion Theme in English Poetry. Dalhousie Review, 22, 1942.
Oman, Carola. Britain against Napoleon. London, 1942.
Quinlan, M. J. Anti-Jacobin Propaganda in England, 1792-94. Journalism Quarterly, 16, 1939.

Speaight, F. Révolution française et romantisme anglais. RHPhC, 1946.
Thompson, J. M. English Witnesses of the French Revolution. Oxford, 1938.
Thudichum, C. Napoleon und die englische Sprache. NSp, 9, 1901.
Yvon, P. Traits d'union normands avec l'Angleterre avant, pendant et après la Révolution. Caen, 1919.
Anon. De l'influence de la Restauration sur la littérature allemande. (GERMANY). Nouvelle Revue Germanique, 27, 1851.
Arnold, E. 1812 im deutschen Volksliede. Leipziger Zt. Wissenschaftl. Beilage, 31, 1912.
Bianquis, G. Les écrivains allemands et la Révolution française. RCC, 1939.
Braubach, M. Die katholischen Universitäten Deutschlands und die französische Revolution. Historische Jb, 149, 1929.
Carnot, H. Echos de la Révolution française en Allemagne. Revue Indépendante, 1845.
Chuquet, A. Les écrivains allemands et la Révolution française. RCC, 18.I. 1894.
Cohn, F. L. The Worship of Napoleon in German Poetry. MLQ, 1, 1940.
Craemer, U. Napoleon in Weimar am 23. Juli, 1807. JbGG, 20, 1934.
Dresch, J. De la Révolution française à la Révolution hitlérienne. Paris, 1946.
Dunan, M. Napoléon dans la littérature allemande contemporaine. "Napoléon", 1926.
Ester, K. d'. Die schöne Literatur und rheinische Presse unter französischer Herrschaft. Kölnische Volkszeitung, Lit. Beilage, 15, 1912.
Gaehtgens zu Ysentorff, H. Napoleon I im deutschen Drama. Frankfurt, 1903.
Gebauer, C. Das französische Element im Theaterleben Magdeburgs während der Fremdherrschaft. Geschichtsblätter für Stadt und Land. (Magdeburg), 1907.
Geiger, L. Franzosenschwärmerei und deutsche Gesinnung, 1815. In: Aus Alt-Weimar. Berlin, 1897.
Gooch, G. P. Germany and the French Revolution. London, 1920.
Hildebrand, R. Aus unserer französischen Zeit. ZDU, 7, 1893.
Hirschstein, H. Die französische Revolution im deutschen Drama und Epos nach 1815. Stuttgart, 1912.
Holzhausen, P. Die Anfänge Bonapartes im Spiegel der zeitgenössischen deutschen Dichtung. Beilage zur Allg. Zt., 234, 1898.
—— Napoleon im deutschen Drama. Bühne und Welt, 2, 1900.
—— Napoleon in der deutschen lyrischen Dichtung. Zeiten und Völker, 1911.
Katt, F. Berliner Theaterverhältnisse zur Franzosenzeit, 1807-08. Deutsche Bühnengenossenschaft, 29, 1900.
Koch, M. Die deutsche Litteratur und die französische Revolution. Deutsches Wochenblatt, 5-6, 1892.
Krieger, H. Frankreich im Urteil der Hamburger Zeitschriften, 1789-1810. Hamburg, 1934.
Landau, P. 1812 in der Dichtung. Aus Kunst und Leben, Beilage der Post, 422, 1912 & in Rhein.-Westfäl. Zt., 1056, 1912.
Landsberg, H. Die französische Revolution im deutschen Drama. National Zt., 286-88, 1900.
Lerminier. De nos constitutions depuis 1789 et des rapports de la France et de l'Allemagne. RDM, 1.XII.1832.
Levi, L. Robespierre dans le théâtre allemand. Ann. Revol., 1908.
Levy-Bruehl. L'Allemagne littéraire et Napoléon I. RB, 1890.
Liensberger, J. Der Tiroler Freiheitskampf im Lichte dramatischer Dichtung. Vorarlberger Volksblatt, 158, 1909.
Niemeyer, E. Die Schwärmerei für Napoleon in der deutschen Dichtung. ALG, 1875.
Raif, A. F. Die Urteile der Deutschen über die französische Nationalität im Zeitalter der Revolution und der deutschen Erhebung. Berlin, 1911.
Rose, J. H. Germany and the French Revolution. Contemporary Rev., 1920.
Rosenthal, E. Waterloo in der deutschen Dichtung. Hannoverland, 1915.
Rovere, J. Les survivances françaises dans l'Allemagne napoléonienne depuis 1815. Paris, 1918.
Rudolf, P. Frankreich im Urteil der Hamburger Zeitschriften in den Jahren 1789-1810. Hamburger Seminar für roman. Sprachen, 1933.
Saint-Mathurin, B. Le culte de Napoléon en Allemagne de 1815 à 1848. Revue des Etudes napoléoniennes, 1917.
Sauer, E. Die französische Revolution von 1789 in zeitgenössischen deutschen Flugschriften und Dichtungen. Weimar. Forschungen, 44, 1913.
Schelling, A. Weimar und die französische Revolution. Wissen & Leben, June, 1921.
Schoemann, M. Weltanschauliche und

stilgeschichtliche Wandlungen im deutschen Napoleondrama. Bonn, 1929.
—— Napoleon in der deutschen Literatur. Berlin, 1931.
Stahl, Sophie. Die Befreiungskriege in Literatur und Kunst 1813-15. Hamburg, 1912.
Stearns, H. E. Germany's Military Heroes of the Napoleonic Era in her Post-War Historical Drama. U. of Michigan, 1939.
Stern, A. Der Einfluss der Französischen Revolution auf das deutsche Geistesleben. Stuttgart, 1928.
Valentin, B. Napoleon und die Deutschen. Berlin, 1925.
Wohlrabe, M. Die Freiheitskriege im Spiegel des Romans und der Dramenliteratur. Leipzig, 1913.
Roche, E. La censure en Hollande pendant la domination française, 1810-13. (HOLLAND). Paris, 1923.
Eckhardt, A. Les Français en Hongrie pendant la Révolution. (HUNGARY). La République hongroise, 1947.
Ciampini, R. Un osservatore italiano della Rivoluzione francese. (ITALY). Firenze, 1934.
Claretie, J. Napoléon Ier et la Comédie française en Italie. RB, 28.III.1896.
Dejob, C. Supplement à un Essai de bibliographie pour servir à l'histoire de l'influence française en Italie de 1796 à 1814. Toulouse, 1893.
Deschamps, G. Les Français à Rome en 1798. Le Temps, 18.II.1900.
Desfeuilles, P. Le goût français à la fin du Consulat et les Italiens d'après la Domenica. NRI, 15.X.1920.
Hazard, P. La Révolution française et les lettres italiennes, 1789-1815. Diss. Lyon. Paris, 1910.
—— L'âme italienne, de la Révolution française au Risorgimento. RDM, 1910.
Isola, M. dell'. Napoléon dans la poésie italienne à partir de 1821. Paris, 1927.
Natali, G. Cultura e poesia in Italia nell' età napoleonica. Torino, 1930.
Omodeo, A. Primato francese e iniziativa italiana. In: Figure e Passioni del Risorgimento. Palermo, 1932.
Paglicci-Brozzi, A. Sul teatro giacobbino ed anti-giacobbino in Italia. Milano, 1887.
Petiet, R. Influence de la Révolution française sur le Risorgimento de l'Unité italienne. NRI, 1922.
Pitre, G. Canti popolari d'Italia su Napoleone I. Palermo, 1897. Cf. GSLI, 30, 1897.
Poggiolini, A. Ammiratori e giudici della Rivoluzione francese. Firenze, 1901.
Rambaud, J. Naples sous Joseph Bonaparte, 1806-08. Paris, 1911.
Sclopis, F. La domination française en Italie, 1800-14. Paris, 1861.
Szyster, B. La Révolution française et les Juifs, 1789-92. (JEWS). Diss. Toulouse, 1929.
Goudzin, N. La Révolution française et la littérature russe. (RUSSIA). In: La littérature soviétique. Moscou, 1946.
Thiry, R. Napoléon en Russie. RP, 15. VII.1898.
Los Santos Olivier, M. Los Españoles y la Revolución francesa. (SPAIN). Madrid, 1914.
Chapuisat, E. La Révolution française vue de la Suisse. (SWITZERLAND). La Révolution française, July, 1939.
Moeckli-Cellier, M. La Révolution française et les écrivains suisses-romands. Neuchâtel, 1932.
Troesch, E. Die helvetische Revolution im Lichte der deutsch-schweizerischen Dichtung. Leipzig, 1911.
Barac, A. Les Conteurs croates et le régime français en Croatie, 1810-14. (YUGOSLAVIA). Zagreb, 1948.
Boppe, A. Documents inédits sur les relations de la Serbie avec Napoléon I. Belgrade, 1888.

2. Influences upon Individual Authors

Anon. John ADAMS on Napoleon and the French. MB, 1934.
Messeri, A. La Rivoluzione francese e V. ALFIERI. Pistoia, 1893.
Bruce, H. L. BLAKE, Carlyle and the French Revolution. Festschrift Charles Gayley. Berkeley, 1922.
Muny, J. M. William Blake and Revolution. Adelphi, 9, 1932.
Dresch, J. BOERNE et son Histoire inédite de la Révolution française. RLC, 2, 1922.
Barker, E. Edmund BURKE et la Révolution française. Revue philosophique 128, 1939.
Luhn, K. Angelsächsische Berichterstattung über die Ereignisse der französischen Revolution bei Burke, Paine, Mackintosh und Young. Frankfurt, 1941.
Mensel, F. Edm. Burke und die französische Revolution. Berlin, 1913.
Bodenstedt, F. Lord BYRONS Ode an Napoleon Bonaparte. Deutsches Museum, 1859.
Brunner, K. Byrons angebliche Hymne

auf den Tod Napoleons. Archiv, 172, 1937.
Eggert, G. Lord Byron und Napoleon. Leipzig, 1933.
Holzhausen, P. Bonaparte, Byron und die Briten. Frankfurt, 1904.
Morley, J. Byron. Fortnightly Review, Dec., 1870.
Wolff, M. J. Byron und Napoleon. ESn, 69, 1934.
Boyer, G. Autour de **CANOVA** et de Napoléon. REI, 1937.
Dalgas, A. La Rivoluzione francese e i Bonaparte nella poesia di **CARDUCCI**. Rev. napoleon., 8, 1911.
Avenel, G. La Révolution française de Th. **CARLYLE**. Nain jaune, 19.V.1867.
Harrold, C. F. Carlyle's Method in The French Revolution. PMLA, 1928.
—— The Translated Passages in Carlyle's French Revolution. JEGPh, 1928.
Lea, F. A. Carlyle and the French Revolution. Adelphi, 18, 1941.
Larivière, C. de. **CATHERINE** II et la Révolution française. Paris, 1893.
Bonnard, G. The Invasion of Switzerland and English Public Opinion: The Background to S. T. **COLERIDGE'S** France: An Ode. ESs, 22, 1940.
Barni, J. **FICHTE** et la Révolution française. Libre Recherche, Jan., 1859.
Delobel, G. Fichte et les idées de la Révolution française. Ann. Revol. May, 1911.
Crino, S. Napoleone Bonaparte nelle odi di Ugo **FOSCOLO** e di Al. Manzoni. Messina, 1902.
Filippini, E. Le redazioni del Sermone foscoliano contro Napoleone. GSLI, 1928.
Goffis, C. F. La leggenda dell' antibonapartismo dei Sepolcri. RLM, 2, 1946.
Ottolini, A. Napoleone nei giudizi del Foscolo. NAnt, 1.X.1921.
Voretzsch, C. **GAUDYS** Kaiserlieder und die Napoleondichtung. PJb, 1895.
Kozlowski, F. Die Stellung **GLEIMS** und seines Freundeskreises zur französischen Revolution. Euphorion, 1904.
Spadoni, G. Luigi **GODARD** e l'Arcadia giacobina e napoleonica. G. M. Crescembeni Gedächtnisschrift. Macerata, 1028.
Anon. **GOETHE** und Napoleon. Illustr. Familienblatt, 10, 1863.
Baldensperger, F. Napoléon et Goethe contre les illusions rationnelles. RB, 21.IV.1934.
Clery, R. de. Goethe et la Révolution française. La Révolution française, July, 1939.
Dowden, E. Goethe and the French Revolution. Fortnightly Review, 1889.
Eyk, O. van. Napoleon im Spiegel der Goetheschen und der Heineschen Lyrik. Amsterdam, 1933.
Fester, R. Goethe und die französische Revolution. DR, 38, 1912.
Fischer, A. Goethe und Napoleon. Frauenfeld, 1899.
Fournier, A. Goethe und Napoleon. Chron. des Wiener Goethe-Vereins, 1896.
Geiger, L. Goethe und die französische Revolution. Beilage zur Allg. Zt., 296, 1895 & 299, 1896.
—— Goethes Unterredung mit Napoleon. ZVL, 10, 1897.
Gerhard, M. Goethes Erleben der französischen Revolution im Spiegel der Natürlichen Tochter. DVLG, 1, 1923.
Hein, N. Goethe in Luxemburg (1792). Luxemburg, 1940.
Kettner, G. Goethes Natürliche Tochter. Berlin, 1912.
Kircheisen, E. M. Napoleon, Goethe et Wieland. Revue d'histoire diplomatique, 1932.
Kroll, E. Französische Forschungen über die Quelle zu Goethes Natürlicher Tochter. Nord und Süd, Jan., 1899.
Lohmann, K. Goethe und Napoleon. Hamburger Nachrichten, 606, 1908.
Loiseau, H. Goethe et la Révolution française. RLC, 12, 1932.
Menge, K. Goethe und Wieland vor Napoleon in Erfurt und Weimar. ZDU, 5, 1891.
Metz, J. R. Goethe bei Napoleon. Gegenwart, 44, 1898.
Müllensiefen, P. Die französische Revolution und Napoleon in Goethes Weltanschauung. JbGG, 1930.
—— Faust als Napoleon. Kommentar zu der Tragödie II. Teil. Stuttgart, 1932.
Muret, M. Napoléon et Goethe. Journal des Débats, 3.VII.1900.
Pigeon, A. Napoléon Ier et le Second Faust de Goethe. Le Livre et l'Image, 1893.
Samuel, R. Goethe, Napoleon, Kleist. PEGS, NS, 14, 1939.
Schoell, A. Goethe und die französische Revolution. In: Goethe in Hauptzügen seines Lebens und Wirkens. Berlin, 1882.
Sklower, S. Entrevue de Napoléon ler et de Goethe. Lille, 1853.
Sorel, A. Une princesse française dans le théâtre de Goethe. Le Temps, 21.VI. 1899.
Steig, R. Bemerkungen zum Problem

Goethe und Napoleon. Euphorion, 6, 1899-1900.
Stresemann, G. Goethe und Napoleon. Deutsche Stimmen, 16.IV.1922.
Ulmann, H. Faust und Napoleon. Beilage zur Allg. Zt., 165, 1892.
Wolff, M. Napoléon, Goethe et Talma. RB, 18.VIII.1900.
Busse, P. G. A. **GRILLPARZER** und Napoleon. JbGrG, 19, 1910.
Korten, H. Th. **HARDY'S** Napoleon-Dichtung, The Dynasts. Ihre Abhängigkeit von Schopenhauer, ihr Einfluss auf G. Hauptmann. Diss. Rostock, 1919.
Dechamps, J. **HAZLITT** et Napoléon. Rev. des Etudes napoléoniennes, Sept., 1939.
Brun, L. **HEBBEL** et Napoléon. RG, 1932.
Anon. Die französische Revolution und die deutsche Philosophie. **HEGELS** Verhältnis zu Franzosentum und Deutschtum. Volk im Werden, 1939.
Hyppolite, J. La signification de la Révolution française dans la Phénoménologie die Hegel. Revue philosophique, 128, 1939.
Stern, A. Hegel et les idées de 1789. Ibid.
Holzhausen, P. H. **HEINE** und Napoleon. Frankfurt, 1903.
Wendel, H. H. Heine et la Révolution française. La Révolution française, 1936.
Stapfer, P. Napoléon le Grand et Napoléon le Petit dans la poésie satirique de Victor **HUGO**. RCC, 8, 1900.
Granier, H. **IFFLANDS** Theaterleitung während der Franzosenzeit, 1807-09. Deutsche Revue, Feb., 1913.
Holzhausen, P. **IMMERMANNS** Verhältniss zu Napoleon I. Beilage zur Allg. Zt., 12.II.1898.
Bernstein, S. **JEFFERSON** and the French Revolution. Science and Society, 7, 1943.
Hazen, C. D. Jefferson in France. In: Contemporary American Opinion of the French Revolution. Baltimore, 1897.
Redslob, R. La paix perpétuelle de **KANT**, la Révolution française et le droit des gens. Madrid, 1933.
Schrecker, P. Kant et la Révolution française. Revue philosophique, 128, 1939.
Catel. Bonaparte und **KLOPSTOCK** in Syrien. Neue Berliner Monatsschrift, 1802.
Leliwa, H. de. Klopstock républicain. RRh, June, 1929.
Minder, R. Klopstock et la Révolution française. Bull. de la Fac. des Lettres de Strasbourg, Jan., 1932.
Vieux, R. La Révolution française jugée par un poète allemand: Essai sur les Odes révolutionnaires de Klopstock. Mélanges H. Lichtenberger. Paris, 1934.
Wilcox, W. B. Lord **LANSDOWNE** on the French Revolution and the Irish Rebellion. Journ. of Mod. History, 17, 1945.
Finsler, G. **LAVATERS** Beziehungen zu Paris in den Revolutionsjahren 1789-95. Neujahrsblatt der Chorherrnstube, 120. Zürich, 1898.
Perroud, C. Lavater et la Révolution française. La Révolution française, 1898.
Hazard, P. **LEOPARDI** et Napoléon. Revue des Etudes napoléoniennes, 1914.
Alfero, G. A. Una eco tedesca del Cinque Maggio di A. **MANZONI**: La Morte di Napoleone, di Adelbert von Chamisso. GSLI, 79, 1922.
Bedarida, H. De quelques adaptations anciennes de l'Ode de Manzoni sur Napoléon, avec une version nouvelle. Crit. & Dante, 1934.
Benvenuti, E. Il Cinque Maggio del Manzoni tradotto di W. Goethe. Marzocco, 16, 1911.
Lesca, G. Postille inedite di A. Manzoni a storici della Rivoluzione francese. NAnt, 1931 & Convivium, 1934.
Meschia, G. A. Ventisette traduzioni in varie lingue del Cinque Maggio. Foligno, 1883.
Morel-Fatio. Une traduction espagnole du Cinque Maggio. Revue critique d'histoire et de litt., 28.III.1881.
Ovidio, F. d'. Il Cinque Maggio in Ispagna. In: Nuovi Studii Manzoniani. Milano, 1908.
Porta, A. Napoleone, Manzoni e Byron. Mélanges Venturi. Pavia, 1923.
Quintavalle, A. Due traduzioni del Cinque Maggio. NAnt, 1929.
Roth, G. Lamartine: L'Ode Bonaparte inspirée par Manzoni. RLC, 5, 1925.
Tasca, G. A. Due poesie in morte di Napoleone (Manzoni e Lamartine). Asti, 1919.
Anon. **MARK TWAIN** et la Révolution française. La Révolution française, 65, 1913.
Bourgin, G. Pour deux sonnets (de Guido **MAZZONI** contre Napoleon I). Mélanges de l'Ecole fr. de Rome, 28, 1908.
Parra-Perez, C. **MIRANDA** et la Révolution française. Paris, 1925.
Porena, M. Vincenzo **MONTI** e Napoleone. NAnt, 1928.
Núñez de Arenas. Don Vincente Maria

SANTIVANEZ: un Madrileño en la Revolución francesa. Rev. de la Bibl. Arch., Museo de Madrid, 2, 1925.
Anon. ...**SCHILLERS** französisches Bürgerrecht. WM, 7, 1860 & Europa, 1865.
Batt, M. Schiller's Attitude towards the French Revolution. JEGPh, 1, 1897.
Baumecker, G. Schiller und die französische Revolution. Berlin, 1939.
Meyer, R. M. Schiller und Robespierre. Nation, 19.XII.1896.
Rieger, K. Schillers Verhältniss zur französischen Revolution. Wien, 1885.
Volpers, R. Friedrich **SCHLEGEL** und Napoleon Bonaparte. Die Kultur, 14 (Wien), 1913.
Brightfield, M. F. **SCOTT**, Hazlitt and Napoleon. UCPPh, 1943.
Sen, A. **SHELLEY** and the French Revolution. In: Studies in Shelley. Calcutta, 1936.
Aubry, O. Mme. de **STAEL**, Napoléon et la France. NL, Jan., 1946.
Gautier, P. Mme. de Staël et Napoléon. Paris, 1902.
Zahn, L. Eine Frau kämpft gegen Napoleon: Das Leben der Mme. de Staël. Berlin, 1939.
Allix, E. La philosophie du droit de F. J. **STAHL** (1802-61) et la philosophie de la Révolution française. Ann. de l'Ecole des Sc. politiques, 1897.
Hellinghaus, O. Graf **STOLBERG** über die französische Revolution und den revolutionären Geist seiner Zeit. Histor-polit. Blätter für das kath. Deutschland, 165, 1920.
Hallberg. La Révolution française jugée par un Allemand (**VARNHAGEN D'ENSE**). Mém. de l'Académie de Toulouse, 9me Sér., 3, 1891.
Morandi, C. Pietro **VERI** e la Rivoluzione francese. Archivio storico lombardo, 1929.
Waal, H. **WIELAND** und Napoleon. Weimar, 1933.
Adams, R. Helen Maria **WILLIAMS** and the French Revolution. In: Wordsworth and Coleridge, Festschrift G. M. Harper. Princeton, 1939.
Woodward, L. D. Une adhérente anglaise de la Révolution française, Hélène-Maria Williams et ses amis. Paris, 1930.
Doll, C. **WORDSWORTH** et la Révolution française. L'Alsace française, 7.IX. 1930.
Logan, J. V. England's Peril and Wordsworth. Sewanee Review, 50, 1942.
Ogawa, Z. Wordsworth and French Revolution. In: Studies in English Literature, 17 (Tokyo), 1937.
Lanzac de Laborie. Un Anglais en France à la veille de la Révolution. (A. **YOUNG**). Correspondant, 10.IV. 1932.
Mathiez, A. La France de 1789 vue par A. Young. Revue pol. et parl., 10.VII. 1931.

EIGHTH PART

English Contributions.

CHAPTER ONE

Generalities.

(See also Emigrants & Refugees, I. IV. 4.)

Anon. Observations sur l'anglomanie dédiées aux peuples du Continent. Le Publiciste, (Fructidor et jours complémentaires) de l'an X.

Boyer, B. B. Insular Contribution to Medieval Literary Tradition on the Continent. CPh, 42, 1948.

Goede, C. A. G. A Foreigner's Opinion of England. Boston, 1822.

Loffelt, A. C. English Actors on the Continent. JbShG, 4, 1869.

Rye, W. B. England as Seen by Foreigners. London, 1865.

Ullmann, S. de. Anglicism and Anglophobia in Continental Literature. ML, 27, 1946.

Vaughan, C. E. The Influence of English Poetry upon the Romantic Revival on the Continent. PBA, 6, 1913-14.

Walpole, Sir H. English Domestic Fiction: Its Influence Abroad. TLS, 7.IX. 1940.

CHAPTER TWO

English Influences upon France.

Anon. French Pictures of the English in the Last Century. The Savages of Europe, 1764. Retrosp. Review, 1, 1852-53.

—— French Translations of English Novels. TLS, 7.VIII.1924.

Angell, J. B. Influence of English Literature upon the French. NAR, 86, 1858.

Ascoli, G. La Grande-Bretagne devant l'opinion française depuis la Guerre de Cent Ans jusqu'à la fin du XVIe siècle. Paris, 1927.

—— La Grande Bretagne devant l'opinion française au XVIIe siècle. 2 vols. Paris, 1930.

Bain, M. Les voyageurs français en Ecosse (1770-1830) et leurs curiosités intellectuelles. Paris, 1931.

Baldensperger, F. L'Angleterre et les Anglais vus à travers la littérature française. BURS, 38, 1905.

—— Projet d'établissement d'un théâtre anglais à Paris (1823). RG, 1909.

Barnicoat, C. A. England Seen Through French Eyes. Fortnightly Review, June, 1908.

Bertaut, J. L'anglicisme en France sous la Restauration. RP, 1.V.1918.

—— Le tour d'Angleterre sous la Restauration. Correspondant, 10.X.1920.

Bizet, R. L'influence anglaise sur la littérature contemporaine. AFR, Oct., 1920.

Bonno, G. La Constitution britannique devant l'opinion française de Montesquieu à Bonaparte. Paris, 1932.

—— La culture et la civilisation britanniques devant l'opinion française, de la paix d'Utrecht aux Lettres Philosophiques. Philadelphia, 1948.

Borgerhoff, J. L. Le théâtre anglais à Paris sous la Restauration. Paris, 1912.

Bosières, R. La littérature anglaise en France. RB, 1882.

Boutroux, E. De l'influence de la philosophie écossaise sur la philosophie française. In: Etudes d'histoire de la philosophie. Paris, 1897.

Briggs, E. R. L'incrédulité et la pensée anglaise en France au début du XVIIIe siècle. RHLF, 61, 1934.

Brüch, J. Die Anglomanie in Frankreich. Stuttgart, 1941.

Chantin, N. P. Biographie dramatique des principaux artistes anglais venus à Paris, précis de souvenirs historiques du théâtre anglais à Paris en 1827-28. Paris, 1828.

Davidson, A. F. Des caractères anglais dans les romans français. Macmillan's Mag., 1883.

Davray, H. D. English Literature in France. Academy, 22.VIII.1903.

—— L'activité intellectuelle de l'Angleterre d'après l'ancien Mercure de France (1662-1778). MF, 1.IV.1937.

Devonshire, M. G. The English Novel in France, 1830-70. London, 1929. Cf. TLS, 2.I.1930.

Draper, F. W. M. The Rise and Fall of the French Romantic Drama, with Special Reference to the Influence of Shakespeare, Scott, and Byron. London, 1923.

Fiévée, J. Lettres sur l'Angleterre. Paris, 1802.

Fiquet du Bocage. Lettre sur le théâtre anglais (avec une traduction de l'Avare, comédie de Shadwell, et de la Femme de campagne, comédie de Wycherley). 2 vols. Paris, 1752.

Fontainas, A. How English Writers Have Influenced French Literature. Fortnightly Rev., 1925.

Fougeret de Monbron. Préservatif contre l'anglomanie. Minorque, 1757.

Gaudin, L. S. Les Lettres anglaises dans l'Encyclopédie. New York, 1942.

Geikie, A. A French Impression of Scotland and the Scots in the Year 1784. Transactions of the Franco-Scottish Soc., 1907.

Givry, G. de. De l'influence anglaise sur la littérature française au XIXe siècle. The Green Leaf, 15.III.1927.

Grey, R. French Critics and English Women-Writers. AFR, 1920.

Grubbs, H. A. La Grande-Bretagne devant l'opinion française. Paris, 1930.

Guyot, Y. The Influence of English Thought on the French Mind. Fortnightly Review, July, 1908.

Harpe, Jacqueline de la. Le Journal des Savants et l'Angleterre, 1702-89. UCPPh, 1941.

Hillebrand, K. Französische Studien englischer Zeitgenossen. In: Zeiten, Völker und Menschen. Strassburg, 1892.

Jäckel, H. Der Engländer im Spiegel der französischen Literatur von der Romantik bis zum Weltkrieg. Breslau, 1932.

Johnson, W. B. The English in French Folklore. Contemporary Review, 1928.

Jones, E. Les voyageurs français en Angleterre de 1815 à 1830. Paris, 1930.

Jusserand, J. J. French Ignorance of English Literature in Tudor Times. NC, 1898.

Langlois, C. V. Les Anglais du moyen âge dans la littérature française. Revue historique, 52, 1893.

Laski, H. The English Constitution and French Public Opinion, 1789-94. Politica, 3, 1938.

Leblond, M. A. Les Anglais dans le roman français moderne. La Revue, 15.XI.1903.

Lee, S. The Beginning of French Translation from the English. Transactions of the Bibliographical Society. London, 1907.

Legouis, E. The Appeal of English Letters to a French Student. Oxford U.P., 1930.

Leighton, R. M. The Tradition of the English Constitution in France on the Eve of the Revolution. Diss. Cornell, 1941.

Liebermann, F. Franzosen über Engländer im 13. Jahrhundert. Archiv, 110, 1903.

Liljegren, S. B. Quelques romans anglais source partielle d'une religion moderne. Mélanges Baldensperger. Paris, 1930.

Lovering, S. L'activité intellectuelle de l'Angleterre d'après l'ancien Mercure de France. Paris, 1930.

Lux, J. Les Anglais dans les comédies françaises du XVIIe siècle. RB, 27.V. & 10.VI.1911.

McWilliam, N. French Impressions of English Character (1668-95). FQ, Dec., 1920.

Miller, M. M. Science and Philosophy as Precursors of the English Influence in France: A Study of the Choix des anciens journaux. PMLA, 1930.

—— The English People as Portrayed in Certain French Journals, 1700-1760. MPh, May, 1937.

Morand, P. Les personnages anglais dans la littérature d'imagination en France, du douzième à la fin du dix-huitième siècle. AFR, Sept., 1920.

Mortimer, R. La France et la littérature anglaise. RHPhC, 1946.

Murray, J. A Sixteenth-Century French Traveller in Scotland. French Studies, 2.

Nerval, G. de. Les acteurs anglais à Paris. L'Artiste, 22.XII.1844. Cf. also La France musicale, 19.I.1856.

Nodier, C. Sur le théâtre anglais à Paris. MF, 1827.

Offor, R. A Collection of Books in the University Library, Leeds, Printed Before the XIXth Century Containing Translations from English into French. Proc. of the Leeds Philos. and Lit. Soc., 4, 1936.

Partridge, E. The French Romantics' Knowledge of English Literature. Paris, 1924.

Pasquet, D. La découverte de l'Angleterre au XVIIIe siècle. RP, 15.XII.1920 & 1.I.1921.

Pinto, V. de S. The English Romantics and France. Spectator, 4.I.1946.

Potez, H. Le romantisme français et l'influence anglaise. La Quinzaine, Oct., 1899.

Quarrell, W. H. A Frenchman in London, 1789. N&Q, 189, 1945.

Reesink, H. J. L'Angleterre et la littérature anglaise dans les trois plus anciens périodiques français de Hollande. Paris, 1931.

Remusat, C. de. L'Angleterre vue de

l'ancienne France. In: L'Angleterre au XVIIIe siècle. Paris, 1856.
Renard, G. L'influence de l'Angleterre sur la France. Nouvelle Revue, 35, 1883.
Reynaud, L. Le Romantisme: ses origines anglo-germaniques. Paris, 1926.
Roe, F. C. French Travellers in Britain. London, 1928.
—— Les Français en Ecosse: jadis et aujourd'hui. FQ, 1938.
Rosières, R. La littérature anglaise en France de 1750 à 1800. RB, 19.VIII. 1882.
Sichel, J. Die englische Literatur im Journal étranger. Diss. Heidelberg, 1907.
Smith, M. A. L'influence des lakistes sur les romantiques français. Paris, 1920.
Streeter, H. W. The Eighteenth Century English Novel in French Translation. A Bibliographical Study. New York, 1936.
Tallentyne, S. G. Some French Impressions of England. Monthly Review, Dec., 1906.
Ternant, A. de. English and Americans in French Fiction. Gentleman's Mag., Sept., 1896.
Ullman, S. An XVIIIth Century Comedy on Anglomania in France. ML, 22, 1940.
Varia. Influence anglaise en Savoie. Intermédiaire, Aug.-Nov. 1925.
—— Littérature anglaise traduite en français. Le Navire d'Argent, 1925.
Wade, I. O. The Clandestine Organization and Diffusion of Philosophic Ideas in France from 1700 to 1750. Princeton, 1938.
Weise, O. Franzosen gegen England. Französische Aeusserungen. Berlin, 1940.
Wolfe, H. English Bards and French Reviewers. Monthly Criterion, Jan., 1927.
Wüscher, G. Der Einfluss der englischen Balladenpoesie auf die französische Literatur von 1765 bis 1840. Zürich, 1891.
Yates, F. A. English Actors in Paris During Shakespeare's Life-Time. RES, 1, 1925.

CHAPTER THREE

English Influences upon (and English Comedians in) Germany.

Anon. Ueber die Anglomanie zu Berlin. Berlin, 1786.
—— Englische Litteratur in Deutschland. Europa, 42, 1855. And in: Grenzboten, 23, 1864.
—— Zur Geschichte der englischen Komödianten. Europa, 1865.
—— Zur Geschichte der englischen Komödianten. Zs. für Bücherfreunde, 4, 1900.
—— Die Engländer im Urteile deutscher Dichter und Denker. Freiburger Zt., 54-55, 1901.
Angell, J. B. Influence of the English Literature on the German. NAR, 84, 1857.
Arns, K. Englische Stoffe im modernen deutschen Drama. ZFEU, 23, 1924.
—— Deutsches Englandschrifttum im ersten und zweiten Weltkrieg. NM, 14.
Baesecke, A. Das Schauspiel der englischen Komödianten in Deutschland; seine dramatische Form und seine Entwicklung. Halle, 1935.
Baumgarten, O. Die Bedeutung des englischen Einflusses für die deutsche praktische Theologie. Zs. f. prakt. Theologie, 1897.
Beam, J. N. Die ersten deutschen Uebersetzungen englischer Lustspiele im 18. Jahrhundert. Diss. Jena. Theatergeschichtl. Forschungen, Hamburg, 1906.
Boas, F. S. English Literature in Germany. Literature, 12.V.1900.
Bolte, J. Die Singspiele der englischen Komödianten und ihrer Nachfolger in Deutschland. Theatergeschichtl. Forschungen. Hamburg, 1893. Cf. ESn, 18.
—— Englische Komödianten in Münster und Ulm. JbShG, 36, 1900.
Born, M. Die englischen Ereignisse der Jahre 1685-90 im Lichte der gleichzeitigen Flugschriftenliteratur Deutschlands. Diss. Bonn, 1914.
Brandl, A. Englische Komödianten in Frankfurt. JbShG, 40, 1904.
Cohn, A. Englische Komödianten in Köln, 1592-1656. JbShG, 21, 1886.
Cook, A. S. Germans in England in the XVIIIth Century. MLN, 4, 1889.
Creizenach, W. Die Schauspiele der englischen Komödianten. Deutsche National-Literatur, 23, 1882-95.
—— Die englischen Comödianten in Frankfurt. JbShG, 18, 1883.
Crueger, J. Englische Komödianten in Strassburg im Elsass. ALG, 16, 1886.
Delius, N. Die englischen Komödianten in Deutschland zu Shakespeares Zeit. Bremer Sonntagsblatt, 9.IV.1865.
Eastlake, A. E. The Influence of English Literature on the German Novel and Drama in the Period from 1880 to 1900. London, 1937.

Eckhardt, E. Deutsche Bearbeitungen älterer englischer Dramen. ESn, 68, 1933.
Edwards, O. Englische Dichtung aus Goethes Zeitalter im Licht deutscher Kunstlehre. Bonn, 1930.
Eloesser, A. Englische Komödianten. Vossische Zt., 170, 1902.
Elsasser, R. Ueber die politischen Bildungsreisen der Deutschen nach England. Heidelberg, 1917.
Elze, K. Die englische Sprache und Litteratur in Deutschland. Dresden, 1864.
Engel, E. Das englische Drama in Deutschland. Türmer, 1901.
Evans, M. B. Traditions of the Elizabethan Stage in Germany. PhQ, 1923.
Fleming, W. Das Schauspiel der Wanderbühne. Leipzig, 1931.
Flindt, E. Ueber den Einfluss der englischen Litteratur auf die deutsche des XVIII. Jahrhunderts. Progr. Charlottenburg, 1897.
Frahne, K. H. Die England-Ideologie der Deutschen. NR, July, 1939.
Fredén, G. A propos du théâtre anglais en Allemagne: l'auteur inconnu des Comédies et Tragédies anglaises de 1620. RLC, 8, 1928.
Harris, C. The English Comedians in Germany before the Thirty Years' War: the Financial Side. PMLA, 22, 1907.
Hartleb, H. Deutschlands erster Theaterbau, eine Geschichte des Theaterlebens und der englischen Komödianten unter Landgraf Moritz dem Gelehrten von Hessen-Kassel. Berlin, 1936.
Hashagen, J. Der Einfluss der angelsächsischen Kultur auf das deutsche Mittelalter. GRM, 26, 1938.
Heine, C. Ueber das englische Drama auf der Weimarer Bühne. ZVL, 1891.
Herz, E. Englische Schauspieler und englisches Schauspiel zur Zeit Shakespeares in Deutschland. Theatergeschichtl. Forschungen. Hamburg, 1903.
Hüsgen, S. H. Das Intellektualfeld in der deutschen Arcadia und in ihrem englischen Vorbild. Diss. Münster, 1936.
Jacobi, J. Das deutsche Nationaldrama im Hinblick auf das englische Nationaldrama zu Shakespeares Zeit. Archiv, 58, 1877.
Kelly, J. A. England and the Englishmen in German Literature of the Eighteenth Century. Columbia U.P., 1921.
—— German Visitors to English Theatres in the XVIIIth Century. Princeton, 1937.
Koch, M. Ueber die Beziehungen der englischen Litteratur zur deutschen im 18. Jahrhundert. Leipzig, 1883.
—— Zur Geschichte der englischen Einwirkungen auf die deutsche Litteratur im XVIII. Jahrhundert. ZVL, 4, 1891.
Koennecke, G. Neue Beiträge zur Geschichte der englischen Comödianten. ZVL, 1, 1887.
Krauss, R. Die englischen Komödianten im heutigen Württemberg. Württembergische Vierteljahrshefte f. Landesgeschichte, N.F., 6, 1898 & 7, 1900.
Lensehan, T. England in deutscher Beleuchtung. Halle, 1907.
Maas, H. Die Kindertruppen, ein Kapitel aus der Geschichte der englischen Theatergesellschaften in dem Zeitraume von 1559-1642. Diss. Göttingen, 1903.
Matheson, P. E. German Visitors to England, 1770-95, and their Impressions. Oxford, 1931.
Meissner, J. Die englischen Comödianten zur Zeit Shakespeares in Oesterreich. Wien, 1884.
Metz, R. Die philosophischen Strömungen der Gegenwart in Grossbritannien. Leipzig, 1935.
Meyer, C. F. Englische Komödianten am Hofe des Herzogs Philip Julius von Pommern-Wolgast. JbShG, 38, 1902.
Meyer, R. M. Die Engländer in der deutschen Litteratur. Nation, 1896.
—— Die Engländer im Urteile deutscher Dichter und Denker. Freiburger Zt., 54-55, 1901.
Muncker, F. Anschauungen vom englischen Staat und Volk in der deutschen Literatur der letzten vier Jahrhunderte. SBAW, 1918 & 1925.
Pascal, R. The Stage of the Englische Komödianten. Three Problems. MLR, 35, 1940.
Philippsthal, R. Deutsche Reisende des 18. Jahrhunderts in England. Festschrift zum 13. Neuphilologentage in Hannover. Berlin, 1908.
Powell, G. H. Anti-English Germany, 1649. The Connoisseur, 1903.
Price, L. M. The Reception of English Literature in Germany. Berkeley, 1932.
Randall, A. W. G. In German Eyes. Literary Review, 1924.
Samson, D. N. English Fiction in Germany. Literature, 4.I.1902.
Schloesser, A. Die englische Literatur

in Deutschland von 1895 bis 1934. Jena, 1937.
Schmidt, W. Die Anglistik im zweiten deutsch-englischen Krieg. NSp, 47.
Schoeffler, H. England in der deutschen Bildung. Leipzig, 1929.
Schultze, S. Englisch-deutsche Uebersetzungslitteratur. Internat. Litteraturberichte, 1898.
Schwarz, F. H. Deutsche Anleihen bei englischen Dramatikern. Jb. des Vereins Schweiz. Gymnasiallehrer, 54, 1925.
Sigmann, L. Die englische Literatur von 1800-1850 im Urteil der zeitgenössischen deutschen Kritik. Heidelberg, 1918. And in: NSp, 30, 1922.
Sittard, J. Die englischen Komödianten in Hamburg. Hamburger Corresp., 141, 142, 160, 1890.
Spira, T. Beiträge zur Geschichte und Aufgabe der englischen Studien in Deutschland. Anglia, 1936.
Spirgatis, M. Englische Litteratur auf der Frankfurter Messe von 1561-1620. In: Sammlung bibliothekswiss. Arbeiten. Leipzig, 1902.
Stahl, E. L. Englische Dramatiker auf der deutschen Bühne. Deutsche Kultur im Leben der Völker, 13, 1938.
Streck, R. Deutschkunde beim Uebersetzen englischer Dichtung. NM, 10, 1939.
Thaler, A. The Travelling Players in Shakespeare's England. MPh, 17, 1919-20.
Tittmann, J. Die Schauspiele der englischen Komödianten in Deutschland. Leipzig, 1880.
Trautmann, K. Englische Comödianten in Nürnberg bis zum Abschlusse des 30 jährigen Krieges. ALG, 14, 1886.
—— Englische Komödianten in Rothenburg ob der Tauber. ZVL, 7, 1894.
Weber, C. A. Die Entwicklung der deutschen Englandwissenschaft. In: Deutschlands Erneuerung (München), Nov., 1942.
Whitman, S. Former Influence of English Thought in Germany. NAR, 1901.
Wicke, Amelie. Die Dichter des Göttingerbundes in ihrem Verhältnis zur englischen Literatur und Aesthetik. Diss. Göttingen, 1929.
Wiem, Irene. Das englische Schrifttum in Deutschland von 1518-1600. Leipzig, 1940.
Willoughby, L. A. On Some German Affinities with the Oxford Movement. MLR, 29, 1934.
Wölcken, F. Shakespeares Zeitgenossen in der deutschen Literatur. Berlin, 1929.
Zart, G. Einfluss der englischen Philosophie seit Bacon auf die deutsche Philosophie des XVIII. Jahrhunderts. Berlin, 1881.
Zimmermann, P. Englische Komödianten in Wolfenbüttel. Festschrift H. Paul. Strassburg, 1902. And in: Braunschweiger Anzeigen, 117-22, 1902.
Zschalig, H. Englische Gedichte in deutschem Gewande. Progr. Dresden, 1896.

CHAPTER FOUR

English Influences Upon Other Countries.

Anon. New Englanders and the Old Home. (AMERICA). Quarterly Review, Jan., 1864.
—— British Men of Letters through American Glasses. Pall Mall Mag., Sept., 1902.
Armond, Anna J. de. Americans in England, 1835-69. Delaware Notes, 17, 1944.
Baker, R. P. A History of English-Canadian Literature to the Confederation: Its Relation to the Literature of Great Britain and the United States. Cambridge, 1920.
Boys, R. C. The English Poetical Miscellany in Colonial America. SPh, 42, 1945.
Breton, M. Le. La tradition britannique aux Etats-Unis. RHPhC, 1934.
Brownell, W. C. English Lecturers in America. Galaxy, 1875.
Bruce, P. A. American Feeling toward England. Westminster Review, Oct., 1900.
Cunningham, W. English Influence in the United States. New York, 1916.
Dickason, D. H. The American Pre-Raphaelites. Art in America, 30, 1942.
Le Clair, R. C. Three American Travelers in England: J. R. Lowell, Henry James and Henry Adams. Diss. U. of Pa., 1944.
Limpus, R. M. American Criticism of British Decadence, 1880-1900. Chicago, 1939.
Marquis, T. G. English-Canadian Literature. Toronto, 1913.
McCutcheon, R. P. The First English Plays in New Orleans. AL, 11, 1941.
Myers, R. M. The Old Dominion Looks to London. A Study of English Lit-

erary Influences upon The Virginia Gazette, 1736-66. Va. Mag. Hist. & Biog., 54, 1946.
Pelham, E. English-Canadian Literature. Cambridge History of English Lit., 14, 1916.
Pound, L. The S. W. Cowboy Songs and the English and Scottish Popular Ballads. MPh, 11, 1913.
Ratcliffe, S. K. English Lecturers in America. Fortnightly Review, Oct., 1935.
Sachse, W. L. The Migration of New Englanders to England, 1640-60. AHR, 53, 1948.
Shockley, M. S. First American Performances of Some English Plays. Festschrift G. F. Reynolds. U. of Colorado, 1945.
—— First American Performances of English Plays in Richmond before 1819. Journal of Southern Hist., 13, 1947.
Smither, N. A History of the English Theatre at New Orleans, 1806-42. Louisiana Hist. Quarterly, 28.
Trent, W. English Culture in Virginia. Johns Hopkins U. Studies in History, 1889.
Parkes, Sir Henry. Australian Views of England. **(AUSTRALIA)**. London, 1869.
Mathesius, V. English Literature and the **CZECHO-SLOVAKS**. London, 1921.
Bolte, J. Englische Komödianten in Dänemark und Schweden. **(DENMARK)**. JbShG, 23, 1888.
Dahl, T. English Influences as Reflected in the Danish Language. Stud. Neoph., 14, 1941-42.
Schütte, G. Anglian Legends in Danish Traditions. Acta Philologica Scandinavica, 16, 1943.
Hansen, A. Engelsk indflydelse paa det hollandske Literatur i det 18. Aarhundrede. **(HOLLAND)**. Dansk Tidskrift, June, 1906.
Pienaar, W. J. B. English Influences in Dutch Literature and Justus van Effen as Intermediary. Cambridge U.P., 1929.
Russell, J. A. Dutch Poetry and English: A Study of the Romantic Revival. Amsterdam, 1939.
Swaen, A. E. H. Engelsche zangwijzen bij hollandsche dichters. NPh, 21-24, 1935-38.
Worp, J. Engelsche letterkunde op ons Tooneel. Tydspieghel. Den Haag, 1887.
Gál, S. Early Travellers from Upper **HUNGARY** in England. Danubian Review, 7, 1939.
Tronchon, H. En guise d'introduction à une bibliographie critique de l'influence anglaise en Hongrie. Revue des Etudes hongroises, 1928.
Anon. The Indian Eye on English Life. **(INDIA)**. Calcutta Review, 105, 1897.
Abdu'L-Latif, S. The Influence of English Literature on Urdu Literature. London, 1924.
Das, H. The Early Indian Visitors to England. Calcutta Review, 12-14, 1924-25.
Mitra, B. English Influence on Bengali Literature. Calcutta Review, 81, 1885.
Graves, A. P. Anglo-Irish Literature. **(IRELAND)**. Cambridge Hist. of English Lit., 14, 1916.
Langenfeldt, G. Anti-Englisches in der irländischen Literatur. Archiv, 162, 1932.
Law, H. Anglo-Irish Literature. Dublin, 1926.
Butti, A. L'anglofobia nella letteratura della Cisalpina e del regno italico. **(ITALY)**. Archivio storico lombardo, 31.XII.1909.
Curatulo, G. E. Il tramonto di una leggenda, la tradizionale amicizia inglese. NAnt, Nov., 1935.
Graf, A. L'anglomania e l'influsso inglese in Italia nel secolo XVIII. Torino, 1911.
Jorio, C. Gl'inglesi visti da un patriota italiano del Risorgimento. Convivium, 13, 1941.
Massarani, T. Poeti inglesi nelle versioni italiane. In: Studi d. lett. e d'arte. Firenze, 1899.
Rebora, P. Antiche testimonianze italiane sulla lingua e cultura inglese. Boll. degli studi inglesi in Italia, 1936.
Richards, P. L. The Italian Novel as Influenced by English Gothic Fiction, 1820-40. Diss. Harvard, 1939.
Yates, F. A. An Italian in Restoration England. JWI, 6, 1943.
Doi, K. The Influence of English Authors on Japanese Literature. **(JAPAN)**. Empire Review, March, 1938.
Tchikawa, S. English Influences on Japanese. Transactions of the Royal Soc. of Literature, N. S., 9, 1930.
Ley, C. D. A Inglaterra e os escritores portugueses. **(PORTUGAL)**. Lisboa, 1939.
Zaluar Nunes, M. Algunas influencias anglo-germanicas nas Viagens na minha terra. Boletim de filologia, 3, 1935.
Grimm, P. Traduceri si imitatiuni românesti diepa literatura engleza. **(RUMANIA)**. Dacoromania, 1922-23.

Anon. The Westernization of **RUSSIA.** The Influence of English Literature. TLS, 13.VI.1942.
Simmons, E. J. English Literature in Russia. HSPhL, 13, 1931.
—— English Literature and Culture in Russia (1553-1840). Harvard U.P., 1935.
Anon. Catalunya i les lletres angleses. **(SPAIN).** Revista, 1935.
Barwick, G. F. Recent English Literature in Spain. Library, N. S., 8, 1907.
Ford, J. D. M. English Influence on Spanish Literature in the Early Part of the Nineteenth Century. PMLA, 16, 1901.
Morán, C. G. Influencia de los escritores romanticos ingleses en el romanticismo español. Madrid, 1923.
Peers, E. A. Minor English Influences on Spanish Romanticism. RH, 62, 1924.
Pfandl, L. Das England-Erlebnis der Spanier in den Jahren 1554-58. In: Gesammelte Aufsätze zur Kulturgeschichte Spaniens. Münster, 1938.
Les, K. M. English Players at the Swedish Court (1592-1600). **(SWEDEN).** MLR, 1931.
Murray, J. J. Sweden and the Jacobites in 1716. HLQ, 8, 1945.
Engel, Claire-Eliane. English Novels in **SWITZERLAND** in the XVIIIth Century. CLS, 14-15, 1944-45.
Vetter, T. Zürich als Vermittlerin englischer Literatur im 18. Jahrhundert. Zürich, 1891.
Wildi, M. Der angelsächsische Roman und der Schweizer Leser. Zürich, 1944.
Fiedler, H. G. The First Link between English and Serbo-Croat Literature. **(YUGOSLAVIA).** SR, 6, 1927.

CHAPTER FIVE

Byron.

1. Influences upon Individual Countries.

Axon, W. E. A. Byron's Influence on European Literature. In: Stray Chapters in Literature, Folklore and Archeology. London, 1888.
Blaze de Bury, H. Lord Byron et le Byronisme. RDM, 15.X.1872.
Chasles, V. E. P. Vie et influence de Byron sur son époque. In: Etudes sur la littérature et les moeurs de l'Angleterre au XIXe siècle. Paris, 1850.
Chiarini, G. Lord Byron nella politica e nella letteratura della prima metà del secolo. NAnt, 34, 1891.
Dupuy, E. La jeunesse des romantiques. Paris, 1905.
Etienne, L. Un retour vers Byron d'après des publications récentes en Angleterre, en France et en Allemagne. RDM, 15.II.1869.
Farinelli, A. Byron e il Byronismo. Bologna, 1924.
Gottschall, R. von. Lord Byron und die Gegenwart. Unsere Zeit, 1866.
Grönert, F. Lord Bqron im Roman. Diss. Erlangen, 1921.
Hugo, V. Lord Byron et ses rapports avec la littérature actuelle. Annales romantiques, 1827-28.
Krug, W. G. Lord Byron als dichterische Gestalt in England, Frankreich, Deutschland und Amerika. Diss. Giessen. Potsdam, 1932.
Muellner, L. Lord Byron in seiner Bedeutung für die Entwicklung der modernen Poesie. Neue Freie Presse, 12754, 1900.
Powell, D. Byron's Foreign Critics. Colorado-Wyoming Journal of Letters, 1939.
Russell, B. Byron and the Modern World. JHI, 1, 1940.
Storoschenko, N. J. Byrons Einfluss auf die europäische Literatur. Iz oblasti literatury, Moskva, 1902.
Veselovskii, A. Studies on Byronism. (In Russian). In: Etiudy i kharakteristiki, Moskva, 1907.
Weddigen, O. Lord Byrons Einfluss auf die europäische Litteratur der Neuzeit. Hannover, 1884 & 1901.
Anon. Lord Byrons Beziehungen zu **AMERIKA.** Beilage zur Allg. Zt., 58-62, 1897.
Jones, J. R. Lord Byron in America. U. of Texas Studies in English, 1940.
Leonard, W. E. Byron and Byronism in America. New York, 1905.
Cajumi, A. Byron e la letteratura francese. **(FRANCE).** Cult., April, 1924.
Clark, W. J. Byron und die romantische Poesie in Frankreich. Leipzig, 1902.
Dargan, E. P. Byron's Fame in France. Virginia Quarterly, 2, 1926.
Estève, E. Byron et le romantisme français, (1812-50). Paris, 1907 & 1929.
Kahn, G. Le byronisme français. Figaro, 19.IV.1924.
Lednicki, W. Byron et les grands maîtres du romantisme français. Revue de Pologne, 1925-26.
Mazure, C. Etude morale sur Lord Byron et sur son influence à l'égard de la littérature contemporaine en France. Revue anglo-française (Poitiers), 1833.

Muoni, G. La leggenda del Byron in Francia. In: Poesia notturna preromantica. Firenze, 1908.
Phillips, W. J. France on Byron. Philadelphia, 1941.
Weddigen, F. H. O. Lord Byrons Einfluss auf die französische Litteratur. Archiv, 69, 1883-84.
Anon. Eine vergessene Byron-Uebersetzung. (**GERMANY**). MLIA, 1880.
—— Byron through German Eyes. TLS, Jan., 1930.
Ackermann, R. Lord Byron. Sein Leben, seine Werke, sein Einfluss auf die deutsche Litteratur. Heidelberg, 1901.
Bader, F. Lord Byron im Spiegel der zeitgenössischen deutschen Dichtung. Archiv, 135, 1916.
Eimer, M. Byron in Germania. Cult., 1924.
Flaischlen, C. Lord Byron in Deutschland. Centralblatt für Bibliothekswesen, 7-8, 1890-91.
Holzhausen, P. Lord Byron und seine deutschen Biographen. Beilage zur Allg. Zt., 74-75, 1903.
Richter, H. Zum hundertsten Jahrestage der Veröffentlichung des Manfred. ESn, 52, 1918.
Schnapp, L. Lord Byron im Spiegel der deutschen Dichtung. Münster, 1923.
Popma, T. Byron en het Byronisme in de Nederlandsche letterkunde. (**HOLLAND**). Amsterdam, 1928.
Schults, U. Het Byronisme in Nederland. Utrecht, 1929.
Bosco, U. Byronismo italiano. (**ITALY**). Cult., 15.IV.1924.
Muoni, G. La fama del Byron e il Byronismo in Italia. Milano, 1903.
—— La leggenda del Byron in Italia. Milano, 1907.
Niccolai, B. Bibliografia di studi inglesi in Italia: Lord Byron. Boll. di studi inglesi in Italia, July, 1937.
Porta, A. Byronismo italiano. Milano, 1928.
Simhart, M. Lord Byrons Einfluss auf die italienische Literatur. Leipzig, 1909.
Stendhal. Lord Byron en Italie et en France. RP, 1830.
Anon. Byrons Don Juan in polnischer Uebersetzung. (**POLAND**). MLIA, 1880.
Lipnicki, E. Byron im Befreiungskampfe der polnischen Nationalliteratur. MLIA, 48, 1877.
Telles, A. Lord Byron em **PORTUGAL**. Lisboa, 1879.
Lo Gatto, E. Byron in **RUSSIA**. Cult., April, 1924.
Maslov, V. I. The Beginning of Byronism in Russia. (In Russian). Kiev, 1915.
Struwe, P. Der Byronismus als Ereignis im russischen Geistesleben. Moskau, 1916.
Veselovskii, A. Byron (and Russia). Moskva, 1902.
Weddigen, O. Byrons Einfluss auf die russische Literatur. Archiv, 69, 1883.
Biller, G. Byron i den svenska litteraturen. (**SCANDINAVIA**). Samlaren, 1912.
Holmberg, O. Beppo-Sommelius. Nya dagl. allehande, 1923.
Holthausen, F. Skandinavische Byron-Uebersetzungen. ESn, 25, 1898.
Skard, S. Byron i norsk litteratur. Edda, 1939.
Lo Gatto, E. Da Lord Byron ai poete slavi. (**SLAVS**). Libri del Giorno, Sept., 1925.
Churchman, P. H. The Beginnings of Byronism in **SPAIN**. RH, 1910.
Peers, E. A. Sidelights on Byronism in Spain. RH, 1920.
—— The Earliest Notice of Byron in Spain. RLC, 2, 1922.
Petrovic, I. M. Lord Bajron kod Jugoslovena. (**YUGOSLAVIA**). Pozarevac, 1931.

2. Influences upon Individual Authors.

Santesson, C. **ATTERBOMS** Byron-dikt. Samlaren, 1933.
Beck, R. G. **BRYNJULFSSON**, an Icelandic Imitator of Childe Harold's Pilgrimage. JEGPh, 1929.
Kaiser. Byrons und C. **DELAVIGNES** Marino Faliero. Progr. Düsseldorf, 1870.
Churchman, P. H. Byron and **ESPRONCEDA**. RH, 20, 1909.
Rycroft, W. S. Espronceda. La influencia de Byron. Bol. bibliografico. Lima, 1926.
Vandegans, A. Anatole **FRANCE** et Byron avant 1873. RLC, 23, 1949.
Sjöholm, S. **FROEDING** och Byron. Edda, 39, 1939.
Sprenger, R. Eine Stelle in Byrons Childe Harold (IV, 140) und **GEIBELS** Tod des Tiberius. ESn, 32, 1903.
Fischer, P. D. **GILDEMEISTERS** Byron-Uebersetzung. MLIA, 1865.
Bowen, A. M. Byron's Influence upon **GOETHE**. Dial, 1900-01.
Wetz, W. Zu Goethes Anzeige des Manfred. ZVL, 16.

Eimer, M. Byron und Ch. D. **GRABBE.** Frankfurter Zt., 15.I.1903.
Wiehr, J. The Relations of Grabbe to Byron. JEGPh, 7, 1908.
Wypfel, L. **GRILLPARZER** und Byron. Zur Entstehungsgeschichte des Trauerspiels Ein treuer Diener seines Herrn. Euphorion, 9-10, 1902-03.
Alexis, W. **HEINES** Tragödien nebst einem lyrischen Intermezzo. Jb. der Litteratur, 31. (Wien), 1825.
Melchior, F. H. Heines Verhältnis zu Lord Byron. Diss. Leipzig, 1902, & Literarhistor. Forschungen, 27, 1903.
Ochsenbein, W. Die Aufnahme Lord Byrons in Deutschland und sein Einfluss auf den jungen Heine. Bern, 1905.
Baker, A. T. Notes on Byron and **HUGO.** FQ, 1932.
Moell, O. Beiträge zur Geschichte der Entstehung der Orientales von V. Hugo. Diss. Heidelberg, 1900.
Rigal, E. Victor Hugo et Byron. RHLF, 1907.
Leitzmann, A. Aus der Frühzeit der Byron-Eindeutschung. **KNEBEL** als Uebersetzer Byrons. Viermonatsschrift der Goethe-Ges., 4, 1940.
Maugain, G. Tradition et nouveautés dans le dernier chant du Pèlerinage d'Harold. **(LAMARTINE).** Mélanges Baldensperger. Paris, 1930.
Treverret, A. de. Lamartine et Lord Byron. Revue de l'Agenais, 16, 1889.
Ludwig, E. Lord Byron und **LASSALLE.** NR, July, 1911.
Estève, E. Byron en France après le romantisme: Le Byronisme de **LECONTE DE LISLE.** RLC, 5, 1925.
Heiss, H. Leconte de Lisles Qain und Byron. ZFSL, 36, 1910.
Mazzuchetti, L. Ugo e Parisina nella cantica giovanile di Giacomo **LEOPARDI.** RI, Dec., 1912.
Monti, G. Giac. Leopardi e Giorgio Byron. In: Studi critici. Firenze, 1887.
Entwistle, W. J. The Byronism of **LERMONTOV'S** A Hero of Our Time. CL, 1, 1949.
Friedrichs, E. Lermontov und Byron. GRM, 1915.
Hanisch, E. Ein Beitrag zum Byronismus Lermontovs. NSp, Oct., 1918.
Harkness, D. J. **LINCOLN** and Byron: Lovers of Liberty. Harrogate (Tenn.), 1941.
Wellek, R. **MACHA** and Byron. SR, 1937.
Zdiechowski, M. Karl Hynek Macha und Byrons Einfluss auf die tschechische Dichtkunst. Anzeiger d. Akad. d. Wissenschaften, Krakau, 1893.
Hermann, L. Une source de la Nuit de Mai **(MUSSET).** NPh, 1924.
Holzamer, W. Ein literarischer Franktireur (der Byron- und Shakespeare-Uebersetzer Al. **NEIDHARDT).** Beilage zur Allg. Zt., 191, 1902.
Dashkevich, N. P. Echoes of Byronism in the Poetry of **PUSHKIN.** (In Russian). In: Pushkin, red. Vengerova, 2, 1908.
Harnack, O. Pushkin und Byron. ZVL, 1, 1888. And in: Essays und Studien. Braunschweig, 1899.
Kozmin, N. Pushkin on Byron. (In Russian). In: Pushkin v mirovoi literature. Leningrad, 1926.
Maslov, V. I. Byronism in Pushkin. (In Russian). In: Sochineniia V. D. Spasova, St. Petersburg, 2, 1889.
Spassowitch, V. Le Byronisme chez Pouchkine et Lermontov. Viestnik Evropy, March, 1888.
Zhirmundskii, V. Byron and Pushkin. (In Russian). Leningrad, 1924 & ZSPh, 3-4, 1926-27.
Jung, A. Lord Byron und George **SAND.** Der Telegraph, 197, 1839.
Palfrey, T. R. Sur une biographie de Byron ayant appartenu à **STENDHAL.** RR, 31, 1940.
Holthausen, F. **TEGNER** und Byron. Archiv, 101, 1898-99.
Beck, R. Grimer **THOMSEN,** a Pioneer Byron Student. JEGPh, 27, 1928.
—— Grimur Thomsen og Byron. In: Logberg (Winnipeg) and Skirmir (Reykjavik), 1937.
Glück, F. Byronismus bei **WAIBLINGER.** Diss. Tübingen, 1922.
Rubin, J. J. **WHITMAN** on Byron, Scott and Sentiment. N&Q, 176, 1939.
Spink, G. W. J. C. von **ZEDLITZ** and Byron. MLR, 26, 1931.

CHAPTER SIX

Carlyle.

1. Influences upon Individual Countries.

Bentley, E. R. The Premature Death of Thomas Carlyle (1795-1945): an Obituary and a Footnote. American Scholar, 15, 1945.
Schapiro, J. S. Thomas Carlyle, Prophet of Fascism. Journal of Mod. History, 17, 1945.

Field. Th. Carlyle (and **AMERICA**). New Englander, Feb., 1850.
Vance, W. S. Carlyle in America before Sartor Resartus. AL, 1936.
—— Carlyle and the American Transcendentalists. Chicago, 1944.
Widger, H. D. Thomas Carlyle in America: His Reputation and Influence. Urbana, 1945.
Taylor, A. C. Carlyle: sa première fortune littéraire en **FRANCE**, (1825-65). Paris, 1929.
Baker, J. E. Carlyle Rules the Reich. (**GERMANY**). SRL, 25, 1933.
Bley, F. Die deutsche Kultur, die deutschen Verleger und Carlyle. Die Zeit, 415, 1902.
Borbein, H. Thomas Carlyle im Lichte des deutschen Schicksals. NM, 1935.
Deimel, T. Carlyle und der Nationalsozialismus. Bonn, 1937.
Seillière, E. L'actualité de Carlyle: un précurseur du national-socialisme. NRC, 1939.
Wippermann, W. Carlyle und das neue Deutschland. Neue Jb. f. deutsche Wissenschaft, 1937.
Anon. Carlyle e la **RUSSIA**. Marzocco, 13.II.1916.

2. Influences upon Individual Authors.

Anon. Carlyle and **EMERSON**. AM, 1883.
Hartwig, G. H. An Immortal Friendship. HJ, 38, 1939-40.
Jessen, J. Carlyle und Emerson. MLIA, 11.VI.1898.
Seillière, E. L'amitié d'Emerson et de Carlyle. Le Temps, 14.XII.1938.
Whipple, E. P. Emerson and Carlyle. NAR, May, 1883.
Wiecki, E. von. Carlyles' Helden und Emersons Repräsentanten, mit Hinweis auf Nietzsches Uebermenschen. Königsberg, 1903.
Grierson, J. H. C. Carlyle and **HITLER**. Cambridge, 1933.
McKeehan, Irene P. Carlyle, Hitler, and Emerson: a Comparison of Political Theories. U. of Colorado Studies, 1942.
Leopold, W. Th. Carlyle and Franz **HORN**. JEGPh, 1929.
Suzannet, A. de. **MERIMEE** et Carlyle. Bull. du Bibliophile, Aug., 1932.
Tourneux, M. Carlyle jugé par **MICHELET**. L'Amateur d'autographes, Jan., 1907.
Roget, F. Carlyle et M. de **MONTLOSIER**. BURS, 1849.
Licciardelli, G. Benito **MUSSOLINI** e Tomasso Carlyle: la nuova aristocrazia. Milano, 1931.
Rebora, P. Carlyle e Mussolini. La Nazione (Firenze), 4.IV.1934.
Bentley, E. R. A Century of Hero Worship: A Study of the Idea of Heroism in Carlyle and **NIETZSCHE**. Philadelphia, 1944.
Duproix, J. J. Carlyle et Nietzsche. BURS, 1907.
Oudinot, G. Thomas Carlyle et Frédéric Nietzsche. MF, Sept., 1899.
Ravenna, G. La teoria dell' eroe in T. Carlyle e Nietzsche. NAnt, 16.VII. 1903.
Richter, K. Carlyle, Nietzsche, Chamberlain. Deutschlands Erneuerung, 21, 1937.
Wilhelmi, J. H. Th. Carlyle und F. Nietzsche: wie sie Gott suchten und was für einen Gott sie fanden. Göttingen, 1897.
Sprenger, R. Zu Fritz **REUTERS** Dorchläuchting. Jb. d. Vereins f. niederd. Sprachforschung, 17, 1891.
Fiedler, H. G. The Friendship of Thomas Carlyle and **VARNHAGEN VAN ENSE**. MLR, 38, 1943.
Anon. Walt **WHITMAN** and Carlyle. New Eclectic, 1, 1868.
Paine, G. The Literary Relations of Whitman and Carlyle, with Especial Reference to their Contrasting Views on Democracy. SPh, 36, 1939.
Rubin, J. J. Whitman and Carlyle: 1846. MLN, 53, 1938.
Smith, F. M. Whitman's Poet-Prophet and Carlyle's Hero. PMLA, 55, 1940.
—— Whitman's Debt to Carlyle's Sartor Resartus. MLQ, 3, 1942.

CHAPTER SEVEN

Defoe.
and the "Robinsonaden."

(See also Utopias I. II. 4., and Voyages I. VII. 1.)

Anon. Russian Translations of Robinson Crusoe. S. P. Eykin, 5, 1843.
—— Uebersetzungen und Nachahmungen von Defoes Robinson Crusoe. ZVL, 1891 ff.
Atkinson, A. A French Desert Island Novel of 1708. PMLA, 36, 1921.
Bergner, G. Le Robinson strasbourgeois (1752). Alsace française, July, 1927.
Robertag, F. Ueber einige den Robinsonaden verwandte Erscheinungen in der

deutschen Litteratur des XVII. Jahrhunderts. Jahresbericht d. Schlesischen Ges. f. vaterländ. Kultur, 50, 1872-73.
Brandl, L. Vordefoesche Robinsonaden in der Weltliteratur. GRM, 5, 1913.
Brueggemann, F. Utopie und Robinsonade. Weimar, 1914.
Dottin, P. Le Robinson suisse. MF, 1924.
—— De Foe et la France. ESs, 13, 1931.
Elissa-Rhaïs, R. Une influence anglaise dans Manon Lescaut: Moll Flanders de Defoe. RLC, 7, 1927.
Flasdieck, H. M. Robinson Crusoe im Lichte der neueren Forschung. DR, 1928.
Forstrom, A. Robinson och Fru Edgren. Festschrift O. Sylwan. Göteborg, 1924.
Fraenkel, L. Robinsons Weg durch die Weltliteratur. LE, 2, 1899.
Greenough, C. N. Defoe in Boston. Publ. of the Colonial Society of Mass., 28, 1935.
Gudde, E. G. Grimmelshausen's Simplizius Simplizissimus and Defoe's Robinson Crusoe. PhQ, 1925.
Hatfield, T. M. Moll Flanders in Germany. JEGPh, 1933.
Hettner, H. Robinson und Robinsonaden. Berlin, 1854.
Hubbard, L. L. The Narrative of the El-Ho Sjouke Gabbes. An Episode . . . by Hendrik Smeeks, 1708. Translated from the Dutch and Compared with the Story of Robinson Crusoe. Ann Arbor, 1921.
Kippenberg, A. Robinsonaden in Deutschland bis zur Insel Felsenburg. Diss. Leipzig, 1892 & Archiv, 90, 1893.
Kleemann, S. Zur Geschichte der Robinsonaden. Euphorion, 1, 1894.
Leisegang, E. Vergessene Robinsonaden. Blätter f. Volksbibliotheken, 13, 1911.
Liebert, H. W. The Swiss Family Robinson: A Bibliographical Note. Yale U. Library Gazette, 22, 1947.
Mann, W. E. Robinson Crusoe en France. Paris, 1916.
Mare, W. de la. Desert Islands and Robinson Crusoe. New York, 1930.
Mertian, H. Le Robinson de la légende. In: Etudes religieuses, historiques et littéraires. Paris, 1862.
Nourrisson, P. Jean-Jacques Rousseau et Robinson Crusoe. Paris, 1931.
Patten, N. van. An Eskimo Translation of Defoe's Robinson Crusoe. Godthaab, Greenland, 1862-1865. Papers of the Bibliographical Society of America, 36, 1942.
Prestel, J. Robinson. In: Fikenscher & Prestel: Jugend und schönes Schrifttum. Anspach, 1925.
Roche, A. J. La source du Tamango de Mérimée. RLC, 14, 1934.
Roetteken, H. Weltflucht und Idylle in Deutschland von 1720 bis zur Insel Felsenburg. I. Robinsonaden. ZVL, 9, 1896.
Scholte, J. H. Die deutsche Robinsonade aus dem Jahre 1669. NPh, 27, 1942.
—— Ueber den Urtext der ältesten deutschen Robinsonade. F&F, 15.
Schott, E. Der erste deutsche Uebersetzer des Robinson. (L. F. Vischer). Blätter d. württembergischen Schwarzwalds, 9, 1902.
Staverman, W. H. Robinson Crusoe in Nederland. Diss. Groningen, 1917 & ESs, 1931.
Ullrich, H. Robinson und Robinsonaden: Bibliographie. Weimar, 1898.
—— Uebersetzungen von Schriften Daniel Defoes. Zs. f. Bücherfreunde, 4, 1900.
—— Die Berechtigung einer neuen Robinson-Uebersetzung. ESn, 36, 1906.
—— Zur Bibliographie der Robinsonaden. Nachträge und Ergänzungen zu meiner Robinson-Bibliographie. Zs. f. Bücherfreunde, 11, 1907.
—— Robinson und die Robinsonaden in der Jugendliteratur. Handbuch d. Pädagogik, 7.
—— Zur Robinson-Literatur. Literaturblatt f. german. & roman. Philol., 1912.
—— Defoes Robinson Crusoe, die Geschichte eines Weltbuches. Leipzig, 1924.
Varia. Robinson Crusoe. ESs, 1931.
Wagner, H. F. Robinson in Oesterreich. Salzburg, 1886.
—— Robinson und die Robinsonaden in unserer Jugendlitteratur. Wien, 1903.
Zobeltitz, F. von. Eine Bibliographie der Robinsonaden. Zs. f. Bücherfreunde, Nov., 1898.

CHAPTER EIGHT

Milton.

(See also Sources, I. V. 2.)

1. Influences upon Individual Countries.

Gertsch, A. Der steigende Ruhm Miltons im 18. Jahrhundert. Köln, Leipzig, 1927.
Parker, W. R. Milton's Contemporary Reputation. Columbus (Ohio), 1940.
Richards, A. E. Milton's Popularity in the 18th Century. MLN, 1926.

Robertson, J. G. Milton's Fame on the Continent. PBA, 1908.
Milligan, B. A. An Early **AMERICAN** Imitator of Milton. AL, 11, 1941.
Bastide, C. Premières mentions du nom de Milton dans une publication française, les Nouvelles ordinaires de Londres, 1650-57. (**FRANCE**). RELV, 1911.
French, J. M. The Burning of Milton's Defensio in France. (1651). MLN, 56, 1941.
Telleen, J. M. Milton dans la littérature française. Paris, 1904.
Bolte, J. Die beiden ältesten Verdeutschungen von Miltons Verlorenem Paradies. (**GERMANY**). ZVL, 1, 1887-88.
Brandl, A. Zur ersten Verdeutschung von Miltons Verlorenem Paradies. Anglia, 1878.
Jenny, G. Miltons Verlorenes Paradies in der deutschen Litteratur des XVIII. Jahrhunderts. Diss. Leipzig, 1890. St. Gallen, 1890. And in: Blätter für literar. Unterhaltung, 1892.
Muncker, F. Miltons Einwirken auf die deutsche Litteratur. In: Klopstock. Stuttgart, 1888.
Schulze, H. G. Miltons Verlorenes Paradies in deutschem Gewand. Bonn, 1928.
Ullrich, H. Deutsche Milton-Uebersetzungen vom 18. Jahrhundert bis zur Gegenwart. Euphorion, 29, 1928.
Walz, J. A. Miltonic Words in the German Poetic Vocabulary: Empyreum, hyazinthene Locken. MDU, 37, 1945-46.
Scherpbier, H. Milton in **HOLLAND**: a Study in the Literary Relations of England and Holland before 1730. Amsterdam, 1934.
Wlislocki, H. von. Miltons erste ungarische Uebersetzung. (**HUNGARY**). ZVL, 4, 1891.
Heltsztynski, S. Milton in **POLAND**. SPh, 26, 1929.
Peers, E. A. Milton in **SPAIN**. SPh, 23, 1926.
Bodmer, J. J. Ablehnung des Verdachtes dass die schweizerische Nation sich habe überreden lassen, an Miltons Verlorenem Paradiese einen Geschmack zu finden. (**SWITZERLAND**). Zürich, 1741.
Bodmer, H. Die Anfänge des zürcherischen Milton. Festschrift M. Bernays. Hamburg, 1893.

2. Influences upon Individual Authors.

Ibershoff, C. H. **BODMER** und Milton. JEGPh, 17, 1918-19.
—— Bodmer and Milton Once More. PMLA, 43, 1928.
Viles, G. B. Comparison of Bodmer's Translation of Milton's Paradise Lost with the Original. Leipzig, 1904.
Haviland, T. P. The Miltonic Quality of **BRACKENRIDGE'S** Poem on Divine Revelation. PMLA, 56, 1941.
Anon. Nisard über **CHATEAUBRIANDS** Uebersetzung von Milton. Blätter zur Kunde der Litteratur des Auslands, 1938.
Baker, A. T. Milton and Chateaubriand. FQ, 1, 1919.
Dick, E. La traduction du Paradis perdu de Chateaubriand. RHLF, 17, 1910.
Wright, R. W. Chateaubriand et Milton. MLR, Oct., 1910.
Fumio Ochi. Milton and **DIODATI**. In: Studies in English Literature, 18. (Tokyo), 1938.
Pollitt, J. D. Ralph Waldo **EMERSON'S** Debt to John Milton. Marshall Review, 3. (Huntington, W. Va.), 1939.
Haviland, T. P. A Measure for the Early **FRENEAU'S** Debt to Milton. PMLA, 55, 1940.
Springer, R. Anklänge an Milton in **GOETHES** Faust. ESn, 18, 1894.
Malone, K. **GRUNDTVIG** on Paradise Lost. PhQ, 20, 1941.
Levy, S. Zu **HEINES** Schöpfungsliedern; Anklänge an Milton. ALG, 1883.
Huebler, F. Milton und **KLOPSTOCK**, mit besonderer Berücksichtigung des Paradise Lost und des Messias. Reichenberg, 1896.
Wolfe, D. M. Milton and **MIRABEAU**. PMLA, 1934.
Manning, C. Milton et **NJEGOS**. Revue des Etudes slaves, 1938.
Durham, F. M. A Possible Relationship Between **POE'S** To Helen and Milton's Paradise Lost. AL, 16, 1945.
John, K. Life of Milton, together with Observations on Paradise Lost, by L. **RACINE** (and Milton in France). London, 1930.
Arnold, M. A French Critic on Milton (E. **SCHERER**). In: Mixed Essays. London, 1879.
Kraeger, H. Milton, **SCHILLER**, Byron. In: Der Byronische Heldentypus. München, 1898.
Johnson, W. G. Skriften om Paradis (by **SPEGEL**) and Milton. JEGPh, 44, 1945.

CHAPTER NINE

Richardson.

1. Influences upon Individual Countries.

Boas, F. S. Richardson's Novels and their Influence. E&S, 1911.
Canby, H. S. Pamela Abroad. MLN, 18, 1903.
Dottin, P. L'accueil fait à Pamela. RAA, 1930.
Purdie, E. Some Adventures of Pamela on the Continental Stage. Festschrift H. G. Fiedler. Oxford, 1938.
Watters, R. E. The Vogue and Influence of Samuel Richardson in **AMERICA**, 1742-1825. Diss. U. of Wisconsin, 1941.
Breton, A. Le. Le roman au dix-huitième siècle. **(FRANCE)**. Paris, 1898.
Facteau, B. A. Les romans de Richardson sur la scène française. Diss. Paris, 1927.
Middendorf. Richardsons Pamela und ihre dramatischen Bearbeitungen in Frankreich. Beilage zur Allg. Zt., 203-04, 1890.
Donner, J. O. E. Richardson in der deutschen Romantik. **(GERMANY)**. ZVL, 10, 1897.
Price, L. M. Richardson and the Moral Weeklies of Germany. Festschrift A. Hohlfeld. Madison, 1925.
—— The Reception of Richardson in Germany. JEGPh, 25, 1926.
Robertson, J. G. The Beginnings of the German Novel. Westminster Review, 142, 1894.
Coe, Ada M. Richardson in **SPAIN**. HR, 1935.

2. Influences upon Individual Authors.

McKillop, A. D. A Letter from S. Richardson to A. C. **CLAIRAUT**. MLN, 63, 1948.
Ducros, L. **DIDEROT**. Paris, 1894.
Taupin, R. Richardson, Diderot et l'art de conter. FR, 12, 1939.
Price, L. M. Richardson, Wetzlar and **GOETHE**. Mélanges Baldensperger. Paris, 1930.
Grimm, C. Encore une fois: La question **MARIVAUX**-Richardson. RLC, 4, 1924.
Schroers, C. Marivaux-Richardson. ESn, 1916.
Swaen, A. E. H. Marianne-Pamela. NPh, 23, 1938.
Wilcox, F. H. **PREVOST'S** Translations of Richardson's Novels. UCPPh, 12, 1927.
Riddershoff, K. Sophie von La **ROCHE**, Schülerin Richardsons und Rousseaus. Diss. Göttingen, 1895.
Anon. Parallèle entre la Clarice de Richardson et la Nouvelle Héloïse de M. **ROUSSEAU**. Journal étranger, Dec., 1761. And in: Variétés littéraires ou Recueil, 3-4, 1768-70.
Schmidt, E. Richardson, Rousseau und Goethe. Jena, 1875 & Berlin, 1902.
Wells, B. W. Richardson and Rousseau. MLN, 11, 1896.
Ettlinger, J. **WIELANDS** Clementina von Porretta und ihr Vorbild. ZVL, 4.
Low, C. B. Wieland and Richardson. MLQ, 7, 1904.
Schmidt, E. Wielands Verhältniss zu Richardson. In: Richardson, Rousseau und Goethe. Berlin, 1902.
Moquette, H. C. M. Over de Romans van **WOLFF EN DEKEN**, beschouwd in verband met de romantische Scheppingen van Richardson. Rotterdam, 1898.

CHAPTER TEN

Scott.

(See also Historical Novels, I. VII. 2.)

1. Influences upon Individual Countries.

Anon. Huitième lettre sur l'histoire: les imitations de W. Scott. Globe, 28.X. 1826.
Charpentier, J. Plaidoyer pour le roman historique. MF, 1933.
Fueter, E. Geschichte der neueren Historiographie. Vol. 5. München, 1911.
Hartland, R. W. Walter Scott et le roman frénétique. Paris, 1929.
Hillhouse, J. T. The Waverley Novels and their Critics. London, Minneapolis, 1936.
Maigron, L. Le roman historique à l'époque romantique; essai sur l'influence de W. Scott. Paris, 1898 & 1912. Cf. QR, 190, 1899.
Maynadier, G. H. Ivanhoe and its Consequences. Barrett Wendell Gedächtnisschrift. Cambridge, (Mass.), 1926.
Munroe, D. Sir Walter Scott and the Development of Historical Study. Queen's Quarterly, 1938.
Schmidt, J. Walter Scott und seine Bedeutung für unsere Zeit. WM, 26, 1869.

Anon. Walter Scott and the Southern States of **AMERICA.** N&Q, 1935.
Eckenrode, H. J. Sir W. Scott and the South. NAR, Oct., 1917.
Anon. Du roman historique en **FRANCE** et en Angleterre. Revue Britannique, Nov., 1834.
—— Scott and his French Pupils. LQHR, 1899.
Baldensperger, F. La grande communion romantique de 1827: sous le signe de W. Scott. RLC, 7, 1927.
Cook, D. The Waverleys in French: Scott's Authorship Revealed in 1822. TLS, 17.VII.1937.
Dargan, E. P. Scott and the French Romanticists. PMLA, 49, 1934.
Devonshire, J. M. The Decline of Sir Walter Scott in France. FQ, 1, 1919.
Hallays, A. Walter Scott et le romantisme français. Journal des Débats, 26.VII. 1898.
Maigron, L. W. Scott et la littérature française. Revue française d'Edimbourg, 1899.
Roth, G. Walter Scott et la France de son temps. Grande Revue, 1932.
Anon. Sir W. Scott und seine deutschen Uebersetzer. **(GERMANY)**. In: Ueberlieferungen zur Geschichte, Literatur und Kunst der Vor- und Mitwelt, herausg. von F. A. Ebert. Dresden, 1827.
Bachmann, F. W. Some German Imitators of Walter Scott. Diss. Chicago, 1933.
Sigmann, L. Scott und die Seeschule in der deutschen Kritik. Diss. Heidelberg, 1917.
Wenger, K. Historische Romane deutscher Romantiker. Bern, 1905.
Vissink, H. Scott and his Influence on Dutch Literature. **(HOLLAND)**. Diss. Amsterdam. Zwolle, 1922.
Anon. Lettera di un romantico sul romanzo storico. **(ITALY)**. Milano, 1831.
Agnoli, G. Gli albori del romanzo storico in Italia e i primi imitatori di Walter Scott. Piacenza, 1906.
Costa, P. Walter Scott in Italia. Corriere d'Italia, 1.X.1921.
Croce, B. Note sulla poesia italiana e straniera del secolo decimo-nono. Walter Scott. Crit., 20.I.1923.
Fassò, L. Saggio di ricerche intorno alla fortuna di Walter Scott in Italia. Atti della R. Accad. di Torino, 41, 1906.
Moscheni, C. Dei moderni romanzi. Lucca, 1828.
Krzyzanowski, J. Walter Scott in **POLAND.** (In Polish). Przegl. Wspolcz, 130, 1933.
Struve, P. Walter Scott and **RUSSIA.** SR, 11, 1933.
Churchman, P. H. & Peers, E. A. A Survey of the Influence of Sir Walter Scott in **SPAIN.** RH, 55, 1922.
Gray, W. F. Scott's Influence in Spain. The W. Scott Quarterly, Oct., 1927.
Núñez de Arenas, M. Simples notas acerca de Walter Scott en España. RH, 1925.
Palencia, A. G. Walter Scott y la censura gubernativa. Rev. del Archivo, Bib. y Museo. Madrid, 1927.
Peers, E. A. Studies in the Influence of Sir Walter Scott in Spain. RH, 58, 1926.
Soldevilla, F. Walter Scott y el renacimiento literario en España. BSS, 1926.
Zellars, G. G. Influencia de Walter Scott en España. RFE, 18, 1931.
Blondal, S. Walter Scott in Swedish Literature. **(SWEDEN)**. The Walter Scott Quarterly, 1928.
Holmberg, O. W. Scott och vi. Litterat. Stockholm, 1924.
Lindström, E. W. Scott och den historiska romanen och novellen i Sverige intill 1850. Diss. Göteborg, 1925.

2. Influences upon Individual Authors.

Fischer, R. Schloss Avalon, der erste historische Roman von W. **ALEXIS.** Diss. Leipzig, 1911.
Korff, H. A. Scott and Alexis. Heidelberg, 1907.
Garnand, H. J. The Influence of Sir Walter Scott on the Works of **BALZAC.** Columbia U.P., 1927.
Gordon, R. K. Sir Walter Scott and the Comédie humaine. MLR, 1928.
Saintsbury, G. Scott and Balzac. Everyman, 18.X.1912.
Iakubovich, D. Preface to **BELKIN'S** Tales and the Story Telling Methods of Walter Scott. (In Russian). In: Pushkin v mirovoi literature. Leningrad, 1926.
—— Reminiscences from Walter Scott in Belkin's Tales. (In Russian). In: Pushkin i ego sovremenniki, 37, 1928.
Kühne, W. Alexander **BRONIKOWSKI** und Walter Scott. ZSPh, 13, 1936.
Rossi, J. Scott and **CARDUCCI.** MLN, 53, 1938.
Rozov, Z. Denis **DAVYDOV** and Walter Scott. Slavonic Yearbook, 19, 1941.
Perrochon, H. Un admirateur suisse de Walter Scott: Emmanuel **DEVELEY.** RLC, 8, 1928.

Latham, E. **DUMAS** and Sir Walter Scott. MF, 1.I.1938.
Klatt, E. Von Scott über **FONTANE** zu Molo. LE, 23, 1921.
Paul, A. Der Einfluss W. Scotts auf die epische Technik Th. Fontaines. Breslau, 1934.
Shears, L. A. The Influence of Walter Scott on the Novels of Theodor Fontane. Columbia U.P., 1922.
Brognoligo. Ivanhoe e i Lombardi alla prima crociata (**GROSSI**). Roma, 1904.
Drescher, M. Die Quellen zu **HAUFFS** Lichtenstein. Diss. Leipzig, 1906.
Eastman, C. W. Wilhelm Hauff's Lichtenstein. Americana-Germanica, 1899-1900.
Thompson, W. W. Hauff's Specific Relation to Walter Scott. PMLA, 1911.
Pierre, F. E. Scott and **HOFFMANN**. MLN, 1930.
Stevenson, R. L. Victor **HUGO'S** Romances. Cornhill Mag., Aug., 1874.
Porterfield, A. W. Ivanhoe Translated by **IMMERMANN**. MLN, Nov., 1913.
Klancar, A. J. Josip **JURCIE**, the Slovene Scott. ASEER, 5, 1946.
Adams, N. B. A Note on **LARRA'S** El Doncel. HR, 9, 1941.
Sells, A. L. **LECONTE DE LISLE** and Sir Walter Scott. French Studies, 1947.
Altrocchi, R. Scott, **MANZONI**, Rovani. MLN, 41, 1926.
Bowen, C. M. Manzoni and Scott. Dublin Review, April, 1925.
Burgada, G. Il talismano di W. Scott e i Promessi sposi. Fanfulla della Domenica, 22, 1900.
Dotti, M. Derivazioni nei Promessi Sposi di A. Manzoni dai Romanzi di Walter Scott. Pisa, 1900.
Ovidio, F. d'. Appunti su Manzoni e W. Scott. Napoli, 1886.
—— Manzoni e Walter Scott. In: Studi Manzoniani. Caserta, 1928.
Zaiotti, P. Del romanzo in generale ed anche dei Promessi Sposi. Bibl. ital., Sept., 1827.
Hewlett, M. **MARK TWAIN** on Sir Walter. Sewanee Review, 29, 1921.
Orians, G. Walter Scott, Mark Twain, and the Civil War. SAQ, 40, 1941.
Thibaudet, A. De Walter Scott à Paul **MORAUD**. NL, 8.X.1932.
Moore, J. R. **POE**, Scott and The Murders in the Rue Morgue. AL, 1936.
—— Poe's Orang-Outang. TLS, 2.IV.1938.
Iakubovich, D. From Notes on **PUSHKIN** and Walter Scott. (In Russian). In: Pushkin i ego sovremenniki, 38-39, 1930.
Lukach, G. Pushkin and Walter Scott. (In Russian). Lit. Krit., 1937.
Hofer, E. Scotts Einfluss auf Ph. J. von **REHFUES'** Roman Scipio Cicala. Progr. Mahr, Weisskirchen, 1909.
McDavid, R. I. Ivanhoe and **SIMMS'** Vasconselos. MLN, 56, 1941.
Augustin-Thierry, A. Walter Scott et Augustin **THIERRY**. Le Figaro, 3.I. 1931.
François, V. E. Sir Walter Scott and A. de **VIGNY**. MLN, 1906.
Adiletta, P. Le fonti del Marco **VISCONTI** in alcuni romanzi storici di W. Scott. Sarno, 1906.

CHAPTER ELEVEN

Shakespeare.

(See also Comparisons, I. V. I. Sources, I. V. 2. & Politics, I. II. 5.)

1. Generalities.

Anon. Shakespeare in Modern Thought. NAR, 85, 1857.
—— Shakespeares Geltung für die Gegenwart. Europa, 1867.
Adler, J. Shakespeare Kritik des XVIII. Jahrhunderts. Diss. Königsberg, 1906.
Babcock, R. W. The Genesis of Shakespeare Idolatry, 1766-99. Chapel Hill (N.C.), 1931.
Chambrun, Clara L. de. Shakespeare Across the Channel. J. Q. Adams Memorial Studies. Washington, 1948.
Du Bois, A. E. Shakespeare and XIXth Century Drama. ELH, 1, 1934.
Duval, G. L'oeuvre shakespearienne, son histoire (1616-1910). Paris, 1911.
Ebisch, W. & Schücking, L. L. Shakespeare Bibliography. Oxford, 1931.
Elcho, R. Shakespeare und die moderne Bühne. Gegenwart, 34, 1873.
Ford, H. L. Shakespeare, 1700-1740. Oxford U.P., 1935.
Herford, C. H. A Sketch of the History of Shakespeare's Influence on the Continent. BRL, 9, 1925.
Hevesi, A. Shakespeare und die moderne Bühne. Pester Lloyd, 314, 1901. Cf. Budapesti Szemle, 242.
Horn, F. Shakespeare und das herrschende ästhetische Prinzip des 17. und 18. Jahrhunderts. Blätter für literar. Unterhaltung, 25-27.I. & 20. III.1831.
Hunt, T. W. Shakespearian Criticism on the Continent. Shakespeariana, 2, 1884-85.

Kilian, E. Shakespeare auf der modernen Bühne. JbShG, 1900-01.
Lancaster, H. C. The Alleged First Foreign Estimate of Shakespeare. MLN, 63, 1948.
Lee, S. Shakespeare and the Modern Stage. New York, 1906.
Legouis, E. La réaction contre la critique romantique de Shakespeare. E&S, 13, 1928.
Merbach, P. A. Shakespeare als Romanfigur. JbShG, 58, 1922.
Naranyana-Menon, C. Shakespeare-Criticism, an Essay in Synthesis. Oxford U.P., 1938.
Pillai, V. K. A. Shakespeare Criticism from the Beginnings to 1765. London, 1933.
Ralli, A. A History of Shakespearian Criticism. 2 vols. Oxford U.P., 1932.
Riedel. Ueber Shakespeares Würdigung in England, Frankreich und Deutschland. Archiv, 48, 1882.
Robertson, J. G. The Knowledge of Shakespeare on the Continent at the Beginning of the XVIIIth Century. MLR, 1, 1906.
Rossi, E. Studien über Shakespeare und das moderne Theater. Leipzig, 1885.
Schiavello, G. La fama dello Shakespeare nel secolo XVIII. Camerino, 1903.
Smith, D. N. Shakespeare in the XVIIIth Century. Oxford, 1928.
Stoll, E. E. Shakespeare Studies, Historical and Comparative in Method. New York, 1927.
Susemihl. Uebersicht der neuren Shakespeare-Literatur. (Deutschland, England, Frankreich). Hallische Jb., 206-209, 1838.
Van Tieghem, P. Shakespeare devant la critique continentale au XVIIIe siècle. Essais et études universitaires, 1945.
—— Adaptations scèniques de Shakespeare sur le continent. RLM, 1, 1946.
—— Le Préromantisme. vol. 3. Paris, 1947.
Wagner, W. Shakespeare und die neueste Kritik. Hamburg, 1874.
Wetz, W. Shakespeare vom Standpunkte der vergleichenden Litteraturgeschichte. Worms, 1890.

2. Hamlet, Lear, Othello and Romeo and Juliet.

(For Falstaff and Shylock, see I. VI. 10.)

Ashe, G. **HAMLET** and Pyrrhus. N&Q, 192, 1947.
Conklin, P. S. A History of Hamlet Criticism, 1601-1821. New York, 1947.
Detter, F. Die Hamletsage. ZDA, 36, 1892.
Fagus. Hamlet de Gascogne ou Shakespeare folkloriste. Minerve française, 15.XI.1919.
Feibleman, J. The Theory of Hamlet. JHI, 7, 1946.
Glunz, H. Das Problem des Hamlet heute. NSp, 47.
Greg, W. W. What Happens in Hamlet? MLR, 1936.
Gutteling, J. F. C. Modern Hamlet Criticism. NPh, 25, 1940.
Monrad, M. J. Hamlet und kein Ende. Philosoph. Monatshefte, 14, 1878.
Müller-Benfey, H. Das Problem des Hamlet. GRM, 1936.
Raven, A. A. A Hamlet Bibliography and Reference Guide, 1877-1935. Chicago U.P., 1937.
Schick, J. Corpus Hamleticum: Hamlet in Sage und Dichtung, Kunst und Musik. Leipzig, 1912 ff. Cf. MLR, 30, 1936.
Schroeder, F. A. Der Ursprung der Hamletsage. GRM, 26, 1938.
Schücking, L. L. Der Sinn des Hamlet. Leipzig, 1935.
Silberschlag, K. Shakespeares Hamlet und seine Beziehungen zu den geschichtlichen Ereignissen und Persönlichkeiten des Shakespeareschen Zeitalters. Deutsches Museum, 1859.
Tannenbaum, S. A. Hamlet and the Gonzago Murders. SAB, 16, 1941.
Witmann, W. Hamlets Bühnenlaufbahn (1601-1877). Leipzig, 1931.
Wolff, E. Hamlet und kein Ende. Frankfurter Zt., 154, 1901.
Yvon, P. Peut-on en finir avec Hamlet? L'Hamlet de Shakespeare et ses commentateurs. Paris, 1932.
Eidam, C. Ueber die Sage vom König **LEAR**. Progr. Würzburg, 1880.
Hammer, J. Note sur l'histoire du roi Lear dans Geoffrey de Monmouth. Latomus, 5, 1946.
Perrett, W. The Story of the King Lear from Geoffrey of Monmouth to Shakespeare. Diss. Jena; Weimar, 1903.
Stoll, E. E. **OTHELLO:** An Historical and Comparative Study. Minneapolis, 1915.
Allen, M. S. Brooke's **ROMEUS AND JULIET** as a Source for the Valentine-Sylvia Plot in The Two Gentlemen of Verona. U. of Texas Studies in English, 1938.
Allen, N. B. Shakespeare and Arthur Brooke. Delaware Notes, 1944.
Axon, E. B. Romeo and Juliet before and

in Shakespeare's Times. London, 1905. And in: Trans. of the Royal Soc. of Lit., 26, 1905.

Brognoligo, G. La leggenda di Giulietta e Romeo. In: Studi di storia letteraria. Roma, 1903.

Cain, H. E. Romeo and Juliet: A Reinterpretation. SAB, 22, 1948.

Colucci, L. La novella di Giulietta e Romeo e le sue fonti classiche. Rassegna nazionale, 27, 1939.

DeJongh, W. F. J. A Borrowing from Caviceo for the Legend of Romeo and Juliet. SAB, 16, 1941.

Fischer, R. Shakespeares Quellen in der Originalsprache: Quellen zu Romeo und Julia. Bonn, 1922.

Fraenkel, L. Untersuchungen zur Stoff- und Quellenkunde von Shakespeares Romeo und Juliet. Berlin, 1890.

—— Untersuchungen zur Entwicklungsgeschichte des Stoffes von Romeo und Julia. ZVL, 3-4, 1890-91.

—— Neue Beiträge zur Geschichte des Stoffes von Romeo und Juliet. ESn, 19, 1894.

Franchetti, A. La Giulietta dello Shakespeare e l'Italia. Bologna, 1889.

Hauvette, H. Reminiscences de Boccace dans une légende célèbre. In: Boccace. Paris, 1914.

Lentzner, K. Zu Romeo und Julia. Anglia, 10, 1887.

Moore, O. H. Le rôle de Boaistuau dans le développement de la légende de Romeo et Juliette. RLC, 9, 1929.

—— The Origins of the Legend of Romeo and Juliet in Italy. Spec., 5, 1930.

—— Da Porto's Deviations from Masuccio. PMLA, 55, 1940.

Porto, L. da. La Novella di Giulietta e Romeo. (Cf. Introduction). Strasbourg, 1936.

Schulze, K. P. Die Entwickelung der Sage von Romeo und Julia. JbShG, 11, 1876.

Stiefel, A. L. Ein weiterer Beitrag zur Romeo- und Julia-Fabel. ZVL, 4, 1891.

—— Bemerkungen zu den Dramatisierungen der Romeo- und Julia-Fabel. Archiv, 127, 1912.

Wolff, M. J. Romeo und Julia bei Shakespeare, Goethe und Lope de Vega. In: William Shakespeare. Leipzig, 1903.

—— Die Tragödie von Romeo und Julietta. JbShG, 47, 1911.

3. Shakespeare in America.

Anon. Shakespeare Celebration in New England, 1864. New England Reg., 1864.

Bristol, F. M. Shakespeare and America. Chicago, 1900.

Cairus, W. B. Shakespeare in America. Edda, 3, 1916.

Chase, M. E. Shakespeare in America. New York, 1939.

Churchill, G. B. Shakespeare in America. JbShG., 42, 1906.

Dunn, E. Shakespeare in America. New York, 1939.

Falk, R. Representative American Criticism of Shakespeare, 1830-85. Diss. U. of Wisconsin, 1940.

Freemantle, A. Shakespeare in America. The Listener, 11.III.1938.

Gaedertz, K. T. Shakespeare in Amerika. MLIA, 1883.

Gates, W. B. Performances of Shakespeare in Ante-Bellum Mississippi. Journal of Miss. Hist., 5, 1943.

Gayley, C. M. Shakespeare and the Formulas of Liberty in America. New York, 1917.

Hoole, W. S. Shakespeare on the Ante-Bellum Charleston Stage. SAB, 21, 1946.

Knortz, K. An American Shakespeare-Bibliography. Boston, 1876.

—— Shakespeare in Amerika. Berlin, 1882.

Law, R. A. Shakespeare and American Scholarship. Twentieth Century English, 1946.

Sherzer, J. American Editions of Shakespeare, 1753-1866. PMLA, 22.

Shockley, M. S. Shakespeare's Plays in the Richmond Theatre, 1819-38. SAB, 15, 1940.

Smith, M. E. Note on Shakespeare in America. SAB, 17, 1942.

Thorndyke, A. Shakespeare in America. Transactions of the British Academy, 13, 1927.

Wallace, C. W. Shakespeare and America. Poetry Review, July, 1914.

Westfall, A. R. American Shakespearean Criticism, 1607-1865. New York, 1939.

—— A New American Shakespeare Allusion. MLN, 63, 1948.

Wilkes, G. Shakespeare from an American Point of View. Including an Inquiry as to his Religious Faith and his Knowledge of Law, with the Baconian Theory Considered. New York, 1877.

Corradini, E. Il **GIULIO CESARE** all' Argentina. NAnt, 205, 1906.
Caprin, G. Il Sogno di Shakespeare all' Argentina (**MIDSUMMER NIGHT'S DREAM**). Marzocco, 15, 1910.
Sprague, A. C. The First American Performance of **RICHARD II**. SAB, 19, 1944.

4. Shakespeare in France.

Anon. Shakespeare in Frankreich. Europa, 1865.
—— Ein französischer Shakespeareroman. Blätter f. litterar. Unterhaltung, 15, 1868.
—— Traduction française de Shakespeare. Intermédiaire des Chercheurs et des Curieux, 10.XII.1882.
—— Shakespeare en France. Ibid. 10. VIII. & 25.IX.1884.
—— Sur la première mention du nom de Shakespeare dans un ouvrage imprimé en français. RHLF, 1894.
—— Some General Characteristics of Shakespearean Criticism in France in the XVIIIth Century. ML, June, 1921.
Baldensperger, F. Notes sur la prononciation française du nom de Shakespeare. Archiv, 115, 1905.
—— Esquisse d'une histoire de Shakespeare en France. In: Etudes d'histoire littéraire, 2me Sér. Paris, 1910.
Barrault, J. L. Shakespeare et les Français. La Revue, 15.XII.1948.
Bertin, G. E. Shakespeare et la France de Voltaire à Gemier. FGB, Dec., 1929.
Blennerhasset, C. Shakespeare in Frankreich. Deutsche Revue, 1900.
Boulenger, J. L'affaire Shakespeare. Paris, 1919.
Brandl, A. Shakespeare in Frankreich. Archiv, 149, 1926.
Buechner, A. Neue französische Werke über Shakespeare. MLIA, 1882.
—— Shakespeare in Paris. MLIA, 7.VI. 1890.
Butterworth, W. Shakespeare's French Critics. Manchester Quarterly, Oct., 1900. And in: Papers of the Manchester Literary Club, 19, 1900.
Chincholle, C. Shakespeare à Paris. Figaro, 15.X.1888.
Coleman, M. Shakespeare et la France. Revue mondiale, 1927.
Coote, H. C. Shakespeare in Paris, 1604. N&Q, 1, 1865.
Courdaveaux, V. Les derniers critiques de Shakespeare en France. Revue contemporaine, 31.VIII.1864.
Courmeaux, E. Destinée de Shakespeare en France. Séances et Travaux de l'Acad. de Reims, 1, 1844-45.
Darmesteter, J. Shakespeare en France. In: Essais de littérature anglaise. Paris, 1883.
Delcourt, J. Shakespeare and France. NC, 79.
Doran, D. Shakespeare en France. NC, 1878 & N&Q, 19.I.1878.
Doumic, R. Shakespeare et la critique française. RDM, 15.X.1904.
Dubeux, A. L'art de traduire Shakespeare: traductions d'autrefois et traductions d' aujourd'hui. RU, July, 1925.
—— Les traductions françaises de Shakespeare. In: Etudes françaises, 15. Paris, 1928.
Ducuing, E. Shakespeare et notre répertoire. Paris, 1847.
Elze, K. Shakespeare in Frankreich. JbShG, 1, 1865.
Engel, J. Shakespeare in Frankreich. JbShG, 34, 1898.
Fierlinger, E. Shakespeare in Frankreich. Progr. Olmütz, 1900.
Galdemar, A. Shakespeare (et son influence générale sur les romantiques français). Le Gaulois, 26.IV.1927.
Gide, A. Shakespeare en francés. Sur (Buenos Aires), Nov., 1938.
Gillet, L. Shakespeare et les poètes romantiques. NL, 28.VI.1930.
Gruen, K. Shakespeare in Frankreich. Deutsches Museum, 1857.
Guillemot, J. Shakespeare sur la scène française. RB, 1892.
Haines, C. M. Shakespeare in France; Criticism: Voltaire to Victor Hugo. London, 1925. Cf. Journal des Débats, 19.IX.1925.
Harrisson, J. A. The Shakespeare Cult in France. Shakespeariana, May, 1884.
Henriot, E. L'affaire Shakespeare. Le Temps, 1.III.1938.
Jagow, C. von. Shakespeare in Frankreich. Der Türmer, 3, 1901.
Jordan, W. G. A Frenchman's Tribute to Shakespeare. Queen's Quarterly, 1932.
Jusserand, J. J. Allusions to Shakespeare in Translations of Old French Novels. Athenaeum, 3160, 1888.
—— Shakespeare en France sous l'Ancien Régime. Paris, 1898. Cr. Journal des Débats, 7.XII.1898.
King, J. C. Shakespeare at the Paris Exhibition. PL, Dec., 1889.
Koszul, A. Pour qu'on joue Shakespeare. BAGB, 1927.
—— Deux représentations shakespear-

iennes à Strasbourg. Bull. de la Faculté des Lettres, Strasbourg, 1937.
Lacroix, A. De l'influence de Shakespeare sur le théâtre français jusqu' à nos jours. Bruxelles, 1856.
Larroumet, G. Shakespeare et le théâtre français. In: Etudes d'histoire et de critique dramatique. Paris, 1892.
Latreille, C. Un épisode de l'histoire de Shakespeare en France. RHLF, 23, 1916.
Lebègue, R. La tragédie shakespearienne en France au temps de Shakespeare. RCC, 38, 1937.
Lee, S. Shakespeare in France. NC, 1899. And in: Shakespeare and the Modern Stage. London, 1906.
Lefranc, A. La question shakespearienne au XVIIIe siècle. RB, 76, 1938.
Lintilhac, E. Shakespeare et le public français. Journal des Elèves de lettres, 16.II.1888.
Loen, A. von. Die Shakespeare-Kenntniss im heutigen Frankreich. Internationale Revue (Wien), 1866.
Longworth Chambrun, A. de. La vogue de Shakespeare en France. Ex Libris, 1923.
—— La vogue de Shakespeare au grand siècle. Revue hebdomadaire, July, 1924.
—— Shakespeare en France. Hommes et Monde, Feb., 1948.
Lotheissen, F. Shakespeare in Frankreich. In: Litteratur & Gesellschaft in Frankreich zur Zeit der Revolution. Wien, 1872.
Lux, J. Shakespeare et l'esprit français. RB, 27.XI.1910.
Mandin, L. Shakespeare trahi par les miroirs. MF, 15.VII.1934.
Mantoux. La jeune France et le vieux Shakespeare. Academy, 1421, 1899.
Monaco, Marion. Shakespeare on the French Stage in the Eighteenth Century. Diss. Bryn Mawr, 1939. And in: Microfilm Abstracts, 5, 1943.
Moraud, M. The Conflict Between the French Classical and the Shakespearian Conception of the Drama. Rice Insittute Pamphlets, (Texas), 15, 1928.
Morhardt, M. A la rencontre de William Shakespeare. MF, 15.VII.1936.
Orsini, N. G. Shakespeare infranciosato. LNI, 20.X.1934.
Pange, Comtesse J. de. Shakespeare en France. Le Gaulois du dimanche, 11. IV.1925.
Pellissier, G. Le drame Shakespearien en France. In: Essais de littérature contemporaine. Paris, 1893.
Proelss, R. Shakespeare in Frankreich. Grenzboten, 3-4, 1881.
Redard, E. Shakespeare dans les pays de langue française. Annales internationales d'histoire. Paris, 1901.
Renaud, J. J. Le théâtre de Shakespeare en France. Grande Revue, 15.XII.1904.
Ritter, G. Shakespeare in Paris. Neue Monatsschrift für Dichtkunst & Kritik, 4, 1876.
Rivers, J. Shakespeare à la française. Library, NS, 6, 1905.
Rosières, R. Shakespeare sur nos théâtres. RB, 7.XII.1889. And in: Recherches sur la poésie contemporaine. Paris, 1896.
Rudwin, M. Shakespeare en France. SAB, 20, 1945.
Servajean, H. Shakespeare en France. RAA, Dec., 1926.
Shackleton, R. Shakespeare in French Translation. ML, 23, 1941.
Smith, F. P. Shakespeare in France. RLC, 17, 1937.
Suarès, A. Shakespeare à Paris. NRF, 1.X.1913.
Varia. Deux siècles d'hommage français à Shakespeare. Comité Franco-Britannique. Paris, 1916.
Vigo-Fazio, I. L. Come Parigi apprezzò Shakespeare. Cultura moderna, 1932.
Wattendorf, L. Essai sur l'influence que Shakespeare a exercée sur la tragédie romantique française. Progr. Coblenz, 1888-89.
Wyzewa, T. de. La résurrection de W. Shakespeare. Figaro, 30.X.1890.
Anon. **HAMLET** in Paris. Blätter f. literar. Unterhaltung, 16, 1868.
Child, T. Hamlet in Paris. AM, 50, 1882. And in PL, Nov., 1890.
Elze, K. Hamlet in Frankreich. JbShG, 1, 1865. And in: Abhandlungen zu Shakespeare. Halle, 1877.
Frey, E. F. Hamlet in Paris. Gegenwart, 52, 1886.
Gottschall, R. von. Hamlet und das Théâtre français. Blätter f. literar. Unterhaltung, 47, 1886.
Laveleye, E. Hamlet à la Comédie française. RB, 25.IX.1886.
Pollock, M. The Hamlet of the Seine. NC, 1886.
Roosebroeck, G. L. van. Hamlet in France in 1663. PMLA, 37, 1922.
Weigand, W. Hamlet in Frankreich. Gegenwart, 23.XI.1889.
Maeterlinck, M. King **LEAR** in Paris. Fortnightly Review, Feb., 1905.
Saur, A. Shakespeares König Lear in

Frankreich bis zum Jahre 1827. Diss. München. Ansbach, 1910.
Strachey, M. King Lear at the Théâtre Antoine. Indep. Review, March, 1906.
Ganderax, L. Two French **MACBETHS.** Shakespeariana, 2, 1885.
Bolte, J. Eine französische Bearbeitung des Kaufmanns von Venedig. (**MERCHANT OF VENICE**). JbShG, 22, 1887.
Chevalier. Première représentation de Shylock à l'Odéon. Le Ménestrel, 51, 1889.
Seymour, C. Shylock in Paris. PL, March, 1890.
Treutel, K. Shakespeares Kaufmann von Venedig in französischer Bühnenbearbeitung. Diss. Rostock, 1901.
Ascoli, G. **OTHELLO** mis au goût français. FGB, 1931.
Child, T. French Versions of the Willow Song. PL, April, 1889.
—— Othello in Paris. PL, Aug., 1889.
Fest, J. Othello in Frankreich. Diss. Erlangen, 1906.
Gilman, Margaret. Othello in French. Paris, 1925.
Boesser, R. Shakespeare's **ROMEO UND JULIA** in französischer Bearbeitung. Diss. Rostock, 1907.
Charlton, H. B. France as Chaperone of Romeo and Juliet. M.K. Pope Festschrift. Manchester, 1939.
Feutry. Les amours infortunées de Juliette et Romeo, nouvelle tirée du théâtre anglais. MF, June, 1752.
Hauvette, H. Une variante française de la légende de Romeo et Juliette. RLC, 1, 1921.
Herold, A. F. Les anciennes adaptations françaises de Romeo et Juliette. MF, 1.I.1911.
Seymour, C. Romeo and Juliet in French. PL, Jan., 1891.
Anon. Shakespeare's **SONNETS** in French. Bookman, Oct., 1900.
Henry, F. Les sonnets de Shakespeare. Paris, 1899.
Nicholson, C. The **TAMING OF THE SHREW** in French. Academy, 1022, 1891.

5. Shakespeare in Germany.

Anon. Die Shakespeare-Litteratur in Deutschland. Vollständiger Catalog von 1762 bis Ende 1851. Cassel, 1852.
—— Shakespeare in Deutschland. Grenzboten, 20, 1861.
—— Die Shakespearewoche. Europa, 1864.
—— Eine Shakespeare-Bearbeitung aus dem XVII. Jahrhundert. Grenzboten, 23, 1864.
—— Shakespeare in Deutschland. Europa, 1865.
—— Shakespeare in Deutschland im XVI. und XVII. Jahrhundert. MLIA, 1.IV. 1865.
—— Shakespeare Aufführungen in München, Karlsruhe und Meiningen. JbShG, 2, 1866-67.
—— Shakespeare auf der deutschen Bühne im XVII. und XVIII. Jahrhundert. Beilage des K. Preuss. Staats-Anzeigers, 42-43, 1870.
Asher, D. Shakespeare in Deutschland. Wissenschaftl. Beilage der Leipziger Zt., 24, 1872.
Assmann. Shakespeare und seine deutschen Uebersetzer. Liegnitz, 1843.
Bauernfeld. Die Wiener Shakespeare-Uebersetzer. Beilage zur Wiener Zt., 45-46, 1877.
Becker, H. Shakespeare in Frankfurt. Die Gesellschaft, 1892.
Benedix, R. Die Shakespearomanie: Zur Abwehr. Stuttgart, 1873.
Benz, R. Shakespeare und der Stil des deutschen Dramas. Masken (Düsseldorf), 18.
Bergmann, A. Einleitung in die Shakespearomanie. Jb. der Grabbe-Ges., 1.
Bernays, M. Zum Studium des deutschen und englischen Shakespeare, 1884. In: Schriften zur Kritik und Litteraturgeschichte, 3. Berlin, 1903.
Biedermann, W. von. Beitrag zu der Frage von der Einbürgerung Shakespeares in Deutschland. Zs. f. deutsche Kulturgeschichte, 1873.
Biltz, C. Ueber den Berliner Shakespeare-Kultus im Allgemeinen und die Aufführungen seiner Königsdramen im Besonderen. Norddeutsche Allg. Zt., 511-13, 1881.
Bodenstedt, F. Ueber einige Shakespeare-Aufführungen in München. JbShG, 2, 1866.
Böhtlingk, A. Shakespeare und unsere Klassiker. Leipzig, 1909-10.
Brandl, A. Shakespeare in Germany. PBA, 1913.
—— Shakespeare auf der englischen Preismedaille der Carls-Schule. JbShG, 55, 1919.
Brüggemann, F. Die Aufnahme Shakespeares auf der Bühne der Aufklärung in den sechziger und siebziger Jahren. Leipzig, 1937.
Cohn, A. Shakespeare in Germany in

the Sixteenth and Seventeenth Centuries. London, Berlin, 1865.
—— Shakespeare-Aufführungen in Breslau, 1692 and 1699. JbShG, 23, 1888.
Conrad, H. Schwierigkeiten der Shakespeare-Uebersetzung. Halle, 1906.
—— Shakespeares Anfänge in Deutschland. Berliner Lokal-Anzeiger, 298, 1908.
Devrient, O. Statistik der Karlsruher Shakespeare-Aufführungen, 1810-72. JbShG, 8, 1873.
Eckardt, L. Shakespeares englische Historien auf der Weimarer Bühne. JbShG, 1, 1865.
Eschenburg, J. J. Ueber Shakespeare. Zürich, 1787.
Fischer, R. Shakespeare und das Burgtheater. Eine Repertoirestudie. JbShG, 37, 1901.
Förster, M. Shakespeare und Deutschland. JbShG, 57, 1921.
Foucher de Careil. Shakespeare en Allemagne. Revue Cont., 31.III.1858.
Fraenkel, L. Die Shakespeare-Forschung und das Shakespeare-Jahrbuch. Gegenwart, 1893.
—— Shakespeare an den deutschen Hochschulen der Gegenwart. JbShG, 32, 1896.
Franz, W. Shakespeare als Kulturkraft in Deutschland und England. Tübingen, 1916.
Frenzel, K. Shakespeare auf der deutschen Bühne. National Zt., 418-20, 1893.
Fresenius, A. Shakespeare auf der deutschen Bühne des XVIII Jahrhunderts. JbShG, 44, 1908.
Fries, A. Ueber den Versstil Shakespeares und seiner Uebersetzer. Berlin, 1916.
Genée, R. Shakespeare-Studien. Ein Wendepunkt in der deutschen Shakespeare-Kritik. Deutsches Museum, 1866.
—— Geschichte der Shakespeare'schen Dramen in Deutschland. Leipzig, 1870.
—— Die Parteien in der deutschen Shakespearekritik. National Zt., 93-95, 1875.
Gericke, R. Statistik der Leipziger Shakespeare-Aufführungen, 1817-71. JbShG, 7, 1872.
—— Beiträge zur Statistik der Shakespeare-Aufführungen deutscher Bühnen. JbShG, 8, 1873.
—— Shakespeare-Aufführungen in Leipzig und Dresden, 1778 bis 1817. JbShG, 12, 1877.
Glaser, A. Ein deutscher Rivale Shakespeares. WM, 9, 1861.
Goldschmidt, K. W. Wir und Shakespeare. LE, 1.I.1907.
Gottschall, R. Ueber (Benedix') Die Shakespearomanie. Leipzig, 1874.
Grabbe, C. D. Ueber die Shakespearomanie. In: Sämtliche Werke. Leipzig, 1908.
Gundolf, F. Shakespeare und der deutsche Geist. Berlin, 1911.
Hagen, A. Shakespeare und Königsberg. JbShG, 15, 1880.
Hart, J. M. Shakespeare in Germany of Today. Putnam's Monthly Mag., Oct., 1870.
Hauffen, A. Shakespeare in Deutschland. Prag, 1893.
Hecker, M. Shakespeares Bild im Spiegel deutscher Dichtung. JbShG, 68, 1932.
Henneberger, A. Die Shakespeare-Aufführungen in Weimar. Grenzboten, 23, 1864.
Hense, C. C. Deutsche Dichter in ihrem Verhältniss zu Shakespeare. JbShG, 1, 5, 6, 1865-71.
Herrig, H. Shakespeares Königsdramen auf der deutschen Bühne. MLIA, 1873.
—— Shakespearomanie und Dramaturgie. MLIA, 1874.
Hirschberg, J. Wirkliche oder scheinbare Entlehnungen aus Shakespeare Dramen. Archiv, 143, 1922.
Joachimi-Dege, Marie. Deutsche Shakespeare-Probleme im 18. Jahrhundert und im Zeitalter der Romantik. Leipzig, 1907.
Jones, O. F. The Treatment of Shakespearian Obscenity by XVIIIth Century German Translators. Diss. Stanford U., 1940.
Keller, W. Shakespeare und die deutsche Jugend. NSp, 45.
Kindermann, H. Shakespeare und das deutsche Volkstheater. JbShG, 72, 1936.
Kluckhohn, P. Die Dramatiker der deutschen Romantik als Shakespeare-Jünger. JbShG, 74, 1938.
Koberstein, A. Shakespeares allmähliches Bekanntwerden in Deutschland und Urtheile über ihn bis zum Jahre 1779. In: Vermischte Aufsätze zur Litteraturgeschichte & Aesthetik. Leipzig, 1858.
—— Shakespeare in Deutschland. JbShG, 1, 1865.
Koehler, R. Einige Bemerkungen und Nachträge zu Albert Cohn's Shakespeare in Germany. JbShG, 1, 1865. And in: Kleinere Schriften, 3. Berlin, 1898.
Kralik, R. von. Shakespeares Beziehungen zu Oesterreich. Kultur, 8, 1907.
Krauss, R. Shakespeares Dramen auf der Stuttgarter Hofbühne. JbShG, 45, 1909.

Kuehne, F. G. Shakespeare auf der englischen und auf der deutschen Bühne. Europa, 11, 1858.
Landsberg, H. Shakespeares Anfänge in Deutschland. Blätter des deutschen Theaters, 3.
Lemcke, L. G. Shakespeare in seinem Verhältniss zu Deutschland. Leipzig, 1864.
Ludwig, A. Deutsche Shakespearewissenschaft im Jubiläumsjahre. LE, 1916.
—— Shakespeare als Held deutscher Dramen. JbShG, 54-55, 1918.
Ludwig, O. Shakespeare Studien. Leipzig, 1926.
Luseke. Shakespeare und das heutige deutsche Laienspiel. JbShG, 1933.
Maass, M. Unsere deutschen Dichterheroen und die sogenannte Shakespearomanie. Thorn, 1874.
Macray, J. Shakespeare in Germany. N&Q, 208, 1865.
Marsop, P. Die Münchener Shakespeare-Bühne. Gegenwart, 1889.
Marx, E. How Shakespeare Became Popular in Germany. Gentleman's Mag., June, 1880.
Meissner, J. Shakespeare in Deutschland. MLIA, 1875.
Melchinger, S. Die Dramaturgie des Sturms und Drangs. Gotha, 1929.
Merschberger. Die Anfänge Shakespeares auf der Hamburger Bühne. Progr. Hamburg, 1890 & JbShG, 25, 1890.
Michel, F. Shakespeare in Deutschland. Frankfurter Zt., 110, 1893.
Moebius, P. Die deutsche Shakespearefeier Leipzig, 1864.
Moltke, M. Die älteren und neueren deutschen Shakespeare-Uebersetzungen. Deutscher Sprachwart, 2, 1867.
—— Shakespeare in Leipzig und Dresden vor 100 Jahren. Wissenschaftl. Beilage der Leipziger Zt., 87-90, 1877.
Müller, J. Shakespeare im Deutschunterricht. ZDK, 53, 1939.
Noire, L. Zwölf Briefe eines Shakespearomanen, Leipzig, 1874.
Nussberger, M. Shakespeare und das deutsche Drama. Schiller als politischer Dichter. Zwei Aufsätze. Zürich, 1917.
Oechelhaeuser, W. Shakespeare auf dem Wiener Burgtheater. JbShG, 4, 1869.
—— Die Würdigung Shakespeares in England und Deutschland. Dessau, 1869. And in: JbShG, 20, 1885.
—— Shakespeareana. Berlin, 1894.
—— Ideen zur Gründung einer deutschen Shakespeare Gesellschaft (1863). JbShG, 58, 1922.
Oehlmann, W. Shakespeares Wert für unsere nationale Litteratur. JbShG, 5, 1870.
Paetow, W. Die erste metrische deutsche Shakespeareübertragung in ihrer Stellung zu ihrer Litteraturepoche. Diss. Bern, 1892.
Pascal, R. Shakespeare in Germany, 1740-1815. Cambridge U. P., 1937.
Perls, A. Shakespeare in Deutschland. In: Streifzüge. Leipzig. 1877.
Piebler, A. Shakespeare Aufführungen der Mannheimer Hof- und Nationalbühne, 1779-1870. JbShG, 9, 1874.
Preston, P. Shakespeare in Heidelberg. Poetry Review, 20, 1929.
Prölss, R. Shakespeare Aufführungen in Dresden, 1816-60. JbShG, 15, 1880.
Ramsey. Shakespeare in Germany. In: Knight's Shakespeare Edition. London, 1843.
Richter, K. A. Shakespeare in Deutschland in den Jahren 1739-70. Oppeln, 1912.
Robertson, J. G. Shakespeare in Germany. MLR, 1.
Roth, W. Shakespeare and Germany. Studies in English Literature, 10, (Tokyo), 1930.
Rothe, H. Shakespeare in Germany. GLL, July, 1937.
Sallwuerk, E. von. Deutsche Shakespeare-Litteratur. LE, 15.IX.1903.
Schlösser, R. Der deutsche Shakespeare. JbShG, 74, 1938.
Schmidt, W. Shakespeare im Leben und in der Wissenschaft des neuen Deutschland. ZNU, 38, 1939.
Schweinshaupt, G. Shakespeares Dramatik in ihrer gehaltischen und formalen Umwandlung auf dem oesterreichischen Theater des 18. Jahrhunderts. Diss. Königsberg, 1938.
Simrock, K. Shakespeare als Vermittler zweier Nationen. Stuttgart, 1843.
Sisson, C. J. The Mythical Sorrows of Shakespeare. PBA, 1934.
Spranger, E. Shakespeare und wir. Internat. Monatsschrift für Wissenschaft, Kunst & Technik, 11, 1917.
Stahl, E. L. Shakespeare und das deutsche Theater. Stuttgart, 1947.
Stahr, A. Shakespeare in Deutschland. In: Prutz' litterarhistor. Taschenbuch, 1843.
Steinert, W. Deutschland und Shakespeare. Akadem. Blätter, 35, 1920.
Stempel, M. Erstaufführungen Shakespearescher Dramen in Deutschland. MLIA, 15.IV.1890.
Stern, A. Ueber Shakespeare in Deutschland. Göttinger Gelehrte Anzeigen, 1872.
Storozhenko. Shakespeare und die deutsche Kritik. (In Russian). In: Opyty izutschenija Schekspira. Moskva, 1902.

Stricker, K. Die Aufnahme Shakespeares am Bremer Stadttheater (1780-1839). JbShG, 54, 1918.
Stroedel, W. Shakespeare auf der deutschen Bühne vom Ende des Weltkrieges bis zur Gegenwart. Weimar, 1938.
Suphan, B. Shakespeare im Anbruch der klassischen Zeit unserer Litteratur. DR, 1889 & JbShG, 25, 1890.
Trautwein von Belle, K. Deutsche Shakespeare-Uebersetzungen, ein Spiegelbild des deutschen Individualismus. MLIA, 1867.
Uhde, H. Der Mannheimer Shakespeare. Diss. Heidelberg. Berlin, 1902.
Ulrici, H. Geschichte des Shakespeare'schen Dramas in Deutschland. In: Shakespeares dramatische Kunst. Leipzig, 1868-69.
Unflad, L. Die Shakespeare-Litteratur in Deutschland. München, 1880.
Vincke, G. von. Shakespeare auf der deutschen Bühne unserer Tage. JbShG, 7, 1872.
—— Die deutsche Bühnenbearbeitung Shakespeares. Gegenwart, 6, 1874.
—— Zur Geschichte der deutschen Shakespeare-Uebersetzungen. JbShG, 16, 1881.
—— Zur Geschichte der deutschen Shakespeare-Bearbeitung. JbShG, 17, 1882.
Vischer, F. Shakespeare in seinem Verhältnis zur deutschen Poesie, insbesondere zur politischen. In: Kritische Gänge, N.F., 2. Stuttgart, 1861.
Wagner, A. Eine Sammlung von Shakespeare-Quartos in Deutschland. Anglia, 25, 1902.
Waldmueller, R. Shakespeare-Uebersetzungen. MLIA, 21, 1873.
Walther, E. Der Einfluss Shakespeares auf die Sturm- und Drangperiode unserer Literatur im XVIII. Jahrhundert. Progr. Chemnitz, 1890. Cf. ZVL, 4, 1890.
Wolff, J. Shakespeare in England und in Deutschland. Internat. Monatsschrift fü Wissenschaft, Kunst & Technik, 10, 1916.
Wundt, M. Shakespeare in der deutschen Philosophie. JbShG, 70, 1934.
Würtenberg, G. Shakespeare in Deutschland. Bielefeld, 1939.
Wurzbach, W. von. Zur Revision des deutschen Shakespeare-Textes. Oesterreich. Rundschau, 7, 1906.

Lederer, M. Zu **ANTONIUS UND KLEOPATRA** in Deutschland. JbShG, 43, 1907.

Anon. Shakespeares Wie es euch gefällt auf der deutschen Bühne. **(AS YOU LIKE IT)**. Grenzboten, 24, 1865.

Krieger, H. Shakespeares **CORIOLAN** und wir. NSp, 47,

Wendheim, M. Shakespeares **CYMBELIN** auf der deutschen Bühne. Bühne & Welt, 15, 1912.

Anon. **HAMLET** seit hundert Jahren in Berlin. JbShG, 13, 1878.
Blaze de Bury, H. Hamlet et ses commentateurs depuis Goethe; les critiques allemands. RDM, 15.III.1868.
Bolte, J. Hamlet als deutsches Puppenspiel. JbShG, 28, 1893.
Bowers, F. T. Alphonsus, Emperor of Germany and the Ur-Hamlet. MLN, 1933.
Corbin, J. The German Hamlet and the Earlier English Versions. HSPhL, 1897.
Creizenach, W. Die Tragödie Der bestrafte Brudermord oder Prinz Hamlet aus Dänemark und ihre Bedeutung für die Kritik des Shakespearschen Hamlet. Berichte der kgl. Sächsischen Ges. der Wissenschaften, 39, 1887.
Daffis, H. Hamlet auf der deutschen Bühne bis zur Gegenwart. Berlin, 1912.
Ehrentreich, A. Bemerkungen zu einem deutschen Hamletroman. NM, 9.
Elze, K. Ueber Hamlet in Deutschland. Leipzig, 1857.
Evans, M. B. Der bestrafte Brudermord, und sein Verhältnis zu Shakespeares Hamlet. In: Theatergesch. Forschungen, Hamburg, 1910.
Kaim, F. Die Gestalt Hamlets im Lichte der deutschen Kritik. Neuphilolog. Centralblatt, 6, 1892.
Litzmann, B. Die Entstehungsgeschichte des ersten deutschen Hamlet. ZVL, 1888.
—— Hamlet in Hamburg, 1625. DR, 70, 1892.
Muralt, A. von. Ein deutsches Shakespeare-Jubiläum (Erstaufführung des Hamlet, 20.IX.1776, in Hamburg). Berliner Neue Nachrichten, 441, 1901.
Pinloche, A. De Shakespearii Hamleto et Germanica tragoedia quae inscribitur: Der bestrafte Brudermord, oder Prinz Hamlet aus Dänemark, quantopere inter se distent. Diss. Paris, 1890.
Remy, M. Hamlet in Berlin. Sonntags-Beilage zur Voss'schen Zt., 50, 1877.
Scholte, J. H. De eerste Hamlet-opvoering in Duitschland. NPh, 2, 1916.
Tanger, G. Der bestrafte Brudermord oder Prinz Hamlet aus Dänemark und sein Verhältnis zu Shakespeares Hamlet. JbShG, 23, 1888.
Weilen, A. von. Hamlet auf der deutschen Bühne bis zur Gegenwart. Berlin, 1908.
Weisstein. Hamlets Einzug in Deutschland. National-Zt., 234, 1902.

Winds, A. Hamlet auf der deutschen Bühne. Berlin, 1909.
Anon. Eine ältere deutsche Bearbeitung von Shakespeares **KOENIG JOHANN** (1801). JbShG, 13, 1878.
Bergmann, A. Probe einer vergessenen **LEAR-Uebersetzung.** JbShG, 72, 1936.
Cohn, A. König Lear 1692 und Titus Andronicus 1699 in Breslau aufgeführt. JbShG, 23, 1888.
Drews, W. König Lear auf der deutschen Bühne bis zur Gegenwart. Berlin, 1932.
Lewes, L. Die Münchener Aufführung des König Lear auf der neueingerichteten Bühne. MLIA, 1889.
Brahm, O. **MACBETH** auf dem deutschen Theater. Nation, 4, 1887-88.
Kilian, E. Maas für Maas als deutsches Bühnenstück. **(MEASURE FOR MEASURE).** JbShG, 1920.
Oechelhäuser, W. Ueber die Darstellung des Sommernachtstraumes auf der deutschen Bühne. **(MIDSUMMER NIGHT'S DREAM).** JbShG, 5, 1870.
Vincke & Elze. Wunderbare Schicksale des Sommernachtstraums. JbShG, 5, 1870.
Bolte, J. Deutsche Verwandte von Shakespeares Viel Lärm um Nichts. **(MUCH ADO ABOUT NOTHING).** JbShG, 21, 1886.
Brunner, K. Die erste deutsche **ROMEO**-Uebersetzung (1758). Archiv, 153, 1928.
Fischer, L. H. Die Sage von Romeo und Julia in deutschen Prosa-Darstellungen des XVII. Jahrhunderts. JbShG, 25, 1890.
Mensel, E. H. Die erste deutsche Romeo-Uebersetzung. Northampton (Mass.), 1933.
Mentzel, E. Ein Meisterwerk Shakespeares in seiner deutschen Bearbeitung. MLIA, 1897.
Miller, Anna E. Die erste deutsche Uebersetzung von Shakespeares Romeo and Juliet. JEGPh, 11, 1912.
Sauer, A. Shakespeares Romeo und Julia in den Bearbeitungen und Uebersetzungen der deutschen Literatur. Diss. Greifswald, 1915.
Wehl, F. Romeo und Julia auf der Berliner Bühne. Europa, 49, 1849.
Wolff, M. J. Die Tragödie von Romio und Julietta. JbShG, 47, 1911.
Anon. Shakespeares **SONETTE** und die deutschen Uebersetzer. MLIA, 73, 1871.
Kahn, L. W. Shakespeares Sonette in Deutschland: Versuch einer literarischen Typologie. Bern, 1935.
Schoen-René, O. E. Shakespeare's Sonnets in Germany, 1787-1939. Diss. Harvard, 1942.
Simrock, K. Uebersetzungen von Shakespeares Gedichten. MLIA, 1867.
Bolte, J. Der Widerspenstigen Zähmung als Görlitzer Schulkomōdie (1678). **(TAMING OF THE SHREW).** JbShG, 27, 1892.
Kōhler, R. (ed.). Kunst über alle Künste, ein bös Weib gut zu machen (1672). Berlin, 1864.
Winds, A. Shakespeares Bezähmte Widerspänstige und ihre deutschen Bearbeitungen. Bühne und Welt, 5, 1903.

6. Shakespeare in Italy.

Angeli, D. La fortuna di Shakespeare in Italia. Marzocco, 21, 1916.
Battaglia, G. Nota sui traduttori italiani di Shakespeare. In: Mosaico, saggi diversi di critica drammatica. Milano, 1845.
Birch, W. J. Shakespeare and his Italian Critics. N&Q, 29.V., 3 & 17.VII.1886.
Butterworth, W. Shakespeare's Italian Critics. Papers of the Manchester Literary Club, 27, 1901. And in: Manchester Quarterly, Oct., 1901.
Cerini, M. Shakespeare e noi. Marzocco, 21, 1916.
Collison-Morley, L. Shakespeare in Italy. Stratford-on-Avon, 1916.
Croce, B. La letteratura shakespeariana in Italia. In: Nuove curiosità storiche. Napoli, 1922.
—— Un viaggiatore in Italia nel settecento apostolo dello Shakespeare. In: Varietà di storia letteraria e civile. Bari, 1931.
Elze, T. Neue italienische Skizzen zu Shakespeare. JbShG, 31, 1895.
Faggi, A. Edizioni italiane di Shakespeare. Marzocco, Sept., 1929.
Ferrando, G. Shakespeare in Italy. SAB, 5, 1930.
Fucilla, J. G. Shakespeare in Italian Criticism. PhQ, 20, 1941.
Gargano, G. S. Shakespeare und die Pflicht Italiens. Marzocco, 11.
—— Traduttori italiani di Shakespeare. Marzocco, 18.VI.1922.
Graf, A. Il teatro inglese in Italia: Shakespeare. In: L'Anglomania e l'influsso inglese in Italia nel secolo XVIII. Torino, 1911.
Hodgson, A. Shakespeare in Italy. The Esquiline, 1890.
Lorenzo, G. de. Italia e Shakespeare. In: Italae vires. Napoli, 1916.
—— Shakespeare e l'Italia. Marzocco, 21, 1916.
Muoni, G. I drammi dello Shakespeare e

la critica romantica italiana (1815-45). Firenze, 1908.
Niccolai, B. Bibliografia degli studi inglesi in Italia: Wm. Shakespeare. Boll. degli studi inglesi in Italia, 1936.
Nulli, S. A. Shakespeare in Italia. Milano, 1918.
Ottolini, A. Traduttori di Shakespeare. Libri del giorno, 1921.
Praz, M. Shakespeare (in Italy). Enciclopedia italiana, 31, 1936.
—— Come Shakespeare è letto in Italia. Riv. ital. del dramma, 2, 1938.
Rebora, P. Shakespeare tradotto in italiano. Leonardo, 5, 1934 & 1947.
—— Comprensione e fortuna di Shakespeare in Italia. CL, 1, 1949.
Reich, B. Fascist Interpretation of Shakespeare. International Literature, 10. 1936.
Robertson, J. G. Shakespeare in Italy. In: Cambridge History of English Literature, 5.
Valgimigli, A. La popolarità di Dante in Italia confronta con Shakespeare. Marzocco, 25.
Anon. La prima traduzione italiana di un dramma di Shakespeare. (Julius **CAESAR**). Marzocco, 13.XI.1932.
Crinò, A. M. La prima traduzione italiana di un dramma di Shakespeare. Rassegna nazionale, 1932.
Anon. Ein italienischer **HAMLET**. (1700). JbShG, 19, 1884.
Keller, W. Zu den italienischen Hamlet-Opern. JbShG, 39, 1903.
Manzi, A. L'istoria d'Amleto sulle scene italiane. Rassegna nazionale, 168, 1909.
Vischer, R. Hamlet in Rom. Litteratur, 33-36, 1874.
Vollhardt, W. Italienische Parallelen zu Shakespeares Hamlet. JbShG, 62, 1926.
Faggi, A. Il personaggio shakespeariano di Iago e due tragedie italiane. (**OTHELLO**). NAnt, 327, 1926.

7. Shakespeare in Other Countries.

Shahani, R. G. Shakespeare through Eastern Eyes. (**ASIA**). London, Paris, 1932.
Henriques, A. Shakespeare i Danmark og i Sverige. (**DENMARK**). Nordisk Tidskrift, 16, 1940.
—— Shakespeare og Danmark indtil 1840. København, 1940.
Rubow, P. V. Shakespeare paa dansk. København, 1932.
Stefansson, J. Shakespeare at Elsinore. Contemporary Review, Jan., 1896.
Hirn, Y. Shakespeare in **FINLAND**. Finsk Tidskrift, April, 1916.
Blackie, J. S. Shakespeare in Modern Greek. (**GREECE**). NC, Dec., 1891.
Boltz, A. Shakespeare in Griechenland. MLIA, 1882 & JbShG, 18, 1883.
Miller, E. Tragédies de Shakespeare traduites en grec. JS, Sept., 1883.
——Shakespeare traduit en grec moderne. RB, 20.X.1883.
Wagner, W. Shakespeare in Griechenland. JbShG, 12, 1877.
Anon. Shakespeare in **HOLLAND**. JbShG, 13, 1878.
Arnold, T. J. Shakespeare-Bibliography in the Netherlands. Bibliographische Adversaria, 4. The Hague, 1879.
Beer, T. H. de. Shakespeare in Dutch. PL, June, 1889.
Bolte, J. Eine holländische Uebersetzung von Shakespeare Taming of the Shrew vom Jahr 1654. JbShG, 26, 1891.
Byvanck, W. G. C. Nederlandsche Shakespeare-Kritik. Gids, July, 1900.
Fraenkel, L. Zur Geschichte von Shakespeares Bekanntwerden in den Niederlanden. ESn, 15, 1891.
Hellwald, E. J. Shakespeare in Holland. Nederlandsch Tydskrift, 1869. And in: Beilage zur Allg. Zt., 77, 1875.
Kok. Bijdragen tot de Shakespeare literatuur in ons land. De Portefeuille, 23, 1883.
Micheels. Hamlet in Holland. L'Enseignement des langues modernes, 6, 1892.
Pannevis, A. Shakespeare en de hedendaagsche nederlandsche uitgaven en vertalingen zijner tooneelstukken. Utrecht, 1863.
Pennink, R. Nederland en Shakespeare: achttiende eeuw en vroege romantiek. s'Gravenhage, 1936.
Schneider, L. Shakespeare in den Niederlanden. JbShG, 26, 1891.
Zuidema, W. Shakespeare en Nederland. Tijdschrift voor nederl. taal en letterkunde, 24, 1905.
Bayer, J. Shakespeare in **HUNGARY**. (In Hungarian). Kisfaludy Tarsasag Evlapjai, Uj Folyam, 23.
Csaszar, E. Shakespeare es a Magyar Költeszet. Budapest, 1917.
Frey, J. Shakespeare in Ungarn. MLIA, 1880.
Haraszti, Z. Shakespeare in Hungary. Boston, 1929.
Marle, T. B. Shakespeare in Budapest. Hungarian Quarterly, 1939.
Yolland, A. Shakespeare in Hungary. Hungarian Quarterly, 1939.
Anon. Note on Shakespeare's Influence in Modern Bengali Literature. (**INDIA**). Bengal Past and Present, 8, 1914.

Legouis, E. La révolte de l'Inde contre Shakespeare. RAA, Feb., 1925.

Einarsson, S. Shakespeare á **ISLANDI.** Winnipeg, 1938.

—— Shakespeare in Iceland: An Historical Survey. ELH, 7, 1940.

Gering, H. Shakespeare in Island. JbShG, 14, 1879.

Jonsson, F. Shakespeare i Island. Edda, 3, 1916.

Hausknecht, E. Shakespeare in **JAPAN.** PL, Oct., 1889.

Hayashi. Shakespeare au Japon. Revue, 1.V.1903.

Piper, K. A. Shakespeare und die Japaner. Der Tag, 431, 1901.

Tannenbaum, S. A. Shakespeare and Japan. SAB, 16.

Calina, Josephina. Shakespeare in **POLAND.** Polish Review, 6, 1946.

Estreicher, S. Shakespeare en Pologne au XVIIIe siècle. (In Polish). Krakov, 1892.

Ziolecki. Shakespeare in Poland, Russia and other Slavonic Countries. Transactions of the Shakespeare-Society, 1880-85.

Richter, E. Eine altportugiesische Version der König Lear-Sage. (**PORTUGAL**). ESn, 29.

Vasconcellos, Caroline Michaelis de. Shakespeare in Portugal. JbShG, 15, 1880.

Beza, M. Shakespeare in **RUMANIA.** London, 1931.

Radulescu, I. H. Les intermédiaires français de Shakespeare en Roumanie. RLC, 18, 1938.

Blum, E. Shakespeare in the USSR. (**RUSSIA**). SAB, 20, 1945.

Dole, N. H. Shakespeare and the Russian Drama. PL, 1889-90.

Friedrichs, E. Shakespeare in Russland. ESn, Shakespeare Gedächtnisheft. Leipzig, 1916.

Herford, C. N. A Russian Shakespearean. Oxford, 1925.

Lazoursky, W. Shakespeare en ukraïnien. (In Russian). Odessa, 1930.

Lebedev, V. A. Sur la connaissance de Shakespeare en Russie jusqu'en 1812. Nouvelles russes, Dec., 1875.

Lirondelle, A. Shakespeare en Russie, 1784-1840. Paris, 1912 & 1927.

Morozov, M. M. Shakespeare on the Soviet Stage. London, 1947.

—— The Study of Shakespeare in the Soviet Union. American Rev. of the Soviet Union, 8, 1947.

Tannenbaum, S. A. Shakespeare in Russia. SAB, 16.

Timofeev, S. Der Einfluss Shakespeares auf das russische Drama. (In Russian). Moskva, 1888.

Wijk, N. van. Der Hamlettypus in der russischen Literatur. De Gids, Dec., 1904.

Zanco, A. Shakespeare in Russia. Annali della Regia Scuola Normale di Pisa, 1938 & Torino, 1945.

Franko, J. Shakespeare bei den **RUTHENEN.** Die Zeit, 36, 1903.

Bryner, C. Shakespeare among the **SLAVS.** ELH, 8, 1941.

Anon. Romeo and Juliet in **SPAIN.** N&Q, 17.XI.1874.

Carrière, M. Shakespeare und die spanischen Dramatiker. JbShG, 6, 1870-71.

Cosens, F. W. Shakespeare in Spain. Athenaeum, 1986, 1865.

Esquerra, R. Shakespeare a Catalunya. Revista, 1935 & Barcelona, 1937.

Hort, G. M. The Shakespeare of Spain. Contemporary Rev., 173, 1948.

López. Shakespeare en Espaňna. Revista hispano-americana, 8, 1882.

Lorenzo y d'Ayot, M. Shakespeare, Lord Byron, como modelos de la juventud literaria. Madrid, 1886.

Martinez, E. J. Shakespeare en España. Revista de Archivos, 1918.

Michaelis, Caroline. Hamlet in Spanien. JbShG, 10, 1874-75.

Par, A. Contribución a la bibliographia española de Shakespeare. Barcelona, 1930.

—— Shakespeare en la literatura española. 2 vols. Madrid, 1935.

—— Representaciones shakespearianas en España. 2 vols. Madrid, 1936-40.

Ruppert y Ujaravi, R. Shakespeare en España. Madrid, 1920. Cf. Literaturblatt f. rom. & germ. Philol., 1923.

Thomas, H. Shakespeare and Spain. Oxford, 1922. And in: Homenaje Menéndez Pidal. Madrid, 1925.

Anon. Shakespeare in Schweden. (**SWEDEN**). JbShG, 12, 1877.

Bolin, W. Hamlet in Schweden. JbShG, 14, 1879.

—— Zur Shakespeare-Litteratur Schwedens. JbShG, 15, 1880.

Nyblom. Shakespeare, hans kommentatores. Svensk Literatur Tidskrift, 1865.

Engel, C. E. Shakespeare in **SWITZERLAND** in the XVIIIth Century. CLS, 17-18, 1945.

Monnier, M. Hamlet à Genève. BURS, Oct., 1876.

Vetter, T. Shakespeare und die deutsche Schweiz. In: Verhandl. der 49. Ver-

sammlung deutscher Philologen in Basel. Leipzig, 1908 & JbShG, 48, 1912.
Fischer, K. Der türkische Hamlet. (TURKEY). Beilage zur Allg. Zt., 110, 1894.
Popovic, V. Shakespeare in Serbia. (YUGOSLAVIA). London, 1928.

8. Shakespeare and Voltaire.

Anon. Shakespeare, Voltaire, Racine. Le Miroir, 5.XI.1821.
—— Voltaire and Shakespeare. Cornhill Mag., 254, 1881.
—— Voltaire et Shakespeare. Intermédiaire des Chercheurs et des Curieux, 25.VIII.1884.
Adams, P. G. How Much of Shakespeare did Voltaire Know? SAB, 16, 1941.
Adolph, K. Voltaire et le théâtre de Shakespeare. Progr. Sorau, 1883.
Babcock, R. W. The English Reaction against Voltaire's Criticism of Shakespeare. SPh, 27, 1930.
Baretti, G. Discours sur Shakespeare et sur M. de Voltaire. Londres, Paris, 1777 & Lanciano, 1911.
Barine, A. Voltaire et Shakespeare. Journal des Débats, 7.I.1903.
Battaglia, G. Voltaire poeta tragico e imitatore di Shakespeare; Shakespeare giudicato da Voltaire; Voltaire e Shakespeare giudicati dal Baretti. In: Mosaico, saggi diversi di critica drammatica. Milano, 1845.
Blaze de Bury, H. Voltaire et Shakespeare. In: Tableaux romantiques de littérature et d'art. Paris, 1878.
Blunt, R. (ed.) Mrs. Montagu, Queen of the Blues, her Letters and Friendships, 1762-1800. 2 vols. London, 1923.
Eberlin. Ueber das Verhältniss Voltaires zu Shakespeare. Archiv, 61, 1879.
Eschenburg, J. J. Shakespeare wider neue voltärische Schmähungen vertheidigt. Deutsches Museum, Jan., 1777.
Faguet, E. Voltaire critique de Shakespeare. RCC, 8-9, 1900-01.
Havens, G. R. Voltaire and English Critics of Shakespeare. Franco-American Pamphlets. (New York), 1944.
Horsley, P. M. George Keate and the Voltaire - Shakespeare Controversy. CLS, 16, 1945.
Humbert, C. Voltaire, ein Bewunderer Shakespeare's. Neue Jb. f. Philologie & Pädagogik. (Leipzig), 1886.
König, W. Voltaire und Shakespeare. JbShG, 10, 1875.
Larroumet, G. Voltaire. L'influence de Shakespeare sur son théâtre. Shakespeare en France à l'époque de Voltaire. RCC, 8, 1900.
Lehmann. Ueber Voltaire's Reformversuch und seine Stelling zu Shakespeare. BBG, 14, 1878.
Lion, H. Voltaire et Shakespeare. In: Les tragédies et les théories dramatiques de Voltaire. Paris, 1896.
Lounsbury, T. R. Shakespeare and Voltaire. London, 1902. Cf. Nation, 6.XI. 1902; Academy, 1600, 1903.
Morandi, L. Voltaire contro Shakespeare, Baretti contro Voltaire. Roma, 1882 & Città di Castello, 1884.
Piccioni, L. Inediti barettiani (Voltaire-Shakespeare). GSLI, 114, 1939.
Rutledge, J. Observations à MM. de l'Académie française au sujet d'une lettre de M. de Voltaire, lue dans cette Académie le 25 août 1776. Paris, 1777.
Schmidt, A. Voltaires Verdienste um die Einführung Shakespeares in Frankreich. Progr. Königsberg, 1864. And in: Gesammelte Abhandlungen. Berlin, 1889.
Serrurier, C. Voltaire et Shakespeare à propos du monologue d'HAMLET. NPh, 5, 1920.
Bertrand, E. Shakespeare et Voltaire. Etude sur l'expression de la jalousie dans OTHELLO et Zaïre. Annales de l'U. de Grenoble, 8, 1896.
Dubedout, E. J. Shakespeare et Voltaire: Othello et Zaïre. MPh, 3, 1906.
Gruenewald, A. Voltaires Zaïre und Shakespeares Othello. Progr. Jagersdorf, 1879.
Linguet, S. N. Comparaison entre Othello et Zaïre. Journal de politique et de littérature, 1-2, 1778.
Ormilly, P. Zaïre et Othello. Revue bordelaise, 16.II. & 1.IV.1880.
Sturm, J. Zaïre und Othello, nebst einer kurzen Darstellung von Voltaires Urtheil über Shakespeare. Progr. Crefeld, 1879.
Yorick (P. C. Ferrigni). Zaïre-Otello. In: Vent' anni al teatro. Firenze, 1885.

9. Shakespeare, Goethe and Schiller.

Anon. Schiller-Byron und Schiller-Shakespeare. Hallische Jb, 312, 1838.
—— Shakespeare, Goethe und Gervinus. Augsburger Allg. Zt., 154, 1850.
—— Shakespeare und Goethe. Unsere Zeit, N.F., 2. (Leipzig), 1866.
—— Shakespeare-Feier bei dem Herrn Rath in Frankfurt. Frankfurter Zt., 81, 1902.
Alford, R. G. Shakespeare in two Ver-

sions of Götz von Berlichingen. PEGS, 5, 1890.
Blackie. Ueber Goethe und Shakespeare. Berliner Tageblatt, 19 & 284, 1890.
Bulthaupt, H. Raum und Zeit bei Shakespeare und Schiller. JbShG, 1900.
Chubb, E. W. Shakespeare's Influence upon Goethe. PL, March, 1905.
Chuquet, A. Goetz de Berlichingen. (Cf. Introduction). Paris, 1885.
Civello, I. Amleto, Faust, Manfredo, Gonsalvo. In: Studi critici. Palermo, 1900.
Deetjen, W. Shakespeare Aufführungen unter Goethes Leitung. JbShG, 68, 1932.
Deye, E. Shakespeare und Schiller. Ein Mahnruf. München, 1931.
Droz, T. Shakespeare et Goethe. Semaine littéraire, 159, 1897.
Duentzer, H. Shakespeare und der junge Goethe. In: Neue Beiträge zur Goetheforschung. Stuttgart, 1891.
Duschinsky, W. Shakespeare'sche Einflüsse auf Schillers Tell. Zs. f. d. österreichischen Gymnasien, 50, 1899.
Eckert, H. Goethes Urteile über Shakespeare aus seiner Persönlichkeit erklärt. Diss. Göttingen, 1918.
Engel, J. F. Spuren Shakespeares in Schillers dramatischen Werken. Progr. Magdeburg, 1901.
Green, B. E. Shakespeare and Goethe. Chattanooga, 1901.
Harnack, O. Ueber Goethes Verhältniss zu Shakespeare. In: Essais und Studien. Braunschweig, 1899.
Huther, A. Goethes Götz von Berlichingen und Shakespeares historische Dramen. Progr. Cottbus, 1893.
Larroumet, G. Shakespeare et Goethe. Temps, chron. théâtr., 1.VII.1899.
Leitzmann, A. Dodd's Beauties of Shakespeare als Quelle für Goethe und Herder. JbShG, 55, 1919.
Lemoinne, J. Etudes critiques: Shakespeare, Goethe et Mirabeau. Paris, 1852.
Leo, F. A. Shakespeare und Goethe. JbShG, 24, 1888-89.
Lerch, E. Goethe und Shakespeare. Berliner Tageblatt, 18.VIII.1918.
Ludwig, A. Zur Aufnahme Shakespeares und Vorbereitung Schillers im deutschen Bühnendrama. Festschrift zum 19. Philologentage. Berlin, 1924.
Ludwig, O. Shakespeare und Schiller. In: Shakespeare-Studien. Leipzig, 1891.
Masson, D. Shakespeare and Goethe. In: Littell's Living Age, 36, 1853. And in: Three Devils. London. 1874.
Meyer-Benfey, H. Goethe's Götz von Berlichingen. Weimar, 1930.
Minor, J. Schiller und Shakespeare. ZDPh, 20, 1888.
—— & Sauer, A. Götz und Shakespeare. In: Studien zur Goethe-Philologie. Wien, 1880.
Morshead, E. D. A. Shakespeare and Goethe. Winchester College Shakespeare-Society. London, 1887.
Niessen, C. Goethe und die romantische Shakespeare-Bühne. Das deutsche Theater Jb, 1923-24.
Petersen, J. Schiller und Shakespeare. Euphorion, 32, 1931.
Richter, H. Goethe und Shakespeare. NSp, 40, 1932.
Rudloff, W. T. Shakespeare, Schiller and Goethe Relatively Considered. London, 1848.
Schlegel, A. W. Etwas über W. Shakespeare bei Gelegenheit Wilhelm Meisters. Horen, 6, 1795-97.
Schöffler, H. Shakespeare und der junge Goethe. JbShG, 1940.
Steck, P. Schiller und Shakespeare. Eine statistische Untersuchung. JbShG, 71, 1935.
Sturtevant, A. M. A New Trace of Shakespeare's Influence upon Schiller's Wallenstein. PMLA, 24, 1909.
Ulrici, H. Ueber Shakespeares dramatische Kunst und sein Verhältnis zu Calderon und Goethe. Halle, 1839.
—— Goethe und Schiller in ihrem Verhältniss zu Shakespeare. Leipzig, 1876.
Vermeil, E. La. jeunesse de Goethe, RCC, 1935-36.
Verschaeve, C. Goethe et Shakespeare. Brugge, 1941.
Wagener, K. B. Shakespeares Einfluss auf Goethe in Leben und Dichtung. Diss. Halle, 1890.
Wahr, F. B. Goethe's Shakespeare. PhQ, 11, 1932.
Westenholz, F. P. von. Goethe über Shakespeare als Bühnendichter. Festschrift Ludwig Geiger. Berlin, 1918.
Jacoby, D. Egmont und Shakespeares Julius **CAESAR**. JbGG, 1891.
Petsch, R. Wilhelm Tell und Julius Caesar. Festgabe L. Geiger. Berlin, 1918.
Schneeberger, H. Die Wechselbeziehung zwischen Schillers Tell und Shakespeares Julius Caesar. Progr. Munnerstadt, 1881-82.
Schmidtmayer, R. Die Wechselbeziehungen zwischen Schillers Tell und Shakespeares Julius Caesar. Progr., 1882.
Ayr, C. L'Ofelia di Shakespeare e la Margherita di Goethe. (**HAMLET**). In: Saggi critici. Livorno, 1894.

Berg, L. Die Beziehungen Hamlets zum Wallenstein. Deutsche Studenten-Zt., 33-34, 1886.

Daffis, H. Goethe und Hamlet. Vossische Zt., Sonntags-Beilage, 13.X.1907.

Diamond, W. Wilhelm Meister's Interpretation of Hamlet. MPh, 23, 1925.

Felsi Marchionni, V. Ofelia e Margherita. In: Scritti letterarie e morali. Fermo, 1894.

Flatter, R. Goethe als Hamlet-Regisseur. NSR, 14, 1946-47.

Friese, H. Zu Goethes Hamleterklärung. ZNU, 37, 1938.

Knortz, K. Hamlet und Faust. Zürich, 1888.

Mortensen, J. Hamlet, Edda, 3, 1916.

Reichlin-Meldegg, C. A. von. Faust und Hamlet. Internationale Revue, 1866.

Riquer, E. de. Ideas estéticas de Goethe a proposito de Hamlet. Barcelona, 1916.

Schellwien, R. Hamlet und Faust, eine Parallele. Philosoph. Monatshefte, 3. (Berlin), 1862.

Schileo, N. Amleto e Faust. In: Pagine raccolte. Treviso, 1915.

Schuetz-Wilson, H. Goethe on Hamlet. London Society, Oct., 1875.

Segrè, C. Goethe e l'Amleto. In: Saggi critici di letterature straniere. Firenze, 1894.

Tomlinson, C. On Goethe's Proposed Alterations in Shakespeare's Hamlet. PEGS, 5, 1889.

Trendelenburg, A. Shakespeare's Faust. Berlin, 1933.

Tuerck, H. Das Wesen des Genius (Faust und Hamlet). Leipzig, 1888.

Winkler, P. Grundzüge einer Parallele zwischen Shakespeares Hamlet und Goethes Faust. Progr. Wasselnheim i.E., 1892.

Wolff, E. Wilhelm Meisters Plan einer Bühnenbearbeitung des Hamlet. Festschrift Ludwig Geiger. Berlin, 1918.

Heuwes. Nahe Verwandtschaft einer Stelle aus Schillers Tell III, 3, und Shakespeares **KOENIG JOHANN.** Lyons Zs. für d. deutschen Unterricht, 5.

Kane, R. J. Tolstoy, Goethe and **KING LEAR.** SAB, 21, 1946.

Beckhaus, H. Shakespeares **MACBETH** und die Schillersche Bearbeitung. Progr. Ostrowo, 1889. Cf. ESn, 16, 1892.

Feldtmeyer, E. Schillers Wallenstein und Shakespeares Macbeth. Progr. Krotoschin, 1865.

Fietkau, H. Schillers Macbeth unter Berücksichtigung des Originals und seiner Quelle. Progr. Königsberg, 1897. englische Original. Progr. Tarnowitz, 1888. Cf. ESn, 16, 1892.

Schatzmann, G. Schillers Macbeth mit dem Originale verglichen. Trautenau, 1889. Cf. ESn, 16, 1892.

Steinweg, K. Zum Macbeth Shakespeares, Schillers und Davenants. NJKA, 2, 1899.

Vincke, G. von. Zu Schiller's Macbeth. JbShG, 4, 1869.

Kohler, J. Shylock und Mephistopheles. (**MERCHANT OF VENICE**). WM, Oct., 1906.

Vincke, G. von. Schillers Bühnenbearbeitung des **OTHELLO**. JbShG, 15, 1880.

Montanari, E. Il **RICCARDO III** shakespeariano e le tragedie giovanili del Goethe e dello Schiller. Rivista abruzzese, 22, 1907.

Hauschild, G. R. Das Verhältnis von Goethes **ROMEO UND JULIA** zu Shakespeares gleichnamiger Tragödie. Progr. Frankfurt, 1907.

Bruggencate, K. Ten. Goethes Faust und Shakespeares **TEMPEST.** Taalstudie, 11, 1891.

Wukadinovic, S. Eine Quelle von Schillers Räubern. (**TWO GENTLEMEN OF VERONA**). Euphorion, 8, 1901.

10. Shakespeare and Wieland, Eschenburg, Schlegel, Tieck.

Bernays, M. Der Schlegel-Tiecksche Shakespeare. JbShG, 1, 1865.

—— Die Entstehungsgeschichte des Schlegelschen Shakespeare. Leipzig, 1872.

Blacker, C. Zu Schlegels Shakespeare Uebersetzung. Anglia Bb., 11.

Brandl, A. Fulda, Heyse und Wilbrandt über die Schlegel-Tieck'sche Shakespeare-Uebersetzung. JbShG, 37, 1901.

Bruder, E. Die erste deutsche Shakespeare Aufführung unter Wieland, 1761. Biberach, 1931.

Conrad, H. Eine neue Revision der Schlegel'schen Shakespeare-Uebersetzung. PJb, 1903.

—— Grundsätze und Vorschläge zur Verbesserung des Schlegel'schen Shakespeare-Textes. JbShG, 39, 1903.

—— In Sachen meiner Revision des Schlegel-Tieck'schen Shakespeare-Textes. Sonntagsbeilage zur Vossischen Zt., 11, 1903.

Delius, N. Die Tieck'sche Shakespearekritik beleuchtet. Bonn, 1846.

Eichler, A. Zur Quellengeschichte und Technik von L. Tiecks Shakespeare-Novellen. ESn, 56, 1922.

Eidam, C. Bemerkungen zu einigen Stel-

Sandmann, B. Schillers Macbeth und das len Shakespeare'scher Dramen, sowie zur Schlegel'schen Uebersetzung. Progr 1900.

—— Shakespeare und Schlegel. Beilage zur Allg. Zt., 33, 1901.

Foerster, M. Nochmals Shakespeare und Schlegel. Beilage zur Allg. Zt., 100, 1901.

Frerking, J. Zwei Shakespearestudien in Tiecks Verkehrter Welt. Euphorion, 17, 1910.

Genee, R. Studien zu Schlegels Shakespeare-Uebersetzung. ALG, 10, 1886.

—— A. W. Schlegel und Shakespeare. Berlin, 1903.

—— Der Schlegel-Tieck'sche Shakespeare und seine Verbesserer. Beilage zur Vossischen Zt., 3-4, 1903.

—— Zur Frage des Schlegel-Tieck'schen Shakespeare. Zeitgeist, 16, 1903.

Gillies, A. Tieck and Shakespeare. JEGPh, 36, 1937.

Groeper, R. Wieland im Lichte seines Verhältnisses zu Shakespeare. Pädagog. Archiv, 1913.

Kilian, E. Zur Geschichte des Schlegel-Tieck'schen Shakespeare. Beilage zur Allg. Zt., 95, 1892.

Koch, M. Ludwig Tiecks Stellung zu Shakespeare. JbShG, 32, 1896.

Koellmann, A. Wieland und Shakespeare. Progr. Remscheid, 1896.

Lazenby, M. The Influence of Wieland and Eschenburg on Schlegel's Shakespeare Translation. Baltimore, 1942. Cf. GR, 1944.

Lerch, E. Shakespeare und Schlegel. Frankfurter Zt., 23.VI.1918.

Luedecke, H. Ludwig Tiecks Shakespeare-Studien. Diss Frankfurt. Zürich, 1917.

—— Shakespeare und der junge Tieck. Neue Zürcher Zt., 23-24.VII.1918.

—— Zur Tieck'schen Shakespeare-Übersetzung. JbShG, 55, 1919.

—— Das Buch über Shakespeare. Handschriftliche Aufzeichnungen von Ludwig Tieck. Halle, 1920.

—— Ludwig Tiecks Shakespeare-Übersetzung. JbShG, 57, 1921.

Meisnest, F. W. Wieland and Shakespeare. MLR, 9, 1914.

Pfeiffer, E. Shakespeares und Tiecks Märchendramen. Bonn. 1934.

Schiller, J. Shakespeare und Schlegel. Beilage zur Allg. Zt., 54, 1900.

Schmidt, E. Wieland und Shakespeare. DLZ, 9.V.1908.

Schnöckelborg, G. A. W. Schlegels Einfluss auf William Hazlitt als Shakespeare-Kritiker. Münster, 1931.

Schrader, H. Eschenburg und Shakespeare. Diss. Marburg, 1911.

Seuffert, B. Wielands, Eschenburgs und Schlegels Shakespeare-Übersetzungen. ALG, 13, 1885.

Simpson, M. Eine Vergleichung der Wieland'schen Shakespeare-Uebersetzung mit dem Originale. Diss. Münster, 1898.

Stadler, E. Wielands Shakespeare. Strassburg, 1910.

Stricker, K. Dorothea Tieck und ihr Schaffen für Shakespeare. JbShG, 72, 1936.

Trautwein von Belle. Der Schlegel-Tieck'sche Shakespeare in neuer Gestalt. MLIA, 1868.

Wetz, W. Zur Beurteilung der sogenannten Schlegel-Tieck'schen Shakespeare-Uebersetzung. ESn, 1901. Cf. Frankfurter Zt., 19.I.1901.

—— Schlegel-Tieck. Zukunft, 11.VIII. 1906.

Zapp, D. Die Schlegel-Tiecksche Shakespeare-Uebersetzung. MLIA, 1869.

Zelak, D. Tieck und Shakespeare. Ein Beitrag zur Geschichte der Shakespearomanie in Deutschland. Progr. Tarnopol & Leipzig, 1902.

Maltzahn, W. von. Julius **CAESAR.** Für die Bühne eingerichtet von A. W. Schlegel. JbShG, 7, 1872.

Horn, E. Zur Geschichte der ersten Aufführung von Schlegels **HAMLET**-Uebersetzung auf dem Königlichen Nationaltheater zu Berlin. JbShG, 51, 1915.

Genee, R. Wieland und Falstaff. **(HENRY V)**. National Zt., 8.IV.1880.

Eddelbuettel, C. Remarks on Tieck's Translation of Shakespeare's **MACBETH.** Progr. Hagen, 1864.

Koester, A. Macbeth. Uebersetzungen von Wieland und Eschenburg und Bearbeitungen von Schiller. In: Schiller als Dramaturg. Berlin, 1891.

Winter, J. W. Dorothea Tiecks Macbeth-Uebersetzung. Berlin, 1938.

Petry, R. Wieland und Shakespeare mit besonderer Berücksichtigung der Uebersetzung des Sommernachtstraums. **(MIDSUMMER NIGHT'S DREAM)**. Progr. Remscheid, 1896.

Wurth, L. Zu Wielands, Eschenburgs und A. W. Schlegels Uebersetzungen des Sommernachtstraums. Progr. Budweis, 1897.

Holtermann, K. Vergleichung der Schlegel'schen und Voss'schen Uebersetzung von Shakespeares **ROMEO UND JULIET**. Progr. Münster, 1892.

Kahn, L. W. Ludig Tieck als Uebersetzer von Shakespeares **SONNETTEN.** GR, 1934.

11. Influences upon Other Authors and Translators.

Brisson, A. Jean **AICARD** et l'odyssée d'Othello. Le Temps, 16.II.1899.
Faggi, A. Il personaggio shakespeariano di Iago e due tragedie italiane. (**ALFIERI**). NAnt, 1926.
Gioberti, V. Parallelo fra l'Alfieri e Shakespeare. In: Scritti letterarii. Torino, 1877.
Pascot, G. Shakespeare e Alfieri. Città del Pieve, 1922.
Spera, G. Alfieri e Shakespeare. Cava dei Tirreni, 1886.
Snolen, N. **ATTERBOM** och Shakespeare. Festschrift O. Sylwan. Göteborg, 1924.
Fouquet, K. Jakob **AYRERS** Sidea, Shakespeares Tempest und das Märchen. Marburg, 1929.
Heinrich, G. Ayrer und Shakespeare. Magyar Shakespeare Tar, 8, 1916.
Luetzelberger, K. Das deutsche Schauspiel und Jacob Ayrer. Album des litter. Vereins Nürnberg, 1867.
—— Jacob Ayrers Phoenizia und Shakespeares Viel Lärm um Nichts. Ibid.
Barbey d'Aurévilly, J. Shakespeare et **BALZAC**. Le Pays, 10.V.1864.
Flat, P. Essais sur Balzac. (Goriot and Lear). Paris, 1893.
Moore, G. Shakespeare et Balzac. RB, Febr. 1910 & Century Monthly Mag., 1914.
Nye, R. B. George **BANCROFT'S** View of Shakespeare. SAB, 18, 1943.
Estève, E. **BANVILLE** et Shakespeare. Mélanges Baldensperger. Paris, 1930.
Yvon, P. L' Henry V de Shakespeare interprété par **BARBEY D'AUREVILLY**. RAA, 1929.
BARETTI: See Voltaire, above.
Anon. Lettre d'un Anglais à M. Fréron, sur la petite comédie des Fausses infidélités de M. **BARTHE**. Année littéraire, 7, 1768.
Baym, M. I. **BAUDELAIRE** and Shakespeare. SAB, 15, 1940.
Freytag, G. **BAUDISSINS** Shakespeare-Uebersetzung und die Shakespeare-Gesellschaft. Sämtl. Werke, 16, 1887.
Kroeplin, H. Für einen Shakespeareuebersetzer: Wolf Graf Baudissin zum 150. Geburtstag. Völkischer Beobachter, 40, 1939.
Shudofsky, M. Sarah **BERNHARDT** on Hamlet. College English, 3.
Storoschenko, N. Shakespeare und **BIELINSKIJ**. (In Russian). Mir Bozhi, 3, 1897. And in: Opyty izucheniia Shekspira, Moskva, 1902.
Boehtlingk, A. **BISMARCK** und Shakespeare. Stuttgart, 1908.
Anon. Shakespeares Sonnette, deutsch von **BODENSTEDT**. Europa, 1862.
Lindau, P. Othello, übersetzt von Fr. Bodenstedt. In: Litterarische Rücksichtslosigkeiten. Leipzig, 1871.
Becker, G. **BODMERS** Sasper. JbShG, 73, 1937.
Elze, K. Bodmers Sasper. JbShG, 1, 1865. And in: Abhandlungen zu Shakespeare. Halle, 1877.
Ibershoff, C. H. Bodmer and Shakespeare. MPh, 15, 1917.
Tobler, G. Bodmers politische Schauspiele. J. J. Bodmer Denksschrift zum 200. Geburtstag. Zürich, 1900.
Frenz, H. Edwin **BOOTH** in Polyglot Shakespeare Performances. GR, 18, 1943.
Sprague, A. C. Edwin Booth's Iago. Theatre Annual, 1947.
Wolff, M. J. (ed.) Caspar Wilhelm von **BORCKES** Julius Caesar. Berlin, 1930.
Anon. Shakespeare und **BOERNE**. JbShG, 33, 1897.
Jacobus, R. P. **BOURGET'S** André Cornelis and Hamlet. Fortnightly Review, Aug., 1895.
Götzinger, E. Das Shakespeare Büchlein des Armen Mannes im Toggenburg, 1780. (U. **BRAEKER**). JbShG, 12, 1877.
Donner, J. O. E. G. **BRANDES** och Shakespeare. Finsk Tidskrift, 102, 1927.
Vogeley, H. **BUECHNER** und Shakespeare. Diss. Marburg. Würzburg, 1934.
Bernays, M. Ein kleiner Nachtrag zu **BUERGERS** Werken. Bruchstück aus Bürgers Uebersetzung des Midsummer Night's Dream. Archiv, 1869.
Ebstein, E. Die Hexenszenen aus Bürgers Macbeth-Uebersetzung im ersten Entwurf. Zs. f. Bücherfreunde, 1912.
Kauenhowen, K. G. A. Bürgers Macbeth-Bearbeitung. Diss. Königsberg. Weida (Thüringen), 1917.
Minor, J. Zu Bürgers Macbeth-Uebersetzung. JbShG, 36, 1900.
CALDERON and Shakespeare: See Parallelisms, I. V. 1.
Scartazzini, G. A. Giulio **CARCANO'S** Shakespeare - Uebersetzung. MLIA, 1879.
Simmons, E. J. **CATHERINE THE GREAT** and Shakespeare. PMLA, 47, 1932.
Platz, H. Houston Stewart **CHAMBERLAIN**, Bayreuth und Shakespeare. NM, 11.
Pierluca, M. Un traduttore di Shake-

speare. (C. CHIARINI). Fanfulla della Domenica, 34, 1912.
Brognoligo, G. Le imitazioni Shakespeariane di Antonio CONTI. Rass. Padovana di Storia, lettere ed arti, 1.
Wolff, M. J. Shakespeare and A. Conti (1720). JEGPh, 37, 1938.
Vandiver, E. P. James Fenimore COOPER and Shakespeare. SAB, 15.
Ruta, E. Il genio di Shakespeare nello studio di B. CROCE. In: Visioni d'Oriente e d' Occidente. Milano, 1924.
Sgroi, C. Il saggio di William Shakespeare di B. Croce. In: Saggi e problemi di critica letteraria. Catania, 1932.
Kilian, E. Die DALBERG'sche Bühnenbearbeitung des Timon von Athen. JbShG, 25, 1890.
—— Dalbergs Bühnenbearbeitungen des Kaufmanns von Venedig und Coriolans. JbShG, 26, 1891.
Deschamps, G. Shakespeare et M. Léon DAUDET. In: La vie et les livres, 4e Sér. Paris, 1897.
Mueller, D. Observations sur les Enfants d'Edouard de DELAVIGNE et sur les rapports de cette tragédie au Richard III de Shakespeare. Progr. Fulda, 1844.
Bernays, M. Nik. DELIUS' Ausgabe der Shakespeare'schen Werke, 1870. In: Schriften zur Kritik und Litteraturgeschichte. Berlin, 1903.
Gilman, Margaret. Le Dissipateur (DESTOUCHES) and Timon of Athens. MLN, 1927.
Davidson, F. A Note on Emily DICKINSON'S Use of Shakespeare. NEQ, 18, 1945.
Anon. Franz von DINGELSTEDT als Bühnenbearbeiter Shakespeares. Allg. litterar. Correspondenz, 8, 1881.
Juergens, W. Dingelstedt, Shakespeare und Weimar. JbShG, 1919.
Schorf, W. Dingelstedts Plan zu einer neuen Shakespeare - Uebersetzung. JbShG, 1940.
Fiorelli, D. DOSTOIEVSKIJ contro Shakespeare. In: Il dramma dell'intelligenza. Roma, 1928.
Anon. De l'Othello de Shakespeare et de DUCIS. Le Catholique, June, 1826.
Dargan, E. P. Shakespeare and Ducis. MPh, 10, 1912.
Downs, B. W. Ducis's Two Hamlets. MLR, 1936.
Dubois, P. F. Macbeth, de Ducis. Globe, 28.II.1826.
Kuehn, C. Ueber Ducis in seiner Beziehung zu Shakespeare. Diss. Jena, 1875.
Malkewitz, G. Ein französischer Shakespearebearbeiter. National-Zt., 483, 1878.
Penning, G. E. Ducis als Nachahmer Shakespeares. Progr. Bremen, 1884.
Le Roux, H. Hamlet, adaptation en vers d'Alexandre DUMAS et de P. Meurice. RB, 14, 1886.
Mauthner, F. Shakespeares Cleopatra und die DUSE. Berliner Tageblatt, 27.IX.1899.
Deetjen, W. Der Sturm als Operntext bearbeitet von EINSIEDEL und Gotter. JbShG, 64, 1928.
Falk, R. P. EMERSON and Shakespeare. PMLA, 56, 1941.
Peery, T. Emerson, the Historical Frame, and Shakespeare. MLQ, 9, 1948.
Baureny, G. L'intrigue du Roi Lear et le roman d'André FAY, Balteky ház. Irodalomtörténeti Közlemények, 65, 1937.
Anon. Kuno FISCHERS Hamlet. JbShG, 33, 1897.
Roessler, C. Kuno Fischer über Shakespeares Hamlet. PJb, Sept., 1896.
Cian, V. Un articolo shakespeariano di Ugo FOSCOLO. GSLI, 91, 1928.
Faggi, A. Il Foscolo e l'Amleto. Marzocco, 10.VI.1928.
—— Ciò che pensava FEDERICO IL GRANDE di Shakespeare. Marzocco, March, 1923.
Volz, G. B. Shakespeare am Hofe Friedrichs des Grossen. DR, 49, 1922.
Wohlrab, M. Ueber die Verwendung von FREYTAGS Technik des Dramas im Unterricht mit besonderer Berücksichtigung von Shakespeares Hamlet. NJKA, 1900.
Valcarenghi, U. GARAVIGLIA interprete di Shakespeare. In: Rievocazioni. Milano, 1932.
Anon. GARIBALDI und Shakespeare. JbShG, 20, 1885.
Schneider, K. GERSTENBERG als Verkünder Shakespeares. JbShG, 58, 1922.
Anon. GERVINUS und sein Vorwort zum Shakespeare. Europa, 28, 1849.
Weigert, A. Shakespeares Macbeth bei Gervinus und Kreyssig. Gegenwart, 11, 1877.
Sgroi, C. Vincenzo GIOBERTI critico di Shakespeare. Rassegna, 1922.
Amico, S. d'. Shakespeare e GOLDONI: Il primo festival teatrale di Venezia. Rassegna dell' istruzione artistica, 5, 1934.
Neri, A. Un giudizio di Carlo Goldoni su Shakespeare. Rivista Europea, March, 1877.

Ortolani, G. Goldoni e Shakespeare. Rivista italiana del dramma, 4, 1940.
Bartmann, H. **GRABBES** Verhältniss zu Shakespeare. Diss. Münster, 1898.
Bolin, W. **GRILLPARZERS** Shakespeare-Studien. JbShG, 18, 1883.
Braun, H. Grillparzers Verhältnis zu Shakespeare. Diss. München. Nürnberg, 1916.
Fries, A. Intime Beobachtungen zu Grillparzers Stil und Versbau. Berlin, 1922.
Glücksmann, H. Grillparzer und Shakespeare. JbGrG, 1938.
Gross, E. Grillparzers Verhältnis zu Shakespeare. JbShG, 51, 1915.
Salinger, H. Shakespeare's Tyranny over Grillparzer. MDU, 31, 1939.
Yates, D. Grillparzer's Hero and Shakespeare's Juliet. MLR, 1926.
Zucker, A. E. Shakespeare and Grillparzer. MLN, 31, 1916.
Eugenio. Luigi **GROTO** and Shakespeare. Gentleman's Mag., Sept., 1800.
Kuery, H. Simon **GRYNAEUS** von Basel 1725-99, der erste deutsche Uebersetzer von Shakespeares Romeo und Julia. Basler Beiträge. Zürich, 1935.
Böhtlingk, A. **GUNDOLFS** Shakespeare in deutscher Sprache: Ein Vademecum. Karlsruhe, 1929.
Salandre, G. Shylock ou le Marchand de Venice par Edmond **HARAUCOURT**. Art et Critique, 21.XII.1889 & RB, 25, 1890 & RDM, 97.
Stirk, S. D. Gerhart **HAUPTMANN** and Hamlet. GLL, 1, 1937.
Voigt, F. A. Gerhard Hauptmann und Shakespeare. GRM, 25, 1937.
—— & Reichart, W. Hauptmann und Shakespeare. Ein Beitrag zur Geschichte des Fortlebens Shakespeares in Deutschland. Breslau, 1938; Goslar, 1947.
Wahr, F. B. The Hauptmann Hamlet. PhQ, April, 1937.
Anon. Ein Urteil **HEBBELS** über Shakespeare. Blätter für literar. Unterhaltung, 1.VIII.1850.
—— Hebbel und die Shakespeare-Manie. Kieler Zt., 28.XI.1902.
Alberts, W. Hebbels Stellung zu Shakespeare. Weimar, Berlin, 1908.
Bartels, A. Hebbel und Shakespeare. Heide (Holstein), 1932.
Brües, O. Hebbel und Shakespeare. Das Nationaltheater, 4. (Berlin), 1931-32.
Graham, P. G. Hebbel's Study of King Lear. Festschrift W. A. Neilson. Northampton (Mass.), 1939.
Keller, W. Eine Bearbeitung des Julius Caesar von Friedrich Hebbel. JbShG, 39, 1903.
Werner, R. M. Hebbels Theaterbearbeitung von Shakespeares Julius Caesar. Zs. f. d. österreichischen Gymnasien, 58, 1907.
Salditt, Maria. **HEGEL'S** Shakespeare-Interpretation. In: Jaspers Philosoph. Forschungen, 5, 1927.
Schalles, E. A. **HEINES** Verhältnis zu Shakespeare (mit einem Arhang über Byron). Diss. Berlin, 1904.
Strecker, K. Heine und Shakespeare. Tägliche Rundschau, Unterhaltungs-Beilage, 40, 1906.
Wadepuhl, W. Heine and Shakespeare. SAB, 21, 1946.
Knight, A. H. J. Herzog **HEINRICH JULIUS** von Braunschweig und Shakespeare. GRM, 25, 1937.
Gates, W. B. O. **HENRY** and Shakespeare. SAB, 19, 1944.
Abramczyk, R. **HERDERS** Anteil an Schlegels Shakespearübersetzung. Vossische Zt., Sonntagsbeilage, 17, 1910.
Gillies, A. Herder's Essay on Shakespeare, Das Herz der Untersuchung. MLR, 32, 1937.
Isaacsen, Hertha. Der junge Herder und Shakespeare. Berlin, 1930.
Joret, C. Herder. Paris, 1875.
Leitzmann, A. Dodds Beauties of Shakespeare als Quelle für Goethe und Herder. JbShG, 55, 1919.
Suphan, B. Herder an Gerstenberg über Shakespeare. Vierteljahrschrift für Litteraturgeschichte, 1889.
Kayser, R. Georg **HERWEGHS** Shakespeare-Auffassung. GQ, 20, 1947.
Hewett-Thayer, H. W. **HOFFMANN'S** Approach to Literature. GR, 16, 1941.
Wehl, F. Shakespeares Komödie der Irrungen in **HOLTEI'S** Bearbeitung. Europa, 45, 1849.
Anon. **HUDSON'S** Edition of Shakespeare. NAR, Jan., 1857.
—— Zur Shakespeare-Feier. (Victor **HUGO**). Europa, 1864.
Barthou, L. Autour du William Shakespeare de Victor Hugo. RP, Aug., 1920.
Daubray, C. Sur le William Shakespeare de Victor Hugo. RdF, 15.III.1937.
Henriot, E. Hugo et William Shakespeare. Le Temps, 14.IX.1937.
Jullien, J. Hugo und Hamlet. MLIA, 35, 1895.
Risi, P. A proposito di William Shakespeare di V. Hugo. Torino, 1865.
St. Albin, E. W. Shakespeare et V. Hugo. Revue Canadienne, 26, 1890.

Warren, A. Shakespeare and Victor Hugo. Spectator, March, 1902.
Arestad, S. **IBSEN** and Shakespeare: A Study in Influence. SS, 19, 1946.
Dickinson, G. L. Shakespeare, Ibsen and Bernard Shaw. Independent Review, July, 1906.
Koht, H. Shakespeare and Ibsen. JEGPh, 44, 1945.
Price, T. R. Ibsen's Dramatic Constructions Compared with Shakespeare's. Shakespeariana, Jan., 1892.
Tissi, S. Analisi di alcuni drammi di Ibsen e dell' Amleto di Shakespeare. In: Al Microscopio psicoanalitico. Milano, 1933.
Waterloo, S. P. Shakespeare and Ibsen. Adelphis, Oct., 1924.
Zucker, A. E. The Courtiers in Hamlet and The Wild Duck. MLN, 54, 1939.
—— Ibsen-Hettner; Coriolanus-Brand. MLN, 1936.
Vincke, G. Die Berliner Hamlet-Aufführung unter **IFFLAND.** JbShG, 21, 1886.
Deetjen, W. **IMMERMANNS** Bearbeitung des Sturms als Operntext. JbShG, 57, 1921.
Vincke, G. Immermanns Einrichtung des Hamlet. JbShG, 21-22, 1886-87.
Wittsack, R. K. L. Immermann der Dramaturg. Berlin, 1914.
Erichsen, V. Hamlet og Søren **KIERKEGAARD.** Edda, 15, 1921.
Oppel, H. Shakespeare und Kierkegaard. JbShG, 76, 1940.
Sprenger, R. "Shade" bei Shakespeare und "Schatten" in E. C. von **KLEISTS** Frühling. ESn, 22, 1895.
Corssen, Meta. Kleists und Shakespeares dramatische Sprache. Diss. Berlin, 1919.
—— Kleists und Shakespeares dramatische Gestalten. JbShG, 58, 1922.
—— Kleist und Shakespeare. Weimar, 1930.
Fischer, O. Macbeth und Penthesilea. Euphorion, 15.
Fries, C. Shakespeare bei Kleist. Archiv, 1935-36.
Harder, H. Shakespeare bei Kleist. Archiv, Dec., 1935.
Hellmann, H. Kleists Prinz von Homburg und Shakespeares Mass für Mass. GRM, 1923.
Schultze-Jahde, K. Kleists Shakespeare Anekdoten. Jb. Kleist Ges., 1925-26.
Wolff, E. Shakespeares Einfluss auf Heinrich von Kleist. Frankfurter Zt., 268-69, 1901.
Jacobowski, L. **KLINGER** und Shakespeare. Ein Beitrag zur Shakespearomanie der Sturm- und Drangperiode. Dresden, Leipzig, 1891.
Lanz, M. Klinger und Shakespeare. Diss. Zürich, 1941.
Chuquet, A. Shakespeare, **KLOPSTOCK** et Mirabeau. RHLF, 1894.
Leitzmann, A. K. **LACHMANN** als Shakespeare-Uebersetzer. JbShG, 1920.
Haak, P. Die ersten französischen Shakespeare Uebersetzungen von **LA PLACE** und Le Tourneur. Diss. Berlin, 1922.
Weilen, A. von. **LAUBE** und Shakespeare. JbShG, 43, 1907.
Looten, C. La première controverse internationale sur Shakespeare entre l'abbé **LEBLANC** et W. Guthrie, 1745-48. Mélanges et travaux, 32, Lille, 1927.
Eckstein, Baron d'. Sur Shakespeare, Rowe, Jane Shore et M. **LEMERCIER.** Drapeau blanc, 12.V.1824.
Stiefel, A. L. Lemercier als Plagiator Shakespeares. ESn, 26, 1899.
Rauch, H. **LENZ** und Shakespeare. Ein Beitrag zur Shakespearomanie der Sturm- und Drangperiode. Berlin, 1892.
Hofmiller, J. **LEO** und Vischer als Shakespeare-Forscher. Beilage zur Allg. Zt., 181, 1901.
Tiessen, E. Herrn F. A. Leo's Verdienste um den Shakespearetext. ESn, 5, 1882.
Crescimone, V. Amleto, Fausto e Giacomo **LEOPARDI.** In: Saggi e conferenze. Roma, 1912.
Mancinelli, N. Un' analogia tra il pessimismo di Leopardi e quello d'Amleto. In: Horae subsecivae. Roma, 1932.
Piccolo, V. Shakespeare e Leopardi. Libri del giorno, Feb., 1922.
Previtera, A. Quelques analogies entre William Shakespeare e Giacomo Leopardi. In: Les harmonies. Messina, 1903.
Reforgiato, V. Amleto, Fausto e Giacomo Leopardi. Catania, 1895.
Anon. Shakespeare und **LESSING.** Europa, 84, 1850.
Henkel, H. Der Blankvers Shakespeares im Drama Lessings, Goethes und Schillers. ZVL, 1, 1888.
Jacoby, D. Emilia Galotti und Shakespeares Othello. Sonntags-Beilage der Vossischen Zt., 26, 1887.
Kettner, G. Lessing und Shakespeare. NJKA, 1907.
Meisnest, F. W. Lessing and Shakespeare. PMLA, 19, 1904.
Rovenhagen, L. Lessings Verhältniss zu Shakespeare. Progr. Aachen, 1867.

Walzel, O. Der Kritiker Lessing und Shakespeare. JbShG, 65, 1929.
Witkowski, G. Aristoteles und Shakespeare in Lessings Hamburgischer Dramaturgie. Euphorion, 2, 1895.
Vandiver, E. P. **LONGFELLOW**, Lamir, Boker and King Lear. SAB, 19, 1944.
Fischer, B. Otto **LUDWIGS** Trauerspielplan Der Landwirt vom Passeier und sein Verhältnis zu den Shakespearestudien. Diss. Greifswald, 1916.
Meyer, R. M. Otto Ludwigs Shakespearestudien. JbShG, 37, 1901.
Mis, L. Les Etudes sur Shakespeare d'O. Ludwig. RG, 1921.
—— Les Etudes sur Shakespeare d'Otto Ludwig exposées dans un ordre méthodique et précédées d'une introduction littéraire. Lille, 1922; Paris, 1929.
Raphael, G. Les Shakespearestudien d'Otto Ludwig et le Shakespeare de Gervinus. Mélanges Andler. Strasbourg, 1924.
Richter, F. Otto Ludwigs Trauerspielplan Tiberius Gracchus und sein Zusammenhang mit den Shakespeare-Studien. Breslau, 1935.
Scherer, W. Otto Ludwigs Shakespearestudien. In: Vorträge. Berlin, 1874.
Stempfe, K. Shakespeare in Deutschland von Otto Ludwig an. Jb. der Philosoph. Fakultät Prag, 1926-27.
Condamin, J. Un royal traducteur de Shakespeare. (**LUIZ OF PORTUGAL**). Extrait de la Revue des Facultés catholiques. Lyon, 1888.
Engel, E. Shakespeares Kaufmann von Venedig ins Portugiesische übersetzt von Dom Luiz König von Portugal. MLIA, 1880.
Decreus, J. Forces constructives dans Hamlet et dans La Princesse Maleine de Maurice **MAETERLINCK**. CLS, 11, 1943.
Mukherji, M. Joyzell and The Tempest. Calcutta Review, 3rd Ser., 57, 1935.
Symons, A. The Belgian Shakespeare: Princess Maleine, The Intruder. Athenaeum, 23.IV.1892.
Brule, A. Une page de **MALLARME** sur Hamlet et Fortinbras. RAA, April, 1925.
Bellezza, P. Una lettera sconosciuta del **MANZONI** sullo Shakespeare. Rassegna nazionale, 1.VIII.1895 & 1.VII. 1896.
—— Gli studi Shakespeariani del Manzoni. GSLI, 31, 1897-98. And in: Irradiazione e riverberi dell'anima italiana. Milano, 1926.
Dragonetti, A. Un giudizio del Manzoni sullo Shakespeare. Italia moderna, 1906.
Faggi, A. Il Macbeth e i Promessi Sposi. Marzocco, 21, 1916.
—— Il Re Lear e i Promessi Sposi. Atti della R. Accad. delle scienze di Torino, 52, 1916-17.
Galletti, A. Manzoni, Shakespeare e Bossuet. Studi di filologia moderna, 4, 1911.
Ovidio, F. d'. Shakespeare e Manzoni. In: Atti della R. Accad. di Napoli, 37, 1906.
Reforgiato, V. Shakespeare e Manzoni. Catania, 1898.
Scarano, N. Amleto e Adelchi. NAnt, 16.IX.1892.
Scherillo, M. Ammiratori ed imitatori dello Shakespeare prima del Manzoni. NAnt, 16.XI.1892.
Holzer, G. **MARK TWAIN** und Shakespeare. Heidelberger Tageblatt, 26.VI. 1909.
Jackson, T. A. Karl **MARX** and Shakespeare. International Literature, Feb., 1936.
Nechkina, M. Shakespeare in K. Marx's Capital. International Literature, March, 1935.
Olson, C. Lear and Moby Dick (**MELVILLE**). Twice a Year, 1, 1938.
Jacoby, D. Der Hamlet-Monolog III, 1, und Lessings Freunde **MENDELSSOHN** und Kleist. JbShG, 25, 1890.
Stern, A. Moses Mendelssohn und Shakespeare. NSR, 22, 1929.
Zollinger, O. Ein französischer Shakespeare-Bearbeiter des XVIII. Jahrhunderts. (L. S. **MERCIER**). JbShG, 38, 1902.
Anon. A French Midsummer Night's Dream: Shakespeare and M. **MEURICE**. Shakespeariana, 2, 1886.
Kraeger, H. Shakespeare-Verse auf der Wanderung in C. F. **MEYERS** Gedichten. ESn, 28, 1900.
Rossetti, W. M. Shakespeare and **MIRABEAU**. N&Q, 12, 1868.
Aicard, J. **MOLIERE** à Shakespeare, prologue en vers. Paris, 1879.
Eyssette, A. Shakespeare chez Molière: Othello à la Comédie Française. Le Gaulois, 25.II.1899.
Kerbaker, M. Sopra un luogo dello Shakespeare imitato da Vincenzo **MONTI**. Atti della R. Accad., Napoli, 13, 1889.
—— Shakespeare e Goethe nei versi di V. Monti. Firenze, 1897.
Pasini, F. V. Monti in difesa dello Shake-

speare. Fanfulla della Domenica, 27, 1905.
Zumbini, B. Sopra un luogo dello Shakespeare imitato dal Monti. In: Studi, Firenze, 1894.
Biller, Clara. Ein spanischer Shakespeare Kritiker (**MORATIN**). JbShG, 7, 1872.
Carreras, L. Refutación de las notas de Moratín contra el Hamlet. In: Retratos a la pluma. Madrid, 1884.
Sauzin, L. Adam Heinrich **MUELLER**. Paris, 1937.
Anon. Shakespeare and **MUSSET**. TLS, 25.IV.1902.
Betbeder-Matibet, Marie. L'influence de Shakespeare sur Musset dans les Comédies et Proverbes. RELV, 1921.
Duval, G. Shakespeare et Musset. Figaro, 8.IV.1911.
Fricke, E. Der Einfluss Shakespeares auf Alfred de Mussets Dramen. Diss. Basel, 1902.
Lafoscade, L. Le théâtre d'Alfred de Musset. Paris, 1902.
Rickey, H. W. Musset shakespearien. Bordeaux, 1932.
Toffanin, G. Musset e Shakespeare. In: Gli ultimi nostri. Forli, 1919.
Child, T. Shakespeare and **NAPOLEON III**. Gentleman's Mag., March, 1885.
Fresenius, A. **NECKER** und Shakespeare. JbShG, 46, 1910.
Kruse, G. R. Shakespeare und Otto **NICOLAI**. JbShG, 46, 1910.
Ludwig, A. **NIETZSCHE** und Shakespeare. JbShG, 56, 1920.
NODIER, C. Pensées de Shakespeare extraites de ses ouvrages. Besançon, 1801.
Rehder, H. **NOVALIS** and Shakespeare. PMLA, 63, 1948.
Willey, N. L. **OEHLENSCHLAEGER'S** Amleth. SS, 17, 1942.
Sarrazin, G. Shakespeare und Orlando **PESCETTI**. ESn, 46, 1913.
Kallenbach, H. **PLATENS** Beziehungen zu Shakespeare. SVL, 8, 1908.
Leitzmann, A. Shakespeare in Platens Tagebüchern. JbShG, 37, 1901.
Hunter, W. B. **POE'S** The Sleeper and Macbeth. AL, 20, 1948.
Bernacki, L. S. A. **PONIATOWSKI** als Shakespeare-Uebersetzer. JbShG, 42, 1906.
Lacroix, A. Shakespeare et M. **PONSARD**. Bruxelles, 1876.
Carpenter, J. C. The Abbé **PREVOST** and Shakespeare. MLR, April, 1915.
Havens, G. R. The Abbé Prévost and Shakespeare. MPh, 17, 1919.
Lerner, N. O. **PUSHKIN'S** Relations to Shakespeare. (In Russian). Zven'ia, 5, 1935.
Pokrovskii, M. Puschkin und Shakespeare. JbShG, 43, 1907.
Dünninger, J. **RAABE** und Shakespeare. GRM, 22, 1934.
Happach. Shakespeares Wirkung auf W. Raabe. Mitteilungen f. d. Ges. der Freunde Raabes, 23, 1933.
Happich. Shakespeares Einfluss auf Deutschland und W. Raabes Beziehungen zu Shakespeare. Ibid., 24, 1934.
Seebass, A. Shakespeare und Raabe. GRM, 22, 1934.
Anon. **RAMON DE LA CRUZ**: Hamlet. Revista contemporanea, Nov., 1900.
Iacuzzi, A.A The Naive Theme in The Tempest as a Link between Thomas Shadwell and Ramón de la Cruz. MLN, 52, 1937.
Tesdorpf, P. & T. Auf Shakespeares Spuren: Henri de **REGNIERS** Gedichtfolge. JbShG, 64, 1920.
Gaucher, M. Le Hamlet de Th. **REINACH**. RB, March, 1880.
Bonghi, R. Shakespeare e **RENAN**. La Tempesta e il Calibano. NAnt, 40, 1878. And in: Horae subsecivae. Roma, 1883.
Minor, J. Ernesto **ROSSI** als Hamlet, Othello, Lear, Macbeth. Deutsche Revue, Jan., 1897.
Zanco, A. Ernesto Rossi interprete e critico shakespeariano. Riv. ital. del dramma, 2, 1938.
Anon. Shakespeare und sein neuester Kritiker (**RUMELIN**). Grenzboten, 25, 1866.
Lamm, M. **RUNEBERGS** Hamlet-tolkning. Skrifter utgivna av Svenska litteratursällskapet i Finland, 1938.
Latreille, C. George **SAND** et Shakespeare. Annales internat. d'histoire, Congrès de Paris, 1901.
Mouly, G. **SARDOU** et Shakespeare. RdF, 1932.
Durian, H. Jocza **SAVITS** und die Münchener Shakespearebühne. Emsdetten, 1937.
Hankiss, J. **SCHELANDRE** et Shakespeare. MLN, 36, 1921.
Gebhard, R. Shakespeare und **SCHOPENHAUER**. JbShG, 47, 1911.
Paulsen, F. Schopenhauser, Hamlet, Mephistopheles. Berlin, 1900.
Wieninger, G. Schopenhauer in seiner Stellung zu Shakespeare. JbShG, 66, 1930.
Kilian, E. **SCHREYVOGELS** Shakespeare-Bearbeitungen. JbShG, 39, 1903.
—— Schreyvogels Romeo und Julia-Bearbeitung. JbShG, 41, 1907.

Hauffen, A. SCHROEDERS Bearbeitung des Kaufmanns von Venedig. Vierteljahrschrift f. Litteraturgeschichte, 5, 1892.
Kauenhowen, K. Zu F. L. Schröders Macbeth-Bearbeitung. Zs. f. Bücherfreunde, 8, 1916.
Vincke, G. Shakespeare und Schröder. JbShG, 11, 1876.
Krauss, R. Ludwig **SCHUBART** als Shakespeare-Uebersetzer. JbShG, 39, 1903.
Lehtonen, J. V. Un passage de Shakespeare dans les Récits de l'enseigne **STAL**. Neuphilolog. Mitteilungen, 25, 1924.
Tomlinson, C. A Modern French Critic of Shakespeare's Comedies (Paul **STAPFER**). N&Q, Feb., 1893.
Fraenkel, L. Karl **STARCKS** Gedanken über Shakespeare, besonders über König Lear. Jahresberichte f. neuere deutsche Litteraturgeschichte, 1898.
Bulman, J. **STRINDBERG** and Shakespeare. London, 1933.
Lang, D. M. **SUMARKOV'S** Hamlet: A Misjudged Russian Tragedy of the Eighteenth Century. MLR, 43, 1948.
Rosenberg, F. Shakespeare in dem Urteil Hippolyte **TAINES**. GRM, 9, 1921.
Linder, S. **TEGNERS** Mjältsjukan och Hamlet. Samlaren, 1936.
Forster, R. **TOLSTOI** contro Shakespeare. Fanfulla della Domenica, 27, 1907.
Kane, R. J. Tolstoy, Goethe and King Lear. SAB, 21, 1946.
Knight, G. W. Shakespeare and Tolstoi. London, 1934.
Wassenberg, R. Tolstois Angriff auf Shakespeare. Diss. Bonn, 1935.
Schücking, L. Eine Anleihe Shakespeares bei **TOURNEUR**. ESn, 50, 1916.
Gebhart, R. Iwan **TURGENJEW** in seinen Beziehungen zu Shakespeare. JbShG, 45, 1909.
Orsini, N. Shakespeare tradotto da **UNGARETTI**. Il Mondo, 1, 1945.
Pellizzi, C. Ungaretti traduttore: I sonetti di Shakespeare. Fiera letteraria, 1, 1946.
Robertis, G. de. Ungaretti traduttore di Shakespeare. Leonardo, 1947.
Underwood, V. P. **VERLAINE** et Coppée traducteurs de Shakespeare. NL, 14.I. 1939.
Anon. Le traduzioni shakespeariane inedite di Alessandro **VERRI**. Marzocco, 4.XII.1932.
Antonucci, G. Le traduzioni shakespeariane inedite di A. Verri. Marzocco, 8. II.1931.
Crinò, A. M. Le traduzioni shakespeariane inedite di A. Verri. Rassegna italiana, 1932.
Giraud, J. Deux souvenirs d'Hamlet et de Faust dans "Paris" d'A. de **VIGNY**. RG, 8, 1912.
Larroumet, G. Théâtre d'Alfred de Vigny: Le More de Venise. RCC, Dec., 1895.
Page. Vigny lecteur de Macbeth et d'Hamlet. Le Français, 1.IV.1919.
Sessely, A. L'influence de Shakespeare sur A. de Vigny. Berne, 1927.
Bayer, J. Friedrich Th. **VISCHER** als Shakespeare-Erklärer. Neue Freie Presse, 29.VIII.1900.
Conrad, H. F. Vischer und Dorothea Tieck als Macbeth-Uebersetzer. Archiv, 106, 1901.
Seliger, P. Vischers Shakespeare-Vorträge. LE, 1.II.1903.
Anon. Shakespeare-Sonetten bij **VONDEL**. Tijdschrift voor nederl. taal en letterkunde, 13, 1894.
Dodgson, E. S. Shakespeare and Vondel. N&Q, 7, 1901.
Sijbrandi, K. Verhandeling over Vondel en Shakespeare als treuerspeldichters. Haarlem, 1841.
Bennett, J. Richard **WAGNER**. The Musical Times, 1890.
Chater, A. G. Shakespeare and Wagner. Temple Bar, 113, 1897.
Gruber, J. **WEISSE** und Shakespeare. ZVL, 1905.
Huettermann, W. Christian Felix Weisse und seine Zeit in ihrem Verhältniss zu Shakespeare. Diss. Bonn, 1912.
Necker, N. **WERDERS** Macbeth-Vorlesungen. Grenzboten, 51, 1885.
Kauenhowen, K. J. K. G. **WERNICHS** Macbeth-Bearbeitung, die erste Aufführung des Macbeth in Berlin, 1778. JbShG, 54, 1918.
Falk, R. P. Critical Tendencies in **R. G. WHITE'S** Shakespeare Commentary. AL, 20, 1948.
—— Shakespeare's Place in Walt **WHITMAN'S** America. SAB, 17, 1942.
Furness, C. J. Walt Whitman's Estimate of Shakespeare. HSPhL, 14, 1932.
Harrison, R. C. Walt Whitman and Shakespeare. PMLA, 44, 1929.

CHAPTER TWELVE

Shelley.

1. Influences upon Individual Countries.

Cameron, K. N. & Frenz, H. The Stage History of Shelley's The Cenci. PMLA, 60, 1945.
Cenci: See also I. VI. 10.
Duhu, J. The Cenci on the Stage, TLS, 24.XI.1945.
Hicks, A. C. An **AMERICAN** Performance of The Cenci. Stanford Studies in Lang. and Lit., 1941.
Power, Julia, Shelley in America in the Nineteenth Century: His Relation to American Critical Thought and His Influence. U. of Nebraska Studies, 1940.
Ackermann, R. Shelley in Frankreich und Italien. **(FRANCE)**. ESn, 17, 1892.
Peyre, H. Shelley et la France: lyrisme anglais et lyrisme français au XIXe siècle. Le Caire, 1935. Cf. RLC, 15, 1935.
Sarrazin, G. Shelley en France. Notebook of the E. S. Soc., 1887.
Stanton, T. Shelley in France. Nation, (New York) 18.VI.1924.
Liptzin, S. Shelley in **GERMANY**. Columbia U.P., 1924.
Dekker, G. De invloed van Keats en Shelley in Nederland gedurende de negentiende eeuw. **(HOLLAND)**. Groningen, 1926.
Kloos, W. Shelley in Nederland. Nieuwe Gids, Sept., 1922 & ESs, 4, 1922.
Ackermann, R. Shelley in Frankreich und Italien. **(ITALY)**. ESn, 17, 1892.
Bini, B. P. B. Shelley nel Risorgimento italiano. Fiume, 1927.
Koszul, A. Inédits italiens de Shelley. RLC, 2, 1922.
Mustacchia, N. Shelley e la sua fortuna in Italia. Catania, 1925.
Varia. Commemorazione di Percy Bysshe Shelley in Roma. Roma, 1893.
Gullon, R. Shelley en vers castillans. **(SPAIN)**. Insula 22 (Madrid), 1947.
Hespelt, E. H. Shelley and Spain. PMLA, 38, 1923.

2. Influences upon Individual Authors.

Anon. **BALZAC** and Shelley. N&Q, 8. VIII.1874.
Baum, P. F. Shelley and the Abbé **BARUEL**. PMLA, 36, 1921.
Lebois, A. L'influence de Shelley sur Elémir **BOURGES**. RLC, 22, 1948.
Marussig, G. Shelley e **DE BOSIS**. NAnt, 1.IX.1928.
Buchwald, O. Die Dramatiker Shelley und **HEBBEL**. Deutsches Museum, 1867.
Morice, C. **LAMARTINE**, Baudelaire, Shelley. Revue contemporaine, Jan., 1886.
Nolva, R. de. Shelley et Lamartine. NRI, 25.I.1922.
Girard, H. Comment Shelley a été révélé à Victor Hugo: La Grève de Samarez de Pierre **LEROUX**. RLC, 2, 1922.
Batault, G. Défense du poète: Shelley (against **MAUROIS**). MF, 1929.
Zanco, A. I Cenci di Shelley e l'imitazione di G. B. **NICCOLINI**. Rivista ital. del dramma, 15.V.1939.
Wilson, A. L. **VERLAINE** and Shelley. PL, 8, 1896.
Chinard, G. Shelley et **VIGNY**: une source possible de la Maison du berger. RLC, 2, 1922.
Cluck, Julia. Elinor **WYLIE'S** Shelley Obsession. PMLA, 56, 1941.

CHAPTER THIRTEEN

Sterne.

1. Influences upon Individual Countries.

Pearce, R. H. Sterne and Sensibility in **AMERICAN** Diaries. MLN, 59, 1944.
Baldwin, C. S. The Literary Influence of Sterne in **FRANCE**. PMLA, 17, 1902.
Barton, F. B. Etude sur l'influence de Sterne en France. Paris, 1911.
Baker, T. S. The Influence of L. Sterne upon **GERMAN** Literature. Americana Germanica, 2, 1900.
Hallamore, G. J. Das Bild Laurence Sternes in Deutschland von der Aufklärung bis zur Romantik. Berlin, 1936.
(Hewett)-Thayer, H. W. Laurence Sterne in Germany. Columbia U. P., 1905.
Rabizzani, G. Sterne in **ITALIA**. Roma, 1920.
Vertsman, I. Lorens Stern. **(RUSSIA)**. In: Literaturnyi Kritik, 7, 1938.

2. Influences upon Individual Authors.

Partridge, E. Deux dettes anglaises de **GAUTIER** (Sterne, Thomson). In: A Critical Medley. Paris, 1926.
Buechner, A. Sternes Koran in Makariens Archiv. **GOETHE** ein Plagiator? Mor-

genblatt für gebildete Leser, 24.IX. 1863.
Duentzer, H. Goethe und Tristram Shandy. ALG, 9, 1880.
Hedain, A. Goethe plagiaire de Sterne. Monde maçonnique, July, 1863.
Loeper, G. von. Noch einmal Goethe und Sterne. Blätter f. literar. Unterhaltung, 1.IV.1869.
Pinger, W. R. R. Laurence Sterne and Goethe. UCPPh, 1920.
Springer, R. Ist Goethe ein Plagiator Lorenz Sternes? Deutsche Museum, 1867. And in: Essays zur Kritik und zur Goethe Literatur. München, 1885.
Ransmeier, J. C. **HEINES** Reisebilder und Sterne. Archiv, 118, 1907.
Vacano, S. Heine und Sterne. Berlin, 1907.
Bauer, F. Sterne'scher Humor in **IMMERMANNS** Münchhausen. Progr. Wien, 1896.
Longo, J. Laurence Sterne und J. G. **JACOBI**. Progr. Wien, 1898.
Hayes, J. C. Laurence Sterne and **JEAN PAUL**. New York, 1942.
Czerny, J. Sterne, Hippel und Jean Paul. Weimar, Berlin, 1904.
Glaesener, H. Laurence Sterne et Xavier de **MAISTRE**. RLC, 7, 1927.
Seidlin, O. Laurence Sterne's Tristram Shandy and Thomas **MANN'S** Joseph the Provider. MLQ, 8, 1947.
Barton, F. B. Laurence Sterne and Charles **NODIER**. MPh, 14, 1916.
Modzalevskij, B. L. **PUSHKIN** and Sterne. (In Russian). Russkij sovremennik, 2, 1924.
Shklovskii, V. Evgenii Onegin. (Pushkin and Sterne). In: Ocherki po poetike Pushkina. Berlin, 1923.
Doernenburg, E. W. **RAABE** und Lawrence Sterne. Mitteilungen f. d. Ges. der Freunde Wilhelm Raabes, 1939-40.
Lang, D. M. Sterne and **RADISHEW**. RLC, 21, 1947.
Bauer, F. Ueber den Einfluss Laurence Sternes auf Chr. M. **WIELAND**. Progr. Karlsbad, 1898-1900.
Behmer, A. Sterne und Wieland. München, 1899.

CHAPTER FOURTEEN

Other English Authors.

Baebler, J. J. Zur Geschichte zweier moralischer Wochenschriften (Die Holländische Bagatelle und das Bernerische Freytagsblättlein). (**ADDISON**). ZVL, 12.
Beauvillé, G. de. Gasparo Gozzi journaliste vénitien du XVIIIe siècle. Paris, 1937.
Carritt, E. F. Addison, Kant and Wordsworth. E&S, 22, 1937.
Cornish, F. F. Goethe and Addison. Transactions of Manchester Goethe Society, 1894.
Eckardt, L. H. Die moralischen Wochenschriften. Grenzboten, 64, 1905.
Fréron, E. Le Spectateur ou le Socrate moderne et le Spectateur français. Ann. Littér., 5, 1755.
Gelobter, H. Le Spectateur von Marivaux und die englischen moralischen Wochenschriften. Diss. Frankfurt, 1936.
Guillemard. Lettre à M. Fréron sur une scène de la tragédie anglaise de Caton d'Utique. Ann. littér., 1765.
Hegnauer, A. G. Der Einfluss von Addisons Cato auf die dramatische Literatur Englands und des Continents in der ersten Hälfte des 18. Jahrhunderts. Diss. Zürich, 1912.
Jacoby, K. Die ersten moralischen Wochenschrift Hamburgs am Anfange des XVIII. Jahrhunderts. Progr. Hamburg, 1888.
Keller, L. Die deutschen Gesellschaften des XVIII. Jahrhunderts und die moralischen Wochenschriften. Monatshefte der Comenius Ges., 9, 1900.
Kurrelmeyer, W. Wieland's Teutscher Merkur and Contemporary English Journals. PMLA, 38, 1923.
Milberg, E. Die deutschen moralischen Wochenschriften des XVIII. Jahrhunderts. Diss. Leipzig, 1889.
Molmenti, P. Gasparo Gozzi. RI, 1923.
Paul, A. Addison's Influence on the Social Reform of his Age. Progr. Hamburg, 1876.
Peterson, H. Notes on the Influence of Addison's Spectator and Marivaux's Spectateur Français upon El Pensador. HR, July, 1936.
Saer, H. A. Notes on the Use of Themes Taken from the Spectator in XVIIIth Century French Plays. ML, 21, 1939.
Segré, C. Lo Spectator dell'Addison e l' Osservatore di Gaspare Gozzi. In: Relazioni letterarie fra Italia e Inghilterra. Firenze, 1911.
Sorani, A. Il centenario dello Spectator. Marzocco, 11.XI.1928.
Treves, Pia. L'Osservatore di Gaspare Gozzi nei suoi rapporti collo Spectator di Giuseppe Addison. Ateneo Veneto, 23, 1900.
Umbach, E. Die deutschen moralischen

Wochenschriften und der Spectator von Addison. Strassburg, 1911.
Vetter, T. Der Spectator als Quelle der Discurse der Maler. Frauenfeld, 1887.
Zanella, G. Giuseppe Addison e Gaspare Gozzi. NAnt, Jan., 1883.
Ten Hoor, G. J. **AKENSIDE'S** The Pleasures of Imagination in Germany. JEGPh, 38, 1939.
Brown, E. K. The French Reputation of M. **ARNOLD**. In: Studies in English. Toronto, 1931.
Mowbray, J. P. Has America Outgrown Matthew Arnold? Critic, May, 1902.
Daiches, D. Jane **AUSTEN**, Karl Marx, and the Aristocratic Dance. American Scholar, 17, 1948.
Dick, E. Eine Quelle Gottfried Kellers. Süddeutsche Monatshefte, Aug., 1910.
Grey, R. English Novels in France. TLS, 30.I.1930.
Lord **BACON**: See also I. II. 4-5.
Dieckmann, H. The Influence of Francis Bacon on Diderot's Interprétation de la nature. RR, 34, 1943-44.
Huet, F. Bacon et J. de Maistre. Nouv. Arch. hist. Gand, 1837.
Levi, A. Il pensiero di Francesco Bacone considerato in relazione con le filosofie della natura del rinascimento e col razionalismo cartesiano. Torino, 1925.
Luc, J. A. de. Bacon tel qu'il est, ou dénonciation d'une traduction française des oeuvres de ce philosophe publiée à Dijon par M. A. de la Salle. Berlin, 1900.
Mueller, M. Bacon in Deutschland. In: Essays. Leipzig, 1872.
Orsini, N. I Saggi di Bacone in Italia. Rinascita, 2, 1939.
Schaub, E. F. Bacon and the Modern Spirit. The Monist, 1930.
Waldberg, F. Baco von Verulams Einfluss auf die deutsche Dichtung. In: Renaissancelyrik. Berlin, 1888.
BARCLAY: See also I. VII. 2.
Collignon, A. Notes historiques, littéraires et bibliographiques sur l'Argénis de Jean Barclay. Paris, 1902.
Kettelhoit, P. Formanalyse der Barclay-Opitzschen Argenis. Diss. Münster, 1934.
Smyth, E. Maurice **BARING** as a Novelist (and France). QR, Oct., 1936.
Anon. Schillers Braut von Messina und **BEAUMONT-FLETCHERS** Rolle, Herzog der Normandie. Zeitung f. d. elegante Welt, 1843.
—— Beaumont and Fletcher in France. TLS, Aug., 1922.
Carter, J. The Lausanne Edition of **BECKFORD'S** Vathek. The Library, 17, 1937.
Hunter, A. O. Le Vathek de William Beckford; Historique des éditions françaises. RLC, 15, 1935.
Jean-Aubry, G. Autour du Vathek de Wm. Beckford. RLC, 16, 1935.
May, M. La jeunesse de William Beckford et la genèse de son Vathek. Diss. Paris, 1928.
Seeber, E. D. Oroonoko in France in the XVIIIth Century. (Aphra **BEHN**). PMLA, 51, 1936.
Cooley, F. Early Danish Criticism of **BEOWULF**. ELH, 7, 1940.
—— Grundtvig's First Translation from Beowulf. SS, 16, 1941.
Jeffery, Harriet M. **BERKELEY'S** Philosophy in Britain and America, from 1800 to the Present. Diss. U. of Colorado, 1942.
Blois, R. E. The American Reputation and Influence of William **BLAKE**. Diss. Boston U., 1941.
Jameson, G. Irish Poets of To-day and Blake. PMLA, 53, 1938.
Lafourcade, G. William Blake et le Marquis de Sade. Confluences, 3, 1943.
Rhodes, S. A. William Blake and Pierre Jean Jouve. RR, April, 1933.
Richter, H. Blake und Hamann. Archiv, 158, 1930.
Saurat, D. Blake and Modern Thought. London, 1929.
Symons, A. Blake et Nietzsche. Fontaine, May, 1947.
Wahl, J. Magie et Romantisme, Notes sur Novalis et Blake. Hermes, 1936.
Collins, C. **BOLINGBROKE** and Voltaire in England. London, 1886.
Hurn, A. S. Voltaire et Bolingbroke. Diss. Paris, 1915.
Torrey, N. L. Bolingbroke and Voltaire: A Fictitious Influence. PMLA, 42, 1927.
Northup, G. T. The Influence of George **BORROW** upon Prosper Mérimée. MPh, July, 1915.
Wright, H. G. Was George Borrow Ever in Denmark? MLR, 1928.
——Influence of George Borrow in Norway and Sweden. MLR, 29, 1934.
Hegeman, D. **BOSWELL** and the Abt Jerusalem: A Note on the Background of Werther. JEGPh, 44, 1945.
Pottle, F. A. Boswell's Life of Johnson: Translations. N&Q, 178, 1940.
Christian, Mildred. A Census of **BRONTE** Manuscripts in the United States. Trollopian, 2-3, 1947-48.
Tas, Jeanne. A Brontë Circle in Holland. Transactions of Brontë Society, 11.
Anon. James Russell Lowell and Robert **BROWNING**. New Englander, Jan., 1870.

—— Mrs. Browning in French. Academy, 20.VI.1903.
Buck, G. Das Nachleben R. Brownings in Kritik und Forschung. GRM, May, 1933.
Du Bos, C. Notes sur Browning en France. Revue critique des idées et des livres, 25.X.1923.
Gosse, E. Browning in France. In: More Books on the Table. London, 1923.
Greer, Louise. Browning Criticism in America. Diss. U. of Va., 1940.
Holmes, S. W. Browning's Sordello in the Light of Jung's Theory of Types. PMLA, 56, 1941.
Phelps, W. L. Browning in Germany. MLN. 1913.
—— Browning in France. MLN, 1916.
Ratchford, Fannie. Browning's Pauline Comes to Texas. Southwest Rev., 28, 1943.
Rostenberg. Leona. Margaret Fuller and Elizabeth Barrett Browning. American N&Q, 2, 1943.
Schneider, F. Browning's The Ring and the Book and Wassermann's Der Fall Maurizius. MLN, 1933.
Stefansson, J. How Browning Strikes a Scandinavian. Browning Society Papers, 13, 1890-91.
Bolte, J. Die Heidelberger Verdeutschung von **BUCHANANS** Tragödie Baptistes. Archiv, 1933.
Lebègue, R. George Buchanan. Son influence en France et au Portugal. Coimbra, 1931.
Helmecke, C. A. **BUCKLE'S** Influence on Strindberg. Diss. Philadelphia, 1924.
Muret, M. Sienkiewicz et **BULWER-LYTTON**. Journal des Débats, 2.IV. 1901.
Price, L. M. Karl Gutzkow and Bulwer Lytton. JEGPh, 16, 1917.
Rigal, E. La genèse d'un drame romantique, Ruy Blas. RHLF, Oct., 1913.
BURKE: See also Politics, I. II. 5.
Braune, F. Edmund Burke in Deutschland. Heidelberg, 1917.
Howard, W. G. Burke Among the Forerunners of Lessing. PMLA, 22, 1907.
Parrel, C. de. Burke et Calonne. FQ, 1929.
Wecter, D. Burke, Franklin and Samuel Petrie. HLQ, 3, 1940.
Kies, P. P. Lessing and **BURNABY**. MLN, 1935.
Anon. **BURNS** in French: The First Translation. The Scotsman, 25.I.1930.
Bakhtine. Lermontof et Robert Burns. In: Années passées, 9, 1908.
Delattre, F. Auguste Angellier et le génie poétique de Robert Burns. EA, 3, 1939.
Foerster, M. Burns und Würzburg. Anglia Bb, 11, 1900.
Jacks, W. Robert Burns in Other Tongues. A Critical Review of the Translations. Glasgow, 1896.
Leclercq, R. Angellier, biographe de Burns. Cahier Angellier, 4, 1927.
Parker, W. Burns, Scott and Turgenev. N&Q, 29.IV.1939.
Power, W. Burns's French Interpreter. Cahier Angellier, 4. (Paris), 1927.
Smith, J. M. & Braunholtz, E. G. W. Burns and Rudel. TLS, 31.V. & 7.XI. 1928.
Wihan, J. Franz Stelzhamer und Robert Burns. Euphorion, 10, 1903.
Zenker, R. Heines achtes Traumbild und Burns Jolly Beggars. ZVL, 7, 1894.
Gabrieli, V. Presentazione italiana di S. **BUTLER**. Civiltà Moderna, 12, 1940.
Ascher, J. Vigny and Thomas **CAMPBELL**. FQ, 1922.
Bird, C. W. A. de Vigny's **CHATTERTON**; a Contribution to the Study of its Genesis and Sources. Los Angeles, 1941.
Gougenheim, G. Une mention de **CHAUCER** en France au XVIe sèicle. RAA, April, 1934.
Hunter, A. C. Le Conte de la Femme de Bath en français au XVIIIe siècle. RLC, 9, 1929.
Kirby, T. A. J. Q. Adams and Chaucer. MLN, 61, 1947.
McGalliard, J. C. Chaucerian Comedy: The Merchant's Tale, Jonson and Molière. PhQ, 25, 1946-47.
Norton, G. M. Chaucer and Balzac. Nation (New York), 21.V.1885.
Spurgeon, C. F. E. Chaucer devant la critique en Angleterre et en France depuis son temps jusqu'à nos jours. Diss. Paris, 1911.
—— Five Hundred Years of Chaucer Criticism and Allusion. Cambridge U.P., 1925.
Whiting, B. J. Emerson, Chaucer and Thomas Warton. AL, 17, 1945.
Woolf, H. B. Thomas Godfrey: Eighteenth-Century Chaucerian. AL, 12, 1941.
—— Chaucer in Colonial America. American N&Q, 3, 1942.
Nelson, R. W. The Reputation of Lord **CHESTERFIELD** in Great Britain and America, 1730-1936. Diss. Northwestern U., 1938.
Cingria, C. A. G. K. **CHESTERTON** et les peuples latins. Lettres françaises, 5, 1942.
Teeten, L. M. Albrecht von Haller and S. **CLARKE**. JEGPh, 1928.
Clark, Mary Elizabeth. Peter Porcupine

in America: The Career of Wm. **COBBETT**, 1792-1800. Philadelphia, 1939.
Iakovlev, N. V. Pushkin and **COLERIDGE.** (In Russian). In: Pushkin v mirovoi literature, 1926.
Porter, N. Coleridge's American Disciples. Bibliotheca sacra, 4, 1847.
Sells, A. L. Zanella, Coleridge, and Shelley. CL, 1950.
Stovall, F. Poe's Debt to Coleridge. U. of Texas Studies in English, 1930.
Whitmer, Anna. American Reaction to the Literary Criticism of S. T. Coleridge, 1830-60. Diss. Ohio State U., 1939.
Hyder, C. K. Wilkie **COLLINS** in America. Festschrift Raphael Dorman O'Leary and Selden Lincoln Whitcomb. U. of Kansas, 1940.
Milley, H. J. W. The Vogue and Influence of Wilkie Collins in England and America. Diss. Yale, 1941.
Rösler, M. **CONGREVES** Double Dealer in deutscher Uebersetzung. NSp, 33, 1925.
Stuart, D. C. The Source of Gresset's Le Méchant. MLN, Feb., 1912.
CONRAD: See Intermediaries, I. IV. 8.
Roth, G. Sainte-Beuve, **CRABBE** et le conte en vers. FQ, 3, 1921.
Clapton, G. T. Baudelaire and Catherine **CROWE.** MLR, 1930.
Hughes, R. Une étape de l'esthétique de Baudelaire: Catherine Crowe. RLC, 17, 1937.
Carrière, J. M. A French Adaptation of Sandford and Merton. (**T. DAY**). MLN, 1935.
Castets, F. Candide de Voltaire, Simplicius de Grimmelshausen, et Candido, dans l'Honnête Courtisane de **DECKER** et Middleton. RLR, 48, 1905.
Houtchens, L. H. Charles **DICKENS** and International Copyright. AL, 13, 1941.
Looten, C. Le centenaire des Pickwick Papers. Les Facultés catholiques de Lille, June, 1936.
Houtschens, C. W. & L. H. Contributions of Early American Journals to the Study of Charles Dickens. MLQ, 6, 1945.
Leacock, S. Charles Dickens and Canada. Queen's Quarterly, 46, 1939.
Peeke, H. L. Charles Dickens in Ohio in 1842. Ohio Archaeological and Historical Quarterly, 1919.
Roe, F. G. Pickwick in America. Connoisseur, 107, 1941.
Burnaud, F. C. Un peu de Pickwick à la française. NC, Aug., 1908.
Heussey, R. Charles Dickens à Paris. Le Livre, 1886.
Maurois, A. Dickens et nous. NL, 24.IV. 1937.
Thackeray, W. M. Dickens in France. Every Saturday, 1867.
Uzanne, O. Charles Dickens en France. Du génie littéraire anglais opposé au génie littéraire français. Le Livre, 1889.
Gummer, E. N. Dickens and Germany. MLR, 1938.
—— Dickens' Works in Germany, 1837-1937. New York, 1940.
Noack, K. Charles Dickens und die deutschen Volksbibliotheken. Blätter f. Volksbibliotheken & Lesehallen, March, 1912.
Vigo-Fazio, L. Dickens in Italia. Le Lettere, 1.III.1920.
Boehm, K. Der Humor bei Daudet in den Tartaringeschichten und bei Dickens in den Pickwickiern. ZFEU, 24, 1925.
Zech, A. Wilhelm Dilthey's Analysis of Charles Dickens. Stanford Studies, 1941.
Church, H. W. Otto Babendick (Frenssen) and David Copperfield. GR, 1936.
Freymond, R. Der Einfluss von Charles Dickens auf Gustav Freytag. Prag, 1912.
Voelk, Vera. Ch. Dickens Einfluss auf G. Freytags Soll und Haben. Jahresbericht des Salzburger Mädchenlyceums, 1908.
Erickson, E. The Influence of Charles Dickens on the Novels of Benito Perez Galdos. Hisp., Dec., 1936.
Dana, H. W. L. Longfellow and Dickens. Publ. of Cambridge Hist. Soc., 28, 1943.
Lueder, F. Die epischen Werke O. Ludwigs und ihr Verhältnis zu Ch. Dickens. Diss. Greifswald, 1910.
Lohre, H. Otto Ludwig und Charles Dickens. Archiv, 124, 1910.
Fox, A. W. Dickens Through French Spectacles. (Maurois). Papers of the Manchester Literary Club, 57, 1932.
Krappe, Edith S. A Possible Source for Poe's The Tell-Tale Heart and The Black Cat. AL, 12, 1940.
Anon. The German Dickens (W. Raabe). TLS, 20.VII.1922.
Doernenberg, E. & Fehse, N. Raabe und Dickens. Magdeburg, 1921.
Geist, H. Fritz Reuters literarische Beziehungen zu Charles Dickens. Erfurt, 1913.
Meyer, R. M. Zu Reuters Stromtid, zwei Quellennachweise. Jb. d. Vereins f. niederdeutsche Sprachforschung, 22, 1896.
Skinner, M. M. Brief Notes on the Indebtedness of Spielhagen to Dickens. JEGPh, 1910.
Atkins, S. A Possible Dickens Influence in Zola. MLQ, 8, 1947.

Hentschel, C. **DISRAELI** and Lassalle. GLL, 2, 1938.

Vallette, J. Un précurseur anglais des poètes contemporains. (**DONNE**). Le Monde, 20.VI.1946.

Baumgartner, M. D. On **DRYDEN'S** Relations to Germany in the 18th Century. U. of Nebraska Studies, 1914.

Eichler, A. Christian Wernickes Hans Sachs und sein Dryden'sches Vorbild Mac Flecknoe. ZVL, 17.

Maillet, A. Dryden et Voltaire. RLC, 18, 1938.

Russell, T. W. Voltaire, Dryden and Heroic Tragedy. New York, 1946.

—— Dryden, inspirateur de Voltaire. RLC, 22, 1948.

Jovy, E. Deux inspirateurs peu connus des Maximes de La Rochefoucauld: Daniel **DYKE** et J. Verneuil. Vitry-le-François, 1910.

Colum, P. Maria **EDGEWORTH** and Ivan Turgenev. British Review, 11, 1915.

Anon. G. **ELIOT** and Emerson. Century Mag., Feb., 1882.

Bisson, L. A. Proust, Bergson, and George Eliot. MLR, 40, 1945.

Fowlie, W. Eliot and Tchelitchew. Accent, 5, 1945.

Godbert, C. W. George Eliot - an Italian Appreciation. (G. Neri). Papers of the Manchester Literary Club, 58, 1932.

Ludlow, J. M. Elise Venner (O. W. Holmes) and Silas Marner. Macmillan's Mag., Aug., 1861.

Pfeiffer, S. George Eliots Beziehungen zu Deutschland. Heidelberg, 1925.

Kies, P. P. The Sources of Lessing's Die Juden. (**FARQUHAR**). PhQ, 1927.

—— Lessing's Intention in Der Dorfjunker. Research Studies, State College of Washington, 11, 1943.

Robertson, J. G. Lessing and Farquhar. MLR, Oct., 1906.

Anon. **FIELDING'S** Danish Translator. (S. Stanley). TLS, 3.IV.1937.

—— Stendhal. Notes sur son exemplaire de Tom Jones, de Fielding. Letteratura, 1937.

Clarke,, C. H. Fielding und der deutsche Sturm und Drang. Diss. Freiburg, 1897. Cf. ESn, 25.

Digeon, A. La condamnation de Tom Jones à Paris. RAA, 1927.

Eaves, T. C. The Publication of the First Translations of Fielding's Tom Jones. Library, 26, 1945.

Krieg, H. J. J. Chr. Bode als Uebersetzer des Tom Jones. Diss. Greifswald, 1909.

Kurrelmeyer, W. A German Version of Joseph Andrews. MLN, 1918.

Price, L. M. The Works of Fielding on the German Stage, 1762-1801. JEGPh, 41, 1942.

Swaen. Fielding and Goldsmith in Leyden. MLR, 1906.

Wood, A. Der Einfluss Fieldings auf die deutsche Literatur. Diss. Heidelberg, 1895.

FLORIO: See Intermediaries, I. IV. 8.

Cazamian, L. M. Lorsqu'un Français lit **GALSWORTHY**. RELV, May, 1925.

Hoch, W. John Galsworthy als Dramatiker in deutscher Beleuchtung. ZNU, 41.

Lancaster, H. C. **GARRICK** at the Comédie Française. MLN, 63, 1948.

Hopkins, A. B. Mrs. **GASKELL** in France, 1849-90. PMLA, 53, 1938.

Anon. Ueber die Uebersetzung der Fabeln des **GAY**. In: Briefe, die neueste Literatur betreffend, 1. Berlin, 1759.

Goulding, S. Eighteenth-Century French Taste and The Beggar's Opera. MLR, 1929.

Kidson, F. The Beggar's Opera, its Pre decessors and Successors. Cambridge U.P., 1923.

Anon. **GIBBON**, Burke et Chateaubriand. Revue Britannique, 2, 1834.

Dick, E. Plagiats de Chateaubriend. Le Voyage en Amérique. Comment Chateaubriand s'est servi de Gibbon. Diss. Berne, 1905.

Dollinger, A. Etudes historiques de Chateaubriand. Paris, 1932.

Perrochon, H. Gibbon et Suzanne Curchod. Gazette de Lausanne, 30.VI.1929.

Powell, L. F. Friedrich von Matthisson on Gibbon. Festschrift H. G. Fiedler. Oxford, 1938.

Briggs, F. **GLOVER'S** Influence on Klopstock, PhQ, Oct., 1922.

Earle, O. The Reputation and Influence of Wm. **GODWIN** in America. Diss. Harvard, 1938.

Brandeis, A. Goethe und **GOLDSMITH**. Chronik des Wiener Goethe-Vereins, 12, 1898.

Carrière, J. M. Notes on A. Berquin's Adaptations from English Poetry. RR, 26, 1935.

Farwick, G. F. Notes from the First French Translation of the Vicar of Wakefield. Library, N.S., 5, 1904.

Ferguson, R. Goldsmith and the Notions "Grille" and "Wandrer" in Werthers Leiden. MLN, 17, 1902.

Friedman, A. Goldsmith and the Marquis d'Argens. MLN, 53.

Hammer, C. Goethe's Estimate of Oliver Goldsmith. JEGPh, 44, 1945.

Knaack, G. Fritz Reuter und O. Goldsmith. ZDU, 13, 1899.
Levy, S. Goethe und Oliver Goldsmith. JbGG, 6, 1885.
Price, L. M. Goldsmith, Sesenheim and Goethe. GR, 1929.
—— The Works of Oliver Goldsmith on the German Stage, 1776-95. MLQ, 5, 1944.
Reding, C. A Study on the Influence of Oliver Goldsmith's Citizen of the World upon the Cartas maruecas of José Cadalso. HR, 1934.
Roberts, W. Goldsmith in France. TLS, 30.XI. & 28.XII.1933.
Roth, G. Goldsmith et A. France. RLC, 2, 1922.
Seeber, E. D. & Remak, H. H. H. The First French Translation of the Deserted Village. MLR, 41, 1946.
Sells, A. L. Oliver Goldsmith's Influence on the French Stage. Durham U. Journal, 33, 1941.
Sollas, H. Goldsmith's Einfluss in Deutschland im 18. Jahrhundert. Diss. Heidelberg, 1903.
Viëtor, K. Goethe, Goldsmith und Merck. Jb. des freien deutschen Hochstifts Frankfurt, 1925.
Walz, J. A. Oliver Goldsmith und Goethes Werther. MLN, 18, 1903.
Weatherly, E. H. Bean Tibbs and Colonel Sellers. (Mark Twain). MLN, 59, 1944.
Williams, J. A. Note on the French Translation of the Vicar of Wakefield. London Mercury, 13, 1925.
Ziegert, M. Goldsmiths Landprediger in Deutschland. Berichte d. freien deutschen Hochstifts zu Frankfurt, 10, 1894.
Zupitza. Oliver Goldsmiths Lustspiel She Stoops to Conquer als Quelle von A. von Winterfelds komischem Roman Der Elephant. Archiv, 85, 1890.
Fulghum, W. B. Whitman's Debt to Joseph **GOSTWICK**. AL, 12, 1941.
Pietsch, K. Zur Frage nach der portugiesischen Uebersetzung von **GOWER'S** Confessio Amantis. Festschrift Manley. Chicago, 1923.
Buchanan, M. A. **GRAY'S** Elegy in Spanish. Nation (New York), 4.IV.1918.
Gloede, O. Thomas Gray und H. Heine. ESn, 17, 1893.
Heckedom. Un plagiaire allemand. (Matthisson). Alsace française, May, 1925.
Martineau, H. Th. Gray, Baudelaire et P. J. Toulet. Yggdrasill, 25.II.1938.
McCain, J. W. Imitations of Gray's Elegy. N&Q, 177, 1939.
Micale, O. Thomas Gray e la sua influenza sulla letteratura italiana. Catania, 1934.
Peers, E. A. The Influence of Young and Gray in Spain. MLR, 21, 1926.
Roth, G. Souvenirs du Cimetière de Campagne de Gray chez Lamartine. RLC, 3, 1923.
Rovillain, E. L. S. Mercier et l'Elegy de Gray. MLN, Nov., 1928.
Zanoboni-Cecchini, L. La prima manifestazione letteraria di Giovanni Berchet. GSLI, 77.
Potez, H. Le premier roman anglais traduit en français. (**GREENE'S** Pandosta, 1615). RHLF, 1904.
Fischer, W. The Merchant Prince of Cornville von S. E. **GROSS** und Rostands Cyrano de Bergerac. Archiv, 133, 1915.
Morgan, A. A Remarkable Lawsuit. (Rostand and Gross). Evening Post, 19.IV.1919.
Muchnic, Helen. Thomas **HARDY** and Thomas Mann. Northampton (Mass.), 1939.
Osawa Mamoru. Hardy and the German Men of Letters. Studies in English Literature. (Tokyo), 1939.
Weber, C. J. Thomas Hardy in America. Colophon, 1, 1940.
—— Thomas Hardy in Maine. Portland, 1942.
—— Thomas Hardy and His New England Editors. NEQ, 15, 1942.
—— Hardy in America: A Study of Thomas Hardy and His American Readers. Waterville (Me.), 1946.
Winslow, D. J. Thomas Hardy: His British and American Critics. Diss. Boston U., 1942.
Liljegren, S. B. A French Draft Constitution of 1792 Modelled on James **HARRINGTON'S** Oceana: Théodore Lesueur, Idées sur l'espèce de gouvernement populaire. With an Introduction on Harrington's Influence in France. Lund, 1932.
Ten Hoor, G. J. James **HARRIS** and the Influences of his Aesthetic Theories in Germany. Diss. U. of Michigan, 1929.
Kies, P. P. Lessing and **HAWKESWORTH**. Research Studies. State College of Washington, 8, 1941.
Hayens, K. Heine, **HAZLITT** and Mrs. Jameson. MLR, 1922.
Anon. La pensée et l'influence de Th. **HOBBES**. Archives de Philosophie, 12, 1937.
Brockdorff, G. von. Fr. M. Klinger und Hobbes. Kiel, 1935.
—— Wahrheit und Wahrscheinlichkeit bei

Hobbes und Condillac. Veröffentlichungen der Hobbes-Ges., 8. (Kiel), 1937.
Lacour-Gayet. Les traductions françaises de Hobbes sous le règne de Louis XIV. Archiv f. Geschichte der Philologie, 12, 1889.
Morize, A. Th. Hobbes et Samuel Sorbière. RG, 1908.
Smyrniadis, B. Les doctrines de Hobbes, Locke et Kant sur le droit d'insurrection. Paris, 1921.
Neumann, W. Die Bedeutung **HOMES** für die Aesthetik und sein Einfluss auf die deutschen Aesthetiker. Diss. Halle, 1894.
Wohlgemuth, J. Henry Homes Aesthetik und ihr Einfluss auf deutsche Aesthetiker. Diss. Rostock, 1893.
Gilman, Margaret. Baudelaire and Th. **HOOD**. RR, July, 1935.
Clemens, C. **HOUSMAN** in America. PL, 49, 1943.
Weber, C. J. Willa Cather Calls on Housman. Colby Library Quarterly (Maine), 1947.
White, W. E. A. Robinson and E. A. Housman. Ibid.
Berger, G. Husserl et **HUME**. Revue internationale de philosophie, 2, 1939.
Erdmann, B. Kant und Hume um 1762. Archiv f. Geschichte der Philosophie, 1. (Berlin), 1888.
Faggi, A. Hume e Magalotti. Atti della R. Acc. delle scienze di Torino, 59, 1923-24.
Laird, J. Opinions récentes sur Hume. Recherches philosophiques, 3, 1934.
Oake, R. B. Did Maupertuis Read Hume's Treatise of Human Nature? RLC, 20, 1940.
Papillon, F. David Hume, précurseur d'Auguste Comte. Philosophie positive, Sept., 1868.
Toynbee, P. Mme. du Deffand and Hume. MLR, Oct., 1929.
Leary, L. Leigh **HUNT** in Philadelphia: An American Literary Incident of 1803. Pa. Mag. Hist. & Biog., 70, 1946.
Aldridge, A. O. A French Critic (C. L. de Villette) of **HUTCHESON'S** Aesthetics. MPh, 45, 1948.
Kanters, R. Aldous **HUXLEY** jugé par Blaise Pascal. Cahiers du Sud, Nov., 1938.
Lang, D. R. Dr. Samuel **JOHNSON** in America: A Study of his Reputation, 1750-1812. Diss. U. of Illinois, 1939.
Lewis, F. R. Dr. Samuel Madden, Dr. Johnson and Benjamin Franklin. Irish Book Lover, 26, 1939.
Piccioni, L. Per le fortune del Rasselas di S. Johnson in Italia. Una versione inedita di G. Baretti. GSLI, 28, 1910.
Powell, L. F. Rasselas. TLS, Feb., 1923.
Saer, H. A Note on Dr. Johnson and Sébastien Mercier. MLR, 36, 1941.
Schinz, A. Les dangers du cliché littéraire: le Dr. Johnson et Jean-Jacques Rousseau. MLN, 57, 1942.
Tinker, C. B. Rasselas in the New World. Yale Review, Oct., 1924.
Arnavon, J. Volpone: de Ben **JONSON** (1605) à Jules Romains (1928). FGB, Sept., 1929.
Grubbs, H. A. An Early French Adaptation of an Elizabethan Comedy; J.-B. Rousseau as an Imitator of Ben Jonson. MLN, 55, 1940.
Richter, H. Ben Jonson's Volpone und sein Erneuerer S. Zweig. JbShG, 63, 1927.
Stanger, H. Der Einfluss Ben Jonsons auf L. Tieck. SVL, 1, 1901-02.
Ten Hoor, G. J. Ben Jonson's Reception in Germany. PhQ, Oct., 1935.
Weiss, A. Zola und Ben Jonson. Beilage zur Allg. Zt., 81, 1895.
Farrell, J. T. **JOYCE** and the Tradition of the European Novel. New York Times Book Rev., 21.I.1945.
Monnier, A. Joyce's Ulysses and the French Public. Kenyon Review, 8, 1946.
Rothman, N. L. Thomas Wolfe and James Joyce: A Study in Literary Influence. In: A Southern Vanguard, (ed. Allen Tate). New York, 1947.
Stahl, E. L. Der englische Vorläufer der Meininger: Charles **KEAN** als Bühnenreformer. Festgabe L. Geiger. Berlin, 1918. Cf. Kölnische Zt., 14 & 21, 1913.
Anon. **KEATS** in France. TLS, 18.IV. 1929.
Ackermann, R. Keats Hymne an Pan in drei deutschen Uebersetzungen. ESn, 27, 1900.
Chivers, T. H. & Perry, M. Keats in Georgia. Georgia Review, 1, 1947.
Dekker, G. De invloed van Keats en Shelley in Nederland gedurende de negentiende eeuw. Groningen, 1926.
Digeon, A. Un hommage oublié d'Anatole France à Keats. RAA, June, 1935.
Marchesi, G. Leopardi e la poesia inglese. Iride, 3, 1899.
Rollins, H. E. Keats' Reputation in America to 1848. Harvard Keats Memorial Studies, 1946.
Wais, K. Mallarmé's Neuschöpfung eines Gedichtes von Keats. ZFSL, 60, 1936.
—— Banville, Chateaubriand, Keats and Mallarmé's Faun. ZFSL, 62, 1938.

Brodmann, C. **KIPLING** im deutschen Gewande. Gegenwart, 2.IV.1898.
Meyerfeld, M. Kipling-Uebersetzungen. LE, 15.VII.1900.
Rice, H. C. Rudyard Kipling in New England. National Review, July, 1938.
Schoenwerth, R. Die niederländischen und deutschen Bearbeitungen von Thomas **KYD'S** Spanish Tragedy. Forschungen, herausg. von Schick & Waldberg. Berlin, 1903.
Worp, J. A. Die Fabel der Spanish Tragedy in einer niederländischen Uebersetzung des Orlando furioso. JbShG, 29-30, 1894.
Barnett, G. P. The First American Review of Charles **LAMB.** PMLA, 61, 1946.
Pfeiffer, K. G. Periodical Criticism of Walter Savage **LANDOR** by his English and American Contemporaries. Diss. U. of N. C., 1940.
Kies, P. P. Lessing and **LEE.** JEGPh, 28, 1929.
Baldensperger, F. Le Moine de **LEWIS** dans la littérature française. JCL, 1903.
Koziol, H. E. T. A. Hoffmanns Die Elixiere des Teufels und M. G. Lewis' The Monk. GRM, 26, 1938.
Pound, Louise. Monk Lewis in Nebraska. SFQ, 9, 1945.
Benn, T. V. Notes sur la fortune du George Barnwell de **LILLO** en France. RLC, 6, 1926.
Genee, R. Lessings bürgerliches Trauerspiel und seine englischen Vorbilder. Vossische Zt. Sonntags-Beilage, 14.I. 1883.
Mead, G. W. Some Direct Influences of Lillo's The London Merchant in France before 1790. Birmingham Southern College Bull., 21, 1928.
Pendell, W. D. The London Merchant and Le Mierre's Barnevelt. MLN, 56, 1941.
Price, L. M. George Barnwell on the German Stage. MDU, 35, 1943.
—— The Bassewitz Translation of the London Merchant, 1752. JEGPh, 43, 1944.
—— George Barnwell Abroad. CL, 2, 1950.
Sandbach, F. Karl Philipp Moritz's Blunt and Lillo's Fatal Curiosity. MLR, 18, 1923.
Walz, J. A. Goethe's Götz von Berlichingen and Lillo's History of George Barnwell. MPh, 3, 1905-06.
Weilen, A. von. Der Kaufmann von London auf deutschen und französischen Bühnen. In: Schippers Beiträge zur Philologie. Wien, 1902.
Bonno, G. The Diffusion and Influence of **LOCKE'S** Essay Concerning Human Understanding in France before Voltaire's Lettres Philosophiques. Proceed. of the Amer. Philos. Soc., 1947.
Broche, G. Locke et Rousseau. In: Une Epoque. Paris, 1905.
Brown, A. John Locke and the Religious Aufklärung. Rev. of Religion, 1949.
—— Locke's Essay and Bodmer and Breitinger. MLQ, 10, 1949.
—— Locke's Tabula Rasa and Gottsched. GR, 24, 1949.
Corwin, R. N. Entwickelung und Vergleichung der Erziehungslehren von John Locke und J. J. Rousseau. Diss. Heidelberg, 1894.
Erdbrügger, G. Die Bedeutung J. Lockes für die Pädagogik Rousseaus. Diss. Würzburg, 1912.
Ernst, F. Der Ursprung der Menschenrechte. NSR, May, 1939.
Ferrari, M. Locke e il Sensismo francese. Modena, 1900.
Krüger, G. Fremde Gedanken in J. J. Rousseaus erstem Discours. Halle, 1891.
Pietsch, T. Ueber das Verhältniss der politischen Theorie Lockes zu Montesquieus Lehre von der Theilung der Gewalten. Diss. Berlin, 1887.
Safter, V. Ein Vergleich der physischen Erziehung bei Locke und Rousseau. Diss. Leipzig, 1889.
Urbach, R. Voltaires Verhältnis zu Newton und Locke. Halle, 1900.
Wilke, G. Die Hauptberührungs- und Unterschiedspunkte J. Lockes und J. J. Rousseaus. Diss. Erlangen, 1898.
Chew, S. C. An English Precursor of Rousseau. (**LYTTLETON**). MLN, 32, 1917.
Bandy, W. T. **MACAULAY** and his Italian Translator. Italica, 25, 1948.
Clark, H. H. The Vogue of Macaulay in America. Transactions Wisconsin Acad., 34, 1942.
Cameron, Margaret M. L'Eassai sur **MACKENZIE** de Chateaubriand. Canada français, 28, 1941.
Kaye, F. B. The Influence of Bernard **MANDEVILLE.** SPh, 19, 1922.
For **MARLOWE'S** Faust: See Goethe's Faust, IV. X. 6.
Bleibtreu, C. Marlowe, Grabbe und Lenz. Wiener Rundschau, 4, 1900.
Hawley, C. A. Gerald **MASSEY** and America. Church History, 8, 1939.

Clapton, G. T. Balzac, Baudelaire et **MATURIN**. FQ, 1930.
Bailey, E. J. G. **MEREDITH** in America. Festschrift J. Morgan Hart. New York, 1910.
Buelow, F. von. Meredith in Deutschland. LE, 1.IX.1904.
Downs, B. W. Meredith and Fontane. GLL, 2, 1938.
Petter, G. B. George Meredith and his German Critics. London, 1939.
Fischer, W. Die Briefe R. Monckton **MILNES** an Varnhagen von Ense (1844-54). Heidelberg, 1922.
Baldensperger, F. **MOORE** et A. de Vigny. MLR, 1, 1906.
Thomas, A. B. Moore en France. Paris, 1911.
Walton, T. A French Disciple of William **MORRIS**: Jean Lahor. RLC, 15, 1935.
Thomas **MORUS**: See also Utopias, I. II. 4-5.
Binder, J. More's Utopia in English: A Note on Translation. MLN, 62, 1947.
Delcourt, J. Saint Thomas More and France. Traditio, 5, 1947.
Fellheimer, J. Silvio Pellico's Tommaso Moro. MLR, 43, 1948.
Kühn, J. Thomas Morus und Rousseau. Histor. Vierteljahrsschrift, 23, 1926.
NEWMAN: See Religion, III. I. 4.
Akar, L. **NEWTON** en France. L'Intermédiaire, 30.I.1940.
Cassirer, E. Newton and Leibniz. Philosoph. Review, 52, 1943.
Ibershoff, C. H. Bodmer and Newton. MLR, 1926.
Mouy, P. Malebranche et Newton. RMM, 1938.
Anon. Extrait de Venise sauvée (**OTWAY**) et comparaison avec le Manilius de La Fosse. MF, Jan., 1747.
Falke, J. Die deutschen Bearbeitungen des Geretteten Venedig von Otway. Diss. Rostock, 1908.
Fellheimer, Jeannette. Michele Leoni's Venezia Salvata, the First Italian Translation of Otway's Tragedy. Ital., 22, 1945.
Roseli. Discours pour la Venise sauvée de La Place. MF, Dec., 1746.
Urban, E. **OWENUS** und die deutschen Epigrammatiker des XVII. Jahrhunderts. Berlin, 1900.
Monrey, G. Marcel Proust, J. Ruskin et W. **PATER**. Le Monde nouveau, Aug., 1926.
Carrière, J. M. Notes on Arnaud Berquin's Adaptations from English Poetry. (**PERCY**). RR, Oct., 1935.
Kircher, E. Volkslied und Volkspoesie in der Sturm- und Drangzeit. Zs. f. deutsche Wortforschung, 1903.
Lohre, H. Von Percy zum Wunderhorn. Berlin, 1902.
Wagener, H. F. Das Eindringen von Percys Reliques in Deutschland. Diss. Heidelberg, 1897.
Sibley, Agnes. Alexander **POPE'S** Prestige in America, 1725-1835. New York, 1949.
Audra, E. Les traductions françaises de Pope (1717-1825), étude de bibliographie. Paris, 1931.
La Harpe, J. de. Pope dans le Journal des Savants. Berkeley, 1933.
MacDonald, W. L. A French Life of Pope. UTQ, 15, 1946.
Rogers, R. W. Critiques on the Essay on Man in France and Germany. ELH, 15, 1948.
Heinzelmann, J. H. Pope in Germany in the Eighteenth Century. MPh, Jan., 1913.
Maack, R. Ueber Popes Einfluss auf die Idylle und das Lehrgedicht in Deutschland. Hamburg, 1895.
Petzet, E. Die deutschen Nachahmungen des Popeschen Lockenraubes. ZVL, 4, 1891.
Beck, R. Alexander Pope and Iceland. Logberg (Winnipeg) & Skirmir (Reykjavik), 1936.
Viglione, F. Una nota all'influsso di Pope sulla letteratura italiana. In: A. V. Cian e suoi scolari. Pisa, 1909.
Helsztynski, S. Pope in Poland. SR, 1928.
Niess, R. J. A Little-Known Spanish Translation of Pope's Essay on Man. HR, 7, 1939.
Branca, V. Alfieri anglomane e due inedite traduzioni dal Pope. Humanitas, 1947.
Anon. Article sur la traduction de l'Essai sur l'homme de Pope, par Castiglioni. Journal étranger, Jan., 1761.
Zanella, G. Al. Pope e Ant. Conti. NAnt, 64, 1882.
Bonnard, G. A. Note on the English Translations of Crousaz' Two Books on Pope's Essay on Man. Lausanne, 1937.
Wagner. Parallèle entre Delille et Pope. Progr. Landshut, 1866.
Levy, S. Einige Parallelen zu Goethe aus Pope. JbGG, 5, 1884.
Frick, A. Ueber Popes Einfluss auf Hagedorn. Progr. Wien, 1901.
Charlier, G. De Pope à Lamartine. Revue de Belgique, Dec., 1906.
Crousaz, J. P. de. Commentaires sur la

traduction en vers de M. l'abbé Du Resnel de l' Essai de M. Pope sur l'Homme. Genève, 1738.
Levy, S. Eine moderne Quelle zu Rückerts Weisheit des Brahmanen. ALG, 1883.
MacClintock, L. Sainte-Beuve and Pope. PMLA, 41, 1926.
Krumpelmann, J. T. Schiller's Hoffnung and Pope's Essay on Man. GR, 1928.
Duchateau, O. Pope et Voltaire. Diss. Greifswald, 1875.
Faguet, E. Jugements de Voltaire sur Pope, Addison, Swift. RCC, 9, 1900.
Havens, G. R. Voltaire's Marginal Comments upon Pope's Essay on Man. MLN, Nov., 1928.
Pachaly, R. Thomas **PRINGLE** und Ferd. Freiligrath. Progr. Freiberg, 1879.
Wukadinovic, S. **PRIOR** in Deutschland. Graz, 1895.
Clapton, G. T. Baudelaire et De **QUINCEY**. Paris, 1931.
Hughes, R. Vers la contrée du rêve. MF, 1.VIII.1939.
Lalou, R. De Thomas de Quincey à Baudelaire. RG, 14, 1923.
Littlefield, W. Alfred de Musset and the English Opium-Eater. Bookman, July, 1902.
Haines, L. F. **READE**, Mill, and Zola: A Study of the Character and Intention of Charles Reade's Realistic Method. SPh, 40, 1943.
H. C. **ROBINSON**: See Intermediaries, I. IV. 8.
Arnould, E. J. F. Richard **ROLLE** and the Sorbonne. Manchester U.P., 1939.
ROSSETTI: See also Intermediaries, I. IV. 8.
Barrès, M. Dante Gabriel Rossetti en France. Le Voltaire, 16.VIII.1886.
Klinnert, A. D. G. Rossetti und Stefan George. Diss. Bonn, 1934.
Luther, A. Rossetti und Maeterlinck. LE, 15.II.1906.
Roosbroeck, G. L. van. Maeterlinck and Rossetti. MLN, Nov., 1919.
Nicolai, F. Beweis, dass das beste in Wielands Johanna Gray aus **ROWE'S** Jane Gray genommen sei. Briefe die neueste Literatur betreffend, 4, 1759.
Schwartz, F. H. Nicholas Rowe, The Fair Penitent. A Contribution and Analysis with a Side-Reference to Richard Beer-Hofmann, Der Graf von Charolais. Bern, 1907.
Wolf, L. Rowe in Deutschland. Diss. Heidelberg, 1910.
Anon. **RUSKIN** en Sorbonne. Le Temps, 11.I.1901.
Audra, E. L'influence de Ruskin en France. RCC, Jan., 1926.
Bisson, L. A. Proust and Ruskin Reconsidered in the Light of the Lettres à une amie. MLR, 39, 1944.
Delattre, F. Ruskin et Bergson. Oxford, 1947.
Guyot, C. Sur Ruskin et Proust. Lettres, 1 (Genève), 1943 & RLC, 21, 1947.
Massis, H. Proust et J. Ruskin. Bull. Mensuel de la Guilde du Libre. (Lausanne), 1941.
Maurois, A. Proust et Ruskin. E&S, 17, 1932.
MacGegan, E. An Early French View of Ruskin. Saint-George, April, 1905.
Murray, J. Marcel Proust et John Ruskin. MF, 1.VII.1926.
Phythian, J. E. A French Estimate of Ruskin. Papers of the Manchester Literary Club, 17, 1898.
Roche, A. J. Proust as Translator of Ruskin. PMLA, 45, 1930.
Souza, S. de. L'influence de Ruskin sur Proust. Diss. Montpellier, 1932.
Iacuzzi, A. The Naïve Theme in the Tempest as a Link between **SHADWELL** and Ramón de la Cruz. MLN, 1937.
Richards, A. S. A Literary Link between Shadwell and Chr. F. Weisse (The Devil of a Wife). PMLA, 21, 1907.
Casati, E. Quelques correspondants français de **SHAFTESBURY**. RLC, 11, 1931.
—— Hérauts et continuateurs de Shaftesbury en France. RLC, 14, 1934.
Cassirer, E. Schiller and Shaftesbury. PEGS, 11, 1935.
Crisafulli, A. S. Parallels to Ideas in the Lettres persanes. PMLA, 1937.
Croce, B. Shaftesbury in Italy. Publ. of the Mod. Human. Research Assoc. Cambridge, 1924.
Elson, C. Wieland and Shaftesbury. Columbia U.P., 1913.
Grudzinski, H. Shaftesburys Einfluss auf Chr. M. Wieland. Mit einer Einleitung über den Einfluss Shaftesburys auf die deutsche Literatur bis 1760. Stuttgart, 1913.
Hatch, I. C. Der Einfluss Shaftesburys auf Herder. SVL, 1, 1901.
Legros, R. P. Diderot et Shaftesbury. MLR, 19, 1924.
Portmann, P. F. Die deutschen Uebersetzungen von Shaftesburys Soliloquy. Willisau (Schweiz), 1942.
Rehorn, F. Ueber das Verhältniss Shaftesburys zu Lessings Laocoon.

Berichte des freien deutschen Hochstifts Frankfurt, 1886-87.

Schultz, F. Die Göttinger Freunde. Journal des freien deutschen Hochstifts, 1926.

Stettner, L. Das philosophische System Shaftesburys und Wielands Agathon. Halle, 1929.

Venturi, F. La jeunesse de Diderot (1713-53). Paris, 1939.

Weiser, C. F. Shaftesbury und das deutsche Geistesleben. Leipzig, 1916.

Bab, J. **SHAWS** Ankunft in Deutschland. Schaubühne, 5, 1909.

Heydet, X. Hermann Bahr et Bernard Shaw. RLV, 1937.

Moore, M. Bernard Shaw et la France. Paris, 1933.

Simmons, E. J. Pushkin and **SHENSTONE**. MLN, Nov., 1930.

Bahlsen, L. **SHERIDANS** Einfluss auf Kotzebue. Berlin, 1889.

Menghini, M. Monti, **SHERLOCK** e Zacchiroli. NAnt, 141, 1895.

Creizenach, W. Eine Tragödie **SHIRLEYS** auf der deutschen Bühne. JbShG, 1911.

Heilley, G. d'. The Gamester en France. Gazette anecdotique, 2, 1877.

Brunhuber, K. Sir Philip **SIDNEYS** Arcadia und ihre Nachläufer. Nürnberg, 1903.

Hainsworth, G. L'Arcadie de Sidney en France. RLC, 10, 1930.

Huesgen, S. H. Das Intellektualfeld in der deutschen Arcadia und in ihrem englischen Vorbild. Diss. Münster, 1936.

Lancaster, H. C. Sidney, Galaut, La Calprenède: an Early Instance of the Influence of English Literature upon French. MLN, Feb., 1927.

Osborn, A. W. Sir Philip Sidney en France. Paris, 1932.

Wallace, M. W. The Reputation of Sir Philip Sidney. Johns Hopkins Alumni Mag., 17, 1931.

Wurmb, A. Die deutsche Uebersetzung von Sidneys Arcadia und Opitz' Verhältnis dazu. Diss. Heidelberg, 1911.

Holthausen, F. **SMOLLETT** und Jean Paul. Archiv, 135, 1916.

Joliat, E. Smollett et la France. Paris, 1935.

—— Millin's Use of Smollett's Travels. RLC, 18, 1938.

Streeter, H. W. Smollett's Novels in France. RR, 1935.

Iakovlev, N. V. Pushkin and **SOUTHEY**. (In Russian). In: Pushkin v mirovoi literature. Leningrad, 1926.

Sousa-Leão, J. de. Southey and Brazil. MLR, 38, 1943.

Wright, H. G. Southey's Relations with Finland and Scandinavia. MLR, 1932.

Didden, R. A German Appreciation of Herbert **SPENCER**. Westminster Rev., 148, 1897.

Fierro, B. Spencer en Bergson. In: Homenage a Bergson. Cordoba (Argentine), 1936.

SPENSER: See also Sources, I. V. 2.

Pienaar, W. J. B. Edmund Spenser and Jonker van der Noot. ESs, 1926.

Arndt, R. Zur Entstehung von Voltaire's Zaïre. (**STEELE**). Marburg, 1906.

Auriant. Une belle histoire de plagiat. (R. L. **STEVENSON** and Maupassant). MF, 1939.

Champion, P. Marcel Schwob et Stevenson. Revue universelle, 1.XII.1926.

Devray, H. D. Stevenson en France. Revue hebdomadaire, April, 1903.

Donce-Brisy, E. R. L. Stevenson dans la littérature française. Bio-bibliographie, 6.VII.1923.

SWIFT: See also Sources, I. V. 2.

Aigner, K. G. W. Rabeners Verhältnis zu Swift. Progr. Pola, 1905.

Caro, J. Lessing und Swift. Studie über Nathan den Weisen. Jena, 1869. Cf. Fischer: Kritische Streitzüge wider die Unkritik. Heidelberg, 1896.

Cooke, Alice L. Some Evidences of Hawthorne's Indebtedness to Swift. Texas Studies in English, 1938.

Crewdson, W. A Japanese Gulliver. NC, Dec., 1913.

Foulet, L. Swift et l'abbé Desfontaines. In: Correspondance de Voltaire (1726-29). Appendix IV. Paris, 1913.

Gloor, G. Swift und die Franzosen. Diss. Zürich, 1922.

Goulding, Sybil. Swift en France au XVIIIe siècle. Paris, 1924. Cf. MLN, 1932.

Jannsen, H. Montesquieus Theorie von der Dreiteilung der Gewalten im Staate auf ihre Quelle zurückgeführt. Gotha, 1878.

Kruuse, J. Swift og Holberg. In: Fem danske studier, København, 1935.

Mueller, W. The Monikins von J. F. Cooper in ihrem Verhältnis zu Gulliver's Travels. Diss. Rostock, 1900.

Philippovic, Vera. Swift in Deutschland. Diss. Zürich, 1903.

Ross, J. F. The Character of Poor Richard: Its Sources and Alterations. PMLA, 55, 1940.

Rovillain, E. E. Jonathan Swift and T. S. Gueulette. MLN, 1929.

Walden, Helen. Jean Paul and Swift. Diss. New York U., 1940.
Amodio, E. **SWINBURNE** e d'Annunzio. Giorn. di Politica e di Letteratura, 16, 1940.
Brown, C. S. More Swinburne-d'Annunzio Parallels. PMLA, 55, 1940.
Delattre, F. A. C. Swinburne et la France. RCC, 1926.
Falzon, P. L. Reminiscences of Swinburne in d'Annunzio. N&Q, 1912.
Mackey, W. F. Verlaine et Swinburne. Le Canada français, 30, 1943.
Bowden, M. **TENNYSON** in France. Manchester, 1930.
Drougard, E. De nouveau sur A Rebours. (Gautier, Mendes, Huysmans). MF, 1.X.1931. And in: Soc. J. K. Huysmans, Oct., 1932.
Eidson, J. O. Tennyson in America: His Reputation and Influence from 1827 to 1858. Athens (Georgia), 1943.
Mallarmé, S. Tennyson vu d'ici. RB, 3, 1892.
Pitollet, C. Les fleurs de Francis Jammes et celles d'Alfred Tennyson. RELV, 56, 1939.
Schmitt, K. Alfred Tennyson in Deutschland. Deutsches Museum, 3, 1853.
Albaugh, Kathryn L. The Influence of W. M. **THACKERAY** on Wilhelm Raabe. Diss. Stanford U., 1941.
Gulliver, H. S. Thackeray in Georgia. Georgia Review, 1, 1947.
Kruger, H. A. Der junge Raabe, Jugendjahre und Erstlingswerke. Leipzig, 1911.
Kurrelmeyer, W. Thackeray and Friedrich von Heyde. MLN, 1933.
Melville, L. Thackeray en France. AFR, Nov., 1919.
Scudder, H. H. Thackeray and N. P. Willis. PMLA, 57, 1942.
Willert, H. Thackeray and Daudet. Archiv, 126, 1911.
Cameron, M. M. L'influence de **THOMSON** sur la poésie descriptive en France, 1759-1810. Paris, 1927.
Davis, R. M. Thomson and Voltaire's Socrate. PMLA, 1934.
Gjerset, F. Der Einfluss von Thomsons Jahreszeiten auf die deutsche Literatur des 18. Jahrhunderts. Heidelberg, 1898.
Halberstadt, B. G. De nederlandsche vertalingen en navolgingen van Thomson's Seasons. Diss. Amsterdam. Leipzig, 1923.
Hirsch, A. L'influence de Thomson en France. RELV, 1925.
Ibershoff, C. H. A German Translation of Passages in Thomson's Seasons. MLN, 1911.
—— Bodmer and Thomson's Seasons. MLN, 41, 1926.
Johnson, W. G. A Swedish Imitator of Thomson. (Dalin). SS, 12, 1933.
—— James Thomson's Influence on Swedish Literature in the 18th Century. Illinois Studies in Lang. and Lit., 1936.
Leglay. De Thomson et de ses traducteurs. Mém. de la Soc. nationale des Sciences et des Arts de Lille, 1849-50.
Partridge, E. A Note on T. Gautier and English Literature. FQ, 1924. And in: A Critical Medley. Paris, 1926.
Stewart, M. C. Traces of Thomson's Seasons in Klopstock's Earlier Works. JEGPh, 1906.
—— B. H. Brockes' Rendering of Thomson's Seasons. JEGPh, 10, 1911.
Walz, J. A. Schillers Spaziergang und Thomson's Seasons. MLN, 1906.
Williams, C. A. James Thomson's Summer and Three of Goethe's Poems. JEGPh, 47, 1948.
Yvon, P. Thomson et ses Saisons en Angleterre et en France. Figaro, 26. IX.1930.
Booth, B. A. **TROLLOPE** in California. HLQ, 3, 1939.
Böttcher, E. Der englische Ursprung des Comte de Boursouffle. (**VANBRUGH**). Rostock, 1906.
WALPOLE: See also Intermediaries, I. IV. 8.
Killen, A. M. Le roman terrifiant ou roman noir de Walpole à Anne Radcliffe et son influence sur la littérature française jusqu'à 1840. Paris, 1923.
Smith, H. E. H. Walpole Anticipates Victor Hugo. MLN, 1926.
Housman, J. E. Izaak **WALTON** and Unamuno. English, 6, 1946.
WESLEY: See Religion, III. I. 4.
Defieber, R. Oscar **WILDE:** Der Mann und sein Werk im Spiegel der deutschen Kritik und sein Einfluss auf die deutsche Literatur. Diss. Heidelberg, 1934.
Lemonnier, L. La condamnation d' O. Wilde et l'opinion française. Revue mondiale, 15.I.1931.
Meyerfeld, M. Oscar Wilde in Deutschland. LE, 1.I.1903.
Reynaud, E. Oscar Wilde à Paris. In: La mêlée symboliste. Paris, 1920.
Saix, G. de. Oscar Wilde chez Maeterlinck. NL, 1945.
Snider, Rose. Oscar Wilde's Progress Down East. NEQ, 13, 1940.
Ritter, O. Dr. **WOLCOT** (Peter Pindar)

und G. A. Bürger. Dr. Wolcot in Deutschland. Archiv, 107, 1902.
Bartlett, Phyllis. Annette and Albertine. (**WORDSWORTH** and Proust). Sewanee Review, 45, 1937.
Bussière, G. & Legouis, E. Le Général Michel Bacharetia de Beaupuy (and Wordsworth). Bull. de la Soc. hist. et arch. du Périgord, 17. Périgueux, 1890.
Cécilia, J. la. Wordsworth et Aug. Comte. Figaro, 25.V.1929.
Foerster, M. Wordsworth, Coleridge and Frederike Brun. Academy, 27.VI.1896.
Howard, L. Wordsworth in America. MLN, 48, 1933.
Leary, L. Wordsworth in America: Addenda. MLN, 58, 1943.
Legouis, E. William Wordsworth and Annette Vallon. London, 1922.
Logan, J. Wordsworth in France. TLS, 20.XI.1937.
Miller, E. A. Wordsworth and W. Müller. Americana Germanica, 3, 1900.
Sélincourt, E. de. Emile Legouis et Wordsworth. In: Hommage à Emile Legouis. EA. Paris, 1938.
Texte, J. William Wordsworth et la poésie lakiste en Francc. RDM, 15.VII. 1896. And in: Etudes de littérature européenne. Paris, 1898.
Pariset, G. Arthur **YOUNG** et ses traducteurs. Révolution française, Jan., 1896.
Baldensperger, F. Young et ses Nuits en France. Etudes d'histoire littéraire, ler Sér., Paris, 1907.
Barnsdorff, J. Youngs Nachtgedanken und ihr Einfluss auf die deutsche Litteratur. Bamberg, 1893.
Bertana, E. Luigi Richni (and Young). Miscell. nuziale Scherillo. Milano, 1904.
Biadego, J. L'origine dei Sepolcri di U. Foscolo. In: Da libri e manoscritti. Verona, 1883.
Bliss, I. S. Young's Night Thoughts in Relation to Contemporary Christian Apologetics. PMLA, 1934.
Cotton, E. Cadalso and his Foreign Sources. BSS, 8, 1931.
Cramer, K. F. Klopstock. Hamburg, 1779-92.
Dimoff, P. Une source anglaise de l'Invention d'A. Chénier. RLC, 1, 1921.
Kind, J. L. Edward Young in Germany. Columbia U.P., 1906.
Montesinos, J. Cadalso o la noche cerada. Cruz y Raya, Rev. de afirmación y negación, April, 1934.
Peers, E. A. The Influence of Young and Gray in Spain. MLR, 1926.
Pettit, H. A Check-List of Young's Night Thoughts in America. Papers Bibliogr. Soc. of America, 42, 1948.
Popovic, P. Branko Magarasevic. Prevodi iz Wielanda i Younga iz 1819. In: Prilozi za knjizevnost, Jezik, istoriju i folklor, 15, 1935.
Steinke, M. W. Edward Young's Conjectures on Original Composition in England and Germany. Diss. Illinois. New York, 1917.
Szyjkowski, M. Les Nuits de Young et la poésie polonaise. (In Polish). Bull. Acad. Sc. de la Pologne, 1915.
Yancey, Myra L. Fernández de Lizardi and his Foreign Sources for Las noches tristes. HR, 9, 1941.

CHAPTER FIFTEEN

The English Language.

Anon. The English Language in America. NAR, Oct., 1860.
Aehle, W. Die Anfänge des Unterrichts in der englischen Sprache, besonders in den Ritterakademien. Hamburg, 1938.
Amero, J. L'anglomanie dans le français, ou les barbarismes anglais usités en France. Paris, 1828.
Bachmann, H. Das englische Sprachgut in den Romanen Jules Verne's. Diss. Greifswald, 1916.
Baker, S. J. The Literature of Pidgin English. American Speech, 19, 1944.
Barbier, P. Loan-Words from English in Eighteenth Century French. MLR, 1921.
Bonnaffé, E. L'anglicisme et l'anglo-américanisme dans la langue française. Paris, 1920.
Brausewetter, E. Die Engländerei in der deutschen Sprache. Internat. Litteraturberichte, 22.III.1900.
Burkhard, A. The Beginnings of the New Poetic Language in Germany. PhQ, 1931.
Carlson, H. G. English Sport Terminology in Scandinavia. Words, 5, 1940.
Darmesteter, J. De l'étude de l'anglais en France. RB, 7.VII.1883.
Dunger, H. Wider die Engländerei in der deutschen Sprache. Berlin, 1900.
Fluegel, E. References to the English Language in the German Literature of the First Half of the XVIth Century. MPh, 1, 1903.
Funke, O. Zum Weltsprachenproblem in England im 17. Jahrhundert. Heidelberg, 1930.

Gelzer, H. Englische Worte im Französischen. Anglia, 67-68, 1943-44.

Goulding, Sybil. Le beau-pére de Rivarol, **Mather Flint**, maître de langue anglaise, à Paris (1740). RLC, 8, 1928.

Hall, R. A. Chinese Pidgin English Grammar and Texts. Journal Amer. Oriental Soc., 64, 1944.

Hippe, M. Vorlesungen über englische Philologie an den Universitäten Deutschlands. ESn, 23-24, 1897.

Hogan, J. J. The English Language in Ireland. Dublin, 1928.

Kerékgyártó, E. English in Hungary: A XVIIth Century Grammar. Hungarian Quarterly, 5, 1939.

Kervigan, A. L'anglais à Paris, histoire humoristique de son introduction dans notre langue et dans nos moeurs. Paris, 1865.

Mathesius, V. English Studies in Czecho-Slovakia. ESs, April, 1923.

Matthews, J. B. The English Language in America. Scribner's Mag., March, 1901.

Meyerfeld, M. Die historischen Lehn- und geflügelten Worte aus dem Englischen. National Zt., 90, 1903.

Orsini, N. G. Gli studi inglesi in Italia nel 1932. Leonardo, Oct., 1933.

Proctor, R. A. English and American English. Gentleman's Mag. N.S., 27, 1881.

Scherer, M. Englisches Sprachgut in der französischen Tagespresse der Gegenwart. Giessener Beiträge, 11, 1923.

Skeat, W. A Rough List of English Words Found in Anglo-French, Especially During the XIIIth and XIVth Centuries. Transactions of the Philolog. Soc., 3, 1880-81. Cf. Romania, 12.

Spira, T. Beiträge zur Geschichte und Aufgabe der englischen Studien in Deutschland. Anglia, Jan., 1936.

Stiven, Agnes B. Englands Einfluss auf den deutschen Wortschatz. Diss. Marburg. Zeulenroda, 1936.

Tardel, H. Das englische Fremdwort in der modernen französischen Sprache. Festschrift Vers. der Phil. Bremen, 1899. Cf. Archiv, 105, 1901.

Thudicum, C. Napoleon und die englische Sprache. NSp, 9, 1901.

Vandaele. Le néologisme exotique. Les emprunts anglais dans le français actuel. Besançon, 1902.

Viëtor, W. Die Aussprache des Englischen nach den deutsch-englischen Grammatiken vor 1750. Heilbronn, 1885.

Walz, J. A. English Influence on the German Vocabulary of the Eighteenth Century. MDU, 35, 1943.

Westphal, J. Englische Ortsnamen im Altfranzösischen. Diss. Strassburg, 1891.

Wilson, C. B. The Grammatical Gender of English Words in German. Americana Germanica, 3, 1899-1900.

CHAPTER SIXTEEN

English Influences upon Individual Authors.

Howitt, W. **ALFIERI** et Rousseau en Angleterre. Revue britannique, March, 1841.

Viglione, F. **L'ALGAROTTI** e l'Inghilterra. Studi di lett. ital., 13. (Napoli), 1919.

Roth, G. Un voyageur français à Londres en 1685 (**ANONYMOUS**). AFR, 1920.

Wehr, I. Ernst Moritz **ARNDT** über England und die Engländer. Hamburger Correspondenz, 5, 1906.

Howie, M. D. Achim von **ARNIM** and Scotland. MLR, 17, 1922.

Jones, K. The Source of Arnim's Owen Tudor. MLN, 1927.

Zwager, N. A Dutch Visitor to England in 1661 (S. P. **ARNOLDINUS**). Tijdschrift voor taal en letteren, 27, 1939.

Horner, E. Das Aufkommen des englischen Geschmackes in Wien und **AYRENHOFFS** Trauerspiel Kleopatra und Antonius. Euphorion, 4, 1895.

Robertson, J. G. Zur Kritik Jacob **AYRERS**. Mit Rücksicht auf Hans Sachs und die englischen Komödianten. Diss. Leipzig, 1892.

Wodick, W. Jacob Ayrers Dramen in ihrem Verhältnis zur einheimischen Literatur und zum Schauspiel der englischen Komödianten. Halle, 1912.

Baldensperger, F. Une suggestion anglaise pour le titre de La Comédie humaine de **BALZAC**. RLC, 1, 1921.

Helm, W. H. Aspects of Balzac. London, 1905.

Bandy, T. **BAUDELAIRE'S** Knowledge of English. This Quarter, Sept., 1929.

Charpentier, J. La poésie britannique et Baudelaire. MF, 147, 1921.

Potez, H. Les sonnets de Baudelaire et la poésie anglaise. RG, Oct., 1909.

Lawton, H. W. Notes sur Jean **BAUDOIN** et sur ses traductions de l'Anglais. RLC, 6, 1926.

Courtines, L. P. **BAYLE'S** Relations with

England and the English. Columbia U.P., 1938.

BARETTI: See also Intermediaries, I. IV. 8.

Piccioni, G. Baretti e la stampa periodica inglese dei suoi tempi. GSLI, 62, 1946.

Murray, J. A Sixteenth-Century French Traveller in Scotland (Jean de **BEAUGUE**). French Studies, Jan., 1948.

Carrière, J. M. **BERQUIN'S** Adaptations from English Periodical Literature. PhQ, July, 1934.

—— Notes on Arnaud Berquin's Adaptations from English Poetry. RR, 1935.

Philipson, P. H. A German Adaptation (**BINZER**) of the Blue Bells of Scotland. MLN, 1910.

BLANC, L. Lettres sur l'Angleterre. Paris, 1865-67. Cf. MLIA, 1866.

BLANQUI, A. Voyage d'un jeune Français en Angleterre et en Ecosse pendant l'automne. Paris, 1822.

Wihan, J. Joh. Chr. **BODE** als Vermittler englischer Geisteswerke in Deutschland. Prag, 1906.

Ibershoff, C. H. **BODMER** as a Literary Borrower. PhQ, 1, 1922.

Vetter, T. Bodmer und die englische Litteratur. Denkschrift zum 200. Geburtstage. Zürich, 1900.

Jespersen, O. **BRANDES** og engelsk Literaturen. Tilskueren, Feb., 1912.

Gustafson, A. T. English Influence in Fredrika **BREMER**. JEGPh, 1931-33.

Ryan, T. **BROWNSON** Speaks of England. Catholic World, 154, 1942.

Harvey, A. E. Martin **BUCER** in England. Diss. Marburg, 1906.

Janelle, P. Strasbourg-Londres en 1549: le voyage de Bucer et Fagius. Alsace française, 27.VIII.1927.

Anon. Ueber **BUERGERS** Quellen und deren Benützung. Neuer Teutscher Merkur, Oct., 1797.

Bloemker, F. Das Verhältnis von Bürgers lyrischer und episch-lyrischer Dichtung zur englischen Literatur. Diss. Münster, 1930.

Bonet-Maury, G. G. A. Bürger et les origines anglaises de la ballade littéraire en Allemagne. Diss. Paris, 1889.

Goetzinger. Ueber die Quellen der Bürgerschen Gedichte. Zürich, 1831.

Gnudi, Martha T. **CARDUCCI'S** Study of English. Ital., 16, 1939.

Anon. Phil. **CHASLES** über die gegenwärtige englische Litteratur. Blätter zur Kunde der Litteratur des Auslands, 1839.

Phillips, E. M. Philarète Chasles, critique et historien de la littérature anglaise. Paris, 1933.

Anon. **CHATEAUBRIAND** in England. Blätter für literar. Unterhaltung, 2. X.1836.

Baldensperger, F. Chateaubriand et l'émigration française à Londres. RHLF, 1907. And in: Etudes d'histoire littéraire, 2. Paris, 1910.

Beranek, V. Chateaubriand über die Engländer und Franzosen. Progr. Bielitz, 1885.

Chérel, A. Autour du Génie du christianisme. Rev. de l'histoire de l'Eglise de France, 1923.

Dempsey, M. A Contribution to the Sources of the Génie du christianisme. Paris, 1928.

Deschamps, J. Chateaubriand en Angleterre. Paris, 1933.

Dick, E. Le séjour de Chateaubriand en Suffolk. RHLF, 15, 1908.

Duchemin, M. Chateaubriand à White Hall. RHLF, 17, 1910.

Miller, M. H. Chateaubriand and English Literature. Baltimore, 1829.

Nisard. Du dernier ouvrage de M. de Chateaubriand. RP, Oct., 1836.

Prescott, W. H. Chateaubriand's Sketches of English Literature. NAR, Oct., 1839.

Reboul, P. La couleur anglaise chez Chateaubriand. Rev. des Sciences hum., 2, 1947.

Roddier, H. Chateaubriand et la Revue d'Edimbourg. RLC, 11, 1931.

Wright, R. W. Quelques sources anglaises de Chateaubriand. RHLF, 17, 1910.

Needham, J. (ed.). The Teacher of Nations: Addresses and Essays in Commemoration of the Visit to England of the Great Czech Educationalist, Jan Amos Komensky, **COMENIUS**, 1641-1941. Cambridge U.P., 1942.

Young, R. F. Comenius in England. Oxford U.P., 1932.

Quigley, H. Italian Criticism in the 18th Century. The Influence of English Philosophy and the Development of Aesthetics Based on Imagination: Antonio **CONTI**. Mélanges Hauvette. Paris, 1934.

Orsini, N. G. **CROCE** e la letteratura inglese. Rassegna d'Italia, 1, 1946.

Cidade, H. A obra poetica do Dr. José Anastácio de **CUNHA**, com um estudio sôbre o anglo-germanismo nos prôtoromanticos portugueses. Coimbra, 1930.

Bartolini, A. Il viaggio di **DANTE** a Oxford, a proposito di un articulo di Gladstone. Roma, 1894.

Cosmo, U. Una nuova fonte dantesca? SM, 1904.
Gladstone, W. E. Did Dante Study in Oxford? NC, June, 1892.
Darmesteter, Mary. James **DARMESTETER** in England. Cosmopolis, Feb., 1896.
Bourchemin, D. Béarnais à Londres: les **DATOURMON.** Bull. de la Soc. de l'hist. du Protestantisme français, 1933.
Huret, J. & Rigaud, J. A. **DAUDET** à Londres. Figaro, 19. & 28.V.1895.
Quarrell, W. H. A Frenchman in London, 1789 (**DECREMPS**) N&Q, 189, 1945.
Morra, U. Sopra una storia italiana della letteratura inglese. (**DE SANCTIS**). Letteratura, Oct., 1937.
Burner, A. Le poète **DESTOUCHES** diplomate. Sa mission à Londres, 1717-23. Rev. d' histoire diplomatique, 1929.
Cru, R. Loyalty. **DIDEROT** as a Disciple of English Thought. New York, 1913.
Gaudin, Lois S. Les Lettres anglaises dans l'Encyclopédie. New York, 1942.
Spink, G. W. English Impressions in **DINGELSTEDT'S** Wanderschaft. MLR, 1929.
Badt, B. A. von **DROSTE-HUELSHOFF,** ihre dichterische Entwicklung und ihr Verhältnis zur englischen Literatur. Breslau, 1909.
Herzfeld, G. Zu Annette von Drostes englischen Quellen. Anglia, 1920.
Nettenheim, Josephine. A. von Droste und die englische Romantik. Jb. der Droste Ges., 1947.
Bertocci, A. P. Charles **DU BOS** and English Literature. New York, 1949.
Bonnerot, L. Ch. Du Bos interprète spirituel de la littérature anglaise. Résurrection. (Toulouse), 1946.
Lang, A. With **DUMAS** in Derbyshire. British Review, Feb., 1914.
Parigot, H. Le Drame d'Alexandre Dumas. Paris, 1898.
Anon. **EMERSON'S** English Traits. Westminster Review, Oct., 1856.
Aynard, J. Les Anglais jugés par Emerson. Journal des Débats, Sept., 1922.
Brittin, N. A. Emerson and the Metaphysical Poets. AL, March, 1936.
Cosman, M. Emerson's English Traits and the English. Mark Twain Quart., 8, 1948.
Davis, M. R. Emerson's Reason and the Scottish Philosophers. NEQ, 17, 1944.
Coleman, A. Influence of English Literature on **FLAUBERT** before 1851. MLN, May, 1911.
FONTANE, T. Journeys to England in Victoria's Early Days, 1844-59. London, 1939.
Neuendorff, O. Fontanes Gang durch die englische Dichtung. Potsdam, 1938.
Rhyn, H. Theodor Fontanes Bearbeitungen altenglischer und altschottischer Balladen. Diss. Bern, 1914.
Stirk, S. D. England and the English in the Letters of Th. Fontane. Proc. of the Leeds Philos. and Liter. Soc., 4, 1936.
Viglione, F. Ugo **FOSCOLO** in Inghilterra. Catania, 1910.
Guillain de Benouville. Alain **FOURNIER.** RB, 6.III.1937.
Hermann, D. La littérature anglaise et l'oeuvre d'Alain Fournier. Présence (Genève), 1936.
Read, C. The English Elements in Benjamin **FRANKLIN.** Pa. Mag. of Hist. and Biog., 64, 1940.
Erbach, W. F. **FREILIGRATHS** Uebersetzungen aus dem Englischen im ersten Jahre seines Schaffens. Diss. Münster, 1908.
Gudde, E. G. Traces of English Influences in Freiligrath's Political and Social Lyrics. JEGPh, 20, 1921.
Liddell, M. F. F. Freiligrath's Debt to English Poets. MLR, 23, 1928.
Roeschen, F. A. Freiligraths Uebersetzungen englischer Dichtungen. Giessen, 1923.
Schwering, J. Unbekannte Jugendgedichte und Uebersetzungen von Ferd. Freiligrath. Beilage zur Allg. Zt., 5.XII. 1896.
Spink, G. W. Freiligrath als Verdeutscher englischer Poesie. Berlin, 1925.
—— Freiligraths Verbannungsjahre in London. Berlin, 1932.
Weddigen, O. Lord Byrons Einfluss auf die europäischen Litteraturen der Neuzeit. Anhang: F. Freiligrath als Vermittler englischer Dichtung in Deutschland. Wald, 1901.
Price, L. M. The Attitude of Gustav **FREYTAG** and Julian Schmid toward English Literature (1848-62). Göttingen, Baltimore, 1915.
Volkenborn, H. **GEIBEL** als Uebersetzer und Nachahmer englischer Dichtungen. Münster, 1910.
Blanck, A. **GEIJER** i England, 1809-10. Stockholm, 1914.
Ward, Phyllis J. Mme. de **GENLIS** in England. RLC, 16, 1936.
Farrell, R. Stefan **GEORGES** Beziehungen zur englischen Dichtung. Berlin, 1937.

Thiel, R. Otto **GILDEMEISTER** als Uebersetzer englischer Dichtungen. Diss. Breslau, 1938.
Alford, R. G. Englishmen at Weimar. English Books in **GOETHE'S** Library. PEGS, 5, 1891.
Boyd, J. Goethe's Knowledge of English Literature. Oxford, 1932.
Brandl, A. Goethe und England. F&F, 8, 1932.
Carr, M. Goethe in his Connection with English Literature. PEGS, 4, 1890.
Deetjen, W. Goethe und Tiecks elisabethanische Studien. JbShG, 65, 1929.
Hayens, K. C. Goethe and English Letters. GLL, 3, 1939.
John, K. Wilhelm Meisters theatralische Sendung und dessen Beziehungen zum englischen humoristischen Roman. GRM, 5, 1913.
Liljegren, S. B. The English Source of Goethe's Gretchen Tragedy. Lund, Oxford, 1937.
Mennie, D. M. A Note on Goethe as a Translator of English Prose, 1820-32. MLR, 1935.
Poeschel, C. & Rodenberg, J. (eds.). Goethe über England und die englische Literatur. Leipzig, 1936.
Sachs, C. Goethes Bekanntschaft mit der englischen Sprache und Literatur. Neuphilolog. Centralblatt, 1905.
Schöffler, H. Die Leiden des jungen Werthers: ihr geistesgeschichtlicher Hintergrund. Frankfurt, 1939.
Vollrath, W. Goethe und Grossbritannien. Erlangen, 1932.
Simmons, E. J. **GOGOL** and English Literature. MLR, 26, 1931.
Loomis, C. G. English Writers in **GOTTSCHED'S** Handlexikon. JEGPh, 42, 1943.
Hay, D. Pietro **GRIFFO:** An Italian in England (1506-12). Italian Studies, 2.
Eder, Beatrice. **GRILLPARZERS** Verhältnis zur englischen Literatur. Diss. Wien, 1934.
Ewen, F. Criticism of English Literature in **GRIMM'S** Correspondance littéraire. SPh, 33, 1936.
Hunter, A. C. Les opinions du Baron Grimm sur le roman anglais. RLC, 12, 1932.
Coffman, Bertha R. The Influence of English Literature on Friedrich von **HAGEDORN.** MPh, 1914-15.
—— A Note on Hagedorn's and Haller's German-English Literary Relations. MLN, 1926.
Jones, H. M. Albrecht von **HALLER** and English Philosophy. PMLA, 40, 1925.
Price, L. M. Albrecht von Haller and English Theology. PMLA, 41, 1926.
Wyplel, L. Englands Einfluss auf die Lehrdichtung Hallers. Progr. 1888.
Voigt, F. A. Gerhart **HAUPTMANN** und England. GRM, 25, 1937.
Anon. **HAWTHORNE** on England. Blackwood's Mag., Nov., 1863.
Hillard, G. S. The English Notebooks of N. Hawthorne. AM, Sept., 1870.
Pryce-Jones, A. Hawthorne in England. Life & Letters Today, 50, 1946.
Stewart, R. (ed.). The English Notebooks. New York, 1941.
Hess, J. A. Heinrich **HEINE'S** Appraisal of John Bull. MLJ, 19, 1934.
Grimm, H. Das Theater des Herzogs **HEINRICH JULIUS VON BRAUNSCHWEIG** zu Wolfenbüttel. WM, 1856.
Knight, A. H. J. The Tragi-Comedies of Duke Heinrich Julius of Brunswick. MLR, 41, 1946.
—— Heinrich Julius, Duke of Brunswick. Oxford, 1948.
Pascal, R. **HERDER** and the Scottish Historical School. PEGS, N.S., 14, 1939.
Schort, L. Herders Beziehungen zur englischen Literatur. Breslau, 1930.
Waag, A. Ueber Herders Uebertragungen englischer Gedichte. Heidelberg, 1892.
Buchholz, J. J. T. **HERMES'** Beziehungen zur englischen Literatur. Diss. Marburg, 1911.
Muskalla, K. J. T. Hermes. Diss. Breslau, 1910.
Weiss, J. J. **HETTNER** et le XVIIIe siècle anglais. Revue contemporaine, March, 1856.
Gilbert, M. E. Hugo von **HOFMANNSTHAL** and England. GLL, 1, 1937.
Lough, J. Baron d'**HOLBACH,** a Prelude to the French Revolution. RHLF, 1936.
Rhoades, L. A. **HOELTYS** Verhältniss zu der englischen Litteratur. Diss. Göttingen, 1892.
Dringenberg, W. Das Englandbild Victor **HUGOS.** Geist der Zeit, 18, 1940.
Filon. Les drames de Victor Hugo et l'histoire d'Angleterre. Journal des Débats, 26.XI.1902.
Thomas, J. H. L'Angleterre dans l'oeuvre de Victor Hugo. Paris, 1934.
Tournier, G. Les points de départ du Cromwell de Victor Hugo. RLC, 7, 1927.
Müller, P. Joh. Chr. **HUETTNERS** Englische Miscellen. Würzburg, 1939.
Wadepuhl, W. Hüttner, a New Source for Anglo-German Relations. GR, 14, 1939.
Ternois, R. Les débuts de l'Anglophilie

en France: Henri **JUSTEL** (1620-93). RLC, 13, 1933.
Baldensperger, F. Louise de **KEROUALLE** et ses quinze ans d'Angleterre. In: Etudes d' histoire littéraire, 3e Sér., Paris, 1939.
Asten-Kinkel, A. Joh. **KINKEL** in England. Deutsche Revue, 26, 1901.
Fischer, W. Des Darmstädter Schriftstellers Johann H. **KUENZEL** (1810-73) Beziehungen zu England. Giessen, 1939.
Charlier, G. Aspects de **LAMARTINE**. Bruxelles, 1937.
Gosse, E. Lamartine and the English Poets. In: More Books on the Table. London, 1923.
Guillemin, H. Les Visions de Lamartine. Paris, 1936.
Séché, L. Les sources littéraires des Méditations. MF, 15.IX.1905.
Havens, G. H. The Abbé **LE BLANC** and English Literature. MPh, 18, 1920.
Nolva, R. de. Les sources anglaises de **LECONTE DE LISLE**. MF, 1.VII. 1922.
Gerhardt, K. I. **LEIBNIZ** in London. The Monist, Oct., 1917.
Clarke, C. H. **LENZ'** Uebersetzungen aus dem Englischen. ZVL, 10, 1897.
Marchesi, G. **LEOPARDI** e la poesia inglese. Iride, 3, 1899.
Olivero, F. La letteratura inglese nei Pensieri di varia filosofia di Leopardi. In: Studi britannici. Torino, 1931.
Vail, C. C. D. Pastor **LESSING'S** Knowledge of English. GR, 20, 1945.
Caro, J. Lessing und die Engländer. Euphorion, 6, 1899.
Kies, P. P. The Sources and Basic Model of Lessing's Miss Sara Sampson. MPh, 24, 1926.
—— Lessing's Early Study of English Drama. JEGPh, 28, 1929.
—— Lessing's Relation to Early English Sentimental Comedy. PMLA, 1932.
Vail, C. C. D. Lessing's Relation to the English Language and Literature. Columbia U. P., 1936.
Betz, G. **LICHTENBERG** as a Critic of the English Stage. JEGPh, 23, 1924.
Hecht, H. Briefe aus Lichtenbergs englischem Freundeskreis. Göttingen, 1925.
Leitzmann, A. Notizen über die englische Bühne aus Lichtenbergs Tagebüchern. JbShG, 42, 1906.
Mare, M. L. & Quarrell, W. H. (eds) Lichtenberg's Visits to England. Oxford, 1938.
Scholte, J. H. Georg Christoph Lichtenberg in England. NPh, 28, 1943.
Le Clair, R. C. Three American Travellers in England: James Russell **LOWELL**, Henry Adams, Henry James. Philadelphia, 1945.
Betz, J. O. **LUDWIGS** Verhältnis zu den Engländern. Frankfurt, 1929.
Waller, E. D. Lorenzo **MAGALOTTI** in England. Italian Studies, 1937.
Holdsworth, F. Joseph de **MAISTRE** et l'Angleterre. Paris, 1936.
Whiting, B. J. The English Proverbs of Stéphane **MALLARME**. RR, 36, 1945.
Graf, A. Il romanticismo del **MANZONI**. Roma, 1896.
Ashbee, H. S. **MARAT** en Angleterre. Acad. des beaux livres, Annales littéraires. Paris, 1890.
Roberts, W. Marat in England. The Bookman. (London), 1893.
McKeithan, D. M. More about **MARK TWAIN'S** War with English Critics of America. MLN, April, 1948.
Morelli, Emilia. **MAZZINI** in Inghilterra. Firenze, 1938 & 1943.
Pinkuss, F. Moses **MENDELSSOHNS** Verhältnis zur englischen Philosophie. Philosoph. Jb. der Gôrres-Ges., 42, 1929.
Ten Hoor, J. Mendelssohn's Relation to English Poetry. PMLA, 1931.
Fredén, G. Friedrich **MENIUS** und das Repertoire der englischen Komödianten in Deutschland. Diss. Upsala. Stockholm, 1938.
Chambon, F. **MERIMEE** et la société anglaise. RLC, 2, 1922.
Connes, G. Introduction à l'édition des Etudes anglo-américaines de Mérimée. Paris, 1930.
Ducreus, J. Opinions de P. Mérimée sur les Anglais. CLS, 23-24, 1946.
Healy, D. Mérimée et les Anglais. Paris, 1946.
Hennig, J. Malvida von **MEYSENBURG** and England. CLS, 23-24, 1946.
Wilson, Claudine J. Francisque **MICHEL** and his Scottish Friends. MLR, 1935.
—— A Frenchman in England: Francisque Michel. RLC, 17, 1937.
Carré, J. M. **MICHELET** et l'Angleterre. RLC, 4, 1924.
Lednicki, W. **MICKIEWICZ** and England. Pologne littéraire, 15.IV.1929.
Windakiewicz, S. The Anglomania of Mickiewicz. SR, 1929.
Dédéyan, C. Les habits anglais de Michel de **MONTAIGNE**. Revue de l'Alliance française, July, 1946.
Anon. **MONTESQUIEU** in England. QR, April, 1903.
Buss, E. Montesquieu and Cartesius. Philos. Monatshefte, Oct., 1869.

Crane, R. S. Montesquieu and British Thought. Journal of Pol. Economy, 49, 1941.
Dedieu, J. Montesquieu et la tradition politique anglaise en France. Paris, 1909 & 1925.
Fletcher, F. T. H. Montesquieu and English Politics. London, 1939.
—— Montesquieu and British Education in the XVIIIth Century. MLR, 38, 1943.
Giovagnoli, R. Vicenzo **MONTI** imitatore. In: Meditazioni di un brontolone. Roma, 1887.
Talva, F. Paul **MORAND** et les Anglais. La Semaine égyptienne, Dec., 1936.
Duncker, A. Landgraf **MORITZ VON HESSEN** und die englischen Komödianten. DR, Aug., 1886.
Meyerfeld, M. Reisen eines Deutschen in England im Jahre 1782 (Karl Ph. **MORITZ**). Die Zeit, 321, 1903.
Zur Linde, O. (ed.). Reisen eines Deutschen in England im Jahre 1782. Berlin, 1903.
Feuillerat, A. H. de La **MORVONNAIS** et la littérature anglaise. Mélanges J. Loth. Annales de Bretagne, 1928.
Horsley, Phyllis M. Comparative Criticism. (**MURALT**). CLS, 10, 1943.
Larat, J. Un voyageur romantique en Angleterre: Charles **NODIER**. AFR, Dec., 1920.
Galland, R. Un poète errant de la Renaissance: Jean van der **NOOT** et l'Angleterre. RLC, 2, 1922.
Eichholz, D. E. A Greek Traveller in Tudor England. (N. **NUCIUS**). G&R, 16, 1947.
Wolle, F. Fitz-James **O'BRIEN** in Ireland and England, 1828-51. AL, 14, 1942.
Vocadlo, O. English Influences on **PALACKY**. SR, 3, 1925.
Potter, S. Palacky a anglické písemnictví. Casopis Matice Moravské, 53, 1929.
Allen, D. C. Dr. Gui **PATIN** Looks at England. SAQ, 42, 1943.
Hager, H. Diary of the Journey of **PHILIP JULIUS DUKE OF STETTIN** through England in the Year 1602. ESn, 18, 1894.
Leigh, R. A. Le Voyage en Angleterre d'Amédée **PICHOT**. RLC, 19, 1939.
Pichot, A. Voyage historique et littéraire en Angleterre et en Ecosse. 3 vols. Paris, 1825. Cf. Globe, 2, 1825.
Zanella, G. **PINDEMONTE** e gli Inglesi. NAnt, 60, 1881.
Hecht, H. (ed.). Thomas **PLATTERS** des Jüngeren Englandfahrt im Jahre 1599. Halle, 1929 & London, 1937.
Battistini, W. Raffaele **POERIO** esule in Inghilterra e le sue relazioni con Luigi de Potter. GSLI, 53, 1935.
Hilton, R. Antonio **PONZ** en Inglaterra. BSS, July, 1936.
Simmons, E. J. La littérature anglaise et **POUCHKINE**. RLC, 17, 1937.
PREVOST: See also Intermediaries, I. IV. 8.
Anderson, P. B. English Drama Transferred to Prévost's Fiction. MLN, March, 1934.
Chew, S. P. Prévost's Mémoires pour servir à l'histoire de la vertu. MLN, 54, 1939.
Cooper, Berenice. The Relation of Le Philosophe anglais by the Abbé Prévost to the Religious Controversies in France and England during the early XVIIIth Century. Transactions of the Wisconsin Academy, 32, 1940.
Engel, Claire E. Des Grieux et Manon ont-ils existé? Revue hebdomadaire, 3.X.1936.
—— Autour du voyage de l'abbé Prévost en Angleterre. RLC, 18, 1938.
——Figures et aventures du XVIIIe siècle: Voyages et découvertes de l'abbé Prévost. Paris, 1939.
Foster, J. The Abbé Prévost and the English Novel. PMLA, 42, 1927.
Havens, G. R. The Abbé Prévost and English Literature. Princeton, 1921.
Hazard, P. Une source anglaise de l'abbé Prévost. MPh, Feb., 1930.
Robertson, M. Introduction à l'édition des Mémoires et aventures d'un homme de qualité. Paris, 1927.
Charlier, G. Athalie et la Révolution d'Angleterre. (**RACINE**). MF, 1931.
Arnold, R. F. Ferdinand **RAIMUND** in England. Wien, 1902.
Tronchon, H. **RENAN** et l'Angleterre. RLC, 7, 1927.
King, G. V. Michel de la **ROCHE** et ses Mémoires littéraires de la Grande-Bretagne (1720 ff). RLC, 15, 1935.
Robertson, J. G. Sophie von La Roche's Visit to England in 1786. MLR, 1932.
Havens, T. B. An English Source of La **ROCHEFOUCAULD'S** Maximes. NC, 1933.
Jovy, E. Deux inspirations inconnues jusqu'ici des Maximes de La Rochefoucauld. Bull. du Bibliophile, 1909.
Anon. A Frenchman in England, 1784. TLS, 23.II.1933.
Marchand, J. François de La Rochefoucauld, voyageur en Ecosse, 1786. Correspondant, 10. & 25.III.1932.

Vallese, T. Paolo **ROLLI** in Inghilterra. Milano, 1938.
Bandy, W. T. **ROUSSEAU'S** Flight from England. RR, 39, 1948.
Courtois, L. Le séjour de J. J. Rousseau en Angleterre. Annales J. J. Rousseau, 6, (Genève), 1910.
Guimbaud, L. J. J. Rousseau à Londres. MF, 16.VII.1912.
SAINT-EVREMOND: See also Intermediaries, I. IV. 8.
Daniels, W. M. Saint-Evremond en Angleterre. Diss. Paris. Versailles, 1907.
Jaspar, M. H. Saint-Evremond à Londres. France Libre, 10, 1945.
Combe, T. G. **SAINTE-BEUVE** poète et les poètes anglais. Bordeaux, 1937.
Craig, H. S. Sainte-Beuve et sa connaissance de l'anglais: quelques précisions. CLS, 8, 1942.
Phillips, E. M. Sainte-Beuve and the English Pre-romantics. Aberystwyth Studies, 1925.
—— Sainte-Beuve and the Lake Poets. FQ, 8, 1926.
—— Sainte-Beuve's Criticism of English Poetry. FQ, 9, 1927.
—— English Friendships of Sainte-Beuve. Bull. of the Mod. Hum. Research Assoc., April, 1927.
—— Sainte-Beuve's Criticism of English Prose. FQ, 13, 1931.
—— Saint-Beuve et les poètes romantiques anglais. RAA, Aug., 1935.
Roth, G. Ce que Sainte-Beuve a su de l'anglais. RG, 12, 1921.
—— Sur les imitations en vers par Sainte-Beuve de poèmes anglais. RG, 13, 1922.
Lafourcade, G. Gabriel **SARRAZIN** critique de la poésie anglaise. EA, May, 1937.
Kelly, J. A. **SCHILLER'S** Attitude towards England. PMLA, 39, 1924.
Sachs, C. Schillers Beziehungen zur englischen Litteratur. Archiv, 30, 1861.
Herzfeld, G. August Wilhelm **SCHLEGEL** in seinen Beziehungen zu englischen Dichtern und Kritikern. Archiv, 138-40, 1919-20.
Schirmer, W. F. A. W. Schlegel und England. JbShG, 75, 1939.
Price, L. M. Christian Heinrich **SCHMID** and his Translations of English Dramas (1767-89). Berkeley, 1942.
Pfenniger, E. **SCHROEDER** als Bearbeiter englischer Stücke. Diss. Zürich, 1920.
SIMOND, L. Voyage d'un Français en Angleterre. Paris, 1816.
Guilloton, V. Autour de la Relation du voyage de S. **SORBIERE** en Angleterre, 1663-64. Northampton (Mass.), 1930.
Morize, A. Sorbière et son Voyage en Angleterre (1664). RHLF, 1907.
Hunter, A. C. J. B. A. **SUARD:** un introducteur de la littérature anglaise en France. Paris, 1925.
Achelis, T. **TAINES** Aufzeichnungen über England. Die Wage, 1906.
Arnould, E. J. Taine et le moyen âge anglais. RLC, 16, 1936.
Looten, C. Le romantisme de Taine, historien de la littérature anglaise. RAA, 1933.
Maurois, A. Taine et l'Angleterre. NL, 2.VI.1928.
Murray, Kathleen. Taine und die englische Romantik. München, 1924.
Olivero, F. La letteratura inglese nella corrispondenza del Taine. L'Erma, 2, 1930-31.
Roe, F. C. Taine et l'Angleterre. Paris, 1923. Cf. AFR, 1923.
Deetjen, W. Goethe und **TIECKS** elisabethanische Studien. JbShG, 65, 1929.
Gillies, A. Ludwig Tieck's English Studies at the University of Göttingen. JEGPh, 36, 1937.
Hewett-Thayer, H. W. Tieck and the Elizabethan Drama. JEGPh, 34, 1935.
Lüdeke, H. Ludwig Tieck und das alte englische Theater. Frankfurt, 1922.
Zeydel, E. H. Ludwig Tieck and England. Princeton, 1931.
—— Ludwig Tieck as a Translator of English. PMLA, 51, 1936.
Cornicelius, M. England in **TREITSCHKES** Darstellung und Urteil. Internat. Monatsschrift f. Wissenschaft, Kunst und Technik, 10, 1916.
Hampe, K. Treitschke in London. Ibid.
Hennig, J. **TRENCK** and Britain. MLR, 41, 1946.
Namer, E. La vita di **VANINI** in Inghilterra (1614). Lecce, 1934.
Jean-Aubry, G. P. **VERLAINE** et l'Angleterre. MF, 15.X.1918 & RP, Oct., 1923.
Bonnefoy, G. Une source anglaise du Stello d'Alfred de **VIGNY.** RLC, 20, 1940.
Gerathwohl, M. A. Alfred de Vigny and Some English Poets on Nature. Fortnightly Review, April, 1913.
Lebbin, E. A. de Vigny's Beziehungen zu England und zur englischen Literatur. Diss. Halle, 1936.
Popova, I. L'originalité de l'oeuvre de Vigny. Diss. Toulouse, 1937.
Anon. Article sur les Lettres anglaises de **VOLTAIRE.** Le Pour et Contre, 1, 1733.

—— Voltaire's Residence in England. NAR, April, 1865.
Baldensperger, F. La chronologie du séjour de Voltaire en Angleterre et les Lettres Philosophiques. Archiv, 1913.
—— Voltaire anglophile avant son séjour d'Angleterre. RLC, 9, 1929.
Ballantyne, A. Voltaire's Visit to England. London, 1893. Cf. Athenaeum, 9.XII.1893 & RHLF, 15.IV.1894.
Brown, H. Voltaire and the Royal Society of London. UTQ, 13, 1943.
Cazes, J. Un carnet de notes de Voltaire. RU, June, 1921.
Dargan, E. P. The Question of Voltaire's Primacy in Establishing the English Vogue. Mélanges Baldensperger. Paris, 1930.
Foulet, L. Le voyage de Voltaire en Angleterre. RHLF, 13, 1906.
Hales. Voltaire in Hampstead. The Hampstead Annual, 1903.
Lanson, G. Deux voyages en Angleterre (Voltaire et César de Saussure). RHLF, 1906.
—— Voltaire et les Lettres philosophiques. RP, 1.VIII.1908.
Larbaud, Valéry. Lettre à deux amis. Commerce, Autumn, 1924.
Sonet, E. Voltaire et l'influence anglaise. Rennes, 1926.
Torrey, N. L. Voltaire's English Notebook. MPh, 1929.
Villemain. Voltaire et la littérature anglaise de la reine Anne. RDM, 10, 1831.
White, F. D. A Sentence from an English Notebook of Voltaire's. MLN, 31, 1916.
Reichalt, K. Richard **WAGNER** und die englische Literatur. Diss. Breslau. Leipzig, 1911.
Vetter, T. Joh. Heinrich **WASER**, ein Vermittler englischer Litteratur. Zürich, 1898.
Bohm, W. Englands Einfluss auf G. R. **WECKHERLIN**. Diss. Göttingen, 1893.
Forster, L. G. R. Weckherlin in England. GLL, 3, 1939.
—— Georg Rudolf Weckherlin; zur Kenntnis seines Lebens in England. Basel, 1944.
—— Sources for G. R. Weckherlin's Life in England: The Correspondence. MLR, 41, 1946.
Gal, S. **WESSELENGI** in England. Hungarian Quarterly, 5, 1939.
Kurrelmeyer, W. **WIELAND'S** Teutscher Merkur and Contemporary English Journals. PMLA, 38, 1923.
Stilgebauer, E. Wieland als Dramatiker. ZVL, 10.
Grossland, J. **ZACHARIAE** and his English Models. Archiv, 120, 1908.
Vizetelly, E. With **ZOLA** in England: a Story of Exile. London, 1899.

NINTH PART

Swiss Contributions.

CHAPTER ONE

General Influences

(See also under Alps. and Genève, in I.VI.10.)

Beck, C. La Suisse vue par les grands écrivains et les voyageurs célèbres. Paris, 1914.

Berlincourt, S. La Suisse dans l'oeuvre des grands poètes romantiques. Berne, 1927.

Breitinger, H. Die Vermittler des deutschen Geistes in Frankreich. Zürich, 1876.

Ermatinger, E. Dichtung und Geistesleben der deutschen Schweiz. München, 1933. Cf. RG, Oct., 1934.

Ernst, F. La tradition médiatrice de la Suisse aux XVIIIe et XIXe siècles. RLC, 6, 1926.

—— Die Schweiz als geistige Mittlerin von Muralt bis Jacob Burckhardt. Zürich, 1932.

Finsler, G. Zürich in der zweiten Hälfte des 18. Jahrhunderts. Zürich, 1884.

Friederich, W.P. Chief Traits of Swiss Literature. SAQ, 1948.

Gisi. Französische Schriftsteller in und von Solothurn (Muralt, Destouches, J. B. Rousseau, Voltaire, Delille). Solothurn, 1898.

Gos, C. Voyageurs illustres en Suisse. Paris, 1937.

Greiner, Trudi. Der literarische Verkehr zwischen der deutschen und welschen Schweiz seit 1848. Bern, 1940.

Guillon, E. & Bettex, G. Le Léman dans la littérature et dans l'art. Paris, 1912

Guinaudeau, O. La Suisse au XVIIIe siècle: les liens spirituels entre Suisses. RLC, 9, 1929.

Guyot, C. Voyageurs romantiques en pays neuchâtelois. Neuchâtel, 1932.

Hornung, J. La littérature de la Suisse française considérée dans son principe religieux et national et dans ses rapports avec les autres littératures de l'Europe. Revue Suisse, 15, 1852.

Jouvenel, B. de. La République des Lettres (Mission de la Suisse). Gazette de Lausanne, 15.II.1947.

Jung, C. G. Die Bedeutung der schweizerischen Linie im Spektrum Europas. NSR, 1928.

Kohler, P. Littératures de la Suisse. Helicon, 1, 1938.

—— Le rôle intellectuel de la Suisse française. In: Périodes et Problémes. Lausanne, 1943.

Korrodi, E. Das Geisteserbe der Schweiz. Zürich, 1929 & 1943.

Locarnini, G. Die literarischen Beziehungen zwischen der italienischen und der deutschen Schweiz. Bern, 1946. Cf. National Zt., 30.III.1947 & Der Kleine Bund, 4.V. 1947.

Loesch, K. C. von. Die Schweiz als Musterland. DR, 1926.

Reynold, G. de. Le doyen Bridel et les origines de la littérature suisse romande. Lausanne, 1909.

—— Bodmer et l'école suisse. Paris, 1913.

—— La Suisse une et diverse. Fribourg, 1924.

—— Défense et illustration de l'esprit suisse. Neuchâtel, 1939.

Rossel, V. Histoire littéraire de la Suisse romande. Genève, 1889.

Rougemont, D. de. Mission ou démission de la Suisse. Neuchâtel, 1940.

Schöffler, H. Das literarische Zürich, 1700-1750. Leipzig, 1925.

Thomas, J. La Suisse et le cosmopolitisme littéraire. Confluences, 2, 1942.

Wehrli, M. Das geistige Zürich im 18. Jahrhundert. Zürich, 1943.

Weilenmann, H. Die vielsprachige Schweiz. Basel, 1925.

Ziegler, H. de. Panorama de la littérature française en Suisse. Le Thyrse, 1939.

Ziehen, E. Philhelvetismus. NSp, 1925.

Grueningen, J. P. The Swiss in the United States. (**AMERICA**). Madison, 1940.

Chicoteau, M. Note sur la Suisse alémanique et les pèlerins anglais de J. Addison à W. Wordsworth. (**ENGLAND**). CLS, 2, 1941.

Funke, O. Switzerland and English Literature. Bern, 1938-40.

Schirmer, G. Die Schweiz im Spiegel englischer und amerikanischer Literatur bis 1848. Zürich, 1929.

Sismondi. Considérations sur Genève dans ses rapports avec l'Angleterre et les Etats protestants. Londres, 1841.

Vetter, T. Zürich als Vermittlerin englischer Litteratur im XVIII. Jahrhundert. Zürich, 1891.

Vreeland, W. Etude sur les rapports littéraires entre Genève et l'Angleterre jusqu' à la publication de la Nouvelle Héloïse. Genève, 1901.

Anon. Gloses et prétextes: ce qu'ils ont dit de la Suisse et des Suisses. (**FRANCE**). Formes et Couleurs, 5-6, 1945.

Baldensperger, F. La Suisse et la littérature française. In: La Suisse et les Français. Paris, 1920.

Moreau, P. Les romantiques français et la Suisse. Revue de l'U. de Lyon, Feb., 1929.

Renard, G. L'influence de la Suisse française sur la France. Lausanne, 1892.
Camenisch, C. Graubünden in der deutschen Dichtung. (**GERMANY**). Leipzig, 1923.
Fleig, H. Die Schweiz im Schrifttum der deutschen Befreiungszeit, 1813-17. Basel, 1942.
Koester, A. Der Zürichsee in der deutschen Dichtung. Leipzig, 1923.
Liebi, A. Das Bild der Schweiz in der deutschen Romantik. Bern, 1946.
Merian, W. Das Berner Oberland in der deutschen Dichtung. Leipzig, 1922.
Schäfer, W. Die Schweiz im deutschen Geistesleben. Berliner Börsen Zt., 64, 1927.
Ziehen, E. Die deutsche Schweizerbegeisterung in den Jahren 1750-1815. Frankfurt 1925.
Zürcher, O. Das Berner Oberland im Lichte der deutschen Dichtung. Leipzig, 1923.
Hennig, J. Irisch-schweizerische Literaturbeziehungen. (**IRELAND**). Die Tat (Zürich) 24.VI.1947.
Cantimori, D. Italiani a Basilea e a Zurigo nel Cinquecento. (**ITALY**). Roma, 1947.
Eberhard, A. Unsere Klassiker in der **TUERKEI**. Neue Zürcher Zt., 17.VI.1947.

CHAPTER TWO

Gessner

1. Influences upon Individual Countries.

Baldensperger, F. L'épisode de Gessner dans la littérature européenne. Salomon Gessner Gedenkbuch. Zürich, 1930.
Reynold, G. de. Un précurseur du romantisme: Gessner et le sentiment de la nature. MF, 1908.
Van Tieghem, P. Les idylles de Gessner et le rêve pastoral dans le préromantisme européen. RLC, 4, 1924.
Kyrre-Olsen, O. Salomon Geszners skrifter i Danmark og Norge. (**DENMARK**). Bergen, 1903.
Reed, Bertha. The Influence of Gessner upon English Literature. (**ENGLAND**). Philadelphia, 1906. CF. MLN, 1908.
Anon. Imité de l'allemand de M. Wieland, de M. de Gerstenberg, de M. Gessner! Etwas Niederschlagendes für die Gallomanie! (**FRANCE**). Deutsches Museum, 1778.
Baldensperger, F. Gessner en France. RHLF, 1903. And in: Etudes d'histoire littéraire, 4e Sér. Paris, 1939.
Broglé, H. Die französische Hirtendichtung in der zweiten Hälfte des 18. Jahrhunderts, dargestellt in ihrem besonderen Verhältnis zu S. Gessner. Leipzig, 1903.
Rauchfuss, A. Der französische Hirtenroman am Ende des 18. Jahrhunderts und sein Verhältnis zu S. Gessner. Diss. Leipzig, 1912.
Horloch, G. L'opera letteraria di S. Gessner e la sua fortuna in **ITALIA**. Castiglione Fiorentino, 1906.
Szyjkowski, M. Le préromantisme en Pologne: le gessnerisme. (**POLAND**). Revue des Etudes slaves, 6, 1925-26.
Borelius, H. Gessners inflytande paa svenska litteraturen. (**SWEDEN**). Samlaren, 22, 1901.

2. Influences upon Individual Authors.

Zanella, D. Salomone Gessner ed Aurelio **BERTOLA**. NAnt, March, 1882.
Blumenthal, F. Lord **BYRON'S** Mystery Cain and its Relation to Milton's Paradise Lost and Gessner's Death of Abel. Progr. Oldenburg, 1891. Cf. ESn, 16.
Becq de Fouquières. Lettres critiques sur A. **CHENIER**. Paris, 1881.
Björkenheim, M. **FLORIAN'S** Estelle. Helsingfors, 1932.
Schwenke, W. Florians Beziehungen zur deutschen Literatur. Diss. Leipzig, 1908.
Weiss, L. Gessner und **KASINCZY**. Lesezirkel Hottingen. (Zürich), 1929-30.
Kerby, W. M. **LEONARD**. Paris, 1925.
Usteri, P. Briefwechsel S. Gessners mit H. **MEISTER**, 1770-79. Archiv, 120, 1908.
Ortiz. Un imitazione rumena dal Gessner e dal Vigny. (C. **NEGRUZZI**). Festschrift Pio Rajna. Firenze, 1911. And in: Varia romanica. Firenze, 1932.
Ernst, F. **TURGOT** und Gessner. NSR, 1930.
Estève, E. Gessner et Alfred de **VIGNY**. RHLF, 17, 1910.
Wittmer, L. Au temps des bergerades: Gessner et **WATELET**. RLC, 2, 1922.

CHAPTER THREE

Rousseau

1. Generalities.

(See also Politics, I. II. 5.)

Babbitt, I. Rousseau and Romanticism. Boston, 1919.
Buffenoir, H. Le prestige de Rousseau. Paris, 1909.
—— J. J. Rousseau et les auteurs de voyages en Suisse. Bull. de l'Institut national genevois, 46, 1924.
Choulguin, A. The Secret of Rousseau's Influence. Prazi, 1930.
Lambeck, H. J. J. Rousseau und seine Neue Héloïse, mit einem vergleichenden Blick auf verwandte Erscheinungen anderer Litteraturen. Progr. Stralsund, 1874.

Lowell, J. R. Rousseau and the Sentimentalists. In: Literary Essays. Boston, 1867.
Matthews, J. W. J. J. Rousseau and the Cosmopolitan Spirit in Literature. London, 1899.
Monnier, M. J. J. Rousseau à l'étranger. BURS, July, 1878.
—— J. J. Rousseau et les étrangers. In: J. J. Rousseau jugé par les Genevois d'aujourd'hui. Genève, 1879.
Mornet, D. L'influence de J. J. Rousseau au XVIIIe siècle. Annales J. J. Rousseau, 8.
Mossner, E. C. Rousseau Hero-Worship: An Unpublished Intimate Record of 1766. MLN, 55, 1940.
Mühll, E. von der. Rousseau et les réformateurs du théâtre. MLN, 55, 1940.
Nourrisson, G. F. Rousseau et le Rousseauisme. Paris, 1903.
Reynold, G. de. J. J. Rousseau et la Suisse. Annales J. J. Rousseau, 1912.
Sadler, M. Rousseau Walks the Earth. UTQ, 6, 1937.
Schinz, A. Le mouvement rousseauiste du dernier quart du siècle. MPh, 1922.
—— Rousseau et les Suisses. In: La Pensée de J. J. Rousseau. Paris. In: 1929.
—— Du succès et de la durée en littérature à propos de Jean-Jacques Rousseau. Mélanges Baldensperger. Paris, 1930.
—— Etat présent des travaux sur J. J. Rousseau. New York, 1941.
Sutton, C. W. H. Farewell to Rousseau. London, 1936.
Vallete, G. J. J. Rousseau genevois. Paris, 1911.
Williams, D. The Influence of Rousseau on Public Opinion, 1760-95. EHR, 1933.

2. Rousseau in England.

Frisch, G. Der revolutionäre Roman in England: seine Beeinflussung durch Rousseau. Diss. Freiburg, 1914.
Gosse, E. Rousseau in England in the Nineteenth Century. Fortnightly Review, July, 1912. And in: Aspects and Impressions. London, 1922.
Johnson, M. L. Contemporary Opinion of Rousseau in English Periodicals. Meredith College Quarterly Bull., 1921-22.
Levaillant, M. Rousseau en Angleterre. NL, 1945.
Schinz, A. Rousseau et les Anglais. In: La pensée de J. J. Rousseau. Paris, 1929.
Sewall, R. B. Rousseau's First Discourse in England. PMLA, 1937.
—— Rousseau's Second Discourse in England from 1755 to 1762. PhQ, 17, 1938.
—— Rousseau's Second Discourse in England and Scotland from 1762 to 1772. PhQ, 18, 1939.
—— An Early Manuscript Translation of Rousseau's Second Discourse. MLN, 56, 1942.
Texte, J. Jean-Jacques Rousseau et les origines du cosmopolitisme littéraire. Etude sur les relations littéraires de la France et de l'Angleterre au XVIIIe siècle. Paris, 1895. London, 1899. Cf. ZFSL, 18, 1896.
Warner, J. H. The Reaction in XVIIIth Century England to Rousseau's Two Discours. PMLA, 1933.
—— A Bibliography of Eithteenth Century English Editions of J. J. Rousseau, with Notes on the Early Diffusion of his Writings. PhQ, 13, 1934.
—— Eighteenth Century English Reactions to the Nouvelle Héloïse. PMLA, 1937.
—— Addenda to the Bibliography of Eighteenth-Century English Editions of J. J. Rousseau. PhQ, 19, 1940.
—— The Basis of J. J. Rousseau's Contemporaneous Reputation in England. MLN, 55, 1940.
—— Emile in Eighteenth-Century England. PMLA, 59, 1944.

3. Rousseau in Germany.

Bals, H. J. J. Rousseau und sein Einfluss auf die Volksschule. Kempten, 1895.
Benrubi, J. Rousseau et le mouvement philosophique et pédagogique en Allemagne. Annales J. J. Rousseau, 1912.
—— Rousseau et les grands représentants de la pensée allemande. In: Leçons faites à l'Ecole des hautes études sociales. Paris, 1912.
Buck, R. Rousseau und die deutsche Romantik. Berlin, 1939.
Fester, R. Rousseau und die deutsche Geschichtsphilosophie. Stuttgart, 1890. Cf. ZVL, 5.
Groeper, R. Rousseau und die deutsche Literatur. ZDU, 26, 1912.
Keller, T. Rousseau in Deutschland. Hamburger Corresp., 325, 1912.
Landau, P. Rousseau und der deutsche Geist. Tagesbote (Brünn), 290, 1912.
Levy-Bruehl. L'influence de J. J. Rousseau en Allemagne. Annales de l'Ecole libre des Sciences polit., 1887.
Mahrenholtz, R. Deutsche Rousseaulitteratur. Krit. Jahresbericht über d. Fortschritte der roman. Philologie, 1890 ff.
Paulsen, F. Rousseaus Einfluss auf die deutsche Bildung. Hilfe, 36, 1906.
Pinloche, A. La réforme de l'éducation en Allemagne au XVIIIe siècle. Paris, 1889.
Schanzenbach, O. Ein Rousseaujünger im Hause Württemberg. Progr. Stuttgart, 1889.

4. Rousseau in Other Countries

Rosenthal, L. Rousseau in Philadelphia. (**AMERICA**). Mag. of American History, 12, 1884.
Spurlin, P. M. Rousseau in America, 1760-1809. FAR, 1948.
Avesnes. Les idées de J. J. Rousseau en **CHINE**. In: En face du Soleil Levant. Paris, 1909.
Dedeck-Héry, E. J. J. Rousseau et le Projet de constitution pour la **CORSE**. Philadelphia, 1932.
McNeil, G. H. The Cult of Rousseau and the French Revolution. (**FRANCE**). JHI, 6, 1945.
Gallas, K. R. La condamnation de l'Emile en **HOLLANDE**. Annales J. J. Rousseau, 17, 1926.
Valkhoff, P. Rousseau in Holland. De nieuwe Taalgids, 7, 1913.
Anon. Rousseau und der Sohn des Ofner Bürgermeisters. (**HUNGARY**). Pester Lloyd, 6.III.1931.
Eckhardt, A. Le Contrat social en Hongrie. Revue des Etudes hongroises, 1924.
Rácz, L. Rousseau dans la littérature hongroise. Annales J. J. Rousseau, 17, 1926.
Cesario, M. L'illuminismo francese in Italia e l'influsso del Rousseau nel pensiero pedagogico italiano. (**ITALY**). Rass. di studi francesi, 1925.
Satta, S. J. J. Rousseau e l'Italia. Fanfulla della Domenica, 29, 1909.
Schiff, M. Editions et traductions italiennes des oeuvres de J. J. Rousseau. Revue des Biliothèques, 17-18, 1907-08.
Forst de Battaglia, O. J. J. Rousseau et la Pologne. (**POLAND**). Pologne littéraire, 15.VII.1928.
Rouff, M. Rousseau et la Pologne. MF, 1.IX.1919.
Szyjkowski, M. Rousseau in XVIIIth Century Poland. (In Polish). Krakov, 1913.
Iorga, N. Rousseau et les **ROUMAINS**. Annales J. J. Rousseau, 17, 1926.
Larivière, C. de. J. J. Rousseau et la **RUSSIE**. Annales J. J. Rousseau, 20, 1931.
Del Rio, A. Algunas notas sobre Rousseau en España. (**SPAIN**) Hisp., 19, 1936.
Spell, J. R. Rousseau's 1750 Discours in Spain. HR, Oct., 1934.
—— A Tentative Bibliography of Spanish Translations of the Works of J. J. Rousseau. HR, 1934.
—— Rousseau in the Spanish World before 1833: A Study in Franco-Spanish Literary Relations. Austin (Texas), 1938.
Pinot, V. Rousseau en Suède. (**SWEDEN**). Revue du XVIIIe siècle, 1914.
Riza, A. J. J. Rousseau dans la littérature turque (1839-1930). (**TURKEY**). Annales J. J. Rousseau, 19, 1929.

5. Rousseau's Influence upon Individual Authors.

Harsazti, Z. John **ADAMS** and Rousseau. AM, 181, 1949.
Howitt, W. **ALFIERI** et Rousseau en Angleterre. Revue britannique, March, 1841.
Oliver, M. S. Un amigo de Rousseau (**ALTUNA**). Hojas del Sabado, 3. Barcelona, 1919.
Schorsch, R. S. Irving **BABBITT** and Rousseauism. Diss. U. of Notre Dame, 1940.
Goessgen, K. Rousseau und **BASEDOW**. Progr. Burg, 1891.
Hahn, G. P. R. Basedow und sein Verhältniss zu Rousseau. Diss. Leipzig, 1885.
Walsemann, A. Die Pädagogik des J. J. Rousseau und J. B. Basedow vom Herbart-Zillerschen Standpunkte verglichen und bearbeitet. Hannover, 1885.
Williams, A. T. The Concept of Equality in the Writings of Rousseau, **BENTHAM** and Kant. Diss. Columbia U., 1907.
Barine, A. George **BRANDES**, ses idées sur J. J. Rousseau. RB, 24, 1883.
Osborn, A. M. Rousseau and **BURKE**: A Study of the Idea of Liberty in XVIIIth Century Political Thought. Oxford U. P., 1940.
Rodari, D. G. G. **BURLAMACCHI** e G. G. Rousseau. Rivista filosofica, 11, 1908.
Del Vecchio. Tra il Burlamaqui e il Rousseau. Cultura contemporanea, 2, 1910.
Horsley, Phyllis. Dr. **BURNEY** and J. J. Rousseau. CLS, 23-24, 1946.
Elze, K. Rousseau und **BYRON**. In: Lord Byron. Berlin, 1886.
Schmidt, O. Rousseau und Byron. Diss. Greifswald. Oppeln, 1890. Cf. ZFSL, 11.
Hartmann, E. J. J. Rousseaus Einfluss auf **CAMPE**. Diss. Erlangen, 1905.
Gos, C. Le cas **CHATEAUBRIAND**–Rousseau et les Alpes. Correspondant, 10.IX. 1928.
Vivier, R. A. **CHENIER**, Rousseau et Foscolo. Mélanges Hauvette. Paris, 1934.
Stephen, L. **COWPER** and Rousseau. Cornhill Mag., 1875.
Sadler, M. Thomas **DAY**: an English Disciple of Rousseau. Cambridge U. P., 1928.
Delpy, G. **FEIJOO** contre J. J. Rousseau. In: Bibliographie des sources françaises de Feijoo. Paris, 1936.
Haymann, F. Weltbürgertum und Vaterlandsliebe in der Staatslehre Rousseaus und **FICHTES**. Berlin, 1924.
Anon. Ueber Lobreden, mit Anwendungen auf **FRIEDRICH DEN GROSSEN** und Rousseau. Deutsches gemeinnütziges Magazin. Leipzig, 1787.
Du Bois-Reymond. Rousseau und Friedrich II. DR, 19, 1879.
Wirz, E. Eine unbekannte Rousseau-Schrift des Malers H. **FUESELI**. Neue Zürcher Zt., 1-8.VIII. & 10-11.IX. 1926.

Rowbotham, A. H. Madame de **GENLIS** and Jean-Jacques Rousseau. MLQ, 3, 1942.

Arrighi, G. L. Le critiche all' Emilio del **GERDIL** e del Capponi. Riv. Pedagogica, 15, 1922.

Melillo, M. Due critici italiani della pedagogia di G. G. Rousseau (S. Gerdil, G. Capponi). Foggia, 1912.

Aron, A. W. The Mature **GOETHE** and Rousseau. JEGPh, 35, 1936.

Benrubi, J. Goethe et Schiller continuateurs de Rousseau. RMM, May, 1912.

Caspars, E. Goethes pädagogische Grundanschauungen im Verhältnis zu Rousseau. Langensalza, 1920.

Deipser, E. Rousseaus Einfluss auf Goethe in pädagogischer Beziehung. Vierteljahrsschrift f. philosoph. Pädagogik, 1920.

Franz, A. Die literarische Portraitzeichnung in Goethes Dichtung und Wahrheit und in Rousseaus Confessions. DVLG, 6, 1928.

Hohenhausen, Elise von. Rousseau, Goethe und Byron; ein kritisch-literarischer Umriss aus ethisch-christlichem Standpunkte. Kassel, 1847.

Merivale, H. Rousseau, Voltaire, and Goethe. In: Historical Studies. London, 1865.

Smith, H. Goethe and Rousseau. PEGS, 1926.

Spickernagel, W. Rousseau und Goethe. Hamburger Nachrichten, 298, 1912.

Woodbridge, B. M. Rousseau and Faust. MLN, 55, 1940.

Torrey, N. L. Rousseau's Quarrel with **GRIMM** and Diderot. Festschrift Albert Feuillerat. New Haven, 1943.

Clark, W. D. A Quotation by **HAZLITT** from Rousseau. MLN, 60, 1945.

Braun, H. W. Rousseaus Einfluss auf die **HEGELSCHE** Staatsphilosophie in ihrer Entwicklung und Vollendung. Diss. Berlin, 1926.

Hänssel, O. Der Einfluss Rousseaus auf die philosophisch-pädagogischen Anschauungen **HERDERS.** Pädagog. Studien, 24, 1902.

Plantiko, O. Rousseaus, Herders und Kants Theorie vom Zukunftsideal der Menschheitsgeschichte. Diss. Greifswald, 1895.

Wolff, H. M. Der junge Herder und die Entwicklungsidee Rousseaus. PMLA, 57, 1942.

Bandy, W. T. A Sidelight on the **HUME**-Rousseau Quarrel. MLN, 63, 1948.

Levy-Bruehl. Quelques mots sur la querelle de Hume et de Rousseau. RMM, May, 1912.

Peoples, M. H. La querelle Rousseau-Hume. Annales J. J. Rousseau, 18, 1927-28.

Pottle, F. A. The Part Played by Horace Walpole and James Boswell in the Quarrel Between Rousseau and Hume. PhQ, 1925.

—— La querelle Rousseau-Hume. Annales J. J. Rousseau, 17, 1926.

Roddier, H. A propos de la querelle Rousseau-Hume: Précisions chronologiques. RHLF, 46, 1939.

—— La querelle Rousseau-Hume. RLC, 18, 1938-39.

Salinger, R. Das Verhältnis Rousseaus zu D. Hume. Vossische Zt. Sonntagsbeilage, 25, 1911.

Schinz, A. La querelle Rousseau-Hume. Annales J. J. Rousseau, 17, 1926.

Zini, Z. Rousseau e Hume. Cultura, 1932.

Braugsch, W. Ueber einige Unterschiede zwischen J. J. Rousseau und **JEAN PAUL.** ZFEU, 13, 1914.

Kommerell, M. Jean Pauls Verhältnis zu Rousseau. Marburg, 1925.

Plath, H. An welchen Punkten kann Jean-Pauls Levana von Rousseau beeinflusst erscheinen? Diss. Erlangen. Heidelberg, 1905.

Cassirer, E. Rousseau, **KANT**, Goethe. Princeton, 1945.

Dieterich, C. Kant und Rousseau. Tübingen, 1878.

Duguit, L. Jean-Jacques Rousseau, Kant et Hegel. Revue du Droit public et de la Science politique. April, 1918.

Hoeffding, H. Rousseaus Einfluss auf die definitive Form der kantischen Ethik. Kant-Studien, 1898.

Menn, M. Immanuel Kants Stellung zu Jean-Jacques Rousseau. Diss. Freiburg, 1894.

Nolen, D. Kant et Rousseau. Revue philosophique, 1880.

Reich, K. Rousseau und Kant. Tübingen, 1936.

Stein, K. H. von. Rousseau und Kant. DR, 56, 1888. And in: Wege nach Weimar, 1907.

Baye & Girardin. **KARAMZIN** et J. J. Rousseau. Paris, 1912.

Faulkner, W. H. **KELLER'S** Der grüne Heinrich: Anna and Judith and their Predecessors in Rousseau's Confessions. U. of Virginia Publications, 1912.

Sewall, R. B. William **KENRICK** as Translator and Critic of Rousseau. PhQ, 20, 1941.

Ayrault, R. Heinrich von **KLEIST.** Paris, 1934.

Wolff, H.M. Kleist's Amazonenstaat im Lichte Rousseaus. PMLA, 1938.

Xylander, O. H. von Kleist und J. J. Rousseau. Berlin, 1937.

Wolff, H. M. Der Rousseaugehalt in **KLINGERS** Drama Das leidende Weib. JEGPh, 39, 1940.

Wyneken, F. A. Rousseaus Einfluss auf Klinger. UCPPh, 1912.

Lienhard, F. **KLOPSTOCK** und Rousseau. Wege nach Weimar, 3, 1907.

Frattini, A. La cultura francese nella formazione del pensiero del **LEOPARDI.** Poesia e verità, 2, 1946.

Patane, A. Leopardi, Foscolo e Rousseau. Athenaeum, 5, 1917.
Ziino, M. Voltaire, Rousseau e i Promessi Sposi. (**MANZONI**). GSLI, 1933.
Rozbroj, H. J. P. **MARAT** (1743-93). Ein Naturforscher und Revolutionär, sein Zusammentreffen in der Geisteswelt mit Goethe, Lamarck, Rousseau. Berlin, 1938.
Murry, J. M. Rousseau and **MARX**. Adelphi, Oct., 1934.
Havens, G. R. Rousseau, **MELON** and Sir William Petty. MLN, 55, 1940.
Matkowski, Z. Les Aïeux de **MICKIEWICZ** et l'Emile de Rousseau. Bull. intern. de l'Acad. des Sciences de Cracovie, Nov., 1906.
Lovejoy, A. O. **MONBODDO** and Rousseau. MPh, 30, 1933.
Altenberger, W. K.Ph. **MORITZ'** pädagogische Ansichten. Ein Beispiel der Wirksamkeit Rousseau'scher Ideen in Deutschland. Leipzig, 1905.
Wolff, H. M. Rousseau, **MOESER** und der Kampf gegen das Rokoko. MDU, 34, 1942.
Schinz, A. Un rousseauiste en Amérique. (J. **NANCREDE**). MLN, 1920.
Benrubi, J. **NIETZSCHE** und Rousseau. Frankfurter Zt., 141, 1910.
Pinot, V. Un disciple de Rousseau: Jean Gabriel **OXENSTIERN**. Le Temps, 14. V.1912.
Clark, H. H. Thomas **PAINE'S** Relation to Voltaire and Rousseau. RAA, 1932.
Hunziker, O. Rousseau und **PESTALOZZI**. Basel, 1885.
Jauss, G. Rousseau und Pestalozzi. Progr. Oberschützen, 1870.
Kramer. A. H. Francke, J. J. Rousseau, H. Pestalozzi. Halle, 1854.
Schneider, K. Rousseau und Pestalozzi, der Idealismus auf deutschem und französischem Boden. Berlin, 1895.
Zoller, F. Pestalozzi et Rousseau. Frankfurt 1881.
Meyer, E. L'abbé de **SAINT-PIERRE**, J. J. Rousseau et Briand-Kellogg. Grande Revue, 1928.
Thiem, E. Wie weit erscheint Chr. G. **SALZMANN** von. J. J. Rousseau beeinflusst? Diss. Erlangen, 1906.
Rocheblave, S. Ce que George **SAND** doit à J. J. Rousseau. Annales J. J. Rousseau, 1935.
Benrubi, J. **SCHILLER** et Rousseau. DR, 157, 1913.
Liepe, W. Der junge Schiller und Rousseau. ZDPh, 51, 1926.
—— Kulturproblem und Totalitätsideal. Zur Entwicklung der Problemstellung von Rousseau zu Schiller. ZDK, 1927.
Schmidt, J. Schiller et Rousseau. Berlin, 1876.
Meyer, H. Rousseau und **SHELLEY**: ein typologischer Vergleich. Diss. Halle, 1935.
Strobel, A. Die Pädagogik **SCHLEIERMACHERS** und Rousseaus. München, 1928.
Jolivet, A. Le rousseauisme d'Auguste **STRINDBERG**. RLC, 13, 1933.
Olay, F. d'. Rousseau et le comte J. **TELEKI**. Gazette de Hongrie, 16.VII.1932.
Dwelshauwers, G. Rousseau et **TOLSTOI**. In: J. J. Rousseau, Leçons faites à l'Ecole des Hautes Etudes Sociales. Paris, 1912.
Gyuris, G. Les vues pessimistes de Rousseau et de Tolstoi sur la culture. (In Hungarian). Pécs, 1930.
Markovitch, M. I. Jean-Jacques Rousseau et Tolstoï. Paris, 1928.
—— Rousseau, Tolstoï, Gandhi. (In Serbian). Letopis Matice Srpske, 1930.
Chapuisat, E. Rousseau et **USTERI**. Révolution française, 14.VI.1910.
Usteri, P. Briefwechsel Rousseaus mit Leonhard Usteri in Zürich. Progr. Zürich, 1886.
Fulchignoni, F. I nemici del teatro. **VOLTAIRE** e la Lettera sugli spettacoli di G. G. Rousseau. Rivista italiana del teatro, 7, 1943.
MacMullan, H. The Satire of **WALKER'S** Vagabond on Rousseau and Godwin. PMLA, 1937.
Klein, T. **WIELAND** und Rousseau. SVL, 3. München, 1903.
Neri, F. II pensiero del Rousseau nelle prime chiose dello **ZIBALDONE**. GSLI, 70, 1917.

CHAPTER FOUR

Mme. de Staël.

1. General Influences.

Anon. Frau von Staël nach der Schilderung einer Engländerin. MLIA, 1866.
Baldensperger, F. A la recherche de l'esprit européen avec Mme. de Staël. Occident et cahiers staëliens, 1930.
Benedetto, L. F. Un attaco contro la Signora di Staël. Marzocco, 28.VI.1931.
Bertaut, J. Mme. de Staël et l'Angleterre. MF, 16.VII.1917.
Chopin, J. Promenades littéraires en Tchécoslovaquie. Grenoble, 1938.
Cordié, C. Un decennio di studi sul Gruppo di Coppet. Paideia, 1, 1946.
Cucchetti, G. Il rifugio di Mme. de Staël (Coppet). RI, 1928.
Dejob, C. Mme. de Staël et l'Italie, avec une bibliographie de l'influence française en Italie de 1795 à 1814. Paris, 1890.
Friedwagner, M. Frau von Staëls Anteil an der romantischen Bewegung in Frankreich. Verhandl. d. IX. Allg. deutschen Neuphil.-Tages, Leipzig, 1901.
—— Frau von Staël und die Romantik in Frankreich, Deutschland und England.

Cernowitzer Allg. Zt. Literar. Beilage, 25.XII.1912.
Gunnell, Doris. Madame de Staël en Angleterre. RHLF, 1913.
Hawkins, R. L. Mme. de Staël and the United States. Harvard U. P., 1930.
Henning, J. L'Allemagne de Mme. de Staël et la polémique romantique. Paris, 1929.
Isidorus (Graf O. H. von Loeben). Deutsche Worte über die Ansichten der Frau von Staël von unserer poetischen Litteratur. Heidelberg, 1814.
Kohler, P. Mme. de Staël et la Suisse. Lausanne 1916.
—— Mme. de Staël au château de Coppet. Lausanne, 1929.
Lanfredini, D. Mme. de Staël e i suoi amici italiani. RLM, June, 1946.
Lenormant. Coppet et Weimar. Mme. de Staël et la grande duchesse Louise. Paris, 1862.
Moench, W. Frau von Staëls Deutschlandbuch und sein Gegenwartswert. NM, May, 1935.
Pellegrini, C. II Sismondi, la Staël e la traduzione italiana di Corinne. Rivista delle Biblioteche e degli Archivi, N. S., 3, 1925.
—— Les idées littéraires de Mme. de Staël et le romantisme français. Ferrara, 1929.
—— II gruppo di Coppet. Annali della R. Scuola Normale Superiore di Pisa. Bologna, 1934.
—— Madame de Staël. II gruppo cosmopolita di Coppet. L'influenza delle sue idee critiche. Firenze, 1938.
Pange, Mme. J. de. Mme. de Staël et les Etats-Unis. RP, 1933.
Traz, R. de. Mme. de Staël et la Suisse. Occident et cahiers staëliens, 2, 1934.
Whitford, R. C. Mme. de Staël's Literary Reputation in England. U. of Illinois Studies, 1918.
—— Mme. de Staël's Literary Reputation in America. MLN, Dec., 1918.
Wickman, J. Madame de Staël i Sverige. Lund, 1911.
Wrangel, E. Madame de Staël i Sverige. Nord. Tidskrift, 1915.

2. Influences upon Individual Authors.

Luzio, A. G. **ACERBI** e la Biblioteca italiana. NAnt, 16. VIII. 1896.
Muoni, G. Ludovico di **BREME** e le prime polemiche intorno a Madama di Staël ed al romanticismo in Italia (1816). Milano, 1902.
Anon. Some Recollections of **BYRON'S** Acquaintance with Mme. de Staël. Murray's Mag., Jan., 1887.
Götze, A. Frau von Staël und **COTTA**. ZFSL, 48, 1926.
Barbi, M. **GIORDANI** o Gherardini contro Madama di Staël? Festschrift R. Renier. Torino, 1912.
Chinard, G. La correspondance de Mme. de Staël avec **JEFFERSON**. RLC, 2, 1922.
Ravasi, S. **LEOPARDI** e Mme. de Staël. Milano, 1910.
Ziino, M. **MANZONI** e Madame de Staël. Conv., 1931.
Breitinger, H. Briefwechsel H. **MEISTERS** und der Frau von Staël. Zürcher Taschenbuch, 1890.
Berti, D. La Staël e **MONTI**. Filotecnico. Torino, 1887.
Bertoni, G. Ancora V. Monti e Madama di Staël. Paraviana, Nov., 1927.
Biadego, G. Monti e la baronessa di Staël. Verona, 1886.
Bustico, G. Madama di Staël nel ricordo di Vincenzo Monti. Rassegna nazionale, 1931.
Foresi, M. L'amicizia passionata della Staël per V. Monti. NAnt, 1.XII.1925.
Ivray, J. d'. Mme. de Staël et V. Monti. Revue mondiale, 15.VIII.1923.
Rava, L. Mme. de Staël e Vincenzo Monti. NAnt, 1928.
Aldridge, A. O. Madame de Staël and Hannah **MORE** on Society. RR, 38, 1947.
Baldensperger, F. Mme. de Staël et Jean de **MUELLER**. BURS, 1912.
NAPOLEON: see IV.VII.25.
Van Tieghem, P. **POUCHKINE** défenseur de Mme. de Staël. RLC, 21, 1947.
Jones, R. A. Une amie anglaise de Mme. de Staël: Miss Fanny **RANDALL**. RLC, 10, 1930.
Carré, J. M. Mme. de Staël et Henry Crabb **ROBINSON**. RHLF, 1912.
Larg. D. G. Mme. de Staël et Henry Crabb Robinson. Fiction et vérité. RLC, 8, 1928.
—— H. C. Robinson and Mme. de Staël. RES, 1929.
Anon. Karl von **VILLERS** und Frau von Staël. Grenzboten, 1899.

CHAPTER FIVE

Other Swiss Authors.

Gonzales Blanco, A. **AMIEL** et Ibsen en Espagne. Hisp., Jan., 1921.
Merian-Genast, E. H.F.Amiel im Spiegel der europäischen Kritik, 1881-1931. Marburg, 1931.
Croce. B. La prima notizia in Italia della Estetica del **BAUMGARTEN** (1756). Critica, 20.VII. 1935.
BODMER: See also Intermediaries, I.IV.8.
Budde, F. Wieland und Bodmer. Berlin, 1910.
Busch, E. Klopstocks Messias und die poetische Theorie von Bodmer und Breitinger. GRM, 29, 1941.
Varia. Johann Jakob Bodmer Denkschrift zum 200. Geburtstage. Zürich, 1900.

Reynold, G. de. Le doyen **BRIDEL** et l'influence de l'Ecole zurichoise dans la Suisse romande. BURS, 1906.
Martin, A. Nietzsche und **BURCKHARDT**. München, 1941.
Neumann, C. Jakob Burckhardt, Deutschland und die Schweiz. Gotha, 1919.
Walzel, O. Jacob Burckhardt und John Ruskin. Basler Zs. f. Geschichte und Altertumskunde, 38, 1941.
CONSTANT: See also Intermediaries, I.IV.8.
Achmatova, Anna. L'Adolphe de B. Constant dans l'oeuvre de Pouchkine. Vremennik I (Les Annales), Acad. des Sciences d'URSS.
Baldensperger, F. Retour à Ellénore ou Légende et Vérité en histoire littéraire. RLC, 17, 1937.
Lonchamp, F. De l'esprit de conquête par Benjamin Constant, bibliographie raisonnée. Bull. du Bibliophile, N. S., 16, 1937.
Romieu, A. Benjamin Constant et l'esprit européen. Paris, 1933.
Tisseau, P. H. L'Adolphe de B. Constant et la Répétition de S. Kierkegaard. RLC, 13, 1933.
Perrochon, H. Gibbon et Suzanne **CURCHOD**. Gazette de Lausanne, 30.VI.1929.
Ochi, F. Milton and **DIODATI**. Studies in English Literature, 18. (Tokyo), 1938.
Wirz, E. Die literarische Tätigkeit des Malers J. H. **FUESSLI**. Diss. Basel, 1912.
Jolivet, A. Strindberg et Jeremias **GOTTHELF**. EG, 3, 1948.
Walter, K. Jeremias Gotthelf und das Elsass. Kolmar, 1941.
Bang, Carol K. **HALLER** and Wieland. MLN, 55, 1940.
Bergmann, E. Neues zum Streit zwischen Haller und La Metrie. Festschrift A. Koster. Leipzig, 1913.
Cunche, G. La renommée de A. de Haller en France: influence du poème des Alpes sur la littérature descriptive au XVIIIe siècle. Diss. Caen, 1918. Neuchâtel, 1921.
Fasola, C. La fama di Albrecht di Haller in Italia alla fine del' 700. Riv. di lett. tedesca, 2, 1908.
Frey, A. Haller und seine Bedeutuug für die deutsche Literatur. Leipzig, 1879.
Teeten, L. M. Albrecht von Haller and L. Clarke. JEGPh, 1928.
Tobler, G. Vincenz B. Tscharner (1728-78), traducteur des poésies de M. de Haller. Bern, 1895.
KELLER: See also Politics, I.II.5.
Anon. Eine Italienerin über Gottfried Keller. MLIA, 1879.
Betz, L. P. Gottfried Keller in der französischen Sorbonne. Neue Zürcher Zt., 15-20.VII.1899. And in: Studien zur vergleichendên Literatur der modernen Zeit. Frankfurt, 1902.
Georgescu-Tistu, N. Gottfried Kellers Siehst du den Stern und Eminescus La Steaua. Bukarest, 1938.
Hochdorf, M. Gottfried Keller im europäischen Gedanken. Zürich, 1919.
Rosenberg, F. Der schlimm-heilige Vitalis von G. Keller und Thais von A. France. Archiv, 1904.
Schmidt, K. E. Gottfried Keller in Frankreich. Frankfurter Zt., July, 1899.
Atkins, S. J. C. **LAVATER** and Goethe: Problems of Psychology and Theology in Werther. PMLA, 63, 1948.
Baldensperger, F. Les théories de Lavater dans la littérature française. Etudes d' histoire littéraire, 2e Sér., Paris, 1910.
Clapton, G. T. Lavater, Gall et Baudelaire. RLC, 13, 1933.
Kuntze, F. Lavater in Dänemark. Grenzboten, 25, 1900.
Larat, J. Un fragment inédit de Charles Nodier, sa Physiognomie inspirée de Lavater. RLC, 1, 1921.
Noordhoek, W. J. Lavater und Holland. NPh, 10, 1924.
Viatte, A. Mme. de Staël et Lavater. RLC, 3, 1923.
—— Quelques épisodes de la propagande illuminée au XVIIIe siècle. RLC, 4, 1924.
Vulliemin, C. C. F. **MEYER** et L. Vulliemin. BURS, Nov., 1899.
Wuest, P. C. F. Meyer in französischem Lichte. Mitteilungen der literarhistor. Ges. Bonn, 11, 1917-18.
Federman, A. J. H. Meyer, Goethes Schweizerfreund, 1760-1832. Leipzig, 1936.
MURALT: See also Intermediaries, I.IV.8.
Brown, F. A. Hamann's Opinion of Muralt. JEGPh, 47, 1948.
Migliorini, B. **PARACELSUS** und sein Einfluss auf den europäischen Wortschatz. Sprachkunde, 1942.
Bobkowska, W. **PESTALOZZI** in Polen. Pologne littéraire, 1927.
Bohnenblust, G. Goethe und Pestalozzi. Bern, 1923.
Payne, J. Pestalozzi: the Influence of his Principles and Practice on Elementary Education. New York, 1877.
Schönebaum, H. Pestalozzi und Herder. AK, 1934.
Schreiber, T. A. First Pestalozzian in the New World. (F. Nef). AGR, 9, 1942.
Wilson, J. B. Antecedents of Brook Farm. NEQ, 15, 1942.
Gyergyai, H. Comment la Hongrie découvrit C. F. **RAMUZ**. Gazette de Lausanne, 31.V.1947.
Muret, M. C. F. Ramuz en France. Journal des Débats, 6.II.1925.
Zoppi, G. Parigi e Ramuz. Rassegna d'Italia, 1, 1946.
SISMONDI: See Intermediaries, I.IV.8.
Cian, V. G. C. L. Sismondi e Federigo Sclopis. Atti dell' Accad. di Torino, 78, 1943.

SPITTELER, C. Meine Beziehungen zu Nietzsche. Süddeutsche Monatshefte, 1908.
Keyzer, W. P. **VINET** en Hollande. Diss. Groningen. Wageningen, 1941.
Avennier, L. Un médecin suisse à Potsdam: **ZIMMERMANN** et Frédéric II. BURS, 1921.
Bouvier, A. K. Zimmermann: un représentant suisse du cosmopolitisme littéraire au XVIIIe siècle. Genève, 1925.
Loomis, G. Thoreau and Zimmermann. NEQ, 10, 1937.
ZSCHOKKE: See Germany, IV.X.12.

CHAPTER SIX

Swiss Influences upon Individual Authors

Sells, Ida E. Marguerite (Matthew **ARNOLD**). MLR, 38, 1943.
Droz, E. Le premier séjour d'Agrippa d' **AUBIGNE** à Genève. BHR, 9, 1947.
François, A. Les Sonnets suisses de Joachim du **BELLAY**. Suivi de Trois tableaux de la Suisse vue par les écrivains français du XVIe siècle. Lausanne, 1946.
Macphail, J. H. **BLAKE** and Switzerland. MLR, 38, 1943.
Amiguet, P. Lord **BYRON** et la Suisse. Le Temps, 15.III.1938.
Choisy, L. F. Byron aux bords du Léman. BURS, 1924.
Engel, Claire-Eliane. Byron et Shelley en Suisse et en Savoie (1816). Chambéry, 1930.
Bouchardy, F. M. et Mme. de **CHATEAUBRIAND** et les Genevois. Genève, 1931.
Guyot, C. M. et Mme. de Chateaubriand à Neuchâtel. Musée Neuchâtelois, 1938.
Moreau, P. Chateaubriand et la Suisse. BURS, 1927.
Lüdeke, H. James Fenimore **COOPER** and the Democracy of Switzerland. ESs, 27, 1946.
Dorian, D. C. Charles **DIODATI** at Geneva. PMLA, 59, 1944.
Bonnard, G. L'importance du deuxième séjour de **GIBBON** à Lausanne dans la formation de l'historien. Mélanges C. Gilliard. Lausanne, 1944. Cf. MLN, 1947.
Schirmer, G. Edward Gibbon und die Schweiz. Festschrift zum 14. Neuphilologentage. Zürich, 1910.
Renner, A. Joh. **GOERRES** in der Schweiz. Schweiz. Rundschau, 1925.
Bohnenblust, G. **GOETHE** und die Schweiz. Frauenfeld, 1932.
Fränkel, J. Goethes Erlebnis der Schweiz. Bern, 1932.
Gattiker, H. Goethe in der oberen Zürichseegegend. Zürich, 1934.
Lutz, H. Goethe und die Schweiz. Bern, 1932.
Perrochon, H. Goethe et le Pays de Vaud. Revue histor. vaudoise, 1933.
Teucher, E. Der ungekannte Goethe. Die Schweiz und Goethe vor 1848. Der Bund (Bern), 28.VIII.1947.
Baechtold, J. **HOELDERLIN** in der Schweiz. Vierteljahrschrift f. Litteraturgeschichte. Weimar, 1888.
Böhm, W. Hölderlin und die Schweiz. Frauenfeld, 1937.
Ienal, E. Das Vorbild von Hölderlins Idylle Kanton Schwyz. Euphorion, 30, 1929.
Mutzner, P. Die Schweiz im Werke Ricarda **HUCHS**. Bern, 1935.
Berend, E. **JEAN PAUL** und die Schweiz. Frauenfeld, 1943.
Giedion-Welcker, C. James **JOYCE** in Zürich. Weltwoche, 18.IV.1941.
Engel, Claire E. George **KEATE** et la Suisse. Zs. z. Schweiz. Geschichte, 1948.
Meyer, C. F. G. **KINKEL** in der Schweiz. MLIA, 3.III.1883.
Faesi, R. Heinrich von **KLEIST** und die Schweiz. Leipzig.
Köster, A. **KLOPSTOCK** und die Schweiz. Leipzig, 1924.
Zürcher, O. Klopstock und die Schweiz. Leipzig, 1922.
Hurter, F. von. Frau von **KRUEDENER** in der Schweiz. Helvetia, 1817.
Hüppy, A. **MARK TWAIN** und die Schweiz. Zürich, 1935.
Forretti, G. **MAZZINI** e l' "Europe centrale." Rassegna storica del Risorgimento, 26, 1939.
Mauerhofer, M. Mazzini et les réfugiés italiens en Suisse. Revue suisse d'histoire, 1932.
Ernst, F. Sébastien **MERCIER** als Freund der Schweiz. NSR, 1933.
Léger, L. **MICKIEWICZ** en Suisse. Le Monde Slave, 2e Sér., 1902.
Clark, W. S. **MILTON** and the Villa Diodati. RES, Jan., 1935.
Guyot, C. Le voyage du Général **MIRANDA** dans la Principauté de Neuchâtel en 1788. Musée neuchâtelois, 1934.
Chapuizat, E. Un Ecossais se promène entre les Alpes et le Jura (John **MOORE**). Gazette de Lausanne, 6.VIII.1947.
Bornoulli, C. **NIETZSCHE** und die Schweiz. Leipzig, 1922.
Salis, R. de. **RILKES** Schweizer Jahre. Leipzig, 1936.
Zermatten, M. Les années valaisannes de Rilke. Lausanne, 1942.
Beer, G. de (ed.) Mme. **ROLAND**: Voyage en Suisse, 1787. Neuchâtel, 1937.

Schazmann, P. E. P. **ROSSI** et la Suisse. Genève, 1939.

Koenig, E. G. John **RUSKIN** und die Schweiz. Bern, 1943.

Ambrière, F. Ce que **SAINTE-BEUVE** doit à Lausanne. NL, 4.XII.1937.

Brousson, J. J. Une journée avec Sainte-Beuve à Lausanne. NL, 6.XI.1937.

Betz, L. P. Die Schweiz in **SCHEFFELS** Leben und Dichten. In: Studien. Zürich 1902.

Monglond, A. **SENANCOUR** en Suisse (1780-1803). RLC, 10, 1930.

Schirmer, G. Der Dichter **SHELLEY** und die Schweiz. Neue Zürcher Zt., 57, 1922.

Reidler, F. W. Cosima **WAGNER** und die Schweiz. NSR, March, 1938.

Ermatinger, E. **WIELAND** und die Schweiz. Leipzig, 1924.

TENTH PART

German Contributions.

CHAPTER ONE

Generalities

(For Early Germanic Influence See II.V.1.)
(See also Sagas I.VI.8 & Emigrants and Refugees, I.IV.4.)

Anon. Etat de la littérature allemande dans les pays étrangers. Revue du Nord, June, 1835.

—— Deutsche Litteratur im Auslande. Neue DR., 1894.

—— Deutsche Litteratur im Auslande. Die Gesellschaft, 10 ff.

—— Deutschland im Urteil des Auslands früher und jetzt. Internat. Monatsschrift f. Wissenschaft, Kunst & Technik, 11, 1917.

Barrès, M. Limites désirables du germanisme littéraire. Bull. de la maison française. New York, 1919.

—— Quelles limites poser au germanisme intellectuel? Revue universelle, 1.I.1922.

Clarke, C. H. Der Deutsche im Ausland. Wissen & Leben, 1.VIII.1919.

Croce, B. II dissidio spirituale della Germania con l'Europa. Bari, 1944.

Curtius, E. R. Der deutsche Geist in Gefahr. Stuttgart, 1932.

Delmont, T. L'intoxication allemande. L' Univers, 9.XII.1917.

Dewey, J. The Mind of Germany. In: Characters and Events. London, 1929.

Eckstein, E. Deutsche Litteratur im Auslande. MLIA, 1885.

Endres, F. Die Verbreitung des Deutschtums über die Erde. Frankfurt 1928.

Feilh, E. Deutschland von draussen gesehen. Berlin, 1939.

Fellerer, K. G. Das deutsche Kirchenlied im Ausland. Münster, 1935.

Friederich, W. P. German Contributions to European Literature. In: Lectures in the Humanities. Chapel Hill, (N. C.), 1949-50.

Hoffmann, K. Das deutsche Element in der modernen Litteratur. In: Zwölf Studien zur Literatur und Ideengeschichte. Charlottenburg, 1908.

Klein, K. K. Literaturgeschichte des Deutschtums im Ausland. Leipzig, 1939.

Lasserre, P. Comment vaincre la pensée allemande. Revue universelle, 15.XI.1920.

Magin-Marrens. Influence germanique dans la civilisation moderne. Mém. de l'Acad. de Stanislas. Nancy, 1843.

Meyer, E. Deutscher Welteinfluss. National-Zt., 11.I.1903.

Meyer, R. M. Deutsche Dramen im Auslande. Wiener Zeit, 1375, 1906.

Miksch, F. Des deutschen Volkes Weltmission im Seelenleben der Völker. Wien, 1926.

Mittner, L. La Germania di fronte all' Europa. NRS, 1944-45.

Montgomery-Silverstope, M. Das romantische Deutschland. Leipzig, 1912.

Morland, J. Enquête sur l'influence allemande hors de France. MF, 1903.

Muehlebrecht, C. Uebersetzungen aus dem Deutschen in die dänische, englische, französische, schwedische, spanische Sprache. Börsenblatt, 128, 130, 269, 270; 1898.

Nagl, J. W. & Zeidler, J. Deutsch-österreichische Literaturgeschichte. 4 vols. Wien, 1899-1937.

Oncken, H. Deutsche geistige Einflüsse in der europäischen Nationalitätenbewegung des 19. Jahrhunderts. DVLG, 7, 1929.

Pirenne, H. De l'influence allemande sur le mouvement historique contemporain. Scientia, June, 1923.

Quinet, E. De la Teutomanie. RDM, 15. XII.1842. Cf. Beilage zur Allg. Zt. 22. XII.1842.

Rohrbach, P. Der deutsche Gedanke in der Welt. Düsseldorf, 1912.

Scherzer, K. Die deutsche Arbeit in aussereuropäischen Ländern. WM, 15, 1864.

Schneider, W. Die auslanddeutsche Dichtung unserer Zeit. Berlin, 1936.

Schoeffer, K. Der deutsche Gedanke in der Welt. Deutsche Verlegerzeitung, 1920.

Spender, S. L'Allemagne et l'Europe. Fontaine, Nov., 1945.

Steinhausen, G. Die Deutschen im Urteil des Auslandes. DR, 1909-10.

Stern, A. Die deutsche Litteratur und das Ausland. Jahresb. f. neuere deutsche Litt. geschichte, 1895 ff.

Stricker, W. Germania, Archiv zur Kenntniss des deutschen Elements in allen Ländern der Erde. Frankfurt, 1847-50.

Taine, H. De l'introduction des idées allemandes en Europe et en Angleterre. Journal des Débats, 6.XI.1860.

Thueming, M. Ausländische Urteile über neue Erscheinungen der deutschen Litteratur. Blätter f. literar. Unterhaltung, 45, 1891.

Weddigen, F. O. Geschichte der Einwirkungen der deutschen Literatur auf die Literaturen der übrigen europäischen Kulturvölker der Neuzeit. Leipzig, 1886.

Wehrli, M. Deutschland in der Kultur des Abendlandes. Civitas, April, 1947.

Wirth, A. Deutsche überseeische Literatur. Internat. Lit. berichte, April, 1897.

CHAPTER TWO

German Influences upon America

Anon. Deutsche Literatur in Nord-Amerika. Blätter z. Kunde der Litteratur des Auslands, 4, 1839.
—— Deutsche Romane in Amerika. MLIA, 1869.
—— Deutsche National- und Kriegslieder in Amerika. MLIA, 1870.
—— La propagande allemande et la conscience américaine. France-Etats-Unis, Nov., 1922.
—— The German Theatre in Milwaukee. Theatre Arts, 28, 1944.
Adams, H. B. The Germanic Origin of New England Towns. Johns Hopkins Studies in History, 1883.
Arciniegas, G. Los Alemanes en la conquista de América. Buenos Aires, 1941; New York, 1943.
Barnstorff, H. German Literature in Translation Published by Poet Lore, 1891-1939. MLJ, 25, 1941.
Baumgarten, E. Amerikanische Philosophie und deutscher Glaube. ZFEU, 1934.
Bernays, C. L. Mittelhochdeutsche Dichtung in den Vereinigten Staaten. MLIA, 1877.
Besser, R. Deutsche Literatur in amerikanischen Zeitschriften. GRM, 2, 1909.
Betz, L. P. Deutsches in der amerikanischen Litteratur. LE, April, 1903.
Busse, K. Deutsch-amerikanische Dichtung. Blätter f. literar. Unterhaltung, 1897.
Conrad, G. Deutschland in Amerika. Zukunft, 18.V.1901.
Cunz, D. The Maryland Germans: A History. Princeton U. P., 1948.
Dahn, F. Deutsche Lieder bei den Amerikanern. MLIA, 1883.
Drescher, M. Deutsche Dichter in Amerika. Jb. der Deutschen in Chicago, 1917.
Dubbs, J. H. Early German Poetry in America. Mercersburg Review, 25, 1878.
Falbisaner, A. Das deutsche Lied in der deutsch-amerikanischen Dichtung. Deutsch-amerikanische Geschichtsblätter, 2, 1902.
Flasche, H. Deutscher Geist in angelsächsischer Geschichtsphilosophie. DVLG, 17, 1939.
Francke, K. Deutsche Cultur in den Vereinigten Staaten, DR, April, 1902.
Frenz, H. The German Drama in the Middle West. AGR, 8, 1942.
Frese, H. Das deutsche Buch in Amerika. Uebersetzungen der Jahre 1918-35. Diss. Marburg. Zeulenroda, 1937.
Goodnight, S. H. German Literature in American Magazines Prior to 1846. Bull. U. of Wisconsin, 1907.
Groth, J. H. C. German Backgrounds of American Transcendentalism: Prolegomena to the Study of Influence. Diss. U. of Washington, 1941.
Haag, A. S. Some German Influences in American Philosophical Thought from 1800-1850. Diss. Boston U., 1939.
Haertel, M. H. German Literature in American Magazines, 1846-80. Bull. U. of Wisconsin, 263, 1908.
Hainebach, H. German Publications in the United States, 1933-45. Bull. New York Publ. Library, 52, 1948.
Hatfield, J. T. German Culture in the United States. Northwestern U. P. (Evanston), 1936.
Hathaway, Lillie. German Literature of the Mid-Nineteenth Century in England and America as Reflected in the Journals of 1840-1914. Boston, 1935.
Hawgood, J. The Tragedy of German America. New York, 1940.
Henkel. The German Influence on the Poetry of England and America in the Course of the XIXth Century. Progr. Eschwege, 1869.
Herbatschek, H. Die Anfänge des deutschen Theaters in Milwaukee. AGR, 13, 1947.
Hewitt, T. B. German Hymns in American Hymnals. GQ, 21,1948.
Hofacker, E. P. German Literature as Reflected in the German-Language Press of St. Louis Prior to 1898. St. Louis, 1946.
Hornaday, C. A. Some German Contributions to American Hymnody. MDU, 32, 1940.
Hoskins, J. P. German Influence on Religious Life and Thought in America During the Colonial Period. Princeton, 1907.
Jantz, H. S. German Thought and Literature in New England, 1620-1820. JEGPh, 41, 1942.
Kaemmerberg, P. Das deutsche Theater in den Vereinigten Staaten. Deutsche Bühne, 19.I.1920.
King, R. Sketches of Early German Influence on Rochester's Theatrical and Musical Life. AGR, 8, 1941.
Klenze, C. von. German Literature in the Boston Transcript, 1830-80. PhQ, 1932.
Knortz, K. Die plattdeutsche Litteratur Nord-Amerikas. In: Folkloristische Streifzüge. Leipzig, 1900.
—— Ein Vorkämpfer für deutsche Philosophie und Litteratur in Amerika. In: Deutsches und Amerikanisches. Glarus, 1894.
Kolbeck, Sister M. O. American Opinion on the Kulturkampf, 1871-82. Washington, 1942.
Konrad, W. R. The Diminishing Influences of German Culture in New Orleans since 1865. Louisiana Historical Quarterly, 24, 1941.

Kuder, M. Die deutschbrasilianische Literatur. Berlin, 1937.
Learned, M. D. The German Impulse in American Literature before 1800. In: Congress of Arts and Sciences, St. Louis Exposition, 3, 1904, Boston, 1906.
Lessing, O. E. Deutsche Literatur in Amerika. Oesterreichische Rundschau, 30, 1912.
Leuchs, A. H. The Early German Theatre in New York, 1840-72. Columbia U. P., 1928.
McConaughy, J. L. Have We an Educational Debt to Germany? Educational Review, May, 1918.
Moehlenbrock, A. H. The German Drama on the New Orleans Stage. Louisiana Historical Quart., 26, 1944.
Morgan, B. Q. Critical Bibliography of German Literature in English Translation, 1481-1927. Stanford U. P., 1938.
—— Sources of German Influences on American Letters. AGR, 10, 1944.
—— Traces of German Influence in American Letters. Ibid.
Olson, Esther M. The German Theater in Chicago. Jb. der deutsch-amerikan. Ges. von Illinois, 1937.
Pochmann, H. A. The Influence of the German Tale on the Short Stories of Irving, Hawthorne and Poe. Diss. U. of N. C., 1930.
Poll, M. Deutsche Litteratur in Amerika. Euphorion, 1897.
——— Bericht über die während der Jahre 1900-1901 in Amerika veröffentlichten Aufsätze über deutsche Litteratur. Euphorion, 9, 1902.
Reichard, H. H. Pennsylvania-German Dialect Writings and Their Writers. Lancaster (Pa.), 1918.
Reichart, W. A. Die Germanistik in Amerika. GRM, 25, 1938.
Robacker, E. F. Pennsylvania German Literature. Changing Trends, 1683-1942. Philadelphia, 1943.
Rosengarten J. G. German Influence in America. Lipp. Mag., April, 1902.
Schaumann, H. Fundamental Characteristics of German-American Lyrics. Diss. Cornell U., 1936.
Schlossmacher, S. Das deutsche Drama im amerikanischen College- und Universitäts-Theater. Emsdetten, 1938.
Schönemann, F. Deutschland in der öffentlichen Meinung Amerikas. ZNU, 36.
Shelley, P. A. The German Heritage of the American Annuals and Giftbooks. Diss. Harvard, 1938.
Spitzer, L. Deutsche Literaturforschung in Amerika. MDU, 37, 1945.
Steiger, E. Noch einige Plaudereien über den Absatz deutscher Bücher und Zeitschriften nach Nord-Amerika. Börsenblatt für die deutsche Buchhandlung, 1902.
Stovall, F. American Idealism. Norman (Okla.), 1943.
Thomas, J. W. The Western Messenger and German Culture. AGR, 11, 1944.
Tschischwitz, B. Das deutsche Theater in Nord-Amerika. Europa, 1866.
Varia. Alemania y el mundo ibero-americano. Alemanha e o mundo ibero-americano. Berlin, 1939.
Waeldler, A. Der Einfluss deutscher Litteratur in Brasilien. MLIA, 1880.
Walz, J. A. German Influence in American Education and Culture. Philadelphia, 1936.
Weddigen, F. H. O. Vermittler des deutschen Geistes in England und Nordamerika. Archiv, 59, 1878.
Wellek, R. The Minor Transcendentalists and German Philosophy. NEQ, 15, 1942.
White, A. D. Some Practical Influence of German Thought upon the United States. Ithaca, 1884.
Wilkens, F. H. Early Influence of German Literature in America. Americana Germanica, 3, 1900.
Witkowski, G. Deutsche Wissenschaft ni Amerika. National-Zt., 504, 1902.
Zapp, A. Ein Amerikaner über deutsches Geistesleben. MLIA, 1881.
Zeydel, E. H. The German Theatre in New York City. Jb. der deutsch-amerikanischen Histor. Ges. von Illinois, 15, 1915.
—— Die germanistische Tätigkeit in Amerika, 1918-26. Euphorion, 29, 1928.
Ziegler, E. D. Translations of German Poetry in American Magazines, 1741-1810. Philadelphia, 1905.
Zimmermann, G. A. Deutsch in Amerika: Beiträge zur Geschichte der deutsch-amerikanischen Literatur. Chicago, 1892.
Zucker, A. E. Bibliographical Notes on the German Language Theater in the United States. MDU, 35, 1943.
—— The History of the German Theater in Baltimore. GR, 18, 1943.

CHAPTER THREE

German Influences upon England

Anon. Englische Urteile über deutsche Literatur. Blätter zur Kunde der Litteratur des Auslands, 1836. And in: Beilage zur Allg. Zt., 25-26.II.1843.
—— Die deutsche Romantik und der englische Geschmack. Blätter zur Kunde der Litteratur des Auslands, 1837.
—— Die deutsche Bühne in London im Jahre 1852. MLIA, 1864.
—— Deutsche Dichtungen in englischen Uebersetzungen. Grenzboten, 28, 1869
—— Die englische Presse über deutsche Litteraturzustände. Europa, 1876.

—— German Influence in English Literature. AM, 1877.
—— German Plays in London. Literature, 13.X.1900.
Arns, K. Zur Kenntnis des deutschen Einflusses im geistigen Leben Englands. Nord & Süd, April, 1919.
Batt, M. The German Story in England About 1826. MPh, Oct., 1907.
Block, M. The British and Foreign Review, or European Quarterly Journal. Ein Beitrag zur Geschichte der Aufnahme deutscher Literatur in England. Zürich, 1921.
Broicher, C. Aaglikanische Kirche und deutsche Philosophie. PJb, 1910.
Bruford, W. H. Germany and the Germans. Eighteenth Century English Traveller's Tales. GLL, 1, 1937.
Colwell, W. A. German Literature in England, 1750-1800. Diss. Harvard, 1906.
Dibelius, W. Englische Berichte über Hamburg und Norddeutschland aus dem 16. bis 18. Jahrhundert. Zs. des Vereins f. hamburgische Geschichte, 19, 1917.
Dunning, W. A. The Political Theories of German Idealists. Political Science Quart., 28, 1913.
Eitner, K. Ein Engländer über deutsches Geistesleben im ersten Drittel dieses Jahrhunderts. Weimar, 1871.
Galinsky, H. Deutsches Schrifttum der Gegenwart in der englischen Kritik der Nachkriegszeit, 1919-35. München, 1938.
Gérard, A. Les tentatives d'influence allemande en Angleterre. RP, May, 1918.
Handschin, C. H. A Bibliography of English Translations of German Novels. Monatshefte f. deutsche Sprache & Pädagogik, 9, 1909.
Harvey, J. L. German Literature in England before 1790. Americana Germanica, 4, 1902.
Herzfeld, G. Zur Geschichte der deutschen Literatur in England. Archiv, 105, 1900 & 110, 1903.
Karpeles, G. Deutsche Klassiker in England. Gegenwart, 1883.
Klatscher, L. Deutsche Klassiker in England. Internat. Litteraturberichte, 11, 1898.
Koeppel, E. Deutsche Strömungen in der englischen Literatur. Strassburg, 1910.
Kornder, T. Der Deutsche im Spiegelbild der englischen Erzählungsliteratur des 19. Jahrhunderts. Erlangen, 1934.
Ludwig, A. Deutschland und Deutsche im englischen Roman des 19. und 20. Jahrhunderts. GRM, 1913.
Margraf, E. Der Einfluss der deutschen Literatur auf die englische am Ende des 18. und im ersten Drittel des 19. Jahrhunderts. Diss. Leipzig, 1901.
Metz, R. England und die deutsche Philosophie. Stuttgart, 1941.
Miller, E. A. Englische Urteile über die deutsche Literatur. Der Türmer, May, 1900.
Morgan, B. Q. A Critical Bibliography of German Literature in English Translation, 1481-1927. With Supplement Embracing the Years 1928-35. Stanford U. P., 1938.
—— & Hohlfeld, A. R. (eds). German Literature in British Magazines, 1750-1860. Wisconsin U.P., 1949. Cf. CL, 2, 1950.
Mossé, F. Poésie saxonne et poésie anglaise à l'époque carolingienne. EG 3, 1948.
Oswald, E. Deutscher Einfluss auf England im XV. Jahrhundert. Beilage zur Allg. Zt., 289-90, 1891.
Passow, A. Deutschlands Einfluss auf die englische Litteratur. MLIA, 1878.
Perry, T. S. German Influence in English Literature. AM, Aug., 1877.
Phillips, T. M. German Philosophy in English Poetry. Papers of the Manchester Literary Club, 45, 1919.
Purdie, E. German Influence on the Literary Ballad in England during the Romantic Revival. PEGS, 3, 1926.
Radczun, W. Das englische Urteil über die Deutschen bis zur Mitte des 17. Jahrhunderts. Berlin, 1933.
Schaible, K. H. Geschichte der Deutschen in England. Strassburg, 1885.
Schirmer, W. F. Der Einfluss der deutschen Literatur auf die englische im 19. Jahrhundert. Halle, 1947.
Scholz, K. Bibliography of English Renditions of Modern German Dramas. German-American Annals, 15, 1917.
Schulze, K. Ein englischer Humorist über Deutschland. Sonntagsblatt, New Yorker Staatszeitung, March, 1903.
Schultz, F. Der Deutsche in der englischen Literatur vom Beginn der Romantik bis zum Ausbruch des Weltkrieges. Halle, 1939.
Schwaninger, C. Die Verdienste der Edinburgh Review um die Verbreitung deutscher Literatur in England, 1802-29. Diss. Zürich, 1921.
Smith, P. Englishmen at Wittenberg in the 16th Century. EHR, 1921.
Stephen, L. The Importation of German. In: Studies of a Biographer. London, 1899.
Stockley, V. German Literature as Known in England. London, 1929.
Stokoe, F. W. German Influence in the English Romantic Period, 1788-1818, with Special Reference to Scott, Coleridge, Shelley and Byron. Cambridge U. P., 1926 & PEGS, 3, 1926.
Süpfle, T. Beiträge zur Geschichte der deutschen Literatur in England im letzten Drittel des 18. Jahrhunderts. ZVL, 6, 1893.
Waddington, M. M. The Development of British Thought from 1820 to 1890 with Special Reference to German Influences. Toronto, 1919.

Weddigen, O. Vermittler des deutschen Geistes in England und Nordamerika. Archiv, 59, 1878.

Weineck, K. Deutschland und der Deutsche im Spiegel der englischen erzählenden Literatur seit 1830. Halle, 1938.

Wenzel, P. Germany and the Germans as Seen by English Novelists of the 19th and 20th Centuries. Bielefeld, 1932.

Witte, K. Die Deutschen im Urteil eines Engländers vor 300 Jahren. National-Zt., 462, 466, 1903.

Zeiger, T. Beiträge zur Geschichte der deutsch-englischen Literaturbeziehungen. Diss. Leipzig & SVL, 1, 1901-02.

CHAPTER FOUR

German Influences upon France

Anon. Die deutsche Literatur (bzw. Philosophie) in Frankreich. Beilage der Allg. Zt., 8.XII.1842; 13,14,25.II & 16.XI.1843; 14.III.1844.

—— Ein französisches Urteil über die deutsche Kunst. Grenzboten, 16, 1857.

—— Deutschland in der Revue des Deux Mondes. MLIA, 1874.

—— Das Deutschtum im Wälschland. Beilage zur Allg. Zt., 15.III.1885.

—— Deutsche Litteratur im Ausland. Neue DR, 1892.

—— Deutschland in der heutigen französischen Literatur. Tägliche Rundschau, Unterhaltungsbeilage, 269, 1912.

Angelloz, J. F. Allemagne, notre souci. MF, 1947.

Antoine, A. Das moderne deutsche Drama in Frankreich. Die Woche, 40, 1904.

Arens, F. Französische Intellektuelle und deutsche Kultur. Der neue Merkur, 3, 1920.

Atkins, S. Germany through French Eyes after the Liberation. GQ, 20, 1947.

Baldensperger, F. L'Allemagne et les Allemands vus à travers la littérature française. BURS, 1907 & 1911.

Baumann, F. Deutschland im Spiegel der französischen Literatur. Post. Sonntagsblatt, 15, 1908.

Berg, L. Deutscher Geist in Frankreich. Gegenwart, 1893.

Bergner, G. Les comédiens allemands à Strasbourg au XVIIIe siècle. Alsace française, 2.X.1926.

Bertaux, F. La littérature allemande en France. Wissen & Leben, 1923.

Betz, L. P. Betrachtungen über den deutschen Einfluss auf die französische Litteratur in der ersten Hälfte dieses Jahrhunderts. In: Heine in Frankreich. Zürich, 1895.

Breitbach, J. Les Français connaissent-ils vraiment la littérature allemande d'aujourd'hui? Revue hebdomadaire, 9.VI.1934.

Carré, J. M. L'Allemagne vue par les écrivains français du XIXe siècle. RRh, 1928-29.

—— Les écrivains français et le mirage allemand. Paris, 1947.

Colombier, P. du. Les lettres allemandes et le public français à propos d'un anniversaire de Goethe. Revue critique des idées et des livres, Feb., 1923.

Courcelle, P. Histoire littéraire des grandes invasions germaniques. Paris, 1948.

Delage, J. Les comédiens allemands à Strasbourg au XVIIIe siècle. RRh, 1927.

Drews, D. Das fränkisch-germanische Bewusstsein des französischen Adels im 18. Jahrhundert. Berlin, 1940.

Duméril, E. Le lied allemand et ses traductions poétiques en France. Paris, 1934.

—— Lieds et ballades germaniques traduits en vers français: essai de bibliographie critique. Paris, 1934. Cf. NL, 1934.

Ehrhard, A. Deutsche Strömungen im französischen Geistesleben der Gegenwart. Oesterreichische Rundschau, 33, 1912.

Eloesser, A. Deutsche Litteratur in Frankreich. Vossische Zt., 3, 1896.

Engel, E. Französische Uebersetzungen deutscher Werke. MLIA, 1880.

—— Deutschlands geistiger Einfluss auf Frankreich. Münchener Neueste Nachrichten, 553, 1902.

Engelmayer, O. Die Deutschlandideologie der Franzosen. Berlin, 1936.

Falconnet, E. De l'influence de la littérature allemande sur la littérature française. Revue du Midi, 6, 1834.

Fauconnet, A. Les études germaniques en France, leur tâche, leur organisation. NSp, 47.

Fligier. Französische Urtheile über die deutsche Litteratur im XVIII. Jahrhundert. Wiener Allg. Zt., 20.VIII.1886.

Friedlaender, L. Französische Urteile über Deutschland. In: Erinnerungen, Reden und Studien. Strassburg, 1905.

Fritzsche, W. L. Deutsche Art in französischer Beleuchtuug. Gegenwart, 24, 1905.

Fuerst, R. Ein Franzose über deutsche Litteratur. Beilage zur Allg. Zt., 169, 1901.

Gaertner, J. Das Journal étranger und seine Bedeutung für die Verbreitung deutscher Literatur in Frankreich. Diss. Heidelberg, 1905.

Geiger, L. Französische Bücher zur deutschen Geistesgeschichte. LE. 5, 1903.

Gide, A. Der Einfluss Deutschlands auf Frankreich. Die literar. Welt, 1929.

Golther, W. Germanisches in der altfranzösischen Dichtung. Krit. Jahresbericht über d. Fortschritte der roman. Philologie, 1890.

Grantoff, O. Deutschland im Lichte Frank-

reichs. Deutsch-französische Rundschau, 1931.
Groth, E. Französische Kritik deutscher Geschichtsforschung. MLIA, 1889.
Guglia, E. Deutsche Litteratur in Frankreich. Grenzboten, 45, 1886.
Hinstorff, C. A. Die Archives littéraires de l'Europe und ihre Stellung zur deutschen Literatur. Progr. Frankfurt 1907.
Hoffmeister, K. Deutschland im Spiegel Frankreichs. Deutsche Akademiker Zt., 18, 1926.
Jacobsen, R. Französische Urteile über deutsche Lyrik. Der Continent, 1, 1907.
Jan, E. von. Deutsches Geistesgut in der französischen Romantik. Zs. f. deutsche Geisteswissenschaft, 1938.
Joseph, M. Die deutschen Universitäten im Urteile französischer Gelehrter (1900-1920). Berlin, 1923.
Jourda, P. L'exotisme dans la littérature française depuis le romantisme: L'Allemagne. RCC, 15.XII.1936.
Kern, F. Der mittelalterliche Deutsche in französischer Ansicht. Historische Zs., 108, 1912.
Klemperer, V. Deutsches Wesen in der französischen Auffassung des 19. und 20. Jahrhunderts. ZDK, 41, 1927.
Koch, M. Geschichte des deutschen Kultureinflusses auf Frankreich. MLIA, 1888.
Kohut, A. Zwei französische Schmähschriften über Deutschland. Gegenwart, 1884.
Krauss, W. Deutschland als Thema der französischen Literatur. DVLG, 11, 1933.
Krieger, H. Der deutsche Dynamismus im Urteil der Franzosen von heute. NM, 5, 1934.
Lavisse, E. Sentiments à l'égard de l'Allemagne. RP, 1.V.1920.
Leuthold, H. Einfluss der deutschen Literatur auf die neuere französische Lyrik. Süddeutsche Zt., Oct., 1859.
Lote, R. Les visages de l'Allemagne à travers la géographie et l'histoire. Annales de l'U. de Grenoble, N. S., 8, 1931.
—— Explication de la littérature allemande. Paris, 1931.
Ludwig, H. Deutsche Romantik im neuen Frankreich. Neue Badische Landes-Zt., 499, 1912.
Mahrenholtz, R. Deutsche Litteratur in französischer Beleuchtung. Blätter für literar. Unterhaltung, 44, 1890.
Mathorez, J. La pénétration allemande en France au XIXe siècle. Revue des Etudes historiques, 1923.
Meissner, F. Der Einfluss des deutschen Geistes auf die französische Litteratur des 19. Jahrhunderts bis 1870. Leipzig, 1893.
Mennell, A. Deutsche Bücher in Frankreich. Gegenwart, 1885.
Meyer, E. Deutschland im Spiegel der modernen französischen Dichtung. WM, 52, 1907.
Monnier, A. & Porson, J. Bibliographie de la littérature allemande traduite en français. Le Navire d'argent, May, 1926.
Müller, O. T. Das Bild vom deutschen Menschen in Frankreich von Mme. de Staël bis Chateaubriant. NSp, 50.
Mundt, T. Deutschland in Frankreich. In: Spazierzüge und Irrfahrten. Altona, 1838.
Noire, L. Die deutsche Litteratur und die Franzosen. Gegenwart, 1887.
Oesterheld, E. Deutschlands Entwicklung im Urteile Frankreichs. Xenien, 1908.
Oswald, E. Ein deutscher Volksdichter für Frankreich. MLIA, 1880.
Ottiker von Leyk. Die deutsche Lyrik in der französischen Uebersetzungslitteratur. Archiv, 1884.
Petersen, F. C. Die Deutschen in Frankreich. Das neue Blatt, 8, 1871.
Pokrandt, A. Deutsche Kultureinflüsse im Frankreich des XIX. Jahrhunderts. Leipzig, 1925.
Reinach, J. De l'influence intellectuelle de l'Allemagne sur la France. RB, 4.V.1878.
Renard, G. L'influence de l'Alllemagne sur la France depuis 1870. Nouvelle Revue, 15.VIII.1884.
Reynaud, L. Les débuts du germanisme en France. MF, April, 1921.
—— L'influence allemande en France au XVIIIe et au XIXe siècle. Paris, 1922.
—— L'opinion française et l'Allemagne. RB, 1939.
Roeder, E. von. Die Rolle der Uebersetzung aus dem Deutschen ins Französische. NM, Nov., 1933.
Rosières, R. La littérature allemande en France de 1750 à 1800. RB, 15.IX.1883.
Rossel, V. La littérature allemande en France au XVIIIe siècle. RHLF, 1895.
Rouge, J. Quelques aspects du romantisme allemand, à la lumière de publications françaises récentes. RG, 1938.
Sattler, Gertrud. Das deutsche Lied in der französischen Romantik. Bern, 1932.
Schmid, I. Einflüsse deutschen Geistes in Frankreich seit dem Kriege 1870-71. Frankfurter Zt., 12.I.1911.
Schneider, G. Ueber den Einfluss der deutschen Litteratur auf Frankreich. MLIA, 1879.
Schneider, H. Deutsche Art und Sitte im Spiegel französischer Reisebeschreibungen aus den Jahren 1830-70. Diss. Köln, 1928.
Schulz, W. Das Deutschlandbild in der französischen Kritik nach 1918. Berlin, 1941.
Semmig, H. Das deutsche Gespenst in Frankreich. Orion, 2, 1863.
Süpfle, T. Ueber den Kultureinfluss Deutschlands auf Frankreich. Progr. Metz, 1882.

——— Geschichte des deutschen Kultureinflusses auf Frankreich. Gotha, 1886 ff. Cf. MLIA, 1886.
——— Französische Studien über die deutsche Litteratur vor Frau von Staël. ZVL, 1, 1887.
Texte, J. Les premiers vulgarisateurs de la littérature allemande en France. RCC, 1896.
——— L'influence allemande dans le romantisme français. In: Etudes de littérature européenne. Paris, 1898.
——— Les origines de l'influence allemande dans la littérature française du XIXe siècle. RHLF, 15.I.1898. Cf. Revue critique, 1898.
Thanlow, G. Wie man in Frankreich mit der deutschen Philosophie umgeht. Kiel, 1852.
Thibaudet, A. Le germanisme et la France. NRF, Sept., 1922.
Thorel, J. Les romantiques allemands et les symbolistes français. Entretiens politiques et littéraires, Sept., 1891.
Tibal, A. L'influence allemande en France au temps du romantisme. Mélanges Andler, Strasbourg, 1924.
Varia. Le romantisme allemand en France; bibliographie. Cahiers du Sud, May, 1937.
Visan, T. de. Le romantisme allemand et le symbolisme français. MF, 15.XII.1910.
Wechssler, E. Einflüsse der altfranzösischen Litteratur auf die altdeutsche. Germanisches in der altfranzösischen Dichtung. Jahresberichte, 1895-96; 1900.
——— Der deutsche Geist in der französischen Literatur des 19. Jahrhunderts von Saint-Martin bis Bergson. DVLG, 2, 1924.
Weidenkaff, K. Die Anschauungen der Franzosen über die geistige Kultur der Deutschen im Verlaufe des 18. und zu Beginn des 19. Jahrhunderts. Diss. Leipzig, 1906.
Wilhelm, J. Deutsche Geistes- und Literatureinflüsse auf Frankreich im 19. Jahrhundert. Deutsche Kultur im Leben der Völker, 13, 1938.
Winkelmann, O. Zur Geschichte des deutschen Theaters in Strassburg unter französischer Herrschaft. Elsässisches Jb, 1898.
Winkler, K. Geschichte der deutschen Litteratur in Frankreich. Rossleben, 1872.
Wittmer, L. L'influence de l'Allemagne en France au XVIIIe et au XIXe siècle: le point de vue suisse. Bull. de l'Institut national genevois, 1924.
Ziemssen, L. Deutsche Dichtung in Frankreich. Gegenwart, 17, 1880.
Zimmermann, K. L. Die Bedeutung der Deutschen in der französischen Literatur des Mittelalters, mit besonderer Berücksichtigung der chansons de geste. RF, 29, 1910.
Zyromski, E. De l'influence de la pensée allemande sur l'esprit français au XIXe siècle. Revue des U. du Midi, 4, 1898.

CHAPTER FIVE

German Influences upon Other Countries.

Jankeff, J. **BULGARIEN** und der deutsche Geist. Europäische Revue, Jan., 1934.
Strauss, A. Die deutsche Litteratur in Bulgarien. ZVL, 7, 1894.
Nadler, J. Das Schrifttum der Sudetendeutschen. (**CZECHOSLOVAKIA.**) Regensburg, 1924.
Nagl, W. Der Kultureinfluss der Deutschen auf den czecho-slavischen Stamm. Alt-Wien, 3, 1894.
Sauer, A. Die deutsche Wissenschaft und Volksbildung in der Tchechoslowakei. Oesterr. Rundschau, 1.IV.1920.
Toischer, W. Zur Geschichte der deutschen Sprache und Litteratur in Böhmen. Mittheilungen d. Vereins f. Geschichte der Deutschen in Böhmen, 13, 1892.
Wolkan, R. Geschichte der deutschen Literatur in Böhmen und in den Sudetenländern. Augsburg, 1925.
Bolte, J. Deutsche Lieder in **DAENEMARK.** SAWB, 20, 1927.
Eaton, J. W. The German Influence in Danish Literature in the Eighteenth Century. Cambridge, 1929.
Paludan, T. Deutsche Wandertruppen in Dänemark. ZDPh, 25.
Weddigen, O. Geschichte der Einwirkungen der deutschen Litteratur auf die Litteratur Dänemarks. Germania, 1899.
Anon. Deutsche Litteratur in Griechenland. (**GREECE.**) Beilage zur Allg. Zt., 38, 1903.
Geelen, A. van. Deutsches Bühnenleben zu Amsterdam in der zweiten Hälfte des 18. Jahrhunderts. (**HOLLAND.**) Nymwegen, 1947.
Hellwald, F. von. Deutscher Einfluss auf die holländische Literatur. MLIA, 1879.
Huizinga, J. Der Einfluss Deutschlands in der Geschichte der niederländischen Kultur. AK, 16, 1925.
Kaakebeen, C. G. De invloed der Duitsche Letteren op de Nederlandsche. Culemborg, 1887.
Menne, K. Der Einfluss der deutschen Litteratur auf die niederländische um die Wende des XVIII. und XIX. Jahrhunderts. Weimar, 1898 & ZDA, 1900.
Osthoff, H. Die Niederländer und das deutsche Lied (1400-1640). Berlin, 1938.
Spoelstra, H. A. C. De invloed van de duitsche letterkunde op de nederlandsche in de tweede helft van de 18e eeuw. Amsterdam, 1931.
Trautwein von Belle, E. Holländische Literatur und Deutschtum. MLIA, 1886.
Wernekke, H. Deutsche Literaturgeschichte in den Niederlanden. MLIA, 1880.
Bleyer, J. La **HONGRIE** et la philologie

allemande au début du XIXe siècle. (In Hungarian). Budapest, 1910.
——— Ueber geistige Rezeption und nationales Schrifttum: Ungarische Literatur und deutscher Einfluss. Festschrift Ermatinger. Frauenfeld, 1933.
Császár, E. Deutsche Elemente in der ungarischen Dichtung des 18. Jahrhunderts. München, 1942.
Galos, R. Contribution aux sources allemandes de la poésie hongroise du XVIIIe siècle. Irodalomtörteneti Közlemenyek, 45, 1937.
Gyorgy, L. Die Uebersetzungen deutscher Romane und Erzählungen in der ungarischen Literatur, 1772-1836. Ungarisches Jb. 8.
Pukársky-Kádár. Geschichte des deutschen Theaters in Ungarn. München, 1933.
Szende, Z. German Influence on Hungarian Culture. GLL, 4, 1939.
Johannesson, A. Literarische Beziehungen Deutschlands zu Island. (ICELAND.) Edda, 18, 1922.
Mohr, W. Entstehungsgeschichte und Heimat der jüngeren Eddalieder südgermanischen Stoffes. ZDA, 75.
Croce, B. Deutsche Kultur in Italien im Zeitalter des Risorgimento. (ITALY.) NSR, 1926.
Debrit, M. La philosophie allemande en Italie, par B. Mazzarella. BURS, 1861.
Dejob, C. Le type de l'Allemand chez les classiques italiens. BI, 1, 1901.
Duprat, P. Les idées allemandes en Italie. RG, 33, 1865.
Fligier. Italienische Urtheile über die deutsche Litteratur im XVIII. Jahrhundert. Wiener Allg. Zt., 25.VIII.1886.
Gamillscheg, E. Immigrazioni germaniche in Italia. Leipzig, 1937.
Giusso, L. La fortuna del germanesimo in Italia. Mercurio, 3, 1946.
Hudal, A. Die deutsche Kulturarbeit in Italien. Münster 1934.
Landau, M. Deutsche Litteratur in italienischem Spiegel. Wiener Zt., 41, 1896.
Lanzky, P. Die deutsche Litteratur in Italien in den beiden letzten Jahrzehnten. MLIA, 1880.
Liebmann, H. Deutsches Land und Volk nach italienischen Berichterstattern der Reformationszeit. Berlin, 1910.
Lohner, Heidi. Deutschlands Anteil an der italienischen Romantik. Bern, 1936.
Ruggiero, G. de. La cultura germanica e noi. La Nuova Europa, 1, 1944.
Sauer, C. M. Deutsche Lyrik in Italien. MLIA, 1881.
Thiemann, T. Deutsche Kultur und Litteratur des XVIII. Jahrhunderts im Lichte der zeitgenössischen italienischen Kritik. Archiv, 72, 1884 & Oppeln, 1886.
Weisbach, W. Das moderne Deutschland im Spiegel italienischer Vorstellungen. PJb, May, 1920.
Zardo, A. La poesia tedesca in Italia nel settecento. NAnt, 16.XI.1927.
Meyen, F. Die norwegischen Uebersetzungen deutscher Schönliteratur, 1841-1941. (NORWAY.) Oslo, 1942.
Brandes, G. Polen und Deutschland. (POLAND.) In: Polen. München, 1898.
Ciechanowska, Z. German Romanticism and Polish Literature. (In Polish.) Krakow, 1936.
Kühne, W. Polnische Bekenntnisse zu deutschen Menschen und zum deutschen Geist. Mitt. der D. Akademie der wissenschaftl. Erforschung und Pflege des Deutschtums, 2, 1936.
Maschke, E. Deutsche Grundlagen in der polnischen Kultur. DR, 1933.
Moser, F. Les romantiques portugais et l'Allemagne. (PORTUGAL.) Paris, 1939.
Rossi, G. C. Aspetti dell'influenza tedesca sul romanticismo portoghese. SG, 5, 1942.
Capesius, B. Die moderne deutsche Dichtung in Rumänien. (RUMANIA.) Der getreue Eckart, 16, 1939.
Radulescu-Motru, C. Rumänien und die deutsche Kultur. Europäische Revue, 1934.
San Giorgiu, I. Deutscher Geist in der rumänischen Literatur. DVLG, 17, 1939.
Anon. Deutsche Lyrik in Russland. (RUSSIA.) Europa, 1856.
——— Deutsche Literatur in Russland. Europa, 1858.
Benz, E. Russische Eschatologie. Studien zur Einwirkung der deutschen Erweckungsbewegung in Russland. Kyrios, 1, 1936.
Billig, J. Der Zusammenbruch des deutschen Idealismus bei den russischen Romantikern. Archiv f. systemat. Philosophie & Soziologie, 34, 1930.
Funck-Brentano. Les sophistes allemands et les nihilistes russes. Paris, 1887.
Gurevich, L. German Romanticism and the Symbolism of our Days. Russkaia Mysl, 4, 1914.
Karawajeva, A. Unser literarischer Nachwuchs. Die Literatur in der Sowjetunion. Spezialnumer der Ges. für kulturelle Verbindung der Sowjetunion mit dem Ausland, 7-8, 1934.
Loewenfeld, R. Deutsche Einflüsse in der russischen Litteratur. MLIA, 63, 1894.
Sazonova, J. The German in Russian Literature. Novosele, 3, 1943. And in: ASEER, 4, 1945.
Schwiefert, F. Das deutsche Buch in Sowjetrussland. Festschrift E. Kuhnert. Berlin, 1928.
Sivers, J. van. Deutsche Dichter in Russland. In: Studien zur Litteraturgeschichte. Berlin, 1855.
Smal-Stockyi, R. Die germanisch-deutschen

Kultureinflüsse im Spiegel der ukrainischen Sprache. Leipzig, 1942.
Steppun, F. German Romanticism and Russian Slavophilism. (In Russian). Russkaia Mysl, 1910.
Veselovskii, A. Deutsche Einflüsse auf das alte russische Theater. Prag, 1876.
Zhirmunskii, V. M. German Romanticism and Contemporary Mysticism. St. Petersburg, 1914.
Anon. Deutsche Dichter im Norden. (**SCANDINAVIA.**) Blätter f. literar. Unterhaltung, 3.XII.1830.
Moeller, C. Deutschland in Scandinavien. Gegenwart, 1902.
Lieb, F. & Cizevskyj, D. Die deutsche Mystik bei den Ostslaven. (**SLAVS.**) ZSPh, 9, 1932.
Matl, J. Die Bedeutung der deutschen Romantik für das nationale Erwachen der Slaven. Deutsche Hefte f. Volksforschung, 4, 1934.
Murko, M. Deutsche Einflüsse auf die Anfänge der slavischen Romantik. Graz, 1897. Cf. Archiv, 119.
Valkhoff, M. Superstrats germanique et slave. NPh, 31, 1947.
Vasmer. Die Einflüsse der deutschen Literatur bei den Slaven. Archiv, 169, 1936.
Fastenrath, J. Deutsche Dichtungen in spanischer Uebersetzung. (**SPAIN.**) MLIA, 1881.
Martin Alonso, N. Motivos alemanes en los clasicos castellanos. Ensayos y Estudios, 2, 1940.
Montolin, M. de. Les influenciès de la cultura alemanya a Catalunya. Revista, 1935.
Post, H. H. L'origine germanique du mot et de l'institution de Hermandad en Espagne. NPh, 26, 1941.
Schmidt-Koch, R. Deutsche Philosophie in spanischer Uebersetzung. Berlin, 1940.
Alker, E. Deutsche Literatur in Schweden. (**SWEDEN.**) Das deutsche Buch, 1937.
Broderius, J. R. German Folk-Songs in Sweden. PhQ, 1929.
Thinfelder, F. Auf deutschen Spuren in der älteren schwedischen Liedliteratur. In: Mitteilungen der Akad. zur wissenschaftl. Erforschung, 1926.
Geilinger, M. Minnesangs Frühling in der Schweiz. (**SWITZERLAND.**) Zürich, 1945.
Wechlin, H. E. Der Aargau als Vermittler deutscher Literatur an die Schweiz (1798-1848). Aarau, 1925.
Anon. Die Bedeutung der deutschen Einflüsse auf die Entstehung der südslavischen Literatur des 19. Jahrhunderts. (**YUGOSLAVIA.**) Deutsche Hefte f. Volks- und Kulturbodenforschung, 1, 1930-31.
Groth, E. Deutsche Kultur in Südosteuropa. ZNU, 39.
Seleskovic. Ueber den deutschen Einfluss auf die südslavische Literatur. Europäische Revue, 10, 1934.
Tropsch, S. Les influences allemandes sur les Illyriens et leurs précurseurs. Le Monde slave, 1935.

CHAPTER SIX

Goethe

1. Generalities

Anon. On the Influence of the Writings of Goethe. Athenaeum, 1832.
Baldensperger, F. La commémoration de la mort de Goethe hors d'Allemagne. RLC, 12, 1932.
——— Goethe et la littérature mondiale. Bull. de l'Association des Amis de l'U. de Liège, 1933.
Barabas, A. von. Goethes Wirkung in der Weltlitteratur. Leipzig, 1903.
Bergmann, A. Das Welt-Echo des Goethejahres. Weimar, 1932.
Bohnenblust, G. Das Erbe Goethes. Lausanne, 1932.
Carossa, H. Wirkungen Goethes in der Gegenwart. In: Goethe, 3, 1938.
——— La significación de Goethe para la actualidad. Ensayos y Estudios 1939.
Carré, J. M. L'Allemagne, la France et l'Angleterre en face de Goethe. RLC, 23, 1949.
Friederich, W. P. Goethe, 1749-1949. Georgia Review, 3, 1949.
Grappe, G. Essai sur le Goethisme. Revue des Idées, 15.X.1906.
Henel, H. Ausländische Goethe-Kritik. DVLG, 12, 1934.
Hirschberg, L. Goethe-Uebersetzungen vor hundert Jahren. Zs. f. Bücherfreunde, 12, 1909.
Hutton, R. H. Goethe and his Influence. In: Literary Essays. London, 1888.
Kaufmann, M. Goethe and Modern Thought. Scottish Review, 18, 1891.
Landgraf, H. Goethe und seine ausländischen Besucher. München, 1932.
Marc, A. En marge de Goethe. Revue du siècle, Jan,. 1934.
Mueller, K. W. Goethes letzte litterarische Thätigkeit, Verhältniss zum Auslande, und Scheiden. Jena, 1832.
Nolte, F. O. Grillparzer, Lessing and Goethe in the Perspective of European Literature. Lancaster (Pa.), 1938.
Nutting. The Over-Estimation of Goethe. Andover Review, July, 1889.
Paschall, C. What Goethe Means to the World. MLF, 1933.
Petersen, J. Goethe im Nachruf. SAWB, 1931.
——— Goethe Verehrung in fünf Jahrzehnten. JbGG, 21, 1935.
Pitrou, R. Le message de Goethe. Le Correspondant, 10.III.1932.

Retté, A. Goethe et l'influence allemande. Européen, 1, 1903.
Robertson, J. G. Goethe and the 20th Century. Cambridge, U. P., 1912.
San Giorgiu, I. Spiritul lui Goethe in literatura universala. Rev. Fundat. Regale, 3, 1935.
Saurat, D. Goethe aujourd'hui. NRF, 1. III.1932.
Suarès, A. Goethe, le grand Européen. Paris, 1932.
Thomas, R. H. Goethe in the Literary Movements of the 20th Century. PEGS, N. S., 14, 1939.
Vermeil, E. Goethe homme du milieu. CL, 1, 1949.
Vulliod, A. Goethe, l'Allemagne et l'Europe. In: Goethe, études publiées par l'U. de Strasbourg. Paris, 1932.
Wenig, C. Goethe in seiner welthistorischen Bedeutung. Weimar, 1857.

2. Faust

(including Marlowe, Calderón, Lessing, etc.)

Anon. Faustlitteratur, 1519-1879. Cat. Ackermann, 66 & 70. München, 1879-80.
——— Ausstellung von Handschriften, Druckwerken, Bildern und Tonwerken zur Faustsage und Faustdichtung veranstaltet vom Freien deutschen Hochstift. Frankfurt, 1893.
Becher, G. Goethes wahre Faust-Form als Lösung des Faust-Rätsels. München, 1940.
Berg, L. Etappen des Faustproblems. Deutsches Wochenblatt, 12, 1901.
Bianquis, Geneviève. Faust à travers quatre siècles. Paris, 1935.
Brown, Beatrice D. Marlowe, Faustus, and Simon Magus. PMLA, 54.
Collin de Plancy, J. Le docteur Faust et autres légendes. Paris, 1889.
Creizenach, W. Geschichte des Volksschauspiels vom Dr. Faust. Halle, 1878.
Delius, F. Marlowe's Faust und seine Quelle. Diss. Göttingen, 1881.
Dieblers, A. Faust- und Wagnerpantomimen in England. Anglia, 7, 1884.
Dumcke, J. Die deutschen Faustbücher. Diss. Leipzig, 1891.
Ellinger, G. Zu den Quellen des Faustbuches von 1587. ZVL, 1.
Ellis-Fermor, Una. The Devil to Pay and the Faust Legend. English, 2.
Engel, K. Zusammenstellung der Faustbücher vom 16. Jahrhundert bis Mitte 1884. Oldenburg, 1885.
Faligan, E. La légende de Faust. Mém. de la Sociéte nat. d'Agriculture. Angers, 24, 1883 & Paris, 1887.
Fischer, K. Die Faustdichtung vor Goethe. In: Goethe-Schriften, 6. Heidelberg, 1909.
Francke, K. Did the Hypnerotomachia Poliphili Influence the Second Part of Faust? HSPhL, 2, 1893.
Fränckel, L. Geschichte der Faustfabel. Euphorion, 2, 1895.
Geissler, H. W. Gestaltungen des Faust: die bedeutendsten Werke der Faustdichtung seit 1587. 3 vols. München, 1927.
Graber, G. Ein Kärntner Spiel vom Doktor Faust. Kärntner Forschungen, 2, 1943.
Green, C. Dr. Faustus: Tragedy of Individualism. Science & Society, 10, 1946.
Greg, W. W. The Damnation of Faustus. MLR, 41, 1946.
Gregori, F. Faust. LE, Jan., 1907.
Gromer, S. Des idées françaises dans Faust. Paris, 1931.
Gronicka, A. de. Thomas Mann's Doktor Faustus: Prolegomena to an Interpretation. GR, 23 1948.
Grutzmacher, R. Goethes Faust. Ein deutscher Mythus. Berlin, 1936.
Hagen, F. H. von der. Ueber die ältesten Darstellungen der Faustsage. Berlin, 1844.
Heilman, R. B. The Tragedy of Knowledge: Marlowe's Treatment of Faustus. Quarterly Rev. of Literature, 2, 1946.
Heinrich, G. Faust. In: Literaturgeschichtliche Aufsätze (In Hungarian). Budapest, 1914.
Heller, O. Faust and Faustus: a Study of Goethe's Relation to Marlowe. St. Louis, 1931. Cf. RLC, 1932.
Henel, H. Faust-Translations and Faust-Mosaics. MDU, 1938.
Heuer, O. Faust in Geschichte, Sage und Dichtung. Berichte des freien deutschen Hochstifts Frankfurt, 1894.
Horner, E. & Komorzynski, E. Zur Geschichte der Fauststoffe. Euphorion, 7, 1900.
House, L. Die Faustsage und der historische Faust. Luxemburg, 1862.
Jacoby, G. Herder als Faust. Leipzig, 1911.
Jantz, H. Goethe's Faust as a Renaissance Man: Sources and Prototypes. CL, 1, 1949.
Jokaff, E. Die Faustsage. Ihre Entstehung und Wandlung bis auf Goethe. Hamburg, 1903.
Kiesewetter, K. Faust in Geschichte und Tradition. Leipzig, 1893.
Kirschbaum, L. Mephistophilis and the Lost Dragon. RES, 18, 1942.
——— Marlowe's Faustus: A Reconsideration. RES, 19, 1943.
Klett, Ada M. Der Streit um Faust II seit 1900. Jena, 1939.
Knauth, P. Die Faustsage in ihrer Entstehung, Verwicklung und Entwicklung. Freiburg, 1881.
Kocher, P. H. The English Faust Book and the Date of Marlowe's Faustus. MLN, 55, 1940.
——— Nashe's Authorship of the Prose Scenes in Faustus. MLQ, 3, 1942.

——— The Early Date for Marlowe's Faustus. MLN, 58, 1943.
Korff, H. A. Faustischer Glaube. Leipzig, 1938.
Korrodi, E. Alte Faustdichtung und Goethes Urfaust. Aufwärts Schwyz, 1, 1906.
Kraus, E. W. Faustiana aus Böhmen. ZVL, 12, 1898.
Krogmann, W. Mephistopheles. Archiv, Oct., 1936.
Kuehnemund, R. Faust and Zarathustra in Our Time. GR, 15, 1940.
Levi, E. Il processo di Faust. Marzocco, 1.III.1931.
——— La risurrezione di Faust. Marzocco, 19.VII.1931.
Levi, R. Faust und Hiob. Nord & Süd, Jan., 1913.
Lichtenberger, E. Faust devant l'Humanité. JbGG, 26, 1905.
Liljegren, S. B. The English Sources of Goethe's Gretchen Tragedy. Lund, 1937.
Lohmeyer, D. Faust und die Welt. Potsdam, 1940.
Maass, E. Ein griechischer Vorläufer des Mephistopheles. JbGG, 1922.
Maddalena, E. La tragedia di Gretchen. NAnt, 1929.
Manacorda, G. Problemi eterni del Faust. NAnt, 16.VII.1931.
Meek, G. J. Faust: The Man and the Myth. Oxford U. P., 1930.
Menza, A. Faust e Giobbe. Catania, 1888.
Meyer, W. Nürnberger Faustgeschichten. SBAW, 1895.
Meyer-Benfey, H. Die Entstehung des Urfaust. PJb, 1923.
——— Lessings Faustpläne. GRM, 1924.
Miller, R. D. The Meaning of Goethe's Faust. Cambridge, 1939.
Mizener, A. The Tragedy of Marlowe's Doctor Faustus. College English, 5, 1943.
Mohr, W. Mephistopheles und Loki. DVLG, 18, 1940.
Morley, H. Marlowe's Faustus and Goethe's Faust. London, 1883.
Muench, W. Die innere Stellung Marlowes zum Volksbuch vom Faust. Bonn, 1879.
Mueller, E. H. Concerning the Regensburg Print of the Volkslied vom Doktor Faust. GQ, 13, 1940.
Müller, G. Geschichte der deutschen Seele. Vom Faustbuch bis Goethes Faust. Freiburg, 1939.
Nessler, N. Die Faustsage und deren Behandlung. Kultu, 7 (Wien), 1906.
——— Zur Entwicklungsgeschichte der Faustsage. Progr. Brogenz, 1916.
Neubert, F. Von Dr. Faustus zu Goethes Faust. Leipzig, 1929.
Novak, B. Die Persönlichkeit Fausts in den Bearbeitungen von Goethe. Diss. Prag, 1925.
Nover, J. Deutsche Sagen in ihrer Entstehung und poetischen Gestaltung. Giessen, 1895.
Obenauer, K. J. Der faustische Mensch. Jena, 1923.
Palmer, P. M. & More, R. P. The Sources of the Faust Tradition, from Simon Magus to Lessing. New York, 1936.
Peter, F. Die Literatur der Faustsage systematisch zusammengestellt. Leipzig, 1857.
Petersen, J. Faustdichtungen nach Goethe. DVLG, 1936.
Petsch, R. Magussage und Faustdichtung. ZDK, 1920. And in: Gehalt und Form. Hamburg, 1925.
——— Goethes Faust und das griechische Altertum. GRM, 1924.
——— Nordisches und Südliches in Goethes Faust. Goethe Vierteljahrsschrift, 1936.
Petzhold, J. Beiträge zur Faustlitteratur. Anzeiger für Bibl. und Bibliothekwissenschaft, 1858-83.
Pitcher, S. M. Some Observations on the 1663 Edition of Faustus. MLN, 56, 1941.
Pniower, O. Goethes Faust, Zeugnisse und Excurse zu seiner Entstehungsgeschichte. Berlin, 1899.
Praz, M. Il dottore Faust: Marlowe e Goethe. Cultura, 1932.
Radermacher, L. Griechische Quellen zur Faustsage. SAWW, 1927.
Rémond, A. & Soula, G. Faust et Saint Sébastien. MF, 1.II.1913.
Richards, A. E. Studies in English Faust Literature. Berlin, 1907.
Ristelhuber, P. Faust dans l'histoire et dans la légende. Paris, 1863.
Rohde, R. Das englische Faustbuch und Marlowes Tragödie. Halle, 1910.
Runge, R. Das Faust-Mephisto-Motiv in deutscher Dichtung. Diss. Bonn, 1933.
Sams, H. W. Faustus and the Reformation. Bull. of the Citadel, 5, 1941.
Sayers, D. L. The Faust Legend and the Idea of the Devil. PEGS, N. S., 15, 1946.
Schade, O. Faust: Vom Aufstieg bis zur Verklärung durch Goethe. Berlin, 1912.
Schmidt, E. Le Faust de Marlowe et ses rapports avec les livres allemands et anglais. Jb. f. roman. & englische Sprache & Litteratur, 1875.
——— Zur Vorgeschichte des Goetheschen Faust. JbGG, 1881-83.
——— Das Verhältniss der deutschen Volksschauspiele zu Marlowes Tragical History of Dr. Faustus. SAWB, 1900.
Steiner, A. The Faust Legend and the Christian Tradition. PMLA, 54, 1939.
Steiner, Olga. Das zeitgeschichtliche Element in den Faustgestaltungen der Stürmer und Dränger. New York, 1942.
Stockmann, A. Die dichterischen Gestaltungen der Faustsage. Stimmen der Zeit, 1929.
Thalmann, M. Weltanschauung im Puppenspiel vom Dr. Faust. PMLA, 52, 1937.
Tille, A. Die deutschen Volkslieder von Doktor Faust. Halle, 1890.

——— Die Faustsplitter in der Litteratur des XVI. bis XVIII. Jahrhunderts nach den ältesten Quellen. Weimar, 1898.
——— Neue Faustsplitter aus dem 16. 17. und 18. Jahrhundert. ZVL, 9, 1896.
Traumann, E. Faustsage und Faustdichtung vor Goethe. In: Goethes Faust. München, 1911.
Unger, R. Von Nathan zu Faust. Basel. 1916.
Vallet, H. E. Le Faust de Lessing. L'Age nouveau, 23.
Velde, A. van der. Marlowes Faust, die älteste dramatische Bearbeitung der Faustsage. Breslau, 1870.
Walz, J. A. Increase Mather and Dr. Faustus, an American Faustsplitter. GR,15,1940.
Warkentin, R. Nachklänge der Sturm- und Drangperiode in der Faustdichtung. München, 1896.
Wehrle. Fausts Persönlichkeit in Geschichte und Dichtung. Progr. Duisburg, 1911.
Wendriner, K. G. Die Faust-Dichtung vor, neben, und nach Goethe. 4 vols. Berlin, 1914.
Witkowski, G. Goethes Faust; mit Kommentar und Erläuterungen. Leipzig, 1929.
Wolf, E. Faust und Luther. Halle, 1912.
Zarncke, F. Bibliographie des Faustbuches. In: Bericht der königl. sächsischen Ges. der Wissenschaften, 1888.

3. Werther and Other Works.

Appell, J. W. Werther und seine Zeit. Oldenburg, 1896.
Atkins, S. P. The Testament of Werther in Poetry and Drama. Harvard U. P., 1949.
Bertaut, J. L'anniversaire de Werther. RRh, 1922.
Boerner, C. G. Werther-Literatur. Leipzig, 1909.
Borghese, G. A. L'attualità del Werther. RI, 1928.
Cora, M. Sul Tasso di Goethe. La Ronda, Oct., 1920.
Feise, E. Zu Entstehungsproblem und Technik von Goethes Werther. JEGPh, 1914.
Flashar, D. Bedeutung, Entwicklung und literarische Nachwirkung von Goethes Mignongestalt. (Wilhelm Meister). Berlin, 1929.
Gaede, W. Goethes Torquato Tasso im Urteil von Mit- und Nachwelt. Diss. München, 1931.
Gugitz, G. Das Wertherfieber in Oesterreich. Wien, 1906.
Hegeman, D. Boswell and the Abt Jerusalem: A Note on the Background of Werther. JEGPh, 44, 1945.
Hermenjat, L. Werther et les frères de Werther. Lausanne, 1892.
Hillebrand, K. Die Wertherkrankheit in Europa. In: Zeiten, Völker und Menschen, 7. Berlin, 1874-85.
Marggraff, H. Goethes Werther im Auslande. Blätter f. literar. Unterhaltung, 46, 1855.
Montégut, E. Werther, types modernes en littérature. RDM, 15.VII.1855.
Morel, L. Les principales imitations de Werther, 1788-1813. Archiv, 121.
Piccoli, V. L'atmosfera del Werther. Illustraz. ital., 59, 1932.
Tiersot, J. Les adaptations scèniques de Werther. Le Livre et l'Image, 1893.
Withington, R. The Letters of Charlotte, an Antidote to Die Leiden des jungen Werthers. PMLA, 27, 1912.

4. Goethe's Influence upon America.

Blankenagel, J. C. An Early American Review of Die Wahlverwandtschaften. JEGPh, 1936.
Cunz, D. Die Marylander Goethe Gesellschaft. MDU, 38, 1946.
Everson, I. G. Goethe's American Visitors. AL, Nov., 1937.
Francke, K. Goethes Vermächtniss an Amerika. Pädagog. Monatshefte, 1900. And in: German Ideals of Today. Boston, 1907.
Geiger, L. Amerikanische Stimmen über Goethe. MLIA, 1888.
Grimm, H. Iphigenie in Amerika. DR, June, 1900.
Grueningen, J. P. von. Goethe in American Periodicals, 1860-1900. PMLA, 50, 1935.
Haney. Goethe in England and America. MLN, 16, 1901.
Hatfield, J. T. Goethe and the Ku-Klux Klan. PMLA, 37, 1922.
Heinemann, W. Goethes Faust in England Amerika. Bibliographische Zusammenstellung. Berlin, 1886.
Holmes, H. A. Una interpretación pampeana de Goethe y Gounod. RIA, 10, 1946.
Klenze, C. von. America and Goethe. Goethe Memorial Volume. Madison, 1932.
——— Das amerikanische Goethebild. Mitteil. der Akad. zur wissenschaftl. Erforschung und zur Pflege des Deutschtums, 1933.
Knortz, K. Goethe in Amerika. In: Goethe und die Wertherzeit. Zürich, 1885.
Leuchs, F. A. H. Goethe on the German-American Stage. GR, 10, 1935.
Lieder, F. W. C. Goethe in England and America. JEGPh, 10, 1911.
Long, O. W. The Attitude of Eminent Englishmen and Americans toward Werther. MPh, 14, 1916.
——— English and American Imitations of Goethe's Werther. MPh, 14, 1916.
——— Werther in America. Festschrift J. A. Walz. Lancaster (Pa.), 1941.
Mackall, L. L. Briefwechsel zwischen Goethe und Amerikanern. JbGG, 25, 1906.

Magyar, F. English Faust Plays on the New York Stage. GQ, 16, 1943.
Morgan, B. Q. Goethe's Faust in Recent Translation. Stanford Studies in Lang. and Lit., 1941.
Muhlberger, J. Goethe und America. Aufbau, 8, 1947.
Neuendorff, H. G. Goethe in Lateinamerika. Viermonatsschrift der Goethe Ges., 5, 1940.
Nordmeyer, H. W. Eine amerikanische Uebersetzung von Goethes Götz. JEGPh, 16, 1917.
Oswald, E. Goethe in England and America. NSp, 1899 & PEGS, 1909.
Reyes, A. Goethe y América. Monterrey, July, 1932.
——— Goethe und Amerika. Deutsche Blätter, 4. Santiago (Chile), 1946.
Schreiber, C. F. Goethe in Amerika. JbGG, 14, 1928.
——— Goethe und Amerika. JbGG, 18, 1932.
Varia. Homenage a Goethe. Anales de la U. de Chile, 1932.
Wadepuhl, W. Goethe und Amerika. Deutsch-amerikan. Geschichtsblätter. Urbana, 1925.
White, H. S. Goethe in Amerika. JbGG, 5, 1884.

5. Goethe's Influence upon England.

Anon. Goethes Faust in England. Blätter zur Kunde der Litteratur des Auslands, 1837.
——— Goethes Faust im englischen Gewande. Signale für die litterar. Welt, 1886.
——— Two New Translations of Faust. Academy, 1889.
——— Articles on English Translations of Goethe's Faust in: Westminster Review, 25; Cornhill Magazine, 26; Blackwood's Mag., 47; Saturday Review, 54-55; Living Age, 115.
——— Goethe in Inghilterra. Cultura, 1932.
Adams, W. D. Goethe in England. In: With Poet and Player. London, 1891.
Alford, R. G. Goethe's Earliest Critics in England. PEGS, 7, 1893.
Baumann, L. Die englischen Uebersetzungen von Goethes Faust. Halle, 1907.
Benson, A. B. English Criticism of the Prologue in Heaven in Goethe's Faust. MPh, 20, 1922.
Bluhm, H. S. The Reception of Goethe's Faust in England after the Middle of the Nineteenth Century. JEGPh, 34, 1935.
Böschenstein, H. Das literarische Goethebild der Gegenwart in England. Breslau, 1934.
Brandl, A. Die Aufnahme von Goethes Jugendwerken in England. JbGG, 3, 1882.
——— Goethe und England. F&F, 31, 1932.
Brown, P. H. The Character of Goethe. QR, April, 1907.
Bruford, W. H. Goethe in England. Geist der Zeit, 16, 1939.
Carr, Mary. Goethe in his Connection with English Literature. PEGS, 4, 1890.
Carré, J. M. Goethe en Angleterre. Paris, 1920. Cf. Journal des Débats, 25.II.1921.
Cazamian, M. L. Le roman et les idées en Angleterre. Paris, 1935.
Chotzner, H. Eine englische Stimme über den alten Goethe. MLIA, 1890.
Cooper, W. A. Translating Goethe's Poems. JEGPh, Oct., 1928.
Courtney, W. L. Faust on the English Stage. Fortnightly Review, 1886.
Dobert, P. Drei neue englische Faustübersetzungen. MLIA, 1881.
Dummer, E. H. Goethe in English. MDU, 36, 1944.
Fiedler, H. G. Goethe's Lyric Poems in English Translation. MLR, 18, 1923.
Gottbrath, K. Der Einfluss von Goethes Wilhelm Meister auf die englische Literatur. München, 1937.
Groeper, R. Goethe und England. Archiv f. Wanderungswesen und Auslandskunde, 11, 1940-41.
Haldane, Viscount. Was ist Goethe den Engländern? Nord & Süd, 1912.
Hauhart, W. F. The Reception of Goethe's Faust in England in the First Half of the Nineteenth Century. New York, 1909.
Hayens, K. C. Goethe and English Letters. GLL, 3, 1939.
Heinemann, W. English Translations and Annotated Editions of Faust. Bibliographer, 2, 1882.
——— Goethes Faust in England und Amerika. Berlin, 1886.
——— The Lyceum Faust. PEGS, 2, 1886.
——— Goethe on the English Stage. PEGS, 4, 1888.
Herzfeld, G. Ein Schotte über Weimar und Goethe. Archiv, 94, 1895.
——— Ein englischer Faustroman und ein englisches Faustdrama. JbGG, 1906.
Hill, C. J. The First English Translator of Werther (1779). MLN, 47, 1932.
Hinz, S. M. Goethe's Lyric Poems in English Translation after 1860. U. of Wisconsin Studies, 26, 1929.
Holland, B. Goethe's Hermann and Dorothea. Dublin Review, July, 1923.
Howe, Susanne. Wilhelm Meister and his English Kinsmen, Apprentices to Life. Columbia U. P., 1930.
Kindt, H. Goethes Faust in England. Gegenwart, 5, 1874.
Lieder, F. W. C. Goethe in England and America. JEGPh, 10, 1911.
Loiseau, H. Goethe et les Anglais. RELV, 42, 1925.
Long, O. W. English Translations of Goethe's Werther. JEGPh, 14, 1915.

——— The Attitude of Eminent Englishmen and Americans toward Werther. MPh, 14, 1916.

——— English and American Imitations of Goethe's Werther. MPh, 14, 1916.

Lovett, R. M. Goethe in English Literature. OC, April, 1932.

Martens, L. Goethe und England. Tägliche Rundschau, 60, 1900.

McKillop, A. A Victorian Faust. PMLA, 40, 1925.

——— The First English Translator of Werther. MLN, 1928.

McLintock, R. The Five Best English Verse Translations of Faust. Manchester Goethe Soc. 1894.

Montgomery, M. The First English Version of Faust Part I and Dichtung und Wahrheit. PEGS, 3, 1926.

Morgan, B. Q. Three Translations of Goethe's Iphigenie auf Tauris. Festschrift A. Hohlfeld. Madison, 1925.

Nicoll, A. Faust on the English Stage. In: Das Buch des Goethe-Lessing Jahres. Braunschweig, 1929.

Norman, F. Goethe und das heutige England. JbGG, 17, 1931.

Oswald, E. Goethe in England and America. NSp, 7, 1899 & PEGS, 1909.

Reed, Lillian E. Fragmentary English Translations of Goethe's Faust. Diss. Yale, 1937.

Robertson, J. G. Goethe und England. GRM, 20, 1932 & JbGG, 18, 1932.

Sanborn, F. B. Goethe's Relation to English Literature. In: Life and Genius of Goethe. Boston, 1886. And in: Dudley's Poetry and Philosophy of Goethe. Chicago, 1887.

Simmons, L. Goethe's Lyric Poems in English Translation prior to 1860. Madison, 1919.

Smith, H. An English Translation of Goethe's Clavigo. MLR, 8, 1913.

Stanger, H. Zwei englische Faustübersetzer. Archiv, 106, 1901.

Tait, J. Goethe's Influence in England, 1832-52. Academy, 39, 1891.

——— The Literary Influence of Goethe's Faust in England, 1832-52. Trans. Manchester Goethe Soc., 1894.

Vara, S. Faust im Englischen. Neue Freie Presse, 15825, 1908.

Vollrath, W. Goethe und Grossbritannien. Erlangen, 1932.

Walz, J. A. An English Faustsplitter. MLN, 1927.

Waterhouse, G. A Unique Translation of Goethe's Faust (Urfaust). Discovery, Sept., 1927.

Willoughby, L. A. An Early English Translation of Goethe's Tasso. MLR, 9, 1914.

6. Goethe's Influence upon France.

Anon. French Criticism of Werther. London Mag., 1, 1820.

——— Faust in Paris. Frankfurter Zt., 21.XII.1912.

Arnold, M. A French Critic on Goethe. In: Mixed Essays. London, 1879.

Baldensperger, F. La resistance à Werther dans la littérature française. RHLF, 1901.

——— Notes sur la prononciation française du nom de Goethe. Euphorion, 9, 1902.

——— Le Faust de Goethe et le romantisme français. MF, 41, 1902.

——— Goethe en France. Paris, 1904 & 1920.

——— Bibliographie critique de Goethe en France. Paris, 1907.

——— Quelques lettres inédites de romantiques français à Goethe. RHLF, 1908.

——— Goethe et la Revue des Deux Mondes. Journal des Débats, 2.XII.1929.

——— Goethe et la Légion d'honneur. RP, 39, 1932.

——— Pour une interprétation correcte de l'épisode d'Euphorion. RLC, 12, 1932.

Bettelheim, A. Goethe in Frankreich. JbGG, 7-8, 1886-87.

Betz, L. P. Werther in Frankreich. Bibliographische Studie. Zs. f. Bücherfreunde, 1903.

Bonmariage, S. La gloire française de Goethe. NRC, 1923.

Cart, W. Goethes Faust in französischer Uebersetzung. Leipzig, 1875.

Charléty, S. Le centenaire de Goethe à la Sorbonne. Annales de l'U. de Paris, 1932.

Chassé, C. Goethe et la France. Bull. du livre français, 1932.

Dargan, E. C. Goethe and France. OC, 913, 1932.

Denis, C. Goethe en France: Succès du germanisme, crise du latinisme. Annales de philosophie chrétienne, Dec., 1904.

Ducros, L. Goethe et le romantisme français. Bull. de la Faculté des lettres de Poitiers, Nov., 1886.

Duentzer, H. Goethe nach den Friedensschlüssen mit Frankreich. MLIA. 1872.

Ehrlich, G. Uebersetzungen von Faust-Stellen als Offenbarungen des französischen Geistes. JEGPh, 1936.

Friederiszick, F. K. Goethe vu par la France d'aujourd'hui. RELV, 1933-34.

Geiger, L. Die Braut von Korinth als französisches Drama. Gegenwart, 40, 1888.

Gross, F. Zwei französische Werthergestalten. MLIA, 1886.

——— Werther in Frankreich. Leipzig, 1888.

——— Goethes Faust in Frankreich. Leipzig, 1889.

Heinermann, T. Goethe in Frankreich. Euphorion, 33, 1932.

Heynen, W. Goethe-Forschung in Frankreich. Grenzboten, 25.VII.1917.

Kube, K. H. Goethes Faust in französischer

Auffassung und Bühnendarstellung. Berlin, 1932.
Langkavel, Martha. Die französischen Uebertragungen von Goethes Faust. Diss. Zürich. Strassburg, 1902.
Lasserre, P. Faust en France. RP. 1.XII.1926 & Paris, 1929.
Leitzmann, A. Verkannte französische Uebersetzungen aus Schiller und Goethe. GRM, 12, 1924.
Lichtenberger, H. Goethe et la France. NL, 9.IV.1932. And in: JbGG, 18, 1932.
Lindau, P. Goethes Faust in Frankreich. Gegenwart, 4, 1873.
Lindau, H. Französische Aufklärungen über Goethes Faust. Frankfurter Zt., 51, 1906.
Loiseau, H. Goethe et la France. Neuchâtel, 1930.
——— Goethe en France. GRM, 20, 1932. And in: Deutsch-franz. Rundschau, 1932.
Lowenthal. Goethe et la France. Revue mondiale, 1927.
Luebke, W. Eine französische Faustübersetzung. Beilage zur Allg. Zt., 31, 1893.
Morel, L. Hermann et Dorothée en France. RHLF, 12, 1905.
——— Werther au théâtre en France. Archiv, 118, 1907.
——— Les principales traductions de Werther et les jugements de la critique (1776-1872). Archiv, 119, 1907.
——— La fortune de Werther en France dans la poésie et le roman (1778-1816). Archiv, 125.
Oeftering, W. E. Werther traduit de l'allemand en 1801. GRM, 25, 1937.
Prodhomme, J. G. Les premières traductions françaises de Goethe. MF, 1931.
Rosenberg, F. Goethes Braut von Korinth in Frankreich. Archiv, 138, 1920.
Ross, Flora E. Goethe in Modern France: with Special Reference to Barrès, Bourget, Gide. Illinois Studies in Languages and Litterature. Urbana, 1937.
Schmidt, K. E. Faust in Frankreich. Die Zeit, 2028, 1908.
Schotthoefer, F. Der Kampf um Faust und jungfranzösische Mystik. LE, 15.I.1913.
Sondheim, M. Werther und der Weltschmerz in Frankreich. Frankfurt, 1929.
Sproude, M. Quelques contrefaçons françaises de Werther. Journal des Débats, 29.IX.1894.
Steiner, A. A French Faustsplitter of the Seventeenth Century. MLN, 53, 1938.
Suepfle, T. Goethes litterarischer Einfluss auf Frankreich. JbGG, 1887.
——— Goethes Faust in Frankreich. Strassburger Post, 13.VIII.1903.
——— Französische Faustübersetzungen. Beilage zur Allg. Zt., 76, 1903.
Texte, J. Le théâtre de Goethe et de Schiller en France au XVIIIe siècle. RCC, 28.V. 1896.
Tille, A. Goethes Faust in der modernen französischen Kunst. Der Lotse, 47, 1901.
Tronchon, H. Encore Goethe en France. RG, July, 1939.
Urbach, O. Goethe und Frankreich. CFA, 1938.
Wadepuhl, W. Goethes Stellung zur französischen Romantik. Madison, 1924.
Weiss, J. J. Les commentateurs de Werther. In: Sur Goethe. Paris, 1893.
Weisstein, G. Ein französischer Faustcommentar. MLIA, 1882.
Wilmotte, M. Goethe et la France. RFB, 1932.
——— Adieu, Goethe! RFB, 1933.
Wychgram, J. Eine französische Faustübersetzung. Blätter f. literar. Unterhaltung, 12, 1893.
Xantippus. Goethe und die Franzosen. MLIA, 1881.

7. Goethe's Influence upon Other Countries.

Anon. Werther in Kurland. (**BALTIC.**) Baltische Monatsschrift, 35, 1888.
——— Goethe in esthnischer Sprache. In: L'Estonie littéraire, 1932.
Petersen, O. von. Goethe und der baltische Osten. Reval, 1930.
——— Goethes Wirkung auf das baltische Geistesleben. Goethe, 4, 1939.
Pierard, L. Goethe et la Belgique. (**BELGIUM.**) Le Flambeau, 1932.
Eischer, O. Goethe et les Tchèques. (**CZECHOSLOVAKIA.**) L'Europe centrale, 19. & 26.III.1932.
Urzidil, J. Goethe in Boehmen. PJb, 1931.
Brandes, G. Goethe in **DAENEMARK.** JbGG, 2, 1881.
Michaelis, S. Goethes Faust in Dänemark. Deutsch-nord. Jb, 1929.
Schweitzer, P. Eine dänische Uebersetzung des Faust. MLIA, 53, 1882.
Koskinen, K. Goethe in **FINNLAND.** ZDPh, 57, 1932.
Ramsay, J. Werthers Lidanden; Wiborg. Finsk Tidskrift, Feb., 1915.
Anon. Vier niederländische Uebersetzungen von Goethes Faust. (**HOLLAND.**) MLIA, 1871.
Hooft, B. H. van T. Das holländische Volksbuch vom Dr. Faust. 's Gravenhage, 1926.
Menne, K. Goethes Werther in der niederländischen Literatur. Leipzig, 1905.
Scholte, J. H. Goethe und Holland. Mitteilungen d. Akademie zur wissenschaftl. Erforschung. & Pflege des Deutschtums, 1932. And in: JbGG, 18, 1932.
Van der Laan, J. E. Goethe in de nederlandsche Letterkunde. Amsterdam, 1933.
Bleyer, J. Goethe in Ungarn. (**HUNGARY.**) JbGG, 18, 1932.
Petz, G. Goethes Beziehungen zu Ungarn. Deutsch-ungar. Heimatblatt, 4, 1932.
Pukansky-Kadar, J. Goethes Faust auf der

ungarischen Bühne. Ungarische Jb., 14, 1934.
Sashegyi, O. A. Werther útja magyarországon. Archivum philologicum, 67, 1943.
Trostler, J. Goethe und die neue ungarische Literatur. Deutsch-ungar. Heimatblatt, 4, 1932.
Waterhouse, G. Goethe, Giesecke, and Dublin. (**IRELAND.**) Proceed. of the Royal Irish Acad., 50, 1943.
Anon. Werther in **ITALIA.** Critica, 37, 1939.
Beutler, E. Römische Goethefeiern. Frankfurter Zt., 13.IV.1932.
Bulle, O. Goethe e l'Italia. NAnt, 25, 1890.
Chiesa, M. W. Goethe negli scrittori Trentini. Studi Trentini di Scienze storiche, 13, 1933.
Croce, B. Il Goethe e la critica italiana. Critica, 20.XI.1918.
——— Vecchi giudizi italiani sul Faust. Critica, 1935.
——— Intorno a un' antologia di traduzioni italiane delle liriche del Goethe. Critica, 37, 1939.
——— Werther in Italia (1797). Critica, 37, 1939.
Emma. Due traduzioni del Fausto. NAnt, 23, 1873.
Fasola, G. Goethes Werke in italienischen Uebersetzungen. JbGG, 16, 1895.
——— Goethe è popolare in Italia? Riv. di lett. ted., 3, 1909.
——— Goethe und sein italienisches Publikum. JbGG, 1909.
Geiger, L. Goethes Beziehungen zu Italien. Die Nation, 16, 1891.
Imperatori, G. Goethe e gli scrittori d'Italia. Udine, 1937.
Kaden, W. Unser Faust bei den Italienern. Die Gegenwart, 1878. And in: Italienische Gipsfiguren. Oldenburg, 1881.
Luebke, W. Mephisto in Italien. Die Gegenwart, 1879.
Meyer, E. Goethe e i romantici italiani. Antologia, 20. (Firenze), 1825.
Michéa, R. Goethe au pays des lazaroni. Mélanges Jules Legras. Paris, 1939.
Pompeati, A. Traduzioni da Goethe. Marzocco, 29.V.1932.
Steiner, A. An Italo-German Faustsplitter of 1621. MLN, 54, 1939.
Stranik, E. Goethe und die italienische Kritik. Freie Welt, 23.X.1926.
Tecchi, B. Libri italiani su Goethe nel primo centenario della nascita. Rassegna nazionale, 1932-33.
Thiemann, T. Die Aufnahme der Goetheschen Werke in Italien. In: Deutsche Kultur und Litteratur des XVIII. Jahrhunderts im Lichte der zeitgenössischen italienischen Kritik. Oppeln, 1886.
Tschudy, U. de. Goethe e la critica italiana. Tevere, 3.III.1932.
Zaniboni, E. La Italienische Reise del Goethe e la sua fortuna in Italia. Fanfulla della Domenica. 1.I.1906.
Kimura, K. Goethe in **JAPAN.** Berlin, 1942.
Glasenapp, O. von. Goethe im **ORIENT.** DR, June, 1925.
Witt, B. Goethe und der Osten. Ostdeutsche Monatshefte, 1932.
Anon. Goethes Einfluss auf die polnische Literatur. (**POLAND.**) Die Wage, 1915.
Bratanek. F. T. (ed.) Zwei Polen in Weimar. Wien, 1870.
Ciechanowska, Zofia. Die Anfänge der Goethe-Kenntnis in Polen. GS, 1932-33.
——— L'oeuvre de Goethe et le romantisme polonais. Bull. de l'Acad. polonaise, 1932.
——— Das Goethe-Jahr in Polen. GS, 2, 1933.
——— Goethe in Polish Literature. SR, 12, 1933.
——— Poland and Goethe. SR, 1933-34.
German. Eine polnische Uebersetzung der Iphigenie. MLIA, 1880.
Karpeles, G. Goethe in Polen. Berlin, 1890.
Klingsland, Z. S. La Pologne à Weimar. NL, 15.XI.1932.
Kurtzmann, L. Goethes Beziehungen zu polnischen Dichtern. MLIA, 1879.
Lipnicki, E. Zur Goethe-Litteratur in Polen. Augsburger Allg. Zt., 19, 1882.
Salles, A. Les relations polonaises de Goethe. Télégramme de Toulouse, 5.VI.1932.
Smogorzewski, C. Goethe et la Pologne. La Pologne, 1932.
Sternbach, H. Goethes Faust im polnischen Gewande. GS, 2, 1932-33.
Tardowski, J. von. Goethe und Polen, Polen und Goethe. JbGG, 19, 1933.
Cordeiro Ramos, G. A lauda faustiana na literatura portuguesa e espanhola. (**PORTUGAL.**) In: O Fausto de Goethe. Coimbra, 1916.
Engel, E. Goethes Faust in Portugal. MLIA, 17, 1880.
Feder, E. Faust in Portuguese Garb. BA, 18, 1944.
Reinhardstoettner, K. von. Goethes Faust in Portugal. In: Aufsätze & Abhandlungen. Berlin, 1887.
Gherghel, I. Goethe dans la littérature roumaine. Avec une vue d'ensemble sur l'influence allemande en général. (**RUMANIA.**) Bucarest, 1931. Cf. RLC, 1934.
——— Bibliografie critica despre Goethe in literatura romana. Revista Germanistilor Romani, 5, 1936.
Munteano, B. Goethe et l'influence allemande en Roumanie. L'Europe centrale, 27.I.1934.
Buchstab, B. Les traductions de Goethe en russe. Bibliographie. (**RUSSIA.**) In: Literaturnoe Nasledstvo. Moskva, 1932.
Bem, A. Der russische Antiwertherismus. GS, 2, 1932-33.
Bittner. Die Faustsage im russischen Schrifttum. ZDPh, 35.

Borchardt, M. Goethes Würdigung in Russland. 1828.
Durylin, S. Russian Writers with Goethe in Weimar. (In Russian). In: Literaturnoe Nasledstvo, 4-6. Moskva, 1932.
Frank, S. Goethe in Russland. GS, 2, 1932-33.
Gorlin, M. Goethe in Russland. ZSPh, 9-10, 1932-33.
Harnack, O. Goethes Beziehungen zu russischen Schriftstellern. ZVL, 3, 1889-90. And in: Essays und Studien. Braunschweig, 1889. Cf. PL, 2, 1890.
Jagoditsch, R. Goethe und seine russischen Zeitgenossen. GS, 1, 1931-32.
——— Goethe in der zeitgenössischen russischen Literatur. GS, 2, 1932-33.
Kallasch, W. W. Goethes Beziehungen zu Russland. (In Russian). In: Pod znamenem nauki. Moskva, 1902.
Koenig, H. Goethe in Russland. Frankfurter Telegraph, April, 1837.
Pogodin, A. Goethe in Russland. GS, 1, 1931-32.
Rozanov, M. N. Goethe in Russian Translations. Geteana, 1, 1932.
Schiller, F. P. Goethe and his Time. Geteana, 1, 1932.
Serguievsky, J. Goethe dans la critique russe. In: Literaturnoe Nasledstvo. Moskva, 1932.
Sipovski, V. D. L'influence de Werther sur le roman russe du XVIIIe siècle. Journal du Ministère de l'instr. publique, Jan., 1906.
Volkov. Goethe dans le théâtre russe. In: Literaturnoe Nasledstvo. Moskva, 1932.
Wahl, H. Russische Weisheitsfreunde bei Goethe und im Goethehaus. Goethe, 3, 1937.
Zabel, E. Goethe und Russland. JbGG, 8, 1921.
Zhirmunskii, V. Goethe in Russian Poetry. In: Literaturnoe Nasledstvo, 4-6, 1932.
——— Goethe in Russian Literature. (In Russian). Leningrad, 1937.
Zoubov, V. La littérature russe sur Goethe. In: Literaturnoe Nasledstvo. Moskva, 1932. Cf. RLC, 14, 1934.

Borelius, H. Goethe und **SKANDINAVIEN.** GRM, 20, 1932.

Masaryk, T. G. & Lunacharsky, A. V. Slav Verdicts on Goethe. (**SLAVS.**) SR, 11, 1932.

Matl, J. Goethe bei den Slaven. Jb. f. Kultur & Geschichte der Slaven, 1932.

Varia. Goethe und die Slaven. GS, 1932-33.

Wukadinovic, S. Goethe und die slavische Welt. JbGG, 18, 1932.

Bertrand, J. J. A. Goethe en Espagne. (**SPAIN.**) Mélanges Baldensperger. Paris, 1930.

Brachfeld, O. Goethe en Espagne. RLC, 12, 1932.

Farinelli, A. Guillaume de Humboldt et l'Espagne: Goethe et l'Espagne. Torino, 1924 & Paris, 1936.
Montoline, M. de. Goethe en la literatura catalana. Barcelona, 1935.
Morente, G. Goethe und die hispanische Welt. JbGG, 18, 1932.
Suarez de Urbina, J. Algunas influencias del Fausto de Goethe en España. Revista de Cultura y Vida Universitaria. (Zaragoza), 1927.
Anon. Goethe in Svezia. (**SWEDEN.**) Cultura, 1932.
Graef, H. G. Goethe und Schweden. In: Goethe Skizzen. Leipzig, 1924.
Wrangel, E. Werther und das Wertherfieber in Schweden. JbGG, 1908.
Bohnenblust, G. Goethe und die Schweiz. (**SWITZERLAND.**) Frauenfeld, 1932.
Reynold, G. de. Goethe, Schiller et la Suisse. Voile latine, July, 1905.
Strich, F. Goethe und die Schweiz. CL, 1, 1949.
Milovic, J. Goethes Einfluss auf die serbokroatische Literatur. (**YUGOSLAVIA.**) Geist der Zeit, 4.IV.1939.
Trivunac, M. Goethe et les Yougoslaves. RLC, 12, 1932.
——— Das Goethejahr in Jugoslavien. GS, 2, 1933.
Warnier, R. Goethe et les Yougoslaves. L'Europe centrale, 30.IV.1932.

8. Goethe's Influence upon Individual Authors.

Schweinfurth, P. Goethe et Seroux d'**AGINCOURT.** RLC, 12, 1932.
Bouvier, B. **AMIEL** et le Faust de Goethe. Mélanges Baldensperger, Paris, 1930.
Thomson, O. R. H. **ANDREYEV'S** Anathema and the Faust Legend. NAR, Dec., 1911.
Guglia, E. Die römischen Elegien des Gabriele d'**ANNUNZIO** und ihr Verhältnis zu Goethe. Chronik des Wiener Goethe-Vereins, 15, 1902.
Anon. Goethe and Matthew **ARNOLD.** Comtemporary Review, Aug., 1881.
Orrick, J. B. Matthew Arnold and Goethe. PEGS, 4, 1927.
Preisinger, H. Matthew Arnold on Goethe. Trans. Manchester Goethe Soc., 1894.
White, H. C. Matthew Arnold and Goethe. PMLA, 36, 1921.
Black, Greta A. P. J. **BAILEY'S** Debt to Goethe's Faust in his Festus. MLR, 28, 1932.
Baldensperger, F. **BALZAC** sur les pas de Goethe l'Européen. BURS, 1927.
Krappe, A. H. Goethe et Balzac. Neuphilol. Mitteilungen, 40, 1940.
Weisstein, G. Ein französischer Goethefresser (**BARBEY D'AUREVILLY.**) MLIA, 7, 1881.
Baldensperger, F. L'appel goethéen chez Maurice **BARRES.** RLC, 5, 1925.

Chappey, J. M. Barrès, Goethe et l'Austrasie. RP, 15.VII.1925.

Koehler, R. Goethe und der italienische Dichter Domenico **BATACCHI.** Bericht der königl. sächs. Ges. f. Wissenschaften 1890. And in: Kleinere Schriften, 3. Berlin, 1898.

Glayton, V. The Relation of Joseph by **BITAUBE** to Goethe's Hermann und Dorothea. RR, 1937.

Hennig, J. John Stuart **BLACKIE'S** Translation of Goethe's Jahrmarktsfest zu Plundersweilen. MLQ, 8, 1947.

Anon. Henri **BLAZE** über Goethe und den zweiten Teil des Faust. Blätter zur Kunde der Litt. des Auslands, 1839.

——— Edition française des Oeuvres lyriques de Goethe publiée par Blaze de Bury. RDM, 1.VII.1843.

Langkavel, M. Blazes Uebersetzung des 2. Teiles von Goethes Faust. Festschrift Morf. Halle, 1905.

Lerminier. Le Faust de Goethe, traduction de Henri Blaze. La poésie allemande et l'esprit français. RDM, 15.VI.1846.

Trivunac, M. Janko **BORISLAVIC,** K. S. Gjalskog i Goethe. Misao, 38, 1932.

Reed, Lillian E. **BORROW'S** Translation of the Walpurgisnacht. JEGPh, 44, 1945.

Speck, W. A. George Borrow and Goethe's Faust. PMLA, 41, 1926.

Steiner, A. Ein vergessener Epigone Werthers in Frankreich. (**BRIDEL.**) Archiv, 165, 1934.

Rhyme, O. P. **BROWNING** and Goethe. MLN, 44, 1929.

Bangs, A. R. Mephistopheles in England. (**BULWER.**) PMLA, 1932.

Goldhan, A. H. Ueber die Einwirkung des Goetheschen Werther und Wilhelm Meister auf die Entwicklung Edward Bulwers. Leipzig, 1895. Cf. Anglia, 16.

Althaus, F. On the Personal Relations between Goethe and **BYRON.** PEGS, 1888. And in: Beilage zur Allg. Zt., 24-25, 1888.

Brandl, A. Goethe und Byron. Oesterreichische Rundschau, 1, 1883.

——— Goethes Verhältnis zu Byron. JbGG, 20, 1899.

Eimer, M. Schopenhauer als Abgesandter Goethes an Byron. ESn, 49, 1916.

Garnett, R. Note on a Mistranslation of Goethe's in Byron's Manfred. PEGS, 2, 1886.

Holl, K. Goethes Vollendung in ihrer Beziehung zu Byron und Carlyle. GRM, 9, 1920-21.

Knobbe, A. Die Faust-Idee in Lord Byrons Dichtungen. Progr. Stralsund, 1906.

Koch, J. Goethe und Byron. Archiv, 1933.

Krummel, C. G. Byron and Goethe. SAQ, 22, 1923.

Matenko, P. The Goethe, Schiller, and Byron Translations of the Saaling Album. MLQ, 6, 1945.

Mazzini, G. Byron e Goethe. (1839). RI, 1907.

Mickiewicz, A. Goethe et Byron. In: Mélanges, 5, 1872. Cf. MLIA, 1879.

Robertson, J. G. Goethe and Byron. PEGS, 2, 1925.

Rose, W. From Goethe to Byron: the Development of Weltschmerz in German Literature. New York, 1924.

Sand, G. Essai sur le drame fantastique: Goethe, Byron, Mickiewicz. RDM, 20, 1839.

Schanz, J. Byrons Verhältnis zu Goethe. Wiener Blätter f. Musik, Theater & Kunst, 26-29, 1857.

Sinzheimer, S. Goethe und Lord Byron. Eine Darstellung der persönlichen und literarischen Verhältnisse mit Berücksichtigung des Faust und Manfred. München, 1894.

Strich, F. Goethe und Byron. Horen, 5, 1929.

Valentin, V. Goethes Verhältniss zu Lord Byron. Berichte d. freien deutschen Hochstifts Frankfurt, 1900.

Werner, J. Die persönlichen und litterarischen Wechselbeziehungen zwischen Goethe und Byron. Ibid. 1885-86.

Pfund, H. W. George Henry **CALVERT,** Admirer of Goethe. Festschrift J. A. Walz. Lancaster (Pa.), 1941.

CAMPO, E. del. Faust. Adapted from the Spanish and Rendered into English Verse by Walter Owen. Buenos Aires, 1943.

Mari, M. **CARDUCCI** e Goethe. Archiginnasio, 1934.

Schönfeld, P. Ein italienisches Urtheil über Goethes Gretchen. MLIA, 1881.

Anon. Letters by E. Oswald, J. A. Froude and Goethe (**CARLYLE** & Goethe.) Academy, 20.II.1880.

——— Carlyle and Goethe. Academy, 20. XI.1887.

——— Goethe and Carlyle. All Year Round, 40 & 59.

——— The Goethe-Carlyle Correspondence. AM, 59, 1887.

——— Correspondence between Goethe and Carlyle. Blackwood's Mag., July, 1887.

——— Goethe and Carlyle, a Comparison. Temple Bar, 86.

Baumann, E. D. Goethe en Carlyle. De 20. Eeuw, Dec., 1905.

Baumgarten, O. Carlyle und Goethe. Tübingen, 1906.

Boyesen, H. H. Goethe and Carlyle. In: Essays on German Literature. London, 1892.

Brie, F. Carlyle und Goethes Symbolum. Anglia, 66, 1942.

Flügel, E. Zu Goethes Verhältniss zu Carlyle. Grenzboten, 44, 1885.

——— Der Briefwechsel zwischen Goethe und Carlyle. Grenzboten, 46, 1887.

Francke, K. Carlyle and Goethe's Symbolum. PhQ, 1927.

Geiger, L. Goethe und Carlyle. Gegenwart, 1887.

Grimm, H. Goethe und Carlyles Briefwechsel. DR, 4, 1887.

Henriot, E. Goethe, Carlyle et Thackeray. Europe nouvelle, 15.X.1921.

Hernried, E. Goethes Verhältnis zu Carlyle. Der Morgen, 26. (Wien), 1911.

Hohlfeld, A. R. The Poems in Carlyle's Translation of Wilhelm Meister. MLN, 36, 1921.

Holl, K. Goethes Vollendung in ihrer Beziehung zu Byron und Carlyle. GRM, 9, 1921.

Kellner, L. Goethe und Carlyle. Nation, 25-26. 1896, And in: Englische Literatur im Zeitalter der Königin Viktoria. Leipzig, 1909.

Mackinnon, J. Carlyle and Goethe. In: Leisure Hours in the Study. London, 1897.

Meisels, S. Carlyle und Goethe. Die Wage, 10, 1907.

Mueller, M. Goethe and Carlyle. Contemporary Review, 1886 & London, 1886.

——— Carlyles persönliche Beziehungen zu Goethe. Berichte d. freien deutschen Hochstiftes Frankfurt 16, 1900.

Oswald, E. Goethe und Carlyle. MLIA, 1882.

——— Carlyle-Goethe-Froude. MLIA, 1886.

Plagens, H. Carlyles Weg zu Goethe. Berlin 1938.

Saenger, S. Thomas Carlyle und Goethe. Carlyle's Goetheporträt. Berlin, 1907.

Schreiber, C. F. Carlyle's Goethe Mask. Yale U. Library Gazette, 18, 1944.

Schröder, R. Thomas Carlyles Abhandlungen über den Goetheschen Faust. Archiv, 1896.

Thomas, C. Carlyle's Indebtedness to Goethe. Nation, 44, 1891.

Wagner, A. Goethe, Carlyle, Nietzsche and the German Middle Class. MDU, 31, 1939.

Schneider, F. Goethe, Heine und Emilio **CASTELAR.** PhQ, 1928.

Ruland, K. Goethe und **CASTELLI.** In: Festgabe zur Enthüllung des Wiener Goethe-Denkmals. Wien, 1900.

Bianquis, G. Le premier traducteur français de l'histoire de Faust (Palma **CAYET**). H&R, 2, 1935.

Kraus, E. W. Goethe a **CECHY.** Praha, 1896.

Cooper, W. A. Goethe's Tasso (and the Abbé de **CHARME**). JEGPh, 15, 1916.

Baldensperger, F. Les deux rencontres manquées entre Goethe et **CHATEAUBRIAND.** RLC, 23, 1949.

Dédéyan, C. Goethe et Chateaubriand. RLC, 23, 1949.

Soblik, P. Werther und René. Diss. Greifswald, 1916.

Delp, W. E. Goethe's Tasso in the Light of **CHEKOV.** CLS, 12, 1944-45.

Francke, K. Goethe and **COGSWELL.** Harvard Monthly, 10.

Anon. **COLERIDGE** über Goethes Faust. Blätter zur Kunde der Litteratur des Auslands, 1836.

Calvert, G. H. Coleridge, Shelley, Goethe. Boston, 1880.

Schreiber, C. F. Coleridge to Boosey—Boosey to Coleridge. (Faust). Yale U. Library Gazette, 22, 1947.

Betz, L. P. Benjamin **CONSTANT'S** Adolphe; ein westschweizerischer Wertherroman. In: Studien. Frankfurt, 1902.

Haas, A. Benjamin Constants Gespräche mit Goethe (1804). Euphorion, 7, 1900.

Chambon, F. Les correspondants de Victor **COUSIN:** Goethe. L'amateur d'autogr., 15.IX.1902.

Bergel, L. **CROCE** as a Critic of Goethe. CL, 1, 1949.

Anon. Alphonse **DAUDET** und Goethe. MLIA, 1879.

Morris, M. Goethe und Daudet. JbGG, 24, 1903.

Rousseaux, A. Goethe et Léon Daudet. Revue universelle, 1.VIII.1932.

Baldensperger, F. Notes biographiques sur l'un des premiers correspondants français de Goethe: le lieutenant **DEMARS.** RG, 1912.

Heinrich, A. Charles **DICKENS** und die Faust Outlines. Anglia, 49, 1926.

Hennig, J. Note on Dickens and Goethe. CLS, 23-24, 1946.

Propper, M. V. Goethe und eine Romanfigur **DOSTOJEVSKIJS.** GS, 2, 1932-33.

Weidle, W. Goethe et Dostoievsky. Le Mois, 1938.

Anon. Professor **DOWDEN** on Goethe. Archiv, 5.VI.1886.

——— Goethe und Alexandre **DUMAS.** Vossische Zt., 27.X.1900.

Herrig, H. Alexandre Dumas' Faust Vorrede. Ein Epilog. MLIA, 1873.

James, H. Alexandre Dumas and Goethe. Nation, 17, 1873.

Anon. **DWIGHT'S** Versions from Goethe and Schiller. NAR, April, 1839.

Braun, F. A. Goethe as Viewed by **EMERSON.** JEGPh, 15, 1916.

Goodnight, S. S. Emerson's Opinion of Goethe. German-American Annals, May, 1903.

Hagboldt, P. Emerson's Goethe. GR & OC, 1932.

Hopkins, V. C. The Influence of Goethe on Emerson's Aesthetic Theory. PhQ, 27, 1948.

Sakman, P. Emersons Goethebild. JbGG, 14, 1928.

Thomas, C. Emersons Verhältnis zu Goethe. JbGG, 24, 1903.

Wahr, F. B. Emerson and Goethe. Ann Arbor, 1915.

Lang, F. M. **EMINESCU** als Dichter und Denker. Cluj, 1928.
Buzzini, L. G. **FLAUBERT** et Goethe. RB, 18.X.1930.
Degoumois, L. Flaubert à l'école de Goethe. Genève, 1925.
Dumesnil, R. Deux des maîtres de Flaubert: Balzac et Goethe. In: En marge de Flaubert. Paris, 1928.
Martin du Gard, M. Sur le Faust d'Ed. **FLEG.** NL, 3.VI.1937.
Acquarone, J. Ugo **FOSCOLO.** Revue Européenne, 1.X.1860.
Bianchi, L. Werther e Jacopo Ortis, Melfi, 1924.
Deubner, F. Quelques remarques sur Werther de Goethe et Ultime Lettere di Jacopo Ortis de Foscolo. Wiesbaden, 1892.
Graf, A. Rileggendo le Ultime lettere di Jacopo Ortis. NAnt, 57, 1895.
Marpillero, G. Werther, Ortis e il Leopardi. GSLI, 36, 1900.
Pieper, K. Werther und Jacopo Ortis. Archiv, 47, 1925.
Zschech, F. Ugo Foscolos Ortis und Goethes Werther. ZVL, 3, 1889-90.
——— Der italienische Wertherroman Ugo Foscolos. Hamburg. Corresp., Lit. Beilage 3, 1906.
——— Sografis Komödie Werther und Ugo Foscolos Letzte Briefe des Jacopo Ortis. GRM, Nov., 1911.
Zumbini, B. Werther e Jacopo Ortis. Atti della R. Accad. di Napoli, 23, 1906. And in: Studi di letteratura comparata. Bologna, 1931.
Aron, A. W. A. **FRANCE** and Goethe. Festschrift A. R. Hohlfeld. Madison, 1925.
Fauconnet, A. Anatole France et Goethe: La Fiancée de Corinthe. MF, 1927.
Braun, F. A. Margaret **FULLER** and Goethe. New York, 1910.
——— Margaret Fuller's Translation and Criticism of Goethe's Tasso. JEGPh, 13, 1914.
Slochower, H. Margaret Fuller and Goethe. GR, 7, 1932.
Grillet, C. Goethe et **GAUTIER.** Grande Revue, 1932.
Poulet, G. Théophile Gautier et le second Faust. RLC, 22, 1948.
Werin, A. **GEIJER** och Goethe. Skrifter utgivna av Svenska litteratursällskapet i Finland, 1938.
Anon. **GIBSON'S** Translations of Goethe's Poems. Saturday Review, 57, 1884.
Baldensperger, F. André **GIDE** antigoethéen. RLC, 13, 1933.
La Harpe, Jacqueline de. Goethe, Gide, and Valéry. CL, 1, 1949.
Robertson, J. G. R. P. **GILLIES** and Goethe. MLR, 4, 1908.
Tronchon, H. Goethéenne d'Alsace: une correspondance d'Albert **GRUEN** sur Faust. Alsace française, 1932.
Boileau, D. A Few Remarks on Mr. **HAYWARD'S** English Prose Translation of Goethe's Faust. London, 1834.
Long, O. W. Frederic **HEDGE.** Portland (Me.), 1940.
Anon. Goethe and Victor **HUGO;** a Comparison. National Review, (London), 1900.
Baldensperger, F. Goethe et Hugo juges et parties. MF, 1.IX.1907.
Hers, J. A. Goethe's Egmont as a Possible Source of Hugo's Hernani. MPh, 27, 1929.
Jäckel, K. Goethe und Victor Hugo. ZFSL, 57, 1933.
Rouault, J. Au sujet de Goethe et de V. Hugo. Eurydice, 1933.
Serre, A. Le sublime Goethe et Victor Hugo. Paris, 1880.
Vaughan, E. Goethe and Hugo. BRL, 10, 1926.
Andrews, A. **IBSEN'S** Peer Gynt and Goethe's Faust. JEGPh, 13, 1914.
Petersen, J. Faust und Brand. Hamlet. Zwei Vorträge. Gotha, 1890.
Zucker, A. E. Goethe and Ibsen's Button-Moulder. PMLA, 57, 1941.
Church, H. W. Henry **IRVING** and Goethe's Faust. GR, 1928.
Kelley, C. P. The Early Development of Henry **JAMES.** U. of Illinois Studies in Language & Lit., 15, 1931.
Ermatinger, E. Gottfried **KELLER** und Goethe. PMLA, 1949.
Kahn, L. W. Goethes Iphigenie, Kleists Amphitryon und **KIERKEGAARD.** MDU, 39, 1947.
Oppel, H. Kierkegaard und Goethe. DVLG, 16, 1938.
Ezban, S. Pierre **LASSERRE,** Goethe et Nietzsche. RR, 38, 1947.
Trivunac, M. O Verteru. (L. K. **LAZAREVICA.**) SKG, 24-25, 1910.
Borgese, G. A. **LEOPARDI** Wertheriano e l'Omero di Ugo Foscolo. Mélanges Baldensperger. Paris, 1930.
Marpillero, G. Werther, Ortis e il Leopardi. GSLI, 36, 1900.
Evans, D. O. Une supercherie littéraire, le Werther français de Pierre **LEROUX.** RLC, 18, 1938.
Buechner, A. Eine französische Goethestudie. (Ernest **LICHTENBERGER.**) MLIA, 1882.
Nordmeyer, H. W. Zu Goethes Faust in England: J. G. **LOCKHART.** JEGPh, 17, 1918.
Anon. **LONGFELLOW'S** Golden Legend. Blackwood's Mag., Feb., 1852.
Chamberlin, W. A. Longfellow's Attitude toward Goethe. MPh, 16, 1918-19.
Kip, H. Z. The Origin of Longfellow's The Arrow and the Song. PhQ, 1930.
Long, O. W. Goethe and Longfellow. GR, 7, 1932.
Varenne, G. Goethe et Claude **LORRAIN.** RLC, 12, 1932.

Wurfl, G. **LOWELL'S** Debt to Goethe. State College (Pa.), 1936.

Bencze, E. La Tragédie de l'homme est-elle le Faust hongrois? (**MADACH.**) RLC, 14, 1934.

Hankiss, J. La Tragédie de l'homme. Revue des Etudes hongroises, 1935.

Beaumont, J. **MANZONI** and Goethe. Italian Studies, 7, 1939.

Lauber, K. G. Goethe und die Manzoniforschung. Hochland, 36, 1938.

Sacchi, E. Manzoni e Goethe. NAnt, 16. X.1919.

Sinigaglia, L. Relazioni di Goethe e Manzoni. Riv. contempor., 3. (Firenze), 1888. Cf. JbGG, 9, 1888.

Speyer, O. Manzoni und Goethe. Grenzboten, 15, 1889.

Zumbini, B. L'Egmont e il Conte di Carmagnola. Fanfulla della Domenica, 1890.

Bertrand, J. J. A. Goethe en Catalogne: J. **MARAGALL.** RLC, 12, 1932.

Montoliu, M. de. Maragall i Goethe. La Revista, 1932.

Siebenschein, H. Goethe und **MASARYK.** Bern, 1948.

Mehring, S. Faust im Französischen. (Pierre **MASCLAUX.**) LE, 15.XII.1910.

Krusemeyer, M. Der Einfluss Goethes auf George **MEREDITH.** ESn, 59, 1925.

Federmann, A. J. H. **MEYER,** Goethes Schweizer Freund, 1760-1823. Leipzig, 1936.

Brandes, G. Goethe und **MICKIEWICZ.** In: Polen. München, 1898.

Ciechanowska, Z. Mickiewicz a Goethe. Lwow, 1925.

Ettlinger, A. Goethe und Mickiewicz. Beilage zur Allg. Zt., 196, 1900.

Meller, E. Die Begegnung zweier Dichterfürsten (Goethe & Mickiewicz). Union, 282-83. (Prag), 1912.

Loewe, P. Goethe und der Sarajlija **MILUTINOWITSCH.** Wiener Fremdenblatt, 82, 1903.

Hamburger, L. Ein französischer Faust. (Marc **MONNIER.**) MLIA, 1879.

Anon. Goethe und der italienische Dichter Vincenzo **MONTI.** Grenzboten, 44, 1902.

Kerbaker, M. Shakespeare e Goethe nei versi di V. Monti. Firenze, 1897.

Rascher, J. F. L. **MORRISON'S** Production of Goethe's Faust. GR, 1929.

Karpeles, G. **NAPOLEON III.** als Goetheübersetzer. JbGG, 21, 1900.

Krüper, A. Ein Noffo von Pandit **NEHRU** als Faustübersetzer. NSp, 48.

Anon. Gérard de **NERVALS** Faust. Neue Zürcher Zt., 11.I.1947.

Betz, L. P. W. von Goethe und Gérard de Nerval. JbGG, 1897.

Nerval, Gérard de. Les deux Faust de Goethe (avant-propos par F. Baldensperger). In: Oeuvres complètes. Paris, 1932.

Montégut, E. Charles **NODIER.** In: Nos morts contemporains. Paris, 1884.

Bobé, L. Goethe og **OEHLENSCHLAEGER.** Tilskueren, 1931.

Schmidt, R. Goethe og Oehlenschläger. In: Fra liv og literatur. Kjøbenhavn, 1887.

Sergel, A. Oehlenschläger in seinen persönlichen Beziehungen zu Goethe, Tieck und Hebbel. Rostock, 1907.

Bem, A. Zitate aus Goethe und Schiller bei N. O. **OGAREV.** GS. 2, 1932-33.

Hennig, J. Goethe's Friendship with Anthony **O'HARA.** MLR, 39, 1944.

Jaeck, E. G. John **OXENFORD** as a Translator. JEGPh, 13, 1914.

Arndt. K. J. **POE'S** Politian and Goethe's Mignon. MLN, 1934.

Braunhard. Fragments du Faust de Goethe, traduits en vers par le prince de **POLIGNAC.** Progr. Arnstadt, 1860.

Hentschel, C. John Cowper **POWYS** and the Gretchen-Cult. Festschrift Ekwall. Uppsala, 1942.

Albert, H. Eine neue Faust Uebersetzung (**PRADES.**) Frankfurter Zt., 1896.

Bem, A. Faust in **PUSHKIN'S** Works. (In Russian.) Slavia, 13, 1934-35.

Berkov, P. N. Werther in Puskins Onegin. GS. 2, 1932-33.

Felkner. Pouchkine et Goethe. In: Hommage à Pouchkine. La Semaine egyptienne, 1937.

Frank, J. G. Pushkin and Goethe. SEER, 26, 1947-48.

Hoffmann, A. Puschkin und seine Beziehungen zu Goethe. St. Petersburger Zt., Montagsblatt, 428, 1912.

Keefer, L. Pushkin and Goethe. MLN, 56, 1941.

Legras, J. Pouchkine et Goethe. RLC, 17, 1937.

Rozov, V. A. Puskin i Gete. In: Universitetskiia Izvestiia, 48, 1908.

Mayer, Ellen. Begegnungen eines Engländers mit Goethe. (**ROBINSON.**) DR, Aug., 1899.

Morse, B. J. Crabb Robinson und Goethe in England. ESn, 67, 1932.

Norman, F. Henry Crabb Robinson and Goethe. PEGS, 6-7, 1930-31.

Anon. Ed. **ROD'S** Estimate of Goethe. Academy, 1897.

Dowden, E. Rod against Goethe. Saturday Review, 81, 1895.

Maehly, J. Goethe in französischer Beleuchtung. Internationale Litteraturberichte, 13-14, 1898.

Schott, S. Ed. Rod's Goethe Buch. Beilage zur Allg. Zt., 130, 1898.

McClain, W. H. Goethe as Romain **ROLLAND'S** Campagnon de route. GR, 19, 1945.

Anon. **SABATIERS** Uebersetzung des Faust. Grenzboten, 1893.

Gluemer, Claire von. François Sabatiers Faustübersetzung. Kölnische Zt., 248, 1893.

Papst, T. L. Eine französische Faust-Uebersetzung. Die Tat, 154, 1947.
Schmidt, L. Frankreichs Faust. MLIA, 1893.
Caro, E. Goethe et Geoffroy **SAINT-HILAIRE.** RDM, 1.XI.1865.
Morel, L. **SAINTE BEUVE,** la littérature allemande et Goethe. RHLF, 15, 1908 & Paris, 1908.
Hankiss, J. Les sept cordes de la lyre ou le Faust français. (G. **SAND**). Mélanges Baldensperger, Paris, 1930.
Mueller, W. George Sands Romane in ihrem Verhältnis zu den Goetheschen. Diss. Bern, 1912.
Croce, B. Di Giovita **SCALVINI,** dei suoi manoscritti inediti e dei suoi giudizi sul Goethe. Critica, 38, 1940.
Anon. Edm. **SCHERER** on Goethe. QR, 145, 1877.
Spach, L. Verunglimpfung Goethes in der Académie française: Goethe und Edm. Scherer. In: Zur Geschichte der modernen französischen Litteratur, Strassburg 1877.
Thomas, C. On Scherers Essay on Goethe. Nation, 1886.
Reuber, K. Albert **SCHWEITZER** und Goethe. Die christliche Welt, 46, 1932.
Bernays, M. Beziehungen Goethes zu Walter **SCOTT.** Zur neueren Literaturgeschichte, 1. (Stuttgart), 1895.
MacIntosh, W. Scott and Goethe: German Influence on the Writings of Sir Walter Scott. Glasgow, 1924.
Marcovitch, M. Walter Scott et Goethe. Strauan Pregled, 1933.
Needler, G. H. Goethe and Scott. Queen's Quarterly, July, 1923.
Neubuerger, E. Goethe und Walter Scott. In: Nachklänge. Frankfurt, 1900.
Olivero, F. Sulla traduzione di W. Scott del Goetz von Berlichingen. In: Saggi di letteratura inglese. Bari, 1913.
Roesel, L. K. Die literarischen und persönlichen Beziehungen Sir Walter Scotts zu Goethe. Leipzig, 1901.
Ruff, W. W. Scott and the Erl-King. ESn, 69, 1934.
Krueger, M. Goethes Geschwister und **SCRIBE'S** Rodolphe ou frère et soeur. Progr. Görlitz, 1899.
Buck, P. M. Goethe and **SHELLEY.** In: Goethe Memorial Volume. Madison, 1932.
Imelmann, R. Shelleys Alastor und Goethe. ZVL, 17, 1909.
Vail, C. C. D. Shelley's Translations from Goethe. GR, 23, 1948.
Zupitza. Zu einer Stelle in Shelleys Uebersetzung der Walpurgisnacht aus dem I. Theil von Goethes Faust. Archiv, 94, 1895.
Kahn-Wallerstein, C. Aus Frédéric **SORETS** Weimarer Zeit. NSR, 1946.
Lindau, P. Goethes Briefe an Soret. Stuttgart, 1877. Cf. RB, 28.IV.1877.
Schmidt, P. Ein bischöfliches Wort über Goethe als Erzieher (Mgr. J. L. **SPALDING**). Litterarische Warte, 4, 1903.
Anon. Goethe, Schiller and Mme. de **STAEL.** Academy, 143, 1830.
Caro, E. Mme. de Staël et Goethe à Weimar (1803). Séances et Trav. de l'Acad. des Sc. mor. et pol., 114. Paris, 1880.
Carlyle, T. Schiller, Goethe and Mme. de Staël. Frazer Mag., 1832. And in: Essays, 2.
Henriot, E. Goethe et **STENDHAL.** Le Temps, 7.VIII.1923.
Vermale, F. L'influence de Goethe sur Stendhal. Annales de l'U. de Grenoble, 14, 1937.
Anon. **TAYLORS** Uebersetzung des Goetheschen Faust. Gegenwart, 12, 1872.
Andrews, W. P. On the Translation of Faust. AM, 1890.
Frenz, H. Bayard Taylor and the Reception of Goethe in America. JEGPh, 41, 1942.
Haskell, J. Bayard Taylor's Translation of Goethe's Faust. New York, 1908.
Krumpelmann, J. T. The Genesis of Bayard Taylor's Translation of Goethe's Faust. JEGPh, 42, 1943.
Prahl, A. J. Bayard Taylor and Goethe. MLQ, 7, 1946.
Rassow, M. Ellen Key, **TEGNER** und Goethe. Stunden mit Goethe, 2, 1906.
Asher, D. Lord **TENNYSON** and Goethe. PEGS, 4, 1890.
Anon. Goethe and **THACKERAY.** The Bookman, 1901.
Henriot, E. Goethe, Carlyle et Thackeray. L'Europe nouvelle, 4, 1921.
Sochaczewer, H. Thackeray and Goethe. TLS, 6.VII, 1946.
Vulpius, W. Thackeray in Weimar. Century Illustr. Monthly Mag., April, 1897.
Walter, E. Goethe und Thackeray. Zs. für deutsche Sprache, 13 (Tokyo), 1910.
Ryder, F. G. George **TICKNOR'S** Sorrows of Young Werther. CL, 1, 1949.
Bode, W. **TOLSTOIS** Urteile über Goethe. Stunden mit Goethe, 8, 1911.
Mann, T. Goethe und Tolstoi. Aachen, 1923 & Berlin, 1932.
Pelaez. Un giudizio del **TOMMASEO** sul Goethe. Fanfulla della Domenica, 36, 1904.
Bem, A. Faust bei **TURGENEV.** GS, 2, 1932-33.
Rosenkranz, E. Turgenev und Goethe. GS, 2, 1932-33.
Jirat, V. J. K. **TYL** und Goethes Faust. GS, 2, 1932-33.
Schmid, G. Goethe und **UWAROW.** Russische Revue, 28, 1888.
Mauthner, F. Ein neuer französischer Faust. (A. **VACQUERIE'S** Futura.) Deutschland, 1890.
Baldensperger, F. Paul **VALERY** extragoethéen. Le Monde français, Feb., 1947.
Bémol, M. Goethe et Valéry. RLC, 21, 1947.
Blanchot, M. Valéry et Faust. L'Arche, Nov., 1946.

Maulnier, T. Le Faust de Valéry. In: Hommes et mondes, Nov., 1946.
Renéville, R. de. Le Faust de P. Valéry. La Nef, Oct., 1946.
Steiner, H. Goethe und Valéry. MDU, 40, 1948.
Valéry, P. Discours en l'honneur de Goethe. NRF, 1.VI.1932.
——— Mon Faust. Fontaine, April, 1947.
Dalmeyda, G. Goethes Tasso und **VIGNYS** Chatterton. JbGG, 23, 1902.
Dervitz, H. Goethe und Ch. de **VILLERS**. Wissenschaftl. Blätter der Hamburger Nachrichten, 1913.
Jirat, V. Zur Frage Goethe und **VRCHLICKY**. GS. 1, 1931-32.
Baldensperger, F. Un goethéen français d'Alsace: Jean-Jacques **WEISS**. Alsace française, 20.III.1932.
Fairley, B. Goethe and **WORDSWORTH**. PEGS, 1934.
Heller, O. Goethe and Wordsworth. MLN, 14, 1899.
Mensch, R. A. J. Goethe and Wordsworth. PEGS, 7, 1893.

CHAPTER SEVEN

Hegel

1. General Influences.

Janev, J. Bibliographie der ausländischen Hegel-Literatur. In: Literarische Berichte auf dem Gebiete der Philosophie. Erfurt, 1930.
Kroner, R. Die interantionale Bedeutung Hegels. Inter Nationes, 1, 1931.
Marcuse, H. Hegel and the Rise of Modern Social Theory. Oxford U. P., 1941.
Rosenthal, J. Hegel and Contemporary Thought. Symposium, April, 1932.
Harmon, F. B. The Social Philosophy of the St. Louis Hegelians. (**AMERICA**.) New York, 1943.
Hoffmann, F. Die hegelsche Philosophie in St. Louis in den Vereinigten Staaten Nordamerikas. Philosophische Monatshefte, 7, 1871-72.
Pochmann, H. A. The Hegelization of the West. AGR, 9, 1943.
Ryan, J. H. Hegelianism in America. Riv. di filosofia neo-scolastica, 23, Suppl.
Walz, J. The St. Louis School of Philosophy. AGR, 4.
Anon. Ein englischer Interpret Hegels. (**ENGLAND**.) MLIA, 1865.
Muirhead, J. H. How Hegel Came to England. Mind, 36, 1927.
Walker, L. J. Hegelianism in Great-Britain. Riv. di filosofia neo-scolastica, 23, Suppl.
Salomaa, J. E. Die Anfänge des Hegelianismus in **FINNLAND**. Kantstudien, 39, 1934.
Forest, A. L'hegélianisme en **FRANCE**. Riv. di filosofia neo-scolastica, 23, Suppl.
Grenier, J. Sur l'hegélianisme en France. NRF, April, 1937.
Saisset, E. Travaux publiés en France sur Kant, Fichte, Schelling, et Hegel. RDM, 15.II.1846.
Wahl, J. Commémoration du centenaire de la mort de Hegel dans les revues philosophiques françaises. Revue d'Allemagne, 1932.
Zyromski, E. Les caractères généraux de la littérature française au XIXe siècle: I. La méthode hegélienne et l'esprit français. Rev. des Lettres françaises et étrangères. Annales des U. du Midi, 1, 1899.
Caroli, G. Hegel in **ITALIA**. In: Matemica e panteismo. Bologna, 1864.
Croce, B. Documenti inediti sull'hegelismo napoletano. Critica, 20.V.1906.
Gentile, G. I primordii dell'hegelismo in Italia. Critica, 20.III.1912.
——— Hegel e il pensiero italiano. Leonardo, 1933.
Jones, W. T. The Revolution in Italian Thought. British Review, June, 1915.
Lucia, V. de. Hegel in Italia. Vasto, 1891.
Mazzantini, C. Lo Hegelismo in Italia. Riv. di filosofia neo-scolastica, 23, Suppl.
Pflaum, C. D. Der Geist Hegels in Italien. Archiv f. Geschichte der Philosophie, 16, 1910.
Piano, U. L. L'hegelismo a Napoli. Potenza, 1903.
Siciliani, P. Gli hegeliani in Italia. Riv. bolognese, 2, 1868.
Bar, A. Die ersten Einflüsse Hegels in der polnischen Zeitschriftenliteratur. (**POLAND**.) GS, 1, 1931-32.
Chizhevskii, D. I. Studies on the History of Philosophy in the Ukraine: Hegel and Schelling. (**RUSSIA**.) Praha, 1931.
——— Hegel in Russia. (In Russian). Paris, 1939.
Gancikoff, L. L'hegelismo in Russia. Riv. di filosofia neo-scolastica, 23, Suppl.
Iakovenko, B. Aus der Geschichte der russischen Philosophie. Prag, 1935.
——— Geschichte des Hegelianismus in Russland. Prag, 1939.
Janeff, J. Zur Geschichte des russischen Hegelianismus. DVLG, 10, 1932.
Chizhevskii, D. I. Hegel bei den Slaven. (**SLAVS**.) Reichenberg i. B., 1934.
Kulling, J. Hegel och reaktionen mot romantiken i Sverige. (**SWEDEN**.) Edda, 4, 1938.

2. Influences upon Individual Authors.

Laziczius, J. von. Hegels Einfluss auf V. **BELINSKIJ.** ZSPh., 5, 1929.
Dieterich, K. **BUCKLE** und Hegel. PJb, 32, 1873.
Liatskii, E. **CHERNYSHEVSKII** and the Teachers of his Ideas. (In Russian). Sovremennyi Mir, 10, 1910.
Kühne, W. Graf August **CIESZKOWSKI,** ein Schüler Hegels und des deutschen Geistes. Leipzig, 1938.
Knoop, B. V. **COUSIN,** Hegel und die französische Romantik. Einfluss und Wirkungen. Diss. München, 1932.
Antoni, C. **CROCE** e Hegel. Rassegna d' Italia, 1, 1946.
Miranda, L. Da Hegel a Croce. Bari, 1921.
Ritchie, D. G. **DARWIN** and Hegel. London, 1894.
Croce, B. Vestigi di critica hegeliana nella critica del **DE SANCTIS.** Cultura, 1.V. 1912.
——— Per lo studio del pensiero del De Sanctis. Atti della R. Accad. Pontaniana, 42. Napoli, 1912.
——— Fr. De Sanctis und die deutsche Geistesarbeit. Internat. Monatsschrift, June, 1912.
De Sanctis, F. Critica del principio dell' estetica hegeliana. In: Pagine sparse, publ. by B. Croce. Bari, 1934.
Haushalter, W. M. Mrs. **EDDY** Purloins from Hegel. Boston, 1936.
Pochmann, H. A. **EMERSON** and the St. Louis Hegelians. AGR, 10, 1944.
Croce, B. L'abate **GIOACCHINO DI FIORE** e Hegel. Critica, 20.V.1934.
Evans, D. O. The Hegelian Idea in Hernani (**HUGO.**) MLN, 63, 1948.
Bense, M. Hegel und **KIERKEGAARD:** eine prinzipielle Untersuchung. Köln, 1948.
Collins, J. Kierkegaard's Critique of Hegel. Thought, 18, 1943.
Lowith, K. L'achèvement de la philosophie classique par Hegel et sa dissolution chez Marx et Kierkegaard. Recherches philosophiques, 4, 1934-35.
Ramsey, P. Existenz and the Existence of God: Kierkegaard and Hegel. Journal cf Religion, 28, 1948.
Wahl, J. Hegel et Kierkegaard. Revue philosophique, Nov., 1931.
Souday, P. Hegel et **MAURRAS.** Paris-Midi, 14.I.1916.
Dockhorn, K. Charles **MORGAN** und Hegel. ESn, 74, 1940.
Townsend, H. G. The Pragmatism of **PEIRCE** and Hegel. Philosophical Review, July, 1928.
Poiton, E. Les disciples de Hegel en France: **RENAN.** Revue nationale, 10.I.1864.
Spaventa, B. Hegel confutato da **ROSMINI.** Cimento, May, 1855.
Engel, O. Der Einfluss Hegels auf die Bildung der Gedankenwelt **TAINES.** Stuttgart, 1920.
Poiton, E. Les disciples de Hegel en France: Taine. Revue nationale, 10.XI.1836.
Rosca, D. D. L'influence de Hegel sur Taine, théoricien de la connaissance et de l'art. Diss. Paris, 1928.
Gindre de Mancy, C. La philosophie hegélienne en France: une théologie nouvelle. (**VACHEROT.**) Revue européenne, 7, 1860.
Gregorovius, F. Der Hegelianer Augusto **VERA** (1887). In: Kleine Schriften zur Geschichte & Kultur, 3. Leipzig, 1892.
Rosenkranz, K. Hegels Naturphilosophie und ihre Bearbeitung durch den italienischen Philosophen A. Vera. Berlin, 1868.
Boatright, M. C. **WHITMAN** and Hegel. U. of Texas Studies in English, 9, 1929.
Parsons, Olive W. Whitman the Non-Hegelian. PMLA, 58, 1943.

CHAPTER EIGHT

Heine

1. General Influences.

Berendsohn, Heine and Our Times. Contemporary Review, Dec., 1939.
Betz, L. P. Heinrich Heine. Ein Weltdichter und ein Dichter der Welt. In: Studien. Frankfurt, 1902.
Kieft, P. Heine in westeuropäischer Beurteilung. Seine Kritiker in Frankreich, England und Holland. Diss. Amsterdam. Zutphen, 1938.
Kohut, A. Heinrich Heine als Romanfigur. Akadem. Bücherschau, 1913.
Mehring, S. H. Heine und seine Lobredner. Nation, 46-47, 1906.
Zendrini, B. Enrico Heine e i suoi interpreti. NAnt, 27-28, 1874.
Sachs, H. B. Heine in **AMERICA.** Philadelphia, 1916.
Fastenrath, J. Heine in Südamerika. MLIA, 1880.
Anon. Englisches Urteil über H. Heine. (**ENGLAND.**) Blätter zur Kunde der Literatur des Auslands, 1, 1836.
Chotzner, H. Ein modernes englisches Urtheil über H. Heine. MLIA, 1890.
Elster, E. Heine in England. MLIA, 1897.
Guttmann, B. Heine in England. Frankfurter Zt., 158, 1912.
Hatscher, L. Englische Bücher über Heine und Schopenhauer. MLIA, 90, 1876.
Kellner, L. Heine in England. Neues Wiener Tagblatt, 23.XII.1897.
Liptzin, S. Heinrich Heine, Hellenist and Cultural Pessimist: A Late Victorian Legend. PhQ, 22, 1942-43.
——— Heinrich Heine and the Early Victorians. MDU, 35, 1943.

——— Heinrich Heine, Blackguard and Apostate: A Study of the Earliest English Attitude towards Him. PMLA, 58, 1943.
——— Heine, the Bard of Democracy: A Contemporary English Legend. GQ, 17, 1944.
——— Heine, the Continuator of Goethe: A Mid-Victorian Legend. JEGPh, 43, 1944.
Lux, J. Heine et la critique anglaise. RB, 13.I.1912.
Seibel, G. English Heine Translations. Pittsburgh Gazette, April, 1906.
Waldmueller, R. Eine englische Uebersetzung von Heines Buch der Lieder. MLIA, 1883.
Winternitz, M. H. Heine in England. Die Zeit, 1900.
Wormley, S. L. Heine in England. Chapel Hill (N. C.), 1943.
Alesius, M. Heine in Frankreich. (**FRANCE.**) Internat. Litteraturberichte, 27.III.1895.
Betz, L. P. Heine in Frankreich. Zürich, 1895.
Bonnerot, J. & Hirth, F. Heine en France. RLC, 17, 1937.
Bourget, P. Heine in der französischen Literatur. Neue Freie Presse, 14902, 1906.
Elster, E. Heine in Frankreich. Blätter f. litterar. Unterhaltung, 1895.
Franzos, K. E. Heine in Frankreich. Deutsche Dichtung, 15.I.1895.
——— Zum Kapitel: Heine in Frankreich. Deutsche Dichtung, 1902.
Hess, J. A. Heinrich Heine and the French. MLJ, 1931.
Laur, E. Die erste französische Ausgabe von Heines Werken. Zs. f. Bücherfreunde, 1902.
Rod, E. La póesie de Henri Heine et son influence en France. BURS, July, 1897.
Schill, E. Les traductions françaises de l'Intermezzo de H. Heine. Paris, 1928.
Seipgens. Eine französische Heine-Uebersetzung. MLIA, 1884.
Walzel, O. F. Heine in Frankreich. Zeit, 26.I.1895.
Kohut, A. Heine in Ungarn. (**HUNGARY.**) MLIA, 1885.
Anon. Heinrich Heine in Italien. (**ITALY.**) MLIA, 1879.
Bonardi, C. Enrico Heine nella letteratura italiana. Livorno, 1907.
Breitinger, H. Die italienischen Heine-Uebersetzer. Gegenwart, 7.VI.1879.
Coronini, C. Zwei italienische Heineübersetzungen. MLIA, 1883.
Kaden, W. Heines Ratcliff in Neapel. Gegenwart, Beilage 9, 1876.
Nassen, J. Heine in Italien (Bibliographio). In: H. Heines Familienleben. Fulda, 1895.
Nossing, Anne F. Heine in Italia nel secolo decimonono. New York, 1948.
Schmidt, L. Heines Reisebilder in italienischer Uebersetzung. MLIA, 19.I.1895.
Vivanti-Lindau, A. Heines William Ratcliff auf dem Teatro Manzoni in Mailand. Gegenwart, 7, 1875.
Karpeles, G. Heine und die Polen. (**POLAND.**) Pester Lloyd, 152, 1907.
Reinhardstoettner, K. von. H. Heine in **PORTUGAL.** Münchener Neueste Nachrichten, 38, 1891.
Adam, G. Heine in **RUMAENIEN.** Aus Fremden Zungen, 2, 1902.
Icaciuc, N. H. Heine in der rumänischen Literatur. Cernauti, 1926.
Berendsohn, W. A. Der lebendige Heine im germanischen Norden. (**SCANDINAVIA.**) Kopenhagen, 1935.
Bazan, E. P. Fortuna española de Heine. (**SPAIN.**) Rev. de España, 110, 1886.
Fastenrath, J. Heine in Spanien. MLIA, 1886.

2. Influences upon Individual Authors.

Karpeles, G. Heine und **ANDERSEN.** Pester Lloyd, 93, 1905.
Anon. **BAUDELAIRE** und Heine. Neue Freie Presse, 13477, 1902.
Cordier, H. Baudelaire et Heine. Bull. du Bibliophile, 1901.
Bonardi, C. Enrico Heine nell'opera di Giosuè **CARDUCCI.** Sassari, 1903.
——— Heine e Carducci. Rivista mens. di lett. ted., 1, 1907.
Anon. **CHIARINIS** italienischer Atta Troll. MLIA, 1878.
Simon-Baumann, L. George **ELIOT** über Heinrich Heine. Anglia, 1931.
Bonardi, C. **FOGAZZARO** e Heine. Critica, 11, 1913.
Svanberg, N. **FROEDING** och Heine. Nysvenska Studier, 1921.
Gladding, B. **HOUSMAN'S** More Poems, VII, and Dehmel's Trost. MLN, 56, 1941.
Haber, T. B. Heine and Housman. JEGPh, 43, 1944.
Salinger, H. Housman's Last Poems XXX and Heine's Lyrisches Intermezzo 62. MLN, 54, 1939.
Legras, J. Heine et Michel **LERMONTOF.** Revue des U. du Midi, 1895.
Huebener, T. **LONGFELLOW'S** Estimate of Heine. GQ, 21,1948.
Polak, K. **MASARYK** und Heine. GS. 3, 1935.
Bescon, Y. Notes sur un traducteur de H. Heine. (**MILLIOT-MADERAN.**) RELV, 1933.
Anon. Aug. **NEFFTZER** et H. Heine. Le Temps, 27.I.1938.
Betz, L. P. Henri Heine et Eugène **RENDUEL.** RHLF, 3, 1896.
Hirth, F. George **SAND** und der Charmante Gott. Das Goldene Tor, 2.
Rosenberg, R. P. Heine and George Sand. JEGPh, 35, 1936.
Black, G. A. James **THOMSON:** his Translations of Heine. MLR, 1936.
Feuchtwanger, L. Heine und O. **WILDE.** Der Spiegel, 1, 1908.

Kernahan, C. Wilde and Heine. Dublin Mag., 1940.
Brix, H. Heine and Chr. **WINTHER.** Analyser og Problemer, 2, 1935.
Wells, W. Humbert **WOLFE:** A Modern English Heine. Sewanee Rev., 49, 1941.
Engel, E. Il canzoniere di Heine von B. **ZENDRINI.** Gegenwart, 1877.
——— Bernardino Zendrini, der Heine-Uebersetzer. MLIA, 1879.
Martini, F. Heine e Zendrini. Milano, 1885.

CHAPTER NINE

Hoffmann

1. General Influences.

Drougard, E. Encore les Elixirs du diable. RLC, 15, 1935.
Mainland, W. F. The Legacy of Hoffmann. GLL, 1, 1937.
Wells, A. L. E. T. A. Hoffmann: Notes on His Life, Work, and Influence. Manitoba Arts Review, 1, 1940.
Zylstra, H. E. T. A. Hoffmann in England and **AMERICA.** Diss. Harvard, 1940.
Gudde, E. G. E.Th.A. Hoffmann's Reception in **ENGLAND.** PMLA, 1926-27.
Horn, W. Ueber das Komische im Schauerroman: E. T. A. Hoffmanns Elixiere des Teufels und ihre Beziehungen zur englischen Literatur. Archiv, 146, 1923-24.
Anon. Hoffman in Frankreich. (**FRANCE.**) Blätter für literar. Unterhaltung, 8.III. 1830. Cf. Der Freimüthige oder Berliner Conversationsblatt, 15.V.1830.
——— Ein deutscher Romantiker in Frankreich. Europa, 1874.
Braak, S. Introduction à une étude sur l'influence d'Hoffmann en France. NPh, 23, 1938.
Breuillac, M. Hoffmann en France. RHLF, 13, 1906.
Champfleury. De l'introduction des Contes d'Hoffmann en France. Athenaeum français, 19.XI.1853.
Hoffmann, E. E. T. A. Hoffmann et la littérature française. Jahresbericht der Armenschule Dresden, 1913.
Pankalla, G. E. T. A. Hoffmann und Frankreich. GRM, 27, 1939.
Pommier, J. (& Baldensperger, F.) Pour les débuts de Hoffmann en France. RLC, 13, 1933.
Schoenherr, K. Die Bedeutung E. T. A. Hoffmanns für die Entwicklung des musikalischen Gefühls in der französischen Romantik. Diss. München, 1931.
Thurau, G. E. T. A. Hoffmanns Erzählungen in Frankreich. Festschrift Oscar Schade. Königsberg, 1896.
Weise, K. O. Die Wirkung einer Synästhesie Hoffmanns in Frankreich. Archiv, 170, 1936.
Gorlin, M. Hoffmann en **RUSSIE.** RLC, 15, 1935.
Rodzevic, S. E. T. A. Hoffmann and Russian Romanticism. (In Russian). Russkii Filologicheskii Vestnik, 1917.
Schneider, F. Hoffman en España. (**SPAIN.**) Festschrift Bonilla y San Martin. Madrid, 1927.
Ljungdorff, V. E. T. A. Hoffmann i Sverige. (**SWEDEN.**) Edda, 1920.

2. Influences upon Individual Authors.

Bayer, R. von. En causant avec **BALZAC.** RRh, 1928.
Giraud, J. Charles **BAUDELAIRE** et Hoffmann le fantastique. RHLF, 26, 1919.
Pommier, J. Baudelaire et Hoffmann. Mélanges Vianey. Paris, 1935.
Ludwig, A. Hoffmann und **DUMAS;** ein Beitrag zu Hoffmanns Schicksalen in Frankreich. Archiv, 1929.
Guichard, L. Un emprunt de **GAUTIER** à Hoffmann. RLC, 21, 1947.
Payr, B. Gautier und Hoffmann. Diss. Leipzig, 1927. Berlin, 1932.
Gorlin, N. N. V. **GOGOL** und E. T. A. Hoffmann. Diss. Berlin. Leipzig, 1933.
Smith, F. P. Un conte fantastique chez **IRVING,** Borel et Dumas Père. RLC, 18, 1938.
Martin, M. Un aventurier intellectuel sous la Restauration et la Monarchie de Juillet: le Dr. **KOREFF.** Paris, 1925.
Marsan, J. Nouvelles et fantaisies de Gérard de **NERVAL.** Paris, 1928.
Cobb, P. The Influence of E. T. A. Hoffmann in the Tales of E. A. **POE.** Chapel Hill (N. C.) 1908.
Gruener, G. Notes on the Influence of E. T.A. Hoffmann upon E. A. Poe. PMLA, 19, 1904.
Smith, G. P. Poe's Metzengerstein. MLN, 1933.
Stein, S. **PUSKIN** i Hoffmann. Tartu, 1937.
Anon. George **SAND** und E. T. A. Hoffmann. MLIA, 6.III.1864.
Drougard, E. Hoffmann et **VILLIERS DE L'ISLE-ADAM.** RLC, 15, 1935.

CHAPTER TEN

Kant

1. General Influences.

Delbos, V. De Kant aux Postkantiens. Paris, 1940.
Gorceix, S. Du nouveau sur un vieux projet de paix perpétuelle. MF, I.V.1934.
Kabir, H. Z. A. Kant and the Modern Mind. Calcutta Review, 72, 1939.

de Kant et la critique littéraire. Revue de l'U. du Midi, 1896.
Creighton, J. E. **AMERICAN** Current Literature on Kant. Kantstudien, 3, 1899.
Anon. Kants Philosophie in **ENGLAND** Hannover, 1797.
——— Urteile der Engländer über Kants Philosophie. Neuer Teutscher Merkur, June, 1799.
——— English Translation of Kant's Critic of Pure Reason. NAR, July, 1839.
Abel, K. Max Müllers englische Ausgabe von Kants Kritik der reinen Vernunft. MLIA, 1882.
Carritt, E. F. The Sources and Effects in England of Kant's Philosophy of Beauty. The Monist, 1925.
Duncan, G. M. English Translations of Kant's Writings. Kantstudien, 1898 & 1906.
Mahaffy, J. P. & Bernard, J. J. Kant's Critical Philosophy for English Readers. London,1872.
Munteano, B. Kant en Angleterre. RLC, 1933-34.
Pfleiderer, E. Kantischer Kritizismus und englische Philosophie. Halle, 1881.
Schmitt-Wendel, K. Kants Einfluss auf die englische Ethik. Berlin, 1912.
Ware, H. G. An English Note on Klopstock and Kant. MLR, 1928.
Watson, J. Kant and his English Critics. Glasgow, 1881.
Wellek, R. Immanuel Kant in England, 1793-1838. Princeton, 1931.
Wentscher, E. Englische Wege zu Kant. Leipzig, 1931.
Bouglé, C. Spiritualisme et Kantisme en **FRANCE.** RP, I.V.1934.
Counson, A. De la légende de Kant chez les romantiques français. Mélanges Kurth, Liège, 1908.
Heine, H. Kant in Frankreich. In: Werke, 6. Paris, 1855.
Laporte, J. Kant et la poésie française. RdF, 15.V.1924.
Picavet, F. La philosophie de Kant en France de 1773 à 1814. In: La Critique de la Raison Pratique. Paris, 1921.
Vallois, M. La formation de l'influence kantienne en France. Paris, 1925.
Verneaux, R. Les sources cartésiennes et kantiennes de l'idéalisme français. Paris, 1936.
Honecker, M. Immanuel Kants Philosophie in den romanischen Ländern. Philosoph. Jb. der Görresgesellschaft, 37, 1924.
Cicchitti Suriani, F. I primordii del Kantismo in Italia. (**ITALY.**) Roma, 1892.
Eberty, G. Kant in Italien. MLIA, 1880.
Werner, K. Kant in Italien. SAWW, 1881. Cf. DLZ, 1882.
Petrovici, J. Kant und das rumänische Denken. (**RUMANIA.**) Archiv f. d. Geschichte der Philosophie & Soziologie, 31, 1927.
Braun, J. Die slavische messianistische Philosophie als Entwicklung und Vollendung der deutschen philosophischen Systeme Kants und seiner Nachfolger. (**SLAVS.**) GS, 3, 1935.
Lutoslawski, W. Kant in Spanien. (**SPAIN.**) Kantstudien, 1, 1896.
Munteano, B. Episodes Kantiens en Suisse et en France sous le Directoire. (**SWITZERLAND.**) RLC, 15, 1935.

2. Influences upon Individual Authors.

Palagy, M. Kant und **BOLZANO.** Eine kritische Parallele. Halle, 1902.
Anon. Kant et M. **BRUNETIERE.** Le Temps, 1.IV.1899.
Bos, C. Le Kantisme de **CARLYLE.** Archiv f. Geschichte der Philosophie, 15, 1902.
Cazamian, L. Carlyle et le Kantisme. RELV, Dec., 1913.
Harrold, C. F. Carlyle's Interpretation of Kant. PhQ, 7, 1928.
Storrs, M. The Relation of Carlyle to Kant and Fichte. Bryn Mawr, 1929 & MPh, 1930.
Howard, C. **COLERIDGE'S** Idealism: A Study of his Relationship to Kant and to the Cambridge Platonists. Boston, 1924.
Lovejoy, A. O. Coleridge and Kant's Two Worlds. ELH, 7, 1940.
Nidecker, H. Notes marginales de S. T. Coleridge. RLC, 7, 1927.
Winckelmann, E. Coleridge und die Kantische Philosophie. Erste Einwirkung des deutschen Idealismus in England. Leipzig, 1933. Cf. Archiv, Oct., 1935.
Ewald, O. Kant und **IBSEN.** Oesterreichische Rundschau, 7, 1906.
Rüfner, V. Herbert **SPENCER,** der Kant Englands. GRM, 16, 1928.
Ollion, E. Charles de **VILLERS** et Kant. U. catholique. Lyon, Oct., 1906.
Seward, G. C. Die theoretische Philosophie William **WHEWELLS** und der kantische Einfluss. Diss. Tübingen, 1938.
Paneth, F. A. Thomas **WRIGHT** of Durham and Immanuel Kant. Durham U. Journal, 33, 1941.

CHAPTER ELEVEN

Schiller

1. General Influences.

Dähne, W. Schiller im Drama und Festspiel. Meiningen, 1909.
Hirsch, F. E. Schiller im Roman und Drama. Zs. f. Bücherfreunde, N. F., 1 & Breslauer Zt., 783, 1914.
Kipka, K. Schillers Maria Stuart im Auslande. SVL, 5, 1905.
Zyromski, E. L'esthétique transcendentale

Ludwig, A. Schiller und die Nachwelt. Berlin, 1909.
Richter, W. Schiller und die Nachwelt. In: Deutsche Beiträge. Chicago U. P., 1947.
Robertson, J. G. Schiller after a Century. Edinburgh, 1905.
Rullmann, W. Die Bearbeitungen, Fortsetzungen und Nachahmungen von Schillers Räubern (1782-1802). Schriften der Ges. f. Theatergeschichte, 15. Berlin, 1910.
Anon. American Versions of Schiller's William Tell. (**AMERICA.**) NAR, 1840.
Barnstorff, H. German and American Interest in Schiller, 1918-39. GQ, 13, 1940.
Bockstahler, O. L. Schiller in Canada. MLF, 25, 1940-41.
Brede, C. Schiller on the Philadelphia Stage to the Year 1830. German American Annals, July, 1905.
Ende, A. von. Schiller und die Amerikaner. LE. 15.IV.1907.
Parry, E. C. Friedrich Schiller in America. Philadelphia, 1905.
Stecher, J. Schiller en **BELGIQUE.** Liège, 1860.
Bobé, L. Schiller und **DAENEMARK.** Euphorion, 12, 1905.
Anon. Schiller in **ENGLAND.** Europa, 1862.
Anderson, J. P. Bibliography of Schiller (in England). In: H. Nevinson's Life of Schiller. London, 1889.
Cooke, M. W. Schiller's Robbers in England. MLR, 11, 1915-16.
Dummer, E. H. Schiller in English. MDU, 35, 1943.
Ewen, F. The Prestige of Schiller in England, 1788-1859. Columbia U. P., 1932.
Freytag, L. Schillers W. Tell in englischer Uebersetzung. MLIA, 1881.
Gaupp, O. Die Engländer über Schiller und die deutsche Literatur. Münchener Neueste Nachrichten, 444, 1905.
Krause, G. Schiller in England. Vossische Zt., 215, 1905.
Perring, H. An English Criticism of Schiller's Robbers (1792). German American Annals, 1903.
Rea, T. Schiller's Dramas and Poems in England. London, 1906.
Smith, H. Two English Translations of Schiller's Wallenstein. MLR, 9, 1914.
Ulrich. Ueber das Schillersche Lied von der Glocke und seine Uebersetzung in das Französische und Englische. Progr., 1871.
Waterhouse, G. Schiller's Räuber in England before 1800. MLR, July, 1935.
Willoughby, L. A. English Translations and Adaptations of Schiller's Robbers. MLR, 16, 1921.
——— Schiller's Kabale und Liebe in English Translation. PEGS, 1, 1924.
——— Schiller in England and Germany. PEGS, 11, 1935.
Baldensperger, F. Notes sur les représentations en province de Robert, chef de brigands. (**FRANCE.**) Euphorion, 10, 1903.
——— Les aspects successifs de Schiller dans le romantisme français. Euphorion, 12, 1905.
——— A propos d'une continuation française du Geisterseher de Schiller. RG, 1907.
Bécart, A. J. Poésies de Schiller, mises en vers français. In: Etudes Schilleriennes, 1861.
Cornil, C. La fortune de Schiller en Allemagne et en France. RG, 25, 1929.
Cosacl. Le théâtre de Schiller imité et traduit en France. Progr. Danzig, 1858.
Dubois, P. F. L'imitation de Schiller. Le Globe, 3.V. & 25.X.1828.
Eggli, E. Schiller et le romantisme français. 2 vols. Paris, 1927.
Kohn, M. Schiller vor 100 Jahren in Frankreich. Zs. f. lateinlose höhere Schulen, 7, 1895.
Landau, M. L'Enfant prodigue und Die Räuber. ZVL, 2, 1880.
Ludwig, A. Zu Schiller in Frankreich. Archiv, N. S., 55, 1929.
Maas, M. Remarques grammaticales et littéraires sur deux traductions de la Cloche de Schiller. Progr. Neu-Braunschweig, 1859.
Morel, L. Le théâtre de Schiller en France. Progr. Zürich, 1897.
Richter, K. Schiller und seine Räuber in der französischen Revolution. Grüneberg, 1865.
Smelmann, S. Schillerphilologie in Frankreich. Gegenwart, 12, 1877.
Trautwein von Belle, E. Schillers Theater in neuer französischer Uebersetzung. MLIA, 1870.
Ulrich. Ueber das Schillersche Lied von der Glocke und seine Uebersetzung in das Französische und Englische. Progr., 1871.
Wolff, T. Die Räuber in Paris. Berliner Tageblatt, 62, 1902.
Arnold, R. F. & Prjatelg, J. Schiller-Uebersetzungen in Ungarn. (**HUNGARY.**) Zs. f. die oesterreichischen Gymnasien, 1905.
Anon. Deutsche Literatur in Italien. (**ITALY.**) Beilage zur Allg. Zt., 14.I.1844.
Fasola, E. Schillers Werke in italienischer Uebersetzung. Euphorion, 8, 1901.
——— et al. Bibliografia Schilleriana. Riv. di lett. tedesca, 2, 1908 & 5, 1911.
Foa, A. Schiller giudicato dai primi romantici italiani. Riv. di letteratura tedesca, 1, 1907.
Mazzuchetti, Lavinia. Schiller in Italia. Milano, 1913.
Piltz, O. Schiller in Italien. Berliner Courier 108, 1905.
Szyjkowski, M. Schiller en Pologne. (**POLAND.**) Mémoires de l'Acad. polonaise, 1915.
Gherghel, J. Schiller in literatura romana. (**RUMANIA.**) Bucuresti, 1935.
Passage, C. E. The Influence of Schiller in **RUSSIA**, 1800-1840. ASEER, 5, 1946.
Peterson, O. P. Schiller in Russland, 1785-1805. New York, 1934.

—— Schiller und die russischen Dichter und Denker des 19. Jahrhunderts, 1805-81. New York, 1939.
Estelrich, J. L. Poesías líricas de Schiller traducidas. (**SPAIN.**) Homenaje a Menéndez y Pelayo. Madrid, 1899.

2. Influences upon Individual Authors

Perrochon, H. H. F. **AMIEL** traducteur de Schiller. RLC, 5, 1925.
Trautwein von Belle, E. Schillers Trauerspiele, französisch von Theodor **BRAUN.** MLIA, 1867.
Wernekke, H. Eine französische Uebersetzung Schillerscher Dramen. MLIA, 1881.
Anon. Schiller's Homage of the Arts by Charles T. **BROOKS.** NAR, April, 1847.
—— Deutsche Literatur in England (**BULWER** als Uebersetzer Schillers). Beilage zur Allg. Zt., 7.IV.1844.
Böddeker, K. Ueber Bulwers Uebersetzungen Schiller'scher Gedichte im Vergleich mit den Originalen. Archiv, 49, 1872.
Maurer, K. W. George **BUTLER** und ein unveröffentlichter Brief Schillers in England. Archiv, Oct., 1936.
Anon. Schiller-**BYRON** und Schiller-Shakespeare. Hallische Jb, 312, 1838.
Schanz, J. Schiller, Platen, Byron. Leipzig, 1865.
Conrad, H. **CARLYLE** und Schiller. Vierteljahrschrift f. Litteraturgeschichte, 1889.
Hildebrand, A. Carlyle und Schiller. Progr. Berlin, 1913.
Kraeger, H. Schiller und Carlyle. Deutsche Monatsschrift, July, 1905.
Küchler, F. Carlyle und Schiller. Diss. Leipzig, 1902 & Anglia, 1903.
Machule, P. **COLERIDGE'S** Wallenstein-Uebersetzung. ESn, 31, 1902.
Markall, L. L. Coleridge Marginalia on Wieland and Schiller. MLR, 1924.
Roscher, H. F. G. Die Wallensteinübersetzung von Samuel T. Coleridge. Leipzig, 1905.
Cyzevskyj, D. Schiller und die Brüder Karamazov (**DOSTOIEVSKI**). ZSPh, 6, 1929.
Anon. Amour et Intrigue, drame de Schiller, traduit par M. Alex. **DUMAS.** RDM, 1.VII.1847.
Fouquet, F. Schiller et M. Alexandre Dumas fils. In: A travers la Vie. Paris, 1896.
Gerhardt, L. Schillers Werke in der Beleuchtung eines französischen Zeitgenossen (**DUVAU**). Zs. f. Bücherfreunde, 1905-06.
Borelius, H. **GEIJER** och Schiller. Samlaren, 1905.
Perrochon, H. Une amie vaudoise de Mme. Schiller: Jeanne **HUC-MAZELET.** Lausanne, 1938.
Pappritz, R. Schiller und Victor **HUGO.** NSp, 9, 1901.
Poirot, J. A. A propos de Victor Hugo. Mém. de la Société néophil. à Helsingfors, 1902.
Baldensperger, F. Schiller et Camille **JORDAN.** RG, 1905.
Krappe, A. H. O Sopro de Deus. (Guerra **JUNQUEIRO**). MLN, 40, 1945.
Neumann, F. W. **KARAMZINS** Verhältnis zu Schiller. ZSPh, 9, 1932.
Reichert, H. W. A Comparison of the Philosophies of Schiller and **KELLER.** MDU, 39, 1947.
Cernobajev, D. Der Irydion (**KRASINSKI**) und Schillers Fiesko. ZSPh, 4, 1927.
Doberenz, H. **LA MARTELIERE** und seine Bearbeitung Schillerscher Dramen auf dem Theater der französischen Revolution. Progr. Lobau i. S., 1883.
Scholl, J. W. **LONGFELLOW** and Schillers Lied von der Glocke. MLN, Feb., 1913.
Chiappelli, A. Il **MANZONI** e lo Schiller. Marzocco, 20.IX.1931.
Giraud, J. Alfred de **MUSSET** et Schiller. RHLF, 1907.
Zardo, A. G. B. **NICCOLINI** e F. Schiller. Padova, 1883.
Varneke, B. **POGODIN** and Schiller (in Russian). Slavia, 5, 1926.
Bormann, W. Zwei Schillerpreise und François **PONSARD.** ZVL, 10, 1897.
Holl, K. **SHERIDAN'S** Verses to the Memory of Garrick and Schiller's Prolog zum Wallenstein. MLN, April, 1914.
Nilsson. A. Schillers inflytande på **TEGNER** och Tegnérs samtida. Samlaren, 1905.
Stallknecht, N. P. **WORDSWORTH'S** Ode to Duty and the Schöne Seele. PMLA, 52, 1937.

CHAPTER TWELVE

Other German Authors

Dalgren, L. E. Ernst Moritz **ARNDT** och Sverige. Vastervik, 1920.
Cohn, A. F. Schwedisch-deutsche Romantik. Malla, Montgomery und B. von **ARNIM.** Deutsch-Nordische Jb., 1926.
Bailey, M. L. Milton and Jakob **BOEHME.** A Study of German Mysticism in Seventeenth-Century England. New York, 1914.
Close, K. J. Böhmes Aufnahme in England. Archiv, 148, 1925.
Hobhouse, S. Isaac Newton and Jacob Boehme. Philosophia, 2, 1937.
Labry, R. L'enseignement d'I. G. Schwartz, Rose-Croix, professeur à l'Université de Moscou, et son influence. Mélanges J. Legras. Paris, 1939.
Snyder, A. D. Coleridge on Böhme. PMLA, 45, 1930.
Struck, W. Der Einfluss Jakob Böhmes auf die englische Literatur des 17. Jahrhunderts. Berlin, 1936.

Wormhoudt, A. L. William Law and Jacob Boehme. Diss. U. of Iowa, 1943.
BOERNE: See Intermediaries, I.IV.8.
Fraustadt, F. Ueber das Verhältniss von Barclays Ship of Fools zur lateinischen, französischen und deutschen Quelle. (**BRANT**). Breslau, 1894.
Pompen, F. A. The English Versions of the Ship of Fools: a Contribution to the History of the Early French Renaissance in England. London, 1925. Cf. MPh, 1926.
Rosenberg, R. P. Problems in Translation with Reference to Dantons Tod. (**BUECHNER**). GQ, 15, 1942.
—— Georg Büchner's Early Reception in America. JEGPh, 44, 1945.
Anon. **BUERGERS** Lenore in England. Beilage zur Allg. Zt., 54, 1901.
Baldensperger, F. La Lénore de Bürger dans la littérature française. Etudes d'histoire littéraire, 1. Sér. Paris, 1907.
Berchet, G. Lettera semiseria di Grisostomo sul Cacciatore feroce e sulla Eleonora di Bürger. Milano, 1816.
Brandl, A. Lenore in England. In: Erich Schmidts Charakteristiken. Berlin, 1886.
Cipolla, F. Aleardi e Bürger. Riv. mens. di letteratura tedesca, 2, 1908.
Colwell, W. B. An Eighteenth Century Translation of Bürger's Leonore. MLN, 24, 1909.
Emerson, O. F. Scott's Early Translations from Bürger. JEGPh, 14, 1915.
—— The Earliest English Translations of Bürger's Leonore: a Study in English and German Romanticism. Western Reserve U. Bull. Cleveland, 1915.
Eschenburg, J. J. Leonore, eine Ballade von Bürger, in drei englischen Uebersetzungen. (Stanley, Spencer, Pye). Göttingen, 1797.
Greg, W. W. English Translations of Lenore. Mod. Quarterly of Lang. and Lit., 2-3, 1899-1900.
Grudzinski, S. Lenore in Polen: eine litterarhistorische Abhandlung. Bochnia, 1890.
Herzfeld, G. Zur Geschichte von Bürgers Lenore in England. Archiv, 106, 1901.
Luzzato, L. Bürger e Manzoni. Fanfulla della Domenica, 27.X.1912.
Parsons, C. O. Scott's Translation of Bürger's Das Lied von der Treue. JEGPh, 33, 1934.
Roberts. Bürgers Lenore. Atheneum, 3823, 1901.
CHAMISSO: See also Intermediaries. I.IV.8.
Bisson, L. A. The First French Edition of Peter Schlemihl. Festschrift Fiedler. Oxford, 1938.
Tardel, H. Vergleichende Studien zu Chamissos Gedichten. ZVL, 13, 1899.
DEDEKIND: See Grobianus, I.VI.10.
Gladding, E. B. Housman's More Poems VII and **DEHMEL'S** Trost. MLN, 56, 1941.
Brown, C. S. T. S. Eliot and die **DROSTE**. Sewanee Rev., Oct., 1938.
Fluegel, E. Carlyle und **ECKERMANN**. JbGG, 24.
Dean, Ruth J. **ELIZABETH**, Abbess of Schönau, and Roger of Ford. MPh, 41, 1943-44.
FICHTE: See also Politics, I.II.5.
Bourdeau, J. Fichte et Mme. de Staël. Journal des Débats, 12.XII.1924.
Janet, P. Fichte et Maine de Biran. RB, 6.VI.1874.
Maggiore, G. Fichte e Gioberti. In: Pagine dell' ora. Milano, 1918.
Perego, L. L'idealismo etico di Fichte e il socialismo contemporaneo. Modena, 1911.
Saisset, E. Travaux publiés en France sur Kant, Fichte, Schelling et Hegel. RDM, 15.II.1846.
Storrs, Margaret. The Relation of Carlyle to Kant and Fichte. Bryn Mawr, 1929. Cf. MPh. 1930.
Berg, R. G. Novalis och **FOUQUE** i Sverige. Stockholm, 1908.
Herzfeld, G. Fouqué und Landor, ein merkwürdiges literarisches Motiv. Archiv, 151, 1926.
FREILIGRATH: See also Intermediaries, I.IV.8.
Anon. Freiligrath in Amerika. Amerika, 25.I.1910.
Appelmann, M. Longfellows Beziehungen zu F. Freiligrath. Münster, 1916.
Engel, E. Ferdinand Freiligrath in englischer Uebersetzung. MLIA, 1876.
Learned, M. D. Freiligrath in Amerika. Americana Germanica, 1, 1897.
Hofschlaeger, M. Jörn Uhl in England. (**FRENSSEN**). Hamburg. Nachrichten, Litteraturbeilage, 24, 1905.
Anon. Herrn Prof. **FRIEDELS** Bemühungen für die Ehre der deutschen Bühne zu Paris. Theater Kalender. Gotha, 1785.
FRIEDRICH DER GROSSE: see also Thematology, I.VI.10. & Voltaire, IV.VII.20.
Albrecht. Friedrich der Grosse auf der Bühne des Théâtre français. Leipziger Zt., 157, 1895.
Allard, Emmy. Friedrich der Grosse in der Literatur Frankreichs. In: Beiträge zur Geschichte der romanischen Sprachen mit einem Ausblick auf Italien und Spanien. Halle, 1913.
Ancona, A. d'. Federico il Grande e gl' Italiani. Roma, 1902; Rostock, 1902. Cf. NAnt, 1902.
Ettlinger, L. Carlyle on Portraits of Frederick the Great. MLR, 40, 1945.
Ferrari, G. Poesie italiane sopra l'ultima guerra consecrate alla S. M. R. di Federigo il Grande, re di Prussia. Vicenzia, 1766.
Fraser, Elizabeth M. Un admirateur français de Frédéric II, traducteur de Télémaque en vers latins. RLC, 13, 1933.

Geiger, L. Friedrich der Grosse in französischen Liedern. Gegenwart, 28, 1884.
Haraszti, Z. John Adams on Frederick the Great. MB, 1934.
Jagdhuhn, G. Die Dichtungen Friedrichs des Grossen. RF, 2, 1936.
Knust, H. Der bleibende Wert des Heldenbildes Friedrichs des Grossen von Carlyle. NM, 10, 1939.
Krause, G. Friedrich der Grosse und die deutsche Poesie. Halle, 1884.
Kürenberg, J. von. Der letzte Vertraute Friedrichs des Grossen, Marchese Giordano Lucchesini. Berlin, 1935.
Ludwig, A. Friedrich der Grosse im spanischen Drama. ZVL, 15, 1904.
Magon, L. Eine unbeachtete Fernwirkung von Friedrich des Grossen De la littérature. Beitrag zur Geschichte der geistigen Beziehungen Deutschlands und Schwedens im 18. Jahrhundert. Festschrift A. Sauer. Stuttgart, 1926.
Marcus, H. Friedrichs des Grossen literarische Propaganda in England. Archiv, 151, 1927.
—— Friedrich der Grosse in der englischen Literatur. Leipzig, 1931.
Serban, N. Alfred de Vigny et Frédéric II; étude d'influence littéraire. Paris, 1920.
Valentin, V. Some Interpretations of Frederick the Great. History, 1934.
Ziehen, E. Friedrich der Grosse und die Schweiz. Leipzig, 1924.
Broicher, C. **FRIES** und Coleridge. PJb, Feb., 1912.
Noordhoek, W. J. **GELLERT** und Holland. Diss. Amsterdam, 1928.
Hegemann, D. V. Boswell's Interviews with Gottsched and Gellert. JEGPh, 46, 1947.
Krumpelmann, J. T. **GERSTAECKER'S** Germelshausen and Lerner's Brigadoon. MDU, 40, 1948.
Suepfle, T. Sechs französische Briefe **GOTTSCHEDS** an Baculard d'Arnaud in Dresden. ZVL, 1, 1888.
Anon. Jugements de Byron sur **GRILLPARZER** et Frédéric Schlegel. Nouvelle Revue Germanique, 35, 1831.
Alkalay, E. Ein Franzose als Grillparzer-Biograph. Norddeutsche Allg. Zt., 63, 1902.
Blankenagel, J. C. Carlyle as a Critic of Grillparzer. PMLA, 42, 1927.
Fiedler, H. G. Notes by G. Meredith on Grillparzer's Ahnfrau. MLR, Oct., 1931.
Jerusalem, I. Ein Gedicht Grillparzers in französischer Nachbildung. JbGrG, 18, 1908.
Meyer, E. Grillparzer und Rostand. MLN, 16, 1901.
Necker, M. Ein Franzose (Aug. Ehrhard) über Grillparzer. JbGrG, 1900.
Parsons, C. O. The Influence of Grillparzer on The Heart of Midlothian. (Scott). N&Q, 189, 1945.
Mahrenholtz, R. Frd. Melch. **GRIMM**, der Vermittler des deutschen Geistes in Frankreich. Archiv, 1889.
Dilkey, M. C. & Schneider, H. John Mitchell Kemble and the Brothers Grimm. JEGPh, 40, 1941.
Hennig, J. The Brothers Grimm and T. C. Croker. MLR, 41, 1946.
Kern, H. Over Jacob Grimm en zijn invloed op de ontwikkeling de Nederland taalwetenschap. Germania, 5. (Brussel), 1903.
Schmidt, E. Briefwechsel der Gebrüder Grimm mit nordischen Gelehrten. Berlin, 1885.
Tonnelat, E. Jacob Grimm et les Slaves du Sud. Revue des Etudes slaves, 1935.
Wilson, J. B. Grimm's Law and the Brahmins. NEQ, 16, 1943.
Dietrich, A. Ein französisches Werk über den Simplizissimus von **GRIMMELSHAUSEN**. MLIA, 1883.
Graf, W. Grimmelshausen in Russland. AK, 23, 1933.
Gudde, E. G. Grimmelshausen's Simplicius Simplicissimus and Defoe's Robinson Crusoe. PhQ, April, 1925.
Hennig, J. Simplicius Simplicissimus' British Relations. MLR, 40. 1945.
Johnson, Hildegard B. The Claus **GROTH** Guild of Davenport, Iowa. AGR, 11, 1944.
Penn, H. Franz Presern und Anastasius **GRUEN**. MLIA, 1888.
Richter, H. Blake und **HAMANN**. Archiv, 158, 1930.
Ruttenauer, J. Hamann und die Fürstin Gallitzin. Hochland, 36, 1938.
Gubernatis, A. de. Robert **HAMERLING** e i suoi traduttori italiani. NAnt, 34, 1877.
Friedrich von **HARDENBERG**: See Novalis, below.
Albert, H. Pariser Briefe (**HAUPTMANN** in Paris). Neue DR, 1894.
Benoist-Hanappier, L. Die französische Uebersetzung der Weber. LE, 15.VII.1906.
Brausewetter, E. Zola über Hauptmann und den Zug zur fremden Litteratur. ZFSL, 1894.
Conrad, H. Hauptmann in englischer Auffassung. Deutsche Zs, 3, 1900.
Dummer, E. H. Gerhart Hauptmann and the Chicago Stage. AGR, 6, 1939-40.
Emerson, H. A Criticism of Meltzer's Translations of Hanneles Himmelfahrt and Die versunkene Glocke. GQ, 1948.
Hasenkamp, G. Von Gerhardt Hauptmann zu Paul Claudel. Jb. der Görres-Ges., 1931.
Jolivet, A. La Winterballade de G. Hauptmann et Herr Arnes penningar de S. Lagerlöf. In: Mélanges Ch. Andler. Strasbourg, 1924.
Mauclair, C. La cloche engloutie au théâtre de l'Oeuvre. Revue Encyclopédique, 27. III.1897.

Mueller, I. Gerhart Hauptmann und Frankreich. GRM, 1937.
Ploetz, A. Gerhart Hauptmann in Amerika. Neue DR. 1894.
Remer, P. Hannele in Paris, MLIA, 7, 1894.
Reuter, O. G. Hauptmann in Italien. MLIA, 7.X.1899.
Scholz, A. Gerhart Hauptmanns Florian Geyer in der Literaturgeschichte. GQ, 20, 1947.
Berg, L. **HEBBEL** und Ibsen. Die Gegenwart, 1890.
Bornstein, P. Cosima Wagner als Hebbel-Uebersetzerin. Hannoverscher Courier, 28. XII.1907.
Hildebrant, G. Das Drama Hebbels und Ibsens. Das Provinz-Theater, 17. Hannover-Dohren, 1913.
Kisch, P. Hebbel und die Tschechen. Prag, 1913.
Paoli, R. Gli studi hebbeliani in Italia. Studi Urbinati, 14, 1940.
Renschel, K. Friedrich Hebbel und Théophile Gautier. SVL, 1, 1901.
Wiehr, J. Hebbel und Ibsen in ihren Anschauungen verglichen. Stuttgart, 1908.
Woerner, R. Ibsen und Hebbels Frauengestalten. Vossische Zt., 564, 1909.
Buechner, A. **HEINSE** und Beyle. Deutsches Museum, 1862.
HERDER: See also Politics, I.II.5.
Bittner, K. J. G. Herders Ideen zur Philosophie der Geschichte der Menschheit und ihre Auswirkungen bei den slavischen Hauptstämmen. GS, 2, 1932-33.
Gillies, A. Two English Translations of Herder's Maran Atha. MLR, 40, 1945.
Heydet, X. La fortune de Herder dans les pays de langue anglaise. RELV, 55, 1938.
Janeff, J. Herder als Kulturphilosoph der Slawen. NSp, 46.
Learned, M. D. Herder and America. German-American Annals, 2, 1904.
Tronchon, H. La fortune intellectuelle de Herder en France. Paris, 1920.
—— Herder et les souvenirs anglais de Weimar. RCC, 15.III.1936.
—— Herder et Henri Amiel. RLC, 3, 1923.
Gillies, A. T. O. Churchill: Translator of Herder's Ideen. MLR, 42, 1947.
Tronchon, H. Victor Cousin, prophète de Herder. RG, 1924.
—— Herder et Lamartine. RLC, 1, 1921.
Gillies, A. Herder and Masaryk: Some Points of Contact. MLR, 40, 1945.
Lanson, G. La formation de la méthode historique de Michelet. Revue d'histoire moderne et contemporaine, Oct., 1905.
Schönebaum, H. Pestalozzi und Herder. AK, 24, 1934.
Tronchon, H. Entre la pensée franco-anglaise et la philosophie allemande: les Portalis émigrés et Herder. MLR, 1919.
Wenderoth, O. Der junge Quinet und seine Uebersetzung von Herders Ideen. Diss. Tübingen, 1906.
Tronchon, H. Renan et Hèrder. RCC, 29, 1927.
—— William Taylor de Norwich et Herder, le Platon du monde chrétien. RG, 1936.
Cassirer, E. Thorild und Herder. Theoria, 7, 1941.
Fogle, S. F. Wordsworth and Herder: A Study in Comparative Ideas. Diss. U. of Illinois 1942-43.
Polderman, F. Maeterlinck et **HEYSE**. La Société nouvelle, 18, 1913.
Kroes, H. W. J. **HOFFMANN VON FALLERSLEBEN** als Vorkämpfer deutscher Kultur in Belgien und Holland. Leipzig, 1915.
HOELDERLIN: See also Parallelisms. I.V.1.
Isherwood, C. German Literature in England: Hoelderlin. New Republic, 5.IV.1939.
Reichenberger, A. G. Hölderlins Lyrik in italienischem Gewande. Le lingue estere, 13, 1948.
Seebass, F. Hölderlin in Frankreich. Das Reich, 3, 1919.
Crepet, J. Baudelaire fut-il en relations avec **HUMBOLDT**? MF, 15.IX.1935.
Leitzmann. W. von Humboldt und Frau von Staël. DR, 1916-17.
Geiger, L. Eine englische Uebersetzung von Straussens **HUTTEN**. MLIA, 1875.
Gentile, G. Giovanni Maria Bertini e l'influsso di **JACOBI** in Italia. Critica, 3, 1905.
Altenheim, Margaret R. **JEAN PAUL'S** Reception in the XIXth and XXth Centuries. Diss. New York U., 1938.
Baldensperger, F. Le Songe de Jean-Paul dans le romantisme français. RU, 1909. And in: Alfred de Vigny, contribution à sa biographie intellectuelle. Paris, 1912.
Brewer, E. V. The New England Interest in Jean Paul Friedrich Richter. UCPPh, 27, 1943.
Buechner, A. Jean-Paul Richter in Frankreich. Stuttgart, 1863.
Hella, A. Jean Paul en France. NL, 30. VI.1928.
Trotzki, M. Jean Paul in Russland. ZDPh, 52, 1927.
Breitinger, H. Carlyle, ein Nachahmer Jean Pauls? Gegenwart, 11.VII.1885.
Conrad, H. Carlyle und Jean Paul. Gegenwart, 20, 1891.
Geissendoerffer, T. Carlyle and Jean Paul Richter. JEGPh, 25, 1926.
Pape, H. Jean Paul als Quelle von Thomas Carlyle's Anschauungen und Stil. Diss. Rostock, 1904'
Brinkley, R. Florence. Some Coleridge Notes on Richter and Reimarus. Princeton U. Library Chron., 5, 1943.
—— Some Unpublished Coleridge Marginalia: Richter and Reimarus. JEGPh, 44, 1945.
Rehm, W. Jean Paul und Dostojewski.

Jb. des Freien Deutschen Hochstifts. Halle, 1940.
Blanguérnon, E. Le Songe de Jean-Paul et Théophile Gautier. RU, 15.V.1910.
Béguin, A. Le Songe de Jean-Paul et Victor Hugo. RLC, 14, 1934.
Deiml, O. Der Prosastil H. W. Longfellows. Der Einfluss von Jean Paul auf Longfellows Prosastil. Kronach, 1927.
Brewer, E. V. The Influence of Jean Paul Richter on George Meredith's Conception of the Comic. JEGPh, 29, 1930.
Fehr, B. Quellenstudien zu G. Meredith: Jean Paul Richter und der Essay on Comedy. Archiv, 127, 1911.
Béguin, A. Une amie française de Jean-Paul: Mme. de Monbart (Josephine de Sydow). RLC, 15, 1935.
Christoph, F. Ueber den Einfluss Jean Paul Fr. Richters auf Thomas de Quincey. Progr. Hof, 1899.
Brewer, E. V. A Pre-Carlylean Critic and Translator of Jean Paul Richter. (Crabb Robinson). GR, 4, 1929.
Heydet, X. Hans **JOHST** en France. RELV, 1937.
Daniel-Rops. A French Catholic Looks at **KAFKA**. Thought, 23, 1948.
Sénéchal, C. **KEYSERLING** et M. P. Souday. Europe, 14, 1927.
Anstett, J. J. J. Giraudoux et H. von **KLEIST**. LM, Aug., 1948.
Heynen, W. Kleist und das Ausland. PJb, 1927.
Minde-Pouet, H. H. Kleist als Bühnenheld. Bühne & Welt, 7.
Nardelli. Il Kleist e il Manzoni. RCLI, 6, 1887.
Peck, L. F. An Adaptation of Kleist's Die Familie Schroffenstein (M. G. Lewis). JEGPh, 44, 1945.
Blomquist, G. **KLOPSTOCK** und Schweden. Deutsch-schwedische Blätter, 1924.
Bologna, G. Di alcune relazioni tra il Klopstock e i poeti italiani. Firenze, 1906.
Eaton, J. W. Klopstock and Danish Literature. GR, 1928.
Elovson, H. Per Elgström och Klopstock. Samlaren, 20, 1939.
Fraenkel, L. Ein französisches Werk über Klopstock. Beilage zur Allg. Zt., 49, 1890.
Girard, H. & Poux, P. Klopstock et le romantisme français jusqu'aux Consolations de Sainte-Beuve. RLC, 8, 1928.
Kurrelmeyer, W. Bodmer über Klopstock und den jungen Wieland. MLN, 58, 1943.
Pasini, F. Per la fortuna di Klosptock in Italia. Padua, 1906.
Pierce, F. E. Blake and Klopstock. SPh, 25, 1928.
Rudwin, M. Les sources de Soumet. CLS, 14-15, 1944.
Scherillo, M. L'Arminio di Pindemonte e la poesia bardita. NAnt, 1890.
Shumway, D. B. Egestorff's Translation of Klopstock's Messias, Compared with Other Early Translations. Americana Germanica, 3, 1901.
Texte, J. Klopstock, Wieland et Lessing en France au XVIIIe siècle. RCC, 16.IV.1896.
Walz, J. A. An English Parallel to Klopstock's Hermannsschlacht. MLN, 1906.
Ware, H. G. An English Note on Klopstock and Kant. MLR, 1928.
Wrangel, E. Klopstock und Schweden. Festschrift Henrik Schück, 1905.
Landau, M. Th. **KOERNER** in Italien. Beilage zur Allg. Zt., 267, 1891.
Negri, L. Al. Manzoni e Teodoro Körner. Atti della R. Accad. delle scienze di Torino, 1920.
Bahlsen, L. **KOTZEBUES** Peru Dramen und Sheridans Pizarro. Archiv, 81.
—— Kotzebue et Sheridan. Progr. Berlin, 1893.
Bogdan-Duica. Ueber die rumänischen Uebersetzer Kotzebues. Jahresberichte f. neuere deutsche Litteraturgeschichte, 11, 1903.
Busnelli, M. D. Une devise de Joubert inspirée par Kotzebue. RHLF, 1931.
Butler, E. M. Mansfield Park and Kotzebue's Lovers' Vows. MLR, 1933.
Coleman, A. P. Kotzebue in Russia. GR, 5, 1930.
—— Kotzebue in tschechischer Uebertragung. ZSPh, 11, 1934.
Curcin, M. Kotzebue im Serbokroatischen. ASPh, 1909.
Gillet, J. E. A Forgotten German Creditor of the English Stage. NC, 1912.
Gosch, Marcella. Translators of Kotzebue in England. MDU, 31, 1939.
Koeppel, E. Kotzebue in England. ESn, 13, 1891.
Ludwig, A. Kotzebue und Delavigne. Archiv, 162, 1933.
Munteano, B. L'âme sensible, le génie français et les débuts de Kotzebue en France. RLC, 9, 1929.
Petzet. Kotzebue im französischen Urtheile. Beilage zur Allg. Zt., 104, 1894.
Pink, M. A. Jane Austin and a Forgotten Dramatist. NC, 1927.
Schneider, F. Kotzebue en España. MPh, 25, 1927.
Schott, F. Kotzebue, Deutschland und Russland. Leipzig, 1820.
Sellier, W. Kotzebue in England. Leipzig, 1901.
Stender Petersen, A. Gogol und Kotzebue. ZSPh, 12, 1935.
Suepfle, T. Kotzebue in Frankreich und England. ZVL, 6, 1892.
Thompson, L. F. Kotzebue. A Survey of his Progress in France and England. Paris, 1928.
Hewett-Thayer, H. W. Ferdinand **LASSALLE** in the Novels of Spielhagen and Meredith. GR, 19, 1944.

Anon. Corrispondenza tra Ludovico Ant. Muratori e G. di **LEIBNIZ**. Modena 1892.
Bacharach, A. Shaftesbury's Optimismus und sein Verhältnis zum Leibnizschen. Diss. Strassburg, 1912.
Faggi, A. Montesquieu e Leibnitz. Atti d. R. Accad. di Torino, 69, 1934.
Ferrari, G. M. Il Leibniz giudicato da G. B. Vico. L'Arduo, 30.IV.1921.
Guerrier, W. Leinbnitz in seinen Beziehungen zu Russland und Peter dem Grossen. Petersburg, Leipzig, 1873.
Hazard, P. Voltaire et Leibniz. Académie royale de Belgique, 1937.
Heinemann, F. H. Toland and Leibniz. Philosophical Review, 54, 1945.
Hess, G. Leibniz korrespondiert mit Paris. Hamburg, 1940.
Klibansky, R. Leibniz' Unknown Correspondence with English Scholars and Men of Letters. London, 1941.
László, H. Leibniz et la Russie. Cahiers de littérature comparée. Budapest, 1948.
Moore, C. A. Did Leibniz Influence Pope's Essay? JEGPh, 16, 1917.
Olgiati, F. Il significato storico di Leibniz. Milano, 1929.
Phedon. Leibnitz et Proust. Publicateur de Béziers, 23.II.1924.
Reumont, A. Magliabecchi, Muratori e Leibnitz. Memoria intorno alle relazioni litterarie tra l'Italia e la Germania. In: Beiträge zur italien. Geschichte. Berlin, 1853-57.
Robef, E. Leibniz et Maine de Biran. Diss. Paris, 1925.
LENAU: See also Intermediaries, I.IV.8.
Baker, G. T. Lenau and Young Germany in America. Baltimore, 1897.
Chelard, R. Le poète Lenau et le pangermanisme (Lenau et la Hongrie). MF, Oct., 1902.
Fraenkel, L. Lenau in Frankreich. Beilage zur Allg. Zt., 184, 1902.
Holzer, R. Ein Franzose über Lenau (Jacques Saly-Stern). Neue Freie Presse, 13622, 1902.
Karl, L. Petöfi et Lenau. RLC, 17, 1937.
Montelin, G. Nicolaus Lenau i Danmark och Norge. Nordisk Tidskrift, 16, 1940.
Rossi, G. Nicolas Lenau e la critica italiana. Convivium, 1936.
Strecker, K. Französische Lenaulitteratur. Tägliche Rundschau, 184, 1902.
Anon. **LESSING** in England. MLIA, 1878.
Baker, G. M. An Early English Translation of Miss Sarah Sampson. MLN, 1907.
Balk, F. Lessing auf der niederländischen Bühne bis 1830. Diss. Nijmegen, 1927.
Blind, K. Lessings Nathan der Weise in England. MLIA, 1882 & 1883.
Boltz. Lessing in Griechenland. MLIA, 1880.
Collins, C. Browning and Lessing. London, 1902.
Ducros, L. Le Laocoon de Lessing et la critique contemporaine. Bull. mens. de la Faculté des Lettres. Poitiers, 1884.
Goodnight, S. H. Lessing and Wieland in American Magazines Prior to 1846. German-American Annals, 6, 1908.
Hall, V. Kafka, Lessing, and Vigny. CL, 1, 1949.
Hermann, A. Lessings Nathan in Ungarn. ZVL, 4, 1891.
Mendes dos Remédios. Lessing fabulista na literatura portuguesa. Biblos, 5, 1929.
Kenwood, S. H. Lessing in England. MLR, 9, 1914.
Kinkel, H. Lessings Dramen in Frankreich. Diss. Heidelberg; Darmstadt, 1908.
Lunding, E. Lessing und Kierkegaard. Orbis Litterarum (Copenhagen), 1947.
Matta, G. Como se transforma un drama en 88 años: Emilia Galotti (1772) y G. Gutierrez (1860). La América, 4, 1860-61.
Merbach, P. A. G. E. Lessing als dramatis persona. In: Lessingbuch. Berlin, 1926.
Requadt, P. Lessing, Schlegel, Kierkegaard. NSR, 1929.
Roedder, E. Lessing's Nathan der Weise auf der englischen Bühne. MDU, 34, 1942.
Schmaus, A. Lessings Fabeln bei D. Obradovic. ZSPh, 8, 1931.
Schneider, H. Lessing und Amerika. MDU 1938.
—— Lessing's Miss Sara Sampson: Die erste englische Uebersetzung. PMLA, 54, 1939.
Segré, C. Il Lessing a Torino. NAnt, 1. III.1931.
Texte, J. Klopstock, Wieland et Lessing en France au XVIIIe siècle. RCC, 1896.
Todt, W. Lessing in England, 1767-1850. Heidelberg, 1912.
Vetlesen, A. S. Kierkegaard og G. Chr. **LICHTENBERG**. Edda, 34, 1934.
Gentile, G. Francesco Bonatelli e l'influsso di **LOTZE** in Italia. Critica, 20.I.1907.
—— Carlo Cantoni e l'influsso di Lotze in Italia. Cultura, 20.V.1907.
Kraushaar, O. Lotze's Influence on the Pragmatism and Practical Philosophy of William James. JHI, 1, 1940.
Martin **LUTHER**: See III.I.3.
Gronicka, A. von. Thomas **MANN** and Russia. GR, 20, 1945.
Ordon, E. Thomas Mann's Joseph Cycle and the American Critic. MDU, 35, 1943.
Perl, W. Thomas Mann 1933 bis 1945: Vom deutschen Humanisten zum amerikanischen Weltbürger. New York, 1945.
Rohmer, C. Buddenbrooks and The Forsyte Saga (Galsworthy). Diss. Würzburg, 1933.
Schlappner, M. Thomas Mann im Spiegel der französischen Kritik der Zwischenkriegszeit. Schweizer Annalen, 6-7, 1946-47.
Karl **MARX**: See I.II.5.
Schmid, G. **MATTHISON** und Linné. Berlin, 1935.

Snyder, A. D. Coleridge's Reading of **MENDELSSOHN'S** Morgenstunden und Jerusalem. JEGPh, 28, 1929.
Parsons, C. O. The Possible Origin of Lockhart's Adam Blair (**MUELLNER**). N&Q, 189, 1945.
Pfeiffer-Belli, W. Thomas **MURNER** im Schweizer Glaubenskampf. Münster, 1940.
Bush, D. **MUSAEUS** in English Verse. MLN, 1928.
Herzfeld, G. Eine neue Quelle für Lewis' Monk. Archiv, 104, 1900.
—— Noch einmal die Quelle des Monk. Archiv, 1906.
NIBELUNGEN: See Comparisons, I.V.1. and Thematology, I.VI.10.
Andler, C. Les précurseurs de **NIETZSCHE**. Paris, 1920. Cf. RB, 1.I.1921.
Bianquis, G. Nietzsche en France. Paris, 1929.
Blei, F. Nietzsche in Frankreich. Die Zeit, 459, 1903.
Foerster-Nietzsche, E. Nietzsche in France and England. OC, 34, 1920.
Gaultier, J. de. Nietzsche et la pensée française. MF, Sept., 1904.
Gourmont, J. de. Les Nietzschéennes. MF, 17.VII.1903.
Hartig, P. Nietzsche und die französische Deutschland-Ideologie. NM, Nov., 1937.
Hultsch, P. Das Denken Nietzsches in seiner Bedeutung für England. GRM, 26, 1938.
Lichtenberger, H. Nietzsche in Frankreich. Die Zeit, 1.IX.1900.
—— Nietzsches Einfluss auf die französische Literatur. Bühne & Welt, 9, 1907.
—— Nietzsche et la crise de la culture contemporaine. Nouvelle Revue de Hongrie, Oct., 1935.
Mauclair, C. Nietzsche in Frankreich. Zeitgeist, 31, 1901.
Muret, M. Nietzsche et la littérature européenne. Journal des Débats, 29.III.1902.
—— Nietzsche et la pensée française. Journal des Débats, 4.V.1905.
Petzold, Gertrud von. Nietzsche in englisch-amerikanischer Beurteilung bis zum Ausgang des Weltkrieges. Anglia, 53, 1929.
Prozor, M. Nietzsche en Russie. MF, March, 1901.
Schuré, E. Nietzsche en France et la psychologie de l'Athée. RB, 8.IX.1900.
Seillière, E. Nietzsche dans le roman français. L'Opinion, 25.VII.1908.
Serieyx de Villers. La faillite du surhomme et la psychologie de Nietzsche. Paris, 1920.
Stemplinger, D. Ein deutscher Irrlehrer des Auslandes. Internat. Monatsschrift f. Wissenschaft, Kunst & Technik, 11, 1917.
Wilhelm, J. Friedrich Nietzsche und der französische Geist. Hamburg, 1939.
Albert, H. A propos des Mouettes: Nietzsche et M. Paul Adam. MF, 1.XII.1906 & 1.I.1907.
Cantinelli, R. Un poète Nietzschéen (d' Annunzio). RB, 8.VIII.1903.
Platz, H. Nietzsche und Bourget. NM, May, 1937.
Petzold, Gertrud von. John Davidson und sein geistiges Werden unter dem Einfluss Nietzsches. Leipzig, 1928.
Lang, B. Renée. Andre Gide et Nietzsche: étude chronologique. RR, 34, 1943.
Gelrot, M. Nietzsche and Gorki (in Russian). Russkoe Bogatstvo, 1903.
Albert, H. Nietzsche et Strindberg. MF, 16.IV.1913.
Jolivet, A. Strindberg et Nietzsche. RLC, 19, 1939.
Strecker, K. Nietzsche und Strindberg. München, 1925.
Fey, E. P. Valéry und Nietzsche. NM, 1931.
Berg, R. G. **NOVALIS** och Fouqué i Sverige. Stockholm, 1908,
Braak, S. Novalis et le symbolisme français. NPh, 7, 1922.
Harrold, C. F. Carlyle and Novalis. SPh, 27, 1930.
Matenko, P. Fragments from Longfellow's Workshop: Novalis. GR, 22, 1947.
Rousseaux, A. Hic et nunc, ou de Novalis à André Gide. In: Littérature du vingtième siècle. Paris, 1938.
Seckarev, V. Novalis und Caadaev. ZSPh, 12, 1935.
Steinkopf, Hanna. Novalis et Sénancour. RLC, 15, 1935.
Loomis C. G. Martin **OPITZ** in Seventeenth-Century England. MLQ, 6, 1945.
Weevers, T. Some Unrecorded Dutch Originals of Opitz. NPh, 23, 1937-38.
Anon. August Graf von **PLATEN** in Zürich. Schweizer Bücher Zt. 4, 1947.
Fasola, C. G. Gherardo de Rossi e August von Platen: Bibliografia. Rivista di lett. tedesca, 2, 1908.
Pocsini, F. Carducci e Platen. Pagine triane, 1.
Quarantotto, G. Carducci e un Lied di A. von Platen. Pagine triane, 1.
POSTL (Sealsfield): See Intermediaries, I.IV.8.
Ingers, E. Satiriken **RABENER** och hans svenska bearbetere. Samlaren, 23, 1902-03.
Brinkley, R. Florence. Some Unpublished Coleridge Marginalia: Richter and **REIMARUS**. JEGPh, 44, 1945.
Anon. Eine französische Beurteilung Fritz **REUTERS**. MLIA, 1869.
Maas, M. Fritz Reuter im französischen Gewande. Archiv, 1869.
—— Philarète Chasles über Fritz Reuter. Archiv, 1869.
J. P. F. **RICHTER**: See Jean Paul, above.
Betz, M. **RILKE** in Frankreich. Wien, 1938.
Closs, A. Rilkes Sonette an Orpheus in englischer Uebersetzung. D&V, 39, 1938.

Mises, R. von. Rilke in English: A Tentative Bibliography. Cambridge (Mass.), 1947.
Sachs, G. R. M. Rilke en España. Rev. hispano-moderna, April, 1938.
San Lazzaro, Clementina di. Die Aufzeichnungen des Malte Laurids Brigge von R. M. Rilke in Vergleich mit Jacobsens Niels Lyhne und A. Gides Nourritures Terrestres. GRM, 29, 1941.
Siebels, E. Italienische Rilkeforschung. D&V, 39, 1938.
—— Italienische Rilke-Uebersetzungen. D&V, 39, 1938.
Wood, F. Rilke and D. H. Lawrence. GR, 15, 1940.
Anon. **ROSEGGER** in französischer Beleuchtung. Basler Nachrichten, 217, 1903.
SACHS: See also Sources, I.V.2.
Baberadt, F. Hans Sachs im Andenken der Nachwelt. Halle, 1906.
Eichler, F. Das Nachleben des Hans Sachs vom 16. bis 19. Jahrhundert. Leipzig, 1904.
Kalff, G. Bredero en Hans Sachs. Tijdskrift van Nederl. Taal- en Letterkunde, 6.
Duprat, P. Les idées de **SAVIGNY** en France. Revue Indépendante, 1844.
Gibelin, J. L'esthétique de **SCHELLING** et l'Allemagne de Mme. de Staël. Paris, 1934.
Nidecker, H. Notes marginales de S. T. Coleridge. RLC, 7, 1927.
Schuhl, P. M. Ravaisson, Quinet, Schelling. RMM, 1936.
Setschkareff, W. Schellings Einfluss in der russischen Literatur der 20er und 30er Jahre des 19. Jahrhunderts. Diss. Leipzig, 1939.
Buchbinder, M. George Ohnet und Johann **SCHERR**. MLIA, 30.X.1897.
Baldensperger, F. Extraits de la correspondance des enfants de Mme. de Staël avec A. W. **SCHLEGEL**. RHLF, 1909.
Bertrand, J. J. A. G. Schlegel et la France. RG, 1922.
Helmholtz, A. The Indebtedness of S. T. Coleridge to A. W. Schlegel. Bull. of the U. of Wisconsin, 1907.
Jaeck, Emma G. The Indebtedness of Madame de Staël to A. W. Schlegel. JEGPh, 10, 1911.
Körner, J. Johann Nicolas Böhl von Faber und A. W. Schlegel. NSp, 1929.
Pange, Mme. J. de. Auguste-Guillaume Schlegel et Mme. de Staël. Paris, 1938 & Hamburg, 1940.
Peyroube, J. Aug. Guill. Schlegel et Mme. de Staël. Etudes, 5.XII.1938.
Schnöckelborg, G. A. W. Schlegels Einfluss auf William Hazlitt als Shakespeare-Kritiker. Diss. Münster. Emsdetten, 1931.
Walzel, O. F. Frau von Staël's Buch De l'Allemagne und W. Schlegel. Festgabe R. Heinzel. Weimar, 1898.
Allen, G. W. Sidney Lanier as a Literary Critic. PhQ, 17, 1938.
Bleyer, J. Franz Szechenyi und Friedrich Schlegel. Budapesti Szemle, June, 1912.
Curtius, E. R. Friedrich Schlegel und Frankreich. ZFEU, 31, 1932.
Koerner, J. Friedrich Schlegel und Mme. de Staël. PJb, June, 1934. And in: Friedrich Schlegel. Frankfurt, 1935.
Rühle-Gerstel, A. F. Schlegel und Chamfort. Euphorion, 24, 1923.
Eaton, J. W. Johann Elias Schlegel in Denmark. MLR, 1928.
Berthoud, A. Aug. Sabatier et **SCHLEIERMACHER** Revue de Théologie, 1901-02.
Anon. Eine französische Beurtheilung **SCHOPENHAUERS**. MLIA, 1874.
Baillot, A. De l'influence de Schopenhauer sur la littérature française. Revue des Lettres. (Bordeaux), 1925.
—— L'influence de la philosophie de Schopenhauer en France, 1860-1900. Paris, 1927.
—— Schopenhauer im Urteil seiner französischen Zeitgenossen. Jb. der Schopenhauer-Ges., 19, 1932.
—— La filiation spirituelle de Schopenhauer en France. Jb. der Schopenhauer-Ges., 21, 1934.
—— Schopenhauer et la pensée française contemporaine. Jb. der Schopenhauer-Ges., 23, 1936.
Bourdeau, J. Schopenhauer en Italie. Journal des Débats, 4.XI.1920.
Furreg, E. Schopenhauer und Schweden. Jb. der Schopenhauer-Ges., 26, 1939.
Goodale, R. H. Schopenhauer and Pessimism in Nineteenth Century English Literature. PMLA, 47, 1932.
Guetzlaff. Schopenhauer in Frankreich. MLIA, 1880.
Hatscher, L. Englische Bücher über Heine und Schopenhauer. MLIA, 1876.
Neugebauer, P. Schopenhauer in England, mit besonderer Berücksichtigung seines Einflusses auf die englische Literatur. Diss. Berlin, 1932.
Rydsjo, D. Eine schwedische Schopenhauer-Uebersetzung. Jb. der Schopenhauer-Ges., 18, 1931.
Springer, R. Arthur Schopenhauer vor der französischen Kritik. Deutsches Museum, 1864.
Lux, J. Balzac et Schopenhauer. RB, 16. III.1912.
Bidou, H. Schopenhauer et H. Bataille. Journal des Débats, 1.II.1925.
Antal, J. Bergson und Schopenhauer. Jb. der Schopenhauer-Ges., 3, 1914.
Brockdorff, C. von. Die Wahrheit über Bergson. Berlin, 1916.
Jacoby, G. Henry Bergson und A. Schopen-

hauer. Internationale Monatsschrift, 10, 1916.
Phelps, W. L. Browning, Schopenhauer and More. NAR, Oct., 1917.
Krakowski, E. Le premier disciple de Schopenhauer en France (Challemel-Lacour). MF, 1932.
Croce, B. De Sanctis e Schopenhauer. Atti dell'Accad. pontaniana, 32, 1903.
Frühn, T. Schopenhauers Einfluss auf Mihail Eminescu. Jb. der Schopenhauer Ges., 23, 1936.
Steinbach, A. Thomas Hardy und Schopenhauer. Festschrift Alois Brandl. Leipzig, 1925.
Delavenay, E. Sur un exemplaire de Schopenhauer annoté par D. H. Lawrence. RAA, Feb., 1936.
Balche, A. de. M. Renan et A. Schopenhauer. Odessa, 1870.
Baillot, A. Taine et Schopenhauer. MF, 1.IV.1928.
Armond, F. d'. Thoreau and Schopenhauer. NEQ, 5, 1932.
Baillot, A. De l'influence de Schopenhauer sur la littérature française: Vigny. Revue des Lettres, March, 1925.
Wilkens, F. H. Dr. Charles Burney on **SCHUBART**. Americana Germanica, 1899.
SEALSFIELD: See Intermediaries. I.IV.8.
Anon. **SPINDLER** und die englische Kritik. Blätter für literar. Unterhaltung, 28.VII.1835.
—— **STERNBERGS** Novellen von einem Engländer beurteilt. Blätter zur Kunde der Litteratur des Auslands, 1837.
Contenson, L. de. Le baron de **STEUBEN** et la propagande allemande aux Etats-Unis. Le Correspondant, 10.IV.1931.
Baker, G. M. Graf Friedrich zu **STOLBERG** in England. MLN, 21, 1906.
Cyzecskyj, D. T. Sevcenko una David **STRAUSS**. ZSPh, 8, 1931.
Guttmann, R. David Fr. Strauss (und Renan). Die Wage, 11, 1908.
Olsson, B. D. F. Strauss och Sverige. Svensk. Dagbl., 10.IV.1930.
Raumer, F. von. Schwartz, Strauss, Renan. Leipzig, 1864.
Dummer, E. H. Hermann **SUDERMANN**, A Contributor to American Culture. AGR, 13, 1947.
Elsenhans, P. C. Vom neuesten italienischen Schauspielwesen. Gegenwart, 1895-96.
Hoefer, M. Sudermanns Heimat in London. MLIA, 1895.
Fasola, C. L. **TIECK** in Italia. Riv. mens. di letteratura tedesca, 1, 1907.
Fischer, L. H. L. Tieck und A. Oehlenschläger. In: Aus Berlins Vergangenheit. Berlin, 1891.
Matenko, P. Tieck's Russian Friends. PMLA, 55, 1940.
Vetterlund, F. En sagodikt av Tieck och "Lycksalighetens ö". (Atterbom). Samlaren, 21, 1940.
Zeydel, E. H. George Ticknor and Ludwig Tieck. PMLA, 44, 1929.
—— Washington Irving and Ludwig Tieck. PMLA, 46, 1931.
—— Ludwig Tieck, the German Romanticist. Princeton, 1935.
Betz, L. P. **UHLAND** in Frankreich. LE, July, 1901.
Carofa, A. S. Baldacchini traduttore di Uhland. Riv. di letteratura tedesca, 5, 1911.
Fischer, H. Uhlands Beziehungen zu ausländischen Litteraturen. ZVL, 1, 1887.
Hausknecht, E. Das Glück von Edenhall (Uhland-Longfellow). Archiv, 98, 1897.
Kaeslin, H. Ludwig Uhlands französische Kritiker und Uebersetzer. Progr. Baden (Schweiz), 1900.
Longo, T. Uhland in Italia. Riv. mens. di letteratura tedesca, 1, 1907.
Mahrenholtz, R. Ein italienisches Urteil über Uhland. Archiv, 1887.
Schwabe, T. Uhland in Italien. N. Tageblatt, Unterhaltungsbeilage, 100. Stuttgart, 1912.
Stoeckle, J. H. W. Longfellow, der Uhland Nord-Amerikas. Rhein. Blätter für Erziehung & Unterricht, 1897.
Fischer, W. Charlotte W. Wynn in ihren Beziehungen zu **VARNHAGEN VON ENSE** und R. M. Milnes. GRM, Sept., 1921.
Paludan, J. Hur mag. Johann **VELTENS** skådespelertrupp upptradt i Stockholm. Samlaren, 1890.
Stender-Petersen, A. J. H. **VOSS** und der junge Gogol. Edda, 1920.
Peck, W. E. Shelley, Mary Shelley and Rinaldo Rinaldini (**VULPIUS**), PMLA, 40, 1925.
Arnoux, A. Rencontres avec R. **WAGNER**. Paris, 1927.
Baudelaire, C. Richard Wagner et Tannhaeuser à Paris. Rev. Européenne, April, 1861.
Boschot, A. Un cénacle wagnérien à Paris (1885). RB, 20.V.1922.
Chamberlain, H. S. Richard Wagner et le génie français. RDM, 15.VII.1896.
Dujardin, E. Richard Wagner et les poètes français contemporains. Revue de Genève, Nov., 1886.
Evenepoel, E. Le wagnérisme hors d' Allemagne. Paris, 1891.
Friedlaender, A. H. von. Der Wagner-Cultus in Frankreich. Gegenwart, 29.IX.1900.
Jäckel, K. Richard Wagner in der französischen Literatur. Breslau, 1931-32.
Jacobson, A. Nachklänge Richard Wagners im Roman. Heidelberg, 1932.
Jaloux, E. Richard Wagner und die französische Poesie. Deutsche Musik Zt, 1902.
Kobbe, G. Wagner in America. Review of Reviews, 20, 1899.

Lassus, J. de. L'influence wagnérienne sur le symbolisme français. Vie des Peuples, Dec., 1925.
Malherbe, H. Richard Wagner et notre temps. MF, 15.VII.1936.
Mauclair, C. R. Wagner und das französische Publikum. Wiener Rundschau, 1. I.1900.
Mendès, C. L'oeuvre wagnérienne en France. Paris, 1899.
Moser, M. Richard Wagner in der englischen Literatur des 19. Jahrhunderts. Bern, 1938.
Rosny, J. H. L'influence de Wagner sur notre littérature. Société internationale de musique. 1913.
Rossi, G. C. Il Tristano di Wagner in versi italiani. Convivium, 10, 1938.
Smyth, E. Wagner in London, Fortnightly Review, Sept., 1936.
Werner, R. R. Wagners dramatische Werke in französischer Uebersetzung. Progr. Berlin, 1901-02.
Woolley, G. Richard Wagner et le symbolisme français. Paris, 1931.
Wyzewa, T. de. Littérature wagnérienne en France. RB, 15.IX.1894.
Wyzewa, Isabelle de. L'interprétation esthétique de Wagner en France. Paris, 1934.
Zapp, A. Richard Wagner von einem Spanier beurteilt. MLIA, 1881.
Souday, P. Barrès et Wagner. Paris-Midi, 12.I.1916.
Zamboni, E. Riccardo Wagner e Francesco De Sanctis. Fanfulla della Domenica, 29, 1907.
Jacobs, R. L. Wagner and Judith Gautier. Music and Letters, April, 1937.
Samazeuilh, G. Richard Wagner et Judith Gautier. Le Ménestrel, 23.IX.1932.
Pottecher, M. Jean Jaurès et Richard Wagner. Grande Revue, July, 1932.
Anon. Richard Wagner in Frankreich. (H. Lichtenberger). MLIA, 68, 1899.
Carcassonne, E. Wagner et Mallarmé. RLC, 16, 1936.
Festerling, W. C. Mendès' Beziehungen zu Richard Wagner. Diss. Greifswald, 1913.
Burns, Sister M. Vincentia. The Wagnerian Theory of Art and Its Influence on the Drama of Eugene O'Neill. Diss. U. of Pa., 1943.
Vigneron, R. Structure de Swann: Balzac, Wagner et Proust. FR, 19, 1946.
Anon. Einführung Richard Wagners in Frankreich (Edouard Schuré). MLIA, 1875.
Petzold, B. Edouard Schuré über Richard Wagner und Anderes. Deutsche Revue, July, 1898.
Heydet, X. Richard Wagner et Bernard Shaw. RELV, June, 1937.
Hennequin, E. L'esthétique de Wagner et la doctrine spencérienne. Revue Wagneriénne, 8.XI.1885.
Drougard, E. Richard Wagner et Villiers de l'Isle-Adam. RLC, 14, 1934.

WALTHER VON DER VOGELWEIDE: See also Politics, I.II.5.

Baragiola, A. Ein Gedicht Walthers von der Vogelweide in italienischer Uebersetzung. MLIA, 1882.
Gerstmayer, G. Walter von der Vogelweide im Wandel der Jahrhunderte. Breslau, 1934.
Sprenger, R. Longfellows Walter von der Vogelweide. ZDU, 7, 1893.
Forster, L. G. R. **WECKHERLIN** and the Choyce of a Wife. MLR, 38.
Koltonovskaia, E. The Problem of Sex and its Treatment (in **WEDEKIND** and Artzybashev) (In Russian) Obrazovanie, 1908.
Frey, J. R. America and Franz **WERFEL.** GQ, 19, 1946.
Reinhardstoettner, K. von. Zacharias **WERNERS** Vierundzwanzigster Februar in Spanien. Beilage zur Allg. Zt., 144, 1892
Rotondi, G. Il Corrade di G. Zanella e i 24. Febbraio di Z. Werner. Athenaeum Oct., 1920.
Wismer, E. Der Einfluss des deutschen Romantikers Z. Werner in Frankreich. Diss. Neuchâtel. Affoltern, 1928.
Anon. Traduction d'Obéron, poème de **WIELAND,** par M. Jullien. RDM, 1.V.1843.
Beyer, W. W. Coleridge, Wieland's Oberon and The Ancient Mariner. RES, 15, 1939.
—— Coleridge, Wieland's Oberon and The Wanderings of Cain. RES, 16, 1940.
Colwell, W. A. The First English Translation of Wieland's Oberon. PMLA, 57, 1942. Cf. also MLN, 22, 1907.
Faust, A. B. John Quincy Adams and Wieland. AGR, 5, 1938.
—— Wieland's Oberon translated by John Quincy Adams. Introduction and Notes by A. B. Faust. New York, 1939.
Gillies, A. A Scottish Correspondent of Wieland's and the Importation of German into Scotland (J. Macdonald). MLR, 1935.
Goodnight, S. H. Lessing and Wieland in American Magazines Prior to 1846. German-American Annals, 6, 1908.
Koszé, J. Ueber Wielands Beliebtheit in Ungarn. Deutsch-ungar. Heimatsblatt, 1, 1929.
Kurrelmeyer, W. English Translations of Wieland. MLN, 32, 1917.
—— Bodmer über Klopstock und den jungen Wieland. MLN, 58, 1943.
Mackall, L. L Coleridge Marginalia on Wieland and Schiller. MLR, 1924.
Priebsch, R. Zur Wertschätzung von Wielands Oberon in England. Archiv, 118, 1907.
Texte, J. Klopstock, Wieland et Lessing en France au XVIIIe siècle. RCC, 5, 1896.

Dimoff, P. **WINCKELMANN** et André Chénier. RLC, 21, 1947.
Dellner, J. Den wolffska filosofien och svensk teologi. (**WOLFF**). Stockholm, 1930.
Mincuk, J. Christian Wolff und seine Schule in der Ukraine. GS, 3, 1935.
Götz, J. Die Entwicklung des **WOLFRAM**-Bildes von Bodmer bis zum Tode Lachmanns in der germanistischen und schönen Literatur. Freiburg, 1940.
Raschen, J. F. L. **ZEDLITZ** and Barthelemy: A Study in Literary Relations. GR, 1, 1925-26.
Freedman, Florence B. Walt Whitman and Heinrich **ZSCHOKKE**: A Further Note. AL,15,1943.
Glicksberg, C. J. W. Whitman and H. Zschokke. N&Q, 2.VI.1934.
Hoskins, J. P. Parke Godwin and the Translation of Zschokke's Tales. PMLA, 20, 1905.

CHAPTER THIRTEEN

The German Language.

Anon. The Study of the German Language. What are the Benefits and Dangers Incident to a Minister from the Study of the German Language? Christian Review, (Boston), 1836.
—— New York: Errichtung eines Lehrstuhls für deutsche Literatur. Beilage zur Allg. Zt., 30.VIII.1843.
—— Die deutsche Sprachgrenze nach Belgien, Frankreich und Italien. Europa, 1848.
—— Zur Geschichte der deutschen Sprache in Amerika. MLIA, 1869.
Andler, C. La chaire de langues et littératures d'origine germanique au Collège de France: Philarète Chasles, Guillaume Guizot, Arthur Chuquet. RLC, 7, 1927.
Arbois de Jubainville. La langue franque, le vieux haut-allemand et la langue française. Romania, 1, 1872.
Bartsch, K. Vom germanischen Geist in den romanischen Sprachen. Verhandlungen des Rostocker Philologentages, 1875.
Bass, A. Deutsche Sprachinseln in Südtirol und Oberitalien. Leipzig, 1902.
Behrens, D. Ueber deutsches Sprachgut im Französischen. Giessen, 1924.
Bernhardi, K. Die Sprachgrenze zwischen Deutschland und Frankreich. Kassel, 1871.
Blankenagel, J. C. An Early American Defense of the Study of German. GQ, Nov., 1933.
Bludau, H. Influence des éléments germaniques sur le vieux français proprement dit. Progr. Deutsch-Crone, 1866.
Brandes, H. K. Die Wörter deutschen Stammes in der französischen Sprache. Detmola, 1867.
Brandl, A. Die Bedeutung der deutschen Sprache über See für Deutschlands Welt-Stellung. Beilage zur Allg. Zt., 235, 1902.
Braune, T. Neue Beiträge zur Kenntniss romanischer Wörter deutscher Herkunft. ZRPh, 20, 1896.
Bruckner, W. Charakteristik der germanischen Elemente im Italienischen. Progr. Basel, 1899.
Brunot, F. L'influence germanique sur la langue française du moyen âge. In: Histoire de la langue et de la littérature française. Paris, 1896.
Buechner, A. Der deutsche Unterricht im modernen Frankreich. MLIA, 1891.
Carlson, H. G. Recent American Loan Words from Germany. American Speech, 15, 1940.
Carr, C. T. German Grammars in England in the 19th Century. MLR, Oct., 1935.
Cipriani, C. J. Etude sur quelques noms propres d'origine germanique (en français et en italien). Diss. Angers, 1901.
Dorpalen, A. German Influences on the American Language. AGR, 7, 1941.
Ehlers, L. Die germanischen Elemente des Altfranzösischen. Progr. 1878-79.
Eichler, A. Die deutsche Sprache in Amerika. Leipziger Zt., 147, 1892.
—— Deutsches Kulturgut im modernenglischen Wortschatz. Archiv, 182, 1943.
Gamillscheg, E. Germanisches im Französischen. ZFSL, 1937, Suppl., 15.
Genelin, P. Germanische Bestandtheile des rhätoromanischen Wortschatzes. Progr. Innsbruck, 1901.
Goebel, J. Deutsch in Amerika. Zukunft, 20.VII.1895.
Goguel, E. Les éléments germaniques dans la langue française. Bull. de la Soc. litt. de Strasbourg, 5, 1870.
Goldschmidt, M. Zur Kritik der altgermanischen Elemente im Spanischen. Diss. Bonn, 1887.
—— Germanisches Kriegswesen im Spiegel des romanischen Lehnwortes. Festgabe W. Foerster. Halle, 1902.
Graf, A. E. Germanische und insbesondere deutsche Lehn- und Fremdwörter im Russischen. Posen, Leipzig, 1943.
Gross, F. Germanismen im Pariser Argot. Gegenwart, 14, 1878.
Guenther, S. Deutsche Sprachreste in Südtirol und an der Grenze Italiens. Beilage zur Allg. Zt., 289, 1891.
—— Von der deutsch-italienischen Sprachgrenze. Die Nation, 10, 1891.
Halbfass. Zwei verschollene deutsche Sprachinseln in Piemont. Wissenschaftliche Beilage der Leipziger Zt., 20-22, 1893.
Hottenrott, K. Ueber germanische Wörter im Französischen. Progr. Köln, 1876.
Huebner, E. Altgermanisches in England.

Westdeutsche Zs. f. Geschichte & Kunst, 3, 1884.
Kaestner, W. Die deutschen Lehnwörter im Polnischen. Leipzig, 1939.
Kester, F. F. Deutsch-Amerikanisch. Eine Sprachstudie. NSp, 1902.
Kiepert, H. Die Sprachgrenze in Elsass-Lothringen. Zs. der Ges. für Erdkunde, 9. (Berlin), 1874.
Klaeber, F. Die deutsche Sprache in den Vereinigten Staaten von Amerika. NM, 11, 1940-41.
Kloss, H. Zwei Vorkämpfer germanischen Sprachtums unter den Angelsachsen. ZNS, 1944.
Koenig, K. F. German Loan Words in America, 1930-40. GQ, 18, 1942.
Kornmesser, E. Die französischen Ortsnamen germanischer Abkunft. Diss. Strassburg, 1888.
Koziol, H. Der deutsche Einfluss auf den englischen Wortschatz. Archiv, 178, 1941.
Lange, F. Ein deutsches Seminar für neuere Philologie in London. Grenzboten, 45, 1886.
Lauret, R. Quel profit peut tirer un Français des études germaniques? Marches de l'Est, July, 1910.
Lévy, P. Les romantiques français et la langue allemande. RG, 1938.
Lindau, P. Die deutschen Fremdwörter im Französischen. In: Aus dem modernen Frankreich. Breslau, 1881.
Loeper-Houselle, M. Der deutsche Sprachunterricht im Elsass unter der französischen Regierung. MLIA, 1882.
Luntzer, V. & Melich, J. Deutsche Ortsnamen und Schulwörter des ungarischen Sprachschatzes. Innsbruck, 1900.
Mackel, E. Die germanischen Elemente in der altfranzösischen und altprovenzalischen Sprache. Diss. Greifswald, 1884.
Meyer, J. Aussprache des Hochdeutschen im XVII. Jahrhundert nach französischer Auffassung. Alemannia, 17, 1889.
Neumann, F. Die germanischen Elemente in der provençalischen und französischen Sprache. Diss. Heidelberg, 1876.
Oppel, H. Die Begegnung romanischer Sprache mit germanisch-deutscher Dichtung. D&V, 39.
Pfeiffer, G. Die neugermanischen Bestandteile der französischen Sprache. Stuttgart, 1902.
Pfister, C. La limite des langues française et allemande en Alsace-Lorraine. Nancy, 1890.
Piel, J. M. Os nomes germanicos na toponomia portuguesa. Boletim de filologia, 6.
Pitton, R. Une grammaire allemande en 1783 (Gottsched). Mélanges H. Lichtenberger. Paris, 1934.
Rockwell, L. I. Older German Loan-Words in American English. American Speech, 20, 1945.
Roger, L. La frontière linguistique et la colonisation germanique en Belgique wallonne et en France septentrionale. ZFSL, 63.
Rosa, U. L'elemento tedesco nel dialetto piemontese. In: Postille etimologiche. Torino, 1859.
Schmidt, G. Das Eindringen der hochdeutschen Schriftsprache in der Rigaschen Ratskanzlei. Mitteilungen aus d. balt. Geschichte, 1. (Riga), 1938.
Schulze, M. Die germanischen Elemente der französischen Sprache. Berlin, 1876.
Schweisthal. Remarques sur le rôle de l'élément franc dans la formation de la langue française. Romania, 12, 1883.
Sebeok, T. A. German Travellers and Language in America. American Speech, 18, 1944.
Seelmann, E. Niedersächsische Elemente in in den Ardennen. Krit. Jahresbericht über d. Fortschritte der roman. Philologie, 2, 1891.
Semmig, H. Deutsche Studien in Frankreich. MLIA, 1879.
Smal-Stockyj, R. Die germanisch-deutschen Kultureinflüsse im Spiegel der ukrainischen Sprache. Leipzig, 1942.
Soehns. Germanisches Eigenthum in der Sprache Italiens. Zs. des allg. deutschen Sprachvereins, 1894.
Stephen, L. The Importation of German. In: Studies of a Biographer. New York, 1907.
Taube, E. German Influence on the English Vocabulary in the Nineteenth Century. JEGPh, 39, 1940.
Thierfelder, F. Deutsch als Weltsprache: 1: Grundlagen der deutschen Sprachgeltung in Europa. Berlin, 1938. Cf. Die Tat, 30, 1938.
Thumb, A. Die germanischen Elemente des Neugriechischen. Strassburg, 1902.
Trivunac, M. Deutsche Lehnwortforschung im südslawischen Sprachraum. Belgrad, 1941.
Ulrich, J. Deutsche Verba im Romanischen. ZRPh, 3, 1879.
Vendryes, J. Sur les plus anciens emprunts germaniques en latin. EG, 3, 1948.
Verdam. Mots d'origine germanique repris dans la langue hollandaise sous vêtement français. Taalstudie, 2, 1880.
Viereck, L. German Instruction in American Schools. Report of the Commission of Education. Washington, 1901.
—— Zwei Jahrhunderte deutschen Unterrichts in den Vereinigten Staaten. Braunschweig, 1903.
Vooys, C. G. N. de. Duitse invloed op de Nederlandse woordvoorraad. Verhandeling der Koninklijke Nederlandsche Akad. van Wetenschappen, Amsterdam, 1946.

in der französischen Sprache. Diss. Strassburg, 1885.

Winkler, G. Die niederdeutsche Sprache in Französisch-Flandern und die Sprachgrenze in Belgien. Globus, 59, 1891.

Wirtz, E. Das Deutsche in Frankreich. NSp, 8, 1901.

Witte, H. Zur Geschichte des Deutschthums in Lothringen. Diss. Metz, 1890.

—— Das deutsche Sprachgebiet Lothringens und seine Wandlungen. Forschungen zur deutschen Landes- und Volkskunde, 8, 1894.

Zahn. Deutsche Personennamen in Italien. Anzeiger für Kunde der deutschen Vorzeit, 1883.

Zeydel, E. H. The German Language in the Prussian Academy. PMLA, 41, 1926.

Zimmerli, J. Die deutsch-französische Sprachgrenze im schweizerischen Jura. Diss. Göttingen, 1891.

Anon. Die ganze Literatur über **BYRON'S** deutsche Sprachkenntnisse. ESn, 21, 1895.

Weijden, J. Die Bemühungen des Hl. Petrus **CANISIUS** um den deutschen Sprachgebrauch. NPh, 28, 1943.

Herthum, P. Die germanischen Lehnwörter im Altitalienischen, vor allem in **DANTES** Divina Commedia. Progr. Arnstadt, 1901.

Hibler, L. von. **MARK TWAIN** und die deutsche Sprache. Anglia, 65, 1941.

Klett, Ada M. Meisterschaft, or the True State of Mark Twain's German. AGR, 7, 1940.

Gruener, G. **POE'S** Knowledge of German. MPh, June, 1904.

Thompson, L. F. Ann **RADCLIFFE'S** Knowledge of German. MLR, 1925.

CHAPTER FOURTEEN

German Influences upon Individual Authors.

Cater, H. D. Henry **ADAMS** Reports on a German Gymnasium. AHR, 53, 1947.

Stirk, S. D. John Quincy Adams's Letters on Silesia. NEQ, Sept., 1936.

Novati, F. L'**ALEARDI** a Josephstadt. Riv. stor. del Risorgimento italiano, 3.

Anon. **ALFIERI** et le Martinsberg. Messager d'Alsace-Lorraine, 21.XII.1912.

Vincenti, L. Alfieri e lo Sturm und Drang. Festgabe Karl Vossler. München, 1932.

Hilz, H. H. F. **AMIEL** und die Deutschen. Diss. München, 1929.

Lorenzen, A. Deutsche Beiträge im Stammbuch Hans Christ. **ANDERSENS.** Internat. Litteraturberichte, 9, 1901.

Topse Jensen, H. G. Om Eventyr-Komedien Ole Lukoie. Festskrift Valdemar Vedel. København, 1935.

Joret, C. J. B. Gaspard d'**ANSSE DE VILLOISON** èt la cour de Weimar. RHLF, 1895.

Price, L. M. The Relation of Baculard d'**ARNAUD** to German Literature. MDU, 37, 1945.

Renwanz, J. Matthew **ARNOLD** und Deutschland. Diss. Greifswald, 1927.

Reuscnel, K. M. Arnolds The Forsaken Merman und sein deutsches Vorbild. GRM, 1924.

Fischer, T. Roger **ASCHAM** in Deutschland. In: Drei Studien zur englischen Litteraturgeschichte. Gotha, 1892.

Katterfeld, A. Roger Ascham, sein Leben und die Werke mit besonderer Berücksichtigung der Berichte über Deutschland aus den Jahren 1550-53. Strassburg, 1879.

Risberg, B. Tyska förebilder till dikter af **ATTERBOM.** Upsala, 1892.

Santesson, C. Atterboms ungdomsdikting. Stockholm, 1920.

Albalat, A. **BALZAC** et l'accent allemand. RB, 20-27.IV.1918.

Daudon, R. L'accent allemand dans Balzac. MLN, 1935.

Schopbach, J. Deutschland und die Deutschen im Urteil H. von Balzacs. Giessen, 1923.

Nye, R. B. George **BANCROFT,** Early Critic of German Literature. MLN, 58, 1943.

Beaulieu-Marconnay. Ansichten eines Engländers (**BARING-GOULD**) über Deutschland. MLIA, 1880.

Rhoden, P. R. Der Deutschenfresser Maurice **BARRES.** Der Deutsche, 49, 1922.

Vermeil, E. A propos de Barrès et de l'Allemagne. Alsace française, 1928.

Anon. Uebersetzungen deutscher Lieder ins Englische (**BASKERVILLE**). Grenzboten, 13, 1854.

Huot, P. **BEAUMARCHAIS** en Allemagne. Révélations tirées des archives d'Autriche. Paris, 1869. Cf. MLIA, 1869.

Stapfer, P. Beaumarchais en Allemagne. RB, 3.IV.1880.

Haemel, A. Deutsche Züge in G. A. **BECQUER.** Archiv, 144, 1923.

Fallot, E. Un voyage à la cour de Prusse en 1775 par D. Ch. E. **BERDOT** de Montbéliard. Mem. de la Soc. de Montbéliard, 30, 1903.

Dryssen, C. **BERGSON** und deutsche Romantik. Marburg, 1922.

Habicht, R. Henri Bergson und das deutsche Typenlustspiel. Strassburg, 1935.

Carrière, J. M. **BERQUIN'S** Adaptations from German Dramatic Literature. SPh, 1935.

Flamini, F. Aurelio **BERTOLA** e i suoi studi intorno alla letteratura tedesca. Pisa, 1895. Cf. GSLI, 1896.

Schokker, R. **BILDERDIJK** en Duitschland. Diss. Amsterdam, 1933.

La Chesnais, P. G. **BJOERNSON** et le Germanisme. RP, 15.III.1917.

Laun, A. Französische Uebersetzungen deut-
Walthemath, W. Die fränkischen Elemente

scher Dichter (Henry **BLAZE**). Archiv, 2, 1848.
Finke, H. Mosèn **BORRA** in Deutschland. Homenatge a Antoni Rubió i Lluch. Barcelona, 1936.
Lebois, A. Les sources allemandes de la Nef d'Elémir **BOURGES**. EG, July, 1947.
Anon. Eine besonnene Stimme aus Frankreich über Deutschland. (Edgar **BOURLOTON**). MLIA, 1872.
Geiger, L. Ein Freund Deutschlands? (**BRANDES**). Zukunft, 20, 1911.
Vedel, V. G. Brandes og Tyskland. Tilskueren, Feb., 1912.
Klenze, C. von. Charles Timothy **BROOKS**, Translator from the German and the Genteel Tradition. New York, 1937.
Warfel, H. R. Charles Brockden **BROWN'S** German Sources. MLQ, 1940.
Albrecht, R. Robert **BROWNINGS** Verhältnis zu Deutschland. Diss. München, 1912.
Carrière, M. Giordano **BRUNO** über die Deutschen. DR, 1890.
Herrick, A. H. William C. **BRYANTS** Beziehungen zur deutschen Dichtung. MLN, June, 1917.
Heath, R. The Archtype of the Pilgrim's Progress. (**BUNYAN**). Centemporary Review, 70, 1896.
Gudde, E. G. Aaron **BURR** in Weimar. SAQ, 40, 1941.
Eimer, M. **BYRON'S** persönliche und geistige Beziehungen zu den Gebieten deutscher Kultur. Anglia, 36, 1912.
Joret, C. **CACAULT** écrivain. Annales de Bretagne, 1905.
Hagge, C. W. G. H. **CALVERT'S** Translations from the German. MLN, 57, 1942.
Shumway, D. B. Thomas **CAMPBELL** and Germany. In: Schelling Anniversary Papers. New York, 1923.
Azzolini, Margherita. Giosuè **CARDUCCI** und die deutsche Literatur. Tübingen, 1910.
Bottacchiari, R. Carducci e la Germania. Scuola e Cultura, 1936.
Hunziker, E. Carducci und Deutschland. Aarau, 1927.
Sternberg, F. La poesia neoclassica tedesca e le Odi barbare di G. Carducci. Trieste, 1910.
Wilhelm, J. Carducci e la Germania. Convivium, 13, 1941.
CARLYLE, T. The State of German Literature. ER, 46, 1827.
—— German Playwrights. Foreign Review, 3, 1829.
—— German Literature of the Fourteenth and Fifteenth Centuries. Foreign Quarterly Review, 8, 1831.
—— Lectures on German Literature. Edinburgh, 1837.
Brooks, R. A. E. (ed.) Thomas Carlyle: Journey to Germany, Autumn 1858. New Haven, 1940.
Carr, C. T. Carlyle's Translations from German. MLR, 42, 1947.
Durand, W. De Quincey and Carlyle in Their Relations to the Germans. PMLA, 22, 1907.
Elbertshagen, H. Die Deutschen und T. Carlyle. Kreuzzeitung, Literatur, 49, 1921.
Fehr, B. Der deutsche Idealismus in Carlyles Sartor Resartus. GRM, 5, 1913.
Harrold, C. F. Carlyle and German Thought: 1819-34. New Haven, 1934. Cf. Rivista di Filosofia, 1937.
Kraeger, H. Carlyles Stellung zur deutschen Sprache und Litteratur. Anglia, 22, 1899.
Lotter, K. Carlyle und die deutsche Romantik. Nürnberg, 1932.
Mann, F. M. Th. Carlyle und Deutschland. Die Lichtung, 4, 1907.
Ritter, G. Der deutsche Idealismus in der geistigen Entwicklung Thomas Carlyles. Grenzboten, 1913.
Salomon, R. Notes on Carlyle's Journey to Germany. (Autumn, 1858). MLN, 58, 1943.
Shine, H. Carlyle and the German Philosophy Problem During the Year 1826-27. PMLA, Sept., 1935.
Stewart, H. L. The Alleged Prussianism of Th. Carlyle. International Journal of Ethics, Jan., 1918.
Streuli, W. Thomas Carlyle als Vermittler deutscher Literatur und deutschen Geistes. Zürich, 1895.
Taine, H. De l'introduction des idées allemandes en Europe et en Angleterre. Journal des Débats, 6.XI.1860.
Vaughan, C. E. Carlyle and his German Masters. E&S, 1910.
Wellek, R. Carlyle and German Romanticism. In: Xenia Pragensia, 1929.
—— Carlyle and the Philosophy of History. PhQ, 23, 1944.
Morel, L. L'influence germanique chez Mme. de **CHARRIERE** et chez Benjamin Constant. RHLF, 18, 1911.
Bardoux, J. Les passages du Rhin de M. de **CHATEAUBRIAND**. RRh, 1922.
Diem, H. Das Bild Deutschlands in Chateaubriands Werk. Bern, 1936.
Grillon de Gouix, P. Chateaubriand, ministre de France à Berlin. Revue universelle, 1939-40.
Spiegelberg. Deutschland und Frankreich im Weltbild A. de **CHATEAUBRIANTS**. ZFSL, 64.
Tissot, E. V. **CHERBULIEZ** über Deutschland. Deutsche Revue, May, 1898.
Casper, P. Ein Franzose über die deutsche Literatur. Erwinia, Strassburg, 1909.
Griffith, R. A. A Wildfrau Story in a **CIBBER** Play. PhQ, 1933.
Anon. Jules **CLARETIE** und sein Aufenthalt in Deutschland. ZFSL, July, 1897.
Thomas, J. W. James Freeman **CLARKE**, Apostle of German Culture to America. Diss. Pa. State College, 1942.

Beach, J. W. **COLERIDGE'S** Borrowings from the German. ELH, 9, 1942.
Chambers, E. K. Samuel Taylor Coleridge. A Bibliographical Study. London, 1938.
Dunstan, A. C. The German Influence on Coleridge. MLR, 17-18, 1922-23.
Ferrier, J. F. The Plagiarisms of S. T. Coleridge. Blackwood's Mag., March, 1840.
Haney, J. L. The German Influence on Samuel Taylor Coleridge. Philadelphia, 1902.
Morley, E. J. Coleridge in Germany, 1799. In: Wordsworth and Coleridge. Princeton, 1939.
Pizzo, E. S. S. T. Coleridge als Kritiker. Anglia, 27, 1916.
Richter, H. Die philosophische Weltanschauung von S. T. Coleridge und ihr Verhältnis zur deutschen Philosophie. Anglia, 1920.
Snyder, A. D. Coleridgiana. RES, Oct., 1928.
Willoughby, L. A. Coleridge and his German Contemporaries. PEGS, 1935.
—— Coleridge und Deutschland. GRM, 24, 1936.
Wolff, L. Coleridge et l'Allemagne. RAA, 11, 1933.
Anon. Quelques lettres de B. **CONSTANT** et de Mad. de Staël sur l'Allemagne. RB, March, 1880.
Morel, L. L'influence germanique chez Madame de Charrière et chez Benjamin Constant. RHLF, 1911-12.
Ullmann, Helene. Benjamin Constant und seine Beziehungen zum deutschen Geistesleben. Marburg, 1915.
Beckers, H. V. **COUSIN** über französische und deutsche Philosophie. Stuttgart, 1834.
Bonnefon, P. V. Cousin et l'Allemagne. RB, 26.I.1907.
Willm. M. Victor Cousin et la philosophie allemande. Nouvelle Revue Germanique, 53, 1833.
Chaix-Ruy, J. Benedetto **CROCE** et l'-Allemagne d'aujourd'hui. RLC, 21, 1947.
Vincenti, L. Croce e la letteratura tedesca. Rassegna d'Italia, 1, 1946.
Atkins, S. Sir Herbert **CROFT** and German Literature. MLQ, 5, 1944.
Gummer, E. N. **DICKENS** and Germany. MLR, 33, 1938.
Jacoby, D. **DIDEROT** in Leipzig. Euphorion, 6, 1899-1900.
Schirlitz, E. E. Diderots Beziehungen zur deutschen Literatur. Archiv, 1885.
Lauser, W. Pater **DIDON** über Deutschland. Gegenwart, 1884.
Harder, F. Eine deutsche Anregung zu **DRYDEN'S** Alexander's Feast? ESn, 61, 1927.
Joret, C. Le comte **DUMANOIR** et la cour de Weimar. Paris, 1896.
Parigot, H. Le drame d'Alexandre **DUMAS** (père). Paris, 1898.
Anon. Aus eines Franzmanns Reisebriefen über Deutschland (Victor **DURUY**). Europa, 1864.
Michael, F. A. **DUVAU.** Ein französischer Freund der Weimarer Gesellschaft. Jb. der Sammlung Kippenberg. Weimar, 1924.
Conrad, H. George **ELIOT** über die deutsche Literatur. Gegenwart, 15, 1886.
Eliot, George. Three Months in Weimar. London, 1855.
Pfeiffer, S. George Eliots Beziehungen zu Deutschland. Heidelberg, 1925.
Francke, K. **EMERSON** and German Personality. International Quarterly, Sept., 1903.
Wahr, F. B. Emerson and the Germans. MDU, 33, 1941.
Wellek, R. Emerson and German Philosophy. NEQ, 16, 1943.
San-Giorgu, J. **EMINESCU** und der deutsche Geist. Jena, 1936.
Tchourtchine, M. **FAURIEL** et ses précurseurs en Allemagne. (In Serbian). SKG, 27.
Schwenka, W. **FLORIANS** Beziehungen zur deutschen Literatur. Diss. Leipzig, 1908.
Fey, E. Das Deutschland **FOGAZZAROS.** Archiv, 167, 1935.
Magnino, B. Ugo **FOSCOLO** e i fondatori dello Sturm und Drang. Rassegna italiana, 10, 1927.
Zumbini, B. Di alcune relazioni del Foscolo con la letteratura tedesca. NAnt, 25, 1874.
Victory, B. M. Benjamin **FRANKLIN** and Germany. Americana Germanica, 1915.
Krumm, G. Gustav **FROEDINGS** Verbindungen mit der deutschen Literatur. Diss. Greifswald, 1934.
Schultz, A. Margaret **FULLER.** Transcendentalist and Interpreter of German Literature. MDU, 34, 1942.
Lussky, G. F. **GALDOS'** Acquaintance with German Literature, as Revealed in his Novelas españolas contemporaneas. MLF, 29, 1944.
Meyer, G. Cardinal **GARAMPIS'** litterarische Reise durch Deutschland 1761-63. Centralblatt für Bibliothekwesen, 3, 1891.
Lauret, R. Théophile **GAUTIER** et les romantiques allemands. Alsace française, 11.VI.1927.
Poulain, L. Traces de l'influence allemande dans l'oeuvre de Th. Gautier. Bâle, 1914.
Batt, M. Contributions to the History of English Opinion of German Literature: **GILLIES** and the Foreign Quarterly Review; Gillies and Blackwood's Magazine. MLN, 17-18, 1902-03.
Girardin, P. Robert Pearce Gillies and the Propagation of German Literature in England. 1916.
Kuechler, W. Saint-Marc **GIRARDIN** als Freund Deutschlands. NSp. 25, 1918.
LeSage, L. Jean **GIRAUDOUX'S** Case against Germany. FR, 17, 1944.

Conrad, M. G. Ein französischer Germanophile (Graf von **GOBINEAU**). Berliner Tageblatt, 20.IX.1902.

Deffoux, L. Les origines de Gobineau en Allemagne. MF, 1925.

Gillot, H. Le germanisme de Gobineau. Alsace française, 18.X.1924.

Slender-Petersen. **GOGOL** und die deutsche Romantik. Euphorion, 1922.

Marcus, H. **GOLDSMITH** über Deutschland. Archiv, 149, 1925-26.

Muret, G. Jeremias **GOTTHELF** und seine Beziehungen zu Deutschland. München, 1912.

Geiger, L. Der Abbé **GREGOIRE** in Weimar. ZFSL, 24, 1902.

Gooch, G. P. Lord **HALDANE** (at Göttingen). Contemporary Review, Oct., 1928.

Osawa, M. **HARDY** and the German Men of Letters. Studies in English Literature, 19. (Tokyo), 1939.

Wruck, J. **HARRIS** und die deutsche Philosophie. Internat. Zs. f. Erziehung, 1935.

Reichert, M. Les sources allemandes des oeuvres poétiques d'André van **HASSELT**. Mém. de l'Acad. royale de langue et de litt. françaises de Belgique, 8, 1934.

Anon. Prose Writers of Germany by Fred. H. **HEDGE**. NAR, Oct., 1848.

Wells, R. V. Three Christian Transcendentalists: James Marsh, Caleb Sprague Henry, and Frederic Henry Hedge. Columbia U. P., 1943.

Mary Eleanor, Sister. Hedge's Prose Writers of Germany as a Source of Whitman's Knowledge of German Philosophy. MLN, 61, 1946.

Ruprecht, W. K. Felicia **HEMANS** und die englischen Beziehungen zur deutschen Literatur. Anglia, 48, 1924.

Bulle, F. Franziskus **HEMSTERHUIS** und der deutsche Irrationalismus des 18. Jahrhunderts. Jena, 1912.

Beam, J. N. Charles **HODGE'S** Student Years in Germany. Princeton U. Library Chronicle, 8, 1947.

Paludan, J. **HOLBERGS** Forhold til det aeldre tyske Drama. Historisk Tidskrift. 6, 1890.

Magill, C. P. An English Liberal in Germany, 1840-42. (W. **HOWITT**). GLL, 1, 1937.

Aubert, A. Les Burgraves. (**HUGO**). Revue Indépendante, 7, 1843.

Hartmann, K. A. M. V. Hugo und Deutschland. ZFSL, 1886.

Humbert, C. Victor Hugos Urtheile über Deutschland. ZFSL, 1883.

Nyrop, K. Autour d'une poésie de Victor Hugo. Mélanges Baldensperger. Paris, 1930.

Pommier, J. Un drame rhénan: Les Burgraves. L'Alsace française, 11.V.1930.

Schielries, F. Victor Hugos Urteile über Deutschland. Diss. Königsberg, 1914.

Croce, B. Vittorio **IMBRIANI**: contro l'ammirazione convenzionale per la Germania e per la sua letteratura. Critica, 20.III.1932.

Mele, E. Alcune versioni dal tedesco di V. Imbriani. Riv. d. letteratura tedesca, 2, 1908.

Arens, E. W. **IRVING** im Rheinland. Eichendorff Kalender, 1927-28.

Pochmann, H. A. Irving's German Sources in the Sketch Book. SPh, 27, 1930.

—— Irving's German Tour and its Influence on his Tales. PMLA, 45, 1930.

Kimball, Marie G. Thomas **JEFFERSON'S** Rhine Journey. AGR, 13, 1946.

Boubée, R. Camille **JORDAN** à Weimar. Correspondant, 25.XI. & 10.XII.1901.

—— C. Jordan en Alsace et à Weimar. Paris, 1911.

Milovic, J. Zmaj Jovan **JOVANOVIC** und die deutsche Literatur. ZSPh, 14, 1937.

Jacobsen, A. Charles **KINGSLEYS** Beziehungen zu Deutschland. Heidelberg, 1917.

Kügler, H. **KIPLINGS** Deutschenhass. Die deutsche höhere Schule, 7, 1940.

Gause, F. Frau von **KRUEDENER** in Ost-Preussen. Altpreussische Forschungen, 9, 1932.

Henriot, E. **LAFORGUE** à Berlin. RRh, July, 1924.

Kahn, G. Jules Laforgue in Deutschland. RRh, 1929.

Geiger, L. **LAHARPE** und die deutsche Literatur. Beilage zur Allg. Zt., 171, 1882.

Bobisch, A. **LAMARTINES** Verhältnis zur deutschen Literatur. Diss. Münster, 1917.

Ahrens, L. **LAMENNAIS** und Deutschland. Münster, 1930.

Mannucci, F. L. Giacomo **LEOPARDI**. La storia poetica. Torino, 1934.

Ewen, F. John Gibson **LOCKHART**, Propagandist of German Literature. MLN, 49, 1934.

Trautwein von Belle, E. Der Belgier Ferd. **LOISE** über die neuere Literatur Deutschlands. MLIA, 1879.

Campbell, T. M. **LONGFELLOWS** Wechselbeziehungen zu der deutschen Literatur. Leipzig, 1907.

Goebel, G. Longfellow als Vermittler deutscher Geisteskultur. Hamburg. Correspondent, Blatt 36, 1907.

Hatfield, J. T. New Light on Longfellow, with Special Reference to his Relations to Germany. Boston, 1933.

—— Longfellow and Germany. AGR, 5, 1938.

Kratz, F. Das deutsche Element in den Werken H. W. Longfellows. Progr. Wasserburg, 1902.

Pattee, F. L. Longfellow and German Romance. PL, 17, 1906.

Schönemann, F. Zum Problem: Longfellow und Deutschland. ZNU, 36.

Sieper, E. Studien zu Longfellows Evangeline. NSp, 9, 1901.
Thiergen, O. Longfellow und seine Beziehungen zur deutschen Literatur. ZDU, 6, 1892.
Worden, J. P. Ueber Longfellows Beziehungen zur deutschen Literatur. Halle, 1900. Cf. German-American Annals, 1904.
Richmond, H. M. **MACKENZIE'S** Translations from the German. MLR, 17, 1922.
Rosemeier, H. N. **MACHIAVELLIS** erste Legation zum Kaiser Maximilian und seine drei Schriften über Deutschland. Diss. Kiel, 1894.
Sillib, R. Machiavellis Stellung zu Deutschland. Diss. Heidelberg, 1892.
Uebelhoer, M. Pierre **MACORLAN** oder die deutsche Romantik im französischen Spiegel. RRh, 1928.
Oppeln-Bronikowski, F. von. Maurice **MAETERLINCK** und Deutschland. Propylaen, 18.IV.1913.
Heminghaus, E. H. **MARK TWAIN'S** German Provenience. MLQ, 6, 1945.
Lederer, M. Mark Twain in Vienna. Mark Twain Quarterly, 7, 1945.
Wecter, D. Mark Twain as Translator from the German. AL, 13, 1941.
Lobinger, M. Un précurseur de la littérature comparée: Nicolas **MARTIN**; son style "biedermeyer," ses inspirations allemandes et hongroises. Szeged, 1937.
Momigliano, F. Giuseppe **MAZZINI** e la letteratura tedesca. Riv. d. letteratura tedesca, 2, 1908.
Mabbott, T. O. A Source for the Conclusion of **MELVILLE'S** Moby Dick. N&Q, 181, 1941.
Araquistáin, L. **MENENDEZ Y PELAYO** y la cultura alemana. Jena, 1933.
Dick, E. Deutschland und die Deutschen bei George **MEREDITH.** GRM, 6, 1914.
Galland, R. Quelques traductions inconnues de l'allemand par Meredith. RLC, 3, 1923.
Lees, J. George Meredith's Literary Relations with Germany. MLR, 12, 1917.
Anon. **MICHELET** über Deutschland. Blätter zur Kunde der Litteratur des Auslands, 1839.
Kaegi, W. Michelet und Deutschland. Basel, 1936.
Monod, G. La vie et la pensée de Jules Michelet. Paris, 1923.
Saunova, I. Der deutsche Einfluss auf die Entwicklung der literarischen und aesthetischen Theorien **MICKIEWICZ'** bis zum Jahre 1830. GS. 2-3, 1934-35.
Jantz, H. S. Samuel **MILLER'S** Survey of German Literature (1803). GR, 16, 1941.
Fischer, W. Die persönlichen Beziehungen R. M. **MILNES** zu Deutschland mit besonderer Berücksichtigung seiner Freundschaft zu Varnhagen von Ense. Würzburg, 1918.
Stern, A. **MIRABEAU** in Berlin. DR, 1889.
Hensel, E. **MONTAIGNES** Reise durch Deutschland. Zeitwende, 4, 1928.
Reinhardstoettner, K. von. Michel Montaigne über München. Jb. f. Münchener Geschichte, 2, 1888.
Geiger, L. **MONTESQUIEU** in Berlin. National-Zeitung, 655, 1897.
—— Montesquieu in Wien. Neue Freie Presse, 27.XI.1897.
Beck, C. A. de **MUSSET** und das Germanentum. ZFEU, 10, 1912.
Haape, W. Musset in seinen Beziehungen zu Deutschland und zum deutschen Geistesleben. ZFSL, 34, 1909.
Lafoscade, L. Le théâtre d'Alfred de Musset. Paris, 1902.
Schauffelberger, J. Alfred de Musset und die deutsche Litteratur. Gegenwart, 21. VIII.1897.
Bertaut, J. Gérard de **NERVAL** aux bords du Rhin. RRh, 1922.
Popa, N. Les sources allemandes de deux Filles du Feu, Jemmy et Isis de Gérard de Nerval. RLC, 10, 1930.
Richer, J. Léo Burckart. RLC, 21, 1947.
Baldensperger, F. Quae in **OEHLENSCHLAGERII** carmine Aladdin inscripto e germanicis litteris pendeant. Diss. Nancy, 1899.
Stewart, W. K. Oehlenschlagers Relation to German Romanticism. SS, 2, 1914.
Iturriaga, J. E. La germanofilia de **ORTEGA Y GASSET.** Letras de México, 3, 1941.
Weisstein, G. Ein Franzose am Hofe des Grossen Kurfürsten (Charles **PALIN**). Mittheilungen d. Vereins f. Geschichte Berlins, 1902.
Proesler, H. Walter **PATER** und sein Verhältnis zur deutschen Literatur. Diss. Freiburg, 1917.
Paparelli, G. La Germania di Enea Silvio **PICCOLOMINI.** Italica, 25, 1948.
Wächtler, P. R. Edgar Allan **POE** und die deutsche Romantik. Leipzig, 1911.
Luther, A. **PUSKIN** und deutsche Sprache und Dichtung. RLC, 17, 1937.
Dunn, W. A. Thomas de **QUINCEY'S** Relation to German Literature and Philosophy. Strassburg, 1901.
Durand, W. De Quincey and Carlyle in their Relations to the Germans. PMLA, 22, 1907.
Anon. Edgar **QUINET** et la poésie allemande. Le Temps, 8.X.1897.
Hilger. Quinet à Heidelberg. La Normandie artistique et littéraire, 1897.
Mundt, T. Ein französischer Dichter am Neckar und die deutsche Theologie. In: Spazierzüge und Irrfahrten. Altona, 1839.
Neumann, H. Das Deutschlanderlebnis bei E. Quinet. Hamburg, 1933.
Tronchon, H. Le jeune Edgar Quinet. Paris, 1937.
Heidenheimer, H. Peter **RAVENNAS** in Mainz und sein Kampf mit den Kölner

Dunkelmännern. Westdeutsche Zs. f. Geschichte & Kunst, 1897.
Anon. Ernest **RENAN** über Deutschland und Preussen. MLIA, 1868.
—— Monsieur Renan et l'Allemagne. Wiesbaden, 1879.
Bamberger, L. Renan et l'école historique allemande. Le Temps, 29.XI. & 2.XII. 1869.
Brunet, G. Renan et l'Allemagne. MF, 1. VIII.1919.
Buré, E. Renan et l'Allemagne. New York, 1945.
Homberger, H. Renan und die deutsche Kultur. DR, 19, 1879. Cf. RB, 14.VI.1879.
Lebert, A. Renan et l'Allemagne. Alsace française, 26.VIII.1928.
Lotheissen, F. Renan über Deutschland. MLIA, 1879.
Michaelis, P. E. Renans Stellung zu Deutschland. NM, 3.
Pommier, J. L'initiation d'Ernest Renan aux lettres allemandes. RLC, 15, 1935.
Sorel, G. Le germanisme et l'historicisme de Renan. Critica, 20.III. & 20.V.1931.
Tronchon, H. Renan et la pensée allemande. RCC, 29, 1927.
RIESELBECK, Baron de. Letters d'un voyageur français sur l'Allemagne. Paris, 1785.
Dans, K. Jacques **RIVIERE**, seine Geistesart und Beurteilung des deutschen Wesens. Würzburg, 1937.
Eitner, K. (ed.). Ein Engländer über deutsches Geistesleben im ersten Drittel dieses Jahrhunderts. (H. Crabb **ROBINSON**). Weimar, 1871.
Morley, E. J. Crabb Robinson in Germany, 1800-1805. Oxford, 1929.
Engel, E. Deutsche Dichter und französischer Kritiker (**ROD**). MLIA, 1881.
Gosshans. Romain **ROLLAND** und der germanische Geist. Würzburg, 1937.
Rosenberg, F. Franzosen und Deutsche in Romain Rollands Jean Christophe. GRM, 4, 1915.
Geiger, L. Ein italienischer Jude als Vermittler deutscher Geisteswerke (Samuel **ROMANELLI**). Allg. Zt. des Judentums, 1903.
Willoughby, L. A. Dante Gabriel **ROSSETTI** and German Literature. London, 1912.
Scheid, N. Edm. **ROSTANDS** Entwicklungsgang und seine Beziehungen zur deutschen Litteratur. Frankfurter Brochüren. Hamm i. E., 1903.
Herzfeld, G. Thomas **RUSSELL**, ein früher Vermittler deutscher Literatur in England. Archiv, 136, 1917.
Kuechler, W. **SAINTE-BEUVE** und die deutsche Literatur. ZFSL, 28, 1905.
Lang, B. Renée. Sainte-Beuve et les Allemands. RR, 32, 1941.
Leclercq, M. Sainte-Beuve et l'Allemagne. RFB, 1929.
Morel, L. Sainte-Beuve, la littérature allemande et Goethe. RHLF, 15, 1908 & Paris, 1908.
Thérive, A. Sainte-Beuve et l'Allemagne. Minerve française, 15.X.1919.
Anon. Ein Franzose über unsere Dichter (**SCHURE**). Europa, 1870.
Boehm, G. Eine Geschichte des deutschen Liedes. MLIA, 1868.
Koch, J. Sir W. **SCOTTS** Beziehungen zu Deutschland. GRM, 15, 1927.
Mennie, D. Sir W. Scott's Unpublished Translations of German Plays. MLR, 33, 1938.
Sommerkamp, F. Walter Scotts Kenntnis und Ansicht von deutscher Literatur. Archiv, 1925.
Thomas, W. Walter Scott et la littérature allemande. Mélanges Lichtenberger. Paris, 1934.
SHAW, B. Was ich der deutschen Kultur verdanke. Neue Rundschau, March, 1911.
Cyzevskyj, D. G. S. **SKOVORODA** and German Mysticism. (In Russian). Trudy Russkago Narodnago Universiteta v Prage, 2, 1929.
Teodoroff, E. K. Deutsche Einflüsse auf Pentscho **SLAWEJKOFF**. Diss. München, 1939.
Baseggio, C. La Germania nel pensiero di Mme. de **STAEL** e di E. Heine. RI, 29, 1926.
Bastian, M. Mme. de Staël en Allemagne. Occident et cahiers staëliens, 2, 1934 & Genève, 1939.
Boy-Ed, Ida. Frau von Staël und deutsche Philosophen. Hamburger Nachrichten, Zs. für Wissenschaft, 438, 1921.
Caro, E. Les deux Allemagnes: Mme. de Staël et H. Heine. Séances et Trav. de l'Acad. des Sciences mor. et pol., 97. (Paris), 1872.
Counson, A. Madame de Staël et la pensée allemande. Revue générale, March, 1913.
Croce, B. La Germania della Signora di Staël. Critica, 42, 1944.
Dejob, C. Mad. de Staël et l'Allemagne. RCC, 12.XII.1895.
Geiger, L. Frau von Staël in Berlin (1804). Euphorion, 1, 1894.
Gläsener, H. La révélatrice d'un peuple. Paris, 1921.
Goetze, A. Ein fremder Gast: Frau von Staël in Deutschland, 1803-04. Jena, 1928.
Haussonville, O. d'. Mme. de Staël et l'-Allemagne. Paris, 1928.
Hennig, J. A. L'Allemagne de Mme. de Staël et la polémique romantique. Paris, 1929.
Jaeck, E. G. Madame de Staël and the Spread of German Literature. New York, 1915.
Joret, C. Mme. de Staël et la cour littéraire de Weimar. Annales de la Faculté des Lettres de Bordeaux, 1899-1900.

—— Mad. de Staël à Berlin. RHLF, 9, 1902.
Keil, R. Frau von Staël und die Weimarischen Dichter. Allg. Oseterreichische Literatur-Zt., 10-12.IV. & 1.V.1886.
Kuhn, J. Mme. de Staël à Munich. Occident et Cahiers staëliens, 30.VI.1933.
Larg, D. G. Une exploratricc malgré elle: le premier départ de Mme de Staël pour l'Allemagne. RLC, 6, 1926.
Lauret, R. De l'Allemagne: Mme. de Staël, Gérard de Nerval. Marches de l'Est, 15.XII.1910.
Mönch, W. Frau von Staëls Deutschlandbuch und sein Gegenwartswert. NM, 6, 1935.
Odlozilik, O. Mme. de Staël et la police autrichienne. Revue française de Prague, Jan., 1926.
Pange, Mme. J. de. Le premier voyage de Mme. de Staël en Allemagne. BURS, 1927.
—— Mme. de Staël et la découverte de l'Allemagne. Paris, 1929.
—— La bibliothèque allemande de Mme. de Staël. RLC, 20, 1940.
Schmidt, P. Frau von Staël, die Vermittlerin deutschen Geistes in Frankreich. Grimma, 1877.
Wertheimer, E. Madame de Staël in Wien. Neue Freie Presse, 10684, 1894.
Braun, A. **STENDHAL** in Wien. Neue Freie Presse, 15828, 1908.
Debray, H. Le séjour de Stendhal à Brunswick (1807-08). NRF, 1.IV.1914.
Denizot, M. Les amis allemands de Stendhal. RRh, 7, 1927.
Henriot, E. Stendhal à Iena et à Brunswick. In: Livres et Portraits, 3e sér. Paris, 1927.
Kayser, R. Stendhal in Braunschweig. Deutsch-franz. Rundschau, 1, 1928.
Kontz, A. De Henrico Beyle, sive Stendhal, litterarum germanicorum judice. Diss. Paris, 1899.
Pitollet, C. Stendhal à Brunswick (1807-08). MF, May, 1921.
Schirmer, W. F. Stendhal und Deutschland. Archiv, 133, 1915.
Schurig, A. H. Beyle-Stendhal in Deutschland. Neue Bahnen, 21, 1903-04.
Sénéchal, C. Stendhal et l'Allemagne. Tentatives, Jan., 1924.
Simon, C. Le sillage de Stendhal en Allemagne. RLC, 6, 1926.
Stendhal. Tagebuch in Braunschweig. München, 1920.
Anon. Saint René **TAILLANDIER** über die deutschen Romane. Europa, 36, 1853. And in: MLIA, 77, 1870.
Fritsch, S. Hippolyte **TAINE** und die Deutschen. Der Türmer, 13, 1911.
Jacobowski, L. H. Taine und seine Stellung zu Deutschland. Gegenwart, 1893.
Lerch, E. Taine und der deutsche Geist. Kölnische Zt., 25.IV.1928.
Maury, L. Taine et l'Allemagne. RB, June, 1928.
Poulain, L. Taine et l'Allemagne. BURS, March, 1908.
Anon. Ein Amerikaner (Bayard **TAYLOR**) über deutsche Dichter und Schriftsteller. Europa, 7, 1857.
Prahl, A. J. Bayard Taylor in Germany. GQ, 18, 1945.
Carlyle, T. William Taylors Historic Survey of German Poetry. ER, 1831.
Herzfeld, G. William Taylor von Norwich. Eine Studie über den Einfluss der neueren deutschen Litteratur in England. Halle, 1897.
Fried, L. **TEGNER'S** Nattvagtsbarnen. Edda, 23, 1925.
Frisa, H. Deutsche Kulturverhältnisse in der Auffassung William **THACKERAYS**. Wien, 1908.
MacCarthy, D. Thackeray at Weimar. TLS, 20.VII.1946.
Vulpius, W. Thackerary in Weimar. Century Mag., 53, 1897.
—— Thackeray und Weimar. WM, 65, 1921.
Werner, R. M. Der Einfluss deutscher Literatur auf Thackeray. Progr. Teplitz, 1907.
Cyzevskij, D. **TJUTCEV** und die deutsche Romantik. ZSPh, 4, 1927.
Dukmeyer, F. Die Deutschen in **TOLSTOIS** Schilderungen. Beilage zur Allg. Zt., 111, 1902.
Hahn, H. Wechselbeziehungen zwischen Tolstoi und der deutschen Literatur. ASPh, 35, 1914.
Leixner, O. von. Tolstoj und das Deutschtum. Deutsche Monatsschrift, 1903.
Borkhovski, E. **TURGENJEW** und Deutschland. WM, 89, 1901.
Classen, K. Turgenevs Einstellung zum Deutschtum. Hamburg, 1938.
Brachfeld, C. Juan **VALERA** et l'Autriche-Hongrie. BH, April, 1939.
VETTORI, F. Viaggio (1507) in Allemania. Paris, 1857. Cf. Revue d'histoire diplomatique, 11, 1897.
Küchler, W. Pierre **VIENOT** über Deutschland. NSp, 1932.
Drougard, E. **VILLIERS DE L'ISLE-ADAM** à Munich il y a 70 ans. NL, 29. VII.1939.
Forgues, E. Souvenirs autobiographiques du baron de **VITROLLES.** Paris, 1924.
Noordegraaf, W. G. **VONDEL** und Köln. Joost van den Vondel Festschrift. Jena, 1937.
Falk, R. P. Walt **WHITMAN** and German Thought. JEGPh, 40, 1941.
Flasche, H. Deutscher Geist in angelsächsischer Geschichtsphilosophie. DVLG, 17, 1939.
Fulghum, W. B. Whitman's Debt to Joseph

Gostwick's German Literature. AL, 12, 1941.
Hertel, L. Walt Whitmans Kenntnis deutscher Literatur. GQ, 21, 1948.
Mary Eleanor, Sister. Hedge's Prose Writers of Germany as a Source of Whitman's Knowledge of German Philosophy. MLN, 61, 1946.
Zarek, O. Walt Whitman and German Poetry. Living Age, 10.II.1923.
Bradley, A. C. English Poetry and German Philosophy in the Age of **WORDSWORTH**. Manchester, 1909. And in: A Miscellany. London, 1929.
Herzberg, M. J. William Wordsworth and German Literature. PMLA, 40, 1925.
Stallknecht, N. P. Wordsworth and Philosophy. PMLA, 1929.
Willoughby, L. A. Wordsworth and Germany. Festschrift H. G. Fiedler. Oxford, 1938.
Treimer, K. Germanische Literatureinflüsse auf Julius **ZEYER**. Jb. für Kultur & Geschichte der Slaven, N. F., 9, 1933.

ELEVENTH PART

North and South American Contributions

CHAPTER ONE

Generalities, Latin American Contributions and Inter-American Relations.

1. General Works.

(For American Types, see Thematology, I.VI.11.)

Anon. Young America Abroad. Literary Review, 22.X.1921.

—— American Culture Abroad. CLN, 4, 1946.

Atkinson, W. C. America in Spain. Hisp., 1934.

—— Programme for a School of Latin-American Studies. BSS, 24, 1947.

Baginsky, P. H. Early German Interest in the New World, 1494-1618. AGR, 5, 1939.

—— German Works Relating to America. 1493-1800. New York, 1942.

Beaubien, C. P. Le problème de la survivance française au Canada et les influences américaines. France-Amérique, 30, 1939.

Brooks, J. G. As Others See Us. New York, 1908.

Castro, A. Sobre la relación entre ambas Américas. RIA, 2, 1940.

Chevalier, F. Publications espagnoles récentes relatives à l'Amérique. BH, 48, 1946.

Commager, H. S. America in Perspective: the United States through Foreign Eyes. New York, 1947.

Díez-Canedo, E. Letras de América. Estudios sobre las literaturas continentales. México, 1944.

Durelli, A. J. Le Canada français et l' Amérique latine. FR, 15, 1942.

Englekirk, J. E. Relaciones literarias interamericanas. Memoria del primer Congreso de Lit. Iberoamer., 1940.

—— El hispanoamericanismo y la generación del 98. RIA, 2, 1940.

—— Obras norteamericanas en traducción española. RIA, 8-9, 1944-45.

Ferguson, J. de L. American Literature in Spain. Columbia U. P., 1916.

Flanagan, J. T. & Grismer, R. L. Mexico in American Fiction Prior to 1850. Hisp., 23, 1940-41.

Grainer, J. A. Latin American Belles-Lettres in English Translation: A Selective and Annotated Guide. Washington, 1942.

Humphreys, R. A. The Study of Latin-American History in England. BSS, 24, 1947.

Jones, H. M. The Image of the New World. Festschrift George F. Reynolds, U. of Colorado, 1945.

Jones, W. K. Latin American Writers in English Translation. Washington, 1944.

Kahane, H. R. Historia mexicana en la literatura alemana neo-romantica. Memoria del segundo Congreso de Lit. Iberoamer., 1941.

Lanctot, G. Les Canadiens français et leur voisin du sud. New Haven, 1941.

Leavitt, S. E. Latin-American Literature in the United States. RLC, 11, 1931.

—— Hispano-American Literature in the United States: A Bibliography of Translations and Criticism. Harvard U. P., 1932.

—— Hispanic-American Literature in the United States. Chapel Hill (N. C.), 1935.

—— Latin American Literature in the United States: Retrospect and Prospect. SPh, 1945.

LeFort, E. C. Some Trends in Contemporary Spanish-American Letters: American Motifs. U. of Miami Hispanic-American Studies, 1941.

MacLeish, A. The American Writers and the New World. Yale Review, 31, 1941.

Ortega, J. Mexico's Role in International Intellectual Cooperation. Albuquerque, 1945.

Pane, R. U. A Selected Bibliography of Latin-American Literature in English Translation. MLJ, 26, 1942.

—— Two Hundred Latin American Books in English Translation: A Bibliography. MLJ, 27, 1943.

—— Three Argentine Poets: Jorge Luis Borges, Leopoldo Lugones and Alfonsina Storni. A Bibliography of their Poems in English Translations with Lists of their Works. Bull. of Bibliography, 18, 1946.

—— Cuban Poetry in English. Bull. of Bibliography, 18, 1946.

—— Three Mexican Poets: Sor Juana Inés de la Cruz, Manuel Gutiérrez Nájera and Enrique González Martínez. A Bibliography of their Poems in English Translation. Bull. of Bibliography, 18, 1946.

Peixoto, A. American Social and Literary Influences in Brazil. BA, 1935.

Ratcliff, D. F. Versiones inglesas de cuatro novelas de la revolución mexicana. Memoria del primer Congreso de Lit. Iberoamer., 1940.

Reid, J. T' The Development of Literary Americanismo in Spanish America. U.

of Miami Hispanic-American Studies, 5, 1948.
Remenyi, J. American Writers in Europe. Georgia Review, 2, 1948.
Romero, F. Influencia del descubrimiento de América en las ideas generales. Humanidades, 29, 1946.
Russak, B. Does Europe Want Our Books? Publishers' Weekly, 153, 1948.
Swigart, Beulah H. The Americas as Revealed in the Encyclopédie. Urbana, 1942.
Taxonera, L. de. L'influence des lettres américaines sur la littérature espagnole. Revue de l'Amérique latine, 1924.
Valle, R. H. Algunos franceses en México. Filosofía y Letras, 6. (México), 1943.
Werner, B. E. Der amerikanische Roman und die europäische Spätlese. Schweizer Journal, 1948.
White, G. The Philosophy of American Literature. Boston, 1891.
Wittke, C. The America Theme in Continental European Literatures. Mississippi Valley Historical Review, 28, 1941.
Wogan, D. A literatura argentina no Brasil. RIA, 12, 1947.
Woolsey, A. W. A Contemporary Texas Tragedy Related in Two Mexican Corridos. Hisp., 28, 1945.

2. Individual Authors.

Calveiro, A. V. Rosalia **CASTRO** en América y en Europa. Cultura Gallega, 3. (La Habana) 1938.
Gonzalez, M. P. Rosalia de Castro in ingles. Revista Cubana, 1937.
Fay, E. G. Rubén **DARIO** in New York. MLN, 57, 1942.
Raeders, G. Un grand poète romantique du Brésil à Coimbre: Antonio Gonçalves **DIAS**. Bull. des Etudes Portugaises, 2, 1936.
Reid, J. T. José Antonio **RAMOS** y la literatura norteamericana. RIA, 12, 1947.
Olguín, M. La filosofía de José Antonio Ramos y su afinidad con la del pueblo y los pensadores de los Estados Unidos. RIA, 12, 1947.
Krumtum, J. C. M. Domingo Faustino **SARMIENTO,** the Horace Mann of Argentina. Diss. Oklahoma U., 1936.
Santovenia, E. Sarmiento y sus amigos cubanos. Revista cubana, 13, 1940.
Cuthbertson, H. George **TICKNOR'S** Interest in Spanish-American Literature. Hisp., 1933.

CHAPTER TWO

North American Influences upon England.

Anon. English Travellers of Rank in America. NAR, 74, 1852.
—— American Reputations in England. The Nation, 18.I.1866.
Arber, E. The Three First English Books on America. Birmingham, 1885.
Berger, M. The British Traveller in America, 1836-60. Columbia U. P., 1943.
Bragg, Mary J. American News in English Periodicals, 1783-1800. HLQ, 8, 1945.
Bryant, W. A. Concepts of America and Americans by the English Romantic Poets: 1790-1850. Diss. Vanderbilt U., 1941.
Chace, W. E. The Descent on Democracy: A Study of American Democracy as Observed by British Travelers, 1815-60. Diss. U. of N. C., 1941.
De Golyer, E. The Journey of Three Englishmen Across Texas in 1568. El Paso, 1947.
Dickson, L. The American Novel in England. Publishers' Weekly, 134, 1938.
Gegenheimer, A. F. They Might Have Been Americans. SAQ, 46, 1947.
Gohdes, C. British Interest in American Literature During the Latter Part of the Nineteenth Century as Reflected in Mudie's Select Library. AL, 13, 1942.
—— American Literature in Nineteenth-Century England. Columbia U. P., 1944.
Heilman, R. B. America in English Fiction, 1760-1800. The Influences of the American Revolution. Baton Rouge (La.), 1937.
Hubach, R. R. St. Louis: Host of Celebrated Nineteenth Century British and American Authors. Missouri Hist. Rev., 38, 1944.
Johnson, Louise H. America in the Thought of Leading British Men of Letters, 1830-90. Diss. U. of Wisconsin, 1943.
Ludlow, J. M. The Growth of American Influence over England. AM, 1894.
Messick, Jane L. The English Traveller in America, 1785-1835. New York, 1922.
Mowat, R. B. Americans in England. Boston, 1935.
Nevins, A. American Social History as Recorded through British Travellers. New York, 1923.
—— America through British Eyes. New York, 1948.
Rhodes, H. G. The American Invasion of the London Stage. Cosmopolitan, May, 1902.

CHAPTER THREE

North American Influences upon France.

Anon. La littérature américaine traduite en français. Bibliographie. Le Navire d' argent, 1925-26.
Andrews, C. E. French Authors Take Revenge. Bookman, March, 1931.

Ansermoz-Dubois, F. L'interprétation française de la littérature américaine d'Entre-Deux-Guerres. (1919-39). Lausanne, 1944.
Barthold, A. French Journalists in the United States, 1780-1800. FAR, 3, 1936.
Baudin, M. L'Américain dans le théâtre français. PhQ, 1925.
Bellessort, A. L'américanisme en France. Revue hebdomadaire, April, 1928.
Bernès, H. La littérature des Etats-Unis en France. Revue de Synthèse historique, 29, 1919.
Capitaine, A. La situation économique et sociale des Etats-Unis d'Amérique à la fin du XVIIIe siècle d'après les voyageurs français. Paris, 1926.
Cestre, C. American Literature through French Eyes. Yale Review, Oct., 1920.
Chinard, G. L'exotisme américain dans la littérature française au XVIe siècle. Paris, 1911.
—— L'Amérique et le rêve exotique dans la littérature française au XVIIe et au XVIIIe siècle. Paris, 1913 & 1933.
—— La Déclaration des droits de l'homme et du citoyen et ses antécédents américains. Washington, 1945.
—— L'Amérique d'Abraham Lincoln et la France. Washington, 1945.
Copans, S. J. French Opinion of the United States under the Second Empire. Diss. Brown U., 1942.
Curtis, E. N. The French Assembly of 1848 and American Constitutional Doctrines. Studies in History, Economics and Public Law, 79 (New York), 1917.
Fay, B. L'Amérique et l'esprit scientifique en France à la fin du XVIIIe siècle. RLC, 3, 1923.
—— Bibliographie critique des ouvrages français relatifs aux Etats-Unis, 1770-1880. Paris, 1925.
Fess, G. M. The American Revolution in Creative French Literature (1775-1937). Columbia (Mo.), 1941.
Fonnol, L. L'America nella letteratura francese del 1927. NAnt, 1.II.1928.
Gager, D. French Comment on American Education. Diss. Columbia U., 1925.
Gibson, D. L. The United States as Seen in the Leading French Literary Periodicals, 1900-1930. Diss. U. of Wisconsin, 1939.
Horneber, F. Englisch-amerikanische Litteratur im Lichte französischer Kritik. Munnerstadt, 1897.
Kalfagan, A. The United States in the Post-War Literature of France (1919-31). MLJ, March, 1934.
Lanux, P. de. Young France and New America. New York, 1917.
Lapp, J. C. The New World in French Poetry of the Sixteenth Century. SPh, 45, 1948.
Lynes, C. The Nouvelle Revue Française and American Literature, 1909-40. FR, 19, 1946.
Mahieu, R. G. Enquêteurs français aux Etats-Unis de 1830 à 1837. Paris, 1934.
Maunhart, H. Wie französische Schriftsteller Amerika sehen. ZFEU, 31, 1932.
Mantz, H. E. French Criticism of American Literature. New York, 1917.
McGee, S. L. La littérature américaine dans la Revue des Deux Mondes, 1831-1900. Montpellier, 1927.
McKee, K. N. The Popularity of the American on the French Stage during the Revolution. Proceedings American Philosophical Society, 83, 1940.
Millar, M. F. X. The American and French Revolutions. Thought, 14, 1939.
Monaghan, F. French Travellers in the United States, 1765-1932: A Bibliography. New York, 1933.
Morris, G. D. American Traits as Seen by the French. Mid-West Quarterly, 1915.
O'Brien, J. American Books and French Readers. College English, 1, 1940.
Partridge, E. Early French Remarks on American Literature. MLN, May, 1925.
Peyre, H. La Louisiane dans la littérature française. In: Louisiane et Texas. Paris, 1938.
—— American Literature Through French Eyes. Virginia Quarterly Review, 1947.
Rice, H. C. Seeing Ourselves as the French See Us. FR, 21, 1948.
Rosenthal, L. The Influence of the United States on France in the 18th Century. New York, 1882.
Ryan, L. W. French Travelers in the Southeastern United States, 1775-1800. Bloomington, 1939.
Satre, J. P. American Novelists in French Eyes. AM, 178, 1946.
Simon, J. French Studies in American Literature and Civilization. AL, 6, 1934.
—— L'Amérique telle que l'ont vue les romanciers français (1917-37). EA, 1, 1937.
Smith, Anne W. Criticism of American Life and Letters in the Revue Encyclopédique. Diss. Northwestern U., 1943.
Swigart, Beulah H. The Americas as Revealed in the Encyclopédic. Urbana, 1942.
Weiss, Yvonne. La Louisane dans la littérature française. Diss. Columbia U., 1947.
Yvon, P. Regards français vers l'Amérique. Caen, 1930.

CHAPTER FOUR

North American Influences upon Germany.

Anon. Der Freiheitskampf der Union in der deutschen Litteratur. Litterar. Rundschau, 18.I.1902.

Baginsky, P. B. German Works Relating to America, 1493-1800. New York, 1942.
Binder-Johnson, Hildegard. Der deutsche Amerika-Auswanderer des 18. Jahrhunderts im zeitgenössischen Urteil. Deutsches Archiv f. Landes- und Volksforschung, 1940.
Breffka, C. Amerika in der deutschen Literatur. Köln, 1917.
Desczyk, G. Amerika in der Phantasie deutscher Dichter. Diss. Leipzig, 1923.
Eberhardt, F. Amerika-Literatur. Die wichtigsten seit 1900 in deutscher Sprache erschienenen Werke über Amerika. Leipzig, 1926.
Goebel, J. Amerika in der deutschen Dichtung. FDPh, 1894.
—— Amerika in der Phantasie deutscher Dichter. Jb. der deutsch-amerikanischen Ges. von Illinois. Chicago, 1925.
Hatfield, J. & Hochbaum, E. The Influence of the American Revolution upon German Literature. Americana Germanica, 3, 1899-1900.
Hewett-Thayer, H. W. America and Americans in Recent German Fiction. The Bookman, 43, 1926. Cf. also: The Modern German Novel. Boston, 1924.
King, H. S. Echoes of the American Revolution in German Literature. UCPPh, 14, 1929.
Koch, S. von. The German Approach to America and American Civilization. English Journal, 23, 1934.
Kohn, M. Amerika im Spiegel deutscher Dichtung. Zeitgeist, 32, 1905.
Krokow, L. von. American Characters in German Novels. AM, 1891-92.
Luedeke, H. American Literature in Germany. AL, May, 1936.
Luyster, N. van de. Emigration to America as Reflected in the German Novel of the XIXth Century. Diss. U. of N. C., 1942.
Meyer, H. Nord-Amerika im Urteil des deutschen Schrifttums bis zur Mitte des 19. Jahrhunderts. Hamburg, 1929.
Noe, A. C. von. Recent German Books on America. Papers of the Bibliographical Society of America, 4, 1909.
Pritzel. Amerika in der deutschen Literatur und Kultur. Literar-musikal. Monatshefte, 112, 1921.
Riley, T. A. New England Anarchism in Germany. NEQ, 18, 1945.
Sauer, A. The Influence of North American Literature on German Literature. Congress of Arts and Sciences, St. Louis Exposition, 1904, New York, 1906. And in: JbGrG, 16, 1906.
Schoenemann, F. Der Amerikanismus in deutscher Auffassuug. Literarischer Handweiser, Dec., 1927.
—— Amerikakunde, eine zeitgemässe Forderung. Bremen, 1921.
Schroeder, S. Amerika in der deutschen Dichtung von 1850 bis 1890. Diss. Heidelberg, 1934.
Tower, R. A. Attempts to Interest Germany in Early American Literature. PhQ, 1928.
Wagner, Lydia E. The Reserved Attitude of the Early German Romanticists toward America. GQ, 16, 1943.
Walz, J. A. The American Revolution and German Literature. MLN, 16, 1901.
—— Der Freiheitskampf der Union in der deutschen Literatur. Literar. Rundschau, 18, 1902.
Weber, P. C. America in Imaginative German Literature in the First Half of the Nineteenth Century. Columbia U. P., 1926.
Wehe, W. Das Amerika-Erlebnis in der deutschen Literatur. Geist der Zeit, 17, 1939.
Willer. Ein amerikanischer Geschichtsphilosoph und sein deutscher Uebersetzer. MLIA, 1866.

CHAPTER FIVE

North American Influences upon Other Countries.

(For Influences upon Latin America see Chapter One).

Massip, S. The Discovery of America by the **CHINESE**. Rev. bimestre cubana. And in: Inter-America, June, 1918.
Zylstra, H. A Mid-Nineteenth Century Dutch View of American Life and Letters. (**HOLLAND**). PMLA, 57, 1942.
Goggio, E. **ITALY** and the American War of Independence. RR, 1929.
Menarini. A. Echi dell'italo-americano in Italia. Lingua nostra, 2, 1940.
Torrielli, A. J. Italian Opinion on America as Revealed by Italian Travellers, 1850-1900. Harvard U.P., 1941.
Vaiciulaitis, A. American Writers in **LITHUANIA**. BA, 17, 1943.
Alexandrova, Vera. America and Americans in Soviet Literature. (**RUSSIA**). Russian Review, 2, 1943.
Kamenetsky, B. Two Centuries of Russian Writing on America. Am. Rev. on the Soviet Union, 6, 1945.
Magidoff, R. American Literature in Russia. SRL, 29, 1946.
Pozner, V. American Literature in Russia. The Bulletin; American Writer's Club of Paris, 1928.
Yarmolinsky, A. Russian Americana, Sixteenth to Eighteenth Centuries: A Bibliographical and Historical Study. New York, 1943.

Genzmer, F. Die isländischen Erzählungen von den Winlandfahrten. (**SCANDINAVIA**). Beiträge z. Geschichte d. deutschen Sprache, 67, 1943-44.
Hermannsson, H. The Vinland Sagas. Islandica, 30. (Ithaca), 1944.
Wiener, L. American Influences in the **SLAVIC** Literature. In: Congress of Arts and Sciences, St. Louis Exposition, 1904, New York, 1906.
SPAIN: See also Chapter One, above.
Englekirk, J. E. Obras norteamericanas en traducción española. RIA, 8-9, 1944-45.
Ferguson, J. de L. American Literature in Spain. New York, 1916.
Monguio, L. Lust for Riches (Spanish novel on Gold-Rush). Cal. Hist. Soc. Quart, 27, 1948.
Zarraga, M. de. The United States as Seen by a Spaniard. Inter-America, 2, 1918.
Elovson, H. Amerika i svensk litteratur, 1750-1820. (**SWEDEN**). Lund, 1930.
Johnson, G. An Exiled Swedish Novelist and the Civil War. Journal Ill. Hist. Soc., 1948.
Marjasch, Sonja. Der amerikanische Bestseller. Sein Wesen und seine Verbreitung, unter besonderer Berücksichtigung der Schweiz. (**SWITZERLAND**). Bern, 1946. Cf. MLN, 1947.

Varia. Emerson en France (Philarète Chasles, Daniel Stern et Emile Montégut). RDM, 1844 & 1847 & Revue indépendante, 1846.

CHAPTER SIX

Emerson

1. General Influences.

Cestre, C. Emerson et la France. In: Harvard et la France. Paris, 1936.
Conway, M. D. Emerson at Home and Abroad. Boston, 1882.
Ende, A. van. Emerson-Uebersetzungen. LE, 5, 1903.
Hill, A. S. The Influence of Emerson. HSPhL, 5, 1896.
Jackson, S. L. A Soviet View of Emerson. NEQ, 19, 1946.
Keller, H. Emerson in Frankreich: Wirkungen und Parallelen. Diss. Giessen, 1932.
Maitra, H. Emerson from an Indian Point of View. Harvard Theological Review, 4, 1911.
Mozoomdar, P. C. Emerson as Seen from India. In: Sanborn, The Genius and Character of Emerson. Boston, 1885.
Scudder, T. Emerson's British Lecture Tour, 1847-48. AL, 7, 1935.
Simon, J. Ralph Waldo Emerson in Deutschland (1851-1932). Berlin, 1937.
Spohr, W. Emerson's Influence in Germany. Ethical Record, 4, 1903.
Thayer, W. F. The Influence of Emerson. Boston, 1886.

2. Influences upon Individual Authors.

Burroughs, J. **ARNOLD** on Emerson and Carlyle. Century, April, 1884.
Gilman, Margaret. **BAUDELAIRE** and Emerson. RR, 34, 1943.
Kuhn, H. **CARLYLE**, Ally and Critic of Emerson. Emory U. Quart., 8, 1948.
Holls, F. W. Emerson's Correspondence with H. **GRIMM**. AM, April, 1903.
Osgood, H. **MAETERLINCK** and Emerson. Arena, 15 (Boston), 1896.
Chazin, M. Emerson's Disciple in Belgium: Marie **MALE** (1855-1927). RR, 1933.
Hummel, H. Emerson and **NIETZSCHE**. NEQ, 19, 1946.
Schottlaender, R. Two Dionysians: Emerson and Nietzsche. SAQ, 39, 1940.
Chazin, M. **QUINET**, an Early Discoverer of Emerson. PMLA, 1933.
—— Extracts from Emerson by Edgar Quinet. RLC, 15, 1935.
Howard, B. D. A French Estimate of Emerson (Daniel **STERN**, 1846). NEQ, Sept., 1937.

CHAPTER SEVEN

Poe

1. General Influences.

Ingram, J. H. The Raven by E. A. Poe; with Literary and Historical Commentary. London, 1885.
Mauclair, C. E. A. Poe as Inspirer of Ideas. Fortnightly Review, 1923.
Whitman, S. H. Edgar Poe and his Critics. Providence, 1860.
Wood, C. The Influence of Poe and Lanier on Modern Literature. Southern Literary Messenger, April, 1939.
Englekirk, J. E. The Raven in Spanish **AMERICA**. Spanish Review, 1, 1934.
—— E. A. Poe in Hispanic Literature. New York, 1934.
—— Bibliography of Mexican Versions of Poe, Verse and Prose. PMLA, 1937.
—— My Nightmare, the last Tale by Poe (and Mexican Interest in E. A. Poe). PMLA, 1937.
Erickson, M. E. Three Guatemalan Translators of Poe. Hisp., 25, 1942.
Babler, O. F. **CZECH** Translations of Poe's Raven. N&Q, 192, 1947.
Hutcherson, D. R. Poe's Reputation in **ENGLAND** and America, 1850-1909. AL, 14, 1942.

Betz, L. P. Die französische Moderne im Gefolge Edgar Poes. (**FRANCE**). In: Studien. Frankfurt, 1902.
Cambiaire, C. P. The Influence of Edgar Allan Poe in France. RR, 1926 & New York, 1927.
Chassé, C. Edgar Poe et la France. Figaro, 20.I.1934.
Cottier, J. Il y a cent ans, la France découvrait E. Poe. NL, 24.IV.1947.
Du Bos, C. Poe and the French Mind. Athenaeum, Jan., 1921.
Engel, Claire-Eliane. L'état des travaux sur E. A. Poe en France. MPh, 1932.
Fontainas, A. Edgar Poe et la poésie française. Mfr, 1933.
Lemonnier, L. E. Poe et la critique française de 1845 à 1875. Diss. Paris, 1928.
—— Edgar Poe et les Parnassiens français. RLC, 9, 1929.
—— L'influence d'Edgar Poe sur quelques poètes symbolistes et décadents. MF, 15.VI.1929.
—— L'influence d'Edgar Poe sur quelques conteurs réalistes. RLC, 11, 1931.
— Edgar Poe et les poètes français. NRC, Paris, 1932.
—— L'influence d'Edgar Poe sur les conteurs français symbolistes et décadents. RLC, 13, 1933.
—— Edgar Poe et les conteurs français. Paris, 1947.
Morris, G. D. Cooper et Poe d'après la critique française du dix-neuvième siècle. Paris, 1912.
—— French Criticism of Poe. SAQ, 14, 1915.
Olivéra Jackowska, S. d'. La réhabilitation d'Edgar Poe et ses plus beaux poèmes en vers français. Paris, 1933.
Page, C. H. E. A. Poe in France. Nation, 14.I.1909.
Ransome, A. Edgar Allan Poe, a Critical Study. Postscript: The French View of Poe. London, 1910.
Seylaz, L. Poe et les premiers symbolistes français. Lausanne, 1923.
Babler, O. F. German Translations of Poe's Raven. (**GERMANY**). N&Q, 1.I.1938.
Betz, L. P. Edgar Poe in Deutschland. Zeit, 35, 1903.
Hippe. E. A. Poe in Deutschland. Münster, 1913.
Mabbot, T. O. German Translations of Poe's Raven. N&Q, 174, 1938.
Prezzolini, G. Poe e le lettere italiane. (**ITALY**). Pegaso, 1930.
Trompeo, P. P. Poe a Roma. La Nuova Europa, 2, 1945.
SPAIN: See Spanish America, above.
Keefer, L. E. A. Poe in **RUSSIA**. Baltimore, 1941 & Porto Allegre, 1944.

2. Influences upon Individual Authors.

Lemonnier, L. Edgar A. Poe et Théodore de **BANVILLE**. RLC, 6, 1926.
Yvon, P. **BARBEY D'AUREVILLY** et Poe. Caen, 1927.
Anon. The French Translator of Edgar Poe (**BAUDELAIRE**). Every Saturday, 3, 1871.
Anichkov, E. Baudelaire and Edgar Poe. (In Russian). Sovremennyi Mir, 1909.
Bernard, J. M. A propos d'un sonnet de Baudelaire (E. Poe, Longfellow, Gray). RHLF, 1909.
Betz, L. P. Edgar Poe und Charles Baudelaire. In: Studien. Frankfurt, 1902.
Cestre, C. Poe et Baudelaire. RAA, April, 1934.
Françon, M. Poe et Baudelaire. PMLA, 60, 1945.
Gourmont, R. de. Notes sur E. Poe et Baudelaire. Flegrea (Napoli), 5.VII.1900.
Jones, P. M. Poe, Baudelaire and Mallarmé: A Problem of Literary Judgement. MLR, 39, 1944-45.
—— Poe and Baudelaire: the Affinity. MLR, 40, 1945.
Lemonnier, L. Les traducteurs d'Edgar Poe en France de 1845 à 1875: Charles Baudelaire. Paris, 1928.
—— Baudelaire traducteur du Corbeau. Mfr., 10.XII.1929.
—— Deux versions de Bérénice. In: Enquêtes sur Baudelaire. Paris, 1929.
Michaud, R. Baudelaire et Edgar A. Poe. Une mise au point. RLC, 18, 1938.
Patterson, A. S. L'influence d'E. Poe sur Ch. Baudelaire. Diss. Grenoble, 1903.
Rhodes, S. A. The Influence of Poe on Baudelaire. RR, 18, 1927.
Rooker, J. J. Baudelaire and Poe. TLS, 20.V.1913.
Schinzel, E. Natur und Natursymbolik bei Poe, Baudelaire und den französischen Symbolisten. Düren, 1931.
Stuart, E. Charles Baudelaire and Edgar Poe: a Literary Affinity. NC, 34, 1893.
Norman, H. L. A Possible Source for E. A. **BUTTI'S** Castello del Sogno. MLN, April, 1937.
Johnston, M. C. Ruben **DARIO'S** Acquaintance with Poe. Hisp., 1934.
Hudson, R. L. Poe and **DISRAELI**. AL, Jan., 1937.
Astrov, V. **DOSTOEVSKY** on Edgar Allan Poe. AL, 14, 1942.
Mabbot, T. O. **DUMAS** and Poe. TLS, 21.XI.1929 & 2.I.1930.
Schwartz, W. L. The Influence of E. A. Poe on Judith **GAUTIER**. MLN, 1927.
Kaun, A. Poe and **GOGOL**. SR, 1937.
Auriant. Emile **HENNEQUIN** traducteur d'Edgar Poe. MF, 1935.
Chassé, C. Essai d'une interprétation objective du Tombeau d'Edgar Poe ou

MALLARME traduit par Mallarmé lui-même. RLC, 23, 1949.
Wais, K. E. A. Poe und Mallarmé's Prose pour des Esseintes. Quellenstudien zu Mallarmé. ZFSL, 61, 1937.
Cain, H. E. James Clarence **MANGAN** and the Poe-Mangan Question. Diss. Washington, 1929.
Marvin, F. R. **MAUPASSANT** and Poe. In: The Fireside Papers. Boston, 1915.
Strout, A. Poe and **POULAILLER.** TLS, 8.I.1939.
Sharma, R. B. Poe and **ROSSETTI.** Calcutta Review, 73, 1939.
Fernandat, R. Paul **VALERY** et les Marginalia de Poe. Mfr. 10.VII.1929.
Jones, R. S. The Influence of Edgar Allan Poe on Paul Valéry, Prior to 1900. CLS, 21-22, 1946.
Lemonnier, L. Paul Valéry et Edgar Poe. NL, 24.VIII.1929.
—— L'influence d'Edgar Poe sur **VERLAINE** et Rimbaud. Figaro littéraire, 19.I.1929.
—— L'influence d'Edgar Poe sur **VILLIERS DE L'ISLE-ADAM.** MF, 15.IX.1933.
Olivero, F. E. A. Poe's Influence on the Tales of Villiers de l'Isle-Adam. ZFEU, 13, 1914.
Wyzewa, T. de. Nos maîtres (Poe et Villiers de l'Isle-Adam). Paris, 1895.

CHAPTER EIGHT

Whitman

1. General Influences.

Allen, G. W. Walt Whitman in Comparative Literature. CLN, 2, 1943-44.
Frenz, H. American Literature and World Literature (Whitman in Europe). Ibid.
Hercourt, J. Primauté de Walt Whitman. Genève, 1939
Schyberg, F. Whitman i verdenslitteraturen. In: Walt Whitman. København, 1933.
Anon. A Canadian Interview with Walt Whitman. (**AMERICA**). American N&Q, 3, 1943.
Alegria, F. Walt Whitman en Hispanoamérica. RIA, 8, 1944.
Englekirk, J. E. Notes on Whitman in Spanish America. HR, 6, 1938.
Blodgett, H. Walt Whitman in **ENGLAND.** Cornell Studies in English. (Ithaca), 1934.
Baldensperger, F. Walt Whitman and **FRANCE.** Columbia U. Quarterly, 21, 1919.
Cestre, C. Un intermède de la renommée de W. Whitman en France. RAA, Dec., 1935.
Jones, P. M. On the Track of an Influence in 1913. CLS, 6-7, 1943.
—— Whitman and the Symbolists. French Studies, Jan., 1948.
Pucciani, O. F. The Literary Reputation of Walt Whitman in France. Diss. Harvard U., 1943.
Clark, G. D. Walt Whitman in **GERMANY.** Texas Review, 6, 1921.
Jacobson, Anna. Walt Whitman in Germany since 1914. GR, 1, 1926.
Law-Robertson, H. Walt Whitman in Deutschland. Diss. Giessen, 1935.
Lessing, O. E. Whitman and his German Critics. JEGPh, 9, 1910 & American Collector, 3, 1926.
Riethmueller, R. Walt Whitman and the Germans. German American Annals, N. S., 4, 1906.
Thornstenberg, E. The Walt Whitman Cult in Germany. Sewanee Rev., 19, 1911.
Remenyi, J. Walt Whitman in **HUNGARIAN** Literature. AL, 16, 1944.
McCain, R. Walt Whitman in **ITALY:** A Bibliography. Bull. of Bibliography, 1940 ff.
—— Walt Whitman in Italy. Italica, 20, 1943.
Parry, A. Walt Whitman in **RUSSIA.** American Mercury, 33, 1934.
Allen, G. W. Walt Whitman's Reception in **SCANDINAVIA.** Papers Bibl. Soc. Amer., 40, 1946.
Ferguson, J. Walt Whitman. In: American Literature in **SPAIN.** Columbia U. P., 1916.

2. Influences upon Individual Authors.

Kennedy, W. S. Alfred **AUSTIN** on Whitman. Conservator, March, 1896.
Torres-Rioseco, A. Ruben **DARIO.** Harvard U. P., 1931.
Springer, O. Walt Whitman and Ferdinand **FREILIGRATH.** AGR, 11, 1944.
Rohdes, S. A. The Influence of Walt Whitman on André **GIDE.** RR, 31, 1940.
GILCHRIST, H. An English Woman's Estimate of Walt Whitman. In: Anne Gilchrist, her Life and Writings. London, 1887.
Starr, W. T. Jean **GIONO** and Walt Whitman. FR, 14, 1940.
Ende, Amelia von. Walt Whitman and Arno **HOLZ.** PL, 16, 1905.
Frenz, H. Walt Whitman's Letters to Karl **KNORTZ.** AL, 20, 1948.
Cairns, W. B. **SWINBURNE'S** Opinion of Walt Whitman. AL, 3, 1931.
Monroe, W. S. Swinburne's Recantation of Walt Whitman. RAA, 8, 1931.
Jackson, E. P. Whitman and **TOLSTOI.** Conservator, Jan., 1895.
Jones, P. M. Whitman and **VERHAEREN.**

Aberystwyth Studies (Univ. College, Wales), 2, 1914.
Randall, Huberta F. Whitman and Verhaeren, Priests of Human Brotherhood. FR, 16, 1942.

CHAPTER NINE

Other North American Authors.

Steiner, Pauline & Frenz, H. **ANDERSON** and Stalling's What Price Glory and Carl Zuckmayer's Rivalen. GQ, 20, 1947.
Svendsen, J. K. Anne **BRADSTREET** in England: A Bibliographical Note. AL, 13, 1941.
Chapin, Clara C. **BRYANT** and Some of his Latin American Friends. Bull cf the Pan American Union, Nov., 1944.
Grubbs, H. A. Mallarmé and Bryant. MLN, 62, 1947.
Frenz, H. Bartley **CAMPBELL'S** My Partner in Berlin. GQ, 17, 1944.
Baldensperger, F. James Fenimore **COOPER** in France. Franco-American Pamphlets, 2, (New York), 1940.
Barba, P. A. Balduin Mollhausen, the German Cooper. Americana Germanica, 17, 1914.
Bosset, G. C. Fenimore Cooper et le roman d'aventure en France vers 1830. Paris, 1929.
Clavel, M. Fenimore Cooper and his Critics: American, British and French Criticisms of the Novelist's Early Work. Aix-en-Provence, 1938.
Constantin-Weyer, M. Fenimore Cooper et le Cycle de Bas-de-Cuir. Europe, 15. XI.1927.
Dargan, E. P. Balzac and Cooper: Les Chouans. MPh, April, 1915.
Garzon de la Casa, Maria Luisa. La sombra de Cooper sobre el americanismo de Alencar. Mexico, 1944.
Gibb, M. M. Le roman de Bas-de-Cuir: étude sur F. Cooper et son influence en France. Paris, 1927.
—— Léon Gozlan et Fenimore Cooper. RLC, 10, 1930.
Goggio, E. Cooper's Bravo in Italy. RR, 1929.
Messac, R. F. Cooper et son influence en France. PMLA, Dec., 1928.
Morize, A. Le Bourriquot de Tartarin. MLN, April, 1929.
Morris, G. D. Cooper et Poe d'après la critique française du dix-neuvième siècle. Paris, 1912.
Palfrey, T. R. Cooper and Balzac: The Headman. MPh, 1932.
Partridge, E. Cooper's Influence on the French Romantics. MLR, 1925. And in: A Critical Medley. Paris, 1926.
Wukadinovic, S. Goethes Novelle: Der Schauplatz. Coopersche Einflüsse. Halle, 1909.
Gallup, D. A Bibliographical Check-list of the Writings of T. S. **ELIOT** including his Contributions to Periodicals and Translations of his Work into Foreign Languages. New Haven, 1947.
Ricard, J. F. Les romans de **FAULKNER** en France. Confluences, 1945.
Adams, P. G. Crèvecoeur and **FRANKLIN.** Penn. Hist., 14, 1947.
Chinard, G. Les amitiés américaines de Mme. d'Houdetot, d'après sa correspondance inédite avec B. Franklin et Th. Jefferson. Paris, 1924.
Counson, A. Franklin et Robespierre. Mélanges Baldensperger. Paris, 1930.
Crane, V. W. Benjamin Franklin, Englishman and American. Colver Lectures, Baltimore, 1936.
—— Franklin's Political Journalism in England. Journal Franklin Inst., 233, 1942.
Dvoichenko-Markoff, Eufrosina. Benjamin Franklin, the American Philosophical Society, and The Russian Academy of Science. Proceedings American Philosophical Society, 91, 1947.
Fay, B. Franklin et Mirabeau collaborateurs. RLC, 8, 1928.
—— Les débuts de Franklin en France. RP, 1931.
—— Le triomphe de Franklin en France. RP, 1931.
Goggio, E. Benjamin Franklin and Italy. RR, 1928.
Hale, E. E. Franklin in France. 2 vols. Boston, 1887-88.
Johansson, J. V. Une plaisanterie de B. Franklin employée comme moyen de propagande par Diderot et Raynal. In: Etudes sur D. Diderot. Paris, 1927.
McMaster, J. B. Franklin in France. AM, 1887.
Miller, C. R. D. Franklin and Carli's Lettere Americane. MPh, 1930.
Nolan, J. B. Benjamin Franklin in Scotland and Ireland, 1759 and 1771. Philadelphia, 1938.
Read, C. Dr. Franklin as the English Saw Him. Journal Franklin Inst., 233, 1942.
Eckert, R. P. Robert **FROST** in England. Mark Twain Quarterly, 3, 1940.
Margaret **FULLER:** See also Intermediaries. I.IV.8.
Barbour, F. M. Margaret Fuller and British Reviewers. NEQ, 9, 1936.
Wellisz, L. The Friendship of Margaret Fuller d'Ossoli and Adam Mickiewicz. New York, 1947.
Hobson, J. A. The Influence of Henry **GEORGE** in England. Fortnightly Review, 1897.
Carlson, C. L. Thomas **GODFREY** in England. AL, Nov., 1935.

O'Brien, J. Henry **HARLAND**, an American Forerunner of Proust. MLN, June, 1939.
Kinth, H. Freiligrath and Bret **HARTE**. Gegenwart, 1876.
Anon. George Eliot and **HAWTHORNE**. New British Review, Aug., 1860.
Baldensperger, F. A propos de Nathaniel Hawthorne en France. MLN, 56, 1941.
Faust, Bertha. Hawthorne's Contemporaneous Reputation: A Study of Literary Opinion in America and England, 1828-64. Philadelphia, 1939.
Lemaître, J. La Lettre écarlate de Hawthorne, drame à l'Odéon. Paris, 1901.
Stewart, R. Hawthorne in England. NEQ, March, 1935.
Praz, M. **HEMINGWAY** in Italy. Partisan Review, 15, 1948.
HERSEY, J. Soviet Writers Discuss A Bell for Adano. American Review on the Soviet Union, 7, 1946.
Starrett, V. Oliver Wendell **HOLMES** and Conan Doyle. American N&Q, 1, 1941.
Boll, E. Charles Dickens and Washington **IRVING**. MLQ, 5, 1944.
Brandes, W. W. Raabe und Washington Irving. Mitteilungen für die Ges. der Freunde W. Raabes, 12, Braunschweig, 1923.
Goggio, E. Washington Irving's Works in Italy. RR, 1931.
Kabel, P. Die Quellen für Heines Bimini und Mohrenkönig. Archiv, 117, 1906.
Kirby, T. A. Carlyle and Irving. ELH, 13, 1946.
—— Irving and Moore: A Note on Anglo-American Literary Relations. MLN, 62, 1947.
Morris, G. D. W. Irving's Fiction in the Light of French Criticism. Indiana U. Studies, 3, 1916.
Pacey, W. C. D. Washington Irving and Charles Dickens. AL, 16, 1945.
Plath, O. W. Irvings Einfluss auf W. Hauff. Euphorion, 20, 1913.
Reichart, W. A. Washington Irving as a Source for Borel and Dumas. MLN, 51, 1936.
—— Washington Irving's Friend and Collaborator: Barham John Livius, Esq. PMLA, 56, 1941.
—— Baron von Gumppenberg, Emily Forster and Washington Irving. MLN, May, 1945.
Wegelin, C. Dickens and Irving: The Problem of Influence. MLQ, 7, 1946.
Chinard, G. (ed.). The Letters of Lafayette and **JEFFERSON**. Baltimore, 1929.
—— Sainte-Beuve, Thomas Jefferson et Tocqueville. Princeton, 1943.
—— Jefferson's Influence Abroad. Miss. Valley Hist. Rev., 30, 1943.
Garlick, R. C. Philip Mazzei, Friend of Jefferson. Baltimore, 1934.
Kimball, Marie. Jefferson in Paris, NAR, 248.
Kozlowski, W. M. Niemcewicz en Amérique et sa correspondance inédite avec Jefferson. 1797-1810. RLC, 8, 1928.
Marraro, H. R. Four Versions of Jefferson's Letter to Mazzei. William & Mary Quarterly Hist. Mag., 22, 1942.
Philips, E. Louis Hue Girardin and Nicolas Gouin Dufief, and their Relations with Thomas Jefferson. Baltimore, 1926.
Bourgeois, Y. R. Sidney **LANIER** et le Goffic. RAA, 1931.
Wood, C. The Influence of Poe and Lanier on Modern Literature. Southern Literary Messenger, April, 1939.
Chinard, G. L'Amérique d'Abraham **LINCOLN** et la France. Washington, 1945.
H. W. **LONGFELLOW**: See also Intermediaries. I.IV.8.
Anon. Longfellows Pandora in deutscher Uebersetzung. MLIA, 1878.
Appelmann, M. H. W. Longfellows Beziehungen zu Ferdinand Freiligrath. Münster, 1916.
Baur, F. Jubileum uitgave van Guido Gezelle's volledige Werken. The Song of Hiawatha, overgedicht in't Vlaamsch dor Guido Bezelle. Gand, 1930.
Chinard, G. Les sources d'un poème de Leconte de Lisle. MLN, Jan., 1921.
Englekirk, J. E. Notes on Longfellow in Spanish America. Hisp., 25, 1942.
Estève, E. Longfellow et la France. Brunswick (Me.), 1925.
Gohdes, C. Longfellow and his Authorized British Publishers. PMLA, 55, 1940.
—— A Check-List of Volumes by Longfellow Published in the British Isles during the Nineteenth Century. Bull. of Bibliography, 17, 1940-41.
Hatfield, J. T. The Longfellow-Freiligrath Correspondence. PMLA, 48, 1933.
Hecht, D. Longfellow in Russia. NEQ, 19, 1946.
—— Lavrov and Longfellow. Russian Review, 5, 1946.
Koszul, A. Longfellow et Quinet. Un souvenir de Strasbourg. Mélanges Baldensperger. Paris, 1930.
Martinelli, N. Riflessi della poesia di Longfellow nei carmi latini di G. Pascoli. LNI. 20.VI.1934.
Richards, I. Longfellow in England. PMLA, 1936.
Santullano, L. Longfellow en Villanueva del Pardillo. Rev. hispánica moderna, 5, 1939.
Shelley, P. A. An Exchange of Letters with Longfellow. PMLA, 60, 1945.
Whitman, J. L. Longfellow and Spain. Columbia U. P., 1928.
Horwill, H. W. **LOWELL'S** Influence in England. New England Mag., Nov., 1902.

Hemminghaus, E. H. **MARK TWAIN** in Germany. Columbia U. P., 1939.
Henderson, A. The Interantional Fame of Mark Twain. NAR, Dec., 1910.
Parry, A. Mark Twain in Russia. BA, 15, 1941.
Robertson, S. Mark Twain in Germany. Mark Twain Quarterly, 2, 1937-38.
Roerich, N. Mark Twain in Russia. Mark Twain Quarterly, 3, 1939.
Schoenemann, F. Mark Twain and Adolf Wildbrandt. MLN, 34, 1929.
Simboli, R. Mark Twain from an Italian Point of View. Critic, 44, 1904.
Thaler, C. von. Mark Twain in Deutschland. Gegenwart, 1899.
Davies, D. Coleridge's Marginalia in **MATHER'S** Magnalia. HLQ, 2, 1939.
Loomis, C. An Unnoted German Reference to Increase Mather. NEQ, 14, 1941.
Rice, H. C. Cotton Mather Speaks to France: American Propaganda in the Age of Louis XIV. NEQ, 16, 1943.
Anderson, C. **MELVILLE'S** English Debut. AL, 11, 1939-40.
Privitera, J. F. **O'HENRY** and Anatole France. MLF, 25, 1940.
Anon. Eugene **O'NEILL'S** Plays Abroad. Program Greenwich Village Theatrical Season, 1925-26.
Frenz, H. A List of Foreign Editions and Translations of Eugene O'Neill's Dramas. Bull. of Bibliogr., 18, 1943-46.
—— Eugene O'Neill in Russia. PL, 49, 1943.
—— Eugene O'Neill in France. BA, 18, 1944.
—— Eugene O'Neill on the London Stage. Queen's Quarterly, 54, 1947.
Seibel, G. Thomas **PAINE** in Germany. OC, 34, 1920.
Hausermann, H. W. Yeats' Criticism of Ezra **POUND**. ESs, 30, 1948.
Steiner, A. W. H. **PRESCOTT** and Jakob Wassermann. JEGPh, 24, 1925.
Cory, D. **SANTAYANA** in Europe. AM, 174, 1944.
SEALSFIELD: See Intermediaries. I.IV.8.
Bantz, Elizabeth. Upton **SINCLAIR**: Book Reviews and Criticisms Published in German and French Periodicals and Newspapers. Bull. of Bibliogr., 18, 1943-46.
Besouchet, Lidia. Amando Fontes y **STEINBECK**. Nosotros, 7, 1942.
Burns, W. & Sutcliffe, E. G. Uncle Tom and Charles Reade. (H. Beecher **STOWE**.) AL, 17, 1946.
Harrod, Hazel. Correspondence of Harriet Beecher Stowe and Elizabeth Barrett Browning. Texas Studies in English, 27, 1948.
Lucas, E. E. La littérature antiesclavagiste au XIXe siècle: étude sur Mme. Beecher Stowe et son influence en France. Paris, 1930.
Maclean, G. Edith. Uncle Tom's Cabin in Germany. Diss. Heidelberg. Americana Germanica, 10, 1910.
Berry, E. G. **THOREAU** in Canada. Dalhousie Rev., 23, 1943.
Cosman, M. A Yankee in Canada. Canadian Hist. Rev., 25, 1944.
Frank, W. Bazalgette and Thoreau. Dial, 1, 1925.
Manning, C. A. Thoreau and Tolstoy. NEQ, 16, 1943.
Villard, O. G. Gandhi's New England Background. Common Sense, 11, 1942.
Bishop, M. Chateaubriand Did Not Meet **WASHINGTON**. MLN, 62, 1947.
Carruth, F. W. Washington in Fiction. Bookman, 15, 1902.
Chinard, G. George Washington as the French Knew Him. Princeton, 1940.
—— Vashington ou la liberté du nouveau monde, tragédie . . . par Billardon de Sauvigny. (1791). Princeton, 1941.
Frey, J. R. George Washington in German Fiction. AGR, 12, 1946.
Varia. Washington (and his Influence in Latin America). Bull. of the Panamerican Union. (Washington), 1932.
Lancaster, H. C. Henry Bordeaux and Maud Muller. (**WHITTIER**). MLN, Jan., 1912.
Pusey, W. W. The German Vogue of Thomas **WOLFE**. GR, 23, 1948.

CHAPTER TEN

The American Language.

Anon. Bartlett's Dictionary of Americanisms. NAR, July, 1849.
Apperson, G. L. English Americanisms. Fireside, Dec., 1901.
Baker, S. J. The Influence of American Slang on Australia. American Speech, 18, 1943.
Johnson, W. G. American Loanwords in American Swedish. Festschrift G. Flom. Urbana, 1942.
König, K. Ueberseeische Wörter im Französischen. Halle, 1939.
Krumpelmann, J. T. Charles Sealsfield's Americanisms. American Speech, 16, 1942.
Kurrelmeyer, W. American and Other Loanwords in German. JEGPh, 43, 1944.
Lodge, C. Shakespeare's Americanisms. Harper's Mag., 1894.
Palmer, P. M. Der Einfluss der Neuen Welt auf den deutschen Wortschatz, 1495-1800. Heidelberg, 1933.
—— Neuweltwörter im Deutschen. Heidelberg, 1939.
Schmidt, M. Amerikanismen bei Charles Sealsfield. Bonn, 1937.

Suhl, A. Anglizismen in Thomas Manns Doktor Faustus. MDU, 40, 1948.
White, R. G. British Americanisms. AM, 45, 1880.
—— Some Alleged Americanisms. AM, 52, 1883.

CHAPTER ELEVEN

American Influences upon Individual Authors.

Schons, Dorothy. The Mexican Background of **ALARCON**. PMLA, 57, 1942.
Miller, C. R. D. **ALFIERI** and America. PhQ, 1932.
Tissot, L. Le Mexique vu au siècle dernier par l'écrivain français J. J. **AMPERE**. Terres Latines (Mexico), 1948.
Bell, W. J. Thomas **ANBUREY'S** Travels through America: A Note on XVIIIth Century Plagiarism. Papers of the Bibliograph. Soc. of America, 37, 1943.
Benton, J. Matthew **ARNOLD** on America. Christian Union, 28.IV.1888.
Jones, H. M. Arnold, Aristocracy, and America. AHR, 49, 1944.
Anon. A Frenchman in the United States in 1840 and 1881: De **BACOURT**. AM, 51, 1883.
Meng, J. J. Abbé **BANDOL** in America. Catholic Historical Rev., 1934.
Marsan, J. **BEAUMARCHAIS** et l'Amérique. Paris, 1919.
Pierson, G. W. Tocqueville and **BEAUMONT** in America. Oxford U. P., 1938.
Bertin, G. Joseph **BONAPARTE** en Amérique, 1815-32. Paris, 1893.
Dostert, L. Paul **BOURGET** et les Etats-Unis. Georgetown U. French Review, May, 1936.
Mandat, E. de. M. Paul Bourget en Amérique. Figaro, 1.VI.1895.
Anon. **BOZ** über Amerika. Beilage zur Allg. Zt., 5.XI.1842.
Zeydel, E. H. Sebastian **BRANT** and the Discovery of America. JEGPh, 42, 1943.
Thompson, L. Fredrika **BREMER** as a Critic of American Literature. Edda, 41, 1941.
Baldensperger, F. Le séjour de **BRILLAT-SAVARIN** aux Etats-Unis. RLC, 2, 1922.
Whitridge, A. Brillat-Savarin in America. Anglo-American Review, 1936.
Gidney, L. M. L'influence des Etats-Unis d'Amérique sur **BRISSOT**, Condorcet et Mme. Roland. Paris, 1930.
Broglie, Duc de. Deux Français aux Etats-Unis et dans la Nouvelle-Espagne en 1782. Journal de voyage du prince de **BROGLIE** et lettres du comte de Ségur. Mélanges publiés par la Soc. des bibliophiles français, 1903.
Anon. **BRUNETIERE** en Amérique. Le Temps, 23.II.1897.
Carus, G. Robert **BURNS** and the American Revolution. OC, 1932.
Jones, J. J. Lord **BYRON** on America. Texas Studies in English, 1941.
Duffy, C. Thomas **CAMPBELL** and America. AL, 13, 1942.
Fernández, J. R. Presencia de América en la obra de **CERVANTES**. Atenea, 88, 1947.
Miramón, A. Las Indias a través de Cervantes. Rev. de las Indias, 32, 1947.
Nicolau d'Oliver, L. América en la obra de Cervantes. Cuadernos Americanos, 7, 1948.
Vasconcelos, J. Cervantes y América. RIA, 13, 1947.
Mahr, A. The Visit of the Rurik to San Francisco in 1816. (**CHAMISSO**, Kotzebue). Stanford U. Publ. History, Econ. Polit., 3, 1932.
Anon. Sur le voyage de **CHATEAUBRIAND** en Amérique. American Quarterly Review, Dec., 1827.
Armstrong, E. K. Chateaubriand's America. PMLA, 22, 1907.
Baldensperger, F. Un prédécesseur de René en Amérique: le Florello de Loaisel de Tréogate. Revue de philologie française, 15, 1901.
—— A propos de Chateaubriand en Amérique. RHLF, 1915.
—— Toujours le voyage de Chateaubriand aux Etats-Unis: entre Baltimore et New York. PMLA, 1932.
—— & Carré, J. M. La première histoire indienne de Chateaubriand et sa source américaine. MLR, 1913.
Bédier, J. Chateaubriand en Amérique. Vérité et fiction. RHLF, 8, 1899-1900. And in: Etudes critiques. Paris, 1904.
Bellessort, A. Chateaubriand en Amérique: la sincérité du voyageur, la portée de son oeuvre. Correspondant, 10.III.1920.
Chazin, M. Chateaubriand, le chantre d'-Odérahi. MLN, 1932.
Chinard, G. Une soeur ainée d'Atala, Odérahi. RB, Dec., 1912.
—— L'exotisme américain dans l'oeuvre de Chateaubriand. Paris, 1918.
Cresson, W. P. Chateaubriand and the Monroe Doctrine. NAR, 1923.
Giraud, V. Les Veillées américaines. Contribution à l'histoire des sources d'Atala. RB, 1913.
Haas, J. Chateaubriand's Reise nach Amerika. New-Yorker Staatszeitung, Sonntagsblatt, 15.III.1903.
Hamel, A. G. van. Nog eens Chateaubriand's reis naar Amerika. Gids, 357, 1900 & June, 1901.
Hazard, P. L'auteur d'Odérahi, histoire américaine. RLC, 3, 1923.
—— Chateaubriand et la littérature des Etats-Unis. RLC, 8, 1928.

Herford, C. Norse Myth in English Poetry. BRL, 5, 1918, 75-100.
Jerrold, C. The Balder Myth and Some English Poets. Saga-Book of Viking Club, 3, 1904, 94-116.
Krappe, A. A Viking Legend in England. Anglia 56, 1932, 432-35.
Leach, H. G. Angevin Britain and Scandinavia. Cambridge, Mass., 1921.
Lindsay, J. The Norse Hero in the English 18th Century. Norseman, 4, 1946, 332-40.
Litzenberg, K. The Victorians and the Vikings: A Bibliographical Essay. Michigan Contributions in Modern Philology, 3, 1947. 27 p.
Nordby, C. The Influence of Old Norse Literature upon English Literature. New York, 1901. (Columbia U. Germanic Studies 1), 78 p.
Paris, G. La Poésie du Moyen Age. 2. Ser. Paris, 1895. [Pp. 45-74, L'Esprit normand en Angleterre].
Seaton, E .Literary Relations of England and Scandinavia in the Seventeenth Century. Oxford, 1935. 384 p. 20 pl.
Smith, A. The Early Literary Relations of England and Scandinavia. Saga-Book of Viking Society, 11, 1934, 215-232.
Stedman, D. Some Points of Resemblance between Beowolf and the Grettla (or Grettis Saga). Saga-Book of Viking Society, 8, 1913, 6-28.
Stefánsson, J. Oldnordisk Indvirkning på engelsk Literatur i det attende og nittende århundrede. Nordisk Tidskrift, 1891, 488-503.
Tuschke, L. "Fair Janet" und "Kong Valdemar og hans Søster." Ein Beitrag zur Frage der Beziehungen zwischen englisch - schottischen und skandinavischen Volksballaden. Berlin, 1940.
Wright, H. Studies in Anglo-Scandinavian Literary Relations. Bangor, 1919, 157 p.
Christophersen, P. Early Anglo-Danish Literary Relations. Norseman, 3, 1945, 363-73.
Downs, B. Anglo-Danish Literary Relations 1867-1900. MLR, 39, 262-79.
Lukman, N. British and Danish Traditions. Classica et Mediaevalia, 6, 1944, 72-109.
Nielsen, L. Ældre dansk Litteratur i engelske Biblioteker. NTBB, 15, 1928, 203-16.
Mead, W. Anglo-Finnish Cultural Relations. Norseman, 6, 1948, 376-87.
Burchardt, C. Norwegian Life and Literature. English Accounts and Views especially in the 19th Century. Oxford, 1920. 230 p.
Downs, B. Anglo-Norwegian Literary Relations 1876-1900. MLR 47, 1952, 449-94.
———, Norse Literary Visitors to Britain. Norseman 6, 1948, 421-25.
Haugen, E. Norges litteraere profil i den engelsktalende verden. Vinduet, 6, 1949, 473-79.
Mortensen, J. (ed.). Sverige i England. Göteborg, 1923. [Pp. 291-96, Svensk litteratur.]
Karsten, T. Die alten nordischen und germanischen Völkerbeziehungen **FINNLANDS** im Lichte der neueren Forschung (Bidrag till Kännedom af Finlands Natur och Folk Utgifne af finska Vetenskabs-Societeten, 88), Helsingfors, 1946. 14 p.
Beck, T. Northern Antiquities in French Learning and Literature 1755-1855. A Study in Preromantic Ideas, 2 vols. **(FRANCE)**. New York, 1934-35.
——— Ragnar Lodbrok's Swan Song in the French Romantic Movement. RR, 22, 1931, 218-22.
Carstensen, R. Skandinavisch-romanische Wechselbeziehungen, dargestellt am Beispiel des Lebenswerkes Kristoffer Nyrops. NM, 10, 1939, 365-80.
Castrén, G. Norden i den franska litteraturen. Helsingfors, 1910. 270 p.
Davison, Mother St. G. The Scandinavian Movement in the Contemporary French Theatre. Fordham U. Diss., 16, 1949; 156-60.
Heeren, A. Ueber den Einfluss der Normannen auf die französische Sprache und Litteratur. Göttingen, 1789. 32 p.
Maury, L. L'Imagination scandinave. Paris, 1929. [Pp. 356-67: Le Nord dans la littérature française.]
———, Les Scandinaves et nous. MF, 301, 1947, 440-53, 676-89.
Pinot, V. Le Nord dans la littérature française. Revue scandinave, 2, 1911, 110-24.
Jessen, F. de. Bibliographie de la littérature française relative au Danemark. Paris, 1924. 322 p.
Jóhannesson, A. Menningarsamband Frakku og Islendinga. Reykjavík, 1943.
Blanck, A. La Suède et la littérature française des origines à nos jours. Paris, 1947.
Garling-Palmér, S. Vår litteratur inför fransk publik och kritik. Varia 10, 1907, 451-61.

Batka, R. Altnordische Stoffe und Studien in Deutschland. (**GERMANY**). Euphorion 2, Suppl. 1896, 1-70, and 6, 1899, 66-83.

Bertram, E. Norden und deutsche Romantik. Deutsch-Nordisches Jb., 1927, 61-79.

Boor, H. de. Deutschland und der germanische Norden. Das deutsche Buch 5, 1925, 353-57.

Ehrmann, E. Die bardische Lyrik im achtzehnten Jahrhundert. Diss., Halle, 1892.

Garin, P. Die Skandinaven in der deutschen Literatur. Die Zukunft, 27, 1899, 554-62.

Gerhardt, M. & Hubatsch, D. Deutschland und Skandinavien im Wandel der Jahrhunderte. Bonn, 1950. 482 p.

Golther, W. Die Edda in deutscher Nachbildung. ZVL, 1892, 275-304.

Grimm, W. Über die Entstehung der altdeutschen Poesie und ihr Verhältnis zu der Nordischen. 1808. Repr. in Kleinere Schriften, 1, 1881, 92-170.

Günther, I. Die Einwirkung des skandinavischen Romans auf den deutschen Naturalismus. Diss. (Nordische Studien 14) Greifswald, 1934, 158 p. [Bibliography, 134-158.]

Herrmann, P. Island in der modernen deutschen Dichtung. Mitteilungen der Islandfreunde, 7, 1920-21.

Lawson, M. Nordic Subjects in Popular Annuals of the Romantic Period. GR, 11, 1939, 229-45.

Magon, L. Deutschland und Skandinavien in ihren geistigen Wechselbeziehungen. In: Deutschland und die Kultur der Ostsee . . ed. G. Schreiber. Münster, 1927, 40-126.

Michael, F. Nordische Erzähler in Deutschland. Das deutsche Buch 1, 1921, 4-7.

Mitchell, P. M. Old Norse-Icelandic Litterature in Germany 1789-1849. With a Critical Bibliography. Diss., typescript. Urbana, Ill., 1942. 249 p.

Oppel, H. Studien zur Auffassung des Nordischen in der Goethezeit. Halle, 1944. 243 p.

Pertz, S. Das Wort "Nordisch." Seine Geschichte bis zur Jahrhundertwende. Dresden, 1939. 72 p.

Petersen, C. Deutschland und der Norden in ihren geschichtlich-kulturellen Beziehungen. In: Deutschland und der Norden. Stuttgart, 1935, 30-52.

———, Deutscher und nordischer Geist. Ihre Wechselwirkungen im Verlauf der Geschichte (Schleswig-Holsteinische Universitäts-Ges. 38) Breslau, 1937. 170 p.

Puschnig, A. Die Ragnar Lodbrokssage in der deutschen Literatur. Jahresbericht Oberrealschule Laibach, 1910.

Roos, C. Germania. København 1938. [Pp. 80-95: Drømmen om Norden i tysk Aandsliv.]

Strauss und Torney, L. von. Nordische Literatur und deutsches Geistesleben. Schleswig-holsteinische Zs. f. Kunst & Literatur, I, 1906, 371-80, 408-14.

Strich, F. Mythologie in der deutschen Literatur von Klopstock bis Wagner. Halle, 1910.

Wrangel, E. Tysklands litteratur under 1700 talet före Klopstock och dess förhållande till den svenska. Samlaren, 22, 1901, 47-64.

Zwiegespräch zwischen den Völkern. Deutschland und der Norden. Herausg. von der Nordischen Ges. Lübeck, 1940. [Der erste Teil . . . geschichtlicher Überblick aus Briefen und Lebensbeschreibungen. Der zweite Teil . . . Gegenwärtiges.]

Grossmann, S. Dansk Digtning i Tyskland. Tilskueren, 1917, 542-48.

Magon, L. Ein Jahrhundert geistiger und literarischer Beziehungen zwischen Deutschland und Skandinavien 1750-1850. Vol. 1: Die Klopstockzeit in Dänemark. Dortmund, 1926. 565 p.

Nielsen, L. Ældre dansk Litteratur i tyske Biblioteker. NTBB, 9, 1922, 203-25.

Beyer, H. Sammenhang og brytning mellom tysk och norsk åndsliv. Samtiden, 61, 1952, 225-44.

Meyen, F. Die deutschen Übersetzungen norwegischer Schönliteratur, 1730-1941. Oslo, 1942. 198 p.

Alker, E. Schweden in der deutschen Dichtung. WM, 1926, 398-400.

Berg, R. G. Svenskt i Blätter für literarische Unterhaltung, 1827-45. In: Studier tillägnade G. Bernstrom. Stockholm, 1927. 7-32.

Schröder, E. Deutsch-schwedische und schwedisch-deutsche Kulturbeziehungen in alter und neuer Zeit. Mitteilungen Universitätsbund Göttingen, 1922. 20 p.

Backman, C. P., & Leffler, B. Ungern i kultur och historie. (**HUNGARY**). Stockholm, 1924. [Pp. 83-86, Svensk litteratur i Ungern.]

Leyen, F. von der. Utgardaloke in **IRLAND**. Beiträge z. Gesch. d. dt. Sprache & Lit., 33, 1907, 382-91.

Grimble, I. The King of Norway in Gaelic Folk Lore. Norseman, 8, 1950, 225-30.

Boer-den Hoed, P. De studie van de scandinavische invloeden op de nederlandsche litteratuur. (**NETHERLANDS**). NP, 36, 1952, 234-40.

Rosman, H. Svensk litteratur i Holland. Ord och Bild, 12, 1903, 229-32.

Buceta, E. Más sobre Noruega, símbolo de la oscuridad. (**PORTUGAL**). RFE, 7, 1920, 378-81.

Campos Ferreira Lima, H. de. Portugal e a Suecia. Revista da historia 13, 1925, 208-21.

Belaiew, N. Eymundar Saga and Icelandic Research in **RUSSIA**. Saga-Book of Viking Society, 11, 1934, 93-99.

Briem, B. Alt-Skandinavien in der neueren russischen wissenschaftlichen Literatur (1918-28). Acta philol. scandinavica, 5, 1930, 211-36.

Lindquist, R. Sverige och svenskarna i den ryska folkpoesien. Ord och Bild, 38, 1929, 383-86.

Schlauch, M. Scandinavian Influence on the Slovo. In: Russian Epic Studies, ed. Jakobson & Simmons (Memoirs of American Folklore Society 42) Philadelphia 1947, 99-124.

Interscandinavian Relations.

a. General.

Afzelius, N. Svenska skrifter rörande Island. Gåva till Islands Allting . . . 1930. (Kungl. Bibliotekets Handlinger 42) Uppsala, 1930.

Andersson, O. Den svenska folkvisan i Finland. Nordisk Kultur IX, A. Folkesvisor. Utgjeven av K. Liestøl, 1931. 55-60.

Benson, A. The Old Norse Element in Swedish Romanticism. New York, 1914, 192 p.

Helgason, J. Finland and Iceland. Le Nord, 2, 1939, 455-58.

Elovson, H. Studier i brytningarna i nordisk litteratur omkring 1890. Edda, 36, 1936, 369-449.

Halvorsen, E. Bjørnsons forhold til den norrøne litteratur. Edda, 51, 1951, 211-19.

Klockhoff, O. Studier över 1600-talets svenska dramatik i Sverige och Finland. In: Festskrift H. Pipping. Helsingfors, 1925. 267-90.

Lidén, A. Den norska strömningen i svensk litteratur under 1800-talet. Uppsala, 1926. 311 p.

Nielsen, L. Ældre dansk Litteratur i Norge. NTBB, 10, 1923, 155-66.

———, Ældre dansk Litteratur i Sverige. Ibid, 13, 1926, 72-86.

Nilsson, A. Tre fornnordiska gestalter. Helge, Frithiof och Kung Fjalar. Lund, 1928, 415 p.

Paasche, F. Finnland und Norwegen. Le Nord, 2, 1939, 448-54.

Söderhjelm, W Minna Canth. Några ord om norskt inflytande i finsk litteratur. In: Til Gerhard Gran 9. Dec. 1916, 284-304.

Steffen, R. Den norska kämpavisan och dess genljud i svensk litteratur. Nordisk Tidskrift, 1924, 19-32.

Wallén, E. Nordisk mytologi i svensk Romantik. Stockholm, 1918. 152 p.

b. Individual Authors, General Relations.

Heimer, A. Den danska sagodiktaren i Sverige och bland svenskar. (**H. C. ANDERSEN**). Stockholm, 1925. 205 p.

Birket-Smith, F. **BELLMAN** og Danmark. Ord och Bild, 37, 1928, 289-306, 357-71.

Schoning, O. Bellmans Digtning og dens Indflydelse i Danmark. (Studier fra Sprog og Oldtidsforskning, 63) København, 1904. 60 p.

Salokas, E. Bellmanin runous Soumessa. In: Kirjallisuudentutkijain seuran vuosikirja. Helsinki, 1929, 23-181.

Brandes, E. **BJØRNSON** og den danske Scene. In: Bjørnstjerne Bjørnson. Festskrift. København, 1902, 15-28.

Bull, F. Bjørnson og Norden. Nordens Kalendar 1933, 34-38.

Hirn, Y. Björnson och Finland. ibid. 18-24.

Söderhjelm, W. Björnson i Finland. In: Bjørnson Festskrift. København, 1902, 107-19. [Extended in his: Profiler ur finskt Kulturliv, 1913.]

Key, E. Björnson och Sverige. ibid. 41-69. (Also in E. Key, Verk och Människor, 1910, 229-69.)

Bull, F. Bjørnson og Sverige. In: Bjørnson Studier, Kristiania, 1911 (Smaaskrifter fra det litt. Seminar 7-13.) 171-281.

Knudsen, B. Signalfeiden. ibid. 319-351. [Bjørnson in Denmark.]

Landquist, J. Björnson och Sverige. Nordens Kalendar 1933, 25-33.

Stolpe, S. Björnson och Sverige. Bonniers litt. magasin, 1, 1932, 62-68.

Leijonhufvud, S. Ett bidrag till belysning af Sveriges litterära beröring med Danmark vid slutet af sextonhundratalet. Samlaren 19, 1898, 112-17. [BORDING's poetry in Sweden.]

Ahlenius, H. Georg **BRANDES** i svensk litteratur till och med 1890. Hans ställning och inflytande. Stockholm 1932. 418 p.

Linder, S. Georg Brandes och Norge. Ord och Bild, 15, 1941, 164-70.

Castrén, G. Frans Michael **FRANZÉN** i Finland. Helsingfors, 1902. 377 p.

Thesen, R. Arne **GARBORG** og Sverige. Ord och Bild 15, 1941, 220-28.

Kyrre, H. M. **GOLDSCHMIDT** og Norge. Edda, 1921, 276-91.

Lindbæk, S. **P. A. HEIBERG** og Norge. Edda, 34, 1934, 87-104.

Wildhagen, F. Verner v. **HEIDENSTAM** og Norge. Ord och Bild 15, 1941, 31-36.

Tarkianen, V. **HOLBERG** i Finland. Edda 31, 1931, 60-80.

Ehrencron-Müller, H. Jeppe paa Bjerget i Sverrig. Edda 30, 1930, 667-79.

Warburg, K. Holberg i Sverige jämte meddelanden om hans svenske öfversättare. Göteborg, 1884. 102 p.

Svedfelt, T. Alexander **KIELLAND** och det svenska åttitalet. Edda 31, 1931, 287-312.

Beyer, H. Søren **KIERKEGAARDS** betydning for norsk aandsliv. Edda, 19, 1923, 1-143.

Erichsen, V. Søren Kierkegaards betyding for norsk aandsliv. Edda 19, 1923, 209-429.

Hansen, H. Søren Kierkegaard og Sverige. Nordisk Tidskrift, 1946, 52-59.

Henriksen, Aa. Methods and Results of Kierkegaard Studies in Scandinavia. Copenhagen, 1951. 160 p.

Kabell, Aa. Kierkegaardstudiet i Norden. København, 1948. 329 p.

Oppel, H. Die Nachwirkung Kierkegaards in der nordischen Dichtung. Nordische Rundschau, 9, 1936-38, 145-57.

Pineau, L. Soeren Kierkegaard et la Norvège. RG, 28, 1927, 209-214. [Criticism of H. Beyer, Sören Kierkegaard og Norge, 1924.]

Sjöstedt, N. Søren Kierkegaard och svensk Litteratur från Fredrika Bremer till Hjalmar Söderberg. Göteborg, 1950. 418 p.

Nörregaard, G. Christian **MOLBECH** og Sverige. Nordisk Tidskrift, 17, 1941, 253-63.

Clausen, J. **RUNEBERG** og Danmark. In: J. L. Runebergs Hundraårsminne. Skrifter utgivna af Svenska Litteratursällskapet i Finland 62.) Helsingfors, 1904. 125-34.

Wrangel, E. Runeberg och Sverige. ibid. 55-110.

c. Individual Authors, Individual Relations.

Bo, A. **AKJÆR** og Fröding. Danske Studier 1949-50, 78-84.

Børge, V. August Strindberg og H. C. **ANDERSEN**. København, 1931. 146 p.

Krohn, H. Georg Brandes och Ernst **AHLGREN**. Nya Argus 20, 1927, 51-54.

Linder, S. Ernst Ahlgren och Georg Brandes. Samlaren, N.F. 16, 1935, 57-89.

Paludan, J. Lyksalighedens Ö. **ATTERBOM** og Paludan-Müller. Nordisk Tidskrift, 1900, 173-205.

Thesen, R. Bjørnstjerne **BJØRNSON** og Georg Brandes. Edda 38, 1939, 1-40.

Frisch, P. Gustaf Fröding og hans **Bjørn**sonbillede. Edda 51, 1951, 4-30.

Paludan, J. Geijer og **GRUNDTVIG**. Edda, 1923, 99-117.

Anker, Ø. Bjørnson og Grundtvig inntil 1872. Edda 32, 1932, 273-338.

Schneider, H. Henrik **IBSEN** und Knut Hamsun. D&V, 42, 1942, 1-14.

Aster, E. von. Ibsen und Strindberg. München 1921. 129 p.

Bühler, C. Strindberg und Ibsen. NSp. 31, 1923, 146-53.

Linder, S. Ibsen och Strindberg. Samlaren NF 13, 1932, 52-105.

Petersen, C. Gustav Fröding—Søren **KIERKEGAARD**. Kirke og kultur, 38, 1931, 203-15.

La Chesnais, P. Ibsen disciple de Kierkegaard. Edda 34, 1934, 355-410.

Möhring, W. Ibsen und Kierkegaard. Berlin (Palaestra 160) 1928. 187 p.

Sturtevant, A. **OEHLENSCHLÄGER** and Tegnér's 'Frithiofssaga.' SS, 6, 1920-21, 134-58.

Bæhrendtz, N. Viktor **RYDBERG** och Bjørnstjerne Bjørnson. Edda, 42, 1942, 1-55.

Krogvig, A. August **STRINDBERG** og Björnstjerne Björnson. In: Böker og mennesker. Kristiania, 1919, 150-74.

Sylwan, O. O. P. **STURZEN-BECKER** och Christian Winther. In: Til Gerhard Gran 9. XII. 1916, Kristiania 1916, 215-18.

Bull, F. **TEGNÉR** og Wergeland. ibid. 105-34.

Böök, F. Undset och Tegnér. Kirke og Kultur 33, 1926, 55-61.

Beyer, H. Sigrid **UNDSET** und Selma Lagerlöf. GRM, 20, 1932, 20-27.

IBSEN

General Studies

Dresdner, A. Ibsen als Norweger und Europäer. Jena 1907. 105 p.

Wais, K. Henrik Ibsens Wirkung in Spanien, Frankreich, Italien. Braunschweig, 1933. 84 p. [Four essays previously published.]

Andersen, Annette. Ibsen in **AMERICA.** SS, 14, 1935-37, 63-109, 115-155.

Fife, R. H. & Anstensen, A. Henrik Ibsen on the American Stage. ASR, 16, 1928, 218-28.

Haugen, E. Ibsen i Amerika. En ukjent førsteopførelse og et Ibsenbrev. Edda, 35, 1935, 553-59.

Zucker, A. Southern Critics of 1903 on Ibsen's Ghosts. PQ, 19, 1940, 392-99.

Domet, A. Arabischer Brief. (Ibsen und das arabische Drama). (**ARABIA**). Die Literatur, 1928, 540-43.

Archer, W. Ibsen and English Criticism. (**ENGLAND**). Fortnightly Rev. 46, 1889, 30-37.

———, The Mausoleum of Ibsen. ibid. 54. 1893, 77-91.

Burchardt, C. Ibsen and England. Norseman, 5, 1947, 149-56.

Decker, C. Ibsen's Literary Reputation and Victorian Taste. SP 32, 1935, 632-45.

Downs, B. Ibsen and his British Admirers. Norseman, 6, 1948, 259-62.

Filon, A. Le théâtre anglais contemporain. Ibsen à Londres. Le drame de demain. RDM, 132, 1895, 178-200.

Franc, M. Ibsen in England. Boston, 1919. 195 p.

Huber, R. Ibsens Bedeutung für das englische Drama. Diss., Marburg, 1914. 87 p.

Irvine, W. Shaw's Quintessence of Ibsenism. SAQ, 46, 1947, 252-62.

Qvamme, B. Ibsen og det engelske Teater. Edda, 42, 1942, 113-21.

Shaw, G. B. The Quintessence of Ibsenism. London, 1891.

Stefánsson, J. Henrik Ibsen i England. Nordisk Tidskrift, 1891, 31-39.

Toledano, D. Ibsen en Angleterre. Revue scandinave, 2, 1911, 597-602.

Söderhjelm, W. Ibsen på finska teatern. (**FINLAND**). In: Henrik Ibsen, Festskrift. Bergen 1898, 246-54.

Brandes, G. Henrik Ibsen en **FRANCE.** Cosmopolis, 5, 1897, 112-24.

Darthèze, A. Ibsen et les acteurs français. Revue d'Art dramatique, 13, 1898, 27-35.

Destrez, F. Ibsen et la Critique française. ibid. 36-45.

Lorde, A. de. Bibliographie. ibid. 68-71, 234-35. [On Ibsen in France.]

Lugné-Poe, A. M. Le théâtre d'Ibsen en France. ibid. 15-20.

Lundeberg, O. Ibsen in France. SS, 8, 1924, 93-107.

Mähly, J. Ibsen in Frankreich. Gegenwart 46, 1894, 38-40.

Reque, A. Trois auteurs dramatiques scandinaves Ibsen, Björnson, Strindberg devant la critique française 1889-1901. Paris 1930. 228 p.

Swanson, C. Ibsen and the Comédie-française. SS, 19, 1946-47, 70-78.

———, An Ibsen Theater in Paris: Lugné-Poe and the Théâtre de l'Oeuvre. SS, 17, 1942-43, 133-39.

Tissot, E. Petite histoire du courant Ibsenien en France. La Quinzaine, 41, 1901, 1-23.

Behrendsohn, W. Henrik Ibsen und die deutsche Geisteswelt. (**GERMANY.**) Deutsch-Nordisches Jb. 1928, 1-13.

Berg, L. Henrik Ibsen. Köln, 1901. [Pp. 32-39, Ibsen in Deutschland.]

Ellehauge, M. Ibsens Indflydelse paa de moderne tysk-østrigske Dramatikere. Tilskueren, 45, 1928, 131-44.

Eller, W. Ibsen in Germany, 1870-1900. Boston, 1918. 203 p. [Bibliography 193-97.]

Fischer, E. Ibsen und das Dritte Reich. NSR, 12, 1940, 755-63.

Jacobsohn, S. Ibsen und Berlin. Schaubühne 7. VI. 1906, 654-60.

Litzmann, B. Ibsens Dramen, 1877-1900. Ein Beitrag zur Geschichte des deutschen Dramas im 19. Jahrhundert. Hamburg 1901, 176 p.

Meyer, E. Was bedeutet Ibsens Lebenswerk für das deutsche Volk und für die deutsche dramatische Literatur? Deutsche Monatsschrift f. d. gesamte Leben d. Gegenwart, 6, 1906, 190-204.

Schmidt, F. Ibsen's Influence upon German Literature. PL 17, 1906, 112-18.

Thalmann, M. Henrik Ibsen, ein Erlebnis der Deutschen. Marburg 1928. 66 p.

Varia. Henrik Ibsen, Gedenkblätter zum 75. Geburtstag. Bühne & Welt 5, 1903, 497-528.

Wais, K. Henrik Ibsen und das Problem des Vergangenen im Zusammenhang

der gleichzeitigen Geistesgeschichte. Stuttgart 1931. 281 p.
Wihan, J. Henrik Ibsen und das deutsche Geistesleben. Reichenberg i. B. 1925, 73 p.
Wolff, E. Die deutsche Ibsen-Litteratur (1872-1902). Bühne & Welt, 5, 1903, 566-70, 605-10.
Anon. Enrico Ibsen. (**ITALY**). Marzocco 22, XI. 1906.
Gara, E. Fortuna del Ibsen in Italia. Libri del giorno, 11, 1928, 139-42.
Prieto, M. Ibsen und **PORTUGAL**. Edda, 28, 1928, 129-135.
Krag, E. Ibsen i Russland. (**RUSSIA**). Edda, 28, 1928, 72-95.
Gregersen, H. Ibsen and **SPAIN**. A Study in Comparative Drama. Harvard U. P., 1936, 209 p.
———, Visiting Italian Interpreters of Ibsen in Barcelona and Madrid. HR, 3, 1935, 166-69.
Grol, M. Ibsen na Beogradskoj pozornici. (**SERBIA**). SKG, 47, 1936, 121-34.

Influences upon Individual Authors.

Krijn, S. Ernst **AHLGREN** en Brand. NP 26, 1941, 141-52.
Kalischer, S. Ibsen und **BRAHM**. Deutsche Theater Zs. 2, 23, 24, 26, 29, 1909.
Prampolini, G. **CROCE** e Ibsen. Rassegna d'Italia, 1, 1946, 223-25.
Vries, J. de. Ibsen en de **CUREL**. Onze Eeuw, 24, 1924, 250-69.
Gregersen, H. Ibsen and **ECHEGARAY** HR 1, 1933, 338-40.
Kennedy, R. The Indebtedness of Echegary to Ibsen. Sewanee Rev. 34, 1926, 402-415.
Kirsch, E. Ibsens Peer Gynt und Dietrich **ECKARTS** freie Übertragung. ZDU, 53, 1939, 429-37.
Klenze, H. von. Paul **ERNST** and Hendrick Ibsen. GR, 16, 1941, 134-45.
Maynial, E. Ibsen et **FOGAZZARO**. RLC, 4, 1924, 92-108.
Kröner, J. Die Technik des realistischen Dramas bei Ibsen und **GALSWORTHY** (Diss. München; Beiträge zur engl. Philol. 28) Leipzig 1935, 113 p.
Feise, E. **HAUPTMANNS** Einsame Menschen und Ibsens Rosmersholm. GR, 10, 1935, 145-65.
Gunvaldsen, K. The Master Builder and Die Versunkene Glocke. MDU, 33, 1941, 153-62.
Bucks, D. & Nethercot, A. Ibsen and **HERNE**'s Margaret Fleming. AL, 17, 1946, 311-33.
Kenner, H. **JOYCE** and Ibsen's Naturalism. Sewanee Rev. 59, 1951, 75-96.
MacLeod, V. The Influence of Ibsen on Joyce. PMLA, 60, 1945, 879-98; 62, 1947, 573-80.
Arestad, S. The Iceman Cometh and The Wild Duck. (**O'NEILL**). SS, 20, 1948, 1-11.
Küther, H. Arthur Wing **PINERO** und sein Verhältnis zu Henrik Ibsen. Diss., Münster, 1937. 67 p.
Oulmont, C. Ibsen jugé par **PIRANDELLO**. L'Age Nouveau, 57, 1951, 121-22.
Lamm, M. Ibsen och **SHAW**. Edda, 47, 1947, 130-40.
Lavrin, J. Ibsen and Shaw. In his: Studies in European Literature. London 1929, 80-98.
Tveterås, H. Ibsen og **SNOILSKY**. In: Norvegica; Minneskrift. Oslo, 1933, 119-71.
Jürgensen, H. Henrik Ibsens Einfluss auf Hermann **SUDERMANN**. Diss., Lausanne, 1903. 85 p.
Zucker, A. The Ibsenian Villain in Sudermann's Heimat. GR, 3, 1928, 208-17.
Setterquist, J. Ibsen and **SYNGE**. Studia Neophilologica 24, 1952, 68-154.
Lamm, M. Ibsen och **TJEKOV**. Edda 47, 1947, 119-29.
Barnes, T. **YEATS**, Synge, Ibsen and Strindberg. Scrutiny 5, 1936, 257-62.

STRINDBERG

Ellehauge, M. Ekko fra Strindberg i Verdensteatret. Edda 31, 1931, 313-27.
Herzog, W. Strindberg und unsere Zeit. Forum, 1, 1914, 65-69.
Jacobsen, H. Strindbergs Verdensry. Tilskueren 41, 1924, 338-49, 402-11.
Robertson, J. Essays and Addresses on Literature. London 1935. [Pp. 255-71: Strindberg's Position in European Literature.]
Gassner, J. Strindberg in **AMERICA**. Theatre Arts, 33, 1949, 49-52.
Gustafson, A. Some Early English and American Strindberg Criticism. In: Festschrift G. T. Flom. Urbana, Ill. 1942, 106-24.
Rapp, E. Strindberg Bibliography. Strindberg's Reception in England and America. SS, 23, 1951, 1-22, 49-59, 109-37.
Anon. Strindberg in **ENGLAND**. TLS 30. I. 1930, 65-66.
Dahlström, C. The Parisian Reception of Strindberg's Plays. (**FRANCE**). SS, 19, 1947, 195-207.

———, Strindberg's 'Fadren' and the Théâtre Libre. MLN, 59, 1944, 567-68.

Gravier, M. Strindberg et le théâtre çais contemporain. LM, 1949, 282-91.

See also A. Reque under Ibsen, above.

Burkhard, A. August Strindberg and Modern **GERMAN** Drama. GQ, 6, 1933, 163-74.

Gravier, M. Strindberg et le théâtre naturaliste allemand. EG, 2-4, 1947-48.

———, Strindberg et le théâtre moderne: L'Allemagne. Lyon, 1949, 185 p.

Marcus, C. Strindberg och den tyska vetenskapen. Nordisk Tidskrift, 1924, 435-41.

Sternberg, K. Unsere Zeit und August Strindberg. Glocke 6, 1920-21, 1176-84.

Wiese, L. Strindberg und die junge Generation. Köln, 1921. 16 p.

Wright, H. Rupert **BROOKE** och Strindberg. Forum, 6, 1919, 164-66.

Cohn, A. **HAUPTMANN** und Strindberg. Glocke, 7, 1921, 988-90.

Lavrin, J. **HUYSMANS** and Strindberg. In his: Studies in European Literature. London 1929, 118-30.

Haywood, I. Strindberg's Influence on Eugene **O'NEILL**. PL 39, 1928, 596-604.

Gravier, M. Strindberg et **WEDEKIND**. EG, 3, 1948, 309-318.

Marcuse, L. Theologie des Eros, Strindberg und Wedekind. Blätter des dt. Theaters, 94, 1923, 1-5.

SWEDENBORG

Hotson, C. Early Influence of Swedenborg in Europe. New-Church Review 37, 1930, 16-34.

Lamm, M. Swedenborg en Angleterre. (**ENGLAND**). Revue Bleue, 1936, 118-22.

Viatte, A. Les Swedenborgiens en **FRANCE** de 1820 à 1830. RLC, 11, 1931, 416-50.

Benz, E. Immanuel Swedenborg als geistiger Wegbahner des deutschen Idealismus und der deutschen Romantik. (**GERMANY**). DVLG, 19, 1941, 1-32.

Bernheim, P. **BALZAC** und Swedenborg. (Romanische Studien, 16) Berlin, 1914. 123 p.

Wright, T. Balzac and Swedenborg. New-Church Review 3, 1896, 481-503.

Schorer, M. Swedenborg and **BLAKE**. MP, 36, 1938, 157-78.

Hotson, C. **EMERSON** and the Swedenborgians. SP, 27, 1930, 517-45.

———, Emerson's Biographical Sources for "Swedenborg." SP, 26, 1929, 23-46.

Torbert, J. Emerson and Swedenborg. Texas Review, 2, 1917, 313-26.

Hotson, C. Swedenborg's Influence in America to 1830. (**FRENEAU**). New-Church Review, 37, 1930, 188-207.

Nugent, C. The Influence of Swedenborg upon **GOETHE**. ibid. 7, 1900, 541-47.

Peebles, W. Swedenborg's Influence upon Goethe. GR, 8, 1933, 147-56.

Morris, M. Swedenborg in Faust. Euphorion, 6, 1899, 491-510.

Schlieper, H. Emanuel Swedenborgs System der Naturphilosophie besonders in seiner Beziehung zu Goethe-Herderschen Anschauungen. Diss., Berlin, 1901. 48 p.

Schuchard, G. The Last Scene in Goethe's Faust. PMLA, 64, 1949, 417-44.

Ahlberg, A. **KANT** och Swedenborg. Nordisk Tidskrift, 1919. 386-98.

Benz, E. Swedenborg und **LAVATER**. Zs. f. Kirchengeschichte 57, 1938, 153-216.

Silver, E. **MAETERLINCK** and Swedenborg. New-Church Review 12, 1905, 416-22.

OTHER SCANDINAVIAN AUTHORS

Bredsdorff, E. H. C. **ANDERSEN** og Charles Dickens, København, 1951. 151 p.

Drachmann, A. E. B. Browning and Hans Andersen. Edda 33, 1933, 494-502.

Hersholt, J. (ed.) H. C. Andersen og Horace E. Scudder. En Brevveksling. Efterskrift af H. Topsøe-Jensen. København, 1948. 207 p.

Porterfield, A. **BOJER'S** Conquest of America. Bookman 58, 1923-24, 287-94.

Larson, H. & Haugen, E. **BJÖRNSON** and America. SS, 13, 1933, 1-12.

Sturtevant, A. Bjørnson and America. In: Bjørnson-Studier (Smaaskrifter fra det litt. Seminar 7-13) Kristiania, 1911, 99-113.

Kodicek, J. Bjørnson and Czechoslovakia. Norseman 3, 1945, 265-67.

Rytter, O. Bjørnson and Czechoslovakia. Norseman 2, 1944, 63-67.

See also A. Reque under Ibsen above. (France).

Eeden, W. van. Bjørnson og Nederland. Edda 51, 1951, 268-80.

Sawicki, S. Björnstjerne Björnson und Polen. Edda 32, 1932, 413-22.

Kara-Murza, S. Bjørnson på den russiske scene. Edda 34, 1934, 168-74.
Benson, A. Mark Twain's Contacts with Scandinavia. (**BLICHER.**) SS 14, 1935-37, 159-67.
Haugen, E. Georg **BRANDES** and his American Translators. JEGP 37, 1938, 462-87.
Rouveyse, A. Souvenirs de mon commerce. George Brandes parmi nous. MF, 194, 1927, 568-88.
Anon. Frederika **BREMER** och Amiel. Hertha, 11, 1924, 27-28.
Benson, A. The Essays on Frederika Bremer in the North American Review. PMLA 41, 1926, 747-55.
Krumm, G. Gustaf **FRÖDINGS** Verbindungen mit der deutschen Literatur. (Nordische Studien 16) Greifswald 1934, 195 p.
Behrendsohn, W. Knut **HAMSUNS** Aufnahme in Deutschland. Deutsch-Nordisches Jb., 1929, 85-92.
Ferwerda, S. **HOLBERG** en Holland. Zutphen 1939, 270 p.
Roos, C. Det 18. Aarhundredes tyske Oversættelser af Holbergs Komedier, deres Oprindelse, Karakter og Skæbne. Kjøbenhavn 1922. 284 p.
———, Holberg und die deutsche Komödie. Deutsch-Nordisches Jb., 1928, 27-40.
Stender-Petersen, A. Holberg og den russiske Komedie i det 18de Århundrede. Holberg Aarbog, 1923-25.
Baer, Lydia. Rilke and Jens Peter **JACOBSEN.** PMLA, 54, 1939, 900-32, 1133-80.
———, A Study of Ernst Wiechert with Special Reference to Jens Peter Jacobsen and Rilke. MLQ 5, 1944, 469-80.
di San Lazzaro, C. Die Aufzeichnungen des Malte Laurids Brigge von R. M. Rilke in Vergleich mit Jacobsens Niels Lyhne und A. Gides Nourritures Terrestres. GRM, 29, 1941, 106-17.
Alexander, I. La philosophie existentialiste en France. Ses sources et ses problèmes fondamentaux. (**KIERKEGAARD.**) FS, 1, 1947, 95-114.
Bohlin, T. Sören Kierkegaard und das religiöse Denken der Gegenwart. München, 1923. 178 p.
Brachfeld, O. Kierkegaard en Allemagne. Revue d'Allemagne, 6, 1932, 596-603.
Chestov, L. Kierkegaard et la philosophie existentielle. Traduit du russe. Paris 1936. 384 p.
Hohlenberg, J. Jean-Paul Sartre og hans forhold til Kierkegaard. Samtiden 1947, 310-22.
Jancke, R. Rilke-Kierkegaard. D&V, 39, 1938, 314-29.
Johnson, H. Kierkegaard and Sartre. ASR, 35, 1947, 220-25.
Löwith, K. Kierkegaard und Nietzsche. DVLG, 11, 1933, 43-66. [A comparison.]
Lowrie, W. 'Existence' as Understood by Kierkegaard and/or Sartre. Sewanee Review, 53, 1950, 379-401.
Lunding, E. Adalbert Stifter. Mit einem Anhang (133-50) über Kierkegaard und die existentielle Literaturwissenschaft. Aarhus 1946.
Moore, W. Recent Studies of Kierkegaard. Journal of Theol. Studies, 40, 1939, 225-31.
Mustard, H. Sören Kierkegaard in German Literary Periodicals, 1860-1930. GR, 26, 1951, 83-101.
Mutius, G. von. Kierkegaard und das heutige Deutschland. Deutsch-Nordisches Jb., 1925, 1-13.
Oppel, H. Kierkegaard und die existentielle Literaturwissenschaft. D&V, 38, 1937, 18-29.
Rougemont, D. de et al. Kierkegaard. [Special number of] Foi et Vie, 64, 1934, 601-720. [Articles by Torsten Bohlin, Jean Wahl, Paul Tisseau; selections from Kierkegaard and reviews.]
Rougemont, D. de. Kierkegaard en France. NRF, 46, 1936, 971-76.
Sjestov, L. Kierkegaard og Dostojevski. Gads danske Magasin 1943, 358-78.
Steere, D. Kierkegaard in English. Journal of Religion 24, 1944, 271-78.
Wahl, J. Heidegger et Kierkegaard. Recherches philosophiques 2, 1932-33, 349-70.
Egidy, E. von. Selma **LAGERLÖF** und Ricarda Huch. Kunstwart 41, 1927-28, 283-90, 351-59.
Jolivet, A. La Winterballade de Gerhart Hauptmann et Herr Arnes peningar de Selma Lagerlöf. In: Mélanges C. Andler. Strasbourg, 1924, 163-70.
Eeden, W. van. Lidt om Jonas **LIE** og Nederland. Edda 52, 1952, 347-48.
Croce, B. Il Corregio dell' **OEHLENSCHLAEGER** e Olinto dal Borgo. Critica 26, 1928, 216-20.
Stewart, W. Oehlenschlæger's Relation to German Romanticism. SS, 2, 1914, 1-24.
Eigenbrodt, W. **RUNEBERG** in Deutschland. In J. L. Runebergs Hundra-

årsmine (Skrifter utgifna af Svenska Litteratursällskapet i Finland 62) Helsingfors, 1904. 111-124.

Söderhjelm, W. Profiler ur finskt kultur liv. Helsingfors, 1913. [Pp. 1-71: Runeberg inför utlandet.]

Waenerberg, T. J. L. Runebergs dikter på holländska. Förhandlinger och uppsatser utg. av Svenska Litteratursällskapet i Finland, 16, 1903, 113-27.

Appelmann, A. The Relation of Longfellow's Evangeline to **TEGNÉR**'s Frithiofs Saga. SS 2, 1914-15, 165-80.

———, Longfellow's Evangeline und Tegner's Frithiof-Saga. Anglia, 49, 1925, 153-72.

Balakian, A. The two Axels. FR, 17, 1943, 18-22. [On Tegnér and Villiers de l'Isle-Adam.]

Benson, A. A List of English Translations of the Frithiofs Saga. GR, 1, 1926, 142-67.

Gravier, M. Tegnér et la France. Aubier 1943, 162 p. [Pp. 123-133, Tegnér en France.]

Nordell, O. Concerning English Translations from the Swedish Poem Frithiof's Saga: A Critique. SS 13, 1933-35, 53-66.

Swan, G. The English Versions of Tegnér's Axel, A Bibliographic Sketch. SS, 1, 1911-14, 179-84.

Thorstenberg, E. The Skeleton in Armour and the Frithiof Saga. MLN, 25, 1910, 189-92.

SCANDINAVIAN INFLUENCES UPON INDIVIDUAL AUTHORS

Gülzow, E. Ernst Moritz **ARNDT** in Schweden. Greifswald 1920. 28p.

Petersen, R. Fire Livsbilleder. København, 1894. [Pp. 141-185: Moritz Arndt og hans Forhold til Danmark.]

Wolfram, R. Ernst Moritz Arndt in Dänemark. Deutsch-Nordische Zs., 2, 1929, 125-30.

———, Ernst Moritz Arndt und Schweden. (Forschungen zur neueren Literaturgeschichte, 65) Weimar, 1933. 232p.

Wolters, F. Ernst Moritz Arndt und der Norden. Deutsch-Nordische Zs., 2, 1929, 5-15.

Rasmussen, E. **BLAKE**s revolusjonære forkynnerperiode. Edda 23, 1938, 290-331.

Hustvedt, S. George **BORROW** and his Danish Ballads. JEGP, 22, 1923, 262-70.

Wright, H. George Borrow's Translations from the Scandinavian Languages. Edda 16, 1921, 137-45.

———, **DEFOE**'s Writings on Sweden. RES, 16, 1940, 25-32.

Diederichs, N. Eugen **DIEDERICHS** und sein Verhältnis zum Norden. Deutsch-Nordisches Jb., 1931, 130-35.

Benson, A. The Sources of William **DUNLAP**'s Ella, A Norwegian Tale. SS, 19, 1946, 136-43.

Reuschel, K. Theodor **FONTANE**s nordische Balladen und Bilder. Festschrift Eugen Mogk, Halle, 1924, pp. 335-49.

Krejči, J. Nordische Stoffe bei **FOUQUÉ**. Vierteljahrsschrift für Litteraturgeschichte, 6, 1893, 553-70.

Hirsch, J. Fouqués Held des Nordens. Seine Quellen und seine Komposition. Berlin 1910, 74p.

Pfau, W. Das Altnordische bei **GERSTENBERG**. Vierteljahrsschrift für Litteraturgeschichte, 2, 1889, 161-95.

Döring, P. Der nordische Dichterkreis und die Schleswiger Litteraturbriefe. Sonderburg, 1880. 60p.

Petersens, H. Robert Pearse **GILLIES**, Foreign Quarterly Review och den svenska litteraturen. Samlaren, 14, 1933, 55-106.

Schwarz, I. Friedrich David **GRÄTER**. Ein Beitrag zur Geschichte der germanischen Philologie und zur Geschichte der deutsch-nordischen Beziehungen. Diss., Greifswald, 1935.

Vetterlund, F. Drag ur Amalie v. **HELVIGS** litterära förbindelser med Sverige. Nordisk Tidskrift, 1903, 27-37.

Kirby, W. William **HERBERT** and his Scandinavian Poetry. Saga-Book of Viking Club, 7, 1911, 206-19.

Paasche, F. **HERDER** og den norröne Digtning. Maal og Minne 2, 1910, 121-38.

Nyrop, K. Autor d'une poésie de Victor **HUGO**. In: Mélanges Baldensperger II, 1930, 141-150. [On Hugo's "Après la bataille" in Légende des Siècles.]

Péès, S. L'origine de la couleur locale scandinave dans le "Han d'Islande" de Victor Hugo. RLC, 9, 1929, 261-84.

Scheel, W. **KLOPSTOCK**s Kenntniss des germanischen Alterthums. Vierteljahrsschrift für Litteraturgeschichte, 6, 1893, 186-212.

Eggli, E. Note sur la source scandinave de l'Epée d'Angantyr de **LECONTE DE LISLE**. CLS, 1, 1941.

Vianey, J. Les sources de Leconte de Lisle. (Publ. de la Société des Langues Romanes, 21) Montpellier, 1907.
Hilen, A. **LONGFELLOW** and Scandinavia. A Study of the Poet's Relationship with the Northern Languages and Literatures. New Haven, 1947.
Leighly, J. Inaccuracies in Longfellow's Translation of Tegnér's Nattvardsbarnen. SS, 21, 1949, 170-80.
Nyland, W. Kalevala as a Reputed Source of Longfellow's Song of Hiawatha. AL, 22, 1950, 1-20.
Osborn, C. & S. Schoolcraft-Longfellow-Hiawatha. Lancaster, Pa. 1942, 697p.
Swan, M. Professor Longfellow, Scandinavian Book Buyer. Harvard Library Bull. 4, 1950, 359-73.
Burkhard, A. Thomas **MANN**'s Indebtedness to Scandinavia. PMLA, 45, 1930.
Marcus, C. Thomas Mann und das Nordische. Deutsch-Nordisches Jb., 1930, 88-103.
Maury, L. Xavier **MARMIER** en Scandinavie. MF, 309, 1950, 353-55.
Wiehe, E. Gottlieb **MOHNIKE** als Vermittler und Übersetzer nordischer Literatur. (Nordische Studien, 15) Greifswald 1934. 123p.
Anderson, K. Scandinavian Elements in the Works of William **MORRIS**. Diss., Harvard, 1942.
Blöndal, S. William Morris und Island. Nordische Rundschau, 5, 1932, 160-70.
Hoare, D. The Works of Morris and of Yeats in Relation to Early Saga Literature. Cambridge, 1937. 179p.
Litzenberg, K. William Morris and Scandinavian Literature: A Bibliographical Essay. SS, 13, 1935, 93-105.
———, William Morris as Critic of Old Norse Literature. Edda 40, 1940, 301-20.
———, Allusions to the Elder Edda in the Non-Norse Poems of William Morris. SS, 14, 1935, 17-24.
———, William Morris and the Heimskringla. ibid., 33-39.
———, William Morris and the Burning of Njál. ibid., 40-41.
Benson, A. Scandinavian References in the Works of **POE**. JEGP, 40, 1941, 73-90.
Batho, E. Sir Walter **SCOTT** and the Sagas; Some Notes. MLR, 24, 1929, 409-15.
Lieder, P. Scott and Scandinavian Literature; the Influence of Bartholin and Others. Smith Coll. Studies in Modern Languages, 2, 1920-21, 8-57.
Wright, H. **SOUTHEY'**s Relations with Finland and Scandinavia. MLR, 27, 1932, 149-67.
Wagner, H. **TASSO** und die nordische Heldensage. Euphorion 6, 1899, 1-18.
Benson, A. Bayard **TAYLOR**'s Interest in the Scandinavian North. SS, 7, 1925, 165-84.
———, Scandinavian Influence in the Writings of **THOREAU**. SS, 16, 1940-41, 241-56.
Moestue, W. **UHLAND**s nordische Studien. Berlin, 1902, 63p.
Golther, W. Die sagengeschichtlichen Grundlagen der Ringdichtung Richard **WAGNER**s. Charlottenburg, 1902.
Giese, A. Die Beziehungen Friedrich W. **WEBER**s zur nordischen Dichtung, (Nordische Studien 12) Braunschweig, 1930.
Unwerth, W. von. Christian **WEISE**s Dramen Regnerus und Ulvilda nebst einer Abhandlung zur deutschen und schwedischen Literaturgeschichte. Breslau, 1914, 296 p.
Trube, H. Friedrich G. **WETZEL**s Leben und Werk mit besonderer Berücksichtigung seiner Lyrik. Berlin, 1928.
Allen, G. Walt **WHITMAN**'s Long Journey Motif. JEGP, 38, 1939, 76-95.
Benson, A. Walt Whitman's Interest in Swedish Writers. JEGP, 31, 1932, 332-45.
Hartman, H. **WORDSWORTH**'s Lapland Night. RES, 14, 1938, 189-93.

THIRTEENTH PART

East-European Contributions.

The Slavic and the Danubian Countries: Russia, Bulgaria, Czechoslovakia, Poland, Yugoslavia; also Hungary and Rumania.

CHAPTER ONE

Russian Influences.

(See also Reciprocal Influences, III. III. 3. and Emigrants and Refugees, I. IV. 4.)

Gorki, M. La Russie et la littérature mondiale. Clarté, 6.XI.1920 & Die Glocke, 25. XII.1920.

Griswold, W. M. A Descriptive List of Novels and Tales Dealing with Life in Russia. Cambridge (Mass.), 1892.

Hearn, L. Russian Literature Abroad. Times-Democrat, 6.IX.1885.

Hirschberg, M. Die Weisheit Russlands. Die Bedeutung des russischen Geistes in der Kulturkrise der Gegenwart. Stockholm, 1947.

Kaun, A. Russian Poetic Trends on the Eve of and on the Morning after 1917. Slavonic Yearbook, 20, 1941.

Lemaître, J. De l'influence récente des littératures du Nord. RDM, 1894.

Liubimenko, J. Le rôle comparatif des différents peuples dans la découverte et la description de la Russie. Revue de synthèse historique, Dec., 1929.

Lozinski, G. La première littérature russe: histoire d'un plagiat. Revue des Etudes slaves, 16, 1936.

Ludkewicz, S. Die Sowjetliteratur als Vortrupp der Weltliteratur. In: Die Literatur in der Sowjetunion für kulturelle Verbindung des Sowjet mit dem Ausland, 7-8, 1934.

Pypin, A. N. A Comparative Historical Study in Russian Literature. (In Russian). Vestnik Evropy, Oct., 1875.

Simmons, E. J. The Place of Russia in Comparative Literature. CLN, 1, 1943.

Vogüé, E. M. de. Avant-propos du roman russe. Paris, 1886.

Wilczkowski, C. Grands thèmes et message de la littérature russe. Paris, 1945.

Wright, C. T. H. The Meaning of Russian Literature. QR, Jan., 1921.

Coleman, A. P. A Report on the Status of Russian and Other Slavic and East European Languages in the Educational Institutions of the United States, Canada and Latin AMERICA. New York, 1948.

Daireaux, M. Le roman russe et la littérature hispano-américaine. RLC, 11, 1931.

Martianov, N. N. (ed.). Books Available in English by Russians and on Russia Published in the United States. New York, 1942.

McCullers, C. The Russians Realists and Southern Literature. Decision, 2, 1941.

Posin, A. P. Russian Studies in American Colleges. Russian Review, 7, 1948.

Anon. Les voyageurs anglais en Russie. (ENGLAND). Revue britannique, Dec., 1841.

Armstrong, T. P. Elizabethan Ideas of Russia. N&Q, 7. & 28.XII.1935.

Brewster, Dorothy. The Russian Soul: An English Literary Pattern. American Scholar, 17, 1948.

Decker, C. Victorian Comment on Russian Realism. PMLA, 52, 1937.

Fedorova, Nina. Russian Motives in English Literature. (In Russian). Novosele, 1, 1943.

Lockhart, P. H. B. The First Englishmen in Russia. Fortnightly Review, June, 1928.

Mohrenschildt, D. von. Bibliography of Books in English on Russian Literature, 1917-42. Russian Review, 2, 1942.

—— Russian Literature in English Translation. CLN, 1, 1943.

Osborne, E. A. Early Translations from the Russian. The Bookman, 82-84, 1932-33.

Sola Pinto, V. de. Russian Poetry in English Verse. English, 5, 1944.

Audiberti. Littérature russe et attente française. (FRANCE). La Nef, 2, 1945.

Baldensperger, F. La part de la Russie dans l'acceptation française du subconscient en littérature. PMLA, 61, 1946.

Bloch, J. R. L'Union Soviétique en guerre et les lettres françaises. L'Arche, 1, (Alger), 1944.

Boutchik, V. Bibliographie des oeuvres littéraires russes traduites en français. Paris, 1938.

—— La littérature russe en France. Paris, 1947.

Jourda, P. L'exotisme dans la littérature française depuis le romantisme: La Russie. RCC, 1937.

Kovalewsky, P. Les études littéraires russes en France (1830-1930). Paris, 1933.

Lirondelle, A. Le roman russe en France à la fin du XIXe siècle. RCC, 26, 1925.

Lozinski, G. La Russie dans la littérature française du moyen âge. Revue des Etudes slaves, 1929.

Mohrenschildt, D. von. Russia in the Intellectual Life of XVIIIth Century France. Columbia U. P., 1936.

Petersen, C. W. Französische Bücher über Russland. Gegenwart, 1893.

Ternois, R. Voyageurs français en Russie. Education Nationale, 15. & 22.IV.1948.

Bab, J. Die Russen und wir. (GERMANY). In: Befreiungsschlacht. Stuttgart, 1928.

Behrmann, M. Eine russische Tragödin in Berlin. Gegenwart, 1886.

Bõhme E. & Luther, A. Frühe deutsche Uebersetzungen aus dem Russischen. Philobiblon, 6, 1933.

Frenzel, K. Russische Erzähler in Deutschland. National-Zt., 21.I.1900.

Naumann, G. Der Kaukasus in der deutschen Literatur. St. Petersburger Zt., 309, 1909.

Poritzky, J. E. Die neuere russische Litteratur und ihr Einfluss auf die deutsche. Blätter für Bücherfreunde, 1901.

Sugenheim, S. Russlands Einfluss auf, und Beziehungen zu Deutschland vom Beginne der Alleinregierung Peters I. bis zum Tode Nicolaus I. (1689-1855); nebst einem einleitenden Rückblicke auf die frühere Zeit. Frankfurt, 1856.

Bobrova, E. I. Russian Classical Literature in ITALY in the XIXth Century. In: Russian Literature in the West (In Russian). Acad. of Sciences, Leningrad, 1945.

Messina, G. L. La letteratura sovietica in Italia. ICS, 1947.

Nunziante, F. Gli Italiani in Russia durante il secolo XVIII. NAnt, 16.VII.1929.

Pandolfi, V. Repertorio sovietico e palcoscenico italiano. La Cultura Sovietica, 1, 1945.

Tyrrell, F. H. The Russians in Oriental Literature. (ORIENT). Calcutta Review, 83, 1886.

—— Notices of Russia and the Russians in Oriental Literature. Asiatic Quarterly Review, N.S., 7, 1894.

Portnoff, G. La literatura rusa en España. (SPAIN). New York, 1932.

CHAPTER TWO

Other Slavic and Danubian Influences and their Inter-Relations. Slavic Contributions in General.

1. Generalities.

Barta, S. Relazioni storiche e culturali ungaro-croate. Corvina, 4, 1941.

Bem, A. Russische Schriftsteller in Karlsbad: Orlov, Gogol, Tolstoi, Turgenev. GS,, 3, 1935.

Berkopec, O. Tschechisch-jugoslavische Literaturbeziehungen. (In Czech). Praha, 1940.

Coleman, A. P. How to Interpret to Americans a Culture of Eastern Europe. U. of Pa. Bull., 1946.

Damiani, E. Poeti slavi in una antologia italiana di poeti nel mundo. Europa orientale, 20, 1940.

David, J. J. Vom Slavischen in der deutschen Litteratur. Zeit, 31, 1902.

Derzhavin, K. N. The Russian Narrative Tale and the Beginning of New Bulgarian Literature. (In Russian) In: Russian Literature in the West. Acad. of Sciences, Leningrad, 1945.

Dieterich, K. Die osteuropäischen Literaturen in ihren Hauptströmungen vergleichend dargestellt. Tübingen, 1911.

Egalènes, J. d'. L'apport polonais dans la culture européenne. Messager de Pologne, 1947.

Eichhoff, F. G. Histoire de la langue et de la littérature des Slaves, Russes, Serbes, Bohèmes, Polonais et Lettons, considerées dans leur origine indienne, leurs anciens monuments, et leur état présent. Paris, Genève, 1839.

Frantsev, V. A. Studies in the History of the Czech Renaissance. Russian-Czech Intellectual Relations at the End of the XVIIIth and the Beginning of the First Half of the XIXth Century. (In Russian). Warsaw, 1902.

Galdi, L. L'influsso dell' umanesimo ungherese sui popoli vicini. Corvina, 6, 1943.

Guéorguevitch, K. La poésie populaire serbocroate dans la littérature polonaise. (In Serbian). Belgrade, 1936.

Gyomrei, A. La découverte de la Hongrie. Nouvelle Revue de Hongrie, 1935.

Hadrovics, L. Die ungarischen Vorlagen eines alten kroatischen Dichters. Archivum Europae Centro-orientalis, 5, 1939.

Hankiss, J. Les caractères nationaux et leur représentation. Un exemple: le portrait du Hongrois dans l'opinion occidentale. Revue de synthèse historique, 1932.

Iorga, N. Polonais et Roumains. Bucarest, 1921.

Jirasek, J. Russia and Ourselves. (In Czech). 4 vols. Praha, 1945-46.

Judas, Elizabeth. Russian Influence on Estonian Literature. Los Angeles, 1941.

Kolbuszewski, S. Influence of Czech Culture in Poland in the Middle Ages. SR, July, 1939.

Krumbacher, K. Der Kulturwert des Slawischen und die slawische Philologie in Deutschland. Intern. Wochenschrift f. Wissenschaft, Kunst & Technik, 29.II. & 7.III. 1908. And in: Populäre Aufsätze. Leipzig, 1909.

Labas, A. Gesichtspunkte für die Erschliessung der ungarischen Literatur für das Ausland. DVLG, 11, 1933.

Lednicki, W. Poland and the World. Quarterly Bull. of the Polish Institute of Arts and Sciences, 1-4. New York, 1943.

—— Russian-Polish Cultural Relations. New Europe, Sept., 1944.

—— Panslavism. In F. Gross : European Ideologies. New York, 1948.

Léger, L. La chaire de littératures slaves au Collège de France. In: Russes et Slaves, 2nd. Ser. Paris, 1896.

Máchal, J. Slavic Literatures. (In Czech). 3 vols. Praha, 1922-29.

Markovitch, M. La dette du romantisme à la poésie populaire yougoslave. Helicon, 1, 1938.

Mathesius, V. What Did Our Country Give to Europe and Mankind? (In Czech). 2 vols. Praha, 1939-40.

Mickiewicz, A. De la littérature slave. Revue Indépendante, 7, 1845.

—— Les Slaves. 3 vols. Paris, 1845-49.

Muckermann, F. Gedanken über Polens europäische Aufgabe. Mélanges Zdiechowski. Cracovie, 1934.

Nagy, I. Les relations intellectuelles entre la Pologne et la Hongrie. Nouvelle Revue de Hongrie, 1935.

Nandris, G. The Earliest Contacts Between Slavs and Roumanians. SR, July, 1939.

Privat, E. L'insurrection polonaise de 1830 et ses échos à l'Occident. Diss. Genève, 1918.

Reychman, J. La république de Raguse et la Pologne. Revue d'histoire comparée, 5, 1947.

Ruffini, M. La letteratura romena in Transilvania nel secolo XVI. Rassegna italoromena, 22, 1942.

Savadjian, L. Bibliographie balkanique. Paris, 1935.

Senn, A. The World's Debt to Poland. Bull. of the Polish Institute of Arts and Sciences, 1, 1943.

Skok, P. Slavs on the Mediterranean. Vox Romanica, 4, 1939.

Spaventi, R. Le relazioni culturali cecopolacche all' epoca della rinascita in Boemia. L'Europa Orientale, 22, 1942.

Szyjkowski, Marjan. The Polish Share in the Czech Renaissance. 3 vols. Praha, 1936-46.

Tadra, F. Cultural Relations of Bohemia with Foreign Countries Before the Hussite Wars. (In Czech). Praha, 1897.

Tagliavini, C. L'influsso ungherese sull' antica lessicographia rumena. Revue des Etudes hongroises, Jan. 1928.

Trólsányi, Z. La littérature russe en langue hongroise. Cahiers de littérature comparée. (Budapest), 1948.

Turóczi-Trostler, J. Littérature européenne et littérature hongroise. ibid.

Yakschitch, G. L'Europe et la résurrection de la Serbie (1804-34). Paris, 1907.

Yovanovitch, V. Les Serbes et la mission de la Serbie dans l'Europe d'Orient. Paris, 1870.

2. Individual Authors.

Eckhardt, A. Le premier poète hongrois, Valentin **BALASSI**, et la Pologne. Mélanges Zdziechowski. Cracovie, 1934.

Lednicki, W. **BLOK'S** Polish Poem. Bull. of the Polish Institute of Arts and Sciences in America, 2, 1944.

Belic, J. K. H. **BOROVSKY** and the Slavs. (In Czech). Praha, 1947.

Dvoichenko-Markova, E. **DERZHAVIN** in Moldavian Literature. (In Russian). Novosele, 7-8, 1943-44.

Chekhovich, K. Josef **DOBROVSKY** and the Ukrainian Language. Slavia, 9, 1930.

Hermann, M. **DOSTOIEWSKI** et Przybyszewski. Lille, 1938.

Paul, K. Vuk Stef. **KARADZIC** et les Polonais. Slavia, 4, 1925.

Coleman, A. P. **MICKIEWICZ** and South Russia. Slavic Studies. (Ithaca), 1943.

Garosci, C. A. Mickiewicz e la Russia. Europa orientale, 20, 1940.

Gorlin, M. Les ballades de Mickiewicz et Pushkin. Rev. des Etudes slaves, 19, 1939.

Klancar, A. Mickiewicz and the Slovenes. Sentinel, 5, 1943.
Lednicki, V. Mickiewicz en Russie. Revue de l'U. de Bruxelles, 1929.
—— Mickiewicz, Dostoevsky and Blok. Bull. of the Polish Institute of Arts & Sciences in America, 1, 1942. And in: Slavic Studies. (Ithaca), 1943.
Léger, L. Mickiewicz et Pouchkine. In: Russes et Slaves, 3e. Sér. Paris, 1899.
Markovitch, M. Adam Mickiewicz et la poésie populaire yougoslave. (In Serbian). Prilozi Proucavanju Narodne. Poezije, 1, 1934.
—— Adam Mickiewicz et la poésie populaire des Slaves du sud. L'Echo de Belgrade, 24.IV.1935.
Struve, G. Mickiewicz in Russia. SEER, 26, 1948.
Galdi, L. **PETOEFI** and Eminescu. ASEER, 7, 1948.
Anon. Two Geniuses (**PUSHKIN** & Mickiewicz) (In Russian). Russkaia Mysl, 12, 1906.
Badalic, J. Pouchkine en Yougoslavie. RLC, 17, 1937.
Brtán, R. Pushkin in Slovak Literature. Turciansky Sv. Martin, 1947.
Coleman, A. P. Pushkin and Mickiewicz. In: Centennial Essays for Pushkin. Harvard U.P., 1937.
Dvoichenko-Markova. Influenta lui Pushkin asupra scriitorilor români. Revista fundatiilor regale, 1937.
—— Pushkin and the Rumanian Historical Legend. ASEER, 7, 1948.
Jakobson, R. Polish Scholarship and Pushkin. ASEER, 5, 1946.
Koulakovski, P. Traductions slaves des poèmes de Pouchkine. Varsovie, 1899.
Lednicki, W. Pouchkine et la Pologne. Paris, 1928 & 1936.
—— Pouchkine et Mickiewicz. RLC, 17, 1937.
—— Bits of Table Talk on Pushkin. ASEER, 5, 1946.
Markovitch, M. Pouchkine et Karadjordje. L'Echo de Belgrade, 10.II.1937.
Mitropan, P. Pouchkine chez les Serbes. (In Serbian). Skoplje, 1937.
Orsier, J. François **RACKI** et la Renaissance scientifique et politique de la Croatie. Revue des Idées, 1910.
Pierre, A. **TCHERNYCHEVSKI** dans les Balkans. L'Europe centrale, 21.IX. 1936.
Letty, J. **TOLSTOI** et Masaryk dans les souvenirs de Valentin Boulgakov. L'Europe Centrale, 23.XI.1935.

CHAPTER THREE

East European Influences upon Individual Nations.

(See also Emigrants and Refugees, I. IV. 4.)

Gergely, E. J. Hungarian Drama in New York: American Adaptations, 1908-40. (**AMERICA**). Philadelphia, 1947.
Maslenikov, O. A. Slavic Studies in America, 1939-46. SEER, 25, 1948.
Coleman, Marion M. Contemporary Czech Drama in English Translation. (**ENGLAND**). CLN, 4, 1946.
—— Bulgarian Materials in English. CLN, 4, 1946.
—— Rumanian Materials in English. Bull. of the American Assoc. of Teachers of Slavic & East European Languages, 5, 1947.
Grzebieniowski, T. The Polish Cause in England a Century Ago. SR, 1932.
Janecek, B. Bibliography of Czech Literature in English Translation. Bull. of Bibliography, 16, 1937.
Kleiner, K. Seven Hundred Years of British-Czech Relations. (In Czech). London, 1942.
Reményi, J. Hungarian Publications in English. ASEER, 1947.
Wellek, R. Bohemia in Early English Literature. ASEER, 1943.
Anon. Bibliographie française de la Hongrie. (**FRANCE**). Revue des Etudes hongroises, 1932.
Beresniewicz, C. Essai d'une bibliographie des traductions françaises de la littérature polonaise. Revue des Bibliothèques, April, 1911.
Cukierman, L. Die polenfreundliche Bewegung in Frankreich im Jahre 1830-31. Diss. Zürich, 1926.
Czaikowa, May. Polish Contributions to French Culture. Slavia, 16, 1941.
Haskovec, P. M. French Chapters. (In Czech). Praha, 1930.
Ibrovac, M. Anthologie de la poésie yougoslave des XIXe et XXe siècles. (Cf. Introduction). Paris, 1935.
Iorga, N. La place des Roumains dans les littératures romanes. Bull. de la Section historique de l'Acad. roumaine, 1.I.1920.
—— Les voyageurs français dans l'Orient européen. RCC, 1926-28 & Paris, 1928.
—— Une vingtaine de voyageurs dans l'Orient européen. Paris, 1928.
Jelinek, H. Etudes tchécoslovaques. Paris, 1927.

Karl, L. La Hongrie et les Hongrois dans les chansons de geste. RLR, 51, 1908.
—— Ungarn im national-spanischen und im klassisch-französischen Drama. Budapest, 1916.
Kont, I. L'histoire et la littérature hongroises en France (XVIe siècle à nos jours). Annales de la Société Kisfaludy, Budapest, 1910.
—— La première étude française sur la langue et la littérature hongroises. Mélanges E. Picot. Paris, 1913.
Lorentowicz, J. & Chrumski, A. M. La Pologne en France; essai d'une bibliographie raisonnée. Paris, 1935-38.
Markovitch, M. Un voyageur français en Serbie. (In Serbian). Glasnik Istoriskoy Drustva, 7, 1934.
Morawski, J. La Pologne vue par deux voyageurs français du XVIe siècle. La Pologne, 1.XII.1932.
Pilon, E. La Pologne et nos muses plaintives. MF, 295, 1939.
Poirier, J. Une source hongroise de l'université de France? (Ratio educationis, 1777). Revue des Etudes hongroises, April, 1928.
Popović, P. Essai de bibliographie française de la littérature yougoslave. Le Monde Slave, May 1931.
Radojkovitch, M. L'opinion française et le mouvement illyrien de 1840 à 1848. Paris, 1936.
Révész, E. de. La Hongrie dans la littérature des réfugiés huguenots. Bull. de la Soc. de l'hist. du Protestantisme fr., 1932.
Roque-Ferrier. La Roumanie dans la littérature du Midi de la France. RLR, 1875 & Paris, 1881.
Schoell, F. L. Motifs polonais dans la littérature française. La Pologne, 1931.
Sénéchal, C. La Pologne de 1830 à 1846 dans la poésie romantique française. Paris, 1937.
Sipos, L. The Literary Repercussion in France of the Hungarian Fight for Independence. (In Hungarian). Budapest, 1929.
Skerlitch, J. The French Romanticists and Serbian Popular Poetry. (In Serbian). Mostar, 1908.
Strém, G. La Hongrie à travers les écrivains français. Revue de Hongrie, 1930.
Tronchon, H. La découverte d'une littérature: France et Hongrie. Revue de Hongrie, Aug., 1912.
Anon. Ein deutsches Weihnachtsspiel aus Ungarn. (GERMANY). Europa, 1858.
Arnold, R. F. Geschichte der deutschen Polenliteratur. Halle, 1900.
Berger, K. Die deutsche Polenliteratur und der neuste Ostmarkenroman. LE, 12.
Bianquis, Geneviève. La Pologne dans la poésie allemande (1772-1832). RLC, 23, 1949.
Eckhardt, A. Une école de rhéteurs hongrois à Strasbourg au XVIe siècle. Cahiers de littérature comparée. (Budapest), 1948.
Farkas, G. La littérature hongroise en Allemagne. (In Hungarian). EPhK, 60, 1936.
Glueckmann, H. Ungarische Dichtungen in deutscher Uebertragung. MLIA, 1887.
Hauffen, A. Böhmische Sage und Geschichte in der deutschen Literatur. Deutsche Arbeit, 2 (Prag), 1903.
Kraus, A. Die alte böhmische Sage und Geschichte in der deutschen Litteratur. Zs. f. d. österreichischen Gymnasien, 53, 1902.
—— Die alte tschechische Geschichte in der deutschen Litteratur. (In Czech). Prag, 1902.
Krejcí, F. V. Die alte Geschichte Böhmens in der deutschen Literatur. Die Zeit, 35, (Wien), 1903.
Kurtzmann, L. Polnische Dichter und ihre deutschen Freunde. MLIA, 1880.
Sommerfeld, M. Ein polnischer Freiheitskampf (1830) im deutschen Lied. Hamburger Correspondent, Literar. Beilage, 1, 1917.
Timm, B. Die Polen in den Liedern deutscher Dichter. Lissa, 1907.
Tropsch, S. Les traductions allemandes des nos poésies populaires. Rad. Jugoslavenske Akademije, 166. Agram, 1906.
Trostler, J. Ungarische Stoffe in der deutschen Literatur des 17. Jahrhunderts. Ungar. Rundschau, 4, 1915.
—— Ungarns Eintritt in das literarische Bewusstsein Deutschlands. Deutsch-Ungarische Heimatsblätter, 1930.
Vasfi. Deutsche Uebersetzungen ungarischer Poesien. Grenzboten, 10, 1851.
Wolkan, R. Böhmens Antheil an der deutschen Litteratur des XVI. Jahrhunderts. Prag, 1890.
Cronia, A. Bohemia in the History of Italian Culture. (In Czech). (ITALY). Praha, 1936.
Damiani, E. Gli studi polonistici in Italia. Europa Orientale, 21, 1941.
Isopescu, C. Viaggiatori eruditi in Romenia. Osservatore romano, 13.VI.1948.
Jordanov, P. Bibliografia delle publicazioni italiane sulla Bulgaria. Europa Orientale, 22, 1942.

Messina, G. L. Gli studi slavistici in Italia. RLM, 3, 1948.
Ortiz, R. La cultura rumena in Atti del R. Istituto Veneto. ARIV, 99, 1940.
Ruberti, C. Per la storia della filologia romena in Italia. Augustea, 1943.
Takács, G. L'Ungheria, gli Ungheresi ed il culto di S. Stefano nei poemi eroici italiani del seicento. Studi e Documenti italo-ungheresi della R. Acc. d'Ungheria di Roma, 2, 1937.
Brachfeld, O. Motifs hongrois dans l'ancienne littérature et la ballade populaire catalanes. (SPAIN). Budapest, 1930.
Karl, L. Ungarn im national-spanischen und klassisch-französischen Drama. Budapest, 1916.
Wedkiewicz, S. La Suède et la Pologne: Essai d'une bibliographie des publications suédoises concernant la Pologne. (SWEDEN). Stockholm, 1918.

CHAPTER FOUR

Dostoievski.

(See also Reciprocal Influences, III. III. 3. and Slavic-Interrelations, Chapter Two, above.)

1. Generalities.

Anon. Dostoevsky and the Novel (in Europe). TLS, 5.VI.1930.
Bem, A. L. Dostojevsky in the World. (In Russian). Slovansky prehled, 22
Levinson, A. Dostoievsky et le roman occidental. RCC, 1926-27.
Luma. Dostojewski und seine Verkünder. Der Deutschenspiegel, 24.IV.1925.
Riza-Zade, Fatima, Dostojevsky in Western Criticism. (In Russian). Literatura i Marxism, 1929.
Romein, J. M. Dostojewski in de Westersche Kritiek. Haarlem, 1924.
Schiller, F. P. The Dostojevsky-Legend in Western European Criticism. (In Russian). Literatura i Marxism, 1928.
Muchnic, Helen. Dostoevsky's English Reputation. (ENGLAND). Northampton (Mass.), 1939.
Neuschaffer, W. Dostojevskijs Einfluss auf den englischen Roman. Heidelberg, 1935.
Mirsky, S. Dostojevski in Frankreich und England. (FRANCE). Slavische Rundschau, 3, 1931.
Charbonnel, V. Les mystiques dans la littérature (française) présente. Paris, 1897.
Drougard, E. Une réplique française de la Légende du Grand Inquisiteur. Rev. des Etudes slaves, 14, 1934.
Henckel, W. Dostojewskijs Raskolnikow auf der französischen Bühne. MLIA, 1888.
Minssen, H. F. Die französische Kritik und Dostojevski. Hamburg, 1934.
Teitelbaum, S. M. Dostoyevski in France of the 1880's. ASEER, 5, 1946.
Buelow, F. von. Dostojewski in Deutschland. (GERMANY). LE, 1.XI.1906.
Dukmeyer, F. Dostojewskis Einführung in Deutschland. Die Funken, 3, 1906.
Hanswedell, E. Die Kenntnis von Dostojevski und seinen Werken im deutschen Naturalismus und der Einfluss seines Raskolnikoff auf die Epoche von 1880-95. Diss. München, 1924.
Kampmann, T. Dostojewsky in Deutschland. Münster, 1931.
Loewenthal, L. Die Auffassung Dostojewskis im Vorkriegsdeutschland. Zs. für Sozialforschung, 3, 1934.
Noetzel, K. Dostojewski und wir. München, 1920.
Assunto, R. Presenza di Dostojevski. (ITALY). ICS, 29, 1946.

2. Influences upon Individual Authors.

Bellander, G. Dan ANDERSON och Dostojevski. Studiekam, 1927.
Pope, J. C. Prufrock and Raskolnikov. (T. S. ELIOT). AL, 17, 1945.
—— Prufrock and Raskolnikov Again: A Letter from Eliot. AL, 18, 1947.
Richter, F. K. Dostojewski im literarischen Denken Paul ERNSTS. GQ, 17, 1944.
Arnold, G. André GIDE et Dostojevski. NRF, July, 1923.
Fayer, M. H. Gide, Freedom and Dostoevsky. Middlebury (Vt.), 1946.
Gide, A. Dostoievski. Paris, 1923.
Massis, H. André Gide et Dostojevsky. Revue universelle, Nov., 1923.
Vacquier, T. Dostojevsky and Gide. Sewanee Review, 37, 1929.
Coates, W. A. Dostoyevski and Gerhart HAUPTMANN. ASEER, 4, 1945-46.
Fondane, B. HEIDEGGER devant Dostojevski. In: La Conscience malheureuse. Paris, 1936.
Sarraute, N. De Dostoievsky à KAFKA. Les Temps Modernes, Oct., 1947.
Bojenow. Dostoiewski et MAUPASSANT. Archive d'anthropologie crim., Jan., 1903.

Secretan, R. Dostoiewsky a-t-il exercé une influence sur H. de **MONTHERLANT?** NL, 10.IV.1937.
Andler, C. **NIETZSCHE** et Dostoievsky. Paris, 1930.
Bierbaum, O. J. Dostoyeffsky and Nietzsche. HJ, 9, 1911.
Giusti, W. Dostojevski e il pensiero tedesco: Nietzsche. RI, 15.III.1926.
Kheisin, M. Dostoevsky and Nietzsche (in Russian). Mir Bozhii, 6, 1903.
Schubart, W. Dostojewski und Nietzsche. Symbolik ihres Lebens. Luzern, 1946.
Shestov, L. Dostoevsky and Nietzsche (in Russian). Berlin, 1922.
—— La philosophie de la tragédie: Dostoievsky et Nietzsche. Paris, 1926 & Berlin, 1931.
Lavrin, J. Dostojevsky and **PROUST.** SR, 1926-27.
Ortega y Gasset, J. Dostojevsky und Proust. NSR, 20.
Knowlton, E. C. A Russian Influence on **STEVENSON.** MPh, 14, 1916.
Ortolani, A. G. Dostoevsky e Italo **SVEVO.** RLM, 1, 1946.
Frankle, Eleanor. Dostoievsky et **WASSERMANN.** RLC, 19, 1940.

CHAPTER FIVE

Mickiewicz.

(See also Slavic Interrelations, Chapter Two, above.)

Coleman, A. P. Mickiewicz and Northern Balladry. Slavonic Yearbook, 1, 1941.
Kridl, M. Adam Mickiewicz: son rôle dans la littérature polonaise et dans la littérature mondiale. Paris, 1921.
Wellisz, L. Reverberations of Mickiewicz's Genius in **AMERICA.** Bull. of the Polish Institute of Arts and Sciences in America, 3, 1945.
—— Mickiewicz and his American Friends. Polish Review, 6, 1946.
Coleman, A. P. Adam Mickiewicz in English. **(ENGLAND).** Schenectady, 1940.
Lednicki, W. Mickiewicz and England. Pologne littéraire, 1929.
Koczorowski, S. P. Adam Mickiewicz et la pensée française, 1830-1923: témoignages des écrivains français. **(FRANCE).** Paris, 1929.
Kridl, M. Mickiewicz et la France. Pologne littéraire, 1929.
Lednicki, W. Mickiewicz at the Collège de France. Slavonic Yearbook, 1941.
Montfort, H. de. Mickiewicz en France avant 1830. RB, 18.V.1929.
Zaleski, Z. L. Le rayonnement de la Pologne en France après 1830 (autour de l'amitié de Mickiewicz, Michelet et Quinet). La Pologne au Congrès internat. de Bruxelles, 16, 1923.
Maver, G. Mickiewicz in Italia. **(ITALY).** Pologne littéraire, 1929.
Kowalski, J. Les cours d'Adam Mickiewicz à Lausanne. **(SWITZERLAND).** Acad. des Sciences et Lettres de Cracovie, 1928.
Cazin, P. Mickiewicz et **BARRES.** Pologne littéraire, 15.XII.1931.
Mazon, A. Une correspondance; Mickiewicz, Victor **COUSIN,** Cyprien Robert. RLC, 14, 1934.
Wellisz, L. The Friendship of Margaret **FULLER** d'Ossoli and Adam Mickiewicz. New York, 1948.
Topass, J. Mickiewicz, **LAMENNAIS,** Montalembert et leurs rapports idéologiques. Pologne littéraire, 9, 1934.
Karenin, V. Adam Mickiewicz and George **SAND** (in Russian). Vestnik Evropy, 1907.

CHAPTER SIX

Pushkin.

(See also Reciprocal Influences, III. III. 3. and Slavic Interrelations, Chapter Two, above.)

Alekseev, M. Pushkin in the West. (In Russian). In: Pushkin: Vremennik pushinskoy komissii, 3, 1937.
Gorlin, M. Les études pouchkiniennes, 1917-37. RLC, 17, 1937.
Kazanskii, B. West European Criticism on Pushkin (in Russian). Literaturnyi Kritik, 1937.
Lanz, H. Pushkin from an International Point of View. Slavia, 16, 1941.
Lednicki, W. Puszkin, 1837-1937. Cracovie, 1937.
Léger, L. Alexandre Pouchkine. Jugements sur Pouchkine. Revue Encyclopédique, 10.VI.1899.
Mazon, A. Alexandre Pouchkine (1799-1837). RLC, 17, 1937.
Mendheim, M. A. S. Puschkin und seine Uebersetzer. Internat. Litteraturberichte, 1900.
Noyes, G. R. Pushkin in World Literature. (In Russian). Harvard U.P., 1937.
Nusinov, I. Pushkin in World Literature. (In Russian). Moskva, 1941.

Rozanov, I. Pushkin in the Poetry of his Contemporaries. (In Russian) Literaturnoe Nasledstvo, 16-18, 1934.
Struve, G. Poushkine et la littérature européenne. In: Hommage à Poushkine; Les Cahiers du journal des poètes (Bruxelles), 1937.
Tomashevskii, B. Die Puskin-Forschung seit 1914. ZSPh, 1925.
Varia. Pushkin in World Literature. (In Russian). Petersburg, 1924.
—— Pushkin. A Collection of Articles and Essays on the Great Russian Poet. Moscow, 1939.
Vengerov, S. A. Pushkiniana of the XXth Century. (In Russian). In: Pushkin i ego sovremenniki, 5, 1918-1927.
Veselovskii, A. Pushkin and European Poetry (in Russian). Zhizn, 5, 1899.
Weidlé, W. Pouchkine et la littérature européenne. Critique, June, 1947.
Bittner, K. Eine amerikanische Ehrung Puskins. (**AMERICA**). Slavische Rundschau, 1938.
Fredericks, A. Pushkin for Americans. Russian Review, 5, 1946.
Simmons, E. J. Introduction to a Translation of Pushkin. HSPhL, 15, 1933.
Cross, S. H. Pouchkine en Angleterre. (**ENGLAND**). RLC, 17, 1937.
Simmons, E. J. La littérature anglaise et Pouchkine. RLC, 17, 1937.
—— English Translations of Eugene Onegin. SR, 17, 1938.
Jousserandot, L. Pouchkine en **FRANCE**. Le Monde Slave, Jan., 1918.
Legras, J. Les Français en face de Pouchkine. Le Monde Slave, Feb., 1937.
Lozinski, G. La littérature française et Pouchkine. RLC, 17, 1937.
Mongault, H. Pouchkine en France. RLC, 17, 1937.
Tomashevskii, B. Pushkin and the French Literature. (In Russian). Literaturnoe Nasledstvo, 31-32, (Moskva) 1937.
Luther, A. Puskin in Deutschland. (**GERMANY**). RLC, 17, 1937.
Damiani, E. Quel che c' è di Puskin e su Puskin in italiano. (**ITALY**). In: Alessandro Puskin nel primo centenario della morte. Roma, 1937.
—— Due drammi italiani su Puskin. Ibid.
Lo Gatto, E. Puskin in Italia. RLC, 17, 1937.
Mioni, A. B. Puskin e Italia. In: Alessandro Puskin nel primo centenario della morte. Roma, 1937.
Bieghler, E. W. Early Spanish Translations of Pushkin. (**SPAIN**). HR, 6, 1938.
Rozanov, V. **IBSEN** and Pushkin (in Russian). Russkaia Mysl, 8, 1907.
Kogan, L. E. Pushkin in the Translation of **MERIMEE**. (In Russian). In: Pushkin: Vremennik pushinskoy komissii, 4-5, 1939.
Markovitch, M. Pouchkine, Mérimée et la poésie populaire serbe. (In Serbian). Palozi proucavanju Narodne poezije, 1, 1937.
Mongault, H. Mérimée et Pouchkine. Monde Slave, 1930.
Baldensperger, F. Un des premiers traducteurs de Pouchkine en France: Alexandre de **ROGUIER**. RLC, 17, 1937.

CHAPTER SEVEN

Tolstoi.

1. General Influences.

(See also Politics, I. II. 5.)

Anon. Le centenaire de Tolstoi. Chronique des Lettres françaises, Nov., 1928.
Crosby, E. Tolstoi et ses traducteurs. Humanité Nouvelle, Aug., 1900.
Garnett, E. Tolstoi's Place in European Literature. Bookman, March, 1901.
Kirkland, J. Tolstoi and the Russian Invasion of the Realm of Fiction. The Dial, 7, 1886.
Kuelpe, E. Anti-Tolstoi. Baltische Monatsschrift, 54, 1902.
Le Breton, A. La pitié sociale dans le roman. RDM, 15.II.1902.
Le Roux, H. A propos de la Puissance des Ténèbres. RB, 1888.
Parodi, M. I cento anni di L. Tolstoi. I Libri del giorno, Sept. 1928.
Souberbielle, A. Comment on traduit Tolstoi. Revue blanche, 1900.
Lednicki, W. Tolstoy through **AMERICAN** Eyes. SEER, 25, 1948.
Suhrawardy, A. A. An Indian on Tolstoi. (**ASIA**). Calcutta Review, 3rd. Ser., 60, 1936.
Smith, J. A. Tolstoy's Fiction in **ENGLAND** and America. Diss. U. of Illinois, 1939.
Yassukovitch, Antonina. Tolstoi in English, 1878-1929. Bull. of New York Public Library, 33, 1929-30.
Anon. Tolstoi et les écrivains français. (**FRANCE**). Le Temps, 6.V.1898.
Chistiakova, M. Leon Tolstoi and France. (In Russian). Literaturnoe Nasledstvo, 31-32. Moskva, 1937.

Gulacke, K. H. Der Einfluss Tolstois auf das französische Geistesleben. Diss. Bonn. Würzburg, 1934.
Halperine-Kaminsky. La Puissance des Ténèbres sur la scène française. Nouvelle Revue, 50, 1888.
Jagow, E. von. Tolstois Macht der Finsterniss im Théâtre libre. MLIA, 1888.
Jaloux, E. Léo Tolstois Einfluss in Frankreich. Prager Tageblatt, 250, 1903.
Lodine, J. Tolstoi en France. NL, 23.XI.1935.
Motyleva, T. L. Tolstoy in French Literature and Criticism of the XIXth Century. In: Leo Tolstoy and the West. Leningrad, 1945.
Priim, F. I. Leo Tolstoy and the French Novel. (In Russian). In: Russian Literature in the West. Acad. of Science, USSR, Leningrad, 1945.
Reyher, A. Zola und Tolstoi auf den Pariser Bühnen. Gegenwart, 1888.
Selbst, W. Tolstoi und das moderne Drama auf der Pariser Bühne. Baltische Monatsschrift, 35, 1888.
Hahn, H. Wechselbeziehungen zwischen Tolstoi und der deutschen Literatur. (GERMANY). ASPh, 35, 1914.
Noetzel, K. Tolstoi und wir. München, 1910.
Polonskii, G. Tolstoy in Germany (in Russian). Sovremennyi Mir, 10, 1908.
Schmidt, E. H. Leo Tolstoi und seine Bedeutung für unsere Kultur. Leipzig, 1901.
Mark. Tolstoi's Living Corpse on the Italian Stage. (ITALY). Solntse Rossii, 31.III.1913.
Zanetti, A. Tolstoi nelle traduzioni italiane. Cultura, 1.VI.1912.

2. Influences upon Individual Authors.

Hapgood, I. F. Count Toystoy and Gabriele d'ANNUNZIO. Bookman, 3, 1896.
Zhantieva, D. G. GALSWORTHY and Leo Tolstoy. In: Leo Tolstoy and the West (In Russian). Leningrad, 1945.
Markovitch, M. Tolstoi et GANDHI. Paris, 1928.
Kashkin, I. A. HEMINGWAY and Tolstoy. In: Leo Tolstoy and the West. Leningrad, 1945.
Elias, J. Henrik IBSEN und Die Macht der Finsternis. Festgabe L. Geiger. Berlin, 1918.
Red'ko, A. Tolstoy and Ibsen (in Russian). Russkoe Bogatstvo, 1907 & 1910.
Purin, C. M. Tolstoi und KROEGER: eine Darstellung ihrer literarischen Beziehungen. Festschrift A. R. Hohlfeld. Madison, 1925.
Faguet, E. Tolstoi et MAUPASSANT. RB, 13.VI.1896.
Chestov. L'idée de bien chez Tolstoi et NIETZSCHE. Paris, 1923.
Claparède, H. Evocation: Tolstoi, Nietzsche, Rilke. Genève, 1944.
Davis, Helen E. Tolstoy and Nietzsche. New York, 1929.
Glasenapp, G. von. Tolstoi und Nietzsche. Baltische Monatsschrift, 1895.
Lavrin, J. Tolstoi and Nietzsche. SR, 4, 1925.
Petrone, I. F. Nietzsche et L. Tolstoi. Critica, 1, 1903.
Shestov, L. Good in the Teaching of Tolstoy and Nietzsche. (in Russian). Berlin, 1922.
Butler, E. M. RILKE and Tolstoy. MLR, 35, 1940.
Motyleva, T. L. R. ROLLAND and Tolstoy. In: Leo Tolstoy and the West (in Russian). Leningrad, 1945.
Tolstoi, G. Tolstoi et VOGUE. NL, 23. XI.1935.
Faguet, E. Tolstoi et ZOLA. RB, 23.V. 1896.

CHAPTER EIGHT

Other East European Authors.

Reviczky, Gyula von. Janos ARANY in deutscher Uebersetzung. MLIA, 1880.
Koyré, A. Russia's Place in the World: Peter CHAADEEV and the Slavophiles. SR, March, 1927.
Grigoriev, A. L. CHEKHOV in the West. In: Russian Literature in the West. Acad. of Sciences, Leningrad, 1945.
Jacoubet, E. K. Mansfield et Tchekhov. EA, 2, 1938-39.
Kogan, P. A. Chekhov among European Humorists (in Russian). Russkaia Mysl, 1906.
Mirsky, D. S. Chekhov and the English. Monthly Criterion, 6, 1927.
Muffang, M. Katherine Mansfield. Diss. Paris, 1937.
Nabokoff, C. Chekhov on the English Stage. Contemporary Review, June, 1926.
Bittner, K. J. A. COMENIUS und G. W. Leibnitz. ZSPh, 6, 1929.
Hunziker, O. Comenius and Pestalozzi. In: Heinrich Pestalozzi. Winterthur, 1927.
Kvacala, J. Die pädagogische Reform des Comenius in Deutschland bis zum Ausgange des 17. Jahrhunderts. Mon. germ. Paed., 26-27.

Kvet, F. B. Leibnitz und Comenius. Abhandl. der K. Böhmischen Ges. der Wiss., 1857.
Young, R. F. Comenius in England. Oxford U.P., 1932.
Joseph CONRAD: See Intermediaries, I. IV. 8.
Szent-Ivámyi, B. von. Matthias CORVINUS in der deutschen Literatur. Ungarische Jb., 20.
Vil'Chur. Kazak EVSTAF'EV, an Ambassador of Russian Culture in America. Novoe Russkoe Slovo, 21.IX.1935.
Chudakov, V. GOGOL and European Literature. (In Russian). Kievskiia universitetskiia Izvestiia, 3,8,10, 1908.
Cournos, J. The First Extensive Studies in English of Gogol and Pushkin. New York Evening Post, Literary Suppl., 12.VI.1926.
Mongault, H. Gogol et Mérimée. RLC, 10, 1930.
Adam, G. GORKI in Deutschland. LE, 4, 1901-02.
—— Gorki-Uebersetzungen. LE, 5, 1903.
Alekseev, V. M. Gorkii in China. Uchenye zapiski Instituta inostrannykh iazykov Krasnoi armii, 1, 1945.
Fox, R. M. Maxim Gorky and the English Standpoint. Fortnighty Review, Oct., 1926.
Poole, E. Maxim Gorky in New York. SEER, 22, 1944.
Elekes, L. HUNYADI, Hero of Danubian Europe. Hungarian Quarterly, 6, 1940.
Damiani, E. Aleko KONSTANTINOV cinquent' anni dopo la morte. RLM, 2, 1947.
Gaffney, M. C. KOSCIUSKO'S Gift to Jefferson. Poland-America, 1932.
Zaleski, Z. L. La légende de Kosciusko: Mickiewicz et Michelet. Rev. des Etudes slaves, 6, 1926.
Janossey, D. A. Great Britain and KOSSUTH. Archivium Europae centro-orientalis, 3, 1937.
Wagner, A. M. Undivine Comedy: Zygmunt KRASINSKI and German Expressionism. ASEER, 6, 1948.
Hecht, D. LAVROV, Chaikovski, and the United States. ASEER, 5, 1946.
Nikolaus LENAU: See Intermediaries, I. IV. 8.
Dukmeyer, F. Die Einführung LERMONTOVS in Deutschland und des Dichters Persönlichkeit. Berlin, 1925.
Heifetz, A. Lermontov in English. Bibliography. New York Public Library, 1942.
Hankiss, J. LISZT écrivain et la littérature européenne. RLC, 17, 1937.
Anon. E. MADACH et la Tragédie de l'homme devant les universités françaises. Revue des Etudes hongroises, 1934.
Bidou, H. Un cri de détresse: La Tragédie de l'homme. Revue des Etudes hongroises, 1934. Cf. le Temps, 7.III.1934.
Hankiss, J. Une tragédie de l'homme, l'Adam hongrois. Revue des Etudes hongroises, 1935.
Montanaro, E. G. La Tragedia dell' uomo, di Madách. La Brigata (Malta), 1935.
Boutakova, V. J. Jugements d'un critique allemand sur MAIAKOVSKY. (In Russian). Vladikavkaj, 1931.
Anon. Fremdländische Dichtungen in deutschem Gewande. (A. PETOEFI). Europa, 1858.
—— Alex. Petöfis Lieder. Europa, 14, 1860.
—— Eine neue Uebersetzung Petöfischer Gedichte. MLIA, 1878.
—— Petöfi dans la correspondance d'Amiel. Revue des Etudes hongroises, 1928.
Barabas, A. von. Petöfi und Nietzsche. Pester Lloyd, 237, 1908.
—— Ein Nietzsche-Problem. Hamburger Fremdenblatt, 270, 1912.
Cifalinò, G. La fortuna di Petöfi in Italia. Corvina, 5, 1942.
—— G. Cassone, apostolo italiano di Petöfi. Corvina, 6, 1943.
Hankiss, J. Petöfi et les poètes français. RLC, 2, 1922.
Kastner, J. Traductions oubliées d'Amiel. Revue des Etudes hongroises, 1928.
Kont, I. Petöfi in Frankreich. Ungarische Rundschau, 2. (Leipzig), 1913.
Leffler, B. L'influence de Petöfi sur le plus grand poète lyrique suédois. Debreceni Szemle, 9, 1937.
Lelkes, E. Petöfi en France. Nouvelle Revue de Hongrie, March, 1939.
Leukei, H. et al. Petöfi dans la littérature universelle (Allemagne, France, Italie, Espagne, Angleterre, Scandinavie). Bibliothèque Petöfi, 27-28. Budapest.
Mallon, O. Petöfi dem Sonnengott. Ein bisher unbekanntes Gedicht Bettina von Arnims. Archiv, 157, 1930.
Opitz, T. Petöfi und seine deutschen Uebersetzer. MLIA, 1866.
Paloczy, L. Petöfi in Italien. MLIA, 1880.
Elsberg, I. SHCHEDRIN and World Literature. Literaturnyi Kritik, 1940.
Manning, C. A. Taras SHEVCHENKO as a World Poet. Ukrainian Quarterly, 1, 1945.

Kosko, M. La fortune de Quo Vadis en France. (SIENKIEWICZ). Paris, 1935.
Muret, M. Sienkiewicz, Hauptmann, d'Annunzio. Journal des Débats, 20.II.1902.
Nobilis, Sister M. Sienkiewicz and the American Poles. Sodalis, (Orchard Lake, Michigan), 1944.
Schoell, F. L. Du discrédit de Sienkiewicz en France. L'Europe centrale, 23.XI.1935.
Lalou, R. **SIEROSZEWSKI** et Norvid en France. NL, 15.XI.1932.
Brewster, P. G. Jurgen and Figures of Earth and the Russian **SKAZKI**. AL, 13, 1942.
Anon. Iwan **TURGENIEW** in Deutschland. Europa, 1872.
Borostyany, F. Turgenjeff und seine französischen Freunde. Pester Lloyd, 5, 1902.
Eichholtz, J. Turgenev in der deutschen Kritik bis zum Jahre 1883. GS., 1, 1931-32.
Gettmann, R. A. Turgenev in England and America. Urbana, 1941. Cf. Russian Rev. 1, 1941, Madison Quarterly, 2, 1942 & JEGPh, 41, 1942.
Gorlin, M. Turgenev's Unpublished Letters to Du Camp, Flaubert and de Goncourt. (In Russian). Literaturnoe Nasledstvo, 31-32. Moskva, 1937.
Halperine-Kaminski, E. Ivan Tourguéneff d'après sa correspondance avec ses amis français (G. Flaubert, G. Sand, Zola, Maupassant, Taine, Renan, Th. Gautier, Sainte-Beuve, Clarétie, etc.). Paris, 1902.
Haumant, E. Le premier séjour de Tourguénef en France. Journal des Débats 12.VIII.1896.
Kleman, M. I. S. Turgenev and Prosper Mérimée. (In Russian) Literaturnoe Nasledstvo, 31-32. Moskva, 1937.
Lerner, D. The Influence of Turgenev on Henry James. Slavonic Yearbook, 20, 1941.
Martin, Clara B. Turgeneff and his Translators. Nation, 26. (New York), 1878.
Noyes, G. S. Turgeneff and his Translators. Nation, 78, 1904.
Parturier, M. Ivan Tourguéniev et Maxime du Camp. RLC 21, 1947.
Seznec, J. Lettres de Tourguéneff à Henry James. CL, 1, 1949.
Whibley, C. Ivan Turgenev (In England). NAR, 1902.
Mazon, A. **VUK** et l'Europe. RCC, 39, 1937-38.

CHAPTER NINE

East European Influences upon Individual Authors.

Armeanca, E. Juliette **ADAM** et la Hongrie. Revue Roumaine de Transylvanie, 1935.
Krappe, A. H. The Source of Pedro Antonio de **ALARCON'S** El extranjero. HR, 11, 1943.
Berkov, P. N. **ALOPAEUS'** Vorlesung über russische Poesie in Göttingen im Jahre 1769. GS, 2, 1932-33.
Altszyler, Hélène. Les Polonais dans l'oeuvre de **BALZAC**. RHLF, 1918.
Korwin-Piotrowska, S. de. Balzac et le monde slave. Paris, 1933.
—— L'Etrangère, Eveline Hanska de Balzac. Paris, 1938.
Hastings, W. S. Une dédicace de Honoré de Balzac: à Maria. RLC, 15, 1935.
Topass, J. J. Les Polonais dans l'oeuvre de Balzac. Le Monde slave, April, 1925.
Birkás, G. La Hongrie vue par un savant français en 1818 (**BEUDANT**). Revue des Etudes hongroises, July, 1933.
Schwab, R. Antécédents hongrois des romans d'Elémir **BOURGES**. Revue des Etudes hongroises, 1937.
Coleman, A. P. John **BOWRING** and the Poetry of the Slavs. Proceedings American Philosophical Society, 84, 1941.
Sova, M. Sir John Bowring (1792-1872) and the Slavs. SEER, 21, 1944.
Eckardt, J. **CAGLIOSTRO** in Mitau. Baltische Monatsschrift, 1864.
Hallays, A. **CHATEAUBRIAND** en Bohême. Journal des Débats, 27.IX.1912.
Kubinova, M. Chateaubriand à Prague en 1833. L'Europe centrale, 3.VI.1933.
Thomas, L. Chateaubriand en Bohême. Marches de l'Est, 25.II.1913.
Anon. **CHESTERTON** en Pologne: son emploi du temps, ses discours. Pologne littéraire, 15.X.1928.
Spiller, R. E. F. **COOPER** and Lafayette: Friends of Polish Freedom, 1830-32. AL, March, 1935.
Markovitch, M. Le Monténégrin d'Alphonse **DAUDET**. (In Serbian). Letopis Matice Srpske, 1934.
—— Un roman yougoslave de Daudet. (In Serbian). Strani Pregled, 1935.
—— Alphonse Daudet et les Serbes. RLC, 21, 1947.
Bilbassov. **DIDEROT** à Petersbourg. (In Russian). Petersbourg, 1884.
Proal, L. Les prédictions de Diderot, J. J. Rousseau et Condillac sur la Russie. MF, Aug., 1918.

Mazon, A. Claude **FAURIEL** et les poèmes prétendus anciens de Russie et de Bohême. Rev. des Etudes slaves, 21, 1944.

Yovanovitch, V. M. Claude Fauriel et la poésie populaire serbe. (In Serbian). SKG, 1. & 16.II.1910.

Amelung, F. Der Dichter Paul **FLEMING** und seine Beziehungen zu Reval. Baltische Monatschrift, 28, 1881.

Gerhardt, D. Paul Fleming und Russland. GS, 4, 1936.

Begey, M. B. **FOGAZZARO** and Messianic Currents from Poland. (In Polish). In: Przeglad Wspolczesny, Cracow, 1938.

Anon. Paul **FORT** à Prague. Revue française de Prague, 1929.

Donskaia, S. Anatole **FRANCE** and Russian Literature. In: Russian Literature in the West. Leningrad, 1945.

Coquart, A. Théophile **GAUTIER** et la Russie. Le Monde slave, July, 1936.

Krappe, A. H. La source polonaise du conte Jettatura de Théophile Gautier. Neuphilol. Mitteilungen, 39, 1938.

Sipos, L. Les traducteurs français des chants nationaux hongrois: d'Auguste de **GERANDO** à Alexandre Dumas. Etudes hongroises, 14-15, 1937.

Ehrentreich, A. André **GIDE** über Russland. Archiv, 172, 1937.

Ward, B. André Gide on Soviet Russia. Contemporary Review, May, 1938.

Bartsch, K. **GOETHE** und das serbische Versmass. Gegenwart, 41, 1883.

Curcin, M. Goethe and Serbo-Croat Ballad Poetry. SR, 1932.

Gesemann, G. Der Klaggesang der edlen Frauen des Asan-Aga: zu Goethes Gedächtnis. Slav. Rundschau, 4, 1932.

Jilek, H. Goethe und der slavische Südosten. Jena, 1941.

Kraus, A. Goethe and Bohemia. (In Czech). Praha, 1893 & 1896.

Lucerna, Camilla. Die südslavische Ballade von Asan-Agas Gattin und ihre Nachbildung durch Goethe. Berlin, 1905.

Miklositch, F. Ueber Goethes Klagegesang von der edlen Frauen des Asan Aga. Wien, 1883.

Milović, J. M. Uebertragungen slavischer Volkslieder aus Goethes Briefnachlass. Leipzig, 1940.

—— Goethe, seine Zeitgenossen und die serbokroatische Volkspoesie. Leipzig, 1941.

—— Talvjs erste Uebertragungen für Goethe. Leipzig, 1941.

Murko, M. Goethes Beziehungen zur serbischen Volkspoesie. Chronik des Wiener Goethe-Vereins, 10, 1899.

—— Das Original von Goethes Klaggesang von der edlen Frauen des Asan Aga in der Literatur und im Volksmunde durch 150 Jahre. GS, 3-4, 1935-36 & Brünn, 1937.

Preisinger, H. Goethe and the Servian Folk-Song. Transactions of the Manchester Goethe-Society, 1886-93. Warrington, 1894.

Wahl, H. Russische Weisheitsfreunde bei Goethe und im Goethehaus. In: Goethe, 2, 1937.

Wendel, H. Die Welt der Südslaven im Spiegel Goethes. Jb. des freien deutschen Hochstifts, Frankfurt, 1926.

Ehrhard, A. La Bohême dans l'oeuvre dramatique de **GRILLPARZER.** RG, 1933.

Paunel, E. J. La route danubienne et de Dobrogea de Grillparzer en 1843. (In Rumanian). Analele Dobrogei, 16, 1935.

Rechzeh, G. Grillparzer und die Slaven. Diss. München. Weimar, 1929.

Tonnelat, E. J. **GRIMM** et les Slaves du Sud. Revue des Etudes slaves, 15, 1935.

Tropsch, S. Jakob Grimm als Uebersetzer serbo-kroatischer Volkslieder. Euphorion, 16, 1924.

Luther, A. Russland im Schaffen Henry von **HEISELERS.** GS, 3, 1935.

Keefer, F. W. **HERDER'S** Russian Utopia. MLN, 1936.

Wegner, A. Herder und das lettische Volkslied. Langensalza, 1928.

Arnold, R. F. **HOLTEI** und der deutsche Polen-Cultus. Festgabe R. Heinzel. Weimar, 1898.

Zatocil, L. Ueber die Bedeutung der alttschechischen Tkadleecek für die Ackermannsforschung. **(JOHANNES VON SAAZ).** Slavische Rundschau, 10.

Petrovitch, S. Le voyage de **LAMARTINE** en Serbie en 1833. (In Serbian). SKG, 30.

Kuthe, O. H. **LAUBES** Roman Die Krieger im Zusammenhang mit der Polenbegeisterung im Jahre 1830. Marburg, 1925.

Bittner, K. Slavica bei G. W. von **LEIBNIZ.** GS, 1, 1932.

Letty, J. H. **LENORMAND** parle à Prague. L'Europe centrale, 14.XII.1935.

LOTI, P. Fleurs d'ennui. Pasquala Ivanovitch. Voyage au Monténégro. Suleima. Paris, 1926.

Stepanov, M. Joseph de **MAISTRE** in Russia. (In Russian). Literaturnoe Nasledstvo, 29-30. Moskva, 1937.

Humbert, J. Le voyage de **MARMONT** en Hongrie et en Transylvanie. L'Europe centrale, 18.XI.1933.
Cahen, G. **MERIMEE** et la Russie. RHLF, 1921.
Matvieev, P. Mêrimée et ses rapports avec la littérature russe. (In Russian). Novoe Vremia, 25.X. & 6.XI.1894.
Mérimée, P. La Guzla, ou choix de poésies illyriques, recueillies dans la Dalmatie, la Bosnie, la Croatie et l'Herzégovine. Paris, 1827.
Mongault, H. Introduction aux Etudes de littérature russe de Mérimée. In: Ouvres complètes de Mérimée. Paris, 1931.
—— Mérimée et l'histoire russe. Le Monde slave, Aug., 1932.
Yovanovitch, V. M. Gousle Prospera Merimea on ingleskoi Kgnijevnosti. SKG, 16.XII.1906.
—— La Guzla de Mérimée. Diss. Grenoble. Paris, 1911.
Lozinski, G. Le général **MIRANDA** en Russie. Le Monde slave, 1933.
Dimitz, A. Charles **NODIER** in seinen Beziehungen zu Krain. Laibacher Wochenblatt, 210-14, 1884.
Dollot, R. Les romans illyriens de Charles Nodier. RLC, 11, 1931.
Larat, J. La tradition et l'exotisme dans l'oeuvre de Charles Nodier (1780-1844) ; étude sur les origines du romantisme français. Paris, 1923.
Maixter, R. Charles Nodier en Illyrie. Revue des Etudes slaves, 4, 1924.
Mounot, A. La Slovenie et Charles Nodier. Bull. trimestriel de l'Acad. de Besançon, 1924.
Pisani, P. Charles Nodier rédacteur du "Télégraphe de Laybach." Bulletin critique, 1887.
Skerlitch, J. Les romantiques français et la poésie populaire serbe: Charles Nodier. (In Serbian). SKG, 16.V. & 1.VI.1904.
Banfi, F. Versioni e studi ungheresi di P. E. **PAVOLINI**. Europa Orientale, 23, 1943.
Coleman, A. P. James Gates **PERCIVAL** and Slavonic Culture. Slavia, 16, 1941.
Tóth, B. Edgar **QUINET** et la Hongrie. Revue des Etudes hongroises, 1928. And in: Debreceni Szemle, May, 1928.
Valjavec, F. **RANKE** und der Süd-Osten. München, 1935.
Frank, S. Rainer Maria **RILKE** und die russische Geistesart. GS, 2, 1932-33.
Soloveitchik, S. & Gladding, E. B. Rilke's Original Russian Poems. MLN, 62, 1947.
Wunderlich, Eva C. Slavonic Traces in Rilke's Geschichten vom Lieben Gott. GR, 22, 1947.
McClain, W. H. Romain **ROLLAND** and Russia. RR, 39, 1948.
Yovanovitch, V. La comtesse de **ROSENBERG** et ses Morlaques. (In Serbian). Belgrade, 1913.
Ganche, E. George **SAND** et les Polonais. La Pologne littéraire et artistique, 1. XII.1926.
Anon. A Polish Source for **SHAKESPEARE**. MB, 15, 1940.
Draper, J. W. Shakespeare's Illyria. RES, 17, 1941.
Ehrsam, T. G. Poland in the Works of Shakespeare. Nowy Swiat, Jan., 1935.
Grégoire, H. Une source bulgare de la Tempête de Shakespeare. L'Europe orientale, 10.X.1934.
—— La Tempête de Shakespeare et les peuples balkaniques. L'Europe centrale, 25.V.1935.
—— The Bulgarian Origins of The Tempest of Shakespeare. SPh, 37, 1940.
Berkov, P. N. Der Akademiker Jakob **STAHLIN** und seine Materialien zur Geschichte der russischen Literatur. GS, 1, 1931-32.
Knowlton, E. C. A Russian Influence on **STEVENSON**. MPh, 14, 1916.
Prahl, A. J. Bayard **TAYLOR'S** Letters from Russia. HLQ, 9, 1946.
Tagliavini, C. Gli studi ungheresi e ugrofinnici di Emilio **TEZA**. Corvina, 5, 1942.
Studer, Ella. Russisches in der **THIDREKSAGA**. Sprache und Dichtung, Bern, 1931.
Lednicki, W. L. Alfred de **VIGNY** et les Slaves. Bull. of the Polish Institute of Arts & Sciences in America, 1, 1942.
Popvitch, P. Zadig de **VOLTAIRE** et les contes populaires serbes. (In Serbian). SKG, 13.
Tchorovitch, V. Encore sur Zadig de Voltaire et les contes populaires serbes. (In Serbian). SKG, 13.